T0038062

Merriam-Webster's
Intermediate
Thesaurus

Merriam-Webster's
Intermediate
Thesaurus

Merriam-Webster, Incorporated
Springfield, Massachusetts

A GENUINE MERRIAM-WEBSTER

The name *Webster* alone is no guarantee of excellence. It is used by a number of publishers and may serve mainly to mislead an unwary buyer.

Merriam-Webster™ is the name you should look for when you consider the purchase of dictionaries or other fine reference books. It carries the reputation of a company that has been publishing since 1831 and is your assurance of quality and authority.

Library of Congress Cataloging-in-Publication Data

Names: Merriam-Webster, Inc.
Title: Merriam-Webster's intermediate thesaurus.
Other titles: Intermediate thesaurus
Description: Springfield, Massachusetts : Merriam-Webster, Incorporated, [2023] | Audience: Ages 10–14. | Summary: "Merriam-Webster's Intermediate Thesaurus is geared towards students grades 5–8, ages 10–14. This reference contains over 150,000 word choices across 19,000 main entries, which feature definitions, usage examples, synonym lists, related word lists, near-antonym lists, and antonym lists"—Provided by publisher.
Identifiers: LCCN 2022042952 | ISBN 9780877796787 (hardcover)
Subjects: LCSH: English language—Synonyms and antonyms—Juvenile literature. | LCGFT: Thesauri (Dictionaries)
Classification: LCC PE1591 .M4788 2023 | DDC 423/.12—dc23/eng/20220919
LC record available at https://lccn.loc.gov/2022042952

Printed in Italy

1st Printing   Grafica Veneta, Trebaseleghe (PD)   June 2023

Preface

Merriam-Webster's Intermediate Thesaurus is specially designed for students aged 11 to 14 who want to enlarge their vocabularies and learn more about the rich variety of the English language. The vocabulary of the thesaurus is largely based upon that of *Merriam-Webster's Intermediate Dictionary*, which is likewise intended for use primarily by middle-school students. We recommend that students turn to the dictionary whenever they need a better understanding of the meaning of any words used in the thesaurus.

Merriam-Webster's Intermediate Thesaurus provides over 150,000 words from which the user may choose. In creating this thesaurus, Merriam-Webster editors have drawn on years of experience with a thesaurus format that is at once easy to use, broad in its scope, and especially helpful to the user in the selection of the right word. We believe that this thesaurus will also prove to be highly useful as a vocabulary builder.

We envision a user of this thesaurus to be someone who is engaged in the always challenging task of putting thoughts into words, and who feels dissatisfied with their original choice of a word. Being conscientious, our hypothetical writer embarks on a search for a word which is close in meaning to the original word but which differs from it in tone, connotation, level of formality, or range of application. To accomplish this end, our writer is in many cases best served by a thesaurus that offers not only a large and comprehensive selection of words to choose from, but also some guidance as to which words, out of many possibilities with similar meanings, are words that really do have the same meaning as the word originally chosen. This thesaurus provides such guidance by grouping the true synonyms together and by stating explicitly the meaning that is shared by all of the synonyms in each group.

Of course, not every user of the thesaurus will be looking for a word that means exactly the same as the word they already had in mind. We have therefore supplemented our lists of synonyms with lists of "related words"—words which don't exactly match the meaning shared by the words listed as synonyms but which are similar enough in meaning that they are likely to be of interest to the user. Similarly, we know that users are not always looking for true antonyms, and so we have endeavored, under the rubric of "near antonyms," to supplement the antonyms with words that are only approximately opposite in meaning to the synonyms.

To aid the user in making a selection from this large stock of offerings, we have provided a sentence or phrase that illustrates a typical context for every synonym listed in this book. The inclusion of a sample sentence or phrase at every synonym is intended to provide guidance about how individual synonyms are used, in the hope that this will help the user choose the most appropriate one.

The thesaurus format is intended to encourage and facilitate students in finding the right word, which results in writing of greater precision and clarity. The word *thesaurus* literally means "treasury" in Latin, and we hope that the treasure trove of words contained in these pages will enhance the user's interest in and appreciation of the English language. We urge both students and teachers to read carefully the following sections entitled Introduction and Using Your Thesaurus in order to make the most of what the book has to offer. The Introduction contains an informative discussion of what distinguishes a synonym from a related word, an antonym from a near antonym. The Using Your Thesaurus section explains in detail the organization of the thesaurus and discusses the differences between the two basic types of entries. Study of this section is especially important.

Merriam-Webster's Intermediate Thesaurus was edited by Serenity H. Carr. Credit for editing also goes to Em Vezina and Linda Wood, who worked on *Merriam-Webster's School Thesaurus*, upon which much of this new revision of the *Intermediate Thesaurus* is based. The entire project was supervised by Em Vezina, who also handled the task of cross-reference. Daniel Brandon and Anne E. McDonald handled data entry and data-file processing and contributed essential technical assistance in a number of other ways. Sarah S. Carragher served as editor in charge of production, guiding the book through its typesetting stages. Proofreaders included Faith A. Bell, Faith de Castro, Carin A. Helfer, Diana M. Jones, Benjamin T. Korzec, Michael D. Metivier, and Emily D. Villanueva.

Introduction

Synonyms

The English language contains a wealth of words, and perhaps no other language has as many synonyms. A carefully chosen synonym can add variety and precision to the work of any writer, whether that writer is a professional or a student.

So, just what are synonyms? Put simply, synonyms are words that mean the same thing. Words that are only somewhat similar in meaning—but do not mean the same thing—are not true synonyms. They are merely related words, and they belong in a different category. In this thesaurus a word is classified as a synonym if and only if it shares with another word at least one basic meaning.

Here's an example of how we arrived at the basic meaning shared by a group of words. The word *fort* is defined in *Merriam-Webster's Intermediate Dictionary* as "a strong or fortified place."

Since a person using *fort* as the starting point in their search for the right word is probably dissatisfied with that term, the word they are seeking will most likely come under a broader or more basic meaning. We can phrase that more basic meaning as: "a structure or place from which one can resist attack." The list of synonyms for *fort—bastion, castle, citadel, fastness, fortification, fortress, hold, stronghold*—can all be said to share this basic meaning. None of these words share identically worded definitions, but they do have in common a basic meaning that allows them to be regarded as synonyms.

If a word is more limited in scope than the basic meaning given at a main entry, then it cannot be regarded as a synonym for that word group. Hence, the words *battlement* and *bulwark* are entered only as related words at *fort,* as they refer to specific kinds of defensive structures.

Related Words

Often thesaurus users are not looking for something that means exactly the same as the word they already have in mind. To help in this situation, the *Intermediate Thesaurus* includes lists of words whose meanings are close to the synonymy group and are likely to be of interest to the user. These related words do not qualify as synonyms because they have meanings that differ from the basic meaning shared by the members of the synonymy group. For example, the word *funny* has the meaning of "causing or intended to cause laughter." A person who is making "funny faces" is causing, or at least trying to cause, others to laugh. *Witty,* although closely related to *funny,* has a slightly different meaning: "given to or marked by mature intelligent humor." A witty person is someone who has a habit of making clever remarks that display a grown-up sense of humor. Because of the close relationship between *funny* and *witty,* many, if not all, of the words listed as synonyms at *witty* are given as related words at *funny.* Thesaurus users are encouraged to go from one related entry to another when searching for just the right word for their purpose.

Some words are not true synonyms of anything, but because they are so fundamentally useful, they have been included in this thesaurus among the lists of related words and in places where they are likely to be most helpful. For example, the word *ballast,* which refers to any type of "heavy material used to make a ship steady," is too narrow in meaning to have any synonyms of its own. It is related to the more general term *load,* however, and so, fittingly, it is included as a related word at the entry for the noun *load.*

Antonyms

An antonym is a word whose meaning is directly opposite to another word's meaning. Fundamental to this thesaurus's concept of an antonym is the notion of negation. An antonym has a meaning that completely cancels out another word's meaning. *Short* and *tall* are complete opposites. Something cannot be both short and tall at the same time, and both words suggest about the same degree of deviation from the norm or average for height. *Good* and *evil* are another pair of exact opposites. Logically, something cannot be both *good* and *evil* in the same way and at the same time.

Words that are only opposite in some aspect of their meaning cannot be said to be true antonyms. For example, *sad,* which means "causing unhappiness," is not a true antonym of *funny,* which means "causing or intended to cause laughter." The opposite of unhappiness is happiness, and there are things that make people happy without generating laughter. Similarly, *hurt,* which means "to feel or cause physical pain," is not an antonym of *heal,* which means "to restore to a healthy condition." The exact opposite of "to feel or cause physical pain" would be "to feel or cause physical pleasure." *Hurt* and *heal* are certainly contrary words, but they differ in their focus and in what they suggest. Pairs of words like *hurt* and *heal* are better regarded as near antonyms.

In this thesaurus, pairs of true antonyms generally fall into three basic classes: (1) words that are mutually exclusive and have no middle ground between them, as *dead* and *alive,* or *perfect* and *imperfect;* (2) words that are on opposite ends of some spectrum, as *maximum* and *minimum,* or *huge* and *tiny;* (3) words that in effect reverse or undo one another, as *assemble* and *disassemble,* or *prove* and *disprove.*

Near Antonyms

Near antonyms are words that do not qualify as antonyms under the strict definition used for this thesaurus but which are clearly in marked contrast with the members of a synonym group. Just as a user may not be seeking a word that is exactly synonymous with another, they may not be seeking a word that is exactly opposite. The user may simply want a word that lies somewhere on the opposite side of the spectrum of meaning. *Afraid* is not so exactly opposite to *courageous* as *cowardly* is, but *afraid* and *courageous* certainly have markedly contrasting meanings and can be considered near antonyms of each other.

Phrases

This thesaurus also includes phrases that, taken as a whole, are synonymous with individual words. Some of these are fixed phrases that contain a word that is entered in the dictionary at its own alphabetical place but is never, or almost never, used except in a fixed phrase. For example, *in jeopardy* appears as a synonymous phrase at *liable* because a person liable (that is, "exposed") to something dangerous or undesirable is a person "in jeopardy." The word *jeopardy* is normally used with this meaning only in the phrase *in jeopardy.*

Idioms constitute the other major class of word combinations that are entered under the heading of phrases. Idioms are phrases that have a figurative meaning that is different from the literal meaning one would get if one were to piece together the meanings of the individual components of the phrase. For example, the phrase *make good* is virtually meaningless if one attempts to piece together the literal meanings of *make* and *good.* As a fixed phrase, however, *make good* means "to reach a desired level of accomplishment" and is a synonym of *succeed.*

Verbal Illustrations

Verbal illustrations play a key role in helping users decide which word best suits their purposes. Members of a synonym group of course have the same core meaning, but typically they differ in their nuances, connotations, level of formality, and range of application. For a description of something that is "very pleasing to look at," one's choices include the following adjectives: *aesthetic, attractive, beauteous, beautiful, comely, cute, fair, fetching, good, goodly, gorgeous, handsome, knockout, lovely, pretty, ravishing, seemly, sightly, stunning,* and *taking.* The thesaurus user is faced with the challenge of deciding which of these words is best for describing, say, a sunset or a city square. To help guide users, each member of a synonym group has been provided with a distinctive verbal illustration that shows how the word is appropriately and typically used:

⟨Sunsets in Hawaii are just *gorgeous.*⟩

⟨a *handsome* man with finely chiseled features⟩

⟨a *knockout* sports car that's the talk of the neighborhood⟩

⟨The hotel offers a *ravishing* view of the ocean.⟩

⟨had never seen such a *taking* city as Venice⟩

In some cases the thesaurus user may decide, after reviewing all of the verbal illustrations for a synonym group, that they still have not found the word that precisely meets their need. The user should then consider the entry's list of related words:

> ***related words*** alluring, appealing, charming, cunning, delightful, engaging, fascinating, glamorous (*also* glamourous), prepossessing; elegant, exquisite, glorious, magnificent, resplendent, splendid, statuesque, sublime, superb; flawless, perfect, radiant; dainty, delicate; personable, pleasant, presentable; prettyish; desirable, dishy, dollish, foxy, pulchritudinous, seductive; hunky; arresting, eye-catching, flamboyant, flashy, glossy, showstopping, showy, slick, snazzy, splashy, striking; photogenic, telegenic

These supplementary words, which are quite close in meaning to the members of the synonym list, are intended to expand the user's options. Some related words are too specific in meaning to be members of any synonym group; some other related words are members of synonym lists at other entries. Thesaurus users should regard the lists of related words as departure points for further exploration.

Lastly, users of this thesaurus are urged to consult it in conjunction with a good dictionary. The preferred companion dictionary would of course be *Merriam-Webster's Intermediate Dictionary*. Regardless of which dictionary is used, thesaurus users should consult a dictionary before attempting to use a word with which they were previously unfamiliar.

Using Your Thesaurus

Every user of *Merriam-Webster's Intermediate Thesaurus* is encouraged to read the following information because a thorough understanding of the *Thesaurus*'s scope, philosophy, and structure is essential to its effective use.

Scope of Merriam-Webster's Intermediate Thesaurus

This thesaurus is intended to be a tool for the conscientious writer who is seeking the precisely right word. It is therefore centered on the general vocabulary of the English language. It is this part of the language that is rich with words that have special nuances, distinctive connotations, and varying degrees of formality. As a consequence, the user generally will not find words that belong to science, technology, or other specialized fields. Obsolete and extremely rare terms have also been omitted, as these would do little to help the writer seeking genuinely useful words. Lastly, words that have been labeled as *vulgar, obscene, disparaging, offensive,* or *nonstandard* in Merriam-Webster's online dictionary, *Merriam-Webster.com*, have been disregarded.

Entry Order

The boldface word or phrase at the beginning of a thesaurus entry is called a **headword**. Headwords appear in alphabetical order for ease of use. Alphabetization is by first letter, then second letter, and so on, regardless of any spaces or hyphens that may separate those letters:

make *vb*

make–believe *adj*

make out *vb*

make over *vb*

Maker *n*

makeshift *adj*

When a headword contains a numeral, the numeral is alphabetized as though it were a spelled-out word:

anywise

A1 *adj*

apace *adv*

Homographs are words that are spelled exactly the same but are different parts of speech or have entirely different etymologies (word origins). Homographs that are different parts of speech are simply entered as separate headwords:

bat *n* **1** a hard strike with a part of the body or an instrument

bat *vb* **1** to deliver a blow to (someone or something) . . .

bear *n* **1** a dull, unpleasant, or difficult piece of work

bear *vb* **1** to bring forth from the womb

If two or more homographs are the same part of speech, they are entered as separate headwords and are grouped together and numbered:

¹list *n* a record of a series of items (as names or titles) usually arranged according to some system

²list *n* the act of positioning or an instance of being positioned at an angle

³list *n* a long narrow piece of material

¹list *vb* **1** to make a list of

²list *vb* to set or cause to be at an angle

As discussed below under the heading "Some Notes about Verbs," verbs that are customarily used in combination with a preposition or an adverb appear as headwords in this thesaurus in either of two ways: with the verb followed by the preposition or adverb in parentheses, or with both the verb and its companion preposition or adverb. Simple verbs are listed first, followed by verbs with parenthetical prepositions or adverbs, which are in turn followed by the boldface verb-adverb or verb-preposition combinations:

talk *vb*

talk (into) *vb*

talk (to) *vb*

talkative *adj*

talk down (to) *vb*

talker *n*

talk over *vb*

When headwords are compound words, a closed compound (one without a space or hyphen) is entered before a hyphenated compound, and a hyphenated compound is entered before an open compound (one with an intervening space):

nosedive *n*

nose–dive *vb*

open–air *adj*

open air *n*

Plural Nouns

Some nouns are always pluralized or are pluralized when they are used with certain meanings. When a thesaurus entry for a noun includes no senses that are used in the singular, the plural form is given as the headword:

leavings *pl n* a remaining group or portion ⟨The *leavings* of the banquet were packed up and delivered to a shelter for the homeless.⟩ — see REMAINDER 1

When a noun is often or usually, but not always, used in the plural form, the singular form is used for the headword, and the plural follows, introduced by the label *often* or *usually*:

shallow *n, usually* **shallows** *pl* a place where a body of water (as a sea or river) is shallow ⟨We waded through the *shallows* looking for tadpoles.⟩ — see SHOAL

When such a noun appears in a list of synonyms, related words, etc., it is shown as a plural form with parentheses around the final *s* or *es*:

shoal *n* a place where a body of water (as a sea or river) is shallow ⟨The *shoals* of Nantucket Island are famous as the final resting place of many ill-fated ships.⟩ **synonyms** ford, shallow(s)

When a noun is used in the singular form in one sense and in the plural form in another, the singular form is given as the headword. The plural form is indicated at the appropriate sense or senses:

provision *n* **1** something upon which the carrying out of an agreement or offer depends ⟨We loaned them the car with the *provision* that they refill the gas tank before returning it.⟩ — see CONDITION 2
2 provisions *pl* substances intended to be eaten ⟨We gave them ample *provisions* so they would not get hungry on the trip.⟩ — see FOOD 1

Variants

An alternate spelling or form of a headword is called a **variant**. Variants are shown in boldface type immediately after the headword and are introduced by *or* or *also*. The label *or* means

that the variant is as common, or nearly as common, as the headword. As long as the variants are equally common, the headword is the spelling that comes first alphabetically.

theater *or* **theatre** *n*

OK *or* **okay** *vb*

However, if one of the spellings is used slightly more frequently than the other, the more common one is shown first even if it does not fall first alphabetically:

goody *or* **goodie** *n*

A variant that is introduced by the label *also* is considerably less common than the headword:

among *also* **amongst** *prep*

facade *also* **façade** *n*

naught *also* **nought** *n*

When two variants are separated from the headword by *also* but from each other by *or*, it means that both variants are considerably less common than the headword:

bogey *also* **bogie** *or* **bogy** *n*

Variants are also shown in the word lists within the entries:

zero *n* **1** the numerical symbol 0 or the absence of number or quantity represented by it ⟨Anything multiplied by *zero* comes out to *zero*.⟩
synonyms aught, cipher, goose egg, naught (*also* nought), nil, nothing, oh, zilch, zip

Capitalization

When an entry word is capitalized in ordinary writing, it is entered in this thesaurus with a capital letter. Other entries begin with a lowercase letter.

Almighty *n* **1** the being worshipped as the creator and ruler of the universe ⟨The worshippers gave thanks to the *Almighty*.⟩ — see DEITY 2

Some words have special meanings when capitalized that they do not have without a capital letter. This thesaurus shows the use of the capital with such entries by putting the label *cap* at the appropriate sense.

pandemonium *n* **1** a state of noisy, confused activity ⟨Christmas morning at our house is always marked by *pandemonium*.⟩ — see COMMOTION

2 *cap* the place of punishment for the wicked after death ⟨a surrealist painting in which all the torments of *Pandemonium* are vividly depicted⟩ — see HELL 1

Parts of Speech

Every headword is followed by one of the following abbreviated part-of-speech labels: *adj* (adjective), *adv* (adverb), *conj* (conjunction), *interj* (interjection), *n* (noun), *prep* (preposition), *pron* (pronoun), or *vb* (verb). Plural nouns are followed by the *pl n* label.

Kinds of Entries

This thesaurus consists of two types of entries: **main entries** and **cross entries**. Each main entry provides a full treatment of a group of synonyms and is located at the alphabetical place of one of the most important words in the group. The cross entries, which are shorter than the main entries, can be found at the alphabetical place of each of the synonyms listed at the main entries. Every headword with its part-of-speech label is followed by either one or more main entries, one or more cross entries, or a combination of the two. If there is more than one meaning treated at a given headword, all the main entries will come first, followed by all the cross entries, and each will begin with a boldface sense number.

A main entry always includes a statement of the core meaning shared by the members of a synonym group. It is by this means that the user knows in what sense the members of the group are being treated as synonyms. This statement of shared meaning is followed by a verbal illustration for the headword. The illustration is followed by a list of synonyms as well as such related words, phrases, near antonyms, and antonyms as may exist for that meaning.

famous *adj* **1** widely known ⟨a book about some of the most *famous* people of the last century⟩
synonyms celebrated, famed, noted, notorious, prominent, renowned, star, visible, well-known
related words fabled, fabulous, legendary; infamous; distinguished, eminent, exceptional, great, illustrious, leading, notable, noteworthy, outstanding, preeminent, prestigious, remarkable, supereminent, superior; important, significant; acknowledged, recognized, respected; favorite, popular, preferred
near antonyms insignificant, unimportant; inconspicuous; undistinguished, unexceptional; unpopular
antonyms anonymous, nameless, obscure, uncelebrated, unknown, unsung

Every word in the list of synonyms at each main entry is entered at its own alphabetical place as a cross entry. The statement of shared meaning

that appears at the main entry will be shown at the cross entry as well. This is done so that the user who is looking at the cross entry will know whether the main entry treats the sense that they are interested in. The statement of shared meaning is followed by a verbal illustration for that particular synonym. The cross entry does not repeat the synonyms, related words, phrases, near antonyms, or antonyms given at the main entry. Instead, at the end of the cross entry, there is a reference that points the user to the appropriate main entry:

celebrated *adj* widely known ⟨a *celebrated* author making an appearance at a talk show⟩ — see FAMOUS 1

fade *vb* **1** to cease to be visible ⟨The departing ship gradually *faded* over the horizon.⟩ — see DISAPPEAR **2** to make white or whiter by removing color ⟨Years of harsh sunlight had *faded* the car, which was once fire-engine red.⟩ — see WHITEN **3** to lose bodily strength or vigor ⟨began to *fade* after a long, hard day⟩ — see WEAKEN 2

Cross-References

A **cross-reference** is a direction at the end of a cross entry that tells the user where the main entry for that particular shared meaning is located. If there is more than one sense at the headword referred to in the cross-reference, the cross-reference will include the relevant sense number. If there is more than one numbered homograph for a headword, the cross-reference will include the correct homograph number as well:

pain *vb* to feel or cause physical pain ⟨My poor head was *paining* so from all that racket.⟩ — see HURT 1

ranking *n* **1** a scheme of rank or order ⟨In one *ranking* of the best places to live, San Francisco surpassed all other cities in the U.S.⟩ — see ³SCALE 1

Cross-references are always between words having the same part of speech. In the above example, for instance, the cross-reference is to the first sense of the third homograph for the noun *scale,* which is of course the same part of speech as *ranking:*

³scale *n* **1** a scheme of rank or order ⟨a student who scored very highly on a standard intelligence *scale*⟩
synonyms graduation, hierarchy, ladder, ordering, ranking

Special Usage Labels

Occasionally words in this thesaurus will bear italicized usage labels. The following labels indicate that a word is limited to regional use: *British, Midland, Scottish, Southern,* and *West.* All of these designations may be used in combination with one another (as *Southern & Midland*) or qualified by the word *chiefly*. Three other labels that have been used for this thesaurus are *dialect, slang,* and *archaic*. The label *dialect* indicates that a word occurs in several regional varieties of American or British English and that the pattern of its usage is too complicated to be concisely labeled. The stylistic label *slang* indicates that the word is used most appropriately in very informal contexts. The temporal label *archaic* indicates that the word is nowadays used only in special contexts, such as poetry or historical fiction:

> **cop** *vb, slang*
>
> **creek** *n* . . . **2** *chiefly British*
>
> **kirk** *n, chiefly Scottish*
>
> **plumb** *adv* . . . **2** *chiefly dialect*

When a headword has multiple senses and a usage label applies to one or more of them but not to all of them, the label will come after the appropriate sense numbers:

> **jack** *n* **1** *slang* something (as pieces of stamped metal or printed paper) customarily and legally used as a medium of exchange, a measure of value, or a means of payment ⟨I'd buy that watch, but I don't have the *jack* right now.⟩ — see MONEY 1
> **2** a piece of cloth with a special design that is used as an emblem or for signaling ⟨a Portuguese ship flying the national *jack*⟩ — see FLAG 1

In the word lists at main entries, special usage labels appear in square brackets immediately after the words to which they apply:

> **car** *n* a self-propelled passenger vehicle on four wheels ⟨every teenager's dream of getting a driver's license and a first *car*⟩
> **synonyms** auto, automobile, machine, motor, motorcar, motor vehicle, wheels [*slang*]

Shared Meanings

Every entry contains a statement of the meaning shared by members of a synonym group. This shared meaning is the "thing" that is referred to when we say that two or more words "mean the same thing" and thus qualify as synonyms. The statement of shared meaning follows the part-of-speech label in single-sense entries and the sense number in multisense entries. Sometimes there are parenthetical elements within these statements of shared meaning, as in the following entry:

> **payment** *n* . . .
> **2** something (as money) that is given or received in return for goods or services ⟨Our *payment* for all the

work we did barely covered our expenses.⟩ ⟨We finally mailed our last car *payment* last week.⟩
> **synonyms** compensation, consideration, pay, recompense, remittance, remuneration, requital

The parenthetical element is intended to suggest the usual range of application of a group of words, but it should not be interpreted as a strict limitation of a word's application.

Some Notes about Verbs

Verbs that have a given meaning only when they are followed by a particular word appear as headwords in this thesaurus in one of several ways. Sometimes both the verb and the following adverb or preposition are shown in boldface:

> **burn out** *vb* to use up all the physical energy of ⟨Working 12-hour days at that job just *burned* me *out*.⟩

Sometimes the verb is shown followed by an adverb, preposition, or other word in parentheses:

> **comply (with)** *vb* **1** to act according to the commands of ⟨The guards rushed to *comply with* the warden's orders.⟩
> **knock (about)** *vb* to move about from place to place aimlessly ⟨We *knocked about* from town to town, looking for a place to stay.⟩
> **leg (it)** *vb* to go on foot ⟨The car was in the shop so we had to *leg it* to work for a couple of days.⟩

And sometimes both styles are combined:

> **hold off (on)** *vb* to assign to a later time ⟨We *held off on* accepting the invitation in the hopes that something better would come along.⟩

If there are two words inside the parentheses and they are separated by *or,* then either word can be used with the verb:

> **fit (in** *or* **into)** *vb* to put among or between others ⟨Do you think that you can *fit* this picture *into* the album?⟩ ⟨I can *fit* you *in* between my two o'clock and three o'clock appointments.⟩

A verb that has a parenthesized element when shown as a headword has that same parenthesized element when the verb appears in a word list. Users who encounter such a verb in a list should remember that the complete verb combination must be used for it to match the shared meaning of its synonym group:

> **obey** *vb* to act according to the commands of . . .
> **synonyms** adhere (to), comply (with), conform (to), follow, mind, observe

When the statement of shared meaning calls for a direct object, all of the members of a synonym group will take a direct object. If the statement of shared meaning does not call for a direct object, then none of the synonyms will take an object. One frequent clue that the members of a word group take an object is the fact that the statement of shared meaning ends with a preposition:

> **constitute** *vb* **1** to be all the substance of ⟨Nine players *constitute* a baseball team.⟩

Not all verbs requiring an object are worded this way, however, so the user may need to study the verbal illustration to determine the need for a direct object. A check of the verbal illustration at a verb's cross entry may be needed for further confirmation.

Verbal Illustrations

Every synonym in this thesaurus is illustrated with an example of its typical use. This **verbal illustration** appears after the statement of shared meaning and is set off by angle brackets. The word being illustrated is italicized in each verbal illustration.

> **fight** *vb* **1** to oppose (someone) in physical conflict ⟨a proud people who have fiercely *fought* all invaders of their homeland⟩
> **hold back** *vb* **1** to create difficulty for the work or activity of ⟨The only thing *holding* Jill *back* from joining the swim team is lack of transportation.⟩

Synonyms Used in Defining

The central word in a dictionary definition is known as the defining term, and every definition has to have one. Likewise, each statement of shared meaning in this thesaurus includes a defining term:

> **gadget** *n* an interesting and often novel device with a practical use ⟨She tried out a new *gadget* for weeding the garden.⟩
> **synonyms** appliance, contraption, contrivance, gimmick, gizmo (*also* gismo), jigger

In the above example, the noun *device* is the defining term. If *device* had not been used as the defining term, it could have been included with good justification in the list of synonyms. However, since it was in fact used as the defining term, *device* was omitted from the list in accordance with our practice of not using a word both as a defining term and as a synonym at the same main entry.

Related Words

The cornerstone of every entry in this thesaurus is the list of synonyms. For the vast majority of main entries, an often generous supply of related words is provided to supplement the synonyms. The lists of related words are meant to suggest to the user an array of paths that might be taken in search of the precisely right word. The number of related words often exceeds that of the synonyms because related words do not have to match the synonyms' shared meaning; they need only relate to some aspect of that statement of shared meaning. Where appropriate, related words are divided into subgroups which are separated by semicolons. Words within each subgroup are usually closer in meaning to each other than to members of neighboring subgroups. The subgroups are generally presented in order of most relevant to least relevant.

> **conceited** *adj* having too high an opinion of oneself ⟨a *conceited* basketball player who was always too busy even to sign autographs⟩
> **synonyms** assured, complacent, consequential, egoistic (*also* egoistical), egotistic (*or* egotistical), important, overweening, pompous, prideful, proud, self-conceited, self-important, self-satisfied, smug, stuck-up, vain, vainglorious
> **related words** blusterous, blustery, boastful, bombastic, braggart, bragging, braggy, cocky, swaggering; arrogant, cavalier, disdainful, haughty, high-hat, lofty, lordly, masterful, self-assertive, supercilious, superior, toplofty (*also* toploftical), uppish, uppity; domineering, high-handed, imperious; highfalutin (*also* hifalutin), holier-than-thou, pretentious; overconfident, presuming, presumptuous; confident, self-assured, self-confident; self-adulatory, self-congratulatory, self-contented, self-gratulatory; self-applauding, self-dramatizing, self-glorifying, self-promoting; self-affected, self-centered, self-engrossed, selfish; condescending, patronizing

Phrases

The heading **phrases** is reserved for expressions that, taken as a whole, are synonymous with their entry's synonym group. These expressions are shown in a list of their own but do not have their own cross entries and thus do not have verbal illustrations in this thesaurus. These expressions are often colorful figures of speech that add interest and variety to one's writing, but the writer is advised to look up unfamiliar expressions in a dictionary before attempting to use them.

Near Antonyms

Just as related words are not exact synonyms, near antonyms are not exact antonyms. Not every synonym group will have near antonyms, but in general they are more plentiful than exact antonyms. As is the case with related words, near antonyms are typically divided into subgroups separated by semicolons. And as with related words, near antonyms are generally listed in order of relevancy.

> **maintenance** *n* the act or activity of keeping something in an existing and usually satisfactory condition ⟨I was hired to perform basic *maintenance* until the property could be sold.⟩
> **synonyms** conservation, conserving, preservation, preserving, upkeep
> **related words** support, sustaining; care, custody, guardianship; defense, guarding, protection, safeguarding, safekeeping
> **near antonyms** dereliction, disregard, ignoring, inattention, neglect, negligence; damage, demolition, destruction, harm, hurt, injury, ruin, ruination

Antonyms

The words in a main entry's antonym list are exactly opposite in meaning to the headword and its list of synonyms. A true antonym is a word whose meaning completely cancels out another word's meaning. True antonyms do not exist for many words in this thesaurus. There are no words that completely cancel out the shared meaning at *car*: "a self-propelled passenger vehicle on four wheels." There is no word in English that essentially means "not a car." A word like *truck* may be used in contradistinction to car, but *truck* and *car* are not antonyms. In this thesaurus words listed as antonyms are given their own cross entries only if they appear as synonyms at some other entry. The word *torrid* has its own cross entry; the cross-reference is to *hot* 1, where the word is a synonym, and not to *cold* 1, where it is an antonym.

At most main entries all of the members of an antonym list are synonyms of each other. At some entries, however, while all the listed antonyms are opposite in meaning to the synonym group, they are not opposite in exactly the same way. The following is an example of such an entry:

> **colorful** *adj* marked by a variety of usually vivid colors ⟨the *colorful* markings on butterflies⟩
> **synonyms** motley, multicolored, polychromatic, polychrome, varicolored, varied, variegated . . .
> **antonyms** colorless; monochromatic, monochromic, self-colored, solid

The opposite meaning of "marked by a variety of usually vivid colors" is "not marked by a variety of usually vivid colors." All of the words in the antonym list fit that meaning. The word *colorless* means "lacking an addition of color." The other antonyms, *monochromatic, monochromic, monotone, self-colored,* and *solid,* mean "having or consisting of a single color" and so, of course, are not synonyms of *colorless.* Antonyms that are not synonymous with each other are separated by semicolons.

A Note Regarding the Number of Times a Word Will Appear in an Entry

In this thesaurus no word will appear in more than one list at any single main entry. The general vocabulary of the English language has a plethora of words with more than one sense. One sense of a multisense word in *Merriam-Webster's Intermediate Dictionary* might be exactly synonymous with a thesaurus entry's statement of shared meaning. Another sense of that same multisense word might be properly regarded as being no more than closely related to it. To avoid confusion, this thesaurus enters such words only in the entry's synonym list and not in the list of related words as well. For example, the much-used word *nice* is in the synonym list at *pleasant,* where the shared meaning is "giving pleasure or contentment to the mind or senses." *Nice* can also be found in the synonym list at *amiable,* where the shared meaning is "having an easygoing and pleasing manner especially in social situations." Since *amiable* is in the list of related words at *pleasant,* one might expect to find *nice* there as well. But finding the same word at two places in the same entry would be confusing for many users, so *nice* is included only in the list of synonyms.

Sometimes multisense words have meanings that are opposite to one another—or nearly so. For example, *Merriam-Webster's Intermediate Dictionary* defines one sense of *nervy* as "showing calm courage," or the equivalent of "fearless," and another sense of the word as "excitable, nervous." Thus, at the thesaurus entry for *nervous,* where the shared meaning for the first given sense is "feeling or showing uncomfortable feelings of uncertainty," *nervy* appears alongside of *jittery, jumpy, tense, uneasy, uptight* and several other synonyms. The list of near antonyms for this same sense of *nervous* includes *confident, self-assured, self-confident,* and *sure. Nervy* might well have been added to the list, in light of the fact that it has a sense meaning "showing calm courage." *Nervy* was omitted from the list of near antonyms to avoid unnecessary confusion.

Guide Words

Guide words are boldface words that are separated by a dot and placed at the top of each page. They are there to indicate the alphabetical range of entries on that page, thereby facilitating the user's search for entries. The first guide word is the headword of the first entry beginning on that page, and the second guide word is the headword of the page's final entry.

A

aback *adv* without warning ⟨completely taken *aback* by the neighbors' announcement that they were moving⟩ — see UNAWARES

abaft *adv* near, toward, or in the stern of a ship or the tail of an aircraft ⟨The lookout in the crow's nest warned that there was an enemy frigate *abaft* and bearing down hard on their ship.⟩ — see AFT

abaft *prep* at, to, or toward the rear of ⟨A school of porpoises swam *abaft* the fishing boat.⟩ — see BEHIND 1

abandon *n* carefree freedom from constraint ⟨She added spices to the stew with complete *abandon*.⟩
synonyms abandonment, ease, lightheartedness, naturalness, spontaneity, spontaneousness, unrestraint
related words ardor, enthusiasm, exuberance, fervor, spirit, warmth, zeal, zealotry, zealousness; carelessness, heedlessness, impulsiveness, indiscretion, insouciance, recklessness, thoughtlessness; unself-consciousness; casualness, offhandedness; excess, indulgence, licentiousness, permissiveness, wantonness, wildness; blank check, free hand
near antonyms embarrassment, reserve, reticence, self-consciousness, uneasiness; inhibition, repression, self-restraint, suppression; carefulness, discreetness, discretion, heedfulness; discipline, self-control, self-denial, self-discipline, willpower
antonyms constraint, restraint

abandon *vb* 1 to give (oneself) over to something especially unrestrainedly ⟨more than ready to *abandon* himself to a life of complete idleness for the duration of his vacation⟩
synonyms deliver, give up, indulge, surrender, yield
related words overdo, overindulge; bask, luxuriate, revel, roll, wallow
near antonyms abstain (from), eschew, forbear, forgo (*also* forego), refrain (from); check, inhibit, restrain
antonyms deny
2 to cause to remain behind ⟨He *abandoned* the group that he had been hiking with and struck out on his own.⟩ — see LEAVE 1
3 to put an end to (something planned or previously agreed to) ⟨The bad weather forced NASA to *abandon* the launch.⟩ — see CANCEL 1
4 to stop doing (something) permanently ⟨customs that were *abandoned* decades ago⟩ — see QUIT 2

abandoned *adj* 1 left unoccupied or unused ⟨She consciously avoided walking past the *abandoned* house, with its broken windows and sagging porch.⟩
synonyms derelict, deserted, desolate, disused, forgotten, forsaken, rejected, vacant, vacated, void
related words ignored, neglected, unattended, untended; castaway, cast-off, discarded, jettisoned, junked, refuse, waste; godforsaken, miserable, shabby, wretched; empty, idle
near antonyms reclaimed, recovered, redeemed, rescued, retrieved, salvaged, saved; reconditioned, rehabbed, rehabilitated, restored; repeopled
2 showing no signs of being under control ⟨wild, *abandoned* dancing that shocked the staid chaperones at the school dance⟩ — see RAMPANT 1

abandonment *n* 1 carefree freedom from constraint ⟨She sang at the top of her lungs with complete *abandonment* in the shower.⟩ — see ABANDON
2 the act of abandoning ⟨The law says *abandonment* by the owner of any building for more than a year entitles the city to sell it.⟩ — see DERELICTION 1

3 the act of putting an end to something planned or previously agreed to ⟨The park commissioner cited cost considerations as the main reason for the project's *abandonment*.⟩ — see CANCELLATION

abase *vb* 1 to lower in character, dignity, or quality ⟨He was unwilling to *abase* himself by pleading guilty to a crime that he did not commit.⟩ — see DEBASE 1
2 to reduce to a lower standing in one's own eyes or in others' eyes ⟨I certainly don't *abase* myself when I do good, honest manual labor.⟩ — see HUMBLE

abash *vb* to throw into a state of self-conscious distress ⟨messing up in front of an audience *abashed* her.⟩ — see EMBARRASS 1

abashment *n* the emotional state of being made self-consciously uncomfortable ⟨He spoke with a touch of *abashment* about his mistake.⟩ — see EMBARRASSMENT 1

abate *vb* 1 to grow less in scope or intensity especially gradually ⟨Interest in the author's home *abated* as her novels waned in popularity.⟩ — see DECREASE 2
2 to make smaller in amount, volume, or extent ⟨A couple of aspirin should *abate* the pain.⟩ — see DECREASE 1
3 to put an end to by formal action ⟨asked the appellate court to *abate* the lower court's ruling⟩ — see ABOLISH 1
4 to take away (an amount or number) from a total ⟨The assessor's office *abated* the taxes on the property.⟩ — see SUBTRACT

abatement *n* 1 something that is or may be subtracted ⟨entitled to a tax *abatement*⟩ — see DEDUCTION 1
2 the amount by which something is lessened ⟨There's been a significant *abatement* in noise from the floor above since the upstairs neighbors installed carpets.⟩ — see DECREASE

abbey *n* a residence for men under religious vows ⟨The monks in the *abbey* grow all their own vegetables.⟩ — see MONASTERY

abbreviate *vb* to make less in extent or duration ⟨He had to *abbreviate* his vacation in France in order to attend to a family emergency.⟩ — see SHORTEN

abbreviation *n* a shortened version of a written work ⟨a recording of musical *abbreviations* that introduces the listener to the great composers⟩ — see ABRIDGMENT

abdicate *vb* to give up (as a position of authority) formally ⟨The revolutionary government forced Nicholas II to *abdicate* the Russian throne.⟩
synonyms cede, relinquish, renounce, resign, step down (from), surrender
related words abjure, deny, disavow, disclaim, disown, waive; forsake, give up, hand over, yield; abandon, desert, quit, vacate
near antonyms appropriate, arrogate, assume, claim, confiscate; seize, take over, usurp, wrest; defend, guard, protect, safeguard, secure

abdomen *n* the part of the body between the chest and the pelvis ⟨a tiny birthmark on the baby's *abdomen*, right next to her belly button⟩ — see STOMACH 1

abduct *vb* to carry away (as a person) forcibly or unlawfully ⟨He claimed he had been *abducted* by aliens.⟩ — see KIDNAP

aberrant *adj* 1 being out of the ordinary ⟨a year of *aberrant* weather—record rainfall in the summer, record heat in the autumn⟩ — see EXCEPTIONAL 1
2 departing from some accepted standard of what is normal ⟨*Aberrant* behavior can be a sign of rabies in a wild animal.⟩ — see DEVIANT

aberration *n* something that is different from what is ordinary or expected ⟨There are some slight *aberrations* in the type due to the nature of old printing presses.⟩ — see ANOMALY 1

abet *vb* **1** to bring (something volatile or intense) into being ⟨the discovery that erosion *abetted* the forest's decline⟩ — see INCITE 1
2 to provide (someone) with what is useful or necessary to achieve an end ⟨Car thieves are often unwittingly *abetted* by owners foolishly leaving the keys in the ignition.⟩ — see HELP 1

abetment *n* an act or instance of helping ⟨an *abetment* of the crime⟩ — see HELP 1

abettor *also* **abetter** *n* **1** one associated with another in wrongdoing ⟨The man who drove the getaway car in the bank robbery was arrested as an aider and *abettor*.⟩ — see ACCOMPLICE
2 someone associated with another to give assistance or moral support ⟨Without all the neighborhood kids as *abettors*, I would never have gotten all my chickens back in their coop.⟩ — see ALLY

abeyance *n* a state of temporary inactivity ⟨Our weekend plans were held in *abeyance* until we could get a weather forecast.⟩
synonyms doldrums, dormancy, holding pattern, latency, moratorium, quiescence, suspense, suspension
related words inaction, inertia, inertness, motionlessness; impasse, standstill; coma, hibernation, hypnosis, repose, rest, sleep, slumber; recess, recession, remission; idleness, layoff
near antonyms recommencement, renewal, resumption, resuscitation
antonyms continuance, continuation

abhor *vb* to dislike strongly ⟨He *abhors* the way people leave their trash at the picnic sites in the park.⟩ — see HATE

abhorrence *n* **1** something or someone that is hated ⟨Driving in heavy traffic is a particular *abhorrence* of mine.⟩ — see HATE 2
2 a very strong dislike ⟨my firm *abhorrence* of all forms of hypocrisy⟩ — see HATE 1

abhorrent *adj* **1** causing intense displeasure, disgust, or resentment ⟨He considers it *abhorrent* the way she keeps her dogs penned up all the time.⟩ — see OFFENSIVE 1
2 feeling or showing open dislike for someone or something regarded as undeserving of respect or concern ⟨She's *abhorrent* of the nonsense that the tabloid media pass off as news.⟩ — see CONTEMPTUOUS 1

abidance *n* **1** the following of a custom, rule, or law ⟨The FDA requires strict *abidance* by food manufacturers of its definitions for certain terms used on product labels.⟩ — see OBSERVANCE 1
2 uninterrupted or lasting existence ⟨the reassuring *abidance* of their friendship through times both good and bad⟩ — see CONTINUATION

abide *vb* **1** to continue to be in a place for a significant amount of time ⟨He refused to *abide* where it was clear that he wasn't wanted.⟩ — see ¹STAY 1
2 to have a home ⟨the charming fantasy that fairies *abide* in the cup-shaped flowers dotting the woodland floor⟩ — see LIVE 1
3 to put up with (something painful or difficult) ⟨cannot *abide* being in huge crowds⟩ — see BEAR 2
4 to remain indefinitely in existence or in the same state ⟨The village's once-honored ways no longer *abide* and now exist only in the memories of a few elders.⟩ — see CONTINUE 1

abiding *adj* having an existence or validity that does not change or diminish ⟨I have an *abiding* interest in animal welfare—it's not just a phase I'm going through.⟩

synonyms ageless, continuing, dateless, enduring, eternal, everlasting, immortal, imperishable, lasting, ongoing, perennial, perpetual, timeless, undying
related words ceaseless, endless, permanent; changeless, constant, stable, stationary, steady, unchanging, unvarying
near antonyms antiquated, archaic, dated, obsolete, outdated, outmoded, out-of-date, outworn, passé

ability *n* the physical or mental power to do something ⟨As a result of the accident the once-vigorous athlete lost the *ability* to walk.⟩
synonyms capability, capacity, competence, competency, faculty
related words aptitude, aptness, endowment, equipment, facility, gift, knack, talent; address, adroitness, deftness, dexterity, hand, skill; gray matter, instinct, intelligence, ken, reason, understanding; might, potency, staying power; adequacy, effectiveness, effectualness, fitness, form, influence, resourcefulness, usefulness; means, resources, wherewithal
near antonyms helplessness, impotence, paralysis, powerlessness, weakness; defectiveness, deficiency, inadequacy, ineffectiveness, ineffectuality, ineffectualness, inefficaciousness, inefficacy, uselessness; debilitation, disablement, impairment, incapacitation
antonyms disability, inability, incapability, incapableness, incapacity, incompetence, ineptitude, ineptness

abjure *vb* **1** to solemnly or formally reject or go back on (as something formerly adhered to) ⟨The woman *abjured* some long-held beliefs when she converted to another religion.⟩
synonyms recant, renege, renounce, repeal, repudiate, retract, take back, unsay, withdraw
related words contradict, deny, disavow, disclaim, disown, gainsay, negate, negative; abandon, bolt, forsake, give up, relinquish, spurn, surrender; disagree (with), disprove, dispute, rebut, refute; back down, back off, backtrack; disallow, recall, revoke
near antonyms acknowledge, admit, affirm, assert, avow, claim, contend, declare, maintain, proclaim, profess, state, vouch, vow; back, confirm, defend, endorse (*also* indorse), espouse, maintain, support, uphold; accept, adopt, embrace
antonyms adhere (to)
2 to resist the temptation of ⟨a strict religious sect that *abjures* the luxuries, comforts, and conveniences of the modern world⟩ — see FORBEAR

ablaze *adj* **1** being on fire ⟨The entire block was *ablaze* by the time firefighters arrived.⟩
synonyms afire, aflame, blazing, burning, combusting, fiery, flaming, ignited, inflamed (*also* enflamed), kindled
related words aglow, flickering, glowing, live, smoldering (*or* smouldering); broiling, hot, piping hot, red-hot, roasting, scalding, scorching, searing, sizzling; burned (*or* burnt), charred, incinerated, scorched, seared, singed
near antonyms choked, damped, dead, doused (*also* dowsed), extinguished, quenched, smothered, snuffed (out), stamped (out), suffocated
2 filled with much light ⟨That night the ballroom, *ablaze* with light, looked very different from the curtained room it usually was by day.⟩ — see BRIGHT 2

able *adj* having the required skills for an acceptable level of performance ⟨looking for an *able* and reliable assistant⟩ — see COMPETENT 1

able–bodied *adj* enjoying health and vigor ⟨Every *able-bodied* citizen volunteered to help.⟩ — see HEALTHY 1

ably *adv* in a skillful or expert manner ⟨*ably* maneuvered the boat up to the dock⟩ — see WELL 3

abnormal *adj* **1** being out of the ordinary ⟨a completely *abnormal* school day, because half of the kids were out sick⟩ — see EXCEPTIONAL 1

2 departing from some accepted standard of what is normal ⟨We noticed his *abnormal* breathing and took him to the emergency room.⟩ — see DEVIANT

abnormality *n* **1** a person, thing, or event that is far from normal ⟨The *abnormalities* in the tree's leaves are caused by disease.⟩ — see FREAK 1

2 something that is different from what is ordinary or expected ⟨Let the vet know if you notice any *abnormalities* in your pet's behavior.⟩ — see ANOMALY 1

abode *n* the place where one lives ⟨Welcome to my humble *abode*.⟩ — see HOME 1

abolish *vb* **1** to put an end to by formal action ⟨The U.S. *abolished* slavery by constitutional amendment on December 6, 1865.⟩

synonyms abate, abrogate, annul, avoid, cancel, dissolve, invalidate, negate, null, nullify, quash, repeal, rescind, vacate, void

related words countermand, override, overrule, overturn, veto; abort, call, call off, drop, recall, retract, reverse, revoke, suspend, withdraw; ban, enjoin, forbid, outlaw, prohibit; disallow, dismiss, reject; annihilate, break down, eliminate, eradicate, liquidate, remove, throw out, write off

phrases do away with, set aside

near antonyms enact, lay down, legislate; establish, found, institute; formalize, legalize, legitimate, legitimize, validate; pass, ratify; allow, approve, authorize, clear, endorse (*also* indorse), permit, sanction, warrant; command, decree, mandate, order, prescribe

2 to destroy all traces of ⟨If only there were a way that we could *abolish* hatred and intolerance.⟩ — see ANNIHILATE 1

abominable *adj* causing intense displeasure, disgust, or resentment ⟨Your table manners are *abominable!*⟩ — see OFFENSIVE 1

abominate *vb* to dislike strongly ⟨I *abominate* this hot, humid weather!⟩ — see HATE

abomination *n* **1** something or someone that is hated ⟨Some of the town's residents declared the ultramodern new building to be an *abomination*.⟩ — see HATE 2

2 a very strong dislike ⟨The townspeople have such an *abomination* of taxes that they have even voted down increases that would have given their schools badly needed funds.⟩ — see HATE 1

aboriginal *adj* belonging to a particular place by birth or origin ⟨The *aboriginal* peoples of northern Alaska are known as Inupiats.⟩ — see NATIVE 1

aboriginal *n* a member of the first people to inhabit a region ⟨The band's distinctive sound comes from instruments used for centuries by the *aboriginals*.⟩ — see ABORIGINE

aborigine *n* a member of the first people to inhabit a region ⟨The *aborigines* had no immunity against the raft of diseases brought by the invaders.⟩

synonyms aboriginal

near antonyms alien, foreigner

antonyms nonnative

abort *vb* to put an end to (something planned or previously agreed to) ⟨had to *abort* the mission to Mars when they lost contact with the satellite⟩ — see CANCEL 1

abortion *n* the act of putting an end to something planned or previously agreed to ⟨The *abortion* of the space mission caused the whole space program to be reexamined.⟩ — see CANCELLATION

abortive *adj* producing no results ⟨an *abortive* attempt to recover the sunken pirate ship⟩ — see FUTILE

abound *vb* to be copiously supplied ⟨a city that *abounds* with art museums and private galleries⟩

synonyms brim, bristle, bulge, burst, bustle, buzz, crawl, hum, overflow, swarm, teem

near antonyms lack, need, want

abounding *adj* possessing or covered with great numbers or amounts of something specified ⟨a city *abounding* with inviting parks⟩ — see RIFE

about *adv* **1** on all sides or in every direction ⟨people standing *about* waiting for a salesclerk to assist them⟩ — see AROUND 1

2 toward the opposite direction ⟨He turned *about* and saw the dog following him.⟩ — see AROUND 2

3 very close to but not completely ⟨I'm *about* finished.⟩ — see ALMOST

about *prep* **1** having to do with ⟨a poignant story *about* a young man who goes off to war⟩

synonyms apropos, apropos of, concerning, of, on, regarding, respecting, touching, toward (*or* towards)

related words over

phrases in regard to, in respect to, in view of, with regard to, with respect to

2 close to ⟨*About* the hedge there was a picket fence.⟩ — see AROUND 1

3 in random positions within the boundaries of ⟨sparrows hopping *about* the lawn near the bird feeder⟩ — see AROUND 2

above *adv* to or in a higher place ⟨We eventually got used to the planes constantly flying *above*.⟩

synonyms aloft, over, overhead

related words skyward, upward (*or* upwards)

near antonyms underneath

antonyms below, beneath, under

above *n* a dwelling place of perfect happiness for the soul after death ⟨She wrote about being visited by an angel from *above*.⟩ — see HEAVEN 1

above *prep* higher than ⟨One minute our kite was *above* the telephone wires; the next minute it was tangled in them.⟩

synonyms over

related words atop

near antonyms underneath

antonyms below, beneath, under

abracadabra *n* **1** a spoken word or set of words believed to have magic power ⟨Originally, an *abracadabra* was a cryptogram of the word "abracadabra" that was repeated in diminishing form until it disappeared entirely—supposedly just like the targeted evil or misfortune.⟩ — see SPELL 1

2 unintelligible or meaningless talk ⟨After some *abracadabra* the spiritualist announced that we had made contact with "the other side."⟩ — see GIBBERISH 1

abrade *vb* **1** to damage or diminish by continued friction ⟨Ropes *abraded* by the rocks were a huge danger to the climbers.⟩

synonyms chafe, erode, fray, frazzle, fret, gall, rasp, rub, wear

related words file, grate, graze, grind, nibble, sandblast, sandpaper, scour, scrape, scuff, shave; reduce, rub out, wear out, wipe (away); bite, break down, break up, chew, corrode, decompose, disintegrate, dissolve, eat; hone, sharpen, whet

2 to make sore by continued rubbing ⟨skin *abraded* by shaving⟩ — see CHAFE 1

3 to damage by rubbing against a sharp or rough surface ⟨The yacht's once-flawless wooden hull had been badly *abraded* by years of rough dockings.⟩ — see SCRAPE 2

abrasion *n* an area of skin roughened or worn away by harsh rubbing against another surface ⟨walked away from the accident with only minor *abrasions*⟩

synonyms bruise, graze, scrape

related words bedsore, gall

abreast *adj* having information especially as a result of study or experience ⟨keeping *abreast* of the latest developments⟩ — see FAMILIAR 2

abridge *vb* to make less in extent or duration ⟨The library's hours have been drastically *abridged* to cut costs.⟩ — see SHORTEN

abridgment *or* **abridgement** *n* a shortened version of a written work ⟨This Italian-English pocket dictionary is an *abridgment* of the hardback edition.⟩
    synonyms abbreviation, condensation, digest
    related words abstract, brief, capsule, outline, overview, précis, recap, recapitulation, résumé (*or* resume *also* resumé), review, sketch, sum, summarization, summary, summation, survey, syllabus, synopsis, wrap-up
    near antonyms amplification, elaboration, enlargement, expansion

abrogate *vb* to put an end to by formal action ⟨The Congress *abrogated* the old treaty.⟩ — see ABOLISH 1

abrupt *adj* **1** being or characterized by direct, brief, and potentially rude speech or manner ⟨The policeman's *abrupt* manner discouraged me from trying to claim that I hadn't seen the red light.⟩ — see BLUNT 1
    2 having an incline approaching the perpendicular ⟨The gentle, rolling hills gradually give way to high mountains with *abrupt* sides.⟩ — see STEEP 1
    3 not expected ⟨His *abrupt* reappearance seems to have caught everyone off guard.⟩ — see UNEXPECTED

abruptly *adv* with great suddenness ⟨The car in front stopped *abruptly*, and we almost hit it.⟩ — see SHORT

abscond *vb* to get free from a dangerous or confining situation ⟨The burglar was trying to *abscond* with the jewels when he tumbled down the stairs.⟩ — see ESCAPE 1

absence *n* **1** a state of being without something necessary, desirable, or useful ⟨The *absence* of volunteers is putting the program in jeopardy.⟩ — see NEED 1
    2 the fact or state of being absent ⟨In the *absence* of ferry service to the island, the ecotourists had to charter a plane.⟩ — see LACK 1

absent *adj* **1** not at a certain place ⟨Three students were *absent* because of the flu.⟩
    synonyms away, missing, out
    related words AWOL, truant; departed, gone, retired; abroad, vacationing
    near antonyms accompanying, attending, participating
    antonyms here, in, present
    2 not present or in evidence ⟨The city's usual stir of activity was conspicuously *absent* due to the report of an escaped lion from the zoo.⟩
    synonyms lacking, missing, nonexistent, wanting
    related words dead, departed, extinct, lost, perished, vanished; defunct, done, expired, finished, lapsed, obsolete, over, passé; inadequate, insufficient, rare, scarce, sparse, uncommon
    near antonyms active, alive, animate, living, thriving; current, going, prevailing, uncanceled; common, prevalent; apparent, conspicuous, evident, obvious, plain
    antonyms existent, present
    3 lost in thought and unaware of one's surroundings or actions ⟨seemed *absent* when I told him you were coming because he nodded but didn't say anything⟩ — see ABSENTMINDED 1

absent *prep* not having ⟨*Absent* a significant source of investment funds, the fledgling company continues to struggle.⟩ — see WITHOUT 1

absentminded *adj* **1** lost in thought and unaware of one's surroundings or actions ⟨I was so *absentminded* I lost track of the time.⟩
    synonyms absent, abstracted, distracted, preoccupied
    related words absorbed, daydreaming, dreaming, dreamy, engrossed, faraway, intent, pensive, rapt; heedless, inattentive, insensible, oblivious, unaware, unconscious, unheeding, unknowing, unmindful, unthinking, unwary, unwitting, vacant; befogged, befuddled, bewildered, confused, dazed, flighty, foggy, forgetful, forgetting, hazy, muddled, scatterbrained, unfocused (*also* unfocussed)
    near antonyms alive, attentive, aware, conscious, engaged, heedful, mindful, observant, observing, openeyed, sharp, vigilant, wary, watchful, wide-awake; clearheaded
    antonyms alert
    2 inclined to forget what one has learned or to do what one should ⟨an *absentminded* uncle who some years sends me two birthday checks⟩ — see FORGETFUL

absolute *adj* **1** exercising power or authority without interference by others ⟨an *absolute* monarchy⟩
    synonyms arbitrary, autocratic (*also* autocratical), despotic, dictatorial, tyrannical (*also* tyrannic), tyrannous
    related words authoritarian, jackbooted, oppressive, totalitarian; antidemocratic, antirepublican; high-handed; domineering, imperious, masterful; all-powerful, almighty, omnipotent; autonomous, self-governing, selfruling, sovereign (*also* sovran); unconditional, unlimited
    near antonyms circumscribed, restrained, restricted; constitutional, lawful; democratic, republican
    antonyms limited
    2 having no exceptions or restrictions ⟨Ironing is an *absolute* bore.⟩ ⟨I want the *absolute* truth.⟩
    synonyms all-out, arrant, blank, categorical (*also* categoric), clean, complete, consummate, dead, deadly, definite, downright, dreadful, fair, flat, out-and-out, outright, perfect, plumb, profound, pure, rank, regular, sheer, simple, stark, thorough, thoroughgoing, total, unadulterated, unalloyed, unconditional, unmitigated, unqualified, utter, very
    related words authentic, classic, genuine, real, veritable; constant, endless, eternal, perpetual, undying, unremitting; extreme, unrestricted; confirmed, habitual, hopeless, inveterate; extraordinary, frightful, horrible, huge, main, superlative, supreme, surpassing, terrible, terrific
    near antonyms doubtful, dubious, equivocal, qualified, questionable, restricted, uncertain
    3 being entirely without fault or flaw ⟨a formal living room decorated with *absolute* taste⟩ — see PERFECT 1
    4 free from added matter ⟨*absolute* alcohol⟩ — see PURE 1
    5 serving to put an end to all debate or questioning ⟨*absolute* proof of her innocence⟩ — see CONCLUSIVE 1

absolution *n* release from the guilt or penalty of an offense ⟨The jury's verdict of "not guilty" was *absolution* in the eyes of the law.⟩ — see PARDON

absolve *vb* to free from a charge of wrongdoing ⟨With her sad eyes, I couldn't help but *absolve* my puppy of chewing my shoes.⟩ — see EXCULPATE

absorb *vb* **1** to take in (something liquid) through small openings ⟨Most of the spilled water was *absorbed* by the tablecloth.⟩
    synonyms drink, imbibe, soak (up), sponge, suck (up), take up
    related words gulp, guzzle, quaff, sip, slurp, swallow, swig, swill
    2 to hold the attention of ⟨Chatting on the phone doesn't *absorb* me so much that I can't do something else at the same time.⟩ — see ENGAGE 1
    3 to make a part of a body or system ⟨The large corporation *absorbed* smaller businesses in takeovers.⟩ — see EMBODY 1
    4 to make complete use of ⟨Cleaning the house *absorbed* the rest of his energy.⟩ — see DEPLETE 1

5 to put up with (something painful or difficult) ⟨Somehow she managed to *absorb* whatever hardships life offered.⟩ — see BEAR 2

absorbed *adj* having the mind fixed on something ⟨Lori was so *absorbed* in her book that she didn't hear the bell ring.⟩ — see ATTENTIVE 1

absorbent *also* **absorbant** *adj* able to soak up liquids especially readily ⟨highly *absorbent* material that is really good for wiping off automobiles⟩
synonyms bibulous, spongy, thirsty
related words osmotic
antonyms nonabsorbent

absorbing *adj* holding the attention or provoking interest ⟨Shell collecting can be so *absorbing* that you don't notice the tide coming in.⟩ — see INTERESTING

absorption *n* a focusing of the mind on something ⟨He forgot to return the phone call due to his *absorption* in setting up the new computer system.⟩ — see ATTENTION 1

abstain (from) *vb* to resist the temptation of ⟨The patient had to *abstain from* solid food before her surgery.⟩ — see FORBEAR

abstemious *adj* given to or marked by restraint in the satisfaction of one's appetites ⟨Being *abstemious* diners, they avoid restaurants with all-you-can-eat buffets.⟩
synonyms abstinent, continent, sober, temperate
related words ascetic (*also* ascetical), austere; disciplined, self-controlled, self-disciplined
near antonyms gluttonous, greedy, rapacious, voracious; self-pleasing, sensual

abstinent *adj* given to or marked by restraint in the satisfaction of one's appetites ⟨I grew up in a family where *abstinent* behavior was expected and self-indulgence was discouraged.⟩ — see ABSTEMIOUS

abstract *adj* **1** dealing with or expressing a quality or idea ⟨The book deals with *abstract* matters such as honesty and integrity on the job.⟩
synonyms conceptual, ideal, metaphysical, theoretical (*also* theoretic)
related words conjectural, hypothetical, speculative; cosmic (*also* cosmical), intellectual, mental, spiritual; ethereal, immaterial, incorporeal, insubstantial, nonmaterial, nonphysical, unsubstantial; impalpable, imperceptible, insensible, intangible; impractical, romantic, unreal, utopian, visionary
near antonyms material, physical; appreciable, detectable, discernible (*also* discernable), noticeable, observable, palpable, perceptible, sensible, substantial, tangible, visible; defined, definite, distinct; actual, factual, real
antonyms concrete, nonabstract
2 using elements of form (as color, line, or texture) with little or no attempt at creating a realistic picture ⟨Cubism is a style of *abstract* art in which natural forms are broken up into geometric shapes.⟩
synonyms nonobjective, nonrealistic
related words expressionist, expressionistic, impressionist, impressionistic; symbolist, symbolistic
near antonyms lifelike, natural
antonyms figurative, nonabstract, objective, realistic

abstract *n* **1** a short statement of the main points ⟨The scientist wrote a bare-bones *abstract* of his research and conclusions.⟩ — see SUMMARY
2 a visible representation of something abstract (as a quality) ⟨a recent college valedictorian who's been hailed as the very *abstract* of what's right with today's young people⟩ — see EMBODIMENT

abstract *vb* **1** to draw the attention or mind to something else ⟨Personal problems *abstracted* him so persistently that he struggled to keep his mind on his work.⟩ — see DISTRACT 1

2 to make into a short statement of the main points (as of a report) ⟨I took the 135-page report and *abstracted* it in three short paragraphs.⟩ — see SUMMARIZE

abstracted *adj* lost in thought and unaware of one's surroundings or actions ⟨The man on the train seemed somewhat *abstracted*, and he did indeed forget to get off at his stop.⟩ — see ABSENTMINDED 1

abstruse *adj* difficult for one of ordinary knowledge or intelligence to understand ⟨You're not the only one who finds Einstein's theory of relativity *abstruse*.⟩ — see PROFOUND 1

absurd *adj* **1** conceived or made without regard for reason or reality ⟨*absurd* claims of having been abducted by UFO's⟩ — see FANTASTIC 1
2 showing or marked by a lack of good sense or judgment ⟨an *absurd* rule that bicycles are not allowed in the park⟩ — see FOOLISH 1
3 so foolish or pointless as to be worthy of scornful laughter ⟨It's *absurd* to expect to make a killing in the stock market overnight.⟩ — see RIDICULOUS 1

absurdity *n* **1** a foolish act or idea ⟨the *absurdity* of putting a squirrel on a leash⟩ — see FOLLY 1
2 lack of good sense or judgment ⟨the *absurdity* of such a complicated plan⟩ — see FOOLISHNESS 1

abundance *n* **1** a considerable amount ⟨an *abundance* of flowers for the wedding⟩ ⟨I grew up with an *abundance* of cousins.⟩ — see LOT 2
2 an amount or supply more than sufficient to meet one's needs ⟨We have an *abundance* of food, so eat as much as you want.⟩ — see PLENTY 1

abundant *adj* **1** being more than enough without being excessive ⟨volunteers providing *abundant* help⟩ — see PLENTIFUL
2 possessing or covered with great numbers or amounts of something specified ⟨a savory soup that is *abundant* with kale, potatoes, and linguica⟩ — see RIFE

abuse *n* **1** harsh insulting language ⟨Hometown fans hurled *abuse* at the visiting team.⟩
synonyms fulmination, invective, vitriol, vituperation
related words blasphemy, curse; epithet, insult, putdown, slur; expletive, swearword; aspersion, bad-mouthing, belittlement, disparagement, revilement, vilification; castigation, chastisement, criticism, excoriation, opprobrium, rebuke, reprimand, reproof; broadside, diatribe, harangue, polemic, tirade
near antonyms acclaim, applause, commendation, praise; compliments, congratulations, endearments, felicitations; adulation, blarney, flattery, overpraise, soft soap
2 incorrect or improper use ⟨The furniture had received a lot of *abuse* from the generations of kids in the family.⟩ — see MISUSE

abuse *vb* **1** to inflict physical or emotional harm upon ⟨adopted a dog that had been *abused*⟩
synonyms bully, ill-treat, ill-use, maltreat, manhandle, mishandle, mistreat, misuse
related words molest, outrage, violate; harm, hurt, injure, oppress, persecute, torment, torture; burn, victimize, wrong; beat (up), mess (up), rough (up), work (over)
phrases take apart
near antonyms care (for), cherish, foster, nurture; baby, cater (to), coddle, favor, gratify, humor, indulge, mollycoddle, pamper, spoil
2 to criticize harshly and usually publicly ⟨a demanding, difficult patient who constantly *abuses* the nurses and aides⟩ — see ATTACK 2
3 to put to a bad or improper use ⟨If you *abuse* your baseball bat by using it to hammer nails, don't expect it to last long.⟩ — see MISAPPLY

4 to take unfair advantage of ⟨He *abused* his parents' trust.⟩ — see EXPLOIT 1

abusive *adj* marked by harsh insulting language ⟨He invariably launches *abusive* attacks against anyone who dares to challenge him.⟩
synonyms invective, opprobrious, scurrilous, truculent
related words affronting, insulting, offending, offensive, outrageous, outraging; coarse, crude, dirty, filthy, foul, foulmouthed, gross, indecent, nasty, obscene, pottymouthed, vulgar; contemptuous, disdainful, scornful; defamatory, libelous (*or* libellous), scandalous, slanderous; maligning, traducing, vilifying; hateful, malevolent, malicious, spiteful; immoderate, intemperate, unbridled, unrestrained
near antonyms moderate, temperate; deferential, respectful; civil, courteous, gracious, mannerly, polite; discreet, judicious, tempered; laudatory, praiseful

abut *vb* to be adjacent to ⟨Our land *abuts* a nature preserve, so we see a lot of wildlife.⟩ — see ADJOIN 1

abutting *adj* having a border in common ⟨The new neighbors promptly erected fences between their property and the *abutting* properties.⟩ — see ADJACENT

abysmal *adj* extending far downward ⟨tried to see into the *abysmal* reaches of the cave⟩ — see DEEP 1

abyss *n* an immeasurable depth or space ⟨Looking down at the dark ocean from the ship's rail, the cruise passenger felt as though he was staring into an *abyss*.⟩
synonyms chasm, deep, gulf, ocean
related words cleft, crevasse, crevice, fissure; cavern, hole, hollow, pit; breadth, expanse, extent, reach, spread, stretch; emptiness, vacancy, vacuum, void

academic *also* **academical** *adj* **1** of or relating to schooling or learning especially at an advanced level ⟨"If you spent more time in *academic* pursuits and less time in social ones, you could easily make good grades," the dean told Valerie.⟩
synonyms educational, intellectual, scholarly, scholastic
related words bookish, nerdy, pedantic, professorial, tweedy; curricular; educative, instructive; collegiate, graduate, postgraduate
near antonyms extracurricular
antonyms nonacademic, noneducational, unacademic, unscholarly
2 existing only as an assumption or speculation ⟨Your arguments are merely *academic*—such a worst-case scenario is unlikely to ever occur.⟩ — see THEORETICAL 1

academy *n* a place or establishment for teaching and learning ⟨a military *academy*⟩ ⟨an *academy* of the fine arts⟩ — see SCHOOL

accede *vb* to give or express one's approval (as to a proposal) ⟨The teacher finally *acceded* to their pleas for more time to complete the project.⟩
synonyms acquiesce, agree, assent, come round, consent
related words adopt, embrace, espouse; abide, bear (with), endure, stand, suffer, tolerate; stomach, swallow, take; bow, knuckle under, relent, submit, succumb, yield
near antonyms rebuff, refuse, reject, scorn, spurn; deny, gainsay
antonyms dissent

accelerate *vb* **1** to become greater in extent, volume, amount, or number ⟨Toy purchases *accelerate* dramatically during the holiday season.⟩ — see INCREASE 2
2 to cause to move or proceed fast or faster ⟨We *accelerated* preparations as the wedding date approached.⟩ — see HURRY 1
3 to make greater in size, amount, or number ⟨The company *accelerated* its advertising purchases even as

the economy appeared to be in recession.⟩ — see INCREASE 1

accent *n* a special notice or importance given to something ⟨Although we dutifully carried binoculars on our bird walk, the *accent* was on recognizing birds by their song.⟩ — see EMPHASIS 1

accent *vb* to indicate the importance of by centering attention on ⟨The town's promotional literature *accents* its vital role in American history.⟩ — see EMPHASIZE 1

accentuate *vb* **1** to indicate the importance of by centering attention on ⟨Let's *accentuate* the saxophones during this piece by having the sax players stand up.⟩ — see EMPHASIZE 1
2 to make markedly greater in measure or degree ⟨The warm weather *accentuated* my spring fever.⟩ — see INTENSIFY
3 to make more apparent ⟨The new bedspread *accentuates* the blue tones of the wallpaper.⟩ — see EMPHASIZE 2

accentuation *n* a special notice or importance given to something ⟨The school's *accentuation* on math skills has resulted in its students being among the highest math scorers in the state.⟩ — see EMPHASIS 1

accept *vb* **1** to agree to receive whether willingly or reluctantly ⟨Some merchants in town will *accept* Canadian coins.⟩ — see TAKE 2
2 to have a favorable opinion of ⟨Most of the employees *accepted* the new work schedule.⟩ — see APPROVE (OF)
3 to regard as right or true ⟨The treatment is now *accepted* by many doctors.⟩ — see BELIEVE 1
4 to take to or upon oneself ⟨*accepted* the responsibility of sending out the invitations⟩ — see ASSUME 1
5 to put up with (something painful or difficult) ⟨He *accepted* the setback without complaint.⟩ — see BEAR 2

acceptability *n* the quality or state of meeting one's needs adequately ⟨The *acceptability* of a broken key or two on a secondhand piano might depend on which keys are broken.⟩ — see SUFFICIENCY

acceptable *adj* of a level of quality that meets one's needs or standards ⟨They found the accommodations *acceptable*.⟩ — see ADEQUATE

acceptably *adv* in a satisfactory way ⟨The previous renters had left the cottage's kitchen *acceptably* clean.⟩ — see WELL 1

access *n* **1** a sudden experiencing of a physical or mental disorder ⟨A sudden *access* of hay fever was making him feel miserable.⟩ — see ATTACK 2
2 the means or right of entering or participating in ⟨In the evening the only *access* to the building is through the side door.⟩ — see ENTRANCE 1

access *vb* to go or come in or into ⟨The bank's new system makes it easier to *access* your account information.⟩ — see ENTER 1

accessible *adj* **1** being within the financial means of most people ⟨a store offering stylish clothes at *accessible* prices⟩
synonyms affordable, popular
related words budget, cheap, discount, inexpensive, low; moderate, modest, reasonable
near antonyms costly, dear, expensive, high
2 possible to get ⟨The website is not *accessible* without your password.⟩ — see AVAILABLE 1
3 situated within easy reach ⟨The elevator makes the upper floors *accessible* to the disabled.⟩ — see CONVENIENT

accessory *adj* available to supply something extra when needed ⟨Most phone services offer *accessory* features such as call-waiting.⟩ — see AUXILIARY

accessory *also* **accessary** *n* **1** something that is not nec-

essary in itself but adds to the convenience or performance of the main piece of equipment ⟨We bought a new car with lots of high-tech *accessories*.⟩
synonyms accoutrement (*or* accouterment), adapter (*also* adaptor), adjunct, appendage, appliance, attachment, option
related words accompaniment, additive, complement, supplement; auxiliary, subsidiary; amenity, extra, filler, frill, incidental, luxury, nonessential, nonnecessity; appurtenances, bells and whistles, equipment, furnishings, paraphernalia, trappings; adornment, decoration, embellishment, enhancement, ornament, trim, trimming
near antonyms essential, necessity, requirement, requisite
2 one associated with another in wrongdoing ⟨The driver of the getaway car was charged as an *accessory* in the robbery case.⟩ — see ACCOMPLICE

accident *n* **1** a chance and usually sudden event bringing loss or injury ⟨She was involved in a minor *accident* on her way home from work.⟩
synonyms casualty, mischance, mishap
related words calamity, cataclysm, catastrophe, deathblow, disaster, tragedy; bummer, knock, misadventure, misfortune; collision, crack-up, crash, smashup, wreck
near antonyms boon, break, godsend, miracle, strike, windfall; fortune, luck, serendipity
2 the uncertain course of events ⟨You shouldn't leave it to *accident* to decide where you'll be lodging in the course of your trip across the country.⟩ — see CHANCE 1

accidental *adj* **1** happening by chance ⟨Finding the gold was all the more remarkable because its discovery was entirely *accidental*.⟩
synonyms casual, chance, fluky (*also* flukey), fortuitous, inadvertent, incidental, unintended, unintentional, unplanned, unpremeditated, unwitting
related words coincidental; freak, odd; aimless, arbitrary, desultory, haphazard, random; uncertain, unexpected, unforeseeable, unforeseen; coerced, forced, involuntary; unconscious, unprompted
near antonyms certain, destined, expected, fixed, foreordained, foreseeable, foreseen, inevitable, predestined, predetermined, predictable, preordained, prescribed, sure; conscious, freewill, knowing, unforced, voluntary, volunteer, willful (*or* wilful)
antonyms calculated, deliberate, intended, intentional, planned, premeditated, premeditative, set
2 not being a vital part of or belonging to something ⟨We're considering the painting's merit as a work of art, its commercial value being entirely *accidental* as far as we're concerned.⟩ — see EXTRINSIC

acclaim *n* public acknowledgment or admiration for an achievement ⟨Many people were involved in the search, but the person who actually found the missing girl got all the *acclaim*.⟩ — see GLORY 1

acclaim *vb* to declare enthusiastic approval of ⟨She has long been *acclaimed* by the critics for her realistic acting.⟩
synonyms accredit, applaud, cheer, crack up, hail, laud, praise, salute, tout
related words bravo, clap, rise (to); ballyhoo; approve, commend, endorse (*also* indorse), favor, recommend, root (for), support; celebrate, eulogize, extol (*also* extoll), glorify, magnify, sing; adulate, belaud, flatter, overpraise; deify, idolize
phrases doff one's hat to (*or* doff one's cap to)
near antonyms belittle, disparage, put down; blame, censure, reprehend, reprobate; admonish, chide, criti-

cize, rebuke, reprimand, reproach, reprove; castigate, excoriate, keelhaul, lambaste (*or* lambast), skewer, vilify
antonyms knock, pan, slam

acclamation *n* enthusiastic and usually public expression of approval ⟨The young piano prodigy has received *acclamation* from audiences worldwide.⟩ — see APPLAUSE 1

acclimate *vb* to change (something) so as to make it suitable for a new use or situation ⟨never could *acclimate* himself to a nine-to-five office job⟩ — see ADAPT

acclimatize *vb* to change (something) so as to make it suitable for a new use or situation ⟨She had lived through several northern winters before she fully *acclimatized* her wardrobe.⟩ — see ADAPT

accolade *n* **1** a formal expression of praise ⟨For their exceptional bravery the firefighters received *accolades* from both local and national officials.⟩ — see ENCOMIUM
2 public acknowledgment or admiration for an achievement ⟨Winning the Nobel Prize for Physics is generally regarded as the highest *accolade* for a physicist.⟩ — see GLORY 1
3 something given in recognition of achievement ⟨a screen performance that won virtually every *accolade* that the film world has to offer⟩ — see AWARD 1

accommodate *vb* **1** to make or have room for ⟨The back seat *accommodates* three people comfortably.⟩
synonyms fit, hold, take
related words carry, contain, seat; enclose (*also* inclose), encompass, enfold; harbor, house
2 to bring to a state free of conflicts, inconsistencies, or differences ⟨Let's *accommodate* the difference in their voices by moving the mike closer to Sarah, whose voice is softer.⟩ — see HARMONIZE 2
3 to change (something) so as to make it suitable for a new use or situation ⟨We *accommodated* the lectern to the height of the guest speaker, who turned out to be quite tall.⟩ — see ADAPT
4 to do a service or favor for ⟨couldn't *accommodate* everyone who wanted a free T-shirt⟩ — see OBLIGE 1
5 to provide with living quarters or shelter ⟨They were able to *accommodated* all ten of their overnight guests.⟩ — see HOUSE 1

accommodating *adj* willing to do a favor ⟨an *accommodating* waiter who readily honored our request to make substitutions in our order⟩
synonyms accommodative, friendly, indulgent, obliging
related words helpful, solicitous; considerate, thoughtful; agreeable, amenable, complaisant, gracious; lenient, permissive

accommodation *n* **1** *usually* **accommodations** *pl* a place to sleep and related amenities for the temporary use of a tourist or traveler ⟨a resort offering a wide range of *accommodations*⟩
synonyms lodging
related words berth, shelter; crash pad
2 the act or practice of each side giving up something in order to reach an agreement ⟨The twins each made an *accommodation* in how to decorate their shared room.⟩ — see CONCESSION 1
3 something that adds to one's ease of living ⟨The village provides public *accommodations* for tourists' needs.⟩ — see COMFORT 2

accommodative *adj* willing to do a favor ⟨Owing to the efforts of an *accommodative* desk clerk, we were moved to a quieter section of the hotel.⟩ — see ACCOMMODATING

accompaniment *n* something that is found along with something else ⟨The sound of crickets was the perfect *accompaniment* to our summer evenings on the porch.⟩
synonyms attendant, companion, concomitant, corollary

related words accessory (*also* accessary), adjunct, appendage; complement, supplement; counterpart, fellow, mate; consequence, follow-up; fixings, trimmings

accompany *vb* **1** to go along with in order to provide assistance, protection, or companionship ⟨Children using the pool must be *accompanied* by a parent at all times.⟩
synonyms attend, chaperone (*or* chaperon), companion, company, convoy, escort, see, squire
related words walk; associate, consort, pal (around); team (up); defend, guard, protect; bring, conduct, guide, lead, pilot, steer, usher; follow, shadow, tag, tag along, tail; hang (around), hover (over)
near antonyms abandon, desert, ditch, dump, forsake
2 to occur or exist at the same time ⟨A general feeling of weariness often *accompanies* a cold.⟩ — see COINCIDE 1

accompanying *adj* present at the same time and place ⟨Call the phone number in the *accompanying* booklet for more information.⟩ — see COINCIDENT 1

accomplice *n* one associated with another in wrongdoing ⟨The thief and his *accomplices* were eventually caught and brought to justice.⟩
synonyms abettor (*also* abetter), accessory (*also* accessary), cohort, confederate
related words collaborationist, collaborator, informant, informer; evidence, state's evidence; companion, comrade, crony, henchman, partner; conspirator, plotter, traitor; gangster, mobster, racketeer

accomplish *vb* to carry through (as a process) to completion ⟨You've *accomplished* your assigned task with your usual efficiency.⟩ — see PERFORM 1

accomplished *adj* **1** having or showing a taste for the fine arts and gracious living ⟨A year as an exchange student in Europe had transformed her into an *accomplished* young woman.⟩ — see CULTIVATED
2 having or showing exceptional knowledge, experience, or skill in a field of endeavor ⟨an *accomplished* performance of a difficult violin concerto⟩ ⟨a delicate eye operation that only the most *accomplished* surgeon would attempt⟩ — see PROFICIENT
3 not capable of being challenged or proved wrong ⟨It is an *accomplished* fact that 10th century Norsemen established settlements in Newfoundland.⟩ — see IRREFUTABLE

accomplishment *n* **1** a successful result brought about by hard work ⟨Our biggest *accomplishment* this week was finishing the living room makeover.⟩
synonyms achievement, acquirement, attainment, baby, coup, success, triumph
related words blockbuster, hit, jackpot, megahit, miracle, smash, winner; conquest, gain, victory, win; skill; deed, feat, performance; arrival, completion, consummation, culmination, execution, fruition, fulfillment (*or* fulfilment), implementation, realization
phrases a feather in one's cap
near antonyms botch, mess, muddle, shambles; bummer, bust, catastrophe, debacle (*also* débâcle), disaster, dud, failure, fiasco, fizzle, flop, washout; disappointment, letdown, loss, setback
2 the doing of an action ⟨Your prompt *accomplishment* of this urgent project is much appreciated.⟩ — see COMMISSION 2
3 the state of being actual or complete ⟨a long, difficult project whose *accomplishment* we wondered if we would ever see⟩ — see FRUITION
4 a high level of taste and enlightenment as a result of extensive intellectual training and exposure to the arts ⟨a man of *accomplishment* acquired through world travel⟩ — see CULTURE 1

accord *n* **1** a formal agreement between two or more na-

tions or peoples ⟨hoped to bring about a peace *accord* between the warring nations⟩ — see TREATY
2 a state of consistency ⟨This undated map doesn't seem to be in *accord* with the current layout of the streets.⟩ — see CONFORMITY 1
3 an arrangement about action to be taken ⟨The judges have reached an *accord*: the match will have to be replayed.⟩ — see AGREEMENT 2
4 the state of being of one opinion about something ⟨Is everyone in *accord* about where to go for lunch?⟩ — see AGREEMENT 1
5 the act or power of making one's own choices or decisions ⟨She did not move to a different workstation of her own *accord*.⟩ — see FREE WILL

accord *vb* **1** to be in agreement on every point ⟨He claims that the newspaper's quote does not *accord* with what he actually said.⟩ — see CHECK 1
2 to give the ownership or benefit of (something) formally or publicly ⟨They were *accorded* certain favors because of their age.⟩ — see CONFER 1

accordance *n* a state of consistency ⟨Make sure the fundraiser is in *accordance* with the school rules.⟩ — see CONFORMITY 1

accordingly *adv* for this or that reason ⟨The application deadline was yesterday; *accordingly*, only applications mailed before midnight can be considered.⟩ — see THEREFORE

account *n* **1** a relating of events usually in the order in which they happened ⟨Newspaper reporters must strive to provide an accurate *account* of what happened.⟩
synonyms chronicle, commentary (*usually* commentaries), history, narration, narrative, record, report, story
related words deposition, documentation, testament, testimony, witness; annals, blog, journal, log, logbook, memoir; anecdote, tale, yarn; saga; recital, recitation; case history, case study
2 a presentation of an artistic work (as a piece of music) from a particular point of view ⟨The pianist gave an *account* of the sonata that revealed a very mature understanding of the work.⟩
synonyms interpretation, performance, reading
related words reworking, variation
3 a record of goods sold or services performed together with the costs due ⟨Please add this meal to my restaurant *account*.⟩ — see ¹BILL 1
4 a sum of money set aside for a particular purpose ⟨After paying the tuition, there was still money left for books in her special *account* for college expenses.⟩ — see FUND 1
5 the capacity for being useful for some purpose ⟨All the planning came to no *account* when the event was abruptly cancelled.⟩ — see USE 2
6 the relative usefulness or importance of something as judged by specific qualities ⟨The position of publicity agent for a star is of considerable *account* in Hollywood.⟩ — see WORTH 1
7 a careful weighing of the reasons for or against something ⟨Take into *account* the potential problems that come with keeping a horse.⟩ — see CONSIDERATION 1
8 a feeling of great approval and liking ⟨The girl held her grandmother, a pioneer in aviation, in high *account*.⟩ — see ADMIRATION 1
9 a person who buys a product or uses a service from a business ⟨The company sends out holiday cards to all its *accounts*.⟩ — see CUSTOMER 1
10 a statement given to explain a belief or act ⟨He could offer no credible *account* for why he had been absent.⟩ — see REASON 1
11 something (as a belief) that serves as the basis for an-

other thing ⟨For that *account* alone you should agree that the system needs overhauling.⟩ — see REASON 2

12 the quality or state of being important ⟨Where we go for dinner is of no *account* to me.⟩ — see IMPORTANCE

account *vb* to think of in a particular way ⟨*account* themselves lucky to be alive⟩ — see CONSIDER 1

account (for) *vb* to give the reason for or cause of ⟨could not *account for* the huge difference in price between the two practically identical handbags⟩ — see EXPLAIN 2

accountable *adj* being the one who must meet an obligation or suffer the consequences for failing to do so ⟨The owner was held *accountable* for his dog's biting of the child.⟩ — see RESPONSIBLE 1

accoutre *or* **accouter** *vb* to provide (someone) with what is needed for a task or activity ⟨hikers *accoutred* with walking sticks, water bottles, trail maps, and compasses⟩ — see FURNISH 1

accoutrement *or* **accouterment** *n* **1** something that is not necessary in itself but adds to the convenience or performance of the main piece of equipment ⟨This vacuum cleaner has all of the *accoutrements* for cleaning furniture as well as floors.⟩ — see ACCESSORY 1

2 accoutrements *or* **accouterments** *pl* items needed for the performance of a task or activity ⟨The kit has all the *accoutrements* that the home pastry chef could ever want.⟩ — see EQUIPMENT

accredit *vb* **1** to explain (something) as being the result of something else ⟨The film buff *accredits* his good choice of movies to reading a reviewer who seldom steers him wrong.⟩ — see CREDIT 1

2 to give official or legal power to ⟨took a course that *accredited* her to teach first aid⟩ — see AUTHORIZE 1

3 to declare enthusiastic approval of ⟨He's generally *accredited* as the finest American dramatist of the postwar generation.⟩ — see ACCLAIM

4 to give official acceptance of as satisfactory ⟨Thus far the board has refused to *accredit* the school.⟩ — see APPROVE

accreditation *n* the granting of power to perform various acts or duties ⟨the only body empowered with the *accreditation* of medical schools in the state⟩ — see COMMISSION 1

accretion *n* **1** a mass or quantity that has piled up or that has been gathered over a period of time ⟨a thick *accretion* of ice in the freezer⟩ — see ACCUMULATION 1

2 something added (as by growth) ⟨*Accretions* of lime have thickened the cave's stalactites and stalagmites over the centuries.⟩ — see INCREASE 1

accrual *n* something added (as by growth) ⟨I had an *accrual* of $100 through interest on my savings account last year.⟩ — see INCREASE 1

accumulate *vb* **1** to become greater in extent, volume, amount, or number ⟨The number of orders through the website is really *accumulating*.⟩ — see INCREASE 2

2 to bring together in one body or place ⟨finally *accumulated* enough donated books to hold a book sale⟩ — see GATHER 1

3 to gradually form into a layer, pile, or mass ⟨clouds *accumulating* on the western horizon⟩ — see COLLECT 2

accumulating *n* the act or process of becoming greater in number ⟨the *accumulating* of newspapers in the basement over the years⟩ — see MULTIPLICATION

accumulation *n* **1** a mass or quantity that has piled up or that has been gathered over a period of time ⟨a vast *accumulation* of evidence about the dangers of smoking⟩

synonyms accretion, assemblage, collection, gathering

related words agglomerate, assortment, conglomerate, conglomeration, hodgepodge, hotchpotch, jumble, medley, mélange, mishmash, mix, mixture, motley, potpourri;

agglomeration, clutter, hash, heap, litter, mass, pile; aggregate, aggregation, sum, totality; backlog, cache, fund, hoard, inventory, kitty, nest egg, reserve, stock, stockpile, store, supply

2 the act or process of becoming greater in number ⟨The *accumulation* of leaves on the ground is proceeding at a much faster rate than my raking.⟩ — see MULTIPLICATION

accuracy *n* the quality or state of being very accurate ⟨Obviously, with brain surgery the *accuracy* of the incision is incredibly important.⟩ — see PRECISION

accurate *adj* **1** being in agreement with the truth or a fact or a standard ⟨an *accurate* count of the number of people coming to the wedding reception⟩ — see CORRECT 1

2 following an original exactly ⟨an *accurate* translation of the original story⟩ — see FAITHFUL 2

3 meeting the highest standard of accuracy ⟨an *accurate* thermometer⟩ ⟨*accurate* measurements⟩ — see PRECISE 1

accuse *vb* to make a claim of wrongdoing against ⟨She was *accused* of lying on the employment application.⟩

synonyms charge, impeach, incriminate, indict

related words blame, call (on), castigate, censure, condemn, criticize, damn, denounce, fault, impugn, reproach, reprobate; chide, rebuke, reprove, tax; appeal, arraign, book, cite, summon; sue, try; frame, implicate, inculpate, inform (against), name, report; recriminate, retaliate

near antonyms advocate, champion, defend; excuse, forgive, justify, pardon, remit, shrive

antonyms absolve, acquit, clear, exculpate, exonerate, vindicate

accustom *vb* to impart knowledge of a new thing or situation to ⟨the task of *accustoming* new recruits to shipboard life⟩ — see ACQUAINT 1

accustomed *adj* being in the habit or custom ⟨Josh was not *accustomed* to eating so late.⟩

synonyms given, habituated, used, wont

related words apt, inclined, liable, likely, prone; hardened, inured; experienced, practiced (*or* practised), seasoned, veteran; addicted, hooked

near antonyms unapt, unlikely; averse, disinclined, opposed; inexperienced, new, unseasoned; disaccustomed, weaned

antonyms unaccustomed, unused, unwonted

ace *adj* having or showing exceptional knowledge, experience, or skill in a field of endeavor ⟨an *ace* computer programmer⟩ — see PROFICIENT

ace *n* **1** a person with a high level of knowledge or skill in a field ⟨Bill took a few lessons with a tennis *ace* to improve his backhand.⟩ — see EXPERT

2 a very small amount ⟨not an *ace* of truth in what she said⟩ — see PARTICLE 1

3 a very small distance or degree ⟨I came within an *ace* of being chosen for the part.⟩ — see HAIR 1

ache *n* a sharp unpleasant sensation usually felt in some specific part of the body ⟨a dull pounding *ache* in his head⟩ — see PAIN 1

ache *vb* to feel or cause physical pain ⟨My feet *ache* from all that walking.⟩ — see HURT 1

ache (for) *vb* **1** to have sympathy for ⟨His heart *ached for* the lost dog.⟩ — see PITY

2 to have an earnest wish to own or enjoy ⟨*aching for* some quiet time to himself⟩ — see DESIRE 1

achievable *adj* capable of being done or carried out ⟨I think that retirement at 55 is an *achievable* goal.⟩ — see POSSIBLE 1

achieve *vb* **1** to obtain (as a goal) through effort ⟨finally *achieved* stardom⟩

synonyms attain, bag, gain, hit, log, make, notch (up), rack up, score, win

related words acquire, capture, carry, draw, garner, get, land, make, obtain, procure, realize, secure; amount (to), approach, equal, match, measure up (to), meet, rival, tie, touch; beat, excel, outdo, surpass, top

near antonyms fall short (of), miss; fail (at); lose

2 to carry through (as a process) to completion ⟨He *achieved* his purpose of restoring the old theater.⟩ — see PERFORM 1

achievement *n* **1** a successful result brought about by hard work ⟨This improvement in your time for a 10K road race is quite an *achievement!*⟩ — see ACCOMPLISHMENT 1

2 the doing of an action ⟨What you're asking is the *achievement* of a miracle.⟩ — see COMMISSION 2

3 the state of being actual or complete ⟨You should be proud of the *achievement* of your goals.⟩ — see FRUITION

Achilles' heel *n* a vulnerable point ⟨This year, the team's *Achilles' heel* is pitching.⟩

synonyms back, chink, underbelly

related words downfall, ruin

aching *adj* **1** causing or feeling bodily pain ⟨my poor, *aching* back⟩ — see PAINFUL 1

2 expressing or suggesting mourning ⟨another one of those *aching* country songs⟩ — see MOURNFUL 1

achy *adj* causing or feeling bodily pain ⟨unable to play in tomorrow's football game because of an *achy* right knee⟩ — see PAINFUL 1

acid *adj* **1** causing or characterized by the one of the basic taste sensations that is produced chiefly by acids ⟨an *acid*-tasting medicine⟩ — see SOUR 1

2 having or showing a habitually bad temper ⟨an *acid* personality that offends most people⟩ — see ILL-TEMPERED

3 marked by the use of wit that is intended to cause hurt feelings ⟨a cultural gadfly known for an *acid* tongue that spares no one⟩ — see SARCASTIC

acidic *adj* **1** causing or characterized by the one of the basic taste sensations that is produced chiefly by acids ⟨The *acidic* flavor of lemon goes nicely with broiled fish.⟩ — see SOUR 1

2 marked by the use of wit that is intended to cause hurt feelings ⟨Her often *acidic* reviews have ruffled more than a few toques in the restaurant kitchens of New York.⟩ — see SARCASTIC

acidity *n* **1** a harsh or sharp quality ⟨I detected a certain *acidity* in the way he responded.⟩ — see EDGE 1

2 biting sharpness of feeling or expression ⟨The *acidity* of their relationship was well known to their mutual acquaintances.⟩ — see ACRIMONY 1

acidness *n* **1** a harsh or sharp quality ⟨There's an irritating *acidness* to the writer's comments on just about everything.⟩ — see EDGE 1

2 biting sharpness of feeling or expression ⟨The *acidness* in his remarks hurt her to the core.⟩ — see ACRIMONY 1

acknowledge *vb* to accept the truth or existence of (something) usually reluctantly ⟨The teen finally had to *acknowledge* that she'd outgrown her favorite shoes.⟩ — see ADMIT 1

acknowledgment *or* **acknowledgement** *n* **1** a formal recognition of an achievement or praiseworthy deed ⟨an *acknowledgment* to the food committee for the delicious refreshments⟩ — see COMMENDATION 1

2 an open declaration of something (as a fault or the commission of an offense) about oneself ⟨a surprising *acknowledgment* that he had been faking his injury⟩ — see CONFESSION

acme *n* **1** the highest part or point ⟨The *acme* of their basketball season was their hard-won victory over last year's state champs.⟩ — see HEIGHT 1

2 the most perfect type or example ⟨a movie that has come to be regarded as the *acme* of the Hollywood musical⟩ — see QUINTESSENCE 1

acoustic *or* **acoustical** *adj* of, relating to, or experienced through the sense of hearing ⟨Is a bird's *acoustic* organ similar to a human's?⟩ — see AUDITORY

acquaint *vb* **1** to impart knowledge of a new thing or situation to ⟨Mr. King spent the first week of the summer internship *acquainting* everyone with the new computers.⟩

synonyms accustom, familiarize, initiate, introduce, orient, orientate

related words wont; apprise, brief, clue (in), fill in, inform; educate, enlighten, ground, instruct, school, train, verse; expose, present, subject; advise, tell, tip (off), warn, wise (up); reacquaint

2 to give information to ⟨His sailor friend *acquainted* him with the latest navigational aids for weekend yachtsmen.⟩ — see ENLIGHTEN 1

3 to make (one person) known (to another) socially ⟨hoping that someone would *acquaint* them with the new neighbors⟩ — see INTRODUCE 1

acquaintance *n* knowledge gained by personal experience ⟨Tiffany's *acquaintance* with goats is limited to a long-ago visit to a petting zoo when she was three.⟩

synonyms cognizance, familiarity

related words association, experience, exposure, intimacy, involvement; initiation, introduction; awareness, comprehension, conception, inkling, notion, understanding; education, enlightenment, grounding, information, instruction, learning, schooling, training

near antonyms callowness, greenness, ignorance, inexperience

antonyms unfamiliarity

acquainted *adj* having information especially as a result of study or experience ⟨would like to see students become *acquainted* with all the services that the university has to offer⟩ — see FAMILIAR 2

acquiesce *vb* to give or express one's approval (as to a proposal) ⟨They *acquiesced* to their opponents' demands.⟩ — see ACCEDE

acquiescence *n* a readiness or willingness to yield to the wishes of others ⟨Good manners demanded our cheerful *acquiescence* to our host's plans for dinner.⟩ — see COMPLIANCE 1

acquiescent *adj* receiving or enduring without offering resistance ⟨She was not as *acquiescent* about sharing her room as her parents seemed to think she should be.⟩ — see PASSIVE

acquirable *adj* possible to get ⟨Cooking is an *acquirable* skill for anyone.⟩ — see AVAILABLE 1

acquire *vb* **1** to come to have gradually ⟨From years of working two jobs, he has *acquired* the ability to get by on only a few hours of sleep a day.⟩ — see DEVELOP 2

2 to receive as return for effort ⟨*acquired* a reputation for always arriving at his friends' house just as they were sitting down to dinner⟩ — see EARN 1

acquirement *n* a successful result brought about by hard work ⟨the contention that the candidate's *acquirements* in the business world would stand him in good stead in the political arena⟩ — see ACCOMPLISHMENT 1

acquisitive *adj* having or marked by an eager and often selfish desire especially for material possessions ⟨*Acquisitive* developers are trying to tear down the historic home and build a shopping mall.⟩ — see GREEDY 1

acquisitiveness *n* an intense selfish desire for wealth or possessions ⟨The queen's *acquisitiveness* would not be satisfied until she owned the largest diamond in the world.⟩ — see GREED

acquit *vb* **1** to free from a charge of wrongdoing ⟨*acquitted* of the robbery charge after proving he was nowhere near the scene of the crime⟩ — see EXCULPATE

2 to manage the actions of (oneself) in a particular way ⟨The king promised handsome rewards to all who *acquitted* themselves well in the battle.⟩ — see BEHAVE

acquittal *n* a setting free from a charge of wrongdoing ⟨confidently predicted that his client's trial would result in a full *acquittal*⟩

synonyms clearing, exculpation, exoneration, vindication

related words absolution, condonation, forgiveness, pardon, remission; atonement, expiation

near antonyms accusation, arraignment, impeachment, incrimination, indictment; castigation, censure, condemnation, denunciation

antonyms conviction

acrid *adj* **1** having or showing deep-seated resentment ⟨There have been *acrid* relations between the two families ever since they fought over that strip of land.⟩ — see BITTER 1

2 marked by the use of wit that is intended to cause hurt feelings ⟨Phillipa's *acrid* comments about the new employee's clothes were disgraceful.⟩ — see SARCASTIC

acridness *n* **1** a harsh or sharp quality ⟨an *acridness* in her voice when she said she hoped that we would get what we deserve⟩ — see EDGE 1

2 biting sharpness of feeling or expression ⟨Over the years the *acridness* he felt toward his stepfather softened somewhat.⟩ — see ACRIMONY 1

acrimonious *adj* having or showing deep-seated resentment ⟨an *acrimonious* parting between the two former friends⟩ — see BITTER 1

acrimoniousness *n* a harsh or sharp quality ⟨*acrimoniousness* lay beneath his words, which on their face seemed harmless enough⟩ — see EDGE 1

acrimony *n* **1** biting sharpness of feeling or expression ⟨She responded with such *acrimony* that he never brought the subject up again.⟩

synonyms acidity, acidness, acridness, asperity, bile, bitterness, cattiness, tartness, virulence, vitriol

related words gruffness, harshness, hostility, relentlessness, severity, sternness, vehemence; crossness, discourteousness, iciness, impoliteness, incivility, nastiness, rudeness, sourness, surliness, ungraciousness; anger, animosity, gall, jaundice, malevolence, malice, rancor, scorn, spite, spleen, venom, vindictiveness; jealousy, pique, resentment, sour grapes

near antonyms civility, cordiality, courtesy, diplomacy, geniality, graciousness, kindness, politeness, tactfulness; compassion, softness, sweetness, sympathy, warmth; oiliness, smoothness, suaveness, suavity, unctuousness, urbanity

2 a harsh or sharp quality ⟨The *acrimony* of his parting words shocked everyone in the office.⟩ — see EDGE 1

acrobat *n* **1** one who performs feats of physical strength, balance, and agility on special apparatus ⟨a child who is a natural *acrobat* with a superb sense of balance⟩

synonyms gymnast

related words exerciser, tumbler; contortionist, equilibrist; aerialist, ropedancer, ropewalker, trampoliner, trampolinist, trapeze artist, trapezist

2 a person who dexterously and expediently changes or adopts opinions ⟨a political *acrobat* whose opinion on any issue is whatever will get the most votes⟩

synonyms opportunist, temporizer

related words self-seeker; conniver, machinator, plotter, schemer

across *adv* from one side to the other of an intervening space ⟨They reached *across* to shake hands.⟩ — see OVER 1

across *prep* **1** to the opposite side of ⟨We rowed *across* the lake.⟩

synonyms athwart, over, through

related words around, round; beyond, past

2 in random positions within the boundaries of ⟨sheep scattered *across* the field⟩ — see AROUND 2

act *n* **1** a performance regularly presented by an individual or group ⟨In his nightclub *act* he impersonates a veritable galaxy of movie stars.⟩

synonyms bit, number, routine, turn

2 a display of emotion or behavior that is insincere or intended to deceive ⟨She was putting on an *act* when she said she was sorry.⟩ — see MASQUERADE

3 a rule of conduct or action laid down by a governing authority and especially a legislature ⟨The Americans with Disabilities *Act* requires public buildings to have wheelchair access.⟩ — see LAW 1

4 something done by someone ⟨It's *acts* such as this—lying about having to work late—that make me feel like I can't trust you.⟩ — see ACTION 1

act *vb* **1** to present a portrayal or performance of ⟨A local student *acted* the part of Tiny Tim in our theater company's production of *A Christmas Carol*.⟩

synonyms do, impersonate, interpret, perform, play, portray

related words depict, dramatize, render, represent; act out, enact, pantomime, playact, role-play, take on; overact, overplay, underplay; ape, clown, ham, imitate, masquerade, mime, mimic, pose (as); star (in); coact, costar

2 to produce a desired effect ⟨The painkiller *acted* surprisingly quickly.⟩

synonyms operate, perform, take, work

related words behave, react, respond; affect, influence, sway; pan out, redound, result

phrases take effect, take hold

near antonyms backfire; fizzle

3 to give the impression of being ⟨always *acting* helpless, just to get attention⟩ — see SEEM

4 to have a certain purpose ⟨The tail feathers of woodpeckers *act* as props while the birds excavate tree trunks for insects.⟩ — see FUNCTION

5 to present a false appearance of ⟨If you *act* confident long enough, you'll begin to actually feel it.⟩ — see FEIGN

6 to pretend to be (what one is not) in appearance or behavior ⟨always giving advice and *acting* the expert⟩ — see IMPERSONATE 1

act (toward) *vb* to behave toward in a stated way ⟨I would never *act toward* my boss that way.⟩ — see TREAT 1

acting *adj* serving in a position for the time being ⟨She will serve as *acting* president of the university until a permanent replacement can be found.⟩

synonyms interim, provisional, temporary

related words alternate, backup, make-do, makeshift, proxy, stopgap, substitute

antonyms long-term, permanent

action *n* **1** something done by someone ⟨Judge people by their *actions*, not by their words.⟩

synonyms act, deed, doing, exploit, feat, thing

related words accomplishment, achievement, attainment; adventure, experience; emprise, enterprise, initiative, undertaking; handiwork, performance, work; stunt, trick; activity, dealing; maneuver, measure, move, operation, procedure, proceeding, step, tactic; coaction

2 the unfolding of events in a dramatic or literary work ⟨The mystery writer displays a sure hand in managing the novel's complicated but never incoherent *action*.⟩
synonyms plot, story
related words subplot; arc, development; design, outline, plan, scheme; argument, subject, theme
3 a court case for enforcing a right or claim ⟨The man filed an *action* in district court.⟩ — see LAWSUIT
4 active fighting during the course of a war ⟨The battalion saw *action* soon after it arrived.⟩ — see COMBAT 1
5 actions *pl* the way or manner in which one conducts oneself ⟨Observing the *actions* of mice in various controlled settings helps scientists understand the effects of certain drugs.⟩ — see BEHAVIOR
6 readiness to engage in daring or difficult activity ⟨The wilderness was tamed by men and women of *action*.⟩ — see ENTERPRISE 2
action figure *n* a small figure often of a human being used especially as a child's plaything ⟨a collection of *action figures* of his favorite superheroes⟩ — see DOLL 1
activate *vb* to cause to function ⟨The thermostat is set to *activate* the heating system only when the temperature drops below 65 degrees.⟩
synonyms actuate, crank (up), drive, move, run, set off, spark, start, touch off, trigger, turn on
related words kick over, turn over; charge, electrify, energize, fire, fuel, generate, power, push; discharge, launch, release, switch, trip; reactivate; arouse, excite, kick-start, stimulate, vitalize; ignite, incite, instigate, provoke, quicken, stir up; accelerate, speed (up), step up
near antonyms arrest, brake, check, cut off, draw up, halt, jam, stall, stick, stop; decelerate, repress, slow, stunt, suppress
antonyms cut, cut out, deactivate, kill, shut off, turn off
active *adj* **1** being in effective operation ⟨The abandoned factory had not been *active* for years.⟩
synonyms alive, functional, functioning, going, live, living, on, operating, operational, operative, running, working
related words effective, effectual; employable, operable, usable (*also* useable), viable, workable; performing, producing, productive, serving, useful, yielding; astir, bustling, busy, dynamic, flourishing, humming, roaring, thriving
phrases in commission (*or* into commission), in force, in gear, on line
near antonyms deactivated, decommissioned; ineffective, ineffectual, useless; inoperable, unusable, unworkable; arrested, asleep, dormant, fallow, idle, inert, latent, lifeless, nonproductive, quiescent, sleepy, stagnating, unproductive, vegetating
antonyms broken, dead, inactive, inoperative, nonactivated, nonfunctional, nonfunctioning, nonoperating, nonoperational, nonoperative
2 having much high-spirited energy and movement ⟨The fish are *active* today, but we still haven't caught anything.⟩ — see LIVELY 1
3 involved in often constant activity ⟨All morning the crowd at the coffeehouse kept the waitstaff pretty *active*.⟩ — see BUSY 1
activity *n* energetic movement of the body for the sake of physical fitness ⟨The man had to restrict his *activity* after the surgery.⟩ — see EXERCISE 1
actor *n* **1** one who acts professionally (as in a play, movie, or television show) ⟨My sister went to drama school to become an *actor*.⟩
synonyms impersonator, mummer, player, trouper
related words barnstormer, enactor, entertainer, performer; actress, starlet; lead, leading lady, leading man,

star; coactor, costar; extra, spear-carrier, walk-on; monologuist (*or* monologist); prima donna, scene-stealer; double, understudy; comedian; tragedian, tragedienne; ham, imitator, impressionist, mime, mimic, pantomime, pantomimist, poser; buffoon, clown, harlequin, stooge, zany
antonyms nonactor
2 one who takes part in something ⟨Benjamin Franklin was a major *actor* in many of the events leading up to the founding of our nation.⟩ — see PARTICIPANT
act out *vb* to behave badly ⟨The boy resorted to *acting out* in order to get attention.⟩ — see MISBEHAVE
actual *adj* existing in fact and not merely as a possibility ⟨The *actual* outcome of the election was quite different from what everybody had expected.⟩
synonyms concrete, effective, existent, factual, genuine, real, true, very
related words attested, authenticated, confirmed, demonstrated, established, proven, substantiated, valid, validated, verified; incontestable, incontrovertible, indisputable, indubitable, inescapable, irrefutable, undeniable, unquestionable; believable, convincing, literal, realistic, unmistakable, verifiable; authentic, bona fide, real-life, real-world; absolute, certain, final, hard, objective, palpable, positive, substantial, tangible; authoritative
near antonyms alleged, assumed, reputed, supposed; conceived, envisaged, envisioned, imagined, pictured, visualized; chimerical (*also* chimeric), fabled, fanciful, fictional, fictitious, illusory, legendary; fabricated, fake, imaginary, invented, made-up, make-believe, pretend, romantic; abstract, symbolic, unreal; virtual
antonyms conjectural, hypothetical, ideal, inexistent, nonexistent, platonic, possible, potential, suppositional, theoretical (*also* theoretic)
actuality *n* **1** the fact of being or of being real ⟨The *actuality* of the Abominable Snowman is not taken seriously by scientists.⟩ — see EXISTENCE
2 the quality of being actual ⟨The *actuality* of equal opportunity depends on more than just having laws that supposedly ensure it.⟩ — see FACT 1
3 the state of being actual or complete ⟨The *actuality* of space travel would never have been believed a hundred years ago.⟩ — see FRUITION
4 something that actually exists ⟨These estimated tax revenues, from casinos that have yet to be built, are being treated as *actualities*.⟩ — see FACT 2
actualize *vb* to come into existence ⟨Several years passed before any profits from the enterprise *actualized*.⟩ — see BEGIN 2
actually *adv* **1** to tell the truth ⟨*Actually*, I'd rather spend the evening at home.⟩
synonyms admittedly, frankly, honestly, indeed, really, truly, truthfully, verily
related words absolutely, certainly, indisputably, indubitably, realistically, undoubtedly, unquestionably, veritably
phrases as a matter of fact, in actuality, in fact, in point of fact, in reality, in truth, to be sure
2 in actual fact ⟨I call her Aunt Emily, but she is *actually* my cousin, not my aunt.⟩ — see VERY 2
actuate *vb* **1** to cause to function ⟨a light *actuated* by a motion detector⟩ ⟨The alarm system *actuates* the door locks.⟩ — see ACTIVATE
2 to set or keep in motion ⟨Hearing depends on sound vibrations that *actuate* the complex mechanism of that sensory organ, the ear.⟩ — see MOVE 2
act up *vb* **1** to behave badly ⟨The two-year-old was *acting up* in the store so much that her dad had to take her outside.⟩ — see MISBEHAVE
2 to engage in attention-getting playful or boisterous be-

havior ⟨You should have seen the boys *acting up* when they put on their costumes.⟩ — see CUT UP

acuity *n* the state or quality of being able to sense slight impressions or differences ⟨a worrisome deterioration in the *acuity* of his hearing over the years⟩
synonyms acuteness, delicacy, keenness, perceptiveness, sensitiveness, sensitivity, sharpness
related words hyperacuity, hypersensitiveness, hypersensitivity, oversensitiveness, oversensitivity, supersensitivity; accuracy, exactitude, exactness, fineness

acumen *n* exceptional discernment and judgment especially in practical matters ⟨She had the business *acumen* to know that the market for sportswear was becoming oversaturated.⟩
synonyms astuteness, caginess (*also* cageyness), canniness, foxiness, hardheadedness, intelligence, keenness, sharpness, shrewdness, wit
related words discernment, insight, perception, perceptiveness, perceptivity, sagaciousness, sagacity, sageness, sapience, wisdom; artfulness, artifice, craft, craftiness, cunning, deviousness, guile, slickness, slyness, sneakiness, subtleness, subtlety, wiliness; brain(s), gray matter, intellect, reason, sense
near antonyms artlessness, greenness, guilelessness, ingenuousness, innocence, naïveté (*also* naivete *or* naiveté), simpleness, simplicity, unsophistication, unworldliness; brainlessness, density, doltishness, dopiness, dumbness, fatuity, foolishness, half-wittedness, mindlessness, oafishness, obtuseness, senselessness, slowness, stupidity, stupidness, vacuity, witlessness

acute *adj* **1** able to sense slight impressions or differences ⟨Dogs, with their *acute* sense of smell, are used for finding toxic substances undetectable by humans.⟩
synonyms delicate, fine, keen, perceptive, quick, sensitive, sharp
related words accurate, clear, discerning, good, piercing, precise, receptive, sensible, subtle; hair-trigger, hyperacute, hypersensitive, oversensitive, supersensitive
near antonyms bad, deadened, dimmed, dull, dulled, fading; dead, insensible, insensitive, numb; imprecise, inaccurate
2 needing immediate attention ⟨famine caused by an *acute* shortage of grain⟩
synonyms burning, compelling, critical, crying, dire, imperative, imperious, instant, pressing, urgent
related words demanding, extreme, immediate, insistent, intense; crucial, grave, life-and-death (*also* life-or-death), serious, severe, vital; dangerous, explosive, hazardous, perilous, precarious, unstable
near antonyms incidental, low-pressure, minor, negligible, trivial, unimportant; nonthreatening, safe, stable
antonyms noncritical, nonurgent
3 extreme in degree, power, or effect ⟨experiencing *acute* distress over the misunderstanding with her best friend⟩ — see INTENSE 1

acuteness *n* **1** a harsh or sharp quality ⟨Judging by the *acuteness* in his tone when he congratulated me, I think he was actually quite resentful that I won.⟩ — see EDGE 1
2 the state or quality of being able to sense slight impressions or differences ⟨The *acuteness* of the bird's eyesight is amazing.⟩ — see ACUITY

ad *n* a published statement informing the public of a matter of general interest ⟨Did you see the *ads* for cheap round-trip flights to Florida?⟩ — see ANNOUNCEMENT

adage *n* an often stated observation regarding something from common experience ⟨that old *adage*, "the early bird gets the worm"⟩ — see SAYING

adamant *adj* sticking to an opinion, purpose, or course of action in spite of reason, arguments, or persuasion ⟨She remained *adamant* about getting the actor's autograph even after he had disappeared backstage.⟩ — see OBSTINATE

adapt *vb* to change (something) so as to make it suitable for a new use or situation ⟨It always takes freshmen a little while to *adapt* themselves to high school.⟩
synonyms acclimate, acclimatize, accommodate, adjust, condition, conform, doctor, edit, fashion, fit, put, shape, suit, tailor
related words readapt, readjust; customize, gear, match, model, pattern; correct, harmonize, square, tune; establish, root, settle; acquaint, familiarize, orient, orientate; equip, prepare, prime, rehearse; harden, inure, season, toughen; alter, convert, make over, modify, recast, reclaim, recycle, redesign, redevelop, redo, reengineer, refashion, refigure, refit, refocus, reinvent, rejigger, remake, remodel, revamp, revise, rework, transform; accustom, condition, naturalize; ready, season; bend; fiddle (with), fine-tune, phase, register, regulate, rig
near antonyms misadjust

adaptable *adj* **1** able to do many different kinds of things ⟨an activities director who's *adaptable* to any kind of situation⟩ — see VERSATILE
2 capable of being readily changed ⟨The caterer's menu is *adaptable* to specific dietary needs, such as vegan, kosher, or low-fat.⟩ — see FLEXIBLE 1

adapter *also* **adaptor** *n* something that is not necessary in itself but adds to the convenience or performance of the main piece of equipment ⟨*Adapters* for the food mixer include a meat grinder and an ice cream maker.⟩ — see ACCESSORY 1

add *vb* **1** to join (something) to a mass, quantity, or number so as to bring about an overall increase ⟨The band recently *added* a saxophonist and a keyboard player to its ranks.⟩ ⟨*Add* another cup of flour to the mixture.⟩
synonyms adjoin, annex, append, tack (on)
related words affix, attach, fasten, fix, graft, hitch, tag, tie; infuse, inject, insert, introduce; aggrandize, amplify, augment, beef (up), boost, compound, enlarge, escalate, expand, extend, increase, multiply, raise, swell; elongate, lengthen, prolong, protract; enhance, heighten, intensify, magnify; complement, supplement, supply; enforce, strengthen; maximize
near antonyms detach, disconnect, disjoin, separate, unfasten; amputate, cut, excise, lop (off), sever; contract, decrease, diminish, lessen, lower, reduce; abbreviate, abridge, curtail, shorten; compress, condense, constrict, cut back, retrench
antonyms abate, bate, deduct, knock off, remove, subtract, take off
2 to combine (numbers) into a single sum ⟨When she *added* all the phone charges herself, she discovered an error in her bill.⟩
synonyms cast (up), foot (up), sum, total
related words calculate, cipher, compute, figure, reckon, table, tabulate, tally, work out; divide, multiply, subtract; count, enumerate, number, tell; recompute, refigure
phrases put together

add (to) *vb* to make greater in size, amount, or number ⟨The need to be back home before 5:00 p.m. *adds to* the difficulty of arranging the trip.⟩ — see INCREASE 1

added *adj* resulting in an increase in amount or number ⟨Ever since his mother got sick, he's had the *added* responsibility of getting his little sister ready for school.⟩ — see ADDITIONAL

addendum *n* **1** a part added at the end of a book or periodical ⟨There's an *addendum* from the author to explain certain stylistic choices that she made.⟩

synonyms supplement
related words coda, epilogue (*also* epilog), postlude; conclusion, ending, finale; accompaniment, addition, complement, postscript; follow-up, sequel
antonyms foreword, introduction, preface, prologue (*also* prolog)
2 something added (as by growth) ⟨With each new *addendum* the list of demands simply got more absurd.⟩ — see INCREASE 1

addict *n* **1** a person who regularly uses drugs especially illegally ⟨an inspiring story about *addicts* who seek help and manage to kick their habit⟩
synonyms user
2 a person with a strong and habitual liking for something ⟨science-fiction *addicts* who eagerly await each new installment in the series⟩ — see FAN

addition *n* **1** a smaller structure added to a main building ⟨a new *addition* to the library providing space for an expanded video collection⟩ — see ANNEX
2 something added (as by growth) ⟨The cache of old stamps I found in the discarded desk was a huge *addition* to my stamp collection.⟩ — see INCREASE 1
3 the act or process of becoming greater in number ⟨How do you account for the *addition* of more paint stains on your shirt after you put on a smock?⟩ — see MULTIPLICATION

additional *adj* resulting in an increase in amount or number ⟨There turned out to be *additional* reasons for her unauthorized absence.⟩
synonyms added, another, else, farther, fresh, further, more, other
related words accessory, adjunct, collateral, extraneous, peripheral, side, supplemental, supplementary; new; excess, extra, plus, spare, surplus; complementary, contributory
near antonyms fewer, less

additionally *adv* in addition to what has been said ⟨The diet recommends fruit juice for breakfast and, *additionally*, fresh fruit once a day.⟩ — see MORE 1

additive *adj* produced by a series of additions of identical or similar things ⟨Certain medications have *additive* effects when taken in conjunction with each other that one doesn't see when any one is used alone.⟩ — see CUMULATIVE

addle *vb* to throw into a state of mental uncertainty ⟨I was *addled* by the time change.⟩ — see CONFUSE 1

addled *adj* **1** having undergone organic breakdown ⟨*addled* eggs found on a long abandoned hen's nest⟩ — see ROTTEN 1
2 suffering from mental confusion ⟨One of the more *addled* audience members confused Ghana with Guyana.⟩ — see DIZZY 2

address *n* **1** a usually formal discourse delivered to an audience ⟨George Washington's Farewell *Address*⟩ — see SPEECH 1
2 the way or manner in which one conducts oneself ⟨a gentleman with all the poise and social *address* that one would expect⟩ — see BEHAVIOR

address *vb* **1** to deal with (something) usually skillfully or efficiently ⟨The problem will only get worse if you don't *address* it now.⟩ — see HANDLE 1
2 to occupy (oneself) diligently or with close attention ⟨Please *address* yourself to what I'm saying and not to your phone.⟩ — see APPLY 2
3 to transmit information or requests to ⟨You may *address* the manager about your problems tomorrow.⟩ — see CONTACT

adduce *vb* to give as an example ⟨In support of a 12-month school year, the committee *adduced* data from other school districts.⟩ — see QUOTE 1

add up (to) *vb* **1** to be the same in meaning or effect ⟨Whether we take the 4:00 train or the 4:15 bus, it *adds up to* the same thing: they both get us back too late.⟩ — see AMOUNT (TO) 2
2 to have a total of ⟨Even if we pool all our money, it won't *add up to* enough to rent a beach house for a week.⟩ — see AMOUNT (TO) 1

adept *adj* having or showing exceptional knowledge, experience, or skill in a field of endeavor ⟨He's an *adept* pitcher, and the team is lucky to have him.⟩ — see PROFICIENT

adept *n* a person with a high level of knowledge or skill in a field ⟨He's an *adept* at political intrigue and power politics.⟩ — see EXPERT

adeptly *adv* in a skillful or expert manner ⟨*adeptly* sank the ball in the basket with a hook shot⟩ — see WELL 3

adeptness *n* subtle or imaginative ability in inventing, devising, or executing something ⟨Her *adeptness* at thinking on her feet makes her a formidable debater.⟩ — see SKILL 1

adequacy *n* the quality or state of meeting one's needs adequately ⟨The fire department sent someone to determine the *adequacy* of the building's evacuation plan.⟩ — see SUFFICIENCY

adequate *adj* of a level of quality that meets one's needs or standards ⟨This old computer is probably *adequate* if you just want to do some word processing.⟩
synonyms acceptable, all right, decent, fine, good, OK (*or* okay), passable, respectable, satisfactory, serviceable, tolerable
related words agreeable, bearable, endurable, sufferable; average, fair, indifferent, mediocre, middling, minimal; common, ordinary, run-of-the-mill, run-of-the-mine (*or* run-of-mine), second-rate, so-so; standard, unexceptional; appropriate, correct, due, fitting, meet, proper, right, seemly, suitable, useful, worthy; gratifying, satisfying
phrases up to snuff
near antonyms disagreeable, disreputable, improper, indecent, objectionable, unfit, unsuitable, unworthy, useless, wrong; bad, cheap, defective, faulty, imperfect, incomplete, lamentable, pitiful, shoddy; dissatisfying; insufficient, meager (*or* meagre), mean, niggardly, poor, scanty, shabby, short, skimpy, spare, stingy; insufferable, intolerable, unbearable, unendurable; atrocious, execrable, miserable, vile, wretched; exceptional, exquisite, extreme, fancy, first-class, high-grade, matchless, maximized, maximum, optimal, optimum, peerless, preeminent, premium, special, supreme, unmatched, unparalleled; A1, bang-up, banner, capital, classic, crackerjack, dandy, divine, fabulous, fine, first-rate, grand, great, heavenly, jim-dandy, keen, marvelous (*or* marvellous), mean, neat, nifty, noble, par excellence, prime, sensational, splendid, stellar, sterling, superb, superior, superlative, supernal, swell, terrific, tip-top, top, top-notch, unsurpassed, wonderful
antonyms deficient, inadequate, insufficient, lacking, unacceptable, unsatisfactory, wanting

adequately *adv* **1** in a satisfactory way ⟨We weren't completely bowled over by the performance, but the band certainly played more than *adequately*.⟩ — see WELL 1
2 in or to a degree or quantity that meets one's requirements or satisfaction ⟨*adequately* provided with candles and freshwater in case of a power outage⟩ — see ENOUGH 1

adhere *vb* to hold to something firmly as if by adhesion ⟨Everyone started calling her "Cookie" when she was little and the name *adhered*.⟩ — see STICK 1

adhere (to) *vb* **1** to give steadfast support to ⟨Our coach *adheres to* the belief that we can win this game if we just have a positive attitude.⟩

synonyms cling (to), hew (to), keep (to), stand by, stick (to *or* with)

related words cleave (to); advocate, back, champion, confirm, defend, endorse (*also* indorse), espouse, support, uphold; accept, adopt, cherish, cultivate, embrace, follow, foster, heed; bolster, boost, buttress, enforce

phrases abide by, hold to, live up to

near antonyms abandon, desert, forsake, give up, relinquish, spurn, surrender; recall, recant, reconsider, renege, renounce, retract, revoke, take back, unsay, withdraw; disagree (with), disprove, dispute, rebut, refute; contradict, deny, disavow, disclaim, disown, gainsay, negate, negative, repudiate; back down, back off, backtrack

antonyms defect (from)

2 to act according to the commands of ⟨*adhere to* the terms of the deceased's will⟩ — see OBEY

adherence *n* **1** a physical sticking to as if by glue ⟨You'd think these refrigerator magnets would have better *adherence*—they fall off every time I open the door.⟩ — see ADHESION 1

2 the following of a custom, rule, or law ⟨*Adherence* to convention requires that the couple send out formal wedding invitations.⟩ — see OBSERVANCE 1

adherent *adj* tending to adhere to objects upon contact ⟨The bandage is made from a mildly *adherent* fiber.⟩ — see STICKY 1

adherent *n* one who follows the opinions or teachings of another ⟨one of the philosopher's *adherents*⟩ — see FOLLOWER 1

adhesion *n* **1** a physical sticking to as if by glue ⟨discourages the use of photo albums that keep the pictures in place by *adhesion* to the pages⟩

synonyms adherence, bonding, cling

related words clumping, cohesion; adhesiveness, attachment, cohesiveness, tenacity; cementing, gluing (*also* glueing)

antonyms unsticking

2 adherence to something to which one is bound by a pledge or duty ⟨She has always shown steadfast *adhesion* to psychiatry's code of ethics.⟩ — see FIDELITY

adhesive *adj* tending to adhere to objects upon contact ⟨She walked barefoot through *adhesive*, clayey mud.⟩ — see STICKY 1

adhesive *n* a substance used to stick things together ⟨She prefers envelopes coated with *adhesive* so that she doesn't have to do any licking.⟩ — see GLUE

adieu *n* an expression of good wishes at parting ⟨We bid our *adieus* and were off.⟩ — see GOOD-BYE

adipose *adj* containing animal fat especially in unusual amounts ⟨Seals have a thick layer of *adipose* tissue, which acts as insulation against the cold and contributes to buoyancy as well.⟩ — see FATTY

adjacent *adj* having a border in common ⟨Their house is *adjacent* to a wooded park.⟩

synonyms abutting, adjoining, bordering, contiguous, flanking, flush, fringing, joining, juxtaposed, neighboring, skirting, touching, verging

related words approximate, close, closest, immediate, near, nearby, nearest, next-door, nigh; attached, communicating, connected, connecting, interconnecting, joined, linked, united; bounding, circumjacent, embracing, encircling, enclosing (*also* inclosing), fencing, rimming, surrounding; peripheral, tangent, tangential; encompassing

near antonyms apart, detached, disconnected, discrete, free-standing, isolate, isolated, removed, separate, single, unattached, unconnected, unlinked; away, distant, far, faraway, far-off, farthest, remote; discontinuous, noncontinuous; broken up, disjoined, dissevered, dissociat-

ed, disunited, divided, divorced, parted, ramified, resolved, severed, split, sundered, uncoupled, unyoked

antonyms nonadjacent, noncontiguous

adjoin *vb* **1** to be adjacent to ⟨The bedroom of their apartment *adjoins* their neighbor's living room.⟩

synonyms abut, border (on), flank, fringe, join, neighbor, skirt, touch, verge (on)

related words attach (to), communicate (with), connect (with), link (with); bound, embrace, encircle, enclose (*also* inclose), fence, line, margin, rim, surround; contact, converge, meet

2 to join (something) to a mass, quantity, or number so as to bring about an overall increase ⟨After the dictionary writer's talk, the principal *adjoined* a few remarks about her own love of words.⟩ — see ADD 1

adjoining *adj* having a border in common ⟨The cows had broken through the fence and were grazing in the *adjoining* field.⟩ — see ADJACENT

adjourn *vb* to bring to a formal close for a period of time ⟨The meeting was *adjourned* by the chairperson until further notice.⟩

synonyms recess, suspend

related words break off, disband, discontinue, disperse, intermit, interrupt; defer, hold off, postpone, put off, reserve, shelve, table; dissolve, end, halt, stop, terminate; break up, close, conclude, wind up, wrap up; abort, call, call off, drop, recall, repeal, rescind, revoke; abrogate, annul, invalidate, negate, nullify, quash, void

near antonyms inaugurate, launch, open; carry on, continue, draw out, extend, proceed, prolong; renew, reopen, resume; assemble, call, convene, convoke, muster, rally, summon

adjudge *vb* to give an opinion about (something at issue or in dispute) ⟨His version of what had happened was generally *adjudged* to be completely fictitious.⟩ — see JUDGE 1

adjudicate *vb* to give an opinion about (something at issue or in dispute) ⟨When we asked the salesclerk to *adjudicate* our disagreement, she agreed with me that the white shoes looked better.⟩ — see JUDGE 1

adjunct *n* **1** a person who helps a more skilled person ⟨serving as an *adjunct* to the congressional delegation on its fact-finding mission⟩ — see HELPER

2 something that is not necessary in itself but adds to the convenience or performance of the main piece of equipment ⟨You can spend a lot on camera accessories, but this nifty little battery recharger is the one *adjunct* that will pay for itself.⟩ — see ACCESSORY 1

adjure *vb* **1** to give advice to ⟨Their coach *adjured* them not to break the laws of any of the countries they would be visiting.⟩ — see ADVISE 1

2 to issue orders to (someone) by right of authority ⟨He *adjured* his followers to remain faithful to the cause.⟩ — see COMMAND 1

adjust *vb* to change (something) so as to make it suitable for a new use or situation ⟨After going on the night shift, he found it difficult to *adjust* his sleep schedule.⟩ ⟨*Adjust* the amount of sugar in the recipe to your taste.⟩ — see ADAPT

adjustable *adj* capable of being readily changed ⟨quantities that are easily *adjustable* if you're cooking for a larger crowd⟩ — see FLEXIBLE 1

adjutant *n* a person who helps a more skilled person ⟨The senator's *adjutants* and aides always arrive ahead of him on the campaign trail.⟩ — see HELPER

ad–lib *adj* made or done without previous thought or preparation ⟨not bad for an *ad-lib* comedy routine⟩ — see EXTEMPORANEOUS

ad–lib *vb* to perform, make, or do without preparation

⟨She had to *ad-lib* constructing a piñata because she'd never actually seen it being done.⟩ — see IMPROVISE

administer *vb* **1** to give out (something) to appropriate individuals ⟨The principal *administers* discipline fairly when students break the rules.⟩

synonyms allocate, apportion, deal (out), dispense, distribute, mete (out), parcel (out), portion, prorate

related words admeasure, allot, allow, appropriate, assign, dish out, divide, divvy (up), dollop (out), lot, measure (out), part, proportion, ration, redistribute, set, share (out), split; bestow, disburse, furnish, issue, provide, share, supply; circulate, disperse, disseminate, scatter, spread; chip in, contribute, donate, pledge; reallocate, reapportion

near antonyms decline, deny, deprive (of), disallow, refuse, reject, withhold; pinch, skimp, stint

antonyms misallocate

2 to carry out effectively ⟨Local officials should see that the fair housing laws are rigorously *administered*.⟩ — see ENFORCE

3 to look after and make decisions about ⟨The lieutenant governor *administers* the affairs of the state in the absence of the governor.⟩ — see CONDUCT 1

administration *n* **1** lawful control over the affairs of a political unit (as a nation) ⟨the fair and just *administration* of the U.S. territories⟩ — see RULE 2

2 the act or activity of looking after and making decisions about something ⟨*Administration* of the funds was left in the hands of a committee.⟩ — see CONDUCT 1

administrative *adj* suited for or relating to the directing of things ⟨Among his other *administrative* duties is the appointment of transit authority officials.⟩ — see EXECUTIVE

administrator *n* a person who manages or directs something ⟨a hospital *administrator*⟩ — see EXECUTIVE

admirable *adj* deserving of high regard or great approval ⟨It's *admirable* the way she helps her elderly neighbor with chores and errands every Saturday.⟩

synonyms applaudable, commendable, creditable, laudable, meritorious, praiseworthy

related words deserving, worthy; awesome, distinctive, distinguished, excellent, honorable, impressive, noteworthy, noticeable, outstanding, redoubtable, reputable, respectable; precious, valuable; delightful, enjoyable, pleasing, satisfying; ethical, good, high-minded, moral, noble, principled

near antonyms base, contemptible, deplorable, despicable, detestable, dirty, infamous, lousy, nasty, notorious, pitiable, pitiful, scabby, scummy, scurvy, sorry, unlikable, unworthy, vile, worthless, wretched; disgraceful, dishonorable, disreputable, ignominious, low, mean, scandalous, seamy, shady, shameful, shocking, sordid, unethical, unsavory

antonyms censurable, discreditable, illaudable, reprehensible

admiration *n* **1** a feeling of great approval and liking ⟨She won *admiration* for her courage.⟩

synonyms account, appreciation, esteem, estimation, favor, regard, respect

related words appetite, fancy, fondness, like, love, partiality, preference, relish, shine, taste, use; acclamation, adoration, adulation, approbation, deference, homage, honor, idolatry, infatuation, lionization, praise, reverence, veneration, worship; delight, enjoyment; amazement, awe, wonder, wonderment; enthusiasm, interest, passion; bias, prejudice; affection, attachment, devotion, passion

near antonyms condemnation, disapproval, disdain, opprobrium, scorn; disappointment, discontent, disenchantment, disgruntlement, disillusionment, displeasure,

indignation, unhappiness; aversion, contempt, disfavor, disgust, disinclination, dislike, disliking, disregard, distaste; hate, hatred, loathing, nausea, repugnance, repulsion, revulsion; abomination, antipathy; deprecation, displeasure, dissatisfaction

antonyms disfavor

2 the rapt attention and deep emotion caused by the sight of something extraordinary ⟨Onlookers gaped in *admiration* as one flower-bedecked float after another paraded past them.⟩ — see WONDER 2

admire *vb* to think very highly or favorably of ⟨I *admire* the way you handled such a touchy situation.⟩

synonyms appreciate, consider, esteem, regard, respect

related words acclaim, accredit, applaud, approve, commend, compliment, credit, praise; delight (in), enjoy, relish, revel (in), savor (*also* savour); dig, fancy, favor, groove (on), like, love; adore, adulate, canonize, deify, dote (on), hallow, idolize, revere, reverence, venerate, worship; cherish, love, prize, treasure, value

phrases set store by (*or* on)

near antonyms abhor, abominate, despise, detest, execrate, hate, loathe; condemn, decry, deplore, disapprove, discount, discountenance, disdain, disfavor, dislike, dismiss, disregard, scorn, vilify

admiring *adj* expressing approval ⟨The smartly dressed couple drew *admiring* glances.⟩ — see FAVORABLE 1

admissible *adj* that may be permitted ⟨Using direct quotations without naming your source is not *admissible*.⟩ — see PERMISSIBLE

admission *n* **1** an open declaration of something (as a fault or the commission of an offense) about oneself ⟨By his own *admission*, his cooking is not the greatest.⟩ — see CONFESSION

2 the means or right of entering or participating in ⟨no *admission* unless accompanied by an adult⟩ — see ENTRANCE 1

admit *vb* **1** to accept the truth or existence of (something) usually reluctantly ⟨The host of the talk show eventually *admitted* that she hadn't actually read the book.⟩ ⟨You can't bring yourself to *admit* your mistakes.⟩

synonyms acknowledge, agree, allow, concede, confess, grant, own (up to)

related words disburden, unburden, unload; affirm, avow, confirm, profess; accept, recognize, yield; announce, break, broadcast, communicate, declare, disclose, divulge, impart, proclaim, publish, reveal, spill, tell, unveil; betray, blab, expose, give away, inform, leak, rat, squeal, talk, tattle, tip (off), warn, wise (up)

phrases come clean (about)

near antonyms disallow, disavow, disclaim, disown; contradict, dispute, gainsay, negate, negative; rebut, refute, reject, repudiate; conceal, cover (up), hide, obscure, veil; kid (oneself)

antonyms deny

2 to offer entrance (as to a place, school, or privilege) to ⟨She was *admitted* to Harvard.⟩

synonyms enter, take

related words entertain, welcome; fellowship; confirm, ratify

near antonyms decline, disallow, disapprove, dismiss, refuse, reject; blackball, blacklist, ostracize; banish, deport, exile, expel, oust, throw out

antonyms ban, bar

3 to make an acknowledgment of something unpleasant as true or valid ⟨I *admit* to some suspicions about the new neighbors.⟩ — see CONFESS 1

admittance *n* the means or right of entering or participating in ⟨*Admittance* to the country club requires sponsorship from a current member.⟩ — see ENTRANCE 1

admittedly *adv* to tell the truth ⟨*Admittedly*, I should not have lost my temper like that.⟩ — see ACTUALLY 1

admixture *n* a distinct entity formed by the combining of two or more different things ⟨an *admixture* of rose petals and lavender for a fragrant potpourri⟩ — see BLEND

admonish *vb* **1** to criticize (someone) so as to correct a fault ⟨The ranger *admonished* her for littering.⟩ — see REBUKE 1
2 to give advice to ⟨My physician is always *admonishing* me to eat more healthy foods.⟩ — see ADVISE 1

admonishing *adj* serving as or offering a warning ⟨Mom shot an *admonishing* glance at me just as I was about to spill the beans.⟩ — see CAUTIONARY

admonishment *n* **1** an opinion suggesting a wise or proper course of action ⟨wintertime *admonishments* about remembering to wear a coat and hat⟩ — see ADVICE
2 the act or an instance of telling beforehand of danger or risk ⟨That near miss with the guardrail was all the *admonishment* I needed to slow down.⟩ — see WARNING 1

admonition *n* **1** an opinion suggesting a wise or proper course of action ⟨a heartfelt *admonition* to the graduates to make the most of their lives⟩ — see ADVICE
2 the act or an instance of telling beforehand of danger or risk ⟨He ignored the ranger's *admonitions* and took the road over the mountain, only to be stranded by the blizzard.⟩ — see WARNING 1

admonitory *adj* serving as or offering a warning ⟨*Admonitory* articles abound around Halloween, warning parents of the hazards of trick-or-treating.⟩ — see CAUTIONARY

ado *n* a state of noisy, confused activity ⟨a bride-to-be caught up in the usual prenuptial *ado*⟩ — see COMMOTION

adolescent *adj* **1** being in the early stage of life, growth, or development ⟨an *adolescent* sheepdog, who hasn't quite gotten the hang of keeping the sheep huddled together⟩ — see YOUNG
2 having or showing the annoying qualities (as silliness) associated with children ⟨We would hope that the college students had outgrown such *adolescent* behavior.⟩ — see CHILDISH
3 lacking in adult experience or maturity ⟨They took a group of *adolescent* recruits and turned them into professional warriors.⟩ — see CALLOW

adopt *vb* to take for one's own use (something originated by another) ⟨We *adopted* some of the local customs.⟩
synonyms borrow, embrace, espouse, take on, take up
related words domesticate, naturalize; appropriate, arrogate, take over, usurp; absorb, assimilate, incorporate, quote; cherish, prize, treasure; cultivate, follow, heed, honor; use, utilize; bring up, foster, nurture, raise, rear; affect, assume, copy, imitate, pretend, put on, simulate
phrases pick up on
near antonyms abandon, forsake, give up, relinquish, surrender; reject, renounce, repudiate, spurn; discard, jettison, junk, throw away, throw out

adorable *adj* having qualities that tend to make one loved ⟨What an *adorable* old lady, so kind and sweet!⟩ ⟨an *adorable* little cottage⟩ — see LOVABLE

adore *vb* **1** to feel passion, devotion, or tenderness for ⟨an attentive, solicitous husband who clearly *adores* his wife⟩ — see LOVE 2
2 to love or admire too much ⟨The teen *adores* her older sister so much that she cannot see her faults.⟩ — see IDOLIZE
3 to offer honor or respect to (someone) as a divine power ⟨worshippers *adoring* the deity⟩ — see WORSHIP 1
4 to take pleasure in ⟨I *adore* those earrings—wherever did you get them?⟩ — see ENJOY 1

adoring *adj* **1** feeling or showing love ⟨*adoring* grandparents who love to spoil their grandchildren⟩ — see LOVING 1
2 reflecting great admiration or devotion ⟨the *adoring* attention of the girls' gymnastics team when our local Olympic hero spoke to them⟩ — see WORSHIPFUL

adorn *vb* to make more attractive by adding something that is beautiful or becoming ⟨The Sultan's tent was richly *adorned* with thick tapestries and gleaming gold candlesticks.⟩ — see DECORATE

adorning *adj* serving to add beauty ⟨*Adorning* garlands of greenery can be seen all over the mansion.⟩ — see DECORATIVE

adornment *n* something that decorates or beautifies ⟨The only *adornment* in the sparely furnished bedroom was a small portrait of the poet Walt Whitman.⟩ — see DECORATION 1

adroit *adj* accomplished with trained ability ⟨With an *adroit* flick of the wrist, she flipped the omelet into the air and landed it squarely back in the pan.⟩ — see SKILLFUL 1

adroitly *adv* in a skillful or expert manner ⟨The captain *adroitly* navigated his vessel through the treacherous waters.⟩ — see WELL 3

adroitness *n* **1** mental skill or quickness ⟨He shows a remarkable *adroitness* in identifying birds the moment they land at the feeder.⟩ — see DEXTERITY 1
2 subtle or imaginative ability in inventing, devising, or executing something ⟨With the *adroitness* of a magician, she twisted the balloons into the shape of a monkey.⟩ — see SKILL 1

adulate *vb* **1** to love or admire too much ⟨The entire family *adulates* their team's quarterback.⟩ — see IDOLIZE
2 to praise too much ⟨a business executive who surrounds herself with assistants who spend all their time *adulating* her⟩ — see FLATTER 1

adulation *n* **1** excessive admiration of or devotion to a person ⟨the pathetic *adulation* of the leader of the cult by her misguided followers⟩ — see WORSHIP
2 excessive praise ⟨More objective critics have observed that the artist never deserved the *adulation* heaped upon his mediocre paintings.⟩ — see FLATTERY

adulatory *adj* **1** overly or insincerely flattering ⟨an office flunky who can be counted on to make an *adulatory* response to the boss's every suggestion⟩ — see FULSOME 1
2 reflecting great admiration or devotion ⟨an *adulatory* eulogy delivered at a beloved teacher's retirement party⟩ — see WORSHIPFUL

adult *adj* **1** relating to or typical of adults; displaying proper maturity ⟨an *adult* reaction to the issue⟩
synonyms grown-up, mature
near antonyms childish, infantile, kiddish
antonyms adolescent, immature
2 fully grown or developed ⟨insects that are butterflies in their *adult* stage⟩ — see MATURE 1

adult *n* a fully grown person ⟨At the beach, the *adults* sat under broad umbrellas while the children splashed in the water.⟩
synonyms grown-up
related words middle-ager; ancient, elder, gaffer, graybeard, oldster, old-timer, senior, senior citizen
near antonyms child, cub, kid, moppet, tad, toddler, tot; baby, infant; adolescent, juvenile, minor, youngster, youth; preteen, preteenager, teen, teenager, teener, teenybopper, tween

adulterant *n* something that is or that makes impure ⟨concerned about *adulterants* in the town's water supply coming from the discharge from the factory⟩ — see IMPURITY 1

adulterate *adj* containing foreign or lower-grade substances ⟨The pharmacist was convicted of selling *adulterate* drugs in order to maximize profits.⟩ — see IMPURE 1

adulterate *vb* to alter (something) for the worse with the addition of foreign or lower-grade substances ⟨The company was fined for *adulterating* its "all beef" frankfurters with cereal.⟩

synonyms cut, dilute, extend, lace, sophisticate, thin, weaken

related words load; befoul, contaminate, corrupt, defile, dirty, envenom, foul, infect, poison, pollute, soil, spoil, sully, taint; cheapen, debase, degrade; manipulate, misrepresent, tamper (with); counterfeit, fake, falsify, fudge; doctor, spike; moderate, qualify, temper

near antonyms fertilize, lard; augment, supplement; decontaminate, purify; clarify, clean, cleanse, distill (*also* distil), filter, flush, leach, pasteurize, purge, refine; better, enhance, improve; compact, concentrate, condense

antonyms enrich, fortify, richen, strengthen

adulterated *adj* containing foreign or lower-grade substances ⟨The outbreak of food poisoning was traced to *adulterated* ground beef.⟩ — see IMPURE 1

adultery *n* a sexual encounter or relationship between a married person and someone other than their spouse ⟨accusations of *adultery*⟩

synonyms infidelity, unfaithfulness

related words promiscuity; disloyalty, faithlessness, falseness, inconstancy, perfidiousness, perfidy, treachery; affair (*also* affaire), fling, love, love affair, romance; intrigue; attachment, infatuation; entanglement, flirtation; liaison, passion

near antonyms allegiance, constancy, dedication, devotedness, devotion, fealty, loyalty, steadfastness

antonyms faithfulness, fidelity

adulthood *n* the state of being fully grown or developed ⟨The period between childhood and *adulthood* is called adolescence.⟩ — see MATURITY

advance *n* **1** forward movement in time or place ⟨During her long convalescence, the housebound woman was barely aware of the *advance* of the seasons.⟩

synonyms advancement, furtherance, going, headway, march, onrush, passage, process, procession, progress, progression

related words current, drift, flow, flux, stream, way; advent, approach, arrival, coming, nearing; bound, jump, leap, step, stride; impetus, momentum

near antonyms ebb, reflux; retraction, return, reversal, reverse

antonyms recess, recession, regress, regression, retreat, retrogression

2 an instance of notable progress in the development of knowledge, technology, or skill ⟨Under her new teacher, the aspiring violinist has made noticeable *advances* in her technique in just a few weeks.⟩

synonyms advancement, breakthrough, enhancement, improvement, refinement

related words quantum leap; amelioration, boost, heightening, increase, melioration, strengthening, upgrade, uplift, upswing, uptrend, upturn; betterment, development, elaboration, evolution, expansion, gestation, growth, maturation, perfection, ripening; civilization, edification, education, enlightenment; renascence, revival; innovation, invention

near antonyms breakdown, collapse, crash; hindrance, impediment, stumbling block; decadence, decay, decline, decrease, degeneration, descent, deterioration, diminishment, downgrade, ebbing, failing, flagging, languishment, lapse, lessening, reduction, sinking, slowing, weak-

ening, worsening; detriment, disablement, drawback, glitch, impairment, shortcoming

antonyms setback

advance *vb* **1** to give to another for temporary use with the understanding that it or a like thing will be returned ⟨*advanced* her some cash with the understanding that the amount would be deducted from her first paycheck⟩ — see LEND

2 to help the growth or development of ⟨great thinkers who did much to *advance* modern science⟩ — see FOSTER 1

3 to move forward along a course ⟨As the technology *advances*, electronic devices keep getting smarter.⟩ — see GO 1

4 to move higher in rank or position ⟨Within six months he was *advanced* to the position of headwaiter.⟩ — see PROMOTE 1

5 to set before the mind for consideration ⟨Let me explain my reasons for *advancing* this proposal.⟩ — see PROPOSE 1

6 to move closer to ⟨I *advanced* cautiously toward the snarling dog.⟩ — see COME 1

advanced *adj* being far along in development ⟨An *advanced* civilization, among the first anywhere to use the plow, developed on the banks of the Nile River thousands of years ago.⟩

synonyms developed, evolved, forward, high, higher, improved, late, progressive, refined

related words precocious; full-blown, full-fledged, full-scale; aged, mature, matured, perfected, ripe, ripened; civilized, educated, enhanced, enlightened; contemporary, current, latest, leading-edge, mod, modern, new, newest, newfangled, new-fashioned, novel, now, present-day, recent, space-age, supermodern, ultramodern, up-to-date; avant

near antonyms green, immature, underdeveloped, undersized (*also* undersize), underweight, unripe, unripened; uncivilized, uneducated; early, embryonic, germinal, primeval, primordial; antediluvian, antiquated, antique, dated, fusty, hoary, musty, Neanderthal (*or* Neandertal), obsolete, old, oldfangled, old-fashioned, old-time, out-of-date, outworn, passé, past

antonyms backward, low, lower, nonprogressive, primitive, rude, rudimentary, undeveloped

advancement *n* **1** a raising or a state of being raised to a higher rank or position ⟨The young man's rapid *advancement* in the company came as no surprise to those who knew him.⟩

synonyms ascent, creation, elevation, preference, preferment, promotion, rise, upgrade

related words aggrandizement, ennoblement, exaltation, glorification, magnification

near antonyms deposition, dethronement, discharge, dismissal, expulsion, impeachment, ouster, overthrow, removal, suspension, unmaking, unseating; downfall, fall

antonyms abasement, comedown, degradation, downgrade, reduction

2 an instance of notable progress in the development of knowledge, technology, or skill ⟨Science has made huge *advancements* in the field of genetics in recent years.⟩ — see ADVANCE 2

3 forward movement in time or place ⟨wondered why we hadn't made any *advancement* in the long checkout line for at least 10 minutes⟩ — see ADVANCE 1

advantage *n* **1** the more favorable condition or position in a competition ⟨Your experience volunteering at the hospital will put you at an *advantage* when you're applying for a job there.⟩

synonyms better, bulge, drop, edge, jump, pull, stead, upper hand, vantage

related words allowance, head start, lead, margin, odds, start; ascendancy (*also* ascendency), command, dominance, mastery, predominance, superiority, supremacy, transcendence, transcendency; precedence, preference, prerogative, privilege, seniority; break, foothold, opportunity; benefit, blessing, boon, felicity, godsend, manna, windfall

near antonyms detriment, stranglehold; disparity, imbalance, inequality, unevenness; disability, failing, impairment, shortcoming; bar, catch, check, clog, crimp, embarrassment, hindrance, hitch, hurdle, impediment, interference, let, manacle, obstacle, obstruction, rub, shackle, stop, trammel; lurch, setback

antonyms disadvantage, drawback, handicap, liability, minus, penalty, strike

2 a thing that helps ⟨had all the *advantages* of being born into a wealthy and powerful family⟩ — see HELP 2

advantage *vb* to provide with something useful or desirable ⟨There's no question that that bicycle racer was significantly *advantaged* by a great set of genes.⟩ — see BENEFIT

advantageous *adj* promoting or contributing to personal or social well-being ⟨a trade agreement that is *advantageous* to both countries⟩ — see BENEFICIAL

advent *n* the act of coming upon a scene ⟨With the *advent* of the mass-produced automobile, the need for a better system of roads and highways soon became apparent.⟩ — see ARRIVAL

adventure *n* **1** an exciting or noteworthy event that one experiences firsthand ⟨Our quiet hike turned into quite an *adventure* when we encountered a bear and her cub.⟩

synonyms experience, exploit, happening, time

related words escapade, lark, ploy; act, action, deed, doing, feat; episode, occasion; baptism, ordeal, test, trial, tribulation; enterprise, risk, venture; expedition, exploration, mission, performance, quest; stunt

near antonyms bore, bummer, bust, downer, drag

2 a risky undertaking ⟨a bold *adventure* in deep-sea exploration that could imperil the submarine and its crew⟩ — see GAMBLE

adventure *vb* **1** to place in danger ⟨The man *adventured* all his savings in a very risky investment scheme.⟩ — see ENDANGER

2 to take a chance on ⟨If I had to *adventure* a guess, I'd say she's about 35.⟩ — see RISK 1

adventuresome *adj* inclined or willing to take risks ⟨They're not inclined to be *adventuresome* when it comes to foreign travel, preferring guided bus tours that stick to the beaten path.⟩ — see BOLD 1

adventurous *adj* inclined or willing to take risks ⟨Let's be *adventurous* and take a bus into the city for New Year's Eve this year.⟩ — see BOLD 1

adversary *adj* marked by opposition or ill will ⟨There was a long history of *adversary* dealings between the two nations.⟩ — see HOSTILE 1

adversary *n* **1** one that is hostile toward another ⟨Our old cat seemed to consider the new kitten an *adversary*.⟩ — see ENEMY

2 one that takes a position opposite another in a competition or conflict ⟨Our *adversaries* in tomorrow's meet are from one of the top schools in the league.⟩ — see OPPONENT 1

adverse *adj* **1** opposed to one's interests ⟨All the *adverse* publicity really caused the movie star's popularity to suffer.⟩

synonyms counter, disadvantageous, hostile, inimical, negative, prejudicial, unfavorable, unfriendly, unsympathetic, untoward

related words bad, baleful, baneful, evil; damaging, deleterious, destructive, detrimental, fatal, harmful, hurtful,

ill, injurious, lethal, malignant, murderous, noxious, pernicious, poisonous, ruinous, threatening, troublesome, unhealthy, wounding; dangerous, hazardous, imperiling (*or* imperilling), jeopardizing, perilous, risky, unsafe; defamatory, offensive, scathing, slanderous; antagonistic, antipathetic, inhospitable, intolerant, uncongenial, uncooperative; competing, conflicting, counteracting, countering, opposing, resistant, resisting

near antonyms beneficial, good, helpful, propitious, useful; harmless, innocent, innocuous, inoffensive, nondestructive, nonfatal, nonlethal, nonthreatening; unresistant; tolerant, understanding; affable, agreeable, amiable, amicable, benign, benignant, complying, congenial, cordial, friendly, hospitable

antonyms advantageous, favorable, friendly, positive, supportive, sympathetic, well-disposed

2 causing or capable of causing harm ⟨The *adverse* effects of the drug are too severe to allow it to be marketed.⟩ — see HARMFUL

adversity *n* **1** bad luck or an example of this ⟨Many people came face-to-face with life-altering *adversity* when the stock market crashed.⟩ — see MISFORTUNE

2 something that is a cause for suffering or special effort especially in the attainment of a goal ⟨Some overcame all the *adversities* of the Great Depression and rebuilt their fortunes.⟩ — see DIFFICULTY 1

advert (to) *vb* to make reference to or speak about briefly but specifically ⟨When our hosts *adverted to* the lateness of the hour we took the hint, and prepared to leave.⟩ — see MENTION 1

advertise *vb* to make known openly or publicly ⟨I wouldn't *advertise* my bad credit rating to the whole world if I were you.⟩ — see ANNOUNCE

advertisement *n* a published statement informing the public of a matter of general interest ⟨an *advertisement* for special low fares to Florida and Cancún during spring break⟩ — see ANNOUNCEMENT

advice *n* an opinion suggesting a wise or proper course of action ⟨We got some good *advice* from the vet about dealing with our dog's habit of chasing cars.⟩

synonyms admonishment, admonition, counsel, guidance, input

related words recommendation, suggestion; hint, pointer, tip; feedback, information; answer, solution; advisement, consideration, thought; alarm (*also* alarum), alert, caution, cautioning, expostulation, forewarning, remonstrance, remonstration, urging, warning; judgment (*or* judgement), observation, verdict; assistance, briefing, coaching, direction, instruction, mentoring, priming, prompting, teaching, tutoring; interference, kibitzing (*also* kibbitzing), meddling; moralizing, pontificating, preaching; exhortation, lecture, lesson, sermon, speech

advisable *adj* suitable for bringing about a desired result under the circumstances ⟨It's never *advisable* to ride double on a bicycle.⟩ — see EXPEDIENT

advise *vb* **1** to give advice to ⟨a popular guidance counselor who has been *advising* students about their college plans for two decades⟩

synonyms adjure, admonish, counsel

related words alert, caution, forewarn, warn; brief, clue (in), fill in, inform, tell, wise (up); coach, direct, guide, instruct, lead, mentor, shepherd, show, teach, tutor; direct, pilot, steer; acquaint, apprise, familiarize; convince, encourage, induce, persuade, talk (into); beg, exhort, implore, prevail (upon), urge; propose, recommend, suggest

2 to put (something) forward as one's choice for a wise or proper course of action ⟨She *advised* calling ahead for a reservation at the new restaurant.⟩

synonyms counsel, recommend, suggest

related words advocate, back, champion, espouse, favor, support; exhort, urge; advance, offer, propose, submit

3 to exchange viewpoints or seek advice for the purpose of finding a solution to a problem ⟨The doctor *advised* with his partner before recommending the patient's treatment.⟩ — see CONFER 2

4 to give information to ⟨We *advised* her as to the best way to get to the art museum by public transportation.⟩ — see ENLIGHTEN 1

5 to give notice to beforehand especially of danger or risk ⟨He *advised* us not to invest our money in what looked like a pyramid scheme.⟩ — see WARN

advised *adj* decided on as a result of careful thought ⟨an *advised* financial decision⟩ — see DELIBERATE 1

advisedly *adv* with full awareness of what one is doing ⟨I'm calling him a traitor, and I use that term *advisedly*.⟩ — see INTENTIONALLY

advisement *n* a careful weighing of the reasons for or against something ⟨We'll take that matter under *advisement* and get back to you later.⟩ — see CONSIDERATION 1

adviser *or* **advisor** *n* a person who gives advice especially professionally ⟨Our financial *adviser* had some words of caution about buying a second home.⟩ — see CONSULTANT

advocate *n* **1** a person who actively supports or favors a cause ⟨Mark Twain, Noah Webster, and President Theodore Roosevelt are among past *advocates* of a reformed spelling system.⟩ — see EXPONENT 1

2 a person whose profession is to conduct lawsuits for clients or to advise about legal rights and obligations ⟨With such a strong case against him, he's going to need the best *advocate*.⟩ — see LAWYER

advocate *vb* to promote the interests or cause of ⟨environmentalists *advocating* agricultural methods designed to slow the destruction of rain forests⟩ — see SUPPORT 1

aegis *also* **egis** *n* **1** means or method of defending ⟨has no claim to the land under the *aegis* of the law⟩ — see DEFENSE 1

2 the financial support and general guidance for an undertaking ⟨a medical study that was questioned by many because it was done under the *aegis* of a major pharmaceutical company⟩ — see AUSPICE 1

aesthetic *also* **esthetic** *or* **aesthetical** *or* **esthetical** *adj* very pleasing to look at ⟨an *aesthetic* arrangement of the floral decorations⟩ — see BEAUTIFUL 1

affability *n* the state or quality of having a pleasant or agreeable manner in socializing with others ⟨First Lady Dolley Madison was beloved by the nation for her *affability* toward people from all walks of life.⟩ — see AMIABILITY 1

affable *adj* **1** having a relaxed, casual manner ⟨As the show's *affable* host, she keeps the freewheeling gabfest from getting out of hand.⟩ — see EASYGOING 1

2 having an easygoing and pleasing manner especially in social situations ⟨As an experienced event planner, he knows that having an *affable* emcee is critical.⟩ — see AMIABLE

3 showing a natural kindness and courtesy especially in social situations ⟨a welcoming, *affable* host⟩ — see GRACIOUS 1

affair *n* **1** *also* **affaire** a brief romantic relationship ⟨an *affair* between two singles spending the summer at the same beach resort⟩
synonyms fling, love, love affair, romance
related words intrigue, liaison; dalliance, hanky-panky; attachment, infatuation; entanglement, flirtation; idyll (*also* idyl), passion; calf-love, puppy love

2 a social gathering ⟨The annual country club dance is a really fancy *affair*.⟩ — see PARTY 1

3 something produced by physical or intellectual effort ⟨The lead float in the parade was a pretty impressive *affair*, a giant eagle's head with equally huge wings.⟩ — see PRODUCT 1

4 something that happens ⟨The whole *affair* from start to finish took a total of 15 minutes.⟩ — see EVENT 1

5 something to be dealt with ⟨It's none of your *affair* whom I'm going out with tonight.⟩ — see MATTER 2

¹affect *vb* **1** to act upon (a person or a person's feelings) so as to cause a response ⟨Their son claims that scary movies don't *affect* him in the least.⟩
synonyms impact, impress, influence, move, reach, strike, sway, tell (on), touch
related words carry away, dazzle, enrapture, enthrall (*or* enthral), entrance, ravish, transport; bias, color; inspire, stir; engage, interest, involve, penetrate, pierce; afflict, agitate, bother, concern, discomfort, discompose, disquiet, distress, disturb, fluster, harry, perturb, pester, plague, smite, strain, stress, trouble, try, upset, worry, wring; allure, attract, bewitch, captivate, charm, enchant, fascinate
phrases get to
near antonyms bore, jade, pall, tire, weary; underwhelm

2 to be the business or affair of ⟨Fortunately, hurricane season doesn't *affect* the West Coast.⟩ — see CONCERN 2

²affect *vb* to present a false appearance of ⟨She *affected* complete unawareness that we were talking about her, though she must have overheard.⟩ — see FEIGN

affectation *n* the quality or state of appearing or trying to appear more important or more valuable than is the case ⟨a woman of great *affectation* at the company⟩ — see PRETENSE 1

affected *adj* **1** lacking in natural or spontaneous quality ⟨*affected* laughter at the boss's jokes⟩ ⟨an *affected* southern accent⟩ — see ARTIFICIAL 1

2 self-consciously trying to present an appearance of grandeur or importance ⟨With her pinkie extended, the four-year-old held her tiny teacup in an *affected* manner.⟩ — see PRETENTIOUS 1

3 having a liking or affection ⟨an apprentice who was well *affected* to learning⟩ — see FOND 1

affectedness *n* the quality or state of appearing or trying to appear more important or more valuable than is the case ⟨She bowed and sat down at the piano with a degree of *affectedness* that was laughable.⟩ — see PRETENSE 1

affecting *adj* having the power to affect the feelings or sympathies ⟨the *affecting* final scene in the play, when the children are reunited with their father⟩ — see MOVING

affection *n* **1** a feeling of strong or constant regard for and dedication to someone ⟨an elderly couple showing their *affection* for each other by little acts of kindness⟩ — see LOVE 1

2 a habitual attraction to some activity or thing ⟨I'm rooting for the team that's behind—just my natural *affection* for the underdog, I guess.⟩ — see INCLINATION 1

affectionate *adj* feeling or showing love ⟨an *affectionate* child who gives hugs and kisses freely⟩ — see LOVING 1

affianced *adj* pledged in marriage ⟨The *affianced* couple are much-sought-after guests for this year's holiday parties.⟩ — see ENGAGED 1

affiliate *n* a local unit of an organization ⟨Our local scout troop is an *affiliate* of a national organization.⟩ — see CHAPTER 1

affiliated *adj* having a close connection like that between family members ⟨Costuming and set design are *affiliated* arts, both requiring research into the period of the play or film.⟩ — see RELATED

affiliation *n* the state of having shared interests or efforts (as in social or business matters) ⟨The Little League team, despite its name, the Northern Dynamites, has no *affiliation* with the Northern Dynamite Company.⟩ — see ASSOCIATION 1

affinity *n* **1** a habitual attraction to some activity or thing ⟨always had an *affinity* for nurturing living things⟩ — see INCLINATION 1

2 the fact or state of having something in common ⟨a study showing an *affinity* between exercise and emotional well-being⟩ — see CONNECTION 1

affirm *vb* **1** to state as a fact usually forcefully ⟨unwilling to *affirm* without further study that the painting is an original Rembrandt⟩ — see CLAIM 1

2 to state clearly and strongly ⟨Our business partner *affirmed* his trust in us, and we in turn promised not to let him down.⟩ — see ASSERT 1

affirmation *n* a solemn and often public declaration of the truth or existence of something ⟨a sworn *affirmation* that he had never acted as a spy for the enemy⟩ — see PROTESTATION

affix *vb* to cause (something) to hold to another ⟨*Affix* a first-class stamp to the envelope.⟩ — see FASTEN 1

afflict *vb* to cause persistent suffering to ⟨The South was *afflicted* by a severe drought.⟩ ⟨He's been *afflicted* by nightmares ever since the accident.⟩

synonyms agonize, anguish, bedevil, beset, besiege, curse, harrow, persecute, plague, rack, torment, torture
related words assail, attack; badger, dog, hound, pursue, ride; aggravate, agitate, annoy, bother, bug, chafe, distress, disturb, exasperate, gall, get, grate, gripe, hagride, harry, irk, irritate, molest, nettle, peeve, pester, pique, put out, rasp, rile, vex; discomfort, discompose, disquiet, fluster, grieve, perturb, strain, stress, trouble, try, upset, worry; crush, oppress, overpower, overwhelm, smite, strike, tyrannize, victimize; hurt, pain, pang, prick, smart, stab, sting, wring; martyr
near antonyms abet, aid, assist, help; deliver, release, relieve, reprieve; comfort, console, content, quiet, solace, soothe, succor

afflicting *adj* hard to accept or bear especially emotionally ⟨the *afflicting* sight of extensive erosion at her favorite beach⟩ — see BITTER 2

affliction *n* **1** a state of great suffering of body or mind ⟨She listened with deep *affliction* as her daughter told her about the trouble.⟩ — see DISTRESS 1

2 deep sadness especially for the loss of someone or something loved ⟨felt such great *affliction* over the destruction of the beautiful old home⟩ — see SORROW

3 a source of harm or misfortune ⟨Drought has been the farmer's *affliction*.⟩ — see BANE 1

4 a source of persistent emotional distress ⟨She suffered from *afflictions* that her therapist had studied.⟩ — see DEMON 2

5 something that causes loss or pain ⟨Loss of habitat is an *affliction* on wildlife.⟩ — see INJURY 1

affluent *adj* having goods, property, or money in abundance ⟨He is *affluent* and can afford to send his children to the best schools.⟩ — see RICH 1

afford *vb* to have enough money for ⟨We can't *afford* new clothes this month.⟩
synonyms go, swing
related words cover; expend, finance, outlay, pay (for), spring (for); pick up, purchase, take; acquire, get, obtain, procure, secure; bid, offer; bankroll, endow, subsidize, underwrite

affordable *adj* **1** being within the financial means of most people ⟨Once those electronic devices became *affordable*, sales skyrocketed.⟩ — see ACCESSIBLE 1

2 costing little ⟨They've added some *affordable* options.⟩ — see CHEAP 1

affront *n* an act or expression showing scorn and usually intended to hurt another's feelings ⟨She took it as an *affront* that she wasn't asked to attend.⟩ — see INSULT

affront *vb* to cause hurt feelings or deep resentment in ⟨I did not mean to *affront* you when I told you I didn't need your help.⟩ — see INSULT

aficionado *also* **afficionado** *n* a person with a strong and habitual liking for something ⟨an *aficionado* of the sci-fi series who has seen all the movies several times⟩ — see FAN

afield *adv* off the desired or intended path or course ⟨How did we get so far *afield* from the subject we intended to discuss?⟩ — see WRONG

afire *adj* being on fire ⟨a tract of the forest all *afire*⟩ — see ABLAZE 1

aflame *adj* being on fire ⟨The kindling in the wood stove was *aflame* as soon as I held a match to it.⟩ — see ABLAZE 1

aflutter *adj* feeling or showing uncomfortable feelings of uncertainty ⟨Jonathan was all *aflutter* about proposing to Shelley that evening.⟩ — see NERVOUS 1

afoot *adj* being in progress or development ⟨Plans are *afoot* for a new sports stadium in the city.⟩ — see ONGOING 1

afraid *adj* filled with fear or dread ⟨Melissa is *afraid* of flying, so she takes a train from Boston to visit her brother in Chicago.⟩
synonyms aghast, alarmed, fearful, frightened, horrified, hysterical, scared, scary, shocked, spooked, terrified, terrorized
related words chicken, fainthearted, fearsome, shrinking, shy, timid, timorous, tremulant, tremulous; agitated, anxious, disconcerted, disquieted, disturbed, jittery, jumpy, nervous, panicked, panicky, panic-stricken, perturbed, skittish, uneasy, upset, worried; phobic; appalled, dismayed, startled; cowed, daunted, intimidated, unnerved; coward, cowardly, craven, lily-livered; careful, cautious, heedful, prudent, unadventurous, wary
near antonyms adventuresome, adventurous, audacious, bold, daredevil, daring, dashing, gutsy, plucky, spirited, spunky, venturesome, venturous; brave, courageous, gallant, hardy, heroic (*also* heroical), intrepid, lionhearted, manful, stalwart, stout, stouthearted, valiant, valorous; assured, collected, composed, confident, cool, sanguine, sure, unperturbed; dauntless, resolute, undaunted
antonyms fearless, unafraid

afresh *adv* yet another time ⟨The applause broke out *afresh* when the band reappeared on stage.⟩ — see AGAIN 1

aft *adj* being at or in the part of something opposite the front part ⟨The *aft* part of the cruise ship turned out to be the noisier section.⟩ — see BACK

aft *adv* near, toward, or in the stern of a ship or the tail of an aircraft ⟨After transferring the controls to the copilot, the captain went *aft* to see what the disturbance was.⟩
synonyms abaft, astern
related words after, back, backward (*or* backwards), behind, rearward (*also* rearwards)
near antonyms ahead, before
antonyms forward

after *adj* **1** being at or in the part of something opposite the front part ⟨I had heard that the *after* section of the cruise ship had nicer cabins.⟩ — see BACK

2 being, occurring, or carried out at a time after something else ⟨In *after* years the government set up a special fund for veterans of the war.⟩ — see SUBSEQUENT

after *adv* following in time or place ⟨Upon seeing *The Nut-cracker* for the first time, and for a long time *after*, Irma wanted to play the part of the Mouse King.⟩
  synonyms afterward (*or* afterwards), later, subsequently, thereafter
  related words next; hereafter, presently, since, soon, then, thereupon; hereinbelow, infra
  near antonyms heretofore, theretofore
  antonyms ahead, antecedently, anteriorly, before, beforehand, previously
after *prep* subsequent to in time or order ⟨The brass band came right *after* the mayor in the parade.⟩
  synonyms behind, below, following, next to, past
  related words since
  near antonyms toward (*or* towards)
  antonyms ahead of, before, ere, of, previous to, prior to, to
aftereffect *n* a condition or occurrence traceable to a cause ⟨He's suffering the *aftereffects* of his injury.⟩ — see EFFECT 1
afterlife *n* 1 a later period of one's life ⟨Written in *afterlife*, his memoirs reveal a kinder, more forgiving man.⟩ — see AGE 3
  2 unending existence after death ⟨hoping to join her deceased parents in the *afterlife*⟩ — see ETERNITY 2
aftermath *n* a condition or occurrence traceable to a cause ⟨The surgery was successful, but she now had to deal with its *aftermath*: a huge bill.⟩ — see EFFECT 1
afterward *or* **afterwards** *adv* following in time or place ⟨We'll go to the game, then have supper *afterward*.⟩ — see AFTER
again *adv* 1 yet another time ⟨Now I have to mop the floor *again* because you didn't wipe your feet.⟩
  synonyms afresh, anew, over
  related words always, consistently, constantly, continuously, endlessly, ever, evermore, forever, incessantly, invariably, perpetually, unfailingly; continually, frequently, oft, often, oftentimes (*or* ofttimes); recurrently, repeatedly; freshly, newly
  near antonyms ne'er, never; infrequently, little, rarely, seldom, unusually; intermittently, occasionally, periodically, sometimes, sporadically
  antonyms nevermore
  2 in addition to what has been said ⟨A green pillow will go fine with my living room; *again*, the best colors are blues and greens.⟩ — see MORE 1
  3 just the opposite being true ⟨I might take swimming lessons this summer; then *again*, I might not.⟩ — see CONTRARIWISE
against *prep* in or into contact with ⟨He leaned *against* the fence and it collapsed.⟩ ⟨unwittingly rubbed his leg *against* some poison ivy⟩
  synonyms on, upon
  related words alongside, next, next to; upside
agape *adj* having or showing signs of eagerly awaiting something ⟨At the sound of the sleigh bells the children were all *agape*, waiting for Santa to appear.⟩ — see EXPECTANT 1
age *n* 1 an extent of time associated with a particular person or thing ⟨The Bronze *Age* marks the beginning of the use of metal by ancient peoples.⟩
  synonyms day, epoch, era, period, time
  related words cycle, generation, year; bit, space, span, spell, stretch, while; date
  2 a long or seemingly long period of time ⟨It took *ages* for the clerk to ring up three items.⟩
  synonyms eon (*or* aeon), cycle, eternity, forever, long, moon
  related words infinity; lifetime

near antonyms flash, instant, jiffy, minute, moment, second, shake, split second, trice, twinkle, twinkling, wink; microsecond, nanosecond
  3 a later period of one's life ⟨stoically endures all of the aches and pains that come with *age*⟩
  synonyms afterlife, evening
  related words sunset, twilight; anecdotage; golden years, oldness, seniority; adulthood, majority, maturity, middle, middle age, midlife, ripeness
  near antonyms youth
  antonyms springtime
age *vb* to become mature ⟨As your cat *ages* and becomes less active, you should change her diet.⟩ — see MATURE
aged *adj* 1 being of advanced years and especially past middle age ⟨a community center for the *aged*⟩ — see ELDERLY
  2 dating or surviving from the distant past ⟨a forest of *aged* and gnarled oaks⟩ — see ANCIENT 1
ageless *adj* having an existence or validity that does not change or diminish ⟨a seemingly *ageless* athlete⟩ — see ABIDING
agency *n* 1 a large unit of a governmental, business, or educational organization ⟨the federal *agency* charged with enforcing laws and regulations regarding food safety⟩ — see DIVISION 2
  2 something used to achieve an end ⟨By what *agency* do you plan to acquire this fortune?⟩ — see AGENT 1
agenda *n* a listing of things to be presented or considered (as at a concert or play) ⟨Unless your proposal is on the meeting's *agenda*, it won't be addressed.⟩ — see PROGRAM 1
agent *n* 1 something used to achieve an end ⟨The whitening *agent* in the detergent is chlorine bleach.⟩ ⟨They see themselves as *agents* of social change.⟩
  synonyms agency, instrument, instrumentality, machinery, means, medium, organ, vehicle
  related words determinant, expedient, factor, influence, ingredient, mechanism, tool; weapon; activator, animator, catalyst, driver, energizer, executor, generator, impetus, incentive, inspiration, instigation, instigator, launcher, mover, power, stimulus, trigger; antecedent, cause, occasion, reason; subagency, subagent
  2 a person who acts or does business for another ⟨The sports *agent* negotiated a record-breaking contract for the baseball player.⟩
  synonyms attorney, commissary, delegate, deputy, envoy, factor, procurator, proxy, rep, representative
  related words ambassador, diplomat, diplomatist, emissary, foreign minister, legate, plenipotentiary; alternate, backup, pinch hitter, relief, replacement, stand-in, sub, substitute, surrogate, understudy; informer, operative, spy; distributor, manager; arbiter, arbitrator, conciliator, go-between, intercessor, intermediary, interposer, liaison, mediator, middleman, peacemaker; mouthpiece, point man, point person, prophet, speaker, spokesman, spokesperson
  3 a person sent on a mission to represent another ⟨an *agent* of the Crown⟩ — see AMBASSADOR
  4 a person who tries secretly to obtain information for one country in the territory of another usually unfriendly country ⟨an *agent* feeding information about enemy troop movements⟩ — see SPY
age-old *adj* dating or surviving from the distant past ⟨*age-old* customs and beliefs⟩ — see ANCIENT 1
agglomerate *n* an unorganized collection or mixture of various things ⟨The Holy Roman Empire was an ever-varying *agglomerate* of central European states that managed to survive for 1,000 years.⟩ — see MISCELLANY 1
agglomerate *vb* to form into a round compact mass

⟨Breakfast cereal consisting of *agglomerated* clusters of wheat, rice, and nuts stays crunchy in milk.⟩ — see WAD

agglomeration *n* an unorganized collection or mixture of various things ⟨Her packed suitcase was an *agglomeration* of random articles of clothing from her closet.⟩ — see MISCELLANY 1

aggrandize *vb* **1** to assign a high status or value to ⟨a movie that *aggrandizes* the bad guys⟩ — see EXALT 1
2 to make greater in size, amount, or number ⟨a generous grant, enabling the library to significantly *aggrandize* its collection of movies⟩ — see INCREASE 1

aggravate *vb* to disturb the peace of mind of (someone) especially by repeated disagreeable acts ⟨It really *aggravates* me when I arrive 10 minutes before the stated closing time, and the store's closed already.⟩ — see IRRITATE 1

aggravating *adj* causing annoyance ⟨There's nothing so *aggravating* as a blaring car alarm that no one is paying any attention to.⟩ — see ANNOYING

aggravation *n* **1** something that is a source of irritation ⟨Drivers distracted by cell phones was one *aggravation* we didn't need.⟩ — see ANNOYANCE 3
2 the act of making unwelcome intrusions upon another ⟨The neighbors' constant *aggravations* prompted us to move out of town.⟩ — see ANNOYANCE 1
3 the feeling of impatience or anger caused by another's repeated disagreeable acts ⟨She informed her children that she didn't need the extra *aggravation* of hearing them fight in the back seat while they were stuck in traffic.⟩ — see ANNOYANCE 2

aggregate *n* a complete amount of something ⟨Numerous episodes of pilferage, taken in the *aggregate*, can really add up to a significant sum.⟩ — see WHOLE

aggregate *vb* to have a total of ⟨Over time, her petty thefts *aggregated* a significant shortfall in the company's books.⟩ — see AMOUNT (TO) 1

aggression *n* **1** an inclination to fight or quarrel ⟨dangerous dogs showing *aggression* towards others⟩ — see BELLIGERENCE
2 the act or action of setting upon with force or violence ⟨An act of *aggression* brought the country to war.⟩ — see ATTACK 1

aggressive *adj* **1** having or showing a bold forcefulness in the pursuit of a goal ⟨If you don't take a more *aggressive* approach to this yard pretty soon, the weeds are going to take over completely.⟩
synonyms ambitious, assertive, enterprising, fierce, go-getting, high-pressure, in-your-face, militant, self-assertive
related words argumentative, bellicose, belligerent, combative, contentious, discordant, disputatious, gladiatorial, militant, pugnacious, quarrelsome, trigger-happy, truculent, warlike; hyperaggressive, overambitious; dynamic, energetic, enterprising, gung ho, hustling, strenuous, vigorous; emphatic, obtrusive; adventuresome, adventurous, daring, dashing, emboldened, gutsy, venturesome, venturous; audacious, bold, brash, brassy, cheeky, cocksure, cocky, confident, determined, forward, impudent, insolent, overconfident, presumptuous, unapologetic, unsubdued, unyielding; bare-knuckle (*also* bare-knuckled *or* bare-knuckles), scrappy
near antonyms easygoing, laid-back, relaxed; acquiescent, amenable, compliant, deferential, docile, resigned, submissive, tractable, yielding; cowering, cringing, groveling (*or* grovelling), shrinking; bashful, demure, diffident, humble, lowly, meek, mild, modest, mousy (*or* mousey), overmodest, passive, quiet, reserved, retiring, shy, subdued, timid, unobtrusive; obsequious, subservient

antonyms ambitionless, low-pressure, nonassertive, unaggressive, unambitious, unassertive, unenterprising
2 feeling or displaying eagerness to fight ⟨a kindergarten teacher who discourages *aggressive* behavior, like pushing, by rewarding those children who wait their turn⟩ — see BELLIGERENT
3 marked by or uttered with forcefulness ⟨an *aggressive* campaign to win the vote⟩ — see EMPHATIC 1

aggressiveness *n* **1** readiness to engage in daring or difficult activity ⟨Because of the mayor's *aggressiveness* in tackling problems, there have been significant changes for the better.⟩ — see ENTERPRISE 2
2 the quality or state of being forceful (as in expression) ⟨He has the *aggressiveness* one needs to pursue a career in show business.⟩ — see VEHEMENCE 1
3 an inclination to fight or quarrel ⟨Male bettas, known for their *aggressiveness*, are best raised alone.⟩ — see BELLIGERENCE

aggressor *n* one that starts armed conflict against another especially without reasonable cause ⟨These pocket-size states had formed an alliance to deter potential *aggressors*.⟩
synonyms invader, raider
related words initiator, instigator; ambusher, forayer, pillager, plunderer; hawk, jingo, militant, militarist, warmonger; belligerent, cobelligerent, combatant
near antonyms defender; dove, pacifist, peacemaker; nonbelligerent

aggrieved *adj* having a feeling that one has been wronged or thwarted in one's ambitions ⟨a line of *aggrieved* ticketholders, demanding a refund for the cancelled concert⟩ — see DISCONTENTED

aghast *adj* filled with fear or dread ⟨I stood there, *aghast*, as the vile monster made its way toward me.⟩ — see AFRAID

agile *adj* moving easily ⟨the expressive movements of *agile* dancers⟩ ⟨*agile* herons wading in the marsh⟩ — see GRACEFUL 1

agility *n* ease and grace in physical activity ⟨a gymnast whose *agility* on the parallel bars has won him several medals⟩ — see DEXTERITY 2

aging *or* **ageing** *adj* being of advanced years and especially past middle age ⟨More and more middle-aged adults must care for *aging* parents.⟩ — see ELDERLY

agitate *vb* **1** to cause (as a liquid) to move about in a circle especially repeatedly ⟨This room could use a ceiling fan to *agitate* the stuffy air a bit.⟩ — see STIR 1
2 to trouble the mind of; to make uneasy ⟨There's no need to *agitate* the patient about little things.⟩ — see DISTURB 1
3 to make a series of small irregular or violent movements ⟨Set the washing machine so it will *agitate* for four minutes before going into the rinse cycle.⟩ — see SHAKE 1
4 to talk about (an issue) usually from various points of view and for the purpose of arriving at a decision or opinion ⟨a question which has been *agitated* by the legislature time and time again⟩ — see DISCUSS

agitated *adj* **1** being in a state of increased activity or agitation ⟨All ferry crossings were cancelled because of the *agitated* waters around the islands.⟩ — see FEVERISH 1
2 feeling overwhelming fear or worry ⟨By the time they finally showed up, long after midnight, we'd become so *agitated* that we never did get to sleep that night.⟩ — see FRANTIC 1

agitating *adj* marked by or causing agitation or uncomfortable feelings ⟨No more *agitating* waits to find out sports scores—get them instantly online!⟩ — see NERVOUS 2

agitation *n* **1** a state of wildly excited activity or emotion ⟨knew immediately, from the horses' *agitation*, that something terrible was happening⟩ — see FRENZY
2 an uneasy state of mind usually over the possibility of an anticipated misfortune or trouble ⟨He spoke with increasing *agitation* about the exam.⟩ — see ANXIETY 1

agitator *n* a person who stirs up public feelings especially of discontent ⟨a political *agitator*⟩
synonyms demagogue (*also* demagog), exciter, firebrand, fomenter, incendiary, inciter, instigator, rabble-rouser
related words demonstrator, marcher, objector, picketer, protester (*or* protestor); advocate, apostle, backer, booster, champion, exponent, persuader, promoter, proponent, reformer, reformist, supporter; alarmist, extremist, insurgent, insurrectionist, radical, rebel, revolter, revolutionary, revolutionist, subversive, troublemaker; prodder, prompter, provoker; agent provocateur
near antonyms peacemaker, reconciler, uniter

aglow *adj* having or being an outward sign of good feelings (as of love, confidence, or happiness) ⟨all *aglow* as she was awarded first place in the spelling bee⟩ — see RADIANT 1

agog *adj* **1** having or showing signs of eagerly awaiting something ⟨parents *agog* for the latest news from the children away at college⟩ — see EXPECTANT 1
2 showing urgent desire or interest ⟨all *agog* to get started on their journey⟩ — see EAGER

agonize *vb* **1** to cause persistent suffering to ⟨The teen got into more trouble, further *agonizing* her poor mother.⟩ — see AFFLICT
2 to feel deep sadness or mental pain ⟨*agonized* for days over whether she'd done the right thing⟩ — see GRIEVE

agonizing *adj* **1** hard to accept or bear especially emotionally ⟨The wait was *agonizing*.⟩ — see BITTER 2
2 intensely or unbearably painful ⟨The soldier died an *agonizing* death.⟩ — see EXCRUCIATING 1

agonizingly *adv* with feelings of bitterness or grief ⟨She *agonizingly* made the decision to have her beloved cat put to sleep.⟩ — see HARD 2

agony *n* **1** a situation or state that causes great suffering and unhappiness ⟨Waiting all those hours to hear the jury's verdict was pure *agony*.⟩ — see HELL 2
2 a state of great suffering of body or mind ⟨the *agony* of never knowing what happened to her dog⟩ — see DISTRESS 1
3 a sudden intense expression of strong feeling ⟨The announcement that the war was over unleashed a mass *agony* of joy.⟩ — see OUTBURST 1

agrarian *adj* engaged in or concerned with agriculture ⟨an *agrarian* community⟩ ⟨the nation's *agrarian* history⟩ — see AGRICULTURAL

agree *vb* **1** to have or come to the same opinion or point of view ⟨My husband and I *agree* on just about every aspect of child-rearing.⟩
synonyms coincide, concur
related words accede (to), accept, acquiesce, assent (to), comply (with), consent (to), go (by); affiliate, ally, associate, unite; collaborate, cooperate, get along, get on
phrases see eye to eye
near antonyms clash, collide, conflict; bicker, counter, dispute, dissent, diverge, fall out, object, oppose, protest, quarrel, resist, rival; dissociate, separate, split
antonyms differ, disagree
2 to come to an arrangement as to a course of action ⟨Since we couldn't *agree*, we tossed a coin to decide the matter.⟩
synonyms bargain, contract, covenant
related words come around, come round; underwrite; arrange, settle
phrases come to terms, strike a bargain

near antonyms differ, dissent; cancel, renege, revoke; argue, contest, dispute, object
antonyms disagree
3 to accept the truth or existence of (something) usually reluctantly ⟨finally *agreed* that the paint job was sloppy and would have to be redone⟩ — see ADMIT 1
4 to be in agreement on every point ⟨The robber's story didn't *agree* with the cop's report on the incident.⟩ — see CHECK 1
5 to form a pleasing relationship ⟨This warm climate seems to *agree* with you.⟩ — see HARMONIZE 1
6 to give or express one's approval (as to a proposal) ⟨We'll have to get the author to *agree* to the revisions before the article can be published.⟩ — see ACCEDE

agreeable *adj* **1** being to one's liking ⟨Is the zoo an *agreeable* alternative for everyone, since the aquarium is closed?⟩ — see SATISFACTORY 1
2 giving pleasure or contentment to the mind or senses ⟨We put on some *agreeable* music for dinner.⟩ — see PLEASANT 1
3 having an easygoing and pleasing manner especially in social situations ⟨an *agreeable* art teacher who lets me do pretty much whatever I want⟩ — see AMIABLE
4 having or marked by agreement in feeling or action ⟨the belief that these new security measures are not *agreeable* with our core concepts of personal freedom⟩ — see HARMONIOUS 3

agreeableness *n* the state or quality of having a pleasant or agreeable manner in socializing with others ⟨The impression that the couple give to first-time visitors is one of natural *agreeableness*.⟩ — see AMIABILITY 1

agreeably *adv* in a pleasing way ⟨an *agreeably* warm day, just right for a picnic⟩ — see WELL 5

agreement *n* **1** the state of being of one opinion about something ⟨We were in *agreement* about one thing at least: that we'd never worked so hard in all our lives.⟩
synonyms accord, concurrence, consensus, unanimity, unison
related words adhesion, assent, consent; acceptance, acquiescence, concession, embrace, embracement; approbation, approval, favor; alliance, collaboration, collusion, complicity, conspiracy; compliance, concert, concertedness, concord, concordance, conformity, consonance, harmony, oneness, solidarity, understanding, union; empathy, rapport, sympathy
phrases meeting of minds
near antonyms discord, dissension (*also* dissention); dissent, opposition, resistance; disapprobation, disapproval, disfavor
antonyms conflict, disagreement
2 an arrangement about action to be taken ⟨We finally reached an *agreement* regarding a fair division of the housework.⟩
synonyms accord, bargain, compact, contract, convention, covenant, deal, disposition, pact, settlement, understanding
related words charter, treaty; binder, pledge, promise; alliance, association, entente, entente cordiale, league, partnership; acceptance, approval, assent, concurrence, consent, OK (*or* okay)
3 a state of consistency ⟨The amount in column A needs to be in *agreement* with the total receipts minus expenses.⟩ — see CONFORMITY 1

agricultural *adj* engaged in or concerned with agriculture ⟨He grew up in an *agricultural* community and farming was still in his blood.⟩
synonyms agrarian, farming
related words agronomic; bucolic, pastoral, pastoralist; garden; country, rural, rustic (*also* rustical)

near antonyms metro, metropolitan, urban; industrial, industrialized
antonyms nonagricultural

agriculture *n* the science or occupation of cultivating the soil, producing crops, and raising livestock ⟨The forest was cut down, and the land given over to *agriculture*.⟩
synonyms farming, husbandry
related words cultivation, culture, farmwork, gardening, horticulture, tillage; animal husbandry, mixed farming, pastoralism; sharecropping

agriculturist *or* **agriculturalist** *n* a person who cultivates the land and grows crops on it ⟨*agriculturists* who adhere to the organization's standards of organic farming⟩ — see FARMER

agronomist *n* a person who cultivates the land and grows crops on it ⟨an *agronomist* specializing in soil management⟩ — see FARMER

aground *adj* resting on the shore or bottom of a body of water ⟨The villagers came to stare at the foreign ship that was *aground* on their beach and at the strangely dressed sailors on board.⟩
synonyms beached, grounded, stranded
related words landed

ah *interj* how surprising, doubtful, or unbelievable ⟨*Ah*— so that's the way it is!⟩ — see NO

aha *interj* how surprising, doubtful, or unbelievable ⟨*Aha*! So the money was never missing in the first place!⟩ — see NO

ahead *adv* **1** so as to precede something in order of time ⟨Call *ahead* for reservations.⟩
synonyms before, beforehand, previously
related words early, prematurely; first, first off, now; presently, shortly, soon
phrases in advance
near antonyms behind, next, subsequently
antonyms after, afterward (*or* afterwards), later
2 toward a point ahead in space or time ⟨I went *ahead* to get a place in the check-out line while she went for the eggs and milk.⟩ — see ONWARD 1
3 toward or at a point lying in advance in space or time ⟨The line moved *ahead* at a snail's pace.⟩ — see ALONG

ahead of *prep* **1** earlier than ⟨always arrives at school *ahead of* the bus⟩ ⟨We were cautioned not to fill out any of the test answers *ahead of* time.⟩ — see BEFORE 1
2 preceding in space ⟨The three lost children emerged from the forest, with the family dog walking proudly *ahead of* them.⟩ — see BEFORE 2

aid *n* **1** a person who helps a more skilled person ⟨Jack is his mother's preferred *aid* in the kitchen.⟩ — see HELPER
2 a thing that helps ⟨A dictionary is a handy *aid* for working crossword puzzles.⟩ — see HELP 2
3 an act or instance of helping ⟨The clerk asked if she needed any *aid* carrying out her purchases.⟩ — see HELP 1

aid *vb* to provide (someone) with what is useful or necessary to achieve an end ⟨I sought to *aid* her in her search for a dachshund puppy by looking online.⟩ — see HELP 1

aide *n* a person who helps a more skilled person ⟨The nurse's *aide* will bring you an extra pillow.⟩ ⟨He served as an *aide* in his father's senatorial campaign.⟩ — see HELPER

ail *n* an abnormal state that disrupts a plant's or animal's normal bodily functioning ⟨Half of the staff is out sick with the usual wintertime *ails*.⟩ — see DISEASE

ail *vb* to trouble the mind of; to make uneasy ⟨parents who were at a loss to explain what was *ailing* their normally vivacious daughter⟩ — see DISTURB 1

ailing *adj* **1** chronically or repeatedly suffering from poor health ⟨When his *ailing* wife had to go to a nursing home, he visited her every day.⟩ — see SICKLY 1
2 temporarily suffering from a disorder of the body ⟨He was *ailing* from some sort of infection in his eye that made it look all red and puffy.⟩ — see SICK 1

ailment *n* an abnormal state that disrupts a plant's or animal's normal bodily functioning ⟨She suffers from a chronic back *ailment*.⟩ — see DISEASE

aim *n* something that one hopes or intends to accomplish ⟨The main *aim* of a trip to the city is to shop for school clothes, but we always go to the artisans' market, too.⟩ — see GOAL

aim *vb* **1** to point or turn (something) toward a target or goal ⟨The new system is *aimed* at reducing costs.⟩
synonyms bend, cast, direct, head, hold, level, pinpoint, set, train
related words sight; bear, face; concentrate, focus; incline, orient, steer
near antonyms avert, curve, deflect, detour, divert, rechannel, shunt, sidetrack
2 to have in mind as a purpose or goal ⟨He *aimed* to have his paper all done in time to go to the movies.⟩ — see INTEND 1

aimless *adj* lacking a definite plan, purpose, or pattern ⟨This *aimless* walking through stores isn't going to get your shopping done.⟩ — see RANDOM

aimlessly *adv* without definite aim, direction, rule, or method ⟨We wandered *aimlessly* through the forest until we were hopelessly lost.⟩ — see HIT OR MISS

air *n* **1** a rhythmic series of musical tones arranged to give a pleasing effect ⟨played a lively *air* on his fiddle⟩ — see MELODY
2 a slight or gentle movement of air ⟨We sailed into the bay on a light *air* and just in time to enjoy a spectacular sunset.⟩ — see BREEZE 1
3 a special quality or impression associated with something ⟨Naomi's the only person I know who can wear old jeans and a T-shirt with an *air* of elegance.⟩ — see AURA 1
4 airs *pl* a display of emotion or behavior that is insincere or intended to deceive ⟨Ever since she joined the country club she's been putting on *airs* of being too "high society" for us ordinary folks.⟩ — see MASQUERADE

air *vb* to make known (as an idea, emotion, or opinion) ⟨He suggested we *air* any complaints about the seating arrangements to the person who actually planned the event.⟩ — see EXPRESS 1

airdrome *n* a place from which aircraft operate that usually has paved runways and a terminal ⟨helicopters taking off from a military *airdrome* near Moscow⟩ — see AIRPORT

airfield *n* a place from which aircraft operate that usually has paved runways and a terminal ⟨The passenger jet made an emergency landing at an abandoned *airfield*.⟩ — see AIRPORT

airman *n* one who flies or is qualified to fly an aircraft or spacecraft ⟨Her grandfather was an *airman* who flew in the Korean War.⟩ — see PILOT

airplane *n* a vehicle for traveling through the air that has fixed wings for lift ⟨She joined the military to learn to fly an *airplane*.⟩
synonyms plane
related words airbus, airliner, air taxi, liner; aircraft, air-cushion vehicle, airframe, airship, ship; jet, jetliner, superjet, supersonic, supersonic transport, trijet, turbojet, turboprop; aerospace plane, rocket plane; bomber, fighter, jump jet, torpedo bomber, torpedo plane, warplane; amphibian, seaplane; biplane, lightplane

airport *n* a place from which aircraft operate that usually has paved runways and a terminal 〈the *airport* nearest us has plane service on only one major airline〉
synonyms airdrome, airfield, field
related words air base, air park, helipad, heliport, jetport; airstrip, landing field, landing strip, runway; launchpad, pad

airy *adj* **1** resembling air in lightness 〈The bakery's lemon pies are famous for their *airy* meringues.〉
synonyms ethereal, fluffy, gossamer, gossamery, light
related words dainty, delicate, downy, feathery, flimsy, gauzelike, gauzy, insubstantial, tender, wispy; buoyant, lighter-than-air, lightweight, rarefied, unsubstantial, weightless; pillowy
near antonyms firm, solid, substantial; bulky, burdensome, cumbersome, hefty, hulking, lumpish, ponderous, unwieldy, weighty
antonyms heavy, leaden
2 open to the free circulation of air 〈a pleasant, *airy* room〉
synonyms breezy
related words atmosphered, vented
near antonyms close, stifling, suffocating
antonyms breathless, stuffy, unventilated
3 located at a greater height than average or usual 〈*airy* mountain villages〉 — see HIGH 3
4 having much high-spirited energy and movement 〈The *airy* revelry of their latest album is a departure from the slower and more somber music of the band's previous work.〉 — see LIVELY 1
5 satisfying or pleasing because of fineness or mildness 〈an *airy* cologne that would be appropriate to wear to the office〉 — see DELICATE 1

akin *adj* **1** having a close connection like that between family members 〈Foxes are closely *akin* to dogs.〉 — see RELATED
2 having qualities in common 〈Mathematics and computer programming are *akin* in that they both require logical thinking.〉 — see ALIKE

alacritous *adj* having or showing the ability to respond without delay or hesitation 〈His *alacritous* response to every request is "Right away, mate!"〉 — see QUICK 1

alacrity *n* cheerful readiness to do something 〈Having just acquired his driver's license that morning, he agreed with *alacrity* to drive his cousin to the airport.〉
synonyms amenability, goodwill, willingness
related words celerity, quickness, rapidity, speed, speediness, swiftness; dispatch, promptitude, promptness; ardor, avidity, eagerness, enthusiasm, exuberance, fervor, keenness, relish, zeal, zest; agreeableness, geniality, good-naturedness, heartiness, warmth; open-mindedness, receptiveness, receptivity, responsiveness
near antonyms leisureliness, pokiness, slowness, sluggishness; apathy, disinterestedness, halfheartedness, indifference, lukewarmness, perfunctoriness; delay, dilatoriness, doubt, equivocation, hesitance, hesitancy, hesitation, reluctance, reservation, reticence, uncertainty, vacillation; disinclination, indisposition, recalcitrance, resistance, unwillingness; antipathy, averseness, aversion

à la mode *also* **a la mode** *adj* being in the latest or current fashion 〈We discovered that what is *à la mode* for teens to wear in the U.S. isn't all that different from what they wear in Europe.〉 — see STYLISH

alarm *also* **alarum** *n* **1** suspicion or fear of future harm or misfortune 〈observed with *alarm* the man staggering toward the edge of the cliff〉 — see APPREHENSION 1
2 the act or an instance of telling beforehand of danger or risk 〈In a daring midnight ride Paul Revere gave the *alarm* that British troops were approaching.〉 — see WARNING 1

3 the emotion experienced in the presence or threat of danger 〈filled with *alarm* when the flood waters reached their front steps〉 — see FEAR 1

alarm *also* **alarum** *vb* **1** to strike with fear 〈I don't want to *alarm* you, but I think you should know there's a bear on your back porch.〉 — see FRIGHTEN
2 to trouble the mind of; to make uneasy 〈*alarmed* at the skyrocketing cost of home heating fuel〉 — see DISTURB 1

alarmed *adj* filled with fear or dread 〈I was *alarmed* to see how sick he is.〉 — see AFRAID

alarming *adj* causing fear 〈an *alarming* rise in her fever〉 — see FEARFUL 1

albeit *conj* in spite of the fact that 〈She felt that her script was still too long, *albeit* it was much shorter than any of her previous scripts.〉 — see ALTHOUGH

album *n* a collection of writings 〈a special anniversary *album* of his poetry published 100 years after his death〉 — see ANTHOLOGY

alcohol *n* a distilled beverage that can make a person drunk 〈After his daughter was born, the man never again touched *alcohol*.〉
synonyms drink, intoxicant, liquor, moonshine, spirits
antonyms nonintoxicant

alcoholic *n* a person who makes a habit of getting drunk 〈a program to help *alcoholics*〉 — see DRUNK

alcove *n* a hollowed-out space in a wall 〈an ancient vase in an *alcove* and a sculpture of Achilles on a stand in the museum's Greek Hall〉 — see NICHE 1

alert *adj* **1** paying close attention usually for the purpose of anticipating approaching danger or opportunity 〈She needed to stay *alert* throughout the train ride so as not to miss her stop.〉
synonyms attentive, awake, observant, open-eyed, vigilant, watchful, wide-awake
related words alive, aware, conscious, sensitive; cognizant, heedful, keen, mindful, observing, regardful, sharp, sharp-eyed; hyperalert, hypervigilant, sleepless, wakeful; careful, cautious, wary; prepared, ready
phrases on guard, on one's toes, on the alert, on the ball, on tiptoe
near antonyms absent, absentminded, absorbed, abstracted, daydreaming, dazed, distracted, dreaming, dreamy, engrossed, faraway, insensible, oblivious, preoccupied; sleeping, unaware, unconscious, unknowing, unwitting; careless, heedless, inattentive, unheeding, unmindful, unthinking, unwary; unprepared, unready
antonyms asleep
2 having or showing a close attentiveness to avoiding danger or trouble 〈warned us to be *alert* to the presence of pickpockets on the crowded bus〉 — see CAREFUL 1
3 having or showing quickness of mind 〈an *alert* and well-trained sheep dog who can handle difficult situations〉 — see INTELLIGENT 1
4 having or showing the ability to respond without delay or hesitation 〈an *alert* force of commandos, ready to go on a mission at a moment's notice〉 — see QUICK 1

alert *n* **1** the act or an instance of telling beforehand of danger or risk 〈the white flash of the doe's raised tail, giving the "danger" *alert* to her fawns〉 — see WARNING 1
2 the state of being constantly attentive and responsive to signs of opportunity, activity, or danger 〈The doctor told the patient to be on the *alert* for any signs of infection.〉 — see VIGILANCE

alert *vb* to give notice to beforehand especially of danger or risk 〈An officer *alerted* us to the possibility that the roads would be flooded and we might have to take a detour.〉 — see WARN

alertness *n* **1** a close attentiveness to avoiding danger 〈We drove through the fog with extra *alertness*, as the road signs repeatedly warned of deer and moose crossings.⟩ — see CAUTION 1

2 the state of being constantly attentive and responsive to signs of opportunity, activity, or danger ⟨The deer maintained their *alertness* even as they grazed.⟩ — see VIGILANCE

alias *n* **1** a descriptive or familiar name given instead of or in addition to the one belonging to an individual ⟨a dressmaker whom everyone knows as "Bet," her adopted *alias* in the dressmaking business that she named after Betsy Ross⟩ — see NICKNAME

2 a fictitious or assumed name ⟨the English author Eric Blair, better known under the *alias* of George Orwell⟩ — see PSEUDONYM

alibi *n* an explanation that frees one from fault or blame ⟨a student who always has a very creative *alibi* for undone homework or late papers⟩ — see EXCUSE

alien *adj* **1** being, relating to, or characteristic of a country other than one's own ⟨a traveler observing *alien* customs⟩ — see FOREIGN 1

2 not being a vital part of or belonging to something ⟨It's completely *alien* to her nature to wish evil on anyone.⟩ — see EXTRINSIC

alienate *vb* **1** to cause to change from friendly or loving to unfriendly or uncaring ⟨Her position on the issue *alienated* many former supporters.⟩ — see ESTRANGE

2 to give over the legal possession or ownership of ⟨Landowners have a right to *alienate* their right of ownership—in other words, they can sell the land if they want to.⟩ — see TRANSFER 1

alienation *n* the loss of friendship or affection ⟨After years of *alienation* from her family, she became reconciled with them when her father fell ill.⟩ — see ESTRANGEMENT

alight *adj* filled with much light ⟨We approached the clearing, *alight* with torches, and observed a reenactment of ancient rites by Druids.⟩ — see BRIGHT 2

alight *vb* **1** to come to rest after descending from the air ⟨A flock of eight swans circled above, then *alighted* on the pond.⟩
synonyms land, light, perch, roost, settle, touch down
related words belly-land, crash-land
near antonyms arise, ascend, climb, rise; float, fly, glide, plane, soar, wing; hang, hover
antonyms blast off, take off

2 to come down from something (as a vehicle) ⟨As she *alighted* from the train, she momentarily lost her footing.⟩
synonyms descend, disembark, light
related words deplane, detrain
near antonyms board, climb (aboard), mount; enplane (*also* emplane), entrain
antonyms embark

alike *adj* having qualities in common ⟨All the houses in the neighborhood are *alike* in that they all have a one-car garage and a fenced-in backyard.⟩
synonyms akin, analogous, comparable, correspondent, corresponding, like, matching, parallel, resembling, similar, such, suchlike
related words commensurate, proportionate; tantamount, virtual; allied, kin, kindred, relatable, related; approaching, approximating, close, coextensive, coincident, conformable, conforming, consistent, consonant, duplicate, equal, equivalent, identical, indistinguishable, me-too, redundant, same, selfsame, synonymous, twin; entire, homogeneous, homogenous, unchanging, uniform, unvaried, unvarying
phrases on the order of
near antonyms disparate, distinct, distinguishable, non-

equivalent, noninterchangeable; variable, varied, varying; imprecise, inaccurate, inexact; unconnected, unrelated
antonyms different, dissimilar, diverse, unakin, unlike

alike *adv* in like manner ⟨regulations that are disapproved of by teachers and students *alike*⟩ — see ALSO 1

alikeness *n* the quality or state of having many qualities in common ⟨Since they're identical twins, you shouldn't be so surprised at the *alikeness* of their personal tastes.⟩ — see SIMILARITY 1

alive *adj* **1** having or showing life ⟨After crashing into the plate glass window the little bird was not only still *alive*, it seemed merely dazed.⟩
synonyms animate, breathing, live, living, quick
related words active, animated, dynamic, lively, thriving, vibrant, vigorous, vital, vivacious; current, existent, existing, extant, going, prevailing, surviving; resurrected
near antonyms dying, fading, moribund; stillborn; reposing, resting; ghostlike, ghostly, ghosty, zombielike; absent, extinct, fallen, finished, gone, lapsed, lost, nonexistent, perished, terminated, vanished; barren, desert
antonyms asleep, breathless, cold, dead, deceased, defunct, departed, expired, lifeless, nonliving

2 marked by much life, movement, or activity ⟨The mall was *alive* with holiday shoppers.⟩
synonyms animated, astir, brisk, bustling, busy, buzzing, flourishing, happening, humming, lively, rousing, stirring, thriving, vibrant
related words abounding, crowded, overflowing, populous, swarming, teeming, thronging
antonyms asleep, dead, inactive, lifeless, sleepy

3 being in effective operation ⟨kept the cause of peace *alive* despite setbacks⟩ — see ACTIVE 1

4 having being at the present time ⟨insists that her new boyfriend is the sweetest guy *alive*⟩ — see EXTANT 1

5 having specified facts or feelings actively impressed on the mind ⟨*alive* to the need for major improvements in the school system⟩ — see CONSCIOUS 1

all *adj* not divided or scattered among several areas of interest or concern ⟨You need to focus *all* your attention on this matter.⟩ — see WHOLE 1

all *adv* **1** to a full extent or degree ⟨We are *all* out of milk.⟩ ⟨I was *all* ready to leave at least ten minutes ago.⟩ — see FULLY 1

2 for each one ⟨The score is three *all*.⟩ — see APIECE

all *pron* every person ⟨A joyous holiday to one and *all*!⟩ — see EVERYBODY

Allah *n* the being worshipped as the creator and ruler of the universe ⟨Muslims worship *Allah*.⟩ — see DEITY 2

all–around *also* **all–round** *adj* **1** not limited or specialized in application or purpose ⟨an *all-around* garden rake that adjusts for any raking task, from raking lawns to delicate flower beds⟩ — see GENERAL 4

2 relating to the main elements and not to specific details ⟨This saw has the top rating for *all-around* performance, but for small detail work it might not be your best choice.⟩ — see GENERAL 2

3 able to do many different kinds of things ⟨an *all-around* player, as skilled on the pitcher's mound as he is at the batting plate⟩ — see VERSATILE

all around *adv* with everyone or everything taken into account at the same time ⟨*All around*, she's our best athlete.⟩
synonyms altogether, collectively, inclusively, overall, together
related words broadly, generally, liberally, loosely; all over, completely, comprehensively, encyclopedically, entirely, exhaustively, fully, thoroughly, totally, wholly
phrases across the board, all in all, in the aggregate, on the whole

near antonyms minutely; literally, restrictedly, strictly; alone, categorically, distinctly, exclusively, fractionally, individually, separately, singly, singularly, solely, solitarily

allay *vb* to make more bearable or less severe ⟨A gentle breeze would *allay* the heat.⟩ — see HELP 2

all but *adv* very close to but not completely ⟨Dinner is *all but* on the table, so don't go anywhere.⟩ — see ALMOST

allege *vb* to state as a fact usually forcefully ⟨She *alleged* that the organization was engaged in fraud.⟩ — see CLAIM 1

allegiance *n* adherence to something to which one is bound by a pledge or duty ⟨torn between his *allegiance* to his native country and the opportunities a sports career overseas could offer⟩ — see FIDELITY

allegory *n* a story intended to teach a basic truth or moral about life ⟨Dr. Seuss's story "The Sneetches" is a telling *allegory* about tolerance for people's differences.⟩
synonyms fable, parable
related words beast fable, bestiary; morality play; legend, myth, mythology, narrative, tale

allergic *adj* having a natural dislike for something ⟨a lover of the outdoors who claims to be *allergic* to desk jobs⟩ — see ANTIPATHETIC 1

allergy *n* a strong feeling of not liking or approving ⟨I think my brother has an *allergy* to work.⟩ — see DISLIKE 1

alleviate *vb* to make more bearable or less severe ⟨A car pool *alleviates* some of the stress of driving the kids to and from school every day.⟩ — see HELP 2

alleviation *n* reduction of or freedom from pain ⟨hoping a couple of aspirin would provide some *alleviation* of the pain in his shoulder⟩ — see EASE 1

alliance *n* 1 a formal agreement between two or more nations or peoples ⟨The smaller countries signed an *alliance* pledging to protect one another against the belligerent behemoth in their midst.⟩ — see TREATY
2 an association of persons, parties, or states for mutual assistance and protection ⟨an *alliance* between the former enemies⟩ — see CONFEDERACY
3 the state of having shared interests or efforts (as in social or business matters) ⟨In *alliance* with booksellers, the nation's schools are promoting National Reading Month.⟩ — see ASSOCIATION 1

allied *adj* having a close connection like that between family members ⟨people with foreign language fluency and an *allied* skill such as the ability to relate to people from different cultures⟩ — see RELATED

all-important *adj* impossible to do without ⟨that *all-important* item for a successful birthday party: a fancily decorated cake with candles⟩ — see ESSENTIAL 1

allocate *vb* 1 to give as a share or portion ⟨not enough computers to *allocate* one to every student⟩ — see ALLOT
2 to give out (something) to appropriate individuals ⟨*allocated* the housework in such a way that the older kids got more than the younger ones⟩ — see ADMINISTER 1
3 to keep or intend for a special purpose ⟨sliced the strawberries after first *allocating* all the nicest ones for the top of the cake⟩ — see DEVOTE 1

allocation *n* 1 a sum of money allotted for a specific use by official or formal action ⟨Recognizing the importance of the arts in the health of a city, the council increased the *allocation* for the city's annual jazz festival.⟩ — see APPROPRIATION 1
2 the act or process of giving out something to each member of a group ⟨The *allocation* of Halloween candy became my job when I was too old to go trick-or-treating myself.⟩ — see DISTRIBUTION 1

allot *vb* to give as a share or portion ⟨Each speaker was *allotted* five minutes to present his or her opinion in the debate.⟩
synonyms allocate, allow, apportion, assign, distribute, lot, ration
related words admeasure, administer, deal, dispense, divide, measure, mete (out), meter, parcel (out), part, portion, prorate, share (out), split; accord, award, give, grant; earmark, reserve; chip in, contribute, donate; reallocate, reapportion, reassign, redistribute
near antonyms deny, deprive (of); keep, retain, stint, withhold; appropriate, arrogate, confiscate

allotment *n* 1 a sum of money allotted for a specific use by official or formal action ⟨The library budget was reduced, while *allotments* for city officials' travel expenses were increased.⟩ — see APPROPRIATION 1
2 something belonging to, due to, or contributed by an individual member of a group ⟨Every kindergartner received colored paper, scissors, and an *allotment* of paste to make paper chains.⟩ — see SHARE 1
3 the act or process of giving out something to each member of a group ⟨The *allotment* of exhibition space at the annual trade show is always fraught with politics and infighting.⟩ — see DISTRIBUTION 1

all-out *adj* 1 having no exceptions or restrictions ⟨Grandpa got the *all-out* support of the family when he decided to remarry at age 72.⟩ — see ABSOLUTE 2
2 trying all possibilities ⟨an *all-out* effort to break open the door⟩ — see EXHAUSTIVE 1

all out *adv* with all power or resources being used ⟨Emma went *all out* for her New Year's Eve party—she even had fireworks!⟩ — see FULL BLAST

all over *adv* 1 in every place or in all places ⟨I've looked *all over*—even outside—and I can't find my other shoe.⟩ — see EVERYWHERE
2 to a full extent or degree ⟨His writing style is his mentor's *all over*.⟩ — see FULLY 1

allow *vb* 1 to give permission for or to approve of ⟨Flash photography is not *allowed* inside the museum.⟩
synonyms have, permit, suffer
related words authorize, commission, license (*also* licence); accede (to), acquiesce, agree (to), assent (to), consent (to), OK (*or* okay), warrant; accord, concede, grant, sanction, vouchsafe; admit, brook, condone, countenance, endure, support, tolerate
phrases stand for
near antonyms hinder, impede, obstruct; censure, deny, disallow, disapprove, interdict, refuse, reject, revoke, suppress, withhold; deplore, discountenance, disfavor, dislike, frown (at *or* on), grudge; check, curb, keep, repress, restrain
antonyms ban, enjoin, forbid, prohibit, proscribe, veto
2 to give permission to ⟨a boarding school that does not *allow* students to go on weekend trips without written permission⟩
synonyms leave, let, permit
related words authorize, commission, empower, license (*also* licence); approve, endorse (*also* indorse), sanction; free, liberate, release; cater (to), give in (to), humor, indulge
near antonyms deter, discourage; bar, block, constrain, curb, frustrate, hold back, impede, inhibit, obstruct, prevent
antonyms enjoin, forbid, prohibit
3 to fail to prevent (some behavior on someone's part) especially from neglect or indifference ⟨Only a lazy gardener would *allow* the weeds to grow that high.⟩
synonyms let, permit, suffer, tolerate
related words brush (aside *or* off), condone, disregard,

ignore, overlook, shrug off, wink (at); excuse, forgive, pardon; brook, cater (to), give in (to), humor, indulge
phrases put up with
near antonyms forbid, prohibit; curb, deter, discourage, frustrate, hold back, impede, inhibit, interfere (with)
antonyms bar, block, constrain, prevent
4 to accept the truth or existence of (something) usually reluctantly ⟨I'll *allow* I probably said more than I should have.⟩ — see ADMIT 1
5 to give as a share or portion ⟨We *allowed* each camper one book of matches.⟩ — see ALLOT
6 to make able or possible ⟨A patient's canceled appointment *allowed* the doctor to squeeze in a few extra phone calls.⟩ — see ENABLE 1
7 to make a statement of one's opinion ⟨He *allowed* that their new house looked very nice.⟩ — see REMARK 1
allowable *adj* that may be permitted ⟨International travel without a passport isn't *allowable*.⟩ — see PERMISSIBLE
allowance *n* **1** something belonging to, due to, or contributed by an individual member of a group ⟨As the shortage progressed, each family's *allowance* of fuel was reduced.⟩ — see SHARE 1
2 the approval by someone in authority for the doing of something ⟨Without the official *allowance* of the school board, no organization can hold its meetings on school property.⟩ — see PERMISSION
alloyed *adj* containing foreign or lower-grade substances ⟨*Alloyed* aluminum, containing either copper or silicon, is much stronger than pure aluminum for cookware.⟩ — see IMPURE 1
all-powerful *adj* having unlimited power or authority ⟨That country's monarch was never an *all-powerful* ruler, but one who shared power with a parliament.⟩ — see OMNIPOTENT
all-purpose *adj* not limited or specialized in application or purpose ⟨an *all-purpose* tool⟩ — see GENERAL 4
all right *adj* **1** being to one's liking ⟨It's *all right* with me if you wear jeans to the party.⟩ — see SATISFACTORY 1
2 not exposed to the threat of loss or injury ⟨As soon as we heard the rescue helicopter, we knew we were *all right*.⟩ — see SAFE 1
3 of a level of quality that meets one's needs or standards ⟨It wasn't a great meal, but it was *all right*.⟩ — see ADEQUATE 1
4 conforming to a high standard of morality or virtue ⟨He's an *all right* guy, so if he says that's the way it happened, I believe him.⟩ — see GOOD 2
all right *adv* **1** in a satisfactory way ⟨If everything goes *all right*, I should be back in a day or two.⟩ — see WELL 1
2 used to express agreement ⟨*All right*, I'll try one tiny bite of octopus.⟩ — see YES
3 without any question ⟨He was there *all right*—I saw him sitting in the back row.⟩ — see INDEED 1
allude *vb* to convey an idea indirectly ⟨Mrs. Simons *alluded* to some health problems, without being specific.⟩ — see HINT
allure *n* the power of irresistible attraction ⟨The nostalgic *allure* of America's Wild West still attracts vacationers to ghost towns.⟩ — see CHARM 2
allure *vb* **1** to attract or delight as if by magic ⟨He was so *allured* by his sister's college roommate that before long he was asking her for a date.⟩ — see CHARM 1
2 to lead away from a usual or proper course by offering some pleasure or advantage ⟨*Allured* by the promise of big bucks, he decided to have a go at a job on the trading floor of the stock market.⟩ — see LURE
allurement *n* **1** something that persuades one to perform an action for pleasure or gain ⟨For him the *allurement* of gambling is not the prospect of getting rich but rather the excitement of the game.⟩ — see LURE 1

2 the act or pressure of giving in to a desire especially when ill-advised ⟨difficult to ignore the *allurements* of the links on the website⟩ — see TEMPTATION 1
alluring *adj* having an often mysterious or magical power to attract ⟨The *alluring* beauty of the swans on the lake held us spellbound.⟩ — see FASCINATING 1
ally *n* someone associated with another to give assistance or moral support ⟨In trying to convince his parents to send him to soccer camp, the youngster had a strong *ally* in his coach.⟩
synonyms abettor (*also* abetter), backer, confederate, supporter, sympathizer
related words empathizer, well-wisher; accessory (*also* accessary), accomplice, coalitionist, collaborationist, collaborator; adjunct, assistant, coadjutor, helper; associate, cohort, colleague, fellow, partner; buddy, chum, companion, comrade, confidant, crony, familiar, friend, intimate, mate, pal
near antonyms belittler, detractor; adversary, enemy, foe, opponent
ally *vb* to form or enter into an association that furthers the interests of its members ⟨The area's small grape growers have *allied* and formed a cooperative that will help them get the best prices.⟩
synonyms associate, band (together), club, coalesce, cohere, confederate, conjoin, cooperate, federate, league, unite
related words cabal, collaborate, gang up, hang together, team (up); incorporate, organize, unionize; affiliate; amalgamate, combine, conglomerate, consolidate, converge, group, join, merge; knot, link, tie, wed
phrases close ranks, pull together
near antonyms detach, disengage, dissolve, disunite, divorce, part, segregate, separate, sever, split, sunder; alienate, estrange, fall out
antonyms break up, disband
almighty *adj* **1** extreme in degree, power, or effect ⟨the *almighty* shock that we got when we received the bill⟩ — see INTENSE 1
2 having unlimited power or authority ⟨When we are young, we want our parents to be *almighty* and to be able to make everything right when something goes wrong.⟩ — see OMNIPOTENT
almighty *adv* to a great degree ⟨That's an *almighty* large pumpkin you've grown there.⟩ — see VERY 1
Almighty *n* the being worshipped as the creator and ruler of the universe ⟨The worshippers gave thanks to the *Almighty*.⟩ — see DEITY 2
almost *adj* being such only when compared to something else ⟨Burdened with impossibly high expectations, the movie came to be regarded as an *almost* failure.⟩ — see COMPARATIVE
almost *adv* very close to but not completely ⟨We were *almost* finished with dinner when an unexpected visitor showed up.⟩ ⟨There were *almost* enough seats for everybody on the bus.⟩
synonyms about, all but, fairly, more or less, most, much, near, nearly, next to, nigh, practically, virtually, well-nigh
related words appreciably, by and large, chiefly, largely, mainly, mostly; kind of, partially, partly, somewhat; approximately, around, roughly
phrases as good as, just about, pretty much, within an inch of
near antonyms absolutely, altogether, completely, entirely, fully, plain, quite, thoroughly; totally, utterly, well, wholly; barely, hardly, scarcely
alms *pl n* a gift of money or its equivalent to a charity, humanitarian cause, or public institution ⟨He believes

that giving *alms* to the poor is a moral duty.⟩ — see CONTRIBUTION

almsgiving *n* the giving of necessities and especially money to the needy ⟨good works such as *almsgiving*, tending the sick and visiting the imprisoned⟩ — see CHARITY 1

aloft *adv* to or in a higher place ⟨The ease with which he can hold a ballerina *aloft* with one hand is awesome.⟩ — see ABOVE

alone *adj* **1** not being in the company of others ⟨No one realized the boy was *alone* in his room so they all left for the movies without him.⟩
synonyms lone, lonely, lonesome, single, solitary, solo, unaccompanied
related words unattended, unchaperoned; forlorn, friendless; cloistered, disassociated, hermetic (*also* hermetical), insulated, isolate, isolated, remote, retired, secluded, withdrawn; quarantined, segregated, separated, sequestered; separate, unattached, unconnected, unlinked; detached, disconnected, disjointed, dissociated, disunited, divided; abandoned, adrift, deserted, desolate, forgotten, forsaken, lorn, neglected
phrases on one's own
near antonyms attended, chaperoned, escorted; adjacent, adjoining, communicating, contiguous, neighboring, next-door; attached, connected, coupled, linked
antonyms accompanied
2 being the one or ones of a class with no other members ⟨He is *alone* among the actors of his generation in his exceptional ability to play both comedic and serious parts.⟩ — see ONLY 2

alone *adv* **1** without aid or support ⟨Completely new to the big city, she nevertheless managed to find her way home *alone*.⟩
synonyms independently, single-handedly, singly, solely, unaided, unassisted
related words individually, separately; solo
phrases by one's own bootstraps, on one's own, on one's own hook, on one's own initiative
near antonyms collectively, conjointly, cooperatively, hand in hand, jointly, mutually, together; en masse
2 for nothing other than ⟨He would willingly play professional baseball for the sheer enjoyment *alone*.⟩ — see SOLELY 1

along *adv* toward or at a point lying in advance in space or time ⟨Traffic was inching *along* at a snail's pace.⟩ ⟨Work on the project is moving right *along*.⟩
synonyms ahead, forth, forward, forwards, on, onward (*also* onwards)
related words before
near antonyms back, backward (*or* backwards), behind, rearward (*also* rearwards)

aloof *adj* having or showing a lack of friendliness or interest in others ⟨The new kid was really not so *aloof* as we thought him at first, just painfully shy.⟩ — see COOL 1

aloud *adv* with one's normal voice speaking the words ⟨The mischievous teacher likes to call on the sleepiest-looking students to read *aloud* from the textbook.⟩
synonyms audibly, out, out loud
related words verbally, vocally; discernibly, distinctly, distinguishably, perceptibly, plainly; blatantly, bloody murder, boisterously, clamorously, loudly, lustily, mightily, noisily, resonantly, resoundingly, stridently, thunderously, uproariously, vociferously
near antonyms faintly, feebly, low, noiselessly, quietly, softly
antonyms inaudibly, silently, soundlessly, voicelessly

alp *n* an elevation of land higher than a hill ⟨an adventurer who has scaled *alps*, explored ocean depths, and flown into the stratosphere⟩ — see MOUNTAIN 1

alpha *n* the point at which something begins ⟨Money is not the *alpha* and omega of life's purpose.⟩ — see BEGINNING

alright *adj* **1** being to one's liking ⟨an *alright* movie, but I wouldn't pay to see it again⟩ — see SATISFACTORY 1
2 not exposed to the threat of loss or injury ⟨We got the plane's nose back up, and after that we were *alright*.⟩ — see SAFE 1

alright *adv* **1** in a satisfactory way ⟨The audition for the orchestra position seemed to go *alright*, but one never knows.⟩ — see WELL 1
2 used to express agreement ⟨*Alright*, you can buy me lunch, but next time it's my treat.⟩ — see YES
3 without any question ⟨She passed the test *alright*—she had the highest score in the class!⟩ — see INDEED 1

also *adv* **1** in like manner ⟨We stayed at a historic London hotel, the same establishment that had *also* welcomed our grandparents many years ago.⟩
synonyms alike, correspondingly, likewise, similarly, so
related words equally, equivalently, identically
phrases as well
near antonyms conversely, inversely, oppositely, vice versa; diversely, unequally, variously
antonyms differently, dissimilarly, otherwise
2 in addition to what has been said ⟨I'd like a motorcycle for my birthday; *also*, I'd like a new smart phone.⟩ — see MORE 1

alter *vb* **1** to make different in some way ⟨Can't you *alter* your plans just slightly so we can leave 10 minutes earlier?⟩ — see CHANGE 1
2 to remove the sex organs of ⟨She contends that cats and dogs that have been *altered* make better pets.⟩ — see NEUTER

alterable *adj* capable of being readily changed ⟨If my vacation plans were *alterable*, I'd change them.⟩ — see FLEXIBLE 1

alteration *n* the act, process, or result of making different ⟨There's been an *alteration* in the intended route of our bird walk.⟩ — see CHANGE 1

altercation *n* an often noisy or angry expression of differing opinions ⟨Judging from all the slamming and banging, I'd say there was some sort of *altercation* going on next door.⟩ — see ARGUMENT 1

alter ego *n* **1** a person who has a strong liking for and trust in another ⟨Over the years the state's other senator became his *alter ego* as well as his political ally.⟩ — see FRIEND 1
2 something or someone that strongly resembles another ⟨The hero of the novel is clearly the author's *alter ego*.⟩ — see IMAGE 1

alternative *n* the power, right, or opportunity to choose ⟨There's no *alternative*: we must cross the stream to reach our destination.⟩ — see CHOICE 1

although *also* **altho** *conj* in spite of the fact that ⟨*Although* I've been to his house several times, I still can't remember how to get there.⟩
synonyms albeit, as, howbeit, notwithstanding, though, when, whereas, while
related words but

altitude *n* **1** the distance of something or someone from bottom to top ⟨The *altitude* of the highest mountain in the U.S. is only about two thirds that of the highest mountain in the world.⟩ — see HEIGHT 3
2 *usually* **altitudes** *pl* an area of high ground ⟨The air is thinner at higher *altitudes*.⟩ — see HEIGHT 4

altogether *adv* **1** for the most part ⟨*Altogether*, I'd say we had a pretty good time.⟩ — see CHIEFLY
2 to a full extent or degree ⟨I was not *altogether* prepared for such bad news.⟩ — see FULLY 1

3 with everyone or everything taken into account at the same time ⟨We spent six months in Europe *altogether*.⟩ — see ALL AROUND

altruistic *adj* having or showing a concern for the welfare of others ⟨I'm not being *altruistic* in giving you these books, since I was going to have to lug them with me if you hadn't come along.⟩ — see CHARITABLE 1

always *adv* **1** on every relevant occasion ⟨Although we never intend more than an afternoon visit, she *always* insists we stay for dinner.⟩
synonyms aye (*also* ay), consistently, constantly, continually, ever, forever, incessantly, invariably, perpetually, unfailingly
related words commonly, frequently, oft, often, oftentimes (*or* ofttimes), recurrently, repeatedly; continuously, steadily, uninterruptedly, unremittingly; dependably, generally, habitually, normally, ordinarily, regularly, routinely, typically, usually; inevitably; eternally, everlastingly
phrases at every turn
near antonyms intermittently, occasionally, periodically, sometimes, sporadically; infrequently, rarely, seldom, unusually; variously
antonyms ne'er, never
2 whatever else is done or is the case ⟨You can *always* take a cab if the buses aren't running.⟩
synonyms anyhow, anyway
phrases at all events, at any rate, at least, in any case, in any event
3 for all time ⟨I will love you *always*.⟩ — see EVER 1

amain *adv* with great effort or determination ⟨conflicting ideals that social philosophers have struggled *amain* to reconcile⟩ — see HARD 1

amalgam *n* a distinct entity formed by the combining of two or more different things ⟨a building that is an *amalgam* of traditional and modern architectural styles⟩ — see BLEND

amalgamate *vb* to turn into a single mass or entity that is more or less the same throughout ⟨Silver *amalgamated* with mercury was used for tooth fillings.⟩ — see BLEND 1

amalgamated *adj* made from the joining of two or more parts or elements ⟨The *Amalgamated* Clothing and Textile Workers Union was formed from the merger of the clothing workers' and textile workers' unions.⟩ — see COMPOSITE

amalgamation *n* a distinct entity formed by the combining of two or more different things ⟨An *amalgamation* of peat moss and vermiculite is a good medium for starting vegetable seedlings.⟩ — see BLEND

amass *vb* **1** to bring together in one body or place ⟨*amassed* a truckload of donations in the course of their canned food drive⟩ — see GATHER 1
2 to gradually form into a layer, pile, or mass ⟨Over the last month a huge mound of paperwork has *amassed* on my desk.⟩ — see COLLECT 2

amateur *adj* lacking or showing a lack of expert skill ⟨In every room there were *amateur* watercolors.⟩ — see AMATEURISH

amateur *n* **1** a person who regularly or occasionally engages in an activity as a pastime rather than as a profession ⟨an *amateur* photographer who has won a number of photo contests⟩
synonyms dabbler, dilettante, nonprofessional, potterer, putterer
related words generalist, general practitioner, jack-of-all-trades; aficionado (*also* afficionado), buff, devotee, enthusiast, fan
antonyms authority, expert, pro, professional, specialist
2 a person who lacks experience and competence in an art or science ⟨a homemade doghouse that looked like it was built by an *amateur* who hadn't mastered basic carpentry⟩
synonyms hack, inexpert
related words beginner, freshman, greenhorn, kid, learner, neophyte, newcomer, novice, rookie, tenderfoot, tyro
near antonyms maestro, virtuoso, whiz, wizard; old hand, old-timer, vet, veteran
antonyms ace, adept, crackerjack (*also* crackajack), craftsman, expert, hand, master, past master, shark, sharp

amateurish *adj* lacking or showing a lack of expert skill ⟨That's an *amateurish* wallpapering job—the pattern doesn't match at the seams.⟩
synonyms amateur, dilettante, inexperienced, inexpert, nonprofessional, unprofessional, unskilled, unskillful
related words curbstone, uninitiated, unprepared, unqualified, unschooled, untaught, untrained, untutored; awkward, clumsy, heavy-handed; crude, defective, faulty, flawed, primitive, unfinished, unpolished; beginning, entry-level, fresh, green, new, raw, unseasoned, untested, untried, would-be; incapable, incompetent, talentless, unfit, ungifted, untalented; avocational, nonprofessional
near antonyms able, accomplished, capable, competent, dexterous (*also* dextrous), gifted, handsome, proficient, skilled, skillful, talented; experienced, practiced (*also* practised), seasoned, veteran; educated, fitted, initiated, knowledgeable, prepared, qualified, schooled, taught, trained, tutored, versed; all-around (*also* all-round), ambidextrous, versatile, well-rounded; finished, polished, slick
antonyms ace, adept, consummate, crackerjack, expert, master, masterful, masterly, professional, virtuosic, virtuoso

amatory *adj* of, relating to, exciting, or expressing sexual attraction or desire ⟨*amatory* letters that kept their love alive during the years they were apart⟩ — see EROTIC

amaze *vb* to make a strong impression on (someone) with something unexpected ⟨Your ability to remember names and faces *amazes* me.⟩ — see SURPRISE 1

amazed *adj* **1** affected with sudden and great wonder or surprise ⟨You'd be *amazed* at the destruction one small squirrel can cause inside a house.⟩ — see THUNDERSTRUCK
2 filled with amazement or wonder ⟨A visitor cannot help but be *amazed* by the size of the Great Pyramid.⟩ — see OPENMOUTHED

amazement *n* **1** the rapt attention and deep emotion caused by the sight of something extraordinary ⟨The crowd watched in *amazement* as the runner broke yet another world record.⟩ — see WONDER 2
2 the state of being strongly impressed by something unexpected or unusual ⟨Imagine Dorothy's *amazement* when she discovered that the Wizard of Oz was just an ordinary man.⟩ — see SURPRISE 2

amazing *adj* **1** causing a strong emotional reaction because of unexpectedness ⟨It was rather *amazing* that the store let me return the sweater after I'd worn and even washed it.⟩ — see SURPRISING 1
2 causing wonder or astonishment ⟨The *amazing* feats of the circus acrobats simply enthralled the audience.⟩ — see MARVELOUS 1

ambassador *n* a person sent on a mission to represent another ⟨a beloved entertainer who has often been sent abroad by the president as his country's goodwill *ambassador*⟩
synonyms agent, delegate, emissary, envoy, legate, minister, representative

related words ambassadress; attaché, chargé d'affaires, consul, deputy, diplomat, foreign minister, proxy; apostle, evangelist, missionary; courier, messenger; mouthpiece, spokesperson

ambiguity *n* the quality or state of having a veiled or uncertain meaning ⟨The *ambiguity* of his message left me wondering what to do.⟩ — see OBSCURITY 1

ambiguous *adj* having an often intentionally veiled or uncertain meaning ⟨The exact reason for the change in plans is *ambiguous*, but I suspect it has something to do with money.⟩ — see OBSCURE 1

ambiguousness *n* the quality or state of having a veiled or uncertain meaning ⟨The *ambiguousness* of her "I'll come if I can" left us wondering if we should find someone to take her place.⟩ — see OBSCURITY 1

ambition *n* 1 eager desire for personal advancement ⟨"Talent without *ambition* will not make you a star," the singer's voice coach liked to remind her.⟩

synonyms aspiration, go-getting

related words determination, diligence, drive, energy, enterprise, go, hustle, industry, initiative, motivation, push; aggression, competitiveness, killer instinct; opportunism, overambitiousness, pretentiousness, pushiness; assertiveness, daring, spirit; ardor, avidity, eagerness, keenness, passion; avarice, greed, hunger

near antonyms apathy, halfheartedness, indifference, unconcern; idleness, indolence, inertia, laziness, shiftlessness, sloth

2 readiness to engage in daring or difficult activity ⟨the *ambition* shown by the undersea explorers of the Mariana Trench, the deepest in the world⟩ — see ENTERPRISE 2

3 something that one hopes or intends to accomplish ⟨His *ambition* is to study international business, then get a job overseas.⟩ — see GOAL

ambitious *adj* 1 having a strong desire for personal advancement ⟨an *ambitious* child actor and his even more ambitious mother, who will do anything to get him in commercials⟩

synonyms aspiring, go-getting, hard-driving, self-seeking

related words determined, diligent, driving, dynamic, enterprising, gung ho, hungry, hustling, industrious, motivated, scrappy, venturesome, venturous; animated, lively, spirited; ardent, avid, eager, energetic, impassioned, keen, raring, vigorous; aggressive, assertive, highflying, opportunistic, overambitious, pretentious, self-assertive; competing, competitive, rival, rivalrous

near antonyms apathetic, disinterested, indifferent, uneager, unenthusiastic, unexcited, uninterested; casual, easygoing, lackadaisical, lazyish; halfhearted, lukewarm, tepid; lazy, lethargic, listless, shiftless, sluggish, spiritless; unaggressive, unassertive

antonyms ambitionless, unambitious

2 having or showing a bold forcefulness in the pursuit of a goal ⟨Cleaning up the vacant lot in one weekend was an *ambitious* undertaking.⟩ — see AGGRESSIVE 1

ambrosial *adj* 1 having a pleasant smell ⟨the *ambrosial* air of a greenhouse filled with orchids⟩ — see FRAGRANT

2 very pleasing to the sense of taste ⟨a platter heaped with exotic and *ambrosial* tropical fruits⟩ — see DELICIOUS 1

ambush *n* 1 a setup in which hidden attackers lie in wait ⟨Revolutionaries laid in *ambush* for the king along the route his carriage would travel.⟩

synonyms surprise (*also* surprize), trap

related words assault, attack, charge, sally; capture, entrapment, mousetrap, snare; hunting, stalking

2 a device or scheme for capturing another by surprise ⟨a resistance leader who was the victim of an *ambush*⟩ — see TRAP 1

ambush *vb* to lie in wait for and attack by surprise ⟨The king's enemies planned to *ambush* the royal coach on the way to Paris and capture the king.⟩

synonyms surprise (*also* surprize), waylay

related words assail, assault, attack, storm, strike; jump, mug, pounce (on), tackle; charge, sally; capture, ensnare, entrap, mousetrap, net, snare, trap; hunt, prey (on *or* upon), stalk

ameliorate *vb* to make better ⟨social legislation that must be given credit for *ameliorating* the lot of millions of deprived people⟩ — see IMPROVE

amenability *n* 1 a desire or disposition to please ⟨Our circle of friends tends to take advantage of Will's *amenability*, usually not even bothering to ask him what he wants to do.⟩ — see COMPLAISANCE

2 cheerful readiness to do something ⟨Our cat Figaro hasn't shown much *amenability* to going outside now that the weather's cold.⟩ — see ALACRITY

amenable *adj* 1 having a desire or inclination (as for a specified course of action) ⟨Whatever you decide to do, I'm *amenable*—just let me know.⟩ — see WILLING 1

2 readily giving in to the command or authority of another ⟨Our normally balky cat becomes the most *amenable* of creatures when confronted with the strange environment of the veterinary clinic.⟩ — see OBEDIENT

3 being the one who must meet an obligation or suffer the consequences for failing to do so ⟨Even our nation's highest leaders must remain *amenable* to the law.⟩ — see RESPONSIBLE 1

amend *vb* 1 to make better ⟨trying to *amend* the situation of the striking workers by supplying them with minimal food supplies⟩ — see IMPROVE

2 to remove errors, defects, deficiencies, or deviations from ⟨The Bill of Rights was adopted in an effort to *amend* a constitution that seemed to many to be deficient in guaranteeing individual rights.⟩ — see CORRECT 1

3 to change one's behavior or character for the better ⟨The judge had heard the defendant promise before that he would *amend*.⟩ — see REFORM 2

amendment *n* a change designed to correct or improve a written work ⟨The article as written requires only one factual *amendment*.⟩ — see CORRECTION 1

amenity *n* 1 an act or utterance that is a customary show of good manners ⟨They exchanged the usual *amenities* before settling down to business.⟩ — see CIVILITY 1

2 something adding to pleasure or comfort but not absolutely necessary ⟨We don't need an expensive hotel with all the *amenities*—just a place to sleep.⟩ — see LUXURY 1

3 something that adds to one's ease of living ⟨That campground has so many of the *amenities* of home that it is best left to those who only like to pretend they are camping.⟩ — see COMFORT 2

4 the state or quality of having a pleasant or agreeable manner in socializing with others ⟨The nurse's natural *amenity* puts the patients at ease.⟩ — see AMIABILITY 1

amiability *n* 1 the state or quality of having a pleasant or agreeable manner in socializing with others ⟨The waitress's *amiability* is what makes eating at the diner so much fun.⟩

synonyms affability, agreeableness, amenity, amiableness, geniality, good-naturedness, good-temperedness, graciousness, niceness, personableness, pleasantness, sweetness

related words amenability, complaisance, mellowness, sweetness and light; amicability, amicableness, amity, cordiality, friendliness; gentleness, kindliness, kindness;

cheerfulness, cheeriness, sunniness; civility, considerateness, consideration, courteousness, courtesy, politeness, thoughtfulness; attractiveness, delightfulness, enjoyableness, likability, likableness, pleasingness
near antonyms boorishness, discourtesy, impoliteness, incivility, rudeness, ungraciousness; cantankerousness, churlishness, crankiness, fussiness, grouchiness, grumpiness, irascibility, irritability, peevishness, petulance, testiness; contentiousness, contrariness, orneriness, querulousness; hostility, unfriendliness; sourness
antonyms disagreeableness, unpleasantness
2 a desire or disposition to please ⟨We had never met our cousin before and were pleased by her *amiability*.⟩ — see COMPLAISANCE
amiable *adj* having an easygoing and pleasing manner especially in social situations ⟨The owner of the inn is an *amiable*, talkative woman who treats guests like family.⟩
synonyms affable, agreeable, genial, good-natured, good-tempered, gracious, mellow, nice, pleasant, sweet, well-disposed
related words amicable, cordial, friendly, neighborly; benign, gentle, kind; cheerful, cheery, sunny; companionable, conversable, sociable; civil, considerate, courteous, polite, thoughtful; accommodating, amenable, obliging; attractive, delightful, enjoyable, likable (*or* likeable)
near antonyms boorish, discourteous, ill-mannered, impolite, inconsiderate, rude, surly, uncivil, unkind, unmannerly, unsociable; bearish, cantankerous, choleric, churlish, crabby, cranky, dyspeptic, fussy, grouchy, grumpy, ill-humored, irascible, irritable, peevish, petulant, quick-tempered, snappish, testy, touchy; argumentative, contentious, contrary, ornery, querulous; unappealing, unattractive; sour, vinegary
antonyms disagreeable, ill-natured, ill-tempered, unamiable, ungenial, ungracious, unpleasant
amiableness *n* the state or quality of having a pleasant or agreeable manner in socializing with others ⟨The dance instructor's natural *amiableness* puts new students immediately at ease.⟩ — see AMIABILITY 1
amicable *adj* **1** having or marked by agreement in feeling or action ⟨The contract negotiations between the hotel workers and management were reasonably *amicable*.⟩ — see HARMONIOUS 3
2 having or showing kindly feeling and sincere interest ⟨finds his coworkers at his new job just as *amicable* as he ever could have hoped⟩ — see FRIENDLY 1
amid *or* **amidst** *prep* **1** in or into the middle of ⟨Having grown up *amid* farmers and ranchers, Keith still thinks of himself as a country boy at heart.⟩ — see AMONG
2 in the course of ⟨He joined the team *amidst* a winning season.⟩ — see DURING
amiss *adj* **1** having a fault ⟨That engine noise indicates that something is clearly *amiss*.⟩ — see FAULTY
2 not appropriate for a particular occasion or situation ⟨Official recognition would not be *amiss* after that spectacular effort.⟩ — see INAPPROPRIATE
amiss *adv* **1** in a mistaken or inappropriate way ⟨I hope that my suggestion was not taken *amiss*.⟩ — see WRONGLY
2 off the desired or intended path or course ⟨The reenactment of the Wright Brothers' first flight went *amiss* when the plane stopped short in a mud puddle.⟩ — see WRONG
amity *n* kindly concern, interest, or support ⟨a youth club fostering *amity* among the city's many and diverse ethnic groups⟩ — see GOODWILL 1
ammunition *n* means or method of defending ⟨She had the *ammunition* to prove her case.⟩ — see DEFENSE 1
amnesty *n* release from the guilt or penalty of an offense ⟨The president of France traditionally grants *amnesty* to specially selected prisoners on Bastille Day.⟩ — see PARDON
amok *or* **amuck** *adv* in a confused and reckless manner ⟨Ms. Baker returned to the classroom to find an escaped mouse and her students running *amok*.⟩ — see HELTER-SKELTER 1
among *also* **amongst** *prep* in or into the middle of ⟨A gull landed *among* the burgers-and-fries eaters at the outdoor snack bar, clearly looking for handouts.⟩
synonyms amid (*or* amidst), mid, midst, through
related words between, betwixt
phrases in the thick of
near antonyms from, out of
amorous *adj* of, relating to, exciting, or expressing sexual attraction or desire ⟨Male birds engage in *amorous* behavior—nest-building, singing, showing off their plumage—in order to attract females.⟩ — see EROTIC
amorphous *adj* having no definite or recognizable form ⟨*amorphous* lumps of clay magically transformed by a skilled potter's hands into works of art⟩ — see FORMLESS 1
amount *n* a given or particular mass or aggregate of matter ⟨We'll need a large *amount* of food to feed the whole hockey team.⟩
synonyms measure, quantity, volume
related words coefficient, degree; body, portion; many, number
amount (to) *vb* **1** to have a total of ⟨The expenses of the trip *amounted to* nearly double what we'd budgeted for.⟩
synonyms add up (to), aggregate, come (to), number, sum (to *or* into), total
related words average, equal, measure, reach; compose, comprise, constitute, make up
phrases clock in at
2 to be the same in meaning or effect ⟨It makes no difference whether you're going to the game or the movies, for it *amounts to* the same thing—that you can't babysit.⟩
synonyms add up (to), come (to), correspond (to), emulate, equal
related words approach, match, measure (up), meet, rival, touch; connote, denote, express, import, mean, signify, smack (of), spell, suggest
ample *adj* **1** being more than enough without being excessive ⟨There's *ample* time to order a pizza before the show.⟩ — see PLENTIFUL
2 more than adequate or average in capacity ⟨I like to curl up to read in the most *ample* chair in the room.⟩ — see SPACIOUS
amplify *vb* **1** to express more fully and in greater detail ⟨After filing a report of missing luggage, he was asked to *amplify* a bit as to the circumstances.⟩ — see EXPAND 1
2 to make greater in size, amount, or number ⟨The number of donors was significantly *amplified* by the promise of thank-you gifts.⟩ — see INCREASE 1
3 to make markedly greater in measure or degree ⟨A fox's large ears serve to *amplify* such sounds as little critters skittering among stones.⟩ — see INTENSIFY
amplitude *n* an area over which activity, capacity, or influence extends ⟨The *amplitude* of Thomas Jefferson's interests—government, architecture, agriculture, science, philosophy—is truly awesome.⟩ — see RANGE 2
amply *adv* in a generous manner ⟨*amply* rewarded the boy who had found her necklace⟩ — see WELL 2
amulet *n* something worn or kept to bring good luck or keep away evil ⟨A small cross made of goat bone was worn in the Middle Ages as an *amulet* to ward off evil.⟩ — see CHARM 1

amuse *vb* to cause (someone) to pass the time agreeably occupied ⟨The older girl *amused* her four-year-old sister at the family reunion by showing her off to all the relatives.⟩
   synonyms disport, divert, entertain, regale, solace
   related words absorb, busy, distract, engage, engross, immerse, interest, involve, occupy; beguile, bewitch, captivate, charm, delight, enchant, enthrall (*or* enthral), fascinate; grip, hypnotize, intrigue, mesmerize; coddle, gratify, humor, indulge, mollycoddle, pamper, please, pleasure, spoil; appease, comfort, conciliate, console, content, mollify, oblige, pacify, placate, propitiate, soothe
   near antonyms bore, jade; drain, enervate, exhaust, fatigue, tire, wear, wear out, weary; aggravate, annoy, bother, bug, chafe, disturb, exasperate, fret, gall, grate, harry, irk, nettle, peeve, perturb, pester, pique, upset, vex

amusement *n* the act or activity of providing pleasure or amusement especially for the public ⟨With the opening of Disneyland in 1955, the film producer Walt Disney greatly expanded his *amusement* empire.⟩ — see ENTERTAINMENT 1

amusing *adj* providing amusement or enjoyment ⟨Grandma told an *amusing* story about Dad when he was little.⟩ — see FUN

analgesic *n* something (as a drug) that relieves pain ⟨The doctor prescribed an *analgesic* and rest for my injured knee.⟩ — see PAINKILLER

analogous *adj* having qualities in common ⟨The telescope's lenses are *analogous* to a person's glasses.⟩ — see ALIKE

analysis *n* **1** the separation and identification of the parts of a whole ⟨Researchers took the sample to the lab for *analysis*.⟩
   synonyms anatomizing, assay, breakdown, dissection
   related words assessment, diagnosis, evaluation, examination, inspection, investigation, muster, scrutiny; arrangement, assortment, cataloging (*or* cataloguing), categorization, classification, codification, indexing; enumeration, inventory, itemization, tabulation; division, reduction, segmentation, separation, subdivision
   near antonyms agglomeration, aggregation, amalgamation, assimilation, coalescence, conglomeration, consolidation, integration, unification
   2 a series of explanations or observations on something (as an event) ⟨She gave a thorough *analysis* of the main character's motives.⟩ — see COMMENTARY 1

analytic *or* **analytical** *adj* according to the rules of logic ⟨He presented a very *analytical* argument for the defendant's innocence.⟩ — see LOGICAL 1

analyze *vb* to identify and examine the basic elements or parts of (something) especially for discovering interrelationships ⟨We'll *analyze* the park's ecosystem before deciding whether snowmobiling should be allowed.⟩
   synonyms anatomize, assay, break down, cut, dissect
   related words assess, diagnose, evaluate, examine, inspect, investigate, scrutinize; arrange, assort, catalog (*or* catalogue), categorize, classify, codify, diagram, enumerate, index, order, schematize, sort, tabulate; divide, reduce, segment, separate, subdivide
   near antonyms agglomerate, aggregate, amalgamate, assimilate, coalesce, conglomerate, consolidate, integrate, synthesize, unify

anarchic *also* **anarchical** *adj* not restrained by or under the control of legal authority ⟨The citywide blackouts caused *anarchic* confusion.⟩ — see LAWLESS 1

anarchy *n* a state in which there is widespread wrongdoing and disregard for rules and authority ⟨the *anarchy* that the country experienced after the dictator drained the treasury and fled the country⟩
   synonyms lawlessness, misrule
   related words anarchism; commotion, tumult, uproar; chaos, confusion, disarray, disorder, disorganization; disruption, disturbance, havoc, riot, strife, turbulence, turmoil, unrest, upheaval; mutiny, rebellion, revolution, uprising; criminality, outlawry
   near antonyms law, law-abidingness, lawfulness, legality, legitimacy, rule; calmness, harmony, order, orderliness, peace, peaceableness, peacefulness, quiet, tranquillity (*or* tranquility)

anathema *n* **1** a prayer that harm will come to someone ⟨The owner uttered an *anathema* before driving the would-be robber from his shop.⟩ — see CURSE 1
   2 something or someone that is hated ⟨Development of the property was *anathema* to the conservationists.⟩ — see HATE 2

anatomize *vb* to identify and examine the basic elements or parts of (something) especially for discovering interrelationships ⟨If you *anatomize* the problem, you'll discover its cause.⟩ — see ANALYZE

anatomizing *n* the separation and identification of the parts of a whole ⟨Your *anatomizing* of the situation is quite insightful.⟩ — see ANALYSIS 1

ancestor *n* **1** a person who is several generations earlier in an individual's line of descent ⟨Bridie's Irish *ancestors* immigrated to the United States in the 19th century during the Great Potato Famine.⟩
   synonyms father, forebear (*also* forbear), forefather, grandfather
   related words ancestress, foremother, grandmother, matriarch; patriarch; ancestry, antecedents, roots
   near antonyms children, family, issue, lineage, offspring, posterity, progeny, seed, stock; daughter, heir, inheritor, scion, son, successor
   antonyms descendant (*also* descendent)
   2 something belonging to an earlier time from which something else was later developed ⟨Pinball machines—the *ancestors* of today's video games—go back to the 19th century.⟩
   synonyms antecedent, archetype, daddy, foregoer, forerunner, precursor, predecessor, prototype
   related words model, original; originator, sire; father, mother
   near antonyms by-product, derivative, offshoot, outgrowth, spin-off; daughter, son
   antonyms descendant (*also* descendent)

ancestry *n* the line of ancestors from whom a person is descended ⟨She traced her Khmer *ancestry* as far back as the 16th century.⟩
   synonyms birth, blood, bloodline, breeding, descent, extraction, family tree, genealogy, line, lineage, origin, parentage, pedigree, stock, strain
   related words heredity, succession; family, house; kin, kindred, relations, relatives; race
   near antonyms offspring; child, heir, inheritor, son, successor
   antonyms issue, posterity, progeny, seed

anchor *n* **1** one who reads and introduces news reports on a news program ⟨The news *anchor* coordinated the reports of the correspondents from around the state.⟩ — see ANCHORPERSON
   2 something or someone to which one looks for support ⟨My best friend has been my *anchor* throughout this crisis.⟩ — see DEPENDENCE 2

anchor *vb* **1** to put securely in place or in a desired position ⟨They used ropes and sandbags to *anchor* the hot-air balloon to the ground.⟩ — see FASTEN 2
   2 to stop at or near a place along the shore ⟨We'll *anchor* at Praia, Cape Verde.⟩ — see LAND 1

anchorage *n* a part of a body of water protected and deep enough to be a place of safety for ships ⟨We sailed into a quiet *anchorage* to wait out the storm.⟩ — see HARBOR 1

anchorperson *n* one who reads and introduces news reports on a news program ⟨The new *anchorperson* did an admirable job of dealing with the late-breaking news story.⟩

synonyms anchor

related words anchorman, anchorwoman, coanchor; broadcaster, commentator, telecaster; correspondent, foreign correspondent, journalist, newshound, newsie, newsman, newswoman, reporter, stringer

ancient *adj* **1** dating or surviving from the distant past ⟨Rome's *ancient* ruins remain carefully preserved even in the midst of the bustle of the modern city.⟩

synonyms aged, age-old, antediluvian, antique, dateless, hoar, hoary, immemorial, old, venerable

related words aging (*or* ageing), mature; antiquated, archaic, dated, fusty, geriatric, medieval (*also* mediaeval), moldy, obsolete, outmoded, out-of-date, passé; old-fashioned, old-time, old-world, retro; durable, enduring, lasting, long-lived, permanent; ageless, hallowed, time-honored, timeless, time-tested, traditional, tried, tried-and-true; classic, classical; prehistoric (*also* prehistorical), primeval, primordial

near antonyms fresh, vernal, young, youthful; contemporary, current, latest, mod, novel, present-day, ultramodern; untested, untried; brand-new, unused, unworn

antonyms modern, new, recent

2 being of advanced years and especially past middle age ⟨I used to think that age 40 was *ancient* until I turned 40 myself.⟩ — see ELDERLY

3 relating to or occurring near the beginning of a process, series, or time period ⟨The *ancient* Inca built a vast network of roads.⟩ — see EARLY 1

ancient *n* a person of advanced years ⟨*Ancients* in the tribe are accorded great respect and valued for their wisdom.⟩ — see SENIOR CITIZEN

anecdote *n* a brief account of something interesting that happened especially to one personally ⟨He told us once again that *anecdote* about the dog and the bike.⟩ — see STORY 2

anesthetic *n* something (as a drug) that relieves pain ⟨The dentist waited until the *anesthetic* took effect.⟩ — see PAINKILLER

anew *adv* yet another time ⟨He junked what he had written and began the essay *anew*.⟩ — see AGAIN 1

angel *n* **1** an innocent or gentle person ⟨would like to think that her child is a perfect *angel*⟩ — see LAMB

2 one that announces or indicates the later arrival of another ⟨looking forward to seeing those red-breasted *angels* of the spring—robins⟩ — see FORERUNNER 1

3 one that helps another with gifts or money ⟨Over the years the industrialist frequently served as the symphony orchestra's anonymous *angel*.⟩ — see BENEFACTOR

anger *n* an intense emotional state of displeasure with someone or something ⟨The patient managed to stifle his *anger* when the receptionist put him on hold for the third time.⟩

synonyms angriness, furor, fury, indignation, irateness, ire, mad, madness, outrage, rage, spleen, wrath, wrathfulness

related words aggravation, annoyance, exasperation, irritation, vexation; acrimoniousness, acrimony, animosity, antagonism, antipathy, bile, bitterness, contempt, embitterment, enmity, grudge, hostility, rancor; envy, jaundice, jealousy, pique, resentment; malevolence, malice, spite, vengefulness, venom, vindictiveness, virulence, vitriol; belligerence, contentiousness, contrariness,

crankiness, disputatiousness, hot-headedness, irascibility, irritability, orneriness, pugnaciousness, pugnacity, querulousness; blowup, flare, flare-up, outburst; chafe, dander, dudgeon, huff, pet, rise, ruffle, temper; air rage, road rage; delirium, heat, passion, warmth

phrases slow burn

near antonyms calmness, forbearance, patience

antonyms delight, pleasure

anger *vb* to make angry ⟨It's virtually impossible to *anger* Mrs. Peterson—she's the most easygoing person I've ever known.⟩

synonyms enrage, incense, inflame (*also* enflame), infuriate, ire, madden, outrage, rankle, rile, roil

related words affront, aggravate, annoy, cross, exasperate, get, huff, irritate, nettle, offend, peeve, pique, provoke, put out, ruffle, vex; antagonize, embitter, envenom

phrases get one's goat, rub the wrong way

near antonyms allay, assuage, relieve; comfort, console, soothe; appease, conciliate, mollify, pacify, placate; calm, lull, quiet, settle; beguile, bewitch, captivate, charm, disarm, enchant

antonyms delight, gratify, please

angered *adj* feeling or showing anger ⟨*Angered* residents demanded to know why their street hadn't been plowed three days after the snowstorm.⟩ — see ANGRY

angle *n* **1** a certain way in which something appears or may be regarded ⟨From this *angle*, that car looks gray, not brown.⟩ — see ASPECT 1

2 a way of looking at or thinking about something ⟨What's your *angle* on the problem?⟩ — see PERSPECTIVE 1

3 something that curves or is curved ⟨The road around the peninsula is all *angles* and hairpin turns.⟩ — see BEND 1

angle *vb* to set or cause to be at an angle ⟨*Angle* the camera this way and the Leaning Tower of Pisa will look straight.⟩ — see LEAN 1

angling *n* the act of positioning or an instance of being positioned at an angle ⟨His *angling* of the picture made everything else on the wall look crooked.⟩ — see TILT

angriness *n* an intense emotional state of displeasure with someone or something ⟨His constant *angriness* makes him unpleasant to work with.⟩ — see ANGER

angry *adj* feeling or showing anger ⟨There's no reason to get *angry* just because your team lost.⟩

synonyms angered, apoplectic, choleric, enraged, foaming, fuming, furious, hot, incensed, indignant, inflamed (*also* enflamed), infuriate, infuriated, irate, ireful, livid, mad, outraged, rabid, rankled, riled, roiled, sore, steaming, wrathful, wroth

related words ranting, raving, stormy; bristling, bristly, burning, cross, passionate, seething, sizzling, smoldering (*or* smouldering), worked up, wrought (up); acrid, acrimonious, antagonistic, antipathetic, bitter, embittered, inimical, malevolent, piqued, rancorous, resentful, spiteful, vengeful, vindictive, virulent; antisocial, cold, cool, disagreeable, disapproving, distant, frigid, icy, ill-tempered, sorehead (*or* soreheaded), sulky, unfriendly, unpleasant; bearish, cantankerous, churlish, crabby, cranky, dyspeptic, fretful, fussy, grouchy, grumpy, ill-humored, irascible, irritable, peevish, perturbed, petulant, put out, quick-tempered, snappish, testy, touchy; argumentative, belligerent, contentious, contrary, disputatious, ornery, pugnacious, quarrelsome, querulous

phrases bent out of shape, blue in the face, fit to be tied, hopping mad, hot under the collar, in a fume, in a huff, in a pet

near antonyms accepting, accommodating, obliging; agreeable, amenable, complaisant; amicable, cordial,

friendly; content, happy, satisfied; empathetic, sympathetic, tolerant, understanding; calm, pacific, peaceable, placid, serene, tranquil, unembittered; affable, amiable, easygoing, genial, good-natured, good-tempered, kind, pleasant, sweet
antonyms delighted, pleased

anguish *n* **1** a state of great suffering of body or mind ⟨As a new teacher, she was in real *anguish* over the decision to report the cheating.⟩ — see DISTRESS 1
2 deep sadness especially for the loss of someone or something loved ⟨Words can't express my *anguish* at losing my cat.⟩ — see SORROW

anguish *vb* **1** to cause persistent suffering to ⟨*anguished* by fear⟩ — see AFFLICT
2 to feel deep sadness or mental pain ⟨I *anguished* over the loss of my father for years afterwards.⟩ — see GRIEVE

anguished *adj* expressing or suggesting mourning ⟨an *anguished* cry⟩ ⟨We offered words to console the *anguished* widow.⟩ — see MOURNFUL 1

animal *adj* of or relating to the human body ⟨had intellectual as well as *animal* needs⟩ — see PHYSICAL 1

animal *n* one of the lower animals as distinguished from human beings ⟨We saw a lot of *animals* at the wildlife refuge.⟩
synonyms beast, brute, creature, critter
related words biped, quadruped; carnivore, herbivore, insectivore; invertebrate, vertebrate; domestic animal, pet; livestock, stock

animate *adj* **1** having much high-spirited energy and movement ⟨an *animate* dance routine that will really get the blood pumping⟩ — see LIVELY 1
2 having or showing life ⟨I had a dream about a sandwich that becomes *animate*.⟩ — see ALIVE 1

animate *vb* to give life, vigor, or spirit to ⟨Mr. Clark *animates* history for his sixth graders by frequently showing up for class dressed like some famous historical figure.⟩
synonyms brace, energize, enliven, fire, invigorate, jazz (up), liven (up), pep (up), quicken, spike, stimulate, vitalize, vivify, zip (up)
related words arouse, awake, awaken, raise, rouse, stir, wake (up); activate, actuate, drive, impel, motivate, motive, move, propel; charge, electrify, galvanize; excite, ferment, foment, incite, inflame (*also* enflame), instigate, kindle, provoke, set off, spark, trigger, turn on, whip (up); abet, boost, buoy, cheer, embolden, fortify, hearten, infuse, inspire, lift, rally, steel, strengthen; reactivate, reanimate, reawake, reawaken, recreate, reenergize, refresh, refreshen, regenerate, reinvigorate, rejuvenate, rekindle, renew, restimulate, resurrect, resuscitate, revitalize, revive
near antonyms burn out, debilitate, do in, drain, enervate, enfeeble, exhaust, fatigue, kayo, sap, tucker (out), undermine, wash out, weaken, wear, wear out, weary; check, curb, inhibit, jade, quell, quench, repress, restrain, slow, still, stunt, suppress; daunt, demoralize, discourage, dishearten, dispirit
antonyms damp, dampen, deaden, dull, kill

animated *adj* **1** having much high-spirited energy and movement ⟨an *animated* group of girls loudly running down the hall⟩ — see LIVELY 1
2 marked by much life, movement, or activity ⟨an *animated* marketplace full of vendors and holiday shoppers⟩ — see ALIVE 2

animatedly *adv* in a quick and spirited manner ⟨The children *animatedly* raced into the gymnasium.⟩ — see GAILY 2

animately *adv* in a quick and spirited manner ⟨Sue began talking *animately* about her favorite subject: horses.⟩ — see GAILY 2

animation *n* the quality or state of having abundant or intense activity ⟨The *animation* of any city depends upon an abundance of street-level restaurants, shops, and places of entertainment.⟩ — see VITALITY 1

animosity *n* a deep-seated ill will ⟨His open *animosity* towards us made our meeting very uncomfortable.⟩ — see ENMITY

annals *pl n* an account of important events in the order in which they happened ⟨Shakespeare used his *annals* of the reigns of English kings as a source.⟩ — see HISTORY 1

annex *n* a smaller structure added to a main building ⟨a new *annex* that will serve as the permanent home for the school library⟩
synonyms addition, extension, penthouse
related words arm, ell, wing

annex *vb* to join (something) to a mass, quantity, or number so as to bring about an overall increase ⟨plans to *annex* the supply room so as to make the classroom bigger⟩ — see ADD 1

annihilate *vb* **1** to destroy all traces of ⟨The landlord hired an exterminator to *annihilate* the ant infestation.⟩
synonyms abolish, black out, blot out, cancel, clean (up), efface, eradicate, expunge, exterminate, extirpate, liquidate, obliterate, root (out), rub out, snuff (out), stamp (out), wipe out
related words decimate, demolish, destroy, devastate, ravage; dismantle, flatten, mow (down), raze, tear down; ruin, total, waste, wreck; blast, blow up, dash, smash; atomize, consume, devour, dissolve, fragment, powder, pulverize, shatter, splinter; doom, finish, kill, kill off, terminate, zap; cancel, cut, discard, ditch, eject, excise, expel, jettison, oust, throw out
near antonyms conserve, preserve, protect, save; build, construct, create, fabricate, fashion, forge, form, frame, make, manufacture, shape; fix, mend, patch, rebuild, recondition, reconstruct, renew, renovate, repair, restore, revamp
2 to bring to a complete end the physical soundness, existence, or usefulness of ⟨The fire *annihilated* parts of the forest.⟩ — see DESTROY 1
3 to defeat by a large margin ⟨We didn't just win; we absolutely *annihilated* them!⟩ — see WHIP 2

annihilation *n* the state or fact of being rendered nonexistent, physically unsound, or useless ⟨activists who seek the *annihilation* of all forms of injustice⟩ — see DESTRUCTION 1

announce *vb* to make known openly or publicly ⟨The excited couple *announced* to everyone within hearing distance that they were expecting.⟩
synonyms advertise, blare, blaze, broadcast, declare, enunciate, flash, give out, herald, placard, post, proclaim, promulgate, publicize, publish, release, sound, trumpet
related words bark, call (off *or* out), cry; bill, billboard, bulletin; knell, ring, toll; blurb, feature, pitch, plug, promote, puff; disseminate, spread; disclose, divulge, introduce, manifest, report, reveal, show; advise, apprise, hand down, inform, notify; communicate, impart, intimate
phrases beat the drum (for *or* about), run with
near antonyms conceal, hush (up), silence, suppress, withhold; recall, recant, retract, revoke

announcement *n* a published statement informing the public of a matter of general interest ⟨An *announcement* was in today's paper regarding the merger of the two banks.⟩
synonyms ad, advertisement, bulletin, communiqué, notice, notification, posting, release
related words broadside, brochure, circular, fly sheet, handbill, handout; bill, billboard, placard, playbill, poster,

show bill, sign; broadcast, cablecast, newscast, telecast; advertising, billing, blurb, commercial, message, pitch, plugola, spot, word; communication, dispatch, report; annunciation, declaration, edict, proclamation, promulgation, pronouncement; ballyhoo, boost, buildup, campaign, plug, promo, promotion, propaganda, publicity

annoy *vb* to disturb the peace of mind of (someone) especially by repeated disagreeable acts ⟨The kids unknowingly *annoyed* their neighbor by walking across his lawn.⟩ — see IRRITATE 1

annoyance *n* **1** the act of making unwelcome intrusions upon another ⟨They have an unlisted number in the hopes that it will reduce the constant *annoyance* by telemarketers.⟩
synonyms aggravation, bedevilment, bugging, disturbance, harassment, harrying, pestering, teasing, vexation
related words molestation, offense (*or* offence), persecution, provocation, torment, torture; devilment, deviltry, mischief
2 the feeling of impatience or anger caused by another's repeated disagreeable acts ⟨Carlene made known her *annoyance* at having to pick up her sister's dirty clothes.⟩
synonyms aggravation, bother, exasperation, frustration, grief, irritation, vexation
related words agitation, discomfort, displeasure, distress, disturbance, upset; irritability, irritableness, peeve, perturbation, pet, pique, resentment, snappishness, trouble; anger, angriness, chafe, dander, dudgeon, gall, huff, indignation, irateness, ire, outrage, umbrage
near antonyms delight, pleasure
3 something that is a source of irritation ⟨flashing ads, visual clutter, and other *annoyances* that are the price for free information on the Internet⟩
synonyms aggravation, bother, bugbear, exasperation, frustration, hassle, headache, inconvenience, irk, irritant, nuisance, peeve, pest, rub, ruffle, thorn, trial, vexation
related words discomfort, fleabite, pinprick; affront, insult, offense (*or* offence); upset, worry; affliction, albatross, burden, cross, curse, menace, millstone, plague, sore; anxiety, plight, predicament, tribulation, trouble; pet peeve, problem; annoyer, disturber, mischief, offender; pandora's box
near antonyms delight, joy, pleasure
4 one who is obnoxiously annoying ⟨Younger brothers can be an *annoyance* sometimes.⟩ — see NUISANCE 1

annoyer *n* one who is obnoxiously annoying ⟨a bratty *annoyer* who wouldn't leave me alone⟩ — see NUISANCE 1

annoying *adj* causing annoyance ⟨My brother has the *annoying* habit of eating all the pickles and leaving a jar full of pickle juice in the refrigerator.⟩
synonyms aggravating, bothersome, chafing, disturbing, exasperating, frustrating, galling, irksome, irritating, maddening, nettling, peeving, pestiferous, pestilent, pesty, rankling, riling, vexatious, vexing
related words burdensome, discomforting, displeasing, disquieting, distressing, importune, inconveniencing; angering, enraging, infuriating; brattish, bratty, mischievous, offensive, troublesome, upsetting; distractive, painful, stressful, tiresome, troubling, trying, worrisome; biting, grating, jangling, jarring, spiny, thorny
near antonyms delightful, pleasing

annuity *n* a sum of money allotted for a specific use by official or formal action ⟨His grandmother's will provided him with an *annuity* of $5,000 a year to be used for school expenses.⟩ — see APPROPRIATION 1

annul *vb* **1** to balance with an equal force so as to make ineffective ⟨Unfortunately, his arrogant attitude *annuls* the many generous favors he does for people.⟩ — see OFFSET

2 to put an end to by formal action ⟨plans to *annul* their marriage⟩ — see ABOLISH 1

anoint *vb* to rub an oily or sticky substance over ⟨It's best to *anoint* the wound with antiseptic to prevent infection.⟩ — see SMEAR 1

anomalous *adj* **1** being out of the ordinary ⟨That was an *anomalous* year for the housing industry, so the number of starts is anything but typical.⟩ — see EXCEPTIONAL 1
2 departing from some accepted standard of what is normal ⟨an *anomalous* burst of anger from this usually easygoing person⟩ — see DEVIANT

anomaly *n* **1** something that is different from what is ordinary or expected ⟨Her C grade is an *anomaly*, as she's never made anything except A's and B's before.⟩
synonyms aberration, abnormality, oddity, oddment, rarity
related words curiosity, peculiarity, singularity; accident, phenomenon, quirk, vagary; distortion, mutation, variation; difference, disparity, inconsistence, inconsistency; error, mistake; contradiction, paradox
near antonyms norm, ordinary, usual
2 a person, thing, or event that is far from normal ⟨Snow in July is an *anomaly* in most of the northern hemisphere.⟩ — see FREAK 1

anon *adv* at or within a short time ⟨Be ready—we will begin our Yuletide Boar's Head Feast *anon*.⟩ — see SHORTLY 2

anonymity *n* the quality or state of being mostly or completely unknown ⟨Oddly enough we like the *anonymity* of being a part of an enormous crowd.⟩ — see OBSCURITY 2

anonymous *adj* **1** known but not named ⟨I heard the news from a person who will remain *anonymous*.⟩ — see CERTAIN 1
2 not named or identified by a name ⟨a beautiful manuscript illuminated by an *anonymous* medieval monk⟩ — see NAMELESS 1

another *adj* resulting in an increase in amount or number ⟨Add *another* thing to the shopping list.⟩ — see ADDITIONAL

answer *n* **1** something spoken or written in reaction especially to a question ⟨the standard *answer* of "Fine, thank you" when asked, "How are you?"⟩
synonyms comeback, rejoinder, reply, response, retort, return
related words back talk, banter, repartee; acknowledgment (*or* acknowledgement), comment, communication, correspondence, feedback, non sequitur, observation, reaction, remark; defense, explanation, justification, plea, rebuttal, refutation
near antonyms challenge, charge, cross-examination, grilling, interrogation, interrogatory, quiz; poll, questionnaire, survey
antonyms inquiry, query, question
2 something attained by mental effort and especially by computation ⟨The *answers* to the odd-numbered problems are at the back of the book.⟩
synonyms result, solution
related words conclusion, determination, explanation, finding; clue, key
3 action or behavior that is done in return to other action or behavior ⟨A shrug of the shoulders was her *answer* to the complaint.⟩ — see REACTION

answer *vb* **1** to speak or write in reaction to a question or to another reaction ⟨He didn't *answer* right away when the teacher asked for his thoughts.⟩
synonyms rejoin, reply, respond, retort, return, riposte
related words acknowledge, comment, communicate, correspond, react, remark; counter, defend, deny, explain, field, rebut, refute

near antonyms challenge, cross-examine, examine, grill, interrogate, pump, quiz; poll, query, survey
antonyms ask, inquire, question
2 to be in agreement on every point ⟨Sorry, I haven't seen anyone *answering* to that description.⟩ — see CHECK 1
3 to do what is required by the terms of ⟨I don't have a ladle as such, but will this spoon *answer* the purpose?⟩ — see FULFILL 1
4 to find an answer for through reasoning ⟨Try to *answer* this riddle.⟩ — see SOLVE
answerable *adj* **1** being the one who must meet an obligation or suffer the consequences for failing to do so ⟨You are *answerable* for your own conduct at all times.⟩ — see RESPONSIBLE 1
2 capable of having the reason for or cause of determined ⟨They say this equation is not *answerable*.⟩ — see SOLVABLE
antagonism *n* a deep-seated ill will ⟨The *antagonism* between them seems to be waning as they come to understand each other.⟩ — see ENMITY
antagonist *n* **1** one that is hostile toward another ⟨Please name the novel's hero and his *antagonist*.⟩ — see ENEMY
2 one that takes a position opposite another in a competition or conflict ⟨his *antagonist* in the boxing match⟩ — see OPPONENT 1
antagonistic *adj* marked by opposition or ill will ⟨countries that have been *antagonistic* towards each other for centuries⟩ — see HOSTILE 1
antagonize *vb* to implant bitter feelings in ⟨Everything he said just *antagonized* the other side even more.⟩ — see EMBITTER
antecedent *adj* going before another in time or order ⟨I'd like to follow up on an *antecedent* question from another reporter.⟩ — see PREVIOUS
antecedent *n* **1** someone or something responsible for a result ⟨What are the *antecedents* of the American Revolutionary War?⟩ — see CAUSE 1
2 something belonging to an earlier time from which something else was later developed ⟨The typewriter is the *antecedent* of the computer keyboard.⟩ — see ANCESTOR 2
antedate *vb* to go or come before in time ⟨Dinosaurs *antedate* cavemen by millions of years.⟩ — see PRECEDE
antediluvian *adj* dating or surviving from the distant past ⟨Archaeologists found evidence in the Middle East of an *antediluvian* people previously unknown to history.⟩ — see ANCIENT 1
antediluvian *n* a person with old-fashioned ideas ⟨an *antediluvian* who still insists on paper bills instead of electronic⟩ — see FOGY
anterior *adj* **1** being at or in the forward part or surface of something ⟨The *anterior* chamber of the eye is bounded in front by the cornea.⟩ — see FRONT
2 going before another in time or order ⟨fossils from an *anterior* geologic age⟩ — see PREVIOUS
anthem *n* a religious song ⟨fervently sang an *anthem* of praise to the Lord⟩ — see HYMN 1
anthology *n* a collection of writings ⟨an *anthology* of American short stories⟩
synonyms album, compilation, miscellany
related words almanac, digest, garland, symposium; casebook, sourcebook; archives, library, miscellanea
antic *adj* **1** causing or intended to cause laughter ⟨*antic* shenanigans that made me nearly fall over with laughter⟩ — see FUNNY 1
2 given to good-natured joking or teasing ⟨an *antic* group of kids at summer camp⟩ — see PLAYFUL
antic *n* a playful or mischievous act intended as a joke

⟨We'll have no more of your *antics*, so just settle down.⟩ — see PRANK
anticipate *vb* **1** to believe in the future occurrence of (something) ⟨I *anticipate* that we'll be seeing you for New Year's.⟩ — see EXPECT
2 to realize or know about beforehand ⟨I *anticipated* this unhelpful response.⟩ — see FORESEE
anticipated *adj* being in accordance with the prescribed, normal, or logical course of events ⟨The *anticipated* date of delivery is July 14th.⟩ — see DUE 2
anticipatory *adj* having or showing signs of eagerly awaiting something ⟨The boy couldn't control his *anticipatory* excitement as he boarded the flight to Orlando.⟩ — see EXPECTANT 1
antipathetic *adj* **1** having a natural dislike for something ⟨a series of adventure books that turned boys who had been *antipathetic* to reading into avid readers⟩
synonyms allergic, averse
related words afraid, disinclined, loath (*also* loth *or* loathe), reluctant, unwilling; antagonistic, hostile, intolerant, negative, opposed, opposing, resistant, resisting, uncongenial, unfriendly, unsympathetic; disgusted, nauseated, repelled, repulsed, revolted, shocked, squeamish, turned off
phrases down on
near antonyms friendly, sympathetic, tolerant, understanding; admiring, appreciative, charmed, delighted, fond, pleased, tickled
2 marked by opposition or ill will ⟨The mayor has always had an openly *antipathetic* relationship with the local press.⟩ — see HOSTILE 1
antipathy *n* **1** a deep-seated ill will ⟨I feel no *antipathy* towards any of my opponents in the tournament.⟩ — see ENMITY
2 something or someone that is hated ⟨Cruelty to animals is one of my most deeply felt *antipathies*.⟩ — see HATE 2
antipodal *adj* being as different as possible ⟨Love is *antipodal* to hate.⟩ — see OPPOSITE
antipode *n* something that is as different as possible from something else ⟨Though twins, the two sisters are *antipodes* in personality.⟩ — see OPPOSITE
antipodean *adj* being as different as possible ⟨Since freedom and equality are often *antipodean* goals, a democratic society must find ways of striking a balance between the two.⟩ — see OPPOSITE
antiquated *adj* having passed its time of use or usefulness ⟨saw an *antiquated* hand-cranked rope-making machine at the textiles museum⟩ — see OBSOLETE
antique *adj* **1** dating or surviving from the distant past ⟨studied shards from *antique* pots made by the Pueblos of the Southwest⟩ — see ANCIENT 1
2 pleasantly reminiscent of an earlier time ⟨loved to collect *antique* sugar tongs⟩ — see OLD-FASHIONED 1
antique *n* something belonging to or surviving from an earlier period ⟨Their house is filled with rare *antiques*, including a collection of 19th-century dolls.⟩
synonyms relic
related words artifact, fossil; antiquities, ruins; hangover, remains, remnant, trace, vestige
antisocial *adj* having or showing a lack of friendliness or interest in others ⟨She's not *antisocial*, just extremely shy.⟩ — see COOL 1
antithesis *n* something that is as different as possible from something else ⟨True love for another is the *antithesis* of the desire to control that person's life.⟩ — see OPPOSITE
antithetical *adj* being as different as possible ⟨spiritual concerns and ideals that are *antithetical* to the materialism embraced by modern society⟩ — see OPPOSITE

anxiety *n* **1** an uneasy state of mind usually over the possibility of an anticipated misfortune or trouble 〈Dorothy's *anxiety* about her brother's operation kept her awake all night.〉
synonyms agitation, anxiousness, apprehension, apprehensiveness, care, concern, disquiet, fear, nervousness, solicitude, sweat, uneasiness, worry
related words strain, stress, tension; alarm (*also* alarum), anguish, consternation, desperateness, desperation, discomfort, discomposure, dismay, distraction, distress, disturbance, edginess, hand-wringing, jitters, jumpiness, panic, tremor; angst, fearfulness, torment, upset, vexation; cold feet, doubt, dread, foreboding, incertitude, misgiving, presentiment, suspense, uncertainty; compunction, qualm, scruple
near antonyms calm, calmness, content, contentment, ease, easiness, peace, peacefulness, placidity, placidness, quiet, quietude, sereneness, serenity, tranquillity (*or* tranquility); comfort, consolation, relief, solace
antonyms unconcern
2 the emotion experienced in the presence or threat of danger 〈The newly discovered virus is creating considerable *anxiety* in the public at large.〉 — see FEAR 1

anxious *adj* **1** feeling or showing uncomfortable feelings of uncertainty 〈was *anxious* about the play tryouts scheduled for the following day〉 — see NERVOUS 1
2 marked by or causing agitation or uncomfortable feelings 〈The whole crowd seemed to make an *anxious* gasp as the home team almost fumbled the ball.〉 — see NERVOUS 2
3 showing urgent desire or interest 〈I'm *anxious* for my birthday party.〉 — see EAGER

anxiousness *n* an uneasy state of mind usually over the possibility of an anticipated misfortune or trouble 〈Don't be overcome with *anxiousness* about things that may never happen.〉 — see ANXIETY 1

any *adj* being one of a group 〈*Any* person who comes in the store today is eligible for the discount.〉 — see EACH

anyhow *adv* **1** in spite of everything 〈Even though it's raining, I'm going to the golf course *anyhow*.〉 — see REGARDLESS
2 without definite aim, direction, rule, or method 〈clothes that were hurriedly stuffed *anyhow* into the suitcase〉 — see HIT OR MISS
3 whatever else is done or is the case 〈Your mother called and said you don't need to stop by, but I think you should *anyhow*.〉 — see ALWAYS 2

anymore *adv* at the present time 〈They don't sell that kind of sandwich *anymore*.〉 — see NOW 1

anyway *adv* **1** in spite of everything 〈I know I really can't afford it, but I'm buying that new car *anyway*.〉 — see REGARDLESS
2 without definite aim, direction, rule, or method 〈Do it *anyway* you feel like!〉 — see HIT OR MISS
3 whatever else is done or is the case 〈Pack an extra sweater *anyway*, as you never know when you might end up needing it.〉 — see ALWAYS 2

anywise *adv* **1** in any way or respect 〈nor is it *anywise* important what you wear to the party〉 — see AT ALL
2 without definite aim, direction, rule, or method 〈He just stuffed his newly cleaned clothes *anywise* back into the drawers.〉 — see HIT OR MISS

A1 *adj* of the very best kind 〈An *A1* mom deserves only the very best Mother's Day card.〉 — see EXCELLENT

apace *adv* with great speed 〈The end of another year is hastening *apace*.〉 — see FAST 1

apart *adv* into parts or pieces 〈The fancy new adjustable rake came *apart* the first time I tried to use it.〉
synonyms asunder, piecemeal

phrases to pieces
antonyms together

apartment *n* **1** a room or set of rooms in a private house or a block used as a separate dwelling place 〈a spacious six-room *apartment* that occupies the entire upper floor of a two-family house〉
synonyms digs, lodgings, suite, tenement
related words condo, condominium, duplex, duplex apartment, efficiency, efficiency apartment, floor-through, garden apartment, penthouse, railroad flat, salon, studio, studio apartment, triplex, walk-up; gallery, wing; apartment building, apartment house, tenement house
2 an area within a building that has been set apart from surrounding space by a wall 〈The museum sets aside this large central *apartment* to display special exhibitions.〉 — see ROOM 2

apathetic *adj* **1** having or showing a lack of interest or concern 〈People of conscience cannot be *apathetic* about the great suffering in this world.〉 — see INDIFFERENT 1
2 not feeling or showing emotion 〈The prisoner gave nothing more than an *apathetic* gaze to his interrogators.〉 — see IMPASSIVE 1

apathy *n* **1** a lack of emotion or emotional expressiveness 〈People have shown a surprising *apathy* toward these problems.〉
synonyms impassivity, insensibility, numbness, phlegm
related words bloodlessness, callosity, callousness, coolness, halfheartedness, hard-heartedness, hardness, heartlessness, imperturbability, insensitivity, obduracy; blankness, deadness, emptiness, vacancy; aloofness, detachment, indifference, unconcern; stiffness, woodenness
near antonyms compassion, empathy, pity, sympathy; receptiveness, receptivity, responsiveness, sensitivity; solicitude, understanding, warmth; hand-wringing, histrionics, hysteria, hysterics, melodrama; vehemence
antonyms emotion, feeling, sensibility
2 lack of interest or concern 〈Her poor grades are proof enough of her *apathy* concerning all academic matters.〉 — see INDIFFERENCE

ape *vb* to use (someone or something) as the model for one's speech, mannerisms, or behavior 〈The younger boys thought it was funny to *ape* their older brothers.〉 — see IMITATE 1

aper *n* a person who adopts the appearance or behavior of another especially in an obvious way 〈They're just no-talent *apers* of whatever pop star has the current number one record.〉 — see COPYCAT

aperture *n* a place in a surface allowing passage into or through a thing 〈You can adjust the *aperture* on this camera's lens by pushing this button.〉 — see HOLE 1

apex *n* **1** the highest part or point 〈She reached the *apex* of fame, only to find it wasn't what she expected.〉 — see HEIGHT 1
2 the last and usually sharp or tapering part of something long and narrow 〈the *apex* of the spear〉 — see POINT 2

aphorism *n* an often stated observation regarding something from common experience 〈What does the *aphorism* "Hindsight is 20/20" mean?〉 — see SAYING

apiece *adv* for each one 〈When you figure that they usually sell for six dollars *apiece*, you're getting quite a bargain.〉
synonyms all, each, per, per capita
related words apart, discretely, independently, individually, respectively, separately, singly
phrases a pop, a shot, a throw
near antonyms aggregately, altogether, collectively, together

apish *adj* using or marked by the use of something else as a basis or model ⟨Whenever I smiled, the baby would respond with an *apish* grin.⟩ — see IMITATIVE 1

aplomb *n* 1 evenness of emotions or temper ⟨You've handled a difficult situation with perfect *aplomb*.⟩ — see EQUANIMITY
2 great faith in oneself or one's abilities ⟨carried herself with the dignity and *aplomb* of a born leader⟩ — see CONFIDENCE 1

apologetic *adj* feeling sorrow for a wrong that one has done ⟨was profusely *apologetic* after accidentally breaking a treasured plate⟩ — see CONTRITE

apoplectic *adj* feeling or showing anger ⟨The coach was *apoplectic* when the ref called a foul.⟩ — see ANGRY

apostate *n* 1 a person who abandons a cause or organization usually without right ⟨An *apostate* from communism, he later became one of its harshest critics.⟩ — see RENEGADE
2 one who betrays a trust or an allegiance ⟨He became an *apostate* to liberalism after he had gotten wealthy.⟩ — see TRAITOR

apostle *n* a person who actively supports or favors a cause ⟨a fervent *apostle* of universal health care⟩ — see EXPONENT 1

apothecary *n* 1 a person who prepares drugs according to a doctor's prescription ⟨In olden days the *apothecary* had few drugs that actually cured anything, most substances being little more than pain relievers.⟩ — see DRUGGIST
2 a retail store where medicines and miscellaneous articles are sold ⟨The historic village boasts an old-fashioned *apothecary* that's been there for almost a century and a half.⟩ — see DRUGSTORE

appall *also* **appal** *vb* to cause an unpleasant surprise for ⟨Conditions inside the house overrun with cats simply *appalled* animal control officers.⟩ — see SHOCK 1

appalling *adj* 1 causing intense displeasure, disgust, or resentment ⟨Opening your mouth to show me your half-chewed food is absolutely *appalling*.⟩ — see OFFENSIVE 1
2 extremely disturbing or repellent ⟨We drove by an *appalling* accident on the highway.⟩ — see HORRIBLE 1

apparatus *n* items needed for the performance of a task or activity ⟨The hospital's operating rooms boast the very latest medical *apparatus*.⟩ — see EQUIPMENT

apparel *n* covering for the human body ⟨a sale on summer *apparel* for women⟩ — see CLOTHING

apparel *vb* to outfit with clothes and especially fine or special clothes ⟨a designer who regularly *apparels* several of the presenters at the Oscar ceremonies⟩ — see CLOTHE 1

apparent *adj* 1 appearing to be true on the basis of evidence that may or may not be confirmed ⟨At the start of the investigation, the *apparent* cause of the accident was mechanical failure.⟩
synonyms assumed, evident, ostensible, presumed, reputed, seeming, supposed
related words demonstrable, external, outward, superficial, visible; conceivable, plausible, possible, supposable; likely, probable; clear, distinct, manifest, obvious, plain; deceptive, delusive, delusory, illusive, illusory, imaginary; misleading, specious; fake, faked, feigned, phony (*also* phoney), pretended, pseudo, put-on; alleged, claimed, professed, purported, so-called
near antonyms inapparent; implausible, impossible, improbable, inconceivable, unlikely; actual, authenticated, confirmed, corroborated, established, genuine, real, substantiated, sure, valid, validated, verified
2 capable of being seen ⟨As the fog lifts, the town in the valley below us will become more *apparent*.⟩ — see VISIBLE 1

3 not subject to misinterpretation or more than one interpretation ⟨It's *apparent* from the smile on her face that she got a part in the play.⟩ — see CLEAR 2

apparently *adv* to all outward appearances ⟨*Apparently*, her husband didn't know the cake was for the raffle, since he helped himself to a piece.⟩
synonyms evidently, ostensibly, presumably, seemingly, supposedly
related words externally, outwardly, visibly; believably, credibly; likely, presumedly, probably; conceivably, maybe, mayhap, perchance, perhaps, possibly, professedly, supposably; allegedly, purportedly, reportedly, reputedly; distinctly, manifestly, obviously, plainly, self-evidently; assuredly, surely
phrases on the surface
near antonyms implausibly, impossibly, improbably, incredibly

apparition *n* the soul of a dead person thought of especially as appearing to living people ⟨an eccentric who claimed to have photographed an *apparition* in her very own house⟩ — see GHOST 1

appeal *n* 1 an earnest request ⟨Red Cross officials made an *appeal* to the public to donate desperately needed blood.⟩ — see PLEA 1
2 the power of irresistible attraction ⟨That new actress has a certain indescribable *appeal*.⟩ — see CHARM 2

appeal (to) *vb* to make a request to (someone) in an earnest or urgent manner ⟨When supplies at the food bank ran desperately low, officials *appealed to* the public for some much-needed replacements.⟩ — see BEG

appealing *adj* having an often mysterious or magical power to attract ⟨The idea of living on Mars is *appealing* to space enthusiasts.⟩ — see FASCINATING 1

appear *vb* 1 to come into view ⟨A police car *appeared* just as I ran a red light.⟩
synonyms come out, materialize, show, show up, turn up, unfold
related words reappear, resurface; bulk, loom; arrive, come; dawn, debut; arise, blossom, bob (up), break, break out, crop (up), emerge, erupt, issue, outcrop, rise, shoot (up), spring (up), surface; happen, occur; reappear, rematerialize
near antonyms depart, leave, retire, withdraw
antonyms clear, disappear, dissolve, evanesce, evaporate, fade, go (away), melt (away), vanish
2 to give the impression of being ⟨It *appears* that he doesn't hear you.⟩ — see SEEM
3 to come into existence ⟨The benefits of the exercise program should *appear* almost immediately.⟩ — see BEGIN 2
4 to get to a destination ⟨a friend who daily manages to *appear* at our door just as dinner is being served⟩ — see COME 2

appearance *n* 1 the outward form of someone or something especially as indicative of a quality ⟨the dignified *appearance* of this world leader⟩ ⟨the college's manicured lawns and well-groomed *appearance* in general⟩
synonyms aspect, dress, figure, garb, look, mien, outside, presence
related words air, bearing, behavior, comportment, demeanor, deportment, manner, poise, pose; carriage, posture, stance; cast, shape, turn; color, coloring, complexion; countenance, face, features, physiognomy, visage
phrases cut of one's jib
2 outward and often deceptive indication ⟨Can't you at least give the *appearance* of listening to what I say?⟩
synonyms face, guise, name, outward, seeming, semblance, show
related words air, effect, impression; hint, implication,

resemblance, suggestion; affectation, demonstration, display, fiction, image, imitation, imposture, likeness, make-believe (*also* make-belief), pose, pretense (*or* pretence), representation, simulation; cloak, disguise, exterior, facade (*also* façade), front, gloss, mask, masquerade, shape, shell, surface, veneer
phrases first blush
3 the act of coming upon a scene ⟨His *appearance* at the party caused considerable speculation.⟩ — see ARRIVAL

appease *vb* to lessen the anger or agitation of ⟨Playing a game often *appeases* an upset toddler.⟩ — see PACIFY 1

appeasing *adj* tending to lessen or avoid conflict or hostility ⟨We had been feuding with the people next door, so inviting them to the party was intended as an *appeasing* gesture.⟩ — see PACIFIC 1

appellation *n* a word or combination of words by which a person or thing is regularly known ⟨a twisting road that deserved the *appellation* "Sidewinder Lane"⟩ — see NAME 1

append *vb* to join (something) to a mass, quantity, or number so as to bring about an overall increase ⟨*Append* the prefix "un-" to each of these words.⟩ — see ADD 1

appendage *n* something that is not necessary in itself but adds to the convenience or performance of the main piece of equipment ⟨Pasta makers became the must-have *appendage* for tabletop mixers.⟩ — see ACCESSORY 1

appertain *vb* **1** to be the property of a person or group of persons ⟨the doctrine that the swath of land between the Atlantic and the Pacific naturally *appertained* to the United States⟩ — see BELONG 2
2 to have a relation or connection ⟨List some of the things *appertaining* to public health.⟩ — see APPLY 1

appetite *n* **1** a need or desire for food ⟨Don't eat before dinner, as it will spoil your *appetite*.⟩ — see HUNGER 1
2 a strong wish for something ⟨an *appetite* for adventure⟩ — see DESIRE 1
3 positive regard for something ⟨The couple has expensive *appetites*.⟩ — see LIKING
4 urgent desire or interest ⟨an athlete with an *appetite* for in-your-face competition⟩ — see EAGERNESS

appetizing *adj* very pleasing to the sense of taste ⟨That dish looks very *appetizing*.⟩ — see DELICIOUS 1

applaud *vb* to declare enthusiastic approval of ⟨I *applaud* your decision to take that advanced course⟩ — see ACCLAIM

applaudable *adj* deserving of high regard or great approval ⟨the *applaudable* goal of working one's way through college⟩ — see ADMIRABLE

applauding *adj* expressing approval ⟨a student encouraged by his teacher's *applauding* comments⟩ — see FAVORABLE 1

applause *n* **1** enthusiastic and usually public expression of approval ⟨A design for a statue of the college's founder has received nothing but *applause* from students and faculty alike.⟩
synonyms acclamation, cheer, cheering, ovation, plaudit(s), rave(s)
related words clapping; bravo, hail, hurrah (*also* hooray *or* hoorah), hosanna; acclaim, accolade, citation, commendation, compliment, encomium, eulogy, homage, paean, panegyric, salutation, tribute; praise
near antonyms boo, hiss, hoot, jeer, raspberry, smirk, sneer, snicker, snigger, snort, whistle; gibe (*or* jibe), putdown, taunt
antonyms booing, hissing
2 public acknowledgment or admiration for an achievement ⟨a heroic effort by the fire department that deserves the *applause* of everyone in the city⟩ — see GLORY 1

appliance *n* **1** an interesting and often novel device with a practical use ⟨Since the invention of the cork, all manner of *appliances* have been invented for the extraction of these sometimes troublesome stoppers.⟩ — see GADGET
2 something that is not necessary in itself but adds to the convenience or performance of the main piece of equipment ⟨an *appliance* that allows the machine to be used as a sander⟩ — see ACCESSORY 1

applicability *n* the fact or state of being pertinent ⟨We have to question the *applicability* of much of the information he has included in his report.⟩ — see PERTINENCE

applicable *adj* **1** capable of being put to use or account ⟨Is that information *applicable* in this case?⟩ — see PRACTICAL 1
2 having to do with the matter at hand ⟨That comment isn't *applicable* to our discussion.⟩ — see PERTINENT
3 meeting the requirements of a purpose or situation ⟨a knack for selecting the most *applicable* word⟩ — see FIT 1

applicant *n* one who seeks an office, honor, position, or award ⟨We have numerous *applicants* for the job.⟩ — see CANDIDATE

application *n* the act or practice of employing something for a particular purpose ⟨Protecting the floor from being scraped by chairs' legs is not the intended *application* of tennis balls, but it's a handy one.⟩ — see USE 1

apply *vb* **1** to have a relation or connection ⟨Does your rule about calling home *apply* to me as well?⟩
synonyms appertain, bear, pertain, refer, relate
related words affect, concern, interest, involve, touch; associate, connect, couple, interrelate, link, tie in; deal (with); treat
phrases have to do with
2 to occupy (oneself) diligently or with close attention ⟨Sam *applied* himself to writing thank-you letters to everyone who'd helped sponsor him for the charity walk.⟩
synonyms address, bend, buckle, devote, give
related words readdress, reapply; knuckle down, set (to), settle (down); busy, commit, concern, engage, involve; exert, exhaust, put out, spend, strain, stress, tax, trouble, wear out; carry on, pitch in, plunge (in); grind, hump, hustle, peg (away), plod, plow, plug (away), work
phrases get cracking, get one's act together, get with it, turn one's hand (*or* turn a hand)
near antonyms dally, dawdle, dillydally, fiddle (around), idle, monkey (around), play, potter (around), putter (around), trifle
3 to put a layer of on a surface ⟨*Apply* the ointment liberally.⟩ — see SPREAD 2
4 to put into action or service ⟨*Apply* the laws of motion to this physics problem.⟩ — see USE 1
5 to bring to bear especially forcefully or effectively ⟨*Apply* pressure to the area to stop the bleeding.⟩ — see EXERT
6 to carry out effectively ⟨a police officer *applying* the law⟩ — see ENFORCE

appoint *vb* **1** to decide upon (the time or date for an event) usually from a position of authority ⟨At the *appointed* hour we were in our places.⟩
synonyms designate, fix, name, set
related words adopt, assign, choose, determine, establish, opt (for), pick, pin (down), prefer, select, settle, single (out), specify; arrange, coordinate, orchestrate; advertise, announce, declare, publish
2 to pick (someone) by one's authority for a specific position or duty ⟨He was *appointed* to the council on national security.⟩
synonyms assign, attach, commission, constitute, designate, detail, name, place

related words authorize, delegate, deputize; anoint, consecrate, create, inaugurate, induct, install, instate, institute, invest, make, ordain; crown, enthrone, throne; choose, destine, draft, elect, handpick, select, single (out), vote (in)

near antonyms blackball, depose, dethrone, displace, eject, evict, oust, overthrow, remove, throw out, uncrown, unmake, unseat

antonyms discharge, dismiss, expel, fire

appointment *n* **1** the state or fact of being chosen for a position or duty ⟨His *appointment* to the Board of Health came as a surprise.⟩

synonyms assignment, commission, designation

related words billet, gig, job, office, place, position, situation, spot, station; authorization, delegation, deputation, placement, ranking; anointing, anointment, induction, installation, installment (*also* instalment), instating, investiture, investment, ordination; choice, choosing, destination, election, nomination, picking, selection, singling (out)

near antonyms blackball, rejection; deposition, dethronement, ejection, eviction, ouster, overthrow, removal

antonyms discharge, dismissal, dismission, expulsion, firing

2 an agreement to be present at a specified time and place ⟨I have a dental *appointment* for two o'clock tomorrow afternoon.⟩ — see ENGAGEMENT 2

3 an assignment at which one regularly works for pay ⟨Meg loved her latest *appointment* as an aide at the governor's office.⟩ — see JOB 1

4 appointments *pl* the movable articles (such as tables and chairs) in a room ⟨The yacht's staterooms have the most luxurious *appointments* imaginable.⟩ — see FURNITURE

apportion *vb* **1** to give as a share or portion ⟨*apportioned* the profits according to years of service with the company⟩ — see ALLOT

2 to give out (something) to appropriate individuals ⟨*apportioned* the grant money to the winners of the competition⟩ — see ADMINISTER 1

apportionment *n* the act or process of giving out something to each member of a group ⟨The *apportionment* of the estate will happen this Friday.⟩ — see DISTRIBUTION 1

apposite *adj* having to do with the matter at hand ⟨Ken enriched his essay on patriotism with some very *apposite* quotations from famous people on the subject.⟩ — see PERTINENT

appraisal *n* **1** an opinion on the nature, character, or quality of something ⟨She gave us a positive *appraisal* of his artistic talents.⟩ — see ESTIMATION 1

2 the act of placing a value on the nature, character, or quality of something ⟨The *appraisal* of the house's value took place yesterday.⟩ — see ESTIMATE 1

appraise *vb* to make an approximate or tentative judgment regarding ⟨Let's take a moment to *appraise* the current situation.⟩ — see ESTIMATE 1

appraisement *n* **1** an opinion on the nature, character, or quality of something ⟨offered us her *appraisement* of the band's latest album⟩ — see ESTIMATION 1

2 the act of placing a value on the nature, character, or quality of something ⟨He was too harsh in his *appraisement* of us.⟩ — see ESTIMATE 1

appreciable *adj* able to be perceived by a sense or by the mind ⟨There doesn't seem to be any *appreciable* difference between this piece and that one.⟩ — see PERCEPTIBLE

appreciate *vb* **1** to become greater in extent, volume, amount, or number ⟨The value of that antique should *appreciate* over time.⟩ — see INCREASE 2

2 to hold dear ⟨I *appreciate* my parents more than I can express.⟩ — see LOVE 1

3 to have a clear idea of ⟨I hope you *appreciate* just how much that collector's comic book costs.⟩ — see COMPREHEND 1

4 to think very highly or favorably of ⟨Many great artists and musicians have not been *appreciated* in their own lifetimes.⟩ — see ADMIRE

appreciation *n* **1** a feeling of great approval and liking ⟨my *appreciation* of her great contributions to sports⟩ — see ADMIRATION 1

2 acknowledgment of having received something good from another ⟨If you can do that, you'll have our heartfelt *appreciation*.⟩ — see THANKS

3 the knowledge gained from the process of coming to know or understand something ⟨a course intended to give students an *appreciation* of abstract art⟩ — see COMPREHENSION

appreciative *adj* **1** expressing approval ⟨His latest novel has received a number of *appreciative* reviews.⟩ — see FAVORABLE 1

2 feeling or expressing gratitude ⟨very *appreciative* after we helped him change his flat tire⟩ — see GRATEFUL 1

appreciativeness *n* acknowledgment of having received something good from another ⟨a note expressing their *appreciativeness* of all that we had done for them⟩ — see THANKS

apprehend *vb* **1** to have a clear idea of ⟨Do you *apprehend* the importance of this discovery?⟩ — see COMPREHEND 1

2 to take or keep under one's control by authority of law ⟨the agency charged with *apprehending* criminals who have violated federal law⟩ — see ARREST 1

apprehended *adj* taken and held prisoner ⟨an *apprehended* criminal⟩ — see CAPTIVE

apprehension *n* **1** suspicion or fear of future harm or misfortune ⟨The hikers entered the dark cave with a great deal of *apprehension*.⟩

synonyms alarm (*also* alarum), apprehensiveness, dread, foreboding, misgiving

related words agitation, anxiety, anxiousness, concern, disquiet, distress, disturbance, fearfulness, uneasiness; scruple, worry; doubt, incertitude, mistrust, suspiciousness, uncertainty, wariness; defeatism, pessimism; foreknowledge, premonition, presage, presentiment

near antonyms excitement, hope, hopefulness; confidence, optimism, sanguinity

2 the act of taking into one's control by authority of law ⟨*Apprehension* of the burglar set the neighborhood at ease.⟩ — see ARREST 1

3 an uneasy state of mind usually over the possibility of an anticipated misfortune or trouble ⟨We felt a great deal of *apprehension* about the trip and about arriving safely.⟩ — see ANXIETY 1

4 the knowledge gained from the process of coming to know or understand something ⟨a good *apprehension* of how computer systems work⟩ — see COMPREHENSION

apprehensiveness *n* **1** an uneasy state of mind usually over the possibility of an anticipated misfortune or trouble ⟨Her *apprehensiveness* about starting college is keeping her awake at night.⟩ — see ANXIETY 1

2 suspicion or fear of future harm or misfortune ⟨My *apprehensiveness* about raw fish disagreeing with me is keeping me from even trying sushi.⟩ — see APPREHENSION 1

apprentice *n* **1** a person who helps a more skilled person ⟨Tom decided to be an *apprentice* to an electrician after he graduated.⟩ — see HELPER

2 a person who is just starting out in a field of activity ⟨Aware that she's only an *apprentice* in the medical field,

she readily defers to her more experienced colleagues.⟩
— see BEGINNER

apprise *vb* to give information to ⟨Let me *apprise* you of the current situation.⟩ — see ENLIGHTEN 1

approach *n* **1** an established course for traveling from one place to another ⟨We will take the standard landing *approach* from the south.⟩ — see PASSAGE 1
2 the means or procedure for doing something ⟨That's a different *approach* to knitting, but it seems to work.⟩ — see METHOD

approach *vb* **1** to come near or nearer ⟨The parade's *approaching*! I can hear the band playing!⟩
synonyms close, draw on, near, nigh
related words arrive, attain, come, gain, hit, land, make, reach, show up, turn up, waltz (up); creep up, sneak up; adjoin, border, touch, verge
near antonyms clear out, depart, exit, go, leave, light out, quit, remove, run away, shove (off), take off, walk out
antonyms back (up *or* away), recede, retire, retreat, withdraw
2 to move closer to ⟨*Approach* the bull with caution.⟩ — see COME 1
3 to come near or nearer to in character or quality ⟨His store-bought dessert doesn't even *approach* your homemade version of it.⟩ — see APPROXIMATE

approaching *adj* being soon to appear or take place ⟨The *approaching* holiday has everyone in a state of excitement.⟩ — see FORTHCOMING 1

approbation *n* an acceptance of something as satisfactory ⟨That plan has the *approbation* of the school board.⟩ — see APPROVAL

appropriate *adj* meeting the requirements of a purpose or situation ⟨I don't think jeans and a T-shirt are *appropriate* attire for a wedding.⟩ — see FIT 1

appropriate *vb* **1** to take or make use of under a guise of authority but without actual right ⟨Archaeologists wrongfully *appropriated* artifacts excavated at ancient sites for their museums.⟩
synonyms arrogate, commandeer, convert, expropriate, pirate, preempt, press, seize, take over, usurp
related words annex, attach, claim, confiscate, impound, repossess, sequester; assume, collar, grab, grasp, snatch, steal, wrench, wrest; despoil, loot, pillage; encroach, infringe, invade, occupy, preoccupy, trespass; embezzle, misapply, misappropriate, misuse
2 to take (something) without right and with an intent to keep ⟨You can't just *appropriate* somebody's term paper and put your name on it!⟩ — see STEAL 1

appropriately *adv* in a manner suitable for the occasion or purpose ⟨Make sure you greet your elders *appropriately*.⟩ — see PROPERLY

appropriateness *n* the quality or state of being especially suitable or fitting ⟨Visitors remarked on the *appropriateness* of window boxes on the cottage, noting they gave it a quaint, cheerful look.⟩
synonyms aptness, felicitousness, felicity, fitness, fittingness, propriety, rightness, seemliness, suitability, suitableness
related words agreeableness, compatibility, congruity, harmoniousness; applicability, bearing, connection, justifiability, materiality, pertinence, relevance, relevancy, validity; acceptability, adequacy, adequateness, convenience, satisfactoriness, serviceableness, usefulness
near antonyms disagreeableness, incompatibility, incongruence, incongruity, incongruousness, inexpedience, inexpediency, inharmoniousness, unbecomingness; inapplicability, irrelevance, irrelevancy; meaninglessness, pointlessness
antonyms impropriety, inappositeness, inappropriate-ness, inaptness, infelicity, unfitness, unsuitability, wrongness

appropriation *n* **1** a sum of money allotted for a specific use by official or formal action ⟨The National Park Service received an increased *appropriation* for wildlife management.⟩
synonyms allocation, allotment, annuity, grant, subsidy
related words aid, assistance, block grant, grant-in-aid, set-aside; foreign aid, relief, state aid; advance, allowance, benefit, bequest, endowment, fund, legacy, stipend, trust, trust fund
2 the unlawful taking or withholding of something from the rightful owner under a guise of authority ⟨the insurgents' *appropriation* of the building for their headquarters⟩
synonyms seizure
related words annexation, assumption, attachment, confiscation, grab, repossession, sequestration; embezzlement, misapplication, misappropriation, misuse, theft; despoilment, looting, pillaging; encroachment, infringement, piracy; invasion, occupation, preoccupancy, trespass; dispossession, ejection, stripping

approval *n* an acceptance of something as satisfactory ⟨Does this poster I made for the recital meet with your *approval*?⟩
synonyms approbation, blessing, favor, imprimatur, OK (*or* okay)
related words backing, cachet, endorsement (*also* indorsement), finalization, formalization, nod, ratification, sanction, support, thumbs-up, vote; benediction, goodwill; acceptation, agreement, assent, concurrence, consent; countenance, liking, satisfaction
phrases clean bill of health, pat on the back
near antonyms refusal, rejection, repudiation; dislike, dissatisfaction; censure, condemnation, criticism, denunciation, deprecation, depreciation, disparagement, opprobrium, reprehension, reproach, reprobation
antonyms disapprobation, disapproval, disfavor

approve *vb* to give official acceptance of as satisfactory ⟨As soon as the pond project was *approved*, the bulldozers were at the site.⟩
synonyms accredit, authorize, clear, confirm, finalize, formalize, OK (*or* okay), ratify, sanction, warrant
related words accept, acknowledge, affirm; certify, endorse (*also* indorse), validate; bless, canonize, sanctify; initial, rubber-stamp, sign, sign off (on); allow, enable, legalize, license (*also* licence), pass, permit; reapprove
near antonyms ban, enjoin, forbid, interdict, prohibit, proscribe; disregard, ignore, neglect, overlook; rebuff, rebut, refuse, spurn
antonyms decline, deny, disallow, disapprove, negative, reject, turn down, veto

approve (of) *vb* to have a favorable opinion of ⟨We don't *approve of* people who stand in the "12 items or less" lane with 13 items.⟩
synonyms accept, care (for), countenance, favor, OK (*or* okay), subscribe (to)
related words acclaim, applaud, laud, praise, salute; back (up), concur (in), stand by, support, sustain, uphold; bear, endure, tolerate; assent (to), consent (to); commend, recommend; enjoy, like
phrases go for, hold with, take kindly to
near antonyms blacklist, censure, condemn, criticize, damn, denounce, deprecate, depreciate, disparage, reprehend, reprobate; dislike, mind; detest, hate, loathe; dissent (from), object (to), oppose
antonyms disapprove (of), discountenance, disfavor

approving *adj* expressing approval ⟨The play did not receive a single *approving* notice.⟩ — see FAVORABLE 1

approximate *adj* **1** being such only when compared to something else ⟨The movie's an *approximate* success, if you can overlook the overblown publicity that preceded it.⟩ — see COMPARATIVE

2 not precisely correct ⟨Police could only give us an *approximate* count of the number of people who attended the air show.⟩ — see INEXACT 1

approximate *vb* to come near or nearer to in character or quality ⟨Rob's violin performance last night didn't even *approximate* what he's really capable of when he's not feeling sick.⟩

synonyms approach, compare (with), measure up (to), stack up (against *or* with)

related words add up (to), amount (to), come (to); duplicate, equal, match; mirror, parallel, reflect; border (on), verge (on)

phrases hold a candle to

apropos *adj* having to do with the matter at hand ⟨The actor announced to reporters that he would regard as *apropos* only questions about the movie and would ignore inquiries about his private life.⟩ — see PERTINENT

apropos *prep* having to do with ⟨He makes a number of telling observations *apropos* the current political situation.⟩ — see ABOUT 1

apropos of *prep* having to do with ⟨*Apropos of* our earlier conversation, here's that file I mentioned.⟩ — see ABOUT 1

apt *adj* **1** having a tendency to be or act in a certain way ⟨That dog is *apt* to run off if you don't put him on a leash.⟩ — see PRONE 1

2 meeting the requirements of a purpose or situation ⟨"Gingerbread" is certainly an *apt* description for that house with all the ornate trim.⟩ — see FIT 1

aptitude *n* **1** a habitual attraction to some activity or thing ⟨an elfish toddler with an *aptitude* for mischief⟩ — see INCLINATION 1

2 a special and usually inborn ability ⟨Clara has an *aptitude* for math.⟩ — see TALENT

aptness *n* **1** an established pattern of behavior ⟨an unfortunate *aptness* to interrupt people in mid sentence⟩ — see TENDENCY 1

2 the quality or state of being especially suitable or fitting ⟨I'd question the *aptness* of that goofy sympathy card.⟩ — see APPROPRIATENESS

aquatic *adj* living, lying, or occurring below the surface of the water ⟨a lifelong fascination with sharks and other fearsome *aquatic* creatures⟩ — see UNDERWATER

aqueduct *n* an open man-made passageway for water ⟨marveled at the ancient Roman *aqueducts* that still carry water to distant villages⟩ — see CHANNEL 1

arbiter *n* a person who impartially decides or resolves a dispute or controversy ⟨The dean of student affairs is the proper *arbiter* when a student disputes a grade.⟩ — see JUDGE 1

arbitrary *adj* **1** having or showing a tendency to force one's will on others without any regard to fairness or necessity ⟨an *arbitrary* piano teacher who makes all her students do the same exercises over and over again⟩

synonyms dictatorial, high-handed, imperious, peremptory, willful (*or* wilful)

related words arrogant, commanding, demanding, dominant, domineering, haughty, imperative, lordly, masterful, overbearing, presumptuous; authoritarian, autocratic (*also* autocratical), despotic, totalitarian, tyrannical (*also* tyrannic), tyrannous; capricious, changeable, erratic, inconsistent, mercurial, whimsical; biased, inequitable, partisan, prejudiced, unequal, unfair, unjust, unrealistic, unreasonable; unconscionable, unethical, unprincipled, unscrupulous

near antonyms balanced, disinterested, dispassionate, equal, equitable, evenhanded, fair, impartial, just, nonpartisan, objective; rational, reasonable, understanding; unbiased, unprejudiced; ethical, honorable, irreproachable, law-abiding, moral, principled, unimpeachable

2 lacking a definite plan, purpose, or pattern ⟨The order of the names of the 10 semifinalists is entirely *arbitrary*.⟩ — see RANDOM

3 exercising power or authority without interference by others ⟨a nation with no tradition of democracy, only a long history of *arbitrary* rulers⟩ — see ABSOLUTE 1

arbitrate *vb* to give an opinion about (something at issue or in dispute) ⟨He will *arbitrate* the dispute between the company and the labor union.⟩ — see JUDGE 1

arbitrator *n* a person who impartially decides or resolves a dispute or controversy ⟨The couple finally agreed to let the salesclerk be the final *arbitrator* and tell them which shirt looked best.⟩ — see JUDGE 1

arc *n* something that curves or is curved ⟨The stars seemed to align themselves into one vast glittering *arc*.⟩ — see BEND 1

arc *vb* to turn away from a straight line or course ⟨The ball *arced* toward the batter and nearly hit him.⟩ — see CURVE 1

arch *adj* **1** coming before all others in importance ⟨Since the start of her acting career her parents have steadfastly remained her *arch* supporters.⟩ — see FOREMOST 1

2 tending to or exhibiting reckless playfulness ⟨The *arch* look on the girl's face betrayed her as the one who had tricked the babysitter into believing that the house was haunted.⟩ — see MISCHIEVOUS 1

arch *n* something that curves or is curved ⟨The limestone *arch* is a natural formation that is the product of many years of erosion.⟩ — see BEND 1

arch *vb* **1** to cause to turn away from a straight line ⟨The cat *arched* her back whenever she was stroked.⟩ — see BEND 1

2 to turn away from a straight line or course ⟨The path gradually *arches* off into the woods.⟩ — see CURVE 1

archaic *adj* having passed its time of use or usefulness ⟨The school needs to update its *archaic* computer system.⟩ — see OBSOLETE

archetypal *also* **archetypical** *adj* **1** constituting, serving as, or worthy of being a pattern to be imitated ⟨St. Peter's basilica in Rome is considered by some art historians to be the *archetypal* structure in the baroque style.⟩ — see MODEL

2 having or showing the qualities associated with the members of a particular group or kind ⟨The movie's hero is pretty *archetypal*, lacking in any distinctive qualities that would distinguish him from countless other masked avengers.⟩ — see TYPICAL 1

archetype *n* **1** something belonging to an earlier time from which something else was later developed ⟨The abacus is sometimes cited as the *archetype* of the modern digital calculator.⟩ — see ANCESTOR 2

2 something from which copies are made ⟨*Beowulf* is considered by some scholars to be the *archetype* for medieval British heroic tales.⟩ — see ORIGINAL

archive *n* a place where books, periodicals, and records are kept for use but not for sale ⟨asked that the rare book be brought from the *archive*⟩ ⟨sent the novelist's letters to the *archive* for preservation⟩ — see LIBRARY 1

arctic *adj* **1** having a low or subnormal temperature ⟨the *arctic* air of deep winter⟩ — see COLD 1

2 lacking in friendliness or warmth of feeling ⟨received the usual *arctic* reception from her in-laws at Thanksgiving⟩ — see COLD 2

ardent *adj* **1** having or expressing great depth of feeling ⟨made *ardent* declarations of love⟩ — see FERVENT 1

2 showing urgent desire or interest ⟨an *ardent* science-fiction fan who has read virtually all of his favorite author's many works⟩ — see EAGER
3 having a notably high temperature ⟨Under an *ardent* sun the band of bedouins made their way across the sandy wastes.⟩ — see HOT 1

ardor *n* **1** depth of feeling ⟨candidates for citizenship reciting the oath of allegiance to the United States with all the *ardor* that they could muster⟩
synonyms emotion, enthusiasm, fervency, fervidness, fervor, fire, heat, intensity, passion, vehemence, violence, warmth
related words emotionalism, emotionality, histrionics, mawkishness, melodrama, sappiness, sentimentality; eagerness, earnestness, excitement, keenness, zest; fanaticism, fever, hot-bloodedness, infatuation, mania, obsession, zeal; compassion, responsiveness, sentiment, sympathy; torridity, torridness
near antonyms aloofness, calmness, collectedness, composure, detachedness, reserve, reservedness, reticence, taciturnity; apathy, indifference, stoicism, stoniness, unconcern; stiffness, woodenness; chilliness, coolness, frigidity, frigidness
antonyms impassivity, insensibility, insensibleness, insensitiveness, insensitivity
2 urgent desire or interest ⟨His *ardor* for leaving home cooled as he began to realize how much he'd miss his family.⟩ — see EAGERNESS
3 intense sexual desire ⟨a musical passage composed to convey the tragic lovers' *ardor*⟩ — see LUST 1

arduous *adj* **1** requiring considerable physical or mental effort ⟨Climbing Mount Everest is an *arduous*, exhausting challenge.⟩ — see HARD 2
2 requiring much time, effort, or careful attention ⟨the *arduous* task of doing the research for my term paper⟩ — see DEMANDING 1

arduously *adv* with great effort or determination ⟨Our guides *arduously* made their way through the dense jungle.⟩ — see HARD 1

area *n* **1** a part or portion having no fixed boundaries ⟨I last saw your dog over in that general *area*.⟩ — see REGION 1
2 a region of activity, knowledge, or influence ⟨a top researcher in the *area* of human genetics⟩ — see FIELD 2

arena *n* **1** a large room or building for enclosed public gatherings ⟨We watched the hockey game in the new sports *arena*.⟩ — see HALL 3
2 a region of activity, knowledge, or influence ⟨has a lot of influence in the local business *arena*⟩ — see FIELD 2

argot *n* the special terms or expressions of a particular group or field ⟨They used the *argot* of figure skaters.⟩ — see TERMINOLOGY

argue *vb* **1** to state (something) as a reason in support of or against something under consideration ⟨I *argued* that a bake sale would make a lot less money than a car wash.⟩
synonyms assert, contend, maintain, plead, reason
related words adduce, cite, mention; claim, insist; affirm, aver, avouch, avow; advance, give, offer, propose, submit; advise, counsel, recommend, suggest, urge; convince, persuade; advocate, champion, defend, enforce, espouse, support; explain, justify, rationalize; consider, debate, discuss; confute, counter, disprove, rebut, refute
2 to express different opinions about something often angrily ⟨They started *arguing* about money.⟩
synonyms bicker, brawl, dispute, fall out, fight, hassle, jar, quarrel, quibble, row, scrap, spat, squabble, tiff, wrangle
related words challenge, dare, defy; clash, contend, contest, tangle; cavil, fuss, nitpick; consider, debate, discuss; kick, object, protest

phrases bandy words, butt heads, lock horns, mix it up
near antonyms coexist, get along; accept, agree, assent, concur, consent
3 to cause (someone) to agree with a belief or course of action by using arguments or earnest requests ⟨I *argued* my boss into letting me telecommute for four days a week.⟩ — see PERSUADE
4 to talk about (an issue) usually from various points of view and for the purpose of arriving at a decision or opinion ⟨candidates *arguing* foreign policy in a nationally televised debate⟩ — see DISCUSS
5 to give evidence or testimony to the truth or factualness of ⟨The security video *argues* that it was a taller man who entered the building.⟩ — see CONFIRM 1

arguer *n* a person who takes part in a dispute ⟨He's in demand on the Sunday morning political shows because he's an eager and indefatigable *arguer*.⟩ — see DISPUTANT

argument *n* **1** an often noisy or angry expression of differing opinions ⟨They settled an *argument* that started in class.⟩
synonyms altercation, bicker, brawl, controversy, cross fire, disagreement, dispute, falling-out, fight, hassle, misunderstanding, quarrel, row, scrap, spat, squabble, tiff, wrangle
related words clash, run-in, skirmish, tangle, tussle; feud, vendetta; attack, contention, dissension (*also* dissention); debate, difference, disputation; fuss, objection, protest, protestation; fisticuffs, fracas, fray, free-for-all, melee (*also* mêlée); catfight
2 a statement given to explain a belief or act ⟨He gave a solid *argument* for the redeeming value of the shockingly violent movie.⟩ — see REASON 1
3 an exchange of views for the purpose of exploring a subject or deciding an issue ⟨The president of the Senate has allotted a week for the *argument* of the treaty.⟩ — see DISCUSSION 1
4 an idea or opinion that is put forth in a discussion or debate ⟨It's my *argument* that we have too many problems here on earth to concern ourselves with trips to Mars.⟩ — see CONTENTION 1

argumentative *adj* **1** given to arguing ⟨He's too *argumentative* to be part of a project in which teamwork is critical.⟩
synonyms contentious, disputatious, quarrelsome, scrappy
related words aggressive, bellicose, belligerent, combative, gladiatorial, militant, pugnacious, truculent, warlike; fractious, surly; balky, contrary, ornery, perverse, restive, wayward; disobedient, froward, insubordinate, intractable, recalcitrant, refractory; hardheaded, headstrong, mulish, obdurate, obstinate, pigheaded, resistant, self-willed, stubborn, unbending, uncompromising, uncooperative, unreasonable, unyielding, willful (*or* wilful); acidic, bearish, bilious, cantankerous, captious, choleric, crabby, cranky, cross, disagreeable, dyspeptic, fretful, grouchy, grumpy, ill-humored, ill-natured, ill-tempered, irascible, irritable, peevish, pettish, petulant, querulous, rude, snappish, snappy, splenetic, testy, touchy, waspish; battling, fighting, warring; controversial
near antonyms affable, amiable, amicable, benevolent, cordial, easygoing, friendly, genial, good-natured, good-tempered, gracious, ingratiating, pleasant, sociable; acquiescent, agreeable, amenable, complaisant, compliant, complying, conciliatory, cooperative, obliging; docile, obedient, submissive, tractable; pacific, peaceable, peaceful
2 feeling or displaying eagerness to fight ⟨an *argumentative* and brash young wrestler⟩ — see BELLIGERENT

arid *adj* **1** causing weariness, restlessness, or lack of interest ⟨an *arid* speech about duty and responsibility⟩ — see BORING
2 marked by little or no precipitation or humidity ⟨*arid* wastelands unfit for human habitation⟩ — see DRY 1
arise *vb* **1** to leave one's bed ⟨The travelers *arose* before dawn and were on their way as the sun came up.⟩
synonyms get up, rise, turn out, uprise
related words arouse, awake, awaken, bestir, stir, wake
near antonyms catnap, doze, drop off, lie up, nap, nod, rest, sleep, slumber, snooze; bunk, perch, roost, settle; couch, flop (down), lie (down), recline
antonyms bed (down), retire, turn in
2 to come to one's attention especially gradually or unexpectedly ⟨Note in your report any problems that *arise* while you are conducting the experiment.⟩
synonyms crop (up), emerge, materialize, spring (up), surface
related words appear, come out, show up, turn up; chance, come, come about, fall out, go (on), go off, hap, happen, occur, pass, transpire; interfere, interpose, intervene, intrude
3 to come into existence ⟨It is not known exactly how mammals *arose*, but scientists date the earliest mammals to the Triassic period.⟩ — see BEGIN 2
4 to move or extend upward ⟨Slowly the hot-air balloon *arose*, and the round-the-world flight was begun.⟩ — see ASCEND
aristocracy *n* **1** the highest class in a society ⟨At one time in China only the *aristocracy* could own land.⟩
synonyms elite, gentility, gentry, nobility, upper class, upper crust
related words A-list, beautiful people, café society, Four Hundred (*or* 400), glitterati, jet set, society; carriage trade, plutocracy
near antonyms commoners, (the) crowd, (the) masses, peasantry, peonage, (the) people, plebeians, (the) populace, (the) public, rank and file; bourgeoisie, middle class, working class; dregs, (the) herd, (the) mob, rabble, rabblement, riffraff, scum, trash
antonyms proletarians, proletariat
2 individuals carefully selected as being the best of a class ⟨Membership in the society is reserved for the literary world's *aristocracy*.⟩ — see ELITE 1
aristocratic *adj* of high birth, rank, or station ⟨She never lets people forget about her *aristocratic* origins.⟩ — see NOBLE 1
arithmetic *n* the act or process of performing mathematical operations to find a value ⟨I haven't actually done the *arithmetic* yet, but I suspect we're losing money on the deal.⟩ — see CALCULATION
¹**arm** *n* a portable weapon from which a shot is discharged by gunpowder ⟨soldiers grabbing their *arms* and helmets and heading into battle⟩ — see GUN 1
²**arm** *n* **1** a large unit of a governmental, business, or educational organization ⟨a company that needs to beef up its marketing *arm* if it wants to compete in today's business world⟩ — see DIVISION 2
2 a part of a body of water that extends beyond the general shoreline ⟨This *arm* of the Atlantic is surprisingly peaceful, as the stronger ocean currents do not reach this far.⟩ — see GULF 1
3 an area of land that juts out into a body of water ⟨Maine has so many long, narrow *arms* that jut out into the ocean that early coastal settlers found it much easier to travel by sea.⟩ — see ²CAPE
4 the right or means to command or control others ⟨Few criminals manage to permanently escape the long *arm* of the law.⟩ — see POWER 1

armada *n* a group of vehicles traveling together or under one management ⟨an *armada* of ships sailing up the coast⟩ — see FLEET
armed forces *pl n* the combined army, air force, and navy of a nation ⟨Our nation's *armed forces* are stationed throughout the world.⟩
synonyms colors, military, service, troops
related words GIs (*or* GI's), men-at-arms, rank and file, servicemen, servicewomen, soldiers, soldiery; force; militia, reserves; armor, defense
near antonyms civilians, noncombatants
armistice *n* a temporary stopping of fighting ⟨Both sides in the conflict agreed to an *armistice* during the solemn holy days.⟩ — see TRUCE
armor *n* **1** means or method of defending ⟨The skunk's primary *armor* is the foul-smelling fluid that it can eject.⟩ — see DEFENSE 1
2 something that encloses another thing especially to protect it ⟨The crab's *armor* makes it difficult prey for some smaller predators.⟩ — see ¹CASE 1
armory *n* a place where military arms are stored ⟨The soldier was sent to the *armory* for a new weapon.⟩
synonyms arsenal, depot, dump, magazine
related words fort, fortress, stronghold; repository, storehouse, warehouse
army *n* **1** a large body of men and women organized for land warfare ⟨In 218 B.C., Hannibal crossed the Alps with an intimidating *army* of people and, most famously, a number of elephants.⟩
synonyms array, battalion, host, legion
related words militia, national guard, standing army; infantry, ranks, regulars, soldiers, troopers, troops
2 a great number of persons or creatures massed together ⟨a vast *army* of loyal fans in line for the band's farewell concert⟩ — see CROWD 1
3 a group of people working together on a task ⟨An *army* of volunteers cleaned up the riverfront.⟩ — see GANG 1
aroma *n* **1** a sweet or pleasant smell ⟨I love the *aroma* of bread baking in the oven.⟩ — see FRAGRANCE
2 the quality of a thing that makes it perceptible to the sense organs in the nose ⟨the ripe *aroma* of a sweatshirt that's in dire need of laundering⟩ — see SMELL 1
3 a special quality or impression associated with something ⟨the *aroma* of power that pervades the government building⟩ — see AURA 1
aromatic *adj* having a pleasant smell ⟨*Aromatic* flowers can add greatly to the ambience of a room.⟩ — see FRAGRANT
around *adj* having being at the present time ⟨She's generally regarded as one of the most talented singers *around*.⟩ — see EXTANT 1
around *adv* **1** on all sides or in every direction ⟨He looked *around*.⟩ ⟨Butterflies were flying all *around*.⟩
synonyms about, round
related words all over, everyplace, everywhere; abroad, hereabouts (*or* hereabout); around, here and there
2 toward the opposite direction ⟨She turned *around* and saw him.⟩
synonyms about, back, backward (*or* backwards), round
related words behind, down, downward (*or* downwards), rearward (*also* rearwards); obversely, reversely; across, athwart, counter, counterclockwise
near antonyms clockwise, deasil
3 at, within, or to a short distance or time ⟨Our dog usually stays *around* our yard.⟩ ⟨He'll be getting in *around* 6:00.⟩ — see NEAR 1
4 from beginning to end ⟨a team that plays all year *around*⟩ — see THROUGH 1

around *prep* **1** close to ⟨I wouldn't stand *around* those rocks—there could be snakes under them!⟩
synonyms about, by, near, next to, nigh
related words alongside, beside; across, along, at; circa; toward (*or* towards)
phrases next door to
2 in random positions within the boundaries of ⟨Huge, strangely shaped rocks were scattered *around* the canyon floor.⟩
synonyms about, across, over, round, through, throughout
related words on

arouse *vb* **1** to cause to stop sleeping ⟨The rooster's crow *aroused* me from my deep sleep.⟩ — see WAKE 1
2 to cease to be asleep ⟨We set the alarm so we would *arouse* at 5:00 a.m.⟩ — see WAKE 2
3 to rouse to strong feeling or action ⟨The court's controversial decision *aroused* many to call for a constitutional amendment.⟩ — see PROVOKE 1

arrange *vb* **1** to come to an agreement or decision concerning the details of ⟨*Arrange* a time for the meeting.⟩ ⟨*Arrange* money matters for your trip.⟩
synonyms decide, fix, set, settle
related words contract, pledge, promise; blueprint, calculate, chart, concert, design, draft, frame, intrigue, lay out, maneuver, map (out), plan, program (*also* programme), schematize, scheme, shape, square away, work out; choose, conclude, determine, figure, opt, resolve; affirm, approve, authorize, clear, confirm, OK (*or* okay), sanction, warrant; close, complete, end, finalize, finish, round (off *or* out), wind up, wrap up; bargain, deal, dicker, haggle, horse-trade, negotiate
phrases dispose of
near antonyms abort, call, call off, drop, recall, repeal, rescind, revoke; differ (over), disagree (with); counter, debate, object, oppose, protest, resist; contest, dispute
2 to put into a particular arrangement ⟨*Arrange* the flowers so that the taller ones are at the center of the bouquet.⟩ — see ORDER 1
3 to bring about through discussion and compromise ⟨I'll *arrange* your free movie pass with the cinema's manager.⟩ — see NEGOTIATE 1
4 to work out the details of (something) in advance ⟨We need to *arrange* our European vacation so that we can get the best deals.⟩ — see PLAN 1

arrangement *n* **1** a method worked out in advance for achieving some objective ⟨They will work out an *arrangement* for repayment of the loan.⟩ — see PLAN 1
2 the way in which something is sized, arranged, or organized ⟨an artistic *arrangement* of the vases on the shelf⟩ — see FORMAT 1
3 the way in which the elements of something (as a work of art) are arranged ⟨The close *arrangement* of the figures in the family portrait is meant to be symbolic of their close emotional attachment.⟩ — see COMPOSITION 3
4 the way objects in space or events in time are arranged or follow one another ⟨The ill-advised *arrangement* of works in the piano recital resulted in pieces of similar mood being played back-to-back.⟩ — see ORDER 1

arrant *adj* having no exceptions or restrictions ⟨That statement is complete and *arrant* nonsense.⟩ — see ABSOLUTE 2

array *n* **1** a number of things considered as a unit ⟨an *array* of baseball gloves in the corner of his room⟩ — see GROUP 1
2 a usually small number of persons considered as a unit ⟨a motley *array* of travelers waiting for the bus⟩ — see GROUP 2
3 dressy clothing ⟨dressed in festive *array* for the city's annual New Year's Eve celebration⟩ — see FINERY
4 the way objects in space or events in time are arranged or follow one another ⟨a marching band's carefully choreographed *array*⟩ — see ORDER 1
5 a large body of men and women organized for land warfare ⟨Feudal lords depended upon their *array* for defense.⟩ — see ARMY 1

array *vb* **1** to make more attractive by adding something that is beautiful or becoming ⟨a hotel lobby *arrayed* with fresh cut flowers⟩ — see DECORATE
2 to outfit with clothes and especially fine or special clothes ⟨*arrayed* in a wedding dress that has been handed down in the family for generations⟩ — see CLOTHE 1
3 to put into a particular arrangement ⟨He *arrayed* his baseball cards in order of their rarity and consequent monetary value.⟩ — see ORDER 1

arrest *n* **1** the act of taking into one's control by authority of law ⟨There were only two *arrests* during the massive protest.⟩
synonyms apprehension, bust [*slang*], collar, pinch
related words raid; house arrest; capture, entrapment, seizure; captivity, confinement, enchainment, hold, immurement, imprisonment, incarceration, restraint; rearrest; remand
near antonyms emancipation, liberation, release
antonyms discharge
2 the stopping of a process or activity ⟨"Hemostasis" is the technical term for *arrest* of bleeding.⟩ — see END 1

arrest *vb* **1** to take or keep under one's control by authority of law ⟨The inept robber was promptly *arrested* by the off-duty policeman he had tried to hold up.⟩
synonyms apprehend, bust [*slang*], collar, nab, nail, pick up, pinch, restrain, seize
related words bag, capture, catch, get, grab, grapple, hook, land, snap (up), snare, snatch, trap; commit, confine, detain, hold, immure, imprison, incarcerate, intern, jail, jug, lock (up); bind, enchain, fetter, handcuff, manacle, shackle, trammel; rearrest; remand
near antonyms emancipate, free, liberate, loose, loosen, release, spring; unbind, unchain
antonyms discharge
2 to bring (something) to a standstill ⟨Cryogenics is based on the idea that extreme cold can almost *arrest* molecular motion.⟩ — see ¹HALT 1
3 to hold the attention of as if by a spell ⟨The sight of the daredevil walking a tightrope between high-rises *arrested* area pedestrians and motorists alike.⟩ — see ENTHRALL 1

arrested *adj* taken and held prisoner ⟨a line of *arrested* suspects waiting to be booked on a variety of charges⟩ — see CAPTIVE

arresting *adj* **1** holding the attention or provoking interest ⟨an *arresting* story⟩ — see INTERESTING
2 likely to attract attention ⟨At seven feet tall, he's an *arresting* figure in any crowd.⟩ — see NOTICEABLE

arrival *n* the act of coming upon a scene ⟨Spring's late *arrival* meant we were still skiing in mid-April.⟩ ⟨The groom blamed his belated *arrival* for the wedding on a huge traffic snarl.⟩
synonyms advent, appearance, coming
related words approach, entrance, ingress; beginning, birth, commencement, dawn, dawning, debut (*also* début), genesis, inception, morning, onset, start
near antonyms dissipation, dissolution, evaporation, fadeaway, fading, melting, passing, vanishing; clearing out, egress, leaving, retirement, retreat, withdrawal; emigration, evacuation, exodus
antonyms decamping, decampment, departing, departure, disappearance, exit, exiting, farewell, going, leave-taking, parting, quitting

arrive *vb* **1** to get to a destination ⟨When will the guests *arrive*?⟩ — see COME 2

2 to reach a desired level of accomplishment ⟨The actress knew she'd *arrived* when she received an Oscar nomination.⟩ — see SUCCEED 2

arrogance *n* an exaggerated sense of one's importance that shows itself in the making of excessive or unjustified claims ⟨In his *arrogance* the president of the club made all the arrangements for the annual banquet without consulting the members.⟩

synonyms assumption, consequence, haughtiness, huffiness, imperiousness, loftiness, lordliness, masterfulness, pompousness, presumptuousness, pretense (*or* pretence), pretension, pretentiousness, self-importance, superciliousness, superiority

related words authoritativeness, bossiness, dominance, high-handedness; condescension, disdain, scorn; chest-thumping, self-assertion, snobbery, snobbishness, snobbism, snootiness; cheek, cheekiness, impertinence, impudence, sauciness; boastfulness, bombast, bravado, strut, swagger, triumphalism, vaingloriousness, vainglory; cockiness, complacence, conceit, egoism, egotism, pride, pridefulness, self-assumption, self-centeredness, self-complacency, self-conceit, self-content, self-contentment, self-opinion, self-partiality, self-satisfaction, smugness, vanity; superiority complex

near antonyms bashfulness, demureness, retiringness, shyness; diffidence, self-distrust, self-doubt, timidity, timidness; lowliness, meekness, mousiness, passiveness, passivity, submissiveness; quietness, reserve, reservedness

antonyms humility, modesty, unassumingness, unpretentiousness

arrogant *adj* having a feeling of superiority that shows itself in an overbearing attitude ⟨The *arrogant* young lawyer elbowed his way to the head of the line of customers, declaring that he was too busy to wait like everybody else.⟩

synonyms cavalier, haughty, highfalutin (*also* hifalutin), high-handed, high-hat, imperious, important, lofty, lordly, masterful, overweening, peremptory, pompous, presuming, presumptuous, pretentious, self-assertive, supercilious, superior, uppish, uppity

related words authoritarian, bossy, dominant, dominating, domineering, pontificating; condescending, disdainful, patronizing; impertinent, impudent, saucy; blusterous, blustery, boastful, bombastic, braggart, bragging, braggy, cocky, swaggering, vain, vainglorious; complacent, conceited, egocentric, egoistic (*also* egoistical), egotistic (*or* egotistical), prideful, proud, self-affected, self-applauding, self-centered, self-complacent, self-conceited, self-pleased, self-satisfied, smug, stuck-up; self-flattering, self-promoting; brash, forward, uninhibited, unreserved; extroverted (*also* extraverted), immodest

near antonyms bashful, cowering, cringing, demure, diffident, introverted, mousy (*or* mousey), overmodest, self-critical, self-doubting, sheepish, shrinking, shy, subdued, timid; acquiescent, compliant, deferential, meek, passive, submissive, unaggressive, unassertive, unassuming, unobtrusive, yielding; quiet, reserved, retiring

antonyms humble, lowly, modest, unarrogant, unpretentious

arrogate *vb* to take or make use of under a guise of authority but without actual right ⟨She *arrogated* the corner office without obtaining prior approval.⟩ — see APPROPRIATE 1

arsenal *n* a place where military arms are stored ⟨sent the ordnance officer to the *arsenal* for weapons⟩ — see ARMORY

arsonist *n* a person who deliberately and unlawfully sets fire to a building or other property ⟨They finally caught the *arsonist*, but only after he'd set fire to four barns.⟩

synonyms firebug, incendiary

related words pyromaniac; flamer, igniter (*also* ignitor), immolator, inflamer

art *n* **1** an occupation requiring skillful use of the hands ⟨one of the country's finest practitioners of the *art* of cabinetmaking⟩ — see CRAFT 1

2 subtle or imaginative ability in inventing, devising, or executing something ⟨There is an *art* to skateboarding.⟩ — see SKILL 1

artery *n* a passage cleared for public vehicular travel ⟨There's an accident on the main *artery* into town, so I'll be late.⟩ — see WAY 1

artful *adj* **1** clever at attaining one's ends by indirect and often deceptive means ⟨The *artful* lawyer got the witness to admit he had been lying.⟩

synonyms beguiling, cagey (*also* cagy), crafty, cunning, cute, designing, devious, foxy, guileful, shrewd, slick, sly, subtle, tricky, wily

related words astute, facile, glib, sharp; crooked, deceitful, deceptive, dishonest, fraudulent, knavish, Machiavellian, oblique, serpentine, shady, shifty, slippery, sneaky, treacherous, underhand, underhanded, unscrupulous; backhanded, double-dealing, hypocritical, insincere, left-handed, mealy, mealymouthed, smooth-tongued, two-faced; circuitous, circular, roundabout; clandestine, concealed, covert, furtive, hugger-mugger, secret, stealthy, surreptitious, undercover; calculating, plotting

near antonyms obvious, open, patent, plain, public, unconcealed; aboveboard, candid, direct, forthright, frank, honest, natural, outspoken, plainspoken, real, simple, sincere, straightforward, unaffected, unpretending, unpretentious, unvarnished; childlike, impressionable, simpleminded, unsophisticated, unworldly; unforced, unstudied; trustful, trusting

antonyms artless, guileless, ingenuous, innocent, undesigning

2 showing a noteworthy use of the imagination and creativity especially in inventing ⟨That kitchen gadget is an *artful* tool for extracting cherry pits.⟩ — see CLEVER 1

3 accomplished with trained ability ⟨That was an *artful* way to handle a very delicate situation.⟩ — see SKILLFUL 1

artfulness *n* **1** skill in achieving one's ends through indirect, subtle, or underhanded means ⟨With well-practiced *artfulness*, he convinced his mother he was sick enough to stay home from school but not sick enough for a visit to the doctor's office.⟩ — see CUNNING 1

2 subtle or imaginative ability in inventing, devising, or executing something ⟨Building a ship model requires a painstaking *artfulness* I don't have.⟩ — see SKILL 1

article *n* a short piece of writing typically expressing a point of view ⟨I read an *article* extolling the benefits of vegetarianism.⟩ — see ESSAY 1

articulate *adj* able to express oneself clearly and well ⟨The television crew covering the science fair were looking for photogenic and *articulate* students to explain their projects on the air.⟩

synonyms eloquent, fluent, well-spoken

related words facile, glib, smooth-tongued, voluble; expressive, outspoken, verbal, vocal; blabby, chatty, garrulous, loquacious, talkative, verbose

near antonyms faltering, halting, hesitant, maundering, mumbling, muttering, sputtering, stammering, stumbling, stuttering; mute, speechless, tongueless, tongue-tied, voiceless

antonyms inarticulate, ineloquent

articulate *vb* **1** to utter clearly and distinctly ⟨She uses a very measured tone and *articulates* every syllable when speaking in public.⟩

synonyms enunciate
related words express, pronounce, say, speak, talk, tell, utter, verbalize, vocalize, voice; speak out, speak up
near antonyms falter, grunt, halt, hesitate, maunder, splutter, sputter, stammer, stumble, stutter; mouth, mumble, murmur, mutter, whisper; breathe, drawl, gasp
2 to convey in appropriate or telling terms ⟨an essay that masterfully *articulates* the case for a greater commitment to space exploration⟩ — see PHRASE
3 to express (a thought or emotion) in words ⟨I'm not *articulating* my thoughts very well.⟩ — see SAY 1

articulateness *n* the art or power of speaking or writing in a forceful and convincing way ⟨The public was swayed by his *articulateness* in stating his position.⟩ — see ELOQUENCE

articulation *n* **1** an act, process, or means of putting something into words ⟨Her boyfriend's *articulation* of his feelings for her was touching.⟩ — see EXPRESSION 1
2 the clear and accurate pronunciation of words especially in public speaking ⟨You will have to work on your *articulation* if you want to be an announcer on TV.⟩ — see DICTION 1

artifice *n* **1** a clever often underhanded means to achieve an end ⟨He used the *artifice* of saying his grandmother had died so that he could get the last seat on the plane.⟩ — see TRICK 1
2 skill in achieving one's ends through indirect, subtle, or underhanded means ⟨Using their *artifice*, the Greeks crafted a hollow wooden horse to hide inside and thereby gained entry into the city of Troy.⟩ — see CUNNING 1
3 subtle or imaginative ability in inventing, devising, or executing something ⟨a painting that could only have been created with the *artifice* of a master⟩ — see SKILL 1
4 the inclination or practice of misleading others through lies or trickery ⟨a crook who is a master of *artifice* and manipulation⟩ — see DECEIT 1
5 the use of clever underhanded actions to achieve an end ⟨The whole story was just an *artifice* to get out of trouble.⟩ — see TRICKERY

artificer *n* a person whose occupation requires skill with the hands ⟨The oil tycoon insisted that the best stone masons, cabinetmakers, and *artificers* in every other craft be employed to create a mansion of unequalled splendor.⟩ — see ARTISAN

artificial *adj* **1** lacking in natural or spontaneous quality ⟨Their *artificial* smiles did not make us feel welcome.⟩
synonyms affected, assumed, bogus, contrived, factitious, fake, false, feigned, forced, mechanical, mock, phony (*also* phoney), plastic, pretended, pseudo, put-on, sham, simulated, strained, unnatural
related words automatic, canned, concocted, fabricated, labored, manufactured, pat, unauthentic, unreal, unrealistic; double-dealing, empty, facile, hollow, hypocritical, insincere, left-handed, mealy, mealymouthed, two-faced, unctuous; histrionic, melodramatic, overacted, overdone, theatrical (*also* theatric); cute, cutesy, genteel, goody-goody, mincing, overrefined, simpering; conventional, formal, impersonal, inflexible, rigid, stiff, stylized, wooden; artful, calculated, conscious, cultivated, deliberate, premeditated, studied
near antonyms authentic, bona fide, real, realistic, right, true; honest, ingenuous, sincere, unpretending; easy, effortless, smooth; extemporaneous, impromptu, impulsive, instinctive, unconscious, unprompted, unrehearsed, unstudied
antonyms artless, genuine, natural, spontaneous, unaffected, uncontrived, unforced
2 not being or expressing what one appears to be or express ⟨the familiar sight of the award winner accepting

the *artificial* congratulations of the other nominees⟩ — see INSINCERE
3 being such in appearance only and made with or manufactured from usually cheaper materials ⟨*artificial* fruit made from wax⟩ — see IMITATION
4 produced by humans rather than natural processes ⟨I find that *artificial* sweeteners often have an odd aftertaste.⟩ — see SYNTHETIC 1

artillery *n* large firearms (as cannons or rockets) ⟨The enemy attacked with heavy *artillery*.⟩
synonyms guns, ordnance
related words ammunition, armament, arms, munitions, weaponry, weapons

artisan *n* a person whose occupation requires skill with the hands ⟨We visited a re-created 19th-century New England village that features an array of *artisans*—a cooper, a carpenter, a blacksmith, a potter, a glassblower.⟩
synonyms artificer, craftsman, handicrafter, tradesman
related words craftswoman; artist, maker; journeyman, master; operative, shaper, smith, technician, wright; workman

artist *n* a person with a high level of knowledge or skill in a field ⟨a pitcher who is a strikeout *artist*⟩ — see EXPERT

artistic *adj* of or relating to the fine arts ⟨Funding for *artistic* endeavors is crucial if the city is to survive and prosper.⟩ — see CULTURAL

artistry *n* subtle or imaginative ability in inventing, devising, or executing something ⟨the high level of *artistry* involved in painting miniatures⟩ — see SKILL 1

artless *adj* **1** free from any intent to deceive or impress others ⟨a genuine and *artless* girl⟩ — see GUILELESS
2 hastily or roughly constructed ⟨*Artless* though it may be, our homemade doghouse has a certain charm to it.⟩ — see RUDE 1

artlessly *adv* without any attempt to impress by deception or exaggeration ⟨*artlessly* commented that the food was okay⟩ — see NATURALLY 3

artlessness *n* the quality or state of being simple and sincere ⟨The *artlessness* of young children should be cherished while it lasts.⟩ — see NAÏVETÉ 1

as *conj* **1** at or during the time that ⟨He slipped *as* he was walking to his car.⟩ — see WHEN 1
2 for the reason that ⟨He stayed home, *as* he had no car.⟩ — see SINCE
3 in spite of the fact that ⟨Silly *as* it sounds, that's exactly the way that it happened.⟩ — see ALTHOUGH
4 the way it would be or one would do if ⟨His face looked *as* he'd gotten a terrible shock.⟩ — see AS IF

ascend *vb* to move or extend upward ⟨The path *ascended* so steeply at one point that we had to scramble up on our hands and knees.⟩
synonyms arise, aspire, climb, lift, mount, rise, soar, thrust, up, uprise, upturn
related words surge, tower; boost, elevate, raise, uplift, upraise; balloon, blast off, take off, zoom; crest, scale, surmount, top; cant, incline, lean, list, recline, slant, slope, tilt, tip
near antonyms dive, nose-dive, plummet, sink, slide
antonyms decline, descend, dip, drop, fall (off), plunge

ascendancy *also* **ascendency** *n* controlling power or influence over others ⟨the *ascendancy* of the government⟩ — see SUPREMACY 1

ascension *n* the act or an instance of rising or climbing up ⟨Her *ascension* from the freshman to the varsity team was evidence of how much she had improved in one season.⟩ — see ASCENT 1

ascent *n* **1** the act or an instance of rising or climbing up ⟨Our plane broke through some heavy low clouds during its *ascent* and leveled off once we were above them.⟩

synonyms ascension, climb, rise, rising, soar

related words boost, hike, increase, raise; elevation, hoist, levitation, raising, takeoff; heave, thrust, upheaval, uplifting, upraising, upsurge, upsweep, upswing, uptrend, upturn, upwelling

near antonyms plop, plummeting, sinking; decline, decrease, down; comedown, downfall, downgrade

antonyms descent, dip, dive, drop, fall, nosedive, plunge

2 an upward slope ⟨We'd reached the final *ascent* of the trail to the summit.⟩

synonyms hill, rise, upgrade, uphill, uprise

related words cant, diagonal, grade, gradient, inclination, incline, lean, pitch, rake, tilt; climb, hump, mound, ridge, swell

near antonyms basin, depression, hollow

antonyms declension, decline, descent, dip, downgrade, fall, hang, hanging

3 a raising or a state of being raised to a higher rank or position ⟨his long, gradual *ascent* into the ranks of management⟩ — see ADVANCEMENT 1

ascertain *vb* **1** to come to an awareness of ⟨I was quickly able to *ascertain* that the puppy was lost.⟩ — see DISCOVER 1

2 to come upon after searching, study, or effort ⟨They *ascertained* that their old colonial-era house had once functioned as a tavern.⟩ — see FIND 1

ascribe *vb* to explain (something) as being the result of something else ⟨*ascribed* their stunning military victory to good intelligence beforehand⟩ — see CREDIT 1

aseptic *adj* free from filth, infection, or dangers to health ⟨Patients with compromised immune systems must be treated in *aseptic* environments.⟩ — see SANITARY

ashamed *adj* suffering from or expressive of a feeling of responsibility for wrongdoing ⟨She was *ashamed* that she had lied to the interviewer.⟩ ⟨wearing a very *ashamed* look⟩ — see GUILTY

ashen *adj* lacking a healthy skin color ⟨still looking *ashen* from his bout with the flu⟩ — see PALE 2

ashes *pl n* the portion or bits of something left over or behind after it has been destroyed ⟨A new and more splendid city was built on the *ashes* of the old.⟩ — see REMAINS 1

ashy *adj* lacking a healthy skin color ⟨Paramedics knew she was in shock because she was *ashy* and shaking.⟩ — see PALE 2

aside from *prep* not including ⟨*Aside from* the C in geometry, he made all A's this term.⟩ — see EXCEPT

as if *conj* the way it would be or one would do if ⟨She looked *as if* she wanted to ask one more question before we left.⟩

synonyms as, as though, like

asinine *adj* showing or marked by a lack of good sense or judgment ⟨It was *asinine* to run into the street like that.⟩ — see FOOLISH 1

asininity *n* **1** a foolish act or idea ⟨a serious journalist who refuses to take part in the *asininity* of reporting celebrity gossip as real news⟩ — see FOLLY 1

2 lack of good sense or judgment ⟨the *asininity* of the decision⟩ — see FOOLISHNESS 1

ask *vb* **1** to put a question or questions to ⟨My coworkers *asked* me all about my trip to Machu Picchu.⟩

synonyms grill, inquire (of), interrogate, query, question, quiz

related words besiege, bombard, cross-examine, cross-question, examine, pump; poll, survey

near antonyms rejoin, retort; comment, observe, remark; avoid, duck

antonyms answer, reply, respond

2 to make a request of ⟨*Ask* the salesclerk for assistance.⟩

synonyms request, solicit

related words appeal (to), beg, beseech, conjure, entreat, implore, importune, invite, petition, plead (to), pray, supplicate; demand, enjoin, exact, press, require

phrases call on (*or* upon)

near antonyms coerce, compel, constrain, force, oblige, require

3 to set or receive as a price ⟨They are only *asking* $300 for that antique grandfather clock.⟩ — see CHARGE 1

4 to request the presence or participation of ⟨We've been *asked* to the awards dinner.⟩ — see INVITE 1

ask (for) *vb* **1** to make a request for ⟨Don't be afraid to *ask for* help if you need it.⟩

synonyms call (for), desire, plead (for), quest, request, seek, solicit, sue (for)

related words apply (for), beg (for), claim, clamor (for), importune, urge, wish (for); demand, enjoin, exact, insist (on), petition (for), press (for), require, requisition; invite

2 to act so as to make (something) more likely ⟨You are *asking for* trouble if you don't study for the test.⟩ — see COURT 1

3 to give a request or demand for ⟨The surgeon *asked for* the scalpel.⟩ — see ORDER 2

askance *also* **askant** *adv* with distrust ⟨We looked *askance* at the dealer's assertion that the car had never been in an accident.⟩

synonyms distrustfully, doubtfully, doubtingly, dubiously, mistrustfully, sideways, skeptically, suspiciously

related words hesitantly, hesitatingly, incredulously, questioningly, quizzically, unbelievingly; guardedly, warily; captiously, critically, cynically, deprecatingly, disapprovingly, disparagingly, negatively, reproachfully, reproachingly, reprovingly, unfavorably; anxiously, apprehensively, uncomfortably, uneasily

phrases with a grain of salt

near antonyms favorably; confidently, sanguinely; credulously, uncritically, unquestioningly

antonyms trustfully, trustingly

askew *adj* inclined or twisted to one side ⟨His hat was *askew* because of the wind.⟩ — see AWRY

aslant *adj* inclined or twisted to one side ⟨That picture is *aslant*—would you mind straightening it?⟩ — see AWRY

asleep *adj* **1** being in a state of suspended consciousness ⟨I was sound *asleep* when the phone rang.⟩

synonyms dormant, dozing, napping, resting, sleeping, slumbering

related words drowsy, nodding, sleepy, slumberous (*or* slumbrous), somnolent; dreaming, reposing; hypnotized, mesmerized; semiconscious; sleepwalking, somnambulant

phrases at rest

near antonyms aware, conscious; sleepless; aroused, astir, awakened, roused, up, wakened; reawakened, revived

antonyms awake, sleepless, wakeful, wide-awake

2 lacking in sensation or feeling ⟨After sitting cross-legged all afternoon, I arose only to discover that my right foot was *asleep*.⟩ — see NUMB 1

aspect *n* **1** a certain way in which something appears or may be regarded ⟨Depending on what *aspect* of college life you consider most important, there are several colleges which might be good for you.⟩

synonyms angle, facet, hand, phase, side

related words air, appearance, character, color, complexion, condition, face, look, semblance, shape, state, visage; period, stage, step; outlook, perspective, position, posture, shoes, slant, stance, standpoint, view, viewpoint; interpretation, reading, translation; article, case, component, count, detail, dimension, element, factor, instance, item, matter, part, particular, point, regard, respect

2 the outward form of someone or something especially as indicative of a quality ⟨He has the *aspect* of a man used to taking charge.⟩ — see APPEARANCE 1

3 the state or fact of facing a particular direction ⟨The harbor's northern *aspect* means that vessels are often exposed to strong winds.⟩ — see EXPOSURE 2

asperity *n* **1** a harsh or sharp quality ⟨doesn't like the *asperity* of most experimental music⟩ — see EDGE 1

2 biting sharpness of feeling or expression ⟨She responded with such *asperity* that we knew she was deeply offended by the question.⟩ — see ACRIMONY 1

3 something that is a cause for suffering or special effort especially in the attainment of a goal ⟨He overcame his share of *asperities* on the road to success.⟩ — see DIFFICULTY 1

asperse *vb* to make untrue and harmful statements about ⟨How dare you *asperse* the character of our dedicated teacher!⟩ — see SLANDER

aspersing *n* the making of false statements that damage another's reputation ⟨She has refused to take part in the mean-spirited *aspersing* in which so many political candidates indulge.⟩ — see SLANDER

aspirant *n* one who seeks an office, honor, position, or award ⟨an unusually large pool of qualified *aspirants* for the scholarship⟩ — see CANDIDATE

aspiration *n* **1** eager desire for personal advancement ⟨A combination of *aspiration* and hard work made her the top female tennis player in the state.⟩ — see AMBITION 1

2 something that one hopes or intends to accomplish ⟨College is his immediate *aspiration* after he graduates from high school.⟩ — see GOAL

aspire *vb* **1** to have in mind as a purpose or goal ⟨*Aspire* to great deeds, and you have a better chance of doing good deeds.⟩ — see INTEND 1

2 to move or extend upward ⟨a tower *aspiring* towards the heavens⟩ — see ASCEND

aspiring *adj* having a strong desire for personal advancement ⟨an *aspiring* young pianist eager to win the prestigious competition⟩ — see AMBITIOUS 1

ass *n* a sturdy and patient domestic mammal that is used especially to carry things ⟨The farm kept a few *asses* for hauling hay in and out of the field.⟩ — see DONKEY 1

assail *vb* **1** to criticize harshly and usually publicly ⟨The union organizers *assailed* the chemical company for failing to provide a safe working environment.⟩ — see ATTACK 2

2 to take sudden, violent action against ⟨a village *assailed* by invaders from the north⟩ — see ATTACK 1

assassin *n* a person who kills another person ⟨shot down by an unknown *assassin*⟩

synonyms cutthroat, homicide, killer, murderer

related words bravo, hit man, triggerman; butcher, executioner, massacrer, slaughterer, slayer; murderess

assault *n* the act or action of setting upon with force or violence ⟨The teen was arrested for his *assault* of the bystander.⟩ — see ATTACK 1

assault *vb* to take sudden, violent action against ⟨arrested for *assaulting* a police officer⟩ — see ATTACK 1

assay *n* the separation and identification of the parts of a whole ⟨A metallurgist did an *assay* on the metal and determined it contained nickel.⟩ — see ANALYSIS 1

assay *vb* **1** to identify and examine the basic elements or parts of (something) especially for discovering interrelationships ⟨The company *assayed* a sample of the rock to see if it contained gold in quantities worth mining.⟩ — see ANALYZE

2 to make an effort to do ⟨*assaying* the task of writing his autobiography⟩ — see ATTEMPT

assemblage *n* **1** a body of people come together in one

place ⟨an *assemblage* of onlookers at the construction site⟩ — see GATHERING 1

2 a mass or quantity that has piled up or that has been gathered over a period of time ⟨We tried to sort through the *assemblage* of ripped wrapping paper and boxes for the missing toy.⟩ — see ACCUMULATION 1

3 a number of things considered as a unit ⟨an *assemblage* of brass candlesticks on the table⟩ — see GROUP 1

4 an organized group of objects acquired and maintained for study, exhibition, or personal pleasure ⟨donated his *assemblage* of 18th-century miniature paintings to the museum⟩ — see COLLECTION 1

assemble *vb* **1** to come together into one body or place ⟨The graduates were told to *assemble* in the cafeteria an hour before the ceremony.⟩

synonyms cluster, collect, concentrate, conglomerate, congregate, convene, converge, forgather (*or* foregather), gather, meet, rendezvous

related words affiliate, ally, associate, band (together), caucus, club, collaborate, confederate, conjoin, consolidate, consort, cooperate, couple, federate, gang up, join, merge, unite; reassemble, reconvene, regather, remeet

phrases get together

near antonyms depart, leave, take off; disjoin, dissociate, disunite

antonyms break up, disband, disperse, split (up)

2 to form by putting together parts or materials ⟨It took a lot more time to *assemble* the model train set than the box said it would.⟩ — see BUILD

3 to bring together in assembly by or as if by command ⟨We *assembled* the club members to decide who would be traveling with whom on the trip.⟩ — see CONVOKE

4 to bring together in one body or place ⟨The caterer *assembled* an assortment of fancy desserts for the reception.⟩ — see GATHER 1

assembly *n* **1** a body of people come together in one place ⟨the usual *assembly* of early morning commuters waiting at the train station⟩ — see GATHERING 1

2 a body of persons gathered for religious worship ⟨The preacher addressed the *assembly* in somber tones.⟩ — see CONGREGATION 1

3 a coming together of a number of persons for a specified purpose ⟨Attendance at the awards *assembly* is mandatory.⟩ — see MEETING 1

assent *vb* to give or express one's approval (as to a proposal) ⟨Are we to conclude from your silence that you *assent*?⟩ — see ACCEDE

assert *vb* **1** to state clearly and strongly ⟨a superpatriot who is never afraid to *assert* her allegiance to flag and country⟩

synonyms affirm, aver, avouch, avow, declare, guarantee, lay down, profess

related words advance, advertise, boost, plug, promote, publicize; announce, blaze, call, proclaim, pronounce, say; accent, accentuate, emphasize, stress, underline, underscore; advocate, champion, defend, espouse, support, uphold; assure, convince, persuade; explain, justify, rationalize; reaffirm, reassert

near antonyms minimize, understate; disregard, ignore, neglect, overlook

2 to state (something) as a reason in support of or against something under consideration ⟨*asserted* that a new roof would be necessary if the school was to remain open⟩ — see ARGUE 1

3 to state as a fact usually forcefully ⟨He vigorously *asserted* that what passes for art these days is absolute rubbish.⟩ — see CLAIM 1

assertion *n* **1** a solemn and often public declaration of the truth or existence of something ⟨The *assertion* that all people have certain unalienable rights is set forth in the Declaration of Independence.⟩ — see PROTESTATION

2 an idea or opinion that is put forth in a discussion or debate ⟨She made the *assertion* that gravity affects light.⟩ — see CONTENTION 1

assertive *adj* **1** having or showing a bold forcefulness in the pursuit of a goal ⟨Some reef fish are *assertive* in defending their territory.⟩ — see AGGRESSIVE 1

2 marked by or uttered with forcefulness ⟨After months of *assertive* declarations that he would not run for president, he announced he was running.⟩ — see EMPHATIC 1

assertiveness *n* the quality or state of being forceful (as in expression) ⟨The *assertiveness* with which he voices his opinions intimidates some people.⟩ — see VEHEMENCE 1

assess *vb* **1** to establish or apply as a charge or penalty ⟨The utility company will *assess* a fee if your payment is late.⟩ — see IMPOSE

2 to make an approximate or tentative judgment regarding ⟨Let's step back and *assess* the situation.⟩ — see ESTIMATE 1

assessment *n* **1** a charge usually of money collected by the government from people or businesses for public use ⟨hated paying the annual *assessment* on his car⟩ — see TAX

2 an opinion on the nature, character, or quality of something ⟨I'm far too quiet, in the *assessment* of my new boss.⟩ — see ESTIMATION 1

3 the act of placing a value on the nature, character, or quality of something ⟨We may have been too hasty in our *assessment* of the value of the property.⟩ — see ESTIMATE 1

assiduity *n* attentive and persistent effort ⟨This project has been successful only through the *assiduity* of a lot of people.⟩ — see DILIGENCE

assiduous *adj* involved in often constant activity ⟨the fascinating sight of *assiduous* ants carrying food into the anthill⟩ — see BUSY 1

assiduously *adv* with great effort or determination ⟨*assiduously* pursued a law degree when continuing to work full-time during the day⟩ — see HARD 1

assiduousness *n* attentive and persistent effort ⟨With painstaking *assiduousness* investigators finally cracked the case of the stolen works of art.⟩ — see DILIGENCE

assign *vb* **1** to give a task, duty, or responsibility to ⟨I *assigned* the class with the task of finding something in the state constitution they felt needed changing.⟩ — see ENTRUST 1

2 to give as a share or portion ⟨Each new employee is *assigned* a cubicle and a computer.⟩ — see ALLOT

3 to give over the legal possession or ownership of ⟨He *assigned* all rights to and royalties from the song to a third party.⟩ — see TRANSFER 1

4 to pick (someone) by one's authority for a specific position or duty ⟨The mayor *assigned* the panel with the task of luring a major sports franchise to the city.⟩ — see APPOINT 2

assignment *n* **1** a piece of work that needs to be done regularly ⟨His first newspaper *assignment* was writing obituaries.⟩ — see CHORE 1

2 a specific task with which a person or group is charged ⟨The spy team's *assignment* was to steal the enemy's plans.⟩ — see MISSION

3 something assigned to be read or studied ⟨Have you read the *assignment* for tomorrow?⟩ — see LESSON

4 the state or fact of being chosen for a position or duty ⟨Her *assignment* to the board of directors was a point of considerable pride for her.⟩ — see APPOINTMENT 1

assimilate *vb* **1** to describe as similar ⟨*assimilated* the 19th-century American captains of industry and com-

merce to the medieval barons who exorbitantly taxed shipping along the Rhine⟩ — see COMPARE 1

2 to have a clear idea of ⟨I'm still trying to *assimilate* the doctor's diagnosis of my heart condition.⟩ — see COMPREHEND 1

3 to make a part of a body or system ⟨Social workers will need time to *assimilate* the new arrivals into the community.⟩ — see EMBODY 1

assist *n* an act or instance of helping ⟨With an *assist* from his dad, the youngster built a doghouse any canine would be proud to call home.⟩ — see HELP 1

assist *vb* to provide (someone) with what is useful or necessary to achieve an end ⟨You can *assist* families in need by donating old clothes in good condition.⟩ — see HELP 1

assistance *n* an act or instance of helping ⟨Thank you for your *assistance* in helping me change my flat tire.⟩ — see HELP 1

assistant *n* a person who helps a more skilled person ⟨the chief *assistant* to the director⟩ — see HELPER

associate *n* **1** a person frequently seen in the company of another ⟨A number of his *associates* were members of organized crime, so he was a person of interest to the FBI.⟩

synonyms cohort, companion, compatriot, comrade, crony, fellow, hobnobber, mate

related words colleague, coworker, equal, peer, workmate; accomplice, affiliate, ally, collaborator, confederate, half, partner; buddy, chum, confidant, familiar, friend, hearty, intimate, pal; countryman; classmate, housemate, messmate, playfellow, playmate, roommate (*also* roomie), schoolmate, shipmate, teammate; attendant, escort; hanger-on, leech, parasite

2 a fellow worker ⟨my *associates* at the office⟩ — see COLLEAGUE

associate *vb* **1** to come or be together as friends ⟨a couple who joined the nature club in order to *associate* with like-minded people⟩

synonyms chum, company, consort, fraternize, hobnob, pal (around), run, sort, travel

related words affiliate, ally, attach, band, bond, club, collaborate, confederate, conjoin, connect, cooperate, couple, gang, get along, get on, group, interrelate, join, knot, league, link, mingle, mix, rally, relate, side, socialize, team, tie, wed; befriend, friend

phrases be friends with, fall in with, keep company (with), rub elbows (with) *or* rub shoulders (with), take up with

near antonyms avoid, cold-shoulder, shun, snub; alienate, estrange; break up, disband, disperse, split (up); disjoin, dissociate, disunite, divorce, sever, split, sunder

2 to think of (something) in combination ⟨She still *associates* that place with the carefree days of her youth.⟩

synonyms connect, correlate, identify, link, relate

related words compare, equate, liken; group, join, lump (together), tie (together)

near antonyms contrast, differentiate, discriminate, distinguish, separate, set off

3 to come together to form a single unit ⟨The elements hydrogen and oxygen *associate* to form molecules of water.⟩ — see UNITE 1

4 to form or enter into an association that furthers the interests of its members ⟨nations deciding to *associate* in order to remove trade barriers⟩ — see ALLY

5 to take part in social activities ⟨You should try to *associate* with people your own age.⟩ — see SOCIALIZE

association *n* **1** the state of having shared interests or efforts (as in social or business matters) ⟨The public television station is producing the series in *association* with a foundation for the arts.⟩

synonyms affiliation, alliance, collaboration, confederation, connection, cooperation, hookup, liaison, linkup, partnership, relation, relationship, tie-up, union
related words business, dealings, interaction; exchange, interconnection, interrelation, mutualism, reciprocity, symbiosis; integration, unification; affinity, attachment, closeness, intimacy, rapport, sympathy; kinship, oneness, solidarity, togetherness, unity; companionship, company, fellowship; bed, cahoots, league
near antonyms breakup, dissolution, disunion; division, parting, separation, severance, split; alienation, divorce, estrangement
antonyms disaffiliation, dissociation
2 a group of persons formally joined together for some common interest ⟨All *associations* meeting on town property must be registered with and approved by the registrar's office.⟩
synonyms board, brotherhood, chamber, club, college, congress, council, fellowship, fraternity, guild (*also* gild), institute, institution, league, order, organization, society, sodality
related words collective, commune, community, cooperative; alliance, bloc, camp, coalition, partnership; body, cadre, group; circle, clan, clique, coterie, junta, lot, set; crew, outfit, party, squad, team; branch, chapter, local; faithful, fold, membership; sisterhood, sorority; cabal, confederacy, conspiracy; band, gang, ring; cartel, combine, syndicate
3 the fact or state of having something in common ⟨What's the *association* between cat hair and my allergic reaction to certain proteins?⟩ — see CONNECTION 1
assort *vb* **1** to arrange or assign according to type ⟨*Assort* these butterfly specimens according to geographic origin.⟩ — see CLASSIFY 1
2 to form a pleasing relationship ⟨Somewhat surprisingly, the collection of ancient Egyptian art *assorts* rather well with the museum's modern design.⟩ — see HARMONIZE 1
assorted *adj* consisting of many things of different sorts ⟨a box of *assorted* chocolates⟩ — see MISCELLANEOUS
assortment *n* **1** an unorganized collection or mixture of various things ⟨an *assortment* of nails at the bottom of my tool box⟩ — see MISCELLANY 1
2 the quality or state of being composed of many different elements or types ⟨We were disappointed in the small clothing store's lack of *assortment*.⟩ — see VARIETY 1
assuage *vb* **1** to make more bearable or less severe ⟨a mother cooing to her toddler and *assuaging* his fear of the dark⟩ — see HELP 2
2 to put a complete end to (a physical need or desire) ⟨That huge meal certainly *assuaged* my hunger.⟩ — see SATISFY 1
3 to lessen the anger or agitation of ⟨Nothing would *assuage* the angry parent except the prompt dismissal of the teacher who had used corporal punishment.⟩ — see PACIFY 1
assume *vb* **1** to take to or upon oneself ⟨We promised to *assume* responsibility for any damage to the flower beds caused by the volleyball game in the backyard.⟩
synonyms accept, bear, shoulder, take over, undertake
related words adopt, embrace, take up; advocate, back, champion, endorse (*also* indorse), espouse, stand by, support, uphold; accede, acquiesce, agree, assent, consent; reaccept, reassume
near antonyms abjure, recant, renounce, retract, take back, unsay, withdraw; decline, refuse, reject, spurn, turn down; abstain (from), forbear, refrain (from); avoid, bypass, detour; abandon, forsake, give up, relinquish, surrender; back down, back off, backtrack

antonyms disavow, disclaim, disown, repudiate
2 to take as true or as a fact without actual proof ⟨Everyone *assumed*, wrongly, that someone else was bringing dessert.⟩
synonyms postulate, premise, presume, presuppose, say, suppose
related words accept, believe, credit, swallow; conclude, deduce, gather, infer, judge, take; conjecture, figure, guess, surmise, suspect, think; conceive, dream, fancy, imagine, perceive, preconceive; speculate, theorize; affirm, allege, assert, aver, avouch, avow, claim, contend, declare, insist, maintain, profess
phrases take for granted
near antonyms challenge, disagree (with), disbelieve, discount, discredit, dispute, distrust, doubt, mistrust, question, wonder (about); deny, disavow, disclaim, disown, reject, repudiate; belie, confute, disprove, rebut, refute
3 to form an opinion from little or no evidence ⟨As I just *assumed* it was too late to go out, I didn't think to ask.⟩ — see GUESS 1
4 to present a false appearance of ⟨She *assumed* an air of nonchalance even though she was wildly ecstatic she won the award.⟩ — see FEIGN
5 to provide with a paying job ⟨She was *assumed* as partner by the prestigious law firm.⟩ — see EMPLOY 1
assumed *adj* **1** appearing to be true on the basis of evidence that may or may not be confirmed ⟨an *assumed* connection between the two species that has yet to be confirmed by fossil findings⟩ — see APPARENT 1
2 lacking in natural or spontaneous quality ⟨The sales-clerk's *assumed* friendliness vanished as soon as I assured her I was just looking.⟩ — see ARTIFICIAL 1
assumption *n* **1** something taken as being true or factual and used as a starting point for a course of action or reasoning ⟨Your argument is faulty because it's based on erroneous *assumptions*.⟩
synonyms given, postulate, premise (*also* premiss), presumption, presupposition, supposition
related words hypothesis, proposition, theory, thesis; axiom, truism, verity; belief, canon, doctrine, dogma, gospel, law; precept, principle, rule, standard, tenet; basis, foundation, ground; conclusion, deduction, inference; affirmation, assertion, avouchment, declaration
2 an exaggerated sense of one's importance that shows itself in the making of excessive or unjustified claims ⟨His air of *assumption* tended to put people off rather quickly.⟩ — see ARROGANCE
assurance *n* **1** a state of mind in which one is free from doubt ⟨I can state with complete *assurance* that no harm will ever come to you.⟩ — see CONFIDENCE 2
2 great faith in oneself or one's abilities ⟨Her *assurance* was evident in the way she carried herself onto the playing field.⟩ — see CONFIDENCE 1
assure *vb* **1** to ease the grief or distress of ⟨friends trying to choose just the right words to *assure* the grieving parents⟩ — see COMFORT
2 to make sure, certain, or safe ⟨security measures that *assured* our safety⟩ — see ENSURE
assured *adj* **1** having or showing a mind free from doubt ⟨a candidate who seemed very *assured* of the outcome of the election⟩ — see CERTAIN 2
2 having or showing great faith in oneself or one's abilities ⟨an *assured* attorney, who dominates any courtroom proceeding⟩ — see CONFIDENT 1
3 having too high an opinion of oneself ⟨He's rather *assured* for a moviemaker with one hit movie to his name.⟩ — see CONCEITED
assuredly *adv* without any question ⟨I am most *assuredly* the person you are looking for.⟩ — see INDEED 1

assuredness *n* a state of mind in which one is free from doubt ⟨the complete *assuredness* with which the basketball player would sink the shot⟩ — see CONFIDENCE 2

astern *adv* near, toward, or in the stern of a ship or the tail of an aircraft ⟨If you turn around and look *astern*, you'll see dolphins following the boat.⟩ — see AFT

as though *conj* the way it would be or one would do if ⟨The applause was so great it was *as though* the preschooler's dance class had been the Bolshoi Ballet.⟩ — see AS IF

astir *adj* marked by much life, movement, or activity ⟨The mall was *astir* with throngs of holiday shoppers.⟩ — see ALIVE 2

astonish *vb* to make a strong impression on (someone) with something unexpected ⟨The news that you and she broke up absolutely *astonishes* me.⟩ — see SURPRISE 1

astonished *adj* **1** affected with sudden and great wonder or surprise ⟨I was *astonished* at seeing a cow wandering down Main Street.⟩ — see THUNDERSTRUCK
2 filled with amazement or wonder ⟨grandparents *astonished* at how much their grandchildren had grown in the past year⟩ — see OPENMOUTHED

astonishing *adj* **1** causing a strong emotional reaction because of unexpectedness ⟨gave us the *astonishing* news they were getting married⟩ — see SURPRISING 1
2 causing wonder or astonishment ⟨an *astonishing* view of the Grand Canyon that few tourists get to see⟩ — see MARVELOUS 1

astonishment *n* **1** the rapt attention and deep emotion caused by the sight of something extraordinary ⟨the Midwesterner's *astonishment* at seeing the ocean for the first time⟩ — see WONDER 2
2 the state of being strongly impressed by something unexpected or unusual ⟨The suddenness of the thunderstorm left the picnickers in a state of *astonishment*.⟩ — see SURPRISE 2

astound *vb* to make a strong impression on (someone) with something unexpected ⟨It *astounds* me that you flew all the way out here just for my birthday.⟩ — see SURPRISE 1

astounded *adj* **1** affected with sudden and great wonder or surprise ⟨We were *astounded* to realize that we were holding the winning lottery ticket.⟩ — see THUNDERSTRUCK
2 filled with amazement or wonder ⟨By the *astounded* look on their faces, I could tell they'd never heard the story before.⟩ — see OPENMOUTHED

astounding *adj* **1** causing a strong emotional reaction because of unexpectedness ⟨the *astounding* sight of their cat returning home after having been missing for two years⟩ — see SURPRISING 1
2 causing wonder or astonishment ⟨experiencing the *astounding* sight of the aurora borealis for the first time⟩ — see MARVELOUS 1

astral *adj* **1** of or relating to the stars ⟨I gave the astronomy students the assignment of charting *astral* movement for the next month.⟩ — see STELLAR 1
2 standing above others in rank, importance, or achievement ⟨After his film became an unexpected blockbuster, the director was suddenly welcome in the most *astral* circles of Hollywood society.⟩ — see EMINENT

astray *adv* off the desired or intended path or course ⟨I think we were led *astray* by the unfortunate similarity of the two names.⟩ — see WRONG

astronomical *also* **astronomic** *adj* unusually large ⟨A googol is an *astronomical* number, and the whimsical coinage of the name was intended to suggest that fact.⟩ — see HUGE

astronomically *adv* to a large extent or degree ⟨Their battalion was *astronomically* outnumbered by enemy forces.⟩ — see GREATLY 2

astute *adj* having or showing a practical cleverness or judgment ⟨a police detective known to be an *astute* judge of character⟩ — see SHREWD 1

astuteness *n* exceptional discernment and judgment especially in practical matters ⟨a political observer renowned for her *astuteness*⟩ — see ACUMEN

asunder *adv* into parts or pieces ⟨The environmental organization was torn *asunder* by bitter rivalries.⟩ — see APART

as well as *prep* in addition to ⟨She is good at basketball *as well as* softball.⟩ — see BESIDES 1

asylum *n* **1** a place where mentally ill people are cared for ⟨She volunteered to play piano for the residents of the state *asylum* on weekends.⟩ — see INSTITUTION 2
2 something (as a building) that offers cover from the weather or protection from danger ⟨The embassy serves as an *asylum* for that country's nationals in need of help.⟩ — see SHELTER

at all *adv* in any way or respect ⟨wasn't *at all* pleased with the way the family portrait came out⟩
synonyms anywise, ever, half
related words somehow, someway (*also* someways); remotely

athirst *adj* showing urgent desire or interest ⟨Everyone was *athirst* for any news at all about family members.⟩ — see EAGER

athwart *adv* **1** from one side to the other of an intervening space ⟨After it enters the Gulf of Mexico, the hurricane is predicted to advance *athwart* to the Texas coastline.⟩ — see OVER 1
2 in a line or direction running from corner to corner ⟨We hung the twisted strips of crepe paper *athwart* to the floor and ceiling so that they formed giant crosses on all four walls.⟩ — see CROSSWISE

athwart *prep* to the opposite side of ⟨*Athwart* the road was farmland as far as the eye could see.⟩ — see ACROSS 1

atmosphere *n* **1** a special quality or impression associated with something ⟨The fireplace and cozy armchairs give the bookstore the *atmosphere* of a comfortable home.⟩ — see AURA 1
2 the circumstances, conditions, or objects by which one is surrounded ⟨liked the quiet and scholarly *atmosphere* of his prep school⟩ — see ENVIRONMENT

atom *n* a very small piece ⟨Give me just one *atom* of information about the novel's surprise ending.⟩ — see BIT 1

atomic *adj* very small in size ⟨made *atomic* adjustments to the clock's mechanism to keep it from whirring as it ran⟩ — see TINY

atomize *vb* to reduce to fine particles ⟨This medication for athlete's foot is *atomized* so that it can be sprayed on from an aerosol can.⟩ — see POWDER

atone (for) *vb* to make up for (an offense) ⟨He tried to *atone for* his thoughtlessness with a heartfelt apology.⟩ — see EXPIATE

atrocious *adj* **1** extremely disturbing or repellent ⟨an *atrocious* crime that shocked even hardened members of the police force⟩ — see HORRIBLE 1
2 extremely unsatisfactory ⟨The picture quality on the pirated DVD was *atrocious*.⟩ — see WRETCHED 1
3 having or showing the desire to inflict severe pain and suffering on others ⟨the *atrocious* treatment of prisoners at the camps⟩ — see CRUEL 1

atrociousness *n* **1** the quality of inspiring intense dread or dismay ⟨George Orwell's novel *1984* captures the *atrociousness* of tyranny.⟩ — see HORROR 1
2 the state or quality of being utterly evil ⟨the unspeakable *atrociousness* of the genocide⟩ — see ENORMITY 1

3 disposition to willfully inflict pain and suffering on others ⟨the king's *atrociousness* in dealing with rivals to the throne⟩ — see CRUELTY

atrocity *n* **1** the quality of inspiring intense dread or dismay ⟨the *atrocity* of war⟩ — see HORROR 1
2 the state or quality of being utterly evil ⟨was appalled by the *atrocity* of the attack on innocents⟩ — see ENORMITY 1
3 disposition to willfully inflict pain and suffering on others ⟨Wars often unleash a level of *atrocity* that would be unimaginable in peacetime.⟩ — see CRUELTY

attach *vb* **1** to cause (something) to hold to another ⟨You can *attach* the buttons to the puppet with fabric glue.⟩ — see FASTEN 1
2 to pick (someone) by one's authority for a specific position or duty ⟨*attached* the colonel to the new regiment⟩ — see APPOINT 2
3 to take ownership or control of (something) by right of one's authority ⟨*attached* the house for nonpayment of property taxes⟩ — see CONFISCATE

attached *adj* having a liking or affection ⟨was rather *attached* to her old stuffed animals⟩ — see FOND 1

attachment *n* **1** a feeling of strong or constant regard for and dedication to someone ⟨I doubt that there's any permanent *attachment* between the two of them.⟩ — see LOVE 1
2 something that is not necessary in itself but adds to the convenience or performance of the main piece of equipment ⟨We bought a grinder *attachment* for the kitchen mixer.⟩ — see ACCESSORY 1
3 adherence to something to which one is bound by a pledge or duty ⟨an unflinching *attachment* to the marriage, through times both good and bad⟩ — see FIDELITY

attack *n* **1** the act or action of setting upon with force or violence ⟨The USS Constitution was nicknamed "Old Ironsides" after its oaken hull successfully withstood a British *attack*.⟩
synonyms aggression, assault, attempt, blitz, blitzkrieg, charge, descent, offense (*or* offence), offensive, onset, onslaught, raid, rush, strike
related words ambush; counteraggression, counterattack, counteroffensive; sally, sortie; envelopment, flanking; breakthrough, foray, incursion, invasion; pillage, ravage, sack; air raid, bombardment, bombing; siege, storm; barrage, cannonade, fusillade, hail, salvo, volley
near antonyms defense, defensive, guard, shield; opposition, resistance; protection, security, shelter
2 a sudden experiencing of a physical or mental disorder ⟨Malaria is characterized by periodic *attacks* of chills and fever.⟩
synonyms access, bout, case, fit, seizure, siege, spell, turn
related words recurrence, relapse; brainstorm, convulsion, pang, paroxysm, spasm, throe; agitation, frenzy; breakdown, collapse, prostration
near antonyms arrest, relief, remission

attack *vb* **1** to take sudden, violent action against ⟨Our dog unexpectedly *attacked* the mailman.⟩
synonyms assail, assault, beset, charge, descend (on *or* upon), jump (on), pounce (on *or* upon), raid, rush, storm, strike
related words bum-rush, gang up (on), mob, swarm; mug, rob; ambush, surprise (*also* surprize), waylay; blitz, bomb, bombard; barrage, cannon, cannonade; bang away (at), batter, buffet, plaster; beleaguer, besiege, press; harry, loot, pillage, plunder, ravage, sack; foray, invade, overrun; envelop, flank
phrases beat up on, fly at, go at, light into, pitch into, round on, set at, set upon, tear into

near antonyms cover, defend, guard, protect, secure, shield
2 to criticize harshly and usually publicly ⟨The mayor and all his aides were *attacked* mercilessly in the press when the scandal erupted.⟩
synonyms abuse, assail, bash, belabor, blast, castigate, excoriate, jump (on), lambaste (*or* lambast), savage, scathe, slam, vituperate
related words berate, harangue, harry, revile, scold, whip; blaspheme, curse, execrate, imprecate, profane; affront, insult, slur; asperse, bad-mouth, belittle, blackguard, disparage, put down; libel, slander, traduce, vilify; chastise, chide, criticize, lace (into), rebuke, reprimand, reproof; fulminate, lash (out)
phrases beat up on, light into, sail into, tie into
near antonyms acclaim, commend, compliment, hail, laud, praise
3 to start work on energetically ⟨Courtney *attacked* the huge mess in her room with determination and enthusiasm.⟩
synonyms tackle
related words address, approach, face; buckle (down to), concentrate (on), focus (on), knuckle down (to), zero (in on); pitch in, plunge (in), settle (down); pursue, take up, undertake
phrases go at, have at, light into, pitch into, sail into, tear into
near antonyms avoid, evade, shun; dally, dawdle, dillydally, fiddle (around), fool, idle, lag, mess, monkey (around), play, poke, potter (around), putter (around), trifle

attain *vb* **1** to obtain (as a goal) through effort ⟨They *attained* mastery of the painting technique.⟩ — see ACHIEVE 1
2 to receive as return for effort ⟨With hard work she will inevitably *attain* success in her chosen profession.⟩ — see EARN 1

attainable *adj* **1** capable of being done or carried out ⟨Set *attainable* goals, not impracticable ones.⟩ — see POSSIBLE 1
2 possible to get ⟨I don't know if those blue jeans are *attainable* overseas.⟩ — see AVAILABLE 1

attainment *n* **1** a successful result brought about by hard work ⟨First place in the state journalism competition is quite an *attainment*.⟩ — see ACCOMPLISHMENT 1
2 the state of being actual or complete ⟨The *attainment* of man's age-old dream of flying was at last realized in 1903 by Orville and Wilbur Wright.⟩ — see FRUITION

attempt *n* **1** an effort to do or accomplish something ⟨It took several *attempts* before we made good ice cream with an old-fashioned hand-cranked ice cream freezer.⟩
synonyms bid, crack, endeavor, essay, fling, go, offer, pass, shot, stab, trial, try, whack, whirl
related words striving, struggle, throes, undertaking; trial and error
2 the act or action of setting upon with force or violence ⟨survived several *attempts* on his life⟩ — see ATTACK 1

attempt *vb* to make an effort to do ⟨After *attempting*—and failing—to start the lawn mower on my own, I finally succeeded with a neighbor's help.⟩ ⟨Don't even *attempt* walking on your broken foot.⟩
synonyms assay, endeavor, essay, seek, strive, try
related words fight, strain, struggle, toil, trouble, work; aim, aspire, hope; assume, take up, undertake
phrases have a go at, shoot at (*or* shoot for), try one's hand (at)
near antonyms drop, give up, quit

attend *vb* **1** to go along with in order to provide assistance, protection, or companionship ⟨A passel of assistants *attend* the movie star wherever she goes.⟩ — see ACCOMPANY 1

2 to pay attention especially through the act of hearing ⟨I'm sorry, but all the noise means I'm having a hard time *attending* to the conversation.⟩ — see LISTEN

3 to take charge of especially on behalf of another ⟨A visiting nurse *attends* Grandpa three days a week.⟩ — see ²TEND 1

4 to occur or exist at the same time ⟨all the pomp and circumstance that *attend* the opening of the Olympic Games⟩ — see COINCIDE 1

attendant *adj* **1** coming as a result ⟨dreaded the coming flu season and the *attendant* flood of school absences⟩ — see RESULTANT

2 present at the same time and place ⟨the foreign dignitary's visit and the *attendant* press coverage about it⟩ — see COINCIDENT 1

attendant *n* **1** one that accompanies another for protection, guidance, or as a courtesy ⟨They let the hotel *attendant* help them with their bags.⟩ — see ESCORT

2 something that is found along with something else ⟨Disease is the inevitable *attendant* of poor sanitation.⟩ — see ACCOMPANIMENT

attending *adj* **1** being within the confines of a specified place ⟨a surprise inspection of the barracks and all *attending* recruits⟩ — see PRESENT 2

2 present at the same time and place ⟨He dislikes flying and all of its *attending* inconveniences.⟩ — see COINCIDENT 1

attention *n* **1** a focusing of the mind on something ⟨I need your full *attention* right now.⟩

synonyms absorption, concentration, engrossment, enthrallment, immersion

related words fixation, obsession, preoccupation; alertness, application, awareness, consideration, heedfulness, intentness, raptness, regard; contemplation, meditation, pondering, rumination

near antonyms absence, absentmindedness, abstractedness, detachment, distraction, obliviousness, remoteness, unawareness, unconsciousness, withdrawal; indifference, mindlessness, unconcern; befuddlement, bewilderment, confusion

antonyms inattention

2 a state of being aware ⟨Several parents brought to the committee's *attention* the deteriorating condition of the playground.⟩

synonyms awareness, cognizance, ear, eye, heed, knowledge, note, notice, observance, observation

related words hyperawareness, hyperconsciousness; advisement, care, concern, consideration, regard, watch; apprehension, discernment, grasp, mind, perception, recognition, thought, understanding

near antonyms disregard, neglect, obliviousness, unawareness

3 an act or utterance that is a customary show of good manners ⟨She enjoyed his old-school *attentions*.⟩ — see CIVILITY 1

attentive *adj* **1** having the mind fixed on something ⟨Susan became particularly *attentive* when the sportscaster turned to women's tennis, her favorite sport.⟩

synonyms absorbed, deep, engrossed, enthralled, focused (*also* focussed), immersed, intent, observant, rapt

related words engaged, interested, intrigued, involved; hypnotized, mesmerized; alert, alive, conscious, open-eyed, watchful, wide-awake

phrases all ears

near antonyms daydreaming, dreamy, faraway, foggy, hazy, lost, oblivious, preoccupied, remote; apathetic, disinterested, uninterested

antonyms absent, absentminded, abstracted, distracted, inattentive, inobservant, unabsorbed, unfocused (*also* unfocussed)

2 given to or made with heedful anticipation of the needs and happiness of others ⟨an *attentive* neighbor who helps out whenever and wherever she spots a need⟩ — see THOUGHTFUL 1

3 paying close attention usually for the purpose of anticipating approaching danger or opportunity ⟨If only for your own safety, you need to stay *attentive* when you are hunting.⟩ — see ALERT 1

attentiveness *n* the state of being constantly attentive and responsive to signs of opportunity, activity, or danger ⟨Your *attentiveness* prevented a potentially bad accident.⟩ — see VIGILANCE

attest *vb* **1** to declare (something) to be true or genuine ⟨The appraiser *attests* that the lamp is indeed an original Tiffany.⟩ — see CERTIFY 1

2 to make a solemn declaration under oath for the purpose of establishing a fact ⟨an eyewitness who will *attest* to my innocence⟩ — see TESTIFY

3 to give evidence or testimony to the truth or factualness of ⟨I'll *attest* that she was at the party.⟩ — see CONFIRM 1

attestation *n* something presented in support of the truth or accuracy of a claim ⟨The fact that he spent hours standing in line for the sequel should be *attestation* enough that he's a die-hard fan of the movie series.⟩ — see PROOF

attire *n* covering for the human body ⟨needed some suitable *attire* for the job interview⟩ — see CLOTHING

attire *vb* to outfit with clothes and especially fine or special clothes ⟨men *attired* in tuxedos for the awards banquet⟩ — see CLOTHE 1

attorney *n* **1** a person who acts or does business for another ⟨talked to the count's *attorney* about buying land from his estate⟩ — see AGENT 2

2 a person whose profession is to conduct lawsuits for clients or to advise about legal rights and obligations ⟨finished law school and became an *attorney*⟩ — see LAWYER

attraction *n* something that attracts interest ⟨a park with the world's fastest roller coaster and other *attractions*⟩ — see MAGNET

attractive *adj* **1** having an often mysterious or magical power to attract ⟨World travel has always been very *attractive* to me.⟩ — see FASCINATING 1

2 very pleasing to look at ⟨Generally the star of a TV commercial is an *attractive* person.⟩ — see BEAUTIFUL 1

attractiveness *n* **1** the power of irresistible attraction ⟨She had a certain *attractiveness* that came from her witty conversation.⟩ — see CHARM 2

2 the qualities in a person or thing that as a whole give pleasure to the senses ⟨The *attractiveness* of the Greek countryside has inspired poets since ancient times.⟩ — see BEAUTY 1

attribute *n* something that sets apart an individual from others of the same kind ⟨List the *attributes* of a mammal.⟩ — see CHARACTERISTIC

attribute *vb* **1** to explain (something) as being the result of something else ⟨*attributed* the quick rescue to the well-trained police force⟩ — see CREDIT 1

2 to give the reason for or cause of ⟨*attributes* his improved grades to a new study method⟩ — see EXPLAIN 2

attrition *n* a gradual weakening, loss, or destruction ⟨took the machinery out of operation since *attrition* had led to the main mechanism's breaking⟩ — see CORROSION

atypical *adj* **1** being out of the ordinary ⟨The postal service delivered the package with *atypical* speed.⟩ — see EXCEPTIONAL 1

2 departing from some accepted standard of what is normal ⟨Since that's an *atypical* response for an infant, you might want to have her hearing tested.⟩ — see DEVIANT

audacious *adj* **1** displaying or marked by rude boldness ⟨The candidate leveled *audacious* charges against his opponent.⟩ — see NERVY 1
2 foolishly adventurous or bold ⟨an *audacious* effort to start a business with no real plan or funding⟩ — see FOOLHARDY 1
3 inclined or willing to take risks ⟨*audacious* adventurers risking everything they had for a shot at glory⟩ — see BOLD 1

audacity *n* shameless boldness ⟨I can't believe he had the *audacity* to tell me to shut up!⟩ — see EFFRONTERY

audibly *adv* with one's normal voice speaking the words ⟨Don't mumble your lines—speak *audibly* so the audience can hear you.⟩ — see ALOUD

audit *n* a close look at or over someone or something in order to judge condition ⟨An energy *audit* of our house showed that we were losing lots of heat and needed to upgrade the insulation.⟩ — see INSPECTION

audit *vb* to look over closely (as for judging quality or condition) ⟨*audited* the equipment to make sure that everything was in working order⟩ — see INSPECT

auditorium *n* a large room or building for enclosed public gatherings ⟨Officials will hold the town meeting in the high school *auditorium*.⟩ — see HALL 3

auditory *adj* of, relating to, or experienced through the sense of hearing ⟨I have a bad *auditory* memory—unless I see a word in writing, and not just hear it, I forget it easily.⟩
synonyms acoustic (*or* acoustical), aural, auricular
related words audiovisual; audible, clear, discernible (*also* discernable), distinct, distinguishable, heard, perceptible
near antonyms faint, feeble, imperceptible, inaudible, indistinct, indistinguishable; low, noiseless, quiet, silent, soft, soundless
antonyms nonauditory

aught *n* the numerical symbol 0 or the absence of number or quantity represented by it ⟨For dates, the year is automatically listed as a pair of *aughts*, so the user has to scroll down to the correct figure.⟩ — see ZERO 1

augment *vb* to make greater in size, amount, or number ⟨Our volleyball team was *augmented* by some of the exchange team's players.⟩ — see INCREASE 1

augmentation *n* something added (as by growth) ⟨*Augmentations* to the benefits package over the years have resulted in a total of 12 paid holidays for employees.⟩ — see INCREASE 1

augur *n* one who predicts future events or developments ⟨ancient Roman *augurs* who predicted the future by reading the flight of birds⟩ — see PROPHET 1

augur *vb* **1** to show signs of a favorable or successful outcome ⟨The extended interview *augurs* well for your acceptance into that law school.⟩ — see BODE
2 to tell of or describe beforehand ⟨The fortune-teller *augured* nothing but a series of calamities for me.⟩ — see FORETELL

auguring *n* a declaration that something will happen in the future ⟨It's a good thing that people don't remember the tabloid's *augurings* a year later, since very few come to pass.⟩ — see PREDICTION

augury *n* **1** a declaration that something will happen in the future ⟨a yearbook *augury* that of all the graduates, he would be the most likely to succeed⟩ — see PREDICTION
2 something believed to be a sign or warning of a future event ⟨Some people believe that a broken mirror is an *augury* of seven years' bad luck.⟩ — see OMEN

august *adj* **1** having or showing a formal and serious or reserved manner ⟨The head of the bank is an *august* dark-haired gentleman.⟩ — see DIGNIFIED
2 large and impressive in size, grandeur, extent, or conception ⟨an *august* golden anniversary celebration for the company⟩ — see GRAND 1

augustness *n* **1** a dignified bearing or appearance befitting someone of royal status ⟨The opera star carries herself with the *augustness* of a queen.⟩ — see MAJESTY 1
2 impressiveness of beauty on a large scale ⟨the *augustness* of the Lincoln Memorial in our nation's capital⟩ — see MAGNIFICENCE

auld lang syne *n* the events or experience of former times ⟨Let us bid farewell to *auld lang syne* and welcome in the new year.⟩ — see PAST

aura *n* **1** a special quality or impression associated with something ⟨The monastery perched high on a mountaintop had an *aura* of unreality and mystery about it.⟩
synonyms air, aroma, atmosphere, climate, flavor, mood, note, odor, smell, temper, vibration(s)
related words mystique, romance; feel, feeling, sensation, sense, spirit; attribute, character, characteristic, image, mark, notion, peculiarity, picture, property, trait; color, illusion, overtone, semblance, suggestion, tone
2 a spiritual force that is held to emanate from or give animation to living beings ⟨alternative medical treatments that rely on the practitioner's ability to detect a patient's *aura*⟩ — see ENERGY 1

aural *adj* of, relating to, or experienced through the sense of hearing ⟨a quiet room for people seeking relief from the overload of *aural* stimulus just outside⟩ — see AUDITORY

au revoir *n* an expression of good wishes at parting ⟨The noise of the street was so loud that the quieter *au revoirs* of her friends went unheard.⟩ — see GOOD-BYE

auricular *adj* of, relating to, or experienced through the sense of hearing ⟨had *auricular* proof that the sun was up, as the birds began chirping⟩ — see AUDITORY

auspice *n* **1** **auspices** *pl* the financial support and general guidance for an undertaking ⟨a program for innovators that is under the *auspices* of a national corporation⟩
synonyms aegis (*also* egis), backing
related words bankrolling, endowment, financing, funding, subsidy; encouragement, fosterage; aid, assistance, help
2 something believed to be a sign or warning of a future event ⟨interpreted the teacher's smile as an *auspice* that he would get an A on his presentation⟩ — see OMEN

auspicious *adj* **1** having qualities which inspire hope ⟨It was an *auspicious* time to open a new business.⟩ — see HOPEFUL 1
2 pointing toward a happy outcome ⟨began the season with an *auspicious* win against their strongest football rival⟩ — see FAVORABLE 2

austere *adj* **1** given to exacting standards of discipline and self-restraint ⟨an *austere* conductor who is as tough on himself as he is on the orchestra⟩ — see SEVERE 1
2 harsh and threatening in manner or appearance ⟨an *austere* fortress at the top of some formidable cliffs⟩ — see GRIM 1

authentic *adj* **1** being exactly as appears or as claimed ⟨The signature on the old document was determined to be *authentic*.⟩
synonyms bona fide, genuine, honest, real, right, true
related words actual, historical, original; lawful, legal, legitimate; identifiable, recognizable, verifiable; proven, substantiated, validated, verified; incontestable, incontrovertible, indisputable, indubitable, irrefutable, undeniable, undoubted, unmistakable, unquestionable; veri-

table, very; accurate, correct, proper; pure, unadulterated, unalloyed
phrases for real
near antonyms artificial, factitious, imitation, man-made, simulated, synthetic, unnatural; concocted, fabricated, manufactured; deceptive, delusive, delusory, misleading
antonyms bogus, counterfeit, fake, false, mock, phony (*also* phoney), pseudo, sham, spurious, suppositious, supposititious, unauthentic, unreal
2 following an original exactly ⟨an *authentic* reconstruction of the Parthenon as it is believed to have looked when first built⟩ — see FAITHFUL 2
authentically *adv* in actual fact ⟨People are surprised to learn that he is an *authentically* certified graduate of clown college.⟩ — see VERY 2
authenticate *vb* **1** to declare (something) to be true or genuine ⟨A jeweler *authenticated* the diamond as real.⟩ — see CERTIFY 1
2 to give evidence or testimony to the truth or factualness of ⟨We require more than simply your word to *authenticate* this story.⟩ — see CONFIRM 1
author *n* **1** a person who creates a written work ⟨a brilliant novel by a first-time *author*⟩
synonyms pen, penman, scribe, writer
related words auteur, belletrist (*also* belle-lettrist), wordsmith; coauthor, coscenarist, cowriter; ghostwriter, hack, hatchet man, scribbler, wordmonger; biographer, hagiographer; autobiographer, memoirist, memorialist; fabulist, fictioneer, fictionist, novelist, romancer, storyteller; essayist, pamphleteer, satirist; dramatist, playwright, scenarist, screenwriter, scriptwriter; bard, poet, rhymer, versifier; blogger, columnist, journalist, newspaperman, reporter, sportswriter
phrases man of letters, woman of letters
antonyms nonauthor
2 a person who establishes a whole new field of endeavor ⟨the *author* of modern genetics⟩ — see FATHER 2
3 *cap* the being worshipped as the creator and ruler of the universe ⟨Let us thank the *Author* of our being for all the blessings He has bestowed.⟩ — see DEITY 2
author *vb* to compose and set down on paper the words of ⟨*authored* a new biography of Thomas Jefferson⟩ — see WRITE 1
authoritarian *adj* **1** fond of ordering people around ⟨grew up with an *authoritarian* older sister who thought she was in charge of everything⟩ — see BOSSY
2 given to exacting standards of discipline and self-restraint ⟨an *authoritarian* coach who runs football practice like it's boot camp⟩ — see SEVERE 1
authoritative *adj* **1** being the most accurate and apparently thorough ⟨This book is considered the most *authoritative* source on that subject.⟩ — see DEFINITIVE 1
2 having power over the minds or behavior of others ⟨After a couple of *authoritative* critics panned the movie, the other reviewers rushed to say how awful it was.⟩ — see INFLUENTIAL 1
3 fond of ordering people around ⟨He's very *authoritative* for someone who doesn't actually outrank us.⟩ — see BOSSY
authority *n* **1** a person with a high level of knowledge or skill in a field ⟨the leading *authority* on neural anatomy⟩ — see EXPERT
2 lawful control over the affairs of a political unit (as a nation) ⟨The sheriff had *authority* over the whole county.⟩ — see RULE 2
3 the power to direct the thinking or behavior of others usually indirectly ⟨speaks with a persuasive *authority* on matters of public health⟩ — see INFLUENCE 1
4 the right or means to command or control others ⟨By

the *authority* vested in me, I now pronounce you married.⟩ — see POWER 1
5 something (as a belief) that serves as the basis for another thing ⟨I had good *authority* to believe that the information was correct.⟩ — see REASON 2
6 something mentioned in a text as providing related and especially supporting information ⟨She cited several passages in the report as *authority* for her conclusions.⟩ — see REFERENCE 1
7 the capacity to persuade ⟨a strict grammarian whose pronouncements carried plenty of *authority* with my third-grade English teacher⟩ — see COGENCY 1
authorization *n* **1** the approval by someone in authority for the doing of something ⟨You will need the *authorization* of the council before you can act.⟩ — see PERMISSION
2 the granting of power to perform various acts or duties ⟨His *authorization* to go ahead with the project was finally given.⟩ — see COMMISSION 1
3 the right to act or move freely ⟨granted *authorization* to enter the military facility⟩ — see FREEDOM 2
authorize *vb* **1** to give official or legal power to ⟨Only the school nurse is *authorized* to give any necessary shots.⟩
synonyms accredit, certify, commission, empower, enable, invest, license (*also* licence), qualify, vest, warrant
related words approve, clear, credential, endorse (*also* indorse), OK (*or* okay), sanction; affirm, confirm, validate; inaugurate, induct, initiate, install, instate, swear in; allow, let, permit; enfranchise, entitle, privilege
near antonyms ban, bar, block, constrain, deny, disallow, disbar, discourage, disenfranchise, disfranchise, exclude, hinder, hold back, impede, inhibit, obstruct, prevent, shut out, stop; enjoin, forbid, interdict, outlaw, prohibit, proscribe, veto
antonyms disqualify
2 to give a right to ⟨This pass will *authorize* you to go backstage.⟩ — see ENTITLE 1
3 to give official acceptance of as satisfactory ⟨a system for sound reproduction that has been *authorized* as meeting the electronic industry's highest standards⟩ — see APPROVE
authorized *adj* ordered or allowed by those in authority ⟨an *authorized* biography of the former president⟩ — see OFFICIAL
auto *n* a self-propelled passenger vehicle on four wheels ⟨The *auto* gave people a level of mobility that they had never known before.⟩ — see CAR
autocracy *n* a system of government in which the ruler has unlimited power ⟨The Magna Carta is historically important because it signified the British rejection of *autocracy* and constituted the first formal restraining of the power of the monarch.⟩ — see DESPOTISM
autocrat *n* one who rules over a people with a sole, supreme, and usually hereditary authority ⟨The townspeople preferred benevolent *autocrats* to lead them.⟩ — see MONARCH 1
autocratic *also* **autocratical** *adj* **1** exercising power or authority without interference by others ⟨Democracy is supposed to protect the people against the rise of *autocratic* rulers.⟩ — see ABSOLUTE 1
2 fond of ordering people around ⟨an *autocratic* boss who is under the delusion that he's still an army colonel⟩ — see BOSSY
autograph *vb* to write one's name on (as a document) ⟨The boy asked the baseball player to *autograph* the bill of his cap.⟩ — see SIGN
automated *adj* designed to replace or decrease human labor and especially physical labor ⟨an *automated* car wash⟩ — see LABORSAVING
automatic *adj* **1** done instantly and without conscious

thought or decision ⟨Carl's *automatic* use of the brakes narrowly averted a collision.⟩

synonyms instinctive, instinctual, involuntary, mechanical, robotic, spontaneous

related words conditioned, natural, Pavlovian, reactive, reflex, simple, subliminal, unconscious, unforced, visceral; blind, inadvertent, unintended, unintentional, unwilling, unwitting; abrupt, quick, ready, sudden; ad-lib, extemporaneous, extempore, impromptu, improvised, offhand, offhanded, snap, spur-of-the-moment, unconsidered, unplanned, unpremeditated, unprepared, unprompted, unreasoned, unrehearsed, unstudied; casual, chance, chancy, haphazard, hasty, hit-or-miss, impetuous, impulsive, mindless, random, rash

near antonyms calculated, conscious, cultivated, deliberate, designed, intended, intentional, predetermined, prepared, projected, refined, rehearsed, volitional, voluntary, willful (*or* wilful); advised, aforethought, careful, considered, foresighted, forethoughtful, measured, meticulous, reasoned, studied, thoughtful

antonyms nonmechanical

2 designed to replace or decrease human labor and especially physical labor ⟨liked the ease of *automatic* bill payment⟩ — see LABORSAVING

automobile *n* a self-propelled passenger vehicle on four wheels ⟨I browsed the classified ads for used *automobiles* for sale.⟩ — see CAR

automobile *vb* to travel by a motorized vehicle ⟨I would rather *automobile* across the country than fly over it at 35,000 feet.⟩ — see DRIVE 2

automobilist *n* a person who travels by automobile ⟨With the introduction of affordable, mass-produced cars, more and more people left their horses at home and became *automobilists*.⟩ — see MOTORIST

autonomous *adj* not being under the rule or control of another ⟨an *autonomous* territory⟩ — see FREE 1

autonomy *n* **1** the act or power of making one's own choices or decisions ⟨The director agreed to make the film only on the condition that she be given complete *autonomy* for the casting.⟩ — see FREE WILL

2 the state of being free from the control or power of another ⟨The 13 British colonies made the momentous decision to seek *autonomy*.⟩ — see FREEDOM 1

autopsy *n* examination of a dead body especially to find out the cause of death ⟨The *autopsy* revealed an advanced stage of cancer.⟩

synonyms postmortem, postmortem examination

related words dissection

near antonyms biopsy, vivisection

auxiliary *adj* available to supply something extra when needed ⟨The auditorium has an *auxiliary* cooling system used only on particularly sweltering days.⟩

synonyms accessory, peripheral, supplemental, supplementary

related words backup, makeshift, substitute; added, additional, another, further; complementary, contributory; adjuvant, assistant, assisting, helping, supportive; secondary, subordinate, subservient, subsidiary; dispensable, excess, nonessential, superfluous, surplus, unessential

near antonyms basic, fundamental, primary, prime; all-important, essential, imperative, indispensable, integral, necessary, needed, needful, required, requisite, vital

antonyms chief, main, principal

avail *n* the capacity for being useful for some purpose ⟨Although I appreciate the concern, your help would be of little *avail* in this situation.⟩ — see USE 2

avail *vb* to provide with something useful or desirable ⟨All your begging will not *avail* you in the least.⟩ — see BENEFIT

available *adj* **1** possible to get ⟨The nursery's orchids are *available* by mail order only.⟩ ⟨Fare information is readily *available* on the website.⟩

synonyms accessible, acquirable, attainable, obtainable, procurable

related words getatable, reachable; appropriable, purchasable, rentable; furnished, provided, supplied; common, omnipresent, prevalent, ubiquitous, universal, widespread; free, free-for-all, open, public, unrestricted

phrases at the ready, on hand, on file, on tap

near antonyms limited, off-limits, restricted; deficient, lacking, missing, rare, scarce, uncommon

antonyms inaccessible, unattainable, unavailable, unobtainable

2 capable of or suitable for being used for a particular purpose ⟨My car is *available* should you need a way to get to the mall.⟩ — see USABLE 1

avarice *n* an intense selfish desire for wealth or possessions ⟨The bank official's embezzlement was motivated by pure *avarice*.⟩ — see GREED

avaricious *adj* having or marked by an eager and often selfish desire especially for material possessions ⟨an *avaricious* scheme to con the elderly couple out of thousands of dollars⟩ — see GREEDY 1

avariciousness *n* an intense selfish desire for wealth or possessions ⟨Their all-consuming *avariciousness* blinds them to the suffering of people just beyond their doorstep.⟩ — see GREED

avenge *vb* to punish in kind the wrongdoer responsible for ⟨a play about a prince who struggles to *avenge* his father's death⟩

synonyms redress, requite, retaliate, revenge

related words castigate, fix, get, penalize, punish, scourge; chasten, chastise, correct, discipline; right; compensate, pay (back), recompense, repay

phrases get even (for)

near antonyms absolve, condone, excuse, forgive, pardon, remit

avenger *n* one who inflicts punishment in return for an injury or offense ⟨a novel about a man who becomes the obsessed *avenger* of his sister's death⟩ — see NEMESIS 1

avenue *n* **1** a passage cleared for public vehicular travel ⟨a city famous for its broad, tree-lined *avenues*⟩ — see WAY 1

2 an established course for traveling from one place to another ⟨The two main *avenues* available to those joining in the California gold rush were the trail across the Southwest desert or the hazard-filled loop around Central and South America.⟩ — see PASSAGE 1

aver *vb* **1** to state as a fact usually forcefully ⟨He was tearfully *averring* his innocence.⟩ — see CLAIM 1

2 to state clearly and strongly ⟨The teen *averred* that she didn't need any help choosing her own clothes.⟩ — see ASSERT 1

average *adj* **1** being about midway between extremes of amount or size ⟨not a Chihuahua or a Saint Bernard, but a dog of more *average* dimensions⟩ — see MIDDLE 1

2 being of the type that is encountered in the normal course of events ⟨just an *average* day at the office⟩ — see ORDINARY 1

3 having or showing the qualities associated with the members of a particular group or kind ⟨The company's marketing people want to interview *average* teenagers to see what kinds of clothes appeal to them.⟩ — see TYPICAL 1

average *n* what is typical of a group, class, or series ⟨My cat's a cut above the *average* when it comes to being a finicky eater.⟩

synonyms norm, normal, par, standard

related words golden mean, mean, median, middle;

commonplace, ordinary, rule, run, status quo, usual; exemplar, representative

near antonyms abnormality, anomaly, rarity

averse *adj* having a natural dislike for something ⟨I'm not *averse* to broccoli if it's cooked right.⟩ — see ANTIPATHETIC 1

averseness *n* a strong feeling of not liking or approving ⟨our dog's strong *averseness* to getting a bath⟩ — see DISLIKE 1

aversion *n* 1 a dislike so strong as to cause stomach upset or queasiness ⟨I simply have this ingrained *aversion* to the sight of bloodshed.⟩ — see DISGUST

2 a strong feeling of not liking or approving ⟨couldn't overcome her *aversion* to her brother-in-law and pointedly avoided his company⟩ — see DISLIKE 1

3 something or someone that is hated ⟨Clichés should be the pet *aversion* of every good writer.⟩ — see HATE 2

avert *vb* to keep from happening by taking action in advance ⟨Her careful planning *averted* disaster.⟩ — see PREVENT

averting *n* the act or practice of keeping something from happening ⟨The *averting* of forest fires can be helped by the clearing of dry underbrush.⟩ — see PREVENTION

aviator *n* one who flies or is qualified to fly an aircraft or spacecraft ⟨The solo flight from New York to Paris by the *aviator* Charles Lindbergh captured the imagination of people around the world.⟩ — see PILOT

avid *adj* 1 having or marked by an eager and often selfish desire especially for material possessions ⟨stared at the array of jewels with an *avid* glint in his eye⟩ — see GREEDY 1

2 showing urgent desire or interest ⟨an *avid* baseball card collector⟩ — see EAGER

avidity *n* 1 an intense selfish desire for wealth or possessions ⟨treasure hunters spurred on by their *avidity*⟩ — see GREED

2 urgent desire or interest ⟨In her *avidity* to express her opinions, she frequently and unthinkingly interrupts people.⟩ — see EAGERNESS

avoid *vb* 1 to get or keep away from (as a responsibility) through cleverness or trickery ⟨trying to *avoid* writing thank-you notes for the gifts he didn't like⟩ — see ESCAPE 2

2 to put an end to by formal action ⟨We asked the court to *avoid* the contract because it was signed under duress.⟩ — see ABOLISH 1

avoidance *n* the act or a means of getting or keeping away from something undesirable ⟨Her habitual *avoidance* of conflict makes talking about problems with her difficult.⟩ — see ESCAPE 2

avoirdupois *n* the amount that something weighs ⟨The coach limited his recruiting to linebackers of a certain *avoirdupois*.⟩ — see WEIGHT 1

avouch *vb* 1 to declare (something) to be true or genuine ⟨a note from my doctor *avouching* that my medical condition did not disqualify me from playing in the game⟩ — see CERTIFY 1

2 to state as a fact usually forcefully ⟨The man *avouched* that he had never cheated on his taxes in his life.⟩ — see CLAIM 1

3 to state clearly and strongly ⟨She tends to *avouch* her opinions in such a way as to imply that anyone who thinks otherwise is wrong.⟩ — see ASSERT 1

avouchment *n* a solemn and often public declaration of the truth or existence of something ⟨Your *avouchment* of his good intentions means he won't be disciplined.⟩ — see PROTESTATION

avow *vb* 1 to state as a fact usually forcefully ⟨They *avowed* that the colonization of Mars in our lifetime is not only possible but probable.⟩ — see CLAIM 1

2 to state clearly and strongly ⟨They *avowed* their undying love for each other.⟩ — see ASSERT 1

avowal *n* 1 a solemn and often public declaration of the truth or existence of something ⟨The candidate felt compelled to make an *avowal* of his patriotism.⟩ — see PROTESTATION

2 an open declaration of something (as a fault or the commission of an offense) about oneself ⟨her own *avowal* that she was to blame for the accident⟩ — see CONFESSION

await *vb* 1 to believe in the future occurrence of (something) ⟨Members of the sect are confidently *awaiting* the imminent end of the world.⟩ — see EXPECT

2 to remain in place in readiness or expectation of something ⟨Crowds had been *awaiting* in the streets for hours.⟩ — see WAIT

awaited *adj* being in accordance with the prescribed, normal, or logical course of events ⟨At the *awaited* moment the President walked up to the lectern and began his address to the nation.⟩ — see DUE 2

awake *adj* 1 not sleeping or able to sleep ⟨was *awake* until 3:00 a.m.⟩ — see WAKEFUL

2 paying close attention usually for the purpose of anticipating approaching danger or opportunity ⟨*awake* to the possibility of fortunes to be made⟩ — see ALERT 1

awake *vb* 1 to cause to stop sleeping ⟨*awoke* the boys for breakfast⟩ — see WAKE 1

2 to cease to be asleep ⟨At the sound of breaking glass she *awoke* with a start.⟩ — see WAKE 2

awaken *vb* 1 to cause to stop sleeping ⟨Be quiet or you'll *awaken* the kids.⟩ — see WAKE 1

2 to cease to be asleep ⟨Guests at the B and B usually *awaken* to the smell of fresh pancakes.⟩ — see WAKE 2

award *n* 1 something given in recognition of achievement ⟨Faye received the highest *award* in the 16 and under category for her poem.⟩

synonyms accolade, decoration, distinction, honor, plume, premium, prize

related words badge, crown, cup, laurel, medal, order, plaque, plate, ribbon; applause, bravo, encomium, eulogy, homage, paean, panegyric, plaudit, tribute; citation, commendation, compliment, honorable mention

2 a position arrived at after consideration ⟨In their *award* the board of arbitrators declared that both writers deserved screen credit for their contributions to the final screenplay.⟩ — see DECISION 1

award *vb* 1 to give something as a token of gratitude or admiration for a service or achievement ⟨We will *award* the top three contestants in the essay competition.⟩ — see REWARD

2 to give the ownership or benefit of (something) formally or publicly ⟨The jury *awarded* damages to the defendant.⟩ — see CONFER 1

aware *adj* having specified facts or feelings actively impressed on the mind ⟨As she was being wheeled out of surgery, she became dimly *aware* that her parents were in the room.⟩ — see CONSCIOUS 1

awareness *n* a state of being aware ⟨While strolling in the big city, maintain an *awareness* of what's going on around you.⟩ — see ATTENTION 2

awash *adj* 1 containing, covered with, or thoroughly penetrated by water ⟨The streets were *awash* from the heavy rains.⟩ — see WET 1

2 possessing or covered with great numbers or amounts of something specified ⟨The literary review is currently *awash* in submissions and will not be accepting any more until next year.⟩ — see RIFE

away *adj* 1 not close in time or space ⟨the store is far *away* from here⟩ ⟨Summer vacation is still three months *away*.⟩ — see DISTANT 1

2 not at a certain place ⟨He's *away* right now, but he should be back at the office next week.⟩ — see ABSENT 1

away *adv* from this or that place ⟨Don't walk *away* while I'm still talking to you.⟩

synonyms down, hence, off, out

related words apart, elsewhere; abroad, afield, astray

awe *n* the rapt attention and deep emotion caused by the sight of something extraordinary ⟨was in *awe* of the sinewy Olympic runners⟩ — see WONDER 2

awed *adj* filled with amazement or wonder ⟨She gave the nationally known golfer an *awed* look.⟩ — see OPEN-MOUTHED

awesome *adj* **1** causing wonder or astonishment ⟨the *awesome* power of the sea⟩ — see MARVELOUS 1

2 of the very best kind ⟨The food at the Sunday brunch was just *awesome*.⟩ — see EXCELLENT

awestruck *also* **awestricken** *adj* **1** affected with sudden and great wonder or surprise ⟨The crowds were *awestruck* by the aerial feats of the stunt pilots.⟩ — see THUNDERSTRUCK

2 filled with amazement or wonder ⟨*awestruck* by the majesty of the Sierra Nevada Mountains⟩ — see OPENMOUTHED

awful *adj* **1** causing intense displeasure, disgust, or resentment ⟨That's an *awful* thing to say about someone.⟩ — see OFFENSIVE 1

2 causing wonder or astonishment ⟨the *awful* power of Niagara Falls⟩ — see MARVELOUS 1

3 extremely disturbing or repellent ⟨Spare me the *awful* details of the murder.⟩ — see HORRIBLE 1

4 extremely unsatisfactory ⟨I can't believe I spent good money to see that movie—it was *awful!*⟩ — see WRETCHED 1

awful *adv* to a great degree ⟨That's *awful* sweet of you!⟩ — see VERY 1

awfully *adv* to a great degree ⟨I'm *awfully* sorry.⟩ — see VERY 1

awfulness *n* the quality of inspiring intense dread or dismay ⟨The *awfulness* of the car accident can scarcely be described.⟩ — see HORROR 1

awkward *adj* **1** lacking social grace and assurance ⟨preteens feeling *awkward* at their first formal dance⟩

synonyms clumsy, gauche, graceless, inelegant, rustic (*also* rustical), stiff, stilted, uncomfortable, uneasy, ungraceful, wooden

related words angular, gawky, lubberly, ungainly; boorish, clownish, uncouth; abashed, discomfited, discomforted, discomposed, disconcerted, discountenanced, embarrassed; self-conscious; agitated, chagrined, dismayed, disquieted, distressed, disturbed, fazed, flustered, jittery, jumpy, mortified, nervous, perturbed, rattled, unsettled, upset; diffident, insecure, meek, modest, self-doubting, timid, unassertive, unassuming, unpretentious

near antonyms assured, calm, collected, composed, confident, cool, placid, poised, secure, self-assured, self-confident, self-possessed, serene, tranquil, undisturbed, unperturbed

antonyms graceful, suave, urbane

2 showing or marked by a lack of skill and tact (as in dealing with a situation) ⟨The *awkward* handling of the seating arrangements at the wedding reception resulted in many hurt feelings.⟩

synonyms botched, bungling, clumsy, fumbled, inept, inexpert, maladroit

related words amateur, amateurish, crude, green, incompetent, ineffectual, inefficient, inexperienced, unpolished, unprofessional, unskilled, unskillful; careless, sloppy, tacky, tactless; ill-advised, ineffective, ineffectual, misdirected, misguided

near antonyms able, accomplished, adept, capable, clever, competent, consummate, crackerjack, expert, masterful, masterly, polished, professional, proficient, skilled, skillful, talented; diplomatic, easy, effortless, gracious, smooth, tactful

antonyms adroit, deft, dexterous (*also* dextrous), facile

3 causing embarrassment ⟨the *awkward* situation of having to listen as your host and hostess quarrel loudly in the next room⟩

synonyms discomfiting, disconcerting, disturbing, embarrassing, flustering, uncomfortable

related words confusing, difficult, disagreeable, impossible, inconvenient, intolerable, troublesome, unpleasant, unwieldy; unsettling; debasing, degrading, demeaning, humbling, humiliating, mortifying

near antonyms agreeable, comfortable, convenient, pleasing

4 causing difficulty, discomfort, or annoyance ⟨Our surprise guests came at a very *awkward* time.⟩ — see IN-CONVENIENT 1

5 difficult to use or operate especially because of size, weight, or design ⟨That manual can opener is *awkward* to hold.⟩ — see CUMBERSOME

6 having or showing an inability to move in a graceful manner ⟨an *awkward* person who is always tripping over herself⟩ — see CLUMSY 2

7 lacking or showing a lack of nimbleness in using one's hands ⟨an *awkward* catch of a fly ball⟩ — see CLUMSY 1

awning *n* a raised covering over something for decoration or protection ⟨stayed under the *awning* outside the shop during the rainstorm⟩ — see CANOPY

awry *adj* inclined or twisted to one side ⟨The shutters that still remained on the run-down old house were all *awry*.⟩

synonyms askew, aslant, cockeyed, crazy, crooked, listing, lopsided, oblique, pitched, skewed, slanted, slanting, slantwise, tilted, tipping, uneven

related words asymmetrical (*or* asymmetric), unbalanced, unsymmetrical; contorted, disordered, distorted, irregular

phrases out of plumb (*or* off plumb)

near antonyms ordered, orderly, regular, uniform; balanced, symmetrical (*or* symmetric)

antonyms even, level, straight

awry *adv* off the desired or intended path or course ⟨Their plans for an outdoor wedding went *awry* when they got a freak hailstorm the night before.⟩ — see WRONG

¹aye *also* **ay** *adv* **1** on every relevant occasion ⟨I *aye* thought that she was the loveliest woman I ever laid eyes on.⟩ — see ALWAYS 1

2 for all time ⟨a friendship that will *aye* endure⟩ — see EVER 1

²aye *also* **ay** *adv* used to express agreement ⟨*Aye*, you're right about that!⟩ — see YES

B

babble *n* unintelligible or meaningless talk ⟨The baby's good-natured *babble* and random gurglings were cute, but not very helpful in determining what he wanted.⟩ — see GIBBERISH 1

babble *vb* 1 to speak rapidly, inarticulately, and usually unintelligibly ⟨in such a rush to tell us the news that she just *babbled*⟩
synonyms chat, chatter, drivel, drool, gabble, gibber, jabber, prattle, sputter
related words blabber, blither, gab, jaw, patter, prate, rattle, run on, tittle-tattle, troll, yak (*also* yack); maunder, mouth, mumble, murmur, mutter; stammer, stutter; screech, shout, shriek
near antonyms articulate, enunciate, pronounce
2 to engage in casual or rambling conversation ⟨The little girls *babbled* contentedly for the whole ride home.⟩ — see CHAT 1

babbler *n* a person who talks constantly ⟨Spending too much time with that *babbler* gives me a headache.⟩ — see CHATTERBOX

babe *n* 1 a person who is just starting out in a field of activity ⟨I was just a *babe* when I started my political career.⟩ — see BEGINNER
2 a recently born person ⟨a *babe* in arms, too young even to crawl⟩ — see BABY 1

babel *n* 1 a place of uproar or confusion ⟨On opening day the area's newest big-box store was an incredible *babel*.⟩ — see MADHOUSE
2 loud, confused, and usually inharmonious sound ⟨the *babel* of languages and accents that can be heard at the city's farmers' market every weekend⟩ — see NOISE 1

babushka *n* a scarf worn on the head ⟨an elderly Russian woman with a *babushka*⟩ — see BANDANNA

baby *n* 1 a recently born person ⟨The *baby* is just learning to sit up, so be careful.⟩
synonyms babe, child, infant, newborn
related words cherub; foundling, nursling, suckling; preemie (*also* premie); bantling, kid, kiddo, moppet, toddler, tot; boy, nipper, tad; juvenile, minor, youngster, youth; brat, imp, squirt, urchin, whippersnapper; girl, hoyden, tomboy
near antonyms adult, grown-up; elder, graybeard, oldster, old-timer, senior, senior citizen
2 a successful result brought about by hard work ⟨a small film that was a labor of love and the *baby* that the director was proudest of⟩ — see ACCOMPLISHMENT 1
3 a person who makes frequent complaints usually about little things ⟨Don't be such a *baby*—you'll get your turn.⟩ — see CRYBABY

baby *vb* to treat with great or excessive care ⟨He *babied* his car, faithfully washing it every week.⟩
synonyms coddle, dandle, indulge, mollycoddle, nurse, pamper, spoil
related words cater (to), humor; content, delight, gladden, gratify, mother, oblige, please, satisfy; appease, mollify, pacify, placate, soothe
near antonyms control, discipline, restrain; oppress; neglect, overlook, slight; molest, outrage, violate; harm, hurt, injure, oppress, persecute, torment, torture, victimize
antonyms abuse, ill-treat, ill-use, maltreat, manhandle, mishandle, mistreat, misuse

babyish *adj* having or showing the annoying qualities (as silliness) associated with children ⟨The boy now thinks that playing with blocks is a rather *babyish* activity.⟩ — see CHILDISH

babysitter *n* a person employed to care for a young child or children ⟨a *babysitter* who is a great favorite with the kids because she's always thinking of fun things to do⟩ — see NURSE

back *adj* being at or in the part of something opposite the front part ⟨She carried all the presents in the *back* door, as the children were playing in the front yard.⟩
synonyms aft, after, hind, hinder, hindmost, posterior, rear, rearward
related words dorsal
near antonyms ventral
antonyms anterior, forward, front

back *adv* 1 toward the opposite direction ⟨She turned *back* for one last comment.⟩ — see AROUND 2
2 toward the rear ⟨She turned around and looked *back* toward him.⟩ — see BACKWARD 1

back *n* 1 a behind part or surface ⟨The *back* of the page was blank.⟩ — see REAR 1
2 a vulnerable point ⟨a candidate needing a loyal aide who can be relied upon to always watch his *back*⟩ — see ACHILLES' HEEL

back *vb* 1 to promote the interests or cause of ⟨She enthusiastically *backed* the plan to renovate and upgrade the school's facilities.⟩ — see SUPPORT 1
2 to provide (someone) with what is useful or necessary to achieve an end ⟨A number of influential people have already agreed to *back* the candidate.⟩ — see HELP 1
3 to provide evidence or information for (as a claim or idea) ⟨The author needs to *back* her thesis with more facts.⟩ — see SUPPORT 4

back away *vb* to move back or away (as from something difficult, dangerous, or disagreeable) ⟨I *backed away* from the snake very slowly and carefully.⟩ — see RETREAT 1

backbone *n* 1 a column of bones supporting the trunk of a vertebrate animal ⟨We found the *backbone* of a fish lying on the beach.⟩ — see SPINE
2 the strength of mind that enables a person to endure pain or hardship ⟨It takes *backbone* to keep the family farm running.⟩ — see FORTITUDE

back down *vb* to break a promise or agreement ⟨If you *back down* about dinner again, I'm not going to agree to another date.⟩ — see RENEGE 1

backdrop *n* the physical conditions or features that form the setting against which something is viewed ⟨Visitors dine at the restaurant with a dramatic stretch of the Pacific Ocean as a jaw-dropping *backdrop*.⟩ — see BACKGROUND 1

backer *n* 1 a person who actively supports or favors a cause ⟨*Backers* of prison reform held a rally in front of the statehouse.⟩ — see EXPONENT 1
2 a person who takes the responsibility for some other person or thing ⟨All financial *backers* will be expected to offer some input into the company's decisions.⟩ — see SPONSOR
3 someone associated with another to give assistance or moral support ⟨The student's *backers* spoke at the school board meeting on her behalf.⟩ — see ALLY

backfire *vb* to have the reverse of the desired or expected effect ⟨My plan to throw her a surprise party *backfired* when she ended up planning a getaway for her birthday.⟩
synonyms boomerang

related words collapse, flop, flunk, fold, wash out; flounder, struggle; decline, slip, slump, wane

near antonyms succeed; flourish, prosper, thrive

background *n* **1** the physical conditions or features that form the setting against which something is viewed ⟨They got married on a mountain top with the sunset as *background*.⟩

synonyms backdrop, ground

related words scene, scenery, set, stage; environment, milieu, setting, surroundings

near antonyms foreground; center, focal point, focus, heart

2 the place and time in which the action for a portion of a dramatic work (as a movie) is set ⟨The *background* of that movie is the World War II era.⟩ — see SCENE 1

backhanded *adj* not being or expressing what one appears to be or express ⟨"Your work is surprisingly good" is a bit of a *backhanded* compliment.⟩ — see INSINCERE

backing *n* **1** an act or instance of helping ⟨The teacher's *backing* on the science project was invaluable.⟩ — see HELP 1

2 the financial support and general guidance for an undertaking ⟨The museum exhibition would not have been possible without corporate *backing*.⟩ — see AUSPICE 1

back of *prep* at, to, or toward the rear of ⟨The equipment shed is a concrete structure *back of* the school.⟩ — see BEHIND 1

back off *vb* to break a promise or agreement ⟨You'd better not *back off* on your promise to do all the planning for the party.⟩ — see RENEGE 1

backpack *n* a soft-sided case designed for carrying belongings especially on the back ⟨Anna stuffed her *backpack* with so many books that she could barely lift it.⟩ — see PACK 1

backside *n* the part of the body upon which someone sits ⟨Our *backsides* were sore after sitting on those hard benches for so long.⟩ — see BUTTOCKS

backslider *n* a person who has sunk below the normal moral standard ⟨The evangelist was determined to win back the *backsliders* who had fallen away.⟩ — see DEGENERATE

back talk *n* disrespectful or argumentative talk given in response to a command or request ⟨His mother sent him to his room because of his constant *back talk*.⟩

synonyms cheek, impertinence, impudence, insolence, mouth, sass, sauce

related words comeback, rejoinder, retort, riposte, wisecrack; cuteness, discourtesy, disrespect, guff, impoliteness, nonsense, rudeness, tactlessness; audacity, boldness, brazenness; coarseness, crassness, vulgarity; abruptness, bluffness, brusqueness, crossness, curtness, gruffness, surliness

near antonyms civility, cordiality, courtesy, diplomacy, politeness, tactfulness; consideration, gallantry, gentility, graciousness, smoothness, suaveness, suavity; deference, respect; affability

backup *n* **1** a crowded mass (as of cars) that impedes or blocks movement ⟨There was the inevitable *backup* of travelers trying to pass through airport security.⟩ — see JAM 1

2 a person or thing that takes the place of another ⟨You didn't get the lead position, but you can be the *backup* to the chosen singer.⟩ — see SUBSTITUTE

backward *adj* **1** directed, turned, or done toward the back ⟨A *backward* turn on ice skates is hard to learn because you can't see where you're going.⟩

synonyms rearward, retrograde

related words reverse, reversed; aft, after, hind, posterior, rear; astern, sternforemost

near antonyms forward

2 not comfortable around people ⟨Curiously, the quiet, *backward* man opened up when around other introverts.⟩ — see SHY 2

backward *or* **backwards** *adv* **1** toward the rear ⟨Looking *backward*, we could see the town receding in the distance.⟩

synonyms back, rearward (*also* rearwards)

related words astern, sternforemost; counterclockwise, left-handed, left-handedly, retrograde, reversely

near antonyms before

antonyms ahead, along, forth, forward, forwards, on, onward (*also* onwards)

2 toward the opposite direction ⟨The loud noise prompted him to glance *backward* to see what was happening.⟩ — see AROUND 2

backwater *n* a rural region that forms the edge of the settled or developed part of a country ⟨a distant *backwater* that didn't even have electricity at that time⟩ — see FRONTIER 2

backwoods *pl n* a rural region that forms the edge of the settled or developed part of a country ⟨He lived far out in the *backwoods* and raised hogs for a living.⟩ — see FRONTIER 2

bad *adj* **1** falling short of a standard ⟨A *bad* first attempt at making pie resulted in a soggy, inedible mess.⟩

synonyms bush, crummy (*also* crumby), deficient, dissatisfactory, ill, inferior, lame, lousy, off, paltry, poor, punk, sour, substandard, unacceptable, unsatisfactory, wanting, wretched, wrong

related words abysmal, atrocious, awful, brutal, deplorable, detestable, disastrous, dreadful, execrable, horrendous, horrible, pathetic, stinky, terrible, unspeakable; defective, faulty, flawed; egregious, flagrant, gross; bum, cheesy, coarse, common, crappy [*slang*], cut-rate, junky, lesser, low-grade, mediocre, miserable, reprehensible, rotten, rubbishy, second-rate, shoddy, sleazy, trashy; abominable, odious, vile; useless, valueless, worthless; inadequate, insufficient, lacking, meager (*or* meagre), mean, niggardly, scanty, shabby, short, skimp, skimpy, spare, stingy; miscreant, scurrilous, villainous; counterfeit, fake, phony (*also* phoney), sham

phrases below par (*or* under par)

near antonyms classic, classical; A1, bang-up, banner, capital, choice, crackerjack, dandy, divine, excellent, exceptional, fabulous, fine, first-class, first-rate, grand, great, heavenly, high-test, jim-dandy, keen, marvelous (*or* marvellous), mean, neat, nifty, noble, par excellence, perfect, premium, prime, sensational, slick, splendid, stellar, sterling, superb, superior, superlative, supernal, swell, terrific, tip-top, top, top-notch, unsurpassed, wonderful; better, exceptional, fancy, high-grade, special, sufficient; average, fair, mediocre, middling, minimal, so-so, unexceptional; suitable, useful, worthy; gratifying, satisfying

antonyms acceptable, adequate, all right, decent, fine, OK (*or* okay), passable, respectable, satisfactory, standard, tolerable

2 not conforming to a high moral standard; morally unacceptable ⟨Stealing is just plain *bad*.⟩

synonyms dark, evil, immoral, iniquitous, nefarious, rotten, sinful, unethical, unlawful, unrighteous, unsavory, vicious, vile, villainous, wicked, wrong

related words base, contemptible, despicable, dirty, disreputable, evil-minded, ignoble, ill, low, mean, snide, sordid; atrocious, cruel, infamous, nasty; blamable, blameworthy, censurable, objectionable, obscene, offensive, reprehensible; corrupt, debased, debauched, degenerate, depraved, dissolute, libertine, loose, perverted, reprobate, sick, unhealthy; defiling, noxious, pernicious, ugly, ungodly, unwholesome; banned, barred, condemned, discouraged, forbidden, illegal, interdicted, outlawed, prohibited, proscribed, unauthorized, unclean; disallowed; execrable, lousy, miserable, wretched; errant, erring, fallen, unprincipled, unscrupulous; improper, incorrect, indecent, indecorous, naughty, unbecoming, unseemly, vulgar; dishonest, dishonorable

near antonyms elevated, high, high-minded, law-abiding, legitimate, lofty, noble, principled, reputable, scrupulous; allowed, authorized, legal, licensed, permissible, permitted; approved, endorsed (*also* indorsed), sanctioned; abetted, encouraged, promoted, supported; clean, correct, decent, decorous, exemplary, proper, seemly; blameless, commendable, creditable, guiltless, legitimate; chaste, immaculate, incorruptible, innocent, inoffensive, irreproachable, perfect, pure, spotless, uncorrupted, unerring, unfallen, unobjectionable, venerable, wholesome; esteemed, respected, upstanding, worthy

antonyms decent, ethical, good, honest, honorable, just, moral, right, righteous, sublime, upright, virtuous
3 causing or capable of causing harm ⟨Sitting too close to the television is said to be *bad* for the eyes.⟩ — see HARMFUL
4 engaging in or marked by childish misbehavior ⟨The children were *bad*, so they didn't get dessert.⟩ — see NAUGHTY
5 feeling unhappiness ⟨Hearing about the world's miseries always makes him feel *bad*.⟩ — see SAD 1
6 having a fault ⟨a letter written in *bad* French⟩ — see FAULTY
7 having undergone organic breakdown ⟨I think the milk has turned *bad*.⟩ — see ROTTEN 1
8 not giving pleasure to the mind or senses ⟨The air in the damp basement had a very *bad* smell.⟩ — see UNPLEASANT
9 of low quality ⟨She bought *bad* shoes that fell apart within a week.⟩ — see CHEAP 2
10 temporarily suffering from a disorder of the body ⟨I've been feeling *bad* all week with this cold.⟩ — see SICK 1
11 having no legal or binding force ⟨All known claims on the property were dismissed by the court as *bad*.⟩ — see NULL 1
bad *adv* in an unsatisfactory way ⟨You didn't do too *bad* on the treadmill test.⟩ — see BADLY 1
bad *n* that which is morally unacceptable ⟨There's *bad* and good in all people.⟩ — see EVIL
badly *adv* **1** in an unsatisfactory way ⟨I'm afraid you performed quite *badly* in our last rehearsal.⟩
synonyms bad, deficiently, inadequately, poorly, unacceptably, unsatisfactorily, wretchedly
related words abysmally, atrociously, awfully, damnably, deplorably, detestably, disastrously, dreadfully, execrably, horrendously, horribly, horrifically, rottenly, terribly; unbearably; inappropriately, incorrectly, indecently, reprehensibly, unsuitably, vulgarly; naughtily; egregiously, flagrantly, grossly; miserably, shoddily, sleazily, trashily, unspeakably; abominably, odiously, vilely; inferiorly, insufficiently, meagerly, meanly, niggardly, scantily, scantly, shabbily, skimpily, sparely, stingily
near antonyms appropriately, congruously, correctly, decorously, felicitously, fittingly, meetly, rightly, seemly, suitably; exactly, faithfully, ideally, precisely; satisfyingly
antonyms acceptably, adequately, all right, fine, good, nicely, OK (*or* okay), passably, satisfactorily, so-so, tolerably, well
2 to a great degree ⟨Blood donors are *badly* needed this time of year.⟩ — see VERY 1

bad–mouth *vb* to express scornfully one's low opinion of ⟨She promptly *bad-mouthed* that awful movie to everyone she knew.⟩ — see DECRY 1
badness *n* the state or quality of being utterly evil ⟨The villain's complete *badness* made him a good foil for the unfailingly virtuous hero.⟩ — see ENORMITY 1
baffle *vb* **1** to prevent from achieving a goal ⟨The language barrier *baffled* everyone and discouraged us from attempting another teleconference.⟩ — see FRUSTRATE 1
2 to throw into a state of mental uncertainty ⟨They were *baffled* by the wording of the clause in the insurance policy.⟩ — see CONFUSE 1
bafflement *n* a state of mental uncertainty ⟨His complete *bafflement* as to the point of the joke was in itself funny.⟩ — see CONFUSION 1
bag *n* **1** a container made of a flexible material (as paper or plastic) ⟨She carries her towel and other supplies to the beach in a bright, colorful *bag* slung over her arm.⟩
synonyms poke [*chiefly Southern & Midland*], pouch, sack
related words carryall, portmanteau, traveling bag; bundle, pack, package, packet, parcel; backpack, barracks bag, duffel bag, haversack, knapsack, rucksack, satchel, tote; handbag, pocketbook, purse, tote bag; ditty bag, flight bag, garment bag, kit bag, shopping bag, work bag
2 a container for carrying money and small personal items ⟨She put a pad and pen in her *bag*.⟩ — see PURSE
bag *vb* **1** to extend outward beyond a usual point ⟨The shirt *bagged* at the waist.⟩ — see BULGE 1
2 to take physical control or possession of (something) suddenly or forcibly ⟨I *bagged* a deer while hunting last weekend.⟩ — see CATCH 1
3 to give up (a job or office) ⟨If the supervisor says one more nasty thing to me, I'm going to *bag* this stupid job.⟩ — see QUIT 1
4 to obtain (as a goal) through effort ⟨She *bagged* a full fellowship at one of the nation's leading universities.⟩ — see ACHIEVE 1
5 to receive as return for effort ⟨*bagged* an acting nomination for a truly inspired performance⟩ — see EARN 1
bail out *vb* **1** to leave a place often for another ⟨If the meeting seems like it will never end, find an excuse to *bail out*.⟩ — see GO 2
2 to remove from danger or harm ⟨The government *bailed out* the savings and loan industry.⟩ — see SAVE 2
bait *n* **1** something used to attract animals to a hook or into a trap ⟨Cheese is the traditional *bait* for trapping mice.⟩
synonyms decoy, lure
related words ambush, net, trap; hook, snare, troll; plug; scent, spinner, stool pigeon; appeal, attraction, call, draw, incentive, pull; enticement, seducement, seduction, temptation; entanglement, entrapment
near antonyms repellent (*also* repellant)
2 something that persuades one to perform an action for pleasure or gain ⟨The promise of free vacation is surefire *bait* to get people to agree to be chaperones for school trips.⟩ — see LURE 1
bait *vb* **1** to attack repeatedly with mean put-downs or insults ⟨The coach trained his players to keep their cool when members of the opposing team *baited* them.⟩ — see TEASE 2
2 to lead away from a usual or proper course by offering some pleasure or advantage ⟨The investment scheme cunningly *baits* the greedy and the unscrupulous.⟩ — see LURE
baiter *n* **1** a person who causes repeated emotional pain, distress, or annoyance to another ⟨a journalist known as a *baiter* of political candidates⟩ — see TORMENTOR

2 one that tries to get a person to give in to a desire ⟨My sister is quite the mischievous *baiter*, always offering candy even though she knows I'm on a diet.⟩ — see TEMPTER

balance *n* **1** a condition in which opposing forces are equal to one another ⟨In order to determine the weight of that beaker, you need to get the two pans of the scale in perfect *balance*.⟩
synonyms counterpoise, equilibrium, equipoise, poise
related words counterbalance, offset; firmness, fixedness, security, stability, steadiness
near antonyms changeability, inconstancy, insecurity, instability, mutability, precariousness, shakiness, unsteadiness, volatility
antonyms disequilibration, disequilibrium, imbalance, nonequilibrium, unbalance
2 a balanced, pleasing, or suitable arrangement of parts ⟨The *balance* of the landscaping is in keeping with the symmetry of so many 18th-century mansions.⟩ — see HARMONY 1
3 a device for measuring weight ⟨Use a *balance* to make sure you get the amounts precisely correct.⟩ — see ¹SCALE
4 a force or influence that makes an opposing force ineffective or less effective ⟨The *balance* to the mountain of complaints are the many letters of praise that we also receive.⟩ — see COUNTERBALANCE
5 a remaining group or portion ⟨and the *balance* of the contestants should stand in that last corner⟩ — see REMAINDER 1

balance *vb* **1** to make equal in amount, degree, or status ⟨We tried to *balance* the total amount of money spent on gifts for each child.⟩ — see EQUALIZE
2 to show uncertainty about the right course of action ⟨His tendency to *balance* and waffle on certain hot-button issues may hurt him in the general election.⟩ — see HESITATE
3 to give what is owed for ⟨She had to *balance* her account with the store.⟩ — see PAY 2

balanced *adj* **1** having full use of one's mind and control over one's actions ⟨No *balanced* person would believe that aliens are about to take over.⟩ — see SANE
2 having the parts agreeably related ⟨A *balanced* arrangement of the furniture made the room look more spacious.⟩ — see HARMONIOUS 2

bald *adj* **1** lacking a usual or natural covering ⟨Trees that are *bald* in the winter aren't the best for giving a home year-round privacy.⟩ — see NAKED 2
2 free from all additions or embellishment ⟨Try to avoid the *bald* statement "You're wrong!" when trying to reason with someone.⟩ — see PLAIN 1
3 not subject to misinterpretation or more than one interpretation ⟨Her angry neighbor's *bald* accusations offended her.⟩ — see CLEAR 2

baleful *adj* **1** being or showing a sign of evil or calamity to come ⟨a dark, *baleful* sky portending a tornado⟩ — see OMINOUS
2 causing or capable of causing harm ⟨She contends that the violent content of so much of popular entertainment is a *baleful* influence on our society.⟩ — see HARMFUL
3 likely to cause or capable of causing death ⟨a medicine that is beneficial in small doses but *baleful* in large⟩ — see DEADLY 1

balk *n* something that makes movement or progress difficult ⟨The extravagant centerpiece on the table proved to be a *balk* to the flow of the diners' conversation.⟩ — see ENCUMBRANCE
balk *vb* to prevent from achieving a goal ⟨The young man refused to be *balked* in achieving his goals.⟩ — see FRUSTRATE 1

balky *adj* given to resisting authority or another's control ⟨a *balky* toddler who only seemed to know the word "no" when told to do something⟩ — see DISOBEDIENT

¹ball *n* **1** a more or less round body or mass ⟨the little rubber *ball* used in racquetball⟩ ⟨a *ball* of string⟩
synonyms globe, orb, sphere
related words globule; ellipse, loop, oval, spheroid; circle, ring, round; chunk, clump, gob, hunk, lump, nugget, wad
near antonyms block, rectangle, square
2 a usually round or cone-shaped little piece of lead made to be fired from a firearm ⟨found a cache of musket *balls* while excavating the old fort⟩ — see BULLET

²ball *n* a social gathering for dancing ⟨a *ball* to celebrate the inauguration⟩ — see DANCE

ball *vb* to form into a round compact mass ⟨*balled* up the paper and threw it at the garbage can⟩ — see WAD

ballad *n* a short musical composition for the human voice often with instrumental accompaniment ⟨a haunting *ballad* about lost love and loneliness⟩ — see SONG 1

balloon *vb* **1** to become greater in extent, volume, amount, or number ⟨the number of students who stay home sick *balloons* every winter⟩ — see INCREASE 2
2 to extend outward beyond a usual point ⟨The paper bag *ballooned* and blew away as the wind lifted it skyward.⟩ — see BULGE 1

ballot *n* **1** a piece of paper indicating a person's preferences in an election ⟨We collected all of the *ballots* from the students voting for class president.⟩
synonyms vote
related words aye (*also* ay), yea; nay, no; blackball; referendum; ticket; absentee ballot, Australian ballot, secret ballot, short ballot, write-in
2 the right to formally express one's position or will in an election ⟨He believes that even convicted felons should have the *ballot*.⟩ — see VOTE 1

ballyhoo *n* **1** a state of noisy, confused activity ⟨It turned out that the *ballyhoo* was the result of a movie being filmed on the street.⟩ — see COMMOTION
2 information released to the media that is designed to gain public attention or support for a person, business, or cause ⟨the usual *ballyhoo* intended to fill the seats at megaplexes around the country⟩ — see PUBLICITY

ballyhoo *vb* **1** to praise or publicize lavishly and often excessively ⟨That reviewer always *ballyhoos* any book by one of his pet authors.⟩ — see TOUT 1
2 to provide publicity for ⟨Technology companies usually spend big bucks *ballyhooing* their new generation of devices.⟩ — see PUBLICIZE 1

balminess *n* lack of good sense or judgment ⟨Only sheer *balminess* would possess someone to invest in that loser of a stock.⟩ — see FOOLISHNESS 1

balmy *adj* **1** marked by temperatures that are neither too high nor too low ⟨a *balmy* spring day⟩ — see CLEMENT 1
2 not harsh or stern especially in nature or effect ⟨A pleasant, *balmy* breeze was all that stirred the wildflowers growing near the shore.⟩ — see GENTLE 1
3 showing or marked by a lack of good sense or judgment ⟨the *balmy* notion that he could rely on winning the lottery⟩ — see FOOLISH 1

balustrade *n* a protective barrier consisting of a horizontal bar and its supports ⟨an ornately carved *balustrade* for the staircase⟩ — see RAILING

ban *n* **1** a prayer that harm will come to someone ⟨a father's *ban* upon his ungrateful son⟩ — see CURSE 1
2 an order that something not be done or used ⟨a quiet seaside resort with a *ban* on noise after midnight⟩ — see PROHIBITION 2

ban *vb* **1** to order not to do or use or to be done or used

⟨The company absolutely *bans* smoking within its buildings.⟩ — see FORBID

2 to prevent the participation, consideration, or inclusion of ⟨The university *banned* those caught in the cheating scandal from graduation ceremonies.⟩ — see EXCLUDE

banal *adj* **1** lacking in qualities that make for spirit and character ⟨the sort of *banal* story that appeals to readers not looking for intellectual stimulation⟩ — see WISHY-WASHY 1

2 used or heard so often as to be dull ⟨Please find new ways of phrasing your thoughts instead of relying on *banal* expressions.⟩ — see STALE 1

banality *n* an idea or expression that has been used by many people ⟨We exchanged *banalities* about the weather.⟩ — see COMMONPLACE

¹band *n* **1** a circular strip ⟨a *band* of cloth tied around his wrist⟩ — see ¹RING 2

2 something that physically prevents free movement ⟨The dog was forced to wear a *band* around its muzzle until it learned not to nip people.⟩ — see BOND 1

3 a line or long narrow section differing in color from the background ⟨Skunks have a *band* of white down their backs.⟩ — see ¹STRIPE 1

²band *n* **1** a usually large group of musicians playing together ⟨the school's marching *band*⟩ ⟨a boy *band*⟩
synonyms orchestra, philharmonic, symphony, symphony orchestra
related words brass band, chamber orchestra; brasses, strings, woodwinds; combo, ensemble, group; company, troupe; duo, octet, quartet (*also* quartette), quintet, septet, sextet, trio

2 a group of people working together on a task ⟨A *band* of volunteer searchers found the lost child.⟩ — see GANG 1

3 a usually small number of persons considered as a unit ⟨a *band* of explorers⟩ — see GROUP 2

4 a number of things considered as a unit ⟨a *band* of songbirds⟩ — see GROUP 1

band *vb* **1** to encircle or bind with or as if with a belt ⟨*banded* the waist of the dress with a speckled belt⟩ — see GIRD 1

2 to gather into a tight mass by means of a line or cord ⟨*banded* the newspapers together for delivery⟩ — see TIE 1

3 to make stripes on ⟨*banded* the sleeves of the robe with strips of contrasting material⟩ — see STRIPE

band (together) *vb* **1** to participate or assist in a joint effort to accomplish an end ⟨We're *banding together* to oppose the construction of one of those big-box stores in our town.⟩ — see COOPERATE 1

2 to form or enter into an association that furthers the interests of its members ⟨Small farmers *banded together* to oppose the interests of the agricultural giants.⟩ — see ALLY

bandage *vb* to cover with a bandage ⟨Her mother always *bandages* her scraped knees very carefully.⟩
synonyms bind, dress, swathe
related words attend, care (for), doctor, medicate, minister (to), nurse, treat; cure, heal, mend, rehabilitate, remedy
near antonyms unbandage

bandanna *or* **bandana** *n* a scarf worn on the head ⟨She uses her colorful print *bandanna* to keep the hair out of her eyes.⟩
synonyms babushka, do-rag, handkerchief, kerchief, mantilla
related words shawl

bandwagon *n* a series of activities undertaken to achieve a goal ⟨We tried to get everyone on the *bandwagon* about forming a neighborhood crime watch.⟩ — see CAMPAIGN

bandy *vb* to talk about (an issue) usually from various points of view and for the purpose of arriving at a decision or opinion ⟨*bandied* around the idea of going out to dinner for their anniversary⟩ — see DISCUSS

bane *n* **1** a source of harm or misfortune ⟨Regarding the new laborsaving machinery as a *bane*, the 19th-century Luddites went about destroying it in protest.⟩
synonyms affliction, curse, nemesis, scourge
related words hex, jinx; danger, hazard, menace, peril, risk, threat, trouble; booby trap, catch, pitfall, snag
near antonyms advantage, aid, assistance, gift, help, relief, support; comfort, consolation, solace; delight, joy, pleasure; armor, defense, guard, protection, safeguard, safety, security, shield
antonyms benefit, blessing, boon, felicity, godsend, good, manna, windfall

2 a substance that by chemical action can kill or injure a living thing ⟨a plant that is believed to be the *bane* of the wolf⟩ — see POISON

baneful *adj* causing or capable of causing harm ⟨Environmentalists fear the development will have a *baneful* effect on wildlife.⟩ — see HARMFUL

bang *adv* without delay ⟨The reform movement was just beginning when it *bang* ran into opposition.⟩ — see IMMEDIATELY

bang *n* **1** a hard strike with a part of the body or an instrument ⟨delivered a sharp *bang* that rattled the door⟩ — see ¹BLOW

2 a loud explosive sound ⟨A sudden *bang* made the cat jump.⟩ — see CLAP 1

3 a pleasurably intense stimulation of the feelings ⟨Emily tried to get the most *bang* for her money at the attractions at the county fair.⟩ — see THRILL

bang *vb* **1** to come into usually forceful contact with something ⟨The toy car *banged* into the wall and stopped.⟩ — see HIT 2

2 to deliver a blow to (someone or something) usually in a strong vigorous manner ⟨idly *banged* trees with a stick⟩ — see HIT 1

3 to shove into a closed position with force and noise ⟨stomped off to his room and *banged* the door⟩ — see SLAM 1

bangle *n* an ornament worn on a chain around the neck or wrist ⟨wore a bracelet with small silver *bangles* on it⟩ — see PENDANT

bang–up *adj* of the very best kind ⟨You did a *bang-up* job on this sales report.⟩ — see EXCELLENT

banish *vb* **1** to force to leave a country ⟨In the old days, criminals were sometimes *banished* to distant lands.⟩
synonyms deport, displace, exile, expatriate, transport
related words dismiss, eject, eliminate, evict, exclude, expel, expulse, oust, run out, throw out; excommunicate, ostracize, reject, repudiate, spurn
near antonyms naturalize, repatriate; accept, admit, take in; entertain, harbor, house, shelter

2 to drive or force out ⟨permanently *banished* the troublemakers from the youth recreational center⟩ — see EJECT 1

banishment *n* the forced removal from a homeland ⟨Punishment for opposing the king included *banishment*.⟩ — see EXILE 1

banister *also* **bannister** *n* a protective barrier consisting of a horizontal bar and its supports ⟨a much-needed new *banister* for the rickety staircase⟩ — see RAILING

¹bank *n* **1** a number of things considered as a unit ⟨a *bank* of telephones set up for the telethon⟩ — see GROUP 1

2 a series of people or things arranged side by side ⟨a *bank* of elevators⟩ — see ¹ROW 1

²**bank** *n* a pile or ridge of granular matter (as sand or snow) ⟨a *bank* of dirt that the construction workers left behind⟩

synonyms bar, drift, mound

related words snowbank, snowdrift; embankment, sandbar; heap, hill, mass, mountain, stack, tuft

bank *vb* **1** to form into a pile or ridge of earth ⟨*banked* sand into little mounds on the beach⟩ — see MOUND 1

2 to put in an account ⟨She always *banks* half of her paycheck.⟩ — see DEPOSIT 1

bankroll *n* available money ⟨My total *bankroll* right now is $2,000.⟩ — see FUND 2

bankroll *vb* to provide money for ⟨Several corporations *bankrolled* the Broadway musical.⟩ — see FINANCE 1

bankrupt *adj* utterly lacking in something needed, wanted, or expected ⟨Despite another brainstorming session, they found themselves *bankrupt* of ideas.⟩ — see DEVOID 1

bankrupt *vb* to cause to lose one's fortune and become unable to pay one's debts ⟨Several bad investments *bankrupted* him.⟩ — see RUIN 1

banned *adj* that may not be permitted ⟨At one time books, movies, and plays could use "*banned* in Boston" as a selling point.⟩ — see IMPERMISSIBLE

banner *adj* of the very best kind ⟨It's been a *banner* year for the petroleum business.⟩ — see EXCELLENT

banner *n* **1** a piece of cloth with a special design that is used as an emblem or for signaling ⟨The boat flew a bright red *banner* for the seaport's harbor festival.⟩ — see FLAG 1

2 an attention-getting word or phrase used to publicize something (as a campaign or product) ⟨After the near accident, the nuclear power station is now operating under the *banner* of "safety first."⟩ — see SLOGAN

banning *n* the act of ordering that something not be done or used ⟨The *banning* of the use of foul language at town council meetings was long overdue.⟩ — see PROHIBITION 1

banquet *n* a large fancy meal often accompanied by ceremony or entertainment ⟨prepared a celebratory *banquet* for the graduating class⟩ — see FEAST 1

banquet *vb* to entertain with a fancy meal ⟨Townspeople *banqueted* the returning troops at the military base.⟩ — see FEAST 1

bantam *adj* of a size that is less than average ⟨a *bantam* comedian who is known to fellow performers for his big heart⟩ — see SMALL 1

banter *n* good-natured teasing or exchanging of clever remarks ⟨Members of the panel were known for their brilliant and witty *banter*.⟩

synonyms chaff, give-and-take, jesting, joshing, raillery, repartee

related words barb, crack, dig, gag, jest, joke, laugh, pleasantry, quip, sally, waggery, wisecrack, witticism; drollness, facetiousness, funniness, hilariousness, humorousness, richness; fooling, kidding, mocking, razzing, ribbing, ridiculing; humor, wit, wordplay; nothings; chatter, chitchat, gossip, small talk

banter *vb* to make jokes ⟨The teacher *bantered* pleasantly with the students at the school dance.⟩ — see JOKE 1

bantering *adj* marked by or expressive of mild or good-natured teasing ⟨the gently *bantering* tone of the couple's conversation⟩ — see QUIZZICAL

baptism *n* the process or an instance of being formally placed in an office or organization ⟨the *baptism* of the new members of the college fraternity⟩ — see INSTALLATION 1

baptize *vb* **1** to give a name to ⟨*baptized* the child "Anne"⟩ — see NAME 1

2 to put into an office or welcome into an organization with special ceremonies ⟨The new sisters will be *baptized* with special initiation rites at the sorority house.⟩ — see INSTALL 1

bar *n* **1** a straight piece (as of wood or metal) that is longer than it is wide ⟨All of the prison's windows are partially covered with steel *bars*.⟩

synonyms billet, rod

related words arbor, beam, board, crossbar, crossbeam, girder; band, strip; bloom, ingot, slab, stick

2 a line or long narrow section differing in color from the background ⟨The cat had a *bar* of white down her throat.⟩ — see ¹STRIPE 1

3 a pile or ridge of granular matter (as sand or snow) ⟨More than one boater has run aground on that treacherous *bar* of sand in the river.⟩ — see ²BANK

4 a place of business where alcoholic beverages are sold to be consumed on the premises ⟨a *bar* that serves meals as well as drinks⟩ — see BARROOM

5 an assembly of persons for the administration of justice ⟨The younger judge brought a fresh viewpoint to the *bar*.⟩ — see COURT 3

6 something that makes movement or progress difficult ⟨The complication of the molecule is the biggest *bar* to reproducing it.⟩ — see ENCUMBRANCE

7 something set up as an example against which others of the same type are compared ⟨We need to raise the *bar* for what is acceptable behavior in this situation.⟩ — see STANDARD 1

bar *prep* not including ⟨Everyone in the company is invited, *bar* none.⟩ — see EXCEPT

bar *vb* **1** to make stripes on ⟨*barred* the fence with white strips⟩ — see STRIPE

2 to order not to do or use or to be done or used ⟨The judge *barred* the jurors from talking to reporters.⟩ — see FORBID

3 to prevent the participation, consideration, or inclusion of ⟨The student was *barred* from competing in the tournament after failing to meet eligibility requirements in time.⟩ — see EXCLUDE

4 to disallow entry into (a place) by means of a physical barrier at the entry point ⟨The bikeway was *barred* by a huge fallen tree.⟩ — see CLOSE (OFF)

barb *n* an act or expression showing scorn and usually intended to hurt another's feelings ⟨Bill delivered one last *barb* as he stalked away.⟩ — see INSULT

barbarian *adj* not civilized ⟨people who were regarded as *barbarian* by the ancient Romans⟩ — see UNCIVILIZED

barbarian *n* an uncivilized person ⟨an ancient city that was invaded by *barbarians*⟩ — see HEATHEN 2

barbaric *adj* **1** having or showing the desire to inflict severe pain and suffering on others ⟨a *barbaric* dictator who suppressed his own people with no qualms⟩ — see CRUEL 1

2 not civilized ⟨the *barbaric* forebears of modern mankind⟩ — see UNCIVILIZED

barbarity *n* disposition to willfully inflict pain and suffering on others ⟨accused their enemy of *barbarity*⟩ — see CRUELTY

barbarous *adj* **1** having or showing the desire to inflict severe pain and suffering on others ⟨a *barbarous* form of punishment⟩ — see CRUEL 1

2 not civilized ⟨shocked them with his *barbarous* behavior⟩ — see UNCIVILIZED

bard *n* a person who writes poetry ⟨a *bard* best known for a series of love poems to his raven-haired beloved⟩ — see POET

bardic *adj* having qualities suggestive of poetry ⟨"Now the trumpet summons us again" is one of the many *bardic* phrases in President Kennedy's inaugural address.⟩ — see POETIC

bare *adj* **1** being this and no more ⟨impoverished people who can no longer afford the *bare* necessities⟩ — see MERE
2 free from all additions or embellishment ⟨Do you want to know the *bare* truth?⟩ — see PLAIN 1
3 lacking a usual or natural covering ⟨The ground was *bare*, without a trace of grass.⟩ — see NAKED 2
4 lacking or shed of clothing ⟨The toddler liked to run around *bare*.⟩ — see NAKED 1
5 lacking contents that could or should be present ⟨The cupboard was *bare*—not a thing to eat.⟩ — see EMPTY 1
6 utterly lacking in something needed, wanted, or expected ⟨The cupboard was *bare* of baking supplies.⟩ — see DEVOID 1

bare *vb* to make known (as information previously kept secret) ⟨She finally *bared* the secret that she had kept to herself for so long.⟩ — see REVEAL 1

barefaced *adj* not subject to misinterpretation or more than one interpretation ⟨a *barefaced* challenge for a fight⟩ — see CLEAR 2

barely *adv* by a very small margin ⟨We *barely* made it to the wedding on time.⟩ — see JUST 2

bareness *n* the quality or state of being empty ⟨The stark *bareness* of the refrigerator suggested it was time to go shopping.⟩ — see VACANCY 2

barf *vb* to discharge the contents of the stomach through the mouth ⟨The movie's in-your-face violence made us want to *barf*.⟩ — see VOMIT

bargain *n* **1** something bought or offered for sale at a desirable price ⟨Those shoes were a *bargain* because the store was going out of business.⟩
synonyms buy, deal, steal
related words clearance, closeout, markdown; bonus, freebie (*or* freebee), gift, giveaway, premium, present; boon, windfall
near antonyms overcharge, rip-off, soaking; markup, surcharge; extravagance, luxury
2 an arrangement about action to be taken ⟨The coworkers made a *bargain* that one would help the other next week.⟩ — see AGREEMENT 2

bargain *vb* **1** to talk over or dispute the terms of a purchase ⟨They *bargained* with the car salesman for half an hour before settling on a price.⟩
synonyms deal, dicker, haggle, horse-trade, negotiate, palter
related words argue, bicker, clash, fight, hassle, quarrel, quibble, squabble, wrangle; comparison shop, shop (around); barter, exchange, trade; hawk, peddle; buy, purchase
phrases cut a deal, wheel and deal
2 to come to an arrangement as to a course of action ⟨I really hadn't *bargained* on buying a whole case of Girl Scout cookies, just a couple of boxes.⟩ — see AGREE 2
3 to bring about through discussion and compromise ⟨*bargained* the price of the painting down to a figure that the artist could still live with⟩ — see NEGOTIATE 1

barge *vb* to move heavily or clumsily ⟨The big man *barged* into the room.⟩ — see LUMBER 1

¹**bark** *vb* to remove the natural covering of ⟨*Barking* a tree will probably kill it.⟩ — see PEEL

²**bark** *vb* to speak sharply or irritably ⟨The new supervisor found that speaking to people with a civil tongue got better results than *barking* at them.⟩ — see SNAP 1

bark *n* a boat equipped with one or more sails ⟨He took a small *bark* out on the lake.⟩ — see SAILBOAT

baron *n* a person of rank, power, or influence in a particular field ⟨a media *baron* who owns several cable networks⟩ — see MAGNATE

baronial *adj* large and impressive in size, grandeur, extent, or conception ⟨a *baronial* mansion with dozens of spacious, luxurious rooms⟩ — see GRAND 1

barrage *n* a rapid or overwhelming outpouring of many things at once ⟨The teacher's rapid-fire *barrage* of homework assignments went by too fast for me to write them all down.⟩
synonyms blitz, blitzkrieg, bombardment, cannonade, flurry, fusillade, hail, salvo, shower, storm, volley
related words broadside, earful; avalanche, burst, cataclysm, cataract, deluge, discharge, engulfment, flood, flood tide, flush, gush, inundation, outburst, outflow, outpouring, overflow, rash, spate, surge, torrent; current, river, stream, tide; excess, glut, overabundance, overage, overkill, overmuch, oversupply, superabundance, superfluity, surfeit, surplus
near antonyms dribble, drip, trickle

barrage *vb* to attack with a rapid or overwhelming outpouring of many things at once ⟨The star athlete was *barraged* with requests for an autograph.⟩ — see BOMBARD 2

barred *adj* **1** having stripes ⟨A tabby is a *barred* cat, often with black stripes.⟩ — see STRIPED
2 that may not be permitted ⟨Smoking is *barred* inside the restaurant.⟩ — see IMPERMISSIBLE

barrel *n* **1** a considerable amount ⟨A visit to an amusement park should be a *barrel* of laughs.⟩ — see LOT 2
2 a metal container in the shape of a cylinder ⟨a trash *barrel*⟩ — see CAN 1
3 an enclosed wooden vessel for holding beverages ⟨*barrels* of fine wine aging in the winery's cellar⟩ — see CASK

barrel *vb* to proceed or move quickly ⟨Faced with a firm deadline, we *barreled* through the project at a furious pace.⟩ — see HURRY 2

barren *adj* **1** producing inferior or only a small amount of vegetation ⟨If the fields aren't allowed to lie idle once every few years, they will become *barren*.⟩
synonyms dead, desolate, impoverished, infertile, poor, stark, unproductive, waste
related words bleak, inhospitable, lifeless; uncultivable, untillable; bankrupted, consumed, debilitated, depleted, diminished, drained, dried-up, enfeebled, exhausted, expended, lessened, reduced, spent, used up; arid, desert, droughty, dry, rainless, sere (*also* sear), thirsty, waterless; baked, dehydrated, parched, sunbaked
near antonyms arable, tillable; green, sylvan, verdant
antonyms fertile, fruitful, lush, luxuriant, productive, rich
2 not able to produce fruit or offspring ⟨The pear tree appears to be *barren*.⟩ — see STERILE 1
3 producing no results ⟨That line of investigation proved *barren*, so the police tried other avenues.⟩ — see FUTILE
4 utterly lacking in something needed, wanted, or expected ⟨Their proposal for revitalizing the downtown business district is utterly *barren* of useful ideas.⟩ — see DEVOID 1

barren *n* land that is uninhabited or not fit for crops ⟨lived out in the *barrens* where it was impossible to grow anything⟩ — see WASTELAND

barricade *n* a physical object that blocks the way ⟨The police put up *barricades* to block off the parade route.⟩ — see BARRIER

barricade *vb* to disallow entry into (a place) by means of a physical barrier at the entry point ⟨The city *barricaded* the flooded streets.⟩ — see CLOSE (OFF)

barrier *n* a physical object that blocks the way ⟨There was a big *barrier* plastered with signs saying "Keep Out" around the trash compactor.⟩
synonyms barricade, fence, hedge, wall

related words bar, pale, paling; block, chain, clog, crimp, deterrent, drag, embarrassment, encumbrance, handicap, hindrance, hurdle, impediment, inhibition, interference, let, obstacle, obstruction, roadblock, stop, stumbling block, trammel; fetter, hobble, manacle, shackle(s); constraint, curb, restraint, snag; buffer, bulwark, bumper, cushion, dam, fender, pad, rampart
near antonyms door, doorway, entrance, entry, entryway, gate, portal; break, gap, pass

barring *n* the act of ordering that something not be done or used ⟨Most of the restaurant's customers applauded the *barring* of the use of cell phones in the dining room.⟩ — see PROHIBITION 1

barring *prep* not including ⟨We'll be there, *barring* rain or some other unexpected problem.⟩ — see EXCEPT

barroom *n* a place of business where alcoholic beverages are sold to be consumed on the premises ⟨*barrooms* closed down during Prohibition⟩
synonyms bar, pub, saloon, tavern
related words brewpub, cabaret, nightclub, speakeasy, sports bar

barter *n* a giving or taking of one thing of value in return for another ⟨According to our *barter* agreement, I do all of the mechanical work on my neighbor's car, and he does all of my snow removal.⟩ — see EXCHANGE 1

base *adj* not following or in accordance with standards of honor and decency ⟨a *base* and sneaky act that is a clear violation of international law⟩ — see IGNOBLE 2

base *n* **1** an immaterial thing upon which something else rests ⟨the firm belief that complete trust is the *base* of any successful marriage⟩
synonyms basis, bedrock, bottom, cornerstone, footing, foundation, ground, groundwork, keystone, root, underpinning, warp
related words anchorage, bed, brace, bulwark, buttress, framework, mount, shore, stay, substratum, substructure, support; assumption, justification, premise (*also* premiss), presumption, presupposition, rationale, supposition, theory, thesis, warrant; backbone, center, core, cornerstone, eye, focus, heart, hub, keystone, nucleus, seat; essence, quintessence, soul, touchstone
2 a place from which an advance (as for military operations) is made ⟨The army's *base* of attack was kept top secret.⟩
synonyms bridgehead, foothold
related words staging area, staging ground; beachhead, camp, center, footing, front, headquarters, installation, station; airbase, bastion, fastness, fortress, stronghold; battlefront, field; toehold
3 a thing or place that is of greatest importance to an activity or interest ⟨The *base* of the industry is California's Silicon Valley.⟩ — see CENTER 1
4 the lowest part, place, or point ⟨The *base* of the mountain extends over a huge area.⟩ — see BOTTOM 3
5 the place from which a commander runs operations ⟨The army *base* is three miles down the road.⟩ — see COMMAND 1

base *vb* to find a basis ⟨She *based* her argument on careful research.⟩
synonyms ground, hang, predicate, rest
related words establish, found; assume, postulate, premise, presume, presuppose, suppose

baseborn *adj* belonging to the class of people of low social or economic rank ⟨In the Middle Ages, a *baseborn* person simply had to accept his or her station in life.⟩ — see IGNOBLE 1

basement *n* **1** a room or set of rooms below the surface of the ground ⟨We store our bicycles in the *basement* during the winter.⟩ — see CELLAR

2 the lowest part, place, or point ⟨The *basement* of the outdoor fountain needs a lot of restoration work.⟩ — see BOTTOM 3

bash *n* **1** a hard strike with a part of the body or an instrument ⟨He hasn't been the same ever since he received that *bash* on his head.⟩ — see ¹BLOW
2 a social gathering ⟨I'm throwing a New Year's *bash* this year.⟩ — see PARTY 1

bash *vb* **1** to come into usually forceful contact with something ⟨The car *bashed* into the tree with glass-shattering force.⟩ — see HIT 2
2 to deliver a blow to (someone or something) usually in a strong vigorous manner ⟨The home renovator *bashed* the old walls with sledgehammers.⟩ — see HIT 1
3 to strike repeatedly ⟨The angry child kept *bashing* her toy with a hammer until it broke.⟩ — see BEAT 1
4 to criticize harshly and usually publicly ⟨movie critics *bashing* the remake of the classic film⟩ — see ATTACK 2

bashful *adj* not comfortable around people ⟨a *bashful* child who hid in his room whenever there were visitors in the house⟩ — see SHY 2

basic *adj* of or relating to the simplest facts or theories of a subject ⟨You'll need a *basic* knowledge of computers for the job.⟩ — see ELEMENTARY

basically *adv* for the most part ⟨Your answer is *basically* correct.⟩ — see CHIEFLY

basics *pl n* general or basic truths on which other truths or theories can be based ⟨If you don't learn the *basics* of algebra now, you'll never master calculus.⟩ — see PRINCIPLES 1

basis *n* an immaterial thing upon which something else rests ⟨The sole *basis* for the rumor is someone's overactive imagination.⟩ — see BASE 1

bask *vb* to refrain from labor or exertion ⟨We blissfully *basked* at the seashore over the long holiday.⟩ — see REST 1

bass *adj* having a low musical pitch or range ⟨a man with an impressive *bass* voice⟩ — see DEEP 2

bastion *n* a structure or place from which one can resist attack ⟨The rebel army retreated to its *bastion* in the mountains to regroup.⟩ — see FORT

bat *n* **1** a hard strike with a part of the body or an instrument ⟨a sharp *bat* with a rolled-up newspaper and that fly was a goner⟩ — see ¹BLOW
2 a heavy rigid stick used as a weapon or for punishment ⟨villagers armed with only *bats* and sticks⟩ — see CLUB 1

bat *vb* **1** to deliver a blow to (someone or something) usually in a strong vigorous manner ⟨*batted* the lamp off the table with one strike⟩ — see HIT 1
2 to strike repeatedly ⟨The boy *batted* the piñata until it finally broke open.⟩ — see BEAT 1
3 to move about from place to place aimlessly ⟨On Sunday afternoons we'd pile into Father's car and *bat* around the countryside.⟩ — see WANDER 1

batch *n* **1** a number of things considered as a unit ⟨a *batch* of essays to correct⟩ — see GROUP 1
2 a usually small number of persons considered as a unit ⟨Please send in the next *batch* of applicants.⟩ — see GROUP 2

bath *n* **1** a great flow of water or of something that overwhelms ⟨After a night in that tropical heat I was practically drowning in a *bath* of sweat.⟩ — see FLOOD
2 a room furnished with a fixture for flushing body waste ⟨retired to the upstairs *bath* to freshen up⟩ — see TOILET

bathe *vb* **1** to flow along or against ⟨The cool waters of the North Atlantic *bathe* the island's shores.⟩ — see WASH 1
2 to make wet ⟨*Bathe* your contact lenses with the solution before inserting them.⟩ — see WET
3 to supply with light ⟨The walls of the canyon were

bathed with the warm rays of the setting sun.⟩ — see IL-LUMINATE 1

bathed *adj* containing, covered with, or thoroughly penetrated by water ⟨covered the victim's burns with *bathed* bandages⟩ — see WET 1

bathroom *n* a room furnished with a fixture for flushing body waste ⟨Everyone should use the *bathroom* before we leave on the long trip.⟩ — see TOILET

battalion *n* a large body of men and women organized for land warfare ⟨The nation's *battalions* were forced to fight on two fronts simultaneously.⟩ — see ARMY 1

batter *vb* **1** to strike repeatedly ⟨Firefighters *battered* the door until it came down.⟩ — see BEAT 1
2 to use bombs or artillery against ⟨Planes *battered* the city.⟩ — see BOMBARD 1

battery *n* **1** a number of things considered as a unit ⟨a *battery* of tests to determine the cause of the medical disorder⟩ — see GROUP 1
2 a usually small number of persons considered as a unit ⟨A *battery* of specialists worked on the problem until it was fixed.⟩ — see GROUP 2

battle *n* **1** a forceful effort to reach a goal or objective ⟨Getting through medical school was an uphill *battle*, but she succeeded.⟩ — see STRUGGLE 1
2 a physical dispute between opposing individuals or groups ⟨a *battle* between rival male lions⟩ — see FIGHT 1
3 active fighting during the course of a war ⟨soldiers who returned to *battle*⟩ — see COMBAT 1
4 an earnest effort for superiority or victory over another ⟨The chess game was a real *battle* between two of the world's best players.⟩ — see CONTEST 1

battle *vb* **1** to engage in a contest ⟨The two teams, which have long been archrivals, will *battle* on the court for the state championship.⟩ — see COMPETE
2 to enter into contest or conflict with ⟨The two top-seeded tennis players *battled* each other for almost three hours.⟩ — see ENGAGE 2
3 to oppose (someone) in physical conflict ⟨boxers *battling* for the title⟩ — see FIGHT 1
4 to strive to reduce or eliminate ⟨We must *battle* hunger and poverty wherever they exist.⟩ — see FIGHT 2

bauble *n* a small object displayed for its attractiveness or interest ⟨The girls picked up some cheap *baubles* at the fair.⟩ — see KNICKKNACK

bawdiness *n* the quality or state of being obscene ⟨a medieval tale noted for its *bawdiness*⟩ — see OBSCENITY

bawdy *adj* **1** depicting or referring to sexual matters in a way that is unacceptable in polite society ⟨a book once banned as *bawdy*⟩ — see OBSCENE 1
2 hinting at or intended to call to mind matters regarded as indecent ⟨a *bawdy* limerick that mischievous storytellers love to recite⟩ — see SUGGESTIVE 1

bawl *vb* **1** to shed tears often while making meaningless sounds as a sign of pain or distress ⟨He *bawled* for days after his teddy bear was lost.⟩ — see CRY 1
2 to speak so as to be heard at a distance ⟨The mover was *bawling* for help as the refrigerator was about to slip out of his hands.⟩ — see CALL 1

bawl out *vb* to criticize (someone) severely or angrily especially for personal failings ⟨He got loudly *bawled out* by the boss.⟩ — see SCOLD

¹**bay** *n* one of the parts into which an enclosed space is divided ⟨The garage has three separate *bays* for cars.⟩ — see COMPARTMENT

²**bay** *n* a part of a body of water that extends beyond the general shoreline ⟨The *bay* is a favorite cruising ground for weekend yachtsmen.⟩ — see GULF 1

bay *vb* **1** to speak so as to be heard at a distance ⟨The crowd was *baying* for the match to begin.⟩ — see CALL 1

2 to make a long loud mournful sound ⟨The beagle *bayed* whenever someone walked by.⟩ — see HOWL 1

bazaar *n* an establishment where goods are sold to consumers ⟨We wandered around the *bazaar* looking to buy gifts.⟩ — see SHOP 1

be *vb* **1** to have life ⟨stories that begin with the familiar line "once upon a time there *was* a beautiful maiden"⟩
synonyms breathe, exist, live, subsist
related words abide, continue, endure, hold on, hold up, keep (on), kick, last, lead, persist, rule, run on, survive; move; flourish, prosper, thrive
near antonyms disappear, evaporate, vanish; cease, desist, discontinue, end, quit, stop; abate, die (down), ebb, let up, moderate, subside, wane
antonyms depart, die, expire, pass away, perish, succumb
2 to occupy a place or location ⟨We'll *be* there waiting for you.⟩ — see STAND 1
3 to take or have a certain position within a group arranged in vertical classes ⟨Our school's football team *is* first in its division.⟩ — see RANK 1
4 to take place ⟨The party *is* next Saturday.⟩ — see HAPPEN

be (to) *vb* to behave toward in a stated way ⟨You need to *be* nice *to* your brother.⟩ — see TREAT 1

beach *n* the usually sandy or gravelly land bordering a body of water ⟨She loves walking along the *beach*, looking for shells that the waves cast up.⟩
synonyms sand(s), strand
related words seaboard, seacoast, seashore, seaside; coast, coastland, coastline, shore, shoreline; oceanfront, shorefront, waterfront; bank, riverbank, riverfront, riverside; esplanade

beached *adj* resting on the shore or bottom of a body of water ⟨The *beached* whale had to be helped back out to sea.⟩ — see AGROUND

beacon *n* something that provides illumination ⟨The floodlit skyscraper is one of the city's most beloved nighttime *beacons*.⟩ — see LIGHT 2

beacon *vb* to supply with light ⟨A lone lighthouse *beacons* the entrance to the island's only harbor.⟩ — see ILLUMINATE 1

beak *n* **1** the jaws of a bird together with their hornlike covering ⟨The bird cracked the walnut shell with its *beak* and ate the nut.⟩
synonyms bill, nib
related words mouth; muzzle; mandible, maw, maxilla
2 the part of the face bearing the nostrils and nasal cavity ⟨The man's prominent *beak* gives him a somewhat aquiline appearance.⟩ — see NOSE 1

beam *n* a narrow sharply defined line of light radiating from an object ⟨We'll need a flashlight that casts a broader *beam* in order to really see anything.⟩ — see SHAFT 1

beam *vb* **1** to emit rays of light ⟨A lighthouse has *beamed* from this site since the 1790s.⟩ — see SHINE 1
2 to express an emotion (as amusement) by curving the lips upward ⟨My father *beamed* when I showed him my new car.⟩ — see SMILE 1

beaming *adj* **1** giving off or reflecting much light ⟨The orchestra began its season of outdoor concerts under a *beaming* moon.⟩ — see BRIGHT 1
2 having or being an outward sign of good feelings (as of love, confidence, or happiness) ⟨Mom's *beaming* face shone with love as we all gathered for a family photo.⟩ — see RADIANT 1

bear *n* **1** a dull, unpleasant, or difficult piece of work ⟨The upcoming kitchen renovation sounds like a real *bear*.⟩ — see CHORE 2

2 an irritable and complaining person ⟨You've been a real *bear* lately—are you having a bad week?⟩ — see GROUCH 1

bear *vb* **1** to bring forth from the womb ⟨Fortunately, she turned out to be able to *bear* children after all.⟩
synonyms deliver, drop, have, mother, produce
related words labor; breed, multiply, propagate, reproduce, spawn; beget, father, generate, get, sire; calve, kid, kindle, kitten, litter, pup, whelp
phrases give birth to
near antonyms abort, lose, miscarry
2 to put up with (something painful or difficult) ⟨I can't *bear* the thought of losing a loved one.⟩
synonyms abide, absorb, accept, brook, countenance, endure, go, hack, handle, meet, pocket, stand, stick out, stomach, support, sustain, sweat out, take, tolerate
related words allow, permit, suffer, swallow; reconcile (to); acquiesce, agree (with *or* to), assent (to), capitulate, consent (to), respect, submit (to), yield (to)
phrases live with, lump (it), stand for, tough out (it)
near antonyms decline, dismiss, refuse, reject, repudiate, spurn, turn down; combat, contest, fight, oppose, resist; avoid, bypass, circumvent, dodge, elude, escape, evade, miss; abstain (from), forbear, refrain (from)
3 to have a relation or connection ⟨I just found another fact that *bears* on this issue.⟩ — see APPLY 1
4 to go on a specified course or in a certain direction ⟨The road *bears* left after the second traffic light.⟩ — see HEAD 1
5 to hold up or serve as a foundation for ⟨The wooden bridge will only *bear* one truck at a time.⟩ — see SUPPORT 3
6 to keep in one's mind or heart ⟨I'm not one to *bear* grudges.⟩ — see HARBOR 1
7 to manage the actions of (oneself) in a particular way ⟨She *bore* herself well in her first public speaking event.⟩ — see BEHAVE
8 to support and take from one place to another ⟨The rescue team came *bearing* much-needed food and supplies.⟩ — see CARRY 1
9 to take to or upon oneself ⟨I *bear* some responsibility for the mishap.⟩ — see ASSUME 1
10 to wear or have on one's person ⟨the right to *bear* arms⟩ — see CARRY 2
11 to be positioned along a certain course or in a certain direction ⟨The path will *bear* north after that marked tree.⟩ — see RUN 3
12 to have as a requirement ⟨The patient's condition *bears* watching.⟩ — see NEED 1
13 to have within ⟨gold-*bearing* ore⟩ — see CONTAIN 1
14 to occupy a place or location ⟨A hot, humid air mass is now *bearing* just south of the Gulf Coast.⟩ — see STAND 1
15 to produce as revenue ⟨an interest-*bearing* savings account⟩ — see YIELD 2

bear (down on) *vb* to push steadily against with some force ⟨You need to *bear down on* that cap a bit to get it to latch tightly.⟩ — see ²PRESS 1

bearable *adj* capable of being endured ⟨The pain from a sprained ankle is annoying but *bearable*.⟩
synonyms endurable, sufferable, supportable, sustainable, tolerable
related words livable (*also* liveable), survivable; acceptable, adequate, admissible, allowable, permissible, reasonable, satisfactory
near antonyms agonizing, appalling, awful, bad, cruel, dire, dreadful, excruciating, frightful, ghastly, grisly, gruesome (*also* grewsome), harrowing, harsh, hideous, horrendous, horrible, horrid, horrifying, lurid, macabre,

monstrous, nasty, nightmarish, painful, rotten, shocking, terrible, tormenting, torturous, unfortunate, vicious, vile, wretched; unacceptable; acute, extreme, intense, piercing; abhorrent, deplorable, distasteful, loathsome, nauseating, obnoxious, offensive, repugnant, repulsive, revolting, sickening; abominable, evil, foul, heinous, noxious, odious, unspeakable
antonyms insufferable, insupportable, intolerable, unbearable, unendurable, unsupportable

beard *vb* to oppose (something hostile or dangerous) with firmness or courage ⟨a man of integrity who was never afraid to *beard* more powerful forces⟩ — see FACE 2

bearing *n* **1** the fact or state of being pertinent ⟨These new facts have some *bearing* on the case.⟩ — see PERTINENCE
2 the fact or state of having something in common ⟨I don't see any *bearing* between the quality of this ice cream and its rather exorbitant price.⟩ — see CONNECTION 1
3 the way or manner in which one conducts oneself ⟨always retained his military *bearing*, even after he entered politics⟩ — see BEHAVIOR

bearish *adj* **1** emphasizing or expecting the worst ⟨Some studio execs are *bearish* about this summer's box office.⟩ — see PESSIMISTIC 1
2 having or showing a habitually bad temper ⟨a *bearish* recluse who ordered everyone to stay off his property⟩ — see ILL-TEMPERED

bear out *vb* to give evidence or testimony to the truth or factualness of ⟨The newly discovered evidence *bore out* the prosecutor's theory.⟩ — see CONFIRM 1

beast *n* **1** a mean, evil, or unprincipled person ⟨She's a real *beast* to anyone who makes the mistake of crossing her.⟩ — see VILLAIN
2 a person whose behavior is offensive to others ⟨He always has to act like a *beast* whenever things don't go his way.⟩ — see JERK 1
3 one of the lower animals as distinguished from human beings ⟨a frigid night that was fit for neither man nor *beast*⟩ — see ANIMAL
4 a dull, unpleasant, or difficult piece of work ⟨Controlling the state's vast bureaucracy has always been a *beast*.⟩ — see CHORE 2

beastly *adv* to a great degree ⟨It's *beastly* hot today!⟩ — see VERY 1

beat *adj* depleted in strength, energy, or freshness ⟨Can we pick this up tomorrow, because I'm *beat*?⟩ — see WEARY 1

beat *n* **1** a hard strike with a part of the body or an instrument ⟨delivered one hard *beat* on the drums⟩ — see ¹BLOW
2 a rhythmic expanding and contracting ⟨a single *beat* of the heart⟩ — see PULSATION
3 the recurrent pattern formed by a series of sounds having a regular rise and fall in intensity ⟨moved to the *beat* of the music⟩ — see RHYTHM
4 a very small space of time ⟨Within a *beat* he was on the phone complaining about an error in his bill.⟩ — see INSTANT

beat *vb* **1** to strike repeatedly ⟨He *beat* the dusty rug with a stick.⟩
synonyms bash, bat, batter, belabor, belt, birch, bludgeon, buffet, club, drub, flog, hammer, hide, lace, lash, lick, maul, mess (up), paddle, pelt, pommel, pound, pummel, rough (up), slate, slog, switch, tan, thrash, thump, wallop, whale, whip
related words assail, assault, attack, beset, box, bust, chop, clobber, clout, crack, cudgel, cuff, descend (on *or* upon), hit, jump (on), knock, lam, paste, pounce (on *or* upon), punch, raid, rush, slam, slap, smack, smash, sock, spank, storm, swat, swipe, thwack, whack; cane, cowhide,

flagellate, horsewhip, leather, pistol-whip, rawhide, scourge, strap; gore, lacerate, wound; maim, mangle, mutilate
phrases beat up on
2 to achieve a victory over 〈She always *beats* everyone at checkers, but she's not as good at chess.〉
synonyms best, conquer, defeat, dispatch, get, get around, lick, master, overbear, overcome, overmatch, prevail (over), skunk, subdue, surmount, take, trim, triumph (over), upend, win (against), worst
related words sweep; edge (out); annihilate, blow out, bomb, break, bury, clobber, cream, crush, drub, finish, flatten, overwhelm, rout, skin, slaughter, smoke [*slang*], snow under, thrash, trounce, upset, wallop, wax [*slang*], whip; cap, excel, flourish, score, succeed; knock off, overpower, overthrow, subjugate, unseat, vanquish; ace (out), better, eclipse, exceed, excel, outdistance, outdo, outfight, outshine, outstrip, overtop, surpass, top, transcend
phrases get the better of, knock for a loop
near antonyms fall, give up, go down, go under; collapse, fail, flop, flunk, fold, wash out
antonyms lose (to)
3 to be greater, better, or stronger than 〈This new animated feature sure *beats* everything else that's ever been done in animation.〉 — see SURPASS 1
4 to expand and contract in a rhythmic manner 〈The patient's heart *beats* roughly 60 times per minute.〉 — see PULSATE
5 to move or cause to move with a striking motion 〈The bird's wings *beat* strongly as it soared in the air.〉 — see FLAP
6 to prevent from achieving a goal 〈You *beat* me to it!〉 — see FRUSTRATE 1
7 to shape with a hammer 〈Medieval artisans *beat* iron into exquisite swords.〉 — see HAMMER 1
8 to shine with a bright harsh light 〈The tropical sun *beat* down on our heads without mercy.〉 — see GLARE 1
9 to strike or cause to strike lightly and usually rhythmically 〈*beat* the drum in a marching rhythm〉 — see ¹TAP
10 to throw into a state of mental uncertainty 〈It *beats* me how that slipup happened.〉 — see CONFUSE 1
11 to avoid having to comply with (something) especially through cleverness 〈He spends all of his time trying to *beat* the system.〉 — see CIRCUMVENT 1
12 to reduce to fine particles 〈Years of pounding had *beaten* the pebbles to a fine dust.〉 — see POWDER
13 to rob by the use of trickery or threats 〈The screenwriter has filed a lawsuit, accusing the production company of *beating* him out of his share of the film's net profits.〉 — see FLEECE
beater *n* one that defeats an enemy or opponent 〈No one likes to see the *beater* of our team in the play-offs.〉 — see VICTOR 1
beating *n* **1** a rhythmic expanding and contracting 〈He wears a pacemaker to help maintain a regular *beating* of his heart.〉 — see PULSATION
2 failure to win a contest 〈She took a *beating* and ended up in second place.〉 — see DEFEAT 1
beau *n* **1** a male romantic companion 〈Her new *beau* brought flowers when he picked her up for their first date.〉 — see BOYFRIEND
2 a man extremely interested in his clothing and personal appearance 〈In his youth the monarch had been a flashy *beau* before ascending to the throne.〉 — see DANDY 1
beau ideal *n* **1** someone of such unequaled perfection as to deserve imitation 〈She is the *beau ideal* of the devoted public servant.〉 — see IDEAL 1
2 the most perfect type or example 〈Frank Lloyd Wright's most famous architectural creation, Falling Wa-

ter, is widely regarded as the *beau ideal* of a building in harmony with its setting.〉 — see QUINTESSENCE 1
beauteous *adj* very pleasing to look at 〈a *beauteous* sunset〉 — see BEAUTIFUL 1
beauteousness *n* the qualities in a person or thing that as a whole give pleasure to the senses 〈the *beauteousness* of the starlit evening〉 — see BEAUTY 1
beautiful *adj* **1** very pleasing to look at 〈a *beautiful* arrangement of flowers〉
synonyms aesthetic (*also* esthetic *or* aesthetical *or* esthetical), attractive, beauteous, comely, cute, fair, fetching, good, goodly, gorgeous, handsome, knockout, lovely, pretty, ravishing, seemly, sightly, stunning, taking
related words alluring, appealing, charming, cunning, delightful, engaging, fascinating, glamorous (*also* glamourous), prepossessing; elegant, exquisite, glorious, magnificent, resplendent, splendid, statuesque, sublime, superb; flawless, perfect, radiant; dainty, delicate; personable, pleasant, presentable; prettyish; desirable, dishy, dollish, foxy, pulchritudinous, seductive; hunky; arresting, eye-catching, flamboyant, flashy, glossy, showstopping, showy, slick, snazzy, splashy, striking; photogenic, telegenic
near antonyms abhorrent, abominable, bad, disagreeable, dreadful, foul, frightful, ghastly, horrible, loathsome, nasty, nauseating, objectionable, offensive, repellent (*also* repellant), repugnant, repulsive, revolting, shocking, sickening, terrible, vile; unappealing, unappetizing, unimposing, unpleasant, unprepossessing; frumpish, frumpy, unbecoming, unshapely
antonyms grotesque, hideous, homely, ill-favored, plain, ugly, unaesthetic, unattractive, unbeautiful, uncute, unhandsome, unlovely, unpleasing, unpretty, unshapely
2 of the very best kind 〈You've done a *beautiful* job of illustrating that children's story.〉 — see EXCELLENT
beautifulness *n* the qualities in a person or thing that as a whole give pleasure to the senses 〈the *beautifulness* of the seacoast〉 — see BEAUTY 1
beautify *vb* to make more attractive by adding something that is beautiful or becoming 〈*beautified* the roadside landscape by planting flowers〉 — see DECORATE
beautifying *adj* serving to add beauty 〈She added one last *beautifying* ornament to the wreath and hung it on the door.〉 — see DECORATIVE
beauty *n* **1** the qualities in a person or thing that as a whole give pleasure to the senses 〈The *beauty* of the landscape was enough to take your breath away.〉
synonyms attractiveness, beauteousness, beautifulness, comeliness, cuteness, fairness, gorgeousness, handsomeness, looks, loveliness, prettiness, sightliness
related words allure, appeal, attraction, fascination, glamour (*also* glamor); charm, delightfulness, elegance, exquisiteness, gloriousness, radiance, radiancy, resplendence, sublimeness, sublimity, superbness; foxiness, lusciousness, nubility, pulchritude, seductiveness, sex appeal, sexiness, shapeliness, tastiness; flawlessness, perfection; daintiness, delicacy; flamboyance, flashiness, glossiness, showiness, slickness, splashiness
near antonyms disagreeableness, dreadfulness, foulness, ghastliness, horribleness, loathsomeness, nastiness, offensiveness, repellency, repulsiveness, terribleness, vileness; blemish, flaw, imperfection
antonyms grotesqueness, hideousness, homeliness, plainness, ugliness, unattractiveness, unbecomingness, unloveliness, unsightliness
2 a lovely woman 〈Grandmother was a *beauty* in her younger days.〉
synonyms enchantress, goddess, honey, knockout, queen, stunner

related words belle, charmer; cover girl; cutie-pie, dish, doll, pretty; coquette, femme fatale, siren, temptress
3 something very good of its kind ⟨That fish is a *beauty*!⟩ — see JIM-DANDY

because *conj* for the reason that ⟨I simply can't go to work today *because* I don't feel well.⟩ — see SINCE

because of *prep* as the result of ⟨I was late for work *because of* the snowstorm, which made driving a nightmare.⟩
synonyms due to, owing to, through, with
phrases on account of

beckon *vb* to direct or notify by a movement or gesture ⟨I *beckoned* the bashful child to come closer.⟩ — see MOTION

becloud *vb* **1** to make (something) unclear to the understanding ⟨Don't *becloud* the discussion by raising unrelated issues.⟩ — see CONFUSE 2
2 to make dark, dim, or indistinct ⟨The smog from the city's steel mills was once so oppressive that it *beclouded* the local landscape even at noon.⟩ — see CLOUD 1

beclouded *adj* **1** covered over by clouds ⟨a gloomy, *beclouded* sky that aptly matched our mood⟩ — see OVERCAST
2 filled with or dimmed by fine particles (as of dust or water) in suspension ⟨The water was so *beclouded* by mud that I couldn't see the bottom.⟩ — see HAZY 1

become *vb* to eventually have as a state or quality ⟨Many people *became* sick with the flu.⟩ ⟨With the arrival of autumn the days *become* crisper and breezier.⟩
synonyms come, get, go, grow, run, turn, wax
related words alter, change, metamorphose, modify, mutate, transfigure, transform
near antonyms abide, be, continue, linger, remain, stay

becoming *adj* meeting the requirements of a purpose or situation ⟨That's a particularly *becoming* dress for the dance.⟩ — see FIT 1

bed *n* **1** a place set aside for sleeping ⟨The sofa in the living room will be your *bed* for the night.⟩
synonyms bunk, pad, rack, sack
related words bedstead, futon, mattress, pallet; bunk bed, cot, couch, daybed, feather bed, four-poster, hammock, Murphy bed, shakedown, sleigh bed, sofa, sofa bed, studio couch, trundle bed, water bed; bassinet, cradle, crib
2 the surface upon which a body of water lies ⟨some prospectors supposedly found gold in the *bed* of that mountain stream⟩ — see BOTTOM 2
3 a natural periodic loss of consciousness during which the body restores itself ⟨I always brush my teeth and floss before going to *bed*⟩ — see SLEEP 1

bed *vb* **1** to go to one's bed in order to sleep ⟨The campers all *bedded* down for the night around 9:00 p.m.⟩
synonyms crash [*slang*], retire, turn in
related words bunk, perch, roost, settle; doze, drop off, nap, nod, sleep, slumber, snooze; couch, lie (down), recline
phrases hit the hay (*or* sack)
near antonyms arouse, awake, awaken, rouse, wake, waken; bestir, stir; reawake, reawaken; shift, stir
antonyms arise, get up, rise, uprise
2 to set solidly in or as if in surrounding matter ⟨a walkway of flagstones firmly *bedded* in the earth⟩ — see ENTRENCH

bedaub *vb* to rub an oily or sticky substance over ⟨He *bedaubed* his sunburn with aloe.⟩ — see SMEAR 1

bedazzle *vb* **1** to hold the attention of as if by a spell ⟨Don't let their promises of immense riches *bedazzle* you.⟩ — see ENTHRALL 1
2 to overpower with light ⟨The theater's enormous chandelier *bedazzled* me as a child.⟩ — see DAZZLE

bedazzling *adj* giving off or reflecting much light ⟨*bedazzling* decorations that added to the holiday cheer⟩ — see BRIGHT 1

bedeck *vb* **1** to make more attractive by adding something that is beautiful or becoming ⟨*bedecked* the house with hundreds of miniature lights for the party⟩ — see DECORATE
2 to outfit with clothes and especially fine or special clothes ⟨The groom and best man arrived *bedecked* in tuxedos.⟩ — see CLOTHE 1

bedevil *vb* to cause persistent suffering to ⟨A lingering cold *bedeviled* me for over a month.⟩ — see AFFLICT

bedevilment *n* the act of making unwelcome intrusions upon another ⟨Constant *bedevilments* from a pesty neighbor kept me from finishing my work.⟩ — see ANNOYANCE 1

bedim *vb* to make dark, dim, or indistinct ⟨The view from the mountain's summit is often *bedimmed* by haze.⟩ — see CLOUD 1

bedizen *vb* to make more attractive by adding something that is beautiful or becoming ⟨a banquet table *bedizened* with flowers⟩ — see DECORATE

bedizened *adj* elaborately and often excessively decorated ⟨a *bedizened* dress once worn by a queen⟩ — see ORNATE 1

bedlam *n* **1** a place where mentally ill people are cared for ⟨French physician Philippe Pinel was instrumental in the transformation of *bedlams* from filthy dumps to well-ordered, humane institutions.⟩ — see INSTITUTION 2
2 a place of uproar or confusion ⟨There's no way I can get any reading done in this *bedlam*, so I'm going to the library.⟩ — see MADHOUSE

bedraggled *adj* **1** containing, covered with, or thoroughly penetrated by water ⟨The cat was all *bedraggled* and fit to be tied after her bath.⟩ — see WET 1
2 not clean ⟨found flood victims in *bedraggled* clothes⟩ — see DIRTY 1

bedrock *n* an immaterial thing upon which something else rests ⟨My religious faith is the *bedrock* of my life.⟩ — see BASE 1

bedspread *n* a decorative cloth used as a top covering for a bed ⟨a beautiful *bedspread* that is a reproduction of an 18th-century design⟩ — see COUNTERPANE

beef *n* **1** an expression of dissatisfaction, pain, or resentment ⟨I had to deal with an angry customer with a *beef* about our service.⟩ — see COMPLAINT 1
2 muscular strength ⟨a heavyweight wrestler with a good deal of *beef*⟩ — see MUSCLE 1

beef *vb* to express dissatisfaction, pain, or resentment usually tiresomely ⟨He tends to stand around and *beef* for hours about any slight, real or imagined.⟩ — see COMPLAIN

beef (up) *vb* **1** to increase the ability of (as a muscle) to exert physical force ⟨*beefed up* the walls with iron bars⟩ — see STRENGTHEN 1
2 to make markedly greater in measure or degree ⟨will *beef up* security for the next few days while the president is in town⟩ — see INTENSIFY

beefy *adj* strongly and heavily built ⟨a *beefy* man who worked in a warehouse all his life⟩ — see ¹HUSKY 1

beer belly *n* an enlarged or bulging abdomen ⟨doing crunches to flatten his *beer belly*⟩ — see POTBELLY

beetle *vb* to extend outward beyond a usual point ⟨Houses in the town commonly have second stories that *beetle* over the ground floors, and the overhang is known as a "bump."⟩ — see BULGE 1

befall *vb* to take place ⟨Whatever *befalls*, we'll make the best of it and carry on.⟩ — see HAPPEN

befit *vb* to be fitting or proper ⟨spoke politely of the deceased, as *befitted* the occasion⟩ — see DO 1

befitting *adj* **1** following the established traditions of refined society and good taste ⟨Many voters feel that the governor has not acted in a *befitting* manner for someone who serves as the state's chief executive.⟩ — see PROPER 1
2 meeting the requirements of a purpose or situation ⟨a *befitting* reply to a civil question⟩ — see FIT 1

befog *vb* **1** to make (something) unclear to the understanding ⟨The professor's convoluted explanation only *befogged* the textbook's presentation of this scientific principle.⟩ — see CONFUSE 2
2 to make dark, dim, or indistinct ⟨The morning murk *befogged* our view of the harbor.⟩ — see CLOUD 1
3 to throw into a state of mental uncertainty ⟨completely *befogged* by the sudden change of subject⟩ — see CONFUSE 1

befogged *adj* **1** filled with or dimmed by fine particles (as of dust or water) in suspension ⟨The *befogged* air of the construction site was so clogged with dust that I started coughing.⟩ — see HAZY 1
2 suffering from mental confusion ⟨Became hopelessly *befogged* after trying to understand the assembly instructions for the furniture.⟩ — see DIZZY 2

before *adv* so as to precede something in order of time ⟨Their arrival was completely expected because a messenger had gone *before*.⟩ — see AHEAD 1

before *prep* **1** earlier than ⟨Since I'm a faster runner, I got there *before* him.⟩
synonyms ahead of, ere, of, previous to, prior to, to
related words till, until, up to
phrases in advance of
near antonyms next, next to, since
antonyms after, following
2 preceding in space ⟨The children always insisted on running *before* their parents.⟩
synonyms ahead of
related words against
phrases in advance of, in front of
antonyms after, following

beforehand *adv* **1** before the usual or expected time ⟨If you arrive *beforehand*, we won't be entirely prepared yet.⟩ — see EARLY
2 so as to precede something in order of time ⟨If you get ready *beforehand*, you won't have to rush at the last minute.⟩ — see AHEAD 1

befoul *vb* **1** to make dirty ⟨Unsightly mud and slush *befouls* the family car every winter.⟩ — see DIRTY
2 to make unfit for use by the addition of something harmful or undesirable ⟨a limit on pollutants that *befoul* drinking water⟩ — see CONTAMINATE

befuddle *vb* to throw into a state of mental uncertainty ⟨Most of the applicants were *befuddled* by the wording of one of the questions on the driving test.⟩ — see CONFUSE 1

befuddled *adj* suffering from mental confusion ⟨an overabundance of statistics that left readers *befuddled*⟩ — see DIZZY 2

befuddlement *n* a state of mental uncertainty ⟨The library patron was in obvious *befuddlement* over where to find the appropriate references.⟩ — see CONFUSION 1

beg *vb* to make a request to (someone) in an earnest or urgent manner ⟨She *begged* her children to be careful.⟩
synonyms appeal (to), beseech, besiege, entreat, implore, importune, petition, plead (to), pray, solicit, supplicate
related words cadge, mooch, sponge; ask, desire, request, sue; claim, coerce, command, compel, demand, force, insist, require; freeload
phrases call on (*or* upon)
near antonyms hint, imply, intimate, suggest; appease,

conciliate, gratify, mollify, oblige, pacify, placate, please, satisfy; comfort, console, content, quiet

beget *vb* **1** to be the cause of (a situation, action, or state of mind) ⟨One change in the natural environment will *beget* others.⟩ — see EFFECT
2 to become the father of ⟨The racehorse *begot* several Kentucky Derby winners.⟩ — see FATHER

begetter *n* a person who establishes a whole new field of endeavor ⟨Michael Faraday is widely hailed as one of the *begetters* of electromagnetism, the field of study that sparked a technological revolution.⟩ — see FATHER 2

beggar *n* a person who lives by public begging ⟨the pitiful *beggars* who roamed the streets⟩
synonyms mendicant, panhandler
related words bohemian, bum, drifter, hobo, tramp, vagabond, vagrant; guttersnipe, urchin, waif; miserable, pauper; cadger, hanger-on, leech, moocher, parasite, schnorrer, sponge, sponger; dependent; derelict, idler

beggared *adj* lacking money or material possessions ⟨The family was completely *beggared* after the stock market crash.⟩ — see POOR 1

beggary *n* the state of lacking sufficient money or material possessions ⟨people who are homeless and living in *beggary*⟩ — see POVERTY 1

begin *vb* **1** to take the first step in (a process or course of action) ⟨She *began* walking to work for exercise.⟩
synonyms commence, embark (on *or* upon), enter (into *or* upon), get off, kick off, launch, open, start, strike (into)
related words create, generate, inaugurate, initiate, innovate, invent, originate; adopt, embrace, take on, take up; establish, father, found, institute, organize, pioneer, set up; spawn; get around (to), get down (to), get round (to)
phrases get going, get to, set about
near antonyms cease, desist, discontinue, halt, knock off, lay off, quit, stop; close, complete; abandon, forsake, leave; abolish, demolish, destroy, exterminate, extinguish, phase out
antonyms conclude, end, finish, terminate
2 to come into existence ⟨The storm *began* late in the day and lasted all night.⟩
synonyms actualize, appear, arise, break, commence, dawn, engender, form, materialize, originate, set in, spring, start
related words be, breathe, exist, live, subsist; arrive, emerge; coalesce, cohere, shape (up); continue, endure, last, persist, survive
near antonyms conclude, desist, discontinue, finish, halt, quit, terminate; disappear, dissolve, evaporate, vanish; depart, die, expire, pass away, perish
antonyms cease, end, stop
3 to be responsible for the creation and early operation or use of ⟨The religious sect was *begun* by a small breakaway faction.⟩ — see FOUND

beginner *n* a person who is just starting out in a field of activity ⟨Although our son is only a *beginner* at swimming, he is making excellent progress.⟩
synonyms apprentice, babe, colt, cub, fledgling, freshman, greenhorn, neophyte, newbie, newcomer, novice, punk, recruit, rookie, tenderfoot, tyro
related words amateur, dabbler, dilettante; learner, student, trainee; candidate, entrant, probationer
near antonyms expert, master, pro, professional
antonyms old hand, old-timer, vet, veteran

beginning *adj* **1** coming before the main part or item usually to introduce or prepare for what follows ⟨The *beginning* part of the book is about his childhood.⟩ — see PRELIMINARY
2 of or relating to the simplest facts or theories of a sub-

ject ⟨a course in *beginning* geology for nonscience majors⟩ — see ELEMENTARY

beginning *n* the point at which something begins ⟨The actual *beginning* of the universe is still under debate, with some scientists continuing to uphold the big bang theory.⟩

synonyms alpha, birth, commencement, dawn, genesis, inception, incipiency, launch, morning, onset, outset, start, threshold

related words drawing board, first base, ground zero, square one; creation, founding, inauguration, initiation, institution, origination; cradle, origin, root, source, spring, well; dawning, opening; advent, appearance, arrival, debut (*also* début), emergence; childhood, infancy, youth

near antonyms cessation, closing, closure, completion, finale, finish, period, stop, termination, windup

antonyms close, conclusion, end, ending, omega

begone *vb* to leave a place often for another ⟨In his frustration the beleaguered actor cried out to the autograph seekers, "*Begone* and let me finish my meal in peace!"⟩ — see GO 2

begrime *vb* to make dirty ⟨Years of spattered mud had thoroughly *begrimed* the mailbox by the side of the road.⟩ — see DIRTY

beguile *vb* 1 to attract or delight as if by magic ⟨The magician effortlessly *beguiled* and amazed the children.⟩ — see CHARM 1

2 to cause to believe what is untrue ⟨*beguiled* her into believing that yet another worthless item would enhance her life⟩ — see DECEIVE

3 to lead away from a usual or proper course by offering some pleasure or advantage ⟨was *beguiled* by the promise of easy money⟩ — see LURE

beguiling *adj* 1 clever at attaining one's ends by indirect and often deceptive means ⟨a smart and *beguiling* child who can manipulate her parents with alarming ease⟩ — see ARTFUL 1

2 tending or having power to deceive ⟨the *beguiling* allure of fame⟩ — see DECEPTIVE 1

behave *vb* to manage the actions of (oneself) in a particular way ⟨If the children *behave* themselves properly, they'll get extra time at recess.⟩

synonyms acquit, bear, carry, comport, conduct, demean, deport, quit

related words check, collect, compose, constrain, contain, control, curb, handle, inhibit, quiet, repress, restrain; moderate, modulate, temper; act, impersonate, play

near antonyms act up, carry on, cut up, misbehave, misconduct

behavior *n* the way or manner in which one conducts oneself ⟨Usually the enfant terrible, he's promising to be on his best *behavior* for the party.⟩

synonyms actions, address, bearing, comportment, conduct, demeanor, deportment

related words etiquette, form, manners, mores, proprieties; p's and q's; amenity, civility, courtesy, decorum, politeness; air, carriage, poise, pose, posture, presence; aspect, look, mien; formality, protocol, rules; custom, habit, pattern, practice (*also* practise), trick, wont; convention, fashion, form, mode, style; affectation, attribute, characteristic, mark, trait; distinctiveness, oddity, peculiarity, singularity, strangeness, uniqueness, weirdness

behead *vb* to cut off the head of ⟨Mary, Queen of Scots, was *beheaded* for plotting against Queen Elizabeth.⟩ — see DECAPITATE

behemoth *n* something that is unusually large and powerful ⟨a corporate *behemoth* endangering small businesses⟩ — see GIANT

behest *n* a statement of what to do that must be obeyed by those concerned ⟨I only made the change at the author's *behest*.⟩ — see COMMAND 1

behind *adj* not arriving, occurring, or settled at the due, usual, or proper time ⟨The required work was *behind*, so now we're running late.⟩ — see LATE 1

behind *n* the part of the body upon which someone sits ⟨cleaned the baby's *behind*⟩ — see BUTTOCKS

behind *prep* 1 at, to, or toward the rear of ⟨She preferred to be *behind* the lead hikers, who were always too much in a rush to enjoy the scenery.⟩

synonyms abaft, back of

phrases in back of

near antonyms ahead of

antonyms before

2 subsequent to in time or order ⟨We arrived *behind* them.⟩ — see AFTER

behindhand *adj* not arriving, occurring, or settled at the due, usual, or proper time ⟨The response was *behindhand*, just like everything else the company did.⟩ — see LATE 1

behold *vb* 1 to have a clear idea of ⟨to anyone who *beholds* the immense complexity of life on earth⟩ — see COMPREHEND 1

2 to make note of (something) through the use of one's eyes ⟨I opened the window blinds and *beheld* snow everywhere.⟩ — see SEE 1

beholden *adj* being under obligation for a favor or gift ⟨Not wanting to be *beholden* to anyone, he insisted on paying his own way.⟩

synonyms indebted, obligated, obliged

related words appreciative, grateful, thankful

being *n* 1 a member of the human race ⟨There isn't a nicer *being* on the planet than her.⟩ — see HUMAN

2 one that has a real and independent existence ⟨New parents are typically in awe at having created this separate *being*.⟩ — see ENTITY

3 the quality or qualities that make a thing what it is ⟨Music is such a large part of her *being* that she could never give up performing.⟩ — see ESSENCE 1

belabor *vb* 1 to criticize harshly and usually publicly ⟨There's no need to *belabor* other people's flaws when you're hardly perfect yourself.⟩ — see ATTACK 2

2 to strike repeatedly ⟨He *belabored* his broken down car in frustration.⟩ — see BEAT 1

belated *adj* not arriving, occurring, or settled at the due, usual, or proper time ⟨a *belated* birthday card⟩ — see LATE 1

belatedness *n* the quality or state of being late ⟨The *belatedness* of the payment resulted in us being charged overdue fees.⟩ — see LATENESS

belch *vb* to violently throw out or off (something from within) ⟨The volcano *belched* lava and ash for days.⟩ — see ERUPT 1

beleaguer *vb* to surround (as a fortified place) with armed forces for the purpose of capturing or preventing commerce and communication ⟨*beleaguered* the castle for months⟩ — see BESIEGE 1

belie *vb* 1 to give a misleading impression of ⟨His bright smile *belied* his actual mood, which was really one of great sadness.⟩

synonyms misrepresent

related words contradict; camouflage, cloak, conceal, counterfeit, disguise, hide, mask, obscure; color, deceive, distort, falsify, garble, mislead, misrender, misreport, twist; dissemble, feign, pretend

near antonyms bare, demonstrate, disclose, discover, evince, exhibit, expose, reveal; flaunt, parade, show off

antonyms betray, represent

2 to prove to be false 〈The latest information *belies* the old theory.〉 — see DISPROVE

3 to keep secret or shut off from view 〈The security council issued false assurances that *belied* the true gravity of the situation.〉 — see ¹HIDE 2

belief *n* **1** mental conviction of the truth of some statement or the reality of some being or phenomenon 〈a *belief* in UFO's led him to relentlessly scan the nighttime skies〉

synonyms credence, credit, faith

related words axiom, law, precept, principle, tenet; assurance, certainty, certitude, conviction, positiveness, sureness; confidence, dependence (*also* dependance), reliance, trust; hope; doctrine, dogma, philosophy; fanaticism, insistence

phrases article of faith

near antonyms distrust, mistrust, skepticism, suspicion, uncertainty

antonyms disbelief, discredit, doubt, nonbelief, unbelief
2 an idea that is believed to be true or valid without positive knowledge 〈It's my *belief* that the sky is blue because our eyes perceive the color blue easily.〉 — see OPINION 1

believable *adj* worthy of being accepted as true or reasonable 〈She had a *believable* excuse for missing the deadline.〉

synonyms credible, creditable, likely, plausible, probable
related words cogent, compelling, conclusive, convincing, decisive, effective, forceful, persuasive, satisfying, strong, telling; acceptable, cogitable, conceivable, imaginable, possible, practical, reasonable; dependable, reliable, trustworthy; sophistic (*or* sophistical), specious
near antonyms absurd, doubtful, dubious, fantastic (*also* fantastical), flimsy, outlandish, preposterous, questionable, ridiculous; impossible, inconceivable, unimaginable, unthinkable; skeptical, suspect, suspicious, uncertain, unsure; hopeless, unworkable, useless
antonyms far-fetched, implausible, improbable, incredible, unbelievable, unlikely, unplausible

believe *vb* **1** to regard as right or true 〈Only the most naive car buyer would have *believed* the salesman's claim that the dealership was actually losing money on the deal.〉

synonyms accept, buy, credit, swallow, take, trust
related words account, accredit, understand; assume, presume, suppose; conclude, deduce, infer
phrases set store by (*or* on)
near antonyms distrust, doubt, mistrust, question, suspect; challenge, dispute
antonyms disbelieve, discredit, reject
2 to have as an opinion 〈Despite the horrors she witnessed and endured, Anne Frank steadfastly *believed* that "people are really good at heart."〉

synonyms conceive, consider, deem, esteem, feel, figure, guess, hold, imagine, judge, reckon [*chiefly dialect*], suppose, think
related words regard, view; accept, perceive; depend, rely, trust; assume, presume, presuppose, surmise; conclude, deduce, infer
near antonyms distrust, doubt, mistrust, question, suspect; disbelieve, discredit, reject

belittle *vb* to express scornfully one's low opinion of 〈Critics *belittled* the action star's acting ability.〉 — see DECRY 1

belittlement *n* the act of making a person or a thing seem little or unimportant 〈an unconscionable *belittlement* of his assistant in public〉 — see DEPRECIATION

belittling *adj* intended to make a person or thing seem of little importance or value 〈There's no need for *belittling* comments about your brother's trumpet playing.〉 — see DEROGATORY

bellicose *adj* feeling or displaying eagerness to fight 〈*bellicose* hockey players who seem to spend more time fighting than playing〉 — see BELLIGERENT

bellicosity *n* an inclination to fight or quarrel 〈The candidate criticized her opponent's *bellicosity* as irresponsible.〉 — see BELLIGERENCE

belligerence *n* an inclination to fight or quarrel 〈The dominant male lion was able to withstand the *belligerence* of younger challengers.〉

synonyms aggression, aggressiveness, bellicosity, combativeness, contentiousness, defiance, disputatiousness, fight, militancy, pugnacity, scrappiness, truculence
related words antagonism, fierceness, hostility, hyperaggressiveness, unfriendliness; imperialism, jingoism, militarism; acidity, biliousness, captiousness, crankiness, crossness, disagreeableness, fractiousness, fretfulness, grouchiness, grumpiness, huffiness, irascibility, irritability, irritableness, orneriness, peevishness, pettishness, petulance, querulousness, rudeness, surliness, testiness, waspishness
phrases chip on one's shoulder
near antonyms antiaggression, anti-imperialism, antimilitarism; affability, amiability, amicability, benevolence, cordiality, friendliness, geniality, graciousness, pleasantness, sociability; gentleness, kindliness, mildness; amenability, complaisance, placability
antonyms nonaggression, pacifism

belligerent *adj* feeling or displaying eagerness to fight 〈The player became quite *belligerent* and was thrown out of the game.〉

synonyms aggressive, argumentative, bellicose, combative, contentious, discordant, disputatious, gladiatorial, militant, pugnacious, quarrelsome, scrappy, truculent, warlike
related words antagonistic, fierce, hostile, hot-tempered; acidic, bearish, bilious, bristly, choleric, crabby, cranky, cross, disagreeable, dyspeptic, fractious, fretful, grouchy, grumpy, ill-humored, ill-natured, ill-tempered, irascible, irritable, ornery, peevish, pettish, petulant, prickly, querulous, rude, snappish, snappy, surly, testy, touchy, ugly, waspish; savage, vicious; battling, fighting, warring
phrases on the warpath
near antonyms anti-imperialist, antimilitarist, unwarlike; affable, amiable, amicable, benevolent, complaisant, conciliatory, cordial, easygoing, friendly, genial, good-natured, good-tempered, gracious, ingratiating, kindhearted, obliging, pleasant, sociable; calm, quiet, relaxed, serene, tranquil; benign, gentle, kindly, mild
antonyms nonaggressive, nonbelligerent, pacific, peaceable, peaceful, unbelligerent, uncombative, uncontentious

bellow *vb* **1** to make a long loud deep noise or cry 〈The cow *bellowed* for her calf.〉 — see ROAR 1
2 to speak so as to be heard at a distance 〈The sergeant was *bellowing* orders.〉 — see CALL 1

belly *n* **1** a need or desire for food 〈As dinnertime approached he could think only of his *belly*.〉 — see HUNGER 1
2 an enlarged or bulging abdomen 〈vowed to get rid of his *belly* in time to attend his class reunion〉 — see POTBELLY
3 the part of the body between the chest and the pelvis 〈a baby with a round little *belly*〉 — see STOMACH 1
4 the seat of one's deepest thoughts and emotions 〈In my *belly* I knew that he wasn't telling the truth, as the details of his story just didn't add up.〉 — see CORE 1

belly *vb* **1** to extend outward beyond a usual point 〈The sails slowly *bellied* as the wind picked up.〉 — see BULGE 1
2 to move slowly with the body close to the ground

⟨Recruits were forced to *belly* over the obstacle course under simulated enemy fire.⟩ — see CRAWL 1

bellyache *n* abdominal pain especially when focused in the digestive organs ⟨Eating too many apples will give you a *bellyache*.⟩ — see STOMACHACHE

bellyache *vb* to express dissatisfaction, pain, or resentment usually tiresomely ⟨tired of the kids *bellyaching* every time they're asked to mow the lawn or take out the trash⟩ — see COMPLAIN

bellyacher *n* **1** a person who makes frequent complaints usually about little things ⟨one of the biggest *bellyachers* about the lousy coffee at work⟩ — see CRYBABY
2 an irritable and complaining person ⟨There's always at least one *bellyacher* who doesn't like the food on the cruise ship.⟩ — see GROUCH 1

belong *vb* **1** to have or be in a usual or proper place ⟨Your shoes *belong* in the closet, not in the middle of the living room where people will trip on them.⟩
synonyms go
related words place, stay; fit (in)
2 to be the property of a person or group of persons ⟨Those textbooks *belong* to the school system and not to the students.⟩
synonyms appertain, pertain
related words have, hold, own, possess

beloved *adj* granted special treatment or attention ⟨Her *beloved* cat sleeps in its own little bed.⟩ — see DARLING 1

beloved *n* a person with whom one is in love ⟨searching for some incredibly romantic spot in which to ask his *beloved* to marry him⟩ — see SWEETHEART

below *adv* **1** in or to a lower place ⟨The skipper climbed *below* to fix the engine.⟩
synonyms beneath, under, underneath
related words beside, near, nearby
near antonyms aloft, overhead
antonyms up
2 toward or in a lower position ⟨When rock climbing I just know that if I look *below*, I'll become paralyzed with fear.⟩ — see DOWN 1

below *prep* **1** in a lower position than ⟨For the photo she sat *below* everyone else, on the floor actually.⟩
synonyms beneath, under
related words underneath
antonyms above, over
2 subsequent to in time or order ⟨He put his own needs *below* those of his children.⟩ — see AFTER

¹**belt** *n* **1** a hard strike with a part of the body or an instrument ⟨delivered a shattering *belt* to the rock with a hammer⟩ — see ¹BLOW
2 the portion of a serving of a beverage that is swallowed at one time ⟨took a *belt* from the flask⟩ — see DRINK 2

²**belt** *n* **1** a strip of flexible material (as leather) worn around the waist ⟨a drugstore cowboy who loves his fancily decorated *belt*⟩
synonyms cummerbund (*also* cumberbund), girdle, sash
related words band, waistband; circle, loop, ribbon, ring; baldric, bandolier (*or* bandoleer), Sam Browne belt
2 a broad geographical area ⟨That part of the country is sometimes called "the farm *belt*" because of the number of farms there.⟩ — see REGION 2

belt *vb* **1** to deliver a blow to (someone or something) usually in a strong vigorous manner ⟨*belted* the baseball out of the park⟩ — see HIT 1
2 to encircle or bind with or as if with a belt ⟨*belted* the little boy's pants tightly so they would stay up⟩ — see GIRD 1
3 to strike repeatedly ⟨*belted* the punching bag relentlessly⟩ — see BEAT 1

4 to proceed or move quickly ⟨The boy went *belting* along on his skateboard.⟩ — see HURRY 2

bemoan *vb* **1** to feel or express sorrow for ⟨*bemoaned* the death of his wife by writing a series of poignant letters addressed to her⟩ — see LAMENT 1
2 to feel sorry or dissatisfied about ⟨a think piece *bemoaning* the coarsening of our society over the last several decades⟩ — see REGRET

bemoaning *adj* expressing or suggesting mourning ⟨She always seems to have a *bemoaning* expression on her face.⟩ — see MOURNFUL 1

bemuse *vb* **1** to hold the attention of ⟨a public that is *bemused* by the shenanigans of celebrities⟩ — see ENGAGE 1
2 to throw into a state of mental uncertainty ⟨The stage mishap momentarily *bemused* the actress.⟩ — see CONFUSE 1

bench *n* **1** a public official having authority to decide questions of law ⟨appealed to the *bench* for leniency⟩ — see JUDGE 2
2 an assembly of persons for the administration of justice ⟨A ruling from the *bench* is expected any day now.⟩ — see COURT 3

benchmark *n* something set up as an example against which others of the same type are compared ⟨This prize-winning biography will be the *benchmark* against which all others will be judged in future years.⟩ — see STANDARD 1

bend *n* **1** something that curves or is curved ⟨It's hard to see around that *bend* in the road, so be careful.⟩
synonyms angle, arc, arch, bow, crook, curvature, curve, turn, wind
related words warp; circle, ring, ringlet, round; coil, curl, curlicue (*also* curlycue); buckle, flexure, fold, loop, spiral, swirl, twist, winding; incurvature, reflection; decline, inclination, incline, slope; corner, turnoff; dogleg, hairpin
2 the act of positioning or an instance of being positioned at an angle ⟨did knee *bends* for exercise⟩ — see TILT

bend *vb* **1** to cause to turn away from a straight line ⟨She *bent* the blade of the knife when she got it jammed in the drawer.⟩
synonyms arch, bow, crook, curve, hook, swerve
related words arc, round; incurvate, incurve, inflect, reflect; deflect, divert; entwine, swirl, turn, twine, twist, veer, warp; coil, curl, enroll (*also* enrol), loop, spiral; dent, dimple; meander, wave, weave, wind; decline, incline, slope
antonyms straighten, unbend, uncurl
2 to occupy (oneself) diligently or with close attention ⟨*bent* herself to the task for the rest of the day⟩ — see APPLY 2
3 to point or turn (something) toward a target or goal ⟨*bent* all of his efforts toward making his first documentary film⟩ — see AIM 1
4 to turn away from a straight line or course ⟨The stream *bends* slightly to the east.⟩ — see CURVE 1
5 to change so much as to create a wrong impression or alter the meaning of ⟨attorneys *bending* the facts to put their client in the most favorable light⟩ — see GARBLE
6 to cause (something) to hold to another ⟨*bend* a leash to the dog's collar⟩ — see FASTEN 1

bending *adj* marked by a long series of irregular curves ⟨The river takes a long *bending* path to the sea.⟩ — see CROOKED 1

beneath *adv* in or to a lower place ⟨a ranch house with all of the rooms on one floor and a combined basement and garage *beneath*⟩ — see BELOW 1

beneath *prep* in a lower position than ⟨sat *beneath* him, on the floor, for the group photo⟩ — see BELOW 1

benediction *n* **1** a prayer calling for divine care, protection, or favor 〈The priest offered a *benediction* for the new recruits.〉 — see BLESSING 1

2 something that provides happiness or does good for a person or thing 〈The library's silence was a welcome *benediction* to someone, like me, who needed to concentrate.〉 — see BLESSING 2

benefaction *n* a gift of money or its equivalent to a charity, humanitarian cause, or public institution 〈The generous *benefaction* from an anonymous donor meant the animal shelter could stay open.〉 — see CONTRIBUTION

benefactor *n* one that helps another with gifts or money 〈An anonymous *benefactor* gave the school a dozen new computers.〉
synonyms angel, donator, donor, patron
related words benefactress, patroness; philanthropist; altruist, bestower, contributor, giver; helper, subscriber, supporter; guardian angel, protector, savior (*or* saviour)
near antonyms beneficiary, donee, giftee, recipient

beneficence *n* a gift of money or its equivalent to a charity, humanitarian cause, or public institution 〈The town library stays open primarily through *beneficences* from concerned residents.〉 — see CONTRIBUTION

beneficent *adj* **1** having or marked by sympathy and consideration for others 〈a *beneficent* couple who are regular volunteers at a homeless shelter〉 — see HUMANE 1

2 having or showing a concern for the welfare of others 〈a *beneficent* effort to help out the needy〉 — see CHARITABLE 1

3 promoting or contributing to personal or social well-being 〈Cultural activities have a *beneficent* effect on a community that can't be measured in dollars and cents.〉 — see BENEFICIAL

beneficial *adj* promoting or contributing to personal or social well-being 〈Tutoring can often be as *beneficial* and rewarding for the tutor as for the student receiving the help.〉
synonyms advantageous, beneficent, benignant, favorable, friendly, good, helpful, kindly, profitable, salutary
related words gratifying, rewarding, satisfying; auspicious, promising, propitious; advisable, desirable, healthful, healthy, salubrious, salutiferous, wholesome; gainful, lucrative, remunerative; ameliorative, amelioratory, bettering, constructive, supportive
near antonyms damaging, deleterious, harmful, injurious
antonyms bad, disadvantageous, unfavorable, unfriendly, unhelpful, unprofitable

benefit *n* **1** a thing that helps 〈It would be a real *benefit* if you could keep track of what you have already bought.〉 — see HELP 2

2 something that provides happiness or does good for a person or thing 〈The meal service is a great *benefit* to the elderly.〉 — see BLESSING 2

benefit *vb* to provide with something useful or desirable 〈His summer internship *benefited* him in two ways: by giving him some tuition funds and by offering vital work experience.〉
synonyms advantage, avail, help, profit, serve
related words succeed, work (for); aid, assist; better, improve; content, delight, gladden, gratify, please, satisfy; bless
near antonyms hinder, impede; damage, harm, hurt, impair, injure; afflict, distress, upset

benevolence *n* **1** an act of kind assistance 〈Self-effacing as well as selfless, he refused all public acknowledgement of his many *benevolences* to the community.〉 — see FAVOR 1

2 kindly concern, interest, or support 〈Her *benevolence*

towards her employees was such that she actually let one live in her home temporarily.〉 — see GOODWILL 1

benevolent *adj* **1** having or marked by sympathy and consideration for others 〈a *benevolent* willingness to provide veterinary services to low-income families at greatly reduced prices〉 — see HUMANE 1

2 having or showing a concern for the welfare of others 〈a *benevolent* businessman who has donated money and time to helping young people〉 — see CHARITABLE 1

benighted *adj* lacking in education or the knowledge gained from books 〈the poor *benighted* souls who do not know the joys of reading〉 — see IGNORANT 1

benign *adj* **1** not causing or being capable of causing injury or hurt 〈Around campus he's known as a real character, but one whose eccentricities are entirely *benign*.〉 — see HARMLESS

2 not harsh or stern especially in nature or effect 〈basking under a *benign* sun on a day in early spring〉 — see GENTLE 1

benignant *adj* **1** having or marked by sympathy and consideration for others 〈a *benignant* understanding of the daily struggles of the economically disadvantaged〉 — see HUMANE 1

2 promoting or contributing to personal or social well-being 〈firmly believes that religion is a *benignant* force in society〉 — see BENEFICIAL

bent *n* **1** a habitual attraction to some activity or thing 〈the perfect gift for a person of a literary *bent*〉 — see INCLINATION 1

2 a special and usually inborn ability 〈Having a decided *bent* for languages, he picked up Italian in no time.〉 — see TALENT

bent (on *or* **upon)** *adj* fully committed to achieving a goal 〈a bride-to-be *bent on* having the perfect wedding〉 — see DETERMINED 1

benumb *vb* to reduce or weaken in strength or feeling 〈A succession of personal tragedies had *benumbed* him to all grief.〉 — see DULL 1

benumbed *adj* lacking in sensation or feeling 〈My *benumbed* ears took a few minutes to warm up after the frigid air outside.〉 — see NUMB 1

bequeath *vb* to give by means of a will 〈Having no heir, he *bequeathed* his fortune to charity.〉 — see LEAVE 2

bequest *n* something that is or may be inherited 〈left small *bequests* to all of her nieces and nephews〉 — see INHERITANCE

berate *vb* to criticize (someone) severely or angrily especially for personal failings 〈There's no need to *berate* someone for making a mistake during the first day on the job.〉 — see SCOLD

bereaved *adj* suffering the death of a loved one 〈The grief of the *bereaved* parents seemed to be without limit.〉
synonyms bereft
related words orphaned, widowed; distressed, grieving, melancholy, miserable, mournful, mourning, sad, sorrowing, suffering, unhappy, upset; bemoaning, crying, lamenting, wailing, weeping

bereft *adj* **1** suffering the death of a loved one 〈Friends tried to comfort the *bereft* widow.〉 — see BEREAVED

2 utterly lacking in something needed, wanted, or expected 〈a cheap motel completely *bereft* of all amenities〉 — see DEVOID 1

berserk *adv* in a confused and reckless manner 〈the familiar scene in horror movies where everyone runs *berserk* as the monster destroys everything in sight〉 — see HELTER-SKELTER 1

berth *n* an assignment at which one regularly works for pay 〈found a *berth* at a travel agency〉 — see JOB 1

beseech *vb* to make a request to (someone) in an earnest or urgent manner ⟨The lawyer ardently *beseeched* the jury to give her client justice.⟩ — see BEG

beseeching *adj* asking humbly ⟨a *beseeching* letter from his parents asking him to bring the grandchildren for a long overdue visit⟩ — see SUPPLIANT

beset *vb* 1 to cause persistent suffering to ⟨He's been *beset* by a lack of self-confidence virtually his entire life.⟩ — see AFFLICT

2 to take sudden, violent action against ⟨The unsuspecting tourists were suddenly *beset* by robbers.⟩ — see ATTACK 1

besetting *adj* caused by or suggestive of an irresistible urge ⟨that woman's *besetting* need to meddle in the affairs of others⟩ — see COMPULSIVE

beside *prep* 1 in addition to ⟨I'll need one more helper *beside* all of you.⟩ — see BESIDES 1

2 not including ⟨I need four books *beside* this one.⟩ — see EXCEPT

besides *adv* in addition to what has been said ⟨"*Besides*," Dan exclaimed, "Who are you to tell me what to do?"⟩ — see MORE 1

besides *prep* 1 in addition to ⟨*Besides* me, there are five people working on this project.⟩

synonyms as well as, beside, beyond, over and above

related words plus; including

phrases along with, at that, together with

near antonyms except (*also* excepting); less, minus, wanting

2 not including ⟨The book is 800 pages long *besides* the bibliography.⟩ — see EXCEPT

besiege *vb* 1 to surround (as a fortified place) with armed forces for the purpose of capturing or preventing commerce and communication ⟨Armies *besieged* the castle for six months before it finally fell.⟩

synonyms beleaguer, blockade, invest

related words barricade, block, cut off, dam, encircle; assail, assault, attack, beset; confine, insulate, isolate, quarantine

phrases lay siege to

near antonyms emancipate, free, liberate, release, rescue

2 to cause persistent suffering to ⟨a family *besieged* by worries about the faltering economy⟩ — see AFFLICT

3 to make a request to (someone) in an earnest or urgent manner ⟨The class *besieged* their teacher with pleas for more time to complete the assignment.⟩ — see BEG

besmear *vb* to rub an oily or sticky substance over ⟨*besmeared* the mirror with jelly⟩ — see SMEAR 1

besmirch *vb* to make dirty ⟨The puppies *besmirched* the white carpet with their dirty paws.⟩ — see DIRTY

besmirched *adj* not clean ⟨I wiped the toddler's *besmirched* face with a damp cloth.⟩ — see DIRTY 1

bespatter *vb* to wet or soil by striking with something liquid or mushy ⟨Vehicle after passing vehicle *bespattered* the sides of my once-clean car with that wintry slush.⟩ — see SPLASH 2

bespeak *vb* 1 to arrange to have something (as a hotel room) held for one's future use ⟨*bespoke* the rental car weeks in advance of their trip⟩ — see RESERVE 1

2 to make known (something abstract) through outward signs ⟨Her expression throughout the meeting *bespoke* great boredom.⟩ — see SHOW 2

3 to serve as a sign or symptom of ⟨her impressive virtuosity as a pianist *bespeaks* years of diligent practice⟩ — see INDICATE 1

best *n* 1 dressy clothing ⟨They wore their *best* to the wedding.⟩ — see FINERY

2 individuals carefully selected as being the best of a class ⟨Only the *best* will go on to the finals.⟩ — see ELITE 1

best *vb* to achieve a victory over ⟨At last she's *bested* her card-playing mother at the game of hearts.⟩ — see BEAT 2

bestow *vb* 1 to make a present of ⟨*bestowed* a new car on their son for graduation⟩ — see GIVE 1

2 to provide with living quarters or shelter ⟨Eventually the refugee family was *bestowed* in its own apartment.⟩ — see HOUSE 1

bestrew *vb* to cover by or as if by scattering something over or on ⟨The flower girl delightedly *bestrewed* the aisle with rose petals.⟩ — see SCATTER 2

bet *n* 1 the money or thing risked on the outcome of an uncertain event ⟨She offered the *bet* of a free lunch if her team won the World Series.⟩

synonyms stake, wager

related words collateral; handle, jackpot, kitty, pool, pot

2 a person or thing that is chosen ⟨Your best *bet* would be the scenic route along the coast.⟩ — see CHOICE 2

bet *vb* to risk (something) on the outcome of an uncertain event ⟨I foolishly *bet* a month's allowance on the World Series.⟩

synonyms gamble, go, lay, play, put, stake, wager

related words bid, offer; adventure, chance, hazard, speculate, venture; endanger, imperil, jeopardize

bête noire *n* 1 something or someone that causes fear or dread especially without reason ⟨Doing my own tax return is the *bête noire* that haunts me every April.⟩ — see BOGEY 1

2 something or someone that is hated ⟨In that organization's view, society's number one *bête noire* should be the drunk driver of a motor vehicle.⟩ — see HATE 2

betide *vb* to take place ⟨We will be happy in our new home, whatever may *betide*.⟩ — see HAPPEN

betoken *vb* to serve as a sign or symptom of ⟨The humor in his writing *betokens* a warm and compassionate heart.⟩ — see INDICATE 1

betray *vb* 1 to be unfaithful or disloyal to ⟨Childhood friends of movie stars often *betray* them by telling their secrets to the supermarket tabloids.⟩

synonyms cross, double-cross, sell (out)

related words give away; inform (on), rat (on), snitch (on), tell (on), turn in

phrases go back on, stab in the back

near antonyms defend, guard, protect, safeguard, save, shield

antonyms stand by

2 to make known (something abstract) through outward signs ⟨His face *betrayed* his exasperation with his nosy neighbor.⟩ — see SHOW 2

3 to lead away from a usual or proper course by offering some pleasure or advantage ⟨She was *betrayed* by a false show of friendship into lending the money.⟩ — see LURE

betrayal *n* the act or fact of violating the trust or confidence of another ⟨the terrible *betrayal* of having her best friend reveal her confidences to others⟩

synonyms business, disloyalty, double cross, faithlessness, falseness, falsity, infidelity, perfidy, sellout, treachery, treason, unfaithfulness

related words abandonment, desertion; deceit, double-dealing, duplicity, guile, two-facedness; fraud, informing, lying, snitching, talebearing, trickery

near antonyms dependability, reliability, trustworthiness; defense, protection, safeguard, shield

antonyms allegiance, devotion, faithfulness, fealty, fidelity, loyalty, staunchness, steadfastness

betrayer *n* 1 a person who provides information about another's wrongdoing ⟨The arrested criminal vowed that he would get his revenge on his *betrayer*.⟩ — see INFORMER

2 one who betrays a trust or an allegiance ⟨The *betrayer* of Anne Frank's family in Amsterdam has never been identified for certain.⟩ — see TRAITOR

betrothal *n* the act or state of being engaged to be married ⟨The couple's *betrothal* lasted four years.⟩ — see ENGAGEMENT 1

betrothed *adj* pledged in marriage ⟨a splendid party in honor of the *betrothed* couple⟩ — see ENGAGED 1

betrothed *n* the person to whom one is engaged to be married ⟨He gazed lovingly at his *betrothed* throughout the dinner.⟩
synonyms fiancé, fiancée, intended
related words admirer, beau, beloved, boyfriend, darling, dear, favorite, fellow, flame, girlfriend, honey, love, lover, steady, swain, sweet, sweetheart, sweetie pie, valentine; bride

better *adv* to a greater or higher extent ⟨He knows property law *better* than anyone else.⟩ — see MORE 2

better *n* **1** one who is above another in rank, station, or office ⟨Be polite to your *betters* and to those below you in equal measure.⟩ — see SUPERIOR
2 the more favorable condition or position in a competition ⟨She got the *better* of her opponents very early in the race.⟩ — see ADVANTAGE 1

better *vb* **1** to be greater, better, or stronger than ⟨This year's profits should *better* last year's by a wide margin.⟩ — see SURPASS 1
2 to make better ⟨They are trying to *better* the lives of working people.⟩ — see IMPROVE

better half *n* the person to whom another is married ⟨"Allow me to introduce you to my *better half*, Joan."⟩ — see SPOUSE

bettor *or* **better** *n* one that bets (as on the outcome of a contest or sports event) ⟨Thousands of *bettors* were at the racetrack last weekend.⟩
synonyms gambler, wagerer
related words high roller, piker; dicer; bluffer, sharper, speculator; bookmaker, handicapper, oddsmaker, tipster

beverage *n* a liquid suitable for drinking ⟨Would anyone like a *beverage* with their snack?⟩ — see DRINK 1

bewail *vb* to feel or express sorrow for ⟨He invariably spends more time *bewailing* his predicament than trying to fix it.⟩ — see LAMENT 1

bewailing *adj* expressing or suggesting mourning ⟨The doctor assured us that my father was fine and that there was no need for the *bewailing* looks on our faces.⟩ — see MOURNFUL 1

beware (of) *vb* to be cautious of or on guard against ⟨*Beware of* that parrot because it bites!⟩
synonyms guard (against), mind, watch out (for)
related words attend, heed, mark, note, notice; behold, discern, observe, perceive, see, watch
phrases be on the lookout for, keep one's eyes open for (*or* keep one's eyes peeled for)
near antonyms discount, disregard, ignore, miss, overlook

bewilder *vb* to throw into a state of mental uncertainty ⟨The change in policy seems to have *bewildered* many of our customers.⟩ — see CONFUSE 1

bewildered *adj* suffering from mental confusion ⟨The *bewildered* dog wandered aimlessly around the playground.⟩ — see DIZZY 2

bewilderment *n* a state of mental uncertainty ⟨She stared at them in *bewilderment* and shock.⟩ — see CONFUSION 1

bewitch *vb* **1** to cast a spell on ⟨a Wiccan who believes that it is indeed possible to *bewitch* someone⟩
synonyms charm, enchant, hex, overlook, spell
related words curse, jinx, possess, voodoo; attract, be-

guile, captivate, fascinate, mesmerize, spellbind; entice, lure, seduce, tempt
near antonyms bless
2 to attract or delight as if by magic ⟨an animated film that *bewitches* children and adults alike⟩ — see CHARM 1

bewitched *adj* being or appearing to be under a magic spell ⟨the *bewitched* princess who could be awakened only by a kiss⟩ — see ENCHANTED

bewitching *adj* having an often mysterious or magical power to attract ⟨a *bewitching* city that tourists flock to⟩ — see FASCINATING 1

bewitchment *n* **1** a spoken word or set of words believed to have magic power ⟨a story full of magical potions and *bewitchments*⟩ — see SPELL 1
2 the power to control natural forces through supernatural means ⟨While stuck in traffic, I could have used a bit of *bewitchment* to clear the road of other drivers.⟩ — see MAGIC 1

beyond *adv* at or to a greater distance or more advanced point ⟨the dream that someday we will journey to the outer reaches of our solar system and *beyond*⟩ — see FARTHER

beyond *n* unending existence after death ⟨Who knows how we'll fare in the *beyond*?⟩ — see ETERNITY 2

beyond *prep* **1** on or to the farther side of ⟨The arrow flew *beyond* the fence and into the woods.⟩
synonyms over, past
related words outside
phrases on the far side of
near antonyms inside
2 out of the reach or sphere of ⟨Letting you have the day off is *beyond* my authority.⟩
synonyms outside, outside of, without
related words except (*also* excepting)
near antonyms inside
antonyms within
3 in addition to ⟨*Beyond* the asking price of the house, there's also the cost of fixing up this "handyman's dream"⟩ — see BESIDES 1

bias *adv* in a line or direction running from corner to corner ⟨made of fabric cut *bias*⟩ — see CROSSWISE

bias *n* **1** an attitude that always favors one way of feeling or acting especially without considering any other possibilities ⟨He has a powerful *bias* towards sentimentality, which comes through even in his grittier stories.⟩
synonyms favor, one-sidedness, partiality, partisanship, ply, prejudice
related words chauvinism, cronyism, favoritism, nepotism; self-opinionatedness, self-partiality; bent, inclination, leaning, penchant, predilection, predisposition, proclivity, propensity, tendency; preconception, prejudgment, prepossession; bigotry, partisanship
near antonyms calm, detachment, indifference; aversion, dislike, distaste, hate
antonyms impartiality, neutrality, objectivity, open-mindedness, unbiasedness
2 a habitual attraction to some activity or thing ⟨From her youth she revealed a strong *bias* toward a life of the mind.⟩ — see INCLINATION 1

bias *vb* to cause to have often negative opinions formed without sufficient knowledge ⟨bad reviews *biased* her against the movie, even though it starred one of her favorite actors.⟩ — see PREJUDICE

biased *adj* inclined to favor one side over another ⟨The refs are *biased* towards the home team.⟩ — see PARTIAL 1

Bible *n* a book made up of the writings accepted by Christians as coming from God ⟨She received a lovely *Bible* as a First Communion gift.⟩
synonyms Book, Good Book, Holy Writ, Scripture

bibulous *adj* able to soak up liquids especially readily ⟨special drying cloths that are so *bibulous* that they can absorb 10 times their weight in water⟩ — see ABSORBENT

bicker *n* an often noisy or angry expression of differing opinions ⟨After a prolonged *bicker*, they finally managed to find a movie that both of them were interested in seeing.⟩ — see ARGUMENT 1

bicker *vb* to express different opinions about something often angrily ⟨You can stop *bickering*—we've chosen a place to go.⟩ — see ARGUE 2

bickerer *n* a person who takes part in a dispute ⟨Though *bickerers* when young, the brothers get on quite well now.⟩ — see DISPUTANT

bid *n* an effort to do or accomplish something ⟨a dramatic film that is widely regarded as the comedian's last-ditch *bid* to be taken seriously as an actor⟩ — see ATTEMPT 1

bid *vb* **1** to issue orders to (someone) by right of authority ⟨The children did as they were *bidden*.⟩ — see COMMAND 1
2 to request the presence or participation of ⟨As company president, I *bid* you all to come to our annual holiday party!⟩ — see INVITE 1

bide *vb* **1** to remain indefinitely in existence or in the same state ⟨He *bides* in the same job he's had for 30 years.⟩ — see CONTINUE 1
2 to remain in place in readiness or expectation of something ⟨I promise you that if you *bide* yet a little longer, all will come to pass just as you desire.⟩ — see WAIT

big *adj* **1** having great meaning or lasting effect ⟨There will be a *big* meeting to resolve the issue.⟩ — see IMPORTANT 1
2 of a size greater than average of its kind ⟨bought a *big* apple to quench his raging appetite⟩ — see LARGE
3 having, characterized by, or arising from a dignified and generous nature ⟨How *big* of you to give your subordinates most of the credit.⟩ — see NOBLE 2
4 having an abundance of some characteristic quality (as flavor) ⟨coffee with a *big* bold taste⟩ — see FULL-BODIED
5 coming before all others in importance ⟨The *big* story that year was the presidential election.⟩ — see FOREMOST 1
6 enjoying widespread favor or approval ⟨Jackets with very wide lapels were *big* that year.⟩ — see POPULAR 1
7 containing unborn young within the body ⟨a mare *big* with a foal⟩ — see PREGNANT 1

big *n* one of high position or importance within a group ⟨With that new promotion he's now one of the *bigs* in the company.⟩ — see BIG SHOT

bight *n* a part of a body of water that extends beyond the general shoreline ⟨The *bight* known as the Bay of Fundy is known for its fast-running tides.⟩ — see GULF 1

big leaguer *n* one of high position or importance within a group ⟨The once-tiny ad agency is now a *big leaguer* that attracts clients on the A-list.⟩ — see BIG SHOT

bigness *n* the quality or state of being large in size ⟨The sheer *bigness* of the 50-pound pumpkin made us want to buy it.⟩ — see LARGENESS

bigot *n* one who stubbornly or intolerantly adheres to his or her own opinions and prejudices ⟨an incorrigible *bigot* who hasn't entertained a new thought in years⟩
synonyms partisan (*also* partizan), sectarian
related words fanatic, purist; nationalist; racialist, racist, supremacist; chauvinist, sexist
near antonyms freethinker, latitudinarian

bigoted *adj* unwilling to grant other people social rights or to accept other viewpoints ⟨a demagogue with *bigoted* followers⟩ — see INTOLERANT 2

big shot *n* one of high position or importance within a group ⟨a meeting at which all of the *big shots* in the company were present⟩
synonyms big, big leaguer, bigwig, heavy, kingpin, nabob, wheel
related words baron, czar (*also* tsar *or* tzar), king, magnate, mogul, prince, tycoon; VIP
near antonyms inferior, subordinate, underling; mediocrity, obscurity
antonyms lightweight, nobody, nonentity, nothing, shrimp, twerp, whippersnapper, zero, zilch

bigwig *n* one of high position or importance within a group ⟨interviewed by several *bigwigs* on the hospital's staff⟩ — see BIG SHOT

bile *n* biting sharpness of feeling or expression ⟨With considerable *bile*, the author recounts a difficult period in his life.⟩ — see ACRIMONY 1

¹**bill** *n* **1** a record of goods sold or services performed together with the costs due ⟨Why is the electric *bill* so high this month?⟩
synonyms account, check, invoice, statement, tab
related words receipt, reckoning; document, ledger, record; charge, cost, expense, fee, price, rate, toll; score, tally
2 a piece of printed paper used as money in the United States ⟨The $5 *bill* has a picture of Abraham Lincoln on the front.⟩
synonyms greenback, note
related words paper money, scrip; buck, smacker [*slang*]; C-note, fifty, five, one, ten, tenner, twenty, two; cash, chips, currency, dough, legal tender, lucre, money, pelf; check, draft, money order
3 a sheet bearing an announcement for posting in a public place ⟨posted a *bill* advertising the new play⟩ — see POSTER
4 the amount owed at a bar or restaurant or the slip of paper stating the amount ⟨Although they were all working adults, their father still insisted on paying the *bill* whenever they went out to eat.⟩ — see CHECK 1
5 a rule of conduct or action laid down by a governing authority and especially a legislature ⟨the fair housing *bill* of the 1960s⟩ — see LAW 1

²**bill** *n* **1** the jaws of a bird together with their hornlike covering ⟨Parrots have very strong *bills* so they can break open nuts.⟩ — see BEAK 1
2 the projecting front part of a hat or cap ⟨The hat was blue, but the *bill* was red.⟩ — see VISOR

¹**billet** *n* a straight piece (as of wood or metal) that is longer than it is wide ⟨a stack of gold *billets* in the vault⟩ — see BAR 1

²**billet** *n* an assignment at which one regularly works for pay ⟨He found a *billet* at one of the leading brokerage houses in New York.⟩ — see JOB 1

billet *vb* to provide with living quarters or shelter ⟨Every colonial household was expected to *billet* a British soldier.⟩ — see HOUSE 1

billow *n* a moving ridge on the surface of water ⟨The great *billows* created by the ocean storm threatened to swamp the fishing boat.⟩ — see WAVE

billow *vb* to extend outward beyond a usual point ⟨The curtains in the open windows *billowed* in the summer wind.⟩ — see BULGE 1

billy *n* a heavy rigid stick used as a weapon or for punishment ⟨Police officers often carry a *billy*.⟩ — see CLUB 1

billy club *n* a heavy rigid stick used as a weapon or for punishment ⟨Rapping the shoes of the sleeping vagrant with his *billy club*, the policeman told him to move on.⟩ — see CLUB 1

bin *n* a covered rectangular container for storing or transporting things ⟨a storage *bin* for hats and gloves⟩ — see CHEST

binary *adj* consisting of two members or parts that are usually joined ⟨A *binary* star is a system of two stars that revolve around each other under their mutual gravitation.⟩ — see DOUBLE 1

bind *n* **1** a difficult, puzzling, or embarrassing situation from which there is no easy escape ⟨With our vacation week fast approaching, and no arrangements for the care of our pets, we were in a serious *bind*.⟩ — see PREDICAMENT

2 something that physically prevents free movement ⟨The burglar was held in a makeshift *bind* until the law officers could arrive.⟩ — see BOND 1

bind *vb* **1** to confine or restrain with or as if with chains ⟨The prisoner was *bound* by the wrists.⟩

synonyms chain, enchain, fetter, handcuff, manacle, shackle, trammel

related words bit, hobble, hog-tie, iron, lash, secure, tie, truss; attach, fasten, join, link; confine, constrain, curb, hamper, hinder, impede; limit, restrict; entangle, tangle

near antonyms emancipate, free, liberate, loose, release, rescue; undo, unfasten, untangle, untie; detach, disengage

antonyms unbind, unfetter, unshackle

2 to cover with a bandage ⟨*Bind* the wound to stop the bleeding.⟩ — see BANDAGE

3 to gather into a tight mass by means of a line or cord ⟨*Bind* the asparagus spears carefully before packing the bunches.⟩ — see TIE 1

binge *n* **1** a time or instance of carefree fun ⟨a shopping *binge* at the mall⟩ — see FLING 1

2 a social gathering ⟨What should we wear to this *binge* at the country club?⟩ — see PARTY 1

binge *vb* to take part in drunken revelry ⟨a program designed to educate college students about the dangers of *bingeing*⟩ — see CAROUSE

biography *n* a history of a person's life ⟨An unauthorized *biography* of the actor gave him some serious headaches.⟩

synonyms life, memoir

related words autobiography; hagiography; psychobiography; tell-all; chronicle, history, past, story; character sketch, profile

bipartite *adj* consisting of two members or parts that are usually joined ⟨separated the *bipartite* rock⟩ — see DOUBLE 1

birch *vb* **1** to strike repeatedly with something long and thin or flexible ⟨a Dickens character cruelly *birched* as punishment⟩ — see WHIP 1

2 to strike repeatedly ⟨threatened to *birch* the pranksters if he ever caught them⟩ — see BEAT 1

bird *n* a member of the human race ⟨They're a couple of tough old *birds* who can manage without any interference from their grandchildren.⟩ — see HUMAN

birdman *n* one who flies or is qualified to fly an aircraft or spacecraft ⟨In the early days of aviation, *birdmen* would travel around the country in their biplanes, putting on flying shows.⟩ — see PILOT

bird's–eye *adj* relating to the main elements and not to specific details ⟨a *bird's-eye* look at the current situation in that part of the world⟩ — see GENERAL 2

birth *adj* being such by blood and not by adoption or marriage ⟨the *birth* mother⟩ — see NATURAL 3

birth *n* **1** the act or instance of being born ⟨Almost from *birth*, he showed all the marks of future greatness.⟩

synonyms nativity

related words creation, genesis, origination, rise; accouchement, bearing, childbearing, labor, parturition; begetting, breeding, fathering, generation, mothering,

parenting, reproduction, siring, spawning; fatherhood, maternity, motherhood, parenthood, paternity

near antonyms abortion, miscarriage; stillbirth

2 the line of ancestors from whom a person is descended ⟨a man of noble *birth*⟩ — see ANCESTRY

3 the point at which something begins ⟨That 12-second flight by Orville Wright marked the *birth* of aviation.⟩ — see BEGINNING

birthplace *n* a place of origin ⟨Montgomery, Alabama, is considered the *birthplace* of the civil rights movement.⟩

synonyms cradle, home, motherland

related words hometown; country, nativity, old country, roots

birthright *n* **1** something that is or may be inherited ⟨believed that the house was her *birthright*⟩ — see INHERITANCE

2 something to which one has a just claim ⟨The promotion is his *birthright*, after the work he put in.⟩ — see RIGHT 1

bisect *vb* to divide by passing through or across ⟨Draw a line that *bisects* the triangle.⟩ — see INTERSECT

bit *n* **1** a very small piece ⟨She left only a *bit* of the broccoli on her plate.⟩

synonyms atom, crumb, dribble, fleck, flyspeck, grain, granule, molecule, morsel, mote, nubbin, nugget, particle, patch, scrap, scruple, snip, snippet, speck, tittle

related words ace, dab, dash, driblet, drop, iota, jot, lick, minim, mite, modicum, nutshell, ounce, pinch, shred, smidgen (*also* smidgeon *or* smidgin *or* smidge), spot, strain, streak, suspicion, taste, touch, trace, whisper, whit; bite, mouthful, nibble, tidbit (*also* titbit); fragment, part, portion, section; chip, flake, shard, shiver, sliver, splinter; clipping, paring, shaving; smithereens

near antonyms chunk, gob, hunk, lump, slab; abundance, barrel, bucket, bushel, deal, heaps, loads, mass, mountain, peck, pile, pot, profusion, quantity, raft, scads, stack, volume, wad, wealth

2 a broken or irregular part of something that often remains incomplete ⟨*bits* of cookie scattered on the table⟩ — see FRAGMENT

3 a very small amount ⟨I'll have only a *bit* of food right now.⟩ — see PARTICLE 1

4 an indefinite but usually short period of time ⟨This will only take a *bit*.⟩ — see WHILE 1

5 a performance regularly presented by an individual or group ⟨known for a comedic *bit* in which she portrayed a very nervous student driver⟩ — see ACT 1

6 something that is pleasing to eat because it is rare or a luxury ⟨Wielding silver trays, the servers offered partygoers a variety of exotic-looking *bits*.⟩ — see DELICACY 1

bite *n* **1** a harsh or sharp quality ⟨The soup has a peppery *bite*.⟩ — see EDGE 1

2 a small piece or quantity of food ⟨had only a *bite* to eat before rushing off⟩ — see MORSEL 1

3 an uncomfortable degree of coolness ⟨weather with a *bite* that suggested winter was right around the corner⟩ — see CHILL

bite (at) *vb* to consume or wear away gradually ⟨The waves were *biting at* the sand castle I had worked so hard on.⟩ — see EAT 2

bite (on) *vb* to crush or grind with the teeth ⟨She tends to *bite on* her pencils when she thinks hard.⟩

synonyms champ, chew, chomp (on), crunch (on), gnaw (on), masticate

related words ruminate; munch, nosh, snack; consume, eat, ingest, swallow; bolt, devour, gobble (up or down), gorge, gulp, scarf, scoff, snack, wolf; nip, pick (at); gum, mumble

phrases sink one's teeth into

biting *adj* **1** causing intense discomfort to one's skin ⟨a *biting* wind that only the toughest football fans were willing to endure⟩ — see CUTTING 1

2 marked by the use of wit that is intended to cause hurt feelings ⟨made *biting* comments about her opponent⟩ — see SARCASTIC

bitter *adj* **1** having or showing deep-seated resentment ⟨a *bitter* attitude about always having to work on Saturday⟩
synonyms acrid, acrimonious, embittered, hard, rancorous, resentful, sore
related words disaffected, discontented, disgruntled, malcontent; contemptuous, cynical, disdainful, misanthropic, scornful; angry, cruel, harsh, mad, rough, savage, vehement, vicious, virulent; acid, caustic, cutting, mordant, sarcastic, trenchant
near antonyms caring, forgiving, gentle, kind, kindhearted, loving, sweet, sympathetic, tender, warm, warmhearted
antonyms unbitter

2 hard to accept or bear especially emotionally ⟨Discovering that he had been cut from the crew team was a *bitter* disappointment.⟩
synonyms afflicting, agonizing, cruel, excruciating, galling, grievous, harrowing, harsh, heartrending, hurtful, painful, tormenting, torturous
related words insufferable, insupportable, intolerable, unacceptable, unbearable, unendurable, unsupportable; appalling, awful, bad, dire, dreadful, ghastly, horrible, miserable, nasty, rotten, severe, terrible, vile, wretched; acute, extreme, intense, piercing
near antonyms bearable, endurable, supportable, sustainable, tolerable; livable (*also* liveable), sufferable, survivable; acceptable, allowable, reasonable
antonyms gratifying, pleasing, sweet

3 causing intense discomfort to one's skin ⟨A *bitter* wind was stinging the faces of the skiers.⟩ — see CUTTING 1

4 difficult to endure ⟨a *bitter* lesson about money and friendship⟩ — see HARSH 1

5 having a low or subnormal temperature ⟨a *bitter* February day for this part of the country⟩ — see COLD 1

6 uncomfortably cool ⟨a *bitter*, rainy day⟩ — see CHILLY 1

7 expressing or suggesting mourning ⟨a *bitter* cry of grief⟩ — see MOURNFUL 1

8 not giving pleasure to the mind or senses ⟨They had to face the *bitter* truth about their chances of winning the election.⟩ — see UNPLEASANT

bitterly *adv* with feelings of bitterness or grief ⟨The child cried *bitterly* after her goldfish died.⟩ — see HARD 2

bitterness *n* **1** a deep-seated ill will ⟨He still harbored an implacable *bitterness* against the company that had fired him.⟩ — see ENMITY

2 a harsh or sharp quality ⟨The *bitterness* of the coffee suggested that it had been reheated.⟩ — see EDGE 1

3 an uncomfortable degree of coolness ⟨There's a *bitterness* in the air, so let's build a fire in the fireplace.⟩ — see CHILL

4 biting sharpness of feeling or expression ⟨complained with great *bitterness* about the unfair treatment he had received⟩ — see ACRIMONY 1

bitty *adj* very small in size ⟨a little *bitty* chick that I could hold in my hand⟩ — see TINY

bivouac *n* a place where a group of people live for a short time in tents or cabins ⟨soldiers setting up a *bivouac* by the stream⟩ — see CAMP 1

bivouac *vb* **1** to live in a camp or the outdoors ⟨The army *bivouacked* for the night by the lake.⟩ — see CAMP (OUT)

2 to provide with living quarters or shelter ⟨Residents who lost power were *bivouacked* in the school.⟩ — see HOUSE 1

bizarre *adj* **1** conceived or made without regard for reason

or reality ⟨a *bizarre* invention that no one could figure out how to use⟩ — see FANTASTIC 1

2 different from the ordinary in a way that causes curiosity or suspicion ⟨I heard the most *bizarre* story.⟩ — see ODD 2

blab *vb* **1** to engage in casual or rambling conversation ⟨frequently calls her best friend and *blabs* for an hour⟩ — see CHAT 1

2 to relate sometimes questionable or secret information of a personal nature ⟨He *blabs* a lot, so never share a secret with him.⟩ — see GOSSIP

blabber *n* **1** a person who talks constantly ⟨a *blabber* who always catches me on my way out the door⟩ — see CHATTERBOX

2 unintelligible or meaningless talk ⟨new parents who enjoy listening to their baby's *blabber*⟩ — see GIBBERISH 1

blabbermouth *n* a person who talks constantly ⟨can't get a word in with that *blabbermouth* around⟩ — see CHATTERBOX

blabby *adj* fond of talking or conversation ⟨She is a sweet woman, but so *blabby* that you need to escape her after a while.⟩ — see TALKATIVE

black *adj* **1** having the color of soot or coal ⟨a little *black* Scottish terrier⟩
synonyms ebony, pitch-black, pitch-dark, pitchy, raven, sable
related words dark, dusky, inky; blackish
near antonyms bright, brilliant, light, pale, palish
antonyms white

2 causing or marked by an atmosphere lacking in cheer ⟨The Friday of the stock market crash was indeed a *black* day for the country.⟩ — see GLOOMY 1

3 being without light or without much light ⟨a *black*, moonless night⟩ — see DARK 1

4 not clean ⟨After working on the car, the mechanic's hands were *black* with grime.⟩ — see DIRTY 1

black *n* a time or place of little or no light ⟨a serial killer who always did his evil deeds in the *black* of night⟩ — see DARK 1

blackball *vb* to reject by or as if by a vote ⟨She was *blackballed* by the sorority.⟩ — see NEGATIVE 1

blacken *vb* **1** to make dirty ⟨*blackened* the towels with their dirty hands⟩ — see DIRTY

2 to make untrue and harmful statements about ⟨The politician maliciously *blackened* his opponent's reputation.⟩ — see SLANDER

3 to make dark, dim, or indistinct ⟨Thick smoke from the forest fires *blackened* the sky for many miles.⟩ — see CLOUD 1

4 to grow dark ⟨The auditorium *blackened* suddenly, and a spotlighted performer appeared alone on stage.⟩ — see DARKEN 2

blackened *adj* not clean ⟨The church's *blackened* ceiling is the result of centuries of candle smoke.⟩ — see DIRTY 1

blackening *n* the making of false statements that damage another's reputation ⟨The *blackening* of the senator's reputation disgusted voters.⟩ — see SLANDER

blackmailer *n* a person who gets money from another by using force or threats ⟨The *blackmailer* threatened to tell the media about the mayor's arrest as a teenager.⟩ — see RACKETEER

blackness *n* a time or place of little or no light ⟨Strange nocturnal noises emanated from the forbidding *blackness* of the forest.⟩ — see DARK 1

blackout *n* a temporary state of unconsciousness ⟨Even though you experienced only a brief *blackout*, you still ought to be checked by a doctor.⟩ — see FAINT

black out *vb* **1** to destroy all traces of ⟨Certain passages of the story were *blacked out*.⟩ — see ANNIHILATE 1

2 to grow dark ⟨With the delivery of the knockout punch, the screen *blacks out*, and in the next scene the boxer wakes up in the hospital.⟩ — see DARKEN 2

3 to lose consciousness ⟨*blacked out* after hitting her head on the beam⟩ — see FAINT

blade *n* **1** a hand weapon with a length of metal sharpened on one or both sides and usually tapered to a sharp point ⟨dueled with *blades* rather than guns⟩ — see SWORD

2 an instrument with a metal length that has a sharp edge for cutting ⟨used a small *blade* to cut the rope⟩ — see KNIFE

blahs *pl n* the state of being bored ⟨I've just been stuck in the *blahs* lately.⟩ — see BOREDOM

blamable *adj* deserving reproach or blame ⟨An honest mistake is hardly a *blamable* offense.⟩ — see BLAME-WORTHY

blame *n* **1** responsibility for wrongdoing or failure ⟨willingly accepted the *blame* for not seeing that the kitchen was properly cleaned⟩
synonyms culpability, fault, guilt, rap
related words blameworthiness, complicity, guiltiness, sinfulness; accusation, censure, condemnation, denunciation, finger-pointing, reproach; regret, remorse, self-reproach, shame
antonyms blamelessness, faultlessness, guiltlessness, innocence

2 the state of being held as the cause of something that needs to be set right ⟨*Blame* for the school's poor performance in standardized tests was attributed to several factors.⟩ — see RESPONSIBILITY 1

blame *vb* to express one's unfavorable opinion of the worth or quality of ⟨More concerned with pleasing audiences, the playwright has always claimed to be indifferent to whether critics praise his comedies or *blame* them without mercy.⟩ — see CRITICIZE

blameless *adj* free from guilt or blame ⟨An investigation of the accident proved them *blameless*.⟩ — see INNOCENT 2

blamelessness *n* the quality or state of being free from guilt or blame ⟨Your *blamelessness* in this incident is obvious, so you won't be punished.⟩ — see INNOCENCE 1

blameworthy *adj* deserving reproach or blame ⟨We were all equally *blameworthy*, whether we had openly approved the free-speech restrictions or simply kept quiet about them.⟩
synonyms blamable, censurable, culpable, reprehensible, reproachable
related words bad, guilty, sinful, wicked; foolish, irresponsible, reckless; chargeable, disciplinable, impeachable, indictable, punishable; criminal, illegal, illicit, unlawful; illegitimate, improper, wrongful
phrases at fault
near antonyms flawless, perfect, pure; guiltless, innocent
antonyms blameless, faultless, impeccable, irreproachable

blanch *vb* to make white or whiter by removing color ⟨A good washing with bleach should *blanch* these yellowed sheets.⟩ — see WHITEN

blanched *adj* lacking a healthy skin color ⟨looking *blanched* and feeble after a long illness⟩ — see PALE 2

bland *adj* not harsh or stern especially in nature or effect ⟨*bland* food that was good for babies⟩ — see GENTLE 1

blandish *vb* to get (someone) to do something by gentle urging, special attention, or flattery ⟨*blandished* the dog into obeying her by praising her repeatedly⟩ — see COAX

blank *adj* **1** not expressing any emotion ⟨The teacher knew no one was paying attention when she looked out and saw all those *blank* faces.⟩
synonyms deadpan, empty, expressionless, impassive, inexpressive, numb, stolid, vacant

related words dull, vacuous, vague, vapid; enigmatic (*also* enigmatical), impenetrable, inscrutable, mysterious; motionless, static, still, wooden; reserved, restrained, reticent, taciturn; aloof, apathetic, cold, cool, detached, indifferent, phlegmatic, unresponsive
near antonyms engaged, interested, responsive; active, alive, animated, bright, busy, dynamic, effervescent, energetic, expansive, exuberant, lively, vivacious; eloquent, revealing, revelatory; emotional, melodramatic, theatrical (*also* theatric), unreserved, unrestrained
antonyms demonstrative, expressive

2 lacking contents that could or should be present ⟨The page of instructions actually turned out to be *blank*.⟩ — see EMPTY 1

3 having no exceptions or restrictions ⟨his *blank* refusal to even consider my request⟩ — see ABSOLUTE 2

blank *n* **1** a piece of paper with information written or to be written on it ⟨handed him an employment *blank* to fill out⟩ — see FORM 2

2 empty space ⟨a *blank* on the form for the patient's insurance policy number⟩ — see VACANCY 1

blanket *adj* belonging or relating to the whole ⟨a *blanket* promise of amnesty for everyone with overdue library books⟩ — see GENERAL 1

blanket *n* something that covers or conceals like a piece of cloth ⟨A *blanket* of fog concealed the view of the harbor.⟩ — see CLOAK 1

blanket *vb* **1** to form a layer over ⟨Leaves *blanketed* all of the land around the house.⟩ — see COVER 2

2 to keep secret or shut off from view ⟨*blanketed* the secret memo from the news media⟩ — see ¹HIDE 2

3 to cause to cease burning ⟨Firefighters managed to *blanket* the fire with foam.⟩ — see EXTINGUISH 1

blankness *n* empty space ⟨A conspicuous *blankness* surrounds the figure of the woman, for the artist is trying to suggest her deep isolation and loneliness.⟩ — see VACANCY 1

blare *n* loud, confused, and usually inharmonious sound ⟨The *blare* of horns arising from the long line of cars behind him did nothing to help the motorist get his car started again.⟩ — see NOISE 1

blare *vb* to make known openly or publicly ⟨Headlines *blared* their championship.⟩ — see ANNOUNCE

blaring *adj* marked by a high volume of sound ⟨A car drove by and woke us up with *blaring* music.⟩ — see LOUD 1

blarney *n* **1** excessive praise ⟨She was charmed by his *blarney*.⟩ — see FLATTERY

2 language, behavior, or ideas that are absurd and contrary to good sense ⟨His excuse was his usual *blarney* about how he'd love to help out but he was just so darned busy.⟩ — see NONSENSE 1

blarney *vb* **1** to get (someone) to do something by gentle urging, special attention, or flattery ⟨Attendants at the nursing home sometimes have to *blarney* the patients to take their medicine.⟩ — see COAX

2 to praise too much ⟨an eager, young assistant who *blarneys* the boss⟩ — see FLATTER 1

blaspheme *vb* to use offensive or indecent language ⟨shocked that someone would *blaspheme* in church⟩ — see SWEAR 1

blasphemous *adj* not showing proper reverence for the holy or sacred ⟨a book denounced as *blasphemous*⟩ — see IRREVERENT

blasphemy *n* an act of great disrespect shown to God or to sacred ideas, people, or things ⟨In the 17th century the Quakers were persecuted for beliefs and practices that older churches regarded as *blasphemies*.⟩
synonyms defilement, desecration, impiety, irreverence, sacrilege

related words cursing, swearing; affront, insult; violation; corruption, debasement, pollution; sin, trespass
near antonyms consecration, purification, sanctification; reverence, veneration
antonyms adoration, glorification, worship
blast *n* **1** a loud explosive sound ⟨A sharp *blast* of the horn startled the other driver.⟩ — see CLAP 1
2 a sudden brief rush of wind ⟨A surprise *blast* stole the umbrella right out of his hands.⟩ — see GUST 1
3 the act or an instance of exploding ⟨The *blast* destroyed the building completely.⟩ — see EXPLOSION 1
4 a social gathering ⟨a weekend *blast*⟩ — see PARTY 1
blast *vb* **1** to cause to break open or into pieces by or as if by an explosive ⟨The highway engineers will have to *blast* that hill in order to put a road through here.⟩
synonyms blow, blow up, burst, demolish, explode, pop, shatter, smash
related words annihilate, decimate, destroy; ruin, wreck; detonate, discharge; fragment, splinter
near antonyms collapse, implode
2 to cause (a projectile) to be driven forward with force ⟨artillery that could *blast* cannonballs from hundreds of yards away⟩ — see SHOOT 1
3 to cause a weapon to release a missile with great force ⟨The recruits were all *blasting* away at the target range.⟩ — see SHOOT 2
4 to criticize harshly and usually publicly ⟨*blasted* the new governor for every little misstep⟩ — see ATTACK 2
5 to proceed or move quickly ⟨*blasted* down the road in a sports car⟩ — see HURRY 2
blasting *adj* marked by a high volume of sound ⟨listened to a *blasting* car radio whenever he drove⟩ — see LOUD 1
blasting *n* a directed propelling of a missile by a firearm or artillery piece ⟨The next *blasting* by the artillery scored a direct hit.⟩ — see SHOT 1
blatant *adj* **1** engaging in or marked by loud and insistent cries especially of protest ⟨a *blatant* clamor for change⟩ — see VOCIFEROUS
2 very noticeable especially for being incorrect or bad ⟨I take off points for *blatant* spelling errors.⟩ — see EGREGIOUS
blaze *n* **1** a sudden intense expression of strong feeling ⟨She felt a *blaze* of resentment upon hearing that she had been passed over for promotion.⟩ — see OUTBURST 1
2 the steady giving off of the form of radiation that makes vision possible ⟨temporarily blinded by the *blaze* of dozens of camera lights⟩ — see LIGHT 1
¹blaze *vb* to make known openly or publicly ⟨The White House didn't waste a minute in *blazing* the lower unemployment figures.⟩ — see ANNOUNCE
²blaze *vb* **1** to be on fire especially brightly ⟨The house *blazed* for over three hours in the late-night fire.⟩ — see BURN 1
2 to shine with a bright harsh light ⟨The spotlight *blazed* through my window.⟩ — see GLARE 1
3 to proceed or move quickly ⟨A champion skier went *blazing* down the ski slope at a record pace.⟩ — see HURRY 2
blazing *adj* **1** being on fire ⟨The *blazing* logs in the fireplace cast a warm glow on our holiday party.⟩ — see ABLAZE 1
2 having or expressing great depth of feeling ⟨a *blazing* speech affirming the value of every individual in this world⟩ — see FERVENT 1
bleach *vb* to make white or whiter by removing color ⟨*bleached* the stained shirt back to its original white⟩ — see WHITEN
bleak *adj* **1** causing or marked by an atmosphere lacking in cheer ⟨a *bleak* outlook for the team for the rest of the season⟩ — see GLOOMY 1

2 marked by wet and windy conditions ⟨It was a dark and *bleak* wintry day.⟩ — see FOUL 1
3 uncomfortably cool ⟨a *bleak* December morning⟩ — see CHILLY 1
bleakness *n* an uncomfortable degree of coolness ⟨The morning *bleakness* prompted me to get a fire going.⟩ — see CHILL
bleary *adj* **1** depleted in strength, energy, or freshness ⟨disoriented, *bleary* passengers departing from the red-eye⟩ — see WEARY 1
2 not seen or understood clearly ⟨The *bleary* outline of a fishing boat could just be seen through the fog.⟩ — see FAINT 1
bleed *vb* **1** to feel deep sadness or mental pain ⟨Her heart *bleeds* at her friend's misfortune.⟩ — see GRIEVE
2 to flow forth slowly through small openings ⟨Pitch was *bleeding* from cuts in the tree bark.⟩ — see EXUDE
3 to remove (liquid) gradually or completely ⟨We'll *bleed* water from the radiators.⟩ — see DRAIN 1
4 to rob by the use of trickery or threats ⟨The scammers *bled* the elderly couple of their life savings.⟩ — see FLEECE
bleed (for) *vb* to have sympathy for ⟨The young man *bleeds for* those less fortunate than he is.⟩ — see PITY
blemish *n* something that spoils the appearance or completeness of a thing ⟨The first mirror had a *blemish* on its surface, so we took it back to the store.⟩
synonyms blotch, defect, deformity, disfigurement, excrescence, fault, flaw, imperfection, mar, mark, pockmark, scar
related words abnormality, distortion, irregularity, malformation; bug, glitch; blot, blur, spot, stain, taint; damage, defacement, impairment, injury; failing, weakness
near antonyms adornment, decoration, embellishment, enhancement, ornament
blemish *vb* **1** to affect slightly with something morally bad or undesirable ⟨A single indiscretion *blemished* his reputation for years.⟩ — see TAINT 1
2 to reduce the soundness, effectiveness, or perfection of ⟨A scratch *blemished* the finish on the car.⟩ — see DAMAGE 1
¹blench *vb* to draw back in fear, pain, or disgust ⟨She *blenched* from the horrible sight.⟩ — see FLINCH
²blench *vb* to make white or whiter by removing color ⟨We'll have to *blench* the sheets with bleach to restore that snow-white look.⟩ — see WHITEN
blend *n* a distinct entity formed by the combining of two or more different things ⟨That fabric is a cotton and polyester *blend*, so it shouldn't shrink as much as pure cotton.⟩
synonyms admixture, amalgam, amalgamation, combination, composite, compound, fusion, intermixture, meld, mix, mixture
related words half-and-half; absorption, blending, coalescence, coalition, commingling, commixture, homogenization, immingling, immixture, integration, interfusion, intermingling, mergence, merging, mingling; assortment, hash, hodgepodge, hotchpotch, jumble, medley, mélange, mishmash, motley, patchwork, potpourri, variety; accumulation, aggregation, conglomeration
near antonyms component, constituent, element, ingredient
blend *vb* **1** to turn into a single mass or entity that is more or less the same throughout ⟨*Blend* the ingredients for the brownies very thoroughly to eliminate lumps in the batter.⟩
synonyms amalgamate, combine, commingle, composite, concrete, fuse, homogenize, incorporate, integrate, intermingle, intermix, meld, merge, mingle, mix
related words add, admix, beat (in), cut in, fold, stir,

toss; coalesce, compound, emulsify; conjoin, join, knit, link, unite; intertwine, interweave, weave

near antonyms cleave, disjoin, disunite, divide, divorce, part, rupture, sever, sunder; disperse, dissolve, scatter; detach, disengage, split

antonyms break down, break up, separate, unmix

2 to form a pleasing relationship ⟨The colors *blend* nicely in that rug.⟩ — see HARMONIZE 1

bless *vb* **1** to make holy through prayers or ritual ⟨The priest *blessed* the water.⟩

synonyms consecrate, hallow, sanctify

related words baptize, canonize, spiritualize; chasten, cleanse, purify; expurgate; commit, dedicate, devote; reconsecrate

near antonyms defile, desecrate, profane; dirty, foul, pollute, soil, taint, violate; blaspheme, curse, cuss, damn, execrate; condemn, damn, punish

2 to proclaim the glory of ⟨*Bless* the name of God.⟩ — see PRAISE 1

3 to furnish freely or naturally with some power, quality, or attribute ⟨*blessed* with a knack for glib conversation⟩ — see ENDOW 1

blessed *also* **blest** *adj* **1** of, relating to, or being God ⟨a prayer to the *blessed* Savior⟩ — see HOLY 3

2 set apart or worthy of veneration by association with God ⟨Statues honoring an array of *blessed* saints are scattered throughout the cathedral.⟩ — see HOLY 2

3 giving pleasure or contentment to the mind or senses ⟨the *blessed* sight of home after a long journey⟩ — see PLEASANT 1

blessedness *n* **1** a feeling or state of well-being and contentment ⟨The proud parents can scarcely describe the *blessedness* of having four healthy children.⟩ — see HAPPINESS 1

2 the quality or state of being spiritually pure or virtuous ⟨Mother Teresa's renowned *blessedness* made her an obvious candidate for sainthood.⟩ — see HOLINESS

blessing *n* **1** a prayer calling for divine care, protection, or favor ⟨said a *blessing* before the meal⟩

synonyms benediction

related words Godspeed; appeal, entreaty, grace, intercession, orison, petition, plea, prayer, supplication; sanctification

phrases laying on of hands

antonyms anathema, curse, execration, imprecation, malediction

2 something that provides happiness or does good for a person or thing ⟨Winning the lottery shortly after being laid off was an unexpected *blessing*.⟩

synonyms benediction, benefit, boon, felicity, godsend, good, manna, windfall

related words grace, mercy; favor, kindness; advantage, aid, assistance, gift, help, relief, support; comfort, consolation, solace; bonus, extra, lagniappe; delight, joy, pleasure

near antonyms hex, jinx; bother, irritant, nuisance, pest; disadvantage; cross, misery, trial, tribulation

antonyms affliction, bane, curse, evil, plague, scourge

3 an acceptance of something as satisfactory ⟨They got married with their parents' *blessing*.⟩ — see APPROVAL

4 the act of making something holy through religious ritual ⟨the *blessing* of the bread⟩ — see CONSECRATION

blind *adj* lacking the power of sight ⟨Our old *blind* cat kept walking into walls and furniture.⟩

synonyms eyeless, sightless, stone-blind

related words blinded, blindfold, blindfolded, unsighted; gravel-blind, purblind

near antonyms observant, observing, seeing; clear-sighted; gimlet-eyed, lynx-eyed, sharp-eyed

antonyms sighted

blind *vb* to overpower with light ⟨The bright lights in the TV studio momentarily *blinded* the quiz show contestants.⟩ — see DAZZLE

blink *vb* **1** to shine with light at regular intervals ⟨You must stop at a *blinking* red light.⟩

synonyms flash, twinkle, wink

related words flare, flicker, glance, glimmer, glint, glisten, glister, glitter, scintillate, shimmer, spark, sparkle

2 to rapidly open and close one's eyes ⟨I *blinked* for a few seconds after the camera flashed.⟩ — see WINK 1

3 to cease resistance (as to another's arguments, demands, or control) ⟨For two days the nations stood on the brink of war, until one finally *blinked*.⟩ — see YIELD 3

4 to look long and hard in wonder or surprise ⟨He stood *blinking* at the ridiculous scene before him in utter disbelief.⟩ — see GAPE

bliss *n* **1** a dwelling place of perfect happiness for the soul after death ⟨believed in the promise of eternal *bliss*⟩ — see HEAVEN 1

2 a feeling or state of well-being and contentment ⟨the enviable *bliss* of a happily married couple⟩ — see HAPPINESS 1

blissful *adj* experiencing pleasure, satisfaction, or delight ⟨a *blissful* cat who obviously loves being stroked⟩ — see GLAD 1

blissfulness *n* a feeling or state of well-being and contentment ⟨the *blissfulness* that only a full stomach and a warm bed can bring⟩ — see HAPPINESS 1

blistering *adj* **1** extreme in degree, power, or effect ⟨Even after a *blistering* attack from the enemy, the fortress held.⟩ — see INTENSE 1

2 moving, proceeding, or acting with great speed ⟨a major-league pitcher known for his *blistering* fastballs⟩ — see FAST 1

blithe *adj* **1** having or showing a good mood or disposition ⟨a *blithe*, obedient child⟩ — see CHEERFUL 1

2 having or showing freedom from worries or troubles ⟨He has a *blithe* attitude about ever having to earn a living because he knows there's a trust fund in his future.⟩ — see CAREFREE

blithesome *adj* **1** having or showing a good mood or disposition ⟨a *blithesome* girl who never seems to be sad or angry⟩ — see CHEERFUL 1

2 indicative of or marked by high spirits or good humor ⟨a *blithesome* and silly joke among old friends⟩ — see MERRY

blitz *n* **1** a rapid or overwhelming outpouring of many things at once ⟨a multimedia *blitz* of advertisements for the summer blockbuster⟩ — see BARRAGE

2 the act or action of setting upon with force or violence ⟨a massive aerial *blitz*⟩ — see ATTACK 1

3 a series of activities undertaken to achieve a goal ⟨an all-out advertising *blitz* to promote the new phone⟩ — see CAMPAIGN

blitz *vb* to use bombs or artillery against ⟨In 1940 and 1941 the German air force *blitzed* London night after horrible night.⟩ — see BOMBARD 1

blitzkrieg *n* **1** a rapid or overwhelming outpouring of many things at once ⟨The survivors of the crash were confronted with a *blitzkrieg* of questions from the media.⟩ — see BARRAGE

2 the act or action of setting upon with force or violence ⟨The war began with a *blitzkrieg* that was designed to shock the enemy into submission.⟩ — see ATTACK 1

blitzkrieg *vb* to use bombs or artillery against ⟨The Germans were determined to *blitzkrieg* London until the British surrendered.⟩ — see BOMBARD 1

blob *n* **1** a small uneven mass ⟨flicked a *blob* of jelly on the toast and began to spread it around⟩ — see LUMP 1

2 the quantity of fluid that falls naturally in one rounded mass ⟨got a *blob* of honey on his sweater⟩ — see DROP 1

bloc *n* **1** a group of people acting together within a larger group ⟨A whole *bloc* of students got together to complain.⟩ — see FACTION

2 an association of persons, parties, or states for mutual assistance and protection ⟨the *bloc* that the United States and most of western Europe formed during the Cold War⟩ — see CONFEDERACY

block *n* **1** a number of things considered as a unit ⟨bought a *block* of stocks⟩ — see GROUP 1

2 something that makes movement or progress difficult ⟨constant bickering that is only a *block* to the completion of the project⟩ — see ENCUMBRANCE

3 *slang* the upper or front part of the body that contains the brain, the major sense organs, and the mouth ⟨threatened to knock his *block* off⟩ — see HEAD 1

4 a group of people acting together within a larger group ⟨a more conservative *block* within the political party⟩ — see FACTION

5 an association of persons, parties, or states for mutual assistance and protection ⟨a *block* of oil-producing nations⟩ — see CONFEDERACY

block *vb* **1** to close up so that no empty spaces remain ⟨*block* up the opening in the wall where a window once was⟩ — see FILL 2

2 to prevent passage through by filling with something ⟨One of the patient's arteries was *blocked*.⟩ — see CLOG 1

blockade *n* the cutting off of an area by military means to stop the flow of people or supplies ⟨It was the *blockade* of all the enemy's major ports that finally won the war.⟩

synonyms investment, siege

related words counterblockade; containment, encirclement, encompassment; confinement, insulation, isolation, quarantine, seclusion, segregation, sequestration; incarceration, internment

blockade *vb* **1** to disallow entry into (a place) by means of a physical barrier at the entry point ⟨The police *blockaded* the whole area around city hall.⟩ — see CLOSE (OFF)

2 to surround (as a fortified place) with armed forces for the purpose of capturing or preventing commerce and communication ⟨*blockaded* the city until it surrendered⟩ — see BESIEGE 1

blockbuster *n* **1** a person or thing that is successful ⟨The movie is expected to be the biggest *blockbuster* of the summer.⟩ — see HIT 1

2 something that is unusually large and powerful ⟨a *blockbuster* of a fighter plane⟩ — see GIANT

blockhead *n* a stupid person ⟨I feel like a *blockhead* for forgetting your birthday.⟩ — see IDIOT

blond *or* **blonde** *adj* of a pale yellow or yellowish brown color ⟨The little boy's *blond* hair darkened to brown as he grew older.⟩

synonyms fair, flaxen, golden, sandy, straw, tawny

related words ash-blond (*or* ash-blonde), blondish, strawberry blonde (*or* strawberry blond), towheaded; gold, light, white

near antonyms black-a-vised, brown, dark, olive, swart; black, ebony, raven

blood *n* **1** a group of persons who come from the same ancestor ⟨In his mind, *blood* came before anything else, and he would not betray his brother.⟩ — see FAMILY 1

2 the line of ancestors from whom a person is descended ⟨She was determined to be of royal *blood*.⟩ — see ANCESTRY

3 the seat of one's deepest thoughts and emotions ⟨In your *blood* you know this business deal just isn't right.⟩ — see CORE 1

4 the taking of another person's life ⟨called for *blood*⟩ — see HOMICIDE 1

bloodline *n* the line of ancestors from whom a person is descended ⟨came from a *bloodline* that could be traced back to the 12th century⟩ — see ANCESTRY

bloodstained *adj* smeared or stained with blood ⟨I had to throw away the *bloodstained* washcloth after a particularly bad nosebleed.⟩ — see BLOODY 1

bloodthirsty *adj* eager for or marked by the shedding of blood, extreme violence, or killing ⟨The Goths were feared as wild and *bloodthirsty*.⟩

synonyms bloody, homicidal, murdering, murderous, sanguinary, sanguine

related words barbaric, barbarous, brutal, cold-blooded, cruel, heartless, inhumane, sadistic, savage, vicious, wanton; antagonistic, ferocious, fierce, gladiatorial, hostile; aggressive, assertive, bellicose, belligerent, combative, contentious, discordant, pugnacious, quarrelsome, scrappy, truculent, violent; merciless, pitiless, ruthless; bloodstained, fell, gory, grim; despiteful, hateful, malevolent, malicious, malign, malignant, mean, nasty, spiteful

near antonyms appeasing, conciliatory, disarming, mollifying, pacific, pacifying, peaceable, peaceful, peacemaking, placating, placative, propitiatory; unaggressive, unassertive; benign, benignant, compassionate, goodhearted, humane, kind, kindhearted, sympathetic, tenderhearted; tender, warm, warmhearted; clement, lenient, merciful; affable, amiable, amicable, benevolent, gentle, kindly; submissive, surrendering, yielding

bloody *adj* **1** smeared or stained with blood ⟨After the fall, her elbow was all *bloody*.⟩

synonyms bloodstained, gory

related words bloodred, carmine, crimson, incarnadine, red, reddish, ruby, sanguine, sanguineous; sanguinary

2 eager for or marked by the shedding of blood, extreme violence, or killing ⟨a *bloody* battle⟩ — see BLOODTHIRSTY

bloody *vb* to reduce the soundness, effectiveness, or perfection of ⟨The politician's reputation was permanently *bloodied* by the rumors of corruption.⟩ — see DAMAGE 1

bloom *n* **1** a state or time of great activity, thriving, or achievement ⟨a handsome young man in the full *bloom* of youth⟩

synonyms blossom, flower, flush, heyday, high noon, prime

related words Indian summer; blooming, blossoming, efflorescence, flowering; acme, apex, climax, meridian, peak, pinnacle, summit, zenith; glory, grandeur, splendor; silver age; comeback, recovery, revival

near antonyms decay, decline, downfall; bottom; shriveling (*or* shrivelling), wilting, withering

2 a rosy appearance (of the cheeks) ⟨After a snowball fight, she came inside with a *bloom* on her cheeks.⟩

synonyms blush, color, flush

related words brightness, brilliance, glow; pinkness, reddishness, redness, rosiness, ruddiness, sanguineness

near antonyms paleness, pallidness, pallor, pastiness, wanness, whiteness; greenishness, greenness, sallowness

3 the usually showy plant part that produces seeds ⟨The rosebush produces *blooms* only in midsummer.⟩ — see FLOWER 1

bloom *vb* **1** to produce flowers ⟨Forsythias only *bloom* at the beginning of spring.⟩

synonyms blossom, blow, flower, unfold

related words leave; open

near antonyms dry up, fade, shrivel, wilt, wither; die, drop, expire, perish

2 to develop a rosy facial color (as from excitement or embarrassment) ⟨She arrived at the house, *blooming* from her vigorous walk.⟩ — see BLUSH

blooming *adj* having a healthy reddish skin tone ⟨the *blooming* faces of children at play in the great outdoors⟩ — see RUDDY

blossom *n* **1** a state or time of great activity, thriving, or achievement ⟨in the full *blossom* of her career as a writer⟩ — see BLOOM 1
2 the usually showy plant part that produces seeds ⟨The marigolds are finally showing *blossoms*.⟩ — see FLOWER 1

blossom *vb* to produce flowers ⟨The fruit tree seemed to *blossom* overnight once the warm spring weather arrived.⟩ — see BLOOM 1

blot *n* a mark of guilt or disgrace ⟨The bribery scandal was a *blot* on his reputation.⟩ — see STAIN 1

blotch *n* **1** a small area that is different (as in color) from the main part ⟨a dog with a single small *blotch* of black⟩ — see SPOT 1
2 something that spoils the appearance or completeness of a thing ⟨That cell tower is another *blotch* on the landscape.⟩ — see BLEMISH

blotch *vb* to mark with small spots especially unevenly ⟨My pen leaked and *blotched* my shirt pocket.⟩ — see SPOT 1

blotched *adj* having blotches of two or more colors ⟨a *blotched* black-and-white rabbit⟩ — see PIED

blot out *vb* **1** to destroy all traces of ⟨*blotted out* all evidence of tampering with the files⟩ — see ANNIHILATE 1
2 to keep secret or shut off from view ⟨Bushes *blotted out* the shed from our view.⟩ — see ¹HIDE 2

¹**blow** *n* a hard strike with a part of the body or an instrument ⟨He was dizzy for the rest of the day after the *blow* to his head.⟩
synonyms bang, bash, bat, beat, belt, bop, box, buffet, bust, chop, clap, clip, clout, crack, cuff, dab, hack, hit, hook, knock, lash, lick, pelt, plump, poke, pound, punch, rap, slam, slap, slug, smack, smash, sock, spank, stinger, stripe, stroke, swat, swipe, switch, thud, thump, thwack, wallop, whack
related words counter, counterblow, counterstroke; body blow, hand, kick, knee, left, one-two, rabbit punch, right, right-hander, roundhouse, shiver, sidewinder, sucker punch, swing, uppercut; cruncher, kayo, knockdown, knockout, KO; battering, beating, bludgeoning, clobbering, cudgeling (*or* cudgelling), drubbing, hammering, lambasting, licking, pasting, pounding, pummeling (*also* pummelling), thrashing; flogging, whip, whipping

²**blow** *n* a sudden brief rush of wind ⟨The ocean *blows* that sweep over the island are so strong that only the hardiest shrubs can grow there.⟩ — see GUST 1

¹**blow** *vb* **1** to breathe hard, quickly, or with difficulty ⟨That horse was really *blowing* after the race.⟩ — see GASP
2 to use up carelessly ⟨Each year he *blows* his holiday bonus on a trip to Las Vegas.⟩ — see WASTE 1
3 to break open or into pieces usually because of internal pressure ⟨A huge crater was formed when the volcano last *blew*.⟩ — see EXPLODE 1
4 to cause to break open or into pieces by or as if by an explosive ⟨The burglar *blew* the safe open.⟩ — see BLAST 1
5 to proceed or move quickly ⟨That car *blew* past us as if we were standing still.⟩ — see HURRY 2
6 to make or do (something) in a clumsy or unskillful way ⟨He keeps *blowing* every job interview that comes his way.⟩ — see BOTCH
7 to praise or express pride in one's own possessions, qualities, or accomplishments often to excess ⟨another self-made millionaire *blowing* about how much he'd achieved⟩ — see BOAST 1

²**blow** *vb* to produce flowers ⟨longing for a grassy field in some far-off land where the wildflowers *blow*⟩ — see BLOOM 1

blow (out) *vb* to let or force out of the lungs ⟨*blew out* a smoke ring and began to tell us a good yarn⟩ — see EXHALE 1

blowout *n* a social gathering ⟨staged a huge *blowout* for Halloween⟩ — see PARTY 1

blowup *n* **1** an outburst or display of excited anger ⟨The boss had another *blowup* when someone fouled up the copy machine.⟩ — see TANTRUM
2 the act or an instance of exploding ⟨The last *blowup* of the volcano flattened trees for miles around.⟩ — see EXPLOSION 1

blow up *vb* **1** to become very angry ⟨She *blew up* at everybody after a very long and very bad day.⟩
synonyms flare (up)
related words anger, fulminate, rage, rant, rave, snap, snarl, sputter, storm, tee off, vent, vituperate; bristle, burn, foam, fume, glare, glower, seethe, sizzle, smolder (*or* smoulder), steam, warm; burst, explode, flare (out), flash, inflame (*also* enflame), madden
phrases blow a gasket, blow one's cool, blow one's stack, blow one's top, fly into a rage, fly off the handle, forget oneself, go ballistic, have a fit, hit the ceiling, hit the roof, lose one's cool, lose one's temper
near antonyms chill out [*slang*], cool (off *or* down), relax; hush, quiet (down)
antonyms calm (down), simmer down
2 to break open or into pieces usually because of internal pressure ⟨The building *blew up* because of a gas leak.⟩ — see EXPLODE 1
3 to cause to break open or into pieces by or as if by an explosive ⟨*blew up* the biggest rocks and then cleared them away⟩ — see BLAST 1

blowy *adj* marked by strong wind or more wind than usual ⟨a *blowy* day that resulted in most of the fall foliage being knocked off the trees⟩ — see ¹WINDY 1

blubber *vb* to shed tears often while making meaningless sounds as a sign of pain or distress ⟨The poor child was *blubbering* because she had fallen and skinned her knee.⟩ — see CRY 1

bludgeon *n* a heavy rigid stick used as a weapon or for punishment ⟨Guards armed with *bludgeons* roamed the compound.⟩ — see CLUB 1

bludgeon *vb* **1** to deliver a blow to (someone or something) usually in a strong vigorous manner ⟨*bludgeoned* the door with an iron bar⟩ — see HIT 1
2 to strike repeatedly ⟨used a shield to avoid being *bludgeoned*⟩ — see BEAT 1

blue *adj* **1** depicting or referring to sexual matters in a way that is unacceptable in polite society ⟨shocked at the *blue* banter she heard on the radio⟩ — see OBSCENE 1
2 feeling unhappiness ⟨A cold, dreary day always leaves me *blue*.⟩ — see SAD 1

blue *n* **1** the expanse of air surrounding the earth ⟨The plane flew off into the *blue*.⟩ — see SKY 1
2 the whole body of salt water that covers nearly three-fourths of the earth ⟨pirate ships that sailed the *blue* in search of treasure⟩ — see OCEAN 1

blueprint *n* a method worked out in advance for achieving some objective ⟨an ambitious young man with a remarkably detailed *blueprint* for becoming a millionaire by the age of 25⟩ — see PLAN 1

blueprint *vb* to work out the details of (something) in advance ⟨*blueprinted* the schedule of events for the festival right down to the last detail⟩ — see PLAN 1

blues *pl n* a state or spell of low spirits ⟨Failing the driving test gave me the *blues* for the rest of the day.⟩ — see SADNESS

bluff *adj* being or characterized by direct, brief, and potentially rude speech or manner ⟨He's a *bluff* but goodhearted teacher.⟩ — see BLUNT 1

bluff *n* a steep wall of rock, earth, or ice ⟨fossils embedded in a stone *bluff* that date from the Jurassic period⟩ — see CLIFF

bluff *vb* **1** to cause to believe what is untrue ⟨I *bluffed* the interviewer into believing that I could really speak French.⟩ — see DECEIVE

2 to present a false appearance of ⟨The basketball player *bluffed* a shot, then passed instead.⟩ — see FEIGN

blunder *n* an unintentional departure from truth or accuracy ⟨fixed a minor *blunder* in the advertising flyer⟩ — see ERROR 1

blunder *vb* **1** to make a mistake ⟨Even though the prosecution had *blundered* several times in presenting its case, it ultimately prevailed.⟩ — see ERR 1

2 to proceed or act clumsily or ineffectually ⟨*blundered* his way through an acceptance speech⟩ — see FLOUNDER 1

blunt *adj* **1** being or characterized by direct, brief, and potentially rude speech or manner ⟨He values honesty and is quite *blunt* about telling people what he thinks.⟩

synonyms abrupt, bluff, brusque (*also* brusk), crusty, curt, downright, short, snippy, unceremonious

related words gruff, rough, snappish; candid, direct, forthright, foursquare, frank, free-spoken, open, outspoken, plain, plainspoken, point-blank, straightforward; artless, discourteous, disrespectful, impertinent, impolite, inconsiderate, insensitive, rude, tactless; brief, closemouthed, laconic, reserved, reticent, terse, tight-lipped; earnest, honest, sincere; coarse, crass, crude, low, uncouth, vulgar

near antonyms civil, considerate, courteous, diplomatic, gracious, polite, politic, smooth, suave, tactful; loquacious, talkative, voluble; long-winded, prolix, verbose; courtly, cultivated, gallant, genteel, polished, refined

antonyms circuitous, mealymouthed

2 lacking sharpness of edge or point ⟨A *blunt* knife won't open that package.⟩ — see DULL 1

blunt *vb* to reduce or weaken in strength or feeling ⟨The mushy music *blunted* the effect of the movie's final tragic scene.⟩ — see DULL 1

blunted *adj* lacking sharpness of edge or point ⟨The *blunted* saw was worthless for fine woodworking.⟩ — see DULL 1

blur *vb* **1** to make (something) unclear to the understanding ⟨an article for the layman that *blurs* the distinction between the two kinds of cholesterol⟩ — see CONFUSE 2

2 to make dark, dim, or indistinct ⟨Evening shadows *blurred* the view of the valley from the overlook.⟩ — see CLOUD 1

blurry *adj* not seen or understood clearly ⟨a *blurry* image in the foreground of the photograph⟩ — see FAINT 1

blurt (out) *vb* to utter with a sudden burst of strong feeling ⟨"I'm hungry!" the toddler *blurted out*.⟩ — see EXCLAIM

blush *n* a rosy appearance (of the cheeks) ⟨a baby with a healthy *blush*⟩ — see BLOOM 2

blush *vb* to develop a rosy facial color (as from excitement or embarrassment) ⟨She *blushed* when she realized she had mistaken his name.⟩

synonyms bloom, color, crimson, flush, glow, redden

related words incarnadine, rouge, ruddle; abash, chagrin, discomfit, disconcert, embarrass, faze, humiliate, mortify

phrases turn color

bluster *n* **1** boastful speech or writing ⟨All the *bluster* in the campaign speech was intended to hide a lack of specifics.⟩ — see BOMBAST 1

2 loud, confused, and usually inharmonious sound ⟨I can't work with all the *bluster* in here.⟩ — see NOISE 1

3 a state of noisy, confused activity ⟨a mayor who got things done without a lot of *bluster* and self-serving publicity⟩ — see COMMOTION

bluster *vb* to talk loudly and wildly ⟨The rude customer *blustered* and yelled threats about lawsuits, but eventually left.⟩ — see RANT

blustery *adj* marked by strong wind or more wind than usual ⟨*blustery* weather causing leaves to blow off trees⟩ — see ¹WINDY 1

board *n* **1** a group of persons formally joined together for some common interest ⟨She sits on the advisory *board*.⟩ — see ASSOCIATION 2

2 a leg-mounted piece of furniture with a broad flat top designed for the serving of food ⟨In preparation for the governor's visit, the taverner arranged an array of fancy dishes and silverware on the inn's finest *board*.⟩ — see TABLE 1

board *vb* **1** to provide food or meals for ⟨housed and *boarded* many foster children over the years⟩ — see FEED 1

2 to provide with living quarters or shelter ⟨We *boarded* the stray cat until a permanent home could be found.⟩ — see HOUSE 1

boarder *n* one who rents a room or apartment in another's house ⟨a *boarder* who paid $100 per week for a room and meals⟩ — see TENANT 1

boast *n* an asset that brings praise or renown ⟨The school's *boast* was a winning football team.⟩ — see GLORY 2

boast *vb* **1** to praise or express pride in one's own possessions, qualities, or accomplishments often to excess ⟨He *boasted* about his latest killing in real estate so I thought he should be the one to pay for dinner.⟩

synonyms blow, brag, crow, swagger

related words bluster, harangue, puff; pride; gush; exult, glory, rejoice; brandish, display, exhibit, expose, flaunt, glorify, parade, show off; magnify, maximize

phrases blow smoke

near antonyms belittle, deprecate, diminish, discount, laugh off, minimize, play down, pooh-pooh (*also* pooh), shrug off; bemoan, lament, mourn, regret

2 to have within ⟨The hotel *boasts* nearly 50 rooms.⟩ — see CONTAIN 1

boaster *n* someone who boasts ⟨I'm tired of hearing about that *boaster's* new car⟩ — see BRAGGART

boat *n* **1** a small buoyant structure for travel on water ⟨Paddling the little *boat* across the lake is great exercise.⟩

synonyms bottom, craft, vessel, watercraft

related words catboat, ketch, sailboat, schooner, yacht; canoe, catamaran, dhow, dinghy, dink, dory, dugout, flatboat, garvey, gig, johnboat, kayak, outrigger, paddleboat, pontoon, pram, punt, raft, rowboat, sampan, scow, scull, shallop, shell, skiff, surfboat, umiak, wherry; cruiser, inboard, motorboat, outboard, powerboat; houseboat, riverboat; auxiliary, bumboat, cutter, jolly boat, launch, lifeboat, longboat, tender, yawl; barge, hoy, keelboat; towboat, tug, tugboat; ferry, ferryboat, gondola, taxi, water taxi; banker, hooker, lugger, scalloper, seiner, shrimper, trawler, whaleboat, whaler, workboat; cockleshell, tub; airboat, air-cushion vehicle, hovercraft; hydrofoil, hydroplane; assault boat, PT boat, torpedo boat

2 a large craft for travel by water ⟨You'll have to take a passenger *boat* to get to the island.⟩ — see SHIP

boat *vb* to travel on water in a vessel ⟨*boated* to the picnic site on an island in the bay⟩ — see SAIL 1

boatload *n* a considerable amount ⟨a *boatload* of publicity for the new handheld devices⟩ — see LOT 2

¹bob *vb* to make (something) shorter or smaller with the use of a cutting instrument ⟨*bobbed* her waist-length hair⟩ — see CLIP 1

²**bob** *vb* **1** to make short up-and-down movements ⟨a family of ducks *bobbing* on the water⟩ — see NOD

2 to deliver a blow to (someone or something) usually in a strong vigorous manner ⟨He playfully *bobbed* his brother on the nose to get his attention.⟩ — see HIT 1

bobble *n* an unintentional departure from truth or accuracy ⟨She's terrified that she'll make some silly *bobble* during the important presentation.⟩ — see ERROR 1

bobble *vb* **1** to make or do (something) in a clumsy or unskillful way ⟨The first baseman *bobbled* the catch, so the runner was safe.⟩ — see BOTCH

2 to make short up-and-down movements ⟨The little doll's head *bobbled* when you poked it.⟩ — see NOD

bode *vb* to show signs of a favorable or desirable outcome ⟨Her natural gift for reading *boded* well for her future in school.⟩

synonyms augur, forebode (*also* forbode), promise

related words forecast, foretell, predict, presage, prognosticate, prophesy; forewarn, warn; anticipate, divine, foreknow, foresee; betoken, foreshadow, harbinger, portend, prefigure, presignify; indicate, signify; allude, connote, hint, imply, insinuate, intimate, suggest

phrases bid fair

bodiless *adj* not composed of matter ⟨Ghosts are supposed to be *bodiless*.⟩ — see IMMATERIAL 1

bodily *adj* of or relating to the human body ⟨The old man suffered from a number of *bodily* ailments.⟩ — see PHYSICAL 1

boding *n* something believed to be a sign or warning of a future event ⟨Among some ancient peoples, solar eclipses were often seen as celestial *bodings* of earthly calamities.⟩ — see OMEN

body *vb* to represent in visible form ⟨abstract sculpture that *bodies* forth the artist's aesthetic of minimalism⟩ — see EMBODY 2

body *n* **1** the main or greater part of something as distinguished from its subordinate parts ⟨The *body* of the novel was quite good, even if the beginning was a bit slow.⟩

synonyms bulk, chief, core, generality, main, mass, staple, weight

related words majority; aggregate, amount, sum, total, totality, whole; bottom, essence, essentiality, marrow, meat, nature, pith, quintessence, root, soul, stuff, substance; center, heart, hub, middle, nucleus, nut, seat; affair, argument, burden, crux, focus, gist, nub, pitch, point, purport; matter, motif, subject, text, theme, topic

near antonyms accessory (*also* accessary), adjunct, appendage, extension, offshoot; component, constituent, element, ingredient; division, part, piece, section, segment; angle, aspect, facet, feature, quality, side

2 a distinct and separate portion of matter ⟨To the early explorers the Atlantic was a gigantic and forbidding *body* of water.⟩

synonyms mass

related words aggregate, amount, bulk, quantity, volume; item, object, thing; material, stuff, substance; totality, whole

3 a group of people acting together within a larger group ⟨feared that there was a *body* of extremists within the party⟩ — see FACTION

4 a group of people sharing a common interest and relating together socially ⟨a hangout where, it seems, much of the student *body* can be found on a Saturday night⟩ — see GANG 2

5 a member of the human race ⟨the most intelligent *body* in this entire place⟩ — see HUMAN

6 a usually small number of persons considered as a unit ⟨A *body* of security men accompany the president at all times.⟩ — see GROUP 2

bog *n* spongy land saturated or partially covered with water ⟨got a shoe stuck in the *bog*⟩ — see SWAMP

bog (down) *vb* to place in conflict or difficulties ⟨We were *bogged down* by the endless changes, and of course finished late.⟩ — see EMBROIL

bogey *also* **bogie** *or* **bogy** *n* **1** something or someone that causes fear or dread especially without reason ⟨Parallel parking has long been a *bogey* for many new drivers.⟩

synonyms bête noire, bugaboo, bugbear, dread, hobgoblin, ogre

related words apparition, ghost, phantasm (*also* fantasm), phantom, poltergeist, shade, specter (*or* spectre), spirit, spook, wraith; banshee, bogeyman (*also* bogyman), demon (*or* daemon), devil, fiend, ghoul, imp, incubus; fright, horrible, horror, monster, monstrosity, terror; bane, curse, enemy, plague, scourge, torment; abomination, anathema

2 the soul of a dead person thought of especially as appearing to living people ⟨The child believed *bogeys* lived in the closet.⟩ — see GHOST 1

bogus *adj* **1** being such in appearance only and made with or manufactured from usually cheaper materials ⟨For that price, you're only going to get furniture covered in *bogus* leather and not the real stuff.⟩ — see IMITATION

2 being such in appearance only and made or manufactured with the intention of committing fraud ⟨The "designer" watches sold on the street are usually *bogus*.⟩ — see COUNTERFEIT 1

3 lacking in natural or spontaneous quality ⟨There was often a lot of *bogus* conviviality at the company's parties.⟩ — see ARTIFICIAL 1

bohemian *n* a person who does not conform to generally accepted standards or customs ⟨He spent a few years living as a *bohemian* in the artists' quarter of the city.⟩ — see NONCONFORMIST 1

boil *vb* **1** to be excited or emotionally stirred up with anger ⟨The crowd *boiled* at the speaker's ranting.⟩

synonyms burn, foam, fume, rage, rankle, seethe, sizzle, steam, storm

related words fulminate, rant, rave; smolder (*or* smoulder); bristle, flare (up), inflame (*also* enflame); chafe, fret, stew; agitate, convulse, roil, shake

phrases see red

2 to cook in a liquid heated to the point that it gives off steam ⟨*Boil* the potatoes until they are tender before you try to mash them.⟩

synonyms coddle, parboil, poach, simmer, stew

related words scald; braise, fricassee, pressure-cook, smother, steam; reboil

3 to be in a state of violent rolling motion ⟨The sea *boiled* and frothed during the storm.⟩ — see SEETHE 1

boisterous *adj* being rough or noisy in a high-spirited way ⟨The fans at the baseball game became particularly *boisterous* after the home run.⟩

synonyms knockabout, rambunctious, raucous, rollicking, rowdy

related words carnival, carnivalesque, raffish, raucous, riotous, rowdyish, ruffianly; stormy, tempestuous, turbulent, violent; headstrong, intractable, obstreperous, recalcitrant, uncontrollable, uncontrolled, undisciplined, ungovernable, uninhibited, unmanageable, unreserved, unrestrained, unruly, wild, willful (*or* wilful); bubbly, buoyant, effervescent, exuberant, high-spirited, impassioned, lively, sprightly, vivacious; clamorous, loudmouthed, noisy, openmouthed, strident, vociferous; howling, screaming, yelling *phrases* wild and woolly

near antonyms sedate, sober, solemn, somber (*or* sombre), staid; decorous, dignified, proper, seemly; calm, hushed, noiseless, peaceful, placid, quiet, restrained, serene, silent, soundless, tranquil; collected, composed, constrained, controlled, imperturbable, inhibited, self-controlled, unflappable, unruffled; moderate, reasonable, subdued, temperate; impassive, phlegmatic, stoic (*or* stoical), stolid; depressed; aloof, detached, indifferent

antonyms orderly

bold *adj* **1** inclined or willing to take risks ⟨Our youngest brother was the *boldest* one in the family, instantly taking to everything from skiing to skateboarding.⟩

synonyms adventuresome, adventurous, audacious, daring, dashing, emboldened, enterprising, gutsy, hardy, nerved, nervy, venturesome, venturous

related words brash, daredevil, foolhardy, heedless, hotheaded, impetuous, imprudent, impulsive, incautious, madcap, overbold, overconfident, rash, reckless, thoughtless, wild; brave, courageous, dauntless, fearless, gallant, greathearted, heroic (*also* heroical), intrepid, lionhearted, stalwart, stout, stouthearted, swashbuckling, unafraid, undaunted, valiant, valorous; gritty, plucky, spirited, spunky; hasty, headlong, precipitate; absurd, asinine, balmy, brainless, foolish, half-witted, harebrained, scatterbrained, silly, wacky (*also* whacky), witless; unnecessary; dumb, idiotic (*also* idiotical), moronic, stupid; irrational, unreasonable

near antonyms chickenhearted, coward, cowardly, craven, lily-livered, milk-livered, milky, shy, timid, timorous; careful, cautious, heedful, prudent, wary; overcareful, overcautious; affrighted, afraid, alarmed, fainthearted, fearful, frightened, horrified, scared, shocked, spooked, startled, terrified, terrorized; unnerved; calm, cool, levelheaded, rational, reasonable, sage, sane, sensible, sound, wise; appalled, concerned, dismayed, upset, worried

antonyms unadventurous, unenterprising

2 displaying or marked by rude boldness ⟨Would it be too *bold* of me to suggest a change?⟩ — see NERVY 1

3 likely to attract attention ⟨an interior decorator who likes to use *bold* colors⟩ — see NOTICEABLE

4 showing a lack of proper social reserve or modesty ⟨a *bold* child who interrupts the adults at his parents' parties⟩ — see PRESUMPTUOUS 1

5 having an incline approaching the perpendicular ⟨The advanced climbers chose a *bold* cliff to test themselves.⟩ — see STEEP 1

6 feeling or displaying no fear by temperament ⟨the *bold* explorers who will someday journey to other planets⟩ — see BRAVE 1

bold–faced *adj* displaying or marked by rude boldness ⟨The child proceeded to tell a *bold-faced* lie despite the evidence right in front of us.⟩ — see NERVY 1

bolster *vb* **1** to hold up or serve as a foundation for ⟨used additional beams to *bolster* the ceiling⟩ — see SUPPORT 3

2 to provide evidence or information for (as a claim or idea) ⟨A couple of tournament wins would *bolster* the extravagant claims that have been made on behalf of the young golfer.⟩ — see SUPPORT 4

bolt *vb* **1** to move suddenly and sharply (as in surprise) ⟨I *bolted* as I read the winning lottery numbers.⟩ — see START 1

2 to proceed or move quickly ⟨The cat *bolted* for the food dish the minute he spied it.⟩ — see HURRY 2

3 to hasten away from something dangerous or frightening ⟨The rabbit *bolted* when it saw the fox approaching.⟩ — see RUN 2

4 to utter with a sudden burst of strong feeling ⟨*bolted* out the answer without thinking⟩ — see EXCLAIM

5 to swallow or eat greedily ⟨The way you *bolted* those hot dogs, it's no wonder you're feeling a little queasy.⟩ — see GOBBLE

bomb *n* something that has failed ⟨Her tell-all book was a *bomb* that landed on the remainder tables with a thud.⟩ — see FAILURE 3

bomb *vb* **1** to attack with a rapid or overwhelming outpouring of many things at once ⟨Following the reporter's outburst, viewers *bombed* the television station with an unprecedented number of complaints.⟩ — see BOMBARD 2

2 to be unsuccessful ⟨The chichi restaurant *bombed* bigtime, lasting only six months.⟩ — see FAIL 2

3 to defeat by a large margin ⟨It's no surprise that the inexperienced baseball team got totally *bombed* in its first game.⟩ — see WHIP 2

4 to use bombs or artillery against ⟨The enemy has *bombed* the city again.⟩ — see BOMBARD 1

bombard *vb* **1** to use bombs or artillery against ⟨The Allies *bombarded* Germany for a great many months during World War II.⟩

synonyms batter, blitz, blitzkrieg, bomb, cannonade, shell

related words rake, strafe; assail, assault, attack, devastate, hit, pound, ravage, strike

2 to attack with a rapid or overwhelming outpouring of many things at once ⟨Reporters *bombarded* the company spokesman with sharp questions.⟩

synonyms barrage, bomb

related words examine, grill, interrogate, pump, query, question, quiz; debrief; cross-examine; annoy, hound, pester; flood, inundate

bombardment *n* a rapid or overwhelming outpouring of many things at once ⟨The *bombardment* of so many instructions meant that I missed some of the information.⟩ — see BARRAGE

bombast *n* **1** boastful speech or writing ⟨We had little interest in being subjected to the speaker's *bombast*.⟩

synonyms bluster, brag, braggadocio, gas, grandiloquence, hot air, rant

related words oratory, rhapsody, rhetoric; turgidity, wind; bloviation, verbosity, windiness; babble, blab, chatter, drivel, gabble, gibber, gibberish, jabber, prattle; jawing, patter, prating, yammering; egotism, self-conceit, self-importance, swagger

2 language that is impressive-sounding but not meaningful or sincere ⟨You need less *bombast* and more substance in this speech.⟩ — see RHETORIC 1

bombastic *adj* marked by the use of impressive-sounding but mostly meaningless words and phrases ⟨a *bombastic* speech intended to impress the voters in her congressional district⟩ — see RHETORICAL 1

bombshell *n* something that makes a strong impression because it is so unexpected ⟨Discovering that I had a long-lost sister was an absolute *bombshell*.⟩ — see SURPRISE 1

bona fide *adj* being exactly as appears or as claimed ⟨a *bona fide* war hero⟩ — see AUTHENTIC 1

bond *n* **1** something that physically prevents free movement ⟨Before they could release the captive, they had to undo a number of *bonds*.⟩

synonyms band, bind, bracelet, chain, cuff(s), fetter, handcuff(s), irons, ligature, manacle(s), shackle

related words captivity, confinement, constraint, curb, enchainment, hindrance, immurement, imprisonment, incarceration, restraint, restriction; entanglement, net, trammel, trap; collar, straitjacket (*also* straightjacket); fastener, hobble, hold, hold-down, holding, tie

2 a uniting or binding force or influence ⟨The *bond* of

love between them was so strong that even death could not break it.⟩
synonyms cement, cord, knot, ligature, link, tie
related words attachment, connection, fastening, hook-up, joint, linkage, linkup, tie-up, union, yoke; affection, fondness, sympathy; fetter, handcuff, manacle, shackle, trammel; constraint, curb, hampering, limit, limitation, restraint, restriction
near antonyms detaching, disengaging, parting, separation; unbinding, unfastening, unfettering, untying (*or* untieing); emancipation, freedom, liberation, release
3 a formal agreement to fulfill an obligation ⟨signed a *bond* to repay the money⟩ — see GUARANTEE 1
4 a substance used to stick things together ⟨What type of *bond* works best on ceramics?⟩ — see GLUE
bond *vb* to form a close personal relationship ⟨a man attempting to *bond* with his new and mistrustful stepson⟩ — see COMMUNE
bondage *n* the state of being enslaved ⟨people freed from *bondage*⟩ — see SLAVERY
bonding *n* a physical sticking to as if by glue ⟨This epoxy has good *bonding* for glass and ceramics.⟩ — see ADHESION 1
bone *adv* to a great degree ⟨grew up in a backwoods area that was *bone* poor⟩ — see VERY 1
bone *n* **1** a habitual attraction to some activity or thing ⟨He hasn't a competitive *bone* in his body.⟩ — see INCLINATION 1
2 bones *pl* a small cube marked on each side with one to six spots and usually played in pairs in various games ⟨The pirates decided their captives' fate with a toss of the *bones*.⟩ — see DIE
3 usually **bones** *pl* the seat of one's deepest thoughts and emotions ⟨I could feel in my *bones* that I had just met my future wife.⟩ — see CORE 1
4 bones *pl* a dead body ⟨requested that his *bones* be buried in the country of his birth⟩ — see CORPSE
bone (up) *vb* to use the mind to acquire knowledge ⟨I suggest you *bone up* a bit before the next exam.⟩ — see STUDY 1
bonus *n* something given in addition to what is ordinarily expected or owed ⟨This job offers a nice yearly *bonus* in addition to the salary.⟩
synonyms dividend, extra, gratuity, gravy, lagniappe, perquisite, tip
related words pension; bestowal, presentation; benefaction, beneficence, benevolence, bounty, charity, generosity, largesse (*also* largess), philanthropy; contribution, donation, gift, offering, present; grant, subsidy; boon, manna, windfall; favor, freebie (*or* freebee), giveaway, premium; award, prize, reward; fringe benefit, icing
bon voyage *n* an expression of good wishes at parting ⟨Everyone said their *bon voyages* as the happy couple left on a cruise for their honeymoon.⟩ — see GOOD-BYE
boo *n* a vocal sound made to express scorn or disapproval ⟨The referee's questionable call was greeted with a chorus of *boos*.⟩ — see CATCALL
booby *n* a person who lacks good sense or judgment ⟨What kind of *booby* goes out into the snow barefoot?⟩ — see FOOL 1
booby trap *n* **1** a usually concealed explosive device designed to go off when disturbed ⟨Luckily, the bomb squad didn't find any *booby traps*.⟩
synonyms mine
related words land mine; torpedo; bomb, explosive; hazard, pitfall, snare, trap; ambush, net, web
2 a danger or difficulty that is hidden or not easily recognized ⟨He noticed the *booby trap* in the interviewer's question just a little too late.⟩ — see PITFALL 1

book *n* **1** a set of printed sheets of paper bound together between covers and forming a work of fiction or nonfiction ⟨I bought another new *book* yesterday, and I can't wait to read it.⟩
synonyms tome, volume
related words hardback, hardcover, paper, paperback, paperbound, pocket book, pocket edition, softback, softcover, trade book, trade edition; folio, quarto; guidebook, handbook, how-to, manual; catalog (*or* catalogue), cyclopedia (*also* cyclopaedia), dictionary, encyclopedia; monograph, primer, text, textbook, tract, treatise; novel, novelette, pulp; album, almanac, anthology, casebook, chapbook, nonbook, omnibus, picture book
2 *cap* a book made up of the writings accepted by Christians as coming from God ⟨He offered to swear on the *Book* that everything had happened just as he said.⟩ — see BIBLE
3 information not generally available to the public ⟨what's the *book* on the new company president?⟩ — see DOPE 1
book *vb* to arrange to have something (as a hotel room) held for one's future use ⟨We *booked* a conference room for the meeting next week.⟩ — see RESERVE 1
bookish *adj* suggestive of the vocabulary used in books ⟨"Fealty" is a *bookish* synonym for "loyalty."⟩
synonyms erudite, learned, literary
related words academic (*also* academical), donnish, inkhorn, pedantic, scholastic; belletristic (*also* belle-lettristic); highbrow, intellectual; educated, schooled; elevated, eloquent, formal, high-flown, lofty, majestic, stately, towering; bombastic, declamatory, florid, flowery, grandiloquent, highfalutin (*also* hifalutin), pompous, stilted
near antonyms chatty, conversational; familiar, informal; slangy; illiterate
antonyms colloquial, nonliterary, unbookish
booklet *n* a short printed publication with no cover or with a paper cover ⟨There's an instruction *booklet* next to the copy machine.⟩ — see PAMPHLET
bookworm *n* a person devoted to intellectual or academic pursuits ⟨a *bookworm* who prefers reading to just about any other activity⟩ — see NERD 1
boom *n* a loud explosive sound ⟨the nerve-jangling *boom* of a car backfiring⟩ — see CLAP 1
boom *vb* **1** to become greater in extent, volume, amount, or number ⟨Orders for the next generation phone are *booming*.⟩ — see INCREASE 2
2 to make a long loud deep noise or cry ⟨The cannons *boomed* throughout the night.⟩ — see ROAR 1
boomerang *vb* to have the reverse of the desired or expected effect ⟨The well-meaning gesture *boomeranged*, since he ended up being offended by it.⟩ — see BACKFIRE
booming *adj* **1** marked by a high volume of sound ⟨a *booming* bass drum⟩ — see LOUD 1
2 marked by vigorous growth and well-being especially economically ⟨a *booming* business that has grown every year since it was founded⟩ — see PROSPEROUS 1
boon *adj* likely to seek or enjoy the company of others ⟨I and my *boon* companions celebrated that afternoon's victory on the gridiron with a night at a local dance club.⟩ — see CONVIVIAL
boon *n* **1** a thing that helps ⟨The couple's generous donation was a great *boon* to the charity's fund-raising campaign.⟩ — see HELP 2
2 an act of kind assistance ⟨a softhearted man who finds it hard to deny any *boon*, whether it be for friend or stranger⟩ — see FAVOR 1
3 something granted as a special favor ⟨At the prep school, seniors are given certain *boons* that make them the envy of underclassmen.⟩ — see PRIVILEGE

4 something that provides happiness or does good for a person or thing ⟨The unexpected rain was a *boon* for the farmers who had been struggling with drought.⟩ — see BLESSING 2

boondocks *pl n* the open rural area outside of big towns and cities ⟨a former city girl who was still adjusting to life in the *boondocks*⟩ — see COUNTRY 2

boor *n* a person whose behavior is offensive to others ⟨a loudmouthed *boor* who embarrassed his family at every social event they attended⟩ — see JERK 1

boorish *adj* having or showing crudely insensitive or impolite manners ⟨*boorish* behavior, such as yelling for service in restaurants⟩ — see CLOWNISH

boost *n* **1** an act or instance of helping ⟨She always liked to give struggling families in the neighborhood a *boost*.⟩ — see HELP 1

2 something added (as by growth) ⟨a sudden *boost* in sales⟩ — see INCREASE 1

3 something that arouses action or activity ⟨According to the President, a tax cut is just the *boost* that the economy needs.⟩ — see IMPULSE 1

boost *vb* **1** to lift with effort ⟨*boosted* the child into her car seat⟩ — see HEAVE 1

2 to make greater in size, amount, or number ⟨a promotion that *boosted* the number of interested customers milling about the showroom⟩ — see INCREASE 1

3 to make markedly greater in measure or degree ⟨Let's *boost* the volume on the radio so everyone can hear.⟩ — see INTENSIFY

4 to move from a lower to a higher place or position ⟨*boosted* the box onto the top shelf⟩ — see RAISE 1

booster *n* a person who actively supports or favors a cause ⟨*Boosters* for the sports team will be attending the game and carrying large signs.⟩ — see EXPONENT 1

boot (out) *vb* to drive or force out ⟨The theater manager *booted out* the audience members who were making a disturbance.⟩ — see EJECT 1

bootleg *n* illegally produced liquor ⟨Getting caught with *bootleg* during Prohibition could have resulted in a jail sentence.⟩ — see MOONSHINE 1

bootless *adj* producing no results ⟨a *bootless* effort to get tickets to the sold-out game⟩ — see FUTILE

booty *n* valuables stolen or taken by force ⟨No one knows where Captain Kidd hid his *booty*, but that hasn't deterred hopeful adventurers from looking for it for the last 300 years.⟩ — see LOOT

bop *n* a hard strike with a part of the body or an instrument ⟨A *bop* to the television set sometimes fixes it.⟩ — see ¹BLOW

bop *vb* to deliver a blow to (someone or something) usually in a strong vigorous manner ⟨The Three Stooges frequently *bopped* each other for laughs.⟩ — see HIT 1

border *n* **1** the line or relatively narrow space that marks the outer limit of something ⟨a rug with a fancily embroidered *border*⟩

synonyms bound, boundary, brim, circumference, compass, confines, edge, end, frame, fringe, hem, margin, perimeter, periphery, rim, skirt, skirting, verge

related words ambit; crest, curb, cusp; ceiling, maximum; demarcation, extent, limitation, measure, mere, restriction, termination; borderland, frontier, march, outskirts, pale, selvage; lap; shore

near antonyms center, core, heart; inner, inside, interior, middle, within

2 a region along the dividing line between two countries ⟨People who live on an international *border* get used to carrying a passport.⟩ — see FRONTIER 1

border *vb* to serve as a border for ⟨That velvet *bordered* the sleeves on this shirt, until it fell off.⟩

synonyms bound, edge, frame, fringe, margin, rim, skirt

related words hem, trim; circumscribe, define, delineate, demarcate, outline, silhouette, sketch, trace; circle, compass, encircle, enclose (*also* inclose), girdle, girth, loop, ring, round, surround, wall; check, confine, control, curb, limit, restrain, restrict

border (on) *vb* **1** to come very close to being ⟨That comment *borders on* insubordination, and you should be more careful in the future.⟩

synonyms verge (on)

related words approach, near; appear, look, resemble, seem, suggest; approximate, compare (with), measure up (to), stack up (against *or* with)

2 to be adjacent to ⟨That state *borders on* three others.⟩ — see ADJOIN 1

bordering *adj* having a border in common ⟨a country that trades with *bordering* nations⟩ — see ADJACENT

borderland *n* a region along the dividing line between two countries ⟨I grew up on the *borderland*, so I speak both languages.⟩ — see FRONTIER 1

¹**bore** *vb* **1** to make a hole or series of holes in ⟨Some woodpecker *bored* holes in our tree in the backyard.⟩ — see PERFORATE

2 to force one's way ⟨With some effort, she *bored* through the throng of screaming fans.⟩ — see ²PRESS 4

²**bore** *vb* to make weary and restless by being dull or monotonous ⟨The professor's lifeless and unimaginative teaching style *bored* the students.⟩

synonyms jade, tire, weary

related words pall; burn out, do in, drain, enervate, exhaust, fatigue, tucker (out), wash out, wear, wear out; debilitate, disable, enfeeble; demoralize, discourage, dishearten, dispirit

phrases put to sleep

near antonyms activate, animate, energize, enliven, excite, galvanize, invigorate, stimulate, strengthen, vitalize; amuse, entertain; allure, attract, beguile, bewitch, captivate, charm, enchant, hypnotize, mesmerize; monopolize, preoccupy; busy, immerse, involve, occupy; rally, rouse, stir

antonyms absorb, busy, engage, engross, enthrall (*or* enthral), fascinate, grip, interest, intrigue

bore *n* someone or something boring ⟨For once, the graduation speaker wasn't a real *bore*.⟩ — see DRAG 1

bored *adj* having one's patience, interest, or pleasure exhausted ⟨I was completely *bored* during that speech.⟩ — see WEARY 2

boredom *n* the state of being bored ⟨She spent that whole meeting in a state of complete *boredom*, waiting for lunch.⟩

synonyms blahs, doldrums, ennui, listlessness, restlessness, tedium, weariness

related words cheerlessness, dispiritedness, joylessness, melancholy; languor, lassitude, lifelessness, torpidity; dullness (*also* dulness), monotonousness, monotony, sameness; apathy, indifference, unconcern

near antonyms beguilement, bewitchment, captivation, enchantment, fascination; absorption, engagement, engrossment, immersion, involvement; animation, excitement, invigoration, stimulation; amusement, entertainment; diversion, relief

boring *adj* causing weariness, restlessness, or lack of interest ⟨I wish this book weren't so *boring*; I keep falling asleep whenever I try to read it.⟩

synonyms arid, colorless, drab, dreary, dry, dull, dusty, flat, heavy, humdrum, jading, leaden, monochromatic, monotonous, numbing, old, pedestrian, ponderous, slow, stale, stodgy, stuffy, stupid, tame, tedious, tiresome, tiring, uninteresting, wearisome, weary, wearying

related words aseptic, barren, blah, dullish, pleasureless, prosaic, prosy, soggy, spiritless; blank, gray (also grey), pallid, pedantic, sterile, suspenseless, undramatic, uneventful, unexciting, unimaginative, uninspiring, unnewsworthy, unrewarding, unsensational, unspectacular; annoying, bothersome, irksome, irritating; longsome; palling; draining, enervating, exhausting, fatiguing, wearing; debilitating, enfeebling; demoralizing, discouraging, disheartening, dispiriting; common, commonplace, ordinary, tepid, unexceptional, unsurprising, vapid; cumbersome, lumbering, plodding, poky (or pokey)

near antonyms amazing, astonishing, astounding, awesome, eye-opening, fabulous, marvelous (or marvellous), sensational, surprising, wonderful, wondrous; animating, breathtaking, electrifying, energizing, enlivening, exciting, exhilarating, galvanizing, hair-raising, inspiring, invigorating, rip-roaring, rousing, stimulating, stirring, thrilling; amusing, diverting, entertaining; moving, poignant, touching; alluring, attracting, attractive, beguiling, bewitching, captivating, charming, enchanting, enthralling, entrancing, fascinating; mesmerizing, spellbinding; suspenseful; arresting, provocative, tantalizing

antonyms absorbing, engaging, engrossing, gripping, interesting, intriguing, involving, riveting

born adj **1** being such from birth or by nature ⟨A born artist and largely self-taught, John Singleton Copley was producing accomplished portraits by the time he was in his late teens.⟩ — see NATURAL 1
2 belonging to a particular place by birth or origin ⟨a born Texan and very proud of it⟩ — see NATIVE 1

borrow vb to take for one's own use (something originated by another) ⟨borrowed the basic plot from a book of tales, but put her personal stamp on the story⟩ — see ADOPT

bosom adj closely acquainted ⟨promised to remain bosom friends for the rest of their lives⟩ — see FAMILIAR 1

bosom n the seat of one's deepest thoughts and emotions ⟨His friend's misfortune pained him to his very bosom.⟩ — see CORE 1

bosom vb to surround or cover closely ⟨an old cottage bosomed by overgrown shrubbery⟩ — see ENFOLD 1

boss n the person (as an employer or supervisor) who tells people and especially workers what to do ⟨Every morning the boss hands out a list of top-priority tasks.⟩
synonyms captain, chief, foreman, head, kingpin, leader, master, taskmaster
related words directress, mistress; administrator, commander, director, executive, general, governor, hierarch, higher-up; leadman, manager, overseer, principal, skipper, standard-bearer, steward, straw boss, superintendent, superior, supervisor; dominator, overlord, potentate, ruler, sovereign (also sovran); figurehead; baron, czar (also tsar or tzar), king, magnate, mogul, president, prince; bigwig, top dog, top gun; cohead, coleader; employer; micromanager; subchief, subdirector; bellwether
near antonyms dependent, inferior, junior, secondary, subject, subordinate, underling

boss vb **1** to be in charge of ⟨She bossed that project for years, until she was promoted again.⟩
synonyms captain, handle, head, overlook, oversee, superintend, supervise
related words administer, command, control, direct, guide, manage, order, run, shepherd, show, steer; monitor, preside (over); govern, rule
phrases call the shots (of), call the tune (for), ride herd on, watch over
2 to exercise authority or power over ⟨bossed the entire job site for a year⟩ — see GOVERN 1
3 to serve as leader of ⟨bossed the entire team of electricians on the construction project⟩ — see LEAD 2

boss (around) vb to issue orders to (someone) by right of authority ⟨That regional manager certainly likes to boss people around.⟩ — see COMMAND 1

bossy adj fond of ordering people around ⟨I don't want to work with him because he's so bossy and always runs roughshod over me.⟩
synonyms authoritarian, authoritative, autocratic (also autocratical), despotic, dictatorial, domineering, imperious, masterful, overbearing, peremptory, tyrannical (also tyrannic), tyrannous
related words arrogant, assumptive, disdainful, fastuous, haughty, highfalutin (also hifalutin), high-hat, important, lofty, lordly, overweening, presuming, presumptuous, pretentious, proud, supercilious, superior, toplofty (also toploftical), uppish, uppity; commanding, controlling, dictating, regimental; arbitrary, high-handed, imperial; directorial; aggressive, assertive, self-assertive; imperative; conceited, pompous, vain; all-powerful, almighty, omnipotent; firm, stern
near antonyms humble, meek, modest, unassuming; amenable, docile, obedient, tractable; indecisive, irresolute; acquiescent, compliant, passive, resigned, submissive, yielding

botch vb to make or do (something) in a clumsy or unskillful way ⟨The first time we tried to make a cake, we botched the job completely.⟩
synonyms blow, bobble, bungle, butcher, dub, flub, fluff, foozle, foul up, fumble, louse up, mangle, mess (up), muff, murder, screw up
related words blunder, muddle, piffle; blemish, damage, flaw, harm, hurt, impair, injure, mar, mutilate, ruin, spoil, vitiate; destroy, wreck; mishandle, mismanage
near antonyms ameliorate, better, enhance, help, improve, meliorate, rectify, refine, reform, remedy; doctor, fix, patch, recondition, renovate, repair, revamp

botched adj showing or marked by a lack of skill and tact (as in dealing with a situation) ⟨a botched attempt at an apology⟩ — see AWKWARD 2

bother n **1** a state of noisy, confused activity ⟨The whole household was in a bother, as our overnight guests were expected to arrive any minute.⟩ — see COMMOTION
2 one who is obnoxiously annoying ⟨Sorry again to be a bother, but I still need help.⟩ — see NUISANCE 1
3 something that is a source of irritation ⟨Returning damaged goods is a real bother.⟩ — see ANNOYANCE 3
4 the feeling of impatience or anger caused by another's repeated disagreeable acts ⟨never let his personal bothers interfere with his responsibilities at work⟩ — see ANNOYANCE 2

bother vb **1** to thrust oneself upon (another) without invitation ⟨I am never going to get this work done if people don't stop wandering into the room and bothering me!⟩
synonyms bug, chivy (or chivvy), disturb, intrude (upon), pester
related words inconvenience, trouble; aggravate, annoy, bedevil, chafe, devil, dog, dun, exasperate, fret, gall, get, grate, hassle, irk, irritate, nettle, peeve, persecute, pique, put out, rankle, rasp, rile, roil, torment, vex, worry; beleaguer, beset, besiege; distress, plague; afflict, provoke; anger, antagonize, enrage, incense, inflame (also enflame), infuriate, madden, outrage; agitate, perturb; butt in, cut in (on), obtrude; encroach, infringe, invade, trespass
near antonyms disregard, forget, ignore, leave, slight; appease, conciliate, disarm, mollify, oblige, placate; delight, gladden, gratify, please, satisfy; comfort, console, content
2 to disturb the peace of mind of (someone) especially by repeated disagreeable acts ⟨It bothers me when obviously sick people go to concerts and spend the whole time coughing and sneezing.⟩ — see IRRITATE 1

3 to experience concern or anxiety ⟨Just get the basic concept right and don't *bother* about the details.⟩ — see WORRY 1

4 to trouble the mind of; to make uneasy ⟨Her child's persistent sore throat *bothered* her.⟩ — see DISTURB 1

bothersome *adj* causing annoyance ⟨a *bothersome* habit of dropping trash on the floor right next to the garbage can⟩ — see ANNOYING

bottleneck *n* a crowded mass (as of cars) that impedes or blocks movement ⟨A *bottleneck* inevitably forms at the start of a construction zone when the highway narrows from three to two lanes.⟩ — see JAM 1

bottom *adj* of, relating to, or located at the bottom ⟨was sitting on the *bottom* step of the stairway⟩

synonyms low

related words below, lower, low-grade, lowly, nether, under; lowered, low-lying, sunken

near antonyms higher, loftier, upper; elevated, escalated, heightened, jacked (up), lifted, raised, uplifted, upraised

antonyms highest, loftiest, top, topmost, upmost, uppermost

bottom *n* **1** the side or part facing downward from something ⟨That side of the shelf is supposed to be the *bottom*, so turn it over before you assemble the bookcase.⟩

synonyms underbelly, underbody, underpart, underside, undersurface

related words belly, sole, toe; base, floor, foot, ground, seat, underpinning; undercarriage

near antonyms acme, apex, climax, crest, crown, culmination, height, high-water mark, meridian, peak, pinnacle, roof, summit; cusp, head, point, tip, tip-top, zenith

antonyms face, top

2 the surface upon which a body of water lies ⟨My missing fishing pole is probably lying on the *bottom* of the lake.⟩

synonyms bed, floor

related words riverbed; base, basement, foundation, ground

near antonyms surface

3 the lowest part, place, or point ⟨sliding all the way to the *bottom* of the snow-covered slope⟩

synonyms base, basement, foot, rock bottom

related words basis, bed, bedrock, foundation, ground, groundwork, keystone, seat, underpinning; depth, nadir, zero

near antonyms acme, apex, climax, crest, culmination, height, meridian, peak, pinnacle, summit, tip, tip-top, zenith

antonyms head, top, vertex

4 the part of the body upon which someone sits ⟨The baby fell backwards onto her *bottom*.⟩ — see BUTTOCKS

5 a small buoyant structure for travel on water ⟨The cargo will be carried by a local *bottom*.⟩ — see BOAT 1

6 an immaterial thing upon which something else rests ⟨The *bottom* of his thesis is the assumption that people are fundamentally good.⟩ — see BASE 1

bottomless *adj* **1** being or seeming to be without limits ⟨The wealthy couple are generous hosts, providing a *bottomless* supply of food and drink.⟩ — see INFINITE

2 extending far downward ⟨a *bottomless* pit⟩ — see DEEP 1

bough *n* a major outgrowth from the main stem of a woody plant ⟨A tree *bough* fell on my car during the windstorm.⟩ — see BRANCH 1

boulevard *n* a passage cleared for public vehicular travel ⟨The city is celebrated for its broad, tree-lined *boulevards*.⟩ — see WAY 1

bounce *n* active strength of body or mind ⟨At 90, there's still a *bounce* in his step.⟩ — see VIGOR 1

bounce *vb* **1** to drive or force out ⟨The bar doesn't hesitate to *bounce* customers for getting rowdy.⟩ — see EJECT 1

2 to strike and fly off at an angle ⟨Most of my shots *bounce* off the rim of the basket.⟩ — see GLANCE 1

3 to let go from office, service, or employment ⟨I'll *bounce* you if I catch you talking that way again!⟩ — see DISMISS 1

4 to set before the mind for consideration ⟨We *bounced* several script suggestions off the producers.⟩ — see PROPOSE 1

5 to move with a light springing step ⟨The girl *bounced* excitedly alongside her parents as they hurried toward the entrance to the amusement park.⟩ — see SKIP 1

bounce (back) *vb* to regain a former or normal state ⟨Once the cleanup from the hurricane is completed, business owners are hoping that tourism quickly *bounces back*.⟩ — see RECOVER 2

bouncing *adj* **1** enjoying health and vigor ⟨a *bouncing* new baby in the family⟩ — see HEALTHY 1

2 having much high-spirited energy and movement ⟨a *bouncing* dance routine that should be good for an aerobics class⟩ — see LIVELY 1

¹bound *n* **1** a real or imaginary point beyond which a person or thing cannot go ⟨You can buy as much as you want, within the *bounds* of reason.⟩ — see LIMIT 1

2 the line or relatively narrow space that marks the outer limit of something ⟨colored outside the *bounds* of the drawing⟩ — see BORDER 1

²bound *n* an act of leaping into the air ⟨The kangaroo took one giant *bound* and was gone.⟩ — see JUMP 1

¹bound *vb* **1** to mark the limits of ⟨The country is *bounded* by water on two sides.⟩ — see LIMIT 2

2 to serve as a border for ⟨Being *bounded* on all sides by the Alps has helped Switzerland maintain its neutrality.⟩ — see BORDER

²bound *vb* **1** to move with a light springing step ⟨The child giggled and *bounded* off to play with her friends.⟩ — see SKIP 1

2 to propel oneself upward or forward into the air ⟨A rabbit *bounded* down the garden path.⟩ — see JUMP 1

bound *adj* fully committed to achieving a goal ⟨I am *bound* and determined to write a novel before I turn 30.⟩ — see DETERMINED 1

boundary *n* **1** a real or imaginary point beyond which a person or thing cannot go ⟨Parents have to set *boundaries* for their children, and the children want them to.⟩ — see LIMIT 1

2 the line or relatively narrow space that marks the outer limit of something ⟨That chalk line marks the *boundary* of our playing field.⟩ — see BORDER 1

bounded *adj* having distinct or certain limits ⟨In their paintings the Impressionists played down *bounded* figures and concentrated on the subtle, fleeting effects of light.⟩ — see LIMITED 1

boundless *adj* being or seeming to be without limits ⟨Her *boundless* energy and enthusiasm make her a natural for the job.⟩ — see INFINITE

bounteous *adj* **1** being more than enough without being excessive ⟨offered a *bounteous* reward for finding the lost ring⟩ — see PLENTIFUL

2 giving or sharing in abundance and without hesitation ⟨a *bounteous* king who made sure all his subjects were well-fed⟩ — see GENEROUS 1

bountiful *adj* **1** being more than enough without being excessive ⟨a *bountiful* supply of apples for the harvest festival⟩ — see PLENTIFUL

2 giving or sharing in abundance and without hesitation ⟨a *bountiful* host who makes sure that everyone has plenty to eat at his dinners⟩ — see GENEROUS 1

bountifully *adv* in a generous manner ⟨Grandma makes sure that everyone in the family is *bountifully* supplied with her hand-knit sweaters and scarves.⟩ — see WELL 2

bountifulness *n* the quality or state of being generous ⟨Because of the restaurant owner's *bountifulness*, a number of homeless people were fed that day.⟩ — see LIBERALITY

bounty *n* **1** something offered or given in return for a service performed ⟨A *bounty* was offered for information leading to the capture of the criminal.⟩ — see REWARD

2 the quality or state of being generous ⟨Her *bounty* at Halloween was known throughout the neighborhood.⟩ — see LIBERALITY

3 the total amount collected or obtained especially at one time ⟨the record-breaking *bounty* from this year's corn harvest⟩ — see HAUL 1

bouquet *n* **1** a bunch of flowers ⟨I bought my wife a nice *bouquet* for her birthday.⟩

synonyms nosegay, posy

related words boutonniere, corsage; arrangement; garland, lei

2 a sweet or pleasant smell ⟨This wine has a good *bouquet*.⟩ — see FRAGRANCE

3 an admiring personal remark ⟨a performance that attracted *bouquets* as well as brickbats⟩ — see COMPLIMENT 1

bout *n* **1** a competitive encounter between individuals or groups carried on for amusement, exercise, or in pursuit of a prize ⟨Undoubtedly the team's best wrestler, he hasn't lost a *bout* yet.⟩ — see GAME 1

2 a sudden experiencing of a physical or mental disorder ⟨She's currently suffering from a *bout* of the flu.⟩ — see ATTACK 2

¹bow *vb* **1** to cease resistance (as to another's arguments, demands, or control) ⟨The mayor *bowed* to the will of the voters.⟩ — see YIELD 3

2 to give up and cease resistance (as to a liking, temptation, or habit) ⟨*bowed* to the craving for fresh coffee⟩ — see YIELD 1

²bow *vb* **1** to turn away from a straight line or course ⟨The river *bows* gently to the north before it reaches the sea.⟩ — see CURVE 1

2 to cause to turn away from a straight line ⟨You'll have to gently *bow* the strip of wood in order to fit it in.⟩ — see BEND 1

bow *n* something that curves or is curved ⟨Her full lips form a pair of perfect *bows*.⟩ — see BEND 1

bowed *adj* **1** bending downward or forward ⟨The *bowed* branches of the weeping willow offered some protection from the rain.⟩ — see NODDING

2 directed down ⟨With *bowed* heads the mourners recited a prayer for the repose of her soul.⟩ — see DOWNCAST 1

bowing *adj* bending downward or forward ⟨The *bowing* blossoms indicated that the petunia plant desperately needed water.⟩ — see NODDING

bowl *n* a large usually roofless building for sporting events with tiers of seats for spectators ⟨a new *bowl* for the football team⟩ — see STADIUM

bowl *vb* **1** to move or proceed smoothly and readily ⟨*bowling* along in my spiffy new car⟩ — see FLOW 2

2 to proceed or move quickly ⟨*bowled* through the test and was the first one to hand it in⟩ — see HURRY 2

bowl (down *or* over) *vb* to strike (someone) so forcefully as to cause a fall ⟨The exuberant dog *bowled over* several children.⟩ — see FELL 1

bowled over *adj* affected with sudden and great wonder or surprise ⟨I was *bowled over* when the appraiser told me what the painting was worth.⟩ — see THUNDERSTRUCK

¹box *n* **1** a covered rectangular container for storing or transporting things ⟨filled a whole *box* with books⟩ — see CHEST

2 a boxlike container for holding a dead body ⟨Grandpa said he wanted to be buried in a simple pine *box*.⟩ — see COFFIN

²box *n* a hard strike with a part of the body or an instrument ⟨suffered a *box* on the ear⟩ — see ¹BLOW

box *vb* to deliver a blow to (someone or something) usually in a strong vigorous manner ⟨threatened to *box* his ears⟩ — see HIT 1

boxer *n* one that engages in the sport of fighting with the fists ⟨That *boxer* is quite famous for being the youngest heavyweight champion ever.⟩

synonyms fighter, prizefighter, pugilist

related words slugger; bantamweight, cruiserweight, featherweight, flyweight, light heavyweight, lightweight, middleweight, superheavyweight, welterweight

boy *n* **1** a male person who has not yet reached adulthood ⟨A giggling little *boy* ran by.⟩

synonyms lad, laddie, nipper, shaver, sonny, stripling, tad, youth

related words adolescent, juvenile, kid, kiddo, minor, moppet, teenager, tween, youngster; brat, gamin, guttersnipe, imp, squirt, urchin, whippersnapper; schoolboy; toddler, tot

2 a male romantic companion ⟨They really like their daughter's new *boy*.⟩ — see BOYFRIEND

boyfriend *n* a male romantic companion ⟨her *boyfriend* always brings her flowers for Valentine's Day⟩

synonyms beau, boy, fellow, man, old man, swain

related words admirer, crush, steady; suitor, wooer; beloved, darling, dear, favorite, flame, honey, love, lover, significant other, soul mate, squeeze [*slang*], sweet, sweetheart, sweetie pie, valentine; fancy man, gigolo; date, escort; husband; fiancé, intended

brace *n* **1** a structure that holds up or serves as a foundation for something else ⟨wore a *brace* for the injured knee⟩ — see SUPPORT 1

2 two things of the same or similar kind that match or are considered together ⟨I bagged a *brace* of pheasants.⟩ — see PAIR

brace *vb* **1** to give life, vigor, or spirit to ⟨The pep talk *braced* the team up for the second half.⟩ — see ANIMATE

2 to hold up or serve as a foundation for ⟨Several boards *braced* the wall.⟩ — see SUPPORT 3

3 to prepare (oneself) mentally or emotionally ⟨She *braced* herself for the job interview.⟩ — see FORTIFY 1

bracelet *n* something that physically prevents free movement ⟨Putting the handcuffs on the jewel thief, the detective asked him how he liked those *bracelets*.⟩ — see BOND 1

bracing *adj* having a renewing effect on the state of the body or mind ⟨a chilly but *bracing* day⟩ — see TONIC 1

bracket *n* one of the units into which a whole is divided on the basis of a common characteristic ⟨They're in the same income *bracket*.⟩ — see CLASS 2

bracket *vb* to describe as similar ⟨Should Mozart be *bracketed* with Hayden?⟩ — see COMPARE 1

brackish *adj* **1** disagreeable or disgusting to the sense of taste ⟨The office coffee is often some *brackish* brew that's been sitting around for a couple of hours.⟩ — see DISTASTEFUL 1

2 of, relating to, or containing salt ⟨The river becomes *brackish* as we approach the tidemark.⟩ — see SALTY 1

brag *n* **1** boastful speech or writing ⟨For all his *brag* about skiing, he actually does very little.⟩ — see BOMBAST 1

2 someone who boasts ⟨She's always been an annoying *brag*.⟩ — see BRAGGART

brag *vb* to praise or express pride in one's own possessions, qualities, or accomplishments often to excess ⟨She *bragged* that she was richer than anyone else in the state.⟩ — see BOAST 1

braggadocio *n* boastful speech or writing ⟨His *braggadocio* hid the fact that he was insecure.⟩ — see BOMBAST 1

braggart *n* someone who boasts ⟨a *braggart* who was always talking about how much money he made⟩
synonyms boaster, brag, bragger, swaggerer
related words blusterer; self-advertiser, self-dramatizer, self-promoter

bragger *n* someone who boasts ⟨She's a tiresome *bragger* who should be ignored.⟩ — see BRAGGART

braid *n* a length of something formed of three or more strands woven together ⟨Until she was 15, she had a *braid* that reached to her knees.⟩
synonyms lace, lacing, plait, plat
related words cornrow, dreadlock, pigtail, queue; braiding

braid *vb* to form into a braid ⟨They taught each other how to *braid* yarn into bracelets.⟩
synonyms plait, plat, pleat
related words interlace, interweave, weave

brain *n* 1 a very smart person ⟨The president promised to have the best *brains* working on the problem.⟩ — see GENIUS 1
2 *often* **brains** *pl* the ability to learn and understand or to deal with problems ⟨You have the *brains* to figure out that problem on your own.⟩ — see INTELLIGENCE 1
3 the part of a person that feels, thinks, perceives, wills, and especially reasons ⟨I'd love to get inside his *brain* and experience the world as he experiences it.⟩ — see MIND 1

brainless *adj* 1 not having or showing an ability to absorb ideas readily ⟨a teacher who affirms that there are no *brainless* students⟩ — see STUPID 1
2 showing or marked by a lack of good sense or judgment ⟨a *brainless* decision to talk on her cell phone while weaving in and out of traffic⟩ — see FOOLISH 1

brainlessness *n* 1 lack of good sense or judgment ⟨had the inexplicable *brainlessness* to sell his car for half of what it was worth⟩ — see FOOLISHNESS 1
2 the quality or state of lacking intelligence or quickness of mind ⟨The turkey is one bird that has often been cited for its *brainlessness*.⟩ — see STUPIDITY 1

brainstorm *vb* to engage in an exchange of information or ideas ⟨They *brainstormed* about ways to raise money for their organization.⟩ — see COMMUNICATE 2

brainy *adj* having or showing quickness of mind ⟨a *brainy* student who was recruited by the top colleges⟩ — see INTELLIGENT 1

brake *n* a thick patch of shrubbery, small trees, or underbrush ⟨built a small shelter in the *brake* to watch for deer⟩ — see THICKET

brake *vb* to cause to move or proceed at a less rapid pace ⟨I *braked* the car sharply when someone pulled out in front of us.⟩ — see SLOW

braking *n* a usually gradual decrease in the pace or level of activity of something ⟨There's always a *braking* in sales after lunch.⟩ — see SLOWDOWN

brambly *adj* having leaves or branches which are likely to cause a scratch ⟨Be careful of the *brambly* blackberry bushes.⟩ — see SCRATCHY 1

branch *n* 1 a major outgrowth from the main stem of a woody plant ⟨I loved climbing among the *branches* of that old tree.⟩
synonyms bough, limb
related words branchlet, offshoot, outgrowth, shoot, spur; spray, sprig

2 a local unit of an organization ⟨a bank with many neighborhood *branches*⟩ — see CHAPTER 1
3 a large unit of a governmental, business, or educational organization ⟨the two *branches* of the U.S. Congress⟩ — see DIVISION 2

branch *vb* to extend outwards from or as if from a central point ⟨Threads *branched* from the center of the spider web.⟩ — see RADIATE 1

branch (out) *vb* to go or move in different directions from a central point ⟨The vine *branched out* as it climbed the trellis.⟩ — see SEPARATE 2

brand *n* 1 a device (as a word) identifying the maker of a piece of merchandise and legally reserved for the exclusive use of that person or company ⟨a company that was sued for using a name that was very similar to a rival's *brand*⟩ — see TRADEMARK 1
2 a mark of guilt or disgrace ⟨had a reputation bearing the *brand* of traitor⟩ — see STAIN 1
3 a hand weapon with a length of metal sharpened on one or both sides and usually tapered to a sharp point ⟨On the battlefield lies our hero, slain by some fell *brand*.⟩ — see SWORD

brand *vb* to produce a vivid impression of ⟨The exact words my father spoke on my graduation day are *branded* in my memory.⟩ — see ENGRAVE 2

brand–new *adj* 1 being in an original and unused or unspoiled state ⟨His car is so well cared for that three years later it still looks *brand-new*.⟩ — see FRESH 1
2 recently made and never used before ⟨a *brand-new* phone still in its original packaging⟩ — see NEW 3

brash *adj* 1 displaying or marked by rude boldness ⟨a *brash* request to get something for free⟩ — see NERVY 1
2 foolishly adventurous or bold ⟨That *brash* motorcyclist likes to show off by riding on only one wheel.⟩ — see FOOLHARDY 1
3 showing poor judgment especially in personal relationships or social situations ⟨He was reprimanded for his *brash* comments to the media about the team's coaching staff.⟩ — see INDISCREET

brashness *n* shameless boldness ⟨For sheer *brashness* it would be hard to beat the customer who wanted a refund on merchandise bought elsewhere.⟩ — see EFFRONTERY

brass *n* shameless boldness ⟨They had the *brass* to demand a refund for something they had broken themselves!⟩ — see EFFRONTERY

brassiness *n* shameless boldness ⟨The *brassiness* with which he would blame his mistakes on others left me speechless.⟩ — see EFFRONTERY

brassy *adj* displaying or marked by rude boldness ⟨A *brassy* customer arrived late and still insisted on being taken first.⟩ — see NERVY 1

brave *adj* 1 feeling or displaying no fear by temperament ⟨Despite considerable risk to their own safety, the *brave* team of rescuers rushed into the collapsed building.⟩
synonyms bold, courageous, dauntless, doughty, fearless, gallant, greathearted, gutsy, heroic (*also* heroical), intrepid, lionhearted, manful, stalwart, stout, stouthearted, undaunted, valiant, valorous
related words determined, firm, game, gamy (*or* gamey), gritty, plucky, resolute, Spartan, undeterred, undismayed, unflinching, unswerving; mettlesome, spirited, spunky; adventuresome, adventurous, audacious, daring, dashing, hardy, venturesome, venturous; foolish, half-witted; brash, brazen, daredevil, foolhardy, heedless, hotheaded, impetuous, imprudent, impulsive, incautious, madcap, overbold, overconfident, rash, reckless, thoughtless, wild; hasty, headlong, precipitate; comforted, emboldened, encouraged, heartened, reassured, unafraid

near antonyms diffident, mousy (*or* mousey), scary, shy, skittish, timid; anxious, nervous; careful, cautious, heedful, prudent, unadventurous; afraid, agitated, disconcerted, disquieted, disturbed, frightened, horrified, panicked, panic-stricken, perturbed, scared, shocked, spooked, startled, terrified, terrorized, unnerved, upset; appalled, concerned, dismayed, worried; unmanly, weak, wimpy
antonyms chicken, chickenhearted, chicken-livered, coward, cowardly, craven, dastardly, fainthearted, fearful, lily-livered, nerveless, spineless, spiritless, timorous, uncourageous, ungallant, unheroic, weakhearted, yellow
2 of the very best kind ⟨The gourmet food shop is off to a *brave* start.⟩ — see EXCELLENT
brave *vb* to oppose (something hostile or dangerous) with firmness or courage ⟨a soldier who *braved* enemy fire to rescue her wounded comrade⟩ — see FACE 2
bravery *n* **1** dressy clothing ⟨children in their Sunday *bravery*⟩ — see FINERY
2 strength of mind to carry on in spite of danger ⟨It took great *bravery* to rescue the dogs trapped in the burning building.⟩ — see COURAGE
brawl *n* **1** a rough and often noisy fight usually involving several people ⟨They were thrown out of the party after starting a *brawl*.⟩
synonyms fracas, fray, free-for-all, melee (*also* mêlée), row, ruckus, ruction
related words battle, clash, combat, conflict, contest, fisticuffs, handgrips, hassle, scrap, scrimmage, scuffle, skirmish, struggle, tussle; horseplay, roughhousing; altercation, argument, dispute, kickup, quarrel, spat, squabble, tiff, wrangle
2 an often noisy or angry expression of differing opinions ⟨The controversial plan prompted a *brawl* at the school board meeting.⟩ — see ARGUMENT 1
brawl *vb* to express different opinions about something often angrily ⟨loudly *brawling* over politics⟩ — see ARGUE 2
brawn *n* muscular strength ⟨an actor who is famous for his *brawn*⟩ — see MUSCLE 1
brawny *adj* **1** having muscles capable of exerting great physical force ⟨The store manager always asked the *brawniest* person there to do the heavy lifting.⟩ — see STRONG 1
2 marked by a well-developed musculature ⟨*brawny* arms that weren't developed in the gym but by years of work in the construction business⟩ — see MUSCULAR 1
3 strongly and heavily built ⟨a tough little boy who's going to be a *brawny* man someday⟩ — see ¹HUSKY 1
brazen *adj* displaying or marked by rude boldness ⟨a *brazen* demand for special treatment just because she's rich⟩ — see NERVY 1
brazen *vb* to oppose (something hostile or dangerous) with firmness or courage ⟨a filmmaker willing to *brazen* the criticism that such a film was sure to provoke⟩ — see FACE 2
brazenness *n* shameless boldness ⟨She had the *brazenness* to expect us to let her copy our work.⟩ — see EFFRONTERY
breach *n* **1** a failure to uphold the requirements of law, duty, or obligation ⟨Failure to deliver on time was a *breach* of the contract.⟩
synonyms infraction, infringement, transgression, trespass, violation
related words misconduct, misdemeanor, misfeasance, misprision, offense (*or* offence), sin, wrong; disregard, forgetting, ignoring, nonobservance, overlooking; delinquency, dereliction, neglect; encroachment, intrusion, invasion
near antonyms respecting, upholding

antonyms noninfringement, observance
2 a breaking of a moral or legal code ⟨Cheating on the exam was a serious *breach* of the military academy's honor code.⟩ — see OFFENSE 1
3 an open space in a barrier (as a wall or hedge) ⟨The cat got out of the yard through a *breach* in the hedge.⟩ — see GAP 1
breach *vb* to fail to keep ⟨a builder being sued by a homeowner for *breaching* a contract⟩ — see VIOLATE 1
bread *n* **1** *slang* something (as pieces of stamped metal or printed paper) customarily and legally used as a medium of exchange, a measure of value, or a means of payment ⟨I'll buy that tomorrow, when I get some *bread*.⟩ — see MONEY
2 substances intended to be eaten ⟨supplied his charges with *bread* and a place to stay⟩ — see FOOD
breadbasket *n, slang* the part of the body between the chest and the pelvis ⟨got hit right in the *breadbasket*⟩ — see STOMACH 1
breadth *n* **1** a wide space or area ⟨A great *breadth* of land awaited those who were brave and hardy enough to settle it.⟩ — see EXPANSE
2 an area over which activity, capacity, or influence extends ⟨The *breadth* of his knowledge on the subject is awesome.⟩ — see RANGE 2
break *n* **1** a momentary halt in an activity ⟨The band came back on stage after a short *break*.⟩ — see PAUSE 1
2 a period during which the usual routine of school or work is suspended ⟨Most of the students at the boarding school are going home for winter *break*.⟩ — see VACATION
3 an open space in a barrier (as a wall or hedge) ⟨The rancher repaired the *break* in the fence where the horse had gotten through.⟩ — see GAP 1
4 a favorable combination of circumstances, time, and place ⟨In classic fashion, her big *break* came when, as an understudy, she took over for an ailing star.⟩ — see OPPORTUNITY
5 the act or an instance of getting free from danger or confinement ⟨a desperate *break* from prison⟩ — see ESCAPE 1
break *vb* **1** to cause to separate into pieces usually suddenly or forcibly ⟨I hated telling her that I had *broken* her favorite glass vase.⟩
synonyms break up, bust, dismember, disrupt, fracture, fragment, rive
related words atomize, crush, grind, powder, pulverize, reduce; blast, blow up, burst, detonate, explode; crack, pop, shatter, shiver, smash; chip, sliver, splinter, split; implode; destroy, ruin, wreck
near antonyms doctor, fix, heal, mend, patch, rebuild, recondition, reconstruct, renovate, repair
2 to bring (as an action or operation) to an immediate end ⟨The final vote *broke* the deadlock.⟩ — see STOP 1
3 to bring to a lower grade or rank ⟨The captain was *broken* to lieutenant commander for disobeying a direct order from his group commander.⟩ — see DEMOTE
4 to change (as a secret message) from code into ordinary language ⟨Alan Turing and the Bletchley Park mathematicians *broke* the Enigma code being used by the Nazis.⟩ — see DECODE 1
5 to come to a temporary halt in one's activity ⟨She *broke* from her ruminations to find that it was already dinnertime.⟩ — see PAUSE
6 to cut into and turn over the sod of (a piece of land) using a bladed implement ⟨Farmers once *broke* fields with horse-drawn plows.⟩ — see PLOW 1
7 to fail to keep ⟨had *broken* his promise not to share their conversation with anyone⟩ — see VIOLATE 1

8 to find an answer for through reasoning ⟨Professor Bates *broke* the problem when she realized that it was possible to synthesize the necessary compounds.⟩ — see SOLVE

9 to reduce the soundness, effectiveness, or perfection of ⟨I *broke* a tooth on the hard candy⟩ — see DAMAGE 1

10 to stop functioning ⟨After working for 30 years, the pump simply *broke* one day.⟩ — see FAIL 1

11 to hasten away from something dangerous or frightening ⟨The herd of gazelles *broke* when they saw the lions racing toward them from the ridge above.⟩ — see RUN 2

12 to use up all the physical energy of ⟨The trek up the mountain just about *broke* me.⟩ — see EXHAUST 1

13 to become known ⟨The story *broke* just yesterday.⟩ — see GET OUT 1

14 to cause to lose one's fortune and become unable to pay one's debts ⟨Another bad investment could *break* him.⟩ — see RUIN 1

15 to come into existence ⟨The crisis had passed, and a new day was *breaking*.⟩ — see BEGIN 2

16 to depart abruptly from a straight line or course ⟨The running back *broke* to his left before running out of bounds.⟩ — see SWERVE 1

17 to diminish the price or value of ⟨distressing economic news that will *break* many energy stocks⟩ — see DEPRECIATE 1

18 to go beyond the limit of ⟨The temperature tomorrow might *break* the previous record.⟩ — see EXCEED 1

19 to penetrate the surface (as of water) from below ⟨Dolphins were *breaking* all around the boat.⟩ — see BROACH 1

breakable *adj* easily broken ⟨Careful—those dishes are *breakable*.⟩ — see FRAGILE 1

breakdown *n* **1** a mental or nervous collapse ⟨If you don't ease your workload, you're going to have a *breakdown*.⟩
synonyms crack-up
related words frazzle, freak-out, meltdown; alarm (*also* alarum), anxiety, apprehension, disquiet; excitability, nervousness; disturbance; agitation, discomposure, perturbation; basket case
near antonyms aplomb, calmness, composure, coolness, imperturbability, placidity, self-possession, sereneness, serenity, tranquillity (*or* tranquility)

2 the process by which dead organic matter separates into simpler substances ⟨Turning the compost pile helps speed the *breakdown*.⟩ — see CORRUPTION 1

3 the separation and identification of the parts of a whole ⟨I want a detailed *breakdown* of the statistics.⟩ — see ANALYSIS 1

break down *vb* **1** to arrange or assign according to type ⟨When presented with the pile of files, the first thing he did was to *break* them *down* by month, order within the month, and region.⟩ — see CLASSIFY 1

2 to go through decomposition ⟨The enamel of a human tooth will begin to *break down* when exposed to sugar for too long.⟩ — see DECAY 1

3 to identify and examine the basic elements or parts of (something) especially for discovering interrelationships ⟨If we *break* the problem *down* into what appear to be three aspects of it, we'll have a better chance of solving it.⟩ — see ANALYZE

4 to stop functioning ⟨The computer finally *broke down* and had to be replaced.⟩ — see FAIL 1

5 to yield to mental or emotional stress ⟨began to *break down* when he realized that he was on the verge of bankruptcy⟩ — see CRACK 2

6 to take apart ⟨The crew was *breaking down* the party tent when we arrived.⟩ — see DISASSEMBLE 1

7 to cause to break with violence and much noise ⟨Firefighters had to *break down* the wall to rescue the kitten.⟩ — see SMASH 1

break in *vb* **1** to enter a house or building by force usually with illegal intent ⟨The burglars *broke in* by smashing a window.⟩
synonyms burglarize
related words invade, trespass; hold up, loot, plunder, rip off, rob, stick up; ransack, rifle; despoil, devastate, maraud, pillage, ravage, sack

2 to cause a disruption in a conversation or discussion ⟨Midway through the news story a reporter *broke in* with an update.⟩ — see INTERRUPT

breakneck *adj* moving, proceeding, or acting with great speed ⟨the *breakneck* production of naval vessels during World War II⟩ — see FAST 1

break off *vb* **1** to bring (as an action or operation) to an immediate end ⟨The judge *broke off* court proceedings until after lunch.⟩ — see STOP 1

2 to come to an end ⟨Talks between the two sides *broke off* when one began making unreasonable demands.⟩ — see CEASE 1

break out *vb* to develop suddenly and violently ⟨A fire *broke out* in the kitchen.⟩ — see ERUPT 2

breakthrough *n* an instance of notable progress in the development of knowledge, technology, or skill ⟨Alexander Fleming's discovery of penicillin was one of medicine's great *breakthroughs*, for penicillin became the first antibiotic to successfully combat bacterial infections in humans.⟩ — see ADVANCE 2

breakup *n* the act or process of a whole separating into two or more parts or pieces ⟨The *breakup* of the Soviet Union and the collapse of communism pretty much signaled the end of the Cold War.⟩ — see SEPARATION 1

break up *vb* **1** to cease to exist or cause to cease to exist as a group or organization ⟨The band *broke up* when their arguments over money grew too stressful.⟩ — see DISBAND 1

2 to come to an end ⟨The meeting *broke up* when all the business for the day had been completed.⟩ — see CEASE 1

3 to set or force apart ⟨He *broke up* the rocks in the old stone wall with a crowbar, sending them tumbling to the ground.⟩ — see SEPARATE 1

4 to yield to mental or emotional stress ⟨likely to *break up* under pressure⟩ — see CRACK 2

5 to bring (as an action or operation) to an immediate end ⟨Police arrived at the scene and immediately *broke up* the fracas.⟩ — see STOP 1

6 to cause to separate into pieces usually suddenly or forcibly ⟨*Break up* the feta cheese and spread it over the salad.⟩ — see BREAK 1

7 to show mirth with an explosive vocal sound ⟨If you *break up* during the skit, the audience will know that you're in on the joke.⟩ — see LAUGH 1

breast *n* the seat of one's deepest thoughts and emotions ⟨Deep in his *breast*, he knew that his father had a great love for him that did not need to be expressed in words.⟩ — see CORE 1

breast *vb* to oppose (something hostile or dangerous) with firmness or courage ⟨*breasted* the diagnosis with fortitude and optimism⟩ — see FACE 2

breath *n* **1** a momentary halt in an activity ⟨Let's all take a *breath* before continuing this discussion.⟩ — see PAUSE 1

2 a slight or gentle movement of air ⟨A sweet *breath* caressed her cheek as she sat in the garden.⟩ — see BREEZE 1

3 an almost imperceptible sign of something ⟨The mornings are already getting warmer, and there is a *breath* of spring in the air.⟩ — see HINT 2

breathe *vb* **1** to inhale and exhale air ⟨Sometimes it gets so hot in here that it's hard to even *breathe*.⟩
synonyms respire
related words blow (out), draw, expire, inbreathe, inspire; gasp, huff, pant, puff, suspire, wheeze; sniff, snore, snort, snuffle, whiff
near antonyms asphyxiate, choke, gag, smother, suffocate; garrote (*or* garotte), stifle, strangle, throttle
2 to have life ⟨As long as I *breathe*, you will have a place to stay.⟩ — see BE 1

breathe (out) *vb* to let or force out of the lungs ⟨leaned back in his chair and *breathed out* the smoke from his pipe⟩ — see EXHALE 1

breather *n* a momentary halt in an activity ⟨We took a *breather* from the seemingly endless task.⟩ — see PAUSE 1

breathing *adj* having or showing life ⟨realized that he didn't need a comic-book superhero, since he had a real, *breathing* hero in his father⟩ — see ALIVE 1

breathless *adj* **1** lacking fresh air ⟨The room was hot and *breathless*.⟩ — see STUFFY 1
2 moving, proceeding, or acting with great speed ⟨ran at a *breathless* pace to get help⟩ — see FAST 1
3 no longer living ⟨carried the *breathless* body of his beloved dog back home⟩ — see DEAD 1

breathtaking *adj* causing great emotional or mental stimulation ⟨a truly *breathtaking* view of the majestic waterfall⟩ — see EXCITING 1

breech *n* **1** the part of the body upon which someone sits ⟨Plant yourselves on your *breeches* on that bench and listen to what I have to say.⟩ — see BUTTOCKS
2 breeches *pl* an outer garment covering each leg separately from waist to ankle ⟨The mounted riders look striking in their red coats and white *breeches*.⟩ — see PANTS

breed *n* a number of persons or things that are grouped together because they have something in common ⟨People like them are a rare *breed*.⟩ — see SORT 1

breed *vb* **1** to bring forth offspring ⟨Rabbits will *breed* very frequently unless they're kept separated.⟩ — see PROCREATE
2 to bring to maturity through care and education ⟨He was *bred* to a life in the military by his father, himself an army captain.⟩ — see BRING UP 1
3 to be the cause of (a situation, action, or state of mind) ⟨This habit of favoring one employee over the others will *breed* resentment.⟩ — see EFFECT
4 to engage in sexual intercourse ⟨Sheep usually *breed* in the fall.⟩ — see COPULATE
5 to set permanently in the consciousness or mind-set ⟨parents who *breed* in their children a deep respect for people of all classes⟩ — see IMPLANT 1

breeding *n* the line of ancestors from whom a person is descended ⟨a family of good *breeding* that is well respected in the community⟩ — see ANCESTRY

breeze *n* **1** a slight or gentle movement of air ⟨A warm spring *breeze* ruffled our hair.⟩
synonyms air, breath, puff, waft, zephyr
related words current, draft, whiff; sea breeze; blast, blow, flurry, gale, headwind, northeaster, norther, northwester, southeaster, southwester, tailwind, westerly, wind; squall, tempest, tornado, windstorm; airflow
near antonyms calm
2 something that is easy to do ⟨That assignment will be a *breeze*.⟩ — see CINCH

breeze *vb* **1** to move or proceed smoothly and readily ⟨We *breezed* through the line for customs at the airport.⟩ — see FLOW 2
2 to proceed or move quickly ⟨The doctor *breezed* past the people in the waiting room, apparently on his way to an emergency.⟩ — see HURRY 2

breezy *adj* **1** having a relaxed, casual manner ⟨a *breezy* tour guide who remains completely unfazed no matter what the mishap⟩ — see EASYGOING 1
2 marked by strong wind or more wind than usual ⟨A *breezy* day usually finds the waters of the bay studded with sail.⟩ — see ¹WINDY 1
3 open to the free circulation of air ⟨Let's sit on the front porch; it's *breezier* there.⟩ — see AIRY 2

brevity *n* **1** the condition of being short ⟨the *brevity* of youth⟩
synonyms briefness, conciseness, shortness
related words abbreviation, abridgment (*or* abridgement), compression, condensation, contraction, curtailment; decreasing, diminishing, lessening, reducing, shortening, shrinking; abruptness, brusqueness, curtness; compendiousness, crispness, laconism, pithiness, succinctness, tautness, terseness; littleness, minuteness, smallness, tininess
near antonyms extensiveness; elongating, elongation, extending, extension, prolongation, prolonging, protraction, stretching; expansion, growth, spread; diffuseness, long-windedness, prolixity, talkativeness, talkiness, verboseness, volubility, wordiness; bigness, bulkiness, greatness, heftiness, largeness
antonyms lengthiness
2 the quality or state of being marked by or using only few words to convey much meaning ⟨the remarkable *brevity* of Emily Dickinson's poems⟩ — see SUCCINCTNESS

brew *vb* **1** to bring (something volatile or intense) into being ⟨They accused her of deliberately trying to *brew* dissension within the rank and file.⟩ — see INCITE 1
2 to be about to happen ⟨There's trouble *brewing* in the department.⟩ — see LOOM

bribable *adj* open to improper influence and especially bribery ⟨They soon found out that the prosecutor was not *bribable*.⟩ — see VENAL

bribe *n* something given or promised in order to improperly influence a person's conduct or decision ⟨That judge refused a huge *bribe* to dismiss the charges against the wealthy defendant.⟩
synonyms fix, sop
related words kickback, payoff; slush fund; incentive, incitement, instigation, motivation, provocation, spur, stimulation, stimulus; boost, encouragement, goad, inducement; allurement, bait, enticement, lure, seduction, temptation, turn-on; flattery, persuasion; decoy, snare, trap

bribe *vb* to influence someone with a bribe ⟨*bribed* the inspectors to look the other way⟩
synonyms buy, corrupt, have, pay off, square
related words fix, tamper (with); abase, debase, debauch, defile, degrade, demean, deprave, dishonor, pervert, poison, profane, subvert, taint, warp; allure, bait, beguile, entice, lead on, lure, seduce, tempt; motivate, provoke, spur, stimulate; goad, induce; flatter, persuade; snare, trap
phrases get at, grease the hand of (*or* grease the palm of), oil the hand of (*or* oil the palm of)

bridal *n* a ceremony in which two people are united in matrimony ⟨an old-fashioned country *bridal*⟩ — see WEDDING

bridgehead *n* a place from which an advance (as for military operations) is made ⟨established a *bridgehead* on the beach before beginning the land invasion⟩ — see BASE 2

bridle *vb* to keep from exceeding a desirable degree or level (as of expression) ⟨Try to *bridle* your criticism next time so that it is helpful and not hurtful.⟩ — see CONTROL 1

brief *adj* **1** marked by the use of few words to convey much information or meaning ⟨a *brief* description of the situation⟩ — see CONCISE

2 not lasting for a considerable time ⟨Fortunately, the meeting was *brief*.⟩ — see SHORT 2
3 lasting only for a short time ⟨a *brief* flash of light⟩ — see MOMENTARY
brief *n* **1** a short statement of the main points ⟨a one-page *brief* of the intelligence report⟩ — see SUMMARY
2 a specific task with which a person or group is charged ⟨The soldiers' *brief* was to secure the village from enemy attacks.⟩ — see MISSION
brief *vb* to give information to ⟨The lieutenant *briefed* his superior officers on the state of the enemy's fortifications.⟩ — see ENLIGHTEN 1
briefly *adv* in a few words ⟨Tell us *briefly* why you chose this position.⟩ — see SHORTLY 1
briefness *n* **1** the condition of being short ⟨The *briefness* of the instructions rendered them less than helpful.⟩ — see BREVITY 1
2 the quality or state of being marked by or using only few words to convey much meaning ⟨In this case the *briefness* of the essay is not a drawback because it says all that needs to be said and does so with eloquence.⟩ — see SUCCINCTNESS
brig *n* a place of confinement for persons held in lawful custody ⟨The captain ordered that the prisoner be thrown into the *brig* immediately.⟩ — see JAIL
bright *adj* **1** giving off or reflecting much light ⟨In the desert the sun was so *bright* that it hurt my eyes.⟩ ⟨The moon is *bright* tonight.⟩
synonyms beaming, bedazzling, brilliant, clear, dazzling, effulgent, glowing, incandescent, lambent, lucent, lucid, luminous, lustrous, radiant, refulgent, shining, shiny, splendid
related words ablaze, ardent, blazing, burning, combusting, fiery, flaming, red-hot; agleam, aglitter, blinding, coruscant, flashing, flickering, glancing, glaring, gleaming, glimmering, glinting, glistening, glistering, glittering, scintillant, scintillating, shimmering, shimmery, sparkling, sunny, twinkling, winking; burnished, polished, shined; superbright, ultrabright
near antonyms blackened, dark, darkened, darkish, darkling, darksome, dimmed, dusky, gloomy, murky, obscure, obscured, pitch-black, pitch-dark, somber (*or* sombre); tenebrous; cloudy, shadowlike, shadowy, shady; gray (*also* grey), leaden, pale, palish
antonyms dim, dull, lackluster, unbright, unbrilliant
2 filled with much light ⟨The display windows of department stores are especially *bright* during the holidays.⟩
synonyms ablaze, alight, brightened, illuminated, illumined, light, lightsome
related words floodlit (*also* floodlighted), highlighted, spotlighted (*or* spotlit); ignited, kindled; moonlit, shiny, sunlit, sunny, sunshiny
near antonyms gloomy, somber (*or* sombre); cloudy, murky, obscured, shadowlike, shadowy; gray (*also* grey), leaden, pale; lightproof
antonyms blackened, dark, darkened, darkish, darkling, dimmed, dusk, dusky, pitch-black, pitch-dark, tenebrous
3 having or showing a good mood or disposition ⟨always walks into work with a *bright* smile on his face⟩ — see CHEERFUL 1
4 having or showing quickness of mind ⟨a company that is always looking for *bright*, ambitious college graduates⟩ — see INTELLIGENT 1
5 having qualities which inspire hope ⟨predicted a *bright* future for the young math whiz⟩ — see HOPEFUL 1
6 pointing toward a happy outcome ⟨All the signs are *bright* right now for an economic boom.⟩ — see FAVORABLE 2
7 serving to lift one's spirits ⟨a *bright* and beautiful

morning to begin planting our garden⟩ — see CHEERFUL 2
8 standing above others in rank, importance, or achievement ⟨a *bright* new star on the music scene⟩ — see EMINENT
9 having or being an outward sign of good feelings (as of love, confidence, or happiness) ⟨a room full of summer interns with *bright*, eager faces⟩ — see RADIANT 1
10 not stormy or cloudy ⟨We'll have a picnic on the next *bright* day.⟩ — see FAIR 1
brighten *vb* to become glad or hopeful ⟨The glum soccer player started to *brighten* upon being told that his injury would not jeopardize his career.⟩ — see CHEER (UP) 1
brightened *adj* filled with much light ⟨The *brightened* room is now a much more cheerful place for the recuperating patients.⟩ — see BRIGHT 2
brightness *n* the quality or state of having or giving off light ⟨The *brightness* of the sunshine made me squint after an afternoon spent in a darkened movie theater.⟩ — see BRILLIANCE 1
brilliance *n* **1** the quality or state of having or giving off light ⟨The *brilliance* of the lights was so intense that I couldn't keep my eyes open for a time.⟩
synonyms brightness, brilliancy, candor, dazzle, effulgence, illumination, lightness, luminosity, luster (*or* lustre), radiance, refulgence, splendor
related words blaze, flare, flash, flicker, light; fluorescence, incandescence, luminescence; burnish, gloss, polish, sheen, shine, shininess; fire, flame, glare, glow; flash, gleam, glimmer, glint, glisten, glitter, scintillation; shimmer, sparkle, twinkle
near antonyms dimness, gloominess, somberness; cloudiness, haziness, murkiness, obscureness, obscurity; colorlessness, grayness, lackluster, paleness, shadiness, shadowiness
antonyms blackness, dark, darkness, dullness (*also* dulness), duskiness
2 impressiveness of beauty on a large scale ⟨The *brilliance* of the palace is really quite staggering.⟩ — see MAGNIFICENCE
brilliancy *n* the quality or state of having or giving off light ⟨The *brilliancy* of the diamond is shown to good effect by the museum's lighting.⟩ — see BRILLIANCE 1
brilliant *adj* **1** giving off or reflecting much light ⟨A *brilliant* chandelier graces the hotel lobby.⟩ — see BRIGHT 1
2 having or showing quickness of mind ⟨a *brilliant* boy who left for college at the age of 16⟩ — see INTELLIGENT 1
3 likely to attract attention ⟨a *brilliant* example of efficient management⟩ — see NOTICEABLE
brilliant *n* a usually valuable stone cut and polished for ornament ⟨The diamond cutter set out an array of *brilliants* to show the various ways the diamond could be cut.⟩ — see GEM 1
brim *n* **1** the line or relatively narrow space that marks the outer limit of something ⟨The *brim* of the teacup was banded with gold.⟩ — see BORDER 1
2 the projecting front part of a hat or cap ⟨touched the *brim* of his cap by way of salute⟩ — see VISOR
brim *vb* **1** to be copiously supplied ⟨a secondhand bookstore that was *brimming* with bargains⟩ — see ABOUND
2 to put into (something) as much as can be held or contained ⟨I *brimmed* the glass with milk, and now I'm sure to spill it.⟩ — see FILL 1
brimful *adj* containing or seeming to contain the greatest quantity or number possible ⟨a book *brimful* of stories about people who overcome childhood adversities to achieve great things⟩ — see FULL 1
brimming *adj* containing or seeming to contain the greatest quantity or number possible ⟨bins *brimming* with

coffee beans from a wide array of tropical localities⟩ — see FULL 1

brine *n* the whole body of salt water that covers nearly three-fourths of the earth ⟨For hundreds of years people from Atlantic Canada have made their living from the *brine.*⟩ — see OCEAN 1

bring *vb* 1 to be the cause of (a situation, action, or state of mind) ⟨Reuniting with her friend *brought* her great joy.⟩ — see EFFECT

2 to cause (someone) to agree with a belief or course of action by using arguments or earnest requests ⟨Nothing will ever *bring* her to admit she's wrong.⟩ — see PERSUADE

3 to have a price of ⟨The antique will probably *bring* at least $1000 at auction.⟩ — see COST

bring about *vb* to be the cause of (a situation, action, or state of mind) ⟨I promise: making one mistake will not *bring about* the apocalypse.⟩ — see EFFECT

bring up *vb* 1 to bring to maturity through care and education ⟨It takes an immense commitment and a lot of love to *bring up* a child.⟩

synonyms breed, foster, nourish, nurse, raise, rear

related words father, mother; attend, care (for), cradle, cultivate, mind, minister (to), nurture, watch; discipline, educate, instruct, mentor, school, teach, train, tutor; edify, enlighten, indoctrinate; feed, provide (for), supply; advance, forward, further, promote; prepare; direct, guide, lead, shepherd, show

near antonyms abuse, ill-treat, ill-use, maltreat, mishandle, mistreat; ignore, neglect; harm, hurt, injure

2 to present or bring forward for discussion ⟨I hate to *bring* this *up*, but we're running short of money.⟩ — see INTRODUCE 2

3 to bring (something) to a standstill ⟨I wasn't expecting the operator to *bring up* the carnival ride so suddenly.⟩ — see ¹HALT 1

brininess *n* the quality or state of being salty ⟨The *brininess* of the soup rendered it inedible.⟩ — see SALTINESS

briny *adj* of, relating to, or containing salt ⟨a *briny* liquid that is often used to make pickles⟩ — see SALTY 1

brisk *adj* 1 having much high-spirited energy and movement ⟨a *brisk* exercise that many athletes use to warm up⟩ — see LIVELY 1

2 moving, proceeding, or acting with great speed ⟨We moved at a *brisk* walk through the exhibit.⟩ — see FAST 1

3 marked by much life, movement, or activity ⟨*brisk* trading on the stock market⟩ — see ALIVE 2

briskly *adv* with great speed ⟨She strode off *briskly* to deal with the problem.⟩ — see FAST 1

briskness *n* the quality or state of having abundant or intense activity ⟨The *briskness* of the shopping scene at the mall makes it a good candidate for our next store.⟩ — see VITALITY 1

bristle *n* a thin, flexible structure that resembles a hair ⟨a hairbrush with plastic *bristles*⟩ — see HAIR 2

bristle *vb* 1 to be copiously supplied ⟨a recent college grad thrilled to be starting a new life in a city *bristling* with possibilities⟩ — see ABOUND

2 to express one's anger usually violently ⟨The man *bristled* at the accusation, and threatened to file a lawsuit.⟩ — see RAGE 1

bristly *adj* covered with or as if with hair ⟨Although pigs look hairless, they're actually *bristly* creatures.⟩ — see HAIRY 1

britches *pl n* an outer garment covering each leg separately from waist to ankle ⟨a traditional riding outfit consisting of red jacket, tan *britches*, and black boots⟩ — see PANTS

brittle *adj* 1 having a texture that readily breaks into little

pieces under pressure ⟨a *brittle* cracker that turned into crumbs in my pocket⟩ — see CRISP 1

2 lacking in friendliness or warmth of feeling ⟨a *brittle* apology that was anything but heartfelt⟩ — see COLD 2

broach *vb* 1 to penetrate the surface (as of water) from below ⟨The immense whale *broaching* was a magnificent sight.⟩

synonyms break, surface

related words emerge, rise

near antonyms dive, drop, drown, founder, plunge, sink, submerge, submerse

2 to present or bring forward for discussion ⟨*broached* the topic of plans for next year's parade⟩ — see INTRODUCE 2

broad *adj* 1 having a greater than usual measure across ⟨an unusually *broad* expanse of water in the island-dotted lake⟩ — see WIDE 1

2 having considerable extent ⟨Her *broad* knowledge of American politics makes her a much-sought-after guest on talk shows.⟩ — see EXTENSIVE

3 not subject to misinterpretation or more than one interpretation ⟨I gave them a *broad* hint that it was time to leave.⟩ — see CLEAR 2

4 relating to the main elements and not to specific details ⟨a *broad* overview of the topic⟩ — see GENERAL 2

broadcast *vb* 1 to cause to be known over a considerable area or by many people ⟨*broadcast* the information only to people who needed to know⟩ — see SPREAD 1

2 to make known openly or publicly ⟨Please don't *broadcast* this news, as it's not being publicly announced yet.⟩ — see ANNOUNCE

broadly *adv* to a large extent or degree ⟨The new policy is *broadly* applicable.⟩ — see GREATLY 2

broad–minded *adj* 1 not bound by traditional ways or beliefs ⟨a *broad-minded* philosophy of parenting⟩ — see LIBERAL 1

2 willing to consider new or different ideas ⟨We have to be *broad-minded* on this issue, since traditional solutions no longer work.⟩ — see OPEN-MINDED 1

broadside *adv* with one side faced forward ⟨One car hit the other *broadside* and crushed the passenger door.⟩ — see SIDEWAYS 1

brochure *n* a short printed publication with no cover or with a paper cover ⟨They handed out *brochures* giving practical hints about environment-friendly practices that every family can adopt.⟩ — see PAMPHLET

broiling *adj* having a notably high temperature ⟨The office was *broiling* because the air conditioning was on the blink.⟩ — see HOT 1

broke *adj* lacking money or material possessions ⟨too *broke* to afford even a used car⟩ — see POOR 1

broken *adj* 1 having an uneven edge or outline ⟨The broken rim of the antique vase greatly reduces its value.⟩ — see RAGGED 1

2 not having a level or smooth surface ⟨That portion of the hiking trail consists of a long, *broken* mountain ridge.⟩ — see UNEVEN 1

brokenhearted *adj* feeling unhappiness ⟨She was *brokenhearted* when their friendship ended.⟩ — see SAD 1

brood *vb* to cover and warm eggs as the young inside develop ⟨Don't disturb the hen while she's *brooding.*⟩ — see SET 1

brook *n* a natural body of running water smaller than a river ⟨There are tiny fish and frogs in that *brook.*⟩ — see CREEK 1

brook *vb* to put up with (something painful or difficult) ⟨I will not *brook* insults from my own employees.⟩ — see BEAR 2

brooklet *n* a natural body of running water smaller than a river ⟨A little *brooklet* trickled past the house.⟩ — see CREEK 1

brotherhood *n* **1** a group of persons formally joined together for some common interest ⟨They're a *brotherhood* of retired war veterans.⟩ — see ASSOCIATION 2
2 the body of people in a profession or field of activity ⟨a family that has been part of the *brotherhood* of police officers for four generations⟩ — see CORPS
3 the feeling of closeness and friendship that exists between companions ⟨the *brotherhood* that existed between the medical missionaries and the villagers they served⟩ — see COMPANIONSHIP
4 kindly concern, interest, or support ⟨In a display of *brotherhood*, other writers rushed to the defense of the jailed journalist.⟩ — see GOODWILL 1

brotherly *adj* of, relating to, or befitting brothers ⟨the *brotherly* love that exists between the members of the scout troop⟩ — see FRATERNAL

browbeat *vb* to make timid or fearful by or as if by threats ⟨I refuse to be *browbeaten* into making unnecessary changes.⟩ — see INTIMIDATE

brownie *n* an imaginary being usually having a small human form and magical powers ⟨Some people believe that *brownies* will clean your house if you leave them milk.⟩ — see FAIRY

browse *vb* **1** to feed on grass or herbs ⟨Cows *browsing* in fields are a common sight along that stretch of the road.⟩ — see ¹GRAZE
2 to take a quick or hasty look ⟨*browsed* through the stacks looking for interesting books⟩ — see GLANCE 2

bruise *n* **1** a bodily injury in which small blood vessels are broken but the overlying skin is not ⟨She got quite a big *bruise* from walking into the corner of the table.⟩ — see CONTUSION
2 an area of skin roughened or worn away by harsh rubbing against another surface ⟨*bruises* caused by ill-fitting hiking boots⟩ — see ABRASION

bruit (about) *vb* to make (as a piece of information) the subject of common talk without any authority or confirmation of accuracy ⟨Please don't *bruit* allegations *about* without confirming them first.⟩ — see RUMOR

brush *n* a brief clash between enemies or rivals ⟨The two advance parties had a *brush*, but no one was wounded.⟩ — see ENCOUNTER

¹**brush** *vb* to move or proceed smoothly and readily ⟨a pop star *brushing* past a crowd of autograph seekers⟩ — see FLOW 2

²**brush** *vb* to pass lightly across or touch gently especially in passing ⟨Spiderwebs *brushed* her cheek as she walked through the basement.⟩
synonyms graze, kiss, nudge, shave, skim
related words bump, contact, scrape, sideswipe, strike, sweep, swipe, touch; bounce, carom, glance, rebound, ricochet, skip; caress, cuddle, fondle, love, pat, pet, stroke; miss, skirt
near antonyms bang, bash, bump, clash, collide, crash, hit, impact, impinge, knock, punch, ram, slam, slap, smack, smash, swipe, thud, thwack, whack

brush (aside *or* **off)** *vb* to dismiss as of little importance ⟨*brushed off* their complaints as the whining of people who were never satisfied⟩ — see EXCUSE 1

brush–off *n* treatment that is deliberately unfriendly ⟨The mayor tends to give anyone under voting age the *brush-off*.⟩ — see COLD SHOULDER

brushwood *n* a thick patch of shrubbery, small trees, or underbrush ⟨cleared away the *brushwood* in order to build a shed⟩ — see THICKET

brusque *also* **brusk** *adj* being or characterized by direct, brief, and potentially rude speech or manner ⟨a *brusque*

and unhelpful reply from the clerk in the hardware store⟩ — see BLUNT 1

brutal *adj* **1** difficult to endure ⟨*brutal* hard labor in the hot sun⟩ — see HARSH 1
2 having or showing the desire to inflict severe pain and suffering on others ⟨a *brutal* military ruler⟩ — see CRUEL 1

brutality *n* disposition to willfully inflict pain and suffering on others ⟨accused the arresting officer of *brutality*⟩ — see CRUELTY

brute *adj* having or showing the desire to inflict severe pain and suffering on others ⟨used *brute* force on the enemy⟩ — see CRUEL 1

brute *n* **1** one of the lower animals as distinguished from human beings ⟨It is a fundamental sense of right and wrong that separates us from the *brutes*.⟩ — see ANIMAL
2 a mean, evil, or unprincipled person ⟨Only a *brute* would be so vicious.⟩ — see VILLAIN

bubble *vb* to flow in a broken irregular stream ⟨The soapy water *bubbled* down the drain.⟩ — see GURGLE

bubbly *adj* joyously unrestrained ⟨offered their *bubbly* congratulations to the expectant parents⟩ — see EXUBERANT

buccaneer *n* someone who engages in robbery of ships at sea ⟨*buccaneers* who preyed upon treasure-laden ships in the Caribbean⟩ — see PIRATE

buck *n* **1** a man extremely interested in his clothing and personal appearance ⟨a vain *buck* who spends an hour before the bathroom mirror every morning⟩ — see DANDY 1
2 an adult male human being ⟨found some strong young *bucks* to help move the furniture⟩ — see MAN 1
3 **bucks** *pl* something (as pieces of stamped metal or printed paper) customarily and legally used as a medium of exchange, a measure of value, or a means of payment ⟨That car costs big *bucks*.⟩ — see MONEY

buck *vb* **1** to move or cause to move with a sharp quick motion ⟨The car *bucked* and stalled.⟩ — see JERK 1
2 to refuse to give in to ⟨*bucked* the trend to outdo everyone else and just wore the same clothes they had in previous years⟩ — see RESIST
3 to shift possession of (something) from one person to another ⟨*Buck* each box to the next person in line, and the last person will stack them in the storeroom.⟩ — see PASS 1

buckaroo *also* **buckeroo** *n* a hired hand who tends cattle or horses at a ranch or on the range ⟨a rip-roaring *buckaroo* of the Old West⟩ — see COWBOY

bucket *n* **1** a considerable amount ⟨made *buckets* of money in the stock market⟩ — see LOT 2
2 a round container that is open at the top and outfitted with a handle ⟨carried water from the well in a *bucket*⟩ — see PAIL

bucket *vb* to lift out with something that holds liquid ⟨*Bucketing* water from the well, we raced to put out the fire.⟩ — see DIP 2

buckle *vb* **1** to fall down or in as a result of physical pressure ⟨The flimsy bridge *buckled* under the weight of the caravan of trucks.⟩ — see COLLAPSE 1
2 to occupy (oneself) diligently or with close attention ⟨He *buckled* himself down and finished the assignment in record time.⟩ — see APPLY 2

bucolic *adj* of, relating to, associated with, or typical of open areas with few buildings or people ⟨a *bucolic* region where farms are still common⟩ — see RURAL

buddy *n* a person who has a strong liking for and trust in another ⟨My old college *buddy* is the one person I can always turn to.⟩ — see FRIEND 1

budge *vb* **1** to cease resistance (as to another's arguments, demands, or control) ⟨Despite hours of intense pressure, she refused to *budge* from her position.⟩ — see YIELD 3

2 to change one's position ⟨He finally *budged* from his beach blanket when the tide started swirling up around him.⟩ — see MOVE 3

3 to change the place or position of ⟨The bureau was so heavy that two people couldn't *budge* it.⟩ — see MOVE 1

budget *adj* costing little ⟨a *budget* phone plan for people on fixed incomes⟩ — see CHEAP 1

budget *n* **1** a sum of money set aside for a particular purpose ⟨We've spent a little more than our *budget* this year.⟩ — see FUND 1

2 the number of individuals or amount of something available at any given time ⟨The tour group had a whole *budget* of requests.⟩ — see SUPPLY

budget *vb* to work out the details of (something) in advance ⟨The vacationers carefully *budgeted* how they would spend their limited time in Italy.⟩ — see PLAN 1

buff *n* a person with a strong and habitual liking for something ⟨He's such a film *buff* that he owns over 3,000 movies.⟩ — see FAN

buff *vb* **1** to make smooth by friction ⟨She learned to *buff* semiprecious stones in order to make her own jewelry.⟩ — see GRIND 1

2 to make smooth or glossy usually by repeatedly applying surface pressure ⟨The janitor *buffed* the lobby floor until it shone.⟩ — see POLISH 1

buffed *adj* having a shiny surface or finish ⟨a beautiful, *buffed* antique table⟩ — see GLOSSY

buffer *n* **1** one who works with opposing sides in order to bring about an agreement ⟨It took a friend serving as a *buffer* between the feuding siblings to get them to speak to one another again.⟩ — see MEDIATOR

2 something that serves as a protective barrier ⟨The bubble wrap acts as a *buffer* for the tablet during shipping.⟩ — see CUSHION

buffer *vb* to lessen the shock of ⟨During my walk an umbrella and thick coat *buffered* the freezing rain.⟩ — see CUSHION

¹**buffet** *n* a hard strike with a part of the body or an instrument ⟨delivered a powerful *buffet* to the punching bag⟩ — see ¹BLOW

²**buffet** *n* a storage case typically having doors and shelves ⟨A *buffet* completed the kitchen set.⟩ — see CABINET

buffet *vb* to strike repeatedly ⟨Fierce winds *buffeted* the small sailboat.⟩ — see BEAT 1

buffoon *n* a comically dressed performer (as at a circus) who entertains with playful tricks and ridiculous behavior ⟨The young princess giggled at the antics of the *buffoon*.⟩ — see CLOWN 1

bug *n* **1** a person with a strong and habitual liking for something ⟨a camera *bug* who loves taking candid shots at fairs and festivals⟩ — see FAN

2 an abnormal state that disrupts a plant's or animal's normal bodily functioning ⟨I can't go to work today because I've caught some *bug* that's going around.⟩ — see DISEASE

bug *vb* **1** to disturb the peace of mind of (someone) especially by repeated disagreeable acts ⟨These incessant phone calls are really starting to *bug* me.⟩ — see IRRITATE 1

2 to thrust oneself upon (another) without invitation ⟨I hate to *bug* you, but could you help me move this table?⟩ — see BOTHER 1

bugaboo *n* something or someone that causes fear or dread especially without reason ⟨Doing one's tax returns are a real *bugaboo* for some people.⟩ — see BOGEY 1

bugbear *n* **1** something or someone that causes fear or dread especially without reason ⟨Communism was once the nation's biggest *bugbear*.⟩ — see BOGEY 1

2 something that is a source of irritation ⟨She hated all the *bugbears* of modern life, especially those long commutes to work.⟩ — see ANNOYANCE 3

bugging *n* the act of making unwelcome intrusions upon another ⟨This perpetual *bugging* has got to stop!⟩ — see ANNOYANCE 1

build *n* the type of body that a person has ⟨She has an athletic *build*.⟩ — see PHYSIQUE

build *vb* to form by putting together parts or materials ⟨He spent hours *building* a model airplane from a kit.⟩

synonyms assemble, construct, erect, fabricate, make, make up, piece, put up, raise, rear, set up

related words carpenter, fashion, forge, frame, hammer, handcraft, manufacture, produce, shape; prefabricate; begin, create, generate, inaugurate, initiate, innovate, invent, originate; constitute, establish, father, found, institute, organize; conceive, concoct, contrive, cook (up), design, devise, imagine, think (up); reassemble, rebuild, reconstruct, redevelop, retrofit; jerry-build, rig (up), throw up; combine, unite

phrases put together

near antonyms demolish, destroy, devastate, flatten, level, pulverize, raze, ruin, ruinate, shatter, smash, wreck; blow up, explode; detach, disengage; disconnect, disjoin, disunite, divide, separate

antonyms demount, disassemble, dismantle, dismember, knock down, strike, take down, tear down

building *n* something built as a dwelling, shelter, or place for human activity ⟨English class will be in that big stone *building* over there.⟩

synonyms edifice, structure

related words construction, erection; bungalow, cabin, chalet, cottage, house, lodge; hovel, hut, shack, shanty, shed; castle, château, estate, hall, manor, mansion, palace, pile, villa; skyscraper, tower

building block *n* one of the parts that make up a whole ⟨Historically the infantry division has been a basic *building block* of armies.⟩ — see ELEMENT 1

bulge *n* **1** a part that sticks out from the general mass of something ⟨several *bulges* in the old vinyl flooring⟩

synonyms bunch, jut, overhang, projection, protrusion, protuberance, swell

related words blob, bump, dilatation, hump, knob, knot, knurl, lump, nub, obtrusion, puff, snag, swelling; block, piece, portion, section; enlargement, escalation, expansion, increase; hill, mound

near antonyms crater, hole, well; basin, bowl, dip, valley; furrow, groove, trench, trough; dimple, gouge, impression, notch, pocket

antonyms cavity, concave, concavity, dent, depression, dint, hollow, indentation, pit, recess

2 the more favorable condition or position in a competition ⟨Somehow she got the *bulge* on him in the race for the statehouse.⟩ — see ADVANTAGE 1

bulge *vb* **1** to extend outward beyond a usual point ⟨The sides of the returning camper's suitcase *bulged* with a month's worth of dirty laundry.⟩

synonyms bag, balloon, beetle, belly, billow, bunch, jut, overhang, poke, pouch, pout, project, protrude, stand out, start, stick out, swell

related words blow up, inflate; dilate, distend, expand; mushroom, snowball; elongate, extend, lengthen, stretch

near antonyms compress, condense, constrict, contract, shrink

2 to be copiously supplied ⟨This guidebook to San Francisco positively *bulges* with useful information.⟩ — see ABOUND

bulk *n* **1** the largest part or quantity of something ⟨Agriculture makes up the *bulk* of the country's economy.⟩ — see MAJORITY 1

2 the main or greater part of something as distinguished from its subordinate parts ⟨The cookie lost a few crumbs, but the *bulk* of it remained.⟩ — see BODY 1
3 the total amount of measurable space or surface occupied by something ⟨Due to its *bulk*, we were unable to get the bookcase into the backseat of the car.⟩ — see ¹SIZE
bulkiness *n* the quality or state of being large in size ⟨The box wasn't heavy, but its *bulkiness* made it awkward to carry.⟩ — see LARGENESS
bulky *adj* of a size greater than average of its kind ⟨*Bulky* packages might cost more to mail.⟩ — see LARGE
¹**bull** *n* an order publicly issued by an authority ⟨The superintendent's office issued a *bull* banning the use of cell phones during school hours.⟩ — see EDICT 1
²**bull** *n, slang* language, behavior, or ideas that are absurd and contrary to good sense ⟨a guy who's always trying to sell some sucker a line of *bull*⟩ — see NONSENSE 1
bull *vb* to force one's way ⟨The beleaguered governor *bulled* through the crowd of reporters without answering a single question.⟩ — see ²PRESS 4
bulldoze *vb* **1** to force one's way ⟨I *bulldozed* through the crowd at the arena, urgently trying to find the bathroom.⟩ — see ²PRESS 4
2 to make timid or fearful by or as if by threats ⟨one of those gatherings at which high-pressure sales reps try to *bulldoze* naive people into buying time-shares⟩ — see INTIMIDATE
bullet *n* a usually round or cone-shaped little piece of lead made to be fired from a firearm ⟨fired a *bullet*⟩
synonyms ball, pellet
related words ammunition, cap, cartridge, charge, dumdum, gunshot, lead, load, missile, pop, projectile, round, shell, shot, slug
near antonyms blank
bulletin *n* **1** a publication that appears at regular intervals ⟨picks up a church *bulletin* every week⟩ — see JOURNAL
2 a published statement informing the public of a matter of general interest ⟨The program was interrupted by a news *bulletin*.⟩ — see ANNOUNCEMENT
bullheadedness *n* a steadfast adherence to an opinion, purpose, or course of action in spite of reason, arguments, or persuasion ⟨*Bullheadedness* runs in that family.⟩ — see OBSTINACY
bully *adj* of the very best kind ⟨That's a *bully* idea for reviving the town's retail center.⟩ — see EXCELLENT
bully *n* a person who teases, threatens, or hurts more vulnerable persons ⟨The school has a procedure for reporting problems with *bullies*.⟩
synonyms hector, intimidator
related words antagonist, enemy; abuser, baiter, giber (*or* jiber), harrier, heckler, mocker, needler, oppressor, persecutor, ridiculer, taunter, tease, teaser, torturer; goon, mug, rough, roughneck, rowdy, ruffian, tough, toughie (*also* toughy)
bully *vb* **1** to inflict physical or emotional harm upon ⟨The kindergarten teacher explained why it was wrong to *bully* classmates.⟩ — see ABUSE 1
2 to make timid or fearful by or as if by threats ⟨a manager who *bullied* employees⟩ — see INTIMIDATE
bulwark *vb* to drive danger or attack away from ⟨vowed to use any means necessary to *bulwark* the country⟩ — see DEFEND 1
bum *adj* of low quality ⟨That was *bum* advice that you got from that salesperson.⟩ — see CHEAP 2
¹**bum** *n* the part of the body upon which someone sits ⟨slipped and fell on his *bum*⟩ — see BUTTOCKS
²**bum** *n* a homeless wanderer who may beg or steal for a living ⟨I feel sorry for *bums* and occasionally give them money.⟩ — see TRAMP

bum *vb* to spend time doing nothing ⟨spent most of the summer just *bumming* around the house⟩ — see IDLE
bum (out) *vb* to make sad ⟨That sort of news really *bums* me *out*.⟩ — see DEPRESS 1
bummer *n* **1** something (as a situation or event) that is depressing ⟨Boy, breaking your leg right before vacation is a *bummer*.⟩ — see DOWNER
2 something that disappoints ⟨The cancellation of the office party was a total *bummer*.⟩ — see DISAPPOINTMENT 2
3 something that has failed ⟨That start-up company proved to be a real *bummer*.⟩ — see FAILURE 3
bump *n* **1** a small rounded mass of swollen tissue ⟨That's a nasty *bump* on your arm where you hit the table.⟩
synonyms knot, lump, node, nodule, swelling
related words growth, tumor, wart; hump, hunch; bruise, contusion; blister, boil; blob, chunk, clod, clump, gob, gobbet, hunk, knob, nub, nubble, nugget, wad
2 the act or an instance of bringing to a lower grade or rank ⟨The *bump* in rank was punishment for insubordination.⟩
synonyms reduction
related words disrating, downgrade; dismissal, firing, layoff, sacking; abasement, debasement, humiliation
3 a forceful coming together of two things ⟨I felt the *bump* of the other car, but there was no damage to either vehicle.⟩ — see IMPACT 1
bump *vb* to come into usually forceful contact with something ⟨The boat *bumped* against the pier.⟩ — see HIT 2
bumper *adj* **1** of the very best kind ⟨It's been a *bumper* year for movies aimed at intelligent adults.⟩ — see EXCELLENT
2 unusually large ⟨a *bumper* crop of pumpkins that year⟩ — see HUGE
bumper *n* something that serves as a protective barrier ⟨Cars have *bumpers* to protect them from damage in minor collisions.⟩ — see CUSHION
bumpkin *n* an awkward or simple person especially from a small town or the country ⟨The actor cultivated an image as just a country *bumpkin*.⟩ — see HICK
bumpy *adj* **1** marked by a series of sharp quick motions ⟨a *bumpy* ride over a badly rutted road⟩ — see JERKY 1
2 not having a level or smooth surface ⟨The *bumpy* road made the jeep bounce all over.⟩ — see UNEVEN 1
bunch *n* **1** a group of people sharing a common interest and relating together socially ⟨That *bunch* goes out to lunch together every Friday.⟩ — see GANG 2
2 a number of things considered as a unit ⟨bought a *bunch* of grapes⟩ — see GROUP 1
3 a usually small number of persons considered as a unit ⟨A small *bunch* of people were sent to clean up the place.⟩ — see GROUP 2
4 a part that sticks out from the general mass of something ⟨a *bunch* in the blanket⟩ — see BULGE 1
5 a considerable amount ⟨I have a *bunch* of thoughts on the matter, so grab a notepad.⟩ — see LOT 2
bunch *vb* **1** to extend outward beyond a usual point ⟨The dress *bunches* a bit at the waist.⟩ — see BULGE 1
2 to gather into a closely packed group ⟨The slow service caused the customers at the pick-up counter to *bunch* up.⟩ — see ²PRESS 3
bundle *n* **1** a considerable amount ⟨a bundle of *plans* for the winter carnival⟩ — see LOT 2
2 a wrapped or sealed case containing an item or set of items ⟨a *bundle* of newspapers⟩ — see PACKAGE 1
3 a very large amount of money ⟨He dropped a *bundle* on that new sports car.⟩ — see FORTUNE 2
bundle *vb* **1** to cause to move or proceed fast or faster ⟨The tour guide *bundled* us off before we had a chance to ask any questions.⟩ — see HURRY 1

2 to proceed or move quickly ⟨Students came *bundling* out of the building when the fire alarm went off.⟩ — see HURRY 2

bung *vb* to close up so that no empty spaces remain ⟨We had *bunged* up the moving van so much that we couldn't have possibly squeezed in one more thing.⟩ — see FILL 2

bungle *vb* to make or do (something) in a clumsy or unskillful way ⟨She *bungled* the job the first time she tried to do it.⟩ — see BOTCH

bungling *adj* showing or marked by a lack of skill and tact (as in dealing with a situation) ⟨a *bungling* attempt to relieve the tension in the room⟩ — see AWKWARD 2

¹**bunk** *n* a place set aside for sleeping ⟨crawled into their *bunks* and went to sleep immediately⟩ — see BED 1

²**bunk** *n* language, behavior, or ideas that are absurd and contrary to good sense ⟨The idea that the Great Wall of China is visible from the moon is pure *bunk*.⟩ — see NONSENSE 1

bunk *vb* to provide with living quarters or shelter ⟨*bunked* the guest in the spare room⟩ — see HOUSE 1

buoy (up) *vb* to fill with courage or strength of purpose ⟨The sudden improvement in his health *buoyed* him *up*.⟩ — see ENCOURAGE 1

buoyant *adj* **1** having or showing a good mood or disposition ⟨All the fans were *buoyant* the day after the big win in the play-offs.⟩ — see CHEERFUL 1

2 joyously unrestrained ⟨She gave him a *buoyant* hug and kiss upon meeting him at the airport.⟩ — see EXUBERANT

¹**burden** *n* **1** a mass or quantity of something taken up and carried, conveyed, or transported ⟨The early settlers often used horses to carry their *burdens*.⟩ — see LOAD 1

2 something one must do because of prior agreement ⟨The *burden* of homework prevented the youngster from joining his friends at the game.⟩ — see OBLIGATION 1

²**burden** *n* a part of a song or hymn that is repeated every so often ⟨had some trouble coming up with a *burden* for the song⟩ — see CHORUS 2

burden *vb* **1** to place a weight or burden on ⟨*burdened* the dog with a little backpack⟩ — see LOAD 1

2 to make sad ⟨She refuses to let everyday problems *burden* her.⟩ — see DEPRESS 1

burdensome *adj* **1** difficult to endure ⟨the *burdensome* living conditions that the early settlers had to endure⟩ — see HARSH 1

2 requiring much time, effort, or careful attention ⟨the *burdensome* task of finishing the tax return⟩ — see DEMANDING 1

bureau *n* a large unit of a governmental, business, or educational organization ⟨the federal revenue *bureau*⟩ — see DIVISION 2

bureaucrat *n* a worker in a government agency ⟨left the private sector and became a government *bureaucrat*⟩
synonyms functionary, public servant
related words clerk, officeholder, official, officiary; employee (*also* employe), hand, hireling, jobholder, underling, worker

burg *n* a thickly settled, highly populated area ⟨moved from a small town into a much bigger *burg*⟩ — see CITY

burgeon *also* **bourgeon** *vb* **1** to become greater in extent, volume, amount, or number ⟨The trout population in the stream is *burgeoning* now that the water is clean.⟩ — see INCREASE 2

2 to grow vigorously ⟨The spring flowers *burgeoned* once the warm weather set in for good.⟩ — see THRIVE 1

burgher *n* a person who lives in a town on a permanent basis ⟨The university provides job's for many of the local *burghers*.⟩
synonyms citizen, townie (*or* towny), villager

related words townswoman; cliff dweller, denizen, dweller, habitant, inhabitant, national, native, occupant, resident, resider, subject; town, townsfolk, townspeople; suburbanite, urbanite
near antonyms alien, foreigner, guest, nonnative, tourist, transient, visitor; gownsman
antonyms noncitizen

burglarize *vb* **1** to enter a house or building by force usually with illegal intent ⟨The Watergate scandal began when Republican operatives *burglarized* the Democratic Party's headquarters in Washington, D.C.⟩ — see BREAK IN 1

2 to remove valuables from (a place) unlawfully ⟨Before they were caught, the thieves had *burglarized* dozens of houses around the city.⟩ — see ROB

burial *n* **1** the act or ceremony of putting a dead body in its final resting place ⟨The children wanted to give the dead bird a proper *burial* in the backyard.⟩
synonyms burying, entombing, entombment, interment, interring, sepulture
related words embalmment, funeral; immurement, inurnment; reburial, reinterment
near antonyms cremation
antonyms disinterment, exhumation, unearthing

2 a final resting place for a dead person ⟨Archaeologically significant artifacts, such as stone tools, have been discovered in Neanderthal *burials*.⟩ — see GRAVE 1

burlesque *n* a work that imitates and exaggerates another work for comic effect ⟨It is interesting to note that the first novel ever written in English was followed by a *burlesque* of it.⟩ — see PARODY 1

burlesque *vb* to copy or exaggerate (someone or something) in order to make fun of ⟨The comics *burlesqued* the candidates.⟩ — see MIMIC 1

burly *adj* strongly and heavily built ⟨A *burly* delivery man brought the furniture.⟩ — see ¹HUSKY 1

burn *vb* **1** to be on fire especially brightly ⟨All evening long we just sat there, contentedly watching the campfire *burn*.⟩
synonyms blaze, combust, flame, glow
related words catch; fire, ignite, kindle; flare (up), light (up); flicker, gutter, waver; bake, char, cook, melt, roast, scorch; smolder (*or* smoulder), spark, sputter; beam, brighten, radiate; beat (down), flash, glare, gleam, glimmer, glint, glisten, glitter, scintillate, shimmer, shine, sparkle, twinkle
phrases go up in flames

2 to set (something) on fire ⟨It is not a good idea to try to *burn* old papers in the sink.⟩
synonyms fire, ignite, inflame (*also* enflame), kindle, light
related words immolate; char, scorch; bake, cook; ash, cremate, incinerate, kiln; set off; brighten, illuminate, illumine, irradiate, lighten, radiate; scald, scathe, sear; reignite, rekindle, relight; bank, stoke
near antonyms choke, smother, suffocate; stamp (out); blacken, darken, dim, dull, obscure
antonyms douse (*also* dowse), extinguish, put out, quench, snuff (out)

3 to be excited or emotionally stirred up with anger ⟨He came home *burning* with anger because of a reprimand at work.⟩ — see BOIL 1

4 to shine with a bright harsh light ⟨The bright streetlight outside our motel room *burned* all night long.⟩ — see GLARE 1

5 to cause to believe what is untrue ⟨He's been *burned* before, so he's careful to double-check such claims now.⟩ — see DECEIVE

6 to make complete use of ⟨heedlessly *burning* the country's resources without any concern for future generations⟩ — see DEPLETE 1

burnable *adj* capable of catching or being set on fire ⟨Don't put something so *burnable* as a towel next to the stove.⟩ — see COMBUSTIBLE

burned–out *or* **burnt–out** *adj* depleted in strength, energy, or freshness ⟨I'm feeling so *burned-out* that I can't wait for vacation.⟩ — see WEARY 1

burning *adj* **1** being on fire ⟨A firefighter must be that rare soul who rushes into a *burning* house, not away from it.⟩ — see ABLAZE 1

2 having a notably high temperature ⟨I couldn't walk on the *burning* sand barefoot.⟩ — see HOT 1

3 having or expressing great depth of feeling ⟨the *burning* enthusiasm of that candidate's campaign workers⟩ — see FERVENT 1

4 needing immediate attention ⟨Once again the media ignored the *burning* issues and focused on fluff.⟩ — see ACUTE 2

burnish *n* brightness created by light reflected from a surface ⟨After some much-needed polishing, the silver tea set had a brilliant *burnish*.⟩ — see SHINE 1

burnish *vb* to make smooth or glossy usually by repeatedly applying surface pressure ⟨*burnished* the floor of the ballroom to a soft luster⟩ — see POLISH 1

burnished *adj* having a shiny surface or finish ⟨Bright *burnished* metal is used extensively in that boutique's decor.⟩ — see GLOSSY

burnout *n* a complete depletion of energy or strength ⟨People in that job often suffer *burnout* and have to retire at a relatively early age.⟩ — see FATIGUE

burn out *vb* to use up all the physical energy of ⟨Working 12-hour days at that job just *burned* me *out*.⟩ — see EXHAUST 1

burro *n* a sturdy and patient domestic mammal that is used especially to carry things ⟨used a *burro* to carry the supplies⟩ — see DONKEY 1

burrow *n* the shelter or resting place of a wild animal ⟨The chipmunk retreated to its *burrow* to have its babies.⟩ — see DEN 1

burst *n* **1** a sudden and usually temporary growth of activity ⟨a sudden *burst* of energy at the end of the race⟩ — see OUTBREAK 1

2 a sudden intense expression of strong feeling ⟨a *burst* of anger that startled the other members on the panel⟩ — see OUTBURST 1

3 the act or an instance of exploding ⟨One *burst* after another could be heard in the distance.⟩ — see EXPLOSION 1

burst *vb* **1** to break open or into pieces usually because of internal pressure ⟨The turnover's crust *burst* when the filling expanded.⟩ — see EXPLODE 1

2 to cause to break open or into pieces by or as if by an explosive ⟨He finally *burst* the piñata open with one mighty swing of the bat.⟩ — see BLAST 1

3 to be copiously supplied ⟨a young singer/dancer who seems to be *bursting* with energy and talent⟩ — see ABOUND

burst (forth) *vb* to develop suddenly and violently ⟨Hives *burst forth* on the child's arms and face whenever she goes near that plant.⟩ — see ERUPT 2

bursting *adj* containing or seeming to contain the greatest quantity or number possible ⟨The store was *bursting* with bargain hunters on the day of the big sale.⟩ — see FULL 1

bursting *n* the act or an instance of exploding ⟨narrowly escaped the *bursting* of the car's gas tank⟩ — see EXPLOSION 1

bury *vb* **1** to place (a dead body) in the earth, a tomb, or the sea ⟨He died on Tuesday and was *buried* on Friday.⟩

synonyms entomb, inter, lay

related words immure, inurn; enshrine; conceal, cover, ensconce, hide; obscure, shade, shield; cloak, curtain, enshroud, shroud; rebury, reinter; coffin

near antonyms burn, cremate; bare, disclose, discover, display, exhibit, expose, reveal, show; uncoffin

antonyms disinter, exhume, unearth

2 to put into a hiding place ⟨He *buried* his face in his hands.⟩ — see ¹HIDE 1

3 to defeat by a large margin ⟨If we don't work harder, the other softball team will *bury* us.⟩ — see WHIP 2

burying *n* the act or ceremony of putting a dead body in its final resting place ⟨All the grandchildren attended the *burying* of their grandfather in his homeland.⟩ — see BURIAL 1

bush *adj* falling short of a standard ⟨a hopelessly *bush* effort at creating a romantic comedy⟩ — see BAD 1

bush *n* a rural region that forms the edge of the settled or developed part of a country ⟨a guide who specializes in taking adventurous tourists through the *bush*⟩ — see FRONTIER 2

bushed *adj* depleted in strength, energy, or freshness ⟨I'm *bushed* after a day of moving boxes from the cellar to the attic.⟩ — see WEARY 1

bushel *n* a considerable amount ⟨picked up a *bushel* of decorations at the after-Christmas sale⟩ — see LOT 2

business *n* **1** transactions or economic support provided by customers ⟨Only places that are equal opportunity employers will get my *business*.⟩

synonyms custom

related words marketplace, trade, traffic; free trade; affairs, dealings, horse-trading; merchandising, retailing, wholesaling

2 a commercial or industrial activity or organization ⟨Most of the local *businesses* belong to the association.⟩ — see ENTERPRISE 1

3 something to be dealt with ⟨We have one piece of *business* remaining for today's meeting.⟩ — see MATTER 2

4 the buying and selling of goods especially on a large scale and between different places ⟨The store is now open for *business*.⟩ — see COMMERCE 1

5 the action for which a person or thing is specially fitted or used or for which a thing exists ⟨Plants going about the *business* of photosynthesis provide the Earth with a renewable source of oxygen.⟩ — see ROLE

6 a region of activity, knowledge, or influence ⟨If you want a medical malpractice lawyer, he's the best in the *business*.⟩ — see FIELD 2

7 a specific task with which a person or group is charged ⟨The interrogators demanded to know what *business* the suspect had in the restricted area at that time of night.⟩ — see MISSION

8 the act or fact of violating the trust or confidence of another ⟨He's been giving his partner the *business* for years.⟩ — see BETRAYAL

bust *n* **1** a hard strike with a part of the body or an instrument ⟨delivered a *bust* to the boxer's chops⟩ — see ¹BLOW

2 something that has failed ⟨The first movie was a hit, but the sequel was an unexpected *bust*.⟩ — see FAILURE 3

3 *slang* the act of taking into one's control by authority of law ⟨The police made a big *bust* last night.⟩ — see ARREST 1

bust *vb* **1** to bring to a lower grade or rank ⟨The commander threatened to *bust* her for failing to salute.⟩ — see DEMOTE

2 to cause to lose one's fortune and become unable to pay one's debts ⟨Gambling is a dangerous habit that has *busted* many unfortunate souls.⟩ — see RUIN 1

3 to cause to separate into pieces usually suddenly or forcibly ⟨He dropped his phone and *busted* it.⟩ — see BREAK 1

4 to deliver a blow to (someone or something) usually in a strong vigorous manner ⟨Watch your mouth or I'll *bust* you in the nose.⟩ — see HIT 1

5 *slang* to take or keep under one's control by authority of law ⟨The cops *busted* them for creating a nuisance.⟩ — see ARREST 1

6 to use up all the physical energy of ⟨I had to *bust* my butt in order to get the project done on time.⟩ — see EXHAUST 1

bustle *n* a state of noisy, confused activity ⟨I couldn't concentrate in all the *bustle* of the student lounge.⟩ — see COMMOTION

bustle *vb* **1** to be copiously supplied ⟨On Saturdays the city's downtown *bustles* with activity as a farmers' market sets up shop.⟩ — see ABOUND

2 to proceed or move quickly ⟨The hostess *bustled* about, taking care of last-minute preparations for the party.⟩ — see HURRY 2

bustling *adj* **1** involved in often constant activity ⟨A *bustling* greeter was there to welcome guests to the grand opening.⟩ — see BUSY 1

2 marked by much life, movement, or activity ⟨a *bustling* shopping center during the holiday season⟩ — see ALIVE 2

busy *adj* **1** involved in often constant activity ⟨The deadline is in two days, so everyone at work has been extremely *busy*.⟩

synonyms active, assiduous, bustling, diligent, employed, engaged, industrious, laborious, occupied, sedulous, working

related words knee-deep, swamped; animated, astir, buzzing, flourishing, happening, humming, lively, thriving, vibrant; absorbed, concentrating, engrossed, focused (*also* focussed), immersed, intent, preoccupied; alive, functional, functioning, going, living, operating, operational, operative, running; energetic, vigorous; hardworking; indefatigable, tireless, untiring

near antonyms free; asleep, dormant, latent, lifeless, quiescent, sleepy; inert, passive; dead, dull, slow; inoperative, nonoperating

antonyms idle, inactive, unbusy, unoccupied

2 marked by much life, movement, or activity ⟨the *busy*, often hectic floor of the New York Stock Exchange⟩ — see ALIVE 2

3 thrusting oneself where one is not welcome or invited ⟨She's one of those *busy* production facilitators—always concerned about other people's work and never her own.⟩ — see INTRUSIVE

busy *vb* to hold the attention of ⟨The video game *busied* the child for hours.⟩ — see ENGAGE 1

busybody *n* a person who meddles in the affairs of others ⟨That *busybody* across the street is always telling me how to tend to my own garden.⟩

synonyms interferer, interloper, intruder, kibitzer (*also* kibbitzer), meddler

related words gaper, gawker, gazer, peeper, peeping Tom, prier (*also* pryer), rubberneck, rubbernecker, snoop, snooper, spy; blabber, discloser, gossip, prattler, revealer, teller; betrayer, talebearer, tattler, tattletale, telltale; snake, sneak; informant, informer, snitcher, squealer, stool pigeon

but *adv* nothing more than ⟨She is *but* a child and too young to understand such things.⟩ — see JUST 3

but *conj* if it were not for the fact that ⟨I would have said something *but* I was too chicken.⟩ — see EXCEPT

but *prep* not including ⟨brought everything *but* the kitchen table to the campground⟩ — see EXCEPT

butcher *n* someone who bungles an effort ⟨The newest intern on the campaign is a *butcher* when it comes to writing press releases.⟩

synonyms screwup

related words incompetent, muddler

near antonyms ace, adept, crackerjack (*also* crackajack), expert, maestro, master, virtuoso, wizard

butcher *vb* **1** to kill on a large scale ⟨The barbarians *butchered* the monks in the monasteries.⟩ — see MASSACRE

2 to make or do (something) in a clumsy or unskillful way ⟨The new piano student *butchered* the piece.⟩ — see BOTCH

butchery *n* the killing of a large number of people ⟨the *butchery* that took place during the war⟩ — see MASSACRE

¹**butt** *n* the part of the body upon which someone sits ⟨Did you just sit on your *butt* all day?⟩ — see BUTTOCKS

²**butt** *n* **1** a person or thing that is made fun of ⟨The social outcast got tired of being the *butt* of everyone's jokes.⟩ — see LAUGHINGSTOCK

2 a person or thing that is the object of abuse, criticism, or ridicule ⟨Usually the U.S. Congress is the *butt* of the radio commentator's scathing wit.⟩ — see TARGET 1

³**butt** *n* an enclosed wooden vessel for holding beverages ⟨a *butt* of hard cider that we had pressed ourselves⟩ — see CASK

butterflies *pl n* a sense of panic or extreme nervousness ⟨Even experienced actors sometimes get *butterflies* before a performance.⟩ — see JITTERS

butt in *vb* to interest oneself in what is not one's concern ⟨Please stop *butting in* on my personal life!⟩ — see INTERFERE

buttocks *pl n* the part of the body upon which someone sits ⟨She slipped in the mud puddle and hit the ground square on her *buttocks*.⟩

synonyms backside, behind, bottom, breech, bum, butt, can, cheeks, fanny, hams, haunches, posterior, rear, rump, seat, tail

related words beam, stern

buttress *n* **1** something or someone to which one looks for support ⟨Our mother had always been the *buttress* of our family in trying times.⟩ — see DEPENDENCE 2

2 a structure that holds up or serves as a foundation for something else ⟨After the wall collapsed, the construction company agreed to rebuild it with a *buttress*.⟩ — see SUPPORT 1

buttress *vb* **1** to hold up or serve as a foundation for ⟨A brace *buttressed* the wall.⟩ — see SUPPORT 3

2 to provide evidence or information for (as a claim or idea) ⟨A mass of circumstantial evidence *buttresses* the prosecutor's case.⟩ — see SUPPORT 4

buy *n* something bought or offered for sale at a desirable price ⟨Four cartons of ice cream for 10 dollars is a real *buy*.⟩ — see BARGAIN 1

buy *vb* **1** to get possession of (something) by giving money in exchange for ⟨I really want to *buy* that new book, but I don't have enough money right now.⟩

synonyms pick up, purchase, take

related words acquire, gain, garner, get, obtain, procure, secure, win; finance, pay (for), spring (for); barter (for), deal (for), dicker (over), exchange (for), haggle (for), negotiate (about), trade (for); bargain (with), chaffer (with), horse-trade (with), palter (with); bid, offer; rebuy, repurchase

near antonyms deal (in), market, merchandise (*also* merchandize), retail, sell, vend

2 to influence someone with a bribe ⟨There were rumors that the mobster had *bought* the judge.⟩ — see BRIBE

3 to regard as right or true ⟨If you *buy* that story, then I have a bridge in Brooklyn you might be interested in.⟩ — see BELIEVE 1

buzz *n* **1** a communication by telephone ⟨Give me a *buzz* when you decide.⟩ — see CALL 3

2 a monotonous sound like that of an insect in motion ⟨The motor made a soft *buzz*.⟩ — see HUM

3 information or opinion that is widely disseminated without any authority or confirmation of accuracy ⟨The *buzz* is that this movie will be the blockbuster of the summer.⟩ — see RUMOR

buzz *vb* **1** to be copiously supplied ⟨For months the area has been *buzzing* with rumors that a megacorporation plans to locate its headquarters here.⟩ — see ABOUND

2 to proceed or move quickly ⟨We've been *buzzing* around all morning getting ready for the meeting with the VIPs from the head office.⟩ — see HURRY 2

3 to fly, turn, or move rapidly with a fluttering or vibratory sound ⟨The little plane *buzzed* past the crowd.⟩ — see WHIR

buzzing *adj* marked by much life, movement, or activity ⟨The arena is really *buzzing* tonight.⟩ — see ALIVE 2

by *adv* at, within, or to a short distance or time ⟨The library is close *by*.⟩ — see NEAR 1

by *prep* **1** along the way of ⟨went *by* the woods to get to the summer cottage⟩

synonyms through, via

related words across, along, alongside, beyond, near, nearby, over; below, beneath, under, underneath; outside, past; throughout

phrases by way of

2 using the means or agency of ⟨We tried to convince them *by* reason.⟩

synonyms in, per, through, via, with

phrases by dint of, by means of, by virtue of (*or* in)

3 close to ⟨that house is right *by* the ocean⟩ — see AROUND 1

4 in the course of ⟨She attends college *by* day and works *by* night.⟩ — see DURING

by–and–by *n* time that is to come ⟨We shall meet again in the *by-and-by*.⟩ — see FUTURE 1

by and large *adv* for the most part ⟨*By and large*, that information is accurate.⟩ — see CHIEFLY

bygone *adj* no longer existing ⟨elderly people reminiscing about *bygone* fashions⟩ — see EXTINCT

bylaw *n* a statement spelling out the proper procedure or conduct for an activity ⟨The club's *bylaws* bar any member whose annual dues remain unpaid from voting in the election.⟩ — see RULE 1

bypass *vb* **1** to avoid by going around ⟨We can *bypass* the traffic jam if we take this other road.⟩ — see DETOUR 1

2 to fail to give proper attention to ⟨a serious news event that was *bypassed* by the media⟩ — see NEGLECT 1

3 to avoid having to comply with (something) especially through cleverness ⟨You can *bypass* the graduation requirements if you do enough extra credit.⟩ — see CIRCUMVENT 1

by–product *n* something that naturally develops or is developed from something else ⟨Hydrogen is one *by-product* of that chemical reaction.⟩ — see DERIVATIVE

byword *n* **1** an often stated observation regarding something from common experience ⟨Mom's favorite *byword* is "You can get more flies with honey than with vinegar."⟩ — see SAYING

2 the most perfect type or example ⟨Nationally, Beverly Hills' Rodeo Drive has become a *byword* for luxury retailing.⟩ — see QUINTESSENCE 1

C

cab *n* an automobile that carries passengers for a fare usually determined by the distance traveled ⟨called a *cab* to get back to the hotel⟩ — see TAXICAB

cabal *n* a group involved in secret or criminal activities ⟨a conspiracy theory about the existence of an international *cabal* devoted to world domination⟩ — see ¹RING 1

cabaret *n* a bar or restaurant offering special nighttime entertainment (as music, dancing, or comedy acts) ⟨a singing superstar who got her start singing in the *cabarets* of New York City⟩ — see NIGHTCLUB

cabin *n* **1** a small, simply constructed, and often temporary dwelling ⟨a small *cabin* that hikers along the Appalachian Trail use for overnight stays⟩ — see SHACK

2 an often small house for recreational or seasonal use ⟨kept a *cabin* in the mountains for vacations during skiing season⟩ — see COTTAGE

3 one of the parts into which an enclosed space is divided ⟨an airplane *cabin*⟩ — see COMPARTMENT

cabinet *n* a storage case typically having doors and shelves ⟨The most precious knickknacks were kept in a *cabinet* with glass doors.⟩

synonyms buffet, closet, console, cupboard, hutch, locker, press, sideboard

related words bookcase, breakfront, chest, china closet, secretary, showcase, vitrine; dresser, pie safe; armoire, clothespress, wardrobe

cabinetwork *n* the movable articles (such as tables and chairs) in a room ⟨18th-century *cabinetwork* from Newport, Rhode Island, is among the most prized of all American furniture.⟩ — see FURNITURE

cable *n* a length of braided, flexible material that is used for tying or connecting things ⟨a mass of *cables* connecting the audio and video components⟩ — see CORD 1

cache *n* **1** a collection of things kept available for future use or need ⟨a *cache* of medical supplies in case of emergency⟩ — see STORE 1

2 a supply stored up and often hidden away ⟨The squirrel kept a *cache* of nuts in the hollow of the tree.⟩ — see HOARD 1

cache *vb* **1** to put (something of future use or value) in a safe or secret place ⟨an eccentric who *cached* money in odd places, such as under the boards of the floor⟩ — see HOARD

2 to put into a hiding place ⟨He *cached* his fishing pole behind a shrub until he could return.⟩ — see ¹HIDE 1

caching *n* the placing of something out of sight ⟨the *caching* of holiday gifts in the weeks before Christmas⟩ — see CONCEALMENT 1

cackle *n* **1** an explosive sound that is a sign of amusement ⟨erupted in a high-pitched *cackle* at the absurdity of the suggestion⟩ — see LAUGH 1

2 friendly, informal conversation or an instance of this

⟨The constant *cackle* of his seat companion made the long flight seem even longer.⟩ — see CHAT 1

cackle *vb* **1** to engage in casual or rambling conversation ⟨The friends had a lot to catch up on and spent two hours *cackling* on the phone.⟩ — see CHAT 1
2 to show mirth with an explosive vocal sound ⟨She *cackled* with glee when her tax-evading neighbor finally got caught.⟩ — see LAUGH 1

cackler *n* a person who talks constantly ⟨steadfastly avoids that *cackler* in the lunchroom, who doesn't mind wasting other people's time⟩ — see CHATTERBOX

cacophonous *adj* marked by or producing a harsh combination of sounds ⟨the *cacophonous* chaos on the floor of the New York Stock Exchange⟩ — see DISSONANT

cacophony *n* loud, confused, and usually inharmonious sound ⟨the *cacophony* of a pet store full of animals⟩ — see NOISE 1

cad *n* a person whose behavior is offensive to others ⟨He's the type of *cad* who readily bad-mouths every girl who's ever dumped him.⟩ — see JERK 1

cadaver *n* a dead body ⟨medical students who train by using *cadavers*⟩ — see CORPSE

cadaverous *adj* **1** lacking a healthy skin color ⟨Everyone always looks *cadaverous* in the winter.⟩ — see PALE 2
2 suffering extreme weight loss as a result of hunger or disease ⟨A tall, *cadaverous* man led us into the library.⟩ — see EMACIATED

caddy *n* a covered rectangular container for storing or transporting things ⟨an antique tea *caddy* from the colonial period⟩ — see CHEST

cadence *n* the recurrent pattern formed by a series of sounds having a regular rise and fall in intensity ⟨The soothing *cadence* of the lecturer's voice nearly put me to sleep.⟩ — see RHYTHM

cadenced *adj* marked by or occurring with a noticeable regularity in the rise and fall of sound ⟨a very *cadenced* voice, as one would expect of an instructor in a meditation class⟩ — see RHYTHMIC

café *also* **cafe** *n* **1** a bar or restaurant offering special nighttime entertainment (as music, dancing, or comedy acts) ⟨The *café* presents nationally known jazz performers in an intimate setting.⟩ — see NIGHTCLUB
2 a public establishment where meals are served to paying customers for consumption on the premises ⟨They met at a little *café* in Paris.⟩ — see RESTAURANT

cage *n* an enclosure with an open framework for keeping animals ⟨He regularly changed the bedding in his hamster's *cage*.⟩
synonyms coop, corral, hutch, pen, pound
related words kennel, run; stockade; cote, dovecote (*also* dovecot), henhouse; fold, sheepfold; pigpen; aquarium, terrarium; live-box; fence

cage *vb* to close or shut in by or as if by barriers ⟨*caged* the rabbit at night so she wouldn't wake everyone up⟩ — see ENCLOSE 1

cagey *also* **cagy** *adj* **1** clever at attaining one's ends by indirect and often deceptive means ⟨a *cagey* old politician who is exceptionally skilled at getting federal money for his district⟩ — see ARTFUL 1
2 slow to begin or proceed with a course of action because of doubts or uncertainty ⟨When it came time to sign the contract, he suddenly got *cagey* about taking on the job.⟩ — see HESITANT

caginess *also* **cageyness** *n* **1** exceptional discernment and judgment especially in practical matters ⟨Most consumers should possess sufficient *caginess* to see through that scam.⟩ — see ACUMEN
2 skill in achieving one's ends through indirect, subtle, or underhanded means ⟨The lawyer's celebrated *caginess*

makes her the first choice for many litigants.⟩ — see CUNNING 1

cajole *vb* to get (someone) to do something by gentle urging, special attention, or flattery ⟨*cajoled* her into doing his math homework for him⟩ — see COAX

cake *n* **1** a small usually rounded mass of minced food that has been fried ⟨The rich, tender *cakes* of crabmeat had been lightly fried.⟩
synonyms croquette, cutlet, fritter, patty (*also* pattie)
related words stick
2 something that is easy to do ⟨Today's assignment is *cake* compared to yesterday's.⟩ — see CINCH

cake *vb* to cover with a hardened layer ⟨shoes *caked* with dried mud⟩ — see ENCRUST

calamitous *adj* **1** bringing about ruin or misfortune ⟨A *calamitous* decision not to sell their products online ruined the business.⟩ — see FATAL 1
2 causing or tending to cause destruction ⟨a *calamitous* flood that destroyed the town's central business district⟩ — see DESTRUCTIVE 1

calamity *n* a sudden violent event that brings about great loss or destruction ⟨This latest breakdown of the car is inconvenient, but not a *calamity*.⟩ — see DISASTER 1

calculate *vb* **1** to determine (a value) by doing the necessary mathematical operations ⟨The family has been *calculating* what a week at the beach resort would end up costing.⟩
synonyms cipher, compute, figure, reckon, work out
related words add up, average, sum, tally, total; add, divide, multiply, subtract; deduct, factor (in *or* into *or* out), figure in; figure out, solve (for); count, itemize, number; calibrate, gauge (*also* gage), measure, scale; appraise, assess, estimate, evaluate, rate, value; recalculate, recompute, refigure
2 to decide the size, amount, number, or distance of (something) without actual measurement ⟨I *calculate* that this job will take another two days to finish.⟩ — see ESTIMATE 2
3 to work out the details of (something) in advance ⟨*calculated* the best route to take to the coast⟩ — see PLAN 1
4 to have in mind as a purpose or goal ⟨I *calculate* to run a marathon from start to finish—even if it kills me.⟩ — see INTEND 1
5 to place reliance or trust ⟨We know we can *calculate* on you following through, whatever the assignment.⟩ — see DEPEND 2

calculated *adj* decided on as a result of careful thought ⟨took a *calculated* risk and got in on the ground floor of the new enterprise⟩ — see DELIBERATE 1

calculation *n* the act or process of performing mathematical operations to find a value ⟨By my *calculation*, it should take me a month to save up for the weekend getaway.⟩
synonyms arithmetic, ciphering, computation, figures, figuring, number crunching, numbers, reckoning
related words addition, division, multiplication, subtraction; calibration, measurement, mensuration; appraisal, assessment, estimation, evaluation, valuation

calendar *n* a listing of things to be presented or considered (as at a concert or play) ⟨The *calendar* of upcoming events at the state fair will be available tomorrow.⟩ — see PROGRAM 1

caliber *or* **calibre** *n* degree of excellence ⟨Musicians of the highest *caliber* perform at that concert hall.⟩ — see QUALITY 1

call *n* **1** a natural vocal sound made by an animal ⟨a ranger who could immediately identify the *call* of every creature in the forest⟩
synonyms cry, note

related words bark, bay, bellow, bray, cackle, calling, caw, cheep, chirp, cluck, coo, crake, croak, crow, grunt, honk, hoot, howl, low, meow (*also* miaow), mew, moo, neigh, oink, peep, quack, roar, screech, squall, squawk, squeak, squeal, trumpet, tu-whit tu-whoo, twitter, whinny, yelp, yip, yowl

2 a coming to see another briefly for social or business reasons ⟨We paid a *call* on the new neighbors the day after they moved in.⟩
synonyms visit, visitation
related words stopover; get-together, meeting, rendezvous, tryst

3 a communication by telephone ⟨Give me a *call* as soon as you arrive, so I'll know you got there safely.⟩
synonyms buzz, ring
related words callback, cold call, conference call, message, toll call, voice mail

4 an act or instance of asking for information ⟨put out a *call* for background information about the suspect⟩ — see QUESTION 2

5 an entitlement to something ⟨You have no *call* to insult people.⟩ — see CLAIM 1

6 a position arrived at after consideration ⟨I told you my preference for a cruise destination, but it's your *call*.⟩ — see DECISION 1

7 the state of being sought after especially for purchase ⟨There's not much *call* for woodstoves in this part of the country.⟩ — see DEMAND 2

call *vb* **1** to speak so as to be heard at a distance ⟨We could hear someone *calling* for help from the other side of the wall.⟩
synonyms bawl, bay, bellow, cry, holler, roar, shout, sound off, thunder, vociferate, yell
related words crow, whoop; scream, screech, shriek, shrill, squeak, squeal; howl, wail, yowl; hail; speak out, speak up
near antonyms breathe, mumble, murmur, mutter, whisper

2 to make a telephone call to ⟨Use this cell phone to *call* me if there's an emergency.⟩
synonyms dial, phone, telephone
related words beep, buzz; call in; cold-call

3 to make a brief visit ⟨The hospital posts the hours during which friends and relatives may *call*.⟩
synonyms come by, pop (in), stop (by *or* in), visit
related words barge (in); look up, see; bop (into), happen (by); frequent, haunt, resort (to)

4 to put an end to (something planned or previously agreed to) ⟨The game was *called* on account of rain.⟩ — see CANCEL 1

5 to think of in a particular way ⟨I wouldn't quite *call* that cheating, but it's not entirely ethical either.⟩ — see CONSIDER 1

6 to utter one's distinctive animal sound ⟨The dog *called* whenever it flushed a quail.⟩ — see CRY 2

7 to bring together in assembly by or as if by command ⟨We *called* all the night workers in for a meeting.⟩ — see CONVOKE

8 to decide the size, amount, number, or distance of (something) without actual measurement ⟨Let's *call* that five feet for now, and we'll measure it out later.⟩ — see ESTIMATE 2

9 to demand or request the presence or service of ⟨rushed to *call* a repairman when the furnace broke⟩ — see SUMMON 1

10 to give a name to ⟨We've decided to *call* the kitten "Molly."⟩ — see NAME 1

11 to request the doing of by virtue of one's authority ⟨The union president is refusing to *call* a strike.⟩ — see COMMAND 2

12 to tell of or describe beforehand ⟨Somehow the political pundit *called* the race results within a mere percentage point.⟩ — see FORETELL

call (for) *vb* **1** to ask for (something) earnestly or with authority ⟨With an eye to the expected rush, the manager *called for* additional waiters.⟩ — see DEMAND 1
2 to make a request for ⟨*called for* someone to help with planning the club's party⟩ — see ASK (FOR) 1

call (on *or* **upon)** *vb* to make a social call upon ⟨Lots of well-wishers *called on* the new parents in the weeks following the birth of their first child.⟩ — see VISIT 1

caller *n* a person who visits another ⟨A number of *callers* have been by since they heard you weren't feeling well.⟩ — see GUEST 1

calligraphy *n* writing done by hand ⟨She specializes in scrollwork with beautiful *calligraphy*.⟩ — see HANDWRITING 2

calling *n* **1** the act of putting an end to something planned or previously agreed to ⟨The *calling* of the match was a disappointment to both players.⟩ — see CANCELLATION
2 the activity by which one regularly makes a living ⟨I think my true *calling* will be as a commercial artist.⟩ — see OCCUPATION

calling off *n* the act of putting an end to something planned or previously agreed to ⟨The *calling off* of the senior prom is not going to go over well.⟩ — see CANCELLATION

call off *vb* **1** to draw the attention or mind to something else ⟨She was about to tell me the big news when her attention was *called off* by the arrival of another guest.⟩ — see DISTRACT 1
2 to put an end to (something planned or previously agreed to) ⟨*called off* the party after half of those invited couldn't make it⟩ — see CANCEL 1

callous *adj* having or showing a lack of sympathy or tender feelings ⟨The *callous* comment "It's just a fish," when the boy's pet died, made him cry.⟩ — see HARD 1

callow *adj* lacking in adult experience or maturity ⟨a story about a *callow* youth who learns the value of hard work and self-reliance⟩
synonyms adolescent, green, immature, inexperienced, juvenile, puerile, raw, unfledged, unformed, unripe, unripened
related words babyish, childish, infantile, infantilized, infantine; boyish, girlish, kiddish, young, youngish, youthful; ingenuous, innocent, naive (*or* naïve), tender; unknowing, unseasoned, unsophisticated, untrained, untried
phrases wet behind the ears
near antonyms advanced, precocious; knowing, savvy, sophisticated, worldly, worldly-wise
antonyms adult, experienced, grown-up, mature, ripe

calm *adj* **1** free from storms or physical disturbance ⟨After a stormy night of high winds and driving rains, the day dawned on a *calm* sea.⟩
synonyms halcyon, hushed, peaceful, placid, quiet, serene, still, stilly, tranquil, untroubled
related words balmy, clement, equable, gentle, mild, moderate, temperate; clear, cloudless, fair, rainless, sunny, sunshiny, windless
near antonyms blizzardy (*also* blizzardly), blustery, squally, windy; extreme, foul, intemperate, nasty, severe
antonyms agitated, angry, inclement, restless, rough, stormy, tempestuous, turbulent, unquiet, unsettled

2 free from emotional or mental agitation ⟨Bystanders tried to help the injured person remain *calm* while they waited for the ambulance to arrive.⟩
synonyms collected, composed, cool, coolheaded, equal, level, limpid, peaceful, placid, sedate, self-possessed,

serene, smooth, tranquil, undisturbed, unperturbed, unruffled, unshaken, untroubled, unworried

related words even, even-keeled, steady, well-adjusted, well-balanced; imperturbable, nerveless, unflappable, unshakable; centered, disciplined, equable, self-contained, self-controlled; affable, breezy, devil-may-care, easygoing, happy-go-lucky, laid-back, loosey-goosey, mellow; carefree, nonchalant, unconcerned; assured, confident, self-assured; aloof, detached, dispassionate, indifferent; bovine, impassive, phlegmatic, sober, stolid; relaxed, relieved, tranquilized (*also* tranquillized)

phrases at peace

near antonyms anxious, distressed, uneasy, unquiet, unsettled, worried; jittery, jumpy, nervous, restless, skittish, tense; high-strung, unstable, uptight

antonyms agitated, discomposed, disturbed, flustered, perturbed, unglued, unstrung, upset

3 free from disturbing noise or uproar ⟨The restaurant became much *calmer* once the rowdy tour group had left.⟩ — see QUIET 1

calm *n* **1** a state of freedom from storm or disturbance ⟨Vacationing city dwellers who are tired of the hustle and bustle enjoy the *calm* of the secluded mountain village.⟩

synonyms calmness, hush, peace, peacefulness, placidity, quiet, quietness, quietude, repose, restfulness, sereneness, serenity, still, stillness, tranquillity (*or* tranquility)

related words lull, pause, respite; silence; mildness, soothingness, comity, concord, harmony; casualness, easygoingness, informality, laid-backness, relaxedness

near antonyms clamor, din, noise, racket

antonyms bustle, commotion, hubbub, hurly-burly, pandemonium, tumult, turmoil, unrest, uproar

2 freedom from disquieting or oppressive thoughts or emotions ⟨The batter always exudes an aura of *calm*, even in clutch situations.⟩ — see PEACE 2

calm *vb* **1** to free from distress or disturbance ⟨The president's reassuring words did much to *calm* the public during the national emergency.⟩

synonyms compose, lull, quiet, settle, soothe, still, tranquilize (*also* tranquillize)

related words appease, conciliate, hush, mollify, pacify, placate; allay, alleviate, assuage, ease, lay, mitigate, quell, relax, relieve, solace; narcotize, sedate, stupefy

near antonyms aggravate, heighten, intensify; arouse, excite, foment, incite, rouse, stir (up), work up

antonyms agitate, discompose, disquiet, disturb, key (up), perturb, upset, vex

2 to gain emotional or mental control of ⟨He *calmed* himself before beginning his speech accepting the award.⟩ — see COLLECT 1

calm (down) *vb* to become still and orderly ⟨The sea finally *calmed down*, making it safe for small craft to venture forth once again.⟩ — see QUIET 1

calming *adj* tending to calm the emotions and relieve stress ⟨a *calming* glass of warm milk⟩ — see SOOTHING 1

calmness *n* **1** a state of freedom from storm or disturbance ⟨The unusual *calmness* of the lake gave its surface a strikingly glassy appearance.⟩ — see CALM 1

2 evenness of emotions or temper ⟨Her resolute *calmness* in a crisis serves her well as a doctor in the emergency room.⟩ — see EQUANIMITY

3 freedom from disquieting or oppressive thoughts or emotions ⟨a teacher who handles even the most vexing situations with a clearheaded *calmness*⟩ — see PEACE 2

camaraderie *n* the feeling of closeness and friendship that exists between companions ⟨pizza parties that are intended to foster *camaraderie* between the varsity and junior varsity players⟩ — see COMPANIONSHIP

camouflage *n* clothing put on to hide one's true identity or imitate someone or something else ⟨The soldiers must wear protective jungle *camouflage* while on patrol.⟩ — see DISGUISE 1

camouflage *vb* to change the dress or looks of so as to conceal true identity ⟨*camouflaged* himself so as not to be spotted by the deer he was hunting⟩ — see DISGUISE 1

camp *n* **1** a place where a group of people live for a short time in tents or cabins ⟨Red Cross workers arrived at the refugee *camp*.⟩

synonyms bivouac, campground, campsite, encampment

related words colony, plantation, settlement; jungle, shantytown; concentration camp, prison camp; barracks, cantonment, installation, post

2 a small, simply constructed, and often temporary dwelling ⟨a hunter's *camp* deep in the woods⟩ — see SHACK

3 an often small house for recreational or seasonal use ⟨Years ago the wealthy industrialists built some rather grand *camps* along the lake.⟩ — see COTTAGE

camp *vb* to provide with living quarters or shelter ⟨Some out-of-town delegates to the convention were *camped* in university dorms.⟩ — see HOUSE 1

camp (out) *vb* to live in a camp or the outdoors ⟨Rather than stay in motels, my family usually *camps out* when we're on vacation.⟩

synonyms bivouac, encamp

related words sleep out, tent; bed (down); backpack, caravan

phrases rough it

campaign *n* a series of activities undertaken to achieve a goal ⟨an all-out *campaign* to bring a minor league baseball team to the city⟩

synonyms bandwagon, blitz, cause, crusade, drive, movement, push

related words assault, attack, maneuver, march, offensive; action, bid, enterprise, initiative, mission, project, undertaking

campaigner *n* one who seeks an office, honor, position, or award ⟨an experienced *campaigner* who knows that one televised mistake can put an end to one's candidacy⟩ — see CANDIDATE

camper *n* a motor vehicle that is specially equipped for living while traveling ⟨The family loaded up the *camper* and headed off for the tour of several national parks.⟩

synonyms caravan, motor home, recreational vehicle, RV, trailer

related words house trailer, mobile home; coach, van

campground *n* a place where a group of people live for a short time in tents or cabins ⟨At last the weary vacationers pulled into a *campground* for the night.⟩ — see CAMP 1

campsite *n* a place where a group of people live for a short time in tents or cabins ⟨The *campsite* at least offers shower and bathroom facilities.⟩ — see CAMP 1

can *n* **1** a metal container in the shape of a cylinder ⟨The shelter stores huge *cans* of water for an emergency.⟩

synonyms barrel, canister (*also* cannister), drum, tin

related words bucket, pail; tin can

2 the part of the body upon which someone sits ⟨He slipped on the ice and landed on his *can*.⟩ — see BUTTOCKS

can *vb* **1** *slang* to bring (as an action or operation) to an immediate end ⟨*Can* the chatter, or I'm kicking you out of this library.⟩ — see STOP 1

2 to let go from office, service, or employment ⟨The cashier was summarily *canned* for stealing from the registers.⟩ — see DISMISS 1

canal *n* an open man-made passageway for water ⟨The Panama *Canal* opened a much easier and shorter passageway from the Atlantic to the Pacific.⟩ — see CHANNEL 1

cancel *vb* **1** to put an end to (something planned or previously agreed to) ⟨Please call to *cancel* your appointment with the dentist if you can't make it.⟩
synonyms abandon, abort, call, call off, drop, recall, repeal, rescind, revoke, scrap, scrub
related words abrogate, annul, invalidate, nullify, void, write off; recant, retract, take back, withdraw; countermand, reverse; break off, discontinue, end, halt, stop, terminate; hold back, interrupt, suspend; give up, relinquish, surrender
near antonyms engage, pledge, promise; begin, commence, initiate, start; take on, take up, undertake
antonyms continue, keep
2 to put an end to by formal action ⟨The agreement can be *canceled* by either side with a formal written notice.⟩ — see ABOLISH 1
3 to show (something written) to be no longer valid by drawing a cross over or a line through it ⟨*canceled* the check and wrote a new one⟩ — see X (OUT)
4 to destroy all traces of ⟨His heartfelt apology *canceled* any lingering animosity between them.⟩ — see ANNIHILATE 1

cancel (out) *vb* to balance with an equal force so as to make ineffective ⟨Unfortunately, this one bad decision will *cancel out* a long record of accomplishment.⟩ — see OFFSET

canceler *or* **canceller** *n* a force or influence that makes an opposing force ineffective or less effective ⟨Bright decorative accents proved to be a *canceler* of the apartment's monotone color scheme.⟩ — see COUNTERBALANCE

cancellation *also* **cancelation** *n* the act of putting an end to something planned or previously agreed to ⟨Bad weather forced the *cancellation* of dozens of flights.⟩
synonyms abandonment, abortion, calling, calling off, dropping, recall, repeal, rescission, revocation
related words neutralization, voidance; ending, halting, stopping, termination; giving up, relinquishment, surrender; reversal, rollback
near antonyms beginning, commencement, initiation; engagement, undertaking
antonyms continuation

candid *adj* **1** free in expressing one's true feelings and opinions ⟨a *candid* person who never hesitates to speak up⟩ — see FRANK
2 marked by justice, honesty, and freedom from bias ⟨a *candid* listing of the advantages and disadvantages of each medical insurance plan⟩ — see FAIR 2

candidate *n* one who seeks an office, honor, position, or award ⟨Each *candidate* for town council was allowed to speak at the candidates' forum.⟩
synonyms applicant, aspirant, campaigner, contender, expectant, hopeful, prospect, seeker
related words competitor, contestant, entrant, entry, favorite, qualifier; dark horse, spoiler, stalking horse; crown prince, favorite son; claimant, pretender
near antonyms incumbent, officeholder; awardee, honoree, inductee; dropout
antonyms noncandidate

candidness *n* the free expression of one's true feelings and opinions ⟨*Candidness* is something that we claim to admire—except when we are on the receiving end of a brutally honest assessment.⟩ — see CANDOR 1

candor *n* **1** the free expression of one's true feelings and opinions ⟨an interview in which the members of the rock band speak with *candor* about their recent squabbling⟩
synonyms candidness, directness, forthrightness, frankness, honesty, openheartedness, openness, outspokenness, plainness, straightforwardness
related words earnestness, sincerity, sobriety; artlessness, genuineness, naïveté (*also* naivete *or* naiveté), simplicity, unsophistication; communicativeness, freedom, license (*or* licence), unrestrainedness, unrestraint
near antonyms circuitousness, evasiveness, secretiveness; inhibition, reserve, restraint, reticence, shyness; diplomacy, tact
antonyms dissembling, dissimulation, indirection
2 the quality or state of having or giving off light ⟨The desert sun shone down on the intrepid travelers with fiery *candor*.⟩ — see BRILLIANCE 1

cane *n* a heavy rigid stick used as a weapon or for punishment ⟨In the past, some teachers would resort to the *cane* when students misbehaved.⟩ — see CLUB 1

canine *n* a domestic mammal that is related to the wolves and foxes ⟨In the minds of some, the winner of this prestigious dog show has a fair claim to the title of King of the *Canines*.⟩ — see DOG 1

canister *also* **cannister** *n* a metal container in the shape of a cylinder ⟨She put the homemade cookies in a fancy *canister* to give as gifts.⟩ — see CAN 1

canned *adj* using or marked by the use of something else as a basis or model ⟨There's a *canned* quality to the screenplay that reminds you of countless other action movies.⟩ — see IMITATIVE 1

canniness *n* **1** exceptional discernment and judgment especially in practical matters ⟨negotiates business deals with all of the proverbial *canniness* of an old-time horse trader⟩ — see ACUMEN
2 skill in achieving one's ends through indirect, subtle, or underhanded means ⟨the *canniness* with which she negotiated her contract⟩ — see CUNNING 1

cannonade *n* a rapid or overwhelming outpouring of many things at once ⟨The director of the sporting event was greeted at the scene with a *cannonade* of complaints.⟩ — see BARRAGE

cannonade *vb* to use bombs or artillery against ⟨The artillery *cannonaded* the enemy encampment all night.⟩ — see BOMBARD 1

canny *adj* having or showing a practical cleverness or judgment ⟨a *canny* card player, good at psyching out opponents⟩ — see SHREWD 1

canon *n* **1** a statement or body of statements concerning faith or morals proclaimed by a church ⟨Members of the church must abide by its *canons*.⟩ — see DOCTRINE 1
2 a record of a series of items (as names or titles) usually arranged according to some system ⟨the *canon* of plays that are attributed to William Shakespeare⟩ — see ¹LIST
3 a collection or system of rules of conduct ⟨The *Model Rules of Professional Conduct* are a lawyer's *canon*.⟩ — see CODE

canonize *vb* **1** to love or admire too much ⟨a singing star so *canonized* by his fans that they refuse to believe anything bad about him⟩ — see IDOLIZE
2 to assign a high status or value to ⟨those movie buffs who have *canonized* Steven Spielberg as filmdom's preeminent director⟩ — see EXALT 1

canopy *n* a raised covering over something for decoration or protection ⟨Trees line both sides of the garden path, with their foliage forming a leafy *canopy* for walkers.⟩
synonyms awning, ceiling, cover, roof, tent
related words marquee; arbor, pergola; screen, shade, shelter, shield, sunshade, umbrella; canvas (*also* canvass), fly

¹cant *n* the degree to which something rises up from a position level with the horizon ⟨a steep *cant* of the riverbank at that turn in the river⟩ — see SLANT 1

²**cant** *n* **1** the pretending of having virtues, principles, or beliefs that one in fact does not have ⟨Many accused the evangelist of *cant*, since his lavish lifestyle seemed to bear little resemblance to what he was preaching.⟩ — see HYPOCRISY

2 the special terms or expressions of a particular group or field ⟨the colorful *cant* used by movie producers and publicity agents in Hollywood⟩ — see TERMINOLOGY

cant *adj* running in a slanting direction ⟨The *cant* buttresses on the interior walls are made of solid oak.⟩ — see DIAGONAL

cant *vb* to set or cause to be at an angle ⟨carefully *canted* the ladder against the wall⟩ — see LEAN 1

cantankerous *adj* having or showing a habitually bad temper ⟨a *cantankerous* regular customer that the employees all avoided⟩ — see ILL-TEMPERED

canted *adj* running in a slanting direction ⟨an odd little house, built with deliberately *canted* windows and not one right angle⟩ — see DIAGONAL

canticle *n* a religious song ⟨The monks offered up a *canticle* at dawn on Easter morning.⟩ — see HYMN 1

canvas *also* **canvass** *n* a picture created with oil paint ⟨One *canvas* by Picasso is worth more money than most of us can imagine.⟩ — see PAINTING

canvass *also* **canvas** *vb* **1** to go around and approach (people) with a request for opinions or information ⟨We *canvassed* people all over town, asking if they would be interested in participating in a recycling program.⟩

synonyms poll, solicit, survey

related words interrogate, question; feel (out), sound (out)

near antonyms report

2 to talk about (an issue) usually from various points of view and for the purpose of arriving at a decision or opinion ⟨*canvassed* all the items on the agenda⟩ — see DISCUSS

canyon *also* **cañon** *n* a narrow opening between hillsides or mountains that can be used for passage ⟨As the scouts made their way through the *canyon*, they marveled at the sheer walls of rock on both sides.⟩

synonyms defile, flume, gap, gorge, gulch, gulf, notch, pass, ravine

related words abyss, chasm, cleft, crevasse, crevice, fissure; dale, dell, glen, hollow, shut-in, vale, valley; basin, floodplain, kettle; arroyo, coulee, draw, gully (*also* gulley), gutter, trench, trough

¹**cap** *n* a small mass containing medicine to be taken orally ⟨I prefer to take my medicine as *caps* rather than in liquid form.⟩ — see PILL 1

²**cap** *n* **1** a covering for the head usually having a shaped crown ⟨grabbed a *cap* and plopped it on his head before running out⟩ — see HAT

2 a piece placed over an open container to hold in, protect, or conceal its contents ⟨I can't find the *cap* to the milk bottle.⟩ — see COVER 1

3 a real or imaginary point beyond which a person or thing cannot go ⟨A *cap* on player salary expenditures was suggested as a way to keep small market teams competitive.⟩ — see LIMIT 1

cap *vb* to set bounds or an upper limit for ⟨The senator will propose a bill to *cap* prices for home heating oil.⟩ — see LIMIT 1

cap (off) *vb* to bring to a triumphant conclusion ⟨*capped off* the baseball season with 10-0 shutout⟩ — see CROWN

capability *n* **1** a skill, an ability, or knowledge that makes a person able to do a particular job ⟨The nature of the tasks to which you are assigned will depend on your *capabilities*.⟩ — see QUALIFICATION 1

2 the physical or mental power to do something ⟨the natural *capability* some people seem to have for teaching⟩ — see ABILITY

3 something that can develop or become actual ⟨There are great *capabilities* in the property, either as a bed-and-breakfast or as a private home.⟩ — see POTENTIAL

capable *adj* having the required skills for an acceptable level of performance ⟨a *capable* and efficient editor⟩ — see COMPETENT 1

capably *adv* in a skillful or expert manner ⟨The summer intern performed all assigned tasks at the television station *capably* and quickly.⟩ — see WELL 3

capacious *adj* more than adequate or average in capacity ⟨That car has a *capacious* trunk that makes it a good choice for families.⟩ — see SPACIOUS

capacity *n* **1** the largest number or amount that something can hold ⟨The seating *capacity* of the school auditorium is 800 people.⟩

synonyms complement, volume

related words burden, fill, load, measure; area, room, space, stowage

2 an assignment at which one regularly works for pay ⟨served in the *capacity* of the network's White House correspondent for a year⟩ — see JOB 1

3 the action for which a person or thing is specially fitted or used or for which a thing exists ⟨Dad offered advice in his *capacity* as a lawyer.⟩ — see ROLE

4 the physical or mental power to do something ⟨Not everyone has the *capacity* for learning higher math.⟩ — see ABILITY

caparison *n* **1** dressy clothing ⟨attended the masquerade ball in the *caparison* of an Indian maharaja⟩ — see FINERY

2 something that decorates or beautifies ⟨horses dressed in Old-West *caparison* for the parade⟩ — see DECORATION 1

caparison *vb* **1** to outfit with clothes and especially fine or special clothes ⟨Used to seeing him in a T-shirt and jeans, we were startled by the sight of the youth *caparisoned* for the prom in a tuxedo.⟩ — see CLOTHE 1

2 to make more attractive by adding something that is beautiful or becoming ⟨The state's rolling hills are even more becoming when they are *caparisoned* in the glorious colors of autumn.⟩ — see DECORATE

¹**cape** *n* a sleeveless garment worn so as to hang over the shoulders, arms, and back ⟨The mysterious figure wrapped his *cape* tightly around his shoulders.⟩

synonyms cloak, frock, mantle

related words burnoose (*or* burnous), capelet, capuchin, cowl, domino, joseph, manta, mantelet, mantilla, poncho, roquelaure, tippet; serape (*or* sarape), shawl, stole, wrap

²**cape** *n* an area of land that juts out into a body of water ⟨Residents fled the *cape* as the hurricane roared up the coast.⟩

synonyms arm, headland, peninsula, point, promontory, spit

related words breakwater, jetty

caper *n* a playful or mischievous act intended as a joke ⟨long-ago college *capers* that have become more rollicking and daring with each recounting⟩ — see PRANK

caper *vb* to play and run about happily ⟨As summer drew to a close, the children spent their days wistfully *capering* on the beach.⟩ — see FROLIC 1

capital *adj* **1** coming before all others in importance ⟨The *capital* goal of the effort is to assimilate the new immigrants.⟩ — see FOREMOST 1

2 of the very best kind ⟨a truly *capital* idea, which I highly endorse⟩ — see EXCELLENT

capital *n* **1** a thing or place that is of greatest importance to an activity or interest ⟨During the 1980s Silicon Valley became the *capital* of the computer industry.⟩ — see CENTER 1

2 the total of one's money and property ⟨invested nearly all of their *capital* in the new business⟩ — see WEALTH 1

capitalize *vb* to provide money for ⟨Several investors agreed to *capitalize* the new venture.⟩ — see FINANCE 1

capitalize (on) *vb* to take unfair advantage of ⟨*capitalized on* her coworker's absence to take full credit for the joint project⟩ — see EXPLOIT 1

capitol *n* the building in which a state legislature meets ⟨The legislators were called to the *capitol* for an emergency session.⟩

synonyms statehouse

related words meetinghouse; chamber, hall; house, senate

capitulate *vb* **1** to cease resistance (as to another's arguments, demands, or control) ⟨One side finally *capitulated* when it became clear that they couldn't win the argument.⟩ — see YIELD 3

2 to yield to the control or power of enemy forces ⟨The city reluctantly *capitulated* to the invaders after a three-day siege.⟩ — see FALL 2

capitulating *n* the usually forced yielding of one's person or possessions to the control of another ⟨The tug-of-war will continue until the *capitulating* of one side or the other.⟩ — see SURRENDER

capitulation *n* the usually forced yielding of one's person or possessions to the control of another ⟨Her sudden *capitulation* surprised everyone; she usually debated for hours.⟩ — see SURRENDER

caprice *n* **1** a sudden impulsive and apparently unmotivated idea or action ⟨An out-of-character *caprice* led him to take the day off from work and go to the beach.⟩ — see WHIM

2 an inclination to sudden illogical changes of mind, ideas, or actions ⟨His knack for picking winning lottery numbers owes more to *caprice* than to a canny assessment of odds.⟩ — see WHIMSICALITY

capricious *adj* **1** likely to change frequently, suddenly, or unexpectedly ⟨*capricious* weather that was balmy one day and freezing cold the next⟩ — see FICKLE 1

2 prone to sudden illogical changes of mind, ideas, or actions ⟨a *capricious* cat who was friendly one minute and standoffish the next⟩ — see WHIMSICAL

capriciousness *n* an inclination to sudden illogical changes of mind, ideas, or actions ⟨The client's *capriciousness* frustrated the building contractor to no end.⟩ — see WHIMSICALITY

capsize *vb* to turn on one's side or upside down ⟨A huge wave out of nowhere caused our little sailboat to *capsize*.⟩

synonyms overturn, turn over, upset

related words invert, overset, overthrow, pitchpole, topple, upend; careen, heel, lean, list, tilt, tip; collapse, fall, founder, give

phrases turn turtle

near antonyms straighten (up); erect, raise

antonyms right

capsule *adj* marked by the use of few words to convey much information or meaning ⟨*capsule* reviews of the latest offerings at the multiplex⟩ — see CONCISE

capsule *n* **1** a small mass containing medicine to be taken orally ⟨took an antibiotic *capsule* three times a day for a week⟩ — see PILL 1

2 something that encloses another thing especially to protect it ⟨a *capsule* containing all sorts of items from our era that is to be opened 100 years from now⟩ — see ¹CASE 1

capsule *vb* to reduce in size or volume by or as if by pressing parts or members together ⟨newscasts that *capsule* complex, important stories into one-minute bits for easy digestion by viewers⟩ — see COMPRESS 1

captain *n* **1** a person in overall command of a ship ⟨The *captain* is responsible for everything that happens to the ship in the course of a voyage.⟩

synonyms commander, skipper

related words sea captain; master, pilot; commanding officer; admiral, commodore, vice admiral; mate, officer

near antonyms crew, crewman, crewmate

2 one in official command especially of a military force or base ⟨the *captain* of the largest army ever marshaled for battle in this country⟩ — see COMMANDER 1

3 the person (as an employer or supervisor) who tells people and especially workers what to do ⟨We only do what the *captain* tells us to, so it's not our fault when things don't work out.⟩ — see BOSS

4 a person of rank, power, or influence in a particular field ⟨a fascinating magazine article profiling the *captains* of the American auto industry⟩ — see MAGNATE

captain *vb* **1** to be in charge of ⟨If you do well on this, you'll be asked to *captain* the next mission.⟩ — see BOSS 1

2 to exercise authority or power over ⟨*captained* the project for a few days while the boss was out of town⟩ — see GOVERN 1

3 to serve as leader of ⟨You did a good job of *captaining* the team.⟩ — see LEAD 2

caption *n* **1** an explanation or description accompanying a pictorial illustration ⟨For the school yearbook, funny *captions* were written for snapshots showing a typical day at school.⟩

synonyms legend

related words key; closed-captioning, subtitle, translation; motto, slogan

2 a word or series of words often in larger letters placed at the beginning of a passage or at the top of a page in order to introduce or categorize ⟨The textbook features cleverly worded *captions* to capture the reader's attention.⟩ — see HEADING

captious *adj* given to making or expressing unfavorable judgments about things ⟨a *captious* and cranky eater who's never met a vegetable he didn't hate⟩ — see CRITICAL 1

captivate *vb* to attract or delight as if by magic ⟨The clown *captivated* the toddlers with his balloon tricks.⟩ — see CHARM 1

captivating *adj* having an often mysterious or magical power to attract ⟨a *captivating* performance by the young singing sensation⟩ — see FASCINATING 1

captivation *n* the power of irresistible attraction ⟨By some mysterious method of *captivation*, the therapist is able to evoke a response from even the shiest of children.⟩ — see CHARM 2

captive *adj* taken and held prisoner ⟨The *captive* soldiers were treated humanely by the guards.⟩

synonyms apprehended, arrested, captured, caught, imprisoned, incarcerated, interned, jailed

related words bound, enslaved, indentured; ensnared, trapped; abducted, kidnapped (*also* kidnaped); subdued, subjugated; occupied

phrases behind bars

near antonyms unconfined, unrestrained; delivered, emancipated, enfranchised, freed, liberated, paroled, released

antonyms free

captive *n* one that has been taken and held in confinement ⟨The *captives* in the concentration camp had devised a daring plan of escape.⟩

synonyms capture, internee, prisoner
related words coprisoner; convict, jailbird; arrestee; abductee, kidnappee (*or* kidnapee)
near antonyms custodian, guard, guardian, jailer (*also* jailor), keeper, marshal (*also* marshall), warden; abductor, kidnapper (*also* kidnaper)
antonyms captor

captivity *n* the act of confining or the state of being confined ⟨The wildlife refuge raises endangered species in *captivity* and then releases them into the wild.⟩ — see INTERNMENT

capture *n* one that has been taken and held in confinement ⟨A Spanish treasure ship was the most valuable *capture* ever taken by that privateer.⟩ — see CAPTIVE

capture *vb* **1** to receive as return for effort ⟨The movie's producers *captured* several awards for their work.⟩ — see EARN 1
2 to take physical control or possession of (something) suddenly or forcibly ⟨*captured* the cat just as it was about to escape out the front door⟩ — see CATCH 1

captured *adj* taken and held prisoner ⟨a *captured* raccoon tested for rabies⟩ — see CAPTIVE

car *n* a self-propelled passenger vehicle on four wheels ⟨every teenager's dream of getting a driver's license and a first *car*⟩
synonyms auto, automobile, machine, motor, motorcar, motor vehicle, wheels [*slang*]
related words coach, jitney, microbus, minibus, minivan, omnibus, van; convertible, fastback, hardtop, hatchback, notchback, ragtop, sports car, sport-utility vehicle, station wagon, SUV, town car, wagon, woody (*or* woodie); compact, coupe (*or* coupé), intermediate, limousine, mini, minicar, sedan, subcompact, V-8; gas-guzzler, land yacht; muscle car, stock car, turbocar; beater, crate, flivver, junker; cream puff; phaeton, roadster, tin lizzie, touring car; hybrid

caravan *n* **1** a group of vehicles traveling together or under one management ⟨a funeral *caravan* slowly making its way down the street⟩ — see FLEET
2 a motor vehicle that is specially equipped for living while traveling ⟨bought a *caravan* and drove cross-country to California⟩ — see CAMPER

carbon copy *n* **1** something or someone that strongly resembles another ⟨The child is a *carbon copy* of his father.⟩ — see IMAGE 1
2 something that is made to look exactly like something else ⟨a clothing company that makes *carbon copies* of designer duds⟩ — see COPY

carcass *n* a dead body ⟨the *carcass* of a squirrel that had been run over⟩ — see CORPSE

card *n* **1** a list of foods served at or available for a meal ⟨The diners asked if there were any specials on the *card* for the evening.⟩ — see MENU 1
2 a person (as a writer) noted for or specializing in humor ⟨You're really a *card*, but save the jokes for after class.⟩ — see HUMORIST

cardinal *adj* coming before all others in importance ⟨the *cardinal* rule of medicine: do no harm⟩ — see FOREMOST 1

care *n* **1** strict attentiveness to what one is doing ⟨Reading the report with more *care* the second time, she detected several errors.⟩
synonyms carefulness, closeness, conscientiousness, heed, heedfulness, meticulousness, pains, scrupulousness
related words advertence, advertency, attention, concentration, focus, observance, observation; alertness, vigilance, watchfulness; dutifulness, punctiliousness, responsibility; bother, effort, painstaking, trouble; exactness, particularity, precision

near antonyms inadvertence, inadvertency, inattention, inobservance
antonyms heedlessness, inattentiveness, negligence
2 attention accompanied by protectiveness and responsibility ⟨That's an extremely valuable violin, so handle it with *care*.⟩
synonyms solicitude
related words concern, considerateness, consideration, kindness, thoughtfulness; babying, coddling, pampering
near antonyms inconsiderateness, inconsideration, thoughtlessness, unconcern, unkindness
antonyms carelessness
3 a close attentiveness to avoiding danger ⟨Take *care* while crossing the street.⟩ — see CAUTION 1
4 an uneasy state of mind usually over the possibility of an anticipated misfortune or trouble ⟨on vacation, without a *care* in the world⟩ — see ANXIETY 1
5 responsibility for the safety and well-being of someone or something ⟨While you're under my *care*, you'll do as you're told.⟩ — see CUSTODY
6 the duty or function of watching or guarding for the sake of proper direction or control ⟨You'll have *care* of the project from its beginning to its completion.⟩ — see SUPERVISION 1
7 the act or activity of looking after and making decisions about something ⟨She stepped up and took over the *care* of the bank after her father retired.⟩ — see CONDUCT 1

care *vb* to have an interest or concern for ⟨a teacher who *cares* what happens to her students long after they leave her classroom⟩
synonyms mind, watch
related words attend, heed, regard; note, notice, observe; empathize (with), feel (for), sympathize (with)
near antonyms disregard, ignore, overlook

care (for) *vb* **1** to take charge of especially on behalf of another ⟨Will you *care for* the lawn while we're gone?⟩ — see ²TEND 1
2 to attend to the needs and comforts of ⟨He is *caring for* his mother while she's sick.⟩ — see NURSE 1
3 to have a favorable opinion of ⟨I don't really *care for* your tone of voice.⟩ — see APPROVE (OF)
4 to wish to have ⟨I don't particularly *care for* rice cereal, but I'll eat it.⟩ — see LIKE 1
5 to show partiality toward ⟨She generally doesn't *care for* war movies.⟩ — see PREFER 1

careen *vb* **1** to make a series of unsteady side-to-side motions ⟨The sled *careened* as it barreled down the hill.⟩ — see ROCK 1
2 to move forward while swaying from side to side ⟨He *careened* unsteadily to the couch after hitting his head.⟩ — see STAGGER 1
3 to proceed or move quickly ⟨Sounding its siren, an ambulance *careened* through the intersection.⟩ — see HURRY 2

career *vb* to proceed or move quickly ⟨She *careered* off to the class she'd almost forgotten.⟩ — see HURRY 2

carefree *adj* having or showing freedom from worries or troubles ⟨passengers on a luxury cruise ship enjoying a *carefree* vacation⟩ ⟨*carefree* college students on spring break⟩
synonyms blithe, debonair, devil-may-care, happy-go-lucky, insouciant, lighthearted, lightsome, unconcerned
related words blasé (*also* blase), breezy, cavalier, nonchalant; casual, easygoing, informal, laid-back, low-pressure, relaxed, unfussy
near antonyms earnest, grave, serious, serious-minded, somber (*or* sombre); careful, cautious, heedful, wary; anxious, concerned, upset, worried; long-suffering, overburdened, sorrowful

antonyms careworn

careful *adj* **1** having or showing a close attentiveness to avoiding danger or trouble ⟨*Careful* drivers slow down on slick or icy roadways.⟩
synonyms alert, cautious, circumspect, conservative, considerate, gingerly, guarded, heedful, safe, wary
related words advertent, attentive, awake, observant, regardful, vigilant, watchful; hypercautious; foresighted, foresightful, forethoughtful, provident, thoughtful; cagey (*also* cagy), calculating, canny, shrewd; deliberate, slow; ultracareful, ultracautious
near antonyms bold, brash, impetuous, rash, reckless, venturesome; asleep, inattentive, regardless; inconsiderate, thoughtless; lax, neglectful, negligent, remiss; imprudent, indiscreet, injudicious; absentminded, forgetful; inadvertent, unintentional, unplanned
antonyms careless, heedless, incautious, unguarded, unmindful, unsafe, unwary
2 taking, showing, or involving great care and effort ⟨That furniture maker was known to be a most *careful* worker, so his output was small.⟩ — see PAINSTAKING

carefulness *n* **1** a close attentiveness to avoiding danger ⟨Her natural *carefulness* keeps her from having car accidents and the high insurance premiums that go with them.⟩ — see CAUTION 1
2 strict attentiveness to what one is doing ⟨A degree of *carefulness* is required to get the details just right.⟩ — see CARE 1

careless *adj* **1** not paying or showing close attention especially for the purpose of avoiding trouble ⟨a *careless* reporter who often doesn't get his facts straight⟩ ⟨a *careless* mistake that caused the plane to crash⟩
synonyms heedless, incautious, mindless, unguarded, unsafe, unwary
related words bold, impetuous, rash, reckless; inattentive, regardless; blithe, inconsiderate, thoughtless; absentminded, forgetful, unmindful; lax, neglectful, negligent, remiss, slipshod; imprudent, indiscreet, injudicious; inadvertent, unintentional, unplanned
near antonyms attentive, observant, vigilant, watchful; foresighted, forethoughtful, provident; calculating, shrewd; considerate, thoughtful; ultracareful, ultracautious
antonyms alert, cautious, circumspect, gingerly, guarded, heedful, safe, wary
2 failing to give proper care and attention ⟨a *careless* effort that made an unnecessary mess⟩ — see NEGLIGENT

carelessness *n* failure to take the care that a cautious person usually takes ⟨The only errors you made were from *carelessness*, not lack of knowledge.⟩ — see NEGLIGENCE 1

caress *vb* to touch or handle in a tender or loving manner ⟨gently *caressed* her hair⟩ — see FONDLE

caretaker *n* a person who takes care of a property sometimes for an absent owner ⟨hired a *caretaker* for the mansion during the winter months⟩ — see CUSTODIAN 1

cargo *n* a mass or quantity of something taken up and carried, conveyed, or transported ⟨We put all of our *cargo* on the pack animals and began our journey through the canyon.⟩ — see LOAD 1

caricature *n* **1** a poor, insincere, or insulting imitation of something ⟨That TV network's reporting is a mere *caricature* of real journalism.⟩ — see MOCKERY 1
2 a work that imitates and exaggerates another work for comic effect ⟨The artist creates *caricatures* of famous paintings by replacing humans with cats.⟩ — see PARODY 1
3 the representation of something in terms that go beyond the facts ⟨The mayor has presented only a *caricature* of his opponent's views.⟩ — see EXAGGERATION

caricature *vb* to copy or exaggerate (someone or something) in order to make fun of ⟨*caricatured* the supervisor's distinctive walk⟩ — see MIMIC 1

carnage *n* the killing of a large number of people ⟨The appalling *carnage* in that war-torn country requires that the outside world intervene.⟩ — see MASSACRE

carnal *adj* **1** having to do with life on earth especially as opposed to that in heaven ⟨The preacher warned those who were interested only in *carnal* pursuits.⟩ — see EARTHLY
2 of or relating to the human body ⟨a missionary who tends to the *carnal* needs of the people as well as to their spiritual concerns⟩ — see PHYSICAL 1
3 pleasing to the physical senses ⟨*carnal* attractions of that gambling mecca in the desert⟩ — see SENSUAL

carnival *n* a time or program of special events and entertainment or amusement ⟨the town's annual Fourth of July *carnival*⟩ — see FESTIVAL

carol *n* a religious song ⟨sang *carols* at the Christmas Eve service⟩ — see HYMN 1

carol *vb* **1** to produce musical sounds with the voice ⟨She *caroled* with glee when she heard the good news.⟩ — see SING 1
2 to proclaim the glory of ⟨landscape photographs that *carol* the majesty and monumentality of Yosemite Valley⟩ — see PRAISE 1

caroler *or* **caroller** *n* one who sings ⟨those feathered *carolers* outside my window every morning⟩ — see SINGER

carom *vb* to strike and fly off at an angle ⟨A ball *caromed* off the wall.⟩ — see GLANCE 1

carouse *vb* to take part in drunken revelry ⟨a night of feasting and *carousing*⟩
synonyms binge, wassail
related words drink, guzzle

carp *n* an expression of dissatisfaction, pain, or resentment ⟨The usual *carp* about that restaurant is that the service is slow.⟩ — see COMPLAINT 1

carp *vb* **1** to express dissatisfaction, pain, or resentment usually tiresomely ⟨Someone who *carps* and whines about everything is a pain.⟩ — see COMPLAIN
2 to make often peevish criticisms or objections about matters that are minor, unimportant, or irrelevant ⟨*carped* about the order of names on the wedding invitations⟩ — see QUIBBLE 1

carper *n* a person given to harsh judgments and to finding faults ⟨Eventually, almost everyone learned to avoid the ski school's resident *carper*.⟩ — see CRITIC 1

carpet *vb* to form a layer over ⟨Leaves *carpeted* the lawn.⟩ — see COVER 2

carping *adj* given to making or expressing unfavorable judgments about things ⟨a peevish and *carping* manager who is not popular with the staff⟩ — see CRITICAL 1

carriage *n* **1** a horse-drawn wheeled vehicle for carrying passengers ⟨a museum with a large collection of beautiful, old *carriages*⟩
synonyms equipage, rig
related words buckboard, cab, cabriolet, carryall, chaise, chariot, coach, coupé (*or* coupe), dogcart, four-in-hand, gig, go-cart, hackney (*or* hackney coach), hansom (*or* hansom cab), jaunting car, landau, phaeton, post chaise, roadster, rockaway, stage, stagecoach, stanhope, surrey, tandem, trap, troika, victoria; turnout
2 a general way of holding the body ⟨Her Ladyship's *carriage* is upright and regal.⟩ — see POSTURE 1

carry *vb* **1** to support and take from one place to another ⟨Each camper must be able to *carry* his or her own backpack.⟩
synonyms bear, cart, convey, ferry, haul, lug, pack, tote, transport

related words deliver, hand over, transfer; forward, send, ship, transmit; bring, fetch, take; move, remove, shift

2 to wear or have on one's person ⟨I always *carry* a camera with me so as to never miss a great shot.⟩
synonyms bear, pack
related words flaunt, show off, sport; display, exhibit, parade, show

3 to bring before the public in performance or exhibition ⟨All of the television networks will *carry* the president's speech.⟩ — see PRESENT 1

4 to have as part of a whole ⟨The idea of equality *carries* with it a number of other concepts.⟩ — see INCLUDE 1

5 to hold up or serve as a foundation for ⟨erected a trellis to *carry* the vine⟩ — see SUPPORT 3

6 to receive as return for effort ⟨*carried* off the award for best picture of the year⟩ — see EARN 1

7 to manage the actions of (oneself) in a particular way ⟨During that difficult time the grieving parents *carried* themselves with unfailing grace and dignity.⟩ — see BE-HAVE

carryall *n* a bag carried by hand and designed to hold a traveler's clothing and personal articles ⟨took only a small *carryall* on the plane⟩ — see TRAVELING BAG

carry away *vb* to fill with overwhelming emotion (as wonder or delight) ⟨The beauty of the music *carried* him *away*.⟩ — see ENTRANCE

carry on *vb* **1** to behave badly ⟨a toddler crying and *carrying on* in the store⟩ — see MISBEHAVE
2 to continue despite difficulties, opposition, or discouragement ⟨She bravely *carried on* despite the loss of her husband.⟩ — see PERSEVERE
3 to look after and make decisions about ⟨*carries on* a business that was opened 75 years ago⟩ — see CONDUCT 1

carry out *vb* to carry through (as a process) to completion ⟨*carried out* the task efficiently and cheerfully⟩ — see PERFORM 1

cart *n* a wheeled usually horse-drawn vehicle used for hauling ⟨a *cart* piled up with hay⟩
synonyms wagon, wain
related words dray, jolt-wagon [*Midland*], oxcart, spring wagon, wagonette; barrow, hand truck, pushcart, tram, truck, wheelbarrow

cart *vb* to support and take from one place to another ⟨*carted* a knapsack filled with books from class to class⟩ — see CARRY 1

cartel *n* a number of businesses or enterprises united for commercial advantage ⟨a *cartel* of oil-producing nations that controls production and influences prices⟩
synonyms combination, combine, syndicate, trust
related words chain, conglomerate, megacorporation; association, guild (*also* gild), organization, partnership, pool, union; big business

cartoon *n* **1** a picture using lines to represent the chief features of an object or scene ⟨a political *cartoon* mocking the state legislature⟩ — see DRAWING
2 a series of drawings that tell a story or part of a story ⟨reading the *cartoons* in the Sunday newspaper⟩ — see COMIC STRIP
3 a poor, insincere, or insulting imitation of something ⟨In this biopic the life of a complex man is reduced to a *cartoon*.⟩ — see MOCKERY 1

carve *vb* to create a three-dimensional representation of (something) using solid material ⟨*carved* a statue out of rare marble⟩ — see SCULPT

cascade *n* a fall of water usually from a great height ⟨The river forms a series of *cascades* as it drops a total of 200 feet in elevation.⟩ — see WATERFALL

¹**case** *n* **1** something that encloses another thing especially to protect it ⟨Those binoculars come with their own *case*.⟩

synonyms armor, capsule, casing, cocoon, cover, covering, housing, hull, husk, jacket, pod, sheath, shell
related words cartridge, cassette (*also* casette); bark; carapace, house, mail, panoply, plate, plating, shield; cuticle, hide, skin; envelope, package, wrapper; backing, coating, coverture, facing
2 a covered rectangular container for storing or transporting things ⟨a handy little cosmetics *case* that matches the rest of her luggage⟩ — see CHEST

²**case** *n* **1** an individual awaiting or under medical care and treatment ⟨Her doctor wishes that all of his *cases* were as cooperative as she is.⟩ — see PATIENT
2 one of a group or collection that shows what the whole is like ⟨This is a perfect *case* of people jumping to the wrong conclusion before all the facts are known.⟩ — see EXAMPLE
3 something that actually exists ⟨This has never been the *case* before.⟩ — see FACT 2
4 a statement given to explain a belief or act ⟨You'll get a chance to make your *case*, but unless you're very convincing, your request will be denied.⟩ — see REASON 1
5 a sudden experiencing of a physical or mental disorder ⟨a young boy suffering from a *case* of bronchitis⟩ — see ATTACK 2
6 something that might happen ⟨It may be the *case* that the cause of the fire will forever remain a mystery.⟩ — see EVENT 2
7 something that requires thought and skill for resolution ⟨That's a tough *case* to solve.⟩ — see PROBLEM 1

cash *n* something (as pieces of stamped metal or printed paper) customarily and legally used as a medium of exchange, a measure of value, or a means of payment ⟨went to the ATM to get more *cash*⟩ — see MONEY

cashier *vb* **1** to let go from office, service, or employment ⟨He was abruptly *cashiered* after money was found missing from the safe.⟩ — see DISMISS 1
2 to get rid of as useless or unwanted ⟨The company is giving away a clutter of computers that have recently been *cashiered* for obsolescence.⟩ — see DISCARD

cash in (on) *vb* to take unfair advantage of ⟨Some observers thought the lawyers were *cashing in on* the tragedy.⟩ — see EXPLOIT 1

casing *n* something that encloses another thing especially to protect it ⟨The egg of this bird has an unusually hard *casing*.⟩ — see ¹CASE 1

cask *n* an enclosed wooden vessel for holding beverages ⟨*casks* of wine that had been in the castle for many years⟩
synonyms barrel, butt, hogshead, keg, pipe, puncheon
related words cistern, tub, vat; can, drum

casket *n* **1** a boxlike container for holding a dead body ⟨bought a beautiful *casket* when her grandmother died⟩ — see COFFIN
2 a covered rectangular container for storing or transporting things ⟨a small *casket* of jewels⟩ — see CHEST

cast *n* **1** a declaration that something will happen in the future ⟨Stock market analysts offered an optimistic *cast* for the coming year.⟩ — see PREDICTION
2 a property that becomes apparent when light falls on an object and by which things that are identical in form can be distinguished ⟨The walls had a slight yellowish *cast*.⟩ — see COLOR 1
3 an instance of looking especially briefly ⟨a mischievous *cast* in his eye when we asked what our destination would be⟩ — see LOOK 2
4 facial appearance regarded as an indication of mood or feeling ⟨His face took on a proud *cast* when we asked how his son was faring.⟩ — see LOOK 1
5 the outward appearance of something as distinguished

from its substance ⟨the lovely *cast* of the baby's features⟩ — see FORM 1

cast *vb* **1** to throw or give off ⟨Spermaceti candles, made from whale oil, are known to *cast* an exceptionally bright light.⟩ — see EMIT 1
2 to point or turn (something) toward a target or goal ⟨*cast* her eyes skyward for signs of the rescue plane⟩ — see AIM 1
3 to put (something) into proper and usually carefully worked out written form ⟨Please *cast* the letter of complaint as politely as possible.⟩ — see COMPOSE 1
4 to send through the air especially with a quick forward motion of the arm ⟨*cast* a rock into the stream⟩ — see THROW 1

cast (off) *vb* to get rid of as useless or unwanted ⟨She decided to *cast off* many of her possessions and live more simply.⟩ — see DISCARD

cast (up) *vb* to combine (numbers) into a single sum ⟨had worked as a clerk in a countinghouse, mainly *casting up* long columns of figures every day⟩ — see ADD 2

cast about (for) *vb* to go in search of ⟨*cast about for* an answer to the question⟩ — see SEEK 1

cast around (for) *vb* to go in search of ⟨*cast around for* a last minute replacement for the lead actor in the movie⟩ — see SEEK 1

castaway *n* one who is cast out or rejected by society ⟨One theory is that Easter Island was first settled by *castaways* from Polynesia.⟩ — see OUTCAST

caste *n* one of the segments of society into which people are grouped ⟨a member of the upper *caste*⟩ — see CLASS 1

castigate *vb* **1** to criticize (someone) severely or angrily especially for personal failings ⟨*castigated* him for his constant tardiness⟩ — see SCOLD
2 to criticize harshly and usually publicly ⟨a newspaper editorial *castigating* the city council for approving the project in the first place⟩ — see ATTACK 2
3 to inflict a penalty on for a fault or crime ⟨a judge who believes in *castigating* criminals to the full extent of the law⟩ — see PUNISH

castigating *adj* inflicting, involving, or serving as punishment ⟨a *castigating* task that succeeds in doing nothing more than making the lives of the inmates miserable⟩ — see PUNITIVE

castigation *n* suffering, loss, or hardship imposed in response to a crime or offense ⟨The loss of his father's trust was the harshest *castigation* that the boy could have possibly received for having told the lie.⟩ — see PUNISHMENT

castigator *n* **1** a person given to harsh judgments and to finding faults ⟨Even Broadway's most famously caustic *castigator* liked the play.⟩ — see CRITIC 1
2 one who inflicts punishment in return for an injury or offense ⟨The principal seems to enjoy his role as the tireless *castigator* of classroom pranksters.⟩ — see NEMESIS 1

castle *n* **1** a structure or place from which one can resist attack ⟨The implacable attackers placed the *castle* under a prolonged siege.⟩ — see FORT
2 a large impressive residence ⟨The mining tycoon built a magnificent *castle* on the hill overlooking the town.⟩ — see MANSION

castoff *n* one who is cast out or rejected by society ⟨a *castoff* who later became a famous poet⟩ — see OUTCAST

casual *adj* **1** not designed to be worn only on special occasions ⟨a restaurant where people in *casual* clothes are always welcome⟩
synonyms everyday, informal, workaday
related words relaxed, sporty; dressed down; shabby, sloppy, slovenly, unkempt

near antonyms best; dressed up; chic, elegant, fashionable, smart, stylish; neat, tidy, trim; semiformal
antonyms dressy, formal, noncasual
2 happening by chance ⟨a *casual* meeting with the next-door neighbors on a beach in Hawaii⟩ — see ACCIDENTAL 1
3 having or showing a lack of interest or concern ⟨only a *casual* examination of the bicycle before buying it⟩ — see INDIFFERENT 1
4 lacking in steadiness or regularity of occurrence ⟨a *casual* attendance at their son's hockey games⟩ — see FITFUL

casualness *n* lack of interest or concern ⟨Her *casualness* distressed everyone who took the issue seriously.⟩ — see INDIFFERENCE

casualty *n* **1** a person or thing harmed, lost, or destroyed ⟨The old tree was a *casualty* of the storm.⟩
synonyms fatality, loss, prey, victim
related words loser, underdog; martyr, sacrifice; collateral damage; murderee
near antonyms gainer, victor, victim; harmer, injurer; assassin, killer, murderer
2 a chance and usually sudden event bringing loss or injury ⟨*casualties* at sea that sometimes resulted in great losses of men or even of entire ships⟩ — see ACCIDENT 1

cat *n* a small domestic animal known for catching mice ⟨The family's *cat* did an exemplary job of keeping the house and yard free of all rodents.⟩
synonyms feline, house cat, kitty, puss, pussy
related words mouser; kit, kitten; alley cat, tabby; gib, tomcat

cataclysm *n* **1** a great flow of water or of something that overwhelms ⟨an ancient *cataclysm* that may have been the basis for the Flood described in the Bible⟩ — see FLOOD
2 a sudden violent event that brings about great loss or destruction ⟨The earthquake that struck Lisbon in 1755, killing 30,000 people, was one of the greatest *cataclysms* ever recorded.⟩ — see DISASTER 1
3 a violent disturbance (as of the political or social order) ⟨a social *cataclysm* that gave rise to a new world order⟩ — see CONVULSION

cataclysmal *or* **cataclysmic** *adj* **1** bringing about ruin or misfortune ⟨a *cataclysmal* decision to plunge the nation into war⟩ — see FATAL 1
2 causing or tending to cause destruction ⟨a *cataclysmal* landslide that virtually wiped out the village⟩ — see DESTRUCTIVE 1
3 marked by sudden or violent disturbance ⟨The French Revolution was one of the great *cataclysmal* events in modern history.⟩ — see CONVULSIVE 1

catacomb *n, usually* **catacombs** *pl* an underground burial chamber ⟨explored the *catacombs* looking for evidence about burial customs of that ancient society⟩ — see CRYPT

catalog *or* **catalogue** *n* a record of a series of items (as names or titles) usually arranged according to some system ⟨a *catalog* of music album titles⟩ — see ¹LIST 1

catalog *or* **catalogue** *vb* to put (someone or something) on a list ⟨*cataloged* the latest additions to the collection⟩ — see ¹LIST 2

catamount *n* a large tawny cat of the wild ⟨found the footprints of a *catamount* on the mountain trail⟩ — see COUGAR

catapult *vb* to send through the air especially with a quick forward motion of the arm ⟨*catapulted* a pumpkin into the next yard⟩ — see THROW 1

cataract *n* **1** a fall of water usually from a great height ⟨The roaring *cataract* is one of the park's most majestic sights.⟩ — see WATERFALL

2 a great flow of water or of something that overwhelms ⟨In spring the melting snows usually produce a *cataract* that inundates the valley.⟩ — see FLOOD

catastrophe *n* **1** a sudden violent event that brings about great loss or destruction ⟨More than one natural *catastrophe* has threatened to destroy their farm over the years.⟩ — see DISASTER 1

2 something that has failed ⟨The movie was a *catastrophe*, nearly bankrupting the studio that produced it.⟩ — see FAILURE 3

catastrophic *adj* bringing about ruin or misfortune ⟨A *catastrophic* tornado destroyed the town's library.⟩ — see FATAL 1

catcall *n* a vocal sound made to express scorn or disapproval ⟨The band's sloppy playing produced only *catcalls* from the crowd.⟩
synonyms boo, hiss, hoot, jeer, raspberry, snort
related words smirk, sneer, snicker, snigger; gibe (*or* jibe), put-down, taunt; whistle
near antonyms applause, clapping
antonyms cheer

catch *n* **1** a danger or difficulty that is hidden or not easily recognized ⟨The *catch* is that you have to come up with the money by tomorrow.⟩ — see PITFALL 1

2 someone or something unusually desirable ⟨Everyone thought the captain of the football team was a real *catch*.⟩ — see PRIZE 1

3 the total amount collected or obtained especially at one time ⟨The total *catch* for our day at the creek was six fish and a crab.⟩ — see HAUL 1

catch *vb* **1** to take physical control or possession of (something) suddenly or forcibly ⟨We tried to *catch* the kitten before she could sneak out the door.⟩
synonyms bag, capture, collar, cop [*slang*], corral, get, grab, grapple, hook, land, nab, nail, net, rap, seize, snag, snap (up), snare, snatch, trap
related words glove, halter, lasso, rope; apprehend, arrest, detain; bay, corner; clasp, clutch, fasten (on), fist, grasp, grip, hold, latch (on *or* onto), secure; rend, wrest; enmesh (*also* immesh), ensnare, entangle, entrap, mesh; abduct, kidnap, spirit (away *or* off)
phrases take hold (of)
near antonyms discharge, free, liberate, release; drop, loosen, unhand
antonyms miss

2 to become affected with (a disease or disorder) ⟨You'll *catch* the flu for sure if you don't get a shot.⟩ — see CONTRACT 1

3 to bring (something) to a standstill ⟨I *caught* myself just as I was about to step into the freshly poured concrete.⟩ — see ¹HALT 1

4 to put securely in place or in a desired position ⟨*caught* back her hair with a barrette⟩ — see FASTEN 2

5 to have a clear idea of ⟨I didn't *catch* the point you were making about our nation's foreign policy.⟩ — see COMPREHEND 1

6 to cause to believe what is untrue ⟨A number of media outlets were *caught* by the woman's hard-luck story.⟩ — see DECEIVE

7 to come upon face-to-face or as if face-to-face ⟨I'll *catch* you at the library tomorrow.⟩ — see MEET 1

8 to make note of (something) through the use of one's eyes ⟨I looked out the window just in time to *catch* the neighbor's dog digging up my flower bed.⟩ — see SEE 1

9 to move fast enough to get even with ⟨Despite the suspect's considerable lead, the fleet-footed police officer was able to *catch* him and make an arrest.⟩ — see OVERTAKE

catching *adj* **1** capable of being passed by physical contact from one person to another ⟨A cold is often *catching* before the symptoms even begin.⟩ — see CONTAGIOUS 1

2 exciting a similar feeling or reaction in others ⟨a *catching* smile that instantly puts patients at ease⟩ — see CONTAGIOUS 2

catch on (to) *vb* **1** to come to an awareness of ⟨She *caught on to* the fact that they were planning a surprise party.⟩ — see DISCOVER 1

2 to have a clear idea of ⟨He finally *caught on to* the concept of phototaxis.⟩ — see COMPREHEND 1

catch up (with) *vb* to move fast enough to get even with ⟨I walked faster to *catch up with* my friends.⟩ — see OVERTAKE

catchy *adj* **1** likely to attract attention ⟨will need a *catchy* slogan to sell the new product, which is actually pretty boring⟩ — see NOTICEABLE

2 requiring exceptional skill or caution in performance or handling ⟨Professor Hartman's exams always include at least one *catchy* question.⟩ — see TRICKY 1

3 lacking in steadiness or regularity of occurrence ⟨She was so winded that her breathing came in *catchy* gasps.⟩ — see FITFUL

categorical *also* **categoric** *adj* having no exceptions or restrictions ⟨a *categorical* denial of the rumors⟩ — see ABSOLUTE 2

categorize *vb* to arrange or assign according to type ⟨*categorized* the questions by topic⟩ — see CLASSIFY 1

category *n* one of the units into which a whole is divided on the basis of a common characteristic ⟨Divide the essays into *categories* based on difficulty of comprehension.⟩ — see CLASS 2

cater *vb* to provide food or meals for ⟨A local firm will *cater* the awards banquet for high school athletes of the year.⟩ — see FEED 1

cater (to) *vb* to give in to (a desire) ⟨The gooey dessert *catered to* the children's sweet tooth.⟩ — see INDULGE 1

catnap *n* a short sleep ⟨A *catnap* left me refreshed enough to face the rest of the day.⟩ — see ¹NAP

catnap *vb* **1** to be in a state of sleep ⟨The children are *catnapping*, so please be quiet.⟩ — see SLEEP 1

2 to sleep lightly or briefly ⟨*catnapped* for 10 minutes and then went back to work⟩ — see NAP 1

catnapping *n* a natural periodic loss of consciousness during which the body restores itself ⟨indulged in some quick *catnapping* between appointments with patients⟩ — see SLEEP 1

cattily *adv* in a mean or spiteful manner ⟨commented *cattily* that the woman onstage was wearing an ugly dress⟩ — see NASTILY

cattiness *n* **1** biting sharpness of feeling or expression ⟨The *cattiness* of the commentary for the televised awards was neither nice nor necessary.⟩ — see ACRIMONY 1

2 the desire to cause pain for the satisfaction of doing harm ⟨There's no reason for saying such hurtful things except sheer *cattiness*.⟩ — see MALICE

catty *adj* having or showing a desire to cause someone pain or suffering for the sheer enjoyment of it ⟨a *catty* remark that served its only purpose: to make someone cry⟩ — see HATEFUL

caught *adj* taken and held prisoner ⟨After seeing how the *caught* soldiers had been treated, we resolved never to be taken alive.⟩ — see CAPTIVE

cause *n* **1** someone or something responsible for a result ⟨the much-debated *causes* of the American Civil War⟩
synonyms antecedent, occasion, reason
related words consideration, determinant, factor; alpha and omega, be-all and end-all; impetus, incentive, inspiration, instigation, stimulus; mother, origin, root, source, spring

near antonyms ramification; denouement (*also* dénouement), repercussion; conclusion, end; by-product, side effect (*also* side reaction)
antonyms aftereffect, aftermath, consequence, corollary, development, effect, fate, fruit, issue, outcome, outgrowth, product, result, resultant, sequel, sequence, upshot
2 a series of activities undertaken to achieve a goal ⟨joined the freedom fighters' *cause* as a young man⟩ — see CAMPAIGN
cause *vb* to be the cause of (a situation, action, or state of mind) ⟨The ice storm *caused* a massive power outage.⟩ — see EFFECT
caustic *adj* marked by the use of wit that is intended to cause hurt feelings ⟨*caustic* movie reviews that serve mainly to show how clever the reviewer is⟩ — see SARCASTIC
caution *n* **1** a close attentiveness to avoiding danger ⟨the extreme *caution* with which the zookeeper handled the snake⟩
synonyms alertness, care, carefulness, cautiousness, chariness, circumspection, heedfulness, prudence, wariness
related words attentiveness, observance, vigilance, watchfulness; foresight, foresightedness, providence; calculation, canniness, deliberateness, deliberation, shrewdness; precaution, safeguard
near antonyms abruptness, hastiness, impetuousness, precipitousness, rashness, suddenness; inconsiderateness, inconsideration, thoughtlessness
antonyms brashness, carelessness, heedlessness, incautiousness, recklessness, unwariness
2 something extraordinary or surprising ⟨How she manages to walk all six dogs at a time is a *caution*.⟩ — see WONDER 1
3 something that tells of approaching danger or risk ⟨This is just a *caution* that the following paragraph practically gives away the entire plot of the movie.⟩ — see WARNING 2
4 the act or an instance of telling beforehand of danger or risk ⟨We heeded the police officer's *caution* about the road ahead.⟩ — see WARNING 1
caution *vb* to give notice to beforehand especially of danger or risk ⟨The doctor *cautioned* that I should still be careful using my sprained wrist for the next several days.⟩ — see WARN
cautionary *adj* serving as or offering a warning ⟨The story of King Midas is a *cautionary* tale about the perils of wishing for something—you just might get it.⟩
synonyms admonishing, admonitory, cautioning, exemplary, premonitory, warning
related words didactic, moralistic, moralizing; advisory, counseling (*or* counselling); punishing, punitive
cautioning *adj* serving as or offering a warning ⟨a *cautioning* story about how envy can destroy a friendship⟩ — see CAUTIONARY
cautious *adj* having or showing a close attentiveness to avoiding danger or trouble ⟨a *cautious* approach to everyday living⟩ — see CAREFUL 1
cautiousness *n* a close attentiveness to avoiding danger ⟨The *cautiousness* of drivers on the icy roadways was largely responsible for the accident-free day.⟩ — see CAUTION 1
cavalcade *n* **1** a group of vehicles traveling together or under one management ⟨the longest *cavalcade* of floats in the history of the parade⟩ — see FLEET
2 a staged presentation often with music that consists of a procession of narrated or enacted scenes ⟨a *cavalcade* presenting major events in the town's history⟩ — see PAGEANT

cavalier *adj* having a feeling of superiority that shows itself in an overbearing attitude ⟨a *cavalier* and pompous boss, indifferent to the feelings of her subordinates⟩ — see ARROGANT
cavalier *n* an honorable and courteous man ⟨a novel about dashing *cavaliers* and gracious ladies⟩
synonyms gentleman
related words Galahad, knight, prince; beau, Beau Brummell, blade, blood, buck, dandy, dude, fop, gallant; captivator, charmer, ladies' man (*also* lady's man), smoothy (*or* smoothie); aristocrat, patrician, swell
cave *n* a naturally formed underground chamber with an opening to the surface ⟨Kentucky's Mammoth *Cave* is actually a series of large chambers on five levels.⟩
synonyms cavern, grot, grotto
related words abyss, chasm, gulf, hollow; crawlway, gallery, subway, tunnel; excavation, mine, pit, shaft, well; bunker, dugout, foxhole; burrow, covert, den, hole, lair, lodge, shelter
cave (in) *vb* **1** to fall down or in as a result of physical pressure ⟨The wall *caved in* when a tree fell on it.⟩ — see COLLAPSE 1
2 to give up and cease resistance (as to a liking, temptation, or habit) ⟨I *caved in* to my bibliomania and bought two more books last week.⟩ — see YIELD 1
cavern *n* a naturally formed underground chamber with an opening to the surface ⟨a *cavern* with beautiful stalactites⟩ — see CAVE
cavil *vb* to make often peevish criticisms or objections about matters that are minor, unimportant, or irrelevant ⟨*caviled* for hours about a single sentence⟩ — see QUIBBLE 1
caviler *or* **caviller** *n* a person given to harsh judgments and to finding faults ⟨the chronic *cavilers* who are going to complain no matter what the mayor does⟩ — see CRITIC 1
caviling *or* **cavilling** *adj* given to making or expressing unfavorable judgments about things ⟨a *caviling* theater critic who has yet to see a play she likes⟩ — see CRITICAL 1
cavity *n* a sunken area forming a separate space ⟨a *cavity* in the lawn where a tree stump had been removed⟩ — see HOLE 2
cavort *vb* to play and run about happily ⟨children *cavorting* on the first sunny day of spring⟩ — see FROLIC 1
cease *n* the stopping of a process or activity ⟨worked without *cease* for the betterment of humanity⟩ — see END 1
cease *vb* **1** to come to an end ⟨The rain finally *ceased*, and we were able to continue the baseball game.⟩
synonyms break off, break up, close, conclude, determine, die, discontinue, elapse, end, expire, finish, go, halt, lapse, leave off, let up, pass, quit, stop, terminate, wind up
related words desist (from), lay off (of), refrain (from); knock off; break down, conk (out), cut out, stall; pause, stay, suspend; abate, peter (out)
phrases bite the dust
near antonyms draw out, extend, prolong, protract
antonyms continue, hang on, persist
2 to bring (as an action or operation) to an immediate end ⟨*Cease* chattering and get down to work, please!⟩ — see STOP 1
cease–fire *n* a temporary stopping of fighting ⟨The two armies declared a *cease-fire* for the holiday.⟩ — see TRUCE
ceaseless *adj* **1** going on and on without any interruptions ⟨There has been *ceaseless* rain for three days.⟩ — see CONTINUOUS

2 lasting forever ⟨promised her *ceaseless* happiness if she would only marry him⟩ — see EVERLASTING 1

ceaselessness *n* uninterrupted or lasting existence ⟨The *ceaselessness* of the noise was as irritating as its loudness.⟩ — see CONTINUATION

cede *vb* **1** to give (something) over to the control or possession of another usually under duress ⟨She reluctantly *ceded* her position as leader.⟩ — see SURRENDER 1

2 to give over the legal possession or ownership of ⟨Spain *ceded* Puerto Rico to the United States as part of the settlement of the Spanish-American War.⟩ — see TRANSFER 1

3 to give up (as a position of authority) formally ⟨The President officially *cedes* his position on the January 20th immediately following the presidential election.⟩ — see ABDICATE

ceiling *n* **1** a real or imaginary point beyond which a person or thing cannot go ⟨There's a *ceiling* on prices.⟩ — see LIMIT 1

2 a raised covering over something for decoration or protection ⟨We sat around the campfire under a *ceiling* of stars.⟩ — see CANOPY

celebrant *n* one who engages in merrymaking especially in honor of a special occasion ⟨All of the *celebrants* at the birthday party received a favor to take home.⟩

synonyms celebrator, merrymaker, reveler (*or* reveller), roisterer

related words bacchanal, binger, carouser, wassailer; cutup, skylarker; noisemaker

antonyms killjoy, party pooper

celebrate *vb* **1** to proclaim the glory of ⟨a personal essay that *celebrates* the single life⟩ — see PRAISE 1

2 to mark with an appropriate practice, rite, or ceremony ⟨a mixed family that *celebrates* both the Christian and Jewish religious holidays⟩ — see KEEP 1

celebrated *adj* widely known ⟨a *celebrated* author making an appearance on a talk show⟩ — see FAMOUS 1

celebration *n* a time or program of special events and entertainment in honor of something ⟨a *celebration* of the company's 100th anniversary⟩ — see FESTIVAL

celebrator *n* one who engages in merrymaking especially in honor of a special occasion ⟨Some rowdy Super Bowl *celebrators* had to be given friendly warnings by the police.⟩ — see CELEBRANT

celebrity *n* **1** a person who is widely known and usually much talked about ⟨*Celebrities* from sports and entertainment attended the opening ceremonies of the Olympic Games.⟩

synonyms figure, icon (*also* ikon), light, luminary, name, notable, notoriety, personage, personality, somebody, standout, star, superstar, VIP

related words favorite, heartthrob, hero; demigod, dignitary, eminence, immortal, monument, pillar, worthy; baron, big shot, bigwig, kahuna, magnate, mogul, nabob, panjandrum

near antonyms lightweight, mediocrity

antonyms nobody, noncelebrity

2 the fact or state of being known to the public ⟨an actor who reportedly feels very uncomfortable with his *celebrity*⟩ — see FAME 1

celerity *n* a high rate of movement or performance ⟨a journalist who writes his well-crafted stories with remarkable *celerity*⟩ — see SPEED 1

celestial *adj* of, relating to, or suggesting heaven ⟨Movie scenes depicting life after death are usually accompanied by *celestial* music.⟩

synonyms ethereal, heavenly, supernal

related words supernatural, unearthly, unworldly; angelic (*or* angelical), beatific, blissful; Olympian, paradisiacal (*or* paradisiac), utopian; cosmic (*also* cosmical), stellar

near antonyms earthly, mundane, terrestrial, worldly; anti-utopian, dystopian

antonyms hellish

cell *n* **1** an area within a building that has been set apart from surrounding space by a wall ⟨a jail *cell*⟩ — see ROOM 2

2 one of the parts into which an enclosed space is divided ⟨*cells* in a honeycomb⟩ — see COMPARTMENT

3 a local unit of an organization ⟨His mission was to locate and infiltrate a terrorist *cell*.⟩ — see CHAPTER 1

cellar *n* a room or set of rooms below the surface of the ground ⟨An amazing array of interesting things were found in the *cellar* of the old house.⟩

synonyms basement

related words cellarage; bunker, crawlway, foundation, hold, vault; cyclone cellar, storm cellar

cement *n* **1** a substance used to stick things together ⟨What kind of *cement* works best on glass and pottery?⟩ — see GLUE

2 a uniting or binding force or influence ⟨She is the *cement* that holds that often quarrelsome group together.⟩ — see BOND 2

cemetery *n* a piece of land used for burying the dead ⟨Many of the soldiers who died in the battle are buried in a *cemetery* nearby.⟩

synonyms graveyard, potter's field

related words catacombs, churchyard; crypt, grave, mausoleum, sepulture, tomb, vault

censor *vb* to remove objectionable parts from ⟨The producers were told that they would have to *censor* their movie if they wanted a PG rating.⟩

synonyms clean (up), expurgate

related words cleanse, purge, purify; abbreviate, edit, shorten; bleep, blip, cut (out), delete, excise, expunge, gut, x (out); black out, repress, silence, suppress; censure, condemn, denounce; examine, review, screen, scrutinize

near antonyms approve, authorize, sanction

censurable *adj* **1** deserving reproach or blame ⟨*censurable* conduct that should get that student expelled⟩ — see BLAMEWORTHY

2 provoking or likely to provoke protest ⟨The *censurable* language on the poster resulted in it being taken down.⟩ — see OBJECTIONABLE

censure *n* an often public or formal expression of disapproval ⟨a rare *censure* of a senator by the full United States Senate for misconduct⟩

synonyms condemnation, denunciation, excoriation, rebuke, reprimand, reproach, reproof, stricture

related words admonishment, admonition, castigation, chastisement, damnation, punishment, remonstrance; business, devil, dressing-down, lash, lecture, lesson, rap, scolding, talking-to, tongue-lashing; belittlement, criticism, deprecation, depreciation, disparagement, pan

near antonyms acclamation, honor, tribute; encomium, eulogy, panegyric, plaudit(s), praise; approval, blessing, sanction

antonyms citation, commendation, endorsement (*also* indorsement)

censure *vb* **1** to express public or formal disapproval of ⟨a vote to *censure* the President for conduct that was unbecoming to his office⟩

synonyms condemn, denounce, rebuke, reprimand, reproach, reprove

related words admonish, chastise; castigate, punish; bawl out, berate, chew out, cut up, dress down, flay, gibbet, jaw, keelhaul, lambaste (*or* lambast), lecture, rail (at *or* against), rate, scold, score, tell off, upbraid; belittle, criticize, deprecate, depreciate, disparage

phrases bring to account, call to account

near antonyms acclaim, applause, hail, honor; eulogize, laud, praise; approve, bless, sanction

antonyms cite, commend, endorse (*also* indorse)

2 to declare to be morally wrong or evil ⟨Our society generally *censures* the taking of another person's life.⟩ — see CONDEMN 1

3 to express one's unfavorable opinion of the worth or quality of ⟨Critics have striven to outdo each other in *censuring* that pop novelist's latest work.⟩ — see CRITICIZE

censurer *n* a person given to harsh judgments and to finding faults ⟨There's more malicious fun in being a *censurer* than in being a celebrator, so many theater critics are the latter.⟩ — see CRITIC 1

center *n* **1** a thing or place that is of greatest importance to an activity or interest ⟨a stretch of coastline that has long been the area's *center* of tourism⟩

synonyms base, capital, central, core, cynosure, eye, focus, ground zero, heart, hub, locus, mecca, nucleus, seat

related words headquarters; happy hunting ground, hive, hot spot, playground, playland; nub, pith; deep, thick; essence, quintessence, soul; attraction, lodestone (*also* loadstone), magnet

phrases where it's at

2 an area or point that is an equal distance from all points along an edge or outer surface ⟨the *center* of the earth⟩

synonyms core, middle, midpoint, midst

related words inside, interior

antonyms perimeter, periphery

center *vb* **1** to bring (something) to a central point or under a single control ⟨*centered* administrative duties under the command of a single person⟩ — see CENTRALIZE

2 to fix (as one's attention) steadily toward a central objective ⟨The students *centered* their attention on final exams.⟩ — see CONCENTRATE 2

central *adj* **1** coming before all others in importance ⟨the *central* theme of the book⟩ — see FOREMOST 1

2 occupying a position equally distant from the ends or extremes ⟨They will hold the conference in the *central* part of the country in order to encourage delegates from both coasts.⟩ — see MIDDLE 1

3 avoiding major social change or extreme political ideas ⟨The candidate appealed to the vast *central* core of the electorate.⟩ — see MODERATE 2

central *n* a thing or place that is of greatest importance to an activity or interest ⟨a health club that has become dating *central* for singles in the area⟩ — see CENTER 1

centralize *vb* to bring (something) to a central point or under a single control ⟨The company decided to *centralize* all of its operations at its Ohio plant.⟩

synonyms center, compact, concentrate, consolidate, unify, unite

related words coordinate, harmonize, integrate, orchestrate; blend, coalesce, combine, fuse, incorporate, merge, reduce; conjoin, join, link; assemble, collect, colligate, gather; reunify, reunite

near antonyms segregate, separate

antonyms decentralize, deconcentrate, spread (out)

cerebral *adj* **1** much given to learning and thinking ⟨a very *cerebral* jurist who has given much thought to what makes our nation's constitution work⟩ — see INTELLECTUAL 1

2 of or relating to the mind ⟨an intelligent young man given to *cerebral* pursuits⟩ — see MENTAL

cerebrum *n* the part of a person that feels, thinks, perceives, wills, and especially reasons ⟨You'll need the patience of a saint and the *cerebrum* of a rocket scientist to figure out the solution to this brainteaser.⟩ — see MIND 1

ceremonial *adj* following or agreeing with established form, custom, or rules ⟨a *ceremonial* presentation of the ambassador's credentials⟩ — see FORMAL 1

ceremonial *n* an oft-repeated action or series of actions performed in accordance with tradition or a set of rules ⟨The funeral of a pope is usually marked by rich pageantry and elaborate *ceremonials*.⟩ — see RITE

ceremonious *adj* **1** marked by or showing careful attention to set forms and details ⟨A century ago everyday life was much more *ceremonious* than today.⟩

synonyms correct, decorous, formal, proper, punctilious, starchy, stiff, stilted

related words sober, solemn, stately; chivalrous, courtly, gallant; genteel, polished, refined; civil, courteous, polite, red-carpet

near antonyms improper, indecorous, unmannerly; discourteous, impolite, rude

antonyms casual, easygoing, informal, laid-back, unceremonious

2 following or agreeing with established form, custom, or rules ⟨the *ceremonious* regalia of the Queen's Guard, the guards of the royal residences in the United Kingdom⟩ — see FORMAL 1

ceremony *n* an oft-repeated action or series of actions performed in accordance with tradition or a set of rules ⟨a beautiful, old-fashioned wedding *ceremony*⟩ — see RITE

certain *adj* **1** known but not named ⟨A *certain* person told me that today is your birthday.⟩

synonyms anonymous, given, one, some, unidentified, unnamed, unspecified

related words particular, specific

near antonyms known, named, specified

2 having or showing a mind free from doubt ⟨I'm *certain* that they'll arrive on time.⟩

synonyms assured, clear, cocksure, confident, doubtless, implicit, positive, sanguine, sure

related words self-assured, self-conceited, self-confident; decisive, resolute, unfaltering, unhesitating, unquestioning, unwavering

near antonyms hesitant, indecisive, vacillating, wavering; diffident, unassuming

antonyms doubtful, dubious, uncertain, unsure

3 having been established and usually not subject to change ⟨A *certain* percentage of the profits will go to charity.⟩ — see FIXED 1

4 impossible to avoid or evade ⟨As he got older, the athlete began to feel the *certain* effects of the aging process on his body.⟩ — see INEVITABLE

5 not likely to fail ⟨Chicken soup is grandma's *certain* cure for pretty much whatever ails you.⟩ — see INFALLIBLE 2

6 not capable of being challenged or proved wrong ⟨Up to this point there's been no *certain* evidence that a crime has been committed.⟩ — see IRREFUTABLE

certainly *adv* without any question ⟨*Certainly*, you can come to the party!⟩ — see INDEED 1

certainty *n* a state of mind in which one is free from doubt ⟨I have full *certainty* that I'll pass the test.⟩ — see CONFIDENCE 2

certificate *n* a written or printed paper giving information about or proof of something ⟨A *certificate* will be awarded to each person who completes the course in lifesaving.⟩

synonyms document, instrument

related words credentials; diploma, parchment; record; warrant, writ; warranty; coupon

certify *vb* **1** to declare (something) to be true or genuine ⟨Experts *certified* the letter as indeed having been written by Abraham Lincoln.⟩

synonyms attest, authenticate, avouch, testify (to), vouch (for), witness

related words guarantee, warrant; affirm, assert, aver, avow, profess, vow

2 to give official or legal power to ⟨*certified* her as a teacher⟩ — see AUTHORIZE 1

3 to give evidence or testimony to the truth or factualness of ⟨Please bring in a doctor's note to *certify* that you were really sick.⟩ — see CONFIRM 1

certitude *n* a state of mind in which one is free from doubt ⟨Believes with *certitude* that he is the best candidate for the job.⟩ — see CONFIDENCE 2

cessation *n* the stopping of a process or activity ⟨The *cessation* of the snowstorm was a relief.⟩ — see END 1

chafe *vb* **1** to make sore by continued rubbing ⟨ill-fitting boots that had badly *chafed* my heels⟩

synonyms abrade, excoriate, fret, gall, irritate

related words graze, scrape, scratch; burn, inflame (*also* enflame); flay, peel, skin

2 to damage or diminish by continued friction ⟨Constant stepping on a rope will gradually *chafe* it, rendering it unsafe for rock climbing.⟩ — see ABRADE 1

3 to disturb the peace of mind of (someone) especially by repeated disagreeable acts ⟨Nothing *chafes* us so much as those telemarketers who call during the dinner hour.⟩ — see IRRITATE 1

¹chaff *n* discarded or useless material ⟨There's a lot of *chaff* in this book, and the reader should be on the alert for it.⟩ — see GARBAGE

²chaff *n* good-natured teasing or exchanging of clever remarks ⟨I got no end of *chaff* about my accent when I was in the military.⟩ — see BANTER

chaff *vb* **1** to make fun of in a good-natured way ⟨*chaffed* her about the brightly colored shirt she had received as a gift⟩ — see TEASE 1

2 to make jokes ⟨a coworker who likes to *chaff* to relieve the tension⟩ — see JOKE 1

chaffing *adj* marked by or expressive of mild or good-natured teasing ⟨a *chaffing* tone to Dad's discussion of my new haircut⟩ — see QUIZZICAL

chafing *adj* causing annoyance ⟨learned to ignore those *chafing* comments⟩ — see ANNOYING

chain *n* **1** a series of things linked together ⟨the *chain* of events that led the American colonies to seek independence from Great Britain⟩

synonyms concatenation, progression, sequence, string, train

related words chain reaction; belt, circle, cycle, vicious circle (*also* vicious cycle); continuum, gamut, gauntlet (*also* gantlet), scale, spectrum; flow, river, stream; file, line, queue, range, row, succession

2 something that makes movement or progress difficult ⟨This community will grow and prosper only after it has thrown off the *chains* of ignorance and prejudice.⟩ — see ENCUMBRANCE

3 something that physically prevents free movement ⟨*chains* on the prisoner's ankles⟩ — see BOND 1

chain *vb* **1** to confine or restrain with or as if with chains ⟨*chaining* up the dog in the backyard⟩ — see BIND 1

2 to put or bring together so as to form a new and longer whole ⟨The prosecutor meticulously and brilliantly *chained* all the evidence together in his closing argument.⟩ — see CONNECT 1

chair *n* **1** a person in charge of a meeting ⟨All questions and comments should be directed to the *chair*.⟩

synonyms chairman, chairperson, moderator, president, speaker

related words chairwoman; cochair, cochairman, cochairperson, cochairwoman, copresident

2 the place of leadership or command ⟨the *chair* of the English department at the university⟩ — see HEAD 2

chairman *n* a person in charge of a meeting ⟨The *chairman* called the meeting to order.⟩ — see CHAIR 1

chairperson *n* a person in charge of a meeting ⟨The *chairperson* will determine the order in which people will speak.⟩ — see CHAIR 1

chalet *n* an often small house for recreational or seasonal use ⟨a mountain *chalet* for weekend getaways⟩ — see COTTAGE

challenge *n* **1** a feeling or declaration of disapproval or dissent ⟨There were no serious *challenges* to the legislative bill, so it passed easily.⟩ — see OBJECTION

2 something that requires thought and skill for resolution ⟨the many *challenges* facing developing countries in the 21st century⟩ — see PROBLEM 1

challenge *vb* **1** to demand proof of the truth or rightness of ⟨Don't hesitate to *challenge* any statement that generalizes about people.⟩

synonyms contest, dispute, impeach, query, question

related words doubt, mistrust; kick (about), object (to), protest; combat, fight, oppose, resist

phrases call in question (*or* call into question)

near antonyms back, defend, support; advocate, champion, promote; abide, endure, stomach, tolerate

antonyms accept, believe, embrace, swallow

2 to invite (someone) to take part in a contest or to perform a feat ⟨I *challenge* you to swim to the other side of the pond.⟩

synonyms dare, defy, stump

related words beard, brave, brazen, breast, confront, face, outbrave

3 to have as a requirement ⟨Having to put up with an overbearing boss *challenges* forbearance.⟩ — see NEED 1

challenged *adj* deprived of the power to perform one or more natural bodily activities ⟨All parts of the sports complex are fully accessible to the physically *challenged*.⟩ — see DISABLED

challenger *n* one who strives for the same thing as another ⟨the third-party *challenger* in the presidential election⟩ — see COMPETITOR

challenging *adj* **1** requiring considerable physical or mental effort ⟨an exceptionally *challenging* brainteaser⟩ — see HARD 2

2 requiring much time, effort, or careful attention ⟨a *challenging* test designed to whittle down the number of contestants⟩ — see DEMANDING 1

chamber *n* **1** an area within a building that has been set apart from surrounding space by a wall ⟨The inner *chamber* is the president's private office.⟩ — see ROOM 2

2 one of the parts into which an enclosed space is divided ⟨If the camera doesn't work, check to see that the battery has been properly installed in its *chamber*.⟩ — see COMPARTMENT

3 a group of persons formally joined together for some common interest ⟨joined the local *chamber* of commerce⟩ — see ASSOCIATION 2

chamber *vb* to provide with living quarters or shelter ⟨*chambered* the lost hikers in the barn until the next morning⟩ — see HOUSE 1

champ *n* the person who comes in first in a competition ⟨the wrestling *champ*⟩ — see CHAMPION 1

champ *vb* to crush or grind with the teeth ⟨kept *champing* a cigar as he barked out orders⟩ — see BITE (ON)

champion *n* **1** the person who comes in first in a competition ⟨the *champion* of the national spelling bee⟩

synonyms champ, victor, winner

related words cochampion, cowinner; placer; finalist, quarterfinalist, semifinalist; medalist (*or* medallist), prizewinner; star, superstar; world-beater

near antonyms loser

2 a person who actively supports or favors a cause 〈She's the biggest *champion* of budget reform in the Congress.〉 — see EXPONENT 1

champion *vb* to promote the interests or cause of 〈He has always *championed* the protection of abused animals.〉 — see SUPPORT 1

championship *n* the position occupied by the one who comes in first in a competition 〈The Yankees have won the *championship* many times.〉 — see CROWN 2

chance *adj* happening by chance 〈a *chance* advantage that I immediately recognized and made full use of〉 — see ACCIDENTAL 1

chance *n* **1** the uncertain course of events 〈Rather than leave everything to *chance*, let's plan how we're going to spend our time in New York City.〉

synonyms accident, circumstance, hazard, luck

related words fortuitousness, fortuity, haphazardry, randomness, uncertainty; happenchance, happenstance; destiny, doom, fate, fortune, lot; danger, peril, risk

near antonyms intent, intention, purpose; design, outline, plan, scheme

2 a favorable combination of circumstances, time, and place 〈This is my one *chance* to succeed.〉 — see OPPORTUNITY

3 a measure of how often an event will occur instead of another 〈The *chance* of being struck by lightning is very low.〉 — see PROBABILITY 2

4 a risky undertaking 〈It's a *chance*, but I think the business will be profitable.〉 — see GAMBLE

chance *vb* **1** to take a chance on 〈I don't think we should *chance* driving in this snowstorm.〉 — see RISK 1

2 to take place 〈There *chanced* to be a beautiful day when we were touring that part of Scotland.〉 — see HAPPEN

chance (upon) *vb* **1** to come upon face-to-face or as if face-to-face 〈I *chanced upon* an old friend as I rounded a corner.〉 — see MEET 1

2 to come upon unexpectedly or by chance 〈I *chanced upon* your mother in the grocery store yesterday.〉 — see HAPPEN (ON *or* UPON)

change *n* **1** the act, process, or result of making different 〈The positive *change* in our students' attitude toward people who are somehow different was a long and gradual process.〉

synonyms alteration, difference, modification, redoing, refashioning, remaking, remodeling, revamping, review, revise, revision, reworking, variation

related words amendment, correction, rectification, reform; conversion, deformation, distortion, metamorphosis, mutation, transfiguration, transformation; oscillation, shift; displacement, replacement, substitution; modulation, regulation, tweak; redesign, redo; aboutface, reversal

antonyms fixation, stabilization

2 the frequent and usually sudden passing from one condition to another 〈There is nothing so constant as *change* itself.〉 — see FLUX 1

3 something (as pieces of stamped metal or printed paper) customarily and legally used as a medium of exchange, a measure of value, or a means of payment 〈She spent quite a chunk of *change* on that car.〉 — see MONEY

change *vb* **1** to make different in some way 〈We've *changed* the look of our living room so it's more fashionable.〉

synonyms alter, make over, modify, recast, redo, refashion, remake, remodel, revamp, revise, rework, vary

related words deform, metamorphose, mutate; regener-ate, revolutionize, transfigure, transform; commute, convert, exchange; rejigger, retool

antonyms fix, freeze, set, stabilize

2 to pass from one form, state, or level to another 〈The weather in New England is constantly *changing*.〉

synonyms fluctuate, mutate, shift, snap, vary

related words metamorphose, morph; better, improve; deteriorate, worsen; turn around; seesaw, teeter, vacillate, waver

antonyms plateau, stabilize

3 to give up (something) and take something else in return 〈Would you mind *changing* your seat so my friends can sit together?〉

synonyms commute, exchange, shift, substitute, swap, switch, trade

related words interchange; displace, replace, supersede; cede, hand over, surrender, yield

changeable *adj* **1** capable of being readily changed 〈an easily *changeable* color scheme for the nursery〉 — see FLEXIBLE 1

2 likely to change frequently, suddenly, or unexpectedly 〈The *changeable* nature of the business is such that you either have too much or too little to do.〉 — see FICKLE 1

changeful *adj* likely to change frequently, suddenly, or unexpectedly 〈a confusingly *changeful* attitude toward where to go on vacation〉 — see FICKLE 1

changeless *adj* not undergoing a change in condition 〈apparently *changeless* mountains〉 — see CONSTANT 1

changelessness *n* the state of continuing without change 〈The *changelessness* of the scenery is actually an illusion.〉 — see CONSTANCY 1

changeover *n* a change in form, appearance, or use 〈the region's *changeover* from an agricultural economy to one based on manufacturing〉 — see CONVERSION 1

changing *adj* not staying constant 〈A *changing* wind made sailing a challenge.〉 — see UNEVEN 2

channel *n* **1** an open man-made passageway for water 〈Water was drained from the swamp through a specially constructed *channel*.〉

synonyms aqueduct, canal, conduit, course, flume, raceway, watercourse, waterway

related words millrace, millstream; floodway, sluice, sluiceway, spillway; swash, tideway, torrent; gutter, trough; river, rivulet, stream

2 a narrow body of water between two land masses 〈the world record for swimming the *channel* between France and Great Britain〉

synonyms narrows, sound, strait

related words arm, bay, gulf, inlet; roads, roadstead; reach, stretch

3 a direct way of passing along information or supplies 〈You need to make arrangements through the proper *channels*.〉 — see PIPELINE

4 a long hollow cylinder for carrying a substance (as a liquid or gas) 〈had to replace the main water *channel*〉 — see PIPE 1

channel *vb* to cause to move to a central point or along a restricted pathway 〈an athletic youth who *channeled* all of his energy into sports〉

synonyms channelize, conduct, direct, funnel, pipe, siphon (*also* syphon)

related words carry, convey, transmit; concentrate, consolidate, focus

channelize *vb* to cause to move to a central point or along a restricted pathway 〈*channelized* all of his resources into winning that state's crucial primary〉 — see CHANNEL

chant *vb* **1** to utter in musical or drawn out tones 〈The frustrated crowd at the rock concert started to *chant*, "We want the show to start!"〉

synonyms intone, sing
related words bellow, belt, roar; chime, chorus
2 to produce musical sounds with the voice ⟨monks *chanting* fervently⟩ — see SING 1

chaos *n* a state in which everything is out of order ⟨The boy's room is in such *chaos* that it looks as though a tornado had struck.⟩
synonyms confusion, disarrangement, disarray, disorder, disorganization, free-for-all, havoc, hell, jumble, mess, messiness, muddle, muss, shambles, tumble, welter
related words anarchy, lawlessness, misrule, riot; knot, snarl, tangle; labyrinth, maze, web; maelstrom, storm; bollix, clutter, litter, mishmash, shuffle; hodgepodge, medley, miscellany, morass, motley
near antonyms method, pattern, plan, system
antonyms order, orderliness

chaotic *adj* lacking in order, neatness, and often cleanliness ⟨a *chaotic* cellar sorely in need of some straightening up⟩ — see MESSY

chaparral *n* a thick patch of shrubbery, small trees, or underbrush ⟨The rabbit darted into the *chaparral*.⟩ — see THICKET

chaperone *or* **chaperon** *vb* to go along with in order to provide assistance, protection, or companionship ⟨Three parents will *chaperone* the students on the school trip.⟩ — see ACCOMPANY 1

chapter *n* **1** a local unit of an organization ⟨Our *chapter* was well represented at the Jaycees' national convention.⟩
synonyms affiliate, branch, cell, council, local
related words arm, division, wing; offshoot, subchapter; lodge, post
2 an individual part of a process, series, or ranking ⟨a fascinating *chapter* in American history⟩ — see DEGREE 1

char *vb* to burn on the surface ⟨I'd like my hamburger *charred*, but not cooked through.⟩ — see SCORCH 1

character *n* **1** a written or printed mark that is meant to convey information to the reader ⟨The pictorial *characters* of the ancient Egyptians had long been a mystery.⟩
synonyms icon (*also* ikon), sign, symbol
related words cipher, letter, numeral; hieroglyph, ideogram, pictogram, pictograph; rune
2 a person of odd or whimsical habits ⟨The junk dealer is certainly a *character*, but he's as honest as they come.⟩ — see ECCENTRIC
3 conduct that conforms to an accepted standard of right and wrong ⟨We need more people of sound *character* in public office.⟩ — see MORALITY 1
4 overall quality as seen or judged by people in general ⟨The general *character* of the business appears to be good.⟩ — see REPUTATION
5 something that sets apart an individual from others of the same kind ⟨one of the distinguishing *characters* of mammals⟩ — see CHARACTERISTIC
6 the set of qualities that make a person different from other people ⟨She regards each of her children as having a distinctive *character* that should be valued for what it is.⟩ — see INDIVIDUALITY 1
7 the set of qualities that makes a person, a group of people, or a thing different from others ⟨The basic *character* of the work requires that an employee be able to work quietly and independently.⟩ — see NATURE 1
8 a member of the human race ⟨You wouldn't believe what kind of *characters* we met on our trip.⟩ — see HUMAN

character *vb* to point out the chief quality or qualities of an individual or group ⟨Formerly *charactered* as "the dark ages," that period of history may not have been quite so benighted as once thought.⟩ — see CHARACTERIZE 1

characteristic *adj* **1** serving to identify as belonging to an individual or group ⟨the *characteristic* taste of licorice⟩
synonyms classic, discriminating, distinct, distinctive, distinguishing, identifying, individual, peculiar, proper, symptomatic, typical
related words idiosyncratic; identifiable, pronounced, unmistakable; general, generic; common, normal, regular, usual; especial, particular, special, specific; archetypal (*also* archetypical), model, paradigmatic
antonyms atypical, nontypical, uncharacteristic, untypical
2 having or showing the qualities associated with the members of a particular group or kind ⟨the *characteristic* loyalty of dogs⟩ — see TYPICAL 1

characteristic *n* something that sets apart an individual from others of the same kind ⟨the ability to speak and other *characteristics* that distinguish human beings from other animals⟩
synonyms attribute, character, criterion, feature, hallmark, mark, marker, note, particularity, peculiarity, point, property, quality, specific, stamp, touch, trait
related words badge, indication, sign; emblem, symbol, token; charm, grace; excellence, merit, virtue; eccentricity, idiosyncrasy, oddity, quirk; individuality, singularity, uniqueness

characterize *vb* **1** to point out the chief quality or qualities of an individual or group ⟨How would you *characterize* the mission of this environmental organization?⟩
synonyms character, define, depict, describe, portray, represent
related words categorize, classify, pigeonhole, type; color, identify, indicate, name, specify; distinguish, individualize, mark, particularize, stamp
2 to be an important feature of ⟨A target-shaped rash *characterizes* Lyme disease.⟩
synonyms distinguish, mark
related words differentiate; customize, individualize, particularize

characterless *adj* lacking strength of will or character ⟨a *characterless* person who never has an opinion of his own⟩ — see WEAK 2

charade *n* a display of emotion or behavior that is insincere or intended to deceive ⟨put on a convincing *charade* to keep her from knowing about the surprise party⟩ — see MASQUERADE

charge *n* **1** a formal claim of criminal wrongdoing against a person ⟨*charges* of burglary that have yet to be proved⟩
synonyms complaint, count, indictment, rap
related words accusation, allegation, plea; crimination; counteraccusation, countercharge; arraignment, impeachment; implication; censure, condemnation, denunciation; incrimination, recrimination
2 a specific task with which a person or group is charged ⟨Your *charge* is to keep everyone else organized and busy.⟩ — see MISSION
3 a statement of what to do that must be obeyed by those concerned ⟨We've received an official *charge* about how to handle the situation.⟩ — see COMMAND 1
4 something one must do because of prior agreement ⟨The first *charge* of our armed forces is to defend this country against enemy attack.⟩ — see OBLIGATION 1
5 the act or action of setting upon with force or violence ⟨the famously disastrous *charge* led by General George Pickett at Gettysburg⟩ — see ATTACK 1
6 the amount of money that is demanded as payment for something ⟨The *charge* for the book will be five dollars.⟩ — see PRICE 1
7 the duty or function of watching or guarding for the sake of proper direction or control ⟨She was given *charge*

of the business during the owner's absence.⟩ — see SU-PERVISION 1

8 a payment made in the course of achieving a result ⟨The *charges* mounted at a dizzying pace as the building project went way over budget.⟩ — see EXPENSE

9 a pleasurably intense stimulation of the feelings ⟨The slopes at this resort aren't particularly challenging and aren't likely to give expert skiers much of a *charge*.⟩ — see THRILL

10 the act or activity of looking after and making decisions about something ⟨He inherited *charge* of the Paris bureau after his supervisor quit.⟩ — see CONDUCT 1

charge *vb* **1** to set or receive as a price ⟨Any shop would *charge* $100 to repair that thing.⟩

synonyms ask, command, demand

related words overcharge, undercharge; bring, fetch, sell (for); discount, mark down, mark up; assess, bill, invoice; price, value

2 to establish or apply as a charge or penalty ⟨*charges* a restocking fee for returned merchandise⟩ — see IMPOSE

3 to give a task, duty, or responsibility to ⟨We're *charging* you with the care of your little sister while we're gone for the evening.⟩ — see ENTRUST 1

4 to issue orders to (someone) by right of authority ⟨*charged* the soldier to keep watch over the prisoner⟩ — see COMMAND 1

5 to make a claim of wrongdoing against ⟨He has not yet been *charged* with any crime.⟩ — see ACCUSE

6 to put into (something) as much as can be held or contained ⟨*charge* a blast furnace with iron ore⟩ — see FILL 1

7 to take sudden, violent action against ⟨plans to *charge* the enemy's fortification at daybreak⟩ — see ATTACK 1

8 to cause a pleasurable stimulation of the feelings of ⟨The players are going into this game still *charged* from their upset victory the week before.⟩ — see THRILL

charged *adj* **1** causing great emotional or mental stimulation ⟨an abstract expressionist who uses a palette of *charged* colors to great effect⟩ — see EXCITING 1

2 having or expressing great depth of feeling ⟨a very *charged* speech that got everyone worked up⟩ — see FERVENT 1

3 serving or likely to arouse a strong reaction ⟨a muralist who creates politically *charged* and often controversial works⟩ — see PROVOCATIVE

chariness *n* a close attentiveness to avoiding danger ⟨He approached the can't-miss investment opportunity with the *chariness* of someone who's been burned before.⟩ — see CAUTION 1

charisma *n* the power of irresistible attraction ⟨a movie star with great *charisma*⟩ — see CHARM 2

charitable *adj* **1** having or showing a concern for the welfare of others ⟨a *charitable* couple who have donated a sizable chunk of their fortune to the local university⟩

synonyms altruistic, beneficent, benevolent, good, humanitarian, philanthropic (*also* philanthropical)

related words selfless, self-sacrificing; bounteous, bountiful, free, freehanded, generous, greathearted, handsome, liberal, magnanimous, munificent, openhanded, openhearted, unselfish, unsparing; compassionate, humane, kind, kindhearted; social-minded

near antonyms self-seeking; cheap, closefisted, niggardly, parsimonious, stingy, tight, tightfisted; pitiless, unfeeling; self-obsessed

antonyms self-centered, selfish

2 giving or sharing in abundance and without hesitation ⟨a *charitable* woman who helped everyone who needed it⟩ — see GENEROUS 1

3 tolerant and kind in the judgment of and expectations

for others ⟨Her best friend, who was inclined towards a more *charitable* interpretation of her actions, let it pass.⟩ — see INDULGENT 1

charity *n* **1** the giving of necessities and especially money to the needy ⟨After amassing a fortune in the computer industry, the brothers devoted themselves to *charity*.⟩

synonyms almsgiving, dole, philanthropy

related words altruism, do-gooding, do-goodism, humanism, humanitarianism; beneficence, benevolence, goodwill; alms, benefaction, contribution, donation; relief, welfare; endowment, fund, grant, subsidy

2 a gift of money or its equivalent to a charity, humanitarian cause, or public institution ⟨donated his mansion and all of its land as a *charity* to the people of his beloved home state⟩ — see CONTRIBUTION

3 kind, gentle, or compassionate treatment especially towards someone who is undeserving of it ⟨Can't you show a little *charity* to a guy who's the first to admit he's not perfect?⟩ — see MERCY 1

4 the capacity for feeling for another's unhappiness or misfortune ⟨His *charity* is such that he's donated much of his fortune.⟩ — see HEART 1

5 kindly concern, interest, or support ⟨Lincoln's famous promise that the period of Reconstruction would be marked by "*charity* for all"⟩ — see GOODWILL 1

charlatan *n* one who makes false claims of identity or expertise ⟨The famed faith healer turned out to be a *charlatan*.⟩ — see IMPOSTOR

charley horse *n* a painful sudden tightening of a muscle ⟨Sam had to stop and rest because of a *charley horse* in his leg.⟩ — see ¹CRAMP

charm *n* **1** something worn or kept to bring good luck or keep away evil ⟨an old cap that I use as a *charm* for whenever I play softball⟩

synonyms amulet, fetish (*also* fetich), mascot, mojo, phylactery, talisman

related words gris-gris (*also* grigri), philter, toadstone; emblem, symbol, token

near antonyms curse, hex, spell

antonyms jinx

2 the power of irresistible attraction ⟨a young singer with the kind of *charm* that turns a performer into a star⟩

synonyms allure, appeal, attractiveness, captivation, charisma, enchantment, fascination, glamour (*also* glamor), magic, magnetism, seductiveness, witchery

related words allurement, attraction, call, lure, seduction; agreeableness, darlingness, delightfulness, niceness, pleasantness, pleasingness, sweetness

near antonyms disagreeableness, distastefulness, obnoxiousness, offensiveness, unpleasantness

antonyms repulsion, repulsiveness

3 a spoken word or set of words believed to have magic power ⟨recited a *charm* to make the prince fall in love with her⟩ — see SPELL 1

4 an ornament worn on a chain around the neck or wrist ⟨a dangling *charm* in the figure of a horse on her bracelet⟩ — see PENDANT

charm *vb* **1** to attract or delight as if by magic ⟨a quaint seaside village that *charms* all who visit it⟩

synonyms allure, beguile, bewitch, captivate, enchant, fascinate, kill, magnetize, wile

related words disarm, draw, entice, lure, pull, seduce, tempt; delight, gratify, please; arrest, enrapture, enthrall (*or* enthral), entrance; appeal (to), interest, intrigue; beckon, court, invite, solicit, woo

near antonyms disgust, offend, repel, revolt; annoy, displease, irk; bore, tire, weary

2 to cast a spell on ⟨In one version of the tale, it is a vengeful fairy who *charms* Sleeping Beauty so that she falls into a sleep for a hundred years.⟩ — see BEWITCH 1

charmed *adj* being or appearing to be under a magic spell ⟨You must be living a *charmed* life if you haven't caught the flu that's going around.⟩ — see ENCHANTED

charming *adj* having an often mysterious or magical power to attract ⟨a *charming* man who had no problem attracting friends⟩ — see FASCINATING 1

chart *n* an illustration of certain features of a geographical area ⟨A *chart* of that section of the coastline will show any possible hazards.⟩ — see MAP

chart *vb* 1 to give an oral or written account of in some detail ⟨The book *charts* the years between the two World Wars.⟩ — see TELL 1

2 to work out the details of (something) in advance ⟨*charted* the entire campaign for governor before she even agreed to run⟩ — see PLAN 1

charter *vb* to take or get the temporary use of (something) for a set sum ⟨Let's *charter* a boat for the day.⟩ — see HIRE 1

charwoman *n* a person hired to perform household or personal services ⟨The upkeep of the estate required several *charwomen*.⟩ — see MAID 1

chase *n* 1 an animal that is hunted or killed ⟨The gazelle is a favorite *chase* of lions.⟩ — see PREY 1

2 the act of going after or in the tracks of another ⟨a high-speed car *chase*⟩ — see PURSUIT

chase *vb* 1 to drive or force out ⟨*chased* the cat out of the garden⟩ — see EJECT 1

2 to go after or on the track of ⟨a dog that likes to *chase* cars⟩ — see FOLLOW 2

3 to seek out (game) for food or sport ⟨Owls often *chase* mice in the dark.⟩ — see HUNT 1

4 to proceed or move quickly ⟨They *chased* all over the place to find the missing child.⟩ — see HURRY 2

chasing *n* the act of going after or in the tracks of another ⟨Despite our determined *chasing*, the rabbit got away.⟩ — see PURSUIT

chasm *n* an immeasurable depth or space ⟨a *chasm* in the ocean floor⟩ — see ABYSS

chaste *adj* 1 free from any trace of the coarse or indecent ⟨As one would expect, the minister's small talk is always *chaste*, even though he likes a joke as much as the next person.⟩

synonyms clean, decent, immaculate, modest, pure, virgin, virginal

related words lily-white, spotless, stainless, unblemished, undefiled, unsoiled, unspotted, unstained, unsullied, untainted, untarnished; decorous, proper, seemly; cultivated, refined, tasteful; harmless, innocent, innocuous, inoffensive

near antonyms blemished, defiled, soiled, spotted, stained, sullied, tainted, tarnished; improper, indecorous, ribald, unseemly; crude, tacky, tasteless, unrefined

antonyms coarse, dirty, filthy, immodest, impure, indecent, obscene, smutty, unchaste, unclean, vulgar

2 free from dirt or stain ⟨The *chaste* white carpet is a key element in the living room's stark, minimalist design.⟩ — see CLEAN 1

chastely *adv* with purity of thought and deed ⟨For living so *chastely* Kateri Tekakwitha became known as the "Lily of the Mohawks."⟩ — see PURELY 1

chasten *vb* 1 to inflict a penalty on for a fault or crime ⟨*chastened* the child a five-minute timeout⟩ — see PUNISH

2 to reduce to a lower standing in one's own eyes or in others' eyes ⟨The unexpected loss to a second-rate player really *chastened* the tournament's top-seeded tennis star.⟩ — see HUMBLE

chasteness *n* the quality or state of being morally pure ⟨Her unchallenged *chasteness* put her on the fast track for sainthood.⟩ — see CHASTITY

chastening *adj* inflicting, involving, or serving as punishment ⟨A *chastening* hour of detention should discourage them from further pranks.⟩ — see PUNITIVE

chastise *vb* 1 to criticize (someone) severely or angrily especially for personal failings ⟨a cold, distant father who rarely paid attention to his children except to *chastise* them⟩ — see SCOLD

2 to inflict a penalty on for a fault or crime ⟨the division of opinion regarding the appropriate way to *chastise* certain crimes⟩ — see PUNISH

chastisement *n* suffering, loss, or hardship imposed in response to a crime or offense ⟨Missing the field trip should be sufficient *chastisement*.⟩ — see PUNISHMENT

chastiser *n* one who inflicts punishment in return for an injury or offense ⟨the highway patrolman who is the committed *chastiser* of those motorists who regard speed limits as no more than suggestions⟩ — see NEMESIS 1

chastising *adj* inflicting, involving, or serving as punishment ⟨a *chastising* lecture on the proper care and feeding of the dog⟩ — see PUNITIVE

chastity *n* the quality or state of being morally pure ⟨a saint who is often held up as a model of *chastity*⟩

synonyms chasteness, innocence, modesty, purity

related words goodness, righteousness, virtue, virtuousness; morality, probity, rectitude; decency, decorum, propriety, seemliness

near antonyms badness, evil, sinfulness, unrighteousness, wickedness; impropriety, indecency, vulgarity

antonyms immodesty, impurity, unchasteness, unchastity

chat *n* 1 friendly, informal conversation or an instance of this ⟨short *chats* between parents and teachers during the school's open house⟩

synonyms cackle, chatter, chitchat, gab, gabfest, gossip, jaw, palaver, patter, rap, schmooze, small talk, table talk, talk, tête-à-tête

related words colloquy, conference, discourse, parley, symposium; debate, dialogue (*also* dialog), exchange, give-and-take; crosstalk, happy talk; yak (*also* yack), yammer

2 talking or a talk between two or more people ⟨a fireside *chat* between two of America's foremost men of letters⟩ — see CONVERSATION

chat *vb* 1 to engage in casual or rambling conversation ⟨The coffeehouse became the favored place to meet friends and *chat* for hours.⟩

synonyms babble, blab, cackle, chatter, converse, gab, gabble, gas, jabber, jaw, palaver, patter, prate, prattle, rap, rattle, run on, schmooze (*or* shmooze), talk, twitter, visit

related words gossip, tattle; descant, discuss, expatiate; yak (*also* yack), yammer

phrases blow smoke, chew the fat (*also* chew the rag), shoot the breeze, talk a blue streak

2 to speak rapidly, inarticulately, and usually unintelligibly ⟨Lost in his own world, the toddler *chatted* happily for hours.⟩ — see BABBLE 1

chat (with) *vb* to communicate with by means of spoken words ⟨*chatting with* the other expectant couples before the start of Lamaze class⟩ — see TALK (TO)

château *n* a large impressive residence ⟨a gorgeous *château* on a hill⟩ — see MANSION

chattel *n* **chattels** *pl* transportable items that one owns ⟨packed up all her *chattels* and moved to a new state⟩ — see POSSESSION 2

chatter *n* 1 friendly, informal conversation or an instance of this ⟨pleasant *chatter* over morning coffee⟩ — see CHAT 1

2 loud, confused, and usually inharmonious sound ⟨The *chatter* of the ship's engine kept us awake all night.⟩ — see NOISE 1

chatter *vb* **1** to engage in casual or rambling conversation ⟨*chattered* idly while waiting in line⟩ — see CHAT 1

2 to speak rapidly, inarticulately, and usually unintelligibly ⟨The parrot *chatters* all day.⟩ — see BABBLE 1

chatterbox *n* a person who talks constantly ⟨My seat companion was a *chatterbox* who never once took a breath during the whole trip.⟩

synonyms babbler, blabber, blabbermouth, cackler, chatterer, conversationalist, gabbler, jabberer, prattler, talker, windbag

related words gossip, talebearer, tattler, tattletale; blatherer, blatherskite; converser, discourser

chatterer *n* a person who talks constantly ⟨That precocious little boy is a real *chatterer*.⟩ — see CHATTERBOX

chatty *adj* **1** having the style and content of everyday conversation ⟨a time when campers were expected to write a *chatty* letter to their folks every week⟩

synonyms colloquial, conversational, gossipy, newsy

related words casual, familiar, informal, intimate, tell-all; digressive, discursive, rambling; communicative, expansive, garrulous, talkative

near antonyms ceremonious, dignified, elevated, formal, solemn, stately

antonyms bookish, literary

2 fond of talking or conversation ⟨a *chatty* older woman who talked to everyone that walked by⟩ — see TALKATIVE

chauvinism *n* excessive favoritism towards one's own country ⟨Their ingrained *chauvinism* has blinded them to their country's faults.⟩

synonyms jingoism, nationalism

related words loyalty, patriotism; nativism, xenophobia

near antonyms internationalism

chauvinist *adj* having or showing excessive favoritism towards one's own country ⟨wrote a history of World War II that was widely criticized for its *chauvinist* slant⟩ — see NATIONALIST 1

chauvinist *n* one who shows excessive favoritism towards his or her country ⟨a *chauvinist* who had never traveled outside the county⟩ — see NATIONALIST

cheap *adj* **1** costing little ⟨E-mail is so popular because it's a *cheap* way to send messages.⟩

synonyms affordable, budget, cut-rate, inexpensive, low, popular, reasonable

related words cheapish, moderate; discount, discounted, fire-sale, lowered, reduced; wholesale; valueless, worthless; supercheap, ultracheap

near antonyms increased; exorbitant, extravagant, overpriced, prohibitive, prohibitory, steep, stiff, superexpensive, unreasonable; luxurious

antonyms costly, dear, deluxe, expensive, high, precious, premium, valuable

2 of low quality ⟨a *cheap* sweater that started to unravel almost as soon as I bought it⟩

synonyms bad, bum, cheesy, coarse, common, cut-rate, execrable, inferior, junky, lousy, low-grade, mediocre, miserable, poor, rotten, rubbishy, second-rate, shoddy, sleazy, terrible, trashy, trumpery, wretched

related words useless, valueless, worthless; indifferent, lackluster, second-class; flashy, garish, gaudy, glitzy, kitsch, kitschy, meretricious, ostentatious, showy, splashy, swank (*or* swanky), tawdry; seedy, shabby, tacky; counterfeit, fake, phony (*also* phoney), sham; supercheap, ultracheap

near antonyms elegant, handsome, tasteful; polished, refined

antonyms excellent, fine, first-class, first-rate, good, high-grade, superior, top-notch

3 giving or sharing as little as possible ⟨a *cheap* coworker who never contributes to the collections taken up in the office⟩ — see STINGY 1

4 arousing or deserving of one's loathing and disgust ⟨That was a *cheap* thing to say to someone who never did you any harm.⟩ — see CONTEMPTIBLE 1

5 involving minimal difficulty or effort ⟨The boxer's early bouts were *cheap* wins, but now he's moving up to the top ranks of boxing.⟩ — see EASY 1

cheapen *vb* **1** to diminish the price or value of ⟨A glutted market *cheapened* cranberries to the point where they were selling for less than what it cost to grow them.⟩ — see DEPRECIATE 1

2 to lower in character, dignity, or quality ⟨a politician who would *cheapen* herself by caving in to lobbyists⟩ — see DEBASE 1

3 to reduce to a lower standing in one's own eyes or in others' eyes ⟨I thought the show *cheapened* the lives of the people it portrayed.⟩ — see HUMBLE

cheapness *n* the quality or practice of being overly sparing with money ⟨His chronic *cheapness* is such that he never takes vacations or replaces old, worn-out household goods.⟩ — see PARSIMONY 1

cheapskate *n* a mean grasping person who is usually stingy with money ⟨A *cheapskate* who lived like a pauper, she was reputedly a wealthy woman at the time of her death.⟩ — see MISER

cheat *n* a dishonest person who uses clever means to cheat others out of something of value ⟨a *cheat* at cards⟩ — see TRICKSTER 1

cheat *vb* **1** to use dishonest methods to achieve a goal ⟨Students who *cheat* on tests end up never knowing anything.⟩

synonyms finagle, fudge

related words crib; color, distort, falsify, misinterpret, misrepresent, misstate, pervert, twist, warp; doctor, fake, tamper (with); elaborate, embellish, embroider, exaggerate, magnify, pad, stretch; dodge, evade, hedge

2 to fall short in satisfying the expectation or hope of ⟨The daredevil survived his plunge over the falls with barely a scratch, having *cheated* death once again.⟩ — see DISAPPOINT

3 to rob by the use of trickery or threats ⟨a despicable confidence man who heartlessly *cheated* elderly people out of their savings⟩ — see FLEECE

cheater *n* a dishonest person who uses clever means to cheat others out of something of value ⟨Gambling casinos have very elaborate means of detecting *cheaters*.⟩ — see TRICKSTER 1

check *n* **1** the amount owed at a bar or restaurant or the slip of paper stating the amount ⟨Diners at that restaurant often look shocked when they receive the *check*.⟩

synonyms bill, tab

related words invoice, receipt; account, reckoning, record, statement; charge, cost, damage, expense, fee, figure; score, tally

2 a close look at or over someone or something in order to judge condition ⟨I made a careful *check* of the antique table before buying it.⟩ — see INSPECTION

3 a record of goods sold or services performed together with the costs due ⟨request a detailed *check* from the company before sending any money⟩ — see ¹BILL 1

4 a small sheet of plastic, paper, or paperboard showing that the bearer has a claim to something (as admittance) ⟨handed over a *check* for his coat⟩ — see TICKET 1

5 something that limits one's freedom of action or choice ⟨The judiciary is intended to be a *check* on the executive and legislative branches of government.⟩ — see RESTRICTION 1

6 an irregular usually narrow break in a surface created by pressure ⟨The network of fine *checks* on the surface would indicate that the painting is quite old.⟩ — see CRACK 1

7 the stopping of a process or activity ⟨The announcement of bad news gave a sudden *check* to the celebration.⟩ — see END 1

check *vb* **1** to be in agreement on every point ⟨Their story of what happened *checks* with the report of the eyewitness.⟩
synonyms accord, agree, answer, cohere, coincide, comport, conform, correspond, dovetail, fit, go, harmonize, jibe, sort, square, tally
related words equal, match, parallel; align (*also* aline), line up, register
phrases fall in with
near antonyms contradict, dispute, gainsay; negate, nullify; clash, conflict, jar
antonyms differ (from), disagree (with)

2 to bring (something) to a standstill ⟨A tree finally *checked* the skidding car.⟩ — see ¹HALT 1

3 to keep from exceeding a desirable degree or level (as of expression) ⟨*Check* your enthusiasm a bit, and think before you marry someone you just met.⟩ — see CONTROL 1

check (out) *vb* to look over closely (as for judging quality or condition) ⟨*Check out* the house and let me know if you think it's worth buying.⟩ — see INSPECT

checklist *n* a record of a series of items (as names or titles) usually arranged according to some system ⟨a *checklist* of things to do before the flight⟩ — see ¹LIST

checkmate *vb* to prevent from achieving a goal ⟨finally *checkmated* the billionaire in his attempt to take over the movie studio⟩ — see FRUSTRATE 1

checkup *n* a close look at or over someone or something in order to judge condition ⟨The vet gave the kitten a *checkup*, then reassuringly declared her in fine health.⟩ — see INSPECTION

cheek *n* **1** disrespectful or argumentative talk given in response to a command or request ⟨Any more *cheek* in this classroom and you'll get a detention.⟩ — see BACK TALK

2 shameless boldness ⟨She had the *cheek* to blame me for the fact that she had forgotten about the staff meeting.⟩ — see EFFRONTERY

3 cheeks *pl* the part of the body upon which someone sits ⟨sat on a blanket to cushion his *cheeks* on the hard bleachers⟩ — see BUTTOCKS

cheekiness *n* shameless boldness ⟨The *cheekiness* of the restaurant's demand that we pay for unordered food was breathtaking.⟩ — see EFFRONTERY

cheeky *adj* displaying or marked by rude boldness ⟨a *cheeky* comment about something that was none of her business⟩ — see NERVY 1

cheep *vb* to make a short sharp sound like a small bird ⟨The toaster *cheeps* to indicate that the toast is done.⟩ — see CHIRP

cheer *n* **1** a mood characterized by high spirits and amusement and often accompanied by laughter ⟨a birthday celebration filled with affection and *cheer*⟩ — see MIRTH

2 a feeling of ease from grief or trouble ⟨The visiting general had some words of *cheer* for each of the hospital's recuperating soldiers.⟩ — see COMFORT 1

3 a state of mind dominated by a particular emotion ⟨Be of good *cheer* in this Christmas season!⟩ — see MOOD 1

4 enthusiastic and usually public expression of approval ⟨All three movies in the series received *cheers* from fans of the novels.⟩ — see APPLAUSE 1

cheer *vb* **1** to declare enthusiastic approval of ⟨Critics and fans alike have *cheered* the latest addition to the author's series of fantasy novels.⟩ — see ACCLAIM

2 to ease the grief or distress of ⟨Let's hope that these flowers will *cheer* my ailing aunt at least a little.⟩ — see COMFORT

cheer (up) *vb* **1** to become glad or hopeful ⟨*Cheer up*—things are bound to get better!⟩
synonyms brighten, lighten, look up, perk (up)
related words rejoice; liven (up), revive; beam, glow, radiate, sparkle; encourage, gladden, hearten
near antonyms despair, despond; brood, fret, mope
antonyms darken, sadden

2 to fill with courage or strength of purpose ⟨The general's speech *cheered up* the troops tremendously.⟩ — see ENCOURAGE 1

cheerful *adj* **1** having or showing a good mood or disposition ⟨a *cheerful* person who is always fun to work with and a pleasure to be around⟩
synonyms blithe, blithesome, bright, buoyant, cheery, chipper, gladsome, lightsome, sunny, upbeat, winsome
related words hopeful, optimistic, rosy, sanguine; animated, chirpy, jaunty, lilting, lively, perky, sprightful, sprightly, vivacious; carefree, careless, cavalier, devil-may-care, easygoing, happy-go-lucky, insouciant, lighthearted, unconcerned; boon, gleeful, jocund, jolly, jovial, merry, mirthful; blissful, delighted, glad, gratified, happy, joyful, joyous, pleased, satisfied, tickled; beaming, grinning, laughing, smiling
near antonyms joyless, sad, unhappy, unsatisfied; dull, lethargic, listless, sluggish, torpid; blue, brokenhearted, crestfallen, dejected, depressed, despondent, disconsolate, disheartened, down, downcast, downhearted, droopy, forlorn, hangdog, inconsolable, low, low-spirited, melancholy, mirthless, sorrowful
antonyms dour, gloomy, glum, morose, saturnine, sulky, sullen

2 serving to lift one's spirits ⟨a hospital with sunny, *cheerful* rooms that are designed to make a patient's stay as pleasant as possible⟩
synonyms bright, cheering, cheery, glad
related words gladdening, heartening, heartwarming; gleaming, radiant, sparkling
near antonyms discouraging, disheartening; colorless, drab, dull, lackluster, lusterless; desolate, dispiriting
antonyms bleak, cheerless, dark, depressing, dismal, dreary, gloomy, gray (*also* grey)

cheerfully *adv* in a cheerful or happy manner ⟨He *cheerfully* announced, "It's a beautiful morning!"⟩ — see GAILY 1

cheerfulness *n* a mood characterized by high spirits and amusement and often accompanied by laughter ⟨His constant *cheerfulness* makes him a pleasure to be around.⟩ — see MIRTH

cheerily *adv* in a cheerful or happy manner ⟨waving *cheerily* as they drove off⟩ — see GAILY 1

cheeriness *n* a mood characterized by high spirits and amusement and often accompanied by laughter ⟨A moment of *cheeriness* interrupted the solemn discussion.⟩ — see MIRTH

cheering *adj* **1** making one feel good inside ⟨the *cheering* sight of a child being reunited with a pet that had been lost⟩ — see HEARTWARMING

2 serving to lift one's spirits ⟨*cheering* words from the doctor that the worst of the treatment was over⟩ — see CHEERFUL 2

cheering *n* enthusiastic and usually public expression of approval ⟨A raucous *cheering* welcomed the newly-weds.⟩ — see APPLAUSE 1

cheerless *adj* causing or marked by an atmosphere lacking in cheer ⟨a dank and *cheerless* castle that was once the site of unspeakable horrors⟩ — see GLOOMY 1

cheery *adj* **1** having or showing a good mood or disposition ⟨a *cheery* grin on the host of the holiday party⟩ — see CHEERFUL 1

2 serving to lift one's spirits ⟨A *cheery*, unexpected compliment can really make another person's day.⟩ — see CHEERFUL 2

cheesy *adj* **1** marked by an obvious lack of style or good taste ⟨*Cheesy* plastic knickknacks lined the fireplace mantel.⟩ — see ¹TACKY 1

2 of low quality ⟨a *cheesy* watch that he bought from a sidewalk vendor preying on tourists⟩ — see CHEAP 2

chef *n* a person who prepares food by some manner of heating ⟨The restaurant hired a famous *chef* to raise the quality of its cuisine.⟩ — see COOK

cherish *vb* **1** to feel passion, devotion, or tenderness for ⟨promised to love and *cherish* each other forever⟩ — see LOVE 2

2 to hold dear ⟨We shall always *cherish* the keepsakes that our grandmother left us.⟩ — see LOVE 1

3 to keep in one's mind or heart ⟨After all these years, she still *cherishes* the memory of her first summer romance.⟩ — see HARBOR 1

cherished *adj* granted special treatment or attention ⟨a *cherished* heirloom that has been in the family for generations⟩ — see DARLING 1

chest *n* a covered rectangular container for storing or transporting things ⟨a *chest* containing almost every tool that the home do-it-yourselfer is likely to need⟩
synonyms bin, box, caddy, case, casket, locker, trunk
related words carton, crate; footlocker, locker, sea chest; coffer, lockbox, safe, safe-deposit box, strongbox; coffin, compartment, vault; canteen; caisson, hope chest; bandbox, hatbox, jewel box, snuffbox

chew *vb* to crush or grind with the teeth ⟨Please *chew* your food thoroughly so you don't choke.⟩ — see BITE (ON)

chew out *vb* to criticize (someone) severely or angrily especially for personal failings ⟨The coach *chews out* even the stars of the team if they fail to show up for practice.⟩ — see SCOLD

chew over *vb* to give serious and careful thought to ⟨yet another senator *chewing over* the idea of running for president⟩ — see PONDER

chewy *adj* not easily chewed ⟨a flavorful but *chewy* piece of meat⟩ — see TOUGH 1

chic *adj* being in the latest or current fashion ⟨a *chic* new hairstyle that makes her look very sophisticated⟩ — see STYLISH

chicanery *n* the use of clever underhanded actions to achieve an end ⟨That candidate only won the election through *chicanery*.⟩ — see TRICKERY

chick *n* a young person who is between infancy and adulthood ⟨Those innocent little *chicks* can scarcely imagine what life has in store for them.⟩ — see CHILD 1

chicken *adj* having or showing a shameful lack of courage ⟨too *chicken* to go through with the stunt⟩ — see COWARDLY

chicken *n* a person who shows a shameful lack of courage in the face of danger ⟨A staunch hawk during the drumbeat for war, he proved to be a *chicken* when it came to actually fighting it.⟩ — see COWARD

chickenhearted *adj* having or showing a shameful lack of courage ⟨too *chickenhearted* to speak up, even though she knew a terrible injustice was being committed⟩ — see COWARDLY

chide *vb* to criticize (someone) so as to correct a fault ⟨She *chided* me for forgetting to offer our guests some refreshments.⟩ — see REBUKE 1

chief *adj* **1** coming before all others in importance ⟨Our *chief* priority this year will be cutting the budget.⟩ — see FOREMOST 1

2 highest in rank or authority ⟨The *chief* administrator will be retiring soon.⟩ — see HEAD

chief *n* **1** the main or greater part of something as distinguished from its subordinate parts ⟨The *chief* of the estate was left to the eldest child.⟩ — see BODY 1

2 the person (as an employer or supervisor) who tells people and especially workers what to do ⟨Our *chief* is out on a business trip right now.⟩ — see BOSS

chiefly *adv* for the most part ⟨Our video collection consists *chiefly* of comedies, but we have a few horror movies.⟩
synonyms altogether, basically, by and large, generally, largely, mainly, mostly, overall, predominantly, primarily, principally, substantially
related words about, more or less, most, much, near, nearly, next to, nigh, practically, some, virtually, well-nigh; broadly, roughly; commonly, frequently, generally, normally, ordinarily, typically, usually; incompletely, partially, partly, rather, somewhat
phrases in general, on the whole
near antonyms completely, entirely, fully, perfectly, thoroughly, totally, wholly; barely, hardly, just, marginally, minimally, scarcely; absolutely, categorically, unqualifiedly

child *n* **1** a young person who is between infancy and adulthood ⟨an imaginative animated film that appeals to adults as well as to *children*⟩
synonyms chick, cub, juvenile, kid, kiddo, moppet, squirt, whelp, youngster, youth
related words adolescent, minor; kindergartner (*also* kindergartener), preschooler, rug rat [*slang*], schoolboy, schoolchild, schoolgirl, schoolkid; babe, baby, bantling, infant, nestling, newborn, toddler, tot, weanling; brat, devil, hellion, imp, monkey, rapscallion, rascal, rogue, urchin, whippersnapper; cherub; preteen, preteenager, subteen, teen, teenager, teener, teenybopper, tween; lad, nipper, shaver, stripling, tad; bobby-soxer, hoyden, tomboy
near antonyms middle-ager; ancient, elder, golden-ager, oldster, old-timer, senior, senior citizen
antonyms adult, grown-up

2 a recently born person ⟨wrapped the *child* in a blanket before taking him outside in the cold⟩ — see BABY 1

3 a condition or occurrence traceable to a cause ⟨Widespread stress is the *child* of the frenetic pace of the modern world.⟩ — see EFFECT 1

childbearing *n* the act or process of giving birth to children ⟨In olden days many women died in *childbearing*.⟩ — see CHILDBIRTH

childbirth *n* the act or process of giving birth to children ⟨women who choose to undergo *childbirth* without the use of anesthetics and other drugs⟩
synonyms childbearing, delivery, labor, parturition, travail
related words birth pang, contraction, pains; pregnancy; abortion, miscarriage; cesarean section (*or* caesarean section), natural childbirth; childbed, confinement, lying-in

childhood *n* the state or time of being a child ⟨Enjoy your *childhood*—it won't last forever!⟩
synonyms youth
related words boyhood, girlhood, toddlerhood; juvenescence; immaturity, juvenility; babyhood, infancy
near antonyms majority; middle age, midlife; sunset
antonyms adulthood

childish *adj* having or showing the annoying qualities (as silliness) associated with children ⟨You almost spoiled the ceremony for everyone with your *childish* giggling.⟩
synonyms adolescent, babyish, immature, infantile, juvenile, kiddish, puerile
related words boyish, brattish, bratty, girlie (*or* girly), girlish; childlike, innocent, naive (*or* naïve), simple, simplistic, unsophisticated
near antonyms unchildlike; cosmopolitan, experienced, knowing, smart, sophisticated, worldly, worldly-wise
antonyms adult, grown-up, mature
child's play *n* **1** something of little importance ⟨The injury is *child's play*, just a scratch.⟩ — see TRIFLE
2 something that is easy to do ⟨Winning the game against those guys will be *child's play*.⟩ — see CINCH
chill *adj* **1** lacking in friendliness or warmth of feeling ⟨were met with a *chill* gaze when they arrived home late from the party⟩ — see COLD 2
2 uncomfortably cool ⟨This *chill* weather is making my teeth chatter.⟩ — see CHILLY 1
3 having a low or subnormal temperature ⟨No one should be coatless on a *chill* night as this.⟩ — see COLD 1
4 causing or marked by an atmosphere lacking in cheer ⟨The house's design may be cutting-edge, but it has a *chill* sterility about it that is anything but homey.⟩ — see GLOOMY 1
chill *n* an uncomfortable degree of coolness ⟨There's a *chill* in the air, so you'd better wear a sweater.⟩
synonyms bite, bitterness, bleakness, chilliness, nip, rawness, sharpness
related words briskness, crispness; frigidity, frigidness, frostiness, gelidity, iciness, wintriness; cold, freeze, snap
near antonyms balminess, warmness, warmth; heat, hotness, sultriness
chill *vb* **1** to cause to lose heat ⟨*Chill* the gelatin for two hours, until it sets.⟩ — see COOL
2 to get rid of nervous tension or anxiety ⟨You want to hang out with us and just *chill* this weekend?⟩ — see RELAX 1
3 to lessen the courage or confidence of ⟨investors *chilled* by the floundering economy⟩ — see DISCOURAGE 1
4 to spend time doing nothing ⟨Instead of going out tonight, let's stay in and *chill*.⟩ — see IDLE
chilliness *n* an uncomfortable degree of coolness ⟨The lingering *chilliness* in the church prompted everyone to put on jackets.⟩ — see CHILL
chilling *adj* uncomfortably cool ⟨a Southern visitor who was not used to the *chilling* air of a Northeast winter⟩ — see CHILLY 1
chill out *vb, slang* **1** to become still and orderly ⟨Stop making that racket, and just *chill out*!⟩ — see QUIET 1
2 to get rid of nervous tension or anxiety ⟨If you don't *chill out*, you're going to get an ulcer.⟩ — see RELAX 1
chilly *adj* **1** uncomfortably cool ⟨those *chilly* nights when a warm fire can be especially comforting⟩
synonyms bitter, bleak, chill, chilling, nipping, nippy, raw, sharp
related words bracing, brisk, crisp, invigorating, rigorous, snappy; arctic, bitter, cold, coolish, freezing, frigid, frosty, glacial, ice-cold, icy, numbing, polar, shivery, wintry (*also* wintery); subfreezing, subzero; frosted, frozen, iced, refrigerated, unheated
near antonyms balmy, warm; lukewarm, tepid; heated, warmed
2 lacking in friendliness or warmth of feeling ⟨a *chilly* glare directed at the person who tried to go to the head of the line⟩ — see COLD 2
3 having a low or subnormal temperature ⟨a *chilly* spring morning⟩ — see COLD 1

chime *n* **1** *usually* **chimes** *pl* a series of short high ringing sounds ⟨the welcoming *chimes* on our doorbell⟩ — see TINKLE
2 peaceful coexistence ⟨firmly believes that science and religion can keep *chime* with one another⟩ — see HARMONY 2
chime *vb* **1** to form a pleasing relationship ⟨The restaurant's manor-house decor *chimes* perfectly with the chef's traditionalist take on haute cuisine.⟩ — see HARMONIZE 1
2 to make the clear sound heard when metal vibrates ⟨The doorbell *chimed* just as we were sitting down to eat.⟩ — see ²RING
3 to say or state again ⟨TV commercial that *chimes* the same message over and over⟩ — see REPEAT 1
chime in *vb* **1** to cause a disruption in a conversation or discussion ⟨"I don't like that show at all," my friend *chimed in*.⟩ — see INTERRUPT
2 to form a pleasing relationship ⟨The illustrations *chimed in* perfectly with the story.⟩ — see HARMONIZE 1
chimera *n* a conception or image created by the imagination and having no objective reality ⟨A monster in the closet would not have been the first *chimera* that the boy had seen in his mind's eye.⟩ — see FANTASY 1
chimerical *also* **chimeric** *adj* not real and existing only in the imagination ⟨For the time being, interplanetary travel remains a *chimerical* feature of life in the 21st century.⟩ — see IMAGINARY
chine *n* a column of bones supporting the trunk of a vertebrate animal ⟨uncovered the *chine* of some animal while digging in the backyard⟩ — see SPINE
chink *n* **1** a vulnerable point ⟨Before the tournament she studied videos of her chief rival, looking for the *chink* in her game.⟩ — see ACHILLES' HEEL
2 an irregular usually narrow break in a surface created by pressure ⟨plugged the *chinks* in the walls with mortar⟩ — see CRACK 1
chink *vb* to make a repeated sharp light ringing sound ⟨In the breeze the flag's chain *chinked* against the flagpole.⟩ — see JINGLE
chip *n* **1** a small flat piece separated from a whole ⟨Wood *chips* were spread over the ground between the plants.⟩
synonyms flake, sliver, splint, splinter
related words bit, disk (*or* disc), fragment, part, particle, portion, scrap, section, shard; flinders, shiver, smithereens; shred, tatter; clipping, paring, shave, shaving, snippet; sheet, slice
near antonyms chunk, hunk, lump, slab
2 a V-shaped cut usually on an edge or a surface ⟨Watch out for the *chip* on the rim of that drinking glass.⟩ — see NOTCH 1
3 **chips** *pl* something (as pieces of stamped metal or printed paper) customarily and legally used as a medium of exchange, a measure of value, or a means of payment ⟨He was in the *chips* after hitting it big in the lottery.⟩ — see MONEY
chip in *vb* to make a donation as part of a group effort ⟨We all *chipped in* and bought pizza for lunch.⟩ — see CONTRIBUTE 1
chipper *adj* having or showing a good mood or disposition ⟨You're awfully *chipper* this morning!⟩ — see CHEERFUL 1
chirp *vb* to make a short sharp sound like a small bird ⟨The sparrows were *chirping* up a storm in the backyard.⟩
synonyms cheep, chirrup, peep, pip, pipe, tweet, twitter
related words cackle, chatter, jabber; sing, trill, warble
chirr *n* a monotonous sound like that of an insect in motion ⟨the *chirr* of dragonflies⟩ — see HUM
chirrup *vb* to make a short sharp sound like a small bird

⟨The kitten *chirruped* insistently for her dinner.⟩ — see CHIRP

chisel *vb* to rob by the use of trickery or threats ⟨ruthlessly *chiseled* other students out of their lunch money⟩ — see FLEECE

chitchat *n* friendly, informal conversation or an instance of this ⟨a bit of *chitchat* over lunch with people we hadn't seen in a while⟩ — see CHAT 1

chivalrous *adj* having, characterized by, or arising from a dignified and generous nature ⟨still engages in *chivalrous* behavior, such as holding doors for people⟩ — see NOBLE 2

chivy *or* **chivvy** *vb* to thrust oneself upon (another) without invitation ⟨a boss with a reputation for *chivying* his workers about every little thing⟩ — see BOTHER 1

chock–full *or* **chockful** *adj* containing or seeming to contain the greatest quantity or number possible ⟨She returned from the buffet with a plate *chock-full* of food.⟩ — see FULL 1

choice *adj* **1** having qualities that appeal to a refined taste ⟨*choice* chocolates for which chocolate lovers are willing to pay extra⟩

synonyms dainty, delicate, elegant, exquisite, fine, rare, select

related words bijou, jewellike; better, exceptional, fancy, high-grade, special; elite, exclusive; classic, excellent, fabulous, first-class, first-rate, grand, great, marvelous (*or* marvellous), noble, outstanding, par excellence, premium, prime, sensational, splendid, stellar, sterling, superb, superior, superlative, supernal, terrific, tip-top, top, top-notch, unsurpassed, wonderful; ultrarare; exclusive, upscale

near antonyms coarse, gross, kitsch, kitschy, lowbrow, raffish, rough, tasteless, uncultivated, uncultured, unpolished, unrefined, vulgar; commercial, mass-produced, popular; common, ordinary; average, lesser, mediocre, run-of-the-mill, run-of-the-mine (*or* run-of-mine), second-class, second-rate; deficient, inferior, low-grade, substandard, unacceptable, unsatisfactory, wanting

2 of the very best kind ⟨Thus far, the pool of applicants for the job has been less than *choice*.⟩ — see EXCELLENT

3 singled out from a number or group as more to one's liking ⟨The restaurant offers a small but *choice* list of vegan entrées.⟩ — see SELECT 1

choice *n* **1** the power, right, or opportunity to choose ⟨You have no *choice*: you have to go to the conference.⟩

synonyms alternative, discretion, election, liberty, option, pick, preference, selection, volition, way

related words determination, free will, will; say, voice, vote; inclination, liking, partiality, penchant, predilection, proclivity, propensity, tendency; discernment, judgment (*or* judgement), perspicacity

near antonyms coercion, duress, force; duty, obligation; Hobson's choice

2 a person or thing that is chosen ⟨my *choice* for best song of all time⟩

synonyms bet, chosen, pick, selection

related words favorite, like, liking, preference; elective, option; appointment, designation, nomination; candidate; preselection

antonyms rejectee

3 individuals carefully selected as being the best of a class ⟨The youth symphony accepts only the *choice* of the city's high school musicians.⟩ — see ELITE 1

4 the act or power of making one's own choices or decisions ⟨The prisoner had no *choice* but to do what he was told.⟩ — see FREE WILL

5 the act or process of selecting ⟨You'll have to make a *choice* eventually.⟩ — see SELECTION 1

choir *n* an organized group of singers ⟨joined the *choir* for next year⟩ — see CHORUS 1

choke *vb* **1** to keep (someone) from breathing by exerting pressure on the windpipe ⟨Let go of my throat—you're *choking* me!⟩

synonyms garrote (*or* garotte), strangle, suffocate, throttle

related words asphyxiate, smother, stifle

near antonyms restore, resuscitate, revive

2 to experience complete or partial blockage of the windpipe ⟨the recommended procedure for helping someone who is *choking*⟩

synonyms gag, suffocate

related words heave, retch, throw up, vomit; asphyxiate, smother, stifle

near antonyms breathe, respire; expire, inspire

3 to be or cause to be killed by lack of breathable air ⟨Thick, black smoke *choked* the trapped firefighters.⟩ — see SMOTHER 1

4 to prevent passage through by filling with something ⟨Overgrown bushes *choked* the narrow alleyway between the buildings.⟩ — see CLOG 1

choke (back) *vb* to refrain from openly showing or uttering ⟨*choked back* a sarcastic reply to an insulting question⟩ — see SUPPRESS 2

choker *n* an ornamental chain or string (as of beads) worn around the neck ⟨a pearl *choker* closely wrapped around her throat⟩ — see NECKLACE

choleric *adj* **1** easily irritated or annoyed ⟨Watch out for the *choleric* librarian at the reference desk.⟩ — see IRRITABLE

2 feeling or showing anger ⟨I absolutely get *choleric* when a telemarketer calls during the dinner hour.⟩ — see ANGRY

chomp (on) *vb* to crush or grind with the teeth ⟨loudly *chomped on* popcorn during the movie⟩ — see BITE (ON)

choose *vb* **1** to decide to accept (someone or something) from a group of possibilities ⟨*Choose* a computer that best suits your needs.⟩

synonyms cull, elect, handpick, name, opt (for), pick, prefer, select, single (out), take

related words preselect; appoint, designate, fix, mark, set, tab, tap; accept, adopt, embrace, espouse; settle (on *or* upon)

near antonyms disapprove, negative, repudiate, spurn; discard, jettison, throw away, throw out

antonyms decline, refuse, reject, turn down

2 to see fit ⟨You can wear whatever you *choose* to the party.⟩

synonyms like, please, want, will, wish

related words ache (for), covet, crave, desire, die (for), fancy, hanker (for), hunger (for), itch (for), long (for), lust (for *or* after), pant (after), pine (for), repine (for), sigh (for), thirst (for), yearn (for); decide, determine, resolve

3 to come to a judgment about after discussion or consideration ⟨*chose* to write on a controversial topic for the local newspaper⟩ — see DECIDE 1

chooser *n* someone with the right or responsibility for making a selection ⟨Among other things, the president must be a good *chooser* of competent individuals, both for his cabinet and for the U.S. Supreme Court.⟩ — see SELECTOR

choosing *n* the act or process of selecting ⟨The *choosing* of a new mayor is left to the voters.⟩ — see SELECTION 1

choosy *or* **choosey** *adj* **1** hard to please ⟨a *choosy* dog who refuses all but the fanciest food⟩ — see FINICKY

2 tending to select carefully ⟨a *choosy* man when it came to clothes for the office⟩ — see SELECTIVE

chop *n* a hard strike with a part of the body or an instrument ⟨delivered a sharp *chop* to his opponent's neck⟩ — see ¹BLOW

chop *vb* to cut into small pieces ⟨*Chop* the onions before adding them to the pot.⟩
synonyms dice, hash, mince
related words chip, grate, grind, kibble, mash, puree (*or* purée), slice; butcher, carve, dissect

chop (down) *vb* to bring down by cutting ⟨We have to *chop down* that tree out front before it falls on the house.⟩ — see FELL 2

choppy *adj* **1** lacking in steadiness or regularity of occurrence ⟨a sharp, *choppy* wind coming off the lake⟩ — see FITFUL
2 marked by a series of sharp quick motions ⟨The old cable car provides a picturesque but *choppy* ride to the mountain's peak.⟩ — see JERKY 1
3 not clearly or logically connected ⟨The plot was intriguing, but the author's style was so *choppy* that I finally gave up in frustration.⟩ — see INCOHERENT 1

chorale *n* **1** a religious song ⟨practiced a *chorale* to perform in church⟩ — see HYMN 1
2 an organized group of singers ⟨a *chorale* that is regarded as being among the best in the state⟩ — see CHORUS 1

chore *n* **1** a piece of work that needs to be done regularly ⟨Everyone in this household is expected to do weekly *chores*.⟩
synonyms assignment, duty, job, task
related words endeavor, enterprise, project, stint, undertaking; care, charge, commission, responsibility; function, mission, office, operation, post; errand; round, route
2 a dull, unpleasant, or difficult piece of work ⟨Cleaning everything out of the attic was a real *chore*.⟩
synonyms bear, beast, headache, job, killer, labor
related words drudgery, grind, heavy lifting; effort, strain, sweat; burden, load, weight; bother, nuisance, trouble
near antonyms breeze, child's play, cinch, duck soup, kid stuff, setup, snap

chortle *n* an explosive sound that is a sign of amusement ⟨The joke provoked a sudden *chortle* from a bystander.⟩ — see LAUGH 1

chortle *vb* to show mirth with an explosive vocal sound ⟨Audiences might *chortle* gently during the movie's amusing bits, but there are few knee-slappers.⟩ — see LAUGH 1

chorus *n* **1** an organized group of singers ⟨the annual Spring program presented by the school's *chorus*⟩
synonyms choir, chorale, consort, glee club
related words ensemble; minstrelsy
2 a part of a song or hymn that is repeated every so often ⟨The whole audience joined in for the *chorus*.⟩
synonyms burden, refrain
related words repeat, response

chosen *adj* singled out from a number or group as more to one's liking ⟨the *chosen* few who are invited to a gathering at the CEO's house at the end of the year⟩ — see SELECT 1

chosen *n* a person or thing that is chosen ⟨Of the five sons in the family, he was his father's *chosen* and thus showered with attention and special gifts.⟩ — see CHOICE 2

chow *n* **1** food eaten or prepared for eating at one time ⟨That evening's *chow* was pretty basic because we were in a hurry.⟩ — see MEAL
2 substances intended to be eaten ⟨There's always at least some *chow* in the house.⟩ — see FOOD

christen *vb* to give a name to ⟨We *christened* the new baby "Ophelia."⟩ — see NAME 1

Christian name *n* a name that is placed before one's family name ⟨Although his *Christian name* is ordinary, his last name is quite distinctive.⟩ — see FORENAME

Christmastide *n* the season celebrating Christmas ⟨May everyone be filled with peace and joy, this *Christmastide*!⟩ — see YULETIDE

Christmastime *n* the season celebrating Christmas ⟨There are always lots of lights on the neighborhood's houses around *Christmastime*.⟩ — see YULETIDE

chronic *adj* being such by habit and not likely to change ⟨a *chronic* smoker who is trying to quit⟩ — see HABITUAL 1

chronicle *n* **1** a relating of events usually in the order in which they happened ⟨a *chronicle* of their adventure on the river⟩ — see ACCOUNT 1
2 an account of important events in the order in which they happened ⟨Only sketchy information about King Arthur can be found in the *chronicles* of ancient England.⟩ — see HISTORY 1

chronicle *vb* to give an oral or written account of in some detail ⟨The book *chronicles* the efforts of two climbers to scale Mount Everest.⟩ — see TELL 1

chronicler *n* a student or writer of history ⟨*chroniclers* who gave often conflicting accounts of battles, depending upon which side they favored⟩ — see HISTORIAN

chronometer *n* a device to measure time ⟨a fancy new *chronometer* that is light-years more advanced than your average wristwatch⟩ — see TIMEPIECE

chubbiness *n* the condition of having an excess of body fat ⟨A bit of *chubbiness* is normal in very small children.⟩ — see CORPULENCE

chubby *adj* having an excess of body fat ⟨The *chubby* baby had slimmed down by the time she was a toddler.⟩ — see FAT 1

chuck *n, chiefly West* substances intended to be eaten ⟨After a long day, the cowboys lined up for some *chuck*.⟩ — see FOOD

chuck *vb* **1** to get rid of as useless or unwanted ⟨After the power outage we reluctantly *chucked* everything that had been sitting in the fridge.⟩ — see DISCARD
2 to give up (a job or office) ⟨I swear, I have half a mind to *chuck* this job and become a hermit!⟩ — see QUIT 1
3 to send through the air especially with a quick forward motion of the arm ⟨*chucked* a wad of paper at his friend's back⟩ — see THROW 1

chuckle *n* an explosive sound that is a sign of amusement ⟨a quick *chuckle* at the funny comment⟩ — see LAUGH 1

chuckle *vb* to show mirth with an explosive vocal sound ⟨Everyone dutifully *chuckled* at the professor's intended jokes.⟩ — see LAUGH 1

chum *n* a person who has a strong liking for and trust in another ⟨college *chums* who go way back⟩ — see FRIEND 1

chum *vb* to come or be together as friends ⟨They always *chum* around together.⟩ — see ASSOCIATE 1

chumminess *n* the state of being in a very personal or private relationship ⟨Her *chumminess* with the boss did not sit well with some of her coworkers.⟩ — see FAMILIARITY 1

chummy *adj* **1** closely acquainted ⟨The neighboring families know each other but are hardly *chummy*.⟩ — see FAMILIAR 1
2 having or showing kindly feeling and sincere interest ⟨She was so *chummy* to me that I sensed that she had put our quarrel behind her.⟩ — see FRIENDLY 1

chump *n* one who is easily deceived or cheated ⟨The guy trying to unload that used car must have thought that I was a *chump*.⟩ — see ¹DUPE

chunk *n* **1** a considerable amount ⟨That new sports car must have cost a real *chunk* of change.⟩ — see LOT 2

2 a small uneven mass ⟨a little *chunk* of dirt⟩ — see LUMP 1

chunky *adj* **1** having small pieces or lumps spread throughout ⟨*Chunky* peanut butter adds an interesting layer of texture when paired with jelly.⟩
  synonyms clumpy, curdy, lumpy, nubbly, nubby
  related words ropy (*also* ropey), thick, viscous; knobbed, knobbly, knobby, lumpish; clabbered, clotted, coagulated, congealed, curdled, gelled, thickened; broken, bumpy, coarse, irregular, jagged, knotted, knotty, pebbly
  antonyms smooth
2 being compact and broad in build and often short in stature ⟨a *chunky* little toddler⟩ — see STOCKY
3 having or being of relatively great depth or extent from one surface to its opposite ⟨a *chunky* piece of bread⟩ — see THICK 1

church *n* **1** a building for public worship and especially Christian worship ⟨a city that is noted for its many historic *churches*⟩
  synonyms kirk [*chiefly Scottish*], tabernacle, temple
  related words abbey, bethel, chapel, minster, mission, oratory, sanctuary, shrine; meetinghouse; mosque, pagoda, shul, synagogue (*also* synagog)
2 a body of persons gathered for religious worship ⟨spoke to the whole *church* at once⟩ — see CONGREGATION 1

churchly *adj* of or relating to a church ⟨refused to discuss *churchly* matters except on Sundays⟩ — see ECCLESIASTICAL

churl *n* **1** an awkward or simple person especially from a small town or the country ⟨As far as he was concerned, anyone from outside the city was a backwater *churl*.⟩ — see HICK
2 a person whose behavior is offensive to others ⟨a *churl* who gets thrown out of parties with remarkable regularity⟩ — see JERK 1

churlish *adj* having or showing crudely insensitive or impolite manners ⟨It would be *churlish* for any dinner guest to express anything but gratitude for his host's generous hospitality.⟩ — see CLOWNISH

churn *vb* **1** to be in a state of violent rolling motion ⟨a *churning* sea made getting to the island a risky undertaking⟩ — see SEETHE 1
2 to cause (as a liquid) to move about in a circle especially repeatedly ⟨*Churn* the cream until it turns into butter.⟩ — see STIR 1

chutzpah *also* **chutzpa** *or* **hutzpah** *or* **hutzpa** *n* shameless boldness ⟨had the *chutzpah* to demand that he be treated as a special case and be given priority in settling his insurance claim⟩ — see EFFRONTERY

cinch *n* something that is easy to do ⟨The clear instructions made setting up the audiovisual system a *cinch*.⟩
  synonyms breeze, cake, child's play, duck soup, picnic, pushover, snap
  related words no-brainer, nothing; sitting duck; gimme, laugher, walkaway
  phrases piece of cake, walk in the park
  near antonyms brainteaser, poser, stumper, toughie (*also* toughy); bother, nuisance, trouble
  antonyms bear, beast, chore, headache, horror show, killer, labor, murder, pain, sticky wicket, stinker [*slang*]

cinch *vb* to make sure, certain, or safe ⟨The team's latest victory *cinches* a trip to the play-offs.⟩ — see ENSURE

cinema *n* **1** the art or business of making a movie ⟨felt that the *cinema* was one of the most challenging and fulfilling forms of artistic expression⟩ — see MOVIE 2
2 a building or part of a building where movies are shown ⟨I got a job cleaning the *cinemas* at the multiplex.⟩ — see THEATER 1

cipher *n* **1** the numerical symbol 0 or the absence of number or quantity represented by it ⟨Remember to put the *cipher* after the decimal point.⟩ — see ZERO 1
2 a person of no importance or influence ⟨It was either write the Great American Novel or be consigned to the status of a *cipher* in the annals of literature.⟩ — see NOBODY

cipher *vb* to determine (a value) by doing the necessary mathematical operations ⟨We were surprised by how much we had spent on the cruise after we had *ciphered* out the grand total.⟩ — see CALCULATE 1

ciphering *n* the act or process of performing mathematical operations to find a value ⟨He wasn't very good at *ciphering*, but he had excellent language skills.⟩ — see CALCULATION

circle *n* **1** something with a perfectly round circumference ⟨A *circle* of columns surrounds the memorial to the fallen heroes.⟩
  synonyms ring, round
  related words circlet, ringlet; ellipse, loop, oval; ball, globe, orb, sphere
2 a circular strip ⟨a decorative *circle* of silver on the rim of the commemorative plate for their 25th wedding anniversary⟩ — see ¹RING 2
3 a group of people sharing a common interest and relating together socially ⟨Pam got together with her social *circle* once a week.⟩ — see GANG 2
4 a series of events or actions that repeat themselves regularly and in the same order ⟨With the birth of a child coming so soon after the death of a grandparent, we were once again reminded of the *circle* of life.⟩ — see CYCLE 1
5 a region of activity, knowledge, or influence ⟨That lies outside the *circle* of our investigation.⟩ — see FIELD 2

circle *vb* **1** to form a circle around ⟨Trees *circle* the little cabin.⟩ — see SURROUND
2 to travel completely around ⟨With a look of extreme frustration, the commander *circled* the new recruit.⟩ — see ENCIRCLE 1

circuitous *adj* **1** not straightforward or direct ⟨We took a *circuitous* route to the airport so as to avoid the massive traffic jam on the highway.⟩ — see INDIRECT
2 using or containing more words than necessary to express an idea ⟨a *circuitous* explanation for what seems like a fairly basic concept⟩ — see WORDY 1

circular *adj* not straightforward or direct ⟨a rather *circular* discussion of the problem that never addresses it directly⟩ — see INDIRECT

circular *n* a short printed publication with no cover or with a paper cover ⟨promptly tosses out those advertising *circulars* that come in the newspaper⟩ — see PAMPHLET

circulate *vb* **1** to cause to be known over a considerable area or by many people ⟨*circulate* the plans for the new stadium around town to get people's reaction⟩ — see SPREAD 1
2 to make (as a piece of information) the subject of common talk without any authority or confirmation of accuracy ⟨He *circulated* a rumor that someone was about to be fired.⟩ — see RUMOR
3 to become known ⟨Rumors are *circulating* around town.⟩ — see GET OUT 1

circumference *n* **1** the distance around a round body ⟨the *circumference* of the earth at the equator⟩
  synonyms girth
  related words ambit, compass; waistline; equator; diameter, radius; perimeter, periphery
2 the line or relatively narrow space that marks the outer limit of something ⟨a silly little matter that's of interest

to no one beyond the *circumference* of this campus〉 — see BORDER 1

circumlocution *n* **1** deliberate evasion in speech 〈Rather than answering the question directly, he resorted to *circumlocution*, which made her suspect that he was hiding something.〉
synonyms equivocation, shuffle
related words quibbling; ambiguity, ambiguousness, equivocalness, murkiness, nebulousness, obscureness, obscurity, opacity
near antonyms candor, directness, forthrightness, frankness, openheartedness, openness, plainness, plumpness, straightforwardness
2 the use of too many words to express an idea 〈Your papers have to be five pages long, but that's five pages of substance, not *circumlocution*.〉 — see VERBIAGE 1

circumlocutory *adj* using or containing more words than necessary to express an idea 〈The studio's statement that "the film's earnings did not live up to expectations" was a *circumlocutory* admission that the movie was a flop.〉 — see WORDY 1

circumnavigate *vb* **1** to travel completely around 〈the first ship to *circumnavigate* the globe〉 — see ENCIRCLE 1
2 to avoid by going around 〈We can *circumnavigate* the traffic jam if we take the next exit.〉 — see DETOUR 1

circumscribe *vb* **1** to set bounds or an upper limit for 〈*circumscribed* his enthusiasm so as not to make the losing side feel worse〉 — see LIMIT 1
2 to mark the limits of 〈Lake Michigan *circumscribes* the city of Chicago on the east.〉 — see LIMIT 2

circumscribed *adj* having distinct or certain limits 〈The powers of that state's governor are so sharply *circumscribed* that often his hands are tied by the state legislature.〉 — see LIMITED 1

circumspect *adj* having or showing a close attentiveness to avoiding danger or trouble 〈She has a reputation for being *circumspect* in making financial decisions.〉 — see CAREFUL 1

circumspection *n* a close attentiveness to avoiding danger 〈*Circumspection* is always good when considering charging someone with cheating.〉 — see CAUTION 1

circumstance *n* **1** a state or end that seemingly has been decided beforehand 〈The condemned traitor seemed indifferent to his *circumstance*.〉 — see FATE 1
2 something that happens 〈Due to unexpected *circumstances*, the test will be postponed.〉 — see EVENT 1
3 the uncertain course of events 〈I was a victim of *circumstance*, for nothing that I could have done would have made a difference.〉 — see CHANCE 1

circumstantial *adj* including many small descriptive features 〈The *circumstantial* account of his surgery told us more than we really wanted to know about the stomach.〉 — see DETAILED 1

circumvent *vb* **1** to avoid having to comply with (something especially through cleverness 〈employees who try to *circumvent* the company's dress code〉
synonyms beat, bypass, dodge, get around, sidestep, skirt
related words avoid, duck, elude, end-run, escape, eschew, evade, outflank, shake, shirk, shun; disobey, disregard, flout, ignore; avert, deflect, divert, obviate, parry, prevent, ward (off)
near antonyms accede (to), acquiesce (to), assent (to); accept, court, embrace, pursue, seek, welcome; catch, contract, incur
antonyms comply (with), follow, keep, obey, observe
2 to avoid by going around 〈*circumvented* the traffic jam by taking an alternate route〉 — see DETOUR 1
3 to travel completely around 〈Most casual joggers will

be able to *circumvent* the reservoir without too much of a strain.〉 — see ENCIRCLE 1

circus *n* **1** a large usually roofless building for sporting events with tiers of seats for spectators 〈The Roman *circus* is believed to have held 50,000 spectators in ancient times.〉 — see STADIUM
2 a place of uproar or confusion 〈With seven kids in the house, it's a *circus* most of the time.〉 — see MADHOUSE

citadel *n* a structure or place from which one can resist attack 〈A massive stone *citadel* continues to command the city of Halifax, Nova Scotia.〉 — see FORT

citation *n* **1** a formal expression of praise 〈The *citation* for the Nobel Prize winner noted his major contributions to quantum theory.〉 — see ENCOMIUM
2 a formal recognition of an achievement or praiseworthy deed 〈a police officer who has received several *citations*〉 — see COMMENDATION 1
3 a passage referred to, repeated, or offered as an example 〈In your paper be sure to include *citations* to back up any points you make about the play.〉 — see QUOTATION

cite *vb* **1** to give as an example 〈*cited* several experts' opinions to back up her argument〉 — see QUOTE 1
2 to make reference to or speak about briefly but specifically 〈*cited* a number of similar instances of people surviving plane crashes〉 — see MENTION 1

citify *vb* to accustom to the ways of the city 〈We've become so *citified* that many people have no idea where their food comes from.〉
synonyms urbanize
related words civilize, cultivate

citizen *n* **1** a person who owes allegiance to a government and is protected by it 〈conscientious *citizens* who regard voting as a duty as well as a right〉
synonyms national, subject
related words compatriot, countryman; inhabitant, native, nonimmigrant, resident
near antonyms foreigner, stranger; immigrant, nonnative
antonyms alien, noncitizen
2 a person who lives in a town on a permanent basis 〈claimed that the good *citizens* of the town were sick of high property taxes〉 — see BURGHER

city *n* a thickly settled, highly populated area 〈commuters who drive every day between their homes in the suburbs and their jobs in the *city*〉
synonyms burg, megalopolis, metropolis, municipality, town
related words borough; urban sprawl; exurb, suburb, suburbia; central city, edge city, garden city; core city, downtown, inner city, midtown

civil *adj* **1** of or relating to a nation 〈The country was not destroyed by outside enemies but by a series of *civil* wars.〉 — see NATIONAL
2 showing consideration, courtesy, and good manners 〈I know you're angry, but please try to be *civil* to each other.〉 — see POLITE 1

civility *n* **1** an act or utterance that is a customary show of good manners 〈After the usual *civilities*, the buyer and seller got down to business.〉
synonyms amenity, attention, courtesy, formality, gesture, pleasantry, politeness
related words honors; ceremony, observance, rite, ritual; decorum, etiquette, form, manners, mores, proprieties; addresses, devoirs, greetings, regards, respects; favor, grace, kindliness, kindness; protocol, rules
2 speech or behavior that is a sign of good manners 〈treated people from all walks of life with the same unfailing *civility*〉 — see POLITENESS 1

civilization *n* **1** the way people live at a particular time and

place ⟨a documentary on the advanced *civilization* created by the Mayas over a thousand years ago⟩
synonyms culture, life, lifestyle, society
related words customs, manners, mores, values; folklore, heritage, legacy, tradition; subculture, subsociety
2 a high level of taste and enlightenment as a result of extensive intellectual training and exposure to the arts ⟨By the 18th century Boston had reached a level of *civilization* sufficiently advanced to support a circle of portrait painters.⟩ — see CULTURE 1

civilized *adj* having or showing a taste for the fine arts and gracious living ⟨a *civilized* older couple who are celebrated for holding dinner parties that are attended by the city's best and brightest⟩ — see CULTIVATED

clack *vb* to make a series of short sharp noises ⟨Her teeth *clacked* because she was freezing while waiting for the bus.⟩ — see RATTLE 1

claim *n* **1** an entitlement to something ⟨I'm announcing my *claim* to that last slice of pizza.⟩
synonyms call, pretense (*or* pretence), pretension, right
related words birthright, prerogative, title; favor, privilege; refusal
near antonyms disclaimer, quitclaim, release, waiver
2 a legal right to participation in the advantages, profits, and responsibility of something ⟨A shareholder has a *claim* in the business.⟩ — see INTEREST 1
3 a solemn and often public declaration of the truth or existence of something ⟨Galileo's *claim* that the moon has a very irregular surface and thus is not the perfect sphere that the ancients had imagined⟩ — see PROTESTATION
4 something that someone insists upon having ⟨Young children make great *claims* on their parents' time.⟩ — see DEMAND 1

claim *vb* **1** to state as a fact usually forcefully ⟨people who *claim* that they have been kidnapped by aliens from other worlds⟩
synonyms affirm, allege, assert, aver, avouch, avow, contend, declare, insist, maintain, profess, protest, purport, warrant
related words announce, broadcast, proclaim; argue, rationalize, reason; confirm, justify, vindicate; defend, persevere, support, uphold; reaffirm, reassert
phrases put forth
near antonyms abandon; disavow, disclaim, disown, negate, negative, reject, repudiate; challenge, dispute, question; confute, disprove, rebut, refute; contradict, counter
antonyms deny, gainsay
2 to ask for (something) earnestly or with authority ⟨After many years had passed, he suddenly appeared to *claim* his inheritance.⟩ — see DEMAND 1
3 to deprive of life ⟨a disease *claims* thousands of Americans each year⟩ — see KILL 1
4 to have as a requirement ⟨Caring for her three small children *claims* virtually all of her time.⟩ — see NEED 1

clairvoyance *n* the power of seeing or knowing about things that are not present to the senses ⟨People who claim to have *clairvoyance* are sometimes asked to help locate missing persons.⟩
synonyms extrasensory perception, sixth sense
related words foreknowledge, foresight, prescience; precognition; telepathy; parapsychology

clamber *vb* to move (as up or over something) often with the help of the hands in holding or pulling ⟨*clambered* over a wall and was never seen again⟩ — see CLIMB 1

clamor *n* **1** a violent shouting ⟨A *clamor* arose from the crowd as the prisoner was brought forward.⟩
synonyms howl, hubbub, hue and cry, hullabaloo, noise, outcry, roar, tumult, uproar

related words clangor, din, racket; outburst, protest
near antonyms mumble, mumbling, murmur, murmuring, rumble, rumbling
2 loud, confused, and usually inharmonious sound ⟨the *clamor* of a dozen people practicing the trumpet at once⟩ — see NOISE 1

clamor (for) *vb* to ask for (something) earnestly or with authority ⟨a dozen customers *clamoring for* service all at once⟩ — see DEMAND 1

clamorous *adj* **1** engaging in or marked by loud and insistent cries especially of protest ⟨a *clamorous* objection to the play that the students have chosen to put on this year⟩ — see VOCIFEROUS
2 full of or characterized by the presence of noise ⟨a *clamorous* kindergarten classroom⟩ — see NOISY 2
3 marked by a high volume of sound ⟨a rock band known for their *clamorous* concerts⟩ — see LOUD 1

clamp *vb* to put securely in place or in a desired position ⟨*clamped* the headphones to her ears and began to listen⟩ — see FASTEN 2

clamp down (on) *vb* to put a stop to (something) by the use of force ⟨the need to *clamp down on* petty crime in the city⟩ — see QUELL 1

clam up *vb* to stop talking ⟨The little girl *clammed up* when the doctor came into the room.⟩ — see SHUT UP 1

clan *n* **1** a group of people sharing a common interest and relating together socially ⟨That *clan* of football fans has parties every weekend on which the New England Patriots play.⟩ — see GANG 2
2 a group of persons who come from the same ancestor ⟨The whole *clan* gets together only for holidays.⟩ — see FAMILY 1

clandestine *adj* undertaken or done so as to escape being observed or known by others ⟨I took a *clandestine* peek at the price tag on the diamond necklace.⟩ — see SECRET 1

clang *n* the loud sound made when metal strikes metal ⟨The horseshoe hit the stake with a satisfying *clang*.⟩
synonyms clangor, clank, clash
related words chime, ding-dong, knell, peal, ping, plink, ring, tintinnabulation; chink, clink, clinkety-clank, jingle, rattle, tinkle, twang; clap, clip-clop, clop, crack, crash, crunch; clump, clunk, thump

clangor *n* **1** loud, confused, and usually inharmonious sound ⟨the *clangor* of pots and pans coming from the kitchen as the cooks threw together an impromptu meal⟩ — see NOISE 1
2 the loud sound made when metal strikes metal ⟨the *clangor* of a battle in the Middle Ages, as steel hit against steel a thousand times⟩ — see CLANG

clangorous *adj* **1** full of or characterized by the presence of noise ⟨grew up in a *clangorous* but warmhearted household⟩ — see NOISY 2
2 making loud, confused, and usually unharmonious sounds ⟨the teen's *clangorous* efforts to learn to play the drums⟩ — see NOISY 1
3 marked by a high volume of sound ⟨a *clangorous* sheet metal factory⟩ — see LOUD 1

clank *n* the loud sound made when metal strikes metal ⟨The car is making a funny *clank*, and this can't be good.⟩ — see CLANG

clannish *adj* bound together by feelings of very close association ⟨a *clannish* family that can be rather cool to outsiders⟩ — see CLOSE-KNIT

clap *n* **1** a loud explosive sound ⟨a *clap* of thunder that woke the whole house up⟩
synonyms bang, blast, boom, crack, crash, pop, report, slam, smash, snap, thunderclap, thwack, whack
related words thunk; clang, clangor, clank, clash;

knock, rap, tap; blare, clamor, howl, hubbub, hue and cry, hullabaloo, outcry, roar, tumult, uproar

2 a hard strike with a part of the body or an instrument ⟨a sharp *clap* to the head of the disrespectful youth⟩ — see ¹BLOW

clap *vb* to deliver a blow to (someone or something) usually in a strong vigorous manner ⟨*clapped* him on the back as a friendly gesture⟩ — see HIT 1

claptrap *n* language, behavior, or ideas that are absurd and contrary to good sense ⟨The idea that you can get a cold from not dressing warmly is *claptrap*.⟩ — see NONSENSE 1

clarification *n* a statement that makes something clear ⟨After that *clarification*, I find I actually agree with you.⟩ — see EXPLANATION 1

clarify *vb* **1** to remove usually visible impurities from ⟨*Clarify* the melted butter by skimming off the milky bits.⟩
synonyms clear, distill (*also* distil), filter, fine, purify
related words process, rectify, refine; clean, cleanse, decontaminate, purge, wash; extract, leach; bolt, screen, sieve, sift; disinfect, sanitize
near antonyms cloud, dull, muddy; contaminate, dirty, soil; defile, pollute, taint; begrime, besmirch, foul, sully

2 to make plain or understandable ⟨It would help if you could *clarify* your position for us.⟩ — see EXPLAIN 1

clarity *n* **1** the state or quality of being easily seen through ⟨mountain streams with water of incredible *clarity*⟩
synonyms clearness, limpidity, limpidness, transparency
related words brightness, brilliance, effulgence, luminosity; resolution, sharpness; apparentness, observability, visibility
near antonyms fogginess, haziness, milkiness, mistiness, murkiness
antonyms cloudiness, opacity, turbidity, turbidness

2 clearness of expression ⟨This explanation of the greenhouse effect is a marvel of *clarity*.⟩ — see SIMPLICITY 2

clash *n* **1** a physical dispute between opposing individuals or groups ⟨a *clash* between rival teams that resulted in some serious injuries⟩ — see FIGHT 1

2 the loud sound made when metal strikes metal ⟨the *clash* of cymbals⟩ — see CLANG

clash *vb* to be out of harmony or agreement usually noticeably ⟨The colors of your shirt and pants *clash*.⟩
synonyms collide, conflict, discord, jar
related words battle, combat, engage, fight, war (against); chafe, gall, grate; differ, disagree, dissent
near antonyms agree, assent, coincide, concur, correspond
antonyms accord, blend, conform (to *or* with), fit, harmonize, match

clash (with) *vb* to oppose (someone) in physical conflict ⟨The heavyweight champ will *clash* with his chief rival in tonight's bout.⟩ — see FIGHT 1

clashing *adj* not being in agreement or harmony ⟨Freedom and equality are often a *clashing* set of ideals.⟩ — see INCONSISTENT 1

clasp *n* the act or manner of holding ⟨Be careful that your *clasp* on the cat isn't too tight, or she could get hurt.⟩ — see HOLD 1

clasp *vb* **1** to put one's arms around and press tightly ⟨Ted *clasped* his long-lost sister and cried without restraint.⟩ — see EMBRACE 1

2 to reach for and take hold of by embracing with the fingers or arms ⟨*clasped* a crayon and began drawing⟩ — see TAKE 1

class *n* **1** one of the segments of society into which people are grouped ⟨a politician who appeals to people of every *class*⟩
synonyms caste, estate, folk, gentry, order, stratum

related words bracket, echelon, grade, layer, level; place, position, rank, standing, status; food chain, grouping, stratification; clan, family, fraternity, people, race, tribe; subcaste

2 one of the units into which a whole is divided on the basis of a common characteristic ⟨a *class* of wireless devices that can be used for Internet access as well as personal communication⟩
synonyms bracket, category, classification, division, family, grade, group, kind, league, order, rank(s), rubric, set, species, type
related words description, feather, ilk, kidney, like, manner, nature, sort; branch, section, speciality, specialty, subclass, subdivision, subgroup, subspecies, variety; breed, race; generation; heading, label, title

3 a number of persons or things that are grouped together because they have something in common ⟨Only a particular *class* of burglar would do that.⟩ — see SORT 1

4 a series of lectures on a subject ⟨took a *class* on modern art⟩ — see COURSE 2

5 degree of excellence ⟨Only horses of great *class* are allowed to enter the Kentucky Derby.⟩ — see QUALITY 1

6 dignified or restrained beauty of form, appearance, or style ⟨an old mansion with tremendous *class*⟩ — see ELEGANCE

7 high position within society ⟨The woman exudes an aura of *class*.⟩ — see RANK 2

class *vb* to arrange or assign according to type ⟨I would *class* that suggestion as helpful, so let's make a note of it.⟩ — see CLASSIFY 1

classic *adj* **1** constituting, serving as, or worthy of being a pattern to be imitated ⟨*classic* designs in furniture that never go out of style⟩ — see MODEL

2 of the very best kind ⟨one of the really *classic* comedies in the history of movies⟩ — see EXCELLENT

3 serving to identify as belonging to an individual or group ⟨the *classic* facial features of the island's inhabitants⟩ — see CHARACTERISTIC 1

4 being the most accurate and apparently thorough ⟨the *classic* study of the alienation of the individual in modern urban society⟩ — see DEFINITIVE 1

classic *n* **1** someone of such unequaled perfection as to deserve imitation ⟨Among people who have devoted themselves to a life of scientific inquiry, Marie Curie is one of the acknowledged *classics*.⟩ — see IDEAL 1

2 something (as a work of art) that is a great achievement and often its creator's greatest achievement ⟨The works of Michelangelo are regarded as *classics* of the sculptor's art.⟩ — see MASTERPIECE

3 the most perfect type or example ⟨His journey of discovery was a *classic* of arduous effort and fierce determination.⟩ — see QUINTESSENCE 1

classical *adj* **1** based on customs usually handed down from a previous generation ⟨the *classical* preparation of a ham for Easter⟩ — see TRADITIONAL 1

2 being the most accurate and apparently thorough ⟨a writer celebrated for his *classical* profiles of eminent Victorians⟩ — see DEFINITIVE 1

classification *n* one of the units into which a whole is divided on the basis of a common characteristic ⟨dinosaur remains that do not fit any existing *classification*⟩ — see CLASS 2

classify *vb* **1** to arrange or assign according to type ⟨*Classify* the baseball cards in your collection on the basis of rarity.⟩
synonyms assort, break down, categorize, class, codify, compartment, digest, distinguish, distribute, grade, group, peg, place, range, rank, separate, sort, type
related words array, dispose, draw up, marshal (*also*

marshall), order, organize, systematize; alphabetize, catalog (*or* catalogue), file, index, list, refer; pigeonhole, shelve; identify, recognize; cull, screen, set, sieve, sift, winnow; clump, cluster; recategorize, reclassify, regroup; subcategorize
near antonyms confuse, disarrange, jumble, lump, mix (up), scramble; misclassify, missort, mistype
2 to put into a particular arrangement ⟨*Classify* the information you got from the Internet by source.⟩ — see ORDER 1

classless *adj* having or showing crudely insensitive or impolite manners ⟨I object not so much to what he did as the *classless* way he did it.⟩ — see CLOWNISH

classy *adj* having or showing elegance ⟨a *classy* seaside resort⟩ — see ELEGANT 1

clatter *n* a state of noisy, confused activity ⟨the *clatter* of a crowded cafeteria⟩ — see COMMOTION

clatter *vb* to make a series of short sharp noises ⟨horses' hooves *clattering* on the pavement⟩ — see RATTLE 1

clattering *adj* full of or characterized by the presence of noise ⟨a huge, *clattering* warehouse⟩ — see NOISY 2

clattery *adj* full of or characterized by the presence of noise ⟨a *clattery* diner serving hordes of hungry workers⟩ — see NOISY 2

clean *adj* **1** free from dirt or stain ⟨Although the soccer team always starts out with *clean* uniforms, they don't stay that way for long.⟩
synonyms chaste, fair, immaculate, pristine, spick-and-span (*or* spic-and-span), spotless, stainless, unsoiled, unstained, unsullied
related words pure, taintless, undefiled, unpolluted, untainted, wholesome; germfree, hygienic, sanitary, sterile; abluted, bleached, cleansed, purified, scrubbed, washed, whitened; milky, snowy, white; flawless, unblemished; bright, shiny, sparkling
near antonyms dingy, greasy, grimy, mucky, muddy, unwashed; defiled, germy, polluted, tainted, unsterile, unsterilized; blackened, discolored
antonyms besmirched, dirty, filthy, foul, grubby, smirched, soiled, spotted, stained, sullied, unclean, uncleaned
2 following or according to the rules ⟨a *clean* check from the other hockey player⟩ — see FAIR 3
3 free from any trace of the coarse or indecent ⟨Only *clean* songs will be permitted for the performances on the last night of summer camp.⟩ — see CHASTE 1
4 trying all possibilities ⟨Police made a *clean* sweep of the area before the governor's arrival.⟩ — see EXHAUSTIVE 1
5 having no exceptions or restrictions ⟨the *clean* joy of running that young children experience⟩ — see ABSOLUTE 2
6 lacking contents that could or should be present ⟨The ship returned with a *clean* hold.⟩ — see EMPTY 1

clean *adv* **1** according to the rules or the law ⟨a boxer who doesn't fight *clean*⟩ — see FAIRLY 2
2 to a full extent or degree ⟨The thief got *clean* away.⟩ — see FULLY 1

clean *vb* **1** to remove the dirt from ⟨We *cleaned* the clothes before donating them to charity.⟩
synonyms cleanse, turn out
related words decontaminate, purge, purify; disinfect, sanitize; brush, comb, dry-clean, dust, mop, muck (out), rinse, scour, scrub, shampoo, sponge, swab, sweep, vacuum, wash, wipe; brighten, deodorize, freshen; pick up, straighten (up), tidy, unclutter; neaten, trim
near antonyms begrime, muddy; defile, pollute, taint; blacken, discolor
antonyms besmirch, dirty, foul, soil, spot, stain, sully

2 to take the internal organs out of ⟨*cleaned* the rabbit before cooking it⟩ — see GUT

clean (up) *vb* **1** to make a place neat and orderly by removing extraneous stuff ⟨You're expected to *clean up* after you use the workroom.⟩
synonyms pick up
related words houseclean, housekeep; clean (off), clean (up), police (up), straighten (up), turn out, unclutter; arrange, order
phrases clean house, set straight
near antonyms clutter, disarrange, mess (up)
2 to remove objectionable parts from ⟨We *cleaned up* the rock star's interview before publishing it in the newspaper.⟩ — see CENSOR
3 to destroy all traces of ⟨hurriedly *cleaned up* the mess that they had created in the kitchen⟩ — see ANNIHILATE 1

cleaner *n* a substance used for cleaning ⟨a kitchen shelf loaded with household *cleaners*⟩
synonyms cleanser, detergent, soap
related words disinfectant, purifier, solvent; scrub, shampoo

cleanse *vb* **1** to free from moral guilt or blemish especially ceremonially ⟨In an elaborate ritual the priestess *cleansed* the gathering of supplicants.⟩ — see PURIFY 1
2 to remove the dirt from ⟨*Cleanse* the wound with soap and water before applying the bandage.⟩ — see CLEAN 1

cleanser *n* a substance used for cleaning ⟨a bathroom *cleanser*⟩ — see CLEANER

cleansing *n* the act or fact of freeing from sin or moral guilt ⟨underwent a *cleansing* before he could enter the temple's most sacred chamber⟩ — see PURIFICATION

clear *adj* **1** easily seen through ⟨the *clear* glass walls of the aquarium's giant ocean tank⟩
synonyms crystalline, limpid, liquid, lucent, pellucid, transparent
related words colorless, uncolored; lucid, semitranslucent, semitransparent, sheer, translucent
near antonyms dark, glazed, tinted; filmy, foggy, hazy, misty, nebulous, smoky (*also* smokey); dense, muddy, murky, turbid
antonyms cloudy, opaque
2 not subject to misinterpretation or more than one interpretation ⟨The meaning of her broad smile was *clear* to the whole class.⟩
synonyms apparent, bald, barefaced, broad, clear-cut, decided, distinct, evident, lucid, luminous, manifest, obvious, open-and-shut, palpable, patent, pellucid, perspicuous, plain, straightforward, transparent, unambiguous, unequivocal, unmistakable
related words digestible, knowable; self-explanatory; clean-cut, simple, tidy, uncomplicated; overt, undisguised; appreciable, perceptible, recognizable, sensible, tangible; discernible (*also* discernable), noticeable, observable, visible; black-and-white, explicit, trenchant, well-defined; clean, decipherable, fair, readable; accessible, coherent, intelligible
near antonyms incomprehensible, unfathomable, unintelligible, unknowable; impalpable, imperceptible, inappreciable, indiscernible, insensible; cloudy, gauzy, gray (*also* grey), hazy, imprecise, indefinite, indeterminate, misty, murky, nebulous, noncommittal, sketchy, slippery, subtle, vague
antonyms ambiguous, clouded, cryptic, dark, enigmatic (*also* enigmatical), equivocal, indistinct, mysterious, nonobvious, obfuscated, obscure, unapparent, unclarified, unclear, unclouded
3 having or showing a mind free from doubt ⟨I need to be absolutely *clear* about what you're saying.⟩ — see CERTAIN 2

4 not stormy or cloudy ⟨Novice pilots can only fly on *clear* days.⟩ — see FAIR 1

5 serving to put an end to all debate or questioning ⟨The evidence is *clear*: he's innocent.⟩ — see CONCLUSIVE 1

6 allowing passage without obstruction ⟨Flooding was widespread, and only some roads are *clear* so far.⟩ — see OPEN 1

7 free from guilt or blame ⟨slept with a *clear* conscience⟩ — see INNOCENT 2

8 giving off or reflecting much light ⟨Spermaceti candles were once highly prized for the *clear* flame that they produced.⟩ — see BRIGHT 1

clear *vb* **1** to rid the surface of (as an area) from things in the way ⟨The early settlers worked hard to *clear* the land for crops.⟩

synonyms free, open, unblock

related words ease, facilitate, loosen (up), smooth, unchoke, unclog, unstop; unclutter; strip

near antonyms clog, close, dam, obstruct, plug, stop; clutter (up)

antonyms block

2 to set (a person or thing) free of something that encumbers ⟨*cleared* the woods of brush⟩ — see RID

3 to give what is owed for ⟨We finally *cleared* the last debt.⟩ — see PAY 2

4 to remove the contents of ⟨*cleared* a drawer so there would be a place to store his clothes⟩ — see EMPTY

5 to remove usually visible impurities from ⟨*cleared* the car windows⟩ — see CLARIFY 1

6 to set free from entanglement or difficulty ⟨*cleared* himself of any involvement in the matter⟩ — see EXTRICATE

7 to make passage through (something) possible by removing obstructions ⟨Plows promptly *cleared* the roads of snow.⟩ — see OPEN 2

8 to free from a charge of wrongdoing ⟨She had once been accused of embezzlement, but an investigation by the bank *cleared* her.⟩ — see EXCULPATE

9 to give official acceptance of as satisfactory ⟨The administration *cleared* the plan, and building should begin shortly.⟩ — see APPROVE

10 to take away from a place or position ⟨*cleared* the dishes from the table⟩ — see REMOVE 2

11 to give information to ⟨Please *clear* my mind about the new arrangement regarding reimbursement for traveling expenses.⟩ — see ENLIGHTEN 1

12 to receive after charges and deductions have been made ⟨*cleared* enough from the house sale to be able to pay off the mortgage⟩ — see ²NET

clear (up) *vb* to make plain or understandable ⟨A simple explanation *cleared* the matter *up*.⟩ — see EXPLAIN 1

clearance *n* the approval by someone in authority for the doing of something ⟨We'll need official *clearance* before publishing this editorial.⟩ — see PERMISSION

clear–cut *adj* **1** not subject to misinterpretation or more than one interpretation ⟨a *clear-cut* case of plagiarism that resulted in her immediate dismissal⟩ — see CLEAR 2

2 so clearly expressed as to leave no doubt about the meaning ⟨*clear-cut* instructions that anyone should be able to follow⟩ — see EXPLICIT

cleared *adj* allowing passage without obstruction ⟨For safety reasons, there must be a *cleared* staircase at all times.⟩ — see OPEN 1

clearheaded *adj* **1** having full use of one's mind and control over one's actions ⟨waited until she was *clearheaded* to make the decision⟩ — see SANE

2 not having one's mind affected by alcohol ⟨woke up *clearheaded* and alert the next morning⟩ — see SOBER 1

clearing *n* **1** a setting free from a charge of wrongdoing

⟨The *clearing* of his good name became his obsession.⟩ — see ACQUITTAL

2 a small area of usually open land ⟨deer browsing in a *clearing* in the woods⟩ — see FIELD 1

clearness *n* the state or quality of being easily seen through ⟨The *clearness* of a diamond is one of the factors used to judge its quality.⟩ — see CLARITY 1

clear out *vb* **1** to cause (members of a group) to move widely apart ⟨The ushers *cleared out* the audience to prepare for the next performance.⟩ — see SCATTER 1

2 to get free from a dangerous or confining situation ⟨Everyone *cleared out* as soon as the fire alarm began sounding.⟩ — see ESCAPE 1

3 to leave a place often for another ⟨The lunch crowd usually *clears out* by 2:00 p.m. at the latest.⟩ — see GO 2

clear–sighted *adj* **1** having or showing a practical cleverness or judgment ⟨a *clear-sighted* businessman who doesn't let sentimentality affect his decisions⟩ — see SHREWD 1

2 having unusually keen vision ⟨A *clear-sighted* person could see for almost 20 miles from the observatory.⟩ — see SHARP-EYED

cleave *vb* to hold to something firmly as if by adhesion ⟨You should resolutely *cleave* to the facts in your report.⟩ — see STICK 1

cleft *n* an irregular usually narrow break in a surface created by pressure ⟨My fishing line managed to get wedged in a *cleft* in the rocks.⟩ — see CRACK 1

clemency *n* kind, gentle, or compassionate treatment especially towards someone who is undeserving of it ⟨The judge chose to show *clemency* to the truly repentant embezzler.⟩ — see MERCY 1

clement *adj* **1** marked by temperatures that are neither too high nor too low ⟨Hawaii is known for its delightfully *clement* climate.⟩

synonyms balmy, equable, genial, gentle, mild, moderate, soft, temperate

related words clear, cloudless, fair, rainless, sunny, sunshiny; calm, halcyon, peaceful, placid, tranquil; delightful, fine, pleasant

near antonyms blustering, blustery, breezy, gusty, rough, squally, stormy, windy; misty, rainy, showery; bleak, cloudy, dismal, foggy, gloomy, gray (*also* grey), hazy, overcast; bitter, dirty, foul, nasty, raw

antonyms harsh, inclement, intemperate, severe

2 tolerant and kind in the judgment of and expectations for others ⟨His *clement* application of authority was a welcome change after years of managerial heavy-handedness.⟩ — see INDULGENT 1

clench *n* the act or manner of holding ⟨Fearful that his suitcase might be stolen, he never once relaxed his *clench* on the handle.⟩ — see HOLD 1

clench *vb* to have or keep in one's hands ⟨*clenched* a tissue in his hands as he told his story of misfortune⟩ — see HOLD 1

clerical *adj* of, relating to, or characteristic of the clergy ⟨*clerical* duties such as providing spiritual counseling⟩

synonyms ministerial, pastoral, priestly, sacerdotal

related words evangelical (*also* evangelic), missionary; apostolic, canonical, diaconal, diocesan, episcopal, papal, patriarchal; churchly, ecclesiastic, ecclesiastical; divine, holy, religious, sacramental; conventual, mendicant, monastic; rabbinic (*or* rabbinical)

antonyms lay, nonclerical, secular, temporal

clerk *n* **1** an official whose job is to keep records ⟨You'll need to get a copy of your birth certificate from the office of the town *clerk*.⟩

synonyms register, registrar, scribe, secretary

related words archivist, bookkeeper, recorder, reporter,

transcriptionist; annalist, chronicler, documenter, historian

2 a person employed to sell goods or services especially in a store ⟨The *clerk* suggested a different brand.⟩ — see SALESPERSON

clever *adj* **1** showing a noteworthy use of the imagination and creativity especially in inventing ⟨an inventor who was constantly coming up with *clever* devices for doing everyday chores⟩

synonyms artful, creative, imaginative, ingenious, innovative, inventive

related words adventurous, fresh, groundbreaking, novel, original, visionary; cleverish, gadgety, gimmicky; convenient, handy, neat, nifty, practical, useful; complex, sophisticated; adroit, deft, dexterous (*also* dextrous), expert, handsome, tricky; brainy, intelligent, sharp, smart

near antonyms dull, pedantic, pedestrian, stodgy; assembly-line, canned, cookie-cutter, derivative, hackneyed, unoriginal; impractical, useless

antonyms uncreative, unimaginative

2 having or showing quickness of mind ⟨A *clever* student figured out a trick to do the assignment faster.⟩ — see INTELLIGENT 1

3 skillful with the hands ⟨The Shakers were *clever* artisans who created many ingenious and highly useful devices.⟩ — see DEXTEROUS 1

4 given to or marked by mature intelligent humor ⟨a *clever* joke that requires a little bit of thought on the part of the listener⟩ — see WITTY

5 having the skill and imagination to create new things ⟨I wonder what *clever* person thought of the digital camera!⟩ — see CREATIVE 1

cleverness *n* **1** mental skill or quickness ⟨It takes real *cleverness* to solve certain brainteasers.⟩ — see DEXTERITY 1

2 subtle or imaginative ability in inventing, devising, or executing something ⟨the undeniable *cleverness* of the negotiator, who managed to get each side to believe that they had won⟩ — see SKILL 1

3 the skill and imagination to create new things ⟨songwriter Cole Porter's overall *cleverness* with words, including his effortless ability to rhyme and pun⟩ — see CREATIVITY 1

cliché *also* **cliche** *adj* used or heard so often as to be dull ⟨a *cliché* tale of betrayal among the fabulously rich⟩ — see STALE 1

cliché *also* **cliche** *n* an idea or expression that has been used by many people ⟨Try to write a love story without resorting to well-worn *clichés*.⟩ — see COMMONPLACE

click *vb* **1** to form a close personal relationship ⟨We just *clicked* from the moment we met.⟩ — see COMMUNE

2 to turn out as planned or desired ⟨Sometimes an idea simply *clicks*.⟩ — see SUCCEED 1

client *n* a person who buys a product or uses a service from a business ⟨a law firm soliciting new *clients* through television advertising⟩ — see CUSTOMER 1

cliff *n* a steep wall of rock, earth, or ice ⟨The *cliff* rises 200 feet from the island's south shore.⟩

synonyms bluff, crag, escarpment, palisade, precipice, scar, scarp

related words butte, hogback, tor; bulwark, embankment; pitch

climate *n* **1** a special quality or impression associated with something ⟨a new school designed to encourage a *climate* of learning⟩ — see AURA 1

2 the circumstances, conditions, or objects by which one is surrounded ⟨It's hard to concentrate in this hectic *climate*.⟩ — see ENVIRONMENT

climax *n* **1** a point in a chain of events at which an impor-

tant change (as in one's fortunes) occurs ⟨The *climax* of the story occurs when the hero discovers the identity of his father.⟩ — see TURNING POINT

2 the highest part or point ⟨the *climax* of her career as a performer⟩ — see HEIGHT 1

climax *vb* to bring to a triumphant conclusion ⟨Organizers *climaxed* the county fair with a pie-eating contest.⟩ — see CROWN

climb *n* the act or an instance of rising or climbing up ⟨a long hard *climb* up the mountain⟩ — see ASCENT 1

climb *vb* **1** to move (as up or over something) often with the help of the hands in holding or pulling ⟨Visitors should use caution when *climbing* over the wet rocks along the shore.⟩

synonyms clamber, scrabble, scramble, swarm

related words shimmy, shin, shinny, skin; ascend, free-climb, get up, mount, scale, summit, surmount; claw, sprawl, struggle

2 to move or extend upward ⟨smoke from the cabin *climbing* in the still mountain air⟩ — see ASCEND

3 to become greater in extent, volume, amount, or number ⟨Complaints to the cable company *climbed* after the changeover.⟩ — see INCREASE 2

clinch *vb* to make final, definite, or beyond dispute ⟨The rain *clinched* the matter: we would have the party indoors.⟩

synonyms decide, determine, nail, settle

related words demonstrate, establish, nail (down), prove, show; affirm, assure, ensure, insure, secure; define, specify, state, stipulate; clarify, clear (up), illuminate; conclude, end, finish

near antonyms confuse, muddle, muddy, unsettle

clincher *n* something (as a fact or argument) that is decisive or overwhelming ⟨The fact that the resort had tennis courts was the *clincher* in our deciding to stay there.⟩

synonyms crusher, topper

related words deathblow, knockout; determinant, factor

phrases ace in the hole

cling *n* a physical sticking to as if by glue ⟨For certain types of materials that plastic wrap has very little *cling*.⟩ — see ADHESION 1

cling *vb* to hold to something firmly as if by adhesion ⟨a dozen magnets *clinging* to the refrigerator⟩ — see STICK 1

cling (to) *vb* **1** to give steadfast support to ⟨continued to *cling to* the old ideas of child rearing long after they had gone out of fashion⟩ — see ADHERE (TO) 1

2 to have or keep in one's hands ⟨*clung to* a pole in the subway car to keep from falling as it lurched along⟩ — see HOLD 1

clink *vb* to make a repeated sharp light ringing sound ⟨coins *clinking* in his pocket as he traipsed down the street⟩ — see JINGLE

clip *n* a hard strike with a part of the body or an instrument ⟨An unexpectedly low branch dealt him a *clip* to the head.⟩ — see ¹BLOW

clip *vb* **1** to make (something) shorter or smaller with the use of a cutting instrument ⟨a mother who's sad to see her little boy's curls *clipped* for the first time⟩

synonyms bob, crop, cut, cut back, dock, lop (off), nip, pare, poll, prune, shave, shear, snip, trim

related words skive, whittle; manicure, mow; pinch, stump; curtail, shorten

near antonyms elongate, extend, lengthen

2 to deliver a blow to (someone or something) usually in a strong vigorous manner ⟨The pitch *clipped* the batter's helmet with enough force to knock it clean off his head.⟩ — see HIT 1

clique *n* a group of people sharing a common interest and relating together socially ⟨That *clique* spends every lunch together.⟩ — see GANG 2

cliquey *adj* bound together by feelings of very close association ⟨found the people at the company to be *cliquey* and unfriendly⟩ — see CLOSE-KNIT

cloak *n* **1** something that covers or conceals like a piece of cloth ⟨the *cloak* of mystery that surrounds the royal family⟩
synonyms blanket, cope, cover, covering, curtain, hood, mantle, mask, pall, robe, shroud, veil, wraps
related words blind, concealer, screen, shield; fig leaf, Trojan horse; camouflage, disguise, facade (*also* façade), face, mask, veneer; gloss, varnish
2 a sleeveless garment worn so as to hang over the shoulders, arms, and back ⟨threw a *cloak* around his shoulders⟩ — see ¹CAPE

cloak *vb* **1** to change the dress or looks of so as to conceal true identity ⟨The biologists *cloaked* their observation post as a thicket of blackberry bushes.⟩ — see DISGUISE 1
2 to keep secret or shut off from view ⟨*cloaked* their military maneuvers from the outside world⟩ — see ¹HIDE 2

clobber *vb* **1** to deliver a blow to (someone or something) usually in a strong vigorous manner ⟨He *clobbered* the ball, sending it in a high arc toward the back wall.⟩ — see HIT 1
2 to defeat by a large margin ⟨They *clobbered* the opposing team.⟩ — see WHIP 2

clock *n* a device to measure time ⟨The *clock* reads 5:00 p.m.⟩ — see TIMEPIECE

clock *vb* to deliver a blow to (someone or something) usually in a strong vigorous manner ⟨I accidentally *clocked* my tennis instructor with my racket.⟩ — see HIT 1

clod *n* **1** a big clumsy often slow-witted person ⟨Despite his imposing size, he's no simple *clod*.⟩ — see OAF 1
2 a small uneven mass ⟨A *clod* of dirt stuck to the bottom of the bucket.⟩ — see LUMP 1
3 the loose surface material in which plants naturally grow ⟨faced with the task of burying his beloved wife in the cold, hard *clod* of the frontier⟩ — see DIRT 1

cloddish *adj* having or showing crudely insensitive or impolite manners ⟨the *cloddish* behavior of the frat boys at the party⟩ — see CLOWNISH

clodhopper *n* **1** an awkward or simple person especially from a small town or the country ⟨a stereotypical depiction of *clodhoppers* visiting the city for the first time⟩ — see HICK
2 a big clumsy often slow-witted person ⟨I do not want that *clodhopper* handling my rare antiques!⟩ — see OAF 1

clog *n* something that makes movement or progress difficult ⟨She's not one to let moral principle be a *clog* upon her conscience.⟩ — see ENCUMBRANCE

clog *vb* **1** to prevent passage through by filling with something ⟨the discovery that a ton of hair was *clogging* the drain in the tub⟩
synonyms block, choke, clot, congest, dam, jam, obstruct, occlude, plug (up), stop (up), stuff
related words bung, cork, stopper, stopple; fill, pack; fur, silt; flood, glut, inundate, overwhelm, swamp
near antonyms excavate, hollow (out), scoop (out); empty, lighten
antonyms clear, free, open (up), unblock, unclog, unstop
2 to create difficulty for the work or activity of ⟨a court system *clogged* by frivolous suits⟩ — see HAMPER

cloister *n* a residence for men under religious vows ⟨monks living in a *cloister* in the country⟩ — see MONASTERY

cloistered *adj* screened or sequestered from view ⟨Behind the stately townhouses lie *cloistered* gardens that the public never sees.⟩ — see SECLUDED

¹**close** *n* an open space wholly or partly enclosed (as by buildings or walls) ⟨a garden in a *close* at the center of the complex⟩ — see COURT 2

²**close** *n* **1** the stopping of a process or activity ⟨at the *close* of the evening⟩ — see END 1
2 the last part of a process or action ⟨managed to conduct the negotiations to a satisfactory *close*⟩ — see FINALE

close *adj* **1** having little space between items or parts ⟨The soldiers marched in *close* formation against the enemy.⟩
synonyms compact, crowded, dense, jam-packed, packed, thick, tight
related words crammed, jammed, overcrowded; massed, pressed, squeezed; airtight, snug; compacted, compressed, condensed, congested; firm, hard, solid; impenetrable, impermeable, impervious
near antonyms commodious, roomy, spacious
antonyms airy, loose, open, uncrowded
2 not being distant in time, space, or significance ⟨My birthday is *close* to Thanksgiving.⟩ ⟨a shopping mall that is very *close* to the highway⟩ ⟨These words are *close* synonyms.⟩
synonyms immediate, near, nearby, neighboring, next-door, nigh
related words abutting, adjacent, adjoining, bordering, contiguous; approaching, coming, forthcoming, oncoming, upcoming; accessible, convenient, handy; close-in, hand-to-hand
phrases at hand, to hand
near antonyms divorced, removed, separated
antonyms away, deep, distant, far, faraway, far-off, remote
3 showing little difference in the standing of the competitors ⟨The election results were so *close* that the votes had to be recounted.⟩
synonyms hairbreadth, narrow, neck and neck, nip and tuck, tight
related words crowded
4 closely acquainted ⟨a small wedding ceremony that was limited to *close* friends⟩ — see FAMILIAR 1
5 given to keeping one's activities hidden from public observation or knowledge ⟨She was as *close* as a stone when it came to talking about her love life.⟩ — see SECRETIVE
6 giving or sharing as little as possible ⟨the kind of folks who are very *close* when charity calls⟩ — see STINGY 1
7 lacking fresh air ⟨a small room with an uncomfortably *close* atmosphere⟩ — see STUFFY 1
8 meeting the highest standard of accuracy ⟨a *close* analysis of the box-office performance of action movies⟩ — see PRECISE 1

close *adv* at, within, or to a short distance or time ⟨The stranded passengers drew *close* for reassurance.⟩ — see NEAR 1

close *vb* **1** to position (something) so as to prevent passage through an opening ⟨Be sure to *close* the gate when you leave.⟩
synonyms shut
related words bar, batten (down), bolt, chain, fasten, latch, lock; plug, seal, stopper; secure; bang, clap, slam
near antonyms unbar, unbolt, unchain, unfasten, unlatch, unlock, unseal
antonyms open
2 to stop the operations of ⟨The merchant will *close* the store if business doesn't improve.⟩
synonyms shut
related words phase out, turn off; extinguish, quell, suppress; gag, muzzle, silence; fail, fold
near antonyms build, expand

antonyms open, start

3 to bring (an event) to a natural or appropriate stopping point ⟨We'll *close* the assembly with the singing of our national anthem.⟩

synonyms complete, conclude, end, finish, round (off *or* out), terminate, wind up, wrap up

related words climax, crown; consummate, perfect; halt, stop, suspend

phrases ring down the curtain (on)

antonyms begin, commence, inaugurate, open, start

4 to come to an end ⟨The third term *closes* on Friday.⟩ — see CEASE 1

5 to come near or nearer ⟨The two groups *closed* with each other from opposite sides of the field.⟩ — see APPROACH 1

close (off) *vb* to disallow entry into (a place) by means of a physical barrier at the entry point ⟨Museum officials *closed off* the west wing after the fire.⟩

synonyms bar, barricade, blockade, guard

related words curtain (off), screen (off); dike, fence, gate, hedge; bolt, lock; obstruct

near antonyms reopen, unblock, unbolt

antonyms open, unbar

closefisted *adj* giving or sharing as little as possible ⟨*closefisted* administrators objecting to legitimate office expenses⟩ — see STINGY 1

close–knit *adj* bound together by feelings of very close association ⟨a *close-knit* family that constantly keeps in touch⟩

synonyms clannish, cliquey

related words bosom, chummy, close, familiar, friendly, intimate, pally, palsy, thick, tight; exclusive; incestuous; forbidding, inhospitable, unfriendly

near antonyms receptive, welcoming

closely *adv* to a close degree ⟨*closely* resembling a normal outfit⟩ — see NEAR 2

closemouthed *adj* **1** given to keeping one's activities hidden from public observation or knowledge ⟨He remained *closemouthed* about their activities.⟩ — see SECRETIVE

2 tending not to speak frequently (as by habit or inclination) ⟨Let's encourage the *closemouthed* children to speak up and not be shy.⟩ — see SILENT 2

closeness *n* **1** the practice or habit of keeping secrets or keeping one's affairs secret ⟨The reporter tried to penetrate her *closeness* about her private life.⟩ — see SECRECY

2 the quality or practice of being overly sparing with money ⟨rebelled against his parents' *closeness* with his allowance⟩ — see PARSIMONY 1

3 the quality or state of being very accurate ⟨The body was too decomposed to estimate the time of death with any great *closeness*.⟩ — see PRECISION

4 the state of being in a very personal or private relationship ⟨The *closeness* of their relationship was a matter of intense speculation among their coworkers.⟩ — see FAMILIARITY 1

5 the state or condition of being near ⟨We were surprised by the *closeness* of everything to our downtown loft.⟩ — see PROXIMITY

6 strict attentiveness to what one is doing ⟨How much you get out of the lecture will depend on the *closeness* with which you listen to it.⟩ — see CARE 1

closer *adj* being the less far of two ⟨The *closer* gas station was also more expensive.⟩ — see NEAR 1

closet *n* **1** a built-in space for storage behind a door ⟨a broom *closet* for the vacuum, carpet sweeper, ironing board, etc.⟩

synonyms cupboard, press

related words larder; cloakroom, coatroom, wardrobe

2 an area within a building that has been set apart from surrounding space by a wall ⟨a huge walk-in *closet*⟩ — see ROOM 2

3 a storage case typically having doors and shelves ⟨a china *closet* in the Hepplewhite style⟩ — see CABINET

closet *vb* to close or shut in by or as if by barriers ⟨He *closeted* himself in his study, vowing not to emerge until he had finished the term paper.⟩ — see ENCLOSE 1

closing *adj* following all others of the same kind in order or time ⟨The orchestra's *closing* piece is traditionally the national anthem.⟩ — see LAST 1

closing *n* the last part of a process or action ⟨A stand-up comedian has to have a strong *closing* if he wants a spirited round of applause.⟩ — see FINALE

closure *n* the stopping of a process or activity ⟨After the *closure* of the region's last copper mine, the population simply withered away.⟩ — see END 1

clot *n* **1** a number of things considered as a unit ⟨A *clot* of daisies occupied one corner of the flower bed.⟩ — see GROUP 1

2 a small uneven mass ⟨*clots* of dirt that were flung up by the horses' hooves⟩ — see LUMP 1

clot *vb* **1** to prevent passage through by filling with something ⟨streets *clotted* by traffic⟩ — see CLOG 1

2 to turn from a liquid into a substance resembling jelly ⟨Scabs form over cuts when your blood starts to *clot*.⟩ — see COAGULATE

cloth *n* a woven or knitted material (as of cotton or nylon) ⟨Cotton canvas was the *cloth* traditionally used for a ship's sails.⟩

synonyms fabric, textile

related words fiber, thread, yarn

clothe *vb* **1** to outfit with clothes and especially fine or special clothes ⟨They liked to *clothe* the twins in identical outfits.⟩

synonyms apparel, array, attire, bedeck, caparison, costume, dress, dress up, garb, garment, get up, gown, invest, rig (out), robe, suit

related words cloak, frock, jacket, mantle, vest; swaddle, swathe, wrap; accoutre (*or* accouter), equip, furnish, outfit, tailor, uniform; dress down, underdress

near antonyms denude, uncover, undrape, unveil

antonyms disarray, disrobe, strip, unclothe, undress

2 to convey in appropriate or telling terms ⟨regulations *clothed* in obscure terminology⟩ — see PHRASE

clothes *pl n* covering for the human body ⟨Put on your warmest *clothes*—it's freezing outside!⟩ — see CLOTHING

clothing *n* covering for the human body ⟨a store that sells both men's and women's *clothing*⟩

synonyms apparel, attire, clothes, dress, duds, garments, gear, raiment, rig, threads, togs, wear

related words wardrobe; array, bravery, caparison, finery, gaiety (*also* gayety), glad rags, pretties, regalia, trim; frippery; tatters; costume, ensemble, frock, garb, getup, guise, livery, outfit; civvies (*also* civies), mufti, couture, ready-to-wear, tailoring; activewear, loungewear, outerwear, playwear, sportswear; nightclothes, sleepwear, smallclothes, underclothes, underwear; haberdashery, menswear

cloud *n* an overspreading element that produces an atmosphere of gloom ⟨All day we were under a *cloud* until we heard the good news.⟩

synonyms darkness, pall, shadow

related words fog, haze, mist, murk; midnight, night; mantle, shroud, veil

cloud *vb* **1** to make dark, dim, or indistinct ⟨the diner's dark interior, *clouded* with smoke and grease⟩

synonyms becloud, bedim, befog, blacken, blur, dark-

en, dim, fog, haze, mist, obscure, overcast, overcloud, overshadow, shadow, shroud
related words adumbrate, blot out, conceal, eclipse, hide, obliterate, screen, shade; camouflage, cloak, cover, curtain, disguise, mask, veil
near antonyms expose, reveal, uncover, unveil
antonyms brighten, illuminate, illumine, light (up), lighten
2 to make (something) unclear to the understanding ⟨Don't *cloud* the issue with obscure statistics.⟩ — see CONFUSE 2
cloudburst *n* a steady falling of water from the sky in significant quantity ⟨The weatherman warned of possible *cloudbursts* in the afternoon.⟩ — see RAIN 1
clouded *adj* **1** covered over by clouds ⟨*Clouded* skies did not diminish our fun.⟩ — see OVERCAST
2 filled with or dimmed by fine particles (as of dust or water) in suspension ⟨With only a *clouded* view of the valley before, we canceled the hang gliding.⟩ — see HAZY 1
cloudless *adj* not stormy or cloudy ⟨playing in the park on a *cloudless* summer day⟩ — see FAIR 1
cloudy *adj* **1** having visible particles in liquid suspension ⟨The water coming out of the faucet was unusually *cloudy*.⟩
synonyms muddy, roiled, turbid
related words dingy, filmy, hazy, scummy, unfiltered; inky, muddied, muddled, murky, puddled, sludgy; opaque
near antonyms clarified, filtered, purified; colorless, transparent, uncolored
antonyms clear, crystalline
2 covered over by clouds ⟨The skies grew *cloudy* and we headed home.⟩ — see OVERCAST
3 filled with or dimmed by fine particles (as of dust or water) in suspension ⟨The room grew *cloudy* with smoke from the fire.⟩ — see HAZY 1
4 causing or marked by an atmosphere lacking in cheer ⟨After his third failed business, he seemed destined to live the rest of his life in a permanently *cloudy* mood.⟩ — see GLOOMY 1
clout *n* **1** a hard strike with a part of the body or an instrument ⟨gave the stubborn handle a solid *clout* to make it turn⟩ — see ¹BLOW
2 the power to direct the thinking or behavior of others usually indirectly ⟨He has a great deal of *clout* in the film industry.⟩ — see INFLUENCE 1
clout *vb* to deliver a blow to (someone or something) usually in a strong vigorous manner ⟨*clouted* the nail with the hammer and drove it all the way into the wood⟩ — see HIT 1
clown *n* **1** a comically dressed performer (as at a circus) who entertains with playful tricks and ridiculous behavior ⟨a *clown* wearing big floppy shoes and a red wig⟩
synonyms buffoon, harlequin, zany
related words cutup, madcap; fool, jester, motley, scaramouch (*or* scaramouche); mime, mimic, mummer, pantaloon; comedian, comedienne, comic, droll, gagman, gagster, humorist, joker, jokester, merry-andrew, second banana, top banana, wag, wit
2 a person whose behavior is offensive to others ⟨You should stay away from that *clown*.⟩ — see JERK 1
clown (around) *vb* to engage in attention-getting playful or boisterous behavior ⟨As a youngster he was always *clowning* around in the classroom.⟩ — see CUT UP 1
clowning *n* wildly playful or mischievous behavior ⟨Our coworker's *clowning* was distracting, but fun to watch.⟩ — see HORSEPLAY
clownish *adj* having or showing crudely insensitive or impolite manners ⟨the *clownish* antics of some of the teenagers at the wedding reception⟩

synonyms boorish, churlish, classless, cloddish, loutish, uncouth
related words coarse, ill-bred, uncultivated, unpolished, unrefined, unsophisticated; tasteless, vulgar; beastly; doltish, oafish, stupid; discourteous, impolite, mannerless, rude, uncivil, ungracious, unmannerly; awkward, ungainly
near antonyms couth, cultivated, polished, refined, sophisticated, well-bred; classy, courtly, genteel, gentlemanly, ladylike; civil, courteous, polite
club *n* **1** a heavy rigid stick used as a weapon or for punishment ⟨They pretended to be knights with wooden swords and *clubs*.⟩
synonyms bat, billy, billy club, bludgeon, cane, cudgel, nightstick, rod, shillelagh (*also* shillalah), staff, truncheon
related words knobkerrie, mace; birch, crabstick, hickory, rattan, stave, switch; beetle, gavel, hammer, mallet, maul, sledgehammer; crook, crosier (*or* crozier), walking stick
2 the meeting place of an organization ⟨The Elks gather at their *club* every Monday evening.⟩
synonyms clubhouse, lodge
related words den, hangout, haunt, hideaway, hideout, lair; camp, headquarters; hall, house, meetinghouse
3 a group of persons formally joined together for some common interest ⟨an alumni *club*⟩ — see ASSOCIATION 2
4 a bar or restaurant offering special nighttime entertainment (as music, dancing, or comedy acts) ⟨a weekly newspaper column devoted to current happenings on the local *club* scene⟩ — see NIGHTCLUB
club *vb* **1** to form or enter into an association that furthers the interests of its members ⟨*clubbed* together to share their love of model rockets⟩ — see ALLY
2 to strike repeatedly ⟨Frustrated, the gardener *clubbed* the inoffensive weed into submission.⟩ — see BEAT 1
clubhouse *n* the meeting place of an organization ⟨We plan to meet at the *clubhouse* each week.⟩ — see CLUB 2
clue *n* a slight or indirect pointing to something (as a solution or explanation) ⟨vainly searched for a *clue* to the answer⟩ — see HINT 1
clue (in) *vb* to give information to ⟨Would you *clue* him *in* on the plan?⟩ — see ENLIGHTEN 1
clump *n* **1** a number of things considered as a unit ⟨Scattered *clumps* of houses were visible from the air.⟩ — see GROUP 1
2 a small uneven mass ⟨a *clump* of dirt⟩ — see LUMP 1
clump *vb* to move heavily or clumsily ⟨a child *clumping* around the house in her father's oversized boots⟩ — see LUMBER 1
clumpy *adj* having small pieces or lumps spread throughout ⟨The soil was a little too *clumpy* to make for a good garden.⟩ — see CHUNKY 1
clumsy *adj* **1** lacking or showing a lack of nimbleness in using one's hands ⟨Diamond cutting is no job for a *clumsy* person.⟩
synonyms awkward, graceless, heavy-handed, left-handed, maladroit, unhandy
related words bunglesome, bungling, gauche, inept, inexpert, unskilled, unskillful
phrases all thumbs
near antonyms expert, masterly, skilled, skillful; coordinated
antonyms deft, dexterous (*also* dextrous), handy, sure-handed
2 having or showing an inability to move in a graceful manner ⟨a *clumsy* bow⟩ ⟨*clumsy* on the dance floor⟩
synonyms awkward, gawky, graceless, ungainly
related words galumphing, lubberly, lumbering, lumpish, shambling, shuffling, unsteady, wobbly (*also* wabbly)

near antonyms light, light-footed (*also* light-foot), lissome (*also* lissom), lithe, nimble, sure-footed
antonyms coordinated, graceful
3 lacking social grace and assurance ⟨felt *clumsy* in the unfamiliar uniform⟩ — see AWKWARD 1
4 showing or marked by a lack of skill and tact (as in dealing with a situation) ⟨a *clumsy* joke⟩ — see AWKWARD 2
5 difficult to use or operate especially because of size, weight, or design ⟨a *clumsy* contraption, but it got the job done⟩ — see CUMBERSOME
6 hastily or roughly constructed ⟨a *clumsy* mock-up of the real thing⟩ — see RUDE 1
cluster *n* **1** a number of things considered as a unit ⟨a *cluster* of stars in the southern sky⟩ — see GROUP 1
2 a usually small number of persons considered as a unit ⟨a small *cluster* of reporters waited by the courthouse door⟩ — see GROUP 2
cluster *vb* **1** to come together into one body or place ⟨The mice *clustered* together into a small burrow.⟩ — see ASSEMBLE 1
2 to gather into a closely packed group ⟨All the cottages are *clustered* on one end of the lake.⟩ — see ²PRESS 3
¹**clutch** *n* **1** a number of things considered as a unit ⟨A *clutch* of medals adorned the general's chest.⟩ — see GROUP 1
2 a usually small number of persons considered as a unit ⟨a *clutch* of people traveling together⟩ — see GROUP 2
²**clutch** *n* **1** a time or state of affairs requiring prompt or decisive action ⟨a football quarterback who always comes through in the *clutch*⟩ — see EMERGENCY
2 the right or means to command or control others ⟨a nation no longer living in the *clutch* of a cruel tyrant⟩ — see POWER 1
clutch *vb* to have or keep in one's hands ⟨He *clutched* the eggs carefully so he wouldn't drop them.⟩ — see HOLD 1
clutter *n* an unorganized collection or mixture of various things ⟨a scrapbook that was a *clutter* of snapshots, diary entries, letters, and newspaper clippings⟩ — see MISCELLANY 1
cluttered *adj* lacking in order, neatness, and often cleanliness ⟨Keeping a *cluttered* workshop makes it hard to find the right tool.⟩ — see MESSY
coach *n* a person who trains performers or athletes ⟨a *coach* who is highly respected by all of the baseball players⟩
synonyms trainer
related words handler, manager; instructor, teacher, tutor; driller, drillmaster; adviser (*or* advisor), counselor (*or* counsellor), guide, mentor
coach *vb* to give advice and instruction to (someone) regarding the course or process to be followed ⟨carefully *coached* us through the home-buying process⟩ — see GUIDE 1
coadjutor *n* a person who helps a more skilled person ⟨He was appointed *coadjutor* to the president.⟩ — see HELPER
coagulate *vb* to turn from a liquid into a substance resembling jelly ⟨The blood *coagulated*, and a scab formed on the wound.⟩
synonyms clot, congeal, gel, jell, jelly, set
related words cake, concrete, firm (up), fix, freeze, harden, solidify; condense, thicken; clump, curd, curdle, gum, lump (up)
near antonyms liquefy (*also* liquify), melt, thaw
coalesce *vb* **1** to come together to form a single unit ⟨Several small townships have *coalesced* into a single metropolis.⟩ — see UNITE 1
2 to form or enter into an association that furthers the interests of its members ⟨The historic preservation movement gained momentum when the two groups *coalesced*.⟩ — see ALLY
coalition *n* **1** a group of people acting together within a larger group ⟨rival *coalitions* struggling for control of the party⟩ — see FACTION
2 an association of persons, parties, or states for mutual assistance and protection ⟨Preservationists formed a *coalition* with the theater owners to preserve these historic structures.⟩ — see CONFEDERACY
coarse *adj* **1** made up of large particles ⟨*Coarse* rock salt was sprinkled on the icy walkway.⟩
synonyms grainy, granular, granulated
related words unfiltered, unrefined; earthy, gravelly, gritty, sandy; pebbly, rocky, stony (*also* stoney); coarse-grained, cracked, kibbled, lumpy, mealy
near antonyms buttery, smooth, velvety; filtered, refined; close-grained, ground, micronized, milled, mulled, pestled, pulverized, reduced, triturated
antonyms dusty, fine, floury, powdery, superfine, ultrafine
2 lacking in refinement or good taste ⟨They were disgusted by his *coarse* manners.⟩
synonyms common, crass, crude, gross, ill-bred, insensible, low, lowbred, lowbrow, raffish, rough, roughneck, rude, rugged, tasteless, uncouth, uncultivated, uncultured, unpolished, unrefined, vulgar
related words boorish, churlish, cloddish, clownish, loutish, ungentlemanly; clumsy, lubberly, lumpish, oafish; inconsiderate, insensitive, thoughtless; countrified (*also* countryfied), provincial, rustic (*also* rustical), unsophisticated; graceless, inelegant, tacky; animallike, barbaric, barbarous, uncivilized; mannerless, unmannerly
near antonyms aristocratic, courtly, patrician; elegant, graceful, restrained; considerate, gracious, sensitive, thoughtful; citified, sophisticated, urbane
antonyms civilized, cultivated, cultured, genteel, polished, refined, smooth, tasteful, ultrarefined, well-bred
3 depicting or referring to sexual matters in a way that is unacceptable in polite society ⟨offended by the *coarse* humor at the celebrity roast⟩ — see OBSCENE 1
4 harsh and dry in sound ⟨a *coarse* laugh⟩ — see HOARSE
5 not having a level or smooth surface ⟨the *coarse* surface of the sandpaper⟩ — see UNEVEN 1
6 of low quality ⟨*coarse* imitations of quality merchandise⟩ — see CHEAP 2
coarseness *n* **1** the quality or state of being obscene ⟨the *coarseness* of the movie's humor⟩ — see OBSCENITY
2 the quality or state of lacking refinement or good taste ⟨There was a *coarseness* about her that really bothered my well-mannered friends.⟩ — see VULGARITY 1
coast *vb* to move or proceed smoothly and readily ⟨*coasting* along easily in the light traffic⟩ — see FLOW 2
coat *n* the hairy covering of a mammal especially when fine, soft, and thick ⟨A poodle's *coat* is often extremely curly.⟩ — see FUR 1
coat *vb* to form a layer over ⟨Thicken the sauce until it will *coat* the back of a spoon.⟩ — see COVER 2
coax *vb* to get (someone) to do something by gentle urging, special attention, or flattery ⟨Trying to *coax* their father into taking them on a ski trip, the kids mentioned what a great skier he is.⟩
synonyms blandish, blarney, cajole, palaver, soft-soap, wheedle
related words adulate, flatter, overpraise; charm, woo; beg, beseech, importune, urge; beguile, cozen, finagle, wangle, wile; entice, lure, seduce, tempt
near antonyms bug, nag, pester, tease; browbeat, bulldoze, bully, cow, intimidate; coerce, compel, constrain, demand, force, make, oblige, require

¹**cock** *n* a fixture for controlling the flow of a liquid ⟨an automobile radiator *cock*⟩ — see FAUCET

²**cock** *n* a quantity of things thrown or stacked on one another ⟨a *cock* of hay⟩ — see ¹PILE 1

³**cock** *n* the act of positioning or an instance of being positioned at an angle ⟨A slight *cock* of his head suggested that he was listening in on our conversation.⟩ — see TILT

cock *vb* to set or cause to be at an angle ⟨*cocked* his head to the side as he listened to her quizzically⟩ — see LEAN 1

cockeyed *adj* **1** inclined or twisted to one side ⟨rakishly wears his hat a little *cockeyed*⟩ — see AWRY
2 showing or marked by a lack of good sense or judgment ⟨a *cockeyed* scheme to build a shopping mall in the middle of nowhere⟩ — see FOOLISH 1

cocksure *adj* **1** displaying or marked by rude boldness ⟨his *cocksure* assertion that he could win⟩ — see NERVY 1
2 showing or having a mind free from doubt ⟨You're always so *cocksure* about everything.⟩ — see CERTAIN 2

cocky *adj* displaying or marked by rude boldness ⟨a *cocky* young actor who thought that he was God's gift to the theater⟩ — see NERVY 1

cocoon *n* **1** something that encloses another thing especially to protect it ⟨He retired to the *cocoon* of his study whenever he'd had enough of the company.⟩ — see ¹CASE 1
2 something that serves as a protective barrier ⟨As the TV had been packed in a *cocoon* of Styrofoam, it arrived in one piece.⟩ — see CUSHION

cocoon *vb* to surround or cover closely ⟨*Cocooned* in puffy down parkas, we braved the bitter cold as best we could.⟩ — see ENFOLD 1

coddle *vb* **1** to cook in a liquid heated to the point that it gives off steam ⟨a hearty, traditional breakfast that included *coddled* eggs⟩ — see BOIL 2
2 to treat with great or excessive care ⟨accused the judiciary of *coddling* criminals⟩ — see BABY

code *n* a collection or system of rules of conduct ⟨Hammurabi was an ancient king of Babylon with a famous *code* of laws⟩ ⟨the tax *code*.⟩
synonyms canon, constitution, decalogue, law
related words discipline, establishment; common law, legislation

codger *n* a person of odd or whimsical habits ⟨just an old *codger* who never harmed anyone⟩ — see ECCENTRIC

codify *vb* **1** to arrange or assign according to type ⟨*Codify* these ancient cultures according to their political structures.⟩ — see CLASSIFY 1
2 to put into a particular arrangement ⟨The rules for the game were *codified* over a hundred years ago.⟩ — see ORDER 1

coequal *adj* resembling another in every respect ⟨The two agencies had *coequal* duties.⟩ — see SAME 1

coequal *n* one that is equal to another in status, achievement, or value ⟨Viewing himself as the *coequal* of the Caesars of ancient Rome, Napoléon surrounded himself with the emblems of classical antiquity.⟩ — see EQUAL

coerce *vb* to cause (a person) to give in to pressure ⟨was *coerced* into signing the document⟩ — see FORCE

coerced *adj* not made or done willingly or by choice ⟨*coerced* participation that couldn't last⟩ — see INVOLUNTARY 1

coercion *n* the use of power to impose one's will on another ⟨A promise obtained by *coercion* is never binding.⟩ — see FORCE 2

coeval *adj* existing or occurring at the same period of time ⟨two stars thought to be *coeval* because they have nearly the same mass and brightness⟩ — see CONTEMPORARY 1

coeval *n* a person who lives at the same time or is about the same age as another ⟨Somewhat surprisingly, Saint Patrick and Attila the Hun were *coevals*.⟩ — see CONTEMPORARY

coexist *vb* to occur or exist at the same time ⟨two nations that should be able to *coexist* without conflict⟩ — see COINCIDE 1

coexistence *n* the occurrence or existence of several things at once ⟨the *coexistence* of dinosaurs and turtles⟩ — see CONCURRENCE 1

coexistent *adj* **1** existing or occurring at the same period of time ⟨the theory that there were two *coexistent* hominids inhabiting that region⟩ — see CONTEMPORARY 1
2 present at the same time and place ⟨a disorder that is often *coexistent* with a deficiency of certain vitamins⟩ — see COINCIDENT 1

coexisting *adj* **1** existing or occurring at the same period of time ⟨*coexisting* but widely separated cultures that had no knowledge of one another⟩ — see CONTEMPORARY 1
2 present at the same time and place ⟨*coexisting* beliefs⟩ — see COINCIDENT 1

coextensive *adj* **1** occupying the same space ⟨South Dakota's Todd County is *coextensive* with the main Rosebud Sioux Reservation.⟩
synonyms coincident
related words allover, overlaying, superimposed, superposed, underlying; conjoining, crisscrossing, intersecting, overlapping; coaxial, concurrent, convergent; conjunctional
near antonyms nonconcurrent, noncongruent
2 existing or occurring at the same period of time ⟨The golden age of Dutch culture was roughly *coextensive* with the Netherlands' reign as a world power.⟩ — see CONTEMPORARY 1

coffer *n* **1** a specially reinforced container to keep valuables safe ⟨kept the jewels in a locked *coffer*⟩ — see SAFE
2 coffers *pl* available money ⟨Let me see what's in the household *coffers* and I'll get back to you about making a donation.⟩ — see FUND 3

coffin *n* a boxlike container for holding a dead body ⟨*Coffins* are said to be the preferred sleeping places of vampires.⟩
synonyms box, casket, pall
related words charnel (*also* charnel house), crypt, sepulture, tomb, vault; urn; body bag

cogency *n* **1** the capacity to persuade ⟨the *cogency* of Thomas Paine's celebrated case for American independence⟩
synonyms authority, conclusiveness, effectiveness, force, forcefulness, persuasion, persuasiveness
related words impact, might, power, punch, strength, weight; believability, credibility, soundness, validity; authoritativeness, definitiveness; influence, sway; appeal, seductiveness
near antonyms invalidity, shakiness, unsoundness; feebleness, powerlessness, weakness
antonyms inconclusiveness, ineffectiveness, ineffectuality, ineffectualness
2 the quality of an utterance that provokes interest and produces an effect ⟨satirical comments of great *cogency*⟩ — see ¹PUNCH 1

cogent *adj* having the power to persuade ⟨The results of the DNA fingerprinting were the most *cogent* evidence for acquittal.⟩
synonyms compelling, conclusive, convincing, decisive, effective, forceful, persuasive, satisfying, strong, telling
related words authoritative, definitive; sound, valid, well-founded; important, significant, weighty; material, pertinent, relevant
near antonyms groundless, invalid, shaky, unfounded,

unsound; inconsequential, insignificant, unimportant; immaterial, irrelevant; feeble, weak

antonyms inconclusive, indecisive, ineffective, unconvincing, unpersuasive

cogitate *vb* to give serious and careful thought to ⟨By the time he finishes *cogitating* what to do with his life, it'll be almost over.⟩ — see PONDER

cognizance *n* **1** a state of being aware ⟨Take *cognizance* of what is happening.⟩ — see ATTENTION 2

2 knowledge gained by personal experience ⟨seemed to have no *cognizance* of last night's events⟩ — see ACQUAINTANCE

cognizant *adj* having specified facts or feelings actively impressed on the mind ⟨not fully *cognizant* of the details of the trade agreement⟩ — see CONSCIOUS 1

cognomen *n* **1** a descriptive or familiar name given instead of or in addition to the one belonging to an individual ⟨richly deserved the *cognomen* of "Butterfingers"⟩ — see NICKNAME

2 a word or combination of words by which a person or thing is regularly known ⟨"Christopher Columbus" is the Latinized *cognomen* of the navigator who was known to his Spanish crewmates as Cristóbal Colón.⟩ — see NAME 1

cohere *vb* **1** to be in agreement on every point ⟨The account in his journal *coheres* with the official report of the battle.⟩ — see CHECK 1

2 to form or enter into an association that furthers the interests of its members ⟨Beset by personal animosities, the people of the neighborhood could not *cohere* into an effective civic association.⟩ — see ALLY

coherence *n* a balanced, pleasing, or suitable arrangement of parts ⟨The house has been expanded and remodeled so many times that now it's a jumbled mess that lacks *coherence*.⟩ — see HARMONY 1

coherent *adj* **1** according to the rules of logic ⟨a *coherent* blueprint to hooking up a home theater system with a minimum of fuss⟩ — see LOGICAL 1

2 not having or showing any apparent conflict ⟨a business venture that is *coherent* with the company's long-range goals⟩ — see CONSISTENT

cohort *n* **1** a person frequently seen in the company of another ⟨It's easier to stick to your work when your *cohorts* do too.⟩ — see ASSOCIATE 1

2 one associated with another in wrongdoing ⟨She and her *cohorts* were arrested for fraud.⟩ — see ACCOMPLICE

coil *vb* to follow a circular or spiral course ⟨a vine *coiling* around a pillar⟩ — see WIND 1

coiling *adj* turning around an axis like the thread of a screw ⟨the *coiling* strands of rope⟩ — see SPIRAL

coinage *n* something (as a device) created for the first time through the use of the imagination ⟨this latest *coinage* from the minds who gave us the MP3 player⟩ — see INVENTION 1

coincide *vb* **1** to occur or exist at the same time ⟨The heaviest snowfall of the season *coincided* with the start of our weeklong ski vacation.⟩

synonyms accompany, attend, coexist, concur

related words chance, hap, happen, transpire

near antonyms antedate, precede, predate; follow, succeed

2 to be in agreement on every point ⟨The two lists *coincide*.⟩ — see CHECK 1

3 to have or come to the same opinion or point of view ⟨Their wishes *coincide* exactly with my desire.⟩ — see AGREE 1

coincidence *n* the occurrence or existence of several things at once ⟨the *coincidence* of the last note of the violin with the sound of the bell⟩ — see CONCURRENCE 1

coincident *adj* **1** present at the same time and place ⟨Sci-entists had no explanation for the *coincident* phenomena.⟩

synonyms accompanying, attendant, attending, coexistent, coexisting, coincidental, concomitant, concurrent

related words contemporaneous, contemporary, simultaneous, synchronous; associated, collateral, connected, linked, related; consequent, resultant, resulting; ensuing, following, subsequent; accidental, casual, chance, fluky (*also* flukey), fortuitous, freak, incident, incidental

near antonyms unassociated, unconnected, unrelated

2 occupying the same space ⟨a study to determine whether the areas with the highest family incomes were *coincident* with the locations having the highest percentage of college graduates⟩ — see COEXTENSIVE 1

3 existing or occurring at the same period of time ⟨*coincident* changes in the region's demographic makeup that were little noted at the time⟩ — see CONTEMPORARY 1

coincidental *adj* **1** existing or occurring at the same period of time ⟨the *coincidental* deaths of John Adams and Thomas Jefferson, both on July 4, 1826⟩ — see CONTEMPORARY 1

2 present at the same time and place ⟨claims a connection between the proliferation of fast-food restaurants and the *coincidental* surge in the rate of obesity⟩ — see COINCIDENT 1

coincidentally *adv* at one and the same time ⟨The final stages of the Napoleonic Wars were fought *coincidentally* with the U.S.-British conflict known as the War of 1812.⟩ — see TOGETHER 1

coincidently *adv* at one and the same time ⟨The outdoor concert is timed so that its rousing finale occurs *coincidently* with the setting of the summer sun.⟩ — see TOGETHER 1

coitus *n* sexual union involving penetration of the vagina by the penis ⟨The act of *coitus* is the natural method by which conception occurs.⟩ — see SEXUAL INTERCOURSE

cold *adj* **1** having a low or subnormal temperature ⟨the *cold* climate of the Yukon⟩ ⟨an unusually *cold* spring that was followed by a sweltering summer⟩

synonyms arctic, bitter, chill, chilly, cool, coolish, freezing, frigid, frosty, glacial, ice-cold, icy, nipping, nippy, numbing, polar, shivery, snappy, wintry (*also* wintery)

related words cryogenic, subfreezing, subzero, ultracold; cutting, keen, penetrating, piercing, sharp; bracing, brisk, crisp, invigorating, rigorous; chilled, cooled, frosted, frozen, iced, refrigerated, unheated

near antonyms lukewarm, tepid; heated, overheated, reheated, warmed; snug, toasty, warm; feverish, flushed, inflamed (*also* enflamed); equatorial, muggy, steamy, summery, tropical

antonyms ardent, blazing, broiling, burning, fervent, fervid, fiery, glowing, hot, igneous, molten, piping hot, red-hot, roasting, scalding, scorching, searing, seething, sizzling, sultry, sweltering, torrid, warming

2 lacking in friendliness or warmth of feeling ⟨The prisoners got only a *cold* stare when they tried to befriend the guard.⟩

synonyms arctic, brittle, chill, chilly, cold-blooded, cool, frigid, frosty, frozen, glacial, icy, unfriendly, unsympathetic, wintry (*also* wintery)

related words bloodless, coldhearted, heartless, kindless, pitiless, uncaring, unfeeling; reserved, soulless, undemonstrative, unemotional, unresponsive; apathetic, indifferent, unenthusiastic, uninterested; aloof, detached, dispassionate, impersonal, standoffish; antisocial, unsociable, unsocial

near antonyms compassionate, kind, kindhearted; demonstrative, emotional, expressive; eager, enthusiastic, passionate

antonyms cordial, friendly, genial, happy, hearty, sympathetic, warm, warm-blooded, warmhearted

3 having or showing a lack of friendliness or interest in others ⟨received a *cold* reception from the hostess⟩ — see COOL 1

4 having lost consciousness ⟨The boxer was out *cold* for a few minutes.⟩ — see UNCONSCIOUS 1

5 causing or marked by an atmosphere lacking in cheer ⟨a *cold* gray sky⟩ — see GLOOMY 1

6 no longer living ⟨Paramedics tried to revive him, but he was already *cold*.⟩ — see DEAD 1

cold *n* a weather condition marked by low temperatures ⟨The *cold* will stay with us for another day, then temperatures should rise.⟩
synonyms freeze, snap
related words cold front; frost; bite, chill, chilliness, chillness, frigidness, nip, wintriness
near antonyms dog days; torridity, torridness
antonyms heat, heat wave

cold–blooded *adj* **1** having or showing a lack of sympathy or tender feelings ⟨a *cold-blooded* criminal⟩ — see HARD 1

2 lacking in friendliness or warmth of feeling ⟨the *cold-blooded* selfishness shown by the miser when confronted by people in need⟩ — see COLD 2

3 not feeling or showing emotion ⟨A *cold-blooded* assessment of the situation showed that the company needed either to lay off workers or go bankrupt.⟩ — see IMPASSIVE 1

4 *or* **coldblood** being offspring produced by parents of different races, breeds, species, or genera ⟨He may not be as fancy as the other horses they own, but that *cold-blooded* gelding is safe and gentle.⟩ — see MIXED 1

cold–shoulder *vb* to deliberately ignore or treat rudely ⟨*cold-shouldered* by his old friends after his family had lost all of its money⟩ — see SNUB 1

cold shoulder *n* treatment that is deliberately unfriendly ⟨At the party the two former friends consciously gave each other the *cold shoulder*.⟩
synonyms brush-off, rebuff, repulse, silent treatment, snub
related words dismissal, kiss-off, rejection; banishment, blackball, ostracism
near antonyms acceptance, embrace, welcome; glad hand, welcome mat
antonyms open arms

coliseum *n* a large usually roofless building for sporting events with tiers of seats for spectators ⟨The local *coliseum* is a standard stop for rock bands on tour.⟩ — see STADIUM

collaborate *vb* to participate or assist in a joint effort to accomplish an end ⟨A trio of museums *collaborated* to mount this once-in-a-lifetime exhibit of van Gogh's major portraits.⟩ — see COOPERATE 1

collaboration *n* **1** the state of having shared interests or efforts (as in social or business matters) ⟨a documentary film on the battle that was produced in *collaboration* with a society of historical reenactors⟩ — see ASSOCIATION 1

2 the work and activity of a number of persons who individually contribute toward the efficiency of the whole ⟨Our *collaboration* produced a better result than any of us could have achieved alone.⟩ — see TEAMWORK

collapse *n* **1** a complete depletion of energy or strength ⟨suffered a mental *collapse* under the strain of studying for his bar exam⟩ — see FATIGUE

2 a falling short of one's goals ⟨The complete *collapse* of the invasion set off a round of finger-pointing and recrimination.⟩ — see FAILURE 2

collapse *vb* **1** to fall down or in as a result of physical pressure ⟨The motel balcony *collapsed* under the weight of so many people.⟩
synonyms buckle, cave (in), crumple, founder, give, go, implode, tumble, yield
related words deflate, flatten, melt; break, break down, conk (out), crash, die, fail, give out, stall; burst, shatter, smash, splinter, split; crack, crumble, pop, snap
phrases give way
near antonyms inflate, rise, swell

2 to be unsuccessful ⟨The legal case *collapsed* in the face of the opposition's evidence.⟩ — see FAIL 2

3 to reduce in size or volume by or as if by pressing parts or members together ⟨The novel *collapses* events from four separate trips into one long odyssey.⟩ — see COMPRESS 1

collar *n* **1** an ornamental chain or string (as of beads) worn around the neck ⟨A simple gold *collar* is all that little black cocktail dress needs.⟩ — see NECKLACE

2 the act of taking into one's control by authority of law ⟨When the crook was finally apprehended, the detective who doggedly checked every single lead got credit for the *collar*.⟩ — see ARREST 1

collar *vb* **1** to take or keep under one's control by authority of law ⟨The guy was *collared* for robbing houses.⟩ — see ARREST 1

2 to take physical control or possession of (something) suddenly or forcibly ⟨She *collared* the boy before he could get into the cookie jar.⟩ — see CATCH 1

colleague *n* a fellow worker ⟨On her first day at work her *colleagues* went out of their way to make her feel welcome.⟩
synonyms associate, coworker
related words equal, fellow, peer; accomplice, ally, cohort, collaborator, confederate, copartner, half, partner; buddy, chum, companion, comrade, crony, pal; compatriot, countryman

collect *vb* **1** to gain emotional or mental control of ⟨Applicants should *collect* their thoughts while waiting to be interviewed.⟩
synonyms calm, compose, contain, control, re-collect, settle
related words hold back, restrain; rally, recover; lull, quiet, soothe, still, tranquilize (*also* tranquillize)

2 to gradually form into a layer, pile, or mass ⟨Dust has been *collecting* under my bed for years.⟩
synonyms accumulate, amass, concentrate, conglomerate, gather, mass, pile (up)
related words clump, lump; bank, drift, ridge
near antonyms disperse, dissipate, scatter

3 to bring together from several sources into a single volume or list ⟨*collected* the author's early short stories, which were originally published in several obscure sci-fi magazines⟩ — see COMPILE

4 to bring together in one body or place ⟨She *collects* antique silverware.⟩ — see GATHER 1

5 to come together into one body or place ⟨A crowd *collected* at the beach as the sun slowly set over the horizon.⟩ — see ASSEMBLE 1

collected *adj* free from emotional or mental agitation ⟨Ann stayed calm and *collected* while she was in the MRI unit.⟩ — see CALM 2

collectedness *n* evenness of emotions or temper ⟨With the *collectedness* of an old pro, the new governor responded to the other hostile questions of the press corps.⟩ — see EQUANIMITY

collection *n* **1** an organized group of objects acquired and maintained for study, exhibition, or personal pleasure ⟨His stamp *collection* has become quite valuable.⟩
synonyms assemblage, library

related words assortment, kaleidoscope, miscellanea, treasure, trove; arsenal, cache, hoard, repertory, reserve, stock, stockpile, store, supply; accumulation, assembly, gathering

near antonyms bric-a-brac, clutter, heap, jumble, litter, pile, ragbag

2 a mass or quantity that has piled up or that has been gathered over a period of time ⟨a *collection* of lint underneath the dryer⟩ — see ACCUMULATION 1

3 a number of things considered as a unit ⟨The historic village boasts an interesting *collection* of gift shops and antique stores.⟩ — see GROUP 1

collective *adj* used or done by a number of people as a group ⟨The cleanup of the neighborhood park was a *collective* effort for which many people should be thanked.⟩

synonyms combined, common, communal, concerted, conjoint, cooperative, joint, multiple, mutual, pooled, public, shared, united

related words bilateral, consensual, reciprocal, symbiotic, synergic, synergistic, two-way; mass, popular; general, generic, universal

near antonyms personal, private; independent, separate, several; esoteric, particular, special, specialized

antonyms exclusive, individual, one-man, one-sided, one-way, single, sole, solitary, unilateral

collectively *adv* with everyone or everything taken into account at the same time ⟨*Collectively*, the firm's partners have 107 years of experience.⟩ — see ALL AROUND

college *n* a group of persons formally joined together for some common interest ⟨a *college* of craftsmen dedicated to preserving the traditional crafts of Appalachia⟩ — see ASSOCIATION 2

collide *vb* **1** to be out of harmony or agreement usually noticeably ⟨The candidate's opinions often *collided* with the party platform.⟩ — see CLASH

2 to come into usually forceful contact with something ⟨Fortunately, I wasn't hurt when my bike *collided* with that fence.⟩ — see HIT 2

collision *n* **1** a forceful coming together of two things ⟨the *collision* of two opposing philosophies regarding the rearing of children⟩ — see IMPACT 1

2 the violent coming together of two bodies into destructive contact ⟨a horrendous car *collision* on the highway⟩ — see CRASH 1

colloquial *adj* **1** used in or suitable for speech and not formal writing ⟨The new coworker's rudeness soon began—to use a *colloquial* expression—to rub me the wrong way.⟩

synonyms conversational, informal, nonliterary, unliterary, vernacular, vulgar

related words dialectal, dialectical (*also* dialectic), nonstandard, regional; incorrect, nongrammatical, substandard, uneducated, unlearned; slang, slangy

near antonyms standard, undialectical; correct, educated, genteel, grammatical, proper

antonyms bookish, formal, learned, literary

2 having the style and content of everyday conversation ⟨a *colloquial* essay on what makes a marriage successful⟩ — see CHATTY 1

colloquy *n* **1** a meeting featuring a group discussion ⟨I attended a *colloquy* on economic globalization.⟩ — see FORUM 1

2 an exchange of views for the purpose of exploring a subject or deciding an issue ⟨The subject of the spirited *colloquy* was the disputed authorship of the plays attributed to Shakespeare.⟩ — see DISCUSSION 1

3 talking or a talk between two or more people ⟨a casual *colloquy* between two old colleagues in the faculty lounge⟩ — see CONVERSATION

collusion *n* a secret agreement or cooperation between two parties for an illegal or dishonest purpose ⟨There was *collusion* between the two companies to fix prices.⟩

synonyms complicity, connivance, conspiracy

related words chicanery, foul play, skulduggery (*or* skullduggery); double-dealing, duplicity; frame-up, setup; conspiration, intrigue, plot, scheme

colonist *n* a person who settles in a new region ⟨Over time the *colonists* began to sense that they were becoming a people unto themselves.⟩ — see FRONTIERSMAN

colonizer *n* a person who settles in a new region ⟨The first *colonizers* of Easter Island must have faced untold challenges.⟩ — see FRONTIERSMAN

colony *n* **1** a settlement in a new country or region ⟨the early history of New York City when it was a Dutch *colony*⟩

synonyms plantation

related words camp, diaspora, exclave, habitation, outpost, post; dependency, mandate, possession, protectorate, territory

2 a group of people with a common interest living in one place ⟨New Hampshire's MacDowell *colony* was founded as a summer residence for writers and composers.⟩ — see COMMUNITY 2

color *n* **1** a property that becomes apparent when light falls on an object and by which things that are identical in form can be distinguished ⟨a shirt that is available in every *color* of the rainbow⟩

synonyms cast, hue, shade, tincture, tinge, tint, tone

related words overtone, undertone; primary color, secondary color, tertiary color; brightness, chroma, chromaticity, contrast, lightness, saturation, value; coloration, coloring, colorway, pigmentation

near antonyms achromatism

2 a substance used to color other materials ⟨added some red *color* to the base paint⟩ — see PIGMENT

3 the hue or appearance of the skin and especially of the face ⟨Her *color* hasn't been good since she got sick.⟩ — see COMPLEXION 1

4 colors *pl* a piece of cloth with a special design that is used as an emblem or for signaling ⟨flew their country's *colors* atop the highest mast on the ship⟩ — see FLAG 1

5 a rosy appearance (of the cheeks) ⟨The stay in the country brought *color* to her cheeks.⟩ — see BLOOM 2

6 colors *pl* the combined army, air force, and navy of a nation ⟨She hopes to carry on the family tradition and serve with the *colors*.⟩ — see ARMED FORCES

7 colors *pl* the set of qualities that makes a person, a group of people, or a thing different from others ⟨We saw his true *colors* during the emergency.⟩ — see NATURE 1

color *vb* **1** to give color or a different color to ⟨She went to a stylist to have her hair *colored*.⟩

synonyms dye, paint, pigment, stain, tincture, tinge, tint

related words brighten, lighten; darken, embrown, tone (down); checker, dapple, daub, fleck, marble, mottle, pattern, polychrome, speck, speckle, streak, striate, stripe, variegate

near antonyms blanch, bleach, whiten

antonyms decolorize

2 to add to the interest of by including made-up details ⟨He gave a highly *colored* version of a rather mundane experience.⟩ — see EMBROIDER

3 to change so much as to create a wrong impression or alter the meaning of ⟨His news reporting is *colored* by his prejudices.⟩ — see GARBLE

4 to develop a rosy facial color (as from excitement or embarrassment) ⟨She *colored* when she realized she had been overheard talking to herself.⟩ — see BLUSH

colorful *adj* marked by a variety of usually vivid colors ⟨the *colorful* markings on butterflies⟩
synonyms motley, multicolored, polychromatic, polychrome, varicolored, varied, variegated
related words brave, bright, brilliant, vibrant; flashy, garish, gaudy, loud, showy, splashy; checkered, dotted, patterned, plaid, plaided, striped; dappled (*also* dapple), marbled, mottled, parti-color (*or* parti-colored), piebald, pied, pinto; flecked, speckled, spotted; barred, brindled (*or* brindle), streaked, striated; bichrome, bicolored (*or* bicolor), dichromatic, trichromatic, tricolor (*or* tricolored), two-tone, two-toned
near antonyms achromatic; bleached, decolorized, faded, washed-out; dull, faint, gray (*also* grey), neutral, pale, pallid, unbrilliant
antonyms colorless; monochromatic, self-colored, solid

coloring *n* **1** a substance used to color other materials ⟨added more *coloring* to the buttercream frosting to get the perfect shade of blue⟩ — see PIGMENT
2 the hue or appearance of the skin and especially of the face ⟨Bright clothes look great with your *coloring*.⟩ — see COMPLEXION 1
3 the representation of something in terms that go beyond the facts ⟨The unexciting facts were given a sensational *coloring* in the local news.⟩ — see EXAGGERATION

colorless *adj* **1** lacking an addition of color ⟨Since we can't decide what color to paint the doghouse, our latest home project remains *colorless* for the time being.⟩
synonyms uncolored, undyed, unpainted, unstained, white
related words clear, limpid, liquid, lucent, pellucid, transparent; bleached, faded, palish, washed-out; dull, faint, gray (*also* grey), neutral, pale, pallid; snow-white, snowy, whited
near antonyms colorful, multicolored, polychromatic, polychrome, varicolored, variegated
antonyms colorized, dyed, hued, painted, pigmented, stained, tinct, tinctured, tinged, tinted
2 causing weariness, restlessness, or lack of interest ⟨page after page of *colorless* prose without even one neat turn of phrase⟩ — see BORING

colossal *adj* unusually large ⟨a *colossal* statue of the town's founder⟩ — see HUGE

colossally *adv* **1** to a great degree ⟨After reading all the praise from critics, I found the play to be *colossally* disappointing.⟩ — see VERY 1
2 to a large extent or degree ⟨the most *colossally* rude person she had ever met⟩ — see GREATLY 2

colosseum *n* a large usually roofless building for sporting events with tiers of seats for spectators ⟨Run 10 laps around the *colosseum*.⟩ — see STADIUM

colossus *n* something that is unusually large and powerful ⟨Leonardo da Vinci remains a *colossus* in the history of art.⟩ — see GIANT

colt *n* a person who is just starting out in a field of activity ⟨a *colt* who looked to the team's more experienced players for advice⟩ — see BEGINNER

coltish *adj* given to good-natured joking or teasing ⟨Off camera the actor is high-spiritedly *coltish*, but turns serious once the camera starts rolling.⟩ — see PLAYFUL

column *n* **1** a series of persons or things arranged one behind another ⟨A *column* of ants stretched between the fallen hot dog and the ant hill.⟩ — see LINE 1
2 an upright shaft that supports an overhead structure ⟨Engraved *columns* supported the arch on either side.⟩ — see PILLAR 1

comb *vb* to look through (as a place) carefully or thoroughly in an effort to find or discover something ⟨*combed* the library for the missing book⟩ — see SEARCH 1

combat *n* **1** active fighting during the course of a war ⟨a soldier who served throughout the war without actually seeing *combat*⟩
synonyms action, battle, field
related words attack, fire, firefight, pitched battle, single combat; hostilities, operations, warfare; duty, service
2 a physical dispute between opposing individuals or groups ⟨The two stags entered a furious *combat* for dominance of the herd.⟩ — see FIGHT 1
3 an earnest effort for superiority or victory over another ⟨the fierce ideological *combat* between the two groups within the party⟩ — see CONTEST 1

combat *vb* **1** to oppose (someone) in physical conflict ⟨a general eager to *combat* the enemy on his own ground⟩ — see FIGHT 1
2 to strive to reduce or eliminate ⟨We must marshal all of our resources to *combat* this disease.⟩ — see FIGHT 2

combative *adj* feeling or displaying eagerness to fight ⟨channeling his naturally *combative* impulses into sports⟩ — see BELLIGERENT

combativeness *n* an inclination to fight or quarrel ⟨The boxer was known more for his unbridled *combativeness* than for his technical skill.⟩ — see BELLIGERENCE

combination *n* **1** a distinct entity formed by the combining of two or more different things ⟨a victory that was due to a *combination* of luck and planning⟩ — see BLEND
2 the act or an instance of joining two or more things into one ⟨the *combination* of mint and chocolate in a delicious dessert⟩ — see UNION 1
3 a number of businesses or enterprises united for commercial advantage ⟨The companies formed a *combination* in an attempt to establish a monopoly in the rubber market.⟩ — see CARTEL
4 an association of persons, parties, or states for mutual assistance and protection ⟨a *combination* of citizens dedicated to fighting higher property taxes⟩ — see CONFEDERACY

combine *n* **1** a number of businesses or enterprises united for commercial advantage ⟨charged that the cable companies had formed an illegal *combine* for the purpose of keeping rates artificially high⟩ — see CARTEL
2 an association of persons, parties, or states for mutual assistance and protection ⟨one of the most notorious *combines* in the history of organized crime⟩ — see CONFEDERACY

combine *vb* **1** to come together to form a single unit ⟨The room's highly varied design elements *combine* to form a harmonious whole.⟩ — see UNITE 1
2 to turn into a single mass or entity that is more or less the same throughout ⟨*Combine* the sugar and flour in a bowl.⟩ — see BLEND 1

combined *adj* used or done by a number of people as a group ⟨a *combined* effort on the part of all of the members⟩ — see COLLECTIVE

combining *n* the act or an instance of joining two or more things into one ⟨enjoys the *combining* of business and pleasure at sales conferences⟩ — see UNION 1

combust *vb* to be on fire especially brightly ⟨Anthracite, which is naturally hard, *combusts* more cleanly than bituminous coal.⟩ — see BURN 1

combustible *adj* capable of catching or being set on fire ⟨Don't store oily rags and other *combustible* materials in a hot attic.⟩
synonyms burnable, fiery, flammable, ignitable (*also* ignitible), inflammable, touchy
related words explosive, incendiary
near antonyms nonexplosive
antonyms fireproof, incombustible, nonburnable, non-

combustible, nonflammable, noninflammable, unburn-able

combusting *adj* being on fire ⟨*Combusting* oxygen tanks turned the fire into a raging inferno.⟩ — see ABLAZE 1

come *vb* **1** to move closer to ⟨*Come* here and sit by the fire.⟩
synonyms advance, approach, near, nigh
related words enter, pop (in)
near antonyms depart, exit, leave
antonyms go, recede (from), retreat, withdraw
2 to get to a destination ⟨When do you think they'll *come*?⟩
synonyms appear, arrive, land, show up, turn up
related words fetch, hit, make, reach; touch down; de-bark, disembark; barge (in), blow in, breeze (in), burst (in *or* into), waltz (in); check in, clock (in)
near antonyms clock (out); flee
antonyms go, leave
3 to eventually have as a state or quality ⟨Your dreams can *come* true.⟩ — see BECOME
4 to take place ⟨Whatever may *come* we'll always be to-gether.⟩ — see HAPPEN
5 to move forward along a course ⟨How is the remodel-ing job *coming*?⟩ — see GO 1

come (to) *vb* **1** to have a total of ⟨Your bill *comes to* $53.74⟩ — see AMOUNT (TO) 1
2 to be the same in meaning or effect ⟨It all *comes to* nothing in the end.⟩ — see AMOUNT (TO) 2
3 to enter the mind of ⟨The actual name of the item didn't *come to* me until I was walking out of the store.⟩ — see OCCUR (TO)

come about *vb* to take place ⟨How did all this *come about*?⟩ — see HAPPEN

come along *vb* to move forward along a course ⟨Our backyard makeover is *coming along* nicely.⟩ — see GO 1

come around *vb* to gain consciousness again ⟨She *came around* surprisingly quickly after falling off the horse.⟩ — see COME TO

comeback *n* **1** a quick witty response ⟨always ready with a *comeback* for every insult⟩ — see RETORT 1
2 something spoken or written in reaction especially to a question ⟨Regardless of the question posed by the pros-ecutor, the witness had a plausible *comeback*.⟩ — see ANSWER 1
3 the process or period of gradually regaining one's health and strength ⟨trying to make a *comeback* after a career-threatening injury⟩ — see CONVALESCENCE

come by *vb* **1** to make a brief visit ⟨*Come by* after work and I'll give you some clothes for the rummage sale.⟩ — see CALL 3
2 to receive as return for effort ⟨A literary award like that isn't easy to *come by*.⟩ — see EARN 1

comedian *n* a person (as a writer) noted for or specializing in humor ⟨struggled to eke out a living as a *comedian* in nightclubs⟩ — see HUMORIST

comedown *n* a loss of status ⟨After a rapid rise to star-dom, the rock band's *comedown* was just as quick.⟩
synonyms decline, demise, descent, down, downfall, fall
related words breakdown, burnout, collapse, crash, meltdown, ruin; defeat, disappointment, reversal, set-back; bottom; abasement, disgrace, humiliation
near antonyms advance, headway, progress; flower, heyday, prime
antonyms aggrandizement, ascent, exaltation, rise, up

come down (with) *vb* to become affected with (a disease or disorder) ⟨I hope that you're not *coming down with* a cold.⟩ — see CONTRACT 1

comedy *n* **1** humorous entertainment ⟨presented a night of *comedy* as part of the weeklong celebrations⟩
synonyms farce, humor, slapstick

related words high comedy, low comedy; burlesque, parody, satire; banter, persiflage, wit; foolery, fun, horse-play, knockabout, monkeyshine(s), shenanigan(s)
2 the amusing quality or element in something ⟨I just don't see the *comedy* in someone flunking a driving test that they really needed to pass.⟩ — see HUMOR 1

comeliness *n* the qualities in a person or thing that as a whole give pleasure to the senses ⟨a verdant countryside of uncommon *comeliness*⟩ — see BEAUTY 1

comely *adj* very pleasing to look at ⟨a brood of *comely* children that any parent would be proud to claim⟩ — see BEAUTIFUL 1

come out *vb* **1** to come to be ⟨In the end everything *came out* OK.⟩
synonyms fall out, pan out, prove, turn out
related words develop, emerge, evolve, germinate, play out, unfold, work out
2 to come into view ⟨*Come out, come out* wherever you are!⟩ — see APPEAR 1
3 to become known ⟨If the truth *comes out*, I'll be in big trouble.⟩ — see GET OUT 1

come round *vb* **1** to gain consciousness again ⟨The medic waved smelling salts under his nose until he *came round*.⟩ — see COME TO
2 to give or express one's approval (as to a proposal) ⟨She's cool to the idea right now, but sooner or later she'll *come round*.⟩ — see ACCEDE

come to *vb* to gain consciousness again ⟨After being in a coma for months, the patient quite unexpectedly *came to*.⟩
synonyms come around, come round, revive
related words pull through, rally, recover; awake, awak-en, wake up
near antonyms black out, faint, pass out

comfort *n* **1** a feeling of ease from grief or trouble ⟨The mourners found *comfort* in their pastor's words.⟩
synonyms cheer, consolation, relief, solace
related words encouragement, inspiration, uplift; assur-ance; alleviation, assuagement, mitigation; contentment, gladness, happiness; commiseration, empathy, sympathy; aid, assistance, help, succor
near antonyms cold comfort; anguish, distress, heart-ache, heartbreak, torment, torture
2 something that adds to one's ease of living ⟨a family campground with all the *comforts* of home⟩
synonyms accommodation, amenity, convenience, lux-ury, nicety
related words bonus, extra; benefit, help, service; de-light, indulgence, joy, pleasure
antonyms burden, millstone, weight
3 reduction of or freedom from pain ⟨a life of *comfort*⟩ — see EASE 1
4 something adding to pleasure or comfort but not abso-lutely necessary ⟨a hotel room featuring an array of do-mestic *comforts*⟩ — see LUXURY 1

comfort *vb* to ease the grief or distress of ⟨The teacher did his best to *comfort* the distraught child.⟩
synonyms assure, cheer, console, reassure, solace, soothe
related words commiserate, condole, empathize, sympa-thize; boost, buoy (up), elevate, lift, uplift; allay, allevi-ate, assuage, relieve; calm, quiet, relax, tranquilize (*also* tranquillize)
near antonyms demoralize, discourage, dishearten; fret, upset, worry; aggravate, intensify, worsen; annoy, irk, ir-ritate; pester
antonyms distress, torment, torture, trouble

comfortable *adj* **1** providing physical comfort ⟨a large, overstuffed chair that is very *comfortable*⟩

synonyms cozy, cushy, easy, snug, soft
related words easeful, relaxing, reposeful, restful; genial, hospitable, inviting, pleasant; commodious, roomy, spacious; homelike, homey (*also* homy), intimate
near antonyms hard, harsh, severe; inhospitable, uninviting, unpleasant
antonyms uncomfortable
2 enjoying physical comfort ⟨Make yourself *comfortable* in the living room while I fix us some snacks.⟩
synonyms cozy, relaxed, snug
related words toasty, warm; content, contented, pleased, satisfied; easeful, peaceful, resting; easygoing, laid-back; undisturbed, unperturbed, untroubled
phrases at ease, at home
near antonyms discontented, displeased, dissatisfied; agitated, disturbed, perturbed, troubled
antonyms uncomfortable
3 being more than enough without being excessive ⟨enjoying retirement with a *comfortable* income⟩ — see PLENTIFUL
comforting *adj* **1** making one feel good inside ⟨the *comforting* smell of fresh bread⟩ — see HEARTWARMING
2 tending to calm the emotions and relieve stress ⟨a long *comforting* soak in a hot bath⟩ — see SOOTHING 1
comforting *n* the giving of hope and strength in times of grief, distress, or suffering ⟨The *comforting* of the sick has always been regarded as one of the major acts of charity.⟩ — see CONSOLATION 1
comfortless *adj* **1** causing discomfort ⟨one of those modern *comfortless* sofas that are more pleasurable to look at than to sit on⟩ — see UNCOMFORTABLE 1
2 causing or marked by an atmosphere lacking in cheer ⟨We spent a night in a sleazy *comfortless* hotel.⟩ — see GLOOMY 1
comic *adj* causing or intended to cause laughter ⟨a *comic* monologue about his misadventures as a first-time camper⟩ — see FUNNY 1
comic *n* **1** a person (as a writer) noted for or specializing in humor ⟨a well-known TV *comic*⟩ — see HUMORIST
2 a series of drawings that tell a story or part of a story ⟨posted an especially funny *comic* by the watercooler⟩ — see COMIC STRIP
3 the amusing quality or element in something ⟨a celebrated humorist who, without fail, could find the *comic* in even the most mundane of situations⟩ — see HUMOR 1
comical *adj* **1** causing or intended to cause laughter ⟨the *comical* antics of the circus clowns⟩ — see FUNNY 1
2 so foolish or pointless as to be worthy of scornful laughter ⟨the *comical* expression on his face when he realized that he had been tricked⟩ — see RIDICULOUS 1
comic strip *n* a series of drawings that tell a story or part of a story ⟨a *comic strip* that is beloved by both children and adults⟩
synonyms cartoon, comic, funny, strip
related words comic book, funny paper(s), graphic novel; animated cartoon, animation; caricature
coming *adj* **1** being soon to appear or take place ⟨a listing of the *coming* attractions⟩ — see FORTHCOMING 1
2 being the one that comes immediately after another ⟨in the *coming* year⟩ — see NEXT
3 of a time after the present ⟨over the *coming* weeks we'll be adding to the staff⟩ — see FUTURE
coming *n* the act of coming upon a scene ⟨The *coming* of the children meant we could finally get the party started.⟩ — see ARRIVAL
comity *n* peaceful coexistence ⟨the *comity* that has always existed among the town's houses of worship⟩ — see HARMONY 2

command *n* **1** a statement of what to do that must be obeyed by those concerned ⟨The captain's *commands* were followed without question.⟩
synonyms behest, charge, commandment, decree, dictate, direction, directive, do, edict, imperative, instruction, order, word
related words demand, requirement; mandate; countermand, counterorder; law, precept, prescript, rule; ordinance, regulation, statute
near antonyms appeal, entreaty, petition, plea, urging; proposal, recommendation, suggestion
2 a highly developed skill in or knowledge of something ⟨a *command* of French that is the result of a year spent in France as an exchange student⟩
synonyms mastership, mastery, proficiency
related words virtuosity; facility, hang; fluency; experience, expertise, know-how, practice (*also* practise), skill(s); acquaintance, familiarity, intimacy
near antonyms incompetence; ignorance, illiteracy, unfamiliarity
3 the place from which a commander runs operations ⟨The general set up his *command* in the old port city.⟩
synonyms base, headquarters
related words home, seat
4 a place from which authority is exercised ⟨central *command*⟩ — see SEAT 1
5 the right or means to command or control others ⟨the army officer in *command* during the attack⟩ — see POWER 1
6 all that can be seen from a certain point ⟨From his mountain perch, the scout had a *command* of the entire valley.⟩ — see VIEW 1
command *vb* **1** to issue orders to (someone) by right of authority ⟨The general *commanded* his troops with Caesar-like imperiousness.⟩
synonyms adjure, bid, boss (around), charge, direct, enjoin, instruct, order, tell
related words ask, petition, request; beg, beseech, entreat; advise, counsel, warn; appoint, assign, authorize, commission; oversee, superintend, supervise; conduct, control, lead, manage; coerce, compel, constrain, force, oblige, require
near antonyms comply (with), follow, keep, observe
antonyms mind, obey
2 to request the doing of by virtue of one's authority ⟨The governor has *commanded* that all state flags be flown at half-mast.⟩
synonyms call, decree, dictate, direct, mandate, ordain, order
related words ask, petition, request; demand, require
phrases call for
near antonyms cancel, countermand, rescind
3 to ask for (something) earnestly or with authority ⟨an act of courage that *commands* the admiration of all who witnessed it⟩ — see DEMAND 1
4 to exercise authority or power over ⟨a cabinet secretary who *commands* the largest department in the federal government⟩ — see GOVERN 1
5 to keep, control, or experience as one's own ⟨Local government does not *command* the resources that are needed to respond to such a huge disaster.⟩ — see HAVE 1
6 to look down on ⟨For centuries an imposing castle has *commanded* that stretch of the river.⟩ — see OVERLOOK 1
7 to serve as leader of ⟨The head of the agency *commands* an army of workers trained to respond to the immediate needs of disaster victims.⟩ — see LEAD 2
8 to set or receive as a price ⟨*commands* a high fee for his decorating services⟩ — see CHARGE 1

commandant *n* one in official command especially of a military force or base ⟨the *commandant* of a naval district⟩ — see COMMANDER 1

commandeer *vb* **1** to take control of (a vehicle) by force ⟨The soldiers *commandeered* civilian vehicles to transport the injured.⟩
synonyms hijack (*also* highjack)
related words carjack, skyjack; appropriate, confiscate, expropriate, seize
2 to take or make use of under a guise of authority but without actual right ⟨*commandeered* all of the equipment, as if the chem lab belonged solely to him⟩ — see APPROPRIATE 1

commander *n* **1** one in official command especially of a military force or base ⟨a surrender of the fort by the *commander* without a single shot having been fired⟩
synonyms captain, commandant, commanding officer
related words commissioned officer, field officer
phrases commander in chief
2 a person in overall command of a ship ⟨the intrepid *commander* of the HMS Surprise⟩ — see CAPTAIN 1

commanding *adj* **1** highest in rank or authority ⟨With the death of the general, he instantly became the *commanding* officer on the field of battle.⟩ — see HEAD
2 likely to attract attention ⟨Even in a room filled with world leaders, he was a *commanding* presence.⟩ — see NOTICEABLE

commanding officer *n* one in official command especially of a military force or base ⟨reported directly to the fort's *commanding officer*⟩ — see COMMANDER 1

commandment *n* a statement of what to do that must be obeyed by those concerned ⟨The boss left behind a list of *commandments* for running the office while he was away.⟩ — see COMMAND 1

commemorate *vb* **1** to be a memorial of ⟨A stone obelisk *commemorates* the Battle of Bunker Hill.⟩
synonyms memorialize
related words celebrate, keep, observe, remember; enshrine, exalt, glorify, honor; bless, consecrate, sanctify, solemnize
near antonyms disgrace, dishonor
2 to mark with an appropriate practice, rite, or ceremony ⟨Let's *commemorate* Martin Luther King Day with readings of some of Dr. King's speeches.⟩ — see KEEP 1

commemorating *adj* serving to preserve the memory of a person, thing, or an event ⟨a *commemorating* reenactment of the Civil War battle on the occasion of its 150th anniversary⟩ — see COMMEMORATIVE

commemorative *adj* serving to preserve the memory of a person, thing, or an event ⟨*commemorative* stamps for the stars of American popular music⟩
synonyms commemorating, memorial, memorializing
related words dedicatory; canonizing, enshrining, exalting, glorifying

commemorative *n* something that serves to keep alive the memory of a person or event ⟨A stamp was issued as a *commemorative* of the event.⟩ — see MEMORIAL

commence *vb* **1** to take the first step in (a process or course of action) ⟨*commence* the festivities⟩ — see BEGIN 1
2 to come into existence ⟨The games *commenced* early in the morning.⟩ — see BEGIN 2

commencement *n* the point at which something begins ⟨There was a large turnout at the *commencement* of the conference, but the numbers dwindled as it progressed.⟩ — see BEGINNING

commend *vb* to put (something) into the possession or safekeeping of another ⟨I *commend* my fate into your hands.⟩ — see GIVE 2

commendable *adj* deserving of high regard or great approval ⟨a *commendable* interest in classical music⟩ — see ADMIRABLE

commendation *n* **1** a formal recognition of an achievement or praiseworthy deed ⟨a firefighter who has been awarded several *commendations* for bravery⟩
synonyms acknowledgment (*or* acknowledgement), citation, mention
related words decoration, medal, ribbon; accolade, award, honor, prize, tribute; dedication
2 a formal expression of praise ⟨a new novel that has received enthusiastic *commendations* from most of the critics⟩ — see ENCOMIUM

commendatory *adj* expressing approval ⟨On the basis of several *commendatory* letters from his teachers, the student was admitted to the advanced studies program.⟩ — see FAVORABLE 1

commensurate *adj* corresponding in size, amount, extent, or degree ⟨Amy was given a job *commensurate* with her abilities and experience.⟩ — see PROPORTIONAL

comment *n* **1** a briefly expressed opinion ⟨just ate the food without offering even a single *comment*⟩ — see REMARK
2 comments *pl* a series of explanations or observations on something (as an event) ⟨The pundit's *comments* on the political events of the previous week were astute as usual.⟩ — see COMMENTARY 1

comment *vb* to make a statement of one's opinion ⟨*commenting* on recent developments in the election⟩ — see REMARK 1

commentary *n* **1** a series of explanations or observations on something (as an event) ⟨The TV anchors provided a running *commentary* on the parade.⟩
synonyms analysis, comment, exposition
related words annotation, explication; note, observation, remark; report, review, write-up
2 *usually* **commentaries** *pl* a relating of events usually in the order in which they happened ⟨The general's *commentaries* on his military campaigns rank among the best firsthand accounts of the war.⟩ — see ACCOUNT 1

commerce *n* **1** the buying and selling of goods especially on a large scale and between different places ⟨a government agency in charge of regulating interstate *commerce*⟩
synonyms business, marketplace, trade, traffic
related words free trade; black market, gray market; dealings, horse-trading; e-tail, merchandising, retailing, wholesaling; bartering
2 doings between individuals or groups ⟨When I was doing outside consulting for the company, I never had much *commerce* with the in-house staff.⟩ — see RELATION 1

commercial *adj* fit or likely to be sold especially on a large scale ⟨the *commercial* fare produced by the Hollywood movie studios⟩
synonyms marketable, salable (*or* saleable)
related words mass-produced, wholesale
antonyms noncommercial, nonsalable, uncommercial, unmarketable, unsalable

commingle *vb* to turn into a single mass or entity that is more or less the same throughout ⟨*commingled* the remaining dry ingredients before adding them to the batter⟩ — see BLEND 1

commiserate (with) *vb* to have sympathy for ⟨We *commiserated with* him but there was little we could do to make the situation better.⟩ — see PITY

commiseration *n* **1** sorrow or the capacity to feel sorrow for another's suffering or misfortune ⟨letters of *commiseration* sent to the hospitalized student⟩ — see SYMPATHY 1

2 the capacity for feeling for another's unhappiness or misfortune ⟨a heartless businessman with no *commiseration* for the less fortunate⟩ — see HEART 1

commissary *n* a person who acts or does business for another ⟨will serve as *commissary* of religious education for the whole diocese⟩ — see AGENT 2

commission *n* **1** the granting of power to perform various acts or duties ⟨President Jefferson's *commission* to Lewis and Clark to explore the Louisiana Territory⟩
synonyms accreditation, authorization, delegation, license (*or* licence), mandate
related words commendation, consignment, entrustment; facilitation, fostering, promotion; commanding, directing, ordering
2 the doing of an action ⟨A single burglar was responsible for the *commission* of all the break-ins.⟩
synonyms accomplishment, achievement, discharge, enactment, execution, fulfillment (*or* fulfilment), implementation, performance, perpetration, pursuance
related words dispatch, expedition; administration, direction, handling, management; application, operation, practice (*also* practise)
antonyms nonfulfillment, nonperformance
3 a select group of persons assigned to consider or take action on some matter ⟨reported to a UN *commission* on the epidemic⟩ — see COMMITTEE
4 the state or fact of being chosen for a position or duty ⟨her *commission* as head of the investigation⟩ — see APPOINTMENT 1

commission *vb* **1** to appoint as one's representative ⟨plans to *commission* a deputy to investigate the matter⟩ — see DELEGATE 1
2 to give official or legal power to ⟨He was *commissioned* lieutenant.⟩ — see AUTHORIZE 1
3 to give a task, duty, or responsibility to ⟨I was *commissioned* to do the biography.⟩ — see ENTRUST 1
4 to pick (someone) by one's authority for a specific position or duty ⟨*commissioned* him to head the office of veterans affairs⟩ — see APPOINT 2

commit *vb* **1** to carry through (as a process) to completion ⟨accused of *committing* a felony⟩ — see PERFORM 1
2 to obligate by prior agreement ⟨We were *committed* to finishing the project.⟩ — see PLEDGE 1
3 to put (something) into the possession or safekeeping of another ⟨Laws *commit* only some power to each official.⟩ — see GIVE 2
4 to put in or as if in prison ⟨*committed* the thieves to prison⟩ — see IMPRISON

commitment *n* **1** adherence to something to which one is bound by a pledge or duty ⟨His frequent absences made others question his *commitment* to the political campaign.⟩ — see FIDELITY
2 something one must do because of prior agreement ⟨They made a *commitment* to pay the bill upon receipt of their order.⟩ — see OBLIGATION 1

committee *n* a select group of persons assigned to consider or take action on some matter ⟨a *committee* in charge of planning the organization's annual holiday party⟩
synonyms commission, panel
related words standing committee, steering committee; subcommittee; delegation, mission; assembly, body, congress, convocation, council, synod

commodious *adj* more than adequate or average in capacity ⟨a house with exceptionally *commodious* closets⟩ — see SPACIOUS

common *adj* **1** often observed or encountered ⟨Horse ranches are a *common* sight in that part of the state.⟩
synonyms commonplace, everyday, familiar, frequent, household, ordinary, routine, ubiquitous, usual

related words normal, regular, standard; mandatory, obligatory; general, universal; ceaseless, constant, continual, continuous, incessant, unceasing; endemic, popular, prevailing, prevalent, rampant; perennial, recurrent, repeated
phrases a dime a dozen
near antonyms aberrant, abnormal, irregular, unnatural; intermittent, occasional, sporadic
antonyms extraordinary, infrequent, rare, seldom, uncommon, unfamiliar, unusual
2 being of the type that is encountered in the normal course of events ⟨just a *common* house cat but an extraordinary friend⟩ — see ORDINARY 1
3 belonging or relating to the whole ⟨facts of *common* knowledge⟩ — see GENERAL 1
4 belonging to the class of people of low social or economic rank ⟨a man of wealth and privilege who mingled without pretense with the *common* folk⟩ — see IGNOBLE 1
5 held by or applicable to a majority of the people ⟨a politician who works not for the special interests but for the *common* good⟩ — see GENERAL 3
6 used or done by a number of people as a group ⟨used a *common* bathroom while at the campground⟩ — see COLLECTIVE
7 of average to below average quality ⟨She has a *common* singing voice that's good enough for performing at those venues.⟩ — see MEDIOCRE 1
8 of low quality ⟨furniture of *common* workmanship that did not justify the high prices⟩ — see CHEAP 2
9 lacking in refinement or good taste ⟨She thought him *common* and ill-bred.⟩ — see COARSE 2

commoners *pl n* the body of the community as contrasted with the elite ⟨The British nobles used to believe that they were fundamentally better than the *commoners*.⟩ — see MASS 1

commonly *adv* according to the usual course of things ⟨Channel catfish are *commonly* found in rivers in the eastern and northern United States.⟩ — see NATURALLY 2

commonness *n* **1** the fact or state of happening often ⟨tardiness of as much *commonness* as the rising of the sun⟩ — see FREQUENCY
2 the quality or state of lacking refinement or good taste ⟨The socialites were appalled by the newcomer's *commonness*.⟩ — see VULGARITY 1

commonplace *adj* **1** being of the type that is encountered in the normal course of events ⟨a *commonplace* occurrence⟩ — see ORDINARY 1
2 often observed or encountered ⟨the large corporate mergers that have become *commonplace*⟩ — see COMMON 1
3 used or heard so often as to be dull ⟨a thriller that uses the *commonplace* plot twist of the evil twin⟩ — see STALE 1

commonplace *n* an idea or expression that has been used by many people ⟨the familiar summertime *commonplace* that "It's not the heat, it's the humidity"⟩
synonyms banality, cliché (*also* cliche), homily, platitude, shibboleth, truism
related words conventional wisdom, party line, routine; inanity; generality, generalization, simplification; adage, proverb, saw, saying; old wives' tale, stereotype
near antonyms profundity

commonsense *adj* based on sound reasoning or information ⟨the *commonsense* interpretation of this so-called mysterious sighting⟩ — see GOOD 1

common sense *n* the ability to make intelligent decisions especially in everyday matters ⟨*Common sense* should tell you to go to the doctor if you're really hurt.⟩
synonyms discreetness, discretion, horse sense, level-

headedness, policy, prudence, sense, sensibleness, wisdom, wit

related words street smarts; farsightedness, forehandedness, foresight, foresightedness, forethoughtfulness, judgment (*or* judgement); brains, gray matter, intelligence; logicality, logicalness, practicality, rationality, rationalness; discernment, discrimination, insight, sagacity, sapience; acumen, astuteness, clearheadedness, keenness, penetration, perspicacity, shrewdness; care, caution, circumspection, premeditation

near antonyms shortsightedness; brainlessness, foolishness, half-wittedness, idiocy, senselessness, stupidity; carelessness, heedlessness; unreasonableness

antonyms imprudence, indiscretion

commonwealth *n* a body of people composed of one or more nationalities usually with its own territory and government ⟨laws that will benefit all the citizens of the *commonwealth*⟩ — see NATION

commotion *n* a state of noisy, confused activity ⟨the *commotion* created when the nation's top pop band arrived in town⟩

synonyms ado, ballyhoo, bluster, bother, bustle, clatter, disturbance, fun, furor, furore, fuss, helter-skelter, hubbub, hullabaloo, hurly-burly, pandemonium, pother, row, ruckus, ruction, rumpus, shindy, squall, stew, stir, storm, to-do, tumult, turmoil, uproar, welter, whirl, williwaw

related words cacophony, clamor, din, howl, hue and cry, noise, outcry, racket, roar; disorder, unrest, upheaval; eruption, flare-up, flurry, flutter, outbreak, outburst; brawl, fracas, fray, hassle, melee (*also* mêlée), scuffle; dither, fever, fret, lather, tizzy

near antonyms calm, hush, peace, quiet, quietude, rest, stillness, tranquillity (*or* tranquility); order, orderliness

communal *adj* used or done by a number of people as a group ⟨The swimming pool is part of the *communal* property of the condo complex⟩ — see COLLECTIVE

commune *vb* to form a close personal relationship ⟨After a week in the wilderness, the scouts were really starting to *commune* with nature.⟩

synonyms bond, click, relate

related words befriend; empathize, identify, sympathize

phrases hit it off

communicable *adj* capable of being passed by physical contact from one person to another ⟨There is no evidence that the virus is *communicable*.⟩ — see CONTAGIOUS 1

communicate *vb* 1 to cause (something) to pass from one to another ⟨The infected cook unknowingly *communicated* the disease to hundreds of people.⟩

synonyms conduct, convey, give, impart, spread, transfer, transfuse, transmit

related words deliver, hand over, surrender, turn over; broadcast, diffuse, disseminate, propagate; hand down, hand on; contaminate, infect, poison

near antonyms catch, come down (with), contract

2 to engage in an exchange of information or ideas ⟨For decades the two medical centers have been *communicating* about cancer research.⟩

synonyms brainstorm, intercommunicate

related words correspond; converse, talk; message; bond, commune, relate; accost, approach, board, contact

3 to make known (something abstract) through outward signs ⟨His voice *communicated* a certain distrust and wariness.⟩ — see SHOW 2

communicate (with) *vb* to transmit information or requests to ⟨*communicating with* other ham radio enthusiasts⟩ — see CONTACT

communication *n* 1 a piece of conveyed information ⟨the latest *communication* from the crew of the space station⟩

synonyms dispatch, message

related words bulletin, communiqué, report; memo, memorandum, notice; epistle, letter, missive, note; electronic mail, e-mail, voice mail; intelligence, news, tidings, word; command, directive, instruction, order

2 the state or fact of being able to exchange information regarding one's current situation ⟨We haven't been in *communication* with him since he left for the Alaskan wilderness.⟩ — see TOUCH 1

communion *n* a friendly relationship marked by ready communication and mutual understanding ⟨gradually established a feeling of *communion* with her fellow physicians⟩ — see RAPPORT

communiqué *n* a published statement informing the public of a matter of general interest ⟨a White House *communiqué*⟩ — see ANNOUNCEMENT

community *n* 1 the people living in a particular area ⟨The whole *community* rallied to the aid of the family who had lost its home.⟩

synonyms neighborhood

related words city, commune, town; denizens, dwellers, inhabitants, residents; citizenry, culture, people, populace, public, society

2 a group of people with a common interest living in one place ⟨a picturesque seacoast village that is known for its sizable *community* of artists⟩

synonyms colony

related words circle, clique, coterie, set, society; band, company, troop; clan, family

3 a group of people sharing a common interest and relating together socially ⟨a large *community* of retired people in the coastal town⟩ — see GANG 2

4 the body of people in a profession or field of activity ⟨members of the medical *community*⟩ — see CORPS

5 the quality or state of having many qualities in common ⟨There's a *community* of aesthetics that makes a very modern-looking gallery an especially appropriate setting for primitive art.⟩ — see SIMILARITY 1

6 the feeling of closeness and friendship that exists between companions ⟨interactive features that are designed to foster a sense of *community* among the visitors to the website⟩ — see COMPANIONSHIP

commutation *n* a giving or taking of one thing of value in return for another ⟨an international *commutation* of food for oil⟩ — see EXCHANGE 1

commute *vb* to give up (something) and take something else in return ⟨*commuting* foreign currency to domestic⟩ — see CHANGE 3

compact *adj* 1 having a consistency that does not easily yield to pressure ⟨a mattress with a *compact* foam core⟩ — see FIRM 2

2 having little space between items or parts ⟨*compact* soil that should provide good support for the plant⟩ — see CLOSE 1

3 marked by the use of few words to convey much information or meaning ⟨*compact* prose without a single wasted word⟩ — see CONCISE

compact *n* 1 a formal agreement between two or more nations or peoples ⟨a five-nation *compact* to control drug traffic⟩ — see TREATY

2 an arrangement about action to be taken ⟨The two made a *compact* never to artificially prolong the other's life in the event of incapacitating illness or injury.⟩ — see AGREEMENT 2

compact *vb* 1 to bring (something) to a central point or under a single control ⟨The media giant decided to *compact* all of its far-flung operations onto a single site.⟩ — see CENTRALIZE

2 to reduce in size or volume by or as if by pressing parts or members together ⟨*Compact* the snow into a tight ball for throwing.⟩ — see COMPRESS 1

compacting *n* the act or process of reducing the size or volume of something by or as if by pressing ⟨the *compacting* of wool fibers into felt⟩ — see COMPRESSION

compactly *adv* in a few words ⟨Write the instructions as *compactly* as possible.⟩ — see SHORTLY 1

compactness *n* the quality or state of being marked by or using only few words to convey much meaning ⟨The *compactness* of his prose requires a close, careful reading.⟩ — see SUCCINCTNESS

compadre *n* a person who has a strong liking for and trust in another ⟨They're longtime *compadres* who have been through a lot together.⟩ — see FRIEND 1

companion *n* 1 a person frequently seen in the company of another ⟨the close *companions* of one's youth⟩ — see ASSOCIATE 1
2 one that accompanies another for protection, guidance, or as a courtesy ⟨Each of the older students was assigned to be the *companion* of a kindergartener on the school trip.⟩ — see ESCORT
3 either of a pair matched in one or more qualities ⟨a sketch that is a *companion* to the original drawing⟩ — see MATE 1
4 something that is found along with something else ⟨the report and its *companion* recommendations for action⟩ — see ACCOMPANIMENT

companion *vb* to go along with in order to provide assistance, protection, or companionship ⟨Movie heroes are often *companioned* by wisecracking sidekicks.⟩ — see ACCOMPANY 1

companionable *adj* 1 having or showing kindly feeling and sincere interest ⟨A *companionable* pat on the back let me know that my shipmates were now my friends.⟩ — see FRIENDLY 1
2 likely to seek or enjoy the company of others ⟨a good club for *companionable* enthusiasts of the great outdoors⟩ — see CONVIVIAL

companionship *n* the feeling of closeness and friendship that exists between companions ⟨The widow's pet cats provided her with *companionship*.⟩
synonyms brotherhood, camaraderie, community, company, comradeship, fellowship, society
related words amity, benevolence, cordiality, friendliness, friendship, goodwill, kindliness; civility, comity, concord, harmony, rapport; charity, generosity; affinity, compassion, empathy, sympathy; chumminess, familiarity, inseparability, intimacy, nearness; affection, devotion, fondness, love
near antonyms forlornness, loneliness, lonesomeness

company *n* 1 an organized group of stage performers ⟨a city that is fortunate enough to have two thriving stage *companies*⟩
synonyms troop, troupe
related words stock company; cast, dramatis personae, ensemble
2 a group of people working together on a task ⟨A *company* of carpenters constructed the frame of the house in no time.⟩ — see GANG 1
3 a commercial or industrial activity or organization ⟨She works for a construction *company*.⟩ — see ENTERPRISE 1
4 the feeling of closeness and friendship that exists between companions ⟨enjoying each other's *company*⟩ — see COMPANIONSHIP
5 a position within view ⟨I would prefer that you not mock your so-called friends while in my *company*.⟩ — see PRESENCE 1

company *vb* 1 to come or be together as friends ⟨In her

sermon the minister noted that Jesus had *companied* with the least privileged and most disadvantaged members of society.⟩ — see ASSOCIATE 1
2 to go along with in order to provide assistance, protection, or companionship ⟨May good fortune *company* you on your journey home!⟩ — see ACCOMPANY 1

comparable *adj* having qualities in common ⟨two *comparable* selections that are hard to choose between⟩ — see ALIKE

comparative *adj* being such only when compared to something else ⟨If you consider the multimillionaire's yearly income, we're living in *comparative* poverty.⟩
synonyms almost, approximate, near, relative
related words alike, comparable, similar; equal, equivalent
near antonyms genuine, real, true
antonyms absolute, complete, downright, out-and-out, outright, perfect, pure, unqualified

compare *vb* 1 to describe as similar ⟨reviews that *compared* the adventure movie to a thrilling ride on a roller coaster⟩
synonyms assimilate, bracket, equate, liken
related words associate, connect, couple, link; allude, refer, relate; equal, match, parallel
antonyms contrast
2 to regard or represent as equal or comparable ⟨*compared* the restaurant's food to the nectar of the gods⟩ — see EQUATE 1

compare (with) *vb* to come near or nearer to in character or quality ⟨Nothing *compares with* the literary achievement of Shakespeare.⟩ — see APPROXIMATE

compartment *n* one of the parts into which an enclosed space is divided ⟨a backpack with many handy *compartments* for storing your electronics⟩
synonyms bay, cabin, cell, chamber, cubicle
related words cubbyhole, pigeonhole; alcove, niche, nook, recess; cabinet, drawer, locker; cavity, hole, hollow; booth, box, crib, loge, stall; bunker, crypt, vault

compartment *vb* to arrange or assign according to type ⟨*Compartment* the responses according to country of origin.⟩ — see CLASSIFY 1

compass *n* 1 a guiding or motivating purpose or principle ⟨a young go-getter who lost his moral *compass* in the course of his quest for fame and fortune⟩
synonyms cynosure, direction, focus
related words benchmark, criterion, grade, mark, measure, par, standard, touchstone, yardstick; aim, ambition, aspiration, dream, goal, intention, object, objective, purpose, target
2 an area over which activity, capacity, or influence extends ⟨within the *compass* of my voice⟩ — see RANGE 2
3 the line or relatively narrow space that marks the outer limit of something ⟨within the *compass* of the city walls⟩ — see BORDER 1

compass *vb* 1 to carry through (as a process) to completion ⟨attempting more than his modest abilities could *compass*⟩ — see PERFORM 1
2 to travel completely around ⟨the great age of exploration, when ships of sail *compassed* the earth⟩ — see ENCIRCLE 1
3 to form a circle around ⟨a mysterious isle, *compassed* by treacherous seas⟩ — see SURROUND
4 to have a clear idea of ⟨The concept that the earth is billions of years old is one that the average mind struggles to *compass*.⟩ — see COMPREHEND 1

compassion *n* 1 sorrow or the capacity to feel sorrow for another's suffering or misfortune ⟨treats the homeless with great *compassion*⟩ — see SYMPATHY 1
2 the capacity for feeling for another's unhappiness or

misfortune ⟨has no *compassion* for people who squander their money⟩ — see HEART 1

compassionate *adj* **1** having or marked by sympathy and consideration for others ⟨a *compassionate* person by nature⟩ — see HUMANE 1

2 having or showing the capacity for sharing the feelings of another ⟨a *compassionate* smile made the refugees feel a little better⟩ — see SYMPATHETIC 1

compatibility *n* peaceful coexistence ⟨the remarkable *compatibility* of roommates from such widely divergent backgrounds⟩ — see HARMONY 2

compatible *adj* **1** having or marked by agreement in feeling or action ⟨didn't think that they'd be *compatible* as roommates⟩ — see HARMONIOUS 3

2 not having or showing any apparent conflict ⟨a theory that is *compatible* with what we already know about early man⟩ — see CONSISTENT

compatriot *n* **1** a person living in or originally from the same country as another ⟨an appeal to all of his *compatriots* to come to their country's aid in its hour of need⟩

synonyms countryman

related words countrywoman; nationalist, patriot; citizen, national, subject; aborigine, native; resident

near antonyms alien, foreigner, immigrant, outsider

2 a person frequently seen in the company of another ⟨doesn't indulge in the lavish lifestyle of his *compatriots* in the movie business⟩ — see ASSOCIATE 1

compel *vb* to cause (a person) to give in to pressure ⟨Public opinion *compelled* her to change her vote on the legislation.⟩ — see FORCE

compelling *adj* **1** having the power to persuade ⟨made a *compelling* argument against military intervention⟩ — see COGENT

2 needing immediate attention ⟨no *compelling* need to raise taxes at this time⟩ — see ACUTE 2

compendious *adj* **1** covering everything or all important points ⟨her *compendious* knowledge of the monarch butterfly⟩ — see ENCYCLOPEDIC

2 marked by the use of few words to convey much information or meaning ⟨a *compendious* summary of the referendum before the voters⟩ — see CONCISE

compensate *vb* **1** to provide (someone) with a just payment for loss or injury ⟨You'll have to *compensate* the neighbors for cutting down their tree.⟩

synonyms indemnify, recompense, recoup, remunerate, requite, satisfy

related words refund, reimburse, repay; redress, remedy, repair; discharge, pay, quit

2 to give (someone) the sum of money owed for goods or services received ⟨I'll *compensate* them well for their efforts.⟩ — see PAY 1

compensate (for) *vb* to balance with an equal force so as to make ineffective ⟨The price of the item has been reduced to *compensate for* a defect.⟩ — see OFFSET

compensation *n* **1** payment to another for a loss or injury ⟨a warehouse worker who received a large *compensation* for his injury while on the job⟩

synonyms damages, indemnification, indemnity, quittance, recompense, recoupment, redress, remuneration, reparation, reprisal(s), requital, restitution, satisfaction

related words amends, atonement, expiation; refund, reimbursement, repayment; settlement; punishment, retaliation

2 something (as money) that is given or received in return for goods or services ⟨fair *compensation* for his work on the project⟩ — see PAYMENT 2

3 the act of offering money in exchange for goods or services ⟨His generous *compensation* was greatly appreciated.⟩ — see PAYMENT 1

compete *vb* to engage in a contest ⟨prizefighters *competing* for the world heavyweight championship⟩

synonyms battle, contend, face off, fight, race, rival, vie

related words challenge, engage, play; jockey, maneuver; try out; train, work

competence *n* the physical or mental power to do something ⟨never questioned his *competence* to finish the task without help⟩ — see ABILITY

competency *n* the physical or mental power to do something ⟨She's proved that she has the *competency* to run a major company.⟩ — see ABILITY

competent *adj* **1** having the required skills for an acceptable level of performance ⟨Any *competent* mechanic should be able to fix that.⟩

synonyms able, capable, equal, fit, good, qualified, suitable

related words accomplished, ace, adept, experienced, expert, master, masterful, masterly, practiced (*also* practised), proficient, seasoned, skilled, skillful, veteran; overqualified; prepared, schooled, trained; apt, ready, willing; all-around (*also* all-round), protean, versatile

phrases on the ball

near antonyms inexperienced, inexpert, unseasoned, unskilled, unskillful; unprepared, unschooled, untrained; beginning, green, new, raw, untested, untried

antonyms incompetent, inept, poor, unfit, unqualified

2 being what is called for by accepted standards of right and wrong ⟨The arbiter has all the necessary information to make a *competent* decision on the matter.⟩ — see JUST 1

competently *adv* in a skillful or expert manner ⟨performed the piece at least *competently*, if not superbly⟩ — see WELL 3

competition *n* **1** a competitive encounter between individuals or groups carried on for amusement, exercise, or in pursuit of a prize ⟨a *competition* between two fierce football rivals⟩ — see GAME 1

2 one who strives for the same thing as another ⟨tried to analyze his major *competition* in the tennis tournament⟩ — see COMPETITOR

3 an earnest effort for superiority or victory over another ⟨the intense *competition* for bragging rights to being the city's best French restaurant⟩ — see CONTEST 1

competitor *n* one who strives for the same thing as another ⟨The *competitors* for this prestigious science award come from the best high schools in the country.⟩

synonyms challenger, competition, contender, contestant, rival

related words archrival; finalist, semifinalist; also-ran, entrant, entry, player; adversary, antagonist, opponent

antonyms noncompetitor

compilation *n* a collection of writings ⟨The poet bound a *compilation* of her best work into a single volume.⟩ — see ANTHOLOGY

compile *vb* to bring together from several sources into a single volume or list ⟨*compiled* the best short stories ever written into one fat book⟩

synonyms collect

related words edit, recompile, redact, redraft, reedit, revamp, revise, rework; accumulate, amass, assemble, collate, gather, group

complacence *n* **1** an often unjustified feeling of being pleased with oneself or with one's situation or achievements ⟨the *complacence* of some of the rich kids at the exclusive private school⟩

synonyms complacency, conceit, conceitedness, ego, egotism, pompousness, pride, pridefulness, self-admiration, self-conceit, self-esteem, self-importance, self-satisfaction, smugness, vaingloriousness, vainglory, vainness, vanity

related words assurance, confidence, self-assurance, self-confidence; self-righteousness; arrogance, disdainfulness, haughtiness, imperiousness, lordliness, self-assertion, snobbishness, superciliousness, superiority; hubris, overconfidence, presumption; pretense (*or* pretence), pretension, pretentiousness; egoism, self-centeredness, selfishness; self-pride, self-respect

near antonyms diffidence, self-doubt; self-disgust, self-hate, self-loathing; altruism, unselfishness; bashfulness, demureness, shyness, timidity, timidness; passiveness, passivity

antonyms humbleness, humility, modesty

2 lack of interest or concern ⟨someone who displayed a startling *complacence* toward his own financial plight⟩ — see INDIFFERENCE

complacency *n* an often unjustified feeling of being pleased with oneself or with one's situation or achievements ⟨a momentary *complacency* that was quickly dispelled by the shock of cold reality⟩ — see COMPLACENCE 1

complacent *adj* **1** having or showing a lack of interest or concern ⟨The auditors were taken aback by his *complacent* response to their findings of fraud.⟩ — see INDIFFERENT 1

2 having too high an opinion of oneself ⟨a *complacent* junior exec who was certain of his indispensability to the company⟩ — see CONCEITED

complain *vb* to express dissatisfaction, pain, or resentment usually tiresomely ⟨the time-honored tradition of new recruits *complaining* about the food in the mess hall⟩

synonyms beef, bellyache, carp, crab, croak, fuss, gripe, grouch, grouse, growl, grumble, grump, holler, kick, moan, murmur, mutter, nag, scream, squawk, squeal, wail, whimper, whine, yammer, yowl

related words object (to), protest, quarrel (with); cavil, quibble; fret, stew, worry; blubber, cry, sob; bemoan, bewail, deplore, lament

phrases kick up a fuss

near antonyms accept, bear, countenance, endure, take, tolerate; applaud, cheer, commend

antonyms crow, delight, rejoice

complainant *n* the person in a legal proceeding who makes a charge of wrongdoing against another ⟨The *complainant* charged that the defendant had broken the ironclad contract that both had signed.⟩

synonyms plaintiff

related words accuser; litigant, party, suitor; appellant, petitioner, pleader

near antonyms accused

antonyms defendant

complainer *n* **1** a person who makes frequent complaints usually about little things ⟨She early on got a reputation as a *complainer* after finding fault with her work space.⟩ — see CRYBABY

2 an irritable and complaining person ⟨a chronic *complainer*⟩ — see GROUCH 1

complaint *n* **1** an expression of dissatisfaction, pain, or resentment ⟨a warning that if there were any more *complaints*, we were turning around and not going to the beach after all⟩

synonyms beef, carp, fuss, grievance, gripe, grouch, grouse, grumble, holler, lament, moan, murmur, plaint, squawk, wail, whimper, whine, yammer

related words challenge, demur, expostulation, kick, objection, protest, quibble, remonstrance, stink

near antonyms commendation, compliment, plaudit; acclaim, applause, praise; approval, endorsement (*also* indorsement), sanction

2 a feeling or declaration of disapproval or dissent ⟨The

condo development proceeded despite the *complaints* of the neighborhood residents.⟩ — see OBJECTION

3 a formal claim of criminal wrongdoing against a person ⟨filed a *complaint* in court⟩ — see CHARGE 1

4 an abnormal state that disrupts a plant's or animal's normal bodily functioning ⟨takes a slew of medicines for his many *complaints*⟩ — see DISEASE

complaisance *n* a desire or disposition to please ⟨took advantage of their *complaisance* to get what she wanted⟩

synonyms amenability, amiability, good-naturedness

related words affability, amicability, amicableness, congeniality, cordiality, friendliness, geniality, sociability; agreeableness, graciousness, pleasantness; kindheartedness, kindliness, warmheartedness; acquiescence, compliance, docility, passivity, submissiveness

near antonyms disagreeableness, sullenness, surliness, ungraciousness; disobedience, intractability, recalcitrance

complement *n* **1** something that serves to complete or make up for a deficiency in something else ⟨With his practicality and her refreshing enthusiasm, they are perfect *complements* to each other.⟩

synonyms supplement

related words addendum, addition; adjunct, annex, appendage, extension; accessory (*also* accessary), accompaniment, appliance, attachment; additive, filler

2 the largest number or amount that something can hold ⟨a full *complement* of sailors on the ship⟩ — see CAPACITY 1

complement *vb* to serve as a completing element to ⟨This silk handkerchief will *complement* your suit very nicely and give it a bit of dash.⟩

synonyms complete, round (off *or* out)

related words finish (off), flesh (out); adorn, beautify, decorate, embellish; better, enhance, improve; constitute, form, make up; enrich, perfect

complementary *adj* related to each other in such a way that one completes the other ⟨The *complementary* contributions of the decorating and cleanup committees were essential to the success of the school dance.⟩

synonyms reciprocal, supplemental, supplementary

related words cooperative, mutual, symbiotic; collective, combined, common, communal, conjoint, joint, shared, united

antonyms noncomplementary, nonreciprocal

complete *adj* **1** not lacking any part or member that properly belongs to it ⟨a *complete* deck of cards⟩

synonyms comprehensive, entire, full, grand, intact, integral, perfect, plenary, total, whole

related words unabridged, uncut, undiminished; all-out, exhaustive, extensive, maximal; full-blooded, full-blown, full-bore, full-fledged, full-on, full-out, full-scale

near antonyms abbreviated, abridged, cut, diminished, reduced

antonyms imperfect, incomplete, partial

2 brought or having come to an end ⟨Your education is never *complete*—there's always something more to learn.⟩

synonyms completed, concluded, done, down, ended, finished, over, terminated, through, up

related words accomplished, achieved, attained, compassed, realized; dead, defunct, extinct, obsolete; expired

phrases out of hand, out of the way

antonyms continuing, incomplete, ongoing, uncompleted, undone, unfinished

3 covering everything or all important points ⟨will present *complete* coverage of the tennis tournament⟩ — see ENCYCLOPEDIC

4 having no exceptions or restrictions ⟨He's a *complete* genius!⟩ — see ABSOLUTE 2

5 trying all possibilities ⟨a *complete* search of the computer file⟩ — see EXHAUSTIVE 1
6 having or showing exceptional knowledge, experience, or skill in a field of endeavor ⟨a riding school that will teach you all skills required of the *complete* equestrian⟩ — see PROFICIENT
complete *vb* **1** to bring (something) to a state where nothing remains to be done ⟨managed to *complete* the assignment with time to spare⟩ — see FINISH 1
2 to serve as a completing element to ⟨The bird's beautiful song simply *completes* its appeal for pet owners.⟩ — see COMPLEMENT
3 to bring (an event) to a natural or appropriate stopping point ⟨The well-attended concert *completed* a great weekend of arts and entertainment events.⟩ — see CLOSE 3
4 to do what is required by the terms of ⟨No payments will be made until the contract is *completed*.⟩ — see FULFILL 1
completed *adj* brought or having come to an end ⟨Unlike most *completed* construction projects, this one came in under budget.⟩ — see COMPLETE 2
completely *adv* **1** to a full extent or degree ⟨She waited until we were *completely* finished before starting the next part.⟩ — see FULLY 1
2 with attention to all aspects or details ⟨an allegation that was *completely* investigated and found to be groundless⟩ — see THOROUGHLY 1
complex *adj* **1** having many parts or aspects that are usually interrelated ⟨This camera is a *complex* instrument that requires careful handling.⟩ ⟨*complex* issues regarding free speech and school discipline⟩
synonyms complicated, convoluted, elaborate, intricate, involved, knotty, labyrinthine, sophisticated
related words overcomplex, overcomplicated; composite, compound, heterogeneous, mixed, multibranched, multifaceted, multifarious, multipart, varied; challenging, difficult, tough; impenetrable, incomprehensible, inexplicable, Kafkaesque, unfathomable, unintelligible
near antonyms oversimplified, simplified, simplistic; homogeneous, uniform, unvaried
antonyms noncomplex, noncomplicated, plain, simple, uncomplicated
2 made or done with great care or with much detail ⟨a *complex* plan for evacuating the city in the event of a natural disaster⟩ — see ELABORATE 1
complex *n* **1** a structure that is designed and built for a particular purpose ⟨an apartment *complex*⟩ — see FACILITY
2 something made up of many interdependent or related parts ⟨a *complex* of government programs designed to assist the needy⟩ — see SYSTEM 1
complex *vb* to make complex or difficult ⟨There's no need to *complex* what should be a simple process for obtaining a building permit.⟩ — see COMPLICATE
complexion *n* **1** the hue or appearance of the skin and especially of the face ⟨a sunscreen for people with very light *complexions*⟩
synonyms color, coloring
related words shade, tint, tone; features, lineaments, looks; countenance, face, visage
2 the set of qualities that makes a person, a group of people, or a thing different from others ⟨changing the *complexion* of the department to reflect changing needs⟩ — see NATURE 1
complexity *n* **1** the state or quality of having many interrelated parts or aspects ⟨The *complexity* of the company's computer system is such that a full-time repairman is needed.⟩

synonyms complicatedness, complication, elaborateness, intricacy, involution, sophistication
related words diversity, heterogeneousness; incomprehensibility, inexplicability
near antonyms simplification; homogeneity, uniformity
antonyms plainness, simpleness, simplicity
2 something that makes a situation more complicated or difficult ⟨the political *complexities* that the secretary-general must deal with⟩ — see COMPLICATION 1
compliance *n* **1** a readiness or willingness to yield to the wishes of others ⟨a strong-willed pop star who is not known for her *compliance*⟩
synonyms acquiescence, compliancy, deference, docility, obedience, submissiveness
related words amenability, amiability, complaisance, good-naturedness; obsequiousness, servility, subservience, subserviency; conformity; cooperativeness, receptiveness, receptivity; humoring, indulgence; acceptance, assent, consent; capitulation, submission, surrender; affability, amicability, congeniality, cordiality, friendliness, geniality, sociability
near antonyms animosity, antipathy, enmity, hostility, ill will
antonyms defiance, disobedience, intractability, recalcitrance
2 a bending to the authority or control of another ⟨an administrator who demands prompt and unquestioning *compliance* from his subordinates⟩ — see OBEDIENCE 1
3 the following of a custom, rule, or law ⟨*compliance* with the statute was far from universal⟩ — see OBSERVANCE 1
compliancy *n* a readiness or willingness to yield to the wishes of others ⟨decided to go against his characteristic *compliancy* and stand up for himself⟩ — see COMPLIANCE 1
compliant *adj* readily giving in to the command or authority of another ⟨a corrupt regime aided by a *compliant* press⟩ — see OBEDIENT
complicate *vb* to make complex or difficult ⟨The need to go to both a PTA conference and condo board meeting really *complicates* tonight's schedule.⟩
synonyms complex, embarrass, entangle, perplex, sophisticate
related words develop, elaborate, expand; intensify, magnify; confound, confuse, mess (up), mix (up), muddle; snarl, tangle
near antonyms abbreviate, cut, shorten; ease, facilitate; disentangle, straighten (out), unravel, untangle; oversimplify
antonyms simplify, streamline
complicated *adj* **1** having many parts or aspects that are usually interrelated ⟨a *complicated* apparatus⟩ — see COMPLEX 1
2 made or done with great care or with much detail ⟨*complicated* plans for redeveloping the riverfront that involve both the private and public sectors⟩ — see ELABORATE 1
complicatedness *n* the state or quality of having many interrelated parts or aspects ⟨The *complicatedness* of the home theater system may require that it be installed by a professional.⟩ — see COMPLEXITY 1
complication *n* **1** something that makes a situation more complicated or difficult ⟨The food allergies of the guests were just another *complication* for the couple trying to plan their wedding reception.⟩
synonyms complexity, difficulty, intricacy
related words aftereffect, ramification, side effect (*also* side reaction); subtlety, technicality; annoyance, bother, headache, inconvenience, matter, trouble

phrases fly in the ointment

2 an abnormal state that disrupts a plant's or animal's normal bodily functioning 〈*Complications* set in after the surgery.〉 — see DISEASE

3 the state or quality of having many interrelated parts or aspects 〈a problem of such irreducible *complication* as to defy any easy solution〉 — see COMPLEXITY 1

complicity *n* a secret agreement or cooperation between two parties for an illegal or dishonest purpose 〈the two major auction houses acting in *complicity* to drive up the prices of art works〉 — see COLLUSION

compliment *n* **1** an admiring personal remark 〈someone who does not know how to accept a *compliment* graciously〉

synonyms bouquet

related words accolade, citation, commendation, encomium, eulogy, homage, paean, panegyric, salutation, tribute, valentine

near antonyms affront, barb, dart, dig, epithet, insult, put-down, slight, slur

2 compliments *pl* best wishes 〈Please extend our *compliments* to the chef for a great meal.〉

synonyms congratulations, felicitations, greetings, regards, respects

related words approval, benediction, blessing, endorsement (*also* indorsement); acknowledgment (*or* acknowledgement), citation, commendation; adulation, flattery, praise; well-wishing

near antonyms dig, gibe (*or* jibe), insult, put-down, taunt

compliment *vb* to express to (someone) admiration for his or her success or good fortune 〈*complimented* her on her election victory〉 — see CONGRATULATE

complimentary *adj* **1** expressing approval 〈The novel received overwhelmingly *complimentary* reviews.〉 — see FAVORABLE 1

2 not costing or charging anything 〈The airline will continue to give out *complimentary* soft drinks on all domestic flights.〉 — see FREE 4

comply (with) *vb* **1** to act according to the commands of 〈The guards rushed to *comply with* the warden's orders.〉 — see OBEY

2 to do what is required by the terms of 〈They were summarily threatened with a lawsuit if they did not *comply with* the contract.〉 — see FULFILL 1

component *n* one of the parts that make up a whole 〈Each set is composed of several distinct *components*.〉 — see ELEMENT 1

comport *vb* **1** to be in agreement on every point 〈an outfit that most definitely does not *comport* with the company's guidelines for dress-down days〉 — see CHECK 1

2 to manage the actions of (oneself) in a particular way 〈The grieving relatives *comported* themselves with grace and dignity during that difficult time.〉 — see BEHAVE

comportment *n* the way or manner in which one conducts oneself 〈the *comportment* of visitors who know that they are in effect their country's goodwill ambassadors〉 — see BEHAVIOR

compose *vb* **1** to put (something) into proper and usually carefully worked out written form 〈*composed* a statement on this hot-button issue that managed to satisfy absolutely no one〉

synonyms cast, craft, draft, draw up, formulate, frame, prepare

related words fabricate, fashion, form, sculpture, shape; couch, express, phrase, state, verbalize, word; author, indite, pen, write; conceive, concoct, devise; build, construct, make; assemble, compound, piece (together); redraft, reformulate, reframe

phrases put together

2 to be all the substance of 〈The earth's crust is *composed* of mostly silicon with several other elements in smaller amounts.〉 — see CONSTITUTE 1

3 to free from distress or disturbance 〈The first order of business was to *compose* the injured pedestrian.〉 — see CALM 1

4 to gain emotional or mental control of 〈She took a deep breath and *composed* herself.〉 — see COLLECT 1

composed *adj* free from emotional or mental agitation 〈stayed *composed* and focused despite all of the distractions〉 — see CALM 2

composer *n* a person who writes musical compositions 〈a versatile *composer* whose works include operas, symphonies, concertos, and sonatas〉

synonyms musician

related words cocomposer; songwriter, tunesmith; symphonist; arranger, orchestrator (*also* orchestrater), scorer; librettist, lyricist, lyrist

composite *adj* made from the joining of two or more parts or elements 〈The movie's special effects included the use of many *composite* photographs.〉

synonyms amalgamated, compound

related words blended, combined, commingled, mingled, mixed; coalescent, fused, integrated; interlaced, intermixed, intertwined, interwoven; cut-and-paste

near antonyms uncombined, unmixed

antonyms noncompound, simple

composite *n* a distinct entity formed by the combining of two or more different things 〈a striking *composite* of two separate images〉 — see BLEND

composite *vb* to turn into a single mass or entity that is more or less the same throughout 〈Wood chips can be *composited* or sold as mulch.〉 — see BLEND 1

composition *n* **1** a literary, musical, or artistic production 〈The *compositions* of Michelangelo include the dome of St. Peter's, the ceiling of the Sistine Chapel, and his monumental statue of David.〉

synonyms number, opus, piece, work

related words classic, magnum opus, masterpiece, pièce de résistance, showpiece; model, outline, sketch

2 a short piece of writing done as a school exercise 〈a teacher who is fond of having her class write *compositions*〉

synonyms paper, theme

related words article, essay, story

3 the way in which the elements of something (as a work of art) are arranged 〈Student photographers learn the importance of *composition* in creating striking images.〉

synonyms arrangement, configuration, design, form, format, getup, layout, makeup, pattern

related words motif, theme

4 a short piece of writing typically expressing a point of view 〈submitted a *composition* to the local newspaper for its special section marking Martin Luther King Day〉 — see ESSAY 1

composure *n* evenness of emotions or temper 〈kept his *composure* in spite of the repeated provocations〉 — see EQUANIMITY

compound *adj* made from the joining of two or more parts or elements 〈a *compound* word〉 — see COMPOSITE

compound *n* a distinct entity formed by the combining of two or more different things 〈mixed the chemicals together to form a new *compound*〉 — see BLEND

compound *vb* **1** to make greater in size, amount, or number 〈We *compounded* our error by waiting too long to call for help.〉 — see INCREASE 1

2 to put or bring together so as to form a new and longer whole 〈the German language's propensity for *compounding* words〉 — see CONNECT 1

comprehend *vb* **1** to have a clear idea of ⟨the age at which children can *comprehend* the difference between right and wrong⟩
synonyms appreciate, apprehend, assimilate, behold, catch, catch on (to), compass, conceive, decipher, decode, dig, discern, get, grasp, know, make, make out, perceive, recognize, register, savvy, see, seize, sense, tumble (to), understand
related words absorb, digest, take in; realize; fathom, penetrate, pierce
phrases pick up on
near antonyms misapprehend, misconceive, misconstrue, misinterpret, misread, mistake, misunderstand
antonyms miss
2 to have a practical understanding of ⟨It took me a while to *comprehend* algebra.⟩ — see KNOW 1
3 to have as part of a whole ⟨The room's view *comprehends* the east beach.⟩ — see INCLUDE 1
comprehension *n* the knowledge gained from the process of coming to know or understand something ⟨the president's *comprehension* of the current economic situation⟩
synonyms appreciation, apprehension, grasp, grip, hold, perception, understanding
related words absorption, assimilation, digestion, uptake; conception, visualization; awareness, enlightenment, realization
near antonyms misapprehension, miscomprehension, misinterpretation, misperception, misunderstanding
antonyms noncomprehension
comprehensive *adj* **1** covering everything or all important points ⟨a *comprehensive* overview of European history since the French Revolution⟩ — see ENCYCLOPEDIC
2 not lacking any part or member that properly belongs to it ⟨a *comprehensive* listing of all the paintings generally attributed to the Dutch artist Rembrandt⟩ — see COMPLETE 1
3 trying all possibilities ⟨*comprehensive* plans for covering just about any conceivable problem⟩ — see EXHAUSTIVE 1
comprehensively *adv* with attention to all aspects or details ⟨No period in American history has been as *comprehensively* studied as the Civil War.⟩ — see THOROUGHLY 1
compress *vb* **1** to reduce in size or volume by or as if by pressing parts or members together ⟨a science textbook that *compresses* a lot of information about anatomy into a few short chapters⟩
synonyms capsule, collapse, compact, condense, constrict, contract, squeeze
related words cram, crowd, jam, jam-pack, pack; abbreviate, abridge, curtail, shorten; downsize, shrink; concentrate, consolidate; simplify, streamline; decrease, diminish, lessen
near antonyms dilate, disperse, dissipate, scatter; distend, inflate, swell
antonyms expand, open, outspread, outstretch
2 to become smaller in size or volume through the drawing together of particles of matter ⟨The substance can *compress* under pressure.⟩ — see CONTRACT 2
compression *n* the act or process of reducing the size or volume of something by or as if by pressing ⟨The *compression* of a long, complicated story into a two-hour movie is never easy.⟩
synonyms compacting, condensation, constriction, contraction, squeeze, squeezing
related words abbreviation, abridgment (*or* abridgement), curtailment, shortening; concentration, consolidation; simplification, streamlining; decreasing, diminishment, lessening

near antonyms dilation, dispersion, dissipation, scattering; distension (*or* distention), swelling
antonyms decompression, expansion
comprise *vb* **1** to be made up of ⟨The mall *comprises* three department stores and 80 smaller shops selling specialized goods.⟩
synonyms consist (of), contain, muster
related words comprehend, embrace, encompass, entail, include, involve, take in; assimilate, embody, incorporate
2 to be all the substance of ⟨At the time, about 100,000 fighting men and women *comprised* our military force in that country.⟩ — see CONSTITUTE 1
compromise *n* the act or practice of each side giving up something in order to reach an agreement ⟨Eventually we reached a *compromise* on the number of hours per week that would be devoted to piano practice.⟩ — see CONCESSION 1
compromise *vb* **1** to place in danger ⟨Officials at the state department were concerned that his statements would *compromise* national security.⟩ — see ENDANGER
2 to reduce the soundness, effectiveness, or perfection of ⟨The deletion of several critical points for space considerations really *compromised* the essay.⟩ — see DAMAGE 1
compulsion *n* the use of power to impose one's will on another ⟨In that class I read books under *compulsion* that I ordinarily wouldn't have considered.⟩ — see FORCE 2
compulsive *adj* caused by or suggestive of an irresistible urge ⟨His *compulsive* clowning around can sometimes be annoying.⟩
synonyms besetting, impulsive, obsessive
related words irrepressible, uncontrollable; automatic, instinctive, involuntary, reflex, spontaneous; conditioned, mechanical; unconscious, unthinking, unwitting; capricious, unpredictable, whimsical
near antonyms unforced, voluntary, willful (*or* wilful); controllable, manageable, resistible
compulsory *adj* forcing one's compliance or participation by or as if by law ⟨*compulsory* retirement at age 70⟩ — see MANDATORY
compunction *n* an uneasy feeling about the rightness of what one is doing or going to do ⟨Throughout her school years she cheated without *compunction*.⟩ — see QUALM
computation *n* the act or process of performing mathematical operations to find a value ⟨We were able to divide the dinner bill fairly with a little *computation*.⟩ — see CALCULATION
compute *vb* to determine (a value) by doing the necessary mathematical operations ⟨For the test we were required to *compute* the answers without using a calculator.⟩ — see CALCULATE 1
comrade *n* **1** a person frequently seen in the company of another ⟨The boy and two of his *comrades* were interviewed by reporters.⟩ — see ASSOCIATE 1
2 a person who has a strong liking for and trust in another ⟨We expect to be *comrades* for the rest of our lives.⟩ — see FRIEND 1
comradeship *n* the feeling of closeness and friendship that exists between companions ⟨Nursing home residents are able to offer each other support and *comradeship*.⟩ — see COMPANIONSHIP
¹con *n* a person convicted as a criminal and serving a prison sentence ⟨I was uneasy with the fact that an ex-*con* was living next door.⟩ — see CONVICT
²con *n* an instance of the use of dishonest methods to acquire something of value ⟨The explanation was so plausible that I never suspected it was all a *con* to make off with my car.⟩ — see FRAUD 1
¹con *vb* **1** to commit to memory ⟨Usually candidates *con*

their entire campaign speech, right down to the jokes they supposedly ad-lib.⟩ — see MEMORIZE

2 to look over closely (as for judging quality or condition) ⟨seemed to be *conning* his face for any sign of interest⟩ — see INSPECT

²**con** *vb* **1** to rob by the use of trickery or threats ⟨a fly-by-night operator who had *conned* hundreds of would-be homeowners out of their hard-earned money⟩ — see FLEECE

2 to cause to believe what is untrue ⟨Ed tried to *con* me into thinking that he had actually won the lottery.⟩ — see DECEIVE

concatenate *vb* **1** to put or bring together so as to form a new and longer whole ⟨*Concatenate* several lists of instructions into a single master file.⟩ — see CONNECT 1

2 to put together into a series by means of or as if by means of a thread ⟨The movie actually *concatenates* into one extended narrative several episodes from various books in the series.⟩ — see THREAD 2

concatenation *n* a series of things linked together ⟨a complicated *concatenation* of events leading to the freak accident⟩ — see CHAIN 1

concave *adj* curved inward ⟨a *concave* lens⟩ — see HOLLOW

concavity *n* a sunken area forming a separate space ⟨Water collected in a shallow *concavity* on the floor of the cave.⟩ — see HOLE 2

conceal *vb* **1** to put into a hiding place ⟨wisely *concealed* the documents in a drawer beneath a false bottom⟩ — see ¹HIDE 1

2 to keep secret or shut off from view ⟨The controls are *concealed* behind a panel.⟩ — see ¹HIDE 2

concealment *n* **1** the placing of something out of sight ⟨Your choice of the oven for the *concealment* of the money was unwise.⟩

synonyms caching, hiding, secretion, stashing

related words burial, burying, entombment, interment, interring

near antonyms disinterment, unearthing

antonyms display, exhibition, exposure, parading, showing

2 a place where a person goes to hide or to avoid others ⟨cave-riddled mountains that offer a multitude of *concealments* where a fugitive could hide indefinitely⟩ — see HIDEOUT

concede *vb* **1** to accept the truth or existence of (something) usually reluctantly ⟨She grudgingly *conceded* his point.⟩ — see ADMIT 1

2 to cease resistance (as to another's arguments, demands, or control) ⟨He *conceded* as soon as it became clear that he could not win.⟩ — see YIELD 3

conceit *n* **1** an elaborate or fanciful way of expressing something ⟨the *conceit* that the crowd at the outdoor rock concert was a vast sea of people waving to the beat of the music⟩

synonyms metaphor

related words device; analogy, circumlocution, code word, crank, dead metaphor, euphemism, simile; mixed metaphor

phrases figure of speech

2 a conception or image created by the imagination and having no objective reality ⟨His dream of swimming in the Olympics is nothing more than a *conceit*.⟩ — see FANTASY 1

3 an often unjustified feeling of being pleased with oneself or with one's situation or achievements ⟨Even though her novels are enormously popular, the writer is more prone to insecurity than to *conceit*.⟩ — see COMPLACENCE 1

conceited *adj* having too high an opinion of oneself ⟨a *conceited* basketball player who was always too busy even to sign autographs⟩

synonyms assured, complacent, consequential, egoistic (*also* egoistical), egotistic (*or* egotistical), important, overweening, pompous, prideful, proud, self-conceited, self-important, self-satisfied, smug, stuck-up, vain, vainglorious

related words blusterous, blustery, boastful, bombastic, braggart, bragging, braggy, cocky, swaggering; arrogant, cavalier, disdainful, haughty, high-hat, lofty, lordly, masterful, self-assertive, supercilious, superior, toplofty (*also* toploftical), uppish, uppity; domineering, high-handed, imperious; highfalutin (*also* hifalutin), holier-than-thou, pretentious; overconfident, presuming, presumptuous; confident, self-assured, self-confident; self-adulatory, self-congratulatory, self-contented, self-gratulatory; self-applauding, self-dramatizing, self-glorifying, self-promoting; self-affected, self-centered, self-engrossed, selfish; condescending, patronizing

near antonyms diffident, self-critical, self-distrustful, self-doubting, self-reproachful, self-reproving; meek, timid, unassertive; down-to-earth, unarrogant, unassuming, unpretentious; bashful, demure, introverted, mousy (*or* mousey), overmodest, retiring, sheepish, shrinking, shy

antonyms egoless, humble, modest, uncomplacent

conceitedness *n* an often unjustified feeling of being pleased with oneself or with one's situation or achievements ⟨She was annoyed by his persistent air of *conceitedness*.⟩ — see COMPLACENCE 1

conceivably *adv* it is possible ⟨We could *conceivably* finish the project next week.⟩ — see PERHAPS

conceive *vb* **1** to form a mental picture of ⟨It takes an idealist to *conceive* a world without war, and an activist to make it happen.⟩ — see IMAGINE 1

2 to have a clear idea of ⟨I cannot *conceive* the reason for such pointless vandalism.⟩ — see COMPREHEND 1

3 to have as an opinion ⟨I just can't *conceive* that he would have lied.⟩ — see BELIEVE 2

concentrate *vb* **1** to increase the amount of (a substance in a mixture) by removing other substances ⟨Prolonged boiling is required to *concentrate* the sap when making maple syrup.⟩

synonyms condense

related words clarify, clean, cleanse, distill (*also* distil), flush, leach, purge, purify, refine; decoct, reduce; compact, harden, solidify; deepen, enhance, heighten, intensify; evaporate, extract, remove; enrich, fortify, richen, strengthen; reconcentrate, recondense

near antonyms adulterate, cut, thin, weaken

antonyms dilute, water (down)

2 to fix (as one's attention) steadily toward a central objective ⟨a president who will try to *concentrate* public attention on the problems of inner cities⟩

synonyms center, fasten, focus, rivet, train

related words aim, direct, home (in on), hone in (on), level, nail, point, set, zero (in on); attend, heed, mind; fixate (on), obsess (over); refocus

3 to bring (something) to a central point or under a single control ⟨time to *concentrate* our efforts on the really important problems that confront us⟩ — see CENTRALIZE

4 to bring together in one body or place ⟨*Concentrate* your forces on the right side of the battlefield.⟩ — see GATHER 1

5 to come together into one body or place ⟨Tourists *concentrated* at the port's duty-free shops.⟩ — see ASSEMBLE 1

6 to gradually form into a layer, pile, or mass ⟨The ozone layer is *concentrated* 20 to 30 miles above the Earth's surface.⟩ — see COLLECT 2

concentrated *adj* **1** having an abundance of some characteristic quality (as flavor) ⟨a *concentrated* mixture of lemonade and iced tea⟩ — see FULL-BODIED

2 not divided or scattered among several areas of interest or concern ⟨When you get a private conference with that financial adviser, you get nothing but his *concentrated* attention.⟩ — see WHOLE 1

concentration *n* a focusing of the mind on something ⟨The noise from the party next door threatened to disturb the law student's *concentration*.⟩ — see ATTENTION 1

concept *n* **1** an idea or statement about all of the members of a group or all the instances of a situation ⟨trying to change the public's *concept* of a nightly newscast⟩ — see GENERALIZATION

2 something imagined or pictured in the mind ⟨a *concept* for a new kind of automobile that could revolutionize the industry⟩ — see IDEA 1

conception *n* **1** an idea or statement about all of the members of a group or all the instances of a situation ⟨the false *conception* that all sharks are dangerous⟩ — see GENERALIZATION

2 something imagined or pictured in the mind ⟨our changing *conceptions* of what constitutes art⟩ — see IDEA 1

conceptual *adj* dealing with or expressing a quality or idea ⟨*Conceptual* thinking is often the most demanding kind of mental activity.⟩ — see ABSTRACT 1

concern *n* **1** a commercial or industrial activity or organization ⟨several banking *concerns* in the area⟩ — see ENTERPRISE 1

2 an uneasy state of mind usually over the possibility of an anticipated misfortune or trouble ⟨The recent drop in profits has caused a great deal of *concern* among shareholders.⟩ — see ANXIETY 1

concern *vb* **1** to have (something) as a subject matter ⟨The book *concerns* the voyages of Arctic explorer Matthew Henson.⟩

synonyms cover, deal (with), pertain (to), treat (of)

related words appertain (to), bear (on *or* upon), refer (to), relate (to); advert (to), allude (to), cite, glance (upon), instance, mention, name, note, notice, quote, specify, touch (upon); offer, present; contain, embrace, encompass, entail, include, incorporate

phrases have to do with

near antonyms exclude, omit; disregard, forget, ignore, neglect, overlook, overpass, pass over, slight, slur (over); brush (aside *or* off), reject, shrug off

2 to be the business or affair of ⟨the problems of air and water pollution that *concern* all of us⟩

synonyms affect, involve, touch

related words appertain (to), apply (to), bear (on), pertain (to), refer (to), relate (to); embroil, ensnare, entangle, implicate

3 to trouble the mind of; to make uneasy ⟨We were greatly *concerned* by reports that yet another previously unknown virus is now posing a threat.⟩ — see DISTURB 1

concerning *prep* having to do with ⟨We had a meeting with the principal today *concerning* the new policy on student-run organizations.⟩ — see ABOUT 1

concert *n* an entertainment featuring singing or the playing of musical instruments ⟨During the summer various groups give *concerts* on the town green.⟩

synonyms musicale

related words performance, presentation; recital, symphony; hootenanny, jam, jam session, sing, songfest; festival, fete (*or* fête), shindig

concert *vb* **1** to bring about through discussion and compromise ⟨warned that the rain forests are in danger of extinction unless the world's industrial powers *concert*

a plan to prevent such an occurrence⟩ — see NEGOTIATE 1

2 to participate or assist in a joint effort to accomplish an end ⟨The governor is eager to *concert* with the federal authorities on this matter.⟩ — see COOPERATE 1

concerted *adj* used or done by a number of people as a group ⟨a victory like that results only from the *concerted* effort of the entire team⟩ — see COLLECTIVE

concession *n* **1** the act or practice of each side giving up something in order to reach an agreement ⟨When trying to get a raise in your salary, it's good to know the art of *concession*.⟩

synonyms accommodation, compromise, give-and-take, negotiation

related words haggle, horse trade; accord, arrangement, bargain, concurrence, consensus, deal, understanding; agreement, settlement; mediation, treaty

2 an open declaration of something (as a fault or the commission of an offense) about oneself ⟨An abject *concession* of guilt from the governor is the only thing that will save her political career.⟩ — see CONFESSION

3 something granted as a special favor ⟨a *concession* to sell their T-shirts at the village fair⟩ — see PRIVILEGE

conciliate *vb* **1** to bring to a state free of conflicts, inconsistencies, or differences ⟨It will be hard to *conciliate* the views of labor and management regarding health benefits.⟩ — see HARMONIZE 2

2 to lessen the anger or agitation of ⟨a principal trying to *conciliate* the parents who did not receive their tickets to the graduation ceremonies⟩ — see PACIFY 1

conciliating *adj* tending to lessen or avoid conflict or hostility ⟨small *conciliating* acts designed to win the trust of the new neighbors⟩ — see PACIFIC 1

conciliator *n* one who works with opposing sides in order to bring about an agreement ⟨His genius as a *conciliator* is that he is able to convince both sides that they got everything they wanted.⟩ — see MEDIATOR

conciliatory *adj* tending to lessen or avoid conflict or hostility ⟨eased the tension with *conciliatory* remarks⟩ — see PACIFIC 1

concise *adj* marked by the use of few words to convey much information or meaning ⟨a *concise* article on violence in the media that manages to say more than most books on the subject⟩

synonyms brief, capsule, compact, compendious, crisp, curt, epigrammatic, laconic, pithy, succinct, summary, terse

related words abrupt, blunt, brusque (*also* brusk), short, snippety, snippy; abbreviated, abridged, condensed, curtailed, shortened; meaty, substantial; meaningful, significant; well-turned

near antonyms redundant, repetitious, tautological, tautologous; enlarged, expanded, supplemented; embellished, embroidered

antonyms circuitous, circumlocutory, diffuse, long-winded, prolix, rambling, verbose, windy, wordy

concisely *adv* in a few words ⟨Since there's little room on the form, you'll have to state *concisely* the reason why you're returning the merchandise.⟩ — see SHORTLY 1

conciseness *n* **1** the condition of being short ⟨We were disappointed by the unexpected *conciseness* of the presentation, since we wanted more details.⟩ — see BREVITY 1

2 the quality or state of being marked by or using only few words to convey much meaning ⟨Many have admired the restrained *conciseness* of Emily Dickinson's poetry.⟩ — see SUCCINCTNESS

conclude *vb* **1** to bring (an event) to a natural or appropriate stopping point ⟨A brief reminder of tonight's game *concluded* the announcements.⟩ — see CLOSE 3

2 to come to an end ⟨The concert *concluded* late in the evening.⟩ — see CEASE 1

3 to bring about through discussion and compromise ⟨*concluded* an economic agreement among the world's leading industrial nations⟩ — see NEGOTIATE 1

4 to come to a judgment about after discussion or consideration ⟨He *concluded* that the reprimand could wait until later.⟩ — see DECIDE 1

5 to form an opinion or reach a conclusion through reasoning and information ⟨*concluded* that only someone with inside information could possibly have known⟩ — see INFER 1

concluded *adj* brought or having come to an end ⟨With another recently *concluded* fiscal year behind us, we are now ready to face new challenges.⟩ — see COMPLETE 2

concluding *adj* following all others of the same kind in order or time ⟨The *concluding* statement will be read by the secretary.⟩ — see LAST 1

conclusion *n* **1** an opinion arrived at through a process of reasoning ⟨the detective's *conclusion* that the perpetrator had to be left-handed⟩

synonyms consequence, deduction, determination, induction, inference

related words decision, deliverance, diagnosis, judgment (*or* judgement), resolution, ruling, verdict; conjecture, guess, surmise; assumption, presumption, supposition

2 a position arrived at after consideration ⟨We came to the *conclusion* that we couldn't go on vacation while the dog was sick.⟩ — see DECISION 1

3 a condition or occurrence traceable to a cause ⟨All their efforts came to no practical *conclusion*.⟩ — see EFFECT 1

4 the last part of a process or action ⟨The *conclusion* of the speech was a farewell to all the graduates.⟩ — see FINALE

5 the stopping of a process or activity ⟨A bell signaled the *conclusion* of the event.⟩ — see END 1

conclusive *adj* **1** serving to put an end to all debate or questioning ⟨The archeological discovery was *conclusive* proof that the Vikings had indeed settled in North America around 1000 A.D.⟩

synonyms absolute, clear, decisive, definitive, last

related words determinate, determinative, incontestable, incontrovertible, indisputable, indubitable, irrefutable, unanswerable, undebatable, undeniable, undisputable, unquestionable; unchallenged, uncontested, undisputed; unambiguous, unequivocal; certain, definite, positive, sure; cogent, compelling, convincing, persuasive, telling

near antonyms debatable, disputable, doubtable, doubtful, moot, problematic (*also* problematical), questionable, refutable; ambiguous, equivocal; debated, disputed

antonyms inconclusive, indecisive, unclear

2 having the power to persuade ⟨a *conclusive* argument for allowing the students to put on a play of their own choosing⟩ — see COGENT

conclusiveness *n* the capacity to persuade ⟨the *conclusiveness* of DNA testing in criminal trials⟩ — see COGENCY 1

concoct *vb* to create or think of by clever use of the imagination ⟨trying to *concoct* an explanation for how the lamp got broken by itself⟩ — see INVENT

concoction *n* something (as a device) created for the first time through the use of the imagination ⟨The first submarine must have seemed like the looniest *concoction* ever to spring from the human mind.⟩ — see INVENTION 1

concomitant *adj* present at the same time and place ⟨An improvement in the facilities led to a *concomitant* improvement in morale.⟩ — see COINCIDENT 1

concomitant *n* something that is found along with something else ⟨Disease is all too often one of the *concomitants* of poverty.⟩ — see ACCOMPANIMENT

concord *n* peaceful coexistence ⟨living in *concord* with people from all walks of life⟩ — see HARMONY 2

concordant *adj* not having or showing any apparent conflict ⟨The movie's opening-weekend gross was fairly *concordant* with box-office returns for that genre.⟩ — see CONSISTENT

concourse *n* a typically long narrow way connecting parts of a building ⟨Airline passengers had to pass through the security checkpoints before being allowed in the *concourse*.⟩ — see HALL 2

concrete *adj* **1** existing in fact and not merely as a possibility ⟨*Concrete* evidence, and not just a theory, must be presented at a trial.⟩ — see ACTUAL

2 relating to or composed of matter ⟨*concrete* objects like rocks and trees⟩ — see MATERIAL 1

3 of a particular or exact sort ⟨While there was a lot of hand-wringing, no one offered a practical, *concrete* plan for the energy shortage.⟩ — see EXPRESS 1

concrete *vb* **1** to become physically firm or solid ⟨The mortar slowly *concreted* in the mold.⟩ — see HARDEN 1

2 to turn into a single mass or entity that is more or less the same throughout ⟨a choral work that *concretes* music and dance into a stunning theatrical experience⟩ — see BLEND 1

concur *vb* **1** to have or come to the same opinion or point of view ⟨I *concur* with your assessment of the political situation.⟩ — see AGREE 1

2 to occur or exist at the same time ⟨the 1960s, a decade in which the Cold War, the race to the moon, the Vietnam War, and the civil rights movement all *concurred*⟩ — see COINCIDE 1

3 to participate or assist in a joint effort to accomplish an end ⟨All sides *concurred* to pass the reform legislation on campaign financing.⟩ — see COOPERATE 1

concurrence *n* **1** the occurrence or existence of several things at once ⟨The *concurrence* of my birthday and the concert by my favorite band made my preference for a birthday present pretty obvious.⟩

synonyms coexistence, coincidence

related words development, happening, occurrence; contemporaneousness, simultaneousness, synchronism, synchrony

near antonyms asynchrony (*or* asynchronism)

2 the state of being of one opinion about something ⟨looked for some sign of *concurrence* among the delegates to the conference⟩ — see AGREEMENT 1

3 the approval by someone in authority for the doing of something ⟨We needed the *concurrence* of the boss before proceeding with the project.⟩ — see PERMISSION

concurrent *adj* **1** existing or occurring at the same period of time ⟨*concurrent* expeditions to the Antarctic that were in a race to reach the South Pole⟩ — see CONTEMPORARY 1

2 present at the same time and place ⟨The postwar period of prosperity and the *concurrent* baby boom are the major topics in this history of the 1950s.⟩ — see COINCIDENT 1

concurrently *adv* at one and the same time ⟨two major trade shows running *concurrently* at the convention center⟩ — see TOGETHER 1

concussion *n* **1** a forceful coming together of two things ⟨The *concussion* of the demolished building coming down was felt for several blocks in all directions.⟩ — see IMPACT 1

2 the violent coming together of two bodies into destructive contact ⟨the theory that such a *concussion*, by a giant asteroid or comet millions of years ago, led to the extinction of the dinosaurs⟩ — see CRASH 1

condemn *vb* **1** to declare to be morally wrong or evil ⟨Their policies and practices were *condemned* as harmful.⟩

synonyms censure, damn, decry, denounce, execrate, reprehend, reprobate

related words attack, blame, blast, criticize, dis (*also* diss) [*slang*], dispraise, fault, knock, pan, slam; belittle, deprecate, disparage; blacklist, excommunicate, ostracize; castigate, chastise, rebuke, reprimand, reproach; admonish, chide, reprove; berate, lambaste (*or* lambast), rake, scold, upbraid, vituperate; curse, imprecate; abhor, abominate, detest, hate, loathe, revile

near antonyms approve, endorse (*also* indorse), sanction; eulogize, exalt, extol (*also* extoll), glorify, laud, praise; acclaim, applaud, commend, hail, salute, tout; consecrate, hallow, sanctify; honor, revere, venerate

antonyms bless

2 to express one's unfavorable opinion of the worth or quality of ⟨a report that *condemns* the working conditions in the factories of many developing countries⟩ — see CRITICIZE

3 to express public or formal disapproval of ⟨The philosopher's works were once *condemned* by the church and placed on its list of forbidden books.⟩ — see CENSURE 1

4 to find or pronounce guilty ⟨The accused was *condemned* by the news media even before the trial began.⟩ — see CONVICT

5 to impose a judicial punishment on ⟨a fair judge who does not rush to *condemn* a felon to life behind bars⟩ — see SENTENCE

condemnation *n* an often public or formal expression of disapproval ⟨a *condemnation* of the war⟩ — see CENSURE

condensation *n* **1** a shortened version of a written work ⟨a *condensation* of the opinion issued by the state's supreme court⟩ — see ABRIDGMENT

2 the act or process of reducing the size or volume of something by or as if by pressing ⟨a staff employed in the *condensation* of magazine articles⟩ — see COMPRESSION

condense *vb* **1** to become smaller in size or volume through the drawing together of particles of matter ⟨Over time the once-fluffy material in the pillow had *condensed* into a lumpy wad.⟩ — see CONTRACT 2

2 to reduce in size or volume by or as if by pressing parts or members together ⟨*Condense* the information into as brief a report as possible.⟩ — see COMPRESS 1

3 to increase the amount of (a substance in a mixture) by removing other substances ⟨*Condense* the milk by heating it.⟩ — see CONCENTRATE 1

condescend *vb* **1** to descend to a level that is beneath one's dignity ⟨I will not *condescend* to name-calling.⟩

synonyms deign, stoop

related words abase, debase, degrade, demean, discredit, disgrace, dishonor, humble, humiliate, lower, shame

near antonyms rise

2 to assume or treat with an air of superiority ⟨wealthy people who tended to *condescend* to their poor relations⟩

synonyms lord (it over), patronize, talk down (to)

related words cold-shoulder, cut, high-hat, slight, snub; queen (it over)

condiment *n* something used to enhance the flavor of cooked or prepared food ⟨The cafeteria's self-serve table has a full array of *condiments*.⟩

synonyms seasoning

related words herb, savory, spice; relish, sauce; flavoring

condition *n* **1** a state of being or fitness ⟨a car that was 10 years old but still in good *condition*⟩

synonyms estate, fettle, form, health, keeping, kilter, order, repair, shape, trim

related words practice (*also* practise); pass, phase, stage; footing, picture, posture, scene, situation, status; rank, standing

near antonyms disorder, disrepair

2 something upon which the carrying out of an agreement or offer depends ⟨You'll get a bonus with the *condition* that we meet our sales forecast.⟩

synonyms contingency, provision, proviso, qualification, reservation, stipulation

related words strings, terms; precondition, prerequisite, requirement, requisite; limitation, modification, restriction; exemption; demand, essential, must, necessity, need

3 an abnormal state that disrupts a plant's or animal's normal bodily functioning ⟨a skin *condition* that prevents me from staying out in the sun for very long⟩ — see DISEASE

4 something necessary, indispensable, or unavoidable ⟨Water is a *condition* for life on Earth.⟩ — see ESSENTIAL 1

5 something that limits one's freedom of action or choice ⟨Their parents placed several *conditions* on their weekend plans.⟩ — see RESTRICTION 1

condition *vb* **1** to bring to a proper or desired state of fitness ⟨the length of time that it takes for runners to *condition* their bodies for a marathon⟩

synonyms season, train

related words fit, prepare, ready; acclimate, acclimatize, accommodate, adapt, adjust, break in, orient, orientate, shape; accustom, familiarize, naturalize; fortify, harden, inure, season, steel, strengthen, toughen

antonyms decondition

2 to change (something) so as to make it suitable for a new use or situation ⟨a family that must *condition* its traditional attitudes regarding child rearing to the realities of modern life⟩ — see ADAPT

conditional *adj* determined by something else ⟨The sale of the house is *conditional* upon the approval of a mortgage for the prospective buyer.⟩ — see DEPENDENT 2

conditioning *n* energetic movement of the body for the sake of physical fitness ⟨The actor went through months of *conditioning* in order to play the role of the buff hero in the action film.⟩ — see EXERCISE 1

condole (with) *vb* to have sympathy for ⟨*condole with* them in their hour of grief⟩ — see PITY

condone *vb* to dismiss as of little importance ⟨He is too quick to *condone* his friend's faults.⟩ — see EXCUSE 1

conduct *n* **1** the act or activity of looking after and making decisions about something ⟨The President left the *conduct* of foreign affairs to the secretary of state.⟩

synonyms administration, care, charge, control, direction, governance, government, guidance, handling, management, operation, oversight, regulation, running, stewardship, superintendence, superintendency, supervision

related words generalship, leadership, rulership; agency; aegis (*also* egis), custody, guardianship, keeping, lap, protection, safekeeping, trust, tutelage, ward; engineering, logistics, machination, manipulation; coadministration, codirection, comanagement

2 the way or manner in which one conducts oneself ⟨a child who has often been scolded for poor *conduct* in public⟩ — see BEHAVIOR

conduct *vb* **1** to look after and make decisions about ⟨The company's president continues to *conduct* the everyday affairs of the software firm he founded many years ago.⟩

synonyms administer, carry on, control, direct, govern,

guide, handle, keep, manage, operate, overlook, oversee, preside (over), regulate, run, steward, superintend, supervise, tend
related words care (for), mind, watch; lead, pilot, steer; guard, protect, safeguard; micromanage, stage-manage; codirect, comanage
phrases watch over
2 to cause to move to a central point or along a restricted pathway ⟨The gutter *conducts* water to the curb, thus protecting the house's basement.⟩ — see CHANNEL
3 to manage the actions of (oneself) in a particular way ⟨*conducted* themselves at the party like perfect ladies and gentlemen⟩ — see BEHAVE
4 to point out the way for (someone) especially from a position in front ⟨a job *conducting* tourists through the historical museum⟩ — see LEAD 1
5 to cause (something) to pass from one to another ⟨a material that *conducts* heat quite efficiently⟩ — see COMMUNICATE 1
conduit *n* **1** a long hollow cylinder for carrying a substance (as a liquid or gas) ⟨the major *conduit* for carrying water to the military base⟩ — see PIPE 1
2 an open man-made passageway for water ⟨Water flowed along the *conduit* to the fountain.⟩ — see CHANNEL 1
confection *n* a food having a high sugar content ⟨Following the main course there were assorted delicious-looking *confections*.⟩ — see SWEET 1
confederacy *n* an association of persons, parties, or states for mutual assistance and protection ⟨a *confederacy* of several small nations who had promised to come to one another's aid if any were attacked⟩
synonyms alliance, bloc, block, coalition, combination, combine, confederation, federation, league, union
related words cabal, conspiracy, junto; cartel, syndicate, trust; faction, front, fusion, side, wing; association, group, organization; affiliation, cooperative, partnership; conference
confederate *n* **1** one associated with another in wrongdoing ⟨The police were able to track down his *confederates* once the thief started talking.⟩ — see ACCOMPLICE
2 someone associated with another to give assistance or moral support ⟨relied on her *confederates* in the medical community for support⟩ — see ALLY
confederate *vb* to form or enter into an association that furthers the interests of its members ⟨The nations *confederated* in order to lower international trade barriers.⟩ — see ALLY
confederation *n* **1** an association of persons, parties, or states for mutual assistance and protection ⟨The smaller nations were forced to form a *confederation* out of self-defense.⟩ — see CONFEDERACY
2 the state of having shared interests or efforts (as in social or business matters) ⟨The big-budget movie was produced by the studio in *confederation* with another in order to lower the risk.⟩ — see ASSOCIATION 1
confer *vb* **1** to give the ownership or benefit of (something) formally or publicly ⟨The British monarch continues to *confer* knighthood on those who are outstanding in their fields of endeavor.⟩
synonyms accord, award, grant, vest
related words bestow, contribute, donate, give, present, show; furnish, provide, supply; extend, offer, proffer; allocate, appropriate, assign; appoint, designate, dub, fix, name, set
near antonyms abort, call, call off, drop, recall, repeal, rescind, revoke; abrogate, annul, invalidate, nullify, void, write off; recant, retract, take back, withdraw
2 to exchange viewpoints or seek advice for the purpose of finding a solution to a problem ⟨My parents are going

to *confer* with a financial adviser about saving for their retirement.⟩
synonyms advise, consult, counsel, parley, treat
related words argue, bandy, bat (around), chew over, debate, deliberate, discuss, dispute, hash (over), moot, palaver, talk, talk over, ventilate; rehash; coach, guide, tutor; recommend, suggest; direct, refer (to)
conference *n* **1** a body of people come together in one place ⟨The *conference* voted to conclude that day's meeting and to resume discussions the next morning.⟩ — see GATHERING 1
2 a meeting featuring a group discussion ⟨a *conference* on the need for international cooperation in combating emerging viruses⟩ — see FORUM 1
3 an exchange of views for the purpose of exploring a subject or deciding an issue ⟨a parent-teacher *conference* to discuss the student's progress in school⟩ — see DISCUSSION 1
confess *vb* **1** to make an acknowledgment of something unpleasant as true or valid ⟨The thief *confessed* to dozens of robberies.⟩
synonyms admit
related words blab, talk, tattle; babble, spill
near antonyms clam up, hush, quiet (down), shut up
2 to accept the truth or existence of (something) usually reluctantly ⟨I had to *confess* it, he had a point.⟩ — see ADMIT 1
confession *n* an open declaration of something (as a fault or the commission of an offense) about oneself ⟨a *confession* that he had been lying all along⟩
synonyms acknowledgment (*or* acknowledgement), admission, avowal, concession
related words self-accusation, self-betrayal, self-revelation; self-incrimination, self-recrimination, self-reproach; affirmation, assertion, avouchment, claim, confirmation, declaration, insistence, profession; allowance; handwringing; betrayal, disclosure, divulgence, giveaway, revelation; announcement, declaration, proclamation, pronouncement; blame, fault, responsibility; contriteness, contrition, penitence, regret, remorse, remorsefulness, repentance, rue
near antonyms denial, disallowance, disclaimer, recantation, rejection, renouncement, repudiation
antonyms disavowal, nonadmission
confidant *n* a person who has a strong liking for and trust in another ⟨She's my *confidant*; I tell her everything without reservation.⟩ — see FRIEND 1
confidence *n* **1** great faith in oneself or one's abilities ⟨a lifelong *confidence* that enabled her to achieve great things despite powerful obstacles⟩
synonyms aplomb, assurance, self-assurance, self-confidence, self-esteem
related words cockiness, complacence, complacency, conceit, conceitedness, ego, egoism, egotism, hubris, overconfidence, pompousness, pride, pridefulness, self-admiration, self-applause, self-assumption, self-complacency, self-conceit, self-consequence, self-content, self-contentment, self-glorification, self-importance, self-opinion, self-partiality, self-satisfaction, smugness, vaingloriousness, vainglory, vanity; calmness, composure, coolness, equanimity; self-poise, self-possession
near antonyms apprehension, doubt, misgiving
antonyms diffidence, insecurity, self-distrust, self-doubt
2 a state of mind in which one is free from doubt ⟨the *confidence* with which the game show contestant answered every question⟩
synonyms assurance, assuredness, certainty, certitude, conviction, face, positiveness, satisfaction, sureness, surety

related words decisiveness, determination, firmness, purposefulness, resoluteness, resolution, resolve

near antonyms hesitancy, hesitation, indecisiveness, irresolution; disbelief, incredulity, unbelief; anxiety, concern, misgiving; distrust, mistrust, suspicion

antonyms doubt, incertitude, nonconfidence, uncertainty

3 firm belief in the integrity, ability, effectiveness, or genuineness of someone or something ⟨As players, we have complete *confidence* in our coach.⟩ — see TRUST 1

4 information shared only with another or with a select few ⟨accused him of betraying an important *confidence*⟩ — see SECRET 1

confident *adj* **1** having or showing great faith in oneself or one's abilities ⟨You'll need to be *confident*—even in the face of rejection—if you want to pursue a career in show business.⟩

synonyms assured, secure, self-assured, self-confident

related words collected, composed, cool, coolheaded, poised, self-possessed, serene, tranquil, unperturbed, unshaken; hopeful, optimistic, rosy, sanguine, upbeat; complacent, conceited, egoistic (*also* egoistical), egotistic (*or* egotistical), important, overweening, pompous, prideful, proud, self-affected, self-applauding, self-centered, self-complacent, self-conceited, self-contented, self-important, self-pleased, self-satisfied; self-promoting, smug, stuck-up, vain, vainglorious; imperturbable, nerveless, unflappable, unself-conscious, unshakable; disciplined, self-collected, self-contained, self-controlled, self-poised; self-reliant, self-sufficient

near antonyms meek, timid, unassertive; humble, modest, unassuming, unpretentious; jittery, jumpy, nervous; bashful, demure, mousy (*or* mousey), overmodest, quiet, reserved, shy; self-critical, self-reproachful, self-reproving

antonyms diffident, insecure, self-distrustful, self-doubting

2 having or showing a mind free from doubt ⟨We were *confident* that the directions we had been given were accurate.⟩ — see CERTAIN 2

confidential *adj* not known or meant to be known by the general populace ⟨Someone leaked *confidential* government information to the press.⟩ — see PRIVATE 1

confiding *adj* having or showing trust in another ⟨a very *confiding* child who is a little too eager to trust total strangers⟩ — see TRUSTING 1

configuration *n* **1** the arrangement of parts that gives something its basic form ⟨The basic *configuration* of the building is that of a geodesic dome.⟩ — see FRAME 1

2 the way in which something is sized, arranged, or organized ⟨a small business computer system in its simplest *configuration*⟩ — see FORMAT 1

3 the way in which the elements of something (as a work of art) are arranged ⟨His photographs have an intentionally loose *configuration*, with no single object intended as the primary center of interest.⟩ — see COMPOSITION 3

4 the outward appearance of something as distinguished from its substance ⟨a birthday cake in the *configuration* of a football⟩ — see FORM 1

confine *vb* **1** to set bounds or an upper limit for ⟨I will *confine* my remarks to the subject we came here to discuss.⟩ — see LIMIT 1

2 to put in or as if in prison ⟨The accused was *confined* until the trial could take place.⟩ — see IMPRISON

confinement *n* **1** the act of confining or the state of being confined ⟨Some wild animals take to *confinement* very poorly.⟩ — see INTERNMENT

2 the act or practice of keeping something (as an activity) within certain boundaries ⟨The *confinement* of com-

mercial development to one stretch of roadway is intended to help preserve the town's rural character.⟩ — see RESTRICTION 2

confines *pl n* **1** a real or imaginary point beyond which a person or thing cannot go ⟨within the *confines* of the city⟩ — see LIMIT 1

2 the line or relatively narrow space that marks the outer limit of something ⟨outside the *confines* of the school walls⟩ — see BORDER 1

3 an area over which activity, capacity, or influence extends ⟨That's beyond the *confines* of my power as dean of the college.⟩ — see RANGE 2

confirm *vb* **1** to give evidence or testimony to the truth or factualness of ⟨several eyewitnesses who can *confirm* the defendant's account of what happened⟩

synonyms argue, attest, authenticate, bear out, certify, corroborate, substantiate, support, validate, verify, vindicate

related words avouch, back (up), testify (to), vouch (for), witness; guarantee, warrant; affirm, assert, aver, avow, declare, profess; demonstrate, document, establish, prove

near antonyms contradict, gainsay; deny, disavow, disclaim; challenge, contest, dispute, question

antonyms disprove, rebut, refute

2 to give official acceptance of as satisfactory ⟨The senate must *confirm* an appointment to an ambassadorship.⟩ — see APPROVE

confirmable *adj* capable of being proven as true or real ⟨The theory was not *confirmable*, and eventually it had to be discarded in favor of one that was.⟩ — see VERIFIABLE

confirmation *n* something presented in support of the truth or accuracy of a claim ⟨He regards the finding as a *confirmation* of the theory that extraterrestrial impacts were responsible for the demise of the dinosaurs.⟩ — see PROOF

confirmatory *adj* serving to give support to the truth or factualness of something ⟨a *confirmatory* test for pregnancy⟩ — see CORROBORATIVE

confirmed *adj* **1** being such by habit and not likely to change ⟨a *confirmed* grouch who never seems to smile⟩ — see HABITUAL 1

2 firmly established over time ⟨a *confirmed* tendency to exaggerate about everything⟩ — see INVETERATE 1

confirming *adj* serving to give support to the truth or factualness of something ⟨In the absence of *confirming* evidence, we should give him the benefit of the doubt.⟩ — see CORROBORATIVE

confiscate *vb* to take ownership or control of (something) by right of one's authority ⟨Anything that might be used as a weapon will be *confiscated* by the security guards.⟩

synonyms attach, expropriate, sequester

related words garnishee; appropriate, arrogate, preempt, usurp; commandeer, seize, take over

near antonyms cede, deliver, forfeit, give up, hand over, release, relinquish, render, surrender, turn over, yield

conflagration *n* **1** a destructive burning ⟨The historic hotel burned to the ground in a horrible *conflagration*.⟩ — see FIRE 1

2 a state of armed violent struggle between states, nations, or groups ⟨What began as a skirmish over disputed territory erupted into a *conflagration* that swept the continent.⟩ — see WAR 1

conflict *n* **1** a lack of agreement or harmony ⟨the *conflict* between absolute freedom and personal responsibility⟩ — see DISCORD

2 a physical dispute between opposing individuals or groups ⟨an armed *conflict* between strikers and strikebreakers⟩ — see FIGHT 1

3 a state of armed violent struggle between states, nations, or groups ⟨The United Nations strives to prevent international *conflicts*.⟩ — see WAR 1

4 an earnest effort for superiority or victory over another ⟨the eternal *conflict* between the forces of good and evil⟩ — see CONTEST 1

conflict *vb* to be out of harmony or agreement usually noticeably ⟨His statement *conflicts* with the facts, as given in the police report.⟩ — see CLASH

conflicting *adj* not being in agreement or harmony ⟨*conflicting* reports from the witnesses at the scene⟩ — see INCONSISTENT 1

confluence *n* the coming together of two or more things to the same point ⟨a happy *confluence* of beautiful weather and spectacular scenery during our vacation⟩ — see CONVERGENCE

conform *vb* **1** to be in agreement on every point ⟨The list *conforms* with the contents of the trunk.⟩ — see CHECK 1

2 to form a pleasing relationship ⟨last-minute changes in the schedule that *conform* with our plans nicely⟩ — see HARMONIZE 1

3 to bring to a state free of conflicts, inconsistencies, or differences ⟨We'll have to *conform* this new rule with existing policy regarding student-run organizations on campus.⟩ — see HARMONIZE 2

4 to change (something) so as to make it suitable for a new use or situation ⟨I can be funny or serious, for I always *conform* my behavior to the situation.⟩ — see ADAPT

conform (to) *vb* to act according to the commands of ⟨an independent-minded person who refuses to *conform to* the dictates of society⟩ — see OBEY

conformable *adj* readily giving in to the command or authority of another ⟨one of the more *conformable* dogs in obedience training⟩ — see OBEDIENT

conformable (to) *adj* not having or showing any apparent conflict ⟨Student conduct must be at all times *conformable to* the principles and values of the school.⟩ — see CONSISTENT

conformation *n* **1** the outward appearance of something as distinguished from its substance ⟨an ice sculpture in the *conformation* of a swan⟩ — see FORM 1

2 the way in which something is sized, arranged, or organized ⟨the regular *conformation* of particles in a crystal⟩ — see FORMAT 1

conformity *n* **1** a state of consistency ⟨The simple lifestyle of the Amish is in *conformity* with their ascetic religious beliefs.⟩

synonyms accord, accordance, agreement, congruity, consonance, harmony, tune

related words compatibility; assimilation, integration; oneness, solidarity, togetherness; affinity, empathy, sympathy

near antonyms contrast, discrepancy, disparateness, disparity, dissimilarity, distinction, distinctiveness, distinctness, diverseness, diversity, unlikeness; deviance, divergence; discord, discordance, dissension (*also* dissention), dissent, dissidence, disunity, friction, strife; variability, variance; incompatibility

antonyms conflict, disagreement, incongruence, incongruity, incongruousness

2 the following of a custom, rule, or law ⟨a community that expected *conformity* to tradition⟩ — see OBSERVANCE 1

confound *vb* **1** to throw into a state of mental uncertainty ⟨We were *confounded* by the app's update, which wasn't at all user-friendly.⟩ — see CONFUSE 1

2 to throw into a state of self-conscious distress ⟨His renewed popularity has *confounded* the critics who said his singing career was dead.⟩ — see EMBARRASS 1

3 to fail to differentiate (a thing) from something similar or related ⟨I think you've *confounded* astrology with astronomy.⟩ — see CONFUSE 3

4 to prove to be false ⟨new discoveries that *confound* much of what archaeologists thought they knew about the Mayan civilization⟩ — see DISPROVE

confront *vb* to oppose (something hostile or dangerous) with firmness or courage ⟨You must *confront* your fear in order to conquer it.⟩ — see FACE 2

confrontation *n* an earnest effort for superiority or victory over another ⟨The softball rivals met in an epic *confrontation* on the last weekend of the summer.⟩ — see CONTEST 1

confuse *vb* **1** to throw into a state of mental uncertainty ⟨The similar-sounding words "censure" and "censor" often *confuse* people.⟩

synonyms addle, baffle, beat, befog, befuddle, bemuse, bewilder, confound, discombobulate, disorient, fox, get, maze, muddle, muddy, mystify, perplex, puzzle, vex

related words stick, stump; abash, discomfit, disconcert, discountenance, embarrass, faze, fluster, mortify, nonplus, rattle; agitate, bother, chagrin, discomfort, discompose, dismay, disquiet, distress, disturb, perturb, stun, unhinge, unsettle, upset; beguile, cozen, deceive, delude, dupe, fool, gull, hoax, hoodwink, humbug, misguide, mislead, snow, string along, take in, trick

phrases blow one's mind, go to one's head

near antonyms assure, reassure, satisfy; enlighten, inform

2 to make (something) unclear to the understanding ⟨Stop *confusing* the issue with irrelevant facts!⟩

synonyms becloud, befog, blur, cloud, fog, muddy

related words complicate, perplex, sophisticate; entangle, snarl, tangle; disarrange, disarray, discompose, dishevel, disorder, disrupt, disturb, jumble, mess (up), muddle, scramble, shuffle, tousle, upset

near antonyms simplify, streamline; disentangle, straighten (out), undo, unravel, unscramble, untangle; decipher, decode; analyze, break down

antonyms clarify, clear (up), illuminate

3 to fail to differentiate (a thing) from something similar or related ⟨A lot of people *confuse* popular fame with enduring achievement.⟩

synonyms confound, mistake, mix (up)

related words lump (together); misapply, miscall, misidentify, misname

antonyms difference, differentiate, discriminate, distinguish, separate

4 to throw into a state of self-conscious distress ⟨She was *confused* by the shocking bluntness of his marriage proposal.⟩ — see EMBARRASS 1

5 to undo the proper order or arrangement of ⟨A sudden burst of wind had hopelessly *confused* the papers on the desk.⟩ — see DISORDER

confused *adj* **1** lacking in order, neatness, and often cleanliness ⟨The cans were lying in a *confused* jumble in the basement.⟩ — see MESSY

2 suffering from mental confusion ⟨I was briefly *confused* after my fall from the horse.⟩ — see DIZZY 2

confusion *n* **1** a state of mental uncertainty ⟨The farmer's driving directions to the fairground just left us in total *confusion*.⟩

synonyms bafflement, befuddlement, bewilderment, distraction, fog, muddle, mystification, perplexity, puzzlement, tangle, whirl

related words abashment, discomfiture, disconcertment, embarrassment, mortification; agitation, chagrin, discomfort, dismay, disquiet, distress, disturbance, perturbation, upset; bother, commotion, dither, flurry, fluster, fuss, stew, turmoil *near antonyms* assurance, certainty, certitude, confidence, conviction, positiveness, sureness

2 a state in which everything is out of order ⟨It was hard to find anything in that *confusion* in the attic.⟩ — see CHAOS

3 the emotional state of being made self-consciously uncomfortable ⟨thrown into speechless *confusion* by the wild accusations⟩ — see EMBARRASSMENT 1

confutation *n* something (as an argument) that serves to disprove ⟨He crafted an elegant *confutation* to the argument that animals do not feel pain.⟩

synonyms disproof, rebuttal, refutation

related words counterargument, counterevidence

near antonyms attestation, confirmation, corroboration, documentation, evidence, substantiation, testament, testimony, validation, witness; authentication, identification, manifestation, verification

antonyms proof

confute *vb* to prove to be false ⟨theories which will eventually be confirmed or *confuted* by experience⟩ — see DISPROVE

congeal *vb* **1** to become physically firm or solid ⟨The surface of the pond *congealed* after several days of frigid temperatures.⟩ — see HARDEN 1

2 to turn from a liquid into a substance resembling jelly ⟨The gravy had already started to *congeal* by the time the waiter served our dinners.⟩ — see COAGULATE

congenial *adj* **1** giving pleasure or contentment to the mind or senses ⟨a couple relaxing in the *congenial* atmosphere of a luxury health spa⟩ — see PLEASANT 1

2 having or marked by agreement in feeling or action ⟨*congenial* traveling companions who made our tour of Italy even more enjoyable than we had anticipated⟩ — see HARMONIOUS 3

congenital *adj* being such from birth or by nature ⟨a *congenital* liar who couldn't speak the truth if his life depended on it⟩ — see NATURAL 1

congest *vb* to prevent passage through by filling with something ⟨The usual weekend traffic *congested* the region's highways.⟩ — see CLOG 1

conglomerate *n* a group of businesses or enterprises under one control ⟨The huge media *conglomerate* owns TV and radio stations, a cable company, and a movie studio.⟩

synonyms empire

related words cartel, combination, combine, syndicate, trust; chain; association, corporation, organization, pool

conglomerate *vb* **1** to come together into one body or place ⟨People *conglomerated* in the downtown streets for an impromptu victory celebration.⟩ — see ASSEMBLE 1

2 to gradually form into a layer, pile, or mass ⟨Over the years the town's discarded junk *conglomerated* at the bottom of the river.⟩ — see COLLECT 2

congratulate *vb* to express to (someone) admiration for his or her success or good fortune ⟨Let me be the first to *congratulate* you on winning the award.⟩

synonyms compliment, felicitate, hug

related words applaud, cheer, commend, hail, salute; extol (*also* extoll), glorify, laud, praise

near antonyms bad-mouth, belittle, cry down, decry, deprecate, depreciate, diminish, discount, disparage, minimize, put down, write off; jeer, mock, ridicule, taunt, tease

congratulations *pl n* best wishes ⟨a gift for you with our *congratulations*⟩ — see COMPLIMENT 2

congregate *vb* **1** to bring together in one body or place ⟨Both captains *congregated* their team members for some pregame strategizing.⟩ — see GATHER 1

2 to come together into one body or place ⟨Pilgrims have

been *congregating* in the town's historic square for centuries.⟩ — see ASSEMBLE 1

congregation *n* **1** a body of persons gathered for religious worship ⟨The whole *congregation* began to sing with great fervor.⟩

synonyms assembly, church

related words flock, laity, parish; communion, confession, denomination, fold, sect; clergy, cloth

2 a body of people come together in one place ⟨A *congregation* of journalists were at the hotel bar, discussing the latest developments.⟩ — see GATHERING 1

congress *n* **1** the highest lawmaking body of a political unit ⟨The national emergency required a special session of *congress*.⟩

synonyms parliament

related words assembly, chamber, council, diet, house, legislative, legislature; general assembly, legislative assembly

2 a coming together of a number of persons for a specified purpose ⟨Following World War I a great *congress* of world leaders took place in Paris to plan the postwar world.⟩ — see MEETING 1

3 a group of persons formally joined together for some common interest ⟨the Canada Trades and Labor *Congress*⟩ — see ASSOCIATION 2

congruity *n* **1** a point which two or more things share in common ⟨The book alleges certain *congruities* between several incidents that were thought to be unrelated.⟩ — see SIMILARITY 2

2 a state of consistency ⟨There's little *congruity* between your professed religious beliefs and your actual behavior.⟩ — see CONFORMITY 1

congruous *adj* **1** having the parts agreeably related ⟨The *congruous* layout of the mansion's formal gardens conveys a sense of both grandeur and intimacy.⟩ — see HARMONIOUS 2

2 not having or showing any apparent conflict ⟨When performing his official duties, the president must be dressed in clothes that are *congruous* with his high position.⟩ — see CONSISTENT

congruously *adv* in a manner suitable for the occasion or purpose ⟨In a *congruously* solemn voice, she recited the oath of office.⟩ — see PROPERLY

conjectural *adj* existing only as an assumption or speculation ⟨a necessarily *conjectural* account of Shakespeare's life, since there is so little hard information⟩ — see THEORETICAL 1

conjecture *n* an opinion or judgment based on little or no evidence ⟨the many *conjectures* about the true identity of Jack the Ripper⟩

synonyms guess, shot, supposition, surmise

related words hypothesis, hypothetical, theory, thesis; dead reckoning, guessing, guesswork, speculation; hunch, intuition; belief, faith

phrases shot in the dark

conjecture *vb* **1** to decide the size, amount, number, or distance of (something) without actual measurement ⟨He *conjectured* that the theater could seat 1000 people more or less.⟩ — see ESTIMATE 2

2 to form an opinion from little or no evidence ⟨You're only *conjecturing* that he was the culprit.⟩ — see GUESS 1

conjoin *vb* **1** to come together to form a single unit ⟨Several streets *conjoin* to form the crossroads known as New York's Times Square.⟩ — see UNITE 1

2 to form or enter into an association that furthers the interests of its members ⟨Small farmers had to *conjoin* in order to compete with the agricultural conglomerates.⟩ — see ALLY

3 to participate or assist in a joint effort to accomplish an end ⟨Government agencies and private charities have *conjoined* to bring relief to the famine-stricken nation.⟩ — see COOPERATE 1

conjoint *adj* used or done by a number of people as a group ⟨Only through the *conjoint* effort of the entire department could we have finished this project on time.⟩ — see COLLECTIVE

conjointly *adv* in or by combined action or effort ⟨The two departments worked *conjointly* to finish the project in less than half the usual time.⟩ — see TOGETHER 2

conjugal *adj* of or relating to marriage ⟨newlyweds still in a rapturous state of *conjugal* happiness⟩ — see MARITAL

conjugate *vb* **1** to come together to form a single unit ⟨biological cells *conjugating* under a microscope⟩ — see UNITE 1

2 to put or bring together so as to form a new and longer whole ⟨*conjugated* polymers in a chemistry lab⟩ — see CONNECT 1

conjunction *n* the coming together of two or more things to the same point ⟨The *conjunction* of the two major highways creates a massive influx of cars into the city.⟩ — see CONVERGENCE

conjuration *n* a spoken word or set of words believed to have magic power ⟨the preposterous claim that he could raise the spirits of the dead with a mystical *conjuration*⟩ — see SPELL 1

conjure (up) *vb* **1** to form a mental picture of ⟨With certain flowers I instantly *conjure up* memories of our Caribbean honeymoon.⟩ — see IMAGINE 1

2 to call into being through the use of one's inner resources or powers ⟨I managed to *conjure up* the courage to ask the boss for a raise.⟩ — see SUMMON 2

conjurer *or* **conjuror** *n* **1** a person skilled in using supernatural forces ⟨In the book the *conjurer* battles a barbarian swordsman.⟩ — see MAGICIAN 1

2 one who practices tricks and illusions for entertainment ⟨a *conjurer* in Las Vegas who must make audiences believe in the impossible eight shows a week⟩ — see MAGICIAN 2

conjuring *n* **1** the power to control natural forces through supernatural means ⟨His attempts at *conjuring* demonstrated the vanity of human wishes.⟩ — see MAGIC 1

2 the art or skill of performing tricks or illusions for entertainment ⟨She's so good at *conjuring* that she's a much-sought-after entertainer at children's parties.⟩ — see MAGIC 2

conk (out) *vb* **1** to lose consciousness ⟨After three days without eating, he simply *conked out*.⟩ — see FAINT

2 to stop functioning ⟨The engine *conked out* just as we were approaching the exact middle of nowhere.⟩ — see FAIL 1

3 to stop living ⟨a list of people whose chief claim to fame is the unusual manner in which they *conked out*⟩ — see DIE 1

connect *vb* **1** to put or bring together so as to form a new and longer whole ⟨*Connect* all the hoses so they'll reach the garden.⟩

synonyms chain, compound, concatenate, conjugate, couple, hitch, hook, interconnect, join, link, yoke

related words articulate, dovetail, integrate, interlock, intermesh; cord, string, wire; cement, coalesce, combine, fuse, unite, weld

near antonyms detach, disengage, divide, part, split; cleave, rupture, sever, sunder

antonyms disconnect, disjoin, disjoint, dissever, disunite, separate, unchain, uncouple, unhitch, unlink, unyoke

2 to come together to form a single unit ⟨The two interstate highways *connect*, so a driver can go from one corner of the state to the other without much trouble.⟩ — see UNITE 1

3 to think of (something) in combination ⟨Opera is popularly *connected* with high society.⟩ — see ASSOCIATE 2

connecting *n* the act or an instance of joining two or more things into one ⟨The *connecting* of the truck to the trailer was easily accomplished.⟩ — see UNION 1

connection *n* **1** the fact or state of having something in common ⟨the endless debate about the *connection* between class size and test scores⟩

synonyms affinity, association, bearing, kinship, liaison, linkage, relation, relationship

related words correlation, interrelation; materiality, pertinence, relevance; bond, link, tie; affiliation, alliance, union; identicalness, sameness; alikeness, community, likeness, resemblance, similarity; accordance, agreement, conformity, congruity, correspondence

near antonyms variability, variance; incompatibility, incongruence, incongruity, incongruousness

2 a place where two or more things are united ⟨There's a problem at the *connection* where the outside wire is hooked up to the inside wiring.⟩ — see JOINT 1

3 an acquaintance who has influence especially in the business or political world ⟨I have a *connection* in Hollywood who might be able to get you a part in a movie.⟩ — see CONTACT 1

4 the act or an instance of joining two or more things into one ⟨That bridge is the only *connection* between the island and the mainland.⟩ — see UNION 1

5 the fact or state of being pertinent ⟨That last comment of yours has no *connection* with what we've been talking about for the last hour.⟩ — see PERTINENCE

6 the state of having shared interests or efforts (as in social or business matters) ⟨In a truly secular society there is no *connection* between church and state.⟩ — see ASSOCIATION 1

7 an assignment at which one regularly works for pay ⟨He enjoyed self-employment and never wanted a *connection* with a big company.⟩ — see JOB 1

connivance *n* a secret agreement or cooperation between two parties for an illegal or dishonest purpose ⟨I was able to sneak out at night with the *connivance* of a camp counselor.⟩ — see COLLUSION

connive *vb* **1** to secretly sympathize with or pretend ignorance of something improper or unlawful ⟨The principal *connived* at all the school absences that were recorded on the day of the city's celebration of its Super Bowl victory.⟩

synonyms wink

related words brush (aside *or* off), condone, disregard, excuse, forgive, gloss (over), gloze (over), ignore, overlook, pardon, pass over, shrug off, tolerate

near antonyms disapprove (of); deny, disallow, refuse

2 to engage in a secret plan to accomplish evil or unlawful ends ⟨suspects that his coworkers are *conniving* to get him fired⟩ — see PLOT

connoisseur *n* a person with a high level of knowledge or skill in a field ⟨works that are highly prized by *connoisseurs* of art glass⟩ — see EXPERT

connubial *adj* of or relating to marriage ⟨a happy couple celebrating half a century of *connubial* bliss⟩ — see MARITAL

conquer *vb* **1** to bring under one's control by force of arms ⟨Before his final defeat, Napoléon had managed to *conquer* much of Europe.⟩

synonyms dominate, overpower, pacify, subdue, subject, subjugate, subordinate, vanquish

related words annihilate, beat, clobber, crush, defeat, drub, lick, mow (down), overcome, prevail (over), reduce, rout, skunk, smash, thrash, triumph (over), trounce, wallop, whip; enslave; break, clamp down (on), crack down (on), put down, quash, quell, repress, silence, smother, snuff (out), squash, squelch, suppress

near antonyms discharge, emancipate, enfranchise, free, liberate, manumit, release, spring, unbind, uncage, unchain, unfetter

2 to achieve a victory over 〈Love *conquers* all, or so romance novels would have us believe.〉 — see BEAT 2

3 to achieve victory (as in a contest) 〈a coach who doesn't demand that his team *conquer*, whatever the cost〉 — see WIN 1

conqueror *n* one that defeats an enemy or opponent 〈hailed as *conqueror* of the barbarian forces〉 — see VICTOR 1

conquest *n* the act or process of bringing someone or something under one's control 〈the *conquest* of much of North and South America by the Spanish during the 16th century〉

synonyms dominating, domination, overpowering, subduing, subjecting, subjection, subjugating, subjugation, vanquishing

related words triumph, victory, win, winning; beating, defeat, drubbing, licking, shellacking, trimming, trouncing, whipping; enslavement

near antonyms emancipation, enfranchisement, freeing, liberation, manumission, release

conscientious *adj* **1** guided by or in accordance with one's sense of right and wrong 〈Operated on the belief that most people are *conscientious*, the unattended farm stand has a price list and a money drawer for customers to leave payment for their purchases.〉

synonyms ethical, honest, honorable, just, moral, principled, scrupulous

related words decent, good, righteous, right-minded, straight, upright, virtuous; dutiful, observant, respectful; overconscientious; reliable, responsible, solid, tried-and-true, true, trustworthy, trusty; esteemed, law-abiding, reputable, respected, upstanding, worthy

near antonyms bad, evil, evil-minded, immoral, indecent, sinful, unrighteous, wicked; unreliable, untrustworthy; corrupt, debased, debauched, degenerate, depraved, dissolute, perverted, reprobate; atrocious, infamous, villainous; base, low, mean, vicious, vile; iniquitous, nefarious

antonyms cutthroat, dishonest, dishonorable, immoral, unconscionable, unethical, unjust, unprincipled, unscrupulous

2 taking, showing, or involving great care and effort 〈a counselor who serves patients by first being a *conscientious* listener〉 — see PAINSTAKING

conscientiousness *n* strict attentiveness to what one is doing 〈finished the last details with as much *conscientiousness* as the first〉 — see CARE 1

conscious *adj* **1** having specified facts or feelings actively impressed on the mind 〈*conscious* of the fact that my hands were sweating the whole time that I was making my presentation〉

synonyms alive, aware, cognizant, mindful, sensible, sentient, witting

related words alert, attentive, careful, cautious, heedful, observant, open-eyed, regardful, safe, vigilant, wary, watchful, wide-awake; hyperaware, hyperconscious

near antonyms careless, heedless, inattentive, incautious, mindless, unguarded, unheeding, unwary

antonyms insensible, oblivious, unaware, unconscious, unmindful, unwitting

2 made, given, or done with full awareness of what one is doing 〈a *conscious* effort to be more understanding〉 — see INTENTIONAL

consciously *adv* with full awareness of what one is doing 〈She *consciously* chose to take the more dangerous route down the mountain.〉 — see INTENTIONALLY

conscript *n* a person forced or required to enroll in military service 〈As the war continued, the body of enlisted soldiers was supplemented by an increasing number of *conscripts*.〉

synonyms draftee, inductee

related words levy; recruit, rookie

near antonyms enlistee, volunteer

conscript *vb* to pick especially for required military service 〈was *conscripted* into the army shortly after turning 18〉 — see DRAFT 1

consecrate *adj* set apart or worthy of veneration by association with God 〈the *consecrate* gold tablets which Joseph Smith claimed to have found〉 — see HOLY 2

consecrate *vb* **1** to keep or intend for a special purpose 〈a philanthropist who *consecrated* his considerable fortune to an array of charitable causes〉 — see DEVOTE 1

2 to make holy through prayers or ritual 〈The church was *consecrated* in 1856.〉 — see BLESS 1

consecrated *adj* set apart or worthy of veneration by association with God 〈built the cemetery on *consecrated* ground〉 — see HOLY 2

consecration *n* the act of making something holy through religious ritual 〈the *consecration* of the temple〉

synonyms blessing, hallowing, sanctification

related words purification; dedication; adoration, glorification, reverence, veneration, worship

near antonyms debasement, defilement, desecration, impiety, irreverence, sacrilege

consecutive *adj* following one after another without others coming in between 〈The team's winning streak has lasted for seven *consecutive* games.〉

synonyms sequential, straight, succeeding, successional, successive

related words serial; constant, continuous, uninterrupted; ensuing, following, later, next, posterior, subsequent

near antonyms in series

antonyms inconsecutive, nonconsecutive, nonsequential

consensus *n* the state of being of one opinion about something 〈finally reached a *consensus* on how to spend the money that the club had raised〉 — see AGREEMENT 1

consent *n* the approval by someone in authority for the doing of something 〈We had to get our neighbor's *consent* in order to trim the tree from his side.〉 — see PERMISSION

consent *vb* to give or express one's approval (as to a proposal) 〈refused to *consent* to the marriage〉 — see ACCEDE

consequence *n* **1** a condition or occurrence traceable to a cause 〈The flood was an inevitable *consequence* of the prolonged, heavy rains.〉 — see EFFECT 1

2 the quality or state of being important 〈a mistake that was of no great *consequence*〉 — see IMPORTANCE

3 an exaggerated sense of one's importance that shows itself in the making of excessive or unjustified claims 〈a junior executive who strutted around the office with all of the *consequence* of a peacock in pinstripes〉 — see ARROGANCE

4 an opinion arrived at through a process of reasoning 〈I am able to deduce several *consequences* from those premises.〉 — see CONCLUSION 1

consequent *adj* **1** according to the rules of logic 〈The conclusion that you have reached is neither *consequent* nor plausible.〉 — see LOGICAL 1

2 coming as a result 〈Her new job and *consequent* relocation added to the stress.〉 — see RESULTANT

consequential *adj* **1** coming as a result ⟨his daily practice and the *consequential* improvement in performance⟩ — see RESULTANT
2 having great meaning or lasting effect ⟨The American Civil War is often regarded as the nation's most *consequential* event since its founding.⟩ — see IMPORTANT 1
3 having too high an opinion of oneself ⟨For such a *consequential* businessman, he's head of a rather small company.⟩ — see CONCEITED
consequently *adv* for this or that reason ⟨Prices were lowered, and *consequently* complaints were fewer.⟩ — see THEREFORE
conservation *n* **1** the careful maintaining and protection of something valuable especially in its natural or original state ⟨Everyone has a duty to aid in the *conservation* of our nation's wilderness areas.⟩
synonyms preservation
related words care, maintenance, upkeep; salvation, saving; defense, guardianship, guarding, keeping, protection, safeguarding, safekeeping; economy, husbandry, management
near antonyms dereliction, ignoring, neglect, squandering, waste; destruction, ruin; damage, harm, hurt, injury
2 the act or activity of keeping something in an existing and usually satisfactory condition ⟨the *conservation* of the nation's monuments and memorials⟩ — see MAINTENANCE
conservative *adj* **1** tending to favor established ideas, conditions, or institutions ⟨*Conservative* baseball fans consider the new ballpark too modern-looking and plain ugly.⟩
synonyms hidebound, old-fashioned, orthodox, reactionary, traditional, unprogressive
related words conventional, square; devoted, faithful, loyal, staunch (*also* stanch), steadfast, steady, true, true-blue; neoconservative, Tory, ultraright, ultrarightist; dowdy, fogyish (*or* fogeyish), fuddy-duddy, ossified, set, stodgy; right, right-wing; antiliberal, antimodern, antiprogressive, antireform, antirevolutionary
near antonyms anticonventional, antiestablishment, antitraditional, extremist, radical, revolutionary; nonconformist; advanced, contemporary, modern; lefty, radical, ultraleft, ultraleftist, ultraprogressive, ultraradical
antonyms broad-minded, large-minded, liberal, nonconservative, nonconventional, nonorthodox, nontraditional, open-minded, progressive, unconventional, unorthodox
2 not excessively showy ⟨dressing in *conservative* clothing so as to make a good impression at job interviews⟩ — see QUIET 2
3 having or showing a close attentiveness to avoiding danger or trouble ⟨Ed made *conservative* investments, and so he wasn't ruined when the market went into a free fall.⟩ — see CAREFUL 1
conservative *n* a person whose political beliefs are centered on tradition and keeping things the way they are ⟨proposed legislation that was opposed by *conservatives* throughout the state⟩
synonyms reactionary, rightist, Tory
related words right, right-wing; conformist; neocon, neoconservative; diehard, standpatter; fuddy-duddy, square
near antonyms extremist, radical, red, revolutionary, revolutionist; reformer, reformist
antonyms leftist, left-winger, lefty, liberal, progressive
conservatory *n* a glass-enclosed building for growing plants ⟨The college's *conservatory* is entirely devoted to cultivating and displaying orchids.⟩
synonyms greenhouse, hothouse
related words cold frame, hot bed; botanical garden (*also* botanic garden)

conserve *vb* **1** to avoid the wasteful or destructive use of ⟨the need to *conserve* oil and other finite fossil fuels⟩
synonyms husband
related words economize, save, scrimp, skimp; preserve, protect, save; hoard, lay up
near antonyms clean (out), consume, deplete, drain, exhaust, expend, impoverish, spend, use up
antonyms blow, dissipate, fritter (away), lavish, misspend, run through, squander, throw away, waste
2 to keep in good condition ⟨Let's *conserve* our national parks so that they may be enjoyed by future generations.⟩ — see MAINTAIN 1
conserving *n* the act or activity of keeping something in an existing and usually satisfactory condition ⟨the *conserving* of such national treasures as the flag that flew over Fort McHenry during its famous bombardment⟩ — see MAINTENANCE
consider *vb* **1** to think of in a particular way ⟨I *consider* him a very good friend.⟩
synonyms account, call, count, esteem, hold, rate, reckon, regard, set down, view
related words believe, deem, feel, sense, think; conceive, fancy, imagine; allow (for), provide (for), regard
phrases take for
2 to give serious and careful thought to ⟨carefully *considering* our options⟩ — see PONDER
3 to have as an opinion ⟨*consider* the price too high⟩ — see BELIEVE 2
4 to think very highly or favorably of ⟨Her well-*considered* novels have seldom been best sellers.⟩ — see ADMIRE
considerable *adj* **1** sufficiently large in size, amount, or number to merit attention ⟨the *considerable* number of auto accidents that resulted from the surprise snowstorm⟩
synonyms good, goodly, handsome, healthy, largish, major, respectable, significant, sizable (*or* sizeable), substantial, tidy
related words big, bulky, hefty, hulking, outsize (*also* outsized), oversize (*or* oversized), voluminous; astronomical (*also* astronomic), bumper, colossal, elephantine, enormous, gigantic, great, herculean, huge, immense, jumbo, king-size (*or* king-sized), mammoth, massive, monstrous, monumental, prodigious, titanic, tremendous, whopping
near antonyms measly, minute, paltry, petty, picayune, picayunish, piddling, puny, trifling, trivial, unimportant; meager (*or* meagre), slight; little, small, tiny, undersized (*also* undersize); bitty, diminutive, miniature, pint-size (*or* pint-sized), pocket, pocket-size (*also* pocket-sized), pygmy, smallish
antonyms inconsequential, inconsiderable, insignificant, insubstantial, negligible, nominal
2 of a size greater than average of its kind ⟨a house with a *considerable* barn in back⟩ — see LARGE
considerably *adv* to a large extent or degree ⟨home electronic devices that have fallen *considerably* in price⟩ — see GREATLY 2
considerate *adj* **1** given to or made with heedful anticipation of the needs and happiness of others ⟨a kindly woman who is very *considerate* of other people's feelings⟩ — see THOUGHTFUL 1
2 having or showing a close attentiveness to avoiding danger or trouble ⟨You need to develop a more *considerate* temperament and learn to think before you speak.⟩ — see CAREFUL 1
considerately *adv* with good reason or courtesy ⟨He *considerately* made breakfast for all of the exhausted rescue workers.⟩ — see WELL 4

consideration *n* **1** a careful weighing of the reasons for or against something ⟨After much *consideration* we decided to make an offer on the house.⟩
synonyms account, advisement, debate, deliberation, reflection, study, thought
related words contemplation, meditation, pondering, rumination; agonizing, hesitation, indecision; premeditation
antonyms short shrift
2 something (as money) that is given or received in return for goods or services ⟨Since it was pro bono work, no *consideration* was given.⟩ — see PAYMENT 2

considered *adj* decided on as a result of careful thought ⟨My *considered* opinion is that this is the best movie I've ever seen.⟩ — see DELIBERATE 1

consign *vb* **1** to cause to go or be taken from one place to another ⟨*consigned* the prisoner to the dungeon⟩ — see SEND
2 to put (something) into the possession or safekeeping of another ⟨The deliveryman had *consigned* our package to a next-door neighbor.⟩ — see GIVE 2

consist (of) *vb* to be made up of ⟨Those cookies *consist of* flour, butter, sugar, chocolate, and vanilla.⟩ — see COMPRISE 1

consistency *n* the degree to which a fluid can resist flowing ⟨Beat the egg whites until they take on the *consistency* of whipped cream.⟩
synonyms density, thickness, viscosity
related words compactness, firmness, solidity; ropiness, stickiness

consistent *adj* not having or showing any apparent conflict ⟨The clothes you wear to work must be *consistent* with the company's dress code.⟩
synonyms coherent, compatible, concordant, conformable (to), congruous, consonant, correspondent (with *or* to), harmonious, nonconflicting
related words self-consistent; appropriate, befitting, felicitous, fit, fitting, meet, proper, right, suitable
phrases of a piece
near antonyms improper, inappropriate, inapt, infelicitous, unsuitable
antonyms conflicting, conflictive, incompatible, incongruous, inconsistent, inharmonious, noncompatible

consistently *adv* on every relevant occasion ⟨He *consistently* brings a sandwich for lunch.⟩ — see ALWAYS 1

consolation *n* **1** the giving of hope and strength in times of grief, distress, or suffering ⟨the *consolation* of the grieving family by their friends⟩
synonyms comforting, consoling, solace, solacing
related words commiseration, compassion, condolence, feeling, sympathy; counseling (*or* counselling); humanity, kindheartedness, kindliness, kindness, mercy, pity
2 a feeling of ease from grief or trouble ⟨the *consolation* that our favorite foods give us when we're having a bad day⟩ — see COMFORT 1

console *n* a storage case typically having doors and shelves ⟨A custom-built walnut *console* holds all of their home-theater components.⟩ — see CABINET

console *vb* to ease the grief or distress of ⟨the military officer who must *console* the bereaved at a soldier's funeral⟩ — see COMFORT

consolidate *vb* **1** to bring (something) to a central point or under a single control ⟨plans to *consolidate* several branches into one regional office⟩ — see CENTRALIZE
2 to make markedly greater in measure or degree ⟨Another win would *consolidate* their hold on first place in their division.⟩ — see INTENSIFY

consolidation *n* the act or an instance of joining two or more things into one ⟨the *consolidation* of several intelligence agencies into one super agency⟩ — see UNION 1

consoling *n* the giving of hope and strength in times of grief, distress, or suffering ⟨The responsibility for the *consoling* of the families of the firefighters fell to the mayor.⟩ — see CONSOLATION 1

consonance *n* **1** a balanced, pleasing, or suitable arrangement of parts ⟨At present, the living room lacks *consonance* because all of the furniture is on one side.⟩ — see HARMONY 1
2 a state of consistency ⟨In good writing there is always *consonance* of thought and expression, as the use of simple words for simple thoughts.⟩ — see CONFORMITY 1

consonant *adj* **1** having the parts agreeably related ⟨The temples and palaces of ancient Greece are among the most *consonant* buildings in architectural history.⟩ — see HARMONIOUS 2
2 not having or showing any apparent conflict ⟨His gentle behavior is *consonant* with his expressed belief in pacifism.⟩ — see CONSISTENT

[1]**consort** *n* **1** a usually small number of persons considered as a unit ⟨A *consort* of doctors attended the case.⟩ — see GROUP 2
2 an organized group of singers ⟨hired a *consort* of madrigal singers to perform at the wedding reception⟩ — see CHORUS 1

[2]**consort** *n* the person to whom another is married ⟨It is the queen's eldest son and not her *consort* who is next in line for the throne.⟩ — see SPOUSE

consort *vb* **1** to come or be together as friends ⟨At college she began *consorting* with activists, eventually becoming one herself.⟩ — see ASSOCIATE 1
2 to form a pleasing relationship ⟨The restaurant's sophisticated menu *consorts* seamlessly with its sleek, modern ambience.⟩ — see HARMONIZE 1

conspicuous *adj* **1** likely to attract attention ⟨The seven-foot-tall basketball player is *conspicuous* in any crowd.⟩ — see NOTICEABLE
2 very noticeable especially for being incorrect or bad ⟨*conspicuous* bureaucratic waste that upsets taxpayers⟩ — see EGREGIOUS

conspiracy *n* **1** a group involved in secret or criminal activities ⟨Members of the *conspiracy* recognized each other by a secret handshake.⟩ — see [1]RING 1
2 a secret agreement or cooperation between two parties for an illegal or dishonest purpose ⟨a *conspiracy* among the leading manufacturers to fix prices⟩ — see COLLUSION
3 a secret plan for accomplishing evil or unlawful ends ⟨Several generals were engaged in a *conspiracy* to overthrow the government.⟩ — see PLOT 1

conspire *vb* **1** to engage in a secret plan to accomplish evil or unlawful ends ⟨*conspired* to replace the leader with someone more easily influenced⟩ — see PLOT
2 to participate or assist in a joint effort to accomplish an end ⟨Foul weather and airline foul-ups seemed to be *conspiring* to ruin our vacation.⟩ — see COOPERATE 1

constabulary *n* a body of officers of the law ⟨All members of the local *constabulary* were on the alert for the escaped convict.⟩ — see POLICE 2

constancy *n* **1** the state of continuing without change ⟨There's the mistaken notion that there is *constancy* in language—words do indeed change their meanings over time.⟩
synonyms changelessness, fixedness, immutability, invariability, stability, steadiness, unchangeableness
related words consistency, regularity, sameness, uniformity; durability, enduringness, lastingness, permanence
near antonyms inconsistence, inconsistency, irregularity, unevenness
antonyms capriciousness, changeability, changeable-

ness, fickleness, instability, mutability, unpredictability, unsteadiness, variability, variableness, volatileness, volatility

2 adherence to something to which one is bound by a pledge or duty ⟨soldiers serving with *constancy* and devotion to country⟩ — see FIDELITY

3 the strength of mind that enables a person to endure pain or hardship ⟨It takes determination and *constancy* to get through law school.⟩ — see FORTITUDE

constant *adj* **1** not undergoing a change in condition ⟨Change is the only *constant* thing in the world of fashion.⟩
synonyms changeless, stable, stationary, steady, unchanging, unvarying
related words fast, fixed, hard-and-fast, immutable, inflexible, invariable, unalterable, unchangeable; established, set, settled; ceaseless, continuing, durable, enduring, lasting, permanent
phrases on an even keel (*also* on even keel)
near antonyms adaptable, alterable, changeable, flexible, mutable, variable; ephemeral, evanescent, fleeting, momentary, transient, transitory; phantasmagoric (*or* phantasmagorical)
antonyms capricious, changeful, changing, fickle, fluctuating, fluid, inconstant, mercurial, skittish, uncertain, unpredictable, unsettled, unstable, unsteady, varying, volatile

2 appearing or occurring repeatedly from time to time ⟨I get *constant* headaches during humid weather.⟩ — see REGULAR 1

3 firm in one's allegiance to someone or something ⟨*constant* friends during times both good and bad⟩ — see FAITHFUL 1

constantly *adv* **1** many times ⟨phone calls *constantly* interrupting my work⟩ — see OFTEN

2 on every relevant occasion ⟨Stay *constantly* on guard until the danger of forest fire is past.⟩ — see ALWAYS 1

constituent *n* one of the parts that make up a whole ⟨The soil contained all of the necessary *constituents* for growing crops.⟩ — see ELEMENT 1

constitute *vb* **1** to be all the substance of ⟨Nine players *constitute* a baseball team.⟩
synonyms compose, comprise, form, make up
related words embody, epitomize, incarnate, incorporate, integrate, materialize, personify, substantiate; complement, complete, supplement; fill (out), flesh (out)

2 to be responsible for the creation and early operation or use of ⟨A fund was *constituted* to help needy students attend the prep school.⟩ — see FOUND

3 to pick (someone) by one's authority for a specific position or duty ⟨the legally *constituted* authorities with jurisdiction in this matter⟩ — see APPOINT 2

4 to put into effect through legislative or authoritative action ⟨charged with enforcing such regulations as are *constituted* by the government⟩ — see ENACT

constitution *n* **1** the set of qualities that makes a person, a group of people, or a thing different from others ⟨the question of whether violent conflict is part of the *constitution* of human society⟩ — see NATURE 1

2 the type of body that a person has ⟨That marathon runner is known more for her strong *constitution* than for her speed.⟩ — see PHYSIQUE

3 a collection or system of rules of conduct ⟨Our society's *constitution* requires that every member in good standing pay yearly dues.⟩ — see CODE

4 a rule of conduct or action laid down by a governing authority and especially a legislature ⟨The *constitution* against murder is universal among civilized societies.⟩ — see LAW 1

constitutional *adj* being a part of the innermost nature of a person or thing ⟨He has a *constitutional* dislike of controversy.⟩ — see INHERENT

constitutional *n* a relaxed journey on foot for exercise or pleasure ⟨I went for my evening *constitutional* in the park.⟩ — see WALK 1

constitutionally *adv* by natural character or ability ⟨I'm afraid that I'm *constitutionally* incapable of carrying a tune.⟩ — see NATURALLY 1

constrain *vb* **1** to cause (a person) to give in to pressure ⟨*constrained* by conscience to tell only the truth⟩ — see FORCE

2 to keep from exceeding a desirable degree or level (as of expression) ⟨*constrained* his anger at the needless interruption⟩ — see CONTROL 1

constraint *n* **1** the checking of one's true feelings and impulses when dealing with others ⟨In civilized society people do not just say or do whatever they feel like—they exercise some *constraint*.⟩
synonyms discipline, discretion, inhibition, repression, reserve, restraint, self-control, self-restraint, suppression
related words command, control, mastery, possession; self-censorship, self-containment, self-denial, self-discipline, self-government, will, willpower; composure, self-poise, self-possession; aloofness, detachedness, distance; bashfulness, modesty, shyness; reticence, silence, taciturnity
near antonyms self-abandonment; unrestrainedness; gratification, indulgence, overindulgence, self-indulgence; candor, frankness
antonyms disinhibition, incontinence

2 something that limits one's freedom of action or choice ⟨put legal *constraints* on the board's activities⟩ — see RESTRICTION 1

3 the use of power to impose one's will on another ⟨Parental *constraint* over children can take several different forms.⟩ — see FORCE 2

constrict *vb* **1** to become smaller in size or volume through the drawing together of particles of matter ⟨The vessel *constricted*, thereby reducing the flow of blood.⟩ — see CONTRACT 2

2 to reduce in size or volume by or as if by pressing parts or members together ⟨*constricted* the opening with a clamp⟩ — see COMPRESS 1

constriction *n* the act or process of reducing the size or volume of something by or as if by pressing ⟨Dan tried to ease the tie's *constriction* of his neck.⟩ — see COMPRESSION

construct *vb* **1** to create or think of by clever use of the imagination ⟨He managed to *construct* a theory that fits all the facts.⟩ — see INVENT

2 to form by putting together parts or materials ⟨*constructed* a hydroelectric dam across the river⟩ — see BUILD

construction *n* **1** something put together by arranging or connecting an array of parts ⟨The swing set turned out to be a more complicated *construction* than the "some assembly required" warning suggested.⟩
synonyms structure
related words arrangement, assembly; configuration, frame, framework, shell, skeleton

2 a statement that makes something clear ⟨Could you give us your *construction* of this clause in the contract?⟩ — see EXPLANATION 1

constructive *adj* having a role in deciding something's final form ⟨His experiences as an exchange student played a *constructive* part in the course that his life would take.⟩ — see FORMATIVE

construe *vb* to make plain or understandable ⟨the role of the justices of the Supreme Court in *construing* the constitution⟩ — see EXPLAIN 1

consult *n* an exchange of views for the purpose of exploring a subject or deciding an issue ⟨It was time for a change of her investments, which called for a *consult* with her financial advisor.⟩ — see DISCUSSION 1

consult *vb* **1** to exchange viewpoints or seek advice for the purpose of finding a solution to a problem ⟨will *consult* with several experts on the disease before deciding which course of treatment to pursue⟩ — see CONFER 2

2 to use or seek out as a source of aid, relief, or advantage ⟨I often *consult* the dictionary when I am uncertain of a word's exact meaning.⟩ — see RESORT (TO) 1

consultant *n* a person who gives advice especially professionally ⟨a *consultant* in public relations to a number of large corporations⟩

synonyms adviser (*also* advisor), counsel, counselor (*or* counsellor)

related words authority, expert, pro, professional, specialist; confidant; cabinet, kitchen cabinet; sounding board

near antonyms counselee

consume *vb* **1** to destroy all trace of ⟨Massive fires had *consumed* hundreds of square miles of forest.⟩

synonyms devour, eat (up)

related words gut; deplete, drain, exhaust, expend, spend, use up; annihilate, decimate, demolish, desolate, devastate, do in, pulverize, raze, ruin, shatter, smash, tear down, waste, wreck; annihilate, blot out, eradicate, exterminate, extinguish, extirpate, obliterate, remove, rub out, stamp (out), wipe out

near antonyms conserve, preserve, protect, save; build, construct, erect, put up, raise

2 to make complete use of ⟨The mining company *consumed* all of the local mineral resources and then moved on.⟩ — see DEPLETE 1

3 to take in as food ⟨hungry enough to *consume* most of the pie⟩ — see EAT 1

consummate *adj* **1** having or showing exceptional knowledge, experience, or skill in a field of endeavor ⟨*Consummate* cabinetmakers, they produced desks and chests of drawers that are now regarded as masterpieces of American furniture.⟩ — see PROFICIENT

2 having no exceptions or restrictions ⟨a *consummate* liar who has practically made mendacity an art form⟩ — see ABSOLUTE 2

3 of the greatest or highest degree or quantity ⟨a ballerina renowned for her *consummate* grace⟩ — see ULTIMATE 1

consummate *vb* to bring (something) to a state where nothing remains to be done ⟨willing to do whatever it takes to *consummate* a business deal⟩ — see FINISH 1

consummation *n* **1** the last part of a process or action ⟨The signing of the contract marked the *consummation* of six months of negotiations.⟩ — see FINALE

2 the state of being actual or complete ⟨The opening of the performing arts center brought to *consummation* years of planning.⟩ — see FRUITION

contact *n* **1** an acquaintance who has influence especially in the business or political world ⟨an intern who got her summer job in the governor's office through *contacts*⟩

synonyms connection

related words in, insider; big shot, bigwig, somebody, VIP; arbiter, arbitrator, conciliator, go-between, intercessor, intermediary, interposer, mediator, middleman, peacemaker

2 the state or fact of being able to exchange information regarding one's current situation ⟨She had moved to the other side of the country, but continued to stay in *contact* with her closest friends.⟩ — see TOUCH 1

contact *vb* to transmit information or requests to ⟨You can *contact* me at this number.⟩

synonyms address, communicate (with), get, reach

related words get through (to); acquaint, advise, apprise, brief, clue, enlighten, familiarize, fill in, inform, instruct, notify, tell, wise (up); buzz, call, phone, telephone; keep up (with)

phrases get hold of, get in touch with (*or* keep in touch with), touch base (with)

contagious *adj* **1** capable of being passed by physical contact from one person to another ⟨chicken pox, measles, German measles, and other *contagious* diseases⟩

synonyms catching, communicable, pestilent, transmittable

related words infectious, infective

near antonyms noninfectious

antonyms noncommunicable

2 exciting a similar feeling or reaction in others ⟨The enthusiasm of the new club members was *contagious*.⟩

synonyms catching, infectious, spreading

related words palpable, perceptible, tangible; irresistible (*also* irresistable), overpowering, overwhelming; disarming, endearing, fetching, inviting, winning, winsome

contain *vb* **1** to have within ⟨The top drawer of the cabinet *contains* my stamp collection.⟩

synonyms bear, boast, hold

related words accommodate, fit, take; case, encase, enclose (*also* inclose), encompass; harbor, house, lodge, shelter

2 to have as part of a whole ⟨The contract *contains* several new clauses.⟩ — see INCLUDE 1

3 to be made up of ⟨The recipe *contains* several parts.⟩ — see COMPRISE 1

4 to gain emotional or mental control of ⟨Kay could hardly *contain* herself when she heard that she had won the scholarship.⟩ — see COLLECT 1

5 to keep from exceeding a desirable degree or level (as of expression) ⟨frantic efforts to *contain* the spread of the disease⟩ — see CONTROL 1

container *n* something into which a liquid or smaller objects can be put for storage or transportation ⟨Save the plastic *containers* from the deli for other uses.⟩

synonyms holder, receptacle, vessel

related words carrier; cartridge; basket, bin, box, caddy, carton, case, casket, crate, handbasket, locker, trunk; bag, hamper, pocket, sack; warmer; basin, bottle, bowl, bucket, can, jar, jug, keg, kettle, kit, pack, pail, pitcher, pot, tub, vat

contaminant *n* something that is or that makes impure ⟨a filter to remove *contaminants* from the drinking water⟩ — see IMPURITY 1

contaminate *vb* to make unfit for use by the addition of something harmful or undesirable ⟨a supply of drinking water that was *contaminated* by a toxic waste dump⟩

synonyms befoul, defile, foul, poison, pollute, taint

related words infect; begrime, besmirch, blacken, dirty, foul up, grime, mire, muddy, smirch, smudge, soil, stain, sully; corrupt, rot, spoil; adulterate, doctor; dilute

near antonyms clarify, clean, cleanse, clear, distill (*also* distil), purge; filter; disinfect, sanitize, sterilize

antonyms decontaminate, purify

contaminated *adj* containing foreign or lower-grade substances ⟨The hospitals had no choice but to throw out the *contaminated* blood supply.⟩ — see IMPURE 1

contemplate *vb* **1** to give serious and careful thought to ⟨She *contemplated* the problem for several hours before reaching a decision.⟩ — see PONDER

2 to have in mind as a purpose or goal ⟨He waited patiently, *contemplating* revenge all the while.⟩ — see INTEND 1

contemplation *n* long or deep thinking about spiritual matters ⟨the decision to enter a monastery and to spend one's life in prayer and *contemplation*⟩

synonyms meditation

related words brown study, daydreaming, navel-gazing, reflection, retrospection, reverie, study, trance, woolgathering; deliberation, pondering, rumination

contemplative *adj* given to or marked by long, quiet thinking ⟨a *contemplative* person who likes to go on solitary walks⟩ ⟨the *contemplative* life of the monks at the abbey⟩

synonyms meditative, melancholy, pensive, reflective, ruminant, thoughtful

related words introspective, retrospective, self-reflective; earnest, grave, sedate, serious, serious-minded, severe, sober, solemn, somber (*or* sombre), weighty; philosophical (*also* philosophic); analytic (*or* analytical), logical, rational; deliberate, purposeful; absentminded, abstracted, preoccupied

near antonyms featherbrained, flighty, flippant, frivolous, goofy, harebrained, light-headed, scatterbrained; brainless, mindless, silly, thoughtless, unthinking

antonyms unreflective

contemporaneous *adj* existing or occurring at the same period of time ⟨*contemporaneous* accounts of the battle from officers on both sides⟩ — see CONTEMPORARY 1

contemporaneously *adv* at one and the same time ⟨Mozart was writing music *contemporaneously* with Haydn.⟩ — see TOGETHER 1

contemporary *adj* 1 existing or occurring at the same period of time ⟨the absurd notion that early cave dwellers were *contemporary* with the dinosaurs⟩

synonyms coeval, coexistent, coexisting, coextensive, coincident, coincidental, concurrent, contemporaneous, simultaneous, synchronous

related words accompanying, attendant, attending, concomitant, incident

antonyms asynchronous, noncontemporary, nonsimultaneous, nonsynchronous

2 being or involving the latest methods, concepts, information, or styles ⟨a magazine devoted to *contemporary* fashions⟩ — see MODERN

contemporary *n* a person who lives at the same time or is about the same age as another ⟨Abraham Lincoln and Charles Darwin were exact *contemporaries*, actually being born on the same day in 1809.⟩

synonyms coeval

related words accompaniment, companion, concomitant; coordinate, counterpart, equal, equivalent, match, peer, rival

contempt *n* open dislike for someone or something considered unworthy of one's concern or respect ⟨my undying *contempt* for people who abuse animals⟩

synonyms despite, despitefulness, disdain, scorn

related words abhorrence, abomination, execration, hate, hatred, loathing, lovelessness; cattiness, hatefulness, invidiousness, malevolence, malice, maliciousness, malignancy, malignity, meanness, spite, spitefulness; aversion, disgust, distaste, horror, odium, repugnance, repulsion, revulsion; animosity, antagonism, antipathy, bitterness, enmity, gall, grudge, hostility, jealousy, pique, resentment; bile, jaundice, rancor, spleen, venom, vindictiveness, virulence, vitriol; aspersion, belittlement, deprecation, depreciation, detraction, diminishment, disparagement; derision, mockery, ridicule; abuse, invective, vituperation; censure, condemnation, denunciation

near antonyms acceptance, tolerance; adoration, adulation, deference, deification, glorification, idolatry, idolization, lionization, reverence, veneration, worship; affection, fancy, fondness, liking, love

antonyms admiration, esteem, estimation, favor, regard, respect

contemptible *adj* 1 arousing or deserving of one's loathing and disgust ⟨the *contemptible* thieves who stole the clothing intended for needy children⟩

synonyms cheap, deplorable, despicable, dirty, grubby, lame, lousy, mean, nasty, paltry, pitiable, pitiful, scabby, scummy, scurvy, sneaking, sorry, wretched

related words abhorrent, abominable, condemnable, detestable, execrable, hateful, loathsome, odious; reptilian, repugnant, repulsive, revolting, revulsive; discreditable, disgraceful, dishonorable, disreputable, ignominious, shameful; base, ignoble, low, shabby, sordid, squalid, vile; blamable, censurable, reprehensible, reproachable; cowardly, craven, dastardly; unethical, unprincipled, unscrupulous

near antonyms high-minded, honest, honorable, noble, principled, redoubtable, reputable, right-minded, scrupulous, upright; ethical, good, moral, right, righteous, virtuous

antonyms admirable, commendable, creditable, laudable, meritorious, praiseworthy

2 deserving pitying scorn (as for inadequacy) ⟨a *contemptible* attempt at science fiction by someone with no understanding of the genre⟩ — see PITIFUL 1

3 not following or in accordance with standards of honor and decency ⟨the *contemptible* behavior of the hikers who littered the trail⟩ — see IGNOBLE 2

contemptuous *adj* 1 feeling or showing open dislike for someone or something regarded as undeserving of respect or concern ⟨loutish tourists who are *contemptuous* of the ways and traditions of their host countries⟩

synonyms abhorrent, disdainful, scornful

related words bold-faced, brash, brassy, brazen, cheeky, cocky, discourteous, disrespectful, fresh, impertinent, impudent, insolent, sassy, saucy; arrogant, cavalier, highfalutin (*also* hifalutin), high-handed, high-hat, pretentious, uppish, uppity; haughty, lofty, lordly, prideful, sniffish, supercilious; pompous, self-important, superior; catty, cruel, despiteful, hateful, malevolent, malicious, malign, malignant, mean, nasty, spiteful

near antonyms deferential, regardful, respectful; accepting, tolerant; courteous, polite

antonyms admiring, applauding, appreciative, approving

2 intended to make a person or thing seem of little importance or value ⟨*contemptuous* comments about the baseball team's pathetic showings⟩ — see DEROGATORY

contend *vb* 1 to engage in a contest ⟨two traditional rivals *contending* for the championship⟩ — see COMPETE

2 to state (something) as a reason in support of or against something under consideration ⟨*contended* that the senator's considerable experience made her the best candidate⟩ — see ARGUE 1

3 to state as a fact usually forcefully ⟨*contended* that his opponent was wrong about practically everything⟩ — see CLAIM 1

contend (with) *vb* 1 to deal with (something) usually skillfully or efficiently ⟨a multitude of problems to *contend with* as soon as she returned to the office⟩ — see HANDLE 1

2 to strive to reduce or eliminate ⟨medical researchers who daily *contend with* disease⟩ — see FIGHT 2

contender *n* 1 one who seeks an office, honor, position, or award ⟨a strong *contender* for the mayoral position⟩ — see CANDIDATE

2 one who strives for the same thing as another ⟨several *contenders* competing for the title of the city's best Italian restaurant⟩ — see COMPETITOR

content *adj* feeling that one's needs or desires have been met ⟨Are you *content* with your present salary?⟩
  synonyms contented, gratified, happy, pleased, satisfied
  related words blissful, delighted, glad, joyful, joyous, jubilant, rejoicing, tickled; ecstatic, elated, enraptured, euphoric, overjoyed, rapturous, thrilled; appeased, mollified, pacified, placated
  near antonyms disaffected, disgruntled, displeased, unsatisfied; aggrieved, anguished, brokenhearted, dejected, depressed, despondent, disconsolate, discouraged, disheartened, dispirited, downcast, downhearted
  antonyms discontent, discontented, displeased, dissatisfied, malcontent, malcontented, unhappy

¹**content** *n* **1** a major object of interest or concern (as in a discussion or artistic composition) ⟨Although I appreciate the poem's lyrical qualities, I don't understand its *content*.⟩ — see MATTER 1
  2 the amount of something (as subject matter) included ⟨Judging from the table of *contents*, I'd have to say that this book covers most of the major topics in American history.⟩ — see COVERAGE
  3 the idea that is conveyed or intended to be conveyed to the mind by language, symbol, or action ⟨The speech was filled with fine words but devoid of any real *content*.⟩ — see MEANING 1

²**content** *n* the feeling experienced when one's wishes are met ⟨slept to her heart's *content* on weekends⟩ — see PLEASURE 1

content *vb* to give satisfaction to ⟨a person easily contented by life's simple pleasures⟩ — see PLEASE 1

contented *adj* feeling that one's needs or desires have been met ⟨Having eaten her fill, the *contented* cat settled down before the fire.⟩ — see CONTENT

contentedness *n* the feeling experienced when one's wishes are met ⟨the look of *contentedness* on the sleeping child's face⟩ — see PLEASURE 1

contention *n* **1** an idea or opinion that is put forth in a discussion or debate ⟨My *contention* is that today's lower batting averages are the result of better pitching.⟩
  synonyms argument, assertion, thesis
  related words conjecture, guess, hunch, hypothesis, speculation, surmise, theory; proposal, proposition; assumption, presupposition, supposition; position, stand; case, explanation, rationale, reason
  2 an earnest effort for superiority or victory over another ⟨Several athletes are in heated *contention* for the award.⟩ — see CONTEST 1

contentious *adj* **1** feeling or displaying eagerness to fight ⟨The Tartars were a *contentious* people who terrorized much of Asia and eastern Europe during the Middle Ages.⟩ — see BELLIGERENT
  2 given to arguing ⟨a tiresomely *contentious* person who likes to argue for the sake of arguing⟩ — see ARGUMENTATIVE 1

contentiousness *n* an inclination to fight or quarrel ⟨His natural tendency towards *contentiousness* made him a poor choice for a diplomatic post.⟩ — see BELLIGERENCE

contentment *n* the feeling experienced when one's wishes are met ⟨a couple of golden-agers looking over their life together with a feeling of *contentment* and accomplishment⟩ — see PLEASURE 1

contest *n* **1** an earnest effort for superiority or victory over another ⟨the eternal *contest* between the forces of good and the forces of evil⟩
  synonyms battle, combat, competition, conflict, confrontation, contention, duel, face-off, grapple, match, rivalry, strife, struggle, sweepstakes (*also* sweep-stake), tug-of-war, war, warfare
  related words horse race; showdown; clash, collision, discord, friction; argument, controversy, debate, disagreement, disputation, dispute, dissension (*also* dissention), quarrel, row, wrangle
  near antonyms concord, harmony, peace
  2 a competitive encounter between individuals or groups carried on for amusement, exercise, or in pursuit of a prize ⟨a *contest* for the gold medal in diving⟩ — see GAME 1
  3 a physical dispute between opposing individuals or groups ⟨What mighty *contests* have been waged on trivial matters!⟩ — see FIGHT 1

contest *vb* to demand proof of the truth or rightness of ⟨vowed to *contest* the claim in court⟩ — see CHALLENGE 1

contestant *n* one who strives for the same thing as another ⟨Three *contestants* will compete on live TV for the cash prize.⟩ — see COMPETITOR

contiguity *n* the state or condition of being near ⟨Because of the *contiguity* of the mall to the border, it attracts many shoppers from out of state.⟩ — see PROXIMITY

contiguous *adj* having a border in common ⟨Connecticut and Massachusetts are *contiguous* states.⟩ — see ADJACENT

continent *adj* given to or marked by restraint in the satisfaction of one's appetites ⟨a strict religious sect that expects its adherents to be *continent*⟩ — see ABSTEMIOUS

continent *n* one of the great divisions of land on the globe or the main part of such a division ⟨Asia is one of the *continents* of the eastern hemisphere.⟩ — see MAINLAND

contingency *n* **1** something that might happen ⟨agencies trying to provide for every *contingency* in a national emergency⟩ — see EVENT 2
  2 something upon which the carrying out of an agreement or offer depends ⟨an offer to buy the house, with the *contingency* that it pass inspection⟩ — see CONDITION 2

contingent *n* **1** a body of persons chosen as representatives of a larger group ⟨The local Scout troop traditionally sends a large *contingent* to the jamboree.⟩
  synonyms delegation
  related words embassy, legation, mission; band, company, crew, detachment, gang, outfit, party, squad, team
  2 something that might happen ⟨Officials in charge of managing the national emergency tried to prepare for every *contingent*, no matter how improbable.⟩ — see EVENT 2

contingent (on *or* **upon)** *adj* determined by something else ⟨The train's scheduled departure is *contingent on* the prompt fixing of the mechanical fault.⟩ — see DEPENDENT 2

continual *adj* **1** going on and on without any interruptions ⟨The castaways hoped that the *continual* broadcast of the distress signal would eventually attract attention.⟩ — see CONTINUOUS
  2 occurring or appearing at intervals ⟨a history of *continual* invasions from countries to the west⟩ — see INTERMITTENT 1

continually *adv* **1** many times ⟨He grew up in a time when children were *continually* being told to mind their manners.⟩ — see OFTEN
  2 on every relevant occasion ⟨The computer program *continually* updates the file with new information.⟩ — see ALWAYS 1

continuance *n* **1** the period during which something exists, lasts, or is in progress ⟨The feud between the two families was bitter and of long *continuance*.⟩ — see DURATION 1
  2 uninterrupted or lasting existence ⟨the *continuance* of hunger in the world despite some valiant efforts to solve the problem⟩ — see CONTINUATION

continuation *n* uninterrupted or lasting existence ⟨The *continuation* of high unemployment has cost the government much support.⟩
synonyms abidance, ceaselessness, continuance, durability, duration, endurance, persistence, subsistence
related words drawing out, elongation, extension, lengthening, prolongation, prolonging, stretching; enduringness, permanence; survival
near antonyms abridgment (*or* abridgement), curtailment, cutback, shortening
antonyms cessation, close, discontinuance, discontinuity, end, ending, expiration, finish, stoppage, surcease, termination

continue *vb* **1** to remain indefinitely in existence or in the same state ⟨The heavy snow *continued* throughout the night.⟩
synonyms abide, bide, endure, hold on, hold up, keep up, last, persist, remain, run on
related words linger, stay, stick around, tarry; carry through, prevail, survive
near antonyms abate, die (down), ebb, let up, moderate, subside, wane
antonyms cease, close, conclude, desist, die, discontinue, end, expire, finish, lapse, leave off, pass, quit, stop, terminate, wind up
2 to begin again or return to after an interruption ⟨We'll *continue* this discussion after we've eaten.⟩ — see RESUME

continuing *adj* **1** going on and on without any interruptions ⟨the *continuing* success of the chain as it opens stores around the country⟩ — see CONTINUOUS
2 having an existence or validity that does not change or diminish ⟨the public's *continuing* interest in every aspect of the lives of celebrities⟩ — see ABIDING

continuous *adj* going on and on without any interruptions ⟨The batteries provide enough power for up to five hours of *continuous* use.⟩
synonyms ceaseless, continual, continuing, incessant, perpetual, running, unbroken, unceasing, uninterrupted, unremitting
related words dateless, deathless, endless, eternal, everlasting, immortal, interminable, permanent, undying, unending; changeless, constant, stable, steady, unchanging, unvarying; durable, enduring, lasting, persistent; imperishable, indestructible
near antonyms intermittent, periodic, periodical, recurrent, recurring; alternate, alternating, cyclic (*or* cyclical), rhythmic (*or* rhythmical), seasonal, serial; erratic, fitful, irregular, occasional, spasmodic, sporadic, spotty, unsteady
antonyms discontinuous, noncontinuous

contort *vb* to twist (something) out of a natural or normal shape or condition ⟨The acrobat is able to *contort* his body so that it almost looks like a pretzel.⟩
synonyms deform, distort, screw, squinch, torture, warp
related words deface, disfigure; wrench, wrest, wring; coil, curl, loop, spiral, twine, wind, wreathe
near antonyms straighten, unbend, uncurl

contortion *n* the twisting of something out of its natural or normal shape or condition ⟨The comedian is renowned for his seemingly endless variety of facial *contortions*.⟩
synonyms deformation, distortion, screwing, squinching, torturing, warping
related words defacement, deformity, disfigurement, malformation

contour *n* a line that traces the outer limits of an object or surface ⟨a car with flowing *contours*⟩ — see OUTLINE 1

contract *n* **1** a formal agreement to fulfill an obligation ⟨accused her of breaking their *contract* by not completing the job on budget⟩ — see GUARANTEE 1
2 an arrangement about action to be taken ⟨a *contract* outlining what needed to be done by each person⟩ — see AGREEMENT 2

contract *vb* **1** to become affected with (a disease or disorder) ⟨Before vaccines were developed, people lived in fear of *contracting* polio.⟩
synonyms catch, come down (with), get, sicken (with), take
related words break out (with); die (from), succumb (to); fail, languish, sink, waste (away), weaken, wilt, wither, worsen
near antonyms gain, heal, mend, recoup, recover, recuperate, snap back; rally, rebound, recover (from), shake (off)
2 to become smaller in size or volume through the drawing together of particles of matter ⟨Metal *contracts* at low temperatures.⟩
synonyms compress, condense, constrict, shrink
related words collapse, deflate, flatten; dry up, shrivel, wilt, wither; abate, decrease, diminish, dwindle, lessen; recede, retreat, withdraw
near antonyms accumulate, grow, increase; balloon, inflate, puff (up)
antonyms balloon, expand, snowball, swell
3 to reduce in size or volume by or as if by pressing parts or members together ⟨*Contract* the calf muscles in your legs.⟩ — see COMPRESS 1
4 to come to an arrangement as to a course of action ⟨The farmer *contracted* for delivery of the hay by the first of July.⟩ — see AGREE 2

contraction *n* the act or process of reducing the size or volume of something by or as if by pressing ⟨Most substances undergo *contraction* when cooled.⟩ — see COMPRESSION

contradict *vb* **1** to make an assertion that is contrary to one made by (another) ⟨No matter what I say, you always have to *contradict* me!⟩
synonyms disagree (with), gainsay
related words challenge, contest, dispute, question; confute, rebut, refute; cross, fight, oppose, resist
near antonyms confirm, corroborate, substantiate, verify; attest, authenticate, avouch, certify, testify (to), vouch (for), witness
antonyms concur (with)
2 to declare not to be true ⟨His account *contradicted* the story that they had gotten earlier.⟩ — see DENY 1

contradiction *n* **1** someone or something with qualities or features that seem to conflict with one another ⟨A professional organizer for others with a messy house of his own, he was a living *contradiction*.⟩
synonyms incongruity, paradox
related words conundrum, enigma, mystery, mystification, puzzle, puzzlement, riddle
2 a refusal to confirm the truth of a statement ⟨The actress's *contradiction* of the rumor that she was quitting the show caused quite a stir.⟩ — see DENIAL 2

contradictory *adj* being as different as possible ⟨*contradictory* predictions regarding stock prices that were of no help to investors at all⟩ — see OPPOSITE

contraption *n* an interesting and often novel device with a practical use ⟨built a *contraption* for automatically buttering toast⟩ — see GADGET

contrariness *n* refusal to obey ⟨cursed the *contrariness* of her beloved mutt when it refused to come back inside the house⟩ — see DISOBEDIENCE

contrariwise *adv* just the opposite being true ⟨The runner is hardly a novice; *contrariwise*, this is his fifth racing event this year.⟩

synonyms again, conversely

phrases if anything, on the contrary, to the contrary

near antonyms even, indeed, nay, true, truly, verily, yea

contrary *adj* **1** being as different as possible ⟨The other jurors seemed sure the defendant was guilty, but I came to the *contrary* conclusion.⟩ — see OPPOSITE

2 engaging in or marked by childish misbehavior ⟨a *contrary* child who wouldn't behave⟩ — see NAUGHTY

3 given to resisting authority or another's control ⟨The *contrary* soldier is facing a court-martial for insubordination.⟩ — see DISOBEDIENT

contrary *n* something that is as different as possible from something else ⟨the admonition that we should not return hate with hate, but rather with its *contrary*—love⟩ — see OPPOSITE

contrast *n* the quality or state of being different ⟨The *contrast* between the two approaches to the problem could not be greater.⟩ — see DIFFERENCE 1

contrast *vb* to be unlike; to not be the same ⟨Her depressed mood today *contrasts* sharply with her good spirits yesterday.⟩ — see DIFFER 1

contribute *vb* **1** to make a donation as part of a group effort ⟨Would you like to *contribute* to the Thanksgiving fund for needy families?⟩

synonyms chip in, kick in, pitch in

related words bestow, donate, give, present; award, confer, dole (out), endow; afford, furnish, provide

2 to make a present of ⟨*contributes* money to a variety of worthy causes⟩ — see GIVE 1

contribution *n* a gift of money or its equivalent to a charity, humanitarian cause, or public institution ⟨*Contributions* for the victims of the earthquake began pouring in.⟩

synonyms alms, benefaction, beneficence, charity, donation, philanthropy

related words offering, tithe; bequest, endowment, legacy; aid, assistance, dole, handout, relief, welfare; grant, subsidy; benevolence, bestowal, largesse (*also* largess), present, presentation

contrite *adj* feeling sorrow for a wrong that one has done ⟨Being *contrite* is not enough to spare you a detention if you're caught skipping class.⟩

synonyms apologetic, penitent, regretful, remorseful, repentant, rueful, sorry

related words ashamed, shamefaced, sheepish; dolorous, grieving, lugubrious, mournful, plaintive, sorrowful, wailing, weeping, woeful

near antonyms cruel, merciless, pitiless, ruthless, unmerciful; shameless, unashamed

antonyms impenitent, remorseless, unapologetic, unrepentant

contriteness *n* a feeling of responsibility for wrongdoing ⟨His determination to make things right again was seen as a sign of his sincere *contriteness*.⟩ — see GUILT 1

contrition *n* a feeling of responsibility for wrongdoing ⟨I'd like to forgive her, but I'm not sure her expression of *contrition* is sincere.⟩ — see GUILT 1

contrivance *n* **1** an interesting and often novel device with a practical use ⟨a new *contrivance* for cleaning computer keyboards⟩ — see GADGET

2 something (as a device) created for the first time through the use of the imagination ⟨Despite the many modern *contrivances* for saving time and labor, we seem to have less leisure and energy than ever before.⟩ — see INVENTION 1

3 the ability to form mental images of things that either are not physically present or have never been conceived or created by others ⟨In that writer's hands, narrative *contrivance* can often deteriorate into pointless gimmickry.⟩ — see IMAGINATION 1

contrive *vb* **1** to create or think of by clever use of the imagination ⟨*contrived* abstract metal sculptures using old household utensils⟩ — see INVENT

2 to engage in a secret plan to accomplish evil or unlawful ends ⟨The mischievous boys were always *contriving* and trying to pull the prank that would be the talk of the school.⟩ — see PLOT

3 to plan out usually with subtle skill or care ⟨*contrived* a way of planning the surprise party without their catching on to it⟩ — see ENGINEER

contrived *adj* lacking in natural or spontaneous quality ⟨the *contrived* applause of a TV studio audience that has been told when to clap⟩ — see ARTIFICIAL 1

contriver *n* one who creates or introduces something new ⟨a *contriver* of yet another piece of exercise equipment⟩ — see INVENTOR

control *n* **1** a mechanism for adjusting the operation of a device, machine, or system ⟨The *controls* for the player are well marked.⟩

synonyms regulator

related words actuator; button, dial, key, knob, lever, push button, selector, switch

2 the ability to direct the course of something ⟨After the tail fell off, the plane went out of the pilot's *control*.⟩ ⟨firefighters keeping *control* of the blaze⟩

synonyms grasp, hand(s)

related words clutch, grip, hold, mastery; arm, command, dominion, helm, sway; authority, domination, jurisdiction, might, power; administration, direction, governance, government, guidance, management, operation, oversight, regulation, running, superintendence, supervision

near antonyms helplessness, weakness; impotence, impotency, powerlessness

3 the act or activity of looking after and making decisions about something ⟨*Control* of manufacturing operations was given to a new manager with fresh ideas.⟩ — see CONDUCT 1

4 the fact or state of having (something) at one's disposal ⟨took *control* of the process of selecting candidates for the scholarship⟩ — see POSSESSION 1

5 the right or means to command or control others ⟨Teachers are responsible for the students under their *control*.⟩ — see POWER 1

control *vb* **1** to keep from exceeding a desirable degree or level (as of expression) ⟨You must learn to *control* your temper.⟩

synonyms bridle, check, constrain, contain, curb, govern, hold, inhibit, keep, measure, regulate, rein (in), restrain, rule, tame

related words bottle (up), choke (back), hold back, mince, muffle, pocket, repress, sink, smother, squelch, stifle, strangle, suppress, swallow; arrest, interrupt, stop; block, hamper, handcuff, hinder, impede, obstruct; gag, muzzle, silence

near antonyms liberate, loose, loosen, unleash; air, express, take out, vent

antonyms lose

2 to gain emotional or mental control of ⟨He *controlled* himself only with the greatest difficulty in the face of his opponent's insulting remarks.⟩ — see COLLECT 1

3 to exercise authority or power over ⟨Circumstances often *control* the choices we make in life.⟩ — see GOVERN 1

4 to look after and make decisions about ⟨During the period that she *controlled* the company it was highly profitable.⟩ — see CONDUCT 1

controversy *n* **1** an often noisy or angry expression of differing opinions ⟨the seemingly imperishable *controversy* over the issue⟩ — see ARGUMENT 1

2 variance of opinion on a matter ⟨There is considerable *controversy* regarding the team's decision to trade the star pitcher.⟩ — see DISAGREEMENT 1

contusion *n* a bodily injury in which small blood vessels are broken but the overlying skin is not ⟨suffered multiple *contusions* as a result of a car accident⟩
synonyms bruise
related words abrasion, bump, lump, scrape, scratch; black eye; discoloration

conundrum *n* something hard to understand or explain ⟨the *conundrum* of how an ancient people were able to build such massive structures without the benefit of today's knowledge and technology⟩ — see MYSTERY

convalesce *vb* to become healthy and strong again after illness or weakness ⟨the long months that the soldier spent in the hospital slowly *convalescing*⟩
synonyms gain, heal, mend, rally, recoup, recover, recuperate, snap back
related words come around, come round, come to, improve, pick up, revive; cheer (up), perk (up); pull through, survive; recruit
near antonyms ail, collapse, sicken; decline, degenerate, deteriorate, fade, fail, languish, sink, waste (away), weaken, wilt, wither, worsen; regress, relapse

convalescence *n* the process or period of gradually regaining one's health and strength ⟨Her release from the hospital was followed by a long *convalescence* at home.⟩
synonyms comeback, healing, mending, rally, recovery, recuperation, rehabilitation, snapback
related words resuscitation, revival; survival
near antonyms decline, degeneration, deterioration, fading, failing, languishing, sinking, wasting (away), weakening, wilting, withering, worsening; regression, relapse

convene *vb* **1** to bring together in assembly by or as if by command ⟨*convened* the members of the council for an emergency session⟩ — see CONVOKE
2 to come together into one body or place ⟨The conventioneers *convened* in the auditorium to hear the guest speaker.⟩ — see ASSEMBLE 1

convenience *n* something that adds to one's ease of living ⟨a house with all the modern *conveniences* that buyers have come to expect⟩ — see COMFORT 2

convenient *adj* situated within easy reach ⟨The shopping mall is *convenient* to all of the area's major highways.⟩
synonyms accessible, handy, reachable
related words close, near, nearby, nigh; abutting, adjacent, adjoining; approachable, attainable, getatable, obtainable; ultraconvenient
phrases at hand, to hand
near antonyms away, distant, far, faraway, far-off, remote, removed; unapproachable, unattainable, unavailable, unobtainable
antonyms inaccessible, inconvenient, unhandy, unreachable, untouchable

convention *n* **1** a coming together of a number of persons for a specified purpose ⟨attended a *convention* of mathematicians in California⟩ — see MEETING 1
2 a formal agreement between two or more nations or peoples ⟨an international *convention* banning the spread of nuclear weapons⟩ — see TREATY
3 an arrangement about action to be taken ⟨The Geneva *Convention* details proper treatment of prisoners of war.⟩ — see AGREEMENT 2
4 an inherited or established way of thinking, feeling, or doing ⟨Our instructions for the paper said to follow standard *convention* for footnotes.⟩ — see TRADITION 1

conventional *adj* **1** accepted, used, or practiced by most people ⟨*Conventional* wisdom holds that an incumbent

president has an overwhelming advantage over his opponent.⟩ — see CURRENT 1
2 based on customs usually handed down from a previous generation ⟨The couple decided not to have a *conventional* wedding.⟩ — see TRADITIONAL 1
3 following or agreeing with established form, custom, or rules ⟨*Conventional* courtesy demands that the bridal couple send written thank-you notes for their gifts.⟩ — see FORMAL 1

converge *vb* to come together into one body or place ⟨Hungry students *converged* on the cafeteria almost as soon as the class bell rang.⟩ — see ASSEMBLE 1

convergence *n* the coming together of two or more things to the same point ⟨the *convergence* of the city's major arteries on a single rotary⟩
synonyms confluence, conjunction, meeting
related words combination, combining, connecting, connection, consolidation, coupling, joining, junction, juncture, linking, merging, unification, union
antonyms divergence

conversant *adj* having information especially as a result of study or experience ⟨a world traveler who is highly *conversant* with the customs of foreign cultures⟩ — see FAMILIAR 2

conversation *n* talking or a talk between two or more people ⟨Thomas Jefferson was celebrated for his brilliant, wide-ranging *conversations* with a host of friends and acquaintances.⟩
synonyms chat, colloquy, converse, dialogue (*also* dialog), discourse, discussion, exchange
related words banter, chaff, cross fire, give-and-take, persiflage, raillery, repartee; conference, parley; babble, chatter, chitchat, gabfest, gossip, palaver, prate, prattle, rap, small talk, table talk; roundtable, symposium; debate, deliberation

conversational *adj* **1** fond of talking or conversation ⟨The antiques dealer is not the *conversational* sort, so customers should not expect any impromptu chats.⟩ — see TALKATIVE
2 having the style and content of everyday conversation ⟨struck a very *conversational* tone in his reports of his travels through foreign countries⟩ — see CHATTY 1
3 used in or suitable for speech and not formal writing ⟨She uses *conversational* language instead of more stilted expressions in her campaign speeches.⟩ — see COLLOQUIAL 1

conversationalist *n* a person who talks constantly ⟨She was known as a compulsive *conversationalist*, so much so that it was often impossible to stop her once she got going.⟩ — see CHATTERBOX

converse *n* talking or a talk between two or more people ⟨Ideally, the college classroom should be a place of intellectual *converse* between student and teacher.⟩ — see CONVERSATION

converse *vb* to engage in casual or rambling conversation ⟨Jurors are not allowed to *converse* while the attorneys go off to one side to confer with the judge.⟩ — see CHAT 1

converse (with) *vb* to communicate with by means of spoken words ⟨In a press conference, the president is not just addressing reporters—he's *conversing with* the public.⟩ — see TALK (TO)

conversely *adv* just the opposite being true ⟨She cannot stand sugary food; *conversely*, her husband is fond of sweets.⟩ — see CONTRARIWISE

conversion *n* **1** a change in form, appearance, or use ⟨The *conversion* of the spare bedroom into a home office was easily accomplished.⟩
synonyms changeover, metamorphosis, transfiguration, transformation

related words shift, transition; alteration, modification; accommodation, adaptation, conformation; reconstruction, reconversion, redo, redoing, refashioning, reformation, remaking, remodeling, revamping, revision, reworking, variation; deformation, disfigurement, distortion, mutation, transmutation; displacement, replacement, substitution, supplantation
2 the act of reasoning or pleading with someone to accept a belief or course of action ⟨was convinced by her *conversion* to Buddhism⟩ — see PERSUASION 1
convert *n* **1** a person who has recently been persuaded to join a religious sect ⟨The *converts* were the most vocal and fervent worshippers in the church.⟩
synonyms neophyte, proselyte
related words regenerate; newcomer, novice, recruit; catechumen
2 one who follows the opinions or teachings of another ⟨The British biologist T. H. Huxley was one of the earliest *converts* to Darwin's theory of evolution.⟩ — see FOLLOWER 1
convert *vb* **1** to persuade to change to one's religious faith ⟨young missionaries who go door-to-door trying to convert people⟩
synonyms proselyte, proselytize
related words missionize; brainwash, influence, sway; propagate
near antonyms secularize; dissuade
2 to change in form, appearance, or use ⟨The old factory was *converted* into an apartment building.⟩
synonyms make over, metamorphose, transfigure, transform
related words adjust, alter, modify, recast; redesign, redo, reengineer, refashion, regenerate, remake, remodel, revamp, revise, rework, vary; deform, disfigure, distort, mutate, transmogrify; displace, replace, substitute, supplant
3 to cause (someone) to agree with a belief or course of action by using arguments or earnest requests ⟨Many who used to insist that global warming was a myth have since been *converted*.⟩ — see PERSUADE
4 to take or make use of under a guise of authority but without actual right ⟨The bailee *converted* the goods to his own use.⟩ — see APPROPRIATE 1
convey *vb* **1** to cause (something) to pass from one to another ⟨He intends to personally *convey* the message to the governor.⟩ — see COMMUNICATE 1
2 to support and take from one place to another ⟨conveying a package to his relatives⟩ — see CARRY 1
3 to give over the legal possession or ownership of ⟨Upon her death, the house will be *conveyed* to a predesignated charity.⟩ — see TRANSFER 1
conveyance *n* something used to carry goods or passengers ⟨The covered wagon was the major *conveyance* that transported settlers and their belongings across the frontier.⟩
synonyms transport, transportation, vehicle
related words carrier, hauler, mover
convict *n* a person convicted as a criminal and serving a prison sentence ⟨a warning that the three escaped *convicts* were armed and dangerous⟩
synonyms con, jailbird
related words lifer, trusty; parolee, probationer; captive, capture, inmate, internee, prisoner
convict *vb* to find or pronounce guilty ⟨An accused person is presumed innocent until *convicted* in a court of law.⟩
synonyms condemn
related words accuse, arraign, charge, impeach, indict; censure, damn, denounce, rebuke, reprimand, reproach, reprove; admonish, castigate, chastise; penalize, punish, sentence

near antonyms cite, commend, endorse (*also* indorse); approve, bless, sanction
antonyms absolve, acquit, clear, exculpate, exonerate, vindicate
conviction *n* **1** a state of mind in which one is free from doubt ⟨spoke with *conviction* about her political beliefs⟩ — see CONFIDENCE 2
2 an idea that is believed to be true or valid without positive knowledge ⟨He held deep *convictions* about life after death.⟩ — see OPINION 1
convince *vb* to cause (someone) to agree with a belief or course of action by using arguments or earnest requests ⟨We *convinced* him to keep silent about our activities until we could spring the surprise.⟩ — see PERSUADE
convincing *adj* having the power to persuade ⟨convincing evidence for the guilt of the accused⟩ — see COGENT
convincing *n* the act of reasoning or pleading with someone to accept a belief or course of action ⟨It will take a great deal of *convincing* to make them see our point of view.⟩ — see PERSUASION 1
convivial *adj* likely to seek or enjoy the company of others ⟨The hiking club attracts a wide range of *convivial* people who share a love of the outdoors.⟩
synonyms boon, companionable, extroverted (*also* extraverted), gregarious, outgoing, sociable, social
related words cordial, forthcoming, friendly, hospitable; affable, genial, gracious; agreeable, amiable, congenial, kindly, neighborly; animated, jaunty, jolly, jovial, lively, peppy, perky, pert, spirited, sprightful, sprightly, vivacious; communicative, expansive, garrulous, talkative; bright, buoyant, cheerful, chipper, effervescent, upbeat; bubbly, exuberant, high-spirited; colonial
near antonyms misanthropic; aloof, cold, cool, detached, distant, frosty, remote, reserved, standoffish; mum, mute, reticent, silent, taciturn
antonyms antisocial, insociable, introverted, nongregarious, reclusive, unsociable, unsocial
conviviality *n* **1** joyful or festive activity ⟨fondly remembers the many evenings spent in *conviviality* with her basketball teammates⟩ — see MERRYMAKING
2 the quality or state of being social ⟨His *conviviality*, warmth, and good nature are irresistible.⟩ — see SOCIABILITY
convocation *n* **1** a body of people come together in one place ⟨the first speaker to address the *convocation*⟩ — see GATHERING 1
2 a coming together of a number of persons for a specified purpose ⟨called for an immediate *convocation* of the council⟩ — see MEETING 1
convoke *vb* to bring together in assembly by or as if by command ⟨They *convoked* a meeting of the delegates.⟩
synonyms assemble, call, convene, muster, summon
related words rally; call in, call out, call up, knell; amass, collect, gather, group, round up; reassemble, reconvene
near antonyms break up, dissolve
convoluted *adj* having many parts or aspects that are usually interrelated ⟨a *convoluted* explanation that left the listeners even more confused than they were before⟩ — see COMPLEX 1
convoy *vb* to go along with in order to provide assistance, protection, or companionship ⟨will *convoy* the shipment to its destination in the war zone⟩ — see ACCOMPANY 1
convulse *vb* to make a series of small irregular or violent movements ⟨convulsing with laughter⟩ — see SHAKE 1
convulsion *n* a violent disturbance (as of the political or social order) ⟨The Russian Revolution was one of the major *convulsions* of the 20th century.⟩
synonyms cataclysm, earthquake, paroxysm, storm, tempest, tumult, upheaval, uproar

related words insurgency, insurrection, mutiny, overthrow, overturn, rebellion, revolt, revolution, subversion, unrest, uprising, upset; fit, seizure, spasm; eruption, flare-up, outbreak, outburst; bluster, bustle, coil, commotion, furor, furore, fuss, hubbub, hullabaloo, hurlyburly, pandemonium, rout, row, ruckus, ruction, rumpus, shindy, squall, stew, stir, to-do, turmoil, welter, williwaw; quaking, rocking, shaking, trembling

convulsive *adj* **1** marked by sudden or violent disturbance ⟨The assassination of Martin Luther King was one of the most *convulsive* events of the 1960s.⟩
synonyms cataclysmal (*or* cataclysmic), stormy, tempestuous, tumultuous, turbulent
related words fitful, spasmodic, sporadic; boisterous, clamorous, furious, noisy, riotous
near antonyms calm, peaceful, placid, serene, tranquil, undisturbed, unperturbed, unshaken, untroubled
2 marked by bursts of destructive force or intense activity ⟨After a day of *convulsive* trading, the stock market was down 300 points.⟩ — see VIOLENT 1

cook *n* a person who prepares food by some manner of heating ⟨the hearty meals prepared by the *cook* at summer camp⟩
synonyms chef, cooker
related words baker; barbecuer, griller

cook *vb* **1** to change so much as to create a wrong impression or alter the meaning of ⟨It turns out the pharmaceutical researcher had *cooked* her data.⟩ — see GARBLE
2 to take place ⟨wondered what was *cooking* when several police cars pulled up to their neighbor's house⟩ — see HAPPEN

cook (up) *vb* to create or think of by clever use of the imagination ⟨*cooked up* a scheme to get out of doing the dishes⟩ — see INVENT

cooker *n* **1** an appliance that prepares food for consumption by heating it ⟨a portable gas-fired *cooker* that's perfect for camping trips⟩
synonyms cookstove, range
related words broiler, fryer (*also* frier), microwave, microwave oven, oven, roaster, rotisserie, stove, toaster, toaster oven
2 a person who prepares food by some manner of heating ⟨Dad was the traditional *cooker* of the big Sunday breakfast.⟩ — see COOK

cookery *n* the art or style of preparing food (as in a specified region) ⟨an introduction to Mexican *cookery*⟩
synonyms cooking, cuisine
related words haute cuisine; gastronomy

cooking *n* the art or style of preparing food (as in a specified region) ⟨a TV show that teaches viewers the basics of French *cooking*⟩ — see COOKERY

cookstove *n* an appliance that prepares food for consumption by heating it ⟨a small *cookstove* that would be appropriate for an apartment⟩ — see COOKER 1

cool *adj* **1** having or showing a lack of friendliness or interest in others ⟨The locals were *cool* towards outsiders.⟩ ⟨The schoolmaster's *cool* manner did not encourage chitchat.⟩
synonyms aloof, antisocial, cold, detached, distant, dry, frosty, remote, standoffish, unbending, unsociable
related words indrawn, introverted, nongregarious, reclusive, reserved, unsocial, withdrawn; misanthropic; apathetic, hard, indifferent, unconcerned; clinical, dispassionate, impersonal, professional; disinterested, incurious, uninterested; reticent, silent, taciturn, uncommunicative; diffident, shy, timid; cliquey
near antonyms boon, companionable, convivial, extroverted (*also* extraverted), gregarious, outgoing; communicative, expansive, garrulous, talkative; affable, genial, gracious, hospitable; agreeable, amiable, congenial, kindly, neighborly
antonyms cordial, friendly, sociable, social, warm
2 free from emotional or mental agitation ⟨In a crisis keep a *cool* head, even if no one else does.⟩ — see CALM 2
3 having a low or subnormal temperature ⟨a *cool* basement that would be perfect for storing wine⟩ — see COLD 1
4 lacking in friendliness or warmth of feeling ⟨directed a *cool* glance at the student who was sneaking into class late⟩ — see COLD 2
5 *slang* being in the latest or current fashion ⟨always dressed in *cool* clothes⟩ — see STYLISH
6 *slang* of the very best kind ⟨a really *cool* garage band that's starting to get some attention from the music industry⟩ — see EXCELLENT

cool *n* **1** the absence of emotional involvement ⟨The judge's customary *cool* stood him in good stead during the sensational trial.⟩
synonyms detachment
related words equitability, equitableness, fairness; disinterestedness, impartiality, objectivity, unbiasedness; balance, rationality, rationalness, reasonability, reasonableness; calm, calmness, peace, peacefulness, placidity, quiet, quietness, quietude, repose, restfulness, sereneness, serenity, tranquillity (*or* tranquility); reserve, undemonstrativeness, unresponsiveness; apathy, indifference
near antonyms emotionalism; bias, favor, one-sidedness, partiality, partisanship, prejudice
2 the quality or state of being fashionable ⟨I envy you your *cool*.⟩
synonyms coolness, fashionableness, hip, modishness
related words chic, chicness, dapperness, elegance, poshness, smartness, style, swank, swankiness; class, grace, gracefulness, majesty, stateliness; artfulness, polish, sophistication, taste, tastefulness
near antonyms flashiness, garishness, gaudiness, gracelessness, grotesqueness, tackiness, tastelessness, tawdriness
antonyms unfashionableness
3 evenness of emotions or temper ⟨Despite the flood of insults, the fledgling stand-up comic never lost his *cool*.⟩ — see EQUANIMITY

cool *vb* to cause to lose heat ⟨*Cool* your drinks in the icy mountain stream.⟩
synonyms chill, refrigerate
related words air-condition; freeze, frost, quick-freeze, supercool; ventilate
near antonyms bake, boil, steam; heat-treat, temper; microwave
antonyms heat, toast, warm

coolheaded *adj* free from emotional or mental agitation ⟨a *coolheaded* response to the crisis⟩ — see CALM 2

coolish *adj* having a low or subnormal temperature ⟨I made the mistake of wearing shorts on a *coolish* day.⟩ — see COLD 1

coolness *n* **1** evenness of emotions or temper ⟨His *coolness* under pressure makes him everyone's first choice to head a project with an ironclad deadline.⟩ — see EQUANIMITY
2 the quality or state of being fashionable ⟨Some people worry about the *coolness* of their clothes.⟩ — see COOL 2

coop *n* an enclosure with an open framework for keeping animals ⟨a chicken *coop*⟩ — see CAGE

coop (up) *vb* to close or shut in by or as if by barriers ⟨restless kids *cooped up* in the house on a rainy day⟩ — see ENCLOSE 1

cooperate *vb* **1** to participate or assist in a joint effort to accomplish an end ⟨Conservation groups *cooperated*

with state authorities to find a humane way to manage the area's overpopulation of deer.⟩
synonyms band (together), collaborate, concert, concur, conjoin, conspire, join, league, team (up), unite
related words connive; affiliate, ally, associate, combine, confederate, hang together, interface
phrases make common cause, play ball, pull together
2 to form or enter into an association that furthers the interests of its members ⟨Several industrialized nations *cooperated* in a trade agreement to reduce or eliminate tariffs.⟩ — see ALLY
cooperation *n* **1** the state of having shared interests or efforts (as in social or business matters) ⟨a series of televised announcements made in *cooperation* with the tobacco companies warning about the hazards of smoking⟩ — see ASSOCIATION 1
2 the work and activity of a number of persons who individually contribute toward the efficiency of the whole ⟨Everyone's *cooperation* will make the project go much faster.⟩ — see TEAMWORK
cooperative *adj* used or done by a number of people as a group ⟨a *cooperative* space project undertaken by Russia and the U.S.⟩ — see COLLECTIVE
coordinate *n* one that is equal to another in status, achievement, or value ⟨The Nobel Memorial Award for Economic Science is universally regarded as the *coordinate* of the original Nobel Prizes for peace, literature, medicine, physics, and chemistry.⟩ — see EQUAL
coordinate *vb* **1** to bring to a state free of conflicts, inconsistencies, or differences ⟨*coordinating* the plans for the surprise party⟩ — see HARMONIZE 2
2 to form a pleasing relationship ⟨very meticulous hosts, who make sure that every aspect of their dinner parties —table settings, food, flowers—*coordinates* right down to the last detail⟩ — see HARMONIZE 1
coordination *n* the work and activity of a number of persons who individually contribute toward the efficiency of the whole ⟨an operation requiring precise *coordination* among all branches of the armed forces⟩ — see TEAMWORK
cop *n* a member of a force charged with law enforcement at the local level ⟨A *cop* stopped her for speeding.⟩ — see OFFICER 1
cop *vb, slang* to take physical control or possession of (something) suddenly or forcibly ⟨Some concertgoers rushed pell-mell through the doors so that they could *cop* the seats down front.⟩ — see CATCH 1
copacetic *also* **copasetic** *or* **copesetic** *adj* being to one's liking ⟨Don't worry, because I assure you that everything's *copacetic*.⟩ — see SATISFACTORY 1
cope *n* something that covers or conceals like a piece of cloth ⟨committed their nefarious deeds under the dark *cope* of night⟩ — see CLOAK 1
cope *vb* to meet one's day-to-day needs ⟨a young man learning to *cope* on his own at college⟩ — see GET ALONG 1
cope (with) *vb* to deal with (something) usually skillfully or efficiently ⟨*coped with* the latest foul-up gracefully⟩ — see HANDLE 1
copious *adj* pouring forth in great amounts ⟨A *copious* rush of words just poured out of the two friends who hadn't seen each other in years.⟩ — see PROFUSE
cop—out *n* the act or a means of getting or keeping away from something undesirable ⟨I think that saying you're sick is just a *cop-out* to get out of going to work.⟩ — see ESCAPE 2
cop out *vb* to break a promise or agreement ⟨Don't *cop out* on your promise to pay for the damage.⟩ — see RENEGE 1
coppice *n* a thick patch of shrubbery, small trees, or un-

derbrush ⟨The deer bounded off into the *coppice*.⟩ — see THICKET
copse *n* a thick patch of shrubbery, small trees, or underbrush ⟨A small *copse* of trees shaded the back of the house.⟩ — see THICKET
copulate *vb* to engage in sexual intercourse ⟨the time of year when deer in the wild are likely to *copulate*⟩
synonyms breed, mate, sleep
related words fornicate
copulation *n* sexual union involving penetration of the vagina by the penis ⟨Female pandas are receptive to *copulation* for a short time once a year.⟩ — see SEXUAL INTERCOURSE
copy *n* something that is made to look exactly like something else ⟨a *copy* of the famous painting "Washington Crossing the Delaware"⟩
synonyms carbon copy, dummy, dupe, duplicate, duplication, facsimile, imitation, mock, reduplication, replica, replication, reproduction
related words counterfeit, fake, forgery, knockoff, phony (*also* phoney), rip-off, sham; miniature, mock-up, simulation; reconstruction, re-creation; image, likeness, semblance, shadow; impression, imprint, print; approximation, reincarnation; extra, reserve, spare
antonyms archetype, original, prototype
copy *vb* **1** to make an exact likeness of ⟨For the movie, set designers *copied* the Oval Office in the White House down to the smallest detail.⟩
synonyms copycat, duplicate, imitate, reduplicate, render, replicate, reproduce
related words counterfeit, fake, forge, knock off, rip off; mimic, simulate; reconstruct, re-create
near antonyms create, imagine, initiate, invent
antonyms originate
2 to use (someone or something) as the model for one's speech, mannerisms, or behavior ⟨She's always *copying* her older sister.⟩ — see IMITATE 1
copycat *n* a person who adopts the appearance or behavior of another especially in an obvious way ⟨Every pop star who makes it big soon has a whole cluster of *copycats*.⟩
synonyms aper, copyist, echo, follower, imitator
related words parrot; ape, emulator, impersonator, impressionist, mimic
copycat *vb* **1** to make an exact likeness of ⟨Foreign manufacturers *copycatted* the products.⟩ — see COPY 1
2 to use (someone or something) as the model for one's speech, mannerisms, or behavior ⟨A performer who *copycats* another never rises to the level of true stardom.⟩ — see IMITATE 1
copyist *n* **1** a person who adopts the appearance or behavior of another especially in an obvious way ⟨He prides himself on being an innovator in fashion, and not a mere *copyist*.⟩ — see COPYCAT
2 one who writes from dictation or copies manuscripts ⟨Some scholars argue that the vexing passage reflects a misreading of the text by an early *copyist*.⟩ — see SCRIBE 1
cord *n* **1** a length of braided, flexible material that is used for tying or connecting things ⟨a vacuum cleaner with an extra long *cord*⟩
synonyms cable, lace, lacing, line, rope, string, wire
related words guy, halyard, lanyard, stay; bungee cord, whipcord
2 a uniting or binding force or influence ⟨the *cords* of trust and affection that exist between the longtime friends⟩ — see BOND 2
cordial *adj* **1** having or showing kindly feeling and sincere interest ⟨a *cordial* inquiry about her mother's health⟩ — see FRIENDLY 1

2 showing a natural kindness and courtesy especially in social situations ⟨a *cordial* hostess who makes sure everyone is comfortable⟩ — see GRACIOUS 1

3 having a renewing effect on the state of the body or mind ⟨He insisted that a *cordial* cup of tea would be just the thing for someone suffering from a cold.⟩ — see TONIC 1

cordiality *n* kindly concern, interest, or support ⟨Everyone appreciated the *cordiality* and thoughtfulness of the welcoming committee.⟩ — see GOODWILL 1

core *n* **1** the seat of one's deepest thoughts and emotions ⟨In my very *core* I knew that an injustice was being committed.⟩

synonyms belly, blood, bone(s), bosom, breast, gut, heart, heartstrings, inside, quick, soul

related words conscience, mind

2 a thing or place that is of greatest importance to an activity or interest ⟨The capitol building is the *core* of the political life of the state.⟩ — see CENTER 1

3 the central part or aspect of something under consideration ⟨At last, we come to the *core* of the issue that has been dividing us.⟩ — see CRUX

4 the main or greater part of something as distinguished from its subordinate parts ⟨A starfish can even survive the division of its *core* into two parts; both halves then regenerate.⟩ — see BODY 1

5 an area or point that is an equal distance from all points along an edge or outer surface ⟨The mountain rises from ground that is almost precisely at the island's *core*.⟩ — see CENTER 2

corker *n* something very good of its kind ⟨That last race was a real *corker*!⟩ — see JIM-DANDY

corkscrew *adj* turning around an axis like the thread of a screw ⟨an angelic child with beautiful *corkscrew* curls⟩ — see SPIRAL

corkscrew *vb* to follow a circular or spiral course ⟨The trail *corkscrews* through dense woods to the top of the steep hill.⟩ — see WIND 1

corn *n* something (as a work of literature or music) that is too sentimental ⟨a story about a lost puppy that was pure *corn*⟩

synonyms mush, schmaltz (*also* schmalz), sludge, slush

related words claptrap, drivel, rubbish

corner *n* **1** a difficult, puzzling, or embarrassing situation from which there is no easy escape ⟨The writers have gotten themselves into a *corner* on that TV show.⟩ — see PREDICAMENT

2 a place where roads meet ⟨We'll meet at the *corner* tomorrow.⟩ — see CROSSROAD 1

3 a point in a chain of events at which an important change (as in one's fortunes) occurs ⟨The president believes that we have turned a *corner* in the war on the disease.⟩ — see TURNING POINT

cornerstone *n* an immaterial thing upon which something else rests ⟨A concern for basic human rights was the *cornerstone* of the president's foreign policy.⟩ — see BASE 1

cornet *n* something shaped like a hollow cone and used as a container ⟨*cornets* of pastry dough that were baked and later filled with cream⟩

synonyms cornucopia, horn

related words funnel, tube

cornucopia *n* **1** an abundant source ⟨Even to the technology-addicted children, the old-fashioned toy chest was a *cornucopia* of delights.⟩ — see MINE 1

2 an amount or supply more than sufficient to meet one's needs ⟨The rabbits found a *cornucopia* of food in the vegetable garden.⟩ — see PLENTY 1

3 something shaped like a hollow cone and used as a container ⟨a *cornucopia* filled with fruits and vegetables in celebration of the harvest⟩ — see CORNET

corny *adj* appealing to the emotions in an obvious and tiresome way ⟨*corny* violin music during the movie's love scenes⟩

synonyms gooey, maudlin, mawkish, mushy, saccharine, sappy, schmaltzy, sentimental, sloppy, slushy, sugarcoated, sugary, wet

related words dreamy, misty-eyed, moonstruck, moony, nostalgic; feel-good, fuzzy; melodramatic, soap-operatic, soapy, sudsy; flat, insipid, soft-boiled, tasteless, vapid, watery; cutesy

near antonyms unadulterated, unvarnished; antisentimental, cynical, hard-boiled, hard-edged, hardheaded

antonyms unsentimental

corollary *n* **1** a condition or occurrence traceable to a cause ⟨One *corollary* of the rise of the Internet was a massive makeover of the publishing industry.⟩ — see EFFECT 1

2 something that is found along with something else ⟨Increased taxes—or expanding deficits—are the inevitable *corollary* to any new government spending program.⟩ — see ACCOMPANIMENT

coronet *n* a decorative band or wreath worn about the head as a symbol of victory or honor ⟨The prince wore a small gold *coronet* to denote his rank.⟩ — see CROWN 1

corporal *adj* of or relating to the human body ⟨started to suffer the *corporal* ailments that come with advancing age⟩ — see PHYSICAL 1

corporeal *adj* of or relating to the human body ⟨*corporeal* cravings such as hunger and thirst⟩ — see PHYSICAL 1

corps *n* the body of people in a profession or field of activity ⟨a reporter who is widely respected throughout the press *corps*⟩

synonyms brotherhood, community, fellowship, fraternity, sodality, vocation

related words calling, profession; association, club, federation, guild (*also* gild), organization, society

corpse *n* a dead body ⟨The startling discovery of a *corpse* required a call to the police.⟩

synonyms bones, cadaver, carcass, remains, stiff

related words mummy; carnage, carrion; ashes; deceased, decedent

corpulence *n* the condition of having an excess of body fat ⟨The doctor warned that the patient's *corpulence* was unhealthy.⟩

synonyms chubbiness, fat, fatness, fleshiness, grossness, obesity, plumpness, portliness, pudginess, rotundity, weight

related words bulkiness, heaviness; huskiness, stoutness; brawniness, burliness; endomorphy

near antonyms fitness, trimness; gauntness, scrawniness, skinniness, weediness

antonyms leanness, reediness, slenderness, slimness, svelteness, thinness

corpulent *adj* having an excess of body fat ⟨A *corpulent*, elegantly dressed opera singer came out and sang, and we knew it was over.⟩ — see FAT 1

corral *n* an enclosure with an open framework for keeping animals ⟨The horses live in our *corral*, along with a cow.⟩ — see CAGE

corral *vb* **1** to close or shut in by or as if by barriers ⟨*corralled* everyone in the conference room for a speech by the CEO⟩ — see ENCLOSE 1

2 to take physical control or possession of (something) suddenly or forcibly ⟨I *corralled* a scattering of stray pens and quickly stuffed them in the drawer to tidy up the desk.⟩ — see CATCH 1

3 to bring together in one body or place ⟨Let's *corral* all the members of the tour group in the lounge.⟩ — see GATHER 1

correct *adj* **1** being in agreement with the truth or a fact or a standard ⟨a real brainteaser with only one *correct* solution to it⟩
synonyms accurate, exact, good, precise, proper, right, so, true, veracious
related words legitimate, logical, sound, valid; errorless, faultless, flawless, impeccable, inerrant, infallible, letter-perfect, perfect; rigorous, strict, stringent
phrases on target, on the money
near antonyms defective, faulty, flawed, imperfect
antonyms false, improper, inaccurate, incorrect, inexact, off, untrue, wrong
2 following the established traditions of refined society and good taste ⟨made sure to wear *correct* dress for the state dinner at the White House⟩ — see PROPER 1
3 marked by or showing careful attention to set forms and details ⟨the *correct* method for folding the American flag⟩ — see CEREMONIOUS 1
correct *vb* **1** to remove errors, defects, deficiencies, or deviations from ⟨More time will be needed to *correct* the computer program.⟩
synonyms amend, debug, emend, rectify, reform, remedy
related words redraft, redraw, restyle, revise, rework, rewrite; cut, shorten; redress, right; ameliorate, better, improve; perfect, polish, touch up; fix, mend, repair; adjust, modulate, regulate; alter, change, modify
near antonyms damage, harm, hurt, impair, injure, mar, spoil; aggravate, worsen
2 to balance with an equal force so as to make ineffective ⟨Hopefully the young entrepreneur's professionalism will serve to *correct* his partner's extreme enthusiasm in the eyes of investors.⟩ — see OFFSET
3 to inflict a penalty on for a fault or crime ⟨an insensitive boss who liked to *correct* subordinates in front of their colleagues⟩ — see PUNISH
correctable *adj* capable of being corrected ⟨a design with some minor, *correctable* faults⟩ — see REMEDIABLE
correcting *adj* inflicting, involving, or serving as punishment ⟨She questions the value of such *correcting* measures as taking away recess from young children.⟩ — see PUNITIVE
correction *n* **1** a change designed to correct or improve a written work ⟨The copy editor's *corrections* were marked in red.⟩
synonyms amendment, emendation
related words cut, deletion; addition, amplification, supplement; alteration, modification, revision; improvement, renovation; clarification, explanation, explication
2 suffering, loss, or hardship imposed in response to a crime or offense ⟨received a severe *correction* after the third offense⟩ — see PUNISHMENT
correctional *adj* inflicting, involving, or serving as punishment ⟨Dad threatened to take *correctional* measures if the household chores were not done.⟩ ⟨the state's largest *correctional* institution⟩ — see PUNITIVE
corrective *adj* **1** serving to raise or adjust something to some standard or proper condition ⟨Eyeglasses are called *corrective* lenses by the department of motor vehicles.⟩
synonyms rectifying, remedial, remedying, reformative, reformatory
related words reparative, restorative; beneficial, helpful, salutary, wholesome; antidotal, counteractive, counterbalancing
2 inflicting, involving, or serving as punishment ⟨a *corrective* sentence of five years' hard labor⟩ — see PUNITIVE
corrective *n* **1** a force or influence that makes an opposing force ineffective or less effective ⟨A substantial outflow

of people proved to be the necessary *corrective* for the spiraling cost of housing.⟩ — see COUNTERBALANCE
2 something that corrects or counteracts something undesirable ⟨The President's speech was intended to be a *corrective* to the country's anxiety.⟩ — see CURE 1
correctly *adv* in a manner suitable for the occasion or purpose ⟨dressed *correctly* for an appearance in court⟩ — see PROPERLY
correlate *vb* to think of (something) in combination ⟨a demanding father who always *correlated* success with hard work⟩ — see ASSOCIATE 2
correspond *vb* **1** to engage in an exchange of written messages ⟨old friends who have been *corresponding* for years⟩
synonyms write
related words communicate, intercommunicate; airmail, e-mail, telegraph; mail, post; answer, reply
2 to be in agreement on every point ⟨The menu for the wedding banquet *corresponds* exactly with everyone's special requests.⟩ — see CHECK 1
correspond (to) *vb* **1** to be the exact counterpart of ⟨The British chancellor of the exchequer *corresponds to* the U.S. secretary of the treasury.⟩ — see MATCH 1
2 to be the same in meaning or effect ⟨"Shut up" and "please be quiet" may *correspond to* each other in meaning, but please use the more polite phrase.⟩ — see AMOUNT (TO) 2
correspondence *n* **1** a point which two or more things share in common ⟨The *correspondence* in hair color is about all that the siblings have in common.⟩ — see SIMILARITY 2
2 the quality or state of having many qualities in common ⟨The best friends' *correspondence* in looks is so striking that they could pass for twins.⟩ — see SIMILARITY 1
3 communications or parcels sent or carried through the postal system ⟨Piles of unanswered *correspondence* littered the office of the reclusive author.⟩ — see MAIL
correspondent *adj* having qualities in common ⟨Reading and writing are actually *correspondent* activities.⟩ — see ALIKE
correspondent *n* a person employed by a newspaper, magazine, or radio or television station to gather, write, or report news ⟨A *correspondent* just filed a new report on the coup.⟩ — see REPORTER
correspondent (with *or* to) *adj* not having or showing any apparent conflict ⟨The new regulation regarding cell phones is *correspondent with* existing policy on the use of electronic devices.⟩ — see CONSISTENT
corresponding *adj* having qualities in common ⟨Solving a crime and diagnosing a disease are *corresponding* tasks: they both require a meticulous search for clues.⟩ — see ALIKE
correspondingly *adv* in like manner ⟨If you're nice to someone, they'll probably be *correspondingly* polite.⟩ — see ALSO 1
corridor *n* **1** a broad geographical area ⟨The urban *corridor* along the state's eastern coast is considerably more liberal than the rural areas to the west.⟩ — see REGION 2
2 a typically long narrow way connecting parts of a building ⟨The long, sterile *corridors* give the government building a forbidding air.⟩ — see HALL 2
corroborate *vb* **1** to give evidence or testimony to the truth or factualness of ⟨The witnesses *corroborated* the policeman's testimony.⟩ — see CONFIRM 1
2 to provide evidence or information for (as a claim or idea) ⟨My personal experience does not *corroborate* your faith in the essential goodness of people.⟩ — see SUPPORT 4

corroborating *adj* serving to give support to the truth or factualness of something ⟨*corroborating* information on the activities of the terrorists⟩ — see CORROBORATIVE

corroboration *n* something presented in support of the truth or accuracy of a claim ⟨That's a serious charge, so you certainly should have *corroboration* for it.⟩ — see PROOF

corroborative *adj* serving to give support to the truth or factualness of something ⟨The results of the DNA fingerprinting were all the *corroborative* evidence the jury needed to convict.⟩
synonyms confirmatory, confirming, corroborating, corroboratory, substantiating, supporting, supportive, verifying, vindicating
related words auxiliary, supplementary; beneficial, helpful
near antonyms contradictory, contrary, counter, opposing
antonyms confuting, disproving, refuting

corroboratory *adj* serving to give support to the truth or factualness of something ⟨offered *corroboratory* testimony for the defendant's alibi⟩ — see CORROBORATIVE

corrode *vb* to consume or wear away gradually ⟨Water slowly *corrodes* iron.⟩ — see EAT 2

corrosion *n* a gradual weakening, loss, or destruction ⟨the *corrosion* of family values that is often brought on by great wealth⟩
synonyms attrition, erosion, waste
related words breakdown, decay, decomposition, disintegration, dissolution
near antonyms gain, increase
antonyms buildup

corrupt *adj* having or showing lowered moral character or standards ⟨*corrupt* businessmen who are out to fleece the public⟩ ⟨*corrupt* business practices that should be investigated⟩
synonyms debased, debauched, decadent, degenerate, degraded, demoralized, depraved, dissipated, dissolute, libertine, loose, perverse, perverted, reprobate, sick, unclean, unwholesome, warped
related words crooked, cutthroat, dishonest, unethical, unprincipled, unscrupulous; contaminated, spoiled, tainted; bad, evil, immoral, iniquitous, miscreant, nefarious, sinful, vicious, wicked
near antonyms incorruptible; ethical, honest, principled; good, moral, righteous, virtuous
antonyms pure, uncorrupt, uncorrupted

corrupt *vb* 1 to go through decomposition ⟨A dead mouse *corrupting* in the walls produced a terrible smell.⟩ — see DECAY 1
2 to lower in character, dignity, or quality ⟨the adage that power *corrupts* honest people⟩ — see DEBASE 1
3 to influence someone with a bribe ⟨He bragged about having *corrupted* half of the officials on the city council.⟩ — see BRIBE

corrupted *adj* having undergone organic breakdown ⟨*corrupted* corpses that sickened the animal control officers sent to investigate⟩ — see ROTTEN 1

corruptible *adj* open to improper influence and especially bribery ⟨There's a rumor that that judge is eminently *corruptible*.⟩ — see VENAL

corruption *n* 1 the process by which dead organic matter separates into simpler substances ⟨The ancient Egyptians used special preservatives to spare their dead from complete *corruption*.⟩
synonyms breakdown, decay, decomposition, putrefaction, rot, spoilage
related words crumbling, disintegration, dissolution; curdling, moldering, souring
near antonyms growth, maturation, ripening

2 a sinking to a state of low moral standards and behavior ⟨The *corruption* of the upper classes eventually led to the fall of the Roman empire.⟩
synonyms corruptness, debasement, debauchery, decadence, degeneracy, degeneration, degradation, demoralization, depravity, dissipatedness, dissipation, dissoluteness, perversion
related words evil, immorality, sinfulness, villainy, wickedness; filth, gangrene, rot, squalor
near antonyms goodness, morality, righteousness, virtue
3 immoral conduct or practices harmful or offensive to society ⟨Socrates was put to death because the ancient Athenians believed he was spreading *corruption* to their youth.⟩ — see VICE 1

corruptness *n* a sinking to a state of low moral standards and behavior ⟨Such *corruptness* in government threatens our democratic institutions.⟩ — see CORRUPTION 2

corsair *n* someone who engages in robbery of ships at sea ⟨No one knows the fate of the *corsair's* treasure-filled ship.⟩ — see PIRATE

cortege *also* **cortège** *n* 1 a body of employees or attendants who accompany and wait on a person ⟨The movie star's *cortege* included her stylist, personal assistant, and press agent.⟩
synonyms following, retinue, suite, train
related words crew, personnel, staff; court; assistant, attendant, helper, retainer
2 a body of individuals moving along in an orderly and often ceremonial way ⟨The funeral *cortege* of mourners stretched for three city blocks.⟩
synonyms parade, procession
related words progress; column, line, string, train

cosmetics *pl n* preparations intended to beautify the face ⟨I need to buy some fresh *cosmetics* to use for the wedding.⟩ — see MAKEUP 1

cosmic *also* **cosmical** *adj* unusually large ⟨predicted that the war would forever be regarded as a *cosmic* error⟩ — see HUGE

cosmopolitan *adj* having a wide and refined knowledge of the world especially from personal experience ⟨a college student who now seems conspicuously *cosmopolitan* after spending his junior year abroad⟩ — see WORLDLY-WISE

cosmopolitan *n* a person with the outlook, experience, and manners thought to be typical of big city dwellers ⟨As someone who had lived in Paris for a year as an exchange student, she seemed very much the *cosmopolitan* to her old classmates.⟩
synonyms metropolitan, slicker, sophisticate
related words urbanite; worldling
antonyms bumpkin, hick, provincial, rustic, yokel

cosmos *n* the whole body of things observed or assumed ⟨an essay that ponders the place of humankind in the vast *cosmos*⟩ — see UNIVERSE

cost *n* 1 a payment made in the course of achieving a result ⟨The newlyweds spared no *cost* in building the kitchen of their dreams.⟩ — see EXPENSE
2 the amount of money that is demanded as payment for something ⟨We can't afford the *cost* of a house just yet, so we're renting an apartment.⟩ — see PRICE 1
3 the loss or penalty involved in achieving a goal ⟨She completed the project, but at the *cost* of her health.⟩ — see PRICE 2

cost *vb* to have a price of ⟨The raffle tickets *cost* a dollar each.⟩
synonyms bring, fetch, go (for), run, sell (for)
related words list (for); amount (to), come (to), total; command, exact; ask, demand

costly *adj* commanding a large price ⟨Running is one sport that does not require a lot of *costly* equipment.⟩

synonyms dear, expensive, extravagant, high, precious, premium, valuable

related words exorbitant, overpriced, prohibitive, sky-high, steep, stiff, unaffordable, uneconomic (*or* uneconomical), unreasonable; deluxe, luxurious, sumptuous

near antonyms moderate, reasonable; valueless, worthless; discounted

antonyms cheap, inexpensive

costume *n* **1** clothing chosen as appropriate for a specific situation ⟨A tuxedo is the only acceptable *costume* for men attending a formal event.⟩ — see OUTFIT 1

2 clothing put on to hide one's true identity or imitate someone or something else ⟨Halloween *costumes* that caricature some of the "celebrities" created by the media over the past year⟩ — see DISGUISE 1

costume *vb* to outfit with clothes and especially fine or special clothes ⟨the days when people, *costumed* in their Sunday best, would parade along the grand avenue on Easter⟩ — see CLOTHE 1

coterie *n* a group of people sharing a common interest and relating together socially ⟨a *coterie* of old friends who attend all of the home games of the high school basketball team⟩ — see GANG 2

cotillion *also* **cotillon** *n* a social gathering for dancing ⟨young men hoping to meet the women of their dreams at the *cotillion*⟩ — see DANCE

cottage *n* an often small house for recreational or seasonal use ⟨For a month every summer we rent a *cottage* on the ocean.⟩

synonyms cabin, camp, chalet, lodge

related words dacha; bungalow, cot; hut, shack, shanty

cottony *adj* **1** covered with or as if with hair ⟨That gray, *cottony* spot on the bread is mold.⟩ — see HAIRY 1

2 smooth or delicate in appearance or feel ⟨fluffy, *cottony* hair⟩ — see SOFT 2

couch *n* a long upholstered piece of furniture designed for several sitters ⟨Find yourself a place on the *couch* and make yourself at home.⟩

synonyms davenport, divan, lounge, settee, sofa

related words lounger, love seat; daybed, sofa bed, studio couch; banquette, bench, ottoman

couch *vb* **1** to convey in appropriate or telling terms ⟨I'm trying to *couch* this delicately: I don't think we should date anymore.⟩ — see PHRASE

2 to lie low with the limbs close to the body ⟨We found him *couched* behind the partition.⟩ — see CROUCH

cougar *n* a large tawny cat of the wild ⟨In many regions, suburban developments have encroached upon the habitat of the *cougar*.⟩

synonyms catamount, mountain lion, panther, puma

council *n* **1** a coming together of a number of persons for a specified purpose ⟨a war *council* attended by the top commanders of each of the armed services⟩ — see MEETING 1

2 a group of persons formally joined together for some common interest ⟨The neighborhood *council* decided to campaign for a new park.⟩ — see ASSOCIATION 2

3 a meeting featuring a group discussion ⟨summoned to a *council* to discuss ways that the state could improve medical care for the elderly⟩ — see FORUM 1

4 a local unit of an organization ⟨The two small scout *councils* were merged into one.⟩ — see CHAPTER 1

5 an exchange of views for the purpose of exploring a subject or deciding an issue ⟨an unscheduled *council* in the judge's chambers⟩ — see DISCUSSION 1

counsel *n* **1** a person whose profession is to conduct lawsuits for clients or to advise about legal rights and obligations ⟨If you cannot afford *counsel*, one will be provided for you.⟩ — see LAWYER

2 an opinion suggesting a wise or proper course of action ⟨I suggest you take the teacher's *counsel*.⟩ — see ADVICE

3 a person who gives advice especially professionally ⟨The toy manufacturer hired a public relations *counsel* to do some damage control.⟩ — see CONSULTANT

4 an exchange of views for the purpose of exploring a subject or deciding an issue ⟨She approved the move after a *counsel* with her advisers.⟩ — see DISCUSSION 1

counsel *vb* **1** to exchange viewpoints or seek advice for the purpose of finding a solution to a problem ⟨concerned parents *counseling* about concussions caused by sports⟩ — see CONFER 2

2 to give advice and instruction to (someone) regarding the course or process to be followed ⟨Every year the admissions officer *counsels* thousands of students about the process of applying to college.⟩ — see GUIDE 1

3 to give advice to ⟨Perhaps a psychologist would be better qualified to *counsel* you.⟩ — see ADVISE 1

4 to put (something) forward as one's choice for a wise or proper course of action ⟨I would *counsel* caution and deliberation in this sensitive matter.⟩ — see ADVISE 2

counselor *or* **counsellor** *n* **1** a person who gives advice especially professionally ⟨a young couple going to a marriage *counselor*⟩ — see CONSULTANT

2 a person whose profession is to conduct lawsuits for clients or to advise about legal rights and obligations ⟨The judge summoned the *counselors* to the bench.⟩ — see LAWYER

count *n* **1** a total number obtained or recorded by noting each thing as it was being added ⟨My *count* for the number of bird species and subspecies that visited the sanctuary that weekend was 43.⟩

synonyms tale, tally

related words score; amount, gross, sum, total, whole; recount

2 a formal claim of criminal wrongdoing against a person ⟨She's been charged with two *counts* of larceny.⟩ — see CHARGE 1

count *vb* **1** to find the sum of (a collection of things) by noting each one as it is being added ⟨*Count* the baseball gloves in the storage locker to see if there are enough to go around.⟩

synonyms enumerate, number, tell

related words add (up), tally, total; calculate, compute, reckon, table, tabulate; check, mark, tick (off); recount

2 to be of importance ⟨Punctuality and a neat appearance *count* during a job interview.⟩ — see MATTER

3 to place reliance or trust ⟨I'm *counting* on you to show up tomorrow to help me move.⟩ — see DEPEND 2

4 to think of in a particular way ⟨I'm not sure I'd *count* that as a serious effort.⟩ — see CONSIDER 1

count (out) *vb* to prevent the participation, consideration, or inclusion of ⟨I don't feel well, so *count* me *out* for the party tonight.⟩ — see EXCLUDE

countenance *n* **1** facial appearance regarded as an indication of mood or feeling ⟨a pleasant *countenance* that puts visitors at ease⟩ — see LOOK 1

2 the front part of the head ⟨a pretty *countenance*⟩ — see FACE 1

3 evenness of emotions or temper ⟨The EMT's purposeful *countenance* was in stark contrast to everyone else's hysteria.⟩ — see EQUANIMITY

countenance *vb* **1** to have a favorable opinion of ⟨I don't *countenance* such behavior in children of any age.⟩ — see APPROVE (OF)

2 to put up with (something painful or difficult) ⟨*countenanced* the delays and inconveniences of traveling by air with good grace⟩ — see BEAR 2

counter *adj* opposed to one's interests ⟨I was unprepared for such a strong *counter* campaign by opponents of the legislative bill.⟩ — see ADVERSE 1

counter *n* **1** a force or influence that makes an opposing force ineffective or less effective ⟨Guidance at home is the best *counter* to the pernicious allure of popular culture.⟩ — see COUNTERBALANCE

2 something that is as different as possible from something else ⟨Her version of the accident was almost the exact *counter* of what actually happened.⟩ — see OPPOSITE

counter *vb* to strive to reduce or eliminate ⟨efforts to *counter* poverty in every sector of our country⟩ — see FIGHT 2

counteract *vb* to balance with an equal force so as to make ineffective ⟨This medication will *counteract* the symptoms but it won't kill the infection.⟩ — see OFFSET

counteraction *n* a force or influence that makes an opposing force ineffective or less effective ⟨The wind serves as a *counteraction* to gravity, making it possible for a kite to remain airborne.⟩ — see COUNTERBALANCE

counterattack *n* an attack made to counter an enemy's attack ⟨Suddenly the tide of battle turned, and the rebels, who had been falling back, made a furious *counterattack*.⟩

synonyms counteroffensive

related words sally, sortie; blitzkrieg, charge; assault, attack, offensive, onslaught

counterbalance *n* a force or influence that makes an opposing force ineffective or less effective ⟨The author's humor is a good *counterbalance* to the book's serious subject matter.⟩

synonyms balance, canceler (*or* canceller), corrective, counter, counteraction, counterpoise, counterweight, equipoise, neutralizer, offset

related words trade-off; ballast, weight

counterbalance *vb* to balance with an equal force so as to make ineffective ⟨A hearty dinner might *counterbalance* missing lunch.⟩ — see OFFSET

counterfeit *adj* **1** being such in appearance only and made or manufactured with the intention of committing fraud ⟨*counterfeit* currency that had been passed all over town⟩

synonyms bogus, fake, false, forged, inauthentic, phony (*also* phoney), sham, spurious, unauthentic

related words artificial, factitious, imitation, man-made, mimic, mock, simulated, substitute, synthetic; dummy, nonfunctioning, ornamental; cultured, fabricated, manufactured; deceptive, delusive, misleading

near antonyms natural; actual, true, valid

antonyms authentic, bona fide, genuine, real, unfaked

2 not being or expressing what one appears to be or express ⟨When it comes to the poor, his compassion is so *counterfeit*.⟩ — see INSINCERE

counterfeit *n* an imitation that is passed off as genuine ⟨The will as well as the other documents turned out to be *counterfeits*.⟩ — see FAKE 1

counterfeit *vb* **1** to imitate or copy especially in order to deceive ⟨an expert at *counterfeiting* money⟩ — see FAKE 1

2 to present a false appearance of ⟨managing to *counterfeit* a happy expression while visiting a sick friend⟩ — see FEIGN

counteroffensive *n* an attack made to counter an enemy's attack ⟨The army launched a *counteroffensive* at dawn.⟩ — see COUNTERATTACK

counterpane *n* a decorative cloth used as a top covering for a bed ⟨a beautiful *counterpane* that was a family heirloom⟩

synonyms bedspread, coverlet, spread

related words comforter, puff, quilt; bedclothes, bedding, clothes

counterpart *n* **1** one that is equal to another in status, achievement, or value ⟨She worked with her *counterpart* in the other office to get the job done.⟩ — see EQUAL

2 something or someone that strongly resembles another ⟨The daughter is her mother's *counterpart* in somewhat reduced form.⟩ — see IMAGE 1

counterpoise *n* **1** a condition in which opposing forces are equal to one another ⟨a musical piece with a *counterpoise* of loud and soft passages⟩ — see BALANCE 1

2 a force or influence that makes an opposing force ineffective or less effective ⟨The happiness brought by a new baby was a timely *counterpoise* to the grief occasioned by a death in the family.⟩ — see COUNTERBALANCE

counterpoise *vb* to balance with an equal force so as to make ineffective ⟨Her overall healthiness largely *counterpoised* the virulence of the infection.⟩ — see OFFSET

countersign *n* a word or phrase that must be spoken by a person in order to pass a guard ⟨The guard demanded the *countersign*.⟩ — see PASSWORD

counterweight *n* a force or influence that makes an opposing force ineffective or less effective ⟨Hard work can often be a *counterweight* to lack of experience.⟩ — see COUNTERBALANCE

countless *adj* too many to be counted ⟨I've told you *countless* times not to do that!⟩

synonyms innumerable, myriad, numberless, uncountable, uncounted, unnumbered, untold

related words endless, infinite, unlimited, vast; many, multitudinous, numerous

phrases beyond number

near antonyms finite, limited

antonyms countable, enumerable, numberable

country *adj* of, relating to, associated with, or typical of open areas with few buildings or people ⟨plain *country* living among unpretentious people⟩ — see RURAL

country *n* **1** the land of one's birth, residence, or citizenship ⟨a great love for my *country*⟩

synonyms fatherland, home, homeland, motherland, sod

related words old country; community, neighborhood

2 the open rural area outside of big towns and cities ⟨out in the *country*, where the air is fresh and the rivers are clean⟩

synonyms boondocks, countryside, sticks

related words exurbia; backwater, backwoods, bush, frontier, hinterland, up-country; wild, wilderness

phrases middle of nowhere

near antonyms conurbation, megalopolis, urban sprawl

3 a body of people composed of one or more nationalities usually with its own territory and government ⟨Usually in time of war, the whole *country* unites behind the president.⟩ — see NATION

countryman *n* **1** a person living in or originally from the same country as another ⟨I met a fellow Canadian *countryman* while traveling in France.⟩ — see COMPATRIOT 1

2 an awkward or simple person especially from a small town or the country ⟨Though neither well-educated nor well-dressed, the *countryman* presented the farmers' case before the state legislature.⟩ — see HICK

countryside *n* the open rural area outside of big towns and cities ⟨Everyone hates to see the *countryside* ruined by new developments.⟩ — see COUNTRY 2

coup *n* a successful result brought about by hard work ⟨Winning that big contract was a real *coup*.⟩ — see ACCOMPLISHMENT 1

couple *n* **1** a small number ⟨There are only a *couple* of errors in the computer program.⟩ — see FEW

2 two things of the same or similar kind that match or are considered together ⟨a *couple* of socks⟩ — see PAIR

couple *vb* **1** to come together to form a single unit ⟨At Pittsburgh, the Allegheny and Monongahela Rivers *couple* to form the Ohio.⟩ — see UNITE 1

2 to put or bring together so as to form a new and longer whole ⟨If you *couple* the two extension cords, the connection should be long enough to reach the next room.⟩ — see CONNECT 1

coupling *n* **1** a place where two or more things are united ⟨the *coupling* between two train cars⟩ — see JOINT 1

2 the act or an instance of joining two or more things into one ⟨credited with the *coupling* of several existing ideas into a single thesis⟩ — see UNION 1

coupon *n* a small sheet of plastic, paper, or paperboard showing that the bearer has a claim to something (as admittance) ⟨a book of discount *coupons*⟩ — see TICKET 1

courage *n* strength of mind to carry on in spite of danger ⟨the moral *courage* to speak out against injustice when no one else will⟩

synonyms bravery, courageousness, daring, dauntlessness, doughtiness, fearlessness, gallantry, greateartedness, guts, hardihood, heart, heroism, intrepidity, intrepidness, nerve, stoutness, valor, virtue

related words backbone, fiber, fortitude, grit, mettle, pluck, pluckiness, spunk, temper; determination, perseverance, resolution; endurance, stamina, stomach, tenacity; audacity, boldness, brazenness, cheek, effrontery, gall, temerity

near antonyms cold feet, faintheartedness, fearfulness, mousiness, timidity, timorousness; feebleness, softness, weakness; impotence, ineffectualness; hesitation, indecision, indecisiveness, irresolution

antonyms cowardice, cowardliness, cravenness, dastardliness, poltroonery, spinelessness

courageous *adj* feeling or displaying no fear by temperament ⟨the *courageous* decision to quit rather than obey an illegal order⟩ — see BRAVE 1

courageousness *n* strength of mind to carry on in spite of danger ⟨The soldiers' exceptional *courageousness* was credited with saving the mission from near disaster.⟩ — see COURAGE

courier *n* one that carries a message or does an errand ⟨A *courier* just delivered a package for you.⟩ — see MESSENGER

course *n* **1** a way of acting or proceeding ⟨The president's usual *course* has been to obtain advice from several people and then make a decision.⟩

synonyms line, policy, procedure, program

related words blueprint, design, plan, scheme, strategy; intent, intention, purpose; approach, direction, method, path, pathway, tack

2 a series of lectures on a subject ⟨a *course* on American history from the colonial period to the present⟩

synonyms class

related words elective, refresher; clinic, institute, seminar, survey course; minicourse; core, curriculum

phrases course of study

3 a usually fixed or ordered series of actions or events leading to a result ⟨set out on the *course* that would lead to a college degree⟩ — see PROCESS 1

4 the direction along which something or someone moves ⟨The river follows a southeasterly *course* to the ocean.⟩ — see PATH 1

5 an open man-made passageway for water ⟨The Erie Canal was replaced by a much larger *course*, the New York State Barge Canal.⟩ — see CHANNEL 1

course *vb* **1** to go after or on the track of ⟨After *coursing* the conspirators for months, the federal agents closed in and made the arrests.⟩ — see FOLLOW 2

2 to make one's way through, across, or over ⟨blood *coursing* through my veins⟩ — see TRAVERSE

3 to proceed or move quickly ⟨racehorses *coursing* down the track⟩ — see HURRY 2

court *n* **1** the residence of a ruler ⟨Hampton *Court* was the imposing residence of King Henry VIII.⟩

synonyms palace

related words castle, château, estate, mansion, villa

2 an open space wholly or partly enclosed (as by buildings or walls) ⟨The art museum boasts a glass-sided *court* that is filled with an array of greenery and sculpture.⟩

synonyms close, courtyard, enclosure (*also* inclosure), patio, quadrangle, yard

related words atrium, galleria, peristyle; forecourt, place, plaza, square; gallery [*Southern & Midland*], porch, stoop; deck, sundeck

3 an assembly of persons for the administration of justice ⟨This *court* is now called to order.⟩

synonyms bar, bench, forum, tribunal

related words criminal court, judicatory, judicature, judiciary; high court, supreme court; court-martial, drumhead court-martial; inquisition, kangaroo court

phrases court of law

4 a public official having authority to decide questions of law ⟨If it please the *court*, I'd like to approach the bench.⟩ — see JUDGE 2

court *vb* **1** to act so as to make (something) more likely ⟨You're *courting* disaster if you keep playing with matches.⟩

synonyms ask (for), invite, woo

related words angle (for), fish (for); hunt, search, seek; provoke, tempt

phrases look for

2 to go on dates that may eventually lead to marriage ⟨They *courted* for a year before getting married.⟩

synonyms date

related words attend, gallant, romance, spark, woo; escort, see, take out

phrases go steady, keep company, make love

courteous *adj* showing consideration, courtesy, and good manners ⟨Their customer service department always gives *courteous* responses, even to rude people.⟩ — see POLITE 1

courteously *adv* with good reason or courtesy ⟨*courteously* suggested that we try other bookstores⟩ — see WELL 4

courteousness *n* speech or behavior that is a sign of good manners ⟨a gentleman of unfailing *courteousness*⟩ — see POLITENESS 1

courtesy *n* **1** an act of kind assistance ⟨did me the *courtesy* of loaning me his jacket⟩ — see FAVOR 1

2 an act or utterance that is a customary show of good manners ⟨The greeting "How are you?" is often intended as no more than a *courtesy*.⟩ — see CIVILITY 1

3 speech or behavior that is a sign of good manners ⟨a woman who responds to every situation with *courtesy* and kindness⟩ — see POLITENESS 1

courting *n* the series of social engagements shared by a couple looking to get married ⟨After two years of *courting*, they finally married.⟩ — see COURTSHIP

courtliness *n* dignified or restrained beauty of form, appearance, or style ⟨There's a *courtliness* to rococo furniture that makes you feel like you should be wearing fine clothes and sipping champagne.⟩ — see ELEGANCE

courtly *adj* having or showing elegance ⟨His *courtly* manners made him a good choice for the ambassadorship.⟩ — see ELEGANT 1

courtship *n* the series of social engagements shared by a couple looking to get married ⟨a long-married couple who look back on their whirlwind *courtship* with fondness and laughter⟩

synonyms courting, dating, suit

related words suit, wooing; affair (*also* affaire), love affair, romance; betrothal, engagement

courtyard *n* an open space wholly or partly enclosed (as by buildings or walls) 〈a series of lunchtime concerts in the museum's open-air *courtyard*〉 — see COURT 2

cove *n* a part of a body of water that extends beyond the general shoreline 〈a secluded *cove* that smugglers once used〉 — see GULF 1

covenant *n* **1** a formal agreement between two or more nations or peoples 〈The two countries signed a peace *covenant* that, it was hoped, would put an end to decades of bitter conflict.〉 — see TREATY
2 a formal agreement to fulfill an obligation 〈I had to sign a *covenant* that I would return the rental car on time.〉 — see GUARANTEE 1
3 an arrangement about action to be taken 〈the *covenant* that existed among neighbors in olden times whereby they would quickly respond to the call to help put out one another's house fires〉 — see AGREEMENT 2

covenant *vb* **1** to come to an arrangement as to a course of action 〈The parties *covenanted* to renew the lease.〉 — see AGREE 2
2 to make a solemn declaration of intent 〈The home buyers had to *covenant* that they would restore and keep the house for at least 10 years in exchange for a low mortgage rate.〉 — see PROMISE 1

cover *n* **1** a piece placed over an open container to hold in, protect, or conceal its contents 〈Where's the *cover* for the cookie jar?〉
synonyms cap, lid, top
related words hood, roof; capsule, case, casing, covering, housing, jacket, sheath, shell
2 means or method of defending 〈provided *cover* while their comrades ran for safety〉 — see DEFENSE 1
3 something that encloses another thing especially to protect it 〈put the restaurant menus in clear plastic *covers* so that they would last longer〉 — see ¹CASE 1
4 a raised covering over something for decoration or protection 〈All of the exhibits at the fair are under *cover*, so the weather won't be a factor.〉 — see CANOPY
5 something that covers or conceals like a piece of cloth 〈Under *cover* of darkness, they escaped.〉 — see CLOAK 1

cover *vb* **1** to serve as a replacement usually for a time only 〈A friend *covered* for me as a hospital volunteer while my family went on vacation.〉
synonyms fill in, pinch-hit, stand in, sub, substitute, take over
related words understudy; relieve, spell; double (as)
2 to form a layer over 〈By morning a foot of snow *covered* the ground.〉
synonyms blanket, carpet, coat, overlay, overlie, overspread, sheet
related words enclose (*also* inclose), enshroud, envelop, enwrap, mantle, shawl, shroud, swathe, wrap; cloak, clothe, curtain, veil; circle, encircle, encompass
3 to place a protective layer over 〈Better *cover* your skin with sunblock if you don't want a sunburn.〉
synonyms screen, shield
related words cloak, clothe, veil; pall; canopy, cap, crown; disguise, mask, obscure
near antonyms bare, expose, uncover
4 to have (something) as a subject matter 〈This section of the book *covers* kitchen makeovers for the enterprising do-it-yourselfer.〉 — see CONCERN 1
5 to keep secret or shut off from view 〈*covered* the foxhole with grass and leaves〉 — see ¹HIDE 2
6 to make one's way through, across, or over 〈We usually manage to *cover* a lot of ground in a single day.〉 — see TRAVERSE

7 to pay continued close attention to (something) for a particular purpose 〈I'll *cover* the reception desk while you take a break.〉 — see MONITOR
8 to drive danger or attack away from 〈*covered* the wounded soldier until he could be rescued from the downed chopper〉 — see DEFEND 1

cover (up) *vb* to keep from being publicly known 〈The governor vainly tried to *cover up* the growing scandal.〉 — see SUPPRESS 1

coverage *n* the amount of something (as subject matter) included 〈The biographical dictionary's *coverage* is limited to people no longer living.〉
synonyms content
related words compass, gamut, range, scope, sweep; membership, participation

covering *n* **1** something that covers or conceals like a piece of cloth 〈With the commotion on the dance floor as a *covering*, we were able to slip out undetected.〉 — see CLOAK 1
2 something that encloses another thing especially to protect it 〈The plastic *coverings* on lamp shades should be removed.〉 — see ¹CASE 1

coverlet *n* a decorative cloth used as a top covering for a bed 〈bought a beautiful new *coverlet* to match the sheets〉 — see COUNTERPANE

covert *adj* **1** screened or sequestered from view 〈a *covert* little hideaway that provides a lot of privacy〉 — see SECLUDED
2 undertaken or done so as to escape being observed or known by others 〈a *covert* operation to provide aid to the rebels〉 — see SECRET 1

covert *n* **1** a place where a person goes to hide or to avoid others 〈We set up a *covert* from which to watch wildlife without being detected.〉 — see HIDEOUT
2 a thick patch of shrubbery, small trees, or underbrush 〈The rabbit rushed to the safety of the nearest *covert*.〉 — see THICKET

covet *vb* to have an earnest wish to own or enjoy 〈I've been *coveting* that sleek sports car in the showroom for some time now.〉 — see DESIRE 1

coveting *adj* having or marked by an eager and often selfish desire especially for material possessions 〈a *coveting* glance at the precious jewels〉 — see GREEDY 1

covetous *adj* **1** having or marked by an eager and often selfish desire especially for material possessions 〈One aggressive bargain hunter rushed to make a *covetous* grab for the last marked-down TV.〉 — see GREEDY 1
2 having or showing mean resentment of another's possessions or advantages 〈The expensive car drew many *covetous* looks.〉 — see ENVIOUS

covetousness *n* **1** a painful awareness of another's possessions or advantages and a desire to have them too 〈His *covetousness* for his neighbors' things spoils any enjoyment he might have of his own possessions.〉 — see ENVY
2 an intense selfish desire for wealth or possessions 〈An insatiable *covetousness* made her work long hours so that she could afford expensive things.〉 — see GREED

cow *vb* to make timid or fearful by or as if by threats 〈A sharp glare *cowed* the child into being quiet.〉 — see INTIMIDATE

coward *n* a person who shows a shameful lack of courage in the face of danger 〈The soldiers who ran as soon as the first shots were fired were branded as *cowards*.〉
synonyms chicken, craven, cur, dastard, funk, poltroon, recreant, sissy
related words defeatist, quitter; cream puff, milquetoast, pushover, weakling, wimp; snake, sneak
near antonyms daredevil
antonyms hero, stalwart, valiant

cowardice *n* a shameful lack of courage in the face of danger ⟨the *cowardice* shown by political leaders who were willing to give the Nazis whatever they wanted⟩
synonyms cowardliness, cravenness, dastardliness, spinelessness
related words diffidence, faintheartedness, fearfulness, timidity, timorousness; carefulness, cautiousness, wariness; bashfulness, shyness; feebleness, softness, weakness
near antonyms audacity, boldness, brazenness; backbone, fiber, fortitude, grit, mettle, pluck, spunk; determination, perseverance, resolution; endurance, stamina, tenacity
antonyms bravery, courage, courageousness, daring, dauntlessness, doughtiness, fearlessness, gallantry, greatheartedness, guts, hardihood, heart, heroism, intrepidity, intrepidness, nerve, stoutness, valiance, valor, virtue

cowardliness *n* a shameful lack of courage in the face of danger ⟨The soldier was court-martialed for *cowardliness* under fire.⟩ — see COWARDICE

cowardly *adj* having or showing a shameful lack of courage ⟨a *cowardly* bully who picks on the weak and defenseless⟩ ⟨vile charges that were made in a *cowardly*, unsigned letter⟩
synonyms chicken, chickenhearted, craven, dastardly, lily-livered, poltroon, pusillanimous, recreant, spineless, unheroic, yellow
related words diffident, fainthearted, fearful, timid, timorous; afraid, frightened, scared; careful, cautious, wary; bashful, coy, shy; feeble, soft, unmanly, weak
near antonyms audacious, bold, brazen, cheeky, nervy; plucky, spirited, spunky; determined, resolute
antonyms brave, courageous, daring, dauntless, doughty, fearless, gallant, greathearted, gutsy, hardy, heroic (*also* heroical), intrepid, lionhearted, stalwart, stout, stouthearted, valiant, valorous

cowboy *n* a hired hand who tends cattle or horses at a ranch or on the range ⟨*Cowboys* were rounding up the cattle for branding.⟩
synonyms buckaroo (*also* buckeroo), cowhand, cowman, cowpoke, cowpuncher, wrangler
related words cowgirl; caballero [*chiefly Southwest*], gaucho, vaquero; horseman, horsewoman; cattleman, rancher, stockman; cowherd, drover, herder, herdsman

cower *vb* to draw back or crouch down in fearful submission ⟨After some time in the animal shelter, the rescued dog finally stopped *cowering* when approached.⟩
synonyms cringe, grovel, quail
related words flinch, recoil, shrink, squinch; blanch, blench, whiten; fawn, kowtow, toady

cowhand *n* a hired hand who tends cattle or horses at a ranch or on the range ⟨We need to hire a new *cowhand* to help out.⟩ — see COWBOY

cowhide *vb* to strike repeatedly with something long and thin or flexible ⟨was *cowhiding* the horse until the sheriff intervened⟩ — see WHIP 1

cowman *n* a hired hand who tends cattle or horses at a ranch or on the range ⟨an expert *cowman* who can round up the livestock in no time⟩ — see COWBOY

coworker *n* a fellow worker ⟨My *coworkers* and I often send facetious e-mails to one another.⟩ — see COLLEAGUE

cowpoke *n* a hired hand who tends cattle or horses at a ranch or on the range ⟨It takes a long time to train a good *cowpoke*.⟩ — see COWBOY

cowpuncher *n* a hired hand who tends cattle or horses at a ranch or on the range ⟨*cowpunchers* hanging out and telling stories during branding time⟩ — see COWBOY

coy *adj* 1 affecting shyness or modesty ⟨Not wanting him to know that she was interested in him, she acted very *coy* at the dance.⟩
synonyms demure, kittenish
related words flirtatious, flirty, girlish; goody-goody, overmodest, priggish, prim, prudish
antonyms uncoy

2 not comfortable around people ⟨a *coy* toddler who hides whenever anyone comes to the house⟩ — see SHY 2

cozen *vb* 1 to cause to believe what is untrue ⟨*cozened* by the warm weather into thinking winter was over⟩ — see DECEIVE

2 to rob by the use of trickery or threats ⟨*cozened* scores of people by persuading them to hand over funds that he would "invest"⟩ — see FLEECE

cozener *n* a dishonest person who uses clever means to cheat others out of something of value ⟨He was a "career" *cozener* who had worked one racket or another his whole life.⟩ — see TRICKSTER 1

cozy *adj* 1 enjoying physical comfort ⟨The cat looked very *cozy*, all cuddled up in the blankets.⟩ — see COMFORTABLE 2

2 providing physical comfort ⟨a coffeehouse with soft, *cozy* chairs⟩ — see COMFORTABLE 1

crab *n* an irritable and complaining person ⟨You're always such a *crab* in the morning!⟩ — see GROUCH 1

crab *vb* 1 to express dissatisfaction, pain, or resentment usually tiresomely ⟨Their two-year-old whined and *crabbed* for the whole car trip.⟩ — see COMPLAIN

2 to reduce the soundness, effectiveness, or perfection of ⟨She *crabbed* the blossoming romance by becoming moody and demanding.⟩ — see DAMAGE 1

crabby *adj* 1 easily irritated or annoyed ⟨a *crabby* old dog who snapped at passersby⟩ — see IRRITABLE

2 given to complaining a lot ⟨a bunch of *crabby* kids who don't want to do any work⟩ — see FUSSY 1

crack *adj* having or showing exceptional knowledge, experience, or skill in a field of endeavor ⟨known as one of the college's *crack* tennis players⟩ — see PROFICIENT

crack *n* 1 an irregular usually narrow break in a surface created by pressure ⟨A pebble struck the car's windshield and left a spidery *crack* in it.⟩
synonyms check, chink, cleft, cranny, crevice, fissure, rift, split
related words crevasse; craze, hairline; fracture, rupture; breach, gap, opening; cut, gash, incision, slit

2 a hard strike with a part of the body or an instrument ⟨A disciplinary *crack* on the hand with a ruler was once common in schoolrooms.⟩ — see ¹BLOW

3 a loud explosive sound ⟨The tree fell with a sharp *crack*.⟩ — see CLAP 1

4 an effort to do or accomplish something ⟨This is my first *crack* at painting.⟩ — see ATTEMPT 1

5 something said or done to cause laughter ⟨A whispered *crack* made the whole back row start laughing.⟩ — see JOKE 1

6 a person of odd or whimsical habits ⟨That conspiracy theorist has been labeled a *crack*.⟩ — see ECCENTRIC

crack *vb* 1 to break suddenly with an explosive sound ⟨The tree branch unexpectedly *cracked* under our weight.⟩
synonyms pop, snap
related words rend, rive, split; crackle, hiss, sizzle, sputter; burst, explode, shatter; clack, clatter, click

2 to yield to mental or emotional stress ⟨After hours of tough questioning the suspect finally *cracked* and blurted out a confession.⟩
synonyms break down, break up, freak (out)
related words choke

phrases blow one's cool, fall apart, go off the deep end, go to pieces, lose it

3 to change (as a secret message) from code into ordinary language ⟨The United States military used the Navajo language as a code during World War II, and the enemy never *cracked* it.⟩ — see DECODE 1

4 to deliver a blow to (someone or something) usually in a strong vigorous manner ⟨*cracked* the log with an ax⟩ — see HIT 1

5 to find an answer for through reasoning ⟨I've been mulling this riddle, but I just can't *crack* it.⟩ — see SOLVE

6 to cause to go insane or as if insane ⟨*Cracked* by years in solitary confinement, the prisoner could only maunder incoherently.⟩ — see CRAZE

crackbrain *n* a person of odd or whimsical habits ⟨a *crackbrain* who wore bedroom slippers to the grocery store⟩ — see ECCENTRIC

crack down (on) *vb* to put a stop to (something) by the use of force ⟨The government *cracked down on* political demonstrations with unprecedented brutality.⟩ — see QUELL 1

crackerjack *adj* **1** having or showing exceptional knowledge, experience, or skill in a field of endeavor ⟨a *crackerjack* photographer who gets the news photo that is reprinted around the world⟩ — see PROFICIENT

2 of the very best kind ⟨a *crackerjack* book on the history of rock music⟩ — see EXCELLENT

crackerjack *also* **crackajack** *n* **1** a person with a high level of knowledge or skill in a field ⟨a young prospect who's supposed to be a *crackerjack* on the baseball diamond⟩ — see EXPERT

2 something very good of its kind ⟨The cheese maker's aged cheddar is a real *crackerjack*.⟩ — see JIM-DANDY

crackpot *n* a person of odd or whimsical habits ⟨Even though he's kind of a *crackpot*, he's never hurt anyone.⟩ — see ECCENTRIC

crack-up *n* **1** a mental or nervous collapse ⟨A *crack-up* required him to take a year off from work.⟩ — see BREAKDOWN 1

2 the violent coming together of two bodies into destructive contact ⟨Two people were injured in a serious *crack-up* on the interstate.⟩ — see CRASH 1

crack up *vb* **1** to declare enthusiastic approval of ⟨That sports car isn't all it's *cracked up* to be.⟩ — see ACCLAIM

2 to praise or publicize lavishly and often excessively ⟨The movie is being *cracked up* as the blockbuster of the summer.⟩ — see TOUT 1

3 to show mirth with an explosive vocal sound ⟨Try not to *crack up* at your own punch lines—it's funnier if you keep a straight face.⟩ — see LAUGH 1

cradle *n* **1** a place of origin ⟨Philadelphia is known as "the *cradle* of liberty" because it was there that the Declaration of Independence was signed.⟩ — see BIRTHPLACE

2 a point or place at which something is invented or provided ⟨The 1848 meeting at Seneca Falls, New York, is often regarded as the *cradle* of the women's suffrage movement.⟩ — see SOURCE 1

craft *n* **1** an occupation requiring skillful use of the hands ⟨The *craft* of cabinetmaking was much admired in colonial times.⟩

synonyms art, handcraft, handicraft, trade

related words skill; calling, occupation, profession, vocation

2 a small buoyant structure for travel on water ⟨borrowed a *craft* to get across the river⟩ — see BOAT 1

3 the inclination or practice of misleading others through lies or trickery ⟨never hesitated to resort to *craft* to get what she wanted in life⟩ — see DECEIT 1

4 skill in achieving one's ends through indirect, subtle, or underhanded means ⟨Celebrated in political circles for his *craft*, he's the legislator who knows how to get bills passed.⟩ — see CUNNING 1

5 subtle or imaginative ability in inventing, devising, or executing something ⟨a really ingenious household appliance that shows a lot of *craft* on the part of its inventors⟩ — see SKILL 1

craft *vb* to put (something) into proper and usually carefully worked out written form ⟨spent hours *crafting* the perfect letter of recommendation for her prize student⟩ — see COMPOSE 1

craftiness *n* **1** skill in achieving one's ends through indirect, subtle, or underhanded means ⟨Other antique dealers envied her for her *craftiness* in getting people to sell their treasures for a song.⟩ — see CUNNING 1

2 the inclination or practice of misleading others through lies or trickery ⟨According to the confidence man's credo of *craftiness*, "There's a sucker born every minute."⟩ — see DECEIT 1

craftsman *n* a person whose occupation requires skill with the hands ⟨If you want good work, hire a *craftsman*.⟩ — see ARTISAN

crafty *adj* clever at attaining one's ends by indirect and often deceptive means ⟨a *crafty* real estate broker who got people to sell their property at bargain prices⟩ — see ARTFUL 1

crag *n* a steep wall of rock, earth, or ice ⟨A menacing *crag* overhangs the hiking trail.⟩ — see CLIFF

craggy *adj* having an uneven edge or outline ⟨Goats scrambled nimbly up the *craggy* side of the mountain.⟩ — see RAGGED 1

cram *vb* **1** to fit (people or things) into a tight space ⟨tried to *cram* one more book into the backpack⟩ — see CROWD 1

2 to put into (something) as much as can be held or contained ⟨*crammed* his mouth with candy⟩ — see FILL 1

3 to fill with food to capacity ⟨one of those eating contests in which competitors attempt to *cram* themselves with as many hot dogs as they can in three minutes⟩ — see GORGE 1

4 to swallow or eat greedily ⟨The thoughtless guest *crammed* a dinner that had taken hours to prepare.⟩ — see GOBBLE

crammed *adj* containing or seeming to contain the greatest quantity or number possible ⟨The auditorium is usually *crammed* when that candidate makes an appearance.⟩ — see FULL 1

¹cramp *n* a painful sudden tightening of a muscle ⟨I was suddenly awakened by a *cramp* in my leg.⟩

synonyms charley horse, crick, spasm

related words contraction, jerk, pang, stitch, twinge, twitch

²cramp *n* something that makes movement or progress difficult ⟨a public ordinance that was seen as just another *cramp* on business⟩ — see ENCUMBRANCE

cramp *vb* to create difficulty for the work or activity of ⟨Having to constantly entertain guests at the summer cottage was really *cramping* my writing efforts.⟩ — see HAMPER

crane *vb* to move from a lower to a higher place or position ⟨*craned* her head to see the roof⟩ — see RAISE 1

cranium *n* the case of bone that encloses the brain and supports the jaws of vertebrates ⟨The *cranium* of a Neanderthal is striking for its brow ridges.⟩ — see SKULL

crank *n* **1** a person of odd or whimsical habits ⟨She's a bit of a *crank*, but still a good-hearted person.⟩ — see ECCENTRIC

2 an irritable and complaining person ⟨He's always a *crank* until he has his morning coffee.⟩ — see GROUCH 1

3 a sudden impulsive and apparently unmotivated idea or action 〈His endless and unpredictable *cranks* made spending time with him exhausting.〉 — see WHIM

crank (up) *vb* to cause to function 〈*Crank up* the engine to see if it will start.〉 — see ACTIVATE

crankiness *n* readiness to show annoyance or impatience 〈Overtired children are often prone to *crankiness*.〉 — see PETULANCE

cranky *adj* **1** difficult to use or operate especially because of size, weight, or design 〈managed to get the *cranky* old car to the salvage yard〉 — see CUMBERSOME
2 easily irritated or annoyed 〈The baby was *cranky* after not being fed for hours.〉 — see IRRITABLE
3 given to complaining a lot 〈passengers growing *cranky* about the flight delays〉 — see FUSSY 1
4 different from the ordinary in a way that causes curiosity or suspicion 〈That's just another of his *cranky* theories about the CIA.〉 — see ODD 2

cranny *n* an irregular usually narrow break in a surface created by pressure 〈One climbing shoe got wedged into a *cranny* on the face of the cliff.〉 — see CRACK 1

crash *n* **1** the violent coming together of two bodies into destructive contact 〈the fiery *crash* of two jumbo jets in midair〉
synonyms collision, concussion, crack-up, smash, smashup, wreck
related words accident; demolishment, destruction, ruin
2 a falling short of one's goals 〈She refused to be discouraged by the *crash* of her first business venture.〉 — see FAILURE 2
3 a loud explosive sound 〈the *crash* of cymbals〉 — see CLAP 1
4 a forceful coming together of two things 〈a story about the *crash* of two alien cultures and the unfortunate consequences〉 — see IMPACT 1

crash *vb* **1** to cause to break with violence and much noise 〈*crashed* the vase against the wall〉 — see SMASH 1
2 to come into usually forceful contact with something 〈The speeding car *crashed* into the tree with horrifying results.〉 — see HIT 2
3 to stop functioning 〈My computer *crashed* yet again!〉 — see FAIL 1
4 to force one's way 〈Fleeing animals *crashed* through the woods.〉 — see ²PRESS 4
5 to go to a lower level especially abruptly 〈Sales of that phone have *crashed* since the competing version came out.〉 — see DROP 2
6 *slang* to go to one's bed in order to sleep 〈I'm so exhausted that I'm just going to *crash* as soon as we get home.〉 — see BED 1
7 *slang* to reside as a temporary guest 〈I'm going to *crash* at my sister's apartment when I'm in New York.〉 — see VISIT 2

crass *adj* lacking in refinement or good taste 〈a loudmouthed jerk given to rude jokes and *crass* comments〉 — see COARSE 2

crassness *n* the quality or state of lacking refinement or good taste 〈The *crassness* of the observation shocked everyone into silence.〉 — see VULGARITY 1

crave *vb* to have an earnest wish to own or enjoy 〈*craves* ice cream at all hours of the day〉 — see DESIRE 1

craven *adj* having or showing a shameful lack of courage 〈a *craven* refusal to deliver the unwelcome news personally〉 — see COWARDLY

craven *n* a person who shows a shameful lack of courage in the face of danger 〈a *craven* who ran away and left everyone else behind to deal with the crisis〉 — see COWARD

cravenness *n* a shameful lack of courage in the face of

danger 〈It was sheer *cravenness* to avoid the consequences of your actions.〉 — see COWARDICE

craving *n* a strong wish for something 〈a pregnant woman with a *craving* for pickles〉 — see DESIRE 1

crawl *vb* **1** to move slowly with the body close to the ground 〈the time we had to *crawl* through a narrow passageway from one cave to another〉
synonyms belly, creep, grovel, slide, slither, snake, worm, wriggle
related words crouch, squat; edge, inch, nose; skulk, sneak, steal, tiptoe
2 to move slowly 〈The weekend traffic on the road to the beach just *crawled*.〉
synonyms creep, drag, inch, limp, nose, ooze, plod, poke, slouch
related words lumber, shamble, shuffle, tramp, trudge
near antonyms float, glide, sail; hurry, tear
antonyms fly, race, speed, whiz (*or* whizz), zip
3 to move or act slowly 〈The deadline is fast approaching, so this is no time to *crawl*.〉 — see DELAY 1
4 to be copiously supplied 〈Something must be up, as city hall is *crawling* with reporters.〉 — see ABOUND

crawler *n* someone who moves slowly or more slowly than others 〈He's always the *crawler* who makes everyone else late.〉 — see SLOWPOKE

crawling *adj* moving or proceeding at less than the normal, desirable, or required speed 〈The *crawling* pace of the narrative is really frustrating.〉 — see SLOW 1

craze *n* a practice or interest that is very popular for a short time 〈If history is any guide, this latest diet for losing weight is just another *craze*.〉 — see FAD

craze *vb* to cause to go insane or as if insane 〈horses *crazed* by the stable fire〉
synonyms crack, derange, frenzy, madden, unbalance, unhinge, unstring
related words agitate, bother, confuse, discompose, disquiet, distract, disturb, perturb, unsettle, upset; annoy, irritate, vex
near antonyms calm, quiet, relax, settle, soothe, tranquilize (*also* tranquillize)

crazy *adj* **1** conceived or made without regard for reason or reality 〈The mansion is a *crazy* construction of several different styles.〉 — see FANTASTIC 1
2 showing urgent desire or interest 〈*crazy* for the latest entertainment news〉 — see EAGER
3 different from the ordinary in a way that causes curiosity or suspicion 〈likes *crazy* hair colors, like blue and pink〉 — see ODD 2
4 inclined or twisted to one side 〈Surrounded by *crazy* stacks of books, she began writing her paper.〉 — see AWRY
5 marked by a long series of irregular curves 〈We walked down a *crazy* path deep in the woods to a secluded swimming hole.〉 — see CROOKED 1

crazy (about *or* **over)** *adj* filled with an intense or excessive love for 〈He's just *crazy about* that new drummer.〉 — see ENAMORED (OF)

creak *n* a harsh grating sound 〈the *creak* of a floorboard〉 — see RASP

cream *n* individuals carefully selected as being the best of a class 〈The school accepts only the *cream* of the world's young violinists.〉 — see ELITE 1

cream *vb* **1** to bring to a complete end the physical soundness, existence, or usefulness of 〈The head-on collision *creamed* the brand-new car in an instant.〉 — see DESTROY 1
2 to defeat by a large margin 〈The novice player was *creamed* in her first tennis tournament.〉 — see WHIP 2

crease *n* a small fold in a soft and otherwise smooth

surface ⟨Rolling, rather than folding, your clothes when you pack will usually prevent a lot of *creases*.⟩ — see WRINKLE 1

crease *vb* to develop creases or folds ⟨Her face *creased* with worry.⟩ — see WRINKLE 1

create *vb* to be the cause of (a situation, action, or state of mind) ⟨It was your negligence that *created* this mess.⟩ — see EFFECT

creation *n* **1** something (as a device) created for the first time through the use of the imagination ⟨Dr. Frankenstein was divinely proud of his *creation*, at least at first.⟩ — see INVENTION 1
2 the whole body of things observed or assumed ⟨an unshakable belief in a primal source, a fount of all *creation*⟩ — see UNIVERSE
3 a raising or a state of being raised to a higher rank or position ⟨the *creation* of an unprecedented number of new cardinals by the pope⟩ — see ADVANCEMENT 1

creative *adj* **1** having the skill and imagination to create new things ⟨Thomas Edison's status as perhaps America's greatest *creative* genius⟩
synonyms clever, imaginative, ingenious, innovative, inventive, original
related words gifted, inspired, talented; resourceful; fecund, fertile, fruitful, generative, germinal, productive, prolific
near antonyms imitative, uninspired; infertile, unproductive; talentless
antonyms uncreative, unimaginative, uninventive, unoriginal
2 showing a noteworthy use of the imagination and creativity especially in inventing ⟨always coming up with *creative* ways to use hamburger⟩ — see CLEVER 1

creativeness *n* the skill and imagination to create new things ⟨a child with the *creativeness* to build his own figure of a superhero out of the parts of several toys⟩ — see CREATIVITY 1

creativity *n* **1** the skill and imagination to create new things ⟨The arts and crafts fair showed the remarkable *creativity* of local artists and artisans.⟩
synonyms cleverness, creativeness, imagination, imaginativeness, ingeniousness, ingenuity, invention, inventiveness, originality
related words fecundity, fertility, fruitfulness, productiveness, productivity, prolificacy, prolificity, prolificness; resourcefulness; genius, giftedness, talent; fire, inspiration
near antonyms dryness, dullness (*also* dulness)
2 the ability to form mental images of things that either are not physically present or have never been conceived or created by others ⟨While his imaginary friend is a little annoying, you have to admire his *creativity* in thinking her up.⟩ — see IMAGINATION 1

creator *n* **1** a person who establishes a whole new field of endeavor ⟨Although some people see Freud as the *creator* of psychology, that isn't really true.⟩ — see FATHER 2
2 *cap* the being worshipped as the creator and ruler of the universe ⟨She humbly gave thanks to her *Creator* for each new day.⟩ — see DEITY 2

creature *n* **1** a member of the human race ⟨We must try to be kind to our fellow *creatures*.⟩ — see HUMAN
2 one of the lower animals as distinguished from human beings ⟨The deepest parts of the ocean are filled with strange *creatures*.⟩ — see ANIMAL

credence *n* **1** firm belief in the integrity, ability, effectiveness, or genuineness of someone or something ⟨I'm afraid I don't put much *credence* in common gossip.⟩ — see TRUST 1
2 mental conviction of the truth of some statement or

the reality of some being or phenomenon ⟨a foolish theory that, incredibly, once had wide *credence* among educated people⟩ — see BELIEF 1

credentials *pl n* a skill, an ability, or knowledge that makes a person able to do a particular job ⟨She certainly has the *credentials* for the position.⟩ — see QUALIFICATION 1

credible *adj* worthy of being accepted as true or reasonable ⟨It's at least a *credible* explanation.⟩ — see BELIEVABLE

credit *n* **1** the right to take possession of goods before paying for them ⟨Because of their reputation for not paying their bills, no store will extend the family *credit*.⟩
synonyms trust
related words installment plan, layaway; charge account, credit line
2 an asset that brings praise or renown ⟨Your intelligence and dedication are a *credit* to you, our choice for teacher of the year.⟩ — see GLORY 2
3 mental conviction of the truth of some statement or the reality of some being or phenomenon ⟨I give full *credit* to this report.⟩ — see BELIEF 1
4 public acknowledgment or admiration for an achievement ⟨She deserves all the *credit*, since she did all the work.⟩ — see GLORY 1
5 the power to direct the thinking or behavior of others usually indirectly ⟨Despite his legal woes, he has not yet lost all his *credit* with the administration.⟩ — see INFLUENCE 1

credit *vb* **1** to explain (something) as being the result of something else ⟨Hal has to *credit* his success in picking winning lottery numbers to pure luck.⟩
synonyms accredit, ascribe, attribute, impute, lay, put down
related words blame, charge, father (on), impute (to), pin (on); assign, refer; associate, attach, connect, link
2 to regard as right or true ⟨I simply cannot *credit* that story about the boy who was supposedly raised by wolves.⟩ — see BELIEVE 1

creditable *adj* **1** deserving of high regard or great approval ⟨a *creditable* effort, even if it didn't succeed completely⟩ — see ADMIRABLE
2 worthy of being accepted as true or reasonable ⟨Let's look for a scientifically *creditable* explanation before going off into the realm of the supernatural.⟩ — see BELIEVABLE

credo *n* **1** a body of beliefs and practices regarding the supernatural and the worship of one or more deities ⟨The *credo* of the ancient Egyptians involved a variety of polytheism.⟩ — see RELIGION 1
2 the basic beliefs or guiding principles of a person or group ⟨We must abide by the simple *credo* that "The customer is always right."⟩ — see CREED 1

credulity *n* readiness to believe the claims of others without sufficient evidence ⟨The quack pushing the phony medicine was taking advantage of the *credulity* of people hoping for miracle cures.⟩
synonyms credulousness, gullibility, naïveté (*also* naivete *or* naiveté), simpleness
related words artlessness, simplicity, unsophistication, unwariness, unworldliness; belief, credibility, faith, trust
near antonyms sophistication, worldliness; distrust, mistrust, suspicion, suspiciousness, wariness; doubt, uncertainty
antonyms incredulity, skepticism

credulousness *n* readiness to believe the claims of others without sufficient evidence ⟨Her well-known *credulousness* makes her an easy target for practical jokes.⟩ — see CREDULITY

creed *n* **1** the basic beliefs or guiding principles of a person or group ⟨Central to the *creed* of this organization of medical volunteers is the belief that health care is a basic human right.⟩

synonyms credo, doctrine, dogma, gospel, ideology (*also* idealogy), philosophy, testament

related words manifesto; metaphysic, theory; axiom, tenet, watchword

2 a body of beliefs and practices regarding the supernatural and the worship of one or more deities ⟨The Amish live by a strict *creed* that rejects many of the values and practices of modern society.⟩ — see RELIGION 1

creek *n* **1** a natural body of running water smaller than a river ⟨the shallow *creek* that runs in back of our house⟩

synonyms brook, brooklet, rill, rivulet, run [*chiefly Midland*], streamlet

related words arroyo, fresh, freshet, runoff; coulee, slough (*also* slew *or* slue), stream, wash; canal, channel, cut, gut, kill, millrace, millstream, race, watercourse, waterway; affluent, branch, confluent, distributary, influent

2 *chiefly British* a part of a body of water that extends beyond the general shoreline ⟨explored many of the *creeks* along the Cornwall coast of England⟩ — see GULF 1

creep *n* a person whose behavior is offensive to others ⟨Leave me alone, you *creep*!⟩ — see JERK 1

creep *vb* **1** to advance gradually beyond the usual or desirable limits ⟨Water *crept* slowly over the top of the tub and onto the floor.⟩ — see ENCROACH

2 to move or act slowly ⟨That Friday afternoon we were just *creeping*, waiting for the buzzer to sound so that we could start the long weekend.⟩ — see DELAY 1

3 to move slowly with the body close to the ground ⟨The kitten *crept* silently across the floor before suddenly pouncing on the mouse.⟩ — see CRAWL 1

4 to move slowly ⟨The class hour seems to *creep* by.⟩ — see CRAWL 2

creeping *adj* moving or proceeding at less than the normal, desirable, or required speed ⟨At this *creeping* pace of progress we'll never have the float ready for the parade.⟩ — see SLOW 1

creepy *adj* **1** fearfully and mysteriously strange or fantastic ⟨a fascinating but *creepy* stage show by an offbeat magician⟩ — see EERIE

2 marked by or causing agitation or uncomfortable feelings ⟨a *creepy* aura about the abandoned farmhouse—as though something horrific had happened there⟩ — see NERVOUS 2

crest *n* **1** the highest part or point ⟨At that point the filmmaker was at the *crest* of his critical acclaim, which included winning an Oscar.⟩ — see HEIGHT 1

2 the line formed when two sloping surfaces come together along their topmost edge ⟨The hiking party reached the *crest* of the mountain just as it began to thunder.⟩ — see RIDGE

crestfallen *adj* feeling unhappiness ⟨She was *crestfallen* when she found out that she hadn't got the job.⟩ — see SAD 1

crevice *n* an irregular usually narrow break in a surface created by pressure ⟨Steam escaped from a long *crevice* in the volcano.⟩ — see CRACK 1

crew *n* **1** a group involved in secret or criminal activities ⟨When one smuggler turned informant, the police were able to nab the leader and his *crew*.⟩ — see ¹RING 1

2 a group of people working together on a task ⟨We'll need the whole *crew* to stay late tomorrow.⟩ — see GANG 1

crick *n* a painful sudden tightening of a muscle ⟨I got a *crick* in my neck from sleeping while sitting up.⟩ — see ¹CRAMP

crime *n* **1** activities that are in violation of the laws of the state ⟨a promise by the president to step up the war against *crime*⟩

synonyms criminality, lawbreaking, lawlessness

related words outlawry; gangsterism, hooliganism, racketeering; malfeasance, misconduct; wrongdoing; evil, immorality, sin, wickedness; corruption, depravity; malefaction, misdeed, misdoing, offense (*or* offence), transgression, trespass

2 a regrettable or blameworthy act ⟨It's a *crime* to waste food, so give the rest of the pizza to me.⟩

synonyms disgrace, pity, shame, sin

related words outrage, scandal

3 a breaking of a moral or legal code ⟨Anyone who commits a *crime* should expect to be punished for it.⟩ — see OFFENSE 1

criminal *adj* contrary to or forbidden by law ⟨People should know with certainty that *criminal* behavior will be punished.⟩ — see ILLEGAL 1

criminal *n* a person who has committed a crime ⟨car thieves, pickpockets, burglars, and other *criminals*⟩

synonyms crook, culprit, lawbreaker, malefactor, miscreant, offender

related words accomplice, principal; desperado, outlaw; convict, jailbird; perp, perpetrator; evildoer, gallows bird, misdoer, misfeasor, sinner, transgressor, trespasser, villain, wrongdoer; blackhander, gangster, hoodlum, hooligan, mobster, racketeer, thug; enforcer, gun, gunman, hit man, triggerman; backslider, recidivist, relapser, repeater; accused, arrestee, defendant, detainee, fish, suspect

near antonyms gangbuster

criminality *n* activities that are in violation of the laws of the state ⟨trying to lower the city's rate of *criminality*⟩ — see CRIME 1

crimp *n* **1** a small fold in a soft and otherwise smooth surface ⟨A small *crimp* in the dollar bill prevented it from being accepted by the bill changer.⟩ ⟨He made a tiny little *crimp* in the corner of the Queen of Spades.⟩ — see WRINKLE 1

2 something that makes movement or progress difficult ⟨The strike could put a real *crimp* in the production schedule.⟩ — see ENCUMBRANCE

crimson *vb* to develop a rosy facial color (as from excitement or embarrassment) ⟨He *crimsoned* the minute he realized the foolishness of what he'd said.⟩ — see BLUSH

cringe *vb* **1** to draw back in fear, pain, or disgust ⟨gruesome crime scene photos that made several jurors *cringe*⟩ — see FLINCH

2 to draw back or crouch down in fearful submission ⟨The puppy *cringed* at the thunderclap.⟩ — see COWER

crinkle *n* a small fold in a soft and otherwise smooth surface ⟨Little *crinkles* at the corners of his mouth showed whenever he smiled.⟩ — see WRINKLE 1

crinkle *vb* **1** to make small sounds usually by rubbing or moving ⟨a paper seat cover that *crinkles* with every move⟩

synonyms rustle

related words crackle, crepitate; creak, squeak; whoosh; babble, gurgle, murmur, sigh, whisper

2 to create (as by crushing) an irregular mass of creases in ⟨*crinkled* the candy wrapper up and threw it away⟩ — see CRUMPLE 1

3 to develop creases or folds ⟨Her forehead *crinkled* in consternation when her guests failed to arrive on time.⟩ — see WRINKLE 1

cripple *vb* **1** to cause severe or permanent injury to ⟨The car crash may have *crippled* two people for life.⟩ — see MAIM

2 to reduce the soundness, effectiveness, or perfection of ⟨The collision so severely *crippled* the ship that it had to be towed into port.⟩ — see DAMAGE 1

3 to render powerless, ineffective, or unable to move ⟨a wave of strikes *crippled* that nation's steel industry⟩ — see PARALYZE 1

crisis *n* a time or state of affairs requiring prompt or decisive action ⟨The governor responded swiftly and surely to the *crisis*.⟩ — see EMERGENCY

crisp *adj* **1** having a texture that readily breaks into little pieces under pressure ⟨The bag of *crisp* cookies had a lot of crumbs on the bottom.⟩

synonyms brittle, crispy, crumbly, flaky (*also* flakey), friable, short

related words crackly, crisped, crispened, crunchy, crusty; breakable, delicate, fragile

near antonyms elastic, flexible, pliable, pliant, resilient; strong, sturdy, tough

2 being clean and in good order ⟨a pretty, *crisp* bedspread for the guest room⟩ — see NEAT 1

3 marked by the use of few words to convey much information or meaning ⟨He issued a series of *crisp* orders.⟩ — see CONCISE

crisply *adv* in a few words ⟨The teacher *crisply* commanded the rubbernecking students to direct their attention forward.⟩ — see SHORTLY 1

crispness *n* the quality or state of being marked by or using only few words to convey much meaning ⟨The *crispness* of the writing is such that this writer says more in nine paragraphs than some others say in nine pages.⟩ — see SUCCINCTNESS

crispy *adj* having a texture that readily breaks into little pieces under pressure ⟨The *crispy* potato chips snapped satisfyingly in my mouth.⟩ — see CRISP 1

criterion *n* **1** something set up as an example against which others of the same type are compared ⟨One *criterion* for grading these essays will be their conformity to the rules of traditional grammar.⟩ — see STANDARD 1

2 something that sets apart an individual from others of the same kind ⟨An exceptionally high degree of physical risk is the preeminent *criterion* of an extreme sport.⟩ — see CHARACTERISTIC

critic *n* **1** a person given to harsh judgments and to finding faults ⟨The president's hard-core *critics* are going to attack him no matter what he does.⟩

synonyms carper, castigator, caviler (*or* caviller), censurer, faultfinder, nitpicker

related words condemner (*or* condemnor), denouncer; belittler, decrier, denigrator, derider, detractor; crucifier; hairsplitter, pettifogger, quibbler; admonisher, haranguer, railer, ranter, rebuker, reproacher, reprover, scold, upbraider; bellyacher, complainer, crybaby, fusser, griper, grouch, grouser, grumbler, whiner

near antonyms commender, praiser

2 a person who makes or expresses a judgment on the quality of offerings in some field of endeavor ⟨The restaurant *critic* said that the fries at that fast-food outlet were the worst she'd ever eaten.⟩

synonyms reviewer

related words analyst, annotator, columnist, commentator; appraiser, evaluator, judge, referee

critical *adj* **1** given to making or expressing unfavorable judgments about things ⟨They are often *critical* of the mayor's policies.⟩

synonyms captious, carping, caviling (*or* cavilling), faultfinding, hypercritical, overcritical

related words discerning, discriminating, judicious; demanding, exacting, fastidious, finicky, fussy, nitpicky, particular, picky; pettifogging, quibbling; harsh, merciless, uncharitable, unforgiving

near antonyms undiscriminating; undemanding, unfussy; charitable, forgiving

antonyms uncritical

2 needing immediate attention ⟨This problem isn't *critical*, so we can go home now and tend to it in the morning.⟩ — see ACUTE 2

3 of the greatest possible importance ⟨This is the *critical* exam that will largely determine your college career.⟩ — see CRUCIAL

4 impossible to do without ⟨*critical* information for an informed medical diagnosis⟩ — see ESSENTIAL 1

criticism *n* an essay evaluating or analyzing something ⟨Every *criticism* of the movie has noted that there are major holes in its plot.⟩

synonyms notice, review

related words column, commentary, editorial, punditry; appraisal, assessment, evaluation; analysis, examination, opinion, outline, study, survey

criticize *vb* to express one's unfavorable opinion of the worth or quality of ⟨people who *criticize* every single idea that the principal has for improving the school⟩

synonyms blame, censure, condemn, denounce, fault, knock, pan, reprehend

related words skewer, tweak; assail, attack, blast, clobber, slam, slash; nick (at), snipe (at); beef, bellyache, carp, cavil, complain, crab, croak, fuss, gripe, grouse, growl, grumble, kick, kvetch, moan, murmur, mutter, quibble, whine; admonish, chide, drub, rebuke, reprimand, reproach, reprove; berate, castigate, crucify, excoriate, flay, gibbet, hammer, keelhaul, lambaste (*or* lambast), lash, pillory, scold, upbraid; bad-mouth, belittle, decry, deride, discommend, disparage, put down

phrases come down hard (on), find fault (with), take to task

near antonyms approve, commend, endorse (*also* indorse), recommend, sanction

antonyms extol (*also* extoll), laud, praise

critter *n* one of the lower animals as distinguished from human beings ⟨She's so fond of every kind of *critter* that she ought to be a veterinarian.⟩ — see ANIMAL

croak *vb* **1** to express dissatisfaction, pain, or resentment usually tiresomely ⟨The cranky patient was always *croaking* to the nurses about something.⟩ — see COMPLAIN

2 *slang* to stop living ⟨I wouldn't go around saying your great-grandmother "*croaked*."⟩ — see DIE 1

3 *slang* to deprive of life ⟨"I *croaked* the old bugger," he bragged.⟩ — see KILL 1

4 *slang* to put to death deliberately ⟨The gangster threatened to *croak* anyone who ratted him out.⟩ — see MURDER 1

croaking *adj* harsh and dry in sound ⟨a *croaking* voice from smoking too many cigarettes⟩ — see HOARSE

crockery *n* articles made of baked clay ⟨a display of beautifully hand-painted *crockery* on the kitchen countertop⟩

synonyms earthenware, pottery, stoneware

related words ceramics; china, ironstone china, porcelain, redware

crony *n* **1** a person frequently seen in the company of another ⟨The criminal's *cronies* were also closely questioned about the illegal gambling operation.⟩ — see ASSOCIATE 1

2 a person who has a strong liking for and trust in another ⟨Only my *cronies* can call me by my nickname.⟩ — see FRIEND 1

crook *n* **1** a person who has committed a crime ⟨A guy on the radio was raving about how all politicians are basically *crooks*.⟩ — see CRIMINAL

2 something that curves or is curved ⟨carried the baby in the *crook* of her arm⟩ — see BEND 1

crook *vb* **1** to cause to turn away from a straight line ⟨*crooked* a finger⟩ — see BEND 1

2 to turn away from a straight line or course ⟨The road suddenly *crooked* to the left.⟩ — see CURVE 1

crooked *adj* **1** marked by a long series of irregular curves ⟨A long, *crooked* line of people had formed in front of the ticket booth.⟩

synonyms bending, crazy, curled, curling, curved, curving, devious, serpentine, sinuous, tortuous, twisted, twisting, winding, windy

related words zigzag, zigzagging; circling, coiled, coiling, corkscrew, looping, spiral, spiraling (*or* spiralling), swirling; circuitous, indirect, roundabout; rambling, wandering; irregular, jagged, uneven

near antonyms direct, linear

antonyms straight, straightaway

2 given to or marked by cheating and deception ⟨the common belief that gambling casinos are often *crooked* businesses⟩ — see DISHONEST 2

3 inclined or twisted to one side ⟨The photo on that wall is *crooked*.⟩ — see AWRY

4 marked by, based on, or done by the use of dishonest methods to acquire something of value ⟨a *crooked* scheme to bill the government for medical services never performed⟩ — see FRAUDULENT 1

crookedness *n* the inclination or practice of misleading others through lies or trickery ⟨For sheer *crookedness* it would be hard to beat the used-car dealer who sold me that lemon.⟩ — see DECEIT 1

crop *n* **1** the quantity of an animal or vegetable product gathered at the end of a season ⟨The wheat *crop* is going to be exceptionally large this year.⟩

synonyms harvest

related words return, yield; cut, cutting

2 a usually small number of persons considered as a unit ⟨The school's latest *crop* of graduates is its most academically gifted so far.⟩ — see GROUP 2

crop *vb* **1** to look after or assist the growth of by labor and care ⟨a family that's been *cropping* potatoes on that piece of land for generations⟩ — see GROW 1

2 to make (something) shorter or smaller with the use of a cutting instrument ⟨grass *cropped* short by repeated grazing⟩ ⟨*cropped* the painting to fit the frame⟩ — see CLIP 1

crop (up) *vb* to come to one's attention especially gradually or unexpectedly ⟨A new issue has just *cropped up* in the campaign.⟩ — see ARISE 2

cropper *n* a falling short of one's goals ⟨More than a few people were glad to see the smug skater come a *cropper* at the national championships.⟩ — see FAILURE 2

croquette *n* a small usually rounded mass of minced food that has been fried ⟨a fish *croquette*⟩ — see CAKE 1

cross *adj* **1** being offspring produced by parents of different races, breeds, species, or genera ⟨raises both purebred and *cross* lambs⟩ — see MIXED 1

2 easily irritated or annoyed ⟨She was *cross* all day because of a nagging headache.⟩ — see IRRITABLE

cross *n* **1** a test of faith, patience, or strength ⟨Dyslexia is just my *cross* to bear, and I accepted it long ago.⟩ — see TRIAL 1

2 an offspring of parents with different genes especially when of different races, breeds, species, or genera ⟨The mare is an Arabian-Thoroughbred *cross*.⟩ — see HYBRID

cross *vb* **1** to be unfaithful or disloyal to ⟨I'll get even with you for *crossing* me.⟩ — see BETRAY 1

2 to divide by passing through or across ⟨There's a light where that street *crosses* Main Street.⟩ — see INTERSECT

3 to make one's way through, across, or over ⟨You may have to *cross* some woods on the way.⟩ — see TRAVERSE

4 to enter the mind of ⟨The idea did *cross* me that he might be pulling my leg.⟩ — see OCCUR (TO)

cross (out) *vb* to show (something written) to be no longer valid by drawing a cross over or a line through it ⟨*Cross out* the old phone number and write in the new one.⟩ — see X (OUT)

crossbred *adj* being offspring produced by parents of different races, breeds, species, or genera ⟨a beautiful *crossbred* dog who had the pleading eyes of a beagle and the body of a greyhound⟩ — see MIXED 1

crossbred *n* an offspring of parents with different genes especially when of different races, breeds, species, or genera ⟨a puppy that was clearly a *crossbred* of a beagle and a dachshund⟩ — see HYBRID

crossbreed *n* an offspring of parents with different genes especially when of different races, breeds, species, or genera ⟨a Siamese *crossbreed* who was atypically black, but had the build and voice of a Siamese⟩ — see HYBRID

cross fire *n* an often noisy or angry expression of differing opinions ⟨Viewers tune in to witness the weekly *cross fire* between the liberal and conservative commentators.⟩ — see ARGUMENT 1

crossing *n* **1** a journey over water in a vessel ⟨an uneventful *crossing* from the United States to Britain⟩ — see SAIL

2 a place where roads meet ⟨Turn left at the next *crossing* and then stay on that road for two miles.⟩ — see CROSSROAD 1

crossness *n* readiness to show annoyance or impatience ⟨a librarian who had a reputation for chronic *crossness*⟩ — see PETULANCE

crossroad *n* **1** *usually* **crossroads** *pl* a place where roads meet ⟨The fast-food chain has a restaurant at practically every *crossroads*.⟩

synonyms corner, crossing, intersection, junction

related words cloverleaf, interchange, overpass, underpass; circle, rotary, traffic circle

2 *usually* **crossroads** *pl* a time or state of affairs requiring prompt or decisive action ⟨We've come to a *crossroads*, and we have to make a decision.⟩ — see EMERGENCY

cross section *n* a number of things selected from a group to stand for the whole ⟨a television ratings service that monitors the viewing of a representative *cross section* of the general population⟩ — see SAMPLE 1

crossways *adv* in a line or direction running from corner to corner ⟨The van had been deliberately parked *crossways* so as to take up both parking spaces.⟩ — see CROSSWISE

crosswise *adv* in a line or direction running from corner to corner ⟨First cut the sandwiches *crosswise* and then trim the crusts.⟩

synonyms athwart, bias, crossways, obliquely, transversely

related words across

phrases on the bias, on the diagonal

near antonyms lengthwise, longitudinally

crotchet *n* an odd or peculiar habit ⟨Her one *crotchet* is a fondness for eating cookies while soaking in the tub.⟩ — see IDIOSYNCRASY

crotchetiness *n* readiness to show annoyance or impatience ⟨the understandable *crotchetiness* of an overworked teacher⟩ — see PETULANCE

crotchety *adj* easily irritated or annoyed ⟨I get *crotchety* after a long day at work.⟩ — see IRRITABLE

crouch *vb* to lie low with the limbs close to the body ⟨The cat *crouched* in the bushes, waiting for the right moment to pounce on the chipmunk.⟩

synonyms couch, huddle, hunch, scrunch, squat, squinch

related words curl up

crow *vb* **1** to feel or express joy or triumph ⟨Being the home of the new Super Bowl champs was the first thing that city residents had to *crow* about in a very long time.⟩ — see EXULT

2 to praise or express pride in one's own possessions, qualities, or accomplishments often to excess ⟨The in-your-face *crowing* by some of the winning athletes at the Olympics was embarrassing.⟩ — see BOAST 1

crowd *n* **1** a great number of persons or creatures massed together ⟨A huge *crowd* of fans was on hand to greet the returning World Series champions.⟩
synonyms army, crush, drove, flock, herd, horde, host, legion, mass, mob, multitude, press, rout, swarm, throng
related words masses, rabble, rabblement, riffraff; gaggle; heap, mountain, pile; jam

2 a group of people sharing a common interest and relating together socially ⟨the fashionable *crowd* at the polo tournament⟩ — see GANG 2

3 the body of the community as contrasted with the elite ⟨No national leader was ever more loved by the *crowd*.⟩ — see MASS 1

crowd *vb* **1** to fit (people or things) into a tight space ⟨*crowded* all the boats into the harbor before the storm struck⟩
synonyms cram, crush, jam, ram, sandwich, squeeze, stuff, wedge
related words fill, heap, jam-pack, load, pack

2 to move upon or fill (something) in great numbers ⟨Cars *crowded* the roads over the long holiday weekend.⟩
synonyms flock, mob, swarm, throng
related words beset, infest, invade, overrun; clog, dam, jam, obstruct, plug (up)

3 to gather into a closely packed group ⟨Everyone *crowded* around to see the baby being shown off by his proud parents.⟩ — see ²PRESS 3

crowded *adj* **1** containing or seeming to contain the greatest quantity or number possible ⟨We kept circling around the *crowded* parking lot at the mall.⟩ — see FULL 1

2 having little space between items or parts ⟨a *crowded* design that made the bedroom wallpaper a little overwhelming⟩ — see CLOSE 1

crown *n* **1** a decorative band or wreath worn about the head as a symbol of victory or honor ⟨the *crown* of laurel leaves that is traditionally placed on the winner of the marathon⟩
synonyms coronet, diadem
related words tiara; garland, laurel

2 the position occupied by the one who comes in first in a competition ⟨his lifelong dream of someday winning the heavyweight boxing *crown*⟩
synonyms championship, title

3 the highest part or point ⟨covered in mud from the soles of his feet to the *crown* of his head⟩ — see HEIGHT 1

crown *vb* to bring to a triumphant conclusion ⟨The Olympic Games were *crowned* by spectacular closing ceremonies.⟩
synonyms cap (off), climax, culminate
related words complete, conclude, finish, round (off *or* out), terminate, wrap up

crucial *adj* of the greatest possible importance ⟨Water is *crucial* to our survival.⟩
synonyms critical, key, pivotal, vital
related words decisive, life-and-death (*also* life-or-death), weighty; basic, elementary, fundamental, essential, indispensable, necessary, requisite; pressing, urgent
near antonyms inconsequential, insignificant, minor, trivial, unimportant

crucible *n* a test of faith, patience, or strength ⟨soldiers who had withstood the *crucible* of war⟩ — see TRIAL 1

crude *adj* **1** being such as found in nature and not altered by processing or refining ⟨A sizable spill of *crude* oil along a coastline is the worst kind of environmental disaster.⟩
synonyms native, natural, raw, rude, undressed, unprocessed, unrefined, untreated
related words undeveloped; semifinished, unfinished, unpolished; uncooked; impure, unfiltered
phrases in the raw, in the rough
near antonyms filtered, pure, purified
antonyms dressed, processed, refined, treated

2 belonging to or characteristic of an early level of skill or development ⟨the *crude* stone tools that those prehistoric peoples used⟩ — see PRIMITIVE 1

3 depicting or referring to sexual matters in a way that is unacceptable in polite society ⟨*Crude* jokes offended many in the audience.⟩ — see OBSCENE 1

4 lacking in refinement or good taste ⟨Any discussion of one's money is considered *crude* by the club's blue-blooded members.⟩ — see COARSE 2

5 hastily or roughly constructed ⟨a *crude* hut that was constructed by some shipwrecked sailors⟩ — see RUDE 1

crudeness *n* **1** the quality or state of being obscene ⟨The blatant *crudeness* of the remark first made him blush and then made him angry.⟩ — see OBSCENITY

2 the quality or state of lacking refinement or good taste ⟨The lowbrow *crudeness* of the commentary at the fashion show horrified her.⟩ — see VULGARITY 1

cruel *adj* **1** having or showing the desire to inflict severe pain and suffering on others ⟨a *cruel* dictator who imprisoned anyone who dared to speak out against him⟩ ⟨*Cruel* and unusual punishments are forbidden by the U.S. Constitution.⟩
synonyms atrocious, barbaric, barbarous, brutal, brute, fiendish, heartless, inhuman, inhumane, sadistic, savage, truculent, vicious, wanton
related words merciless, pitiless, ruthless, stonyhearted, unfeeling; fell, ferocious, grim; bloodthirsty, cutthroat, murderous, sanguinary, sanguine; catty, despiteful, hateful, malevolent, malicious, malign, malignant, mean, nasty, spiteful, vindictive; draconian, draconic, hard-handed, harsh, heavy-handed, oppressive
phrases red in tooth and claw
near antonyms tender, warm, warmhearted; charitable, clement, lenient, merciful, pitying; pacific, peaceable, peaceful
antonyms benign, benignant, compassionate, good-hearted, humane, kind, kindhearted, sympathetic, tenderhearted

2 difficult to endure ⟨the *cruel* climate of the Arctic⟩ — see HARSH 1

3 hard to accept or bear especially emotionally ⟨the *cruel* situation of being orphaned at an early age⟩ — see BITTER 2

4 having or showing a desire to cause someone pain or suffering for the sheer enjoyment of it ⟨My cat seems *cruel* when she catches a mouse, but it's her nature.⟩ — see HATEFUL

cruelty *n* disposition to willfully inflict pain and suffering on others ⟨Centuries after he ravaged Europe, Attila the Hun remains notorious for his *cruelty*.⟩
synonyms atrociousness, atrocity, barbarity, brutality, heartlessness, inhumanity, sadism, savageness, savagery, truculence, viciousness, wantonness
related words hard-heartedness, mercilessness, pitilessness, ruthlessness, unfeelingness; ferociousness, ferocity, fierceness, grimness; bloodlust, bloodthirstiness, murderousness, sanguineness, sanguinity; cattiness, hatefulness, malevolence, maliciousness, malignity, meanness, nasti-

ness, spitefulness; hardhandedness, harshness, heavy-handedness, oppressiveness
near antonyms warmheartedness, warmness, warmth; charitableness, clemency, leniency, mercifulness, mercy, pity
antonyms compassion, good-heartedness, humanity, kindheartedness, kindness, sympathy
cruise *n* a journey over water in a vessel ⟨took a luxury *cruise* for their first wedding anniversary⟩ — see SAIL
cruise *vb* 1 to move about from place to place aimlessly ⟨The girls happily *cruised* around the mall for hours.⟩ — see WANDER 1
2 to move or proceed smoothly and readily ⟨She's been *cruising* through her daily physical therapy with remarkable ease.⟩ — see FLOW 2
3 to travel on water in a vessel ⟨*cruised* to the Bahamas in their yacht⟩ — see SAIL 1
crumb *n* 1 a very small amount ⟨There is not a *crumb* of proof to support that claim.⟩ — see PARTICLE 1
2 a very small piece ⟨Eating pretzels in bed got *crumbs* between the sheets.⟩ — see BIT 1
crumble *vb* to become worse or of less value ⟨The stock of the energy company *crumbled* after the revelations of fraud and mismanagement.⟩ — see DETERIORATE 1
crumbly *adj* having a texture that readily breaks into little pieces under pressure ⟨a *crumbly* shortbread cookie⟩ — see CRISP 1
crummy *also* **crumby** *adj* falling short of a standard ⟨The dry cleaners did a *crummy* job of pressing my suit.⟩ — see BAD 1
crumple *vb* 1 to create (as by crushing) an irregular mass of creases in ⟨*crumpled* the piece of paper and angrily threw it in the wastebasket⟩
synonyms crinkle, rumple, scrunch, wrinkle
related words corrugate, crease, crimp, fold, pleat, pucker, ruck; crisp, ripple, ruffle; contract, furrow, knit; mess (up), muss (up)
near antonyms even, iron, press, straighten; unfold; tidy
antonyms flatten, iron out, smooth, smoothen, uncrumple
2 to fall down or in as a result of physical pressure ⟨The box *crumpled* when I accidentally dropped a brick on it.⟩ — see COLLAPSE 1
crunch *n* 1 a falling short of an essential or desirable amount or number ⟨a severe energy *crunch* that resulted in long lines at the gas pumps⟩ — see DEFICIENCY
2 a time or state of affairs requiring prompt or decisive action ⟨a player who's always good in a *crunch*, like when we need a goal to win the soccer match⟩ — see EMERGENCY
crunch *vb* to press or strike against or together so as to make a scraping sound ⟨I could hear the bicycle gears *crunch* as I shifted the derailleur.⟩ — see GRIND 2
crunch (on) *vb* to crush or grind with the teeth ⟨She *crunched on* a carrot while watching TV.⟩ — see BITE (ON)
crusade *n* a series of activities undertaken to achieve a goal ⟨a grassroots *crusade* for spending more money on our public schools⟩ — see CAMPAIGN
crusader *n* one who is intensely or excessively devoted to a cause ⟨a *crusader* for improved safety in coal mines⟩ — see ZEALOT
crush *n* 1 a strong but often short-lived liking for another person ⟨Sue fondly remembers the *crush* that she had on a boy one summer long ago.⟩
synonyms infatuation, passion
related words fixation, obsession; affection, devotion, fondness, love; craze, fad, rage, vogue
2 a great number of persons or creatures massed togeth-

er ⟨The huge *crush* in the store must have far exceeded safety limits.⟩ — see CROWD 1
crush *vb* 1 to cause to become a pulpy mass ⟨dark-colored grapes that will be *crushed* to make red wine⟩
synonyms mash, pulp, squash
related words press, squeeze; beat, pound, powder, pulverize
2 to put a stop to (something) by the use of force ⟨The government is doing everything to *crush* the latest guerrilla uprising.⟩ — see QUELL 1
3 to reduce to fine particles ⟨*crushed* the baby's medicine tablet and mixed it with applesauce⟩ — see POWDER
4 to subject to incapacitating emotional or mental stress ⟨The terrible news of her death simply *crushed* the entire family.⟩ — see OVERWHELM 1
5 to apply external pressure on so as to force out the juice or contents of ⟨After *crushing* the grapes, let the skins soak in the juice in order to extract some color.⟩ — see ²PRESS 2
6 to fit (people or things) into a tight space ⟨Everything from his apartment was *crushed* into the back of the truck.⟩ — see CROWD 1
7 to put one's arms around and press tightly ⟨She tearfully *crushed* the child to her breast.⟩ — see EMBRACE 1
crusher *n* something (as a fact or argument) that is decisive or overwhelming ⟨The *crusher* was that we would be out of town that weekend in any event.⟩ — see CLINCHER
crusty *adj* being or characterized by direct, brief, and potentially rude speech or manner ⟨a *crusty* old fisherman who doesn't care to have his picture taken with silly tourists⟩ — see BLUNT 1
crux *n* the central part or aspect of something under consideration ⟨The *crux* of the problem is that the school's current budget is totally inadequate.⟩
synonyms core, essence, gist, heart, meat, net, nub, nubbin, nucleus, pith, pivot, point, root, sum
related words course, direction, drift, tenor; body, content, substance; hypothesis, proposition, purport, subject, theme, thesis
phrases sum and substance, the long and short (*or* the long and the short)
cry *n* 1 a loud vocal expression of strong emotion ⟨The boy let out a joyful *cry* when his lost dog returned home.⟩ — see SHOUT
2 a natural vocal sound made by an animal ⟨the lonesome *cry* of a coyote⟩ — see CALL 1
3 an attention-getting word or phrase used to publicize something (as a campaign or product) ⟨"A chance to change America" was the *cry* on which the candidate was hoping to win the White House.⟩ — see SLOGAN
4 an earnest request ⟨The king was deaf to their *cries*.⟩ — see PLEA 1
5 a sudden short emotional utterance ⟨*Cries* of disbelief greeted the announcement of the surprise winner for best picture.⟩ — see EXCLAMATION
cry *vb* 1 to shed tears often while making meaningless sounds as a sign of pain or distress ⟨Some kids started to *cry* even before the doctor had given them their shot.⟩
synonyms bawl, blubber, sob, weep
related words grieve, keen, lament, mourn; howl, scream, squall, wail, yowl; mewl, pule, whimper, whine; sniffle, snivel; groan, moan, sigh
2 to utter one's distinctive animal sound ⟨We knew that we were getting very close to the ocean when we could hear sea gulls *crying*.⟩
synonyms call, sing
3 to speak so as to be heard at a distance ⟨We heard someone *cry* "Wait!" but the train pulled away anyway.⟩ — see CALL 1

cry (out) *vb* to utter with a sudden burst of strong feeling ⟨"I can't stand it!" he *cried out.*⟩ — see EXCLAIM

crybaby *n* a person who makes frequent complaints usually about little things ⟨car trips that were often spoiled by a couple of *crybabies* in the back seat⟩
synonyms baby, bellyacher, complainer, fusser, griper, grumbler, whiner
related words bawler, bleater, moaner, screamer, squawker, wailer, weeper; crab, grump, malcontent
near antonyms happy camper

cry down *vb* to express scornfully one's low opinion of ⟨She *cried down* any party to which she wasn't invited.⟩ — see DECRY 1

crying *adj* needing immediate attention ⟨a *crying* need for more activities for young people in this town⟩ — see ACUTE 2

crypt *n* an underground burial chamber ⟨The old church's *crypt* is the final resting place for the president and his beloved wife.⟩
synonyms catacomb(s), vault
related words mausoleum, sepulture, tomb

cryptic *adj* 1 being beyond one's powers to know, understand, or explain ⟨puzzled by the *cryptic* e-mail message left on his computer⟩ — see MYSTERIOUS 1
2 having an often intentionally veiled or uncertain meaning ⟨The oracle offered only *cryptic* predictions that could be interpreted any number of different ways.⟩ — see OBSCURE 1

crystalline *adj* easily seen through ⟨We could see fish swimming beneath the *crystalline* ice of the frozen lake.⟩ — see CLEAR 1

crystallize *also* **crystalize** *vb* to take on a definite form ⟨After months of planning, the project is finally starting to *crystallize.*⟩ — see FORM 1

cub *n* 1 a person who is just starting out in a field of activity ⟨the kind of big story that can propel a *cub* reporter into the stratosphere of the newspaper world⟩ — see BEGINNER
2 a young person who is between infancy and adulthood ⟨assigned to teach a bunch of young *cubs* how to play baseball⟩ — see CHILD 1

cubicle *n* one of the parts into which an enclosed space is divided ⟨data entry clerks busily typing in *cubicles*⟩ — see COMPARTMENT

cuddle *vb* to lie close ⟨kittens *cuddling* in a basket⟩ — see NUZZLE

cudgel *n* a heavy rigid stick used as a weapon or for punishment ⟨A farmer armed with a *cudgel* drove us off his land.⟩ — see CLUB 1

¹**cue** *n* a slight or indirect pointing to something (as a solution or explanation) ⟨Taking a *cue* from nature, scientists are developing safe and effective insecticides using insect hormones.⟩ — see HINT 1

²**cue** *n* a series of persons or things arranged one behind another ⟨The *cue* to get tickets to the concert moved with agonizing slowness.⟩ — see LINE 1

¹**cuff** *n* a hard strike with a part of the body or an instrument ⟨The mama cat would give her kittens a *cuff* with a paw whenever they played too rough.⟩ — see ¹BLOW

²**cuff** *n, usually* **cuffs** *pl* something that physically prevents free movement ⟨The policeman snapped the *cuffs* on and led the prisoner away to the car.⟩ — see BOND 1

cuisine *n* the art or style of preparing food (as in a specified region) ⟨spent several years in Tuscany mastering Italian *cuisine*⟩ — see COOKERY

cull *n* something separated from a group or lot for not being as good as the others ⟨The unbruised apples will be packed in bags, and the *culls* will be used for cider.⟩
synonyms discard, reject, rejection, second

related words castaway, throwaway; hand-me-down, white elephant; rubbish, scrap, trash, waste

cull *vb* to decide to accept (someone or something) from a group of possibilities ⟨*culled* the best short stories from the author's body of writings⟩ — see CHOOSE 1

culminate *vb* to bring to a triumphant conclusion ⟨*culminated* the school year with a trip to New York⟩ — see CROWN

culmination *n* the highest part or point ⟨an acting performance that was seen as the *culmination* of a brilliant career on the stage⟩ — see HEIGHT 1

culpability *n* responsibility for wrongdoing or failure ⟨cannot find *culpability* where there is neither knowledge that a crime has been committed nor evidence of intent to commit a crime⟩ — see BLAME 1

culpable *adj* deserving reproach or blame ⟨She's more *culpable* than the other children because she's old enough to know better.⟩ — see BLAMEWORTHY

culprit *n* a person who has committed a crime ⟨The police caught the *culprit* a mere two blocks from the scene of the crime.⟩ — see CRIMINAL

cult *n* 1 a group of people showing intense devotion to a cause, person, or work (as a film) ⟨Long after it had gone off the air, the TV series continued to have a huge *cult.*⟩
synonyms following
related words discipleship; fandom
2 a body of beliefs and practices regarding the supernatural and the worship of one or more deities ⟨an ancient *cult* that centered on the worship of the earth as the source of all life⟩ — see RELIGION 1

cultivate *vb* 1 to come to have gradually ⟨*cultivated* a taste for opera in order to fit in with his new circle of friends⟩ — see DEVELOP 2
2 to help the growth or development of ⟨*cultivated* a passion for learning among his students over the years⟩ — see FOSTER 1
3 to look after or assist the growth of by labor and care ⟨She *cultivates* her own vegetables in a small backyard garden.⟩ — see GROW 1
4 to work by plowing, sowing, and raising crops on ⟨We ought to *cultivate* the field out back.⟩ — see FARM

cultivated *adj* having or showing a taste for the fine arts and gracious living ⟨The museum's annual gala for charity attracts not only a very wealthy, but also a very *cultivated* crowd.⟩
synonyms accomplished, civilized, cultured, genteel, polished, refined
related words cerebral, highbrow, high-toned, intellectual, intellectualist; bourgeois, middlebrow; educated, erudite, knowledgeable, learned, literate, scholarly, well-read; civil, courteous, mannerly, polite, well-bred; cosmopolitan, sophisticated, urbane; hypercivilized, over-civilized, oversophisticated
near antonyms ignorant, illiterate, uneducated, unlettered; lowbrow, unintelligent; coarse, ill-bred, ill-mannered; backwoods, provincial, rustic (*also* rustical); inelegant, polyester, unsophisticated; boorish, churlish, cloddish, clownish, crude, uncouth, vulgar
antonyms barbaric, barbarous, philistine, uncivilized, uncultured, ungenteel, unpolished, unrefined

cultivation *n* a high level of taste and enlightenment as a result of extensive intellectual training and exposure to the arts ⟨People of *cultivation* appreciate the special experience that only live theater can provide.⟩ — see CULTURE 1

cultivator *n* a person who cultivates the land and grows crops on it ⟨encountered an indigenous people who were experienced *cultivators* of the soil as well as highly skilled craftsmen⟩ — see FARMER

cultural *adj* of or relating to the fine arts ⟨With its many museums, theaters, and opera and ballet companies, the city is a *cultural* paradise.⟩
synonyms artistic
related words aesthetic (*also* esthetic *or* aesthetical *or* esthetical), tasteful
near antonyms nonaesthetic
antonyms nonartistic, noncultural

culture *n* **1** a high level of taste and enlightenment as a result of extensive intellectual training and exposure to the arts ⟨Because of its wide reputation as a place of *culture*, Boston became known as "the Athens of America."⟩
synonyms accomplishment, civilization, cultivation, polish, refinement
related words education, erudition, intellectualism, intellectuality, knowledge, learning, scholarship; cosmopolitanism, sophistication, urbanity; gentility, manners; class, elegance, grace, taste; civility, courteousness, courtesy, politeness
near antonyms ignorance, illiteracy; parochialism, provincialism, rusticity, unsophistication; boorishness, churlishness, clownishness, coarseness, crudeness, vulgarity
antonyms barbarianism, barbarism, philistinism
2 the way people live at a particular time and place ⟨a study of ancient Anasazi *culture* as it existed in the canyons of the American Southwest⟩ — see CIVILIZATION 1

culture *vb* to look after or assist the growth of by labor and care ⟨*culture* bacteria in laboratory dishes⟩ — see GROW 1

cultured *adj* having or showing a taste for the fine arts and gracious living ⟨the most highly *cultured* period of the country's long history⟩ — see CULTIVATED

cumbersome *adj* difficult to use or operate especially because of size, weight, or design ⟨a long-handled wrench that is too *cumbersome* for tight spots, such as under the sink⟩
synonyms awkward, clumsy, cranky, cumbrous, ponderous, ungainly, unhandy, unwieldy
related words uncontrollable, unmanageable; bulky, elephantine, heavy, hulking, massive
near antonyms functional, practicable, practical, serviceable, useful
antonyms handy

cumbrous *adj* difficult to use or operate especially because of size, weight, or design ⟨It took two people to haul the *cumbrous* machine into the garage.⟩ — see CUMBERSOME

cummerbund *also* **cumberbund** *n* a strip of flexible material (as leather) worn around the waist ⟨A *cummerbund* is the perfect accessory for a man's tuxedo.⟩ — see ²BELT 1

cumulative *adj* produced by a series of additions of identical or similar things ⟨The *cumulative* scores will determine the winner.⟩
synonyms additive, incremental
related words gradual, step-by-step, stepwise; increscent, progressive; accruable, accrued, aggregated, amassed, built-up, compiled, conglomerated
near antonyms regressive

cunning *adj* **1** clever at attaining one's ends by indirect and often deceptive means ⟨a *cunning*, underhanded plan to win the election by preying on people's fears and prejudices⟩ — see ARTFUL 1
2 skillful with the hands ⟨Only the most *cunning* cabinetmaker could have crafted such a beautifully proportioned chest of drawers.⟩ — see DEXTEROUS 1

cunning *n* **1** skill in achieving one's ends through indirect, subtle, or underhanded means ⟨the *cunning* with which

Tom Sawyer was able to get others to whitewash the fence for him⟩
synonyms artfulness, artifice, caginess (*also* cageyness), canniness, craft, craftiness, deviousness, foxiness, guile, slickness, slyness, sneakiness, subtleness, subtlety, wiliness
related words calculation, care, design; savvy, sharpness, shrewdness; cleverness, ingeniousness, ingenuity, inventiveness; ease, facility, finesse; deceitfulness, duplicity, shiftiness, underhandedness
2 subtle or imaginative ability in inventing, devising, or executing something ⟨the unmatched *cunning* of the scout who led them safely through the trackless wilderness⟩ — see SKILL 1
3 the inclination or practice of misleading others through lies or trickery ⟨used *cunning* and subterfuge to work her way up the corporate ladder⟩ — see DECEIT 1

cup *n* a round vessel equipped with a handle and designed for drinking ⟨a large *cup* that can hold almost a pint of hot chocolate⟩
synonyms mug
related words beaker, stein, tankard; chalice, goblet; demitasse, noggin; teacup

cupboard *n* **1** a built-in space for storage behind a door ⟨The colonial dining room features a double-door corner *cupboard* for the family's finest china.⟩ — see CLOSET 1
2 a storage case typically having doors and shelves ⟨Dishes go in the *cupboard* next to the sink.⟩ — see CABINET

cupidity *n* an intense selfish desire for wealth or possessions ⟨Reports of great treasure in the Indies inflamed the *cupidity* of Columbus's crew.⟩ — see GREED

cur *n* **1** a person who shows a shameful lack of courage in the face of danger ⟨denounced as *curs* those officers who deserted their posts⟩ — see COWARD
2 a person whose behavior is offensive to others ⟨Only a *cur* would abandon his friends.⟩ — see JERK 1

curb *n* something that limits one's freedom of action or choice ⟨These international regulations act as a *curb* on the plundering of a nation's archaeological treasures.⟩ — see RESTRICTION 1

curb *vb* to keep from exceeding a desirable degree or level (as of expression) ⟨Try to *curb* your curiosity when it comes to your neighbors' business.⟩ — see CONTROL 1

curdy *adj* having small pieces or lumps spread throughout ⟨*curdy* cottage cheese⟩ — see CHUNKY 1

cure *n* **1** something that corrects or counteracts something undesirable ⟨A fun hobby is always a good *cure* for boredom.⟩
synonyms corrective, remedy
related words cure-all, elixir, panacea; answer, solution; aid, help, relief, succor; medicine, palliative
2 a substance or preparation used to treat disease ⟨researchers tirelessly working to find a *cure* for cancer⟩ — see MEDICINE

cure *vb* **1** to bring about recovery from ⟨Do you have anything that will *cure* my headache?⟩
synonyms heal, mend, remedy
related words allay, alleviate, assuage, relieve; palliate, soothe; ease, lighten, moderate, temper; doctor, nurse; medicate, treat; diagnose
near antonyms aggravate, worsen; misdiagnose, overdiagnose, underdiagnose
2 to restore to a healthy condition ⟨The antibiotic *cured* the sick boy of the bacterial infection.⟩ — see HEAL 1

cure–all *n* something that cures all ills or problems ⟨Raising a young person's self-esteem is not the *cure-all* that some people think.⟩
synonyms elixir, panacea

related words magic bullet, silver bullet; corrective, cure, remedy; miracle drug, wonder drug

curio *n* **1** a small object displayed for its attractiveness or interest ⟨Be careful of the fragile *curios* on the end tables.⟩ — see KNICKKNACK

2 something strange or unusual that is an object of interest ⟨a museum's collection of *curios* brought back from the Far East by 19th-century traders⟩ — see CURIOSITY 2

curiosity *n* **1** an eager desire to find out about things that are often none of one's business ⟨Our neighbor's *curiosity* about what we were doing last night was really offensive.⟩

synonyms curiousness, inquisitiveness, nosiness

related words attentiveness, concern, interest, regard, wonderment; inquiry, interrogation, prying, questioning; interference, intrusiveness, meddlesomeness, obtrusiveness, officiousness; eavesdropping, rubbernecking

near antonyms apathy, disinterestedness, disregard, indifference, unconcern

2 something strange or unusual that is an object of interest ⟨The museum's *curiosities* include items constructed entirely out of toothpicks.⟩

synonyms curio, exotic, oddity, oddment, rarity

related words marvel, prodigy, rara avis, rare bird, wonder; abnormality, anomaly, freak, monster, monstrosity; malformation, mutant, mutation

3 a small object displayed for its attractiveness or interest ⟨an assortment of *curiosities* from around the world that the family picked up during various vacations⟩ — see KNICKKNACK

4 an odd or peculiar habit ⟨Charles Dickens typically endowed his characters with an array of endearing *curiosities*.⟩ — see IDIOSYNCRASY

curious *adj* **1** interested in what is not one's own business ⟨*Curious* neighbors peered out of their windows as the new people moved in.⟩

synonyms inquisitive, nosy (*or* nosey), prying, snoopy

related words interfering, intrusive, meddlesome, meddling, obtrusive, officious; inquisitional, inquisitorial, questioning, quizzical; concerned, interested

near antonyms apathetic, disinterested, indifferent, unconcerned, uninterested

antonyms incurious, uncurious

2 different from the ordinary in a way that causes curiosity or suspicion ⟨That's a pretty *curious* coincidence.⟩ — see ODD 2

3 noticeably different from what is generally found or experienced ⟨That is one of the most *curious* paintings I've ever seen.⟩ — see UNUSUAL 1

curiousness *n* an eager desire to find out about things that are often none of one's business ⟨Children have a natural *curiousness* about everything.⟩ — see CURIOSITY 1

curl *n* a length of hair that forms a loop or series of loops ⟨a little girl with beautiful shining *curls*⟩

synonyms ringlet

related words crimp, wave; perm, permanent, set; lock, tress

curl *vb* to follow a circular or spiral course ⟨An inviting path for joggers *curls* around the reservoir.⟩ — see WIND 1

curled *adj* **1** forming or styled into loops ⟨The strokes of the capital letters were elaborately *curled*.⟩ — see CURLY

2 marked by a long series of irregular curves ⟨a *curled* and complicated route through a series of caves⟩ — see CROOKED 1

curling *adj* marked by a long series of irregular curves ⟨a *curling* labyrinth designed to discourage grave robbers from ever finding the inner burial chamber⟩ — see CROOKED 1

curl up *vb* to sit or recline comfortably or cozily ⟨I love to *curl up* in a big chair with a book.⟩ — see SNUGGLE 1

curly *adj* forming or styled into loops ⟨the boy's naturally *curly* locks⟩

synonyms curled

related words crimped, crimpy, crisp, frizzled, frizzy, kinky, waved, wavy

near antonyms lank, limp; straightened

antonyms straight, uncurled

curmudgeon *n* an irritable and complaining person ⟨Only a *curmudgeon* would object to the nursing home's holiday decorations.⟩ — see GROUCH 1

currency *n* something (as pieces of stamped metal or printed paper) customarily and legally used as a medium of exchange, a measure of value, or a means of payment ⟨I prefer to carry only paper *currency*, as coins are too heavy.⟩ — see MONEY

current *adj* **1** accepted, used, or practiced by most people ⟨*Current* wisdom on parenting favors allowing children lots of self-expression.⟩

synonyms conventional, customary, going, popular, prevailing, prevalent, standard, stock, usual

related words average, common, everyday, normal, ordinary; regular, routine; ubiquitous, universal, widespread; accustomed, wonted; fashionable, in, modish, stylish

near antonyms abnormal, exceptional, extraordinary, uncommon

antonyms nonstandard, unconventional, unpopular, unusual

2 being or involving the latest methods, concepts, information, or styles ⟨*Current* therapies for treating cancer have success rates that were undreamed of only a few decades ago.⟩ — see MODERN

3 existing or in progress right now ⟨the *current* fundraising effort⟩ — see PRESENT 1

current *n* **1** a prevailing or general movement or inclination ⟨The *currents* of fashion are always changing.⟩ — see TREND 1

2 noticeable movement of air in a particular direction ⟨curtains that were being lightly lifted by a fresh *current* from the open window⟩ — see ¹WIND 1

currently *adv* at the present time ⟨We're *currently* working on three separate projects.⟩ — see NOW 1

curse *n* **1** a prayer that harm will come to someone ⟨uttered a *curse* upon his persecutor from the scaffold⟩

synonyms anathema, ban, execration, imprecation, malediction

related words censure, condemnation, damnation, denunciation, excommunication; hex, jinx, mojo, spell, voodoo; pox

near antonyms citation, commendation, endorsement (*also* indorsement)

antonyms benediction, benison, blessing

2 a source of harm or misfortune ⟨Intolerance of personal differences is a *curse* of humanity.⟩ — see BANE 1

curse *vb* **1** to ask a divine power to send harm or evil upon ⟨I *curse* whoever had the idea of having annoying salespeople call up innocent people to sell them things they don't want.⟩

synonyms imprecate

related words condemn, damn, denounce, execrate, reprobate; hex, jinx, voodoo; darn (*also* durn), dash; cuss (out), fulminate (against), rail (against), revile

near antonyms applaud, commend, congratulate

antonyms bless

2 to cause persistent suffering to ⟨Misfortunes and problems seem to have *cursed* everyone ever associated with that house.⟩ — see AFFLICT

3 to use offensive or indecent language ⟨You'll have to put a quarter in the jar every time you *curse*.⟩ — see SWEAR 1

4 to use profane or obscene language at or about ⟨She *cursed* him for showing up late again.⟩ — see DAMN 1

cursorily *adv* with excessive or careless speed ⟨*cursorily* glanced over the report before tossing it to one side⟩ — see HASTILY 1

cursory *adj* acting or done with excessive or careless speed ⟨Your essays require more than a *cursory* effort at proofreading.⟩ — see HASTY 1

curt *adj* **1** being or characterized by direct, brief, and potentially rude speech or manner ⟨She was offended by the *curt* reply to her well-meaning question.⟩ — see BLUNT 1

2 marked by the use of few words to convey much information or meaning ⟨On a daily basis she e-mailed to her commanders *curt* reports on the situation.⟩ — see CONCISE

curtail *vb* to make less in extent or duration ⟨*curtailed* the school day because of the stormy weather⟩ — see SHORTEN

curtain *n* **1** something that covers or conceals like a piece of cloth ⟨There has long been a *curtain* of secrecy surrounding that religious sect.⟩ — see CLOAK 1

2 curtains *pl* pieces of cloth hung to darken, decorate, or divide a room ⟨The kittens keep climbing the *curtains*.⟩ — see DRAPERY

3 curtains *pl* the permanent stopping of all the vital bodily activities ⟨It'll be *curtains* for us if we're caught.⟩ — see DEATH 1

curtain *vb* to keep secret or shut off from view ⟨She dropped her head and in shame *curtained* her face with her hair.⟩ — see ¹HIDE 2

curvature *n* something that curves or is curved ⟨*Curvature* of the spine is called scoliosis.⟩ — see BEND 1

curve *n* something that curves or is curved ⟨the bold *curve* of the racing yacht's hull⟩ — see BEND 1

curve *vb* **1** to turn away from a straight line or course ⟨After following a straight path most of the way down the mountain, the ski trail abruptly *curves* to the right.⟩
synonyms arc, arch, bend, bow, crook, hook, round, sweep, swerve, trend, wheel
related words circle, coil, curlicue, curl, loop, spiral; turn, twist, wind; deviate, veer
antonyms straighten

2 to cause to turn away from a straight line ⟨*curved* the wood to make a bow⟩ — see BEND 1

curved *adj* marked by a long series of irregular curves ⟨a *curved* strip of metal that had sheared off during the collision⟩ — see CROOKED 1

curving *adj* marked by a long series of irregular curves ⟨The *curving* shoreline on the island's south side is a beachcomber's paradise.⟩ — see CROOKED 1

cushion *n* something that serves as a protective barrier ⟨used a blanket as a *cushion* between the two tables in the moving van⟩
synonyms buffer, bumper, cocoon, fender, pad
related words baffle, muffler; padding; safeguard, shield; barricade, cordon

cushion *vb* to lessen the shock of ⟨A substantial nest egg helped to *cushion* the sudden loss of her job.⟩
synonyms buffer, gentle, soften
related words baffle, dampen, deaden, dull; moderate, modulate, temper; allay, alleviate, assuage, ease; lighten, mitigate, relieve
near antonyms heighten, intensify, sharpen

cushy *adj* providing physical comfort ⟨a big *cushy* chair that's perfect for watching television⟩ — see COMFORTABLE 1

cusp *n* **1** an interval of time just before the onset of something ⟨medical researchers who are on the *cusp* of a major breakthrough⟩ — see POINT 3

2 the last and usually sharp or tapering part of something long and narrow ⟨the *cusp* of a fang⟩ — see POINT 2

cuss *vb* to use offensive or indecent language ⟨The little girl clapped her hands over her ears when her brother started *cussing*.⟩ — see SWEAR 1

custodian *n* **1** a person who takes care of a property sometimes for an absent owner ⟨The *custodian* made his usual rounds of the building to make sure that everything was OK.⟩
synonyms caretaker, guardian, janitor, keeper, warden, watchman
related words curator; sexton, steward

2 a person or group that watches over someone or something ⟨served as *custodian* of the prisoner until he could be turned over to federal authorities⟩ — see GUARD 1

3 someone that protects ⟨We must regard ourselves as *custodians* of the Earth so that its natural resources may be enjoyed by many generations to come.⟩ — see PROTECTOR

custody *n* responsibility for the safety and well-being of someone or something ⟨the government department having *custody* of all official state gifts⟩
synonyms care, guardianship, keeping, safekeeping, trust, ward
related words control, governorship, hand(s), management, superintendence, supervision

custom *adj* made or fitted to the needs or preferences of a specific customer ⟨That business tycoon wears only *custom* suits.⟩ — see CUSTOM-MADE

custom *n* **1** a usual manner of behaving or doing ⟨It is my *custom* to have half a bagel and coffee for breakfast.⟩ — see HABIT 1

2 an inherited or established way of thinking, feeling, or doing ⟨The *custom* around here is that the bride's family pays for the wedding.⟩ — see TRADITION 1

3 transactions or economic support provided by customers ⟨That restaurant certainly lost my *custom* after they were cited for health code violations.⟩ — see BUSINESS 1

customary *adj* **1** accepted, used, or practiced by most people ⟨The *customary* response to the greeting "How are you?" is "Fine, thanks!"⟩ — see CURRENT 1

2 based on customs usually handed down from a previous generation ⟨the *customary* toasting of the bride and groom at their wedding reception⟩ — see TRADITIONAL 1

customer *n* **1** a person who buys a product or uses a service from a business ⟨The store greatly values its regular *customers*.⟩
synonyms account, client, guest, patron
related words consumer, end user, user; buyer, correspondent, purchaser; browser, prospect, shopper, window-shopper; bargainer, haggler; regular
near antonyms merchant, seller, vendor (*also* vender); shopkeeper, tradesman; black marketer (*or* black marketeer), fence

2 a member of the human race ⟨He's one tough *customer*, so you'd better not cross him.⟩ — see HUMAN

customized *adj* made or fitted to the needs or preferences of a specific customer ⟨a *customized* car for a physically challenged person⟩ — see CUSTOM-MADE

custom–made *adj* made or fitted to the needs or preferences of a specific customer ⟨an odd-sized window that will require the purchase of *custom-made* curtains⟩
synonyms custom, customized, tailored, tailor-made
related words particular, special, specialized; custom-built; made-to-measure
antonyms mass-produced, ready-made

cut *n* **1** a piece that has been separated from the whole by cutting ⟨Choose *cuts* of meat that have very little visible fat.⟩

synonyms cutting, slice

related words chop, cutlet; length, part, portion, section, segment; chunk, hunk, lump; clipping, paring, shaving, sliver, snippet, splinter

2 an individual part of a process, series, or ranking ⟨One of the new recruits is a *cut* above the rest in intelligence.⟩ — see DEGREE 1

3 something belonging to, due to, or contributed by an individual member of a group ⟨I received my *cut* of the profits from the garage sale.⟩ — see SHARE 1

4 an act or expression showing scorn and usually intended to hurt another's feelings ⟨Completely ignoring her was the unkindest *cut* of all.⟩ — see INSULT

cut *vb* **1** to penetrate with a sharp edge (as a knife) ⟨I *cut* my hand on a piece of broken glass.⟩

synonyms gash, incise, rip, shear, slash, slice, slit

related words crosscut, hacksaw, saw, scissor; cleave, rive, split; pierce, stab; bruise, butcher, hack, haggle, lacerate, mangle; rend, tear; carve, chip, chisel, notch; anatomize, dissect, section; chop, dice, mince; amputate, cut off, sever

2 to fail to attend ⟨a warning that she had been *cutting* too many classes without valid excuses⟩

synonyms miss, skip

related words ignore, neglect, pass over

phrases absent oneself, play hooky

antonyms attend, show up (for)

3 to deliberately ignore or treat rudely ⟨The snobbish lady *cut* anyone who didn't meet her standards of wealth and social standing.⟩ — see SNUB 1

4 to make (something) shorter or smaller with the use of a cutting instrument ⟨When you *cut* the pad, make it a little smaller than the carpet.⟩ — see CLIP 1

5 to shorten the standing leafy plant cover of ⟨You need to *cut* the lawn very soon—before it becomes a jungle.⟩ — see MOW 1

6 to alter (something) for the worse with the addition of foreign or lower-grade substances ⟨The fruit juice was so *cut* with water that it was barely a fruit-flavored drink.⟩ — see ADULTERATE

7 to depart abruptly from a straight line or course ⟨*cut* towards the goal, eluding a defender⟩ — see SWERVE 1

8 to divide by passing through or across ⟨A long mountain range virtually *cuts* that country in half.⟩ — see INTERSECT

9 to identify and examine the basic elements or parts of (something) especially for discovering interrelationships ⟨Whichever way you *cut* it, we won't be seeing any profits from the business for at least three years.⟩ — see ANALYZE

cut (across) *vb* to make one's way through, across, or over ⟨*Cut across* the field on the way to school.⟩ — see TRAVERSE

cut (down) *vb* to bring down by cutting ⟨We need to *cut down* that dying tree.⟩ — see FELL 2

cut back *vb* **1** to make (something) shorter or smaller with the use of a cutting instrument ⟨We need to *cut back* the bushes a bit so that the house number is visible from the street.⟩ — see CLIP 1

2 to make less in extent or duration ⟨*cut back* the meeting so everyone could leave early for the long weekend⟩ — see SHORTEN

cute *adj* **1** clever at attaining one's ends by indirect and often deceptive means ⟨She's very nice, but she's not afraid to get *cute* when there's something she wants.⟩ — see ARTFUL 1

2 making light of something usually regarded as serious or sacred ⟨We're having a serious discussion here, so cut the *cute* remarks.⟩ — see FLIPPANT

3 very pleasing to look at ⟨a *cute* baby that no one could resist cooing over⟩ — see BEAUTIFUL 1

cuteness *n* the qualities in a person or thing that as a whole give pleasure to the senses ⟨That kitten's *cuteness* is simply overwhelming!⟩ — see BEAUTY 1

cut in *vb* to cause a disruption in a conversation or discussion ⟨a stranger *cut in* with unsolicited advice on how we could fix our relationship⟩ — see INTERRUPT

cutlet *n* a small usually rounded mass of minced food that has been fried ⟨a breaded veal *cutlet*⟩ — see CAKE 1

cut off *vb* **1** to bring (as an action or operation) to an immediate end ⟨The majority party *cut off* debate and forced a vote on the bill.⟩ — see STOP 1

2 to set or keep apart from others ⟨The dog *cut off* the one sheep that had to be sheared.⟩ — see ISOLATE

cut out *vb* **1** to stop functioning ⟨The engine abruptly *cut out.*⟩ — see FAIL 1

2 to bring (as an action or operation) to an immediate end ⟨Now *cut* that *out*, or I'm turning this car around!⟩ — see STOP 1

3 to leave a place often for another ⟨After a few minutes of their brainless conversation I was ready to *cut out.*⟩ — see GO 2

4 to take the place of ⟨This ambitious new friend of hers seems to be *cutting out* people that she's known for years.⟩ — see REPLACE 1

cut–rate *adj* **1** costing little ⟨opted for a *cut-rate* insurance policy because we didn't need anything more⟩ — see CHEAP 1

2 of low quality ⟨a *cut-rate* motel that looked like the kind at which people in horror movies always end up⟩ — see CHEAP 2

cutter *n* an instrument with a metal length that has a sharp edge for cutting ⟨a fabric *cutter*⟩ — see KNIFE

cutthroat *adj* not guided by or showing a concern for what is right ⟨*cutthroat* business practices intended to drive competitors out of business⟩ — see UNPRINCIPLED

cutthroat *n* a person who kills another person ⟨While traveling the ancient Silk Road, traders were constant prey to *cutthroats* and thieves.⟩ — see ASSASSIN

cutting *adj* **1** causing intense discomfort to one's skin ⟨a frigid day with a *cutting* wind that made it seem even colder⟩

synonyms biting, bitter, keen, penetrating, piercing, raw, sharp, shrewd, smarting, stinging

related words brisk, invigorating, nippy, snappy; needlelike, prickly, tingling; caustic

near antonyms balmy, gentle, mild, soothing

2 having an edge thin enough to cut or pierce something ⟨the *cutting* side of the sword blade⟩ — see SHARP 1

3 marked by the use of wit that is intended to cause hurt feelings ⟨Her *cutting* comments really upset me, and we haven't spoken since.⟩ — see SARCASTIC

cutting *n* a piece that has been separated from the whole by cutting ⟨a bag full of grass *cuttings*⟩ — see CUT 1

cut up *vb* to engage in attention-getting playful or boisterous behavior ⟨high-spirited cousins who *cut up* at every family gathering⟩

synonyms act up, clown (around), horse around, monkey (around), show off, skylark

related words carry on, misbehave; roughhouse; caper, cavort, disport, frisk, frolic, gambol, lark, rollick, romp; carouse, revel, roar, wassail

cycle *n* **1** a series of events or actions that repeat themselves regularly and in the same order ⟨the *cycle* of birth, growth, decline, and death that is experienced by all life forms⟩

synonyms circle, round, wheel

related words pattern, syndrome; course, development,

progression, run; beat, loop, ring; revolution, rotation, turn, turnover; chain, sequence, series, string, succession, train

2 a long or seemingly long period of time ⟨Years, centuries, and *cycles* will pass before I budge on that issue!⟩ — see AGE 2

cynic *n* a person who distrusts other people and believes that everything is done for selfish reasons ⟨a *cynic* who believes that nobody does a good deed without expecting something in return⟩

synonyms misanthrope, pessimist

related words doubter, negativist, skeptic; belittler, critic, derider, detractor, scoffer; malcontent; defeatist, quitter

near antonyms optimist, Pollyanna, positivist; idealist, sentimentalist

cynical *adj* having or showing a deep distrust of human beings and their motives ⟨so *cynical* that he can't understand why anyone would volunteer to help out at a homeless shelter⟩

synonyms misanthropic, pessimistic

related words distrustful, mistrustful, negativist, negativistic, skeptical, suspicious; derisive, mocking, sardonic, scornful; defeatist, fatalistic, negative; ironic (*also* ironical), sarcastic; jaded, sophisticated, worldly-wise; hard-bitten, hard-boiled, hardcase, hard-edged, unsentimental

near antonyms trustful, trusting, unsuspicious; cheerful, optimistic, positive, positivist, positivistic, rose-colored; ingenuous, innocent, naive (*or* naïve), unsophisticated; impractical, romantic; maudlin, mushy, saccharine, sappy, sentimental

antonyms uncynical

cynosure *n* **1** a guiding or motivating purpose or principle ⟨with an unwavering commitment to equal rights for all as his only *cynosure*⟩ — see COMPASS 1

2 a thing or place that is of greatest importance to an activity or interest ⟨That company is the *cynosure* for anyone wishing to make it in the music business.⟩ — see CENTER 1

czar *also* **tsar** *or* **tzar** *n* a person of rank, power, or influence in a particular field ⟨a showbiz *czar* who is said to be able to make or break a career⟩ — see MAGNATE

D

dab *n* **1** a quick thrust ⟨One more quick *dab* of the brush and he would be finished with his painting.⟩ — see ¹POKE 1

2 a very small amount ⟨She added a *dab* of sesame oil to the dressing before pouring it on the salad.⟩ — see PARTICLE 1

3 a hard strike with a part of the body or an instrument ⟨A bear can knock a man down with a simple *dab* of his paw.⟩ — see ¹BLOW

dabbler *n* a person who regularly or occasionally engages in an activity as a pastime rather than as a profession ⟨He was a *dabbler*, learning the basics of many arts but mastering none.⟩ — see AMATEUR 1

dad *n* a male human parent ⟨My *dad* does most of the cooking.⟩ — see FATHER 1

daddy *n* **1** a male human parent ⟨I stopped calling my father "*Daddy*" because I thought it sounded childish.⟩ — see FATHER 1

2 something belonging to an earlier time from which something else was later developed ⟨Cook's Tours can be considered the *daddy* of all organized travel tours.⟩ — see ANCESTOR 2

daffy *adj* showing or marked by a lack of good sense or judgment ⟨Their *daffy* antics made generations of movie audiences laugh.⟩ — see FOOLISH 1

daft *adj* showing or marked by a lack of good sense or judgment ⟨a *daft* plan, doomed to failure and ridicule⟩ — see FOOLISH 1

daftness *n* lack of good sense or judgment ⟨His *daftness* won him the vote for senior class clown.⟩ — see FOOLISHNESS 1

daily *adj* occurring, done, produced, or appearing every day ⟨They made their *daily* stop at the coffee shop after work to relax before dinner.⟩

synonyms day-to-day, diurnal

related words alternate, cyclic (*or* cyclical), intermittent, periodic, recurrent, recurring, regular; ceaseless, continual, continuing, continuous, everlasting, frequent, incessant, perpetual, unbroken, unceasing, uninterrupted, unremitting

near antonyms monthly, weekly, yearly; erratic, infrequent, irregular; occasional, spasmodic, sporadic; interrupted

daintiness *n* the state or quality of having a delicate structure ⟨We were impressed by the *daintiness* of the etching on the crystal vase.⟩ — see DELICACY 2

dainty *adj* **1** hard to please ⟨You can't afford to be *dainty* about food when you're starving.⟩ — see FINICKY

2 having qualities that appeal to a refined taste ⟨The *dainty* hors d'oeuvres were delicious, but not terribly filling.⟩ — see CHOICE 1

3 satisfying or pleasing because of fineness or mildness ⟨a set of *dainty* teacups⟩ — see DELICATE 1

4 very pleasing to the sense of taste ⟨the sort of *dainty* finger foods that might be served at afternoon tea⟩ — see DELICIOUS 1

dainty *n* something that is pleasing to eat because it is rare or a luxury ⟨The wedding guests were treated to a variety of *dainties*.⟩ — see DELICACY 1

dais *n* a level usually raised surface ⟨The speaker took his place at the front of the *dais*.⟩ — see PLATFORM

dale *n* an area of lowland between hills or mountains ⟨a hunting lodge in a secluded *dale* in the country⟩ — see VALLEY

dalliance *n* activity engaged in to amuse oneself ⟨an extremely serious scientist who is not much given to *dalliance* or idle chitchat⟩ — see PLAY 1

dallier *n* someone who moves slowly or more slowly than others ⟨The *dalliers* began to hurry when they realized a violent storm was brewing.⟩ — see SLOWPOKE

dally *vb* **1** to engage in activity for amusement ⟨He spent his college years *dallying*, seemingly determined to acquire as little knowledge as possible.⟩ — see PLAY 1

2 to move or act slowly ⟨Don't *dally* on the way to the interview.⟩ — see DELAY 1

3 to show a sexual attraction for someone just for fun ⟨twenty-somethings who spent the summer *dallying* with the group renting the neighboring beach house⟩ — see FLIRT 1

4 to spend time doing nothing ⟨I kept *dallying* at my desk until I couldn't put off doing my work any longer.⟩ — see IDLE

dallying *adj* moving or proceeding at less than the normal, desirable, or required speed ⟨The *dallying* diners seemed oblivious to the fact that other customers were impatiently waiting for tables.⟩ — see SLOW 1

dam *n* a bank of earth constructed to control water ⟨The river backed up behind the *dam* until it formed a new lake.⟩

synonyms dike, embankment, head, levee

related words breakwater, jetty, seawall; breastwork, bulwark, earthwork, rampart; canal, channel, ditch, gutter, trough; lock; barricade, barrier, block; floodgate, sluice; barrage, milldam, weir

dam *vb* **1** to prevent passage through by filling with something ⟨Ice floes were *damming* the river.⟩ — see CLOG 1

2 to close up so that no empty spaces remain ⟨*dam* up the pipes⟩ — see FILL 2

damage *n* **1** something that causes loss or pain ⟨The collision did a great deal of *damage* to her car.⟩ — see INJURY 1

2 damages *pl* a sum of money to be paid as a punishment ⟨ordered by the court to pay $1000 in punitive *damages*⟩ — see FINE

3 damages *pl* payment to another for a loss or injury ⟨The company was forced to pay millions in *damages* to the permanently disabled worker.⟩ — see COMPENSATION 1

4 the amount of money that is demanded as payment for something ⟨She winced when she saw the *damage* after the family's shopping spree.⟩ — see PRICE 1

damage *vb* **1** to reduce the soundness, effectiveness, or perfection of ⟨The burst pipe *damaged* the entire city's water supply.⟩

synonyms blemish, bloody, break, compromise, crab, cripple, deface, disfigure, flaw, harm, hurt, impair, injure, mar, spoil, vitiate

related words deteriorate, enervate, enfeeble, undermine, weaken; erode, scour, wash out, wear (away); tarnish; dent, ding, dint; botch, queer; lacerate, wound; disable, hamstring, lame, maim, mangle, mutilate, torment, torture; annihilate, bang up, bash, batter, clobber, crush, dash, decimate, demolish, desolate, destroy, devastate, do in, pulverize, raze, ruin, scourge, shatter, smash, tear down, total, waste, wipe out, wreck

near antonyms cure, heal, help, rectify, rehabilitate, remedy; edit, remodel, revise; ameliorate, better, enhance, enrich, improve, meliorate, perfect, refine

antonyms doctor, fix, mend, patch, rebuild, recondition, reconstruct, renovate, repair, revamp

2 to cause bodily damage to ⟨His knee was badly *damaged* in the accident, and he walked with a limp for months.⟩ — see INJURE 1

damaging *adj* causing or capable of causing harm ⟨the *damaging* effects of the sun on unprotected skin⟩ — see HARMFUL

dame *n* **1** a dignified usually elderly woman of some rank or authority ⟨As the grand *dames* of local society, they determined which charities received support.⟩ — see MATRIARCH

2 a woman of high birth or social position ⟨The lords and *dames* of the shire eagerly awaited the royal visit.⟩ — see GENTLEWOMAN

damn *vb* **1** to use profane or obscene language at or about ⟨*damned* the car for once again breaking down⟩

synonyms curse

related words imprecate, maledict; criticize, reprove; admonish, chide, rebuke, reprimand, reproach; blame, censure, reprehend, reprobate

near antonyms bless, extol (*also* extoll), glorify, laud, magnify, praise; acclaim, applaud, commend, compliment, hail, salute

2 to declare to be morally wrong or evil ⟨a heresy that was quickly *damned* by a hastily called church council⟩ — see CONDEMN 1

3 to impose a judicial punishment on ⟨*damned* him to life in prison without the possibility of parole⟩ — see SENTENCE

damp *adj* **1** containing or characterized by an uncomfortable amount of moisture ⟨The *damp* air made 85 degrees feel like 105.⟩ — see HUMID

2 slightly or moderately wet ⟨Marks can usually be removed with a *damp* cloth.⟩ — see MOIST

damp *n* the amount of water suspended in the air in tiny droplets ⟨We bought a dehumidifier for the basement when the *damp* down there began causing mold to grow.⟩ — see MOISTURE

damp *vb* **1** to deprive of emotional or intellectual vitality ⟨He refused to let the setbacks *damp* his drive for success.⟩ — see DEHYDRATE 1

2 to make or become slightly or moderately wet ⟨*Damp* the shirt slightly before ironing it.⟩ — see MOISTEN

3 to reduce or weaken in strength or feeling ⟨Nothing seemed to *damp* their love for the home team.⟩ — see DULL 1

dampen *vb* **1** to make or become slightly or moderately wet ⟨*Dampen* a paper towel with water and use it to clean up the mess.⟩ — see MOISTEN

2 to reduce or weaken in strength or feeling ⟨The oppressive heat *dampened* our spirits.⟩ — see DULL 1

3 to deprive of emotional or intellectual vitality ⟨Nothing could *dampen* their enthusiasm.⟩ — see DEHYDRATE 1

damper *n* a device on a musical instrument that deadens or softens its tone ⟨The pianist used the *damper* pedal on the piano for the quiet passages.⟩ — see MUTE

dampness *n* the amount of water suspended in the air in tiny droplets ⟨The *dampness* in the basement caused some things to mold.⟩ — see MOISTURE

damsel *n* a young unmarried woman ⟨Knights are celebrated in fairy tales for rescuing *damsels* in distress.⟩ — see GIRL 1

dance *n* a social gathering for dancing ⟨Who are you taking to the *dance* on Saturday night?⟩

synonyms ball, cotillion (*also* cotillon), formal, hop, prom

related words blowout, celebration, event, festival, festivity, fete (*or* fête), gala, masquerade, mixer, party, reception, shindig, soiree (*or* soirée); hoedown, square dance

dance *vb* **1** to perform a series of usually rhythmic bodily movements to music ⟨She can't resist *dancing* to her favorite music.⟩

synonyms foot (it), hoof (it), step

related words prance, strut, trip; boogie (*also* boogy *or* boogey), bop, fox-trot, gavotte, jig, jitterbug, jive, mambo, polka, shag, shimmy, shuffle, tango, tap-dance, twist, waltz; tread

phrases shake a leg, trip the light fantastic

2 to make an irregular series of quick, sudden movements ⟨The lithe boxer *danced* around the ring, staying just out of the reach of his opponent.⟩ — see FLIT

dandle *vb* to treat with great or excessive care ⟨The college president is a past master at *dandling* wealthy alumni.⟩ — see BABY

dandy *adj* of the very best kind ⟨That's a *dandy* new racing bike.⟩ — see EXCELLENT

dandy *n* **1** a man extremely interested in his clothing and personal appearance ⟨a *dandy* whose hair was always perfect⟩
synonyms beau, buck, dude, fop, gallant
related words blade, cavalier, dasher; clotheshorse, swell
near antonyms slob, sloven
2 something very good of its kind ⟨That new phone is a *dandy*.⟩ — see JIM-DANDY
danger *n* **1** the state of not being protected from injury, harm, or evil ⟨We were unaware of the *danger* that lay ahead.⟩
synonyms distress, endangerment, imperilment, jeopardy, peril, risk, trouble
related words exposure, liability, openness, vulnerability; precariousness, threat; susceptibility, susceptibleness; defenselessness, helplessness, weakness
near antonyms preservation, salvation; defense, protection; exemption, immunity, impunity, inviolability, invulnerability
antonyms safeness, safety, secureness, security
2 something that may cause injury or harm ⟨willing to face the *dangers* of the Arctic in quest of the Northwest Passage⟩
synonyms hazard, menace, peril, pitfall, risk, threat, trouble
related words snare, trap; booby trap
near antonyms guard, protection, safeguard, shield, ward; asylum, harbor, haven, refuge, retreat, shelter
dangerous *adj* **1** involving potential loss or injury ⟨The soldiers were specially selected to go on a *dangerous* mission behind enemy lines.⟩
synonyms grave, grievous, hazardous, jeopardizing, menacing, parlous, perilous, risky, serious, threatening, unhealthy, unsafe, venturesome
related words dicey, insecure, precarious, treacherous, uncertain; ultrahazardous; chance, haphazard, random; adverse, bad, baleful, baneful, deleterious, detrimental, evil, harmful, hurtful, ill, inimical, injurious, malignant, nasty, noxious, pernicious, pestilent; deadly, deathly, destructive, dire, fatal, fateful, lethal, mortal, murderous
near antonyms advantageous, beneficial, good; ultrasafe
antonyms harmless, innocent, innocuous, nonhazardous, nonthreatening, safe, unthreatening
2 causing or capable of causing harm ⟨the common knowledge that smoking is *dangerous* to one's health⟩ — see HARMFUL
dangle *vb* to place on an elevated point without support from below ⟨He *dangled* the string in front of the cat, hoping that it was in the mood for play.⟩ — see HANG 1
dangling *adj* extending freely from a support from above ⟨There was a *dangling* banner in one corner of the room.⟩ — see DEPENDENT 1
dank *adj* slightly or moderately wet ⟨Vegetables tended to go bad quickly in the *dank* cellar.⟩ — see MOIST
dapper *adj* being strikingly neat and trim in style or appearance ⟨Grandpa looked very *dapper* in his best suit.⟩ — see SMART 1
dapple *n* a small area that is different (as in color) from the main part ⟨The clouds threw *dapples* of shadow over the quiet street.⟩ — see SPOT 1
dapple *vb* to mark with small spots especially unevenly ⟨Sunlight *dappled* the canopy of vines over our heads.⟩ — see SPOT 1
dappled *also* **dapple** *adj* **1** marked with spots ⟨a *dappled* fawn⟩ — see SPOTTED 1
2 having blotches of two or more colors ⟨a forest that was vibrant with the *dappled* foliage of autumn⟩ — see PIED

dare *vb* **1** to invite (someone) to take part in a contest or to perform a feat ⟨I *dare* you to repeat that to my face!⟩ ⟨He *dared* his friend to race to the end of the block.⟩ — see CHALLENGE 2
2 to oppose (something hostile or dangerous) with firmness or courage ⟨Every day the old fisherman *dared* the elements to make his meager living.⟩ — see FACE 2
daredevil *adj* **1** foolishly adventurous or bold ⟨His *daredevil* stunts are sure to end in disaster someday.⟩ — see FOOLHARDY 1
2 having or showing a lack of concern for the consequences of one's actions ⟨a *daredevil* driver who thinks that drag racing on city streets is a harmless game⟩ — see RECKLESS 1
daredevil *n* a person who seeks out very dangerous or foolhardy adventures with no apparent fear ⟨That little *daredevil* has broken an arm and an ankle this year alone.⟩
synonyms devil, madcap, madman
related words berserk (*or* berserker), cowboy
daring *adj* inclined or willing to take risks ⟨*daring* acrobats who risk life and limb every day for the entertainment of the crowds at the circus⟩ — see BOLD 1
daring *n* strength of mind to carry on in spite of danger ⟨Skydiving requires both skill and *daring*.⟩ — see COURAGE
dark *adj* **1** being without light or without much light ⟨It gets *dark* earlier in the winter.⟩
synonyms black, darkened, darkish, darkling, darksome, dim, dimmed, dusk, dusky, gloomy, murky, obscure, obscured, pitch-black, pitch-dark, pitchy, somber (*or* sombre)
related words crepuscular, twilit; moonless, starless; cloudy, dull, dulled, lackluster; shadowlike, shadowy, shady; gray (*also* grey), leaden, pale; beclouded, befogged, clouded, foggy, misty, smoggy, soupy
near antonyms ablaze, agleam, aglitter, alight, beaming, beamy, effulgent, glaring, glowing, incandescent, lambent, radiant, relucent, resplendent, shining, sparkling, ultrabright; glossy, lustrous, shiny; floodlit (*also* floodlighted), highlighted, spotlighted (*or* spotlit); moonlit, moony, starlit, sunlit
antonyms bright, brightened, brilliant, illuminated, illumined, light, lightsome, lucent, lucid, luminous
2 causing or marked by an atmosphere lacking in cheer ⟨Those were *dark* days for many businesses.⟩ — see GLOOMY 1
3 given to keeping one's activities hidden from public observation or knowledge ⟨The actor was always quite *dark* about his life before his arrival in Hollywood.⟩ — see SECRETIVE
4 having an often intentionally veiled or uncertain meaning ⟨The superhero was not daunted by the villain's *dark* threats.⟩ — see OBSCURE 1
5 lacking in education or the knowledge gained from books ⟨a *dark* period in European history when people lived in ignorance, fear, and want⟩ — see IGNORANT 1
6 not conforming to a high moral standard; morally unacceptable ⟨*dark* deeds that resulted in the Russian czar being known to history as Ivan the Terrible⟩ — see BAD 2
dark *n* **1** a time or place of little or no light ⟨I have a bad habit of running into tables in the *dark*.⟩
synonyms black, blackness, darkness, dusk, gloaming, gloom, murk, night, semidarkness, shade, shadows, twilight, umbra
related words midnight; blackout, brownout, dimout; shadiness, umbrage; dullness (*also* dulness), somberness; cloudiness, fogginess, haziness, mistiness, murkiness;

dimness, faintness, gloominess, grayness, paleness; half-light

near antonyms moonlight, starlight, sunlight; effulgence, radiance, radiancy, shine, sunshine; incandescence, luminescence, luminosity

antonyms blaze, brightness, brilliance, day, daylight, glare, glow, light, lightness

2 the time from sunset to sunrise when there is no visible sunlight ⟨We were going to wait until *dark* to go trick-or-treating.⟩ — see NIGHT 1

darken *vb* **1** to take on a gloomy or forbidding look ⟨His face slowly *darkened* as we told him the sad news.⟩

synonyms gloom, glower, lower (*also* lour)

related words frown, scowl; glare, stare; brood, mope, pet, pout, sulk; anger, bristle, fume, rage, steam, storm; intimidate, menace, threaten

antonyms brighten, cheer (up), lighten, perk (up)

2 to grow dark ⟨The sky *darkened* as a storm moved in.⟩

synonyms blacken, black out, dusk

related words dim, fade, wane; gloom, lower (*also* lour)

near antonyms dawn; beam, glow, radiate, shine

antonyms brighten, light, lighten

3 to make dark, dim, or indistinct ⟨Years of accumulated grime have *darkened* the painting until it can barely be seen.⟩ — see CLOUD 1

4 to affect slightly with something morally bad or undesirable ⟨The scandal *darkened* his otherwise sterling reputation.⟩ — see TAINT 1

darkened *adj* being without light or without much light ⟨Wanting to surprise her, we waited in the *darkened* room for her to get home.⟩ — see DARK 1

darkening *adj* causing or marked by an atmosphere lacking in cheer ⟨a *darkening* sky that seemed to match our downcast spirits⟩ — see GLOOMY 1

darkish *adj* being without light or without much light ⟨The *darkish* galleries do not show off the museum's paintings to their best advantage.⟩ — see DARK 1

darkling *adj* being without light or without much light ⟨the *darkling* valleys of Transylvania, where tales of vampires have long existed⟩ — see DARK 1

darkness *n* **1** a time or place of little or no light ⟨He escaped under cover of *darkness*.⟩ — see DARK 1

2 the quality or state of having a veiled or uncertain meaning ⟨the *darkness* of certain passages in the book⟩ — see OBSCURITY 1

3 the time from sunset to sunrise when there is no visible sunlight ⟨Let's wait for *darkness* before telling ghost stories.⟩ — see NIGHT 1

4 an overspreading element that produces an atmosphere of gloom ⟨The *darkness* of that period of my life was soon over.⟩ — see CLOUD

darksome *adj* being without light or without much light ⟨a pile of *darksome* ruins in the heart of the forest⟩ — see DARK 1

darling *adj* **1** granted special treatment or attention ⟨They poured gifts and affection on their *darling* child.⟩

synonyms beloved, cherished, dear, favored, favorite, fond, loved, pet, precious, special, sweet

related words admired, adored, appreciated, esteemed, relished, revered; prized, treasured; preferred

near antonyms abhorred, abominated, despised, detested, disdained, disfavored, disliked, execrated, hated, loathed, unfavorite; abandoned, forgotten, ignored; alienated, estranged

antonyms unbeloved

2 having qualities that tend to make one loved ⟨a *darling* child who everyone cooed over⟩ — see LOVABLE

3 giving pleasure or contentment to the mind or senses ⟨What a *darling* set of dishes!⟩ — see PLEASANT 1

darling *n* **1** a person or thing that is preferred over others ⟨For a while that candidate was the *darling* of the news media and could do no wrong.⟩ — see FAVORITE

2 a person with whom one is in love ⟨Anything you say, *darling*!⟩ — see SWEETHEART

darn *n* the smallest amount or part imaginable ⟨Nobody gave a *darn* about us when we were poor, but now that we are rich, we have friends we never knew about!⟩ — see JOT

darn *vb* to close up with a series of interlacing stitches ⟨In the old days, holes in socks had to be *darned* by hand.⟩ — see SEW

dart *n* an act or expression showing scorn and usually intended to hurt another's feelings ⟨The *darts* flew fast and furiously when the two former friends bumped into each other at the party.⟩ — see INSULT

dart *vb* to make an irregular series of quick, sudden movements ⟨The housefly *darted* about the room until it found an open window and flew out.⟩ — see FLIT

dash *n* active strength of body or mind ⟨The cavalry officer's *dash* and enthusiasm inspired his men to follow him into battle.⟩ — see VIGOR 1

dash *vb* **1** to go at a pace faster than a walk ⟨One sprinter *dashed* to the finish line in record-breaking time.⟩ — see RUN 1

2 to proceed or move quickly ⟨We *dashed* about in a panic, trying to get everything organized before the guests were scheduled to arrive.⟩ — see HURRY 2

3 to send through the air especially with a quick forward motion of the arm ⟨He *dashed* water in his face in an attempt to wake up.⟩ — see THROW 1

4 to wet or soil by striking with something liquid or mushy ⟨Our clothes were *dashed* with the mud of passing cars.⟩ — see SPLASH 2

5 to cause (something liquid or mushy) to move along in sheets ⟨A sudden jolt *dashed* the hot coffee onto the driver's lap.⟩ — see SPLASH 2

6 to make sad ⟨She's not one to be *dashed* by setbacks.⟩ — see DEPRESS 1

dashing *adj* inclined or willing to take risks ⟨the *dashing* heroes in stories about the American West⟩ — see BOLD 1

dashingly *adv* in a strikingly neat and trim manner ⟨a handsome young man *dashingly* dressed in a tuxedo for the prom⟩ — see SMARTLY

dastard *n* a person who shows a shameful lack of courage in the face of danger ⟨The villain of the story is a *dastard* indeed.⟩ — see COWARD

dastardliness *n* a shameful lack of courage in the face of danger ⟨the *dastardliness* of the enemy's surprise attack⟩ — see COWARDICE

dastardly *adj* having or showing a shameful lack of courage ⟨His *dastardly* conduct in a critical moment haunted him for the rest of his life.⟩ — see COWARDLY

date *n* **1** an agreement to be present at a specified time and place ⟨I have a *date* to meet my financial consultant at seven o'clock.⟩ — see ENGAGEMENT 2

2 the period during which something exists, lasts, or is in progress ⟨the short *date* of our vacation⟩ — see DURATION 1

date *vb* **1** to go on a social engagement with ⟨I don't want to *date* him—I'd rather just be friends.⟩

synonyms take out

related words accompany, escort, see; court, woo

2 to go on dates that may eventually lead to marriage ⟨We *dated* for two years before we got engaged.⟩ — see COURT 2

dated *adj* having passed its time of use or usefulness ⟨His jokes are awfully *dated*, referring to things that happened years ago.⟩ — see OBSOLETE

dateless *adj* **1** dating or surviving from the distant past ⟨*dateless* artifacts left by an obscure people of the distant past⟩ — see ANCIENT 1

2 lasting forever ⟨the *dateless* cycle of the seasons⟩ — see EVERLASTING 1

3 having an existence or validity that does not change or diminish ⟨It is because of their *dateless* themes that the plays of Shakespeare are still performed today.⟩ — see ABIDING

dating *n* the series of social engagements shared by a couple looking to get married ⟨Their *dating* started after being introduced by friends.⟩ — see COURTSHIP

datum *n* a single piece of information ⟨Let's begin our discussion of this matter with a *datum* from actual experience.⟩ — see FACT 3

daub *vb* **1** to make dirty ⟨a tablecloth *daubed* with too many spills to ignore any longer⟩ — see DIRTY

2 to rub an oily or sticky substance over ⟨He begins his nightly transformation into a circus clown by *daubing* greasepaint on his face.⟩ — see SMEAR 1

daunt *vb* to lessen the courage or confidence of ⟨The raging inferno didn't *daunt* the firefighters for a moment.⟩ — see DISCOURAGE 1

dauntless *adj* feeling or displaying no fear by temperament ⟨*dauntless* heroes who are inclined to rush to danger, not away from it⟩ — see BRAVE 1

dauntlessness *n* strength of mind to carry on in spite of danger ⟨the inspiring *dauntlessness* of the soldiers who led the charge up the hill⟩ — see COURAGE

davenport *n* a long upholstered piece of furniture designed for several sitters ⟨We seated ourselves on the *davenport* while we waited for him to get ready.⟩ — see COUCH

dawdle *vb* **1** to move or act slowly ⟨If you continue to *dawdle*, we'll be late for sure.⟩ — see DELAY 1

2 to spend time doing nothing ⟨accused the city council of *dawdling* even as the city's infrastructure continued to crumble⟩ — see IDLE

dawdler *n* someone who moves slowly or more slowly than others ⟨We encouraged the *dawdlers* to pick up the pace.⟩ — see SLOWPOKE

dawdling *adj* moving or proceeding at less than the normal, desirable, or required speed ⟨The *dawdling* pace of the movie was really making us restless.⟩ — see SLOW 1

dawn *n* **1** the first appearance of light in the morning or the time of its appearance ⟨We stayed up talking until *dawn*.⟩

synonyms dawning, day, daybreak, daylight, light, morn, morning, sun, sunrise, sunup

related words daytime; forenoon

near antonyms dark, darkness, midnight, night, nighttime; midday; dusk, evening, eventide, gloaming, twilight

antonyms nightfall, sundown, sunset

2 the point at which something begins ⟨the *dawn* of civilization⟩ — see BEGINNING

dawn *vb* to come into existence ⟨A smile *dawned* on his face as he got the joke.⟩ — see BEGIN 2

dawn (on) *vb* to enter the mind of ⟨It finally *dawned on* me that I had been going the wrong way.⟩ — see OCCUR (TO)

dawning *n* the first appearance of light in the morning or the time of its appearance ⟨the cold, gray *dawning* of a wintry day⟩ — see DAWN 1

day *n* **1** the hours of light between one night and the next ⟨During the *day*, we like to go play ball in the park.⟩

synonyms daylight, daytime

related words light, sunlight, sunshine; dawn, dawning, daybreak, forenoon, morn, morning, sunrise; noon; dusk, evening, gloaming, nightfall, sundown, sunset, twilight

near antonyms black, blackness, dark, darkness

antonyms night, nighttime

2 an extent of time associated with a particular person or thing ⟨the brief but glorious *day* of the clipper ship⟩ — see AGE 1

3 the first appearance of light in the morning or the time of its appearance ⟨At the break of *day* I was relieved to realize that I had survived another night in the wilderness.⟩ — see DAWN 1

daybreak *n* the first appearance of light in the morning or the time of its appearance ⟨I always seem to wake up at *daybreak*, regardless of what the clock says.⟩ — see DAWN 1

daydream *n* a conception or image created by the imagination and having no objective reality ⟨I hoped that one day world peace would be a reality and not just a *daydream*.⟩ — see FANTASY 1

daydreaming *n* the state of being lost in thought ⟨If you're bored while traveling, *daydreaming* is a common state to be in.⟩ — see REVERIE

daylight *n* **1** the first appearance of light in the morning or the time of its appearance ⟨*Daylight* was just breaking when we stumbled out of bed.⟩ — see DAWN 1

2 the hours of light between one night and the next ⟨There isn't a lot of *daylight* left, so we'd better get home soon.⟩ — see DAY 1

3 daylights *pl* the normal or healthy condition of the mental abilities ⟨nearly scared the *daylights* out of him with that scream⟩ — see MIND 2

daytime *n* the hours of light between one night and the next ⟨It's a lot easier to find your way to a new place in the *daytime*.⟩ — see DAY 1

day–to–day *adj* occurring, done, produced, or appearing every day ⟨the *day-to-day* routine of commuting to work⟩ — see DAILY

daze *n* a state of mental confusion ⟨She was in a *daze* for a minute after being hit on the head by a volleyball.⟩ — see HAZE 2

daze *vb* **1** to make senseless or dizzy by a blow ⟨The fall *dazed* him for a moment, causing him to become disoriented.⟩ — see STUN 1

2 to overpower with light ⟨a skier *dazed* by the glare from the snow⟩ — see DAZZLE

dazed *adj* suffering from mental confusion ⟨The *dazed* goalie could only watch as the winning shot went flying past him.⟩ — see DIZZY 2

dazzle *n* the quality or state of having or giving off light ⟨the *dazzle* of the stars on a cold but clear winter's night⟩ — see BRILLIANCE 1

dazzle *vb* to overpower with light ⟨Skiers were *dazzled* by the glare off of the slopes of freshly packed snow.⟩

synonyms bedazzle, blind, daze

related words confuse, overpower, overwhelm, stun

dazzling *adj* giving off or reflecting much light ⟨the attraction that the *dazzling* lights of Broadway have for many young performers⟩ — see BRIGHT 1

deactivate *vb* to cause to stop functioning ⟨*Deactivate* the machine carefully, or you'll risk an electric shock.⟩

synonyms kill, shut off, turn off

related words flick (off); dismantle, mothball, phase out; arrest, brake, chock, cut off, draw up, halt, jam, stall, stick

near antonyms charge, electrify, energize, fire, fuel, generate, power, push; discharge, launch, release, switch, trip; reactivate

antonyms activate, actuate, crank (up), drive, move, propel, run, set off, spark, start, touch off, trigger, turn on

dead *adj* **1** no longer living ⟨I inherited this heirloom from my *dead* great-grandfather.⟩

synonyms breathless, cold, deceased, defunct, departed, fallen, gone, late, lifeless, low

related words extinct; dying, fading, moribund; still-born; finished, lapsed, terminated; insensate, nonliving; done, done for
phrases bitten the dust
near antonyms animated; dynamic, lively, thriving, vibrant, vital, vivacious; active, functioning, operative, running
antonyms alive, animate, breathing, going, live, living, quick
2 lacking in gaiety, movement, or animation ⟨The store is often *dead* after 4:00 p.m.⟩
synonyms slow
related words lethargic, sluggish, torpid; dormant, fallow, free, idle, inactive, inert, inoperative, latent, off, vacant
near antonyms abounding, overflowing, swarming, teeming, thronging
antonyms alive, animated, astir, bustling, busy, buzzing, flourishing, humming, lively, thriving, vibrant
3 depleted in strength, energy, or freshness ⟨A long day of traveling left them just *dead*.⟩ — see WEARY 1
4 having no exceptions or restrictions ⟨There was a *dead* silence following that incredibly moving performance.⟩ — see ABSOLUTE 2
5 lacking in sensation or feeling ⟨My foot was *dead* after I absentmindedly sat on it for an hour.⟩ — see NUMB 1
6 no longer existing ⟨the *dead* Babylonian culture⟩ — see EXTINCT
7 not being in a state of use, activity, or employment ⟨local coal mines that have been *dead* for years⟩ — see INACTIVE 2
8 of, relating to, or suggestive of death ⟨fell into a *dead* faint upon hearing the news⟩ — see DEATHLY 1
9 producing inferior or only a small amount of vegetation ⟨the *dead* wastes of the far country to the west⟩ — see BARREN 1
dead *adv* **1** in a direct line or course ⟨The finish line is *dead* ahead.⟩ — see DIRECTLY 1
2 to a full extent or degree ⟨I'm *dead* certain that's the one I want.⟩ — see FULLY 1
dead *n* the state of being dead ⟨It's impossible to raise someone from the *dead*.⟩ — see DEATH 2
deaden *vb* **1** to deprive of emotional or intellectual vitality ⟨An excess of detail *deadens* much of the mystery novel's suspense.⟩ — see DEHYDRATE 1
2 to reduce or weaken in strength or feeling ⟨A couple of aspirins *deadened* the headache.⟩ — see DULL 1
dead heat *n* a situation in which neither participant in a contest, competition, or struggle comes out ahead of the other ⟨The horses crossed the finish line in a *dead heat*.⟩ — see TIE 1
deadlock *n* a point in a struggle where neither side is capable of winning or willing to give in ⟨The jury sent a note to the judge that it was hopelessly stuck in a *deadlock*.⟩ — see IMPASSE 1
deadly *adj* **1** likely to cause or capable of causing death ⟨The doctors were alarmed about the outbreak of the *deadly* new virus.⟩
synonyms baleful, deathly, fatal, fell, killer, lethal, mortal, murderous, pestilent, terminal, vital
related words baneful, deleterious, destructive, harmful, injurious, noxious, pernicious, truculent; infectious, infective, poisonous, sublethal, toxic, virulent; dangerous, grave, grievous, hazardous, jeopardizing, menacing, parlous, perilous, risky, serious, threatening, ugly, unhealthy, unsound; bloody, internecine, sanguinary, sanguine
near antonyms beneficial, restorative, salubrious, salutary; alleviative, corrective, remedial, tonic; advantageous, beneficial, useful; nonpoisonous, nontoxic, safe

antonyms healthful, healthy, nonfatal, nonlethal, wholesome
2 having no exceptions or restrictions ⟨A *deadly* silence followed the announcement.⟩ — see ABSOLUTE 2
3 of, relating to, or suggestive of death ⟨A *deadly* pallor spread across her face as the tragic news gradually sank in.⟩ — see DEATHLY 1
deadly *adv* to a great degree ⟨I'm *deadly* serious about making an offer on the house.⟩ — see VERY 1
deadness *n* the state of being dead ⟨They believe in an afterlife that transcends *deadness* in the grave.⟩ — see DEATH 2
deadpan *adj* not expressing any emotion ⟨He delivered the joke in such a *deadpan* voice that we thought at first that he was serious.⟩ — see BLANK 1
deadwood *n* discarded or useless material ⟨Much of the material in the file cabinets is just *deadwood*.⟩ — see GARBAGE
deafening *adj* marked by a high volume of sound ⟨a DJ blasting *deafening* music⟩ — see LOUD 1
¹**deal** *n* a considerable amount ⟨There is a great *deal* of work to be done.⟩ — see LOT 2
²**deal** *n* **1** an arrangement about action to be taken ⟨We made a *deal* to cooperate on the next assignment.⟩ — see AGREEMENT 2
2 the transfer of ownership of something from one person to another for a price ⟨We closed the *deal* for the house last week.⟩ — see SALE
3 a formal agreement to fulfill an obligation ⟨If the other party backs out of the *deal* after it's signed, you can sue.⟩ — see GUARANTEE 1
4 position with regard to conditions and circumstances ⟨We don't yet know what the *deal* is with the new manager.⟩ — see SITUATION 1
5 something bought or offered for sale at a desirable price ⟨The phone you found online is a great *deal* especially if you don't pay for shipping and handling.⟩ — see BARGAIN 1
deal *vb* **1** to carry on the business of buying and selling goods or other property ⟨That store *deals* in used furniture.⟩ — see TRADE 1
2 to talk over or dispute the terms of a purchase ⟨You're going to have to learn how to *deal* if you want to buy a car at a fair price.⟩ — see BARGAIN 1
deal (in) *vb* to offer for sale to the public ⟨The company *deals in* virtually all types of insurance.⟩ — see MARKET
deal (out) *vb* to give out (something) to appropriate individuals ⟨Volunteers along the race route *dealt out* drinks and snacks to the runners.⟩ — see ADMINISTER 1
deal (with) *vb* **1** to behave toward in a stated way ⟨It's important to *deal with* others fairly.⟩ — see TREAT 1
2 to have (something) as a subject matter ⟨This textbook *deals with* the history of France.⟩ — see CONCERN 1
dealer *n* **1** a buyer and seller of goods for profit ⟨a *dealer* in fine fabrics⟩ — see MERCHANT
2 the person in a business deal who hands over an item in exchange for money ⟨If both the *dealer* and the buyer are happy, then the item sold at a fair price.⟩ — see VENDOR
dealings *pl n* doings between individuals or groups ⟨I've had *dealings* with those guys before.⟩ — see RELATION 1
dean *n* the senior member of a group ⟨The *dean* of the Aspen ski instructors oversaw the training of the rescue team.⟩
synonyms elder, elder statesman, senior
related words better, superior; old hand, old-timer, vet, veteran
near antonyms inferior, subordinate, underling; beginner, colt, fledgling, freshman, greenhorn, neophyte, newbie, newcomer, novice, recruit, rookie, tenderfoot, tyro
antonyms baby, junior

dear *adj* **1** commanding a large price ⟨Caviar has always been among the *dearest* of foods.⟩ — see COSTLY

2 granted special treatment or attention ⟨spared no expense when caring for and feeding her *dear* little dog⟩ — see DARLING 1

3 having qualities that tend to make one loved ⟨a *dear* friend that I would do anything for⟩ — see LOVABLE

dear *n* a person with whom one is in love ⟨I love you, *dear*.⟩ — see SWEETHEART

dearth *n* **1** a falling short of an essential or desirable amount or number ⟨There was a *dearth* of usable firewood at the campsite.⟩ — see DEFICIENCY

2 the fact or state of being absent ⟨The *dearth* of salesclerks at the shoe store annoyed us.⟩ — see LACK 1

death *n* **1** the permanent stopping of all the vital bodily activities ⟨We were all saddened by the *death* of our dog.⟩

synonyms curtains, decease, demise, dissolution, doom, end, exit, expiration, fate, grave, passage, passing, quietus, sleep

related words casualty, fatality; martyrdom, self-destruction, self-murder, self-slaughter, suicide; annihilation, destruction, ending, extermination, ruin; assassination, execution, massacre, slaughter

near antonyms existence, life; creation, genesis, origination, rise

antonyms birth, nativity

2 the state of being dead ⟨*Death* is one of the few constants in the universe.⟩

synonyms dead, deadness, grave, lifelessness, sleep

related words mortality

near antonyms immortality; life span, lifetime

antonyms existence, life

3 the act of ceasing to exist ⟨the *death* of videotape⟩

synonyms demise, expiration, termination

related words dispersion, dissolution; cessation, close, conclusion, decease, discontinuance, doom, end, ending, finish, halt, lapse, passing, quietus, shutdown, shutoff, stop, stoppage, surcease; suicide; annihilation, destruction, ruin

near antonyms existence, persistence, prolongation; inauguration, initiation, institution, origination

antonyms alpha, beginning, birth, commencement, creation, dawn, genesis, inception, incipiency, launch, morning, onset, outset, start

4 something that is the cause of one's ultimate failure or loss of life ⟨That muscle car will be the *death* of him yet.⟩ — see DOWNFALL 1

5 the killing of a large number of people ⟨do not yet know the extent of *death* from the storm⟩ — see MASSACRE

deathless *adj* lasting forever ⟨an author who craved *deathless* fame⟩ — see EVERLASTING 1

deathly *adj* **1** of, relating to, or suggestive of death ⟨his *deathly* pallor⟩

synonyms dead, deadly, mortal

related words cadaverous; ghostlike, ghostly, phantom, spectral; inactive, inert, inoperative, lifeless, quiescent, still; macabre; baleful, fatal, fateful, fell, killer, lethal, murderous, pestilent

near antonyms active, alive, animate, breathing, live, living; animated, bouncing, brisk, energetic, frisky, jaunty, jazzy, lively, peppy, perky, pert, racy, snappy, spanking, sparky, spirited, sprightful, sprightly, springy, vigorous, vital, vivacious, zippy; able-bodied, chipper, fit, hale, healthy, hearty, robust, sound, well, whole, wholesome

2 likely to cause or capable of causing death ⟨Smallpox is one *deathly* disease that medical science has been able to conquer.⟩ — see DEADLY 1

debacle *also* **débâcle** *n* **1** a sudden violent event that brings about great loss or destruction ⟨the financial *debacle* that was the stock market crash of 1929⟩ — see DISASTER 1

2 something that has failed ⟨The movie, which some had predicted would be a blockbuster, turned out to be the summer's biggest *debacle* at the multiplexes.⟩ — see FAILURE 3

debar *vb* to prevent the participation, consideration, or inclusion of ⟨The judge *debarred* all of the reporters from the courtroom.⟩ — see EXCLUDE

debark *vb* to go ashore from a ship ⟨The seasick passengers *debarked* as soon as the ship dropped anchor.⟩ — see DISEMBARK 1

debase *vb* **1** to lower in character, dignity, or quality ⟨We *debase* ourselves when we adopt the moral code and behavior of our despised enemies.⟩

synonyms abase, cheapen, corrupt, debauch, degrade, demean, demoralize, deprave, deteriorate, lessen, pervert, poison, profane, subvert, vitiate, warp

related words befoul, begrime, contaminate, defile, dilute, dirty, pollute, taint, thin, weaken; descend; disgrace, dishonor, humble, humiliate, shame, take down; blemish, damage, deface, destroy, flaw, harm, hurt, impair, mar, ruin, spoil, stain, tarnish, wreck; depreciate, downgrade

near antonyms dignify, exalt, honor; ameliorate, amend, better, enhance, enrich, improve, meliorate, perfect; clarify, clean, cleanse, purify, refine, restore; respect

antonyms elevate, ennoble, uplift

2 to reduce to a lower standing in one's own eyes or in others' eyes ⟨Our failure to win a single game completely *debased* us.⟩ — see HUMBLE

debased *adj* having or showing lowered moral character or standards ⟨a book that examines the *debased* character of the criminal mind⟩ — see CORRUPT

debasement *n* a sinking to a state of low moral standards and behavior ⟨the *debasement* of professional sports to a shamelessly commercial enterprise⟩ — see CORRUPTION 2

debatable *adj* **1** open to question or dispute ⟨It's always *debatable* which college football team is really number one, since there's more than one ranking system.⟩

synonyms disputable, doubtable, doubtful, moot, negotiable, questionable

related words contradictable, refutable; debated, disputed; dubious, iffy, inconclusive, indecisive, problematic (*also* problematical), shaky, uncertain; academic (*also* academical), hypothetical, speculative, theoretical (*also* theoretic); ambiguous, equivocal

near antonyms irrefutable; definite; unambiguous, unequivocal; absolute, clear, conclusive, decisive; uncontested, undisputed

antonyms accomplished, certain, incontestable, incontrovertible, indisputable, indubitable, positive, questionless, settled, sure, unanswerable, undebatable, undeniable, unquestionable

2 giving good reason for being doubted, questioned, or challenged ⟨the *debatable* wisdom of staying up so late⟩ — see DOUBTFUL 2

debate *n* **1** a careful weighing of the reasons for or against something ⟨After much *debate*, I decided to get the chocolate ice cream.⟩ — see CONSIDERATION 1

2 variance of opinion on a matter ⟨There was a great deal of *debate* over the need for cutting costs by eliminating some programs.⟩ — see DISAGREEMENT 1

3 an exchange of views for the purpose of exploring a subject or deciding an issue ⟨There was no *debate* over the expenditures before the vote.⟩ — see DISCUSSION 1

debate *vb* **1** to give serious and careful thought to ⟨still *debating* what to do⟩ — see PONDER

2 to talk about (an issue) usually from various points of view and for the purpose of arriving at a decision or opinion ⟨We *debated* the advantages versus the disadvantages of the proposed waterfront development.⟩ — see DISCUSS

debater *n* a person who takes part in a dispute ⟨The *debater* was unable to come up with a convincing rebuttal for his opponent's argument.⟩ — see DISPUTANT

debauch *vb* to lower in character, dignity, or quality ⟨The long stay at the port had *debauched* the ship's crew to the point where they no longer acted like naval professionals.⟩ — see DEBASE 1

debauched *adj* having or showing lowered moral character or standards ⟨a *debauched* society⟩ — see CORRUPT

debaucher *n* a person who has sunk below the normal moral standard ⟨In his youth the man had been a *debaucher* of the worst sort.⟩ — see DEGENERATE

debauchery *n* **1** immoral conduct or practices harmful or offensive to society ⟨a Roman emperor's descent into *debauchery*⟩ — see VICE 1

2 a sinking to a state of low moral standards and behavior ⟨The minister decried what he called the *debauchery* of society.⟩ — see CORRUPTION 2

debilitate *vb* to diminish the physical strength of ⟨an illness that *debilitates* most patients⟩ — see WEAKEN 1

debilitated *adj* lacking bodily strength ⟨The rehab facility offers therapy for *debilitated* residents.⟩ — see WEAK 1

debilitation *n* **1** a gradual sinking and wasting away of mind or body ⟨the *debilitation* caused by the virus⟩ — see DECLINE 1

2 the quality or state of lacking physical strength or vigor ⟨attributed the patient's general *debilitation* to an iron deficiency⟩ — see WEAKNESS 1

debility *n* the quality or state of lacking physical strength or vigor ⟨Our grandmother's *debility* is due in large part to her advanced age.⟩ — see WEAKNESS 1

debonair *adj* **1** having or showing freedom from worries or troubles ⟨His *debonair* dismissal of my inquiry concerning his financial situation led me to believe that nothing was wrong.⟩ — see CAREFREE

2 having or showing very polished and worldly manners ⟨The *debonair* gentleman charmed everyone in the room.⟩ — see SUAVE

debris *n* **1** discarded or useless material ⟨the unsightly *debris* left after mining operations had ceased⟩ — see GARBAGE

2 the portion or bits of something left over or behind after it has been destroyed ⟨The demolition workers cleared away all of the *debris* from the demolished building.⟩ — see REMAINS 1

debt *n* **1** something (as money) which is owed ⟨He filed for bankruptcy when his *debts* exceeded his assets.⟩

synonyms liability (*usually* liabilities), obligation, score

related words bond, delinquency; default, embarrassment

near antonyms quietus, quittance, repayment

2 a breaking of a moral or legal code ⟨Will you forgive us our *debts*?⟩ — see OFFENSE 1

debug *vb* to remove errors, defects, deficiencies, or deviations from ⟨The computer program ran much faster after it was *debugged*.⟩ — see CORRECT 1

debunk *vb* **1** to prove to be false ⟨a website that *debunks* urban legends⟩ — see DISPROVE

2 to reveal the true nature of ⟨The investigative reporter easily *debunked* the charlatan's claims of clairvoyance.⟩ — see EXPOSE 1

decadence *n* **1** a change to a lower state or level ⟨a sym-

bol of the *decadence* of their once-mighty civilization⟩ — see DECLINE 2

2 a sinking to a state of low moral standards and behavior ⟨The book condemns society's *decadence*.⟩ — see CORRUPTION 2

decadent *adj* **1** having lost forcefulness, courage, or spirit ⟨Social critics claimed that their culture had become *decadent* and weak.⟩ — see EFFETE 1

2 having or showing lowered moral character or standards ⟨Opponents of gambling casinos claim that gambling is a *decadent* form of entertainment.⟩ — see CORRUPT

decadent *n* a person who has sunk below the normal moral standard ⟨avant-garde artists who were scorned by the bourgeoisie as talentless *decadents*⟩ — see DEGENERATE

decalogue *n* a collection or system of rules of conduct ⟨the *decalogue* for scouting known as the Scout Oath⟩ — see CODE

decamping *n* the act of leaving a place ⟨the mass *decamping* for the mountains or the shore by city dwellers that occurs every summer weekend⟩ — see DEPARTURE 1

decampment *n* the act of leaving a place ⟨The simultaneous *decampment* of tens of thousands of sports fans from the stadium created the inevitable traffic jam.⟩ — see DEPARTURE 1

decapitate *vb* to cut off the head of ⟨Charles I of England was *decapitated* in 1649.⟩

synonyms behead, guillotine, head

related words prune, shorten, trim; scalp

decay *n* **1** a gradual sinking and wasting away of mind or body ⟨Daily exercise will slow the physical *decay* that usually accompanies growing older.⟩ — see DECLINE 1

2 the process by which dead organic matter separates into simpler substances ⟨the cycle by which the *decay* of dead plants on the forest floor provides soil and nutrients for the next generation of plants⟩ — see CORRUPTION 1

decay *vb* **1** to go through decomposition ⟨The logs *decayed* on the rain forest floor.⟩ ⟨The atom of plutonium *decayed* in the test chamber.⟩

synonyms break down, corrupt, decompose, disintegrate, fester, foul, molder, putrefy, rot, spoil

related words sour, turn; contaminate, defile, pollute, taint; addle, curdle, ferment; mortify; rust; crumble, decline, degenerate, descend, deteriorate, dilapidate, sink, wither

phrases fall apart, go to seed (*or* run to seed)

near antonyms age, develop, grow, mature, ripen; refresh, renew, restore; cleanse, purify; assemble, compose, integrate; ameliorate, better, improve, meliorate

2 to become worse or of less value ⟨The restaurant's standards for food and service had *decayed* over the years.⟩ — see DETERIORATE 1

3 to lose bodily strength or vigor ⟨Having reached her 80s, the woman could sense that her body was *decaying*.⟩ — see WEAKEN 2

decayed *adj* **1** having lost forcefulness, courage, or spirit ⟨a candidate who vehemently rejects the idea that liberalism is a *decayed* political philosophy⟩ — see EFFETE 1

2 having undergone organic breakdown ⟨We routinely throw all *decayed* or unwanted organic matter into our compost heap.⟩ — see ROTTEN 1

decaying *n* a gradual sinking and wasting away of mind or body ⟨the *decaying* of muscle mass from inactivity⟩ — see DECLINE 1

decease *n* the permanent stopping of all the vital bodily activities ⟨In the event of the *decease* of the president, the vice president will assume the office.⟩ — see DEATH 1

deceased *adj* no longer living ⟨grieving relatives of the *deceased* man⟩ — see DEAD 1

deceit *n* **1** the inclination or practice of misleading others through lies or trickery ⟨a rise to power that was marked by treachery and *deceit*⟩

synonyms artifice, craft, craftiness, crookedness, cunning, deceitfulness, dishonesty, dissembling, dissimulation, double-dealing, duplicity, fakery, foxiness, fraud, guile, wiliness

related words equivocation, lying, mendacity, prevarication; chicanery, fraudulence, hanky-panky, skulduggery (*or* skullduggery), subterfuge, swindling, trickery, wile; falsehood, falsity, fib, untruth; hypocrisy, insincerity, sanctimoniousness, two-facedness; artfulness, caginess (*also* cageyness), deviousness, shrewdness; treacherousness, underhandedness, unscrupulousness; covertness, furtiveness, secrecy, shadiness, sneakiness, stealthiness; oiliness, shiftiness, slickness, slipperiness, slyness, smoothness

near antonyms candidness, candor, directness, frankness, openness, plainness; honesty, probity; dependability, reliability, reliableness, solidity, trustiness, trustworthiness; decency, goodness, incorruptibility, integrity, righteousness, truthfulness, uprightness, virtuousness

antonyms artlessness, forthrightness, good faith, guilelessness, ingenuousness, sincerity

2 the tendency to tell lies ⟨She's completely free of *deceit*.⟩ — see DISHONESTY 1

deceitful *adj* **1** marked by, based on, or done by the use of dishonest methods to acquire something of value ⟨charged the store owner with *deceitful* practices⟩ — see FRAUDULENT 1

2 tending or having power to deceive ⟨The *deceitful* salesman neglected to mention some important information about the used car.⟩ — see DECEPTIVE 1

deceitfulness *n* **1** the inclination or practice of misleading others through lies or trickery ⟨Her *deceitfulness* about the long-term effects of her weight-loss program was finally exposed.⟩ — see DECEIT 1

2 the tendency to tell lies ⟨His lifelong *deceitfulness* began when he was young.⟩ — see DISHONESTY 1

deceive *vb* to cause to believe what is untrue ⟨He went to great lengths to *deceive* his family about the nature of his new job at the mall.⟩

synonyms beguile, bluff, burn, catch, con, cozen, delude, dupe, fool, gaff, gull, have, hoax, hoodwink, humbug, misguide, misinform, mislead, snow, spoof, string along, take in, trick

related words kid, put on, tease; bleed, cheat, chisel, defraud, diddle, euchre, flam, fleece, hustle, mulct, rook, shortchange, skin, squeeze, stick, sting, swindle

phrases do a number on, lead one down the garden path (*also* lead one up the garden path), pull one's leg, pull the wool over one's eyes

near antonyms debunk, expose, reveal, show up, uncloak, uncover, unmask; disclose, divulge, tell, unveil; disabuse, disenchant, disillusion

antonyms undeceive

deceiving *adj* tending or having power to deceive ⟨The *deceiving* nature of most flat maps of the globe causes some people to believe erroneously that Greenland is actually bigger than South America.⟩ — see DECEPTIVE 1

decelerate *vb* to cause to move or proceed at a less rapid pace ⟨She *decelerated* the car as we entered the school zone.⟩ — see SLOW

deceleration *n* a usually gradual decrease in the pace or level of activity of something ⟨Demand for our product is dropping, so I have ordered a *deceleration* of production.⟩ — see SLOWDOWN

decency *n* **1** socially acceptable behavior ⟨The standards of basic *decency* called for them to help the older lady with her groceries.⟩

synonyms decorum, form, propriety

related words etiquette; civility, courteousness, courtesy, gentilesse, gentility, graciousness, mannerliness, politeness, politesse; dignity, grace, refinement; discretion, prudence; appropriateness, correctitude, correctness, decorousness, fitness, rightness, seemliness; attention, attentiveness, care, carefulness; character, goodness, highmindedness, honesty, honor, integrity, morality, probity, rectitude, righteousness, straightness, uprightness, virtue, virtuousness

near antonyms coarseness, crudeness, gracelessness; discourtesy, impoliteness, incivility, vulgarity; imprudence, indiscretion; badness, evil, immorality, wickedness; debauchery, degeneracy, degradation, depravity, perversion; crookedness, dishonesty, underhandedness, unscrupulousness

antonyms impropriety, indecency

2 conduct that conforms to an accepted standard of right and wrong ⟨expected all of their children to be models of *decency*⟩ — see MORALITY 1

decent *adj* **1** conforming to a high standard of morality or virtue ⟨as *decent* and kind a couple as you could ever hope to meet⟩ — see GOOD 2

2 following the accepted rules of moral conduct ⟨demanded nothing less than *decent* behavior by the troops serving overseas⟩ — see HONORABLE 1

3 following the established traditions of refined society and good taste ⟨We were asked to wait a *decent* interval before making the announcement.⟩ — see PROPER 1

4 free from any trace of the coarse or indecent ⟨Students were warned that their skits could be funny but still had to remain *decent*.⟩ — see CHASTE 1

5 of a level of quality that meets one's needs or standards ⟨He did a *decent* job on the project, but there's still room for improvement.⟩ — see ADEQUATE

deceptive *adj* **1** tending or having power to deceive ⟨In his *deceptive* answer about the vehicle's history, the salesman said that the used car had never been hit by another car.⟩

synonyms beguiling, deceitful, deceiving, deluding, delusive, delusory, fallacious, false, misleading, specious

related words artful, crafty, cunning, devious, foxy, guileful, shady, shifty, slick, sly, sneaking, sneaky, subtile, subtle, trick, trickish, tricky, underhand, underhanded, wily; crooked, defrauding, dishonest, dissembling, double-dealing, faithless, fast, fraudulent, knavish, lying, mendacious, untrustworthy, untruthful; bogus, counterfeit, fake, feigned, forged, phony (*also* phoney), sham, spurious; insidious, perfidious, treacherous; artificial, backhanded, hypocritical, insincere, left-handed, two-faced

near antonyms candid, direct, foursquare, frank, free-spoken, open, openhearted, outspoken, plain, plainspoken, straight; clarifying, elucidative, explanatory; revealing, revelatory; honest, trustworthy, truthful

antonyms aboveboard, forthright, nondeceptive, straightforward

2 given to or marked by cheating and deception ⟨a mail-order firm indicted for *deceptive* business practices⟩ — see DISHONEST 2

decide *vb* **1** to come to a judgment about after discussion or consideration ⟨They *decided* to go out for pizza after the movie was over.⟩

synonyms choose, conclude, determine, figure, name, opt, resolve, settle (on *or* upon)

related words decree, rule; cull, elect, handpick, pick, prefer, select, single (out); adjudge, adjudicate, arbitrate,

find, judge, referee, rule (on), umpire; chew over, cogitate, consider, contemplate, debate, deliberate, entertain, meditate, mull (over), ponder, question, ruminate, study, think (about *or* over), weigh
near antonyms abstain, decline, refuse, reject, turn down; delay, halt, hesitate, stall, temporize; shilly-shally, vacillate, waver
2 to give an opinion about (something at issue or in dispute) ⟨The judge *decided* that the defendant was not liable for damages.⟩ — see JUDGE 1
3 to come to an agreement or decision concerning the details of ⟨They waited for their captors to *decide* their fate.⟩ — see ARRANGE 1
4 to make final, definite, or beyond dispute ⟨The huge sum that they were offering *decided* the matter: we would sell the house.⟩ — see CLINCH
5 to form an opinion or reach a conclusion through reasoning and information ⟨The commanding officer *decided* that the soldier was indeed telling the truth.⟩ — see INFER 1
decided *adj* not subject to misinterpretation or more than one interpretation ⟨The home team had a *decided* advantage.⟩ — see CLEAR 2
decidedness *n* firm or unwavering adherence to one's purpose ⟨For two years he pursued the presidential nomination with an undeviating *decidedness*.⟩ — see DETERMINATION 1
decimate *vb* to bring to a complete end the physical soundness, existence, or usefulness of ⟨The army's attack *decimated* the enemy's defenses beyond repair.⟩ — see DESTROY 1
decimation *n* the state or fact of being rendered nonexistent, physically unsound, or useless ⟨the virtual *decimation* of the trees by the invasive moth species⟩ — see DESTRUCTION 1
decipher *vb* **1** to change (as a secret message) from code into ordinary language ⟨We *deciphered* the hidden message to find out when we were supposed to meet.⟩ — see DECODE 1
2 to have a clear idea of ⟨a convoluted thriller, the plot of which I was never able to actually *decipher*⟩ — see COMPREHEND 1
decision *n* **1** a position arrived at after consideration ⟨After much deliberation, we made a *decision* about what to have on our pizza.⟩
synonyms award, call, conclusion, deliverance, determination, diagnosis, judgment (*or* judgement), opinion, resolution, verdict
related words behest, charge, commandment, decree, dictate, directive, edict, instruction, mandate, order, word; last word, say-so; adjudication, disposition, doom, finding, ruling, sentence; choice, option, selection; consensus; belief, conviction, eye, feeling, mind, notion, persuasion, sentiment, view
near antonyms deadlock, draw, halt, stalemate, stand-off, tie
2 firm or unwavering adherence to one's purpose ⟨acted with swift *decision*⟩ — see DETERMINATION 1
decisive *adj* **1** fully committed to achieving a goal ⟨Only a team with a *decisive* attitude is going to win a state championship.⟩ — see DETERMINED 1
2 having the power to persuade ⟨a lawyer who knows how to construct the kind of *decisive* argument that sways a jury⟩ — see COGENT
3 serving to put an end to all debate or questioning ⟨the *decisive* finding of the investigator regarding the cause of the accident⟩ — see CONCLUSIVE 1
decisiveness *n* firm or unwavering adherence to one's purpose ⟨moved with speed and *decisiveness* in investigating the charges⟩ — see DETERMINATION 1

deck *vb* to make more attractive by adding something that is beautiful or becoming ⟨*Deck* the halls with boughs of holly.⟩ — see DECORATE
declaim *vb* **1** to give a formal often extended talk on a subject ⟨Over the last two centuries some of the most illustrious personages of their times have *declaimed* in the town's historic lyceum.⟩ — see TALK 1
2 to talk as if giving an important and formal speech ⟨He *declaimed* at some length about the nation's obligation to spread democratic values around the world.⟩ — see ORATE 1
declamation *n* a usually formal discourse delivered to an audience ⟨inspired *declamations* about the global triumph of democracy within our lifetimes⟩ — see SPEECH 1
declaration *n* a solemn and often public declaration of the truth or existence of something ⟨Once the delegates had made the *declaration* that the colonies were henceforth independent of Great Britain, their fate was sealed.⟩ — see PROTESTATION
declare *vb* **1** to make known openly or publicly ⟨She chose to *declare* her presidential aspirations at her college alma mater.⟩ — see ANNOUNCE
2 to state as a fact usually forcefully ⟨She would *declare* her innocence to the whole world if she could.⟩ — see CLAIM 1
3 to state clearly and strongly ⟨Our guest enthusiastically *declared* that the pie was the best he had ever eaten.⟩ — see ASSERT 1
4 to make known (something abstract) through outward signs ⟨Though she was silent, her expression *declared* her unwillingness to go along with the others.⟩ — see SHOW 2
declension *n* **1** a change to a lower state or level ⟨a *declension* in her acting career from leading roles to cameos eventually⟩ — see DECLINE 2
2 a downward slope ⟨From this region to the seacoast there's a gentle *declension* of the landscape.⟩ — see DECLINE 3
decline *n* **1** a gradual sinking and wasting away of mind or body ⟨Doctors tried to slow the patient's *decline*.⟩
synonyms debilitation, decay, decaying, degeneration, descent, deterioration, ebbing, enfeeblement, weakening
related words exhaustion; drooping, flagging, limping; regression, relapse, setback
near antonyms invigoration, strengthening; progress; rejuvenation, rejuvenescence
antonyms comeback, improvement, rally, recovery, recuperation, rehabilitation, revitalization, snapback
2 a change to a lower state or level ⟨the *decline* of the Roman Empire⟩
synonyms decadence, declension, degeneracy, degeneration, degradation, descent, deterioration, downfall, downgrade, ebb, eclipse, fall
related words dark age, sunset; decay, rotting, spoiling; breakup, crumbling, decomposition, disintegration, dissolution; abasement, debasement; depreciation, lessening; decimation, demolishment, demolition, desolation, destruction, havoc, ruin, ruination; abatement, decrease, decrement, de-escalation, deflation, diminishment, diminution, dip, downslide, downtrend, downturn, drop, loss, lowering, reduction, sag, shrinkage, slip, slump
near antonyms advancement, development, evolution, growth; blossoming, flourishing, flowering; renewal, restoration, revitalization; heightening; accretion, accrual, addendum, addition, augmentation, boost, enhancement, gain, increase, increment, raise, supplement
antonyms ascent, rise, upswing
3 a downward slope ⟨The bicyclist lost control on the unexpectedly steep *decline*.⟩

synonyms declension, descent, dip, downgrade, fall, hang, hanging

related words basin, depression, hollow

near antonyms grade, gradient, hill, inclination, incline, lean, pitch, rake, tilt

antonyms acclivity, ascent, rise, upgrade, uphill, uprise

4 a loss of status ⟨The engagement at the small club was an unmistakable sign of the rock band's *decline*.⟩ — see COMEDOWN

5 the amount by which something is lessened ⟨a huge *decline* in the value of the artwork after its authenticity was questioned⟩ — see DECREASE

decline *vb* **1** to show unwillingness to accept, do, engage in, or agree to ⟨He *declined* the invitation to the party.⟩ ⟨She *declined* to participate in the soccer game.⟩

synonyms disapprove, negative, pass, refuse, reject, reprobate, repudiate, spurn, throw out, turn down

related words disdain, rebuff, scorn, scout; overrule, veto; forbid, prohibit, proscribe; dismiss, ignore; abstain (from), forbear, refrain (from); deny, disavow, disclaim, dispute, gainsay; stick; abjure, recant, renounce, retract, take back, unsay, withdraw; avoid, bypass, detour; contradict, deny, disown, negate; disagree (with), disprove, dispute, rebut, refute; back down, back off, backtrack; disallow, recall, renege, revoke

phrases turn one's back on

near antonyms condone, countenance, swallow, tolerate; adopt, embrace, take, welcome; accede, acquiesce, agree, assent, consent; choose, handpick, select; espouse, support

antonyms accept, agree (to), approve

2 to be unwilling to grant ⟨*declined* our request to hold a party⟩ — see DENY 2

3 to go to a lower level especially abruptly ⟨New-car sales *declined* to their lowest level in years.⟩ — see DROP 2

4 to become worse or of less value ⟨His reputation as a writer began to *decline* not long after his death.⟩ — see DETERIORATE 1

5 to grow less in scope or intensity especially gradually ⟨The winds should *decline* as soon as the cold front passes.⟩ — see DECREASE 2

6 to lead or extend downward ⟨The bike path *declines* toward the riverbank and then follows the river for several miles.⟩ — see DESCEND 1

declined *adj* bending downward or forward ⟨We awaited our punishment with *declined* heads.⟩ — see NODDING

declining *adj* bending downward or forward ⟨The *declining* flowers perked up with the gentle rainfall.⟩ — see NODDING

decode *vb* **1** to change (as a secret message) from code into ordinary language ⟨The agents worked into the night to *decode* the intercepted message from the enemy spy.⟩

synonyms break, crack, decipher

related words descramble, unscramble; render, translate; dope (out), figure out, puzzle (out), solve, unravel, work, work out

near antonyms garble, jumble (up), mix (up)

antonyms cipher, code, encipher, encode, encrypt

2 to have a clear idea of ⟨I was never able to *decode* the strange relationship that existed between those two people.⟩ — see COMPREHEND 1

decolorize *vb* to make white or whiter by removing color ⟨The sample was *decolorized* before being examined under a microscope.⟩ — see WHITEN

decompose *vb* to go through decomposition ⟨Detectives needed to know how long it would take a corpse to *decompose* to that advanced state.⟩ — see DECAY 1

decomposed *adj* having undergone organic breakdown ⟨the *decomposed* remains of an old tree trunk⟩ — see ROTTEN 1

decomposition *n* the process by which dead organic matter separates into simpler substances ⟨The unmistakable smell of *decomposition* led us to some fruit that had fallen behind the refrigerator.⟩ — see CORRUPTION 1

decorate *vb* to make more attractive by adding something that is beautiful or becoming ⟨*decorated* the mansion's hallways with priceless paintings and luxurious tapestries⟩

synonyms adorn, array, beautify, bedeck, bedizen, caparison, deck, do, doll up, dress, embellish, enrich, garnish, grace, ornament, trim

related words accessorize, dress up, trap, trick (out); brighten, freshen, smarten; boss, chase; braid, embroider, feather, figure, filigree, fillet, flounce, frill, fringe, furbelow, garland, hang, lace, ribbon, swag, wreathe; appliqué, gild, paint

near antonyms simplify, streamline; bare, denude, dismantle, display, expose, reveal, strip, uncover; uglify

antonyms blemish, deface, disfigure, mar, scar, spoil

decoration *n* **1** something that decorates or beautifies ⟨Traditionally the family puts lots of *decorations* on and around the Christmas tree.⟩

synonyms adornment, caparison, embellishment, frill, garnish, ornament, trim

related words apparel, bells and whistles, blazonry, bric-a-brac, chichi, emblazonry, filigree, finery; flounce, flourish, furbelow, ruffle; enhancement, enrichment, improvement; appliqué, embossment, embroidery, fancywork; bedizenment, gilt, glitter; design, figure, pattern; furnishings, regalia, trappings

near antonyms blemish, defacement, disfigurement, scar; blot, spot, stain

2 something given in recognition of achievement ⟨an army veteran proudly wearing his old military *decorations*⟩ — see AWARD 1

decorative *adj* serving to add beauty ⟨A necklace of *decorative* flowers was planted along the path to the cottage.⟩

synonyms adorning, beautifying, embellishing, ornamental

related words alluring, appealing, attractive, charming, delightful, glamorous (*also* glamourous), pleasing, prepossessing; beauteous, beautiful, comely, fair, gorgeous, handsome, lovely, pretty, stunning; detailed, elaborate, fancy, ornate

antonyms functional, utilitarian

decorous *adj* **1** following the established traditions of refined society and good taste ⟨We were asked to be on our most *decorous* behavior at the formal event.⟩ — see PROPER 1

2 marked by or showing careful attention to set forms and details ⟨the oppressively *decorous* standards of a royal court⟩ — see CEREMONIOUS 1

decorum *n* socially acceptable behavior ⟨High standards of *decorum* are usually required when visiting the memorial.⟩ — see DECENCY 1

decoy *n* something used to attract animals to a hook or into a trap ⟨We set the *decoy* afloat in the marsh and from the blind waited for the ducks to arrive.⟩ — see BAIT 1

decoy *vb* to lead away from a usual or proper course by offering some pleasure or advantage ⟨tacky souvenir shops to which first-time tourists had been *decoyed* into spending their hard-earned money⟩ — see LURE

decrease *n* the amount by which something is lessened ⟨The average *decrease* in the price of milk was five cents per gallon.⟩

synonyms abatement, decline, decrement, dent, depression, diminishment, diminution, drop, fall, loss, reduction, shrinkage

related words deduction, subtraction; downturn, slip, slump; curtailment, cut, cutback, retrenchment, shortening

near antonyms accretion, accrual, accumulation, addition, supplement; continuation, extension; upswing, uptrend, upturn

antonyms boost, enlargement, gain, increase, increment, raise, rise

decrease *vb* 1 to make smaller in amount, volume, or extent ⟨Workers *decreased* the volume of water flowing through the pipes in order to prevent an overflow.⟩

synonyms abate, de-escalate, dent, deplete, diminish, downsize, drop, dwindle, ease, knock down, lessen, lower, reduce

related words compress, condense, constrict, contract; abbreviate, abridge, clip, crop, curtail, cut, cut back, cut down, dock, nick, pare, prune, retrench, shorten, slash, trim, truncate, whittle; deflate, shrink; minimize; moderate, modify, modulate, qualify; deprive, strip

near antonyms blow up, dilate, distend, inflate, swell; elongate, extend, lengthen, prolong, protract; add (to), complement, supplement; enhance, heighten, intensify; redouble

antonyms aggrandize, amplify, augment, boost, enlarge, escalate, expand, increase, raise

2 to grow less in scope or intensity especially gradually ⟨The force of the wind slowly *decreased* until the flowers were standing upright again.⟩

synonyms abate, decline, de-escalate, diminish, dwindle, ease, ebb, fall, lessen, let up, lower, moderate, pall, recede, relent, remit, shrink, subside, taper, taper off, wane

related words compress, condense, constrict, contract; evaporate, fade (away), fritter (away), give out, melt (away), peter (out), tail (off), vanish; slacken, slow (down); alleviate, relax; flag, sink, weaken; cave (in), collapse, deflate

near antonyms appear, emerge, show up; blow up, distend, elongate, lengthen

antonyms accumulate, balloon, build, burgeon (*also* bourgeon), enlarge, escalate, expand, grow, increase, intensify, mount, mushroom, pick up, rise, snowball, soar, swell, wax

decree *n* 1 a statement of what to do that must be obeyed by those concerned ⟨The boss doesn't give out many *decrees*, but he does expect those that are issued to be fully obeyed.⟩ — see COMMAND 1

2 an order publicly issued by an authority ⟨a *decree* issued by the state's supreme court to the legislature⟩ — see EDICT 1

decree *vb* to request the doing of by virtue of one's authority ⟨The new supervisor *decreed* that thenceforth coffee breaks would have a 15-minute limit.⟩ — see COMMAND 2

decrement *n* the amount by which something is lessened ⟨Each *decrement* in amount is limited to one third of the previous total.⟩ — see DECREASE

decry *vb* 1 to express scornfully one's low opinion of ⟨Scientists were quick to *decry* the claims of the psychic.⟩

synonyms bad-mouth, belittle, cry down, deprecate, depreciate, diminish, discount, dismiss, disparage, minimize, play down, put down, run down, write off

related words discommend; abuse, scold; disapprove (of), dislike; censure, condemn, criticize, denounce, reprehend, reprobate; asperse, defame, malign, rip, slander, slur, traduce, vilify; discredit, disgrace

phrases dump on

near antonyms approve, countenance, endorse (*also* indorse), favor, recommend, sanction; commend, compliment, eulogize

antonyms acclaim, applaud, exalt, extol (*also* extoll), glorify, laud, magnify, praise

2 to declare to be morally wrong or evil ⟨environmentalists *decrying* the failure of humans as guardians of the planet⟩ — see CONDEMN 1

decrying *adj* intended to make a person or thing seem of little importance or value ⟨the usual *decrying* remarks about the clothes that the stars wore to the awards ceremony⟩ — see DEROGATORY

dedicate *vb* to keep or intend for a special purpose ⟨a young attorney who has decided to *dedicate* her career to helping the poor receive justice⟩ — see DEVOTE 1

dedication *n* adherence to something to which one is bound by a pledge or duty ⟨Her *dedication* to the ideals of the organization is indeed admirable.⟩ — see FIDELITY

deduce *vb* to form an opinion or reach a conclusion through reasoning and information ⟨I can *deduce* from the simple observation of your behavior that you're trying to hide something from me.⟩ — see INFER 1

deducible *adj* being or provable by reasoning in which the conclusion follows necessarily from given information ⟨The killer's identity is clearly *deducible* from the clues scattered throughout the novel.⟩ — see DEDUCTIVE

deduct *vb* to take away (an amount or number) from a total ⟨After *deducting* taxes, what's left is your net pay for the week.⟩ — see SUBTRACT

deduction *n* 1 something that is or may be subtracted ⟨Contestants get a *deduction* from their scores for every incorrect guess.⟩

synonyms abatement, discount, reduction

related words giveback, kickback, rebate; dent, depreciation; decline, decrement, diminishment, diminution, drop, fall, loss; forfeit, forfeiture, penalty

near antonyms accretion, accrual, augmentation, boost, gain, increase, increment, raise, rise; appreciation

antonyms addition

2 the act or an instance of taking away from a total ⟨the *deduction* of the amount awarded to the plaintiff in order to pay the legal fees⟩ — see SUBTRACTION

3 an opinion arrived at through a process of reasoning ⟨His impressive *deduction* of the correct answer from only a few hints.⟩ — see CONCLUSION 1

deductive *adj* being or provable by reasoning in which the conclusion follows necessarily from given information ⟨a judgment reached through *deductive* logic⟩

synonyms deducible, derivable, inferable (*also* inferrible), reasoned

related words conjectural, hypothetical, purported, supposed, suppositional; logical, rational

near antonyms inducible, inductive; absolute, categorical (*also* categoric), definite, explicit, express; instinctive, intuitive; illogical, irrational

antonyms nondeductive

deed *n* 1 an act of notable skill, strength, or cleverness ⟨Traditionally heroes have been celebrated for their great *deeds* in song and story.⟩ — see FEAT 1

2 something done by someone ⟨*Deeds* always carry greater weight than words.⟩ — see ACTION 1

deed *vb* to give over the legal possession or ownership of ⟨The philanthropist unexpectedly *deeded* his entire fortune to the animal shelter.⟩ — see TRANSFER 1

deem *vb* to have as an opinion ⟨I *deem* it fitting that we mark this solemn occasion with a moment of silence.⟩ — see BELIEVE 2

deep *adj* 1 extending far downward ⟨lowered their bucket down a *deep* well⟩ ⟨The ax made a *deep* cut into the wood.⟩

synonyms abysmal, bottomless, profound

related words abyssal, unfathomable; boundless, endless, immeasurable, infinite, limitless, measureless, unlimited, vast

near antonyms depthless, two-dimensional; even, flat, flush, horizontal, level, plane, smooth; finite, limited, measured, restricted

antonyms shallow, shoal, skin-deep, superficial, surface

2 having a low musical pitch or range ⟨The tour guide had an impressively *deep* voice.⟩

synonyms bass, grave, low, throaty

related words boomy, tubby; gruff, hoarse, husky, rough, smoky (*also* smokey)

near antonyms squeaking, squeaky, squealing, thin; earsplitting, penetrating, piercing, strident; peeping, tinny

antonyms acute, high, high-pitched, piping, sharp, shrill, treble

3 being beyond one's powers to know, understand, or explain ⟨a *deep*, dark secret that he took to his grave⟩ — see MYSTERIOUS 1

4 difficult for one of ordinary knowledge or intelligence to understand ⟨Her poetry is now regarded as sentimental and not very *deep*.⟩ — see PROFOUND 1

5 having an often intentionally veiled or uncertain meaning ⟨one of those *deep* lines in the poem that can be interpreted in any number of different ways⟩ — see OBSCURE 1

6 extreme in degree, power, or effect ⟨I fell into a *deep* sleep after taking the potion.⟩ — see INTENSE 1

7 firmly established over time ⟨a *deep* devotion to obtaining justice for all, even society's most disadvantaged⟩ — see INVETERATE 1

8 having considerable extent ⟨an economist with a *deep* understanding of the forces that propel the global economy⟩ — see EXTENSIVE

9 having the mind fixed on something ⟨I was so *deep* in the mystery novel that I didn't hear the doorbell.⟩ — see ATTENTIVE 1

10 not close in time or space ⟨an episode in her *deep* past that she had never spoken about⟩ — see DISTANT 1

deep *n* **1** the most intense or characteristic phase of something ⟨the kind of cold weather that we usually have only in the *deep* of winter⟩ — see THICK

2 the whole body of salt water that covers nearly three-fourths of the earth ⟨sailors exploring the farther reaches of the briny *deep*⟩ — see OCEAN 1

3 an immeasurable depth or space ⟨the belief that somewhere in the *deep* of outer space humankind will meet its ultimate destiny⟩ — see ABYSS

deepen *vb* to make markedly greater in measure or degree ⟨This book really *deepens* our knowledge of how the brain works.⟩ — see INTENSIFY

deep–rooted *adj* firmly established over time ⟨He had had a *deep-rooted* fear of the dark from the time he was a small child.⟩ — see INVETERATE 1

deep–seated *adj* firmly established over time ⟨He has *deep-seated* convictions about religion that no one is ever going to change.⟩ — see INVETERATE 1

de–escalate *vb* **1** to make smaller in amount, volume, or extent ⟨First, the mediator tried to *de-escalate* the tension in the room.⟩ — see DECREASE 1

2 to grow less in scope or intensity especially gradually ⟨The fighting *de-escalated* as the peace talks progressed.⟩ — see DECREASE 2

deface *vb* **1** to deliberately cause the damage or destruction of another's property ⟨The principal vowed to punish whoever *defaced* the statue in front of the school.⟩ — see VANDALIZE

2 to reduce the soundness, effectiveness, or perfection of ⟨Years of wear had *defaced* the fine engraving on the coins.⟩ — see DAMAGE 1

defacement *n* deliberate damaging or destroying of another's property ⟨The *defacement* of the school's property ended up costing hundreds of dollars.⟩ — see VANDALISM

defacer *n* a person who damages or destroys property on purpose ⟨So far the police have no leads on the identity of the *defacer* of the street signs.⟩ — see VANDAL

defamation *n* the making of false statements that damage another's reputation ⟨accused the news reporter of *defamation* of character⟩ — see SLANDER

defamatory *adj* causing or intended to cause unjust injury to a person's good name ⟨*defamatory* remarks that were published in the newspaper⟩ — see LIBELOUS

defame *vb* to make untrue and harmful statements about ⟨Of course I want to win the election, but I refuse to *defame* my opponent in order to do so.⟩ — see SLANDER

defaming *n* the making of false statements that damage another's reputation ⟨the callous *defaming* of the popular actress by the unscrupulous tabloid reporter⟩ — see SLANDER

default *n* the nonperformance of an assigned or expected action ⟨a *default* in the repayment of a bank loan⟩ — see FAILURE 1

defeat *n* **1** failure to win a contest ⟨still getting over their *defeat* in the basketball game earlier that week⟩

synonyms beating, drubbing, licking, loss, lump, overthrow, rout, shellacking, trimming, trouncing, whipping

related words collapse, debacle (*also* débâcle), failure, fiasco, fizzle, flop, nonsuccess, setback, upset; lurch, shutout, washout, whitewash

near antonyms accomplishment, achievement; blowout, landslide, romp, sweep, walkaway, walkover

antonyms success, triumph, victory, win

2 a falling short of one's goals ⟨truly disheartened by the *defeat* of his plans to revitalize downtown⟩ — see FAILURE 2

defeat *vb* to achieve a victory over ⟨They *defeated* their archrivals easily and moved into the next round of the play-offs.⟩ — see BEAT 2

defeatist *adj* emphasizing or expecting the worst ⟨Your *defeatist* attitude is depressing everyone else on the team!⟩ — see PESSIMISTIC 1

defeatist *n* one who emphasizes bad aspects or conditions and expects the worst ⟨We told her that if she was going to be such a *defeatist*, she should keep her thoughts to herself.⟩ — see PESSIMIST 1

defect *n* something that spoils the appearance or completeness of a thing ⟨The statue has a slight *defect* on the base, so it's being sold at a discount.⟩ — see BLEMISH

defect (from) *vb* to leave (a cause or party) often in order to take up another ⟨Soldiers *defected from* the rebel army en masse as the failure of their cause became apparent.⟩

synonyms desert, rat (on)

related words abandon, abdicate, abjure, apostatize, cut off, disown, forsake, quit, reject, renounce, repudiate, spurn; renege; depart, go, leave, withdraw

phrases go back on, jump ship, run out on, walk out on

near antonyms adhere (to), cling (to), stick (to *or* with); cherish, cultivate, foster

defective *adj* having a fault ⟨We promptly took the *defective* phone back to the store for a replacement.⟩ — see FAULTY

defector *n* a person who abandons a cause or organization usually without right ⟨The *defector* requested political asylum.⟩ — see RENEGADE

defend *vb* **1** to drive danger or attack away from ⟨a solemn oath to *defend* the mother country at any cost⟩

synonyms bulwark, cover, fence, guard, keep, protect, safeguard, screen, secure, shield, ward
related words avert, prevent; oppose, resist, withstand; battle, contend, fight, war; conserve, preserve, save
phrases stand up for
near antonyms bombard, storm; beset, besiege, overrun; capitulate, cave, submit, yield
antonyms assail, assault, attack
2 to continue to declare to be true or proper despite opposition or objections ⟨She will *defend* her friends to the bitter end.⟩ — see MAINTAIN 2
defendable *adj* **1** capable of being defended against physical attack ⟨That nation has long insisted on having borders that it regards as *defendable*.⟩ — see TENABLE 1
2 capable of being defended with good reasoning against verbal attack ⟨He decided to argue the side he considered more *defendable* in the debate.⟩ — see TENABLE 2
defender *n* someone that protects ⟨He's a staunch *defender* of human rights.⟩ — see PROTECTOR
defense *n* **1** means or method of defending ⟨Thorns are a rose's *defense* against grazing animals.⟩
synonyms aegis (*also* egis), ammunition, armor, cover, guard, protection, safeguard, screen, security, shield, wall, ward
related words arm, armament, munitions, weapon, weaponry; fastness, fort, fortress, palisade, stronghold
near antonyms aggression, assault, attack, offense (*or* offence), offensive
2 an explanation that frees one from fault or blame ⟨There's absolutely no *defense* for your actions.⟩ — see EXCUSE
defenseless *adj* lacking protection from danger or resistance against attack ⟨The lack of warm clothing left the hikers *defenseless* against the unexpected cold snap.⟩ — see HELPLESS 1
defenselessness *n* the quality or state of having little resistance to some outside agent ⟨Our utter *defenselessness* against the rising floodwaters quickly became apparent.⟩ — see SUSCEPTIBILITY
defensible *adj* **1** capable of being defended against physical attack ⟨The pioneers retreated to a *defensible* hillside to take a stand against the raiders.⟩ — see TENABLE 1
2 capable of being defended with good reasoning against verbal attack ⟨In hindsight, her actions are *defensible*.⟩ — see TENABLE 2
defensive *adj* intended to resist or prevent attack or aggression ⟨a *defensive* alliance among the small nations against the aggressors⟩
synonyms protective
related words deterrent, preventive; safe, secure
near antonyms aggressive, bellicose, belligerent, combative, contentious, in-your-face, militant, pugnacious, quarrelsome, scrappy, truculent, warlike
antonyms offensive
defensive *n* a position of readiness to oppose actual or expected attack ⟨Their unexpectedly harsh words put him on the *defensive*.⟩
synonyms guard
related words alert, lookout, qui vive, watch
antonyms offensive
defer *vb* to assign to a later time ⟨We agreed to *defer* a discussion of the issue until we had more information.⟩ — see POSTPONE
deference *n* a readiness or willingness to yield to the wishes of others ⟨The sycophantic *deference* with which the hotel treats celebrity guests.⟩ — see COMPLIANCE 1
deferential *adj* marked by or showing proper regard for another's higher status ⟨The class listened with *deferential* attention.⟩ — see RESPECTFUL

deferentially *adv* in a manner showing no signs of pride or self-assertion ⟨behaved *deferentially* when approaching someone in authority⟩ — see LOWLY
defiance *n* **1** refusal to obey ⟨She was held in contempt for her *defiance* of the court order.⟩ — see DISOBEDIENCE
2 the inclination to resist ⟨A week of obedience training cured the dog of its *defiance* of its owners.⟩ — see RESISTANCE 1
3 an inclination to fight or quarrel ⟨The protesters stood their ground, sure of their cause and full of *defiance*.⟩ — see BELLIGERENCE
defiant *adj* given to resisting authority or another's control ⟨The *defiant* puppy refused to let go of the football.⟩ — see DISOBEDIENT
deficiency *n* a falling short of an essential or desirable amount or number ⟨The disease may be caused by a nutritional *deficiency*.⟩
synonyms crunch, dearth, deficit, failure, famine, inadequacy, insufficiency, lack, paucity, pinch, poverty, scantiness, scarceness, scarcity, shortage, want
related words absence, omission; meagerness, poorness, skimpiness; necessity, need, privation
near antonyms bountifulness, copiousness; excess, overabundance, oversupply, surfeit, surplus
antonyms abundance, adequacy, amplitude, opulence, plenitude, plenty, sufficiency, wealth
deficient *adj* **1** lacking some necessary part ⟨A diet *deficient* in calcium can lead to weak bones.⟩ — see INCOMPLETE
2 falling short of a standard ⟨Woefully *deficient* eyesight kept him out of military service.⟩ — see BAD 1
3 not coming up to an expected measure or meeting a particular need ⟨too *deficient* in experience to handle the situation by himself⟩ — see SHORT 3
deficiently *adv* in an unsatisfactory way ⟨The road to the mountain lodge is so *deficiently* marked that we had a terrible time finding it.⟩ — see BADLY 1
deficit *n* a falling short of an essential or desirable amount or number ⟨a growing *deficit* in the number of hours devoted to sleep⟩ — see DEFICIENCY
defile *n* a narrow opening between hillsides or mountains that can be used for passage ⟨The cattle, once they were cornered in the *defile*, were quickly rounded up.⟩ — see CANYON
defile *vb* **1** to make unfit for use by the addition of something harmful or undesirable ⟨The lake has been *defiled* by pollutants.⟩ — see CONTAMINATE
2 to treat (a sacred place or object) shamefully or with great disrespect ⟨Art conservators were careful not to do anything that might *defile* the holy relic.⟩ — see DESECRATE
defilement *n* **1** an act of great disrespect shown to God or to sacred ideas, people, or things ⟨For two centuries the Christian monasteries in England suffered *defilements* at the hands of Viking invaders.⟩ — see BLASPHEMY
2 something that is or that makes impure ⟨considered billboards *defilements* of the landscape⟩ — see IMPURITY 1
define *vb* **1** to draw or make apparent the outline of ⟨The glass skyscraper's sleek silhouette was strikingly *defined* by the setting sun to its west.⟩ — see OUTLINE 1
2 to mark the limits of ⟨The river *defines* the town on the south.⟩ — see LIMIT 2
3 to point out the chief quality or qualities of an individual or group ⟨a woman who is *defined* by her unswerving loyalty to her friends⟩ — see CHARACTERIZE 1
4 to give the rules about (something) clearly and exactly ⟨Let me *define* the task so that there is no doubt in your minds about what needs to be done.⟩ — see PRESCRIBE
defined *adj* having distinct or certain limits ⟨well *defined*

guidelines on the range of activities in which the intelligence agency can engage⟩ — see LIMITED 1

definite *adj* **1** having distinct or certain limits ⟨There should be a *definite* scope to your paper.⟩ — see LIMITED 1
2 so clearly expressed as to leave no doubt about the meaning ⟨a *definite* instruction not to let anyone in the house while the parents were out for the evening⟩ — see EXPLICIT
3 having no exceptions or restrictions ⟨The house is a *definite* bargain by today's standards.⟩ — see ABSOLUTE 2

definitely *adv* without any question ⟨That is *definitely* the kind of dog we're looking to adopt.⟩ — see INDEED 1

definitive *adj* **1** being the most accurate and apparently thorough ⟨the *definitive* biography on the 16th president⟩
synonyms authoritative, classic, classical
related words conclusive, decisive; approved, official, sanctioned; accurate, correct; complete, comprehensive, exhaustive, thorough
2 serving to put an end to all debate or questioning ⟨a *definitive* answer that put an immediate end to the discussion⟩ — see CONCLUSIVE 1
3 so clearly expressed as to leave no doubt about the meaning ⟨the insurance company's *definitive* statement on the types of surgical operations that are covered⟩ — see EXPLICIT
4 constituting, serving as, or worthy of being a pattern to be imitated ⟨Dashiell Hammett's Sam Spade is often cited as the *definitive* hard-boiled private detective.⟩ — see MODEL

deflect *vb* to change the course or direction of (something) ⟨The wind *deflected* the Frisbee just as I was about to lunge for it.⟩ — see TURN 2

deform *vb* to twist (something) out of a natural or normal shape or condition ⟨The tree's trunk was *deformed* by the adjacent boulder.⟩ — see CONTORT

deformation *n* the twisting of something out of its natural or normal shape or condition ⟨the *deformation* of the steel girders under the enormous weight of the bridge⟩ — see CONTORTION

deformed *adj* badly or imperfectly formed ⟨His first sculpture looked more like a *deformed* rabbit than a galloping horse.⟩ — see MALFORMED

deformity *n* something that spoils the appearance or completeness of a thing ⟨a condition that causes *deformity* of the fingernails⟩ — see BLEMISH

defraud *vb* to rob by the use of trickery or threats ⟨Senior citizens generally were too smart to fall for the fast-talking salesman's attempts to *defraud* them.⟩ — see FLEECE

defrauder *n* a dishonest person who uses clever means to cheat others out of something of value ⟨The state's department of consumer protection has to contend with *defrauders* of every ilk.⟩ — see TRICKSTER 1

defrauding *adj* marked by, based on, or done by the use of dishonest methods to acquire something of value ⟨Every new technology has brought with it a raft of *defrauding* schemes that make full use of it.⟩ — see FRAUDULENT 1

defrosted *adj* freed from a frozen state by exposure to warmth ⟨I tossed a *defrosted* steak under the broiler for dinner.⟩ — see THAWED

deft *adj* **1** accomplished with trained ability ⟨a photographer known for her *deft* use of lighting⟩ — see SKILLFUL 1
2 skillful with the hands ⟨The *deft* jeweler quickly attached the diamond to its mount on the gold band.⟩ — see DEXTEROUS 1

deftness *n* **1** ease and grace in physical activity ⟨the effortless *deftness* with which he plays the piano⟩ — see DEXTERITY 2
2 subtle or imaginative ability in inventing, devising, or

executing something ⟨With *deftness* and aplomb she managed to keep the bickering relatives apart for the duration of the reception.⟩ — see SKILL 1

defunct *adj* **1** no longer existing ⟨A stack of brochures and a few faded placards are all that remain of the *defunct* organization.⟩ — see EXTINCT
2 no longer living ⟨a *defunct* species that we know only through fossil remains⟩ — see DEAD 1

defy *vb* **1** to go against the commands, prohibitions, or rules of ⟨She *defied* conventional wisdom and invested in the startup company.⟩ — see DISOBEY
2 to invite (someone) to take part in a contest or to perform a feat ⟨After missing the target, she *defied* her boyfriend to do better.⟩ — see CHALLENGE 2
3 to oppose (something hostile or dangerous) with firmness or courage ⟨a rescue team willing to *defy* the raging storm⟩ — see FACE 2
4 to refuse to give in to ⟨a bicyclist who regularly *defies* illness and infirmity in order to compete in races⟩ — see RESIST

degeneracy *n* **1** a change to a lower state or level ⟨the sad *degeneracy* of the city's downtown⟩ — see DECLINE 2
2 a sinking to a state of low moral standards and behavior ⟨the *degeneracy* of the family into a gang of petty thieves⟩ — see CORRUPTION 2

degenerate *adj* **1** having lost forcefulness, courage, or spirit ⟨a *degenerate* society in which people had no sense of being citizens, only consumers⟩ — see EFFETE 1
2 having or showing lowered moral character or standards ⟨a movie about a gang of *degenerate* criminals⟩ — see CORRUPT

degenerate *n* a person who has sunk below the normal moral standard ⟨a *degenerate* who is uninterested in anything but his own gratification⟩
synonyms backslider, debaucher, decadent, deviate, libertine, pervert, profligate, rake
related words bankrupt, delinquent, derelict, incorrigible; blackguard, cad, heel, knave, miscreant, rascal, reprobate, rogue, scoundrel, villain; lecher, playboy, playgirl
near antonyms saint

degenerate *vb* to become worse or of less value ⟨Over the years the community-minded organization *degenerated* into just a social club.⟩ — see DETERIORATE 1

degeneration *n* **1** a change to a lower state or level ⟨the organization's *degeneration* from a movement for political reform to just another political party⟩ — see DECLINE 2
2 a gradual sinking and wasting away of mind or body ⟨the troubling *degeneration* of his memory⟩ — see DECLINE 1
3 a sinking to a state of low moral standards and behavior ⟨the general *degeneration* that characterized so many old mining towns⟩ — see CORRUPTION 2

degradation *n* **1** a change to a lower state or level ⟨There has been a slight *degradation* in the car's performance.⟩ — see DECLINE 2
2 a sinking to a state of low moral standards and behavior ⟨the belief that moral *degradation* is an unmistakable sign of a nation in decline⟩ — see CORRUPTION 2

degrade *vb* **1** to bring to a lower grade or rank ⟨the view that such a system *degrades* doctors to the status of medical employees who ultimately are not in charge of their patients' health care⟩ — see DEMOTE
2 to lower in character, dignity, or quality ⟨*degrading* the school's animal mascot with a silly costume⟩ — see DEBASE 1
3 to reduce to a lower standing in one's own eyes or in others' eyes ⟨The players *degraded* themselves with their crude antics off the field.⟩ — see HUMBLE

degraded *adj* having or showing lowered moral character or standards ⟨Some residents felt that the city's festivities for Mardi Gras had become *degraded*.⟩ — see CORRUPT

degrading *adj* intended to make a person or thing seem of little importance or value ⟨Tom made *degrading* comments about his so-called friend behind his back.⟩ — see DEROGATORY

degree *n* 1 an individual part of a process, series, or ranking ⟨They worked on the project by *degrees* and eventually it got done.⟩

synonyms chapter, cut, grade, inch, notch, peg, phase, place, point, stage, step

related words angle, aspect, facet, side; amount, measure, plane; decrement, increment

2 the placement of someone or something in relation to others in a vertical arrangement ⟨a second-*degree* burn⟩ — see RANK 1

dehydrate *vb* 1 to deprive of emotional or intellectual vitality ⟨a job that he claimed *dehydrated* his soul⟩

synonyms damp, dampen, deaden, enervate

related words burn out, debilitate, do in, drain, enfeeble, exhaust, fatigue, sap, tucker (out), undermine, weaken, wear, wear out; daunt, demoralize, discourage, dishearten, dispirit

near antonyms arouse, rouse, stir; charge, electrify, galvanize; excite, ferment, fire, foment, incite, inflame (*also* enflame), instigate, kindle, provoke, spark, trigger, whip (up); abet, boost, buoy, cheer, embolden, fortify, hearten, inspire, lift

antonyms brace, energize, enliven, invigorate, quicken, stimulate, vitalize, vivify

2 to make dry ⟨bought a dehumidifier in order to *dehydrate* the damp basement⟩ — see DRY 1

deification *n* excessive admiration of or devotion to a person ⟨the instant *deification* by the press of the war hero⟩ — see WORSHIP

deify *vb* 1 to love or admire too much ⟨materialistic people who *deify* money⟩ — see IDOLIZE

2 to offer honor or respect to (someone) as a divine power ⟨Some ancient pagans *deified* such objects of nature as trees and rivers.⟩ — see WORSHIP 1

3 to assign a high status or value to ⟨Fans *deified* the team's quarterback.⟩ — see EXALT 1

deifying *adj* reflecting great admiration or devotion ⟨the *deifying* descriptions of military heroes that are often published in wartime⟩ — see WORSHIPFUL

deign *vb* to descend to a level that is beneath one's dignity ⟨I wouldn't *deign* to answer that absurd accusation.⟩ — see CONDESCEND 1

deity *n* 1 a being having superhuman powers and control over a particular part of life or the world ⟨To the ancient Greeks, Zeus was the *deity* who ruled over the sky and weather, and Poseidon was god of the sea.⟩

synonyms divinity, god

related words angel, demigod, demon (*or* daemon), devil, spirit, supernatural

2 *cap* the being worshipped as the creator and ruler of the universe ⟨We prayed to the *Deity* for guidance.⟩

synonyms Allah, Almighty, Author, Creator, Divinity, Everlasting, Father, God, Godhead, Jehovah, Maker, Providence, Supreme Being

3 the quality or state of being divine ⟨the repudiation of the claim of *deity* by the Japanese emperor after the end of World War II⟩ — see DIVINITY 1

dejected *adj* feeling unhappiness ⟨The *dejected* players slowly made their way back to the locker room, where they could mourn their defeat in private.⟩ — see SAD 1

dejection *n* a state or spell of low spirits ⟨I find that a walk outside often works wonders when trying to overcome *dejection*.⟩ — see SADNESS

delay *n* an instance or period of being prevented from going about one's business ⟨There was a *delay* for our boarding while the airplane unloaded incoming passengers.⟩

synonyms detainment, holding pattern, holdup, wait

related words deferment, deferral, postponement; reprieve, respite; foot-dragging, hesitation, lag, pause, setback, slowdown

near antonyms haste, rush; dispatch, promptitude, promptness

delay *vb* 1 to move or act slowly ⟨She ordered the kids to stop *delaying* and to get to bed.⟩

synonyms crawl, creep, dally, dawdle, dillydally, drag, lag, linger, loiter, mope, poke, shilly-shally, tarry

related words fiddle (around), monkey (around), play, potter (around), putter (around), trifle; idle, loaf, loll, lounge; ease, inch, lumber, plod, saunter, shuffle, stagger, stroll; decelerate, slow (down *or* up); filibuster, procrastinate, stall, temporize

phrases drag one's feet (*also* drag one's heels), drop behind, fall behind, hang fire, mark time, take one's time

near antonyms bowl, breeze, dart, hump, hurtle, hustle, scramble, stampede; gallop, jog, run, sprint, trot; accelerate, quicken, speed (up); fast-forward, outpace, outrun, outstrip, overtake

antonyms barrel, bolt, career, course, dash, fly, hasten, hotfoot (it), hurry, race, rip, rocket, run, rush, scoot, scud, scurry, speed, tear, whirl, whisk, whiz (*or* whizz), zip

2 to assign to a later time ⟨Our guests *delayed* their departure until after dinner.⟩ — see POSTPONE

delectable *adj* 1 giving pleasure or contentment to the mind or senses ⟨a *delectable* melody to listen to after a hard day⟩ — see PLEASANT 1

2 very pleasing to the sense of taste ⟨A *delectable* roast turkey lay on the table.⟩ — see DELICIOUS 1

delectable *n* something that is pleasing to eat because it is rare or a luxury ⟨a gourmet shop filled with *delectables* for every palate⟩ — see DELICACY 1

delectably *adv* in a pleasing way ⟨a *delectably* witty comedy⟩ — see WELL 5

delectation *n* 1 a source of great satisfaction ⟨tourists enjoying the *delectations* of this tropical paradise for the first time⟩ — see DELIGHT 1

2 the feeling experienced when one's wishes are met ⟨A musical concert was presented for the *delectation* of the guests.⟩ — see PLEASURE 1

delegate *n* 1 a person sent on a mission to represent another ⟨The *delegate* had a list of concerns to discuss with the country's new prime minister.⟩ — see AMBASSADOR

2 a person who acts or does business for another ⟨The real estate developer sent a *delegate* to the town meeting to represent his interests.⟩ — see AGENT 2

delegate *vb* 1 to appoint as one's representative ⟨He *delegated* his son to go pick up the tickets for him.⟩

synonyms commission, depute, deputize

related words assign, charge; appoint, designate, name

near antonyms abrogate; abdicate

2 to put (something) into the possession or safekeeping of another ⟨a manager who is reluctant to *delegate* authority to subordinates⟩ — see GIVE 2

delegation *n* 1 a body of persons chosen as representatives of a larger group ⟨A *delegation* from the local scout troop is being sent to the national jamboree.⟩ — see CONTINGENT 1

2 the granting of power to perform various acts or duties ⟨the *delegation* by the president to the secretary of state

of complete control of the nation's foreign policy⟩ — see COMMISSION 1

delete *vb* to show (something written) to be no longer valid by drawing a cross over or a line through it ⟨The teacher *deleted* the last line of the student's essay, wisely sensing that it lessened the impact.⟩ — see X (OUT)

deleterious *adj* causing or capable of causing harm ⟨Nicotine has long been recognized as a *deleterious* substance.⟩ — see HARMFUL

deletion *n* something left out ⟨One of the *deletions* from the final cut of the movie turned out to be my one line of dialogue.⟩ — see OMISSION

deliberate *adj* **1** decided on as a result of careful thought ⟨The judge made a *deliberate* decision to impose the minimum sentence.⟩

synonyms advised, calculated, considered, knowing, measured, reasoned, studied, thoughtful, thought-out, weighed

related words aforethought, premeditated, prepense; educated, informed; intentional, purposeful; designed, intended, planned, projected; careful, meticulous; foresighted, forethoughtful, provident, prudent

near antonyms half-cocked, ill-advised; chance, haphazard, hit-or-miss, random; aimless, desultory, purposeless; hasty, hurried, rushed; abrupt, impetuous, sudden; automatic, extemporaneous, impromptu, instinctive, spontaneous

antonyms casual, unadvised, uncalculated, unconsidered, unstudied

2 made, given, or done with full awareness of what one is doing ⟨a *deliberate* act of vandalism⟩ — see INTENTIONAL

deliberate *vb* to give serious and careful thought to ⟨The jury *deliberated* the case for three days before returning a verdict.⟩ — see PONDER

deliberately *adv* with full awareness of what one is doing ⟨*deliberately* chose to break the rules⟩ — see INTENTIONALLY

deliberation *n* **1** a careful weighing of the reasons for or against something ⟨gave the matter full *deliberation* before reaching a decision⟩ — see CONSIDERATION 1

2 an exchange of views for the purpose of exploring a subject or deciding an issue ⟨There was a great deal of *deliberation* among the representatives about the wording of the public statement.⟩ — see DISCUSSION 1

delicacy *n* **1** something that is pleasing to eat because it is rare or a luxury ⟨presented with a plate of national *delicacies* while they waited for the queen⟩

synonyms bit, dainty, delectable, goody (*or* goodie), tidbit (*also* titbit), treat, viand

related words morsel; dessert, junket, sweet, sweetmeat

2 the state or quality of having a delicate structure ⟨We never cease to marvel at the *delicacy* of a snowflake.⟩

synonyms daintiness, exquisiteness, fineness, fragility

related words diaphanousness, flimsiness, insubstantiality, wispiness; brittleness, crumbliness, friability

near antonyms firmness, solidity; strength

antonyms coarseness, crudeness, roughness, rudeness

3 the tendency to be or state of being squeamish ⟨The urgent need for blood prompted many people to overcome their habitual *delicacy* and become first-time donors.⟩

synonyms qualmishness, queasiness, squeamishness

related words daintiness, fastidiousness, finicalness, finickiness, fussiness

near antonyms boldness

antonyms indelicacy

4 the quality or state of being very accurate ⟨The *delicacy* of the watch movement is incredible.⟩ — see PRECISION

5 the quality or state of lacking physical strength or vigor ⟨All of her life the shy poet gave the appearance of extreme *delicacy*.⟩ — see WEAKNESS 1

6 the state or quality of being able to sense slight impressions or differences ⟨The *delicacy* of the sensor is such that it will be affected by the slightest vibration.⟩ — see ACUITY

delicate *adj* **1** satisfying or pleasing because of fineness or mildness ⟨A heavy sauce would spoil the *delicate* flavor of this fish.⟩

synonyms airy, dainty, exquisite, refined, subtle

related words choice, elegant, extraordinary, incomparable, peerless, preeminent, prime, rare, select, superior, superlative, supreme, unsurpassed; picked, selected; fine, fragile, frail

near antonyms coarse, crude, rough; common, ordinary; average, fair, indifferent, mediocre, medium, middling, run-of-the-mill, second-rate

antonyms robust, strong, sturdy

2 able to sense slight impressions or differences ⟨Only a person with *delicate* taste buds could tell the difference between these two wines.⟩ — see ACUTE 1

3 accomplished with trained ability ⟨the *delicate* handling of a difficult diplomatic situation⟩ — see SKILLFUL 1

4 easily broken ⟨*delicate* glassware that must be carefully wrapped for shipping⟩ — see FRAGILE 1

5 easily injured without careful handling ⟨the *delicate* ecosystem of the wetlands⟩ — see TENDER 1

6 hard to please ⟨a cat of *delicate* tastes⟩ — see FINICKY

7 having qualities that appeal to a refined taste ⟨*delicate* perfumes that connoisseurs of scents appreciate⟩ — see CHOICE 1

8 lacking bodily strength ⟨a *delicate* child who was never allowed to play sports⟩ — see WEAK 1

9 made or done with extreme care and accuracy ⟨*delicate* measurements that are only possible using the latest technology⟩ — see FINE 2

10 meeting the highest standard of accuracy ⟨extremely *delicate* instruments such as an atomic clock⟩ — see PRECISE 1

11 not harsh or stern especially in nature or effect ⟨A *delicate* breeze was floating in from the open window.⟩ — see GENTLE 1

12 requiring exceptional skill or caution in performance or handling ⟨a *delicate* situation that must be treated carefully⟩ — see TRICKY 1

delicious *adj* **1** very pleasing to the sense of taste ⟨The family sat down to a *delicious* Thanksgiving dinner.⟩

synonyms ambrosial, appetizing, dainty, delectable, flavorful, luscious, lush, palatable, savory (*also* savoury), scrumptious, succulent, tasteful, tasty, toothsome, yummy

related words digestible, eatable, edible; delightful, heavenly, pleasing; agreeable, gratifying, pleasant; satisfying; choice, delicate, exquisite, rare

near antonyms banal, boring, commonplace, tedious; noisome, smelly, stinky; noxious, unwholesome; miserable, wretched; abhorrent, abominable, awful, detestable, disagreeable, foul, horrid, nauseating, offensive, repellent (*also* repellant), repugnant, repulsive, sickening, unpleasant

antonyms distasteful, flat, flavorless, insipid, stale, tasteless, unappetizing, unpalatable, unsavory, yucky (*also* yukky)

2 giving pleasure or contentment to the mind or senses ⟨A *delicious* breeze gave us welcome relief from the tropical heat.⟩ — see PLEASANT 1

deliciously *adv* in a pleasing way ⟨a *deliciously* told anecdote⟩ — see WELL 5

deliciousness *n* the quality of being delicious ⟨The fancy feast was *deliciousness* itself.⟩

   synonyms lusciousness, palatability, savor (*also* savour), savoriness, tastiness

   related words digestibility, edibility, edibleness; daintiness, delicacy

   antonyms distastefulness, flatness, insipidity, staleness, tastelessness, unpalatability

delight *n* **1** a source of great satisfaction ⟨The opportunity for travel was one of the major *delights* of the couple's golden years.⟩

   synonyms delectation, feast, joy, kick, manna, pleasure, treat

   related words amusement, diversion, entertainment, fun, recreation; comfort, relief, solace; gratification, indulgence; ambrosia

2 someone or something that provides amusement or enjoyment ⟨With his great sense of humor and bubbly personality, he is a *delight* to be around.⟩ — see FUN 1

3 the feeling experienced when one's wishes are met ⟨We were filled with *delight* at the sight of everyone in the family together at last for the holidays.⟩ — see PLEASURE 1

delight *vb* **1** to feel or express joy or triumph ⟨They *delighted* in seeing their team win the championship after so many years.⟩ — see EXULT

2 to give satisfaction to ⟨The news that you had won the Pulitzer *delighted* us beyond words.⟩ — see PLEASE 1

delight (in) *vb* to take pleasure in ⟨I've been *delighting in* your company, so I was wondering if we might have another date.⟩ — see ENJOY 1

delighted *adj* experiencing pleasure, satisfaction, or delight ⟨We're *delighted* to meet you finally!⟩ — see GLAD 1

delightful *adj* **1** giving pleasure or contentment to the mind or senses ⟨a *delightful* rendition of our favorite song⟩ — see PLEASANT 1

2 providing amusement or enjoyment ⟨We had a *delightful* time at the party.⟩ — see FUN

delightfully *adv* in a pleasing way ⟨a *delightfully* silly song about dancing bears⟩ — see WELL 5

delimit *vb* to mark the limits of ⟨The highway *delimits* the eastern edge of the downtown area.⟩ — see LIMIT 2

delineate *vb* **1** to draw or make apparent the outline of ⟨The cat's curled-up shape was softly *delineated* by the glow of the fire.⟩ — see OUTLINE 1

2 to give a representation or account of in words ⟨The story does a remarkable job of *delineating* the emotions that new parents feel.⟩ — see DESCRIBE 1

delineated *adj* producing a mental picture through clear and impressive description ⟨The finely *delineated* characters of the novel will seem real to the reader.⟩ — see GRAPHIC 1

delineation *n* **1** a picture using lines to represent the chief features of an object or scene ⟨his simple but striking *delineations* of Dutch landscapes⟩ — see DRAWING 1

2 a vivid representation in words of someone or something ⟨a finely wrought *delineation* of a young couple's first experience with love⟩ — see DESCRIPTION 1

delinquency *n* **1** the nonperformance of an assigned or expected action ⟨We received a notice informing us of our *delinquency* in paying our utility bill.⟩ — see FAILURE 1

2 the quality or state of being late ⟨*Delinquency* of our mortgage payment meant that we would have to pay a surcharge.⟩ — see LATENESS

delinquent *adj* not arriving, occurring, or settled at the due, usual, or proper time ⟨The bank was annoyed because our check was *delinquent*.⟩ — see LATE 1

deliquesce *vb* to go from a solid to a liquid state ⟨a rotting tomato slowly *deliquescing* in the hot summer sun⟩ — see LIQUEFY

delirious *adj* **1** feeling overwhelming fear or worry ⟨We were *delirious* with anxiety until he finally made it home.⟩ — see FRANTIC 1

2 marked by great and often stressful excitement or activity ⟨rushing about in a *delirious* state during the holidays⟩ — see FURIOUS 1

delirium *n* a state of wildly excited activity or emotion ⟨The team's victory sent fans into *delirium*.⟩ — see FRENZY

deliver *vb* **1** to free from the penalties or consequences of sin ⟨*Deliver* us from evil.⟩ — see SAVE 1

2 to remove from danger or harm ⟨The passengers waited for the rescue ship to *deliver* them.⟩ — see SAVE 2

3 to give (something) over to the control or possession of another usually under duress ⟨*delivered* up the ransom money⟩ — see SURRENDER 1

4 to put (something) into the possession of someone for use or consumption ⟨The inn endeavors to *deliver* the luxuries that its guests have come to expect.⟩ — see FURNISH 2

5 to put (something) into the possession or safekeeping of another ⟨*delivered* the artifacts to the museum⟩ — see GIVE 2

6 to turn out as planned or desired ⟨Finally, a summer blockbuster that *delivers*!⟩ — see SUCCEED 1

7 to bring forth from the womb ⟨She *delivered* four healthy babies.⟩ — see BEAR 1

8 to give (oneself) over to something especially unrestrainedly ⟨He *delivered* himself over to the Lord.⟩ — see ABANDON 1

deliverance *n* **1** the saving from danger or evil ⟨They prayed for *deliverance* from the drought.⟩ — see SALVATION

2 a position arrived at after consideration ⟨The jury's *deliverance* shocked the courtroom.⟩ — see DECISION 1

deliverer *n* **1** a person who delivers goods to customers usually over a regular local route ⟨We eagerly took the food and tipped the *deliverer*.⟩ — see DELIVERYMAN

2 one that saves from danger or destruction ⟨The surviving passengers thanked their *deliverers* profusely.⟩ — see SAVIOR

delivery *n* **1** a freeing from an obligation or responsibility ⟨The school bell signaled our *delivery* from math class.⟩ — see RELEASE 1

2 the act or process of giving birth to children ⟨Her second *delivery* took only three hours.⟩ — see CHILDBIRTH

deliveryman *n* a person who delivers goods to customers usually over a regular local route ⟨The *deliveryman* dropped off a package for us while we were at the store.⟩

   synonyms deliverer

   related words delivery boy; bearer, carrier, courier, go-between, liaison, messenger

delude *vb* to cause to believe what is untrue ⟨We *deluded* ourselves into thinking that the ice cream wouldn't affect our diet.⟩ — see DECEIVE

deluding *adj* tending or having power to deceive ⟨the *deluding* appearance of the surface of the river, which is actually quite fast-moving⟩ — see DECEPTIVE 1

deluge *n* **1** a great flow of water or of something that overwhelms ⟨a *deluge* of thanks and appreciation for the returning troops⟩ — see FLOOD

2 a steady falling of water from the sky in significant quantity ⟨The exiting moviegoers were caught in the *deluge* without umbrellas.⟩ — see RAIN 1

deluge *vb* to cover with a flood ⟨*deluged* with requests for help⟩ — see FLOOD

delusion *n* **1** a conception or image created by the imagination and having no objective reality ⟨The patient is suffering from *delusions* and hallucinations.⟩ — see FANTASY 1

2 a false idea or belief ⟨He appears to suffer from the *delusion* that he'll be able to finish on time.⟩ — see FALLACY 1

delusive *adj* tending or having power to deceive ⟨*delusive* promises of high-paying jobs for low-skilled workers⟩ — see DECEPTIVE 1

delusory *adj* tending or having power to deceive ⟨the *delusory* notion that wealth invariably brings happiness⟩ — see DECEPTIVE 1

deluxe *adj* showing obvious signs of wealth and comfort ⟨a classy hotel with truly *deluxe* accommodations⟩ — see LUXURIOUS

delve (into) *vb* to search through or into ⟨We uncovered many interesting stories as we *delved into* the history of the house we were restoring.⟩ — see EXPLORE 1

delving *n* a systematic search for the truth or facts about something ⟨We didn't want to pry and did as little personal *delving* as possible.⟩ — see INQUIRY 1

demagogue *also* **demagog** *n* a person who stirs up public feelings especially of discontent ⟨a politician who is just a *demagogue* preying upon people's fears and prejudices⟩ — see AGITATOR

demand *n* **1** something that someone insists upon having ⟨The store refused the customer's *demand* for a refund.⟩
synonyms claim, dun, requisition, ultimatum
related words desire, request, want, wish; drive, need, requirement, stipulation; basic, essential, must; imposition; condition, provision

2 the state of being sought after especially for purchase ⟨a steadily declining *demand* for film cameras⟩
synonyms call, market, request
related words bear market, bull market; buyer's market, seller's market

3 something necessary, indispensable, or unavoidable ⟨We are very confident that our new employee is fully equal to the *demands* of the job.⟩ — see ESSENTIAL 1

demand *vb* **1** to ask for (something) earnestly or with authority ⟨The losing party *demanded* a recount of the votes cast in the election.⟩
synonyms call (for), claim, clamor (for), command, enjoin, exact, insist (on), press (for), quest, stipulate (for)
related words ask, plead (for), request, want; cry (for), necessitate, need, require, take, warrant; requisition; impose; badger, dun, hound
near antonyms give up, relinquish, surrender, yield

2 to have as a requirement ⟨a task that *demands* one's unremitting attention⟩ — see NEED 1

3 to set or receive as a price ⟨superstars who *demand* millions for appearing in a movie⟩ — see CHARGE 1

demanding *adj* **1** requiring much time, effort, or careful attention ⟨The *demanding* assignment kept them working all night long.⟩
synonyms arduous, burdensome, challenging, exacting, grueling (*or* gruelling), laborious, onerous, taxing, toilsome
related words difficult, formidable, hard, herculean, rough, rugged, stiff, strenuous, tough; oppressive, trying; rigid, rigorous, severe, stern, strict, stringent
near antonyms easy, effortless, facile, simple, smooth
antonyms light, nondemanding, unchallenging, undemanding

2 hard to please ⟨He will play before a *demanding* audience of music critics, who are not easily impressed.⟩ — see FINICKY

3 requiring considerable physical or mental effort ⟨the *demanding* task of reading and grading student compositions⟩ — see HARD 2

demarcate *vb* to mark the limits of ⟨A yellow line *demarcated* the county on the road map.⟩ — see LIMIT 2

demarcation *n* the state of being kept distinct ⟨The lines of *demarcation* between art and entertainment are often blurry.⟩ — see SEPARATION 2

¹**demean** *vb* **1** to lower in character, dignity, or quality ⟨It *demeans* the political process to demand that candidates make promises that everyone knows are unrealistic.⟩ — see DEBASE 1

2 to reduce to a lower standing in one's own eyes or in others' eyes ⟨His statement was not meant to *demean* the group's hard work.⟩ — see HUMBLE

²**demean** *vb* to manage the actions of (oneself) in a particular way ⟨I shall endeavor to *demean* myself with utmost respect when our president comes to visit.⟩ — see BEHAVE

demeaning *adj* intended to make a person or thing seem of little importance or value ⟨demanded an apology for his *demeaning* comments⟩ — see DEROGATORY

demeanor *n* the way or manner in which one conducts oneself ⟨Her warm *demeanor* made us feel at home.⟩ — see BEHAVIOR

demerit *n* a defect in character ⟨My typing has the advantage of speed but the *demerit* of inaccuracy.⟩ — see FAULT 1

demesne *n* **1** a part or portion having no fixed boundaries ⟨the vast and frozen *demesne* of the northern tundra⟩ — see REGION 1

2 the area around and belonging to a building ⟨The mansion's huge *demesne* covers more than 100 acres.⟩ — see GROUND 1

demilitarization *n* the reduction or elimination of a country's armed forces or weapons ⟨the *demilitarization* that occurred in the aftermath of World War II⟩ — see DISARMAMENT

demilitarize *vb* to reduce the size and strength of the armed forces of ⟨The two nations agreed to *demilitarize* themselves reciprocally.⟩ — see DISARM 1

demise *n* **1** the permanent stopping of all the vital bodily activities ⟨He inherited all of the estate upon the sudden *demise* of his grandfather.⟩ — see DEATH 1

2 the act of ceasing to exist ⟨the gradual *demise* of the Roman Empire over the course of several centuries⟩ — see DEATH 3

3 a loss of status ⟨After her *demise* as the doyenne of New York society, the mere mention of her name was regarded as a faux pas.⟩ — see COMEDOWN

demise *vb* to stop living ⟨our much beloved, recently *demised* leader⟩ — see DIE 1

democracy *n* government in which the supreme power is held by the people and used by them directly or indirectly through representation ⟨Under our *democracy* the people have some control over their lives by being able to select their own political leaders.⟩
synonyms republic, self-government, self-rule
related words pure democracy; home rule, self-determination; autonomy, sovereignty (*also* sovranty)
near antonyms despotism, dictatorship, monarchy, monocracy, totalitarianism, tyranny

democratic *adj* of, relating to, or favoring political democracy ⟨The *democratic* system ensures that every citizen's voice is heard.⟩
synonyms popular, republican, self-governing, self-ruling
related words representative; libertarian, nontotalitarian
near antonyms autocratic (*also* autocratical), despotic,

dictatorial, monarchal (*or* monarchial), monarchical (*also* monarchic), tyrannical (*also* tyrannic)
antonyms nondemocratic, undemocratic

demolish *vb* **1** to destroy (as a building) completely by knocking down or breaking to pieces 〈Developers *demolished* the old warehouse to make room for the new shopping mall.〉
synonyms level, raze, tear down
related words blow up; abolish, annihilate, crack up, crush, dash, decimate, destroy, devastate, devour, dissolve, do in, eradicate, extirpate, finish, flatten, obliterate, overturn, pulverize, ravage, ruin, scourge, smash, total, unmake, waste, wipe out, wreck
near antonyms build, construct, erect, put up, raise; rebuild, renew, renovate, restore; create, fabricate, fashion, forge, form, make, manufacture, shape
2 to bring to a complete end the physical soundness, existence, or usefulness of 〈The old barn was *demolished* by the heavy snow that had piled upon the roof.〉 — see DESTROY 1
3 to cause to break open or into pieces by or as if by an explosive 〈The children *demolished* the piñata.〉 — see BLAST 1

demolishment *n* the state or fact of being rendered nonexistent, physically unsound, or useless 〈the *demolishment* of the old building〉 — see DESTRUCTION 1

demolition *n* the state or fact of being rendered nonexistent, physically unsound, or useless 〈Several condemned buildings around the city are undergoing *demolition* as part of the revitalization program.〉 — see DESTRUCTION 1

demon *or* **daemon** *n* **1** an evil spirit 〈Only in rare cases is the ancient rite of exorcism performed to cast out a troublesome *demon*.〉
synonyms devil, fiend, ghost, ghoul, imp
related words incubus, nightmare, succubus; genie, jinni (*or* jinn *also* djinni *or* djinn); apparition, banshee, bogey (*also* bogie *or* bogy), bugbear, familiar, genius, phantasm (*also* fantasm), phantom, poltergeist, shade, shadow, specter (*or* spectre), spirit, spook, vision, wraith; brownie, dwarf, elf, faerie (*also* faery), fairy, fay, gnome, goblin, gremlin, hobgoblin, kobold, leprechaun, pixie (*also* pixy), puck, sprite, troll; monster, ogre
near antonyms angel
2 a source of persistent emotional distress 〈a man who was finally able to conquer the *demons* of his past〉
synonyms affliction, terror, torment
related words bête noire, bogey (*also* bogie *or* bogy), bugaboo, bugbear, hobgoblin, ogre

demoniac *also* **demoniacal** *adj* of, relating to, or worthy of an evil spirit 〈The naturalist described the wolverine as having *demoniac* energy.〉 — see FIENDISH 1

demonic *also* **demonical** *adj* of, relating to, or worthy of an evil spirit 〈The villain in the movie cackled with *demonic* laughter.〉 — see FIENDISH 1

demonstrable *adj* capable of being proven as true or real 〈As a serious scientist, she is only interested in *demonstrable* phenomena.〉 — see VERIFIABLE

demonstrate *vb* **1** to gain full recognition or acceptance of 〈You must *demonstrate* your scientific thesis before a jury of your professional peers.〉 — see ESTABLISH 1
2 to show the existence or truth of by evidence 〈The paleontologist hopes to *demonstrate* that dinosaurs once existed in central Peru by unearthing the fossil evidence.〉 — see PROVE 1
3 to make known (something abstract) through outward signs 〈The babysitter's actions during the emergency *demonstrate* beyond doubt her general dependability.〉 — see SHOW 2

4 to make plain or understandable 〈A few striking facts should *demonstrate* the complex nature of our topic.〉 — see EXPLAIN 1
5 to show or make clear by using examples 〈The visiting physicist *demonstrated* very graphically several basic scientific principles.〉 — see ILLUSTRATE 1

demonstration *n* **1** a mass meeting for the purpose of displaying or arousing support for a cause or person 〈Students organized a *demonstration* to protest the change in university policy.〉 — see RALLY 2
2 an outward and often exaggerated indication of something abstract (as a feeling) for effect 〈Tina staged a grand *demonstration* of her love for her husband with a candlelight-and-champagne Valentine's Day dinner.〉 — see SHOW 1

demonstrative *adj* **1** showing feeling freely 〈My grandmother was always very *demonstrative* when we visited, showering us with hugs and kisses.〉
synonyms effusive, emotional, uninhibited, unreserved, unrestrained
related words dramatic, histrionic, hyperemotional, melodramatic, theatrical (*also* theatric); gushing, maudlin, mawkish, mushy, schmaltzy, sentimental; communicative, expansive; extroverted (*also* extraverted), outgoing; affectionate, feeling, intense, loving, passionate, sensitive, soulful, warm; blunt, candid, frank, outspoken, plain
near antonyms constrained; quiet, reticent, silent, taciturn; bashful, modest, retiring, shy; introverted, self-directed; aloof, detached, dispassionate, impassive, indifferent, phlegmatic, stolid, unconcerned, unfeeling; chilly, cold, frigid, glacial, hard-boiled, hard-edged, icy, unfriendly
antonyms inhibited, reserved, restrained, undemonstrative, unemotional
2 having or expressing great depth of feeling 〈a *demonstrative* welcome for the returning troops by their families and friends〉 — see FERVENT 1

demoralization *n* **1** a sinking to a state of low moral standards and behavior 〈Steps were taken to address the *demoralization* at the company.〉 — see CORRUPTION 2
2 the state of being discouraged 〈The officers struggled to combat the *demoralization* of the troops as their tour of duty grew longer.〉 — see DISCOURAGEMENT

demoralize *vb* **1** to deprive of courage or confidence 〈The sight of the forbidding cliffs was not enough to *demoralize* the intrepid climbers.〉 — see UNNERVE 1
2 to lessen the courage or confidence of 〈We refused to be *demoralized* by our humiliating defeat and vowed to come roaring back the following week.〉 — see DISCOURAGE 1
3 to lower in character, dignity, or quality 〈a justice system *demoralized* by corruption〉 — see DEBASE 1

demoralized *adj* having or showing lowered moral character or standards 〈a *demoralized* profession that had lost the integrity that once made it great〉 — see CORRUPT

demote *vb* to bring to a lower grade or rank 〈The court-martial's decision was to *demote* the officer responsible for the failed mission.〉
synonyms break, bust, degrade, downgrade, reduce
related words can, cashier, dismiss, downsize, fire, lay off, sack; abase, debase, demean, humble, humiliate, lower
near antonyms hire
antonyms advance, elevate, promote, raise

demount *vb* to take apart 〈Soldiers were expected to be able to *demount* and reassemble their weapons.〉 — see DISASSEMBLE 1

demur *n* a feeling or declaration of disapproval or dissent

⟨We accepted his offer to pay for our dinners without *demur*.⟩ — see OBJECTION

demur *vb* to present an opposing opinion or argument ⟨Don't hesitate to *demur* to the idea if you have any qualms.⟩ — see OBJECT

demure *adj* **1** affecting shyness or modesty ⟨We were not fooled by her *demure* self-deprecation.⟩ — see COY 1

2 not comfortable around people ⟨Hesitant and *demure*, she hardly spoke a word at the banquet table.⟩ — see SHY 2

3 not having or showing any feelings of superiority, self-assertiveness, or showiness ⟨schoolchildren all wearing *demure* uniforms⟩ — see HUMBLE 1

demureness *n* the absence of any feelings of being better than others ⟨Her excessive *demureness* will be to her disadvantage if she wants a career in show business.⟩ — see HUMILITY

den *n* **1** the shelter or resting place of a wild animal ⟨The foxes hid in their *den* until the bear finally left the area.⟩
synonyms burrow, hole, house, lair, lodge
related words nest; territory

2 a place where a person goes to hide or to avoid others ⟨an abandoned building that is often used as a *den* by the city's petty criminals⟩ — see HIDEOUT

denial *n* **1** an unwillingness to grant something asked for ⟨Our supervisor's *denial* of unpaid personal leave got mixed reactions from the staff.⟩
synonyms disallowance, nay, no, refusal, rejection
related words rebuff, repudiation, repulse, spurn; negative; ban, veto; deterrence, discouragement, repression, suppression
near antonyms acceptance, acquiescence, agreement, assent, authorization, clearance, concurrence, consent, leave, license (*or* licence), permission, sanction, sufferance; imprimatur, seal, stamp
antonyms allowance, approval, grant, OK (*or* okay)

2 a refusal to confirm the truth of a statement ⟨The senator issued a flat *denial* of the accusation against her.⟩
synonyms contradiction, disallowance, disavowal, disclaimer, negation, rejection, repudiation
related words disproof, rebuttal, refutation; negative
near antonyms concession, confession; affirmation, assertion, declaration; attestation, corroboration, documentation, substantiation, testament, testimony, validation
antonyms acknowledgment (*or* acknowledgement), admission, avowal, confirmation

denizen *n* **1** someone who regularly spends time in a particular place ⟨one of those muscular *denizens* of the gym⟩
synonyms familiar, frequenter, rat, regular
related words client, customer, guest, patron; addict, aficionado (*also* afficionado), buff, bug, devotee, enthusiast, fan, fanatic, fancier, fiend, freak, lover, maniac, nut

2 one who lives permanently in a place ⟨The polar bear is an iconic *denizen* of the snowy Arctic.⟩ — see INHABITANT

denominate *vb* to give a name to ⟨King Macbeth of Scotland was *denominated* the Red King.⟩ — see NAME 1

denomination *n* a word or combination of words by which a person or thing is regularly known ⟨a variety of creative works that today come under the *denomination* of "art"⟩ — see NAME 1

denotation *n* **1** a word or combination of words by which a person or thing is regularly known ⟨"Soul" is the common *denotation* for that mysterious force within the human body that gives it life and yet is separate from it.⟩ — see NAME 1

2 the idea that is conveyed or intended to be conveyed to

the mind by language, symbol, or action ⟨Although most people exercise for fitness, the *denotation* of the term "fitness" varies from exerciser to exerciser.⟩ — see MEANING 1

denotative *adj* indicating something ⟨A willingness to tutor other students in this course will be seen as *denotative* of the student's mastery of it.⟩ — see INDICATIVE

denote *vb* **1** to communicate or convey (as an idea) to the mind ⟨a flashing red light that *denotes* danger⟩ — see MEAN 1

2 to serve as a sign or symptom of ⟨The well-kept yard *denotes* a homeowner with a sense of responsibility for the well-being of his neighborhood.⟩ — see INDICATE 1

denoting *adj* indicating something ⟨An arrow is a common *denoting* symbol for direction.⟩ — see INDICATIVE

denounce *vb* **1** to declare to be morally wrong or evil ⟨The church council *denounced* the bishop's teachings, officially declaring them to be heresy.⟩ — see CONDEMN 1

2 to express one's unfavorable opinion of the worth or quality of ⟨*denounced* the shoddy merchandise that the local shops were foisting on tourists⟩ — see CRITICIZE

3 to express public or formal disapproval of ⟨The governor has *denounced* the court's decision and vows to press for a constitutional amendment.⟩ — see CENSURE 1

dense *adj* **1** having little space between items or parts ⟨the *dense* soil in the garden⟩ — see CLOSE 1

2 not having or showing an ability to absorb ideas readily ⟨She accused him of being *dense* when he didn't seem to understand her at first.⟩ — see STUPID 1

denseness *n* the quality or state of lacking intelligence or quickness of mind ⟨complained about the *denseness* of the shipping clerks who had misplaced his order⟩ — see STUPIDITY 1

density *n* **1** the degree to which a fluid can resist flowing ⟨Molasses has greater *density* than room-temperature water.⟩ — see CONSISTENCY

2 the quality or state of lacking intelligence or quickness of mind ⟨He was frustrated by their *density* as he tried to explain.⟩ — see STUPIDITY 1

dent *n* **1** a sunken area forming a separate space ⟨There was a big *dent* in the car's hood where something had hit it.⟩ — see HOLE 2

2 the amount by which something is lessened ⟨A little belt-tightening would at least make a small *dent* in our credit-card debt.⟩ — see DECREASE

dent *vb* to make smaller in amount, volume, or extent ⟨Hopefully this vacation won't *dent* our bank account too much.⟩ — see DECREASE 1

dented *adj* curved inward ⟨The *dented* car fender bore silent testament to an accident that no one in the family was owning up to.⟩ — see HOLLOW

denuded *adj* lacking a usual or natural covering ⟨the *denuded* trees left behind after the forest fire had passed⟩ — see NAKED 2

denunciation *n* an often public or formal expression of disapproval ⟨the official *denunciation* of the congresswoman's actions before the full house⟩ — see CENSURE

deny *vb* **1** to declare not to be true ⟨The congressman *denied* all charges of wrongdoing.⟩
synonyms contradict, disallow, disavow, disclaim, disown, gainsay, negate, negative, refute, reject, repudiate
related words traverse; challenge, confute, disprove, rebut; disagree (with), dispute
near antonyms accept, adopt, embrace, espouse; affirm, announce, assert, aver, claim, declare, maintain, profess, submit; authenticate, corroborate, substantiate, validate, verify
antonyms acknowledge, admit, allow, avow, concede, confirm, own

2 to be unwilling to grant ⟨The director *denied* access to the top secret files to all but those with a need to know.⟩ **synonyms** decline, disallow, disapprove, negative, refuse, reject, reprobate, withhold
related words ban, enjoin, forbid, prohibit, proscribe, veto; rebuff, repel, spurn; check, constrain, curb, hold, keep, repress, restrain, restrict; hinder, impede, obstruct
near antonyms afford, furnish, give, provide, supply; authorize, commission, license (*also* licence); accede (to), acquiesce, agree (to), assent (to), consent (to), warrant; accord, sanction, vouchsafe
antonyms allow, concede, grant, let, OK (*or* okay), permit

3 to refuse to acknowledge as one's own or as one's responsibility ⟨He *denied* that the signature on the document was his.⟩ — see DISCLAIM 1

depart *vb* **1** to leave a place often for another ⟨I'll sing one more song before I *depart.*⟩ — see GO 2
2 to stop living ⟨a special tribute for those members of the motion picture academy who have *departed* over the past year⟩ — see DIE 1

departed *adj* **1** no longer existing ⟨A few crumbling ruins are all that remain of that *departed* civilization.⟩ — see EXTINCT
2 no longer living ⟨our dear *departed* friend⟩ — see DEAD 1

departing *n* the act of leaving a place ⟨His *departing* was accompanied by tears and heartfelt good wishes.⟩ — see DEPARTURE 1

department *n* **1** a large unit of a governmental, business, or educational organization ⟨the *Department* of the Interior⟩ — see DIVISION 2
2 a region of activity, knowledge, or influence ⟨That's not my *department*, but maybe I can help you anyway.⟩ — see FIELD 2

departure *n* **1** the act of leaving a place ⟨His sudden *departure* left them wondering if they'd upset him.⟩
synonyms decamping, decampment, departing, exit, exiting, farewell, going, leave, leave-taking, lighting out, outgo, parting, quitting, walking out
related words flight, retirement, retreat, running away, withdrawal; diaspora, emigration, evacuation, exodus; embarkation, embarkment; disembarkation, egress; abandonment, forsaking, relinquishment
near antonyms coming; approach, entrance, ingress
antonyms advent, appearance, arrival
2 a turning away from a course or standard ⟨Any *departure* from our traditional Thanksgiving meal was met with cries of disapproval.⟩ — see DIVERGENCE 2

depend *vb* **1** to be determined by, based on, or subject (to) ⟨Whether or not we play baseball will *depend* on how much rain we get.⟩
synonyms hang, hinge, ride, turn
related words base, establish, found, rest, stay; ground
2 to place reliance or trust ⟨I know I can always *depend* on you for help when I really need it.⟩
synonyms calculate, count, lean, reckon, rely
related words commit, entrust (*also* intrust), trust
phrases bank on, call on (*or* upon), figure on, look to, stand on
near antonyms distrust, mistrust, question, suspect

dependability *n* worthiness as the recipient of another's trust or confidence ⟨Her *dependability* as a friend, in good times and bad, is legendary.⟩ — see RELIABILITY

dependable *adj* worthy of one's trust ⟨They're seeking a *dependable* person to look after their summer home in the off-season.⟩
synonyms good, reliable, responsible, safe, secure, solid, steady, sure, tried, tried-and-true, true, trustworthy, trusty

related words constant, devoted, faithful, fast, loyal, staunch (*also* stanch), steadfast, true-blue; honest, sincere, single-minded; infallible, unerring; bedrock, firm, sound, strong; effective, telling; attested, authenticated, confirmed, proven, valid, validated, verified; blameless, faultless, guiltless, impeccable, inerrant, irreproachable, unimpeachable, unquestionable
near antonyms disloyal, faithless, false, fickle, inconstant, perfidious, recreant, traitorous, treacherous, unfaithful, untrue; deceitful, dishonest, lying, mendacious, untruthful
antonyms uncertain, undependable, unreliable, unsafe, untrustworthy

dependence *also* **dependance** *n* **1** the quality or state of needing something or someone ⟨a baby's total *dependence* upon his or her parents for every one of life's needs⟩
synonyms dependency, reliance
related words reciprocity, relativity; confidence, credence, faith, stock, trust
near antonyms autonomy, self-determination, sovereignty (*also* sovranty)
antonyms independence, self-reliance, self-sufficiency, self-support
2 something or someone to which one looks for support ⟨Ultimately rice became the chief *dependence* in that state.⟩
synonyms anchor, buttress, mainstay, pillar, reliance, standby
related words backbone, sinew(s), spine; right hand; bolsterer, crutch, stay; anchorage, harbor, refuge

dependency *n* the quality or state of needing something or someone ⟨She teased about his heavy *dependency* on coffee to get him moving in the morning.⟩ — see DEPENDENCE 1

dependent *adj* **1** extending freely from a support from above ⟨The *dependent* willow branches swayed in the gentle breeze.⟩
synonyms dangling, hanging, pendent (*or* pendant), pendulous
related words drooping, flagging, lolling, sagging, wilting
2 determined by something else ⟨Our going to the movies tonight is *dependent* on whether or not we have any money left after we eat out.⟩
synonyms conditional, contingent (on *or* upon), subject (to), tentative
related words liable, open, susceptible; limited, modified, qualified, restricted; debatable, disputable, doubtable, doubtful, iffy, problematic (*also* problematical), questionable, shady, shaky, suspect, uncertain
near antonyms absolute, all-out, arrant, categorical (*also* categoric), complete, consummate, out-and-out, outright, perfect, simple, total, ultimate, unadulterated, unalloyed, unconditional, unequivocal, unmitigated, unqualified, utter; basic, fundamental, primary
antonyms independent, unconditional

depict *vb* **1** to give a representation or account of in words ⟨This letter from an eyewitness *depicts* the battle in greater detail than any other account.⟩ — see DESCRIBE 1
2 to point out the chief quality or qualities of an individual or group ⟨The report *depicted* him as a reliable assistant and an employee who could be entrusted with any task.⟩ — see CHARACTERIZE 1
3 to present a picture of ⟨The painting *depicts* a pastoral landscape on a summer day.⟩ — see PICTURE 1

depiction *n* a vivid representation in words of someone or something ⟨The set piece of the novel is a *depiction* of

the battle that makes readers feel like they were there.⟩
— see DESCRIPTION 1

deplete *vb* **1** to make complete use of ⟨Miners *depleted* the vein of copper ore after only a few months.⟩
synonyms absorb, burn, consume, devour, drain, exhaust, expend, play out, spend, use up
related words abate, decrease, de-escalate, diminish, downsize, dwindle, lessen, lower, reduce; eat, use; bankrupt, clean (out), impoverish; cripple, debilitate, disable, enfeeble, sap, undermine, weaken; dry up, empty; blow, dissipate, fritter (away), guzzle, lavish, misspend, run through, squander, throw away, waste
phrases run out of
near antonyms augment, enlarge, increase; bolster, enforce, fortify, strengthen; rebuild, repair, restore, revive; conserve, preserve, save
antonyms renew, replace
2 to make smaller in amount, volume, or extent ⟨Drought *depleted* the water reserves.⟩ — see DECREASE 1

deplorable *adj* **1** arousing or deserving of one's loathing and disgust ⟨We will not tolerate such *deplorable* behavior.⟩ — see CONTEMPTIBLE 1
2 of a kind to cause great distress ⟨condemned the *deplorable* conditions in which the family was living⟩ — see REGRETTABLE

deplore *vb* **1** to feel or express sorrow for ⟨a statement from the company *deploring* the unintended damage to the environment⟩ — see LAMENT 1
2 to feel sorry or dissatisfied about ⟨Ed *deplored* the fact that his guests were seeing his apartment at its messiest.⟩ — see REGRET

deploring *adj* expressing or suggesting mourning ⟨a *deploring* look on his face long after the funeral had ended⟩ — see MOURNFUL 1

deport *vb* **1** to force to leave a country ⟨*deported* them back to their country of birth⟩ — see BANISH 1
2 to manage the actions of (oneself) in a particular way ⟨Nora *deported* herself appropriately at the ceremony.⟩ — see BEHAVE

deportation *n* the forced removal from a homeland ⟨the *deportation* of the Jews from Spain in 1492⟩ — see EXILE 1

deportee *n* a person forced to emigrate for political reasons ⟨The *deportee* vowed that he would someday return to a liberated nation.⟩ — see ÉMIGRÉ 1

deportment *n* the way or manner in which one conducts oneself ⟨Her *deportment* during the hearing was a model of self-restraint and class.⟩ — see BEHAVIOR

depose *vb* **1** to remove from a position of prominence or power (as a throne) ⟨A military junta *deposed* the dictator after he had bankrupted the country.⟩
synonyms dethrone, displace, oust, uncrown, unmake, unseat, unthrone
related words can, cashier, discharge, dismiss, fire, muster out, remove, retire, sack; overthrow, subvert, supplant, topple, usurp; banish, boot (out), bounce, chase, drum (out), eject, expel, extrude, rout, run off, throw out
near antonyms baptize, inaugurate, induct, initiate, install, instate, invest; appoint, designate, elect
antonyms crown, enthrone, throne
2 to make a solemn declaration under oath for the purpose of establishing a fact ⟨She was nervous when the time to *depose* before the jury finally arrived.⟩ — see TESTIFY
3 to arrange something in a certain spot or position ⟨*deposed* her fan and gloves on the dressing table⟩ — see PLACE 1

deposit *n* **1** matter that settles to the bottom of a body of liquid ⟨a *deposit* of silt on the river bed⟩

synonyms deposition, dregs, grounds, precipitate, sediment
related words lees; ooze, silt, sludge; dross, slag, waste
2 a collection of things kept available for future use or need ⟨a *deposit* of spare parts⟩ — see STORE 1
3 a sum of money set aside for a particular purpose ⟨made a *deposit* at the bank every week⟩ — see FUND 1

deposit *vb* **1** to put in an account ⟨We quickly *deposited* the check in a bank account.⟩
synonyms bank
related words cache, hoard, lay away, reserve, salt away, save, squirrel (away), stash, store, stow; invest
near antonyms remove, take out; disburse, expend, give, lay out, pay, spend
antonyms withdraw
2 to arrange something in a certain spot or position ⟨*deposited* their luggage at the foot of the hotel bed⟩ — see PLACE 1

deposition *n* matter that settles to the bottom of a body of liquid ⟨several types of *deposition* on the bottom of the lake⟩ — see DEPOSIT 1

depository *n* a building for storing goods ⟨a book *depository*⟩ — see STOREHOUSE

depot *n* **1** a building for storing goods ⟨a distribution *depot* for auto parts⟩ — see STOREHOUSE
2 a place where military arms are stored ⟨The guns and ammunition were stored in a *depot* in Concord.⟩ — see ARMORY

deprave *vb* to lower in character, dignity, or quality ⟨the belief that consumerism *depraves* society as a whole⟩ — see DEBASE 1

depraved *adj* having or showing lowered moral character or standards ⟨the *depraved* actions of a few troubled individuals⟩ — see CORRUPT

depravedness *n* the state or quality of being utterly evil ⟨The prosecutor argued that the crimes in their utter *depravedness* called for a severe punishment.⟩ — see ENORMITY 1

depravity *n* **1** a sinking to a state of low moral standards and behavior ⟨a chapter on the *depravity* of the king and his court⟩ — see CORRUPTION 2
2 immoral conduct or practices harmful or offensive to society ⟨He was sinking into a life of *depravity*.⟩ — see VICE 1
3 the state or quality of being utterly evil ⟨the *depravity* of the demons and devils in many tales of horror⟩ — see ENORMITY 1

deprecate *vb* **1** to express scornfully one's low opinion of ⟨Movie critics *deprecated* the comedy as boring.⟩ — see DECRY 1
2 to hold an unfavorable opinion of ⟨*deprecates* TV sitcoms as childish and simpleminded⟩ — see DISAPPROVE (OF)

deprecation *n* **1** refusal to accept as right or desirable ⟨Considering that he's a member of the old school, his *deprecation* of contemporary manners isn't surprising.⟩ — see DISAPPROVAL
2 the act of making a person or a thing seem little or unimportant ⟨She resorted to *deprecation* of the old methods in promoting her new plans.⟩ — see DEPRECIATION

depreciate *vb* **1** to diminish the price or value of ⟨A faded finish will really *depreciate* your car when you decide to trade it in.⟩
synonyms break, cheapen, depress, downgrade, lower, mark down, reduce, sink, write off
related words debase, demonetize; underprice; abridge, compress, contract, de-escalate, deflate, downsize, dwindle, lessen, moderate, shrink

near antonyms bloat, blow up, inflate; overestimate, overprice, overrate, overvalue

antonyms appreciate, enhance, mark up, upgrade

2 to express scornfully one's low opinion of ⟨dared to *depreciate* Shakespeare, saying his works have no relevance for modern audiences⟩ — see DECRY 1

depreciation *n* the act of making a person or a thing seem little or unimportant ⟨A *depreciation* of the role of minorities in the building of the nation was once a common feature of history books.⟩

synonyms belittlement, deprecation, detraction, diminishment, disparagement, put-down

related words aspersion, backbiting, calumny, defamation, libel, slander, vilification; derision, mockery, ridicule; abuse, invective, vituperation; censure, condemnation, criticism, denouncement, denunciation; de-emphasis, minimization, soft-pedaling

near antonyms acclaim, praise; approbation, approval, blessing, commendation; puffery

antonyms aggrandizement, ennoblement, exaltation, glorification, magnification

depreciative *adj* intended to make a person or thing seem of little importance or value ⟨the usual *depreciative* comments by the troops about the food in the mess hall⟩ — see DEROGATORY

depreciatory *adj* intended to make a person or thing seem of little importance or value ⟨a customer making *depreciatory* remarks about the quality of the service at the restaurant⟩ — see DEROGATORY

depress *vb* **1** to make sad ⟨The thought of once again failing the bar exam *depressed* me.⟩

synonyms bum (out), burden, dash, oppress, sadden

related words ail, distress, trouble; afflict, torment, torture; daunt, demoralize, discourage, dishearten, dismay, dispirit, unnerve; agitate, bother, concern, discomfort, discompose, disquiet, disturb, freak (out), perturb, undo, unhinge, unsettle, upset, worry

near antonyms animate, enliven, invigorate; assure, comfort, console, reassure, solace, soothe; excite, inspire, stimulate; elate, exhilarate; encourage, hearten; delight, gratify, please; boost, elevate, lift, uplift

antonyms brighten, buoy, cheer (up), gladden, lighten, rejoice

2 to cause to fall intentionally or unintentionally ⟨Construction workers *depressed* the roadbed in order to make way for an overpass.⟩ — see DROP 1

3 to diminish the price or value of ⟨The glut of wheat on the market has *depressed* that commodity for most of the past year.⟩ — see DEPRECIATE 1

4 to push steadily against with some force ⟨*depressed* the lever to start the machine⟩ — see ²PRESS 1

depressed *adj* **1** curved inward ⟨The *depressed* sections of the highway under the overpasses constantly get flooded during heavy rainstorms.⟩ — see HOLLOW

2 feeling unhappiness ⟨I was *depressed* and didn't feel much like going to the party.⟩ — see SAD 1

3 kept from having the necessities of life or a healthful environment ⟨a *depressed* group of people⟩ — see DEPRIVED

depressing *adj* **1** causing or marked by an atmosphere lacking in cheer ⟨the *depressing* atmosphere of the empty mall⟩ — see GLOOMY 1

2 causing unhappiness ⟨more *depressing* news about the famine overseas⟩ — see SAD 2

depression *n* **1** a period of decreased economic activity ⟨During the 1930s the U.S. suffered a great *depression*.⟩

synonyms recession, slump

related words bust, crash, panic; stagnation; downdraft, downswing, downtrend, downturn, slowdown

near antonyms development, growth; advancement, progress; rally, recovery

antonyms boom

2 a state or spell of low spirits ⟨She called her friend to see if a sympathetic ear would relieve his *depression*.⟩ — see SADNESS

3 a sunken area forming a separate space ⟨The water generally collects in the patchwork of *depressions* in the city plaza.⟩ — see HOLE 2

4 the amount by which something is lessened ⟨a *depression* in the number of new homes being built⟩ — see DECREASE

deprivation *n* the state of being robbed of something normally enjoyed ⟨the concern of some that there has been a *deprivation* of rights⟩ — see PRIVATION

deprived *adj* kept from having the necessities of life or a healthful environment ⟨a program to help *deprived* children⟩

synonyms depressed, disadvantaged, underprivileged

related words beggared, broke, destitute, impecunious, impoverished, indigent, needy, penniless, penurious, poor, poverty-stricken, unprivileged; bankrupt, bankrupted, insolvent; pinched, reduced, straitened

near antonyms blessed (*also* blest), fortunate, lucky; affluent, flush, loaded, moneyed (*also* monied), opulent, rich, wealthy, well-heeled, well-off, well-to-do; coddled, indulged, pampered, spoiled; comfortable, propertied, prosperous, successful; flourishing, prospering, thriving

antonyms advantaged, privileged

depth *n* **1** distance measured from the top to the bottom of something ⟨Be sure to check the *depth* of the water before diving off the dock.⟩

synonyms drop

related words lowness; draft, sounding

near antonyms shallowness; altitude, elevation, height, stature

2 the quality of being great in extent (as of insight) ⟨The *depth* of the poet's understanding of human nature has given his works a timeless appeal.⟩

synonyms profoundness, profundity

related words discernment, perception, perceptiveness, perceptivity, sagacity, sapience, sense, sensibility, wisdom; braininess, brightness, brilliance, intellect, intelligence, judgment (*or* judgement), reason, sense, smartness, wit; acuity, acuteness, keenness, penetration, perspicacity, sensitivity, sharpness

near antonyms shallowness, superficiality; brainlessness, idiocy, imbecility, mindlessness, simpleness, stupidity, witlessness; illogic, irrationality, unreasonableness, unsoundness

3 the most intense or characteristic phase of something ⟨I was in the *depths* of thought when I was interrupted.⟩ — see THICK

4 the most extreme or advanced point ⟨Even in the *depth* of the Great Depression people never lost hope.⟩ — see HEIGHT 2

depthless *adj* lacking significant physical depth ⟨crossed the brook at its most *depthless* point⟩ — see SHALLOW 1

depute *vb* to appoint as one's representative ⟨The governor has the authority to *depute* anyone he wants.⟩ — see DELEGATE 1

deputize *vb* to appoint as one's representative ⟨He *deputized* a local citizen to take charge of the situation while he went for reinforcements.⟩ — see DELEGATE 1

deputy *n* **1** a person who acts or does business for another ⟨The club president sent a *deputy* to the conference to vote on our behalf.⟩ — see AGENT 2

2 a person who helps a more skilled person ⟨a *deputy* supervisor to help out with routine tasks⟩ — see HELPER

derange *vb* **1** to cause to go insane or as if insane ⟨Being stranded at night on a lonely road would *derange* anyone.⟩ — see CRAZE

2 to undo the proper order or arrangement of ⟨The room was all *deranged* by the rambunctious children.⟩ — see DISORDER

derangement *n* an act or instance of the order of things being disturbed ⟨the *derangement* of the carefully organized event by an unexpected incident⟩ — see UPSET

derelict *adj* **1** failing to give proper care and attention ⟨The guards were judged *derelict* in their duty.⟩ — see NEGLIGENT

2 left unoccupied or unused ⟨an old *derelict* mansion that was rumored to be haunted⟩ — see ABANDONED 1

dereliction *n* **1** the act of abandoning ⟨the *dereliction* of the cause by its leader⟩
synonyms abandonment, desertion, forsaking
related words defection; discard, dumping, jettisoning
near antonyms retention; recoupment, repossession, retrieval
antonyms reclamation

2 failure to take the care that a cautious person usually takes ⟨The ski area was not held responsible for the injury on account of the skier's own manifest *dereliction*.⟩ — see NEGLIGENCE 1

3 the nonperformance of an assigned or expected action ⟨Both sentries were to be court-martialed for *dereliction* of duty.⟩ — see FAILURE 1

4 a defect in character ⟨believes that society is guilty of a moral *dereliction* if it does not care for those unable to care for themselves⟩ — see FAULT 1

deride *vb* to make (someone or something) the object of unkind laughter ⟨My brothers *derided* our efforts, but were forced to eat their words when we won first place.⟩ — see RIDICULE

derision *n* **1** a person or thing that is made fun of ⟨In the 19th century any supporter of women's rights could expect to become a *derision* to her neighbors.⟩ — see LAUGHINGSTOCK

2 the making of unkind jokes as a way of showing one's scorn for someone or something ⟨Her absurd behavior on the awards show became a source of *derision* for comedians.⟩ — see RIDICULE

derisive *adj* so foolish or pointless as to be worthy of scornful laughter ⟨the *derisive* performances of some of the singers on the talent show⟩ — see RIDICULOUS 1

derisory *adj* **1** intended to make a person or thing seem of little importance or value ⟨The *derisory* term "the boob tube" is sometimes used when referring to television.⟩ — see DEROGATORY

2 so foolish or pointless as to be worthy of scornful laughter ⟨The pawnbroker offered what I regarded as a *derisory* amount for the diamond ring.⟩ — see RIDICULOUS 1

derivable *adj* being or provable by reasoning in which the conclusion follows necessarily from given information ⟨The solution was easily *derivable* from the clues we were given.⟩ — see DEDUCTIVE

derivative *adj* taken or created from something original or basic ⟨a *derivative* style that she took from earlier painters⟩ — see SECONDARY 1

derivative *n* something that naturally develops or is developed from something else ⟨The whole field of industrial robots is a *derivative* of technology developed for the space program.⟩
synonyms by-product, offshoot, outgrowth, spin-off
related words descendant (*also* descendent); aftermath, consequence, corollary, development, fruit, growth, issue, outcome, product, result, sequel, sequence, upshot;

denouement (*also* dénouement), repercussion; aftereffect, side effect (*also* side reaction); copy, duplicate, facsimile, replica, reproduction
near antonyms archetype, original, prototype; antecedent, cause, determinant, occasion, reason
antonyms origin, root, source

derive *vb* to form an opinion or reach a conclusion through reasoning and information ⟨From the summit, he was able to *derive* his location from the position of several prominent landmarks.⟩ — see INFER 1

derogatory *adj* intended to make a person or thing seem of little importance or value ⟨The team's fans made *derogatory* remarks about their rivals.⟩
synonyms belittling, contemptuous, decrying, degrading, demeaning, depreciative, depreciatory, derisory, disdainful, disparaging, scornful, slighting, uncomplimentary
related words aspersing, defamatory, insulting, libelous (*or* libellous), maligning, slandering, slanderous, vilifying; abusive, opprobrious, scurrilous; catty, cruel, despiteful, hateful, malevolent, malicious, malign, malignant, mean, nasty, spiteful, unkind, virulent; critical, denunciative, denunciatory; acrimonious, bitter, envious, jaundiced, jealous, rancorous, resentful; acrid, caustic, scathing, venomous
near antonyms admiring, adulatory, applauding, approving, friendly, positive; appreciative, respectful; kind, kindhearted, kindly, sympathetic, unmalicious, warm, warmhearted
antonyms commendatory, complimentary, laudative, laudatory

descant *vb* **1** to give a formal often extended talk on a subject ⟨an English professor who loves to *descant* on his beloved Shakespeare⟩ — see TALK 1

2 to produce musical sounds with the voice ⟨The soprano *descanted* above the melody line.⟩ — see SING 1

descend *vb* **1** to lead or extend downward ⟨The pathway *descends* to the river bank.⟩
synonyms decline, dip, drop, fall, plunge, sink
related words angle, cant, cock, heel, incline, lean, list, recline, slant, slope, tilt, tip
near antonyms even, flatten, level, plane, smooth, straighten
antonyms arise, ascend, climb, mount, rise, uprise, upsweep, upturn

2 to become worse or of less value ⟨The order of the classroom *descended* into chaos when the teacher left the room.⟩ — see DETERIORATE 1

3 to go to a lower level especially abruptly ⟨Leaves slowly *descended* from the branches in the gentle autumn wind.⟩ — see DROP 2

4 to come down from something (as a vehicle) ⟨The driver *descended* from the truck's cab.⟩ — see ALIGHT 2

descend (on *or* **upon)** *vb* to take sudden, violent action against ⟨A pair of seagulls *descended* on the unguarded lunch.⟩ — see ATTACK 1

descendant *also* **descendent** *adj* bending downward or forward ⟨the *descendant* branches of a weeping willow⟩ — see NODDING

descending *adj* bending downward or forward ⟨the dancer's *descending* head⟩ — see NODDING

descent *n* **1** the act or process of going to a lower level or altitude ⟨The airplane began its gradual *descent* to the landing field.⟩
synonyms dip, dive, down, drop, fall, nosedive, plunge
related words comedown, decline, downfall, downgrade; plummeting, sinking
near antonyms advance, headway, progress, progression; betterment, improvement

antonyms ascent, climb, rise, rising, soaring, upswing, upturn

2 a gradual sinking and wasting away of mind or body ⟨the family patriarch's heartbreaking *descent* into infirmity and senility⟩ — see DECLINE 1

3 a change to a lower state or level ⟨the nation's rapid *descent* into anarchy after the revolution⟩ — see DECLINE 2

4 a loss of status ⟨For throwing the game, the ballplayer underwent a huge *descent* in the eyes of the fans.⟩ — see COMEDOWN

5 a sudden attack on and entrance into hostile territory ⟨the lightning *descent* of the invading army on that unsuspecting border town⟩ — see RAID 1

6 the act or action of setting upon with force or violence ⟨the *descent* of the voracious locusts on the wheat fields⟩ — see ATTACK 1

7 the line of ancestors from whom a person is descended ⟨a person of Finnish *descent*⟩ — see ANCESTRY

8 a downward slope ⟨On bicycle tours the ascents always seem to outnumber the *descents*.⟩ — see DECLINE 3

describe *vb* **1** to give a representation or account of in words ⟨He tried to *describe* the dream he had last night as accurately as he could.⟩

synonyms delineate, depict, draw, image, paint, picture, portray, render, sketch

related words characterize, define, label, qualify, represent; demonstrate, illustrate; narrate, recite, recount, rehearse, relate, report, tell; display, exhibit, show; hint, suggest; draft, outline, silhouette, trace, vignette; summarize, sum up, touch off; redescribe, reimage

near antonyms color, distort, falsify, garble, misdescribe, misrepresent, misstate, pervert, twist, warp

2 to give an oral or written account of in some detail ⟨a biography of Washington that *describes* the decisive Battle of Yorktown at great length⟩ — see TELL 1

3 to point out the chief quality or qualities of an individual or group ⟨How would you *describe* the people you encountered on your trip?⟩ — see CHARACTERIZE 1

description *n* **1** a vivid representation in words of someone or something ⟨We immediately recognized the man from our cousin's *description* of him.⟩

synonyms delineation, depiction, picture, portrait, portrayal, sketch, vignette

related words account, anecdote, chronicle, narrative, report, story, tale, yarn; demonstration, exemplification, illustration; clarification, elucidation, explanation, explication, exposition

2 a number of persons or things that are grouped together because they have something in common ⟨fixes small appliances and other things of that *description*⟩ — see SORT 1

descry *vb* **1** to come upon after searching, study, or effort ⟨We couldn't *descry* the reasons for his sudden departure.⟩ — see FIND 1

2 to make note of (something) through the use of one's eyes ⟨I could just *descry* the ship coming over the horizon.⟩ — see SEE 1

desecrate *vb* to treat (a sacred place or object) shamefully or with great disrespect ⟨Vandals *desecrated* the tombstones with graffiti.⟩

synonyms defile, profane, violate

related words blaspheme, curse, swear; befoul, contaminate, foul, poison, pollute, soil, sully, taint; affront, defame, insult, offend, outrage

near antonyms bless, consecrate, dedicate, hallow, sanctify; honor, respect; cleanse, purge, purify

desecration *n* an act of great disrespect shown to God or to sacred ideas, people, or things ⟨a *desecration* of the ancient tomb⟩ — see BLASPHEMY

¹**desert** *n* land that is uninhabited or not fit for crops ⟨We were lost in the *desert* for days without food.⟩ — see WASTELAND

²**desert** *n, usually* **deserts** *pl* suffering, loss, or hardship imposed in response to a crime or offense ⟨The robbers got their just *deserts*.⟩ — see PUNISHMENT

desert *vb* **1** to leave (a cause or party) often in order to take up another ⟨The volunteer became disillusioned with his candidate and *deserted* to a political rival.⟩ — see DEFECT (FROM)

2 to cause to remain behind ⟨*deserted* her friends at the food court for some independent shopping⟩ — see LEAVE 1

deserted *adj* left unoccupied or unused ⟨We had the *deserted* beach all to ourselves.⟩ — see ABANDONED 1

deserter *n* a person who abandons a cause or organization usually without right ⟨We had orders to find and capture the *deserters* before they could reveal our location.⟩ — see RENEGADE

desertion *n* the act of abandoning ⟨The soldiers were demoted for *desertion* of their posts.⟩ — see DERELICTION 1

deserve *vb* to be or make worthy of (as a reward or punishment) ⟨The team really *deserved* that victory after the way they played.⟩ — see EARN 2

deserved *adj* being what is called for by accepted standards of right and wrong ⟨a well *deserved* promotion for a hard worker⟩ — see JUST 1

deserving *adj* having sufficient worth or merit to receive one's honor, esteem, or reward ⟨scholarships awarded to *deserving* students⟩ — see WORTHY

desex *vb* to remove the sex organs of ⟨*desexed* the baby chickens destined for market⟩ — see NEUTER

design *n* **1** a method worked out in advance for achieving some objective ⟨She always achieves her objective by *design* rather than by luck.⟩ — see PLAN 1

2 a secret plan for accomplishing evil or unlawful ends ⟨The thief had devised an elaborate *design* to get the invaluable artwork.⟩ — see PLOT 1

3 something that one hopes or intends to accomplish ⟨My *design* in writing to you is to ask for your support.⟩ — see GOAL

4 a unit of decoration that is repeated all over something (as a fabric) ⟨The curtains have a lovely floral *design*.⟩ — see PATTERN 1

5 the way in which the elements of something (as a work of art) are arranged ⟨The *design* of the building's lobby encourages the free flow of traffic.⟩ — see COMPOSITION 3

design *vb* **1** to have in mind as a purpose or goal ⟨Early on she had *designed* to a top position in a major insurance company.⟩ — see INTEND 1

2 to work out the details of (something) in advance ⟨The manager *designed* a better layout for the factory floor to improve efficiency.⟩ — see PLAN 1

designate *vb* **1** to decide upon (the time or date for an event) usually from a position of authority ⟨the *designated* time for the meeting⟩ — see APPOINT 1

2 to pick (someone) by one's authority for a specific position or duty ⟨He has yet to *designate* his successor as head of the firm.⟩ — see APPOINT 2

3 to give a name to ⟨He was *designated* "Air Jordan" by his fans.⟩ — see NAME 1

designation *n* **1** a word or combination of words by which a person or thing is regularly known ⟨We've never given the homemade gadget a proper *designation*.⟩ — see NAME 1

2 the state or fact of being chosen for a position or duty ⟨Her *designation* as the running mate was greeted with enthusiasm.⟩ — see APPOINTMENT 1

designedly *adv* with full awareness of what one is doing ⟨The puzzle was *designedly* difficult to decipher.⟩ — see INTENTIONALLY

designer *adj* being or involving the latest methods, concepts, information, or styles ⟨That car manufacturer is claiming that their new models are the last word in *designer* technology.⟩ — see MODERN

designer *n* one who creates or introduces something new ⟨credited as the *designer* of the first sneaker specifically intended for distance running⟩ — see INVENTOR

designing *adj* clever at attaining one's ends by indirect and often deceptive means ⟨a scheme devised by a group of greedy and *designing* people⟩ — see ARTFUL 1

desirable *adj* suitable for bringing about a desired result under the circumstances ⟨a *desirable* location for the new house⟩ — see EXPEDIENT

desire *n* **1** a strong wish for something ⟨A *desire* for adventure and excitement prompted him to move abroad.⟩
synonyms appetite, craving, drive, hankering, hunger, itch, longing, passion, pining, thirst, urge, yearning, yen
related words compulsion, impulse, impulsion, will, zeal; liking, love, taste, weakness; eagerness, impatience; want, wish; necessity, need, requirement; obsession; acquisitiveness, avarice, avariciousness, avidity, covetousness, cupidity, greed, greediness, rapaciousness, rapacity; mania
near antonyms abhorrence, abomination, allergy, averseness, aversion, disfavor, disgust, disinclination, dislike, disliking, distaste, hatred, loathing, nausea, repugnance, repulsion, revulsion; apathy, indifference, insouciance, nonchalance, unconcern
2 an earnest request ⟨At the delegate's *desire*, the voice vote on the controversial measure was followed by an actual roll call.⟩ — see PLEA 1

desire *vb* **1** to have an earnest wish to own or enjoy ⟨He greatly *desired* a new mountain bike for his next birthday.⟩
synonyms ache (for), covet, crave, die (for), hanker (for *or* after), hunger (for), itch (for), long (for *or* after), pant (after), pine (for), repine (for), sigh (for), thirst (for), want, wish (for), yearn (for)
related words spoil (for); adore, delight (in), dig, enjoy, fancy, groove (on), like, love, relish, revel (in); favor, prefer; admire, appreciate, cherish, prize, treasure, value
phrases set one's heart on
near antonyms abhor, abominate, despise, detest, execrate, hate, loathe; decline, refuse, reject, spurn
2 to make a request for ⟨The host *desires* a response to the dinner invitation by tomorrow.⟩ — see ASK (FOR) 1

desirous *adj* showing urgent desire or interest ⟨Management is very *desirous* of finishing the project on time and within budget.⟩ — see EAGER

desirousness *n* urgent desire or interest ⟨Her *desirousness* for advancement in the corporation is such that she works harder than anyone.⟩ — see EAGERNESS

desist (from) *vb* to bring (as an action or operation) to an immediate end ⟨ordered to *desist from* using the copyrighted music⟩ — see STOP 1

desk *n* a large unit of a governmental, business, or educational organization ⟨the city *desk* of a prominent newspaper⟩ — see DIVISION 2

desolate *adj* **1** causing or marked by an atmosphere lacking in cheer ⟨a *desolate* house abandoned many years ago⟩ — see GLOOMY 1
2 sad from lack of companionship or separation from others ⟨He was less *desolate* after adopting a rescue dog.⟩ — see LONESOME 1
3 left unoccupied or unused ⟨a *desolate* mining town that had its brief heyday more than a century ago⟩ — see ABANDONED 1

4 producing inferior or only a small amount of vegetation ⟨wild, *desolate* plains on which only the hardiest could survive⟩ — see BARREN 1

desolate *vb* to bring to a complete end the physical soundness, existence, or usefulness of ⟨The passage of time slowly *desolated* the ancient city.⟩ — see DESTROY 1

desolation *n* **1** a state or spell of low spirits ⟨A visit from an old friend eased his *desolation*.⟩ — see SADNESS
2 land that is uninhabited or not fit for crops ⟨looked out over the vast untamed *desolation* to the north⟩ — see WASTELAND
3 the state of being unattended to or not cared for ⟨the *desolation* of the abandoned garden⟩ — see NEGLECT 1
4 the state or fact of being rendered nonexistent, physically unsound, or useless ⟨The photos captured a scene of utter *desolation*.⟩ — see DESTRUCTION 1

despair *n* **1** utter loss of hope ⟨The endless drought drove the farmers to *despair*.⟩
synonyms desperation, despond, despondency, forlornness, hopelessness
related words blue devils, blues, dejection, depression, desolation, disconsolateness, dispiritedness, doldrums, dolor, downheartedness, dreariness, dumps, gloom, gloominess, joylessness, melancholy, mopes, oppression, sadness, sorrow, unhappiness; self-despair, self-pity; dolefulness, woefulness; agony, distress, pain; misery, woe, wretchedness; cynicism, pessimism; acceptance, resignation
phrases slough of despond
near antonyms cheer, cheerfulness, sunniness; optimism; gaiety (*also* gayety), glee, gleefulness, jollity, joviality, lightheartedness, merriment, mirth, mirthfulness; bliss, blissfulness, ecstasy, elation, euphoria, exhilaration, exuberance, exultation, gladness, happiness, joy, joyfulness, joyousness, jubilation, rapture, rapturousness
antonyms hope, hopefulness
2 the state of being discouraged ⟨The other team's temporary lead caused some momentary *despair*.⟩ — see DISCOURAGEMENT

despair *vb* to lose all hope or confidence ⟨We *despaired* when we saw how little time we had left to complete our project.⟩
synonyms despond
related words give up, surrender, yield; darken, sadden; agonize, bleed, grieve, hurt, mourn, sorrow, suffer; discourage, dishearten, dispirit
phrases lose heart
near antonyms exult, rejoice; assure, encourage, hearten, reassure; hope
antonyms brighten, cheer (up), perk (up)

despairing *adj* **1** emphasizing or expecting the worst ⟨*despairing* predictions regarding the effects of global overpopulation⟩ — see PESSIMISTIC 1
2 feeling or showing no hope ⟨*Despairing* applicants need to be reminded that most students are eventually accepted somewhere.⟩ — see DESPONDENT 1

desperation *n* utter loss of hope ⟨The robbery was an act of *desperation*.⟩ — see DESPAIR 1

despicable *adj* **1** arousing or deserving of one's loathing and disgust ⟨a *despicable* traitor⟩ — see CONTEMPTIBLE 1
2 not following or in accordance with standards of honor and decency ⟨his *despicable* behavior toward those less fortunate⟩ — see IGNOBLE 2
3 deserving pitying scorn (as for inadequacy) ⟨a *despicable* attempt at making a movie comedy⟩ — see PITIFUL 1

despise *vb* **1** to dislike strongly ⟨I *despise* anchovies on pizza, and I refuse to eat them!⟩ — see HATE
2 to ignore in a disrespectful manner ⟨a traitor hated and *despised* by the whole community⟩ — see SCORN 2

despite *n* **1** open dislike for someone or something considered unworthy of one's concern or respect ⟨pointedly ignored his false friend out of *despite*⟩ — see CONTEMPT
2 the desire to cause pain for the satisfaction of doing harm ⟨Sheer *despite* was the sole reason for her hurtful comments.⟩ — see MALICE
3 the negative result caused by something that creates difficulty for achieving success ⟨baffled as to why working-class voters would vote in *despite* of their own economic interests⟩ — see DISADVANTAGE 2

despite *prep* without being prevented by ⟨We went to the party *despite* the bad weather outside.⟩
synonyms notwithstanding, with
phrases in defiance of, in despite of, in spite of

despiteful *adj* having or showing a desire to cause someone pain or suffering for the sheer enjoyment of it ⟨*despiteful* treatment of his poor relations during their visit⟩ — see HATEFUL

despitefully *adv* in a mean or spiteful manner ⟨a theater critic known for his *despitefully* negative reviews⟩ — see NASTILY

despitefulness *n* open dislike for someone or something considered unworthy of one's concern or respect ⟨the undisguised *despitefulness* with which the fashion designer announces his "10 worst" list⟩ — see CONTEMPT

despoil *vb* to search through with the intent of committing robbery ⟨The burglars *despoiled* the art museum in search of treasures they thought they could sell.⟩ — see RANSACK 1

despond *n* **1** a state or spell of low spirits ⟨He sank into a *despond* after losing the championship.⟩ — see SADNESS
2 utter loss of hope ⟨Finding a new job rescued him from a deep *despond*.⟩ — see DESPAIR 1

despond *vb* to lose all hope or confidence ⟨We must not *despond* even though we live in trying times.⟩ — see DESPAIR

despondency *n* **1** a state or spell of low spirits ⟨in *despondency* because he couldn't seem to settle into a lasting relationship⟩ — see SADNESS
2 the state of being discouraged ⟨In their *despondency* they seemingly forgot that losing teams can become winning teams in a single season.⟩ — see DISCOURAGEMENT
3 utter loss of hope ⟨She never once gave into *despondency* and self-pity during her long recovery from her injuries in the car crash.⟩ — see DESPAIR 1

despondent *adj* **1** feeling or showing no hope ⟨After four days and still no sign of the lost kitty, the boy grew *despondent*.⟩
synonyms despairing, forlorn, hopeless
related words blue, brokenhearted, crestfallen, dejected, depressed, disconsolate, doleful, down, downcast, downhearted, gloomy, glum, hangdog, heartbroken, heartsick, heartsore, inconsolable, joyless, low, low-spirited, melancholy, miserable, mournful, sad, saddened, sorrowful, sorry, unhappy, woebegone, woeful, wretched; disappointed, discouraged, disheartened, dispirited; accepting, resigned
near antonyms ecstatic, elated, enraptured, entranced, euphoric, exhilarated, exuberant, exultant; blithe, blithesome, jocund, jolly, jovial, lightsome, merry, mirthful; encouraged, heartened; animated, jaunty, lively, perky, sprightful, sprightly, vivacious; blissful, buoyant, cheerful, cheery, chipper, delighted, glad, gladdened, gladsome, gleeful, happy, joyful, joyous, jubilant, sunny, upbeat
antonyms hopeful, optimistic
2 feeling unhappiness ⟨feeling *despondent* after learning a close friend was moving away⟩ — see SAD 1

despot *n* a person who uses power or authority in a cruel,

unjust, or harmful way ⟨a *despot* who was finally overthrown⟩
synonyms dictator, oppressor, tyrannizer, tyrant
related words autarch, autocrat, monocrat; authoritarian, potentate, totalitarian; overlord, warlord; boss, captain, chief, dominator, kingpin, leader, master, overlord, ruler; king, monarch, prince, queen, sovereign (*also* sovran); baron, czar (*also* tsar *or* tzar), magnate, mogul, tycoon; disciplinarian, discipliner, enforcer, martinet, taskmaster
phrases man on horseback

despotic *adj* **1** exercising power or authority without interference by others ⟨a nation ruled by a series of *despotic* rulers⟩ — see ABSOLUTE 1
2 fond of ordering people around ⟨The *despotic* coach demands that his players obey him without question.⟩ — see BOSSY

despotism *n* a system of government in which the ruler has unlimited power ⟨By the end of the 20th century many countries around the world had rejected *despotism* in favor of democracy.⟩
synonyms autocracy, dictatorship, totalitarianism, tyranny
related words monarchism, monarchy, monocracy; Communism, fascism, Nazism; domination, oppression
near antonyms democracy, self-government, self-rule; freedom, self-determination; autonomy, sovereignty (*also* sovranty)

destine *vb* to determine the fate of in advance ⟨His extreme height seemed to *destine* him for a career in basketball.⟩
synonyms doom, fate, foredoom, foreordain, ordain, predestine, predetermine, preordain
related words predestinate; augur, forecast, foretell, predict, presage, prognosticate, prophesy; preconceive, prejudge; condemn, sentence; bode, forebode (*also* forbode), portend; anticipate, divine, foreknow, foresee

destiny *n* a state or end that seemingly has been decided beforehand ⟨I just knew that it wasn't my *destiny* to end up in a dead-end job.⟩ — see FATE 1

destitute *adj* **1** lacking money or material possessions ⟨a program to house *destitute* families⟩ — see POOR 1
2 utterly lacking in something needed, wanted, or expected ⟨a lingering drought and a sky *destitute* of rain clouds⟩ — see DEVOID 1

destitution *n* the state of lacking sufficient money or material possessions ⟨an orphan who rose from *destitution* to wealth and fame⟩ — see POVERTY 1

de-stress *vb* to get rid of nervous tension or anxiety ⟨He watches classic movie comedies as a way to *de-stress*.⟩ — see RELAX 1

destroy *vb* **1** to bring to a complete end the physical soundness, existence, or usefulness of ⟨They practically *destroyed* the safe in order to get at the money inside.⟩ ⟨Their poor scores on the final exam *destroyed* any chance they might have had to pass the course.⟩
synonyms annihilate, cream, decimate, demolish, desolate, devastate, do in, extinguish, pulverize, raze, rub out, ruin, shatter, smash, tear down, total, waste, wreck
related words beat, best, clobber, conquer, crush, defeat, drub, lick, master, overbear, overcome, overmatch, prevail (over), rout, scotch, skunk, subdue, surmount, thrash, trim, triumph (over), trounce, wallop, whip, win (against); blast, blow up, break, cripple, damage, deface, deteriorate, disfigure, disintegrate, dissolve, harm, impair, injure, mangle, mar, mutilate, spoil, vitiate; erode, scour, wash out, wear (away); dilapidate, disassemble, dismantle, gut, take down, undo, unmake; blot out, efface, eradicate, expunge, exterminate, extirpate, liqui-

date, obliterate, remove, root (out), snuff (out), stamp (out), wipe out; despoil, havoc, loot, pillage, plunder, ravage, sack, trample, trash, vandalize

near antonyms doctor, fix, mend, patch, recondition, repair, revamp; create, invent; assemble, fabricate, fashion, forge, form, frame, make, manufacture, produce, shape; bring about, constitute, establish, father, found, institute, organize; conserve, preserve, protect, save; rebuild, reconstruct, remodel, renovate, restore

antonyms build, construct, erect, put up, raise, rear, set up

2 to bring destruction to (something) through violent action 〈Wildfires *destroyed* thousands of acres in forests across the state.〉 — see RAVAGE

3 to deprive of life 〈Regrettably, the veterinarian was forced to *destroy* the injured horse.〉 — see KILL 1

destruction *n* **1** the state or fact of being rendered nonexistent, physically unsound, or useless 〈The storm resulted in the *destruction* of their tree house.〉

synonyms annihilation, decimation, demolishment, demolition, desolation, devastation, extermination, extinction, havoc, loss, obliteration, ruin, ruination, wastage, wreckage

related words depredation, despoilment, despoliation; breakup, collapse, disintegration, dissolution; assassination, execution, massacre, slaughter; dismantlement, effacement, eradication

near antonyms rescue, salvage, salvation, saving; conservation, preservation, protection; reclamation, reconstruction, re-creation, refurbishment, regeneracy, remodeling, renovation, restoration

antonyms building, construction, erection, raising

2 something that is the cause of one's ultimate failure or loss of life 〈an economic system that ended up being the *destruction* of the empire〉 — see DOWNFALL 1

destructive *adj* **1** causing or tending to cause destruction 〈The *destructive* storm blew down trees all over town.〉

synonyms calamitous, cataclysmal (*or* cataclysmic), devastating, disastrous, ruinous

related words baleful, deadly, deathly, fatal, lethal, mortal, murderous, pestilent, poisonous, virulent, vital; deleterious, detrimental, harmful, pernicious

near antonyms preservative, protective; constructive, creative, formative, productive; harmless, innocent, innocuous, inoffensive; ameliorative, helpful, useful; healthful, healthy, nonfatal, nonlethal, salubrious, wholesome

antonyms nondestructive

2 bringing about ruin or misfortune 〈technology used for *destructive* ends〉 — see FATAL 1

desultorily *adv* without definite aim, direction, rule, or method 〈I sat watching the movie, *desultorily* eating popcorn.〉 — see HIT OR MISS

desultory *adj* **1** lacking a definite plan, purpose, or pattern 〈a *desultory* search for something of interest on TV〉 — see RANDOM

2 passing from one topic to another 〈a *desultory* discussion about the news of the day〉 — see DISCURSIVE

detached *adj* **1** having or showing a lack of friendliness or interest in others 〈a *detached* observer at company parties, taking it all in and saying very little〉 — see COOL 1

2 not physically attached to another unit 〈a *detached* garage on the side of the house〉 — see SEPARATE 2

detachment *n* **1** lack of favoritism toward one side or another 〈The judge showed commendable *detachment* when deciding the controversial case.〉

synonyms disinterestedness, equity, fairness, impartiality, justice, neutrality, objectivity

related words apathy, indifference, unconcern; broadmindedness, open-mindedness, tolerance; straddling

near antonyms chauvinism, nepotism; subjectiveness, subjectivity; bent, inclination, leaning, penchant, predilection, predisposition, proclivity, propensity, tendency; preconception, prejudgment

antonyms bias, favor, favoritism, nonobjectivity, onesidedness, partiality, partisanship, prejudice

2 a small military unit with a special task or function 〈The general sent a *detachment* ahead to scout the enemy's position.〉

synonyms detail

related words commando, firing squad, outpost, paratroops, patrol, picket, rear guard, sentry, watch; battalion, command, company, corps, division, regiment, squad, squadron, troop, wing

3 the absence of emotional involvement 〈His *detachment* allowed him a clearer perspective on the case.〉 — see COOL 1

detail *n* **1** a separate part in a list, account, or series 〈Every *detail* was accounted for.〉 — see ITEM 1

2 a single piece of information 〈didn't leave out a single *detail* in his police report on the burglary〉 — see FACT 3

3 a small military unit with a special task or function 〈The officer sent out a *detail* to patrol the perimeter of the compound.〉 — see DETACHMENT 2

4 a specific task with which a person or group is charged 〈The soldier was placed on guard *detail*.〉 — see MISSION

detail *vb* **1** to assign to a place or position 〈Once again he was *detailed* to guard duty.〉 — see ²POST

2 to pick (someone) by one's authority for a specific position or duty 〈The new assistant was *detailed* to accompany the boss on the business trip.〉 — see APPOINT 2

3 to specify one after another 〈*detailed* all of the reasons that the plan was a bad idea〉 — see ENUMERATE 1

detailed *adj* **1** including many small descriptive features 〈a *detailed* report on all the activities that their Scout troop had been involved in over the past year〉

synonyms circumstantial, elaborate, full, minute, particular, particularized, thorough

related words enumerated, inventoried, itemized, listed, numerated; delineated, specific, specified; abundant, copious; comprehensive, encyclopedic, exhausting, exhaustive, inclusionary, inclusive, in-depth, omnibus, panoramic, thoroughgoing; distinct, explicit, sharp; mapped (out); descriptive, graphic (*also* graphical), picturesque, vivid

near antonyms brief, compact, concise, crisp, pithy, short, succinct, terse; ambiguous, indeterminate, nebulous, sketchy, vague; bird's-eye, broad, general, nonspecific, overall, unspecified

antonyms compendious, summary

2 made or done with great care or with much detail 〈a *detailed* miniature of the royal palace〉 — see ELABORATE 1

detainment *n* an instance or period of being prevented from going about one's business 〈The returning vacationers' *detainment* at the border only lasted a few minutes.〉 — see DELAY

detect *vb* to come upon after searching, study, or effort 〈I can *detect* just a hint of lemon in the soup.〉 — see FIND 1

detectable *adj* able to be perceived by a sense or by the mind 〈There was a barely *detectable* hum coming from the refrigerator.〉 — see PERCEPTIBLE

detection *n* the act or process of sighting or learning the existence of something for the first time 〈My *detection* of the scent of baked apple pie led me to the kitchen.〉 — see DISCOVERY 1

detective *n* a person not on the police force who investigates criminal or illicit activity or searches for missing persons 〈The code used by the serial killer in his letters to the police was actually cracked by an amateur *detective*.⟩

synonyms investigator, operative, sleuth

related words shadow, tail, tracer, tracker; fed, Federal, G-man, narc (*or* nark) [*slang*], plainclothesman

detector *n* a device that detects some physical quantity and responds usually with a transmitted signal ⟨a motion *detector* to thwart burglaries⟩ — see SENSOR

deter *vb* to steer (a person) from an activity or course of action ⟨We tried to *deter* him from choosing colleges based only on where his friends were applying.⟩ — see DISCOURAGE 2

detergent *n* a substance used for cleaning ⟨Add the *detergent* to the washing machine before putting in the clothes.⟩ — see CLEANER

deteriorate *vb* 1 to become worse or of less value ⟨The garden slowly *deteriorated* after months of neglect.⟩

synonyms crumble, decay, decline, degenerate, descend, ebb, regress, retrograde, rot, sink, worsen

related words abate, de-escalate, diminish, downsize, dwindle, recede, wane; break down, corrupt, decompose, degrade, dilapidate, disintegrate, molder, putrefy; sour, spoil; lessen, lower, reduce; debilitate, undermine; droop, fail, fall, flag, lag, languish, run down, sag, slip, waste (away), weaken, wilt

phrases go to pot, go to seed (*or* run to seed)

near antonyms better, upgrade; enhance, enrich, fortify, heighten, intensify, strengthen; advance, develop, march, proceed, progress

antonyms ameliorate, improve, meliorate

2 to lower in character, dignity, or quality ⟨childish name-calling that merely *deteriorates* what should be a serious discussion on an important issue⟩ — see DEBASE 1

deterioration *n* 1 a gradual sinking and wasting away of mind or body ⟨muscle *deterioration* resulting from prolonged disuse⟩ — see DECLINE 1

2 a change to a lower state or level ⟨a *deterioration* in the quality of food at that once-thriving restaurant⟩ — see DECLINE 2

determinate *adj* 1 having been established and usually not subject to change ⟨a *determinate* order of succession to the throne⟩ — see FIXED 1

2 having distinct or certain limits ⟨Contestants have a *determinate* length of time to answer the questions.⟩ — see LIMITED 1

determination *n* 1 firm or unwavering adherence to one's purpose ⟨a fierce *determination* to succeed⟩

synonyms decidedness, decision, decisiveness, firmness, granite, purposefulness, resoluteness, resolution, resolve

related words doggedness, obduracy, obstinacy, perseverance, persistence, persistency, stubbornness, tenaciousness, tenacity; certainty, certitude, confidence, sureness; alacrity, eagerness, gameness, readiness; backbone, fortitude, grit, iron, pluck, sand

near antonyms doubt, incertitude, indetermination, uncertainty; aversion, disinclination, indisposition, reluctance, unwillingness

antonyms hesitation, indecision, indecisiveness, irresoluteness, irresolution, vacillation

2 a position arrived at after consideration ⟨a *determination* by the judge regarding an appropriate sentence⟩ — see DECISION 1

3 an opinion arrived at through a process of reasoning ⟨his *determination* of the truth of the matter⟩ — see CONCLUSION 1

determine *vb* 1 to give an opinion about (something at issue or in dispute) ⟨A three-member panel will *determine* the case.⟩ — see JUDGE 1

2 to come to a judgment about after discussion or consideration ⟨trying to *determine* which direction we were facing⟩ — see DECIDE 1

3 to come upon after searching, study, or effort ⟨We failed to *determine* the answer to the riddle.⟩ — see FIND 1

4 to come to an end ⟨Your participation in the savings plan *determines* with the termination of your employment here.⟩ — see CEASE 1

5 to make final, definite, or beyond dispute ⟨Your choice of college could *determine* the rest of your life.⟩ — see CLINCH

determined *adj* 1 fully committed to achieving a goal ⟨His *determined* opponent would not be bluffed or shaken.⟩

synonyms bent (on *or* upon), bound, decisive, firm, hellbent (on *or* upon), intent, out, purposeful, resolute, resolved, set, single-minded

related words bitter, vehement; certain, cocksure, confident, positive, sure; earnest, serious; steady, unfaltering, unhesitating, unswerving, unwavering; adamant, adamantine, dogged, hard, hardened, hardheaded, headstrong, immovable, implacable, inflexible, mulish, obdurate, persistent, pertinacious, perverse, pigheaded, rigid, self-willed, stubborn, tenacious, unbending, uncompromising, unrelenting, unyielding, willful (*or* wilful)

phrases on one's mettle

near antonyms distrustful, doubtful, dubious, mistrustful, skeptical, suspicious, uncertain, unconvinced, undecided, unsettled, unsure; disinclined, indisposed, loath (*also* loth *or* loathe), reluctant

antonyms faltering, hesitant, indecisive, irresolute, undetermined, unresolved, vacillating, wavering

2 showing no signs of slackening or yielding in one's purpose ⟨a *determined* effort to finish first in the race⟩ — see UNYIELDING 1

determinedly *adv* with great effort or determination ⟨*Determinedly* unhip, the restaurant serves old-fashioned comfort food.⟩ — see HARD 1

deterrent *n* something that makes movement or progress difficult ⟨The homeowner put up a fence around his garden as a *deterrent* for animals.⟩ — see ENCUMBRANCE

detest *vb* to dislike strongly ⟨I *detest* pepperoni, and wouldn't eat it if you paid me!⟩ — see HATE

detestable *adj* not following or in accordance with standards of honor and decency ⟨the *detestable* actions of a villain⟩ — see IGNOBLE 2

dethrone *vb* to remove from a position of prominence or power (as a throne) ⟨The nation's last monarch was *dethroned* in a popular uprising many years ago.⟩ — see DEPOSE 1

detonate *vb* to break open or into pieces usually because of internal pressure ⟨a bomb *detonated* in the desert⟩ — see EXPLODE 1

detonation *n* the act or an instance of exploding ⟨There was a series of *detonations* around the base of the condemned building, causing it to come crashing down in a matter of minutes.⟩ — see EXPLOSION 1

detour *n* a turning away from a course or standard ⟨The conversation took a *detour* on to another topic.⟩ — see DIVERGENCE 2

detour *vb* 1 to avoid by going around ⟨We had to *detour* the construction zone in order to get to the stadium.⟩

synonyms bypass, circumnavigate, circumvent, skirt

related words leapfrog; avoid, dodge, duck, elude, escape, eschew, evade, flee, shake, shun

near antonyms confront, face, meet; accept, court, embrace, pursue, seek, welcome

2 to change one's course or direction ⟨We had to *detour* for a few miles around the section of highway under construction.⟩ — see TURN 3

detraction *n* the act of making a person or a thing seem little or unimportant ⟨Her *detraction* of every new idea was annoying to the other club members.⟩ — see DEPRECIATION

detriment *n* **1** something that causes loss or pain ⟨Opponents of casino gambling claim that it is a *detriment* to society at large.⟩ — see INJURY 1

2 the negative result caused by something that creates difficulty for achieving success ⟨The requirement that runners wear shoes for the race worked to his *detriment* since he was used to running barefoot.⟩ — see DISADVANTAGE 2

detrimental *adj* causing or capable of causing harm ⟨There were serious concerns that the factory's waste was *detrimental* to the local environment.⟩ — see HARMFUL

devastate *vb* **1** to bring destruction to (something) through violent action ⟨Chicago was *devastated* by a fire in 1871.⟩ — see RAVAGE

2 to bring to a complete end the physical soundness, existence, or usefulness of ⟨crops *devastated* by disease⟩ — see DESTROY 1

3 to subject to incapacitating emotional or mental stress ⟨We were *devastated* by the awful news.⟩ — see OVERWHELM 1

devastating *adj* causing or tending to cause destruction ⟨a *devastating* blow to our morale⟩ — see DESTRUCTIVE 1

devastation *n* the state or fact of being rendered nonexistent, physically unsound, or useless ⟨the sheer *devastation* of the forest by fire⟩ — see DESTRUCTION 1

develop *vb* **1** to gradually become clearer or more detailed ⟨The facts of what had happened slowly *developed* over the next few days.⟩

synonyms elaborate, evolve, unfold

related words advance, fare, forge, get along, get on, march, proceed, progress; blossom, grow, mature, ripen; materialize; emerge, play out

2 to come to have gradually ⟨The youngster *developed* a taste for green olives.⟩

synonyms acquire, cultivate, form

related words absorb, adopt, embrace, take in, take on; gain, get, obtain; achieve, attain, reach; foster, nourish, nurture, promote

near antonyms abandon, desert, forsake; cast, discard, ditch, dump, fling (off *or* away), jettison, junk, reject, scrap, shed, shuck (off), slough (*also* sluff), throw away, throw out, unload

antonyms lose

3 to become mature ⟨The wine is *developing* nicely in the new oak barrels.⟩ — see MATURE

4 to express more fully and in greater detail ⟨Marketing people *developed* the initial idea into a complete promotional campaign.⟩ — see EXPAND 1

developed *adj* being far along in development ⟨a highly *developed* society with a rigid class system⟩ — see ADVANCED

developer *n* one who creates or introduces something new ⟨the *developer* of software that is used the world over⟩ — see INVENTOR

development *n* **1** the act or process of going from the simple or basic to the complex or advanced ⟨the *development* of an idea into a marketable product⟩

synonyms elaboration, evolution, expansion, growth, progress, progression

related words advancement, betterment, improvement, perfection, refinement; incubation, maturation, maturing, ripening; blossoming, flourishing, flowering; addition, augmentation, enhancement, supplementation; emergence, evolvement, metamorphosis

near antonyms backslide, lapse, relapse; decadence, decay, decaying, declension, decline, degeneracy, degeneration, degradation, descent, deterioration, devaluation, downfall, downgrade, ebbing, falling, weakening

antonyms regress, regression, retrogression, reversion

2 a condition or occurrence traceable to a cause ⟨a *development* that the writers of the law never anticipated or intended⟩ — see EFFECT 1

3 the process of becoming mature ⟨a tulip's *development* from a bulb into a flower⟩ — see MATURATION

deviant *adj* departing from some accepted standard of what is normal ⟨a study of *deviant* behavior⟩

synonyms aberrant, abnormal, anomalous, atypical, deviate, irregular, unnatural, untypical

related words unrepresentative; extraordinary, preternatural; rare, uncommon, uncustomary, unusual, unwonted; bizarre, curious, far-out, funny, kinky, odd, outlandish, out-of-the-way, quirky, remarkable, screwy, strange, wacky (*also* whacky), way-out, weird, wild; eccentric, freakish, idiosyncratic, nonconformist, unconventional, unorthodox; extraordinary, preternatural; rare, uncommon, uncustomary, unusual, unwonted; odd, peculiar, strange

near antonyms common, commonplace, everyday, familiar, ordinary, routine, run-of-the-mill, run-of-the-mine (*or* run-of-mine), unexceptional, unremarkable, workaday; customary, usual, wonted; archetypal (*also* archetypical), average, characteristic, representative

antonyms natural, normal, regular, standard, typical

deviant *n* a person who does not conform to generally accepted standards or customs ⟨branded as social *deviants* by a society that did not value self-expression⟩ — see NONCONFORMIST 1

deviate *adj* departing from some accepted standard of what is normal ⟨a *deviate* response to the situation⟩ — see DEVIANT

deviate *n* a person who has sunk below the normal moral standard ⟨warned him to stay away from that *deviate*⟩ — see DEGENERATE

deviate *vb* to change one's course or direction ⟨sailors forced to *deviate* from their course in order to avoid the storm⟩ — see TURN 3

device *n* **1** a clever often underhanded means to achieve an end ⟨used every *device* and stratagem he knew to keep the party a surprise⟩ — see TRICK 1

2 an article intended for use in work ⟨The salesclerk tried to sell me a new *device* for grooming cats.⟩ — see IMPLEMENT

3 devices *pl* a habitual attraction to some activity or thing ⟨Left to her own *devices* she'd eat at a fast-food restaurant every night of the week.⟩ — see INCLINATION 1

devil *n* **1** *cap* the supreme personification of evil often represented as the ruler of hell ⟨The *Devil* is traditionally seen as a being who relentlessly tempts people to commit evil.⟩

synonyms fiend, Lucifer, Satan, serpent

related words deuce, dickens; Mephistopheles

2 an evil spirit ⟨acted as if possessed by some *devil*⟩ — see DEMON 1

3 a member of the human race ⟨That poor *devil* never did achieve his dream.⟩ — see HUMAN

4 an appealingly mischievous person ⟨Why, you little *devil!*⟩ — see SCAMP 1

5 a mean, evil, or unprincipled person ⟨He's a *devil* to everyone he does business with.⟩ — see VILLAIN

6 a person who seeks out very dangerous or foolhardy adventures with no apparent fear ⟨Originally snowboarders were regarded as *devils* on the slopes.⟩ — see DAREDEVIL

devilfish *n* any of several extremely large rays ⟨They saw a *devilfish* when they went scuba diving in the Caribbean, but it swam away quickly.⟩
synonyms manta, manta ray, sea devil
related words ray, skate

devilish *adj* 1 going beyond a normal or acceptable limit in degree or amount ⟨That's a *devilish* amount of bad luck for any person to have to endure.⟩ — see EXCESSIVE
2 of, relating to, or worthy of an evil spirit ⟨a *devilish* plan to sabotage the other party's political convention⟩ — see FIENDISH 1
3 tending to or exhibiting reckless playfulness ⟨a *devilish* grin that told us he was up to something⟩ — see MIS-CHIEVOUS 1

devilishly *adv* beyond a normal or acceptable limit ⟨a *devilishly* clever scheme to make money⟩ — see TOO 1

devilishness *n* playful, reckless behavior that is not intended to cause serious harm ⟨The children always concoct some sort of *devilishness* on Halloween.⟩ — see MISCHIEF 1

devil–may–care *adj* 1 having a relaxed, casual manner ⟨a *devil-may-care* golfer who knows that it's only a game⟩ — see EASYGOING 1
2 having or showing a lack of concern for the consequences of one's actions ⟨The *devil-may-care* speed with which he drives his sports car is going to cause a lot of grief someday.⟩ — see RECKLESS 1
3 having or showing freedom from worries or troubles ⟨the *devil-may-care* attitude that some people have about needlessly contributing to global warming⟩ — see CARE-FREE

devilment *n* playful, reckless behavior that is not intended to cause serious harm ⟨His *devilment* at school remains the stuff of local legend.⟩ — see MISCHIEF 1

devilry *or* **deviltry** *n* 1 playful, reckless behavior that is not intended to cause serious harm ⟨children always getting into some *devilry*⟩ — see MISCHIEF 1
2 the power to control natural forces through supernatural means ⟨superstitious villagers who were quick to attribute an unexpected occurrence to *devilry*⟩ — see MAGIC 1

devious *adj* 1 clever at attaining one's ends by indirect and often deceptive means ⟨We left it to our most *devious* friends to find out the latest information.⟩ — see ARTFUL 1
2 marked by a long series of irregular curves ⟨a *devious* trail through the swampland⟩ — see CROOKED 1

deviousness *n* skill in achieving one's ends through indirect, subtle, or underhanded means ⟨His *deviousness* was almost as terrible as his lack of scruples.⟩ — see CUN-NING 1

devise *vb* to create or think of by clever use of the imagination ⟨She quickly *devised* a new scheme when the first one failed.⟩ — see INVENT

deviser *n* one who creates or introduces something new ⟨Melvil Dewey was the *deviser* of a new system for organizing books.⟩ — see INVENTOR

devoid *adj* 1 utterly lacking in something needed, wanted, or expected ⟨The so-called comedy is totally *devoid* of intelligence, originality, and even laughs.⟩
synonyms bankrupt, bare, barren, bereft, destitute, void
related words blank, empty, innocent, stark, vacant, wanting; deficient, fragmental, fragmentary, incomplete, insufficient, partial, short; absent, missing
near antonyms furnished, provided, supplied; brimming, bulging, bursting, chock-full (*or* chockful), crammed, crowded, fat, jammed, jam-packed, loaded, packed, saturated, stuffed; abounding, swarming, teeming, thick, thronging
antonyms filled, flush, fraught, full, replete, rife

2 lacking contents that could or should be present ⟨The picnic jug was completely *devoid* of juice after only a few minutes.⟩ — see EMPTY 1

devote *vb* 1 to keep or intend for a special purpose ⟨I conscientiously *devote* several hours every weekend to playing with my dog.⟩
synonyms allocate, consecrate, dedicate, earmark, reserve, save
related words bless, hallow, sanctify; commit, consign, entrust (*also* intrust); apply, bestow, employ, use
phrases set apart, set aside
near antonyms ignore, neglect; misapply, misuse
2 to occupy (oneself) diligently or with close attention ⟨Planning a diplomatic career, she's been intensely *devoting* herself to the study of foreign languages in college.⟩ — see APPLY 2

devoted *adj* 1 feeling or showing love ⟨a *devoted* couple who enjoy sharing their lives with one another⟩ — see LOVING 1
2 firm in one's allegiance to someone or something ⟨remembered her most *devoted* friends in her will⟩ — see FAITHFUL 1

devotedness *n* 1 a feeling of strong or constant regard for and dedication to someone ⟨the heartwarming *devotedness* that the newlywed couple felt for each other⟩ — see LOVE 1
2 adherence to something to which one is bound by a pledge or duty ⟨the kind of *devotedness* that only a dog can show for its master⟩ — see FIDELITY

devotee *n* a person with a strong and habitual liking for something ⟨a *devotee* of stamp collecting⟩ — see FAN

devotion *n* 1 a feeling of strong or constant regard for and dedication to someone ⟨Albert Schweitzer was world-renowned for his *devotion* to his fellow man.⟩ — see LOVE 1
2 adherence to something to which one is bound by a pledge or duty ⟨the knight's fierce *devotion* to his lord⟩ — see FIDELITY
3 belief and trust in and loyalty to God ⟨a people of deep spirituality and indomitable *devotion*⟩ — see FAITH 1

devotional *adj* of, relating to, or used in the practice or worship services of a religion ⟨a religious bookstore with an extensive stock of *devotional* literature⟩ — see RELI-GIOUS 1

devour *vb* 1 to destroy all trace of ⟨A series of devastating storms *devoured* the beach on the south side of the island.⟩ — see CONSUME 1
2 to make complete use of ⟨a medical emergency that *devoured* their savings⟩ — see DEPLETE 1
3 to swallow or eat greedily ⟨The hungry dogs *devoured* their food.⟩ — see GOBBLE

devout *adj* 1 firm in one's allegiance to someone or something ⟨*Devout* Red Sox fans never lost faith during the long World Series drought.⟩ — see FAITHFUL 1
2 showing a devotion to God and to a life of virtue ⟨*devout* monks living a life of prayer and solitude⟩ — see HOLY 1

devoutness *n* the quality or state of being spiritually pure or virtuous ⟨an inspiring figure of *devoutness* who devoted her life to helping the poor⟩ — see HOLINESS

dexterity *n* 1 mental skill or quickness ⟨the ambassador showed great *dexterity* in his handling of the touchy situation.⟩
synonyms adroitness, cleverness, finesse, sleight
related words faculty, knack, talent; competence, competency, efficiency, expertise, know-how, proficiency; ingeniousness, ingenuity, resourcefulness; savvy, sharpness, shrewdness; artfulness, artifice, caginess (*also* cageyness), canniness, craft, craftiness, cunning, devious-

ness, foxiness, guile, slickness, slyness, sneakiness, subtleness, wiliness

near antonyms inadequacy, incompetence, ineptitude, ineptness; brainlessness, denseness, density, doltishness, dopiness, dullness (*also* dulness), dumbness, fatuity, foolishness, mindlessness, obtuseness, senselessness, simpleness, slowness, stupidity, stupidness, witlessness

2 ease and grace in physical activity ⟨The juggler needed lots of *dexterity* in order to keep all five balls in the air at the same time.⟩

synonyms agility, deftness, nimbleness, sleight, spryness

related words coordination; flexibility, gracefulness, limberness, litheness, loose-jointedness, suppleness; handiness, sure-handedness; sure-footedness; adeptness, adroitness, finesse

near antonyms disability, inability, incapability, incapacity; debilitation, disablement, impairment, incapacitation; unhandiness

antonyms awkwardness, clumsiness, gaucheness, gawkiness, gawkishness, gracelessness, ham-handedness, heavy-handedness, klutziness, ungainliness

dexterous *also* **dextrous** *adj* **1** skillful with the hands ⟨The *dexterous* watchmaker was able to repair the antique watch's delicate gears and parts.⟩

synonyms clever, cunning, deft, handy

related words agile, flexible, graceful, limber, lissome (*also* lissom), lithe, lithesome, nimble, spry; coordinated; able, adept, capable, competent, expert, masterful, masterly, proficient, qualified, skilled, skillful, sure-handed; double-jointed, loose-jointed

near antonyms awkward, bungling, clumsy, fumbling, gauche, gawky, graceless, stiff, stilted, uncomfortable, uneasy, ungainly, ungraceful, wooden; incapable, incompetent, inept, inexpert, maladroit

antonyms handless, heavy-handed, unhandy

2 accomplished with trained ability ⟨*dexterous* handling of a potentially embarrassing situation⟩ — see SKILL-FUL 1

diabolical *or* **diabolic** *adj* of, relating to, or worthy of an evil spirit ⟨The police quickly mobilized to track down the *diabolical* criminal.⟩ — see FIENDISH 1

diabolicalness *n* the state or quality of being utterly evil ⟨the *diabolicalness* of the criminal's actions⟩ — see ENORMITY 1

diadem *n* a decorative band or wreath worn about the head as a symbol of victory or honor ⟨Miss America's *diadem* was auctioned off for charity.⟩ — see CROWN 1

diagnosis *n* a position arrived at after consideration ⟨My *diagnosis* of the situation is that immediate action needs to be taken.⟩ — see DECISION 1

diagonal *adj* running in a slanting direction ⟨The *diagonal* design ran up the wall all the way from the lower left to the upper right-hand corner.⟩

synonyms cant, canted, inclined, leaning, listing, oblique, pitched, slant, slanted, slantwise, sloped, sloping, tilted, tilting

near antonyms horizontal, level; plumb, up-and-down, vertical; parallel, perpendicular

diagonal *n* the degree to which something rises up from a position level with the horizon ⟨The ramp was set at a low *diagonal* to make it easier to ascend.⟩ — see SLANT 1

diagram *n* something that visually explains or decorates a text ⟨The explanation of the process of photosynthesis is accompanied by a very useful *diagram*.⟩ — see ILLUS-TRATION 1

dial *vb* to make a telephone call to ⟨*dialed* 911 and asked for the police⟩ — see CALL 2

dialect *n* the special terms or expressions of a particular group or field ⟨The promotional team for the new tech-

nology used a *dialect* full of words that the press found difficult to follow.⟩ — see TERMINOLOGY

dialogue *also* **dialog** *n* **1** an exchange of views for the purpose of exploring a subject or deciding an issue ⟨calling for an international *dialogue* on human rights⟩ — see DISCUSSION 1

2 talking or a talk between two or more people ⟨coworkers having a short *dialogue* about politics at the watercooler before heading back to work⟩ — see CONVERSATION

diametric *or* **diametrical** *adj* being as different as possible ⟨That husband and wife have seemingly *diametric* personalities, but somehow their marriage works.⟩ — see OPPOSITE

diarrhea *n* abnormally frequent intestinal evacuations with more or less fluid stools ⟨I was taken with severe *diarrhea* while attending the conference.⟩

synonyms flux, Montezuma's revenge, runs

related words dysentery; scour(s)

diatribe *n* a long angry speech or scolding ⟨He was forced to sit through a long *diatribe* after he came home late once too often.⟩ — see TIRADE

dice *n* a small cube marked on each side with one to six spots and usually played in pairs in various games ⟨She anxiously rolled the *dice*, hoping to win the jackpot.⟩ — see DIE

dice *vb* to cut into small pieces ⟨I quickly *diced* some peppers and onions and threw them into the stew.⟩ — see CHOP

dicker *n* a giving or taking of one thing of value in return for another ⟨I was hoping to make a *dicker* with another collector of vinyl records.⟩ — see EXCHANGE 1

dicker *vb* to talk over or dispute the terms of a purchase ⟨They *dickered* over the price of the car for a few minutes.⟩ — see BARGAIN 1

dictate *n* a statement of what to do that must be obeyed by those concerned ⟨a starchily worded *dictate* from on high concerning the company's dress code⟩ — see COMMAND 1

dictate *vb* to request the doing of by virtue of one's authority ⟨*dictated* that the terms of surrender be negotiated by his senior staff⟩ — see COMMAND 2

dictator *n* a person who uses power or authority in a cruel, unjust, or harmful way ⟨The *dictator* had a fierce stranglehold on the country.⟩ — see DESPOT

dictatorial *adj* **1** exercising power or authority without interference by others ⟨a *dictatorial* leader with total control over people's lives⟩ — see ABSOLUTE 1

2 fond of ordering people around ⟨It's no surprise that the *dictatorial* manager is highly unpopular among employees.⟩ — see BOSSY

3 having or showing a tendency to force one's will on others without any regard to fairness or necessity ⟨Even the teachers chafed under the *dictatorial* rule of the principal.⟩ — see ARBITRARY 1

dictatorship *n* a system of government in which the ruler has unlimited power ⟨a revolution that only ended up replacing one *dictatorship* with another⟩ — see DESPOTISM

diction *n* **1** the clear and accurate pronunciation of words especially in public speaking ⟨Shakespearean actors with very good *diction*⟩

synonyms articulation, enunciation

related words elocution, expression, utterance; speech, wording

2 the way in which something is put into words ⟨the spare *diction* that is the hallmark of the poetry of Robert Frost⟩ — see WORDING 1

dictionary *n* a reference book giving information about

the meanings, pronunciations, uses, and origins of words listed in alphabetical order ⟨Try to develop the habit of going to the *dictionary* whenever you encounter an unfamiliar word.⟩
synonyms lexicon, wordbook
related words gloss, glossary, thesaurus, vocabulary
die *n* a small cube marked on each side with one to six spots and usually played in pairs in various games ⟨He rolled the *die*, hoping for a six.⟩
synonyms bones, dice
die *vb* **1** to stop living ⟨The king *died* of old age after a long and fruitful reign.⟩
synonyms conk (out), croak [*slang*], demise, depart, drop, end, exit, expire, fall, go, pass (on), pass away, part, perish, succumb
related words predecease; consume, disappear, dry up, fade, fail
phrases bite the dust, buy it (*or* buy the farm), give up the ghost, kick the bucket
near antonyms come to, revive; linger; be, exist, subsist; flourish, prosper, thrive
antonyms breathe, live
2 to come to an end ⟨The storm *died* just as dawn was breaking over the horizon.⟩ — see CEASE 1
3 to stop functioning ⟨Fortunately, when the engine *died* we were only two blocks from home.⟩ — see FAIL 1
die (for) *vb* to have an earnest wish to own or enjoy ⟨I'd *die for* some ice cream right now.⟩ — see DESIRE 1
differ *vb* **1** to be unlike; to not be the same ⟨My brother and I *differ* markedly in the way we handle money.⟩
synonyms contrast, vary
related words deviate, diverge, divide, fluctuate, separate
near antonyms accord, agree, conform, correspond
antonyms compare, match
2 to have a different opinion ⟨After much arguing, we simply have agreed to *differ* about the issue.⟩ — see DISAGREE
difference *n* **1** the quality or state of being different ⟨the *difference* between right and wrong⟩
synonyms contrast, disagreement, discrepancy, disparateness, disparity, dissimilarity, distance, distinction, distinctiveness, distinctness, diverseness, diversity, unlikeness
related words deviance, divergence; differentiability, discriminability, distinguishability; change, modification, variation; variability, variance; anomalousness, incompatibility, incongruence, incongruity, incongruousness, nonconformity
near antonyms identicalness, identity; accordance, agreement, conformity, congruity, correspondence, parallelism, similitude; equality, equivalence, equivalency; homogeneity, homogeneousness, uniformity
antonyms alikeness, analogousness, analogy, community, likeness, resemblance, sameness, similarity
2 variance of opinion on a matter ⟨We must try to settle our *differences* without fighting.⟩ — see DISAGREEMENT 1
3 the act, process, or result of making different ⟨It won't make any *difference* which one you choose.⟩ — see CHANGE 1
difference *vb* to understand or point out the difference in ⟨You must *difference* what is necessary from what is simply desired.⟩ — see DISTINGUISH 1
different *adj* **1** being not of the same kind ⟨How are plantains *different* from bananas?⟩
synonyms disparate, dissimilar, distant, distinct, distinctive, distinguishable, diverse, other, unlike, unalike
related words divers, miscellaneous, mixed, several, sundry, variant, varied; differentiable, discriminable; al-

ternate, alternative, individual, particular, peculiar, single; disproportionate, divergent, unequal
near antonyms equal, selfsame; equivalent, tantamount; akin, analogous, comparable, homological, homologous, related; homogeneous, homogenous, uniform
antonyms alike, identical, indistinguishable, kin, kindred, like, parallel, same, similar
2 not the same or shared ⟨My brother and I sleep in *different* rooms.⟩ — see SEPARATE 1
differential *adj* favoring, applying, or being unequal treatment of different classes of people ⟨did away with *differential* pay scales for men and women doing the same work⟩ — see DISCRIMINATORY
differentiate *vb* to understand or point out the difference in ⟨It was hard at first to *differentiate* between the two styles of music.⟩ — see DISTINGUISH 1
differently *adv* in a different way ⟨We do things *differently* around here.⟩ — see OTHERWISE
difficult *adj* **1** requiring considerable physical or mental effort ⟨*difficult* questions on the exam that required analytical thinking⟩ — see HARD 2
2 requiring exceptional skill or caution in performance or handling ⟨It's a *difficult* situation when two of your friends are quarreling and you're trying to stay out of it.⟩ — see TRICKY 1
difficulty *n* **1** something that is a cause for suffering or special effort especially in the attainment of a goal ⟨the many *difficulties* that he encountered on the road from poor orphan to head of a major corporation⟩
synonyms adversity, asperity, hardness, hardship, rigor
related words discomfort, inconvenience, nuisance; affliction, trial, tribulation; knock, misfortune, mishap, tragedy; bar, catch, check, clog, crimp, embarrassment, handicap, hindrance, hitch, hurdle, impediment, interference, let, manacle, obstacle, obstruction, rub, shackle, snag, stop, trammel; block, chain, deterrent, encumbrance, fetter, inhibition; hump
near antonyms advantage, break, opportunity
2 something that makes a situation more complicated or difficult ⟨There was a minor *difficulty* when we realized that the store had already closed.⟩ — see COMPLICATION 1
3 a feeling or declaration of disapproval or dissent ⟨The only *difficulty* I have with the dress is its color—does it come in anything besides purple?⟩ — see OBJECTION
4 variance of opinion on a matter ⟨The business partners found a way to iron out their *difficulties*.⟩ — see DISAGREEMENT 1
diffident *adj* not comfortable around people ⟨For someone who makes a living performing for other people, the actress is remarkably *diffident* in real life.⟩ — see SHY 2
diffuse *adj* using or containing more words than necessary to express an idea ⟨a *diffuse* speech that took a great deal of time to make a very small point⟩ — see WORDY 1
diffuseness *n* the use of too many words to express an idea ⟨I was bored by the *diffuseness* of the Victorian novel I was trying to read.⟩ — see VERBIAGE 1
dig *n* **1** a quick thrust ⟨I gave him a *dig* in the ribs with my elbow.⟩ — see ¹POKE 1
2 an act or expression showing scorn and usually intended to hurt another's feelings ⟨got in a couple of *digs* about lawyers⟩ — see INSULT
3 digs *pl* a room or set of rooms in a private house or a block used as a separate dwelling place ⟨You can check out my new *digs* on the north side of town.⟩ — see APARTMENT 1
dig *vb* **1** to hollow out or form (something) by removing earth ⟨A backhoe *dug* a hole in the backyard to make a swimming pool.⟩
synonyms excavate, shovel

related words dredge; burrow, claw, grub; dig in; scoop, spade; delve; mine, quarry

near antonyms fill (in); smooth (out *or* over)

2 to take pleasure in ⟨I really *dig* bluegrass music.⟩ — see ENJOY 1

3 to have a clear idea of ⟨Can you *dig* what I'm saying?⟩ — see COMPREHEND 1

4 to urge or push forward with or as if with a pointed object ⟨Every time I stopped paying attention, he'd *dig* me in the ribs.⟩ — see PROD 1

dig (into) *vb* to search through or into ⟨We anxiously *dug into* the old records that we found in the 19th-century house that we were restoring.⟩ — see EXPLORE 1

dig (through) *vb* to look through (as a place) carefully or thoroughly in an effort to find or discover something ⟨I roughly *dug through* the closet looking for my shoes⟩ — see SEARCH 1

digest *n* **1** a short statement of the main points ⟨a *digest* of yesterday's departmental meeting⟩ — see SUMMARY

2 a shortened version of a written work ⟨On the ballot there will be a *digest* of the proposed law that is to be submitted for voter approval.⟩ — see ABRIDGMENT

digest *vb* **1** to arrange or assign according to type ⟨This volume *digests* the state's laws for easy reference by local authorities.⟩ — see CLASSIFY 1

2 to make into a short statement of the main points (as of a report) ⟨I *digested* the results of my experiments into a few pages.⟩ — see SUMMARIZE

diggings *pl n* the place where one lives ⟨He hasn't been seen around these *diggings* lately.⟩ — see HOME 1

digit *n* a character used to represent a mathematical value ⟨You only need to fill in the last two *digits* of the year in which you were born.⟩ — see NUMBER 1

dignified *adj* having or showing a formal and serious or reserved manner ⟨assumed a *dignified* stance⟩ ⟨*dignified* funeral services for the fallen firefighters⟩

synonyms august, distinguished, imposing, portly, solemn, staid, stately

related words decorous, proper, seemly; grave, grim, sober, somber (*or* sombre); aristocratic, elegant, elevated, handsome, lordly, majestic, noble

near antonyms coarse, crass, crude, improper, indecent, uncouth, unseemly, vulgar

antonyms flighty, frivolous, giddy, goofy, silly, undignified

dignify *vb* to assign a high status or value to ⟨Our graduation ceremony was *dignified* by a visit from the mayor.⟩ — see EXALT 1

dignity *n* high position within society ⟨The archbishop is very conscious of his *dignity*.⟩ — see RANK 2

digression *n* a departure from the subject under consideration ⟨The professor's frequent and extended *digressions* are the stuff of campus legend.⟩ — see TANGENT

digressive *adj* passing from one topic to another ⟨a *digressive* lecture on current events around the world⟩ — see DISCURSIVE

dike *n* **1** a bank of earth constructed to control water ⟨an elaborate system of *dikes* built to protect the lowlands from the relentless onslaught of the sea⟩ — see DAM

2 a long narrow channel dug in the earth ⟨Water flowed along the *dike* to the small pond.⟩ — see DITCH

dilapidated *adj* showing signs of advanced wear and tear and neglect ⟨a *dilapidated* car that had seen better days⟩ — see SHABBY 1

dilapidation *n* the state of being unattended to or not cared for ⟨The sad *dilapidation* of the old downtown movie theater has finally prompted local preservationists to mount a restoration campaign.⟩ — see NEGLECT 1

dilatory *adj* moving or proceeding at less than the normal, desirable, or required speed ⟨She tends to be *dilatory* about returning e-mails.⟩ — see SLOW 1

dilemma *n* **1** a situation in which one has to choose between two or more equally unsatisfactory choices ⟨faced with a *dilemma* whether to cancel his vacation or miss the wedding⟩

synonyms quandary

related words deadlock, impasse, quagmire, stalemate, standoff; knot, problem; bind, difficulty, fix, hole, jam, pickle, pinch, plight, predicament, spot

near antonyms breeze, cinch, duck soup, snap

2 a difficult, puzzling, or embarrassing situation from which there is no easy escape ⟨With home prices in a free fall, sellers were in a terrible *dilemma*.⟩ — see PREDICAMENT

dilettante *adj* lacking or showing a lack of expert skill ⟨Many *dilettante* efforts could be seen at the sidewalk art show.⟩ — see AMATEURISH

dilettante *n* a person who regularly or occasionally engages in an activity as a pastime rather than as a profession ⟨A *dilettante* at heart, she was never willing to commit the time and effort that ballet demands.⟩ — see AMATEUR 1

diligence *n* attentive and persistent effort ⟨Through the *diligence* and ingenuity of a devoted group of citizens, the playground was reopened.⟩

synonyms assiduity, assiduousness, industriousness, industry

related words application, attentiveness, attention, care, concentration; doggedness, perseverance, persistence, tenacity, tirelessness; bother, effort, effortfulness, pains, painstaking, trouble

near antonyms carelessness, negligence, slackness; idleness, indolence, laziness

diligent *adj* involved in often constant activity ⟨a student who has been unceasingly *diligent* in pursuit of a degree in mathematics⟩ — see BUSY 1

diligently *adv* with great effort or determination ⟨working *diligently* to finish his documentary in time for the film festival⟩ — see HARD 1

dillydally *vb* **1** to move or act slowly ⟨Don't *dillydally* on the way to the store.⟩ — see DELAY 1

2 to spend time doing nothing ⟨restaurant employees who, during the slow periods, would rather be doing something instead of just *dillydallying*⟩ — see IDLE

dillydallying *adj* moving or proceeding at less than the normal, desirable, or required speed ⟨The *dillydallying* congress hadn't passed any legislation, and the term was almost over.⟩ — see SLOW 1

dilute *adj* **1** not containing very much of some important element ⟨a *dilute* acid that's safe to handle in the classroom⟩ — see WEAK 3

2 containing foreign or lower-grade substances ⟨a *dilute* solution of ammonia⟩ — see IMPURE 1

dilute *vb* to alter (something) for the worse with the addition of foreign or lower-grade substances ⟨The pharmacist was convicted of *diluting* prescription drugs.⟩ — see ADULTERATE

diluted *adj* **1** not containing very much of some important element ⟨To clean the bird feeder, soak it in a solution of *diluted* bleach.⟩ — see WEAK 3

2 containing foreign or lower-grade substances ⟨a *diluted* solution of sulfuric acid⟩ — see IMPURE 1

dim *adj* **1** being without light or without much light ⟨a *dim*, windowless room in the basement⟩ — see DARK 1

2 lacking a surface luster or gloss ⟨Over time, exposure to ultraviolet light will make bright pigments turn *dim*.⟩ — see MATTE

3 not seen or understood clearly ⟨I have only a *dim* knowledge of the subject.⟩ — see FAINT 1

dim *vb* to make dark, dim, or indistinct ⟨The storm clouds *dimmed* our view of the city from the airplane.⟩ — see CLOUD 1

dimension *n* **1** the total amount of measurable space or surface occupied by something ⟨The mansion is as great in *dimension* as it is in splendor.⟩ — see ¹SIZE
2 dimensions *pl* an area over which activity, capacity, or influence extends ⟨The vast *dimensions* of the subject will require years of study.⟩ — see RANGE 2

diminish *vb* **1** to express scornfully one's low opinion of ⟨He tends to *diminish* any rival's accomplishments with snide remarks.⟩ — see DECRY 1
2 to make smaller in amount, volume, or extent ⟨The state's blood supplies were severely *diminished* by the two consecutive disasters.⟩ — see DECREASE 1
3 to grow less in scope or intensity especially gradually ⟨The sound of the train *diminished* as our distance from it increased.⟩ — see DECREASE 2

diminishment *n* **1** the act of making a person or a thing seem little or unimportant ⟨The comment was not meant as a *diminishment* of his contribution to the project.⟩ — see DEPRECIATION
2 the amount by which something is lessened ⟨There was a sharp *diminishment* in our savings after the college tuition bill was paid.⟩ — see DECREASE

diminution *n* the amount by which something is lessened ⟨a *diminution* of 60 percent over the course of the month⟩ — see DECREASE

diminutive *adj* of a size that is less than average ⟨a single *diminutive* shrub on the edge of the lawn⟩ — see SMALL 1

diminutive *n* a living thing much smaller than others of its kind ⟨dik-diks, the *diminutives* of the antelope family⟩ — see DWARF 1

diminutiveness *n* the quality or state of being little in size ⟨the *diminutiveness* of many of the girls on the gymnastics team⟩ — see SMALLNESS

dimmed *adj* being without light or without much light ⟨a *dimmed* lounge where students like to rest and sleep⟩ — see DARK 1

din *n* loud, confused, and usually inharmonious sound ⟨There's always a great *din* from the cafeteria during lunch.⟩ — see NOISE 1

din *vb* to say or state again ⟨safety lessons *dinned* into us over and over⟩ — see REPEAT 1

dine *vb* **1** to take a meal ⟨They *dined* elegantly at the city's finest restaurant before taking in a show downtown.⟩
synonyms eat, fare, feed, partake, refresh
related words banquet, feast, repast; chow (down), dig in; glut, gorge, gormandize, overeat, overfeed, pig out; graze, nibble, nosh, pick, snack; board, mess, dine out; breakfast, lunch, sup; picnic
phrases break bread
near antonyms diet, fast
2 to entertain with a fancy meal ⟨The advertising agency lavishly wines and *dines* prospective clients.⟩ — see FEAST 1

diner *n* a public establishment where meals are served to paying customers for consumption on the premises ⟨We'll just grab a quick hamburger at the local *diner*.⟩ — see RESTAURANT

dinghy *n* a boat equipped with one or more sails ⟨We went sailing on the secluded lake in a little two-person *dinghy*.⟩ — see SAILBOAT

dinginess *n* the state or quality of being dirty ⟨She was appalled by the *dinginess* of the hotel room.⟩ — see DIRTINESS

dingy *adj* not clean ⟨The bed sheets were pretty *dingy* so we threw them in the laundry pile.⟩ — see DIRTY 1

dinky *adj* of a size that is less than average ⟨recent college graduates crowding into a *dinky* New York City apartment⟩ — see SMALL 1

dinner *n* a large fancy meal often accompanied by ceremony or entertainment ⟨There will be a celebratory *dinner* at a local restaurant for the entire team.⟩ — see FEAST 1

dinnerware *n* dishes used for eating or serving food or drink ⟨We received three sets of *dinnerware* as wedding gifts.⟩ — see TABLEWARE 2

dinning *adj* making loud, confused, and usually unharmonious sounds ⟨*Dinning* honks and beeps arose from cars stuck in the massive traffic jam.⟩ — see NOISY 1

dint *n* a sunken area forming a separate space ⟨left a small *dint* in the car's fender⟩ — see HOLE 2

dip *n* **1** a downward slope ⟨Marathoners have one last *dip* before the race course levels off and the finish line comes into view.⟩ — see DECLINE 3
2 the act or process of going to a lower level or altitude ⟨The city's population has taken a slight *dip* since the last census.⟩ — see DESCENT 1

dip *vb* **1** to sink or push (something) briefly into or as if into a liquid ⟨First *dip* a paper towel in water.⟩ ⟨She *dipped* a hand into her pocket and pulled out a piece of candy.⟩
synonyms douse (*also* dowse), duck, dunk, immerse, souse, sop, submerge, submerse
related words bathe, moisten, soak, steep, wet; drench, drown, flood; dive, plunge, thrust
2 to lift out with something that holds liquid ⟨carefully *dipped* water from the bucket to the kettle⟩
synonyms bucket, lade, ladle, scoop, spoon
related words deplete, drain, eliminate, empty, exhaust; bleed, draw (off); dish, slop; decant, draw, pump, siphon (*also* syphon), suction
near antonyms pour; fill
3 to go to a lower level especially abruptly ⟨The temperature *dipped* a bit in the evening.⟩ — see DROP 2
4 to lead or extend downward ⟨Slow down, the road *dips* here.⟩ — see DESCEND 1
5 to take a quick or hasty look ⟨I *dipped* into the book, but I didn't have a chance to study it thoroughly.⟩ — see GLANCE 2

diplomacy *n* the ability to deal with others in touchy situations without offending them ⟨That candidate is thought to lack the *diplomacy* necessary in dealing with people of power and influence.⟩ — see TACT

diplomatic *adj* having or showing tact ⟨a *diplomatic* attempt at preventing any hurt feelings⟩ — see TACTFUL

dipper *n* a utensil with a bowl and a handle that is used especially in cooking and serving food ⟨The metal *dipper* left in the stew pot was too hot to touch.⟩ — see SPOON

dire *adj* **1** being or showing a sign of evil or calamity to come ⟨a *dire* forecast of a plunge in stock prices⟩ — see OMINOUS
2 causing fear ⟨a series of *dire* tremors that hinted at a huge volcanic eruption⟩ — see FEARFUL 1
3 needing immediate attention ⟨a *dire* need for food and medicine⟩ — see ACUTE 1
4 causing or marked by an atmosphere lacking in cheer ⟨With stock prices steadily falling, these are *dire* days on the trading floor.⟩ — see GLOOMY 1

direct *adj* **1** done or working without something else coming in between ⟨a zoologist whose works are based entirely on her *direct* observation of animals in the wild⟩ ⟨The virus was the *direct* cause of the disease.⟩
synonyms firsthand, immediate, primary
related words clinical, empirical (*also* empiric); efficient; hands-on
antonyms indirect, secondhand

2 free in expressing one's true feelings and opinions ⟨Our coach is very *direct*, never hesitating for a moment to tell a player whenever he isn't performing up to snuff.⟩ — see FRANK

3 going straight to the point clearly and firmly ⟨clear and *direct* instructions that left no room for misinterpretation⟩ — see STRAIGHTFORWARD 1

4 free from irregularities or digressions in course ⟨This road provides the most *direct* route to your destination.⟩ — see STRAIGHT 1

direct *adv* in a direct line or course ⟨flew *direct* to the coast⟩ — see DIRECTLY 1

direct *vb* **1** to cause to move to a central point or along a restricted pathway ⟨The aqueduct *directs* the water into an artificial lake.⟩ — see CHANNEL

2 to issue orders to (someone) by right of authority ⟨Our tour guide *directed* us to wait in front of the building until she could rejoin us.⟩ — see COMMAND 1

3 to request the doing of by virtue of one's authority ⟨The caretaker *directed* that all of the windows be closed before we left.⟩ — see COMMAND 2

4 to look after and make decisions about ⟨The music teacher *directs* both the student orchestra and the marching band.⟩ — see CONDUCT 1

5 to point or turn (something) toward a target or goal ⟨We quickly *directed* our attention toward the noise coming from the rear.⟩ — see AIM 1

6 to point out the way for (someone) especially from a position in front ⟨The guide *directed* the tour through the museum with commendable efficiency and expertise.⟩ — see LEAD 1

direction *n* **1** a statement of what to do that must be obeyed by those concerned ⟨We were given very specific *directions* for the first part of the exam.⟩ — see COMMAND 1

2 the act or activity of looking after and making decisions about something ⟨working under the close *direction* of the engineering supervisor⟩ — see CONDUCT 1

3 a guiding or motivating purpose or principle ⟨a life that seemed to lack any *direction*⟩ — see COMPASS 1

4 a prevailing or general movement or inclination ⟨Some people worry about the overall *direction* that political discourse has taken.⟩ — see TREND 1

directive *n* **1** a statement of what to do that must be obeyed by those concerned ⟨The company president regularly issues *directives* intended for all staff members.⟩ — see COMMAND 1

2 an order publicly issued by an authority ⟨a presidential *directive*⟩ — see EDICT 1

3 a written communication giving information or directions ⟨a growing stack of unread *directives* from the company's senior vice president⟩ — see MEMORANDUM 1

directly *adv* **1** in a direct line or course ⟨We went *directly* to the site without stopping to pick up extra supplies.⟩
synonyms dead, direct, due, plumb, plump, right, straight, straightway
phrases as the crow flies
near antonyms circuitously, deviously, veeringly
antonyms indirectly

2 in an honest and direct manner ⟨The instructor deals with her art students very *directly*, always telling them the plain truth.⟩ — see STRAIGHTFORWARD 1

3 in the same words ⟨quoted *directly* from the statute⟩ — see VERBATIM

4 without delay ⟨In case of a medical emergency, do not try to contact your doctor but instead go *directly* to the hospital.⟩ — see IMMEDIATELY

5 at or within a short time ⟨Dinner should be ready *directly*.⟩ — see SHORTLY 2

directness *n* the free expression of one's true feelings and opinions ⟨His *directness* is much appreciated by his patients.⟩ — see CANDOR 1

director *n* a person who manages or directs something ⟨The new *director* of the company plans to make a number of changes in daily operations.⟩ — see EXECUTIVE

directorial *adj* suited for or relating to the directing of things ⟨an applicant with a number of *directorial* positions on his résumé⟩ — see EXECUTIVE

direful *adj* **1** being or showing a sign of evil or calamity to come ⟨The stock market crash was the first *direful* indication of the dark days to come.⟩ — see OMINOUS

2 causing fear ⟨We heard the *direful* howling of the wolves during the night.⟩ — see FEARFUL 1

dirge *n* a composition expressing one's grief over a loss ⟨Bagpipes played a haunting *dirge* at the funeral for the fallen leader.⟩ — see LAMENT 2

dirt *n* **1** the loose surface material in which plants naturally grow ⟨Dig into the *dirt* to a depth of about three inches.⟩
synonyms clod, earth, ground, soil
related words blackland, clay, kaolin, muck, mud; dust, gravel, sand; humus, loam, topsoil; alluvium, colluvium, loess, marl, sediment, shingle, silt; mull; subsoil, substratum

2 the solid part of our planet's surface as distinguished from the sea and air ⟨He tripped and planted his face in the *dirt*.⟩ — see EARTH 2

3 foul matter that mars the purity or cleanliness of something ⟨There's some *dirt* on your shoes.⟩ — see FILTH 1

4 solid matter discharged from an animal's alimentary canal ⟨Tread carefully, as there's cow *dirt* all over the pasture.⟩ — see DROPPING 1

dirtiness *n* the state or quality of being dirty ⟨The health inspector took the manager to task over the general *dirtiness* of the restaurant.⟩
synonyms dinginess, dustiness, filthiness, foulness, griminess, grubbiness, nastiness, smuttiness, soilage, squalidness, uncleanliness, uncleanness
related words discoloration, staining; impurity; messiness, mussiness, sloppiness, untidiness; insanitation, squalor; muddiness, sootiness
near antonyms purity
antonyms cleanliness, spotlessness

dirty *adj* **1** not clean ⟨After working in the factory all day, his clothes are very *dirty*.⟩
synonyms bedraggled, besmirched, black, blackened, dingy, dusty, filthy, foul, grimy, grubby, grungy, mucky, muddy, nasty, smutty, soiled, sordid, stained, sullied, unclean, uncleanly
related words contaminated, defiled, germy, impure, polluted, tainted; insanitary, uncleaned, unsanitary, unsterile, unsterilized, unwashed; greasy, gunky; littered, messed, messy, muddled, mussed, mussy, rumpled, scruffy, sloppy, slovenly, unkempt, untidy; raunchy, scuzzy [*slang*], shabby, sleazy, squalid
near antonyms clear, limpid, pure; cleaned, cleansed, combed, groomed, neat, ordered, orderly, tidy; bleached, purified, whitened; bright, flawless, perfect, shiny, sparkling, unspotted, untouched; taintless, unblemished, undefiled, unpolluted, untainted, virgin, wholesome
antonyms clean, immaculate, spick-and-span (*or* spic-and-span), spotless, stainless, ultraclean, unsoiled, unstained, unsullied

2 depicting or referring to sexual matters in a way that is unacceptable in polite society ⟨a *dirty* joke⟩ — see OBSCENE 1

3 marked by wet and windy conditions ⟨They were unknowingly sailing into *dirty* weather.⟩ — see FOUL 1

4 not being in accordance with the rules or standards of what is fair in sport ⟨The school is known for the *dirty* football it plays.⟩ — see FOUL 2

5 not following or in accordance with standards of honor and decency ⟨accused the other campaign of playing *dirty* tricks⟩ — see IGNOBLE 2

6 arousing or deserving of one's loathing and disgust ⟨Laying off longtime employees was a *dirty* way for the company for reduce labor costs.⟩ — see CONTEMPT-IBLE 1

7 open to improper influence and especially bribery ⟨a movie about a *dirty* cop paid to protect a mafioso⟩ — see VENAL

dirty *vb* to make dirty ⟨She *dirtied* her new sneakers when she splashed in the puddle.⟩

synonyms befoul, begrime, besmirch, blacken, daub, foul, grime, mire, muck, muddy, smirch, smudge, soil, stain, sully

related words contaminate, defile, pollute, taint; discolor; confuse, disarrange, disarray, dishevel, disorder, draggle, jumble, mess, muddle

near antonyms decontaminate, purge, purify; disinfect, sanitize; brush, dry-clean, dust, mop, rinse, scour, scrub, sweep, wash, wipe; brighten, deodorize, freshen, renew; straighten (up)

antonyms clean, cleanse

disable *vb* **1** to cause severe or permanent injury to ⟨*disabled* by an injury⟩ — see MAIM

2 to render powerless, ineffective, or unable to move ⟨*disabled* the controls for unauthorized users⟩ — see PARALYZE 1

disabled *adj* deprived of the power to perform one or more natural bodily activities ⟨an entrance for *disabled* customers⟩

synonyms challenged, exceptional, impaired

related words special-needs; halt, paralyzed, quadriplegic; immobile, immobilized; ailing, diseased, ill, incapacitated, sick, unfit, unhealthy, unsound, unwell; blind, deaf, hard of hearing, mute

near antonyms bouncing, chipper, fit, hale, healthy, hearty, robust, sound, well, whole, wholesome

antonyms able-bodied, abled, nondisabled, unimpaired

disabuse *vb* to free from mistaken beliefs or foolish hopes ⟨Let me *disabuse* you of your foolish notions.⟩ — see DISILLUSION

disadvantage *n* **1** a feature of someone or something that creates difficulty for achieving success ⟨Their lack of height was a *disadvantage* on the basketball court.⟩

synonyms drawback, handicap, liability, minus, negative, strike

related words albatross, millstone, stranglehold; disability, impairment; failing, shortcoming; bar, catch, check, clog, crimp, embarrassment, hindrance, hitch, hurdle, impediment, interference, let, manacle, obstacle, obstruction, rub, shackle, stop, trammel

near antonyms vantage; head start, jump, lead, margin, start; ascendancy (*also* ascendency), better, command, control, drop, mastery, predominance, superiority, supremacy, transcendence, upper hand; prerogative, privilege; break, opportunity; aid, assistance, help

antonyms advantage, edge, plus

2 the negative result caused by something that creates difficulty for achieving success ⟨Intense pretrial publicity worked to our *disadvantage*.⟩

synonyms despite, detriment, disfavor, penalty

related words deficit, deprivation, expense, loss; damage, harm, hurt, injury; prejudice

near antonyms gain

antonyms advantage, favor

disadvantaged *adj* kept from having the necessities of life or a healthful environment ⟨*disadvantaged* families struggling to get by⟩ — see DEPRIVED

disadvantageous *adj* opposed to one's interests ⟨Such an arrangement with the wholesalers would be *disadvantageous* for small farmers.⟩ — see ADVERSE 1

disaffect *vb* **1** to cause to change from friendly or loving to unfriendly or uncaring ⟨a candidate winning over *disaffected* voters⟩ — see ESTRANGE

2 to make discontented ⟨The troops were *disaffected* by the extension of their tours of duty.⟩ — see DISCONTENT

disaffection *n* the loss of friendship or affection ⟨widespread *disaffection* with the governor's administration in its final year⟩ — see ESTRANGEMENT

disagree *vb* to have a different opinion ⟨The leader thought we were still headed north on the trail, but I *disagreed*.⟩

synonyms differ, dissent

related words clash, collide, conflict, contrast; counter, debate, object, oppose, protest, resist; contest, dispute; argue, bicker, fall out, quarrel

phrases take issue

near antonyms accede, accept, acquiesce, comply, consent, defer; affiliate, ally, associate, collaborate, come round, compromise, cooperate, get along, side

antonyms agree, assent, concur

disagree (with) *vb* to make an assertion that is contrary to one made by (another) ⟨She *disagreed with* me when I said that the jacket was dark blue.⟩ — see CONTRADICT 1

disagreeable *adj* **1** having or showing a habitually bad temper ⟨I've never known her to be *disagreeable*.⟩ — see ILL-TEMPERED

2 not giving pleasure to the mind or senses ⟨a *disagreeable* smell coming from the closet⟩ — see UNPLEASANT

disagreeing *adj* not being in agreement or harmony ⟨*disagreeing* accounts of what happened⟩ — see INCONSISTENT 1

disagreement *n* **1** variance of opinion on a matter ⟨There was some *disagreement* about what color the missing sweater actually was.⟩

synonyms controversy, debate, difference, difficulty, disputation, dispute, dissension (*also* dissention)

related words clash, collision, conflict, confliction, discord; combat, contention, strife, struggle; altercation, argument, bicker, falling-out, fight, kickup, misunderstanding, quarrel, set-to

near antonyms acceptance, compliance; concord, peace

antonyms accord, agreement, consensus, harmony, unanimity

2 an often noisy or angry expression of differing opinions ⟨A loud *disagreement* started as soon as we tried to order pizza for everyone.⟩ — see ARGUMENT 1

3 the quality or state of being different ⟨There is some *disagreement* between the accounts on the sequence of events.⟩ — see DIFFERENCE 1

disallow *vb* **1** to declare not to be true ⟨*disallowing* the philosophical concept of free will⟩ — see DENY 1

2 to be unwilling to grant ⟨*disallowed* the defendant's request for a new trial⟩ — see DENY 2

disallowance *n* **1** an unwillingness to grant something asked for ⟨The taxpayer was notified of the *disallowance* of his claim for medical expenses.⟩ — see DENIAL 1

2 a refusal to confirm the truth of a statement ⟨a categorical *disallowance* of all charges⟩ — see DENIAL 2

disappear *vb* to cease to be visible ⟨The stranger *disappeared* into the mists, never to be seen again.⟩

synonyms dissolve, evanesce, evaporate, fade, flee, fly, melt, sink, vanish *related words* blank (out), clear, disperse, dissipate, dissolve, dry up; blur, dim

phrases drop out of sight

near antonyms arrive, break out, come out, emerge, issue, loom, show up

antonyms appear, materialize

disappoint *vb* to fall short in satisfying the expectation or hope of 〈They were *disappointed* by the outcome of the big game.〉

synonyms cheat, dissatisfy, fail, let down

related words bum (out), chagrin, discontent, disgruntle, displease, distress, upset; disenchant, disillusion; deceive, delude, mock

near antonyms fulfill (*or* fulfil); gladden

antonyms content, gratify, satisfy

disappointment *n* **1** the emotion felt when one's expectations are not met 〈We felt keen *disappointment* when our offer on the house was rejected.〉

synonyms dismay, dissatisfaction, frustration, letdown

related words crestfallenness, discontent, discontentedness, discontentment, disgruntlement, displeasure; disenchantment, disillusionment; blues, dejectedness, dejection, depression, desolateness, desolation, despondency, disconsolateness, distress, doldrums, dolefulness, dolor, downheartedness, dreariness, dumps, gloom, gloominess, joylessness, melancholy, mopes, oppression, sadness, sorrow, unhappiness; chagrin, discomfiture

near antonyms fulfillment (*or* fulfilment); bliss, felicity, gladness, happiness, joy

antonyms content, contentedness, contentment, gratification, satisfaction

2 something that disappoints 〈After all the publicity and high expectations, the sequel to the movie blockbuster was a huge *disappointment*.〉

synonyms bummer, letdown

related words anticlimax, failure, fiasco, fizzle; lemon, loser

near antonyms success, winner; relief

disapprobation *n* refusal to accept as right or desirable 〈There was widespread *disapprobation* of the plan to combine the two school districts.〉 — see DISAPPROVAL

disapproval *n* refusal to accept as right or desirable 〈Thus far, every one of her choices for college has met with her parents' *disapproval*.〉

synonyms deprecation, disapprobation, discountenance, disfavor, dislike, displeasure

related words distaste; rejection, thumbs-down; blame, censure, condemnation, criticism, denunciation, dispraise, opprobrium, reprehension, reproach, reprobation; antagonism, antipathy, hostility; belittlement, disparagement, objection, opposition

near antonyms acclaim, commendation, praise; endorsement (*also* indorsement), sanction, thumbs-up; empathy, sympathy

antonyms approbation, approval, favor

disapprove *vb* **1** to be unwilling to grant 〈The committee *disapproved* the proposal to allow casino gambling in the state.〉 — see DENY 2

2 to show unwillingness to accept, do, engage in, or agree to 〈*disapproved* the first set of blueprints submitted by the firm〉 — see DECLINE 1

disapprove (of) *vb* to hold an unfavorable opinion of 〈My sister *disapproves of* my decision.〉

synonyms deprecate, discountenance, disfavor, dislike, reprove, tsk-tsk

related words object (to), pooh-pooh (*also* pooh), reject, reprehend, reprobate, scorn; censure, condemn, criticize, denounce, discommend; chide, rebuke, reproach, scold

phrases look down one's nose (on)

near antonyms endorse (*also* indorse), sanction, support; adore, delight (in), dig, enjoy, fancy, groove (on), love, relish, revel (in)

antonyms approve, favor

disarm *vb* **1** to reduce the size and strength of the armed forces of 〈The defeated nation was *disarmed* so that it would never again be a threat to international order.〉

synonyms demilitarize

related words demobilize

near antonyms equip, reequip, weapon; embattle, mechanize, mobilize

antonyms arm, militarize

2 to lessen the anger or agitation of 〈Her future father-in-law was totally *disarmed* by her easy charm.〉 — see PACIFY 1

disarmament *n* the reduction or elimination of a country's armed forces or weapons 〈The ambassador spoke at length about the possible unilateral *disarmament* of his country.〉

synonyms demilitarization

related words demobilization

near antonyms equipment, reequipment; mobilization

antonyms armament, militarization

disarming *adj* **1** having qualities that tend to make one loved 〈a thoroughly *disarming* little rascal who can talk his way out of any trouble〉 — see LOVABLE

2 likely or intended to win one's affection 〈There's a *disarming* lack of pretension about the girl.〉 — see INGRATIATING

3 tending to lessen or avoid conflict or hostility 〈The salesperson's *disarming* smile made me forget why I was angry.〉 — see PACIFIC 1

disarrange *vb* to undo the proper order or arrangement of 〈The wind had hopelessly *disarranged* my hair.〉 — see DISORDER

disarranged *adj* lacking in order, neatness, and often cleanliness 〈a *disarranged* collection of sports memorabilia scattered about the room〉 — see MESSY

disarrangement *n* a state in which everything is out of order 〈The *disarrangement* of the files makes it almost impossible to find anything.〉 — see CHAOS

disarray *n* a state in which everything is out of order 〈The boys' bedroom was in its usual *disarray*.〉 — see CHAOS

disarray *vb* to undo the proper order or arrangement of 〈She had accidentally *disarrayed* her sister's closet, leaving a telltale sign of borrowing without permission.〉 — see DISORDER

disarrayed *adj* lacking in order, neatness, and often cleanliness 〈a *disarrayed* pile of rugs in the attic〉 — see MESSY

disassemble *vb* **1** to take apart 〈You can *disassemble* the bookcase for easy storage.〉

synonyms break down, demount, dismantle, dismember, knock down, take down

related words detach, disengage; break up, disaggregate, disarticulate, disconnect, disjoin, disjoint, dissever, disunite, divide, separate

near antonyms build, erect, pitch; combine, unite

antonyms assemble, construct

2 to go off in different directions and cease to exist as a body or unified whole 〈The class was slow to *disassemble*, many waiting around to ask the instructor some questions.〉 — see DISPERSE 1

disaster *n* **1** a sudden violent event that brings about great loss or destruction 〈Hurricanes are natural *disasters*.〉

synonyms calamity, cataclysm, catastrophe, debacle (*also* débâcle), tragedy

related words collapse, crash, meltdown; Armageddon, doomsday, end-time; convulsion, paroxysm, upheaval; accident, casualty, fatality; misadventure, mischance,

misfortune, mishap; blast, blow, double whammy, one-two (*or* one-two punch)
near antonyms godsend, manna, windfall
2 something that has failed ⟨An utter *disaster*, the play opened and closed on the same night.⟩ — see FAILURE 3
disastrous *adj* **1** bringing about ruin or misfortune ⟨a split-second, *disastrous* decision that I would forever regret⟩ — see FATAL 1
2 causing or tending to cause destruction ⟨The building was destroyed by a *disastrous* fire.⟩ — see DESTRUCTIVE 1
disavow *vb* **1** to declare not to be true ⟨*disavowed* the testimony that she had given earlier in the trial⟩ — see DENY 1
2 to refuse to acknowledge as one's own or as one's responsibility ⟨The government will *disavow* any knowledge of your mission.⟩ — see DISCLAIM 1
disavowal *n* a refusal to confirm the truth of a statement ⟨The mayor's *disavowal* of the rumor that the school was being closed put our minds at rest.⟩ — see DENIAL 2
disband *vb* **1** to cease to exist or cause to cease to exist as a group or organization ⟨The university *disbanded* the committee after the report had been submitted.⟩ ⟨The rock group *disbanded* upon finishing their farewell tour.⟩
synonyms break up, disperse, dissolve
related words demobilize
near antonyms incorporate; consolidate; hang together
antonyms band, join, unite
2 to cause (members of a group) to move widely apart ⟨The police tried to *disband* the crowd after the fireworks display was over.⟩ — see SCATTER 1
disbandment *n* an act or process in which something scatters or is scattered ⟨the *disbandment* of the crowd at the end of the outdoor rock concert⟩ — see SCATTERING 1
disbelief *n* refusal to accept something as true ⟨Their story explaining their absence was met with *disbelief*.⟩
synonyms incredulity, unbelief
related words discredit, distrust, doubt, mistrust, skepticism, suspicion, uncertainty; denial, rejection, repudiation, unfaith
near antonyms acceptance, conviction, faith; trust
antonyms belief, credence, credit
disbelieve *vb* to think not to be true or real ⟨Many *disbelieved* the medium's claims that she could communicate with the spirits of the dead.⟩
synonyms discredit, negate
related words deny, reject, repudiate; distrust, doubt, mistrust, suspect; debunk, disprove, refute; deride, pooh-pooh (*also* pooh), scoff (at)
near antonyms trust
antonyms accept, believe, credit, swallow
disbeliever *n* a person who is always ready to doubt or question the truth or existence of something ⟨The usual *disbelievers* refused to accept the scientists' findings.⟩ — see SKEPTIC
disbelieving *adj* inclined to doubt or question claims ⟨The senator stated her case before a *disbelieving* press corps.⟩ — see SKEPTICAL 1
disburden *vb* **1** to empty or rid of cargo ⟨*disburdened* the oil tanker before it could leak any more oil⟩ — see UNLOAD 1
2 to set (a person or thing) free of something that encumbers ⟨The movie theater was a place where we could *disburden* ourselves of our cares for a couple of hours.⟩ — see RID
disburse *vb* to hand over or use up in payment ⟨The foundation *disburses* money to many worthy causes.⟩ — see SPEND 1
disbursement *n* **1** a payment made in the course of

achieving a result ⟨substantial *disbursements* for research and development⟩ — see EXPENSE
2 the act of offering money in exchange for goods or services ⟨the *disbursement* of the foundation's funds to several cancer research centers⟩ — see PAYMENT 1
3 the act or process of giving out something to each member of a group ⟨the agency whose responsibilities included the *disbursement* of strains of the virus to medical research labs around the country⟩ — see DISTRIBUTION 1
discard *n* something separated from a group or lot for not being as good as the others ⟨Toss all of your *discards* in the garbage.⟩ — see CULL
discard *vb* to get rid of as useless or unwanted ⟨You should *discard* an old, torn sweater.⟩
synonyms cashier, cast (off), chuck, ditch, dump, fling (off *or* away), jettison, junk, lose, pitch, reject, scrap, shed, shuck (off), throw away, throw out, toss, unload
related words abandon, abdicate, desert, forsake; dismiss; abolish, annihilate, eliminate, eradicate, expunge, exterminate, extinguish, extirpate, liquidate, remove, root (out), stamp (out), wipe out
phrases dispose of, set aside
near antonyms adopt, embrace, take on; employ, use, utilize; hold, hold back, keep, retain
discarding *n* the getting rid of whatever is unwanted or useless ⟨the daily *discarding* of all unwanted e-mail⟩ — see DISPOSAL 1
discern *vb* **1** to make note of (something) through the use of one's eyes ⟨I was barely able to *discern* the garden gate through the mist.⟩ — see SEE 1
2 to understand or point out the difference in ⟨too young to *discern* between right and wrong⟩ — see DISTINGUISH 1
3 to have a clear idea of ⟨We're still trying to *discern* the meaning of that cryptic remark.⟩ — see COMPREHEND 1
discernible *also* **discernable** *adj* able to be perceived by a sense or by the mind ⟨*discernible* differences in the two authors' writing styles⟩ — see PERCEPTIBLE
discerning *adj* having or showing deep understanding and intelligent application of knowledge ⟨a *discerning* critic of modern art⟩ — see WISE 1
discernment *n* the ability to understand inner qualities or relationships ⟨the *discernment* to know when someone is a true friend⟩ — see WISDOM 1
discharge *n* **1** a directed propelling of a missile by a firearm or artillery piece ⟨the thunderous *discharge* of the cannons⟩ — see SHOT 1
2 a freeing from an obligation or responsibility ⟨a full *discharge* from responsibility for the accident⟩ — see RELEASE 1
3 the termination of the employment of an employee or a work force often temporarily ⟨She was resentful over what she felt was a wrongful *discharge*.⟩ — see LAYOFF
4 the doing of an action ⟨aided in the *discharge* of his duties by a capable assistant⟩ — see COMMISSION 2
discharge *vb* **1** to cause (a projectile) to be driven forward with force ⟨Robert Goddard was the first to *discharge* a rocket containing an instrument package.⟩ — see SHOOT 1
2 to empty or rid of cargo ⟨docks for *discharging* containerships⟩ — see UNLOAD 1
3 to give what is owed for ⟨*discharge* a debt in full⟩ — see PAY 2
4 to release (as from slavery or confinement) ⟨*discharged* the prisoners upon the signing of the peace treaty⟩ — see FREE 1
5 to throw or give off ⟨The mighty river *discharges* its waters into the ocean.⟩ — see EMIT 1

6 to cause a weapon to release a missile with great force ⟨felt a strong recoil as the rifle *discharged*⟩ — see SHOOT 2
7 to let go from office, service, or employment ⟨Ten workers were *discharged* when their stealing was discovered.⟩ — see DISMISS 1

disciple *n* one who follows the opinions or teachings of another ⟨a circle of dedicated *disciples* who conscientiously wrote down everything the prophet said⟩ — see FOLLOWER 1

disciplinary *adj* inflicting, involving, or serving as punishment ⟨called for *disciplinary* actions in response to the unacceptable behavior⟩ — see PUNITIVE

discipline *n* **1** a region of activity, knowledge, or influence ⟨You must choose a *discipline* to focus on in college.⟩ — see FIELD 2
2 suffering, loss, or hardship imposed in response to a crime or offense ⟨Harsh *discipline* was imposed to keep order within the ranks.⟩ — see PUNISHMENT
3 the checking of one's true feelings and impulses when dealing with others ⟨She lacks the *discipline* that's essential for a job in customer relations.⟩ — see CONSTRAINT 1

discipline *vb* to inflict a penalty on for a fault or crime ⟨The pranksters were *disciplined* for their stunt.⟩ — see PUNISH

disciplining *adj* inflicting, involving, or serving as punishment ⟨*disciplining* actions taken in response to the rowdiness⟩ — see PUNITIVE

disclaim *vb* **1** to refuse to acknowledge as one's own or as one's responsibility ⟨He *disclaimed* any part in the prank.⟩
synonyms deny, disavow, disown, repudiate
related words contradict, disallow, gainsay, negate, negative, refuse, reject; challenge, confute, criticize, disprove, rebut, refute; dispute, question; abdicate, abjure, recant, renounce, retract
phrases wash one's hands of
near antonyms accept, adopt, embrace, espouse; admit, concede, confess, grant; affirm, announce, assert, aver, declare, maintain, profess, submit; authenticate, confirm, corroborate, substantiate, validate, verify
antonyms acknowledge, avow, claim, own, recognize
2 to declare not to be true ⟨Her spokesperson flatly *disclaimed* the marriage rumor circulating in the press.⟩ — see DENY 1

disclaimer *n* **1** a document containing a declaration of an intentional giving up of a right, claim, or privilege ⟨The school requires student athletes to sign a *disclaimer* in the event they are injured during competition.⟩ — see WAIVER
2 a refusal to confirm the truth of a statement ⟨the intelligence agency's pro forma *disclaimer* of any involvement in the incident⟩ — see DENIAL 2

disclose *vb* to make known (as information previously kept secret) ⟨The informer *disclosed* all sorts of details about the secret organization.⟩ — see REVEAL 1

disclosure *n* the act or an instance of making known something previously unknown or concealed ⟨He offered full *disclosure* of the companies he owns stock in.⟩ — see REVELATION

discombobulate *vb* to throw into a state of mental uncertainty ⟨Our grandmother seems a bit *discombobulated* by all of this birthday fuss.⟩ — see CONFUSE 1

discomfit *vb* **1** to prevent from achieving a goal ⟨Constant interruptions *discomfited* her in her attempt to finish the speech.⟩ — see FRUSTRATE 1
2 to throw into a state of self-conscious distress ⟨He was *discomfited* by the awkward situation of having his ex-girlfriend meet his current one.⟩ — see EMBARRASS 1

discomfiting *adj* causing embarrassment ⟨the *discomfiting* scrutiny of an audience of music critics⟩ — see AWKWARD 3

discomfiture *n* the emotional state of being made self-consciously uncomfortable ⟨blushed and lowered her eyes in evident *discomfiture*⟩ — see EMBARRASSMENT 1

discomfort *vb* to trouble the mind of; to make uneasy ⟨The harsh criticism of his musical talent did not *discomfort* him in the least.⟩ — see DISTURB 1

discomforting *adj* **1** causing discomfort ⟨a *discomforting* perch on the thin balcony rail⟩ — see UNCOMFORTABLE 1
2 causing worry or anxiety ⟨The layoff rumors created a *discomforting* situation for the workers.⟩ — see TROUBLESOME

discommode *vb* to cause discomfort to or trouble for ⟨The breakdown of her car didn't *discommode* her seriously.⟩ — see INCONVENIENCE

discommoding *adj* causing difficulty, discomfort, or annoyance ⟨the thoroughly unpleasant and *discommoding* experience of changing a flat tire in the rain⟩ — see INCONVENIENT

discompose *vb* **1** to trouble the mind of; to make uneasy ⟨*discomposed* by the tone of the message left on his voice mail⟩ — see DISTURB 1
2 to undo the proper order or arrangement of ⟨The wind *discomposed* her carefully arranged papers.⟩ — see DISORDER

discomposing *adj* causing worry or anxiety ⟨a *discomposing* response to our routine query about her health⟩ — see TROUBLESOME

disconcert *vb* to throw into a state of self-conscious distress ⟨We were *disconcerted* by the unexpected changes to the program.⟩ — see EMBARRASS 1

disconcerting *adj* causing embarrassment ⟨a *disconcerting* habit of chewing with his mouth open⟩ — see AWKWARD 3

disconnect *vb* to set or force apart ⟨*disconnected* the two parts of the light fixture⟩ — see SEPARATE 1

disconnected *adj* **1** not clearly or logically connected ⟨a *disconnected* narrative of her time in the hospital⟩ — see INCOHERENT 1
2 not physically attached to another unit ⟨a *disconnected* computer terminal⟩ — see SEPARATE 2

disconsolate *adj* **1** causing or marked by an atmosphere lacking in cheer ⟨She spent her last days in the *disconsolate* environs of a hospital ward.⟩ — see GLOOMY 1
2 feeling unhappiness ⟨She was utterly *disconsolate* when her best friend moved away.⟩ — see SAD 1

disconsolateness *n* a state or spell of low spirits ⟨his *disconsolateness* over the loss of his dog⟩ — see SADNESS

discontent *adj* having a feeling that one has been wronged or thwarted in one's ambitions ⟨a novel about a woman who is *discontent* with her small-town life⟩ — see DISCONTENTED

discontent *n* the condition of being dissatisfied with one's life or situation ⟨The rebels worked to stir up *discontent* among the citizens.⟩
synonyms discontentedness, discontentment, disgruntlement, displeasure, dissatisfaction
related words bitterness, resentment; aggrievement, disquiet, perturbation, uneasiness; blues, dejection, depression, desolateness, desolation, despondency, disconsolateness, doldrums, dolefulness, dolor, downheartedness, dreariness, dumps; misery, sadness, sorrow, unhappiness, wretchedness
near antonyms bliss, felicity, gladness, happiness, joy, lightheartedness; exultation, jubilation, triumph
antonyms contentedness, contentment, pleasure, satisfaction

discontent *vb* to make discontented ⟨The ongoing lack of decent food *discontented* the soldiers in the rebel army.⟩
synonyms disaffect, disgruntle, displease, dissatisfy
related words alienate, estrange; aggrieve, agitate, discompose, disquiet, disturb, perturb, upset; annoy, irk, irritate, nettle, peeve; depress, sadden
near antonyms delight, gladden, tickle; calm, soothe, tranquilize (*also* tranquillize)
antonyms content, gratify, please, satisfy

discontented *adj* having a feeling that one has been wronged or thwarted in one's ambitions ⟨He was becoming increasingly *discontented* with his job.⟩
synonyms aggrieved, discontent, disgruntled, displeased, dissatisfied, malcontent
related words disappointed, disenchanted, disillusioned, frustrated, unfulfilled; disquieted, disturbed, perturbed, upset; dejected, depressed, despairing, despondent, disconsolate, doleful, down, downcast, downhearted, forlorn, hangdog, inconsolable, joyless, low-spirited, miserable, mournful, sad, sorrowful, unhappy
phrases out of joint
near antonyms blissful, delighted, glad, happy, joyful, joyous; elated, exultant, jubilant, triumphant
antonyms content, contented, gratified, pleased, satisfied

discontentedness *n* the condition of being dissatisfied with one's life or situation ⟨He was left with a vague feeling of *discontentedness* even after he got the car he had always wanted.⟩ — see DISCONTENT

discontentment *n* the condition of being dissatisfied with one's life or situation ⟨widespread *discontentment* with the way the club was being run⟩ — see DISCONTENT

discontinuance *n* the stopping of a process or activity ⟨the possible *discontinuance* of one of the town's big holiday traditions⟩ — see END 1

discontinue *vb* 1 to bring (as an action or operation) to an immediate end ⟨Once the symptoms disappeared, the treatment was *discontinued*.⟩ — see STOP 1
2 to stop doing (something) permanently ⟨We have *discontinued* the manufacture of that item.⟩ — see QUIT 2
3 to come to an end ⟨Publication of the magazine will *discontinue* at the end of the year.⟩ — see CEASE 1

discontinuity *n* 1 an open space in a barrier (as a wall or hedge) ⟨microscopic *discontinuities* in the connecting wires⟩ — see GAP 1
2 a break in continuity ⟨a noticeable *discontinuity* in the flow of the story⟩ — see GAP 2

discontinuous *adj* lacking in steadiness or regularity of occurrence ⟨The novel captures the *discontinuous* nature of a soldier's life: long stretches of boredom interrupted by flashes of activity.⟩ — see FITFUL

discord *n* a lack of agreement or harmony ⟨The *discord* between two of the members threatened to tear our team of researchers apart.⟩
synonyms conflict, discordance, dissension (*also* dissention), dissent, dissidence, disunion, disunity, division, friction, schism, strife, variance, war, warfare
related words clash, collision, competition, contention; altercation, argument, bicker, brawl, debate, disagreement, dispute, divide, fissure; falling-out, fight, hassle, jar, mix-up, quarrel, row, run-in, scrap, spat, squabble, tiff, wrangle; incompatibility, incongruence, incongruity, incongruousness, inconsistence, inconsistency, inconsonance, inharmoniousness; animosity, antagonism, antipathy, cold war, enmity, hostility, ill will, rancor
near antonyms concurrence, cooperation
antonyms accord, agreement, concord, concordance, harmony, peace

discord *vb* to be out of harmony or agreement usually noticeably ⟨The testimony he gave on the stand *discorded* with his earlier statements.⟩ — see CLASH

discordance *n* 1 a lack of agreement or harmony ⟨There was a real *discordance* between the tough guys that the actor played in the movies and the nice person that he was in real life.⟩ — see DISCORD
2 loud, confused, and usually inharmonious sound ⟨the jarring *discordance* coming from the garage where the band was rehearsing⟩ — see NOISE 1

discordant *adj* 1 marked by or producing a harsh combination of sounds ⟨*discordant* tones coming from the poorly tuned instrument⟩ — see DISSONANT
2 making loud, confused, and usually unharmonious sounds ⟨the *discordant* cries of gulls fighting over the fishing boat's castoffs⟩ — see NOISY 1
3 feeling or displaying eagerness to fight ⟨a *discordant* family that benefited from counseling⟩ — see BELLIGERENT
4 not being in agreement or harmony ⟨the difficult task of bringing together *discordant* elements⟩ — see INCONSISTENT 1

discount *n* something that is or may be subtracted ⟨a *discount* of 20% from the original price⟩ — see DEDUCTION 1

discount *vb* 1 to dismiss as of little importance ⟨Even while acknowledging the primacy of the director, we should not *discount* the contributions of all the others who worked on the film.⟩ — see EXCUSE 1
2 to express scornfully one's low opinion of ⟨We shouldn't *discount* their contributions to our fund-raising efforts.⟩ — see DECRY 1

discountenance *n* refusal to accept as right or desirable ⟨made known his long-standing *discountenance* of the method⟩ — see DISAPPROVAL

discountenance *vb* 1 to hold an unfavorable opinion of ⟨She *discountenanced* changes made to the traditional model.⟩ — see DISAPPROVE (OF)
2 to throw into a state of self-conscious distress ⟨The political party was *discountenanced* by the actions of a few of its overly zealous members.⟩ — see EMBARRASS 1

discourage *vb* 1 to lessen the courage or confidence of ⟨I didn't let losing *discourage* me from trying again.⟩
synonyms chill, daunt, demoralize, dishearten, dismay, dispirit, frustrate, unnerve
related words browbeat, bully, cow, intimidate; depress, sadden, weigh; afflict, try; damp, dampen, deaden; distress, trouble; bother, irk, vex, worry; debilitate, enfeeble, undermine, weaken; frighten, horrify, scare
phrases throw cold water on
near antonyms buoy (up), cheer, gladden; animate, enliven, invigorate; enforce, fortify, strengthen; assure, reassure; boost, energize, excite, galvanize, inspire, lift, provoke, quicken, rally, stimulate, stir
antonyms embolden, encourage, hearten, nerve, steel
2 to steer (a person) from an activity or course of action ⟨The higher fines may help *discourage* drivers from speeding on the highway.⟩
synonyms deter, dissuade, inhibit
related words divert; unsell; repel
near antonyms egg (on), exhort, goad, prod, urge; impel, induce, prompt
antonyms encourage, persuade

discouragement *n* the state of being discouraged ⟨I tried desperately to avoid *discouragement* after failing the bar exam twice.⟩
synonyms demoralization, despair, despondency, disheartenment, dismay, dispiritedness
related words blues, dejection, depression, dumps, gloom, melancholy, mopes; defeatism, pessimism, resignation
near antonyms optimism, sanguinity
antonyms encouragement

discourse *n* talking or a talk between two or more people ⟨Thomas Jefferson is said to have been able to participate in knowledgeable *discourse* on a breathtaking array of subjects.⟩ — see CONVERSATION

discourse *vb* **1** to give a formal often extended talk on a subject ⟨The guest lecturer *discoursed* at some length on the long-term results of the study.⟩ — see TALK 1

2 to talk as if giving an important and formal speech ⟨grandly *discoursed* as though he were an expert on every subject⟩ — see ORATE 1

discourteous *adj* showing a lack of manners or consideration for others ⟨We wouldn't tolerate anything so *discourteous* as the interruption of another speaker during a discussion.⟩ — see IMPOLITE

discourteousness *n* rude behavior ⟨a campaign to try to remedy the increasing *discourteousness* of the state's drivers⟩ — see DISCOURTESY

discourtesy *n* rude behavior ⟨The courtiers shuddered at the *discourtesy* shown to the king.⟩
synonyms discourteousness, disrespect, impertinence, impoliteness, impudence, incivility, inconsiderateness, inconsideration, insolence, rudeness, ungraciousness
related words audacity, boldness, brashness, brassiness, forwardness, sauciness, shamelessness; boorishness, caddishness, churlishness, clownishness, crudeness, loutishness, vulgarity; abruptness, brusqueness, crustiness, curtness, gruffness, sharpness; crabbedness, crossness, disagreeableness, grumpiness, sullenness, surliness; impropriety, inappropriateness, incorrectness, indecency, unfitness, unsuitability; arrogance, conceit, conceitedness, presumption, pretense (*or* pretence), pretension, pretentiousness
near antonyms humility, meekness, modesty; deference, dutifulness, respectfulness, submissiveness; acceptability, appropriateness, correctness, decency, decorousness, fitness, goodness, propriety, respectability, respectableness, rightness, seemliness, suitability, suitableness; affability, cordiality, friendliness, geniality, hospitality, kindness; felicitousness, grace, gracefulness
antonyms civility, considerateness, consideration, courtesy, gentility, graciousness, politeness, politesse, thoughtfulness

discover *vb* **1** to come to an awareness of ⟨I was startled to *discover* that my keys were missing.⟩
synonyms ascertain, catch on (to), find out, hear, learn, realize, see, wise (up)
related words hit (on *or* upon), tumble (to); descry, detect, encounter, espy, see, spot; calculate, dope (out), figure out, find, puzzle (out); discern, mind, note, observe, perceive; divine
phrases get wind of
near antonyms miss, overlook; disregard, ignore; forget, unlearn; blanket, blot out, cloak, conceal, cover, curtain, enshroud, hide, mask, occult, screen, shroud, veil
2 to come upon after searching, study, or effort ⟨We hope to *discover* the reason for his headaches.⟩ — see FIND 1
3 to make known (as information previously kept secret) ⟨*discovered* to his friend that he had lost most of his money⟩ — see REVEAL 1

discovery *n* **1** the act or process of sighting or learning the existence of something for the first time ⟨the *discovery* of a new species of frog⟩
synonyms detection, finding, spotting, unearthing
related words awareness, espial, notice; disclosure, exposure, revelation, uncovering, unveiling; creation, invention; exploration; rediscovery
near antonyms disappearance, loss; concealment, hiding

2 something discovered ⟨His many zoological *discoveries* include several species of birds.⟩
synonyms find
related words pay dirt, strike; breakthrough

discredit *n* the state of having lost the esteem of others ⟨To his everlasting *discredit*, the coach was found to have placed bets against his own team.⟩ — see DISGRACE 1

discredit *vb* **1** to reduce to a lower standing in one's own eyes or in others' eyes ⟨The prosecutor *discredited* the witness by pointing out her inconsistent statements.⟩ — see HUMBLE
2 to think not to be true or real ⟨I *discredit* the story that the old inn is haunted.⟩ — see DISBELIEVE
3 to prove to be false ⟨The pseudoscience of phrenology has been thoroughly *discredited*.⟩ — see DISPROVE

discreditable *adj* not respectable ⟨the *discreditable* conduct of sore losers⟩ — see DISREPUTABLE

discreet *adj* **1** having or showing good judgment and restraint especially in conduct or speech ⟨He was very *discreet*, only saying what was necessary.⟩
synonyms intelligent, judicious, prudent
related words cautious, circumspect, cozy; forehanded, foresighted, foresightful, forethoughtful; discerning, discriminating, sage, sane, sapient, senseful, sensible, wise; canny, provident; astute, perspicacious, sagacious, shrewd
near antonyms careless, heedless, incautious, rash; improvident, shortsighted; foolish, unwise
antonyms imprudent, indiscreet, injudicious
2 not readily seen or noticed ⟨With a *discreet* gesture, she signalled to her husband that she was ready to leave the party.⟩ — see UNOBTRUSIVE

discreetness *n* the ability to make intelligent decisions especially in everyday matters ⟨I appreciated her *discreetness* in keeping the information to herself.⟩ — see COMMON SENSE

discrepancy *n* the quality or state of being different ⟨The *discrepancy* of the calculations of my bill by the hotel and myself was a matter of concern.⟩ — see DIFFERENCE 1

discrepant *adj* not being in agreement or harmony ⟨widely *discrepant* conclusions on the impact the real estate development would have on the local environment⟩ — see INCONSISTENT 1

discrete *adj* not physically attached to another unit ⟨several *discrete* sections to this vast medical complex, including a college of pharmacology and a research center⟩ — see SEPARATE 2

discreteness *n* the state of being kept distinct ⟨The *discreteness* of the sonnets is given visual emphasis by having each one on a separate page.⟩ — see SEPARATION 2

discretion *n* **1** the ability to make intelligent decisions especially in everyday matters ⟨We'll rely on your *discretion* in handling the accusation.⟩ — see COMMON SENSE
2 the power, right, or opportunity to choose ⟨Ambassadorships are generally regarded as subject to the president's *discretion*.⟩ — see CHOICE 1
3 the checking of one's true feelings and impulses when dealing with others ⟨In that job you'll be expected to show *discretion* and act like a professional at all times.⟩ — see CONSTRAINT 1

discretionary *adj* subject to one's freedom of choice ⟨*Discretionary* spending on luxuries dropped dramatically last year.⟩ — see OPTIONAL

discriminate *vb* to understand or point out the difference in ⟨The human eye can *discriminate* between very slight gradations of color.⟩ — see DISTINGUISH 1

discriminating *adj* **1** favoring, applying, or being unequal treatment of different classes of people ⟨posted the rules against *discriminating* practices in the hiring of employees⟩ — see DISCRIMINATORY

2 serving to identify as belonging to an individual or group ⟨A *discriminating* feature of poison ivy is a compound leaf with three mitten-shaped leaflets.⟩ — see CHARACTERISTIC 1

discrimination *n* the state of being kept distinct ⟨In her mind there did not exist a *discrimination* between the imaginary and the real.⟩ — see SEPARATION 2

discriminative *adj* favoring, applying, or being unequal treatment of different classes of people ⟨fighting laws which were grossly *discriminative*⟩ — see DISCRIMINATORY

discriminatory *adj* favoring, applying, or being unequal treatment of different classes of people ⟨a company that was fined for its *discriminatory* practices⟩

synonyms differential, discriminating, discriminative

related words biased, inequitable, partial, partisan, prejudiced, prejudicial, unequal, unfair, unjust; clubby, selective; segregative

near antonyms equal, equitable, fair, just; impartial, neutral, objective, unbiased, uncolored, unprejudiced

antonyms nondiscriminatory

discursive *adj* passing from one topic to another ⟨The speaker's *discursive* style made it difficult to understand his point.⟩

synonyms desultory, digressive, leaping, maundering, rambling, wandering

related words circuitous, deviating, devious, indirect, roundabout

near antonyms coherent, consistent, logical; direct, focused (*also* focussed), straightforward, undeviating

discuss *vb* to talk about (an issue) usually from various points of view and for the purpose of arriving at a decision or opinion ⟨We *discussed* the new proposal for the school stadium.⟩

synonyms agitate, argue, bandy, canvass (*also* canvas), debate, dispute, moot, talk over

related words review, speak (about), talk (about); broach, introduce, propound, raise, stir up; forge, talk out, thrash (out); chew over, consider, deliberate, weigh

discussion *n* **1** an exchange of views for the purpose of exploring a subject or deciding an issue ⟨The *discussion* about the club budget went on for hours.⟩

synonyms argument, colloquy, conference, consult, council, counsel, debate, deliberation, dialogue (*also* dialog), give-and-take, palaver, parley, talk

related words bull session, chat room, forum, meeting, roundtable, seminar, skull session (*also* skull practice), symposium, talkathon; chat, conversation, rap, words; discourse; bargaining, consultancy, negotiation, pourparler

2 talking or a talk between two or more people ⟨*discussions* around the watercooler at work⟩ — see CONVERSATION

disdain *n* open dislike for someone or something considered unworthy of one's concern or respect ⟨showing undisguised *disdain* for the other employees⟩ — see CONTEMPT

disdain *vb* to show contempt for ⟨*disdained* the deserter as a coward⟩ — see SCORN 1

disdainful *adj* **1** feeling or showing open dislike for someone or something regarded as undeserving of respect or concern ⟨a *disdainful* attitude toward authority⟩ — see CONTEMPTUOUS 1

2 having or displaying feelings of scorn for what is regarded as beneath oneself ⟨*disdainful* of manual labor of any kind⟩ — see PROUD 1

3 intended to make a person or thing seem of little im-

portance or value ⟨*disdainful* remarks regarding the accommodations⟩ — see DEROGATORY

disease *n* an abnormal state that disrupts a plant's or animal's normal bodily functioning ⟨They caught a rare *disease* while they were traveling.⟩

synonyms ail, ailment, bug, complaint, complication, condition, disorder, fever, ill, illness, infirmity, malady, sickness, trouble

related words contagion, contagious disease; contagium, infection; attack, bout, fit, spell; debility, decrepitude, feebleness, frailness, lameness, sickliness, unhealthiness, unsoundness, unwellness, weakness; malaise, matter, pip; pest, pestilence, plague

near antonyms fitness, healthiness, heartiness, robustness, soundness, wholeness, wholesomeness; fettle, shape

antonyms health, wellness

disembark *vb* **1** to go ashore from a ship ⟨The cruise passengers *disembarked* as soon as they got to the terminal in Miami.⟩

synonyms debark, land

related words beach; anchor, dock, put in

near antonyms board, get (on); weigh (anchor)

antonyms embark

2 to come down from something (as a vehicle) ⟨Before you *disembark*, make sure you haven't left anything on your seat.⟩ — see ALIGHT 2

disembowel *vb* to take the internal organs out of ⟨Ancient Roman prophets would *disembowel* animals in order to read the future from their entrails.⟩ — see GUT

disenchant *vb* to free from mistaken beliefs or foolish hopes ⟨If you thought that you could pass this course without doing any work, let me be the first to *disenchant* you.⟩ — see DISILLUSION

disencumber *vb* **1** to empty or rid of cargo ⟨We *disencumbered* our pack animals as soon as we made camp that night.⟩ — see UNLOAD 1

2 to set (a person or thing) free of something that encumbers ⟨a simple statement of the terms of the contract *disencumbered* of legal jargon⟩ — see RID

disencumbered *adj* no longer burdened with something unpleasant or painful ⟨The paying off of my loan left me feeling delightfully *disencumbered*.⟩ — see FREE 2

disengage *vb* to set free from entanglement or difficulty ⟨sought to *disengage* myself from the embarrassing situation⟩ — see EXTRICATE

disentangle *vb* **1** to separate the various strands of ⟨It took forever to *disentangle* the knot.⟩ — see UNRAVEL 1

2 to set free from entanglement or difficulty ⟨the years that it took to *disentangle* ourselves from our troubles after someone started using our social security numbers⟩ — see EXTRICATE

disfavor *n* **1** a strong feeling of not liking or approving ⟨Bob made no attempt to hide his *disfavor* of the changes.⟩ — see DISLIKE 1

2 refusal to accept as right or desirable ⟨Their suggestion was met with *disfavor* by virtually all of the other club members.⟩ — see DISAPPROVAL

3 the negative result caused by something that creates difficulty for achieving success ⟨The defendant certainly acted to his own *disfavor* with his frequent outbursts.⟩ — see DISADVANTAGE 2

disfavor *vb* **1** to feel dislike for ⟨a style of stage acting that is *disfavored* by most theatergoers today⟩ — see DISLIKE 1

2 to hold an unfavorable opinion of ⟨polls showing that the proposed law is highly *disfavored* by most voters⟩ — see DISAPPROVE (OF)

disfigure *vb* to reduce the soundness, effectiveness, or perfection of ⟨The statue was seriously *disfigured* by years of exposure to the elements.⟩ — see DAMAGE 1

disfigurement *n* something that spoils the appearance or completeness of a thing ⟨a plastic surgeon who occasionally donates his services to treat the *disfigurements* of needy children⟩ — see BLEMISH

disgorge *vb* to violently throw out or off (something from within) ⟨The volcano *disgorged* lava in a spectacular nighttime show.⟩ — see ERUPT 1

disgrace *n* **1** the state of having lost the esteem of others ⟨The students who cheated were in *disgrace* with their schoolmates.⟩
synonyms discredit, dishonor, disrepute, ignominy, infamy, odium, opprobrium, reproach, shame
related words scandal; contempt, despite, disdain, scorn; deprecation, disapprobation, disapproval, disfavor; abasement, debasement, debasing, degradation, dust, humbling, humiliation; blot, brand, shadow, slur, smirch, spot, stain, stigma, taint
near antonyms admiration, appreciation, estimation, regard; awe, fear, reverence; fame, glory, renown, repute
antonyms esteem, honor, respect
2 a cause of shame ⟨The exposure of his criminal record was a huge *disgrace* for the councilman.⟩
synonyms dishonor, opprobrium, reflection, reproach, scandal
related words blot, brand, slur, smirch, spot, stain, stigma, taint
near antonyms boast, glory, jewel, pride, treasure
antonyms credit, honor
3 a regrettable or blameworthy act ⟨It's a *disgrace* to let all the leftover food from the banquet go to waste, so let's deliver it to the homeless shelter.⟩ — see CRIME 2

disgrace *vb* to reduce to a lower standing in one's own eyes or in others' eyes ⟨*disgraced* by the shameful actions of their leader⟩ — see HUMBLE

disgraceful *adj* not respectable ⟨*disgraceful* disruptions at the graduation ceremonies⟩ — see DISREPUTABLE

disgruntle *vb* **1** to cause to change from friendly or loving to unfriendly or uncaring ⟨an employee *disgruntled* by the boss's shabby treatment⟩ — see ESTRANGE
2 to make discontented ⟨a crew *disgruntled* by a long voyage that provided no opportunity for recreation onshore⟩ — see DISCONTENT

disgruntled *adj* having a feeling that one has been wronged or thwarted in one's ambitions ⟨She has to deal with *disgruntled* customers all day long.⟩ — see DISCONTENTED

disgruntlement *n* **1** the condition of being dissatisfied with one's life or situation ⟨a survey showing the extent of people's *disgruntlement* with the company's service⟩ — see DISCONTENT
2 the loss of friendship or affection ⟨feelings of neglect that inevitably lead to *disgruntlement* among employees⟩ — see ESTRANGEMENT

disguise *n* **1** clothing put on to hide one's true identity or imitate someone or something else ⟨Mardi Gras revelers dressed in a colorful array of outlandish *disguises*.⟩
synonyms camouflage, costume, guise
related words domino, mask, veil, visor (*also* vizor), vizard; costumery, dress, getup, outfit, rig; coloring, makeup, paint
2 a display of emotion or behavior that is insincere or intended to deceive ⟨Somehow, he managed to put on a *disguise* of happiness as he watched his secret crush marry someone else.⟩ — see MASQUERADE

disguise *vb* **1** to change the dress or looks of so as to conceal true identity ⟨The spies *disguised* themselves as harmless tourists.⟩
synonyms camouflage, cloak, dress up, mask
related words blanket, blot out, conceal, cover, curtain,
enshroud, hide, obscure, occult, screen, shroud, veil; affect, assume, counterfeit, dissemble, dissimulate, feign, pose, pretend, sham, simulate; act, fake, impersonate, masquerade, play; gild, gloss (over), varnish, whitewash
near antonyms display, exhibit, expose, flaunt, parade, show, uncloak, unclothe, uncover, undrape, unveil; bare, betray, disclose, discover, divulge, expose, reveal
antonyms unmask
2 to keep secret or shut off from view ⟨That investigative reporter usually does a good job of *disguising* her true motives for interviewing a person.⟩ — see ¹HIDE 2

disgust *n* a dislike so strong as to cause stomach upset or queasiness ⟨We turned from the grisly scene with *disgust*.⟩
synonyms aversion, distaste, horror, loathing, nausea, repugnance, repulsion, revulsion
related words abhorrence, abomination, antipathy, execration, hate, hatred; allergy, averseness, disapproval, disfavor, disinclination, dislike, disliking, displeasure
near antonyms appetite, bent, fancy, favor, fondness, like, liking, love, partiality, penchant, predilection, preference, propensity, relish, shine, taste, use

disgust *vb* to cause to feel disgust ⟨The smell of the greasy food *disgusted* me.⟩
synonyms nauseate, put off, repel, repulse, revolt, sicken, turn off
related words displease, distress; appall (*also* appal), disquiet, horrify; affront, insult, offend, outrage, shock
phrases turn one's stomach
near antonyms allure, attract, beguile, bewitch, captivate, charm, disarm, draw, enchant, entice, fascinate, lure, pull, seduce, tempt; delight, gratify, please, rejoice, tickle; enrapture, enthrall (*or* enthral), entrance; appeal (to), interest, intrigue

disgusted *adj* filled with disgust ⟨The *disgusted* diners left after discovering the dirty condition of the restaurant.⟩ — see SICK 2

dish *n* **1** a usually circular utensil for holding something (as food) ⟨We threw all of the ingredients for the salsa into a *dish* and mixed them together.⟩
synonyms vessel
related words bowl, casserole, charger, cup, plate, platter, salver, saucer, server, tray, waiter
2 a physically attractive person ⟨Grandpa said he still thinks Grandma is a *dish*.⟩ — see DOLL 2
3 information or opinion that is widely disseminated without any authority or confirmation of accuracy ⟨the latest Hollywood *dish*⟩ — see RUMOR

dish *vb* to relate sometimes questionable or secret information of a personal nature ⟨a DJ who *dishes* all the celebrity gossip⟩ — see GOSSIP

dishearten *vb* to lessen the courage or confidence of ⟨We were *disheartened* by the news.⟩ — see DISCOURAGE 1

disheartenment *n* the state of being discouraged ⟨our excusable *disheartenment* in the face of overwhelming odds against winning the game⟩ — see DISCOURAGEMENT

dishevel *vb* to undo the proper order or arrangement of ⟨Decorations for the garden wedding had been *disheveled* by the wind.⟩ — see DISORDER

disheveled *or* **dishevelled** *adj* lacking in order, neatness, and often cleanliness ⟨He got his suit pressed so he wouldn't look so *disheveled*.⟩ — see MESSY

dishonest *adj* **1** telling or containing lies ⟨I think he is being *dishonest* about how much he knows.⟩ ⟨*dishonest* statements on the claims form⟩
synonyms lying, mendacious, untruthful
related words erroneous, fallacious, false, misleading, untrue; double-dealing, hypocrite, hypocritical, insincere, mealymouthed, smooth-tongued, two-faced; perjurious

near antonyms candid, open, plainspoken, straightforward; earnest, sincere, true; conscientious, moral, principled, scrupulous; dependable, reliable, trustworthy, trusty; decent, ethical, honorable, just, respectable, righteous, right-minded, straight, upright, upstanding, virtuous
antonyms honest, truthful, veracious
2 given to or marked by cheating and deception ⟨*dishonest* car dealers who roll back mileage gauges⟩ ⟨*dishonest* business deals that landed him in jail⟩
synonyms crooked, deceptive, double-dealing, fast, fraudulent, guileful, rogue, shady, sharp, shifty, underhand, underhanded
related words unconscionable, unethical, unprincipled, unscrupulous; deceitful, deceiving, deluding, delusive, delusory, false; artful, beguiling, cagey (*also* cagy), crafty, cunning, foxy, slick, sly, subtle, wily; defrauding, devious, furtive, slippery, sneaking, sneaky, trickish, tricky; insidious, perfidious, treacherous
near antonyms conscientious, decent, ethical, honorable, just, scrupulous, upright; forthright, straightforward
antonyms aboveboard, honest, straight
3 marked by, based on, or done by the use of dishonest methods to acquire something of value ⟨*dishonest* appraisals of art works⟩ — see FRAUDULENT 1
dishonesty *n* **1** the tendency to tell lies ⟨If you gain a reputation for *dishonesty*, no one will believe you even when you're telling the truth.⟩
synonyms deceit, deceitfulness, falsehood, mendacity, untruthfulness
related words artifice, craft, craftiness, crookedness, cunning, dissembling, dissimulation, double-dealing, duplicity, fakery, foxiness, guile, insincerity, trickishness, wiliness; falseness; hypocrisy
near antonyms honor, incorruptibility; candidness, candor, frankness, good faith, sincerity, straightforwardness; dependability, reliability, reliableness, trustworthiness; accuracy, objectivity; authenticity, correctness, genuineness; credibility
antonyms honesty, integrity, probity, truthfulness, veraciousness, veracity, verity
2 the inclination or practice of misleading others through lies or trickery ⟨the use of *dishonesty* in their advertisements⟩ — see DECEIT 1
dishonor *n* **1** the state of having lost the esteem of others ⟨a person of integrity who would never bring *dishonor* upon himself⟩ — see DISGRACE 1
2 a cause of shame ⟨Your expulsion for cheating is a *dishonor* to this family.⟩ — see DISGRACE 2
dishonor *vb* to reduce to a lower standing in one's own eyes or in others' eyes ⟨*dishonored* herself by fixing the results of her medical research⟩ — see HUMBLE
dishonorable *adj* **1** not following or in accordance with standards of honor and decency ⟨resorted to *dishonorable* tactics in order to win⟩ — see IGNOBLE 2
2 not respectable ⟨*dishonorable* conduct shown by some people while visiting foreign countries⟩ — see DISREPUTABLE
disillusion *vb* to free from mistaken beliefs or foolish hopes ⟨We were *disillusioned* when we saw how the movie star acted in real life.⟩
synonyms disabuse, disenchant, undeceive
related words sophisticate; advise, apprise, clue (in), fill in, wise (up); debunk, expose, refute, show up, uncloak, uncover, unmask; disclose, divulge, spill, tell, unveil
near antonyms beguile, bluff, cozen, delude, dupe, fool, gull, hoax, hoodwink, kid, misguide, misinform, mislead, misrepresent, snow, take in, trick

disinclination *n* **1** a lack of willingness or desire to do or accept something ⟨It's an understatement to say that our dog shows a *disinclination* to get into the car to go to the vet.⟩ — see RELUCTANCE
2 a strong feeling of not liking or approving ⟨a strong *disinclination* for Brussels sprouts⟩ — see DISLIKE 1
disinclined *adj* slow to begin or proceed with a course of action because of doubts or uncertainty ⟨*disinclined* to pay his friends a visit without calling first⟩ — see HESITANT
disintegrate *vb* **1** to go through decomposition ⟨Fallen leaves slowly *disintegrate* over the course of the winter.⟩ — see DECAY 1
2 to reduce to fine particles ⟨Exposure to the elements is gradually *disintegrating* the ancient temple's irreplaceable friezes.⟩ — see POWDER
disinter *vb* to remove from place of burial ⟨The Egyptian mummy was carefully *disinterred* in hopes that it would yield secrets about the Old Kingdom.⟩ — see EXHUME
disinterested *adj* **1** having or showing a lack of interest or concern ⟨His boss seemed completely *disinterested* in his project proposal.⟩ — see INDIFFERENT 1
2 marked by justice, honesty, and freedom from bias ⟨a judge who is widely respected for his *disinterested* decisions⟩ — see FAIR 2
disinterestedness *n* **1** lack of favoritism toward one side or another ⟨The *disinterestedness* with which the newspaper reports stories earns it the respect and trust of the community.⟩ — see DETACHMENT 1
2 lack of interest or concern ⟨A fair measure of the level of *disinterestedness* in the proceedings was the near-constant yawning by both participants and observers.⟩ — see INDIFFERENCE
disjoin *vb* to set or force apart ⟨*disjoined* the two drinking glasses, which were stuck together, only with the greatest difficulty⟩ — see SEPARATE 1
disjoint *vb* **1** to set or force apart ⟨*disjointed* the parts of a chicken for frying⟩ — see SEPARATE 1
2 to undo the proper order or arrangement of ⟨The author deliberately *disjoints* his narrative in favor of a more impressionistic account of the war.⟩ — see DISORDER
disjointed *adj* not clearly or logically connected ⟨She could hardly follow their *disjointed* conversation.⟩ — see INCOHERENT 1
dislike *n* **1** a strong feeling of not liking or approving ⟨I have a strong *dislike* for olives.⟩
synonyms allergy, averseness, aversion, disfavor, disinclination, disliking
related words disgust, distaste, loathing, nausea, repugnance, repulsion, revulsion; abhorrence, abomination, antipathy, execration, hate, hatred; deprecation, disapproval, displeasure, dissatisfaction; jaundice
near antonyms affection, attachment, devotedness, devotion, love, passion; bent, leaning, penchant, predilection, propensity, tendency
antonyms appetite, favor, fondness, like, liking, partiality, preference, relish, shine, taste, use
2 refusal to accept as right or desirable ⟨the public's general *dislike* of negative campaign ads⟩ — see DISAPPROVAL
dislike *vb* **1** to feel dislike for ⟨The two dogs *disliked* each other the first time they met, and never did become friends.⟩
synonyms disfavor
related words abhor, abominate, detest, execrate, hate, loathe; condemn, despise, scorn; cringe (at), disapprove (of), mind, object (to), shy (from *or* away from)
near antonyms admire, appreciate, cherish, esteem, regard, respect; adore, deify, idolize, revere, reverence,

venerate, worship; prize, treasure, value; savor (*also* savour); dote (on), idolize; favor, prefer
antonyms adore, cotton (to), delight (in), dig, enjoy, fancy, groove (on), like, love, relish, revel (in)
2 to hold an unfavorable opinion of ⟨I *dislike* the governor's heavy-handed way of pushing his agenda.⟩ — see DISAPPROVE (OF)
disliking *n* a strong feeling of not liking or approving ⟨I had taken an instant *disliking* to the new neighbors.⟩ — see DISLIKE 1
dislocate *vb* **1** to change the place or position of ⟨*dislocated* his shoulder in the accident⟩ — see MOVE 1
2 to undo the proper order or arrangement of ⟨The company's entire structure was *dislocated* by the merger.⟩ — see DISORDER
dislocation *n* an act or instance of the order of things being disturbed ⟨The slightest *dislocation* in her daily routine bothered the elderly woman.⟩ — see UPSET
disloyal *adj* not true in one's allegiance to someone or something ⟨It would be *disloyal* to abandon them.⟩ — see FAITHLESS
disloyalty *n* **1** lack of faithfulness especially to one's husband or wife ⟨She knew rumors of her husband's *disloyalty* were not true.⟩ — see INFIDELITY 1
2 the act or fact of violating the trust or confidence of another ⟨His *disloyalty* to the company led to his dismissal.⟩ — see BETRAYAL
dismal *adj* **1** causing or marked by an atmosphere lacking in cheer ⟨a suitably *dismal* setting for a haunted house⟩ — see GLOOMY 1
2 causing unhappiness ⟨the *dismal* failure of our hopes for the championship⟩ — see SAD 2
3 extremely unsatisfactory ⟨The quarterback's *dismal* performance suggested that he had not fully recovered from his recent injury.⟩ — see WRETCHED 1
dismantle *vb* to take apart ⟨Let's *dismantle* the table for easier transport.⟩ — see DISASSEMBLE 1
dismay *n* **1** the emotion felt when one's expectations are not met ⟨filled with *dismay* at not making the finals⟩ — see DISAPPOINTMENT 1
2 the state of being discouraged ⟨In my *dismay* I failed to realize that there would be other chances.⟩ — see DISCOURAGEMENT
dismay *vb* **1** to lessen the courage or confidence of ⟨The imposing climb up the mountain did not *dismay* them.⟩ — see DISCOURAGE 1
2 to trouble the mind of; to make uneasy ⟨parents who became increasingly *dismayed* by their son's frequent ear infections⟩ — see DISTURB 1
dismember *vb* **1** to cause to separate into pieces usually suddenly or forcibly ⟨quickly *dismembered* the old toolshed and hauled it off to the dump⟩ — see BREAK 1
2 to take apart ⟨*dismembered* the stage settings after the last performance⟩ — see DISASSEMBLE 1
dismiss *vb* **1** to let go from office, service, or employment ⟨Several employees were recently *dismissed*.⟩
synonyms bounce, can, cashier, discharge, fire, muster out, release, remove, retire, sack, terminate, turn off
related words downsize, excess, furlough, lay off, trim; boot (out), chuck (out), drum (out), throw out, unseat; separate
phrases send packing, show the door (one)
near antonyms keep; reemploy, rehire; contract, subcontract; recruit
antonyms employ, engage, hire, retain, take on
2 to drive or force out ⟨The sick boy's nurse *dismissed* the visitors so he could get some rest.⟩ — see EJECT 1
3 to express scornfully one's low opinion of ⟨Critics *dismissed* his music as mere noise.⟩ — see DECRY 1

dismissal *n* the termination of the employment of an employee or a work force often temporarily ⟨numerous *dismissals* from the company during the economic slump⟩ — see LAYOFF
disobedience *n* refusal to obey ⟨They gave up on training the dog to fetch because of his constant *disobedience*.⟩
synonyms contrariness, defiance, frowardness, insubordination, intractability, rebellion, rebelliousness, recalcitrance, refractoriness, unruliness, waywardness, willfulness
related words civil disobedience, noncooperation; discourteousness, disrespect, impertinence, impoliteness, impudence, inconsiderateness, inconsideration, insolence, rudeness, ungraciousness; doggedness, hardheadedness, mulishness, obduracy, obstinacy, peevishness, pertinaciousness, pertinacity, perversity, self-will, stubbornness, tenaciousness, tenacity; knavery, mischievousness, naughtiness
near antonyms amenability, amiability; submissiveness, subservience, subserviency; trainability; deference, docility, dutifulness
antonyms compliance, obedience, submission, subordinateness, subordination, tractability, tractableness
disobedient *adj* given to resisting authority or another's control ⟨The *disobedient* child refused to take a nap.⟩
synonyms balky, contrary, defiant, froward, insubordinate, intractable, obstreperous, rebel, rebellious, recalcitrant, refractory, restive, ungovernable, unruly, untoward, wayward, willful (*or* wilful)
related words noncooperative, uncooperative; insurgent, mutinous; adamant, adamantine, dogged, hardheaded, headstrong, immovable, implacable, inflexible, mulish, obdurate, obstinate, opinionated, peevish, pertinacious, pigheaded, rigid, self-willed, stubborn, unbending, uncompromising, unrelenting, unyielding; fractious, restive, uncontrollable, unmanageable, wild; perverse, resistant, wrongheaded; bad, disorderly, errant, misbehaving, mischievous, naughty; undisciplined; discourteous, disrespectful, ill-bred, ill-mannered, ill-natured, impertinent, impolite, impudent, inconsiderate, insolent, ornery, rude, uncivil, uncouth, ungracious, unmannerly
near antonyms acquiescent, agreeable, amiable, cooperative, deferential, obliging; yielding; behaved, disciplined, well-bred; courteous, polite, respectful; kowtowing, obsequious, subservient; decorous, mannerly, orderly, proper; controllable, governable, manageable, trainable
antonyms amenable, compliant, conformable, docile, obedient, ruly, submissive, tractable
disobey *vb* to go against the commands, prohibitions, or rules of ⟨students who *disobey* their teachers and use cell phones in class⟩ ⟨drivers who consistently *disobey* traffic laws⟩
synonyms defy, mock, rebel (against)
related words disoblige; mutiny (against), revolt (against); disregard, ignore, overlook, overpass, pass over, tune out; brush off, dismiss, flout, pooh-pooh (*also* pooh), reject, scoff (at), scorn, shrug off, wink (at); breach, break, infringe, transgress, violate; buck, combat, contest, dispute, fight, oppose, resist, withstand
near antonyms capitulate (to), concede (to), defer (to), serve, stoop (to), submit (to), surrender (to), yield (to); cooperate (with); keep, observe; accede (to), acquiesce (to), agree (to), assent (to), oblige; attend, hear, heed, listen (to), mark, note, notice, regard, watch
antonyms comply (with), conform (to), follow, mind, obey
disoblige *vb* to cause discomfort to or trouble for ⟨Kay didn't want to *disoblige* her relatives by spending the night at their place.⟩ — see INCONVENIENCE

disobliging *adj* causing difficulty, discomfort, or annoyance ⟨a friend with the *disobliging* habit of never having the cash to pay his fair share of the restaurant check⟩ — see INCONVENIENT 1

disorder *n* **1** a state in which everything is out of order ⟨the general *disorder* of the room after the guests left the party⟩ — see CHAOS

2 an abnormal state that disrupts a plant's or animal's normal bodily functioning ⟨afflicted all her life with a nervous *disorder*⟩ — see DISEASE

disorder *vb* to undo the proper order or arrangement of ⟨Be careful not to *disorder* the carefully arranged contents of the dresser.⟩

synonyms confuse, derange, disarrange, disarray, discompose, dishevel, disjoint, dislocate, disorganize, disrupt, disturb, hash, jumble, mess (up), mix (up), muddle, muss, rumple, scramble, shuffle, tousle, tumble, upset

related words embroil, entangle, snarl, tangle; agitate, perturb, stir (up), unsettle; clutter

near antonyms align (*also* aline), line, line up, queue; classify, codify, methodize, systematize, systemize; adjust, fix; make up; unscramble

antonyms arrange, array, dispose, draw up, marshal (*also* marshall), order, organize, range, regulate, straighten (up), tidy

disordered *adj* lacking in order, neatness, and often cleanliness ⟨The doctor's *disordered* clothing was obviously thrown on in a hurry.⟩ — see MESSY

disorderly *adj* **1** not restrained by or under the control of legal authority ⟨*Disorderly* mobs roamed the streets after the fall of the city.⟩ — see LAWLESS 1

2 lacking in order, neatness, and often cleanliness ⟨*disorderly* piles of clothes on various tables about the room⟩ — see MESSY

disorganization *n* a state in which everything is out of order ⟨All of her notes were in a state of *disorganization*.⟩ — see CHAOS

disorganize *vb* to undo the proper order or arrangement of ⟨those unexpected problems that can *disorganize* an entire plan⟩ — see DISORDER

disorient *vb* to throw into a state of mental uncertainty ⟨hikers *disoriented* by the sudden change in direction⟩ — see CONFUSE 1

disown *vb* **1** to declare not to be true ⟨He steadfastly *disowned* that he was guilty.⟩ — see DENY 1

2 to refuse to acknowledge as one's own or as one's responsibility ⟨Her parents threatened to *disown* her if she didn't go back to school.⟩ — see DISCLAIM 1

disparage *vb* to express scornfully one's low opinion of ⟨Voters don't like ads in which the candidates *disparage* each other.⟩ — see DECRY 1

disparagement *n* the act of making a person or a thing seem little or unimportant ⟨*disparagement* of his car as a clunker⟩ — see DEPRECIATION

disparaging *adj* intended to make a person or thing seem of little importance or value ⟨We heard no *disparaging* comments about the musical performers.⟩ — see DEROGATORY

disparate *adj* being not of the same kind ⟨She was interested in such *disparate* subjects as chemistry and anthropology.⟩ — see DIFFERENT 1

disparateness *n* the quality or state of being different ⟨The *disparateness* of their notions of an ideal vacation may indicate that they would not make compatible traveling companions.⟩ — see DIFFERENCE 1

disparity *n* the quality or state of being different ⟨an enormous *disparity* in the lives of the rich and the poor⟩ — see DIFFERENCE 1

dispassionate *adj* marked by justice, honesty, and freedom from bias ⟨*Dispassionate* refereeing is all that we ask.⟩ — see FAIR 2

dispatch *n* **1** a message on paper from one person or group to another ⟨a soldier sending daily *dispatches* to friends and family back home⟩ — see ¹LETTER

2 a piece of conveyed information ⟨The general sent a *dispatch* to headquarters.⟩ — see COMMUNICATION 1

dispatch *vb* **1** to cause to go or be taken from one place to another ⟨*dispatched* a messenger with urgent news⟩ — see SEND

2 to deprive of life ⟨The exterminator *dispatched* the termites with professional efficiency.⟩ — see KILL 1

3 to put to death deliberately ⟨was forced to *dispatch* the injured animal⟩ — see MURDER 1

4 to achieve a victory over ⟨They *dispatched* the other team without breaking a sweat.⟩ — see BEAT 2

dispel *vb* to cause (members of a group) to move widely apart ⟨The sudden downpour *dispelled* the throng of street revelers.⟩ — see SCATTER 1

dispensable *adj* not needed by the circumstances or to accomplish an end ⟨a new invention that renders the old methods *dispensable*⟩ — see UNNECESSARY

dispensation *n* the act or process of giving out something to each member of a group ⟨the emergency *dispensation* of medicine to the sick⟩ — see DISTRIBUTION 1

dispense *vb* to give out (something) to appropriate individuals ⟨A conscientious pharmacist never *dispenses* pills to people without assurances that they understand the instructions.⟩ — see ADMINISTER 1

dispersal *n* an act or process in which something scatters or is scattered ⟨the *dispersal* of plant seeds in the forests through natural means⟩ — see SCATTERING 1

disperse *vb* **1** to go off in different directions and cease to exist as a body or unified whole ⟨The crowd *dispersed* once the show ended.⟩

synonyms disassemble, dissipate, dissolve, scatter

related words branch (out), break up, disband, diverge, divide, fork, separate, spill; clear, disappear, evanesce, evaporate, fade, flee, go (away), melt

near antonyms congregate, gather, meet

2 to cause (members of a group) to move widely apart ⟨The family of the lost kitty *dispersed* searchers to all corners of the neighborhood.⟩ — see SCATTER 1

3 to cease to exist or cause to cease to exist as a group or organization ⟨The campaign staff *dispersed* almost immediately after the election.⟩ — see DISBAND 1

dispersion *n* an act or process in which something scatters or is scattered ⟨the *dispersion* of energy from a source⟩ — see SCATTERING 1

dispirit *vb* to lessen the courage or confidence of ⟨*dispirited* by the overwhelming amount of information needed to write the report⟩ — see DISCOURAGE 1

dispiritedness *n* **1** a state or spell of low spirits ⟨experienced a period of general *dispiritedness* after moving away from her childhood home⟩ — see SADNESS

2 the state of being discouraged ⟨the *dispiritedness* experienced by the losing team in the Super Bowl⟩ — see DISCOURAGEMENT

displace *vb* **1** to change the place or position of ⟨The slight tremor *displaced* the dishes on the shelves, but didn't do any real damage.⟩ — see MOVE 1

2 to force to leave a country ⟨World War II *displaced* people all over Europe.⟩ — see BANISH 1

3 to take the place of ⟨inefficient methods *displaced* by newer ones⟩ — see REPLACE 1

4 to remove from a position of prominence or power (as a throne) ⟨The CEO was summarily *displaced* after the hostile takeover.⟩ — see DEPOSE 1

displacement *n* the forced removal from a homeland ⟨the *displacement* of Jews from the land of their ancestors⟩ — see EXILE 1

display *n* 1 a public showing of objects of interest ⟨a *display* of paintings by masters of French Impressionism⟩ — see EXHIBITION 1

2 an outward and often exaggerated indication of something abstract (as a feeling) for effect ⟨a *display* of heartfelt sympathy⟩ — see SHOW 1

display *vb* 1 to present so as to invite notice or attention ⟨*Display* the best items at the front of the showcase.⟩ — see SHOW 1

2 to make known (something abstract) through outward signs ⟨an actress who can *display* a great range of emotion⟩ — see SHOW 2

displease *vb* to make discontented ⟨Her coworkers' tendency to pry *displeased* her.⟩ — see DISCONTENT

displeased *adj* having a feeling that one has been wronged or thwarted in one's ambitions ⟨feeling vaguely *displeased* by the way his internship was going⟩ — see DISCONTENTED

displeasing *adj* not giving pleasure to the mind or senses ⟨The new hotel is a *displeasing* mix of architectural styles.⟩ — see UNPLEASANT

displeasure *n* 1 refusal to accept as right or desirable ⟨Fans showed their *displeasure* by loudly booing the umpire.⟩ — see DISAPPROVAL

2 the condition of being dissatisfied with one's life or situation ⟨His *displeasure* with his job intensified as the years wore on.⟩ — see DISCONTENT

disport *vb* 1 to cause (someone) to pass the time agreeably occupied ⟨*disported* themselves with silly games while they waited in the airport⟩ — see AMUSE

2 to engage in activity for amusement ⟨a full-service resort where vacationers may *disport* at a variety of indoor and outdoor activities⟩ — see PLAY 1

3 to play and run about happily ⟨The puppies *disported* in the backyard while we ate on the patio.⟩ — see FROLIC 1

4 to present so as to invite notice or attention ⟨Football fans triumphantly *disported* the sports memorabilia they had just won.⟩ — see SHOW 1

disposal *n* 1 the getting rid of whatever is unwanted or useless ⟨Trash *disposal* is on Wednesday in our neighborhood.⟩

synonyms discarding, disposition, dumping, jettison, junking, removal, riddance, scrapping, throwing away

related words clearance, clearing; decimation, demolishment, demolition, destruction

near antonyms accumulation, acquirement, collection, deposit, gathering

2 the way objects in space or events in time are arranged or follow one another ⟨the *disposal* of troops along the ridge⟩ — see ORDER 1

dispose *vb* 1 to arrange something in a certain spot or position ⟨looking for the perfect spot to *dispose* the new knickknack⟩ — see PLACE 1

2 to put into a particular arrangement ⟨The nurse *disposed* the surgical instruments in the exact order in which they would be needed.⟩ — see ORDER 1

disposed *adj* having a desire or inclination (as for a specified course of action) ⟨a dog that is *disposed* to bite⟩ — see WILLING 1

disposition *n* 1 one's characteristic attitude or mood ⟨He has a cheerful *disposition* and is very rarely depressed.⟩

synonyms grain, nature, temper, temperament

related words cheer, frame, habit, humor, inclination, mode, spirit; angle, mind-set, outlook, perspective, slant, standpoint, viewpoint; emotion, feeling, heart, passion, sentiment, spirit; strain; belief, conviction, judgment (or judgement), mind, notion, opinion, persuasion, view; expression, tone, vein; character, identity, individuality, makeup, mettle, personality, selfhood, self-identity, setup

2 a habitual attraction to some activity or thing ⟨a woman with a *disposition* to help others⟩ — see INCLINATION 1

3 the getting rid of whatever is unwanted or useless ⟨We'll have to find some means for the *disposition* of all of this junk.⟩ — see DISPOSAL 1

4 the way objects in space or events in time are arranged or follow one another ⟨planned the *disposition* of events at her wedding with a precision that military commanders would envy⟩ — see ORDER 1

5 an arrangement about action to be taken ⟨All that remains is a *disposition* regarding the ownership of the house⟩ — see AGREEMENT 2

disproof *n* something (as an argument) that serves to disprove ⟨The DNA evidence was all the *disproof* needed to overturn the wrongful conviction.⟩ — see CONFUTATION

disprove *vb* to prove to be false ⟨Magellan's circumnavigation of the globe *disproved* any lingering notions that the earth is flat.⟩

synonyms belie, confound, confute, debunk, discredit, falsify, rebut, refute

related words overthrow, overturn; challenge, contest, query, question; doubt, mistrust; debate, discuss, hash (over), moot, talk over

phrases give the lie to

near antonyms document, evidence, evince, record, show, support, witness; back (up), buttress, corroborate, substantiate; adduce, attest, authenticate, certify, identify; demonstrate, display, illustrate, manifest

antonyms confirm, establish, prove, validate, verify

disputable *adj* 1 giving good reason for being doubted, questioned, or challenged ⟨a speech full of *disputable* generalizations⟩ — see DOUBTFUL 2

2 open to question or dispute ⟨All *disputable* claims must be referred to the committee.⟩ — see DEBATABLE 1

disputant *n* a person who takes part in a dispute ⟨There were only three *disputants* in the argument, but they made enough noise for a dozen.⟩

synonyms arguer, bickerer, debater, disputer, fighter, quarreler (*or* quarreller), squabbler, wrangler

related words advocate, codefendant, defendant, plaintiff, pleader; challenger, contender, contestant, skirmisher; fusser, nitpicker, pettifogger, quibbler

disputation *n* variance of opinion on a matter ⟨a heated *disputation* over the true authorship of the poem popularly known as "The Night Before Christmas"⟩ — see DISAGREEMENT 1

disputatious *adj* 1 feeling or displaying eagerness to fight ⟨The refs enforced a new rule designed to constrain *disputatious* players.⟩ — see BELLIGERENT

2 given to arguing ⟨a *disputatious* professor who could give you an argument on just about anything⟩ — see ARGUMENTATIVE 1

disputatiousness *n* an inclination to fight or quarrel ⟨The stubborn *disputatiousness* of the committee members kept them from getting much accomplished.⟩ — see BELLIGERENCE

dispute *n* 1 variance of opinion on a matter ⟨a *dispute* over the proper pronunciation of "nuclear"⟩ — see DISAGREEMENT 1

2 an often noisy or angry expression of differing opinions ⟨After much *dispute*, the school committee decided that all backpacks would have to be stored in lockers during class hours.⟩ — see ARGUMENT 1

dispute *vb* 1 to demand proof of the truth or rightness of

⟨a whole slew of relatives eager to *dispute* his claim to being the sole heir⟩ — see CHALLENGE 1

2 to express different opinions about something often angrily ⟨hometown fans *disputing* with visiting fans over which had the better team⟩ — see ARGUE 2

3 to talk about (an issue) usually from various points of view and for the purpose of arriving at a decision or opinion ⟨In an extended session the city council *disputed* the need for a new high school.⟩ — see DISCUSS

disputer *n* a person who takes part in a dispute ⟨In debate she's a dogged *disputer* who never gives an inch.⟩ — see DISPUTANT

disquiet *n* **1** a disturbed or uneasy state ⟨a period of *disquiet* before the results of the close election were confirmed⟩ — see UNREST

2 an uneasy state of mind usually over the possibility of an anticipated misfortune or trouble ⟨I was filled with *disquiet* by the news.⟩ — see ANXIETY 1

disquiet *vb* to trouble the mind of; to make uneasy ⟨We were *disquieted* by the strange noises we heard outside our tent at night.⟩ — see DISTURB 1

disquieting *adj* **1** causing worry or anxiety ⟨*disquieting* news of troubles in town⟩ — see TROUBLESOME

2 marked by or causing agitation or uncomfortable feelings ⟨With a *disquieting* voice she asked me to investigate the strange noise coming from the basement.⟩ — see NERVOUS 2

disregard *n* lack of interest or concern ⟨The judge found that the statements were made in reckless *disregard* of the truth.⟩ — see INDIFFERENCE

disregard *vb* **1** to ignore in a disrespectful manner ⟨He *disregarded* the advice of his family and quit school.⟩ — see SCORN 2

2 to fail to give proper attention to ⟨*disregarded* the posted warnings of avalanche danger and went skiing anyway⟩ — see NEGLECT 1

3 to dismiss as of little importance ⟨This essay is so good that I can safely *disregard* a couple of spelling errors.⟩ — see EXCUSE 1

disrepair *n* the state of being unattended to or not cared for ⟨The old house was in such *disrepair* that the roof had caved in.⟩ — see NEGLECT 1

disreputable *adj* not respectable ⟨a *disreputable* Internet retailer that had a record of hundreds of complaints for shoddy merchandise and slow refunds⟩

synonyms discreditable, disgraceful, dishonorable, ignominious, infamous, notorious, shady, shameful, shoddy, shy

related words bad, criminal, immoral, seamy, sordid, unethical, unsavory, wicked; base, contemptible, despicable, detestable, dirty, low, mean, miserable, vile, wretched; evil, iniquitous, nefarious, rotten, sinful, unrighteous, vicious, villainous, wrong; corrupt, debased, debauched, degenerate, depraved, dissolute, gamy (*or* gamey), libertine, loose, perverted, reprobate

near antonyms decent, ethical, good, honest, just, moral, noble, principled, righteous, upright, upstanding; esteemed, prestigious, reputed, respected; authorized, legal, licensed, permissible, permitted; approved, endorsed (*also* indorsed), sanctioned; clean, correct, decorous, exemplary, proper, seemly

antonyms honorable, reputable, respectable

disrepute *n* the state of having lost the esteem of others ⟨a once proud name fallen into *disrepute*⟩ — see DISGRACE 1

disrespect *n* rude behavior ⟨treated the resort's service workers with haughty *disrespect*⟩ — see DISCOURTESY

disrespect *vb* **1** to cause hurt feelings or deep resentment in ⟨I didn't mean to *disrespect* the other players when I said she was the star of the team.⟩ — see INSULT

2 to show contempt for ⟨The player once again *disrespected* fans by refusing to sign autographs.⟩ — see SCORN 1

disrespectful *adj* showing a lack of manners or consideration for others ⟨Being four hours late is *disrespectful* of the people you promised to meet.⟩ — see IMPOLITE

disrobe *vb* to remove clothing from ⟨The doctor instructed the patient to *disrobe* himself before the examination.⟩ — see UNDRESS 1

disrobed *adj* lacking or shed of clothing ⟨a statue of a partially *disrobed* warrior⟩ — see NAKED 1

disrupt *vb* **1** to cause to separate into pieces usually suddenly or forcibly ⟨Frost heaves *disrupted* the pavement on the road.⟩ — see BREAK 1

2 to undo the proper order or arrangement of ⟨The arrival of a baby in the household would totally *disrupt* their established routine.⟩ — see DISORDER

disruption *n* an act or instance of the order of things being disturbed ⟨The flat tire resulted in an unfortunate *disruption* of the schedule for our road trip.⟩ — see UPSET

dissatisfaction *n* **1** the condition of being dissatisfied with one's life or situation ⟨We're aware of a growing *dissatisfaction* among group members.⟩ — see DISCONTENT

2 the emotion felt when one's expectations are not met ⟨She felt keen *dissatisfaction* at the hurried job the house painters had done.⟩ — see DISAPPOINTMENT 1

dissatisfactory *adj* falling short of a standard ⟨This report is completely *dissatisfactory* on several counts.⟩ — see BAD 1

dissatisfied *adj* having a feeling that one has been wronged or thwarted in one's ambitions ⟨The store prides itself on never allowing a customer to walk away *dissatisfied*.⟩ — see DISCONTENTED

dissatisfy *vb* **1** to fall short in satisfying the expectation or hope of ⟨a restaurant serving portions that will not *dissatisfy* even the heartiest eater⟩ — see DISAPPOINT

2 to make discontented ⟨He was *dissatisfied* with his job.⟩ — see DISCONTENT

dissect *vb* to identify and examine the basic elements or parts of (something) especially for discovering interrelationships ⟨Let's *dissect* the plot of this thriller to see what makes it thrilling.⟩ — see ANALYZE

dissection *n* the separation and identification of the parts of a whole ⟨the book's *dissection* of the causes of the Great Depression⟩ — see ANALYSIS 1

dissemble *vb* **1** to present a false appearance of ⟨He *dissembled* happiness at the news that his old girlfriend was getting married—to someone else.⟩ — see FEIGN

2 to take on a false or deceptive appearance ⟨Children learn to *dissemble* at a surprisingly early age.⟩ — see PRETEND 1

dissembling *n* **1** the inclination or practice of misleading others through lies or trickery ⟨a crafty child given to frequent *dissembling* to get what she wants⟩ — see DECEIT 1

2 the pretending of having virtues, principles, or beliefs that one in fact does not have ⟨In the end the preacher's smarmy *dissembling* is discovered, and he is exposed as a fraud.⟩ — see HYPOCRISY

disseminate *vb* to cause to be known over a considerable area or by many people ⟨The Internet enables us to *disseminate* information more quickly than in the past.⟩ — see SPREAD 1

dissension *also* **dissention** *n* **1** a lack of agreement or harmony ⟨Religious *dissension* threatened to split the colony.⟩ — see DISCORD

2 variance of opinion on a matter ⟨continued *dissension* among historians on the exact spot of Columbus's first landing⟩ — see DISAGREEMENT 1

dissent *n* **1** a lack of agreement or harmony ⟨considerable *dissent* within the party's rank and file⟩ — see DISCORD
2 departure from a generally accepted theory, opinion, or practice ⟨The chief justice joined in the *dissent* from the majority opinion.⟩ — see HERESY
dissent *vb* to have a different opinion ⟨Anyone who *dissented* was encouraged to speak out while they had the chance.⟩ — see DISAGREE
dissenter *n* a person who believes, teaches, or advocates something opposed to accepted beliefs ⟨a society that prized conformity very highly and treated *dissenters* of any kind very harshly⟩ — see HERETIC 1
dissenting *adj* deviating from commonly accepted beliefs or practices ⟨There were a few *dissenting* voices in the group.⟩ — see HERETICAL
disservice *n* unfair or inadequate treatment of someone or something or an instance of this ⟨You do a great *disservice* to the professionals at the day-care center when you refer to them as "babysitters."⟩
synonyms inequity, injury, injustice, raw deal, shaft, unfairness, unjustness, wrong
related words affront, indignity, insult, offense (*or* offence), outrage, put-down, slight, slur; beef, complaint, grievance
near antonyms cricket
antonyms equitableness, equity, fairness, justice
dissever *vb* to set or force apart ⟨placed the *dissevered* pieces of chicken in the roasting pan⟩ — see SEPARATE 1
dissidence *n* **1** a lack of agreement or harmony ⟨Political *dissidence* had plagued the country for years.⟩ — see DISCORD
2 departure from a generally accepted theory, opinion, or practice ⟨After abstract art became established, its proponents became just as intolerant of *dissidence* as earlier schools of art had been.⟩ — see HERESY
dissident *adj* deviating from commonly accepted beliefs or practices ⟨*dissident* elements within the organization⟩ — see HERETICAL
dissident *n* a person who believes, teaches, or advocates something opposed to accepted beliefs ⟨The conference drew political *dissidents* of every ilk.⟩ — see HERETIC 1
dissimilar *adj* being not of the same kind ⟨a place where people with *dissimilar* backgrounds can interact⟩ — see DIFFERENT 1
dissimilarity *n* the quality or state of being different ⟨The effectiveness of a metaphor largely depends upon the superficial *dissimilarity* of the two things being compared.⟩ — see DIFFERENCE 1
dissimulate *vb* to take on a false or deceptive appearance ⟨As an actress she had been trained to *dissimulate*, so she had no trouble hiding her true feelings offstage as well.⟩ — see PRETEND 1
dissimulation *n* **1** the inclination or practice of misleading others through lies or trickery ⟨We were sure his promises were sincere and not just *dissimulation*.⟩ — see DECEIT 1
2 the pretending of having virtues, principles, or beliefs that one in fact does not have ⟨She refused to indulge in *dissimulation* simply to be popular.⟩ — see HYPOCRISY
dissipate *vb* **1** to cause (members of a group) to move widely apart ⟨*dissipated* the enemy forces with unremitting artillery fire⟩ — see SCATTER 1
2 to use up carelessly ⟨*dissipated* the family fortune in reckless business ventures⟩ — see WASTE 1
3 to go off in different directions and cease to exist as a body or unified whole ⟨The fog should *dissipate* once the sun comes out in full force.⟩ — see DISPERSE 1
dissipated *adj* having or showing lowered moral character or standards ⟨a brilliant but *dissipated* writer⟩ — see CORRUPT

dissipatedness *n* a sinking to a state of low moral standards and behavior ⟨a novel chronicling the *dissipatedness* of a generation born to great wealth⟩ — see CORRUPTION 2
dissipation *n* **1** a sinking to a state of low moral standards and behavior ⟨the wasting of a once promising life in *dissipation*⟩ — see CORRUPTION 2
2 an act or process in which something scatters or is scattered ⟨the *dissipation* of the clouds by the early morning winds⟩ — see SCATTERING 1
dissociate *vb* to set or force apart ⟨attempts to *dissociate* herself from her troubled past⟩ — see SEPARATE 1
dissolute *adj* having or showing lowered moral character or standards ⟨literature dealing with the *dissolute* and degrading aspects of human experience⟩ — see CORRUPT
dissoluteness *n* a sinking to a state of low moral standards and behavior ⟨the growing *dissoluteness* of the Roman nobles as the empire declined⟩ — see CORRUPTION 2
dissolution *n* **1** the act or process of a whole separating into two or more parts or pieces ⟨the *dissolution* of the empire into a patchwork of petty kingdoms⟩ — see SEPARATION 1
2 the permanent stopping of all the vital bodily activities ⟨a disease that brought about his *dissolution*⟩ — see DEATH 1
dissolve *vb* **1** to cease to be visible ⟨as the mist *dissolved* in the morning sun⟩ — see DISAPPEAR
2 to cease to exist or cause to cease to exist as a group or organization ⟨The company formally *dissolved* three months after declaring bankruptcy.⟩ — see DISBAND 1
3 to put an end to by formal action ⟨The king simply *dissolved* parliament.⟩ — see ABOLISH 1
4 to go off in different directions and cease to exist as a body or unified whole ⟨The clouds gradually *dissolved*, and the sun came out.⟩ — see DISPERSE 1
dissonant *adj* marked by or producing a harsh combination of sounds ⟨A *dissonant* chorus of noises arose from the busy construction site.⟩
synonyms cacophonous, discordant, inharmonious, unmelodious, unmusical
related words blaring, clanging, clangorous, clashing, clattering, dinning, grating, harsh, jangling, jangly, jarring, metallic, noisy, raspy, raucous, scratching, screeching, shrill, squeaky, strident; disagreeable, unpleasant, unpleasing; atonal, off-key, tuneless; resounding, sonorous; clamorous, uproarious
near antonyms euphonious, mellifluent, mellifluous, mellow, melodic, sweet, tuneful; resonant, sonorous; quavering, trilling, warbling; agreeable, appealing, pleasant; cadenced, lilting, lyric, lyrical, rhythmic (*or* rhythmical)
antonyms harmonious, harmonizing, melodious, musical
dissuade *vb* to steer (a person) from an activity or course of action ⟨tried to *dissuade* her from going⟩ — see DISCOURAGE 2
distance *n* **1** the space or amount of space between two points, lines, surfaces, or objects ⟨The *distance* between the earth and the sun is about 93 million miles.⟩
synonyms lead, length, remove, spacing, spread, stretch, way
related words altitude, area, breadth, depth, height, rise, space, volume, width; extension, extent; cast, range, reach, scope, shot, sweep, throw; drop, fall, flight, haul; berth, clearance
2 a wide space or area ⟨a region marked by great, featureless *distances*⟩ — see EXPANSE

3 the quality or state of being different ⟨The brothers' personalities are like the *distance* between night and day.⟩ — see DIFFERENCE 1

distant *adj* **1** not close in time or space ⟨The *distant* towers were barely visible in the fog.⟩
synonyms away, deep, far, faraway, far-flung, far-off, remote, removed
related words apart, devious, isolated, lonesome, obscure, odd, outlying, out-of-the-way, retired, secluded, secret, sequestered
near antonyms adjacent, adjoining, contiguous
antonyms close, near, nearby, nigh
2 having or showing a lack of friendliness or interest in others ⟨was *distant* and distracted all throughout the interview⟩ — see COOL 1
3 being not of the same kind ⟨a marriage between two people from very *distant* cultures⟩ — see DIFFERENT 1

distaste *n* a dislike so strong as to cause stomach upset or queasiness ⟨usually views abstract paintings with *distaste*⟩ — see DISGUST

distasteful *adj* **1** disagreeable or disgusting to the sense of taste ⟨Cod-liver oil is so *distasteful* that it's worse than anything it cures.⟩
synonyms brackish, unappetizing, unpalatable, unsavory, yucky (*also* yukky)
related words abominable, awful, bad, filthy, foul, horrible, loathsome, nasty, nauseating, noisome, obnoxious, offensive, repellent (*also* repellant), repugnant, repulsive, revolting, shocking, sickening; bland, flat, flavorless, insipid, savorless, tasteless
near antonyms appealing, attractive, flavorful, piquant, rich
antonyms appetizing, delectable, delicious, palatable, savory (*also* savoury), tasty, toothsome, yummy
2 not giving pleasure to the mind or senses ⟨Please don't ask me to discuss such a *distasteful* topic.⟩ — see UNPLEASANT
3 causing intense displeasure, disgust, or resentment ⟨the *distasteful* nature of his job as a bill collector⟩ — see OFFENSIVE 1

distill *also* **distil** *vb* **1** to fall or let fall in or as if in drops ⟨The basement walls *distill* water every time it rains heavily.⟩ — see DRIP
2 to remove usually visible impurities from ⟨*Distill* the water before pouring it in the steam iron.⟩ — see CLARIFY 1

distinct *adj* **1** being not of the same kind ⟨two *distinct* approaches to the same problem⟩ — see DIFFERENT 1
2 not subject to misinterpretation or more than one interpretation ⟨a person with a *distinct* Scottish accent⟩ — see CLEAR 2
3 of a particular or exact sort ⟨I left *distinct* instructions on how to work the washer.⟩ — see EXPRESS 1
4 serving to identify as belonging to an individual or group ⟨one of the *distinct* traits of a preliterate society⟩ — see CHARACTERISTIC 1

distinction *n* **1** exceptionally high quality ⟨a shop selling goods of *distinction*⟩ — see EXCELLENCE 1
2 a quality that gives something special worth ⟨It has the *distinction* of being the oldest house in the city.⟩ — see EXCELLENCE 2
3 public acknowledgment or admiration for an achievement ⟨I did all of the work, and the other guy got all the *distinction*.⟩ — see GLORY 1
4 the fact or state of being above others in rank or importance ⟨A number of physicians of national *distinction* serve on the staff of the teaching hospital.⟩ — see EMINENCE 1
5 something given in recognition of achievement ⟨Kate

won a number of *distinctions* in her long career as an actress.⟩ — see AWARD 1
6 the quality or state of being different ⟨The *distinction* between the two photographic prints escapes me.⟩ — see DIFFERENCE 1
7 the state of being kept distinct ⟨the *distinction* between liberty and license⟩ — see SEPARATION 2

distinctive *adj* **1** being not of the same kind ⟨She seems to alternate between two *distinctive* musical styles.⟩ — see DIFFERENT 1
2 serving to identify as belonging to an individual or group ⟨the *distinctive* odor of a barnyard⟩ — see CHARACTERISTIC 1

distinctiveness *n* the quality or state of being different ⟨the pronounced *distinctiveness* of his style of playing the violin⟩ — see DIFFERENCE 1

distinctness *n* the quality or state of being different ⟨The *distinctness* of Jane Austen's writing makes it easy to recognize on a test.⟩ — see DIFFERENCE 1

distinguish *vb* **1** to understand or point out the difference in ⟨Even at such a young age, he could *distinguish* the calls of various birds.⟩
synonyms difference, differentiate, discern, discriminate, separate
related words contradistinguish; comprehend, grasp, know, understand; divide, part, sever; demarcate, set off
near antonyms confound, lump (together), mingle
antonyms confuse, mistake, mix (up)
2 to be an important feature of ⟨muffin recipes *distinguished* by their ease and simplicity⟩ — see CHARACTERIZE 2
3 to find out or establish the identity of ⟨I learned at an early age to *distinguish* the sound of a piano in an orchestra.⟩ — see IDENTIFY 1
4 to make note of (something) through the use of one's eyes ⟨I could barely *distinguish* the garden gate through the mist.⟩ — see SEE 1
5 to arrange or assign according to type ⟨Please *distinguish* the specimens by acidity.⟩ — see CLASSIFY 1

distinguishable *adj* **1** able to be perceived by a sense or by the mind ⟨an evening star easily *distinguishable* by the naked eye⟩ — see PERCEPTIBLE
2 being not of the same kind ⟨Snowflakes are *distinguishable* from each other under a microscope.⟩ — see DIFFERENT 1

distinguished *adj* **1** having or showing a formal and serious or reserved manner ⟨Heads turned as the well-dressed, *distinguished* couple strode through the hotel lobby.⟩ — see DIGNIFIED
2 standing above others in rank, importance, or achievement ⟨a *distinguished* astronomer who is widely respected in the field⟩ — see EMINENT

distinguishing *adj* serving to identify as belonging to an individual or group ⟨a novice birder still learning the *distinguishing* features of various finches⟩ — see CHARACTERISTIC 1

distort *vb* **1** to change so much as to create a wrong impression or alter the meaning of ⟨The coach's message was so *distorted* after passing through so many people that it was unintelligible.⟩ — see GARBLE
2 to twist (something) out of a natural or normal shape or condition ⟨If you keep *distorting* your face like that, someday it's going to freeze in that position.⟩ — see CONTORT

distorted *adj* badly or imperfectly formed ⟨a *distorted* tree trunk⟩ — see MALFORMED

distortion *n* the twisting of something out of its natural or normal shape or condition ⟨a *distortion* of the car chassis resulting from collision⟩ — see CONTORTION

distract *vb* **1** to draw the attention or mind to something else ⟨We were *distracted* from our discussion by the noise outside.⟩
synonyms abstract, call off, divert
related words amuse, beguile, entertain; stray, wander
near antonyms concentrate, focus
2 to trouble the mind of; to make uneasy ⟨*distracted* by the looming tax deadline⟩ — see DISTURB 1

distracted *adj* **1** feeling overwhelming fear or worry ⟨She's been *distracted* about her son ever since he left on that polar expedition.⟩ — see FRANTIC 1
2 lost in thought and unaware of one's surroundings or actions ⟨The *distracted* driver rear-ended the pickup truck that had stopped for the red light.⟩ — see ABSENT-MINDED 1
3 suffering from mental confusion ⟨Even after two days, he was still *distracted* by the jet lag.⟩ — see DIZZY 2

distraction *n* **1** a state of mental uncertainty ⟨In my *distraction* I forgot where I was.⟩ — see CONFUSION 1
2 a state of wildly excited activity or emotion ⟨driven to *distraction* by the constant chatter⟩ — see FRENZY
3 the act or activity of providing pleasure or amusement especially for the public ⟨Sledding is a fun and inexpensive winter *distraction*.⟩ — see ENTERTAINMENT 1
4 someone or something that provides amusement or enjoyment ⟨a harmless *distraction* for children at the playground⟩ — see FUN 1

distraught *adj* feeling overwhelming fear or worry ⟨a child *distraught* by the loss of her teddy bear⟩ — see FRANTIC 1

distress *n* **1** a state of great suffering of body or mind ⟨The upcoming bar exam is causing us considerable *distress*.⟩ ⟨The survivors were in extreme *distress* after having been stranded on the island for a week.⟩
synonyms affliction, agony, anguish, hurt, misery, pain, rack, strait(s), torment, torture, travail, tribulation, woe
related words discomfort; cross, crucible, trial; heartache, heartbreak, joylessness, sadness, sorrow, unhappiness; emergency, pinch; asperity, difficulty, hardship, rigor; ache, pang, smarting, soreness, stitch, throe, twinge; danger, jeopardy, trouble
near antonyms comfort, consolation, solace; alleviation, assuagement, ease, relief; peace, security; well-being
2 the state of not being protected from injury, harm, or evil ⟨a ship in *distress*⟩ — see DANGER 1

distress *vb* to trouble the mind of; to make uneasy ⟨Don't let all the bad news *distress* you.⟩ — see DISTURB 1

distressful *adj* **1** marked by or causing agitation or uncomfortable feelings ⟨the *distressful* period during which we waited to learn who had made the cut⟩ — see NERVOUS 2
2 of a kind to cause great distress ⟨the *distressful* living conditions in the refugee camp⟩ — see REGRETTABLE

distressing *adj* **1** causing worry or anxiety ⟨I heard some *distressing* news.⟩ — see TROUBLESOME
2 of a kind to cause great distress ⟨the *distressing* death of our favorite actor⟩ — see REGRETTABLE
3 marked by or causing agitation or uncomfortable feelings ⟨the *distressing* habit of constantly fiddling with her hair⟩ — see NERVOUS 2

distribute *vb* **1** to arrange or assign according to type ⟨We'll *distribute* the assignments according to seniority.⟩ — see CLASSIFY 1
2 to give as a share or portion ⟨We're committed to *distributing* the school's limited scholarship money so that it benefits more students.⟩ — see ALLOT
3 to give out (something) to appropriate individuals ⟨I *distributed* pamphlets on recycling to everyone in the neighborhood.⟩ — see ADMINISTER 1

distribution *n* **1** the act or process of giving out something to each member of a group ⟨Aid workers oversaw the *distribution* of medicine.⟩
synonyms allocation, allotment, apportionment, disbursement, dispensation, division, issuance
related words reallocation, reapportionment, redistribution, redivision, repartition; division, partition, separation
2 the way objects in space or events in time are arranged or follow one another ⟨The *distribution* of those stars has long suggested the form of a dipper.⟩ — see ORDER 1

district *n* an area (as of a city) set apart for some purpose or having some special feature ⟨Independence Hall in Philadelphia's historic *district*⟩
synonyms neighborhood, quarter, section
related words belt, zone; department, division, part; ward; area, locality, place, region; barrio, enclave, ghetto, hood (*or* 'hood)

distrust *n* a feeling or attitude that one does not know the truth, truthfulness, or trustworthiness of someone or something ⟨The psychic's bold claims were greeted with *distrust*.⟩ — see DOUBT

distrust *vb* to have no trust or confidence in ⟨We instinctively *distrust* those phone calls that tell us we have won a free vacation or car.⟩
synonyms doubt, mistrust, question, suspect
related words disbelieve, discount, discredit, negate
near antonyms bank (on *or* upon), count (on *or* upon), depend (on *or* upon), rely (on *or* upon)
antonyms trust

distrustful *adj* **1** inclined to doubt or question claims ⟨She was *distrustful* of the caller's claim that she'd won a free vacation.⟩ — see SKEPTICAL 1
2 not feeling sure about the truth, wisdom, or trustworthiness of someone or something ⟨naturally *distrustful* of politicians who claim to have all the answers⟩ — see DOUBTFUL 1

distrustfully *adv* with distrust ⟨I read the stories in the tabloids *distrustfully*.⟩ — see ASKANCE

distrustfulness *n* a feeling or attitude that one does not know the truth, truthfulness, or trustworthiness of someone or something ⟨one voter who usually listens to campaign promises with an air of *distrustfulness*⟩ — see DOUBT

disturb *vb* **1** to trouble the mind of; to make uneasy ⟨The news *disturbed* us.⟩
synonyms agitate, ail, alarm (*also* alarum), bother, concern, discomfort, discompose, dismay, disquiet, distract, distress, exercise, flurry, frazzle, freak (out), fuss, perturb, undo, unhinge, unsettle, upset, worry
related words aggravate, anger, bug, chafe, chivy (*or* chivvy), exasperate, fret, gall, get, grate, harry, irk, irritate, nettle, peeve, pester, pique, put off, put out, rile, vex; bedevil, haunt, plague; abash, confound, confuse, discomfit, disconcert, discountenance, embarrass, faze, fluster, jar, mortify, nonplus, rattle, shake up; daunt, demoralize, discourage, dishearten, dispirit, unnerve
near antonyms allay, alleviate, assuage; appease, conciliate, mollify, pacify, placate, propitiate
antonyms calm, compose, quiet, settle, soothe, tranquilize (*also* tranquillize)
2 to change the place or position of ⟨The items on her desk had been *disturbed* by someone.⟩ — see MOVE 1
3 to undo the proper order or arrangement of ⟨Her careful filing system is sure to be *disturbed* during the move.⟩ — see DISORDER
4 to thrust oneself upon (another) without invitation ⟨I'm sorry to *disturb* you while you're working.⟩ — see BOTHER 1

5 to cause discomfort to or trouble for ⟨Please do not *disturb* yourself—I'll get my own drink.⟩ — see INCONVENIENCE

disturbance *n* **1** a state of noisy, confused activity ⟨I went to investigate the *disturbance* outside.⟩ — see COMMOTION
2 an act or instance of the order of things being disturbed ⟨caused a *disturbance* in the carefully ordered proceedings⟩ — see UPSET
3 the act of making unwelcome intrusions upon another ⟨The assistant apologized for the *disturbance* and got straight to the point.⟩ — see ANNOYANCE 1

disturbing *adj* **1** causing annoyance ⟨a *disturbing* visit by the next-door neighbor while I was trying to study⟩ — see ANNOYING
2 causing embarrassment ⟨There was a *disturbing* silence as I struggled to remember her name.⟩ — see AWKWARD 3
3 causing worry or anxiety ⟨a *disturbing* trend in the nation's energy consumption⟩ — see TROUBLESOME
4 marked by or causing agitation or uncomfortable feelings ⟨The car made a *disturbing* noise.⟩ — see NERVOUS 2

disunion *n* **1** a lack of agreement or harmony ⟨a country troubled by political *disunion*⟩ — see DISCORD
2 the act or process of a whole separating into two or more parts or pieces ⟨an organization headed toward *disunion*⟩ — see SEPARATION 1

disunite *vb* to set or force apart ⟨She attempted to *disunite* the members of the group by vicious gossip.⟩ — see SEPARATE 1

disunited *adj* disagreeing with each other ⟨The *disunited* members of the committee couldn't accomplish anything.⟩ — see DIVIDED

disunity *n* a lack of agreement or harmony ⟨troubling signs of *disunity* within the normally peaceful organization⟩ — see DISCORD

disuse *n* lack of use ⟨Since the car has experienced years of *disuse*, starting it up won't be easy.⟩
synonyms idleness, inactivity
related words abandonment, desertion, neglect; abeyance, dormancy, latency, quiescence
antonyms use

disused *adj* left unoccupied or unused ⟨a *disused* warehouse that had been refurbished into apartments⟩ — see ABANDONED 1

ditch *n* a long narrow channel dug in the earth ⟨After skidding on the ice, our car went right into the *ditch*.⟩
synonyms dike, gutter, trench, trough
related words culvert, drain, draw, gully (*also* gulley), ravine; drill, furrow

ditch *vb* **1** to end a usually intimate relationship with ⟨He *ditched* the band to start up a new one.⟩
synonyms dump, leave
related words brush (aside *or* off), cold-shoulder, cut, high-hat, slight, snub; abandon, desert, forsake, maroon, quit
phrases kiss good-bye
near antonyms hook up (with), take; befriend, latch (on *or* onto)
2 to get rid of as useless or unwanted ⟨We *ditched* the old table at the town dump.⟩ — see DISCARD

dither *n* **1** a state of nervous or irritated concern ⟨They're in a *dither* over what to do next.⟩ — see FRET
2 a sense of panic or extreme nervousness ⟨We were all in a *dither* while we waited for the test results.⟩ — see JITTERS

dither *vb* to show uncertainty about the right course of action ⟨We *dithered* all afternoon over whether to go to

the park or to the movies and ended up doing neither.⟩ — see HESITATE

dithery *adj* feeling or showing uncomfortable feelings of uncertainty ⟨an expectant father in a high state of *dithery* alarm⟩ — see NERVOUS 1

ditty *n* a short musical composition for the human voice often with instrumental accompaniment ⟨sung a little *ditty* in a minor key⟩ — see SONG 1

diurnal *adj* occurring, done, produced, or appearing every day ⟨a love as constant and certain as the *diurnal* tides⟩ — see DAILY

divan *n* a long upholstered piece of furniture designed for several sitters ⟨Whenever I stayed over at their house I usually slept on the *divan* in the living room.⟩ — see COUCH

dive *n* **1** an act or instance of diving ⟨The penguin took a *dive* off of the ice sheet.⟩
synonyms pitch, plunge
related words dip, immersion, submersion; fall, plump, slip, spill, stumble, tumble; descent, drop; belly flop, jackknife, swan dive
near antonyms jump, leap
2 the act or process of going to a lower level or altitude ⟨Stock prices took a long, steady *dive*.⟩ — see DESCENT 1

dive *vb* **1** to cast oneself head first into deep water ⟨The children liked to *dive* off the dock.⟩
synonyms pitch, plunge, sound
related words dip, immerse, submerge; belly flop, plump, plunk (*or* plonk)
near antonyms surface
2 to go to a lower level especially abruptly ⟨Sales figures for existing homes *dived* dramatically when mortgage rates skyrocketed.⟩ — see DROP 2

diverge *vb* **1** to change one's course or direction ⟨The deer abruptly *diverged* from its intended path the moment it spied the waiting lynx.⟩ — see TURN 3
2 to go or move in different directions from a central point ⟨At that point the road and the railroad tracks *diverge*.⟩ — see SEPARATE 2

divergence *n* **1** a movement in different directions away from a common point ⟨a growing *divergence* of opinion⟩
synonyms separation
related words difference, disagreement, discrepancy, disparateness, disparity, dissidence, dissimilarity, distinction, distinctiveness, distinctness, diversity, unlikeness
phrases parting of the ways
near antonyms accord, agreement; likeness, similarity
antonyms convergence
2 a turning away from a course or standard ⟨Any *divergence* from the community's strict moral code was met with social ostracism.⟩
synonyms departure, detour, diversion
related words regression, retrogression, reversion
near antonyms adherence

divers *adj* being of many and various kinds ⟨The state fair offers *divers* amusements for the whole family.⟩ — see MANIFOLD

diverse *adj* being not of the same kind ⟨a movement supported by people with *diverse* interests but one common goal⟩ — see DIFFERENT 1

diverseness *n* **1** the quality or state of being composed of many different elements or types ⟨The *diverseness* of the offerings at the art fair made judging a challenge.⟩ — see VARIETY 1
2 the quality or state of being different ⟨The *diverseness* of the two top movies in the running for Best Picture could not be more striking.⟩ — see DIFFERENCE 1

diversion *n* **1** someone or something that provides amusement or enjoyment ⟨A scavenger hunt was organized as a *diversion* for the guests at the party.⟩ — see FUN 1

2 the act or activity of providing pleasure or amusement especially for the public ⟨Movies and television became two of the most popular and influential *diversions* of the 20th century.⟩ — see ENTERTAINMENT 1

3 a turning away from a course or standard ⟨carefully weighed testimony that did not contain the slightest *diversion* from the truth⟩ — see DIVERGENCE 2

diversity *n* **1** the quality or state of being composed of many different elements or types ⟨The *diversity* of plant life on that tropical island is staggering.⟩ — see VARIETY 1

2 the quality or state of being different ⟨There's considerable *diversity* in the platforms for the two major parties.⟩ — see DIFFERENCE 1

divert *vb* **1** to cause (someone) to pass the time agreeably occupied ⟨a light comedy to *divert* the tired business executive⟩ — see AMUSE

2 to change the course or direction of (something) ⟨The bike race was *diverted* around the construction zone.⟩ — see TURN 2

3 to draw the attention or mind to something else ⟨trying to *divert* the child with a toy while the doctor was giving her a shot⟩ — see DISTRACT 1

diverting *adj* providing amusement or enjoyment ⟨Some tall and *diverting* tales were told by the festival's roving storyteller.⟩ — see FUN

divide *vb* **1** to set or force apart ⟨Volunteers *divided* the donated groceries into several dozen piles.⟩ — see SEPARATE 1

2 to go or move in different directions from a central point ⟨The group *divided* based on those who wanted to go swimming and those who didn't.⟩ — see SEPARATE 2

divided *adj* disagreeing with each other ⟨The club members are sharply *divided* on the need for more fund-raising.⟩

synonyms disunited, split

related words balkanized, fractionalized, fractionated; cohesionless, factious

phrases at loggerheads, at odds

antonyms unanimous, undivided, united

dividend *n* something given in addition to what is ordinarily expected or owed ⟨The reward money was an unexpected *dividend* for our good deed.⟩ — see BONUS

divider *n* something that divides, separates, or marks off ⟨placed a *divider* across the gym so we could have two activities going on at once⟩ — see DIVISION 1

divine *adj* **1** of the very best kind ⟨How about a piece of the most *divine* apple pie I've ever tasted!⟩ — see EXCELLENT

2 of, relating to, or being God ⟨For these *divine* gifts let us be truly thankful.⟩ — see HOLY 3

divine *vb* to realize or know about beforehand ⟨It was easy to *divine* their intention to get married.⟩ — see FORESEE

diviner *n* one who predicts future events or developments ⟨Somehow the *diviner* failed to foresee her own misfortunes with the law.⟩ — see PROPHET 1

divinity *n* **1** the quality or state of being divine ⟨Henry David Thoreau felt the presence of *divinity* in every part of nature.⟩

synonyms deity, godhead, godhood

related words blessedness, godliness, holiness, piousness, saintliness

2 a being having superhuman powers and control over a particular part of life or the world ⟨a modest temple built for one of the minor *divinities* in ancient Greek mythology⟩ — see DEITY 1

3 *cap* the being worshipped as the creator and ruler of the universe ⟨Communal worship of the *Divinity* was expected of every member of the colony.⟩ — see DEITY 2

divisible *adj* capable of being split into two or more parts or pieces ⟨easily *divisible* into enough pieces for everyone⟩ — see SEPARABLE

division *n* **1** something that divides, separates, or marks off ⟨We poked our heads over the *division* between the yards to see what the fuss was about.⟩

synonyms divider, partition, separation

related words barrier, fence, wall; border, boundary, limit

2 a large unit of a governmental, business, or educational organization ⟨She was transferred to another *division* in the company.⟩

synonyms agency, arm, branch, bureau, department, desk, office, service

related words subdepartment, subdivision

3 one of the units into which a whole is divided on the basis of a common characteristic ⟨one of the major *divisions* of birds⟩ — see CLASS 2

4 the act or process of a whole separating into two or more parts or pieces ⟨The assembly line was a major development in the *division* of labor among workers.⟩ — see SEPARATION 1

5 the act or process of giving out something to each member of a group ⟨the person in charge of the *division* of the profits among the business partners⟩ — see DISTRIBUTION 1

6 a lack of agreement or harmony ⟨We're trying to resolve the *division* between our two countries.⟩ — see DISCORD

divorce *vb* to set or force apart ⟨In your head you need to *divorce* your wishes and fantasies from the realities of the world as it is.⟩ — see SEPARATE 1

divulge *vb* to make known (as information previously kept secret) ⟨We tried to make him *divulge* the name of the winner, but he wouldn't budge.⟩ — see REVEAL 1

divulgence *n* the act or an instance of making known something previously unknown or concealed ⟨The government strictly prohibits the *divulgence* of classified information.⟩ — see REVELATION

dizzy *adj* **1** having a feeling of being whirled about and in danger of falling down ⟨I felt very *dizzy* after I got off of the roller coaster.⟩

synonyms giddy, light-headed, reeling, whirling

related words faint, weak; addled, befuddled, confused, dazed, groggy

near antonyms clearheaded; stable, steady

2 suffering from mental confusion ⟨He felt *dizzy* from trying to remember all of the dates and names that were sure to be asked on the test.⟩

synonyms addled, befogged, befuddled, bewildered, confused, dazed, distracted, dopey (*also* dopy), shell-shocked, silly, stunned, stupefied

related words senseless, unconscious

phrases at sea, out of it

near antonyms alert, conscious

antonyms clearheaded

3 moving, proceeding, or acting with great speed ⟨prices climbing at a *dizzy* rate⟩ — see FAST 1

4 lacking in seriousness or maturity ⟨moved from playing *dizzy* comedic parts to serious dramatic roles⟩ — see GIDDY 1

do *n* **1** a social gathering ⟨It's supposed to be some sort of fancy *do*.⟩ — see PARTY 1

2 a statement of what to do that must be obeyed by those concerned ⟨issued a long list of *dos* and don'ts before we even started the project⟩ — see COMMAND 1

do *vb* **1** to be fitting or proper ⟨That outfit just won't *do* for the wedding.⟩
synonyms befit, go, serve, suit
related words satisfy, suffice; function, work
phrases fill the bill (*or* fit the bill)
2 to be enough ⟨Even half of that amount of sugar will *do*.⟩ — see SERVE 2
3 to carry through (as a process) to completion ⟨*Do* as much as you can and leave the rest.⟩ — see PERFORM 1
4 to make more attractive by adding something that is beautiful or becoming ⟨We *did* the living room in French provincial style.⟩ — see DECORATE
5 to meet one's day-to-day needs ⟨I'm *doing* just fine⟩ — see GET ALONG 1
6 to be the cause of (a situation, action, or state of mind) ⟨This neighborhood cleanup effort might just *do* some good.⟩ — see EFFECT
7 to copy or exaggerate (someone or something) in order to make fun of ⟨The laughing partygoers begged their host to *do* George Bush again.⟩ — see MIMIC 1
8 to move forward along a course ⟨How are you *doing* with the house restoration?⟩ — see GO 1
9 to present a portrayal or performance of ⟨He's *done* Hamlet on the stage many times.⟩ — see ACT 1
10 to rob by the use of trickery or threats ⟨*did* them out of their savings with surprising ease⟩ — see FLEECE
11 to take place ⟨Nothing's ever *doing* in this boring little town.⟩ — see HAPPEN

doable *adj* capable of being done or carried out ⟨The assignment will be just barely *doable* in the time allowed.⟩ — see POSSIBLE 1

docile *adj* readily giving in to the command or authority of another ⟨a *docile* young pony that went wherever it was led⟩ — see OBEDIENT

docility *n* a readiness or willingness to yield to the wishes of others ⟨dogs bred for *docility* instead of aggressiveness⟩ — see COMPLIANCE 1

dock *n* a structure used by boats and ships for taking on or landing cargo and passengers ⟨The boat remained tied up at the *dock* for a week, waiting for the weather to clear.⟩
synonyms float, jetty, landing, levee, pier, quay, wharf
related words berth, mooring, slip; dockyard, marina, quayage, shipyard, wharfage

¹**dock** *vb* **1** to make less in extent or duration ⟨The editorial was *docked* by about a hundred words to make it fit on the page.⟩ — see SHORTEN
2 to make (something) shorter or smaller with the use of a cutting instrument ⟨The boxer's tail was *docked* soon after birth.⟩ — see CLIP 1

²**dock** *vb* to stop at or near a place along the shore ⟨The cruise ship *docked* at the first port of call early the next morning.⟩ — see LAND 1

docket *n* a listing of things to be presented or considered (as at a concert or play) ⟨on the Broadway *docket* for the early part of this season⟩ — see PROGRAM 1

dockworker *n* one who loads and unloads ships at a port ⟨The *dockworkers* spent all afternoon taking crates off of the ship.⟩
synonyms longshoreman, stevedore

doctor *n* a person specially trained in healing human medical disorders ⟨We called a *doctor* as soon as we realized the baby was sick.⟩
synonyms medic, physician
related words family doctor, family physician, family practitioner, general practitioner; anesthesiologist, dermatologist, gynecologist, internist, neurologist, ob-gyn, obstetrician, ophthalmologist, orthopedist, pathologist, pediatrician (*also* pediatrist), physiatrist, podiatrist, radi-

ologist, urologist; attending, clinician, hospitalist; specialist; plastic surgeon, surgeon; intern (*also* interne), resident; aidman, nurse, nurse-practitioner; EMT, paramedic (*also* paramedical); physical therapist, physiotherapist
antonyms nondoctor, nonphysician

doctor *vb* **1** to give medical treatment to ⟨a pledge to *doctor* the burn victims until they were whole again⟩
synonyms treat
related words cure, heal, mend, rehabilitate, remedy; attend, care (for), dose, drug, hospitalize, minister (to), nurse
2 to put into good shape or working order again ⟨spends his spare time *doctoring* old cars⟩ — see MEND 1
3 to change (something) so as to make it suitable for a new use or situation ⟨slightly *doctored* his standard campaign speech for a collegiate audience⟩ — see ADAPT

doctrine *n* **1** a statement or body of statements concerning faith or morals proclaimed by a church ⟨the Catholic Church's *doctrine* on the Eucharist⟩
synonyms canon, dogma
related words canon law; belief, conviction, tenet; credo, creed, ideology (*also* idealogy), philosophy, theology; axiom, precept, principle; symbol
2 the basic beliefs or guiding principles of a person or group ⟨the *doctrine* of quantum physicists⟩ — see CREED 1

document *n* **1** a piece of paper with information written or to be written on it ⟨filled out the *documents* for a bank loan⟩ — see FORM 2
2 a written or printed paper giving information about or proof of something ⟨Have your *documents* ready as you approach the border.⟩ — see CERTIFICATE

document *vb* to show the existence or truth of by evidence ⟨He tried in vain to *document* a link between ancient civilizations and extraterrestrials.⟩ — see PROVE 1

documentary *adj* restricted to or based on fact ⟨a *documentary* film on the early history of jazz⟩ — see FACTUAL 1

documentation *n* something presented in support of the truth or accuracy of a claim ⟨The archaeologist presented convincing *documentation* of her theory at the conference.⟩ — see PROOF

dodder *vb* to move forward while swaying from side to side ⟨was *doddering* down the walk outside the nursing home⟩ — see STAGGER 1

dodge *n* a clever often underhanded means to achieve an end ⟨just another *dodge* to get out of working in the yard⟩ — see TRICK 1

dodge *vb* **1** to move suddenly aside or to and fro ⟨*dodging* through the crowd on his way to the exit⟩
synonyms duck, sidestep, weave, zigzag
related words avoid, elude, escape, evade, parry, shirk, skirt; deflect, turn; slide, slip
2 to avoid having to comply with (something) especially through cleverness ⟨always trying to *dodge* the landlord's rule prohibiting pets⟩ — see CIRCUMVENT 1
3 to get or keep away from (as a responsibility) through cleverness or trickery ⟨*dodged* the horde of paparazzi by leaving through the service entrance⟩ — see ESCAPE 2

dodger *n* a dishonest person who uses clever means to cheat others out of something of value ⟨one of the most artful *dodgers* in the annals of American crime⟩ — see TRICKSTER 1

dodging *n* the act or a means of getting or keeping away from something undesirable ⟨the governor's repeated *dodging* of tough questions at the press conference⟩ — see ESCAPE 2

dodo *n* a stupid person ⟨She called him a *dodo* after he lost the money.⟩ — see IDIOT

doff *vb* to rid oneself of (a garment) ⟨The blazing sun soon had the men *doffing* their jackets.⟩ — see REMOVE 1

dog *n* **1** a domestic mammal that is related to the wolves and foxes ⟨a *dog* who needs a loving home⟩
synonyms canine, doggy (*or* doggie), hound, pooch
related words cur, mongrel, mutt; bitch; lapdog, pup, puppy, puppy dog, whelp; bandog, bird dog, coonhound, courser, gundog, hunter, sheepdog, sled dog, watchdog, wolf dog, wolfhound; guide dog, police dog, working dog
2 a person whose behavior is offensive to others ⟨Don't speak to me, you *dog!*⟩ — see JERK 1

dog *vb* **1** to go after or on the track of ⟨star athletes being *dogged* by fans when they're out in public⟩ — see FOLLOW 2
2 to subject (someone) to constant scoldings and sharp reminders ⟨tired of constantly having to *dog* their son about cleaning his room⟩ — see NAG 1

dog–eared *adj* showing signs of advanced wear and tear and neglect ⟨an old *dog-eared* copy of a beloved book⟩ — see SHABBY 1

dogged *adj* **1** continuing despite difficulties, opposition, or discouragement ⟨a madman who spent his life in *dogged* pursuit of power⟩ — see PERSISTENT
2 sticking to an opinion, purpose, or course of action in spite of reason, arguments, or persuasion ⟨Your *dogged* adherence to a really lame argument is embarrassing.⟩ — see OBSTINATE
3 showing no signs of slackening or yielding in one's purpose ⟨a *dogged* search for the missing piece of the puzzle⟩ — see UNYIELDING 1

doggedness *n* a steadfast adherence to an opinion, purpose, or course of action in spite of reason, arguments, or persuasion ⟨Being an effective detective requires *doggedness* as well as cleverness.⟩ — see OBSTINACY

dogging *n* the act of going after or in the tracks of another ⟨the merciless *dogging* of the Hollywood couple by the press⟩ — see PURSUIT

doggy *or* **doggie** *n* a domestic mammal that is related to the wolves and foxes ⟨What a good little *doggy!*⟩ — see DOG 1

dogma *n* **1** a statement or body of statements concerning faith or morals proclaimed by a church ⟨Catholic *dogma*⟩ — see DOCTRINE 1
2 the basic beliefs or guiding principles of a person or group ⟨The Golden Rule encompasses a *dogma* that can serve all mankind.⟩ — see CREED 1

do in *vb* **1** to bring to a complete end the physical soundness, existence, or usefulness of ⟨a business venture that was *done in* by poor planning⟩ — see DESTROY 1
2 to deprive of life ⟨The early frost *did in* all of our tender plants.⟩ — see KILL 1
3 to put to death deliberately ⟨was *done in* by some traitor⟩ — see MURDER 1
4 to use up all the physical energy of ⟨The long day of hard work really *did me in.*⟩ — see EXHAUST 1
5 to rob by the use of trickery or threats ⟨too savvy an investor to be *done in* by preposterous claims of astronomical returns⟩ — see FLEECE

doing *n* something done by someone ⟨Is that mess in the kitchen your *doing?*⟩ — see ACTION 1

doldrums *pl n* **1** a state of temporary inactivity ⟨The theater scene is usually in the *doldrums* during the summer.⟩ — see ABEYANCE
2 a state or spell of low spirits ⟨The team had been in the *doldrums* ever since losing the championship.⟩ — see SADNESS
3 the state of being bored ⟨in the *doldrums* while we waited for something to happen⟩ — see BOREDOM

dole *n* the giving of necessities and especially money to the needy ⟨a weekly *dole* provided to hard up folks⟩ — see CHARITY 1

doleful *adj* **1** expressing or suggesting mourning ⟨a *doleful* expression on their faces as they said good-bye to the friends they had made over the summer⟩ — see MOURNFUL 1
2 feeling unhappiness ⟨the visibly *doleful* players, heartbroken about their loss⟩ — see SAD 1

dolefulness *n* **1** a state or spell of low spirits ⟨With the resigned *dolefulness* of an athlete who knows his playing days are over, he cleared out his locker for the last time.⟩ — see SADNESS
2 deep sadness especially for the loss of someone or something loved ⟨a period of *dolefulness* for the grieving family⟩ — see SORROW

doll *n* **1** a small figure often of a human being used especially as a child's plaything ⟨There was a row of *dolls* along the shelf in the bedroom.⟩
synonyms action figure, dolly, puppet
related words rag doll; figure, figurine; handpuppet, marionette
2 a physically attractive person ⟨Her new boyfriend is a real *doll!*⟩
synonyms dish, fox, knockout
related words beauty, eyeful, goddess, lovely, stunner; beefcake, hunk, stud

doll up *vb* **1** to make more attractive by adding something that is beautiful or becoming ⟨If you were to *doll up* those Shaker-style rooms, you'd ruin their simple elegance.⟩ — see DECORATE
2 to put on one's best or formal clothes ⟨Kim got all *dolled up* for the party.⟩ — see DRESS UP 1

dolly *n* a small figure often of a human being used especially as a child's plaything ⟨My kid sister was always playing with her *dollies*.⟩ — see DOLL 1

dolor *n* deep sadness especially for the loss of someone or something loved ⟨Her sad poems grew out of a deep *dolor* that lasted for months.⟩ — see SORROW

dolorous *adj* expressing or suggesting mourning ⟨*dolorous* ballads of death and regret⟩ — see MOURNFUL 1

dolt *n* a stupid person ⟨He's always jokingly calling his best friend a *dolt*.⟩ — see IDIOT

doltish *adj* not having or showing an ability to absorb ideas readily ⟨My friends laughed at my *doltish* ignorance of how to use chopsticks.⟩ — see STUPID 1

doltishness *n* the quality or state of lacking intelligence or quickness of mind ⟨He acted with uncharacteristic *doltishness*.⟩ — see STUPIDITY 1

domain *n* a region of activity, knowledge, or influence ⟨a museum director who is one of the most powerful figures in the art *domain*⟩ — see FIELD 2

domestic *adj* **1** of or relating to a household or family ⟨The surest way to maintain *domestic* peace and harmony is to have everyone pitch in on chores.⟩
synonyms familial, household
related words homelike, homely, homey (*also* homy); residential
antonyms nondomestic, nonfamilial
2 changed from the wild state so as to become useful and obedient to humans ⟨*domestic* animals in a barnyard⟩ — see TAME 1
3 belonging to a particular place by birth or origin ⟨The *domestic* bird population has been virtually wiped out by the brown tree snake.⟩ — see NATIVE 1

domestic *n* a person hired to perform household or personal services ⟨Working as a team, the couple hired themselves out as *domestics* for wealthy homeowners.⟩ — see MAID 1

domesticated *adj* changed from the wild state so as to

become useful and obedient to humans ⟨The *domesticated* horses are kept in a corral.⟩ — see TAME 1

domicile *n* the place where one lives ⟨Welcome to my *domicile*, humble though it may be!⟩ — see HOME 1

domicile *vb* to provide with living quarters or shelter ⟨The university *domiciles* students in a variety of buildings in and around its urban campus.⟩ — see HOUSE 1

dominance *n* **1** controlling power or influence over others ⟨Although Napoléon had achieved *dominance* over the European continent, Great Britain still ruled the waves.⟩ — see SUPREMACY 1

2 the fact or state of being above others in rank or importance ⟨the professor's *dominance* in the field of ancient Greek history⟩ — see EMINENCE 1

dominant *adj* coming before all others in importance ⟨the *dominant* authority on the English language⟩ — see FOREMOST 1

dominate *vb* **1** to bring under one's control by force of arms ⟨By 1941 Hitler had *dominated* much of Europe.⟩ — see CONQUER 1

2 to look down on ⟨The ruined fortress *dominates* the town.⟩ — see OVERLOOK 1

dominating *n* the act or process of bringing someone or something under one's control ⟨the gradual *dominating* of Europe by a few ruling families⟩ — see CONQUEST

domination *n* **1** controlling power or influence over others ⟨auction houses battling for *domination* in the high-end art market⟩ — see SUPREMACY 1

2 the act or process of bringing someone or something under one's control ⟨the Spanish *domination* of the Americas in the 16th century⟩ — see CONQUEST

domineering *adj* fond of ordering people around ⟨The younger children in the family were controlled by a *domineering* older sister.⟩ — see BOSSY

dominion *n* **1** controlling power or influence over others ⟨The U.S. has *dominion* over the island.⟩ — see SUPREMACY 1

2 the right or means to command or control others ⟨The butler was granted *dominion* over the housekeepers.⟩ — see POWER 1

don *vb* to place on one's person ⟨She *donned* her best gown for the ball.⟩ — see PUT ON 1

donate *vb* to make a present of ⟨We plan to *donate* all the profits from the rummage sale to charity.⟩ — see GIVE 1

donation *n* **1** a gift of money or its equivalent to a charity, humanitarian cause, or public institution ⟨a generous *donation* to the orphanage from an anonymous benefactor⟩ — see CONTRIBUTION

2 something given to someone without expectation of a return ⟨A chocolate cake was my *donation* to the office party.⟩ — see GIFT 1

donator *n* one that helps another with gifts or money ⟨a frequent *donator* of funds to research foundations⟩ — see BENEFACTOR

done *adj* **1** brought or having come to an end ⟨The demanding job was finally *done*.⟩ — see COMPLETE 2

2 depleted in strength, energy, or freshness ⟨After bicycling 30 miles we were completely *done*.⟩ — see WEARY 1

3 no longer existing ⟨He said the day of the circus big top is *done*.⟩ — see EXTINCT

donkey *n* **1** a sturdy and patient domestic mammal that is used especially to carry things ⟨We put our bags on the *donkey* and headed down the canyon.⟩

synonyms ass, burro, jackass

related words jack, jennet, jenny; hinny, mule; pack animal

2 a stupid person ⟨They called him a *donkey* when he refused to go along with their plans.⟩ — see IDIOT

donor *n* one that helps another with gifts or money ⟨a list of *donors* in the charitable foundation's annual report⟩ — see BENEFACTOR

doom *n* **1** a state or end that seemingly has been decided beforehand ⟨a prophet of *doom* predicting another recession⟩ — see FATE 1

2 the permanent stopping of all the vital bodily activities ⟨the story of a mysterious creature that lures travelers to their *doom*⟩ — see DEATH 1

doom *vb* **1** to determine the fate of in advance ⟨Tom had always felt that he was *doomed* to remain single forever.⟩ — see DESTINE

2 to impose a judicial punishment on ⟨*doomed* the murderer to life in prison without the possibility of parole⟩ — see SENTENCE

door *n* **1** a barrier by which an entry is closed and opened ⟨We locked the *door* to the room so that no one could get in.⟩

synonyms gate, hatch, portal

related words double door, Dutch door, French door, lattice, portcullis, postern, revolving door, storm door, trapdoor, wicket

2 the opening through which one can enter or leave a structure ⟨a steady stream of visitors through the front *door*⟩

synonyms doorway, entrance, gate, gateway, way

related words hatch, hatchway

3 the means or right of entering or participating in ⟨Education unlocks the *door* to advancement.⟩ — see ENTRANCE 1

doorkeeper *n* a person who tends a door ⟨The *doorkeeper* held the door open for us so we didn't have to put down our packages.⟩

synonyms doorman, gatekeeper

doorman *n* a person who tends a door ⟨We tipped the hotel *doorman* for getting us a cab.⟩ — see DOORKEEPER

doorway *n* **1** the means or right of entering or participating in ⟨the *doorway* to a life of luxury and leisure⟩ — see ENTRANCE 1

2 the opening through which one can enter or leave a structure ⟨He stood in the *doorway* until we finally invited him in.⟩ — see DOOR 2

dope *n* **1** information not generally available to the public ⟨The stool pigeon gave us the *dope* on their deal.⟩

synonyms book, inside, lowdown, scoop, tip

related words dirt, dish, gossip, rumor, story; hint, pointer; information, intelligence, news, tidings, word

near antonyms ancient history, open secret

2 a stupid person ⟨I locked my keys in the car—I'm such a *dope*!⟩ — see IDIOT

dope (out) *vb* to find an answer for through reasoning ⟨We tried to *dope out* the answer from the little information we had been given.⟩ — see SOLVE

dopey *also* **dopy** *adj* **1** not having or showing an ability to absorb ideas readily ⟨a sweet but *dopey* little dog who never learned any tricks⟩ — see STUPID 1

2 suffering from mental confusion ⟨We were still *dopey* from having all those facts and figures thrown at us.⟩ — see DIZZY 2

dopiness *n* the quality or state of lacking intelligence or quickness of mind ⟨amused by the sheer *dopiness* of the movie's plot⟩ — see STUPIDITY 1

do–rag *n* a scarf worn on the head ⟨wearing a nylon *do-rag*⟩ — see BANDANNA

dork *n, slang* a stupid person ⟨Mom, I look like a *dork* in these clothes.⟩ — see IDIOT

dorky *adj, slang* not having or showing an ability to absorb ideas readily ⟨We teased dad for looking so *dorky* in his high school prom picture.⟩ — see STUPID 1

dormancy *n* **1** a state of temporary inactivity ⟨Some volcanoes have eruptive cycles marked by long stretches of *dormancy*.⟩ — see ABEYANCE

2 lack of action or activity ⟨a fighting force that could be roused instantly from *dormancy* to action⟩ — see INACTION

dormant *adj* **1** being in a state of suspended consciousness ⟨The bears lay *dormant* in their den during the winter.⟩ — see ASLEEP 1

2 not being in a state of use, activity, or employment ⟨The engine lay *dormant* in the garage until we found a use for it.⟩ — see INACTIVE 2

dot *n* a small area that is different (as in color) from the main part ⟨There was just a *dot* on the tablecloth where the food had spattered.⟩ — see SPOT 1

dot *vb* **1** to cover by or as if by scattering something over or on ⟨a hillside *dotted* with wildflowers⟩ — see SCATTER 2

2 to mark with small spots especially unevenly ⟨the practice of some chefs of positioning a small portion of food in the center and *dotting* the rest of the plate with sauce⟩ — see SPOT 1

dote (on) *vb* to love or admire too much ⟨*doted on* her only grandchild⟩ — see IDOLIZE

dotted *adj* marked with spots ⟨a *dotted* tie that didn't go with his striped shirt at all⟩ — see SPOTTED 1

dotty *adj* showing or marked by a lack of good sense or judgment ⟨It would be *dotty* to turn the offer down.⟩ — see FOOLISH 1

double *adj* **1** consisting of two members or parts that are usually joined ⟨an egg with a *double* yolk⟩

synonyms binary, bipartite, dual, duplex, twin, twofold

related words mated, paired

near antonyms unpaired

antonyms single

2 being twice as great or as many ⟨After it was ranked the best in the country, the college had *double* the usual number of applicants.⟩

synonyms twofold

3 not being or expressing what one appears to be or express ⟨She's known for speaking with a *double* tongue, so I doubt that her concern is very heartfelt.⟩ — see INSINCERE

double *adv* to two times the amount or degree ⟨raced to his side *double* quick⟩ — see DOUBLY

double *n* something or someone that strongly resembles another ⟨He looks so much like you that he could be your *double*.⟩ — see IMAGE 1

double *vb* **1** to make twice as great or as many ⟨We *doubled* our investment in six months.⟩

synonyms duplicate, redouble

related words compound, multiply; accumulate, balloon, build (up), burgeon (*also* bourgeon), enlarge, escalate, expand, increase, mount, mushroom, proliferate, rise, snowball, swell, wax

2 to lay one part over or against another part of ⟨*Double* the wet cloth and place it on the patient's forehead.⟩ — see FOLD 1

double–cross *vb* to be unfaithful or disloyal to ⟨She promised to share the profits but then *double-crossed* us.⟩ — see BETRAY 1

double cross *n* the act or fact of violating the trust or confidence of another ⟨Politics is full of *double crosses* and backbiting.⟩ — see BETRAYAL

double–crosser *n* one who betrays a trust or an allegiance ⟨We knew he was a *double-crosser* so we didn't tell him our real plans.⟩ — see TRAITOR

double–dealing *adj* **1** marked by, based on, or done by the use of dishonest methods to acquire something of value ⟨*double-dealing* business practices that are being investigated by the state's attorney general⟩ — see FRAUDULENT 1

2 not being or expressing what one appears to be or express ⟨The *double-dealing* salesman never told me that the car had been in an accident and repaired.⟩ — see INSINCERE

3 given to or marked by cheating and deception ⟨The *double-dealing* team owners were pitting the two cities against one another, both of whom badly wanted the franchise.⟩ — see DISHONEST 2

double–dealing *n* the inclination or practice of misleading others through lies or trickery ⟨a go-between suspected of *double-dealing*⟩ — see DECEIT 1

double–talk *n* **1** language marked by abstractions, jargon, euphemisms, and circumlocutions ⟨The reporter listened to the senator's *double-talk* for about 30 seconds, and then repeated the question.⟩ — see GIBBERISH 2

2 unintelligible or meaningless talk ⟨The man on the sidewalk rattled off some *double-talk*, shoved the petition in my face, and before I realized it, I had added my signature to the list.⟩ — see GIBBERISH 1

doubly *adv* to two times the amount or degree ⟨We did the test again to be *doubly* sure of the results.⟩

synonyms double, twice, twofold

doubt *n* a feeling or attitude that one does not know the truth, truthfulness, or trustworthiness of someone or something ⟨From the beginning I had my *doubts* about the investment scheme.⟩

synonyms distrust, distrustfulness, incertitude, misgiving, mistrust, mistrustfulness, query, reservation, skepticism, suspicion, uncertainty

related words disbelief, incredulity, unbelief; anxiety, concern, paranoia, wariness; compunction, qualm, scruple, tremor

near antonyms credence, faith

antonyms assurance, belief, certainty, certitude, confidence, conviction, sureness, surety, trust

doubt *vb* to have no trust or confidence in ⟨I *doubt* that I'll have time to finish.⟩ — see DISTRUST

doubtable *adj* **1** giving good reason for being doubted, questioned, or challenged ⟨Her argument rested entirely upon some highly *doubtable* logic.⟩ — see DOUBTFUL 2

2 open to question or dispute ⟨That his wartime exploit happened at all is very *doubtable*.⟩ — see DEBATABLE 1

doubter *n* a person who is always ready to doubt or question the truth or existence of something ⟨There will always be some hard-core *doubters* of the government's denial of the UFO incident.⟩ — see SKEPTIC

doubtful *adj* **1** not feeling sure about the truth, wisdom, or trustworthiness of someone or something ⟨He was *doubtful* about the decision to complete the project despite its mounting problems.⟩

synonyms distrustful, dubious, mistrustful, skeptical, suspicious, uncertain, unconvinced, undecided, unsettled, unsure

related words equivocal; diffident, insecure; halting, hesitant, indecisive, irresolute, vacillating, wavering; conflicted

phrases on the fence

near antonyms assured, confident, sanguine, self-assured; decisive, determined, resolute

antonyms certain, convinced, positive, sure

2 giving good reason for being doubted, questioned, or challenged ⟨The election results were highly *doubtful*, so an investigation was begun.⟩

synonyms debatable, disputable, doubtable, dubious, equivocal, fishy, problematic (*also* problematical), queer, questionable, shady, shaky, suspect, suspicious *related words* alleged, so-called, supposed; moot; ambiguous, open, unclear; uncertain, undecided, undetermined; far-fetched, flimsy, improbable, unlikely, weak

near antonyms decisive, definitive; clear, obvious, open-and-shut, positive

antonyms certain, incontestable, indisputable, indubitable, questionless, sure, undeniable, undoubted, unproblematic, unquestionable

3 not likely to be true or to occur ⟨Our winning the championship increasingly looks like a *doubtful* outcome.⟩ — see IMPROBABLE

4 open to question or dispute ⟨a *doubtful* claim to the property⟩ — see DEBATABLE 1

doubtfully *adv* with distrust ⟨We followed our guide *doubtfully*, keeping our eyes open at all times.⟩ — see ASKANCE

doubting *adj* inclined to doubt or question claims ⟨*Doubting* viewers will wonder if there's anything real about that so-called reality show.⟩ — see SKEPTICAL 1

doubtingly *adv* with distrust ⟨We looked at her *doubtingly* as she told the story of her life.⟩ — see ASKANCE

doubtless *adj* having or showing a mind free from doubt ⟨another one of his *doubtless* predictions that will never come true⟩ — see CERTAIN 2

doubtless *adv* **1** without any question ⟨She is *doubtless* the smartest person in the class.⟩ — see INDEED 1

2 by reasonable assumption ⟨*Doubtless* you have heard this story before, but I'll tell it anyway.⟩ — see PROBABLY

dough *n* something (as pieces of stamped metal or printed paper) customarily and legally used as a medium of exchange, a measure of value, or a means of payment ⟨I didn't have to spend a lot of *dough* for a new phone.⟩ — see MONEY

doughtiness *n* strength of mind to carry on in spite of danger ⟨a new recruit with all of the *doughtiness* of the finest soldiers who ever saw battle⟩ — see COURAGE

doughty *adj* feeling or displaying no fear by temperament ⟨the *doughty* heroes of old⟩ — see BRAVE 1

dour *adj* harsh and threatening in manner or appearance ⟨He had a *dour* expression on his face.⟩ — see GRIM 1

¹**douse** *vb* to rid oneself of (a garment) ⟨In those days a gentleman would *douse* his hat when going indoors.⟩ — see REMOVE 1

²**douse** *also* **dowse** *vb* **1** to cause to cease burning ⟨You should *douse* the campfire before leaving in the morning.⟩ — see EXTINGUISH 1

2 to make wet ⟨The heavy rains thoroughly *doused* the tourists strolling the town streets.⟩ — see WET

3 to sink or push (something) briefly into or as if into a liquid ⟨*Douse* the grapes in water to remove any grit.⟩ — see DIP 1

doused *also* **dowsed** *adj* containing, covered with, or thoroughly penetrated by water ⟨shook the water out of her thoroughly *doused* hair⟩ — see WET 1

dove *n* **1** a person who opposes war or warlike policies ⟨The *doves* were in favor of using the surplus to improve the nation's schools and not its weapons systems.⟩

synonyms pacifist

related words peacemaker

near antonyms militarist; chauvinist, nationalist

antonyms hawk, jingo, warmonger

2 an innocent or gentle person ⟨He's a *dove* who wouldn't hurt a fly.⟩ — see LAMB

dovetail *vb* to be in agreement on every point ⟨The research *dovetails* with other similar studies.⟩ — see CHECK 1

dowager *n* a dignified usually elderly woman of some rank or authority ⟨The estate is owned by a wealthy *dowager*.⟩ — see MATRIARCH

dowdily *adv* in a careless or unfashionable manner ⟨dressed hurriedly and *dowdily* to go do her workout⟩ — see SLOPPILY

dowdy *adj* **1** lacking neatness in dress or person ⟨She played a *dowdy* old woman in the film.⟩ — see SLOPPY 1

2 marked by an obvious lack of style or good taste ⟨the *dowdy*, beat-up furniture at the cheap motel⟩ — see ¹TACKY 1

down *adj* **1** brought or having come to an end ⟨eight *down* and two to go⟩ — see COMPLETE 2

2 directed down ⟨a *down* escalator⟩ — see DOWNCAST 1

3 feeling unhappiness ⟨feeling a bit *down*⟩ — see SAD 1

4 temporarily suffering from a disorder of the body ⟨*down* with the flu⟩ — see SICK 1

5 not being in working order ⟨My computer is *down*.⟩ — see INOPERABLE 1

down *adv* **1** toward or in a lower position ⟨The stairs went *down* to the basement.⟩

synonyms below, downward (*or* downwards), over

related words facedown; low; downgrade, downstairs

near antonyms aloft

antonyms up, upward (*or* upwards), upwardly

2 from this or that place ⟨came *down* from New York for the weekend⟩ — see AWAY

¹**down** *n* a soft airy substance or covering ⟨a comforter filled with goose *down*⟩ — see FUZZ

²**down** *n* **1** something (as a situation or event) that is depressing ⟨Lately it's been one *down* after another in my life.⟩ — see DOWNER

2 the act or process of going to a lower level or altitude ⟨suffered with a psychological disorder in which she alternated between emotional ups and *downs*⟩ — see DESCENT 1

3 a loss of status ⟨experienced the ups and *downs* of a career in showbiz⟩ — see COMEDOWN

³**down** *n, usually* **downs** *pl* a broad area of level or rolling treeless country ⟨hold a festival on the *downs*⟩ — see PLAIN 1

down *vb* **1** to strike (someone) so forcefully as to cause a fall ⟨*downed* his opponent with one stunning blow⟩ — see FELL 1

2 to take into the stomach through the mouth and throat ⟨*downing* slices of pizza and guzzling bottles of soda⟩ — see SWALLOW 1

3 to reject by or as if by a vote ⟨All attempts to ban plastic shopping bags had been *downed* by the town council.⟩ — see NEGATIVE 1

downcast *adj* **1** directed down ⟨Her *downcast* gaze made us realize that she was shy.⟩

synonyms bowed, down, downward, lowered

near antonyms elevated, lifted, raised, uplifted, upward

2 feeling unhappiness ⟨I'm always a little *downcast* on rainy days.⟩ — see SAD 1

downer *n* something (as a situation or event) that is depressing ⟨That story was a real *downer*.⟩

synonyms bummer, down

related words bore, drag; accident, fatality, mishap, woe; calamity, catastrophe, debacle (*also* débâcle), misfortune, tragedy

near antonyms pick-me-up, trip

antonyms upper

downfall *n* **1** something that is the cause of one's ultimate failure or loss of life ⟨An insatiable love of money would be their *downfall*.⟩

synonyms death, destruction, ruin, ruination

related words bane, curse, torment; Achilles' heel, tragic flaw

phrases kiss of death

2 a change to a lower state or level ⟨the gradual *downfall* of the Roman Empire⟩ — see DECLINE 2

3 a loss of status ⟨an ill-advised speech that proved to be the cause of the candidate's *downfall*⟩ — see COMEDOWN

4 a steady falling of water from the sky in significant quantity ⟨We ducked under an overhang to shelter ourselves from the sudden *downfall*.⟩ — see RAIN 1

downgrade *n* **1** a change to a lower state or level ⟨a singing career on the *downgrade*⟩ — see DECLINE 2

2 a downward slope ⟨The gentle *downgrade* of the parking area is designed for drainage.⟩ — see DECLINE 3

downgrade *vb* **1** to bring to a lower grade or rank ⟨Increased automation resulted in many jobs in the factory being *downgraded*.⟩ — see DEMOTE

2 to diminish the price or value of ⟨The company's filing for bankruptcy *downgraded* the stock to the point where it was selling for pennies a share.⟩ — see DEPRECIATE 1

downhearted *adj* feeling unhappiness ⟨*downhearted* because his best friend was taking a job out of state⟩ — see SAD 1

downheartedness *n* a state or spell of low spirits ⟨His *downheartedness* lasted until he got a new job.⟩ — see SADNESS

downpour *n* a steady falling of water from the sky in significant quantity ⟨The *downpour* was so heavy that we were soaked by the time we got to the car.⟩ — see RAIN 1

downright *adj* **1** being or characterized by direct, brief, and potentially rude speech or manner ⟨Rural folks are often known for their *downright* speech, as they are generally not ones to beat around the bush.⟩ — see BLUNT 1

2 having no exceptions or restrictions ⟨That's a *downright* lie, and you know it!⟩ — see ABSOLUTE 2

downsize *vb* to make smaller in amount, volume, or extent ⟨The company *downsized* its overseas operations in an attempt to cut costs.⟩ — see DECREASE 1

down–to–earth *adj* **1** not having or showing any feelings of superiority, self-assertiveness, or showiness ⟨We were all impressed by how *down-to-earth* the movie star turned out to be.⟩ — see HUMBLE 1

2 willing to see things as they really are and deal with them sensibly ⟨a *down-to-earth* guidance counselor who is frank in telling students which colleges they're likely to get into⟩ — see REALISTIC 1

downward *adj* directed down ⟨the hawk's *downward* flight⟩ — see DOWNCAST 1

downward *or* **downwards** *adv* toward or in a lower position ⟨At this point the river flows gently *downward* to the sea.⟩ — see DOWN 1

downwind *adj* being in the direction that the wind is blowing ⟨We were *downwind* of the deer, so it couldn't smell us.⟩

synonyms leeward

antonyms upwind, windward

downy *adj* smooth or delicate in appearance or feel ⟨the *downy* surface of a ripe peach⟩ — see SOFT 2

doze *n* a short sleep ⟨a brief *doze* in the sun⟩ — see ¹NAP

doze *vb* **1** to be in a state of sleep ⟨likes to *doze* through those lazy summer afternoons⟩ — see SLEEP 1

2 to sleep lightly or briefly ⟨She *dozed* fitfully in the car but never fell completely asleep.⟩ — see NAP 1

dozer *n* one who sleeps ⟨The abrupt stop wakened the *dozers* on the bus.⟩ — see SLEEPER

dozing *adj* being in a state of suspended consciousness ⟨The *dozing* dog was running—at least in his dream.⟩ — see ASLEEP 1

dozing *n* a natural periodic loss of consciousness during which the body restores itself ⟨*Dozing* is a natural response to the stifling heat of summer.⟩ — see SLEEP 1

drab *adj* causing weariness, restlessness, or lack of interest

⟨The new city hall promises to be another *drab* pile of masonry for the town.⟩ — see BORING

draft *n* **1** a mass or quantity of something taken up and carried, conveyed, or transported ⟨the *draft* of an average-sized oil tanker⟩ — see LOAD 1

2 the portion of a serving of a beverage that is swallowed at one time ⟨Leo took a long *draft* of the water before putting his glass down.⟩ — see DRINK 2

3 noticeable movement of air in a particular direction ⟨Do you feel a *draft* from beneath the door?⟩ — see ¹WIND 1

draft *vb* **1** to pick especially for required military service ⟨My grandfather was *drafted* to fight in the war.⟩

synonyms conscript, levy

related words impress, press; enlist, enroll (*also* enrol), recruit; call up; sign up, volunteer

near antonyms discharge, muster out

2 to put (something) into proper and usually carefully worked out written form ⟨*Draft* a letter to the local newspaper giving your views on the problem.⟩ — see COMPOSE 1

3 to remove (liquid) gradually or completely ⟨Remember to *draft* the water from the pool so that we can close it up for the winter.⟩ — see DRAIN 1

draftee *n* a person forced or required to enroll in military service ⟨The massive mobilization required *draftees* to be rushed through training.⟩ — see CONSCRIPT

drag *n* **1** someone or something boring ⟨That lecture was such a *drag* that half of the audience fell asleep.⟩

synonyms bore, drip

related words bummer, downer; pill

near antonyms blast, kick, rush, upper

2 a passage cleared for public vehicular travel ⟨the main *drag* in town⟩ — see WAY 1

3 something that makes movement or progress difficult ⟨a *drag* on the economy⟩ — see ENCUMBRANCE

4 the portion of a serving of a beverage that is swallowed at one time ⟨took a deep *drag* of coffee before speaking his piece⟩ — see DRINK 2

5 a person who spoils the pleasure of others ⟨C'mon, don't be a *drag*—let's stay out a little longer.⟩ — see KILLJOY

6 clothing chosen as appropriate for a specific situation ⟨attending the Renaissance fair in medieval *drag*⟩ — see OUTFIT 1

drag *vb* **1** to cause to follow by applying steady force on ⟨The deliveryman *dragged* the barrels over against the wall.⟩ — see PULL 1

2 to move or act slowly ⟨One of the climbers was beginning to *drag*.⟩ — see DELAY 1

3 to move slowly ⟨The play *dragged* and seemed to take forever to get to its predictable conclusion.⟩ — see CRAWL 2

dragger *n* someone who moves slowly or more slowly than others ⟨We quickly left the *draggers* behind and sprinted up the hill.⟩ — see SLOWPOKE

dragging *adj* moving or proceeding at less than the normal, desirable, or required speed ⟨a mysterious, cloaked figure with a strange, *dragging* walk⟩ — see SLOW 1

drain *vb* **1** to remove (liquid) gradually or completely ⟨We *drained* the water from the tank before cleaning it.⟩

synonyms bleed, draft, draw (off), pump, siphon (*also* syphon), tap

related words suck; clear, empty, evacuate, exhaust, vacate, vacuate, void; decant; deplete; clean, flush, purge

near antonyms bathe, douse (*also* dowse), drench, soak, souse, wash, water, wet; deluge, drown, flood, inundate, overflow; submerge, swamp

antonyms fill

2 to make complete use of ⟨virtually *drained* the country's natural resources⟩ — see DEPLETE 1
3 to use up all the physical energy of ⟨The long hike *drained* us.⟩ — see EXHAUST 1

drained *adj* depleted in strength, energy, or freshness ⟨We were completely *drained* after shoveling snow all afternoon.⟩ — see WEARY 1

drainpipe *n* a pipe or channel for carrying off water from a roof ⟨Our *drainpipe* is always getting clogged with leaves.⟩ — see GUTTER 1

drama *n* **1** the public performance of plays ⟨He has been interested in *drama* from the first time he ever saw a play.⟩
synonyms dramatics, stage, theater (*or* theatre), theatricals
related words boards; acting, footlights; entertainment, showbiz, show business; amusement, distraction, diversion, recreation; exhibition, pageant, pageantry, presentation, production, show
2 a written work in which the story is told through speech and action that is intended to be acted out on stage ⟨wrote a police *drama* that really captured the speech of cops and criminals⟩ — see PLAY 2

dramatic *adj* **1** having the general quality or effect of a stage performance ⟨the basketball player's *dramatic* announcement of his sudden retirement⟩
synonyms histrionic, melodramatic, theatrical (*also* theatric)
related words affected, emotional, emotionalistic, sensational; actorish, actorly, actressy, dramaturgic (*or* dramaturgical), ham; amazing, astonishing, astounding, awesome, exciting, eye-opening, fabulous, marvelous (*or* marvellous), surprising, wonderful, wondrous; overdramatic
near antonyms matter-of-fact, monotonous, uneventful, unexciting; uninspiring, unnewsworthy, unrewarding, unsensational, unspectacular; common, commonplace, ordinary, stale, unexceptional
antonyms undramatic
2 given to or marked by attention-getting behavior suggestive of stage acting ⟨Oh, don't be so *dramatic*, and just tell us what happened!⟩ — see THEATRICAL 1
3 likely to attract attention ⟨a *dramatic* drop in the temperature overnight⟩ — see NOTICEABLE 1

dramatics *pl n* the public performance of plays ⟨Todd took part in *dramatics* while a student at the local university.⟩ — see DRAMA 1

dramatization *n* a written work in which the story is told through speech and action that is intended to be acted out on stage ⟨a *dramatization* of a true story⟩ — see PLAY 2

drapery *n* pieces of cloth hung to darken, decorate, or divide a room ⟨The *drapery* for the picture window matched the color of the furniture in the center of the room.⟩
synonyms curtains, drapes
related words hanging(s), shade, tapestry, window shade

drapes *pl n* pieces of cloth hung to darken, decorate, or divide a room ⟨We hung new *drapes* in the living room to match the new color scheme.⟩ — see DRAPERY

draw *n* **1** a situation in which neither participant in a contest, competition, or struggle comes out ahead of the other ⟨The game ended in a *draw*.⟩ — see TIE 1
2 something that attracts interest ⟨City leaders hoped that the new waterfront development would be a big *draw* for tourists.⟩ — see MAGNET
3 the act or an instance of applying force on something so that it moves in the direction of the force ⟨The archers held the bow at full *draw*.⟩ — see PULL 1

draw *vb* **1** to make a representation of by producing lines on a surface ⟨See if you can *draw* the bowl of fruit.⟩
synonyms picture
related words caricature, cartoon; crayon, pencil; outline, profile; scrawl, scribble, sketch
2 to cause to follow by applying steady force on ⟨Draw a chair up to the fire and sit with us.⟩ — see PULL 1
3 to give a representation or account of in words ⟨a writer who *draws* characters with lifelike clarity⟩ — see DESCRIBE 1
4 to receive as return for effort ⟨*draws* a hefty weekly salary⟩ — see EARN 1
5 to take away from a place or position ⟨Draw her aside so we can ask a quick question.⟩ — see REMOVE 2
6 to take the internal organs out of ⟨plucking and *drawing* a chicken⟩ — see GUT
7 to shape with a hammer ⟨*drew* the metal into a thin sheet by pounding it⟩ — see HAMMER 1

draw (off) *vb* to remove (liquid) gradually or completely ⟨*drew off* the fat from the top of the drippings⟩ — see DRAIN 1

drawback *n* a feature of someone or something that creates difficulty for achieving success ⟨This plan has only one *drawback*: it's unworkable.⟩ — see DISADVANTAGE 1

drawing *n* a picture using lines to represent the chief features of an object or scene ⟨With an economy of lines, he created a vivid *drawing* of the tree.⟩
synonyms cartoon, delineation, sketch
related words contour, figure, outline, silhouette; caricature, illustration; depiction, image, likeness, portrait, representation; engraving, etch, etching; aquatint, charcoal, line drawing, pastel, watercolor; blueprint

drawing out *n* the act of making longer ⟨the tedious *drawing out* of wool into thread that was required before weaving⟩ — see EXTENSION 1

draw on *vb* **1** to be the cause of (a situation, action, or state of mind) ⟨The general's imprudent remarks *drew on* a public rebuke by the secretary of defense.⟩ — see EFFECT
2 to come near or nearer ⟨Night *draws on*, so we should hurry home.⟩ — see APPROACH 1

draw out *vb* to make longer ⟨The reporter tried to *draw out* the interview.⟩ — see EXTEND 1

draw up *vb* **1** to bring (something) to a standstill ⟨She *drew* the car *up* in front of the house.⟩ — see ¹HALT 1
2 to put into a particular arrangement ⟨*drew up* the troops into a line along the ridge⟩ — see ORDER 1
3 to put (something) into proper and usually carefully worked out written form ⟨Draw up a proposal and submit it to the committee for approval.⟩ — see COMPOSE 1

dread *adj* causing fear ⟨Every ship on the Spanish Main was terrified of running into the *dread* pirate.⟩ — see FEARFUL 1

dread *n* **1** suspicion or fear of future harm or misfortune ⟨the *dread* felt by people awaiting bad news⟩ — see APPREHENSION 1
2 the emotion experienced in the presence or threat of danger ⟨We were filled with *dread* when we saw the rapids we would be rafting down.⟩ — see FEAR 1
3 something or someone that causes fear or dread especially without reason ⟨Speaking in public is a perennial *dread* for many people.⟩ — see BOGEY 1

dreadful *adj* **1** causing fear ⟨a *dreadful* storm⟩ — see FEARFUL 1
2 causing intense displeasure, disgust, or resentment ⟨a *dreadful* performance⟩ — see OFFENSIVE 1
3 extremely disturbing or repellent ⟨*dreadful* news of a fire⟩ — see HORRIBLE 1
4 extreme in degree, power, or effect ⟨the *dreadful* heat of the desert⟩ — see INTENSE 1

5 having no exceptions or restrictions ⟨They made a *dreadful* mess of the kitchen.⟩ — see ABSOLUTE 2

dreadfulness *n* the quality of inspiring intense dread or dismay ⟨The *dreadfulness* of an oncoming avalanche can scarcely be described.⟩ — see HORROR 1

dream *n* **1** a conception or image created by the imagination and having no objective reality ⟨His invention is only a *dream* right now, but someday it might be a reality.⟩ — see FANTASY 1

2 something that one hopes or intends to accomplish ⟨My *dream* is to open my own restaurant.⟩ — see GOAL

3 something very good of its kind ⟨The Alaskan cruise exceeded their wildest expectations—it was a *dream* of a vacation.⟩ — see JIM-DANDY

dream *vb* to form a mental picture of ⟨I *dreamed* that I was living on that proverbial desert island in the South Pacific.⟩ — see IMAGINE 1

dreamer *n* one whose conduct is guided more by the image of perfection than by the real world ⟨a *dreamer* who believes in ending wars⟩ — see IDEALIST

dreamily *adv* in a pleasing way ⟨Our date at the restaurant went *dreamily* until the check arrived.⟩ — see WELL 5

dreamy *adj* **1** giving pleasure or contentment to the mind or senses ⟨a beach resort that is a perfectly *dreamy* place to relax⟩ — see PLEASANT 1

2 tending to calm the emotions and relieve stress ⟨the kind of *dreamy* music I want after a hard day at work⟩ — see SOOTHING 1

drear *adj* causing or marked by an atmosphere lacking in cheer ⟨It was a *drear* morning in January when I went to take my driving test.⟩ — see GLOOMY 1

dreariness *n* a state or spell of low spirits ⟨My own *dreariness* seemed to match the dismal weather we were having.⟩ — see SADNESS

dreary *adj* **1** causing or marked by an atmosphere lacking in cheer ⟨Sam vowed that he would never take a desk job working in a *dreary* office.⟩ — see GLOOMY 1

2 causing unhappiness ⟨Families struggled through *dreary* economic times in the 1930s.⟩ — see SAD 2

3 causing weariness, restlessness, or lack of interest ⟨another *dreary* lecture to suffer through⟩ — see BORING

dredge *vb* to look through (as a place) carefully or thoroughly in an effort to find or discover something ⟨I've been *dredging* my memory bank, and I simply can't remember her name.⟩ — see SEARCH 1

dredge (up) *vb* to come upon after searching, study, or effort ⟨I might be able to *dredge up* some old baby clothes to donate.⟩ — see FIND 1

dregs *pl n* matter that settles to the bottom of a body of liquid ⟨poured the *dregs* into the sink⟩ — see DEPOSIT 1

drench *vb* **1** to make wet ⟨We were *drenched* by the sudden rainstorm.⟩ — see WET

2 to wet thoroughly with liquid ⟨When using the carpet shampooer, wet but do not *drench* the carpet.⟩ — see SOAK 1

drenched *adj* containing, covered with, or thoroughly penetrated by water ⟨The *drenched* tourists straggled into the visitors' center.⟩ — see WET 1

dress *adj* relating to or suitable for wearing to an event requiring elegant dress and manners ⟨The naval commander wore his *dress* uniform to the ball.⟩

synonyms dressy, formal

related words costume, costumey; chic, dapper, fashionable, in, modish, natty, sharp, smart, snappy, stylish; custom-made, fitted, tailored; black-tie, evening, white-tie; semiformal

near antonyms street; dowdy, outmoded, styleless, unfashionable, unstylish; frowsy (*or* frowzy), grungy,

sloppy, sloven, slovenly, unkempt, untidy; disheveled (*or* dishevelled), messy, mussy, rumpled, wrinkled

antonyms casual, informal, sportif, sporty

dress *n* **1** a garment with a joined blouse and skirt usually worn by a woman or girl ⟨What a lovely *dress* you're wearing today!⟩

synonyms frock, gown

related words chemise, coatdress, granny dress, housedress, jumper, kimono, kirtle, minidress, Mother Hubbard, muumuu, overdress, sack, sheath, shift, shirtdress, shirtwaist, sundress, sweaterdress, tea gown

2 clothing chosen as appropriate for a specific situation ⟨a bagpiper in full Scottish Highlander *dress*⟩ — see OUTFIT 1

3 covering for the human body ⟨a businessman who is very conservative in his *dress*⟩ — see CLOTHING

4 the outward form of someone or something especially as indicative of a quality ⟨another version of the Cinderella story but in modern-romance *dress*⟩ — see APPEARANCE 1

dress *vb* **1** to cover with a bandage ⟨First wash and then *dress* the wound.⟩ — see BANDAGE

2 to make more attractive by adding something that is beautiful or becoming ⟨Let's *dress* up the room with some greenery for the holiday party.⟩ — see DECORATE

3 to make smooth or glossy usually by repeatedly applying surface pressure ⟨*Dress* the granite block to be used as the headstone on all four sides.⟩ — see POLISH 1

4 to outfit with clothes and especially fine or special clothes ⟨*dressed* the young girl in satin and lace⟩ — see CLOTHE 1

5 to put on one's best or formal clothes ⟨We don't usually *dress* for dinner.⟩ — see DRESS UP 1

6 to look after or assist the growth of by labor and care ⟨*Dress* the beans by applying fertilizer once a week.⟩ — see GROW 1

dress down *vb* to criticize (someone) severely or angrily especially for personal failings ⟨*dressed down* for boorish behavior at the dance⟩ — see SCOLD

dressing *n* **1** a medicated covering used to heal an injury ⟨Nurses put a *dressing* over his cuts so they wouldn't get infected.⟩

synonyms plaster, poultice

related words cream, liniment, lotion, ointment, unguent

2 a savory fluid food used as a topping or accompaniment to a main dish ⟨tangy salad *dressing*⟩ — see SAUCE 1

dress up *vb* **1** to put on one's best or formal clothes ⟨We always like to *dress up* when going to parties.⟩

synonyms doll up, dress

related words preen, primp, prink, smarten (up); accessorize; apparel, array, attire, bedeck, bedizen, caparison, clothe, costume, deck, dude (up), garb, garment, invest, rig (out), robe, suit, tog (out *or* up)

2 to change the dress or looks of so as to conceal true identity ⟨*dressed up* store bought pound cake with fresh fruit and whipped cream⟩ — see DISGUISE 1

3 to outfit with clothes and especially fine or special clothes ⟨The girls were *dressed up* in skirts or dresses.⟩ — see CLOTHE 1

dressy *adj* relating to or suitable for wearing to an event requiring elegant dress and manners ⟨shopping for a *dressy* handbag for a New Year's Eve party⟩ — see DRESS

dribble *n* a very small piece ⟨Donations were coming in *dribbles*.⟩ — see BIT 1

dribble *vb* **1** to fall or let fall in or as if in drops ⟨water *dribbling* over the lip of the fountain⟩ — see DRIP

2 to flow in a broken irregular stream ⟨Rainwater *dribbling* along the partially clogged gutter.⟩ — see GURGLE

3 to let saliva or some other substance flow from the mouth ⟨The baby *dribbled* all down her bib.⟩ — see DROOL 1

driblet *n* **1** a very small amount ⟨money doled out in *driblets* to the workers⟩ — see PARTICLE 1

2 the quantity of fluid that falls naturally in one rounded mass ⟨Rain leaked through the roof in solitary *driblets* here and there.⟩ — see DROP 1

drift *n* **1** a pile or ridge of granular matter (as sand or snow) ⟨Deep *drifts* of snow blocked our driveway.⟩ — see ²BANK

2 a prevailing or general movement or inclination ⟨the steady *drift* of the population away from large cities⟩ — see TREND 1

3 the idea that is conveyed or intended to be conveyed to the mind by language, symbol, or action ⟨You should expect a visit from someone you know well, if you get my *drift*.⟩ — see MEANING 1

drift *vb* **1** to move or proceed smoothly and readily ⟨casual conversation *drifting* from one topic to another⟩ — see FLOW 2

2 to rest or move along the surface of a liquid or in the air ⟨The boat *drifted* along on the current.⟩ — see FLOAT 1

3 to move about from place to place aimlessly ⟨spent several years *drifting* from town to town, picking up odd jobs whenever he needed cash⟩ — see WANDER 1

drifter *n* a person who roams about without a fixed route or destination ⟨The *drifter* just packed up and moved on to the next town.⟩ — see NOMAD

drill *n* **1** an established and often automatic or monotonous series of actions followed when engaging in some activity ⟨Shuttling the kids between extracurricular activities is all part of the suburban *drill*.⟩ — see ROUTINE 1

2 something done over and over in order to develop skill ⟨doing vocabulary *drills* all afternoon in preparation for the test⟩ — see EXERCISE 2

¹**drill** *vb* **1** to make a hole or series of holes in ⟨the nerve-jangling sound when a dentist *drills* a tooth⟩ — see PERFORATE

2 to strike with a missile from a gun ⟨*drilled* the target from 100 yards away⟩ — see SHOOT 3

²**drill** *vb* to put or set into the ground to grow ⟨He *drills* soybeans in the same rows with corn.⟩ — see PLANT 1

drink *n* **1** a liquid suitable for drinking ⟨We went inside to have a *drink* after mowing the lawn.⟩

synonyms beverage, drinkable, libation, potable, quencher

related words potion; pop, soda, soda pop, soft drink; nectar; alcohol, brew, intoxicant, liquor, spirits; mix, mixer

2 the portion of a serving of a beverage that is swallowed at one time ⟨The thirsty soldier took a long *drink* from his canteen.⟩

synonyms belt, draft, drag, gulp, nip, quaff, shot, sip, slug, snort, sup, swallow, swig, swill

related words drop

3 a distilled beverage that can make a person drunk ⟨You have to be at least 21 to get a *drink*.⟩ — see ALCOHOL

drink *vb* **1** to swallow in liquid form ⟨The doctor wants her to *drink* lots of water before the examination.⟩

synonyms gulp, guzzle, hoist, imbibe, quaff, sip, slurp, sup, swig, swill, toss (down *or* off)

related words lap, lick, suck; consume, down, kill, mouth (down); nip, tipple; pledge, toast, wine

2 to partake excessively of alcoholic beverages ⟨It's illegal to *drink* and drive.⟩

synonyms guzzle

related words carouse, revel; imbibe, nip

near antonyms abstain

3 to take in (something liquid) through small openings ⟨The hot surface of the porous rock *drank* water like a sponge.⟩ — see ABSORB 1

drinkable *adj* suitable for drinking ⟨had to boil the water to make it *drinkable*⟩ — see POTABLE

drinkable *n* a liquid suitable for drinking ⟨The thoughtful hostess offered her guests an assortment of *drinkables*.⟩ — see DRINK 1

drip *n* **1** someone or something boring ⟨He's well-meaning, but kind of a *drip*.⟩ — see DRAG 1

2 the quantity of fluid that falls naturally in one rounded mass ⟨The faucet leaked one *drip* after another no matter what I did to try to fix it.⟩ — see DROP 1

drip *vb* to fall or let fall in or as if in drops ⟨Water from the leaky roof was *dripping* all over the floor.⟩

synonyms distill (*also* distil), dribble, drop, trickle

related words drizzle, sprinkle; flow, pour, roll, run, stream; cascade, gutter, ripple; bleed, exude, ooze, seep, weep; discharge

near antonyms gush, spout, spurt

dripping *adj* containing, covered with, or thoroughly penetrated by water ⟨*dripping* shoes left on the porch to dry⟩ — see WET 1

drive *n* **1** a passage cleared for public vehicular travel ⟨raced our motorcycles along the *drive*⟩ — see WAY 1

2 a series of activities undertaken to achieve a goal ⟨a fund-raising *drive* for the school's marching band⟩ — see CAMPAIGN

3 a strong wish for something ⟨a *drive* to succeed in the television news business⟩ — see DESIRE 1

4 active strength of body or mind ⟨Senior citizens who exercise regularly are more likely to have the *drive* to keep up with their grandchildren.⟩ — see VIGOR 1

5 readiness to engage in daring or difficult activity ⟨a great opportunity for a sales representative who is full of *drive*⟩ — see ENTERPRISE 2

drive *vb* **1** to urge, push, or force onward ⟨Cowboys *drove* the herd of cattle from San Antonio to San Francisco.⟩

synonyms herd, punch, run

related words shepherd; wrangle; exhort, flog, goad, hound, press, prick, prod, prompt, scourge, spur, whip

2 to travel by a motorized vehicle ⟨I'm going to *drive* across the country—want to come?⟩

synonyms automobile, motor, tool

related words roll, wheel; joyride; chauffeur, hack, taxi; ride; drag, race

3 to apply force to (someone or something) so that it moves in front of one ⟨*drove* the plunger into the opening⟩ — see PUSH 1

4 to cause (a person) to give in to pressure ⟨The corrupt governor was *driven* out of office.⟩ — see FORCE

5 to cause to function ⟨machinery *driven* by waterpower⟩ — see ACTIVATE

6 to set or keep in motion ⟨This motor *drives* the gears, which then turn the shaft.⟩ — see MOVE 2

7 to proceed or move quickly ⟨The runner *drove* past the finish line and then came to a dead stop.⟩ — see HURRY 2

drivel *n* **1** language, behavior, or ideas that are absurd and contrary to good sense ⟨I'm not going to waste my time reading this *drivel*.⟩ — see NONSENSE 1

2 unintelligible or meaningless talk ⟨My roommate talks in her sleep, but it's just *drivel*.⟩ — see GIBBERISH 1

drivel *vb* **1** to let saliva or some other substance flow from the mouth ⟨The panting dog *driveled* on my hand.⟩ — see DROOL 1

2 to speak rapidly, inarticulately, and usually unintelligibly ⟨What's he *driveling* about now?⟩ — see BABBLE 1

driver *n* a person who travels by automobile ⟨Fans arriving by public transportation will find the south entrance most convenient, but *drivers* will have a choice of entrances.⟩ — see MOTORIST

drizzle *n* a light or fine rain ⟨The intermittent *drizzle* was just heavy enough to spoil all of our outdoor activities.⟩
synonyms mist, sprinkle
related words precipitation, rainfall, shower
near antonyms cloudburst, deluge, downpour, storm; rainstorm, thunderstorm; monsoon

droll *adj* causing or intended to cause laughter ⟨told a *droll* story to keep us entertained⟩ — see FUNNY 1

droll *n* a person (as a writer) noted for or specializing in humor ⟨the *drolls* of late-night TV talk shows⟩ — see HUMORIST

drollness *n* the amusing quality or element in something ⟨the *drollness* of the speaker's approach to a touchy subject⟩ — see HUMOR 1

¹**drone** *n* a lazy person ⟨Those *drones* just lie around while we do all the work.⟩ — see LAZYBONES

²**drone** *n* a monotonous sound like that of an insect in motion ⟨heard the *drone* of an airplane overhead⟩ — see HUM

drone *vb* to fly, turn, or move rapidly with a fluttering or vibratory sound ⟨the sound of *droning* bees all around us⟩ — see WHIR

drool *n* the fluid that is secreted into the mouth by certain glands ⟨The baby left a puddle of *drool* on my shirt.⟩ — see SALIVA

drool *vb* 1 to let saliva or some other substance flow from the mouth ⟨The dog *drooled* when we put the steak down on the floor.⟩
synonyms dribble, drivel, salivate, slaver, slobber
related words water; expectorate, spit; foam, froth, splutter; sputter
2 to make an exaggerated display of affection or enthusiasm ⟨financial advisors *drooling* over the new investment strategy⟩ — see GUSH 2
3 to speak rapidly, inarticulately, and usually unintelligibly ⟨Stop *drooling*, slow down, and take a deep breath, because I can't understand you.⟩ — see BABBLE 1

droop *n* the extent to which something hangs or dips below a straight line ⟨Tighten the line at the top of the banner so there won't be so much *droop*.⟩ — see SAG

droop *vb* 1 to be limp from lack of water or vigor ⟨The flowers *drooped* on their stalks in the blazing sun.⟩
synonyms flag, hang, loll, sag, wilt
related words slouch, slump; cave (in), collapse, crumple, drop, fall, sink, subside, yield
near antonyms distend; rise, straighten, unbend, uncurl
2 to lose bodily strength or vigor ⟨As the afternoon wore on, we started to *droop*.⟩ — see WEAKEN 2

drooping *adj* bending downward or forward ⟨faded, *drooping* banners lining the walls of the old gym⟩ — see NODDING

droopy *adj* 1 bending downward or forward ⟨the *droopy* heads of tired fans riding home on the bus⟩ — see NODDING
2 not stiff in structure ⟨a *droopy* stalk of celery⟩ — see LIMP 1
3 feeling unhappiness ⟨looking *droopy* and miserable while standing in the pouring rain⟩ — see SAD 1

drop *n* 1 the quantity of fluid that falls naturally in one rounded mass ⟨A *drop* of water fell from the leaky faucet every few seconds.⟩
synonyms blob, driblet, drip, droplet, glob, globule
related words gobbet; dewdrop, raindrop, tear, teardrop; spatter; dribble, trickle
2 distance measured from the top to the bottom of something ⟨a *drop* of 10 feet from the roof to the ground⟩ — see DEPTH 1

3 the act or process of going to a lower level or altitude ⟨The sudden *drop* of the plane really shook up the passengers.⟩ — see DESCENT 1
4 the amount by which something is lessened ⟨a huge *drop* in pressure⟩ — see DECREASE
5 the more favorable condition or position in a competition ⟨got the *drop* on his opponent very early in the wrestling match⟩ — see ADVANTAGE 1

drop *vb* 1 to cause to fall intentionally or unintentionally ⟨I *dropped* the fly ball.⟩ ⟨*Drop* the anchor.⟩
synonyms depress, lower, throw
related words flatten, floor, level; knock down, topple; plop, plunk down; bobble, bungle, foozle, fumble; immerse, sink, submerge
antonyms lift, pick up, raise
2 to go to a lower level especially abruptly ⟨Although they start out high, prices for home electronics eventually *drop*.⟩
synonyms crash, decline, descend, dip, dive, fall, lower, nose-dive, plummet, plunge, sink, tumble
related words abate, decrease, de-escalate, die (down), diminish, droop, dwindle, ebb, lessen, let up, moderate, subside, taper off, wane; recede, retreat
near antonyms accumulate, balloon, build, burgeon (*also* bourgeon), enlarge, escalate, expand, grow, increase, intensify, mushroom, pick up, snowball, swell, wax
antonyms arise, ascend, lift, mount, rise, soar, spike, up
3 to bring (as an action or operation) to an immediate end ⟨*Drop* what you're doing and come here.⟩ — see STOP 1
4 to stop doing (something) permanently ⟨I *dropped* my calculus class and took biology instead.⟩ — see QUIT 2
5 to lead or extend downward ⟨The roller coaster tracks *drop* suddenly, so get ready.⟩ — see DESCEND 1
6 to put an end to (something planned or previously agreed to) ⟨*dropped* that plan in favor of another⟩ — see CANCEL 1
7 to bring forth from the womb ⟨The cow *dropped* her calf early this morning.⟩ — see BEAR 1
8 to strike (someone) so forcefully as to cause a fall ⟨The boxer *dropped* his opponent with a single well-aimed blow.⟩ — see FELL 1
9 to fail to win, gain, or obtain ⟨The local hockey team has *dropped* two out of the last three contests.⟩ — see LOSE 2
10 to fall or let fall in or as if in drops ⟨The cold glass *dropped* condensation.⟩ — see DRIP
11 to hand over or use up in payment ⟨I *dropped* $50 on these shoes.⟩ — see SPEND 1
12 to make reference to or speak about briefly but specifically ⟨He would ever so "casually" *drop* the names of celebrities he knew personally.⟩ — see MENTION 1
13 to make smaller in amount, volume, or extent ⟨With these icy road conditions, drivers should be *dropping* their speed.⟩ — see DECREASE 1
14 to stop living ⟨During the Black Death people all over Asia and Europe were *dropping* like flies.⟩ — see DIE 1

droplet *n* the quantity of fluid that falls naturally in one rounded mass ⟨There were only a few *droplets* left in the canteen.⟩ — see DROP 1

dropping *n* 1 droppings *pl* solid matter discharged from an animal's alimentary canal ⟨The only bad part about owning a rabbit was cleaning the *droppings* out of the litter box every night.⟩
synonyms dirt, dung, excrement, excreta, feces, slops, waste
related words night soil, stool; dunghill, guano, manure, midden, muck; spoor; sewage, sewerage; coprolite

2 the act of putting an end to something planned or previously agreed to ⟨The *dropping* of an act from the talent show should bring it to an end on time.⟩ — see CANCELLATION

dross *n* discarded or useless material ⟨got rid of the *dross* before closing up the shop⟩ — see GARBAGE

droughty *adj* marked by little or no precipitation or humidity ⟨a *droughty* region that could never support settlements⟩ — see DRY 1

drove *n* **1** a great number of persons or creatures massed together ⟨People flocked to the annual festival in *droves*.⟩ — see CROWD 1
2 a group of domestic animals assembled or herded together ⟨a *drove* of cattle⟩ — see HERD 1

drown *vb* **1** to cover with a flood ⟨whole villages *drowned* by the overflowing river⟩ — see FLOOD
2 to wet thoroughly with liquid ⟨She *drowned* the carpet with shampoo, and so it took forever to dry.⟩ — see SOAK 1
3 to make wet ⟨cooked pasta *drowned* in marinara sauce⟩ — see WET

drowse *n* a short sleep ⟨I was just falling into a *drowse* when you called.⟩ — see ¹NAP

drowse *vb* to sleep lightly or briefly ⟨picnickers *drowsing* in the shade of an oak tree⟩ — see NAP 1

drowsiness *n* the quality or state of desiring or needing sleep ⟨We tried to fight our *drowsiness* but fell asleep anyway.⟩ — see SLEEPINESS

drowsy *adj* **1** desiring or needing sleep ⟨The *drowsy* students shuffled into the first-period class.⟩ — see SLEEPY 1
2 tending to cause sleep ⟨listened to *drowsy* music while waiting in the dentist's office⟩ — see HYPNOTIC

drub *vb* **1** to strike repeatedly ⟨The old lady was *drubbing* the would-be purse snatcher when the police arrived on the scene.⟩ — see BEAT 1
2 to defeat by a large margin ⟨We *drubbed* our traditional football rivals.⟩ — see WHIP 2

drubbing *n* failure to win a contest ⟨We took a terrible *drubbing* in last night's basketball game.⟩ — see DEFEAT 1

drudge *n* a person who does very hard or dull work ⟨worked like a *drudge* at a low-paying job that had few benefits⟩
synonyms drudger, grub, grubber, grunt, laborer, peon, plugger, slogger, toiler, worker
related words workhorse; serf
near antonyms shirker; drone, idler, lazybones, loafer, slouch, slug, sluggard

drudge *vb* to devote serious and sustained effort ⟨factory workers who must *drudge* all day at repetitive tasks⟩ — see LABOR

drudger *n* a person who does very hard or dull work ⟨a youth striving to become something more than just a *drudger* working at some dead-end job⟩ — see DRUDGE

drudgery *n* very hard or unpleasant work ⟨Cleaning up the little cabin was *drudgery*, but we enjoyed using it all summer.⟩ — see TOIL

drug *n* a substance or preparation used to treat disease ⟨prescribed a *drug* to treat the bacterial infection⟩ — see MEDICINE

druggist *n* a person who prepares drugs according to a doctor's prescription ⟨She got her prescription for antibiotics filled by the *druggist*.⟩
synonyms apothecary, pharmacist
related words pharmacologist

drugstore *n* a retail store where medicines and miscellaneous articles are sold ⟨We picked up her medicine and some toothpaste at the *drugstore*.⟩
synonyms apothecary, pharmacy
related words dispensary; sick bay

drum *n* a metal container in the shape of a cylinder ⟨an oil *drum*⟩ — see CAN 1

drum *vb* to strike or cause to strike lightly and usually rhythmically ⟨absentmindedly *drumming* his fingers on the table⟩ — see ¹TAP

drum (out) *vb* to drive or force out ⟨*drummed out* of the service for conduct unbecoming an officer⟩ — see EJECT 1

drunk *adj* being under the influence of alcohol ⟨a wedding guest who got a little *drunk*⟩
synonyms drunken, inebriate, inebriated, intoxicated
related words bleary-eyed; debauched, dissipated, dissolute; alcoholic, bibulous
near antonyms abstemious, abstinent, dry, temperate, teetotal; clearheaded, cool, level, steady
antonyms sober, straight

drunk *n* a person who makes a habit of getting drunk ⟨got a reputation as a *drunk*⟩
synonyms alcoholic, drunkard, inebriate
near antonyms teetotalist

drunkard *n* a person who makes a habit of getting drunk ⟨In Mark Twain's classic novel, Huck Finn's father is a *drunkard*.⟩ — see DRUNK

drunken *adj* being under the influence of alcohol ⟨*drunken* revelers taking taxis home instead of driving⟩ — see DRUNK

dry *adj* **1** marked by little or no precipitation or humidity ⟨the *dry* climate of the American Southwest⟩
synonyms arid, droughty, sere (*also* sear), thirsty, waterless
related words air-dry; bone-dry, hyperarid, ultradry; baked, dehydrated, parched, sunbaked; rainless; desert
near antonyms awash, bathed, doused (*also* dowsed), drenched, dripping, saturated, soaked, soaking, sodden, soggy, sopping, soppy, soused, washed, watered, waterlogged, watery; deluged, drowned, flooded, inundated, overflowed; submerged, swamped; hydrated
antonyms damp, dank, humid, moist, wet
2 causing weariness, restlessness, or lack of interest ⟨a very *dry* topic for a lecture at a museum of natural history⟩ — see BORING
3 having or showing a lack of friendliness or interest in others ⟨a *dry* temperament that suited him well in a desk job that required no interaction with the customers⟩ — see COOL 1

dry *vb* **1** to make dry ⟨The wind quickly *dried* their clothes.⟩
synonyms dehydrate, parch, scorch, sear
related words dehumidify; drain; evaporate; mummify, shrivel, wither, wizen; air-dry, bake
near antonyms bathe, deluge, douse (*also* dowse), drench, drown, flood, inundate, overflow, saturate, soak, sop, souse; damp, dampen, humidify, moisten; rehydrate; dip, dunk, submerge, swamp
antonyms hydrate, wash, water, wet
2 to lose liveliness, force, or freshness ⟨His creative talents were just *drying* on the vine in that small, provincial town.⟩ — see WITHER 1

dryad *n* a mythical goddess represented as a young woman and said to live outdoors ⟨*Dryads* were said to live within trees, their lives ending when the life of the tree ended.⟩ — see NYMPH

dry run *n* a private performance or session in preparation for a public appearance ⟨We had time for just one *dry run* of the play before opening night.⟩ — see REHEARSAL

dual *adj* consisting of two members or parts that are usually joined ⟨*dual* axles⟩ — see DOUBLE 1

dub *vb* **1** to give a name to ⟨I've *dubbed* my car "Rusty," which pretty much describes it.⟩ — see NAME 1
2 to make or do (something) in a clumsy or unskillful

way ⟨He *dubbed* his first attempt at homemade yogurt, but he got it reasonably right on the second.⟩ — see BOTCH

dubious *adj* **1** giving good reason for being doubted, questioned, or challenged ⟨Any letter bearing the signature of Sherlock Holmes would be of *dubious* authenticity, to say the least.⟩ — see DOUBTFUL 2
2 slow to begin or proceed with a course of action because of doubts or uncertainty ⟨I'm *dubious* about our plan to go hang gliding without having had any training.⟩ — see HESITANT
3 not likely to be true or to occur ⟨made the *dubious* claim of being of royal blood⟩ — see IMPROBABLE
4 not feeling sure about the truth, wisdom, or trustworthiness of someone or something ⟨I'm *dubious* about a diet that claims I can eat all I want and still lose weight.⟩ — see DOUBTFUL 1

dubiously *adv* with distrust ⟨The young girl approached the camel *dubiously*.⟩ — see ASKANCE

duck *n* a member of the human race ⟨Her coworkers regard her as something of an odd *duck*.⟩ — see HUMAN

duck *vb* **1** to get or keep away from (as a responsibility) through cleverness or trickery ⟨They managed to *duck* the issue.⟩ — see ESCAPE 2
2 to move suddenly aside or to and fro ⟨*Duck* behind a pillar before they see us!⟩ — see DODGE 1
3 to sink or push (something) briefly into or as if into a liquid ⟨*ducked* his head underwater⟩ — see DIP 1

ducking *n* the act or a means of getting or keeping away from something undesirable ⟨the *ducking* of a difficult question⟩ — see ESCAPE 2

duck soup *n* something that is easy to do ⟨Hooking up this home theater should be *duck soup*—right?⟩ — see CINCH

duct *n* a long hollow cylinder for carrying a substance (as a liquid or gas) ⟨air *ducts* to provide ventilation⟩ — see PIPE 1

dud *n* **1** something that has failed ⟨Our first attempt was a complete *dud*, so we had to start over.⟩ — see FAILURE 3
2 duds *pl* covering for the human body ⟨Those are some pretty fancy *duds* you're wearing.⟩ — see CLOTHING
3 duds *pl* transportable items that one owns ⟨You have one hour to pack up your *duds* and clear out of here.⟩ — see POSSESSION 2

dude *n* **1** a man extremely interested in his clothing and personal appearance ⟨a *dude* given to sporting expensive suits and flashy jewelry⟩ — see DANDY 1
2 an adult male human being ⟨OK, *dude*, whatever you say!⟩ — see MAN 1

dudgeon *n* the feeling of being offended or resentful after a slight or indignity ⟨stomped off in high *dudgeon* after having his honor questioned⟩ — see PIQUE

due *adj* **1** having reached the date at which payment is required ⟨The loan is *due* next April.⟩
synonyms mature
related words delinquent, outstanding, overdue, owed, owing, receivable, unpaid, unsettled; payable
near antonyms cleared, liquidated, paid (off *or* up), repaid, settled; prepaid
antonyms undue
2 being in accordance with the prescribed, normal, or logical course of events ⟨Their train is *due* to arrive in half an hour.⟩
synonyms anticipated, awaited, expected, scheduled, slated
near antonyms behind, behindhand, belated, delinquent, dilatory, late, latish, overdue, tardy; early, premature, untimely; unanticipated, unforeseen, unlooked-for
3 being what is called for by accepted standards of right

and wrong ⟨All the participants in the trial are required to treat the judge with *due* respect.⟩ — see JUST 1

due *adv* **1** as stated or indicated without the slightest difference ⟨The island lies *due* south of the headland.⟩ — see EXACTLY 1
2 in a direct line or course ⟨a plane flying *due* east⟩ — see DIRECTLY 1

due (to) *adj* coming as a result ⟨success that is *due to* hard work⟩ — see RESULTANT

duel *n* an earnest effort for superiority or victory over another ⟨a *duel* for the title of captain of the team⟩ — see CONTEST 1

due to *prep* as the result of ⟨Evening classes were cancelled *due to* heavy snow.⟩ — see BECAUSE OF

dull *adj* **1** lacking sharpness of edge or point ⟨The *dull* knife just bounced off the skin of the tomato without cutting it.⟩
synonyms blunt, blunted, dulled, obtuse
related words dullish; rounded, smooth; even, flat, flattened, level
near antonyms jagged, needlelike, prickly, spiked, spikelike, spiky (*also* spikey); spiny; jabbing, lacerating, piercing, scratching, stabbing; ultrasharp
antonyms cutting, edged, edgy, ground, honed, keen, pointed, sharp, sharpened, whetted
2 causing weariness, restlessness, or lack of interest ⟨There's never a *dull* moment around here!⟩ — see BORING
3 covered over by clouds ⟨*Dull* skies plagued most of our vacation days at the beach.⟩ — see OVERCAST
4 lacking a surface luster or gloss ⟨A good polish should restore that car's *dull* finish.⟩ — see MATTE
5 lacking intensity of color ⟨That canvas shirt should fade to an attractive, *dull* red over time.⟩ — see PALE 1
6 not having or showing an ability to absorb ideas readily ⟨not a single *dull* student in the class⟩ — see STUPID 1
7 not loud in pitch or volume ⟨a *dull* roar from the distance⟩ — see SOFT 1
8 slow to move or act ⟨a *dull* market for luxury goods this holiday season⟩ — see INACTIVE 1

dull *vb* **1** to reduce or weaken in strength or feeling ⟨The aspirin *dulled* his headache and he was soon feeling better.⟩
synonyms benumb, blunt, damp, dampen, deaden, numb
related words muffle, mute, tone (down); decrease, diminish, lessen, let up (on), lower, reduce, subdue; debilitate, enfeeble, weaken; dwindle, recede, subside, taper (off), wane; alleviate, ease, lighten; abate, moderate
near antonyms amplify, augment, beef (up), boost, consolidate, deepen, enhance, heighten, intensify, magnify, redouble, step up, strengthen; animate, arouse, stimulate
antonyms sharpen, whet
2 to make white or whiter by removing color ⟨The painting's once-vivid colors have been *dulled* by time.⟩ — see WHITEN

dulled *adj* **1** lacking a surface luster or gloss ⟨It might be best to paint the exposed pipes with a *dulled* enamel.⟩ — see MATTE
2 lacking intensity of color ⟨The *dulled* colors and brownish tones are characteristic of this painter's works.⟩ — see PALE 1
3 lacking sharpness of edge or point ⟨the *dulled* blade of a knife that had been stored in a drawer full of miscellaneous utensils⟩ — see DULL 1

dullness *also* **dulness** *n* the quality or state of lacking intelligence or quickness of mind ⟨the *dullness* of the characters in the movie⟩ — see STUPIDITY 1

dumb *adj* **1** deliberately refraining from speech ⟨The mayor has chosen to remain *dumb* about her position on the matter.⟩ — see SILENT 1

2 not having or showing an ability to absorb ideas readily ⟨I'm not *dumb* enough to believe that.⟩ — see STUPID 1

3 tending not to speak frequently (as by habit or inclination) ⟨He prefers to remain *dumb*, and replies in monosyllables if really pressed.⟩ — see SILENT 2

dumbbell *n* a stupid person ⟨I feel like a *dumbbell* for making such a careless mistake.⟩ — see IDIOT

dumbfound *also* **dumfound** *vb* to make a strong impression on (someone) with something unexpected ⟨The surprise ending will *dumbfound* even the most seasoned mystery reader.⟩ — see SURPRISE 1

dumbfounded *also* **dumfounded** *adj* **1** affected with sudden and great wonder or surprise ⟨*dumbfounded* by the realization that he had just won the grand prize in the multistate lottery⟩ — see THUNDERSTRUCK

2 filled with amazement or wonder ⟨*dumbfounded* visitors to the Grand Canyon⟩ — see OPENMOUTHED

dumbfounding *also* **dumfounding** *adj* causing a strong emotional reaction because of unexpectedness ⟨the *dumbfounding* sight of the race car driver walking away from that horrific crash⟩ — see SURPRISING 1

dumbness *n* **1** incapacity for or restraint from speaking ⟨the determined *dumbness* of the accountants who tally the votes for the Academy Awards⟩ — see SILENCE 1

2 the quality or state of lacking intelligence or quickness of mind ⟨The movie's *dumbness* is actually what makes it funny.⟩ — see STUPIDITY 1

dummy *adj* being such in appearance only and made with or manufactured from usually cheaper materials ⟨The *dummy* shutters on the house are actually made of vinyl and are for decoration only.⟩ — see IMITATION

dummy *n* **1** a stupid person ⟨She's in love with you, you *dummy*.⟩ — see IDIOT

2 a three-dimensional representation of the human body used especially for displaying clothes ⟨The *dummies* were arranged in the store window as if they were acting out scenes.⟩ — see MANNEQUIN 1

3 something that is made to look exactly like something else ⟨For the movie, the props department made a *dummy* of the spacecraft used in the actual mission.⟩ — see COPY

dump *n* **1** a place where discarded materials (as trash) are dumped ⟨All of the used packaging eventually ends up in the *dump*.⟩

synonyms landfill, sanitary landfill

related words dustbin, dustheap, junkyard, kitchen midden, midden; transfer station; mess, pigpen, pigsty, sty

2 a place where military arms are stored ⟨a daring raid on the ammunition *dump*⟩ — see ARMORY

3 a dirty or messy place ⟨I'm sorry the place is such a *dump*.⟩ — see PIGPEN

dump *vb* **1** to end a usually intimate relationship with ⟨I can't believe you got *dumped*.⟩ — see DITCH 1

2 to get rid of as useless or unwanted ⟨Just *dump* the trash on the curb and go back inside.⟩ — see DISCARD

dumping *n* the getting rid of whatever is unwanted or useless ⟨the *dumping* of last year's fashions by the garment manufacturers⟩ — see DISPOSAL 1

dumps *pl n* a state or spell of low spirits ⟨I've been down in the *dumps* all week.⟩ — see SADNESS

dumpy *adj* **1** being compact and broad in build and often short in stature ⟨clothing for *dumpy* physiques⟩ — see STOCKY

2 showing signs of advanced wear and tear and neglect ⟨We could only find rooms at a *dumpy* motel on the outskirts of the city.⟩ — see SHABBY

dun *n* something that someone insists upon having ⟨It's

probably not a good idea to ignore a loan shark's *dun* for repayment.⟩ — see DEMAND 1

dunce *n* a stupid person ⟨He's here on scholarship, so he's no *dunce*.⟩ — see IDIOT

dung *n* solid matter discharged from an animal's alimentary canal ⟨Researchers tracked the wild gorillas by following the piles of *dung*.⟩ — see DROPPING 1

dunk *vb* to sink or push (something) briefly into or as if into a liquid ⟨*dunking* a cookie in milk⟩ — see DIP 1

duo *n* two things of the same or similar kind that match or are considered together ⟨The shy boy and his outgoing friend make an unlikely *duo*.⟩ — see PAIR

¹**dupe** *n* one who is easily deceived or cheated ⟨The swindler was able to escape with all of the *dupe's* money.⟩

synonyms chump, gull, pigeon, pushover, sap, sucker, tool

related words mark, target, victim; butt, derision, laughingstock, mock, mockery; booby, dodo, fool, goose, halfwit, jackass, monkey, nincompoop, ninny, nitwit, simp, simpleton, turkey, yo-yo; loser; blockhead, dolt, dope, dumbbell, dummy, dunce, idiot, imbecile, moron

near antonyms cheat, cheater, cozener, defrauder, dodger, hoaxer, shark, sharper, slicker, swindler, trickster

²**dupe** *n* something that is made to look exactly like something else ⟨He built a *dupe* of the original model, which is locked in a vault.⟩ — see COPY

dupe *vb* to cause to believe what is untrue ⟨We were *duped* into thinking the dummy was a real alien.⟩ — see DECEIVE

duplex *adj* consisting of two members or parts that are usually joined ⟨a *duplex* apartment with all of the bedrooms on the second floor⟩ — see DOUBLE 1

duplicate *adj* resembling another in every respect ⟨*duplicate* copies of the portrait that were painted by the artist himself⟩ — see SAME 1

duplicate *n* **1** something or someone that strongly resembles another ⟨doll carriages that are *duplicates* of baby carriages⟩ — see IMAGE 1

2 something that is made to look exactly like something else ⟨a *duplicate* of a house key⟩ — see COPY

duplicate *vb* **1** to make an exact likeness of ⟨art students trying to *duplicate* paintings in the museum's collection as part of their training⟩ — see COPY 1

2 to make or do again ⟨We were unable to *duplicate* the experiment in our own lab.⟩ — see REPEAT 4

3 to make twice as great or as many ⟨The recipe can be easily *duplicated* in order to feed a large family.⟩ — see DOUBLE 1

duplication *n* **1** something or someone that strongly resembles another ⟨In adulthood he became sort of a living *duplication* of his late father.⟩ — see IMAGE 1

2 something that is made to look exactly like something else ⟨a *duplication* of an ancient Chinese vase for the mass market⟩ — see COPY

3 the act of saying or doing over again ⟨Let's avoid *duplication* of effort on this group project if we can.⟩ — see REPEAT

duplicity *n* the inclination or practice of misleading others through lies or trickery ⟨We were lucky not to be taken in by his *duplicity*.⟩ — see DECEIT 1

durability *n* uninterrupted or lasting existence ⟨the *durability* of the novel's popularity since it was first published in the 1930s⟩ — see CONTINUATION

duration *n* **1** the period during which something exists, lasts, or is in progress ⟨You should gradually increase the *duration* of your workout.⟩

synonyms continuance, date, life, life span, lifetime, run, standing, time

related words spell, stretch; span, tenure, term; hitch, tour, turn; half-life; age, longevity
2 uninterrupted or lasting existence ⟨scientists warning that the very *duration* of our civilization depends upon finding a solution to this major environmental problem⟩ — see CONTINUATION

duress *n* the use of power to impose one's will on another ⟨complied with the order only under *duress*⟩ — see FORCE 2

during *prep* in the course of ⟨We took notes *during* class.⟩
synonyms amid (*or* amidst), by, over, pending, through, throughout

dusk *adj* being without light or without much light ⟨Under a *dusk* sky, the campers wearily bedded down for the night.⟩ — see DARK 1

dusk *n* **1** the time from when the sun begins to set to the onset of total darkness ⟨We stopped playing at *dusk*, since it was getting too dark to see the ball.⟩
synonyms evening, eventide, gloaming, night, nightfall, sundown, sunset, twilight
related words dark, darkness, nighttime
near antonyms day, daytime, light; forenoon
antonyms dawn, dawning, daybreak, daylight, morn, morning, sunrise, sunup
2 a time or place of little or no light ⟨legends of fearsome beasts living in the *dusk* of the great forest⟩ — see DARK 1
3 partial darkness due to the obstruction of light rays ⟨the forbidding *dusk* of Germany's famed Black Forest⟩ — see SHADE 1

dusk *vb* to grow dark ⟨a *dusking* room⟩ — see DARKEN 2

dusky *adj* being without light or without much light ⟨in the *dusky* depths of the dungeon⟩ — see DARK 1

dust *n* **1** discarded or useless material ⟨the piles of *dust* that future archaeologists will sift through for insights into our civilization⟩ — see GARBAGE
2 the solid part of our planet's surface as distinguished from the sea and air ⟨dived for the ball and landed in the *dust*⟩ — see EARTH 2

dust *vb* to defeat by a large margin ⟨The inexperienced sprinter somehow *dusted* the field of veterans.⟩ — see WHIP 2

dustiness *n* the state or quality of being dirty ⟨We were glad for a shower after the *dustiness* of the hike.⟩ — see DIRTINESS

dusty *adj* **1** consisting of very small particles ⟨*dusty* soil⟩ — see FINE 1
2 not clean ⟨old *dusty* clothes⟩ — see DIRTY 1
3 causing weariness, restlessness, or lack of interest ⟨I almost fell asleep reading that *dusty* book of memoirs.⟩ — see BORING

dutiful *adj* marked by or showing proper regard for another's higher status ⟨The family took *dutiful* care of their ailing relative.⟩ — see RESPECTFUL

duty *n* **1** a charge usually of money collected by the government from people or businesses for public use ⟨The shop at the airport charges no *duty* on tourist memorabilia.⟩ — see TAX
2 a piece of work that needs to be done regularly ⟨the regular *duties* of a lifeguard⟩ — see CHORE 1

3 something one must do because of prior agreement ⟨I must obey the call of *duty* and serve my country.⟩ — see OBLIGATION 1

dwarf *n* **1** a living thing much smaller than others of its kind ⟨Shetland ponies are the *dwarfs* of the horse world.⟩
synonyms diminutive, midget, mite, peewee, pygmy (*also* pigmy), runt, scrub, shrimp
related words nubbin; mini, miniature; bantam; half-pint
near antonyms whale, whopper
antonyms behemoth, colossus, giant, jumbo, leviathan, mammoth, monster, titan
2 an imaginary being usually having a small human form and magical powers ⟨Snow White and the seven *dwarfs*⟩ — see FAIRY

dwarf *vb* to hold back the normal growth of ⟨shrubs *dwarfed* by the lack of water⟩ — see STUNT

dwarfish *adj* of a size that is less than average ⟨a *dwarfish* people living deep in the rain forest⟩ — see SMALL 1

dwell *vb* **1** to continue to be in a place for a significant amount of time ⟨*dwelling* with a farm family as an exchange student in France⟩ — see ¹STAY 1
2 to have a home ⟨The ancient Greek gods were believed to *dwell* on Mount Olympus.⟩ — see LIVE 1

dweller *n* one who lives permanently in a place ⟨the kinds of nuisances that city *dwellers* are all too familiar with⟩ — see INHABITANT

dwelling *n* the place where one lives ⟨the simple *dwellings* in which the Pilgrims spent the first winter at Plymouth⟩ — see HOME 1

dwindle *vb* **1** to make smaller in amount, volume, or extent ⟨The long winter *dwindled* our supply of firewood to practically nothing.⟩ — see DECREASE 1
2 to grow less in scope or intensity especially gradually ⟨As the work day goes on, my energy *dwindles*.⟩ — see DECREASE 2

dye *n* a substance used to color other materials ⟨soaked the fabric in blue *dye*⟩ — see PIGMENT

dye *vb* to give color or a different color to ⟨*dyed* her hair a startling red⟩ — see COLOR 1

dyestuff *n* a substance used to color other materials ⟨Indigo is a *dyestuff* originally from India.⟩ — see PIGMENT

dying *adj* nearly dead ⟨We watered the *dying* plants just in time.⟩ — see MORIBUND

dynamic *adj* **1** having active strength of body or mind ⟨a *dynamic* new challenger for the title of heavyweight champion⟩ — see VIGOROUS 1
2 marked by or uttered with forcefulness ⟨a *dynamic* speech expressing her party's goals and values⟩ — see EMPHATIC 1

dynamically *adv* in a vigorous and forceful manner ⟨presented her ideas so *dynamically* that the other committee members were instantly won over by her proposal⟩ — see HARD 3

dyspeptic *adj* having or showing a habitually bad temper ⟨As might be expected, the newspaper's resident curmudgeon took a *dyspeptic* view of the whole affair.⟩ — see ILL-TEMPERED

E

each *adj* being one of a group ⟨*Each* park visitor receives a free souvenir.⟩
 synonyms any, every
 related words all; several; particular; respective, specific
 phrases each and every
 near antonyms neither
each *adv* for each one ⟨raffle tickets selling for a dollar *each*⟩ — see APIECE
eager *adj* showing urgent desire or interest ⟨Tom was *eager* to try out his new pair of skis.⟩
 synonyms agog, anxious, ardent, athirst, avid, crazy, desirous, enthusiastic, excited, great, greedy, gung ho, hot, hungry, impatient, keen, nuts, raring, solicitous, thirsty, voracious, wild
 related words engaged, interested; happy, hung up, obsessed; ambitious, appetent, covetous, craving, hankering, longing, pining; breathless, restive, restless; amenable, disposed, game, glad, inclined, ready, unreluctant, willing
 phrases champing at the bit, chomping at the bit
 near antonyms casual, incurious, insouciant, nonchalant, unconcerned, uninterested; aloof, detached, disinterested; impassive, stolid; halfhearted, lackadaisical, languid, languorous, lukewarm, spiritless; averse, disinclined, hesitant, loath (*also* loth *or* loathe), reluctant, unwilling
 antonyms apathetic, indifferent, uneager, unenthusiastic
eagerness *n* urgent desire or interest ⟨students with an *eagerness* to learn⟩
 synonyms appetite, ardor, avidity, desirousness, enthusiasm, excitement, hunger, impatience, keenness, lust, thirst
 related words alacrity, quickness; ambition, zest; appetence, fervency, passion, warmth, zeal; amenability, readiness, willingness
 near antonyms casualness, insouciance, nonchalance, unconcern; aloofness, detachment; impassivity, languor; halfheartedness, lukewarmness
 antonyms apathy, indifference
ear *n* a state of being aware ⟨I'm trying to get the boss's *ear* in order to ask for a raise in my pay.⟩ — see ATTENTION 2
earliest *adj* coming before all others in time or order ⟨The *earliest* computers were massive machines that practically filled up a room.⟩ — see FIRST 1
early *adj* **1** relating to or occurring near the beginning of a process, series, or time period ⟨*early* birds of the Jurassic period⟩
 synonyms ancient, primal, primeval, primitive, primordial
 related words embryonic, germinal, infant; aged, age-old, antediluvian, antiquated, antique, dateless, hoary, old, prehistoric (*also* prehistorical); obsolete, outmoded, out-of-date, passé
 near antonyms advanced, complex, developed, evolved, high, higher; full-blown, full-fledged, full-scale
 antonyms late
 2 occurring before the usual or expected time ⟨We had an *early* dinner so as not to miss the concert.⟩
 synonyms inopportune, precocious, premature, unseasonable, untimely
 related words unanticipated, unexpected, unforeseen, unlooked-for; abrupt, sudden

 near antonyms behindhand, belated, delinquent, latish, overdue, slow, tardy; anticipated, expected; delayed, detained, postponed
 antonyms late
early *adv* before the usual or expected time ⟨That year spring arrived *early*.⟩
 synonyms beforehand, inopportunely, precociously, prematurely, unseasonably
 related words immediately, instantly, presently, promptly, pronto, punctually; apropos, betimes, seasonably
 antonyms late, tardily
earmark *vb* to keep or intend for a special purpose ⟨The earnings from my second job have been *earmarked* for a down payment on a car.⟩ — see DEVOTE 1
earn *vb* **1** to receive as return for effort ⟨I *earn* pocket money by mowing lawns.⟩
 synonyms acquire, attain, bag, capture, carry, come by, draw, gain, garner, get, knock down, land, make, obtain, procure, realize, reap, secure, win
 related words clear, gross, net; accomplish, achieve, notch (up), score; accumulate, amass, draw, rack up; catch, pick up; annex, occupy, take over; reacquire, reattain, recapture, regain, remake
 near antonyms accord, give, grant, pay; give up, hand over, part (with), relinquish, surrender, yield
 antonyms forfeit, lose
 2 to be or make worthy of (as a reward or punishment) ⟨You've *earned* the afternoon off after all that hard work.⟩
 synonyms deserve, merit, rate
 related words entitle, qualify
earnest *adj* not joking or playful in mood or manner ⟨I'll accept only an *earnest* apology from you.⟩ — see SERIOUS 1
earnest *n* a mental state free of jesting or trifling ⟨I am in deadly *earnest* about this marriage proposal.⟩ — see EARNESTNESS
earnestness *n* a mental state free of jesting or trifling ⟨practiced the art of acting with great *earnestness*⟩
 synonyms earnest, graveness, gravity, intentness, seriousness, soberness, sobriety, solemnity, staidness
 related words gravitas, humorlessness; decisiveness, deliberation, determination, firmness, purposefulness, resoluteness, resolve; absorption, attentiveness, concentration, engrossment, enthrallment, immersion, intensity
 near antonyms lightness, shallowness, superficiality; dalliance; cheerfulness, gaiety (*also* gayety), glee, high-spiritedness, merriment, mirth
 antonyms facetiousness, flightiness, flippancy, frivolity, frivolousness, levity, lightheartedness, lightness, play, unseriousness
earnings *pl n* **1** an increase usually measured in money that comes from labor, business, or property ⟨*earnings* from babysitting jobs that are being put away for college⟩ — see INCOME 1
 2 the amount of money left when expenses are subtracted from the total amount received ⟨After subtracting what we spent on music and refreshments, the *earnings* from our charity gala were still impressive.⟩ — see PROFIT 1
earshot *n* range of hearing ⟨Babysitters should remain within *earshot* of young children.⟩
 synonyms hail, hearing, sound
 related words volume; distance, sight

earsplitting *adj* marked by a high volume of sound ⟨the *earsplitting* noise coming from the jackhammers at the construction site⟩ — see LOUD 1

earth *n* **1** the celestial body on which we live ⟨environmentalists who are committed to preserving the *earth*⟩
synonyms globe, planet, world
related words cosmos, creation, nature, universe; ball, orb, sphere; macrocosm, microcosm, microcosmos
2 the solid part of our planet's surface as distinguished from the sea and air ⟨After the long flight, I was glad to feel the *earth* under my feet.⟩
synonyms dirt, dust, ground, land, soil, terra firma
related words continent, zone; island, isthmus, mainland, peninsula
3 the loose surface material in which plants naturally grow ⟨Set the plants deep enough into the *earth* so that they'll be sure to take root.⟩ — see DIRT 1
4 a very large amount of money ⟨It'll cost the *earth* to repair that porcelain vase, so make sure that it's worth it.⟩ — see FORTUNE 2

earthenware *n* articles made of baked clay ⟨a wide array of hand-painted *earthenware* available at the craft fair⟩ — see CROCKERY

earthlike *adj* consisting or suggestive of earth ⟨The basket of garden-fresh mushrooms had that typically *earthlike* smell.⟩ — see EARTHY 1

earthly *adj* having to do with life on earth especially as opposed to that in heaven ⟨*earthly* delights⟩
synonyms carnal, fleshly, material, mundane, temporal, terrestrial, worldly
related words animal, bodily, corporal, corporeal, physical; daily, diurnal
near antonyms celestial, Elysian, empyreal, empyrean, supernal; metaphysical; devotional, divine, religious, sacred, spiritual, utopian; extraterrestrial; ethereal, supernatural
antonyms heavenly, nontemporal, unearthly, unworldly

earthquake *n* **1** a shaking of the earth ⟨The San Andreas Fault is notorious for its *earthquakes*.⟩
synonyms quake, shake, tremor
related words aftershock, foreshock, shock; cataclysm, convulsion, upheaval; seaquake
2 a violent disturbance (as of the political or social order) ⟨a candidate causing a political *earthquake*⟩ — see CONVULSION

earthy *adj* **1** consisting or suggestive of earth ⟨the unmistakably *earthy* aroma of a greenhouse⟩
synonyms earthlike, loamy
related words clayey, dusty, muddy, sandy, silty
2 willing to see things as they really are and deal with them sensibly ⟨The dog trainer was *earthy*, no-nonsense, and blunt—with us, as well as our dog.⟩ — see REALISTIC 1

ease *n* **1** reduction of or freedom from pain ⟨The sunburn medication brought me instant *ease*.⟩
synonyms alleviation, comfort, release, relief
related words appeasement, assuagement, decrease, diminishment, mitigation, moderation, mollification; calming, salving, soothing
near antonyms discomfort, unrest; agony, anguish, misery, suffering, torment, torture; ache, pain, pang, prick, smart, sting, stitch, throe, tingle, twinge
2 carefree freedom from constraint ⟨a gymnast who can handle even the most demanding moves on the parallel bars with total *ease*⟩ — see ABANDON
3 freedom from activity or labor ⟨The dream of every lottery player is a life of fabulous luxury and everlasting *ease*.⟩ — see ¹REST 1

ease *vb* **1** to free from obstruction or difficulty ⟨measures intended to *ease* the flow of traffic during rush hour⟩
synonyms facilitate, grease, loosen (up), smooth, unclog

related words accelerate, expedite, hasten, hurry, quicken, rush, speed; advance, forward, further, promote; abet, aid, assist, help, improve; disentangle, straighten (out), untangle; simplify, streamline
phrases pave the way (for)
near antonyms hinder, impede; retard; aggravate, worsen; perplex, sophisticate
antonyms complicate
2 to make less taut ⟨The rock climber *eased* the rope a little so that his fellow climber had room to maneuver.⟩ — see SLACKEN 1
3 to make more bearable or less severe ⟨grandmother's firm belief that there are few ailments that chicken soup won't *ease*⟩ — see HELP 2
4 to make smaller in amount, volume, or extent ⟨The chair of the Federal Reserve has promised to *ease* interest rates.⟩ — see DECREASE 1
5 to grow less in scope or intensity especially gradually ⟨New investments in the region have *eased* since the rise in interest rates.⟩ — see DECREASE 2

easily *adv* **1** without difficulty ⟨a skater who *easily* executes even the most difficult jumps⟩
synonyms easy, effortlessly, facilely, fluently, freely, handily, lightly, painlessly, readily, smoothly, well
related words ably, adeptly, adroitly, competently, dexterously, efficiently, expertly, masterfully, proficiently, skillfully; instinctively, intuitively, naturally, spontaneously
phrases in a breeze, no sweat [*slang*], without ado, without a hitch
near antonyms awkwardly, clumsily, gracelessly, hamhandedly, ineptly, maladroitly, unskillfully; meticulously, painfully, painstakingly, thoroughly; assiduously, diligently, indefatigably, industriously, intensely, intently, mightily, sedulously, tirelessly
antonyms arduously, hardly, laboriously, strenuously
2 without any question ⟨We *easily* have enough people to get the project under way.⟩ — see INDEED 1

easy *adj* **1** involving minimal difficulty or effort ⟨a minor problem with an *easy* solution⟩
synonyms cheap, effortless, facile, fluent, fluid, light, painless, ready, royal, simple, smooth, soft
related words idiotproof, mindless, quick, straightforward, unchallenging, uncomplicated; apparent, clear, clear-cut, distinct, evident, manifest, obvious, open-and-shut, palpable, patent, perspicuous, plain, transparent, unambiguous, unequivocal, unmistakable
near antonyms burdensome, exhausting, onerous, oppressive, painful, stressful, taxing, troublesome; abstruse, complex, complicated, intricate, involved, knotty, problematic (*also* problematical), recondite
antonyms arduous, demanding, difficult, exacting, formidable, grueling (*or* gruelling), hard, herculean, killer, labored, laborious, murderous, rough, severe, stiff, strenuous, toilful, toilsome, tough
2 readily taken advantage of ⟨people who are *easy* prey for scam artists⟩
synonyms exploitable, gullible (*also* gullable), naive (*or* naïve), susceptible, trusting, unwary, wide-eyed
related words credulous, overcredulous, trustful, uncritical, unsuspecting, unsuspicious; artless, genuine, guileless, innocent, simple, unsophisticated, unworldly; malleable, pliable, pliant; deceivable; acquiescent, agreeable, amiable, obliging; yielding
near antonyms critical, cynical, mistrustful, skeptical, suspicious, wary; sophisticated; clear-sighted, hardheaded; shrewd, street-smart, streetwise
3 providing physical comfort ⟨my favorite *easy* chair for watching TV⟩ — see COMFORTABLE 1
4 tolerant and kind in the judgment of and expectations

for others ⟨Despite her *easy* approach to discipline, she had a remarkably well-behaved class.⟩ — see INDULGENT 1

easy *adv* without difficulty ⟨We can make the trip in four hours *easy*.⟩ — see EASILY 1

easygoing *adj* **1** having a relaxed, casual manner ⟨Counselors at the summer camp are pretty *easygoing*.⟩
synonyms affable, breezy, devil-may-care, happy-go-lucky, laid-back, low-pressure, mellow
related words carefree, casual, lackadaisical, nonchalant, unaffected, unconcerned, unfussy, unperturbed, untroubled, unworried; familiar, homey (*also* homy), informal; flexible, lax, lenient, permissive, pliable, pliant, soft; accessible, approachable; imperturbable, nerveless, unflappable, unshakable; amicable, companionable, comradely, cordial, genial, hail-fellow-well-met, hearty, neighborly, warm, warmhearted
near antonyms ceremonious, decorous, formal, rigid, strict; anxious, distressed, worried; jittery, jumpy, nervous, skittish, tense
antonyms high-strung, uptight
2 not bound by rigid standards ⟨Some people are pretty *easygoing* about housekeeping.⟩
synonyms flexible, lax, loose, relaxed, slack, unrestrained, unrestricted
related words careless, derelict, heedless, irresponsible, lazy, neglectful, negligent, remiss, slipshod, sloppy, sloven, slovenly, unfussy
near antonyms constrained, restrained, restricted, tight; careful, conscientious, exact, fussy, meticulous, painstaking, punctilious, scrupulous; implacable, inflexible
antonyms hard, harsh, rigid, rigorous, severe, stern, strict

eat *vb* **1** to take in as food ⟨Having gone all day without food, we greedily *ate* the hamburgers.⟩
synonyms consume, ingest, put down
related words digest, down, mouth (down), swallow; bolt, chow (down on), devour, glut (on), gobble (up *or* down), gorge, gulp, scoff, slop, snarf (down), swill, wolf; chew, gnaw (at *or* on), gum, lap, lick, nibble (on), nurse, pick (at); relish, savor (*also* savour), taste; banquet, dine, fare, feast, gormandize, pig out, regale; dispatch, polish off; breakfast, lunch, sup; munch, nosh, snack
2 to consume or wear away gradually ⟨The pot's protective coating was *eaten* away by the acid.⟩
synonyms bite (at), corrode, erode, fret, nibble
related words break down, break up, decompose, disintegrate, dissolve; decimate, destroy, devastate, ruin, waste, wreck
near antonyms freshen, recreate, refresh, refreshen, regenerate, rejuvenate, renew, restore, revitalize, revive
3 to take a meal ⟨Where's the best place to *eat* in this town?⟩ — see DINE 1
4 to disturb the peace of mind of (someone) especially by repeated disagreeable acts ⟨It really *eats* me the way people go to national parks to enjoy nature—and then leave their litter behind.⟩ — see IRRITATE 1

eat (up) *vb* **1** to receive or accept gladly or readily ⟨Predictably, moviegoers *ate up* the sequel to last summer's blockbuster.⟩ — see WELCOME
2 to destroy all trace of ⟨The surf created by a powerful hurricane could really *eat up* what's left of the island's eastern beach.⟩ — see CONSUME 1

eatable *adj* suitable for use as food ⟨a survival course in which you learn which wild plants are *eatable*⟩ — see EDIBLE

eatables *pl n* substances intended to be eaten ⟨The buffet table aboard the cruise ship always had a tempting array of *eatables*.⟩ — see FOOD

eavesdrop (on) *vb* to listen to (another in private conversation) ⟨a nosy traveler who likes to *eavesdrop on* his fellow airline passengers⟩
synonyms listen in (on), overhear
related words bug, tap, wiretap; monitor, snoop, spy, surveil; attend, hear, hearken, heed, mind

eaves trough *n* a pipe or channel for carrying off water from a roof ⟨rain so heavy that the *eaves trough* couldn't handle it⟩ — see GUTTER 1

ebb *n* a change to a lower state or level ⟨a surprising *ebb* in the quality of workmanship⟩ — see DECLINE 2

ebb *vb* **1** to become worse or of less value ⟨The fortunes of the town slowly *ebbed* as factory after textile factory closed.⟩ — see DETERIORATE 1
2 to grow less in scope or intensity especially gradually ⟨The howling winds *ebbed* as the hurricane moved into the interior.⟩ — see DECREASE 2

ebbing *n* a gradual sinking and wasting away of mind or body ⟨Seniors who stay active can keep at bay some of the *ebbing* of the memory that can come with advanced years.⟩ — see DECLINE 1

ebony *adj* having the color of soot or coal ⟨The *ebony* appliances look very sleek and modern.⟩ — see BLACK 1

eccentric *adj* different from the ordinary in a way that causes curiosity or suspicion ⟨His *eccentric* decorating style isn't going over well with the neighbors.⟩ — see ODD 2

eccentric *n* a person of odd or whimsical habits ⟨an *eccentric* who designed his house to look like a Scottish castle⟩
synonyms character, codger, crack, crackbrain, crackpot, crank, flake, kook, nut, oddball, oddity, screwball, weirdo, zany
related words bohemian, maverick, nonconformist, quixote; coot, geezer; curio, rarity; freak
phrases odd duck, piece of work
near antonyms conformer, conformist, follower, sheep

eccentricity *n* an odd or peculiar habit ⟨One of the woman's *eccentricities* was her lifelong habit of reading while soaking in the bathtub for hours.⟩ — see IDIOSYNCRASY

ecclesiastic *adj* of or relating to a church ⟨a council to make final determinations on *ecclesiastic* matters⟩ — see ECCLESIASTICAL

ecclesiastical *adj* of or relating to a church ⟨*ecclesiastical* laws that have been in existence for centuries⟩
synonyms churchly, ecclesiastic
related words blessed (*also* blest), consecrated, divine, hallowed, holy, religious, sacramental, sacred, sacrosanct, sanctified; apostolic, canonical, clerical, episcopal, evangelical (*also* evangelic), ministerial, papal, pastoral, patriarchal, priestly, rabbinic (*or* rabbinical), sacerdotal
near antonyms lay, profane, secular, temporal; nonclerical; nondenominational, nonsectarian
antonyms nonchurch, nonecclesiastical

echelon *n* the placement of someone or something in relation to others in a vertical arrangement ⟨Jobs in the upper *echelons* of the company pay quite well indeed.⟩ — see RANK 1

echo *n* **1** a person who adopts the appearance or behavior of another especially in an obvious way ⟨a younger sister who was her *echo* all the while that they were growing up⟩ — see COPYCAT
2 a tiny often physical indication of something lost or vanished ⟨A few stone carvings are the only *echoes* that remain of a once-mighty civilization.⟩ — see VESTIGE 1

echo *vb* **1** to continue or be repeated in a series of reflected sound waves ⟨Laughter *echoed* across the lake.⟩ — see REVERBERATE
2 to say after another ⟨They *echoed* in a singsong voice everything she said.⟩ — see REPEAT 3

eclectic *adj* consisting of many things of different sorts

⟨The museum's *eclectic* collection has everything from a giraffe skeleton to medieval musical instruments.⟩ — see MISCELLANEOUS

eclipse *n* a change to a lower state or level ⟨the *eclipse* of the town from a grand seaside resort to a tacky tourist trap⟩ — see DECLINE 2

eclipse *vb* to be greater, better, or stronger than ⟨The brilliant young pianist now *eclipsed* even his own mentor in musical artistry.⟩ — see SURPASS 1

economical *adj* careful in the management of money or resources ⟨We have to be *economical* in our use of the camp's limited supply of electricity.⟩ — see FRUGAL

economize *vb* to avoid unnecessary waste or expense ⟨In tough times people learn how to *economize*.⟩
synonyms pinch, save, scrimp, skimp, spare
related words conserve, husband, maintain, manage, preserve; scrape; cut back, cut down, retrench; hoard, lay up
phrases pinch pennies
near antonyms blow, dissipate, fritter (away), lavish, misspend, run through, spend, squander, throw away; splurge
antonyms waste

economizing *adj* careful in the management of money or resources ⟨*Economizing* drivers aren't so affected by every hike in the price of gasoline.⟩ — see FRUGAL

economy *n* careful management of material resources ⟨People on fixed incomes are used to practicing *economy*.⟩
synonyms frugality, husbandry, parsimony, providence, scrimping, skimping, thrift
related words conservation, saving; miserliness, stinginess; belt-tightening, retrenchment; discretion, forehandedness, prudence; austerity, moderation, restraint, temperance
near antonyms extravagance, improvidence, lavishness, prodigality, squandering
antonyms wastefulness

ecstasy *n* a state of overwhelming usually pleasurable emotion ⟨Actors are typically in *ecstasy* upon winning an Oscar.⟩
synonyms elation, euphoria, exhilaration, heaven, high, intoxication, paradise, rapture, rhapsody, swoon, transport
related words exaltation; blessedness, bliss, blissfulness, delight, enchantment, felicity, gladness, happiness, joy, joyfulness, joyousness, pleasure; reverie, trance; inspiration; fervor, frenzy, madness, passion; cheer, cheerfulness, exuberance, glee, gleefulness, jubilance, jubilation, lightheartedness
near antonyms misery, sadness, unhappiness, woe, wretchedness; blues, dejection, desolation, despair, despondency, disconsolateness, disheartenment, dispiritedness, doldrums, downheartedness, dreariness, dumps, forlornness, gloom, gloominess, heartsickness, melancholy, mopes
antonyms depression

ecstatic *adj* experiencing or marked by overwhelming usually pleasurable emotion ⟨a football player who was *ecstatic* upon receiving a full athletic scholarship to the college of his choice⟩
synonyms elated, elevated, enraptured, entranced, euphoric, exhilarated, giddy, intoxicated, rapt, rapturous, rhapsodic (*also* rhapsodical)
related words enchanted, exultant, glorying, jubilant, rejoicing, triumphant; enthusiastic, excited, gung ho, thrilled; blissed-out, blissful, delighted, glad, gratified, happy, joyful, joyous, pleased, satisfied, tickled
phrases on cloud nine, over the moon

near antonyms blue, brokenhearted, crestfallen, dejected, despondent, disconsolate, disheartened, doleful, down, downcast, downhearted, forlorn, gloomy, glum, hangdog, heartbroken, heartsick, heartsore, inconsolable, joyless, low, low-spirited, melancholy, miserable, mournful, sad, saddened, sorrowful, sorry, unhappy, woebegone, woeful, wretched
antonyms depressed

Eden *n* an often imaginary place or state of utter perfection and happiness ⟨Some of the first Europeans to explore Polynesia thought that they had indeed discovered a tropical *Eden*.⟩ — see PARADISE 1

edge *n* **1** a harsh or sharp quality ⟨Her comments had a sarcastic *edge*.⟩
synonyms acidity, acidness, acridness, acrimoniousness, acrimony, acuteness, asperity, bite, bitterness, harshness, keenness, poignancy, pungency, roughness, sharpness, tartness
related words ginger, punch, spice; raucousness, severeness, severity, shrillness, virulence, vitriol; cattiness, maliciousness; pointedness, thorniness
near antonyms gentleness, kindliness
antonyms mildness, softness
2 the line or relatively narrow space that marks the outer limit of something ⟨The design along the *edge* of the plate is badly worn.⟩ — see BORDER 1
3 the more favorable condition or position in a competition ⟨My big feet give me something of an *edge* in swimming.⟩ — see ADVANTAGE 1
4 the power to produce a desired result ⟨The utter lack of enforcement provisions totally blunts the *edge* of the law.⟩ — see EFFICACY
5 an interval of time just before the onset of something ⟨Researchers are on the *edge* of a medical breakthrough.⟩ — see POINT 3

edge *vb* **1** to make sharp or sharper ⟨If you *edge* the tip of that stick, it should be a fine skewer for roasting marshmallows.⟩ — see SHARPEN
2 to serve as a border for ⟨pavement *edging* the flower bed⟩ — see BORDER

edged *adj* having an edge thin enough to cut or pierce something ⟨Always store your finely *edged* knives in a knife block.⟩ — see SHARP 1

edgewise *adv* with one side faced forward ⟨You can squeeze through the narrow passage between the two caves if you go *edgewise*.⟩ — see SIDEWAYS 1

edginess *n* a state of nervousness marked by sudden jerky movements ⟨The *edginess* of the basketball players in the moments before the start of the tournament was apparent.⟩ — see JUMPINESS

edgy *adj* **1** feeling or showing uncomfortable feelings of uncertainty ⟨With an *edgy* voice the spelling-bee contestant started to spell the difficult word.⟩ — see NERVOUS 1
2 having an edge thin enough to cut or pierce something ⟨Be careful as you walk along the beach—those broken clam shells are *edgy* enough to cut your feet.⟩ — see SHARP 1
3 serving or likely to arouse a strong reaction ⟨a director known for his *edgy*, over-the-top satires on modern life⟩ — see PROVOCATIVE

edible *adj* suitable for use as food ⟨*edible* plant products⟩
synonyms eatable, esculent
related words absorbable, chewable, digestible, ingestible, swallowable; nourishing, nutritious, nutritive; appetizing, delicious, flavorful, palatable, savory (*also* savoury), succulent, tasty, toothsome, toothy
near antonyms indigestible, nondigestible, nonnutritious, undigestible
antonyms inedible, nonedible, uneatable

edibles *pl n* substances intended to be eaten ⟨Even if the storm turns out to be a blizzard, there are enough *edibles* in the refrigerator to last us a week.⟩ — see FOOD

edict *n* **1** an order publicly issued by an authority ⟨The school board's *edict* put a new student dress code into effect.⟩
synonyms bull, decree, directive, fiat, ruling
related words call, conclusion, decision, deliverance, determination, diagnosis, judgment (*or* judgement), opinion, resolution, verdict; announcement, declaration, dictum, manifesto, proclamation, pronouncement; canon, encyclical
2 a statement of what to do that must be obeyed by those concerned ⟨this household's *edict* of long standing: no video games until all homework has been completed⟩ — see COMMAND 1

edifice *n* **1** a large, magnificent, or massive building ⟨The U.S. Capitol is one of our nation's most impressive *edifices*.⟩
synonyms hall, palace, tower
related words construction, erection, structure; castle, château, countryseat, estate, hacienda, manor, manor house, mansion, showplace, villa; mausoleum, memorial, monument
2 something built as a dwelling, shelter, or place for human activity ⟨The first *edifices* built by the colonists were primitive huts with walls of dried mud and roofs covered with thatch.⟩ — see BUILDING
3 the arrangement of parts that gives something its basic form ⟨The *edifice* of the argument is quite simple, once you get past the fancy language.⟩ — see FRAME 1

edify *vb* to provide (someone) with moral or spiritual understanding ⟨a family-oriented show that tried to *edify* the television audience as well as entertain it⟩ — see ENLIGHTEN 2

edit *vb* **1** to prepare for publication by correcting, rewriting, or updating ⟨The publisher *edited* a new version of its best-selling school dictionary.⟩
synonyms redraft, revamp, revise, rework
related words perfect, polish, touch up; copyedit, read; amend, annotate, correct, emend, rectify; fact-check; collect, compile; get out, issue, print, publish; abridge, redact
2 to change (something) so as to make it suitable for a new use or situation ⟨The restaurant chef has *edited* several of his gourmet dishes for preparation by the home cook.⟩ — see ADAPT

educate *vb* **1** to cause to acquire knowledge or skill in some field ⟨a revered professor of astronomy who is credited with *educating* many of today's leading astronomers⟩ — see TEACH
2 to provide (someone) with moral or spiritual understanding ⟨the belief that parents *educate* their children by example⟩ — see ENLIGHTEN 2

educated *adj* **1** having or displaying advanced knowledge or education ⟨an *educated* work force⟩
synonyms erudite, knowledgeable, learned, literate, scholarly, well-read
related words civilized, cultivated, cultured; cerebral, highbrow, intellectual; polished, refined, well-bred; academic (*also* academical), bookish, didactic, didactical, inkhorn, pedantic, professorial; informed, instructed, schooled, skilled, trained; homeschooled; briefed, enlightened, informed, versed
near antonyms uncivilized, uncultivated, uncultured; lowbrow, semiliterate, unintellectual; ill-bred, unpolished, unrefined; uninformed, unknowledgeable; uninstructed, unschooled, untaught, untutored; semiliterate, undereducated

antonyms benighted, dark, ignorant, illiterate, uneducated, unlearned, unlettered, unscholarly
2 having or showing exceptional knowledge, experience, or skill in a field of endeavor ⟨a violinist caressing the instrument with an *educated* touch⟩ — see PROFICIENT

education *n* **1** the act or process of imparting knowledge or skills to another ⟨a teacher who devoted herself to the *education* of children with special needs⟩
synonyms instruction, schooling, teaching, training, tutelage, tutoring
related words didactics, pedagogics, pedagogy; higher education, higher learning; coaching, conditioning, cultivation, preparation, readying; development, direction, guidance, nurturance, nurturing; edification, enlightenment, improvement; apprenticeship
2 the understanding and information gained from being educated ⟨a person whose extensive *education* was obvious to all who met him⟩
synonyms erudition, knowledge, learnedness, learning, scholarship
related words culture, edification, enlightenment; reading; bookishness, pedantry
near antonyms functional illiteracy
antonyms ignorance, illiteracy, illiterateness

educational *adj* **1** providing useful information or knowledge ⟨We found the talk on easy ways for families to recycle household products very *educational*.⟩ — see INFORMATIVE
2 of or relating to schooling or learning especially at an advanced level ⟨The community college strives to meet the *educational* needs of the residents of its urban location.⟩ — see ACADEMIC 1

educative *adj* providing useful information or knowledge ⟨College students discover that what they experience outside the classroom can be just as *educative* as anything that happens within.⟩ — see INFORMATIVE

educator *n* a person whose occupation is to give formal instruction in a school ⟨She decided at a fairly young age that there is no more rewarding career than that of an *educator*.⟩ — see TEACHER

educe *vb* to draw out (something hidden, latent, or reserved) ⟨The gift of a puppy finally *educed* a response from the shy boy.⟩
synonyms elicit, evoke, inspire, raise
related words drag, dredge (up), extort, extract, pull, wangle, wrest, wring; coax (out), gain, get, obtain, procure, secure; bare, disclose, discover, divulge, evince, expose, reveal, uncloak, uncover, unmask, unveil
phrases call forth
near antonyms disregard, forget, ignore, miss, neglect, overlook, overpass, pass over

eerie *also* **eery** *adj* fearfully and mysteriously strange or fantastic ⟨*Eerie* noises would occasionally come from locked rooms in the castle.⟩
synonyms creepy, haunting, spooky, uncanny, unearthly, weird
related words ghastly, ghostlike, ghostly, ghoulish, spectral; bizarre, curious, odd, outlandish, outré, peculiar, quaint, quirky; unaccustomed, uncommon, unusual; metaphysical, preternatural, supernatural; enigmatic (*also* enigmatical), inscrutable, mysterious, puzzling
near antonyms common, commonplace, everyday, normal, ordinary, prosaic, routine, typical, unexceptional, unremarkable, usual; natural; expected, familiar, predictable

efface *vb* to destroy all traces of ⟨When the supply ship finally arrived, it discovered that virtually all evidence of the colony at Roanoke had been *effaced*.⟩ — see ANNIHILATE 1

effect *n* **1** a condition or occurrence traceable to a cause ⟨Better health is always one of the *effects* of improved hygiene.⟩

synonyms aftereffect, aftermath, child, conclusion, consequence, corollary, development, fate, fruit, issue, outcome, outgrowth, product, result, resultant, sequel, sequence, upshot

related words ramification; denouement (*also* dénouement), echo, implication, repercussion; afterclap, afterglow, aftershock; by-product, fallout, offshoot, ripple, side effect (*also* side reaction), spin-off

phrases matter of course

near antonyms consideration, determinant, factor; base, basis, foundation, ground, groundwork; impetus, incentive, inspiration, instigation, stimulus; mother, origin, root, source, spring

antonyms antecedent, cause, occasion, reason

2 the power to bring about a result on another ⟨Friendship has a profound *effect* on our lives.⟩

synonyms impact, influence, mark, repercussion, sway

related words authority, clout, prestige, pull, weight; command, domination, dominion, mastery; consequence, importance, significance; sovereignty (*also* sovranty), supremacy

near antonyms helplessness, impotence, impotency, powerlessness, weakness

3 effects *pl* transportable items that one owns ⟨The family packed up its household *effects* and moved to Florida.⟩ — see POSSESSION 2

effect *vb* to be the cause of (a situation, action, or state of mind) ⟨classroom discussions designed to *effect* a change in racial attitudes⟩

synonyms beget, breed, bring, bring about, cause, create, do, draw on, effectuate, engender, generate, induce, make, occasion, produce, prompt, result (in), spawn, translate (into), work, yield

related words conduce (to), contribute (to); decide, determine; begin, establish, father, found, inaugurate, initiate, innovate, institute, introduce, launch, pioneer, set, set up, start; advance, cultivate, develop, encourage, forward, foster, further, nourish, nurture, promote; enact, render, turn out

phrases bring forth, give rise to

near antonyms impede, limit, restrict; clamp down (on), crack down (on), crush, dampen, put down, quash, quell, repress, smother, squash, squelch, stifle, subdue, suppress; arrest, check, control, curb, inhibit, rein (in), restrain, retard; abolish, demolish, destroy, extinguish, liquidate, quench

effective *adj* **1** producing or capable of producing a desired result ⟨an *effective* treatment of the once-dreaded disease⟩

synonyms effectual, efficacious, efficient, fruitful, operative, potent, productive

related words hyperefficient, ultraefficient; adequate, capable, competent; accomplished, adept, consummate, experienced, expert, masterly, practiced (*also* practised), proficient, skilled, skillful, versed, veteran, virtuoso; cogent, convincing, killer, sound, striking, telling, valid; active, dynamic; useful, working; applicable, feasible, functional, practicable, practical, realizable, usable (*also* useable), workable

near antonyms incapable, incompetent, inexperienced, inexpert, unqualified, unseasoned, unskilled, unskillful; abortive, bootless, futile, vain; empty, hollow, idle, pointless, unavailing, unprofitable, unsuccessful; inoperative, worthless

antonyms fruitless, ineffective, ineffectual, inefficient, inoperative, unfruitful, unproductive, useless

2 having the power to persuade ⟨made an *effective* argument in favor of the proposal⟩ — see COGENT

3 existing in fact and not merely as a possibility ⟨made the mistake of confusing the plant's production capacity with its *effective* output⟩ — see ACTUAL

effectiveness *n* **1** the capacity to persuade ⟨The "guilty" verdict was all the proof needed of the *effectiveness* of the prosecutor's closing argument.⟩ — see COGENCY 1

2 the power to produce a desired result ⟨The huge upsurge in sales pretty much demonstrated the *effectiveness* of the new ad campaign.⟩ — see EFFICACY

3 the quality of an utterance that provokes interest and produces an effect ⟨Your writing lacks *effectiveness* because practically every sentence is in the passive voice.⟩ — see ¹PUNCH 1

effectual *adj* producing or capable of producing a desired result ⟨found an *effectual* remedy for the condition⟩ — see EFFECTIVE 1

effectualness *n* the power to produce a desired result ⟨The *effectualness* of that new treatment has yet to be proven.⟩ — see EFFICACY

effectuate *vb* to be the cause of (a situation, action, or state of mind) ⟨the hope that the greater social interaction between the freshmen and the upper classmen will *effectuate* greater school spirit⟩ — see EFFECT

effeminate *adj* of or relating to a man who has or displays qualities traditionally considered more suitable for women ⟨He had a high and somewhat *effeminate* voice.⟩

synonyms effete, womanish

related words feminine, girlish, girlie (*or* girly), womanlike, womanly; old-maidish, overnice, prissy, spinsterish; dandyish, dudish, foppish, sappy; camp, campy

antonyms manlike, manly, mannish, masculine, virile

effervescent *adj* joyously unrestrained ⟨Candidates for positions on the cheerleading squad should have naturally *effervescent* personalities.⟩ — see EXUBERANT

effete *adj* **1** having lost forcefulness, courage, or spirit ⟨the soft, *effete* society that marked the final years of the Roman empire⟩

synonyms decadent, decayed, degenerate, overripe, washed-up

related words overrefined, precious; decaying, declining, dying, failing, waning; debilitated, enervate, enervated, enfeebled, feeble, frail, languid, sapped, soft, wasted, weak, weakened, wimpy; dissolute, immoral; debased, debauched, degraded, demoralized, depraved, dissipated, dissolute

antonyms undecadent

2 lacking bodily strength ⟨The outdoor adventure program takes *effete* youths from comfortable suburbs and turns them into hardy campers.⟩ — see WEAK 1

3 lacking strength of will or character ⟨The governor is too *effete* to take on the powerful special interests that really run this state.⟩ — see WEAK 2

4 of or relating to a man who has or displays qualities traditionally considered more suitable for women ⟨a slightly more *effete* style of clothing⟩ — see EFFEMINATE

efficacious *adj* producing or capable of producing a desired result ⟨Taking a cookie break while studying is one of the most *efficacious* ways of rejuvenating the mind that I have ever discovered.⟩ — see EFFECTIVE 1

efficaciousness *n* the power to produce a desired result ⟨the *efficaciousness* of exercise in improving overall well-being⟩ — see EFFICACY

efficacy *n* the power to produce a desired result ⟨We questioned the *efficacy* of the alarms in actually preventing auto theft.⟩

synonyms edge, effectiveness, effectualness, efficaciousness, efficiency, productiveness

related words ability, capability, capacity; potency, puissance, strength

near antonyms inability, inadequacy, incompetence

antonyms ineffectiveness, ineffectuality, ineffectualness, inefficiency

efficiency *n* the power to produce a desired result ⟨the proven *efficiency* of meditation to reduce stress⟩ — see EFFICACY

efficient *adj* producing or capable of producing a desired result ⟨That manual lawn mower is not a very *efficient* tool for doing a huge yard.⟩ — see EFFECTIVE 1

effort *n* the active use of energy in producing a result ⟨The finished parade float was well worth the *effort*.⟩

synonyms elbow grease, exertion, expenditure, labor, pains, sweat, trouble, while, work

related words drudgery, grind, slog, strain, toil, travail; dint, energy; force, might, muscle, power, puissance; attempt, endeavor, essay, fling, go, pass, shot, stab, trial, try, whack

near antonyms adroitness, ease, facility, fluency, smoothness; dormancy, idleness, inaction, inactivity, indolence, inertia, languor, laziness, quiescence

effortless *adj* involving minimal difficulty or effort ⟨Using an automatic dishwasher is not quite as *effortless* as I would like—you still have to put the dishes away.⟩ — see EASY 1

effortlessly *adv* without difficulty ⟨The pizza worker flung the round of dough into the air and *effortlessly* caught it.⟩ — see EASILY 1

effrontery *n* shameless boldness ⟨The little squirt had the *effrontery* to deny eating any cookies, even with the crumbs still on his lips.⟩

synonyms audacity, brashness, brass, brassiness, brazenness, cheek, cheekiness, chutzpah (*also* chutzpa *or* hutzpah *or* hutzpa), face, gall, nerve, nerviness, pertness, presumption, presumptuousness, sauce, sauciness, temerity

related words arrogance, assurance, cockiness, confidence, hardihood, overconfidence, sanguinity, self-assurance, self-confidence; discourteousness, disrespect, impertinence, impoliteness, impudence, incivility, inconsiderateness, inconsideration, insolence, rudeness, ungraciousness; back talk, sass; swagger, swash

near antonyms bashfulness, diffidence, faintheartedness, hesitancy, modesty, shyness, timidity, timidness, timorousness; civility, courteousness, courtesy, gentility, graciousness, mannerliness, manners

effulgence *n* the quality or state of having or giving off light ⟨The exceptional *effulgence* of the harvest moon is always a striking sight.⟩ — see BRILLIANCE 1

effulgent *adj* giving off or reflecting much light ⟨The stars always seem more *effulgent* when viewed in the country, far away from the distracting lights of the city.⟩ — see BRIGHT 1

effusive *adj* showing feeling freely ⟨Often *effusive* no matter what the occasion, they are even more so at weddings and funerals.⟩ — see DEMONSTRATIVE 1

egg (on) *vb* to try to persuade (someone) through earnest appeals to follow a course of action ⟨Though exhausted, I was *egged on* by spectators to finish the marathon.⟩ — see URGE

egghead *n* a person with strong intellectual interests ⟨a scientist who embraced the reputation of being an *egghead*⟩ — see INTELLECTUAL

ego *n* **1** a reasonable or justifiable sense of one's worth or importance ⟨I have enough *ego* not to want to give up easily in any contest or competition.⟩ — see PRIDE 1

2 an often unjustified feeling of being pleased with oneself or with one's situation or achievements ⟨a star athlete with a refreshing lack of *ego*⟩ — see COMPLACENCE 1

egocentric *adj* overly concerned with one's own desires, needs, or interests ⟨The novel's *egocentric* main character journeys to "find herself."⟩

synonyms egoistic (*also* egoistical), egotistic (*or* egotistical), self-centered, selfish, self-seeking

related words inner-directed; complacent, conceited, overweening, pompous, prideful, proud, self-complacent, self-conceited, self-contented, self-directed, self-glorifying, self-important, self-pleased, self-satisfied, smug, vain, vainglorious

near antonyms altruistic, beneficent, benevolent, charitable, generous, greathearted, humanitarian, magnanimous, philanthropic (*also* philanthropical), self-giving, self-sacrificing; other-directed; diffident, self-doubting; self-reflective

antonyms self-forgetful, self-forgetting, selfless, unselfish

egoism *n* excessive interest in oneself ⟨Because of her *egoism*, she never gave a thought to asking how the others felt.⟩

synonyms egotism, self-centeredness, self-interest, selfishness, self-regard

related words complacence, complacency, conceit, conceitedness, ego, pompousness, pride, pridefulness, self-admiration, self-conceit, self-esteem, self-importance, self-indulgence, self-partiality, self-respect, self-satisfaction, self-sufficiency, smugness, vaingloriousness, vainglory, vainness, vanity; self-assumption, self-consequence, self-content, self-contentment, self-glorification

near antonyms altruism, generosity, magnanimity, self-sacrifice; detachment, disinterestedness, fairness, impartiality, neutrality, objectivity; self-flagellation; self-annihilation, self-immolation

antonyms self-abandonment, self-forgetfulness, selflessness, unselfishness

egoistic *also* **egoistical** *adj* **1** having too high an opinion of oneself ⟨He was so *egoistic* he thought everyone was coming just to see him.⟩ — see CONCEITED

2 overly concerned with one's own desires, needs, or interests ⟨They're too *egoistic* to even give a thought to becoming involved in something that benefits the whole community.⟩ — see EGOCENTRIC

egotism *n* **1** an often unjustified feeling of being pleased with oneself or with one's situation or achievements ⟨For someone who has won a Nobel Prize in physics, he is remarkably without *egotism*.⟩ — see COMPLACENCE 1

2 excessive interest in oneself ⟨*Egotism* is not something that winners of the Nobel Prize for peace usually have time for.⟩ — see EGOISM

egotistic *or* **egotistical** *adj* **1** having too high an opinion of oneself ⟨The *egotistic* pro quarterback was always too busy to sign autographs, forgetting that the fans had paid good money to see him play.⟩ — see CONCEITED

2 overly concerned with one's own desires, needs, or interests ⟨He resolved to be less *egotistic* and devote his time to helping others.⟩ — see EGOCENTRIC

egregious *adj* very noticeable especially for being incorrect or bad ⟨The student's theme was marred by a number of *egregious* errors in spelling.⟩

synonyms blatant, conspicuous, flagrant, glaring, gross, obvious, patent, pronounced, rank, striking

related words arresting, clear, distinct, dramatic, emphatic, evident, eye-catching, marked, notable, noticeable, outstanding, plain, prominent, remarkable, salient, showy, splashy; absolute, arrant, downright, out-and-out, outright, sheer, stark, utter; detectable, discernible (*also* discernable), observable, perceptible, visible; abom-

inable, atrocious, awful, deplorable, execrable, heinous, lousy, monstrous, outrageous
near antonyms imperceptible, inconspicuous, unnoticeable, unobtrusive; inconsequential, inconsiderable, insignificant, slight, small, trifling, trivial; concealed
egress *n* a place or means of going out ⟨The only *egress* from the nightclub was a dark, narrow stairway to the street below.⟩ — see EXIT 1
ejaculate *vb* to utter with a sudden burst of strong feeling ⟨"Eureka!" the Greek mathematician Archimedes is said to have *ejaculated* upon discovering a method for determining the purity of gold.⟩ — see EXCLAIM
ejaculation *n* a sudden short emotional utterance ⟨Ned uttered a profane *ejaculation* upon stubbing his toe in the dark.⟩ — see EXCLAMATION
eject *vb* 1 to drive or force out ⟨We summarily *ejected* the unwanted guest from our party.⟩
synonyms banish, boot (out), bounce, chase, dismiss, drum (out), expel, extrude, oust, out, rout, run off, throw out, turn out
related words deport, displace, evict, exile, expatriate, ostracize, read out, shut out; can, cashier, defenestrate, discharge, fire, muster out, release, remove, retire, sack, terminate
phrases give one the gate [*slang*], send packing
near antonyms accept, admit, take, take in; welcome; entertain, harbor, house, lodge, shelter
2 to violently throw out or off (something from within) ⟨a nebula *ejecting* streams of gas⟩ — see ERUPT 1
elaborate *adj* 1 made or done with great care or with much detail ⟨*elaborate* festivities for the 200th anniversary of the town's founding⟩
synonyms complex, complicated, detailed, fancy, intricate, involved, sophisticated
related words elegant, exquisite, grand, magnificent, ornate, splendid; chichi, extravagant, exuberant, fancified, flamboyant, frilly, gimmicked (up), grandiose, ostentatious, overwrought, showy, souped-up; Byzantine, convoluted, involute, involuted, labyrinthine
near antonyms modest, plain, uncomplicated; bald, bare, naked, unadorned, undecorated, unvarnished
antonyms simple, unfancy, unsophisticated
2 including many small descriptive features ⟨the *elaborate* world known as Middle Earth that J.R.R. Tolkien created in his richly imagined novels⟩ — see DETAILED 1
3 having many parts or aspects that are usually interrelated ⟨plans for an *elaborate* center for sports, entertainment, and shopping⟩ — see COMPLEX 1
elaborate *vb* to gradually become clearer or more detailed ⟨as mankind's understanding of the universe has *elaborated*⟩ — see DEVELOP 1
elaborate (on) *vb* 1 to add to the interest of by including made-up details ⟨My friend tends to *elaborate on* his hiking experiences, turning an ordinary walk in the woods into a hair-raising adventure.⟩ — see EMBROIDER
2 to express more fully and in greater detail ⟨The candidate for governor refused to *elaborate on* how she would balance the state's budget.⟩ — see EXPAND 1
elaborateness *n* the state or quality of having many interrelated parts or aspects ⟨The *elaborateness* of the parade is such that a virtual army of people spend the whole year working on it.⟩ — see COMPLEXITY 1
elaboration *n* 1 the act or process of going from the simple or basic to the complex or advanced ⟨the *elaboration* of the Internet from an exclusive computer network into a worldwide communications network of colossal proportions⟩ — see DEVELOPMENT 1
2 the representation of something in terms that go beyond the facts ⟨The eyewitness was deemed unreliable

because of his obvious *elaboration* of what he had actually seen.⟩ — see EXAGGERATION
elapse *vb* to come to an end ⟨In those coin-operated binoculars at scenic areas your viewing time seems to *elapse* almost before it has begun.⟩ — see CEASE 1
elastic *adj* 1 able to revert to original size and shape after being stretched, squeezed, or twisted ⟨*elastic* rubber bands⟩
synonyms flexible, resilient, rubberlike, rubbery, springy, stretch, stretchable, supple
related words adaptable, ductile, kneadable, malleable, plastic, pliable, pliant; limber, lissome (*also* lissom), lithe, lithesome, willowy
near antonyms compact, firm, hard, solid, unyielding; brittle, crisp, crumbly, flaky (*also* flakey), friable, short
antonyms inelastic, inflexible, nonelastic, rigid, stiff
2 capable of being readily changed ⟨When vacationing, we generally have very *elastic* daily sightseeing plans.⟩ — see FLEXIBLE 1
elate *vb* to fill with great joy ⟨The winning of the state basketball championship *elated* the whole town.⟩
synonyms elevate, enrapture, exhilarate, intoxicate, transport
related words commove, excite, inspire, stimulate, uplift; content, delight, gladden, gratify, please, rejoice, satisfy, warm
near antonyms demoralize, discourage, dishearten, dispirit; distress, oppress, sadden
antonyms depress
elated *adj* experiencing or marked by overwhelming usually pleasurable emotion ⟨She was *elated* upon learning that she had been accepted by her first-choice college.⟩ — see ECSTATIC
elation *n* a state of overwhelming usually pleasurable emotion ⟨Most people can't imagine the kind of *elation* that comes with winning a super lottery's grand prize, but they're dying to find out.⟩ — see ECSTASY
elbow *vb* to force one's way ⟨the sort of greedy person who is always the first to *elbow* to the front of the buffet table at every party⟩ — see ²PRESS 4
elbow grease *n* the active use of energy in producing a result ⟨With a little polish and a lot of *elbow grease*, I was able to make the old silver teapot shine again.⟩ — see EFFORT
elder *n* 1 a person of advanced years ⟨There's a lot you can learn from your *elders*.⟩ — see SENIOR CITIZEN
2 one who is above another in rank, station, or office ⟨As your *elder* in the company, he is within his rights to tell you what to do.⟩ — see SUPERIOR
3 one who is older than another ⟨She is my *elder* by two years.⟩ — see SENIOR 1
4 the senior member of a group ⟨As the *elder* of the contingent of living former presidents, he was accorded a place of highest honor at the ceremonies.⟩ — see DEAN
elderly *adj* being of advanced years and especially past middle age ⟨*Elderly* people who stay active are usually the healthiest and the happiest.⟩
synonyms aged, aging (*or* ageing), ancient, geriatric, long-lived, old, older, senior
related words centenarian, nonagenarian, octogenarian, septuagenarian, sexagenarian; oldish; adult, grown-up, mature, middle-aged; pensioned, retired, superannuated; venerable; decrepit, doddering, senile, tottery; overage (*also* overaged)
phrases long in the tooth, of a certain age
near antonyms ageless; youngish; adolescent, immature, juvenile, preteen, puerile; minor, underage; callow, green, inexperienced, raw; babyish, childish, childlike, infantile, infantine, kiddish
antonyms young, youthful

elder statesman *n* the senior member of a group ⟨The *elder statesman* of the White House correspondents is finally retiring after nearly a half century of service.⟩ — see DEAN

elect *adj* singled out from a number or group as more to one's liking ⟨This *elect* body of students represents the best that the nation's high schools have to offer.⟩ — see SELECT 1

elect *n* individuals carefully selected as being the best of a class ⟨The members of this all-American team are the *elect* of collegiate football.⟩ — see ELITE 1

elect *vb* to decide to accept (someone or something) from a group of possibilities ⟨I've *elected* to study French as my foreign language.⟩ — see CHOOSE 1

election *n* **1** the act or process of selecting ⟨The *election* of a major is something that every college student has to do at some point.⟩ — see SELECTION 1
2 the power, right, or opportunity to choose ⟨At the country inn, breakfast in bed is entirely at the *election* of the guest.⟩ — see CHOICE 1

elective *adj* subject to one's freedom of choice ⟨a plastic surgeon who mainly does face-lifting and other kinds of *elective* surgery⟩ — see OPTIONAL

electric *adj* causing great emotional or mental stimulation ⟨Dr. King's "I Have a Dream" speech was one of the truly *electric* moments in American oratory.⟩ — see EXCITING 1

electrify *vb* to cause a pleasurable stimulation of the feelings of ⟨Marian Anderson *electrified* audiences with her soaring operatic voice.⟩ — see THRILL

electrifying *adj* causing great emotional or mental stimulation ⟨Polls ranked the U.S. hockey team's victory in 1980 as one of the most *electrifying* moments in Olympic history.⟩ — see EXCITING 1

elegance *n* dignified or restrained beauty of form, appearance, or style ⟨the *elegance* of the hotel's French furnishings⟩
synonyms class, courtliness, elegancy, fineness, grace, gracefulness, handsomeness, majesty, refinement, stateliness
related words augustness, brilliance, gloriousness, glory, grandeur, grandness, lavishness, luxuriance, luxuriousness, luxury, magnificence, nobility, nobleness, opulence, ornateness, plushiness, plushness, resplendence, richness, splendor, sumptuousness; artfulness, chic, polish, sophistication, taste, tastefulness; classicism, dignity, exquisiteness, restraint, simplicity; affectedness, grandiosity, ostentation, ostentatiousness, pretentiousness, showiness
near antonyms coarseness, crudeness, flamboyance, flashiness, garishness, gaudiness, glitz, grotesqueness, grotesquerie (*also* grotesquery), kitsch, tastelessness, tawdriness, vulgarity
antonyms gracelessness, inelegance

elegancy *n* dignified or restrained beauty of form, appearance, or style ⟨There's a certain *elegancy* about this hotel that other places in Las Vegas don't have.⟩ — see ELEGANCE

elegant *adj* **1** having or showing elegance ⟨The bride's *elegant* gown received nothing but praise.⟩
synonyms classy, courtly, fine, graceful, handsome, majestic, refined, stately, tasteful
related words august, baronial, gallant, glorious, grand, heroic (*also* heroical), imposing, lavish, luxurious, magnificent, monumental, noble, ornate, proud, regal, rich, royal, splendid, superb; artful, genteel, polished, sophisticated; classic, conservative, exquisite, quiet, restrained, simple, understated; aristocratic, patrician; à la mode (*also* a la mode), chic, fashionable, in, modish, posh,

sharp, sleek, smart, snappy, stylish, swagger, swank (*or* swanky); affected, grandiose, ostentatious, pretentious, recherché
near antonyms cheesy, coarse, crude, flamboyant, flashy, garish, gaudy, glitzy, grotesque, loud, raffish, splashy, tacky, tawdry, ticky-tacky (*also* ticky-tack); rough-edged, rude, trashy, uncouth, uncultivated, uncultured, unpolished, unrefined, vulgar
antonyms dowdy, graceless, inelegant, styleless, tasteless, unfashionable, unhandsome, unstylish
2 having qualities that appeal to a refined taste ⟨prepared an *elegant* dinner for the honored guests⟩ — see CHOICE 1

elegiac *also* **elegiacal** *adj* causing or marked by an atmosphere lacking in cheer ⟨The sight of an old ruined church or castle can be a pleasantly *elegiac* experience.⟩ — see GLOOMY 1

elegy *n* a composition expressing one's grief over a loss ⟨"O Captain! My Captain!" is Walt Whitman's *elegy* on the death of President Lincoln.⟩ — see LAMENT 2

element *n* **1** one of the parts that make up a whole ⟨A free press is an essential *element* of a democracy.⟩
synonyms building block, component, constituent, factor, ingredient, member
related words basis, part and parcel; detail, item, particular, point; aspect, characteristic, facet, feature, trait; division, fragment, particle, partition, piece, portion, section, sector, segment; subcomponent
near antonyms aggregate, composite, compound, mass; sum, summation, total, totality; admixture, amalgam, amalgamation, blend, combination, intermixture, mix, mixture
antonyms whole
2 elements *pl* general or basic truths on which other truths or theories can be based ⟨The *elements* of mathematics can be traced back to Euclid.⟩ — see PRINCIPLES 1
3 a region of activity, knowledge, or influence ⟨She felt most in her *element* in the mathematics section of the exam.⟩ — see FIELD 2

elemental *adj* of or relating to the simplest facts or theories of a subject ⟨Even if you're not planning on becoming a scientist, you should have an *elemental* knowledge of chemistry.⟩ — see ELEMENTARY

elementary *adj* of or relating to the simplest facts or theories of a subject ⟨students who do not have even an *elementary* knowledge of geography⟩
synonyms basic, beginning, elemental, essential, fundamental, introductory, rudimentary, underlying
related words primal, primary, prime, simple; crude, primeval, primitive, primordial, rude, uncomplicated; preliminary, preparatory; crucial, important, key
near antonyms complex, sophisticated; complicated, convoluted, detailed, elaborate, extensive, intricate; developed, evolved, high, higher, refined
antonyms advanced

elephantine *adj* unusually large ⟨The wedding reception was held under an *elephantine* tent on the great lawn.⟩ — see HUGE

elevate *vb* **1** to fill with great joy ⟨Seeing their son graduate from college was one of the most *elevating* moments in their lives.⟩ — see ELATE
2 to move from a lower to a higher place or position ⟨the old trick of using a fat phone book to *elevate* a child to a more comfortable position at the table⟩ — see RAISE 1
3 to move higher in rank or position ⟨She was *elevated* to department chair.⟩ — see PROMOTE 1
4 to assign a high status or value to ⟨a decade in which greed and selfishness were *elevated* to the rank of virtues⟩ — see EXALT 1

elevated *adj* **1** being positioned above a surface ⟨an *elevated* monorail that transports visitors all over the theme park⟩
synonyms lifted, raised, uplifted, upraised
related words aerial; erect, perpendicular, standing, upright, upstanding, vertical
near antonyms low, low-lying, short, squat
antonyms sunken
2 very dignified in form, tone, or style ⟨the *elevated* language of Lincoln's Gettysburg Address⟩
synonyms eloquent, formal, high-flown, lofty, majestic, stately, towering
related words affected, bombastic, declamatory, florid, flowery, grandiloquent, grandiose, highfalutin (*also* hifalutin), oratorical, pompous, pretentious, rhetorical (*also* rhetoric), stilted; cultured, refined; classy, courtly, fine, graceful, tasteful; aristocratic, genteel, patrician; correct, educated, grammatical, proper; academic (*also* academical), bookish, learned, literary
near antonyms casual, colloquial, conversational, informal, nonformal, slangy, unbookish, unliterary, vernacular; coarse, common, crass, crude, gross, ill-bred, indecent, lowbred, lowbrow, rough, rude, tasteless, uncouth, uncultivated, uncultured, unpolished, unrefined, vulgar; incorrect, substandard, uneducated, unlearned
antonyms ineloquent, low, undignified
3 being at a higher level than average ⟨For the next several days temperatures will be a little *elevated* for this time of year.⟩ — see HIGH 2
4 having, characterized by, or arising from a dignified and generous nature ⟨The offspring of this very wealthy family have been instilled with the *elevated* notion that they should devote their lives to public service.⟩ — see NOBLE 2
5 located at a greater height than average or usual ⟨From their *elevated* position the machine gunners had a commanding view of the whole battlefield.⟩ — see HIGH 3
6 experiencing or marked by overwhelming usually pleasurable emotion ⟨She's been in an *elevated* mood all week after hearing that she got the promotion.⟩ — see ECSTATIC
elevation *n* **1** a raising or a state of being raised to a higher rank or position ⟨The appointment of Sandra Day O'Connor marked the first *elevation* of a woman to the U.S. Supreme Court.⟩ — see ADVANCEMENT 1
2 an area of high ground ⟨Little Round Top is one of the most visited *elevations* in the entire Gettysburg National Military Park.⟩ — see HEIGHT 4
3 the distance of something or someone from bottom to top ⟨The *elevation* of Angel Falls is 979 meters, making it the world's highest waterfall.⟩ — see HEIGHT 3
4 the most extreme or advanced point ⟨Some people contend that Western civilization reached its *elevation* in Greece around 400 B.C.⟩ — see HEIGHT 2
elf *n* an imaginary being usually having a small human form and magical powers ⟨*Elves* are often portrayed as rather mischievous.⟩ — see FAIRY
elfin *adj* having an often mysterious or magical power to attract ⟨The heroine in the story has an *elfin* charm.⟩ — see FASCINATING 1
elfish *adj* given to good-natured joking or teasing ⟨an *elfish* comedian who often played wisecracking sidekicks⟩ — see PLAYFUL
elicit *vb* to draw out (something hidden, latent, or reserved) ⟨The role *elicited* the actress's flair for comedy that previous directors had overlooked.⟩ — see EDUCE
eliminate *vb* to prevent the participation, consideration, or inclusion of ⟨The stiff entry fee is intended to *eliminate* less-than-serious competitors.⟩ — see EXCLUDE

elite *n* **1** individuals carefully selected as being the best of a class ⟨The winners of this science award represent the *elite* of our high schools.⟩
synonyms aristocracy, best, choice, cream, elect, fat, flower, pick, pride, prime, upper crust
related words establishment, gentry, nobility, quality, society, top, top drawer, upper class
phrases cream of the crop, Hall of Fame
near antonyms commoners, herd, masses, mob, multitude, rank and file, unwashed
2 the highest class in a society ⟨The country's *elite* owned or controlled most of the wealth.⟩ — see ARISTOCRACY 1
elixir *n* something that cures all ills or problems ⟨warned that casino gambling would not be an *elixir* for all of the region's economic woes⟩ — see CURE-ALL
elocution *n* the art of speaking in public eloquently and effectively ⟨the oft-told story that he practiced *elocution* by learning to speak with a mouth full of pebbles⟩ — see ORATORY 1
elongate *vb* to make longer ⟨These exercises can *elongate* your leg muscles.⟩ — see EXTEND 1
elongate *or* **elongated** *adj* of great extent from end to end ⟨The giraffe's *elongate* neck is thought to be the result of natural selection.⟩ — see LONG 1
elongation *n* the act of making longer ⟨the *elongation* of artificial fibers in the manufacturing process⟩ — see EXTENSION 1
eloquence *n* the art or power of speaking or writing in a forceful and convincing way ⟨the *eloquence* of Martin Luther King's "I Have a Dream" speech⟩
synonyms articulateness, poetry, rhetoric
related words expression, expressiveness; declamation, elocution, oratory; cogency, force, forcefulness, meaningfulness, persuasion, persuasiveness; ardor, emotion, fervency, fervidness, fervor, heat, intensity, passion, power, vehemence, warmth
phrases gift of gab
antonyms inarticulateness
eloquent *adj* **1** able to express oneself clearly and well ⟨An *eloquent* writer and speaker, Elizabeth Cady Stanton was one of the founders of the women's rights movement.⟩ — see ARTICULATE
2 clearly conveying a special meaning (as one's mood) ⟨In an *eloquent* gesture, the defeated general was graciously given back his sword at the surrender ceremonies.⟩ — see EXPRESSIVE
3 very dignified in form, tone, or style ⟨President Kennedy's *eloquent* inaugural address is often credited with inspiring a whole generation.⟩ — see ELEVATED 2
else *adj* resulting in an increase in amount or number ⟨Is there anything *else* you would like to add to your list?⟩ — see ADDITIONAL
else *adv* in a different way ⟨If you could do it over again, how *else* would you have done it?⟩ — see OTHERWISE
elucidate *vb* to make plain or understandable ⟨colored charts that really help to *elucidate* the points made in the text⟩ — see EXPLAIN 1
elucidation *n* a statement that makes something clear ⟨The candidate issued *elucidations* of his earlier statements.⟩ — see EXPLANATION 1
elucidative *adj* serving to explain ⟨Most editions of Shakespeare's plays now have *elucidative* footnotes to help the modern reader.⟩ — see EXPLANATORY
elude *vb* to get or keep away from (as a responsibility) through cleverness or trickery ⟨the millionaire had been *eluding* his fair share of taxes for years before getting caught⟩ — see ESCAPE 2
eluding *n* the act or a means of getting or keeping away from something undesirable ⟨The disease's *eluding* of a

cure ended with the development of the new drug.〉 —
see ESCAPE 2

elusive *adj* hard to find, capture, or isolate 〈The giant
squid is one of the ocean's most *elusive* inhabitants.〉
synonyms evasive, fugitive
related words cagey (*also* cagy), shifty; ephemeral, evanescent, fleeting, impermanent, momentary, passing,
short-lived, temporary, transient, transitory; inaccessible, inconvenient, unapproachable, unattainable, unavailable, unobtainable, unreachable, untouchable
near antonyms accessible, approachable, attainable,
available, convenient, obtainable, reachable

elvish *adj* tending to or exhibiting reckless playfulness
〈With *elvish* glee the children on the swing went higher
and higher.〉 — see MISCHIEVOUS 1

Elysium *n* **1** a dwelling place of perfect happiness for the
soul after death 〈The Roman citizens were comforted by
their belief that their beloved leader was now experiencing the joys of *Elysium*.〉 — see HEAVEN 1
2 an often imaginary place or state of utter perfection
and happiness 〈The universal dream that there exists
somewhere an earthly *Elysium* where people live trouble-
free lives.〉 — see PARADISE 1

emaciated *adj* suffering extreme weight loss as a result of
hunger or disease 〈As she recovered, she grew less *emaciated*.〉
synonyms cadaverous, gaunt, haggard, skeletal, wasted
related words lank, lanky, rawboned, scraggy, scrawny,
sinewy, skinny, spare, thin; starved, underfed, undernourished; famished, hungry, starving; shriveled (*or*
shrivelled), withered, wizened
near antonyms beefy, brawny, burly, fit, hale, healthy,
hearty, husky; chubby, corpulent, fat, fleshy, heavyset,
obese, overweight, plump, portly, pudgy, roly-poly, rotund, stocky, thickset, tubby; flabby, soft

emancipate *vb* to release (as from slavery or confinement)
〈Under the cover of darkness animal rights activists
emancipated the inhabitants of the mink ranch.〉 — see
FREE 1

emancipation *n* the act of setting free from slavery 〈a
book discussing the *emancipation* of enslaved people〉 —
see LIBERATION

emasculate *vb* to deprive of courage or confidence 〈Being
eliminated early in one's very first tournament can be an
emasculating experience.〉 — see UNNERVE 1

embankment *n* a bank of earth constructed to control water 〈The *embankment* is steep, so be careful walking
along the ridge.〉 — see DAM

embargo *n* an order that something not be done or used
〈There's a standing *embargo* against the use of foul language in this house.〉 — see PROHIBITION 2

embark (on *or* **upon)** *vb* to take the first step in (a process
or course of action) 〈She's eager to finish college and to
embark upon a career in teaching.〉 — see BEGIN 1

embarrass *vb* **1** to throw into a state of self-conscious distress 〈The modest young soldier was *embarrassed* by the
public praise for his heroism.〉
synonyms abash, confound, confuse, discomfit, disconcert, discountenance, faze, fluster, mortify, nonplus, rattle
related words agitate, bother, chagrin, discomfort, discompose, dismay, disquiet, distress, disturb, perturb, put
off, put out, unhinge, unsettle, upset; debase, degrade,
demean, humble, humiliate, shame
near antonyms calm, comfort, console, relieve, soothe;
buoy, cheer, embolden, encourage, hearten; assure, reassure
2 to create difficulty for the work or activity of 〈A lot of
this paperwork is unnecessary and just *embarrasses* the
organization.〉 — see HAMPER

3 to make complex or difficult 〈He claims that the new
government regulations will needlessly *embarrass* the operations of small businesses in the state.〉 — see COMPLI-
CATE

embarrassing *adj* causing embarrassment 〈An *embarrassing* failure of memory inauspiciously marked my first appearance as an actor.〉 — see AWKWARD 3

embarrassment *n* **1** the emotional state of being made
self-consciously uncomfortable 〈experienced the great
embarrassment of tripping while on stage〉
synonyms abashment, confusion, discomfiture, fluster,
mortification
related words agitation, bother, chagrin, discomfort,
discomposure, dismay, disquiet, distress, disturbance,
perturbation, uneasiness, upset; disgrace, ignominy,
shame; debasement, degradation, humiliation, mortification; humble pie
phrases egg on one's face
near antonyms aplomb, assurance, composure, confidence, coolness, equanimity, poise, self-assurance, self-
confidence, self-possession
2 something that makes movement or progress difficult
〈A big suitcase filled with clothes proved to be more an
embarrassment than a convenience on my trip.〉 — see
ENCUMBRANCE

embed *also* **imbed** *vb* to set solidly in or as if in surrounding matter 〈The nails were solidly *embedded* in those old
plaster walls.〉 — see ENTRENCH

embellish *vb* **1** to add to the interest of by including made-
up details 〈The story of the comic marriage proposal was
embellished as it passed from one generation to the next
in the family.〉 — see EMBROIDER
2 to make more attractive by adding something that is
beautiful or becoming 〈The walls of the French restaurant are *embellished* with scenes of Parisian life.〉 — see
DECORATE

embellishing *adj* serving to add beauty 〈The chef tends to
overuse sprigs of parsley and other *embellishing* garnish-
es on dishes that don't need them.〉 — see DECORATIVE

embellishment *n* **1** something that decorates or beautifies
〈A colorful mobile is just the *embellishment* that the
soon-to-be nursery needs.〉 — see DECORATION 1
2 the representation of something in terms that go beyond the facts 〈The actor's penchant for *embellishment*
suggests that his memoirs would be more appropriately
shelved in the fiction section.〉 — see EXAGGERATION

embitter *vb* to implant bitter feelings in 〈They refused to
let the unfortunate incident *embitter* them.〉
synonyms antagonize, envenom
related words aggravate, anger, enrage, incense, infuriate, madden; alienate, disaffect, disgruntle, estrange, set
(against); curdle, sour
near antonyms endear, ingratiate; appease, assuage,
mollify, pacify, placate, propitiate

embittered *adj* having or showing deep-seated resentment
〈Gradually the *embittered* woman realized that her lingering feelings of hatred were slowly destroying her.〉 —
see BITTER 1

emblem *n* a device, design, or figure used as an identifying
mark 〈The state uses a beehive as its *emblem*.〉
synonyms ensign, hallmark, logo, symbol, trademark
related words attribute, icon (*also* ikon), pictograph;
logogram, logograph; badge, coat of arms, cognizance,
crest, insignia, monogram; colophon, stamp, token

emblematic *also* **emblematical** *adj* having the function or
meaning of an object or figure that stands for something
else 〈The dove is *emblematic* of the organization's mission to bring some peace to a troubled world.〉 — see
SYMBOLIC

embodiment *n* a visible representation of something abstract (as a quality) ⟨Mother Theresa was often regarded as the *embodiment* of selfless devotion to others.⟩
synonyms abstract, epitome, genius, icon (*also* ikon), image, incarnation, manifestation, personification
related words concretization, exemplification, personalization, realization, substantiation; essence, quintessence, soul; archetype, exemplar, model, paradigm, pattern; reincarnation

embody *vb* **1** to make a part of a body or system ⟨They must *embody* their ideas in substantial institutions if they are to survive.⟩
synonyms absorb, assimilate, incorporate, integrate
related words amalgamate, blend, combine, commingle, fuse, intermingle, merge, mingle; acculturate, accustom, condition, enculturate, naturalize
2 to represent in visible form ⟨George Washington *embodied* so many of the virtues that Americans hold dear.⟩
synonyms body, epitomize, express, incarnate, incorporate, manifest, materialize, personalize, personify, substantiate
related words actualize, concretize, realize; exemplify, illustrate, image, objectify, symbolize, typify
antonyms disembody

embolden *vb* to fill with courage or strength of purpose ⟨His poor showing in his first swim meet just *emboldened* him to train even harder.⟩ — see ENCOURAGE 1

emboldened *adj* inclined or willing to take risks ⟨Not too surprisingly, rock climbing tends to attract the more *emboldened* seekers of outdoor adventure.⟩ — see BOLD 1

embosom *vb* **1** to surround or cover closely ⟨a villa that has been *embosomed* by the verdant hills of northern Italy for three centuries⟩ — see ENFOLD 1

embower *vb* to surround or cover closely ⟨Over the years grapevines have completely *embowered* the summerhouse in the garden.⟩ — see ENFOLD 1

embrace *vb* **1** to put one's arms around and press tightly ⟨Upon being finally reunited, the overjoyed father *embraced* his son.⟩
synonyms clasp, crush, enfold, grasp, hug, strain
related words clamp, cling, cradle, grab, grip, hold; bosom, embosom, encircle, entwine, envelop; fold, lock, twine, wrap; cuddle, fondle, nestle, nuzzle, pat, pet, snuggle, stroke
2 to surround or cover closely ⟨The stone walls that *embrace* the monastery serve to symbolize its function as a retreat from an unquiet world.⟩ — see ENFOLD 1
3 to take for one's own use (something originated by another) ⟨Rap music came to be *embraced* by people who were far removed from where it originated.⟩ — see ADOPT
4 to receive or accept gladly or readily ⟨The exchange student was gratified to be so quickly *embraced* by people of the small rural community.⟩ — see WELCOME
5 to have as part of a whole ⟨A course in social studies can *embrace* everything from sociology to civics and economics.⟩ — see INCLUDE 1
6 to form a circle around ⟨a sleepy village *embraced* by low hills⟩ — see SURROUND

embroider *vb* to add to the interest of by including made-up details ⟨Dad likes to *embroider* his fishing stories.⟩
synonyms color, elaborate (on), embellish, exaggerate, magnify, pad, stretch
related words dress up; amplify, enhance, expand, flesh (out); fudge, hedge; overdo, overdraw, overemphasize, overplay, overstate; emphasize, stress; caricature; satirize
near antonyms belittle, minimize, play down, understate

embroidering *n* the representation of something in terms that go beyond the facts ⟨With considerable *embroidering* the owners of the bed-and-breakfast have turned a few odd incidents into a full-blown legend of ghostly apparitions.⟩ — see EXAGGERATION

embroidery *n* **1** decorative stitching done on cloth with the use of a needle ⟨She's been able to turn her skill at *embroidery* into a second business selling decorative cushions at craft fairs.⟩ — see NEEDLEWORK
2 the representation of something in terms that go beyond the facts ⟨It's doubtful that she ever told an anecdote without considerable *embroidery*.⟩ — see EXAGGERATION

embroil *vb* to place in conflict or difficulties ⟨The town has been *embroiled* in controversy over the building of the huge shopping mall.⟩
synonyms bog (down), mire
related words enmesh (*also* immesh), ensnare, entangle, entrap, snare, tangle, trap
near antonyms emancipate, free, liberate, release

emend *vb* to remove errors, defects, deficiencies, or deviations from ⟨The first printout quickly revealed that our computer program needed to be *emended*.⟩ — see CORRECT 1

emendation *n* a change designed to correct or improve a written work ⟨The governor's numerous *emendations* to the speechwriter's first draft left not one sentence untouched.⟩ — see CORRECTION 1

emerge *vb* to come to one's attention especially gradually or unexpectedly ⟨Problems *emerged* almost as soon as the contractor began the excavation for the swimming pool.⟩ — see ARISE 2

emergency *n* a time or state of affairs requiring prompt or decisive action ⟨an alert, quick-thinking girl who is good to have around in an *emergency*⟩
synonyms clutch, crisis, crossroad(s), crunch, exigency, extremity, head, juncture, zero hour
related words contingency, possibility; climax, turning point; happening, landmark, milestone; condition, pass, situation, strait; deadlock, impasse, stalemate; corner, fix, hole, hot water, jam, last ditch, pinch, predicament, scrape, spot; eleventh hour, last minute
phrases moment of truth, point of no return

emigrant *n* one that leaves one place to settle in another ⟨a city with *emigrants* from many lands⟩
synonyms émigré (*also* emigré), immigrant, migrant, settler
related words defector, deportee, evacuee, exile, expatriate, refugee, relocatee, repatriate; alien, foreigner, illegal, noncitizen, nonnative; colonist, newcomer, squatter; migrator, pilgrim, pioneer, trekker
near antonyms aborigine, native; citizen, habitant, inhabitant, national, resident
antonyms nonimmigrant

émigré *also* **emigré** *n* **1** a person forced to emigrate for political reasons ⟨The revolution resulted in a flood of *émigrés* into neighboring countries.⟩
synonyms deportee, evacuee, exile, expatriate, refugee
related words alien, fugitive; castoff, outcast, pariah; loyalist, patriot
2 one that leaves one place to settle in another ⟨The *émigrés* moved into many different nations.⟩ — see EMIGRANT

eminence *n* **1** the fact or state of being above others in rank or importance ⟨the *eminence* of the Nobel Prize in the field of awards and prizes⟩
synonyms distinction, dominance, noteworthiness, preeminence, primacy, superiority, supremacy, transcendence
related words celebrity, fame, famousness, glory, honor,

renown, reputation, repute; megastardom, stardom, superstardom; greatness, illustriousness, nobleness, notableness; ascendancy (*also* ascendency), authority, domination, dominion; influence, power, prestige, weight; infamy, notoriety
near antonyms inferiority, mediocrity; obscureness, obscurity
2 an area of high ground ⟨The old citadel sits on an *eminence* with a commanding view of the city.⟩ — see HEIGHT 4

eminent *adj* standing above others in rank, importance, or achievement ⟨Many *eminent* surgeons are on the hospital's staff.⟩
synonyms astral, bright, distinguished, illustrious, luminous, noble, notable, noteworthy, outstanding, preeminent, prestigious, redoubtable, signal, star, superior
related words celebrated, exalted, famed, famous, glorious, honored, renowned, reputable; infamous, notorious; dominant, paramount, predominant
near antonyms insignificant, minor, unimportant; average, inferior, mediocre; obscure, uncelebrated, unsung

emissary *n* **1** a person sent on a mission to represent another ⟨Most of the industrialized nations of the world sent *emissaries* to the conference on global warming.⟩ — see AMBASSADOR
2 a person who tries secretly to obtain information for one country in the territory of another usually unfriendly country ⟨The embassy's staff likely contains at least one *emissary* who reports to the home country's chief of intelligence.⟩ — see SPY

emit *vb* **1** to throw or give off ⟨nuclei that *emit* gamma rays⟩
synonyms cast, discharge, evolve, exhale, expel, give out, irradiate, issue, radiate, release, shoot, throw out, vent
related words eliminate, evacuate, excrete, exude, ooze, secrete; eject, erupt, gush, jet, pour, spew, spout, spray, spurt, squirt
near antonyms absorb, soak (up), sponge, suck (up), take up
2 to send forth using the vocal chords ⟨I was so scared I couldn't *emit* a peep.⟩ — see UTTER 1

emolument *n* the money paid regularly to a person for labor or services ⟨The annual *emolument* for the director of the charity is officially only one dollar.⟩ — see WAGE

emotion *n* **1** a subjective response to a person, thing, or situation ⟨My *emotions* after hearing the good news went from complete surprise to overwhelming joy.⟩ — see FEELING 1
2 depth of feeling ⟨The *emotion* that the singer is able to instill in "Amazing Grace" is truly stirring.⟩ — see ARDOR 1

emotional *adj* **1** having or expressing great depth of feeling ⟨Worship at revival meetings often takes a markedly *emotional* form.⟩ — see FERVENT 1
2 having the power to affect the feelings or sympathies ⟨In one *emotional* scene in the movie the boy must say goodbye to his extraterrestrial friend.⟩ — see MOVING
3 showing feeling freely ⟨The fact that he is not a very *emotional* person does not mean that he is not a loving, caring father.⟩ — see DEMONSTRATIVE 1

emphasis *n* **1** a special notice or importance given to something ⟨a college with a long-established *emphasis* on sports⟩
synonyms accent, accentuation, stress, weight
related words attention, concentration, focus; consequence, import, moment, note, significance, value, worth; precedence, primacy, priority; consideration, heed, regard

near antonyms minimization, underemphasis; disregard, indifference
antonyms de-emphasis
2 the quality or state of being forceful (as in expression) ⟨The *emphasis* with which my parents issued the warning about smoking left no doubt that they were serious.⟩ — see VEHEMENCE 1

emphasize *vb* **1** to indicate the importance of by centering attention on ⟨supermarket tabloids that *emphasize* sensational news stories⟩
synonyms accent, accentuate, feature, highlight, illuminate, point (up), press, stress
related words focus, identify, pinpoint; advertise, boost, plug, promote, publicize; overplay
phrases bear down on, make much of
near antonyms tone (down), underemphasize, understate; belittle, discount, disparage, minimize
antonyms de-emphasize, play down
2 to make more apparent ⟨The long drapes *emphasize* the height of the ceiling.⟩
synonyms accentuate, stress, underline, underscore
related words amplify, beef (up), boost, strengthen; augment, deepen, enhance, enlarge, heighten, magnify, maximize, supplement; enliven, jazz (up)
near antonyms decrease, diminish, lessen, minimize, reduce, subdue, tone (down), understate, weaken
antonyms de-emphasize

emphatic *adj* **1** marked by or uttered with forcefulness ⟨The governor issued an *emphatic* denial of all charges.⟩
synonyms aggressive, assertive, dynamic, energetic, forceful, full-blooded, muscular, resounding, strenuous, vehement, vigorous, violent
related words decided, insistent, marked, pointed; absolute, categorical (*also* categoric), clear, plain, unambiguous, unequivocal; arresting, compelling, conspicuous, impelling, noticeable, striking
near antonyms guarded, mild, weak, wishy-washy; ambiguous, equivocal, halting, hesitant; understated
antonyms nonassertive, nonemphatic, unemphatic
2 likely to attract attention ⟨With all of the decorative fishing nets, lobster pots, and oars, the seafood restaurant's nautical theme was a little too *emphatic* for my taste.⟩ — see NOTICEABLE

empire *n* a group of businesses or enterprises under one control ⟨The media mogul's *empire* consists of newspapers, TV stations, and cable companies.⟩ — see CONGLOMERATE

empirical *also* **empiric** *adj* **1** based on observation or experience ⟨guidelines for raising children that are based on *empirical* evidence⟩
synonyms experimental, objective, observational
related words actual, factual, genuine, hard, material, real; accepted, established, tried, tried-and-true; indisputable, undeniable; demonstrable, provable, verifiable
near antonyms conjectural, hypothetical, speculative; unproven, unsubstantiated; metaphysical, transcendentalist, visionary
antonyms nonempirical, theoretical (*also* theoretic), unempirical
2 capable of being proven as true or real ⟨an *empirical* fact⟩ — see VERIFIABLE

employ *n* the state of being provided with a paying job ⟨While you're under our *employ*, you can't do outside work for our competitors.⟩ — see HIRE 1

employ *vb* **1** to provide with a paying job ⟨a new factory that will *employ* 500 people⟩
synonyms assume, engage, hire, pay, place, recruit, retain, take on
related words reemploy, reengage, rehire; apprentice,

contract, job, partner, subcontract; enlist; advance, promote, upgrade; keep (on); headhunt, scout
near antonyms furlough, lay off, lock out
antonyms can, discharge, dismiss, fire, sack
2 to put into action or service ⟨She's looking for a job in which she can *employ* her considerable writing skills.⟩ — see USE 1

employable *adj* capable of or suitable for being used for a particular purpose ⟨This wall map of the bay is for decoration only—it's not *employable* for actual navigation.⟩ — see USABLE 1

employed *adj* involved in often constant activity ⟨insisted that the children be *employed* in some useful activity, even during school vacations⟩ — see BUSY 1

employee *also* **employe** *n* one who works for another for wages or a salary ⟨an employer who was loved and admired by generations of *employees*⟩
synonyms hand, hireling, jobholder, retainer, worker
related words assistant, cog, flunky (*also* flunkey *or* flunkie), subordinate, underling, yes-man; drudge, grub, hack, jobber, laborer, toiler; nine-to-fiver, wage earner, wageworker, workingman, workingwoman, workman, workwoman; associate, colleague, coworker; temp, temporary
near antonyms boss, superior, supervisor
antonyms employer

employment *n* **1** the act or practice of employing something for a particular purpose ⟨the *employment* of charcoal in sketching⟩ — see USE 1
2 the activity by which one regularly makes a living ⟨His regular *employment* is that of a restaurant waiter, but he always identifies himself as an actor.⟩ — see OCCUPATION
3 the state of being provided with a paying job ⟨The parents tried to convey to their children the joys of meaningful *employment*.⟩ — see HIRE 1

emporium *n* an establishment where goods are sold to consumers ⟨an *emporium* for home electronic equipment filled with stuff I didn't know I needed but now desperately want⟩ — see SHOP 1

empower *vb* **1** to give official or legal power to ⟨the federal agency *empowered* to collect taxes⟩ — see AUTHORIZE 1
2 to make able or possible ⟨workshops in financial management to *empower* workers to plan for their retirement⟩ — see ENABLE 1

emptiness *n* **1** a need or desire for food ⟨the *emptiness* that usually sets in about three o'clock in the afternoon⟩ — see HUNGER 1
2 empty space ⟨There in the vast *emptiness* of the desert was a long-abandoned jeep.⟩ — see VACANCY 1
3 the quality or state of being empty ⟨The *emptiness* of the interior of the isolated house just made it seem all the more eerie.⟩ — see VACANCY 2

empty *adj* **1** lacking contents that could or should be present ⟨The refrigerator is *empty*, so we'll have to eat out.⟩
synonyms bare, blank, clean, devoid, stark, vacant, vacuous, void
related words barren, hollow; available, clear, free, open; unfilled, unfurnished; unattended, uninhabited, unoccupied; abandoned, deserted, emptied, forsaken, vacated; depleted, drained, dry, exhausted
near antonyms complete; replete; furnished, provided, supplied; filled, occupied; flush, overflowing, packed, teeming
antonyms full
2 feeling a desire or need for food ⟨As the long car trip wore on, we all started to feel a little *empty*.⟩ — see HUNGRY 1

3 having no meaning ⟨Her apology was just an *empty* gesture.⟩ — see MEANINGLESS
4 having no usefulness ⟨an *empty* task that was assigned just to keep us busy⟩ — see WORTHLESS
5 producing no results ⟨All of the leads in the missing-person case were turning up *empty*.⟩ — see FUTILE
6 not expressing any emotion ⟨a crowd of *empty* faces⟩ — see BLANK 1

empty *vb* to remove the contents of ⟨*Empty* the room before starting to paint the ceiling.⟩
synonyms clear, evacuate, vacate, void
related words deplete, drain, eliminate, exhaust, waste; bleed, draw (off); clean, flush, purge, scour, sweep
antonyms fill, load

emulate *vb* **1** to be the same in meaning or effect ⟨What they offered at the new resort didn't begin to *emulate* the kind of pampering we were used to getting at the resort that closed down.⟩ — see AMOUNT (TO) 2
2 to use (someone or something) as the model for one's speech, mannerisms, or behavior ⟨a pro athlete who has often said that children should *emulate* their parents—not him⟩ — see IMITATE 1

emulative *adj* using or marked by the use of something else as a basis or model ⟨Right now she's an *emulative* singer, not having yet created a style of her own.⟩ — see IMITATIVE 1

enable *vb* **1** to make able or possible ⟨My new glasses *enable* me to read the fine print.⟩
synonyms allow, empower, let, permit
related words fit, prepare, qualify, ready; approve, endorse (*also* indorse), sanction; condition, equip
near antonyms inhibit, preclude; disallow, enjoin, forbid, prohibit
antonyms prevent
2 to give official or legal power to ⟨a law that would *enable* the authorities to use wiretaps without obtaining court orders⟩ — see AUTHORIZE 1

enact *vb* to put into effect through legislative or authoritative action ⟨Congress *enacts* all laws relating to foreign trade and immigration.⟩
synonyms constitute, lay down, legislate, make, ordain, pass
related words reenact, repass; bring about, effect; allow, authorize, permit, sanction; decree, dictate, proclaim; administer, execute; approve, confirm, ratify
near antonyms abolish, abrogate, annul, cancel, invalidate, kill, nullify; overturn, reverse, void
antonyms repeal, rescind, revoke

enactment *n* **1** a rule of conduct or action laid down by a governing authority and especially a legislature ⟨As a result of an *enactment* by Congress, this breathtaking canyon will be permanently protected from development.⟩ — see LAW 1
2 the doing of an action ⟨The *enactment* of the crime is never actually shown on screen.⟩ — see COMMISSION 2

enamored (of) *adj* filled with an intense or excessive love for ⟨I became completely *enamored of* the city and its people.⟩
synonyms crazy (about *or* over), enraptured (by), gone (on), infatuated (with), mad (about), nuts (about)
related words hung up (on), obsessed; foolish, silly, wild; bewitched, captivated, charmed, enchanted, entranced, fascinated
phrases stuck on, sweet on
near antonyms cool, detached, unenchanted, unimpressed; disenchanted, disillusioned; heart-free

encamp *vb* **1** to live in a camp or the outdoors ⟨The hike will take several days, and we plan to *encamp* along the trail.⟩ — see CAMP (OUT)

2 to provide with living quarters or shelter ⟨the locations where Napoleon's troops were *encamped*⟩ — see HOUSE 1

encampment *n* a place where a group of people live for a short time in tents or cabins ⟨a recreational area that will serve as this year's *encampment* for the Scouts' jamboree⟩ — see CAMP 1

encapsulate *vb* to make into a short statement of the main points (as of a report) ⟨Can you *encapsulate* the president's speech in about a paragraph?⟩ — see SUMMARIZE

encapsulation *n* a short statement of the main points ⟨didn't have time to read the full news article, just the *encapsulation* on the second page⟩ — see SUMMARY

encase *vb* to close or shut in by or as if by barriers ⟨Ice *encased* the trees after the storm.⟩ — see ENCLOSE 1

enchain *vb* to confine or restrain with or as if with chains ⟨He stopped being *enchained* by fear.⟩ — see BIND 1

enchant *vb* **1** to attract or delight as if by magic ⟨The child actress *enchanted* audiences with her bubbly personality.⟩ — see CHARM 1

2 to cast a spell on ⟨Out of spite, the jealous queen *enchanted* her chief rival for the title of the fairest one of all.⟩ — see BEWITCH 1

3 to hold the attention of as if by a spell ⟨The tales about the young wizard have *enchanted* children around the globe.⟩ — see ENTHRALL 1

enchanted *adj* being or appearing to be under a magic spell ⟨an *enchanted* isle of the South Pacific⟩

synonyms bewitched, charmed, entranced, magic, magical, spellbound

related words jinxed; dreamy, fairy, fairylike; fantastic (*also* fantastical), miraculous, utopian, wondrous; hypnotized, mesmerized; bedazzled, captivated, fascinated

enchanter *n* a person skilled in using supernatural forces ⟨In Shakespeare's play an *enchanter* creates a storm at sea that causes his rivals to be cast upon the shores of his magical isle.⟩ — see MAGICIAN 1

enchanting *adj* having an often mysterious or magical power to attract ⟨Visitors have long found the Highlands of Scotland to be an *enchanting* place.⟩ — see FASCINATING 1

enchantment *n* **1** a spoken word or set of words believed to have magic power ⟨stories about magic potions and *enchantments*⟩ — see SPELL 1

2 the power of irresistible attraction ⟨He writes about the *enchantments* of sailing.⟩ — see CHARM 2

3 the power to control natural forces through supernatural means ⟨There are people even today who claim to be skilled in *enchantment*.⟩ — see MAGIC 1

enchantress *n* **1** a woman believed to have often harmful supernatural powers ⟨In Homer's *Odyssey*, an *enchantress* turns some of Odysseus's men into swine.⟩ — see WITCH 1

2 a woman whom men find irresistibly attractive ⟨Scarlett O'Hara is one of literature's most celebrated *enchantresses*.⟩ — see SIREN

3 a lovely woman ⟨an *enchantress* of the silver screen whose legend has only grown over the years⟩ — see BEAUTY 2

encircle *vb* **1** to travel completely around ⟨communication satellites *encircling* the earth⟩

synonyms circle, circumnavigate, circumvent, compass, girdle, girth, orbit, ring, round

related words circumambulate, cross, traverse

2 to form a circle around ⟨Immediately after announcing their engagement, the couple was *encircled* by their applauding friends.⟩ — see SURROUND

enclose *also* **inclose** *vb* **1** to close or shut in by or as if by barriers ⟨dogs who spend the day *enclosed* in small cages⟩

synonyms cage, closet, coop (up), corral, encase, envelop, fence (in), hedge, house, immure, include, pen, wall (in)

related words bound, circumscribe, confine, contain, limit, restrict; encircle, encompass, enfold, enframe, frame, ring, surround; armor, cocoon, encapsulate, encapsule, encyst, ensheathe, ensphere, enwomb

2 to form a circle around ⟨In a show of support, the women rushed to *enclose* their distraught friend.⟩ — see SURROUND

3 to surround or cover closely ⟨The house was *enclosed* by a high hedge that shielded it from public view.⟩ — see ENFOLD 1

enclosure *also* **inclosure** *n* an open space wholly or partly enclosed (as by buildings or walls) ⟨a fenced-in *enclosure* where the sheep are allowed to graze unattended⟩ — see COURT 2

encomium *n* a formal expression of praise ⟨the *encomiums* bestowed on a teacher at her retirement ceremonies⟩

synonyms accolade, citation, commendation, eulogy, homage, hymn, paean, panegyric, salutation, tribute

related words award, decoration, dedication, honor, prize; acclaim, acclamation, laudation; applause, plaudit(s); bravo; approval, cachet, compliment, recommendation

near antonyms censure, condemnation, denunciation, indictment, rebuke, reprimand, reproof; admonition, correction, harangue, lecture, sermon

encompass *vb* **1** to form a circle around ⟨A necklace of sapphire-blue lakes *encompasses* the town.⟩ — see SURROUND

2 to have as part of a whole ⟨The district *encompasses* most of the downtown area.⟩ — see INCLUDE 1

3 to surround or cover closely ⟨A fog of mystery has long *encompassed* the organization.⟩ — see ENFOLD 1

encounter *n* a brief clash between enemies or rivals ⟨an *encounter* between fans of the rival teams⟩

synonyms brush, hassle, run-in, scrape, skirmish

related words argument, fight, quarrel, row, spat, squabble, tiff; battle, brawl, fray, wrangle

encounter *vb* **1** to come upon face-to-face or as if face-to-face ⟨quite unexpectedly *encountered* our next-door neighbor while vacationing in Europe⟩ — see MEET 1

2 to come upon unexpectedly or by chance ⟨We *encountered* a host of unforeseen problems during the restoration of our 200-year-old house.⟩ — see HAPPEN (ON or UPON)

3 to enter into contest or conflict with ⟨They *encountered* opponents of the plan at the meeting.⟩ — see ENGAGE 2

encourage *vb* **1** to fill with courage or strength of purpose ⟨a pep talk that *encouraged* the team to get out there and do their best⟩

synonyms buoy (up), cheer (up), embolden, hearten, inspire, steel

related words animate, enliven, invigorate; enforce, fortify, strengthen; assure, reassure; boost, energize, excite, galvanize, provoke, quicken, rally, stimulate, stir

near antonyms demoralize, depress, sadden; debilitate, enfeeble, hamstring, undermine, weaken; intimidate, psych (out)

antonyms daunt, discourage, dishearten, dispirit

2 to help the growth or development of ⟨asserted that the government should be *encouraging* small businesses⟩ — see FOSTER 1

3 to rouse to strong feeling or action ⟨The movie's special effects *encourage* audiences to sit on the edge of their seats.⟩ — see PROVOKE 1

4 to try to persuade (someone) through earnest appeals to follow a course of action ⟨My parents *encouraged* me to try out again for the team.⟩ — see URGE

encouragement *n* something that arouses action or activity ⟨The huge rebates that the auto companies were offering were all the *encouragement* I needed to buy a new car.⟩ — see IMPULSE 1

encouraging *adj* **1** having qualities which inspire hope ⟨*encouraging* signs that the economy is improving⟩ — see HOPEFUL 1

2 making one feel good inside ⟨the *encouraging* story of a young girl who overcame great social and physical obstacles to become an outstanding athlete⟩ — see HEARTWARMING

3 pointing toward a happy outcome ⟨We're off to an *encouraging* start on this project.⟩ — see FAVORABLE 2

encroach *vb* to advance gradually beyond the usual or desirable limits ⟨Each year the sea continues to *encroach* upon the island's beaches.⟩
synonyms creep, inch, worm
related words snake, sneak; entrench (*also* intrench), impinge, infringe, intrude, invade; overpass, overreach, overrun, overshoot, overstep

encrust *also* **incrust** *vb* to cover with a hardened layer ⟨My boots were *encrusted* with mud.⟩
synonyms cake, rime
related words besmear, coat, smear, spread; cover, daub; coagulate, congeal, harden

encumber *vb* **1** to create difficulty for the work or activity of ⟨the claim that regulations *encumber* doctors, taking time away from the actual practice of medicine⟩ — see HAMPER
2 to place a weight or burden on ⟨Don't *encumber* your pack animal so much that it can hardly move.⟩ — see LOAD 1

encumbrance *n* something that makes movement or progress difficult ⟨Without the *encumbrance* of a heavy backpack, I could sprint along the trail.⟩
synonyms balk, bar, block, chain, clog, cramp, crimp, deterrent, drag, embarrassment, fetter, handicap, hindrance, hurdle, impediment, inhibition, interference, manacle, obstacle, obstruction, shackles, stop, stumbling block, trammel
related words catch, hitch, rub, snag; barrier, blockade, blockage, brick wall, stone wall; arrest, bit, brake, check, constraint, curb, hobble, rein, restraint; embargo, stoppage; delay, holdup, stall; burden, cumber, load; danger, hazard, peril, reef; adversity, difficulty, disadvantage, drawback, hardship
near antonyms catalyst, goad, impetus, incentive, spur, stimulant, stimulus; advantage, break, edge; aid, assistance, benefit, boost, help

encyclopedic *adj* covering everything or all important points ⟨a tour guide with an *encyclopedic* knowledge of New York City and its people⟩
synonyms compendious, complete, comprehensive, exhaustive, full, global, inclusive, in-depth, omnibus, panoramic, thorough, universal
related words broad, encyclical, general, inclusionary, overall; cosmic (*also* cosmical), extensive, far, far-reaching, grand, large, vast, wide; blanket, unrestricted
near antonyms circumscribed, limited, narrow, restricted, specialized; exact, precise; individual, singular, specific; incomplete, patchy, sketchy

end *n* **1** the stopping of a process or activity ⟨got a drink at the *end* of practice⟩
synonyms arrest, cease, cessation, check, close, closure, conclusion, discontinuance, ending, expiration, finish, halt, lapse, offset, shutdown, shutoff, stay, stop, stoppage, surcease, termination

related words phaseout; abeyance, break, interruption, layoff, letup, moratorium, pause, standstill, suspension
near antonyms extension, persistence, prolongation
antonyms continuance, continuation

2 a real or imaginary point beyond which a person or thing cannot go ⟨I'm at the *end* of my patience.⟩ — see LIMIT 1

3 an unused or unwanted piece or item typically of small size or value ⟨A couple of *ends* of wallpaper were all that was left after we finished papering the room.⟩ — see ¹SCRAP 1

4 something that one hopes or intends to accomplish ⟨In this case the *ends* definitely do not justify the means.⟩ — see GOAL

5 the last and usually sharp or tapering part of something long and narrow ⟨a child's pair of scissors with blunt *ends*⟩ — see POINT 2

6 the last part of a process or action ⟨The project wasn't yet over, but we were definitely at the beginning of the *end*.⟩ — see FINALE

7 the line or relatively narrow space that marks the outer limit of something ⟨The *ends* of his shirt cuffs were badly frayed.⟩ — see BORDER 1

8 the permanent stopping of all the vital bodily activities ⟨How the explorers met their *end* is unknown.⟩ — see DEATH 1

9 something belonging to, due to, or contributed by an individual member of a group ⟨Keep up your *end* of the bargain.⟩ — see SHARE 1

end *vb* **1** to bring (an event) to a natural or appropriate stopping point ⟨Let's *end* the meeting in half an hour.⟩ — see CLOSE 3

2 to bring (as an action or operation) to an immediate end ⟨Her speech *ended* the ceremony.⟩ — see STOP 1

3 to come to an end ⟨a book so good that you hate to see it *end*⟩ — see CEASE 1

4 to stop living ⟨a great general, who *ended* on the field of battle⟩ — see DIE 1

endanger *vb* to place in danger ⟨a reckless use of fireworks that *endangered* the lives of many people⟩
synonyms adventure, compromise, gamble (with), hazard, imperil, jeopardize, menace, peril, risk, venture
related words intimidate, threaten; expose; subject; chance, wager
near antonyms guard, protect, shelter, shield; preserve, resume, save

endangered *adj* being in a situation where one is likely to meet with harm ⟨a daring attempt to rescue the *endangered* passengers from the burning boat⟩ — see LIABLE 1

endangerment *n* the state of not being protected from injury, harm, or evil ⟨I didn't think I would be subject to any *endangerment* if I simply dangled my legs over the rock ledge.⟩ — see DANGER 1

endearing *adj* **1** having qualities that tend to make one loved ⟨All my friends find kittens and puppies *endearing*.⟩ — see LOVABLE

2 likely or intended to win one's affection ⟨His impish sense of humor is one of his more *endearing* traits.⟩ — see INGRATIATING

endeavor *n* an effort to do or accomplish something ⟨the hope that this latest *endeavor* will yield much information about the atmosphere of the planet⟩ — see ATTEMPT 1

endeavor *vb* **1** to devote serious and sustained effort ⟨The trapped climber *endeavored* mightily to get the boulder to budge.⟩ — see LABOR

2 to make an effort to do ⟨Our club is forever *endeavoring* to find ways to raise more money for activities.⟩ — see ATTEMPT

ended *adj* brought or having come to an end ⟨The recently *ended* season was one of the best that the baseball team ever had.⟩ — see COMPLETE 2

endemic *adj* belonging to a particular place by birth or origin ⟨The fish is not an *endemic* species of the lake, and it is rapidly devouring the native trout population.⟩ — see NATIVE 1

ending *n* 1 the last part of a process or action ⟨Their efforts had a successful *ending*.⟩ — see FINALE
2 the stopping of a process or activity ⟨The best part about any dental procedure is its *ending*.⟩ — see END 1

endless *adj* 1 being or seeming to be without limits ⟨From the promontory visitors can look out over an *endless* sea.⟩ — see INFINITE
2 lasting forever ⟨The *endless* roar is what I remember most about Niagara Falls.⟩ — see EVERLASTING 1

endorse *also* **indorse** *vb* to promote the interests or cause of ⟨an increase in the number of parents who *endorse* the idea of school uniforms⟩ — see SUPPORT 1

endow *vb* 1 to furnish freely or naturally with some power, quality, or attribute ⟨a young performer *endowed* with a great singing voice⟩
synonyms bless, endue (*or* indue), favor, gift, invest
related words equip, provide, supply; bestow (on *or* upon), clothe, confer (on), cover; accord, award, grant; empower, enable, enhance, enrich, heighten; bequeath, will
near antonyms strip; deplete, drain, exhaust; skimp, stint
2 to furnish (as an institution) with a regular source of income ⟨a wealthy businessman who *endowed* several museums⟩
synonyms finance, fund, subsidize
related words establish, found, organize; bequeath, contribute, donate, support, underwrite; award, grant; back, promote, sponsor; capitalize, invest (in)
near antonyms draw; subsist
antonyms defund, disendow
3 to provide money for ⟨The program to bring the arts to youths is *endowed* by a grant from the federal government.⟩ — see FINANCE 1

endowment *n* a special and usually inborn ability ⟨an athlete's physical *endowments*⟩ — see TALENT

endue *or* **indue** *vb* 1 to cause (as a person) to become filled or saturated with a certain quality or principle ⟨professional soldiers *endued* with an ironclad sense of duty and honor⟩ — see INFUSE
2 to furnish freely or naturally with some power, quality, or attribute ⟨She's always been *endued* with an unquenchable optimism.⟩ — see ENDOW 1

endurable *adj* capable of being endured ⟨A flu shot is never pleasant, but I find the momentary pain entirely *endurable*.⟩ — see BEARABLE

endurance *n* uninterrupted or lasting existence ⟨We need to assure the *endurance* of this tradition.⟩ — see CONTINUATION

endure *vb* 1 to come to a knowledge of (something) by living through it ⟨an elderly couple who have *endured* the ups and downs of a half century of married life⟩ — see EXPERIENCE
2 to put up with (something painful or difficult) ⟨At some point we all have to *endure* the loss of a beloved pet.⟩ — see BEAR 2
3 to remain indefinitely in existence or in the same state ⟨The fashion business is built on change, since nobody expects a particular clothing style to *endure*.⟩ — see CONTINUE 1

enduring *adj* having an existence or validity that does not change or diminish ⟨science fiction's *enduring* fascination with worlds beyond our own⟩ — see ABIDING

enemy *n* one that is hostile toward another ⟨a beloved minister with no known *enemies*⟩
synonyms adversary, antagonist, foe, hostile, opponent
related words archenemy, archfoe, nemesis; combatant, invader; competitor, emulator, rival
near antonyms buddy, chum, compadre, crony, fellow, hail-fellow, hail-fellow-well-met, hearty, hobnobber, mate, musketeer, pal; abettor (*also* abetter), accomplice, ally, collaborator, colleague, comrade, confederate, friendly, partner; adherent, disciple, follower; backer, benefactor, exponent, supporter, sympathizer, well-wisher
antonyms friend

energetic *adj* 1 having active strength of body or mind ⟨A lifelong fitness fanatic, he remained *energetic* well into his 80s.⟩ — see VIGOROUS 1
2 having much high-spirited energy and movement ⟨trying to find the right music for an *energetic* aerobics routine⟩ — see LIVELY 1
3 marked by or uttered with forcefulness ⟨The salesperson gave us an *energetic* sales pitch, talking excitedly about the amazing features of this year's cars.⟩ — see EMPHATIC 1

energetically *adv* in a vigorous and forceful manner ⟨The crew worked *energetically* to get the parade float done on time.⟩ — see HARD 3

energize *vb* to give life, vigor, or spirit to ⟨a teacher who knows how to *energize* history lessons with little-known but interesting facts about long-ago people⟩ — see ANIMATE

energized *adj* made or become fresh in spirits or vigor ⟨After a refreshing lunch, we felt *energized* and ready to hit the bike trail once again.⟩ — see NEW 4

energy *n* 1 a spiritual force that is held to emanate from or give animation to living beings ⟨Many Eastern cultures believe in the significance of life *energy* in the healing process.⟩
synonyms aura, vibration(s)
related words inner light, light, nature, soul, spirit; élan vital, life, lifeblood
2 active strength of body or mind ⟨For a woman of advanced years, she has remarkable *energy*.⟩ — see VIGOR 1
3 something with a usable capacity for doing work ⟨Some of the power needs of the house are provided by solar *energy*.⟩ — see FUEL
4 the ability to exert effort for the accomplishment of a task ⟨I'm so tired that I don't think I have the *energy* to take another step.⟩ — see POWER 2

enervate *vb* 1 to deprive of emotional or intellectual vitality ⟨He decided to quit the job that so *enervated* him.⟩ — see DEHYDRATE 1
2 to diminish the physical strength of ⟨The surgery really *enervated* me for weeks afterwards.⟩ — see WEAKEN 1

enervated *adj* 1 lacking bodily energy or motivation ⟨As the heat wave wore on, everyone really started to feel *enervated*.⟩ — see LISTLESS
2 lacking bodily strength ⟨Months of recovery in the hospital had rendered him *enervated* and unfit.⟩ — see WEAK 1

enfeeble *vb* to diminish the physical strength of ⟨Long periods of being confined to a hospital bed will *enfeeble* anyone.⟩ — see WEAKEN 1

enfeebled *adj* lacking bodily strength ⟨The *enfeebled* old woman now needs a companion to help her with everyday tasks.⟩ — see WEAK 1

enfeeblement *n* 1 a gradual sinking and wasting away of mind or body ⟨Daily exercise can help to halt some of the *enfeeblement* that comes with advanced years.⟩ — see DECLINE 1
2 the quality or state of lacking physical strength or vigor ⟨A lot of the *enfeeblement* I've experienced since the ac-

cident is being gradually diminished by daily physical therapy.⟩ — see WEAKNESS 1

enfold *vb* **1** to surround or cover closely ⟨Darkness began to *enfold* the house on the hill.⟩
synonyms bosom, cocoon, embosom, embower, embrace, enclose (*also* inclose), encompass, enshroud, envelop, enwrap, invest, involve, lap, mantle, muffle, shroud, swathe, veil, wrap
related words curtain; embed (*also* imbed), encase; swaddle; blanket, overlay, overspread; camouflage, cloak, disguise, mask; circle, encircle
near antonyms bare, denude, expose, strip
2 to put one's arms around and press tightly ⟨The winner *enfolded* the huge bouquet of roses in her arms and thanked the judges.⟩ — see EMBRACE 1

enforce *vb* to carry out effectively ⟨The duty of the police is to *enforce* the law.⟩
synonyms administer, apply, execute, implement
related words bring about, effect, effectuate; discharge, fulfill (*or* fulfil), render; cite; enact, legislate; honor, observe, uphold; promulgate
near antonyms disregard, ignore, neglect

enfranchise *vb* to release (as from slavery or confinement) ⟨In a way, modern labor-saving appliances *enfranchised* people, giving them much more leisure time.⟩ — see FREE 1

enfranchisement *n* **1** the act of setting free from slavery ⟨The Emancipation Proclamation was merely the first step in the full *enfranchisement* of enslaved people.⟩ — see LIBERATION
2 the right to formally express one's position or will in an election ⟨She was a leader in the movement for the *enfranchisement* of women.⟩ — see VOTE 1

engage *vb* **1** to hold the attention of ⟨The challenging game *engaged* us all evening.⟩
synonyms absorb, bemuse, busy, engross, enthrall (*or* enthral), enwrap, fascinate, grip, immerse, interest, intrigue, involve, occupy
related words allure, attract, beguile, bewitch, captivate, charm, enchant, obsess; hypnotize, mesmerize; distract, preoccupy; hog, monopolize
phrases catch one's eye
near antonyms bore, jade, pall, tire, weary
2 to enter into contest or conflict with ⟨The troops were prepared to *engage* the enemy.⟩
synonyms battle, encounter, face, meet, take on
related words emulate, rival; contend, fight, oppose
near antonyms elude, escape, evade; retreat
3 to obligate by prior agreement ⟨We can't go to the dance because we're already *engaged* to attend a piano recital.⟩ — see PLEDGE 1
4 to provide with a paying job ⟨The wealthy couple are looking to *engage* a handyman to take care of the estate.⟩ — see EMPLOY 1
5 to take or get the temporary use of (something) for a set sum ⟨The group of friends have *engaged* a chauffeured limousine for the prom.⟩ — see HIRE 1

engaged *adj* **1** pledged in marriage ⟨The *engaged* couple make a charming pair.⟩
synonyms affianced, betrothed
related words committed
antonyms unattached
2 involved in often constant activity ⟨I'm *engaged* right now, so call back some other time.⟩ — see BUSY 1

engagement *n* **1** the act or state of being engaged to be married ⟨The fun couple recently announced their *engagement*.⟩
synonyms betrothal, espousal
antonyms disengagement

2 an agreement to be present at a specified time and place ⟨a lifelong practice of marking all of my *engagements* on a weekly calendar⟩
synonyms appointment, date, rendezvous, tryst
related words arrangement; invitation; get-together, meeting; call, visit; schedule
3 the state of being provided with a paying job ⟨His *engagement* as a caddie at the golf club was his first work experience.⟩ — see HIRE 1

engaging *adj* **1** having an often mysterious or magical power to attract ⟨The inventor has an *engaging* aura that is hard to describe.⟩ — see FASCINATING 1
2 holding the attention or provoking interest ⟨a movie with an *engaging* story that will hold your interest for a couple of hours⟩ — see INTERESTING

engender *vb* **1** to be the cause of (a situation, action, or state of mind) ⟨a suggestion to go out for pizza that *engendered* a lot of interest⟩ — see EFFECT
2 to come into existence ⟨feelings of confidence and independence that were only just beginning to *engender* within her⟩ — see BEGIN 2

engine *n* a device that changes energy into mechanical motion ⟨a car with a 200-horsepower *engine*⟩
synonyms machine, motor
related words converter, transformer; appliance, mechanism; equipment, tool; mill

engineer *n* a person who designs and guides a plan or undertaking ⟨the *engineer* of a movement to eradicate hunger⟩
synonyms mastermind
related words builder, maker, producer; captain, commander, director, handler, leader, manager, quarterback; contriver, designer, formulator, originator, spawner; arranger, hatcher, organizer, planner, plotter, schemer; machinator, maneuverer; developer, generator, inaugurator, initiator, inspirer, instituter (*or* institutor), pioneer

engineer *vb* to plan out usually with subtle skill or care ⟨The mayor *engineered* an agreement to have a major league team play in our city.⟩
synonyms contrive, finagle, finesse, frame, machinate, maneuver, manipulate, mastermind, negotiate, wangle
related words arrange, concert, conclude, work out; angle (for), compass, intrigue, plot, scheme; connive; brew, concoct, cook (up), hatch; captain, command, conduct, direct, handle, manage, quarterback, run; gerrymander
near antonyms blow, bobble, botch, bungle, butcher, flub, fumble, louse up, mangle, mess (up), mishandle, muff

engrave *vb* **1** to cut (as letters or designs) on a hard surface ⟨*engraved* the birth and death dates on the tombstone⟩
synonyms etch, grave, incise, inscribe
related words carve, chisel, sculpt, sculpture; chase, groove, notch; score, trace; affix, impress
2 to produce a vivid impression of ⟨a scar that forever *engraved* the killer's face in the witness's mind⟩
synonyms brand, etch, impress, imprint, ingrain (*also* engrain)
related words imbue, implant, inculcate, infuse; fix, set, stamp
near antonyms blot out, expunge, obliterate

engross *vb* to hold the attention of ⟨a mystery story that will *engross* readers all the way to the surprise ending⟩ — see ENGAGE 1

engrossed *adj* having the mind fixed on something ⟨I was too *engrossed* in the book to notice the time.⟩ — see ATTENTIVE 1

engrossing *adj* holding the attention or provoking interest

⟨an *engrossing* lecture on the behavior of some of the lesser known deep-sea creatures⟩ — see INTERESTING

engrossment *n* a focusing of the mind on something ⟨My *engrossment* in the video game made me lose track of time.⟩ — see ATTENTION 1

engulf *vb* to cover with a flood ⟨High waves from the hurricane *engulfed* large areas of the coastal community.⟩ — see FLOOD

enhance *vb* **1** to make better ⟨Some shrubbery would really *enhance* the curb appeal of that house.⟩ — see IMPROVE

2 to make markedly greater in measure or degree ⟨Fresh chilies *enhanced* the spiciness of the dish.⟩ — see INTENSIFY

enhancement *n* an instance of notable progress in the development of knowledge, technology, or skill ⟨the phenomenal *enhancements* that have been made in home electronic equipment⟩ — see ADVANCE 2

enigma *n* something hard to understand or explain ⟨How the pyramids were built has long been an *enigma*.⟩ — see MYSTERY

enigmatic *also* **enigmatical** *adj* **1** being beyond one's powers to know, understand, or explain ⟨The discovery of the abandoned ship in mid ocean remains one of the most *enigmatic* episodes in seafaring history.⟩ — see MYSTERIOUS 1

2 having an often intentionally veiled or uncertain meaning ⟨the *Mona Lisa's enigmatic* smile⟩ — see OBSCURE 1

enjoin *vb* **1** to ask for (something) earnestly or with authority ⟨Police *enjoined* the community's full cooperation in finding the culprits.⟩ — see DEMAND 1

2 to issue orders to (someone) by right of authority ⟨Undeterred, the captain *enjoined* his crew to sail at full speed.⟩ — see COMMAND 1

3 to order not to do or use or to be done or used ⟨The judge *enjoined* them from selling the property.⟩ — see FORBID

enjoining *n* the act of ordering that something not be done or used ⟨the *enjoining* of the use of all electronics during the test⟩ — see PROHIBITION 1

enjoy *vb* **1** to take pleasure in ⟨We still *enjoy* seeing movies on the big screen.⟩

synonyms adore, delight (in), dig, fancy, groove (on), like, love, relish, revel (in), savor (*also* savour)

related words admire, appreciate, cherish, revere, venerate, worship; prize, treasure, value; devour, eat (up), feast (on); dote (on), idolize; cotton (to), favor, prefer; indulge (in), luxuriate (in), wallow (in)

phrases be partial to, get a kick out of (*or* get a charge out of), go for, have a soft spot for, take to

near antonyms abhor, abominate, detest, dislike, hate, loathe; condemn, despise, scorn

2 to keep, control, or experience as one's own ⟨a country where the people *enjoy* the highest living standards in the world⟩ — see HAVE 1

enjoyable *adj* **1** giving pleasure or contentment to the mind or senses ⟨The great food, service, and atmosphere made for a most *enjoyable* dinner.⟩ — see PLEASANT 1

2 providing amusement or enjoyment ⟨The theme park's great variety of attractions mean that every member of the family will have an *enjoyable* time.⟩ — see FUN

enjoyment *n* **1** the fact or state of having (something) at one's disposal ⟨a scenic walkway along the ocean shore that is intended for the *enjoyment* of all⟩ — see POSSESSION 1

2 the feeling experienced when one's wishes are met ⟨This new video game should provide countless hours of *enjoyment*.⟩ — see PLEASURE 1

enlarge *vb* **1** to become greater in extent, volume, amount,

or number ⟨As the number of students in the school *enlarges*, more teachers will have to be hired.⟩ — see INCREASE 2

2 to make greater in size, amount, or number ⟨With a new member of the family on the way, maybe we should consider *enlarging* the house.⟩ — see INCREASE 1

3 to release (as from slavery or confinement) ⟨a wild animal *enlarged* from a trap⟩ — see FREE 1

enlighten *vb* **1** to give information to ⟨The lecturer at the planetarium *enlightened* us about the latest astronomical discoveries.⟩

synonyms acquaint, advise, apprise, brief, clear, clue (in), familiarize, fill in, hip, inform, instruct, tell, verse, wise (up)

related words advertise, alert, notify; announce (to), disclose (to); assure, certify, convince, reassure, warrant; educate, lecture, school, teach, tutor; disabuse, disenchant, disillusion, undeceive

phrases keep posted (one), let know (one)

near antonyms misinform, mislead

2 to provide (someone) with moral or spiritual understanding ⟨Many people around the world have been *enlightened* by the teachings of Gautama Buddha.⟩

synonyms edify, educate, illuminate, illumine, inspire, nurture

related words elevate, ennoble, enrich, ensoul, lift, uplift; better, improve, regenerate, renew, transform; exalt, glorify, transfigure

near antonyms confuse, perplex, puzzle; becloud, cloud, darken, obscure

enlist (in) *vb* to become a member of ⟨Young men and women were *enlisting in* the navy in greater numbers.⟩ — see ENTER 2

enliven *vb* to give life, vigor, or spirit to ⟨In most instances it's a good idea to *enliven* a speech with a joke or two.⟩ — see ANIMATE

enmesh *also* **immesh** *vb* to catch or hold as if in a net ⟨They spent years *enmeshed* in lawsuits.⟩ — see ENTANGLE 2

enmity *n* a deep-seated ill will ⟨*Enmity* had existed between the two families for generations.⟩

synonyms animosity, antagonism, antipathy, bitterness, gall, grudge, hostility, jaundice, rancor

related words blood feud, feud, score, vendetta; hate, hatred, loathing; vindictiveness, virulence, vitriol; alienation, disaffection, estrangement; conflict, coolness, discord, friction, strain, tension; inhospitableness, unfriendliness; malice, malignancy, malignity, spite, spitefulness, venom

near antonyms amiability, amicability, civility, cordiality, friendliness, hospitality, neighborliness; comity, empathy, friendship, goodwill, sympathy, understanding

antonyms amity

ennoble *vb* to assign a high status or value to ⟨The heroic actions of firefighters *ennobles* the profession of fire fighting in the public mind.⟩ — see EXALT 1

ennui *n* the state of being bored ⟨the kind of *ennui* that comes from having too much time on one's hands and too little will to find something productive to do⟩ — see BOREDOM

enormity *n* **1** the state or quality of being utterly evil ⟨the *enormity* of the crimes committed by the Nazis⟩

synonyms atrociousness, atrocity, badness, depravedness, depravity, diabolicalness, evilness, heinousness, hideousness, monstrosity, sinfulness, vileness, wickedness

related words accursedness, baseness, cursedness, devilishness, execrableness, hellishness; corruption, decadence, degeneracy, perverseness; immorality; infamy, notoriety

near antonyms morality; chasteness, innocence, purity
antonyms goodness, righteousness, virtuousness
2 the quality or state of being very large ⟨The *enormity* of the canyon can only be grasped by taking a trip through its entire length.⟩ — see IMMENSITY
enormous *adj* unusually large ⟨That pumpkin is so *enormous* that it has to be a record holder.⟩ — see HUGE
enormously *adv* **1** to a great degree ⟨an *enormously* entertaining film⟩ — see VERY 1
2 to a large extent or degree ⟨The neighbors have been *enormously* helpful while we've tried to get settled.⟩ — see GREATLY 2
enormousness *n* the quality or state of being very large ⟨The *enormousness* of the mall is such that one could shop at a different store for every day of the year.⟩ — see IMMENSITY
enough *adv* **1** in or to a degree or quantity that meets one's requirements or satisfaction ⟨The elevator is big *enough* to hold everyone.⟩
synonyms adequately, satisfactorily, sufficiently, suitably
related words acceptably, fairly, moderately, passably, tolerably; meetly, properly, rightly, seemly; agreeably, satisfyingly, abundantly, amply, optimally, plenteously, plentifully; commensurately, proportionately
antonyms inadequately, insufficiently, unsatisfactorily
2 to some degree or extent ⟨I can play the piano well *enough*, but I have no hope for a musical career.⟩ — see FAIRLY 1
3 to a full extent or degree ⟨I think we've prepared *enough* to feel confident.⟩ — see FULLY 1
enrage *vb* to make angry ⟨The fact that the auto garage bungled the repair and then overcharged him simply *enraged* the customer.⟩ — see ANGER
enraged *adj* feeling or showing anger ⟨He had an *enraged* look on his face.⟩ — see ANGRY
enrapture *vb* **1** to fill with great joy ⟨*enraptured* upon learning that he would be attending college on a full sports scholarship⟩ — see ELATE
2 to fill with overwhelming emotion (as wonder or delight) ⟨This classic ballet never fails to *enrapture* audiences young and old.⟩ — see ENTRANCE
enraptured *adj* experiencing or marked by overwhelming usually pleasurable emotion ⟨the *enraptured* look on the fans' faces during the band's concerts⟩ — see ECSTATIC
enraptured (by) *adj* filled with an intense or excessive love for ⟨She was *enraptured by* her new puppy.⟩ — see ENAMORED (OF)
enrich *vb* **1** to make better ⟨A truly great book can *enrich* your life.⟩ — see IMPROVE
2 to make more attractive by adding something that is beautiful or becoming ⟨The church's magnificent interior is *enriched* with stunningly beautiful murals.⟩ — see DECORATE
enroll *also* **enrol** *vb* **1** to add (a person) to a list or roll as a participant or member ⟨The community college will *enroll* anyone who has a GED or high school diploma.⟩
synonyms inscribe, list, matriculate, register
related words enlist, impanel, induct; conscript, draft, muster; book, schedule; check in
near antonyms check off; exclude, expel, expunge, reject; omit, overlook
2 to put (someone or something) on a list ⟨Can I *enroll* you on the list of volunteers?⟩ — see ¹LIST 2
enroll (in) *vb* to become a member of ⟨She *enrolled in* the engineering course.⟩ — see ENTER 2
enrollment *also* **enrolment** *n* the number of individuals registered ⟨The school's *enrollment* currently stands at 500.⟩ — see REGISTRATION

ensconce *vb* **1** to establish or place comfortably or snugly ⟨The kids had contentedly *ensconced* themselves on the couch before the TV.⟩ ⟨happily *ensconced* in her new home⟩
synonyms install, lodge, nestle, perch, roost, settle
related words deploy, fix, locate, park, plant, position, set, situate, station; anchor, bivouac, camp, camp (out); burrow, curl up, dig in; harbor, house
2 to put into a hiding place ⟨I *ensconced* the spare house key in a place where no one would think to look.⟩ — see ¹HIDE 1
enshrine *vb* to assign a high status or value to ⟨Some teachers tend to *enshrine* their personal preferences as sacred rules of English grammar.⟩ — see EXALT 1
enshroud *vb* **1** to keep secret or shut off from view ⟨The criminal organization uses a strictly enforced vow of silence to *enshroud* its villainous doings.⟩ — see ¹HIDE 2
2 to surround or cover closely ⟨A dense fog *enshrouded* the bridge spanning the harbor.⟩ — see ENFOLD 1
ensign *n* **1** a device, design, or figure used as an identifying mark ⟨that *ensign* of Halloween, the jack-o-lantern⟩ — see EMBLEM
2 a piece of cloth with a special design that is used as an emblem or for signaling ⟨Fittingly, the organization promoting the welfare of marine life features a dolphin on its *ensign*.⟩ — see FLAG 1
enslavement *n* the state of being enslaved ⟨Having known the misery of *enslavement* firsthand, Frederick Douglass went on to devote his life to the cause of making others free.⟩ — see SLAVERY
ensnare *vb* to catch or hold as if in a net ⟨Parked just out of view, the state trooper was lying in wait to *ensnare* unwary speeders.⟩ — see ENTANGLE 2
ensuing *adj* **1** being the one that comes immediately after another ⟨Business was slow in the restaurant's first year, but the *ensuing* year saw a much-needed increase.⟩ — see NEXT
2 being, occurring, or carried out at a time after something else ⟨the discovery of gold and the *ensuing* rush of prospectors⟩ — see SUBSEQUENT
ensure *vb* to make sure, certain, or safe ⟨regulations that *ensure* the wholesomeness of our food⟩
synonyms assure, cinch, guarantee, guaranty, insure, secure
related words attest, certify, vouch, warrant, witness; pledge, promise, swear
near antonyms enfeeble, undermine, weaken
entail *vb* to have as part of a whole ⟨A lavish wedding *entails* extensive planning.⟩ — see INCLUDE 1
entangle *vb* **1** to twist together into a usually confused mass ⟨In the process of taking down the Christmas tree, we managed to *entangle* the string of lights into a hopeless mess of wires.⟩
synonyms interlace, intertwine, interweave, knot, snarl, tangle
related words jumble, scrabble, scramble; braid, entwine, entwist, plait, twine, weave, wind, wreathe, writhe
near antonyms unknot, unravel, unscramble
antonyms disentangle, unsnarl, untangle, untwine, untwist
2 to catch or hold as if in a net ⟨The swindler gradually became *entangled* in a web of lies.⟩
synonyms enmesh (*also* immesh), ensnare, entrap, mesh, net, snare, tangle, trap
related words bag, birdlime, capture, collar; embroil, implicate, involve, mire
near antonyms detach, disengage, extricate; clear, free, liberate
antonyms disentangle, untangle

3 to make complex or difficult ⟨The history of Alexander the Great is *entangled* by variant accounts of his exploits.⟩ — see COMPLICATE

entanglement *n* something that catches and holds ⟨His life is greatly complicated by his legal *entanglements*.⟩ — see WEB 1

enter *vb* **1** to go or come in or into ⟨The hikers *entered* the cave with considerable caution.⟩
synonyms access, penetrate, pierce
related words barge (in), breeze (in), burst (in *or* into), waltz (in); pop (in); stray (into), wander (into); crash, encroach, gate-crash, infiltrate, infringe, intrude, invade, trespass
phrases set foot in, step into
antonyms depart, exit, leave
2 to become a member of ⟨patriotic young men and women *entering* the armed services⟩ ⟨debutantes *entering* society⟩
synonyms enlist (in), enroll (in), join, sign on (for), sign up (for)
related words reenlist, reenroll, reenter, rejoin, re-up
near antonyms drop out, quit, withdraw
antonyms demit
3 to put (someone or something) on a list ⟨New voters fill out a form and elections officials *enter* their names into the database.⟩ — see ¹LIST 2
4 to offer entrance (as to a place, school, or privilege) to ⟨The club *enters* only five new members a year.⟩ — see ADMIT 2

enter (into *or* upon) *vb* to take the first step in (a process or course of action) ⟨a series of counseling sessions intended to help young couples about to *enter into* the trials and tribulations of marriage⟩ — see BEGIN 1

enterprise *n* **1** a commercial or industrial activity or organization ⟨The booming economy witnessed the launch of many small *enterprises*.⟩
synonyms business, company, concern, establishment, firm, house, interest, outfit
related words conglomerate, corporation; association, cartel, chain, combine, syndicate, trust; agency, dealer, outlet
2 readiness to engage in daring or difficult activity ⟨the *enterprise* shown by the early developers and promoters of personal computers⟩
synonyms action, aggressiveness, ambition, drive, go, hustle, initiative
related words grit, pluck, snap, spirit, spunk, starch; killer instinct, overambitiousness; assertiveness, self-reliance; energy, hardihood, pep, vigor, vitality
near antonyms inactivity, inertia, passivity; diffidence, faintheartedness, timidity; hesitation, reluctance; indolence, laziness
3 a risky undertaking ⟨The general viewed the proposed invasion as a military *enterprise* that offered no easy way out.⟩ — see GAMBLE

enterprising *adj* **1** having or showing a bold forcefulness in the pursuit of a goal ⟨The company is claiming that there will be huge financial rewards for *enterprising* sales representatives.⟩ — see AGGRESSIVE 1
2 inclined or willing to take risks ⟨*Enterprising* people of vision were responsible for the boom in technological industries.⟩ — see BOLD 1

entertain *vb* **1** to cause (someone) to pass the time agreeably occupied ⟨*Entertain* the kids while I go and prepare dinner.⟩ — see AMUSE
2 to give serious and careful thought to ⟨Have you ever *entertained* the thought that you could be wrong?⟩ — see PONDER
3 to keep in one's mind or heart ⟨I don't *entertain* the

hope of ever getting a plum job like that.⟩ — see HARBOR 1

entertaining *adj* providing amusement or enjoyment ⟨a list of *entertaining* things to do on a snow day⟩ — see FUN

entertainment *n* **1** the act or activity of providing pleasure or amusement especially for the public ⟨We didn't stay for the featured *entertainment* because we don't care for comedy acts.⟩ ⟨The film is purely for *entertainment* and not meant to be taken seriously.⟩
synonyms amusement, distraction, diversion, recreation
related words nightlife, show business; delectation, delight, enjoyment, joy, mirth; gratification, relaxation, relief, satisfaction; exhibition, performance, presentation, presentment, production, show; escapism
2 someone or something that provides amusement or enjoyment ⟨What do you do for *entertainment* in this town?⟩ — see FUN 1

enthrall *or* **enthral** *vb* **1** to hold the attention of as if by a spell ⟨*Enthralled* by the flickering fire in the hearth, we lost all track of time.⟩
synonyms arrest, bedazzle, enchant, fascinate, grip, hypnotize, mesmerize, spellbind
related words enrapture, entrance, thrill; beguile, bewitch, charm; absorb, engage, engross, involve
2 to fill with overwhelming emotion (as wonder or delight) ⟨For years these master magicians have been *enthralling* audiences with their astounding illusions.⟩ — see ENTRANCE
3 to hold the attention of ⟨a play that will *enthrall* you for two hours⟩ — see ENGAGE 1

enthralled *adj* having the mind fixed on something ⟨gave her speech to several hundred *enthralled* listeners⟩ — see ATTENTIVE 1

enthralling *adj* holding the attention or provoking interest ⟨an *enthralling* account of life in the scientific community in Antarctica⟩ — see INTERESTING

enthrallment *n* a focusing of the mind on something ⟨The child's *enthrallment* with the new toy lasted about 30 minutes.⟩ — see ATTENTION 1

enthrone *vb* to assign a high status or value to ⟨The literary world has *enthroned* Shakespeare for so long that his preeminence among writers seems unassailable.⟩ — see EXALT 1

enthuse *vb* to make an exaggerated display of affection or enthusiasm ⟨She *enthused* over the gifts presented by her young children.⟩ — see GUSH 2

enthusiasm *n* **1** a practice or interest that is very popular for a short time ⟨His current *enthusiasm* is long distance running.⟩ — see FAD
2 urgent desire or interest ⟨In my *enthusiasm* to get going, I forgot to pack any foul-weather clothing.⟩ — see EAGERNESS
3 depth of feeling ⟨spoke about wildlife conservation with evident *enthusiasm*⟩ — see ARDOR 1

enthusiast *n* a person with a strong and habitual liking for something ⟨Skiing *enthusiasts* can't wait for the first snowfall of the season.⟩ — see FAN

enthusiastic *adj* showing urgent desire or interest ⟨As soon as the gates to the concert area opened, *enthusiastic* fans rushed to get the best seats.⟩ — see EAGER

enthusiastically *adv* in an enthusiastic manner ⟨Sportswriters have praised this new pitching find *enthusiastically*.⟩ — see SKY-HIGH

entice *vb* to lead away from a usual or proper course by offering some pleasure or advantage ⟨Every commercial seemed to be for some tempting snack specifically designed to *entice* me.⟩ — see LURE

enticement *n* **1** something that persuades one to perform an action for pleasure or gain ⟨The hospital often offers T-shirts or caps as *enticements* for people to donate blood.⟩ — see LURE 1

2 the act or pressure of giving in to a desire especially when ill-advised ⟨The *enticement* of the party buffet was just too great to ignore for very long.⟩ — see TEMPTATION 1

entire *adj* **1** not divided or scattered among several areas of interest or concern ⟨This matter is important, so please give me your *entire* attention.⟩ — see WHOLE 1

2 not lacking any part or member that properly belongs to it ⟨The *entire* team needs to be present for the photograph.⟩ — see COMPLETE 1

entirely *adv* to a full extent or degree ⟨Are you *entirely* aware of what you're doing with that thing?⟩ — see FULLY 1

entitle *vb* **1** to give a right to ⟨The card *entitles* my grandmother to the discount for senior citizens.⟩

synonyms authorize, privilege, qualify

related words empower, enable, enfranchise, license (*also* licence); approve, endorse (*also* indorse); allow, let, permit; accredit, certificate, certify, ratify; legitimize, sanction, validate, warrant

near antonyms disable, disempower, disenfranchise; decertify; disallow, forbid, proscribe; delegitimize, invalidate, nullify

antonyms disqualify

2 to give a name to ⟨Apart from the obvious, she couldn't decide what to *entitle* her painting of a vase with flowers.⟩ — see NAME 1

entity *n* one that has a real and independent existence ⟨the question of whether extrasensory perception will ever be a scientifically recognized *entity*⟩

synonyms being, existent, individual, individuality, integer, object, reality, something, substance, thing

related words body, subject; material, matter, quantity, stuff

near antonyms nonentity

entomb *vb* to place (a dead body) in the earth, a tomb, or the sea ⟨A number of Boston's historic notables are *entombed* in the Old Granary Burying Ground.⟩ — see BURY 1

entombing *n* the act or ceremony of putting a dead body in its final resting place ⟨The *entombing* of the pharaohs in the pyramids must have been a magnificent sight.⟩ — see BURIAL 1

entombment *n* the act or ceremony of putting a dead body in its final resting place ⟨the *entombment* of President Kennedy in Arlington National Cemetery⟩ — see BURIAL 1

entrails *pl n* the internal organs of the body ⟨In ancient Rome predictions of future events would sometimes be based on an examination of the *entrails* of a sacrificial animal.⟩ — see GUT 1

entrance *n* **1** the means or right of entering or participating in ⟨*Entrance* to the club is by invitation only.⟩

synonyms access, admission, admittance, door, doorway, entrée (*or* entree), entry, gateway, ingress, key, passport, ticket

related words approval, authorization, permission, qualification; open door, welcome mat

near antonyms discharge, dismissal, ejection, expulsion, ouster, rejection, removal

2 the opening through which one can enter or leave a structure ⟨When you come, use the *entrance* on the right side of the building.⟩ — see DOOR 2

entrance *vb* to fill with overwhelming emotion (as wonder or delight) ⟨a production of *The Nutcracker* ballet that will *entrance* audiences⟩

synonyms carry away, enrapture, enthrall (*or* enthral), rap, rapture, ravish, transport

related words delight, gladden, gratify, please, satisfy; bewitch, captivate, charm, enchant, fascinate; elate, excite, exhilarate, stir

phrases knock dead, knock one's socks off

entranced *adj* **1** being or appearing to be under a magic spell ⟨a view that leaves visitors *entranced* and speechless⟩ — see ENCHANTED

2 experiencing or marked by overwhelming usually pleasurable emotion ⟨the *entranced* look on her face⟩ — see ECSTATIC

entrancing *adj* having an often mysterious or magical power to attract ⟨Travelers to India say that it has an *entrancing* beauty that is hard to describe.⟩ — see FASCINATING 1

entrap *vb* to catch or hold as if in a net ⟨a string of inconsistent statements and outright lies that finally *entrapped* the witness⟩ — see ENTANGLE 2

entreat *vb* to make a request to (someone) in an earnest or urgent manner ⟨She began her letter by *entreating* me to forgive the belatedness of her reply.⟩ — see BEG

entreating *adj* asking humbly ⟨It was hard to refuse such amusingly *entreating* kids raising funds.⟩ — see SUPPLIANT

entreaty *n* an earnest request ⟨Our *entreaties* to give us another few minutes to answer the test questions fell on deaf ears.⟩ — see PLEA 1

entrée *or* **entree** *n* the means or right of entering or participating in ⟨*Entrée* to the country club is through sponsorship by someone who is already a member.⟩ — see ENTRANCE 1

entrench *also* **intrench** *vb* to set solidly in or as if in surrounding matter ⟨a father who *entrenched* in our minds the belief that hard work pays off⟩

synonyms bed, embed (*also* imbed), fix, impact, implant, ingrain (*also* engrain), lodge, root

related words imbue, infuse; beat (into), drive (into); establish, place, put, settle, stick

near antonyms eliminate, eradicate; eject, expel; detach, disconnect, disengage, remove

antonyms dislodge, root (out), uproot

entrenched *also* **intrenched** *adj* firmly established over time ⟨I have an *entrenched* dislike of mimes.⟩ — see INVETERATE 1

entrust *also* **intrust** *vb* **1** to give a task, duty, or responsibility to ⟨We *entrusted* our financial adviser with the investment of our savings.⟩

synonyms assign, charge, commission, task, trust

related words confer, impose; commit, consign, delegate, recommend, repose; allocate, allot; authorize, empower, invest

2 to put (something) into the possession or safekeeping of another ⟨We *entrusted* our pets to the care of our neighbor while we went on vacation.⟩ — see GIVE 2

entry *n* **1** the entrance room of a building ⟨Please wait in the *entry* while I get the person you want.⟩ — see HALL 1

2 the means or right of entering or participating in ⟨believed that a college education was one's *entry* to a life of prosperity⟩ — see ENTRANCE 1

entryway *n* the entrance room of a building ⟨a small *entryway* to receive visitors⟩ — see HALL 1

entwine *vb* **1** to cause to twine about one another ⟨marveled at how the vines had delicately and intricately *entwined* themselves on the trellis⟩ — see INTERTWINE 1

2 to follow a circular or spiral course ⟨The quick-growing vine was soon *entwining* around the fence post.⟩ — see WIND 1

enumerate *vb* **1** to specify one after another ⟨She pro-

ceeded to *enumerate* the reasons why she would be the best candidate.⟩
synonyms detail, itemize, list, numerate, recite, reel off, rehearse, tick (off)
related words outline; tabulate, tally; catalog (*or* catalogue), inventory; chart, diagram, graph; calculate, compute, estimate, figure, reckon; cite, mention, name
near antonyms generalize
2 to find the sum of (a collection of things) by noting each one as it is being added ⟨There were more birds hovering about the bird feeder than I could possibly *enumerate*.⟩ — see COUNT 1
3 to make a list of ⟨Let's *enumerate* the top ten reasons why Top Ten lists have gotten out of hand.⟩ — see ¹LIST 1

enunciate *vb* **1** to utter clearly and distinctly ⟨*Enunciate* your words, and then you won't have to repeat them so often.⟩ — see ARTICULATE 1
2 to make known openly or publicly ⟨Today the President *enunciated* a new foreign policy.⟩ — see ANNOUNCE
3 to express (a thought or emotion) in words ⟨a paper that *enunciates* the goals of the environmental organization⟩ — see SAY 1
enunciation *n* the clear and accurate pronunciation of words especially in public speaking ⟨a radio announcer who is known for his very careful *enunciation*⟩ — see DICTION 1
envelop *vb* **1** to close or shut in by or as if by barriers ⟨A cloud of silence *enveloped* the library.⟩ — see ENCLOSE 1
2 to surround or cover closely ⟨Mist *enveloped* the mountains.⟩ — see ENFOLD 1
envenom *vb* to implant bitter feelings in ⟨thoughtless, self-indulgent antics that only managed to *envenom* his teammates⟩ — see EMBITTER
envenomed *adj* containing or contaminated with a substance capable of injuring or killing a living thing ⟨The *envenomed* spines of these tropical fishes make them a particular hazard of coral reefs.⟩ — see POISONOUS
envious *adj* having or showing mean resentment of another's possessions or advantages ⟨a family that is *envious* of their neighbors' big house⟩
synonyms covetous, invidious, jaundiced, jealous, resentful
related words begrudging, grudging; avaricious, grasping, greedy, rapacious; distrustful, suspicious; malicious, petty, spiteful
phrases eating one's heart out, green with envy
near antonyms generous, kind, kindhearted; altruistic, benevolent, charitable; well-meaning
antonyms unenvious
enviousness *n* a painful awareness of another's possessions or advantages and a desire to have them too ⟨Lisa's *enviousness* of Debra's athletic achievements was obvious to all of their friends.⟩ — see ENVY
environment *n* the circumstances, conditions, or objects by which one is surrounded ⟨the joys of growing up in the *environment* that a vibrant city offers⟩
synonyms atmosphere, climate, environs, medium, milieu, setting, surround, surroundings
related words location, place, position, space; backdrop, background; element; situation, status; habitat
environs *pl n* **1** the districts adjacent to a city ⟨The city and its *environs* total about a million in population.⟩
synonyms outskirts, suburbia
related words country, countryside, exurbia
near antonyms downtown, inner city, midtown
2 an adjoining region or space ⟨You can get just about any kind of ethnic food in the *environs* of the university.⟩
synonyms neighborhood

related words environment, surround, surroundings
3 the circumstances, conditions, or objects by which one is surrounded ⟨grew up in the *environs* of a big city⟩ — see ENVIRONMENT
envisage *vb* to form a mental picture of ⟨I'm trying to *envisage* you on a surfboard.⟩ — see IMAGINE 1
envoy *n* **1** a person sent on a mission to represent another ⟨The president sent the secretary of state as a personal *envoy* to gain the support of the country's allies.⟩ — see AMBASSADOR
2 a person who acts or does business for another ⟨One of the students was chosen as the club's *envoy* in meetings with the principal.⟩ — see AGENT 2
envy *n* a painful awareness of another's possessions or advantages and a desire to have them too ⟨Their exotic vacation inspired *envy* among their friends.⟩
synonyms covetousness, enviousness, invidiousness, jealousy, resentment
related words animosity, enmity, hatred, ill will; malice, maliciousness, spitefulness
near antonyms benevolence, goodwill, kindness, sympathy
enwrap *vb* **1** to hold the attention of ⟨*Enwrapped* in my own thoughts, I failed to notice the coworker standing outside my cubicle.⟩ — see ENGAGE 1
2 to surround or cover closely ⟨An air of serenity *enwraps* the leafy arboretum.⟩ — see ENFOLD 1
eon *or* **aeon** *n* a long or seemingly long period of time ⟨It's been *eons* since I saw a movie at the multiplex.⟩ ⟨glaciers that formed *eons* ago⟩ — see AGE 2
ephemeral *adj* lasting only for a short time ⟨The autumnal blaze of colors is always to be treasured, all the more so because it is so *ephemeral*.⟩ — see MOMENTARY
epicure *n* a person with refined tastes in food and wine ⟨an *epicure* who opened her own restaurant⟩
synonyms epicurean, gourmand, gourmet
related words connoisseur, dilettante; foodie
near antonyms glutton, gorger, guzzler, hog, overeater, stuffer, swiller, trencherman
epicurean *n* a person with refined tastes in food and wine ⟨an *epicurean* with a beautifully equipped kitchen⟩ — see EPICURE
epigram *n* an often stated observation regarding something from common experience ⟨Benjamin Franklin's famous *epigram*, "Remember that time is money"⟩ — see SAYING
epigrammatic *adj* marked by the use of few words to convey much information or meaning ⟨Oscar Wilde's *epigrammatic* observation, "In America the young are always ready to give to those who are older than themselves the full benefits of their inexperience"⟩ — see CONCISE
episode *n* something that happens ⟨She had a brief *episode* of brain fog and couldn't focus on her homework.⟩ — see EVENT 1
episodic *also* **episodical** *adj* **1** appearing in parts or numbers that follow regularly ⟨The long novel was filmed for television as an *episodic* movie that was shown over the course of five evenings.⟩ — see SERIAL
2 lacking in steadiness or regularity of occurrence ⟨Malaria is characterized by *episodic* attacks of chills and fever.⟩ — see FITFUL
epistle *n* a message on paper from one person or group to another ⟨the *epistles* of Saint Paul to various communities of early Christians⟩ — see ¹LETTER
epithet *n* **1** a descriptive or familiar name given instead of or in addition to the one belonging to an individual ⟨King Richard I of England was given the very laudatory *epithet* "the Lion-Hearted."⟩ — see NICKNAME
2 an act or expression showing scorn and usually intend-

ed to hurt another's feelings ⟨The school has a strict ban against the use of *epithets*.⟩ — see INSULT

epitome *n* **1** a short statement of the main points ⟨The golden rule is often cited as the *epitome* of moral conduct: "Do unto others as you would have them do unto you."⟩ — see SUMMARY

2 a visible representation of something abstract (as a quality) ⟨He was the *epitome* of style.⟩ — see EMBODIMENT

3 the most perfect type or example ⟨Mahatma Gandhi is often cited as the *epitome* of a resolute reformer who uses nonviolence to bring about social and political change.⟩ — see QUINTESSENCE 1

epitomize *vb* **1** to make into a short statement of the main points (as of a report) ⟨His personal code of behavior on the playing field is *epitomized* by his favorite saying, "Cheaters never win."⟩ — see SUMMARIZE

2 to represent in visible form ⟨The Parthenon in Athens *epitomizes* the ancient Greek ideal of architectural beauty.⟩ — see EMBODY 2

epoch *n* an extent of time associated with a particular person or thing ⟨Sir Isaac Newton is usually credited with establishing the *epoch* of modern science.⟩ — see AGE 1

equable *adj* marked by temperatures that are neither too high nor too low ⟨An area with an *equable* climate would be our first choice for a place in which to settle.⟩ — see CLEMENT 1

equal *adj* **1** marked by justice, honesty, and freedom from bias ⟨the basic belief that everyone is entitled to *equal* opportunity in employment⟩ — see FAIR 2

2 resembling another in every respect ⟨As far as I can see, except for the high price, the store-brand jacket is *equal* to the jacket with the designer label.⟩ — see SAME 1

3 having the required skills for an acceptable level of performance ⟨looking for someone *equal* to the challenge of running a large state university⟩ — see COMPETENT 1

4 free from emotional or mental agitation ⟨He proceeded, in an *equal* tone, to recount the disturbing events of the day.⟩ — see CALM 2

equal *n* one that is equal to another in status, achievement, or value ⟨a basketball player who truly has no *equal* in his sport⟩

synonyms coequal, coordinate, counterpart, equivalent, fellow, like, match, parallel, peer, rival

related words analogue (*or* analog); double, half, mate, twin; associate, colleague, companion, copartner, partner; competitor

equal *vb* **1** to produce something equal to (as in quality or value) ⟨No one has *equaled* Shakespeare's plays.⟩

synonyms match, meet, tie

related words beat, better, eclipse, excel, outdistance, outdo, outshine, outstrip, overtop, surpass, top, transcend; amount (to), approach, touch; approximate, keep up, measure up (to), parallel, rival, stack up (against *or* with)

2 to be the same in meaning or effect ⟨She said the beach was so beautiful it *equalled* paradise.⟩ — see AMOUNT (TO) 2

3 to be the exact counterpart of ⟨In the British system a public school *equals* an American prep school.⟩ — see MATCH 1

equality *n* the state or fact of being exactly the same in number, amount, status, or quality ⟨They demanded *equality* in pay.⟩ — see EQUIVALENCE

equalize *vb* to make equal in amount, degree, or status ⟨a plan to *equalize* educational opportunities for all the state's children, rich and poor alike⟩

synonyms balance, equate, even, level

related words equilibrate, equipoise; accommodate, adjust, compensate, fit; counterbalance; homogenize, normalize, regularize, standardize; democratize

near antonyms disequilibrate

equanimity *n* evenness of emotions or temper ⟨an Olympic diver who always displays remarkable *equanimity* on the platform⟩

synonyms aplomb, calmness, collectedness, composure, cool, coolness, countenance, equilibrium, imperturbability, placidity, repose, self-possession, serenity, tranquillity (*or* tranquility)

related words assurance, confidence, poise, self-assurance, self-confidence; easygoingness, laid-backness

near antonyms alarm (*also* alarum), anxiety, anxiousness, apprehension, apprehensiveness, care, concern, disquiet, solicitude, uneasiness, worry; excitability, excitableness, nervousness; disturbance

antonyms agitation, discomposure, perturbation

equate *vb* **1** to regard or represent as equal or comparable ⟨a value system that *equates* money with success⟩

synonyms compare, liken

related words associate, connect, correlate, identify, join, link, match, relate; group, lump (together); assort, categorize, class, classify, grade, group, sort

near antonyms differentiate, discern, discriminate, distinguish, separate

2 to describe as similar ⟨I don't *equate* material wealth with happiness.⟩ — see COMPARE 1

3 to make equal in amount, degree, or status ⟨You'll stop running up debts when you start *equating* what you spend with what you earn.⟩ — see EQUALIZE

equatorial *adj* being near the equator ⟨a lush *equatorial* rain forest that is threatened by rampant development⟩ — see LOW 1

equilibrium *n* **1** a condition in which opposing forces are equal to one another ⟨We must find an *equilibrium* between commercial development and conservation of our natural treasures.⟩ — see BALANCE 1

2 evenness of emotions or temper ⟨The announcement that I'd won left me speechless, and several minutes passed before I recovered my *equilibrium*.⟩ — see EQUANIMITY

equine *n* a large hoofed domestic animal that is used for carrying or drawing loads and for riding ⟨One of the more esteemed *equines* of modern times was the racehorse Seabiscuit.⟩ — see HORSE

equip *vb* **1** to make competent (as by training, skill, or ability) for a particular office or function ⟨Years of service in the congress and in the cabinet *equipped* her better than most people for the office of the presidency.⟩ — see QUALIFY 2

2 to provide (someone) with what is needed for a task or activity ⟨a visit to a ski shop to *equip* ourselves for a week of skiing in the Rockies⟩ — see FURNISH 1

equipage *n* a horse-drawn wheeled vehicle for carrying passengers ⟨For their old-fashioned wedding, the couple arrived at the church in a Victorian-era *equipage*, complete with costumed driver.⟩ — see CARRIAGE 1

equipment *n* items needed for the performance of a task or activity ⟨The *equipment* for the polar expedition included ships, instruments, sleds, dogs, and provisions.⟩

synonyms accoutrements (*or* accouterments), apparatus, gear, hardware, material(s), matériel (*or* materiel), outfit, paraphernalia, stuff, tackle

related words accessories, appurtenances, attachments, fittings; baggage, belongings, impedimenta; appliances, facilities, instruments, machinery, tools; apparel, attire, habiliments, raiment, trappings; armamentarium, armory, arsenal, battery; assets, resources

equipoise *n* **1** a condition in which opposing forces are equal to one another ⟨When participating in any dangerous sport, one should maintain an *equipoise* between fearless boldness and commonsense caution.⟩ — see BALANCE 1

2 a force or influence that makes an opposing force ineffective or less effective ⟨One's frugality is a much-needed *equipoise* to the other's spendthrift ways.⟩ — see COUNTERBALANCE

equitable *adj* marked by justice, honesty, and freedom from bias ⟨The will calls for an *equitable* distribution of the estate's assets among the four children.⟩ — see FAIR 2

equity *n* **1** lack of favoritism toward one side or another ⟨The judge considered both sides of the argument with *equity*.⟩ — see DETACHMENT 1

2 the practice of giving to others what is their due or an instance of this ⟨Basic to the notion of *equity* is the principle that all people are of equal standing in the eyes of the law.⟩ — see JUSTICE 1

equivalence *n* the state or fact of being exactly the same in number, amount, status, or quality ⟨moviegoers who mistakenly believe that there is an *equivalence* between the personality of an actor and that of his character⟩
synonyms equality, equivalency, par, parity, sameness
related words compatibility, correlation, correspondence; alikeness, community, likeness, parallelism, resemblance, similarity, similitude; exchangeability, interchangeability; identicalness, identity
near antonyms difference, disagreement, discrepancy, disparateness, disparity, distinction, distinctiveness, distinctness, divergence, diverseness, diversity; incompatibility; dissimilarity, unlikeness
antonyms imparity, inequality, nonequivalence

equivalency *n* the state or fact of being exactly the same in number, amount, status, or quality ⟨As long as there's a rough *equivalency* in the armaments of the two countries, neither is likely to attack the other.⟩ — see EQUIVALENCE

equivalent *n* one that is equal to another in status, achievement, or value ⟨That huge mansion is the *equivalent* of five ordinary houses.⟩ — see EQUAL

equivocal *adj* **1** giving good reason for being doubted, questioned, or challenged ⟨The evidence that this latest diet really results in lasting weight loss is certainly *equivocal*.⟩ — see DOUBTFUL 2

2 having an often intentionally veiled or uncertain meaning ⟨He responded to the reporters' questions with *equivocal* answers.⟩ — see OBSCURE 1

equivocalness *n* the quality or state of having a veiled or uncertain meaning ⟨The intriguing *equivocalness* of her statement kept everyone guessing.⟩ — see OBSCURITY 1

equivocate *vb* to avoid giving a definite answer or position ⟨The candidate *equivocated* as long as he could on controversial issues.⟩
synonyms fudge, hedge, pussyfoot
related words yo-yo; dodge, duck, elude, eschew, evade, shake, shirk, shun, sidestep, skirt; bypass, circumvent; cavil, quibble; straddle
phrases beat around the bush (*or* beat about the bush), hem and haw, straddle the fence

equivocation *n* **1** deliberate evasion in speech ⟨His answers were filled with *equivocation*.⟩ — see CIRCUMLOCUTION 1

2 the quality or state of having a veiled or uncertain meaning ⟨the *equivocation* of the last line of the poem, "That is all ye know on earth, and all ye need to know"⟩ — see OBSCURITY 1

era *n* an extent of time associated with a particular person or thing ⟨The introduction of the mass production of cars on an assembly line ushered in the *era* of the automobile.⟩ — see AGE 1

eradicate *vb* to destroy all traces of ⟨the successful effort to *eradicate* smallpox around the globe⟩ — see ANNIHILATE 1

ere *prep* earlier than ⟨an old typewriter that was a relic of that ancient time *ere* the invention of word processors⟩ — see BEFORE 1

erect *adj* rising straight up ⟨a column still *erect* among the ancient ruins⟩
synonyms perpendicular, plumb, raised, standing, upright, upstanding, vertical
related words elevated, lifted, upended, upraised; semierect; freestanding, stand-alone
near antonyms prostrate, supine; diagonal, hanging, sagging, slant, slanted, slanting, slanty
antonyms flat, recumbent

erect *vb* **1** to fix in an upright position ⟨We need to *erect* our tent before the sun goes down.⟩
synonyms pitch, put up, raise, rear, set up, upend, upraise
related words brace, buttress, prop (up), shore (up), support; boost, crane, elevate, heave, heft, heighten, hike, hoist, jack (up), lift, perk (up), pick up, up, uphold, uplift
near antonyms demolish, flatten, knock down, level, raze, tear down

2 to form by putting together parts or materials ⟨We'd better *erect* some sort of shelter before these woods are in total darkness.⟩ — see BUILD

ergo *adv* for this or that reason ⟨According to that line of reasoning, the eyewitness couldn't identify the aircraft, *ergo* it must have been from another planet.⟩ — see THEREFORE

erode *vb* **1** to consume or wear away gradually ⟨the fear that inflation will continue to *erode* people's savings⟩ — see EAT 2

2 to damage or diminish by continued friction ⟨The winds and desert sands have *eroded* much of the original surface of these ancient monuments.⟩ — see ABRADE 1

erosion *n* a gradual weakening, loss, or destruction ⟨The *erosion* of the banks along the river worries flood experts.⟩ — see CORROSION

erotic *also* **erotical** *adj* of, relating to, exciting, or expressing sexual attraction or desire ⟨the *erotic* aspects of the fairy tale⟩
synonyms amatory, amorous, sexy
related words carnal, fleshly, sensual, sensuous; lascivious, lewd, lustful, obscene, prurient, suggestive, titillating; dirty, filthy, foul, gross, indecent, nasty, ribald, vulgar; fetishistic, perversive
near antonyms clean, decent, decorous, polite, proper, seemly; innocuous, inoffensive

err *vb* **1** to make a mistake ⟨We badly *erred* when we calculated the driving distance.⟩
synonyms blunder, flub, fluff, foul up, fumble, louse up, mess (up), screw up, stumble, trip
related words nod; bobble, botch, bungle, butcher, foozle, mangle, mishandle, muff, murder; miscalculate, misconceive, miscount, miscue, misdeem, misjudge, mistake; misconstrue, misinterpret, misunderstand
phrases drop the ball, lay an egg

2 to commit an offense ⟨When we *err*, we must be willing to accept the consequences.⟩ — see OFFEND 1

errant *adj* **1** engaging in or marked by childish misbehavior ⟨He blamed the prank on *errant* students.⟩ — see NAUGHTY

2 traveling from place to place ⟨the *errant* gunslinger as a standard character in western novels⟩ — see ITINERANT

erratic *adj* **1** lacking a definite plan, purpose, or pattern ⟨So far your effort to land a summer job has been very *erratic*.⟩ — see RANDOM

2 lacking in steadiness or regularity of occurrence ⟨Because of your *erratic* attendance at practice, you're in danger of being cut from the team.⟩ — see FITFUL

3 not staying constant ⟨Business at the fast-food restaurant has been so *erratic* lately that the manager never knows how much staff to have on hand.⟩ — see UNEVEN 2

4 different from the ordinary in a way that causes curiosity or suspicion ⟨Its *erratic* punctuation made me wonder if the email was a scam from a foreign country.⟩ — see ODD 2

erratically *adv* without definite aim, direction, rule, or method ⟨The police officer pulled over the driver, who had been driving very *erratically*.⟩ — see HIT OR MISS

erroneous *adj* not being in agreement with what is true ⟨a news article about the new virus that was filled with much *erroneous* information⟩ — see FALSE 1

erroneously *adv* in a mistaken or inappropriate way ⟨People *erroneously* believed that the disease was contagious.⟩ — see WRONGLY

erroneousness *n* the quality or state of being false ⟨The *erroneousness* of so much that is printed in the tabloids is amazing.⟩ — see FALLACY 2

error *n* **1** an unintentional departure from truth or accuracy ⟨A report on the incident contained several unfortunate *errors*.⟩

synonyms blunder, bobble, fault, flub, fluff, fumble, gaff, gaffe, goof, inaccuracy, lapse, miscue, misstep, mistake, oversight, screwup, slip, slipup, stumble, trip

related words bloomer, blooper, boner, howler, pratfall; foul-up, snafu; misapprehension, miscomprehension, misconception, misconstruction, miscue, misdescription, misinterpretation, misjudgment, misreading, misstatement, misunderstanding

near antonyms accuracy, correctness, exactitude, exactness, preciseness, precision, strictness; inerrancy, infallibility, perfection

2 a breaking of a moral or legal code ⟨He acknowledged the *error* of his ways and asked for forgiveness.⟩ — see OFFENSE 1

3 a false idea or belief ⟨repeating an *error* in citing that statistic⟩ — see FALLACY 1

erstwhile *adj* having been such at some previous time ⟨My *erstwhile* friend ignored me when I ran into her at the mall.⟩ — see FORMER 1

erudite *adj* **1** having or displaying advanced knowledge or education ⟨The most *erudite* people in medical research attended the conference.⟩ ⟨an *erudite* lecture on the latest discoveries in astronomy⟩ — see EDUCATED 1

2 suggestive of the vocabulary used in books ⟨the *erudite* language of a textbook on philosophy⟩ — see BOOKISH

erudition *n* the understanding and information gained from being educated ⟨a scientist of impressive *erudition* but with a down-to-earth manner⟩ — see EDUCATION 2

erupt *vb* **1** to violently throw out or off (something from within) ⟨The volcano *erupted* clouds of poisonous gas and tons of hot ash.⟩

synonyms belch, disgorge, eject, expel, jet, spew, spout, spurt

related words gush, pour, squirt, stream, surge; exhale, issue, release, shoot, spit, spring, vent; discharge, emit, fire; cast, fling, heave, hurl, launch, pitch, toss

near antonyms bottle (up), contain, restrain, shut (in *or* up)

2 to develop suddenly and violently ⟨A fire *erupted*, and flames soon engulfed the room.⟩

synonyms break out, burst (forth), explode, flame, flare (up)

related words rocket, skyrocket; balloon, burgeon (*also* bourgeon), mount, multiply, mushroom, proliferate, snowball, swell, wax; blow up, detonate, touch off

eruption *n* **1** a sudden intense expression of strong feeling ⟨a great *eruption* of glee as it suddenly dawned on her that she had won⟩ — see OUTBURST 1

2 the act or an instance of exploding ⟨The *eruption* of the volcano Krakatoa was one of the most violent in global history.⟩ — see EXPLOSION 1

escalate *vb* **1** to become greater in extent, volume, amount, or number ⟨The war between the two countries *escalated*.⟩ — see INCREASE 2

2 to make greater in size, amount, or number ⟨The president promised to *escalate* the government's program to combat the dreaded disease.⟩ — see INCREASE 1

escalated *adj* being at a higher level than average ⟨For a time there was an *escalated* interest in the scientist's life story.⟩ — see HIGH 2

escapade *n* a playful or mischievous act intended as a joke ⟨Their *escapades* at the prep school became the stuff of boarding-school legend.⟩ — see PRANK

escape *n* **1** the act or an instance of getting free from danger or confinement ⟨a daring prison *escape*⟩

synonyms break, flight, getaway, lam, rout, slip

related words jailbreak; deliverance, liberation, redemption, release, rescue, salvation

near antonyms captivity, confinement, immurement, imprisonment, incarceration, internment; custody, hold, holding, retention; endangerment, hazard, imperilment, jeopardy, peril, risk, trouble

2 the act or a means of getting or keeping away from something undesirable ⟨the reading of science-fiction novels as an *escape* from reality⟩

synonyms avoidance, cop-out, dodging, ducking, eluding, evasion, out, shaking, shunning

related words bypassing, circumvention, runaround, sidestepping, skirting; averting, precluding, prevention

near antonyms abidance, endurance, submission, toleration

escape *vb* **1** to get free from a dangerous or confining situation ⟨Everyone managed to *escape* from the burning building in time.⟩

synonyms abscond, clear out, flee, fly, get out, lam, run away, run off

related words avoid, elude, evade, lose, shun; decamp, depart, elope, exit, go, leave, move, quit, sally (forth), shove (off), take off, walk out; disentangle, extricate; emancipate, enfranchise, free, liberate, loose, loosen, redeem, release, rescue, spring

phrases break free

near antonyms abide, dwell, hang around, linger, remain, stay, stick around, tarry; return

2 to get or keep away from (as a responsibility) through cleverness or trickery ⟨a judge who is determined not to let criminals *escape* punishment⟩

synonyms avoid, dodge, duck, elude, evade, finesse, get around, shake, shirk, shun

related words miss; avert, deflect, divert, obviate, parry, prevent, ward (off); ban, bar, debar, eliminate, except, exclude, preclude, rule out; bypass, circumvent, skirt; foil, fox, frustrate, outfox, outsmart, outwit, overreach, thwart

phrases fight shy of, keep clear of, stay clear of, steer clear of

near antonyms accept, court, embrace, pursue, seek, welcome; catch, contract, incur

escarpment *n* a steep wall of rock, earth, or ice ⟨The castle sits atop an *escarpment* that for hundreds of years made it virtually invulnerable to attack.⟩ — see CLIFF

escort *n* one that accompanies another for protection, guidance, or as a courtesy ⟨The mayor served as the senator's *escort* for her tour of the city.⟩
  synonyms attendant, companion, guard, guide
  related words chaperone (*or* chaperon), squire; shadow, sidekick; conductor, leader, pilot; convoy, courier, honor guard

escort *vb* to go along with in order to provide assistance, protection, or companionship ⟨A student from the college *escorted* my parents and me on our tour of the campus.⟩ — see ACCOMPANY 1

esculent *adj* suitable for use as food ⟨Harvesting wild mushrooms is no business for amateurs, since some of the *ésculent* ones closely resemble poisonous varieties.⟩ — see EDIBLE

esoteric *adj* **1** difficult for one of ordinary knowledge or intelligence to understand ⟨Metaphysics is such an *esoteric* subject that most people are content to leave it to the philosophers.⟩ — see PROFOUND 1
  2 not known or meant to be known by the general populace ⟨He gave up stardom for some *esoteric* reason.⟩ — see PRIVATE 1

especial *adj* **1** being out of the ordinary ⟨a candidate who handled the stunning defeat with *especial* grace⟩ — see EXCEPTIONAL 1
  2 of a particular or exact sort ⟨With a very ordinary lawn, we don't have any *especial* need for a gardener.⟩ — see EXPRESS 1

especially *adv* **1** in the specific case of one person or thing as distinguished from others ⟨All employees, but *especially* the administrative assistants, will need to learn to use the new phone system.⟩
  synonyms particularly
  related words individually, personally; restrictively, selectively
  phrases in especial, in particular
  near antonyms broadly, widely
  antonyms generally
  2 to a great degree ⟨That university is *especially* strong in the sciences.⟩ — see VERY 1

espionage *n* the secret gathering of information on others ⟨the acts of *espionage* on behalf of the Confederacy carried on by Belle Boyd and Rose Greenhow⟩
  synonyms spying
  related words counterespionage, counterintelligence, intelligence; cloak-and-dagger; observation, reconnaissance, surveillance; bugging, eavesdropping, wiretapping

espousal *n* **1** a ceremony in which two people are united in matrimony ⟨The expected *espousal* of the Hollywood actor and the singing superstar should attract the elite of show business.⟩ — see WEDDING
  2 the act or state of being engaged to be married ⟨They chose to have an extended *espousal*.⟩ — see ENGAGEMENT 1

espouse *vb* **1** to give in marriage ⟨a couple happy to *espouse* their daughter to their best friends' son⟩ — see MARRY 2
  2 to take as a spouse ⟨Dan heeded his father's advice to *espouse* someone with whom he had common interests.⟩ — see MARRY 3
  3 to take for one's own use (something originated by another) ⟨The new theory has been *espoused* by many leading physicists.⟩ — see ADOPT

esprit *n* active strength of body or mind ⟨The dance company has an infectious *esprit* that captivates audiences.⟩ — see VIGOR 1

espy *vb* to make note of (something) through the use of one's eyes ⟨Out of the corner of my eye I *espied* the squirrel making another raid on the bird feeder.⟩ — see SEE 1

essay *n* **1** a short piece of writing typically expressing a point of view ⟨school *essays* on what it means to be a patriot⟩
  synonyms article, composition, paper, theme
  related words column, commentary, editorial, feature, report, review, write-up; dissertation, thesis; tract, treatise; discourse, discussion, study
  2 an effort to do or accomplish something ⟨My first *essay* at baking a cake did not go well.⟩ — see ATTEMPT 1
  3 a procedure or operation carried out to resolve an uncertainty ⟨a little homemade *essay* to determine the easiest way to strip the paint from the bookcase⟩ — see EXPERIMENT

essay *vb* to make an effort to do ⟨He had been in gymnastics for some time before he even considered *essaying* that move.⟩ — see ATTEMPT

essence *n* **1** the quality or qualities that make a thing what it is ⟨The belief that power ultimately rests with the people is the very *essence* of democracy.⟩
  synonyms being, essentiality, nature, quintessence, soul, stuff, substance
  related words heart, spirit; center, core, marrow, pith, seat; embodiment, epitome, incarnation, manifestation, personification; aspect, attribute, feature, property; gist, nub
  phrases name of the game
  2 the central part or aspect of something under consideration ⟨presented the *essence* of weeks of testimony in a 20-minute appeal to the jury⟩ — see CRUX

essential *adj* **1** impossible to do without ⟨A well-stocked public library is *essential* for the well-being of a community.⟩
  synonyms all-important, critical, imperative, indispensable, integral, necessary, needed, needful, required, requisite, vital
  related words prerequisite; compulsory, mandatory, nonelective, obligatory; consequential, crucial, important, major, material, meaningful, momentous, significant, substantial, weighty; basic, central, fundamental, key, organic; insistent, persistent, pressing, urgent
  phrases of the essence
  near antonyms undesired, unwanted; inconsequential, insignificant, unimportant; excess, external, extra, extraneous, superfluous, surplus
  antonyms dispensable, needless, nonessential, unessential, unnecessary, unneeded
  2 of or relating to the simplest facts or theories of a subject ⟨Anyone with an *essential* knowledge of human biology can follow the documentary.⟩ — see ELEMENTARY
  3 being a part of the innermost nature of a person or thing ⟨an unquenchable belief in the *essential* goodness of most people⟩ — see INHERENT

essential *n* **1** something necessary, indispensable, or unavoidable ⟨The *essentials* for success include a willingness to work and the right attitude.⟩
  synonyms condition, demand, must, necessary, necessity, need, needful, requirement, requisite
  related words precondition, prerequisite; advantage, edge, plus
  near antonyms amenity, comfort, extra, extravagance, frill, indulgence, luxury, superfluity, surplus, surplusage
  antonyms nonessential, nonnecessity
  2 essentials *pl* general or basic truths on which other truths or theories can be based ⟨This will be just an introduction to the *essentials* of computer programming.⟩ — see PRINCIPLES 1

essentiality *n* the quality or qualities that make a thing what it is ⟨Physical strength or endurance is the *essentiality* that makes activity a sport and not just a game.⟩ — see ESSENCE 1

establish *vb* **1** to gain full recognition or acceptance of ⟨a first novel that *established* him as one of the most promising writers of his generation⟩
synonyms demonstrate, prove, show, substantiate
related words attest, authenticate, bear out, document, evidence, support, sustain, uphold; confirm, corroborate, justify, validate, verify
near antonyms confute, discredit, invalidate, rebut, refute
antonyms disprove
2 to show the existence or truth of by evidence ⟨The developers haven't *established* that there's a need for another shopping center in town.⟩ — see PROVE 1
3 to be responsible for the creation and early operation or use of ⟨*established* the first school in the nation⟩ — see FOUND

establisher *n* a person who establishes a whole new field of endeavor ⟨Alfred Stieglitz is often credited as the *establisher* of photography as an art form.⟩ — see FATHER 2

establishment *n* **1** a building, room, or suite of rooms occupied by a service business ⟨one of the best dining *establishments* in the city⟩ — see PLACE 2
2 a commercial or industrial activity or organization ⟨New business *establishments* sprang up all over.⟩ — see ENTERPRISE 1
3 a public organization with a particular purpose or function ⟨The proposed change in pollution standards was supported by environmental *establishments* across the board.⟩ — see INSTITUTION 1
4 a structure that is designed and built for a particular purpose ⟨The city boasts a host of outstanding medical *establishments*.⟩ — see FACILITY

estate *n* **1** a large impressive residence ⟨The *estates* of multimillionaires line the shores of this ocean resort.⟩ — see MANSION
2 a state of being or fitness ⟨The mayor pronounced the city's schools to be in their best *estate* ever.⟩ — see CONDITION 1
3 one of the segments of society into which people are grouped ⟨the passionate belief that a society is judged by how well it treats and cares for those in the lowest *estate*⟩ — see CLASS 1
4 a piece of land and its buildings used to grow crops or raise livestock ⟨a huge coffee *estate* in Brazil⟩ — see FARM

esteem *n* a feeling of great approval and liking ⟨an athlete who is held in great *esteem* by her peers⟩ — see ADMIRATION 1

esteem *vb* **1** to think of in a particular way ⟨I had *esteemed* the whole affair to be a colossal waste of time.⟩ — see CONSIDER 1
2 to think very highly or favorably of ⟨Although the works of the Impressionist painters are *esteemed* today, they met with scorn when they were introduced.⟩ — see ADMIRE
3 to have as an opinion ⟨I should have *esteemed* it most likely that the business would succeed.⟩ — see BELIEVE 2

esteemed *adj* having a good reputation especially in a field of knowledge ⟨Concerned about his heart, my grandfather went to see an *esteemed* cardiac specialist.⟩ — see RESPECTABLE 1

estimate *n* **1** the act of placing a value on the nature, character, or quality of something ⟨What we owe our war veterans is beyond *estimate*.⟩
synonyms appraisal, appraisement, assessment, estimation, evaluation, reckoning, valuation
related words calculation, computation, measurement;

audit, check, checkup, examination, inspection, review, scan, scrutiny, survey; reassessment, transvaluation; overestimation, overevaluation; underestimation
2 an opinion on the nature, character, or quality of something ⟨The *estimate* of many art specialists is that the painting is a fake.⟩ — see ESTIMATION 1

estimate *vb* **1** to make an approximate or tentative judgment regarding ⟨Experts *estimated* the value of the painting at a million dollars.⟩
synonyms appraise, assess, evaluate, rate, set, value
related words adjudge, deem, judge; ascertain, determine, discover, learn; price, prize; decide, settle; analyze, assay, survey, test; reappraise, reassess, reevaluate, rejudge, revalue; misesteem, misjudge, misprize
2 to decide the size, amount, number, or distance of (something) without actual measurement ⟨We *estimated* the snowfall to be about a foot.⟩
synonyms calculate, call, conjecture, figure, gauge (*also* gage), guess, judge, make, place, put, reckon, suppose
related words conclude, deduce, extrapolate, gather, infer, reason, understand
near antonyms calibrate, measure, scale; compute, work out

estimation *n* **1** an opinion on the nature, character, or quality of something ⟨The teacher's *estimation* of her student's scientific aptitude proved to be well-founded when he won a national science award.⟩
synonyms appraisal, appraisement, assessment, estimate, evaluation, fix, judgment (*or* judgement)
related words aperçu, feeling, impression, notion, perception; confidence, faith, stock, trust; belief, conviction, mind, persuasion, sentiment, view; conjecture, guess, hunch, hypothesis, surmise, theory
2 the act of placing a value on the nature, character, or quality of something ⟨I may have been a little too hasty in my *estimation* of his musical abilities.⟩ — see ESTIMATE 1
3 a feeling of great approval and liking ⟨a show business superstar who enjoys the *estimation* of fans and fellow performers alike⟩ — see ADMIRATION 1

estrange *vb* to cause to change from friendly or loving to unfriendly or uncaring ⟨She *estranged* several of her coworkers when she let her promotion go to her head.⟩
synonyms alienate, disaffect, disgruntle, sour
related words antagonize, embitter, envenom; aggravate, anger, enrage, incense, inflame (*also* enflame), infuriate, madden, outrage, rankle, rile, roil; break up, dissociate, disunite, divide, separate, sever, split, sunder, uncouple, unlink, unyoke; disenchant, disillusion
near antonyms endear, ingratiate; appease, conciliate, disarm, mollify, pacify, placate, propitiate
antonyms reconcile

estrangement *n* the loss of friendship or affection ⟨After years of *estrangement*, the friends put their quarrel behind them.⟩
synonyms alienation, disaffection, disgruntlement, souring
related words antagonism, embitterment, envenoming; breach, breakup, divorce, rift, rupture, schism, separation, split; animosity, antagonism, antipathy, bitterness, hostility, jaundice, rancor; aggravation, furor, fury, incensing, indignation, infuriation, ire, outrage, rage, spleen, wrath; disenchantment, disillusionment
near antonyms endearment, ingratiation; appeasement, conciliation, mollification, pacification, propitiation
antonyms reconcilement, reconciliation

estuary *n* a part of a body of water that extends beyond the general shoreline ⟨The city sits on the shores of a deep *estuary* where the Hudson River meets the Atlantic Ocean.⟩ — see GULF 1

etch *vb* **1** to cut (as letters or designs) on a hard surface ⟨The artist *etched* his landscape on a copper plate.⟩ — see ENGRAVE 1
2 to produce a vivid impression of ⟨In just a few pages the writer *etched* an unforgettable portrait of an early aviation pioneer.⟩ — see ENGRAVE 2
eternal *adj* **1** having an existence or validity that does not change or diminish ⟨a charming fable that presents some *eternal* truths in a fresh way⟩ — see ABIDING
2 lasting forever ⟨the quest for some magic potion that promises *eternal* youth⟩ — see EVERLASTING 1
eternally *adv* for all time ⟨We will be *eternally* grateful for your kind generosity.⟩ — see EVER 1
eternity *n* **1** endless time ⟨the question whether the universe will end someday or continue to exist in *eternity*⟩
synonyms everlasting, infinity, perpetuity
related words boundlessness, endlessness, interminableness, limitlessness, permanence, permanency, timelessness
near antonyms temporariness, transitoriness
2 unending existence after death ⟨a firm belief in the *eternity* of the soul⟩
synonyms afterlife, beyond, hereafter, immortality
related words afterworld, otherworld
3 a long or seemingly long period of time ⟨We waited in line for tickets for an *eternity*.⟩ — see AGE 2
ethereal *adj* **1** not composed of matter ⟨that *ethereal* attribute that every performer should have—charisma⟩ — see IMMATERIAL 1
2 resembling air in lightness ⟨The bakery's scrumptious pastries have a wonderfully *ethereal* consistency.⟩ — see AIRY 1
3 of, relating to, or suggesting heaven ⟨a land of *ethereal* beauty and tranquillity⟩ — see CELESTIAL
ethical *adj* **1** conforming to a high standard of morality or virtue ⟨the *ethical* behavior expected of every member of the police force⟩ — see GOOD 2
2 following the accepted rules of moral conduct ⟨advocated for the *ethical* treatment of animals⟩ — see HONORABLE 1
3 guided by or in accordance with one's sense of right and wrong ⟨*Ethical* writers do not use the words of other writers without giving them proper credit.⟩ — see CONSCIENTIOUS 1
ethics *pl n* the code of good conduct for an individual or group ⟨The *ethics* of scouting require scouts to be loyal, clean, and reverent.⟩
synonyms morality, morals, norms, principles, standards
related words customs, dictates, etiquette, manners, mores, values; beliefs, dogma, faith, tenets
ethnic *adj* of, relating to, or reflecting the traits exhibited by a group of people with a common ancestry and culture ⟨the variety of *ethnic* groups in the U.S.⟩ — see RACIAL
etiquette *n* personal conduct or behavior as evaluated by an accepted standard of appropriateness for a social or professional setting ⟨The couple exhibited poor *etiquette* when they left the party without saying goodbye to the host and hostess.⟩ — see MANNER 1
eulogy *n* a formal expression of praise ⟨Several *eulogies* were given at the special assembly marking the retirement of the company's longtime president.⟩ — see ENCOMIUM
euphonious *adj* **1** having a pleasantly flowing quality suggestive of music ⟨an opera singer with an appropriately *euphonious* name⟩ — see LYRIC 1
2 having a pleasing mixture of notes ⟨The doorbell had a noticeably *euphonious* chime.⟩ — see HARMONIOUS 1

euphoria *n* a state of overwhelming usually pleasurable emotion ⟨A general *euphoria* seemed to engulf the city following the World Series win.⟩ — see ECSTASY
euphoric *adj* experiencing or marked by overwhelming usually pleasurable emotion ⟨The *euphoric* winner was momentarily speechless.⟩ — see ECSTATIC
evacuate *vb* to remove the contents of ⟨*Evacuate* the cupboards completely before spraying the insecticide.⟩ — see EMPTY
evacuee *n* a person forced to emigrate for political reasons ⟨*Evacuees* by the thousands poured into the camps for displaced persons.⟩ — see ÉMIGRÉ 1
evade *vb* to get or keep away from (as a responsibility) through cleverness or trickery ⟨people who use every loophole in the law to *evade* paying taxes⟩ — see ESCAPE 2
evaluate *vb* to make an approximate or tentative judgment regarding ⟨A trained assistant was hired to *evaluate* the needs of the patients waiting to see the doctor.⟩ — see ESTIMATE 1
evaluation *n* **1** an opinion on the nature, character, or quality of something ⟨What's your *evaluation* of her writing ability?⟩ — see ESTIMATION 1
2 the act of placing a value on the nature, character, or quality of something ⟨The *evaluation* of the defendant's mental condition was conducted by a team of psychiatrists.⟩ — see ESTIMATE 1
evanesce *vb* to cease to be visible ⟨The kids' rainy-day gloom *evanesced* the minute they heard that we were going out for ice cream.⟩ — see DISAPPEAR
evanescent *adj* lasting only for a short time ⟨beauty that is as *evanescent* as a rainbow⟩ — see MOMENTARY
evaporate *vb* to cease to be visible ⟨By mid-morning the fog that had enshrouded the island had just *evaporated*.⟩ — see DISAPPEAR
evasion *n* the act or a means of getting or keeping away from something undesirable ⟨Pleading chronic back pain is my standard *evasion* for doing any heavy lifting.⟩ — see ESCAPE 2
evasive *adj* hard to find, capture, or isolate ⟨Believers in Bigfoot have never quite explained how such a large creature can be so *evasive*.⟩ — see ELUSIVE
even *adj* **1** being neither more nor less than a certain amount, number, or extent ⟨The distance to town is an *even* mile.⟩
synonyms exact, flat, precise, round
near antonyms approximate, comparative, near, relative; imprecise
2 having a surface without bends, breaks, or irregularities ⟨Let's find an *even* stretch of ground to pitch our tent.⟩ — see LEVEL 1
3 resembling another in every respect ⟨The teams of the two schools are fairly *even*.⟩ — see SAME 1
4 not varying ⟨Energy demands do not stay *even* throughout the day but peak significantly during the afternoon hours.⟩ — see UNIFORM
even *adv* **1** not merely this but also ⟨The blue whale is a large, *even* enormous animal.⟩
synonyms indeed, nay, truly, verily, yea
related words assuredly, certainly, decidedly, definitely, doubtless, incontestably, incontrovertibly, indisputably, really, surely, truly, undeniably, undoubtedly, unquestionably
phrases in fact, in reality, in truth
2 to a full extent or degree ⟨I will love you *even* to the end of time.⟩ — see FULLY 1
even *vb* **1** to make free from breaks, curves, or bumps ⟨*Even* the filling before adding the top layer of the cake.⟩
synonyms flatten, level, plane, smooth

related words clip, crop, pare, prune, shave, trim; lay, press, spread; card, comb, rake; surface
near antonyms coarsen, rumple, wrinkle; bend; dent, pit
antonyms rough, roughen
2 to make equal in amount, degree, or status ⟨That win *evens* the teams at one game apiece.⟩ — see EQUALIZE

evenhanded *adj* marked by justice, honesty, and freedom from bias ⟨an *evenhanded* assessment of the work⟩ — see FAIR 2

evening *n* **1** a later period of one's life ⟨Now in the *evening* of their lives, the married couple are ready to hand the family business over to the next generation.⟩ — see AGE 3
2 the time from when the sun begins to set to the onset of total darkness ⟨In the *evening* a reddish glow often appears on the mountaintops.⟩ — see DUSK 1

event *n* **1** something that happens ⟨Dinnertime was devoted to talking over the day's *events*.⟩
synonyms affair, circumstance, episode, happening, incident, occasion, occurrence, thing
related words coincidence, freak; landmark, milestone, page, phenomenon, turning point; adventure, experience, time; happenchance, happenstance; accident, crisis, emergency, juncture; achievement, deed, exploit, feat; news, tidings; circus, extravaganza, pageant
2 something that might happen ⟨In the *event* of rain, graduation ceremonies will be held indoors.⟩
synonyms case, contingency, contingent, eventuality, possibility
related words probability; accident, chance, hazard, risk
3 a competitive encounter between individuals or groups carried on for amusement, exercise, or in pursuit of a prize ⟨Figure skating is usually one of the most popular *events* in the winter Olympics.⟩ — see GAME 1
4 a social gathering ⟨The mayor's evenings are often tied up with one *event* after another.⟩ — see PARTY 1

eventful *adj* having great meaning or lasting effect ⟨The first moon landing was universally regarded as an *eventful* moment in human history.⟩ — see IMPORTANT 1

eventide *n* the time from when the sun begins to set to the onset of total darkness ⟨*Eventide* was their favorite time for enjoying a quiet respite in the backyard.⟩ — see DUSK 1

eventuality *n* **1** something that can develop or become actual ⟨A cure for that disease seems like a certain *eventuality*—it's just a matter of time.⟩ — see POTENTIAL
2 something that might happen ⟨A full-force hurricane on the day of the picnic was one *eventuality* that we hadn't planned on.⟩ — see EVENT 2

eventually *adv* at a later time ⟨Stop whining about how long it's taking us—we'll get there *eventually*!⟩ — see YET 1

ever *adv* **1** for all time ⟨The name of Benedict Arnold will *ever* be linked with treason.⟩
synonyms always, aye (*also* ay), eternally, everlastingly, evermore, forever, forevermore, permanently, perpetually
related words enduringly, long, perennially
phrases for good (*also* for good and all), for keeps
antonyms ne'er, never, nevermore
2 in any way or respect ⟨How can we *ever* repay what you've done for us?⟩ — see AT ALL
3 on every relevant occasion ⟨The boy and his *ever* present dog were a common sight around the village.⟩ — see ALWAYS 1
4 to a great degree ⟨Boy, was I *ever* embarrassed!⟩ ⟨It's been *ever* so long since we've seen you.⟩ — see VERY 1

everlasting *adj* **1** lasting forever ⟨Valentines typically express the giver's *everlasting* love and devotion.⟩

synonyms ceaseless, dateless, deathless, endless, eternal, immortal, permanent, perpetual, undying, unending
related words durable, enduring, lasting, long-lived, persistent, stubborn; imperishable, indefeasible, indestructible, indissoluble, inexpungible; timeless; abiding, stable, standing, steadfast, steady, unfailing, unfaltering; continual, continuing, continuous, incessant, unbroken, unceasing, uninterrupted, unremitting
near antonyms ephemeral, evanescent, fleeting, fugitive, momentary, passing, short-lived, transitory; interim, provisional, short-term
antonyms impermanent, mortal, temporary, transient
2 having an existence or validity that does not change or diminish ⟨Shakespeare's plays are still being performed 400 years later because they deal with *everlasting* truths and universal emotions.⟩ — see ABIDING

everlasting *n* **1** endless time ⟨that special bond that has existed between mother and child from *everlasting*⟩ — see ETERNITY 1
2 *cap* the being worshipped as the creator and ruler of the universe ⟨people who believe that the magnificence of the natural world is proof of the existence of the *Everlasting*⟩ — see DEITY 2

everlastingly *adv* for all time ⟨The sacrifices made by our brave soldiers on this battlefield will be *everlastingly* remembered.⟩ — see EVER 1

evermore *adv* for all time ⟨He promised to love her *evermore*, if only she would consent to be his wife.⟩ — see EVER 1

every *adj* being one of a group ⟨*Every* man here must decide for himself whether to go or to stay.⟩ — see EACH

everybody *pron* every person ⟨*Everybody* must do what his or her conscience dictates.⟩
synonyms all, everyone
related words anybody, anyone; somebody, someone
phrases each and everyone, one and all
antonyms nobody, none, no one

everyday *adj* **1** being of the type that is encountered in the normal course of events ⟨We're just an *everyday* family, with a dog and a cat and bills to pay.⟩ — see ORDINARY 1
2 having to do with the practical details of regular life ⟨Even the richest man in town has to do such *everyday* tasks as brushing his teeth.⟩ — see MUNDANE 1
3 not designed to be worn only on special occasions ⟨*Everyday* clothes will be fine for this party.⟩ — see CASUAL 1
4 often observed or encountered ⟨The book provides solutions to *everyday* problems.⟩ — see COMMON 1

everyone *pron* every person ⟨There's plenty of food for *everyone*.⟩ — see EVERYBODY

everyplace *adv* in every place or in all places ⟨I can't be *everyplace* at once, so somebody has to help me.⟩ — see EVERYWHERE

everywhere *adv* in every place or in all places ⟨Freedom and happiness are the goals of people *everywhere*.⟩
synonyms all over, everyplace, throughout
related words every which way; right and left
phrases all over the place (*or* map), far and near, in every corner (*or* quarter), on all hands (*or* on every hand)

evidence *n* something presented in support of the truth or accuracy of a claim ⟨Do you have any *evidence* that this bike is yours?⟩ — see PROOF

evident *adj* **1** appearing to be true on the basis of evidence that may or may not be confirmed ⟨The *evident* cause of the accident was icy road conditions.⟩ — see APPARENT 1
2 not subject to misinterpretation or more than one interpretation ⟨She rose with the *evident* intention of saying something.⟩ — see CLEAR 2

evidently *adv* to all outward appearances ⟨She was *evidently* dissatisfied with her job and abruptly quit.⟩ — see APPARENTLY

evil *adj* **1** causing or capable of causing harm ⟨She drank an *evil* potion.⟩ — see HARMFUL
2 not conforming to a high moral standard; morally unacceptable ⟨Their *evil* deeds rank among the worst in history.⟩ — see BAD 2
3 causing intense displeasure, disgust, or resentment ⟨She refused to eat olives or anything which had their *evil* flavor.⟩ — see OFFENSIVE 1

evil *n* that which is morally unacceptable ⟨Our free will allows us to choose between good and *evil*.⟩
synonyms bad, evildoing, ill, immorality, iniquity, sin, villainy, wrong
related words atrociousness, atrocity, badness, balefulness, darkness, depravedness, devilishness, diabolism, enormity, evilness, heinousness, satanism, sinfulness, vileness, wickedness; devilry (*or* deviltry); cancer, canker, decay, rot, squalor; corruption, debauchery, degeneracy, depravity, indecency, malefaction, perversion, pervertedness, scurrility, scurrilousness; abomination, anathema, taboo (*also* tabu)
near antonyms decency, goodness, honesty, integrity, probity, rectitude, uprightness; righteousness, virtuousness
antonyms good, morality, right, virtue

evildoer *n* **1** a person who commits moral wrongs ⟨If good people stand by and do nothing, *evildoers* will triumph.⟩
synonyms malefactor, sinner, wrongdoer
related words criminal, crook, felon, lawbreaker, miscreant, misdoer, misfeasor, offender, reprobate, transgressor, villain; corrupter (*also* corruptor)
near antonyms angel, innocent, saint
2 a mean, evil, or unprincipled person ⟨Voldemort is one of the most notorious *evildoers* in all of children's literature.⟩ — see VILLAIN

evildoing *n* that which is morally unacceptable ⟨a book that ponders the question of the presence of *evildoing* in a universe controlled by a benevolent Supreme Being⟩ — see EVIL

evilness *n* the state or quality of being utterly evil ⟨the *evilness* of the crimes⟩ — see ENORMITY 1

evince *vb* to make known (something abstract) through outward signs ⟨He *evinced* an interest in art at an early age.⟩ — see SHOW 2

eviscerate *vb* to take the internal organs out of ⟨The ancient Egyptians would *eviscerate* the bodies of the dead as part of the process of mummifying them.⟩ — see GUT

evocative *adj* provoking a memory or mental association ⟨The Italian-American restaurant is decorated in a manner *evocative* of the charming outdoor cafés in Italy.⟩ — see SUGGESTIVE 2

evoke *vb* to draw out (something hidden, latent, or reserved) ⟨The old family photographs we found in the attic *evoked* a wealth of warm memories.⟩ — see EDUCE

evolution *n* the act or process of going from the simple or basic to the complex or advanced ⟨the *evolution* of motion pictures from short, silent reels into a medium of mass entertainment and an art form⟩ — see DEVELOPMENT 1

evolve *vb* **1** to gradually become clearer or more detailed ⟨As the governor's plans for the reform of state government *evolved*, objections from various groups inevitably arose.⟩ — see DEVELOP 1
2 to throw or give off ⟨Baking soda and citric acid react with each other and *evolve* carbon dioxide.⟩ — see EMIT 1

evolved *adj* being far along in development ⟨Whether this is an *evolved* technology or one still in its infancy is a matter of debate.⟩ — see ADVANCED

ewer *n* a handled container for holding and pouring liquids that usually has a lip or a spout ⟨a silver *ewer* in the elaborately ornamented style favored by the Victorians⟩ — see PITCHER

exact *adj* **1** being in agreement with the truth or a fact or a standard ⟨Maybe I wasn't being very *exact* when I said I had done it a million times—but it sure seemed like it!⟩ — see CORRECT 1
2 being neither more nor less than a certain amount, number, or extent ⟨The *exact* number of passengers on that airplane was 147.⟩ — see EVEN 1
3 following an original exactly ⟨an *exact* replica of an airplane flown by the Tuskegee Airmen⟩ — see FAITHFUL 2
4 made or done with extreme care and accuracy ⟨The company stresses that its optical telescopes are *exact* instruments and should not be handled as toys.⟩ — see FINE 2
5 meeting the highest standard of accuracy ⟨In order for the blind to fit properly, we must have the *exact* measurements of the window.⟩ — see PRECISE 1

exact *vb* **1** to ask for (something) earnestly or with authority ⟨Every war inevitably *exacts* the greatest sacrifice possible from some of the nation's best and brightest.⟩ — see DEMAND 1
2 to establish or apply as a charge or penalty ⟨vowed to *exact* a heavy fine from any hockey player engaging in such outrageous behavior on the ice⟩ — see IMPOSE
3 to get (as money) by the use of force or threats ⟨That loan shark can be counted upon to *exact* repayment of his loan by whatever means necessary.⟩ — see EXTORT

exacting *adj* **1** hard to please ⟨He was shocked when his normally *exacting* supervisor complimented him on a job well done.⟩ — see FINICKY
2 not allowing for any exceptions or loosening of standards ⟨the prep school's *exacting* standards for admission⟩ — see RIGID 1
3 requiring considerable physical or mental effort ⟨The new recruits had to adjust themselves to the *exacting* discipline of military life.⟩ — see HARD 2
4 requiring much time, effort, or careful attention ⟨Writing will always be an *exacting* task.⟩ — see DEMANDING 1

exactitude *n* the quality or state of being very accurate ⟨After its opening weekend, a movie's final box office gross can be estimated with considerable *exactitude*.⟩ — see PRECISION

exactly *adv* **1** as stated or indicated without the slightest difference ⟨We will meet at *exactly* six o'clock.⟩
synonyms due, full, just, precisely, right, sharp, smack-dab, squarely
phrases on the button, on the nose
2 in the same manner ⟨He wants to be *exactly* like his father.⟩ — see JUST 1
3 in the same words ⟨a plagiarism suit alleging that one historian had copied large segments of another's text *exactly*⟩ — see VERBATIM
4 without any relaxation of standards or precision ⟨Follow the rules *exactly* and you won't get into trouble.⟩ — see STRICTLY
5 to a full extent or degree ⟨She listened to the advice, then did *exactly* what she wanted to anyway.⟩ — see FULLY 1
6 used to express agreement ⟨"Are you calling me a liar?" "*Exactly*."⟩ — see YES

exactness *n* the quality or state of being very accurate ⟨The *exactness* of the bathroom scale isn't such that you could use it in business.⟩ — see PRECISION

exaggerate *vb* **1** to add to the interest of by including made-up details ⟨The American colonist John Smith is believed by many historians to have *exaggerated* his adventures.⟩ — see EMBROIDER

2 to describe or express in too strong terms ⟨It would be impossible to *exaggerate* the importance of this entrance exam.⟩ — see OVERSTATE

exaggeration *n* the representation of something in terms that go beyond the facts ⟨Their *exaggeration* was such that a rainstorm became a hurricane.⟩

synonyms caricature, coloring, elaboration, embellishment, embroidering, embroidery, hyperbole, magnification, overstatement, padding, stretching

related words amplification, enhancement; fabrication, misrepresentation; fudging, hedging; puffery; superlative

near antonyms belittlement, disparagement, minimizing, poor-mouthing

antonyms meiosis, understatement

exalt *vb* **1** to assign a high status or value to ⟨Popular support and media hype have *exalted* Super Bowl Sunday to the level of a national holiday.⟩

synonyms aggrandize, canonize, deify, dignify, elevate, ennoble, enshrine, enthrone, glorify, magnify

related words boost, lift, promote, raise, upgrade, uplift; heighten, intensify; idealize, romanticize, sanitize, sugarcoat; acclaim, extol (*also* extoll), honor, laud, praise

near antonyms belittle, decry, depreciate, disparage, minimize

antonyms abase, degrade, demean, humble, humiliate

2 to proclaim the glory of ⟨monstrous, gaudy gambling palaces that seem to *exalt* the very notion of excess⟩ — see PRAISE 1

exam *n* a set of questions or problems designed to assess knowledge, skills, or intelligence ⟨The *exam* will cover everything we have studied this term.⟩ — see EXAMINATION 1

examination *n* **1** a set of questions or problems designed to assess knowledge, skills, or intelligence ⟨Applicants to the prep school are required to take a demanding *examination*.⟩

synonyms exam, quiz, test

related words aptitude test, intelligence test, placement test; pretest, retest; board(s), midterm, midyear; catechism; audition; final; checkup, inspection, review

2 a systematic search for the truth or facts about something ⟨an *examination* into the extent of forest regeneration⟩ — see INQUIRY 1

3 a close look at or over someone or something in order to judge condition ⟨Even a hasty *examination* will tell any jeweler that that is not a real diamond.⟩ — see INSPECTION

examine *vb* **1** to put a series of questions to ⟨The defense attorney was eager to *examine* her star witness.⟩

synonyms grill, interrogate, pump, query, question, quiz

related words debrief; cross-examine, cross-question; annoy, hound, pester; canvass (*also* canvas), poll

phrases give the third degree to, pick the brains of

2 to look over closely (as for judging quality or condition) ⟨The customer painstakingly *examined* the antique piece of furniture from top to bottom before purchasing it.⟩ — see INSPECT

3 to search through or into ⟨a groundbreaking study that *examined* the benefits of weight training⟩ — see EXPLORE 1

example *n* one of a group or collection that shows what the whole is like ⟨a structure that is a fine *example* of contemporary architecture⟩

synonyms case, exemplar, illustration, instance, prototype, representative, sample, specimen

related words archetype, classic, locus classicus, paradigm; cross section, microcosm; evidence, indication, manifestation, sign

phrases case in point

exasperate *vb* to disturb the peace of mind of (someone) especially by repeated disagreeable acts ⟨Small children can *exasperate* their parents with endless questions about why this or that is so.⟩ — see IRRITATE 1

exasperating *adj* causing annoyance ⟨those *exasperating* details that come with almost any job⟩ — see ANNOYING

exasperation *n* **1** something that is a source of irritation ⟨Add people who use cell phones inconsiderately to the list of daily *exasperations*.⟩ — see ANNOYANCE 3

2 the feeling of impatience or anger caused by another's repeated disagreeable acts ⟨my rising *exasperation* with these constant interruptions⟩ — see ANNOYANCE 2

excavate *vb* to hollow out or form (something) by removing earth ⟨Workmen are *excavating* a long tunnel that will eventually replace the aboveground expressway.⟩ — see DIG 1

exceed *vb* **1** to go beyond the limit of ⟨The lawyers argued that the court had clearly *exceeded* its authority.⟩

synonyms break, outrun, overpass, overreach, overrun, overshoot, overstep, surpass, transcend

related words encroach, entrench (*also* intrench), infringe, invade, trespass; overdo, overutilize, overwork

2 to be greater, better, or stronger than ⟨Her knowledge of the team's statistics *exceeds* that of anyone else I know.⟩ — see SURPASS 1

exceeding *adj* being out of the ordinary ⟨She accepted the apology with *exceeding* graciousness.⟩ — see EXCEPTIONAL 1

exceedingly *also* **exceeding** *adv* to a great degree ⟨The salesclerk was *exceedingly* patient with one customer who couldn't make up his mind.⟩ — see VERY 1

excel *vb* to be greater, better, or stronger than ⟨The special effects in this new sci-fi extravaganza *excel* any that we've seen previously.⟩ — see SURPASS 1

excellence *n* **1** exceptionally high quality ⟨The annual awards honor *excellence* in children's literature.⟩

synonyms distinction, excellency, greatness, perfection, preeminence, superbness, superiority, supremacy

related words faultlessness, flawlessness, impeccability; goodness, value, worth; consequence, importance

near antonyms averageness, badness, crumminess, inferiority, mediocrity, ordinariness, worthlessness

2 a quality that gives something special worth ⟨The particular *excellence* of down in clothing and sleeping bags is its lightness.⟩

synonyms distinction, excellency, grace, merit, value, virtue

related words advantage, edge, plus, superiority

near antonyms blemish, defect, failing, fault, flaw; drawback, minus, negative

antonyms deficiency, demerit, disvalue

excellency *n* **1** a quality that gives something special worth ⟨claimed that granite has so many *excellencies* as material for countertops that it is well worth the high price⟩ — see EXCELLENCE 2

2 exceptionally high quality ⟨The *excellency* of the violins crafted by Stradivarius is beyond dispute.⟩ — see EXCELLENCE 1

excellent *adj* of the very best kind ⟨Fast-food fans rate this chain's fries as *excellent*.⟩

synonyms A1, awesome, bang-up, banner, beautiful, brave, bully, bumper, capital, choice, classic, cool [*slang*], crackerjack, dandy, divine, fabulous, famous, fantastic, fine, first-class, first-rate, grand, great, groovy, heavenly, hot, immense, jim-dandy, lovely, marvelous (*or*

marvellous), mean, neat, nifty, noble, par excellence, prime, prize, quality, sensational, splendid, stellar, sterling, superb, superior, superlative, supernal, swell, terrific, tip-top, top, top-notch, top-of-the-line, unsurpassed, wonderful
related words acceptable, adequate, all right, decent, good, OK (*or* okay), passable, satisfactory, tolerable; better, exceptional, fancy, high-grade, high-test, premium, select, special, superfine; classical, standard, traditional
phrases out of this world, too much
near antonyms bad, inferior, low-grade, substandard, unsatisfactory; mediocre, middling, second-class, second-rate
antonyms atrocious, awful, execrable, lousy, pathetic, poor, rotten, terrible, vile, wretched

except *vb* **1** to present an opposing opinion or argument ⟨I must *except* to your remark that there are no great novelists currently living.⟩ — see OBJECT
2 to prevent the participation, consideration, or inclusion of ⟨We'll have to *except* members who haven't paid their club dues from voting in the election.⟩ — see EXCLUDE

except *also* **excepting** *conj* if it were not for the fact that ⟨I'd go, *except* it's too far.⟩
synonyms but, only, saving, yet

except *also* **excepting** *prep* not including ⟨The store is open daily *except* Sundays.⟩
synonyms aside from, bar, barring, beside, besides, but, except for, excluding, exclusive of, other than, outside, outside of, save, saving

except for *prep* not including ⟨*Except for* newscasts, I hardly watch any television at all.⟩ — see EXCEPT

exceptionable *adj* provoking or likely to provoke protest ⟨As long as the language is not *exceptionable*, people can post any comments they want on the website.⟩ — see OBJECTIONABLE

exceptional *adj* **1** being out of the ordinary ⟨An *exceptional* amount of snow fell in March.⟩
synonyms aberrant, abnormal, anomalous, atypical, especial, exceeding, extraordinary, freak, odd, peculiar, phenomenal, rare, singular, uncommon, uncustomary, unique, unusual, unwonted
related words conspicuous, notable, noticeable, outstanding, prominent, remarkable, salient, striking; bizarre, deviant, eccentric, freakish, monstrous, oddball, outlandish, quaint, strange, weird; incomprehensible, inconceivable, incredible, unimaginable, unthinkable
near antonyms everyday, familiar, frequent
antonyms common, customary, normal, ordinary, typical, unexceptional, unextraordinary, usual
2 deprived of the power to perform one or more natural bodily activities ⟨Her experience working with *exceptional* children was rewarding and inspiring.⟩ — see DISABLED
3 having or showing quickness of mind ⟨a special school for *exceptional* children⟩ — see INTELLIGENT 1

excerpt *n* a part taken from a longer work ⟨He'll read an *excerpt* from the novel at the book signing.⟩
synonyms extract, passage
related words clip, snippet, sound bite; citation, quotation; locus classicus; sample, selection

excess *adj* being over what is needed ⟨Any *excess* food from the party will be donated to a shelter for the homeless.⟩ — see SPARE 1

excess *n* the state or an instance of going beyond what is usual, proper, or needed ⟨a new television season with an *excess* of sitcoms⟩
synonyms fat, overabundance, overage, overflow, overkill, overmuch, oversupply, redundancy, superabundance, superfluity, surfeit, surplus

related words abundance, bounty, plentitude, plenty, profusion, sufficiency; overproduction, overstock
near antonyms dearth, lack, scarcity, want
antonyms deficiency, deficit, insufficiency

excessive *adj* going beyond a normal or acceptable limit in degree or amount ⟨nerdy hackers who spend an *excessive* amount of time sitting in front of their computers⟩
synonyms devilish, exorbitant, extravagant, extreme, fancy, immoderate, inordinate, insane, intolerable, lavish, overdue, overmuch, overweening, steep, stiff, towering, unconscionable, undue, unmerciful
related words boundless, endless, immeasurable, infinite, limitless; unbearable, unjustifiable, unwarranted; improper, inappropriate, thick, unseemly; unrestrained
phrases a bit much, over the top
near antonyms deficient, inadequate, insufficient; minimal, minimum
antonyms middling, moderate, modest, reasonable, temperate

excessively *adv* beyond a normal or acceptable limit ⟨Noise from the party was *excessively* loud.⟩ — see TOO 1

exchange *n* **1** a giving or taking of one thing of value in return for another ⟨*Exchanges* of commemorative pins are common among Olympic athletes.⟩
synonyms barter, commutation, dicker, swap, trade, trade-off, truck
related words replacement, substitution; reciprocation, recompense, requital; bargain, deal, horse trade, negotiation, transaction; bargaining, dealing, dickering, haggling, horse trading; logrolling
2 talking or a talk between two or more people ⟨We had a brief *exchange* with the bride and groom as we went through the receiving line.⟩ — see CONVERSATION

exchange *vb* to give up (something) and take something else in return ⟨I'd like to *exchange* this sweater for one in a larger size.⟩ — see CHANGE 3

excitable *adj* easily excited by nature ⟨an *excitable* child who enjoys being outside⟩
synonyms flighty, fluttery, high-strung, hyperactive, jittery, jumpy, nervous, skittish, spasmodic, spooky
related words hot-blooded, mercurial, temperamental, unstable, volatile, volcanic; anxious, edgy, flibbertigibbety, nervy, tense, uptight; emotional, emotionalistic, hypersensitive, intense, sensitive, soulful
near antonyms calm, collected, cool, serene, tranquil; easy, easygoing, laid-back, relaxed
antonyms imperturbable, nerveless, unexcitable, unflappable, unshakable

excite *vb* **1** to cause a pleasurable stimulation of the feelings of ⟨For some reason the first snowfall of the season never fails to *excite* us.⟩ — see THRILL
2 to rouse to strong feeling or action ⟨The trailers *excited* a lot of interest in the movie.⟩ — see PROVOKE 1

excited *adj* **1** being in a state of increased activity or agitation ⟨*Excited* trading on the stock exchange followed in the wake of the favorable economic report.⟩ — see FEVERISH 1
2 showing urgent desire or interest ⟨Everyone was *excited* about the upcoming family vacation.⟩ — see EAGER

excitement *n* **1** something that arouses a strong response from another ⟨There were few *excitements* of any kind on our very uneventful trip back home.⟩ — see PROVOCATION 1
2 urgent desire or interest ⟨In our *excitement* to get going, we forgot to make sure that all of the lights in the house had been turned off.⟩ — see EAGERNESS

exciter *n* a person who stirs up public feelings especially of discontent ⟨Many of the *exciters* of the so-called "tax revolt" were actually campaign workers for one of the gubernatorial candidates.⟩ — see AGITATOR

exciting *adj* **1** causing great emotional or mental stimulation ⟨an *exciting*, come-from-behind victory for the underdogs in the last game of the World Series⟩
synonyms breathtaking, charged, electric, electrifying, exhilarating, galvanizing, hair-raising, inspiring, rip-roaring, rousing, stimulating, stirring, thrilling
related words arresting, interesting, intriguing, provocative, tantalizing, titillating; absorbing, engrossing, gripping, riveting; moving, poignant, touching; enchanting, enthralling, fascinating, spellbinding; dynamic, energetic, high-voltage, lively, lusty
near antonyms boring, tedious, tiresome; dreary, dull, humdrum, monotonous, uninteresting
antonyms unexciting
2 serving or likely to arouse a strong reaction ⟨And what *exciting* news have you for us today?⟩ — see PROVOCATIVE

exclaim *vb* to utter with a sudden burst of strong feeling ⟨The whole team *exclaimed* with one voice, "We won!"⟩
synonyms blurt (out), bolt, cry (out), ejaculate
related words blunder, leak; bellow, crow, holler, hoot, howl, roar, shout, whoop, yowl; aah (*also* ah), ooh; interject

exclamation *n* a sudden short emotional utterance ⟨The good news was greeted with a chorus of joyous *exclamations*.⟩
synonyms cry, ejaculation, interjection
related words aah (*also* ah), ooh; holler, hoot, howl, shout, whoop, yell, yelp, yowl; scream, screech, shriek, squall, squeak, squeal

exclude *vb* to prevent the participation, consideration, or inclusion of ⟨You can share files with some people on the network while *excluding* others.⟩
synonyms ban, bar, count (out), debar, eliminate, except, rule out, shut out
related words blackball, blacklist, excommunicate, ostracize; banish, deport, exile, expel, oust, throw out; obviate, preclude, prevent, prohibit; deter, stave off, ward (off); check off, disregard; comb (out), weed (out)
phrases close one's doors to
near antonyms accept, embrace, entertain, take in, welcome; unban
antonyms admit, include

excluding *prep* not including ⟨*Excluding* me, plan on five guests for dinner tonight.⟩ — see EXCEPT

exclusive *adj* **1** belonging only to the one person, unit, or group named ⟨Residents of the apartment complex have *exclusive* use of the pool.⟩ — see SOLE 1
2 not divided or scattered among several areas of interest or concern ⟨During interviews she always gives the job applicant her *exclusive* attention.⟩ — see WHOLE 1
3 being in the latest or current fashion ⟨an *exclusive* designer gown of the sort that shows up on red carpets⟩ — see STYLISH

exclusively *adv* for nothing other than ⟨His best paintings are the ones that he did *exclusively* for the sheer pleasure they gave him.⟩ — see SOLELY 1

exclusive of *prep* not including ⟨There is a sale on all merchandise *exclusive of* jewelry.⟩ — see EXCEPT

excoriate *vb* **1** to criticize harshly and usually publicly ⟨The mayor had hardly been in office for a month before she was being *excoriated* for problems of very long standing.⟩ — see ATTACK 2
2 to make sore by continued rubbing ⟨The new shoes had badly *excoriated* his heels.⟩ — see CHAFE 1

excoriation *n* an often public or formal expression of disapproval ⟨the judge's *excoriation* of the lawyer's incompetent defense⟩ — see CENSURE

excrement *n* solid matter discharged from an animal's alimentary canal ⟨an ordinance that requires dog walkers to remove their animal's *excrement* from city streets⟩ — see DROPPING 1

excrescence *n* **1** an abnormal mass of tissue ⟨concerned about the weird *excrescence* that seemed to be developing on his hand⟩ — see GROWTH 1
2 something that spoils the appearance or completeness of a thing ⟨Local residents regard the hulking apartment building as a hideous *excrescence* on their once-lovely street.⟩ — see BLEMISH

excreta *pl n* solid matter discharged from an animal's alimentary canal ⟨The cage badly needed to be cleaned of the rabbit's *excreta*.⟩ — see DROPPING 1

excruciating *adj* **1** intensely or unbearably painful ⟨He finally visited the doctor when the pain became *excruciating*.⟩
synonyms agonizing, harrowing, racking, tormenting, torturing, torturous, wrenching
related words acute, exquisite, extreme, fierce, intense, vehement, violent; biting, cutting, penetrating, piercing, sharp, shooting, smarting, stabbing, stinging, tearing, tingling
2 difficult to endure ⟨the *excruciating* heat that the settlers faced as they crossed the deserts of the Southwest⟩ — see HARSH 1
3 hard to accept or bear especially emotionally ⟨Most *excruciating* of all was the endless wait for news.⟩ — see BITTER 2
4 extreme in degree, power, or effect ⟨their *excruciating* grief⟩ — see INTENSE 1

exculpate *vb* to free from a charge of wrongdoing ⟨I will present evidence that will *exculpate* my client.⟩
synonyms absolve, acquit, clear, exonerate, vindicate
related words atone (for), expiate; discharge, liberate, redeem, release, unburden; condone, excuse, whitewash; forgive, pardon, remit; avenge, redress, revenge
near antonyms accuse, arraign, charge, impeach, indict; convict
antonyms criminate, incriminate

exculpation *n* a setting free from a charge of wrongdoing ⟨evidence that might bring about the *exculpation* of the defendant⟩ — see ACQUITTAL

excursion *n* **1** a short trip for pleasure ⟨Our weekend *excursions* have encompassed virtually all parts of our home state.⟩
synonyms jaunt, junket, outing, ramble, sally, spin
related words journey, travel(s), voyage; tour; expedition, odyssey, safari; detour; hike, peregrination, trek, walk; pilgrimage
2 a departure from the subject under consideration ⟨The professor's frequent and sometimes far-ranging *excursions* in his lectures are the stuff of campus legend.⟩ — see TANGENT

excursionist *n* a person who travels for pleasure ⟨a list of things to do for weekend *excursionists* in the city⟩ — see TOURIST

excusable *adj* worthy of forgiveness ⟨Such minor errors are *excusable*.⟩ — see VENIAL

excuse *n* an explanation that frees one from fault or blame ⟨"A really important phone call" is no *excuse* for not paying proper attention to one's driving.⟩
synonyms alibi, defense, justification, plea, reason
related words color, guise, pretense (*or* pretence), pretext, rationale, rationalization, vindication, whitewash; cop-out, out; acknowledgment (*or* acknowledgement), atonement, confession; extenuation, palliation

excuse *vb* **1** to dismiss as of little importance ⟨More often than not, voters are willing to *excuse* a candidate's youthful indiscretion.⟩

synonyms brush (aside *or* off), condone, discount, disregard, forgive, gloss (over), gloze (over), ignore, overlook, overpass, pardon, pass over, remit, shrug off, whitewash, wink (at)

related words explain, justify, rationalize; absolve, acquit, clear, exculpate, exonerate, vindicate; waive, wave (aside *or* off)

phrases close one's eyes to, forgive and forget

near antonyms heed, mark, mind, note, object (to)

2 to be an acceptable reason for ⟨Having a passenger in labor will generally *excuse* a little disregard for the speed limit.⟩ — see JUSTIFY 1

3 to make (something) seem less bad by offering excuses ⟨He's always *excusing* his chronic lying by claiming that everybody lies.⟩ — see PALLIATE 1

execrable *adj* **1** extremely unsatisfactory ⟨Her *execrable* singing finally brought a complaint from the neighbors.⟩ — see WRETCHED 1

2 of low quality ⟨another souvenir shop selling *execrable* knickknacks⟩ — see CHEAP 2

3 not following or in accordance with standards of honor and decency ⟨a sordid crime that was covered with *execrable* excess by the newspaper tabloids and cable news outlets⟩ — see IGNOBLE 2

execrate *vb* **1** to declare to be morally wrong or evil ⟨Leaders from around the world *execrated* the hostile actions.⟩ — see CONDEMN 1

2 to dislike strongly ⟨Some readers adulate the author while others *execrate* him.⟩ — see HATE

execration *n* **1** a prayer that harm will come to someone ⟨Upon discovering that someone had stolen his golf bag, he let loose a volley of *execrations*.⟩ — see CURSE 1

2 a very strong dislike ⟨a cowardly betrayal that earned him the *execration* of all who had remained loyal to the cause⟩ — see HATE 1

3 something or someone that is hated ⟨The traitor would forever be an *execration* amongst his own people.⟩ — see HATE 2

execute *vb* **1** to carry out effectively ⟨the agency charged with *executing* the nation's environmental laws⟩ — see ENFORCE

2 to carry through (as a process) to completion ⟨When you *execute* this dance step, try to keep your arms a little higher.⟩ — see PERFORM 1

3 to put to death deliberately ⟨During the war those convicted of desertion were summarily *executed*.⟩ — see MURDER 1

execution *n* the doing of an action ⟨The *execution* of this magic trick must be accomplished in one fluid motion.⟩ — see COMMISSION 2

executive *adj* suited for or relating to the directing of things ⟨the *executive* skills needed to manage a large business office⟩

synonyms administrative, directorial, managerial, supervisory

related words bureaucratic, governmental, ministerial, official, parliamentary; regulatory

antonyms nonmanagerial, nonsupervisory

executive *n* a person who manages or directs something ⟨a program that teaches company *executives* how to better manage their staffs⟩

synonyms administrator, director, manager, superintendent, supervisor

related words codirector, comanager, co-organizer; middle manager; boardman, officer, official; commissioner, minister; boss, chief, head, leader, president

exemplar *n* **1** one of a group or collection that shows what the whole is like ⟨The village's Congregational church could serve as an *exemplar* of the white clapboard

church with a steeple that is a fixture in old New England towns.⟩ — see EXAMPLE

2 someone of such unequaled perfection as to deserve imitation ⟨Few of history's heroes were quite the *exemplars* that generations of schoolteachers made them out to be.⟩ — see IDEAL 1

3 the most perfect type or example ⟨The paintings of the French painter Claude Monet are often regarded as *exemplars* of Impressionism.⟩ — see QUINTESSENCE 1

exemplary *adj* **1** constituting, serving as, or worthy of being a pattern to be imitated ⟨As a hospital volunteer you have given *exemplary* service to your community.⟩ — see MODEL

2 serving as or offering a warning ⟨Armies have traditionally used public execution as an *exemplary* punishment for the crime of desertion.⟩ — see CAUTIONARY

exemplify *vb* to show or make clear by using examples ⟨In your review you don't really *exemplify* your points with specific examples from the novel.⟩ — see ILLUSTRATE 1

exemption *n* freedom from punishment, harm, or loss ⟨those motorists who think that they can flout the town's parking regulations with *exemption*⟩ — see IMPUNITY

exercise *n* **1** energetic movement of the body for the sake of physical fitness ⟨The doctor ordered plenty of fresh air and *exercise*.⟩

synonyms activity, conditioning, exertion

related words training, warm-up, workout; toning, trimming; aerobics, athletics, bodybuilding, calisthenics, gymnastics, isometrics, weight lifting

2 something done over and over in order to develop skill ⟨a young piano student dutifully going through the standard finger *exercises*⟩

synonyms drill, practice (*also* practise), routine, training, workout

related words assignment, homework, lesson; brushup, refresher, review

3 the act or practice of employing something for a particular purpose ⟨the *exercise* of one's right to vote⟩ — see USE 1

exercise *vb* **1** to bring to bear especially forcefully or effectively ⟨a senator who consistently *exercises* his clout in Congress to get pork barrel projects for his state⟩ — see EXERT

2 to do over and over so as to become skilled ⟨The only way to *exercise* your writing skills is to do more writing.⟩ — see PRACTICE

3 to put into action or service ⟨commended the firefighters for *exercising* really good judgment in that emergency⟩ — see USE 1

4 to trouble the mind of; to make uneasy ⟨The slightest change in travel plans is enough to get him all *exercised*.⟩ — see DISTURB 1

exert *vb* to bring to bear especially forcefully or effectively ⟨Parental involvement has consistently been shown to *exert* the most influence over a child's success in school.⟩

synonyms apply, exercise, ply, put out, wield

related words employ, use, utilize; abuse, misapply, misuse

exertion *n* **1** energetic movement of the body for the sake of physical fitness ⟨Even moderate *exertion* has been shown to have health benefits.⟩ — see EXERCISE 1

2 the active use of energy in producing a result ⟨The number of blueberries that we were finding was hardly worth the *exertion*.⟩ — see EFFORT

exfoliate *vb* to cast (a natural bodily covering or appendage) aside ⟨a soap that promises to help me *exfoliate* all that dry, flaky skin I've apparently been carrying around⟩ — see SHED 1

exhale *vb* **1** to let or force out of the lungs ⟨Before answering, the suspect *exhaled* a cloud of cigarette smoke.⟩
synonyms blow (out), breathe (out), expel, expire
related words expectorate
antonyms inbreathe, inspire
2 to throw or give off ⟨The lilacs were *exhaling* a sweet fragrance that virtually filled the room.⟩ — see EMIT 1
exhaust *vb* **1** to use up all the physical energy of ⟨The long day at the county fair had *exhausted* everyone.⟩
synonyms break, burn out, bust, do in, drain, fatigue, frazzle, kill, outwear, tire, tucker (out), wash out, wear, wear out, weary
related words debilitate, enervate, enfeeble, sap, waste, weaken
phrases wear to a frazzle
near antonyms activate, energize, invigorate, rejuvenate, strengthen, vitalize; relax, rest, unwind
2 to make complete use of ⟨We had been at the theme park barely two hours, and we were on the verge of *exhausting* our spending money.⟩ — see DEPLETE 1
exhausted *adj* depleted in strength, energy, or freshness ⟨The *exhausted* runner crossed the finish line and just collapsed.⟩ — see WEARY 1
exhaustion *n* a complete depletion of energy or strength ⟨With all of the work and activity that the holiday season brings, we were on the point of *exhaustion*.⟩ — see FATIGUE
exhaustive *adj* **1** trying all possibilities ⟨After an *exhaustive* search of our house, we still hadn't found the cat.⟩
synonyms all-out, clean, complete, comprehensive, full-scale, out-and-out, thorough, thoroughgoing, total
related words broad, extensive, far-reaching, in-depth, wide; general, global, inclusive, methodical (*also* methodic), systematic; no-holds-barred, unhampered, unrestrained
near antonyms aimless, desultory, haphazard, hit-or-miss, random; cursory, shallow, slipshod, superficial; limited, narrow, restricted
2 covering everything or all important points ⟨an *exhaustive* survey of the nation's eating habits⟩ — see ENCYCLOPEDIC
exhaustively *adv* with attention to all aspects or details ⟨The psychic's claims were *exhaustively* examined by scientific experts and found to be without merit.⟩ — see THOROUGHLY 1
exhibit *n* a public showing of objects of interest ⟨a touring *exhibit* of national treasures from the Smithsonian Institution⟩ — see EXHIBITION 1
exhibit *vb* to present so as to invite notice or attention ⟨These naturalists take their birds of prey on tour and *exhibit* them before groups of schoolchildren.⟩ — see SHOW 1
exhibition *n* **1** a public showing of objects of interest ⟨an *exhibition* of valuable and fascinating artifacts from a recovered pirate ship⟩
synonyms display, exhibit, exposition, fair, show
related words demonstration, performance, presentation, production; pageant; auction, offering, presentment, sale
2 an outward and often exaggerated indication of something abstract (as a feeling) for effect ⟨For the benefit of the crowd, the professional wrestler made a great *exhibition* of ferocity.⟩ — see SHOW 1
exhilarate *vb* **1** to cause a pleasurable stimulation of the feelings of ⟨were *exhilarated* by hang gliding⟩ — see THRILL
2 to fill with great joy ⟨The climactic moment of commencement ceremonies usually *exhilarates* graduates and proud parents alike.⟩ — see ELATE

exhilarated *adj* experiencing or marked by overwhelming usually pleasurable emotion ⟨The winner's *exhilarated* glow was seen in newspaper photographs around the globe.⟩ — see ECSTATIC
exhilarating *adj* causing great emotional or mental stimulation ⟨No recording can capture the *exhilarating* feeling of being at a live concert.⟩ — see EXCITING 1
exhilaration *n* **1** a pleasurably intense stimulation of the feelings ⟨The lavish spectacle results in one *exhilaration* after another.⟩ — see THRILL
2 a state of overwhelming usually pleasurable emotion ⟨the *exhilaration* of victory that spectators get to witness at the Olympic Games⟩ — see ECSTASY
exhort *vb* to try to persuade (someone) through earnest appeals to follow a course of action ⟨The speaker *exhorted* the graduating students to go forth and try to make a difference in the world.⟩ — see URGE
exhume *vb* to remove from place of burial ⟨The remains of John Paul Jones were *exhumed* in Paris and transported with great ceremony to the U.S. Naval Academy.⟩
synonyms disinter, unearth
antonyms bury, entomb, inter, tomb
exigency *n* a time or state of affairs requiring prompt or decisive action ⟨the *exigencies* requiring snap decisions that traders on the stock exchange face every day⟩ — see EMERGENCY
exile *n* **1** the forced removal from a homeland ⟨The *exile* of French settlers from Nova Scotia resulted in the birth of the Cajun community in the U.S.⟩
synonyms banishment, deportation, displacement, expatriation, expulsion
related words ostracism; extradition; diaspora, dispersion, scattering; emigration, migration; evacuation; ethnic cleansing, transportation; dispossession, ejection, ouster
near antonyms repatriation, return; immigration
2 a person forced to emigrate for political reasons ⟨After being overthrown in a coup, the dictator spent the remainder of his life as an *exile* in a string of less-than-welcoming countries.⟩ — see ÉMIGRÉ 1
exile *vb* to force to leave a country ⟨With their conquest of the Moors complete, Ferdinand and Isabella next *exiled* the Jews from Spain.⟩ — see BANISH 1
exist *vb* to have life ⟨Strive to have a full, rich life rather than merely *exist*.⟩ — see BE 1
existence *n* the fact of being or of being real ⟨The *existence* of UFO's is something that people continue to argue about.⟩
synonyms actuality, reality, subsistence
related words genuineness, realness; activity, animation, life; currency, presence, prevalence
near antonyms absence, dearth, lack, want; potentiality, virtuality
antonyms inexistence, nonbeing, nonexistence, unreality
existent *adj* **1** existing in fact and not merely as a possibility ⟨believes that angels are *existent*⟩ — see ACTUAL
2 having being at the present time ⟨The coelacanth is one *existent* fish that was once thought to be entirely extinct.⟩ — see EXTANT 1
existent *n* one that has a real and independent existence ⟨Other worlds are *existents* that are generally taken for granted in works of science fiction.⟩ — see ENTITY
existing *adj* having being at the present time ⟨*Existing* breeds of the turkey that graces our Thanksgiving table are said to bear little resemblance to the gamy birds that the Pilgrims enjoyed.⟩ — see EXTANT 1
exit *n* **1** a place or means of going out ⟨All of the building's *exits* were clearly marked.⟩
synonyms egress, issue, outlet

related words escape, escape hatch, release; gate, mouth, opening, passage, vent

near antonyms access, entrée (*or* entree)

antonyms entrance, entry, entryway, ingress

2 the act of leaving a place ⟨The movie star's quick *exit* through the back of the hotel went unnoticed by the horde of photographers waiting out front.⟩ — see DEPARTURE 1

3 the permanent stopping of all the vital bodily activities ⟨Grandfather's peaceful *exit* was exactly what he said he wanted.⟩ — see DEATH 1

exit *vb* **1** to leave a place often for another ⟨In case of fire, *exit* from the building in a calm and orderly fashion.⟩ — see GO 2

2 to stop living ⟨Granny expressed her wish to *exit* surrounded by family and friends.⟩ — see DIE 1

exiting *n* the act of leaving a place ⟨Their *exiting* of the boring party was swiftly and quietly accomplished.⟩ — see DEPARTURE 1

exodus *n* a flowing or going out ⟨the mass *exodus* from the cities for the beaches and the mountains on most summer weekends⟩ — see OUTFLOW

exonerate *vb* to free from a charge of wrongdoing ⟨The results of the DNA fingerprinting *exonerated* the defendant.⟩ — see EXCULPATE

exoneration *n* a setting free from a charge of wrongdoing ⟨The accused refused a plea bargain, asserting that he was innocent and would settle for nothing less than complete *exoneration*.⟩ — see ACQUITTAL

exorbitant *adj* going beyond a normal or acceptable limit in degree or amount ⟨The cost of our stay was so *exorbitant* you would have thought that we had bought the hotel and not just spent a few nights there.⟩ — see EXCESSIVE

exorbitantly *adv* beyond a normal or acceptable limit ⟨The show was well worth the *exorbitantly* priced concert tickets.⟩ — see TOO 1

exotic *adj* excitingly or mysteriously unusual ⟨the gradual disappearance of *exotic* lands in a culturally homogenized world⟩

synonyms fantastic (*also* fantastical), glamorous (*also* glamourous), marvelous (*or* marvellous), outlandish, romantic, strange

related words colorful, picture-book, picturesque, quaint; alien, foreign; dark, distant, faraway, remote; alluring, captivating, enchanting, fascinating, magical

antonyms familiar, nonexotic, nonglamorous, unexotic, unglamorous, unromantic

exotic *n* something strange or unusual that is an object of interest ⟨The botanical garden boasts an array of horticultural *exotics* from around the world.⟩ — see CURIOSITY 2

expand *vb* **1** to express more fully and in greater detail ⟨an article on the event that the author later *expanded* into a book⟩

synonyms amplify, develop, elaborate (on), flesh (out)

related words add (to), complement, supplement; discourse, expatiate, ramble, run on

near antonyms compress, contract; outline, summarize, sum up

antonyms abbreviate, abridge, condense, shorten

2 to make greater in size, amount, or number ⟨We had to *expand* the list of wedding guests several times in order to accommodate all the relatives Mother wouldn't dream of excluding.⟩ — see INCREASE 1

3 to arrange the parts of (something) over a wider area ⟨a spare leaf for those times when we have to *expand* the dining table to accommodate extra guests⟩ — see OPEN 3

4 to become greater in extent, volume, amount, or number ⟨Water *expands* when it becomes frozen.⟩ — see INCREASE 2

expanse *n* a wide space or area ⟨the great explorers who crossed the vast *expanses* of the seven seas in small ships⟩

synonyms breadth, distance, expansion, extent, field, length, plain, reach, sheet, spread, stretch, waste

related words domain, sphere, territory; compass, range, scope, sweep; gamut, scale, spectrum; depth, emptiness, void; extension, latitude, span; amplitude, immensity, magnitude

expansion *n* **1** something added (as by growth) ⟨The museum's new wing is only the first in a series of *expansions* planned for the next decade.⟩ — see INCREASE 1

2 the act or process of going from the simple or basic to the complex or advanced ⟨the *expansion* of remedial reading classes into a district-wide program using school volunteers for a variety of needs⟩ — see DEVELOPMENT 1

3 a wide space or area ⟨We gazed in awe at the starstrewn *expansion* of nighttime sky above us.⟩ — see EXPANSE

expansive *adj* having considerable extent ⟨As the river nears the end of its long journey to the sea it becomes quite *expansive* in breadth.⟩ — see EXTENSIVE

expatiate *vb* to give a formal often extended talk on a subject ⟨The naturalist is known for her willingness to *expatiate* on any number of issues relating to wildlife and the environment.⟩ — see TALK 1

expatriate *n* a person forced to emigrate for political reasons ⟨While in exile, the deposed king was accompanied by a small band of loyal *expatriates*.⟩ — see ÉMIGRÉ 1

expatriate *vb* to force to leave a country ⟨Members of the deposed dictator's once-feared political party were *expatriated* as well.⟩ — see BANISH 1

expatriation *n* the forced removal from a homeland ⟨Romeo kills Juliet's cousin, Tybalt, resulting in his *expatriation* from Verona.⟩ — see EXILE 1

expect *vb* to believe in the future occurrence of (something) ⟨We *expect* their arrival late this afternoon.⟩

synonyms anticipate, await, hope (for), watch (for)

related words bank on, count (on *or* upon), depend (on *or* upon), rely (on *or* upon), wait (for); envisage, foresee; foretell, predict, prophesy; assume, presume, presuppose; contemplate, eye, view

phrases look for, look forward to

near antonyms doubt, question

expectant *adj* **1** having or showing signs of eagerly awaiting something ⟨*Expectant* crowds gathered at the spot where the President was scheduled to make an appearance.⟩

synonyms agape, agog, anticipatory

related words open-eyed, openmouthed; alert, vigilant, watchful; anxious, athirst, breathless, eager, enthusiastic, raring; impatient, restive, restless

near antonyms apathetic, indifferent, unconcerned, unimpressed, uninterested, unmoved

2 containing unborn young within the body ⟨a medication that should not be taken by *expectant* women without consulting their doctors⟩ — see PREGNANT 1

expectant *n* one who seeks an office, honor, position, or award ⟨college players who were all *expectants* for a draft pick⟩ — see CANDIDATE

expected *adj* being in accordance with the prescribed, normal, or logical course of events ⟨The children did their chores without the *expected* whining.⟩ — see DUE 2

expedient *adj* suitable for bringing about a desired result under the circumstances ⟨We made the *expedient* decision to sell the land to whomever offered the most money.⟩

synonyms advisable, desirable, judicious, politic, prudent, tactical, wise

related words advantageous, beneficial, profitable; useful, utilitarian; feasible, possible, practicable, practical; opportune, seasonable, timely; opportunistic, self-seeking

near antonyms impractical, profitless, unfeasible, unprofitable; inopportune, unseasonable, untimely

antonyms impolitic, imprudent, inadvisable, inexpedient, injudicious, unwise

expedient *n* **1** a temporary replacement ⟨If you're a spectator caught without rainwear at a sporting event, then a plastic garbage bag makes an acceptable, if unfashionable, *expedient*.⟩ — see MAKESHIFT

2 an action planned or taken to achieve a desired result ⟨He vowed to use any *expedient* available to get the project done on time.⟩ — see MEASURE 1

3 something that one uses to accomplish an end especially when the usual means is not available ⟨Since there wasn't a single bandage left in our backpacks, we had to use a bandanna, our only *expedient*.⟩ — see RESOURCE 1

expedition *n* a going from one place to another usually of some distance ⟨an avid mountain climber, always on an *expedition* to some far-off corner of the world⟩ — see JOURNEY

expeditious *adj* having or showing the ability to respond without delay or hesitation ⟨a company that is well-regarded for its *expeditious* handling of any request or complaint⟩ — see QUICK 1

expel *vb* **1** to drive or force out ⟨Animal lover though I am, I was determined to *expel* the uninvited mouse from my room.⟩ — see EJECT 1

2 to throw or give off ⟨Something in a wastebasket was *expelling* a foul odor.⟩ — see EMIT 1

3 to violently throw out or off (something from within) ⟨Ringing and flashing madly, the slot machine *expelled* a bucketful of quarters.⟩ — see ERUPT 1

4 to let or force out of the lungs ⟨I asked the patient to *expel* a deep breath.⟩ — see EXHALE 1

expend *vb* **1** to hand over or use up in payment ⟨Redecoration will have to wait, since we've just *expended* our last dollar in buying the house.⟩ — see SPEND 1

2 to make complete use of ⟨Settlers had to be sure not to *expend* their supply of firewood before the end of the long winter.⟩ — see DEPLETE 1

expenditure *n* **1** a payment made in the course of achieving a result ⟨You'll have to drastically cut back on your clothing *expenditures* if you hope to save anything.⟩ — see EXPENSE

2 the active use of energy in producing a result ⟨the *expenditure* of the nation's military might on wars that may or may not involve the national interest⟩ — see EFFORT

expense *n* a payment made in the course of achieving a result ⟨They spared no *expense* in building the house of their dreams.⟩

synonyms charge, cost, disbursement, expenditure, outgo, outlay

related words overhead; outflow; pocket money, spending money; price, rate, tab, tariff, toll

expensive *adj* commanding a large price ⟨*expensive* clothing that only the truly wealthy can afford⟩ — see COSTLY

expensively *adv* in a luxurious manner ⟨The pop singer's *expensively* decorated mansion was a testament to her commercial success.⟩ — see HIGH

experience *n* **1** knowledge gained by actually doing or living through something ⟨The hospital is looking for nurses with operating-room *experience*.⟩

synonyms expertise, know-how, proficiency, savvy, skills

related words background; command, mastery; acquaintance, conversance, familiarity, intimacy

near antonyms ignorance, unawareness, unfamiliarity

antonyms inexperience

2 an exciting or noteworthy event that one experiences firsthand ⟨related in a book his *experiences* as a roving correspondent for network TV news⟩ — see ADVENTURE 1

experience *vb* to come to a knowledge of (something) by living through it ⟨Have you ever *experienced* the loss of a pet?⟩

synonyms endure, feel, have, know, pass, see, suffer, sustain, taste, undergo, witness

related words encounter, meet; accept; assimilate, digest

phrases go through

experienced *adj* having or showing exceptional knowledge, experience, or skill in a field of endeavor ⟨For this delicate eye operation, seek out an *experienced* eye surgeon.⟩ — see PROFICIENT

experiment *n* a procedure or operation carried out to resolve an uncertainty ⟨Benjamin Franklin's famous *experiment* in which he flew a kite in a thunderstorm to see if lightning and electricity were identical⟩

synonyms essay, experimentation, test, trial

related words trial and error; dry run, shakedown; exercise, practice (*also* practise), rehearsal, tryout, workout; crucible, ordeal; attempt, effort, try

experimental *adj* **1** made or done as an experiment ⟨an *experimental* procedure for patients suffering from hip pain⟩

synonyms pilot, trial

related words exploratory, investigative; preliminary, preparatory, provisional, temporary, tentative; conjectural, hypothetical, speculative, theoretical (*also* theoretic); untested, untried; unproved, unproven

near antonyms accepted, established, standard; tested, tried; advanced, developed; proved, proven; conclusive, decisive, definitive, final, permanent

2 based on observation or experience ⟨asserted that *experimental* knowledge is vastly superior to idle speculation and theorizing⟩ — see EMPIRICAL 1

experimentation *n* a procedure or operation carried out to resolve an uncertainty ⟨physicists discovering the interactions of energy and matter through observation and *experimentation*⟩ — see EXPERIMENT

expert *adj* **1** accomplished with trained ability ⟨To a serious collector, the *expert* carving on the duck decoy justifies its high price.⟩ — see SKILLFUL 1

2 having or showing exceptional knowledge, experience, or skill in a field of endeavor ⟨People interested in laser eye surgery are advised to seek out an *expert* practitioner.⟩ — see PROFICIENT

expert *n* a person with a high level of knowledge or skill in a field ⟨The book was written by an *expert* in the field.⟩

synonyms ace, adept, artist, authority, connoisseur, crackerjack (*also* crackajack), fiend, guru, hand, hotshot, maestro, master, past master, scholar, shark, virtuoso, whiz, wizard

related words pro, professional; consultant, hired gun, specialist; addict, aficionado (*also* afficionado), buff, devotee, enthusiast, fan; craftsman, journeyman; jack-of-all-trades, Renaissance man; mistress

near antonyms apprentice, beginner, neophyte, novice; dabbler, dilettante; nonprofessional

antonyms amateur, inexpert

expertise *n* knowledge gained by actually doing or living through something ⟨new dog owners who were seeking someone with *expertise* in animal obedience⟩ — see EXPERIENCE 1

expertly *adv* in a skillful or expert manner ⟨The apple pie was a traditional but *expertly* made version of an old favorite.⟩ — see WELL 3

expiate *vb* to make up for (an offense) ⟨Yom Kippur is the holy day on which Jews are expected to *expiate* sins committed during the past year.⟩

synonyms atone (for), mend, redeem

related words compensate, recompense, reimburse, remunerate, repay; amend, correct, rectify, redress; propitiate

phrases make amends for, make good for

expiration *n* **1** the act of ceasing to exist ⟨directed that upon her *expiration* her splendid Italian-style villa be given to the public as a museum⟩ — see DEATH 3

2 the stopping of a process or activity ⟨the *expiration* of the offer to sell⟩ — see END 1

3 the permanent stopping of all the vital bodily activities ⟨Upon the *expiration* of the last beneficiary, the trust terminates.⟩ — see DEATH 1

expire *vb* **1** to come to an end ⟨Speakers will not be allowed to continue after their allotted time has *expired*.⟩ — see CEASE 1

2 to let or force out of the lungs ⟨He vows to hold on to that belief until he *expires* his last breath.⟩ — see EXHALE 1

3 to stop living ⟨made one last visit to his homeland and *expired* not long afterwards⟩ — see DIE 1

expired *adj* no longer existing ⟨a wildlife organization dedicated to ensuring that the giant panda not be added to the list of *expired* species⟩ — see EXTINCT

explain *vb* **1** to make plain or understandable ⟨a pamphlet that *explains* the medical procedure in language that any layperson can understand⟩

synonyms clarify, clear (up), construe, demonstrate, elucidate, explicate, expound, get across, illuminate, illustrate, interpret, simplify, spell out

related words decipher, decode; analyze, break down; disentangle, undo, unravel, unscramble, untangle; resolve, solve; define, specify; annotate, commentate, gloss

near antonyms befog, cloud; confound, confuse

antonyms obscure

2 to give the reason for or cause of ⟨Can you *explain* why you're so early?⟩

synonyms account (for), attribute, explain away, rationalize

related words condone, excuse, forgive, justify; absolve, acquit, exculpate, exonerate, vindicate

explainable *adj* capable of having the reason for or cause of determined ⟨Investigators found that the so-called mysterious happenings at the house were entirely *explainable*.⟩ — see SOLVABLE

explain away *vb* **1** to give the reason for or cause of ⟨They tried to *explain away* the delays, citing computer problems.⟩ — see EXPLAIN 2

2 to make (something) seem less bad by offering excuses ⟨Dad tries to *explain away* his forgetfulness, saying he's getting older.⟩ — see PALLIATE 1

explanation *n* **1** a statement that makes something clear ⟨an *explanation* of photosynthesis that most museum visitors will be able to understand⟩

synonyms clarification, construction, elucidation, explication, exposition, illumination, illustration, interpretation

related words paraphrase, restatement, translation; annotation, comment, commentary, epexegesis, gloss; deciphering, decoding; disentanglement, unscrambling; analysis; edification, enlightenment; meaning; demonstration, enactment; justification, rationale, rationalization, reasoning; caution, caveat, warning

2 a statement given to explain a belief or act ⟨When questioned, the neighbors were at a loss for an *explanation* for the family's sudden departure.⟩ — see REASON 1

explanatory *adj* serving to explain ⟨The *explanatory* section has as its heading "What the New Tax Changes Mean."⟩

synonyms elucidative, expository, illuminative, illustrative, interpretative, interpretive

related words analytic (*or* analytical), demonstrative, discursive; exculpatory, exonerative

explicable *adj* capable of having the reason for or cause of determined ⟨The mystery of those strange noises became quite *explicable* once we realized that a colony of bats had taken up residence.⟩ — see SOLVABLE

explicate *vb* to make plain or understandable ⟨The physicist did his best to *explicate* the wave theory of light for the audience of laymen.⟩ — see EXPLAIN 1

explication *n* a statement that makes something clear ⟨Any *explication* of Einstein's theory of relativity probably wouldn't help me much.⟩ — see EXPLANATION 1

explicit *adj* so clearly expressed as to leave no doubt about the meaning ⟨*explicit* instructions about what to do in an emergency⟩

synonyms clear-cut, definite, definitive, express, specific, unambiguous, unequivocal

related words avowed, declared, specified, stated; categorical (*also* categoric), complete, comprehensive, exhaustive, full; certain, sure, unmistakable; clear, distinct, lucid, well-defined; exact, precise; direct, literal, plain, simple, straightforward

near antonyms cryptic, dark, enigmatic (*also* enigmatical), obscure, unclear; imprecise, inaccurate, incorrect, inexact; incomprehensible, unintelligible

antonyms implicit, implied, inferred; ambiguous, circuitous; equivocal, indefinite, unspecific, vague

explicitness *n* **1** careful thoroughness of detail ⟨The *explicitness* of the instructions for how to uninstall the program should make it easy.⟩ — see PARTICULARITY 1

2 clearness of expression ⟨The user's manual is written with such rare *explicitness* that the average consumer actually has a chance of understanding it!⟩ — see SIMPLICITY 2

explode *vb* **1** to break open or into pieces usually because of internal pressure ⟨The container *exploded* when the liquid inside froze.⟩

synonyms blow, blow up, burst, detonate, go off, pop

related words fragment, shatter, smash, splinter; discharge, fire, shoot; balloon, burgeon (*also* bourgeon), mushroom

near antonyms collapse, fizzle

antonyms implode

2 to cause to break open or into pieces by or as if by an explosive ⟨Ignition of leaking gas can *explode* a gas line.⟩ — see BLAST 1

3 to develop suddenly and violently ⟨Their frustration finally *exploded* into anger.⟩ — see ERUPT 2

exploit *n* **1** an act of notable skill, strength, or cleverness ⟨the fanciful *exploits* of the giant lumberjack Paul Bunyan⟩ — see FEAT 1

2 something done by someone ⟨Once famed as an actor, John Wilkes Booth is now remembered for a single *exploit*, his assassination of Lincoln.⟩ — see ACTION 1

3 an exciting or noteworthy event that one experiences firsthand ⟨a memoir recounting three decades of *exploits* as a roving foreign correspondent for TV news⟩ — see ADVENTURE 1

exploit *vb* **1** to take unfair advantage of ⟨the type of person who *exploits* a friend's good nature by constantly sponging off of him⟩

synonyms abuse, capitalize (on), cash in (on), impose (on *or* upon), play (on *or* upon), use, work
related words jerk around, manipulate, mistreat; bleed, cheat, fleece, overcharge, skin, soak, stick; commercialize, commodify
phrases trade on, walk on
2 to control or take advantage of by artful, unfair, or insidious means ⟨a politician willing to *exploit* any national tragedy for political gain⟩ — see MANIPULATE 1
3 to put into action or service ⟨It will be a shame if you don't *exploit* your artistic talent to the fullest.⟩ — see USE 1
exploitable *adj* **1** capable of or suitable for being used for a particular purpose ⟨claimed that solar power is an *exploitable* form of energy that is being underutilized⟩ — see USABLE 1
2 readily taken advantage of ⟨The group opposes commercials on TV shows for kids, believing that young viewers are too *exploitable* by advertisers.⟩ — see EASY 2
exploration *n* a systematic search for the truth or facts about something ⟨an *exploration* into the disappearance of famed aviator Amelia Earhart⟩ — see INQUIRY 1
explore *vb* **1** to search through or into ⟨Communities must *explore* new ways of raising money for their cultural institutions.⟩
synonyms delve (into), dig (into), examine, inquire (into), investigate, look (into), probe, research
related words inspect, sift, study, view; browse, cruise, peruse, scan, skim (through), surf, thumb (through)
phrases check into, check up on
2 to go into or range over for purposes of discovery ⟨We must continue to *explore* the depths of the ocean.⟩
synonyms hunt, probe, prospect, search
related words reconnoiter (*or* reconnoitre), scout; disclose, discover, reveal, unearth; fathom, plumb, sound
explosion *n* **1** the act or an instance of exploding ⟨the *explosion* of the first atomic bomb at Hiroshima⟩
synonyms blast, blowup, burst, bursting, detonation, eruption, outburst
related words discharge, firing, shooting; blowout, flareup; bang, boom, pop; airburst, groundburst
antonyms implosion
2 a sudden intense expression of strong feeling ⟨the *explosion* of patriotic feeling that the country experienced after that momentous event⟩ — see OUTBURST 1
3 an outburst or display of excited anger ⟨The tennis player's expletive-enriched *explosions* on the court tested the patience of officials.⟩ — see TANTRUM
explosive *adj* **1** extreme in degree, power, or effect ⟨There's been an *explosive* interest in the sport since the Olympics.⟩ — see INTENSE 1
2 marked by bursts of destructive force or intense activity ⟨one of the most *explosive* storms to hit that area of the coast in some time⟩ — see VIOLENT 1
exponent *n* **1** a person who actively supports or favors a cause ⟨*Exponents* of space exploration earnestly called for more missions to the outer reaches of the solar system.⟩
synonyms advocate, apostle, backer, booster, champion, friend, herald, paladin, promoter, proponent, supporter
related words loyalist, partisan (*also* partizan), stalwart; adherent, cohort, disciple, follower; applauder, cheerleader, encourager
near antonyms enemy, foe, rival; belittler, critic, faultfinder
antonyms adversary, antagonist, opponent
2 one who brings an art or science to full realization ⟨has long reigned as the nation's leading *exponent* of modern dance⟩
synonyms guru

related words dean, grand old man; ideologue (*also* idealogue), philosopher, theorist; advocate, apostle, backer, booster, champion, promoter, proponent, supporter
expose *vb* **1** to reveal the true nature of ⟨a well-researched article that *exposes* the UFO story as a hoax⟩
synonyms debunk, nail, show up, uncloak, uncover, undress, unmask
related words demolish, discredit, disprove; disclose, divulge, tell, unveil
phrases blow the whistle on
near antonyms conceal, hide, secrete, veil
antonyms camouflage, cloak, disguise, mask
2 to make known (as information previously kept secret) ⟨The documentary claims to *expose* the business as a fraud.⟩ — see REVEAL 1
3 to make known (something abstract) through outward signs ⟨The tight race for the championship *exposed* one team's mean streak.⟩ — see SHOW 2
4 to present so as to invite notice or attention ⟨I didn't want to *expose* my ignorance in front of the others, so I kept silent.⟩ — see SHOW 1
exposed *adj* **1** being in a situation where one is likely to meet with harm ⟨Without our immune systems we'd be *exposed* to all sorts of deadly infections.⟩ — see LIABLE 1
2 lacking a usual or natural covering ⟨The *exposed* electrical wires were a safety hazard.⟩ — see NAKED 2
3 lacking protection from danger or resistance against attack ⟨The soldiers were *exposed* in the open field.⟩ — see HELPLESS 1
exposition *n* **1** a public showing of objects of interest ⟨an *exposition* of flying machines from the early days of aviation⟩ — see EXHIBITION 1
2 a series of explanations or observations on something (as an event) ⟨The nonstop *exposition* of the ceremonies by the TV newscasters was both unnecessary and irritating.⟩ — see COMMENTARY 1
3 a statement that makes something clear ⟨The astronomer's *exposition* of white dwarfs was a little helpful.⟩ — see EXPLANATION 1
expository *adj* serving to explain ⟨an *expository* piece on the workings of the internal-combustion engine⟩ — see EXPLANATORY
expostulation *n* a feeling or declaration of disapproval or dissent ⟨Despite the earnest *expostulations* of his friends, Jack decided to go to a different school.⟩ — see OBJECTION
exposure *n* **1** the state of being left without shelter or protection against something harmful ⟨Some people chronically avoid situations in which there is a high level of *exposure* to germs.⟩
synonyms liability, openness, vulnerability
related words predisposition, susceptibility; defenselessness, helplessness, weakness; danger, jeopardy, peril, risk
near antonyms protection, safeguarding, sheltering, shielding
2 the state or fact of facing a particular direction ⟨This plant will need to be in a room with a southern *exposure*.⟩
synonyms aspect
related words alignment (*also* alinement), arrangement
3 the act or an instance of making known previously unknown or concealed ⟨the *exposure* by the local newspaper of an email scam⟩ — see REVELATION
expound *vb* **1** to make known (as an idea, emotion, or opinion) ⟨a rambling interview in which the celebrated author *expounds* his views on an array of topics⟩ — see EXPRESS 1
2 to make plain or understandable ⟨At the start of the

trial the judge *expounded* the legal difference between libel and slander to the jury.⟩ — see EXPLAIN 1

express *adj* **1** of a particular or exact sort ⟨a trip to the supermarket with the *express* purpose of buying milk⟩
synonyms concrete, distinct, especial, peculiar, precise, set, special, specific
related words lone, only, separate, single, sole, solitary; distinctive, exclusive, individual, unique; limited, restricted; differentiated, specialized; given, specified
near antonyms general, generalized, generic, nonexclusive, universal
antonyms nonspecific
2 so clearly expressed as to leave no doubt about the meaning ⟨Students are not allowed to leave the grounds during school hours unless they have *express* permission from the principal's office.⟩ — see EXPLICIT

express *vb* **1** to make known (as an idea, emotion, or opinion) ⟨In a true democracy, a person can freely *express* his or her views.⟩
synonyms air, expound, give, look, raise, sound, state, vent, ventilate, voice
related words advertise, announce, declare, enunciate, proclaim, say; broadcast, circulate, disseminate, publish; describe, write, write up; sound off, speak out, speak up; chime in; communicate, convey, put across; offer, submit
phrases give air to, put forth
near antonyms censor, restrain, restrict
antonyms stifle, suppress
2 to apply external pressure on so as to force out the juice or contents of ⟨Except as a fun event at festivals, nowadays people do not make wine by *expressing* grapes with their feet.⟩ — see ²PRESS 2
3 to communicate or convey (as an idea) to the mind ⟨An upraised thumb is a gesture *expressing* approval or encouragement.⟩ — see MEAN 1
4 to convey in appropriate or telling terms ⟨Could you *express* your opinion of the book?⟩ — see PHRASE
5 to represent in visible form ⟨Towering spires *express* in glass and steel the optimism of the age.⟩ — see EMBODY 2

expression *n* **1** an act, process, or means of putting something into words ⟨The poem is his *expression* of his wonder of nature.⟩
synonyms articulation, formulation, phrasing, statement, utterance, voice, wording
related words outlet, vent; observation, reflection, remark, thought; speech, tongue
2 facial appearance regarded as an indication of mood or feeling ⟨We could tell by the fans' *expressions* that the team had lost again.⟩ — see LOOK 1
3 a pronounceable series of letters having a distinct meaning especially in a particular field ⟨The *expression* "John Doe" is used in legal proceedings to refer to a person whose actual name is either unknown or being withheld from the public.⟩ — see WORD 1
4 a sequence of words having a specific meaning ⟨The popular *expression* "raining cats and dogs" is meaningless in other languages.⟩ — see PHRASE

expressionless *adj* not expressing any emotion ⟨Veteran poker players invariably have *expressionless* faces, regardless of the hand they're holding.⟩ — see BLANK 1

expressive *adj* clearly conveying a special meaning (as one's mood) ⟨The teacher's *expressive* sigh showed that she had heard that excuse many times before.⟩
synonyms eloquent, meaning, meaningful, pregnant, revealing, revelatory, significant, suggestive
related words graphic (*also* graphical), pictorial, vivid; evocative, redolent, reminiscent; weighty; flavorful, full-bodied, rich
antonyms unexpressive

expressway *n* a passage cleared for public vehicular travel ⟨A baffling maze of high-speed *expressways* encircles the city.⟩ — see WAY 1

expropriate *vb* **1** to take or make use of under a guise of authority but without actual right ⟨land *expropriated* under the regime⟩ — see APPROPRIATE 1
2 to take ownership or control of (something) by right of one's authority ⟨plans by the city to *expropriate* entire blocks of houses in order to bulldoze them for expansion of the airport⟩ — see CONFISCATE

expulsion *n* the forced removal from a homeland ⟨the ruthless *expulsion* of the French-speaking Acadians from Nova Scotia by the British⟩ — see EXILE 1

expunge *vb* to destroy all traces of ⟨Time and the weather have *expunged* any evidence that a thriving community once existed here.⟩ — see ANNIHILATE 1

expurgate *vb* to remove objectionable parts from ⟨The newspaper had to *expurgate* the expletive-laden speech.⟩ — see CENSOR

exquisite *adj* **1** extreme in degree, power, or effect ⟨Jane felt such *exquisite* anger at being betrayed by a so-called friend that she could hardly think straight.⟩ — see INTENSE 1
2 having qualities that appeal to a refined taste ⟨*Exquisite* pen-and-ink drawings of city scenes grace the walls of the formal restaurant.⟩ — see CHOICE 1
3 satisfying or pleasing because of fineness or mildness ⟨Waiters at the wedding reception served *exquisite* hors d'oeuvres from silver trays.⟩ — see DELICATE 1

exquisiteness *n* the state or quality of having a delicate structure ⟨marveled at the *exquisiteness* of the lace on the bride's gown⟩ — see DELICACY 2

extant *adj* **1** having being at the present time ⟨a celebrated author who is generally regarded as America's greatest novelist *extant*⟩
synonyms alive, around, existent, existing, living
related words active, busy, flourishing, functioning, operating, working
near antonyms defunct, destroyed, exterminated; departed, gone, lost; nonexistent; idle, inactive, inert
antonyms dead, extinct
2 existing or in progress right now ⟨When people envisage the future, they often base their predictions on the assumption that *extant* trends will continue indefinitely.⟩ — see PRESENT 1

extemporaneous *adj* made or done without previous thought or preparation ⟨Caught by surprise, I had to make an *extemporaneous* speech at the awards banquet.⟩
synonyms ad-lib, extempore, impromptu, improvised, offhand, offhanded, snap, spur-of-the-moment, unconsidered, unplanned, unpremeditated, unprepared, unrehearsed, unstudied
related words unscripted; automatic, impulsive, instinctive, involuntary, spontaneous; casual, cursive, informal, unauthorized; half-baked, half-cocked, ill-advised
near antonyms deliberate, intended, intentional
antonyms considered, planned, premeditated, premeditative, prepared, rehearsed

extempore *adj* made or done without previous thought or preparation ⟨After the election both candidates admitted that they had made a number of *extempore* remarks that they later regretted.⟩ — see EXTEMPORANEOUS

extemporize *vb* to perform, make, or do without preparation ⟨A good talk show host has to be able to *extemporize* the interviews when things don't go as planned.⟩ — see IMPROVISE

extend *vb* **1** to make longer ⟨Our guests from out of town *extended* their visit by a week.⟩

synonyms draw out, elongate, lengthen, outstretch, prolong, protract, stretch

related words amplify, enlarge, expand, increase; thin

near antonyms decrease, diminish, lessen, reduce; thicken

antonyms abbreviate, abridge, curtail, cut, cut back, shorten

2 to put before another for acceptance or consideration ⟨The couple *extended* an invitation to join them for a get-together at their house after the concert.⟩ — see OFFER 1

3 to arrange the parts of (something) over a wider area ⟨You can *extend* that chaise longue so that it lies completely flat.⟩ — see OPEN 3

4 to be positioned along a certain course or in a certain direction ⟨Our backyard *extends* all the way to that brook.⟩ — see RUN 3

5 to make greater in size, amount, or number ⟨embarked on a series of wars intended to *extend* his empire⟩ — see INCREASE 1

6 to alter (something) for the worse with the addition of foreign or lower-grade substances ⟨The company *extends* its ice cream with thickeners and other additives.⟩ — see ADULTERATE

extended *adj* **1** expressing one thing in terms normally used for another ⟨The word "snake" in its *extended* sense refers to a contemptible or treacherous person.⟩ — see FIGURATIVE

2 having considerable extent ⟨An *extended* portion of the valley is now devoted to the growing of grapes for wine.⟩ — see EXTENSIVE

3 lasting for a considerable time ⟨I've met her, but I have never had an *extended* conversation with her.⟩ — see LONG 2

4 of great extent from end to end ⟨The two armies clashed along an *extended* line of battle that stretched for miles.⟩ — see LONG 1

extended family *n* those who live as a family in one house ⟨Their *extended family* includes a grandmother and widowed aunt.⟩ — see HOUSEHOLD

extension *n* **1** the act of making longer ⟨The board's *extension* of the school year drew howls of protest.⟩

synonyms drawing out, elongation, lengthening, prolongation, prolonging, stretching

antonyms abbreviation, abridgment (*or* abridgement), curtailment, cutback, shortening

2 a smaller structure added to a main building ⟨The new *extension* will connect the house with what is now a freestanding garage.⟩ — see ANNEX

extensive *adj* having considerable extent ⟨a rock hound whose *extensive* reading enables him to identify just about any rock or mineral⟩

synonyms broad, deep, expansive, extended, far-flung, far-reaching, rangy, wide, widespread

related words comprehensive, general, global, inclusive; boundless, endless, infinite, limitless, unlimited; capacious, commodious, roomy, spacious

near antonyms circumscribed, limited, restricted

antonyms narrow

extensively *adv* to a large extent or degree ⟨Several beaches were *extensively* damaged by the hurricane.⟩ — see GREATLY 2

extent *n* **1** a real or imaginary point beyond which a person or thing cannot go ⟨The coach exceeded the *extent* of his authority by exempting some of the players from the requirement.⟩ — see LIMIT 1

2 a wide space or area ⟨the seemingly endless *extent* of the windswept prairies⟩ — see EXPANSE

3 an area over which activity, capacity, or influence extends ⟨The *extent* of this criminal investigation has widened considerably since it began.⟩ — see RANGE 2

4 the total amount of measurable space or surface occupied by something ⟨Looking at the *extent* of the stain on my shirt, you might think that I had spilled a gallon of coffee.⟩ — see ¹SIZE

extenuate *vb* to make (something) seem less bad by offering excuses ⟨They tried to *extenuate* their tardiness with claims of missing the bus.⟩ — see PALLIATE 1

exterior *adj* situated on the outside or farther out ⟨The house's *exterior* walls badly need to be painted.⟩ — see OUTER

exterior *n* an outer part or layer ⟨The *exterior* of the tooth consists of very hard enamel.⟩

synonyms face, outside, shell, skin, surface, veneer

related words facade (*also* façade), front, top; cover, covering, facing; appearance, disguise, guise, mask, semblance, show

antonyms inside, interior

exterminate *vb* to destroy all traces of ⟨Let's hope that the fumigant *exterminates* the whole colony of cockroaches, for any survivors may be resistant to any poison.⟩ — see ANNIHILATE 1

extermination *n* the state or fact of being rendered nonexistent, physically unsound, or useless ⟨The company guarantees total *extermination* of termites.⟩ — see DESTRUCTION 1

external *adj* **1** not being a vital part of or belonging to something ⟨*external* factors affecting their decision⟩ — see EXTRINSIC

2 situated on the outside or farther out ⟨The *external* chambers of the ancient tomb gave little indication of the magnificence of the innermost chamber.⟩ — see OUTER

extinct *adj* no longer existing ⟨A few overgrown ruins are all that remain of that once mighty but now *extinct* civilization.⟩

synonyms bygone, dead, defunct, departed, done, expired, gone, vanished

related words nonexistent; dying, faded, moribund; collapsed, fallen, overthrown; antiquated, dated, obsolete, passé; finished, lapsed, terminated; lost, missing

near antonyms active, dynamic, thriving, vibrant

antonyms alive, existent, existing, extant, living

extinction *n* the state or fact of being rendered nonexistent, physically unsound, or useless ⟨The state's population of moose has been replenished, having once been hunted almost to *extinction*.⟩ — see DESTRUCTION 1

extinguish *vb* **1** to cause to cease burning ⟨The fire in the skillet was quickly *extinguished* by slamming the lid on.⟩

synonyms blanket, douse (*also* dowse), put out, quench, snuff (out)

related words choke, smother, suffocate; blow out, rub out, snub (out), stamp (out), stub

antonyms fire, ignite, inflame (*also* enflame), kindle, light

2 to bring to a complete end the physical soundness, existence, or usefulness of ⟨a last minute comeback that *extinguished* the team's chance to overcome their rivals⟩ — see DESTROY 1

extirpate *vb* to destroy all traces of ⟨the triumph of modern medicine in *extirpating* certain diseases⟩ — see ANNIHILATE 1

extol *also* **extoll** *vb* to proclaim the glory of ⟨campaign literature *extolling* the candidate's military record⟩ — see PRAISE 1

extort *vb* to get (as money) by the use of force or threats ⟨He was arrested for *extorting* bribes.⟩

synonyms exact, wrest, wring

related words bleed, fleece, gouge, skin, squeeze; cheat, racketeer, swindle; coerce, compel, force

extortioner *n* a person who gets money from another by using force or threats ⟨police snaring an *extortioner*⟩ — see RACKETEER

extortionist *n* a person who gets money from another by using force or threats ⟨testified against the *extortionists* in court⟩ — see RACKETEER

extra *adj* being over what is needed ⟨always has *extra* food on hand in the event that unexpected company drops by⟩ — see SPARE 1

extra *adv* to a great degree ⟨The children tried to be *extra* quiet while their mother was recovering.⟩ — see VERY 1

extra *n* **1** an interchangeable part or piece of equipment that is kept on hand for replacement of an original ⟨That printer runs through ink cartridges incredibly fast, so I always keep plenty of *extras* on hand.⟩ — see SPARE

2 something adding to pleasure or comfort but not absolutely necessary ⟨The motel is clean and comfortable, but there are no *extras*.⟩ — see LUXURY 1

3 something given in addition to what is ordinarily expected or owed ⟨As an *extra*, the dealer filled the tank of my new car.⟩ — see BONUS

extract *n* a part taken from a longer work ⟨The anthology includes a long *extract* from the epic poem.⟩ — see EXCERPT

extract *vb* to draw out by force or with effort ⟨*extracted* a splinter from my hand⟩

synonyms prize, pry, pull, root (out), tear (out), uproot, wrest, wring, yank

related words mine, pluck, remove, take (out), withdraw; eke (out), scrounge

near antonyms implant, insert, install; cram, jam, ram, stuff, wedge

extraction *n* the line of ancestors from whom a person is descended ⟨a family of Italian *extraction*⟩ — see ANCESTRY

extraneous *adj* **1** not being a vital part of or belonging to something ⟨The architect's streamlined modern style shuns any sort of *extraneous* ornamentation.⟩ — see EXTRINSIC

2 not having anything to do with the matter at hand ⟨The professor would have covered all of the course material if she had refrained from her *extraneous* remarks on just about everything.⟩ — see IRRELEVANT

extraneousness *n* the quality or state of not having anything to do with the matter at hand ⟨The *extraneousness* of the commentators' remarks became more pronounced as the broadcast dragged on.⟩ — see IRRELEVANCE

extraordinary *adj* **1** being out of the ordinary ⟨The marine is being cited for *extraordinary* courage.⟩ — see EXCEPTIONAL 1

2 noticeably different from what is generally found or experienced ⟨No one noticed anything *extraordinary* about his behavior.⟩ — see UNUSUAL 1

extrapolate *vb* to form an opinion or reach a conclusion through reasoning and information ⟨We can *extrapolate* from past economic recessions the probable course of the current one.⟩ — see INFER 1

extrasensory perception *n* the power of seeing or knowing about things that are not present to the senses ⟨Discouraged by the lack of progress in the case, the police were willing to listen to a woman claiming *extrasensory perception*.⟩ — see CLAIRVOYANCE

extravagance *n* **1** the quality or fact of being free or wasteful in the expenditure of money ⟨Hollywood stars are famous for the *extravagance* of their parties.⟩

synonyms lavishness, prodigality, profusion, wastefulness

related words conspicuous consumption, splurge; bountifulness, generosity, liberality; improvidence, squandering; indulgence, overindulgence, self-indulgence; excess, overkill

near antonyms austerity, moderation, restraint, temperance

antonyms economy, frugality

2 an instance of spending money or resources without care or restraint ⟨The purchase of a new sports car was simply the latest of his *extravagances*.⟩ — see WASTE 1

extravagant *adj* **1** given to spending money freely or foolishly ⟨On my income, I can't afford to be *extravagant*.⟩ — see PRODIGAL

2 going beyond a normal or acceptable limit in degree or amount ⟨The book doesn't quite merit the *extravagant* praise that it has received.⟩ — see EXCESSIVE

3 commanding a large price ⟨surprised her with *extravagant* gifts⟩ — see COSTLY

extravagantly *adv* in a luxurious manner ⟨The ancient Roman emperors lived as *extravagantly* as any rulers in history.⟩ — see HIGH

extreme *adj* **1** most distant from a center ⟨spacecraft that is specially designed to explore the *extreme* edge of our solar system⟩

synonyms farthermost, farthest, furthermost, furthest, outermost, outmost, remotest, ultimate, utmost

related words aftermost, rearmost, sternmost

near antonyms intermediate, medial, median, mid, middle, midmost

antonyms inmost, innermost, nearest

2 being very far from the center of public opinion ⟨Their *extreme* political views attracted only a small band of followers.⟩

synonyms extremist, fanatic (*or* fanatical), rabid, radical, revolutionary, revolutionist, ultra

related words subversive, violent, wild; reactionary

near antonyms conservative, moderate, temperate; conventional, orthodox, traditional; liberal, progressive

antonyms middle-of-the-road, nonrevolutionary, unrevolutionary

3 going beyond a normal or acceptable limit in degree or amount ⟨In their *extreme* zeal the members of the cult are willing to do whatever their leader dictates.⟩ — see EXCESSIVE

extremely *adv* to a great degree ⟨an *extremely* hot day⟩ — see VERY 1

extremist *adj* being very far from the center of public opinion ⟨Their *extremist* views set them apart from the rest of the community.⟩ — see EXTREME 2

extremist *n* a person who favors rapid and sweeping changes especially in laws and methods of government ⟨*Extremists* wanted to do away with everything, even though they had no thought-out plan for what to do afterwards.⟩ — see RADICAL

extremity *n* **1** a time or state of affairs requiring prompt or decisive action ⟨made offers of aid to the refugees, and of asylum in *extremity*⟩ — see EMERGENCY

2 the most extreme or advanced point ⟨At its *extremity* the fever was actually life-threatening.⟩ — see HEIGHT 2

extricate *vb* to set free from entanglement or difficulty ⟨You've woven such a web of lies that it's hard to see how you can *extricate* yourself now.⟩

synonyms clear, disengage, disentangle, free, liberate, release, untangle

related words deliver, redeem, rescue, save; disburden, disencumber, unburden; unravel, unsnarl, untie, untwine

phrases cut loose

near antonyms block, hamper, hinder, impede, obstruct; burden, encumber, load, weigh
antonyms embroil, entangle
extrinsic *adj* not being a vital part of or belonging to something ⟨The fact that the ring belonged to your grandmother is *extrinsic* to its value to a jeweler.⟩
synonyms accidental, alien, extraneous, external, foreign
related words exterior, outside; immaterial, inapplicable, insignificant, irrelevant; nonessential, unessential, unnecessary
near antonyms congenital, deep-seated, inborn, inbred; inside, interior, internal; basic, essential, necessary
antonyms inherent, innate, intrinsic
extroverted *also* **extraverted** *adj* likely to seek or enjoy the company of others ⟨a job in a research lab that is probably not well suited to an *extroverted* person⟩ — see CONVIVIAL
extrude *vb* to drive or force out ⟨the sort of person who is determined to *extrude* every last gob of toothpaste from the tube⟩ — see EJECT 1
exuberance *n* the quality or state of having abundant or intense activity ⟨The *exuberance* of the housing market was an encouraging economic indicator.⟩ — see VITALITY 1
exuberant *adj* joyously unrestrained ⟨*Exuberant* crowds rushed to greet the returning national champions in collegiate basketball.⟩
synonyms bubbly, buoyant, effervescent, frolicsome, high-spirited, vivacious
related words extroverted (*also* extraverted), outgoing, uninhibited; carefree, happy-go-lucky, insouciant, joyful, lighthearted, lively, sprightly; boisterous, raucous, rollicking, rowdy; giddy, light-headed, overexuberant, silly; ecstatic, euphoric, lyric, rapturous; audacious, bold, brash, brazen, impertinent, impudent, insolent, saucy
near antonyms constrained, inhibited, restrained, subdued; impassive, phlegmatic, stoic (*or* stoical), stolid; depressed, dour, glum, morose, surly
antonyms low-spirited, sullen
exuberantly *adv* in an enthusiastic manner ⟨Her last employer sang her praises so *exuberantly* that we just had to hire her.⟩ — see SKY-HIGH
exude *vb* to flow forth slowly through small openings ⟨A sticky resin *exudes* from the bark of the tree.⟩
synonyms bleed, ooze, percolate, seep, strain, sweat, weep
related words dribble, drip, trickle; discharge, emit, give off, vent; flow, spring
near antonyms flood, gush, pour, stream, surge
exult *vb* to feel or express joy or triumph ⟨The winners of the Super Bowl spent the next week *exulting* in their victory.⟩
synonyms crow, delight, glory, joy, rejoice, triumph
related words gloat, preen, swell; boast, brag; flaunt, parade, show off, strut, swagger
phrases kick up one's heels
near antonyms bemoan, bewail, grieve, lament, regret, weep
exultant *adj* having or expressing feelings of joy or triumph ⟨the *exultant* winner of the award for best country artist of the year⟩

synonyms exulting, glorying, jubilant, prideful, proud, rejoicing, triumphant
related words ecstatic, elated, euphoric; arrogant, boastful, cocky; conquering, victorious, winning
near antonyms crestfallen, defeated, dejected, depressed, disconsolate, dispirited, downcast
exulting *adj* having or expressing feelings of joy or triumph ⟨With an *exulting* smile the winner of the race waved to the cheering crowd.⟩ — see EXULTANT
eye *n* **1** a circular strip ⟨Push the drawstring through the metal *eye* and knot it on one end.⟩ — see ¹RING 2
2 a state of being aware ⟨This young actor has the *eye* of every director in Hollywood.⟩ — see ATTENTION 2
3 a thing or place that is of greatest importance to an activity or interest ⟨This wilderness area is at the *eye* of the controversy between conservation and development.⟩ — see CENTER 1
4 an idea that is believed to be true or valid without positive knowledge ⟨In my *eye*, cats make better pets than dogs.⟩ — see OPINION 1
5 an instance of looking especially briefly ⟨All of the guys cast an eager *eye* on the boxes of pizza waiting to be opened.⟩ — see LOOK 2
6 the ability to see ⟨Her *eyes* are diminishing with age.⟩ — see EYESIGHT
7 a fixed intent look ⟨peering through the window with an eager *eye*⟩ — see GAZE
eye *vb* **1** to keep one's eyes on ⟨A lot of his backyard bird watching was spent *eyeing* the squirrels as they depleted the bird feeder of seeds.⟩ — see WATCH 1
2 to make note of (something) through the use of one's eyes ⟨I was starting to believe her tale of woe, until I *eyed* the diamond ring on her finger.⟩ — see SEE 1
3 to give serious and careful thought to ⟨We're *eyeing* the possibility of buying property there.⟩ — see PONDER
eye–catching *adj* likely to attract attention ⟨Brad needs an *eye-catching* slogan for his campaign for president of the student body.⟩ — see NOTICEABLE
eyeless *adj* lacking the power of sight ⟨His failing eyesight makes him fear that he may be *eyeless* in old age.⟩ — see BLIND
eye–opening *adj* **1** causing a strong emotional reaction because of unexpectedness ⟨Hunting for a first apartment in a big city is an *eye-opening* experience for young people.⟩ — see SURPRISING 1
2 causing wonder or astonishment ⟨The movie has some *eye-opening* special effects.⟩ — see MARVELOUS 1
eyesight *n* the ability to see ⟨the keen *eyesight* of a bird of prey⟩
synonyms eye, sight, vision
related words myopia, nearsightedness; farsightedness; astigmatism, diplopia, squint, strabismus; double vision
eyesore *n* something unpleasant to look at ⟨The old abandoned house was a neighborhood *eyesore*.⟩
synonyms fright, horror, mess, monstrosity, sight
related words eye-catcher; blot, smear, smudge, spot, stain
near antonyms vision
eyespot *n* a small area that is different (as in color) from the main part ⟨a tie having *eyespots* of blue on a light gray background⟩ — see SPOT 1

F

fable *n* **1** a story intended to teach a basic truth or moral about life ⟨a *fable* about a man who helps a lion that later spares the man's life⟩ — see ALLEGORY

2 a traditional but unfounded story that gives the reason for a current custom, belief, or fact of nature ⟨According to an ancient *fable* the waters of the mountain spring are the tears of a woman weeping for her lost children.⟩ — see MYTH 1

3 something that is the product of the imagination ⟨grew up reading *fables* about far-off lands and fairy godmothers⟩ — see FICTION

4 a statement known by its maker to be untrue and made in order to deceive ⟨the *fables* that people tell themselves to rationalize their failures and shortcomings⟩ — see LIE

fabled *adj* based on, described in, or being a myth ⟨The *fabled* unicorn continues to be a symbol of elusive and magical beauty.⟩ — see MYTHICAL 1

fabric *n* **1** a woven or knitted material (as of cotton or nylon) ⟨a *fabric* that is supposed to repel rain⟩ — see CLOTH

2 the arrangement of parts that gives something its basic form ⟨The schools are a major part of the *fabric* of our town.⟩ — see FRAME 1

fabricate *vb* **1** to bring into being by combining, shaping, or transforming materials ⟨With a few inexpensive materials from a craft shop, we were able to *fabricate* our own holiday wreath.⟩ — see MAKE 1

2 to create or think of by clever use of the imagination ⟨*fabricated* a daring plan to create an underground explosion that would take the enemy totally by surprise⟩ — see INVENT

3 to form by putting together parts or materials ⟨The house was essentially *fabricated* at the factory and then shipped to the site for assembly.⟩ — see BUILD

4 to make a statement one knows to be untrue ⟨Since he didn't have a good excuse for not having done his homework, he would have to *fabricate* one.⟩ — see ¹LIE

fabrication *n* **1** a statement known by its maker to be untrue and made in order to deceive ⟨Her claim that she had been a nurse during the war proved to be a total *fabrication*.⟩ — see LIE

2 something that is the product of the imagination ⟨The notion that the Colossus of Rhodes could straddle the harbor was a *fabrication* of medieval writers.⟩ — see FICTION

fabricator *n* a person who tells lies ⟨He's been a *fabricator* for so long that it no longer occurs to him to tell the truth.⟩ — see LIAR

fabulous *adj* **1** based on, described in, or being a myth ⟨The city of Phoenix is named after a *fabulous* bird that every 500 years destroys itself with fire, only to rise again from its own ashes.⟩ — see MYTHICAL 1

2 causing wonder or astonishment ⟨the *fabulous* sites of dazzlingly lit Las Vegas⟩ — see MARVELOUS 1

3 not real and existing only in the imagination ⟨a story of a *fabulous* land where the people know nothing of war and live together in perfect harmony⟩ — see IMAGINARY

4 of the very best kind ⟨We had a *fabulous* time on our vacation.⟩ — see EXCELLENT

facade *also* **façade** *n* **1** a forward part or surface ⟨All of the stores in the mall have *facades* that are in keeping with the style of a 19th-century American village.⟩ — see FRONT 1

2 a display of emotion or behavior that is insincere or intended to deceive ⟨She manages to keep a sunny *fa*-

cade even though she's going through rough times.⟩ — see MASQUERADE

3 a deceptively attractive external appearance ⟨The company's *facade* of success collapsed when it was revealed that its financial officers had been cooking the books for years.⟩ — see GLOSS 1

face *n* **1** the front part of the head ⟨His *face* is familiar.⟩

synonyms countenance, kisser [*slang*], mug, puss [*slang*], visage

related words appearance, aspect, features, lineaments, looks, mien, presence; expression, physiognomy

2 a forward part or surface ⟨The *face* of the store building has been altered many times over the years to meet changing tastes and needs.⟩ — see FRONT 1

3 a twisting of the facial features in disgust or disapproval ⟨It's rude to make a *face* when your dinner hostess offers you broccoli.⟩ — see GRIMACE

4 an outer part or layer ⟨A much-needed sandblasting revealed that the *face* of the old stone church is actually a pinkish granite.⟩ — see EXTERIOR

5 facial appearance regarded as an indication of mood or feeling ⟨A rainy day is no excuse for just moping around with a long *face*, so let's do something!⟩ — see LOOK 1

6 outward and often deceptive indication ⟨On the *face* of it, the idea seemed reasonable.⟩ — see APPEARANCE 2

7 a member of the human race ⟨I see they've hired some new *faces*.⟩ — see HUMAN

8 shameless boldness ⟨You have to wonder how anyone has the *face* to ask such a personal question.⟩ — see EFFRONTERY

9 a state of mind in which one is free from doubt ⟨He managed to maintain *face* despite the endless series of crises.⟩ — see CONFIDENCE 2

face *vb* **1** to stand or sit with the face or front toward ⟨The house *faces* the sparkling blue waters of the Pacific Ocean.⟩

synonyms front, look (toward), point (toward)

related words abut, adjoin, border, bound, fringe, margin, meet, neighbor, rim, skirt, touch; command, dominate, overlook; look down (on)

2 to oppose (something hostile or dangerous) with firmness or courage ⟨movie superheroes who are ever ready to *face* danger without blinking an eye⟩

synonyms beard, brave, brazen, breast, confront, dare, defy, outbrave

related words face up (to), front; affront; challenge; encounter, meet; accost, approach, corner; repel, resist, stand, withstand; battle, combat, contend (with), fight, oppose, square (off)

phrases stand up to

near antonyms avoid, eschew, shun; elude, escape, evade, shake

antonyms dodge, duck, funk, shirk, sidestep

3 to cover with something that protects ⟨We decided to *face* our old frame house with aluminum siding.⟩ — see SHEATHE

4 to enter into contest or conflict with ⟨The Boston Red Sox were eager to *face* their traditional rivals, the Yankees, in the play-offs.⟩ — see ENGAGE 2

faceless *adj* not named or identified by a name ⟨*Faceless* gossipmongers had been spreading rumors about the actor for years.⟩ — see NAMELESS 1

face–off *n* an earnest effort for superiority or victory over another ⟨The annual fall *face-off* between these traditional rivals is a big event for both football-mad colleges.⟩ — see CONTEST 1

face off *vb* to engage in a contest ⟨eager to *face off* with her longtime rival⟩ — see COMPETE

facet *n* a certain way in which something appears or may be regarded ⟨There are so many *facets* to Benjamin Franklin: statesman, scientist, inventor, American original.⟩ — see ASPECT 1

facetious *adj* 1 given to or marked by mature intelligent humor ⟨The essay is a *facetious* commentary on the absurdity of war as a solution for international disputes.⟩ — see WITTY
2 making light of something usually regarded as serious or sacred ⟨a *facetious* and tasteless remark⟩ — see FLIPPANT

facetiousness *n* a lack of seriousness often at an improper time ⟨a serious problem that is not a matter for *facetiousness* and lame jokes⟩ — see FRIVOLITY

face–to–face *adv* in person and usually privately ⟨I won't believe that accusation until I meet with him *face-to-face* and ask him myself.⟩ — see TÊTE-À-TÊTE

facile *adj* 1 having or showing a lack of depth of understanding or character ⟨The movie takes a *facile* look at relationships.⟩ — see SUPERFICIAL 2
2 involving minimal difficulty or effort ⟨A few early *facile* victories misled the country into thinking that the war would be short and relatively painless.⟩ — see EASY 1

facilely *adv* without difficulty ⟨She was able to fix the problem quickly and *facilely*.⟩ — see EASILY 1

facilitate *vb* to free from obstruction or difficulty ⟨The software *facilitates* creation of business documents.⟩ — see EASE 1

facility *n* a structure that is designed and built for a particular purpose ⟨The city is known for its outstanding medical *facilities*.⟩
synonyms complex, establishment, installation
related words building, edifice; institute, institution; business, company, concern, outfit

facsimile *n* 1 something or someone that strongly resembles another ⟨The family resemblance is so strong that the boy is virtually a pint-size *facsimile* of his father.⟩ — see IMAGE 1
2 something that is made to look exactly like something else ⟨This is not an antique copy of the Declaration of Independence but a modern *facsimile*.⟩ — see COPY

fact *n* 1 the quality of being actual ⟨Like other scientists, astronomers deal in the realm of *fact*, not speculation.⟩
synonyms actuality, factuality, materiality, reality
related words authenticity, genuineness, truth, verity
near antonyms fancy, fantasy (*also* phantasy), fiction, fictitiousness; dreaminess, surreality
antonyms irreality, unreality
2 something that actually exists ⟨Once considered a wild fantasy, the Internet is now a *fact* of everyday life.⟩
synonyms actuality, case, materiality, reality
related words certainty; circumstance, event, occurrence, phenomenon; element, item, particular, thing
near antonyms eventuality, possibility, potentiality, probability
antonyms fantasy (*also* phantasy), fiction, illusion
3 a single piece of information ⟨a book of little-known *facts* about famous people⟩
synonyms datum, detail, nicety, particular, particularity, point, specific
related words article, item; component, constituent, element, ingredient, member, part; aspect, circumstance, facet, factor; evidence, exhibit; database, information, knowledge
near antonyms error, fallacy, falsehood, inaccuracy, misconception, misstatement, myth

4 facts *pl* a collection of factual knowledge about something ⟨After learning the *facts* on the situation, we decided that something should be done.⟩ — see INFORMATION 1

faction *n* a group of people acting together within a larger group ⟨Several *factions* within the environmental movement have joined forces to save this wilderness area.⟩
synonyms bloc, block, body, coalition, party, sect, set, side, wing
related words splinter, split; crew, gang, pack, team; denomination, persuasion; caucus, movement

factitious *adj* lacking in natural or spontaneous quality ⟨the *factitious* friendliness shown by the hotel's front desk workers⟩ — see ARTIFICIAL 1

factor *n* 1 a person who acts or does business for another ⟨At the auction the high bidder for the painting was actually a *factor* for a wealthy art collector.⟩ — see AGENT 2
2 one of the parts that make up a whole ⟨Price was only one *factor* in my decision to buy the car.⟩ — see ELEMENT 1

factory *n* a building or set of buildings for the manufacturing of goods ⟨The new *factory* will create hundreds of much-needed jobs.⟩
synonyms manufactory, mill, plant, shop, works, workshop
related words sweatshop; atelier, studio, workplace, workroom; yard

factual *adj* 1 restricted to or based on fact ⟨a *factual* biography of George Washington that scoffs at the story about the cherry tree⟩
synonyms documentary, hard, historical, literal, matter-of-fact, nonfictional, objective, true
related words actual, authentic, bona fide, genuine, real, right; documented, established; confirmable, reliable, supportable, sustainable, verifiable; demonstrable, provable; incontestable, incontrovertible, indisputable, irrefutable, undeniable, unquestionable; plain, simple; certain, undoubted
near antonyms hypothetical, speculative, theoretical (*also* theoretic); apocryphal, unauthentic, undocumented; chimerical (*also* chimeric), fabulous, fanciful, fantastic (*also* fantastical), imaginary, imagined, invented, legendary, made-up, make-believe, mythical (*or* mythic), pretend; embroidered; insupportable, unsupportable
antonyms fictional, fictionalized, fictitious, nondocumentary, nonfactual, nonhistorical, unhistorical
2 existing in fact and not merely as a possibility ⟨As a serious scientist, she is only interested in *factual* phenomena and lets others speculate about the hypothetical.⟩ — see ACTUAL

factuality *n* 1 agreement with fact or reality ⟨Some viewers complained that the TV docudrama was short on *factuality* and long on speculation.⟩ — see TRUTH
2 the quality of being actual ⟨Although this account of the discovery seems like it must be fiction, its very *factuality* makes it all the more fascinating.⟩ — see FACT 1

faculty *n* 1 a natural ability of the mind or body ⟨Although they are well into their 80s, the mental *faculties* of this couple are as sharp as ever.⟩ — see POWER 3
2 a special and usually inborn ability ⟨Even when he was still at a young age, John Singleton Copley's artistic *faculties* were readily recognizable.⟩ — see TALENT
3 the physical or mental power to do something ⟨the belief that if someone loses their sight, all of their other physical *faculties* are heightened⟩ — see ABILITY

fad *n* a practice or interest that is very popular for a short time ⟨Once the *fad* for that kind of music had passed, nobody would have been caught dead listening to it.⟩

synonyms craze, enthusiasm, fashion, go, last word, latest, mode, rage, sensation, style, trend, vogue
related words nine days' wonder (*also* nine day wonder); new wave; crush, infatuation; fervor, passion; furor, fuss, hullabaloo, to-do, uproar; bandwagon, crusade, cult, movement; novelty, wrinkle; caprice, fancy, whim
near antonyms classic, standard

faddish *adj* enjoying widespread favor or approval ⟨a *faddish* novelist who impressed some critics, at least for a time⟩ — see POPULAR 1

faddy *adj* enjoying widespread favor or approval ⟨That chef's *faddy* cuisine was all the rage among foodies back in the 1990s.⟩ — see POPULAR 1

fade *vb* **1** to cease to be visible ⟨The departing ship gradually *faded* over the horizon.⟩ — see DISAPPEAR

2 to make white or whiter by removing color ⟨Years of harsh sunlight had *faded* the car, which was once fire-engine red.⟩ — see WHITEN

3 to lose bodily strength or vigor ⟨began to *fade* after a long, hard day⟩ — see WEAKEN 2

faded *adj* lacking intensity of color ⟨Rather than buy *faded* jeans, I get the dark blues and let time and the washing machine do their thing.⟩ — see PALE 1

faerie *also* **faery** *n* an imaginary being usually having a small human form and magical powers ⟨In ancient folklore *faeries* were often portrayed as powerful beings who could wreak havoc on the lives of humans.⟩ — see FAIRY

fail *vb* **1** to stop functioning ⟨My cell phone *failed* just as I was about to call you.⟩
synonyms break, break down, conk (out), crash, cut out, die, give out, stall
related words fizzle, sputter, wheeze; act up, malfunction; jam
antonyms start (up)

2 to be unsuccessful ⟨Despite all the publicity, the movie *failed* miserably at the box office.⟩
synonyms bomb, collapse, flop, flunk, fold, founder, miss, wash out
related words flounder, struggle; decline, sink, slip, slump, wane; crash, crumble, miscarry, misfire; go under; implode, self-destruct
phrases come a cropper, come to grief, come up empty, die on the vine, fall flat, fall on one's face, fall short, lay an egg
near antonyms cook, flourish, prosper, thrive; prevail, triumph, win
antonyms click, deliver, go, go over, pan out, succeed, work out

3 to fall short in satisfying the expectation or hope of ⟨Although the minor-league franchise continues to *fail* local fans, hope springs eternal.⟩ — see DISAPPOINT

4 to lose bodily strength or vigor ⟨Ever since she reached the age of 90, Grandma has been noticeably *failing*.⟩ — see WEAKEN 2

5 to miss the opportunity or obligation ⟨*failed* to mention that he had already been paid for the job⟩ — see NEGLECT 3

failing *n* a defect in character ⟨We could talk about your *failings*, but let's concentrate on your strengths.⟩ — see FAULT 1

failure *n* **1** the nonperformance of an assigned or expected action ⟨Your *failure* to check the batteries in the smoke detector could have tragic results.⟩
synonyms default, delinquency, dereliction, neglect, negligence, oversight
related words carelessness, heedlessness, inadvertence, inadvertency, laxity
near antonyms compliance, discharge, fulfillment (*or* fulfilment)

2 a falling short of one's goals ⟨The *failure* of the school's fund-raising drive was a big disappointment to all.⟩
synonyms collapse, crash, cropper, defeat, fizzle, non-success
related words futility, uselessness; ineffectiveness, ineffectuality, ineffectualness, inefficaciousness, inefficacy; deficiency, inadequacy, insufficiency; disappointment, letdown, setback; insolvency, ruin
near antonyms victory, win
antonyms accomplishment, achievement, success

3 something that has failed ⟨The students' first attempt to build a homemade rocket was a disappointing *failure*.⟩
synonyms bomb, bummer, bust, catastrophe, debacle (*also* débâcle), disaster, dud, fiasco, fizzle, flop, frost, lemon, loser, miss, turkey, washout
related words also-ran, disappointment, dog; botch, hash, mess, muddle, shambles; nonevent; nonstarter
near antonyms corker, crackerjack (*also* crackajack), dandy, jim-dandy, phenomenon
antonyms blockbuster, hit, smash, success, winner

4 a falling short of an essential or desirable amount or number ⟨The *failure* of the potato crop had a devastating effect on the population of Ireland.⟩ — see DEFICIENCY

faint *adj* **1** not seen or understood clearly ⟨After wandering in the woods for hours, we had only a *faint* idea of where we were.⟩
synonyms bleary, blurry, dim, foggy, fuzzy, gauzy, hazy, indefinite, indistinct, indistinguishable, misty, murky, nebulous, obscure, opaque, pale, shadowy, unclear, undefined, undetermined, vague
related words dark, dusky, gloomy; impalpable, inappreciable, intangible; incomprehensible, indiscernible, inexplicable, mysterious, puzzling
near antonyms bright, distinct, evident, obvious, plain; certain, firm, strong, sure
antonyms clear, definite, pellucid

2 lacking bodily strength ⟨I was starting to feel a little *faint* after going so long without food.⟩ — see WEAK 1

faint *n* a temporary state of unconsciousness ⟨Shocking news can cause a person to fall into a *faint*.⟩
synonyms blackout, insensibility, knockout, swim, swoon
related words daze, trance; drowsiness, narcosis, sleep, somnolence

faint *vb* to lose consciousness ⟨the kind of person who *faints* at the sight of blood⟩
synonyms black out, conk (out), pass out, swoon
related words break down, collapse; zonk (out)
antonyms come around, come round, come to, revive

fainthearted *adj* easily frightened ⟨The sport of river rafting is not for those who are *fainthearted*.⟩ — see SHY 1

faintheartedness *n* lack of willingness to assert oneself and take risks ⟨His *faintheartedness* got the better of him, and he backed off from the ski trail intended for experts.⟩ — see TIMIDITY

faintness *n* the quality or state of lacking physical strength or vigor ⟨Once the worst of the illness had passed, his *faintness* subsided.⟩ — see WEAKNESS 1

fair *n* a public showing of objects of interest ⟨a dazzling array of sleek cabin cruisers at the annual boat *fair*⟩ — see EXHIBITION 1

fair *adj* **1** not stormy or cloudy ⟨We prayed for *fair* weather during our vacation at the beach.⟩
synonyms bright, clear, cloudless, sunny, sunshiny, unclouded
related words balmy, clement, gentle, mild, moderate, temperate; calm, halcyon, peaceful, placid, serene, tranquil; fine, pleasant

near antonyms harsh, inclement, severe; blustering, blustery, breezy, gusty; foggy, hazy, misty, murky, soupy
antonyms bleak, cloudy, dirty, foul, nasty, overcast, rainy, raw, rough, squally, stormy, tempestuous, turbulent
2 marked by justice, honesty, and freedom from bias ⟨a commanding officer who enjoyed the respect of his soldiers because his decisions were always *fair*⟩
synonyms candid, disinterested, dispassionate, equal, equitable, evenhanded, impartial, indifferent, just, nonpartisan, objective, square, unbiased, unprejudiced
related words frank, forthright, open, straight, straightforward; balanced, rational, reasonable
near antonyms deceitful, deceptive, dishonest; arbitrary, unconscionable, unreasonable; jaundiced, unfriendly, unsympathetic; distorted, warped
antonyms biased, inequitable, nonobjective, one-sided, partial, partisan, prejudiced, unjust
3 following or according to the rules ⟨a hockey player who is respected for his *fair* play⟩
synonyms clean, legal, sportsmanlike, sportsmanly
related words just, law-abiding; ethical, moral, principled, scrupulous; honorable, irreproachable, unimpeachable
near antonyms immoral, unethical, unprincipled, unrighteous, unscrupulous, vicious, wrong
antonyms dirty, foul, nasty, unfair, unsportsmanlike
4 of light complexion ⟨*Fair* people tend to sunburn easily.⟩
synonyms light
related words ashen, ashy, pale, paled, palish, pallid, pasty, peaked, sallow, sallowish, wan, white
antonyms dark, swart
5 having qualities which inspire hope ⟨As long as the team keeps playing as hard as they can, they have a *fair* chance of winning—no matter what the scoreboard says.⟩ — see HOPEFUL 1
6 of a pale yellow or yellowish brown color ⟨the abundance of people with *fair* hair in Scandinavia⟩ — see BLOND
7 of average to below average quality ⟨For what they charged us, the painters should have done better than a *fair* job of painting the house.⟩ — see MEDIOCRE 1
8 very pleasing to look at ⟨a handsome knight and his *fair* maiden⟩ — see BEAUTIFUL 1
9 having no exceptions or restrictions ⟨It would take a *fair* miracle for that project to be finished on time.⟩ — see ABSOLUTE 2
10 being what is called for by accepted standards of right and wrong ⟨Most thought his dismissal was *fair* since he had been given many chances to clean up his act.⟩ — see JUST 1
11 free from dirt or stain ⟨A handwritten thank-you letter requires nothing less than a sheet of *fair* white paper.⟩ — see CLEAN 1
fair *adv* according to the rules or the law ⟨We expect everyone on this basketball court to play *fair*.⟩ — see FAIRLY 2
fairly *adv* **1** to some degree or extent ⟨For someone without professional training, she sings *fairly* well.⟩
synonyms enough, kind of, like, moderately, more or less, pretty, quite, rather, relatively, something, somewhat, sort of
related words acceptably, passably, tolerably; little, negligibly, nominally, slightly, vaguely; half, halfway, incompletely, part, partially, partly
phrases a bit, after a sort, a little, a mite, a tad, a touch, of sorts (*or* of a sort), to a degree
near antonyms awfully, beastly, deadly, especially, ex-

ceedingly (*also* exceeding), exceptionally, extremely, frightfully, greatly, heavily, highly, hugely, mightily, mortally, particularly, terribly, very; considerably, extensively, significantly, substantially
2 according to the rules or the law ⟨Carson had acquired the land *fairly*.⟩
synonyms clean, fair
related words ethically, high-mindedly, morally, nobly; honorably
near antonyms ignobly, immorally, underhandedly, unethically; dishonorably
antonyms dirty, illegally
3 very close to but not completely ⟨He *fairly* knocked me flat on my face as he ran by.⟩ — see ALMOST
fairness *n* **1** the qualities in a person or thing that as a whole give pleasure to the senses ⟨A city of incomparable *fairness*, Venice has enchanted travelers for centuries.⟩ — see BEAUTY 1
2 lack of favoritism toward one side or another ⟨*Fairness* was certainly uppermost in the elderly woman's mind as she made arrangements for dividing the family heirlooms among her many grandchildren.⟩ — see DETACHMENT 1
fairy *n* an imaginary being usually having a small human form and magical powers ⟨*Fairies* are part of the folklore of many countries and cultures.⟩
synonyms brownie, dwarf, elf, faerie (*also* faery), gnome, goblin, gremlin, hobgoblin, leprechaun, pixie (*also* pixy), puck, sprite, troll
related words little people; changeling; imp; banshee, ghoul, hag, ogre
fairy tale *n* a statement known by its maker to be untrue and made in order to deceive ⟨Did you really see a bear, or are you telling us another one of your *fairy tales*?⟩ — see LIE
faith *n* **1** belief and trust in and loyalty to God ⟨a people who are known for their strong and steadfast *faith*⟩
synonyms devotion, piety, religion
related words devoutness, piousness, religiousness; adoration, reverence, veneration, worship; profession, protestation
near antonyms disbelief, doubt, unbelief, unfaith; agnosticism, know-nothingism
antonyms atheism, godlessness
2 a body of beliefs and practices regarding the supernatural and the worship of one or more deities ⟨The city of Jerusalem is sacred to three *faiths*: Christianity, Islam, and Judaism.⟩ — see RELIGION 1
3 adherence to something to which one is bound by a pledge or duty ⟨After they had to declare bankruptcy, the family found out how much *faith* their friends had.⟩ — see FIDELITY
4 firm belief in the integrity, ability, effectiveness, or genuineness of someone or something ⟨Never having had much *faith* in banks, the old miser kept his money under the mattress.⟩ — see TRUST 1
5 mental conviction of the truth of some statement or the reality of some being or phenomenon ⟨She has complete *faith* that the universe is controlled by a benevolent Supreme Being with a master plan.⟩ — see BELIEF 1
faithful *adj* **1** firm in one's allegiance to someone or something ⟨Fans of the Chicago Cubs are famously *faithful*.⟩
synonyms constant, devoted, devout, fast, good, loyal, pious, staunch (*also* stanch), steadfast, steady, true, true-blue
related words dependable, dutiful, reliable, responsible, solid, tried, tried-and-true, trustworthy, trusty; unfaltering, unhesitating, unwavering; determined, intent, resolute; confirmed, inveterate, sworn; ardent, avid, enthusiastic, fervent, fervid, gung ho, impassioned, passionate, serious

near antonyms irresponsible, undependable, unreliable, untrustworthy; faltering, hesitant, vacillating, wavering; dubious, irresolute, shaky, uncertain; apathetic, dispassionate, uninterested

antonyms disloyal, faithless, false, fickle, inconstant, perfidious, recreant, traitorous, treacherous, unfaithful, untrue

2 following an original exactly ⟨a *faithful* filming of Robert Louis Stevenson's novel *Treasure Island*⟩

synonyms accurate, authentic, exact, precise, right, strict, true, veracious

related words lifelike, realistic; careful, conscientious, meticulous, punctilious, scrupulous; authoritative; bona fide, genuine, real

near antonyms careless, slack, slipshod, slovenly; erroneous, incorrect, invalid, off, unsound, untrue, untruthful, wrong

antonyms corrupt, corrupted, false, imprecise, inaccurate, inauthentic, inexact, loose, unfaithful

faithfulness *n* adherence to something to which one is bound by a pledge or duty ⟨put the *faithfulness* of his disciples to the test⟩ — see FIDELITY

faithless *adj* not true in one's allegiance to someone or something ⟨*faithless* friends who deserted him in his time of need⟩

synonyms disloyal, false, fickle, inconstant, perfidious, recreant, traitorous, treacherous, unfaithful, untrue

related words irresponsible, trustless, undependable, unreliable, untrustworthy; faltering, hesitant, vacillating, wavering; dubious, irresolute, uncertain; apathetic, dispassionate, uninterested

near antonyms dependable, dutiful, reliable, responsible, solid, tried, tried-and-true, trustworthy, trusty; unfaltering, unhesitating, unwavering; determined, intent, resolute; confirmed, inveterate, sworn; ardent, avid, enthusiastic, fervent, fervid, impassioned, passionate

antonyms constant, devoted, devout, faithful, fast, loyal, staunch (*also* stanch), steadfast, steady, true

faithlessness *n* **1** lack of faithfulness especially to one's husband or wife ⟨They promised each other to abstain from *faithlessness.*⟩ — see INFIDELITY 1

2 the act or fact of violating the trust or confidence of another ⟨The former butler's mercenary *faithlessness* shocked and offended the royal family.⟩ — see BETRAYAL

fake *adj* **1** being such in appearance only and made with or manufactured from usually cheaper materials ⟨The dress was adorned with *fake* pearls.⟩ — see IMITATION

2 being such in appearance only and made or manufactured with the intention of committing fraud ⟨arrested for peddling "designer" watches that were *fake*⟩ — see COUNTERFEIT 1

3 lacking in natural or spontaneous quality ⟨The boss's pitiful attempts at humor were met with *fake* laughter.⟩ — see ARTIFICIAL 1

4 not being or expressing what one appears to be or express ⟨the *fake* friendliness of the sales rep⟩ — see INSINCERE

fake *n* **1** an imitation that is passed off as genuine ⟨Experts declared that one of the museum's prized paintings was actually a *fake.*⟩

synonyms counterfeit, forgery, hoax, humbug, phony (*also* phoney), sham

related words copycat, knockoff; copy, facsimile, replica, reproduction; dummy, mock-up; fraud, gaff, imposture, spoof, swindle; simulation, synthetic

near antonyms original

2 one who makes false claims of identity or expertise ⟨A hidden-camera investigation revealed that the so-called psychic was a *fake.*⟩ — see IMPOSTOR

fake *vb* **1** to imitate or copy especially in order to deceive ⟨Pranksters *faked* giant footprints and then claimed that they had seen Bigfoot.⟩

synonyms counterfeit, forge, phony

related words simulate; duplicate, reduplicate, replicate, reproduce; crib, plagiarize; adulterate, doctor, fudge, manipulate, tamper (with); concoct, cook (up), fabricate, invent

2 to present a false appearance of ⟨While running for class president, Dan was not above *faking* friendship with people just to get their votes.⟩ — see FEIGN

3 to perform, make, or do without preparation ⟨If you give me the gist of the plan, I can probably *fake* enough for the speech.⟩ — see IMPROVISE

faker *n* one who makes false claims of identity or expertise ⟨The medium was exposed as a *faker* who was herself making the strange noises that she claimed were from the dead.⟩ — see IMPOSTOR

fakery *n* the inclination or practice of misleading others through lies or trickery ⟨If the product were any good, the company wouldn't have to resort to *fakery* to get people to buy it.⟩ — see DECEIT 1

fall *n* **1** the act of going down from an upright position suddenly and involuntarily ⟨a bad *fall* that resulted in several broken bones⟩

synonyms slip, spill, stumble, tumble

related words pratfall; misstep, trip; descent, dive, plunge, slide; free-fall

2 a change to a lower state or level ⟨Last night's record *fall* in temperature was a sure sign that winter's coming, like it or not.⟩ — see DECLINE 2

3 a loss of status ⟨Being sent back to the minor leagues was quite a *fall* for the once-promising pitcher.⟩ — see COMEDOWN

4 the act or process of going to a lower level or altitude ⟨Jim panicked during his first unassisted *fall* when his parachute's rip cord didn't respond to the first tug.⟩ — see DESCENT 1

5 the amount by which something is lessened ⟨That year the *fall* in prices was 10 cents for a gallon of regular gas.⟩ — see DECREASE

6 *usually* **falls** *pl* a fall of water usually from a great height ⟨Tourists were often soaked by the spray of water from the *falls.*⟩ — see WATERFALL

7 a downward slope ⟨The sharp *fall* of the land sends rivers rushing to the seas.⟩ — see DECLINE 3

fall *vb* **1** to go down from an upright position suddenly and involuntarily ⟨Better sand that walkway before somebody *falls* on the ice.⟩

synonyms slip, stumble, topple, trip, tumble

related words collapse, crumple, drop, plop, plunk (*or* plonk), slump (over); crash, free-fall, nose-dive, plummet, plunge, precipitate, wipe out; slide

antonyms get up, rise, stand (up), uprise

2 to yield to the control or power of enemy forces ⟨The city *fell* to the enemy.⟩

synonyms capitulate, give up, knuckle under, submit, succumb, surrender

related words bow, buckle, cave (in), collapse, give (in); hand over, relinquish; lose; concede, fail, fold

near antonyms buck, defy, fight, oppose, repel, resist, withstand; beat, overcome, win; conquer, prevail, triumph

antonyms endure, stand

3 to go to a lower level especially abruptly ⟨Once the cold front moved in, temperatures quickly *fell.*⟩ — see DROP 2

4 to grow less in scope or intensity especially gradually ⟨Manufacturing in the area is *falling,* and closing signs are going up all over.⟩ — see DECREASE 2

5 to lead or extend downward ⟨The lake bottom *falls* sharply just a few feet from the shoreline, so be careful.⟩ — see DESCEND 1

6 to undergo defeat ⟨Not surprisingly, the novice player *fell* to a much stronger opponent.⟩ — see LOSE 3

7 to commit an offense ⟨Even saints can *fall*.⟩ — see OFFEND 1

8 to stop living ⟨If their brave leader *falls*, the men will continue the fight.⟩ — see DIE 1

fallacious *adj* **1** not using or following good reasoning ⟨It's *fallacious* to say that something must exist because science hasn't proven its nonexistence.⟩ — see ILLOGICAL

2 tending or having power to deceive ⟨consumers who harbor the *fallacious* belief that credit-card spending will never catch up with them⟩ — see DECEPTIVE 1

fallaciousness *n* the quality or state of being false ⟨The *fallaciousness* of that argument will be apparent as soon as we examine it.⟩ — see FALLACY 2

fallacy *n* **1** a false idea or belief ⟨the once-common *fallacy* that the earth is flat⟩

synonyms delusion, error, falsehood, falsity, hallucination, illusion, misbelief, misconception, myth, old wives' tale, untruth

related words factoid; superstition; fiction, pretense (*or* pretence); distortion, inaccuracy, misapprehension, miscomprehension, misinterpretation, misjudgment, misperception, misunderstanding; misinformation, misreport, misrepresentation, misstatement; sophism, sophistry; fib, half-truth, lie, story, tale

antonyms truth, verity

2 the quality or state of being false ⟨The *fallacy* of the notion of spontaneous generation was demonstrated by the Dutch naturalist Leeuwenhoek.⟩

synonyms erroneousness, fallaciousness, falsehood, falseness, falsity, untruth

related words speciousness, spuriousness; delusion; inaccuracy, incorrectness; dishonesty, mendacity, untruthfulness

near antonyms accuracy, actuality, correctness, factuality, factualness, genuineness; credibility, honesty, trustworthiness, truthfulness, veracity

antonyms truth, verity

fall back *vb* to move back or away (as from something difficult, dangerous, or disagreeable) ⟨Resistance was greater than expected, and the invading army was forced to *fall back*.⟩ — see RETREAT 1

fallen *adj* no longer living ⟨Let's take a moment to remember our *fallen* comrades.⟩ — see DEAD 1

fall guy *n* a person or thing taking the blame for others ⟨The sandlot ball players wanted the littlest kid to be the *fall guy* for the broken window, figuring that he'd have the best chance of escaping punishment.⟩ — see SCAPEGOAT

falling–out *n* an often noisy or angry expression of differing opinions ⟨The two friends have been lonely and miserable since they had a *falling-out*.⟩ — see ARGUMENT 1

fall out *vb* **1** to express different opinions about something often angrily ⟨Club members were soon *falling out* about how to spend the money they'd made washing cars.⟩ — see ARGUE 2

2 to come to be ⟨I had planned to have a sports career, but things *fell out* otherwise.⟩ — see COME OUT 1

fallow *adj* not being in a state of use, activity, or employment ⟨The coal mine has been lying *fallow* since the drop in prices made it unprofitable.⟩ — see INACTIVE 2

false *adj* **1** not being in agreement with what is true ⟨Early reports about the explosion contained much *false* information.⟩

synonyms erroneous, inaccurate, incorrect, inexact, invalid, off, unsound, untrue, untruthful, wrong

related words counterfactual; specious, spurious; deceptive, delusive, delusory, distorted, fallacious, fictitious, illusory, misleading; amiss, askew, awry; deceitful, dishonest, fraudulent, lying, mendacious; unconfirmed, unproven, untested; fabricated, invented, made-up, trumped-up

phrases off base

near antonyms confirmed, demonstrated, established, proven, tested; faultless, flawless, impeccable, letter-perfect, perfect

antonyms accurate, correct, errorless, exact, factual, precise, proper, right, sound, true, valid, veracious

2 being such in appearance only and made with or manufactured from usually cheaper materials ⟨George Washington's *false* teeth were not made of wood but of elephant ivory and cow's teeth.⟩ — see IMITATION

3 being such in appearance only and made or manufactured with the intention of committing fraud ⟨The signatures on the documents turned out to be *false*.⟩ — see COUNTERFEIT 1

4 lacking in natural or spontaneous quality ⟨a salesman's *false* smile⟩ — see ARTIFICIAL 1

5 marked by, based on, or done by the use of dishonest methods to acquire something of value ⟨*false* advertising that claimed that the vegetables were organically grown when they weren't⟩ — see FRAUDULENT 1

6 not true in one's allegiance to someone or something ⟨*false* friends who deserted the prizefighter when all his money was gone⟩ — see FAITHLESS

7 tending or having power to deceive ⟨It turned out that the con man had made *false* promises of easy profits.⟩ — see DECEPTIVE 1

falsehood *n* **1** a false idea or belief ⟨The possibility of a perpetual motion machine is one *falsehood* that has been disproved by modern physics.⟩ — see FALLACY 1

2 a statement known by its maker to be untrue and made in order to deceive ⟨several *falsehoods* in the witness's testimony that may be grounds for perjury⟩ — see LIE

3 the quality or state of being false ⟨Scientists eventually demonstrated the *falsehood* of the claim that prehistoric fish did not evolve lungs and legs.⟩ — see FALLACY 2

4 the tendency to tell lies ⟨a cynic who believes that politics are a veritable fount of *falsehood*⟩ — see DISHONESTY 1

falseness *n* **1** lack of faithfulness especially to one's husband or wife ⟨So that their love would never know a moment of *falseness*, Thomas Jefferson promised his dying wife that he would never remarry.⟩ — see INFIDELITY 1

2 the act or fact of violating the trust or confidence of another ⟨She could not believe that her so-called best friend could ever be guilty of such *falseness*.⟩ — see BETRAYAL

3 the quality or state of being false ⟨The *falseness* of your reasoning is so blatant that it's no wonder you reached that absurd conclusion.⟩ — see FALLACY 2

falsify *vb* **1** to change so much as to create a wrong impression or alter the meaning of ⟨Taking that statement completely out of context essentially *falsifies* it, whether that's your intention or not.⟩ — see GARBLE

2 to prove to be false ⟨Telephone records *falsified* his claim that he wasn't home that night.⟩ — see DISPROVE

falsity *n* **1** a false idea or belief ⟨the *falsity* that the stars influence behavior⟩ — see FALLACY 1

2 a statement known by its maker to be untrue and made in order to deceive ⟨The witness was accused of telling *falsities*.⟩ — see LIE

3 lack of faithfulness especially to one's husband or wife ⟨The *falsity* of Guinevere usually figures prominently in medieval and modern tellings of the legend of King Arthur.⟩ — see INFIDELITY 1

4 the act or fact of violating the trust or confidence of another ⟨Despite being offered a fortune to spill the president's secrets, the trusted aide declared that he'd sooner die than be guilty of such *falsity*.⟩ — see BETRAYAL

5 the quality or state of being false ⟨The *falsity* of Columbus's estimate of the earth's circumference was pretty much demonstrated when he made a head-on collision with the western hemisphere.⟩ — see FALLACY 2

falter *vb* **1** to show uncertainty about the right course of action ⟨Martin Luther King, Jr. never once *faltered* in his demand for equal rights.⟩ — see HESITATE

2 to swing unsteadily back and forth or from side to side ⟨The cut tree seemed to *falter* for a moment before crashing to the ground.⟩ — see TEETER 1

faltering *n* a state or an instance of temporary inaction because of uncertainty about the right course of action ⟨When it's so clear that this is the right thing to do, there's no excuse for *faltering*.⟩ — see HESITATION

fame *n* **1** the fact or state of being known to the public ⟨Many go to Hollywood in search of *fame* and fortune.⟩
synonyms celebrity, notoriety, renown
related words infamy; character, mark, name, report, reputability, reputation, repute; cachet, place, position, prestige, rank, standing, stature, status; megastardom, popularity, stardom, superstardom; distinction, eminence, glory, greatness, honor, illustriousness, note, preeminence, prominence, visibility; acclaim, accolade, acknowledgment (*or* acknowledgement), homage, laurels, praise, recognition; adoration, idolization
near antonyms disgrace, dishonor, disrepute, ignominy, odium, opprobrium, shame; inconspicuousness, invisibility; unpopularity
antonyms anonymity, oblivion, obscureness, obscurity

2 overall quality as seen or judged by people in general ⟨He has some *fame* locally as an honest antiques dealer.⟩ — see REPUTATION

famed *adj* widely known ⟨San Francisco's *famed* Golden Gate Bridge⟩ — see FAMOUS 1

familial *adj* of or relating to a household or family ⟨It's a *familial* duty as well as a tradition for everyone in my family to eat dinner together.⟩ — see DOMESTIC 1

familiar *adj* **1** closely acquainted ⟨the little inside jokes that people who have long been *familiar* like to share⟩
synonyms bosom, chummy, close, friendly, intimate, thick, tight
related words clannish, close-knit, tight-knit; affable, boon, companionable, convivial, cordial, genial, gracious, hearty; gregarious, sociable, social; comfortable, cozy, easy, snug; amicable, neighborly; confidential, secretive; adoring, affectionate, dear, devoted, fond, loving, tender, tenderhearted, warm
near antonyms aloof, antisocial, cold, cool, detached, distant, frosty, remote, reserved, standoffish, unfriendly, unsociable, withdrawn
antonyms distant

2 having information especially as a result of study or experience ⟨book editors who are *familiar* with what is being taught in the schools⟩
synonyms abreast, acquainted, conversant, informed, knowledgeable, up, up-to-date, versed
related words alive, aware, cognizant, conscious, heedful, mindful, sensible, sentient
phrases at home, in the know
near antonyms insensible, unaware, unconscious, unmindful; blind, oblivious, unknowing, unwitting; inattentive, unheeding
antonyms ignorant, unacquainted, unfamiliar, uninformed, unknowledgeable

3 often observed or encountered ⟨The woman and her pair of Welsh corgis were a *familiar* sight in the quiet neighborhood.⟩ — see COMMON 1

4 showing a lack of proper social reserve or modesty ⟨Rather too *familiar* for a first-time guest in our home, the woman kept asking how much we paid for this or for that.⟩ — see PRESUMPTUOUS 1

familiar *n* **1** someone who regularly spends time in a particular place ⟨A longtime *familiar* of the gym, she would most likely have been there on the day in question.⟩ — see DENIZEN 1

2 a person who has a strong liking for and trust in another ⟨With old *familiars* the normally reserved writer can be quite warm and funny.⟩ — see FRIEND 1

familiarity *n* **1** the state of being in a very personal or private relationship ⟨The elderly couple enjoys a *familiarity* that is the result of many years of happy marriage.⟩
synonyms chumminess, closeness, inseparability, intimacy, nearness
related words immediacy; affinity, kinship; commitment, devotedness, devotion; affection, attachment, fondness, love, passion; constancy, faithfulness, fidelity; amity, fellowship, friendship, goodwill; affability, conviviality, cordiality, geniality; mutuality; cliquishness, clubbiness
near antonyms aloofness, coolness, remoteness, reserve
antonyms distance

2 a socially improper or unsuitable act or remark ⟨Placing his hand on my shoulder was just one *familiarity* by the car salesman that I did not appreciate.⟩ — see IMPROPRIETY 2

3 knowledge gained by personal experience ⟨The restaurant critic's considerable *familiarity* with restaurant kitchens should stand her in good stead.⟩ — see ACQUAINTANCE

familiarize *vb* **1** to give information to ⟨The general's day-to-day duties included *familiarizing* the president on international developments.⟩ — see ENLIGHTEN 1

2 to impart knowledge of a new thing or situation to ⟨One office worker is assigned with the task of *familiarizing* new staffers with the use of electronic equipment around the office.⟩ — see ACQUAINT 1

family *n* **1** a group of persons who come from the same ancestor ⟨The Adams *family* made remarkable contributions to American life for more than two centuries.⟩
synonyms blood, clan, folks, house, kin, kindred, kinfolk (*or* kinfolks), kinsfolk, line, lineage, people, race, stock, tribe
related words blended family, nuclear family; extended family, household, kith; brood; descendant (*also* descendent), issue, offspring, progeny, scion, seed; clansman, kinsman, kinswoman, relative; dynasty; nation, nationality
near antonyms ancestry, birth, descent, extraction, origin, pedigree

2 one of the units into which a whole is divided on the basis of a common characteristic ⟨the flute, the clarinet, the oboe, and other members of the woodwind *family*⟩ — see CLASS 2

family tree *n* the line of ancestors from whom a person is descended ⟨His *family tree* includes writers, musical composers, and other notables in the arts.⟩ — see ANCESTRY

famine *n* a falling short of an essential or desirable amount or number ⟨There's a *famine* of good general practitioners in many rural areas.⟩ — see DEFICIENCY

famished *adj* **1** feeling a desire or need for food ⟨After a full day of skiing, I was feeling absolutely *famished.*〉 — see HUNGRY 1

2 lacking money or material possessions 〈They held a food drive to help *famished* families in their own community.〉 — see POOR 1

famishment *n* a need or desire for food 〈There's something about outdoor activity that invariably increases one's *famishment.*〉 — see HUNGER 1

famous *adj* **1** widely known 〈a book about some of the most *famous* people of the last century〉

synonyms celebrated, famed, noted, notorious, prominent, renowned, star, visible, well-known

related words fabled, fabulous, legendary; infamous; distinguished, eminent, exceptional, great, illustrious, leading, notable, noteworthy, outstanding, preeminent, prestigious, remarkable, supereminent, superior; important, significant; acknowledged, respected; favorite, popular, preferred

near antonyms insignificant, unimportant; inconspicuous; undistinguished, unexceptional; unpopular

antonyms anonymous, nameless, obscure, uncelebrated, unknown, unsung

2 of the very best kind 〈some truly *famous* Southern-style cooking〉 — see EXCELLENT

fan *n* a person with a strong and habitual liking for something 〈lifelong *fans* of country and western music〉

synonyms addict, aficionado (*also* afficionado), buff, bug, devotee, enthusiast, fanatic, fancier, fiend, fool, freak, head, hound, junkie (*also* junky), lover, maniac, nut, sucker

related words groupie; admirer, amateur, collector, connoisseur, dilettante; authority, expert; adherent, convert, cultist, disciple, follower, hanger-on, votary; advocate, apostle, backer, champion, evangelist, exponent, friend, patron, promoter, proponent, supporter; partisan (*also* partizan), zealot; booster, rooter, well-wisher; faddist

near antonyms nonadmirer; belittler, carper, critic, detractor

antonyms nonfan

fan (out) *vb* **1** to arrange the parts of (something) over a wider area 〈The accordionist smoothly *fanned out* the bellows of his instrument as he played.〉 — see OPEN 3

2 to extend outwards from or as if from a central point 〈Most of the city's subway lines *fan out* from this central station.〉 — see RADIATE 1

fanatic *n* **1** a person with a strong and habitual liking for something 〈Football *fanatics* are pretty much booked up for weekends from Labor Day to Super Bowl Sunday.〉 — see FAN

2 one who is intensely or excessively devoted to a cause 〈Once he joined the movement, he became a *fanatic.*〉 — see ZEALOT

fanatic *or* **fanatical** *adj* being very far from the center of public opinion 〈Because of her *fanatical* views, her friends know better than to discuss the issues with her.〉 — see EXTREME 2

fancier *n* a person with a strong and habitual liking for something 〈Chocolate *fanciers* generally like their favorite confection without the addition of milk or a lot of sugar.〉 — see FAN

fanciful *adj* **1** conceived or made without regard for reason or reality 〈She harbors the *fanciful* notion that she has a talent for singing.〉 — see FANTASTIC 1

2 not real and existing only in the imagination 〈the *fanciful* creatures that J.R.R. Tolkien created for his Middle Earth novels〉 — see IMAGINARY

fancy *adj* **1** made or done with great care or with much detail 〈We're having a little get-together after the concert—nothing *fancy.*〉 — see ELABORATE 1

2 going beyond a normal or acceptable limit in degree or amount 〈I would rather go without than pay the hotel bar's *fancy* prices.〉 — see EXCESSIVE

fancy *n* **1** a conception or image created by the imagination and having no objective reality 〈a writer with a prodigious talent for creating *fancies* that captivate readers young and old〉 — see FANTASY 1

2 a sudden impulsive and apparently unmotivated idea or action 〈Is this a serious interest in music, or just your latest *fancy* that will be forgotten after a week?〉 — see WHIM

3 positive regard for something 〈Now that he's rich he's taken a *fancy* to expensive sports cars.〉 — see LIKING

4 the ability to form mental images of things that either are not physically present or have never been conceived or created by others 〈To fans of Lewis Carroll, the animal creations of his fertile *fancy* are as real as any creature to be found at the zoo.〉 — see IMAGINATION 1

fancy *vb* **1** to form a mental picture of 〈Try to *fancy*, if you can, our mother on an elephant when she was touring India.〉 — see IMAGINE 1

2 to take pleasure in 〈The teacher didn't *fancy* the idea of failing the student, even if he was the class clown.〉 — see ENJOY 1

fanny *n* the part of the body upon which someone sits 〈Be careful on that icy walk, unless you want to fall on your *fanny.*〉 — see BUTTOCKS

fantastic *also* **fantastical** *adj* **1** conceived or made without regard for reason or reality 〈a *fantastic* scheme for getting rich quick〉

synonyms absurd, bizarre, crazy, fanciful, foolish, insane, nonsensical, preposterous, unreal, wild

related words implausible, inconceivable, incredible, unbelievable, unimaginable, unthinkable; extravagant, grotesque; curious, eccentric, far-out, funny, kinky, kooky (*also* kookie), odd, outlandish, out-of-the-way, peculiar, quaint, quirky, screwy, strange, wacky (*also* whacky), way-out, weird; farcical, laughable, ludicrous, ridiculous; nightmarish; dreamlike, surreal

phrases off the wall [*slang*]

antonyms realistic, reasonable

2 excitingly or mysteriously unusual 〈a story about a *fantastic* land filled with unimaginable riches〉 — see EXOTIC

3 not real and existing only in the imagination 〈a science fiction writer who can conjure up *fantastic* worlds and make them seem as real as our own〉 — see IMAGINARY

4 too extraordinary or improbable to believe 〈concocted some *fantastic* story to try to explain why they had returned home so late〉 — see INCREDIBLE

5 fantastic of the very best kind 〈Surfing conditions were simply *fantastic*!〉 — see EXCELLENT

fantasy *vb* to form a mental picture of 〈She regularly *fantasies* exciting adventures.〉 — see IMAGINE 1

fantasy *also* **phantasy** *n* **1** a conception or image created by the imagination and having no objective reality 〈a constant daydreamer who started to believe his own *fantasies*〉

synonyms chimera, conceit, daydream, delusion, dream, fancy, figment, hallucination, illusion, nonentity, phantasm (*also* fantasm), pipe dream, unreality, vision

related words ignis fatuus, mirage, will-o'-the-wisp; idea; concoction, fable, fabrication, fiction, invention; envisaging, imaging, visualization; cloud-cuckoo-land, cloudland, utopia; daymare, nightmare

phrases castle in Spain, castle in the air

near antonyms actuality, fact, reality

2 the ability to form mental images of things that either are not physically present or have never been conceived or created by others ⟨The painter gave free rein to his *fantasy* to create pictures that capture the kind of reality we experience only in our dreams.⟩ — see IMAGINATION 1

3 something that is the product of the imagination ⟨We were coming to the conclusion that the person Karen "saw" in the woods was another one of her *fantasies*.⟩ — see FICTION

far *adj* **1** lasting for a considerable time ⟨the primitive rafts that ancient peoples built for their *far* journeys across the wide expanses of Oceania⟩ — see LONG 2

2 not close in time or space ⟨the dream of someday sending astronauts to explore the *far* reaches of our solar system⟩ — see DISTANT 1

far *adv* to a great degree ⟨the solid advice that if you can't say something good about a person, it is *far* better to say nothing at all⟩ — see VERY 1

faraway *adj* not close in time or space ⟨Growing up in a seaport instilled in the youth a restless desire to travel to *faraway* places.⟩ — see DISTANT 1

farce *n* **1** a poor, insincere, or insulting imitation of something ⟨The recall of a duly elected official for a frivolous reason is not democracy in action but a *farce*.⟩ — see MOCKERY 1

2 humorous entertainment ⟨The rubber-faced, loose-jointed comedian is a master of knockabout *farce*.⟩ — see COMEDY 1

farcical *adj* **1** causing or intended to cause laughter ⟨the *farcical* behavior of the troupe of circus clowns⟩ — see FUNNY 1

2 so foolish or pointless as to be worthy of scornful laughter ⟨the *farcical* routine that a person has to go through to get a refund from that company⟩ — see RIDICULOUS 1

fare *n* substances intended to be eaten ⟨That restaurant is well-known for serving only fresh, seasonal *fare* from local suppliers.⟩ — see FOOD

fare *vb* **1** to meet one's day-to-day needs ⟨The shepherd went to see how the lambs were *faring* on the upper pastures.⟩ — see GET ALONG 1

2 to move forward along a course ⟨Families can be seen *faring* along the road to the campground while driving or towing all manner of conveyance.⟩ — see GO 1

3 to take a meal ⟨Diners at this charming country inn will *fare* sumptuously in an authentic colonial atmosphere.⟩ — see DINE 1

farewell *adj* given, taken, or performed at parting ⟨The singer's *farewell* tour seemed to last almost as long as her entire career.⟩ — see PARTING

farewell *n* **1** an expression of good wishes at parting ⟨The exchange student and her host family said their tearful *farewells*, promising to keep in touch.⟩ — see GOOD-BYE

2 the act of leaving a place ⟨Before making his final *farewell*, the company president personally spoke to as many employees as he could.⟩ — see DEPARTURE 1

3 the act or process of two or more persons going off in different directions ⟨Our *farewell* was rushed, and we didn't say all that we wanted to before heading off to colleges at opposite ends of the country.⟩ — see PARTING 1

far-fetched *adj* not likely to be true or to occur ⟨an exciting thriller, but one with a *far-fetched* plot that no sensible person could believe⟩ — see IMPROBABLE

far-flung *adj* **1** having considerable extent ⟨It could once be said that the sun never set on the *far-flung* British Empire.⟩ — see EXTENSIVE

2 not close in time or space ⟨traveled to *far-flung* towns that had not seen a doctor in years⟩ — see DISTANT 1

farm *n* a piece of land and its buildings used to grow crops

or raise livestock ⟨a *farm* that has been in the same family for five generations⟩

synonyms estate, farmstead, grange, ranch

related words farmland, farmyard; farmhouse, hacienda, homestead, manor, plantation, spread; garden, orchard

farm *vb* to work by plowing, sowing, and raising crops on ⟨We're planning on *farming* 50 acres the first year.⟩

synonyms cultivate, tend, till

related words crop, plant; harvest, reap; harrow, hoe; sharecrop

farmer *n* a person who cultivates the land and grows crops on it ⟨a young *farmer* whose family has been growing wheat for many generations⟩

synonyms agriculturist (*or* agriculturalist), agronomist, cultivator, grower, planter, tiller

related words farmhand, field hand, gleaner, harvester, plowman, reaper; workfolk (*or* workfolks); gentleman farmer, sharecropper, subsistence farmer, tenant farmer, yeoman; homesteader, nester [*West*]; granger; rancher, ranchero, ranchman

antonyms nonfarmer

farming *adj* engaged in or concerned with agriculture ⟨grew up in a small *farming* community⟩ — see AGRICULTURAL

farming *n* the science or occupation of cultivating the soil, producing crops, and raising livestock ⟨Since an ancestor settled there in the 19th century, *farming* has been the only occupation for six generations of the family.⟩ — see AGRICULTURE

farmstead *n* a piece of land and its buildings used to grow crops or raise livestock ⟨Many of the area's proud, old *farmsteads* are still in use.⟩ — see FARM

far-off *adj* not close in time or space ⟨Many a young person has joined the military with the hope of traveling to *far-off* places.⟩ ⟨the impossibility of predicting what life will be like in the *far-off* future⟩ — see DISTANT 1

far-out *adj* different from the ordinary in a way that causes curiosity or suspicion ⟨wearing some *far-out* clothes⟩ — see ODD 2

far-reaching *adj* having considerable extent ⟨To the pioneers the *far-reaching* prairies seemed like an endless sea of grass.⟩ — see EXTENSIVE

farsighted *adj* having or showing awareness of and preparation for the future ⟨*Farsighted* conservationists long ago realized that wilderness areas of breathtaking beauty needed to be protected from future development.⟩ — see FORESIGHTED

farsightedness *n* concern or preparation for the future ⟨Thanks to our *farsightedness*, we had sufficient emergency supplies when the storm knocked out our power.⟩ — see FORESIGHT 2

farther *adj* resulting in an increase in amount or number ⟨For *farther* information on this condition, you should consult your family physician.⟩ — see ADDITIONAL

farther *adv* at or to a greater distance or more advanced point ⟨They had traveled *farther* down the Colorado River than any previous explorers.⟩

synonyms beyond, further, yon, yonder

farthermost *adj* most distant from a center ⟨It's a long trip to a major hospital for residents of the *farthermost* corners of the state.⟩ — see EXTREME 1

farthest *adj* most distant from a center ⟨For privacy and quiet, we requested a hotel room that was *farthest* from the elevator.⟩ — see EXTREME 1

fascinate *vb* **1** to attract or delight as if by magic ⟨For years the zoo's family of giant pandas have *fascinated* visitors.⟩ — see CHARM 1

2 to hold the attention of as if by a spell ⟨I can gaze at the sea for hours, *fascinated* by the never-ending waves crashing upon the shore.⟩ — see ENTHRALL 1

3 to hold the attention of ⟨The subject of artificial intelligence *fascinates* me.⟩ — see ENGAGE 1

fascinating *adj* **1** having an often mysterious or magical power to attract ⟨The *fascinating* paintings of the Renaissance were on display at the museum.⟩

synonyms alluring, appealing, attractive, bewitching, captivating, charming, elfin, enchanting, engaging, entrancing, fetching, glamorous (*also* glamourous), luring, magnetic, seductive

related words absorbing, arresting, engrossing, enthralling, gripping, hypnotic, hypnotizing, mesmerizing, riveting, spellbinding; enticing, tantalizing, tempting; exciting, haunting, interesting, intriguing, titillating; beckoning, inviting, winning; darling, delightful, pleasant, pleasing

near antonyms boring, irksome, tedious, tiresome, wearisome; abhorrent, abominable, appalling, awful, distasteful, hideous, horrendous, horrible, horrid, invidious, loathsome, nauseating, noisome, obnoxious, odious, offensive, shocking, sickening; drab, dreary, dull, flat, humdrum, jading, leaden, monotonous, pedestrian, ponderous

antonyms repellent (*also* repellant), repelling, repugnant, repulsive, revolting, unalluring

2 holding the attention or provoking interest ⟨the *fascinating*—but dubious—legend that Pocahontas rescued John Smith from certain death⟩ — see INTERESTING

fascination *n* the power of irresistible attraction ⟨the *fascination* that the subject of dinosaurs has for most children⟩ — see CHARM 2

fashion *n* **1** a practice or interest that is very popular for a short time ⟨always tried to keep up with the latest *fashion*⟩ — see FAD

2 a distinctive way of putting ideas into words ⟨When angry, he tends to express himself in an unbecoming *fashion*.⟩ — see STYLE 1

3 a usual manner of behaving or doing ⟨It has long been my *fashion* to rise early.⟩ — see HABIT 1

4 the means or procedure for doing something ⟨You can mix the ingredients in any *fashion* you choose—by hand or by machine.⟩ — see METHOD

5 high position within society ⟨an event attended by people of *fashion* from all over the city⟩ — see RANK 2

6 the outward appearance of something as distinguished from its substance ⟨Over the millennia, nature had worked the face of the rocky cliff into the *fashion* of a man's head.⟩ — see FORM 1

fashion *vb* **1** to change (something) so as to make it suitable for a new use or situation ⟨The ex-governor seems to be *fashioning* his political beliefs to win favor with a more conservative national electorate.⟩ — see ADAPT

2 to bring into being by combining, shaping, or transforming materials ⟨For the Christmas pageant the boy's mother was able to *fashion* the length of fabric into something that could pass as a shepherd's outfit.⟩ — see MAKE 1

fashionable *adj* **1** being in the latest or current fashion ⟨a shopping district filled with expensive boutiques selling *fashionable* clothing from the top designers⟩ — see STYLISH

2 enjoying widespread favor or approval ⟨That breed of dog became *fashionable* after it became the preferred dog among Hollywood celebrities.⟩ — see POPULAR 1

fashionableness *n* **1** the state of enjoying widespread approval ⟨The *fashionableness* of that look skyrocketed after it began to show up on some very fashionable people.⟩ — see POPULARITY

2 the quality or state of being fashionable ⟨the *fashionableness* of jeans⟩ — see COOL 2

fast *adj* **1** moving, proceeding, or acting with great speed ⟨The *fast* pace of construction resulted in our new house being done ahead of schedule.⟩

synonyms blistering, breakneck, breathless, brisk, dizzy, fleet, fleet-footed, flying, hasty, hot, lightning, nippy, quick, rapid, rapid-fire, rattling, snappy, speedy, swift, whirlwind, zippy

related words expeditious, prompt, ready; accelerated, hastened, hurried, quickened, rushed; breathtaking; energetic, strenuous, strong, vigorous; high-speed; rush; ultrafast, ultrarapid

near antonyms crawling, dallying, dawdling, dillydallying, dragging, laggard, languid, lingering, plodding, poking, poky (*or* pokey), slowish, sluggish, unhurried; deliberate, leisurely, measured; dilatory, late, tardy; ultraslow

antonyms slow

2 firm in one's allegiance to someone or something ⟨The two girls soon became *fast* and inseparable friends.⟩ — see FAITHFUL 1

3 firmly positioned in place and difficult to dislodge ⟨The rusty, old screws are so *fast* in the fitting that there's no hope of getting them out.⟩ — see TIGHT 2

4 given to or marked by cheating and deception ⟨Rolling back odometers was just one of the *fast* practices that the used-car dealer was guilty of.⟩ — see DISHONEST 2

5 marked by the ability to withstand stress without structural damage or distortion ⟨As the storm approached, we checked to see that every thing on the outside of the house was *fast* and locked in position.⟩ — see STABLE 1

6 not lasting for a considerable time ⟨After a *fast* explanation of the procedure, we were turned loose to do the work.⟩ — see SHORT 2

7 having or showing quickness of mind ⟨I don't know how to operate this machine, but I'm a *fast* learner.⟩ — see INTELLIGENT 1

fast *adv* **1** with great speed ⟨Run as *fast* as you can to get help.⟩

synonyms apace, briskly, fleetly, full tilt, hastily, hot, posthaste, presto, pronto, quick, quickly, rapidly, snappily, soon, speedily, swift, swiftly

related words immediately, promptly, readily; impetuously, impulsively, rashly, recklessly; abruptly, suddenly; energetically, vigorously

phrases a mile a minute, at full throttle, at full tilt, by leaps and bounds, in a hurry, in short order, like a shot, like gangbusters, like wildfire

near antonyms laggardly, lingeringly, ploddingly, sluggishly; deliberately, leisurely; tardily

antonyms slow, slowly

2 to a full extent or degree ⟨Everyone in camp was *fast* asleep within minutes of hitting the sack.⟩ — see FULLY 1

fasten *vb* **1** to cause (something) to hold to another ⟨Use this paper clip to *fasten* your picture to the application form.⟩

synonyms affix, attach, bend, fix

related words adhere, bolt, cinch, clamp, clasp, clench, clinch, clip, glue, hang, harness, hasp, lace, lash, latch, nail, paste, pin, plaster, rivet, screw, shackle, staple, stick, strap, tack, tackle, tie, toggle, yoke; coapt, connect, join, link, unite; reaffix, reattach, refasten, refix, resecure; batten, belay, button

near antonyms break up, disconnect, disjoin, disjoint, dissever, dissociate, disunite, divide, divorce, part, separate, sever, split, sunder, uncouple, unlink, unyoke; loose, loosen; unbind, unfix, unlash, untie

antonyms detach, undo, unfasten, unhook

2 to put securely in place or in a desired position 〈Don't forget to *fasten* all the lines on your tent.〉
synonyms anchor, catch, clamp, fix, hitch, moor, secure, set
related words embed (*also* imbed), entrench (*also* intrench), implant, ingrain (*also* engrain), lodge, stuff, wedge
near antonyms extract, prize, pry, pull, root (out), tear (out), uproot, wrest, yank
antonyms loose, loosen, unfasten, unfix, unloose, unloosen
3 to fix (as one's attention) steadily toward a central objective 〈If you could *fasten* your attention on one task for more than a minute, you just might get something done.〉 — see CONCENTRATE 2
fastidious *adj* hard to please 〈He is very *fastidious* about how he arranges his collection, and woe to anyone who dares to mess around with it.〉 — see FINICKY
fastness *n* **1** a high rate of movement or performance 〈The amazing *fastness* with which the boy took his shower had us wondering if he'd used any water.〉 — see SPEED 1
2 a structure or place from which one can resist attack 〈The guerillas retreated to their network of hidden *fastnesses* deep within the mountains.〉 — see FORT
3 adherence to something to which one is bound by a pledge or duty 〈His uncompromising *fastness* to the cause of freedom was beyond question.〉 — see FIDELITY
fast–track *vb* to cause to move or proceed fast or faster 〈We're going to *fast-track* this project so that the product is in the stores for the holiday shopping season.〉 — see HURRY 1
fat *n* **1** individuals carefully selected as being the best of a class 〈High-end grocery chains will pay very high prices for produce that is the *fat* of the harvest.〉 — see ELITE 1
2 the state or an instance of going beyond what is usual, proper, or needed 〈claimed that there was absolutely no *fat* in the military's budget〉 — see EXCESS
3 the condition of having an excess of body fat 〈an exercise program to help you gain strength and lose *fat*〉 — see CORPULENCE
fat *adj* **1** having an excess of body fat 〈the popular image of Santa Claus as a *fat* man in a red suit〉
synonyms chubby, corpulent, fleshy, full, obese, overweight, plump, portly, pudgy, replete, roly-poly, rotund, round, tubby
related words beefy, bulky, chunky, heavy, heavyset, plumpish, stocky, stout, thick, thickset, weighty; brawny, burly, hefty, husky; dumpy, squat, stubby; hippy; flabby, soft
near antonyms angular, gaunt, lank, lanky, rawboned, sinewy; cadaverous, emaciated, haggard, pinched, skeletal, wasted; puny, scraggy, scrawny, slight; rangy, reedy, spindling, spindly, stringy, svelte, sylphlike, twiggy, waspish, weedy, willowy; anorexic
antonyms lean, skinny, slender, slim, spare, thin
2 containing or seeming to contain the greatest quantity or number possible 〈The lake is so *fat* with trout that you probably could catch fish with a bare hook.〉 — see FULL 1
3 having a greater than usual measure across 〈A set of *fat* encyclopedia volumes once took up the whole shelf.〉 — see WIDE 1
4 having or being of relatively great depth or extent from one surface to its opposite 〈a *fat* slice of watermelon〉 — see THICK 1
5 producing abundantly 〈the *fat* soil in the river's delta〉 — see FERTILE
6 yielding a profit 〈The highly sought-after baseball player signed a *fat* contract that set a record for the major leagues.〉 — see PROFITABLE 1

fatal *adj* **1** bringing about ruin or misfortune 〈I made the *fatal* mistake of sharing my secret with the office's biggest blabbermouth.〉
synonyms calamitous, cataclysmal (*or* cataclysmic), catastrophic, destructive, disastrous, fateful, ruinous, unfortunate
related words hapless, ill-fated, ill-starred, luckless; adverse, baleful, baneful, damaging, deleterious, detrimental, evil, harmful, hurtful, ill, injurious, noxious, pernicious, prejudicial
near antonyms fluky (*also* flukey), fortuitous, fortunate, happy, lucky, providential; auspicious, bright, encouraging, fair, golden, heartening, hopeful, optimistic, promising, propitious, rose-colored, rosy, upbeat
2 likely to cause or capable of causing death 〈That snake's venom is *fatal* unless the victim is given the antidote almost immediately.〉 — see DEADLY 1
fatality *n* a person or thing harmed, lost, or destroyed 〈A number of passengers were injured but there were no *fatalities*.〉 — see CASUALTY 1
fate *vb* to determine the fate of in advance 〈the warning that the lack of an advanced education will *fate* a person to a lifetime of below-average earnings〉 — see DESTINE
fate *n* **1** a state or end that seemingly has been decided beforehand 〈the belief that it was this country's *fate* to extend from sea to sea〉
synonyms circumstance, destiny, doom, fortune, lot, portion
related words accident, chance, happenstance, hazard, luck; predestination; aftereffect, aftermath, conclusion, consequence, development, effect, fruit, issue, outcome, outgrowth, result, resultant, sequel, sequence, upshot
2 a condition or occurrence traceable to a cause 〈The *fate* of the presidential election hinged on a few thousand votes in a single state.〉 — see EFFECT 1
3 the permanent stopping of all the vital bodily activities 〈He met his *fate* in a tragic highway accident.〉 — see DEATH 1
fateful *adj* bringing about ruin or misfortune 〈a *fateful* encounter with a confidence man that they would long regret〉 — see FATAL 1
fathead *n* a stupid person 〈Sorry I was such a *fathead* and I forgot your birthday.〉 — see IDIOT
father *n* **1** a male human parent 〈the special relationship that exists between *fathers* and sons〉
synonyms dad, daddy, old man, pa, papa (*also* poppa), pop, sire
related words paterfamilias, patriarch; father figure, father image; stepfather
2 a person who establishes a whole new field of endeavor 〈Sir Isaac Newton is regarded by many as the *father* of modern science.〉
synonyms author, begetter, creator, establisher, founder, generator, inaugurator, initiator, instituter (*or* institutor), originator, sire
related words cocreator, cofounder; conceiver, contriver, designer, deviser, formulator, innovator, introducer, inventor, spawner; builder, maker, producer; developer, pioneer, researchist; organizer, promoter; encourager, galvanizer, inspiration, inspirer
near antonyms disciple, follower, pupil, student, supporter
3 a person who is several generations earlier in an individual's line of descent 〈Our *fathers* founded this nation on the fundamental belief that no person is entitled to rule by divine right.〉 — see ANCESTOR 1
4 *cap* the being worshipped as the creator and ruler of the universe 〈Let us ask humbly for the blessings of our *Father* in heaven.〉 — see DEITY 2

father *vb* to become the father of ⟨Paul Revere somehow found room in his small house for the large family he had *fathered*.⟩

synonyms beget, get, sire

related words multiply, procreate, propagate, reproduce, spawn; bear, engender, gender, generate, produce

fatherland *n* the land of one's birth, residence, or citizenship ⟨Though they had lived in their adopted country for many years, the immigrant families never broke their ties with the *fatherland* entirely.⟩ — see COUNTRY 1

fathom *vb* to measure the depth of (as a body of water) typically with a weighted line ⟨The pilot had to continually *fathom* the river, which drought conditions had lowered to unprecedented levels.⟩ — see ²SOUND 1

fatigue *vb* to use up all the physical energy of ⟨The rescue workers pressed on, though their efforts to reach the miners had almost completely *fatigued* them.⟩ — see EXHAUST 1

fatigue *n* a complete depletion of energy or strength ⟨The day-long battle against the blaze left firefighters in a state of utter *fatigue*.⟩

synonyms burnout, collapse, exhaustion, frazzle, lassitude, prostration, tiredness, weariness

related words debilitation, debility, disablement, enfeeblement, faintness, feebleness, frailness, frailty, impotence, infirmity, weakness; overfatigue; languor, listlessness; sluggishness, slumber, torpidity; apathy, inertia, passiveness, passivity

near antonyms bounce, dash, drive, energy, ginger, go, liveliness, pep, punch, sap, snap, starch, verve, vigor, vim, vitality, zing, zip; might, muscle, potency, power, puissance, strength; briskness, jauntiness, spiritedness, sprightliness, vivaciousness, vivacity

antonyms refreshment, rejuvenation, rejuvenescence, revitalization

fatigued *adj* depleted in strength, energy, or freshness ⟨The *fatigued* hikers paused for some much-needed fun and frolic in the woodland stream.⟩ — see WEARY 1

fatness *n* the condition of having an excess of body fat ⟨He advised his patients that *fatness* was unhealthy.⟩ — see CORPULENCE

fatty *adj* containing animal fat especially in unusual amounts ⟨*fatty* ground beef that was the cheapest available⟩

synonyms adipose

related words greasy; lardy, rich

near antonyms fibrous, gristly, stringy, tough; nonfat

antonyms defatted, lean

fatuity *n* 1 a foolish act or idea ⟨Building another mall in an area that seems to already have a surplus of them seems like a gross *fatuity*.⟩ — see FOLLY 1

2 lack of good sense or judgment ⟨the *fatuity* of the homeowner who used gasoline to burn a pile of brushwood⟩ — see FOOLISHNESS 1

3 the quality or state of lacking intelligence or quickness of mind ⟨was patient with my *fatuity* when it came to electronics⟩ — see STUPIDITY 1

fatuous *adj* 1 not having or showing an ability to absorb ideas readily ⟨The *fatuous* questions that the audience members asked after the lecture suggested to the oceanographer that they had understood little.⟩ — see STUPID 1

2 showing or marked by a lack of good sense or judgment ⟨Ignoring the avalanche warnings, the *fatuous* skiers continued on their course.⟩ — see FOOLISH 1

faucet *n* a fixture for controlling the flow of a liquid ⟨Don't forget to turn off the *faucet*.⟩

synonyms cock, gate, spigot, stopcock, tap, valve

related words hydrant, spout; petcock

fault *vb* to express one's unfavorable opinion of the worth or quality of ⟨You should look at your own work before *faulting* what others have done.⟩ — see CRITICIZE

fault *n* 1 a defect in character ⟨the common *fault* of being quick to judge others⟩

synonyms demerit, dereliction, failing, foible, frailty, shortcoming, sin, vice, want, weakness

related words blot, spot, stain; blemish, deficiency, flaw, imperfection, minus, nit; Achilles' heel, soft spot; corruption, depravity, evil, immorality, sinfulness, wickedness

phrases feet of clay

near antonyms excellence, perfection; goodness, integrity, morality, probity, rectitude, righteousness

antonyms merit, virtue

2 an unintentional departure from truth or accuracy ⟨There's a *fault* somewhere in the program.⟩ — see ERROR 1

3 responsibility for wrongdoing or failure ⟨Getting the time of the performance wrong was entirely my *fault*.⟩ — see BLAME 1

4 something that spoils the appearance or completeness of a thing ⟨The minor *faults* in the leather are entirely natural and are what gives it a look different from vinyl.⟩ — see BLEMISH

5 the state of being held as the cause of something that needs to be set right ⟨The auto accident was entirely the other driver's *fault*.⟩ — see RESPONSIBILITY 1

faultfinder *n* a person given to harsh judgments and to finding faults ⟨I hate to be a *faultfinder*, but the invitation has a spelling error.⟩ — see CRITIC 1

faultfinding *adj* given to making or expressing unfavorable judgments about things ⟨Publishers now have to produce textbooks that pass muster with a slew of *faultfinding* committees.⟩ — see CRITICAL 1

faultily *adv* in a mistaken or inappropriate way ⟨discovered that the foreign ambassador's statement had been *faultily* translated⟩ — see WRONGLY

faultless *adj* 1 being entirely without fault or flaw ⟨This 18th-century chest of drawers is considered a *faultless* example of early American craftsmanship.⟩ — see PERFECT 1

2 free from guilt or blame ⟨I may have broken my share of things in the past, but in this instance I am entirely *faultless*.⟩ — see INNOCENT 2

faultlessly *adv* without any flaws or errors ⟨At the recital the young piano student performed the sonata *faultlessly*.⟩ — see PERFECTLY 1

faultlessness *n* the quality or state of being free from guilt or blame ⟨The coach assured the disappointed players of their *faultlessness* in the loss.⟩ — see INNOCENCE 1

faulty *adj* having a fault ⟨The cause of the power failure was traced to *faulty* wiring.⟩

synonyms amiss, bad, defective, flawed, imperfect

related words fallible; blemished, broken, crippled, damaged, defaced, disfigured, harmed, hurt, impaired, injured, marred, spoiled, vitiated; deficient, inadequate, incomplete, insufficient, wanting

phrases on the blink

near antonyms complete, entire, intact, whole; unblemished, undamaged, unimpaired, unspoiled

antonyms faultless, flawless, impeccable, perfect

faux *adj* being such in appearance only and made with or manufactured from usually cheaper materials ⟨The kitchen counters were made of *faux* marble.⟩ — see IMITATION

favor *vb* 1 to do a service or favor for ⟨Although she was at the party as a guest, the singer *favored* us with a song.⟩ — see OBLIGE 1

2 to have a favorable opinion of ⟨If this measure will

reduce our property taxes, then I *favor* it.⟩ — see AP-PROVE (OF)

3 to show partiality toward ⟨Older moviegoers tend to *favor* films that have certain extras—like a plot and developed characters.⟩ — see PREFER 1

4 to furnish freely or naturally with some power, quality, or attribute ⟨*favored* with good looks⟩ — see ENDOW 1

favor *n* **1** an act of kind assistance ⟨a good and generous friend who is always doing *favors* for others⟩
synonyms benevolence, boon, courtesy, grace, indulgence, kindness, mercy, service, turn
related words dispensation, waiver; advantage, benefit, blessing, godsend, manna; liberty, license (*or* licence), privilege
near antonyms hindrance, hurdle, impediment, interference, obstacle

2 a feeling of great approval and liking ⟨Entertainers often learn that the *favor* of the public can be fickle indeed.⟩ — see ADMIRATION 1

3 an acceptance of something as satisfactory ⟨Over the years that kind of movie fell out of *favor* with the mass audience.⟩ — see APPROVAL

4 an attitude that always favors one way of feeling or acting especially without considering any other possibilities ⟨Although his own son is on the hockey team that he coaches, Mr. Watkins conscientiously avoids any show of *favor*.⟩ — see BIAS 1

5 positive regard for something ⟨was willing to do just about anything to keep the boss's *favor*⟩ — see LIKING

6 the state of enjoying widespread approval ⟨The pop band fell out of *favor* almost overnight.⟩ — see POPULARITY

favorable *adj* **1** expressing approval ⟨*Favorable* reviews for the movie were widespread.⟩
synonyms admiring, applauding, appreciative, approving, commendatory, complimentary, friendly, good, positive
related words accepting, warm; encomiastic, eulogistic, flattering, laudative, laudatory, panegyrical, praiseful; respectful, supportive, sympathetic; adoring, adulatory, idolizing, worshipful, worshipping (*also* worshiping); advisory, recommendatory
near antonyms captious, carping, caviling (*or* cavilling), censuring, critical, faultfinding, hypercritical, overcritical; belittling, contemptuous, disdainful, disparaging, scornful, slighting
antonyms adverse, depreciative, depreciatory, derogatory, disapproving, inappreciative, negative, unappreciative, uncomplimentary, unfavorable, unflattering, unfriendly

2 pointing toward a happy outcome ⟨*favorable* economic conditions for opening a new business⟩
synonyms auspicious, bright, encouraging, golden, heartening, hopeful, promising, propitious
related words fortuitous, fortunate, happy, lucky, providential; advantageous, beneficial, profitable, prosperous, salutary; idealist, idealistic, romantic, utopian, visionary
near antonyms unfortunate, unhappy, unlucky; calamitous, catastrophic, disastrous, fatal, ruinous; baleful, dark, dire, direful, doomy, foreboding, gloomy, ill, menacing, ominous, portentous, sinister; threatening
antonyms dim, discouraging, disheartening, futureless, hopeless, inauspicious, unfavorable, unpromising, unpropitious

3 promoting or contributing to personal or social well-being ⟨He moved to a region with a milder climate in the hope that it would be more *favorable* to his health.⟩ — see BENEFICIAL

favorably *adv* in a pleasing way ⟨Her violin teacher has been *favorably* impressed with her progress.⟩ — see WELL 5

favored *adj* **1** granted special treatment or attention ⟨The youngest child was also the most *favored*.⟩ — see DARLING 1

2 singled out from a number or group as more to one's liking ⟨For a *favored* few, the restaurant always has a table available, no matter how busy it is.⟩ — see SELECT 1

favorite *adj* **1** granted special treatment or attention ⟨That teacher claims not to have any *favorite* students.⟩ — see DARLING 1

2 singled out from a number or group as more to one's liking ⟨Mint chocolate chip is my *favorite* flavor of ice cream.⟩ — see SELECT 1

3 enjoying widespread favor or approval ⟨a radio station that mostly plays *favorite* songs from the 1960s and 1970s⟩ — see POPULAR 1

favorite *n* a person or thing that is preferred over others ⟨The youngest child was always Mother's *favorite*.⟩
synonyms darling, minion, pet, preference, speed
related words beloved, dear, sweetheart; jewel, prize, treasure
phrases cup of tea
near antonyms abomination, anathema, bête noire, bugbear

fawn *vb* to use flattery or the doing of favors in order to win approval especially from a superior ⟨a student who could not wait to *fawn* over the new teacher⟩
synonyms fuss, kowtow, suck (up), toady
related words drool, gush, slaver, slobber; endear, ingratiate; court, woo; adulate, idolize, worship; blandish, cajole, coax, flatter, overpraise, soft-soap; cower, cringe, grovel; abase, debase, demean; defer, submit, yield
phrases curry favor, kiss up to
near antonyms despise, disdain, scorn; gibe (*or* jibe), jeer, scoff; brave, challenge, defy

fawner *n* a person who flatters another in order to get ahead ⟨Having surrounded himself with *fawners* who gave him only good news, the governor had no idea of the true state of affairs.⟩ — see SYCOPHANT

fay *adj* given to good-natured joking or teasing ⟨a *fay* girl who was popular with the other students⟩ — see PLAYFUL

faze *vb* to throw into a state of self-conscious distress ⟨The collapse of part of the scenery didn't *faze* the actors one bit, and they just carried on.⟩ — see EMBARRASS 1

fealty *n* adherence to something to which one is bound by a pledge or duty ⟨As much as I wanted to back my friend up, my *fealty* to the truth was greater, and I could not lie for him.⟩ — see FIDELITY

fear *vb* to experience concern or anxiety ⟨Her friends *feared* that she was counting too much on getting the job.⟩ — see WORRY 1

fear *n* **1** the emotion experienced in the presence or threat of danger ⟨The sight of the headless horseman filled the schoolmaster with *fear*.⟩
synonyms alarm (*also* alarum), anxiety, dread, fearfulness, fright, horror, panic, scare, terror, trepidation
related words phobia; creeps, jitters, nervousness, willies; pang, qualm, twinge; agitation, apprehension, consternation, discomposure, disquiet, funk, perturbation; concern, dismay, worry; cowardice, faintheartedness, timidity, timorousness
near antonyms aplomb, assurance, boldness, confidence, self-assurance, self-confidence; bravery, courage, courageousness, daring, dauntlessness, doughtiness, fearlessness, fortitude, gallantry, hardihood, intrepidity, intrepidness, stoutness, valor; audacity, guts, nerve

2 an uneasy state of mind usually over the possibility of an anticipated misfortune or trouble ⟨*Fear* for her family's safety drove her to seek help from neighbors she hardly knew.⟩ — see ANXIETY 1

fearful *adj* **1** causing fear ⟨the *fearful* roar of a lion⟩
synonyms alarming, dire, direful, dread, dreadful, fearsome, forbidding, formidable, frightening, frightful, ghastly, hair-raising, horrendous, horrible, horrifying, intimidating, redoubtable, scary, shocking, terrible, terrifying
related words daunting, demoralizing, disconcerting, discouraging, dismaying, disquieting, distressing, disturbing, perturbing, startling, threatening, troubling, trying, unnerving; creepy, eerie (*also* eery), weird; appalling, atrocious, awful, grisly, gruesome (*also* grewsome), hideous, horrid, macabre, monstrous, nightmarish
near antonyms calming, comforting, consoling, inviting, lulling, pacifying, quieting, reassuring, relaxing, soothing, tranquilizing (*also* tranquillizing); nonintimidating, nonthreatening
2 easily frightened ⟨The stray cat that we took in is still *fearful*, even around us.⟩ — see SHY 1
3 extreme in degree, power, or effect ⟨The *fearful* wind and cold simply made being outside a miserable experience.⟩ — see INTENSE 1
4 filled with fear or dread ⟨*Fearful* of venturing out onto the dark highway, the stranded motorist decided to wait in the car for help.⟩ — see AFRAID

fearfulness *n* the emotion experienced in the presence or threat of danger ⟨The veterinarian was adept at easing the *fearfulness* of her animal patients.⟩ — see FEAR 1

fearless *adj* feeling or displaying no fear by temperament ⟨Skydiving is one sport that tends to attract *fearless* types.⟩ — see BRAVE 1

fearlessness *n* strength of mind to carry on in spite of danger ⟨the admirable *fearlessness* shown by the pioneers of the civil rights movement⟩ — see COURAGE

fearsome *adj* **1** causing fear ⟨At night the child would always imagine that there were *fearsome* monsters lurking under his bed.⟩ — see FEARFUL 1
2 extreme in degree, power, or effect ⟨After working all afternoon in the hot sun, I had developed a *fearsome* thirst.⟩ — see INTENSE 1
3 easily frightened ⟨The more *fearsome* of the two children would only peer at the guests from a distance.⟩ — see SHY 1

feasible *adj* capable of being done or carried out ⟨Would it be *feasible* to build a cabin in so short a time?⟩ — see POSSIBLE 1

feast *n* **1** a large fancy meal often accompanied by ceremony or entertainment ⟨They celebrated their 50th wedding anniversary with a *feast* at a fancy banquet hall with their closest friends and family.⟩
synonyms banquet, dinner, feed, spread
related words chow, mess, repast, table; blowout, carnival, festival, fete (*or* fête), gala, party, shindig; festivity; barbecue (*also* barbeque), clambake, cookout, fry, luau, roast; buffet, luncheon
2 a source of great satisfaction ⟨The colorful Mardi Gras parade is a *feast* for the senses.⟩ — see DELIGHT 1
3 an amount or supply more than sufficient to meet one's needs ⟨On the Internet there's a *feast* of information about this historical event.⟩ — see PLENTY 1

feast *vb* **1** to entertain with a fancy meal ⟨The returning war heroes were *feasted* all over the country.⟩
synonyms banquet, dine, junket, regale
related words board, cater, feed, provision; fete (*or* fête), honor, recognize
2 to give satisfaction to ⟨*Feast* your eyes on all the fresh flowers at the farmers' market.⟩ — see PLEASE 1

feat *n* **1** an act of notable skill, strength, or cleverness ⟨Washington's legendary *feat* of tossing a silver dollar across the Rappahannock River⟩
synonyms deed, exploit, number, stunt, trick
related words accomplishment, achievement, attainment, coup, success, triumph; adventure; performance
2 something done by someone ⟨Famously rich, the oil magnate is today remembered less for his *feats* than for his finances.⟩ — see ACTION 1

feather *n* **1** a number of persons or things that are grouped together because they have something in common ⟨The two brothers are sports-obsessed and most of their friends are of the same *feather*.⟩ — see SORT 1
2 dressy clothing ⟨Prom couples strutted into the ballroom in full *feather*.⟩ — see FINERY
3 a state of mind dominated by a particular emotion ⟨You're in fine *feather* today!⟩ — see MOOD 1

featherbrained *adj* lacking in seriousness or maturity ⟨Some *featherbrained* youngsters giggled through the ceremonies.⟩ — see GIDDY 1

feathery *adj* having little weight ⟨The apple pie had a wonderfully *feathery* crust.⟩ — see ¹LIGHT 1

feature *n* something that sets apart an individual from others of the same kind ⟨Perhaps the most striking *feature* of that house is the way it was constructed to fit into its hillside site.⟩ — see CHARACTERISTIC

feature *vb* **1** to indicate the importance of by centering attention on ⟨a restaurant *featuring* an extensive menu of creative American cuisine⟩ — see EMPHASIZE 1
2 to form a mental picture of ⟨I can't *feature* that guy wearing anything other than his usual jeans and T-shirt.⟩ — see IMAGINE 1

feces *pl n* solid matter discharged from an animal's alimentary canal ⟨examined the animal's *feces* for signs of intestinal parasites⟩ — see DROPPING 1

fecund *adj* producing abundantly ⟨The Franklin stove, bifocals, and the lightning rod are just a few of the inventions that we owe to the *fecund* creativity of Benjamin Franklin.⟩ — see FERTILE

federate *vb* to form or enter into an association that furthers the interests of its members ⟨In the years following World War II, the U.S. and the nations of western Europe made the decision to *federate* as the North Atlantic Treaty Organization.⟩ — see ALLY

federation *n* an association of persons, parties, or states for mutual assistance and protection ⟨The new organization is a *federation* of existing organizations that were all dedicated to preserving Civil War battlefields.⟩ — see CONFEDERACY

fed up *adj* having one's patience, interest, or pleasure exhausted ⟨*Fed up* with the noise and bustle of the big city, the family decided to try country life.⟩ — see WEARY 2

fee *n* the amount of money that is demanded as payment for something ⟨My dentist's *fees* seem to increase with every visit.⟩ — see PRICE 1

feeble *adj* lacking bodily strength ⟨He was too *feeble* to take more than a few steps.⟩ — see WEAK 1

feebleness *n* the quality or state of lacking physical strength or vigor ⟨The patient felt a lingering *feebleness* in the weeks following her heart surgery.⟩ — see WEAKNESS 1

feed *n* **1** a large fancy meal often accompanied by ceremony or entertainment ⟨The company barbecue was an elaborate *feed* that was enlivened by country music and dancing.⟩ — see FEAST 1
2 food eaten or prepared for eating at one time ⟨After soccer practice we were all ready for a hot shower and a satisfying *feed*.⟩ — see MEAL

feed *vb* **1** to provide food or meals for ⟨a charity dedicated to *feeding* the hungry⟩
synonyms board, cater, provision, victual

related words serve, wait; nourish, nurture, sustain; banquet, dine, feast, regale; mess; batten, fatten, fill; force-feed, overfeed, surfeit; underfeed; hand-feed, spoon-feed; refeed, reprovision

2 to put (something) into the possession of someone for use or consumption ⟨All week long colleagues have been *feeding* me ideas for a magazine article.⟩ — see FURNISH 2

3 to take a meal ⟨an all-you-can-eat buffet where families can *feed* heartily and fairly inexpensively⟩ — see DINE 1

feed (on, upon, *or* off) *vb* to seize and eat (something) as prey ⟨The flycatcher is a bird that—as its name suggests—*feeds on* winged insects in midair.⟩ — see PREY (ON *or* UPON)

feel *n* an indefinite physical response to a stimulus ⟨the warm *feel* that fine cashmere gives⟩ — see SENSATION 1

feel *vb* **1** to have a vague awareness of ⟨I *feel* trouble brewing in the town.⟩

synonyms perceive, scent, see, sense, smell, taste

related words behold, descry, discern, distinguish, espy, eye, look (at), note, notice, observe, perceive, regard, remark, sight, spy, view, witness; ascertain, catch on (to), discover, find out, hear, learn, realize; anticipate, divine, expect, foreknow, foresee; assume, conjecture, guess, presume, speculate, suppose, surmise, suspect

2 to come into bodily contact with (something) so as to perceive a slight pressure on the skin ⟨Feel this blanket and perceive how soft it is.⟩ — see TOUCH 1

3 to come to a knowledge of (something) by living through it ⟨With the birth of their first child the couple came to *feel* true happiness for the first time.⟩ — see EXPERIENCE

4 to have as an opinion ⟨I just *feel* that we haven't explored all of our options for raising funds.⟩ — see BELIEVE 2

5 to search for something blindly or uncertainly ⟨The sudden blackout had us *feeling* around in the dark for a flashlight.⟩ — see GROPE

6 to give the impression of being ⟨It *felt* like a good idea at the time.⟩ — see SEEM

feel (for) *vb* to have sympathy for ⟨a reminder that during the holidays we should all *feel for* those families who have members serving in the military abroad⟩ — see PITY

feeling *n* **1** a subjective response to a person, thing, or situation ⟨an overall *feeling* of happiness about their new home⟩

synonyms emotion, passion, sentiment

related words impression, perception, sensation, sense; angle, outlook, perspective, standpoint, viewpoint; belief, conviction, judgment (*or* judgement), mind, notion, opinion, persuasion, verdict, view; receptiveness, receptivity, responsiveness, sensibility, sensitiveness, sensitivity

near antonyms insensitiveness, insensitivity, unfeelingness

2 feelings *pl* general emotional condition ⟨a remark that thoughtlessly hurt her *feelings*⟩

synonyms heartstrings, passions, sensibilities

related words cheer, frame, humor, mode, mood, spirit, temper

3 an idea that is believed to be true or valid without positive knowledge ⟨an interesting think piece in which the congresswoman expressed her *feelings* about our nation's most pressing problems⟩ — see OPINION 1

4 an indefinite physical response to a stimulus ⟨that odd *feeling* of forward movement you get when the parked car next to you backs out⟩ — see SENSATION 1

5 sorrow or the capacity to feel sorrow for another's suffering or misfortune ⟨a rich person without much *feeling* for those who are less fortunate⟩ — see SYMPATHY 1

6 the capacity for feeling for another's unhappiness or misfortune ⟨A woman of great *feeling*, the princess wanted to use her status and influence to help the needy.⟩ — see HEART 1

feign *vb* to present a false appearance of ⟨I would never *feign* illness just to get out of a test.⟩

synonyms act, affect, assume, bluff, counterfeit, dissemble, fake, pretend, profess, put on, sham, simulate

related words dissimulate, impersonate, let on, masquerade, play, playact, pose; forge, imitate; camouflage, conceal, disguise, mask; feint; malinger

phrases make believe

feigned *adj* **1** lacking in natural or spontaneous quality ⟨The *feigned* applause that polite people give after a bad concert.⟩ — see ARTIFICIAL 1

2 not being or expressing what one appears to be or express ⟨the *feigned* looks of innocence I got when I asked who had broken the lamp⟩ — see INSINCERE

felicitate *vb* to express to (someone) admiration for his or her success or good fortune ⟨The other pianists rushed to *felicitate* the winner of the piano competition.⟩ — see CONGRATULATE

felicitations *pl n* best wishes ⟨our heartfelt *felicitations* on the start of your new business⟩ — see COMPLIMENT 2

felicitous *adj* **1** giving pleasure or contentment to the mind or senses ⟨A *felicitous* accompaniment to dinner is provided by a harpist on weekends at the restaurant.⟩ — see PLEASANT 1

2 meeting the requirements of a purpose or situation ⟨The museum's restaurant is featuring a French menu as a *felicitous* complement to the current show on French Impressionism.⟩ — see FIT 1

felicitously *adv* in a pleasing way ⟨The evening passed quietly but *felicitously* as we chatted with the other guests at the inn.⟩ — see WELL 5

felicitousness *n* the quality or state of being especially suitable or fitting ⟨Guests remarked on the perfect *felicitousness* of the rose garden as a site for a June wedding.⟩ — see APPROPRIATENESS

felicity *n* **1** a feeling or state of well-being and contentment ⟨Dan told his friends that marriage had brought him a *felicity* that he had never known before.⟩ — see HAPPINESS 1

2 something that provides happiness or does good for a person or thing ⟨The elderly couple counted their grandchildren as their most cherished *felicities*.⟩ — see BLESSING 2

3 the quality or state of being especially suitable or fitting ⟨the telling *felicity* of the epigraphs that precede each chapter of the novel⟩ — see APPROPRIATENESS

feline *n* a small domestic animal known for catching mice ⟨The commercial claims that the product will please the palate of even the most finicky *feline*.⟩ — see CAT

feline *adj* moving easily ⟨The thief was eerily *feline* as he moved stealthily through the darkened rooms.⟩ — see GRACEFUL 1

fell *adj* **1** likely to cause or capable of causing death ⟨planning for distribution of resources in case of some *fell* event⟩ — see DEADLY 1

2 violently unfriendly or aggressive in disposition ⟨Captain Hook was the *fell* nemesis of Peter Pan.⟩ — see FIERCE 1

fell *vb* **1** to strike (someone) so forcefully as to cause a fall ⟨a boxer who was often *felled* in the first round⟩

synonyms bowl (down *or* over), down, drop, floor, knock down, level, mow (down), prostrate

related words kayo, KO; overthrow, topple; bang, bash, belt, bludgeon, clobber, hammer, hit, jab, paste, poke, pound, punch, slam, slap, slog, slug, smack, smite, sock, swat, swipe, thump, thwack, wallop, whack, whale

2 to bring down by cutting ⟨The settlers began the daunting task of *felling* the mighty trees that blanketed the island.⟩

synonyms chop (down), cut (down), hew, mow

related words bulldoze, demolish, flatten, level, raze, tear down

3 to deprive of life ⟨the quest for a cure for malaria, the disease that *felled* so many during the digging of the Panama Canal⟩ — see KILL 1

fellow *n* **1** a male romantic companion ⟨She introduced us to her new *fellow*.⟩ — see BOYFRIEND

2 a person frequently seen in the company of another ⟨The singer's *fellows* could often be found at the club.⟩ — see ASSOCIATE 1

3 an adult male human being ⟨What does a *fellow* have to do to get waited on around here?⟩ — see MAN 1

4 either of a pair matched in one or more qualities ⟨One ice skate isn't much good without its *fellow*.⟩ — see MATE 1

5 one that is equal to another in status, achievement, or value ⟨He is well regarded as a chemist by his *fellows* in the field.⟩ — see EQUAL

fellowship *n* **1** a friendly relationship marked by ready communication and mutual understanding ⟨The new counselor is eager to develop a trustful *fellowship* with the troubled teens at the center.⟩ — see RAPPORT

2 a group of persons formally joined together for some common interest ⟨a *fellowship* of physicians dedicated to administering medical aid without regard to politics⟩ — see ASSOCIATION 2

3 kindly concern, interest, or support ⟨This music festival would not have been a success without the *fellowship* of many people in the community.⟩ — see GOODWILL 1

4 the body of people in a profession or field of activity ⟨She violated just about every ethical principle that the legal *fellowship* holds dear.⟩ — see CORPS

5 the feeling of closeness and friendship that exists between companions ⟨the *fellowship* that exists among members of a college fraternity⟩ — see COMPANIONSHIP

felonious *adj* contrary to or forbidden by law ⟨The investigators found that while his actions were ethically questionable, they were not *felonious*.⟩ — see ILLEGAL 1

female *adj* of, relating to, or marked by qualities traditionally associated with women ⟨The composer's new music calls for *female* voices.⟩ — see FEMININE

female *n* an adult female human being ⟨There are an equal number of males and *females* at the school.⟩ — see WOMAN 1

feminine *adj* of, relating to, or marked by qualities traditionally associated with women ⟨a designer adding *feminine* touches to the clothing collection⟩

synonyms female, womanish, womanlike, womanly

related words girlie (or girly), girlish; effeminate, effete, unmanly; ladylike

near antonyms boyish, hoydenish, tomboyish; male, manlike, manly, mannish, masculine, virile; neuter; hairy-chested, hypermasculine

antonyms unfeminine, unwomanly

fen *n* spongy land saturated or partially covered with water ⟨a day spent trudging through the *fens* in quest of game birds⟩ — see SWAMP

fence *n* a physical object that blocks the way ⟨The only way to prevent motorists from trying to use that unsafe bridge is to put a *fence* across the road leading to it.⟩ — see BARRIER

fence *vb* to drive danger or attack away from ⟨He had worked as a bodyguard, *fencing* a number of pop stars at big events.⟩ — see DEFEND 1

fence (in) *vb* to close or shut in by or as if by barriers ⟨*Fencing in* the yard would keep our dog in as well as keep unwanted stray dogs out.⟩ — see ENCLOSE 1

fend (off) *vb* to drive back ⟨The herd *fended off* the attacking hyenas.⟩ — see REPEL 1

fender *n* something that serves as a protective barrier ⟨Not wanting our brand-new cabin cruiser to get scratched, we put thick rubber *fenders* between it and the dock.⟩ — see CUSHION

feral *adj* living outdoors without taming or domestication by humans ⟨Animal experts discourage homeowners from trying to adopt *feral* animals as pets.⟩ — see WILD 1

ferment *n* a disturbed or uneasy state ⟨The city was in *ferment* as its residents nervously awaited the outcome of the referendum vote.⟩ — see UNREST

ferment *vb* to bring (something volatile or intense) into being ⟨the various social and economic factors that *fermented* the major cultural change during the U.S. during the 1960s⟩ — see INCITE 1

ferocious *adj* **1** extreme in degree, power, or effect ⟨the *ferocious* appetite that athletic teenagers have been known to display⟩ — see INTENSE 1

2 marked by bursts of destructive force or intense activity ⟨*Ferocious* forest fires threatened to destroy hundreds of homes in the scrubland.⟩ — see VIOLENT 1

3 violently unfriendly or aggressive in disposition ⟨The animal is notorious as a *ferocious* predator.⟩ — see FIERCE 1

4 marked by great and often stressful excitement or activity ⟨After a day of *ferocious* trading, the stock market was up 200 points.⟩ — see FURIOUS 1

ferret (out) *vb* to come upon after searching, study, or effort ⟨The reporter *ferreted out* the facts behind the case.⟩ — see FIND 1

ferry *vb* **1** to support and take from one place to another ⟨There are shuttle buses to *ferry* visitors from the parking lots to the fairground.⟩ — see CARRY 1

2 to travel on water in a vessel ⟨We're planning to *ferry* to several islands in the Lesser Antilles.⟩ — see SAIL 1

fertile *adj* producing abundantly ⟨The *fertile* mind of Leonardo da Vinci explored art, architecture, engineering, mathematics, and many other fields.⟩

synonyms fat, fecund, fruitful, lush, luxuriant, productive, prolific, rich

related words bearing, generative, producing, yielding; abounding, abundant, bountiful; copious, generous, liberal, plenteous, plentiful, plenitudinous; blooming, bursting, flourishing, swarming, teeming, thriving; creative, inventive, original

near antonyms meager (or meagre), scant, scanty, skimp, skimpy, spare, sparse

antonyms barren, dead, infertile, sterile, unfruitful, unproductive

fervency *n* depth of feeling ⟨The guest soloist was able to infuse the familiar hymn with a moving *fervency*.⟩ — see ARDOR 1

fervent *adj* **1** having or expressing great depth of feeling ⟨a *fervent* speech that called for tolerance and compassion for those who are different⟩

synonyms ardent, blazing, burning, charged, demonstrative, emotional, fervid, feverish, fiery, flaming, glowing, hot-blooded, impassioned, incandescent, intense, passionate, red-hot, religious, torrid, vehement, warm, warm-blooded

related words gushing, maudlin, mawkish, mushy, saccharine, sappy, schmaltzy, sentimental, sloppy, sugary;

histrionic, melodramatic; enthusiastic, gung ho, keen, zealous; enamored, infatuated, obsessed; uninhibited, unreserved, unrestrained; frenzied, orgiastic, overemotional, overexcited, overheated
phrases on fire
near antonyms detached, dry, impersonal, objective; reserved, undemonstrative
antonyms cold, cool, dispassionate, impassive, unemotional
2 having a notably high temperature ⟨In the thick, *fervent* air of a tropical afternoon, a languor set in.⟩ — see HOT 1

fervid *adj* **1** having or expressing great depth of feeling ⟨At the school board meeting the librarian delivered a *fervid* speech defending the classic novel against would-be censors.⟩ — see FERVENT 1
2 having a notably high temperature ⟨the *fervid* sands of the desert⟩ — see HOT 1

fervidness *n* depth of feeling ⟨The *fervidness* that the actor brought to the part of Romeo made the play fresh all over again.⟩ — see ARDOR 1

fervor *n* depth of feeling ⟨surprised by the *fervor* that her parents' old love letters contained when she discovered them in the attic⟩ — see ARDOR 1

fester *vb* to go through decomposition ⟨Seagulls left the remains of shellfish *festering* on the dock.⟩ — see DECAY 1

festival *n* a time or program of special events and entertainment in honor of something ⟨Tourists flock to the town for its annual strawberry *festival*.⟩
synonyms carnival, celebration, festivity, fete (*or* fête), fiesta, gala, jubilee
related words jamboree, merriment, merrymaking, rejoicing, revel, revelry; exhibit, exhibition, exposition, fair, show

festive *adj* indicative of or marked by high spirits or good humor ⟨We arrived at the Christmas party to find everyone already in a *festive* mood.⟩ — see MERRY

festivity *n* **1** a mood characterized by high spirits and amusement and often accompanied by laughter ⟨Rather than mourn our friend's death we celebrated his life, and his memorial service was more notable for its *festivity* than its funereal gloom.⟩ — see MIRTH
2 a time or program of special events and entertainment in honor of something ⟨Year-long *festivities* will mark the 300th anniversary of the city's founding.⟩ — see FESTIVAL
3 joyful or festive activity ⟨In keeping with their habit of doing everything in a big way, the couple's wedding will entail a whole weekend of *festivity*.⟩ — see MERRYMAKING

fetch *vb* to have a price of ⟨Those old toys that we tossed away are now *fetching* big bucks as antiques.⟩ — see COST

fetching *adj* **1** having an often mysterious or magical power to attract ⟨The woman's *fetching* smile has long made the painting a favorite with visitors to the museum.⟩ — see FASCINATING 1
2 very pleasing to look at ⟨a most *fetching* outfit in which to go skiing⟩ — see BEAUTIFUL 1

fetch up *vb* to bring (something) to a standstill ⟨The driver *fetched up* the horse-drawn carriage in front of the church.⟩ — see ¹HALT 1

fete *or* **fête** *n* **1** a social gathering ⟨The heiress wanted to do something with her life other than shuttle from *fete* to *fete*.⟩ — see PARTY 1
2 a time or program of special events and entertainment in honor of something ⟨The island's annual *fete* is a celebration of the daffodil in all of its springtime beauty.⟩ — see FESTIVAL

fete *or* **fête** *vb* to show appreciation, respect, or affection for (someone) with a public celebration ⟨The returning servicemen and servicewomen were *feted* with a week's worth of celebrations.⟩ — see HONOR

fetid *adj* having an unpleasant smell ⟨That *fetid* cheese from Belgium is definitely an acquired taste.⟩ — see MALODOROUS

fetish *also* **fetich** *n* **1** something about which one is constantly thinking or concerned ⟨Dieting seems to be a *fetish* with some people.⟩ — see FIXATION
2 something worn or kept to bring good luck or keep away evil ⟨an archaeologist discovering an old animal tooth that may have been worn as a *fetish*⟩ — see CHARM 1

fetter *n* **1** something that limits one's freedom of action or choice ⟨a time-honored tradition is fine as long as it doesn't become a *fetter* that prevents us from trying something new⟩ — see RESTRICTION 1
2 something that makes movement or progress difficult ⟨claims that government regulations are unnecessary *fetters* that keep him from achieving his business goals⟩ — see ENCUMBRANCE
3 something that physically prevents free movement ⟨He considered a seat belt a pointless *fetter*—until one saved his life in an auto accident.⟩ — see BOND 1

fetter *vb* **1** to confine or restrain with or as if with chains ⟨a painting depicting prisoners *fettered* with irons⟩ — see BIND 1
2 to create difficulty for the work or activity of ⟨the belief that too many rules and restrictions *fetter* children's creativity⟩ — see HAMPER

fettle *n* a state of being or fitness ⟨A visit to the relatives on the other side of the state revealed them all to be in fine *fettle*.⟩ — see CONDITION 1

fever *n* **1** an abnormal state that disrupts a plant's or animal's normal bodily functioning ⟨Before the days of modern medicine, when death remained a mystery, people said that someone died of a *fever* and left it at that.⟩ — see DISEASE
2 a state of wildly excited activity or emotion ⟨In the *fever* of a political campaign a lot of things get said that never should have been said.⟩ — see FRENZY

feverish *adj* **1** being in a state of increased activity or agitation ⟨scary stories that were the product of a *feverish* imagination⟩
synonyms agitated, excited, frenzied, heated, hectic, hyperactive, overactive, overwrought
related words hyperexcited, overexcited; afire, aflutter, atingle; anxious, dithery, edgy, het up, high-strung, hyped-up, jittery, jumpy, nervous, nervy, perturbed, tense, troubled, uneasy, unquiet, upset, uptight, wired
phrases in a lather, keyed up
near antonyms calm, collected, composed, cool, coolheaded, placid, serene, tranquil, undisturbed, unperturbed, unshaken, untroubled, unworried
2 having or expressing great depth of feeling ⟨The desperate prisoner made a *feverish* appeal for mercy.⟩ — see FERVENT 1
3 marked by great and often stressful excitement or activity ⟨working at a *feverish* pace to get the project done on time⟩ — see FURIOUS 1

few *n* a small number ⟨A *few* of the songs on the album are good, but most are forgettable.⟩
synonyms couple, handful, scatter, scattering, smattering, sprinkle, sprinkling
related words fragment, iota, jot, modicum, particle, scrap, shred, tittle, whit
near antonyms majority, most; abundance, excess, plenty, surplus; deal, gobs, heap, lot, mass, much, peck, pile,

plenitude, plenty, pot, profusion, quantity, raft, reams, slather, stack, wad, wealth
antonyms army, crowd, flock, horde, host, legion, loads, many, mountain, multitude, oodles, scads
fiancé *n* the person to whom one is engaged to be married ⟨couldn't wait to introduce her *fiancé* to all of her relatives⟩ — see BETROTHED
fiancée *n* the person to whom one is engaged to be married ⟨He and his *fiancée* work at the same company.⟩ — see BETROTHED
fiasco *n* something that has failed ⟨Undaunted by his early *fiascoes*, he continued his experiments in rocketry.⟩ — see FAILURE 3
fiat *n* an order publicly issued by an authority ⟨The school principal issued a *fiat* that caps were not to be worn inside the school.⟩ — see EDICT 1
fib *n* a statement known by its maker to be untrue and made in order to deceive ⟨the claim that everyday living would be impossible without at least a few innocent *fibs*⟩ — see LIE
fib *vb* to make a statement one knows to be untrue ⟨Bob *fibbed* and said that he had remembered to water her plants while she was away.⟩ — see ¹LIE
fibber *n* a person who tells lies ⟨research that shows that children learn to become *fibbers* at a remarkably early age⟩ — see LIAR
fiber *n* 1 the strength of mind that enables a person to endure pain or hardship ⟨A person of lesser *fiber* would not have spoken out against such an injustice.⟩ — see FORTITUDE
2 a thin, flexible structure that resembles a hair ⟨The fabric is made from a mix of synthetic *fibers*.⟩ — see HAIR 2
fibrous *adj* resembling or having the texture of a mass of strings ⟨thick, *fibrous* hair that was not easy to comb⟩ — see STRINGY
fickle *adj* 1 likely to change frequently, suddenly, or unexpectedly ⟨a *fickle* friendship that was on and off over the years⟩
synonyms capricious, changeable, changeful, flickery, fluctuating, fluid, inconsistent, inconstant, mercurial, mutable, skittish, temperamental, uncertain, unpredictable, unsettled, unstable, unsteady, variable, volatile
related words aimless, arbitrary, desultory, erratic, haphazard, hit-or-miss, irregular, random, scattered, slapdash, stray; hesitating, shaky, shilly-shally, shilly-shallying, vacillating, wavering; dicey, undependable, unreliable, untrustworthy; adaptable, mobile, protean, versatile
phrases up in the air
near antonyms equable, even, uniform; abiding, durable, lasting, permanent, persistent; dependable, reliable, sure, tried, tried-and-true, true, trustworthy, trusty
antonyms certain, changeless, constant, immutable, invariable, predictable, settled, stable, stationary, steady, unchangeable, unchanging, unvarying
2 not true in one's allegiance to someone or something ⟨When the family's fortune disappeared, so did their *fickle* friends.⟩ — see FAITHLESS
fiction *n* something that is the product of the imagination ⟨Most stories about famous outlaws of the Old West are *fictions* that have little or nothing to do with fact.⟩
synonyms fable, fabrication, fantasy (*also* phantasy), figment, invention
related words anecdote, narrative, novel, story, tale, yarn; fairy tale, falsehood, falsity, fib, lie, mendacity, misrepresentation, prevarication, untruth, whopper; make-believe
near antonyms actuality, realness
antonyms fact, materiality, reality

fictional *adj* not real and existing only in the imagination ⟨The events in the movie seemed so real to some fans that they could not believe that the whole thing was *fictional*.⟩ — see IMAGINARY
fictitious *adj* not real and existing only in the imagination ⟨His wartime exploits turned out to be entirely *fictitious*, as he had never even been in the military.⟩ — see IMAGINARY
fiddle *vb* 1 to make jerky or restless movements ⟨The executive *fiddled* with a pen as she impatiently waited for the meeting to begin.⟩ — see FIDGET
2 to rob by the use of trickery or threats ⟨conscienceless grifters who had spent their lives *fiddling* the naive⟩ — see FLEECE
fiddle (around) *vb* to spend time in aimless activity ⟨We spent the snow day just *fiddling around*.⟩
synonyms goof (around), monkey (around), play, potter (around), putter (around), trifle
related words dally, dawdle, dillydally, idle, loaf, loll, lounge; clown (around), horse around; diddle (with), tinker
near antonyms buckle (down), knuckle down, set (to), settle (down)
fiddle (with) *vb* to handle thoughtlessly, ignorantly, or mischievously ⟨I could tell that someone had been *fiddling with* my smartphone.⟩ — see TAMPER (WITH)
fidelity *n* adherence to something to which one is bound by a pledge or duty ⟨They have never wavered in their *fidelity* to the cause of freedom.⟩
synonyms adhesion, allegiance, attachment, commitment, constancy, dedication, devotedness, devotion, faith, faithfulness, fastness, fealty, loyalty, piety, steadfastness, troth
related words affection, fondness; determination, firmness, resolution; dependability, reliability, trustiness, trustworthiness
near antonyms alienation, disaffection, estrangement, separation
antonyms disloyalty, faithlessness, falseness, falsity, inconstancy, infidelity, perfidiousness, perfidy, treachery, unfaithfulness
fidget *vb* to make jerky or restless movements ⟨Small children are likely to *fidget* in church.⟩
synonyms fiddle, jerk, jig, jiggle, squirm, thrash, toss, twist, twitch, wiggle, wriggle, writhe
related words flit, flutter, twitter; quake, quiver, shake, shiver, shudder, tremble; pace
near antonyms relax, rest, unwind; calm (down), still
fidgets *pl n* a state of nervousness marked by sudden jerky movements ⟨One dental patient in the waiting room had a bad case of the *fidgets*.⟩ — see JUMPINESS
fie *interj* how surprising, doubtful, or unbelievable ⟨Fie! You expect me to believe that sorry excuse?⟩ — see NO
field *n* 1 a small area of usually open land ⟨a *field* that is the frequent site of neighborhood softball games⟩
synonyms clearing, ground, lot, parcel, plat, plot, tract
related words common(s); grass, green, greensward, lawn; glade, grassland, heathland, lea (*or* ley), meadow, moor, pasture, pastureland
2 a region of activity, knowledge, or influence ⟨the first woman to enter the *field* of medicine⟩
synonyms area, arena, business, circle, department, discipline, domain, element, firmament, front, game, line, province, realm, specialty, sphere, walk
related words frontier; study, subject; territory, turf; occupation, profession, pursuit, racket, vocation; ambit, amplitude, breadth, compass, confine, dimension(s), extent, ken, reach, scope, sweep, width; subfield, subspecialty

3 a part or portion having no fixed boundaries ⟨If you set your camera lens to small aperture, the *field* of sharp focus will be quite large.⟩ — see REGION 1

4 a place from which aircraft operate that usually has paved runways and a terminal ⟨Worsham *Field* in Corpus Christi used to be home to a sizable crop dusting operation.⟩ — see AIRPORT

5 a wide space or area ⟨The cemetery's *field* of crosses for the war's fallen seemed to stretch to infinity.⟩ — see EXPANSE

6 active fighting during the course of a war ⟨In the classroom the general had been a brilliant theoretician, but in the *field* he proved to be a wholly incompetent tactician.⟩ — see COMBAT 1

field *vb* to deal with (something) usually skillfully or efficiently ⟨The customers gave the waitress a large tip because she kept smiling as she *fielded* their many requests.⟩ — see HANDLE 1

fiend *n* **1** a mean, evil, or unprincipled person ⟨a crime committed by some *fiend*⟩ — see VILLAIN

2 a person with a strong and habitual liking for something ⟨Comic-book *fiends* seem to have their own little world.⟩ — see FAN

3 an evil spirit ⟨the legend that a *fiend* continues to haunt the castle⟩ — see DEMON 1

4 the supreme personification of evil often represented as the ruler of hell ⟨He swore that not even the *fiend* could tempt him to eat that dessert.⟩ — see DEVIL 1

5 a person with a high level of knowledge or skill in a field ⟨Our in-house computer *fiend* fixed the problem in no time.⟩ — see EXPERT

fiendish *adj* **1** of, relating to, or worthy of an evil spirit ⟨a *fiendish* delight in playing cruel tricks⟩

synonyms demoniac (*also* demoniacal), demonic (*also* demonical), devilish, diabolical (*or* diabolic), satanic

related words hellish; baleful, evil, sinister; malevolent, malicious, malignant; heinous, monstrous; immoral, iniquitous, nefarious, vicious, vile, villainous, wicked; barbarous, cruel, ferocious, inhuman, savage

near antonyms celestial, heavenly; beneficent, benevolent, benign, benignant; godly, holy, sainted, saintly; ethical, good, moral, righteous, virtuous

antonyms angelic (*or* angelical)

2 having or showing the desire to inflict severe pain and suffering on others ⟨He shook with *fiendish* laughter as he concocted his cruel plan.⟩ — see CRUEL 1

fierce *adj* **1** violently unfriendly or aggressive in disposition ⟨The Vikings had a well-earned reputation for being *fierce* warriors.⟩

synonyms fell, ferocious, grim, savage, vicious

related words argumentative, bellicose, belligerent, combative, discordant, disputatious, gladiatorial, militant, pugnacious, scrappy, warlike; bare-knuckle (*also* bare-knuckled *or* bare-knuckles), in-your-face, take-no-prisoners; menacing, threatening; brute, inhuman, inhumane; barbaric, uncivilized, wild; heartless, implacable, merciless, pitiless, relentless, ruthless, unrelenting, wanton; bloodthirsty, bloody, homicidal, murdering, murderous, sanguinary, sanguine; rapacious, ravenous, voracious

near antonyms amicable, companionable, comradely, congenial, cordial, friendly, genial, hearty, warm, warmhearted; compliant, submissive, tame; benign, compassionate, kind, merciful; pacific, peaceable, peaceful; amiable, complaisant, obliging; human, humane; civilized, cultured

antonyms gentle, mild, unaggressive

2 extreme in degree, power, or effect ⟨A *fierce* wind made the frigid temperatures seem even worse.⟩ — see INTENSE 1

3 harsh and threatening in manner or appearance ⟨the *fierce* faces of the players on the opposing hockey team⟩ — see GRIM 1

4 having or showing a bold forcefulness in the pursuit of a goal ⟨a social reformer of *fierce* and fearless determination⟩ — see AGGRESSIVE 1

5 marked by bursts of destructive force or intense activity ⟨*Fierce* fighting raged on the battlefield.⟩ — see VIOLENT 1

6 marked by great and often stressful excitement or activity ⟨*Fierce* early-morning trading sent stocks soaring.⟩ — see FURIOUS 1

fierceness *n* the quality or state of being forceful (as in expression) ⟨The *fierceness* of her denial prompted many people to wonder if maybe she was innocent after all.⟩ — see VEHEMENCE 1

fiery *adj* **1** being on fire ⟨the *fiery* interior of the furnace⟩ — see ABLAZE 1

2 having a notably high temperature ⟨the long, dangerous trek across the *fiery* desert⟩ — see HOT 1

3 having or expressing great depth of feeling ⟨The *fiery* preacher held the members of the revival meeting spellbound.⟩ — see FERVENT 1

4 marked by a lively display of strong feeling ⟨The controversial editorial sparked a page's worth of *fiery* letters to the editor.⟩ — see SPIRITED 1

5 capable of catching or being set on fire ⟨With a *fiery* vapor like that, the lighting of a single match could cause an explosion.⟩ — see COMBUSTIBLE

6 easily irritated or annoyed ⟨The man was known for his *fiery* temper.⟩ — see IRRITABLE

fiesta *n* a time or program of special events and entertainment in honor of something ⟨The city's Latino community holds a series of *fiestas* throughout the summer.⟩ — see FESTIVAL

fight *n* **1** a physical dispute between opposing individuals or groups ⟨When he was young he got into one *fight* after another.⟩

synonyms battle, clash, combat, conflict, contest, fracas, fray, hassle, scrap, scrimmage, scuffle, skirmish, struggle, tussle

related words pitched battle; brawl, free-for-all, melee (*also* mêlée), mix-up, ruckus, ruction; blows, fistfight, fisticuffs, slugfest; confrontation, duel, face-off, joust; altercation, argument, contretemps, controversy, cross fire, disagreement, dispute, falling-out, kickup, misunderstanding, quarrel, row, spat, squabble, tangle, tiff, wrangle; catfight

near antonyms truce

2 a forceful effort to reach a goal or objective ⟨The mayoral candidate pledged to lead a successful *fight* to improve the city's schools.⟩ — see STRUGGLE 1

3 an inclination to fight or quarrel ⟨a tough, streetwise kid with a lot of *fight* in him⟩ — see BELLIGERENCE

4 an often noisy or angry expression of differing opinions ⟨The sisters have their share of *fights*, but they quickly get over them.⟩ — see ARGUMENT 1

fight *vb* **1** to oppose (someone) in physical conflict ⟨a proud people who have fiercely *fought* all invaders of their homeland⟩

synonyms battle, clash (with), combat, scrimmage (with), skirmish (with), war (against)

related words duel, joust; bang, bash, bat, batter, beat, belt, bludgeon, bop, buffet, clobber, hammer, hit, knock, paste, pound, punch, slam, slap, slog, slug, smack, smite, sock, strike, swat, swipe, thump, thwack, wallop, whack, whale; box, spar; brawl; grapple, scuffle, tussle, wrestle; bump, collide

near antonyms give up, submit, surrender

2 to strive to reduce or eliminate ⟨a civil rights leader who dedicated his life to *fighting* prejudice⟩
synonyms battle, combat, contend (with), counter, oppose
related words baffle, checkmate, foil, frustrate, resist, thwart, withstand; confront, defy, face, meet
near antonyms abide, bear, endure, suffer; advocate, back, champion, endorse (*also* indorse), support, uphold
antonyms advance, cultivate, encourage, forward, foster, further, nourish, nurture, promote
3 to engage in a contest ⟨Everyone on that street seems to be *fighting* to see who can create the gaudiest holiday lighting display.⟩ — see COMPETE
4 to express different opinions about something often angrily ⟨If you kids continue to *fight*, I'm turning this car around and we're heading back home!⟩ — see ARGUE 2
5 to refuse to give in to ⟨I tried to *fight* the temptation to eat another cookie—and lost.⟩ — see RESIST
fighter *n* **1** a person engaged in military service ⟨the debate whether to send in more *fighters*⟩ — see SOLDIER
2 one that engages in the sport of fighting with the fists ⟨a program at the community center for training local youths as *fighters*⟩ — see BOXER
3 a person who takes part in a dispute ⟨We kept the two *fighters* apart until they had calmed down and could talk sensibly.⟩ — see DISPUTANT
figment *n* **1** a conception or image created by the imagination and having no objective reality ⟨Unable to find any tracks in the snow the next morning, I was forced to conclude that the shadowy figure had been a *figment* of my imagination.⟩ — see FANTASY 1
2 something that is the product of the imagination ⟨Thus far, the invisible human being has been nothing more than a *figment* of fantasy writers.⟩ — see FICTION
figurative *adj* expressing one thing in terms normally used for another ⟨the *figurative* use of "allergy" to mean "a feeling of dislike"⟩
synonyms extended, metaphoric (*or* metaphorical)
related words allegorical, emblematic (*also* emblematical), symbolic (*also* symbolical)
near antonyms literal; nonsymbolic
antonyms nonfigurative, nonmetaphorical
figure *n* **1** a character used to represent a mathematical value ⟨No doubt the *figures* on the price tags at the jewelry store are so small because the zeroes are so many.⟩ — see NUMBER 1
2 a line that traces the outer limits of an object or surface ⟨We could gradually see the *figure* of a ship coming our way through the fog.⟩ — see OUTLINE 1
3 a person who is widely known and usually much talked about ⟨*Figures* from the worlds of sport and entertainment will be guests at the White House dinner.⟩ — see CELEBRITY 1
4 a small statue ⟨Painted wooden *figures* by untrained artists can be quite valuable on today's antiques market.⟩ — see FIGURINE
5 a three-dimensional representation of the human body used especially for displaying clothes ⟨The museum features a collection of *figures* strikingly attired in suits of medieval armor.⟩ — see MANNEQUIN 1
6 a unit of decoration that is repeated all over something (as a fabric) ⟨upholstered the chair with a fabric embossed with *figures* of fleur-de-lis⟩ — see PATTERN 1
7 something that visually explains or decorates a text ⟨The layout editor could have done a better job of getting the *figures* on the same page as the specific portion of text that they are intended to illustrate.⟩ — see ILLUSTRATION 1
8 the amount of money that is demanded as payment for

something ⟨A number of the paintings at the auction sold at *figures* far higher than had been estimated.⟩ — see PRICE 1
9 the outward appearance of something as distinguished from its substance ⟨The ice sculpture at the banquet was in the *figure* of an eagle spreading its wings.⟩ — see FORM 1
10 the type of body that a person has ⟨an aging athlete who maintained a youthful *figure*⟩ — see PHYSIQUE
11 figures *pl* the act or process of performing mathematical operations to find a value ⟨a person with a good head for *figures*⟩ — see CALCULATION
12 the outward form of someone or something especially as indicative of a quality ⟨Unshaven and dirty, he presents a sorry *figure*.⟩ — see APPEARANCE 1
figure *vb* **1** to come to a judgment about after discussion or consideration ⟨We *figured* that we had better arrive early at the concert in order to get good seats.⟩ — see DECIDE 1
2 to decide the size, amount, number, or distance of (something) without actual measurement ⟨Let's *figure* the juice in the pan to be about a cup and just add it to the mix.⟩ — see ESTIMATE 2
3 to determine (a value) by doing the necessary mathematical operations ⟨The car dealer *figured* that our monthly car payment would be $357.⟩ — see CALCULATE 1
4 to have as an opinion ⟨I *figure* I have as good a chance as anyone.⟩ — see BELIEVE 2
figure out *vb* to find an answer for through reasoning ⟨a book of brainteasers that even a really clever person won't have an easy time *figuring out*⟩ — see SOLVE
figurine *n* a small statue ⟨His collection of *figurines* includes toy soldiers from every war that America has fought.⟩
synonyms figure, statuette
related words doll, dolly, hand puppet, marionette, puppet; bust, figurehead; carving, model, sculpture; dummy, form, manikin (*also* mannikin), mannequin
antonyms colossus
figuring *n* the act or process of performing mathematical operations to find a value ⟨The *figuring* of the cost of the car repair was rushed, and so it bears little resemblance to the actual result.⟩ — see CALCULATION
filch *vb* to take (something) without right and with an intent to keep ⟨Too hungry to wait until the party had started, he *filched* a cookie from the buffet table when no one was looking.⟩ — see STEAL 1
file *n* a series of persons or things arranged one behind another ⟨a long *file* of people waiting to get tickets to the game⟩ — see LINE 1
¹file *vb* to make smooth by friction ⟨beautifully *filed* nails that obviously had been done by a manicurist⟩ — see GRIND 1
²file *vb* to move along with a steady regular step especially in a group ⟨To the strains of that familiar music, this year's graduating class *filed* into the auditorium.⟩ — see MARCH 1
fill *n* soft material that is used to fill the hollow parts of something ⟨We ripped the tag off years ago, so we have no idea what the *fill* in that pillow is.⟩ — see FILLING
fill *vb* **1** to put into (something) as much as can be held or contained ⟨*Fill* the basket with apples.⟩
synonyms brim, charge, cram, heap, jam, jam-pack, load, pack, stuff
related words drench, flood, glut, swamp; bloat, bulk; crowd, crush, mat, press, ram, shove, squash, squeeze; refill, refresh, reload, repack, replenish; overcharge, overfill, overflow, saturate; honeycomb, penetrate

near antonyms lighten; deplete, drain, eliminate, exhaust; bleed, draw (off); clean, flush, purge, scour, sweep
antonyms clear, empty, evacuate, vacate, void
2 to close up so that no empty spaces remain ⟨Before starting to paint, *fill* all the cracks with putty.⟩
synonyms block, bung, dam, pack, plug, stop, stuff
related words choke, clog, close (off), clot, congest, jam, obstruct, occlude; caulk, chink, seal; repack, restuff
near antonyms excavate, hollow (out), scoop (out), shovel
3 to do what is required by the terms of ⟨Orders received by this date will be *filled* in time for early planting.⟩ — see FULFILL 1

filled *adj* containing or seeming to contain the greatest quantity or number possible ⟨*Filled* baskets of every variety of apple were available at the farmers' market.⟩ — see FULL 1

filler *n* soft material that is used to fill the hollow parts of something ⟨The vase was packed in Styrofoam *filler* to protect it during shipping.⟩ — see FILLING

fill in *vb* **1** to give information to ⟨My friend quickly *filled* me *in* on the portion of the movie that I had missed.⟩ — see ENLIGHTEN 1
2 to serve as a replacement usually for a time only ⟨Can you *fill in* for me while I'm on vacation?⟩ — see COVER 1

filling *n* soft material that is used to fill the hollow parts of something ⟨The *filling* for the parka is goose down.⟩
synonyms fill, filler, padding, stuffing
related words packing; interlining, lining, quilting; buffer, bumper, cushion, fender, pad

film *n* **1** a story told by means of a series of continuously projected pictures and a sound track ⟨We watched a *film* on insects in science class.⟩ — see MOVIE 1
2 the art or business of making a movie ⟨Visitors learned about some of the special-effects techniques used in *film*.⟩ — see MOVIE 2

filmy *adj* **1** being of a material lacking in sturdiness or substance ⟨*filmy* cobwebs covering the entryway to the cellar⟩ — see FLIMSY 1
2 very thin and easy to see through ⟨Those *filmy* curtains don't block out enough light.⟩ — see SHEER 1

filter *vb* **1** to pass through a filter ⟨Steep the tea and then *filter* it to get rid of the leaves.⟩ — see STRAIN 2
2 to remove usually visible impurities from ⟨After frying the chicken, we *filtered* the oil and kept it in the refrigerator to use again.⟩ — see CLARIFY 1

filth *n* **1** foul matter that mars the purity or cleanliness of something ⟨The *filth* in the restaurant's kitchen was unbelievable.⟩
synonyms dirt, grime, muck, smut, soil
related words scum, sewage, sewerage, slime, sludge, swill; dross, garbage, junk, litter, refuse, rubbish, scrap, trash, waste
near antonyms cleanliness, cleanness
2 the quality or state of being obscene ⟨films full of *filth* and violence⟩ — see OBSCENITY

filthiness *n* **1** the quality or state of being obscene ⟨The book was banned primarily because of the *filthiness* of the language.⟩ — see OBSCENITY
2 the state or quality of being dirty ⟨the appalling *filthiness* of the oven in the vacated apartment⟩ — see DIRTINESS

filthy *adj* **1** depicting or referring to sexual matters in a way that is unacceptable in polite society ⟨You cannot use such *filthy* language on the public airwaves.⟩ — see OBSCENE 1
2 not clean ⟨You can't go out unless you clean this *filthy* room first.⟩ — see DIRTY 1

filthy *adv* to a great degree ⟨The invention made him *filthy* rich.⟩ — see VERY 1

finagle *vb* **1** to plan out usually with subtle skill or care ⟨Let me look at my schedule and see if I can't *finagle* a visit to the museum.⟩ — see ENGINEER
2 to use dishonest methods to achieve a goal ⟨She'll *finagle* until she gets exactly what she wants.⟩ — see CHEAT 1

final *adj* **1** following all others of the same kind in order or time ⟨This will be my *final* order.⟩ — see LAST 1
2 having been established and usually not subject to change ⟨The wedding date is *final*.⟩ — see FIXED 1

finale *n* the last part of a process or action ⟨The *finale* to the festivities was a grand display of fireworks.⟩
synonyms close, closing, conclusion, consummation, end, ending, finis, finish, windup, wrap-up
related words acme, apex, climax, copestone, crown, culmination, high-water mark, meridian, peak, pinnacle, summit, tip-top, top, zenith; aftermath, anticlimax, coda, epilogue (*also* epilog), postscript; shank, tag end
near antonyms foreword, introduction, preamble, preface, prelude, prologue (*also* prolog)
antonyms beginning, dawn, opening, start

finalize *vb* **1** to bring (something) to a state where nothing remains to be done ⟨We're still *finalizing* our travel plans but hope to have them done by the end of the week.⟩ — see FINISH 1
2 to give official acceptance of as satisfactory ⟨The bank won't *finalize* the loan before Tuesday because of the holiday.⟩ — see APPROVE

finally *adv* at a later time ⟨We're making steady progress and may *finally* finish this project.⟩ — see YET 1

finance *vb* **1** to provide money for ⟨A local business kindly *financed* the high school band's trip to New York City.⟩
synonyms bankroll, capitalize, endow, fund, stake, subsidize, underwrite
related words grubstake; cofinance, refinance; advocate, aid, back, champion, endorse (*also* indorse), patronize, sponsor, support; maintain, nourish, provide (for); clear, defray, discharge, foot, liquidate, pay, pay off, pay up, quit, recompense, settle, spring (for), stand
antonyms defund
2 to furnish (as an institution) with a regular source of income ⟨established a fund to *finance* a visiting lecturer position at the local college⟩ — see ENDOW 2

finances *pl n* available money ⟨will have to take a look at our *finances* to see if we can afford it⟩ — see FUND 2

financial *adj* of or relating to money, banking, or investments ⟨The *financial* world was watching the stock market closely.⟩
synonyms fiscal, monetary, pecuniary, pocket
related words commercial
antonyms nonfinancial

find *n* something discovered ⟨That antique plate was a great garage sale *find*.⟩ — see DISCOVERY 2

find *vb* **1** to come upon after searching, study, or effort ⟨We finally *found* the information after searching dozens of Internet sites.⟩
synonyms ascertain, descry, detect, determine, discover, dredge (up), ferret (out), find out, get, hit (on *or* upon), hunt (down *or* up), learn, locate, root (out), rummage, run down, scare up, scout (up), track (down), turn up
related words espy, sight, spot; look for, search (for *or* out), seek
near antonyms lose, mislay, misplace, misset
antonyms miss, overlook, pass over
2 to come upon unexpectedly or by chance ⟨Hey, I *found* my notebook!⟩ — see HAPPEN (ON *or* UPON)

finding *n* **1** a decision made by a court or tribunal regarding a case it has heard ⟨The appeals court overturned the lower court's *finding* for the plaintiff.⟩ — see SENTENCE

2 the act or process of sighting or learning the existence of something for the first time ⟨The scientists were thrilled with the *finding* of the new fossil.⟩ — see DISCOVERY 1

find out *vb* **1** to come to an awareness of ⟨That was around the time that I *found out* I was adopted.⟩ — see DISCOVER 1

2 to come upon after searching, study, or effort ⟨I *found out* where she lived by asking her friend.⟩ — see FIND 1

fine *adv* in a satisfactory way ⟨You did just *fine* on the stress test.⟩ — see WELL 1

fine *adj* **1** consisting of very small particles ⟨the *fine* sand found on the island's beaches⟩

synonyms dusty, floury, powdery

related words smooth; filtered, pulverized, refined; superfine, ultrafine

near antonyms rough; unfiltered, unrefined; gravelly, gritty, sandy; pebbly, rocky, stony (*also* stoney); lumpy, mealy

antonyms coarse, grainy, granular, granulated

2 made or done with extreme care and accuracy ⟨the *fine* distinction between bravery and recklessness⟩

synonyms delicate, exact, hairline, hairsplitting, minute, nice, refined, subtle

related words nitpicking, quibbling; frivolous, inconsequential, inconsiderable, insignificant, negligible, petty, piddling, trifling, trivial; demanding, exacting, fastidious, finicky, fussy, meticulous, particular, picky

near antonyms apparent, clear, clear-cut, evident, manifest, obvious, open-and-shut, palpable, patent, perspicuous, plain, transparent, unambiguous, unequivocal, unmistakable; broad, indefinite; careless, heedless, incautious, slapdash, slipshod, sloppy

antonyms coarse, inexact, rough

3 being of less than usual width ⟨Use a *fine* line for the outline of the facial features you intend to carve into the pumpkin.⟩ — see NARROW 1

4 being to one's liking ⟨That arrangement is *fine* with me.⟩ — see SATISFACTORY 1

5 free from added matter ⟨That silver is .9600 *fine*.⟩ — see PURE 1

6 meeting the highest standard of accuracy ⟨making the final *fine* measurements⟩ — see PRECISE 1

7 of a level of quality that meets one's needs or standards ⟨I usually buy a different brand but this one is *fine*.⟩ — see ADEQUATE

8 of a size that is less than average ⟨Read the *fine* print.⟩ — see SMALL 1

9 of the very best kind ⟨a *fine* performance of a classic ballet⟩ — see EXCELLENT

10 having qualities that appeal to a refined taste ⟨savored every morsel of the restaurant's *fine* cuisine⟩ — see CHOICE 1

11 able to sense slight impressions or differences ⟨hearing so *fine* that it can seemingly hear the tiniest twig snap⟩ — see ACUTE 1

12 having or showing elegance ⟨a *fine* old structure in the city's historic district⟩ — see ELEGANT 1

fine *n* a sum of money to be paid as a punishment ⟨a $50 *fine* for speeding⟩

synonyms damages, forfeit, forfeiture, mulct, penalty

related words reparations; assessment, award, compensation; indemnity

¹fine *vb* to establish or apply as a charge or penalty ⟨The police will *fine* you for driving with one headlight out.⟩ — see IMPOSE

²fine *vb* to remove usually visible impurities from ⟨materials used to *fine* glass⟩ — see CLARIFY 1

fineness *n* **1** the quality or state of being little in size ⟨The

fineness of the grains of sand enhances the appeal of the beach.⟩ — see SMALLNESS

2 the quality or state of being very accurate ⟨the *fineness* of the telescope's lens and mirror⟩ — see PRECISION

3 the state or quality of having a delicate structure ⟨the *fineness* of the cat's bones⟩ — see DELICACY 2

4 dignified or restrained beauty of form, appearance, or style ⟨There's a *fineness* to the jewelry designs of Fabergé that elevates them to the level of decorative art.⟩ — see ELEGANCE

finery *n* dressy clothing ⟨The guests arrived at the wedding in all their *finery*.⟩

synonyms array, best, bravery, caparison, feather, frippery, full dress, gaiety (*also* gayety), regalia

related words apparel, attire, costume, duds, habiliment(s), rags, raiment, rig, threads, togs, wear

phrases best bib and tucker

near antonyms tatters

finesse *n* mental skill or quickness ⟨maneuvered his opponent to checkmate with his customary *finesse*⟩ — see DEXTERITY 1

finesse *vb* **1** to plan out usually with subtle skill or care ⟨I had to *finesse* the schedule a bit to fit in another patient that afternoon.⟩ — see ENGINEER

2 to get or keep away from (as a responsibility) through cleverness or trickery ⟨He tried to *finesse* the blame for the fiasco, even though he was in charge at the time.⟩ — see ESCAPE 2

finicky *adj* hard to please ⟨Cats have a reputation for being *finicky* eaters.⟩

synonyms choosy (*or* choosey), dainty, delicate, demanding, exacting, fastidious, fussy, nice, particular, picky

related words discerning, discriminating, selective; insightful, knowledgeable; captious, carping, caviling (*or* cavilling), critical, faultfinding, hypercritical, overcritical; careful, meticulous, painstaking, punctilious, scrupulous; queasy (*also* queazy), squeamish; peevish, petulant, prickly, touchy; prim, prissy

near antonyms affable, breezy, carefree, devil-may-care, happy-go-lucky, lackadaisical, laid-back, low-pressure, relaxed; flexible, lax, loose; lenient, permissive; uncritical; indiscriminating, undiscriminating

antonyms undemanding, unfastidious, unfussy

finis *n* the last part of a process or action ⟨If the two countries keep up their arms race, the inevitable *finis* to their rivalry will be their mutual destruction.⟩ — see FINALE

finish *n* **1** the last part of a process or action ⟨A pie-eating contest is the fair's traditional *finish*.⟩ — see FINALE

2 the stopping of a process or activity ⟨an all-out fight right to the *finish*⟩ — see END 1

finish *vb* **1** to bring (something) to a state where nothing remains to be done ⟨We should *finish* the painting of the house by tomorrow.⟩

synonyms complete, consummate, finalize, perfect, polish

related words stick out; accomplish, achieve, effect; carry out, carry through, discharge, do, execute, fulfill (*or* fulfil), perform; ameliorate, amend, better, enhance, enrich, improve, meliorate; machine, refine, round (off *or* out), shine, touch up

near antonyms abandon, desert, discontinue, drop, forsake, quit

2 to bring (an event) to a natural or appropriate stopping point ⟨We'll *finish* the concert before dark.⟩ — see CLOSE 3

3 to come to an end ⟨The three-day race *finished* yesterday.⟩ — see CEASE 1

finished *adj* brought or having come to an end ⟨The

frosting isn't *finished* until you've added all of the decorative roses.⟩ — see COMPLETE 2

finite *adj* **1** having a limit ⟨Our nation's natural resources are abundant, but they are also *finite*.⟩
synonyms limited
related words circumscribed, restricted; definable, defined, definite, determinate, discrete; decided, established, fixed, set; exact, precise, specific; measurable, mensurable, numerable
near antonyms unconfined, unrestricted; immeasurable, indefinite, indeterminate, measureless, undefinable, undefined, unfathomable
antonyms boundless, endless, illimitable, infinite, limitless, unbounded, unlimited
2 having distinct or certain limits ⟨We have a *finite* number of options to consider.⟩ — see LIMITED 1

fire *n* **1** a destructive burning ⟨a number of suspicious *fires* in the neighborhood recently⟩
synonyms conflagration, holocaust, inferno
related words blaze, flare-up; backfire, bonfire, brush fire, campfire, forest fire, wildfire; arson
2 depth of feeling ⟨She has the *fire* in her heart that a run for the White House requires.⟩ — see ARDOR 1
3 a test of faith, patience, or strength ⟨He asked to be sent to the front lines, as he was eager to prove himself in the *fire* of battle.⟩ — see TRIAL 1

fire *vb* **1** to cause (a projectile) to be driven forward with force ⟨police officers *firing* rubber bullets⟩ — see SHOOT 1
2 to cause a weapon to release a missile with great force ⟨Soldiers *fired* at the enemy in panic-stricken disorder.⟩ — see SHOOT 2
3 to give life, vigor, or spirit to ⟨A school outing to the natural history museum *fired* his imagination, and he grew up to become an eminent paleontologist.⟩ — see ANIMATE
4 to let go from office, service, or employment ⟨*fired* him for always showing up late⟩ — see DISMISS 1
5 to send through the air especially with a quick forward motion of the arm ⟨*fired* a pass to the running back⟩ — see THROW 1
6 to set (something) on fire ⟨lit some kindling before attempting to *fire* the logs⟩ — see BURN 2

fire (up) *vb* to rouse to strong feeling or action ⟨The dynamic speaker *fired up* the audience as no one had previously done.⟩ — see PROVOKE 1

firearm *n* a portable weapon from which a shot is discharged by gunpowder ⟨will need a permit to carry a *firearm*⟩ — see GUN 1

firebrand *n* a person who stirs up public feelings especially of discontent ⟨a *firebrand* who urged crowds to protest⟩ — see AGITATOR

firebug *n* a person who deliberately and unlawfully sets fire to a building or other property ⟨After the second suspicious fire, police set a trap for the *firebug*.⟩ — see ARSONIST

fireproof *adj* incapable of being burned ⟨Remember to store valuable papers in a *fireproof* box.⟩ — see INCOMBUSTIBLE

fireside *n* the place where one lives ⟨couldn't wait to get off the plane and back to his comfortable *fireside*⟩ — see HOME 1

fireworks *pl n* an outburst or display of excited anger ⟨Can we have a calm, rational discussion without the usual *fireworks*?⟩ — see TANTRUM

firing *n* a directed propelling of a missile by a firearm or artillery piece ⟨Experts found a flaw in the gun's *firing*.⟩ — see SHOT 1

firm *n* a commercial or industrial activity or organization ⟨merged with another *firm* to become a major player in the brokerage business⟩ — see ENTERPRISE 1

firm *adj* **1** not showing weakness or uncertainty ⟨a friendly fellow with a ready smile and a *firm* handshake⟩
synonyms forceful, hearty, iron, lusty, robust, solid, stout, strong, sturdy, vigorous
related words hard, ironclad, mighty, powerful, tough, unyielding; animated, brisk, energetic, frisky, jaunty, jazzy, lively, peppy, perky, spirited, sprightful, sprightly, springy, vital, vivacious, zippy; assured, certain, confident, sanguine, secure, sure
near antonyms feeble, fragile, frail; limp, listless, spiritless; diffident, insecure, self-doubting; characterless, effete, frail, spineless, weakened, wimpy, wishy-washy
antonyms uncertain, weak
2 having a consistency that does not easily yield to pressure ⟨cold butter that was too *firm* to spread⟩
synonyms compact, hard, rigid, solid, stiff, unyielding
related words compacted, compressed, hardened, indurated, stiffened, tempered; close, dense, heavy, thick, thickset; inelastic, inflexible, ramrod, unbending; compressed, condensed; adamantine, rocklike; sturdy, substantial; impenetrable, impermeable, nonporous
near antonyms loose, scattered, thin; bendable, elastic, flexible, malleable, pliable, pliant, supple; droopy, flaccid, floppy, lank, limp, slack; airy, light; permeable, porous; ultrasoft
antonyms flabby, soft, spongy, squashy, squishy
3 firmly positioned in place and difficult to dislodge ⟨was *firm* in the saddle during the canter⟩ — see TIGHT 2
4 fully committed to achieving a goal ⟨We asked him to reconsider, but he was *firm* in his commitment to the project.⟩ — see DETERMINED 1
5 having been established and usually not subject to change ⟨The selling price of the house is *firm*, so there'll be no dickering.⟩ — see FIXED 1
6 marked by the ability to withstand stress without structural damage or distortion ⟨built on a *firm* foundation, so the house hasn't settled⟩ — see STABLE 1
7 based on sound reasoning or information ⟨He insists that his argument is *firm*.⟩ — see GOOD 1

firm (up) *vb* to become physically firm or solid ⟨Wait for the modeling clay to *firm up* before handling the finished pot.⟩ — see HARDEN 1

firmament *n* **1** the expanse of air surrounding the earth ⟨The stars in the *firmament* twinkled ever so brightly.⟩ — see SKY 1
2 a region of activity, knowledge, or influence ⟨a major figure in the classical music *firmament*⟩ — see FIELD 2

firmly *adv* in a vigorous and forceful manner ⟨Andy stomped his feet *firmly* to get the snow off his boots.⟩ — see HARD 3

firmness *n* **1** firm or unwavering adherence to one's purpose ⟨a woman of remarkable *firmness* in the achievement of the goals she has set for herself⟩ — see DETERMINATION 1
2 the ability to withstand force or stress without being distorted, dislodged, or damaged ⟨Test the *firmness* of the concrete before parking the car on it.⟩ — see STABILITY 1

first *adv* **1** as a substitute ⟨Eat anchovies? I'd eat dirt *first*.⟩ — see INSTEAD
2 by choice or preference ⟨We will not give in, but will fight for our freedom *first*.⟩ — see RATHER 1

first *adj* **1** coming before all others in time or order ⟨the much-studied *first*—and last—voyage of the *Titanic*⟩
synonyms earliest, foremost, inaugural, initial, leadoff, maiden, original, pioneer, premier, virgin
related words ancient, early, primal, primary, prime,

primeval, primitive, primordial; antecedent, preceding, previous

near antonyms advanced, late; consequent, ensuing, following, subsequent, succeeding; penultimate

antonyms final, last, latest, latter, terminal, terminating, ultimate

2 coming before all others in importance ⟨There are a number of reasons we can't go, but the *first* is that we don't have the money.⟩ — see FOREMOST 1

3 highest in rank or authority ⟨auditioned and got *first* clarinet in the band⟩ — see HEAD

first–class *adj* of the very best kind ⟨a *first-class* production of a classic American musical⟩ — see EXCELLENT

firsthand *adj* done or working without something else coming in between ⟨had *firsthand* knowledge of the events of that evening⟩ — see DIRECT 1

firstly *adv* in the beginning ⟨*Firstly*, gather all the ingredients together.⟩ — see ORIGINALLY

first–rate *adj* of the very best kind ⟨wanted a *first-rate* bike and not the cheap model she had been using⟩ — see EXCELLENT

firth *n* a part of a body of water that extends beyond the general shoreline ⟨the *Firth* of Forth in Scotland⟩ — see GULF 1

fiscal *adj* of or relating to money, banking, or investments ⟨gained some *fiscal* knowledge by taking an economics course⟩ — see FINANCIAL

fish *vb* to search for something blindly or uncertainly ⟨Take a minute to *fish* for some change to drop in the donation box.⟩ — see GROPE

fish *n* a member of the human race ⟨He's rather an odd *fish*.⟩ — see HUMAN

fishy *adj* giving good reason for being doubted, questioned, or challenged ⟨Something's *fishy* about the way he's acting.⟩ — see DOUBTFUL 1

fissure *n* an irregular usually narrow break in a surface created by pressure ⟨Lava flows up through a *fissure* in the earth's crust.⟩ — see CRACK 1

fit *adj* **1** meeting the requirements of a purpose or situation ⟨clothing that is *fit* for horseback riding⟩

synonyms applicable, appropriate, apt, becoming, befitting, felicitous, fitted, fitting, good, happy, meet, pretty, proper, right, suitable

related words deserved, just, justified; needed, required, requisite; able, capable, competent, cut out, qualified, trained; pitch-perfect; acceptable, adequate, decent, kosher, satisfactory, serviceable, tolerable; correct, decorous, respectable, seemly; balanced, companionate, congruous, consonant, harmonious; rightful

phrases in order

near antonyms incapable, incompetent, inept, inexpert, unqualified, unskilled, unskillful, untrained; inadequate, intolerable, unacceptable, unsatisfactory; graceless, incorrect, indecorous; incompatible, uncongenial

antonyms improper, inapplicable, inappropriate, inapt, incongruous, indecent, infelicitous, misbecoming, unapt, unbecoming, unfit, unfitting, unhappy, unseemly, unsuitable, wrong

2 being in a state of fitness for some experience or action ⟨*fit* for military service⟩ — see READY 1

3 capable of or suitable for being used for a particular purpose ⟨I don't think those bald tires are *fit* for winter driving.⟩ — see USABLE 1

4 enjoying health and vigor ⟨Eat well and stay *fit*.⟩ — see HEALTHY 1

5 having the required skills for an acceptable level of performance ⟨need to hire someone whose language skills make them *fit* for the job⟩ — see COMPETENT 1

fit *n* **1** a sudden experiencing of a physical or mental disor-

der ⟨She always has a sneezing *fit* on the first day of spring.⟩ — see ATTACK 2

2 a sudden intense expression of strong feeling ⟨helpless *fits* of laughter from the audience⟩ — see OUTBURST 1

3 an outburst or display of excited anger ⟨Ned found out what the car repair would cost and threw a *fit*.⟩ — see TANTRUM

fit *vb* **1** to be in agreement on every point ⟨He *fits* the description exactly.⟩ — see CHECK 1

2 to change (something) so as to make it suitable for a new use or situation ⟨They had to *fit* their spending to their new income level.⟩ — see ADAPT

3 to make competent (as by training, skill, or ability) for a particular office or function ⟨That final computer course should *fit* him for a career in programming.⟩ — see QUALIFY 2

4 to make or have room for ⟨We can *fit* you in the booth if the rest of us squeeze closer together.⟩ — see ACCOMMODATE 1

5 to make ready in advance ⟨I won't have time to *fit* the spare room for the guests.⟩ — see PREPARE 1

fit (in *or* **into)** *vb* to put among or between others ⟨Do you think you can *fit* this picture *into* the album?⟩ ⟨I can *fit* you *in* between my two o'clock and three o'clock appointments.⟩ — see INSERT

fit (out) *vb* to provide (someone) with what is needed for a task or activity ⟨*fitted* the hikers *out* with good boots and heavy socks⟩ — see FURNISH 1

fitful *adj* lacking in steadiness or regularity of occurrence ⟨A night of *fitful* sleep did not leave me feeling well rested the next morning.⟩

synonyms casual, catchy, choppy, discontinuous, episodic (*also* episodical), erratic, intermittent, irregular, occasional, spasmodic, sporadic, spotty, unsteady

related words convulsive, sudden, violent; broken, disconnected, fragmentary, interrupted; aimless, arbitrary, desultory, haphazard, hit-and-miss, hit-or-miss, odd, random, scattered, slapdash, stray; capricious, changeful, changing, flickery, fluctuating, fluid, inconstant, mercurial, mutable, temperamental, uncertain, unpredictable, unsettled, unstable, varying, wavering; changeable, fickle, variable, volatile

near antonyms changeless, equable, even, stable, stationary, uniform; unchanging, unvarying, unwavering; methodical (*also* methodic), orderly, systematic; unrelenting, unremitting

antonyms constant, continuous, habitual, periodic, regular, repeated, steady

fitness *n* **1** the condition of being sound in body ⟨a gymnastics program promoting *fitness* and agility in school-aged children⟩ — see HEALTH 1

2 the quality or state of being especially suitable or fitting ⟨No one questioned her *fitness* for the job.⟩ — see APPROPRIATENESS

fitted *adj* meeting the requirements of a purpose or situation ⟨Her personality is well *fitted* to a desk job.⟩ — see FIT 1

fitting *adj* meeting the requirements of a purpose or situation ⟨It is only *fitting* that you should be the one to take her back to the airport since she flew out to see you.⟩ — see FIT 1

fittingly *adv* in a manner suitable for the occasion or purpose ⟨He was dressed *fittingly* for the prom—all decked out in a spiffy tux.⟩ — see PROPERLY

fittingness *n* the quality or state of being especially suitable or fitting ⟨I trusted their judgment and didn't have to worry about the *fittingness* of their choice for a school play.⟩ — see APPROPRIATENESS

fix *n* **1** a difficult, puzzling, or embarrassing situation from which there is no easy escape ⟨What a *fix* we're in!⟩ — see PREDICAMENT

2 something given or promised in order to improperly influence a person's conduct or decision ⟨The winner was a surprise, and some people suspect a *fix*.⟩ — see BRIBE

3 an opinion on the nature, character, or quality of something ⟨What's your *fix* on the military situation over there?⟩ — see ESTIMATION 1

fix *vb* **1** to arrange something in a certain spot or position ⟨*fixed* my hair so that it would stop falling in my eyes⟩ — see PLACE 1

2 to cause (something) to hold to another ⟨First, you need to *fix* those pieces of wood together.⟩ — see FASTEN 1

3 to come to an agreement or decision concerning the details of ⟨Make sure to *fix* the number of guests with the bride's family before drawing up a list of people from the groom's side.⟩ — see ARRANGE 1

4 to decide upon (the time or date for an event) usually from a position of authority ⟨Have we *fixed* a day for the party yet?⟩ — see APPOINT 1

5 to make ready in advance ⟨Would you mind *fixing* dinner tonight?⟩ — see PREPARE 1

6 to put into good shape or working order again ⟨have to *fix* the car before we can go⟩ — see MEND 1

7 to put securely in place or in a desired position ⟨*fixed* the mittens to the child's snowsuit⟩ — see FASTEN 2

8 to set solidly in or as if in surrounding matter ⟨The image of what Santa Claus looks like is solidly *fixed* in our minds.⟩ — see ENTRENCH

9 to remove the sex organs of ⟨The animal shelter requires a pledge from the adoptive owner that they will have their new pet *fixed*.⟩ — see NEUTER

10 to restore to a healthy condition ⟨It took surgery and months of physical therapy to completely *fix* her bum knee.⟩ — see HEAL 1

fixable *adj* capable of being corrected ⟨Don't worry, that mistake in scheduling is *fixable*.⟩ — see REMEDIABLE

fixation *n* something about which one is constantly thinking or concerned ⟨The band is my latest music *fixation*.⟩
synonyms fetish (*also* fetich), mania, obsession, preoccupation, prepossession
related words monomania; complex, problem, trip; appetite, compulsion, craving, desire, drive, enthusiasm, fascination, fixation, hunger, infatuation, itch, longing, lust, passion, pining, thirst, urge, yearning, yen; idiosyncrasy, quirk; bent, disposition, inclination, leaning, partiality, penchant, predilection, predisposition, proclivity, propensity, tendency
near antonyms apathy, disinterestedness, disregard, indifference, insouciance, nonchalance, unconcern, unconcernedness

fixed *adj* **1** having been established and usually not subject to change ⟨The baseball card dealer's prices were *fixed*, so bargaining was not an option.⟩
synonyms certain, determinate, final, firm, flat, frozen, hard, hard-and-fast, set, settled, stable
related words nonadjustable, noncancelable, nonnegotiable, unchangeable; constant, steady, unchanging, uniform, unwavering; definite, exact, explicit, specific; given, stated, stipulated; dependable, good, reliable, responsible, safe, solid, sure, tried, tried-and-true, true, trustworthy, trusty
near antonyms adjustable, changeable, negotiable; indefinite, open-ended, unspecified; capricious, changeful, flickery, fluctuating, fluid, inconstant, mercurial, mutable, temperamental, uncertain, unpredictable, unsettled, unstable, unsteady, variable, volatile

2 not capable of changing or being changed ⟨Interest accrues at a *fixed* rate.⟩ — see INFLEXIBLE 1

fixedness *n* the state of continuing without change ⟨wasn't comfortable with the *fixedness* of her stare⟩ — see CONSTANCY 1

fizz *n* a sound similar to the speech sound \s\ stretched out ⟨The light bulb burned out with a quick *fizz*.⟩ — see HISS 1

fizz *vb* to make a sound like that of stretching out the speech sound \s\ ⟨soda pop *fizzing* in the glass⟩ — see HISS

fizzle *n* **1** a falling short of one's goals ⟨The home team's unexpected *fizzle* in that last game cost them the championship.⟩ — see FAILURE 2

2 something that has failed ⟨The play was a *fizzle*, opening and closing the same night.⟩ — see FAILURE 3

fizzle *vb* to make a sound like that of stretching out the speech sound \s\ ⟨A pair of fatty burgers *fizzled* on the grill.⟩ — see HISS

fjord *also* **fiord** *n* a part of a body of water that extends beyond the general shoreline ⟨a cruise through the breathtaking *fjords* along the coast of Norway⟩ — see GULF 1

flabbergast *vb* to make a strong impression on (someone) with something unexpected ⟨Your decision to suddenly quit your job *flabbergasts* me.⟩ — see SURPRISE 1

flabbergasted *adj* **1** affected with sudden and great wonder or surprise ⟨I was *flabbergasted* when I heard she was moving out of the state.⟩ — see THUNDERSTRUCK

2 filled with amazement or wonder ⟨responded to the news of his arrival with a *flabbergasted* gasp⟩ — see OPENMOUTHED

flabbergasting *adj* causing a strong emotional reaction because of unexpectedness ⟨the *flabbergasting* sight of the mess that had been left in the kitchen⟩ — see SURPRISING 1

flabby *adj* giving easily to the touch ⟨having *flabby* abdominal muscles can lead to back pain.⟩ — see SOFT 3

flaccid *adj* not stiff in structure ⟨the *flaccid* stalks of celery that had been around for far too long⟩ — see LIMP 1

¹flag *vb* **1** to be limp from lack of water or vigor ⟨flowers *flagging* in the summer heat⟩ — see DROOP 1

2 to lose bodily strength or vigor ⟨We *flagged* as we neared the end of the long mountain trail.⟩ — see WEAKEN 2

²flag *vb* to direct or notify by a movement or gesture ⟨*flagged* the cars into the other parking lot⟩ — see MOTION

flag *n* **1** a piece of cloth with a special design that is used as an emblem or for signaling ⟨The *flags* of both countries were prominently displayed at the treaty signing.⟩
synonyms banner, colors, ensign, guidon, jack, pennant, pennon, standard, streamer
related words bunting, gonfalon; black flag, Jolly Roger, tricolor, union jack, white flag; burgee, semaphore, signaler (*or* signaller)

2 an object intended to give public notice or warning ⟨road crews using handheld stop signs as *flags* at both ends of the highway construction zone⟩ — see SIGNAL 1

flagellate *vb* to strike repeatedly with something long and thin or flexible ⟨Some medieval monks believed it was necessary to *flagellate* themselves in order to keep their desires in check.⟩ — see WHIP 1

flagon *n* a handled container for holding and pouring liquids that usually has a lip or a spout ⟨brought a *flagon* of wine to the table⟩ — see PITCHER

flagrant *adj* very noticeable especially for being incorrect or bad ⟨That was a *flagrant* violation of the rules.⟩ — see EGREGIOUS

flail *vb* **1** to move or cause to move with a striking motion ⟨He started to *flail* his arms wildly when he spied a bat in the house.⟩ — see FLAP
2 to strike repeatedly with something long and thin or flexible ⟨The fish's tail *flailed* the water.⟩ — see WHIP 1
flair *n* a special and usually inborn ability ⟨a person with a *flair* for making friends quickly⟩ — see TALENT
¹**flake** *n* a small flat piece separated from a whole ⟨Sprinkle the cake with coconut *flakes*.⟩ — see CHIP 1
²**flake** *n* a person of odd or whimsical habits ⟨I love my brother even though he's kind of a *flake*.⟩ — see ECCENTRIC
flaky *also* **flakey** *adj* having a texture that readily breaks into little pieces under pressure ⟨a tender but *flaky* crust on the pastry⟩ — see CRISP 1
flamboyance *n* excessive or unnecessary display ⟨The campy *flamboyance* of her costume almost guaranteed she'd win the masquerade pageant.⟩ — see OSTENTATION
flamboyant *adj* **1** likely to attract attention ⟨has a gallery of *flamboyant* gestures that makes him easy to imitate⟩ — see NOTICEABLE
2 excessively showy ⟨the *flamboyant* floats in the Mardi Gras parade⟩ — see GAUDY
flame *n* a person with whom one is in love ⟨Sue decided to look up an old *flame* while she was in town.⟩ — see SWEETHEART
flame *vb* **1** to be on fire especially brightly ⟨Guests gathered around as the Yule log *flamed* brightly in the inn's great stone fireplace.⟩ — see BURN 1
2 to develop suddenly and violently ⟨My anger *flamed* when the usher told my friend to shut up.⟩ — see ERUPT 2
3 to shine with a bright harsh light ⟨The noonday sun *flamed* down on the desert travelers.⟩ — see GLARE 1
4 to shoot forth bursts of light ⟨The actress's ruby necklace *flamed* dazzlingly under the bright lights.⟩ — see FLASH 1
flaming *adj* **1** being on fire ⟨a fancy restaurant serving eye-catching *flaming* desserts⟩ — see ABLAZE 1
2 having or expressing great depth of feeling ⟨a *flaming* speech in support of basic human rights⟩ — see FERVENT 1
flammable *adj* capable of catching or being set on fire ⟨Avoid wearing loose *flammable* clothing when using the blowtorch.⟩ — see COMBUSTIBLE
flank *n* a place, space, or direction away from or beyond a central point or line ⟨painted the name of the ship along its *flank*⟩ — see SIDE 1
flank *vb* to be adjacent to ⟨The tackles *flank* the center on a football team's offensive line.⟩ — see ADJOIN 1
flanking *adj* having a border in common ⟨*flanking* farms that share the same water source⟩ — see ADJACENT
flap *n* a state of wildly excited activity or emotion ⟨There was a major *flap* when area residents found out that the President would be visiting.⟩ — see FRENZY
flap *vb* to move or cause to move with a striking motion ⟨the stirring sight of a huge flock of geese *flapping* their wings⟩
synonyms beat, flail, flop, flutter, whip
related words bang, batter, buffet, knock, pound, smack, spank, thump; flick, flicker, flit; fan, oscillate, sway, swing; undulate, wave; palpitate, pulse, throb
flapjack *n* a flat cake made from thin batter and cooked on both sides (as on a griddle) ⟨For breakfast, there's bacon and *flapjacks* with syrup.⟩ — see PANCAKE
flare *n* **1** a sudden and usually temporary growth of activity ⟨a *flare* in antacid sales around the holidays⟩ — see OUTBREAK 1
2 a sudden intense expression of strong feeling ⟨ended

the quarrel with a stunning *flare* of accusations⟩ — see OUTBURST 1
3 the steady giving off of the form of radiation that makes vision possible ⟨In the darkness the *flare* of a single match might be seen by enemy troops.⟩ — see LIGHT 1
flare *vb* to shine with a bright harsh light ⟨floodlights *flaring* into the forbidding empty spaces surrounding the prison⟩ — see GLARE 1
flare (out) *vb* to arrange the parts of (something) over a wider area ⟨Can we *flare out* the umbrella a little more so that more of the picnic table is sheltered?⟩ — see OPEN 3
flare (up) *vb* **1** to become very angry ⟨Naturally I *flared up* when he insulted me.⟩ — see BLOW UP 1
2 to develop suddenly and violently ⟨The disease tends to *flare up* again if the patient stops taking the medication.⟩ — see ERUPT 2
flare–up *n* **1** a sudden and usually temporary growth of activity ⟨took medication to prevent a *flare-up* of her asthma⟩ — see OUTBREAK 1
2 a sudden intense expression of strong feeling ⟨There's no need for an angry *flare-up*, as we'll take care of the problem immediately.⟩ — see OUTBURST 1
flash *adj* lasting only for a short time ⟨*flash* floods in the local area⟩ — see MOMENTARY
flash *n* **1** a sudden and usually temporary growth of activity ⟨a *flash* of last-minute trips to the grocery store before the onset of the big snowstorm⟩ — see OUTBREAK 1
2 a sudden intense expression of strong feeling ⟨a much-needed *flash* of humor during the otherwise boring lecture⟩ — see OUTBURST 1
3 a very small space of time ⟨The shower will be over in a *flash*.⟩ — see INSTANT
4 something extraordinary or surprising ⟨The new goalie for our hockey team was apparently quite a *flash* in his hometown.⟩ — see WONDER 1
5 excessive or unnecessary display ⟨The expensive clothes, the luxury cars, and other apparent signs of success are all *flash* that belie the fact that the family is up to its ears in debt.⟩ — see OSTENTATION
flash *vb* **1** to shoot forth bursts of light ⟨The actress's diamond necklace *flashed* as she hurried on stage to accept the award.⟩
synonyms flame, glance, gleam, glimmer, glint, glisten, glister, glitter, luster (*or* lustre), scintillate, shimmer, sparkle, twinkle, wink
related words beam, radiate, shine; bedazzle, blind, daze, dazzle; blaze, burn, flare, glare, glow
2 to present so as to invite notice or attention ⟨*flashed* a wad of cash as he paid for his coffee⟩ — see SHOW 1
3 to shine with light at regular intervals ⟨The disco lights *flashed*, and the revelers danced.⟩ — see BLINK 1
4 to make known openly or publicly ⟨*flashed* the news of the royal birth around the world⟩ — see ANNOUNCE
flashiness *n* excessive or unnecessary display ⟨his penchant for *flashiness*, as evidenced by his expensive, specially tailored suits⟩ — see OSTENTATION
flashy *adj* **1** attractively eye-catching in style ⟨I bought a *flashy* new car.⟩ — see JAZZY 1
2 excessively showy ⟨wore *flashy* rings on almost all the fingers of his left hand⟩ — see GAUDY
flat *adj* **1** being neither more nor less than a certain amount, number, or extent ⟨Industrial growth has been a *flat* two percent for each of the last four quarters.⟩ — see EVEN 1
2 causing weariness, restlessness, or lack of interest ⟨a *flat* portrayal of Benjamin Franklin in the new TV series⟩ — see BORING
3 having a surface without bends, breaks, or irregularities ⟨preferred riding her bike on a *flat* road⟩ — see LEVEL 1

4 having been established and usually not subject to change ⟨charged a *flat* rate for overseas calls⟩ — see FIXED 1

5 having no exceptions or restrictions ⟨a *flat* denial of the charges⟩ — see ABSOLUTE 2

6 lacking a surface luster or gloss ⟨used a *flat* paint for the condo's interior walls⟩ — see MATTE

7 lacking in qualities that make for spirit and character ⟨a dull, *flat* reading of the poem⟩ — see WISHY-WASHY 1

8 lacking in taste or flavor ⟨This pasta dish tastes a little *flat*.⟩ — see INSIPID 1

flat *adv* to a full extent or degree ⟨I am *flat* broke this week.⟩ — see FULLY 1

flatten *vb* **1** to make free from breaks, curves, or bumps ⟨*flattened* out the wrinkled paper before attempting to trace the pattern⟩ — see EVEN 1

2 to defeat by a large margin ⟨If you don't understand the rules, you're going to get *flattened* when you try to play.⟩ — see WHIP 2

flatter *vb* **1** to praise too much ⟨The billionaire has an army of assistants who are eager to *flatter* him at every opportunity.⟩

synonyms adulate, blarney, honey, overpraise, puff, soft-soap, stroke

related words blandish, cajole, coax, wheedle; fawn, kowtow, suck (up to), toady; idolize, worship; eulogize, extol (*also* extoll), laud, praise; applaud, commend, compliment; congratulate, felicitate; drool, gush, slaver, slobber; endear, ingratiate; court, romance, woo

near antonyms bad-mouth, belittle, decry, depreciate, disparage, put down

2 to think highly of (oneself) ⟨Don't *flatter* yourself that no one has ever thought of that idea before.⟩ — see PRIDE

flattery *n* excessive praise ⟨a talk show host who is known for charming her guests with disingenuous *flattery*⟩

synonyms adulation, blarney, overpraise, soft soap

related words allurements, blandishments, endearments; caresses, compliments, congratulations, felicitations, greetings, regards, respects; adoration, idolatry, worship; fawning, sycophancy, toadying; cajolement, cajolery, ingratiation, smarm; acclaim, applause, commendation, praise

near antonyms bad-mouthing, belittlement, depreciation, detraction, disparagement, put-down

flatware *n* eating and serving utensils ⟨asked for inexpensive stemware and *flatware* for their wedding⟩ — see TABLEWARE 1

flaunt *vb* to present so as to invite notice or attention ⟨She playfully *flaunted* her engagement ring in front of her relatives.⟩ — see SHOW 1

flaunting *n* an outward and often exaggerated indication of something abstract (as a feeling) for effect ⟨At first, her *flaunting* of her newfound wealth was understandable, but after a while it became tiresome.⟩ — see SHOW 1

flavor *n* **1** a special quality or impression associated with something ⟨a birthday party whose Caribbean decorations gave it a tropical *flavor*⟩ — see AURA 1

2 something (as an herb) that adds an agreeable or interesting taste to food ⟨a dish that incorporates most of the trademark *flavors* of southeast Asia⟩ — see SEASONING 1

3 the property of a substance that can be identified by the sense of taste ⟨We loved the deep *flavor* of the native strawberries.⟩ — see TASTE 1

flavor *vb* to make more pleasant to the taste by adding something intensely flavored ⟨Try *flavoring* the beans with salt and oregano.⟩ — see SEASON 1

flavorful *adj* very pleasing to the sense of taste ⟨makes a *flavorful* broth⟩ — see DELICIOUS 1

flavoring *n* something (as an herb) that adds an agreeable or interesting taste to food ⟨soup made with beef *flavoring*⟩ — see SEASONING 1

flavorless *adj* lacking in taste or flavor ⟨a *flavorless* fruitcake that must have been given as a gift many times over⟩ — see INSIPID 1

flaw *n* something that spoils the appearance or completeness of a thing ⟨I noted the *flaw* in the diamond before I bought it.⟩ — see BLEMISH

flaw *vb* to reduce the soundness, effectiveness, or perfection of ⟨That crack has *flawed* the vase to the extent that its value in the antiques market is greatly reduced.⟩ — see DAMAGE 1

flawed *adj* having a fault ⟨a *flawed* paint job that resulted in some peeling almost as soon as the paint had dried⟩ — see FAULTY

flawless *adj* being entirely without fault or flaw ⟨a *flawless* performance of the piano concerto⟩ — see PERFECT 1

flawlessly *adv* without any flaws or errors ⟨*flawlessly* recited the first 100 digits of pi⟩ — see PERFECTLY 1

flaxen *adj* of a pale yellow or yellowish brown color ⟨fields of *flaxen* wheat waving in the wind⟩ — see BLOND

flay *vb* **1** to criticize (someone) severely or angrily especially for personal failings ⟨He was *flayed* by the media for his thoughtless comments.⟩ — see SCOLD

2 to remove the natural covering of ⟨They *flayed* their kill right there in the forest, taking both the meat and the skin home.⟩ — see PEEL

fleck *n* **1** a small area that is different (as in color) from the main part ⟨flooring tile that is brown with *flecks* of white⟩ — see SPOT 1

2 a very small piece ⟨wiped a *fleck* of cookie off his jacket⟩ — see BIT 1

fleck *vb* to mark with small spots especially unevenly ⟨To achieve the desired effect, *fleck* the canvas with paint simply by flicking the brush close to the surface.⟩ — see SPOT 1

flecked *adj* marked with spots ⟨That *flecked* blue writing paper is so attractive.⟩ — see SPOTTED 1

fledgling *n* a person who is just starting out in a field of activity ⟨At hockey he's still a *fledgling* and needs to work on his basic skating skills.⟩ — see BEGINNER

flee *vb* **1** to cease to be visible ⟨The fog *fled* with the arrival of the dawn.⟩ — see DISAPPEAR

2 to get free from a dangerous or confining situation ⟨a prisoner who *fled* on foot⟩ — see ESCAPE 1

3 to hasten away from something dangerous or frightening ⟨a toddler who *fled* when the ladybug he had been quietly watching suddenly began flying around the room⟩ — see RUN 2

fleece *n* the hairy covering of a mammal especially when fine, soft, and thick ⟨learning how to shear the *fleece* off a sheep⟩ — see FUR 1

fleece *vb* to rob by the use of trickery or threats ⟨swindlers who use the telephone to *fleece* senior citizens out of their savings⟩

synonyms beat, bleed, cheat, chisel, con, cozen, defraud, do, do in, fiddle, gaff, hustle, mulct, pluck, rip off, rook, screw, short, shortchange, skin, squeeze, stick, stiff, sting, swindle, victimize

related words extort, wrench, wrest, wring; clip, gouge, nick, overcharge, soak; exploit; deceive, dupe, fool, gull, trick; rope (in); betray, double-cross; fast-talk

phrases sell a bill of goods to, take for a ride, take to the cleaners

fleecy *adj* covered with or as if with hair ⟨There were signs of the family's *fleecy* poodle all over the upholstery.⟩ — see HAIRY 1

fleet *adj* moving, proceeding, or acting with great speed ⟨a jewel thief said to be light of heart and *fleet* of foot⟩ — see FAST 1

fleet *n* a group of vehicles traveling together or under one management ⟨a *fleet* of buses rolling down the highway⟩
synonyms armada, caravan, cavalcade, line, motorcade, train
related words argosy, convoy, flotilla, navy; column, cortege (*also* cortège), parade, procession

fleet–footed *adj* moving, proceeding, or acting with great speed ⟨The Roman god Mercury was the *fleet-footed* messenger of the gods.⟩ — see FAST 1

fleeting *adj* lasting only for a short time ⟨I had a *fleeting* desire to jump into the cool lake but kept on hiking.⟩ — see MOMENTARY

fleetly *adv* with great speed ⟨horses galloping *fleetly* across the plain⟩ — see FAST 1

fleetness *n* a high rate of movement or performance ⟨Clipper ships were renowned for their *fleetness* on the high seas.⟩ — see SPEED 1

flesh *n* animal and especially mammal tissue used as food ⟨eats no *flesh* of any kind, only fruits, grains, and vegetables⟩ — see MEAT 1

flesh (out) *vb* to express more fully and in greater detail ⟨a lengthy follow-up that *fleshes out* the original report on the military engagement⟩ — see EXPAND 1

fleshiness *n* **1** the condition of having an excess of body fat ⟨The child's *fleshiness* disappeared as he grew into a gangly teenager.⟩ — see CORPULENCE
2 the quality or state of being full of juice ⟨loves the *fleshiness* of ripe watermelon⟩ — see SUCCULENCE

fleshly *adj* **1** having to do with life on earth especially as opposed to that in heaven ⟨a time of year when people shouldn't focus on *fleshly* concerns, but instead on spiritual matters⟩ — see EARTHLY
2 of or relating to the human body ⟨The *fleshly* eye sees the only finished painting, but the mind's eye sees the genius behind its creation.⟩ — see PHYSICAL 1
3 pleasing to the physical senses ⟨returning campers looking forward to all the *fleshly* pleasures of home, including hot showers⟩ — see SENSUAL

fleshy *adj* **1** full of juice ⟨*fleshy* apples, the kind good for making cider⟩ — see JUICY
2 having an excess of body fat ⟨*fleshy* walruses that are graceful when swimming⟩ — see FAT 1

flexible *adj* **1** capable of being readily changed ⟨I'm lucky enough to have a very *flexible* work schedule.⟩
synonyms adaptable, adjustable, alterable, changeable, elastic, fluid, malleable, modifiable, pliable, variable
related words changing, fluctuating, inconstant, unstable, unsteady, varying, versatile
near antonyms constant, stable, steady, unchanging, uniform, unvarying
antonyms established, fixed, immutable, inelastic, inflexible, invariable, nonmalleable, ramrod, set, unadaptable, unalterable, unbudgeable, unchangeable
2 not bound by rigid standards ⟨parents with a *flexible* attitude when it comes to the children's bedtime⟩ — see EASYGOING 2
3 able to bend easily without breaking ⟨The tent was held up by crisscrossing *flexible* rods threaded through the top.⟩ — see WILLOWY
4 able to revert to original size and shape after being stretched, squeezed, or twisted ⟨used a *flexible* plastic for the toy⟩ — see ELASTIC 1

flick *vb* to make an irregular series of quick, sudden movements ⟨The horse's tail *flicked* in restless irritation.⟩ — see FLIT

flick *n* a story told by means of a series of continuously projected pictures and a sound track ⟨We could catch a *flick* together next weekend.⟩ — see MOVIE 1

flicker *vb* to make an irregular series of quick, sudden movements ⟨a dragonfly *flickering* above the salt marsh⟩ — see FLIT

flicker *n* **1** a story told by means of a series of continuously projected pictures and a sound track ⟨As a child, the future director would spend hours sitting in the theater, totally entranced by the *flickers*.⟩ — see MOVIE 1
2 a sudden and usually temporary growth of activity ⟨Usually there's a *flicker* in car sales when the new models come out.⟩ — see OUTBREAK 1
3 an almost imperceptible sign of something ⟨There was a *flicker* of recognition in her eye when I mentioned his name, but she denied knowing him.⟩ — see HINT 2

flickery *adj* likely to change frequently, suddenly, or unexpectedly ⟨Wise political leaders don't try to govern according to *flickery* public opinion.⟩ — see FICKLE 1

flier *also* **flyer** *n* **1** a risky undertaking ⟨willing to take a *flier* on the bold, new venture⟩ — see GAMBLE
2 one who flies or is qualified to fly an aircraft or spacecraft ⟨a hot-air balloon *flier*⟩ — see PILOT

¹flight *n* travel through the air by the use of wings ⟨For centuries people have been fascinated by the *flight* of birds.⟩
synonyms flying
related words aviation; aeronautics; ballooning, gliding, hang gliding, paragliding, skydiving, soaring

²flight *n* the act or an instance of getting free from danger or confinement ⟨a work of 19th-century Romanticism depicting the ancient Israelites' *flight* from Egypt⟩ — see ESCAPE 1

flightiness *n* **1** a lack of seriousness often at an improper time ⟨The principal spoke to the students about their *flightiness* during the ceremony.⟩ — see FRIVOLITY
2 a state of nervousness marked by sudden jerky movements ⟨the *flightiness* of the horses before they were loaded on the trailer⟩ — see JUMPINESS

flighty *adj* **1** easily excited by nature ⟨You have to be quiet while the deer are grazing, as they are *flighty* animals and will run if they hear you.⟩ — see EXCITABLE
2 lacking in seriousness or maturity ⟨*flighty* and giggly preteens at their first dance⟩ — see GIDDY 1

flimsy *adj* **1** being of a material lacking in sturdiness or substance ⟨a *flimsy* scarf that was more for decoration than for warmth⟩
synonyms filmy, frothy, gauzy, gossamer, gossamery, insubstantial, sleazy, unsubstantial
related words dainty, delicate, fine; feeble, fragile, frail; sheer, transparent
near antonyms durable, knockabout, lasting, tough; coarse, heavy, rough, rude
antonyms sturdy, substantial
2 not likely to be true or to occur ⟨"The check is in the mail" is a pretty *flimsy* and tired excuse.⟩ — see IMPROBABLE

flinch *vb* to draw back in fear, pain, or disgust ⟨There are some patients who *flinch* at the mere sight of a needle.⟩
synonyms blench, cringe, quail, recoil, shrink, squinch, wince
related words blanch, pale, whiten; quake, quiver, shake, shudder, tremble; crouch; jerk, start, twitch; recede, retire, retreat, withdraw; falter, hesitate, reel, waver
near antonyms advance, approach, near; beard, challenge, confront, defy, face

fling *n* **1** a time or instance of carefree fun ⟨Most families spend Labor Day weekend having one last summer *fling*.⟩

synonyms binge, frolic, gambol, idyll (*also* idyl), lark, revel, rollick, romp, spree

related words caper, escapade, prank; bender, bust, carouse, souse, toot; antic, monkeyshine(s), shenanigan(s); field day; festivity, merriment, merrymaking

2 an effort to do or accomplish something ⟨Take a *fling* at waterskiing and see how it goes.⟩ — see ATTEMPT 1

3 a brief romantic relationship ⟨They had a summer *fling* before each headed off to college.⟩ — see AFFAIR 1

fling *vb* to send through the air especially with a quick forward motion of the arm ⟨*flinging* rocks into the pond just for the fun of it⟩ — see THROW 1

fling (off *or* **away)** *vb* to get rid of as useless or unwanted ⟨He *flung away* the used matchstick.⟩ ⟨*flinging off* dirty clothes⟩ — see DISCARD

flinty *adj* **1** given to exacting standards of discipline and self-restraint ⟨a *flinty* warrior hardened by years of battle⟩ — see SEVERE 1

2 harsh and threatening in manner or appearance ⟨wrestling opponents intimidating each other with *flinty* stares⟩ — see GRIM 1

flip *adj* making light of something usually regarded as serious or sacred ⟨She made a *flip* comment about my presentation.⟩ — see FLIPPANT

flip *vb* **1** to turn over pages in an idle or cursory manner ⟨*Flip* through this home decorating book to see if there's anything we could use.⟩ — see SKIM 1

2 to change the position of (an object) so that the opposite side or end is showing ⟨*flip* the coin over⟩ — see REVERSE 2

flippancy *n* a lack of seriousness often at an improper time ⟨Many people were offended by the *flippancy* of his responses.⟩ — see FRIVOLITY

flippant *adj* making light of something usually regarded as serious or sacred ⟨He gave a *flippant* response to a serious question.⟩

synonyms cute, facetious, flip, pert, smart, smart-alecky, wise

related words flighty, frivolous; cheeky, cocky, fresh, impertinent, impish, impudent, mischievous, playful, roguish, sassy, saucy, waggish; disrespectful, rude; breezy, casual, glib, inappropriate, thoughtless

near antonyms grave, serious, sober, solemn, somber (*or* sombre)

antonyms earnest, sincere

flirt *vb* **1** to show a sexual attraction for someone just for fun ⟨The servers at that restaurant *flirt* with all the customers.⟩

synonyms dally, trifle

related words vamp; court, mash, woo; josh, kid, put on, razz, rib, tease; fool, lead on, string along; manipulate, play (with)

2 to make an irregular series of quick, sudden movements ⟨lazily watched the butterflies *flirting* among the wildflowers⟩ — see FLIT

flit *vb* to make an irregular series of quick, sudden movements ⟨Bargain hunters at the flea market *flitted* from table to table like hummingbirds in a garden.⟩

synonyms dance, dart, flick, flicker, flirt, flutter, zip

related words dash, fly, sail, shoot, speed, sprint, zing, zoom; scamper, scud, scurry, scuttle, skip, skitter; meander, ramble, roam, wander

near antonyms float, hang, hover

float *n* a structure used by boats and ships for taking on or landing cargo and passengers ⟨The crew put the cargo on the *float* before heading back down the river.⟩ — see DOCK

float *vb* **1** to rest or move along the surface of a liquid or in the air ⟨a canoe *floating* down the river⟩ ⟨particles of dust *floating* in the air⟩

synonyms drift, glide, hang, hover, poise, ride, sail, swim, waft

related words bob, dangle, suspend; buoy; balloon, raft

near antonyms dive, plunge; dip, immerse, submerge, submerse

antonyms settle, sink

2 to move about from place to place aimlessly ⟨lost touch with a childhood friend who spent much of his adult life *floating* from place to place⟩ — see WANDER 1

flock *n* **1** a great number of persons or creatures massed together ⟨a *flock* of obstreperous reporters at the press conference⟩ — see CROWD 1

2 a group of domestic animals assembled or herded together ⟨a *flock* of sheep crossing the road⟩ — see HERD 1

flock *vb* to move upon or fill (something) in great numbers ⟨Vacationers *flocked* to the towns along the shore in order to escape the August heat.⟩ — see CROWD 2

flog *vb* **1** to strike repeatedly with something long and thin or flexible ⟨a sailor *flogged* for attempting mutiny⟩ — see WHIP 1

2 to strike repeatedly ⟨The rancher was fined heavily for *flogging* a horse.⟩ — see BEAT 1

flogger *n* a long thin or flexible tool for striking ⟨a horseman who believes that *floggers* should be used sparingly⟩ — see WHIP

flood *n* a great flow of water or of something that overwhelms ⟨A *flood* nearly wiped out the town.⟩ ⟨a *flood* of messages on my computer⟩

synonyms bath, cataclysm, cataract, deluge, flood tide, inundation, overflow, spate, torrent

related words current, river, stream, tide; cloudburst, discharge, flush, gush, outflow, outpouring; flux, inflow, influx; engulfment, washout; avalanche, blizzard; cascade, waterfall; excess, glut, overabundance, overage, overkill, overmuch, oversupply, superabundance, superfluity, surfeit, surplus

near antonyms dribble, drip, trickle

flood *vb* to cover with a flood ⟨The lowlands were completely *flooded*.⟩ ⟨Angry calls *flooded* the radio station.⟩

synonyms deluge, drown, engulf, gulf, inundate, overflow, overwhelm, submerge, submerse, swamp

related words avalanche, smother; overcome, overrun; flow, flush, gush, pour, sluice, spout, spurt, stream; douse (*also* dowse), drench, soak, wet

near antonyms dehydrate, dry, parch

antonyms drain

flood tide *n* a great flow of water or of something that overwhelms ⟨the *flood tide* of criticism that the company received⟩ — see FLOOD

floor *n* the surface upon which a body of water lies ⟨discovered a new species of crab living on the ocean *floor*⟩ — see BOTTOM 2

floor *vb* **1** to cause an unpleasant surprise for ⟨The news just *floored* me.⟩ — see SHOCK 1

2 to make a strong impression on (someone) with something unexpected ⟨As you might expect, winning the lottery simply *floored* us.⟩ — see SURPRISE 1

3 to strike (someone) so forcefully as to cause a fall ⟨The boxer *floored* his opponent in the second round, winning the fight by a knockout.⟩ — see FELL 1

4 to subject to incapacitating emotional or mental stress ⟨The pushing and shoving at the clearance sale absolutely *floored* me, and I had to leave.⟩ — see OVERWHELM 1

flop *n* something that has failed ⟨The movie is such a *flop* that theaters stopped showing it after a week.⟩ — see FAILURE 3

flop *vb* **1** to throw or set down clumsily or casually ⟨They lazily *flopped* themselves onto the couch to watch the game.⟩ ⟨*flopped* the bag of groceries onto the counter⟩

synonyms plop, plump, plunk (*or* plonk)

related words fling, heave, sling, toss; ensconce, install, plant, settle

2 to be unsuccessful ⟨The attempt to run the ball into the end zone *flopped*, and our team lost by five points.⟩ — see FAIL 2

3 to move or cause to move with a striking motion ⟨a fish *flopping* around on the dock⟩ — see FLAP

floppy *adj* not stiff in structure ⟨My basset hound is always tripping over her long, *floppy* ears.⟩ — see LIMP 1

flora *n* green leaves or plants ⟨a fascination with the lush *flora* of the South⟩ — see GREENERY

floral *adj* of or relating to flowers ⟨bedroom wallpaper with a *floral* pattern⟩

synonyms flowered, flowery

related words florid; abloom, blossomy, floriferous

florid *adj* **1** elaborately and often excessively decorated ⟨a *florid*, gilded mirror that took up most of the wall⟩ — see ORNATE 1

2 full of fine words and fancy expressions ⟨gave a *florid* speech in honor of the queen's visit⟩ — see FLOWERY 1

3 having a healthy reddish skin tone ⟨a jolly man with a *florid* complexion⟩ — see RUDDY

floss *n* a soft airy substance or covering ⟨used cotton *floss* to simulate Santa's beard⟩ — see FUZZ

flounce *n* a strip of fabric gathered or pleated on one edge and used as trimming ⟨a prom dress with small *flounces* along the hem⟩ — see RUFFLE 1

flounder *vb* **1** to proceed or act clumsily or ineffectually ⟨unprepared singers who *floundered* helplessly through the musical number⟩

synonyms blunder, limp, lumber, plod, struggle, stumble, trudge

related words jog, shamble, shuffle; wallow, welter; falter, lurch, reel, stagger, sway, teeter, totter; fumble, muddle

near antonyms coast, fly, glide, kilt, sail, zip, zoom

2 to move heavily or clumsily ⟨The car *floundered* through the heavy wet snow, constantly getting stuck.⟩ — see LUMBER 1

flourish *vb* **1** to grow vigorously ⟨That plant *flourishes* in cool, wet weather.⟩ — see THRIVE 1

2 to reach a desired level of accomplishment ⟨The arts program *flourished* once it received adequate funding.⟩ — see SUCCEED 2

flourishing *adj* **1** having attained a desired end or state of good fortune ⟨a *flourishing* actor in the early years of the talkies⟩ — see SUCCESSFUL 1

2 marked by much life, movement, or activity ⟨a *flourishing* market in sports memorabilia⟩ — see ALIVE 2

3 marked by vigorous growth and well-being especially economically ⟨a *flourishing* community that has become a major beneficiary of the economic boom⟩ — see PROSPEROUS 1

floury *adj* consisting of very small particles ⟨shelves of old books covered with *floury* dust⟩ — see FINE 1

flout *vb* to ignore in a disrespectful manner ⟨an able-bodied motorist openly *flouting* the law and parking in a space reserved for the disabled⟩ — see SCORN 2

flow *vb* **1** to move in a stream ⟨Water was *flowing* over the dam at a tremendous rate.⟩

synonyms pour, roll, run, stream

related words arise, issue, spring; course, race, rush; gush, spout, spurt; deluge, engulf, flood, inundate, overflow, overrun, swamp; cascade, dribble, drip, gutter, ripple, sheet, trickle; flush, wash out

near antonyms clot, coagulate, congeal, gel, harden, set

antonyms back up

2 to move or proceed smoothly and readily ⟨As everyone relaxed, the conversation really started to *flow*.⟩

synonyms bowl, breeze, brush, coast, cruise, drift, glide, roll, sail, skim, slide, slip, stream, sweep, whisk

related words fly, race, rush, speed

near antonyms limp, lumber, plod, stumble, trudge; shamble, shuffle; stamp, stomp, stump, tramp; labor, toil

antonyms flounder, struggle

flower *vb* to produce flowers ⟨The plant will keep *flowering* if you water it and regularly cut off the dead blossoms.⟩ — see BLOOM 1

flower *n* **1** the usually showy plant part that produces seeds ⟨*Flowers* are always a thoughtful gift.⟩

synonyms bloom, blossom

related words floret, floweret (*also* flowerette); bouquet, nosegay, posy; arrangement, boutonniere, corsage, garland, lei, spray, wreath

2 a state or time of great activity, thriving, or achievement ⟨The skiing season is usually in full *flower* by Christmas.⟩ — see BLOOM 1

3 individuals carefully selected as being the best of a class ⟨Without exception, the *flower* of this year's graduating class will be going to prestigious colleges.⟩ — see ELITE 1

flowered *adj* of or relating to flowers ⟨a pretty tablecloth with a *flowered* border⟩ — see FLORAL

flowery *adj* **1** full of fine words and fancy expressions ⟨the *flowery* verses that always appear on valentines⟩

synonyms florid, grandiloquent, highfalutin (*also* hifalutin), high-flown, high-sounding, ornate, rhetorical (*also* rhetoric)

related words affected, fancy-pants, grandiose, pompous, pretentious, stilted; excessive, flattering, fulsome; boastful, bombastic; elevated, eloquent, lofty; bookish, inkhorn, learned

near antonyms prosaic, unpoetic; bald, direct, lean, matter-of-fact, plain, plainspoken, simple, spare, stark, straightforward, unadorned; natural, unaffected, unpretentious

2 of or relating to flowers ⟨Mother's Day cards typically have a *flowery* design on the cover.⟩ — see FLORAL

flowing *adj* capable of moving like a liquid ⟨a *flowing* silk scarf⟩ — see FLUID 1

flub *n* an unintentional departure from truth or accuracy ⟨When she was told her information was wrong, she apologized for the *flub* and immediately corrected it.⟩ — see ERROR 1

flub *vb* **1** to make or do (something) in a clumsy or unskillful way ⟨added too much flour and *flubbed* the gravy⟩ — see BOTCH

2 to make a mistake ⟨At some point in your training you're going to *flub*, so don't let it rattle you.⟩ — see ERR 1

fluctuate *vb* to pass from one form, state, or level to another ⟨Temperatures will *fluctuate* between the low and high 50s today.⟩ — see CHANGE 2

fluctuating *adj* **1** likely to change frequently, suddenly, or unexpectedly ⟨A *fluctuating* stock market makes it hard for investors to know what to do.⟩ — see FICKLE 1

2 not staying constant ⟨Our speed was constantly *fluctuating*, so the figure of 50 miles per hour is just an average.⟩ — see UNEVEN 2

fluent *adj* **1** able to express oneself clearly and well ⟨a very *fluent* speaker who always communicates his points well⟩ — see ARTICULATE

2 capable of moving like a liquid ⟨heated the wax until it was *fluent*, then poured it into the mold⟩ — see FLUID 1

3 involving minimal difficulty or effort ⟨a *fluent* performance of one of the oldest magic tricks in the book⟩ — see EASY 1

fluently *adv* without difficulty ⟨*fluently* negotiates even the most challenging slalom courses⟩ — see EASILY 1

fluff *n* **1** a soft airy substance or covering ⟨His sweater was covered in *fluff*.⟩ — see FUZZ

2 an unintentional departure from truth or accuracy ⟨The flustered newscaster's *fluffs* included a mispronunciation of the town's name.⟩ — see ERROR 1

fluff *vb* **1** to make a mistake ⟨Unnerved by her earlier missteps, the skater *fluffed* on the final jump as well.⟩ — see ERR 1

2 to make or do (something) in a clumsy or unskillful way ⟨I completely *fluffed* the introduction by calling her by the wrong name.⟩ — see BOTCH

fluffy *adj* resembling air in lightness ⟨big *fluffy* pillows⟩ — see AIRY 1

fluid *adj* **1** capable of moving like a liquid ⟨Warm the jam until it is *fluid*, then spread it over the cake.⟩

synonyms flowing, fluent, liquid

related words diluted, thin, watery, weak; semiliquid, semisolid

near antonyms clotted, coagulated, gelatinous, gelled, jelled, jellied, thick; gluey, glutinous, gooey, gummy, viscous

antonyms hard, nonliquid, solid

2 capable of being readily changed ⟨The script is still *fluid* at this point, so be prepared for last-minute rewrites.⟩ — see FLEXIBLE 1

3 involving minimal difficulty or effort ⟨The dance looked smooth and *fluid*, though backstage we could see the dancer gasping for breath and sweating from the effort.⟩ — see EASY 1

4 likely to change frequently, suddenly, or unexpectedly ⟨His arrival plans are *fluid*, so expect him anytime.⟩ — see FICKLE 1

fluky *also* **flukey** *adj* **1** coming or happening by good luck especially unexpectedly ⟨a *fluky* coincidence that kept me safely at home when the blizzard hit⟩ — see FORTUNATE 1

2 happening by chance ⟨the *fluky* selection of consecutive numbers on consecutive days of the lottery⟩ — see ACCIDENTAL 1

flume *n* **1** a narrow opening between hillsides or mountains that can be used for passage ⟨hiked through the *flume* and into the meadow beyond it⟩ — see CANYON

2 an open man-made passageway for water ⟨built a *flume* next to the road for runoff⟩ — see CHANNEL 1

flunk *vb* to be unsuccessful ⟨The movie *flunks*, both as entertainment and as a dramatization of a historical incident.⟩ — see FAIL 2

flunky *also* **flunkey** *or* **flunkie** *n* a person who flatters another in order to get ahead ⟨a rock star who saw through the phonies and the *flunkies*⟩ — see SYCOPHANT

fluorescence *n* the steady giving off of the form of radiation that makes vision possible ⟨studied the *fluorescence* of certain elements⟩ — see LIGHT 1

flurry *n* **1** a sudden and usually temporary growth of activity ⟨a *flurry* of activity on the floor of the stock market as soon as the news spread⟩ — see OUTBREAK 1

2 a sudden brief rush of wind ⟨a *flurry* that scattered the fallen leaves⟩ — see GUST 1

3 a rapid or overwhelming outpouring of many things at once ⟨a patient with a mysterious illness being subjected to a *flurry* of tests⟩ — see BARRAGE

flurry *vb* to trouble the mind of; to make uneasy ⟨*Flurried* by visions of falls and broken bones, the parents wouldn't even allow the child to ride a bike.⟩ — see DISTURB 1

flush *adj* **1** having a healthy reddish skin tone ⟨was *flushed* after getting out of the hot bath⟩ — see RUDDY

2 having a surface without bends, breaks, or irregularities ⟨The *flush* paneling on the door gives it a very plain and dull look.⟩ — see LEVEL 1

3 having active strength of body or mind ⟨a *flush*, healthy man of 65⟩ — see VIGOROUS 1

4 having goods, property, or money in abundance ⟨She's very *flush* now that her business is doing well.⟩ — see RICH 1

5 possessing or covered with great numbers or amounts of something specified ⟨a field *flush* with flowers⟩ — see RIFE

6 having a border in common ⟨The front yard's floral border is *flush* with the sidewalk.⟩ — see ADJACENT

flush *n* **1** a rosy appearance (of the cheeks) ⟨looked for a *flush* on her cheeks as evidence of a fever⟩ — see BLOOM 2

2 a state or time of great activity, thriving, or achievement ⟨was in the *flush* of his youth⟩ — see BLOOM 1

3 a sudden intense expression of strong feeling ⟨a *flush* of patriotic pride⟩ — see OUTBURST 1

flush *vb* **1** to pour liquid over or through in order to cleanse ⟨Use this cleaner to *flush* the drain in the sink.⟩

synonyms irrigate, rinse, sluice, wash, wash out

related words deluge, engulf, flood, inundate, swamp; flow, gush, rush, stream; drench, saturate, soak; douse (*also* dowse), slosh, splash

2 to develop a rosy facial color (as from excitement or embarrassment) ⟨He *flushed* deeply upon hearing the compliment.⟩ — see BLUSH

fluster *n* **1** a state of nervous or irritated concern ⟨All the yelling on the bus put the driver in a *fluster*.⟩ — see FRET

2 the emotional state of being made self-consciously uncomfortable ⟨There was a palpable *fluster* in the audience when I asked my awkward question.⟩ — see EMBARRASSMENT 1

fluster *vb* to throw into a state of self-conscious distress ⟨was *flustered* when her parents dragged out her baby pictures for her new boyfriend⟩ — see EMBARRASS 1

flustering *adj* causing embarrassment ⟨a *flustering* situation that left us all silent⟩ — see AWKWARD 3

flutter *n* a sudden and usually temporary growth of activity ⟨The site saw a *flutter* of construction last month, but nothing's happening now.⟩ — see OUTBREAK 1

flutter *vb* **1** to make an irregular series of quick, sudden movements ⟨a lonely butterfly *fluttering* across the lawn⟩ — see FLIT

2 to move or cause to move with a striking motion ⟨curtains *fluttering* in the breeze⟩ — see FLAP

fluttery *adj* easily excited by nature ⟨a *fluttery* bus driver who was obviously in the wrong line of work⟩ — see EXCITABLE

flux *n* **1** the frequent and usually sudden passing from one condition to another ⟨The English language is always in a state of *flux*.⟩

synonyms change, inconstancy, oscillation

related words metamorphosis, mutation, transformation, transmogrification, transmutation; vacillation, wavering

2 a flowing or coming in ⟨January typically brings a great *flux* of returns to department stores.⟩ — see INFLUX

3 abnormally frequent intestinal evacuations with more or less fluid stools ⟨Civil War doctors noted frequent cases of *flux* in the camps.⟩ — see DIARRHEA

flux *vb* to go from a solid to a liquid state ⟨A solid will *flux* more quickly under pressure.⟩ — see LIQUEFY

fly *vb* **1** to move through the air with or as if with outstretched wings ⟨The Wright brothers realized mankind's age-old wish to *fly*.⟩

synonyms glide, plane, soar, wing

related words drift, float, hang, hover, waft; coast, cruise, sail, sweep; dart, flit, flutter; catapult, jet, orbit, rocket; dive, stoop

2 to get free from a dangerous or confining situation ⟨You must *fly* to safety immediately.⟩ — see ESCAPE 1

3 to proceed or move quickly ⟨Jim *flew* down the concourse to catch his flight.⟩ — see HURRY 2

4 to hasten away from something dangerous or frightening ⟨I approached cautiously, ready to *fly* if necessary.⟩ — see RUN 2

5 to cease to be visible ⟨The morning mist had *flown*, and a sparkling sea lay before us.⟩ — see DISAPPEAR

6 to withstand scrutiny and gain acceptance or approval ⟨The familiar "Because I said so!" is a reason that won't *fly* with most teenagers.⟩ — see WASH 2

flying *adj* **1** acting or done with excessive or careless speed ⟨a *flying* attempt at finishing the work⟩ — see HASTY 1

2 moving, proceeding, or acting with great speed ⟨That car was *flying* as it careened down the streets.⟩ — see FAST 1

flying *n* travel through the air by the use of wings ⟨had never had the slightest fear of *flying*⟩ — see ¹FLIGHT

flyspeck *n* a very small piece ⟨surreptitiously removed a *flyspeck* of dirt from the china⟩ — see BIT 1

foam *n* a light mass of fine bubbles formed in or on a liquid ⟨a steaming cup of hot cocoa with a sprinkling of marshmallows drifting through the *foam*⟩

synonyms froth, head, lather, spume, suds, surf

related words mousse; mist, spindrift, spray; scum

foam *vb* to be excited or emotionally stirred up with anger ⟨The old man *foamed* and raged when they told him he would have to give up the farm.⟩ — see BOIL 1

foaming *adj* feeling or showing anger ⟨Jon was so upset that he was really *foaming*.⟩ — see ANGRY

foamy *adj* covered with, consisting of, or resembling foam ⟨*foamy* milk shakes⟩

synonyms frothy, lathery, sudsy

related words bubbly, effervescent, fizzy, sparkling; soapy

focus *n* **1** a thing or place that is of greatest importance to an activity or interest ⟨In the 19th century Paris was the *focus* of the art world.⟩ — see CENTER 1

2 a guiding or motivating purpose or principle ⟨a wildlife conservation organization that seems to have lost its *focus*⟩ — see COMPASS 1

focus *vb* to fix (as one's attention) steadily toward a central objective ⟨Try to *focus* your attention on the task at hand.⟩ — see CONCENTRATE 2

focused *also* **focussed** *adj* **1** having the mind fixed on something ⟨He was *focused* on the football game and didn't hear me knock.⟩ — see ATTENTIVE 1

2 not divided or scattered among several areas of interest or concern ⟨a *focused* effort to provide shelter for the homeless during the winter⟩ — see WHOLE 1

foe *n* **1** one that is hostile toward another ⟨Are you friend or *foe*?⟩ — see ENEMY

2 one that takes a position opposite another in a competition or conflict ⟨This Saturday our team will go up against our longtime *foes* in a game that will determine the champion of the conference.⟩ — see OPPONENT 1

fog *n* **1** a state of mental confusion ⟨I didn't get enough sleep and now I'm in a *fog*.⟩ — see HAZE 2

2 an atmospheric condition in which suspended particles in the air rob it of its transparency ⟨The *fog* lifted once the sun was out.⟩ — see HAZE 1

3 a state of mental uncertainty ⟨I wandered around in a *fog* after the shocking news.⟩ — see CONFUSION 1

fog *vb* **1** to make (something) unclear to the understanding ⟨extraneous matters that only serve to *fog* the central issue⟩ — see CONFUSE 2

2 to make dark, dim, or indistinct ⟨Time will *fog* memories.⟩ — see CLOUD 1

foggy *adj* **1** filled with or dimmed by fine particles (as of dust or water) in suspension ⟨It's pretty *foggy* outside, so be careful driving home.⟩ — see HAZY 1

2 not seen or understood clearly ⟨could only see a *foggy* outline of the other car in the dark⟩ — see FAINT 1

fogy *also* **fogey** *n* a person with old-fashioned ideas ⟨old *fogies* who said that hip-hop would never last⟩

synonyms antediluvian, fossil, fuddy-duddy, reactionary, stick-in-the-mud

related words conservative, rightist, Tory; mandarin, old hand, old-timer, veteran; old maid

near antonyms liberal, progressive, radical

antonyms hipster, modern, trendy

foible *n* a defect in character ⟨could tolerate my uncle's *foibles* because we loved him dearly⟩ — see FAULT 1

foil *vb* to prevent from achieving a goal ⟨In popular fiction the hero will always *foil* the villain's plans.⟩ — see FRUSTRATE 1

foist *vb* to offer (something fake, useless, or inferior) as genuine, useful, or valuable ⟨shopkeepers who *foist* shoddy souvenirs on unsuspecting tourists⟩

synonyms palm off, pass off, wish

related words entail, force, impose, inflict; counterfeit, fake, forge; distort, falsify, misrepresent

fold *n* a group of people sharing a common interest and relating together socially ⟨ready to welcome their old friend back into the *fold*⟩ — see GANG 2

fold *vb* **1** to lay one part over or against another part of ⟨*Fold* the blanket so that it will fit inside the trunk.⟩

synonyms double

related words overlap, overlay, overlie; collapse; close, shut; plait, pleat

antonyms extend, open, spread, unfold, unroll

2 to be unsuccessful ⟨The business *folded* after just two months.⟩ — see FAIL 2

folder *n* a short printed publication with no cover or with a paper cover ⟨a *folder* offering tips for heating one's home efficiently⟩ — see PAMPHLET

foliage *n* green leaves or plants ⟨decided the office needed more *foliage* and bought a few plants⟩ — see GREENERY

folk *n* **1 folks** *pl* a group of persons who come from the same ancestor ⟨Her *folks* have farmed that land for five generations.⟩ — see FAMILY 1

2 one of the segments of society into which people are grouped ⟨the working-class *folk* with no airs or pretentions⟩ — see CLASS 1

3 folks *pl* human beings in general ⟨C'mon, *folks*, let's get to work!⟩ — see PEOPLE 1

folklore *n* the body of customs, beliefs, stories, and sayings associated with a people, thing, or place ⟨The Scottish Highlands are rich in *folklore*.⟩

synonyms legend, lore, myth, mythology, tradition

related words folklife; information, knowledge, wisdom; anecdote, fable, folktale, old wives' tale, tale, yarn

follow *vb* **1** to come after in time ⟨A wrap-up always *follows* the Super Bowl broadcast.⟩

synonyms postdate, succeed, supervene

related words displace, replace, supersede, supplant; ensue

antonyms antedate, precede, predate

2 to go after or on the track of ⟨Let's *follow* the boys to their hiding place.⟩

synonyms chase, course, dog, hound, pursue, run, shadow, tag, tail, trace, track, trail

related words accompany, chaperone (*or* chaperon), escort; hunt, search (for); seek; eye, observe, watch

phrases run after

near antonyms head

antonyms guide, lead, pilot

3 to act according to the commands of ⟨*Follow* me, and you'll do OK.⟩ — see OBEY
4 to make one's way through, across, or over ⟨We *followed* the path into the garden.⟩ — see TRAVERSE
5 to take notice of and be guided by ⟨Don't *follow* his advice!⟩ — see HEED 1
6 to keep one's eyes on ⟨I stood on the platform and *followed* the departing train until it disappeared from sight.⟩ — see WATCH 1

follower *n* **1** one who follows the opinions or teachings of another ⟨The *followers* of Gandhi have spread his philosophy of nonviolence all over the world.⟩
synonyms adherent, convert, disciple, partisan (*also* partizan), pupil, votary
related words apostle, missionary, proselytizer, soldier; faithful, loyalist; advocate, backer, champion, supporter; protégé, scholar, student; ideologist, ideologue (*also* idealogue), sectarian; admirer, cultist, devotee, enthusiast, fan, idolater (*or* idolator), worshipper (*or* worshiper), zealot; apparatchik, camp follower, flunky (*also* flunkey *or* flunkie), hanger-on, henchman, lackey, lickspittle, minion, stooge, sycophant, toady, yes-man
near antonyms apostate, defector, renegade, traitor, turncoat
antonyms leader
2 a person who adopts the appearance or behavior of another especially in an obvious way ⟨The musician's gritty style inspired a whole generation of *followers*.⟩ — see COPYCAT

following *adj* being the one that comes immediately after another ⟨The *following* morning, I found the cat was gone.⟩ — see NEXT

following *n* **1** a body of employees or attendants who accompany and wait on a person ⟨a prince with a large *following* to do practically everything for him⟩ — see CORTEGE 1
2 a group of people showing intense devotion to a cause, person, or work (as a film) ⟨That rock star attracts quite a *following*.⟩ — see CULT 1
3 the act of going after or in the tracks of another ⟨took part in the *following* of the coyote⟩ — see PURSUIT

following *prep* subsequent to in time or order ⟨*Following* the concert, there will be refreshments in the lobby.⟩ — see AFTER

folly *n* **1** a foolish act or idea ⟨The American purchase of Alaska was originally considered a grand *folly*.⟩
synonyms absurdity, asininity, fatuity, foolery, idiocy, imbecility, inanity, stupidity
related words absurdness, craziness, foolishness, inaneness, madness, senselessness, witlessness; monkeyshine(s), shenanigan(s), tomfoolery; drivel, humbug, nonsense, twaddle; blunder, bungle, flub, goof, howler
near antonyms discretion, forethought, prudence, sagacity, wisdom; brainstorm, inspiration
2 lack of good sense or judgment ⟨In all my *folly*, I didn't think about how my actions would hurt my father.⟩ — see FOOLISHNESS 1
3 language, behavior, or ideas that are absurd and contrary to good sense ⟨enough of this *folly* about moving to the Australian outback⟩ — see NONSENSE 1

foment *vb* to bring (something volatile or intense) into being ⟨Abigail Adams told her husband, John, that if women were not remembered by the new American government, they would "*foment* a Rebellion and will not hold ourselves bound by any Laws in which we have no voice or Representation."⟩ — see INCITE 1

fomenter *n* a person who stirs up public feelings especially of discontent ⟨sent the *fomenters* of the rebellion to prison⟩ — see AGITATOR

fond *adj* **1** having a liking or affection ⟨They discovered they were both *fond* of country music.⟩
synonyms affected, attached, inclined, partial
related words crazy (about *or* over), enamored, enraptured, gone (on), infatuated, mad (about), nuts (about); desirous, eager, enthusiastic, excited, gung ho, keen
phrases big on
near antonyms apathetic, cool, indifferent, uninterested; contemptuous, disdainful, scornful; antagonistic, antipathetic, hostile; alienated, disaffected, disenchanted, estranged
antonyms allergic, averse, disinclined
2 feeling or showing love ⟨Dad gave me a *fond* embrace upon parting.⟩ — see LOVING 1
3 granted special treatment or attention ⟨My *fondest* wish is to see my children happy.⟩ — see DARLING 1

fondle *vb* to touch or handle in a tender or loving manner ⟨a cat who enjoys being *fondled* by his loving owners⟩
synonyms caress, gentle, love, pat, pet, stroke
related words bill, canoodle, cuddle, nestle, nose, nuzzle, snuggle, spoon; feel up, paw; cradle, embrace, enfold, hug; bounce, dandle; knead; baby, coddle, indulge, mollycoddle, pamper, spoil

fondness *n* **1** a feeling of strong or constant regard for and dedication to someone ⟨My *fondness* for you will never fail.⟩ — see LOVE 1
2 positive regard for something ⟨I have a *fondness* for expensive chocolate.⟩ — see LIKING

food *n* substances intended to be eaten ⟨a simple, little restaurant with excellent *food*⟩
synonyms bread, chow, chuck [*chiefly West*], eatables, edibles, fare, foodstuffs, grub, meat, provender, provisions, table, viands, victuals, vittles
related words commissary, rations, supplies; aliment, nutriment; diet, nurture; mess, pap; ensilage, feed, fodder, forage, silage, slop, swill; feast, meal, refreshments, regale, repast, spread; board; dish, plate, platter, serving; finger food, natural food
near antonyms bane, poison, toxin, venom

foodstuffs *pl n* substances intended to be eaten ⟨stocked up on candles and *foodstuffs* before the hurricane⟩ — see FOOD

fool *n* **1** a person who lacks good sense or judgment ⟨Only a *fool* would attempt to climb that mountain unprepared.⟩
synonyms booby, goose, half-wit, nincompoop, ninny, nitwit, simpleton, turkey, yo-yo
related words daredevil; madman, madwoman; blockhead, dodo, dolt, donkey, dope, dork [*slang*], dumbbell, dummy, dunce, fathead, gander, goon, half-wit, idiot, ignoramus, imbecile, know-nothing, moron, numskull (*or* numbskull), pinhead, stock; featherbrain; butt, dupe, laughingstock, mockery, monkey; chump, loser, schlemiel (*also* shlemiel); character, codger, crackbrain, crank, kook, oddball, screwball, weirdo; flibbertigibbet
near antonyms sage, thinker; brain, genius
2 a person formerly kept in a royal or noble household to amuse with jests and pranks ⟨A king's *fool* could get away with saying things that others in the palace couldn't.⟩
synonyms jester, motley
related words buffoon, clown, comedian, comedienne, comic, cutup, droll, harlequin, joker, jokester, madcap, merry-andrew, vice, wag, zany; mime, mummer
3 a person with a strong and habitual liking for something ⟨I'm a *fool* for ice cream—virtually any flavor.⟩ — see FAN

fool *adj* showing or marked by a lack of good sense or judgment ⟨He's always got some *fool* plan or other.⟩ — see FOOLISH 1

fool *vb* **1** to cause to believe what is untrue ⟨I *fooled* him into thinking that we were driving to the store, not to his surprise birthday party.⟩ — see DECEIVE

2 to make jokes ⟨an edgy comedian *fooling* with an appreciative college audience⟩ — see JOKE 1

fool (with) *vb* to handle thoughtlessly, ignorantly, or mischievously ⟨not a good idea to *fool with* power tools before you've read the manual⟩ — see TAMPER (WITH)

foolery *n* **1** a foolish act or idea ⟨Investing in that company would be *foolery*.⟩ — see FOLLY 1

2 wildly playful or mischievous behavior ⟨Let the kids have a little *foolery* once in a while.⟩ — see HORSEPLAY

foolhardy *adj* **1** foolishly adventurous or bold ⟨hikers who were *foolhardy* enough to remain on the summit during a thunderstorm⟩

synonyms audacious, brash, daredevil, madcap, overbold, overconfident, reckless

related words adventuresome, adventurous, bold, daring, venturesome, venturous; hotheaded; impetuous, imprudent, impulsive, incautious, rash; brainless, foolish, harebrained, scatterbrained; careless, heedless, thoughtless; hasty, headlong, precipitate

near antonyms unadventurous, unambitious; fainthearted, fearful, mousy (*or* mousey), scary, shy, skittish, timid, timorous; calm, cool, levelheaded, sensible; chicken, chickenhearted, cowardly, craven, dastardly, lily-livered, pusillanimous, recreant, spineless, unheroic, yellow

antonyms careful, cautious, circumspect, guarded, heedful, prudent, safe, wary

2 having or showing a lack of concern for the consequences of one's actions ⟨It's *foolhardy* to go hiking during late fall without warm clothes.⟩ — see RECKLESS 1

fooling *adj* marked by or expressive of mild or good-natured teasing ⟨ribbed him with *fooling* comments about his old-fashioned taste in music⟩ — see QUIZZICAL

foolish *adj* **1** showing or marked by a lack of good sense or judgment ⟨*foolish* people who thought that the world would end in the year 2000⟩ ⟨a *foolish* scheme that was supposed to make us all rich⟩

synonyms absurd, asinine, balmy, brainless, cockeyed, daffy, daft, dotty, fatuous, fool, half-baked, harebrained, half-witted, inept, jerky, kooky (*also* kookie), nonsensical, nutty, preposterous, sappy, screwball, senseless, silly, simpleminded, stupid, unwise, wacky (*also* whacky), weak-minded, witless, zany

related words airheaded, chowderheaded, chuckleheaded, dense, dim, dim-witted, doltish, dopey (*also* dopy), dorky [*slang*], dull, dumb, dunderheaded, empty-headed, fatuous, feebleminded, idiotic (*also* idiotical), imbecile (*or* imbecilic), knuckleheaded, mindless, moronic, oafish, obtuse, opaque, simple, slow, slow-witted, soft, soft-headed, thoughtless, thick, thickheaded, unintelligent, vacuous, witless; fallacious, illogical, invalid, irrational, unreasonable, unreasoning, unsound, weak; farcical, laughable, ludicrous, ridiculous; buffoonish, clownish; ill-advised, unconsidered, unreasoned

phrases out to lunch

near antonyms brainy, bright, clever, intelligent, smart; logical, rational, reasonable, valid; well-advised

antonyms judicious, prudent, sagacious, sage, sane, sapient, sensible, sound, wise

2 conceived or made without regard for reason or reality ⟨*foolish* attempts to construct a perpetual motion machine⟩ — see FANTASTIC 1

3 lacking importance ⟨The current regulations are cluttered with *foolish* details.⟩ — see UNIMPORTANT

foolishness *n* **1** lack of good sense or judgment ⟨the *foolishness* of going off to search for the fountain of youth⟩

synonyms absurdity, asininity, balminess, brainlessness, daftness, fatuity, folly, imbecility, inanity, madness, nonsensicalness, nuttiness, preposterousness, senselessness, silliness, simplicity, wackiness, witlessness, zaniness

related words denseness, doltishness, dopiness, dullness (*also* dulness), dumbness, feeblemindedness, idiocy, mindlessness, oafishness, obtuseness, simpleness, slowness, stupidity, stupidness, vacuity; fallacy, irrationality, unreasonableness; kookiness, weirdness; laughableness, ludicrousness, ridiculousness

near antonyms logicality, logicalness, rationality, rationalness, reasonability, reasonableness, validity; discernment, insight, perception

antonyms prudence, sagaciousness, sagacity, sageness, sanity, sapience, sensibleness, soundness, wisdom

2 language, behavior, or ideas that are absurd and contrary to good sense ⟨I couldn't listen to another second of their *foolishness*, so I told them to be quiet.⟩ — see NONSENSE 1

3 the quality or state of lacking intelligence or quickness of mind ⟨You didn't fail the test because of any innate *foolishness* but because of a lack of preparation.⟩ — see STUPIDITY 1

foot *n* the lowest part, place, or point ⟨the *foot* of the pedestal⟩ — see BOTTOM 3

foot *vb* to give what is owed for ⟨I'll *foot* the bill for dinner.⟩ — see PAY 2

foot (it) *vb* **1** to go on foot ⟨After the car broke down, we had to *foot it* to the movie.⟩ — see WALK 1

2 to perform a series of usually rhythmic bodily movements to music ⟨We got out onto the dance floor and *footed it* like crazy.⟩ — see DANCE 1

foot (up) *vb* to combine (numbers) into a single sum ⟨Please *foot up* your traveling expenses from this past month.⟩ — see ADD 2

foothold *n* a place from which an advance (as for military operations) is made ⟨Don't let the opposing team push us back down the field and gain a *foothold*.⟩ — see BASE 2

footing *n* **1** an immaterial thing upon which something else rests ⟨Your donations help provide the charity with a firm financial *footing* for its work.⟩ — see BASE 1

2 position with regard to conditions and circumstances ⟨The village's two churches are on a friendly *footing*.⟩ — see SITUATION 1

3 the placement of someone or something in relation to others in a vertical arrangement ⟨You'll have to work hard to get a better *footing* in the company.⟩ — see RANK 1

footloose *adj* **1** not bound, confined, or detained by force ⟨After having been leashed for so long, the suddenly *footloose* dog ran helter-skelter about the yard.⟩ — see FREE 3

2 not held back by rules, duties, or worries ⟨I wished I could be as carefree as that *footloose* toddler.⟩ — see FREEWHEELING

footpath *n* a rough course or way formed by or as if by repeated footsteps ⟨found the *footpath* leading down into the valley⟩ — see TRAIL 1

footprint *n* the mark or impression made by a foot ⟨mysterious *footprints* along the beach⟩

synonyms footstep, step, trace, vestige

related words hoofprint; pug, spoor, track; tread

footstep *n* the mark or impression made by a foot ⟨saw muddy *footsteps* on the just-cleaned stairs⟩ — see FOOTPRINT

foozle *vb* to make or do (something) in a clumsy or unskillful way ⟨*foozled* the attempt to move the couch into the apartment and tore the fabric on the arms⟩ — see BOTCH

fop *n* a man extremely interested in his clothing and

personal appearance ⟨said it was a style for *fops*⟩ — see DANDY 1

for *conj* for the reason that ⟨The bill should be listed as paid, *for* I mailed it in on time.⟩ — see SINCE

forage *vb* to feed on grass or herbs ⟨cows *foraging* in the pasture⟩ — see ¹GRAZE

forage (for) *vb* to go in search of ⟨squirrels *foraging for* acorns⟩ — see SEEK 1

foray *n* a sudden attack on and entrance into hostile territory ⟨made a nighttime *foray* into the enemy camp and took their command post⟩ — see RAID 1

foray (into) *vb* to enter for conquest or plunder ⟨Vikings *foraying into* the village⟩ — see INVADE

forbear *vb* to resist the temptation of ⟨She's old enough to make her own decisions, so we must *forbear* criticizing them.⟩

synonyms abjure, abstain (from), forgo (*also* forego), keep (from), refrain (from)

related words avoid, eschew, shun; check, constrain, curb, inhibit; deny, refuse, reject, repudiate; buck, combat, fight

near antonyms acquiesce (to), capitulate, concede (to), knuckle under (to)

antonyms bow (to), give in (to), submit (to), succumb (to), surrender (to), yield (to)

forbearance *n* 1 the capacity to endure what is difficult or disagreeable without complaining ⟨We thank you for your *forbearance* while we attend to the technical difficulties interrupting the TV program.⟩ — see PATIENCE

2 kind, gentle, or compassionate treatment especially towards someone who is undeserving of it ⟨The judge showed *forbearance*, and gave the first offender a suspended sentence.⟩ — see MERCY 1

forbearing *adj* accepting pains or hardships calmly or without complaint ⟨She was inspired by the *forbearing* patients of the intensive care unit.⟩ — see PATIENT 1

forbid *vb* to order not to do or use or to be done or used ⟨Smoking is *forbidden* throughout the building.⟩ ⟨We *forbid* you to see him.⟩

synonyms ban, bar, enjoin, interdict, outlaw, prohibit, proscribe

related words deter, discourage, dissuade; clamp down (on), crack down (on), crush, put down, quash, quell, repress, silence, snuff (out), squash, squelch, subdue, suppress; halt, preclude, prevent, stop; embargo, exclude, rule out, shut out; debar, disallow, reject, repudiate, veto; bridle, check, curb, inhibit, rein (in), restrain; block, hinder, impede, obstruct; illegalize

near antonyms approve, endorse (*also* indorse), sanction; authorize, license (*also* licence), warrant; abet, advance, cultivate, encourage, forward, further, nourish, nurture, promote, support; bid, command, order; abide, bear, brook, countenance, endure, tolerate

antonyms allow, let, permit, suffer

forbidden *adj* that may not be permitted ⟨Trespassing is *forbidden*.⟩ — see IMPERMISSIBLE 1

forbidding *adj* 1 causing fear ⟨a dark, *forbidding* house, that is reputed to be haunted⟩ — see FEARFUL 1

2 harsh and threatening in manner or appearance ⟨He told us in a *forbidding* voice to stop calling him by that name.⟩ — see GRIM 1

forbidding *n* the act of ordering that something not be done or used ⟨the landlord's *forbidding* of loud music after 10:00 p.m.⟩ — see PROHIBITION 1

force *n* 1 a body of persons at work or available for work ⟨The entire *force* of the shipyard will be needed to get this government order done on time.⟩

synonyms help, manpower, personnel, pool, staff, workforce

related words labor, proletariat, rank and file; band, company, crew, gang, outfit, party, squad, team; employee (*also* employe), helper, hireling, worker

2 the use of power to impose one's will on another ⟨a cruel tyrant who disbanded the parliament and ruled by *force*⟩

synonyms coercion, compulsion, constraint, duress, pressure

related words browbeating, bulldozing, bullying; fear, intimidation, menace, sword, terror, terrorism, threat, violence; might, muscle, potency, puissance, strength; hardheadedness, self-will, willfulness; strain, stress

near antonyms agreement, approval, consent, permission; convincing, persuasion, reason, suasion

3 the ability to exert effort for the accomplishment of a task ⟨got through the college board exams by sheer *force* of will⟩ — see POWER 2

4 the capacity to persuade ⟨Surely you were influenced by the *force* of his arguments?⟩ — see COGENCY 1

5 the quality of an utterance that provokes interest and produces an effect ⟨felt the full *force* of her denunciation of war as a morally acceptable option⟩ — see ¹PUNCH 1

6 the use of brute strength to cause harm to a person or property ⟨threatened to resort to *force* if he wouldn't listen to reason⟩ — see VIOLENCE 1

7 a body of officers of the law ⟨The new police chief will most likely be someone from the *force*.⟩ — see POLICE 2

8 the number of individuals or amount of something available at any given time ⟨the great debate during the Cold War was whether the nation's missile *force* was adequate⟩ — see SUPPLY

force *vb* to cause (a person) to give in to pressure ⟨I had to *force* myself to get up this morning.⟩ ⟨They were *forced* to sell at a lower price.⟩

synonyms coerce, compel, constrain, drive, impel, impress, make, muscle, obligate, oblige, press, pressure

related words browbeat, bulldoze, bully, cow, hector, intimidate; blackmail, high-pressure, menace, shame, terrorize, threaten; drag; badger, hound

phrases twist one's arm

near antonyms allow, let, permit; argue, convince, induce, move, persuade, prevail (on *or* upon), satisfy, talk (into), win (over)

forced *adj* 1 forcing one's compliance or participation by or as if by law ⟨*forced* attendance at orientation sessions⟩ — see MANDATORY

2 lacking in natural or spontaneous quality ⟨I wasn't too excited about their wedding plans and so gave them a *forced* smile.⟩ — see ARTIFICIAL 1

3 not made or done willingly or by choice ⟨Participation in the program was *forced*.⟩ — see INVOLUNTARY 1

forceful *adj* 1 having the power to persuade ⟨made a very *forceful* argument against going to war⟩ — see COGENT

2 marked by or uttered with forcefulness ⟨He kept asking for money until I gave him a very *forceful* and blunt "no."⟩ — see EMPHATIC 1

3 not showing weakness or uncertainty ⟨took a *forceful* stand on the highly controversial issue⟩ — see FIRM 1

4 having power over the minds or behavior of others ⟨a *forceful* speaker whose words moved the audience to tears⟩ — see INFLUENTIAL 1

forcefully *adv* in a vigorous and forceful manner ⟨He shut the door a little too *forcefully* and broke the glass.⟩ — see HARD 3

forcefulness *n* 1 the capacity to persuade ⟨The *forcefulness* of his argument is indisputable.⟩ — see COGENCY 1

2 the quality of an utterance that provokes interest and produces an effect ⟨delivered the punch line with appropriate *forcefulness*⟩ — see ¹PUNCH 1

3 the quality or state of being forceful (as in expression) ⟨Her clenched teeth only added to the *forcefulness* of her words.⟩ — see VEHEMENCE 1

forcibly *adv* in a vigorous and forceful manner ⟨After getting in the ref's face once too often, he was *forcibly* ejected from the game.⟩ — see HARD 3

ford *n* a place where a body of water (as a sea or river) is shallow ⟨didn't attempt getting the horses across the stream until we had reached the *ford*⟩ — see SHOAL

forearm *vb* to prepare (oneself) mentally or emotionally ⟨*forearmed* themselves for the championship game with the help of a sports psychologist⟩ — see FORTIFY 1

forebear *also* **forbear** *n* a person who is several generations earlier in an individual's line of descent ⟨His *forebears* came to America on the *Mayflower*.⟩ — see ANCESTOR 1

forebode *also* **forbode** *vb* to show signs of a favorable or successful outcome ⟨That police car parked outside the house doesn't *forebode* well.⟩ — see BODE

foreboding *adj* being or showing a sign of evil or calamity to come ⟨*Foreboding* war clouds began to gather.⟩ — see OMINOUS

foreboding *n* **1** a feeling that something bad will happen ⟨I have this strange *foreboding* that your ski vacation will not turn out well, so be extra careful.⟩ — see PREMONITION

2 something believed to be a sign or warning of a future event ⟨used to think that if he saw a blackbird fly over his left shoulder it was a *foreboding* of harm⟩ — see OMEN

3 suspicion or fear of future harm or misfortune ⟨a pessimist who is always overcome by a sense of *foreboding* before flying on an airplane⟩ — see APPREHENSION 1

forecast *n* a declaration that something will happen in the future ⟨I want to check the weather *forecast* so I'll know what kind of clothes to pack for the trip tomorrow.⟩ — see PREDICTION

forecast *vb* to tell of or describe beforehand ⟨The station's meteorologist *forecasts* sun for the next five days.⟩ — see FORETELL

forecaster *n* one who predicts future events or developments ⟨a financial *forecaster* who is widely followed by small investors⟩ — see PROPHET 1

forecasting *n* a declaration that something will happen in the future ⟨The construction company's *forecasting* of a September 1 completion date for the new school was wildly optimistic.⟩ — see PREDICTION

foredoom *vb* to determine the fate of in advance ⟨Since the dawn of the ages he was *foredoomed* to become king one day.⟩ — see DESTINE

forefather *n* a person who is several generations earlier in an individual's line of descent ⟨Our *forefathers* bought this farm, and our family has worked it for three generations.⟩ — see ANCESTOR 1

forefront *n* the leading or most important part of a movement ⟨a politician who was in the *forefront* of women's rights⟩
synonyms van, vanguard
related words spearhead; avant-garde

forego *vb* to go or come before in time ⟨If the crowds are any indication of the public's interest in the presidential candidate, then his reputation obviously *foregoes* him.⟩ — see PRECEDE

foregoer *n* **1** one that announces or indicates the later arrival of another ⟨an early November snowfall that appears to be a disconcerting *foregoer* of the harsh winter facing us⟩ — see FORERUNNER 1

2 something belonging to an earlier time from which something else was later developed ⟨Not many people

still have manual typewriters, the *foregoers* to word processors.⟩ — see ANCESTOR 2

foregoing *adj* going before another in time or order ⟨Your *foregoing* statement contradicts your latest one.⟩ — see PREVIOUS

forehanded *adj* having or showing awareness of and preparation for the future ⟨She was *forehanded* enough to stock up on batteries for winter storms.⟩ — see FORESIGHTED

foreign *adj* **1** being, relating to, or characteristic of a country other than one's own ⟨More Americans should take an interest in *foreign* languages.⟩
synonyms alien, nonnative
related words imported, introduced, naturalized, transplanted; external, multicultural, multilateral; foreign-born, nonindigenous; distant, far-off, overseas, remote; bizarre, exotic, outlandish, strange
near antonyms endemic, local; aboriginal, indigenous
antonyms domestic, native

2 not being a vital part of or belonging to something ⟨Pediatricians often have to remove peas or other *foreign* bodies from inside the ears of curious toddlers.⟩ — see EXTRINSIC

foreigner *n* a person who is not native to or known to a community ⟨I can tell by your accent you're a *foreigner* in these parts.⟩ — see STRANGER

foreknow *vb* to realize or know about beforehand ⟨What young person can possibly *foreknow* what life will bring?⟩ — see FORESEE

foreknowledge *n* the special ability to see or know about events before they actually occur ⟨a suspenseful story about a man who has a frightening *foreknowledge* of disasters⟩ — see FORESIGHT 1

foreman *n* the person (as an employer or supervisor) who tells people and especially workers what to do ⟨Tom asked the shift *foreman* if he could take a break.⟩ — see BOSS

foremost *adj* **1** coming before all others in importance ⟨Albert Einstein is regarded by many as the *foremost* figure of the 20th century.⟩
synonyms arch, big, capital, cardinal, central, chief, dominant, first, grand, great, greatest, highest, key, leading, main, master, overbearing, paramount, predominant, preeminent, premier, primal, primary, principal, prior, sovereign (*also* sovran), supreme
related words distinguished, eminent, illustrious, noble, notable, noteworthy, outstanding, prestigious, signal, star, stellar, superior; high-level, senior, top; important, influential, major, mighty, momentous, significant; incomparable, matchless, unequaled (*or* unequalled), unparalleled, unsurpassed; celebrated, famed, famous, renowned
near antonyms inconsequential, inconsiderable, insignificant, minor, negligible, slight, trifling, trivial, unimportant; collateral, inferior, secondary, subordinate, subsidiary
antonyms last, least

2 highest in rank or authority ⟨wanted to speak to the *foremost* supervisor in our department⟩ — see HEAD

3 coming before all others in time or order ⟨When the *foremost* person in line tripped, everyone had to stop.⟩ — see FIRST 1

forename *n* a name that is placed before one's family name ⟨A long string of *forenames* was given to the latest addition to the royal family.⟩
synonyms Christian name, given name
related words appellation, denomination, designation; cognomen, denotation, epithet, handle, nickname, sobriquet (*also* soubriquet), title; alias, nom de plume, pen name, pseudonym; baptismal name

forenoon *n* the time from sunrise until noon ⟨Enjoy the relatively cool *forenoon*, for the afternoon promises to be a scorcher.⟩ — see MORNING 1

foreordain *vb* to determine the fate of in advance ⟨We are such good friends, it's almost like we were *foreordained* to meet.⟩ — see DESTINE

forepart *n* a forward part or surface ⟨moved to the *forepart* of the machine to check the mechanism⟩ — see FRONT 1

forerunner *n* **1** one that announces or indicates the later arrival of another ⟨The return of the swallows is traditionally regarded as a *forerunner* of spring.⟩
synonyms angel, foregoer, harbinger, herald, precursor
related words foreboder, foreshadower, foretaste, forewarning; advertiser, blazoner, crier, proclaimer; courier, messenger, runner; augury, auspice, boding, foreboding, foreshadowing, omen, portent, prefiguring, presage; mark, sign, symptom
2 something belonging to an earlier time from which something else was later developed ⟨We enjoyed the demonstration of the simple hand loom that was the *forerunner* of today's computer-controlled looms.⟩ — see ANCESTOR 2

foresee *vb* to realize or know about beforehand ⟨a freak accident that no one could possibly have *foreseen*⟩
synonyms anticipate, divine, foreknow
related words augur, forecast, foretell, predict, presage, prognosticate, prophesy; envisage, foreshadow, prefigure, visualize; alert, caution, foretoken, forewarn; preview; descry, discern, perceive; apprehend, dread, fear

foreseeing *adj* having or showing awareness of and preparation for the future ⟨Some years ago the senator wrote a *foreseeing* essay on the promise of alternative energies.⟩ — see FORESIGHTED

foreseer *n* one who predicts future events or developments ⟨In Greek mythology Cassandra was a *foreseer* who always accurately predicted misfortune but was never believed.⟩ — see PROPHET 1

foreshadow *vb* to give a slight indication of beforehand ⟨a series of small tremors that *foreshadowed* the massive earthquake the next day⟩
synonyms harbinger, herald, prefigure
related words anticipate, foreknow, foresee; forecast, foretell, predict, prognosticate, prophesy; forewarn; augur, bode, forebode (*also* forbode), portend, presage, promise; allude, connote, hint, imply, insinuate, intimate, suggest

foreshadowing *n* something believed to be a sign or warning of a future event ⟨The hero's strange encounter with a grave digger is often seen as a *foreshadowing* of his own death.⟩ — see OMEN

foresight *n* **1** the special ability to see or know about events before they actually occur ⟨a mysterious woman who claims to have the gift of *foresight*⟩
synonyms foreknowledge, prescience
related words foreboding, premonition, prenotion, presage, presentiment; clairvoyance, extrasensory perception, sixth sense; omniscience; augury, divination
2 concern or preparation for the future ⟨had the *foresight* to realize the global importance of the Internet⟩
synonyms farsightedness, foresightedness, forethought, prescience, providence, vision
related words premeditation; discernment, discretion, insight, perception, perceptiveness, prudence, sagaciousness, sagacity, sageness, sapience, wisdom
near antonyms hindsight
antonyms improvidence, myopia, shortsightedness

foresighted *adj* having or showing awareness of and preparation for the future ⟨the *foresighted* conservationists who worked to create the national park system⟩

synonyms farsighted, forehanded, foreseeing, forethoughtful, forward, prescient, proactive, provident, visionary
related words careful, cautious, heedful; discerning, insightful, perceptive, percipient, prudent, sagacious, sage, sapient, wise
near antonyms careless, heedless, incautious
antonyms half-baked, half-cocked, improvident, myopic, shortsighted

foresightedness *n* concern or preparation for the future ⟨Thanks to your *foresightedness*, we have enough ice and food to last through the blackout.⟩ — see FORESIGHT 2

forest *n* a dense growth of trees and shrubs covering a large area ⟨She owned a little cottage deep in the *forest*.⟩
synonyms timber, timberland, wood(s), woodland
related words brake, brushwood, chaparral, coppice, copse, covert, grove, scrubland, stand, thicket; greenwood, wildwood; woodlot; arboretum, plantation

forestall *vb* to keep from happening by taking action in advance ⟨You can often *forestall* skidding on the ice simply by driving more slowly.⟩ — see PREVENT

forestallment *n* the act or practice of keeping something from happening ⟨By raising the necessary funds, the historical society was able to effect a last-minute *forestallment* of the demolition of the town's oldest house.⟩ — see PREVENTION

foretell *vb* to tell of or describe beforehand ⟨a 16th-century astrologer who, some claim, accurately *foretold* 20th-century events⟩
synonyms augur, call, forecast, predict, presage, prognosticate, prophesy, read
related words alert, caution, forewarn, warn; bode, forebode (*also* forbode), portend, promise; anticipate, divine, foreknow, foresee; announce, declare, herald, proclaim
near antonyms describe, narrate, recite, recount, relate, report, tell

foreteller *n* one who predicts future events or developments ⟨Some regard that 16th-century astrologer as an uncanny *foreteller* of some of the most disastrous events of the 20th century.⟩ — see PROPHET 1

foretelling *n* a declaration that something will happen in the future ⟨the ludicrous *foretellings* of self-styled psychics at the end of each year⟩ — see PREDICTION

forethought *n* concern or preparation for the future ⟨In a show of *forethought*, the city had set up a network of well-supplied emergency shelters to accommodate victims of the hurricane.⟩ — see FORESIGHT 2

forethoughtful *adj* having or showing awareness of and preparation for the future ⟨doctors encouraging people to be *forethoughtful* and get their flu shots in advance of the flu season⟩ — see FORESIGHTED

forever *adv* **1** for all time ⟨We'll be best friends *forever*.⟩ — see EVER 1
2 on every relevant occasion ⟨He is *forever* reminding me to wear my hat and gloves in cold weather.⟩ — see ALWAYS 1

forever *n* a long or seemingly long period of time ⟨It took *forever* to fill out all the forms.⟩ — see AGE 2

forevermore *adv* for all time ⟨a hero that will be praised *forevermore* for his great deeds⟩ — see EVER 1

forewarn *vb* to give notice to beforehand especially of danger or risk ⟨I should *forewarn* you before you come to visit that we have a dog.⟩ — see WARN

forewarning *n* the act or an instance of telling beforehand of danger or risk ⟨We heeded the *forewarning* to stay off the ice until the town had checked to see if it was thick enough.⟩ — see WARNING 1

foreword *n* a short section (as of a book) that leads to or explains the main part ⟨The editor makes some good points in the *foreword* about the author's life, so be sure to read it.⟩ — see INTRODUCTION

forfeit *n* a sum of money to be paid as a punishment ⟨The *forfeit* for each baseball player involved in the brawl was $5,000.⟩ — see FINE

forfeiture *n* a sum of money to be paid as a punishment ⟨The *forfeiture* for early withdrawal of the investment savings will be an amount equal to 10 percent of the investment.⟩ — see FINE

forgather *or* **foregather** *vb* to come together into one body or place ⟨The mayor asked the townsfolk to *forgather* at the war monument for the Memorial Day ceremony.⟩ — see ASSEMBLE 1

¹forge *vb* to move forward along a course ⟨The rescue team *forged* ahead despite the bad weather.⟩ — see GO 1

²forge *vb* **1** to imitate or copy especially in order to deceive ⟨arrested for *forging* the doctor's signature on the prescription⟩ — see FAKE 1
2 to shape with a hammer ⟨loved the artisan look of that hand-*forged* copper pot⟩ — see HAMMER 1

forged *adj* being such in appearance only and made or manufactured with the intention of committing fraud ⟨a *forged* ancient document that didn't fool experts in cartography⟩ — see COUNTERFEIT 1

forgery *n* an imitation that is passed off as genuine ⟨That is a cheap *forgery*, not an authentic Ming Dynasty vase.⟩ — see FAKE 1

forget *vb* **1** to be unable to recall or think of ⟨I *forget* exactly on which street that the house is.⟩
synonyms unlearn
related words lose, miss; blank; misremember; disregard, ignore, neglect, overlook, overpass, pass over, slight, slur (over)
near antonyms remind
antonyms hark back (to), recall, recollect, remember, reminisce (about), think (of)
2 to fail to give proper attention to ⟨She promised not to *forget* her high school friends after she went off to college.⟩ — see NEGLECT 1
3 to leave undone or unattended to especially through carelessness ⟨He *forgot* the pot boiling on the stove.⟩ — see NEGLECT 2
4 to miss the opportunity or obligation ⟨I *forgot* to call on his birthday.⟩ — see NEGLECT 3

forgetful *adj* inclined to forget what one has learned or to do what one should ⟨We become more *forgetful* as we get older.⟩
synonyms absentminded
related words absent, abstracted, lost, oblivious, preoccupied, unmindful; amnesiac (*or* amnesic), senile; befogged, befuddled, bewildered, confused, dazed, muddled, scatterbrained, unfocused (*also* unfocussed); lax, neglectful, negligent, remiss, slack; careless, heedless, inconsiderate, thoughtless; inattentive, insensible, unaware, unconscious, unheeding, unknowing, unthinking
near antonyms alert, attentive, awake, keen, open-eyed, sharp, vigilant, watchful, wide-awake; careful, cautious, circumspect, conscientious, heedful, thoughtful, wary
antonyms retentive

forgetfulness *n* a state of being disregardful or unconscious of one's surroundings, concerns, or obligations ⟨I welcomed the *forgetfulness* of one's worries that only sleep can bring.⟩ — see OBLIVION

forgivable *adj* worthy of forgiveness ⟨Accidentally spilling your coffee on my newspaper is certainly a *forgivable* mishap.⟩ — see VENIAL

forgive *vb* **1** to cease to have feelings of anger or bitterness toward ⟨It is not easy to *forgive* those who have hurt us.⟩
synonyms pardon

related words absolve, acquit, clear, exculpate, exonerate, vindicate; remit, shrive; condone, disregard, excuse, ignore, pass over, shrug off; discharge, liberate, redeem, release, unburden
near antonyms abhor, abominate, despise, detest, dislike, execrate, hate, loathe; avenge, redress, requite, retaliate, revenge; discipline, penalize, punish
2 to dismiss as of little importance ⟨He has so many good qualities that I guess we can *forgive* a slight penchant for exaggeration.⟩ — see EXCUSE 1

forgiveness *n* release from the guilt or penalty of an offense ⟨They asked her *forgiveness* for failing to invite her to the party.⟩ — see PARDON

forgo *also* **forego** *vb* to resist the temptation of ⟨I'll *forgo* the appetizers to save room for dinner.⟩ — see FORBEAR

forgotten *adj* left unoccupied or unused ⟨a *forgotten* doll under the bed⟩ ⟨a long-*forgotten* house down a winding dirt road⟩ — see ABANDONED 1

fork *vb* to go or move in different directions from a central point ⟨The road *forks* up ahead and you'll want to take the right fork.⟩ — see SEPARATE 2

forlorn *adj* **1** feeling unhappiness ⟨She was *forlorn* when she found out the trip had been cancelled.⟩ — see SAD 1
2 sad from lack of companionship or separation from others ⟨a *forlorn* wanderer far from home⟩ — see LONESOME 1
3 causing or marked by an atmosphere lacking in cheer ⟨a *forlorn* little town whose brief economic boom ended decades ago⟩ — see GLOOMY 1
4 feeling or showing no hope ⟨the *forlorn* expression of a candidate who knows that he hasn't a prayer of winning the election⟩ — see DESPONDENT 1

forlornness *n* **1** a state or spell of low spirits ⟨Seemingly nothing could relieve the losing team's *forlornness*.⟩ — see SADNESS
2 utter loss of hope ⟨With the *forlornness* of someone who had been disappointed many times before, he abandoned his quest.⟩ — see DESPAIR 1

form *vb* **1** to take on a definite form ⟨My ideas on the subject are just starting to *form*.⟩
synonyms crystallize (*also* crystalize), jell, shape (up), solidify
related words associate, coalesce, cohere, fuse; combine, conjoin, conjugate, connect, couple, join, link (up), unify, unite
near antonyms break down, decay, decompose, disintegrate
2 to be all the substance of ⟨This one sentence really *forms* the basis of your argument.⟩ — see CONSTITUTE 1
3 to bring into being by combining, shaping, or transforming materials ⟨*formed* the pot out of the clay⟩ — see MAKE 1
4 to come into existence ⟨the new company *formed* from two smaller ones⟩ — see BEGIN 2
5 to come to have gradually ⟨I don't want you beginning skiers to *form* any bad habits.⟩ — see DEVELOP 2

form *n* **1** the outward appearance of something as distinguished from its substance ⟨The wood-carver carved the block of wood into the *form* of a duck.⟩
synonyms cast, configuration, conformation, fashion, figure, geometry, shape
related words contour, outline, profile, silhouette; frame, framework, shell, skeleton; arrangement, design, format, layout, makeup, organization, pattern, plan, setup
near antonyms composition, material, matter, raw material, stuff, substance
2 a piece of paper with information written or to be

written on it ⟨I filled out all the *forms* for applying to the school.⟩
synonyms blank, document, paper
related words instrument, writ; filing; sheet
3 personal conduct or behavior as evaluated by an accepted standard of appropriateness for a social or professional setting ⟨It's bad *form* to throw a tantrum on the court just because you lost a tennis match.⟩ — see MANNER 1
4 a state of being or fitness ⟨After a long season off, the football team is back in good *form*.⟩ — see CONDITION 1
5 a three-dimensional representation of the human body used especially for displaying clothes ⟨put the dress on the *form* to finish pinning it together⟩ — see MANNEQUIN 1
6 an oft-repeated action or series of actions performed in accordance with tradition or a set of rules ⟨We'll use the second *form* in our church missals for today's Lenten service.⟩ — see RITE
7 socially acceptable behavior ⟨displayed good *form* throughout the formal dinner⟩ — see DECENCY 1
8 the means or procedure for doing something ⟨There are established *forms* for voting on motions and amendments at meetings.⟩ — see METHOD
9 the type of body that a person has ⟨He has the big-boned *form* of a linebacker.⟩ — see PHYSIQUE
10 the way in which the elements of something (as a work of art) are arranged ⟨Museumgoers liked the asymmetrical *form* of the mobile.⟩ — see COMPOSITION 3
formal *n* a social gathering for dancing ⟨He asked her to the *formal* at the end of the year.⟩ — see DANCE
formal *adj* **1** following or agreeing with established form, custom, or rules ⟨a *formal* meeting of the board of directors⟩ ⟨a *formal* contract that was legally binding⟩
synonyms ceremonial, ceremonious, conventional, orthodox, regular, routine
related words authorized, official, sanctioned; accepted, correct, decorous, genteel, nice, polite, proper, respectable, seemly; formalistic, ritual, ritualistic; methodical (*also* methodic), orderly, systematic
near antonyms unauthorized, unofficial; graceless, improper, inappropriate, incorrect, indecorous, inept, infelicitous, unapt, unbecoming, unfit, unhappy, unseemly, unsuitable
antonyms casual, freewheeling, informal, irregular, unceremonious, unconventional, unorthodox
2 being something in name or form only ⟨was the *formal* head of the charitable organization though he never attended a single meeting⟩ — see NOMINAL 1
3 marked by or showing careful attention to set forms and details ⟨We gave her a *formal* invitation to dinner.⟩ — see CEREMONIOUS 1
4 relating to or suitable for wearing to an event requiring elegant dress and manners ⟨The dress code is *formal* for tonight's event.⟩ ⟨a shop that rents out *formal* wear⟩ — see DRESS
5 very dignified in form, tone, or style ⟨the *formal* language of the coronation ceremony⟩ — see ELEVATED 2
formality *n* **1** an act or utterance that is a customary show of good manners ⟨Bowing to your guest is a *formality* you don't need to perform for me.⟩ — see CIVILITY 1
2 an oft-repeated action or series of actions performed in accordance with tradition or a set of rules ⟨the *formalities* of signing a will⟩ — see RITE
formalize *vb* **1** to make agree with a single established standard or model ⟨We'll need to *formalize* our research results before we submit our study for review.⟩ — see STANDARDIZE
2 to give official acceptance of as satisfactory ⟨The plan

has yet to be *formalized* by the city council.⟩ — see APPROVE
format *n* **1** the way in which something is sized, arranged, or organized ⟨The book's *format* is very user-friendly.⟩
synonyms arrangement, configuration, conformation, formation, layout, setup
related words design, plan, scheme; composition, constitution, getup, makeup; build, construction, structure
2 the way in which the elements of something (as a work of art) are arranged ⟨This abstract painter bases the *format* of his works on color and its subtle gradations and not line or form.⟩ — see COMPOSITION 3
formation *n* the way in which something is sized, arranged, or organized ⟨geese flying south in a V-*formation*⟩ — see FORMAT 1
formative *adj* having a role in deciding something's final form ⟨a teacher who was a *formative* influence on generations of students⟩
synonyms constructive, productive
related words causal, creative; consequential, influential
antonyms nonconstructive, nonproductive, unproductive
former *adj* **1** having been such at some previous time ⟨The coach is a *former* professional baseball player.⟩
synonyms erstwhile, late, old, onetime, other, past, sometime, whilom
related words bygone, dead, defunct, departed, expired, extinct, gone, long-ago, vanished
near antonyms contemporary, current, extant, ongoing, present, present-day; coming, future, prospective, unborn
2 going before another in time or order ⟨The *former* manual had some errors, but the current version has its own problems.⟩ — see PREVIOUS
formidable *adj* **1** causing fear ⟨a *formidable*, irascible old man who frightened the neighborhood children⟩ — see FEARFUL 1
2 requiring considerable physical or mental effort ⟨Running a marathon is a *formidable* undertaking.⟩ — see HARD 2
formless *adj* **1** having no definite or recognizable form ⟨a *formless* mass of clay that the potter transformed into an attractive bowl⟩
synonyms amorphous, shapeless, unformed, unshaped, unstructured
related words characterless; chaotic, disorganized, incoherent, systemless, unordered, unorganized; dim, fuzzy, hazy, indefinite, indeterminate, indistinct, indistinguishable, murky, nebulous, obscure, unclear, undefined, undetermined, vague
near antonyms coherent, ordered, orderly, organized; clear, decided, definite, distinct
antonyms formed, shaped, shapen, structured
2 not composed of matter ⟨From this *formless* void the universe was supposed to have been created.⟩ — see IMMATERIAL 1
formulaic *adj* using or marked by the use of something else as a basis or model ⟨She thought the plots of most action movies were pretty *formulaic*.⟩ — see IMITATIVE 1
formulate *vb* **1** to convey in appropriate or telling terms ⟨The doctor was trying to *formulate* a good way to tell her that she would need surgery.⟩ — see PHRASE
2 to put (something) into proper and usually carefully worked out written form ⟨a writer planning to *formulate* a response to what he considered a very unfair review of his work⟩ — see COMPOSE 1
formulation *n* an act, process, or means of putting something into words ⟨His letter was a very accurate *formulation* of his thoughts on the matter.⟩ — see EXPRESSION 1

formulator *n* one who creates or introduces something new ⟨the *formulator* of the microcomputer⟩ — see INVENTOR

forsake *vb* to cause to remain behind ⟨She *forsook* acting for a teaching career.⟩ — see LEAVE 1

forsaken *adj* left unoccupied or unused ⟨The *forsaken* paper mill was now a rusting wreck.⟩ — see ABANDONED 1

forsaking *n* the act of abandoning ⟨an irresponsible *forsaking* of his duties⟩ — see DERELICTION 1

fort *n* a structure or place from which one can resist attack ⟨a series of *forts* along the frontier⟩
synonyms bastion, castle, citadel, fastness, fortification, fortress, hold, stronghold
related words battlement, breastwork, bulwark, earthwork, embattlement, parapet, rampart; bunker, dugout; blockhouse, garrison house

forte *n* something for which a person shows a special talent ⟨Doing funny impressions of people has always been my *forte*.⟩
synonyms speciality, specialty, thing
related words area, arena, business, circle, demesne, department, discipline, domain, field, line, province, realm, sphere; element; aptitude, aptness, bent, faculty, flair, genius, gift, knack, talent; pursuit, racket, vocation; inclination, leaning, partiality, penchant, predilection, predisposition, proclivity, propensity, tendency

forth *adv* 1 toward a point ahead in space or time ⟨From that day *forth* we were fast friends.⟩ — see ONWARD 1
2 toward or at a point lying in advance in space or time ⟨Go *forth* into the world with love and hope.⟩ — see ALONG

forthcoming *adj* 1 being soon to appear or take place ⟨Everyone's excited about the *forthcoming* company gala.⟩
synonyms approaching, coming, imminent, impending, nearing, oncoming, pending, upcoming
related words future; anticipated, awaited, expected, foreseen, predicted
phrases at hand, on hand, on tap, to come
near antonyms bygone, erstwhile, foregone, former, old, onetime, other, past, sometime, whilom
antonyms late, recent
2 free in expressing one's true feelings and opinions ⟨It's hard to tell what her views on that hot-button issue exactly are, as she's not very *forthcoming*.⟩ — see FRANK

forthright *adj* 1 free in expressing one's true feelings and opinions ⟨She sometimes was a little too *forthright* for her own good and ended up saying things that inadvertently offended people.⟩ — see FRANK
2 going straight to the point clearly and firmly ⟨I appreciate your *forthright* explanation of the situation.⟩ — see STRAIGHTFORWARD 1

forthrightly *adv* in an honest and direct manner ⟨The police commissioner *forthrightly* and unhesitatingly admitted his mistake.⟩ — see STRAIGHTFORWARD

forthrightness *n* the free expression of one's true feelings and opinions ⟨I valued her *forthrightness* in telling me she didn't like being called "Susie."⟩ — see CANDOR 1

forthwith *adv* without delay ⟨If the fire alarm rings, leave the building *forthwith*.⟩ — see IMMEDIATELY

fortification *n* a structure or place from which one can resist attack ⟨defenders at the border *fortifications* preparing for an attack⟩ — see FORT

fortify *vb* 1 to prepare (oneself) mentally or emotionally ⟨Kelly *fortified* herself for the basketball tournament with a series of confidence-boosting exercises.⟩
synonyms brace, forearm, nerve, poise, psych (up), ready, steel, strengthen
related words arm; harden, inure, season, toughen; bolster, boost, buoy (up), buttress, enforce, prop (up), support, sustain; cheer (up), comfort, embolden, encourage, hearten, inspire; rally, rouse, stir
near antonyms daunt, demoralize, discourage, dishearten, dispirit, psych (out), shake, unnerve; debilitate, enervate, enfeeble, prostrate, sap, soften, tire, undercut, undermine, weaken
2 to increase the ability of (as a muscle) to exert physical force ⟨He downed another granola bar to *fortify* himself for the rest of the bike ride.⟩ — see STRENGTHEN 1
3 to make able to withstand physical hardship, strain, or exposure ⟨Bought lots of warm clothing to *fortify* ourselves against the cold.⟩ — see HARDEN 2

fortitude *n* the strength of mind that enables a person to endure pain or hardship ⟨It was only with the greatest *fortitude* that the Pilgrims were able to survive their first winter in Plymouth.⟩
synonyms backbone, constancy, fiber, grit, guts, pluck, spunk
related words determination, purposefulness, resoluteness, resolution; bravery, courage, courageousness, daring, dauntlessness, doughtiness, fearlessness, gallantry, greatheartedness, intrepidity, intrepidness, nerve, stoutness, valor; endurance, forbearance, stamina, sufferance, tolerance; heart, mettle, spirit; audacity, boldness, brass, cheek, effrontery, gall, hardihood, nerve, nerviness, temerity
near antonyms indecisiveness, irresoluteness, irresolution, vacillation; cowardice, cowardliness, cravenness, dastardliness, faintheartedness, pusillanimity, timidity, timorousness
antonyms spinelessness

fortress *n* a structure or place from which one can resist attack ⟨The boys built a snow *fortress* and then challenged the neighborhood kids to a snowball fight.⟩ — see FORT

fortuitous *adj* 1 coming or happening by good luck especially unexpectedly ⟨Your arrival just before the thunderstorm was *fortuitous*.⟩ — see FORTUNATE 1
2 happening by chance ⟨She firmly believes that the creation of the universe was something other than just the *fortuitous* coming together of particles of matter.⟩ — see ACCIDENTAL 1

fortunate *adj* 1 coming or happening by good luck especially unexpectedly ⟨In a *fortunate* turn of events, the motel had one last vacancy.⟩
synonyms fluky (*also* flukey), fortuitous, happy, lucky, providential
related words convenient, opportune, seasonable, timely; unexpected, unforeseen, unlooked-for; accidental, chance, coincidental, serendipitous; auspicious, bright, encouraging, fair, heartening, hopeful, promising, propitious; benign, favorable, golden, good, halcyon; advantageous, beneficial, profitable
near antonyms inconvenient, inopportune, unseasonable, untimely; anticipated, expected, foreseen; deliberate, intentional, planned; inauspicious, unpromising; calamitous, catastrophic, disastrous
antonyms hapless, ill-fated, ill-starred, luckless, starcrossed, unfortunate, unhappy, unlucky
2 having good luck ⟨Rabbits' feet are seen as making the carrier of them *fortunate*.⟩ — see LUCKY 1

fortunateness *n* success that is partly the result of chance ⟨He attributed his habitual *fortunateness* to the lucky penny that he had long ago stuck in his shoe.⟩ — see LUCK 1

fortune *n* 1 what is going to happen to someone in the time ahead ⟨The telephone psychic proceeded to tell me my *fortune*—at great length.⟩
synonyms future

related words circumstance, destiny, doom, fate, hap, lot, portion; futurities, outlook, prospect
near antonyms present
antonyms past

2 a very large amount of money ⟨The billionaire's huge mansion must have cost a *fortune*.⟩
synonyms bundle, earth, king's ransom, mint, pile, wad
related words heap, pot; bonanza, mine; assets, capital, means, property, riches, wealth, wherewithal; bread [*slang*], cash, chips, currency, dough, gold, jack [*slang*], legal tender, lucre, pelf, tender, wampum
near antonyms petty cash, pin money, pocket money, spending money
antonyms mite, peanuts, pittance, song

3 a state or end that seemingly has been decided beforehand ⟨It was his *fortune* that he should wander in the wilderness before becoming king.⟩ — see FATE 1

4 success that is partly the result of chance ⟨In a streak of good *fortune*, she won the lottery twice that year.⟩ — see LUCK 1

5 the total of one's money and property ⟨The family *fortune* is mostly in rare paintings and real estate.⟩ — see WEALTH 1

fortune–teller *n* one who predicts future events or developments ⟨The carnival's *fortune-teller* should have predicted that I'd pass right by her.⟩ — see PROPHET 1

forty winks *pl n* a short sleep ⟨After turning the boat over to the first mate, the captain went below decks for *forty winks*.⟩ — see ¹NAP

forum *n* **1** a meeting featuring a group discussion ⟨a public *forum* called to find out how residents felt about a large discount store being built in their neighborhood⟩
synonyms colloquy, conference, council, panel, parley, roundtable, seminar, symposium
related words colloquium; caucus, town meeting; assembly, conclave, congregation, congress, consistory, convention, convocation, synod; debate, deliberation; brainstorming; chat room, newsgroup; medium, outlet, platform, venue

2 an assembly of persons for the administration of justice ⟨A jury may have acquitted Lizzie Borden, but she was guilty of murder in the *forum* of public opinion.⟩ — see COURT 3

forward *adj* **1** showing a lack of proper social reserve or modesty ⟨asking very *forward* questions⟩ — see PRESUMPTUOUS 1

2 being at or in the forward part or surface of something ⟨the ship's *forward* deck⟩ — see FRONT

3 being far along in development ⟨believed himself to be very *forward* in his views⟩ — see ADVANCED

4 having or showing awareness of and preparation for the future ⟨She was *forward* enough to start investing in her retirement fund at the age of 18.⟩ — see FORESIGHTED

forward *adv* **1** toward or at a point lying in advance in space or time ⟨If you keep walking *forward*, you'll hit that wall.⟩ — see ALONG

2 toward a point ahead in space or time ⟨From this day *forward*, our two nations will live in peace and harmony.⟩ — see ONWARD 1

forward *vb* to help the growth or development of ⟨Their foundation will help *forward* better relations between young people from those warring nations.⟩ — see FOSTER 1

forwards *adv* toward or at a point lying in advance in space or time ⟨For every step that her campaign takes *forwards*, it seems to take two backwards.⟩ — see ALONG

fossil *n* a person with old-fashioned ideas ⟨said the board of directors was made up of a bunch of old *fossils*⟩ — see FOGY

foster *vb* **1** to help the growth or development of ⟨The head librarian firmly declared that it is indeed the duty of local government to *foster* learning and a love of reading.⟩
synonyms advance, cultivate, encourage, forward, further, incubate, nourish, nurse, nurture, promote
related words advocate, back, champion, endorse (*also* indorse), support, uphold; endow, finance, fund, patronize, stake, subsidize, underwrite; abet, aid, assist; advertise, boost, plug, publicize, tout; agitate (for), campaign (for), work (for)
near antonyms ban, bar, enjoin, forbid, interdict, outlaw, prevent, prohibit, proscribe; repress, snuff (out), squash, squelch, stifle, subdue, suppress; arrest, check, halt, retard; encumber, fetter, hobble, impede, interfere (with), manacle, obstruct, shackle
antonyms discourage, frustrate, hinder, inhibit

2 to bring to maturity through care and education ⟨a greathearted couple *fostering* two adopted children as well as three more of their own⟩ — see BRING UP 1

foul *vb* **1** to make dirty ⟨The mechanic *fouled* the bath towels with axle grease.⟩ — see DIRTY

2 to make unfit for use by the addition of something harmful or undesirable ⟨industrial pollution *fouling* the water supply⟩ — see CONTAMINATE

3 to reduce to a lower standing in one's own eyes or in others' eyes ⟨The minister was irreparably *fouled* by baseless rumors and allegations.⟩ — see HUMBLE

4 to go through decomposition ⟨Unless you want to smell the organic refuse as it *fouls*, locate the compost heap away from the house.⟩ — see DECAY 1

foul *adj* **1** marked by wet and windy conditions ⟨The *foul* weather brought out the windbreakers and rain slickers as everyone braced for a day of rough sailing.⟩
synonyms bleak, dirty, inclement, nasty, raw, rough, squally, stormy, tempestuous, turbulent
related words blowy, blustering, blustery, breezy, gusty, windblown, windswept; cloudy, overcast; rainy, snowy; foggy, hazy, misty, murky, soupy
near antonyms rainless; balmy, calm, halcyon, peaceful, placid, pleasant, serene
antonyms bright, clear, clement, cloudless, fair, sunny, sunshiny, unclouded

2 not being in accordance with the rules or standards of what is fair in sport ⟨an aggressive hockey player who is known for his *foul* play and readiness for a fight⟩
synonyms dirty, illegal, nasty, unfair, unsportsmanlike
related words dishonorable, shabby, shameful; ignoble, low, mean, ungentlemanly; immoral, rotten, unchivalrous, unethical, unjust, unprincipled, unrighteous, unscrupulous
phrases below the belt
near antonyms just, law-abiding; ethical, moral, principled, righteous, scrupulous; honorable, irreproachable, unimpeachable
antonyms clean, fair, legal, sportsmanlike, sportsmanly

3 causing intense displeasure, disgust, or resentment ⟨a *foul* taste that made us gag⟩ — see OFFENSIVE 1

4 depicting or referring to sexual matters in a way that is unacceptable in polite society ⟨That movie features nonstop *foul* language.⟩ — see OBSCENE 1

5 having an unpleasant smell ⟨the *foul* fumes from the paper mill⟩ — see MALODOROUS

6 not clean ⟨*foul* rainwater collecting in the feeding trough⟩ — see DIRTY 1

foulness *n* **1** the quality or state of being obscene ⟨The *foulness* of your language means that your post won't get on the website's bulletin board.⟩ — see OBSCENITY

2 the state or quality of being dirty ⟨The *foulness* of the water made it undrinkable.⟩ — see DIRTINESS

foul play *n* **1** the taking of another person's life ⟨The coroner ruled that there was no evidence of *foul play*.⟩ — see HOMICIDE 1

2 the use of brute strength to cause harm to a person or property ⟨The suspect has a long history of *foul play*, and was once convicted on assault and battery charges.⟩ — see VIOLENCE 1

foul–up *n* an instance of confusion ⟨There was a *foul-up* with our mail order, and not one item arrived as ordered.⟩

synonyms mix-up

related words bobble, botch, bungle, fumble; blunder, error, fault, flub, goof, inaccuracy, lapse, miscue, misstep, mistake, oversight, slip, slipup, stumble; chaos, confusion, disarrangement, disarray, disorder, disorganization, hash, jumble, mess, muddle, shambles

foul up *vb* **1** to make or do (something) in a clumsy or unskillful way ⟨tried not to *foul up* the football play⟩ — see BOTCH

2 to make a mistake ⟨Unfortunately, I *fouled up* and in my e-mail gave everyone the wrong date for the meeting.⟩ — see ERR 1

found *vb* to be responsible for the creation and early operation or use of ⟨John Harvard did not actually *found* the university that now bears his name.⟩

synonyms begin, constitute, establish, inaugurate, initiate, innovate, institute, introduce, launch, pioneer, plant, set up, start

related words author, father, originate; conceive, concoct, contrive, cook (up), create, devise, fabricate, invent, make up, manufacture, produce, think (up); construct, put up; develop, enlarge, expand; endow, finance, fund, subsidize; arrange, organize, systematize

near antonyms abolish, annihilate, annul, nullify; end, finish, halt, stop, terminate; round (off *or* out), wind up, wrap up

antonyms phase out, shut (up)

foundation *n* **1** a public organization with a particular purpose or function ⟨donated to a *foundation* that supported cancer research⟩ — see INSTITUTION 1

2 an immaterial thing upon which something else rests ⟨She had a good enough *foundation* in math to pursue an economics degree.⟩ — see BASE 1

founder *n* a person who establishes a whole new field of endeavor ⟨Maria Montessori was the *founder* of an educational system dedicated to maximizing a child's creative potential.⟩ — see FATHER 2

founder *vb* **1** to be unsuccessful ⟨The theater company *foundered* after its corporate funding dried up.⟩ — see FAIL 2

2 to fall down or in as a result of physical pressure ⟨The structure started to sway and suddenly *foundered*.⟩ — see COLLAPSE 1

foursquare *adj* **1** free in expressing one's true feelings and opinions ⟨I decided it was best to be *foursquare* with him when he asked for my opinion.⟩ — see FRANK

2 going straight to the point clearly and firmly ⟨a *foursquare* evaluation of her performance that didn't mince words⟩ — see STRAIGHTFORWARD 1

3 having four equal sides and four right angles ⟨The design of the *foursquare* Georgian mansion is strongly symmetrical, the wide central hallway being flanked by two rooms on either side.⟩ — see SQUARE 1

foursquare *adv* in an honest and direct manner ⟨Kay asked him *foursquare* if he was ever going to finish the project.⟩ — see STRAIGHTFORWARD

fox *n* a physically attractive person ⟨Both he and his twin sister are *foxes*.⟩ — see DOLL 2

fox *vb* **1** to throw into a state of mental uncertainty ⟨She won't be *foxed* by such telemarketing tricks.⟩ — see CONFUSE 1

2 to get the better of through cleverness ⟨No confidence man will ever *fox* me and get my hard-earned money.⟩ — see OUTWIT

foxiness *n* **1** skill in achieving one's ends through indirect, subtle, or underhanded means ⟨It did not take an incredible amount of *foxiness* on his part to get you to spill the beans.⟩ — see CUNNING 1

2 the inclination or practice of misleading others through lies or trickery ⟨an imposter of such formidable *foxiness* that a movie was made of his entertaining escapades⟩ — see DECEIT 1

3 exceptional discernment and judgment especially in practical matters ⟨lacks the *foxiness* needed to make it in the dog-eat-dog world of show business⟩ — see ACUMEN

foxy *adj* clever at attaining one's ends by indirect and often deceptive means ⟨a *foxy* salesperson⟩ — see ARTFUL 1

foyer *n* **1** a centrally located room in a building that serves as a gathering or waiting area or as a passageway into the interior ⟨Theatergoers crowded the *foyer* during the play's intermission.⟩

synonyms hall, lobby

related words entry, entryway, hallway, vestibule; concourse, corridor, gallery, passageway; antechamber, anteroom, chamber, waiting room

2 the entrance room of a building ⟨Leave your muddy boots in the *foyer* and come into the house.⟩ — see HALL 1

fracas *n* **1** a physical dispute between opposing individuals or groups ⟨The police broke up the *fracas* and threw both combatants in the lockup.⟩ — see FIGHT 1

2 a rough and often noisy fight usually involving several people ⟨police preparing for any *fracas* that might follow the soccer game⟩ — see BRAWL 1

fractionation *n* the act or process of a whole separating into two or more parts or pieces ⟨Originally conceived as one novel, *The Lord of the Rings* underwent a *fractionation* into a trilogy when its publisher feared it was too massive to sell as a single volume.⟩ — see SEPARATION 1

fracture *vb* **1** to cause to separate into pieces usually suddenly or forcibly ⟨*fractured* his arm in the fall⟩ — see BREAK 1

2 to fail to keep ⟨civil liberties that have been *fractured* by the government's actions⟩ — see VIOLATE 1

fragile *adj* **1** easily broken ⟨*fragile* flower petals⟩

synonyms breakable, delicate, frail

related words dainty, fine, gossamer; eggshell, flimsy, slight, tenuous; brittle, crisp, crispy, crumbly, crushable, embrittled, flaky (*also* flakey), friable, shaky, shivery, short; feeble, infirm, soft, spindly, tender, weak; inelastic, inflexible, stiff

near antonyms compact, firm, hard, rigid, solid, substantial, unyielding; elastic, flexible, resilient, rubberlike, rubbery, springy, stretch, stretchable, supple

antonyms nonbreakable, strong, sturdy, tough, unbreakable

2 easily injured without careful handling ⟨Babies are *fragile*, so remember to care for them gently.⟩ — see TENDER 1

3 small in degree ⟨a *fragile* possibility that we might emerge from this fiasco unscathed⟩ — see REMOTE 1

fragility *n* **1** the state or quality of having a delicate structure ⟨We marveled at the *fragility* and yet the surprising strength of the bird's wing bones.⟩ — see DELICACY 2

2 the quality or state of lacking physical strength or vigor ⟨the *fragility* of the abandoned baby bird⟩ — see WEAKNESS 1

fragment *vb* to cause to separate into pieces usually suddenly or forcibly ⟨You can *fragment* that peanut brittle easily, but how it breaks is basically up to the brittle.⟩ — see BREAK 1

fragment *n* a broken or irregular part of something that often remains incomplete ⟨*fragments* of broken glass⟩
synonyms bit, piece, scrap
related words shred, tatter; end, leftover, oddment, remainder, remnant, stub; portion, section, segment; chip, flake, shard, shatter, shiver, sliver, splinter; clipping, paring, shaving; atom, crumb, dribble, fleck, flyspeck, grain, granule, molecule, morsel, mote, nubbin, nugget, particle, patch, scruple, snip, snippet, speck, tittle

fragmental *adj* lacking some necessary part ⟨We will have to settle for a quick, *fragmental* explanation of what happened.⟩ — see INCOMPLETE

fragmentary *adj* lacking some necessary part ⟨The historical record of this pharaoh's life and reign is *fragmentary* at best.⟩ — see INCOMPLETE

fragrance *n* a sweet or pleasant smell ⟨the *fragrance* of lilac trees in full bloom⟩
synonyms aroma, bouquet, incense, perfume, redolence, scent, spice
related words essence, odor
antonyms reek, stench, stink

fragrant *adj* having a pleasant smell ⟨The balsam fir is a favorite as a Christmas tree because it is so *fragrant*.⟩
synonyms ambrosial, aromatic, perfumed, redolent, savory (*also* savoury), scented, sweet
related words flowery, fruity, pungent, spicy; odiferous, odored, odoriferous, odorous; clean, fresh, pure
near antonyms odorless, unscented; fusty, musty, stale; gamy (*or* gamey)
antonyms fetid, foul, malodorous, noisome, putrid, rank, reeking, reeky, skunky, smelly, stenchful, stenchy, stinking, stinky, strong

frail *adj* 1 easily broken ⟨a *frail* eggshell⟩ — see FRAGILE 1
2 easily injured without careful handling ⟨Be careful with your grandmother, as she's very *frail* and a fall would be disastrous.⟩ — see TENDER 1
3 lacking bodily strength ⟨He was *frail* after a long battle with bronchitis.⟩ — see WEAK 1
4 lacking strength of will or character ⟨a *frail* person, easily swayed by others⟩ — see WEAK 2
5 small in degree ⟨a *frail* hope of success⟩ — see REMOTE 1

frailness *n* 1 the quality or state of lacking physical strength or vigor ⟨His *frailness* prevented him from playing football.⟩ — see WEAKNESS 1
2 the quality or state of lacking strength of will or character ⟨Don't take advantage of your younger sister's *frailness* of character.⟩ — see WEAKNESS 2

frailty *n* 1 a defect in character ⟨Selfishness is a common human *frailty*.⟩ — see FAULT 1
2 the quality or state of lacking physical strength or vigor ⟨*Frailty* doesn't affect all elderly people, for many are indeed healthy and strong.⟩ — see WEAKNESS 1
3 the quality or state of lacking strength of will or character ⟨It was hard not to show *frailty* at such a difficult time.⟩ — see WEAKNESS 2

frame *vb* 1 to bring into being by combining, shaping, or transforming materials ⟨*framed* a unique coffee table from an old, discarded chest of drawers⟩ — see MAKE 1
2 to plan out usually with subtle skill or care ⟨a composer *framing* the structure of a song⟩ — see ENGINEER
3 to put (something) into proper and usually carefully worked out written form ⟨You'll need to *frame* your argument well if you're going to win the debate.⟩ — see COMPOSE 1

4 to work out the details of (something) in advance ⟨*framed* a schedule for the project⟩ — see PLAN 1
5 to serve as a border for ⟨Trees *framed* the walkway.⟩ — see BORDER

frame *n* 1 the arrangement of parts that gives something its basic form ⟨Now that the *frame* has been built, we have a better idea of the size of our new house.⟩
synonyms configuration, edifice, fabric, framework, shell, skeleton, structure
related words cage, lattice, network; contour, figure, outline, profile, shape, silhouette; chassis
2 the type of body that a person has ⟨a tall man with a big *frame*⟩ — see PHYSIQUE
3 the line or relatively narrow space that marks the outer limit of something ⟨a white curtain with a blue *frame*⟩ — see BORDER 1

framework *n* the arrangement of parts that gives something its basic form ⟨You've got the *framework* of the story and just need to fill in the details.⟩ — see FRAME 1

franchise *n* the right to formally express one's position or will in an election ⟨The Territory of Wyoming granted women the *franchise* in 1869, a full 51 years before the 19th Amendment granted women the right to vote in all elections.⟩ — see VOTE 1

frank *adj* free in expressing one's true feelings and opinions ⟨Our ballet teacher is very *frank* about telling her students whether she thinks they have the talent for a career in dance.⟩
synonyms candid, direct, forthcoming, forthright, foursquare, free-spoken, honest, open, openhearted, outspoken, plain, plainspoken, straight, straightforward, unguarded, unreserved
related words artless, earnest, guileless, ingenuous, innocent, naive (*or* naïve), natural, real, sincere, unaffected, undesigning, unpretending, unpretentious; outgoing, uninhibited, unrestrained; vocal, vociferous; abrupt, bluff, blunt, brusque (*also* brusk), crusty, curt, gruff, sharp; impertinent, impolite, inconsiderate, rude, tactless, thoughtless, uncivil, ungracious, unmannerly, unsubtle
near antonyms inhibited, reserved, restrained; closemouthed, laconic, quiet, reticent, taciturn, tight-lipped, uncommunicative; diplomatic, politic, tactful; civil, considerate, courteous, polite
antonyms dissembling, uncandid, unforthcoming

frankly *adv* to tell the truth ⟨*Frankly*, I'd rather stay at home than go to the movies tonight.⟩ — see ACTUALLY 1

frankness *n* the free expression of one's true feelings and opinions ⟨Considering her reputation for *frankness*, I knew she would tell me what she really thought of my work.⟩ — see CANDOR 1

frantic *adj* 1 feeling overwhelming fear or worry ⟨The *frantic* student searched all over the school for the lost notebook.⟩
synonyms agitated, delirious, distracted, distraught, frenzied, hysterical (*also* hysteric)
related words alarmed, anxious, disquieted, disturbed, nervous, perturbed, tense, troubled, upset, worried, wrought (up); berserk, demented, deranged, mad, maniacal (*also* maniac), nuclear; ranting, raving
phrases beside oneself
near antonyms calm, peaceful, placid, self-possessed, serene, tranquil; cool, coolheaded, undisturbed, unperturbed, unshaken, untroubled, unworried
antonyms collected, composed, self-collected, self-possessed, unhysterical
2 marked by great and often stressful excitement or activity ⟨The holiday season seems to be moving along at a *frantic* pace.⟩ — see FURIOUS 1

frantically *adv* in a confused and reckless manner ⟨The veterinarian ran *frantically* from room to room looking for the escaped hamster.⟩ — see HELTER-SKELTER 1

fraternal *adj* of, relating to, or befitting brothers ⟨There was a *fraternal* bond between the two boys all throughout their school years.⟩

synonyms brotherly

related words familial, sisterly; chummy, friendly, neighborly

fraternity *n* **1** a group of persons formally joined together for some common interest ⟨a firm believer in community service and a dedicated member of the local *fraternity* of Good Samaritans⟩ — see ASSOCIATION 2

2 the body of people in a profession or field of activity ⟨the *fraternity* of civil engineers⟩ — see CORPS

fraternize *vb* **1** to come or be together as friends ⟨The head coach made it a practice not to *fraternize* with the players.⟩ — see ASSOCIATE 1

2 to take part in social activities ⟨a group of kids *fraternizing* together after school every day⟩ — see SOCIALIZE

fraud *n* **1** an instance of the use of dishonest methods to acquire something of value ⟨Thousands of people lost money when the investment scheme turned out to be a *fraud*.⟩

synonyms con, hustle, scam, sting, swindle

related words cross, fix; Ponzi scheme, pyramid scheme; racket, rip-off; thimblerig, three-card monte; device, dodge, gimmick, jig, ploy, scheme, sleight, stratagem, trick, wile; counterfeit, fake, forgery, hoax, humbug, phony (*also* phoney), sham

2 one who makes false claims of identity or expertise ⟨The self-proclaimed psychic turned out to be a *fraud*.⟩ — see IMPOSTOR

3 the inclination or practice of misleading others through lies or trickery ⟨charges that he had gained control of his elderly mother's estate by *fraud*⟩ — see DECEIT 1

fraudulent *adj* **1** marked by, based on, or done by the use of dishonest methods to acquire something of value ⟨Hoping to get millions from the insurance company, the man made the *fraudulent* claim that he had been seriously injured in the accident.⟩

synonyms crooked, deceitful, defrauding, dishonest, double-dealing, false

related words beguiling, deceiving, deceptive, deluding, delusive, delusory, fallacious, misleading, specious; spurious

near antonyms legitimate, true, valid

antonyms aboveboard, honest, truthful

2 given to or marked by cheating and deception ⟨*fraudulent* citizens who cheat on their taxes⟩ — see DISHONEST 2

fraught *adj* **1** possessing or covered with great numbers or amounts of something specified ⟨Every room in my childhood home is *fraught* with memories.⟩ — see RIFE

2 marked by or causing agitation or uncomfortable feelings ⟨had a *fraught* meeting with his former business partner⟩ — see NERVOUS 2

fray *n* **1** a forceful effort to reach a goal or objective ⟨Another generation of scientists entered the *fray* to find a cure for the disease.⟩ — see STRUGGLE 1

2 a physical dispute between opposing individuals or groups ⟨The referee warned the players that he would not tolerate any *frays*.⟩ — see FIGHT 1

3 a rough and often noisy fight usually involving several people ⟨A *fray* broke out after the soccer match.⟩ — see BRAWL 1

fray *vb* to damage or diminish by continued friction ⟨Constant rubbing against the rock face has badly *frayed* our climbing rope.⟩ — see ABRADE 1

frayed *adj* worn or torn into or as if into rags ⟨She wore a beloved but badly *frayed* flannel shirt.⟩ — see RAGGED 2

frazzle *n* a complete depletion of energy or strength ⟨Months of overtime work have left her worn to a *frazzle*.⟩ — see FATIGUE

frazzle *vb* **1** to damage or diminish by continued friction ⟨Years of use have *frazzled* the cord for the window blinds to the breaking point.⟩ — see ABRADE 1

2 to use up all the physical energy of ⟨Trying to hold down two full-time jobs had completely *frazzled* him.⟩ — see EXHAUST 1

3 to trouble the mind of; to make uneasy ⟨an endless series of dietary warnings that had served only to *frazzle* the general public⟩ — see DISTURB 1

freak *adj* being out of the ordinary ⟨Even weather forecasters seemed surprised by the *freak* hailstorm.⟩ — see EXCEPTIONAL 1

freak *n* **1** a person, thing, or event that is far from normal ⟨That snowstorm in April was a *freak*, since our weather is usually much balmier by then.⟩

synonyms abnormality, anomaly, monster, monstrosity

related words abortion, malformation, miscreation, mutant, mutation; character, crackbrain, crackpot, crank, eccentric, kook, nut, oddball, screwball, weirdo; aberrant, deviant; individualist, maverick, nonconformist; curiosity, peculiarity, singularity; aberration, irregularity, oddity, rarity

near antonyms sample, specimen; commonplace, usual

antonyms average, norm, normal, par, standard

2 a person with a strong and habitual liking for something ⟨I'm a hockey *freak*.⟩ — see FAN

3 a sudden impulsive and apparently unmotivated idea or action ⟨He suddenly had the bizarre *freak* to take a road trip across the country.⟩ — see WHIM

freak (out) *vb* **1** to trouble the mind of; to make uneasy ⟨Don't talk about spiders, as they *freak* me *out*.⟩ — see DISTURB 1

2 to yield to mental or emotional stress ⟨The landlady totally *freaked out* when she saw the mouse run across the hall.⟩ — see CRACK 2

freckle *vb* to mark with small spots especially unevenly ⟨The baker *freckled* the frosting with flakes of coconut.⟩ — see SPOT 1

freckled *adj* marked with spots ⟨a tanned girl with a *freckled* face⟩ — see SPOTTED 1

free *adj* **1** not being under the rule or control of another ⟨The country became *free* after many years under foreign control.⟩

synonyms autonomous, freestanding, independent, self-governing, self-ruling, separate, sovereign (*also* sovran)

related words freeborn; delivered, emancipated, freed, liberated, manumitted, redeemed, released; unconquered, unruled, unsupervised; empowered, enfranchised; democratic, republican

near antonyms bound, captive, conquered, enslaved, fettered, subdued, subjugated; inferior, subordinate, subservient

antonyms dependent, nonautonomous, non-self-governing, subject, unfree

2 no longer burdened with something unpleasant or painful ⟨After our son arrived home safely, we were grateful to be *free* from worry.⟩

synonyms disencumbered, quit, unburdened

related words delivered, freed, liberated, released; unhampered, unimpeded

near antonyms encumbered, handicapped, hindered, hobbled

3 not bound, confined, or detained by force ⟨All of the

animals in the game preserve are *free* to roam all over its vast area.⟩

synonyms footloose, loose, unbound, unconfined, unrestrained

related words escaped; uncaged, unchained, unfettered, unleashed; uncaught; unanchored, unbolted, undone, unfastened, untied; clear, disengaged

phrases at large, at liberty

near antonyms caught; caged, chained, enclosed (*also* inclosed), immured, imprisoned, leashed, penned; anchored, bolted, fastened, fettered, manacled, shackled, tied; kidnapped (*also* kidnaped)

antonyms bound, restrained, unfree

4 not costing or charging anything ⟨Although the museum normally charges admission, on Wednesdays it is *free* to all.⟩

synonyms complimentary, gratis, gratuitous

related words nominal; bestowed, donated, given; pro bono; discretionary, freewill, optional, voluntary; uncompensated, unpaid

phrases on the house

near antonyms paid; costly, dear, expensive, high

5 allowing passage without obstruction ⟨Make sure the pass is *free* before you attempt the trip through the mountains this winter.⟩ — see OPEN 1

6 giving or sharing in abundance and without hesitation ⟨The lottery winner was very *free* with his money.⟩ — see GENEROUS 1

7 not being in a state of use, activity, or employment ⟨This table is *free* if you want to use it.⟩ — see INACTIVE 2

8 showing a lack of proper social reserve or modesty ⟨She's a little too *free* with information about her personal life.⟩ — see PRESUMPTUOUS 1

9 not physically attached to another unit ⟨An arrangement of *free* columns adds interest to the Greco-Roman sculpture garden.⟩ — see SEPARATE 2

free *vb* **1** to release (as from slavery or confinement) ⟨A global crusade to *free* Nelson Mandela from a South African prison had emerged.⟩

synonyms discharge, emancipate, enfranchise, enlarge, liberate, loose, loosen, manumit, release, spring, unbind, uncage, unchain, unfetter

related words bail (out), deliver, parole, ransom, redeem, rescue, save; adrift, disencumber, disengage, disentangle, extricate; unshackle

phrases turn loose

near antonyms handcuff, manacle, shackle, trammel; commit, immure, imprison, incarcerate, intern, jail, lock (up); conquer, enslave, subdue, subjugate

antonyms bind, confine, enchain, fetter, restrain

2 to make passage through (something) possible by removing obstructions ⟨We'll *free* the river by breaking up the ice jam.⟩ — see OPEN 2

3 to rid the surface of (as an area) from things in the way ⟨Would you mind *freeing* up the work area so I can work?⟩ — see CLEAR 1

4 to set (a person or thing) free of something that encumbers ⟨A phone call would *free* your parents from worry.⟩ — see RID

5 to set free from entanglement or difficulty ⟨This plan should *free* us from debt.⟩ — see EXTRICATE

freebie *or* **freebee** *n* something given to someone without expectation of a return ⟨I got this detergent sample as a *freebie* with my new washing machine.⟩ — see GIFT 1

freebooter *n* someone who engages in robbery of ships at sea ⟨The ship was captured by *freebooters* who were looking for gold.⟩ — see PIRATE

freedom *n* **1** the state of being free from the control or power of another ⟨We owe our *freedom* to the untold

numbers of soldiers who have fought in our nation's wars since its founding.⟩

synonyms autonomy, independence, liberty, self-determination, self-government, sovereignty (*also* sovranty)

related words emancipation, enfranchisement, liberation, manumission, release

near antonyms captivity, enchainment, enslavement, immurement, imprisonment, incarceration, internment, subjugation

antonyms dependence (*also* dependance), heteronomy, subjection, unfreedom

2 the right to act or move freely ⟨The youngsters had full *freedom* of the park.⟩

synonyms authorization, free hand, latitude, license (*or* licence), run

related words authority, clutch, command, control, dominion, grip, hold, mandate, mastery, power, sway; range, room, space; blank check, carte blanche

free–for–all *adj* freely available for use or participation by all ⟨The public library has a *free-for-all* lending policy.⟩ — see OPEN 2

free–for–all *n* **1** a rough and often noisy fight usually involving several people ⟨During the play-offs, fans of the opposing teams clashed in the streets in several *free-for-alls*.⟩ — see BRAWL 1

2 a state in which everything is out of order ⟨It was a *free-for-all* when the doors to the arena opened and the crowd rushed in all at once.⟩ — see CHAOS

free hand *n* the right to act or move freely ⟨gave him *free hand* in managing the club⟩ — see FREEDOM 2

freehanded *adj* giving or sharing in abundance and without hesitation ⟨She is very *freehanded* with her friends whenever she gets some extra money.⟩ — see GENEROUS 1

freeing *n* the act of setting free from slavery ⟨a human rights group that works tirelessly for the *freeing* of political prisoners all over the world⟩ — see LIBERATION

freely *adv* **1** of one's own free will ⟨I will *freely* give my life for my country.⟩ — see VOLUNTARILY

2 without difficulty ⟨The horse broke the halter rope quite *freely*.⟩ — see EASILY 1

free–spoken *adj* free in expressing one's true feelings and opinions ⟨I pride myself on being *free-spoken* and feel no hesitancy in telling you my honest opinion on just about anything.⟩ — see FRANK

freestanding *adj* **1** not physically attached to another unit ⟨a *freestanding* air conditioner that doesn't need to be in a window⟩ — see SEPARATE 2

2 not being under the rule or control of another ⟨It's a *freestanding* store, not a franchise.⟩ — see FREE 1

freeway *n* a passage cleared for public vehicular travel ⟨a new driver who's nervous about driving on the *freeway* for the first time⟩ — see WAY 1

freewheeling *adj* not held back by rules, duties, or worries ⟨James Bond has long been the model of the *freewheeling* hero who encounters danger and excitement in every corner of the globe.⟩

synonyms footloose

related words affable, breezy, casual, devil-may-care, easygoing, happy-go-lucky, laid-back, nonchalant, relaxed; unattached, uncommitted; self-abandoned, unbridled, unrestrained; uninhibited; self-assured, self-confident, self-reliant

near antonyms attached, committed, pledged

antonyms tied

freewill *adj* done, made, or given with one's own free will ⟨Our office staff made a *freewill* offering for UNESCO.⟩ — see VOLUNTARY 1

free will *n* the act or power of making one's own choices or decisions ⟨All of the workers at the animal shelter are unpaid and are there of their own *free will*.⟩

synonyms accord, autonomy, choice, self-determination, volition, will

related words election, preference, selection; bent, devices, disposition, inclination, leaning, partiality, penchant, predilection, predisposition, proclivity, propensity, tendency; alternative, discretion, option, pick, way

near antonyms coercion, compulsion, constraint, duress, force, pressure

freeze *n* a weather condition marked by low temperatures ⟨The Midwest will experience an intense *freeze* later in the week.⟩ — see COLD

freeze *vb* to become physically firm or solid ⟨Add antifreeze to the water in the radiator so it won't *freeze* and damage the engine.⟩ — see HARDEN 1

freezing *adj* having a low or subnormal temperature ⟨Why aren't you wearing a coat, as it's *freezing* outside?⟩ — see COLD 1

freight *n* 1 a mass or quantity of something taken up and carried, conveyed, or transported ⟨shipped a large *freight* of steel to the manufacturer⟩ — see LOAD 1
2 the amount of money that is demanded as payment for something ⟨families struggling to pay the *freight* for college⟩ — see PRICE 1

freight *vb* to place a weight or burden on ⟨It took six hours to *freight* the cargo airplane.⟩ — see LOAD 1

frenetic *adj* marked by great and often stressful excitement or activity ⟨the *frenetic* rush to get every member of the cast in place before the curtain went up⟩ — see FURIOUS 1

frenzied *adj* 1 being in a state of increased activity or agitation ⟨the *frenzied* scene at the mall on the day after Thanksgiving⟩ — see FEVERISH 1
2 feeling overwhelming fear or worry ⟨*Frenzied* rescue workers searched through the snow, looking for more victims of the avalanche.⟩ — see FRANTIC 1
3 marked by great and often stressful excitement or activity ⟨the *frenzied* pace of the first week of the new school year⟩ — see FURIOUS 1

frenziedly *adv* in a confused and reckless manner ⟨The *frenziedly* scattering gazelles were fleeing the cheetah.⟩ — see HELTER-SKELTER 1

frenzy *n* a state of wildly excited activity or emotion ⟨In its *frenzy* to flee the danger, the herd thundered across the savannah.⟩

synonyms agitation, delirium, distraction, fever, flap, furor, furore, fury, hysteria, rage, rampage, uproar

related words chaos, confusion, disorder, havoc, pandemonium, turmoil; bedlam, bother, brouhaha, bustle, clamor, clatter, commotion, disturbance, fuss, hoo-ha (*also* hoo-hah), hubbub, hullabaloo, hurly-burly, ruckus, ruction, rumpus, shindy, squall, stew, stir, storm, tempest, to-do, tumult

near antonyms calm, calmness, peace, peacefulness, placidity, quiet, quietude, repose, restfulness, sereneness, serenity, still, stillness, tranquillity (*or* tranquility)

frenzy *vb* to cause to go insane or as if insane ⟨local football fans who were *frenzied* by the fact that their team was going to the Super Bowl⟩ — see CRAZE

frequency *n* the fact or state of happening often ⟨The *frequency* of twins in that family is remarkable.⟩

synonyms commonness, frequentness, prevalence

related words constancy, regularity; appearance, incidence, occurrence

antonyms infrequence, infrequency, rareness, uncommonness, unusualness

frequent *adj* 1 appearing or occurring repeatedly from time to time ⟨Our local multiplex usually has *frequent*

showings of blockbusters, with starting times about every half hour.⟩ — see REGULAR 1
2 often observed or encountered ⟨Finches are *frequent* sights in this part of the country.⟩ — see COMMON 1

frequent *vb* to go to or spend time in often ⟨Like their counterparts elsewhere, the town's teenagers like to *frequent* the local malls.⟩

synonyms haunt, resort (to), visit

related words patronize; attend, take in; infest, invade, overrun, swarm; call (on *or* upon), pop (in), run (in), stop (in *or* by); camp (out in), sojourn (at), stay (at), stop (over), tarry (in)

near antonyms dodge, duck, elude, escape, eschew, evade, shake

antonyms avoid, shun

frequenter *n* 1 a person who visits another ⟨He's a regular *frequenter* of their home.⟩ — see GUEST 1
2 someone who regularly spends time in a particular place ⟨A club *frequenter*, he knows what's hot in music and what's not.⟩ — see DENIZEN 1

frequently *adv* many times ⟨Our oddball uncle *frequently* lets himself into our house without knocking.⟩ — see OFTEN

frequentness *n* the fact or state of happening often ⟨The *frequentness* and the fierceness of the storms that winter were unprecedented.⟩ — see FREQUENCY

fresh *adj* 1 being in an original and unused or unspoiled state ⟨The restaurant uses only really *fresh* ingredients in all of its dishes.⟩

synonyms brand-new, mint, pristine, virgin, virginal

related words unaltered, unblemished, unbruised, uncontaminated, undamaged, undefiled, unharmed, unhurt, unimpaired, uninjured, unmarred, unpolluted, unsoiled, unspoiled, unsullied, untainted, untouched, unworn; new, spick-and-span (*or* spic-and-span)

near antonyms blemished, broken, bruised, damaged, defaced, defiled, disfigured, harmed, hurt, impaired, injured, marred, soiled, sullied, tainted; faded, shopworn, used, worn; contaminated, polluted, spoiled; hand-me-down, second hand

antonyms stale
2 displaying or marked by rude boldness ⟨If you are *fresh* with the art teacher, she'll give you a detention immediately.⟩ — see NERVY 1
3 not known or experienced before ⟨a *fresh* look at the situation⟩ — see NEW 2
4 resulting in an increase in amount or number ⟨She's making *fresh* changes on top of the existing ones.⟩ — see ADDITIONAL

freshen *vb* to bring back to a former condition or vigor ⟨Cool glasses of lemonade *freshened* us after a day of hard work outside.⟩ — see RENEW 1

freshened *adj* made or become fresh in spirits or vigor ⟨The team came back from the locker room *freshened* and ready for the rest of the game.⟩ — see NEW 4

freshly *adv* not long ago ⟨a *freshly*-paved road⟩ — see NEWLY

freshman *n* a person who is just starting out in a field of activity ⟨Our senator is just a *freshman* in Congress.⟩ — see BEGINNER

freshness *n* the quality or appeal of being new ⟨The *freshness* of that teacher's approach makes his classes fun and interesting.⟩ — see NOVELTY 1

fret *vb* 1 to consume or wear away gradually ⟨Over the span of thousands of years, the annual spring runoff *fretted* the rock, forming a deep channel.⟩ — see EAT 2
2 to damage or diminish by continued friction ⟨Don't let the girth *fret* the horse's belly or you won't be able to ride him.⟩ — see ABRADE 1

3 to experience concern or anxiety ⟨Don't *fret* over whether it will be sunny tomorrow, as there's nothing we can do about it.⟩ — see WORRY 1

4 to make sore by continued rubbing ⟨The stiff, starchy collar was *fretting* my neck, and I couldn't wait to change out of that costume.⟩ — see CHAFE 1

fret *n* a state of nervous or irritated concern ⟨One of my customers always gets into a *fret* if I'm so much as 5 minutes late delivering his pizza.⟩

synonyms dither, fluster, fuss, huff, lather, pother, stew, tizzy, twitter

related words bother, dudgeon, pique; alarm (*also* alarum), hand-wringing, panic; ado, agitation, delirium, distraction, furor, hysteria, uproar

friable *adj* having a texture that readily breaks into little pieces under pressure ⟨Sand dollars are *friable*, so handle them carefully.⟩ — see CRISP 1

friary *n* a residence for men under religious vows ⟨The Franciscans left the chapel and went to the *friary* for rest.⟩ — see MONASTERY

friction *n* a lack of agreement or harmony ⟨There was *friction* between the two sides of the family.⟩ — see DISCORD

frictionless *adj* having or marked by agreement in feeling or action ⟨enjoys an easygoing and *frictionless* relationship with her in-laws⟩ — see HARMONIOUS 3

friend *n* **1** a person who has a strong liking for and trust in another ⟨really close *friends* who like to do everything together and are always sharing secrets⟩

synonyms alter ego, buddy, chum, compadre, comrade, confidant, crony, familiar, intimate, pal

related words acquaintance; associate, cohort, colleague, companion, fellow, hearty, hobnobber, partner, peer, sport; blood brother, brother, main man, sister; abettor (*also* abetter), accomplice, ally, collaborator, confederate; pen pal; benefactor, supporter, sympathizer, well-wisher; friendly

near antonyms adversary, antagonist, competitor, opponent, rival; archenemy, nemesis

antonyms enemy, foe

2 a person who actively supports or favors a cause ⟨hopes that the new governor will be a *friend* to environmental causes⟩ — see EXPONENT 1

friendliness *n* kindly concern, interest, or support ⟨The family was overwhelmed by the *friendliness* of the welcoming committee.⟩ — see GOODWILL 1

friendly *adj* **1** having or showing kindly feeling and sincere interest ⟨All of the people in my new department seem *friendly*.⟩ ⟨As a *friendly* gesture, we presented our new neighbors with a plate of homemade cookies.⟩

synonyms amicable, chummy, companionable, cordial, genial, hearty, neighborly, palsy, warm, warmhearted

related words affable, agreeable, approachable, good-natured, good-tempered, gracious, nice, sweet; clubby, convivial, gregarious, hospitable, sociable, social; jolly, jovial, merry; extroverted (*also* extraverted), outgoing; brotherly, fraternal, sisterly; close, familiar, intimate; adoring, affectionate, devoted, fond, loving, tender, tenderhearted

near antonyms alienated, estranged; chilly, cold, cold-blooded, cool, frigid, frosty, glacial, icy, wintry (*also* wintery); unsociable, unsocial; aggressive, argumentative, bellicose, belligerent, combative, contentious, disputatious, pugnacious, quarrelsome, scrappy, truculent; inhospitable, inimical

antonyms antagonistic, hostile, unfriendly

2 closely acquainted ⟨We're *friendly* with our neighbors.⟩ — see FAMILIAR 1

3 expressing approval ⟨a *friendly* sign that our pet project would be approved⟩ — see FAVORABLE 1

4 willing to do a favor ⟨a kid-*friendly* restaurant with high chairs and a special menu for small-fry appetites⟩ — see ACCOMMODATING

5 promoting or contributing to personal or social well-being ⟨The state's attitude towards commercial development is widely regarded as *friendly* to the business community.⟩ — see BENEFICIAL

friendship *n* kindly concern, interest, or support ⟨I appreciate your *friendship* during this difficult time for my family.⟩ — see GOODWILL 1

fright *n* **1** something unpleasant to look at ⟨People in our neighborhood think that that orange and green office building is a hideous *fright*.⟩ — see EYESORE

2 the emotion experienced in the presence or threat of danger ⟨The nightmare so filled me with *fright* that I couldn't get back to sleep.⟩ — see FEAR 1

fright *vb* to strike with fear ⟨a ghastly sight that would *fright* even the most stouthearted soul⟩ — see FRIGHTEN

frighten *vb* to strike with fear ⟨Around the campfire the campers tried to *frighten* one another with ghostly legends and grisly tales.⟩

synonyms alarm (*also* alarum), fright, horrify, panic, scare, shock, spook, startle, terrify, terrorize

related words appall (*also* appal), dismay, floor, jolt, shake, shake up; amaze, astound, awe; chill, daunt, demoralize, dispirit, emasculate, psych (out), undo, unman, unnerve, unstring; discomfort, discompose, disconcert, disquiet, distract, distress, disturb, perturb, unsettle, upset, worry

phrases give one the creeps, make one's flesh creep (*or* crawl)

near antonyms assure, cheer, comfort, console, solace, soothe; embolden, encourage, hearten, inspire, steel

antonyms reassure

frightened *adj* filled with fear or dread ⟨I am *frightened* of the dark.⟩ — see AFRAID

frightening *adj* causing fear ⟨a truly *frightening* movie⟩ — see FEARFUL 1

frightful *adj* **1** causing fear ⟨a *frightful* sound emanated from somewhere deep within the forest⟩ — see FEARFUL 1

2 extremely disturbing or repellent ⟨I couldn't listen to the *frightful* details of the trial.⟩ — see HORRIBLE 1

3 extreme in degree, power, or effect ⟨flew into a *frightful* fit of rage⟩ — see INTENSE 1

frightfully *adv* to a great degree ⟨That coat is *frightfully* expensive, so don't spill anything on it.⟩ — see VERY 1

frightfulness *n* the quality of inspiring intense dread or dismay ⟨I had heard stories about the *frightfulness* of the entrance exams.⟩ — see HORROR 1

frigid *adj* **1** having a low or subnormal temperature ⟨Frigid gusts of wind stung their faces.⟩ — see COLD 1

2 lacking in friendliness or warmth of feeling ⟨The innkeeper gave us a *frigid* and unnecessarily formal welcome.⟩ — see COLD 2

frill *n* **1** a strip of fabric gathered or pleated on one edge and used as trimming ⟨I just had to sew the *frill* onto the bottom of the skirt and the dress was finished.⟩ — see RUFFLE 1

2 something adding to pleasure or comfort but not absolutely necessary ⟨We didn't get any food or drinks on the no-*frills* flight.⟩ — see LUXURY 1

3 something that decorates or beautifies ⟨a birthday cake decorated with *frills* like edible glitter⟩ — see DECORATION 1

fringe *n* the line or relatively narrow space that marks the outer limit of something ⟨was on the *fringes* of the crowd and couldn't see the speaker⟩ — see BORDER 1

fringe *vb* **1** to be adjacent to ⟨The orchestral pit *fringed* the edge of the stage.⟩ — see ADJOIN 1

2 to serve as a border for ⟨Neat rows of red brick *fringe* the estate's flower beds.⟩ — see BORDER

fringing *adj* having a border in common ⟨*fringing* nations engaging in trade over the border⟩ — see ADJACENT

frippery *n* dressy clothing ⟨Couples dressed in their most elegant *frippery* for the big gala at the symphony.⟩ — see FINERY

frisk *vb* to play and run about happily ⟨carefree kids laughing and *frisking* about in their backyard⟩ — see FROLIC 1

friskiness *n* a natural disposition for playful behavior ⟨As your puppy grows older, her *friskiness* will diminish a bit, but this breed is generally very energetic and playful.⟩ — see PLAYFULNESS

frisky *adj* **1** given to good-natured joking or teasing ⟨a *frisky* kid who keeps the class in stitches with his jokes⟩ — see PLAYFUL

2 having much high-spirited energy and movement ⟨The *frisky* colt didn't like to be kept in his stall.⟩ — see LIVE-LY 1

fritter *n* a small usually rounded mass of minced food that has been fried ⟨She loves eating corn *fritters* with maple syrup.⟩ — see CAKE 1

fritter (away) *vb* to use up carelessly ⟨Quit *frittering away* the afternoon playing video games and get some housework done!⟩ — see WASTE 1

fritterer *n* someone who spends money freely or foolishly ⟨a wastrel who had the dubious distinction of being the *fritterer* of one of the largest fortunes ever amassed in America⟩ — see PRODIGAL

frivolity *n* a lack of seriousness often at an improper time ⟨The boys were scolded for joking during the funeral service, which was hardly the time for *frivolity*.⟩

synonyms facetiousness, flightiness, flippancy, frivolousness, levity, light-headedness, lightness, silliness

related words cheer, cheerfulness, festivity, gaiety (*also* gayety), glee, gleefulness, high-spiritedness, hilarity, joviality, lightheartedness, merriment, mirth, mirthfulness; childishness, goofiness, puerility; insignificance, littleness, slightness, smallness, triviality

near antonyms dejection, depression, despondency, dispiritedness, downheartedness, gloom, gloominess, heartsickness, joylessness, melancholy, mopes, moroseness, sadness, sullenness, unhappiness

antonyms earnestness, gravity, seriousness, soberness, solemnity

frivolous *adj* **1** lacking importance ⟨Judges are getting sick of people bringing *frivolous* lawsuits.⟩ — see UNIMPORTANT

2 lacking in seriousness or maturity ⟨a *frivolous* conversation about cat memes⟩ — see GIDDY 1

frivolousness *n* a lack of seriousness often at an improper time ⟨His childish *frivolousness* at the awards ceremony wasn't appreciated by anyone.⟩ — see FRIVOLITY

frock *n* **1** a garment with a joined blouse and skirt usually worn by a woman or girl ⟨Please get into your nicest *frock* and join us at the party.⟩ — see DRESS 1

2 a sleeveless garment worn so as to hang over the shoulders, arms, and back ⟨the man clutched his heavy *frock* as he made his way through the driving rain⟩ — see ¹CAPE

frolic *n* **1** a playful or mischievous act intended as a joke ⟨We listened to the senior citizens share memories of long-ago *frolics*.⟩ — see PRANK

2 a time or instance of carefree fun ⟨We took the long weekend as a three-day *frolic* and spent it at the beach.⟩ — see FLING 1

3 activity engaged in to amuse oneself ⟨firmly believes that childhood should be a time of carefree *frolic*⟩ — see PLAY 1

frolic *vb* **1** to play and run about happily ⟨Scores of swimmers were *frolicking* in the ocean surf along the beach.⟩

synonyms caper, cavort, disport, frisk, gambol, lark, rollick, romp, sport

related words bound, hop, leap, lope, skip, spring, trip, tumble; dance, prance; carouse, revel, roister; carry on, horse around; clown, cut up; joyride, roughhouse, skylark; kite

phrases cut capers, kick up one's heels

near antonyms mope, pout, stew, sulk

2 to engage in activity for amusement ⟨He would rather *frolic* than do yard work any day of the week.⟩ — see PLAY 1

frolicking *n* activity engaged in to amuse oneself ⟨a night of *frolicking* by three soldiers just before they are sent to the war zone⟩ — see PLAY 1

frolicsome *adj* **1** given to good-natured joking or teasing ⟨a *frolicsome* uncle who was a favorite among his relatives⟩ — see PLAYFUL

2 joyously unrestrained ⟨teachers smiling at the *frolicsome* students leaving school for summer vacation⟩ — see EXUBERANT

front *vb* to stand or sit with the face or front toward ⟨The apartment complex *fronts* the ocean.⟩ — see FACE 1

front *adj* being at or in the forward part or surface of something ⟨Visitors use the *front* door, but family knows to go around to the side entrance.⟩

synonyms anterior, forward

related words ventral

near antonyms dorsal

antonyms aft, after, hind, hinder, hindmost, posterior, rear, rearward

front *n* **1** a forward part or surface ⟨The *front* of the church features a magnificent stained-glass window.⟩

synonyms facade (*also* façade), face, forepart

related words outside, skin, surface, veneer

near antonyms innards, inside, interior

antonyms back, rear, rearward, reverse

2 a display of emotion or behavior that is insincere or intended to deceive ⟨That smile is just a *front*—I don't think she actually likes me at all.⟩ — see MASQUERADE

3 a region of activity, knowledge, or influence ⟨Are we making any progress on the marketing *front*?⟩ — see FIELD 2

frontier *n* **1** a region along the dividing line between two countries ⟨the *frontier* on the U.S.-Mexico border⟩

synonyms border, borderland, march

2 a rural region that forms the edge of the settled or developed part of a country ⟨Alaska has been called America's last *frontier*.⟩

synonyms backwater, backwoods, bush, hinterland, up-country

related words boondocks, country, countryside, sticks

phrases (the) back of beyond

frontiersman *n* a person who settles in a new region ⟨The *frontiersmen* were willing to brave harsh living conditions in order to achieve a better life.⟩

synonyms colonist, colonizer, homesteader, pioneer, settler

related words explorer, pathfinder, trailblazer; bushranger, mountain man, woodsman

frost *n* **1** a covering of tiny ice crystals on a cold surface ⟨the wintertime routine of scraping the *frost* off the car's windshield every morning⟩

synonyms hoar, hoarfrost, rime

related words frostwork

2 something that has failed ⟨One sales pitch was a *frost*, but the other was a wild success.⟩ — see FAILURE 3

frost *vb* to disturb the peace of mind of (someone)

especially by repeated disagreeable acts ⟨It was the sales-clerk's high-handed rudeness that really *frosted* me.⟩ — see IRRITATE 1

frosty *adj* **1** having a low or subnormal temperature ⟨a *frosty* autumn that was a sign of the brutal winter that followed⟩ — see COLD 1
2 having or showing a lack of friendliness or interest in others ⟨Her response was *frosty* enough to tell me she didn't appreciate the question.⟩ — see COOL 1
3 lacking in friendliness or warmth of feeling ⟨She gave the telemarketer on the phone a *frosty* "No, thank you" and hung up.⟩ — see COLD 2

froth *n* a light mass of fine bubbles formed in or on a liquid ⟨*froth* on the ocean waves⟩ — see FOAM

frothy *adj* **1** covered with, consisting of, or resembling foam ⟨a *frothy* dessert made of whipped egg whites and fruit puree⟩ — see FOAMY
2 lacking in seriousness or maturity ⟨a *frothy* comedy that didn't challenge the intellect⟩ — see GIDDY 1
3 being of a material lacking in sturdiness or substance ⟨flowing, *frothy* costumes worn by willowy ballerinas⟩ — see FLIMSY 1

froward *adj* **1** engaging in or marked by childish misbehavior ⟨Their *froward* pranks are not appropriate in the workplace.⟩ — see NAUGHTY
2 given to resisting authority or another's control ⟨*froward* students sent to the vice-principal's office⟩ — see DISOBEDIENT
3 given to resisting control or discipline by others ⟨Acting like a *froward* preschooler is not going to get you what you want.⟩ — see UNCONTROLLABLE

frowardness *n* refusal to obey ⟨a horse with a willful disposition and *frowardness* beyond control⟩ — see DISOBEDIENCE

frown *n* a twisting of the facial features in disgust or disapproval ⟨It was clear from the *frown* on the CEO's face that sales were headed in the wrong direction.⟩ — see GRIMACE

frown *vb* to look with anger or disapproval ⟨She was *frowning* when I arrived and I knew she was annoyed.⟩
synonyms glare, gloom, glower, lower (*also* lour), scowl
related words gape, gaze, ogle, stare; grimace, pout, sulk; growl, snarl, sneer, snigger
phrases look daggers (*or* stare daggers)
antonyms beam, grin, smile

frowsy *or* **frowzy** *adj* lacking neatness in dress or person ⟨a *frowsy* struggling artist⟩ — see SLOPPY 1

frozen *adj* **1** firmly positioned in place and difficult to dislodge ⟨The car door was *frozen* ever since an accident had damaged the hinge.⟩ — see TIGHT 2
2 having been established and usually not subject to change ⟨Pay rates will remain *frozen* until the company does better financially.⟩ — see FIXED 1
3 lacking in friendliness or warmth of feeling ⟨He responded to my greeting with a *frozen* "hello" and stared straight ahead.⟩ — see COLD 2

frugal *adj* careful in the management of money or resources ⟨By being *frugal*, the family is able to stretch its monthly budget.⟩
synonyms economical, economizing, provident, scrimping, sparing, thrifty
related words conserving, preserving, saving; forehanded, foresighted, foresightful, prudent; penny-wise; cheap, close, closefisted, mean, niggard, niggardly, parsimonious, penurious, pinching, spare, stingy, stinting, tight, tightfisted
near antonyms improvident, shortsighted; bountiful, charitable, freehanded, generous, liberal, munificent, openhanded, unselfish, unsparing; extravagant, indulgent, lavish

antonyms prodigal, profligate, spendthrift, squandering, thriftless, unthrifty, wasteful

frugality *n* careful management of material resources ⟨Her lifelong *frugality* has enabled her to save enough money to go to college next year.⟩ — see ECONOMY

fruit *n* **1** a condition or occurrence traceable to a cause ⟨One *fruit* of your faithfulness in carrying out your duties will be more rewarding responsibilities.⟩ — see EFFECT 1
2 something produced by physical or intellectual effort ⟨a "miracle drug" that was the *fruit* of years of research and development⟩ — see PRODUCT 1
3 the descendants of a person, animal, or plant ⟨gave thanks for the *fruit* of her womb⟩ — see OFFSPRING

fruitful *adj* **1** producing abundantly ⟨a very *fruitful* tree that gives us plenty of apples every year⟩ — see FERTILE
2 producing or capable of producing a desired result ⟨I hope your efforts to find that missing package are *fruitful*.⟩ — see EFFECTIVE 1

fruition *n* the state of being actual or complete ⟨When she landed the lead in a Broadway play, a lifelong dream was brought to *fruition*.⟩
synonyms accomplishment, achievement, actuality, attainment, consummation, fulfillment (*or* fulfilment), pass, realization
related words success, triumph
near antonyms defeat, failure, fizzle, nonsuccess
antonyms naught (*also* nought), nonfulfillment

fruitless *adj* **1** producing no results ⟨This argument is totally *fruitless*, as neither of us will change our position.⟩ — see FUTILE
2 not able to produce fruit or offspring ⟨a stand of blighted, *fruitless* trees⟩ — see STERILE 1

frustrate *vb* **1** to prevent from achieving a goal ⟨A multitude of conflicting opinions *frustrated* me in my attempt to find a computer that best suits my needs.⟩
synonyms baffle, balk, beat, checkmate, discomfit, foil, thwart
related words bar, block, clog, encumber, fetter, hamper, handicap, hinder, hobble, hold back, impede, inhibit, interfere (with), manacle, obstruct, shackle, tie up, trammel; arrest, check, halt, set back, short-circuit, stall, stop; avert, forestall, obviate, preclude, prevent; negate, neutralize, nullify; counteract, offset; conquer, defeat, overcome
near antonyms abet, aid, assist; ease, facilitate, smooth
antonyms advance, cultivate, encourage, forward, foster, further, nurture, promote
2 to lessen the courage or confidence of ⟨Challenge the math student, but don't *frustrate* him or her with overly difficult problems.⟩ — see DISCOURAGE 1

frustrating *adj* causing annoyance ⟨These daily traffic jams are *frustrating*.⟩ — see ANNOYING

frustration *n* **1** something that is a source of irritation ⟨Bad spelling is a constant *frustration* to language-arts teachers.⟩ — see ANNOYANCE 3
2 the emotion felt when one's expectations are not met ⟨The kids couldn't hide their *frustration* when they couldn't get the electronic toy to work.⟩ — see DISAPPOINTMENT 1
3 the feeling of impatience or anger caused by another's repeated disagreeable acts ⟨the passengers' *frustration* with the delay⟩ — see ANNOYANCE 2

fuddy–duddy *n* a person with old-fashioned ideas ⟨a *fuddy-duddy* who won't even give the new method a chance⟩ — see FOGY

fudge *n* language, behavior, or ideas that are absurd and contrary to good sense ⟨I was starting to realize that Grandpa's tales about when he was a boy were a lot of *fudge*.⟩ — see NONSENSE 1

fudge *vb* **1** to avoid giving a definite answer or position ⟨The candidate wouldn't say whether he was for or against the issue but just *fudged*.⟩ — see EQUIVOCATE

2 to use dishonest methods to achieve a goal ⟨She's been *fudging* on her taxes for years.⟩ — see CHEAT 1

3 to change so much as to create a wrong impression or alter the meaning of ⟨Tom *fudged* the facts about his educational background so he could get the position.⟩ — see GARBLE

fuel *n* something with a usable capacity for doing work ⟨such nonrenewable *fuels* as coal, petroleum, and natural gas⟩

synonyms energy, power

related words kindling, propellant (*also* propellent); force

fugitive *adj* **1** hard to find, capture, or isolate ⟨that *fugitive* trait called artistic creativity⟩ — see ELUSIVE

2 lasting only for a short time ⟨He had *fugitive* thoughts of leaving town after finishing high school but never acted on them.⟩ — see MOMENTARY

3 traveling from place to place ⟨a small *fugitive* circus that traveled the countryside⟩ — see ITINERANT

fulfill *or* **fulfil** *vb* **1** to do what is required by the terms of ⟨The football player must remain with the team one more year to *fulfill* his contract.⟩

synonyms answer, complete, comply (with), fill, keep, meet, redeem, satisfy

related words conclude, consummate, finalize, finish, perfect; accomplish, achieve, bring about, carry out, effect; commit, compass, discharge, execute, make, perform

phrases abide by, make good (*or* make good on)

near antonyms default (on); disregard, forget, ignore, neglect, overlook, overpass, pass over, slight

antonyms breach, break, transgress, violate

2 to carry through (as a process) to completion ⟨You have *fulfilled* your duties most admirably.⟩ — see PERFORM 1

fulfilling *adj* making one feel good inside ⟨The college student had a *fulfilling* job tutoring kids with learning disabilities.⟩ — see HEARTWARMING

fulfillment *or* **fulfilment** *n* **1** the doing of an action ⟨her commendably prompt *fulfillment* of any assignment given her⟩ — see COMMISSION 2

2 the state of being actual or complete ⟨He saw the entire project through, from initial idea to final *fulfillment*.⟩ — see FRUITION

full *adv* **1** to a full extent or degree ⟨waited until it was *full* dark to begin the fireworks display⟩ — see FULLY 1

2 to a great degree ⟨He knew *full* well that what he was doing was wrong.⟩ — see VERY 1

3 as stated or indicated without the slightest difference ⟨*Full* in the center of the square stands an enormous statue of the city's founder.⟩ — see EXACTLY 1

full *n* a complete amount of something ⟨The account is now paid in *full*.⟩ — see WHOLE

full *adj* **1** containing or seeming to contain the greatest quantity or number possible ⟨At the start of the game everyone was *full* of energy and hope.⟩ ⟨The boy's bedroom is *full* of sports trophies and medals.⟩

synonyms brimful, brimming, bursting, chock-full (*or* chockful), crammed, crowded, fat, filled, jammed, jam-packed, loaded, packed, stuffed

related words overcrowded, overfilled, overflowing, overfull, overladen, overloaded, overstuffed; abounding, flush, fraught, replete, rife, swarming, teeming

near antonyms deficient, inadequate, incomplete, insufficient, short, shortish, shy, wanting; depleted, drained, exhausted

antonyms bare, blank, devoid, empty, stark, vacant, void

2 of the highest degree ⟨Even at the age of eighteen he hadn't reached his *full* height.⟩ ⟨a boat going at *full* speed⟩

synonyms greatest, maximum, top, topmost, utmost, utter

related words heightened, high

near antonyms lessened, low

antonyms least, littlest, lowest, minimal, minimum, slightest

3 having one's appetite completely satisfied ⟨Even the heartiest eaters are sure to be *full* when they leave that restaurant.⟩

synonyms replete, sated, satiate, satiated, stuffed, surfeited

related words glutted, gorged, overfed, overfull, overstuffed

near antonyms underfed, undernourished

antonyms empty, famished, hungry, starved, starving

4 covering everything or all important points ⟨a *full* analysis of the problems facing our cities today⟩ — see ENCYCLOPEDIC

5 having an abundance of some characteristic quality (as flavor) ⟨The dessert had a rich, *full* chocolate flavor.⟩ — see FULL-BODIED

6 having an excess of body fat ⟨a *full* face and broad smile⟩ — see FAT 1

7 including many small descriptive features ⟨a very *full* description of the city's cultural offerings⟩ — see DETAILED 1

8 not lacking any part or member that properly belongs to it ⟨a *full* deck of cards⟩ — see COMPLETE 1

full blast *adv* with all power or resources being used ⟨had the heat going *full blast*⟩

synonyms all out, full tilt, tooth and nail

related words completely, comprehensively, detailedly, exhaustively, fully, minutely, roundly, thoroughly, totally; extremely, utterly

phrases full steam ahead, in full career, like crazy, to the hilt

full-blooded *adj* **1** of unmixed ancestry ⟨a *full-blooded* American Indian⟩ — see PUREBRED

2 having a healthy reddish skin tone ⟨Dave had the *full-blooded* complexion of a rugged outdoorsman.⟩ — see RUDDY

3 marked by or uttered with forcefulness ⟨mounted a *full-blooded* attack on his opponent's position⟩ — see EMPHATIC 1

full-blown *adj* fully grown or developed ⟨Before he became a *full-blown* literary sensation, he wrote articles for little journals that paid even littler money.⟩ — see MATURE 1

full-bodied *adj* having an abundance of some characteristic quality (as flavor) ⟨After that huge Sunday brunch, everyone needed a *full-bodied* coffee.⟩

synonyms big, concentrated, full, lusty, muscular, plush, potent, rich, robust, strong

related words heavy; straight, undiluted, unmixed; high-octane, high-test; enriched, fortified; concentrated

near antonyms dilute, diluted, watered-down, watery

antonyms delicate, light, mild, thin, thinned, weak, weakened

full dress *n* dressy clothing ⟨teens in *full dress* for the prom⟩ — see FINERY

full-fledged *adj* fully grown or developed ⟨It was years before he became a *full-fledged* star.⟩ — see MATURE 1

full-scale *adj* trying all possibilities ⟨a *full-scale* search and rescue for the victims of the rock slide⟩ — see EXHAUSTIVE 1

full tilt *adv* **1** with all power or resources being used ⟨During the war the nation's factories were going *full tilt.*⟩ — see FULL BLAST

2 with great speed ⟨The fleeing robber ran *full tilt* down the hill.⟩ — see FAST 1

fully *adv* **1** to a full extent or degree ⟨The apartment comes *fully* furnished.⟩

synonyms all, all over, altogether, clean, completely, dead, enough, entirely, even, exactly, fast, flat, full, heartily, out, perfectly, plumb [*chiefly dialect*], quite, thoroughly, totally, utterly, well, wholly, wide

related words absolutely, categorically, cold, downright, plain, stone-cold, unqualifiedly; basically, by and large, chiefly, generally, largely, mainly, more or less, mostly, overall, predominantly, predominately, primarily, principally, substantially; abundantly, copiously, generously, greatly

phrases all the way, at length, down the line, down to the ground, for fair, in whole, to bits, to pieces, to the hilt, to the max

near antonyms barely, hardly, just, kind of, marginally, minimally, scarcely, slightly, superficially; roughly, somewhat

antonyms half, halfway, incompletely, part, partially, partly

2 with attention to all aspects or details ⟨wanted to be *fully* involved in the project⟩ — see THOROUGHLY 1

fulminate *vb* to talk loudly and wildly ⟨She was embarrassed when her friend began *fulminating* at the restaurant about the service.⟩ — see RANT

fulmination *n* harsh insulting language ⟨a proposal that has been the target of much *fulmination*⟩ — see ABUSE 1

fulsome *adj* **1** overly or insincerely flattering ⟨Not all of the players agreed with the captain's *fulsome* praise for the coach.⟩

synonyms adulatory, gushing, unctuous

related words drooling, slavering, slobbering; sickening; demonstrative, effusive, mushy, uninhibited, unreserved, unrestrained; artificial, backhanded, feigned, hypocritical, insincere, left-handed, mealymouthed, sanctimonious, two-faced; disarming, endearing, ingratiating, winning, winsome; extravagant, lavish, unrestrained; abundant, copious, profuse

near antonyms artless, earnest, genuine, honest, ingenuous, sincere, true, unaffected, unpretending, unpretentious

2 giving or sharing in abundance and without hesitation ⟨survivors who were *fulsome* in their gratitude toward the rescue team⟩ — see GENEROUS 1

3 causing intense displeasure, disgust, or resentment ⟨The author perpetuates some truly *fulsome* stereotypes in her novel.⟩ — see OFFENSIVE 1

fumble *n* an unintentional departure from truth or accuracy ⟨Emma played the entire piano piece without a single *fumble*.⟩ — see ERROR 1

fumble *vb* **1** to make or do (something) in a clumsy or unskillful way ⟨Her assistant *fumbled* the party plans by getting the time wrong on the invitations.⟩ — see BOTCH

2 to search for something blindly or uncertainly ⟨The librarian *fumbled* for the light switch as she entered the dark room.⟩ — see GROPE

3 to make a mistake ⟨Just when it looked like he was going to get away with the ruse, he *fumbled*.⟩ — see ERR 1

fumbled *adj* showing or marked by a lack of skill and tact (as in dealing with a situation) ⟨a *fumbled* attempt to make up⟩ — see AWKWARD 2

fume *vb* **1** to be excited or emotionally stirred up with anger ⟨He sat there, *fuming* at the delay.⟩ — see BOIL 1

2 to express one's anger usually violently ⟨She was *fuming* at me and slammed the door on the way out.⟩ — see RAGE 1

fuming *adj* feeling or showing anger ⟨I was *fuming* after losing the game by a single point.⟩ — see ANGRY

fun *vb* to make jokes ⟨just a couple of old friends *funning* with each other⟩ — see JOKE 1

fun *adj* providing amusement or enjoyment ⟨There were so many *fun* things to do at summer camp that the kids really hated to leave.⟩

synonyms amusing, delightful, diverting, enjoyable, entertaining, pleasurable

related words agreeable, beguiling, nice, pleasant, satisfying, welcome; recreational; antic, comic, comical, droll, farcical, funny, hilarious, humorous, laughable, ludicrous, ridiculous, riotous, risible, uproarious; blithesome, gleeful, happy, jocose, jocund, jolly, jovial, merry, mirthful, sunny; exciting, stimulating, thrilling

near antonyms disagreeable, displeasing, distasteful, uncongenial, unlovely, unpleasant, unpleasing, unwelcome

antonyms boring, drab, dreary, dull, flat, heavy, humdrum, jading, leaden, monotonous, pedestrian, pleasureless, ponderous, stodgy, stuffy, tedious, tiresome, tiring, uninteresting, wearisome, weary, wearying

fun *n* **1** someone or something that provides amusement or enjoyment ⟨Theme parks with their rides, shows, and games are great *fun* for the whole family.⟩

synonyms delight, distraction, diversion, entertainment, pleasure, recreation

related words escape, pastime, time killer; binge, fling, frolic, gambol, lark, revel, rollick, romp, spree; frolicking, rollicking; carousing, conviviality, festivity, gaiety (*also* gayety), hilarity, jollification, jollity, merrymaking, reveling (*or* revelling), revelry; picnic, laugh, riot, scream; activity, game

near antonyms killjoy, party pooper

antonyms bore, bummer, downer, drag

2 an attitude or manner not to be taken seriously ⟨Don't get mad: I was only saying it in *fun*.⟩

synonyms game, jest, play, sport

related words facetiousness, flightiness, flippancy, frivolity, frivolousness, levity, silliness

near antonyms earnestness, gravity, seriousness, soberness, sobriety, solemnity

antonyms earnest

3 activity engaged in to amuse oneself ⟨Dad came outside to where we were playing touch football and joined the *fun*.⟩ — see PLAY 1

4 a state of noisy, confused activity ⟨The *fun* really began when the deer broke out of its pen and started wandering down the street.⟩ — see COMMOTION

function *n* **1** a social gathering ⟨made a brief appearance at the annual holiday *function*⟩ — see PARTY 1

2 an assignment at which one regularly works for pay ⟨What's your *function* in this company?⟩ — see JOB 1

3 the action for which a person or thing is specially fitted or used or for which a thing exists ⟨That machine's *function* is to sort bolts by size.⟩ — see ROLE

function *vb* to have a certain purpose ⟨The heart *functions* as a pump for the blood.⟩

synonyms act, perform, serve, work

related words operate, run; administer, carry on, control, direct, guide, handle, manage, oversee, regulate, supervise

functional *adj* **1** being in effective operation ⟨I don't think that vending machine is *functional*, so don't put money into it.⟩ — see ACTIVE 1

2 capable of being put to use or account ⟨a *functional* knowledge of auto mechanics⟩ — see PRACTICAL 1

3 capable of or suitable for being used for a particular purpose ⟨a very *functional* kitchen utensil for peeling potatoes⟩ — see USABLE 1

functionary *n* **1** a person who holds a public office ⟨spoke to high-ranking *functionaries* at the embassy in the hopes that they could help⟩ — see OFFICIAL

2 a worker in a government agency ⟨the faceless *functionaries* at the Internal Revenue Service⟩ — see BUREAUCRAT

functioning *adj* being in effective operation ⟨looked for a *functioning* washing machine at the laundromat, but the few that weren't broken were in use⟩ — see ACTIVE 1

fund *vb* **1** to furnish (as an institution) with a regular source of income ⟨Her will *funded* a new science center for her beloved alma mater.⟩ — see ENDOW 2

2 to provide money for ⟨Dad advised me to get a job because he wasn't going to *fund* my social life forever.⟩ — see FINANCE 1

fund *n* **1** a sum of money set aside for a particular purpose ⟨Our club has a *fund* for parties—which we like to have as often as possible.⟩

synonyms account, budget, deposit, kitty, nest egg, pool

related words chest, coffer(s); assets, savings, savings account; bankroll, cache, collection, cushion, hoard, pocketbook, reserve, treasure; petty cash, pin money, pocket money, spending money

2 funds *pl* available money ⟨My *funds* were a little low, so I asked for a small advance on my paycheck.⟩

synonyms bankroll, coffers, finances, pocket, resources, wherewithal

related words shirt; bread [*slang*], cash, chips, currency, dough, gold, jack [*slang*], legal tender, lucre, pelf, scratch [*slang*], tender, wampum; assets, capital, deep pockets, fortune, means, opulence, riches, roll, substance, wealth; purse, treasury; cash flow; financing

near antonyms debts, liabilities

3 the number of individuals or amount of something available at any given time ⟨We have a deep *fund* of volunteers to call on when there is an unexpected need for help.⟩ — see SUPPLY

fundamental *adj* of or relating to the simplest facts or theories of a subject ⟨The purpose of the course is to furnish students with *fundamental* knowledge of algebra.⟩ — see ELEMENTARY

fundamentals *pl n* general or basic truths on which other truths or theories can be based ⟨All students at the school of music must take a course in the *fundamentals* of their chosen art.⟩ — see PRINCIPLES 1

funeral *adj* expressing or suggesting mourning ⟨a slow and heavy *funeral* song⟩ — see MOURNFUL 1

funeral director *n* a person who manages funerals and prepares the dead for burial or cremation ⟨The *funeral director* instructed the pallbearers on how to proceed.⟩

synonyms mortician, undertaker

related words embalmer

funereal *adj* causing or marked by an atmosphere lacking in cheer ⟨shivered with cold in the dark and *funereal* Victorian mansion⟩ — see GLOOMY 1

¹funk *n* a strong unpleasant smell ⟨The overpowering *funk* of rotten meat emanated from the garbage bin.⟩ — see STINK 1

²funk *n* a person who shows a shameful lack of courage in the face of danger ⟨He may be a strong, athletic guy, but he's a real *funk* when it comes to donating blood.⟩ — see COWARD

funnel *vb* to cause to move to a central point or along a restricted pathway ⟨*funneled* endless time and money into his misguided pet project⟩ — see CHANNEL

funniness *n* the amusing quality or element in something ⟨The *funniness* of the situation is often lost on the victim of the prank.⟩ — see HUMOR 1

funning *adj* marked by or expressive of mild or good-natured teasing ⟨After he confided to his friends that he had a crush on his science lab partner, they made *funning* comments about the "chemistry" between the two sweethearts.⟩ — see QUIZZICAL

funny *n* **1** a series of drawings that tell a story or part of a story ⟨Reading the Sunday *funnies* is part of my weekend ritual.⟩ — see COMIC STRIP

2 something said or done to cause laughter ⟨Let's can the *funnies*—we've got serious work to do here.⟩ — see JOKE 1

funny *adj* **1** causing or intended to cause laughter ⟨a very *funny* movie that had audiences rolling in the aisles⟩

synonyms antic, comic, comical, droll, farcical, hilarious, humorous, hysterical (*also* hysteric), laughable, ludicrous, ridiculous, riotous, risible, screaming, uproarious

related words amusing, diverting, entertaining; clownish, knockabout, slapstick, slapsticky, zany; facetious, flip, flippant, smart-alecky, snickery; jocular, playful, waggish; campy, jokey (*also* joky); rich, whimsical, witty, wry; blithesome, gleeful, jocose, jocund, jolly, jovial, laughing, merry, mirthful

near antonyms earnest, grave, no-nonsense, sedate, serious, severe, sober, sobersided, solemn, somber (*or* sombre), staid, unsmiling, weighty; affecting, moving, poignant, touching, tragic (*also* tragical); lachrymose, mournful, sad, sorrowful, tearful, woeful

antonyms humorless, lame, unamusing, uncomic, unfunny, unhumorous, unhysterical

2 different from the ordinary in a way that causes curiosity or suspicion ⟨That's *funny*, for I could have sworn I put my keys right here yesterday.⟩ — see ODD 2

3 noticeably different from what is generally found or experienced ⟨That's a *funny*-looking dog—what kind is it?⟩ — see UNUSUAL 1

fur *n* **1** the hairy covering of a mammal especially when fine, soft, and thick ⟨The chinchilla is known for its exceptionally soft *fur*.⟩

synonyms coat, fleece, hair, jacket, pelage, pile, wool

related words undercoat, underfur; hide, leather, pelt, skin

2 a soft airy substance or covering ⟨picked at the *fur* on the chenille pillows⟩ — see FUZZ

3 the outer covering of an animal removed for its commercial value ⟨He made his fortune trading *furs* in the 17th century.⟩ — see HIDE 1

furbelow *n* a strip of fabric gathered or pleated on one edge and used as trimming ⟨She opted for a simple wedding dress that did without all the frills and *furbelows*.⟩ — see RUFFLE 1

furious *adj* **1** marked by great and often stressful excitement or activity ⟨Everyone worked at a *furious* pace in order to get the float ready for the parade.⟩

synonyms delirious, ferocious, feverish, fierce, frantic, frenetic, frenzied, mad, rabid, violent, wild

related words concentrated, high-pressured, intense, intensive, vehement; excessive, exorbitant, extravagant, extreme, immoderate, inordinate, lavish, overmuch, overweening, unconscionable, undue; demented, deranged, irrational, maniacal (*also* maniac)

near antonyms calm, peaceful, placid, quiet, serene, subdued, tranquil, undisturbed, unperturbed, untroubled; moderate, reasonable, temperate; casual, easygoing, low-pressure; balanced, sane, sound

antonyms relaxed

2 extreme in degree, power, or effect ⟨a *furious* storm⟩ — see INTENSE 1

3 feeling or showing anger ⟨a *furious* customer demanding to see the manager⟩ — see ANGRY

4 marked by bursts of destructive force or intense activity ⟨Rioters went on a *furious* rampage.⟩ — see VIOLENT 1

furlough *n* the termination of the employment of an employee or a work force often temporarily ⟨The landscaping company usually has to put most of its personnel on *furlough* during the extremely slow winter months.⟩ — see LAYOFF

furnish *vb* **1** to provide (someone) with what is needed for a task or activity ⟨The art students were *furnished* with brushes, crayons, pencils, and various other art supplies.⟩

synonyms accoutre (*or* accouter), equip, fit (out), gird, outfit, provision, rig, supply

related words stock, store; bestow, contribute, donate, give, present; apportion, deal (out), dispense, distribute, mete (out), parcel (out), portion, prorate; allocate, allot, assign; arm, fortify, prepare

near antonyms strip

2 to put (something) into the possession of someone for use or consumption ⟨We'll gladly *furnish* the food for any out-of-town guests.⟩

synonyms deliver, feed, give, hand, hand over, provide, supply

related words ply (with); administer, allocate, apportion, deal (out), dispense, distribute, mete (out), parcel (out), portion, prorate; assign, cede, deed, make over, transfer

near antonyms conserve, keep up, maintain, preserve, save

antonyms hold (back), keep (back), reserve, retain, withhold

furnishings *pl n* the movable articles (such as tables and chairs) in a room ⟨We moved the *furnishings* out of the room so we could sand down and refinish the wood floor.⟩ — see FURNITURE

furniture *n* the movable articles (such as tables and chairs) in a room ⟨We bought all new *furniture* for our new house.⟩

synonyms appointments, cabinetwork, furnishings, movables (*or* moveables)

related words belongings, chattels, effects, gear, goods, holdings, paraphernalia, possessions, things; case goods

near antonyms built-ins, fixtures

furor *n* **1** a state of noisy, confused activity ⟨The classroom was in a *furor* when the mice escaped from their cage.⟩ — see COMMOTION

2 a state of wildly excited activity or emotion ⟨euphoric children in a gift-opening *furor* on Christmas morning⟩ — see FRENZY

3 an intense emotional state of displeasure with someone or something ⟨Residents were in a *furor* about the new paper mill being constructed within city limits.⟩ — see ANGER

furore *n* **1** a state of noisy, confused activity ⟨The store's going-out-of-business sale caused such a *furore* that security guards had to be called in to restore order.⟩ — see COMMOTION

2 a state of wildly excited activity or emotion ⟨baseball fans in a *furore* as the game stretched to 11 innings⟩ — see FRENZY

furrow *n* a small fold in a soft and otherwise smooth surface ⟨The *furrows* in his usually unwrinkled brow suggested that he was very worried.⟩ — see WRINKLE 1

furrow *vb* **1** to cut into and turn over the sod of (a piece of land) using a bladed implement ⟨We had to *furrow* the field before we could plant the wheat.⟩ — see PLOW 1

2 to develop creases or folds ⟨His brow *furrowed* in concentration as he tried to figure out the math problem.⟩ — see WRINKLE 1

furry *adj* **1** covered with or as if with hair ⟨a *furry* teddy bear that would be so nice to cuddle up with⟩ — see HAIRY 1

2 made of or resembling hair ⟨green *furry* mold on old bread⟩ — see HAIRY 2

further *adj* resulting in an increase in amount or number ⟨I think *further* research is needed before we can say whether that treatment is safe or not.⟩ — see ADDITIONAL

further *adv* **1** at or to a greater distance or more advanced point ⟨Go *further* along this road and you'll see the sign for the highway.⟩ — see FARTHER

2 in addition to what has been said ⟨I'll say nothing *further* at this time.⟩ — see MORE 1

further *vb* to help the growth or development of ⟨She worked hard to *further* her career.⟩ — see FOSTER 1

furtherance *n* forward movement in time or place ⟨The 1965 Civil Rights Act was a major step in the *furtherance* of social justice in the U.S.⟩ — see ADVANCE 1

furthermore *adv* in addition to what has been said ⟨I'm not interested in what you are selling, and *furthermore*, I asked your company not to contact me ever again!⟩ — see MORE 1

furthermost *adj* most distant from a center ⟨a probe that will travel into the *furthermost* reaches of deep space⟩ — see EXTREME 1

furthest *adj* most distant from a center ⟨This belongs in the aisle *furthest* from the cash registers.⟩ — see EXTREME 1

furtive *adj* **1** given to acting in secret and to concealing one's intentions ⟨a *furtive* guy who always seems to be up to something⟩ — see SNEAKY 1

2 undertaken or done so as to escape being observed or known by others ⟨We gave each other *furtive* glances as we watched our friend open the booby-trapped soda.⟩ — see SECRET 1

fury *n* **1** a bad-tempered scolding woman ⟨Tradition has it that Socrates' wife was known as a *fury*.⟩ — see SHREW

2 a state of wildly excited activity or emotion ⟨The sudden appearance of the rock star whipped the crowd of onlookers into a *fury* of excitement.⟩ — see FRENZY

3 an intense emotional state of displeasure with someone or something ⟨He rose in a *fury* and stormed out.⟩ — see ANGER

fuse *vb* **1** to come together to form a single unit ⟨Our two local teams *fused* into a larger regional team.⟩ — see UNITE 1

2 to go from a solid to a liquid state ⟨The lightning strike was so hot it caused the electrical wires to *fuse* and then drip onto the road.⟩ — see LIQUEFY

3 to turn into a single mass or entity that is more or less the same throughout ⟨The many foundries would daily *fuse* copper and zinc to create the brass that made the city famous.⟩ — see BLEND 1

fusillade *n* a rapid or overwhelming outpouring of many things at once ⟨responded calmly to the *fusillade* of criticism leveled at his design for the memorial⟩ — see BARRAGE

fusion *n* a distinct entity formed by the combining of two or more different things ⟨a *fusion* of jazz and classical music⟩ — see BLEND

fuss *n* **1** a feeling or declaration of disapproval or dissent ⟨She made a *fuss* about not being picked for the lead role in the play.⟩ — see OBJECTION

2 a state of nervous or irritated concern ⟨The new parents are always in a *fuss* over whether the baby is dressed warmly enough.⟩ — see FRET

3 a state of noisy, confused activity ⟨The company managed the move into the new building without any undue *fuss*.⟩ — see COMMOTION

4 an expression of dissatisfaction, pain, or resentment ⟨None of the employees made a *fuss* over having to come to work in a snowstorm.⟩ — see COMPLAINT 1

fuss *vb* **1** to express dissatisfaction, pain, or resentment usually tiresomely ⟨The eldest daughter is always *fussing* that she gets stuck with all the chores around the house.⟩ — see COMPLAIN

2 to make an exaggerated display of affection or enthusiasm ⟨fans *fussing* over their favorite rock guitarist⟩ — see GUSH 2

3 to make often peevish criticisms or objections about matters that are minor, unimportant, or irrelevant ⟨the picky eater who *fusses* over the arrangement of food on his plate or who won't eat the rice if it touches the salad⟩ — see QUIBBLE 1

4 to use flattery or the doing of favors in order to win approval especially from a superior ⟨Stop *fussing* over me and just tell me what you want.⟩ — see FAWN

5 to experience concern or anxiety ⟨There is no use in *fussing* over things that you can't control.⟩ — see WORRY 1

6 to trouble the mind of; to make uneasy ⟨You shouldn't let a little thing like that *fuss* you.⟩ — see DISTURB 1

fusser *n* **1** a person who makes frequent complaints usually about little things ⟨Bill sat next to an insufferable *fusser*, who whined during the entire bus trip.⟩ — see CRYBABY

2 an irritable and complaining person ⟨a natural *fusser* who has never had a glimmer of gratitude for anything done for him⟩ — see GROUCH 1

fussy *adj* **1** given to complaining a lot ⟨Predictably, the kids riding in the back were *fussy* passengers, always asking "Are we there yet?"⟩

synonyms crabby, cranky, grouchy, grumpy, querulous
related words restive, restless, uneasy; discontented, disgruntled, displeased, dissatisfied; fretful, nervous, worrisome; cantankerous, choleric, cross, crotchety, irascible, irritable, ornery, peevish, perverse, pettish, petulant, quick-tempered, short-tempered, snappish, snappy, snippy, testy, waspish
near antonyms affable, agreeable, amiable, genial, good-humored, good-natured, good-tempered, gracious, well-disposed; accommodating, complaisant, obliging; easygoing, laid-back, relaxed
antonyms forbearing, long-suffering, patient, stoic (*or* stoical), tolerant, uncomplaining

2 hard to please ⟨Cats have a well-deserved reputation for being *fussy* eaters.⟩ — see FINICKY

3 taking, showing, or involving great care and effort ⟨a *fussy* teacher who reads through papers two and even three times before issuing a grade⟩ — see PAINSTAKING

4 elaborately and often excessively decorated ⟨The room, with its rococo furniture and its overabundance of knickknacks, is just too *fussy* for my taste.⟩ — see ORNATE 1

fusty *adj* having an unpleasant smell ⟨I couldn't stay too long in the *fusty* attic without sneezing.⟩ — see MALODOROUS

futile *adj* producing no results ⟨The prison is so well guarded that all attempts to escape have been *futile*.⟩

synonyms abortive, barren, bootless, empty, fruitless, ineffective, ineffectual, profitless, unavailing, unproductive, unprofitable, unsuccessful, useless, vain
related words hollow, idle, meaningless, pointless, valueless, worthless; hopeless, impossible, lost, no-win, unattainable; inadequate, insufficient, lacking, wanting
phrases in vain, no dice, not worth the candle, of no avail
near antonyms meaningful, worthwhile; adequate, sufficient; applicable, feasible, functional, practicable, practical, realizable, usable (*also* useable), workable
antonyms deadly, effective, effectual, efficacious, efficient, fruitful, potent, productive, profitable, successful, virtuous

future *adj* of a time after the present ⟨We must preserve our national parks in all their glory so that *future* generations can experience the majesty of nature.⟩

synonyms coming, unborn
related words approaching, forthcoming, imminent, impending, nearing, oncoming, pending, upcoming; after, ensuing, later, posterior, subsequent; anticipated, awaited, expected, planned, predicted, projected, prospective; eventual, final, last, ulterior, ultimate
near antonyms ancient, olden; antecedent, anterior, precedent, preceding, previous, prior
antonyms bygone, past

future *n* **1** time that is to come ⟨In the *future*, there may be medical discoveries that are beyond our fondest dreams.⟩

synonyms by-and-by, futurity, hereafter, offing
related words eventuality, finality; posterity
near antonyms yesterday, yesteryear; old, yore; moment, now, present, today
antonyms past

2 what is going to happen to someone in the time ahead ⟨With such a strong academic record, his *future* looks bright.⟩ — see FORTUNE 1

futurist *n* one who predicts future events or developments ⟨Economic *futurists* predict a new world order in which information is the resource that drives a nation's economy.⟩ — see PROPHET 1

futurity *n* time that is to come ⟨We can scarcely imagine what observers in some remote *futurity* will think of civilization as it existed at the dawn of the 21st century.⟩ — see FUTURE 1

fuzz *n* a soft airy substance or covering ⟨a comfortable old sweater with clumps of *fuzz* all over it⟩

synonyms down, floss, fluff, fur, lint, nap, pile
related words batting

fuzzy *adj* **1** made of or resembling hair ⟨wore a *fuzzy* red wig at the Halloween party⟩ — see HAIRY 2

2 not expressed in precise terms ⟨The specifics of the program proposed by the candidate are rather *fuzzy*, perhaps intentionally so.⟩ — see VAGUE 1

3 not seen or understood clearly ⟨We saw a *fuzzy* outline through the fog.⟩ — see FAINT 1

G

gab *vb* to engage in casual or rambling conversation ⟨She spent her lunch period *gabbing* with friends.⟩ — see CHAT 1

gab *n* friendly, informal conversation or an instance of this ⟨a car salesman with the proverbial gift for *gab*⟩ — see CHAT 1

gabble *n* unintelligible or meaningless talk ⟨He claimed he was speaking Arabic, but an Egyptian friend confided that all his murmurings were just *gabble*.⟩ — see GIBBERISH 1

gabble *vb* 1 to engage in casual or rambling conversation ⟨I heard my parents' guests still *gabbling* in the living room late into the night.⟩ — see CHAT 1
2 to speak rapidly, inarticulately, and usually unintelligibly ⟨During the filming of the party scene the extras were told to just *gabble* and act like they were having a great time.⟩ — see BABBLE 1

gabbler *n* a person who talks constantly ⟨She was a real *gabbler* who never let you get a word in edgewise.⟩ — see CHATTERBOX

gabby *adj* fond of talking or conversation ⟨a *gabby* talk-show host known for funny interviews⟩ — see TALKATIVE

gabfest *n* friendly, informal conversation or an instance of this ⟨The slumber party was an all-night *gabfest*.⟩ — see CHAT 1

gad (about) *vb* to move about from place to place aimlessly ⟨He *gads about* town every Saturday, visiting with various shopkeepers and locals.⟩ — see WANDER 1

gadabout *n* a person who roams about without a fixed route or destination ⟨She was a thoughtful *gadabout*, always picking up souvenirs for her friends from wherever her travels took her.⟩ — see NOMAD

gadfly *n* one who is obnoxiously annoying ⟨a sports commentator who was a tactless *gadfly* during post-game interviews with the losing team⟩ — see NUISANCE 1

gadget *n* an interesting and often novel device with a practical use ⟨She tried out a new *gadget* for weeding the garden.⟩
synonyms appliance, contraption, contrivance, gimmick, gizmo (*also* gismo), jigger
related words implement, instrument, tool, utensil; accessory (*also* accessary), adjunct; mechanism, trick; thingummy

gaff *n* 1 a socially improper or unsuitable act or remark ⟨You can expect to make some amusing *gaffs* until you get more familiar with the language.⟩ — see IMPROPRIETY 2
2 an unintentional departure from truth or accuracy ⟨Double-check her writing, as it's typically riddled with *gaffs*.⟩ — see ERROR 1

gaff *vb* 1 to cause to believe what is untrue ⟨a charlatan who *gaffed* senior citizens into thinking he had a cure for their ills⟩ — see DECEIVE
2 to rob by the use of trickery or threats ⟨The operators of the traveling carnival had *gaffed* the gullible with a variety of time-honored ruses.⟩ — see FLEECE

gaffe *n* 1 a socially improper or unsuitable act or remark ⟨He committed a huge *gaffe* when he started drinking from the finger bowl.⟩ — see IMPROPRIETY 2
2 an unintentional departure from truth or accuracy ⟨so-called debates, which were mainly about seeing which candidate made the most *gaffes*⟩ — see ERROR 1

gag *n* 1 something said or done to cause laughter ⟨The movie featured a *gag* involving a chicken driving a car that audiences thought was hysterically funny.⟩ — see JOKE 1
2 a playful or mischievous act intended as a joke ⟨the timeworn *gag* of wearing a lampshade as a hat⟩ — see PRANK

gag *vb* 1 to discharge the contents of the stomach through the mouth ⟨The terrible smell of rotting fish made me *gag*.⟩ — see VOMIT
2 to experience complete or partial blockage of the windpipe ⟨I took a bite that was too large and began to *gag*.⟩ — see CHOKE 2
3 to make jokes ⟨That actor typically mugs and *gags* through his movies.⟩ — see JOKE 1

gage *n* something given or held to assure that the giver will keep a promise ⟨In the old days a sheriff would take *gage* in the form of personal goods from an accused person who then had to appear in court or forfeit the goods.⟩ — see PLEDGE 1

gaiety *also* **gayety** *n* 1 dressy clothing ⟨Attendees of the masquerade ball arrived dressed in all their *gaiety*.⟩ — see FINERY
2 joyful or festive activity ⟨We loved the *gaiety* of the annual harvest festival.⟩ ⟨the *gaiety* of the wedding reception⟩ — see MERRYMAKING
3 a mood characterized by high spirits and amusement and often accompanied by laughter ⟨the *gaiety* of children enjoying an outing at an amusement park⟩ — see MIRTH

gaily *also* **gayly** *adv* 1 in a cheerful or happy manner ⟨We sat around the table, *gaily* joshing each other and laughing about the good old days.⟩
synonyms cheerfully, cheerily, happily, heartily, jocosely, jovially, merrily, mirthfully
related words amusedly, exuberantly, giddily, gigglingly, joyfully, joyously; blithely, blithesomely, breezily, gladly, laughingly, lightheartedly, sunnily; good-humoredly, good-naturedly, jocularly; hopefully, optimistically, sanguinely
near antonyms dejectedly, despondently, disconsolately, dispiritedly, wretchedly; forlornly, mournfully, sorrowfully; dourly, glumly, mirthlessly, sulkily, sullenly; dismally, drearily, gloomily, pessimistically
antonyms bleakly, cheerlessly, darkly, heavily, miserably, morosely, unhappily
2 in a quick and spirited manner ⟨children *gaily* running to the buses on the last day of school⟩
synonyms animatedly, animately, high-spiritedly, lively, pertly, spiritedly, sprightly, trippingly, vivaciously
related words friskily, gamesomely, playfully, skittishly, sportively; briskly, crisply, effervescently, energetically, springily; breezily, dapperly, dashingly, jauntily; agilely, nimbly, spryly
near antonyms halfheartedly, idly, indolently, lazily, lethargically, slothfully; heavily, inactively, listlessly, tiredly, wearily
antonyms dully, inanimately, sluggishly, tardily

gain *n* 1 something added (as by growth) ⟨She attributed her recent *gain* in muscle mass to weight training.⟩ — see INCREASE 1
2 the amount of money left when expenses are subtracted from the total amount received ⟨The company posted a substantial fourth-quarter *gain*, signaling an end to their money-losing ventures.⟩ — see PROFIT 1

3 *usually* **gains** *pl* an increase usually measured in money that comes from labor, business, or property ⟨Net *gains* this year were better than last.⟩ — see INCOME 1

gain *vb* **1** to gradually increase in ⟨Our hopes were raised as the movement *gained* strength.⟩

synonyms gather, grow (in), pick up

related words double (in), triple (in); accrue, accumulate, amass; excite, stimulate; enhance, enlarge, enrich, expand, extend, maximize; boost, elevate, jack (up), mount, ramp (up), step up

near antonyms abate, decline (in), diminish (in), dip, dwindle, fall (in), lessen, taper, taper off

antonyms decrease (in), lose

2 to receive as return for effort ⟨He *gained* her affections with his boyishly shy manner.⟩ — see EARN 1

3 to become healthy and strong again after illness or weakness ⟨is steadily *gaining* after his bout with the flu and will be back on his feet soon⟩ — see CONVALESCE

4 to become greater in extent, volume, amount, or number ⟨The new version of the car *gained* in both width and length compared to the earlier model.⟩ — see INCREASE 2

5 to obtain (as a goal) through effort ⟨He vowed to *gain* control of the company by any means necessary.⟩ — see ACHIEVE 1

6 to cause (someone) to agree with a belief or course of action by using arguments or earnest requests ⟨The political party was able to *gain* some supporters with intense recruitment on college campuses.⟩ — see PERSUADE

gainful *adj* yielding a profit ⟨She graduated from school and went looking for *gainful* employment.⟩ — see PROFITABLE 1

gainsay *vb* **1** to declare not to be true ⟨It can't be *gainsaid* that most people wish they had more time and money.⟩ — see DENY 1

2 to make an assertion that is contrary to one made by (another) ⟨They repeatedly tried to *gainsay* me, though every point I made was backed up by facts.⟩ — see CONTRADICT 1

gal *n* a female romantic companion ⟨Grampa said in the old days the boys would take their *gals* to dance marathons.⟩ — see GIRLFRIEND

gala *n* a time or program of special events and entertainment in honor of something ⟨VIPs attended the *gala* celebrating the reopening of the museum.⟩ — see FESTIVAL

gale *n* a sudden intense expression of strong feeling ⟨The audience responded to the comedian's joke with *gales* of laughter.⟩ — see OUTBURST 1

gall *n* **1** a deep-seated ill will ⟨Her kindly feelings turned to *gall* when she found out her nephew only wanted her money.⟩ — see ENMITY

2 shameless boldness ⟨I can't believe he had the *gall* to ask me how much money I make.⟩ — see EFFRONTERY

gall *vb* **1** to damage or diminish by continued friction ⟨Move that rope so the sharp edge of the hull doesn't *gall* it.⟩ — see ABRADE 1

2 to disturb the peace of mind of (someone) especially by repeated disagreeable acts ⟨It absolutely *galls* me that some millionaires pay no taxes.⟩ — see IRRITATE 1

3 to make sore by continued rubbing ⟨Tie your shoes so they don't *gall* your heels sliding on and off like that.⟩ — see CHAFE 1

gallant *adj* **1** feeling or displaying no fear by temperament ⟨a *gallant* firefighter, rushing into the burning house to save the children⟩ ⟨a *gallant* rescue⟩ — see BRAVE 1

2 having, characterized by, or arising from a dignified and generous nature ⟨a *gallant* knight⟩ ⟨The members of that service club are known for their *gallant* service to the community.⟩ — see NOBLE 2

3 large and impressive in size, grandeur, extent, or conception ⟨a great and *gallant* sailing ship⟩ — see GRAND 1

gallant *n* **1** a man extremely interested in his clothing and personal appearance ⟨He was quite a *gallant*, well-known at the men's shops.⟩ — see DANDY 1

2 a man who courts a woman usually with the goal of marrying her ⟨She had a whole host of *gallants* vying for her hand in marriage.⟩ — see SUITOR 1

gallantly *adv* in a manner befitting a person of the highest character and ideals ⟨*gallantly* offered to personally accompany the lost tourists back to their hotel⟩ — see GREATLY 1

gallantry *n* strength of mind to carry on in spite of danger ⟨The mayor commended the rescuers for their *gallantry*.⟩ — see COURAGE

gallery *n* **1** a building or part of a building in which objects of interest are displayed ⟨We visited an array of art *galleries* while on vacation.⟩ — see MUSEUM

2 a typically long narrow way connecting parts of a building ⟨The guest rooms in the east wing open up onto a long windowed *gallery*.⟩ — see HALL 2

galling *adj* **1** causing annoyance ⟨Her holier-than-thou attitude is *galling*.⟩ — see ANNOYING

2 hard to accept or bear especially emotionally ⟨Losing in the last round of play-offs was *galling* to our home team.⟩ — see BITTER 2

gallivant *also* **galavant** *vb* to move about from place to place aimlessly ⟨We *gallivanted* about the country before returning to school in the fall.⟩ — see WANDER 1

gallivanting *also* **galavanting** *adj* traveling from place to place ⟨The *gallivanting* entertainers stayed in town for a few days, then moved on.⟩ — see ITINERANT

gallop *vb* to go at a pace faster than a walk ⟨He dawdles to school but *gallops* coming home.⟩ — see RUN 1

galore *adj* **1** pouring forth in great amounts ⟨There was food *galore* at our Thanksgiving meal.⟩ — see PROFUSE

2 being more than enough without being excessive ⟨With restaurants *galore*, the city is an epicure's delight.⟩ — see PLENTIFUL

galvanize *vb* to cause a pleasurable stimulation of the feelings of ⟨Theatergoers were *galvanized* by the actor's powerhouse performance as Hamlet.⟩ — see THRILL

galvanizing *adj* causing great emotional or mental stimulation ⟨The presentation on the international aid organization was *galvanizing* and thought-provoking.⟩ — see EXCITING 1

gamble *n* a risky undertaking ⟨It's a *gamble*, but I'm willing to take the risk.⟩

synonyms adventure, chance, enterprise, flier (*also* flyer), speculation, throw, venture

related words bet, hazard, stake, wager; liberty; dark horse, long shot, play

antonyms sure thing

gamble *vb* to risk (something) on the outcome of an uncertain event ⟨a foolish man who *gambled* his life savings on the lottery⟩ — see BET

gamble (on) *vb* to take a chance on ⟨a movie studio willing to *gamble on* a new actress for its summer blockbuster⟩ — see RISK 1

gamble (with) *vb* to place in danger ⟨You don't want to *gamble with* your life, so buckle up.⟩ — see ENDANGER

gambler *n* one that bets (as on the outcome of a contest or sports event) ⟨Marveled at the huge swarm of *gamblers* in the casino.⟩ — see BETTOR

gambol *n* a time or instance of carefree fun ⟨She and her old college roommate headed off for one final European *gambol* before returning to the States to start their separate careers.⟩ — see FLING 1

gambol *vb* to play and run about happily ⟨Dog owners

chat while their pooches *gambol* on the park's great lawn.⟩ — see FROLIC 1

game *adj* having a desire or inclination (as for a specified course of action) ⟨Are you *game* for going out tonight?⟩ — see WILLING 1

game *n* **1** a competitive encounter between individuals or groups carried on for amusement, exercise, or in pursuit of a prize ⟨decided he would indulge in a friendly basketball *game* with his friends before dinner⟩
synonyms bout, competition, contest, event, match, meet, sweepstakes (*also* sweep-stake), tournament, tourney
related words athletics, sport; battle, conflict, scrimmage, skirmish, struggle, tug-of-war, tussle; championship, national(s); final, play-off, semifinal; derby, field day, open, outing; biathlon, decathlon, heptathlon, pentathlon, triathlon; marathon, race, ultramarathon; heat, round, run, set; rally, volley; rubber, runoff, sudden death; dead heat, photo finish, seesaw; classic
2 a method worked out in advance for achieving some objective ⟨The crook told his accomplice, "Here's the *game*: look surprised when the police ask about the money."⟩ — see PLAN 1
3 an attitude or manner not to be taken seriously ⟨For some Internet users posting comments is all a *game*, so just ignore them.⟩ — see FUN 2
4 the activity by which one regularly makes a living ⟨Stand-up comedy is his *game*, and he's one of a handful of people making a decent living at it.⟩ — see OCCUPATION
5 a region of activity, knowledge, or influence ⟨The education *game* simply was no longer of interest to her.⟩ — see FIELD 2

gamut *n* the distance or extent between possible extremes ⟨The actress's work runs the *gamut* from goofy comedies to serious historical dramas.⟩ — see RANGE 3

gander *n* an instance of looking especially briefly ⟨We suggested that they take a *gander* at the display of classic cars.⟩ — see LOOK 2

gang *n* **1** a group of people working together on a task ⟨A *gang* of neighborhood residents spent the weekend cleaning up the park.⟩
synonyms army, band, company, crew, outfit, party, squad, team
related words battalion, corps, troop; force, host, stable, troupe; help, personnel, staff
2 a group of people sharing a common interest and relating together socially ⟨The whole *gang* went out for pizza.⟩ ⟨The school's gamers had their own little *gang*.⟩
synonyms body, bunch, circle, clan, clique, community, coterie, crowd, fold, lot, network, pack, ring, set
related words charmed circle, elite, in-group; club, college, fellowship, guild (*also* gild), league, organization, society; camp, faction, sect, side, tribe; mess, squad; brotherhood, fraternity, order, sisterhood, sodality, sorority; commune; alliance, bloc, coalition, confederation, congress, council, federation, union
3 a group involved in secret or criminal activities ⟨politicians promising to stop the growth of criminal *gangs*⟩ — see ¹RING 1

gangling *adj* being tall, thin and usually loose-jointed ⟨The riders at the barn just loved the *gangling* newborn colt.⟩ — see LANKY

gangly *adj* being tall, thin and usually loose-jointed ⟨a *gangly* teenager who was born to play varsity basketball⟩ — see LANKY

gangster *n* a violent, brutal person who is often a member of an organized gang ⟨Al Capone remains one of the most notorious *gangsters* in American history.⟩ — see HOODLUM

gap *n* **1** an open space in a barrier (as a wall or hedge) ⟨There were several visible *gaps* in the wall where the drywall had pulled away from the wall framing.⟩
synonyms breach, break, discontinuity, gulf, hiatus, hole, interstice, interval, opening, rent, rift, separation, void
related words chink, cleft, crack, cranny, crevice, fissure; notch, slit, split; interspace, pore; abyss, aperture, cavity, chasm, gape, orifice; fracture, rupture, severance
2 a break in continuity ⟨There was a 15-minute *gap* between the two televised sporting events.⟩
synonyms discontinuity, hiatus, interim, interlude, intermission, interruption, interstice, interval
related words interspace, lag, pause, space, time lag, window; bumper; adjournment, discontinuance, lapse, suspension; lull, recess, respite, rest; subinterval
near antonyms continuum, run, stretch; procession, progression
antonyms continuation
3 an incomplete or deficient area ⟨a *gap* in his understanding⟩
synonyms hiatus, hole, space, void
related words defectiveness, detriment, disability, failing, fault, impairment, weakness; deficiency, deficit, imperfection, inadequacy, incompleteness, insufficience, insufficiency, lack, need, shortcoming, shortfall, want
4 a narrow opening between hillsides or mountains that can be used for passage ⟨The scouts thought they were stuck until they found a *gap* in the mountain range that they could hike through.⟩ — see CANYON

gape *n* a fixed intent look ⟨I told him to stop staring, that his rather stupid *gape* was annoying.⟩ — see GAZE

gape *vb* to look long and hard in wonder or surprise ⟨stood *gaping* at the sight⟩
synonyms blink, gawk, gaze, goggle, peer, rubberneck, stare
related words glare, gloat, glower; consider, eye, fixate, observe, regard, watch; leer, ogle; peruse, pore (over), study; outstare, stare down
near antonyms glance, glimpse, peek, peep; browse, dip (into), scan; wink (at)

garb *n* **1** clothing chosen as appropriate for a specific situation ⟨He decided to clothe himself in traditional Scottish *garb* for the celebration.⟩ — see OUTFIT 1
2 the outward form of someone or something especially as indicative of a quality ⟨a fable about personal redemption presented in the *garb* of a conventional horror story⟩ — see APPEARANCE 1

garb *vb* to outfit with clothes and especially fine or special clothes ⟨firefighters *garbed* in protective gear⟩ — see CLOTHE 1

garbage *n* discarded or useless material ⟨The raccoons were looking for leftover food in the family's *garbage*.⟩
synonyms chaff, deadwood, debris, dross, dust, junk, litter, refuse, riffraff, rubbish, scrap, trash, truck, waste
related words sewage, slop, swill, wash; remains, rubble, ruins; dump, scrap heap; lumber, odds and ends, trumpery; jetsam, wreckage; castoff, cull, discard, hand-me-down, reject, throwaway
near antonyms catch, gem, goody (*or* goodie), jewel, pearl, plum, prize, treasure, trove, valuable; booty, find, salvage

garble *vb* to change so much as to create a wrong impression or alter the meaning of ⟨The candidate complained that his views had been deliberately *garbled* by his opponent.⟩
synonyms bend, color, cook, distort, falsify, fudge, misinterpret, misrepresent, misstate, pervert, slant, twist, warp

related words misdescribe, misspeak, mistranslate; belie, camouflage, disguise, dissemble, gloss (over), mask, veil, whitewash; censor; complicate, confound, confuse, mistake, mix (up); mystify, obscure; equivocate, fib, lie, palter, prevaricate

near antonyms clarify, clear (up), explain, illuminate, illustrate, interpret, spell out; decipher

garden *n* a large room or building for enclosed public gatherings ⟨We used to go to Boston's historic *garden* to hear concerts and see basketball games.⟩ — see HALL 3

gargantuan *adj* unusually large ⟨a creature of *gargantuan* proportions⟩ — see HUGE

garish *adj* excessively showy ⟨The wedding guest's thick makeup was *garish* and unnecessary.⟩ — see GAUDY

garishness *n* excessive or unnecessary display ⟨The *garishness* of the enormous statues in the small yard was almost funny.⟩ — see OSTENTATION

garment *vb* to outfit with clothes and especially fine or special clothes ⟨a socialite who was among the most stylishly *garmented* women of her time⟩ — see CLOTHE 1

garments *pl n* covering for the human body ⟨chimney sweeps wearing the traditional *garments* of their trade⟩ — see CLOTHING

garner *vb* 1 to bring together in one body or place ⟨She *garnered* more evidence to support her theory.⟩ ⟨an array of rock bands *garnered* from all over the country by the promoters of the festival⟩ — see GATHER 1

2 to receive as return for effort ⟨a novelist who has *garnered* praise for his literate crime novels⟩ — see EARN 1

garnish *n* something that decorates or beautifies ⟨Added a *garnish* of parsley to the plate before serving it.⟩ — see DECORATION 1

garnish *vb* to make more attractive by adding something that is beautiful or becoming ⟨a chef who never served any dish without first *garnishing* it⟩ — see DECORATE

garrote *or* **garotte** *vb* to keep (someone) from breathing by exerting pressure on the windpipe ⟨was *garroted* by the gangsters⟩ — see CHOKE 1

garrulous *adj* 1 fond of talking or conversation ⟨a *garrulous* boy who was in constant trouble for talking out of turn⟩ — see TALKATIVE

2 using or containing more words than necessary to express an idea ⟨Now that he's advanced in years, Grandpa likes to tell *garrulous*, shaggy-dog accounts of his youthful misadventures.⟩ — see WORDY 1

gas *n* 1 boastful speech or writing ⟨all that *gas* about being the best fisherman in the world⟩ — see BOMBAST 1

2 language that is impressive-sounding but not meaningful or sincere ⟨The candidate's pledge that he'll fight for the common people is just a lot of *gas*.⟩ — see RHETORIC 1

3 active strength of body or mind ⟨The tennis player ran out of *gas* toward the end of the long match.⟩ — see VIGOR 1

gas *vb* to engage in casual or rambling conversation ⟨a group of kids in the mall, *gassing* about their favorite music⟩ — see CHAT 1

gaseous *adj* marked by the use of impressive-sounding but mostly meaningless words and phrases ⟨a pompous professor known for his *gaseous* lectures that often put students to sleep⟩ — see RHETORICAL 1

gash *vb* to penetrate with a sharp edge (as a knife) ⟨Her face had been *gashed* by the rocks as she tumbled down the embankment.⟩ — see CUT 1

gash *n* a long deep cut ⟨The hiker got a *gash* in his knee that required four stitches.⟩

synonyms incision, laceration, rent, rip, slash, slit, tear

related words abrasion, score, scrape, scratch; injury, wound; crack, fracture, rupture, snag

gasp *vb* to breathe hard, quickly, or with difficulty ⟨The runner was audibly *gasping* by the end of the marathon.⟩

synonyms blow, heave, hyperventilate, pant, puff, wheeze

related words choke, gag, gulp, huff; asphyxiate, smother, stifle, strangle; snore, snuffle; exhale, expire

phrases be out of breath

gate *n* 1 a barrier by which an entry is closed and opened ⟨Be sure to latch the *gate* when you leave so the dog doesn't get out.⟩ — see DOOR 1

2 the opening through which one can enter or leave a structure ⟨passed through the *gates* of the walled city⟩ — see DOOR 2

3 a fixture for controlling the flow of a liquid ⟨An attendant opens the *gate* in the lock so the ships can get through the canal.⟩ — see FAUCET

gatekeeper *n* a person who tends a door ⟨Most people in the line have little chance of making it past the club's *gatekeeper* and his velvet rope.⟩ — see DOORKEEPER

gateway *n* 1 something that allows someone to achieve a desired goal ⟨Hopefully, my college degree will be a *gateway* to a high-paying job.⟩ — see PASSPORT 1

2 the means or right of entering or participating in ⟨Denver is the *gateway* to the West.⟩ — see ENTRANCE 1

3 the opening through which one can enter or leave a structure ⟨There are security checkpoints at all of the stadium's *gateways*.⟩ — see DOOR 2

gather *vb* 1 to bring together in one body or place ⟨He *gathered* the leftovers from the table and gave them to the dog.⟩ ⟨Let's *gather* the students and have them line up on the playground before going in from recess.⟩

synonyms accumulate, amass, assemble, collect, concentrate, congregate, corral, garner, group, lump, pick up, round up

related words ball, batch, bunch, cluster, huddle; heap, pile, stack; band, muster, raise, rally; flock, herd, hive, pack, press, swarm, throng; combine, connect, join, link, merge, pool, unite; arrange, collate, compile, organize, systematize

phrases get together

near antonyms break up, disband, disintegrate, dissolve, separate, sever, split (up); dismiss, send

antonyms dispel, disperse, dissipate, scatter

2 to catch or collect (a crop or natural resource) for human use ⟨Late summer is when we *gather* the tomatoes and begin canning them for the winter.⟩ — see HARVEST

3 to come together into one body or place ⟨A crowd *gathered* around the street musician.⟩ ⟨Ask the faculty to *gather* in the lounge for the meeting.⟩ — see ASSEMBLE 1

4 to form an opinion or reach a conclusion through reasoning and information ⟨I *gather* that, since you are back so early, the store was closed?⟩ — see INFER 1

5 to gradually form into a layer, pile, or mass ⟨Fallen leaves *gathered* beneath the huge tree.⟩ — see COLLECT 2

6 to gradually increase in ⟨The movement *gathered* force as election day neared.⟩ — see GAIN 1

7 to call into being through the use of one's inner resources or powers ⟨Somehow she *gathered* the strength to finish the marathon.⟩ — see SUMMON 2

gathering *n* 1 a body of people come together in one place ⟨The President spoke before the *gathering* of student leaders.⟩

synonyms assemblage, assembly, conference, congregation, convocation, meeting, muster

related words company, consort, coterie, gang, pack; caucus, forum, market, panel, rally, symposium, synod; gallery, grandstand, house; crowd, flock, horde, legion, multitude, press, swarm, throng; crush, mob, rabble

2 a coming together of a number of persons for a

specified purpose ⟨I attended a *gathering* for descendants of people who came to America on the Mayflower.⟩ — see MEETING 1

3 a mass or quantity that has piled up or that has been gathered over a period of time ⟨a great *gathering* of dust under the bed⟩ — see ACCUMULATION 1

gauche *adj* lacking social grace and assurance ⟨His loud talking at the opera marked him as *gauche* and uncultured.⟩ — see AWKWARD 1

gaud *n* a small object displayed for its attractiveness or interest ⟨some tacky little *gaud* that they had picked up at a souvenir stand at an amusement park⟩ — see KNICKKNACK

gaudiness *n* excessive or unnecessary display ⟨the *gaudiness* of the velvety wallpaper and cut-glass lamps⟩ — see OSTENTATION

gaudy *adj* excessively showy ⟨*gaudy* decorations on all the doors and windows at festival time⟩
synonyms flamboyant, flashy, garish, glitzy, loud, noisy, ostentatious, splashy, swank (*or* swanky)
related words extravagant, fulsome, overdone, over-the-top, overwrought; bedizened, ornate; fancy, snazzy; blaring, bright, florid, glaring, glittery, overbright; graceless, inelegant, lurid, tacky, tasteless, tawdry, tinselly, vulgar
near antonyms inconspicuous, muted, restrained, subdued, toned (down), unobtrusive; elegant, graceful, tasteful; modest, plain, simple
antonyms conservative, quiet, understated, unflamboyant

gauge *also* **gage** *vb* **1** to decide the size, amount, number, or distance of (something) without actual measurement ⟨Glance over the pattern and try to *gauge* how much fabric you'll need.⟩ — see ESTIMATE 2

2 to find out the size, extent, or amount of ⟨It's very difficult to *gauge* how upset he really is by his controlled reaction.⟩ — see MEASURE 1

gaunt *adj* suffering extreme weight loss as a result of hunger or disease ⟨a *gaunt* patient suffering from the side effects of treatment⟩ — see EMACIATED

gauntlet *also* **gantlet** *n* a test of faith, patience, or strength ⟨Before being adopted, school textbooks must often run the *gauntlet* of several local and state committees.⟩ — see TRIAL 1

gauzy *adj* **1** being of a material lacking in sturdiness or substance ⟨*gauzy* spiderwebs⟩ — see FLIMSY 1

2 very thin and easy to see through ⟨*gauzy* curtains that let plenty of light through⟩ — see SHEER 1

3 not seen or understood clearly ⟨I have only a *gauzy* recollection of those long-ago events.⟩ — see FAINT 1

gawk *n* a big clumsy often slow-witted person ⟨He thought that the linebackers were dumb *gawks* until he got to know them better.⟩ — see OAF 1

gawk *vb* to look long and hard in wonder or surprise ⟨We couldn't help *gawking* at the exotically dressed guests in the hotel lobby.⟩ — see GAPE

gawky *adj* having or showing an inability to move in a graceful manner ⟨the stiff, *gawky* gait of a newborn colt⟩ — see CLUMSY 2

gaze *vb* to look long and hard in wonder or surprise ⟨We just sat there and *gazed* at the panorama before us until it got too dark to see.⟩ — see GAPE

gaze *n* a fixed intent look ⟨her admiring *gaze* at the artwork⟩
synonyms eye, gape, regard, scrutiny, stare
related words glare, glower; contemplation, fixation; attention, observance, observation, surveillance, watch; examination, inspection, perusal, study, survey
near antonyms flash, glance, glimpse, peek, peep, sight; browse, scan

gazette *n* a publication that appears at regular intervals ⟨He picked up the monthly car-buyer's *gazette* when he was in town.⟩ — see JOURNAL

gear *n* **1** items needed for the performance of a task or activity ⟨The rookie grabbed his *gear*, threw on his pads, and headed out to the football field for practice.⟩ — see EQUIPMENT

2 transportable items that one owns ⟨You can store your *gear* in the overhead bin during the flight.⟩ — see POSSESSION 2

3 covering for the human body ⟨the latest in kid *gear*⟩ — see CLOTHING

gel *vb* to turn from a liquid into a substance resembling jelly ⟨The fruit juice should *gel* after you add the pectin.⟩ — see COAGULATE

gem *n* **1** a usually valuable stone cut and polished for ornament ⟨a ring set with diamonds and other precious *gems*⟩
synonyms brilliant, gemstone, jewel, rock [*slang*]
related words bauble, bijou, trinket; birthstone; cameo, solitaire, teardrop; paste, rhinestone, zircon
near antonyms rough

2 someone or something unusually desirable ⟨Her new car is a real *gem*.⟩ ⟨The new teacher is a real *gem*.⟩ — see PRIZE 1

gemstone *n* a usually valuable stone cut and polished for ornament ⟨Traditionally, the *gemstone* for someone born in May is an emerald.⟩ — see GEM 1

genealogy *n* the line of ancestors from whom a person is descended ⟨He has a distinguished *genealogy* that traces back to William the Conqueror.⟩ — see ANCESTRY

general *adj* **1** belonging or relating to the whole ⟨a *general* increase in postage rates⟩ ⟨There's been a *general* improvement in the economy.⟩
synonyms blanket, common, generic, global, overall, universal
related words broad, broadscale, comprehensive, extensive, inclusionary, overarching, pervasive, ubiquitous, wholesale, wide, widespread; aggregate, collective, complete, full, plenary
near antonyms component, constituent; cross-sectional, divisional, fragmentary, partial; local, localized, regional, sectional
antonyms individual, particular

2 relating to the main elements and not to specific details ⟨She gave the *general* impression of being kindhearted.⟩ ⟨a *general* course of study in American history⟩
synonyms all-around (*also* all-round), bird's-eye, broad, nonspecific, overall
related words comprehensive, inclusive; absolute, boundless, expansive, extensive, infinite, panoramic, vast, wide; nonspecific, unlimited, unrestricted, unspecified
near antonyms limited, restricted, specified; distinct, explicit, precise, sharp; comprehensive, elaborate, full, mapped (out), thorough; enumerated, inventoried, itemized, listed; individual, singular; particular
antonyms delineated, detailed, particularized, specific

3 held by or applicable to a majority of the people ⟨It was the *general* opinion that the politician was a liar.⟩ ⟨The *general* mood of the nation was one of hope and optimism.⟩
synonyms common, majority, overall, popular, prevailing, public, ruling, vulgar
related words unanimous, universal; pop; everyday, familiar, household, usual, well-known; dominant, predominant, preponderant; characteristic, typical; pandemic, pervasive, prevalent, rife, widespread; communal, shared

near antonyms rare, strange, unknown, unusual; distinctive, especial, idiosyncratic, peculiar, special, unique; individual, separate, singular

antonyms uncommon, unpopular

4 not limited or specialized in application or purpose ⟨a new kitchen tool of *general* usefulness⟩ ⟨a *general* education⟩

synonyms all-around (*also* all-round), all-purpose, unlimited, unqualified, unrestricted, unspecialized

related words mixed-use, multipurpose; broad, wide; nonspecific, unspecified, vague

near antonyms bounded, circumscribed, definite, demarcated, determinate, finite, qualified; selective

antonyms limited, restricted, specialized, technical

generality *n* **1** an idea or statement about all of the members of a group or all the instances of a situation ⟨The idea that all television is mindless is a gross *generality*.⟩ — see GENERALIZATION

2 the main or greater part of something as distinguished from its subordinate parts ⟨an important but little-known Scottish inventor whose work was never appreciated by the *generality* of the public⟩ — see BODY 1

3 the largest part or quantity of something ⟨The *generality* of that high school's students will go on to college.⟩ — see MAJORITY 1

generalization *n* an idea or statement about all of the members of a group or all the instances of a situation ⟨made several sweeping *generalizations* about cities⟩

synonyms concept, conception, generality, notion, stereotype

related words cliché (*also* cliche), commonplace, platitude, truism; adage, proverb, saw, saying; oversimplification, simplification

generally *adv* **1** according to the usual course of things ⟨After lunch we *generally* go for a walk.⟩ — see NATURALLY 2

2 for the most part ⟨*Generally*, I don't care for raw vegetables.⟩ — see CHIEFLY

generate *vb* to be the cause of (a situation, action, or state of mind) ⟨His rabble-rousing speech *generated* a lot of controversy among local taxpayers.⟩ — see EFFECT

generator *n* a person who establishes a whole new field of endeavor ⟨The French painter Paul Cézanne is considered to be one of the principal *generators* of modern art.⟩ — see FATHER 2

generic *adj* belonging or relating to the whole ⟨"Flu" is sometimes a *generic* term used for any illness caused by a virus.⟩ — see GENERAL 1

generosity *n* the quality or state of being generous ⟨a sidewalk beggar who benefited from the *generosity* of kindhearted passersby⟩ — see LIBERALITY

generous *adj* **1** giving or sharing in abundance and without hesitation ⟨a civic leader who is very *generous* with his money and time⟩

synonyms bounteous, bountiful, charitable, free, free-handed, fulsome, liberal, munificent, open, openhanded, unselfish, unsparing

related words extravagant, handsome, lavish, overgenerous, profuse; altruistic, beneficent, benevolent, hospitable, humanitarian, philanthropic (*also* philanthropical); big, greathearted, largehearted, magnanimous, openhearted; compassionate, good-hearted, kind, kindly, sympathetic

near antonyms mean, petty, small; frugal, spare, sparing, thrifty; stinting; acquisitive, avaricious, avid, coveting, covetous, desirous, grasping, hoggish, mercenary, rapacious; begrudging, envious, grudging, resentful

antonyms cheap, close, closefisted, mingy, niggardly, parsimonious, penurious, selfish, stingy, stinting, tight, tightfisted, uncharitable

2 being more than enough without being excessive ⟨mashed potatoes with a *generous* serving of butter⟩ — see PLENTIFUL

generously *adv* in a generous manner ⟨gave *generously* to several charities⟩ — see WELL 2

genesis *n* the point at which something begins ⟨I was present at the meeting, which was later considered the *genesis* of the new political movement.⟩ — see BEGINNING

genetic *also* **genetical** *adj* genetically passed or capable of being passed from parent to offspring ⟨hemophilia and other *genetic* medical disorders⟩ — see HEREDITARY

genial *adj* **1** having an easygoing and pleasing manner especially in social situations ⟨a *genial* host who makes a point of speaking personally to each and every guest⟩ — see AMIABLE

2 having or showing kindly feeling and sincere interest ⟨*genial* new neighbors who helped us unpack boxes and brought us dinner our first night in the new place⟩ — see FRIENDLY 1

3 showing a natural kindness and courtesy especially in social situations ⟨his *genial* offer to give me his seat on the bus⟩ — see GRACIOUS 1

4 marked by temperatures that are neither too high nor too low ⟨They wanted to move to a more *genial* clime for health reasons.⟩ — see CLEMENT 1

geniality *n* the state or quality of having a pleasant or agreeable manner in socializing with others ⟨Her unforced *geniality* never fails to draw fellow passengers into a conversation with her.⟩ — see AMIABILITY 1

genius *n* **1** a very smart person ⟨The 16-year-old college graduate was considered to be a *genius*.⟩

synonyms brain, intellect, thinker, whiz, wizard

related words polymath, Renaissance man; blue, bluestocking, highbrow, intellectual; sage, savant; egghead, nerd; master, virtuoso

near antonyms ignoramus, illiterate, know-nothing, lowbrow; anti-intellectual, philistine; ass, donkey, fool, jackass; beast, boor, cad, churl, clown, creep, cur, heel, jerk, louse, lout, skunk, snake, stinker

antonyms blockhead, dodo, dolt, dope, dumbbell, dummy, dunce, fathead, goon, half-wit, hammerhead, idiot, imbecile, moron, nitwit, numskull (*or* numbskull), pinhead

2 a special and usually inborn ability ⟨He had a *genius* for remembering long strings of numbers.⟩ ⟨She had a *genius* for saying the right thing, no matter what the social situation.⟩ — see TALENT

3 a habitual attraction to some activity or thing ⟨a *genius* for hiking in remote areas⟩ — see INCLINATION 1

4 the set of qualities that makes a person, a group of people, or a thing different from others ⟨Putting the needs of the individual before those of society is alien to the *genius* of the Japanese people.⟩ — see NATURE 1

5 a visible representation of something abstract (as a quality) ⟨The giant tortoise would seem to be the very *genius* of the unfathomable ancientness that one associates with the Galápagos Islands.⟩ — see EMBODIMENT

gent *n* an adult male human being ⟨ladies and *gents*⟩ — see MAN 1

genteel *adj* **1** following the established traditions of refined society and good taste ⟨a person of *genteel* manners⟩ — see PROPER 1

2 having or showing a taste for the fine arts and gracious living ⟨She grew up in *genteel* old Savannah.⟩ — see CULTIVATED

3 of high birth, rank, or station ⟨prohibited by reason of her *genteel* birth from marrying the man she loved⟩ — see NOBLE 1

4 showing consideration, courtesy, and good manners ⟨his *genteel* gesture of holding the door for people following him⟩ — see POLITE 1

gentile *n* a person who does not worship the God of the Bible ⟨an outreach event to which *gentiles* were invited⟩ — see HEATHEN 1

gentility *n* **1** speech or behavior that is a sign of good manners ⟨He was full of the same *gentility* and grace that marked the rest of the family.⟩ — see POLITENESS 1

2 the highest class in a society ⟨As members of the *gentility*, they felt an obligation to help the less fortunate.⟩ — see ARISTOCRACY 1

gentle *adj* **1** not harsh or stern especially in nature or effect ⟨Use a *gentle* detergent on that delicate silk blouse.⟩ ⟨her *gentle* ways⟩

synonyms balmy, benign, bland, delicate, light, mellow, mild, soft, soothing, tender

related words calm, pacific, peaceful, placid, quiet, serene, tranquil; clement, compassionate, easy, lenient, merciful; buffering, emollient, softening; sleek, slick, smooth

near antonyms exquisite, fierce, intense, powerful, severe; forceful, forcible, savage, violent; roughened, rugged, strong; abrading, irritating, roughening; grim, gruff, rude, stiff; heavy-handed, oppressive, pitiless, tyrannical (*also* tyrannic)

antonyms caustic, coarse, hard, harsh, rough, scathing, stern, ungentle

2 marked by temperatures that are neither too high nor too low ⟨Whisk the egg yolks in a double boiler set over a *gentle* heat.⟩ — see CLEMENT 1

3 of high birth, rank, or station ⟨I loved reading about the days when *gentle* lords and ladies danced at fancy balls.⟩ — see NOBLE 1

4 not loud in pitch or volume ⟨The mother spoke in a *gentle* voice to her child.⟩ — see SOFT 1

gentle *vb* **1** to lessen the anger or agitation of ⟨Employees soon learned that their hot-tempered boss needed to be *gentled* several times a day.⟩ — see PACIFY 1

2 to touch or handle in a tender or loving manner ⟨He soothingly *gentled* his cat's head as she was being treated by the vet.⟩ — see FONDLE

3 to lessen the shock of ⟨Adding a bit of sugar to the salsa will *gentle* the hot spiciness of the chili peppers.⟩ — see CUSHION

gentleman *n* **1** a man of high birth or social position ⟨Many of the signers of the Declaration of Independence were *gentlemen* who were risking everything.⟩

synonyms grandee, nobleman, peer

related words country gentleman, squire; cavalier, chevalier, knight; don, hidalgo, nabob, nawab, seigneur, seignior, sheikh (*or* sheik); baron, baronet, count, duke, earl, esquire, marchese, margrave, marquess (*or* marquis), master, prince, princelet, princeling, raja, viscount; lordship, sire [*archaic*]

near antonyms boor, churl, fellah, peasant, peon; commoner, pleb, plebeian; proletarian

2 an adult male human being ⟨Ladies and *gentlemen*, please take your seats.⟩ — see MAN 1

3 an honorable and courteous man ⟨The host was such a *gentleman* that he offered to call a cab for me.⟩ — see CAVALIER

gentlewoman *n* a woman of high birth or social position ⟨In the 19th century a number of American *gentlewomen* used their wealth and influence to further abolitionism, women's rights, and other worthy causes.⟩

synonyms dame, lady, noblewoman

related words baroness, countess, duchess, marchesa, marchioness, marquise, queen, viscountess; dowager, matriarch, matron, mistress; ladyship

gentry *n* **1** the highest class in a society ⟨poor tenant farmers working for landed *gentry*⟩ — see ARISTOCRACY 1

2 one of the segments of society into which people are grouped ⟨The old-line yachting *gentry* frowns on vulgar displays of wealth.⟩ — see CLASS 1

genuine *adj* **1** being exactly as appears or as claimed ⟨They had a *genuine* van Gogh hanging in their living room.⟩ — see AUTHENTIC 1

2 free from any intent to deceive or impress others ⟨*genuine* compliments about her boss's flair for fashion⟩ — see GUILELESS

3 existing in fact and not merely as a possibility ⟨There's *genuine* value in learning how to do household repairs on one's own.⟩ — see ACTUAL

genuinely *adv* in actual fact ⟨The girl is *genuinely* fond of her older brother.⟩ — see VERY 2

geometry *n* the outward appearance of something as distinguished from its substance ⟨The *geometry* of Sydney's famed opera house is suggestive of some modernistic sailing ship.⟩ — see FORM 1

geriatric *adj* being of advanced years and especially past middle age ⟨He went into nursing to work with *geriatric* patients.⟩ — see ELDERLY

germane *adj* having to do with the matter at hand ⟨My personal opinion isn't *germane* to our discussion of the facts of the case.⟩ — see PERTINENT

germfree *adj* free from filth, infection, or dangers to health ⟨We had to prepare the microscope slides in an isolated and *germfree* environment.⟩ — see SANITARY

gestation *n* the state of containing unborn young within the body ⟨The length of *gestation* for the gray wolf is about 63 days.⟩ — see PREGNANCY

gesticulation *n* a movement of the body or limbs that expresses or emphasizes an idea or feeling ⟨As the argument grew more heated, his *gesticulations* got bigger and wilder.⟩ — see GESTURE 1

gesture *vb* to direct or notify by a movement or gesture ⟨The police officer *gestured* me to the side of the road to tell me my headlight was out.⟩ — see MOTION

gesture *n* **1** a movement of the body or limbs that expresses or emphasizes an idea or feeling ⟨She shrugged her shoulders in a *gesture* of indifference.⟩

synonyms gesticulation, mime, pantomime, sign, signal

related words beck, beckon, flourish, shrug, wave; body language, posture; indication, motion

2 an act or utterance that is a customary show of good manners ⟨He sent a handwritten thank-you note as a *gesture* of his gratitude.⟩ — see CIVILITY 1

get *vb* **1** to acquire complete knowledge, understanding, or skill in ⟨I'm not sure I ever *got* the new math.⟩ — see LEARN 1

2 to become affected with (a disease or disorder) ⟨Don't cough on me—I don't want to *get* your cold!⟩ — see CONTRACT 1

3 to become the father of ⟨Abraham was quite old when he *got* his son Isaac.⟩ — see FATHER

4 to cause (someone) to agree with a belief or course of action by using arguments or earnest requests ⟨We tried to *get* the mayor to let us stage the concert in the town square, but she refused.⟩ — see PERSUADE

5 to come upon after searching, study, or effort ⟨I redid the math problem until I *got* the right answer.⟩ — see FIND 1

6 to disturb the peace of mind of (someone) especially by repeated disagreeable acts ⟨Continuously clearing your throat like that is starting to *get* to me.⟩ — see IRRITATE 1

7 to eventually have as a state or quality ⟨It's going to *get* colder as winter approaches.⟩ — see BECOME

8 to receive as return for effort ⟨He *got* an A on his final paper.⟩ — see EARN 1

9 to have a clear idea of ⟨She was speaking so fast—did you *get* what she said?⟩ — see COMPREHEND 1

10 to take physical control or possession of (something) suddenly or forcibly ⟨The defense tackled the running back and *got* the ball.⟩ — see CATCH 1

11 to leave a place often for another ⟨We hope to *get* away to the Bahamas for a vacation.⟩ — see GO 2

12 to achieve a victory over ⟨You may have won this game, but I'll *get* you next time!⟩ — see BEAT 2

13 to transmit information or requests to ⟨I've been trying all day, but I can't *get* either of them in order to ask the question.⟩ — see CONTACT

14 to put to death deliberately ⟨"I'll *get* you if you talk to the cops," the loan shark warned.⟩ — see MURDER 1

15 to throw into a state of mental uncertainty ⟨What *gets* me is why she would do such a weird thing.⟩ — see CONFUSE 1

get *n* the descendants of a person, animal, or plant ⟨In some animal species, a new mate will refuse to raise another male's *get*.⟩ — see OFFSPRING

get across *vb* to make plain or understandable ⟨What I'm trying to *get across* is that there simply is no money for the project.⟩ — see EXPLAIN 1

get along *vb* **1** to meet one's day-to-day needs ⟨Most college students can *get along* with just a few hours of sleep at night.⟩

synonyms cope, do, fare, get by, get on, make out, manage, shift

related words carry on, contrive, scrape (by *or* through), scrounge; last, survive; eke out, scrape (out), squeeze, wrest, wring; afford, swing

phrases fend for oneself, make do, make ends meet, make shift

near antonyms collapse, fail, fall short, fizzle, flounder; decline, peter (out), slump, wane; give up

2 to move forward along a course ⟨The preparations for the party are *getting along* just fine.⟩ — see GO 1

get around *vb* **1** to achieve a victory over ⟨Somehow, an inexperienced lawyer managed to *get around* the media giant's stable of high-priced legal eagles.⟩ — see BEAT 2

2 to avoid having to comply with (something) especially through cleverness ⟨Somehow she managed to *get around* the rules for paying the sales tax on a car bought out of state.⟩ — see CIRCUMVENT 1

3 to become known ⟨Word of the discovery of gold quickly *got around*.⟩ — see GET OUT 1

4 to get or keep away from (as a responsibility) through cleverness or trickery ⟨Their lawyer has spent months trying to *get around* certain restrictions in the contract.⟩ — see ESCAPE 2

getaway *n* the act or an instance of getting free from danger or confinement ⟨The bank robbers jumped into the waiting car and made their *getaway*.⟩ — see ESCAPE 1

get by *vb* to meet one's day-to-day needs ⟨Working at night paid my college tuition and enabled me to *get by*—but just barely.⟩ — see GET ALONG 1

get off *vb* **1** to leave a place often for another ⟨We told him to *get off* for home before it got dark.⟩ — see GO 2

2 to take the first step in (a process or course of action) ⟨Breakfast helps you *get off* to a good start in the morning.⟩ — see BEGIN 1

get on *vb* **1** to meet one's day-to-day needs ⟨Despite his new job's low pay, he was still *getting on*.⟩ — see GET ALONG 1

2 to move forward along a course ⟨Find out how the marketing department is *getting on* with the new ad campaign.⟩ — see GO 1

get out *vb* **1** to become known ⟨News of the rock star's secret wedding *got out* to the news media.⟩

synonyms break, circulate, come out, get around, leak (out), out, spread

related words develop, transpire, unfold; disclose, reveal, spill, tell

near antonyms hush (up), suppress; conceal, disguise, hide, mask; secrete

2 to get free from a dangerous or confining situation ⟨He tried but couldn't *get out* of the old well without assistance.⟩ — see ESCAPE 1

3 to produce and release for distribution in printed form ⟨a romance novelist who *got* a new book *out* every year⟩ — see PUBLISH 1

get–together *n* **1** a coming together of a number of persons for a specified purpose ⟨I promised to meet friends for lunch after that morning's *get-together* for sales reps.⟩ — see MEETING 1

2 a social gathering ⟨I was invited to a neighborhood *get-together* in the neighbors' backyard.⟩ — see PARTY 1

getup *n* **1** clothing chosen as appropriate for a specific situation ⟨She went to the prom in some elaborately beaded *getup*.⟩ — see OUTFIT 1

2 the way in which the elements of something (as a work of art) are arranged ⟨The menu's *getup* is pretty standard, with appetizers listed first and desserts last.⟩ — see COMPOSITION 1

get up *vb* **1** to leave one's bed ⟨You need to *get* right *up* when the alarm goes off in the morning.⟩ — see ARISE 1

2 to outfit with clothes and especially fine or special clothes ⟨all *got up* in her Sunday best⟩ — see CLOTHE 1

3 to call into being through the use of one's inner resources or powers ⟨I'm still trying to *get up* the energy to reply.⟩ — see SUMMON 2

gewgaw *also* **geegaw** *n* a small object displayed for its attractiveness or interest ⟨Their son had a shelf devoted just to *gewgaws* featuring his favorite team's mascot.⟩ — see KNICKKNACK

ghastliness *n* the quality of inspiring intense dread or dismay ⟨The *ghastliness* of the Holocaust can scarcely be described.⟩ — see HORROR 1

ghastly *adj* **1** extremely disturbing or repellent ⟨a *ghastly* crime that shocked even hard-bitten detectives⟩ — see HORRIBLE 1

2 extreme in degree, power, or effect ⟨I'm afraid that there's been a *ghastly* misunderstanding.⟩ — see INTENSE 1

3 causing fear ⟨a *ghastly* horror story⟩ — see FEARFUL 1

ghost *n* **1** the soul of a dead person thought of especially as appearing to living people ⟨We looked for *ghosts* in the graveyard on Halloween.⟩

synonyms apparition, bogey (*also* bogie *or* bogy), phantasm (*also* fantasm), phantom, poltergeist, shade, shadow, specter (*or* spectre), spirit, spook, sprite, vision, visitant, wraith

related words angel, familiar, genie, genius, jinni (*or* jinn *also* djinni *or* djinn); double, doppelgänger (*or* doppelganger); fetch; incubus, lamia, succubus, zombie (*also* zombi); demon (*or* daemon), devil, fiend, ghoul, imp

2 a tiny often physical indication of something lost or vanished ⟨The down-at-the-heels town house is but a *ghost* of the neighborhood's former grandeur.⟩ — see VESTIGE 1

3 an evil spirit ⟨the vengeful *ghosts* of seamen who were deliberately shipwrecked upon these shores⟩ — see DEMON 1

ghoul *n* an evil spirit ⟨In Arabic folklore, *ghouls* could change their shapes but had one unchanging feature: donkey's hooves for feet.⟩ — see DEMON 1

giant *adj* unusually large ⟨The *giant* sycamore tree that dwarfs our house is almost 250 years old.⟩ — see HUGE

giant *n* something that is unusually large and powerful ⟨The Great Pyramids of Egypt are *giants* among the world's architectural wonders.⟩

  synonyms behemoth, blockbuster, colossus, jumbo, leviathan, mammoth, monster, titan, whale, whopper

  related words amazon, giantess; bulk, hulk; steamroller

  near antonyms lightweight, weakling, wimp, wisp; nonentity, twerp, whippersnapper

  antonyms diminutive, dwarf, half-pint, midget, mite, peewee, pygmy (*also* pigmy), runt, shrimp

gibber *vb* to speak rapidly, inarticulately, and usually unintelligibly ⟨Stop *gibbering*, and pull yourself together!⟩ — see BABBLE 1

gibber *n* unintelligible or meaningless talk ⟨All I could get from her *gibber* was that something had exploded.⟩ — see GIBBERISH 1

gibberish *n* 1 unintelligible or meaningless talk ⟨The lad was so excited he could only talk *gibberish*.⟩

  synonyms abracadabra, babble, blabber, double-talk, drivel, gabble, gibber, jabber, jabberwocky, mumbo jumbo, nonsense, prattle

  related words blah (*also* blah-blah), twaddle; chatter, gab, patter, prate, tattle, twitter; cackle, clack, clatter

  2 language marked by abstractions, jargon, euphemisms, and circumlocutions ⟨All I got from the doctor's *gibberish* was that I had a sore throat, which I already knew.⟩

  synonyms double-talk, gobbledygook (*also* gobbledegook), rigmarole (*also* rigamarole)

  related words bureaucratese, computerese, educationese, governmentese, legalese, Pentagonese, psychobabble, technobabble; bombast, gas, grandiloquence, hot air, oratory, rhetoric, wind

gibe *or* **jibe** *vb* to make (someone or something) the object of unkind laughter ⟨teammates *gibing* each other when one fouls up an important play⟩ — see RIDICULE

giddy *adj* 1 lacking in seriousness or maturity ⟨The *giddy* youngsters continued to laugh, joke, and make faces during the ceremonies.⟩

  synonyms dizzy, featherbrained, flighty, frivolous, frothy, goofy, harebrained, light-headed, puerile, scatterbrained, silly

  related words fatuous, foolish, inane, nonsensical, witless; daffy, daft, fruity; flippant, fluttery, giggly, happy, light, lighthearted, playful; sappy, shallow, superficial

  near antonyms grave, melancholy, somber (*or* sombre), thoughtful; dignified, heavy, no-nonsense, sedate, severe, solemn, staid

  antonyms earnest, serious, serious-minded, sober

  2 having a feeling of being whirled about and in danger of falling down ⟨I love the *giddy* feeling you get riding roller coasters.⟩ — see DIZZY 1

  3 experiencing or marked by overwhelming usually pleasurable emotion ⟨He's clearly *giddy* at the news that his ailing grandfather will be fine.⟩ — see ECSTATIC

gift *n* 1 something given to someone without expectation of a return ⟨We gave him an unusual birthday *gift*.⟩

  synonyms donation, freebie (*or* freebee), giveaway, lagniappe, largess (*also* largesse), present, presentation

  related words alms, benefaction, beneficence, benevolence, charity, contribution, dole, handout, oblation, offering, philanthropy, tithe; grant, subsidy; remembrance, tribute, valentine; bonus, boon, windfall; courtesy, favor, generosity, sacrifice; gratuity, tip; award, prize, reward; dowry; bequest, legacy

  near antonyms advance, loan; bribe, peace offering, sop

  2 a special and usually inborn ability ⟨She has a *gift* for making guests feel right at home.⟩ — see TALENT

gift *vb* to furnish freely or naturally with some power, quality, or attribute ⟨*gifted* with a talent for languages⟩ — see ENDOW 1

gigantic *adj* unusually large ⟨A raccoon got into the trash and now there's a *gigantic* mess in our backyard.⟩ — see HUGE

giggle *n* an explosive sound that is a sign of amusement ⟨I couldn't help but *giggle* at his remark.⟩ — see LAUGH 1

giggle *vb* to show mirth with an explosive vocal sound ⟨We were all joking and *giggling* nervously while waiting for the ceremony to begin.⟩ — see LAUGH 1

gimmick *n* 1 a clever often underhanded means to achieve an end ⟨That free magazine subscription they offer is just a sales *gimmick* to get you to buy their product.⟩ — see TRICK 1

  2 an interesting and often novel device with a practical use ⟨a phone equipped with a fitness monitor and other neat *gimmicks*⟩ — see GADGET

  3 a danger or difficulty that is hidden or not easily recognized ⟨The deal sounds too good to be true, so make sure there aren't any *gimmicks*.⟩ — see PITFALL 1

ginger *n* active strength of body or mind ⟨a 60-year-old with the *ginger* to consider skydiving lessons⟩ — see VIGOR 1

gingerbread *adj* elaborately and often excessively decorated ⟨We marveled at all the woodwork on the historic *gingerbread* cottages that lined the coast.⟩ — see ORNATE 1

gingerly *adj* having or showing a close attentiveness to avoiding danger or trouble ⟨I gave the cork on the bottle of champagne a *gingerly* twist.⟩ — see CAREFUL 1

gingery *adj* 1 having active strength of body or mind ⟨a *gingery* old lobsterman who goes out every day regardless of the weather⟩ — see VIGOROUS 1

  2 marked by a lively display of strong feeling ⟨I got a *gingery* rebuke when I asked the spry old woman if she needed any help crossing the street.⟩ — see SPIRITED 1

gird *vb* 1 to encircle or bind with or as if with a belt ⟨For the celebration of the heroes' return, well-wishers *girded* hundreds of trees with yellow ribbons.⟩ ⟨She *girded* her waist with a delicate sash.⟩

  synonyms band, belt, girdle, girt, girth, wrap

  related words tie up, truss; circle, enwreathe, loop, wind, wreathe; bandage, swathe; chain, cord, enchain, lash, rope, shackle, tape, wire

  near antonyms unbind, unlash, unshackle, untie, unwind

  antonyms ungird, unwrap

  2 to provide (someone) with what is needed for a task or activity ⟨The Spartan warrior *girded* himself for battle with sword and shield.⟩ — see FURNISH 1

  3 to form a circle around ⟨A tall hedge *girds* the exclusive estate and shields it from prying eyes.⟩ — see SURROUND

girdle *n* a strip of flexible material (as leather) worn around the waist ⟨The maiden drew a handkerchief from the *girdle* around her waist and offered it to the knight as a token of affection.⟩ — see ²BELT 1

girdle *vb* 1 to encircle or bind with or as if with a belt ⟨Trees *girdled* the campus, essentially hiding it from view.⟩ ⟨wire *girdling* the bundle of firewood⟩ — see GIRD 1

  2 to travel completely around ⟨an asteroid belt that *girdles* the inner planets of the solar system⟩ — see ENCIRCLE 1

  3 to form a circle around ⟨the rings that famously *girdle* the planet Saturn⟩ — see SURROUND

girl *n* 1 a young unmarried woman ⟨His parents really like the *girl* he's engaged to.⟩

  synonyms damsel, maid, maiden, miss

related words virgin; deb, debutante, ingenue (*or ingénue*); lass, lassie, sister; colleen, mademoiselle, senorita (*or señorita*)

2 a female person who has not yet reached adulthood ⟨When I was a *girl*, I wanted a horse so badly.⟩
synonyms lass, lassie, miss
related words bobby-soxer, junior miss, schoolgirl, teenybopper; gamine, hoyden, pixie (*also* pixy), tomboy
3 a female romantic companion ⟨He sent her a text asking her to be his *girl*.⟩ — see GIRLFRIEND

girlfriend *n* a female romantic companion ⟨He proposed to his *girlfriend* of seven years.⟩
synonyms gal, girl, lady, ladylove, old lady, woman
related words beloved, darling, dear, favorite, flame, honey, love, lover, significant other, sweet, sweetheart, valentine

girt *vb* to encircle or bind with or as if with a belt ⟨His wounded leg was *girted* by bandages.⟩ — see GIRD 1

girth *n* the distance around a round body ⟨a redwood with a *girth* of some 26 feet, making it wide enough for a full-grown man to walk through⟩ — see CIRCUMFERENCE 1

girth *vb* **1** to encircle or bind with or as if with a belt ⟨You'll need to make sure you *girth* the saddle tightly or you'll fall off the horse.⟩ — see GIRD 1
2 to travel completely around ⟨His arms couldn't quite *girth* the stone column.⟩ — see ENCIRCLE 1

gist *n* the central part or aspect of something under consideration ⟨I didn't catch every word between them, but I heard enough to get the *gist* of the conversation.⟩ — see CRUX

give *vb* **1** to make a present of ⟨Math tutors generously *give* their time to help students after school.⟩
synonyms bestow, contribute, donate, give away, present, volunteer
related words chip in, kick in, pitch in, throw in; award, confer, endow, endue (*or* indue), render; furnish, provide; lavish, regale; aid, assist, benefit, help; administer, dish out, dispense, impart, issue, mete (out); extend, offer, put up, tender; sacrifice
phrases give of
near antonyms hold, keep, pocket, retain, withhold; preserve, save; advance, lend, loan; sell
2 to put (something) into the possession or safekeeping of another ⟨I *gave* my camera to my father to hold while I went swimming.⟩
synonyms commend, commit, consign, delegate, deliver, entrust (*also* intrust), hand, hand over, leave, pass, recommend, repose, transfer, transmit, trust, turn over, vest
related words confer, grant; assign, deal (out), dispense, disperse, distribute, divide; hand in, release, relinquish, submit, surrender, turn in, yield; bequeath, hand down, hand on, will; advance, lend, loan; furnish, supply
near antonyms detain, hold back, reserve, withhold; own, possess; accept, take in; occupy, take, take over
antonyms hold, keep, retain
3 to bring before the public in performance or exhibition ⟨The author will *give* a reading from her latest work at 7:00 p.m.⟩ — see PRESENT 1
4 to fall down or in as a result of physical pressure ⟨They loaded the shopping cart with so much food it *gave* under all the weight.⟩ — see COLLAPSE 1
5 to hand over or use up in payment ⟨I wouldn't *give* a nickel for such a run-down car.⟩ — see SPEND 1
6 to make known (as an idea, emotion, or opinion) ⟨She *gave* her opinion on the matter very firmly and unmistakably.⟩ — see EXPRESS 1
7 to occupy (oneself) diligently or with close attention ⟨He totally *gave* himself to his studies in the hopes of winning a scholarship for next year.⟩ — see APPLY 2

8 to produce as revenue ⟨a company that consistently *gives* $30 million in profits to the owner⟩ — see YIELD 2
9 to put (something) into the possession of someone for use or consumption ⟨I *gave* him my e-mail address.⟩ — see FURNISH 2
10 to put before another for acceptance or consideration ⟨She *gave* the committee her grant proposal.⟩ — see OFFER 1
11 to cause (something) to pass from one to another ⟨She *gave* her cold to me, and now I'm so sick that I can barely get out of bed.⟩ — see COMMUNICATE 1

give–and–take *n* **1** an exchange of views for the purpose of exploring a subject or deciding an issue ⟨a *give-and-take* about what we should do Saturday night⟩ — see DISCUSSION 1
2 the act or practice of each side giving up something in order to reach an agreement ⟨Negotiating the terms of the deal will require some *give-and-take* on both sides.⟩ — see CONCESSION 1
3 good-natured teasing or exchanging of clever remarks ⟨We enjoyed the flirty *give-and-take* between the two romantic lead characters.⟩ — see BANTER

giveaway *n* something given to someone without expectation of a return ⟨offering a Caribbean vacation *giveaway* to the millionth customer⟩ — see GIFT 1

give away *vb* **1** to make known (something abstract) through outward signs ⟨The insincerity of his apology was *given away* by that slight smirk on his face.⟩ — see SHOW 2
2 to make a present of ⟨My aunt *gave away* all her potted plants when she moved.⟩ — see GIVE 1

give in *vb* **1** to give up and cease resistance (as to a liking, temptation, or habit) ⟨*Give in* and have some chocolate!⟩ — see YIELD 1
2 to cease resistance (as to another's arguments, demands, or control) ⟨After withstanding hours of begging, their father finally *gave in* and let them go to the amusement park.⟩ — see YIELD 3

given *adj* **1** being in the habit or custom ⟨a quiet man not *given* to loud expressions of emotion⟩ — see ACCUSTOMED
2 having a tendency to be or act in a certain way ⟨She's *given* to exaggeration.⟩ — see PRONE 1
3 known but not named ⟨Candidates for the quiz show must complete the qualifying test within a *given* amount of time.⟩ — see CERTAIN 1

given *n* something taken as being true or factual and used as a starting point for a course of action or reasoning ⟨It's a *given* that television viewers are influenced by advertising, either consciously or subconsciously.⟩ — see ASSUMPTION 1

given name *n* a name that is placed before one's family name ⟨Everyone calls me Jack, but my *given name* is John.⟩ — see FORENAME

give out *vb* **1** to make known openly or publicly ⟨That's information that I'm not prepared to *give out*.⟩ — see ANNOUNCE
2 to throw or give off ⟨This heater *gives out* a funny smell sometimes.⟩ — see EMIT 1
3 to stop functioning ⟨I'm waiting for the fuel pump in my old car to *give out*.⟩ — see FAIL 1

give up *vb* **1** to give (something) over to the control or possession of another usually under duress ⟨He was in so much debt he had to *give up* his house and move into a cheaper apartment.⟩ — see SURRENDER 1
2 to stop doing (something) permanently ⟨I hope you won't *give up* playing the piano.⟩ — see QUIT 2
3 to yield to the control or power of enemy forces ⟨With the prospect of a renewed enemy attack, the regiment reluctantly decided to *give up*.⟩ — see FALL 2

4 to give (oneself) over to something especially unrestrainedly ⟨She *gave* herself *up* completely to her work.⟩ — see ABANDON 1

giving *n* the act of offering money in exchange for goods or services ⟨a diorama about pioneer life at the museum that depicts the *giving* of beads for clothes⟩ — see PAYMENT 1

gizmo *also* **gismo** *n* an interesting and often novel device with a practical use ⟨I found all sorts of interesting woodworking *gizmos* in the garage.⟩ — see GADGET

glacial *adj* **1** having a low or subnormal temperature ⟨A *glacial* weather front coming down from Canada will bring freezing temperatures this weekend.⟩ — see COLD 1
2 lacking in friendliness or warmth of feeling ⟨Her *glacial* manner discouraged him from attempting further conversation.⟩ — see COLD 2

glad *adj* **1** experiencing pleasure, satisfaction, or delight ⟨The man was *glad* to see his old college buddies again, after so long an absence.⟩
synonyms blissful, delighted, gratified, happy, joyful, joyous, pleased, satisfied, thankful, tickled
related words blithe, blithesome, buoyant, cheerful, cheery, gladsome, lighthearted, sunny, upbeat; gleeful, jocund, jolly, jovial, merry, mirthful, smiling; beatific, ecstatic, elated, enraptured, entranced, euphoric, exhilarated, rapturous, rhapsodic (*also* rhapsodical); exuberant, exultant, jubilant, rapt, rejoicing, thrilled; hopeful, optimistic, rosy, sanguine
near antonyms aggrieved, anguished, blue, brokenhearted, dejected, depressed, despondent, disconsolate, disheartened, downcast, downhearted, forlorn, melancholy; doleful, dolorous, lachrymose, mournful, plaintive, sorrowful, sorry, woeful; black, dark, desolate, dispirited, gloomy, glum, grieved, heartbroken, heartsick, miserable, woebegone, wretched
antonyms displeased, dissatisfied, joyless, sad, unhappy, unpleased, unsatisfied
2 having a desire or inclination (as for a specified course of action) ⟨I am *glad* to do the work if it will help the cause.⟩ — see WILLING 1
3 serving to lift one's spirits ⟨Doctors brought *glad* tidings to the reporters awaiting news of the queen's condition.⟩ — see CHEERFUL 2
4 feeling or expressing gratitude ⟨She was *glad* of the offer of a ride home.⟩ — see GRATEFUL 1

gladden *vb* to give satisfaction to ⟨It would *gladden* me to hear you sing again.⟩ — see PLEASE 1

gladdening *adj* making one feel good inside ⟨The overdue change to warm, sunny weather is *gladdening*.⟩ — see HEARTWARMING

gladiatorial *adj* feeling or displaying eagerness to fight ⟨not a reasoned discussion but a shouting match between *gladiatorial* pundits from opposite ends of the political spectrum⟩ — see BELLIGERENT

gladness *n* **1** a feeling or state of well-being and contentment ⟨felt nothing but *gladness* at seeing her best friend beat her out for the award⟩ — see HAPPINESS 1
2 the feeling experienced when one's wishes are met ⟨The children's *gladness* was evident as they rushed over to the new playground.⟩ — see PLEASURE 1

gladsome *adj* having or showing a good mood or disposition ⟨a *gladsome* group of carolers strolling through the city's historic district⟩ ⟨a *gladsome* smile⟩ — see CHEERFUL 1

glamorize *also* **glamourize** *vb* to represent or think of as better than reality would warrant ⟨Most people *glamorize* fame, not thinking of the lack of privacy that accompanies it.⟩ — see IDEALIZE

glamorous *also* **glamourous** *adj* **1** excitingly or mysteriously unusual ⟨the *glamorous* sights and scents of a Turkish market⟩ — see EXOTIC
2 having an often mysterious or magical power to attract ⟨*glamorous* Hollywood celebrities whose every move is breathlessly recorded by the media⟩ — see FASCINATING 1

glamour *also* **glamor** *n* the power of irresistible attraction ⟨the *glamour* of the fashion industry⟩ — see CHARM 2

glance *n* an instance of looking especially briefly ⟨She was about to say something about the surprise, but I silenced her with a *glance*.⟩ — see LOOK 2

glance *vb* **1** to strike and fly off at an angle ⟨The basketball *glanced* off the rim.⟩ ⟨Her wild pitch *glanced* off my shoulder and landed in the dugout.⟩
synonyms bounce, carom, rebound, ricochet, skim, skip
related words brush, graze, nudge, rake, shave, sweep; bump, contact, hit, kiss, touch; sideswipe; reflect
2 to take a quick or hasty look ⟨I just *glanced* at the instructions before assembling the bike.⟩ ⟨He *glanced* over his shoulder to see if she was still there.⟩
synonyms browse, dip, glimpse, glint, peek, skim
related words peep; blink, squint; look over, peruse, scan
near antonyms examine, overlook, oversee, question, survey; study, view; peer, pry; gawk, goggle, rubberneck; leer, ogle
antonyms gaze, stare
3 to shoot forth bursts of light ⟨diamonds *glancing* in the display case⟩ — see FLASH 1

glare *n* the steady giving off of the form of radiation that makes vision possible ⟨the sudden *glare* of the squad car's headlights in my rearview mirror⟩ — see LIGHT 1

glare *vb* **1** to shine with a bright harsh light ⟨The spotlight *glared* down on the suspect as the police questioned him relentlessly.⟩
synonyms beat, blaze, burn, flame, flare
related words beam, glow, radiate; flash, glance, gleam, glimmer, glint, glisten, glister, glitter, scintillate, shimmer, sparkle, twinkle; bedazzle, blind, daze, dazzle
2 to look with anger or disapproval ⟨Don't *glare* at me like that when I tell you "no."⟩ — see FROWN

glaring *adj* very noticeable especially for being incorrect or bad ⟨No one missed the *glaring* spelling error in the title.⟩ — see EGREGIOUS

gleam *n* the steady giving off of the form of radiation that makes vision possible ⟨The door opened a crack and let in a *gleam* of light from the hallway.⟩ — see LIGHT 1

gleam *vb* to shoot forth bursts of light ⟨fine china and stemware *gleaming* in the candlelight⟩ — see FLASH 1

glee *n* a mood characterized by high spirits and amusement and often accompanied by laughter ⟨They were dancing with *glee*.⟩ — see MIRTH

glee club *n* an organized group of singers ⟨My dad sang with the *glee club* in college.⟩ — see CHORUS 1

gleeful *adj* indicative of or marked by high spirits or good humor ⟨the *gleeful* atmosphere that envelops the host city of the Super Bowl⟩ — see MERRY

gleefulness *n* a mood characterized by high spirits and amusement and often accompanied by laughter ⟨the infectious *gleefulness* that permeates the town during its annual Fourth of July celebration⟩ — see MIRTH

glide *vb* **1** to move or proceed smoothly and readily ⟨looking for a college course that he could just *glide* through⟩ — see FLOW 2
2 to move through the air with or as if with outstretched wings ⟨a kite *gliding* on the autumn breeze⟩ — see FLY 1
3 to rest or move along the surface of a liquid or in the air ⟨water striders *gliding* along the surface of the brook⟩ — see FLOAT 1

glimmer *n* **1** a very small amount ⟨a *glimmer* of hope⟩ — see PARTICLE 1

2 an almost imperceptible sign of something ⟨I saw a *glimmer* of recognition in her eyes.⟩ — see HINT 2

glimmer *vb* to shoot forth bursts of light ⟨The waters of the rippling brook *glimmered* in the sun.⟩ — see FLASH 1

glimpse *n* an instance of looking especially briefly ⟨I only got a *glimpse* of him as we drove by.⟩ — see LOOK 2

glimpse *vb* to take a quick or hasty look ⟨He just *glimpsed* at the photo and then turned his attention elsewhere.⟩ — see GLANCE 2

glint *vb* **1** to shoot forth bursts of light ⟨The cat's eyes *glinted* in the moonlight.⟩ — see FLASH 1

2 to take a quick or hasty look ⟨The thief *glinted* around the corner to see if anyone was coming.⟩ — see GLANCE 2

glisten *vb* to shoot forth bursts of light ⟨This seemingly dull opal really *glistens* in full light.⟩ — see FLASH 1

glistening *adj* having a shiny surface or finish ⟨a *glistening* marble table top⟩ — see GLOSSY

glister *vb* to shoot forth bursts of light ⟨The dew *glistered* in the soft light of the early morning.⟩ — see FLASH 1

glitter *vb* to shoot forth bursts of light ⟨The queen's crown *glittered* under the glare of the TV lights.⟩ — see FLASH 1

glitz *n* excessive or unnecessary display ⟨a nice dinner, but without all the *glitz* of folded napkins and fancy china⟩ — see OSTENTATION

glitzy *adj* excessively showy ⟨I think that rhinestone-studded outfit is a little too *glitzy*.⟩ — see GAUDY

gloaming *n* **1** a time or place of little or no light ⟨Fireflies could be seen in the *gloaming*.⟩ — see DARK 1

2 the time from when the sun begins to set to the onset of total darkness ⟨With the *gloaming* came the familiar call of the whip-poor-will.⟩ — see DUSK 1

glob *n* **1** a small uneven mass ⟨I found a *glob* of chewing gum under my theater seat.⟩ — see LUMP 1

2 the quantity of fluid that falls naturally in one rounded mass ⟨Add a *glob* or two of molasses to the batter.⟩ — see DROP 1

global *adj* **1** belonging or relating to the whole ⟨Do a *global* search and replace the misspelling throughout the whole document.⟩ — see GENERAL 1

2 covering everything or all important points ⟨They published a *global* report on the plight of endangered species.⟩ — see ENCYCLOPEDIC

3 having every part of the surface the same distance from the center ⟨One of the fair's more striking pavilions was a *global* structure with a monorail running through its center.⟩ — see ROUND 1

globe *n* **1** a more or less round body or mass ⟨The glassblower shaped the molten mass into a *globe* of remarkable thinness and clarity.⟩ — see ¹BALL 1

2 the celestial body on which we live ⟨New Year's celebrations around the *globe*⟩ — see EARTH 1

globule *n* the quantity of fluid that falls naturally in one rounded mass ⟨fat *globules* of hot wax dripping onto the table⟩ — see DROP 1

gloom *n* **1** a state or spell of low spirits ⟨He has been in a perpetual *gloom* since his dog died.⟩ — see SADNESS

2 a time or place of little or no light ⟨The *gloom* of a rainy night is the perfect setting for a mystery story.⟩ — see DARK 1

gloom *vb* **1** to look with anger or disapproval ⟨We just sat there, *glooming*, as we waited and waited for our dinners to arrive.⟩ — see FROWN

2 to take on a gloomy or forbidding look ⟨He continued to *gloom* over the fact that he had been passed over for promotion to district manager.⟩ — see DARKEN 1

gloominess *n* a state or spell of low spirits ⟨Even in the depths of her *gloominess* she never lost hope entirely.⟩ — see SADNESS

gloomy *adj* **1** causing or marked by an atmosphere lacking in cheer ⟨The cold rain made for a *gloomy* day.⟩

synonyms black, bleak, cheerless, chill, cloudy, cold, comfortless, dark, darkening, depressing, desolate, dire, disconsolate, dismal, drear, dreary, elegiac (*also* elegiacal), forlorn, funereal, glum, godforsaken, gray (*also* grey), lonely, lonesome, lugubrious, miserable, morbid, morose, murky, saturnine, sepulchral, solemn, somber (*or* sombre), sullen, wretched

related words blue, dejected, depressed, despondent, disconsolate, down, droopy, hangdog, inconsolable, low, melancholy, mirthless, sad, unhappy, woebegone, woeful; dim, discomfiting, discouraging, disheartening, dismaying, dispiriting, distressful, distressing, upsetting; hopeless, pessimistic; lamentable, mournful, plaintive, sorrowful; colorless, drab, dull; dour, grim, lowering (*also* louring), lowery (*also* loury), menacing, oppressive, threatening

near antonyms blithe, blithesome, buoyant, jocund, jolly, joyful, joyous, merry, mirthful; encouraging, hopeful, optimistic; lighthearted, lightsome

antonyms bright, cheerful, cheering, cheery, comforting, cordial, festive, heartwarming, sunshiny

2 feeling unhappiness ⟨What's wrong? I've never seen you look so *gloomy*.⟩ — see SAD 1

3 being without light or without much light ⟨That house would be less *gloomy* if some of the overgrown trees and shrubs were cleared away.⟩ — see DARK 1

glorify *vb* **1** to assign a high status or value to ⟨A number of big names were recruited in the hopes that their presence would *glorify* the university's school of medicine in the eyes of the medical world.⟩ — see EXALT 1

2 to offer honor or respect to (someone) as a divine power ⟨Let us now *glorify* the Lord.⟩ — see WORSHIP 1

3 to praise or publicize lavishly and often excessively ⟨fond parents who *glorify* everything that their precious offspring do⟩ — see TOUT 1

4 to proclaim the glory of ⟨The hillsides ablaze in red and gold silently *glorify* New England in the fall.⟩ — see PRAISE 1

5 to represent or think of as better than reality would warrant ⟨Don't let the job title "team spirit coordinator" fool you—he's nothing more than a *glorified* college cheerleader.⟩ — see IDEALIZE

glorious *adj* large and impressive in size, grandeur, extent, or conception ⟨The advent of the printing press in the West ushered in a *glorious* new era of learning.⟩ — see GRAND 1

gloriously *adv* in a pleasing way ⟨The choir rose to the occasion and sang *gloriously*.⟩ — see WELL 5

gloriousness *n* impressiveness of beauty on a large scale ⟨the indisputable *gloriousness* of the Taj Mahal⟩ — see MAGNIFICENCE

glory *vb* to feel or express joy or triumph ⟨The whole city *gloried* in the home team's winning of the World Series.⟩ — see EXULT

glory *n* **1** public acknowledgment or admiration for an achievement ⟨The theater director gave the stage crew all the *glory* for the successful production.⟩

synonyms acclaim, accolade, applause, credit, distinction, homage, honor, laurels, sun

related words celebrity, fame, renown, repute; compliment, encomium, eulogy, panegyric, toast, tribute; acclamation, ovation, plaudit, praise, rave, rhapsody; citation, commendation, note, recommendation; enshrinement, enthronement, exaltation, glorification

2 an asset that brings praise or renown ⟨The new art museum has become the *glory* of the college campus.⟩

synonyms boast, credit, honor, jewel, pride, treasure

related words pièce de résistance, showpiece; attraction, feature, highlight; distinction, excellence, merit, value, virtue
phrases a feather in one's cap
near antonyms disgrace, dishonor; blemish, blot, defect, shame, slur, smirch, smudge, stain, stigma; eyesore, fright, horror, mess
3 impressiveness of beauty on a large scale ⟨He was overwhelmed by the imperial *glory* of Rome.⟩ — see MAGNIFICENCE

glorying *adj* having or expressing feelings of joy or triumph ⟨The Olympic athletes were told to stifle the *glorying* antics and to accept their medals with some measure of humility.⟩ — see EXULTANT

gloss *n* **1** a deceptively attractive external appearance ⟨She used a computer to give her astrological predictions the *gloss* of real science.⟩
synonyms facade (*also* façade), veneer
related words fluff; fig leaf; charade, front, guise, masquerade, pose, semblance, show
2 brightness created by light reflected from a surface ⟨The surface has such a high *gloss* that you can see your face reflected in it.⟩ — see SHINE 1

gloss *vb* to make smooth or glossy usually by repeatedly applying surface pressure ⟨The action of the water will serve to *gloss* the seal's coat.⟩ — see POLISH 1

gloss (over) *vb* **1** to make (something) seem less bad by offering excuses ⟨I don't want to *gloss over* her misbehavior, but keep in mind that she's been under a lot of stress lately.⟩ — see PALLIATE 1
2 to dismiss as of little importance ⟨This biographer tends to *gloss over* his subject's many character flaws.⟩ — see EXCUSE 1

glossy *adj* having a shiny surface or finish ⟨the *glossy* finish on the gym floor⟩ ⟨a sports car with an interior upholstered with *glossy* leather⟩
synonyms buffed, burnished, glistening, lustrous, polished, rubbed, satin, satiny, sleek
related words brushed, eggshell, semigloss, semilustrous; silken, silky, slick, slippery; glassy, glazed, lacquered, shellacked, varnished; gleaming, glittering, reflective, shining
near antonyms lackluster; unvarnished
antonyms dim, dull, flat, lusterless, matte (*also* mat *or* matt)

glow *n* the steady giving off of the form of radiation that makes vision possible ⟨The *glow* of the restaurant's table lamps is especially flattering to diners.⟩ — see LIGHT 1

glow *vb* **1** to be on fire especially brightly ⟨The coals *glowed* red-hot.⟩ — see BURN 1
2 to develop a rosy facial color (as from excitement or embarrassment) ⟨When they found out he had won the tournament, his parents *glowed* with pride.⟩ — see BLUSH

glower *vb* **1** to look with anger or disapproval ⟨baseball fans *glowering* at their TVs as they watched their favorite team lose⟩ — see FROWN
2 to take on a gloomy or forbidding look ⟨The old man just sat in his rocking chair, his face *glowering* at the prospect of unwanted company.⟩ — see DARKEN 1

glowing *adj* **1** giving off or reflecting much light ⟨enjoyed the warmth of the *glowing* fire⟩ — see BRIGHT 1
2 having a healthy reddish skin tone ⟨He was *glowing* after spending an afternoon outside splitting firewood.⟩ — see RUDDY
3 having or being an outward sign of good feelings (as of love, confidence, or happiness) ⟨Her *glowing* face made it evident she'd been offered the job.⟩ — see RADIANT 1
4 having or expressing great depth of feeling ⟨*glowing* declarations of everlasting love⟩ — see FERVENT 1

gloze (over) *vb* **1** to make (something) seem less bad by offering excuses ⟨He tried to *gloze over* his bad test grade by noting that he still had a B average.⟩ — see PALLIATE 1
2 to dismiss as of little importance ⟨We're certainly willing to *gloze over* a couple of minor historical inaccuracies in an otherwise splendid movie.⟩ — see EXCUSE 1

glue *n* a substance used to stick things together ⟨I used *glue* to stick the photo in the album.⟩
synonyms adhesive, bond, cement, size
related words epoxy, epoxy resin, library paste, mucilage, paste, superglue, water glass; dope, gum

gluey *adj* tending to adhere to objects upon contact ⟨Don't overbeat the mashed potatoes, or they will be thick and *gluey* instead of light and fluffy.⟩ — see STICKY 1

glum *adj* **1** causing or marked by an atmosphere lacking in cheer ⟨the usual *glum* waiting room at the tax collector's office⟩ ⟨a cold, *glum* day⟩ — see GLOOMY 1
2 feeling unhappiness ⟨How can you be *glum* after such a great day?⟩ — see SAD 1
3 given to or displaying a resentful silence and often irritability ⟨a chronically *glum* and pouting child⟩ — see SULKY

glut *vb* to fill with food to capacity ⟨I prefer not to watch those nature programs where all they show are predators *glutting* themselves on the kill.⟩ — see GORGE 1

glutinous *adj* tending to adhere to objects upon contact ⟨a bad horror movie from the 1950s about a *glutinous* blob that devoured Manhattan⟩ — see STICKY 1

glutton *n* one who eats greedily or too much ⟨He's such a *glutton* that he ate the whole cake.⟩
synonyms gorger, gormandizer, gourmand, hog, overeater, pig, swiller
related words feaster, trencherman; muncher; guzzler
near antonyms dieter, nibbler, picker

gluttonous *adj* having a huge appetite ⟨*Gluttonous* customers had practically emptied the all-you-can-eat buffet.⟩ — see VORACIOUS 1

gnash *vb* to press or strike against or together so as to make a scraping sound ⟨dogs *gnashing* their teeth⟩ — see GRIND 2

gnaw (on) *vb* to crush or grind with the teeth ⟨a dog *gnawing on* a bone⟩ — see BITE (ON)

gnome *n* an imaginary being usually having a small human form and magical powers ⟨In Europe, *gnomes* are thought to guard underground treasure, so that may be why statues of them are commonly placed in gardens.⟩ — see FAIRY

go *adj* being in a state of fitness for some experience or action ⟨All systems are *go*!⟩ — see READY 1

go *n* **1** a practice or interest that is very popular for a short time ⟨Snowboarding is all the *go*.⟩ — see FAD
2 active strength of body or mind ⟨a healthy six-year-old full of *go*⟩ — see VIGOR 1
3 an effort to do or accomplish something ⟨It took several *goes* to get the car started.⟩ — see ATTEMPT 1
4 readiness to engage in daring or difficult activity ⟨a young executive with the *go* to make this company grow⟩ — see ENTERPRISE 2

go *vb* **1** to move forward along a course ⟨Everything is *going* according to our plans.⟩
synonyms advance, come, come along, do, fare, forge, get along, get on, go off, march, pace, proceed, progress
related words accelerate, fast-forward, speed; approach, near; journey, pass, repair, run, travel, wend; actuate, drive, impel, propel, push; take out
phrases gain ground
near antonyms arrest, balk, block, check, detain, halt, hinder, hold back, impede, nip, obstruct, slow (down *or* up), stem; repress, retard, stunt, suppress; delay, interrupt, stall; cramp, hamper, inhibit; cease, let up, pause
antonyms remain, stand, stay, stop

2 to leave a place often for another ⟨We will *go* on vacation at the end of the year.⟩ ⟨She decided it would be better to *go* before it got any later.⟩
synonyms bail out, begone, clear out, cut out, depart, exit, get, get off, go off, move, part, quit, sally (forth), shove (off), step (along), take off, walk out
related words start, strike out; abscond, decamp, escape, evacuate, flee, fly, get out, run away, scram, skip; light out; abandon, desert, forsake, vacate; emigrate; adjourn, remove, retire, retreat, withdraw
phrases beat it, hit the road, pull stakes (*or* pull up stakes), take a hike (*also* take a walk), take a powder
near antonyms abide, dwell, lodge, remain, settle, stay, tarry; approach, close, near; hit, land, reach
antonyms arrive, come, show up, turn up
3 to be fitting or proper ⟨At Mardi Gras, just about anything *goes*.⟩ — see DO 1
4 to be in agreement on every point ⟨Your account of how the fire started doesn't *go* with what she said.⟩ — see CHECK 1
5 to be positioned along a certain course or in a certain direction ⟨The highway *goes* right along the river.⟩ — see RUN 3
6 to eventually have as a state or quality ⟨The room *went* dark.⟩ — see BECOME
7 to fall down or in as a result of physical pressure ⟨We watched the building *go* after the demolition crew detonated the charges.⟩ — see COLLAPSE 1
8 to have or be in a usual or proper place ⟨These plates *go* in this cabinet.⟩ — see BELONG 1
9 to lose bodily strength or vigor ⟨When you get old, your eyesight starts to *go*.⟩ — see WEAKEN 2
10 to make one's way through, across, or over ⟨I *went* the length of the street before finding an empty parking space.⟩ — see TRAVERSE
11 to occur within a continuous range of variation ⟨Selling prices for houses in that neighborhood generally *go* between one and two million.⟩ — see RUN 4
12 to risk (something) on the outcome of an uncertain event ⟨To play in this game of poker, you have to be willing to *go* at least five dollars per round.⟩ — see BET
13 to come to an end ⟨We were having so much fun that the evening just came and *went*.⟩ — see CEASE 1
14 to have enough money for ⟨I think I can *go* for the new car after all.⟩ — see AFFORD
15 to put up with (something painful or difficult) ⟨I can't *go* the smell of that rotting food for one more minute.⟩ — see BEAR 2
16 to stop living ⟨Her grandmother *went* peacefully last night.⟩ — see DIE 1
17 to turn out as planned or desired ⟨We tried very hard to get the food cooperative to *go*, but it never really worked out.⟩ — see SUCCEED 1
go (for) *vb* to have a price of ⟨Those cars *go for* $35,000.⟩ — see COST
go (to) *vb* to use or seek out as a source of aid, relief, or advantage ⟨When the sales representative refused to help us, we *went to* the store manager.⟩ — see RESORT (TO) 1
goad *n* something that arouses action or activity ⟨The threat of legal action should be a sufficient *goad* to make them fulfill the contract.⟩ — see IMPULSE 1
goad *vb* **1** to try to persuade (someone) through earnest appeals to follow a course of action ⟨She tried to *goad* me into auditioning for the play.⟩ — see URGE
2 to urge or push forward with or as if with a pointed object ⟨*goading* the horse forward into the stall⟩ — see PROD 1
goal *n* something that one hopes or intends to accomplish ⟨Leaving the world a better place than I found it is one of my main *goals*.⟩
synonyms aim, ambition, aspiration, design, dream, end, idea, ideal, intent, intention, mark, meaning, object, objective, plan, point, pretension, purpose, target, thing
related words grail, holy grail; plot, project, scheme; desire, hope, mind, wish; destination, terminus
phrases name of the game
near antonyms means, method, way
goat *n* a person or thing taking the blame for others ⟨used the press as the *goat* for his failing campaign⟩ — see SCAPEGOAT
¹gob *n* **1** a small uneven mass ⟨She grabbed a *gob* of clay from the block and threw it on the pottery wheel.⟩ — see LUMP 1
2 gobs *pl* a considerable amount ⟨He has *gobs* of money.⟩ — see LOT 2
²gob *n* one who operates or navigates a seagoing vessel ⟨Avast, ye *gobs*, and haul anchor!⟩ — see SAILOR
gobbet *n* a small uneven mass ⟨I deftly avoided stepping in a *gobbet* of spit on the sidewalk.⟩ — see LUMP 1
gobble *vb* to swallow or eat greedily ⟨They *gobbled* the sandwiches like they hadn't eaten for days.⟩
synonyms bolt, cram, devour, gorge, gormandize, gulp, scarf, scoff, wolf
related words overeat, pig out, swill
near antonyms nibble, peck, pick
gobbledygook *also* **gobbledegook** *n* language marked by abstractions, jargon, euphemisms, and circumlocutions ⟨Cut through the *gobbledygook* and just tell me what the final cost of the car would be.⟩ — see GIBBERISH 2
go–between *n* **1** one that carries a message or does an errand ⟨I acted as *go-between* between the law office and the courthouse.⟩ — see MESSENGER
2 one who works with opposing sides in order to bring about an agreement ⟨He acted as *go-between* for the two warring nations during the peace process.⟩ — see MEDIATOR
goblin *n* an imaginary being usually having a small human form and magical powers ⟨We dressed up the toddlers like *goblins* for Halloween.⟩ — see FAIRY
god *n* **1** a being having superhuman powers and control over a particular part of life or the world ⟨In some belief systems, natural forces like the wind and the sea were *gods*.⟩ — see DEITY 1
2 *cap* the being worshipped as the creator and ruler of the universe ⟨Let us give thanks to *God*.⟩ — see DEITY 2
goddess *n* a lovely woman ⟨Like any guy in love, he thought his new girlfriend was a *goddess*.⟩ — see BEAUTY 2
godforsaken *adj* causing or marked by an atmosphere lacking in cheer ⟨Who would want to visit such a *godforsaken* place?⟩ — see GLOOMY 1
godhead *n* **1** the quality or state of being divine ⟨In some cultures, the ruler of the people has *godhead* and is worshipped accordingly.⟩ — see DIVINITY 1
2 *cap* the being worshipped as the creator and ruler of the universe ⟨praying to the *Godhead*⟩ — see DEITY 2
godhood *n* the quality or state of being divine ⟨According to Greek myth, Hercules was granted *godhood* after his death.⟩ — see DIVINITY 1
godless *adj* lacking religious emotions, principles, or practices ⟨*godless* ideologies⟩ — see IRRELIGIOUS
godlike *adj* of, relating to, or being God ⟨the *godlike* splendor of creation⟩ — see HOLY 3
godliness *n* the quality or state of being spiritually pure or virtuous ⟨They say that cleanliness is next to *godliness*.⟩ — see HOLINESS
godly *adj* **1** showing a devotion to God and to a life of

virtue ⟨a *godly* and humble man who prayed to be rewarded in the next world⟩ — see HOLY 1

2 of, relating to, or being God ⟨A *godly* voice from the heavens commanded him to build an ark.⟩ — see HOLY 3

godsend *n* something that provides happiness or does good for a person or thing ⟨That holiday bonus has proved to be a *godsend* for my bills.⟩ — see BLESSING 2

Godspeed *n* an expression of good wishes at parting ⟨A hearty *Godspeed* was extended to all the departing troops.⟩ — see GOOD-BYE

go–getter *n* an ambitious person who eagerly goes after what is desired ⟨a *go-getter* with his sights set on the presidency⟩

synonyms hustler, live wire, powerhouse, rustler, self-starter

related words eager beaver; achiever, comer, doer, enterpriser; he-man, individualist; pistol

near antonyms dawdler, idler, loafer, lounger, putterer; goldbrick, malingerer, procrastinator, shirker, slacker; drone, lazybones, sluggard; dallier, laggard, lingerer, loiterer, slowpoke, stick-in-the-mud; daydreamer, dreamer; dropout, quitter

go–getting *adj* **1** having a strong desire for personal advancement ⟨This job is a great opportunity for some *go-getting* young person.⟩ — see AMBITIOUS 1

2 having or showing a bold forcefulness in the pursuit of a goal ⟨a determined newcomer who made a *go-getting* bid for the governorship⟩ — see AGGRESSIVE 1

go–getting *n* eager desire for personal advancement ⟨With all her *go-getting*, she should move quickly up the corporate ladder.⟩ — see AMBITION 1

goggle *vb* to look long and hard in wonder or surprise ⟨Crowds *goggled* at the elaborate costumes and floats in the Mardi Gras parade.⟩ — see GAPE

going *adj* **1** accepted, used, or practiced by most people ⟨What's the *going* price for a good used washing machine?⟩ — see CURRENT 1

2 being in effective operation ⟨He just can't keep his small bookstore *going*.⟩ — see ACTIVE 1

3 having attained a desired end or state of good fortune ⟨Our continued partnership with them is a *going* concern.⟩ — see SUCCESSFUL 1

going *n* **1** forward movement in time or place ⟨I tried to get down the hill quickly, but it was slow *going* with an injured foot.⟩ — see ADVANCE 1

2 the act of leaving a place ⟨She was so absorbed in her TV show she didn't notice his comings or *goings*.⟩ — see DEPARTURE 1

gold *n* something (as pieces of stamped metal or printed paper) customarily and legally used as a medium of exchange, a measure of value, or a means of payment ⟨All the *gold* in the world won't buy happiness.⟩ — see MONEY

golden *adj* **1** having qualities which inspire hope ⟨This may be your *golden* moment to impress a baseball scout, so don't blow it.⟩ — see HOPEFUL 1

2 marked by conspicuously full and rich sounds or tones ⟨She sang in a *golden* alto that filled the concert hall.⟩ — see RESONANT

3 marked by vigorous growth and well-being especially economically ⟨the *golden* age of industrialization⟩ — see PROSPEROUS 1

4 of a pale yellow or yellowish brown color ⟨a *golden* Labrador⟩ — see BLOND

5 pointing toward a happy outcome ⟨That new job is a *golden* opportunity.⟩ — see FAVORABLE 2

golden–ager *n* a person of advanced years ⟨The club offered discounts and special tours for *golden-agers*.⟩ — see SENIOR CITIZEN

golden mean *n* a middle point between extremes ⟨When it comes to money, the *golden mean* is saving some income, while giving yourself a modest spending allowance.⟩ — see MEAN 1

gone *adj* **1** no longer existing ⟨Woolly mammoths have been long *gone*.⟩ — see EXTINCT

2 no longer living ⟨Doctors came to the waiting room to give the sad news that the patient was *gone*.⟩ — see DEAD 1

3 no longer possessed ⟨I put my watch right here on the table, but now it's *gone*.⟩ — see LOST

4 containing unborn young within the body ⟨a woman who's seven months *gone*⟩ — see PREGNANT 1

gone (on) *adj* filled with an intense or excessive love for ⟨I've never seen her so *gone on* anyone before.⟩ — see ENAMORED (OF)

good *adv* in a satisfactory way ⟨Things are going *good* for us.⟩ — see WELL 1

good *n* **1** something that provides happiness or does good for a person or thing ⟨a force for *good*⟩ — see BLESSING 2

2 the state of doing well especially in relation to one's happiness or success ⟨I am doing this for your own *good*.⟩ — see WELFARE

3 goods *pl* products that are bought and sold in business ⟨The store had a hard time selling leftover Easter *goods* that were still on the shelves by Mother's Day.⟩ — see MERCHANDISE

4 goods *pl* a skill, an ability, or knowledge that makes a person able to do a particular job ⟨The hiring committee thinks this latest applicant really has the *goods*.⟩ — see QUALIFICATION 1

5 goods *pl* transportable items that one owns ⟨Before moving to Florida, the couple sold their house and auctioned off their household *goods*.⟩ — see POSSESSION 2

good *adj* **1** based on sound reasoning or information ⟨We had enough information to make a *good* assessment of the situation.⟩

synonyms commonsense, firm, hard, informed, just, justified, levelheaded, logical, rational, reasonable, reasoned, sensible, sober, solid, valid, well-founded

related words actual, real, true; certain, sure; validated, verified; confirmed, corroborated, substantiated; cogent, convincing; colorable, credible, plausible

near antonyms unsubstantiated, unsupported, unwarranted; flimsy, implausible, unconvincing, weak; fallacious, false, misguided, misled

antonyms groundless, illogical, invalid, irrational, nonrational, nonsensical, nonvalid, unfounded, uninformed, unjustified, unreasonable, unreasoned, unsound

2 conforming to a high standard of morality or virtue ⟨a *good* person who seldom did wrong⟩ ⟨*Good* behavior will earn you the respect of others.⟩

synonyms all right, decent, ethical, honest, honorable, just, moral, nice, right, righteous, right-minded, straight, upright, virtuous

related words correct, decorous, proper, seemly; high-minded, noble, principled; commendable, creditable, exemplary, legitimate; esteemed, law-abiding, reputable, respected, upstanding, worthy; blameless, clean, guiltless, immaculate, incorrupt (*also* incorrupted), incorruptible, innocent, inoffensive, irreproachable, unobjectionable; angelic (*or* angelical), pure, scrupulous, spotless, uncorrupted, unerring; goody-goody, moralistic, pharisaical, rectitudinous, sanctimonious, self-righteous

near antonyms improper, incorrect, indecorous, naughty, unbecoming, unseemly; corrupt, debased, debauched, degenerate, depraved, dissolute, libertine, perverted, reprobate; unprincipled, unscrupulous; atrocious, infamous, villainous; base, low, mean, vicious, vile; blameworthy, objectionable, offensive; iniquitous, nefarious; errant, erring, fallen

antonyms bad, dishonest, dishonorable, evil, evil-minded, immoral, indecent, sinful, unethical, unrighteous, wicked, wrong

3 according to the rules of logic ⟨Give me one *good* reason why I shouldn't go.⟩ — see LOGICAL 1

4 being to one's liking ⟨That band's music is *good*.⟩ — see SATISFACTORY 1

5 expressing approval ⟨The critic gave the restaurant a *good* review.⟩ — see FAVORABLE 1

6 firm in one's allegiance to someone or something ⟨a *good* Democrat⟩ — see FAITHFUL 1

7 giving pleasure or contentment to the mind or senses ⟨We had a *good* time at the movies.⟩ — see PLEASANT 1

8 having or showing exceptional knowledge, experience, or skill in a field of endeavor ⟨She's *good* at math.⟩ — see PROFICIENT

9 having sufficient worth or merit to receive one's honor, esteem, or reward ⟨She is *good* enough to win a fellowship.⟩ — see WORTHY

10 having the required skills for an acceptable level of performance ⟨That electrician is *good* at what he does.⟩ — see COMPETENT 1

11 meeting the requirements of a purpose or situation ⟨Those rotten apples aren't *good* to eat.⟩ — see FIT 1

12 sufficiently large in size, amount, or number to merit attention ⟨He had a *good* number of valuable baseball cards in his collection.⟩ — see CONSIDERABLE 1

13 worthy of one's trust ⟨a car that should be *good* for another few years⟩ — see DEPENDABLE

14 being in agreement with the truth or a fact or a standard ⟨If these measurements are *good*, the venetian blind should fit the window perfectly.⟩ — see CORRECT 1

15 very pleasing to look at ⟨These colors look *good* together.⟩ — see BEAUTIFUL 1

16 beneficial to the health of body or mind ⟨Eating a *good* breakfast will provide you with more energy during the day.⟩ ⟨He didn't like broccoli even though he knew it was *good* for him.⟩ — see HEALTHFUL

17 having or showing a concern for the welfare of others ⟨volunteers with *good* intentions⟩ — see CHARITABLE 1

18 of a level of quality that meets one's needs or standards ⟨The food at that restaurant is *good* but not great.⟩ — see ADEQUATE

19 promoting or contributing to personal or social well-being ⟨product packaging that is intended to be *good* for the environment⟩ — see BENEFICIAL

Good Book *n* a book made up of the writings accepted by Christians as coming from God ⟨What does the *Good Book* say about temptation?⟩ — see BIBLE

good–bye *or* **good–by** *n* an expression of good wishes at parting ⟨We said our *good-byes* and headed for home.⟩

synonyms adieu, au revoir, bon voyage, farewell, Godspeed

related words leave-taking, send-off

near antonyms greeting(s), salutation, salute; welcome

antonyms hello

good–hearted *adj* having or marked by sympathy and consideration for others ⟨a *good-hearted* doctor who regularly sees poor patients for free⟩ — see HUMANE 1

good–heartedness *n* the capacity for feeling for another's unhappiness or misfortune ⟨Thanks to the *good-heartedness* of its dedicated volunteers, the soup kitchen has never been understaffed.⟩ — see HEART 1

goodly *adj* **1** of a size greater than average of its kind ⟨$10,000 is a *goodly* reward to offer for a missing wedding ring.⟩ — see LARGE

2 sufficiently large in size, amount, or number to merit attention ⟨A *goodly* number of people gathered to watch the spectacle.⟩ — see CONSIDERABLE 1

3 very pleasing to look at ⟨The smartly dressed soldiers marching snappily along made for a *goodly* sight.⟩ — see BEAUTIFUL 1

good–natured *adj* having an easygoing and pleasing manner especially in social situations ⟨The guests at the party were a *good-natured* bunch.⟩ — see AMIABLE

good–naturedness *n* **1** a desire or disposition to please ⟨His *good-naturedness* makes him an easy person to work with.⟩ — see COMPLAISANCE

2 the state or quality of having a pleasant or agreeable manner in socializing with others ⟨The *good-naturedness* of her response to the friendly teasing made her a hit with the guests.⟩ — see AMIABILITY 1

goodness *n* conduct that conforms to an accepted standard of right and wrong ⟨a person of such unaffected *goodness* that his friends were inspired to lead better lives⟩ — see MORALITY 1

good–tempered *adj* having an easygoing and pleasing manner especially in social situations ⟨Her children were *good-tempered* and well-behaved in public.⟩ — see AMIABLE

good–temperedness *n* the state or quality of having a pleasant or agreeable manner in socializing with others ⟨The volunteer's general *good-temperedness* was infectious and lifted the spirits of those waiting to give blood.⟩ — see AMIABILITY 1

goodwill *n* **1** kindly concern, interest, or support ⟨the long tradition of *goodwill* that exists between the United States and Canada⟩

synonyms amity, benevolence, brotherhood, charity, cordiality, fellowship, friendliness, friendship, kindliness, neighborliness

related words camaraderie, collegiality, community, companionship, company, comradeship; civility, comity, concord, harmony, rapport; charity, generosity; affinity, communion, empathy, kindness, sympathy, tolerance; altruism, philanthropy, selflessness, unselfishness

near antonyms disfavor; animosity, antagonism, antipathy, enmity, hate, hatred, hostility, incivility, malice, rancor; querulousness

antonyms ill will, malevolence, venom

2 cheerful readiness to do something ⟨He took on the task of coaching the soccer team with lots of zeal and *goodwill*.⟩ — see ALACRITY

goody *or* **goodie** *n* something that is pleasing to eat because it is rare or a luxury ⟨couldn't wait to sample the bonbons, tortes, and other *goodies*⟩ — see DELICACY 1

gooey *adj* appealing to the emotions in an obvious and tiresome way ⟨Things get especially *gooey* during the scene in which the lovers are reunited at long last.⟩ — see CORNY

goof *n* **1** an unintentional departure from truth or accuracy ⟨That typo is one of the text's rare *goofs*.⟩ — see ERROR 1

2 a stupid person ⟨Whoops, I forgot to call. What a *goof*.⟩ — see IDIOT

goof (around) *vb* to spend time in aimless activity ⟨We've been *goofing around* long enough; it's time to get some real work done.⟩ — see FIDDLE (AROUND)

goof (off) *vb* to spend time doing nothing ⟨We returned home unannounced and found the babysitter *goofing off*.⟩ — see IDLE

go off *vb* **1** to break open or into pieces usually because of internal pressure ⟨Specialists were able to deactivate the bomb before it *went off*.⟩ — see EXPLODE 1

2 to move forward along a course ⟨The wedding *went off* without so much as a single glitch.⟩ — see GO 1

3 to leave a place often for another ⟨Don't *go off* without telling us where we can find you.⟩ — see GO 2

goofy *adj* lacking in seriousness or maturity ⟨She was making *goofy* faces at us.⟩ — see GIDDY 1

goon *n* **1** a stupid person ⟨Don't be a *goon* and forget mom's birthday again.⟩ — see IDIOT

2 a violent, brutal person who is often a member of an organized gang ⟨The crime boss threatened to send the *goons* after him if he squealed.⟩ — see HOODLUM

goose *n* a person who lacks good sense or judgment ⟨Don't be such a silly *goose*—you're dressed just fine for the party!⟩ — see FOOL 1

goose egg *n* the numerical symbol 0 or the absence of number or quantity represented by it ⟨He was such a bad bowler that his final score was a big, fat *goose egg*.⟩ — see ZERO 1

go over *vb* to turn out as planned or desired ⟨His sales pitch *went over* as expected, and he saw a 200% increase in his commissions.⟩ — see SUCCEED 1

gore *vb* to penetrate or hold (something) with a pointed object ⟨Running with the bulls in Pamplona, Spain, may sound like fun, but the bulls have been known to *gore* runners who get too close.⟩ — see IMPALE

gorge *n* a narrow opening between hillsides or mountains that can be used for passage ⟨Tourists walked the bridge over the *gorge*, marveling at the spectacular drop.⟩ — see CANYON

gorge *vb* **1** to fill with food to capacity ⟨We *gorged* ourselves on the four pies Aunt Martha had brought for Thanksgiving.⟩
synonyms cram, glut, sate, stuff, surfeit
related words gobble, gormandize, pig out; gulp, guzzle; cloy, fill; banquet, feast, regale
near antonyms diet, fast

2 to eat greedily or to excess ⟨The kids began *gorging* on Halloween candy the minute they got back from trick-or-treating.⟩
synonyms gormandize, overeat, pig out, swill
related words devour, glut, sate, stuff, surfeit, wolf; banquet, feast, regale; bolt, cram, gulp, guzzle
phrases load up on
near antonyms nibble, peck, pick, taste

3 to swallow or eat greedily ⟨The ravenous dogs furiously *gorged* the scraps of meat.⟩ — see GOBBLE

gorgeous *adj* very pleasing to look at ⟨Sunsets in Hawaii are just *gorgeous*.⟩ — see BEAUTIFUL 1

gorgeousness *n* **1** the qualities in a person or thing that as a whole give pleasure to the senses ⟨Nothing compares to the *gorgeousness* of the first snow of the winter.⟩ — see BEAUTY 1

2 impressiveness of beauty on a large scale ⟨We were taken aback by the indescribable *gorgeousness* of the Grand Canyon at sunset.⟩ — see MAGNIFICENCE

gorger *n* one who eats greedily or too much ⟨a shark that is such a *gorger* it can't move after devouring a meal⟩ — see GLUTTON

gormandize *vb* **1** to eat greedily or to excess ⟨Everybody tends to *gormandize* on Thanksgiving—it's traditional!⟩ — see GORGE 2

2 to swallow or eat greedily ⟨hungry soccer players who will *gormandize* whatever they happen to find in the fridge⟩ — see GOBBLE

gormandizer *n* one who eats greedily or too much ⟨a *gormandizer* whose enjoyment of food inspired him to become a chef⟩ — see GLUTTON

gory *adj* smeared or stained with blood ⟨He doesn't watch too many movies that feature *gory* violence.⟩ — see BLOODY 1

gospel *n* the basic beliefs or guiding principles of a person or group ⟨Her private *gospel* is to do good cheerfully and without any expectation of reward.⟩ — see CREED 1

gossamer *adj* **1** being of a material lacking in sturdiness or substance ⟨Fairies are usually depicted as wearing *gossamer* or tattered clothing.⟩ — see FLIMSY 1

2 resembling air in lightness ⟨The *gossamer* veil seemed to float about the bride as she walked down the aisle.⟩ — see AIRY 1

3 very thin and easy to see through ⟨I didn't see the *gossamer* spider webs until the sun hit them just right.⟩ — see SHEER 1

gossamery *adj* **1** being of a material lacking in sturdiness or substance ⟨That *gossamery* dress should be washed gently by hand so it doesn't rip.⟩ — see FLIMSY 1

2 resembling air in lightness ⟨a *gossamery* feather floating on the breeze⟩ — see AIRY 1

3 very thin and easy to see through ⟨Use this *gossamery* cheesecloth to strain the liquid out of the cottage cheese.⟩ — see SHEER 1

gossip *n* **1** a person who habitually reveals personal or sensational facts about others ⟨Be careful what you say because he's a terrible *gossip*.⟩
synonyms talebearer, telltale
related words betrayer, blabbermouth, informant, informer, snitcher, squealer, stool pigeon, tattler, tattletale; libeler, scandalmonger

2 friendly, informal conversation or an instance of this ⟨We lingered at the water fountain for a little *gossip*.⟩ — see CHAT 1

3 information or opinion that is widely disseminated without any authority or confirmation of accuracy ⟨Idle *gossip* can really damage a person's reputation even if it is later proven to be false.⟩ — see RUMOR

gossip *vb* to relate sometimes questionable or secret information of a personal nature ⟨a neighbor who loves to *gossip* with others about everyone⟩
synonyms blab, dish, talk, tattle, wag
related words bandy (about), circulate, rumor; blabber, disclose, divulge, reveal, tell; hint, imply, insinuate, intimate, let on, suggest; inform, report, snitch, squeal, tip (off); babble, spill
phrases spill the beans
near antonyms clam up, shut up

gossipy *adj* having the style and content of everyday conversation ⟨This book on the people who have occupied the White House is a little too *gossipy* to qualify as serious history.⟩ — see CHATTY 1

gouge *vb* to charge (someone) too much for goods or services ⟨Since I had forgotten the sunscreen, I was forced to buy it from the concession stand at the beach—where they *gouged* me for it.⟩ — see OVERCHARGE 1

gourmand *n* **1** a person with refined tastes in food and wine ⟨a finicky *gourmand* who vacationed in Europe every year simply for the wine⟩ — see EPICURE

2 one who eats greedily or too much ⟨a *gourmand* who seems to swallow food without even pausing to taste it⟩ — see GLUTTON

gourmet *n* a person with refined tastes in food and wine ⟨Food critics have to be *gourmets* in order to write about food in an informed way.⟩ — see EPICURE

govern *vb* **1** to exercise authority or power over ⟨The president is elected in order to *govern* the country.⟩
synonyms boss, captain, command, control, preside (over), rule
related words conduct, direct, head, lead; administer, manage, micromanage, oversee, regulate, superintend, supervise; dictate, dominate, domineer, lord (it over), master, oppress, reign (over), tyrannize; conquer, subdue, subjugate

2 to keep from exceeding a desirable degree or level (as of expression) ⟨You need to *govern* your speech and be able to communicate your outrage without resorting to shouting.⟩ — see CONTROL 1
3 to look after and make decisions about ⟨The company's finances are *governed* by its chief financial officer.⟩ — see CONDUCT 1
governance *n* **1** lawful control over the affairs of a political unit (as a nation) ⟨After World War II, the four Allied nations shared the *governance* of the territory of postwar Germany under the Allied Control Council.⟩ — see RULE 2
2 the act or activity of looking after and making decisions about something ⟨While a financial advisor can be helpful, the *governance* of your family finances ultimately rests with you.⟩ — see CONDUCT 1
government *n* **1** lawful control over the affairs of a political unit (as a nation) ⟨*government* by the people, for the people⟩ — see RULE 2
2 the act or activity of looking after and making decisions about something ⟨a board involved in the *government* of the distribution of benefits to veterans⟩ — see CONDUCT 1
gown *n* **1** a garment with a joined blouse and skirt usually worn by a woman or girl ⟨a shopping trip to find the perfect *gown* for the wedding⟩ — see DRESS 1
2 a loose pullover garment worn in bed ⟨a warm flannel *gown* for cold nights⟩ — see NIGHTGOWN
gown *vb* to outfit with clothes and especially fine or special clothes ⟨a Renaissance portrait of a queen *gowned* in exotic silks and satins⟩ — see CLOTHE 1
grab *n* an instance of theft ⟨an illegal land *grab*⟩ — see THEFT 2
grab *vb* to take physical control or possession of (something) suddenly or forcibly ⟨Don't *grab* my arm like that!⟩ — see CATCH 1
grace *n* **1** an act of kind assistance ⟨In Victor Hugo's novel, *Les Misérables*, Jean Valjean's decision to go to jail for the man mistaken for him is a *grace* that goes beyond thanks.⟩ — see FAVOR 1
2 dignified or restrained beauty of form, appearance, or style ⟨a beautiful structure that is the epitome of the *grace* that marks the classical style⟩ — see ELEGANCE
3 a quality that gives something special worth ⟨As if taste were not enough, chocolate has the added *grace* of being good for you.⟩ — see EXCELLENCE 2
grace *vb* to make more attractive by adding something that is beautiful or becoming ⟨I hope that you will *grace* our gathering with your presence.⟩ — see DECORATE
graceful *adj* **1** moving easily ⟨The *graceful* ballerina effortlessly leapt across the stage.⟩
synonyms agile, feline, light, light-footed (*also* light-foot), lightsome, lissome (*also* lissom), lithe, lithesome, nimble, spry
related words acrobatic, flexible, limber, loose-jointed, pliable, pliant, supple; adroit, deft, dexterous (*also* dextrous), light-fingered; fleet-footed, sure-footed; athletic, balletic, coordinated
near antonyms inflexible, rigid, stiff; bungling, inept, maladroit
antonyms awkward, clumsy, gawky, graceless, lumbering, ungainly, ungraceful
2 having or showing elegance ⟨sat down in the old plantation home's very *graceful* parlor⟩ — see ELEGANT 1
gracefulness *n* dignified or restrained beauty of form, appearance, or style ⟨a home decorated with all of the *gracefulness* you'd expect of a fashion designer⟩ ⟨impressed by the *gracefulness* of the antebellum mansion⟩ — see ELEGANCE

graceless *adj* **1** lacking or showing a lack of nimbleness in using one's hands ⟨a *graceless* person who was a butterfingers when it came to playing basketball⟩ — see CLUMSY 1
2 lacking social grace and assurance ⟨He was a *graceless* preteen but evolved into a confident teenager.⟩ — see AWKWARD 1
3 not appropriate for a particular occasion or situation ⟨a *graceless* refusal to help during a difficult time⟩ — see INAPPROPRIATE
4 having or showing an inability to move in a graceful manner ⟨Penguins are *graceless* on land but not in the water.⟩ — see CLUMSY 2
5 showing poor judgment especially in personal relationships or social situations ⟨Indifferent to the nuances of constructive criticism, she sometimes says things which are hurtful or *graceless*.⟩ — see INDISCREET
gracious *adj* **1** showing a natural kindness and courtesy especially in social situations ⟨a *gracious* host who goes out of his way to make every guest feel welcome⟩
synonyms affable, cordial, genial, hospitable, sociable
related words agreeable, amiable, benign, benignant, congenial, convivial, friendly, kind, kindly, neighborly; accommodating, obliging; considerate, courteous, polite, thoughtful; cosmopolitan, sophisticated, urbane; approachable, attentive, outgoing
near antonyms boorish, churlish; abrupt, blunt, brusque (*also* brusk), curt, gruff, sharp, snippy; antisocial, disagreeable, discourteous, ill-mannered, impolite, rude, sullen, surly, uncivil, unfriendly, unkind, unmannerly; crabbed, crabby, cross, crusty, grumpy
antonyms inhospitable, ungenial, ungracious, unsociable
2 having an easygoing and pleasing manner especially in social situations ⟨a *gracious* innkeeper whose jokes and laughter made weary travelers feel right at home⟩ — see AMIABLE
3 showing consideration, courtesy, and good manners ⟨He was a *gracious* man, habitually offering his seat on the bus to others.⟩ — see POLITE 1
graciousness *n* **1** speech or behavior that is a sign of good breeding ⟨The children were taught *graciousness* from a young age.⟩ — see POLITENESS 1
2 the state or quality of having a pleasant or agreeable manner in socializing with others ⟨His *graciousness* and wit kept his fellow diners entertained throughout the meal.⟩ — see AMIABILITY 1
gradational *adj* proceeding or changing by steps or degrees ⟨*gradational* increases in altitude⟩ — see GRADUAL
gradationally *adv* by small steps or amounts ⟨By adding the white tint drop by drop, she *gradationally* changed the color from dark red to pink.⟩ — see GRADUALLY
grade *n* **1** an individual part of a process, series, or ranking ⟨just one *grade* removed from completion⟩ — see DEGREE 1
2 degree of excellence ⟨only motor oil of the highest *grade* for his fancy sports car⟩ — see QUALITY 1
3 one of the units into which a whole is divided on the basis of a common characteristic ⟨There are various *grades* of wool to consider when selecting a fabric.⟩ — see CLASS 2
4 something set up as an example against which others of the same type are compared ⟨That painting just doesn't make the *grade*.⟩ — see STANDARD 1
5 the degree to which something rises up from a position level with the horizon ⟨The hill rises at a seven percent *grade*.⟩ — see SLANT 1
grade *vb* **1** to arrange or assign according to type ⟨*Grade* these apples "extra fancy" and those "fancy."⟩ — see CLASSIFY 1

2 to take or have a certain position within a group arranged in vertical classes 〈How would you *grade* your meal on a scale of one to five?〉 — see RANK 1

gradient *n* the degree to which something rises up from a position level with the horizon 〈The path goes up at a pretty steep *gradient* before leveling off.〉 — see SLANT 1

gradual *adj* proceeding or changing by steps or degrees 〈A *gradual* drop in gas prices will take place over the next several months.〉

synonyms gradational, incremental, phased, piecemeal, step-by-step

related words progressive, stepped, tapered; imperceptible, inching; decrescent, increscent

near antonyms acute, sharp; changeable, dynamic, meteoric, volatile

antonyms abrupt, sudden

gradually *adv* by small steps or amounts 〈*gradually* worked his way down the class roster〉 〈Add the sugar to the beaten egg whites *gradually* to make the meringue.〉

synonyms gradationally, little by little, piece by piece, piecemeal

related words increasingly, progressively; fractionally, imperceptibly; slowly

phrases bit by bit, by degrees, inch by inch

near antonyms acutely, sharply, steeply; hastily, precipitously

antonyms abruptly, suddenly

graduation *n* a scheme of rank or order 〈The school had a *graduation* of testing levels into which to divide the students.〉 — see ³SCALE 1

grain *n* **1** a very small piece 〈Just give me a *grain* of information about what to expect on the program.〉 — see BIT 1

2 one's characteristic attitude or mood 〈Cheating, even on my income taxes, goes against my *grain*.〉 — see DISPOSITION 1

grainy *adj* made up of large particles 〈*Grainy* sand kept it off the rankings as one of the nation's best beaches.〉 — see COARSE 1

grand *adj* **1** large and impressive in size, grandeur, extent, or conception 〈the *grand* ceremonies that typically mark the opening of the Olympic Games〉

synonyms august, baronial, gallant, glorious, grandiose, heroic (*also* heroical), imperial, imposing, magnificent, majestic, massive, monumental, noble, proud, regal, royal, splendid, stately

related words colossal, monstrous, prodigious, stupendous, tremendous; kingly, lordly, princely, queenly; awesome, awful, cosmic (*also* cosmical), sublime, wondrous; formidable, impressive, prepossessing, redoubtable; pompous; marvelous (*or* marvellous), superb, terrific, wonderful; extravagant, lavish, luxurious, opulent, palatial, palatine, sumptuous; gorgeous, resplendent, splendiferous; extraordinary, remarkable, sensational, striking; celestial, divine, heavenly

near antonyms lowly, modest, unprepossessing; average, common, mediocre, ordinary, run-of-the-mill, second-rate; mean, meretricious, shabby, sordid; insignificant, measly, paltry, petty, puny, trifling, trivial

antonyms humble, unheroic, unimposing, unimpressive

2 coming before all others in importance 〈We won the *grand* prize.〉 — see FOREMOST 1

3 not lacking any part or member that properly belongs to it 〈The *grand* total comes to $350.〉 — see COMPLETE 1

4 of a size greater than average of its kind 〈In the *grand* ring of the three-ring circus stood the ringmaster.〉 — see LARGE

5 of high birth, rank, or station 〈the *grand* dame of American theater〉 — see NOBLE 1

6 of the very best kind 〈That picnic in the mountains was simply *grand*.〉 — see EXCELLENT

7 unusually large 〈Before them lay a *grand* treeless plain that stretched as far as the eye could see.〉 — see HUGE

grandee *n* a man of high birth or social position 〈Only a Spanish *grandee*—and no one of lesser rank—can address comments to the king and queen of Spain.〉 — see GENTLEMAN 1

grandeur *n* impressiveness of beauty on a large scale 〈We were struck by the *grandeur* of the sun setting over the Golden Gate Bridge.〉 — see MAGNIFICENCE

grandfather *n* a person who is several generations earlier in an individual's line of descent 〈This tradition has been passed down from our pioneer *grandfathers*.〉 — see ANCESTOR 1

grandiloquence *n* **1** boastful speech or writing 〈a heavyweight champion who was famous for his entertaining *grandiloquence* prior to every match〉 — see BOMBAST 1

2 language that is impressive-sounding but not meaningful or sincere 〈the predictably wearisome *grandiloquence* of the speeches at a political convention〉 — see RHETORIC 1

grandiloquent *adj* **1** full of fine words and fancy expressions 〈Poets in the 19th century tended to write poetry filled with *grandiloquent* phrases.〉 — see FLOWERY 1

2 marked by the use of impressive-sounding but mostly meaningless words and phrases 〈At Independence Day celebrations *grandiloquent* speeches by local politicians are as traditional as fireworks.〉 — see RHETORICAL 1

grandiose *adj* **1** large and impressive in size, grandeur, extent, or conception 〈a *grandiose* plan to upgrade the entire interstate highway system in 10 years〉 — see GRAND 1

2 self-consciously trying to present an appearance of grandeur or importance 〈She made some *grandiose* claim that she was the descendant of a French princess.〉 — see PRETENTIOUS 1

grandiosity *n* the quality or state of appearing or trying to appear more important or more valuable than is the case 〈I'd rather be thought of as a person with simple integrity, not a person given to *grandiosity* and exaggeration.〉 — see PRETENSE 1

grandly *adv* **1** in a luxurious manner 〈We were staying at the Plaza Hotel in New York and living rather *grandly*.〉 — see HIGH

2 in a manner befitting a person of the highest character and ideals 〈They had *grandly* offered to pay the entire cost of the treatment at the children's hospital.〉 — see GREATLY 1

grandness *n* **1** impressiveness of beauty on a large scale 〈We wanted to see the Alps in all of their wintertime *grandness*.〉 — see MAGNIFICENCE

2 the quality or state of being large in size 〈Visitors were impressed with the *grandness* of the movie set.〉 — see LARGENESS

grange *n* a piece of land and its buildings used to grow crops or raise livestock 〈Organizers asked the community's farmers to meet at the Howard family *grange* to help raise a new barn.〉 — see FARM

granite *n* firm or unwavering adherence to one's purpose 〈He had the *granite* to see the project out to the end.〉 — see DETERMINATION 1

grant *n* a sum of money allotted for a specific use by official or formal action 〈applied for a federal *grant* to restore the building, one of the oldest and most architecturally significant in the state〉 — see APPROPRIATION 1

grant *vb* **1** to accept the truth or existence of (something) usually reluctantly 〈You will *grant* that she is difficult to work with.〉 — see ADMIT 1

2 to give the ownership or benefit of (something) formally or publicly ⟨By the power vested in me, I *grant* you the keys to the city.⟩ — see CONFER 1

granting *n* the approval by someone in authority for the doing of something ⟨Your *granting* of an interview for this job opening will be much appreciated.⟩ — see PERMISSION

granular *adj* made up of large particles ⟨Icy, *granular* snow makes for terrible skiing—if you can, ski on light, powdery snow.⟩ — see COARSE 1

granulated *adj* made up of large particles ⟨Don't use powdered sugar in that recipe, use *granulated* sugar.⟩ — see COARSE 1

granule *n* a very small piece ⟨Is there one *granule* of truth in that statement?⟩ — see BIT 1

graphic *n* something that visually explains or decorates a text ⟨The use of *graphics* in the text of the dictionary helps to break up the visual monotony of the page.⟩ — see ILLUSTRATION 1

graphic *also* **graphical** *adj* **1** producing a mental picture through clear and impressive description ⟨The report offered many *graphic* details about the earthquake.⟩

synonyms delineated, pictorial, picturesque, visual, vivid

related words depicted, descriptive, expressive; concrete, explicit, specific; faithful, lifelike, natural, photographic, realistic; fresh, incisive, sharp

near antonyms indeterminate, nebulous, obscure, sketchy, unclear, vague; bleary, blurry, dark, dim, faint, foggy, fuzzy, hazy, indefinite, indistinct, indistinguishable, muddy, murky, shadowlike, shadowy; ambiguous, cryptic, dark, enigmatic (*also* enigmatical), equivocal, inscrutable, mysterious

2 consisting of or relating to pictures ⟨He got a degree in *graphic* design.⟩ — see PICTORIAL 1

grapple *n* **1** the act or manner of holding ⟨I was simply unable to break my opponent's viselike *grapple* and lost the wrestling match.⟩ — see HOLD 1

2 an earnest effort for superiority or victory over another ⟨After a *grapple* with his conscience, he confessed to lying.⟩ — see CONTEST 1

grapple *vb* **1** to seize and attempt to unbalance one another for the purpose of achieving physical mastery ⟨two sumo wrestlers *grappling* like a pair of mammoth bears⟩ — see WRESTLE

2 to take physical control or possession of (something) suddenly or forcibly ⟨A crane *grappled* the sunken boat and hoisted it above water.⟩ — see CATCH 1

grapple (with) *vb* to deal with (something) usually skillfully or efficiently ⟨a medical ethicist who *grapples with* extremely difficult questions all the time⟩ — see HANDLE 1

grasp *n* **1** the ability to direct the course of something ⟨She finally felt like her career was within her *grasp*.⟩ — see CONTROL 2

2 the act or manner of holding ⟨During the roller coaster ride, I held the safety bar with a viselike *grasp*.⟩ — see HOLD 1

3 the knowledge gained from the process of coming to know or understand something ⟨I think I finally have a *grasp* of Spanish grammar.⟩ — see COMPREHENSION

grasp *vb* **1** to have a practical understanding of ⟨He just doesn't *grasp* how important it is that he call when he'll be late.⟩ — see KNOW 1

2 to put one's arms around and press tightly ⟨The departing soldier *grasped* his children a little closer than usual.⟩ — see EMBRACE 1

3 to reach for and take hold of by embracing with the fingers or arms ⟨The attendant *grasped* my arm and steered me towards the door.⟩ — see TAKE 1

4 to have a clear idea of ⟨The emergency operator finally *grasped* what he was trying to tell her.⟩ — see COMPREHEND 1

grasping *adj* having or marked by an eager and often selfish desire especially for material possessions ⟨a *grasping* person who wouldn't give a dime to charity⟩ — see GREEDY 1

graspingness *n* an intense selfish desire for wealth or possessions ⟨That period of the 19th century when the *graspingness* of the robber barons knew no bounds is often called the Gilded Age.⟩ — see GREED

grassland *n* a broad area of level or rolling treeless country ⟨stunning pictures of the giraffes and zebras roaming the *grasslands* of Africa⟩ — see PLAIN 1

grate *vb* **1** to disturb the peace of mind of (someone) especially by repeated disagreeable acts ⟨His negative attitude is starting to *grate* on me.⟩ — see IRRITATE 1

2 to pass roughly and noisily over or against a surface ⟨The sled *grated* along the bare pavement.⟩ — see SCRAPE 1

3 to press or strike against or together so as to make a scraping sound ⟨He *grated* the pieces of metal together.⟩ — see GRIND 2

grateful *adj* **1** feeling or expressing gratitude ⟨She was *grateful* for her neighbor's help after she broke her foot.⟩

synonyms appreciative, glad, obliged, thankful

related words beholden, indebted; contented, delighted, gratified, pleased, satisfied, tickled; thanking

near antonyms inhospitable, rude, thoughtless, ungracious

antonyms inappreciative, thankless, unappreciative, ungrateful

2 giving pleasure or contentment to the mind or senses ⟨I'm glad for the *grateful* warmth of the fire on such a cold day.⟩ — see PLEASANT 1

gratefulness *n* acknowledgment of having received something good from another ⟨a note expressing her sincere *gratefulness* for our help⟩ — see THANKS

gratification *n* the feeling experienced when one's wishes are met ⟨Eating good chocolate gives me a sense of intense *gratification*.⟩ — see PLEASURE 1

gratified *adj* **1** experiencing pleasure, satisfaction, or delight ⟨I am deeply *gratified* that you'll be able to come to the wedding.⟩ — see GLAD 1

2 feeling that one's needs or desires have been met ⟨A good meal eaten in excellent company is enough to keep me *gratified* for some time.⟩ — see CONTENT

gratify *vb* **1** to give in to (a desire) ⟨Just *gratify* this one whim of mine.⟩ — see INDULGE 1

2 to give satisfaction to ⟨Your presence at the holiday table would really *gratify* your grandparents.⟩ — see PLEASE 1

gratifying *adj* **1** giving pleasure or contentment to the mind or senses ⟨a spectacular film that is *gratifying* to both the mind and the eyes⟩ — see PLEASANT 1

2 making one feel good inside ⟨Your warm welcome sure is *gratifying* to this tired soul.⟩ — see HEARTWARMING

grating *adj* **1** disagreeable to one's aesthetic or artistic sense ⟨The mix of colors in that painting is terribly *grating*.⟩ — see HARSH 2

2 harsh and dry in sound ⟨With a *grating* voice, she croaked a feeble "hello."⟩ — see HOARSE

gratis *adj* not costing or charging anything ⟨If you sign up today, you get double your order *gratis*.⟩ — see FREE 4

gratitude *n* acknowledgment of having received something good from another ⟨Accept these flowers as a token of my *gratitude*.⟩ — see THANKS

gratuitous *adj* **1** not costing or charging anything ⟨They will throw in a *gratuitous* box of chocolates when you spend $30 or more in their shop.⟩ — see FREE 4

2 not needed by the circumstances or to accomplish an end ⟨That violent scene was completely *gratuitous* and didn't need to be in the movie at all.⟩ — see UNNECESSARY

gratuity *n* **1** a small sum of money given for a service over and above what is due ⟨For parties of eight or more, we automatically add an 18% *gratuity* onto the bill.⟩ — see ²TIP 1

2 something given in addition to what is ordinarily expected or owed ⟨The intern got a $100 *gratuity* in addition to his regular pay.⟩ — see BONUS

grave *adj* **1** having a matter of importance as its topic ⟨This journal focuses on the *grave* issues confronting the nation.⟩ — see SERIOUS 2

2 involving potential loss or injury ⟨Going over Niagara Falls poses a *grave* danger.⟩ — see DANGEROUS 1

3 not joking or playful in mood or manner ⟨When I asked him how his dog was doing, he looked *grave* and said, "Not good."⟩ — see SERIOUS 1

4 having a low musical pitch or range ⟨a *grave* hexachord⟩ — see DEEP 2

grave *vb* to cut (as letters or designs) on a hard surface ⟨He *graved* his initials into the rock face.⟩ — see ENGRAVE 1

grave *n* **1** a final resting place for a dead person ⟨The boy put flowers on his grandmother's *grave*.⟩

synonyms burial, sepulture, tomb

related words catacomb, crypt, mausoleum, vault; cemetery, churchyard, graveyard, potter's field

2 the permanent stopping of all the vital bodily activities ⟨a rock star who found his early *grave* in a plane crash⟩ — see DEATH 1

3 the state of being dead ⟨a terrible fear of the *grave*⟩ — see DEATH 2

gravel *adj* harsh and dry in sound ⟨After his bout with laryngitis, he had a terribly *gravel* voice.⟩ — see HOARSE

gravelly *adj* harsh and dry in sound ⟨His singing voice is *gravelly* and soulful.⟩ — see HOARSE

graveness *n* a mental state free of jesting or trifling ⟨The topic is treated with appropriate *graveness*.⟩ — see EARNESTNESS

gravestone *n* a shaped stone laid over or erected near a grave and usually bearing an inscription to identify and preserve the memory of the deceased ⟨We love to tour old cemeteries and read the hauntingly poetic inscriptions on the *gravestones*.⟩ — see TOMBSTONE

graveyard *n* a piece of land used for burying the dead ⟨Reflecting the Quaker avoidance of personal vanity, the *graveyard* is not marked by so much as a single headstone.⟩ — see CEMETERY

gravid *adj* containing unborn young within the body ⟨The patient is a *gravid* woman in her seventh month.⟩ — see PREGNANT 1

gravity *n* a mental state free of jesting or trifling ⟨He uttered the oath with proper *gravity*.⟩ — see EARNESTNESS

gravy *n* **1** a savory fluid food used as a topping or accompaniment to a main dish ⟨We'll order a large serving of fries with extra *gravy*.⟩ — see SAUCE 1

2 something given in addition to what is ordinarily expected or owed ⟨The bonus I received in addition to my salary was pure *gravy*.⟩ — see BONUS

gray *also* **grey** *adj* **1** of the color gray ⟨The *gray* sky portended snow.⟩

synonyms grayish, leaden, silver, silvery, slate, slaty (*also* slatey), steely

related words achromatic, colorless, neutral; dirty, dull, faded, sad, washed-out; ashen, ashy, chalky, livid, mousy (*or* mousey), pale, palish, white, whitish; chocolate, dun, sandy, sepia; grizzled, hoar, hoary

near antonyms ablaze, bright, deep, rich; colorful, motley, multicolored, polychromatic, polychrome, varicolored, variegated

2 causing or marked by an atmosphere lacking in cheer ⟨a *gray* rainy day⟩ — see GLOOMY 1

grayish *adj* of the color gray ⟨The black stallion and white mare produced a *grayish* filly.⟩ — see GRAY 1

gray matter *n* the ability to learn and understand or to deal with problems ⟨She's got the *gray matter* to figure that equation out.⟩ — see INTELLIGENCE 1

¹graze *vb* to feed on grass or herbs ⟨cows *grazing* in the meadow⟩

synonyms browse, forage, pasture, rustle

related words eat, feed, nibble; range, stock; overgraze

²graze *vb* **1** to damage by rubbing against a sharp or rough surface ⟨I *grazed* my elbow diving for the ball.⟩ — see SCRAPE 2

2 to pass lightly across or touch gently especially in passing ⟨The volleyball just *grazed* my face, so I'm okay.⟩ — see ²BRUSH

graze *n* an area of skin roughened or worn away by harsh rubbing against another surface ⟨a stumble that resulted in nothing more serious than a *graze* on the knee⟩ — see ABRASION

grease *vb* **1** to coat (something) with a slippery substance in order to reduce friction ⟨Make sure you *grease* the pan before you put the batter in.⟩ — see LUBRICATE

2 to free from obstruction or difficulty ⟨Your help might *grease* the complicated adoption proceedings.⟩ — see EASE 1

greased *adj* having or being a surface so smooth as to greatly reduce traction ⟨The floor was *greased* with condensation, and so we slid everywhere we went.⟩ — see SLICK 1

greasy *adj* having or being a surface so smooth as to greatly reduce traction ⟨That wet tarmac road is *greasy* enough to send the car into a skid.⟩ — see SLICK 1

great *adj* **1** having or showing exceptional knowledge, experience, or skill in a field of endeavor ⟨one of the *great* anthropologists⟩ — see PROFICIENT

2 having, characterized by, or arising from a dignified and generous nature ⟨a *great* humanitarian⟩ ⟨*great* acts of charity⟩ — see NOBLE 2

3 lasting for a considerable time ⟨We haven't seen them in a *great* while.⟩ — see LONG 2

4 of a size greater than average of its kind ⟨I saw a *great* moose calmly walking through our backyard.⟩ — see LARGE

5 of the very best kind ⟨This cake is *great*!⟩ — see EXCELLENT

6 showing urgent desire or interest ⟨She's *great* on any type of sport that requires endurance.⟩ — see EAGER

7 coming before all others in importance ⟨He regards global warming as the *great* issue of the day.⟩ — see FOREMOST 1

8 of high birth, rank, or station ⟨a descendant of one of the *great* families of Philadelphia⟩ — see NOBLE 1

great *adv* in a pleasing way ⟨The game was going *great* for the home team.⟩ — see WELL 5

greatcoat *n* a warm outdoor coat ⟨The men donned their *greatcoats* for the ride in the open carriage.⟩ — see OVERCOAT

greatest *adj* **1** coming before all others in importance ⟨the *greatest* achievement in the history of cinema⟩ — see FOREMOST 1

2 of the highest degree ⟨I have the *greatest* respect for the selfless medical missionaries working around the world.⟩ — see FULL 2

greathearted *adj* **1** feeling or displaying no fear by temperament ⟨those *greathearted* ordinary folks who answered their country's call for military service⟩ — see BRAVE 1

2 having, characterized by, or arising from a dignified and generous nature ⟨a *greathearted* program to provide basic necessities to millions of children in war-torn countries⟩ — see NOBLE 2

greatheartedness *n* strength of mind to carry on in spite of danger ⟨It took a special kind of *greatheartedness* for the conscientious objector to remain true to his beliefs.⟩ — see COURAGE

greatly *adv* **1** in a manner befitting a person of the highest character and ideals ⟨As commander of the Union army's first Black regiment, Robert Gould Shaw died as *greatly* as he had lived.⟩
synonyms gallantly, grandly, heroically, high-mindedly, honorably, magnanimously, nobly
related words loftily, venerably; magnificently, majestically; chivalrously; bravely
near antonyms abominably, contemptibly, despicably, detestably, hatefully, nastily, pitiably, sorrily, wretchedly; degenerately
antonyms basely, dishonorably, ignobly
2 to a large extent or degree ⟨Authorities have *greatly* increased the scope of their investigation into the matter.⟩
synonyms astronomically, broadly, colossally, considerably, enormously, extensively, highly, hugely, largely, massively, monstrously, much, sizably, staggeringly, stupendously, tremendously, utterly, vastly
related words appreciably, noticeably, significantly; abundantly, amply, copiously, healthily, plentifully
phrases a lot, by half, no end
near antonyms modestly; fractionally; imperceptibly, infinitesimally, insignificantly, invisibly, microscopically, minutely; barely, hardly, just, minimally, scarcely
antonyms little, negligibly, nominally, slightly
3 to a great degree ⟨I'm not *greatly* bothered by this setback.⟩ — see VERY 1

greatness *n* **1** exceptionally high quality ⟨a poet whose work is of enduring *greatness*⟩ — see EXCELLENCE 1
2 the quality or state of being large in size ⟨The overwhelming *greatness* of the canyon is what visitors first notice.⟩ — see LARGENESS

greed *n* an intense selfish desire for wealth or possessions ⟨Don't let *greed* for riches control you.⟩
synonyms acquisitiveness, avarice, avariciousness, avidity, covetousness, cupidity, graspingness, greediness, rapaciousness, rapacity
related words commercialism, materialism, possessiveness; piggishness; appetite, craving, desire, drive, hankering, hunger, itch, longing, lust, passion, pining, ravenousness, thirst, voracity, yearning, yen; egoism, egotism, self-centeredness, self-interest, selfishness, self-regard
near antonyms contentment, fulfillment (*or* fulfilment), gratification, satisfaction; bounteousness, bountifulness, bounty, charity, generosity, largesse (*also* largess), liberality, magnanimity, openhandedness, openheartedness, unselfishness; altruism, selflessness

greediness *n* **1** an intense selfish desire for wealth or possessions ⟨Her all-consuming *greediness* blinded her to the pain she caused others in her drive to get rich.⟩ — see GREED

greedy *adj* **1** having or marked by an eager and often selfish desire especially for material possessions ⟨a young rocker who was *greedy* for fame and riches⟩ ⟨the *greedy* exploitation of the land by developers⟩
synonyms acquisitive, avaricious, avid, coveting, covetous, grasping, mercenary, rapacious

related words commercialistic, materialistic, philistine; desirous, eager; hoggish, piggish, piggy, swinish; devouring, gluttonous, gobbling, ravenous, voracious; egocentric, egoistic (*also* egoistical), egotistic (*or* egotistical), self-centered, self-seeking; discontent, discontented, malcontent, unsatisfied; begrudging, grudging, resentful
near antonyms nonmaterialistic; altruistic, bounteous, bountiful, charitable, freehanded, generous, greathearted, handsome, liberal, magnanimous, munificent, openhanded, openhearted, selfless, unselfish, unsparing; controlled, moderate, restrained, temperate; content, sated, satisfied
2 having a huge appetite ⟨The *greedy* seagulls will snatch your sandwich right out of your hand.⟩ — see VORACIOUS 1
3 showing urgent desire or interest ⟨He's *greedy* for new assignments that will really challenge him.⟩ — see EAGER

green *adj* **1** covered with a thick, healthy natural growth ⟨fields *green* with meadow grass⟩ — see LUSH 1
2 lacking in adult experience or maturity ⟨a new pitcher who's pretty *green*, even by rookie standards⟩ — see CALLOW
3 lacking in worldly wisdom or informed judgment ⟨In spite of her age, she's still *green* enough to be hoodwinked by fast-talking scammers.⟩ — see NAIVE 1

green *n* **1** green leaves or plants ⟨The lonely soldier dreamt of the fields of *green* that he had wandered in as a youth.⟩ — see GREENERY
2 something (as pieces of stamped metal or printed paper) customarily and legally used as a medium of exchange, a measure of value, or a means of payment ⟨I need to save up some *green* before I can afford that cruise.⟩ — see MONEY

greenback *n* a piece of printed paper used as money in the United States ⟨She threw a few *greenbacks* on the counter to pay for the meal.⟩ — see ¹BILL 2

greenery *n* green leaves or plants ⟨Scottish highlands covered with lush *greenery*.⟩
synonyms flora, foliage, green, herbage, leafage, vegetation, verdure
related words grassland, prairie; underbrush, undergrowth

greenhorn *n* a person who is just starting out in a field of activity ⟨Go easy on him—he's just a *greenhorn* and doesn't have all the experience you do.⟩ — see BEGINNER

greenhouse *n* a glass-enclosed building for growing plants ⟨We needed to move the plants into the *greenhouse* before the first frost killed them.⟩ — see CONSERVATORY

greeting *n* **1** an expression of goodwill upon meeting ⟨The volunteer directed the conference participants towards the coffee after offering them a cheerful *greeting*.⟩ — see HELLO
2 greetings *pl* best wishes ⟨When you see him, give him my sincerest *greetings*.⟩ — see COMPLIMENT 2

gregarious *adj* likely to seek or enjoy the company of others ⟨a *gregarious* child who ran up to every person on the playground and wanted to be their friend⟩ — see CONVIVIAL

gregariousness *n* the quality or state of being social ⟨His natural *gregariousness* serves him well as a salesman.⟩ — see SOCIABILITY

gremlin *n* an imaginary being usually having a small human form and magical powers ⟨During the World Wars, fighter pilots adopted the fanciful notion that *gremlins* were responsible for mechanical failures on their planes.⟩ — see FAIRY

griddle cake *n* a flat cake made from thin batter and

cooked on both sides (as on a griddle) ⟨buckwheat *griddle cakes* served with syrup and butter⟩ — see PANCAKE

grief *n* **1** deep sadness especially for the loss of someone or something loved ⟨Even the gruff grandfather felt a heart-breaking *grief* when the family dog died.⟩ — see SORROW
2 the feeling of impatience or anger caused by another's repeated disagreeable acts ⟨Trying to fix the computer isn't worth the *grief*.⟩ — see ANNOYANCE 2

grievance *n* **1** a lingering ill will towards a person for a real or imagined wrong ⟨This is no place to air your *grievances* against him.⟩ — see GRUDGE 1
2 an expression of dissatisfaction, pain, or resentment ⟨She decided to file a formal *grievance* against the utility company.⟩ — see COMPLAINT 1

grieve *vb* to feel deep sadness or mental pain ⟨We all *grieved* over the lost cat.⟩
synonyms agonize, anguish, bleed, hurt, mourn, sorrow, suffer
related words ache, long (for), pine (away), sigh, smart; rack, torment, torture; bemoan, bewail, deplore, lament, rue; bawl, blubber, cry, groan, howl, keen, moan, sob, take on, wail, weep, yammer, yowl; languish; regret
phrases eat one's heart out, tear one's hair
near antonyms beam, cheer, crow, delight, exult, glory, joy, laugh, ravish, rejoice, triumph; assure, cheer, comfort, commiserate, console, reassure, solace, soothe, sympathize

grieve (for) *vb* to feel or express sorrow for ⟨I *grieve for* your loss.⟩ — see LAMENT 1

grieving *adj* expressing or suggesting mourning ⟨The *grieving* sobs of the widow could be heard throughout the funeral service.⟩ — see MOURNFUL 1

grievous *adj* **1** difficult to endure ⟨The loss of their biggest customer was a *grievous* blow to the business.⟩ — see HARSH 1
2 hard to accept or bear especially emotionally ⟨the *grievous* loss of a loved one⟩ — see BITTER 2
3 involving potential loss or injury ⟨a *grievous* wound that requires a doctor's immediate attention⟩ — see DANGEROUS 1
4 of a kind to cause great distress ⟨The *grievous* cost of the war weighed heavily on the president's mind.⟩ — see REGRETTABLE

grievously *adv* with feelings of bitterness or grief ⟨I was *grievously* disappointed not to be invited to the wedding.⟩ — see HARD 2

grill *n* a public establishment where meals are served to paying customers for consumption on the premises ⟨He headed down to the local *grill* for a burger.⟩ — see RESTAURANT

grill *vb* **1** to put a series of questions to ⟨Police *grilled* the suspect, but had to release him when it became clear he didn't have the information they were looking for.⟩ — see EXAMINE 1
2 to put a question or questions to ⟨*grilled* the children about where the cookies went⟩ — see ASK 1

grim *adj* **1** harsh and threatening in manner or appearance ⟨a *grim* and desolate landscape⟩ ⟨a *grim* and short-tempered shopkeeper who didn't exactly invite friendly conversation⟩
synonyms austere, dour, fierce, flinty, forbidding, gruff, intimidating, lowering (*also* louring), rough, rugged, severe, stark, steely, stern, ungentle
related words bleak, cold, hostile, inhospitable, inimical, unfriendly, unsympathetic; adamant, bound, determined, firm, intent, purposeful, resolute, resolved, steadfast, unflinching; fixed, hard, hardened, hardheaded, immovable, implacable, inflexible, ironhanded, mulish, obdurate, obstinate, rigid, self-willed, set, stiff, stubborn,

unbending, uncompromising, unrelenting, unyielding, willful (*or* wilful); immutable, unchangeable; black, cheerless, dark, gloomy, glum, joyless, moody, morose, sulky, sullen, surly; brooding, grave, humorless, melancholy, serious, sober, sobersided, solemn, somber (*or* sombre), staid, unsmiling
near antonyms bland, meek, mellow, soft, soothing; easy, quiet, tranquil; agreeable, bright, cheerful, inviting, pleasant, pleasing, sweet; glad, happy, lighthearted, merry, mirthful, sunny; featherbrained, flighty, frivolous, giddy, goofy, harebrained, light-headed, playful, scatterbrained, silly
antonyms benign, benignant, gentle, mild, tender
2 difficult to endure ⟨This winter is supposed to be particularly *grim*, so stock up on firewood.⟩ — see HARSH 1
3 showing no signs of slackening or yielding in one's purpose ⟨With *grim* determination, the parents worked long hours to put their children through college.⟩ — see UNYIELDING 1
4 violently unfriendly or aggressive in disposition ⟨*grim* warriors heading into battle⟩ — see FIERCE 1

grimace *vb* to distort one's face ⟨Playgoers *grimaced* at the actor's terrible attempt at a French accent.⟩ — see MUG 1

grimace *n* a twisting of the facial features in disgust or disapproval ⟨He made a *grimace* when he tasted the medicine.⟩
synonyms face, frown, lower (*also* lour), mouth, mug, pout, scowl
related words flinch, squinch, wince; growl, snarl; rictus, simper, smirk; scoff, sneer; glare, glower, look, stare
near antonyms grin, laugh, smile

grime *n* foul matter that mars the purity or cleanliness of something ⟨This new product really cuts through *grime*.⟩ — see FILTH 1

grime *vb* to make dirty ⟨Countless hours of work were needed to clean the floors of the old warehouse that had been *grimed* from a century of use.⟩ — see DIRTY

griminess *n* the state or quality of being dirty ⟨disgusted by the *griminess* in which the previous tenant had left the appliances⟩ — see DIRTINESS

grimy *adj* not clean ⟨This mirror is so *grimy* you can barely see your reflection in it.⟩ — see DIRTY 1

grin *vb* to express an emotion (as amusement) by curving the lips upward ⟨I *grinned* at the kids' fooling around in the pool.⟩ — see SMILE 1

grind *n* **1** a harsh grating sound ⟨The *grind* of ice in the blender sent the cat running from the room.⟩ — see RASP
2 a person devoted to intellectual or academic pursuits ⟨Don't be such a *grind*—go out with your friends and enjoy yourself!⟩ — see NERD 1
3 very hard or unpleasant work ⟨Yard work is a real *grind*.⟩ — see TOIL
4 an established and often automatic or monotonous series of actions followed when engaging in some activity ⟨The daily *grind* of a 50-mile commute was getting old.⟩ — see ROUTINE 1

grind *vb* **1** to make smooth by friction ⟨After they are *ground* and polished, these stones can be used for jewelry.⟩
synonyms buff, file, hone, rasp, rub, sand
related words plane, scrape; sandblast, scour; burnish, dress, gloss, polish, shine, smooth; edge, hone, sharpen, strop, whet; regrind
near antonyms coarsen, rough (up), roughen, scuff
2 to press or strike against or together so as to make a scraping sound ⟨Everyone in the car winced when the driver *ground* the gears trying to shift into second.⟩
synonyms crunch, gnash, grate, grit, scrape, scrunch

related words creak, groan, moan, rasp, scratch, whine; clash, collide, jar

3 to make sharp or sharper ⟨Better *grind* down that ax before you try to cut down that tree.⟩ — see SHARPEN

4 to make smooth or glossy usually by repeatedly applying surface pressure ⟨He used the finest polishing paper available to *grind* down the facets of the diamond before dusting it with a soft cloth.⟩ — see POLISH 1

5 to pass roughly and noisily over or against a surface ⟨The boy idly *ground* the rock against the stone wall.⟩ — see SCRAPE 1

6 to reduce to fine particles ⟨*Grind* whole coffee beans if you want the freshest coffee.⟩ — see POWDER

grinder *n* a large sandwich on a long split roll ⟨I ordered a meatball *grinder* from the beach's concession stand.⟩ — see SUBMARINE

grip *n* **1** a bag carried by hand and designed to hold a traveler's clothing and personal articles ⟨She placed her *grip* in the train's overhead rack and seated herself comfortably.⟩ — see TRAVELING BAG

2 the act or manner of holding ⟨Get a better *grip* on the lid and try to open the jar again.⟩ — see HOLD 1

3 the knowledge gained from the process of coming to know or understand something ⟨He has a good *grip* on basic Spanish grammar and spelling.⟩ — see COMPREHENSION

4 the right or means to command or control others ⟨a tyrant that keeps the masses tightly in his *grip*⟩ — see POWER 1

5 a part by which an implement is held ⟨I bought new pots with heat-resistant *grips*.⟩ — see HANDLE 1

grip *vb* **1** to have or keep in one's hands ⟨She *gripped* the handlebars tightly and raced down the hill.⟩ — see HOLD 1

2 to hold the attention of as if by a spell ⟨That true crime story *gripped* me as much as any whodunit.⟩ — see ENTHRALL 1

3 to hold the attention of ⟨That movie will *grip* any true sports car fan.⟩ — see ENGAGE 1

4 to reach for and take hold of by embracing with the fingers or arms ⟨The baby *gripped* my fingers and wouldn't let go.⟩ — see TAKE 1

gripe *n* an expression of dissatisfaction, pain, or resentment ⟨I would rather not listen to *gripes* about your job.⟩ — see COMPLAINT 1

gripe *vb* **1** to disturb the peace of mind of (someone) especially by repeated disagreeable acts ⟨Constant complaints from the customers *griped* her.⟩ — see IRRITATE 1

2 to express dissatisfaction, pain, or resentment usually tiresomely ⟨Her tendency to *gripe* constantly drove everyone away.⟩ — see COMPLAIN

griper *n* **1** a person who makes frequent complaints usually about little things ⟨He's a *griper* who can find fault with anything.⟩ — see CRYBABY

2 an irritable and complaining person ⟨Driving across the country in four days would make anyone a confirmed *griper*.⟩ — see GROUCH 1

gripping *adj* holding the attention or provoking interest ⟨I found the exhibit on the Holocaust intensely *gripping* and quite moving.⟩ — see INTERESTING

grisliness *n* the quality of inspiring intense dread or dismay ⟨The *grisliness* of the crime scene was too much for the jury.⟩ — see HORROR 1

grisly *adj* extremely disturbing or repellent ⟨He gave some *grisly* testimony during the trial.⟩ — see HORRIBLE 1

grit *n* the strength of mind that enables a person to endure pain or hardship ⟨She was an athlete with true *grit*, continuing her training despite bad weather and an injury.⟩ — see FORTITUDE

grit *vb* to press or strike against or together so as to make

a scraping sound ⟨The crash victim *gritted* his teeth as a way of coping with the pain.⟩ — see GRIND 2

groan *n* **1** a crying out in grief ⟨When the underdogs lost the playoffs, the *groans* of millions of disappointed fans were heard throughout the land.⟩ — see LAMENT 1

2 a long low sound indicating pain or grief ⟨The hiker let out a *groan* when he tried to stand on the sprained ankle.⟩ — see MOAN 1

groan *vb* to utter a moan ⟨We heard someone *groaning* in pain.⟩ — see MOAN 1

groomed *adj* being clean and in good order ⟨The front office is always carefully *groomed* in order to give customers a good first impression.⟩ — see NEAT 1

groove *n* **1** an established and often automatic or monotonous series of actions followed when engaging in some activity ⟨I can't get into the *groove* on Monday morning without a cup of coffee.⟩ — see ROUTINE 1

2 a situation or activity for which a person or thing is best suited ⟨After years of bouncing from job to job, she discovered that her natural *groove* was social work.⟩ — see NICHE 2

groove *vb* **1** to mark with or as if with a line or groove ⟨If you *groove* that piece of wood, we should be able to fit this smaller board into it.⟩ — see SCORE 1

2 to form a pleasing relationship ⟨Surprisingly, his flighty, artistic sensibility and her no-nonsense practicality *groove* together rather well.⟩ — see HARMONIZE 1

groove (on) *vb* to take pleasure in ⟨Thrill-seekers who *groove on* skiing will love snowboarding.⟩ — see ENJOY 1

groovy *adj* of the very best kind ⟨a great movie with *groovy* special effects⟩ — see EXCELLENT

grope *vb* to search for something blindly or uncertainly ⟨She nervously *groped* for her car keys.⟩ ⟨*groping* for the right answer⟩

synonyms feel, fish, fumble, scrabble

related words grabble; cast about, hunt, look, reach, seek (out); capture, clutch, corral, get, grab, nab, nail, seize, snatch; comb, dig (through), dredge, rake, ransack, rifle, rummage, scour

gross *adj* **1** depicting or referring to sexual matters in a way that is unacceptable in polite society ⟨He was thrown out of the game for using *gross* language.⟩ — see OBSCENE 1

2 lacking in refinement or good taste ⟨She refused to mix with what she called "the *gross* masses who are unappreciative of fine art."⟩ — see COARSE 2

3 very noticeable especially for being incorrect or bad ⟨a *gross* mistake that some proofreader should have caught⟩ — see EGREGIOUS

4 causing intense displeasure, disgust, or resentment ⟨The little boy insisted that worms are *gross*.⟩ — see OFFENSIVE 1

grossness *n* **1** the condition of having an excess of body fat ⟨That level of *grossness* is unhealthy.⟩ — see CORPULENCE

2 the quality or state of being obscene ⟨the *grossness* of his language⟩ — see OBSCENITY

3 the quality or state of lacking refinement or good taste ⟨The *grossness* of his table manners disgusted the other wedding guests.⟩ — see VULGARITY 1

grot *n* a naturally formed underground chamber with an opening to the surface ⟨The famous Dead Sea Scrolls were discovered in a long-forgotten *grot* by a shepherd boy.⟩ — see CAVE

grotesque *adj* **1** disagreeable to one's aesthetic or artistic sense ⟨The gaudy, overdecorated interior of the gambling casino was just too *grotesque* for my taste.⟩ — see HARSH 2

2 unpleasant to look at ⟨That bloody Halloween mask is *grotesque*.⟩ — see UGLY 1

grotesque *n* a strange or horrible and often frightening creature ⟨a gallery of *grotesques* from some horror movie⟩ — see MONSTER 1

grotto *n* a naturally formed underground chamber with an opening to the surface ⟨At the heart of the shrine is a small rocky *grotto* into which pilgrims can descend.⟩ — see CAVE

grouch *n* **1** an irritable and complaining person ⟨an uncle who is a real *grouch* when he's sick⟩
synonyms bear, bellyacher, complainer, crab, crank, curmudgeon, fusser, griper, grouser, growler, grumbler, grump, murmurer, mutterer, whiner
related words malcontent, sorehead; grinch, killjoy, party pooper, spoilsport; defeatist, pessimist; faultfinder, kicker, nagger, nitpicker, objector, quibbler, repiner; hypochondriac
near antonyms optimist, Pollyanna; happy camper
2 a state of resentful silence or irritability ⟨Having been proven wrong, he had a *grouch* on for hours afterwards.⟩ — see SULK
3 an expression of dissatisfaction, pain, or resentment ⟨It wouldn't be a workday if we didn't hear his daily *grouch* about the coffee.⟩ — see COMPLAINT 1

grouch *vb* to express dissatisfaction, pain, or resentment usually tiresomely ⟨a woman who likes to *grouch* about how unappreciated she is⟩ — see COMPLAIN

grouchiness *n* readiness to show annoyance or impatience ⟨Sometimes the toddler's *grouchiness* was so cute, I had to hold back a smile.⟩ — see PETULANCE

grouchy *adj* **1** easily irritated or annoyed ⟨A lack of sleep would make anyone *grouchy*.⟩ — see IRRITABLE
2 given to complaining a lot ⟨a *grouchy* kid who refuses to eat his vegetables⟩ — see FUSSY 1

ground *adj* having an edge thin enough to cut or pierce something ⟨a finely *ground* axe⟩ — see SHARP 1

ground *n* **1** **grounds** *pl* the area around and belonging to a building ⟨an escorted tour of the White House and its surrounding *grounds*⟩
synonyms demesne, park, premises (*also* premisses), yard
related words acres, estate, land, lot, parcel, plot, property, real estate, realty; campus; churchyard, dooryard; close, enclosure (*also* inclosure), garden, plaza
2 **grounds** *pl* matter that settles to the bottom of a body of liquid ⟨Strain the coffee to remove the *grounds*.⟩ — see DEPOSIT 1
3 **grounds** *pl* something (as a belief) that serves as the basis for another thing ⟨The proposal was rejected on the *grounds* that it was too costly.⟩ — see REASON 2
4 a small area of usually open land ⟨I'll meet you at the parade *ground* in two hours.⟩ — see FIELD 1
5 an immaterial thing upon which something else rests ⟨argued that equality was the *ground* for the new law⟩ — see BASE 1
6 the loose surface material in which plants naturally grow ⟨I stuck the shovel in the *ground* and went inside for a glass of water.⟩ — see DIRT 1
7 the physical conditions or features that form the setting against which something is viewed ⟨Take her picture against a blue *ground* in order to bring out her blue eyes.⟩ — see BACKGROUND 1
8 the solid part of our planet's surface as distinguished from the sea and air ⟨One of the Nordic creation myths states that the *ground* was formed by the body of the giant Ymir when he was killed by Odin and his brothers.⟩ — see EARTH 2

ground *vb* to find a basis ⟨You're *grounding* your entire case on circumstantial evidence.⟩ — see BASE

grounded *adj* resting on the shore or bottom of a body of water ⟨Once his boat was *grounded*, all he could do was wait for the tide to come back in and raise it off the sand bar.⟩ — see AGROUND

groundless *adj* having no basis in reason or fact ⟨Please stop making *groundless* accusations against people you happen to dislike.⟩ ⟨Fears of a strike proved *groundless*.⟩
synonyms invalid, nonvalid, unfounded, unreasonable, unsubstantiated, unsupported, unwarranted
related words illogical, irrational, nonlogical, unconscionable, unsound; fallacious, false, misled, wrong; gratuitous, uncalled-for, unnecessary; flimsy, implausible, misleading, specious, unconvincing, untenable, weak; ill-advised, unreasoned; inconsistent; absurd, asinine, brainless, fatuous, foolish, half-witted, harebrained, meaningless, nonsensical, preposterous, senseless, silly, simpleminded, stupid, unwise; wacky (*also* whacky)
near antonyms validated, verified; confirmed, corroborated; informed, logical, rational; commonsense, sane, sensible, sober, wise; actual, genuine, real, true; certain, sure; clear, cogent, compelling, convincing, credible, persuasive, plausible, satisfying, solid, sound
antonyms good, hard, just, justified, reasonable, reasoned, substantiated, valid, well-founded

ground plan *n* a method worked out in advance for achieving some objective ⟨Their *ground plan* is first to finish college and then get married.⟩ — see PLAN 1

ground rule *n* a statement spelling out the proper procedure or conduct for an activity ⟨Before the debate begins, let's lay out some *ground rules*.⟩ — see RULE 1

groundwork *n* an immaterial thing upon which something else rests ⟨They had collectively laid the *groundwork* for a new kind of art.⟩ — see BASE 1

ground zero *n* a thing or place that is of greatest importance to an activity or interest ⟨a city that was once *ground zero* for the insurance industry⟩ — see CENTER 1

group *vb* **1** to arrange or assign according to type ⟨You should first *group* the invertebrates by genus.⟩ — see CLASSIFY 1
2 to bring together in one body or place ⟨*Group* the kids together and we'll see who's missing.⟩ — see GATHER 1

group *n* **1** a number of things considered as a unit ⟨Car buffs stood around admiring a *group* of classic cars in the parking lot.⟩
synonyms array, assemblage, band, bank, batch, battery, block, bunch, clot, clump, cluster, clutch, collection, grouping, huddle, knot, lot, muster, package, parcel, passel, set, suite
related words accumulation, aggregate, aggregation, conglomeration; agglomeration, assortment, hodgepodge, jumble, miscellany, mixture, odds and ends, sundries, variety; cycle, run, series, suit
phrases the whole kit and caboodle
near antonyms entity, item, single, unit
2 a usually small number of persons considered as a unit ⟨The next tour *group* was being seated for dinner.⟩
synonyms array, band, batch, battery, body, bunch, cluster, clutch, consort, crop, grouping, huddle, knot, lot, parcel, party, passel
related words assembly, collective, congregation, gathering, muster, organization; circle, clan, clique, coterie, fellowship, gang, ring, round, set; faction, guild (*also* gild), order, school, sect; crew, outfit, phalanx, task force, team; alliance, bloc, coalition, confederacy, confederation, federation, league, union; battalion, squadron; bevy, brood, covey
phrases the whole kit and caboodle
near antonyms individual, single
3 one of the units into which a whole is divided on the basis of a common characteristic ⟨a government that is representative of all social *groups*⟩ — see CLASS 2

grouping *n* **1** a number of things considered as a unit ⟨the standard *grouping* for an average living room: sofa, matching wing chairs, and the inevitable coffee table⟩ — see GROUP 1
2 a usually small number of persons considered as a unit ⟨The next *grouping* of tourists can start the house tour as soon as the last bunch leaves.⟩ — see GROUP 2

grouse *vb* to express dissatisfaction, pain, or resentment usually tiresomely ⟨He hasn't stopped *grousing* since we started this vacation.⟩ — see COMPLAIN

grouse *n* an expression of dissatisfaction, pain, or resentment ⟨a forum in which employees can air their *grouses*⟩ — see COMPLAINT 1

grouser *n* an irritable and complaining person ⟨She had the misfortune of waiting on a table full of *grousers*, who sent her back to the kitchen constantly and then refused to tip her.⟩ — see GROUCH 1

grovel *vb* **1** to draw back or crouch down in fearful submission ⟨peasants *groveling* before the king⟩ — see COWER
2 to move slowly with the body close to the ground ⟨Because of their anatomy, bats can only *grovel* while moving along the ground.⟩ — see CRAWL 1

grow *vb* **1** to look after or assist the growth of by labor and care ⟨a dedicated home gardener who *grows* tomatoes in her small garden every summer⟩
synonyms crop, cultivate, culture, dress, promote, raise, rear, tend
related words breed, produce, propagate; plant, sow; gather, glean, harvest, reap; germinate, quicken, ripen, root
near antonyms kill; dig, extirpate, pick, pluck, pull (up), uproot; cut, hay, mow
2 to become mature ⟨You've *grown* so much since we last saw each other.⟩ — see MATURE
3 to eventually have as a state or quality ⟨He will *grow* angry if we don't answer his question.⟩ — see BECOME

grow (in) *vb* to gradually increase in ⟨You've *grown in* wisdom over the years.⟩ — see GAIN 1

grower *n* a person who cultivates the land and grows crops on it ⟨Orange *growers* in Florida had a bumper crop.⟩ — see FARMER

growl *vb* **1** to express dissatisfaction, pain, or resentment usually tiresomely ⟨He was *growling* about how much work he had to do.⟩ — see COMPLAIN
2 to make a long loud deep noise or cry ⟨The neighbor's dog *growls* every time we pass the house.⟩ — see ROAR 1
3 to make a low heavy rolling sound ⟨I'm sorry my stomach is *growling*, but I'm just really hungry.⟩ — see RUMBLE

growler *n* an irritable and complaining person ⟨We can't figure out why our very happy and optimistic friend is dating that chronic *growler*.⟩ — see GROUCH 1

grown–up *adj* relating to or typical of adults; displaying proper maturity ⟨They're *grown-up* enough to deal with the situation.⟩ — see ADULT 1

grown–up *n* a fully grown person ⟨Once you turn 12, you get to eat with the *grown-ups* at Thanksgiving.⟩ — see ADULT

growth *n* **1** an abnormal mass of tissue ⟨The vet found a *growth* on the dog's neck under her collar.⟩
synonyms excrescence, lump, neoplasm, tumor
related words outgrowth; cancer, carcinoma, lymphoma, malignancy, melanoma, polyp; cyst, tubercle, wart
2 the act or process of going from the simple or basic to the complex or advanced ⟨the *growth* of the gambling industry into an economic mainstay in some locations⟩ — see DEVELOPMENT 1
3 the process of becoming mature ⟨Her reflections and mature behavior certainly demonstrate just how much emotional *growth* took place last summer.⟩ — see MATURATION

grow up *vb* to become mature ⟨Everyone has to *grow up* at some point in their lives.⟩ — see MATURE

grub *n* **1** substances intended to be eaten ⟨After the game, we headed to the diner for some hearty *grub*.⟩ — see FOOD
2 a person who does very hard or dull work ⟨You may have to spend some time working as a *grub* before challenging work comes your way.⟩ — see DRUDGE

grub *vb* to devote serious and sustained effort ⟨*grubbing* away at the yard work before the first snow of the season⟩ — see LABOR

grubber *n* a person who does very hard or dull work ⟨a team of hardworking *grubbers*⟩ — see DRUDGE

grubbiness *n* the state or quality of being dirty ⟨The *grubbiness* and general dilapidation of the old house discouraged potential buyers.⟩ — see DIRTINESS

grubby *adj* **1** not clean ⟨Clean off those *grubby* hands before you touch anything.⟩ — see DIRTY 1
2 arousing or deserving of one's loathing and disgust ⟨That's a *grubby* reason to stop talking to a friend.⟩ — see CONTEMPTIBLE 1

grudge *n* **1** a lingering ill will towards a person for a real or imagined wrong ⟨He's had a *grudge* against her ever since she told on him.⟩
synonyms grievance, resentment, score
related words condemnation; offense (*or* offence), umbrage; complaint; dudgeon, huff, peeve, pique; despite, hatefulness, malevolence, malice, maliciousness, meanness, nastiness, spite, spitefulness, spleen, venom, viciousness; animosity, antagonism, antipathy, bitterness, enmity, hostility, rancor
2 a deep-seated ill will ⟨There's been a *grudge* between the two families for years.⟩ — see ENMITY

grueling *or* **gruelling** *adj* **1** requiring considerable physical or mental effort ⟨Running a marathon is *grueling*.⟩ — see HARD 2
2 requiring much time, effort, or careful attention ⟨Cutting diamonds can be *grueling* work.⟩ — see DEMANDING 1

gruesome *also* **grewsome** *adj* extremely disturbing or repellent ⟨I didn't stick around to hear the *gruesome* details of the car accident.⟩ — see HORRIBLE 1

gruesomeness *n* the quality of inspiring intense dread or dismay ⟨permanently scarred by the sheer *gruesomeness* of what she had witnessed during the war⟩ — see HORROR 1

gruff *adj* **1** harsh and dry in sound ⟨She had a *gruff* speaking voice, but a surprisingly sweet singing voice.⟩ — see HOARSE
2 harsh and threatening in manner or appearance ⟨I didn't exchange one word with the *gruff* mountaineer who sat next to me in the diner.⟩ — see GRIM 1

grumble *n* an expression of dissatisfaction, pain, or resentment ⟨a chorus of moans and *grumbles* when they found out that the overnight camping trip had been cancelled⟩ — see COMPLAINT 1

grumble *vb* **1** to express dissatisfaction, pain, or resentment usually tiresomely ⟨He *grumbled* about how sore his feet were after standing all day.⟩ — see COMPLAIN
2 to make a low heavy rolling sound ⟨heavily loaded trucks *grumbling* as they passed over the steel bridge⟩ — see RUMBLE

grumbler *n* **1** an irritable and complaining person ⟨The tour would have been okay if I hadn't been paired up with a *grumbler* who whined through the whole thing.⟩ — see GROUCH 1

2 a person who makes frequent complaints usually about little things 〈How can you be such a *grumbler* when so much in your life is going well?〉 — see CRYBABY

grump *n* an irritable and complaining person 〈He's a real *grump* in the morning.〉 — see GROUCH 1

grump *vb* **1** to express dissatisfaction, pain, or resentment usually tiresomely 〈Those incessantly *grumping* patients were generally ignored by the nursing home staff.〉 — see COMPLAIN

2 to silently go about in a bad mood 〈He's been *grumping* about the house all morning because the golf tournament got rained out.〉 — see SULK

grumpiness *n* readiness to show annoyance or impatience 〈I don't want your *grumpiness* to spoil the evening.〉 — see PETULANCE

grumpy *adj* **1** easily irritated or annoyed 〈a *grumpy* neighbor whose yard we had long ago learned not to trespass〉 — see IRRITABLE

2 given to complaining a lot 〈The baby's sure to be *grumpy* if she doesn't get her afternoon nap.〉 — see FUSSY 1

grungy *adj* **1** not clean 〈After playing outside, the kids came in *grungy* and in need of a good bath.〉 — see DIRTY 1

2 showing signs of advanced wear and tear and neglect 〈Even though this *grungy* sweatshirt is falling apart, it's still my favorite.〉 — see SHABBY 1

grunt *n* **1** speech that is not clear enough to be understood 〈Preoccupied with what he was doing, the mechanic gave only a *grunt* when I asked when the car would be ready.〉 — see MUMBLE

2 a person who does very hard or dull work 〈We have an opening in the warehouse if you don't mind doing *grunt* work.〉 — see DRUDGE

grunt *vb* to speak softly and unclearly 〈He was so absorbed with the video game that when asked what he wanted for dinner, he just *grunted*.〉 — see MUMBLE

grunting *n* speech that is not clear enough to be understood 〈Dad says he talks in his sleep, but really it's just snorts and *grunting*.〉 — see MUMBLE

guarantee *vb* **1** to assume responsibility for the satisfactory quality or performance of 〈The shop will *guarantee* all work done on the car for 30 days.〉 — see WARRANT 1

2 to make sure, certain, or safe 〈I can *guarantee* that you'll feel better after using my product for 30 days.〉 — see ENSURE

3 to state clearly and strongly 〈I *guarantee* that this movie is better than the last one in the series.〉 — see ASSERT 1

guarantee *n* **1** a formal agreement to fulfill an obligation 〈The contractors gave us a written *guarantee* that the work on the house would be done on time.〉

synonyms bond, contract, covenant, deal, guaranty, surety, warranty

related words oath, pledge, troth, vow, word; accord, bargain, compact, concordat, convention, pact, treaty; assurance, insurance, seal; deposit, pawn, security

2 something given or held to assure that the giver will keep a promise 〈You'll have to give your car keys as a *guarantee* that you'll come back.〉 — see PLEDGE 1

guarantor *n* a person who takes the responsibility for some other person or thing 〈The town police force is the *guarantor* of our safety.〉 — see SPONSOR

guaranty *n* **1** a formal agreement to fulfill an obligation 〈This fridge comes with a money-back *guaranty* of complete customer satisfaction.〉 — see GUARANTEE 1

2 something given or held to assure that the giver will keep a promise 〈Couples exchange engagement rings as a symbolic *guaranty* that they will marry.〉 — see PLEDGE 1

guaranty *vb* **1** to make sure, certain, or safe 〈a house *guarantied* against termite damage〉 — see ENSURE

2 to assume responsibility for the satisfactory quality or performance of 〈a watch *guarantied* to be water-resistant to a depth of 100 feet〉 — see WARRANT 1

guard *n* **1** a person or group that watches over someone or something 〈I checked in with the security *guard* at the gate.〉

synonyms custodian, guardian, keeper, lookout, picket, sentinel, sentry, warden, warder, watch, watcher, watchman

related words patrol, spotter, surveillant, watchdog; bodyguard, convoy, defender, escort, honor guard; gatekeeper

2 a position of readiness to oppose actual or expected attack 〈Be on your *guard* against snakes in the swamp.〉 — see DEFENSIVE

3 a protective device (as on a weapon) to prevent accidental operation 〈I slid the *guard* into place over the chainsaw chain.〉 — see SAFETY 2

4 means or method of defending 〈The boxer's sparring partner managed to get a blow in under his left *guard*.〉 — see DEFENSE 1

5 one that accompanies another for protection, guidance, or as a courtesy 〈The honor *guards* raised their sabers as the happy couple descended the church steps.〉 — see ESCORT

6 someone that protects 〈a battalion of burly *guards* surrounding the celebrity〉 — see PROTECTOR

guard *vb* **1** to drive danger or attack away from 〈Their job is to *guard* the quarterback so he doesn't get sacked.〉 — see DEFEND 1

2 to disallow entry into (a place) by means of a physical barrier at the entry point 〈A fire-breathing dragon *guarded* the entrance to the castle.〉 — see CLOSE (OFF)

guard (against) *vb* to be cautious of or on guard against 〈Unfortunately, you have to *guard against* theft while you're traveling.〉 — see BEWARE (OF)

guarded *adj* having or showing a close attentiveness to avoiding danger or trouble 〈a *guarded* man who knew better than to reveal such delicate information〉 〈*guarded* actions〉 — see CAREFUL 1

guardian *n* **1** a person or group that watches over someone or something 〈The state became his *guardian* when he was put into protective custody.〉 — see GUARD 1

2 a person who takes care of a property sometimes for an absent owner 〈The *guardians* of the summer estate awaited the return of the tycoon.〉 — see CUSTODIAN 1

3 someone that protects 〈The editor defended his newspaper's unrelenting exposure of government corruption, arguing that it is journalism's role to act as a *guardian* of democracy.〉 — see PROTECTOR

guardianship *n* responsibility for the safety and well-being of someone or something 〈He gave the *guardianship* of his estate to his children.〉 〈Dad has *guardianship* of the dogs while I'm away on vacation.〉 — see CUSTODY

guardrail *n* a protective barrier consisting of a horizontal bar and its supports 〈The car ran off the road, but fortunately it only hit the *guardrail*.〉 — see RAILING

guardroom *n* a place of confinement for persons held in lawful custody 〈hauled the prisoners of war into the *guardroom* and sent for the doctor on duty〉 — see JAIL

guess *n* an opinion or judgment based on little or no evidence 〈If you don't know the answer for sure, just make a *guess*.〉 — see CONJECTURE

guess *vb* **1** to form an opinion from little or no evidence 〈Can you *guess* how many people were there?〉

synonyms assume, conjecture, imagine, presume, speculate, suppose, surmise, suspect *related words* conclude, deduce, gather, infer; hypothecate, theorize; believe, conceive, expect, judge, reckon [*chiefly dialect*], take, think

near antonyms demonstrate, document, establish, prove, substantiate, validate; ascertain, determine, find out, learn

2 to decide the size, amount, number, or distance of (something) without actual measurement ⟨I would *guess* the road goes for about two miles before you have to take a left.⟩ — see ESTIMATE 2

3 to have as an opinion ⟨I never would have *guessed* that she was capable of such a thing.⟩ — see BELIEVE 2

guest *n* **1** a person who visits another ⟨We invited the afternoon *guests* to stay for dinner.⟩

synonyms caller, frequenter, visitant, visitor

related words houseguest; company; invitee; crasher, hanger-on

near antonyms denizen, dweller, habitant, inhabitant, occupant, resident, resider; cohost, cohostess, host, hostess

2 a person who buys a product or uses a service from a business ⟨The headwaiter will seat the *guests* as soon as the waitress clears and sets a table for them.⟩ — see CUSTOMER 1

guffaw *n* an explosive sound that is a sign of amusement ⟨He managed to keep a straight face for a minute before he let loose with a loud *guffaw*.⟩ — see LAUGH 1

guidance *n* **1** an opinion suggesting a wise or proper course of action ⟨I sought career *guidance* from the college counselor.⟩ — see ADVICE

2 the act or activity of looking after and making decisions about something ⟨People felt secure under the president's cautious *guidance* of foreign affairs.⟩ — see CONDUCT 1

3 the duty or function of watching or guarding for the sake of proper direction or control ⟨an adviser who undertakes the *guidance* of his students' academic careers⟩ — see SUPERVISION 1

guide *n* one that accompanies another for protection, guidance, or as a courtesy ⟨We followed our *guide* through the dangerous mountain trails.⟩ — see ESCORT

guide *vb* **1** to give advice and instruction to (someone) regarding the course or process to be followed ⟨The pastry chef *guided* her through the creation of the wedding cake, showing her how to ice the layers, fashion the elaborate decorations, and assemble the whole shebang.⟩

synonyms coach, counsel, lead, mentor, pilot, shepherd, show, tutor

related words godfather; direct, engineer, steer, sway; accompany, attend, chaperone (*or* chaperon), convoy, escort, see, squire; oversee, superintend, supervise; drill, train; brief, enlighten, inform; instruct, school, teach, tutor; inculcate, indoctrinate; cultivate, foster, nurture

phrases walk through

2 to look after and make decisions about ⟨Parents thought the new superintendent would *guide* the school system well.⟩ — see CONDUCT 1

3 to point out the way for (someone) especially from a position in front ⟨I would be happy to *guide* you folks to the historic part of town.⟩ — see LEAD 1

guidon *n* a piece of cloth with a special design that is used as an emblem or for signaling ⟨Each army command unit flew a different color *guidon*, though they were all the same shape.⟩ — see FLAG 1

guild *also* **gild** *n* a group of persons formally joined together for some common interest ⟨After his apprenticeship, he was able to join the stonemasons' *guild*.⟩ — see ASSOCIATION 2

guile *n* **1** skill in achieving one's ends through indirect,

subtle, or underhanded means ⟨a shady salesman who usually relies on a combination of quick thinking and *guile*⟩ — see CUNNING 1

2 the inclination or practice of misleading others through lies or trickery ⟨a person so full of *guile* he can't even be trusted to give you the correct time of day⟩ — see DECEIT 1

guileful *adj* **1** clever at attaining one's ends by indirect and often deceptive means ⟨a *guileful* plan to outmaneuver his opponent⟩ — see ARTFUL 1

2 given to or marked by cheating and deception ⟨I received a *guileful* answer when I asked the dealer if the used car had ever been in a collision.⟩ — see DISHONEST 2

guileless *adj* free from any intent to deceive or impress others ⟨She was an easygoing, *guileless* young woman who was comfortable just being herself.⟩

synonyms artless, genuine, honest, ingenuous, innocent, naive (*or* naïve), natural, real, simple, sincere, true, unaffected, unpretending, unpretentious

related words childlike, dewy-eyed, gee-whiz, impressionable, inexperienced, malleable, persuadable, persuasible, simpleminded, unsophisticated, unworldly, wide-eyed; spontaneous, unforced, unstudied; candid, direct, frank, free, free-spoken, open, openhearted, plain, plainspoken, single-minded, straight, straightforward, unguarded; trustful, trusting; exploitable, gullible (*also* gullable), susceptible, unwary

phrases on the level

near antonyms critical, cynical, mistrustful, skeptical, suspicious, wary; cosmopolitan, sophisticated, worldly, worldly-wise; civilized, cultivated, cultured, polished, refined; crooked, deceitful, deceptive, devious, double-dealing, hypocritical, manipulative, two-faced; arch, calculating, canny, crafty, cunning, designing, foxy, knavish, sharp, shifty, shrewd, slick, slippery, sly, subtle, tricky, underhanded, wily; flattering, mealymouthed, smooth, sycophantic, unctuous

antonyms affected, artful, artificial, assuming, dishonest, dissembling, dissimulating, fake, false, guileful, insincere, phony (*also* phoney), pretentious

guilelessly *adv* without any attempt to impress by deception or exaggeration ⟨She's a naturally sweet child, *guilelessly* unaware of how adorable she is.⟩ — see NATURALLY 3

guilelessness *n* the quality or state of being simple and sincere ⟨The small-town boy's *guilelessness* is endearing, but it may not serve him well in the ruthless big city.⟩ — see NAÏVETÉ 1

guillotine *vb* to cut off the head of ⟨French Revolutionary forces captured and *guillotined* countless aristocrats in the chaotic period following the downfall of the monarchy.⟩ — see DECAPITATE

guilt *n* **1** a feeling of responsibility for wrongdoing ⟨He was wracked with *guilt* after he accidentally broke his sister's antique grandfather clock.⟩

synonyms contriteness, contrition, penitence, regret, remorse, remorsefulness, repentance, rue, self-reproach, shame

related words compunction, misgiving, prick, qualm, scruple; blame, culpability, fault; liability, rap, responsibility; chagrin, embarrassment; anguish, distress, grief, sadness, sorrow; bloodguilt, bloodguiltiness; excuses, hand-wringing, mea culpa

antonyms impenitence, remorselessness

2 responsibility for wrongdoing or failure ⟨The chief financial officer was saddled with the *guilt* for the company's failure.⟩ — see BLAME 1

guiltless *adj* free from guilt or blame ⟨If the jury acquits him, he is *guiltless* in the eyes of the law.⟩ — see INNOCENT 2

guiltlessness *n* the quality or state of being free from guilt or blame ⟨Her *guiltlessness* is obvious, since she couldn't possibly have been at the scene of the crime.⟩ — see INNOCENCE 1

guilty *adj* suffering from or expressive of a feeling of responsibility for wrongdoing ⟨She was burdened with a *guilty* conscience after stealing the newspaper from the newsstand.⟩

synonyms ashamed, shamed, shamefaced

related words apologetic, contrite, penitent, remorseful, repentant, sorry; regretful, rueful; penitential; blushing, chagrined, embarrassed, hangdog, sheepish; blamable, blameworthy, culpable

near antonyms impenitent, remorseless, unapologetic, unrepentant; brazen, cheeky, impudent; blameless, guiltless, innocent

antonyms shameless, unashamed

guise *n* **1** a display of emotion or behavior that is insincere or intended to deceive ⟨My new neighbor began seeking my company under the *guise* of friendship, but he turned out to be a chronic moocher.⟩ — see MASQUERADE

2 clothing chosen as appropriate for a specific situation ⟨She felt as though she should be wearing some sort of Germanic *guise*, complete with dirndl, for the fall festival featuring traditional German food and drink.⟩ — see OUTFIT 1

3 clothing put on to hide one's true identity or imitate someone or something else ⟨He snuck into the castle to rescue Ivanhoe in the *guise* of a priest coming to give Ivanhoe his last rites.⟩ — see DISGUISE 1

4 outward and often deceptive indication ⟨The teacher got the kindergartners to do their classroom chores in the *guise* of a game.⟩ — see APPEARANCE 2

gulch *n* a narrow opening between hillsides or mountains that can be used for passage ⟨The *gulch* floods in the spring with the runoff from the mountains, so wait until later in the summer to hike it.⟩ — see CANYON

gulf *n* **1** a part of a body of water that extends beyond the general shoreline ⟨We dipped our feet in the warm waters of the *gulf*.⟩

synonyms arm, bay, bight, cove, creek [*chiefly British*], estuary, firth, fjord (*also* fiord), inlet, loch [*Scottish*]

related words harbor, port, road(s), roadstead; narrow, sound, strait; backwater, slough (*also* slew *or* slue)

2 an immeasurable depth or space ⟨A great *gulf* of time and space separates us from the first inhabitants of North America.⟩ — see ABYSS

3 a narrow opening between hillsides or mountains that can be used for passage ⟨The *gulf* was too wide to cross, so we had to hike down into it and go through it.⟩ — see CANYON

4 an open space in a barrier (as a wall or hedge) ⟨A wide *gulf* in the defensive wall meant the city was in grave danger.⟩ — see GAP 1

5 water moving rapidly in a circle with a hollow in the center ⟨The doomed ship was sucked into the *gulf* and consigned to Davy Jones's locker.⟩ — see WHIRLPOOL

gulf *vb* to cover with a flood ⟨With the administration *gulfed* by so many real problems, it's absurd for the president to concern himself with this nonissue.⟩ — see FLOOD

gull *n* one who is easily deceived or cheated ⟨a *gull* who believed their guarantees of easy money⟩ — see ¹DUPE

gull *vb* to cause to believe what is untrue ⟨We were *gulled* into believing that if we answered the e-mail, we'd somehow become millionaires, but instead we just got put on a list for junk mail.⟩ — see DECEIVE

gullibility *n* readiness to believe the claims of others without sufficient evidence ⟨I kidded her about her well-known *gullibility* by repeatedly offering to sell her a bridge.⟩ — see CREDULITY

gullible *also* **gullable** *adj* readily taken advantage of ⟨He thought his grandmother was *gullible*, but she was sharper than he was in many ways.⟩ — see EASY 2

gulp *n* the portion of a serving of a beverage that is swallowed at one time ⟨The runner took a big *gulp* of water.⟩ — see DRINK 2

gulp *vb* **1** to swallow in liquid form ⟨hastily *gulping* down the last of her tea before rushing out the door⟩ — see DRINK 1

2 to swallow or eat greedily ⟨You never taste your food—you just *gulp* it!⟩ — see GOBBLE

gummy *adj* tending to adhere to objects upon contact ⟨The outside of the bottle was *gummy* with old dribbles of salad oil.⟩ — see STICKY 1

gun *vb* to strike with a missile from a gun ⟨traded stories of the Wild West, when outlaws *gunned* men down⟩ — see SHOOT 3

gun *n* **1** a portable weapon from which a shot is discharged by gunpowder ⟨While her father preferred hunting with a crossbow, she preferred a *gun*.⟩

synonyms arm, firearm, piece, small arm

related words derringer, forty-five (*or* .45), gat [*slang*], handgun, revolver, rod [*slang*], sidearm, six-gun, six-shooter, zip gun; self-loader, semiautomatic; breechloader, culverin, fieldpiece, firelock, flintlock, harquebus (*or* arquebus), matchlock, musket, rifle, shotgun, smoothbore, twenty-two (*or* .22); AK-47, assault rifle, assault weapon, automatic, carbine, machine gun, machine pistol, repeater, submachine gun, tommy gun; speargun

2 guns *pl* large firearms (as cannon or rockets) ⟨The field commander called for the big *guns* to be deployed for the full-scale assault.⟩ — see ARTILLERY

gung ho *adj* showing urgent desire or interest ⟨He was *gung ho* about his accounting class.⟩ — see EAGER

gurgle *vb* to flow in a broken irregular stream ⟨The tiny stream *gurgled* down the rocky slope and joined the larger river at the bottom of the hill.⟩

synonyms bubble, dribble, lap, plash, ripple, splash, trickle, wash

related words eddy, purl, swirl; swash, swish, whish; drip, drop; gush, jet, rush, spew, spout, spurt, squirt

near antonyms run

antonyms pour, roll, stream

guru *n* **1** a person with a high level of knowledge or skill in a field ⟨one of those weather *gurus* that the television networks always drag out whenever there's a big blizzard brewing⟩ — see EXPERT

2 one who brings an art or science to full realization ⟨the fitness *guru* who developed the hot new regimen⟩ — see EXPONENT 2

gush *n* **1** a flowing or going out ⟨The dam burst with a stupendous *gush* of water.⟩ — see OUTFLOW

2 a sudden intense expression of strong feeling ⟨With a *gush* of tears, he told a story about his beloved late grandfather.⟩ — see OUTBURST 1

gush *vb* **1** to flow out in great quantities or with force ⟨The dam cracked and water *gushed* from the break.⟩

synonyms jet, pour, rush, spew, spout, spurt, squirt

related words cascade, issue, roll, run, stream; plash, slosh, splash, wash; surge, swell; flush, sluice; deluge, drown, engulf, flood, inundate, overflow, overwhelm, submerge, submerse, swamp

near antonyms spatter, sprinkle; bleed, exude, leak, ooze, percolate, seep, strain, weep

antonyms dribble, drip, drop, trickle

2 to make an exaggerated display of affection or enthusi-

asm ⟨He *gushed* about his favorite basketball player, calling him "the best there ever was."⟩
synonyms drool, enthuse, fuss, rave, rhapsodize, slobber
related words dote (on); fawn; emote

gushing *adj* **1** overly or insincerely flattering ⟨She heaped disgustingly *gushing* praise on her boss's very modest contribution to the project.⟩ — see FULSOME 1
2 pouring forth in great amounts ⟨The *gushing* water from the opened fire hydrant reduced water pressure to a dangerous level.⟩ — see PROFUSE

gust *n* **1** a sudden brief rush of wind ⟨A *gust* tore her umbrella from her grip and blew it down the street.⟩
synonyms blast, blow, flurry, williwaw
related words breeze, zephyr; current, draft; air, breath, waft; puff, whiff; bluster, gale, hurricane, squall, tempest, tornado, windstorm; northeaster, norther, northerly, northwester, southeaster, southwester, westerly
2 a sudden intense expression of strong feeling ⟨The stressed-out coworker cried out with a *gust* of emotion that we had never witnessed before.⟩ — see OUTBURST 1

gusty *adj* marked by strong wind or more wind than usual ⟨Watch out for *gusty* conditions as the storm blows in.⟩ — see ¹WINDY 1

gut *n* **1 guts** *pl* the internal organs of the body ⟨The student dissected the frog and looked at its *guts* with a mixture of fascination and disgust.⟩
synonyms entrails, innards, inside(s), viscera, vitals
related words bowel(s), intestine(s); chitterlings (*or* chitlins), giblet(s), variety meat
2 guts *pl* strength of mind to carry on in spite of danger ⟨It took a lot of *guts* to rush into that burning building and save her cat.⟩ — see COURAGE
3 guts *pl* the strength of mind that enables a person to endure pain or hardship ⟨She had the *guts* to keep running the race even though she felt like quitting.⟩ — see FORTITUDE
4 the part of the body between the chest and the pelvis ⟨He felt a pain in his *gut*.⟩ — see STOMACH 1
5 an enlarged or bulging abdomen ⟨a bulging *gut* following a large meal⟩ — see POTBELLY
6 the seat of one's deepest thoughts and emotions ⟨The film packs an emotional wallop that the viewer will feel in his *gut*.⟩ — see CORE 1

gut *vb* to take the internal organs out of ⟨You'll need to *gut* the fish and wash it out before you can cook it.⟩
synonyms clean, disembowel, draw, eviscerate

related words bone, dress; cut, excise, extract, remove, withdraw, yank; transplant

gutsy *adj* **1** inclined or willing to take risks ⟨a *gutsy* coach willing to let her team improvise on the court⟩ — see BOLD 1
2 feeling or displaying no fear by temperament ⟨They were *gutsy* enough to attempt a rescue on their own.⟩ — see BRAVE 1

gutter *n* **1** a pipe or channel for carrying off water from a roof ⟨One of his chores is to clean leaves and sticks out of the *gutters* before winter sets in.⟩
synonyms drainpipe, eaves trough, spout, trough, waterspout
related words drain, flume, sluice; conduit, duct; aqueduct
2 a long narrow channel dug in the earth ⟨rainwater running off the road into the *gutters*⟩ — see DITCH

guy *n* **1** a member of the human race ⟨What would you *guys* like to order?⟩ — see HUMAN
2 an adult male human being ⟨He was not the kind of *guy* she ever thought she'd date.⟩ — see MAN 1

guzzle *vb* **1** to swallow in liquid form ⟨He *guzzled* my soda before I could stop him.⟩ — see DRINK 1
2 to partake excessively of alcoholic beverages ⟨*guzzling* a cold one after working outside on a hot day⟩ — see DRINK 2

gym *n* a building or room used for sports activities and exercising ⟨He decided to get up early and go to the *gym* to lift weights.⟩
synonyms gymnasium, spa
related words arena, bowl, coliseum, colosseum, stadium

gymnasium *n* a building or room used for sports activities and exercising ⟨Since it was raining, the kids had recess in the *gymnasium*.⟩ — see GYM

gymnast *n* one who performs feats of physical strength, balance, and agility on special apparatus ⟨the years of training required to become a champion *gymnast*⟩ — see ACROBAT 1

gyrate *vb* to move in circles around an axis or center ⟨The gyroscope got its name for the way the disk inside the instrument *gyrates* around an axis.⟩ — see SPIN 1

gyration *n* a rapid turning about on an axis or central point ⟨I was dizzy from the spirally *gyrations* of the roller coaster.⟩ — see SPIN 1

H

habit *n* **1** a usual manner of behaving or doing ⟨It was his *habit* to rise early.⟩
synonyms custom, fashion, pattern, practice (*also* practise), ritual, trick, way, wont
related words disposition; bent, inclination, proclivity, set, tendency, tenor, turn; bag, convention, form, mode, style; usage, use; deportment, manners, mores; drill, groove, jog trot, regime (*also* régime), regimen, rote, routine, rut; affectation, airs, pose; attribute, characteristic, mark, trait
2 the type of body that a person has ⟨an imposing man of vigorous *habit*⟩ — see PHYSIQUE

habitable *adj* suitable for living in ⟨The frigid Arctic is not *habitable* for amphibians and reptiles—or for humans, either, for that matter.⟩ — see LIVABLE

habitant *n* one who lives permanently in a place ⟨The *habitants* of Indiana are nicknamed "Hoosiers."⟩ — see INHABITANT

habitat *n* the place where a plant or animal is usually or naturally found ⟨A forest in California is set aside to preserve the unique brushy, rugged *habitat* required by nesting California condors.⟩ — see HOME 2

habitation *n* the place where one lives ⟨Even though they spend most of their time at their condo in Florida, they still consider their farmhouse in Nebraska their permanent *habitation*.⟩ — see HOME 1

habitual *adj* **1** being such by habit and not likely to change ⟨She admits she's a *habitual* procrastinator, but she still manages to meet all her deadlines.⟩

synonyms chronic, confirmed, inveterate

related words incorrigible, unreconstructed, unregenerate; born, natural; persistent, regular, repeat, serial, steady, unchanging, unfailing; addicted; accustomed, habituated, used, wonted; deep-rooted, deep-seated, entrenched (*also* intrenched), inbred, inherent, innate, intrinsic; apt, inclined, prone

near antonyms unaccustomed, unused; intermittent, occasional

2 appearing or occurring repeatedly from time to time ⟨Her supervisor warned her that she could be fired for *habitual* tardiness.⟩ — see REGULAR 1

habituated *adj* being in the habit or custom ⟨Not only did the early-morning anchorman become *habituated* to getting up early, he found he actually liked it.⟩ — see ACCUSTOMED

hacienda *n* a large impressive residence ⟨The sugar baron spared no expense in building a grand *hacienda* on his plantation near Cuernavaca.⟩ — see MANSION

hack *adj* used or heard so often as to be dull ⟨The abrupt revelation of an enemy masquerading as a friend is such a *hack* plot twist.⟩ — see STALE 1

¹hack *n* **1** a V-shaped cut usually on an edge or a surface ⟨Smallish *hacks* made in the bark of the trees marked the trail through the forest.⟩ — see NOTCH 1

2 a hard strike with a part of the body or an instrument ⟨completely stunned by a vicious *hack* across the neck⟩ — see ¹BLOW

²hack *n* **1** an automobile that carries passengers for a fare usually determined by the distance traveled ⟨After a week of hailing *hacks* and inhabiting hotels, the sales rep was happy to be home.⟩ — see TAXICAB

2 a person who lacks experience and competence in an art or science ⟨Is he really any good at the piano or just a *hack*?⟩ — see AMATEUR 2

hack *vb* **1** to deal with (something) usually skillfully or efficiently ⟨I have no doubt that she can *hack* a job with that many responsibilities.⟩ — see HANDLE 1

2 to put up with (something painful or difficult) ⟨She's not sure she can *hack* that miserable job much longer.⟩ — see BEAR 2

hackney *adj* used or heard so often as to be dull ⟨She quickly learned to ignore her children's *hackney* complaints like "It isn't fair" and "Why me?"⟩ — see STALE 1

hackney *vb* to use so much as to make less appealing ⟨Advertisers have *hackneyed* the word "revolutionary" so much that it now just means that a product is new.⟩

synonyms stereotype

related words bore, exhaust, overdo; coarsen; deplete, jade, tire, wear out; popularize

hackneyed *adj* used or heard so often as to be dull ⟨It's *hackneyed*, but true—the more you save the more you earn.⟩ — see STALE 1

hag *n* a woman believed to have often harmful supernatural powers ⟨falsely accused of being a *hag* who had caused the plague⟩ — see WITCH 1

haggard *adj* suffering extreme weight loss as a result of hunger or disease ⟨The rescued hiker appeared *haggard* and worn after a week in the woods.⟩ — see EMACIATED

haggle *vb* to talk over or dispute the terms of a purchase ⟨Dan had to *haggle* to get his friend to sell his guitar for 50 bucks.⟩ — see BARGAIN 1

¹hail *n* **1** a heavy fall of objects ⟨A *hail* of small stones warned them of the oncoming avalanche.⟩ — see RAIN 2

2 a rapid or overwhelming outpouring of many things at once ⟨Even under the *hail* of angry questions, the press secretary stayed cool.⟩ — see BARRAGE

²hail *n* range of hearing ⟨Stay within *hail* of the restaurant's front desk so you'll know when your table is ready.⟩ — see EARSHOT

hail *vb* **1** to declare enthusiastic approval of ⟨The museum director *hailed* the artist's new installation as a groundbreaking work of genius.⟩ — see ACCLAIM

2 to demand or request the presence or service of ⟨Let's *hail* a taxi.⟩ ⟨We *hailed* the waiter for the check.⟩ — see SUMMON 1

hair *n* **1** a very small distance or degree ⟨a race that was won by a *hair*⟩

synonyms ace, hairbreadth (*or* hairsbreadth), hairline, inch, step, stone's throw

related words bit, crumb, dab, iota, jot, minim, mite, particle, smidgen (*also* smidgeon *or* smidgin *or* smidge), trace, trifle

near antonyms infinity

2 a thin, flexible structure that resembles a hair ⟨discovered *hairs* on the plant's stem⟩

synonyms bristle, fiber, thread

related words microfiber; cord, rope, string, wire, yarn; fuzz, tuft

3 the hairy covering of a mammal especially when fine, soft, and thick ⟨has no *hair*, but wears a wig⟩ ⟨a coat made of camel's *hair*⟩ — see FUR 1

hairbreadth *adj* showing little difference in the standing of the competitors ⟨a *hairbreadth* victory, but a victory nevertheless⟩ — see CLOSE 3

hairbreadth *or* **hairsbreadth** *n* a very small distance or degree ⟨just missed the bull's-eye by a *hairbreadth*⟩ — see HAIR 1

hairline *adj* **1** being of less than usual width ⟨A *hairline* crack in the mug, almost too small to notice, was enough to make the mug break when filled with hot tea.⟩ — see NARROW 1

2 made or done with extreme care and accuracy ⟨a *hairline* distinction between her rating of certain things as "necessary" and others as "absolutely necessary"⟩ — see FINE 2

3 meeting the highest standard of accuracy ⟨an ultrasensitive telescope that requires *hairline* placement of the lenses⟩ — see PRECISE 1

hairline *n* a very small distance or degree ⟨The controversial measure passed by a *hairline*, the margin of victory being but a single vote.⟩ — see HAIR 1

hair–raising *adj* **1** causing fear ⟨*hair-raising* stories of headless corpses and disembodied screams⟩ — see FEARFUL 1

2 causing great emotional or mental stimulation ⟨a theme park that is legendary for its lightning-fast roller-coaster and other *hair-raising* rides⟩ — see EXCITING 1

hairsplitting *adj* made or done with extreme care and accuracy ⟨Usage experts have attempted to make some *hairsplitting* distinctions between the two words, but most writers blithely ignore them.⟩ — see FINE 2

hairy *adj* **1** covered with or as if with hair ⟨a *hairy* spider⟩

synonyms bristly, cottony, fleecy, furry, hirsute, rough, shaggy, silky, unshorn, woolly (*also* wooly)

related words bearded, bewhiskered, mustachioed (*also* moustachioed), whiskered; stubbled, stubbly; downy, fluffy, fuzzy, linty, nappy

near antonyms beardless, shaved, shaven

antonyms bald, furless, glabrous, hairless, shorn, smooth

2 made of or resembling hair ⟨I found enough *hairy* clumps around the house to make another cat!⟩ ⟨a *hairy* mass of fiberglass insulation⟩

synonyms furry, fuzzy, rough, shaggy, woolly (*also* wooly)

related words downy, fluffy, nappy, puffy; hairlike

3 requiring exceptional skill or caution in performance or handling ⟨Landing on that airstrip is always a *hairy* proposition.⟩ — see TRICKY 1

4 marked by or causing agitation or uncomfortable feelings ⟨The snowstorm made for a *hairy* commute back home that evening.⟩ — see NERVOUS 2

halcyon *adj* **1** free from storms or physical disturbance ⟨fondly recalled the *halcyon* days after graduating from college⟩ — see CALM 1

2 marked by vigorous growth and well-being especially economically ⟨During those early *halcyon* years the company's potential for growth seemed unlimited.⟩ — see PROSPEROUS 1

hale *adj* enjoying health and vigor ⟨still *hale* and strong at 80, often outdoing his younger golfing buddies⟩ — see HEALTHY 1

hale *vb* to cause to follow by applying steady force on ⟨The fishermen *haled* the huge net onto the deck of the ship.⟩ — see PULL 1

half *adj* lacking some necessary part ⟨*half* measures that did nothing but prolong the problem⟩ — see INCOMPLETE

half *adv* **1** in any way or respect ⟨This cut on your arm isn't *half* as bad as it looks.⟩ — see AT ALL

2 in some measure or degree ⟨What you said is only *half* true.⟩ — see PARTLY

half *n* either of a pair matched in one or more qualities ⟨It's the bottom *half* of the ninth inning, and the Yankees are up at bat.⟩ — see MATE 1

half–baked *adj* showing or marked by a lack of good sense or judgment ⟨He's always got some *half-baked* "solution" to a difficult, complex problem.⟩ — see FOOLISH 1

halfhearted *adj* showing little or no interest or enthusiasm ⟨*halfhearted* applause from the audience⟩ — see TEPID 1

halfway *adj* **1** lacking some necessary part ⟨When *halfway* measures, such as posting signs, failed to keep people off the property, a fence was erected.⟩ — see INCOMPLETE

2 occupying a position equally distant from the ends or extremes ⟨By the time she had reached the *halfway* point, she was ready to quit the marathon.⟩ — see MIDDLE 1

halfway *adv* in some measure or degree ⟨That was a *halfway* decent performance of a difficult piece.⟩ — see PARTLY

half–wit *n* **1** a person who lacks good sense or judgment ⟨Some *half-wit* had left the gate open, and all the sheep had gotten loose.⟩ — see FOOL 1

2 a stupid person ⟨Even a *half-wit* knows that ice cream melts if it's not in the freezer.⟩ — see IDIOT

half–witted *adj* **1** not having or showing an ability to absorb ideas readily ⟨The young genius made his peers seem *half-witted* in comparison.⟩ — see STUPID 1

2 showing or marked by a lack of good sense or judgment ⟨Bill had the *half-witted* idea to try to swim across the raging river, and would have drowned if someone hadn't rescued him.⟩ — see FOOLISH 1

hall *n* **1** the entrance room of a building ⟨The dinner guests hung their coats in the *hall*.⟩

synonyms entry, entryway, foyer, hallway, lobby, vestibule

related words antechamber, anteroom, lounge, waiting room; door, doorway, entrance, portal, threshold

2 a typically long narrow way connecting parts of a building ⟨The bedroom is at the end of the *hall*.⟩

synonyms concourse, corridor, gallery, hallway, passageway

related words arcade, breezeway, cloister, loggia

3 a large room or building for enclosed public gatherings ⟨The concert *hall* was full.⟩

synonyms arena, auditorium, garden, theater (*or* theatre)

related words arena theater, music hall, odeum, playhouse, theater-in-the-round; ballroom; lyceum; chamber, house, senate

4 a centrally located room in a building that serves as a gathering or waiting area or as a passageway into the interior ⟨From the main *hall* of the museum, turn left to see the ancient pottery collection and turn right to see the mummies.⟩ — see FOYER 1

5 a large impressive residence ⟨Lord Plentiworth has opened his family's hereditary home, Richley *Hall*, to visitors on Tuesdays.⟩ — see MANSION

6 a large, magnificent, or massive building ⟨On your right, you will see Parliament *Hall*, a splendid example of Georgian architecture.⟩ — see EDIFICE 1

hallmark *n* **1** a device, design, or figure used as an identifying mark ⟨The *hallmark* of the Primrose Pottery Works is the small rose emblem etched on each piece.⟩ — see EMBLEM

2 something that sets apart an individual from others of the same kind ⟨regards kindness and gentleness as the *hallmarks* of a real man⟩ — see CHARACTERISTIC

hallow *vb* to make holy through prayers or ritual ⟨Lincoln's memorable words at the Gettysburg battlefield, "we cannot dedicate—we cannot consecrate—we cannot *hallow*—this ground"⟩ — see BLESS 1

hallowed *adj* **1** deserving honor and respect especially by reason of age ⟨the college's *hallowed* tradition of ringing the chapel bell one hundred times before commencement ceremonies⟩ — see VENERABLE 1

2 set apart or worthy of veneration by association with God ⟨a church erected on one of Christianity's most *hallowed* sites⟩ — see HOLY 2

3 not to be violated, criticized, or tampered with ⟨*hallowed* traditions that bind the present generation with all those that have gone before⟩ — see SACRED 1

hallowing *n* the act of making something holy through religious ritual ⟨the belief that the marriage ceremony is a *hallowing* of the union between two people⟩ — see CONSECRATION

hallucination *n* **1** a conception or image created by the imagination and having no objective reality ⟨Were the voices real, or merely a *hallucination*?⟩ — see FANTASY 1

2 a false idea or belief ⟨the common *hallucination* that gluttony during the holiday season doesn't have consequences⟩ — see FALLACY 1

hallway *n* **1** a typically long narrow way connecting parts of a building ⟨The *hallway* between the bedroom and bathroom was strewn with toys.⟩ — see HALL 2

2 the entrance room of a building ⟨Visitors to the Georgian mansion are received in a handsomely proportioned *hallway* featuring an open staircase.⟩ — see HALL 1

halt *n* **1** a point in a struggle where neither side is capable of winning or willing to give in ⟨Negotiations are at a *halt*, with neither management nor the union budging on the issue of salary limits.⟩ — see IMPASSE 1

2 the stopping of a process or activity ⟨Gardening came to a *halt* during the week of solid rain.⟩ — see END 1

¹halt *vb* **1** to bring (something) to a standstill ⟨Traffic was *halted* by the parade.⟩

synonyms arrest, bring up, catch, check, draw up, fetch up, hold up, stall, stay, still, stop

related words baffle, balk, block, blockade, bottleneck, clog, dam, detain, hinder, hold, hold back, impede, obstruct, snag, stem; conclude, cut off, end, terminate; call,

discontinue, suspend; choke off, rein (in), repress, squash, squelch, stanch (*or* staunch), stunt, suppress
near antonyms carry on, continue, keep (on), keep up, persist, run on; advance, fare, march, move, proceed, progress, wend; actuate, budge, drive, goad, impel, propel, push, spur, stir
2 to bring (as an action or operation) to an immediate end ⟨The private eye abruptly *halted* his surveillance of the building upon being spotted by his subject.⟩ — see STOP 1
3 to come to an end ⟨All filming *halted* when the star of the movie quit in a huff.⟩ — see CEASE 1
²**halt** *vb* **1** to walk while favoring one leg ⟨Even with her twisted ankle, she managed to *halt* along and complete her Walk for Peace.⟩ — see LIMP 1
2 to show uncertainty about the right course of action ⟨The baby took a few steps, *halting* between attempting another and sitting down.⟩ — see HESITATE
hammer *vb* **1** to shape with a hammer ⟨Medieval artisans *hammered* brass into various bowls and trays, which they then embossed with elaborate designs.⟩
synonyms beat, draw, forge, pound
related words chase, planish; fashion, form, knead, model, pat, work; mint, stamp; abate, boast, carve, chisel, cut, grave, hew, knap, sculpt, sculpture
2 to deliver a blow to (someone or something) usually in a strong vigorous manner ⟨*hammer* a nail⟩ ⟨*hammered* the ball for a home run⟩ — see HIT 1
3 to strike repeatedly ⟨I tried *hammering* the door to wake them up.⟩ ⟨The crops were *hammered* with hail.⟩ — see BEAT 1
4 to criticize (someone) severely or angrily especially for personal failings ⟨The critics have long been *hammering* the stage actress for resorting to the same mixed bag of mannerisms over and over.⟩ — see SCOLD
hamper *vb* to create difficulty for the work or activity of ⟨Fallen branches *hampered* the hikers as they made their way along the narrow path.⟩
synonyms clog, cramp, embarrass, encumber, fetter, handcuff, handicap, hinder, hobble, hog-tie, hold back, hold up, impede, inhibit, interfere (with), manacle, obstruct, shackle, stymie, tie up, trammel
related words balk, check, constrain, curb, rein, restrain; bind, chain, halter, leash, tether, tie; arrest, brake, delay, retain, retard; barricade, block, blockade, roadblock; bog (down), mire; choke, smother, stifle, strangle, suffocate; baffle, foil, frustrate, stump, thwart; disrupt, sabotage; muzzle, repress, suppress; confine, hedge (in)
phrases cramp one's style, give a hard time
near antonyms clear, make way, open, unclog, unstop; free, liberate, release, untie; loosen, smooth; encourage, further, promote
antonyms aid, assist, facilitate, help
hams *pl n* the part of the body upon which someone sits ⟨After sitting on my *hams* all day, I could use a good workout.⟩ — see BUTTOCKS
hamstring *vb* to render powerless, ineffective, or unable to move ⟨The downtown development committee claims that it's *hamstrung* by city ordinances protecting historic buildings.⟩ — see PARALYZE 1
hand *n* **1** a certain way in which something appears or may be regarded ⟨On the one *hand*, you would have more storage space in a larger house, but on the other, you would have more rooms to heat.⟩ — see ASPECT 1
2 a place, space, or direction away from or beyond a central point or line ⟨Tall buildings rose on either *hand*.⟩ ⟨nothing but wide open space on either *hand*⟩ — see SIDE 1
3 an arrow-shaped piece on a dial or scale for registering

information ⟨Both *hands* of the clock pointed to 12.⟩ — see POINTER 1
4 one who works for another for wages or a salary ⟨The restaurant always hires several more *hands* for the busy summer season.⟩ — see EMPLOYEE
5 the form or style of a particular person's writing ⟨writes with a flowing, old-fashioned *hand*⟩ — see HANDWRITING 1
6 *usually* **hands** *pl* the ability to direct the course of something ⟨The final decision is in your *hands*.⟩ — see CONTROL 2
7 hands *pl* the fact or state of having (something) at one's disposal ⟨I'd like to get my *hands* on that vintage Cadillac convertible.⟩ — see POSSESSION 1
8 an act or instance of helping ⟨The downstairs tenant gave us a *hand* getting the heavy dresser up the stairs.⟩ — see HELP 1
9 a person with a high level of knowledge or skill in a field ⟨Once she got her own business, the young woman showed that she was quite a *hand* at making money.⟩ — see EXPERT
hand *vb* **1** to put (something) into the possession of someone for use or consumption ⟨His parents *handed* him a number of used household items for his first apartment.⟩ — see FURNISH 2
2 to shift possession of (something) from one person to another ⟨The clerk *handed* her the receipt.⟩ — see PASS 1
3 to put (something) into the possession or safekeeping of another ⟨Mom *handed* me her bundles while she fished for her house keys.⟩ — see GIVE 2
handbag *n* **1** a bag carried by hand and designed to hold a traveler's clothing and personal articles ⟨Joe flies only with a *handbag* so he doesn't have to check his luggage.⟩ — see TRAVELING BAG
2 a container for carrying money and small personal items ⟨Her *handbag* is just big enough to hold her hairbrush and wallet.⟩ — see PURSE
handbook *n* a book used for instruction in a subject ⟨a *handbook* of grammar⟩ — see TEXTBOOK
handcraft *n* an occupation requiring skillful use of the hands ⟨We learned about traditional *handcrafts* like barrel-making and leather-working at the colonial history museum.⟩ — see CRAFT 1
handcuff *n, usually* **handcuffs** *pl* something that physically prevents free movement ⟨The man reluctantly held out his wrists so the policeman could snap on *handcuffs*.⟩ — see BOND 1
handcuff *vb* **1** to confine or restrain with or as if with chains ⟨Peg wanted to take the trip, but was *handcuffed* by her responsibility to watch her ailing father.⟩ — see BIND 1
2 to create difficulty for the work or activity of ⟨the fear that the new mandatory standardized tests will *handcuff* the state's teachers, who will have to specifically tailor their lesson plans for the test⟩ — see HAMPER
handful *n* a small number ⟨Only a *handful* of people signed up for the wintertime hike.⟩ — see FEW
handicap *n* **1** a feature of someone or something that creates difficulty for achieving success ⟨Her natural shyness was not a *handicap* when she played chess.⟩ — see DISADVANTAGE 1
2 something that makes movement or progress difficult ⟨Her uncomfortable shoes became a *handicap* on the walking tour of the city, as she often had to sit and rest her sore feet.⟩ — see ENCUMBRANCE
handicap *vb* to create difficulty for the work or activity of ⟨The baseball player's small size did not *handicap* him in the least.⟩ — see HAMPER
handicraft *n* an occupation requiring skillful use of the

hands ⟨volunteers demonstrating early American *handicrafts*, such as blacksmithing, glassblowing, and weaving⟩ — see CRAFT 1

handicrafter *n* a person whose occupation requires skill with the hands ⟨an accomplished *handicrafter* who cards, spins, and weaves wool from the sheep she raises⟩ — see ARTISAN

handily *adv* without difficulty ⟨Terry *handily* whipped up a fluffy meringue and spread it on the pie.⟩ — see EASILY 1

handiwork *n* something produced by physical or intellectual effort ⟨Proud of his *handiwork*, he was certain that the birdhouse would win first place in its category.⟩ — see PRODUCT 1

handkerchief *n* a scarf worn on the head ⟨She tied a *handkerchief* around her head and set about cleaning out the dust-covered attic.⟩ — see BANDANNA

handle *n* **1** a part by which an implement is held ⟨a set of steak knives with wooden *handles*⟩
synonyms grip
related words bar, handlebar; bow, loop; hilt, shaft; broomstick
2 a word or combination of words by which a person or thing is regularly known ⟨The boxer likes to go by the *handle* "Champ."⟩ — see NAME 1
3 a descriptive or familiar name given instead of or in addition to the one belonging to an individual ⟨Since it seemed decreed that every new firefighter have a *handle*, his was soon "Hulk."⟩ — see NICKNAME

handle *vb* **1** to deal with (something) usually skillfully or efficiently ⟨As host of a live TV talk show, she must *handle* any situation that comes up.⟩
synonyms address, contend (with), cope (with), field, grapple (with), hack, manage, maneuver, manipulate, negotiate, play, swing, take, treat
related words engineer, finesse, jockey; carry out, get off, pull; command, direct, guide, steer; control, micromanage, regulate, run; react (to), respond (to)
phrases come to grips with, have a grip on
near antonyms botch, bungle, foozle, fumble, louse up, mess (up), mishandle, muff, scamp
2 to behave toward in a stated way ⟨*handles* all requests professionally, even when customers are rude⟩ — see TREAT 1
3 to control the mechanical operation of ⟨We learned how to *handle* basic woodworking power tools.⟩ — see OPERATE 1
4 to look after and make decisions about ⟨I'll take care of the flower beds, and you can *handle* all the lawn care.⟩ — see CONDUCT 1
5 to put up with (something painful or difficult) ⟨I can't *handle* much more of this foul weather.⟩ — see BEAR 2
6 to be in charge of ⟨I'll be *handling* the team's workouts while the leader is on vacation.⟩ — see BOSS 1

handling *n* the act or activity of looking after and making decisions about something ⟨The *handling* of proper order in the courtroom is the job of the sergeant at arms.⟩ — see CONDUCT 1

hand over *vb* **1** to give (something) over to the control or possession of another usually under duress ⟨The seller *handed over* the car's title to the buyer.⟩ — see SURRENDER 1
2 to put (something) into the possession of someone for use or consumption ⟨In response to a request for donations, we *handed over* all our extra blankets and pillows to the homeless shelter.⟩ — see FURNISH 2
3 to put (something) into the possession or safekeeping of another ⟨*handed over* their valuables to the desk clerk, who put them in the hotel safe⟩ — see GIVE 2
4 to shift possession of (something) from one person to another ⟨*Hand over* that screwdriver, will you please?⟩ — see PASS 1

handpick *vb* to decide to accept (someone or something) from a group of possibilities ⟨Anna *handpicked* what she considered to be the cutest kitten from the litter.⟩ — see CHOOSE 1

handsome *adj* **1** having or showing elegance ⟨The glass-topped table was a *handsome* addition to the room.⟩ — see ELEGANT 1
2 of a size greater than average of its kind ⟨Mark earns a *handsome* salary as senior vice president of the firm.⟩ — see LARGE
3 very pleasing to look at ⟨a *handsome* man with finely chiseled features⟩ — see BEAUTIFUL 1
4 sufficiently large in size, amount, or number to merit attention ⟨Real estate developers realized a *handsome* profit on that deal.⟩ — see CONSIDERABLE 1

handsomely *adv* in a generous manner ⟨rewarded *handsomely* the kids who had found his lost dog⟩ — see WELL 2

handsomeness *n* **1** dignified or restrained beauty of form, appearance, or style ⟨a modern-style addition that detracts from the *handsomeness* of that neoclassic building⟩ — see ELEGANCE
2 the qualities in a person or thing that as a whole give pleasure to the senses ⟨She never had noticed his *handsomeness* until he got a more becoming haircut.⟩ — see BEAUTY 1

hand–to–mouth *adj* less plentiful than what is normal, necessary, or desirable ⟨Joe survived on a *hand-to-mouth* income that came from any odd job that he could find.⟩ — see MEAGER

handwriting *n* **1** the form or style of a particular person's writing ⟨She immediately recognized the *handwriting* on the envelope as that of her old college roommate.⟩
synonyms hand, penmanship, script
related words scratch, scrawl, scribble; cursive, print, running hand; autograph, John Henry
2 writing done by hand ⟨The columnist laments the decline of fine *handwriting*, as so few people write letters by hand anymore.⟩
synonyms calligraphy, longhand, manuscript, penmanship, script
related words lettering; shorthand, stenography
antonyms print, type, typewriting

handy *adj* **1** situated within easy reach ⟨keeps a box of tissue *handy* whenever she reads *Charlotte's Web* to the children⟩ — see CONVENIENT
2 skillful with the hands ⟨*handy* with a needle and thread⟩ — see DEXTEROUS 1

hang *n* **1** a downward slope ⟨Don't ski that *hang*—it's too dangerous.⟩ — see DECLINE 3
2 the extent to which something hangs or dips below a straight line ⟨There's too much *hang* in the bunting on the parade float—nothing should be touching the ground.⟩ — see SAG

hang *vb* **1** to place on an elevated point without support from below ⟨*Hang* your coats on the coat rack in the hall.⟩
synonyms dangle, sling, suspend, swing
related words hook, mount, pin, tack; garland, string; extend (out), jut, project, stick out; overhang, protrude; cascade, depend, fall; balance, poise
2 to be determined by, based on, or subject (to) ⟨Our plan to go to the amusement park has all been worked out; now it just *hangs* on the weather.⟩ — see DEPEND 1
3 to be limp from lack of water or vigor ⟨As they neared the end of the long, hard march all but the most hardy were *hanging*, and some could barely put one foot in front of the other.⟩ — see DROOP 1

4 to rest or move along the surface of a liquid or in the air 〈*Hanging* just above the horizon was a little pink cloud.〉 — see FLOAT 1

5 to find a basis 〈That's very slim evidence upon which to *hang* a theory.〉 — see BASE

hang (over) *vb* to remain poised to inflict harm, danger, or distress on 〈As long as the possibility of having to move again was *hanging over* them, the family couldn't really settle in.〉 — see THREATEN

hang around *vb* to continue to be in a place for a significant amount of time 〈If you *hang around* until my husband gets home, you can meet him.〉 — see ¹STAY 1

hang back *vb* to show uncertainty about the right course of action 〈She *hung back* until she had more time to consider the decision.〉 — see HESITATE

hangdog *adj* feeling unhappiness 〈"Why do you look so *hangdog* today?" she asked.〉 — see SAD 1

hanger–on *n* a person who is supported by or seeks support from another without making an adequate return 〈Almost overnight, the singer was a star, and almost overnight, he was surrounded by *hangers-on* who wanted something.〉 — see LEECH

hanging *adj* **1** bending downward or forward 〈*Hanging* branches blocked our way for a good part of the trail.〉 — see NODDING

2 extending freely from a support from above 〈Light from a *hanging* chandelier filled the great hall.〉 — see DEPENDENT 1

hanging *n* a downward slope 〈With a steep *hanging* like that, the roofers can't be too careful.〉 — see DECLINE 3

hangout *n* a place for spending time or for socializing 〈A favorite *hangout* of the golden-agers is the local community center.〉

synonyms haunt, rendezvous, resort

related words camp, canteen, club, clubhouse, country club, key club, service club, union; harbor, harborage, haven, nest, refuge, retreat, sanctuary

hanker (for *or* **after)** *vb* to have an earnest wish to own or enjoy 〈*hankering for* some company in his lonely mountain cabin〉 〈*hanker after* a life of leisure〉 — see DESIRE 1

hankering *n* a strong wish for something 〈I've had a *hankering* for pizza with anchovies all afternoon.〉 — see DESIRE 1

hanky–panky *n* the use of clever underhanded actions to achieve an end 〈Dan had to resort to a certain amount of *hanky-panky* to sneak away from the house without his dog seeing him.〉 — see TRICKERY

haphazard *adj* lacking a definite plan, purpose, or pattern 〈The cookies turned out to be good despite our *haphazard* choice of ingredients.〉 — see RANDOM

haphazard *adv* without definite aim, direction, rule, or method 〈Shoes were tossed *haphazard* into the closet.〉 — see HIT OR MISS

haphazardly *adv* without definite aim, direction, rule, or method 〈You should not begin writing *haphazardly*; first, make an outline.〉 — see HIT OR MISS

hapless *adj* having, prone to, or marked by bad luck 〈The *hapless* motorist had barely paid his bill and driven away from the body shop when a truck sideswiped his car.〉 — see UNLUCKY 1

happen *vb* to take place 〈Did anything exciting *happen* over the summer?〉

synonyms be, befall, betide, chance, come, come about, cook, do, occur, pass, transpire

related words break, develop, rise, shape (up); arise, crop (up), materialize, spring (up); intervene; fall out, follow, result, turn out; go off, proceed

phrases come to pass

happen (on *or* **upon)** *vb* to come upon unexpectedly or by chance 〈*happened on* the filming of a movie〉

synonyms chance (upon), encounter, find, hit (upon), light (on *or* upon), meet, stumble (on *or* onto)

related words luck (out, on, onto, *or* into); confront, face; discover, strike, turn up

phrases bump into, come across, run across, run against, run into, run upon

happen (upon) *vb* to come upon face-to-face or as if face-to-face 〈He *happened upon* the hotel manager in the lobby and promptly complained about the room.〉 — see MEET 1

happening *adj* **1** being in the latest or current fashion 〈Those are some *happening* duds, man!〉 — see STYLISH

2 marked by much life, movement, or activity 〈The downtown theater district is a *happening* place this autumn.〉 — see ALIVE 2

3 enjoying widespread favor or approval 〈He's always into whatever's *happening* at the moment.〉 — see POPULAR 1

happening *n* **1** an exciting or noteworthy event that one experiences firsthand 〈The President's visit to the school was a real *happening* for teachers and students alike.〉 — see ADVENTURE 1

2 something that happens 〈gave a detailed account of all the *happenings* of the weekend〉 — see EVENT 1

happily *adv* **1** in a cheerful or happy manner 〈*happily* accepted the invitation to dinner〉 — see GAILY 1

2 in a manner suitable for the occasion or purpose 〈one of those rare occasions on which business and pleasure *happily* mixed〉 — see PROPERLY

happiness *n* **1** a feeling or state of well-being and contentment 〈Her *happiness* was complete when she got her very own house.〉

synonyms blessedness, bliss, blissfulness, felicity, gladness, joy

related words elation, exhilaration, exultation; ecstasy, euphoria, glory, heaven, paradise, rapture, rapturousness, ravishment, transport; delectation, delight, enjoyment, pleasure; cheer, cheerfulness, comfort, exuberance, gaiety (*also* gayety), gladsomeness, glee, gleefulness, jollity, joyfulness, joyousness, jubilance, jubilation, lightheartedness, merriness, mirth; content, contentedness, gratification, satisfaction

near antonyms agony, anguish, desolation, joylessness, sorrow, woe, woefulness; blues, cheerlessness, dejection, depression, desolateness, despondency, disheartenment, dispiritedness, doldrums, downheartedness, gloom, gloominess, melancholy, plaintiveness

antonyms calamity, ill-being, misery, sadness, unhappiness, wretchedness

2 the feeling experienced when one's wishes are met 〈Tom finally found true *happiness* as a doctor in a poor rural area.〉 — see PLEASURE 1

happy *adj* **1** coming or happening by good luck especially unexpectedly 〈a *happy* discovery, finding the letter that would prove her innocence〉 — see FORTUNATE 1

2 experiencing pleasure, satisfaction, or delight 〈made bread for the first time and was *happy* with the tasty result〉 — see GLAD 1

3 feeling that one's needs or desires have been met 〈Diane has been much *happier* ever since she moved.〉 — see CONTENT

4 having good luck 〈the *happy* person who is both appreciated and rewarded for all his hard work〉 — see LUCKY 1

5 meeting the requirements of a purpose or situation 〈The dessert was a *happy* complement to such a fine meal.〉 — see FIT 1

6 having extreme or relentless concern ⟨Poll-*happy* pundits just care about which political candidate is winning, and never about the issues.⟩ — see HUNG UP 1

happy–go–lucky *adj* **1** having a relaxed, casual manner ⟨He is completely *happy-go-lucky* on fishing trips—if he catches something, fine; if he doesn't, that's fine, too.⟩ — see EASYGOING 1

2 having or showing freedom from worries or troubles ⟨She's always had a *happy-go-lucky* disposition.⟩ — see CAREFREE

harangue *n* **1** a long angry speech or scolding ⟨She launched into a long *harangue* about poor customer service without realizing that I wasn't even an employee!⟩ — see TIRADE

2 a usually formal discourse delivered to an audience ⟨the dictator's lengthy *harangue* before a captive audience⟩ — see SPEECH 1

harangue *vb* **1** to give a formal often extended talk on a subject ⟨The eminent professor *harangued* for three hours on his favorite subject.⟩ — see TALK 1

2 to talk as if giving an important and formal speech ⟨a talk-show guest using the interviewer's questions as an opportunity to *harangue* on a variety of pet peeves⟩ — see ORATE 1

harassment *n* the act of making unwelcome intrusions upon another ⟨He owes her a lot of money, so he shouldn't be surprised at her constant *harassment* for a repayment.⟩ — see ANNOYANCE 1

harbinger *n* one that announces or indicates the later arrival of another ⟨His successful job interview was seen as a *harbinger* of better times to come.⟩ — see FORERUNNER 1

harbinger *vb* to give a slight indication of beforehand ⟨the hope that the housing slump does not *harbinger* a general economic recession⟩ — see FORESHADOW

harbor *n* **1** a part of a body of water protected and deep enough to be a place of safety for ships ⟨The tanker stayed in Boston *harbor* three days to undergo repairs.⟩

synonyms anchorage, harborage, haven, port

related words basin, dock, marina, moorage, mooring; arm, bay, bight, cove, estuary, firth, fjord (*also* fiord), gulf, inlet, lagoon, narrow, roads, roadstead; canal, channel, sound, strait; containerport, home port, seaport

2 something (as a building) that offers cover from the weather or protection from danger ⟨Seeking a *harbor* from the drenching rain, we ducked into a café.⟩ — see SHELTER

harbor *vb* **1** to keep in one's mind or heart ⟨He had long *harbored* a grudge against his old employer, who had high-handedly fired him without cause.⟩

synonyms bear, cherish, entertain, have, hold, nurse

related words cultivate, foster, nurture, support, sustain; carry, keep, maintain, preserve, remember, retain, treasure; cleave (to), cling (to), hug, stick (to); brood (about *or* over), fixate (on *or* upon), obsess (about *or* over)

phrases hang on to, hold on to

near antonyms disregard, drop, forget, ignore, neglect, overlook; abjure, decline, deny, disdain, refuse, reject, repudiate, scorn; abandon, desert, discard, forsake, give up, part (with), quit, renounce, throw out; expunge

2 to provide with living quarters or shelter ⟨The woods in our suburb *harbor* deer, foxes, raccoons, and skunks.⟩ — see HOUSE 1

3 to be or provide a shelter for ⟨The little cabin is *harbored* from the wind by a thick growth of pines.⟩ — see SHELTER 1

harborage *n* **1** a part of a body of water protected and deep enough to be a place of safety for ships ⟨The city boasts one of the best deepwater *harborages* on the Atlantic coast.⟩ — see HARBOR 1

2 something (as a building) that offers cover from the weather or protection from danger ⟨The only *harborage* from the storm was a lone tree.⟩ — see SHELTER

hard *adj* **1** having or showing a lack of sympathy or tender feelings ⟨a *hard* man, who never had a kind word for anyone⟩

synonyms callous, cold-blooded, hard-boiled, heartless, inhuman, inhumane, insensate, insensitive, merciless, obdurate, pitiless, remorseless, ruthless, soulless, stony (*also* stoney), take-no-prisoners, thick-skinned, uncharitable, unfeeling, unmerciful, unsparing, unsympathetic

related words boorish, heedless, inconsiderate, thoughtless, uncaring, unfriendly, unloving, unthinking; grim, hard-bitten, harsh, heavy-handed, oppressive, rough, severe, sledgehammer, stern, tough, ungentle; abusive, acrimonious, disagreeable, hateful, ill-natured, ill-tempered, malevolent, malicious, mean, rancorous, spiteful, surly, virulent; barbarous, brutal, cruel, evil-minded, savage, vicious; austere, cold, frosty

near antonyms benevolent, benignant, gentle, kind; clement, indulgent, lenient, mild; cordial, friendly, good-natured, good-tempered, gracious; tolerant, understanding; affectionate, fond, loving

antonyms charitable, compassionate, humane, kindhearted, kindly, merciful, sensitive, softhearted, sympathetic, tender, tenderhearted, warm, warmhearted

2 requiring considerable physical or mental effort ⟨Clearing land is *hard* work.⟩ ⟨a *hard* exam to pass⟩

synonyms arduous, challenging, demanding, difficult, exacting, formidable, grueling (*or* gruelling), heavy, herculean, killer, laborious, murderous, rigorous, rough, rugged, severe, stiff, strenuous, tall, toilsome, tough, uphill

related words abstract, abstruse, complex, complicated, elusive, hairy, insoluble, intricate, involved, knotty, opaque, problematic (*also* problematical), recondite, serious, spiny, stubborn, thorny, ticklish, tricky; bruising, burdensome, exhausting, labored, onerous, oppressive, stressful, taxing, tight, trying; annoying, bothersome, distressing, irksome, troublesome, vexatious; grievous, grim, strict, stringent; brutal, cruel, inhuman, painful

near antonyms achievable, clear, doable, elementary, manageable, uncomplicated; comforting, gentle, painless, relaxed, smooth, soothing; accessible, friendly, idiotproof, user-friendly

antonyms cheap, easy, effortless, facile, light, mindless, simple, soft, undemanding

3 able to withstand hardship, strain, or exposure ⟨They were forced to import sheep of a *harder* stock, one that could thrive in the harsh climate.⟩ — see HARDY 1

4 based on sound reasoning or information ⟨Do you have any *hard* evidence that Bigfoot exists?⟩ — see GOOD 1

5 difficult to endure ⟨the *hard* life of a migrant farm worker⟩ — see HARSH 1

6 extreme in degree, power, or effect ⟨a carpet that withstood years of *hard* wear⟩ — see INTENSE 1

7 given to exacting standards of discipline and self-restraint ⟨a *hard* disciplinarian who is quick to punish the tiniest violation of the rules⟩ — see SEVERE 1

8 having a consistency that does not easily yield to pressure ⟨*hard* candies⟩ ⟨fell on the *hard* floor and bruised her arm⟩ — see FIRM 2

9 having been established and usually not subject to change ⟨There isn't always a *hard* line between right and wrong.⟩ — see FIXED 1

10 having or showing deep-seated resentment ⟨Joe maintained *hard* feelings toward those who had cheated him.⟩ — see BITTER 1

11 sticking to an opinion, purpose, or course of action in spite of reason, arguments, or persuasion ⟨a woman with a *hard* will who never budged from her chosen path⟩ — see OBSTINATE

12 restricted to or based on fact ⟨That newscast is strictly devoted to *hard* news, as the producers prefer to leave the gossip to others.⟩ — see FACTUAL 1

hard *adv* **1** with great effort or determination ⟨We took a much-needed break after working *hard* all week.⟩ ⟨a *hard*-won victory⟩

synonyms amain, arduously, assiduously, determinedly, diligently, hardly, industriously, intensely, intensively, intently, laboriously, mightily, purposefully, sedulously, strenuously

related words animatedly, briskly, dynamically, energetically, feverishly, spiritedly, vehemently, vigorously, zealously; continuously, ploddingly, steadfastly, steadily, unrelentingly, unremittingly; ardently, attentively, conscientiously, earnestly, exhaustively, meticulously, painstakingly, thoroughly; indefatigably, tirelessly, unflaggingly, untiringly, wearilessly; obstinately, stubbornly, willfully

near antonyms casually, desultorily, halfheartedly, indolently, lackadaisically, languidly, lazily, listlessly, shiftlessly, sluggishly, spiritlessly, tiredly, wearily

2 with feelings of bitterness or grief ⟨The boys took the news of their friend's moving away *hard*.⟩

synonyms agonizingly, bitterly, grievously, hardly, mournfully, painfully, regretfully, resentfully, ruefully, sadly, sorely, sorrowfully, unhappily, woefully, wretchedly

related words cheerlessly, dejectedly, despairingly, despondently, disconsolately, dispiritedly, downheartedly, low-spiritedly; darkly, dismally, distressfully, distressingly, dourly, drearily, forlornly, gloomily, glumly, joylessly, mirthlessly, miserably, morosely, pessimistically, somberly, sullenly; acutely, harshly, keenly, piercingly, poignantly, severely, sharply; cruelly, hurtfully, rancorously

near antonyms cheerfully, cheerily, delightedly, gleefully, good-naturedly, lightheartedly, merrily, mirthfully, rejoicingly, sunnily; blithely, blithesomely, calmly, casually, dispassionately, easily, impassively, indifferently, lightly, nonchalantly, stoically, unconcernedly

antonyms blissfully, gladly, happily, joyfully, joyously

3 in a vigorous and forceful manner ⟨The batter hit the ball *hard*, causing it to soar out of bounds.⟩ ⟨The wind blew *hard* all day.⟩

synonyms dynamically, energetically, firmly, forcefully, forcibly, mightily, powerfully, roundly, stiffly, stoutly, strenuously, strongly, sturdily, vigorously

related words hammer and tongs, robustly, roughshod, sharply, vehemently, violently; animatedly, briskly, crisply, eagerly, gamely, heartily, lustily, snappily, spiritedly, spunkily, vivaciously; decidedly, determinedly, directly, emphatically, intensively, intently, purposefully, rigidly, smartly, solidly, squarely, steadfastly, steadily, sturdily, surely; aggressively, assertively, potently

phrases like gangbusters, to beat the band, with a vengeance, with might and main

near antonyms delicately, faintly, frailly, shakily; bloodlessly, halfheartedly, languidly, lazily, listlessly, spiritlessly; impotently, ineffectively, ineffectually, lamely, nervelessly, spinelessly, uncertainly

antonyms feebly, gently, softly, weakly

4 at, within, or to a short distance or time ⟨The groom stood *hard* by, ready to help, as the lady mounted the skittish horse.⟩ — see NEAR 1

5 in a manner so as to cause loss or suffering ⟨The old bicycle has obviously gotten some *hard* use.⟩ — see HARDLY 1

hard–and–fast *adj* **1** having been established and usually not subject to change ⟨The school has *hard-and-fast* rules about attendance.⟩ — see FIXED 1

2 not capable of changing or being changed ⟨*hard-and-fast* beliefs that are the rock-solid foundation of their religion⟩ — see INFLEXIBLE 1

hard–bitten *adj* able to withstand hardship, strain, or exposure ⟨*hard-bitten* journalists⟩ — see HARDY 1

hard–boiled *adj* **1** having or showing a lack of sympathy or tender feelings ⟨a *hard-boiled* detective⟩ — see HARD 1

2 having or showing a practical cleverness or judgment ⟨made the *hard-boiled* business decision to downsize the company, thereby costing thousands of longtime employees their jobs⟩ — see SHREWD 1

hard–core *adj* firmly established over time ⟨*hard-core* habits that will be extremely difficult to change⟩ — see INVETERATE 1

hard–driving *adj* having a strong desire for personal advancement ⟨She's the most *hard-driving* malpractice lawyer I've ever seen.⟩ — see AMBITIOUS 1

harden *vb* **1** to become physically firm or solid ⟨The glue begins to *harden* as soon as it is exposed to air.⟩

synonyms concrete, congeal, firm (up), freeze, set, solidify

related words cake, callus, encrust (*also* incrust); clot, coagulate, jell, jelly, thicken; calcify, crystallize (*also* crystalize), ossify, rigidify; anneal, case-harden, temper

near antonyms deliquesce, dissolve, flux, fuse, melt, smelt, thaw, unfreeze

antonyms liquefy (*also* liquify), soften

2 to make able to withstand physical hardship, strain, or exposure ⟨pioneer women who had been *hardened* by years of living on the plains⟩

synonyms fortify, inure, season, steel, strengthen, toughen

related words acclimate, acclimatize, adapt, adjust; anneal, temper; invigorate, vitalize; immunize; bolster, boost, brace, buttress, enforce, forearm, prop (up), support; break in, limber (up), train; accustom, condition, naturalize

near antonyms emasculate, enervate, enfeeble, exhaust, sap, weaken; cripple, debilitate, hamstring, incapacitate; sensitize

antonyms soften

3 to increase the ability of (as a muscle) to exert physical force ⟨arm muscles that were *hardened* by all the years of casting and hauling fishing nets⟩ — see STRENGTHEN 1

hardened *adj* **1** able to withstand hardship, strain, or exposure ⟨*hardened* from years of military service⟩ — see HARDY 1

2 sticking to an opinion, purpose, or course of action in spite of reason, arguments, or persuasion ⟨*Hardened* cynics regarded those TV shows as being anything but reality-based.⟩ — see OBSTINATE

hardheaded *adj* **1** having or showing a practical cleverness or judgment ⟨a *hardheaded* politician who was guided by practicality over ideology⟩ — see SHREWD 1

2 sticking to an opinion, purpose, or course of action in spite of reason, arguments, or persuasion ⟨Granny remained *hardheaded* about keeping her house and not moving into a nursing home.⟩ — see OBSTINATE

3 willing to see things as they really are and deal with them sensibly ⟨a *hardheaded* principal who understands the pressures teenagers face⟩ — see REALISTIC 1

hardheadedness *n* **1** a steadfast adherence to an opinion, purpose, or course of action in spite of reason, arguments, or persuasion 〈Her unrelenting *hardheadedness* didn't win many friends, but it helped her to get her way most of the time.〉 — see OBSTINACY
2 exceptional discernment and judgment especially in practical matters 〈the *hardheadedness* of a bean counter〉 — see ACUMEN

hardihood *n* **1** active strength of body or mind 〈The 80-year-old grandmother attributes her *hardihood* to having eaten a cup of yogurt every day for the past 50 years.〉 — see VIGOR 1
2 strength of mind to carry on in spite of danger 〈The explorers were driven by an almost reckless *hardihood* in the face of the unknown.〉 — see COURAGE

hard–luck *adj* having, prone to, or marked by bad luck 〈a *hard-luck* ball club that never could get the breaks it needed〉 — see UNLUCKY 1

hardly *adv* **1** in a manner so as to cause loss or suffering 〈The new judge vowed to deal *hardly* with repeat offenders.〉
synonyms hard, harshly, ill, oppressively, roughly, severely, sternly, stiffly
related words callously, cold-bloodedly, hard-heartedly, heartlessly, inhumanely, inhumanly, insensitively, mercilessly, obdurately, pitilessly, ruthlessly, tyrannically, uncharitably, unfeelingly, unmercifully, unsparingly; abusively, brutishly, savagely, viciously; aggressively, assertively, decidedly, determinedly, firmly, grimly, strongly, toughly
near antonyms benevolently, benignantly, considerately, cordially, kindly, lovingly, tenderly; charitably, compassionately, humanely, mercifully, softheartedly, sympathetically, tolerantly, understandingly
antonyms clemently, gently, leniently, lightly, mildly, softly
2 certainly not 〈The news is *hardly* surprising.〉
synonyms ill, no, none, noway (*usually* no way), scarcely
related words near, never, nothing, nowise
phrases by no means, nothing doing, on no account
near antonyms awful, awfully, enormously, exceedingly (*also* exceeding), extremely, greatly, highly, hugely, mightily, mighty, most, quite, terribly, very; assuredly, perfectly, plainly, really, truly, unequivocally, unquestionably, utterly; doubtless, more or less, mostly, rather, slightly, somewhat
antonyms absolutely, certainly, completely, definitely, surely
3 by a very small margin 〈We were *hardly* able to make it back to camp before darkness set in.〉 — see JUST 2
4 with feelings of bitterness or grief 〈His broker did not think that he would take his financial losses so *hardly*.〉 — see HARD 2
5 with great effort or determination 〈The state championship was a *hardly* fought contest between two evenly matched teams.〉 — see HARD 1

hardness *n* **1** something that is a cause for suffering or special effort especially in the attainment of a goal 〈The test questions were rated for *hardness*, a rating of five indicating the most difficult.〉 — see DIFFICULTY 1
2 the quality or state of being demanding or unyielding (as in discipline or criticism) 〈The aunt's *hardness* gradually crumbled under the influence of the little orphan's endearing ways.〉 — see SEVERITY

hardship *n* something that is a cause for suffering or special effort especially in the attainment of a goal 〈Working two jobs was a *hardship* he was willing to endure to get out of debt.〉 — see DIFFICULTY 1

hard up *adj* lacking money or material possessions 〈*hard up* aspiring artists〉 — see POOR 1

hardware *n* items needed for the performance of a task or activity 〈Volunteers gathered together the *hardware* needed to set up a first aid station at the finish line for the marathon.〉 — see EQUIPMENT

hardy *adj* **1** able to withstand hardship, strain, or exposure 〈Chrysanthemums are *hardy* enough to survive a light frost.〉
synonyms hard, hard-bitten, hardened, inured, rugged, stout, strong, sturdy, tough, toughened, vigorous
related words flinty, leathery, resilient, stalwart; durable, enduring, everlasting, immortal, imperishable, lasting, permanent, stable, staunch (*also* stanch), staying, tenacious, unyielding; flourishing, prospering, thriving; able-bodied, brawny, muscular; fit, fortified, hale, healthy, husky, lusty, red-blooded, robust, sound, strapping, virile; annealed, seasoned, tempered
near antonyms emasculated, enervated, enfeebled, exhausted, run-down, sapped, wasted, weakened, worn, worn-out; crippled, debilitated, diseased, incapacitated, infirm, unsound; fragile, frail, puny; resistless, sensitive, susceptible, unresistant, vulnerable, yielding
antonyms delicate, soft, tender, weak
2 inclined or willing to take risks 〈*hardy* souls who pioneered new paths into outer space〉 — see BOLD 1

harebrained *adj* **1** lacking in seriousness or maturity 〈The movie follows the *harebrained* antics of a pair of longtime friends.〉 — see GIDDY 1
2 showing or marked by a lack of good sense or judgment 〈a *harebrained* idea〉 — see FOOLISH 1

hark *vb* to pay attention especially through the act of hearing 〈a line of poetry beginning, "*Hark*! The bells ring."〉 — see LISTEN

hark back (to) *vb* to bring back to mind 〈The new stadium, designed for nostalgic appeal, *harks back to* the intimate ballparks of yore.〉 — see REMEMBER

harlequin *n* a comically dressed performer (as at a circus) who entertains with playful tricks and ridiculous behavior 〈Among the court entertainers waiting to enter the grand hall were masked *harlequins* in brightly colored pantaloons.〉 — see CLOWN 1

harm *n* something that causes loss or pain 〈You were lucky to get up from the fall without *harm*.〉 〈no *harm* in trying〉 — see INJURY 1

harm *vb* **1** to cause bodily damage to 〈The important thing is that no one was *harmed* in the accident.〉 — see INJURE 1
2 to reduce the soundness, effectiveness, or perfection of 〈The company's reputation has been *harmed* by allegations of crooked accounting.〉 — see DAMAGE 1

harmful *adj* causing or capable of causing harm 〈They use a pest control method that is not *harmful* to the environment.〉
synonyms adverse, bad, baleful, baneful, damaging, dangerous, deleterious, detrimental, evil, hurtful, ill, injurious, mischievous, noxious, pernicious, prejudicial, wicked
related words hostile, inimical, unfriendly; contagious, deadly, infectious, infective, pestiferous, pestilent, poisonous, venomous; insidious, menacing, ominous, sinister, threatening; hazardous, imperiling (*or* imperilling), jeopardizing, perilous, risky, unsafe, unsound; nasty, noisome, unhealthful, unhealthy, unwholesome; destructive, fatal, killer, lethal, malignant, ruinous
near antonyms advantageous, beneficial, useful; favorable, good, propitious; healthful, healthy, helpful, palliative, remedial, salubrious, salutary, wholesome; secure, sound; benignant

antonyms benign, harmless, innocent, innocuous, inoffensive, safe

harmless *adj* not causing or being capable of causing injury or hurt ⟨a perfectly *harmless* little spider⟩
synonyms benign, innocent, innocuous, inoffensive, safe
related words healthful, healthy, salubrious, wholesome; benignant; sound, trustworthy; gentle, gracious, mild; nonthreatening, painless, unobjectionable
near antonyms poisonous, venomous; menacing, ominous, sinister, threatening; hazardous, imperiling (*or* imperilling), jeopardizing, perilous, risky, unsafe, unsound; nasty, noisome, unhealthful, unhealthy, unwholesome; offensive, painful, scathing, wounding; deadly, fatal, lethal, ruinous; destructive, insidious, malignant, noxious, pestilent, polluted, tainted
antonyms adverse, bad, baleful, baneful, damaging, dangerous, deleterious, detrimental, evil, harmful, hurtful, ill, injurious, mischievous, noxious, pernicious, prejudicial, wicked

harmonious *adj* **1** having a pleasing mixture of notes ⟨the naturally *harmonious* sounds of a forest glen in springtime⟩
synonyms euphonious, harmonizing, melodious, musical, symphonic, tuneful
related words blending, chiming, flowing, mellifluent, mellifluous; mellow, melodic, sweet; echoing, resonant, sonorous; quavering, trilling, warbling; agreeable, appealing, pleasant; cadenced, lilting, lyric, lyrical, rhythmic (*or* rhythmical), songful, songlike; chordal, homophonic, orchestral, polyphonic (*or* polyphonous), tonal
near antonyms blaring, clanging, clashing, clattering, grating, harsh, jangling, jarring, metallic, raspy, raucous, scratching, screeching, shrill, squeaky, strident; disagreeable, unpleasant, unpleasing; atonal, off-key
antonyms discordant, disharmonious, dissonant, inharmonious, tuneless, unmelodious, unmusical
2 having the parts agreeably related ⟨a *harmonious* arrangement of archways and doorways in the palace courtyard⟩
synonyms balanced, congruous, consonant
related words even, proportioned, regular, symmetrical (*or* symmetric); aesthetic (*also* esthetic *or* aesthetical *or* esthetical), artistic, becoming, elegant, graceful, tasteful; agreeable, felicitous, pleasant, pleasing, satisfying; compatible, coordinated, matched, matching
near antonyms asymmetrical (*or* asymmetric), disordered, irregular, skewed, unequal, uneven, unsymmetrical; distasteful, graceless, inartistic, inelegant, tasteless, unaesthetic, unbecoming, ungraceful, unlovely; disagreeable, displeasing, dissatisfying, infelicitous, unfortunate, unpleasant, unsightly; clashing, conflicting, disunited, incompatible
antonyms disharmonic, disharmonious, incongruous, inharmonic, inharmonious, unbalanced
3 having or marked by agreement in feeling or action ⟨An unusually *harmonious* meeting among the leaders resulted in a quick peace agreement.⟩
synonyms agreeable, amicable, compatible, congenial, frictionless, kindred, unanimous, united
related words pacific, peaceable, peaceful; collaborating, cooperative, symbiotic, synergetic, synergic; sympathetic, tolerant, understanding; affable, amiable, cordial, friendly, genial, neighborly
near antonyms antagonistic, antipathetic, clashing, conflicting, hostile, inimical, unfriendly; belligerent, contentious, quarrelsome; contradicting, contradictory, contrary, opposing, opposite; competing, competitive, rivaling (*or* rivalling)

antonyms disagreeable, discordant, disharmonious, disunited, incompatible, inharmonious, uncongenial
4 not having or showing any apparent conflict ⟨No form of social discrimination can ever be *harmonious* with the basic principles and ideals of our nation.⟩ — see CONSISTENT

harmonize *vb* **1** to form a pleasing relationship ⟨The color of the walls *harmonized* nicely with the blue tones in the carpet.⟩
synonyms agree, assort, blend, chime, chime in, conform, consort, coordinate, groove
related words balance, correlate, correspond, dovetail, hang together, match; meet, parallel; bond, coalesce, cohere, conjoin, fuse, merge, square, tally
near antonyms contradict, contrast, counter, differ, diverge, jar; cancel (out), counteract, negate, offset
antonyms clash, collide, conflict
2 to bring to a state free of conflicts, inconsistencies, or differences ⟨an attempt to *harmonize* the traditional stories about the event with the historical evidence⟩
synonyms accommodate, conciliate, conform, coordinate, key, reconcile
related words adapt, tune; blend, combine, connect, correlate, dovetail, fit, fuse, integrate, join, match, merge, orchestrate, pair, square, suit, synthesize, unify, unite; align (*also* aline), arrange, array, balance, equalize, even, order, proportion, regularize, standardize
near antonyms confuse, disarray, disorder, disorganize, disrupt, disturb, skew, upset; alienate, estrange
antonyms disharmonize
3 to be in agreement on every point ⟨Interrogated in separate rooms, the two burglary suspects gave stories that didn't *harmonize* at all.⟩ — see CHECK 1

harmonizing *adj* having a pleasing mixture of notes ⟨A *harmonizing* chorus of early-morning chirps arose from the bird-laden trees.⟩ — see HARMONIOUS 1

harmony *n* **1** a balanced, pleasing, or suitable arrangement of parts ⟨Her face had an angelic *harmony* that fascinated the leading painters of her day.⟩
synonyms balance, coherence, consonance, proportion, symmetry, symphony, unity
related words coordination, correlation, correspondence, equalization, equilibrium, evenness, order, orderliness, regularity, uniformity
near antonyms confusion, disorganization, disturbance, tension; disconnectedness, disjointedness, incompatibility; irregularity, unevenness
antonyms asymmetry, discordance, disproportion, disunity, imbalance, incoherence, violence
2 peaceful coexistence ⟨the apparent inability of the party's right and left wings to resolve their conflicts and live in *harmony* at least during the convention⟩
synonyms chime, comity, compatibility, concord, peace
related words amity, companionship, compatibleness, congeniality, fellowship, fraternization, friendship; collaboration, reciprocity, symbiosis; agreement, consensus, unanimity; cohesion, cohesiveness, unity; affinity, connection, empathy, kinship, oneness, rapport, solidarity, sympathy, understanding; peacefulness, sereneness, serenity, sweetness and light, tranquillity (*or* tranquility)
near antonyms antagonism, antipathy, enmity, hatred, hostility, unfriendliness; alienation, breach, divorce, estrangement, rupture, schism, severance; dissent, dissidence; anarchy, disorder, disturbance, strife, turmoil
antonyms conflict, discord, dissension (*also* dissention), variance
3 a state of consistency ⟨For once, the kids' idea of a vacation was in perfect *harmony* with their parents' notion of total relaxation.⟩ — see CONFORMITY 1

harness *vb* to put into action or service ⟨Huge dams *harness* the power of water to produce electricity.⟩ — see USE 1

harpoon *vb* to penetrate or hold (something) with a pointed object ⟨She deftly *harpooned* a shrimp with her skewer and held it over the fire.⟩ — see IMPALE

harrow *vb* to cause persistent suffering to ⟨The villagers were *harrowed* by drought.⟩ — see AFFLICT

harrowing *adj* **1** hard to accept or bear especially emotionally ⟨They survived a *harrowing* ordeal.⟩ — see BITTER 2

2 intensely or unbearably painful ⟨a *harrowing* injury⟩ — see EXCRUCIATING 1

harrying *n* the act of making unwelcome intrusions upon another ⟨the *harrying* of the debtor by bill collectors⟩ — see ANNOYANCE 1

harsh *adj* **1** difficult to endure ⟨a *harsh* winter⟩

synonyms bitter, brutal, burdensome, cruel, excruciating, grievous, grim, hard, heavy, inhuman, murderous, onerous, oppressive, rough, rugged, searing, severe, stiff, tough, trying

related words austere, bleak, comfortless, discomforting, forbidding, inhospitable, uncomfortable; rigorous, strict, stringent; agonizing, heartbreaking, heartrending, painful, wretched; crushing, grinding, overwhelming, wearing; insufferable, insupportable, intolerable, unbearable, unendurable; harrowing, tortuous; bad, disagreeable, hostile, unfriendly, unpleasant

near antonyms comfortable, cozy, luxurious, snug; agreeable, friendly, genial, hospitable, pleasant; peaceful, relaxing, reposeful, restful; bearable, endurable, painless, tolerable; balmy, calm, clement, gentle, mild, moderate, temperate

antonyms easy, light, soft

2 disagreeable to one's aesthetic or artistic sense ⟨The *harsh* lighting in the cafeteria makes the food look slightly off-color.⟩

synonyms grating, grotesque, jarring, unaesthetic

related words acid, flashy, garish, gaudy, loud, tawdry; tacky, tasteless, vulgar; inartistic, unartistic; artless, clumsy, crude, graceless, inelegant, rude; uncouth, uncultured, unrefined; gross, obscene, repugnant, repulsive, ugly; disagreeable, unpleasant, unpleasing; blaring, clashing, discordant, disharmonious, dissonant, inharmonious, jangling, off-key, ragged, raspy, raucous, unmelodious, unmusical

near antonyms artful, artistic; attractive, beautiful, becoming, comely; agreeable, appealing, felicitous, good, harmonious, harmonizing, pleasing, seemly; calming, comforting, soothing; softened, subdued; cultured, elegant, graceful, gracious, polished, refined, tasteful

antonyms aesthetic (*also* esthetic *or* aesthetical *or* esthetical)

3 causing discomfort ⟨a *harsh* north wind⟩ — see UNCOMFORTABLE 1

4 given to exacting standards of discipline and self-restraint ⟨a *harsh* judge with little patience for ill-prepared lawyers⟩ — see SEVERE 1

5 hard to accept or bear especially emotionally ⟨the *harsh* reality of failure⟩ ⟨*harsh* words of criticism from her music teacher⟩ — see BITTER 2

6 not giving pleasure to the mind or senses ⟨I winced at the *harsh* sound that the machine was making.⟩ — see UNPLEASANT

harshly *adv* in a manner so as to cause loss or suffering ⟨The league punished the players *harshly* for violating the rules.⟩ — see HARDLY 1

harshness *n* **1** a harsh or sharp quality ⟨There was a *harshness* about her voice that made her an evocative blues singer.⟩ — see EDGE 1

2 the quality or state of being demanding or unyielding (as in discipline or criticism) ⟨I was surprised at the *harshness* of the choirmaster's criticism, since he was usually pretty easygoing.⟩ — see SEVERITY

harum–scarum *adj* having or showing a lack of concern for the consequences of one's actions ⟨a *harum-scarum* dash through the crowded terminal to make the flight⟩ — see RECKLESS 1

harum–scarum *adv* in a confused and reckless manner ⟨Dana tossed everything *harum-scarum* from the closet in a desperate attempt to find her shoes.⟩ — see HELTER-SKELTER 1

harvest *n* the quantity of an animal or vegetable product gathered at the end of a season ⟨We can thank the bountiful *harvest* of 1621 for our traditional feast of turkey and all the trimmings every November.⟩ — see CROP 1

harvest *vb* to catch or collect (a crop or natural resource) for human use ⟨*harvest* salmon from nearby rivers⟩ ⟨Every year we *harvest* corn from our own garden.⟩

synonyms gather, pick, reap

related words fish, seal, shrimp, whale; accumulate, forage, garner; glean; cut, hay, mow; bag, capture, hunt, net, snare, trap; crop, grow, raise

near antonyms plant, seed, sow

hash *n* an unorganized collection or mixture of various things ⟨The docudrama was a *hash* of facts, half-truths, speculation, and pure fiction.⟩ — see MISCELLANY 1

hash *vb* **1** to cut into small pieces ⟨He *hashed* some roast beef, put it in a pie shell, and topped it with a layer of mashed potatoes.⟩ — see CHOP

2 to undo the proper order or arrangement of ⟨The bookkeeper had so *hashed* the figures it took weeks to straighten out the accounts.⟩ — see DISORDER

hassle *n* **1** a brief clash between enemies or rivals ⟨The best way to avoid *hassles* with those aggressive telemarketers is to hang up on them.⟩ — see ENCOUNTER

2 a physical dispute between opposing individuals or groups ⟨A *hassle* broke out after the game.⟩ — see FIGHT 1

3 an often noisy or angry expression of differing opinions ⟨had a huge *hassle* with an airline representative before she got her ticket refunded⟩ — see ARGUMENT 1

4 something that is a source of irritation ⟨It's a *hassle* to find a parking space downtown.⟩ — see ANNOYANCE 3

hassle *vb* **1** to attack repeatedly with mean put-downs or insults ⟨Some spectators were asked to leave for *hassling* the ref.⟩ — see TEASE 2

2 to express different opinions about something often angrily ⟨constantly *hassled* with the chef over the need to cook pork thoroughly⟩ — see ARGUE 2

haste *n* **1** a high rate of movement or performance ⟨I made *haste* to get there on time.⟩ — see SPEED 1

2 excited and often showy or disorderly speed ⟨*Haste* makes waste.⟩ ⟨In her *haste*, she forgot her keys.⟩ — see HURRY 1

hasten *vb* **1** to cause to move or proceed fast or faster ⟨You can *hasten* the activation of yeast with heat.⟩ — see HURRY 1

2 to proceed or move quickly ⟨The contractors *hastened* to complete the project before the deadline.⟩ — see HURRY 2

hastily *adv* **1** with excessive or careless speed ⟨The *hastily* put together report contained a lot of errors.⟩

synonyms cursorily, headlong, hotfoot, hurriedly, pell-mell, precipitately, precipitously, rashly

related words headfirst, headily, hotheadedly, impatiently, impetuously, impulsively, recklessly, thoughtlessly; automatically, glancingly, haphazardly; impromptu, spontaneously; abruptly, suddenly; offhand, offhandedly

phrases on the spur of the moment

near antonyms calculatingly, circumspectly, designedly; falteringly, haltingly, hesitantly, hesitatingly, tentatively; leisurely, slowly
antonyms deliberately, studiedly
2 with great speed ⟨The congresswoman *hastily* made her way towards the waiting elevator.⟩ — see FAST 1
hastiness *n* excited and often showy or disorderly speed ⟨Several council members objected to the *hastiness* with which the proposal was brought to a vote.⟩ — see HURRY 1
hasty *adj* **1** acting or done with excessive or careless speed ⟨Anna later regretted her *hasty* decision to sell her car.⟩
synonyms cursory, flying, headlong, helter-skelter, hurried, overhasty, pell-mell, precipitate, precipitous, rash, rushed
related words breakneck, breathtaking; headstrong, hotheaded, impatient, impetuous, impulsive, madcap, reckless, unadvised; quick, rapid, speedy, swift; horseback, impromptu, makeshift, offhand, offhanded, rush, slapdash, snap, spontaneous, spur-of-the-moment; abrupt, sudden
near antonyms calculated, calculating, measured; circumspect, foresighted, forethoughtful; drawn-out, extended, long-term, prolonged; faltering, hesitant, hesitating, tentative; dallying, dawdling, laggard, leisurely, poky (*or* pokey), shilly-shallying, slow
antonyms deliberate, unhurried, unrushed
2 moving, proceeding, or acting with great speed ⟨We all wish our sick friend a *hasty* recovery.⟩ — see FAST 1
hat *n* a covering for the head usually having a shaped crown ⟨In those days, no properly dressed person left home without a *hat*.⟩
synonyms cap, headdress, headgear, headpiece, lid [*slang*]
related words baseball cap, beret, biretta, boater, bonnet, bowler, cloche, cocked hat, cowboy hat, cowl, derby, fedora, fez, hard hat, helmet, high hat, homburg, hood, miter (*or* mitre), nightcap, panama, pillbox, porkpie hat, service cap, shako, silk hat, skullcap, sombrero, sou'wester, Stetson, stocking cap, stovepipe, sunbonnet, tam, tam-o'-shanter, ten-gallon hat, top hat, topper, toque, tricorne (*or* tricorn), turban, zucchetto
hatch *n* a barrier by which an entry is closed and opened ⟨Watertight *hatches* provided access through the ship's bulkheads.⟩ — see DOOR 1
hatch *vb* to cover and warm eggs as the young inside develop ⟨The mallards and geese have begun *hatching* in their nests down by the pond.⟩ — see SET 1
hate *n* **1** a very strong dislike ⟨*Hate* can sometimes be replaced with tolerance when people meet face to face.⟩
synonyms abhorrence, abomination, execration, hatred, loathing
related words cattiness, despite, despitefulness, hatefulness, invidiousness, malevolence, malice, maliciousness, malignancy, malignity, meanness, spite, spitefulness; aversion, disgust, distaste, horror, odium, repugnance, repulsion, revulsion; animosity, antagonism, antipathy, bitterness, contempt, disdain, enmity, grudge, hostility, jealousy, pique, resentment, scorn; bile, jaundice, rancor, spleen, venom, virulence, vitriol
near antonyms appetite, inclination, liking; admiration, adoration, veneration, worship; acceptance, tolerance; passion, relish, taste
antonyms affection, devotion, fondness, love
2 something or someone that is hated ⟨My one *hate* in gym is square dancing.⟩
synonyms abhorrence, abomination, anathema, antipathy, aversion, bête noire, execration
related words dread, horror, phobia; bogey (*also* bogie

or bogy), bugaboo, bugbear; adversary, enemy; annoyance, grievance, hassle, nuisance, peeve
near antonyms beloved, darling, dear, honey, sweetheart; delight, enjoyment, felicity, joy, pleasure; favorite, like, preference; treasure
antonyms love
hate *vb* to dislike strongly ⟨I *hate* going out in the rain and cold.⟩
synonyms abhor, abominate, despise, detest, execrate, loathe
related words deplore, deprecate, disapprove (of), discountenance, disdain, disfavor, scorn
phrases have it in for
near antonyms desire, fancy, favor, like, prefer; enjoy, relish; admire, adore, approve (of), esteem, hallow, idolize, revere, venerate, worship; cherish, prize, treasure
antonyms love
hateful *adj* having or showing a desire to cause someone pain or suffering for the sheer enjoyment of it ⟨The most *hateful* comments were deleted from the website.⟩
synonyms catty, cruel, despiteful, malevolent, malicious, malign, malignant, mean, nasty, spiteful, vicious, virulent
related words devious, scoundrelly, scurvy, snakelike; acrimonious, bitter, envious, jaundiced, jealous, rancorous, resentful, vindictive; contemptuous, deprecating, derogatory, disdainful, disparaging, mean-spirited, obnoxious, opprobrious, scornful, snide, unkind, unkindly, unloving; baleful, baneful, evil; harsh, hostile, inimical; acrid, caustic, poisonous, scathing, venomous
near antonyms compassionate, good, good-hearted, kind, kindhearted, kindly, sympathetic, warm, warmhearted; affable, agreeable, amiable, cordial, friendly, genial, gracious, nice, pleasant; affectionate, amorous, sweet, tender, tenderhearted; humane; altruistic, highminded, humanitarian, magnanimous, noble, philanthropic (*also* philanthropical)
antonyms benevolent, benign, benignant, loving, unmalicious
hatefully *adv* in a mean or spiteful manner ⟨It's not clear if the comments were made *hatefully* or not.⟩ — see NASTILY
hatefulness *n* the desire to cause pain for the satisfaction of doing harm ⟨Her political commentary seems to be nothing more than an exercise in *hatefulness*.⟩ — see MALICE
hatred *n* a very strong dislike ⟨A lifelong *hatred* of war that inspired him to join a peace movement.⟩ — see HATE 1
haughtiness *n* an exaggerated sense of one's importance that shows itself in the making of excessive or unjustified claims ⟨It was surprising to see such *haughtiness* in someone who had come from such humble origins.⟩ — see ARROGANCE
haughty *adj* **1** having a feeling of superiority that shows itself in an overbearing attitude ⟨He rejected their offer with a tone of *haughty* disdain.⟩ — see ARROGANT
2 having or displaying feelings of scorn for what is regarded as beneath oneself ⟨The student reporter received a *haughty* letter in reply to his request for an interview with the governor.⟩ — see PROUD 1
haul *n* **1** the total amount collected or obtained especially at one time ⟨Our latest trip to collect shells at the beach resulted in quite a *haul*.⟩
synonyms bounty, catch, take, yield
related words bag; earnings, gain, gross, income, net, payoff, proceeds, profit, receipts, return, revenue, winnings; booty, loot, plunder, spoils, swag; appropriation, collection
near antonyms deduction, loss, subtraction

2 a mass or quantity of something taken up and carried, conveyed, or transported ⟨a truck carrying a large *haul* of lumber⟩ — see LOAD 1

3 the act or an instance of applying force on something so that it moves in the direction of the force ⟨The sharp *haul* strained the rope but didn't break it.⟩ — see PULL 1

haul *vb* **1** to cause to follow by applying steady force on ⟨A pair of strong oxen *hauled* the plow.⟩ — see PULL 1

2 to support and take from one place to another ⟨A vast army of trucks *haul* produce across America every day.⟩ — see CARRY 1

haunches *pl n* the part of the body upon which someone sits ⟨squatted down on her *haunches* to get a better shot of the ducks with her camera⟩ — see BUTTOCKS

haunt *n* a place for spending time or for socializing ⟨One of their favorite after-school *haunts* is Joe's Pizza.⟩ — see HANGOUT

haunt *vb* to go to or spend time in often ⟨Much of her time is spent *haunting* antique shops in search of unique knobs for the curio cabinets she builds.⟩ — see FREQUENT

haunting *adj* fearfully and mysteriously strange or fantastic ⟨the *haunting* tones of the Highland bagpipes⟩ — see EERIE

have *vb* **1** to keep, control, or experience as one's own ⟨My uncle *has* a sizable collection of baseball cards.⟩

synonyms command, enjoy, hold, own, possess, retain

related words keep, reserve, withhold; bear, carry; boast, show off, sport

phrases rejoice in

near antonyms abandon, cede, disclaim, disown, hand over, relinquish, renounce, surrender, yield; discard, dump; decline, reject, repudiate, spurn; need, require

antonyms lack, want

2 to agree to receive whether willingly or reluctantly ⟨We decided that I would *have* the job of calling the volunteers on the phone.⟩ ⟨She agreed to *have* him as an assistant.⟩ — see TAKE 2

3 to bring forth from the womb ⟨Her grandmother *had* 5 children.⟩ — see BEAR 1

4 to cause to believe what is untrue ⟨He'd been *had*—the painting was a fake, and he never saw the "art dealer" or his money again.⟩ — see DECEIVE

5 to come to a knowledge of (something) by living through it ⟨I *had* a great time at the party.⟩ ⟨She *had* three operations on her leg.⟩ — see EXPERIENCE

6 to give permission for or to approve of ⟨I will not *have* any more nonsense about a party in celebration of my retirement.⟩ — see ALLOW 1

7 to influence someone with a bribe ⟨an upstanding judge who could not be *had* at any price⟩ — see BRIBE

8 to keep in one's mind or heart ⟨I have never *had* an unkind thought for him.⟩ ⟨Do you *have* an opinion?⟩ — see HARBOR 1

have (to) *vb* to be under necessity or obligation to ⟨I *have to* take out the trash before we can leave.⟩ ⟨Gran *has to* take medicine for her heart.⟩ — see NEED 2

haven *n* **1** a part of a body of water protected and deep enough to be a place of safety for ships ⟨This picturesque cove is one of the most popular *havens* on all of the cape.⟩ — see HARBOR 1

2 something (as a building) that offers cover from the weather or protection from danger ⟨The cross-country skiers hoped desperately to find a cave as a *haven* from the blizzard.⟩ — see SHELTER

havoc *n* **1** a state in which everything is out of order ⟨Computer network problems created *havoc* throughout the office.⟩ — see CHAOS

2 the state or fact of being rendered nonexistent, physi-cally unsound, or useless ⟨The powerful hurricane wreaked *havoc* all along the coast.⟩ — see DESTRUCTION 1

hawk *n* one who urges or attempts to cause a war ⟨The *hawks* voted against reducing the military's budget.⟩ — see WARMONGER

hawk *vb* to sell from place to place usually in small quantities ⟨a determined bootstrapper who went from *hawking* newspapers on the street corner to running a media empire⟩ — see PEDDLE

hawker *n* one who sells things outdoors ⟨street corner *hawkers* selling everything from fake designer purses to original works of art⟩ — see PEDDLER

hazard *n* **1** something that may cause injury or harm ⟨The tumbledown old barn was considered a fire *hazard*.⟩ — see DANGER 2

2 the uncertain course of events ⟨It was only by *hazard* and good fortune that we found our way back to the trail.⟩ — see CHANCE 1

hazard *vb* **1** to place in danger ⟨Just so the tourists could see the sea lions up close, the captain needlessly *hazarded* his ship.⟩ — see ENDANGER

2 to take a chance on ⟨Joe was unwilling to *hazard* landing the plane on the small island, which didn't even have an airfield.⟩ — see RISK 1

hazardous *adj* involving potential loss or injury ⟨a *hazardous* journey across the arctic ice⟩ — see DANGEROUS 1

haze *n* **1** an atmospheric condition in which suspended particles in the air rob it of its transparency ⟨Jim could barely make out the tall buildings through the *haze*.⟩

synonyms fog, mist, murk, reek, smog, soup

related words bank, cloud, fume, miasma, smoke, smother, steam

2 a state of mental confusion ⟨He felt like he was in a *haze* from the jet lag.⟩

synonyms daze, fog, muddle, spin, swoon

related words reverie, trance; befuddlement, bewilderment, perplexity, puzzlement; delirium, malaise, paralysis; cloudiness, fogginess

near antonyms alertness, levelheadedness

¹**haze** *vb* to attack repeatedly with mean put-downs or insults ⟨The comments on the website consisted mostly of two guys *hazing* each other.⟩ — see TEASE 2

²**haze** *vb* to make dark, dim, or indistinct ⟨Unfortunately, smog was *hazing* the view of the distant city skyline.⟩ — see CLOUD 1

hazed *adj* covered over by clouds ⟨*Hazed* skies made the flat landscape look even duller.⟩ — see OVERCAST

hazy *adj* **1** filled with or dimmed by fine particles (as of dust or water) in suspension ⟨*Hazy* skies made it dangerous to fly.⟩ ⟨the *hazy* sunshine so common in August⟩

synonyms beclouded, befogged, clouded, cloudy, foggy, misty, murky, smoggy, soupy

related words overcast, rainy, stormy, thick; dirty, miry, mucky, muddy, slimy, slushy, turbid; smoky (*also* smokey), smudgy, sooty; filmy, milky, opaque

near antonyms bright, clean; clement, fair, sunny, sunshiny; translucent, transparent

antonyms clear, cloudless, limpid, pellucid, unclouded

2 covered over by clouds ⟨When taking landscape photographs, compensate for dull, *hazy* skies by emphasizing colorful features on the ground.⟩ — see OVERCAST

3 not seen or understood clearly ⟨The meaning of "you should" here is *hazy*—does it mean "you are strongly urged" or "you are commanded"?⟩ — see FAINT 1

head *adj* highest in rank or authority ⟨She was *head* editor of the magazine for 17 years.⟩

synonyms chief, commanding, first, foremost, high, lead, leading, preeminent, premier, presiding, primary, prime, principal, supreme, top *related words* high-level, senior; controlling, directing, managing, officiating, overseeing, regnant, reigning, ruling, supervisory; main, major, paramount, predominant, predominate, sovereign (*also* sovran); ascendant (*also* ascendent), dominant, grand, superior, topmost, upmost, upper, uppermost

phrases in charge

near antonyms ancillary, inferior, last, less, lesser, lower, lowly, second, secondary, subordinate, subsidiary; assistant, assisting, coadjutor, deputy, junior, under

head *n* **1** the upper or front part of the body that contains the brain, the major sense organs, and the mouth ⟨I hit my *head* as I went through the low doorway.⟩

synonyms block [*slang*], noddle, noggin, pate, poll

related words cranium, crown, scalp, skull

2 the place of leadership or command ⟨Every year a different parent is placed at the *head* of the troop's cookie drive.⟩

synonyms chair, headship, helm, rein(s)

related words chieftainship, commandership, directorship; forefront, lead, vanguard; captainship, chairmanship, deanship, dictatorship, generalship, governorship, kingship, mastership, mastery, premiership, presidentship, superintendency; dominance, dominion, jurisdiction, sovereignty (*also* sovranty), sway, upper hand; eminence, height, pedestal, pinnacle, seat, throne, top

near antonyms ranks

3 a light mass of fine bubbles formed in or on a liquid ⟨The *head* on the ice cream soda rose a good two inches above the rim of the glass.⟩ — see FOAM

4 a member of the human race ⟨The tour guide counted *heads*, and everyone was present.⟩ — see HUMAN

5 a time or state of affairs requiring prompt or decisive action ⟨The situation came to a *head*, requiring intervention.⟩ — see EMERGENCY

6 the beginning part of a stream ⟨Lake Itasca in Minnesota is the *head* of the Mississippi River.⟩ — see HEADWATER

7 the highest part or point ⟨The man stood at the *head* of the stairs and looked down.⟩ — see HEIGHT 1

8 the normal or healthy condition of the mental abilities ⟨You're out of your *head* if you think you can swim across that river.⟩ — see MIND 2

9 the part of a person that feels, thinks, perceives, wills, and especially reasons ⟨challenged us to put our *heads* together and find a solution to the problem⟩ — see MIND 1

10 the person (as an employer or supervisor) who tells people and especially workers what to do ⟨As *head* of the planning committee, he had the responsibility of appointing someone to look into the parking situation.⟩ — see BOSS

11 a bank of earth constructed to control water ⟨Settlers built a *head* to create a millpond.⟩ — see DAM

12 a room furnished with a fixture for flushing body waste ⟨Give me a chance to visit the *head*, and I'll be all set to go.⟩ — see TOILET

13 a person with a strong and habitual liking for something ⟨She's a total tech *head* who adores home electronics and computers.⟩ — see FAN

14 a word or series of words often in larger letters placed at the beginning of a passage or at the top of a page in order to introduce or categorize ⟨I rechecked to make sure that all the *heads* were in boldface.⟩ — see HEADING

15 a special and usually inborn ability ⟨I have no *head* for remembering names.⟩ — see TALENT

head *vb* **1** to go on a specified course or in a certain direction ⟨I turned around and *headed* for home.⟩

synonyms bear, make

related words aim, bend, direct, point, turn; beeline, light out, put, put out, set off, strike, take off; face, orient, steer; back, come about, come round, cut, incline, put about, reverse, swerve, tack, veer, wheel, yaw

2 to be at the front of ⟨*Heading* the procession at the dog show was a miniature poodle, followed by dogs seemingly of every breed.⟩ — see LEAD 3

3 to be in charge of ⟨She *heads* the hiring committee.⟩ — see BOSS 1

4 to be positioned along a certain course or in a certain direction ⟨The road to riches *headed* north, thought many, as off they went to Alaska to try their luck at panning gold.⟩ — see RUN 3

5 to point or turn (something) toward a target or goal ⟨After a long day at the beach, we *headed* the car toward home.⟩ — see AIM 1

6 to serve as leader of ⟨Robert La Salle *headed* the expedition that claimed Louisiana for the French king.⟩ — see LEAD 2

7 to cut off the head of ⟨*heading* and gutting a fish⟩ — see DECAPITATE

headache *n* **1** a dull, unpleasant, or difficult piece of work ⟨Filling out all the required forms was a real *headache*.⟩ — see CHORE 2

2 something that is a source of irritation ⟨One of the *headaches* of being a band teacher is never knowing if the school's music program will be cut.⟩ — see ANNOYANCE 3

headdress *n* a covering for the head usually having a shaped crown ⟨Most of the acrobats riding the horses wore some sort of fancy *headdress*.⟩ — see HAT

headgear *n* a covering for the head usually having a shaped crown ⟨In some states a helmet is required *headgear* for motorcycle riders.⟩ — see HAT

heading *n* a word or series of words often in larger letters placed at the beginning of a passage or at the top of a page in order to introduce or categorize ⟨The recipe for turkey gumbo is under the *heading* "stews" rather than under "soups."⟩

synonyms caption, head, headline, rubric, title

related words banner, streamer; catch word, guide word, running head; greeting, salutation; superscript, superscription; subhead, subheading, subtitle

headland *n* **1** an area of high ground jutting out into a body of water beyond the line of the coast ⟨The lighthouse, situated on a narrow, rocky *headland*, commands an expansive view of the coast.⟩

synonyms point, promontory

related words cape, foreland, peninsula, spit; breakwater, jetty, levee

2 an area of land that juts out into a body of water ⟨Navigation is notoriously difficult at the southernmost tip of South America, where ships must round the *headland* of Cape Horn.⟩ — see ²CAPE

headline *n* a word or series of words often in larger letters placed at the beginning of a passage or at the top of a page in order to introduce or categorize ⟨I usually just glance at the *headlines* in the morning paper before dashing off to work.⟩ — see HEADING

headlong *adj* acting or done with excessive or careless speed ⟨terrified forest creatures in a *headlong* retreat from the rapidly spreading fire⟩ — see HASTY 1

headlong *adv* **1** with excessive or careless speed ⟨plunged *headlong* into the crowd⟩ — see HASTILY 1

2 without delay ⟨We had barely finished the last project when we went *headlong* into the next one.⟩ — see IMMEDIATELY

headpiece *n* **1** a covering for the head usually having a shaped crown ⟨The bride will be wearing a flowing veil fastened to a pearl-covered *headpiece*.⟩ — see HAT

2 the ability to learn and understand or to deal with problems ⟨She's always had the best *headpiece* of the family.⟩ — see INTELLIGENCE 1

headquarters *pl n* **1** a place from which authority is exercised ⟨The *headquarters* of the newly established United States government was in New York City, the nation's first capital.⟩ — see SEAT 1

2 the place from which a commander runs operations ⟨The scout went straight to the large tent in the center of the camp, correctly assuming that it served as the division's *headquarters*.⟩ — see COMMAND 3

headship *n* **1** the duty or function of watching or guarding for the sake of proper direction or control ⟨While she was in the hospital, the CEO had her most trusted lieutenant assume temporary *headship* of the firm.⟩ — see SUPERVISION 1

2 the place of leadership or command ⟨The person at the *headship* of the firm will face daunting challenges, given the current state of the economy.⟩ — see HEAD 2

headstone *n* a shaped stone laid over or erected near a grave and usually bearing an inscription to identify and preserve the memory of the deceased ⟨Many of the old *headstones* were nearly impossible to read.⟩ — see TOMB-STONE

headstrong *adj* **1** given to resisting control or discipline by others ⟨a *headstrong* child who likes to test the limits of his parents' patience⟩ — see UNCONTROLLABLE

2 sticking to an opinion, purpose, or course of action in spite of reason, arguments, or persuasion ⟨The tenants of the building remain *headstrong* in their determination not to be evicted by the developer.⟩ — see OBSTINATE

headwater *n, usually* **headwaters** *pl* the beginning part of a stream ⟨In the 1800s, Meriwether Lewis and William Clark explored the Missouri River from its mouth to its *headwaters*.⟩

synonyms head, source

related words geyser, headspring, hot spring, spring; branch

headway *n* forward movement in time or place ⟨The ant was making little *headway* carrying a crumb that was about five times his size.⟩ — see ADVANCE 1

heal *vb* **1** to restore to a healthy condition ⟨This ointment will help *heal* the wound.⟩ ⟨*healed* the sick⟩

synonyms cure, fix, mend, rehabilitate, set up

related words attend (to), care (for), doctor, medicate, minister (to), nurse, physic, treat; fortify, rejuvenate, renew, resuscitate, revitalize, revive; alleviate, relieve, remedy, repair

near antonyms cripple, damage, disable, harm, hurt, impair, injure, lacerate, lame, maim, mangle, mutilate, wound; afflict, ail, debilitate, enervate, enfeeble, lay up, sap, sicken, waste, weaken

2 to become healthy and strong again after illness or weakness ⟨Most of the soldiers could go home while they were still *healing* from their wounds.⟩ — see CONVALESCE

3 to bring about recovery from ⟨Time *heals* all wounds, even those of the heart.⟩ — see CURE 1

healing *n* the process or period of gradually regaining one's health and strength ⟨the long period of *healing* following the operation⟩ — see CONVALESCENCE

health *n* **1** the condition of being sound in body ⟨We nursed him back to *health*.⟩

synonyms fitness, healthiness, heartiness, robustness, sap, soundness, wellness, wholeness, wholesomeness

related words fettle, shape; cleanliness, hygiene; hardiness, lustiness, robustiousness, ruggedness, stamina, strength, toughness, vigor, vigorousness, vitality; bloom, flush, flushness; activeness, agility, liveliness, spryness; weal, welfare, well-being

near antonyms debility, decrepitude, feebleness, frailness, infirmity, lameness, sickliness, weakness; ailment, condition, disease, disorder, malady, trouble

antonyms illness, sickness, unhealthiness, unsoundness

2 a state of being or fitness ⟨a country in good economic *health* now that the recession is past⟩ — see CONDITION 1

healthful *adj* beneficial to the health of body or mind ⟨One of the most *healthful* forms of exercise is a brisk walk.⟩

synonyms good, healthy, restorative, salubrious, salutary, tonic, wholesome

related words alleviative, corrective, recuperative, refreshing, rehabilitative, rejuvenescent, remedial; advantageous, useful; aseptic, clean, hygienic, sanitary; nourishing, nutritional, nutritious

near antonyms damaging, deleterious, harmful, injurious, pernicious; infectious, poisonous, sickening, toxic; insanitary, unhygienic, unsanitary

antonyms noxious, unhealthful, unhealthy, unwholesome

healthiness *n* the condition of being sound in body ⟨Healthy teeth are an indication of a horse's overall *healthiness*.⟩ — see HEALTH 1

healthy *adj* **1** enjoying health and vigor ⟨Always active, Grandma has remained *healthy* into her 80s.⟩

synonyms able-bodied, bouncing, fit, hale, hearty, robust, sound, well, whole, wholesome

related words hard, hardy, iron, lusty, rugged, stalwart, strong, sturdy, tough; active, agile, chipper, lively, sprightful, sprightly, spry, vigorous, vital; all right, good, right

phrases in fine fettle, in shape, in the pink

near antonyms decrepit, enfeebled, feeble, infirm, rundown, sickened, sickly, weak, weakened, weakly, wornout; debilitated, halt, incapacitated, lame; delicate, fragile, frail; emaciated, gaunt, haggard, malnourished, undernourished; afflicted, troubled; bad, poorly

antonyms ailing, diseased, ill, sick, unfit, unhealthy, unsound, unwell

2 beneficial to the health of body or mind ⟨The air in here isn't *healthy*.⟩ ⟨ads that promote *healthy* eating habits⟩ — see HEALTHFUL

3 sufficiently large in size, amount, or number to merit attention ⟨a *healthy* turnout of volunteers to plant trees on Arbor Day⟩ — see CONSIDERABLE 1

4 marked by vigorous growth and well-being especially economically ⟨Coming out of a prolonged recession, the restaurant business seemed to be *healthy* again.⟩ — see PROSPEROUS 1

heap *n* **1** a considerable amount ⟨She always has a *heap* of good ideas.⟩ ⟨You're in a *heap* of trouble for missing curfew!⟩ — see LOT 2

2 a quantity of things thrown or stacked on one another ⟨Jess found her shoe under a *heap* of clothes on the floor.⟩ — see ¹PILE 1

heap *vb* **1** to give readily and in large quantities ⟨He was embarrassed by all the praise *heaped* on him.⟩ — see RAIN 2

2 to lay or throw on top of one another ⟨*heaped* the stones in a corner of the yard⟩ — see PILE 1

3 to put into (something) as much as can be held or contained ⟨*heaped* her plate with spaghetti⟩ — see FILL 1

hear *vb* **1** to come to an awareness of ⟨I *heard* your sister is home from the hospital.⟩ — see DISCOVER 1

2 to pay attention especially through the act of hearing ⟨At least *hear* what I have to say before you start disagreeing.⟩ — see LISTEN

hearing *n* range of hearing ⟨Let's make sure she's out of *hearing* before I tell you what I got her for her birthday.⟩ — see EARSHOT

hearken *vb* to pay attention especially through the act of hearing ⟨*Hearken*! I hear the distant beat of the hooves of many horses.⟩ — see LISTEN

heart *n* **1** the capacity for feeling for another's unhappiness or misfortune ⟨She has a big *heart*.⟩
synonyms charity, commiseration, compassion, feeling, good-heartedness, humanity, kindheartedness, kindliness, kindness, mercy, pity, softheartedness, sympathy, warmheartedness
related words feelings, responsiveness, sensibility, sensitivity; affection, love, regard; affinity, empathy, rapport; altruism, benevolence, generosity, goodwill, humanism, humanitarianism, philanthropy; beneficence, benignancy
near antonyms callousness, indifference, unconcern; cruelty, harshness; animosity, antipathy, dislike, hatred, hostility
antonyms coldheartedness, hard-heartedness, inhumanity, mercilessness, pitilessness
2 a thing or place that is of greatest importance to an activity or interest ⟨The *heart* of the village economy was the outdoor market.⟩ — see CENTER 1
3 strength of mind to carry on in spite of danger ⟨The hiker never lost *heart* while she was lost in the woods.⟩ — see COURAGE
4 the central part or aspect of something under consideration ⟨At the *heart* of the problem is the school's outmoded computer system.⟩ ⟨avoided any small talk and got right to the *heart* of the matter⟩ — see CRUX
5 the seat of one's deepest thoughts and emotions ⟨Deep down in her *heart*, she knew he was telling the truth.⟩ — see CORE 1

heartache *n* deep sadness especially for the loss of someone or something loved ⟨the *heartache* she felt when she saw the innocent victims of the war⟩ — see SORROW

heartbreak *n* deep sadness especially for the loss of someone or something loved ⟨I understand the *heartbreak* you must feel over your grandmother's death.⟩ — see SORROW

heartbreaking *adj* **1** causing unhappiness ⟨a *heartbreaking* loss in the final minutes of the game⟩ — see SAD 2
2 of a kind to cause great distress ⟨the *heartbreaking* state of Main Street now that most of the businesses have closed⟩ — see REGRETTABLE
3 deserving of one's pity ⟨a *heartbreaking* attempt to escape that ends in disaster⟩ — see PATHETIC 1

heartbroken *adj* **1** feeling unhappiness ⟨She's not as *heartbroken* over missing out on the trip to New York as I thought she would be.⟩ — see SAD 1
2 expressing or suggesting mourning ⟨a *heartbroken* sob⟩ — see MOURNFUL 1

hearten *vb* to fill with courage or strength of purpose ⟨Thinking we were hopelessly lost, we were *heartened* by the sight of a familiar farmhouse.⟩ — see ENCOURAGE 1

heartening *adj* **1** having qualities which inspire hope ⟨a *heartening* visit to the hospital, where the patient was alert and sitting up⟩ — see HOPEFUL 1
2 making one feel good inside ⟨Hearing how his students still appreciated him after all those years was *heartening* to the music teacher.⟩ — see HEARTWARMING
3 pointing toward a happy outcome ⟨The accomplishments of the first day were a *heartening* start to our renovation of the house.⟩ — see FAVORABLE 2

hearth *n* the place where one lives ⟨All were welcome, friends and strangers alike, to their humble *hearth*.⟩ — see HOME 1

hearthstone *n* the place where one lives ⟨After years

abroad, the eldest son returned to the family *hearthstone*, the old house in Philadelphia.⟩ — see HOME 1

heartily *adv* **1** in a cheerful or happy manner ⟨The players laughed *heartily* at the coach's good-natured quips.⟩ — see GAILY 1
2 to a full extent or degree ⟨I am *heartily* tired of this spring-cleaning.⟩ — see FULLY 1

heartiness *n* the condition of being sound in body ⟨Granddad's *heartiness* on the hike put everyone else to shame—he wouldn't even hear of stopping to rest.⟩ — see HEALTH 1

heartless *adj* **1** having or showing a lack of sympathy or tender feelings ⟨a *heartless* abandonment of animals⟩ — see HARD 1
2 having or showing the desire to inflict severe pain and suffering on others ⟨a *heartless* enemy that takes no prisoners⟩ — see CRUEL 1

heartlessness *n* disposition to willfully inflict pain and suffering on others ⟨the *heartlessness* of whoever abandoned the dog⟩ — see CRUELTY

heartrending *adj* **1** causing unhappiness ⟨I couldn't bear to see the *heartrending* photos.⟩ — see SAD 2
2 hard to accept or bear especially emotionally ⟨a *heartrending* decision to break up⟩ — see BITTER 2
3 of a kind to cause great distress ⟨*heartrending* memories of all the crimes he'd committed and now regretted⟩ — see REGRETTABLE
4 deserving of one's pity ⟨the *heartrending* sight of a starving child holding out his hands for food⟩ — see PATHETIC 1

heartsick *adj* feeling unhappiness ⟨Pa felt *heartsick* over having to give up the family farm.⟩ — see SAD 1

heartsickness *n* a state or spell of low spirits ⟨could not begin to describe the *heartsickness* he felt when he sold the family farm⟩ — see SADNESS

heartsore *adj* feeling unhappiness ⟨a grandmother feeling *heartsore* because she missed her grandchildren so⟩ — see SAD 1

heartstrings *pl n* **1** general emotional condition ⟨She always said she didn't care much for cats, but now the little kitten was tugging at her *heartstrings*.⟩ — see FEELING 2
2 the seat of one's deepest thoughts and emotions ⟨a story that will touch the very *heartstrings* of its readers⟩ — see CORE 1

heartwarming *adj* making one feel good inside ⟨Sarah was deeply touched by the *heartwarming* welcome she received from her relatives in Israel.⟩
synonyms cheering, comforting, encouraging, fulfilling, gladdening, gratifying, heartening, rewarding, satisfying
related words affecting, inspiring, inspiriting, moving, poignant, stirring, touching; edifying, elevating, uplifting; sympathetic, tender; kind, kindly, loving, warm; animating, enlivening, exciting, exhilarating, invigorating, rousing, stimulating, thrilling; pleasing, pleasurable, welcoming
near antonyms cheerless, disappointing, disgruntling, displeasing, dissatisfying, heartbreaking, heartrending, saddening; discomforting, disconcerting, dismaying, distressing, disturbing, upsetting; cold, unfeeling, unfriendly, unkind, unloving, unpleasant
antonyms demoralizing, depressing, discouraging, disheartening, dispiriting

hearty *adj* **1** characterized by unqualified enthusiasm ⟨Their decision to marry at long last has the whole family's *hearty* approval.⟩
synonyms wholehearted
related words single-minded; ardent, avid, eager, enthusiastic, excited, exuberant, fervent, gung ho, impassioned, keen, mettlesome, passionate, raring, vehement,

warm, zealous; animated, energetic, lively, spirited, vigorous; absolute, bona fide, earnest, genuine, sincere, unaffected, undisguised

near antonyms apathetic, disinterested, dispassionate, indifferent, uninterested; lackadaisical, listless, perfunctory, spiritless, uneager, unenthusiastic, unexcited; equivocal, hesitant, qualified, tentative, uncertain; delayed, dilatory, doubtful, hedging, hesitating; forced, reluctant, resistant, reticent, unwilling

antonyms grudging, halfhearted, lukewarm, tepid

2 enjoying health and vigor ⟨You're looking really *hearty* after that month in the clear mountain air!⟩ — see HEALTHY 1

3 having or showing kindly feeling and sincere interest ⟨The mayor gave the assembled volunteers his *hearty* thanks for their restoration of the bandstand on the town square.⟩ — see FRIENDLY 1

4 not showing weakness or uncertainty ⟨I gave the reins a *hearty* tug but the horse wouldn't budge.⟩ — see FIRM 1

hearty *n* one who operates or navigates a seagoing vessel ⟨Gather round me *hearties*, and I'll tell you a sea tale that'll shiver your timbers for sure.⟩ — see SAILOR

heat *n* **1** depth of feeling ⟨Anna informed the doctor, with considerable *heat*, that she had been kept waiting for three hours.⟩ — see ARDOR 1

2 *slang* a body of officers of the law ⟨He thought he was so slick, but the *heat* was onto him in no time.⟩ — see POLICE 2

heat *vb* to cause to have or give off heat to a moderate degree ⟨*heated* water for tea⟩ ⟨*Heat* the oven to 350 degrees before you put the cake in.⟩ — see WARM 1

heated *adj* **1** being in a state of increased activity or agitation ⟨a *heated* discussion about who should pay for the pizza⟩ — see FEVERISH 1

2 having or giving off heat to a moderate degree ⟨Early settlers put *heated* bricks under the blankets to keep warm.⟩ — see WARM 1

heathen *adj* not civilized ⟨old missionaries who mistakenly thought that they were going off to China to tame the *heathen* hordes⟩ — see UNCIVILIZED

heathen *n* **1** a person who does not worship the God of the Bible ⟨a belief held by *heathens*⟩

synonyms gentile, idolater (*or* idolator), pagan

related words atheist, nonbeliever, unbeliever; neo-pagan, polytheist

near antonyms Christian, Jew, Muslim

2 an uncivilized person ⟨considered the people to be *heathens*⟩

synonyms barbarian

related words Neanderthal, primitive

heathenish *adj* not civilized ⟨denouncing the punishment as *heathenish*⟩ — see UNCIVILIZED

heave *vb* **1** to lift with effort ⟨I *heaved* my duffel bag into the bus's overhead compartment.⟩

synonyms boost, heft, hoist, jack (up)

related words elevate, hike, pick up, raise, rear, up, uplift, upraise, uprear

near antonyms depress, drop, lower; sink, submerge, submerse

2 to discharge the contents of the stomach through the mouth ⟨Mike *heaved* as soon as he stepped off the roller coaster.⟩ — see VOMIT

3 to move from a lower to a higher place or position ⟨*heaved* the bucket from the bottom of the well⟩ — see RAISE 1

4 to send through the air especially with a quick forward motion of the arm ⟨*heaved* the brick over the fence⟩ — see THROW 1

5 to breathe hard, quickly, or with difficulty ⟨By the time he reached the top step of the tower, he was *heaving*.⟩ — see GASP

heaven *n* **1** a dwelling place of perfect happiness for the soul after death ⟨We prayed that the souls of the deceased would go to *heaven*.⟩

synonyms above, bliss, Elysium, kingdom come, paradise, sky

related words glory, promised land, Valhalla; afterlife, afterworld, hereafter, otherworld

phrases on high

near antonyms inferno; limbo, purgatory; hades, netherworld, underworld; abyss, pit

antonyms hell, Pandemonium, perdition

2 an often imaginary place or state of utter perfection and happiness ⟨Compared to my old job, this new one is *heaven*!⟩ — see PARADISE 1

3 a state of overwhelming usually pleasurable emotion ⟨She was in *heaven* the day she learned she was one of the finalists for the science scholarship.⟩ — see ECSTASY

4 *usually* **heavens** *pl* the expanse of air surrounding the earth ⟨the starry *heavens*⟩ ⟨The space shuttle gradually disappeared into the *heavens*.⟩ — see SKY 1

heavenly *adj* **1** of the very best kind ⟨I had a *heavenly* time at the dance.⟩ — see EXCELLENT

2 of, relating to, or being God ⟨Do not concern yourself with material possessions, but with things *heavenly*, the prophet admonished.⟩ — see HOLY 3

3 of, relating to, or suggesting heaven ⟨*heavenly* hosts singing "Alleluia!"⟩ — see CELESTIAL

4 giving pleasure or contentment to the mind or senses ⟨The *heavenly* aroma of chocolate fills the shop.⟩ — see PLEASANT 1

heavily *adv* to a great degree ⟨*heavily* spiced sausage⟩ ⟨The family was *heavily* in debt.⟩ — see VERY 1

heaviness *n* **1** the amount that something weighs ⟨The numbers on the back of each sample indicate the *heaviness* of the carpeting material.⟩ — see WEIGHT 1

2 the state or quality of being heavy ⟨The backpack was filled with water bottles that gave it an extra *heaviness*.⟩ — see WEIGHTINESS 1

heavy *adj* **1** having great weight ⟨This trunk full of books is much too *heavy* for one person to lift.⟩

synonyms hefty, massive, ponderous, weighty

related words burdensome, leaden, lumpish; bulky, elephantine, massy, outsize (*also* outsized), voluminous; overweight, top-heavy; solid, substantial; ultraheavy

near antonyms airy, ethereal, feathery, fluffy, gossamer, gossamery; flimsy, insubstantial, slight; lightweight, undersized (*also* undersize), underweight

antonyms light, weightless

2 causing weariness, restlessness, or lack of interest ⟨The study of history doesn't have to be all about dull *heavy* reading and the memorization of dates.⟩ — see BORING

3 containing much seasoning, fat, or sugar ⟨Avoid *heavy* desserts like cheesecake and pecan pie.⟩ — see RICH 2

4 covered up or by clouds ⟨*heavy* skies threatening rain⟩ — see OVERCAST

5 difficult to endure ⟨They are paying a *heavy* price for their mistakes.⟩ — see HARSH 1

6 extreme in degree, power, or effect ⟨*heavy* rains⟩ ⟨The company expects *heavy* losses this year.⟩ — see INTENSE 1

7 having a matter of importance as its topic ⟨We got into a *heavy* discussion about death and the afterlife.⟩ — see SERIOUS 2

8 requiring considerable physical or mental effort ⟨Until we find our groove, it's going to be *heavy* sledding on this project.⟩ — see HARD 2

9 having great power or influence ⟨She's not among the handful of *heavy* critics who can make or break a Broadway show.⟩ — see IMPORTANT 2
10 containing unborn young within the body ⟨The heifer was *heavy* with young and soon would be birthing.⟩ — see PREGNANT 1

heavy *n* **1** a mean, evil, or unprincipled person ⟨He played the *heavy* in film after film.⟩ — see VILLAIN
2 one of high position or importance within a group ⟨In the field of secondary education, she definitely ranks as one of the *heavies*.⟩ — see BIG SHOT

heavy–handed *adj* **1** given to exacting standards of discipline and self-restraint ⟨The gym teacher is *heavy-handed* with the students.⟩ — see SEVERE 1
2 lacking or showing a lack of nimbleness in using one's hands ⟨Kara felt *heavy-handed* and awkward when she held the newborn infant.⟩ — see CLUMSY 1

heavyset *adj* being compact and broad in build and often short in stature ⟨Bob has the *heavyset* build of a weight lifter.⟩ — see STOCKY

heckle *vb* to attack repeatedly with mean put-downs or insults ⟨The players were being *heckled* by the fans.⟩ — see TEASE 2

heckler *n* a person who causes repeated emotional pain, distress, or annoyance to another ⟨The speakers were upset by several *hecklers* in the crowd.⟩ — see TORMENTOR

hectic *adj* being in a state of increased activity or agitation ⟨exhausted from a *hectic* day at the office⟩ — see FEVERISH 1

hectically *adv* in a confused and reckless manner ⟨A moth kept banging *hectically* against the screen, seeking the light on the other side.⟩ — see HELTER-SKELTER 1

hector *n* a person who teases, threatens, or hurts more vulnerable persons ⟨laws penalizing debt collection agencies that operate like *hectors*⟩ — see BULLY

hector *vb* to make timid or fearful by or as if by threats ⟨The judge ordered the attorney to stop *hectoring* the witness.⟩ — see INTIMIDATE

hedge *n* a physical object that blocks the way ⟨The messenger was confronted with a *hedge* of spears held aloft by the castle guards.⟩ — see BARRIER

hedge *vb* **1** to avoid giving a definite answer or position ⟨She kept *hedging* whenever he asked her to support his campaign.⟩ — see EQUIVOCATE
2 to close or shut in by or as if by barriers ⟨The prison was *hedged* by a high stone wall.⟩ — see ENCLOSE 1

heed *n* **1** a state of being aware ⟨took *heed* of the students' learning styles so as to prepare appropriate lessons⟩ — see ATTENTION 2
2 strict attentiveness to what one is doing ⟨Pay *heed* to what you're doing with that knife while you're talking.⟩ — see CARE 1

heed *vb* **1** to take notice of and be guided by ⟨If we had *heeded* the ranger's advice, we might not have gotten lost.⟩
synonyms follow, listen (to), mind, note, observe, regard, watch
related words consider, contemplate, mull, ponder, weigh; comply (with), conform (to), keep, obey, respect; attend (to), hark (to), hear, hearken (to); mark, notice, see
near antonyms brush (aside *or* off), discount, dismiss, gloss (over), gloze (over), neglect, pass over, pooh-pooh (*also* pooh), scorn, shrug off; defy, flout; slight, snub
antonyms disregard, ignore, tune out
2 to pay attention especially through the act of hearing ⟨That boy never *heeds* when I caution him about running with his shoelaces untied.⟩ — see LISTEN

heedful *adj* having or showing a close attentiveness to avoiding danger or trouble ⟨*Heedful* of snakes, we watched our footing while walking through the tall grass to the lake's edge.⟩ — see CAREFUL 1

heedfulness *n* **1** a close attentiveness to avoiding danger ⟨Despite their habitual *heedfulness*, even good drivers can get into accidents.⟩ — see CAUTION 1
2 strict attentiveness to what one is doing ⟨Mom always exercises extreme *heedfulness* when she handles her best china.⟩ — see CARE 1

heedless *adj* not paying or showing close attention especially for the purpose of avoiding trouble ⟨*heedless* drivers who back out of parking spaces without looking⟩ — see CARELESS 1

heedlessness *n* failure to take the care that a cautious person usually takes ⟨The dog's lack of protection against rabies was purely due to his owner's *heedlessness*.⟩ — see NEGLIGENCE 1

heel *n* a person whose behavior is offensive to others ⟨She felt like a *heel* when she found out that she'd blamed the wrong person.⟩ — see JERK 1

heel *vb* to set or cause to be at an angle ⟨The strong gust *heeled* the sailboat almost to the point of capsizing, but we managed to right it.⟩ — see LEAN 1

heft *n* **1** the amount that something weighs ⟨Some synthetic fabrics are nice and warm, but I prefer wool because it has more *heft*.⟩ — see WEIGHT 1
2 the power to direct the thinking or behavior of others usually indirectly ⟨As a former senator, he still had some *heft* in political circles.⟩ — see INFLUENCE 1

heft *vb* **1** to lift with effort ⟨*hefted* his growing son onto his shoulders⟩ — see HEAVE 1
2 to move from a lower to a higher place or position ⟨He *hefted* his baggy gym shorts a little higher.⟩ — see RAISE 1

heftiness *n* **1** the quality or state of being large in size ⟨a restaurant known for the *heftiness* of its portions⟩ — see LARGENESS
2 the state or quality of being heavy ⟨Clerks no longer have to deal with the *heftiness* of paper files now that everything is filed on computers.⟩ — see WEIGHTINESS 1

hefty *adj* **1** having great weight ⟨That's a pretty *hefty* book bag for a tiny person like you!⟩ — see HEAVY 1
2 of a size greater than average of its kind ⟨received a *hefty* donation from the local business association⟩ — see LARGE
3 strongly and heavily built ⟨*Hefty* since childhood, he became a champion wrestler.⟩ — see ¹HUSKY 1

height *n* **1** the highest part or point ⟨Many regard the painting of the Sistine Chapel as the *height* of Michelangelo's career.⟩
synonyms acme, apex, climax, crest, crown, culmination, head, high noon, high-water mark, meridian, noon, noontime, peak, pinnacle, summit, tip-top, top, zenith
related words bloom, blossom, flood tide, flower, glory, heyday, prime; cap, ceiling, roof; extreme, extremity, tip, vertex; high, highlight, highspot
near antonyms abyss, base, foot; minimum
antonyms bottom, rock bottom
2 the most extreme or advanced point ⟨the *height* of arrogance⟩
synonyms depth, elevation, extremity, limit
related words consummation, epitome, quintessence, ultimate
3 the distance of something or someone from bottom to top ⟨The average *height* of the players on the volleyball team is well over six feet.⟩
synonyms altitude, elevation, inches, stature
related words rise; highness, loftiness, tallness

4 an area of high ground ⟨Gulliver, standing on a *height* near the shore, saw an island suspended above the sea.⟩

synonyms altitude(s), elevation, eminence, highland, hill, hump, mound, prominence, rise, upland

related words alp, mount, mountain, peak; butte, mesa, plateau, table, tableland; bluff, cliff, crag, precipice, steep, tor; ridge, sierra; sugarloaf; foothill, hillock, hummock, knob, knoll

near antonyms dale, dell, depression, dingle, glen, hollow, vale, valley; basin, bottom, bottomland, fen, flat, floodplain, plain, tidewater

antonyms lowland

5 the most intense or characteristic phase of something ⟨At the very *height* of the storm, someone knocked on the door.⟩ — see THICK

heighten *vb* **1** to make markedly greater in measure or degree ⟨Several controversial measures have *heightened* parental awareness of the impact of school policy decisions.⟩ — see INTENSIFY

2 to move from a lower to a higher place or position ⟨*heightened* the adjustable shelf a couple of inches⟩ — see RAISE 1

heightened *adj* being at a higher level than average ⟨*heightened* levels of interest⟩ — see HIGH 2

heinousness *n* the state or quality of being utterly evil ⟨The *heinousness* of the Holocaust was only fully realized after the war.⟩ — see ENORMITY 1

heir *n* a person who has the right to inherit property ⟨Upon his death, Mr. Parkworth's property was divided evenly among his *heirs*, four sons and three daughters.⟩

synonyms inheritor, legatee

related words claimant; heir apparent, representative, succeeder, successor; coheir, coheiress, heiress; beneficiary, devisee, grantee; descendant (*also* descendent), scion

heist *n* an instance of theft ⟨It was the largest jewelry *heist* in the city's history.⟩ — see THEFT 2

heist *vb* to take (something) without right and with an intent to keep ⟨A professional burglar was able to *heist* a box of jewelry from the safe in the closet.⟩ — see STEAL 1

helical *adj* turning around an axis like the thread of a screw ⟨Sirius, the brightest star in the heavens, travels a *helical* path through space⟩ — see SPIRAL

hell *n* **1** the place of punishment for the wicked after death ⟨condemned to *hell* for their sins⟩

synonyms Pandemonium, perdition

related words blazes, inferno; purgatory; hades, netherworld, shades, Tartarus, underworld; Sheol; abyss, pit; fire and brimstone, hellfire

near antonyms glory, promised land, Valhalla

antonyms bliss, elysian fields, Elysium, empyrean, heaven, kingdom come, paradise, sky

2 a situation or state that causes great suffering and unhappiness ⟨Picking cotton under the hot summer sun was *hell*.⟩

synonyms agony, horror, misery, murder, nightmare, torment, torture

related words affliction, calvary, cross, curse, ordeal, trial, tribulation; calamity, misfortune, tragedy; gall, thorn; bummer, downer, drag

near antonyms delight, diversion, entertainment, fun, joy, pleasure, recreation; lark, picnic, riot

antonyms heaven, paradise

3 a state in which everything is out of order ⟨All *hell* broke loose when the jury's verdict was announced.⟩ — see CHAOS

hell–bent (on *or* **upon)** *adj* fully committed to achieving a goal ⟨She's *hell-bent on* a career in show business and seems to have the talent and work ethic to succeed.⟩ — see DETERMINED 1

hellion *n* an appealingly mischievous person ⟨The little *hellions* were tearing through the house squirting their water pistols.⟩ — see SCAMP 1

hello *n* an expression of goodwill upon meeting ⟨We said our *hellos* and got right down to business.⟩

synonyms greeting, salutation, salute, welcome

related words ave, hail; amenities, civilities, pleasantries; regards, respects, wishes

antonyms adieu, bon voyage, farewell, Godspeed, goodbye (*or* good-by)

helm *n* the place of leadership or command ⟨She took the *helm* of the university.⟩ — see HEAD 2

helm *vb* to operate or control the course of ⟨a treacherous route for any weekend sailor just learning to *helm* his vessel⟩ — see NAVIGATE 1

help *n* **1** an act or instance of helping ⟨I could use your *help* getting this tire back on the car.⟩

synonyms abetment, aid, assist, assistance, backing, boost, hand, lift, support

related words advancement, encouragement, facilitation, forwarding, furtherance, furthering, nurturance; benefaction, promotion; advice, care, counsel, guidance, mentoring; attendance, attention, hand-holding, service; assuagement, palliation, relief, succor

near antonyms constraint, frustration, inhibition, interference, obstruction, repression, restraint; deterrence, discouragement

antonyms hindrance

2 a thing that helps ⟨The blender is a great *help* for making smoothies.⟩

synonyms advantage, aid, benefit, boon

related words hand, lift, pick-me-up; support; blessing, godsend, windfall; recourse, refuge, resort, resource

near antonyms constraint, inhibitor, liability, obstacle, obstruction, restraint, stranglehold

antonyms disadvantage, drawback, encumbrance, hindrance, impediment, minus

3 a body of persons at work or available for work ⟨It's so hard to get good *help* these days.⟩ — see FORCE 1

help *vb* **1** to provide (someone) with what is useful or necessary to achieve an end ⟨We offered to *help* her when she moved into an apartment.⟩

synonyms abet, aid, assist, back, prop (up), support

related words advance, ease, facilitate, forward, foster, further, launch; champion, endorse (*also* indorse), patronize, promote, sponsor; attend, care (for), comfort, minister (to), succor; sustain; bolster, boost, buttress; advise, counsel, guide, mentor, nurture; bail out, deliver, rescue, save; embolden, encourage, hearten; benefit, favor, oblige, profit, serve

phrases bear a hand, to stand one in good stead

near antonyms balk, bar, block, constrain, hamper, handicap, hold back, impede, inhibit, obstruct, restrain, strangle; baffle, foil, frustrate, inconvenience, interfere, oppose, sabotage, thwart; desert, disappoint, fail, let down; discourage, dishearten; repress, retard, stifle, straiten, stunt; damage, harm, hurt, injure

antonyms hinder

2 to make more bearable or less severe ⟨The new ointment didn't *help* Josh's sunburn one bit.⟩

synonyms allay, alleviate, assuage, ease, mitigate, mollify, palliate, relieve, soothe

related words abate, lighten, moderate, soften, temper; cure, heal, remedy; amend, correct, emend, fix, mend, rectify, reform, repair; ameliorate, better, enhance, enrich, improve, meliorate, perfect, refine

near antonyms harm, hurt, impair, injure; heighten, intensify, sharpen
antonyms aggravate
3 to keep from happening by taking action in advance ⟨They couldn't *help* the way things turned out.⟩ — see PREVENT
4 to provide with something useful or desirable ⟨Being independently wealthy certainly *helped* him during his years as a struggling young artist.⟩ — see BENEFIT
5 to make better ⟨Some minor revisions would *help* this essay immensely.⟩ — see IMPROVE
helper *n* a person who helps a more skilled person ⟨Over the summer Chris worked as a carpenter's *helper*.⟩
synonyms adjunct, adjutant, aid, aide, apprentice, assistant, coadjutor, deputy, helpmate, helpmeet, sidekick
related words attendant, servant; auxiliary, legman, subordinate, underling; employee (*also* employe), hand, help, hireling, laborer, worker; man Friday, right hand; aide-de-camp
helpful *adj* **1** providing service or assistance ⟨a website that I've always found to be *helpful* for finding information on common medical problems⟩
synonyms useful
related words advantageous, beneficial, efficacious, favorable, productive, profitable, salutary; accommodating, obliging
near antonyms ineffective, ineffectual; adverse, disadvantageous, inconvenient, profitless, unfavorable
antonyms unhelpful, useless
2 promoting or contributing to personal or social well-being ⟨It would be *helpful* to have more than one thesaurus in the classroom.⟩ — see BENEFICIAL
helpless *adj* **1** lacking protection from danger or resistance against attack ⟨After the storm we found a *helpless* baby bird that had fallen out of its nest.⟩
synonyms defenseless, exposed, susceptible, undefended, unguarded, unprotected, unresistant, vulnerable
related words indefensible, untenable; uncovered, unsafe; overcome, preyed (on *or* upon); disarmed, passive, resistless, unarmed; feeble, frail, weak; abandoned, marooned
phrases in the lurch
near antonyms defensible; covered, fortified, safe, screened, secure, sheltered; armed, armored; immune, impenetrable, impregnable, invincible, strong, unassailable, unbeatable, unconquerable; almighty, omnipotent
antonyms guarded, invulnerable, protected, resistant, shielded
2 unable to act or achieve one's purpose ⟨We watched, feeling *helpless*, as the vase slipped from her hand and crashed to the floor.⟩ — see POWERLESS
helpmate *n* a person who helps a more skilled person ⟨After several years as a photographer's *helpmate*, the young man decided to pursue his own ambitions in commercial photography.⟩ — see HELPER
helpmeet *n* a person who helps a more skilled person ⟨Exasperated, the army surgeon requested a *helpmeet* who wouldn't faint at the sight of blood.⟩ — see HELPER
helter–skelter *adj* **1** acting or done with excessive or careless speed ⟨a bill that was pushed through committee in a last-minute *helter-skelter* burst of legislative activity⟩ — see HASTY 1
2 lacking a definite plan, purpose, or pattern ⟨papers stacked *helter-skelter* on her desk⟩ — see RANDOM
helter–skelter *adv* **1** in a confused and reckless manner ⟨The sheep ran *helter-skelter* inside their pen when the coyote appeared in their midst.⟩
synonyms amok (*or* amuck), berserk, frantically, frenziedly, harum-scarum, hectically, madly, pell-mell, wild, wildly

related words agitatedly, confusedly, crazily, feverishly, haywire, skittishly, uncontrollably; heedlessly, hotheadedly, recklessly, wantonly; chaotically, riotously, tumultuously, turbulently; aimlessly, haphazard, haphazardly, hit-or-miss, topsy-turvy
near antonyms calmly, composedly, coolly (*also* cooly), imperturbably, peacefully, placidly, self-composedly, self-possessedly, serenely, unconcernedly; meekly, mildly, passively, tamely; methodically, orderly
2 without definite aim, direction, rule, or method ⟨goods arranged *helter-skelter* on the shelves of the variety store⟩ — see HIT OR MISS
helter–skelter *n* a state of noisy, confused activity ⟨the *helter-skelter* of the playground⟩ — see COMMOTION
hem *n* the line or relatively narrow space that marks the outer limit of something ⟨The *hem* of the blouse was gold.⟩ — see BORDER 1
hence *adv* **1** for this or that reason ⟨an endangered orchid species, *hence* illegal to pick⟩ — see THEREFORE
2 from this or that place ⟨The king commanded, "Get thee *hence*, traitor!"⟩ — see AWAY
henceforth *adv* from this point on ⟨*Henceforth*, there will be no more prolonged coffee breaks.⟩
synonyms henceforward, hereafter
related words afterward (*or* afterwards), later, subsequently; hereupon, thereupon
henceforward *adv* from this point on ⟨You have sworn to tell the truth in this court, and *henceforward* you are bound by your oath.⟩ — see HENCEFORTH
henpeck *vb* to subject (someone) to constant scoldings and sharp reminders ⟨She *henpecked* me into seeing a doctor about my cough.⟩ — see NAG 1
herald *n* **1** a person who actively supports or favors a cause ⟨an outspoken *herald* of prison reform⟩ — see EXPONENT 1
2 one that announces or indicates the later arrival of another ⟨the American robin—the *herald* of spring in the North⟩ — see FORERUNNER 1
herald *vb* **1** to give a slight indication of beforehand ⟨The reshuffle of the company's management *heralded* the sweeping changes to come.⟩ — see FORESHADOW
2 to make known openly or publicly ⟨Let's *herald* the great tidings to all the world!⟩ — see ANNOUNCE
herbage *n* green leaves or plants ⟨added some ferns and other *herbage* to the sidewalk planters⟩ — see GREENERY
herculean *adj* **1** requiring considerable physical or mental effort ⟨the *herculean* task of grading 60 student essays over one weekend⟩ — see HARD 2
2 unusually large ⟨a *herculean* banquet table that took eight men to lift it⟩ — see HUGE
herd *n* **1** a group of domestic animals assembled or herded together ⟨the great *herds* of cattle that cowboys once drove across the plains⟩
synonyms drove, flock
related words colony, covey, gaggle, pack, pod, school, swarm
2 the body of the community as contrasted with the elite ⟨Aspire to achieve something, to distinguish yourself from the *herd*.⟩ — see MASS 1
3 a great number of persons or creatures massed together ⟨gearing up for the *herd* of holiday shoppers at the mall on the day after Thanksgiving⟩ — see CROWD 1
herd *vb* to urge, push, or force onward ⟨The guards briskly *herded* us through the museum in order to prevent overcrowding.⟩ — see DRIVE 1
herder *n* a tender of livestock ⟨The nomadic reindeer *herders* of Siberia live in reindeer-skin tents.⟩
synonyms herdsman

related words buckaroo (*also* buckeroo), cowboy, cowgirl, cowhand, cowherd, cowman, cowpoke, cowpuncher, gaucho, ranchero, vaquero; sheepherder, shepherd, shepherdess; goatherd; swineherd; wrangler; drover

herdsman *n* a tender of livestock ⟨A lone *herdsman* stood with his sheep and his dog on the hillside.⟩ — see HERDER

hereafter *adv* from this point on ⟨He is giving up all his worldly goods and *hereafter* will devote his life to the poor.⟩ — see HENCEFORTH

hereafter *n* **1** time that is to come ⟨Dan apologized for being late to the meeting and assured his boss that there would be no such recurrences in the *hereafter*.⟩ — see FUTURE 1

2 unending existence after death ⟨He hoped to be reunited with his deceased wife in the *hereafter*.⟩ — see ETERNITY 2

hereditary *adj* genetically passed or capable of being passed from parent to offspring ⟨Eye and hair color are *hereditary*.⟩

synonyms genetic (*also* genetical), heritable, inborn, inheritable, inherited

related words congenital, inbred, inherent, innate, native, natural

near antonyms acquired

antonyms nonhereditary

heresy *n* departure from a generally accepted theory, opinion, or practice ⟨the *heresy* of asserting that Shakespeare was not a great writer⟩

synonyms dissent, dissidence, heterodoxy, nonconformity

related words error, fallacy, falsehood, misbelief, misconception, myth; apostasy, defection, infidelity, schism, separatism; deviance, iconoclasm, unconventionality; disagreement, discord, dissension (*also* dissention)

near antonyms agreement, conformation, conventionality

antonyms conformity, orthodoxy

heretic *n* **1** a person who believes, teaches, or advocates something opposed to accepted beliefs ⟨Galileo was condemned as a *heretic* for supporting Copernicus's thesis that the earth revolves around the sun and not vice versa.⟩

synonyms dissenter, dissident, nonconformist

related words apostate, defector, renegade; schismatic, sectarian, separationist, separatist; disbeliever, infidel, misbeliever, unbeliever; bohemian, individualist

antonyms conformer, conformist

2 a person who does not conform to generally accepted standards or customs ⟨He's the ultimate *heretic*: a Yankees fan living deep in the heart of the Red Sox Nation.⟩ — see NONCONFORMIST 1

heretical *also* **heretic** *adj* deviating from commonly accepted beliefs or practices ⟨It would be *heretical* to suggest changing the long-standing company policy.⟩

synonyms dissenting, dissident, heterodox, maverick, nonconformist, nonorthodox, out-there, unconventional, unorthodox

related words free-spirited, freethinking, nontraditional; apostate, defecting, renegade; schismatic (*also* schismatical), sectarian, separatist

antonyms conforming, conformist, conventional, orthodox

heretofore *adv* up to this or that time ⟨Having been *heretofore* unwilling to fly, he was forced to make an exception for his brother's out-of-state wedding.⟩ — see HITHERTO

heritable *adj* genetically passed or capable of being passed from parent to offspring ⟨*heritable* characteristics like skin and eye and hair color⟩ — see HEREDITARY

heritage *n* **1** an inherited or established way of thinking, feeling, or doing ⟨Hospitality is a cherished Southern *heritage*.⟩ — see TRADITION 1

2 something that is or may be inherited ⟨This farm is my *heritage* from my father, as it was for him from his father.⟩ — see INHERITANCE

hermit *n* a person who lives away from others ⟨St. Jerome is said to have spent two years as a *hermit* in the desert, searching for inner peace.⟩ — see RECLUSE

hermitage *n* **1** a place where a person goes to hide or to avoid others ⟨The artist's desert *hermitage* was a small adobe house at the end of a long dusty road.⟩ — see HIDEOUT

2 a residence for men under religious vows ⟨Monks in that *hermitage* take a vow of silence.⟩ — see MONASTERY

hero *n* a large sandwich on a long split roll ⟨shared a footlong meatball *hero* with his friend⟩ — see SUBMARINE

heroic *also* **heroical** *adj* **1** feeling or displaying no fear by temperament ⟨a memorial honoring the *heroic* nurses who served in the war⟩ — see BRAVE 1

2 large and impressive in size, grandeur, extent, or conception ⟨an opera production of *heroic* proportions⟩ — see GRAND 1

3 unusually large ⟨a *heroic* statue of Alexander the Great astride his horse⟩ — see HUGE

heroically *adv* in a manner befitting a person of the highest character and ideals ⟨Doctors and nurses worked *heroically* through the night to keep the patient alive.⟩ — see GREATLY 1

heroism *n* strength of mind to carry on in spite of danger ⟨the inspiring *heroism* of the firefighters who risked their lives to save the people trapped in the burning building⟩ — see COURAGE

hesitance *n* **1** a lack of willingness or desire to do or accept something ⟨Sales figures for the month were up, as consumers began to overcome their *hesitance* about purchasing big-ticket items.⟩ — see RELUCTANCE

2 a state or an instance of temporary inaction because of uncertainty about the right course of action ⟨She mistook my *hesitance* to mean I didn't like her poem, but I was trying to come up with appropriate words of praise.⟩ — see HESITATION

hesitancy *n* **1** a lack of willingness or desire to do or accept something ⟨His appointment to the superintendency was confirmed by the school board without the least *hesitancy*.⟩ — see RELUCTANCE

2 a state or an instance of temporary inaction because of uncertainty about the right course of action ⟨His *hesitancy* in pulling over into the next lane while he had a chance resulted in him missing his exit.⟩ — see HESITATION

hesitant *adj* slow to begin or proceed with a course of action because of doubts or uncertainty ⟨He was *hesitant* about committing himself to the oversight of the project, which he knew would be long and difficult.⟩

synonyms cagey (*also* cagy), disinclined, dubious, indisposed, loath (*also* loth *or* loathe), reluctant, reticent

related words uneager, unenthusiastic; averse, unwilling; doubtful, faltering, halting, indecisive, infirm, irresolute, questioning, skeptical, uncertain, undecided, unsure, vacillating, wobbly (*also* wabbly); fainthearted, shy, timid

near antonyms eager, enthusiastic, glad, happy, keen; ready, willing; certain, decided, determined, resolute, sure, unquestioning

antonyms disposed, inclined

hesitate *vb* to show uncertainty about the right course of action ⟨I didn't *hesitate* to tell them that what they were doing was wrong and that I wanted no part of it.⟩

synonyms balance, dither, falter, halt, hang back, scruple, shilly-shally, stagger, teeter, vacillate, waver, wobble (*also* wabble)

related words haw, hem; dally, dawdle, delay, linger, pause, procrastinate, wait; back down, chicken (out); consider, debate, deliberate, ponder, weigh; oscillate, sway; equivocate, hedge, pussyfoot

near antonyms decide; budge, stir; advance, continue
antonyms dive (in), plunge (in)

hesitation *n* a state or an instance of temporary inaction because of uncertainty about the right course of action ⟨Because of one moment's *hesitation*, I missed getting the picture of the elusive butterfly.⟩

synonyms faltering, hesitance, hesitancy, indecision, irresolution, pause, shilly-shally, shilly-shallying, vacillation, wavering, wobbling (*also* wabbling)

related words delay, hawing, procrastination, waiting; misgiving, second thought; consideration, debate, deliberation, doubt, incertitude, indecisiveness, indetermination, uncertainness, uncertainty; avoidance, equivocation; aversion, disinclination, indisposition, reluctance, unwillingness; faintheartedness, shyness, timidity, timidness

near antonyms certainty, certitude, confidence, decisiveness, determination, firmness, resoluteness, resolution, sureness; alacrity, eagerness, readiness

heterodox *adj* **1** deviating from commonly accepted beliefs or practices ⟨a scientist with very *heterodox* theories⟩ — see HERETICAL

2 not rigidly following established form, custom, or rules ⟨Her *heterodox* approach to teaching initially met with some resistance from her peers.⟩ — see INFORMAL 1

heterodoxy *n* departure from a generally accepted theory, opinion, or practice ⟨Copernicus's theory that the earth revolved around the sun was arrant *heterodoxy* at a time when the earth was thought to be the center of the universe.⟩ — see HERESY

heterogeneous *adj* consisting of many things of different sorts ⟨The seating in the hall was a *heterogeneous* collection of old school desk chairs, wood and metal folding chairs, and even a few plush theater seats.⟩ — see MISCELLANEOUS

heterogeneousness *n* the quality or state of being composed of many different elements or types ⟨the ever increasing *heterogeneousness* of the nation's population⟩ — see VARIETY 1

het up *adj* feeling or showing uncomfortable feelings of uncertainty ⟨It won't do you any good to get all *het up* before the tryouts and lose sleep.⟩ — see NERVOUS 1

hew *vb* **1** to bring down by cutting ⟨laboriously *hewed* trees to build their rude log cabins⟩ — see FELL 2

2 to hold to something firmly as if by adhesion ⟨We decided to *hew* to the original plan rather than change everything.⟩ — see STICK 1

hew (to) *vb* to give steadfast support to ⟨no longer was able to *hew to* the party line and so he switched political parties⟩ — see ADHERE (TO) 1

hex *n* **1** a woman believed to have often harmful supernatural powers ⟨people who used to believe that misfortune was caused by evil *hexes* and mischievous sprites⟩ — see WITCH 1

2 something that brings bad luck ⟨There seemed to be a *hex* on him, for all of his business ventures came to naught despite his hard work.⟩ — see JINX

3 a spoken word or set of words believed to have magic power ⟨The wizard had put a *hex* on the evil gnome that turned him to stone.⟩ — see SPELL 1

hex *vb* to cast a spell on ⟨I think our plans have been *hexed* from the start—everything is going wrong.⟩ — see BEWITCH 1

heyday *n* a state or time of great activity, thriving, or achievement ⟨In its *heyday*, the circus was a major form of entertainment for small-town America.⟩ — see BLOOM 1

hiatus *n* **1** an open space in a barrier (as a wall or hedge) ⟨Steam was rising from a *hiatus* in the ground.⟩ — see GAP 1

2 an incomplete or deficient area ⟨a *hiatus* in the law which prevented the district attorney from prosecuting the offenders⟩ — see GAP 3

3 a break in continuity ⟨a three-year *hiatus* before the fifth book in the series appeared⟩ — see GAP 2

hick *n* an awkward or simple person especially from a small town or the country ⟨I felt like a *hick* when I visited the city for the first time.⟩

synonyms bumpkin, churl, clodhopper, countryman, hillbilly, provincial, rustic, yokel

related words boor, clod, clown, gawk, lout, oaf; greenhorn, tenderfoot; backwoodsman, mountaineer

near antonyms slicker, smoothy (*or* smoothie); metropolitan, suburbanite, urbanite

antonyms cosmopolitan, sophisticate

hide *n* **1** the outer covering of an animal removed for its commercial value ⟨Seal *hides* are used by Inuits to make footwear, boats, shelters, bags, and clothing.⟩

synonyms fur, leather, pelt, skin

related words badger, beaver, chamois, chinchilla, ermine, fox, marten, mink, muskrat, otter, Persian lamb, rabbit, raccoon (*also* racoon), sable, seal; bearskin, buckskin, calfskin, coonskin, cowhide, deerskin, doeskin, goatskin, horsehide, kidskin, lambskin, pigskin, rawhide, sealskin, sharkskin, sheep, sheepskin, snakeskin; fleece, mouton; alligator, crocodile

2 the hairless natural covering of an animal prepared for use ⟨boots made of shiny alligator *hide*⟩ — see LEATHER 1

¹**hide** *vb* **1** to put into a hiding place ⟨The thief had *hidden* the stolen jewelry under the floorboards.⟩

synonyms bury, cache, conceal, ensconce, secrete

related words hoard, squirrel (away), stash; entomb, inter

near antonyms bare, expose, reveal, show, uncover, unmask, unveil, unwrap; flaunt, parade, show off; disinter, unearth

antonyms display, exhibit

2 to keep secret or shut off from view ⟨He tried to *hide* his criminal past.⟩ ⟨She *hid* the cat's litter box behind a screen.⟩

synonyms belie, blanket, blot out, cloak, conceal, cover, curtain, disguise, enshroud, mask, obscure, occult, screen, shroud, suppress, veil

related words bury, camouflage, cover (up), smother; gild, gloss (over), varnish, whitewash; becloud, bedim, befog, block, cloud, darken, eclipse, obstruct, occlude, overcast, overshadow, shade

near antonyms present; clarify, illuminate; advertise, air, broadcast, get out, proclaim, publicize, publish, spread

antonyms bare, disclose, display, divulge, expose, reveal, show, uncloak, uncover, unmask, unveil

3 to remain out of sight ⟨He *hid* in the closet during the game of hide-and-seek.⟩

synonyms lie, lurk, repose, skulk

related words slink, sneak; avoid, elude, evade

phrases lie low, sit tight

near antonyms come out, materialize, show up, turn up

antonyms appear

²**hide** *vb* **1** to strike repeatedly ⟨The grizzled quartermaster threatened to *hide* any soldier caught stealing provisions.⟩ — see BEAT 1

2 to strike repeatedly with something long and thin or flexible ⟨threatened to *hide* us if he ever caught us again⟩ — see WHIP 1

hideaway *n* a place where a person goes to hide or to avoid others ⟨The novelist has a little *hideaway* in the country where he goes whenever he wants to do some serious writing.⟩ — see HIDEOUT

hidebound *adj* tending to favor established ideas, conditions, or institutions ⟨The *hidebound* innkeeper refused to see the need for a website, insisting that the inn had done without one for over 150 years.⟩ — see CONSERVATIVE 1

hideous *adj* **1** causing intense displeasure, disgust, or resentment ⟨the *hideous* way in which longtime employees were summarily dismissed⟩ — see OFFENSIVE 1

2 extremely disturbing or repellent ⟨a *hideous* crime that could not be fully described in the newspapers⟩ — see HORRIBLE 1

3 unpleasant to look at ⟨wearing a *hideous* Halloween mask that made the kids all jump with fright⟩ — see UGLY 1

hideousness *n* **1** the quality of inspiring intense dread or dismay ⟨the *hideousness* of the way they carelessly ruined a lovely woodland⟩ — see HORROR 1

2 the state or quality of being utterly evil ⟨The *hideousness* of the defendant's alleged crimes should not prevent him from getting a fair trial.⟩ — see ENORMITY 1

hideout *n* a place where a person goes to hide or to avoid others ⟨Police found the stolen jewels under the floorboards in the thief's *hideout*, a cabin deep in the woods.⟩

synonyms concealment, covert, den, hermitage, hideaway, lair, nest

related words blind, cover, nook, recess; hangout, harbor, harborage, haunt, haven, refuge, retreat, shelter

hiding *n* the placing of something out of sight ⟨Fearing that the enemy would soon be upon them, the museum director oversaw the *hiding* of the most valuable works of art.⟩ — see CONCEALMENT 1

hie *vb* to proceed or move quickly ⟨We had best *hie* home before the snow gets worse.⟩ — see HURRY 2

higgledy–piggledy *adj* lacking in order, neatness, and often cleanliness ⟨The quilt was a *higgledy-piggledy* patchwork of odd-shaped fabric scraps, each of which held a fond memory for the family.⟩ — see MESSY

high *adj* **1** extending to a great distance upward ⟨Mount Everest is the *highest* mountain in the world.⟩

synonyms lofty, tall, towering

related words dominant, dominating, eminent, prominent; elevated, lifted, raised, uplifted, upswept; high-rise, statuesque

near antonyms flat, stubby, stumpy

antonyms low, low-lying, short, squat

2 being at a higher level than average ⟨Gasoline prices are *high* right now.⟩ ⟨a *high* fever⟩ ⟨people with *high* incomes⟩

synonyms elevated, escalated, heightened, increased, jacked (up), raised, up

related words extreme, full, maximized, maximum, peaked, sky-high, utmost; over, overfilled, overflowing, overfull, overlarge, overloaded, oversize (*or* oversized)

near antonyms decreased, depressed, dropped, receded, under

antonyms down, low

3 located at a greater height than average or usual ⟨an eagle's nest *high* on the cliff⟩ ⟨an old house with *high* ceilings⟩

synonyms airy, elevated

related words ascendant (*also* ascendent), ascending, soaring; overhead, overlooking, raised, upheld, uplifted, upraised; topmost, upmost, upper, uppermost, upward

near antonyms depressed, descendant (*also* descendent), descending, down, dropped, fallen, grounded, lowered, sunken; abreast, even, level

antonyms low, low-lying

4 being far along in development ⟨*high* technology⟩ — see ADVANCED

5 commanding a large price ⟨The concert tickets weren't cheap—you don't even want to know how *high* they were.⟩ — see COSTLY

6 having, characterized by, or arising from a dignified and generous nature ⟨She had the *highest* intentions, but her "help" turned out to be a disaster.⟩ — see NOBLE 2

7 highest in rank or authority ⟨*high* government officials⟩ ⟨lord *high* executioner⟩ — see HEAD

high *adv* in a luxurious manner ⟨After he had made a fortune, Philip lived pretty *high*.⟩

synonyms expensively, extravagantly, grandly, large, lavishly, luxuriously, opulently, palatially, richly, sumptuously

related words imposingly, impressively, magnificently, splendidly; grandiosely, ostentatiously, pompously, pretentiously; affluently, comfortably, fine, wealthily; immoderately, indulgently, intemperately, prodigally, wantonly, wastefully

near antonyms unpretentiously; cheaply, economically, frugally, inexpensively, meagerly, poorly, skimpily, sparely, sparingly, thriftily; conservatively, moderately, prudently, reasonably, restrainedly, sensibly, temperately

antonyms austerely, humbly, modestly, plainly, simply

high *n* **1** a state of overwhelming usually pleasurable emotion ⟨It took days for the *high* of the World Series win to wear off.⟩ — see ECSTASY

2 the expanse of air surrounding the earth ⟨V formations of honking geese on *high* mean winter will soon be here.⟩ — see SKY 1

highborn *adj* of high birth, rank, or station ⟨Skeptics have argued that these dramatic masterpieces must have been written by someone more *highborn* than one William Shakespeare of Stratford-upon-Avon.⟩ — see NOBLE 1

highbrow *adj* much given to learning and thinking ⟨finally, a TV series that appeals to a *highbrow* audience⟩ — see INTELLECTUAL 1

highbrow *n* a person with strong intellectual interests ⟨Guests at her elegant dinner parties are a mix of the city's *highbrows* and captains of industry.⟩ — see INTELLECTUAL

higher *adj* being far along in development ⟨an institute of *higher* learning⟩ ⟨*higher* primates, such as the apes⟩ — see ADVANCED

highest *adj* **1** being at a point or level higher than all others ⟨the *highest* grade⟩ ⟨the *highest* flag on the pole⟩ — see TOP 1

2 coming before all others in importance ⟨turned to the *highest* authority for answers⟩ ⟨the *highest* official in the land⟩ — see FOREMOST 1

highfalutin *also* **hifalutin** *adj* **1** full of fine words and fancy expressions ⟨His *highfalutin* paean to the working class failed to win over a crowd that wanted to hear down-to-earth proposals for economic relief.⟩ — see FLOWERY 1

2 having a feeling of superiority that shows itself in an overbearing attitude ⟨Her *highfalutin* relatives made the snide remark that her little house "has that lived-in look"⟩ — see ARROGANT

3 having or displaying feelings of scorn for what is regarded as beneath oneself ⟨He refused to be intimidated by the *highfalutin* manner of the sales staff in the fashionable boutique.⟩ — see PROUD 1

4 self-consciously trying to present an appearance of

grandeur or importance ⟨"Fine Southern cuisine" sounds a bit *highfalutin* for a barbecue shack.⟩ — see PRETENTIOUS 1

high–flown *adj* **1** full of fine words and fancy expressions ⟨She gave a *high-flown* reply instead of a simple "yes" or "no" answer.⟩ — see FLOWERY 1
2 very dignified in form, tone, or style ⟨*high-flown* speeches about the nobleness of their cause⟩ — see ELEVATED 2

high–handed *adj* **1** having a feeling of superiority that shows itself in an overbearing attitude ⟨The manager displayed a *high-handed* demeanor that increasingly demoralized the members of his staff.⟩ — see ARROGANT
2 having or showing a tendency to force one's will on others without any regard to fairness or necessity ⟨That college tends to be rather *high-handed* about whom they accept.⟩ — see ARBITRARY 1

high–hat *adj* having a feeling of superiority that shows itself in an overbearing attitude ⟨Several *high-hat* society types arrived after we did, but they got seated first.⟩ — see ARROGANT

high–hat *vb* **1** to show contempt for ⟨One presidential candidate presents himself as an outsider who has long been *high-hatted* by the Beltway elite.⟩ — see SCORN 1
2 to deliberately ignore or treat rudely ⟨Ed was *high-hatted* by an old college friend who's now a power player on Wall Street.⟩ — see SNUB 1

high jinks *also* **hijinks** *pl n* wildly playful or mischievous behavior ⟨Despite the team's dismal record, the players have won over many fans with their exuberant *high jinks*.⟩ — see HORSEPLAY

highland *n* an area of high ground ⟨the cool, humid *highlands* of the Pacific Northwest⟩ — see HEIGHT 4

highlight *vb* to indicate the importance of by centering attention on ⟨The article *highlights* the accomplishments of astronomer Maria Mitchell.⟩ — see EMPHASIZE 1

highly *adv* **1** to a great degree ⟨She was *highly* satisfied with her personal results for the marathon.⟩ — see VERY 1
2 to a large extent or degree ⟨That is *highly* different from your first idea for a family vacation.⟩ — see GREATLY 2

high–minded *adj* **1** having, characterized by, or arising from a dignified and generous nature ⟨*high-minded* efforts to improve the lives of people who are less fortunate⟩ — see NOBLE 2
2 self-consciously trying to present an appearance of grandeur or importance ⟨She was too *high-minded* to admit publicly to watching trashy movies, but privately she loved them.⟩ — see PRETENTIOUS 1

high–mindedly *adv* in a manner befitting a person of the highest character and ideals ⟨Sal *high-mindedly* gave his colleagues all the credit for the successful completion of the project.⟩ — see GREATLY 1

high noon *n* **1** a state or time of great activity, thriving, or achievement ⟨The *high noon* of the whaling industry occurred in the first half of the 19th century.⟩ — see BLOOM 1
2 the highest part or point ⟨The exhibition showcased works painted at the *high noon* of French Impressionism.⟩ — see HEIGHT 1
3 the middle of the day ⟨The dedication ceremony began at *high noon* with a 21-gun salute.⟩ — see NOON 1

high–pitched *adj* having a high musical pitch or range ⟨the *high-pitched* sound of a siren⟩ — see SHRILL

high–pressure *adj* having or showing a bold forcefulness in the pursuit of a goal ⟨a *high-pressure* salesman who wouldn't take "no" for an answer⟩ ⟨"for a limited time only" and other standbys of *high-pressure* advertising⟩ — see AGGRESSIVE 1

high–sounding *adj* full of fine words and fancy expressions ⟨*high-sounding* speeches full of promises⟩ — see FLOWERY 1

high–spirited *adj* **1** joyously unrestrained ⟨a *high-spirited* crowd loudly cheering the basketball team on⟩ — see EXUBERANT
2 marked by a lively display of strong feeling ⟨The band struck up a *high-spirited* march as the President's motorcade approached.⟩ — see SPIRITED 1

high–spiritedly *adv* in a quick and spirited manner ⟨The teens *high-spiritedly* donned superhero costumes in preparation for the party they were giving at the Children's Hospital.⟩ — see GAILY 2

high–strung *adj* easily excited by nature ⟨A dog that tends to be *high-strung* is not the best pet for young children.⟩ — see EXCITABLE

high–water mark *n* the highest part or point ⟨He hit the *high-water mark* of his acting career when he played Tiny Tim in a school play.⟩ — see HEIGHT 1

highway *n* a passage cleared for public vehicular travel ⟨The four-lane *highway* narrows to two lanes once you leave the city.⟩ — see WAY 1

hijack *also* **highjack** *vb* to take control of (a vehicle) by force ⟨tried to *hijack* a truck⟩ — see COMMANDEER 1

hike *vb* **1** to travel by foot for exercise or pleasure ⟨She *hiked* along the trail around the pond.⟩
synonyms ramble, saunter, stroll, tramp, tromp
related words roam, rove, wander; peregrinate, traipse, traverse, trek, walk; march
2 to move from a lower to a higher place or position ⟨With a determined look, he *hiked* his trousers up and buckled down to work.⟩ — see RAISE 1

hilarious *adj* causing or intended to cause laughter ⟨*hilarious* cartoons that the whole family can enjoy⟩ ⟨the clown's *hilarious* antics⟩ — see FUNNY 1

hilariousness *n* the amusing quality or element in something ⟨The *hilariousness* of the situation only struck us later, and we had a good laugh.⟩ — see HUMOR 1

hilarity *n* a mood characterized by high spirits and amusement and often accompanied by laughter ⟨My attempt to master using chopsticks was a source of great *hilarity* at the restaurant.⟩ — see MIRTH

hill *n* **1** a quantity of things thrown or stacked on one another ⟨The ants made little *hills* of dirt.⟩ — see ¹PILE 1
2 an area of high ground ⟨a town nestled in a valley surrounded by green *hills*⟩ — see HEIGHT 4
3 an upward slope ⟨I got stuck behind a truck going up a *hill* in a no-passing zone.⟩ — see ASCENT 2

hill *vb* to form into a pile or ridge of earth ⟨*hilled* peat moss around the rosebushes to protect them from the freeze⟩ — see MOUND 1

hillbilly *n* an awkward or simple person especially from a small town or the country ⟨In the skit, he was a shy *hillbilly* in love with a city girl.⟩ — see HICK

hind *adj* being at or in the part of something opposite the front part ⟨the frog's long *hind* legs⟩ ⟨the hawk's reddish *hind* feathers⟩ — see BACK

hinder *adj* being at or in the part of something opposite the front part ⟨The animal's case of mange was especially bad in its *hinder* parts.⟩ — see BACK

hinder *vb* to create difficulty for the work or activity of ⟨was not *hindered* by a lack of money because she could use what food she had on hand⟩ — see HAMPER

hindmost *adj* **1** being at or in the part of something opposite the front part ⟨The dance teacher had to keep reminding us to kick our *hindmost* foot when we reversed direction.⟩ — see BACK
2 following all others of the same kind in order or time ⟨The *hindmost* wagon in the caravan had the roughest

ride because of the deep ruts and dust created by the others.⟩ — see LAST 1

hindrance *n* something that makes movement or progress difficult ⟨made a survey of all the *hindrances* to wheelchair access, such as curbs and stairs⟩ — see ENCUMBRANCE

hinge *vb* to be determined by, based on, or subject (to) ⟨The outcome of the game *hinged* on a single play.⟩ — see DEPEND 1

hint *n* **1** a slight or indirect pointing to something (as a solution or explanation) ⟨Can't you give me some *hint* as to where you're taking me?⟩
synonyms clue, cue, indication, inkling, intimation, lead, suggestion
related words breath, flicker, glimmer, glimpse, mention, scent, whiff, wind; hunch, idea, inspiration, notion; allusion, implication, inference; assistance, nod, prompt, tip, tip-off, wink; feeling, foreboding, intuition, premonition, presentiment, suspicion; augury, foreshadower, foretaste, harbinger, omen, portent, prefigurement, presage, symptom
near antonyms answer, solution
2 an almost imperceptible sign of something ⟨There was the slightest *hint* of impatience in her voice.⟩
synonyms breath, flicker, glimmer, suggestion, touch, trace, whiff
related words inkling, intimation, scent, wind; evidence, indication, mark, sign
near antonyms permeation, pervasion, saturation
3 a piece of advice or useful information especially from an expert ⟨some helpful *hints* for cleaning carpet stains⟩ — see ¹TIP 1
4 a very small amount ⟨I detect just a *hint* of mint in the sauce.⟩ — see PARTICLE 1

hint *vb* to convey an idea indirectly ⟨Fay kept *hinting* that she wouldn't mind an invitation to spend the weekend at their beach house.⟩
synonyms allude, imply, indicate, infer, insinuate, intimate, suggest
related words advert, mention, point, refer, signal, signalize, signify; smack (of), smell (of)
near antonyms announce, declare, proclaim; elucidate, explain, spell out; delineate, describe

hinterland *n* a rural region that forms the edge of the settled or developed part of a country ⟨The colonies hugged the coastline, while the *hinterland* remained largely unexplored.⟩ — see FRONTIER 2

hip *adj* **1** being in the latest or current fashion ⟨*hip* sunglasses whose fancy prices will make you squint in disbelief⟩ — see STYLISH
2 having inside information ⟨He wasn't *hip* to what was going on behind the scenes and was taken totally unawares by the company shake-up.⟩ — see WISE 2

hip *n* the quality or state of being fashionable ⟨kids dyeing their hair in pursuit of *hip*⟩ — see COOL 2

hip *vb* to give information to ⟨If you want to get *hipped* on what goes on behind the scenes at a television network, you should read this book.⟩ — see ENLIGHTEN 1

hire *n* **1** the state of being provided with a paying job ⟨He spent most of his career in the *hire* of high-paying defense contractors.⟩
synonyms employ, employment, engagement
related words appointment, assignment, conscription, enlistment, recruitment; tenure; occupation, place, position, post, situation, work
near antonyms discharge, dismissal, firing, removal, sack, severance; suspension; furlough, layoff, leave, liberty, retirement
antonyms joblessness, nonemployment, unemployment

2 the money paid regularly to a person for labor or services ⟨used to mow lawns for *hire*⟩ — see WAGE

hire *vb* **1** to take or get the temporary use of (something) for a set sum ⟨The Youngs *hired* a limousine for their daughter's wedding.⟩
synonyms charter, engage, lease, rent
related words sublease, sublet; arrange (for), bespeak, book, contract (for), order, reserve, sign up (for)
2 to provide with a paying job ⟨The farm *hires* teenagers to pick blueberries in the summer.⟩ — see EMPLOY 1

hireling *n* one who works for another for wages or a salary ⟨I demanded to speak to the store's owner and not one of his *hirelings*.⟩ — see EMPLOYEE

hirsute *adj* covered with or as if with hair ⟨wore a *hirsute* mask as part of his werewolf costume⟩ — see HAIRY 1

hiss *n* **1** a sound similar to the speech sound \s\ stretched out ⟨the *hiss* of air escaping from a balloon⟩
synonyms fizz, sizzle, swish, whish, whiz (*or* whizz)
related words wheeze, whistle, whoosh, zip; sibilance, sibilant
2 a vocal sound made to express scorn or disapproval ⟨There was a chorus of boos and *hisses* from the fans when the umpire called the runner out.⟩ — see CATCALL

hiss *vb* to make a sound like that of stretching out the speech sound \s\ ⟨The frightened kitten *hissed* at us when we tried to pick it up.⟩
synonyms fizz, fizzle, sizzle, swish, whish, whiz (*or* whizz)
related words wheeze, whistle, whoosh, zip; bubble, effervesce; buzz, drone, hum

hissy fit *n* an outburst or display of excited anger ⟨She had a *hissy fit* when I told her she couldn't go.⟩ — see TANTRUM

historian *n* a student or writer of history ⟨*Historians* are still trying to sort out fact from fiction in the story of Kateri Tekakwitha, the Lily of the Mohawks.⟩
synonyms chronicler
related words autobiographer, biographer; archivist, chronologist, genealogist, hagiographer

historical *adj* restricted to or based on fact ⟨a *historical* novel that tells the story of Hannibal's crossing of the Alps through the eyes of a young boy⟩ — see FACTUAL 1

history *n* **1** an account of important events in the order in which they happened ⟨a *history* of the American Civil Rights Movement during the 1960s⟩
synonyms annals, chronicle, record
related words blog, commentary, journal, memoir, reminiscence(s); autobiography, biography, life; legend, narrative, saga, story, tale; archives, documentation, log, register, report; genealogy
2 a relating of events usually in the order in which they happened ⟨We heard the whole *history* of her illness in excruciating detail.⟩ — see ACCOUNT 1
3 the events or experience of former times ⟨*History* has many lessons to teach us, if only we would listen.⟩ — see PAST

histrionic *adj* **1** given to or marked by attention-getting behavior suggestive of stage acting ⟨a penchant for dish throwing, door slamming, and other *histrionic* displays of temper⟩ — see THEATRICAL 1
2 having the general quality or effect of a stage performance ⟨We never tired of his *histrionic* reenactment of how he found money under the floorboards of a house he was renovating.⟩ — see DRAMATIC 1

hit *n* **1** a person or thing that is successful ⟨The new babysitter turned out to be a *hit* with the kids.⟩
synonyms blockbuster, megahit, smash, success, winner
related words crackerjack (*also* crackajack), dandy, jimdandy, pip, prizewinner; gem, jewel, treasure; marvel,

natural, phenomenon, sensation, wonder; coup, triumph, victory

near antonyms disappointment, fizzle, lemon, loser

antonyms bomb, bummer, bust, catastrophe, debacle (*also* débâcle), dud, failure, fiasco, flop, misfire, turkey, washout

2 a hard strike with a part of the body or an instrument ⟨The quarterback can't take too many more *hits* like that and escape permanent injury.⟩ — see ¹BLOW

hit *vb* **1** to deliver a blow to (someone or something) usually in a strong vigorous manner ⟨A good carpenter *hits* a nail just two or three times to drive it in.⟩

synonyms bang, bash, bat, belt, bludgeon, bob, bop, box, bust, clap, clip, clobber, clock, clout, crack, hammer, knock, nail, paste, pound, punch, rap, slam, slap, slog, slug, smack, smite, sock, strike, swat, swipe, thump, thwack, wallop, whack, whale, zap

related words batter, beat, buffet, bung, chop, cuff, drub, lace, lambaste (*or* lambast), lick, mangle, maul, pelt, pepper, pommel, pummel, rough; scuff; bunt, flick, stroke, tap; bump, butt, jab, kick, knee, poke, prod, push, shove, stamp; bowl (down *or* over), cream, deck, fell, floor, knock down, level; rabbit-punch, sucker punch; cane, club, cudgel, flail, flog, lash, sap, slash, sledge, sledgehammer, spear, stab, switch, thrash, whip; brain, conk, skull

phrases hang one on

2 to come into usually forceful contact with something ⟨When she fell on the ice, she *hit* hard and badly bruised her elbow.⟩

synonyms bang, bash, bump, collide, crash, impact, impinge, knock, ram, slam, smash, strike, swipe, thud

related words bounce, carom, clunk, glance, rebound, ricochet, skim, skip; contact, land, touch; brush, graze, kiss, nudge, scrape, shave, sweep; bulldoze, muscle, press, push

near antonyms miss, skirt

3 to obtain (as a goal) through effort ⟨The rock band *hit* the big time with their third album.⟩ — see ACHIEVE 1

hit (on *or* **upon)** *vb* to come upon after searching, study, or effort ⟨The doctor finally *hit on* what was wrong with the pain-wracked patient.⟩ — see FIND 1

hit (upon) *vb* to come upon unexpectedly or by chance ⟨The popular belief is that Sir Isaac Newton *hit upon* his understanding of gravity at the sight of an apple falling from a tree.⟩ — see HAPPEN (ON *or* UPON)

hitch *n* **1** a danger or difficulty that is hidden or not easily recognized ⟨There are always a few *hitches* when you launch a system as complex as this one.⟩ — see PITFALL 1

2 a fixed period of time during which a person holds a job or position ⟨Bill signed on for a three-year *hitch* in the army.⟩ — see TERM 1

hitch *vb* **1** to move or cause to move with a sharp quick motion ⟨The boy kept *hitching* up his pants because they were too big in the waist.⟩ — see JERK 1

2 to put or bring together so as to form a new and longer whole ⟨She escaped out the window by using a makeshift rope of bedsheets and clothing she'd *hitched* together.⟩ — see CONNECT 1

3 to put securely in place or in a desired position ⟨*hitched* the trailer to the back of the car⟩ — see FASTEN 2

4 to travel by securing free rides ⟨He *hitched* across the country after he graduated from college.⟩ — see HITCHHIKE

hitcher *n* one who hitchhikes ⟨never stops for *hitchers* on interstates, where hitchhiking is illegal⟩ — see HITCHHIKER

hitchhike *vb* to travel by securing free rides ⟨a novel in

which the hero undertakes a journey of self-discovery by *hitchhiking* around the country⟩

synonyms hitch, thumb

related words bum; stow away

hitchhiker *n* one who hitchhikes ⟨*hitchhikers* whose car had broken down⟩

synonyms hitcher

related words stowaway

hither *adj* being the less far of two ⟨We began to explore the *hither* bank while our companions crossed the creek to explore the yonder bank.⟩ — see NEAR 1

hitherto *adv* up to this or that time ⟨At the talent show Kyle revealed his *hitherto* unknown gift for doing impressions.⟩

synonyms heretofore, theretofore, yet

related words before, previously

phrases so far, thus far

near antonyms afterward (*or* afterwards), later, subsequently; hereupon, thereupon

antonyms henceforth, henceforward, hereafter, thenceforth, thenceforward (*also* thenceforwards), thereafter

hit–or–miss *adj* lacking a definite plan, purpose, or pattern ⟨a *hit-or-miss* method of finding the answers⟩ — see RANDOM

hit or miss *adv* without definite aim, direction, rule, or method ⟨I was learning Spanish *hit or miss*, mostly just by hearing my friends speak it.⟩

synonyms aimlessly, anyhow, anyway, anywise, desultorily, erratically, haphazard, haphazardly, helter-skelter, irregularly, randomly, willy-nilly

related words arbitrarily, capriciously, carelessly, casually, indiscriminately, informally, offhand, offhandedly, promiscuously, whimsically; accidentally, fortuitously, inadvertently, unconsciously, unintentionally, unwittingly; disconnectedly, disjointedly, fitfully, intermittently, spottily, unpredictably; higgledy-piggledy, topsy-turvy

phrases at random

near antonyms carefully, formally, gingerly, meticulously, orderly, punctiliously; deliberately, intentionally, purposefully, purposely

antonyms methodically

hoagie *also* **hoagy** *n* a large sandwich on a long split roll ⟨I had a steak-and-cheese *hoagie* for the first time in Philadelphia.⟩ — see SUBMARINE

hoar *adj* dating or surviving from the distant past ⟨the *hoar* and crumbling stones of ruined temples⟩ — see ANCIENT 1

hoar *n* a covering of tiny ice crystals on a cold surface ⟨The *hoar*-covered meadow gleamed in the early-morning sun.⟩ — see FROST 1

hoard *n* **1** a supply stored up and often hidden away ⟨Dan keeps a *hoard* of empty yogurt containers in his basement workshop for storing whatnots.⟩

synonyms cache, stash, stockpile, store

related words coffers, deposit, funds, nest egg, savings, sinking fund, treasure; inventory, pool, reserve, stock; provisions, resources; accumulation, assemblage, collection, gathering, harvest; repertory

2 a collection of things kept available for future use or need ⟨She couldn't find one pencil with an eraser in her entire *hoard* of pencil stubs.⟩ — see STORE 1

hoard *vb* to put (something of future use or value) in a safe or secret place ⟨He's been *hoarding* empty yogurt containers all winter, with the intention of using them to start seedlings in the spring.⟩

synonyms cache, lay away, lay up, put by, salt away, squirrel (away), stash, stockpile, store, stow, treasure

related words accumulate, acquire, amass, assemble,

collect, concentrate, garner, gather, pick up, round up, scrape (together); heap, pile, stack; conserve, husband, preserve; bank, coffer, deposit, hold, keep, reserve, retain, save, stock, withhold; bury, conceal, ensconce, secrete

phrases set aside

near antonyms cast, discard, ditch, dump, fling (off *or* away), jettison, throw away, throw out, unload; consume, squander, use up, waste; hand over, relinquish, surrender; blow, dissipate, fritter (away), lavish, misspend, run through, spend; deplete, exhaust, expend, impoverish; dispel, disperse, dissipate, scatter

hoarfrost *n* a covering of tiny ice crystals on a cold surface ⟨The *hoarfrost* formed a delicate swirly pattern on the window.⟩ — see FROST 1

hoarse *adj* harsh and dry in sound ⟨The thirsty man spoke in a *hoarse* whisper.⟩

synonyms coarse, croaking, grating, gravel, gravelly, gruff, husky, rasping, raspy, scratchy, throaty

related words growling, growly, guttural; cacophonous, discordant, grinding, jarring, rough, scraping, scratching; cawing, raucous, screeching, strident; choked, cracked, strained, strangled; dissonant, inharmonious, unmelodious, unmusical

near antonyms gentle, gliding, golden, liquid, mellifluent, mellifluous, mellow, soothing, sweet, tender; satiny, silken, smooth, soft, velvety; euphonious, lyric, lyrical, melodic, melodious, musical

hoary *adj* dating or surviving from the distant past ⟨*Hoary* oak trees with dripping moss and gnarled limbs shaded us from the sun.⟩ — see ANCIENT 1

hoax *n* an imitation that is passed off as genuine ⟨The skeleton of the purported ancient hominid turned out to be a *hoax*.⟩ — see FAKE 1

hoax *vb* to cause to believe what is untrue ⟨a skilled forger who *hoaxed* the art world into believing that the paintings were long-lost Vermeers⟩ — see DECEIVE

hoaxer *n* **1** a dishonest person who uses clever means to cheat others out of something of value ⟨If it sounds too good to be true, you're probably dealing with a *hoaxer* in a boiler room somewhere.⟩ — see TRICKSTER 1

2 one who makes false claims of identity or expertise ⟨His college roommate turned out to be a complete *hoaxer* and not the son of a wealthy shipping tycoon he said he was.⟩ — see IMPOSTOR

hob *n* playful, reckless behavior that is not intended to cause serious harm ⟨Our indoor Frisbee game—my dog's and mine—played *hob* with a couple of lamps and a vase.⟩ — see MISCHIEF 1

hobble *vb* **1** to create difficulty for the work or activity of ⟨We were *hobbled* by the snowstorm from getting to work.⟩ — see HAMPER

2 to walk while favoring one leg ⟨I *hobbled* home with a twisted ankle.⟩ — see LIMP 1

hobgoblin *n* **1** an imaginary being usually having a small human form and magical powers ⟨In Shakespeare's *Midsummer Night's Dream*, Puck is a *hobgoblin* who plays pranks such as spoiling milk and tripping old ladies.⟩ — see FAIRY

2 something or someone that causes fear or dread especially without reason ⟨The fear of success and the pressures that come with it can be more of a *hobgoblin* than the possibility of failure.⟩ — see BOGEY 1

hobnob *vb* **1** to come or be together as friends ⟨Those two have been *hobnobbing* together since freshman year.⟩ — see ASSOCIATE 1

2 to take part in social activities ⟨We spent some time *hobnobbing* with the rich and famous while in Los Angeles.⟩ — see SOCIALIZE

hobnobber *n* a person frequently seen in the company of another ⟨The actor's agent is a *hobnobber* with a lot of big movie producers.⟩ — see ASSOCIATE 1

hobo *n* a homeless wanderer who may beg or steal for a living ⟨kind folks who always gave *hoboes* who came to the farm a meal and then sent them on their way⟩ — see TRAMP

hock *vb* to leave as a guarantee of repayment of a loan ⟨The prince had to *hock* the family jewels to pay his gambling debts.⟩ — see PAWN

hodgepodge *n* an unorganized collection or mixture of various things ⟨The exhibit was a *hodgepodge* of different styles of art.⟩ — see MISCELLANY 1

hog *n* one who eats greedily or too much ⟨The bigger dog was a real *hog* at feeding time.⟩ — see GLUTTON

hoggish *adj* having a huge appetite ⟨was feeling *hoggish* after the hike and ate the whole bag of cookies⟩ — see VORACIOUS 1

hogshead *n* an enclosed wooden vessel for holding beverages ⟨The ship's hold carried 164 *hogsheads* of molasses.⟩ — see CASK

hog–tie *vb* to create difficulty for the work or activity of ⟨Their principals' inflexible demands virtually *hog-tied* the diplomats' efforts to negotiate a peace treaty.⟩ — see HAMPER

hogwash *n* language, behavior, or ideas that are absurd and contrary to good sense ⟨The librarian told us a lot of *hogwash* about how you can go to jail for having overdue books.⟩ — see NONSENSE 1

hoist *vb* **1** to lift with effort ⟨Dockworkers *hoisted* all 164 barrels of molasses out of the ship's hold when it arrived in port.⟩ — see HEAVE 1

2 to move from a lower to a higher place or position ⟨*hoisted* the flag on the flagpole⟩ — see RAISE 1

3 to swallow in liquid form ⟨Make sure you *hoist* some liquids before running.⟩ — see DRINK 1

hold *n* **1** the act or manner of holding ⟨Make sure you have a firm *hold* on the chain saw before you turn it on.⟩

synonyms clasp, clench, grapple, grasp, grip

related words anchorage, purchase; grab, seizure; foothold, footing, toehold; clinch, embrace, hug

near antonyms release, relinquishment

2 a structure or place from which one can resist attack ⟨the ruins of an ancient Roman *hold*⟩ — see FORT

3 the right or means to command or control others ⟨The government has no *hold* over where we live and work.⟩ — see POWER 1

4 the state or fact of being able to exchange information regarding one's current situation ⟨I worry that I won't be able to get *hold* of you in an emergency.⟩ — see TOUCH 1

5 the knowledge gained from the process of coming to know or understand something ⟨I need to get *hold* of the situation before planning a course of action.⟩ — see COMPREHENSION

hold *vb* **1** to have or keep in one's hands ⟨This casserole dish is too hot to *hold*, so grab a potholder.⟩

synonyms clench, cling (to), clutch, grip

related words bear, carry; bag, capture, catch, collar, corral, grab, grapple, hook, land, latch (on *or* onto), nab, nail, seize, snap (up), snare, snatch, take, trap; feel, handle, paw; clasp, embrace, grasp, hug; cradle

phrases hang on to, hold on to

near antonyms drop, give, hand, unclasp, unhand; cede, deliver, give up, hand over, release, relinquish, render, turn over, yield

2 to continue to have in one's possession or power ⟨She, and she alone, *held* the keys to the mysterious chest.⟩ — see KEEP 2

3 to have as an opinion ⟨"We *hold* these truths to be

self-evident, that all men are created equal.") — see BE-LIEVE 2

4 to have within ⟨The mysterious chest *held* an ancient book on magic spells and potions.⟩ — see CONTAIN 1

5 to keep in one's mind or heart ⟨Justin still *held* her close to his heart, though they had long parted.⟩ — see HARBOR 1

6 to keep, control, or experience as one's own ⟨The same family has *held* this piece of land for over 300 years.⟩ — see HAVE 1

7 to make or have room for ⟨The couple needed to rent a hall that would *hold* 300 people.⟩ — see ACCOMMODATE 1

8 to reach for and take hold of by embracing with the fingers or arms ⟨Please *hold* my arm on these slippery stairs.⟩ — see TAKE 1

9 to think of in a particular way ⟨*held* to be the best barbeque in the state⟩ — see CONSIDER 1

10 to keep from exceeding a desirable degree or level (as of expression) ⟨We managed to *hold* our laughter until we got outside.⟩ ⟨*Hold* your temper until you hear the whole story.⟩ — see CONTROL 1

11 to point or turn (something) toward a target or goal ⟨*held* the camera on the performer⟩ — see AIM 1

hold back *vb* **1** to create difficulty for the work or activity of ⟨The only thing *holding* Jill *back* from joining the swim team is lack of transportation.⟩ — see HAMPER

2 to refrain from openly showing or uttering ⟨*held back* her tears until she was alone⟩ — see SUPPRESS 2

holder *n* **1** one who has a legal or rightful claim to ownership ⟨The *holders* of the land gave us permission to camp on it.⟩ — see PROPRIETOR

2 something into which a liquid or smaller objects can be put for storage or transportation ⟨Her hat made a good *holder* for the shells she collected on the beach.⟩ — see CONTAINER

holding *n* **1** a decision made by a court or tribunal regarding a case it has heard ⟨The court's *holding* was based on an interpretation of the First Amendment.⟩ — see SENTENCE

2 *usually* **holdings** *pl* transportable items that one owns ⟨The museum's *holdings* of ancient manuscripts are among the rarest in the world.⟩ — see POSSESSION 2

holding pattern *n* **1** a state of temporary inactivity ⟨Repair work on the bridge was in a *holding pattern* for the duration of the winter.⟩ — see ABEYANCE

2 an instance or period of being prevented from going about one's business ⟨The couple has been trapped in this *holding pattern* for six months, as adoption officials work on the case.⟩ — see DELAY

hold off (on) *vb* to assign to a later time ⟨We *held off on* accepting the invitation in the hopes that something better would come along.⟩ — see POSTPONE

hold on *vb* **1** to remain indefinitely in existence or in the same state ⟨The ancient beliefs still *held on* in remote mountain villages.⟩ — see CONTINUE 1

2 to remain in place in readiness or expectation of something ⟨*Hold on* a minute—it's not your turn!⟩ — see WAIT

hold out *vb* to continue to operate or to meet one's needs ⟨We hoped our supply of firewood would *hold out* until power was restored.⟩ ⟨Luckily, the old outboard motor *held out* till we made it to shore.⟩

synonyms hold up, keep up, last, prevail, survive

related words carry on, cope, endure, fare, get along, get by, get on, go, hang in, make out, manage, persevere; abide, continue, draw out, hang on, hold on, linger, persist, remain, run on, stretch

near antonyms break, break down, collapse, conk (out), crash, cut out, die, expire, stall, stop; run down, wane

antonyms fail, fizzle, give out, peter (out), run out

holdup *n* an instance or period of being prevented from going about one's business ⟨a *holdup* in construction due to the weather⟩ — see DELAY

hold up *vb* **1** to assign to a later time ⟨*held up* mail delivery until we had a permanent address⟩ — see POSTPONE

2 to bring (something) to a standstill ⟨Traffic was *held up* for miles by the accident.⟩ — see ¹HALT 1

3 to create difficulty for the work or activity of ⟨If lack of transportation is the only thing *holding* you *up*, I can give you a ride.⟩ — see HAMPER

4 to continue to operate or to meet one's needs ⟨The air conditioner *held up* this year, but it's not going to make it through another summer.⟩ — see HOLD OUT

5 to remain indefinitely in existence or in the same state ⟨The storm's hurricane-force winds did not *hold up* once it hit the coast.⟩ — see CONTINUE 1

6 to withstand scrutiny and gain acceptance or approval ⟨an argument that won't *hold up* in court⟩ — see WASH 2

hole *n* **1** a place in a surface allowing passage into or through a thing ⟨Line up the pegs on section A with the *holes* in section B and press the two together.⟩

synonyms aperture, opening, orifice, perforation

related words loophole; breach, break, chink, cleft, crack, cranny, crevice, cut, fissure, gash, notch, rent, rift, rupture, slash, slit, split, tear; space; exit, mouth, outlet, pore, vent; entrance, inlet; pinhole, pinprick, punch, puncture; airhole, armhole, buttonhole, keyhole, knothole, peephole, pothole, wormhole

near antonyms fill, filler, filling, patch, plug, seal, stopper; barrier, blockage, obstacle, obstruction

2 a sunken area forming a separate space ⟨Dig a *hole* big enough to plant the tree.⟩

synonyms cavity, concavity, dent, depression, dint, hollow, indentation, pit, recess

related words burrow, cave, cavern, ditch, excavation, furrow, groove, gutter, trench, trough; basin, bowl, valley; alcove, cleft, niche, nook, opening, recess, socket; alveolus, dimple, gouge, impression, imprint, notch, pocket; borehole, chuckhole, crater, posthole, pothole, sinkhole, wallow, water hole, well; abyss, chasm, gulf, vacuity, vacuum, void

near antonyms hill, mound, rise; bump, bunch, hump, lump, swell, swelling, tumor

antonyms bulge, jut, projection, protrusion, protuberance

3 a difficult, puzzling, or embarrassing situation from which there is no easy escape ⟨Bill dug himself into a *hole* by promising to be in two places at the same time.⟩ — see PREDICAMENT

4 a dirty or messy place ⟨When people see my room, they often ask, "How can you live in this *hole*?"⟩ — see PIGPEN

5 an open space in a barrier (as a wall or hedge) ⟨The boy found a *hole* in the chain-link fence big enough to squeeze through.⟩ — see GAP 1

6 the shelter or resting place of a wild animal ⟨watched the snake slither into its *hole*⟩ — see DEN 1

7 an incomplete or deficient area ⟨There's a huge *hole* in your logic.⟩ — see GAP 3

hole *vb* to make a hole or series of holes in ⟨*holed* the cabinet with a drill⟩ — see PERFORATE

holiness *n* the quality or state of being spiritually pure or virtuous ⟨Known throughout the world for his *holiness*, the prophet was visited daily by hundreds of pilgrims.⟩

synonyms blessedness, devoutness, godliness, piety, piousness, sainthood, saintliness, saintship, sanctity

related words asceticism, devotion, morality, prayerfulness, religiousness; priestliness; goodness, rectitude, righ-

teousness, uprightness, virtue, virtuousness; consecration, sacredness
near antonyms blasphemousness, irreverence, sacrilegiousness; depravedness, depravity, evilness, heinousness, monstrosity, sinfulness, vileness, wickedness; hypocrisy, sanctimoniousness, sanctimony
antonyms godlessness, impiety, ungodliness, unholiness

holler *n* **1** a loud vocal expression of strong emotion ⟨I heard a *holler* from somewhere in the woods and ran toward it.⟩ — see SHOUT
2 an expression of dissatisfaction, pain, or resentment ⟨There didn't seem to be a thermostat setting that wouldn't bring a *holler* from somebody.⟩ — see COMPLAINT 1

holler *vb* **1** to express dissatisfaction, pain, or resentment usually tiresomely ⟨another city council meeting with residents *hollering* about the unsatisfactory collection of garbage⟩ — see COMPLAIN
2 to speak so as to be heard at a distance ⟨There's no need to *holler*; I'm in the next room.⟩ — see CALL 1

hollow *adj* curved inward ⟨There's a noticeably *hollow* spot in the mattress where he has been sleeping.⟩
synonyms concave, dented, depressed, indented, recessed, sunken
related words alveolar, cavernous, crescentic, cuplike, cupped, cuppy, recurved; dimpled, pockmarked; compressed, condensed, contracted, diminished, reduced
near antonyms ballooning, blown up, bulbous, enlarged, expanded, extended, jutting, projecting, puffy, risen; domed, global, round, rounded, spherical
antonyms bulging, cambered, convex, protruding, protrusive, protuberant

hollow *n* **1** a sunken area forming a separate space ⟨She made a little *hollow* in her mound of mashed potatoes and filled it with gravy.⟩ — see HOLE 2
2 an area of lowland between hills or mountains ⟨a quaint village nestled in a *hollow* among green hills⟩ — see VALLEY

holocaust *n* **1** a destructive burning ⟨The *holocaust* caused by the ignited chemicals completely destroyed the factory.⟩ — see FIRE 1
2 the killing of a large number of people ⟨As many as 2,000,000 people may have perished in the *holocaust* perpetrated by Cambodia's Khmer Rouge.⟩ — see MASSACRE

holy *adj* **1** showing a devotion to God and to a life of virtue ⟨The *holy* monk spent many hours on his knees in prayer.⟩
synonyms devout, godly, pious, religious, sainted, saintly
related words ascetic (*also* ascetical), prayerful, reverent, reverential, spiritual, worshipful; pietistic, religiose; beatified, blessed (*also* blest), canonized, venerable; angelic (*or* angelical), cherubic; chaste, moral, pure, righteous, upright, virtuous
near antonyms blasphemous, desecrating, irreverent, profane, sacrilegious; nonreligious, secular, unspiritual, worldly; backsliding, unfaithful; evil, immoral, iniquitous, miscreant, sinful, sinning, unrighteous, wicked
antonyms antireligious, faithless, godless, impious, irreligious, ungodly, unholy
2 set apart or worthy of veneration by association with God ⟨The *holy* writings of Judaism.⟩
synonyms blessed (*also* blest), consecrate, consecrated, hallowed, sacred, sacrosanct, sanctified
related words adored, enshrined, glorified, revered, venerated, worshipped (*also* worshiped); ceremonial, liturgical, priestly, religious, ritual, sacramental, spiritual; biblical, scriptural

near antonyms earthly, mundane, profane, secular, temporal, worldly
antonyms deconsecrated, desacralized, unconsecrated, unhallowed
3 of, relating to, or being God ⟨a *holy* relic⟩
synonyms blessed (*also* blest), divine, godlike, godly, heavenly, sacred, supernatural
related words eternal, everlasting, immortal; all-powerful, almighty, omnipotent, omniscient, supreme
near antonyms human, mortal, natural
4 not to be violated, criticized, or tampered with ⟨The time she spends writing every day is *holy* and you'd better not interrupt her.⟩ — see SACRED 1

Holy Writ *n* a book made up of the writings accepted by Christians as coming from God ⟨quotes extensively from *Holy Writ* in his sermons⟩ — see BIBLE

homage *n* **1** a formal expression of praise ⟨The poem is a moving *homage* to all who have served in our nation's armed services.⟩ — see ENCOMIUM
2 public acknowledgment or admiration for an achievement ⟨the unique *homage* that we grant to Olympic athletes⟩ — see GLORY 1

hombre *n* an adult male human being ⟨He's a tough *hombre*.⟩ — see MAN 1

home *n* **1** the place where one lives ⟨As we entered his 34-room mansion, our host playfully exclaimed, "Welcome to my humble *home*!"⟩
synonyms abode, diggings, domicile, dwelling, fireside, habitation, hearth, hearthstone, house, lodging, pad, place, quarters, residence, roof
related words accommodations, housing, nest, shelter; bungalow, cabin, casita, chalet, cottage; duplex, ranch, ranch house, saltbox, split level, townhome, town house, tract house, triplex; apartment, apartment house, condominium, flat, tenement, tenement house, walk-up; penthouse, salon, suite; barracks, billet, boardinghouse, dorm, dormitory, lodging house, lodgment (*or* lodgement), room(s), rooming house; castle, château, countryseat, estate, hall, manor, manor house, mansion, palace, villa; farmhouse, grange, hacienda, homestead; hermitage, parsonage, rectory, vicarage; hovel, hut, hutch, shack, shanty
2 the place where a plant or animal is usually or naturally found ⟨the American South, the *home* of the armadillo⟩
synonyms habitat, niche, range, territory
related words element, environment, environs, haunt, locality, milieu, neighborhood, setting, surroundings
3 the land of one's birth, residence, or citizenship ⟨The U.S. is my *home*.⟩ — see COUNTRY 1
4 those who live as a family in one house ⟨a man who believes that a person's *home* is the most important thing in life⟩ — see HOUSEHOLD
5 a place of origin ⟨Springfield, Massachusetts, is the *home* of basketball, for it was there that the first hoops were hung in 1891.⟩ — see BIRTHPLACE

homeland *n* the land of one's birth, residence, or citizenship ⟨travels every year to Italy, her *homeland* for the first two decades of her life⟩ — see COUNTRY 1

homely *adj* unpleasant to look at ⟨a *homely*, lovable mutt⟩ — see UGLY 1

homesteader *n* a person who settles in a new region ⟨In the 1800s *homesteaders* in search of cheap land and a new life headed to the West in droves.⟩ — see FRONTIERSMAN

homicidal *adj* eager for or marked by the shedding of blood, extreme violence, or killing ⟨a *homicidal* maniac⟩ — see BLOODTHIRSTY

homicide *n* **1** the taking of another person's life ⟨the victim of a *homicide*⟩
synonyms blood, foul play, murder, slaying

related words manslaughter; bloodshed, butchery, carnage, decimation, destruction, massacre, slaughter; assassination, execution, hit; euthanasia, mercy killing; filicide, fratricide, matricide, parricide, patricide, regicide, uxoricide

2 a person who kills another person ⟨Throughout the ages society has stigmatized the *homicide*.⟩ — see ASSASSIN

homily *n* **1** a public speech usually by a member of the clergy for the purpose of giving moral guidance or uplift ⟨Last Sunday's *homily* was about being kind to your neighbors.⟩ — see SERMON

2 an idea or expression that has been used by many people ⟨a TV movie filled with the usual *homilies* about people triumphing over life's adversities⟩ — see COMMONPLACE

homogenize *vb* **1** to make agree with a single established standard or model ⟨plans to *homogenize* the science curriculum in public high schools throughout the state⟩ — see STANDARDIZE

2 to turn into a single mass or entity that is more or less the same throughout ⟨Chain stores and fast-food restaurants have *homogenized* the nation's highways and byways to the point where every place looks like every other place.⟩ — see BLEND 1

Homo sapiens *n* the human race ⟨How far into the outer reaches of the universe will *Homo sapiens* someday be able to go?⟩ — see MANKIND

hone *vb* **1** to make sharp or sharper ⟨*honed* the knife's blade to razor-like sharpness⟩ ⟨*honed* his crossword-puzzle skills by reading the dictionary as though it were a thrilling novel⟩ — see SHARPEN

2 to make smooth by friction ⟨*honed* the edge of the axe until it was amazingly sharp⟩ — see GRIND 1

honed *adj* having an edge thin enough to cut or pierce something ⟨Using a finely *honed* butcher knife will make cutting meat easier.⟩ — see SHARP 1

honest *adj* **1** being in the habit of telling the truth ⟨At least the weatherman is *honest* and doesn't pretend to be able to predict the unpredictable.⟩ — see TRUTHFUL

2 conforming to a high standard of morality or virtue ⟨*honest* and industrious farm folk⟩ — see GOOD 2

3 following the accepted rules of moral conduct ⟨an *honest* customer who tells the cashier she's given him too much change⟩ — see HONORABLE 1

4 free from any intent to deceive or impress others ⟨a person who helps others from an *honest* desire to do good⟩ — see GUILELESS

5 free in expressing one's true feelings and opinions ⟨Appreciate your *honest* friends, who tell you what you need to hear and not what you want to hear.⟩ — see FRANK

6 guided by or in accordance with one's sense of right and wrong ⟨Kay made an *honest* attempt to return the money she had found in the cafeteria.⟩ — see CONSCIENTIOUS 1

7 being exactly as appears or as claimed ⟨a restaurant serving *honest* down-home Southern cooking⟩ — see AUTHENTIC

honestly *adv* to tell the truth ⟨*Honestly*, I haven't the slightest idea what you're talking about.⟩ — see ACTUALLY 1

honesty *n* **1** devotion to telling the truth ⟨George Washington has gone down in history for his *honesty*.⟩

synonyms integrity, probity, truthfulness, veracity, verity

related words honor, honorableness, incorruptibility, rectitude, righteousness, right-mindedness, scrupulosity, scrupulousness, uprightness; artlessness, candidness, candor, forthrightness, frankness, good faith, guileless-

ness, ingenuousness, sincerity, straightforwardness; dependability, reliability, reliableness, trustiness, trustworthiness; accuracy, objectivity; authenticity, correctness, genuineness, truth; credibility

near antonyms artifice, crookedness, dissembling, dissimulation, double-dealing, duplicity, fakery, falseness, falsity, fraudulentness, hypocrisy, insincerity, two-facedness; beguilement, craftiness, cunning, furtiveness, guile, indirection, insidiousness, oiliness, perfidy, slickness, slipperiness, slyness, smoothness, treacherousness, trickery, underhandedness, unscrupulousness, wiliness; equivocation, prevarication; exaggeration, inaccuracy

antonyms deceit, deceitfulness, dishonesty, lying, mendacity, untruthfulness

2 conduct that conforms to an accepted standard of right and wrong ⟨He's known for his *honesty* in business dealings.⟩ — see MORALITY 1

3 faithfulness to high moral standards ⟨She knew she could count on her students' *honesty*, even if she left the classroom for a few moments during the test.⟩ — see HONOR 1

4 the free expression of one's true feelings and opinions ⟨I am speaking with all *honesty* when I say that your apple pie is the best I've ever tasted.⟩ — see CANDOR 1

honey *n* **1** a lovely woman ⟨She's a *honey*, all right.⟩ — see BEAUTY 2

2 something very good of its kind ⟨This morning one of my employees had a real *honey* of an excuse for being late for work.⟩ — see JIM-DANDY

3 a person with whom one is in love ⟨He usually gives his *honey* a dozen red roses on Valentine's Day.⟩ — see SWEETHEART

honey *vb* to praise too much ⟨She knew that the hairstylist was *honeying* her for a reason—the expectation of a generous tip.⟩ — see FLATTER 1

honor *n* **1** faithfulness to high moral standards ⟨The mayor, a man of *honor*, never broke a promise to the voters.⟩

synonyms honesty, integrity, probity, rectitude, righteousness, uprightness

related words blamelessness, character, conscientiousness, decency, fairness, high-mindedness, incorruptibility, justice, morality, nobility, reputability, respectability, right-mindedness, scrupulousness, virtue, virtuousness

near antonyms corruptibility, corruption, corruptness, debasement, debauchery, decadence, degeneracy, degradation, depravity, disgrace, disgracefulness, disreputableness, dissipatedness, dissipation, dissoluteness, perversion, pervertedness, profligacy, shamelessness, venality; criminality, crookedness, dishonesty, immorality, unrighteousness, unscrupulousness; meanness, reprehensibleness, rottenness, sinfulness, vileness, villainy, wickedness, wretchedness

antonyms baseness, dishonor, lowness

2 an asset that brings praise or renown ⟨a dedicated, caring teacher who is an *honor* to the teaching profession⟩ — see GLORY 2

3 public acknowledgment or admiration for an achievement ⟨the *honor* we give to our soldiers on Veterans Day⟩ — see GLORY 1

4 something given in recognition of achievement ⟨has received several *honors* from the Boy Scouts for his many years of service⟩ — see AWARD 1

5 something granted as a special favor ⟨It will be an *honor* for me to show you around the city.⟩ — see PRIVILEGE

honor *vb* to show appreciation, respect, or affection for (someone) with a public celebration ⟨The newlyweds were *honored* with a dinner given by the bride's grandmother.⟩

synonyms fete (*or* fête), recognize

related words acknowledge, cite, commend, compliment, credit, thank; extol (*also* extoll), glorify, laud, praise, tout; acclaim, applaud, cheer, hail, salute; celebrate, commemorate, memorialize, observe; congratulate, felicitate

near antonyms discredit, disgrace, dishonor, humble, humiliate, shame; bad-mouth, defame, libel, malign, slander; boo, hiss, hoot, jeer; censure, condemn, damn, denounce, reprobate; mock, put down, ridicule, slight

honorable *adj* **1** following the accepted rules of moral conduct ⟨The only *honorable* thing to do is to admit that you were wrong and apologize.⟩

synonyms decent, ethical, honest, just, noble, principled, respectable, righteous, upright, upstanding

related words blameless, guiltless, irreproachable, unassailable, unimpeachable; chivalrous, high-minded, rightminded; conscientious, fair, good, incorruptible, moral, reputable, respected, scrupulous, uncorrupted, virtuous

near antonyms bad, corrupt, criminal, crooked, evil, immoral, iniquitous, knavish, mean, nefarious, rascally, reprehensible, roguish, rotten, scoundrelly, sinful; unscrupulous, vile, villainous, wicked, wretched; blamable, blameworthy, censurable, culpable; debased, debauched, decadent, degenerate, degraded, demoralized, depraved, disgraceful, disreputable, dissipated, dissolute, libertine, perverse, perverted, profligate, reprobate, shameful, venal

antonyms base, dishonest, dishonorable, ignoble, low, unethical, unjust, unprincipled, unrighteous, unworthy

2 conforming to a high standard of morality or virtue ⟨It was *honorable* of you to give all the credit to your friend.⟩ — see GOOD 2

3 guided by or in accordance with one's sense of right and wrong ⟨I believe that if I genuinely cannot decide fairly, I should do the *honorable* thing and decline to serve on the panel.⟩ — see CONSCIENTIOUS 1

honorably *adv* in a manner befitting a person of the highest character and ideals ⟨Their sons served *honorably* to preserve freedom for future generations.⟩ — see GREATLY 1

¹hood *n* a violent, brutal person who is often a member of an organized gang ⟨The mob boss sent his toughest *hoods* out on the job.⟩ — see HOODLUM

²hood *n* something that covers or conceals like a piece of cloth ⟨counterfeiters conducting their affairs under a *hood* of secrecy⟩ — see CLOAK 1

hoodlum *n* a violent, brutal person who is often a member of an organized gang ⟨A couple of *hoodlums* held up the convenience store.⟩

synonyms gangster, goon, hood, hooligan, mobster, punk, roughneck, rowdy, ruffian, tough

related words cutthroat, scoundrel, villain; assassin, bandit, bravo, brigand, criminal, crook, desperado, felon, gunman, highwayman, lawbreaker, mafioso, malefactor, offender, outlaw, perp, perpetrator, pirate; pickpocket, racketeer, robber, swindler, thief, vandal

hoodwink *vb* to cause to believe what is untrue ⟨Tom Sawyer famously *hoodwinked* the other boys into thinking there was nothing more enjoyable than whitewashing a fence.⟩ — see DECEIVE

hoof (it) *vb* **1** to go on foot ⟨I *hoofed it* to school when I missed the bus.⟩ — see WALK 1

2 to perform a series of usually rhythmic bodily movements to music ⟨He *hoofs it* from seven to eight every Thursday night with other avid square dancers.⟩ — see DANCE 1

hook *n* a hard strike with a part of the body or an instrument ⟨delivered a hard right *hook* that struck his opponent in the eye⟩ — see ¹BLOW

hook *vb* **1** to cause to turn away from a straight line ⟨The pitcher *hooked* the ball, and the batter missed.⟩ — see BEND 1

2 to put or bring together so as to form a new and longer whole ⟨I *hooked* up three short chains together to make a longer necklace.⟩ — see CONNECT 1

3 to take (something) without right and with an intent to keep ⟨The monkey *hooked* four bananas from the basket and scampered away to enjoy them.⟩ — see STEAL 1

4 to take physical control or possession of (something) suddenly or forcibly ⟨At the clearance sale I *hooked* one of the few remaining digital cameras.⟩ — see CATCH 1

5 to turn away from a straight line or course ⟨Hang the bird feeder on a branch that *hooks* upward.⟩ — see CURVE 1

hookup *n* the state of having shared interests or efforts (as in social or business matters) ⟨The drama club's *hookup* with a local acting company provided several aspiring young actors with experience doing summer theater.⟩ — see ASSOCIATION 1

hooligan *n* a violent, brutal person who is often a member of an organized gang ⟨London bobbies clearing the streets of *hooligans*⟩ — see HOODLUM

hoop *n* a circular strip ⟨made Christmas garlands from *hoops* of red and green construction paper⟩ — see ¹RING 2

hoosegow *n* a place of confinement for persons held in lawful custody ⟨The cops threatened to throw her in the *hoosegow*.⟩ — see JAIL

hoot *n* **1** a loud vocal expression of strong emotion ⟨The courtroom erupted in *hoots* of laughter upon hearing the witness's sarcastic retort.⟩ — see SHOUT

2 a vocal sound made to express scorn or disapproval ⟨He ignored the *hoots* and jeers coming from the back of the crowd and kept on speaking.⟩ — see CATCALL

3 the smallest amount or part imaginable ⟨I don't give a *hoot* what you think!⟩ — see JOT

4 someone or something that is very funny ⟨That stand-up comic is a *hoot*.⟩ — see SCREAM

hop *n* **1** a social gathering for dancing ⟨Back in those days taking someone to the school *hop* was a big deal.⟩ — see DANCE

2 an act of leaping into the air ⟨She made it across the rocky creek in two *hops*.⟩ — see JUMP 1

hop *vb* **1** to move with a light springing step ⟨A rabbit *hopped* across the frozen grass.⟩ — see SKIP 1

2 to propel oneself upward or forward into the air ⟨The bus stopped, a lone passenger *hopped* on, and the driver continued on his way.⟩ — see JUMP 1

hope (for) *vb* to believe in the future occurrence of (something) ⟨He was *hoping for* an A in English.⟩ — see EXPECT

hopeful *adj* **1** having qualities which inspire hope ⟨Economists are offering a *hopeful* forecast for a healthy economy in the coming year.⟩

synonyms auspicious, bright, encouraging, fair, golden, heartening, likely, optimistic, promising, propitious, rose-colored, rosy, upbeat

related words cheering, comforting, reassuring, soothing; assured, confident, decisive, doubtless, positive, sure, unhesitating; beamish, bullish; favorable, good

near antonyms cheerless, comfortless; doubtful, dubious, uncertain; bearish, grim, negative, unfavorable; funereal, glum, gray (*also* grey), miserable, wretched

antonyms bleak, dark, depressing, discouraging, disheartening, dismal, dreary, gloomy, hopeless, inauspicious, pessimistic, unencouraging, unlikely, unpromising, unpropitious

2 pointing toward a happy outcome ⟨In a *hopeful*

response to the ad, several people called to say they'd
seen our lost cat.〉 — see FAVORABLE 2

hopeful *n* one who seeks an office, honor, position, or
award 〈The three mayoral *hopefuls* are going to debate
on local TV.〉 — see CANDIDATE

hopeless *adj* **1** not capable of being cured or reformed 〈a
hopeless optimist who looked for the good in everyone
and everything〉
synonyms incorrigible, incurable, irrecoverable, irredeemable, irremediable, irretrievable, unrecoverable,
unredeemable
related words irreparable, irreversible, uncorrectable;
unencouraging, unpromising; impenitent, unreformed,
unregenerate, unrepentant
near antonyms reversible; encouraging, promising; penitent, regretful, remorseful, repentant, rueful, sorry; correctable, fixable, rectifiable, repairable, reparable, salv-
able, salvageable
antonyms curable, reclaimable, recoverable, reformable, remediable, retrievable, savable (*or* saveable)
2 emphasizing or expecting the worst 〈The poor girl was
feeling *hopeless* about ever finding her lost cat.〉 — see
PESSIMISTIC 1
3 incapable of being solved or accomplished 〈Keeping
this desk organized is *hopeless*.〉 — see IMPOSSIBLE
4 feeling or showing no hope 〈felt confused and *hopeless*
after being laid off〉 — see DESPONDENT 1

hopelessness *n* utter loss of hope 〈a feeling of *hopelessness* among the fans〉 — see DESPAIR 1

horde *n* a great number of persons or creatures massed
together 〈a *horde* of mosquitoes〉 〈*hordes* of shoppers
crowding the stores〉 — see CROWD 1

horn *n* something shaped like a hollow cone and used as a
container 〈musketeers carrying their gunpowder in powder *horns*〉 — see CORNET

horrendous *adj* **1** causing fear 〈A *horrendous* explosion
shook the building.〉 — see FEARFUL 1
2 causing intense displeasure, disgust, or resentment 〈a
horrendous breach of good manners that should not escape censure〉 — see OFFENSIVE 1
3 extremely disturbing or repellent 〈Emergency room
personnel must not flinch even from the most *horrendous* injuries.〉 — see HORRIBLE 1

horrible *adj* **1** extremely disturbing or repellent 〈a *horrible*
car accident〉
synonyms appalling, atrocious, awful, dreadful, frightful, ghastly, grisly, gruesome (*also* grewsome), hideous,
horrendous, horrid, horrifying, lurid, macabre, monstrous, nightmare, nightmarish, shocking, terrible, terrific
related words alarming, bloodcurdling, dire, direful,
fearful, fearsome, forbidding, formidable, frightening,
gut-wrenching, hair-raising, intimidating, redoubtable,
scary, terrifying; abhorrent, deplorable, disagreeable,
distasteful, loathsome, nauseating, noisome, obnoxious,
obscene, offensive, repugnant, repulsive, revolting, sickening; abominable, evil, foul, heinous, noxious, odious,
unspeakable, vile; grotesque, ugly, unsightly
near antonyms agreeable, appealing, attractive, delectable, delicious, delightful, enjoyable, enticing, inviting,
pleasant, pleasing, pleasurable, satisfying, welcome;
cheering, comforting, soothing
2 causing fear 〈a *horrible* scream that made shivers go up
and down our spines〉 — see FEARFUL 1
3 causing intense displeasure, disgust, or resentment 〈I
can never forgive her for the *horrible* way she treated
me.〉 — see OFFENSIVE 1
4 extremely unsatisfactory 〈I'm never going back to that
restaurant; the service was *horrible*!〉 — see WRETCHED 1

horrid *adj* **1** causing intense displeasure, disgust, or resentment 〈accused him of stealing and said mean and *horrid*
things about him〉 — see OFFENSIVE 1
2 extremely disturbing or repellent 〈told a *horrid* story〉
— see HORRIBLE 1

horridness *n* the quality of inspiring intense dread or dismay 〈the *horridness* of the accident〉 — see HORROR 1

horrified *adj* filled with fear or dread 〈He sat rigid in his
seat, *horrified* that the plane would crash.〉 — see AFRAID

horrify *vb* to strike with fear 〈The news of the accident
horrified her.〉 — see FRIGHTEN

horrifying *adj* **1** causing fear 〈a *horrifying* tale of evil〉 —
see FEARFUL 1
2 extremely disturbing or repellent 〈the *horrifying* sight
of a rat in the restaurant〉 — see HORRIBLE 1

horror *n* **1** the quality of inspiring intense dread or dismay
〈It's difficult to even begin to comprehend the *horror* of
the Holocaust.〉
synonyms atrociousness, atrocity, awfulness, dreadfulness, frightfulness, ghastliness, grisliness, gruesomeness,
hideousness, horridness, monstrosity, repulsiveness
related words badness, baseness, depravedness, depravity, diabolicalness, evil, evilness, foulness, heinousness,
immorality, iniquity, invidiousness, sinfulness, ungodliness, viciousness, vileness, wickedness; deplorableness,
despicableness, detestableness, execrableness, hatefulness, loathsomeness, reprehensibleness; creepiness, eeri-
ness, fearfulness, fearsomeness, ghoulishness, scariness;
agony, anguish, hellishness, misery, torment, torture
near antonyms agreeableness, delightfulness, pleasantness, pleasurableness; allurement, appeal, attraction, attractiveness
2 a situation or state that causes great suffering and unhappiness 〈She had never experienced the *horrors* of
war.〉 — see HELL 2
3 something unpleasant to look at 〈Are you really going
to hang that *horror* on the wall?〉 — see EYESORE
4 the emotion experienced in the presence or threat of
danger 〈Imagine my *horror* at finding myself face to face
with a lion on the loose.〉 — see FEAR 1
5 a dislike so strong as to cause stomach upset or queasiness 〈Cat lover or no, she regards cleaning the litter box
with *horror*.〉 — see DISGUST

horse *n* a large hoofed domestic animal that is used for
carrying or drawing loads and for riding 〈The mounted
police stable their *horses* in the city park.〉
synonyms equine, nag, steed
related words colt, foal, gelding, mare, stallion; bronco,
mustang, pony; charger, courser, galloper, hackney,
mount, packhorse, prancer, quarter horse, racehorse,
saddle horse, trotter, workhorse; bay, black, buckskin,
dun, palomino, pinto, roan, skewbald, sorrel; cob, dob-
bin, jade, skate

horse around *vb* to engage in attention-getting playful or
boisterous behavior 〈The boys were *horsing around* on
the boat when one of them fell overboard.〉 — see CUT
UP

horselaugh *n* an explosive sound that is a sign of amusement 〈Even in a crowded auditorium you wouldn't have
trouble picking out his earsplitting *horselaugh*.〉 —
see LAUGH 1

horseplay *n* wildly playful or mischievous behavior 〈When
he saw us spraying each other with the hose instead of
washing the car, Dad yelled, "Cut out the *horseplay*!"〉
synonyms clowning, foolery, high jinks (*also* hijinks),
horsing around, monkeying, roughhouse, roughhousing,
skylarking, tomfoolery
related words childishness, clownishness, foolishness,
funning, jesting, joking, nonsense, silliness, waggery;

boisterousness, rambunctiousness, rowdiness, rowdyism, devilry (*or* deviltry), impishness, knavery, mischief, mischievousness, prankishness, rascality, roguishness, trickery; cavorting, frivolity, frolicking, gamboling (*or* gambolling), merrymaking, playfulness, revelry, roistering, romping, sporting, sportiveness

horse sense *n* the ability to make intelligent decisions especially in everyday matters ⟨Pure *horse sense* should tell you not to play with matches.⟩ — see COMMON SENSE

horse–trade *vb* to talk over or dispute the terms of a purchase ⟨I *horse-traded* with the painter: I did his tax returns, and he did my kitchen.⟩ — see BARGAIN 1

horsewhip *vb* to strike repeatedly with something long and thin or flexible ⟨The pirate threatened to *horsewhip* crew members who challenged his authority.⟩ — see WHIP 1

horsing around *n* wildly playful or mischievous behavior ⟨At the beach there was a lot more *horsing around* on the sand than actual swimming in the water.⟩ — see HORSEPLAY

hose *n* a close-fitting covering for the foot and leg ⟨a reenactor dressed like Benjamin Franklin in waistcoat, breeches, and *hose*⟩ — see STOCKING

hospice *n* a place that provides rooms and usually a public dining room for overnight guests ⟨The monks run a *hospice* for travelers in their mountain retreat.⟩ — see HOTEL

hospitable *adj* showing a natural kindness and courtesy especially in social situations ⟨The family is unfailingly *hospitable* whenever guests show up unexpectedly at their summer cottage.⟩ — see GRACIOUS 1

host *n* **1** a great number of persons or creatures massed together ⟨A *host* of people assembled along the parade route to see the new president.⟩ — see CROWD 1
2 a large body of men and women organized for land warfare ⟨The small band of defenders was no match for the enemy's mighty *host* of thousands.⟩ — see ARMY 1

hostel *n* a place that provides rooms and usually a public dining room for overnight guests ⟨We stayed in *hostels* as we backpacked through Europe.⟩ — see HOTEL

hostelry *n* a place that provides rooms and usually a public dining room for overnight guests ⟨The grande dame of the city's *hostelries*, it has played host to presidents, kings, and Hollywood royalty.⟩ — see HOTEL

hostile *adj* **1** marked by opposition or ill will ⟨Her suggestions were given a *hostile* reception.⟩
synonyms adversary, antagonistic, antipathetic, inhospitable, inimical, jaundiced, mortal, negative, unfriendly, unsympathetic
related words adverse, argumentative, bellicose, belligerent, clashing, combative, conflicting, contentious, contrary, disputatious, militant, opposed, pugnacious, quarrelsome, resisting, scrappy, truculent; antisocial, cold, cool, disagreeable, disapproving, distant, frigid, icy; biased, prejudiced; acrimonious, bitter, despiteful, hateful, malevolent, malicious, malign, malignant, opprobrious, rancorous, spiteful, unloving, vindictive, virulent
near antonyms affable, amiable, amicable, civil, companionable, comradely, convivial, cordial, genial, good-natured, good-tempered, gracious, gregarious, neighborly, pleasant, sociable, social, warm; affectionate, devoted, kind, kindly, loving, nice, sweet; accepting, agreeable, approving, benign, empathetic, favorable, understanding, warmhearted, welcoming
antonyms friendly, hospitable, nonantagonistic, nonhostile, sympathetic
2 opposed to one's interests ⟨The company's president vows to fight the *hostile* takeover by the giant corporation.⟩ — see ADVERSE 1

hostile *n* one that is hostile toward another ⟨Reports of *hostiles* in the area kept the troops on edge.⟩ — see ENEMY

hostility *n* **1** a deep-seated ill will ⟨a lingering *hostility* between the two neighbors ever since they had that property-line dispute⟩ — see ENMITY
2 hostilities *pl* a state of armed violent struggle between states, nations, or groups ⟨Both sides agreed to cease all *hostilities*.⟩ — see WAR 1

hot *adj* **1** having a notably high temperature ⟨The casserole, just out of the oven, was too *hot* to eat.⟩
synonyms ardent, broiling, burning, fervent, fervid, fiery, piping hot, red, red-hot, roasting, scalding, scorching, searing, sultry, superheated, sweltering, torrid
related words blazing, glowing, seething, sizzling; heated, overheated, reheated, warmed; snug, toasty, warm; feverish, flushed, inflamed (*also* enflamed); muggy, steamy, summerlike, summery, tropical
near antonyms chill, chilly, cool, coolish, nippy, snappy; blizzardly, frosty, snowy, subfreezing, subzero, wintry (*also* wintery); chilled, cooled, refrigerated, unheated; benumbed, numb
antonyms arctic, bitter, cold, freezing, frigid, frozen, glacial, ice-cold, iced, icy
2 being or involving the latest methods, concepts, information, or styles ⟨This spring it's the cool shades of lipstick that are *hot*.⟩ — see MODERN
3 enjoying widespread favor or approval ⟨I was surprised to learn that American jazz has long been *hot* in Russia.⟩ — see POPULAR 1
4 marked by bursts of destructive force or intense activity ⟨Your *hot* temper is going to get you in trouble.⟩ ⟨a *hot* battle for first place in the American League⟩ — see VIOLENT 1
5 showing urgent desire or interest ⟨We were *hot* to get the baseball game started and wished it would stop raining.⟩ — see EAGER
6 feeling or showing anger ⟨You don't have to get all *hot* about it!⟩ — see ANGRY
7 moving, proceeding, or acting with great speed ⟨bought a *hot* new car that should tear up the roadways⟩ — see FAST 1
8 of the very best kind ⟨I don't think that's such a *hot* idea.⟩ — see EXCELLENT

hot *adv* with great speed ⟨Workers were working *hot* and heavy to repair the breach in the levee.⟩ — see FAST 1

hot air *n* **1** boastful speech or writing ⟨His taking credit for the rescue was mostly *hot air*, since the boat was actually saved by the Coast Guard.⟩ — see BOMBAST 1
2 language that is impressive-sounding but not meaningful or sincere ⟨Her campaign promise to "fight for the people" showed a taste for stale *hot air*.⟩ — see RHETORIC 1

hot–blooded *adj* having or expressing great depth of feeling ⟨After watching the successful defense of Fort McHenry, Francis Scott Key quickly wrote the *hot-blooded* poem that later became known as "The Star-Spangled Banner."⟩ — see FERVENT 1

hotcake *n* a flat cake made from thin batter and cooked on both sides (as on a griddle) ⟨*Hotcakes* and maple syrup are on the breakfast menu.⟩ — see PANCAKE

hotchpotch *n* an unorganized collection or mixture of various things ⟨Sunday supper was a *hotchpotch* of leftovers.⟩ — see MISCELLANY 1

hotel *n* a place that provides rooms and usually a public dining room for overnight guests ⟨For their 50th anniversary they stayed at one of the finest *hotels* in San Francisco.⟩
synonyms hospice, hostel, hostelry, inn, lodge, public house, tavern

related words B and B, bed-and-breakfast, guesthouse; apartment hotel; accommodations, lodgings, rest; court, motel, motor court, motor inn, motor lodge, resort, spa, tourist court, youth hostel; camp, campground; bunkhouse, dorm, dormitory; boardinghouse, lodging house, rooming house

hotfoot *adv* with excessive or careless speed ⟨lowered his plane *hotfoot* onto a pasture when the engine started to sputter⟩ — see HASTILY 1

hotfoot (it) *vb* to proceed or move quickly ⟨You'd better *hotfoot it* to the bus stop if you're going to catch the bus.⟩ — see HURRY 2

hothouse *n* a glass-enclosed building for growing plants ⟨grows tomatoes in his *hothouse* all winter long⟩ — see CONSERVATORY

hotness *n* the state of enjoying widespread approval ⟨The phenomenal *hotness* of the movie's stars is the driving force behind all of the advance publicity.⟩ — see POPULARITY

hotshot *n* a person with a high level of knowledge or skill in a field ⟨While still in his 20s, he was known on Wall Street as an investment *hotshot*.⟩ — see EXPERT

hot war *n* a state of armed violent struggle between states, nations, or groups ⟨Fortunately, the cool relationship between the two nations never escalated into a *hot war*.⟩ — see WAR 1

hound *n* 1 a domestic mammal that is related to the wolves and foxes ⟨In the yard an old *hound* greeted us with a single bark.⟩ — see DOG 1
2 a person with a strong and habitual liking for something ⟨A camera *hound* even before the baby arrived, he's now become obsessive.⟩ — see FAN
3 a mean, evil, or unprincipled person ⟨a no-good *hound* who betrayed a good friend⟩ — see VILLAIN

hound *vb* 1 to go after or on the track of ⟨The actress was *hounded* by reporters night and day.⟩ — see FOLLOW 2
2 to subject (someone) to constant scoldings and sharp reminders ⟨kept *hounding* his mother to let him drive her car until she gave in⟩ — see NAG 1

hounding *n* the act of going after or in the tracks of another ⟨The rock star eventually couldn't take the constant *hounding* by reporters and fans.⟩ — see PURSUIT

house *n* 1 a commercial or industrial activity or organization ⟨a publishing *house* that specializes in school textbooks⟩ — see ENTERPRISE 1
2 a group of persons who come from the same ancestor ⟨The present British royal family belongs to the *House* of Windsor.⟩ — see FAMILY 1
3 the place where one lives ⟨Come over to my *house* for supper so I can show off my new stove.⟩ — see HOME 1
4 those who live as a family in one house ⟨The whole *house* is in a state of excited anticipation for the holidays.⟩ — see HOUSEHOLD
5 the shelter or resting place of a wild animal ⟨Prairie dogs make their *house* underground.⟩ — see DEN 1

house *vb* 1 to provide with living quarters or shelter ⟨Some of the freshmen were temporarily *housed* in local motels while the new dorm was being finished.⟩
synonyms accommodate, bestow, billet, bivouac, board, bunk, camp, chamber, domicile, encamp, harbor, lodge, put up, quarter, roof, room, shelter, take in
related words ensconce, home, roost, secure, shed, stable, tent; barrack; bed (down)
near antonyms eject, evict
2 to close or shut in by or as if by barriers ⟨The carpenter built casing to *house* the hot water pipes.⟩ — see ENCLOSE 1

house cat *n* a small domestic animal known for catching mice ⟨The *house cat* at the Cheshire Cat Bookstore has

the dual responsibility of being mascot and mouser.⟩ — see CAT

household *adj* 1 of or relating to a household or family ⟨He spent the weekend at home, helping with *household* chores.⟩ — see DOMESTIC 1
2 often observed or encountered ⟨"Ozone" is now a *household* word, thanks to global warming.⟩ — see COMMON 1

household *n* those who live as a family in one house ⟨a *household* that consists of a mom, two kids, and a grandmother⟩
synonyms extended family, home, house, ménage
related words blood, folks, kin, kindred, kinfolk (*or* kinfolks), kinsfolk, kith; brood; nuclear family; clan, community

housekeeper *n* a person hired to perform household or personal services ⟨They hired a *housekeeper* for the new house.⟩ — see MAID 1

housemaid *n* a person hired to perform household or personal services ⟨became both nurse and *housemaid* to the elderly man⟩ — see MAID 1

housing *n* something that encloses another thing especially to protect it ⟨a camera with a waterproof *housing* for taking pictures of coral reefs and other underwater features⟩ — see ¹CASE 1

hovel *n* a small, simply constructed, and often temporary dwelling ⟨a poor man's *hovel*⟩ — see SHACK

hover *vb* to rest or move along the surface of a liquid or in the air ⟨The man claimed that the UFO *hovered* a moment, then spun off into space at incredible speed.⟩ — see FLOAT 1

hover (over) *vb* to remain poised to inflict harm, danger, or distress on ⟨After the first big layoff, the possibility of losing their jobs *hovered over* all of the factory's workers.⟩ — see THREATEN

howbeit *adv* in spite of that ⟨I've never written a poem before; *howbeit*, I feel my first attempt is quite good.⟩ — see HOWEVER

howbeit *conj* in spite of the fact that ⟨Our visit to Niagara Falls was very pleasant, *howbeit* slightly shorter than we had planned.⟩ — see ALTHOUGH

however *adv* in spite of that ⟨I'm all out of eggs; *however*, I can still make us a nice breakfast.⟩
synonyms howbeit, nevertheless, nonetheless, notwithstanding, still, though, withal, yet
related words after all, anyhow, regardless
phrases all the same (*or* just the same), at the same time

howl *n* 1 a crying out in grief ⟨We had to endure the puppy's mournful *howls* on her first night in our house.⟩ — see LAMENT 1
2 a loud vocal expression of strong emotion ⟨*howls* of laughter from the children watching the clown's silly antics⟩ — see SHOUT
3 a violent shouting ⟨He let out a *howl* of protest.⟩ — see CLAMOR 1

howl *vb* 1 to make a long loud mournful sound ⟨Several coyotes began *howling* close by as the sun went down.⟩ ⟨The wind *howled* on the open plain.⟩
synonyms bay, keen, wail, yowl
related words bawl, scream, screech, shriek, shrill, squall, squeal, yell, yelp
2 to cry out loudly and emotionally ⟨The boy *howled* in pain when he stubbed his toe.⟩ — see SCREAM 1

hub *n* a thing or place that is of greatest importance to an activity or interest ⟨Broadway is the *hub* of theater life in New York.⟩ — see CENTER 1

hubbub *n* 1 a state of noisy, confused activity ⟨Imagine all the *hubbub* at the zoo when the lion escaped.⟩ — see COMMOTION

2 a violent shouting ⟨The people who had been waiting for the flight made a huge *hubbub* when they were told that it was cancelled.⟩ — see CLAMOR 1

huckster *n* one who sells things outdoors ⟨*hucksters* outside the stadium selling everything from key chains to life-size cutouts of the quarterback⟩ — see PEDDLER

huddle *n* **1** a coming together of a number of persons for a specified purpose ⟨After an all-night *huddle*, the state legislature finally approved a budget for the coming year.⟩ — see MEETING 1
2 a number of things considered as a unit ⟨We saw a *huddle* of tents that turned out to be a Boy Scout encampment.⟩ — see GROUP 1
3 a usually small number of persons considered as a unit ⟨In the lobby during intermission *huddles* of theatergoers were excitedly discussing the play.⟩ — see GROUP 2

huddle *vb* **1** to gather into a closely packed group ⟨The puppies *huddled* together to keep warm.⟩ — see ²PRESS 3
2 to lie low with the limbs close to the body ⟨The girl *huddled* under her bed during the game of hide-and-seek.⟩ — see CROUCH

hue *n* a property that becomes apparent when light falls on an object and by which things that are identical in form can be distinguished ⟨We decorated the room in *hues* of blue and green.⟩ — see COLOR 1

hue and cry *n* a violent shouting ⟨the *hue and cry* in the classroom when someone let loose a snake⟩ — see CLAMOR 1

huff *n* **1** a state of nervous or irritated concern ⟨Mom was in a *huff* because everyone was running late and was going to miss the school bus.⟩ — see FRET
2 an outburst or display of excited anger ⟨She gets all in a *huff* every time anyone makes the slightest criticism.⟩ — see TANTRUM
3 the feeling of being offended or resentful after a slight or indignity ⟨He left the restaurant in a *huff* after waiting 15 minutes to be seated.⟩ — see PIQUE

huff *vb* to talk loudly and wildly ⟨Demanding to speak to the branch manager, she *huffed* about the rudeness of the bank teller.⟩ — see RANT

huffiness *n* **1** an exaggerated sense of one's importance that shows itself in the making of excessive or unjustified claims ⟨The *huffiness* in his voice put off his coworkers.⟩ — see ARROGANCE
2 readiness to show annoyance or impatience ⟨There's no point in telling her what you think unless you want to put up with her *huffiness*.⟩ — see PETULANCE

hug *vb* **1** to express to (someone) admiration for his or her success or good fortune ⟨She *hugged* herself for having made a killing on the investment.⟩ — see CONGRATULATE
2 to put one's arms around and press tightly ⟨Grandma *hugged* the grandchildren good-bye.⟩ — see EMBRACE 1

huge *adj* unusually large ⟨The old stadium was replaced by a *huge* new one that seats 100,000 spectators.⟩
synonyms astronomical (*also* astronomic), bumper, colossal, cosmic (*also* cosmical), elephantine, enormous, gargantuan, giant, gigantic, grand, herculean, heroic (*also* heroical), immense, jumbo, king-size (*or* king-sized), leviathan, mammoth, massive, mighty, monster, monstrous, monumental, mountainous, oceanic, prodigious, super, titanic, tremendous, vast, vasty, whacking, whopping
related words big, bulky, considerable, extensive, good, goodly, great, gross, handsome, hefty, hulking, largish, major, outsize (*also* outsized), overgrown, oversize (*or* oversized), sizable (*or* sizeable), substantial, tidy, voluminous; august, formidable, grandiose, imposing, lofty, majestic; cavernous, monolithic, overwhelming, staggering, stupendous, towering; boundless, immeasurable, infinite

near antonyms little, mini, petite, pint-size (*or* pint-sized), puny, small, smallish, undersized (*also* undersize); dinky, dwarfish, half-pint
antonyms bantam, bitty, diminutive, infinitesimal, micro, microminiature, microscopic (*also* microscopical), midget, miniature, minuscule, minute, pocket, pygmy, teeny, teeny-weeny, tiny, wee

hugely *adv* **1** to a great degree ⟨a *hugely* popular movie⟩ — see VERY 1
2 to a large extent or degree ⟨This donation has added *hugely* to the library's collection of music manuscripts.⟩ — see GREATLY 2

hugeness *n* the quality or state of being very large ⟨You can only appreciate the *hugeness* of the dome when you see how tiny the people standing under it look.⟩ — see IMMENSITY

hugger–mugger *adj* **1** lacking in order, neatness, and often cleanliness ⟨a *hugger-mugger* presentation of the facts of the case that left everyone confused⟩ — see MESSY
2 undertaken or done so as to escape being observed or known by others ⟨a tale of *hugger-mugger* doings and international espionage⟩ — see SECRET 1

hulk *n* a big clumsy often slow-witted person ⟨The team recruited a 6 foot, 5 inch *hulk* to play offensive tackle.⟩ — see OAF 1

hulking *adj* **1** of a size greater than average of its kind ⟨A heavy, *hulking* stone blocked the way.⟩ — see LARGE
2 strongly and heavily built ⟨I need a strong *hulking* young man to carry out the box of books.⟩ — see ¹HUSKY 1

hull *n* something that encloses another thing especially to protect it ⟨sunflower seed *hulls*⟩ — see ¹CASE 1

hull *vb* to remove the natural covering of ⟨*Hull* the pinto beans before adding them.⟩ — see PEEL

hullabaloo *n* **1** a state of noisy, confused activity ⟨There was a lot of needless *hullabaloo* as the new millennium approached.⟩ — see COMMOTION
2 a violent shouting ⟨There was such a *hullabaloo* in the room that he couldn't hear himself think.⟩ — see CLAMOR 1

hum *n* a monotonous sound like that of an insect in motion ⟨We heard the *hum* of an outboard motor and a few minutes later the small craft came into sight.⟩
synonyms buzz, chirr, drone, purr, thrum, whir (*also* whirr), whiz (*or* whizz), zoom
related words babble, coo, gasp, gurgle, hiss, moan, murmur, rustle, sigh, whisper; whish, zing, zip
near antonyms bawl, howl, roar, scream, screech, shriek, squall, squeal, yelp, yell

hum *vb* **1** to be copiously supplied ⟨The restaurant was *humming* with diners.⟩ — see ABOUND
2 to fly, turn, or move rapidly with a fluttering or vibratory sound ⟨A helicopter *hummed* overhead.⟩ — see WHIR

human *adj* relating to or characteristic of human beings ⟨It's *human* nature to care about what people think of us.⟩
synonyms mortal, natural
related words hominid, humanlike, humanoid
near antonyms angelic (*or* angelical), divine, godlike, preternatural, superhuman, supernatural; immortal, omnipotent, omniscient; animal, beastly, brute; inhuman, robotic
antonyms nonhuman

human *n* a member of the human race ⟨*Humans* are not endowed with a natural defense against the elements, such as fur or a thick hide.⟩
synonyms being, bird, body, character, creature, cus-

tomer, devil, duck, face, fish, guy, head, individual, life, man, mortal, party, person, personage, scout, sort, soul, specimen, stiff, thing, wight
related words hominid, humanoid; brother, fellow, fellowman, neighbor; celebrity, personality, somebody
phrases son of man
near antonyms animal, beast, brute, critter
humane *adj* **1** having or marked by sympathy and consideration for others ⟨*humane* guards who treated the prisoners decently⟩ ⟨The Geneva conventions spelled out standards for the *humane* treatment of prisoners of war.⟩
synonyms beneficent, benevolent, benignant, compassionate, good-hearted, kind, kindhearted, kindly, softhearted, sympathetic, tender, tenderhearted, warmhearted
related words considerate, solicitous, thoughtful; affable, amicable, benign, companionable, comradely, cordial, friendly, genial, gentle, good, good-natured, good-tempered, gracious, mild, neighborly, nice, pleasant, sweet, warm; clement, forbearing, forgiving, lenient, merciful, soft; patient, pitying, tolerant, understanding; altruistic, brotherly, charitable, freehanded, generous, greathearted, humanitarian, liberal, magnanimous, munificent, noble, openhearted, philanthropic (*also* philanthropical), selfless, unselfish, unsparing
near antonyms merciless, pitiless, ruthless, stonyhearted; inconsiderate, insensitive, thoughtless, uncaring, unthinking; grim, hard-boiled, harsh, heavy-handed, severe, stern, tough, unsentimental; hateful, malevolent, malicious, malign, malignant, mean, nasty, spiteful, virulent; antihumanitarian, uncharitable
antonyms atrocious, barbaric, barbarous, brutal, brute, callous, cold-blooded, cruel, fiendish, heartless, inhuman, inhumane, insensate, sadistic, savage, truculent, uncompassionate, unfeeling, unkind, unkindly, unsympathetic, vicious, wanton
2 having or showing the capacity for sharing the feelings of another ⟨the movie's *humane* treatment of a difficult subject⟩ — see SYMPATHETIC 1
humanitarian *adj* having or showing a concern for the welfare of others ⟨*humanitarian* efforts to aid the earthquake victims⟩ — see CHARITABLE 1
humanity *n* **1** human beings in general ⟨All *humanity* can learn from this tragedy.⟩ — see PEOPLE 1
2 the capacity for feeling for another's unhappiness or misfortune ⟨a country known for the *humanity* of its liberal immigration policy⟩ — see HEART 1
3 the human race ⟨In Greek mythology, the gods display many of the weaknesses of *humanity*, such as jealousy, foolishness, and greed.⟩ — see MANKIND
humankind *n* **1** human beings in general ⟨All *humankind* shares the desire for peace.⟩ — see PEOPLE 1
2 the human race ⟨Perhaps someday *humankind* will find the key that unlocks the mystery of the universe.⟩ — see MANKIND
humble *adj* **1** not having or showing any feelings of superiority, self-assertiveness, or showiness ⟨a medical scientist who remained remarkably *humble* even after winning the Nobel Prize⟩
synonyms demure, down-to-earth, lowly, meek, modest, unassuming, unpretentious
related words acquiescent, compliant, deferential, resigned, submissive, unaggressive, unassertive, yielding; cowering, cringing, shrinking; ingenuous, naive (*or* naïve), plain, simple, unaffected; bashful, diffident, introverted, mousy (*or* mousey), overmodest, passive, quiet, reserved, retiring, sheepish, shy, subdued, timid, unobtrusive; self-deprecating, self-deprecatory
near antonyms aggressive, assertive, audacious, bold,

brash, brassy, cheeky, forward, impertinent, impudent, saucy; cocksure, cocky, confident, hubristic, overconfident, self-confident; egocentric, egoistic (*also* egoistical), prideful, self-centered, self-complacent, self-conceited, self-congratulatory, self-important, self-satisfied, smug, stuck-up, swelled-headed; boastful, bombastic, braggy, swaggering, vain, vainglorious; condescending, disdainful, dominant, dominating, domineering, overbearing, patronizing, pontificating; flamboyant, ostentatious, showy; extroverted (*also* extraverted), immodest, outgoing, uninhibited, unreserved
antonyms arrogant, conceited, egotistic (*or* egotistical), haughty, highfalutin (*also* hifalutin), high-handed, high-hat, hoity-toity, imperious, lordly, overweening, peremptory, pompous, presuming, presumptuous, pretentious, self-assertive, supercilious, superior, uppity
2 belonging to the class of people of low social or economic rank ⟨a *humble* peasant girl who claimed she was chosen by God to restore the French king to his throne⟩ — see IGNOBLE 1
humble *vb* to reduce to a lower standing in one's own eyes or in others' eyes ⟨Philip was utterly *humbled* by a crushing defeat in the first round of the state chess tournament.⟩
synonyms abase, chasten, cheapen, debase, degrade, demean, discredit, disgrace, dishonor, foul, humiliate, lower, shame, sink, smirch, take down
related words abash, confound, confuse, discomfit, disconcert, discountenance, embarrass, faze, fluster, mortify, nonplus, rattle; belittle, castigate, criticize, cry down, decry, depreciate, diminish, discount, disparage, minimize, put down, ridicule, write off; bad-mouth, defame, defile, libel, malign, slander; affront, insult; censure, condemn, damn, denounce, execrate, reprehend, reprobate
near antonyms acclaim, applaud, boast, celebrate, cheer, cite, commend, compliment, congratulate, decorate, eulogize, extol (*also* extoll), hail, honor, laud, praise, salute, tout; acknowledge, recognize; highlight; dignify, ennoble, enshrine, enthrone, glorify, magnify; advance, boost, lift, promote, raise, upgrade, uplift; idealize, romanticize
antonyms aggrandize, canonize, deify, elevate, exalt
humbleness *n* the absence of any feelings of being better than others ⟨In a display of true *humbleness* he gave much of the credit for his discovery to others.⟩ — see HUMILITY
humbly *adv* in a manner showing no signs of pride or self-assertion ⟨*humbly* accepted the criticism⟩ — see LOWLY
humbug *n* **1** an imitation that is passed off as genuine ⟨Tests showed that the "old" map of America was a cleverly made *humbug*.⟩ — see FAKE 1
2 language, behavior, or ideas that are absurd and contrary to good sense ⟨Those UFO stories are a lot of *humbug*.⟩ — see NONSENSE 1
3 one who makes false claims of identity or expertise ⟨One *humbug* after another claimed to be the miraculously surviving daughter of the Russian czar.⟩ — see IMPOSTOR
humbug *vb* to cause to believe what is untrue ⟨*humbugged* into believing that the bones were the skeleton of a prehistoric human being⟩ — see DECEIVE
humbuggery *n* language, behavior, or ideas that are absurd and contrary to good sense ⟨a lot of *humbuggery* about a mean old witch that lives in the woods⟩ — see NONSENSE 1
humdrum *adj* causing weariness, restlessness, or lack of interest ⟨She leads a *humdrum* life.⟩ ⟨a *humdrum* meal⟩ — see BORING
humdrum *n* a tedious lack of variety ⟨loathed the *humdrum* of daily life in a small town⟩ — see MONOTONY

humid *adj* containing or characterized by an uncomfortable amount of moisture ⟨The air was so *humid* that our beach towels hanging on the line never really got dry.⟩
synonyms damp, muggy, sticky, sultry
related words steamy, summerlike, summery, sweltering, torrid; semitropical (*also* semitropic), subhumid, subtropical (*also* subtropic), tropic, tropical; close, heavy, oppressive, smothering, stifling, stuffy, suffocating; dank, moist
near antonyms arid, baked, burned (*or* burnt), dehydrated, desert, droughty, dusty, parched, scorched, seared, semiarid, sere (*also* sear), sunbaked, thirsty, waterless
antonyms dry
humidity *n* the amount of water suspended in the air in tiny droplets ⟨The oppressive *humidity* made the hot day seem even hotter.⟩ — see MOISTURE
humiliate *vb* to reduce to a lower standing in one's own eyes or in others' eyes ⟨I hope I don't *humiliate* myself during the presentation.⟩ — see HUMBLE
humility *n* the absence of any feelings of being better than others ⟨Displaying genuine *humility*, the peace activist accepted the Nobel Prize on behalf of all who have worked to end the violence.⟩
synonyms demureness, humbleness, lowliness, meekness, modesty
related words acquiescence, compliance, deference, passivity, submission, submissiveness; ingenuousness, naïveté (*also* naivete *or* naiveté); directness, plainness, simpleness; bashfulness, diffidence, mousiness, quietness, reserve, reservedness, retiringness, sheepishness, shyness, timidity, timidness
near antonyms aggressiveness, assertiveness; boldness, brashness, brassiness, cheek, cheekiness, cockiness, forwardness, overconfidence, swagger, temerity; impertinence, impudence, insolence, nerve, sauciness; boastfulness, chest-thumping, self-centeredness, self-complacency, self-conceit, self-glorification, self-importance, self-satisfaction, vaingloriousness, vanity; condescension, disdain, scorn; flamboyance, ostentation, ostentatiousness, showiness
antonyms arrogance, assumption, conceit, egoism, egotism, haughtiness, huffiness, imperiousness, loftiness, lordliness, pompousness, presumptuousness, pretense (*or* pretence), pretension, pretentiousness, pride, pridefulness, superciliousness, superiority
humming *adj* marked by much life, movement, or activity ⟨The new science center is usually *humming* with school groups on Thursdays.⟩ — see ALIVE 2
humor *n* **1** the amusing quality or element in something ⟨We failed to see any *humor* in his lame jokes.⟩
synonyms comedy, comic, drollness, funniness, hilariousness, humorousness, richness
related words amusement, enjoyment, fun, pleasure; absurdity, irony, laughableness, ludicrousness, ridiculousness; whimsicality, wittiness, wryness; burlesque, caricature, farce, jest, lampoon, parody, satire, slapstick, spoof, takeoff; jocularity, jokiness, playfulness, waggishness
near antonyms agony, anguish, dolor, grief, heartache, heartbreak, misery, sorrow, torment, torture, tribulation, woe; gravity, seriousness, soberness, solemnity, somberness
antonyms pathos
2 humorous entertainment ⟨a screenwriter best known for lowbrow *humor*⟩ — see COMEDY 1
3 a state of mind dominated by a particular emotion ⟨The prospect of going out to dinner put her in a good *humor* all day.⟩ — see MOOD 1
4 a sudden impulsive and apparently unmotivated idea or action ⟨She was seized by a sudden *humor* to contact

an old college friend that she hadn't seen in ages.⟩ — see WHIM
humor *vb* to give in to (a desire) ⟨Sue *humored* her grandfather by listening to his war stories for the hundredth time.⟩ — see INDULGE 1
humorist *n* a person (as a writer) noted for or specializing in humor ⟨Mark Twain is perhaps America's most beloved *humorist*.⟩
synonyms card, comedian, comic, droll, jester, joker, jokester, wag, wit
related words comedienne, entertainer; banterer, cutup, kidder, knockabout, practical joker, prankster, quipster, teaser, wisecracker; buffoon, clown, fool, harlequin, zany; caricaturist, lampooner, parodist, satirist
humorless *adj* not joking or playful in mood or manner ⟨*humorless* people who can't see the lighter side of life⟩ — see SERIOUS 1
humorous *adj* **1** causing or intended to cause laughter ⟨the *humorous* moments in an otherwise somber affair⟩ ⟨"Most *humorous* costume" went to the little baby dressed as a turtle.⟩ — see FUNNY 1
2 given to or marked by mature intelligent humor ⟨The movie's a *humorous* look at love and marriage.⟩ — see WITTY
humorousness *n* the amusing quality or element in something ⟨The *humorousness* of falling on a banana peel is usually lost on the person who falls.⟩ — see HUMOR 1
hump *n* **1** an elevation of land higher than a hill ⟨A cloud-capped *hump* straddles the border separating the two countries.⟩ — see MOUNTAIN 1
2 an area of high ground ⟨The grassy *hump* at the center of the park is a popular sledding spot during the winter.⟩ — see HEIGHT 4
hump *vb* **1** to devote serious and sustained effort ⟨The farmers had to really *hump* to get the harvest in before the rains.⟩ — see LABOR
2 to proceed or move quickly ⟨The boat was really *humping* before the motor started to sputter all of a sudden.⟩ — see HURRY 2
hunch *vb* to lie low with the limbs close to the body ⟨He *hunched* next to a bush to avoid being seen.⟩ — see CROUCH
hung *adj* bending downward or forward ⟨stood penitently before the judge with a *hung* head while he received his sentence⟩ — see NODDING
hunger *n* **1** a need or desire for food ⟨No degree of *hunger* would induce me to eat octopus.⟩
synonyms appetite, belly, emptiness, famishment, munchies, stomach
related words rapaciousness, rapacity, ravenousness, voraciousness, voracity; malnutrition, starvation, undernourishment; craving, sweet tooth; famine, fast, hunger strike; gourmandism, greed, hoggishness
near antonyms fill, glut, repleteness, repletion, satiation, satiety, satisfaction, surfeit
antonyms inappetence
2 a strong wish for something ⟨a *hunger* for knowledge⟩ — see DESIRE 1
3 urgent desire or interest ⟨Joe reads everything he can find on airplanes with a seemingly insatiable *hunger*.⟩ — see EAGERNESS
hunger (for) *vb* to have an earnest wish to own or enjoy ⟨voters *hungering for* honest and upright leadership⟩ — see DESIRE 1
hungry *adj* **1** feeling a desire or need for food ⟨John was still *hungry* after eating only a muffin for breakfast.⟩
synonyms empty, famished, starved, starving
related words rapacious, ravenous, voracious, wolfish; malnourished, underfed, undernourished; gluttonous, gormandizing, greedy, hoggish, piggish, piggy

near antonyms engorged, glutted, gorged, overfed, overfull, overstuffed, replete, stuffed, surfeited
antonyms full, sated, satiate, satiated, satisfied
2 showing urgent desire or interest ⟨*hungry* for the latest news⟩ — see EAGER

hung up *adj* **1** having extreme or relentless concern ⟨parents of a toddler who are already *hung up* about her getting into a good college⟩
synonyms happy, obsessed
related words absorbed, anxious, concerned, distracted, engaged, engrossed, full, involved, knee-deep, occupied, preoccupied, prepossessed, worried; ardent, crazy, dotty, fervent, fervid, feverish, foolish, impassioned, nuts, passionate, silly
near antonyms apathetic, casual, cool, detached, disinterested, dispassionate, incurious, indifferent, insouciant, nonchalant, unconcerned, uncurious, unenthusiastic, uninterested, uninvolved
2 feeling or showing uncomfortable feelings of uncertainty ⟨so *hung up* about having his tax returns audited that he can't sleep⟩ — see NERVOUS 1

hunk *n* a small uneven mass ⟨a thick chowder with *hunks* of potato⟩ — see LUMP 1

hunt *n* an act or process of looking carefully or thoroughly for someone or something ⟨Soon the whole family was involved in the *hunt* for Mom's car keys.⟩ — see SEARCH

hunt *vb* **1** to seek out (game) for food or sport ⟨Native Americans of the plains *hunted* buffalo for food, clothing, and shelter.⟩
synonyms chase, stalk
related words capture, drag, net, snare, trap; dog, ferret, hawk, hound; course, pursue, run, run down, spoor, track, trail; gun (for), harpoon, kill, shoot; poach; cull
2 to go in search of ⟨I spent all afternoon *hunting* a job for the summer.⟩ — see SEEK 1
3 to go into or range over for purposes of discovery ⟨We *hunted* the flea market for bargains.⟩ — see EXPLORE 2

hunt (down *or* **up)** *vb* to come upon after searching, study, or effort ⟨He managed to *hunt down* his ancestors, who arrived back in the 16th century.⟩ — see FIND 1

hunt (through) *vb* to look through (as a place) carefully or thoroughly in an effort to find or discover something ⟨She *hunted through* old birth and marriage records to trace the family tree.⟩ — see SEARCH 1

hunter *n* a person who hunts game ⟨*Hunters* must have a license to shoot deer.⟩
synonyms huntsman
related words huntress, sportsman, sportswoman; archer, gunner; birder, falconer, fowler, hawker; hunter-gatherer, trapper; poacher
antonyms nonhunter

huntsman *n* a person who hunts game ⟨The *huntsman* presented the king with two pheasants for the royal table.⟩ — see HUNTER

hurdle *n* something that makes movement or progress difficult ⟨the many *hurdles* he had to overcome on the road to success⟩ — see ENCUMBRANCE

hurl *vb* **1** to discharge the contents of the stomach through the mouth ⟨That meal was so gross I thought I was going to *hurl*.⟩ — see VOMIT
2 to proceed or move quickly ⟨A fighter jet *hurled* through the sky.⟩ — see HURRY 2
3 to send through the air especially with a quick forward motion of the arm ⟨*hurled* snowballs at each other⟩ — see THROW 1

hurly–burly *n* a state of noisy, confused activity ⟨lost sight of his children in all the *hurly-burly* of the fair⟩ — see COMMOTION

hurried *adj* acting or done with excessive or careless speed ⟨*hurried* shoppers who grab the wrong items⟩ ⟨ate a *hurried* meal⟩ — see HASTY 1

hurriedly *adv* with excessive or careless speed ⟨*hurriedly* dashed off a note to let them know she'd been called away for an emergency⟩ — see HASTILY 1

hurry *n* **1** excited and often showy or disorderly speed ⟨After all her *hurry* to get her report done on time, Elizabeth learned that it wasn't due till the following week.⟩
synonyms haste, hastiness, hustle, precipitation, precipitousness, rush
related words bustle, flurry, flutter, scurry, scuttle, stir, whirl; beeline, dash, scramble, stampede; hotheadedness, impetuosity, impetuousness, impulsiveness, impulsivity, rashness; expedition, expeditiousness, fastness, fleetness, quickness, rapidity, rapidness, speed, speediness, swiftness, velocity
near antonyms dilatoriness, lateness, pokiness, procrastination, slowness; languor, leisureliness, sluggishness; dormancy, inaction, inactivity, inertia, inertness, quiescence
antonyms deliberateness, deliberation
2 a high rate of movement or performance ⟨a person who does everything in a *hurry*⟩ — see SPEED 1

hurry *vb* **1** to cause to move or proceed fast or faster ⟨The new nurses were *hurried* through the orientation program because they were so desperately needed on the ward.⟩
synonyms accelerate, bundle, fast-track, hasten, quicken, rush, speed (up), whisk
related words drive, goad, prod, propel, push, race, spur, stir, urge; aid, dispatch, ease, encourage, expedite, facilitate
near antonyms delay, encumber, fetter, hamper, hinder, hobble, hold back, hold up, impede, interfere (with), manacle, rein (in), restrain, shackle, tie up, trammel; arrest, check, stall, stay, still, stop
antonyms brake, decelerate, retard, slow (down)
2 to proceed or move quickly ⟨If we *hurry*, we'll make the four o'clock train.⟩
synonyms barrel, belt, blast, blaze, blow, bolt, bowl, breeze, bundle, bustle, buzz, careen, career, chase, course, dash, drive, fly, hasten, hie, hotfoot (it), hump, hurl, hurtle, hustle, jet, jump, motor, nip, pelt, race, ram, rip, rocket, run, rush, rustle, scoot, scurry, scuttle, shoot, speed, step, tear, travel, trot, whirl, whisk, zip, zoom
related words dart, flit, scamper, scud, scuffle; stampede, streak, whiz (*or* whizz); gallop, jog, sprint; accelerate, quicken; fast-forward, outpace, outrun, outstrip, overtake
phrases beat it, get a move on, make tracks, shake a leg, step on it
near antonyms dally, dawdle, dillydally, drag, lag, linger, loiter, poke, tarry; lumber, plod, saunter, shuffle, stroll; decelerate, slow (down *or* up)
antonyms crawl, creep, poke

hurt *n* **1** a state of great suffering of body or mind ⟨In her *hurt* she said a lot of things that she didn't really mean.⟩ — see DISTRESS 1
2 something that causes loss or pain ⟨a totally baseless accusation that caused lasting *hurt* to his reputation⟩ — see INJURY 1

hurt *vb* **1** to feel or cause physical pain ⟨My head *hurts*.⟩ ⟨a bad sprain that really *hurts*⟩ ⟨I *hurt* all over.⟩
synonyms ache, pain, smart
related words bite, bleed, burn, chafe, cramp, fester, itch, nag, pinch, pound, rack, sting, swell, throb, tingle, twinge; agonize, anguish, suffer; afflict, harrow, torment, torture
2 to reduce the soundness, effectiveness, or perfection of

⟨Don't worry that you'll *hurt* the new lawn by walking across it.⟩ — see DAMAGE 1

3 to cause bodily damage to ⟨the common belief that reading in poor light *hurts* your eyes⟩ — see INJURE 1

4 to feel deep sadness or mental pain ⟨It *hurt* me to see them go.⟩ — see GRIEVE

hurtful *adj* **1** causing or capable of causing harm ⟨The most *hurtful* thing you can do to this silk dress is put it in the dryer.⟩ — see HARMFUL

2 hard to accept or bear especially emotionally ⟨He said *hurtful* things that she could never forgive.⟩ — see BITTER 2

hurting *adj* causing or feeling bodily pain ⟨A badly *hurting* finger kept her from writing neatly.⟩ — see PAINFUL 1

hurtle *vb* **1** to proceed or move quickly ⟨The probe *hurtled* through space to its destination: Jupiter.⟩ — see HURRY 2

2 to send through the air especially with a quick forward motion of the arm ⟨He *hurtled* his javelin down the field.⟩ — see THROW 1

husband *n* a male partner in a marriage ⟨She and her *husband* just celebrated their 50th wedding anniversary.⟩

synonyms man, old man

related words better half, companion, consort, mate, partner, significant other, spouse; bridegroom; widower; househusband

husband *vb* to avoid the wasteful or destructive use of ⟨Let's *husband* our natural resources so that our children and grandchildren may benefit from them.⟩ — see CONSERVE 1

husbandry *n* **1** careful management of material resources ⟨In accordance with his practice of good *husbandry*, he never buys anything on credit.⟩ — see ECONOMY

2 the science or occupation of cultivating the soil, producing crops, and raising livestock ⟨a family of winemakers whose tradition of vineyard *husbandry* goes back several generations⟩ — see AGRICULTURE

hush *n* **1** a state of freedom from storm or disturbance ⟨The storm passed, and a *hush* fell over the sea.⟩ — see CALM 1

2 the near or complete absence of sound ⟨A *hush* fell over the auditorium as the lights went down.⟩ — see SILENCE 2

hush *vb* **1** to become still and orderly ⟨The whole room *hushed* when the queen made her entrance.⟩ — see QUIET 1

2 to stop talking ⟨Everyone in the courtroom *hushed* when the judge entered.⟩ — see SHUT UP 1

3 to stop the noise or speech of ⟨He tried to *hush* the baby by making a lot of silly faces.⟩ — see SILENCE 1

hush (up) *vb* to keep from being publicly known ⟨The well-connected family was able to *hush up* the scandal so it never reached the papers.⟩ — see SUPPRESS 1

hushed *adj* **1** free from disturbing noise or uproar ⟨The bishop entered the *hushed* interior of the Gothic church.⟩ — see QUIET 1

2 free from storms or physical disturbance ⟨The *hushed* lake was smooth as glass the morning after the storm.⟩ — see CALM 1

3 mostly or entirely without sound ⟨a *hushed* sickroom⟩ — see SILENT 3

4 not known or meant to be known by the general populace ⟨*hushed* negotiations between the two countries⟩ — see PRIVATE 1

husk *n* something that encloses another thing especially to protect it ⟨corn *husks*⟩ ⟨A high stone wall is the *husk* that protects the actor from prying curiosity seekers.⟩ — see ¹CASE 1

husk *vb* to remove the natural covering of ⟨the tedious task of *husking* coconuts⟩ — see PEEL

¹husky *adj* **1** strongly and heavily built ⟨a *husky* weight lifter⟩

synonyms beefy, brawny, burly, hefty, hulking

related words able-bodied, athletic, herculean, mighty, muscle-bound, muscular, powerful, robust, rugged, sinewy, stalwart, stout, strapping, strong, sturdy; chunky, compact, heavy, heavyset, solid, squat, stocky, thickset; chubby, portly, pudgy, roly-poly, tubby

near antonyms lean, light, lightweight, slender, slight, slim, svelte, sylphlike, thin, willowy; gangling, gangly, gaunt, gawky, lanky, reedy, scraggy, scrawny, skinny, spare, stringy, twiggy, waspish, weedy; spidery, wiry; debilitated, delicate, effete, emaciated, enervated, enfeebled, feeble, fragile, frail, infirm, puny, unathletic, weak, weakly, wimpy

2 of a size greater than average of its kind ⟨The neighbors bought a fairly *husky* lawn mower for their small yard.⟩ — see LARGE

²husky *adj* harsh and dry in sound ⟨a voice that was *husky* from an afternoon of cheering on the team⟩ — see HOARSE

hustle *n* **1** excited and often showy or disorderly speed ⟨the *hustle* and bustle of the holiday season⟩ — see HURRY 1

2 readiness to engage in daring or difficult activity ⟨With his characteristic *hustle*, he had everything lined up in two days.⟩ — see ENTERPRISE 2

3 an instance of the use of dishonest methods to acquire something of value ⟨a clever *hustle* that tricked people into revealing their bank account information⟩ — see FRAUD 1

hustle *vb* **1** to devote serious and sustained effort ⟨Everyone really *hustled* to get the magazine out on schedule.⟩ — see LABOR

2 to proceed or move quickly ⟨We'd better *hustle*, or we'll miss the train.⟩ — see HURRY 2

3 to rob by the use of trickery or threats ⟨A customer *hustled* the cashier by getting him all confused while he was making change.⟩ — see FLEECE

hustler *n* an ambitious person who eagerly goes after what is desired ⟨The ad for the sales job claims that for someone who's a real *hustler*, the sky's the limit.⟩ — see GO-GETTER

hut *n* a small, simply constructed, and often temporary dwelling ⟨Smoke rose from a fisherman's *hut* on the shore of the lake.⟩ — see SHACK

hutch *n* **1** a small, simply constructed, and often temporary dwelling ⟨The campers slept in a *hutch* along the river.⟩ — see SHACK

2 a storage case typically having doors and shelves ⟨Mom keeps her best china in a *hutch* in the dining room.⟩ — see CABINET

3 an enclosure with an open framework for keeping animals ⟨The owner took the rabbit out of the *hutch* so the children could pet it.⟩ — see CAGE

hybrid *adj* being offspring produced by parents of different races, breeds, species, or genera ⟨A *hybrid* rose called "American Beauty" was actually first developed in France.⟩ — see MIXED 1

hybrid *n* an offspring of parents with different genes especially when of different races, breeds, species, or genera ⟨A tangelo is a *hybrid* of the tangerine and the grapefruit.⟩

synonyms cross, crossbred, crossbreed, mongrel

related words mule; outcross; half-bred

near antonyms pureblood, purebred, thoroughbred

hygienic *adj* free from filth, infection, or dangers to health ⟨food packaging done under rigidly *hygienic* conditions⟩ — see SANITARY

hymn *n* **1** a religious song ⟨Our Sunday church services always open with a *hymn*.⟩
synonyms anthem, canticle, carol, chorale, psalm, spiritual
related words dirge, lament, requiem; Gloria Patri, paean; mass, oratorio; processional, recessional
2 a formal expression of praise ⟨The documentary on the Shakers is essentially a *hymn* to the simple life.⟩ — see ENCOMIUM

hymn *vb* to proclaim the glory of ⟨During the honeymoon following the inauguration, newspaper articles seemed to *hymn* the president's every move.⟩ — see PRAISE 1

hymnal *n* a book of hymns ⟨*Hymnals* are distributed among the congregation before the church service so everyone can join in the singing.⟩
synonyms hymnbook, psalmody
related words breviary, missal, Psalter; songbook, songster; antiphonal, antiphonary

hymnbook *n* a book of hymns ⟨a worshipper who knew the words of all the church songs and didn't need a *hymnbook*⟩ — see HYMNAL

hyperactive *adj* **1** being in a state of increased activity or agitation ⟨The skyrocketing price of oil resulted in a wildly fluctuating, *hyperactive* stock market.⟩ — see FEVERISH 1
2 easily excited by nature ⟨a new treatment to help some *hyperactive* children⟩ — see EXCITABLE

hyperbole *n* the representation of something in terms that go beyond the facts ⟨"Enough food to feed a whole army" is a common example of *hyperbole*.⟩ — see EXAGGERATION

hypercritical *adj* given to making or expressing unfavorable judgments about things ⟨If you go by what that *hypercritical* reviewer says, you are going to end up seeing very few movies.⟩ — see CRITICAL 1

hyperventilate *vb* to breathe hard, quickly, or with difficulty ⟨He was so nervous he began *hyperventilating*, and the extra oxygen made him dizzy.⟩ — see GASP

hypnosis *n* the art or act of inducing in a person a sleeplike state during which he or she readily follows suggestions ⟨With *hypnosis* there's some question as to just how involuntary the actions of the hypnotized person really are.⟩
synonyms hypnotism, mesmerism
related words autohypnosis, automatism, autosuggestion, self-hypnosis, self-suggestion; bewitchment, enchantment, spellbinding

hypnotic *adj* tending to cause sleep ⟨Her eyes soon grew heavy from the *hypnotic* rhythm of the train's wheels.⟩
synonyms drowsy, narcotic, opiate, slumberous (*or* slumbrous), somnolent
related words depressant, relaxant, sedative, tranquilizing (*also* tranquillizing); calming, comforting, lulling, pacifying, quieting, relaxing, restful, settling, soothing; analgesic, anesthetic, anesthetizing, benumbing, deadening, dulling, numbing; hypnotizing, mesmerizing, stupefying
near antonyms arousing, awakening, energizing, invigorating, rousing, stimulating, wakening, waking; bracing, refreshing, restorative, reviving, stimulative, stimulatory
antonyms stimulant

hypnotism *n* the art or act of inducing in a person a sleep-like state during which he or she readily follows suggestions ⟨Some people have undergone *hypnotism* in order to change certain behaviors.⟩ — see HYPNOSIS

hypnotize *vb* to hold the attention of as if by a spell ⟨The crowd was *hypnotized* by the powerful, eloquent speaker.⟩ — see ENTHRALL 1

hypocrisy *n* the pretending of having virtues, principles, or beliefs that one in fact does not have ⟨the *hypocrisy* of people who claim to care about the environment but ride around in gas-guzzlers⟩
synonyms cant, dissembling, dissimulation, insincerity, piousness
related words deceit, deceitfulness, dishonesty, double-dealing, falsity, perfidy, two-facedness; affectation, affectedness, pretense (*or* pretence), pretension, pretentiousness, sanctimoniousness, self-righteousness, self-satisfaction; duplicity, fakery, falseness, fraudulentness, shamming; artificiality, glibness, oiliness, smoothness, unctuousness
near antonyms candor, directness, forthrightness, frankness, honesty, openheartedness, openness, probity, straightforwardness, truthfulness; artlessness, guilelessness, naturalness, unaffectedness
antonyms genuineness, sincereness, sincerity

hypocritical *adj* not being or expressing what one appears to be or express ⟨It's *hypocritical* to say mean things behind someone's back, and then to act nice when you want something from her.⟩ — see INSINCERE

hypodermic *n* a slender hollow instrument by which material is put into or taken from the body through the skin ⟨He hardly felt it when the nurse stuck the *hypodermic* in his arm.⟩ — see NEEDLE 1

hypodermic needle *n* a slender hollow instrument by which material is put into or taken from the body through the skin ⟨Mike doesn't mind getting shots as long as he doesn't catch sight of the *hypodermic needle*.⟩ — see NEEDLE 1

hypodermic syringe *n* a slender hollow instrument by which material is put into or taken from the body through the skin ⟨The nurse filled a different *hypodermic syringe* for each injection.⟩ — see NEEDLE 1

hypothesis *n* an idea that is the starting point for making a case or conducting an investigation ⟨Working on the *hypothesis* that teenagers function better in the late morning, some high schools are starting classes later.⟩ — see THEORY

hypothetical *adj* existing only as an assumption or speculation ⟨We talked about what we would do in various *hypothetical* emergencies.⟩ — see THEORETICAL 1

hysteria *n* a state of wildly excited activity or emotion ⟨A few of the children started to scream, and soon others joined in the *hysteria*.⟩ — see FRENZY

hysterical *adj* **1** causing or intended to cause laughter ⟨Some of the things little kids come out with are *hysterical*.⟩ — see FUNNY 1
2 feeling overwhelming fear or worry ⟨Leaders counseled the people not to get *hysterical* over the spread of the disease.⟩ — see FRANTIC 1
3 filled with fear or dread ⟨Upon hearing the announcement that a shark had been sighted, *hysterical* beachgoers raced out of the water.⟩ — see AFRAID

I

ice–cold *adj* having a low or subnormal temperature ⟨*ice-cold* hands from hours spent shoveling snow⟩ — see COLD 1

icon *also* **ikon** *n* **1** a written or printed mark that is meant to convey information to the reader ⟨The phone is very user-friendly as it doesn't use any *icons* that you haven't seen a million times before.⟩ — see CHARACTER 1
2 a visible representation of something abstract (as a quality) ⟨cites James Bond as an *icon* of British cool⟩ — see EMBODIMENT
3 a person who is widely known and usually much talked about ⟨a sports bar filled with photos of *icons* from football, basketball, and baseball⟩ — see CELEBRITY 1
4 a two-dimensional design intended to look like a person or thing ⟨Any *icon* of the Deity is regarded as blasphemous.⟩ — see PICTURE 1

icy *adj* **1** having a low or subnormal temperature ⟨an *icy* drink that was especially refreshing on that hot afternoon⟩ — see COLD 1
2 lacking in friendliness or warmth of feeling ⟨She wondered why the salesclerk at the boutique had given her an *icy* glare.⟩ — see COLD 2

idea *n* **1** something imagined or pictured in the mind ⟨My *idea* of the perfect vacation spot is an uncrowded, unspoiled beach.⟩
synonyms concept, conception, image, impression, notion, picture, thought
related words apprehension, premonition, presentiment; preconception, prejudice, prepossession; delusion, hallucination, illusion, phantasm (*also* fantasm); caprice, conceit, fancy, vagary, whim; cognition, observation, perception, reflection; assumption, belief, conclusion, conviction; conjecture, guess, hunch, hypothesis, speculation, supposition, surmise, theory; brainstorm, brain wave, inspiration
near antonyms actuality, fact, reality
2 someone of such unequaled perfection as to deserve imitation ⟨Helen Keller remains my *idea* of a person with indomitable spirit.⟩ — see IDEAL 1
3 something that one hopes or intends to accomplish ⟨The *idea* is to get the information without seeming to be nosy.⟩ — see GOAL

ideal *adj* **1** dealing with or expressing a quality or idea ⟨Honesty is an *ideal* entity that has more admirers than practitioners.⟩ — see ABSTRACT 1
2 not real and existing only in the imagination ⟨He depicts an *ideal* society in which conflict and privation are unknown.⟩ — see IMAGINARY
3 being entirely without fault or flaw ⟨She is an *ideal* candidate for the job.⟩ — see PERFECT 1

ideal *n* **1** someone of such unequaled perfection as to deserve imitation ⟨She's our *ideal* of the concerned, caring physician.⟩
synonyms beau ideal, classic, exemplar, idea, model, nonpareil, paragon
related words role model; embodiment, epitome, incarnation, manifestation, personification; archetype, example, mirror, paradigm, pattern; guideline, principle, rule; gauge (*also* gage), standard, touchstone; essence, quintessence; acme, apex, culmination, peak, pinnacle, summit, zenith; god, hero, icon (*also* ikon), idol
2 the most perfect type or example ⟨The Taj Mahal in India is generally regarded as the *ideal* of Mogul architectural beauty.⟩ — see QUINTESSENCE 1

3 something that one hopes or intends to accomplish ⟨His *ideal* is to make enough money so that he can retire at 50.⟩ — see GOAL

idealist *n* one whose conduct is guided more by the image of perfection than by the real world ⟨An *idealist* sees the best in everyone, regardless of how they behave.⟩
synonyms dreamer, romantic, utopian, visionary
related words daydreamer, fantasizer, woolgatherer; optimist, Pollyanna; do-gooder, reformer; perfectionist
near antonyms cynic, defeatist, pessimist
antonyms pragmatist, realist

idealize *vb* to represent or think of as better than reality would warrant ⟨He had a tendency to *idealize* his heroes and believe they could do no wrong.⟩
synonyms glamorize (*also* glamourize), glorify, romanticize
related words heroicize, heroize; soften; adulate, canonize, deify, idolize; aggrandize, dignify, ennoble, enshrine, enthrone, magnify
near antonyms belittle, decry, deprecate, disparage, minimize, put down
antonyms deglamorize

ideally *adv* without any flaws or errors ⟨an *ideally* executed routine on the parallel bars that earned him perfect scores from the judges⟩ — see PERFECTLY 1

identical *adj* **1** being one and not another ⟨We visited the *identical* place last year.⟩ — see SAME 2
2 resembling another in every respect ⟨*identical* dresses whose only difference is a designer label that fetches a high price⟩ — see SAME 1

identicalness *n* the state of being exactly alike ⟨The *identicalness* of your answers to your friend's suggests that someone copied.⟩ — see IDENTITY 1

identify *vb* **1** to find out or establish the identity of ⟨There's sufficient forensic evidence to allow investigators to *identify* the perpetrator.⟩
synonyms distinguish, pinpoint, single (out)
related words diagnose; determine, find; locate, pick out, place, recognize, spot; check, examine, inspect, investigate, notice, observe, scrutinize; betray, disclose, discover, reveal
phrases put one's finger on
near antonyms camouflage, conceal, disguise, hide; counterfeit, feign, sham, simulate
2 to think of (something) in combination ⟨For some reason, he always *identified* the color red with flowers.⟩ — see ASSOCIATE 2

identifying *adj* serving to identify as belonging to an individual or group ⟨The marching band's striking black-and-silver uniforms serve as its *identifying* mark for thousands of parade spectators.⟩ — see CHARACTERISTIC 1

identity *n* **1** the state of being exactly alike ⟨Although the covers of the two paperback editions of the novel are different, there's a complete *identity* in the texts.⟩
synonyms identicalness, sameness
related words oneness, selfsameness; equality, equivalence; accordance, agreement, conformity, congruity, correspondence, likeness, resemblance, similarity
near antonyms alteration, change, modification, variation; distinction, distinctiveness, distinctness, individuality, separateness, uniqueness, unusualness; deviance, divergence; variance; incompatibility, incongruence, incongruity, incongruousness

antonyms difference, disagreement, discrepancy, disparateness, disparity, dissimilarity, unlikeness

2 the set of qualities that make a person different from other people ⟨Children begin to form their own *identity* at a very young age.⟩ — see INDIVIDUALITY 1

ideology *also* **idealogy** *n* the basic beliefs or guiding principles of a person or group ⟨Members of that sect follow an *ideology* of nonviolence and freely given cooperation.⟩ — see CREED 1

idiocy *n* a foolish act or idea ⟨Trying to get that many people to agree on anything was pure *idiocy*.⟩ — see FOLLY 1

idiom *n* a sequence of words having a specific meaning ⟨The English *idiom* "how are you doing?" is our version of a greeting that in some other languages can be translated as "how are you going?"⟩ — see PHRASE

idiosyncrasy *n* an odd or peculiar habit ⟨His only *idiosyncrasy* is his inveterate wearing of sneakers, even with business suits.⟩

synonyms crotchet, curiosity, eccentricity, mannerism, oddity, peculiarity, quirk, singularity, tic, trick, twist

related words affectation, airs; attribute, characteristic, mark, property, trait; custom, habit, pattern, practice (*also* practise), way, wont; abnormality, neuroticism, perversion, weirdness; disposition, genius, leaning, partiality; bent, inclination, penchant, predilection, predisposition, proclivity, propensity, tendency, turn; character, humor, identity, individuality, nature, personality, temperament

near antonyms conformity, sameness

idiot *n* a stupid person ⟨I really made an *idiot* of myself at the party.⟩

synonyms blockhead, dodo, dolt, donkey, dope, dork [*slang*], dumbbell, dummy, dunce, fathead, goof, goon, half-wit, ignoramus, imbecile, know-nothing, moron, nincompoop, ninny, nitwit, numskull (*or* numbskull), oaf, pinhead, simpleton, stock, turkey, yo-yo

related words booby, buffoon, fool, goose, zany; loser; gawk; featherbrain; beast, boor, cad, clown, creep, heel, jerk, skunk, snake, stinker, villain

near antonyms egghead, intellect, intellectual, sage, thinker, whiz, wizard

antonyms brain, genius

idle *adj* **1** not being in a state of use, activity, or employment ⟨The car was *idle* for two weeks while they went on vacation.⟩ — see INACTIVE 2

2 not easily aroused to action or work ⟨an *idle* employee who always seems to be either on break or at lunch⟩ — see LAZY 1

idle *vb* to spend time doing nothing ⟨She likes to *idle* during the summer and recharge herself.⟩

synonyms bum, chill, dally, dawdle, dillydally, goof (off), kick back, lazy, loaf, loll, lounge

related words fiddle (around), fool, mess, monkey, muck, piddle, play, potter (around), putter (around), trifle; lag, linger, loiter, poke, relax, rest, tarry; mosey, saunter, stroll

phrases kill time, twiddle one's thumbs

near antonyms drudge, grind, grub, hump, hustle, labor, moil, peg, plod, plow, plug, sweat, toil, travail, work; apply, buckle (down); exert, put out

idleness *n* **1** an inclination not to do work or engage in activities ⟨The brothers' innate *idleness* meant that neither did much, either inside or outside their ramshackle cabin.⟩ — see LAZINESS

2 lack of action or activity ⟨A day spent in *idleness* is nice, but a month of doing nothing is boring!⟩ — see INACTION

3 lack of use ⟨The *idleness* of the machine was apparent by its thick layer of dust.⟩ — see DISUSE

idler *n* a lazy person ⟨a group of *idlers* reclining by the pool⟩ — see LAZYBONES

idolater *or* **idolator** *n* a person who does not worship the God of the Bible ⟨a civilization of polytheists and *idolaters*⟩ — see HEATHEN 1

idolatry *n* excessive admiration of or devotion to a person ⟨his *idolatry* of his favorite basketball star⟩ — see WORSHIP

idolization *n* excessive admiration of or devotion to a person ⟨The *idolization* of the playwright continues to this day.⟩ — see WORSHIP

idolize *vb* to love or admire too much ⟨She blindly *idolized* her older sister, refusing to acknowledge her faults.⟩

synonyms adore, adulate, canonize, deify, dote (on), worship

related words appreciate, cherish, esteem, prize, treasure, value; fancy, favor, like, prefer; regard; hallow, respect, revere, venerate; approve, endorse (*also* indorse), support

near antonyms abhor, abominate, despise, detest, disdain, dislike, hate, loathe; belittle, deprecate, disparage, put down

idolizing *adj* reflecting great admiration or devotion ⟨Brian gave his fiancée an *idolizing* glance.⟩ — see WORSHIPFUL

idyll *also* **idyl** *n* a time or instance of carefree fun ⟨Her year as an intern to a movie producer was not the *idyll* that she had expected it to be.⟩ — see FLING 1

ignitable *also* **ignitible** *adj* capable of catching or being set on fire ⟨Gasoline fumes are quite *ignitable*.⟩ — see COMBUSTIBLE

ignite *vb* to set (something) on fire ⟨We tried using newspapers as kindling to *ignite* the logs in the fireplace.⟩ — see BURN 2

ignited *adj* being on fire ⟨The *ignited* fireworks went off all at once.⟩ — see ABLAZE 1

ignoble *adj* **1** belonging to the class of people of low social or economic rank ⟨an *ignoble* child who would one day grow up to be a prince among playwrights⟩

synonyms baseborn, common, humble, inferior, low, lower-class, lowly, mean, plebeian, proletarian, vulgar

related words bourgeois, middle-class; plain, poor, simple, working-class

near antonyms eminent, illustrious, notable, prominent

antonyms aristocratic, genteel, gentle, grand, great, high, highborn, lofty, noble, patrician, upper-class, wellborn

2 not following or in accordance with standards of honor and decency ⟨Such an *ignoble* act is completely unworthy of a military officer.⟩

synonyms base, contemptible, despicable, detestable, dirty, dishonorable, execrable, ignominious, low, mean, nasty, paltry, snide, sordid, vile, wretched

related words bad, evil, foul, immoral, iniquitous, miscreant, wicked, wrong; cruel, vicious; blamable, blameworthy, censurable, reprehensible; corrupt, debased, debauched, degenerate, depraved, dissolute, perverted; atrocious, villainous; unethical, unprincipled, unscrupulous; discreditable, disgraceful, disreputable, shameful, unworthy

near antonyms ethical, honest, just, principled, righteous, right-minded, scrupulous; commendable, excellent, exemplary, good, moral, right; decent, proper, reputable, respectable, seemly; blameless, guiltless; incorruptible, irreproachable; uncorrupted, unerring

antonyms high, high-minded, honorable, lofty, noble, straight, upright, venerable, virtuous

ignominious *adj* **1** not respectable ⟨suffered an *ignominious* defeat⟩ — see DISREPUTABLE

2 not following or in accordance with standards of honor and decency ⟨The cheating students were expelled for their *ignominious* violation of the honor code.⟩ — see IGNOBLE 2

ignominy *n* the state of having lost the esteem of others

⟨He spent the remainder of his life in *ignominy* after being involved in a bribery scandal.⟩ — see DISGRACE 1

ignoramus *n* a stupid person ⟨Only an *ignoramus* would be foiled by the building's security system.⟩ — see IDIOT

ignorance *n* **1** the state of being unaware or uninformed ⟨*Ignorance* of the law is no excuse.⟩

synonyms innocence, obliviousness, unawareness, unfamiliarity

related words callowness, greenness, inexperience, naïveté (*also* naivete *or* naiveté), rawness, simpleness, unsophistication

near antonyms experience, know-how; sophistication

antonyms acquaintance, awareness, cognizance, familiarity

2 the state of being unlearned ⟨"Our foe," said the educator, "is *ignorance*."⟩

synonyms illiteracy

related words functional illiteracy, innumeracy; brainlessness, dumbness, idiocy, imbecility, stupidity; philistinism; foolishness, mindlessness, senselessness, witlessness

near antonyms education, instruction, training; enlightenment, knowledge; erudition, scholarship

antonyms learning

ignorant *adj* **1** lacking in education or the knowledge gained from books ⟨They were *ignorant*, but not stupid.⟩

synonyms benighted, dark, illiterate, rude, simple, uneducated, uninstructed, unlearned, unlettered, unread, unschooled, untaught, untutored

related words functionally illiterate, innumerate, semiliterate, unknowledgeable; artless, lowbrow, philistine, uncultivated, uncultured; callow, green, inexperienced, innocent, naive (*or* naïve); unsophisticated; raw, unskilled, untrained; brainless, dumb, idiotic (*also* idiotical), imbecile (*or* imbecilic), moronic, stupid, witless; foolish, senseless, silly

near antonyms brilliant, intelligent, smart; experienced, expert, trained; erudite, learned, scholarly; cultivated, cultured, highbrow, intellectual; sophisticated; acquainted, aware, familiar

antonyms educated, knowledgeable, literate, schooled, well-read

2 not informed about or aware of something ⟨He was *ignorant* of their wedding plans.⟩

synonyms innocent, insensible, oblivious, unacquainted, unaware, unconscious, uninformed, unknowing, unmindful, unwitting

related words uneducated, unschooled, untaught; absent, absentminded, abstracted, heedless, inattentive, inconscient

phrases in the dark

near antonyms hip, up-to-date; educated, knowledgeable, schooled, taught; heedful, observant; sensitive, sentient

antonyms acquainted, aware, cognizant, conscious, conversant, grounded, informed, knowing, mindful, witting

ignore *vb* **1** to fail to give proper attention to ⟨*Ignoring* your health now will haunt you further down the road.⟩ — see NEGLECT 1

2 to dismiss as of little importance ⟨Although the movie is a cinematic tour de force, one can't *ignore* the fact that it seriously distorts history.⟩ — see EXCUSE 1

ilk *n* a number of persons or things that are grouped together because they have something in common ⟨We're looking for chestnuts and other items of that *ilk* for our autumn decorations.⟩ — see SORT 1

ill *adj* **1** affected with nausea ⟨She grew *ill* from the constant rocking motion of the boat.⟩ — see NAUSEOUS 1

2 causing or capable of causing harm ⟨One of the *ill* effects of winter weather is the rapid spread of germs as people spend more time together indoors.⟩ — see HARMFUL

3 temporarily suffering from a disorder of the body

⟨Since I'm *ill*, I guess that I'll just have to miss that dental appointment.⟩ — see SICK 1

4 falling short of a standard ⟨Such *ill* behavior will not be tolerated.⟩ — see BAD 1

5 being or showing a sign of evil or calamity to come ⟨The mounting injuries appear to be an *ill* omen for this season's championship.⟩ — see OMINOUS

ill *adv* **1** in a manner so as to cause loss or suffering ⟨In those days society treated debtors very *ill*, even going so far as to put them in prison.⟩ — see HARDLY 1

2 certainly not ⟨You can *ill* afford to miss another day of work.⟩ — see HARDLY 2

ill *n* **1** an abnormal state that disrupts a plant's or animal's normal bodily functioning ⟨chicken pox and the other *ills* that were once a fixture of childhood⟩ — see DISEASE

2 that which is morally unacceptable ⟨idealistic people who try to cure all of our society's *ills*⟩ — see EVIL

3 bad luck or an example of this ⟨She does not wish *ill* upon anyone.⟩ — see MISFORTUNE

ill–advised *adj* showing poor judgment especially in personal relationships or social situations ⟨an *ill-advised* decision to loan him money⟩ — see INDISCREET

ill–bred *adj* **1** lacking in refinement or good taste ⟨the *ill-bred* habit of chewing with the mouth open⟩ — see COARSE 2

2 showing a lack of manners or consideration for others ⟨Only an *ill-bred*, conceited person would demand that everyone cater to their whims.⟩ — see IMPOLITE

illegal *adj* **1** contrary to or forbidden by law ⟨It is *illegal* to import these birds into this country.⟩

synonyms criminal, felonious, illegitimate, illicit, lawless, unlawful, wrongful

related words bad, evil, immoral, shameful, sinful, unethical, wicked, wrong; blamable, blameworthy, censurable, reprehensible; banned, barred, contraband, criminalized, disallowed, discouraged, forbidden, interdicted, outlawed, prohibited, proscribed; bootleg, unauthorized, unlicensed, unsanctioned; under-the-counter, under-the-table; corrupt, unprincipled, unscrupulous, villainous

near antonyms ethical, good, just, principled, right, righteous, virtuous; allowed, permitted; authorized, licensed; approved, endorsed (*also* indorsed), sanctioned; abetted, encouraged, promoted, suggested, supported; correct, decent, decorous, proper, seemly

antonyms lawful, legal, legitimate

2 not being in accordance with the rules or standards of what is fair in sport ⟨an *illegal* pass⟩ — see FOUL 2

illegitimate *adj* **1** contrary to or forbidden by law ⟨an *illegitimate* use of campaign contributions for personal expenses⟩ — see ILLEGAL 1

2 not using or following good reasoning ⟨made several *illegitimate* inferences⟩ — see ILLOGICAL

ill–fated *adj* having, prone to, or marked by bad luck ⟨The *ill-fated* trip ended in disaster for all.⟩ — see UNLUCKY 1

ill–favored *adj* unpleasant to look at ⟨an *ill-favored* and yapping little dog⟩ — see UGLY 1

ill–humored *adj* having or showing a habitually bad temper ⟨An *ill-humored* person should probably not take a job that requires dealing with the public.⟩ — see ILL-TEMPERED

illicit *adj* contrary to or forbidden by law ⟨They were arrested for selling *illicit* copies of the software.⟩ — see ILLEGAL 1

illimitable *adj* being or seeming to be without limits ⟨the *illimitable* expanse of the universe⟩ — see INFINITE

illiteracy *n* the state of being unlearned ⟨efforts to reduce *illiteracy*⟩ — see IGNORANCE 2

illiterate *adj* lacking in education or the knowledge gained from books ⟨It was long ago an agricultural society in which most people were *illiterate*.⟩ — see IGNORANT 1

ill–mannered *adj* showing a lack of manners or consideration for others ⟨an *ill-mannered* child who doesn't say "please" or "thank you"⟩ — see IMPOLITE

ill–natured *adj* having or showing a habitually bad temper ⟨an *ill-natured* and unpleasant old horse that sometimes bites⟩ — see ILL-TEMPERED

illness *n* **1** an abnormal state that disrupts a plant's or animal's normal bodily functioning ⟨She suffered from a mysterious *illness* that left her weak and tired all the time.⟩ — see DISEASE
2 the condition of not being in good health ⟨He was prone to *illness* as a child.⟩ — see SICKNESS 1

illogical *adj* not using or following good reasoning ⟨the *illogical* claim that playing basketball makes people taller because one sees so many tall players⟩ ⟨*Illogical* people are likely to believe every sensational claim made online.⟩
synonyms fallacious, illegitimate, inconsequential, invalid, irrational, nonrational, unreasonable, unreasoning, unsound, weak
related words misleading, specious; half-baked, ill-advised, misguided, unconsidered, unreasoned; inconsistent; absurd, asinine, foolish, meaningless, nonsensical, preposterous, reasonless, senseless, silly; odd, peculiar, strange, surreal, unusual, weird; wacky (*also* whacky); disordered, disorganized, rambling, random; unconvincing; inexplicable, unaccountable, unexplainable
near antonyms commonsense, sane, sensible, sober, wise; enlightened, informed, just, justified, reasoned; ordered, organized; clear, cogent, compelling, convincing, credible, persuasive, plausible, satisfying, solid; certain, sure, true; confirmed, corroborated, demonstrated, established, substantiated, validated
antonyms logical, rational, reasonable, sound, valid, well-founded

ill–starred *adj* having, prone to, or marked by bad luck ⟨an *ill-starred* attempt to circumnavigate the earth in a balloon⟩ — see UNLUCKY 1

ill–tempered *adj* having or showing a habitually bad temper ⟨An *ill-tempered* cat will scratch with little provocation.⟩
synonyms acid, bearish, cantankerous, disagreeable, dyspeptic, ill-humored, ill-natured, ornery, splenetic, surly
related words choleric, crabby, cranky, crotchety, fussy, grouchy, grumpy, querulous; irascible, irritable, peevish, peppery, petulant, quick-tempered, short-tempered, snappish, snippy, testy, touchy; argumentative, contentious, contrary; angry, indignant, irate, mad, upset, uptight
near antonyms agreeable, amicable, congenial, friendly, pleasant; benign, gentle, kind, nice, sweet; bubbly, cheerful, cheery, effervescent, exuberant, high-spirited, joyful, lighthearted, lively, vivacious; content, glad, happy; calm, placid, serene; long-suffering, patient, tolerant
antonyms amiable, good-humored, good-natured, good-tempered

ill–treat *vb* to inflict physical or emotional harm upon ⟨Anyone who *ill-treats* their pets should not be allowed to have any.⟩ — see ABUSE 1

illuminate *vb* **1** to supply with light ⟨A floor lamp *illuminates* a living room rather nicely.⟩
synonyms bathe, beacon, illumine, irradiate, light, lighten
related words brighten; beam, beat (down), radiate, shine; enhalo; floodlight; highlight; blaze, burn, fire, flame, glare, glow, ignite, incinerate, kindle; bedazzle, blind, daze, dazzle; gleam, glisten, glitter
near antonyms dim, dull, obscure; cover, shroud, veil; douse (*also* dowse), extinguish, put out, quench, snuff (out)
antonyms blacken, darken
2 to make plain or understandable ⟨The museum's exhibit on the refraction of light really *illuminated* the subject for us.⟩ — see EXPLAIN 1

3 to supplement with pictorial matter for the purpose of explanation or decoration ⟨No one knows for sure the identity of the artist who *illuminated* that medieval manuscript so beautifully.⟩ — see ILLUSTRATE 2
4 to indicate the importance of by centering attention on ⟨The test results *illuminated* the need to focus on math.⟩ — see EMPHASIZE 1
5 to provide (someone) with moral or spiritual understanding ⟨how man is *illuminated* by a higher spirit⟩ — see ENLIGHTEN 2

illuminated *adj* filled with much light ⟨An intensely *illuminated* room is usually needed for producing live television shows.⟩ — see BRIGHT 2

illumination *n* **1** a statement that makes something clear ⟨The candidate's so-called *illuminations* of his views on a number of controversial issues left many voters in the dark.⟩ — see EXPLANATION 1
2 the quality or state of having or giving off light ⟨In that clime the *illumination* of the full moon is such as you can practically read by it.⟩ — see BRILLIANCE 1
3 the steady giving off of the form of radiation that makes vision possible ⟨A steady *illumination* from the flashlight was all I had while changing the tire.⟩ — see LIGHT 1

illuminative *adj* serving to explain ⟨*Illuminative* descriptions of the sights to be seen from the observatory gave us a much better idea of what we were looking at.⟩ — see EXPLANATORY

illumine *vb* **1** to supply with light ⟨Small table lamps *illumine* the inn's dining room in a most romantic way.⟩ — see ILLUMINATE 1
2 to provide (someone) with moral or spiritual understanding ⟨Readers of great literature are both entertained and *illumined*.⟩ — see ENLIGHTEN 2

illumined *adj* filled with much light ⟨*Illumined* display windows in the street's many shops add much to the holiday glow.⟩ — see BRIGHT 2

ill–use *vb* to inflict physical or emotional harm upon ⟨Some of the employees felt the new manager *ill-used* them and they quit.⟩ — see ABUSE 1

illusion *n* **1** a conception or image created by the imagination and having no objective reality ⟨The magician specializes in creating *illusions*, so that people believe they have seen something when they really haven't.⟩ — see FANTASY 1
2 a false idea or belief ⟨He had no *illusions* about how much work the project would require.⟩ — see FALLACY 1

illusionist *n* one who practices tricks and illusions for entertainment ⟨We tried to figure out how the *illusionist* made his assistant disappear from the stage.⟩ — see MAGICIAN 2

illustrate *vb* **1** to show or make clear by using examples ⟨She *illustrated* her point with a story about her experiences as a field anthropologist.⟩
synonyms demonstrate, exemplify, instance
related words adduce, cite, mention, quote; name, specify; analyze, break down; clarify, clear (up), explain, explicate, expound; edify, elucidate, enlighten; illuminate; construe, interpret; simplify, spell out; detail, enumerate, list
near antonyms becloud, blur, cloud, darken, fog, muddy, obscure; confuse, perplex, puzzle
2 to supplement with pictorial matter for the purpose of explanation or decoration ⟨lavishly *illustrated* the book on the artist Caravaggio with color plates⟩
synonyms illuminate
related words image, picture, visualize
3 to make plain or understandable ⟨The recent fire *illustrates* the need for improved safety codes.⟩ — see EXPLAIN 1

illustration *n* **1** something that visually explains or decorates a text ⟨This book on birds has gorgeous *illustrations*.⟩
synonyms diagram, figure, graphic, plate, visual

related words art, artwork; drawing, illumination, image, pictogram, pictograph, picture; caption, key, legend; inset; depiction, pictorialization, portrait, portrayal, representation; clarification, elucidation, explanation, explication, exposition

2 a statement that makes something clear ⟨She gave several *illustrations* until she was understood.⟩ — see EXPLANATION 1

3 a two-dimensional design intended to look like a person or thing ⟨The doctor sketched an *illustration* to explain the procedure to the patient.⟩ — see PICTURE 1

4 one of a group or collection that shows what the whole is like ⟨chose one essay as an *illustration* of the high quality of the collection⟩ — see EXAMPLE

illustrative *adj* serving to explain ⟨an *illustrative* analogy⟩ — see EXPLANATORY

illustrious *adj* standing above others in rank, importance, or achievement ⟨an *illustrious* physicist who is a sure bet for a Nobel Prize⟩ — see EMINENT

image *vb* **1** to present a picture of ⟨In the painting Sacagawea is *imaged* as an intrepid woman pointing the way for Lewis and Clark.⟩ — see PICTURE 1

2 to give a representation or account of in words ⟨The brochure *images* a vacation at the resort in language that makes you want to make a reservation this instant.⟩ — see DESCRIBE 1

3 to reproduce or show (an exact likeness) as a mirror would ⟨The burnished chrome fixtures *imaged* the jewelry store's glittery merchandise.⟩ — see REFLECT 1

4 to form a mental picture of ⟨He *imaged* what the ancient city would have looked like.⟩ — see IMAGINE 1

image *n* **1** something or someone that strongly resembles another ⟨The girl is growing up to be the perfect *image* of her mother.⟩

synonyms alter ego, carbon copy, counterpart, double, duplicate, duplication, facsimile, likeness, match, picture, replica, ringer, spit, twin

related words effigy, portrait, portrayal; companion, fellow, mate; equal, equivalent; analogue (*or* analog), parallel

near antonyms antithesis, converse, opposite, reverse

2 a two-dimensional design intended to look like a person or thing ⟨a cave with prehistoric *images* of wild animals⟩ — see PICTURE 1

3 something imagined or pictured in the mind ⟨a sentimental visit to her childhood home to see if it still matched her mental *image* of the place⟩ — see IDEA 1

4 a visible representation of something abstract (as a quality) ⟨a general who became for many the very *image* of the stoic warrior⟩ — see EMBODIMENT

imaginary *adj* not real and existing only in the imagination ⟨told by the psychologist that it was perfectly normal for their child to have an *imaginary* friend⟩

synonyms chimerical (*also* chimeric), fabulous, fanciful, fantastic (*also* fantastical), fictional, fictitious, ideal, imagined, invented, made-up, make-believe, mythical (*or* mythic), phantasmal, phantom, pretend, unreal, visionary

related words fabled, legendary, romantic; abstract, hypothetical, theoretical (*also* theoretic); unbelievable, unconvincing, unlikely; conceived, envisaged, envisioned, pictured, visualized; daydreamlike, deceptive, delusional, delusive, hallucinatory, illusory, phantasmagoric (*or* phantasmagorical); concocted, fabricated, feigned, fictive; inexistent, nonexistent

near antonyms authentic, genuine, true; factual, verifiable, verified; believable, convincing, realistic; corporeal, material, physical, solid, substantial; palpable, tangible

antonyms actual, existent, existing, real

imagination *n* **1** the ability to form mental images of things that either are not physically present or have never been conceived or created by others ⟨A cartoonist needs a fertile *imagination* in order to create interesting cartoons on demand.⟩

synonyms contrivance, creativity, fancy, fantasy (*also* phantasy), imaginativeness, invention, inventiveness, originality

related words brainstorm, brainstorming, inspiration; fecundity, fertility; ingenuity, resourcefulness; versatility; chimera, daydream, delusion, dream, figment, hallucination, illusion, mirage, phantasm (*also* fantasm), pipe dream; envisaging, visualization

near antonyms literality, literalness

2 the skill and imagination to create new things ⟨She lacks the *imagination* to be anything but an imitator of other directors' cinematic styles.⟩ — see CREATIVITY 1

imaginative *adj* **1** having the skill and imagination to create new things ⟨an *imaginative* child who is always writing short stories about her pet cat⟩ — see CREATIVE 1

2 showing a noteworthy use of the imagination and creativity especially in inventing ⟨We found an *imaginative* gadget that can grind the beans and heat the water to brew coffee.⟩ — see CLEVER 1

imaginativeness *n* **1** the ability to form mental images of things that either are not physically present or have never been conceived or created by others ⟨What sets apart geniuses like Thomas Edison and Ben Franklin from the average person is their keen intellect and restless *imaginativeness*.⟩ — see IMAGINATION 1

2 the skill and imagination to create new things ⟨It took exceptional *imaginativeness* and tireless dedication to invent the airplane.⟩ — see CREATIVITY 1

imagine *vb* **1** to form a mental picture of ⟨She was determined to have the career that she had always *imagined*.⟩

synonyms conceive, conjure (up), dream, envisage, fancy, fantasy, feature, image, picture, see, vision, visualize

related words daydream, stargaze; hallucinate; re-create, reflect, relive, reminisce; contemplate, meditate, ponder, ruminate; concoct, fabricate, invent, make up, manufacture, plan, project; foresee, prefigure

2 to have as an opinion ⟨I *imagine* that's true, but you still have to prove it.⟩ — see BELIEVE 2

3 to form an opinion from little or no evidence ⟨I *imagine* things will change rapidly once we begin.⟩ — see GUESS 1

imagined *adj* not real and existing only in the imagination ⟨She got needlessly upset about *imagined* dangers.⟩ — see IMAGINARY

imbecile *n* a stupid person ⟨Sometimes when those guys get together they act like a bunch of *imbeciles*.⟩ — see IDIOT

imbecility *n* **1** a foolish act or idea ⟨He was pulled over for the sheer *imbecility* of forgetting to turn his headlights on.⟩ — see FOLLY 1

2 lack of good sense or judgment ⟨We were stunned by the *imbecility* of the ideas presented by this once-respected biologist.⟩ — see FOOLISHNESS 1

imbibe *vb* **1** to swallow in liquid form ⟨She *imbibed* several cups of coffee.⟩ — see DRINK 1

2 to take in (something liquid) through small openings ⟨Plants can *imbibe* water through their roots.⟩ — see ABSORB 1

imbue *vb* to cause (as a person) to become filled or saturated with a certain quality or principle ⟨Her work with special needs students *imbued* her with a sense of purpose that she had never known before.⟩ — see INFUSE

imitate *vb* **1** to use (someone or something) as the model for one's speech, mannerisms, or behavior ⟨He's good at *imitating* his father.⟩

synonyms ape, copy, copycat, emulate, mime, mimic

related words ditto, echo, reecho, repeat; burlesque,

caricature, lampoon, mock, parody, travesty; impersonate, perform, play; pantomime

2 to copy or exaggerate (someone or something) in order to make fun of 〈Mom, make him stop *imitating* me!〉 — see MIMIC 1

3 to make an exact likeness of 〈a second-rate artist who was notorious for *imitating* the works of other painters〉 — see COPY 1

imitation *n* something that is made to look exactly like something else 〈challenged me to tell the real roses from the silk *imitations*〉 — see COPY

imitation *adj* being such in appearance only and made with or manufactured from usually cheaper materials 〈The stage production uses only *imitation* diamonds, as real gems would be too expensive.〉

synonyms artificial, bogus, dummy, fake, false, faux, imitative, man-made, mimic, mock, pretend, sham, simulated, substitute, synthetic

related words cultured, manufactured, process; unauthentic; adulterated, designer, doctored, engineered, fudged, juggled, manipulated, tampered (with); concocted, fabricated; counterfeit, deceptive, forged, fraudulent, misleading, phony (*also* phoney); affected, feigned, pinchbeck, pseudo, spurious

near antonyms authentic, bona fide, legitimate, true; premium, quality, valuable; pure, unadulterated

antonyms genuine, natural, real

imitative *adj* **1** using or marked by the use of something else as a basis or model 〈Your writing style tends to be *imitative* of whichever author you've recently read.〉

synonyms apish, canned, emulative, formulaic, mimetic, mimic, unoriginal

related words copied, cribbed, plagiarized; artificial, bogus, factitious, fake, false, imitation, man-made, mock, sham, simulated, substitute, synthetic; duplicated, photocopied, reduplicated, reproduced, transcribed; backup; counterfeit, deceptive, forged, fraudulent, misleading; perfunctory, routine, uninspired

near antonyms authentic, bona fide, legitimate, true; genuine, natural, real; classic, ideal, model

antonyms archetypal (*also* archetypical), original

2 being such in appearance only and made with or manufactured from usually cheaper materials 〈An *imitative* extract never has the flavor of the real thing.〉 — see IMITATION

imitator *n* **1** a person who adopts the appearance or behavior of another especially in an obvious way 〈an Elvis *imitator* in a sequined jumpsuit〉 — see COPYCAT

2 a person who imitates another's voice and mannerisms for comic effect 〈That comedian is a hilarious *imitator* of a surprising array of current celebrities.〉 — see MIMIC 1

immaculate *adj* **1** free from any trace of the coarse or indecent 〈an *immaculate* soul〉 — see CHASTE 1

2 free from dirt or stain 〈somehow managed to keep the white carpet *immaculate*〉 — see CLEAN 1

3 being entirely without fault or flaw 〈a fussy groundskeeper who always manages to restore the football field to an *immaculate* expanse of healthy, well-manicured turf〉 — see PERFECT 1

immaterial *adj* **1** not composed of matter 〈It is only possible to study *immaterial* forces like gravity by observing their effects on the physical world.〉

synonyms bodiless, ethereal, formless, incorporeal, insubstantial, nonmaterial, nonphysical, spiritual, unsubstantial

related words metaphysical, supernatural; impalpable, insensible, intangible; airy, gaseous, gossamery, tenuous, thin, vaporous, wispish

near antonyms animal, carnal, fleshly; detectable, discernible (*also* discernable), noticeable, observable, palpable, sensible, tangible, visible; bulky, heavy, massive, solid

antonyms bodily, corporeal, material, physical, substantial

2 not having anything to do with the matter at hand 〈While undoubtedly upsetting, that story is *immaterial* to the question of why you are late.〉 — see IRRELEVANT

immature *adj* **1** being in the early stage of life, growth, or development 〈*Immature* frogs are called "tadpoles."〉 — see YOUNG

2 having or showing the annoying qualities (as silliness) associated with children 〈an *immature* teenager who still threw tantrums〉 — see CHILDISH

3 lacking in adult experience or maturity 〈Sometimes high school students are still too *immature* to understand the consequences of their actions.〉 — see CALLOW

immeasurable *adj* being or seeming to be without limits 〈the *immeasurable* expanse of the ocean〉 — see INFINITE

immediacy *n* the state or condition of being near 〈The *immediacy* of Christmas is just beginning to dawn on many last-minute shoppers.〉 — see PROXIMITY

immediate *adj* **1** done or occurring without any noticeable lapse in time 〈I felt *immediate* relief after taking the painkiller.〉 — see INSTANTANEOUS

2 done or working without something else coming in between 〈She is my *immediate* superior, so I report to her.〉 — see DIRECT 1

3 done, carried out, or given without delay 〈*Immediate* treatment saved the victim of the massive heart attack.〉 — see PROMPT 1

4 not being distant in time, space, or significance 〈The effect of the change won't be known in the *immediate* future.〉 — see CLOSE 2

5 existing or in progress right now 〈We need to solve the *immediate* problems before working on the more long-term ones.〉 — see PRESENT 1

immediately *adv* without delay 〈If we don't leave *immediately*, we'll be late for the concert.〉

synonyms bang, directly, forthwith, headlong, instantly, now, plumb, presently, promptly, pronto, right, right away, right now, straightaway, straightway

related words away, freely; anon, momentarily, shortly, soon; apace, briskly, fast, fleetly, full-tilt, posthaste, quick, quickly, rapidly, readily, snappily, speedily, swift, swiftly; abruptly, presto, suddenly, unexpectedly; hastily, impetuously, impulsively, rashly, recklessly; exactly, opportunely, punctually, seasonably

phrases at once, in no time, off the bat, on a dime, on the double, on the spot

near antonyms slowly; late, tardily

immemorial *adj* dating or surviving from the distant past 〈the *immemorial* Alps, where once Hannibal's army marched〉 — see ANCIENT 1

immense *adj* **1** unusually large 〈The elephant was simply *immense*, even as elephants go.〉 — see HUGE

2 of the very best kind 〈We had simply an *immense* time at the luxury resort.〉 — see EXCELLENT

immenseness *n* the quality or state of being very large 〈The overwhelming *immenseness* of the stadium made me feel like an ant.〉 — see IMMENSITY

immensity *n* the quality or state of being very large 〈The *immensity* of the mountain was awe-inspiring, especially up close.〉

synonyms enormity, enormousness, hugeness, immenseness, magnitude, massiveness, vastness

related words bigness, extensiveness, greatness, largeness, sizableness, voluminousness, weightiness; awesomeness, grandness, stupendousness, tremendousness; boundlessness, limitlessness; ampleness, capaciousness, commodiousness, spaciousness; extravagance, extremeness, gaudiness, grandiosity

near antonyms littleness, puniness, smallness; triviality

antonyms diminutiveness, minuteness, tininess

immerse *vb* **1** to hold the attention of ⟨That documentary never fails to *immerse* an audience.⟩ — see ENGAGE 1

2 to sink or push (something) briefly into or as if into a liquid ⟨tried to *immerse* the balloon in the water⟩ — see DIP 1

immersed *adj* having the mind fixed on something ⟨The child was so *immersed* in a book that she didn't hear her mother calling.⟩ — see ATTENTIVE 1

immersing *adj* holding the attention or provoking interest ⟨an *immersing* documentary on the array of animal species threatened with extinction⟩ — see INTERESTING

immersion *n* a focusing of the mind on something ⟨A program of complete *immersion* in the language is the only way you're going to learn it.⟩ — see ATTENTION 1

immigrant *n* one that leaves one place to settle in another ⟨European *immigrants* came to North America in the 16th century.⟩ — see EMIGRANT

imminent *adj* **1** giving signs of immediate occurrence ⟨Those clouds mean rain is *imminent*.⟩

synonyms impending, looming, pending, threatening

related words approaching, coming, forthcoming, future, near, nearing, oncoming, upcoming; brewing, gathering; likely, possible, probable; inevitable, unavoidable; lowering, menacing, ominous, portentous; anticipated, awaited, expected, foreseen, predicted

phrases around the corner

near antonyms distant, far-off, remote; eventual, ultimate; bygone, former, past; late, recent

2 being soon to appear or take place ⟨We are awaiting their *imminent* arrival.⟩ — see FORTHCOMING 1

immobile *adj* **1** fixed in a place or position ⟨The patient must remain *immobile* while he is in the MRI unit.⟩ — see STATIONARY 1

2 incapable of moving or being moved ⟨a huge, *immobile* tree of an endangered species that the creators of the theme park decided to make part of the design⟩ — see IMMOVABLE 1

immobilize *vb* to render powerless, ineffective, or unable to move ⟨Town councils felt *immobilized* by the powers newly granted to the state legislature.⟩ — see PARALYZE 1

immoderate *adj* going beyond a normal or acceptable limit in degree or amount ⟨Make sure you don't drive at an *immoderate* speed.⟩ — see EXCESSIVE

immodest *adj* showing a lack of proper social reserve or modesty ⟨an *immodest* proposal for altering the town's traditional character by a newcomer at his first town meeting⟩ — see PRESUMPTUOUS 1

immolate *vb* to give up as an offering to a god ⟨a ceremony in which they *immolated* their cherished possessions so that the gods would send rain⟩ — see SACRIFICE

immolation *n* something offered to a god ⟨ceremonial *immolation* for a good harvest⟩ — see SACRIFICE

immoral *adj* **1** not conforming to a high moral standard; morally unacceptable ⟨considered their actions *immoral*⟩ — see BAD 2

2 not guided by or showing a concern for what is right ⟨Stealing another's words, even over the Internet, remains an *immoral* act.⟩ — see UNPRINCIPLED

immorality *n* **1** immoral conduct or practices harmful or offensive to society ⟨gave stealing and lying as examples of *immorality*⟩ — see VICE 1

2 that which is morally unacceptable ⟨a discussion of the indifference between criminality and *immorality*⟩ — see EVIL

immortal *adj* **1** lasting forever ⟨the age-old quest for *immortal* fame⟩ — see EVERLASTING 1

2 having an existence or validity that does not change or diminish ⟨They vowed that their love was *immortal* and that they'd never part.⟩ — see ABIDING

immortality *n* unending existence after death ⟨Central to most religions is a belief in the *immortality* of the soul.⟩ — see ETERNITY 2

immortalize *vb* to give eternal or lasting existence to ⟨*immortalized* the words "Call me Ishmael" as the novel's opening line⟩ — see PERPETUATE

immovable *adj* **1** incapable of moving or being moved ⟨That boulder is *immovable*, even with a bulldozer.⟩

synonyms immobile, irremovable, nonmotile, nonmoving, unbudging, unmovable

related words motionless, moveless, static, stationary, still; fast, fixed, rooted, steadfast, stuck, wedged

near antonyms portable, removable (*also* removeable), transferable (*also* transferrable), transportable

antonyms mobile, motile, movable (*or* moveable), moving

2 sticking to an opinion, purpose, or course of action in spite of reason, arguments, or persuasion ⟨Despite our excuses and pleas, the police officer was *immovable* on the matter of a hefty fine for speeding.⟩ — see OBSTINATE

immunity *n* freedom from punishment, harm, or loss ⟨The suspect refused to name his partners unless he was granted *immunity*.⟩ — see IMPUNITY

immure *vb* **1** to close or shut in by or as if by barriers ⟨Scientists at the research station in Alaska are *immured* by the frozen wastelands that surround them.⟩ — see ENCLOSE 1

2 to put in or as if in prison ⟨He *immured* himself in his room until he finished his homework.⟩ — see IMPRISON

immurement *n* the act of confining or the state of being confined ⟨The *immurement* of Japanese-Americans continued for the duration of the war.⟩ — see INTERNMENT

immutability *n* the state of continuing without change ⟨The *immutability* of the laws of physics is a myth, since refinements of those laws continue to be made.⟩ — see CONSTANCY 1

immutable *adj* not capable of changing or being changed ⟨*immutable* laws of nature⟩ — see INFLEXIBLE 1

imp *n* **1** an appealingly mischievous person ⟨scooped up the little *imp* and took him to bed⟩ — see SCAMP 1

2 an evil spirit ⟨a story about a crumbling mansion infested with a brood of *imps*⟩ — see DEMON 1

impact *vb* **1** to act upon (a person or a person's feelings) so as to cause a response ⟨The event *impacted* the boy for the rest of his life.⟩ — see ¹AFFECT 1

2 to come into usually forceful contact with something ⟨the damage sustained when a car going 40 miles an hour *impacts* with a brick wall⟩ — see HIT 2

3 to set solidly in or as if in surrounding matter ⟨The fossils of ancient sea creatures were found *impacted* in the rock.⟩ — see ENTRENCH

impact *n* **1** a forceful coming together of two things ⟨The glass shattered immediately upon *impact* with the floor.⟩

synonyms bump, collision, concussion, crash, jar, jolt, jounce, kick, shock, slam, smash, strike, wallop

related words blow, buffet, hit, knock, punch, rap, slap, thump; bashing, battering, bludgeoning, clobbering, hammering, lambasting, licking, pounding, pummeling (*also* pummelling), thrashing; contact, encounter, meeting, touch

2 the power to bring about a result on another ⟨The case had such a powerful *impact* on her that she became a crusader for sentencing reform.⟩ — see EFFECT 2

3 the quality of an utterance that provokes interest and produces an effect ⟨The story has real dramatic *impact*.⟩ — see ¹PUNCH 1

impair *vb* to reduce the soundness, effectiveness, or

perfection of ⟨Already *impaired* by a crack, the windshield shattered upon impact with the baseball.⟩ — see DAMAGE 1

impaired *adj* deprived of the power to perform one or more natural bodily activities ⟨special devices for sight-*impaired* visitors⟩ — see DISABLED

impale *vb* to penetrate or hold (something) with a pointed object ⟨*Impale* a marshmallow or two on that stick and let's start toasting!⟩

synonyms gore, harpoon, jab, lance, peck, pick, pierce, puncture, run through, skewer, spear, spike, spit, stab, stick, transfix

related words spindle; perforate, riddle; bayonet, dirk, gimlet, pike, poniard, prong, quill; pinprick, poke, prick, punch, thrust; cut, knife, slice

impalpable *adj* **1** not capable of being perceived by the sense of touch ⟨The rich colors used in the wall coverings and furniture give the room an *impalpable* warmth.⟩ — see INTANGIBLE

2 not perceptible by a sense or by the mind ⟨Any difference between the two sound systems is *impalpable* to all but the most discerning audiophiles.⟩ — see IMPERCEPTIBLE

impart *vb* to cause (something) to pass from one to another ⟨*imparted* the latest information on the approaching snowstorm⟩ — see COMMUNICATE 1

impartial *adj* marked by justice, honesty, and freedom from bias ⟨an *impartial* evaluation of the job applicant's qualifications⟩ — see FAIR 2

impartiality *n* lack of favoritism toward one side or another ⟨The defense lawyers challenged the *impartiality* of the presiding judge.⟩ — see DETACHMENT 1

impassable *also* **impassible** *adj* impossible to get through or into ⟨The road was *impassable* until snowplows cleared it.⟩ — see IMPENETRABLE 1

impasse *n* **1** a point in a struggle where neither side is capable of winning or willing to give in ⟨Negotiations are at an *impasse*.⟩

synonyms deadlock, halt, stalemate, standoff, standstill

related words dead end; bind, bottleneck, corner, dilemma, fix, hole, jam, morass, pickle, pinch, plight, predicament, quagmire, quandary, spot; difficulty; problem

2 a difficult, puzzling, or embarrassing situation from which there is no easy escape ⟨the impossible *impasse* faced by those who opposed the war but did not want to seem disloyal to the troops⟩ — see PREDICAMENT

impassioned *adj* having or expressing great depth of feeling ⟨an *impassioned* plea for justice⟩ — see FERVENT 1

impassive *adj* **1** not feeling or showing emotion ⟨She remained *impassive* throughout the trial.⟩

synonyms apathetic, cold-blooded, numb, phlegmatic, stoic (*or* stoical), stolid, undemonstrative, unemotional

related words cold, cool, dispassionate, unmoved; calm, collected, composed; imperturbable, unflappable; reserved, reticent, taciturn; bland, blank, deadpan, dry, empty, expressionless, inexpressive, stone-faced, straight-faced, vacant, wooden; enigmatic (*also* enigmatical), impenetrable, inscrutable; aloof, bloodless, detached, indifferent, insensible, unconcerned, unsentimental; impersonal, objective, unresponsive; pitiless, unfeeling; inconsiderate, thoughtless

near antonyms blazing, burning, fiery, flaming, glowing, red-hot; ardent, enthusiastic, gung ho, warm-blooded, zealous; gushing, maudlin, mawkish, mushy, sentimental; dramatic, histrionic, melodramatic, overemotional, overheated; compassionate, responsive, sympathetic; reactive, sensitive

antonyms demonstrative, emotional, fervent, fervid, hot-blooded, impassioned, passionate, vehement

2 not expressing any emotion ⟨an *impassive* expression on the prisoner's face as his sentence was read⟩ — see BLANK 1

impassivity *n* a lack of emotion or emotional expressiveness ⟨the jury's *impassivity* as they heard the testimony⟩ — see APATHY 1

impatience *n* urgent desire or interest ⟨The child's *impatience* for her birthday is charming.⟩ — see EAGERNESS

impatient *adj* **1** showing urgent desire or interest ⟨She was *impatient* to give her presentation before the landmark commission.⟩ — see EAGER

2 unable or unwilling to endure ⟨those airline passengers who are so *impatient* of delays, even for the most obvious of reasons⟩ — see INTOLERANT 1

impeach *vb* **1** to make a claim of wrongdoing against ⟨The company's president has been *impeached* by the Securities and Exchange Commission.⟩ — see ACCUSE

2 to demand proof of the truth or rightness of ⟨questionable methodology that should cause us to *impeach* the findings of this survey⟩ — see CHALLENGE 1

impeccability *n* the quality or state of being free from guilt or blame ⟨The *impeccability* of her moral character and untiring selflessness qualified her for sainthood.⟩ — see INNOCENCE 1

impeccable *adj* **1** being entirely without fault or flaw ⟨The etiquette expert was celebrated for her absolutely *impeccable* manners.⟩ — see PERFECT 1

2 free from guilt or blame ⟨The head of the investigation must be a person of *impeccable* probity and honesty.⟩ — see INNOCENT 2

3 free from sin ⟨the belief that there can be no such thing as an *impeccable* soul⟩ — see INNOCENT 1

impeccably *adv* without any flaws or errors ⟨He speaks French *impeccably*.⟩ — see PERFECTLY 1

impecunious *adj* lacking money or material possessions ⟨They were so *impecunious* that they couldn't afford to give one another even token Christmas gifts.⟩ — see POOR 1

impecuniousness *n* the state of lacking sufficient money or material possessions ⟨Her claims of *impecuniousness* rang false when we noticed the luxuries she had bought for herself.⟩ — see POVERTY 1

impede *vb* to create difficulty for the work or activity of ⟨The construction work *impeded* the smooth running of the office for several months.⟩ — see HAMPER

impediment *n* something that makes movement or progress difficult ⟨tough going for the burros on the canyon trail, even without the added *impediment* of heavy loads⟩ — see ENCUMBRANCE

impel *vb* **1** to set or keep in motion ⟨Gasoline *impels* a car's engine.⟩ — see MOVE 2

2 to cause (a person) to give in to pressure ⟨I felt *impelled* to tell the truth, however painful it might be.⟩ — see FORCE

impend *vb* to be about to happen ⟨For confirmed pessimists some disaster always seems to be *impending*.⟩ — see LOOM

impend (over) *vb* to remain poised to inflict harm, danger, or distress on ⟨Fears of an economic recession *impended over* the stock market.⟩ — see THREATEN

impending *adj* **1** being soon to appear or take place ⟨an *impending* celebration of the 100th anniversary of the college's founding⟩ — see FORTHCOMING 1

2 giving signs of immediate occurrence ⟨an *impending* eruption of the volcano⟩ — see IMMINENT 1

impenetrable *adj* **1** impossible to get through or into ⟨The ancient temple was surrounded by vast stretches of *impenetrable* jungle.⟩

synonyms impassable (*also* impassible), impermeable, impervious, impregnable

related words close, compact, dense, thick, tight; compressed, condensed; sturdy, substantial, tough; firm, frozen, hard, solid, stiff; inflexible, rigid, unbending, unyielding

near antonyms soft, squishy; bendable, elastic, flexible, giving, malleable, pliable, yielding; absorbent, porous
antonyms negotiable, passable, penetrable, permeable
2 being beyond one's powers to know, understand, or explain ⟨an *impenetrable* secret code⟩ — see MYSTERIOUS 1
3 impossible to understand ⟨The textbook's language is completely *impenetrable*, at least to me.⟩ — see INCOMPREHENSIBLE
4 not allowing penetration (as by gas, liquid, or light) ⟨The container of toxic waste has an *impenetrable* seal to prevent leaks.⟩ — see TIGHT 1
impenitent *adj* not sorry for having done wrong ⟨an *impenitent* criminal who said he'd do it all over again, given the chance⟩ — see REMORSELESS 1
imperative *adj* **1** forcing one's compliance or participation by or as if by law ⟨an *imperative* duty to educate children⟩ — see MANDATORY
2 impossible to do without ⟨Proper equipment is *imperative* for the success of this chemical experiment.⟩ — see ESSENTIAL 1
3 needing immediate attention ⟨an *imperative* need for medical supplies⟩ — see ACUTE 2
imperative *n* **1** a statement of what to do that must be obeyed by those concerned ⟨a secretary of defense who was fond of issuing harshly worded *imperatives*⟩ — see COMMAND 1
2 something one must do because of prior agreement ⟨Although he had little taste for the social *imperatives* that come with being governor, he put on a brave face.⟩ — see OBLIGATION 1
imperceptible *adj* not perceptible by a sense or by the mind ⟨a slight difference in hue between the two glasses that's *imperceptible* unless they're placed side by side⟩
synonyms impalpable, inappreciable, indistinguishable, insensible
related words inaudible, intangible; inconspicuous, indistinct, unnoticeable, unseeable, unseen; faint, insignificant, liminal, slender, slight, subtle, trivial; buried, concealed, covert, disguised, obscure, shrouded, unapparent, vague
near antonyms audible, observable, recognizable, tangible, visible; clear, conspicuous, evident, eye-catching, manifest, noticeable, obvious, plain, prominent, striking; apparent, distinct, significant, straightforward
antonyms appreciable, discernible (*also* discernable), palpable, perceptible, ponderable, sensible
imperfect *adj* having a fault ⟨an *imperfect* representation of the circumstances surrounding Paul Revere's famous ride⟩ — see FAULTY
imperfection *n* something that spoils the appearance or completeness of a thing ⟨The shirt was marked down because of a minor *imperfection*.⟩ — see BLEMISH
imperial *adj* large and impressive in size, grandeur, extent, or conception ⟨Peter envisioned an *imperial* city that would rival the capitals of Europe for beauty and magnificence.⟩ — see GRAND 1
imperil *vb* to place in danger ⟨A single mistake could *imperil* the lives of everyone involved in the military operation.⟩ — see ENDANGER
imperilment *n* the state of not being protected from injury, harm, or evil ⟨The city has reduced the number of its firefighters, to the *imperilment* of every homeowner.⟩ — see DANGER 1
imperious *adj* **1** fond of ordering people around ⟨an *imperious* little boy who liked to tell the other scouts what to do⟩ — see BOSSY

2 having a feeling of superiority that shows itself in an overbearing attitude ⟨an *imperious* movie star who barked orders at the waiters⟩ — see ARROGANT
3 having or showing a tendency to force one's will on others without any regard to fairness or necessity ⟨an office administrator with an *imperious* manner that really grates on people⟩ — see ARBITRARY 1
4 needing immediate attention ⟨As the population ages, the need for trained medical workers becomes *imperious*.⟩ — see ACUTE 2
imperiousness *n* an exaggerated sense of one's importance that shows itself in the making of excessive or unjustified claims ⟨The *imperiousness* of that fashion designer irritates everyone around her.⟩ — see ARROGANCE
imperishable *adj* **1** impossible to destroy ⟨Energy is *imperishable*.⟩ — see INDESTRUCTIBLE
2 having an existence or validity that does not change or diminish ⟨the belief that through military glory one could achieve *imperishable* fame⟩ — see ABIDING
impermanent *adj* **1** intended to last, continue, or serve for a limited time ⟨built an *impermanent* structure to serve for the archaeologists' living quarters during the dig⟩ — see TEMPORARY 1
2 lasting only for a short time ⟨a summer romance that was an *impermanent* fancy, quickly forgotten⟩ — see MOMENTARY
impermeable *adj* **1** impossible to get through or into ⟨The wall of security people surrounding the visiting dignitary was *impermeable*.⟩ — see IMPENETRABLE 1
2 not allowing penetration (as by gas, liquid, or light) ⟨An *impermeable* seal on the ancient tomb had preserved the artifacts exceptionally well.⟩ — see TIGHT 1
impermissible *adj* that may not be permitted ⟨Trial juries must be able to discern the difference between a permissible inference and *impermissible* speculation.⟩
synonyms banned, barred, forbidden, interdicted, outlawed, prohibited, proscribed, taboo (*also* tabu)
related words intolerable, unacceptable, unbearable, unendurable; illegal, illegitimate, illicit, improper, inappropriate, unauthorized, unlawful, unlicensed; ineffable, unmentionable; unseemly, unsuitable; objectionable; disallowed, disapproved, discouraged; refused, rejected, revoked, unsanctioned, vetoed; suppressed; precluded, prevented, stopped; excluded, ruled out, shut out; blocked, hindered, impeded, obstructed
near antonyms acceptable, bearable, endurable, tolerable; accepted, accredited, allowed, appropriate, approved, authorized, endorsed (*also* indorsed), lawful, legal, legitimate, licensed, OK (*or* okay), permitted, warranted; accorded, granted, sanctioned, vouchsafed; brooked, condoned, countenanced; encouraged, promoted, supported; commanded, mandatory, ordered, required; proper, seemly, suitable, tolerated, unobjectionable
antonyms allowable, permissible, permissive, sufferable
impersonate *vb* **1** to pretend to be (what one is not) in appearance or behavior ⟨He was arrested for *impersonating* a police officer.⟩
synonyms act, masquerade (as), play, pose (as)
related words ape, copy, imitate, mime, mimic, mock, monkey, parody, travesty; perform, portray
2 to present a portrayal or performance of ⟨Interpreters at the living history museum *impersonate* figures who are known to have actually lived in the colonial town.⟩ — see ACT 1
impersonator *n* **1** a person who imitates another's voice and mannerisms for comic effect ⟨A versatile *impersonator*, he conjures up a glittering array of female stars and divas in the course of his act.⟩ — see MIMIC 1
2 one who acts professionally (as in a play, movie, or

television show) ⟨a gifted *impersonator* who can convincingly portray both heroes and heels⟩ — see ACTOR 1

impertinence *n* **1** disrespectful or argumentative talk given in response to a command or request ⟨He refused to tolerate any *impertinence* from his children.⟩ — see BACK TALK

2 rude behavior ⟨the *impertinence* of deliberately ignoring waiting customers while they finished their conversation⟩ — see DISCOURTESY

3 the quality or state of not having anything to do with the matter at hand ⟨The *impertinence* of that issue renders any discussion of it a waste of our time.⟩ — see IRRELEVANCE

impertinent *adj* **1** displaying or marked by rude boldness ⟨The *impertinent* child had a smart answer for everything.⟩ — see NERVY 1

2 showing a lack of manners or consideration for others ⟨*impertinent* salesmen who telephone people during the dinner hour⟩ — see IMPOLITE

3 not having anything to do with the matter at hand ⟨Your résumé needlessly lists skills that are *impertinent* to the job for which you are applying.⟩ — see IRRELEVANT

imperturbability *n* evenness of emotions or temper ⟨His *imperturbability* in a crisis is legendary among hospital staffers.⟩ — see EQUANIMITY

imperturbable *adj* not easily panicked or upset ⟨The chef was absolutely *imperturbable*—even when the kitchen caught on fire.⟩ — see UNFLAPPABLE

impervious *adj* **1** not allowing penetration (as by gas, liquid, or light) ⟨The material for this coat is supposed to be *impervious* to rain.⟩ — see TIGHT 1

2 impossible to get through or into ⟨The rain forest is *impervious* to all but the most dedicated explorers.⟩ — see IMPENETRABLE 1

impetus *n* something that arouses action or activity ⟨The reward money should be sufficient *impetus* for someone to come forward with information about the robbery.⟩ — see IMPULSE 1

impiety *n* an act of great disrespect shown to God or to sacred ideas, people, or things ⟨Some of the townspeople leveled accusations of *impiety* against him.⟩ — see BLASPHEMY

impinge *vb* to come into usually forceful contact with something ⟨Hail was noisily *impinging* upon the car's exterior.⟩ — see HIT 2

impious *adj* not showing proper reverence for the holy or sacred ⟨an *impious* act that shocked their pious community⟩ — see IRREVERENT

impish *adj* tending to or exhibiting reckless playfulness ⟨The *impish* children rode their bikes at breakneck speeds.⟩ — see MISCHIEVOUS 1

impishness *n* **1** a natural disposition for playful behavior ⟨Her irrepressible *impishness* means that no one is ever safe from her practical jokes.⟩ — see PLAYFULNESS

2 playful, reckless behavior that is not intended to cause serious harm ⟨The boys' *impishness* was easy to forgive, since it caused no real harm.⟩ — see MISCHIEF 1

implacable *adj* **1** sticking to an opinion, purpose, or course of action in spite of reason, arguments, or persuasion ⟨an *implacable* judge who knew in his bones that the cover-up extended to the highest levels of government⟩ — see OBSTINATE

2 showing no signs of slackening or yielding in one's purpose ⟨an *implacable* dedication to the proposition that everyone is entitled to a quality education⟩ — see UNYIELDING 1

implant *vb* **1** to set permanently in the consciousness or mind-set ⟨a music teacher who strove to *implant* within his students a love of the classics⟩

synonyms breed, inculcate, plant, sow

related words drive, hammer, pound; embed (*also* imbed),

entrench (*also* intrench), fix, lodge, root; imbue, infuse, ingrain (*also* engrain), inoculate, invest, steep, suffuse

2 to set solidly in or as if in surrounding matter ⟨The gemstone was poorly *implanted* in the setting, so it was constantly popping out.⟩ — see ENTRENCH

implausible *adj* too extraordinary or improbable to believe ⟨He gave an *implausible* excuse for arriving late.⟩ — see INCREDIBLE

implement *vb* to carry out effectively ⟨*implemented* the evacuation plan without a hitch⟩ — see ENFORCE

implement *n* an article intended for use in work ⟨gardening *implements* such as hoes, spades, and pruners⟩

synonyms device, instrument, tool, utensil

related words apparatus, appliance, mechanism; contraption, contrivance, gadget, gizmo (*also* gismo), jigger; accessory (*also* accessary), accoutrement (*or* accouterment), adjunct, appendage, attachment

implementation *n* the doing of an action ⟨The *implementation* of the idea turned out to be harder than its conception.⟩ — see COMMISSION 2

implicit *adj* **1** understood although not put into words ⟨The *implicit* agreement among members of the outing club is that everyone pays his or her own way on all trips.⟩

synonyms implied, tacit, unexpressed, unspoken, unvoiced, wordless

related words inferred, presumed; construed, interpreted; unannounced, undeclared, unsaid, untold; hinted, insinuated, intimated, suggested

near antonyms apparent, blatant, evident, manifest, obvious, plain, straightforward; unambiguous, unequivocal, unmistakable

antonyms explicit, express, expressed, spoken, stated, voiced

2 having or showing a mind free from doubt ⟨Members of the expedition must have *implicit* trust in their leaders.⟩ — see CERTAIN 2

3 existing only as a possibility and not in fact ⟨There's a risk *implicit* in any extreme sport.⟩ — see POTENTIAL

implied *adj* understood although not put into words ⟨There was an *implied* agreement that they would share the costs.⟩ — see IMPLICIT 1

implode *vb* to fall down or in as a result of physical pressure ⟨a controlled demolition during which the entire building *imploded* in a matter of seconds⟩ — see COLLAPSE 1

implore *vb* to make a request to (someone) in an earnest or urgent manner ⟨The victims of the hurricane *implored* the governor to put the full resources of the state into the relief effort.⟩ — see BEG

imploring *adj* asking humbly ⟨The *imploring* boy tearfully asked the veterinarian to do what he could to save the life of his dog.⟩ — see SUPPLIANT

imply *vb* to convey an idea indirectly ⟨They may have *implied* that they'd help, but they didn't actually say so.⟩ — see HINT

impolite *adj* showing a lack of manners or consideration for others ⟨The librarian was shocked that anyone could be so *impolite* as to continue talking despite repeated warnings to be quiet.⟩

synonyms discourteous, disrespectful, ill-bred, ill-mannered, impertinent, inconsiderate, rude, thoughtless, uncalled-for, uncivil, ungracious, unhandsome, unmannerly

related words arch, audacious, bold, bold-faced, brash, brassy, brazen, cheeky, fresh, impudent, insolent, lippy, sassy, saucy, shameless; boorish, caddish, churlish, clownish, loutish, uncouth, vulgar; abrupt, blunt, brusque (*also* brusk), crusty, curt, gruff, sharp, snippety, snippy; antisocial, crabbed, cross, disagreeable, grumpy, sullen, surly; improper, incorrect, indecent, indecorous, unseemly; arrogant, conceited, haughty, high-handed, imperious, peremptory, pompous, presumptuous, pretentious, supercilious, superior

near antonyms humble, meek, modest, unassertive; deferential, dutiful, respectful, submissive, yielding; acceptable, appropriate, becoming, befitting, correct, decent, decorous, fit, fitting, good, meet, proper, respectable, right, seemly, suitable; affable, cordial, friendly, genial, hospitable, sociable; felicitous, graceful; chivalrous, courtly, gallant; ceremonious; elegant, refined

antonyms civil, considerate, courteous, genteel, gracious, mannerly, polite, thoughtful, well-bred

impoliteness *n* rude behavior ⟨Such flagrant *impoliteness* must never be tolerated.⟩ — see DISCOURTESY

import *n* **1** the quality or state of being important ⟨I can't overemphasize the *import* of this examination on your future academic career.⟩ — see IMPORTANCE

2 the idea that is conveyed or intended to be conveyed to the mind by language, symbol, or action ⟨I didn't understand all the technical jargon, but got the general *import* of the speech.⟩ — see MEANING 1

import *vb* **1** to be of importance ⟨It *imports* little whether you like Grandma's gift; you should have graciously thanked her.⟩ — see MATTER

2 to communicate or convey (as an idea) to the mind ⟨The word "freedom" can *import* different things to different people.⟩ — see MEAN 1

importance *n* the quality or state of being important ⟨A final exam has great *importance*.⟩

synonyms account, consequence, import, magnitude, moment, significance, weight, weightiness

related words celebrity, distinction, eminence, fame, note, noteworthiness, notoriety, preeminence, prominence, renown; store, substance, substantiveness, value, worth, worthiness; gravity, seriousness; authority, control, dominion, mastery, potency, power, sway; mark, name, report, reputation, repute; centrality, essentiality, essentialness; cachet, position, prestige, rank, standing, stature, status; glory, honor, illustriousness

near antonyms paltriness, valuelessness, worthlessness; discredit, disgrace, dishonor, disrepute, ignominy, infamy, odium, opprobrium, shame

antonyms littleness, puniness, slightness, smallness, triviality

important *adj* **1** having great meaning or lasting effect ⟨The discovery of penicillin was a very *important* event in the history of medicine.⟩

synonyms big, consequential, eventful, major, material, meaningful, momentous, monumental, much, significant, substantial, weighty

related words decisive, fatal, fateful, strategic; earnest, grave, heavy, serious, sincere; distinctive, exceptional, impressive, outstanding, prominent, remarkable; valuable, worthwhile, worthy; distinguished, eminent, great, illustrious, noble, notable, noteworthy, outstanding, preeminent, prestigious; famous, notorious, renowned; all-important, central, critical, crucial, essential, key, pivotal, seminal, vital

near antonyms paltry, petty, worthless; anonymous, nameless, obscure, uncelebrated, unknown

antonyms inconsequential, inconsiderable, insignificant, little, minor, negligible, slight, small, trifling, trivial, unimportant

2 having great power or influence ⟨Rachel Carson was an *important* figure in the environmental movement.⟩

synonyms heavy, influential, mighty, potent, powerful, puissant, significant, strong

related words high-level, senior, top; able, capable, competent, effective, efficient; celebrated, distinguished,

dominant, eminent, famed, famous, great, illustrious, noble, notable, noteworthy, notorious, outstanding, preeminent, prestigious, prominent, renowned; dynamic, energetic, forceful, high-powered, robust, vigorous

near antonyms anonymous, nameless, obscure, uncelebrated, unknown; incapable, incompetent, ineffective, inept, inexpert, unfit, unqualified, unskilled, unskillful

antonyms helpless, impotent, insignificant, little, powerless, unimportant, weak

3 having a feeling of superiority that shows itself in an overbearing attitude ⟨an *important* businessman who always expects special treatment wherever he goes⟩ — see ARROGANT

4 having too high an opinion of oneself ⟨Oh, you're so *important*—you think the world revolves around you!⟩ — see CONCEITED

importune *vb* to make a request to (someone) in an earnest or urgent manner ⟨She was always *importuning* people for favors, even when she had no right to ask.⟩ — see BEG

impose *vb* to establish or apply as a charge or penalty ⟨That state now *imposes* a fine for texting while driving.⟩

synonyms assess, charge, exact, fine, lay, levy, put

related words dock, excise, penalize, tax; extort, wrest, wring; bleed, fleece, gouge, skin, squeeze; coerce, compel, force; inflict, wreak

near antonyms abate, diminish, lessen; forgive, release; condone, disregard, excuse, gloss (over), gloze (over), ignore, pardon

antonyms remit

impose (on *or* **upon)** *vb* to take unfair advantage of ⟨Thanks for offering your own bed, but I wouldn't dream of *imposing on* you and will be perfectly happy on the couch.⟩ — see EXPLOIT 1

imposing *adj* **1** having or showing a formal and serious or reserved manner ⟨The president of the bank is exactly the sort of *imposing* figure that one might expect.⟩ — see DIGNIFIED

2 large and impressive in size, grandeur, extent, or conception ⟨The corporation's *imposing* headquarters were designed by one of the nation's cutting-edge architects.⟩ — see GRAND 1

imposition *n* a charge usually of money collected by the government from people or businesses for public use ⟨an *imposition* of 10% on imported goods⟩ — see TAX

impossible *adj* incapable of being solved or accomplished ⟨the seemingly *impossible* problem of world hunger⟩ ⟨Fitting everything in my backpack seemed an *impossible* task.⟩

synonyms hopeless, insoluble, insuperable, unattainable, unsolvable

related words impracticable, impractical, infeasible, unusable, unworkable; debatable, disputable, doubtable, doubtful, dubious, far-fetched, fishy, improbable, problematic (*also* problematical), questionable, shady, shaky, suspect, suspicious, unfeasible, unlikely; implausible, inconceivable, incredible, unbelievable, unimaginable, unthinkable; futile, useless; absurd, fantastic (*also* fantastical), outlandish, preposterous, ridiculous

near antonyms applicable, functional, practicable, practical, reasonable, serviceable, usable (*also* useable), useful, working; likely, probable; acceptable, believable, conceivable, credible, plausible

antonyms achievable, attainable, doable, feasible, possible, realizable, resolvable, soluble, workable

impost *n* a charge usually of money collected by the government from people or businesses for public use ⟨Consumers steadfastly resisted any *impost* on merchandise purchased over the Internet.⟩ — see TAX

impostor *or* **imposter** *n* one who makes false claims of identity or expertise ⟨The man who claimed to be a prince turned out to be an *impostor*.⟩

synonyms charlatan, fake, faker, fraud, hoaxer, humbug, mountebank, phony (*also* phoney), pretender, quack, ringer, sham

related words copycat, imitator, impersonator, mimic; actor, bluffer, counterfeiter, deceiver, dissembler, duper, feigner, misleader, operator, trickster; poseur; cozener, defrauder, dodger, sharper, sharpie (*or* sharpy), skinner, swindler

near antonyms ace, adept, authority, crackerjack (*also* crackajack), expert, maestro, master, past master, professional, virtuoso, whiz, wizard

impotence *n* the lack of sufficient ability, power, or means ⟨The congressional committee's essential *impotence* in exerting any influence was frustrating to its members.⟩ — see INABILITY

impotent *adj* **1** not able to produce fruit or offspring ⟨Most mules are *impotent*.⟩ — see STERILE 1

2 unable to act or achieve one's purpose ⟨an *impotent* ruler who was just a figurehead⟩ — see POWERLESS

impoverished *adj* **1** lacking money or material possessions ⟨the widespread hope that the lottery's record-setting jackpot is won by an *impoverished* family⟩ — see POOR 1

2 producing inferior or only a small amount of vegetation ⟨an *impoverished* field that over the years had been overgrazed⟩ — see BARREN 1

impoverishment *n* the state of lacking sufficient money or material possessions ⟨The gradual loss of manufacturing jobs plunged the area into a level of *impoverishment* it had never known.⟩ — see POVERTY 1

impracticable *adj* not capable of being put to use or account ⟨an *impracticable* plan for dealing with the bears seen roaming in the suburban neighborhood⟩ — see IMPRACTICAL

impractical *adj* not capable of being put to use or account ⟨The flimsy little toy shovel was cute, but completely *impractical* for digging up tree stumps.⟩

synonyms impracticable, inoperable, nonpractical, unusable, unworkable, useless

related words unsuitable; inaccessible, unattainable, unavailable, unobtainable, unreachable; dead, dormant, fallow, free, idle, inactive, inert, inoperative, latent; arrested, interrupted; unrealistic

near antonyms accessible, acquirable, available, obtainable, procurable, reachable; all-around (*also* all-round), handy; active, alive, busy, employed, functioning, operating, operative, running, working

antonyms applicable, feasible, functional, operable, operational, practicable, practical, serviceable, usable (*also* useable), useful, utilizable, workable

imprecate *vb* to ask a divine power to send harm or evil upon ⟨With her dying breath the witch *imprecated* the villagers for their relentless persecution of her.⟩ — see CURSE 1

imprecation *n* a prayer that harm will come to someone ⟨The defiant prisoner continued to hurl *imprecations* and insults at the guards.⟩ — see CURSE 1

imprecise *adj* not precisely correct ⟨3.14 is an *imprecise* approximation of the value of pi.⟩ — see INEXACT 1

impregnable *adj* **1** incapable of being defeated, overcome, or subdued ⟨an *impregnable* fortress that had foiled one invader after another over the centuries⟩ — see INVINCIBLE

2 impossible to get through or into ⟨the castle's supposedly *impregnable* walls⟩ — see IMPENETRABLE 1

impregnate *vb* to wet thoroughly with liquid ⟨*impregnated* the cloth with furniture polish⟩ — see SOAK 1

impress *n* a perceptible trace left by pressure ⟨The stamp left a smudgy *impress* on the paper.⟩ — see PRINT 1

impress *vb* **1** to act upon (a person or a person's feelings)

so as to cause a response ⟨The drummers *impressed* him with the intensity of their musical performance.⟩ — see ¹AFFECT 1

2 to produce a vivid impression of ⟨*impressed* the importance of safe driving habits by displaying photos of car accidents⟩ — see ENGRAVE 2

3 to cause (a person) to give in to pressure ⟨After weeks of nagging, they *impressed* her into going to the masquerade party.⟩ — see FORCE

impression *n* **1** a perceptible trace left by pressure ⟨a shoe *impression* in the dirt that could lead police to the culprit⟩ — see PRINT 1

2 something imagined or pictured in the mind ⟨I had a vague *impression* that the guide would be female.⟩ — see IDEA 1

impressionist *n* a person who imitates another's voice and mannerisms for comic effect ⟨a celebrated *impressionist* who can do enough rapid-fire imitations to populate an entire stage with characters⟩ — see MIMIC 1

impressive *adj* having the power to affect the feelings or sympathies ⟨an *impressive* play about a loving family attempting to lift themselves out of poverty⟩ — see MOVING

imprimatur *n* an acceptance of something as satisfactory ⟨We could not begin the project without the boss's *imprimatur*.⟩ — see APPROVAL

imprint *n* **1** a mark or series of marks left on a surface by something that has passed along it ⟨found an *imprint* on the road where something apparently had been dragged⟩ — see TRACK 1

2 a perceptible trace left by pressure ⟨an *imprint* of a dinosaur's foot embedded in the limestone⟩ — see PRINT 1

imprint *vb* to produce a vivid impression of ⟨That early lesson on the value of honesty permanently *imprinted* itself on my mind.⟩ — see ENGRAVE 2

imprison *vb* to put in or as if in prison ⟨In this society, we try to *imprison* criminals so that they can't do any more harm.⟩

synonyms commit, confine, immure, incarcerate, intern, jail, jug, lock (up)

related words constrain, limit, restrain, restrict, shut; bar, gate; apprehend, arrest, bust [*slang*], capture, catch, detain, nab, pick up, pinch, seize; impress, shanghai; hold, impound, keep; bind, enchain, fetter, handcuff, manacle, shackle, trammel

near antonyms emancipate, enfranchise, manumit, unbind, uncage, unchain, unfetter

antonyms discharge, free, liberate, release

imprisoned *adj* taken and held prisoner ⟨took up the cause of *imprisoned* political dissidents⟩ — see CAPTIVE

imprisonment *n* the act of confining or the state of being confined ⟨The offense is punishable by a fine or *imprisonment*.⟩ — see INTERNMENT

improbable *adj* not likely to be true or to occur ⟨It seems *improbable* that the two writers never met since they traveled in the same social circles.⟩

synonyms doubtful, dubious, far-fetched, flimsy, questionable, unapt, unlikely

related words implausible, impossible, inconceivable, incredible, unbelievable, unimaginable, unthinkable; absurd, bizarre, fantastic (*also* fantastical), foolish, nonsensical, odd, outlandish, preposterous, ridiculous, unreal, wild; outside, remote, slight

near antonyms believable, conceivable, credible, earthly, imaginable, plausible; possible, potential; liable

antonyms likely, probable

impromptu *adj* made or done without previous thought or preparation ⟨Our dinner guest thanked us with an *impromptu* song.⟩ — see EXTEMPORANEOUS

improper *adj* not appropriate for a particular occasion or situation ⟨an *improper* use of slang in a formal piece of writing⟩ — see INAPPROPRIATE

improperly *adv* in a mistaken or inappropriate way ⟨The manufacturer's warranty is no longer valid if the appliance is used *improperly*.⟩ — see WRONGLY

impropriety *n* **1** the quality or state of not being socially proper ⟨The *impropriety* of the song that the campers sang for the visitors was embarrassing.⟩
synonyms inappropriateness, incorrectness, indecency, indelicateness
related words coarseness, crudeness, vulgarity; immodesty, naughtiness; imprudence, indiscreetness, indiscretion; churlishness, discourteousness, disrespect, impertinence, impoliteness, impudence, incivility, inconsiderateness, inconsideration, insolence, rudeness, ungraciousness
near antonyms discretion, prudence; etiquette, form, manners, proprieties; considerateness, consideration, gentility, graciousness, thoughtfulness
antonyms appropriateness, correctness, decency, decorousness, decorum, fitness, propriety, rightness, seemliness, suitability, suitableness
2 a socially improper or unsuitable act or remark ⟨such *improprieties* as asking people how much money they make⟩
synonyms familiarity, gaff, gaffe, indiscretion, solecism
related words blunder, error, flub, fumble, goof, lapse, miscue, misstep, mistake, oversight, slip, slipup, stumble; discourtesy, incivility, offense (*or* offence); foul-up, muff; misapprehension, misconception, misjudgment, misstatement, misunderstanding
near antonyms form, manners, mores, proprieties
antonyms amenity, attention, civility, courtesy, formality, gesture, pleasantry
3 the quality or state of being unsuitable or unfitting ⟨I see no *impropriety* in referring to certain anatomical parts by their standard names.⟩ — see INAPPROPRIATENESS 1

improve *vb* to make better ⟨A little salt would *improve* this bland food.⟩
synonyms ameliorate, amend, better, enhance, enrich, help, meliorate, perfect, refine, upgrade
related words correct, emend, rectify, reform, remediate, remedy; edit, fine-tune, redraft, refurbish, rehab, rehabilitate, revamp, revise, rework; beef (up), boost, fortify, intensify, strengthen; fine, hone, polish; retouch, touch up; sweeten
near antonyms damage, harm, hurt, impair, injure, spoil, tarnish, vitiate; blemish, deface, disfigure, flaw, mar; diminish, lessen, lower, reduce
antonyms worsen

improved *adj* being far along in development ⟨An *improved* version of the software is now available.⟩ — see ADVANCED

improvement *n* an instance of notable progress in the development of knowledge, technology, or skill ⟨There's been a great *improvement* in your handwriting.⟩ — see ADVANCE 2

improvident *adj* not thinking about and providing for the future ⟨the *improvident* view that you don't need to save for retirement⟩
synonyms myopic, shortsighted
related words careless, heedless, imprudent, incautious, injudicious, mindless, unguarded, unsafe, unwary, unwise; extravagant, prodigal, profligate, spendthrift, thriftless, unthrifty; indulgent, lavish, reckless, wasteful
near antonyms careful, judicious, prudent, sensible, wise; economical, economizing, frugal, scrimping, sparing, thrifty; conserving, preserving, saving
antonyms farsighted, forehanded, foreseeing, foresighted, forethoughtful, provident

improvise *vb* to perform, make, or do without preparation ⟨Since the award was a complete surprise, I *improvised* an acceptance speech.⟩
synonyms ad-lib, extemporize, fake
related words concoct, contrive, cook (up), devise, fabricate, hatch, invent, make up, manufacture, think (up); dash (off)
near antonyms arrange, lay, prepare, ready; consider, contemplate, ponder, study; exercise, practice (*also* practise), rehearse

improvised *adj* made or done without previous thought or preparation ⟨stumbled through an *improvised* reply to an unexpected question at the press conference⟩ — see EXTEMPORANEOUS

imprudent *adj* showing poor judgment especially in personal relationships or social situations ⟨a very sweet girl, but so *imprudent* that no one trusts her with a secret⟩ — see INDISCREET

impudence *n* **1** disrespectful or argumentative talk given in response to a command or request ⟨My mother would not tolerate *impudence* from any of us.⟩ — see BACK TALK
2 rude behavior ⟨Their *impudence* irritated everyone at the wedding reception.⟩ — see DISCOURTESY

impudent *adj* displaying or marked by rude boldness ⟨the guest's *impudent* inquiries about the cost of just about everything we had in the house⟩ — see NERVY 1

impulse *n* **1** something that arouses action or activity ⟨The new auto factory was just the *impulse* that the local economy needed.⟩
synonyms boost, encouragement, goad, impetus, incentive, incitement, instigation, momentum, motivation, provocation, spur, stimulant, stimulus, yeast
related words inducement, invitation; antecedent, cause, consideration, grounds, motive, occasion, reason; catalyst, catalyzer, fuel, spark
phrases shot in the arm
antonyms counterincentive, disincentive
2 a habitual attraction to some activity or thing ⟨the universal, fundamental *impulse* of self-preservation⟩ — see INCLINATION 1

impulsive *adj* **1** caused by or suggestive of an irresistible urge ⟨an *impulsive* purchase of a very expensive jacket⟩ — see COMPULSIVE
2 prone to sudden illogical changes of mind, ideas, or actions ⟨He's *impulsive* and often does things he later regrets.⟩ — see WHIMSICAL

impulsiveness *n* an inclination to sudden illogical changes of mind, ideas, or actions ⟨His irrepressible *impulsiveness* sometimes got him into trouble.⟩ — see WHIMSICALITY

impunity *n* freedom from punishment, harm, or loss ⟨She mistakenly believed that she could insult people with *impunity*.⟩
synonyms exemption, immunity
related words aegis (*also* egis), armor, cover, defense, guard, protection, safeguard, safety, security, shield; buffer, bumper, screen; absolution, absolving, dispensation, forgiveness
near antonyms exposure, liability, openness, susceptibility, susceptibleness, vulnerability

impure *adj* **1** containing foreign or lower-grade substances ⟨Be careful, because *impure* motor oil can damage your car's engine.⟩
synonyms adulterate, adulterated, alloyed, contaminated, dilute, diluted, polluted, tainted, thinned, weakened
related words unclarified, unfiltered, unrefined; besmirched, corrupted, debased, defiled, dirtied, fouled, soiled, spoiled, sullied; blended, commingled, incorporated, intermingled, intermixed, merged, mingled, mixed;

coalesced, combined, compounded; cheapened, doctored

near antonyms clarified, filtered, purified, refined, ultrarefined; neat, plain, straight; concentrated, strong; uncombined; pasteurized; sterile, sterilized; clean, immaculate, spotless, stainless, unsoiled, unsullied

antonyms fine, pure, ultrapure, unadulterated, unalloyed, uncontaminated, uncut, undiluted, unmixed, unpolluted, untainted

2 depicting or referring to sexual matters in a way that is unacceptable in polite society ⟨sorry for his *impure* remarks⟩ — see OBSCENE 1

impurity *n* **1** something that is or that makes impure ⟨*Impurities* in the water made it cloudy.⟩

synonyms adulterant, contaminant, defilement, pollutant
related words blot, blotch, spot, stain, taint; dirt, filth, grime, muck, scum, sludge, smut, soil; blemish, defect, disfigurement, fault, flaw; abnormality, imperfection, irregularity
near antonyms clarifier, filter, purifier, refiner; cleanliness, immaculateness, purity

2 the quality or state of being obscene ⟨the *impurity* of the song's lyrics⟩ — see OBSCENITY

impute *vb* to explain (something) as being the result of something else ⟨People often *impute* his silence to unfriendliness and not to the shyness it really represents.⟩ — see CREDIT 1

in *adj* **1** being in the latest or current fashion ⟨the *in* hairstyle this spring⟩ — see STYLISH
2 enjoying widespread favor or approval ⟨The *in* thing to do is not always the right thing to do.⟩ — see POPULAR 1
3 being within the confines of a specified place ⟨The doctor isn't *in* right now.⟩ — see PRESENT 2

in *adv* at, within, or to a short distance or time ⟨The fielders closed *in*.⟩ — see NEAR 1

in *n* the power to direct the thinking or behavior of others usually indirectly ⟨Her years of experience with the federal regulatory agency gives her a tremendous *in* as a lobbyist for the nuclear power industry.⟩ — see INFLUENCE 1

in *prep* using the means or agency of ⟨drawn on the wall *in* crayon⟩ — see BY 2

inability *n* the lack of sufficient ability, power, or means ⟨the apparent *inability* of some young children to sit still⟩
synonyms impotence, inadequacy, incapability, incapacity, incompetence, ineptitude, insufficiency, powerlessness
related words disqualification, inaptitude; ineffectiveness, inefficacy, ineffectualness, inefficaciousness, inefficacy, inefficiency
near antonyms aptitude, bent, endowment, flair, genius, gift, knack, talent; effectiveness, effectualness, efficaciousness, efficiency; fitness, suitability, suitableness; potency, power, puissance, sinew, strength
antonyms ability, adequacy, capability, capacity, competence, competency, potency

inaccessible *adj* hard or impossible to get to or get at ⟨The area is *inaccessible* by car.⟩
synonyms inconvenient, unapproachable, unattainable, unavailable, unobtainable, unreachable, untouchable
related words away, distant, far, faraway, far-off, remote, removed; apart, isolated, out-of-the-way, secluded
near antonyms close, immediate, near, nearby, neighboring, next-door, nigh
antonyms accessible, acquirable, approachable, attainable, convenient, getatable, handy, obtainable, procurable, reachable

inaccuracy *n* an unintentional departure from truth or accuracy ⟨an unfortunate *inaccuracy* in the report⟩ — see ERROR 1

inaccurate *adj* **1** not being in agreement with what is true ⟨He claimed that the TV ratings were *inaccurate* because they didn't take into account all those viewers in health clubs.⟩ — see FALSE 1
2 not precisely correct ⟨The estimate is *inaccurate*, but will do for our purposes.⟩ — see INEXACT 1

inaccurately *adv* in a mistaken or inappropriate way ⟨*inaccurately* reported that she was absent that day⟩ — see WRONGLY

inaction *n* lack of action or activity ⟨As a result of the park department's *inaction*, the city's pools are not ready to open for the summer.⟩
synonyms dormancy, idleness, inactivity, inertness, nonaction, quiescence
related words indolence, inertia, languor, lassitude, laziness, listlessness, shiftlessness, sleepiness, sloth, sluggishness; dallying, loafing, lolling, lounging
near antonyms animateness, briskness, exuberance, jazziness, liveliness, peppiness, robustness, sprightliness, vibrancy, vivacity; assiduity, assiduousness, business, diligence, employment, industriousness, industry, occupation
antonyms action, activeness, activity

inactive *adj* **1** slow to move or act ⟨It's easiest to catch snakes early in the morning, while they're still cold and *inactive*.⟩
synonyms dull, inert, lethargic, quiescent, sleepy, sluggish, torpid
related words ambitionless, apathetic, indolent, languorous, lazy, lazyish, listless, shiftless, slack, slothful, sluggard, sluggardly; dormant, motionless, resting, sedentary, static, still; dead; dopey (*also* dopy), drugged, asleep, drowsy, somnambulant
near antonyms busy, engaged, occupied, working; animated, bouncing, dynamic, energetic, lively, peppy, perky, spirited, sprightly, springy, vigorous, vital, vivacious, zippy; assiduous, diligent, hardworking, industrious, sedulous
antonyms active

2 not being in a state of use, activity, or employment ⟨an *inactive* oil well⟩
synonyms dead, dormant, fallow, free, idle, inert, inoperative, latent, off, unused, vacant
related words abeyant, arrested, interrupted; unoccupied; asleep, lifeless, moribund, quiescent, sleepy; inoperable, unusable, unworkable, useless; dull, slow
phrases at rest, on the shelf, out of commission
near antonyms functional, operable, operational, workable; assiduous, industrious, sedulous; energetic, vigorous; feasible, practical, usable (*also* useable), useful, viable
antonyms active, alive, busy, employed, functioning, going, living, on, operating, operative, running, working

inactivity *n* **1** lack of action or activity ⟨The *inactivity* outside the school led me to think that it must have been vacation week.⟩ — see INACTION
2 lack of use ⟨After weeks of *inactivity*, the car wouldn't start.⟩ — see DISUSE

inadequacy *n* **1** a falling short of an essential or desirable amount or number ⟨The *inadequacy* of our servings was soon apparent, as hungry guests started clamoring for seconds.⟩ — see DEFICIENCY
2 the lack of sufficient ability, power, or means ⟨He tried to blame others in order to hide the *inadequacy* of his leadership.⟩ — see INABILITY

inadequate *adj* not coming up to an expected measure or meeting a particular need ⟨an *inadequate* amount of food on hand for so many unexpected guests⟩ — see SHORT 3

inadequately *adv* in an unsatisfactory way ⟨She did the job quickly, but *inadequately*.⟩ — see BADLY 1

inadvertent *adj* happening by chance ⟨an *inadvertent* encounter with a snake in the brush⟩ — see ACCIDENTAL 1

inadvisable *adj* showing poor judgment especially in personal relationships or social situations ⟨It's *inadvisable* to have public arguments in the hallways.⟩ — see INDISCREET

inane *adj* having no meaning ⟨*inane* and useless phrases⟩ — see MEANINGLESS

inanity *n* **1** a foolish act or idea ⟨Pam quickly realized that her suggestion was an *inanity* and withdrew it.⟩ — see FOLLY 1
2 lack of good sense or judgment ⟨the *inanity* of the winner's comments on the awards show⟩ — see FOOLISHNESS 1

inapplicability *n* the quality or state of not having anything to do with the matter at hand ⟨The professor pointed out the *inapplicability* of the principle to the issue under discussion.⟩ — see IRRELEVANCE

inapplicable *adj* not having anything to do with the matter at hand ⟨The judge refused to allow mention of the defendant's conviction for shoplifting, ruling that it was *inapplicable* to the case at hand.⟩ — see IRRELEVANT

inappreciable *adj* not perceptible by a sense or by the mind ⟨an *inappreciable* change in the temperature⟩ — see IMPERCEPTIBLE

inappropriate *adj* not appropriate for a particular occasion or situation ⟨He wore casual clothes that were *inappropriate* for the interview.⟩
synonyms amiss, graceless, improper, inapt, incongruous, incorrect, indecorous, inept, infelicitous, perverse, unapt, unbecoming, unfit, unhappy, unseemly, unsuitable, untoward, wrong
related words inopportune, unfortunate, unseasonable, untimely; extraneous, immaterial, inapplicable, irrelative, irrelevant; misbecoming, mismatched; incompatible, inconsistent, uncongenial; banned, barred, disallowed; forbidden, interdicted, outlawed, prohibited, proscribed; awkward, gauche, ungraceful; unacceptable, unsatisfactory
phrases out of place, out of the way
near antonyms fortunate, opportune, seasonable, timely; applicable, apposite, apropos, apt, germane, material, pat, pointed, relative, relevant; compatible, congenial, harmonious; allowed, authorized, permitted; approved, endorsed (*also* indorsed), kosher, licensed, sanctioned; abetted, encouraged, promoted, supported; acceptable, adequate, all right, decent, fine, OK (*or* okay), passable, respectable, satisfactory, tolerable; balanced, companionate, congruous, consonant, harmonious
antonyms appropriate, becoming, befitting, correct, decorous, felicitous, fit, fitting, genteel, happy, meet, proper, right, seemly, suitable

inappropriately *adv* in a mistaken or inappropriate way ⟨We were dressed *inappropriately* for the event.⟩ — see WRONGLY

inappropriateness *n* **1** the quality or state of being unsuitable or unfitting ⟨I was angered by the *inappropriateness* of his comments.⟩
synonyms impropriety, inaptness, incorrectness, infelicity, unfitness, wrongness
related words extraneousness, inadequacy, inadmissibility, inapplicability, irrelevance, meaninglessness, pointlessness, senselessness; inauspiciousness, inexpedience, inexpediency, intolerability, undesirability, undesirableness, unsatisfactoriness, uselessness; unbecomingness
near antonyms admissibility, applicability, bearing, connection, materiality, pertinence, pointedness, relevance, relevancy

antonyms appropriateness, aptness, correctness, felicitousness, felicity, fitness, fittingness, propriety, rightness, seemliness, suitability, suitableness
2 the quality or state of not being socially proper ⟨The *inappropriateness* of belching in a restaurant should have been apparent to you.⟩ — see IMPROPRIETY 1

inapt *adj* **1** not appropriate for a particular occasion or situation ⟨an *inapt* but well-meaning attempt to inject some humor into the proceedings⟩ — see INAPPROPRIATE
2 lacking qualities (as knowledge, skill, or ability) required to do a job ⟨I feel *inapt* for the job, but I'll do my best.⟩ — see INCOMPETENT

inaptly *adv* in a mistaken or inappropriate way ⟨The development was *inaptly* named Apple Orchard Condominiums, presumably in honor of what was destroyed in order to build them.⟩ — see WRONGLY

inaptness *n* the quality or state of being unsuitable or unfitting ⟨The *inaptness* of the festive outfit made her stand out among the somberly dressed mourners.⟩ — see INAPPROPRIATENESS 1

inarticulate *adj* unable to speak ⟨The news rendered people *inarticulate* with surprise.⟩ — see MUTE 1

inasmuch as *conj* for the reason that ⟨You should not use that source, *inasmuch as* it is badly out-of-date.⟩ — see SINCE

inaugural *adj* coming before all others in time or order ⟨the *inaugural* event in the city's week long festival honoring the sailing ships⟩ — see FIRST 1

inaugural *n* the process or an instance of being formally placed in an office or organization ⟨attended the *inaugurals* of the city's last three mayors⟩ — see INSTALLATION 1

inaugurate *vb* **1** to be responsible for the creation and early operation or use of ⟨*inaugurated* the college's environmental studies program⟩ — see FOUND
2 to put into an office or welcome into an organization with special ceremonies ⟨The president *inaugurated* the newest member of the club with a welcoming speech.⟩ — see INSTALL 1

inauguration *n* the process or an instance of being formally placed in an office or organization ⟨the pomp and circumstance of a presidential *inauguration*⟩ — see INSTALLATION 1

inaugurator *n* a person who establishes a whole new field of endeavor ⟨the famed *inaugurator* of the assembly line in the production of automobiles⟩ — see FATHER 2

inauspicious *adj* being or showing a sign of evil or calamity to come ⟨This many problems so early in the project is a most *inauspicious* sign.⟩ — see OMINOUS

inauthentic *adj* being such in appearance only and made or manufactured with the intention of committing fraud ⟨an *inauthentic* fossil that was probably made in a factory a few months ago⟩ — see COUNTERFEIT 1

inborn *adj* **1** being a part of the innermost nature of a person or thing ⟨an *inborn* talent for dancing⟩ — see INHERENT
2 genetically passed or capable of being passed from parent to offspring ⟨Certain instincts are *inborn* in mice.⟩ — see HEREDITARY

inbred *adj* being a part of the innermost nature of a person or thing ⟨an *inbred* desire to do good in the world⟩ — see INHERENT

incandescence *n* the steady giving off of the form of radiation that makes vision possible ⟨Candles made from whale oil were once highly prized because they burned with an *incandescence* superior to that of other candles.⟩ — see LIGHT 1

incandescent *adj* **1** giving off or reflecting much light ⟨sitting in darkness, except for the *incandescent* coals of our campfire⟩ — see BRIGHT 1

2 having or expressing great depth of feeling ⟨a speaker *incandescent* with righteous anger⟩ — see FERVENT 1

incantation *n* a spoken word or set of words believed to have magic power ⟨ritual prayers and *incantations*⟩ — see SPELL 1

incapability *n* the lack of sufficient ability, power, or means ⟨the *incapability* of some birds to fly⟩ — see INABILITY

incapable *adj* lacking qualities (as knowledge, skill, or ability) required to do a job ⟨The workers were *incapable* of working fast enough to keep up with the schedule.⟩ — see INCOMPETENT

incapacitate *vb* **1** to render powerless, ineffective, or unable to move ⟨The malfunctioning of a single component can *incapacitate* the engine.⟩ — see PARALYZE 1
2 to cause severe or permanent injury to ⟨The stroke left her completely *incapacitated*.⟩ — see MAIM

incapacity *n* the lack of sufficient ability, power, or means ⟨His *incapacity* for working with numbers doesn't make him a good choice for class treasurer.⟩ — see INABILITY

incarcerate *vb* to put in or as if in prison ⟨The state *incarcerated* over 1900 people last year.⟩ — see IMPRISON

incarcerated *adj* taken and held prisoner ⟨*Incarcerated* residents of that state are still allowed to vote in elections.⟩ — see CAPTIVE

incarceration *n* the act of confining or the state of being confined ⟨He was bored and frustrated by his *incarceration* in the quarantine.⟩ — see INTERNMENT

incarnate *vb* to represent in visible form ⟨the general view that Hitler *incarnated* extreme egotism and indeed evil itself⟩ — see EMBODY 2

incarnation *n* a visible representation of something abstract (as a quality) ⟨She is the very *incarnation* of grace and tactfulness.⟩ — see EMBODIMENT

incautious *adj* not paying or showing close attention especially for the purpose of avoiding trouble ⟨An *incautious* comment got her in political hot water.⟩ — see CARELESS 1

incautiousness *n* failure to take the care that a cautious person usually takes ⟨A mere moment of *incautiousness* can cause an accident.⟩ — see NEGLIGENCE 1

incendiary *n* **1** a person who deliberately and unlawfully sets fire to a building or other property ⟨Firefighters caught the *incendiary*, who was watching the effects of his handiwork.⟩ — see ARSONIST
2 a person who stirs up public feelings especially of discontent ⟨Officials blamed the protests on outside *incendiaries* who were intent on discrediting the government.⟩ — see AGITATOR

incense *n* a sweet or pleasant smell ⟨the heavenly *incense* of spring flowers⟩ — see FRAGRANCE

¹**incense** *vb* to make angry ⟨The insult so *incensed* him that he refused to ever be friends again.⟩ — see ANGER

²**incense** *vb* to fill or infuse with a pleasant odor or odor-releasing substance ⟨The gift shop was heavily *incensed* with a cloying mixture of herbal essences.⟩ — see SCENT 1

incensed *adj* feeling or showing anger ⟨*Incensed* customers demanded that the charges be removed from their bills.⟩ — see ANGRY

incentive *n* something that arouses action or activity ⟨The handsome reward for the missing dog was an *incentive* for me to start looking.⟩ — see IMPULSE 1

inception *n* the point at which something begins ⟨This seemed like a good program at its *inception*, but it isn't working out as planned.⟩ — see BEGINNING

incertitude *n* a feeling or attitude that one does not know the truth, truthfulness, or trustworthiness of someone or something ⟨a growing *incertitude* about the accuracy of the study⟩ — see DOUBT

incessant *adj* going on and on without any interruptions

⟨The *incessant* noise from an outside repair crew was a real distraction during the test.⟩ — see CONTINUOUS

incessantly *adv* on every relevant occasion ⟨She *incessantly* made the same suggestion for a theme whenever anyone mentioned having a party.⟩ — see ALWAYS 1

inch *n* **1** a very small distance or degree ⟨Give them an *inch*, and they'll take a mile!⟩ — see HAIR 1
2 an individual part of a process, series, or ranking ⟨*Inch* by inch, we're making progress toward our fund-raising goal.⟩ — see DEGREE 1
3 inches *pl* the distance of something or someone from bottom to top ⟨made the most of her *inches* by standing on her tiptoes to reach the top shelf⟩ — see HEIGHT 3

inch *vb* **1** to advance gradually beyond the usual or desirable limits ⟨Every year the water *inches* further up the embankments, threatening to permanently engulf the island city.⟩ — see ENCROACH
2 to move slowly ⟨The car *inched* carefully across the snow-covered causeway.⟩ — see CRAWL 2

incident *n* something that happens ⟨The odd little *incident* was reported in the local paper.⟩ — see EVENT 1

incidental *adj* **1** happening by chance ⟨an *incidental* meeting of two ships in the middle of the Atlantic⟩ — see ACCIDENTAL 1
2 lacking importance ⟨We still have to work out a few *incidental* details, but the proposal is largely complete.⟩ — see UNIMPORTANT

incipiency *n* the point at which something begins ⟨From its *incipiency* the city's monthlong festival of the performing arts has been a great success.⟩ — see BEGINNING

incise *vb* **1** to cut (as letters or designs) on a hard surface ⟨*incised* a pattern into the copper plate⟩ — see ENGRAVE 1
2 to penetrate with a sharp edge (as a knife) ⟨*incised* the tree with a sharp ax to get the sap flowing⟩ — see CUT 1

incision *n* a long deep cut ⟨The surgeon made a thin *incision* with the scalpel.⟩ — see GASH

incite *vb* **1** to bring (something volatile or intense) into being ⟨He was arrested for *inciting* a riot.⟩
    synonyms abet, brew, ferment, foment, instigate, pick, provoke, raise, stir (up), whip (up)
    related words advance, cultivate, encourage, forward, foster, further, nourish, nurture, promote, sow, stimulate; detonate, set, set off, trigger; excite, galvanize, inflame (*also* enflame), inspire, motivate, rouse; activate, energize, enliven, fire, invigorate, jazz (up), liven (up), pep (up), quicken, stimulate, vitalize
    phrases set in motion
    near antonyms bridle, check, constrain, curb, discourage, hold, inhibit, regulate, rein (in), restrain, tame; allay, calm, quiet, settle, soothe, still, subdue, tranquilize (*also* tranquillize)
2 to rouse to strong feeling or action ⟨The demagogue's fiery rant *incited* the crowd to become violent.⟩ — see PROVOKE 1

incitement *n* **1** something that arouses a strong response from another ⟨The news was an *incitement* of fear and paranoia.⟩ — see PROVOCATION 1
2 something that arouses action or activity ⟨The approaching deadline was certainly an *incitement* to get going on the assignment.⟩ — see IMPULSE 1

inciter *n* a person who stirs up public feelings especially of discontent ⟨The governor warned that *inciters* of mob violence would be dealt with harshly.⟩ — see AGITATOR

inciting *adj* serving or likely to arouse a strong reaction ⟨a deliberately *inciting* comment questioning someone's patriotism⟩ — see PROVOCATIVE

incivility *n* rude behavior ⟨I won't tolerate *incivility*, and that includes text messaging while I'm speaking.⟩ — see DISCOURTESY

inclement *adj* marked by wet and windy conditions ⟨The weather report warned that the holiday weekend would be spoiled by *inclement* weather.⟩ — see FOUL 1

inclination *n* **1** a habitual attraction to some activity or thing ⟨her natural *inclination* to help people in need⟩
synonyms affection, affinity, aptitude, bent, bias, bone, devices, disposition, genius, impulse, leaning, partiality, penchant, predilection, predisposition, proclivity, propensity, tendency, turn
related words favor, one-sidedness, partisanship, prejudice; endowment, faculty, flair, genius, gift, knack, talent; appetite, fancy, fondness, like, liking, preference, taste; forte, speciality, specialty; convention, custom, habit, pattern, practice (*also* practise), routine, trick, way, wont; eccentricity, idiosyncrasy, oddity, peculiarity, quirk, singularity
near antonyms allergy, averseness, aversion, disfavor, disinclination, dislike, disliking, distaste; detachment, impartiality, neutrality, objectivity; apathy, disinterestedness, indifference, insouciance, nonchalance, unconcern
2 the act of positioning or an instance of being positioned at an angle ⟨The photographer adjusted the *inclination* of the subject's head.⟩ — see TILT
3 the degree to which something rises up from a position level with the horizon ⟨The *inclination* of the hill is gentle, so walking up it isn't too bad.⟩ — see SLANT 1

incline *n* the degree to which something rises up from a position level with the horizon ⟨The steep *incline* of the hill meant that it was impossible to ride a bicycle up it.⟩ — see SLANT 1

incline *vb* **1** to set or cause to be at an angle ⟨carefully *inclined* the ladder against the house⟩ — see LEAN 1
2 to show a liking or proneness (for something) ⟨a good restaurant for diners who *incline* to spicy food⟩ — see LEAN 2

inclined *adj* **1** having a desire or inclination (as for a specified course of action) ⟨We couldn't have convinced him if he weren't already so *inclined*.⟩ — see WILLING 1
2 having a liking or affection ⟨a performer strictly for those *inclined* towards loud music⟩ — see FOND 1
3 having a tendency to be or act in a certain way ⟨a kindly couple who are *inclined* to be helpful to strangers⟩ — see PRONE 1
4 running in a slanting direction ⟨The highway ramps and other *inclined* roadways were treacherous during the ice storm.⟩ — see DIAGONAL

inclining *adj* bending downward or forward ⟨The *inclining* branches of the evergreens seemed almost ready to break under the weight of the heavy snow.⟩ — see NODDING

include *vb* **1** to have as part of a whole ⟨The college application *included* some thought-provoking essay questions.⟩
synonyms carry, comprehend, contain, embrace, encompass, entail, involve, number, subsume, take in
related words comprise, consist (of); bracket; have, hold, own, possess; admit; compose, constitute, form, make; assimilate, embody, incorporate, integrate
near antonyms ban, bar, debar, preclude, prevent, prohibit; deny, refuse, reject; eliminate, except, rule out; lose, mislay, misplace
antonyms exclude, leave (out), omit
2 to close or shut in by or as if by barriers ⟨that inextinguishable spark of liberty that is *included* within every human being⟩ — see ENCLOSE 1

inclusive *adj* covering everything or all important points ⟨a butterfly expert with an *inclusive* knowledge of his subject⟩ — see ENCYCLOPEDIC

inclusively *adv* with everyone or everything taken into account at the same time ⟨For the complete body makeover, a week at the spa costs, *inclusively*, $10,000.⟩ — see ALL AROUND

incognito *adj* not named or identified by a name ⟨An *incognito* source in the CIA was the source of the information.⟩ — see NAMELESS 1

incoherent *adj* **1** not clearly or logically connected ⟨The thriller's *incoherent* plot left movie audiences wondering who did what.⟩
synonyms choppy, disconnected, disjointed, unconnected
related words baffling, bewildering, confounding, confused, confusing, disordered, disorderly, disorganized, muddled, perplexing, puzzling, unorganized; disconcerting, frustrating; fallacious, illogical, inconsistent, invalid, irrational, unsound; absurd, asinine, bizarre, curious, eccentric, foolish, odd, outlandish, outré, peculiar, screwy, strange, unreasonable, unusual, weird; inexplicable, unaccountable, unexplainable
near antonyms ordered, orderly, organized, systematic, systematized; logical, rational, reasonable, sensible, solid, sound, valid; cogent, compelling, convincing, persuasive, plausible, satisfying; clear, clear-cut, lucid, perspicuous, transparent, unambiguous, unequivocal, unmistakable
antonyms coherent, connected
2 consisting of particles that do not stick together ⟨a driveway covered with *incoherent* gravel⟩ — see LOOSE 2

incombustible *adj* incapable of being burned ⟨We keep our important papers in an *incombustible* safe in the basement.⟩
synonyms fireproof, noncombustible, nonflammable, noninflammable
related words nonexplosive
near antonyms ablaze, afire, aflame, blazing, burning, combusting, fiery, flaming, ignited, inflamed (*also* enflamed), kindled; consumable; explosive, incendiary, volcanic
antonyms burnable, combustible, flammable, ignitable (*also* ignitible), inflammable

income *n* **1** an increase usually measured in money that comes from labor, business, or property ⟨Her summer job gave her some extra *income*.⟩
synonyms earnings, gain(s), proceeds, profit, return, revenue, yield
related words windfall; salary, take-home pay, tips, wages; bankroll, capital, finances, funds, money, pocket, pocketbook, resources, wherewithal
near antonyms charge, cost, disbursement, expenditures, expenses, outgo, outlay
2 a flowing or coming in ⟨The *income* of matériel is still hampered by inadequate logistical support.⟩ — see INFLUX

incommode *vb* to cause discomfort to or trouble for ⟨The innkeepers tried to hide how much the request *incommoded* them.⟩ — see INCONVENIENCE

incommoding *adj* causing difficulty, discomfort, or annoyance ⟨such *incommoding* features of air travel as flight delays and time-consuming security screenings⟩ — see INCONVENIENT 1

incommunicable *adj* beyond the power to describe ⟨The vastness of the universe is *incommunicable*.⟩ — see INDESCRIBABLE

incomparable *adj* having no equal or rival for excellence or desirability ⟨the *incomparable* jewel known as the Hope Diamond⟩ — see ONLY 1

incompatible *adj* not being in agreement or harmony ⟨The committee's *incompatible* goals—develop new projects and cut costs—meant that they got very little accomplished.⟩ — see INCONSISTENT 1

incompetence *n* the lack of sufficient ability, power, or means ⟨the astounding *incompetence* of the new assistant⟩ — see INABILITY

incompetent *adj* lacking qualities (as knowledge, skill, or ability) required to do a job ⟨An *incompetent* carpenter had built the deck, and the railings were loose already.⟩
synonyms inapt, incapable, inept, inexpert, unfit, unqualified, unskilled, unskillful
related words ineffective, ineffectual, inefficient; amateurish, callow, green, inexperienced, raw, unprofessional; unequipped, unprepared, untrained; useless, worthless; disqualified, ineligible; wanting
near antonyms prepared, ready, trained; overqualified; accomplished, ace, adept, consummate, crack, experienced, practiced (*also* practised), seasoned, veteran, virtuoso; all-around (*also* all-round), protean, versatile
antonyms able, capable, competent, expert, fit, qualified, skilled, skillful, ultracompetent
incomplete *adj* lacking some necessary part ⟨an *incomplete* puzzle that has several pieces missing⟩
synonyms deficient, fragmental, fragmentary, half, halfway, partial
related words broken, damaged, flawed, impaired, imperfect, injured, marred, spoiled; sketchy, unassembled, uncompleted, unfinished
near antonyms flawless, unbroken, undamaged, unimpaired, uninjured, unmarred; completed, finished
antonyms complete, entire, full, intact, integral, perfect, whole
incompletely *adv* in some measure or degree ⟨a physiological process that is *incompletely* understood at the present time⟩ — see PARTLY
incomprehensible *adj* impossible to understand ⟨Rocket science is *incomprehensible* to most people.⟩
synonyms impenetrable, unfathomable, unintelligible
related words abstruse, enigmatic (*also* enigmatical), esoteric, inscrutable, recondite, unsearchable; cryptic, darkling, deep, mysterious, mystic, oblique, obscure, occult, uncanny; unanswerable, unknowable; baffling, bewildering, confounding, confusing, mystifying, perplexing, puzzling; inconceivable, unimaginable, unthinkable
near antonyms basic, elemental, elementary, essential, fundamental, rudimentary, underlying; coherent, connected, ordered, orderly, organized, systematic, systematized; clear, cogent, compelling, convincing, lucid, pellucid, perspicuous, plain, straightforward
inconceivable *adj* too extraordinary or improbable to believe ⟨the formerly *inconceivable* idea that humans could land on the moon⟩ — see INCREDIBLE
incongruity *n* someone or something with qualities or features that seem to conflict with one another ⟨He is an *incongruity*: a sailor who doesn't know how to swim.⟩ — see CONTRADICTION 1
incongruous *adj* 1 not appropriate for a particular occasion or situation ⟨There's an *incongruous* modernism to the actor's performance in this period piece.⟩ — see INAPPROPRIATE
2 not being in agreement or harmony ⟨*incongruous* theories about the origins of matter⟩ — see INCONSISTENT 1
inconsequential *adj* 1 lacking importance ⟨That's an *inconsequential* problem compared to the other issues.⟩ — see UNIMPORTANT
2 so small or unimportant as to warrant little or no attention ⟨an *inconsequential* error that does nothing to lessen the value of the report⟩ — see NEGLIGIBLE 1
3 not using or following good reasoning ⟨an *inconsequential* line of argument that did little to further the prosecution's case⟩ — see ILLOGICAL
inconsiderable *adj* 1 lacking importance ⟨The duties of the club's vice president are *inconsiderable* by any standard.⟩ — see UNIMPORTANT
2 so small or unimportant as to warrant little or no atten-

tion ⟨an *inconsiderable* number of complaints about the car seat⟩ — see NEGLIGIBLE 1
inconsiderate *adj* showing a lack of manners or consideration for others ⟨She was *inconsiderate* by nature, never bothering to hold the door for the next person.⟩ — see IMPOLITE
inconsiderateness *n* rude behavior ⟨They were embarrassed by the *inconsiderateness* of their children.⟩ — see DISCOURTESY
inconsideration *n* rude behavior ⟨Fortunately, the *inconsideration* and self-centeredness of toddlers is eventually outgrown.⟩ — see DISCOURTESY
inconsistent *adj* 1 not being in agreement or harmony ⟨*Inconsistent* theories make it difficult to settle on one explanation.⟩
synonyms clashing, conflicting, disagreeing, discordant, discrepant, incompatible, incongruous, inharmonious, repugnant
related words irreconcilable; antagonistic, antipodal, antipodean, antithetical, contradictory, contrary, diametric (*or* diametrical), opposing, opposite
phrases at odds, at variance
near antonyms akin, like, similar
antonyms agreeing, compatible, concordant, conformable (to), congruous, consistent, consonant, correspondent (with *or* to), harmonious, nonconflicting
2 likely to change frequently, suddenly, or unexpectedly ⟨An *inconsistent* breeze was our only relief from the heat.⟩ — see FICKLE 1
inconsolable *adj* feeling unhappiness ⟨The child was *inconsolable* when his favorite stuffed animal was lost.⟩ — see SAD 1
inconspicuous *adj* not readily seen or noticed ⟨left an *inconspicuous* scratch on the wall⟩ — see UNOBTRUSIVE
inconstancy *n* 1 lack of faithfulness especially to one's husband or wife ⟨a medieval fable about the immorality of *inconstancy*⟩ — see INFIDELITY 1
2 the frequent and usually sudden passing from one condition to another ⟨The *inconstancy* of public opinion is such that today's hero may be tomorrow's punching bag.⟩ — see FLUX 1
inconstant *adj* 1 likely to change frequently, suddenly, or unexpectedly ⟨Our windjammer sailed wherever the *inconstant* winds took us.⟩ — see FICKLE 1
2 not true in one's allegiance to someone or something ⟨an *inconstant* but always entertaining friend⟩ — see FAITHLESS
incontestable *adj* not capable of being challenged or proved wrong ⟨the *incontestable* statement that every contest has a winner and a loser⟩ — see IRREFUTABLE
incontestably *adv* without any question ⟨You are *incontestably* correct that tomorrow is another day.⟩ — see INDEED 1
incontrovertible *adj* not capable of being challenged or proved wrong ⟨*incontrovertible* facts that left the jury with no choice but to convict⟩ — see IRREFUTABLE
incontrovertibly *adv* without any question ⟨an *incontrovertibly* accurate measurement of the height of the mountain⟩ — see INDEED 1
inconvenience *n* something that is a source of irritation ⟨the *inconvenience* of having to walk everywhere until the car is fixed⟩ — see ANNOYANCE 3
inconvenience *vb* to cause discomfort to or trouble for ⟨He *inconvenienced* his sister by moving into her tiny apartment.⟩
synonyms discommode, disoblige, disturb, incommode, put out, trouble
related words burden, encumber, saddle, weigh; fetter, hamper, hamstring, handicap, hinder, hobble, hold back,

hold up, impede, inhibit, interfere (with), manacle, obstruct, shackle, tie up, trammel; aggravate, anger, annoy, bother, bug, chafe, exasperate, gall, get, irk, nettle, peeve, pique, rile, vex; grate, inflame (*also* enflame), provoke; agitate, perturb, upset

near antonyms abet, aid, assist, help; ease, facilitate, smooth; appease, conciliate, disarm, mollify, pacify, placate; delight, gladden, gratify, please, satisfy; comfort, console, content

antonyms accommodate, favor, oblige

inconvenient *adj* **1** causing difficulty, discomfort, or annoyance ⟨The unexpected visitors showed up at an *inconvenient* time.⟩

synonyms awkward, discommoding, disobliging, incommoding

related words bothersome, burdensome, onerous, troublesome; annoying, disturbing, exasperating, frustrating, galling, irksome, irritating, maddening, riling, vexatious, vexing

near antonyms acceptable, bearable, endurable, sufferable, tolerable; advantageous, desirable, helpful

antonyms convenient, ultraconvenient

2 hard or impossible to get to or get at ⟨For some reason, the homeowners placed the dishes in an *inconvenient* cabinet.⟩ — see INACCESSIBLE

incorporate *vb* **1** to make a part of a body or system ⟨The school administrators decided to *incorporate* technology across the curriculum.⟩ — see EMBODY 1

2 to turn into a single mass or entity that is more or less the same throughout ⟨*incorporated* all the ingredients for the cheesecake mixture⟩ — see BLEND 1

3 to represent in visible form ⟨The one-of-a-kind house *incorporates* the architect's fundamental belief that a structure should be fully integrated into its setting.⟩ — see EMBODY 2

incorporeal *adj* not composed of matter ⟨Ghosts are supposed to be *incorporeal*.⟩ — see IMMATERIAL 1

incorrect *adj* **1** having an opinion that does not agree with truth or the facts ⟨You're *incorrect* about the date of the final exam—it's next Tuesday, not Wednesday.⟩

synonyms mistaken, wrong

related words confused, misguided, misinformed, misled; erroneous, false, inaccurate, inexact, untrue; deceived, deluded, duped, tricked

phrases all wet, full of it

near antonyms informed; accurate, exact, precise, true

antonyms correct, right

2 not appropriate for a particular occasion or situation ⟨chose the *incorrect* military uniform for the treaty ceremony⟩ — see INAPPROPRIATE

3 not being in agreement with what is true ⟨an *incorrect* but not intentionally deceitful statement⟩ — see FALSE 1

incorrectly *adv* in a mistaken or inappropriate way ⟨You *incorrectly* identified the part of speech of one of the words in the sentence.⟩ — see WRONGLY

incorrectness *n* **1** the quality or state of being unsuitable or unfitting ⟨No one cares about the *incorrectness* of your clothes—just come.⟩ — see INAPPROPRIATENESS 1

2 the quality or state of not being socially proper ⟨He's just a little kid and doesn't understand the *incorrectness* of what he said.⟩ — see IMPROPRIETY 1

incorrigible *adj* not capable of being cured or reformed ⟨an *incorrigible* criminal who will spend the rest of his life behind bars⟩ — see HOPELESS 1

increase *n* **1** something added (as by growth) ⟨Shortly after he turned 12, he had a sudden height *increase*.⟩

synonyms accretion, accrual, addendum, addition, augmentation, boost, expansion, gain, increment, more, plus, proliferation, raise, rise, supplement

related words accumulation, assemblage, collection, gathering; complement; continuation, extension, uptrend, upturn; jump, run-up, spike

near antonyms deduction, subtraction

antonyms abatement, decline, decrease, decrement, diminishment, diminution, fall, lessening, loss, lowering, reduction, shrinkage

2 the act or process of becoming greater in number ⟨The *increase* in the number of students enrolled at the school was very gradual.⟩ — see MULTIPLICATION

increase *vb* **1** to make greater in size, amount, or number ⟨We have to *increase* the number of season-ticket holders if the local sports franchise is to survive.⟩

synonyms accelerate, add (to), aggrandize, amplify, augment, boost, compound, enlarge, escalate, expand, extend, multiply, raise, swell, up

related words boom, jump, skyrocket, spike; bump (up), ratchet (up) *also* rachet (up); blow up, dilate, distend, inflate; draw out, elongate, flesh (out), lengthen, prolong, protract, stretch; develop, enhance, heighten, intensify, magnify; complement, supplement; beef (up), strengthen; maximize; accumulate, amass, collect; follow up, parlay

near antonyms abbreviate, abridge, curtail, shorten; compress, condense, constrict, contract; cut back, retrench

antonyms abate, decrease, de-escalate, diminish, downsize, dwindle, lessen, lower, minify, reduce, subtract (from)

2 to become greater in extent, volume, amount, or number ⟨Traffic delays *increased* because of the construction.⟩

synonyms accelerate, accumulate, appreciate, balloon, boom, burgeon (*also* bourgeon), climb, enlarge, escalate, expand, gain, mount, multiply, mushroom, proliferate, rise, snowball, spread, swell, wax

related words jump, rocket, skyrocket, surge; heighten, intensify, redouble; blow up, bulk, distend, inflate, puff (up); crest, peak

antonyms contract, decrease, diminish, dwindle, lessen, recede, wane

increased *adj* being at a higher level than average ⟨an *increased* concentration of sugar in the bloodstream⟩ — see HIGH 2

incredible *adj* too extraordinary or improbable to believe ⟨I find that an *incredible* coincidence.⟩

synonyms fantastic (*also* fantastical), implausible, inconceivable, incredulous, unbelievable, unconvincing, unimaginable, unthinkable

related words debatable, disputable, doubtable, doubtful, dubious, far-fetched, fishy, flimsy, questionable, shaky, suspect, suspicious, unlikely, unreasonable; hopeless, impossible; absurd, comical, farcical, laughable, ludicrous, outlandish, preposterous, ridiculous, risible, silly; indefensible, insupportable, untenable

phrases full of it

near antonyms likely, possible, probable; reasonable; certain, incontestable, indisputable, indubitable, questionless, sure, undeniable, undoubted, unquestionable

antonyms believable, cogitable, conceivable, convincing, credible, creditable, imaginable, plausible, supposable, thinkable

incredibly *adv* to a great degree ⟨The exam was *incredibly* difficult.⟩ — see VERY 1

incredulity *n* refusal to accept something as true ⟨The teacher's *incredulity* about the claims in the essay proved to be well-founded.⟩ — see DISBELIEF

incredulous *adj* **1** inclined to doubt or question claims ⟨*Incredulous* by nature, I'm of course very suspicious of anyone who claims to be able to communicate with the dead.⟩ — see SKEPTICAL 1

2 too extraordinary or improbable to believe ⟨an

incredulous account of alien abduction that the tabloids had a field day with⟩ — see INCREDIBLE

increment *n* something added (as by growth) ⟨added another big *increment* to the sales total this quarter⟩ — see INCREASE 1

incremental *adj* **1** proceeding or changing by steps or degrees ⟨the *incremental* changes to the company's business strategy⟩ — see GRADUAL

2 produced by a series of additions of identical or similar things ⟨the *incremental* total for my collection of baseball cards⟩ — see CUMULATIVE

incriminate *vb* to make a claim of wrongdoing against ⟨In exchange for a reduced sentence, the thief agreed to *incriminate* his accomplice.⟩ — see ACCUSE

incubate *vb* **1** to cover and warm eggs as the young inside develop ⟨The hen *incubated* her eggs for two weeks.⟩ — see SET 1

2 to help the growth or development of ⟨Hopefully, these youthful visits to the museum will *incubate* an enduring love of art.⟩ — see FOSTER 1

inculcate *vb* **1** to cause (as a person) to become filled or saturated with a certain quality or principle ⟨dedicated teachers *inculcating* young minds with a love of learning⟩ — see INFUSE

2 to set permanently in the consciousness or mind-set ⟨parents who *inculcated* in their offspring an abiding belief in giving back to the community⟩ — see IMPLANT 1

incumbent *adj* forcing one's compliance or participation by or as if by law ⟨It is *incumbent* upon you to attend every staff meeting.⟩ — see MANDATORY

incurable *adj* not capable of being cured or reformed ⟨an *incurable* know-it-all at work⟩ — see HOPELESS 1

incurious *adj* having or showing a lack of interest or concern ⟨a quick *incurious* glance at the pile of junk mail⟩ — see INDIFFERENT 1

incursion *n* a sudden attack on and entrance into hostile territory ⟨There were *incursions* from the border every summer.⟩ — see RAID 1

indebted *adj* being under obligation for a favor or gift ⟨thereafter forever felt *indebted* to the producer for giving her her lucky break⟩ — see BEHOLDEN

indecency *n* **1** the quality or state of being obscene ⟨Parents complained about the *indecency* of the movie's language.⟩ — see OBSCENITY

2 the quality or state of not being socially proper ⟨That a remark of such indisputable *indecency* was uttered at a meeting of the school board made everyone gasp.⟩ — see IMPROPRIETY 1

indecent *adj* depicting or referring to sexual matters in a way that is unacceptable in polite society ⟨a book once labeled *indecent*⟩ — see OBSCENE 1

indecision *n* a state or an instance of temporary inaction because of uncertainty about the right course of action ⟨His *indecision* about where to go for dinner, while everyone was getting hungrier by the minute, was frustrating.⟩ — see HESITATION

indecorous *adj* not appropriate for a particular occasion or situation ⟨an *indecorous* joke for a solemn moment in the marriage ceremony⟩ — see INAPPROPRIATE

indeed *interj* how surprising, doubtful, or unbelievable ⟨*Indeed*, you really did shave all your hair off!⟩ — see NO

indeed *adv* **1** without any question ⟨I know that you can *indeed* do better than that!⟩

synonyms all right, alright, assuredly, certainly, definitely, doubtless, easily, incontestably, incontrovertibly, indisputably, plainly, really, so, sure, surely, truly, undeniably, undoubtedly, unquestionably

related words conceivably, likely, perhaps, possibly, probably; obviously, unmistakably

phrases by all means, by all odds, damn well, for certain, for sure

2 not merely this but also ⟨That is not merely a reason, but is *indeed* the entire point.⟩ — see EVEN 1

3 to tell the truth ⟨That woman can be funny—*indeed*, she can be hilarious!⟩ — see ACTUALLY 1

indefatigable *adj* showing no signs of weariness even after long hard effort ⟨an *indefatigable* laborer who can work from sunrise to sunset⟩ — see TIRELESS

indefensible *adj* too bad to be excused or justified ⟨The company took a completely *indefensible* position on the issue.⟩ — see INEXCUSABLE

indefinable *adj* beyond the power to describe ⟨Some *indefinable* quality makes that movie star very appealing.⟩ — see INDESCRIBABLE

indefinite *adj* **1** being or seeming to be without limits ⟨the *indefinite* vastness of the frozen tundra⟩ — see INFINITE

2 not expressed in precise terms ⟨an *indefinite* longing for something new and exciting in her life⟩ — see VAGUE 1

3 not seen or understood clearly ⟨Through the dense fog we could just barely discern the *indefinite* form of another boat.⟩ — see FAINT 1

indelicacy *n* the quality or state of lacking refinement or good taste ⟨The *indelicacy* of their dinner conversation made the other guests wince in embarrassment.⟩ — see VULGARITY 1

indelicateness *n* **1** the quality or state of lacking refinement or good taste ⟨The well-known *indelicateness* of the comedian's humor made him a poor choice for master of ceremonies.⟩ — see VULGARITY 1

2 the quality or state of not being socially proper ⟨Because of the *indelicateness* of the topic, let's avoid it as dinner conversation.⟩ — see IMPROPRIETY 1

indemnification *n* payment to another for a loss or injury ⟨That insurance company is known to be slow when processing claims for *indemnification*.⟩ — see COMPENSATION 1

indemnify *vb* to provide (someone) with a just payment for loss or injury ⟨The company generously *indemnifies* workers who are injured on the job.⟩ — see COMPENSATE 1

indemnity *n* payment to another for a loss or injury ⟨She now lives on a pension and an *indemnity* from her former employer.⟩ — see COMPENSATION 1

indentation *n* **1** a sunken area forming a separate space ⟨The previous occupant's furniture had left some fairly noticeable *indentations* in the carpet.⟩ — see HOLE 2

2 a V-shaped cut usually on an edge or a surface ⟨deep *indentations* along the edge of the leaf⟩ — see NOTCH 1

indented *adj* curved inward ⟨That *indented* area of the mountainside is prone to avalanches.⟩ — see HOLLOW

independence *n* **1** the ability to care for one's self ⟨They tried to foster a sense of *independence* in their children.⟩ — see SELF-SUFFICIENCY

2 the state of being free from the control or power of another ⟨College freshmen often revel in their newfound *independence*.⟩ — see FREEDOM 1

independent *adj* **1** able to take care of oneself or itself without outside help ⟨an *independent* young man who moved out of his parents' house while still a college student⟩ — see SELF-SUFFICIENT

2 not being under the rule or control of another ⟨Finally they are an *independent* people, after centuries of domination by their neighbors.⟩ — see FREE 1

independently *adv* without aid or support ⟨*independently* came to the same conclusion⟩ — see ALONE 1

in–depth *adj* covering everything or all important points ⟨an *in-depth* report on the job market⟩ — see ENCYCLOPEDIC

indescribable *adj* beyond the power to describe ⟨the *indescribable* immensity of Mount Everest⟩

synonyms incommunicable, indefinable, ineffable, inexpressible, nameless, unspeakable, unutterable
related words unsayable; inconceivable, incredible, unbelievable, unimaginable, unthinkable; inexplicable, unexplainable; characterless
near antonyms conceivable, imaginable, thinkable
antonyms communicable, definable, expressible, speakable
indestructible *adj* impossible to destroy ⟨Diamonds are widely considered to be *indestructible* because they are one of the hardest known substances.⟩
synonyms imperishable, inextinguishable
related words incorruptible; deathless, immortal, perpetual, undying; indissoluble, ineffaceable, ineradicable, inexpungible; durable, enduring, everlasting, lasting, permanent, unbreakable; strong, sturdy, tough
near antonyms mortal; impermanent, transient, transitory; breakable, delicate, flimsy, fragile, frail
antonyms destructible, extinguishable, perishable
index *n* an arrow-shaped piece on a dial or scale for registering information ⟨The *index* on the thermometer dropped below zero.⟩ — see POINTER 1
index *vb* to put (someone or something) on a list ⟨*indexed* all the books in the library by category⟩ — see ¹LIST 2
indicate *vb* **1** to serve as a sign or symptom of ⟨His attitude seems to *indicate* that he has little interest in the project.⟩
synonyms bespeak, betoken, denote, mean, signify
related words bode, foreshow, foretell, presage
2 to convey an idea indirectly ⟨Her expression *indicated* that she was uncomfortably cold, but she was too polite to say so.⟩ — see HINT
indication *n* a slight or indirect pointing to something (as a solution or explanation) ⟨There are *indications* that a medical breakthrough in the treatment of the disease is imminent.⟩ — see HINT 1
indicative *adj* indicating something ⟨a wide-eyed look that is *indicative* of his constant curiosity⟩
synonyms denotative, denoting, reflective, significant, signifying, telltale
related words alluding, allusive, referring; characteristic, symptomatic; demonstrative, exhibiting, expressive; symbolic (*also* symbolical); connoting, hinting, implying, suggestive
indicator *n* an arrow-shaped piece on a dial or scale for registering information ⟨You should refill when the *indicator* on the gas gauge shows that there's only a quarter of a tank left.⟩ — see POINTER 1
indict *vb* to make a claim of wrongdoing against ⟨The grand jury could *indict* them for fraud and embezzlement.⟩ — see ACCUSE
indictment *n* a formal claim of criminal wrongdoing against a person ⟨That prosecutor gets an *indictment* for 90% of the cases.⟩ — see CHARGE 1
indifference *n* lack of interest or concern ⟨It's a matter of complete *indifference* to me what you decide to do.⟩
synonyms apathy, casualness, complacence, disinterestedness, disregard, insouciance, nonchalance, unconcern
related words halfheartedness, lukewarmness; carelessness, heedlessness, recklessness, unawareness; listlessness; aloofness, cool, detachment; callosity, callousness, hard-heartedness, hardness, insensitivity; bloodlessness, impassivity, phlegm, stoicism, stolidity
near antonyms attention, attentiveness, awareness, conscientiousness, curiosity, heedfulness, keenness; sensitivity, warmheartedness; bias, partiality, prejudice; ardor, desire, fervency, passion, vehemence, zeal
antonyms concern, interest, regard
indifferent *adj* **1** having or showing a lack of interest or concern ⟨*indifferent* about the result of the football game⟩
synonyms apathetic, casual, complacent, disinterested,

incurious, insensible, insouciant, nonchalant, perfunctory, unconcerned, uncurious, uninterested
related words halfhearted, lukewarm, tepid; aloof, cold, numb, remote, unemotional; callous, insensitive, unfeeling; calm, cool, detached, dispassionate; careless, heedless, mindless; impassive, impervious, phlegmatic, stoic (*or* stoical), stolid; lethargic, listless; unimpressed
near antonyms attentive, aware, conscientious, heedful, mindful; caring, sensitive, warmhearted; ardent, fervent, keen, passionate, warm, zealous
antonyms concerned, interested
2 of average or below average quality ⟨an *indifferent* but drinkable cup of coffee⟩ — see MEDIOCRE 1
3 marked by justice, honesty, and freedom from bias ⟨They believed their art teacher could offer an *indifferent* judgment on their works' merits.⟩ — see FAIR 2
indigence *n* the state of lacking sufficient money or material possessions ⟨There are various state and federal programs to help relieve *indigence*.⟩ — see POVERTY 1
indigenous *adj* **1** belonging to a particular place by birth or origin ⟨the culture of the *indigenous* people of that country⟩ — see NATIVE 1
2 being a part of the innermost nature of a person or thing ⟨the drive to create that is *indigenous* to humanity⟩ — see INHERENT
indigent *adj* lacking money or material possessions ⟨Because he was *indigent*, the court appointed a lawyer to defend him.⟩ — see POOR 1
indignant *adj* feeling or showing anger ⟨The poker player became *indignant* at the accusation of cheating.⟩ — see ANGRY
indignation *n* an intense emotional state of displeasure with someone or something ⟨Her *indignation* at the offensive television show led her to start a grassroots campaign for its cancellation.⟩ — see ANGER
indignity *n* an act or expression showing scorn and usually intended to hurt another's feelings ⟨minor *indignities* such as intentionally mispronouncing a person's name⟩ — see INSULT
indirect *adj* not straightforward or direct ⟨The cab driver took a very *indirect* route to the hotel.⟩ ⟨a long-winded, *indirect* answer to a very simple question⟩
synonyms circuitous, circular, roundabout
related words crooked, serpentine, sinuous, tortuous, twisting, winding; rambling, wandering; circumlocutory, long-winded, prolix, verbose; deceitful, deceptive, devious, dishonest, insidious, misleading, sneaky, underhand, underhanded; calculating, crafty, cunning, subtle, tricky
near antonyms candid, forthright, frank, honest, open, plain, unconcealed, undisguised
antonyms direct, straight, straightforward
indiscreet *adj* showing poor judgment especially in personal relationships or social situations ⟨Telling a friend's secrets is *indiscreet*, and unkind as well.⟩
synonyms brash, graceless, ill-advised, imprudent, inadvisable, injudicious, tactless, unwise
related words dumb, idiotic (*also* idiotical), moronic, stupid; careless, heedless, inconsiderate, mindless, thoughtless; ill-mannered, improper, inappropriate, indecorous, unbecoming, uncivil, unseemly; foolish, harebrained, nonsensical, preposterous, senseless, silly
near antonyms intelligent, logical, rational, sensible, smart, sound; appropriate, becoming, civil, decorous, proper, seemly; sage, sane, sapient
antonyms advisable, discreet, judicious, prudent, tactful, wise
indiscretion *n* a socially improper or unsuitable act or remark ⟨He has been criticized for *indiscretions* in his handling of the situation.⟩ — see IMPROPRIETY 2

indispensable *adj* impossible to do without ⟨Fully aware that he was an *indispensable* assistant, he decided that it was high time that he be paid what he was worth.⟩ — see ESSENTIAL 1

indisposed *adj* **1** slow to begin or proceed with a course of action because of doubts or uncertainty ⟨One person in our reading group is very *indisposed* to suggesting a book.⟩ — see HESITANT

2 temporarily suffering from a disorder of the body ⟨Dave stays home from work whenever he feels the least *indisposed*.⟩ — see SICK 1

indisposition *n* the condition of not being in good health ⟨A brief *indisposition* made her miss the party.⟩ — see SICKNESS 1

indisputable *adj* not capable of being challenged or proved wrong ⟨an *indisputable* fact that is not subject to interpretation⟩ — see IRREFUTABLE

indisputably *adv* without any question ⟨You are *indisputably* correct in your calculations.⟩ — see INDEED 1

indistinct *adj* not seen or understood clearly ⟨I managed to discern a blurry, *indistinct* shadow through the downpour.⟩ — see FAINT 1

indistinguishable *adj* **1** not perceptible by a sense or by the mind ⟨*indistinguishable* differences that can be measured only electronically⟩ — see IMPERCEPTIBLE

2 not seen or understood clearly ⟨*indistinguishable* shapes in the fog⟩ — see FAINT 1

3 resembling another in every respect ⟨a synthetic fabric that supposedly is *indistinguishable* from real silk⟩ — see SAME 1

individual *n* **1** a member of the human race ⟨Every *individual* has value.⟩ — see HUMAN

2 one that has a real and independent existence ⟨Our general concept of what constitutes a chair is based on our experience with many *individuals* that were called chairs.⟩ — see ENTITY

individual *adj* **1** of, relating to, or belonging to a single person ⟨Everyone has his or her own *individual* opinion about the subject, but you will have to work together.⟩
synonyms individualized, particular, peculiar, personal, personalized, private, privy, separate, singular, unique
related words characteristic, distinctive, intimate; identifying, idiosyncratic; especial, express, special, specific; independent, nonconformist, self-directed, self-sufficient; custom, customized, specialized
near antonyms broad, prevailing, prevalent, widespread; common, normal, regular, typical
antonyms general, generic, popular, public, shared, universal

2 not the same or shared ⟨Guest rooms at the inn have *individual* bathrooms.⟩ — see SEPARATE 1

3 serving to identify as belonging to an individual or group ⟨He's got a highly *individual* laugh that I would know anywhere.⟩ — see CHARACTERISTIC 1

individualist *n* a person who does not conform to generally accepted standards or customs ⟨an *individualist* who steadfastly refuses to do what everyone else is doing⟩ — see NONCONFORMIST 1

individuality *n* **1** the set of qualities that make a person different from other people ⟨Her *individuality* showed through in everything she did.⟩
synonyms character, identity, personality, selfhood, self-identity
related words distinctiveness, idiosyncrasy, oneness, peculiarity, separateness, singleness, singularity, uniqueness; disposition, humor, nature, temper, temperament; independence
near antonyms conformity, conventionality

2 one that has a real and independent existence ⟨According to immanentism, God is not so much an *individuality* as an abstract mind or spirit that pervades the world.⟩ — see ENTITY

individualized *adj* of, relating to, or belonging to a single person ⟨an *individualized* plan of study for a gifted student in the class⟩ — see INDIVIDUAL 1

indoctrinate *vb* to cause to acquire knowledge or skill in some field ⟨*indoctrinated* children in proper safety procedures⟩ — see TEACH

indolence *n* an inclination not to do work or engage in activities ⟨A general feeling of *indolence* usually overtakes them during summer vacation.⟩ — see LAZINESS

indolent *adj* not easily aroused to action or work ⟨an *indolent* boy who had to be forced to help out with the chores⟩ — see LAZY 1

indomitable *adj* incapable of being defeated, overcome, or subdued ⟨Her *indomitable* spirit got her through many difficult times.⟩ — see INVINCIBLE

indubitable *adj* not capable of being challenged or proved wrong ⟨the *indubitable* fact that there are no more woolly mammoths or saber-toothed tigers around⟩ — see IRREFUTABLE

induce *vb* **1** to be the cause of (a situation, action, or state of mind) ⟨The medication *induced* labor.⟩ — see EFFECT

2 to cause (someone) to agree with a belief or course of action by using arguments or earnest requests ⟨finally *induced* the eyewitness to the crime to cooperate with the police⟩ — see PERSUADE

inducement *n* the act of reasoning or pleading with someone to accept a belief or course of action ⟨gave up smoking only after a prolonged *inducement* by all the other family members⟩ — see PERSUASION 1

inducing *n* the act of reasoning or pleading with someone to accept a belief or course of action ⟨After the *inducing* of his friends, he decided to go back to school and finish his degree.⟩ — see PERSUASION 1

induct *vb* to put into an office or welcome into an organization with special ceremonies ⟨*inducted* the pitcher into the Baseball Hall of Fame⟩ — see INSTALL 1

inductee *n* a person forced or required to enroll in military service ⟨a new crop of *inductees* produced by the draft⟩ — see CONSCRIPT

induction *n* **1** the process or an instance of being formally placed in an office or organization ⟨The formal *induction* will be tomorrow, but the college president has already started work.⟩ — see INSTALLATION 1

2 an opinion arrived at through a process of reasoning ⟨the scientist's *induction* that magnetism was likely the cause of the phenomenon⟩ — see CONCLUSION 1

indulge *vb* **1** to give in to (a desire) ⟨The grandparents *indulged* the child's wishes to an extent that they never did with their own children.⟩
synonyms cater (to), gratify, humor
related words bask, luxuriate, revel, wallow; coddle, mollycoddle, pamper, spoil; delight, please, pleasure; sate, satiate, satisfy
near antonyms bridle, check, constrain, curb, inhibit, restrain, stifle

2 to give (oneself) over to something especially unrestrainedly ⟨conventioneers who were obviously eager to *indulge* themselves in all of the vices that Las Vegas might offer⟩ — see ABANDON 1

3 to treat with great or excessive care ⟨You *indulge* those grandkids in ways you never did with your own kids.⟩ — see BABY

indulgence *n* **1** an act of kind assistance ⟨She was used to getting every kind of *indulgence* from her doting parents.⟩ — see FAVOR 1

2 something adding to pleasure or comfort but not absolutely necessary ⟨Bubble baths were her one *indulgence*.⟩ — see LUXURY 1

indulgent *adj* **1** tolerant and kind in the judgment of and expectations for others ⟨She was perhaps a bit too *indulgent* with her children, who always seemed to get away with everything.⟩

synonyms charitable, clement, easy, soft

related words accommodating, acquiescent, amenable, obliging; easygoing, laid-back, undemanding

near antonyms demanding; uncharitable, unforgiving; inflexible, intolerant, unbending, uncompromising, unyielding

antonyms hard, harsh, severe, stern, strict

2 willing to do a favor ⟨an *indulgent* clerk who let me try on practically every size-seven shoe the store had⟩ — see ACCOMMODATING

industrious *adj* involved in often constant activity ⟨an *industrious* worker who never seems to sleep⟩ — see BUSY 1

industriously *adv* with great effort or determination ⟨worked *industriously* to complete the project ahead of schedule⟩ — see HARD 1

industriousness *n* attentive and persistent effort ⟨She did twice as much work as anyone else through sheer *industriousness*.⟩ — see DILIGENCE

industry *n* attentive and persistent effort ⟨He isn't the smartest kid in class, but he gets the best grades by determined *industry*.⟩ — see DILIGENCE

inebriate *adj* being under the influence of alcohol ⟨*inebriate* New Year's eve partyers⟩ — see DRUNK

inebriate *n* a person who makes a habit of getting drunk ⟨an *inebriate* taken into police custody⟩ — see DRUNK

inebriated *adj* being under the influence of alcohol ⟨vacationers who were slightly *inebriated*⟩ — see DRUNK

ineffable *adj* beyond the power to describe ⟨An *ineffable* beauty descends upon the canyon as the sun begins to set.⟩ — see INDESCRIBABLE

ineffective *adj* **1** not producing the desired result ⟨an *ineffective* effort to reduce unemployment that only spurred inflation⟩

synonyms ineffectual, inefficient, inexpedient

related words abortive, bootless, fruitless, futile, nonproductive, pointless, profitless, unavailing, unproductive, unprofitable, unsuccessful, useless, worthless

near antonyms availing, beneficial, helpful, productive, profitable, successful, useful, worthwhile

antonyms effective, effectual, efficacious, efficient, expedient, operant, ultraefficient

2 producing no results ⟨an *ineffective* medication that will be denied FDA approval⟩ — see FUTILE

ineffectual *adj* **1** not producing the desired result ⟨An *ineffectual* effort to find the trail again did at least lead them to another stunning view of the canyon.⟩ — see INEFFECTIVE 1

2 producing no results ⟨another *ineffectual* plan⟩ — see FUTILE

inefficient *adj* not producing the desired result ⟨*inefficient* measures to solve the problem⟩ — see INEFFECTIVE 1

inelegant *adj* **1** lacking social grace and assurance ⟨*inelegant* preteens still learning how to act at formal events⟩ — see AWKWARD 1

2 marked by an obvious lack of style or good taste ⟨*inelegant* furniture that looked like it belonged in a budget motel⟩ — see ¹TACKY 1

inept *adj* **1** lacking qualities (as knowledge, skill, or ability) required to do a job ⟨an *inept* editor who misses many errors⟩ — see INCOMPETENT

2 not appropriate for a particular occasion or situation ⟨an *inept* choice of movies for the children⟩ — see INAPPROPRIATE

3 showing or marked by a lack of skill and tact (as in dealing with a situation) ⟨an *inept* effort to become friends with their future son-in-law⟩ — see AWKWARD 2

4 showing or marked by a lack of good sense or judgment ⟨She offers one *inept* suggestion after another.⟩ — see FOOLISH 1

ineptitude *n* the lack of sufficient ability, power, or means ⟨My *ineptitude* on the tennis court made it clear that I should try another sport.⟩ — see INABILITY

inequity *n* **1** the state of being unfair or unjust ⟨the *inequity* of the punishment in relation to the wrongdoing⟩ — see INJUSTICE 1

2 unfair or inadequate treatment of someone or something or an instance of this ⟨the unavoidable *inequities* of any system for distributing benefits⟩ — see DISSERVICE

inert *adj* **1** not being in a state of use, activity, or employment ⟨the *inert*, abandoned factories that are scattered all over that dying city⟩ — see INACTIVE 2

2 slow to move or act ⟨a sleepy, *inert* reptile that is no threat to people when left alone⟩ — see INACTIVE 1

inertia *n* an inclination not to do work or engage in activities ⟨The *inertia* that grips so many of the club's members is the reason why nothing ever gets done.⟩ — see LAZINESS

inertness *n* lack of action or activity ⟨the noticeable *inertness* of the campus on weekends, when most of the students go home⟩ — see INACTION

inescapable *adj* impossible to avoid or evade ⟨Some people believe that your fate is determined at birth and thus *inescapable*.⟩ — see INEVITABLE

inescapably *adv* because of necessity ⟨*Inescapably*, we must take some drastic measures to avoid a catastrophe.⟩ — see NEEDS

inevitable *adj* impossible to avoid or evade ⟨Getting wet is *inevitable* if you are going to try to give your dog a bath.⟩

synonyms certain, inescapable, necessary, sure, unavoidable, unescapable

related words decided, definite, settled; likely, possible, probable; destined, fated, foreordained, predestined, predetermined, preordained; inexorable, relentless, unremitting

phrases in the bag, in the cards (*also* on the cards)

near antonyms preventable (*also* preventible); doubtful, dubious, questionable, shaky, unclear; undecided, unsettled; undependable, unreliable; improbable, unlikely

antonyms avoidable, evadable, uncertain, unsure

inevitably *adv* because of necessity ⟨We must *inevitably* make some sacrifices if we are going to save money.⟩ — see NEEDS

inexact *adj* **1** not precisely correct ⟨A thousand is an *inexact* figure for the number of islands in the St. Lawrence River.⟩

synonyms approximate, imprecise, inaccurate, loose

related words erroneous, false, incorrect, off, wrong; general, indefinable, indefinite, indeterminate, indistinct, undefined, undetermined, unsettled, vague; faulty, flawed, mistaken; specious, distorted, fallacious, misleading; doubtful, dubious, questionable, uncertain; inconclusive, indecisive; debatable, disputable; unconfirmed, unsubstantiated, unsupported

near antonyms certain, incontestable, indubitable, positive, sure, undeniable, unquestionable; correct, errorless, factual, right, sound, true, valid; clear-cut, decisive, definable, defined, definite; incontrovertible, indisputable, irrefutable; absolute, unqualified; confirmed, corroborated, determined, established, substantiated, supported, validated

antonyms accurate, dead, exact, precise, ultraprecise, veracious

2 not being in agreement with what is true ⟨an *inexact* and misleading statement regarding the cost of the service⟩ — see FALSE 1

inexcusable *adj* too bad to be excused or justified ⟨Such rudeness is *inexcusable* and will be punished.⟩
synonyms indefensible, insupportable, unforgivable, unjustifiable, unpardonable, unwarrantable
related words insufferable, intolerable, unbearable, unendurable; abominable, atrocious, heinous, monstrous, outrageous, scandalous, shocking; egregious, flagrant, glaring, gross, rank; unacceptable, untenable; evil, iniquitous, vicious, wicked; base, contemptible, deplorable, despicable, dirty, execrable, ignoble, reprobate, vile, wretched; cruel, nasty; banned, barred, condemned, disallowed, forbidden, interdicted, outlawed, prohibited, proscribed
near antonyms acceptable, tolerable; authorized, legal, permissible; allowed, permitted, tolerated; approved, endorsed (*also* indorsed), sanctioned; abetted, encouraged, promoted, supported; ethical, moral, virtuous
antonyms defensible, excusable, forgivable, justifiable, pardonable, venial

inexhaustible *adj* showing no signs of weariness even after long hard effort ⟨seemingly *inexhaustible* horses that pulled heavy wagons across the wide prairies⟩ — see TIRELESS

inexpedient *adj* not producing the desired result ⟨a nutritionally dubious, *inexpedient* method for losing weight⟩ — see INEFFECTIVE 1

inexpensive *adj* costing little ⟨*inexpensive* but pretty jewelry that can be worn every day⟩ — see CHEAP 1

inexperienced *adj* **1** lacking in adult experience or maturity ⟨an *inexperienced* young man living on his own for the first time⟩ — see CALLOW
2 lacking or showing a lack of expert skill ⟨An *inexperienced* carpenter had obviously built the rough-hewn cabin.⟩ — see AMATEURISH

inexpert *adj* **1** lacking or showing a lack of expert skill ⟨an *inexpert* attempt at putting on an outdoor concert⟩ — see AMATEURISH
2 lacking qualities (as knowledge, skill, or ability) required to do a job ⟨The *inexpert* mechanic only made the problem worse—and charged me a fortune for doing it!⟩ — see INCOMPETENT
3 showing or marked by a lack of skill and tact (as in dealing with a situation) ⟨a well-meaning but *inexpert* attempt to make me feel better⟩ — see AWKWARD 2

inexpert *n* a person who lacks experience and competence in an art or science ⟨The shoddy tiling in the bathroom was a sure sign that it was the work of an *inexpert*.⟩ — see AMATEUR 2

inexplicable *adj* impossible to explain ⟨an *inexplicable* desire for ice cream at two in the morning⟩
synonyms unaccountable, unexplainable
related words indefinable, indescribable, inexpressible, unsayable; cryptic, enigmatic (*also* enigmatical), impenetrable, incomprehensible, inscrutable, mysterious, unfathomable, unknowable; irrational, unreasonable, unsound; foolish, illogical, mindless, senseless; absurd, odd, peculiar, strange, unusual, weird
near antonyms logical, rational, reasonable, tenable; sane, sensible, wise; compelling, convincing, persuasive, plausible, satisfying; confirmed, corroborated, determined, established, explained, substantiated, validated
antonyms accountable, explainable, explicable

inexpressible *adj* beyond the power to describe ⟨overcome by an *inexpressible* awe at the sight of the thunderous waterfall⟩ — see INDESCRIBABLE

inexpressive *adj* not expressing any emotion ⟨Jon kept a

resolutely *inexpressive* face throughout the poker game.⟩ — see BLANK 1

inextinguishable *adj* impossible to destroy ⟨Freedom remains an *inextinguishable* dream for people around the world.⟩ — see INDESTRUCTIBLE

infallible *adj* **1** not being or likely to be wrong ⟨a teacher with an *infallible* memory for names⟩
synonyms unerring, unfailing
related words errorless, faultless, flawless, impeccable; certain, foolproof, inerrant, perfect, sure; dependable, reliable
near antonyms defective, faulty, flawed, imperfect; undependable, unreliable
antonyms fallible
2 not likely to fail ⟨an *infallible* cure for hiccups⟩
synonyms certain, sure, surefire, unfailing
related words dependable, reliable; deadly, unerring
near antonyms doubtful, questionable, uncertain
antonyms fallible

infamous *adj* not respectable ⟨the *infamous* criminal who remains known only by the moniker of "Jack the Ripper"⟩ — see DISREPUTABLE

infamy *n* the state of having lost the esteem of others ⟨Despite her eventual acquittal, she could never completely free herself of the *infamy* of being an accused criminal.⟩ — see DISGRACE 1

infant *n* a recently born person ⟨*Infants* should be kept warm at all times.⟩ — see BABY 1

infantile *adj* having or showing the annoying qualities (as silliness) associated with children ⟨his *infantile* humor⟩ — see CHILDISH

infatuated (with) *adj* filled with an intense or excessive love for ⟨hopelessly *infatuated with* the rock band's lead singer⟩ — see ENAMORED (OF)

infatuation *n* a strong but often short-lived liking for another person ⟨had a brief *infatuation* with the captain of the ski team⟩ — see CRUSH 1

infectious *adj* exciting a similar feeling or reaction in others ⟨an *infectious* giggle that got the whole class laughing⟩ — see CONTAGIOUS 2

infelicitous *adj* not appropriate for a particular occasion or situation ⟨an *infelicitous* comment that drew audible gasps from the guests⟩ — see INAPPROPRIATE

infelicity *n* the quality or state of being unsuitable or unfitting ⟨the *infelicity* of holiday decorations at a funeral home⟩ — see INAPPROPRIATENESS 1

infer *vb* **1** to form an opinion or reach a conclusion through reasoning and information ⟨He *inferred* that she had left because her coat was gone.⟩
synonyms conclude, decide, deduce, derive, extrapolate, gather, judge, make out, reason, understand
related words assume, suppose; conjecture, guess, speculate, surmise; construe, interpret, read; contemplate, philosophize, rationalize, think; ascertain, dope (out), find out
phrases draw a conclusion
2 to convey an idea indirectly ⟨The results *infer* that there might be a problem with one piece of the equipment.⟩ — see HINT

inferable *also* **inferrible** *adj* being or provable by reasoning in which the conclusion follows necessarily from given information ⟨the *inferable* but unstated conclusion of the report⟩ — see DEDUCTIVE

inference *n* an opinion arrived at through a process of reasoning ⟨That seems like a reasonable *inference*, but in this case it happens to be incorrect.⟩ — see CONCLUSION 1

inferior *n* one who is of lower rank and typically under the authority of another ⟨She is nice to her *inferiors* as well as to her superiors.⟩ — see UNDERLING

inferior *adj* **1** situated lower down ⟨creatures that inhabit the dark, *inferior* depths of the ocean⟩
synonyms lower, nether
related words lowest; underlying
near antonyms highest, uppermost; overhanging, overhead
antonyms higher, superior, upper
2 of little or less value or merit ⟨a girl who has always felt *inferior* to her older sister⟩
synonyms mean, minor, secondary, second-class, second-rate
related words junior, lesser, lower, low-level, petty, smaller, subordinate, under; average, common, fair, middling, ordinary; amiss, bad, defective, unsatisfactory, wrong; deficient, inadequate, insufficient, unacceptable; littler, slighter, smaller; jerkwater, one-horse, small-time, two-bit
near antonyms major, more, primary, senior; choice, exceptional, first-class, first-rate, high-grade, premium, prime, select, selected; acceptable, adequate, sufficient
antonyms greater, higher, superior
3 belonging to the class of people of low social or economic rank ⟨a member of the nobility among the *inferior* classes of society⟩ — see IGNOBLE 1
4 falling short of a standard ⟨an *inferior* science textbook that was out-of-date the day that it was published⟩ — see BAD 1
5 having not so great importance or rank as another ⟨An *inferior* officer cannot strike a superior under any circumstances.⟩ — see LESSER
6 of low quality ⟨the *inferior* workmanship of the furniture⟩ — see CHEAP 2
inferno *n* a destructive burning ⟨The intense heat of the raging *inferno* repeatedly drove back the firefighters.⟩ — see FIRE 1
infertile *adj* **1** not able to produce fruit or offspring ⟨An *infertile* cow is of limited use to a farmer.⟩ — see STERILE 1
2 producing inferior or only a small amount of vegetation ⟨Only parched, *infertile* fields remained after months of drought.⟩ — see BARREN 1
infest *vb* to spread or swarm over in a troublesome manner ⟨In desperation, we called in an exterminator because the house was *infested* with ants.⟩
synonyms overrun
related words beset, overspread, overwhelm; abound, crawl, teem; annoy, pester, plague; contaminate, infect
infidelity *n* **1** lack of faithfulness especially to one's husband or wife ⟨warned the young couple of the high cost of dishonesty and *infidelity*⟩
synonyms disloyalty, faithlessness, falseness, falsity, inconstancy, unfaithfulness
related words adultery; betrayal, double-cross, double-dealing, duplicity, sellout, treachery, treason; deceit, lying
near antonyms staunchness, steadfastness; dependability, reliability; honesty, trustworthiness
antonyms allegiance, constancy, devotedness, devotion, faith, faithfulness, fealty, fidelity, loyalty
2 the act or fact of violating the trust or confidence of another ⟨The one thing that the political boss will not forgive is *infidelity*.⟩ — see BETRAYAL
3 a sexual encounter or relationship between a married person and someone other than their spouse ⟨denied accusations of *infidelities*⟩ — see ADULTERY
infiltrate *vb* to introduce in a gradual, secret, or clever way ⟨Over time, undercover agents *infiltrated* the crime ring.⟩ — see INSINUATE 1
infinite *adj* being or seeming to be without limits ⟨the *infinite* expanse of outer space⟩

synonyms bottomless, boundless, endless, illimitable, immeasurable, indefinite, limitless, measureless, unbounded, unfathomable, unlimited
related words abysmal; countless, incalculable, incomputable, innumerable, unmeasured; exhaustless, inexhaustible; extensive, far-flung, immense, vast
near antonyms measurable; depthless, shallow, superficial
antonyms bounded, circumscribed, definite, finite, limited, restricted
infinitesimal *adj* very small in size ⟨a soft drink with only an *infinitesimal* amount of caffeine⟩ — see TINY
infinity *n* endless time ⟨It seemed as though that meeting might extend into *infinity*.⟩ — see ETERNITY 1
infirm *adj* lacking bodily strength ⟨The elderly and *infirm* have to be especially careful during the winter months.⟩ — see WEAK 1
infirmity *n* **1** an abnormal state that disrupts a plant's or animal's normal bodily functioning ⟨an 18th-century quack who specialized in mysterious *infirmities*⟩ — see DISEASE
2 the quality or state of lacking physical strength or vigor ⟨A period of *infirmity* left the athlete completely out of shape.⟩ — see WEAKNESS 1
inflame *also* **enflame** *vb* **1** to make angry ⟨The newspaper editorial *inflamed* her enough to inspire her to dash off a letter to the editor.⟩ — see ANGER
2 to set (something) on fire ⟨A carelessly tossed cigarette *inflamed* the papers in the trash can.⟩ — see BURN 2
inflamed *also* **enflamed** *adj* **1** being on fire ⟨the *inflamed* hillsides in one of the largest wildfires in the state's history⟩ — see ABLAZE 1
2 feeling or showing anger ⟨He gets red-faced when he's *inflamed* enough.⟩ — see ANGRY
inflammable *adj* capable of catching or being set on fire ⟨Some pajamas are made of *inflammable* material, so be careful.⟩ — see COMBUSTIBLE
inflexibility *n* the quality or state of being demanding or unyielding (as in discipline or criticism) ⟨The principal's *inflexibility* in matters of discipline is the stuff of school legend.⟩ — see SEVERITY
inflexible *adj* **1** not capable of changing or being changed ⟨the *inflexible* law of gravity⟩
synonyms fixed, hard-and-fast, immutable, invariable, unalterable, unchangeable
related words changeless, constant, determinate, established, set, settled, stable, steadfast, steady, unaltered, unchanging, unvarying; immovable, unmovable
near antonyms adaptable, adjustable; fickle, fluctuating, inconstant, uncertain, unsettled, unstable, varying; plastic, pliable, pliant, supple, willowy
antonyms alterable, changeable, elastic, flexible, mutable, variable
2 incapable of or highly resistant to bending ⟨Shoes made of *inflexible* plastic hurt my feet.⟩ — see STIFF 1
3 not allowing for any exceptions or loosening of standards ⟨The *inflexible* entry rules for the contest ban anyone who works for the company as well as any of their relatives.⟩ — see RIGID 1
4 sticking to an opinion, purpose, or course of action in spite of reason, arguments, or persuasion ⟨Her *inflexible* father was unmoved by tears and pleading, and he grounded her anyway.⟩ — see OBSTINATE
inflow *n* a flowing or coming in ⟨The *inflow* of new students every September means that there will always be new members for student organizations.⟩ — see INFLUX
influence *vb* to act upon (a person or a person's feelings) so as to cause a response ⟨The news reports of the devastating flood *influenced* a great many people to make contributions for food and supplies.⟩ — see ¹AFFECT 1

influence *n* **1** the power to direct the thinking or behavior of others usually indirectly ⟨a mayor who doesn't hesitate to use her *influence* to get business leaders behind civic improvements⟩
synonyms authority, clout, credit, heft, in, pull, sway, weight
related words counterinfluence; command, dominance, dominion, mastery, predominance, scepter, sovereignty (*also* sovranty), supremacy; consequence, eminence, importance, moment; impact, impress, impression, imprint, mark
near antonyms helplessness, impotence, impotency, powerlessness, weakness
2 the power to bring about a result on another ⟨The basic premise of astrology is that the position of the stars has an *influence* on human affairs.⟩ — see EFFECT 2

influential *adj* **1** having power over the minds or behavior of others ⟨a highly *influential* writer⟩
synonyms authoritative, forceful, weighty
related words cogent, controlling, dominating, masterful; dominant, predominant, regnant, sovereign (*also* sovran), supreme; eminent, important, momentous
near antonyms helpless, impotent, powerless, weak; incapable
2 having great power or influence ⟨A particularly *influential* politician got the team a new ballpark.⟩ — see IMPORTANT 2

influx *n* a flowing or coming in ⟨a sudden *influx* of people into the exurbs⟩
synonyms flux, income, inflow, inrush
related words deluge, flood, flow, inundation, overflow, spate, torrent; rush, stampede; river, stream, tide
near antonyms emigration, exodus, flight
antonyms outflow, outpouring

inform *vb* **1** to give information (as to the authorities) about another's improper or unlawful activities ⟨The police only caught the mastermind of the burglary because his disgruntled partner *informed*.⟩ — see SQUEAL 1
2 to give information to ⟨He chose teaching as a career because it affords the opportunity to *inform* a whole generation of young minds.⟩ — see ENLIGHTEN 1

informal *adj* **1** not rigidly following established form, custom, or rules ⟨An *informal* meeting allowed everyone to get acquainted.⟩
synonyms heterodox, irregular, unceremonious, unconventional, unorthodox
related words unauthorized, unofficial; casual, easygoing, familiar, free and easy, lax, loose, offhand, relaxed
near antonyms correct, decorous, proper; constrained, inhibited, restrained, rigid, stiff, stuffy, uptight
antonyms ceremonial, ceremonious, conventional, formal, orthodox, regular, routine
2 not designed to be worn only on special occasions ⟨chose an *informal* flowery dress⟩ — see CASUAL 1
3 used in or suitable for speech and not formal writing ⟨The use of *informal* language in a scholarly article is really inappropriate.⟩ — see COLLOQUIAL 1

informant *n* a person who provides information about another's wrongdoing ⟨The FBI is working closely with *informants* to find out about the subversive group.⟩ — see INFORMER

information *n* **1** a collection of factual knowledge about something ⟨The network correspondent spent the entire day gathering *information* for her report on the brewing scandal.⟩
synonyms facts
related words findings, intelligence
2 a report of recent events or facts not previously known ⟨What's the latest *information* about the wildfires out in the West?⟩ — see NEWS

informational *adj* providing useful information or knowledge ⟨an *informational* presentation from the company's health care provider⟩ — see INFORMATIVE

informative *adj* providing useful information or knowledge ⟨Some websites for family vacation resorts are very *informative* and some are practically useless.⟩
synonyms educational, educative, informational, instructional, instructive
related words comprehensive, copious, detailed, full; communicatory, edifying, elucidative, explanatory; chatty, gossipy, newsy; availing, beneficial, constructive, helpful, profitable
near antonyms impractical, unhelpful, unusable, useless
antonyms unenlightening, unilluminating, uninformative, uninstructive

informed *adj* **1** based on sound reasoning or information ⟨The expert's *informed* opinion persuaded many fence-sitters to get a flu shot.⟩ — see GOOD 1
2 having information especially as a result of study or experience ⟨People who are *informed* about nutrition have some serious misgivings about this new diet.⟩ — see FAMILIAR 2

informer *n* a person who provides information about another's wrongdoing ⟨The *informer* who told the police about that conspiracy has angered a lot of dangerous people.⟩
synonyms betrayer, informant, rat, snitch, snitcher, squealer, stool pigeon, talebearer, tattler, tattletale, telltale
related words collaborator; blabber, blabbermouth, gossip, leaker; snoop, snooper, spy; notifier

infraction *n* a failure to uphold the requirements of law, duty, or obligation ⟨Speeding is only a minor *infraction*, but vehicular homicide is a serious felony.⟩ — see BREACH 1

infrequent *adj* not often occurring or repeated ⟨a shut-in who made *infrequent* trips to the store⟩
synonyms isolated, occasional, odd, rare, sporadic
related words scarce, scattered, uncommon, unique, unusual; choppy, discontinuous, erratic, fitful, intermittent, irregular, spasmodic, spotty, unsteady
phrases few and far between
near antonyms daily, regular; common, ordinary, routine
antonyms frequent

infrequently *adv* not often ⟨Their grandparents were disappointed that they visited so *infrequently*.⟩ — see SELDOM

infringement *n* a failure to uphold the requirements of law, duty, or obligation ⟨a government action limiting freedom of speech that is an *infringement* of the U.S. Constitution⟩ — see BREACH 1

infuriate *vb* to make angry ⟨The quarterback's careless mistake *infuriated* the coach.⟩ — see ANGER

infuriate *adj* feeling or showing anger ⟨an *infuriate* and relentless opponent⟩ — see ANGRY

infuriated *adj* feeling or showing anger ⟨an *infuriated* correspondent who keeps sending increasingly vicious letters⟩ — see ANGRY

infuse *vb* to cause (as a person) to become filled or saturated with a certain quality or principle ⟨parents who *infuse* their children with a strong sense of responsibility to the community⟩
synonyms endue (*or* indue), imbue, inculcate, ingrain (*also* engrain), inoculate, invest, steep, suffuse
related words animate, charge, enliven, invigorate, leaven; implant, plant; impregnate, permeate, pervade, saturate; deluge, drown, fill, flood, inundate, overwhelm, submerge
near antonyms strip; clear, empty; eliminate, remove, take away

ingenious *adj* **1** having the skill and imagination to create new things ⟨an *ingenious* but rather eccentric inventor⟩ — see CREATIVE 1

2 showing a noteworthy use of the imagination and creativity especially in inventing ⟨A chair that can't tip over is quite *ingenious*.⟩ — see CLEVER 1

ingeniousness *n* the skill and imagination to create new things ⟨hired a new designer whose vision demonstrates a real *ingeniousness*⟩ — see CREATIVITY 1

ingenuity *n* the skill and imagination to create new things ⟨The mystery writer's exceptional *ingenuity* enabled her to devise plots that always had readers guessing to the very end.⟩ — see CREATIVITY 1

ingenuous *adj* **1** free from any intent to deceive or impress others ⟨photographs that capture the *ingenuous* smiles of young children at play⟩ — see GUILELESS

2 lacking in worldly wisdom or informed judgment ⟨the story of an *ingenuous* newcomer to the big city who outwits the slickers at their own game⟩ — see NAIVE 1

ingenuously *adv* without any attempt to impress by deception or exaggeration ⟨Like some other successful business owners, she *ingenuously* claims that she doesn't consider herself a genius, only hardworking.⟩ — see NATURALLY 3

ingenuousness *n* the quality or state of being simple and sincere ⟨His aw-shucks *ingenuousness* endeared him to his sophisticated new friends.⟩ — see NAÏVETÉ 1

ingest *vb* **1** to take in as food ⟨a species of sea star that *ingests* its meal by pushing its stomach out of its body⟩ — see EAT 1

2 to take into the stomach through the mouth and throat ⟨*ingested* the foul-tasting medicine with only the greatest difficulty⟩ — see SWALLOW 1

ingrain *also* **engrain** *vb* **1** to cause (as a person) to become filled or saturated with a certain quality or principle ⟨The journalism professor has long *ingrained* his students with a deep respect for their chosen profession.⟩ — see INFUSE

2 to produce a vivid impression of ⟨The privation he had witnessed forever *ingrained* itself upon the young doctor's memory.⟩ — see ENGRAVE 2

3 to set solidly in or as if in surrounding matter ⟨The Browns tried to *ingrain* traditional values in their children.⟩ — see ENTRENCH

ingrain *adj* being a part of the innermost nature of a person or thing ⟨an *ingrain* skepticism that saves him from falling for every hoax that comes along⟩ — see INHERENT

ingrained *also* **engrained** *adj* being a part of the innermost nature of a person or thing ⟨attitudes that are deeply *ingrained* in the culture⟩ — see INHERENT

ingratiating *adj* likely or intended to win one's affection ⟨One of the children had a most *ingratiating* smile.⟩
synonyms disarming, endearing, winning, winsome
related words adorable, charming, likable (*or* likeable), lovable (*also* loveable); affecting, poignant, touching; adulatory, deferential, effusive, flattering, fulsome, groveling (*or* grovelling), kowtowing, obsequious, sycophantic; drooling, slavering, slobbering; saccharine, soapy, sugary, unctuous
near antonyms alienating, disaffecting, displeasing; repugnant, repulsive; arrogant, disdainful, haughty, insolent, proud, scornful
antonyms unendearing, uningratiating

ingredient *n* one of the parts that make up a whole ⟨One of the *ingredients* in the salad dressing is garlic.⟩ — see ELEMENT 1

ingress *n* the means or right of entering or participating in ⟨With limited *ingress* and egress to the freeway, the stadium is the frequent scene of bottlenecks.⟩ — see ENTRANCE 1

inhabitable *adj* suitable for living in ⟨the search for an *inhabitable* planet⟩ — see LIVABLE

inhabitant *n* one who lives permanently in a place ⟨The *inhabitants* of the town don't like the tourists.⟩
synonyms denizen, dweller, habitant, occupant, resident, resider, tenant
related words aborigine, native; citizen, national, subject; colonist, émigré (*also* emigré), migrant, newcomer, settler; burgher, local, townie (*or* towny), villager
near antonyms alien, foreigner, nonresident; guest, tourist, visitor; defector, emigrant, escaper, evacuee, exile, expatriate, refugee
antonyms transient

inharmonious *adj* **1** not being in agreement or harmony ⟨The resort bans electronic devices because the owners believe that they are *inharmonious* with the quiet and therapeutic atmosphere other guests desire.⟩ — see INCONSISTENT 1

2 marked by or producing a harsh combination of sounds ⟨a deliberately *inharmonious* piece of music in the modern idiom⟩ — see DISSONANT

inherent *adj* being a part of the innermost nature of a person or thing ⟨an *inherent* concept of justice⟩
synonyms constitutional, essential, inborn, inbred, indigenous, ingrain, ingrained (*also* engrained), innate, integral, intrinsic, native, natural
related words basic, deep-rooted, elemental, fundamental; congenital, hereditary, inherited, inmost, inner, interior; internal; characteristic, distinctive, peculiar; habitual, inveterate; normal, regular, typical
phrases in one's blood
near antonyms alien, foreign; accidental, coincidental, incidental; acquired; superficial, surface; exterior, external
antonyms adventitious, extraneous, extrinsic

inherently *adv* by natural character or ability ⟨the commentator's observation that online polls are *inherently* unscientific⟩ — see NATURALLY 1

inheritable *adj* genetically passed or capable of being passed from parent to offspring ⟨Eye color is an *inheritable* trait.⟩ — see HEREDITARY

inheritance *n* something that is or may be inherited ⟨A keen sense of humor was her *inheritance* from her mother.⟩
synonyms bequest, birthright, heritage, legacy, patrimony
related words heirloom; bestowal, gift, offering, present

inherited *adj* genetically passed or capable of being passed from parent to offspring ⟨Hair color is *inherited*.⟩ — see HEREDITARY

inheritor *n* a person who has the right to inherit property ⟨Someday that little boy will become the *inheritor* of one of the largest private fortunes in the country.⟩ — see HEIR

inhibit *vb* **1** to create difficulty for the work or activity of ⟨The cold *inhibited* her from getting much work done that morning.⟩ — see HAMPER

2 to keep from exceeding a desirable degree or level (as of expression) ⟨laws designed to *inhibit* the powers of the intelligence organizations⟩ — see CONTROL 1

3 to steer (a person) from an activity or course of action ⟨Don't let fear of failure *inhibit* you from trying.⟩ — see DISCOURAGE 2

inhibition *n* **1** the checking of one's true feelings and impulses when dealing with others ⟨He has no *inhibitions* when it comes to expressing his opinion.⟩ — see CONSTRAINT 1

2 something that makes movement or progress difficult ⟨Without the *inhibition* of their jackets, the boys were able to wrestle more vigorously.⟩ — see ENCUMBRANCE

inhospitable *adj* marked by opposition or ill will ⟨The proposal received an unexpectedly *inhospitable* response from the city council.⟩ — see HOSTILE 1

inhuman *adj* **1** difficult to endure ⟨*inhuman* living conditions⟩ — see HARSH 1

2 having or showing a lack of sympathy or tender feelings ⟨an *inhuman* indifference to the sufferings of other human beings⟩ — see HARD 1

3 having or showing the desire to inflict severe pain and suffering on others ⟨a classic sociological study showing just how *inhuman* an individual can become when given absolute power over another⟩ — see CRUEL 1

inhumane *adj* **1** having or showing a lack of sympathy or tender feelings ⟨*inhumane* treatment of animals⟩ — see HARD 1

2 having or showing the desire to inflict severe pain and suffering on others ⟨an *inhumane* leader charged with war crimes⟩ — see CRUEL 1

inhumanity *n* disposition to willfully inflict pain and suffering on others ⟨Man's *inhumanity* to man has been a recurring theme in human history.⟩ — see CRUELTY

inimical *adj* **1** marked by opposition or ill will ⟨received an *inimical* response rather than the anticipated support⟩ — see HOSTILE 1

2 opposed to one's interests ⟨laws designed to enhance national security that some regard as *inimical* to cherished freedoms⟩ — see ADVERSE 1

inimitable *adj* having no equal or rival for excellence or desirability ⟨an *inimitable* performer of violin solos⟩ — see ONLY 1

iniquitous *adj* not conforming to a high moral standard; morally unacceptable ⟨zero tolerance at the academy for cheating and other *iniquitous* practices⟩ — see BAD 2

iniquity *n* **1** immoral conduct or practices harmful or offensive to society ⟨exhorted them to avoid such places of *iniquity*⟩ — see VICE 1

2 that which is morally unacceptable ⟨the *iniquity* of slavery⟩ — see EVIL

initial *adj* coming before all others in time or order ⟨You've resolved my *initial* complaint, but now I have a new question.⟩ — see FIRST 1

initially *adv* in the beginning ⟨We *initially* intended to renovate our home from the ground up.⟩ — see ORIGINALLY

initiate *vb* **1** to be responsible for the creation and early operation or use of ⟨no one knows who *initiated* written language⟩ — see FOUND

2 to impart knowledge of a new thing or situation to ⟨*initiated* the new recruits in the unspoken laws of military conduct⟩ — see ACQUAINT 1

3 to put into an office or welcome into an organization with special ceremonies ⟨*initiated* her as Surgeon General before an army of reporters and photographers⟩ — see INSTALL 1

initiation *n* the process or an instance of being formally placed in an office or organization ⟨the *initiation* of the newest members of the local chamber of commerce⟩ — see INSTALLATION 1

initiative *n* readiness to engage in daring or difficult activity ⟨The sentry showed remarkable *initiative* and uncommon bravery in foiling the attack.⟩ — see ENTERPRISE 2

initiator *n* a person who establishes a whole new field of endeavor ⟨As the *initiator* of printing from movable type, Gutenberg revolutionized people's access to written language.⟩ — see FATHER 2

inject *vb* **1** to put among or between others ⟨*injected* one more comment into the body of the text⟩ — see INSERT

injudicious *adj* showing poor judgment especially in personal relationships or social situations ⟨*injudicious* comments that lost him his job⟩ — see INDISCREET

injure *vb* **1** to cause bodily damage to ⟨Ted *injured* himself while skiing.⟩

synonyms damage, harm, hurt, wound

related words batter, bloody, blow out, bruise, contuse, cut, gash, gore, lacerate, scald, scar, scathe, strain, tear; crease, graze, nick; cripple, hamstring, lame, maim, mangle, mutilate; abuse, aggrieve, afflict, maltreat, torment, torture; lay up; blemish, impair, mar, scrape, spoil

near antonyms cure, fix, heal, mend, remedy

2 to reduce the soundness, effectiveness, or perfection of ⟨The agent's treachery has *injured* our national security for years to come.⟩ — see DAMAGE 1

injurious *adj* causing or capable of causing harm ⟨Inaccurate news reports are *injurious* to the public's faith in the media.⟩ — see HARMFUL

injury *n* **1** something that causes loss or pain ⟨The harsh words were the worst *injury* that his father could inflict.⟩

synonyms affliction, damage, detriment, harm, hurt

related words disservice, injustice, outrage, wrong; affront, dart, indignity, insult, offense (*or* offence); beating, crippling, mayhem, mutilation; defacement, disability, disablement, disfigurement, impairment; lesion; rupture, strain; abrasion, chafe, scrape, scratch; bruise, contusion, swelling, wound; bump, concussion; cut, gash, laceration; burn, scald, scar, scathe, sear

near antonyms healing, recovery; cure, fix, remedy

2 unfair or inadequate treatment of someone or something or an instance of this ⟨The state did the rancher an *injury* when it destroyed his herd of cattle without adequate proof that it was diseased.⟩ — see DISSERVICE

injustice *n* **1** the state of being unfair or unjust ⟨The *injustice* of the coach's accusation that I'd been lazy frustrated and angered me.⟩

synonyms inequity, unfairness, unjustness

related words dirtiness, foulness

antonyms equity, fairness, justice

2 unfair or inadequate treatment of someone or something or an instance of this ⟨a group that has long suffered *injustice* at the hands of our judicial system⟩ — see DISSERVICE

inkling *n* a slight or indirect pointing to something (as a solution or explanation) ⟨He did not give the slightest *inkling* that he was planning to quit.⟩ — see HINT 1

inlet *n* a part of a body of water that extends beyond the general shoreline ⟨went fishing in the quiet *inlets* of the coast⟩ — see GULF 1

inn *n* a place that provides rooms and usually a public dining room for overnight guests ⟨We decided to stay at an *inn* rather than keep driving all night.⟩ — see HOTEL

innards *pl n* **1** the internal organs of the body ⟨unpleasant memories of having to examine the *innards* of a frog for science class⟩ — see GUT 1

2 an interior or internal part ⟨Consumers are warned against poking around in the *innards* of the air conditioner.⟩ — see INSIDE 1

innate *adj* being a part of the innermost nature of a person or thing ⟨an *innate* athletic ability that allowed him to excel at just about any sport he tried his hand at⟩ — see INHERENT

innately *adv* by natural character or ability ⟨Anne Frank's memorable belief that most people are *innately* good⟩ — see NATURALLY 1

inner *adj* **1** situated farther in ⟨an *inner* area of the national park that is some distance from the nearest road⟩

synonyms inside, interior, internal, inward

related words inmost, innermost; central, mid, middle, midmost

near antonyms outermost, outmost; surface

antonyms exterior, external, outer, outside, outward

2 of or relating to the mind ⟨The man kept his *inner* life private.⟩ — see MENTAL

innocence *n* **1** the quality or state of being free from guilt or blame ⟨The accused embezzler eventually proved her *innocence* and was released.⟩

synonyms blamelessness, faultlessness, guiltlessness, impeccability

related words decency, goodness, honesty, incorruptibility, integrity, law-abidingness, righteousness, uprightness, virtuousness; morality, virtue; chastity, purity, sinlessness; harmlessness, inoffensiveness

near antonyms blame, fault, responsibility; corruption, criminality, depravity, evil, immorality, reprehensibleness, sinfulness, wickedness; harmfulness, offensiveness

antonyms blameworthiness, culpability, guilt, guiltiness
2 the quality or state of being simple and sincere ⟨The *innocence* of the child's question touched everyone present.⟩ — see NAÏVETÉ 1
3 the state of being unaware or uninformed ⟨In my *innocence* I just assumed that quoted rate was for a week's stay and not for a single night at the health spa.⟩ — see IGNORANCE 1
4 the quality or state of being morally pure ⟨In Melville's novel, the sailor Billy Budd serves as a symbol of absolute *innocence*.⟩ — see CHASTITY

innocent *n* an innocent or gentle person ⟨an *innocent* who is often puzzled by and prey to the evils of the world⟩ — see LAMB

innocent *adj* **1** free from sin ⟨an *innocent* baby⟩
synonyms impeccable, pure
related words chaste, moral, virgin, virtuous; immaculate, spotless, unblemished, unstained, unsullied; decent, ethical, good, honest, honorable, righteous, upright, virtuous; blameless, guiltless

near antonyms lascivious, lewd, lustful, oversexed, unchaste; evil, immoral, iniquitous, reprobate, unrighteous, virtueless, wicked; corrupt, debased, debauched, degenerate, depraved, dissolute, erring, fallen, lost, perverted; condemned, damned

antonyms impure, sinful, sinning
2 free from guilt or blame ⟨The robbery suspect was eventually found to be *innocent*.⟩
synonyms blameless, clear, faultless, guiltless, impeccable, irreproachable

related words absolved, acquitted, cleared, exonerated, vindicated; ethical, law-abiding, moral, righteous, upright, virtuous

phrases in the clear
near antonyms blamable, blameworthy, censurable, culpable, impeachable, indictable, punishable; accused, impeached, indicted; condemned, convicted; hangdog, shamed, shamefaced

antonyms guilty
3 free from any intent to deceive or impress others ⟨an *innocent* offer to sing before the gathering⟩ — see GUILELESS
4 lacking in worldly wisdom or informed judgment ⟨an *innocent* young woman who felt a little out of place among her more sophisticated roommates⟩ — see NAIVE 1
5 not causing or being capable of causing injury or hurt ⟨good-natured teasing that is just *innocent* fun⟩ — see HARMLESS
6 not informed about or aware of something ⟨His surprised expression showed that he was entirely *innocent* of the changes.⟩ — see IGNORANT 2

innocently *adv* **1** without any attempt to impress by deception or exaggeration ⟨"You look nice," she commented *innocently*.⟩ — see NATURALLY 3
2 with purity of thought and deed ⟨Very young children approach the world so *innocently*.⟩ — see PURELY 1

innocuous *adj* not causing or being capable of causing injury or hurt ⟨those *innocuous* lies we must tell every day if society is to remain civil⟩ — see HARMLESS

innovate *vb* to be responsible for the creation and early operation or use of ⟨*innovated* a new system for filing books that dramatically improved efficiency in libraries⟩ — see FOUND

innovation *n* something (as a device) created for the first time through the use of the imagination ⟨The computer is one *innovation* that revolutionized the business world.⟩ — see INVENTION 1

innovative *adj* **1** having the skill and imagination to create new things ⟨an award for the most *innovative* designer of consumer electronics⟩ — see CREATIVE 1
2 showing a noteworthy use of the imagination and creativity especially in inventing ⟨*innovative* automotive technology⟩ — see CLEVER 1

innovator *n* one who creates or introduces something new ⟨Thank goodness for the *innovator* who thought up the remote control.⟩ — see INVENTOR

innumerable *adj* too many to be counted ⟨Our reasons to give thanks are as *innumerable* as the stars.⟩ — see COUNTLESS

inoculate *vb* to cause (as a person) to become filled or saturated with a certain quality or principle ⟨*inoculated* them with the idea that the individual can always make a difference in this world⟩ — see INFUSE

inoffensive *adj* not causing or being capable of causing injury or hurt ⟨an *inoffensive* little joke at the opening of his speech⟩ — see HARMLESS

inoperable *adj* **1** not being in working order ⟨We have several *inoperable* cars on the property.⟩
synonyms down, inoperative, malfunctioning, nonfunctional, nonfunctioning, nonoperating

related words broken; off; deactivated, deadlocked, ineffective, ineffectual, nonproductive, unproductive, unusable, unworkable, useless

phrases on the blink, on the fritz, out of commission
near antonyms effective, effectual, employable, performing, producing, productive, serving, usable (*also* useable), useful, viable, workable

antonyms functional, functioning, operable, operant, operating, operational, operative, running, working
2 not capable of being put to use or account ⟨a delightfully creative but *inoperable* plan for building a theme park in the area⟩ — see IMPRACTICAL

inoperative *adj* **1** not being in a state of use, activity, or employment ⟨Be careful when putting your hands in even an *inoperative* garbage disposal.⟩ — see INACTIVE 2
2 not being in working order ⟨looking for an expert to fix the *inoperative* grandfather clock⟩ — see INOPERABLE 1
3 having no legal or binding force ⟨The decision of the state's supreme court has rendered the law *inoperative*.⟩ — see NULL 1

inopportune *adj* occurring before the usual or expected time ⟨their *inopportune* arrival before the house was cleaned⟩ — see EARLY 2

inopportunely *adv* before the usual or expected time ⟨Our guest dropped in *inopportunely*, before dinner was ready.⟩ — see EARLY

inordinate *adj* going beyond a normal or acceptable limit in degree or amount ⟨an *inordinate* number of complaints about the slow pace of snow removal around the city⟩ — see EXCESSIVE

inordinately *adv* beyond a normal or acceptable limit ⟨taking an *inordinately* long time to finish the house⟩ — see TOO 1

input *n* an opinion suggesting a wise or proper course of action ⟨He solicited *input* from several trusted sources before making the investment.⟩ — see ADVICE

inquest *n* a systematic search for the truth or facts about something ⟨The police conducted an *inquest* into the case.⟩ — see INQUIRY 1

inquire (into) *vb* to search through or into ⟨The principal *inquired into* the possibility of holding graduation at a larger hall.⟩ — see EXPLORE 1

inquire (of) *vb* to put a question or questions to ⟨casually *inquired of* the neighbors the identity of the house's previous owner⟩ — see ASK 1

inquiry *n* 1 a systematic search for the truth or facts about something ⟨an *inquiry* into the origins of the universe⟩
synonyms delving, examination, exploration, inquest, inquisition, investigation, probe, probing, research, study
related words quest; audit, check; checkup, diagnosis, inspection; hearing, interrogation, trial; feeler, query, question; poll, questionary, questionnaire, survey; challenge, cross-examination, grilling, quiz; rehearing, reinvestigation; self-exploration, self-reflection, self-scrutiny
2 an act or instance of asking for information ⟨One student made a hesitant *inquiry* about the assignment.⟩ — see QUESTION 2

inquisition *n* a systematic search for the truth or facts about something ⟨There's no need to conduct an *inquisition* about so trivial a matter.⟩ — see INQUIRY 1

inquisitive *adj* interested in what is not one's own business ⟨an *inquisitive* neighbor⟩ — see CURIOUS 1

inquisitiveness *n* an eager desire to find out about things that are often none of one's business ⟨His irksome *inquisitiveness* made people reluctant to socialize with him.⟩ — see CURIOSITY 1

inroad *n* a sudden attack on and entrance into hostile territory ⟨The army is finally making *inroads* into enemy territory.⟩ — see RAID 1

inrush *n* a flowing or coming in ⟨A sudden *inrush* of air blew my hair back.⟩ — see INFLUX

insane *adj* 1 conceived or made without regard for reason or reality ⟨a completely *insane* plan to build a ball field in the middle of nowhere⟩ — see FANTASTIC 1
2 going beyond a normal or acceptable limit in degree or amount ⟨She saved an *insane* amount of money last year.⟩ — see EXCESSIVE

inscribe *vb* 1 to cut (as letters or designs) on a hard surface ⟨paid a jeweler to *inscribe* their names and wedding date on their wedding rings⟩ — see ENGRAVE 1
2 to add (a person) to a list or roll as a participant or member ⟨*inscribed* the couple in the society of sustaining donors to the museum⟩ — see ENROLL 1
3 to put (someone or something) on a list ⟨*inscribed* his name on the list of those to be commended⟩ — see ¹LIST 2

inscrutable *adj* 1 being beyond one's powers to know, understand, or explain ⟨the many *inscrutable* beliefs of that ancient religion⟩ — see MYSTERIOUS 1
2 having an often intentionally veiled or uncertain meaning ⟨Ancient oracles typically uttered *inscrutable* prophecies that could be interpreted almost any way one chose.⟩ — see OBSCURE 1

insecure *adj* 1 not tightly fastened, tied, or stretched ⟨*Insecure* twine allowed the bundle of newspapers to break open as soon as it was tossed to the ground.⟩ — see LOOSE 1
2 feeling or showing uncomfortable feelings of uncertainty ⟨I always feel *insecure* in situations where I don't know anyone.⟩ — see NERVOUS 1

insecurity *n* the quality or state of not being firmly fixed in position ⟨The *insecurity* of the bookcase made it dangerous for a household with small children who like to climb.⟩ — see INSTABILITY

insensate *adj* 1 lacking animate awareness or sensation ⟨the *insensate* stones⟩
synonyms insensible, senseless, unfeeling
related words lifeless; unconscious
near antonyms aware, cognizant, conscious; animated, lively, vibrant

antonyms animate, feeling, sensate, sensible, sensitive, sentient
2 having or showing a lack of sympathy or tender feelings ⟨an *insensate* boss who refuses to allow time off for funerals⟩ — see HARD 1

insensibility *n* 1 a lack of emotion or emotional expressiveness ⟨an odd *insensibility* to the honor done her⟩ — see APATHY 1
2 a temporary state of unconsciousness ⟨knocked into *insensibility* by the blow to the head⟩ — see FAINT

insensible *adj* 1 having lost consciousness ⟨If a choking person is *insensible*, you should lay them down on their back before performing the Heimlich maneuver.⟩ — see UNCONSCIOUS 1
2 not perceptible by a sense or by the mind ⟨The fragile glass flowers can be damaged by even the most *insensible* tremors.⟩ — see IMPERCEPTIBLE
3 having or showing a lack of interest or concern ⟨City hall remains *insensible* to our complaints about the downtown parking situation.⟩ — see INDIFFERENT 1
4 lacking animate awareness or sensation ⟨Even the canyon's *insensible* rocks seemed to mock the stranded climber's utter helplessness.⟩ — see INSENSATE 1
5 lacking in refinement or good taste ⟨an *insensible* brute upon whom the niceties of life were completely lost⟩ — see COARSE 2
6 not informed about or aware of something ⟨a scientist who usually is so engrossed in his work that he is quite *insensible* of the passage of time⟩ — see IGNORANT 2

insensitive *adj* 1 having or showing a lack of sympathy or tender feelings ⟨an *insensitive* remark that was incredibly rude⟩ — see HARD 1
2 lacking in sensation or feeling ⟨fingers rendered *insensitive* by the cold⟩ — see NUMB 1

inseparability *n* the state of being in a very personal or private relationship ⟨Never seen apart, the two sisters had an *inseparability* that was well-known to their friends.⟩ — see FAMILIARITY 1

insert *vb* to put among or between others ⟨surreptitiously *inserted* the book in its proper place on the shelf⟩
synonyms fit (in *or* into), inject, insinuate, interject, interpolate, interpose, intersperse, introduce
related words cut in, inlay, inset, install; interfile, interline, lard, weave; cram, shove, thrust, wedge; add, append, attach
near antonyms eject, eliminate, exclude, expel, extract, withdraw; deduct, detach, subtract; reject

inside *adj* 1 not known or meant to be known by the general populace ⟨made a stock trade based on *inside* information⟩ — see PRIVATE 1
2 situated farther in ⟨chose the *inside* lane to run around the track⟩ — see INNER 1

inside *n* 1 an interior or internal part ⟨The *inside* of the clock features an amazingly complex mechanism.⟩
synonyms innards, interior, within
related words belly, bowels, guts; stuffing; recesses; center, core, heart
near antonyms border, boundary, brim, edge, end, extremity, fringe, limit, margin, perimeter, periphery, rim; surface
antonyms exterior, outside
2 *usually* **insides** *pl* the internal organs of the body ⟨medical students eager to see what people's *insides* look like⟩ — see GUT 1
3 the seat of one's deepest thoughts and emotions ⟨Not one to share her fears and worries, she keeps it all on the *inside*.⟩ — see CORE 1
4 information not generally available to the public ⟨a person with the *inside* on what really happened at the board meeting⟩ — see DOPE 1

insight *n* the ability to understand inner qualities or relationships ⟨a therapist with real *insight* into people's personalities⟩ — see WISDOM 1

insightful *adj* having or showing deep understanding and intelligent application of knowledge ⟨a critical study featuring an *insightful* analysis of the novelist's recurring themes⟩ — see WISE 1

insignificant *adj* **1** lacking importance ⟨an *insignificant* detail that we can safely ignore⟩ — see UNIMPORTANT
2 so small or unimportant as to warrant little or no attention ⟨The *insignificant* wear on the doll's face does nothing to diminish its considerable value as an antique.⟩ — see NEGLIGIBLE 1

insincere *adj* not being or expressing what one appears to be or express ⟨the *insincere* compliments of a spiteful gossip⟩
synonyms artificial, backhanded, counterfeit, double, double-dealing, fake, feigned, hypocritical, left-handed, mealy, mealymouthed, phony (*also* phoney), pretended, two-faced, unctuous
related words affected, assumed, claptrap, contrived, forced, mechanical, put-on, simulated, strained, unnatural; empty, hollow, meaningless; deceitful, devious, dishonest, false, untruthful; facile, glib, superficial; bogus, sham; facetious, jocular, tongue-in-cheek; canting, pharisaical, pious, sanctimonious, self-righteous, simon-pure
near antonyms direct, forthright, frank, heart-to-heart, open, plain, straightforward
antonyms artless, candid, genuine, honest, sincere, undesigning

insincerity *n* the pretending of having virtues, principles, or beliefs that one in fact does not have ⟨The *insincerity* of the family's professed concern for the environment is pretty much exposed by the gas-guzzler parked in the driveway.⟩ — see HYPOCRISY

insinuate *vb* **1** to introduce in a gradual, secret, or clever way ⟨Years were needed for the agent to *insinuate* himself into the criminal organization.⟩
synonyms infiltrate, slip, sneak, wind, worm, wriggle
related words creep, edge, wiggle; insert, interpolate, interpose, introduce
2 to convey an idea indirectly ⟨Are you *insinuating* that I won by cheating?⟩ — see HINT
3 to put among or between others ⟨quietly *insinuated* herself among the concertgoers raptly listening to the piano solo⟩ — see INSERT

insipid *adj* **1** lacking in taste or flavor ⟨an apple pie with a mushy, *insipid* filling that strongly resembled soggy cardboard⟩
synonyms flat, flavorless, savorless, tasteless, unsavory
related words bland, dilute, thin, watery, weak; plain, unflavored
near antonyms distasteful, loathsome, sickening, unappetizing, unpalatable; mawkish; appetizing, delectable, delicious, palatable, toothsome; keen, piquant, seasoned, spicy; flavored; heavy, rich
antonyms flavorful, sapid, savory (*also* savoury), tasteful, tasty
2 lacking in qualities that make for spirit and character ⟨an *insipid* and somewhat boring movie⟩ — see WISHY-WASHY 1

insist *vb* to state as a fact usually forcefully ⟨She continued to *insist* that she was right, even in the face of overwhelming evidence to the contrary.⟩ — see CLAIM 1

insist (on) *vb* to ask for (something) earnestly or with authority ⟨The director *insisted on* absolute quiet on the set.⟩ — see DEMAND 1

insistence *n* a solemn and often public declaration of the truth or existence of something ⟨a continued *insistence*

that there was a massive cover-up by the government⟩ — see PROTESTATION

insistent *adj* continuing despite difficulties, opposition, or discouragement ⟨Margaret Sanger is remembered as an *insistent* crusader for birth control.⟩ — see PERSISTENT

insolence *n* **1** disrespectful or argumentative talk given in response to a command or request ⟨amazed that parents would tolerate such *insolence* from their children⟩ — see BACK TALK
2 rude behavior ⟨Her frequent displays of *insolence* have lowered her standing among movie fans.⟩ — see DISCOURTESY

insolent *adj* displaying or marked by rude boldness ⟨an appallingly *insolent* reply to a reasonable request⟩ — see NERVY 1

insoluble *adj* incapable of being solved or accomplished ⟨the seemingly *insoluble* mystery concerning the identity of the people who built these ancient structures⟩ — see IMPOSSIBLE

insouciance *n* lack of interest or concern ⟨Amy wandered into the meeting with complete *insouciance* to the fact that she was late.⟩ — see INDIFFERENCE

insouciant *adj* **1** having or showing freedom from worries or troubles ⟨the *insouciant* gaiety of the idle rich⟩ — see CAREFREE
2 having or showing a lack of interest or concern ⟨an *insouciant* attitude about punctuality⟩ — see INDIFFERENT 1

inspect *vb* to look over closely (as for judging quality or condition) ⟨*inspected* the collie before the dog show⟩
synonyms audit, check (out), con, examine, overlook, oversee, review, scan, scrutinize, survey, view
related words notice, observe, watch; comb, peruse, pore (over); analyze, dissect, parse; delve (into), explore, investigate, plumb, probe, research, study
phrases go over
near antonyms skim; glance (at *or* over); miss, overlook

inspection *n* a close look at or over someone or something in order to judge condition ⟨The recruits lined up for an *inspection.*⟩
synonyms audit, check, checkup, examination, review, scan, scrutiny, survey, view
related words analysis, assay, dissection; exploration, investigation, probe, research, study; inquisition, interrogation; once-over, perusal; observation, surveillance, watch; checkout, test-drive, trial run

inspire *vb* **1** to fill with courage or strength of purpose ⟨The rousing campaign speech *inspired* everyone to get out the vote.⟩ — see ENCOURAGE 1
2 to draw out (something hidden, latent, or reserved) ⟨What *inspired* that comment?⟩ — see EDUCE
3 to provide (someone) with moral or spiritual understanding ⟨Great works of visual art can *inspire* us in ways that the written word often cannot.⟩ — see ENLIGHTEN 2

inspiring *adj* causing great emotional or mental stimulation ⟨an *inspiring* idea for a national program in which young people would commit themselves to a year of community service⟩ — see EXCITING 1

instability *n* the quality or state of not being firmly fixed in position ⟨The *instability* of the bridge became tragically apparent when it suddenly collapsed.⟩
synonyms insecurity, precariousness, shakiness, unsteadiness
related words insubstantiality, unsoundness; changeability, inconstancy, mutability; laxness, looseness, slackness
near antonyms firmness, soundness, substantiality
antonyms fastness, fixedness, security, stability, steadiness

install *vb* **1** to put into an office or welcome into an

organization with special ceremonies ⟨*installed* her as the new principal of the high school⟩
synonyms baptize, inaugurate, induct, initiate, instate, invest, seat
related words swear in; consecrate, enshrine; accept, admit, take in; enlist, enroll (*also* enrol)
near antonyms can, discharge, fire, terminate; muster out
2 to establish or place comfortably or snugly ⟨*installed* herself in an easy chair by the fireplace and remained there for the rest of the afternoon⟩ — see ENSCONCE 1

installation *n* **1** the process or an instance of being formally placed in an office or organization ⟨The *installation* of a new president takes place once every four years.⟩
synonyms baptism, inaugural, inauguration, induction, initiation, installment (*also* instalment), investiture, investment
related words enlistment, enrollment (*also* enrolment); promotion
near antonyms discharge, removal
2 a structure that is designed and built for a particular purpose ⟨a massive *installation* that supplies the electrical power needs for the entire state⟩ — see FACILITY

installment *also* **instalment** *n* the process or an instance of being formally placed in an office or organization ⟨attended the *installment* of the new university president⟩ — see INSTALLATION 1

instance *n* one of a group or collection that shows what the whole is like ⟨This is just one *instance* of his repeated failure to do what he promised.⟩ — see EXAMPLE

instance *vb* **1** to give as an example ⟨*instanced* one particular incident as an illustration of their penchant for practical jokes⟩ — see QUOTE 1
2 to make reference to or speak about briefly but specifically ⟨The astronomer *instanced* the latest astronomical research in her presentation on measuring star magnitude.⟩ — see MENTION 1
3 to show or make clear by using examples ⟨I *instanced* the hero's moral courage with several examples from the novel.⟩ — see ILLUSTRATE 1

instant *adj* **1** done or occurring without any noticeable lapse in time ⟨an *instant* response to the cry for help⟩ — see INSTANTANEOUS
2 needing immediate attention ⟨an *instant* need for food supplies⟩ — see ACUTE 2
3 existing or in progress right now ⟨We should be more concerned with *instant* dangers than with those in the far-off future.⟩ — see PRESENT 1

instant *n* a very small space of time ⟨It all happened in an *instant*.⟩
synonyms beat, flash, jiffy, minute, moment, second, shake, split second, trice, twinkle, twinkling, wink
related words snatch, spurt
near antonyms eon (*or* aeon), age, eternity, forever; infinity, lifetime

instantaneous *adj* done or occurring without any noticeable lapse in time ⟨The thunder following the flash of lightning was nearly *instantaneous*.⟩
synonyms immediate, instant, split-second, straightaway
related words summary; fast, hit-and-run, prompt, quick, rapid, speedy, swift
near antonyms dilatory, tardy; slow, sluggish; prolonged, protracted; deferred, delayed

instantly *adv* without delay ⟨showed leadership by reacting *instantly* to the crisis⟩ — see IMMEDIATELY

instantly *conj* just at the moment that ⟨We realized there would be problems *instantly* we saw the final report.⟩ — see WHEN 2

instate *vb* to put into an office or welcome into an organization with special ceremonies ⟨The new secretary of the treasury was *instated* on Monday.⟩ — see INSTALL 1

instead *adv* as a substitute ⟨I was offered a ride, but I chose to walk *instead*.⟩
synonyms first, rather
related words alternately, alternatively
phrases in lieu

instigate *vb* **1** to bring (something volatile or intense) into being ⟨The medical breakthrough *instigated* a whole new field of therapy.⟩ — see INCITE 1
2 to rouse to strong feeling or action ⟨She blamed him for *instigating* the argument.⟩ — see PROVOKE 1

instigating *adj* serving or likely to arouse a strong reaction ⟨an artist who deliberately creates *instigating* works of art that are sure to arouse controversy⟩ — see PROVOCATIVE

instigation *n* **1** something that arouses a strong response from another ⟨Without *instigation* the man suddenly threw a punch.⟩ — see PROVOCATION 1
2 something that arouses action or activity ⟨The promise of windfall profits was all the *instigation* they needed to invest in the scheme.⟩ — see IMPULSE 1

instigator *n* a person who stirs up public feelings especially of discontent ⟨an *instigator* who always managed to be innocently standing by once the trouble began⟩ — see AGITATOR

instinctive *adj* done instantly and without conscious thought or decision ⟨The *instinctive* reaction of a parent is to protect their children.⟩ — see AUTOMATIC 1

instinctual *adj* done instantly and without conscious thought or decision ⟨The birds' *instinctual* response is to fly away when startled.⟩ — see AUTOMATIC 1

institute *n* **1** a group of persons formally joined together for some common interest ⟨founded an *institute* to combat the cruel treatment of animals⟩ — see ASSOCIATION 2
2 a public organization with a particular purpose or function ⟨a scientific *institute* researching a cure for cancer⟩ — see INSTITUTION 1

institute *vb* to be responsible for the creation and early operation or use of ⟨Elizabeth Cady Stanton is generally credited with *instituting* the women's-rights movement in 1848.⟩ — see FOUND

instituter *or* **institutor** *n* a person who establishes a whole new field of endeavor ⟨Henry Ford is known as the *instituter* of the use of the assembly line in auto manufacturing.⟩ — see FATHER 2

institution *n* **1** a public organization with a particular purpose or function ⟨a charitable *institution* devoted to raising funds to feed the hungry⟩
synonyms establishment, foundation, institute
related words body, collective, group; corporation, enterprise; charity, philanthropy; think tank
2 a place where mentally ill people are cared for ⟨Their father was committed to an *institution* after his mental health began to rapidly deteriorate.⟩
synonyms asylum, bedlam
related words hospital; halfway house, home; hospice, sanatorium, sanitarium, sanitorium
3 a group of persons formally joined together for some common interest ⟨an *institution* devoted to studying social problems and proposing solutions for them⟩ — see ASSOCIATION 2

instruct *vb* **1** to cause to acquire knowledge or skill in some field ⟨spent his military career *instructing* young pilots⟩ — see TEACH
2 to give information to ⟨*instructed* everyone in the use of the new computer system⟩ — see ENLIGHTEN 1
3 to issue orders to (someone) by right of authority ⟨The

proctors *instructed* everyone to put their pencils down and hand in their tests.⟩ — see COMMAND 1

instruction *n* **1** a statement of what to do that must be obeyed by those concerned ⟨needed an administrative assistant who was good at following *instructions*⟩ — see COMMAND 1
2 the act or process of imparting knowledge or skills to another ⟨the view that the *instruction* of our nation's youth should be our highest priority⟩ — see EDUCATION 1

instructional *adj* providing useful information or knowledge ⟨an *instructional* video on home repair for do-it-yourselfers⟩ — see INFORMATIVE

instructive *adj* providing useful information or knowledge ⟨an *instructive* demonstration of the proper way to pack a suitcase so your clothes don't arrive in a mess⟩ — see INFORMATIVE

instructor *n* a person whose occupation is to give formal instruction in a school ⟨Carter had spent most of his adulthood as an *instructor* in the local school system.⟩ — see TEACHER

instrument *n* **1** a written or printed paper giving information about or proof of something ⟨A valid will is a legal *instrument*.⟩ — see CERTIFICATE
2 an article intended for use in work ⟨Always choose the right *instrument* for any woodworking job.⟩ — see IMPLEMENT
3 something used to achieve an end ⟨He sees scouting as an *instrument* for building character in young people.⟩ — see AGENT 1
4 one that is or can be used to further the purposes of another ⟨the claim that the scientists are mere *instruments* of the tobacco companies, who pay them to produce findings that are highly suspect⟩ — see ¹PAWN

instrumentalist *n* a person who plays a musical instrument ⟨He excels as a conductor, a composer, and as an *instrumentalist*.⟩ — see MUSICIAN 1

instrumentality *n* something used to achieve an end ⟨Computer literacy is only an *instrumentality* for acquiring an education, and not an end in itself.⟩ — see AGENT 1

insubordinate *adj* given to resisting authority or another's control ⟨The junior officer was court-martialed for being *insubordinate*.⟩ — see DISOBEDIENT

insubordination *n* refusal to obey ⟨was fired for chronic *insubordination*⟩ — see DISOBEDIENCE

insubstantial *adj* **1** being of a material lacking in sturdiness or substance ⟨an *insubstantial* carton that could not possibly stand up during long-distance shipping⟩ — see FLIMSY 1
2 not composed of matter ⟨Energy is *insubstantial*.⟩ — see IMMATERIAL 1

insufferable *adj* more than can be put up with ⟨an *insufferable* bore whose only topic of conversation is himself⟩ — see UNBEARABLE

insufficiency *n* **1** a falling short of an essential or desirable amount or number ⟨dealt with the school's *insufficiency* of art supplies by buying materials out of her own pocket⟩ — see DEFICIENCY
2 the lack of sufficient ability, power, or means ⟨her alleged *insufficiency* for the job⟩ — see INABILITY

insufficient *adj* not coming up to an expected measure or meeting a particular need ⟨There's been an *insufficient* number of volunteers for the job, so I'll have to select someone.⟩ — see SHORT 3

insular *adj* not broad or open in views or opinions ⟨an *insular* community that is not receptive of new ideas, especially from outsiders⟩ — see NARROW 2

insulate *vb* to set or keep apart from others ⟨tried to *insulate* their children from the often disturbing news in the mass media⟩ — see ISOLATE

insulation *n* the state of being alone or kept apart from others ⟨She had grown up in such rural *insulation* that she found the busy streets of New York quite overwhelming.⟩ — see ISOLATION

insult *n* an act or expression showing scorn and usually intended to hurt another's feelings ⟨Panelists on that political talk show simply exchange *insults*, not ideas.⟩
synonyms affront, barb, cut, dart, dig, epithet, indignity, name, offense (*or* offence), outrage, personality, poke, put-down, sarcasm, slap, slight, slur
related words catcall, gibe (*or* jibe), jeer, mock, quip, sneer, taunt; abuse, invective, vituperation; disapproval, opprobrium; disgrace, dishonor, shame; attack, criticism, knock, slam, swipe; torment, torture
near antonyms accolade, commendation, compliment; acclaim, applause, praise; adulation, flattery

insult *vb* to cause hurt feelings or deep resentment in ⟨*insulted* their hosts by casually remarking about the outdated look of their home⟩
synonyms affront, disrespect, offend, outrage, slap, slight, wound
related words cut, snub; displease, distress, disturb, hurt, pain, trouble, upset; jeer, mock, ridicule, sneer (at), taunt; defame, disparage, libel, malign, revile, slander, slur, smear; oppress, persecute, torment, torture
near antonyms acclaim, applaud, approve, hail; commend, compliment, eulogize, praise; adulate, flatter; exalt, glorify, honor; delight, gratify, please, satisfy

insuperable *adj* **1** incapable of being defeated, overcome, or subdued ⟨The building project ran into *insuperable* financial difficulties and had to be scrapped.⟩ — see INVINCIBLE
2 incapable of being solved or accomplished ⟨*Insuperable* problems have arisen which make it very unlikely that we will ever finish this project.⟩ — see IMPOSSIBLE

insupportable *adj* **1** more than can be put up with ⟨His *insupportable* arrogance is more than anyone should have to bear.⟩ — see UNBEARABLE
2 too bad to be excused or justified ⟨The organization's actions have been denounced as morally *insupportable*.⟩ — see INEXCUSABLE

insure *vb* to make sure, certain, or safe ⟨Management took steps to *insure* the timely completion of the project.⟩ — see ENSURE

insurgency *n* open fighting against authority (as one's own government) ⟨The *insurgency* has continued for three years.⟩ — see REBELLION 1

insurgent *adj* taking part in a rebellion ⟨Any *insurgent* soldiers will be dealt with harshly.⟩ — see REBELLIOUS 1

insurgent *n* a person who rises up against authority ⟨*insurgents* trying to gain control of the city⟩ — see REBEL

insurmountable *adj* incapable of being defeated, overcome, or subdued ⟨the familiar story of the underdog who ultimately triumphs despite *insurmountable* odds⟩ — see INVINCIBLE

insurrection *n* open fighting against authority (as one's own government) ⟨the famous *insurrection* led by Spartacus opposing slavery in ancient Rome⟩ — see REBELLION 1

insurrectionary *adj* taking part in a rebellion ⟨a small *insurrectionary* force that was soundly defeated by the loyalists⟩ — see REBELLIOUS 1

insurrectionary *n* a person who rises up against authority ⟨only a small band of *insurrectionaries* who were willing to stand up to the dictator⟩ — see REBEL

insurrectionist *n* a person who rises up against authority ⟨a secret meeting of *insurrectionists*⟩ — see REBEL

intact *adj* not lacking any part or member that properly belongs to it ⟨It's rare to find such an old chess set that is *intact*.⟩ — see COMPLETE 1

intangible *adj* not capable of being perceived by the sense of touch ⟨*intangible* forces like gravity⟩
synonyms impalpable
related words bodiless, immaterial, incorporeal, insubstantial, unsubstantial; ethereal, spiritual, unreal
near antonyms corporeal, physical; embodied, material, real, solid, substantial
antonyms palpable, tactile, tangible, touchable
integer *n* **1** a character used to represent a mathematical value ⟨Three is a positive *integer*.⟩ — see NUMBER 1
2 one that has a real and independent existence ⟨an event that is seen as the point at which the gay rights movement became an *integer* and not just a smattering of protests⟩ — see ENTITY
integral *adj* **1** being a part of the innermost nature of a person or thing ⟨a car dealer respected for his *integral* honesty and straightforwardness with customers⟩ — see INHERENT
2 impossible to do without ⟨She's an *integral* member of the team of archaeologists at that dig.⟩ — see ESSENTIAL 1
3 not lacking any part or member that properly belongs to it ⟨a prep school that adheres to the belief that athletics are essential to an *integral* life⟩ — see COMPLETE 1
integrate *vb* **1** to make a part of a body or system ⟨*integrate* the new developments into our understanding of the disease⟩ — see EMBODY 1
2 to turn into a single mass or entity that is more or less the same throughout ⟨*Integrate* the powders thoroughly before adding them to the liquid.⟩ — see BLEND 1
integrity *n* **1** conduct that conforms to an accepted standard of right and wrong ⟨Tom demonstrated that he was a man of *integrity* by taking full responsibility for his actions.⟩ — see MORALITY 1
2 devotion to telling the truth ⟨Her *integrity* is such that she tells the truth even when people least want to hear it.⟩ — see HONESTY 1
3 faithfulness to high moral standards ⟨a politician of great honesty and *integrity*⟩ — see HONOR 1
intellect *n* **1** a very smart person ⟨one of the finest *intellects* of our time⟩ — see GENIUS 1
2 the ability to learn and understand or to deal with problems ⟨a child of great *intellect* as well as artistic talent⟩ — see INTELLIGENCE 1
intellectual *adj* **1** much given to learning and thinking ⟨As the daughter of college professors, she's used to being around *intellectual* people.⟩
synonyms cerebral, highbrow, nerdy
related words cultivated, cultured; erudite, learned, literate, scholarly, well-read; academic (*also* academical), bookish, professorial; didactic, high-toned, hyperintellectual, pedantic; educated, schooled; brainy, bright, brilliant, clever, intelligent, quick-witted, smart
near antonyms uncultivated, uncultured; ignorant, illiterate, uneducated, unlettered, unread; dumb, foolish, idiotic (*also* idiotical), moronic, slow, stupid, unintelligent; benighted, unenlightened
antonyms anti-intellectual, lowbrow, nonintellectual, philistine
2 of or relating to the mind ⟨*intellectual* pursuits such as reading and studying⟩ — see MENTAL
3 of or relating to schooling or learning especially at an advanced level ⟨Research that shows that people from very *intellectual* backgrounds are happiest with spouses having comparable educations.⟩ — see ACADEMIC 1
intellectual *n* a person with strong intellectual interests ⟨He discovered that in politics a reputation for being an *intellectual* was regarded as a liability.⟩
synonyms egghead, highbrow, nerd
related words bluestocking; Brahmin, mandarin, sage; brain, genius, intellect, thinker, whiz, wizard

near antonyms blockhead, dolt, dope, dumbbell, dummy, dunce, fathead, half-wit, imbecile, moron, nitwit, pinhead, simpleton
antonyms anti-intellectual, lowbrow, philistine
intellectuality *n* the ability to learn and understand or to deal with problems ⟨One doesn't need the *intellectuality* of a rocket scientist to understand the problem.⟩ — see INTELLIGENCE 1
intelligence *n* **1** the ability to learn and understand or to deal with problems ⟨High scores on this test supposedly demonstrate great *intelligence*.⟩
synonyms brain(s), gray matter, headpiece, intellect, intellectuality, mentality, reason, sense
related words eggheadedness, highbrowism, intellectualism; braininess, brilliance; acumen, alertness, apprehension, astuteness, discernment, discriminability, insight, judgment (*or* judgement), perception, perspicacity; common sense, horse sense, mother wit; aptitude, talent; sagacity, sapience, wisdom, wit; head, mind, skull
near antonyms denseness, density, doltishness, dopiness, dullness (*also* dulness), dumbness, fatuity, feeblemindedness, foolishness, half-wittedness, idiocy, imbecility, senselessness, simpleness, slowness, stupidity
2 a report of recent events or facts not previously known ⟨usually received the latest *intelligence* about how the war was going⟩ — see NEWS
3 exceptional discernment and judgment especially in practical matters ⟨As head of the customer service department, he has handled complaints and disputes with unfailing *intelligence* and good humor.⟩ — see ACUMEN
intelligent *adj* **1** having or showing quickness of mind ⟨Proud parents typically insist that their children are *intelligent* way beyond their years.⟩ ⟨His *intelligent* response to the emergency averted a disaster.⟩
synonyms alert, brainy, bright, brilliant, clever, exceptional, fast, keen, nimble, quick, quick-witted, sharp, sharp-witted, smart
related words apt, ingenious, resourceful; acute, astute, discerning, insightful, knowing, perceptive, percipient, perspicacious, sagacious, sapient, savvy, wise; cerebral, erudite, genial, highbrow, knowledgeable, learned, literate, scholarly, well-read; creative, inventive, judicious, prudent, sage, sane, sapient, sensible, sound, wise; crafty, cunning, foxy, shrewd, wily; logical, rational, reasonable
near antonyms feebleminded, simpleminded; ignorant, illiterate, lowbrow, nonintellectual, unacademic, uneducated, uninformed, unintellectual, untaught, unthinking; absurd, asinine, balmy, cockeyed, daffy, daft, dotty, fool, half-baked, harebrained, nonsensical, preposterous, sappy, screwball, wacky (*also* whacky), zany
antonyms airheaded, boneheaded, brainless, bubbleheaded, chuckleheaded, dense, dim, dim-witted, doltish, dopey (*also* dopy), dorky [*slang*], dull, dumb, dunderheaded, empty-headed, fatuous, half-witted, knuckleheaded, mindless, obtuse, opaque, senseless, simple, slow, slow-witted, soft, softheaded, stupid, thick, thickheaded, thick-witted, unintelligent, vacuous, weak-minded, witless
2 having the ability to reason ⟨There is some debate over whether dolphins are *intelligent* animals.⟩ — see RATIONAL 1
3 having or showing good judgment and restraint especially in conduct or speech ⟨an *intelligent* response that satisfied everyone⟩ — see DISCREET 1
intemperate *adj* showing no signs of being under control ⟨a comment on the website that revealed an *intemperate* anger⟩ — see RAMPANT 1
intend *vb* **1** to have in mind as a purpose or goal ⟨an aspiring entrepreneur who *intends* to revolutionize the biotech industry⟩

synonyms aim, aspire, calculate, contemplate, design, look, mean, meditate, plan, propose, purport, purpose

related words dream, hope, wish; consider, debate, mull (over), ponder; attempt, endeavor, strive, struggle, try; plot, scheme; accomplish, achieve, effect, execute, perform

phrases figure on

2 to communicate or convey (as an idea) to the mind ⟨Lawyers for both sides argued for days about what was *intended* by a particular phrase in the law.⟩ — see MEAN 1

intended *n* the person to whom one is engaged to be married ⟨After a bit of debate, she and her *intended* have finally picked out a wedding site.⟩ — see BETROTHED

intended *adj* made, given, or done with full awareness of what one is doing ⟨You may feign innocence, but I know that that last remark was an *intended* dig.⟩ — see INTENTIONAL

intense *adj* **1** extreme in degree, power, or effect ⟨the *intense* cold of the polar regions⟩

synonyms acute, almighty, blistering, deep, dreadful, excruciating, explosive, exquisite, fearful, fearsome, ferocious, fierce, frightful, furious, ghastly, hard, heavy, intensive, keen, profound, terrible, vehement, vicious, violent

related words accentuated, concentrated, deepened; emphasized, enhanced, heightened, intensified, magnified; exhaustive, thorough; harsh, rigorous, severe

near antonyms feeble, weak; shallow, superficial; moderated, qualified; alleviated, eased, lightened, toned (down); abated, decreased, diminished, lessened, reduced, subdued

antonyms light, moderate, soft

2 having or expressing great depth of feeling ⟨an *intense* actor who favors edgy film roles⟩ — see FERVENT 1

intensely *adv* **1** with great effort or determination ⟨Rosa struggled *intensely* to master the language of her adopted country.⟩ — see HARD 1

2 to a great degree ⟨The senate race was *intensely* close.⟩ — see VERY 1

intensify *vb* to make markedly greater in measure or degree ⟨*intensified* her efforts to preserve the town's historic buildings and landmarks⟩

synonyms accentuate, amplify, beef (up), boost, consolidate, deepen, enhance, heighten, magnify, redouble, step up, strengthen

related words broaden, enlarge, expand, extend, lengthen; accelerate, hasten, quicken; emphasize, point (up), sharpen, stress; augment, enforce, restrengthen, supplement; maximize; enliven, jazz (up); aggravate

near antonyms decrease, diminish, lessen, let up (on), reduce, subdue, tone (down), weaken; dwindle, recede, subside, taper (off), wane; alleviate, ease, lighten

antonyms abate, moderate

intensity *n* **1** depth of feeling ⟨Peter spoke with great *intensity* and eloquence on the need to combat racism.⟩ — see ARDOR 1

2 the quality or state of being forceful (as in expression) ⟨The *intensity* of the actor's performance had theatergoers on the edge of their seats.⟩ — see VEHEMENCE 1

intensive *adj* extreme in degree, power, or effect ⟨an *intensive* effort to prevent a discount store from opening in town⟩ — see INTENSE 1

intensively *adv* with great effort or determination ⟨labored *intensively* in order to get the film ready for its premiere⟩ — see HARD 1

intent *adj* **1** fully committed to achieving a goal ⟨*intent* on finishing her sculpture in time for the group show⟩ — see DETERMINED 1

2 having the mind fixed on something ⟨He was so *intent* on his work that he didn't hear the dog bark.⟩ — see ATTENTIVE 1

intent *n* **1** something that one hopes or intends to accomplish ⟨I'm sorry that I hurt your feelings; that wasn't my *intent*.⟩ — see GOAL

2 the idea that is conveyed or intended to be conveyed to the mind by language, symbol, or action ⟨The wording was a little unclear, but I think I grasped the *intent*.⟩ — see MEANING 1

intention *n* **1** something that one hopes or intends to accomplish ⟨Her *intention* is to climb the highest peak in each of the 50 states.⟩ — see GOAL

2 the idea that is conveyed or intended to be conveyed to the mind by language, symbol, or action ⟨She was uncertain of the *intention* of his frantic gesturing.⟩ — see MEANING 1

intentional *adj* made, given, or done with full awareness of what one is doing ⟨I'm fairly sure that your "accidental" cutting down of my rosebush was really *intentional*.⟩

synonyms conscious, deliberate, intended, knowing, purposeful, set, voluntary, willful (*or* wilful), witting

related words designed, planned; conscious; advised, calculated, considered, measured, reasoned, studied, thoughtful, weighed; premeditated, premeditative, prepense; discretionary, elective, optional, volunteer

near antonyms inadvertent, unwitting; accidental, chance, haphazard, hit-or-miss, incidental, random; aimless, desultory, purposeless; abrupt, impetuous, sudden; coerced, forced, involuntary; compulsory, mandatory, necessary, nonelective, obligatory, ordered, required; extemporaneous, impromptu, impulsive, instinctive, spontaneous, unforced, unpremeditated

antonyms nondeliberate, nonpurposive, unintentional

intentionally *adv* with full awareness of what one is doing ⟨The witness *intentionally* gave misleading answers to the questions.⟩

synonyms advisedly, consciously, deliberately, designedly, knowingly, purposefully, purposely, willfully, wittingly

related words calculatedly, studiedly; voluntarily, willingly; premeditatedly

phrases on purpose

near antonyms accidentally; haphazardly, randomly; involuntarily, unwillingly; impulsively, instinctively, spontaneously

antonyms inadvertently, unconsciously, unintentionally, unknowingly, unwittingly

intently *adv* with great effort or determination ⟨*intently* studied his notes just before the exam⟩ — see HARD 1

intentness *n* a mental state free of jesting or trifling ⟨studied the dance steps with obvious *intentness*⟩ — see EARNESTNESS

inter *vb* to place (a dead body) in the earth, a tomb, or the sea ⟨The soldier was *interred* with great honors at Arlington National Cemetery.⟩ — see BURY 1

interaction *n* doings between individuals or groups ⟨She guessed from the friendly *interaction* that they were close to the other parents in the organization.⟩ — see RELATION 1

intercede *vb* to act as a go-between for opposing sides ⟨asked an old friend of the family to *intercede* in the bitter dispute over the inheritance⟩ — see INTERVENE

intercessor *n* one who works with opposing sides in order to bring about an agreement ⟨Eventually, they hired an *intercessor*, because they were getting nowhere on their own.⟩ — see MEDIATOR

intercommunicate *vb* to engage in an exchange of information or ideas ⟨The two agencies will need to *intercommunicate* better if the nation is ever to become truly secure.⟩ — see COMMUNICATE 2

interconnect *vb* to put or bring together so as to form a new and longer whole ⟨We *interconnected* all of our audio and video components to get the full home theater experience.⟩ — see CONNECT 1

intercourse *n* **1** doings between individuals or groups ⟨the unspoken rules of social *intercourse*⟩ — see RELATION 1 **2** sexual union involving penetration of the vagina by the penis ⟨had a discussion with their teenage child about safe *intercourse*⟩ — see SEXUAL INTERCOURSE

interdict *n* an order that something not be done or used ⟨the principal's *interdict* against cell phones in the classroom⟩ — see PROHIBITION 2

interdict *vb* to order not to do or use or to be done or used ⟨The state legislature moved to *interdict* the use of radar-detection devices by motorists.⟩ — see FORBID

interdicted *adj* that may not be permitted ⟨an *interdicted* hold in wrestling⟩ — see IMPERMISSIBLE

interdicting *n* the act of ordering that something not be done or used ⟨the *interdicting* against and punishment of bullying at school⟩ — see PROHIBITION 1

interdiction *n* **1** an order that something not be done or used ⟨a written *interdiction* against the use of electronic devices during examinations⟩ — see PROHIBITION 2 **2** the act of ordering that something not be done or used ⟨The recent *interdiction* against open fires on the beach has riled summer revelers.⟩ — see PROHIBITION 1

interest *vb* to hold the attention of ⟨The book didn't *interest* me, so I ended up watching the parade of people on the sidewalk.⟩ — see ENGAGE 1

interest *n* **1** a legal right to participation in the advantages, profits, and responsibility of something ⟨All of the workers at the food cooperative have an *interest* in it.⟩ **synonyms** claim, share, stake **related words** co-ownership, ownership, part, partnership, possession, title **2** the state of doing well especially in relation to one's happiness or success ⟨Make no mistake: she's determined to act in her own *interest* in this business deal.⟩ — see WELFARE **3** a commercial or industrial activity or organization ⟨a multinational corporation with *interests* on every continent⟩ — see ENTERPRISE 1

interesting *adj* holding the attention or provoking interest ⟨This is one of the most *interesting* books I've read all year.⟩ **synonyms** absorbing, arresting, engaging, engrossing, enthralling, fascinating, gripping, immersing, intriguing, involving, riveting **related words** breathtaking, electric, electrifying, exciting, exhilarating, galvanizing, inspiring, rousing, stimulating, stirring, thrilling; provocative, tantalizing; emphatic, showy, splashy, striking; curious, odd, unusual, weird; amazing, astonishing, astounding, eventful, eye-opening, fabulous, marvelous (*or* marvellous), surprising, wonderful, wondrous; amusing, entertaining **near antonyms** tiresome, tiring, wearisome, wearying; sterile, unexciting; dreary, humdrum, pedestrian; demoralizing, discouraging, disheartening, dispiriting **antonyms** boring, drab, dry, dull, heavy, monotonous, tedious, uninteresting

interfere *vb* to interest oneself in what is not one's concern ⟨a strong resentment of outsiders who attempted to *interfere* with their traditional ways of doing things⟩ **synonyms** butt in, intrude, meddle, mess, nose, obtrude, poke, pry, snoop **related words** intercede, interpose, intervene; barge (in), chisel (in), encroach, infringe, invade, trespass; fiddle, fool, monkey, play, tamper **near antonyms** avoid, eschew, shun; disregard, ignore, neglect, overlook

interfere (with) *vb* to create difficulty for the work or activity of ⟨He claims that the federal regulations *interfere with* his business and are of no benefit to anyone.⟩ — see HAMPER

interference *n* something that makes movement or progress difficult ⟨Without the *interference* of the rain, we could have made good time on that road trip.⟩ — see ENCUMBRANCE

interferer *n* a person who meddles in the affairs of others ⟨an *interferer* who always needs to know what everyone is doing⟩ — see BUSYBODY

interfering *adj* thrusting oneself where one is not welcome or invited ⟨She made a decision on her own and ignored her *interfering* relatives.⟩ — see INTRUSIVE

interim *adj* **1** intended to last, continue, or serve for a limited time ⟨Putting up some students in local motels is obviously just an *interim* solution to the college's housing shortage.⟩ — see TEMPORARY 1 **2** serving in a position for the time being ⟨will serve as *interim* head of the police department until the investigation is completed⟩ — see ACTING

interim *n* a break in continuity ⟨There was a brief *interim* in the proceedings while everyone got organized.⟩ — see GAP 2

interior *n* an interior or internal part ⟨The *interior* of the computer was clogged with dust.⟩ — see INSIDE 1

interior *adj* **1** of or relating to the mind ⟨The novel's characters have plenty of adventures, but their *interior* lives are never explored.⟩ — see MENTAL **2** situated farther in ⟨I was given a windowless *interior* office.⟩ — see INNER 1

interject *vb* to put among or between others ⟨She occasionally *interjected* comments into the conversation.⟩ — see INSERT

interjection *n* a sudden short emotional utterance ⟨A chorus of angry *interjections* greeted the announcement that our flight would be delayed.⟩ — see EXCLAMATION

interlace *vb* **1** to cause to twine about one another ⟨*interlaced* strands of her hair for a new look⟩ — see INTERTWINE 1 **2** to scatter or set here and there among other things ⟨She *interlaced* jokes between the serious passages in the speech.⟩ — see THREAD 1 **3** to twist together into a usually confused mass ⟨I've *interlaced* the cables on my audio-video system so confusingly that I've no idea what connects what.⟩ — see ENTANGLE 1

interloper *n* a person who meddles in the affairs of others ⟨Summer residents were regarded as *interlopers* who had no deep commitment to the town's welfare.⟩ — see BUSYBODY

interlude *n* a break in continuity ⟨There was a brief *interlude* in the performance while the stagehands shifted scenery.⟩ — see GAP 2

intermediary *adj* occupying a position equally distant from the ends or extremes ⟨The bridal couple were regally ensconced in *intermediary* seats at the head table.⟩ — see MIDDLE 1

intermediary *n* one who works with opposing sides in order to bring about an agreement ⟨In the past he's served as an *intermediary* in several negotiations.⟩ — see MEDIATOR

intermediate *adj* **1** being about midway between extremes of amount or size ⟨With a compact being too small and a van too large, we settled on an *intermediate*-sized sedan.⟩ — see MIDDLE 2 **2** occupying a position equally distant from the ends or extremes ⟨Although the party activists tend to back candidates with somewhat extreme views, ordinary voters generally prefer the *intermediate* aspirant.⟩ — see MIDDLE 1

intermediate *n* one who works with opposing sides in order to bring about an agreement ⟨an *intermediate* between the workers and the employer⟩ — see MEDIATOR

intermediate *vb* to act as a go-between for opposing sides ⟨If the secretary-general chooses to *intermediate* in this dispute, he'll need all of his diplomatic skills just to get both sides in the same room.⟩ — see INTERVENE

interment *n* the act or ceremony of putting a dead body in its final resting place ⟨an *interment* in a private cemetery⟩ — see BURIAL 1

intermingle *vb* to turn into a single mass or entity that is more or less the same throughout ⟨Thoroughly *intermingle* the different kinds of candy so that each bag will get a good assortment.⟩ — see BLEND 1

intermission *n* a break in continuity ⟨an awkward *intermission* between speeches⟩ — see GAP 2

intermittent *adj* **1** occurring or appearing at intervals ⟨*Intermittent* showers had me opening and closing my umbrella all day long.⟩

synonyms continual, periodic, periodical, recurrent, recurring

related words alternate, alternating, cyclic (*or* cyclical), rhythmic (*or* rhythmical), seasonal, serial; erratic, fitful, irregular, occasional, spasmodic, sporadic, spotty, unsteady

near antonyms eternal, everlasting, interminable, perpetual

antonyms constant, continuous, incessant, unceasing

2 lacking in steadiness or regularity of occurrence ⟨The breadwinner's *intermittent* employment put the family in a difficult position financially.⟩ — see FITFUL

intermix *vb* to turn into a single mass or entity that is more or less the same throughout ⟨*intermixed* the ingredients just until there were no more lumps in the batter⟩ — see BLEND 1

intermixture *n* a distinct entity formed by the combining of two or more different things ⟨The building is an intriguing *intermixture* of classical and modern elements.⟩ — see BLEND

intern *vb* to put in or as if in prison ⟨Some Polish citizens were *interned* in Russian camps during World War II.⟩ — see IMPRISON

internal *adj* **1** situated farther in ⟨Somehow grave robbers hadn't managed to locate and enter the *internal* chambers of the Egyptian tomb.⟩ — see INNER 1

2 of or relating to the mind ⟨the never-ending *internal* monologue of the novel's main character⟩ — see MENTAL

interned *adj* taken and held prisoner ⟨The soldiers daringly rescued their *interned* comrades without the loss of a single life.⟩ — see CAPTIVE

internee *n* one that has been taken and held in confinement ⟨All *internees* were released upon the cessation of hostilities.⟩ — see CAPTIVE

internment *n* the act of confining or the state of being confined ⟨The *internment* of Americans of Japanese descent during World War II is one of the more shameful chapters in United States history.⟩

synonyms captivity, confinement, immurement, imprisonment, incarceration, prison

related words bondage, enslavement, servitude; restraint, restriction; arrest, capture, entrapment; custody, detainment, house arrest; detention, hold

near antonyms emancipation, liberation, manumission, redemption, release; freedom, independence, liberty

interpenetrate *vb* to spread throughout ⟨With tie-dyeing, the dye does not *interpenetrate* the entire fabric.⟩ — see PERMEATE

interpolate *vb* to put among or between others ⟨*interpolated* a new paragraph into the online encyclopedia article⟩ — see INSERT

interpose *vb* **1** to act as a go-between for opposing sides ⟨an elder statesman who has *interposed* a number of times in international conflicts⟩ — see INTERVENE

2 to cause a disruption in a conversation or discussion ⟨I hate to *interpose*, but could you tell me what you meant by that last remark?⟩ — see INTERRUPT

3 to put among or between others ⟨The new system has *interposed* a barrier between doctors and their patients.⟩ — see INSERT

interposer *n* one who works with opposing sides in order to bring about an agreement ⟨I hope that we can resolve this dispute by ourselves, without the help of some outside *interposer*.⟩ — see MEDIATOR

interpret *vb* **1** to make plain or understandable ⟨a passage in the poem that scholars haven't been able to *interpret* to everyone's satisfaction⟩ — see EXPLAIN 1

2 to present a portrayal or performance of ⟨The actor *interpreted* the role of Fletcher Christian in a challengingly new way.⟩ — see ACT 1

interpretation *n* **1** a statement that makes something clear ⟨That's one possible *interpretation* of that cryptic remark.⟩ — see EXPLANATION 1

2 a presentation of an artistic work (as a piece of music) from a particular point of view ⟨a sensitive *interpretation* of a piece that is a touchstone for violinists⟩ — see ACCOUNT 2

interpretative *adj* serving to explain ⟨The book was annotated with *interpretative* commentary.⟩ — see EXPLANATORY

interpretive *adj* serving to explain ⟨an edition of Shakespeare's plays with many *interpretive* footnotes that students should find very helpful⟩ — see EXPLANATORY

interring *n* the act or ceremony of putting a dead body in its final resting place ⟨Fittingly, the *interring* took place on a gloomy, rainy day.⟩ — see BURIAL 1

interrogate *vb* **1** to put a question or questions to ⟨*interrogated* him about where he'd gone the night before⟩ — see ASK 1

2 to put a series of questions to ⟨Police *interrogated* the murder suspect for hours on end.⟩ — see EXAMINE 1

interrupt *vb* to cause a disruption in a conversation or discussion ⟨It's rude to *interrupt* when someone is making an important point.⟩

synonyms break in, chime in, cut in, interpose, intrude

related words barge (in), bother, horn in; add, contribute, put in

interruption *n* **1** a break in continuity ⟨an *interruption* in cable service during the lightning storm⟩ — see GAP 2

2 a momentary halt in an activity ⟨a brief *interruption* in the discussion while we all got coffee⟩ — see PAUSE 1

intersect *vb* to divide by passing through or across ⟨A dry streambed *intersects* the trail at several points.⟩

synonyms bisect, cross, cut

related words crisscross

intersection *n* a place where roads meet ⟨Take a left turn at the next *intersection*.⟩ — see CROSSROAD 1

intersperse *vb* **1** to scatter or set here and there among other things ⟨For variety, *intersperse* some photos among the other decorations on the wall.⟩ — see THREAD 1

2 to put among or between others ⟨*intersperses* some fascinating factoids about famous players between his profiles of the nation's ball parks.⟩ — see INSERT

interstice *n* **1** a break in continuity ⟨There's an occasional *interstice* in the tedium, but most of the novel is boring.⟩ — see GAP 2

2 an open space in a barrier (as a wall or hedge) ⟨pesky weeds growing in the *interstices* between the flagstones⟩ — see GAP 1

intertwine *vb* **1** to cause to twine about one another ⟨*intertwined* two different colors of yarn⟩

synonyms entwine, interlace, interweave, lace, ply, twist, weave, wreathe, writhe
related words braid, plait, blend, fuse, join, link, mix
near antonyms disentangle, uncoil, untangle, untwine, unwind
2 to twist together into a usually confused mass ⟨*Intertwining* yarn is usually a bad idea, because you'll never get it all sorted out again.⟩ — see ENTANGLE 1
interval *n* **1** a break in continuity ⟨There were *intervals* of thousands of years between the major ice ages.⟩ — see GAP 2
2 an open space in a barrier (as a wall or hedge) ⟨Unable to find my way out of the maze, I cheated and squeezed through a convenient *interval* in the hedge.⟩ — see GAP 1
intervene *vb* to act as a go-between for opposing sides ⟨I *intervened* in the argument before any real harm was done.⟩
synonyms intercede, intermediate, interpose, mediate
related words butt in, interfere, intrude, meddle, obtrude, pry, snoop; arbitrate, moderate, negotiate, referee; barge (in), bother; break (in), chime in, cut in; infringe, invade, trespass
near antonyms stand by; avoid, eschew, shun; disregard, ignore, overlook
interweave *vb* **1** to cause to twine about one another ⟨We *interweaved* garlands of red and gold beads and wrapped them around the Christmas tree.⟩ — see INTERTWINE 1
2 to scatter or set here and there among other things ⟨The author artfully *interweaves* excerpts from soldiers' letters into his history of the Vietnam War.⟩ — see THREAD 1
3 to twist together into a usually confused mass ⟨In our play the kitten and I managed to *interweave* the skeins of yarn into a hopeless tangle.⟩ — see ENTANGLE 1
intimacy *n* the state of being in a very personal or private relationship ⟨There can be both rewards and regrets from *intimacy* with another person.⟩ — see FAMILIARITY 1
intimate *adj* **1** closely acquainted ⟨*intimate* friends who can practically finish each other's sentences⟩ — see FAMILIAR 1
2 not known or meant to be known by the general populace ⟨They trusted each other enough to share some *intimate* thoughts.⟩ — see PRIVATE 1
intimate *n* a person who has a strong liking for and trust in another ⟨Usually quite aloof in public, he's actually quite relaxed with his *intimates*.⟩ — see FRIEND 1
intimate *vb* to convey an idea indirectly ⟨She's trying to *intimate* that there was more going on than anyone knew.⟩ — see HINT
intimation *n* a slight or indirect pointing to something (as a solution or explanation) ⟨The newscaster could not resist giving a slight *intimation* that the voting was going contrary to predictions.⟩ — see HINT 1
intimidate *vb* to make timid or fearful by or as if by threats ⟨Refusing to be *intimidated* by the manager's harsh stare, I demanded my money back.⟩
synonyms browbeat, bulldoze, bully, cow, hector
related words bluster; affright, alarm (*also* alarum), frighten, horrify, scare, shock, spook, startle, terrify; menace, terrorize, threaten; badger, hound; bludgeon, coerce, compel, constrain, force, make, oblige, press, pressure, push around; demoralize, psych (out), unman, unnerve; discompose, disconcert, disquiet, distress, disturb, perturb, upset
phrases pick on
near antonyms cheer, comfort, console, reassure, solace, soothe; embolden, encourage, hearten, steel; convince, persuade
intimidating *adj* **1** causing fear ⟨the *intimidating* prospect of the college entrance exams⟩ — see FEARFUL 1

2 harsh and threatening in manner or appearance ⟨an *intimidating* bodyguard keeping the fans away from the rock star⟩ — see GRIM 1
intimidator *n* a person who teases, threatens, or hurts more vulnerable persons ⟨The loan shark hired an *intimidator* to make sure that he got all that was owed him.⟩ — see BULLY
intolerable *adj* **1** more than can be put up with ⟨This stifling heat is *intolerable*.⟩ — see UNBEARABLE
2 going beyond a normal or acceptable limit in degree or amount ⟨the *intolerable* haste with which the press passed judgment on the accused⟩ — see EXCESSIVE
intolerant *adj* **1** unable or unwilling to endure ⟨*Intolerant* of fools, she is not an easy person to work for.⟩
synonyms impatient
related words uncompromising, unforgiving, unyielding; complaining, fussing, griping, grumbling, kvetching, protesting, whining
near antonyms accepting, forgiving, long-suffering, resigned, uncomplaining, willing; indulgent
antonyms abiding, enduring, forbearing, patient, tolerant
2 unwilling to grant other people social rights or to accept other viewpoints ⟨*intolerant* people who callously deny others the very rights that they take for granted⟩
synonyms bigoted, narrow, narrow-minded, prejudiced, small-minded
related words conservative, hidebound, old-fashioned, reactionary; blindfolded, blinkered, insular, parochial, provincial; biased, one-sided, partial, partisan
near antonyms extreme, progressive, radical; impartial, objective, unbiased
antonyms broad-minded, liberal, open-minded, tolerant, unprejudiced
intone *vb* to utter in musical or drawn out tones ⟨"The day is begun," the narrator *intoned*.⟩ — see CHANT 1
intoxicant *n* a distilled beverage that can make a person drunk ⟨a religious denomination that strictly forbids the use of all *intoxicants*⟩ — see ALCOHOL
intoxicate *vb* **1** to cause a pleasurable stimulation of the feelings of ⟨The stunning spectacle of this Las Vegas show is sure to *intoxicate* spectators.⟩ — see THRILL
2 to fill with great joy ⟨She was *intoxicated* by the news that she'd gotten the job of her dreams.⟩ — see ELATE
intoxicated *adj* **1** being under the influence of alcohol ⟨State police warned that there would be zero tolerance for *intoxicated* drivers over the long holiday weekend.⟩ — see DRUNK
2 experiencing or marked by overwhelming usually pleasurable emotion ⟨the *intoxicated* moment when she found out that she'd won the award⟩ — see ECSTATIC
intoxication *n* a state of overwhelming usually pleasurable emotion ⟨the *intoxication* felt by two people who have just fallen in love⟩ — see ECSTASY
intractability *n* refusal to obey ⟨The dog's frustrating *intractability* forced the family to try obedience training by a professional.⟩ — see DISOBEDIENCE
intractable *adj* **1** given to resisting authority or another's control ⟨an *intractable* child who deliberately does the opposite of whatever he is told⟩ — see DISOBEDIENT
2 given to resisting control or discipline by others ⟨Cats are by nature fairly *intractable* animals.⟩ — see UNCONTROLLABLE
intrepid *adj* feeling or displaying no fear by temperament ⟨an *intrepid* explorer who probed parts of the rain forest never previously attempted⟩ — see BRAVE 1
intrepidity *n* strength of mind to carry on in spite of danger ⟨He managed to get back to camp, despite the grizzly bears, through sheer *intrepidity*.⟩ — see COURAGE

intrepidness *n* strength of mind to carry on in spite of danger ⟨a globe-trotting journalist of remarkable *intrepidness* who never flinches from any challenge life has to offer⟩ — see COURAGE

intricacy *n* **1** something that makes a situation more complicated or difficult ⟨just now learning the *intricacies* of owning one's own business⟩ — see COMPLICATION 1
2 the state or quality of having many interrelated parts or aspects ⟨The *intricacy* of the puzzle requires close concentration.⟩ — see COMPLEXITY 1

intricate *adj* **1** having many parts or aspects that are usually interrelated ⟨an *intricate* machine that requires some training to use it properly⟩ — see COMPLEX 1
2 made or done with great care or with much detail ⟨an *intricate* hairstyle that requires far too much maintenance to suit my taste⟩ — see ELABORATE 1

intrigue *n* a secret plan for accomplishing evil or unlawful ends ⟨The *intrigue* was quickly discovered, and the would-be thieves were arrested.⟩ — see PLOT 1

intrigue *vb* **1** to engage in a secret plan to accomplish evil or unlawful ends ⟨evidence that the leading manufacturers had *intrigued* to keep prices artificially high⟩ — see PLOT
2 to hold the attention of ⟨The mystery story *intrigued* me so that I read it in one sitting.⟩ — see ENGAGE 1

intriguing *adj* holding the attention or provoking interest ⟨an *intriguing* concept that should engender much debate among climatologists⟩ — see INTERESTING

intrinsic *adj* being a part of the innermost nature of a person or thing ⟨the question of whether people have an *intrinsic* sense of right and wrong⟩ — see INHERENT

intrinsically *adv* by natural character or ability ⟨He's worked hard to be good at baseball, as he's not *intrinsically* athletic.⟩ — see NATURALLY 1

introduce *vb* **1** to make (one person) known (to another) socially ⟨A friend *introduced* them, and they wound up getting married.⟩
synonyms acquaint, present
related words address, greet, hail, meet
2 to present or bring forward for discussion ⟨After about 20 minutes the moderator *introduced* a new topic for the debate.⟩
synonyms bring up, broach, moot, place, raise
related words allude (to), cite, mention, name, refer (to); offer, propose, suggest; air, express, speak (of), talk (about), vent, ventilate; interject, interrupt; debate, discuss, thrash (out *or* over)
near antonyms censor, hush (up), quiet, silence, suppress
3 to be responsible for the creation and early operation or use of ⟨Luther Burbank *introduced* the idea of plant breeding, developing over 800 new varieties of fruits, vegetables, grains, and grasses.⟩ — see FOUND
4 to impart knowledge of a new thing or situation to ⟨*introduced* everyone to the company's new phone system⟩ — see ACQUAINT 1
5 to put among or between others ⟨Let's *introduce* a new variable to the equation.⟩ — see INSERT

introducer *n* one who creates or introduces something new ⟨The *introducer* of the ballpoint pen was a man by the name of John Loud.⟩ — see INVENTOR

introduction *n* a short section (as of a book) that leads to or explains the main part ⟨A leading biologist wrote the *introduction* to that new textbook.⟩
synonyms foreword, preamble, preface, prelude, prologue (*also* prolog)
related words beginning, commencement, initiation, opening, origin, origination, outset, start
near antonyms postscript; aftermath; cessation, close, closing, conclusion, end, finale, finish, termination
antonyms epilogue (*also* epilog)

introductory *adj* **1** coming before the main part or item usually to introduce or prepare for what follows ⟨an *introductory* paragraph to the chapter on evolution⟩ — see PRELIMINARY
2 of or relating to the simplest facts or theories of a subject ⟨an *introductory* course in computer programming⟩ — see ELEMENTARY

introverted *adj* not comfortable around people ⟨a quiet, *introverted* child who likes to sit at home and read books⟩ — see SHY 2

intrude *vb* **1** to cause a disruption in a conversation or discussion ⟨Forgive me for *intruding*, but I think I know where that restaurant is.⟩ — see INTERRUPT
2 to interest oneself in what is not one's concern ⟨the story of a would-be matchmaker who *intrudes* into the lives of her friends⟩ — see INTERFERE

intrude (upon) *vb* to thrust oneself upon (another) without invitation ⟨A man with an opinion on everything, he doesn't hesitate to *intrude upon* whoever happens to be standing by.⟩ — see BOTHER 1

intruder *n* a person who meddles in the affairs of others ⟨This is my project, not yours, so don't be an *intruder*.⟩ — see BUSYBODY

intruding *adj* thrusting oneself where one is not welcome or invited ⟨a relentlessly *intruding* child who likes to interrupt adult conversations simply to get attention⟩ — see INTRUSIVE

intrusive *adj* thrusting oneself where one is not welcome or invited ⟨She's that proverbially *intrusive* neighbor who never knocks before coming in.⟩
synonyms busy, interfering, intruding, meddlesome, meddling, nosy (*or* nosey), obtrusive, officious, presuming, presumptuous, prying, snoopy
related words bold, brazen, impertinent, impudent, insolent, rude; invading, trespassing; curious, inquisitive, annoying, harassing; overbearing
near antonyms hands-off; uninvolved; quiet, reclusive, reserved, reticent, retiring, silent, taciturn, withdrawn; inhibited, restrained, subdued
antonyms unobtrusive

inundate *vb* to cover with a flood ⟨Water from the overflowing bathtub *inundated* the bathroom floor.⟩ — see FLOOD

inundation *n* a great flow of water or of something that overwhelms ⟨The family's shed was washed away in the last *inundation*.⟩ — see FLOOD

inure *vb* to make able to withstand physical hardship, strain, or exposure ⟨The hardship of army training *inured* her to the rigors of desert warfare.⟩ — see HARDEN 2

inured *adj* able to withstand hardship, strain, or exposure ⟨the weather-beaten, *inured* faces of farmers⟩ — see HARDY 1

invade *vb* to enter for conquest or plunder ⟨a superpower that had a tendency to *invade* and take over smaller and weaker countries⟩
synonyms foray (into), overrun, raid
related words despoil, loot, maraud, pillage, plunder, ransack, ravage, sack, strip; conquer, crush, dominate, overcome, overpower, overwhelm, subdue, subject, subjugate, vanquish; assail, assault, attack, beset, charge, rush, storm, strike; battle, clash (with), combat, fight, war (with); encroach, infringe, trespass; beleaguer, besiege, blockade, invest; garrison, occupy
near antonyms defend, guard, protect, safeguard, shield, ward; defy, oppose, repel, resist, withstand; capitulate (to), cede (to), submit (to), surrender (to), yield (to)

invader *n* one that starts armed conflict against another especially without reasonable cause ⟨Vigilant defenders at the border were quick to repel the *invaders*.⟩ — see AGGRESSOR

¹invalid *adj* chronically or repeatedly suffering from poor health ⟨an old and now *invalid* woman who rarely gets out anymore⟩ — see SICKLY 1

²invalid *adj* **1** having no legal or binding force ⟨The treaty is *invalid* once one side violates it.⟩ — see NULL 1

2 not being in agreement with what is true ⟨That's an *invalid* assumption on your part.⟩ — see FALSE 1

3 not using or following good reasoning ⟨an argument which has one untrue premise is *invalid*⟩ — see ILLOGICAL

4 having no basis in reason or fact ⟨an *invalid* claim that can be easily disproved by the facts⟩ — see GROUNDLESS

invalidate *vb* to put an end to by formal action ⟨Those nations eventually *invalidated* their trade agreement.⟩ — see ABOLISH 1

invariability *n* the state of continuing without change ⟨The *invariability* of the weather around here gets boring sometimes.⟩ — see CONSTANCY 1

invariable *adj* not capable of changing or being changed ⟨an *invariable* interest rate⟩ — see INFLEXIBLE 1

invariably *adv* on every relevant occasion ⟨He *invariably* orders the same thing every time we go to that restaurant.⟩ — see ALWAYS 1

invariant *adj* not varying ⟨an *invariant* value⟩ — see UNIFORM

invasion *n* a sudden attack on and entrance into hostile territory ⟨the *invasion* of the Soviet Union by Germany during World War II⟩ — see RAID 1

invective *n* harsh insulting language ⟨hurled curses and *invective* at the driver who heedlessly cut them off in traffic⟩ — see ABUSE 1

invective *adj* marked by harsh insulting language ⟨a sharp, *invective* e-mail⟩ — see ABUSIVE

invent *vb* to create or think of by clever use of the imagination ⟨They *invented* an explanation for the broken vase that would satisfy their grandmother.⟩

synonyms concoct, construct, contrive, cook (up), devise, fabricate, make up, manufacture, think (up)

related words design, hatch, produce; daydream, dream; conceive, envisage, imagine, picture, vision, visualize; adlib, extemporize, improvise

phrases come up with

near antonyms copy, copycat, duplicate, imitate, mimic, reduplicate, replicate, reproduce

invented *adj* not real and existing only in the imagination ⟨a daydreamer who lives mostly in her *invented* magic kingdom⟩ — see IMAGINARY

invention *n* **1** something (as a device) created for the first time through the use of the imagination ⟨His clever *invention* made people's lives easier.⟩

synonyms coinage, concoction, contrivance, creation, innovation, wrinkle

related words contraption, device, gadget, gizmo (*also* gismo), novelty; design, product, work; dream, fantasy (*also* phantasy), picture, vision; conception, imagining, origination

near antonyms carbon copy, copy, dupe, duplicate, duplication, facsimile, imitation, reduplication, replica, replication, reproduction

2 something that is the product of the imagination ⟨Unsurprisingly, the story about being kidnapped by aliens was pure *invention*.⟩ — see FICTION

3 the ability to form mental images of things that either are not physically present or have never been conceived or created by others ⟨A writer with great *invention*, she is able to create on the page worlds that don't exist but certainly seem like they could.⟩ — see IMAGINATION 1

4 the skill and imagination to create new things ⟨A per-

son of seemingly endless *invention*, Thomas Edison held a world-record 1,093 patents.⟩ — see CREATIVITY 1

inventive *adj* **1** showing a noteworthy use of the imagination and creativity especially in inventing ⟨*inventive* electronic games⟩ ⟨*inventive* ways to use leftovers⟩ — see CLEVER 1

2 having the skill and imagination to create new things ⟨An *inventive* youth, he devised an automatic feeding system for his dog.⟩ — see CREATIVE 1

inventiveness *n* **1** the ability to form mental images of things that either are not physically present or have never been conceived or created by others ⟨The artist's fertile *inventiveness* allows her to put on canvas landscapes that have never been trod by mortal feet.⟩ — see IMAGINATION 1

2 the skill and imagination to create new things ⟨the contention that, in order to prosper, cities must attract young, well-educated people of great *inventiveness* in both the arts and high technology⟩ — see CREATIVITY 1

inventor *n* one who creates or introduces something new ⟨the *inventor* of the electric light bulb⟩

synonyms contriver, designer, developer, deviser, formulator, innovator, introducer, originator

related words author, begetter, creator, establisher, father, founder, generator, inaugurator, initiator, instituter (*or* institutor), sire; groundbreaker, pioneer, planner; builder, maker, producer; dreamer

near antonyms aper, copier, copycat, duplicator, imitator, mimic

inventory *vb* to make a list of ⟨Would you *inventory* the supplies in the back room?⟩ — see ¹LIST 1

inventory *n* the number of individuals or amount of something available at any given time ⟨The dealership has an unusually large *inventory* of pre-owned vehicles.⟩ — see SUPPLY

invert *vb* to change the position of (an object) so that the opposite side or end is showing ⟨If you *invert* the coin, there's a picture of a buffalo on the back.⟩ — see REVERSE 2

invertebrate *adj* lacking strength of will or character ⟨an *invertebrate* response to a serious situation⟩ — see WEAK 2

invest *vb* **1** to cause (as a person) to become filled with or saturated with a certain quality or principle ⟨*invested* the film with his own enthusiasm for the wonders of flight⟩ — see INFUSE

2 to furnish freely or naturally with some power, quality, or attribute ⟨a woman *invested* with the strong desire to make the world a better place⟩ — see ENDOW 1

3 to give official or legal power to ⟨*invested* him with power of attorney⟩ — see AUTHORIZE 1

4 to outfit with clothes and especially fine or special clothes ⟨a fashion designer who has *invested* several winners of the best actress award⟩ — see CLOTHE 1

5 to put into an office or welcome into an organization with special ceremonies ⟨The beloved actor was finally *invested* as a knight by the queen.⟩ — see INSTALL 1

6 to surround (as a fortified place) with armed forces for the purpose of capturing or preventing commerce and communication ⟨The city was mercilessly *invested* for an entire year, but never fell.⟩ — see BESIEGE 1

7 to surround or cover closely ⟨Nightfall *invested* the land.⟩ — see ENFOLD 1

investigate *vb* to search through or into ⟨experts *investigating* new ways of dealing with the problem⟩ — see EXPLORE 1

investigation *n* a systematic search for the truth or facts about something ⟨Officials launched an extensive *investigation* of the plane crash.⟩ — see INQUIRY 1

investigator *n* a person not on the police force who investigates criminal or illicit activity or searches for missing persons ⟨The *investigator* in charge of the case was touted as an expert at tracing stolen art.⟩ — see DETECTIVE

investiture *n* the process or an instance of being formally placed in an office or organization ⟨the *investiture* of a new member of parliament⟩ — see INSTALLATION 1

investment *n* **1** the cutting off of an area by military means to stop the flow of people or supplies ⟨The *investment* of Cuba was one of the decisive moments in the Cuban Missile Crisis.⟩ — see BLOCKADE

2 the process or an instance of being formally placed in an office or organization ⟨The *investment* of a new diocesan bishop is typically a grand and solemn occasion.⟩ — see INSTALLATION 1

inveterate *adj* **1** firmly established over time ⟨He has an *inveterate* tendency to tell some very tall tales.⟩

synonyms confirmed, deep, deep-rooted, deep-seated, entrenched (*also* intrenched), hard-core, rooted, settled

related words firm, fixed, frozen, hard, hard-and-fast, immutable, irradicable, set, unalterable, unchangeable; embedded (*also* imbedded), implanted, inculcated, instilled; inborn, inbred, ingrained (*also* engrained), inherent, innate, integral, intrinsic, natural; accustomed, chronic, customary, habitual, regular, typical, usual; abiding, enduring, lifelong, persistent, persisting

near antonyms brief, ephemeral, fleeting, impermanent, interim, momentary, provisional, short-lived, short-term, temporary, transient

2 being such by habit and not likely to change ⟨The man is an *inveterate* liar who only rarely tells the truth.⟩ — see HABITUAL 1

invidious *adj* having or showing mean resentment of another's possessions or advantages ⟨Inevitably, his remarkable success attracted the *invidious* attention of the other sales representatives.⟩ — see ENVIOUS

invidiousness *n* a painful awareness of another's possessions or advantages and a desire to have them too ⟨She pretended to be happy for her friend's good fortune, but there was an unmistakable *invidiousness* about her supposedly heartfelt congratulations.⟩ — see ENVY

invigorate *vb* to give life, vigor, or spirit to ⟨The fresh air and sunshine *invigorated* the children after a long winter indoors.⟩ — see ANIMATE

invigorated *adj* made or become fresh in spirits or vigor ⟨an *invigorated* worker returning from a relaxing vacation⟩ — see NEW 4

invigorating *adj* having a renewing effect on the state of the body or mind ⟨An *invigorating* breeze made our afternoon sail all the more enjoyable.⟩ — see TONIC 1

invincible *adj* incapable of being defeated, overcome, or subdued ⟨an *invincible* wrestler who has never lost a match⟩

synonyms impregnable, indomitable, insuperable, insurmountable, invulnerable, unbeatable, unconquerable

related words inviolable, unassailable, unbreachable, untouchable; armored, defended, guarded, protected, safe, safeguarded, secure, shielded; unbeaten, unbowed, unconquered, undefeated, unsubdued

near antonyms exposed, imperiled (*or* imperilled), insecure, liable, open, susceptible, unguarded, unprotected, unsafe; defenseless, helpless, powerless, weak

antonyms superable, surmountable, vincible, vulnerable

inviolable *adj* not to be violated, criticized, or tampered with ⟨a person with *inviolable* moral standards⟩ ⟨an *inviolable* trust between lawyer and client⟩ — see SACRED 1

invite *vb* **1** to request the presence or participation of ⟨She's *invited* only select friends to visit her new house.⟩

synonyms ask, bid

related words solicit; beckon, call, summon

2 to act so as to make (something) more likely ⟨You're

just *inviting* ridicule by making such outrageous claims.⟩ — see COURT 1

invoice *n* a record of goods sold or services performed together with the costs due ⟨The *invoice* stated that we owed $1500.⟩ — see ¹BILL 1

involuntary *adj* **1** not made or done willingly or by choice ⟨My long stays on the sidelines during our football games were strictly *involuntary*.⟩

synonyms coerced, forced, unintended, unintentional, unwilling

related words accidental, unplanned, unpremeditated; automatic, impulsive, instinctive, spontaneous, unprompted; inadvertent, unconscious, unknowing, unwitting

near antonyms advised, conscious, considered, knowing, planned, premeditated, premeditative, purposeful; volitional; self-imposed, self-inflicted

antonyms deliberate, freewill, intentional, unforced, voluntary, willful (*or* wilful), willing

2 done instantly and without conscious thought or decision ⟨Breathing is *involuntary*.⟩ — see AUTOMATIC 1

3 forcing one's compliance or participation by or as if by law ⟨the abolition of *involuntary* servitude by civilized society⟩ — see MANDATORY

involution *n* the state or quality of having many interrelated parts or aspects ⟨The *involution* of the thriller's plot made it hard to follow.⟩ — see COMPLEXITY 1

involve *vb* **1** to be the business or affair of ⟨This isn't something that *involves* you, so don't worry about it.⟩ — see CONCERN 2

2 to have as part of a whole ⟨A tragic play usually *involves* a number of plot devices, including the hero's fatal flaw.⟩ — see INCLUDE 1

3 to hold the attention of ⟨Her blissful daydream so completely *involved* her that she never heard the knock on the door.⟩ — see ENGAGE 1

4 to surround or cover closely ⟨became *involved* in a growing, cheering crowd⟩ — see ENFOLD 1

involved *adj* **1** having many parts or aspects that are usually interrelated ⟨a remarkably *involved* story for a writer so young⟩ — see COMPLEX 1

2 made or done with great care or with much detail ⟨very *involved* descriptions of every last detail of the lavish wedding⟩ — see ELABORATE 1

involving *adj* holding the attention or provoking interest ⟨an *involving* book that you won't be able to put down⟩ — see INTERESTING

invulnerable *adj* incapable of being defeated, overcome, or subdued ⟨The team seems *invulnerable* this season.⟩ — see INVINCIBLE

inward *adj* situated farther in ⟨moved towards the *inward* room for more privacy⟩ — see INNER 1

in–your–face *adj* having or showing a bold forcefulness in the pursuit of a goal ⟨an *in-your-face* attitude that sometimes puts people off⟩ — see AGGRESSIVE 1

iota *n* the smallest amount or part imaginable ⟨There's not an *iota* of doubt regarding the defendant's guilt.⟩ — see JOT

irascibility *n* readiness to show annoyance or impatience ⟨His natural *irascibility* tends to make people leave him alone.⟩ — see PETULANCE

irascible *adj* easily irritated or annoyed ⟨forced to endure a memorably *irascible* boss on her first job after college⟩ — see IRRITABLE

irate *adj* feeling or showing anger ⟨The big increase in cable rates prompted a flood of *irate* calls and letters.⟩ — see ANGRY

irateness *n* an intense emotional state of displeasure with someone or something ⟨His *irateness* was such that we worried about his blood pressure.⟩ — see ANGER

ire *n* an intense emotional state of displeasure with

someone or something ⟨The patronizing comment from the snooty waiter roused her *ire*.⟩ — see ANGER

ire *vb* to make angry ⟨Nothing *ires* him more than having to wait for his dinner.⟩ — see ANGER

ireful *adj* feeling or showing anger ⟨*ireful* expressions on the faces of the protesters of the tax increase⟩ — see ANGRY

irk *vb* to disturb the peace of mind of (someone) especially by repeated disagreeable acts ⟨She *irked* her friend by chewing her gum loudly during the movie.⟩ — see IRRITATE 1

irk *n* something that is a source of irritation ⟨One of the teacher's major *irks* is a cell phone that rings during a lecture.⟩ — see ANNOYANCE 3

irksome *adj* causing annoyance ⟨the *irksome* habit of leaving all the kitchen cabinet doors open⟩ — see ANNOYING

iron *adj* not showing weakness or uncertainty ⟨He had an *iron* determination to succeed on Wall Street.⟩ — see FIRM 1

irons *pl n* something that physically prevents free movement ⟨They clapped the prisoner in *irons*.⟩ — see BOND 1

irradiate *vb* 1 to supply with light ⟨The light from a galaxy of flashing signs *irradiates* the heart and soul of Las Vegas.⟩ — see ILLUMINATE 1
2 to throw or give off ⟨*irradiating* an aura of supreme confidence on the playing field⟩ — see EMIT 1

irrational *adj* not using or following good reasoning ⟨He has an *irrational* fear of cats.⟩ — see ILLOGICAL

irrecoverable *adj* 1 not capable of being cured or reformed ⟨an *irrecoverable* spendthrift⟩ — see HOPELESS 1
2 not capable of being repaired, regained, or undone ⟨One computer file proved to be *irrecoverable* after the crash.⟩ — see IRREPARABLE

irredeemable *adj* 1 not capable of being cured or reformed ⟨resigned to the fact that his in-laws are *irredeemable* practical jokers⟩ — see HOPELESS 1
2 not capable of being repaired, regained, or undone ⟨the *irredeemable* loss of innocence that the war brought about⟩ — see IRREPARABLE

irrefutable *adj* not capable of being challenged or proved wrong ⟨the *irrefutable* reply of "Because I like it!"⟩
synonyms accomplished, certain, incontestable, incontrovertible, indisputable, indubitable, positive, sure, unanswerable, undeniable, unquestionable
related words unambiguous, unequivocal; absolute, clear, conclusive, decisive, definite; uncontested, uncontradicted, undisputed, unquestioned
near antonyms debated, disputed; doubtful, dubious, iffy, inconclusive, indecisive, uncertain; ambiguous, equivocal; hypothetical, speculative, theoretical (*also* theoretic)
antonyms answerable, contradictable, debatable, disputable, doubtable, moot, negotiable, problematic (*also* problematical), questionable, refutable

irregular *adj* 1 departing from some accepted standard of what is normal ⟨It was a bank customer's slightly *irregular* behavior that made people suspicious.⟩ — see DEVIANT
2 lacking in steadiness or regularity of occurrence ⟨*irregular* mail delivery to the island⟩ — see FITFUL
3 not having a level or smooth surface ⟨Although the moon looks smooth from here, it actually has a very bumpy and *irregular* surface.⟩ — see UNEVEN 1
4 not rigidly following established form, custom, or rules ⟨The request is *irregular*, but I'll allow it.⟩ — see INFORMAL 1
5 not staying constant ⟨*irregular* gusts of wind⟩ — see UNEVEN 2

irregularly *adv* without definite aim, direction, rule, or method ⟨attended class only *irregularly*⟩ — see HIT OR MISS

irrelevance *n* the quality or state of not having anything to do with the matter at hand ⟨The *irrelevance* of the comment brought conversation to a standstill.⟩
synonyms extraneousness, impertinence, inapplicability
related words inappropriateness, inaptness, unfitness, unsuitability; inaneness, inanity, meaninglessness, pointlessness, uselessness
near antonyms appropriateness, aptness, fitness, suitability, suitableness; importance, significance; usefulness
antonyms applicability, bearing, connection, materiality, pertinence, relevance, relevancy

irrelevant *adj* not having anything to do with the matter at hand ⟨*irrelevant* questions that merely disrupted the classroom lesson⟩
synonyms extraneous, immaterial, impertinent, inapplicable
related words incidental, peripheral, tangent, tangential; dead, moot; inconsequential, insignificant, unimportant; empty, inane, meaningless, pointless, senseless, useless; inappropriate, inapt, unsuitable
phrases beside the point, neither here nor there
near antonyms important, meaningful, significant; sensible, useful; appropriate, apt, fit, suitable
antonyms applicable, apposite, apropos, germane, material, pertinent, pointed, relative, relevant

irreligious *adj* lacking religious emotions, principles, or practices ⟨raised in an *irreligious* family⟩
synonyms godless, nonreligious
related words churchless, unchurched; heathen, pagan, paganish, ungodly, unholy; agnostic, atheistic (*or* atheistical); unconsecrated, unhallowed; profane, secular, temporal, worldly
near antonyms devout, God-fearing, godly, holy, pious, prayerful, reverent, saintly, worshipful, worshipping (*also* worshiping); blessed (*also* blest), consecrated, hallowed, sacred, sacrosanct, sanctified; devotional, spiritual
antonyms religious

irremediable *adj* 1 not capable of being cured or reformed ⟨the firm belief that no convicted criminal is *irremediable*⟩ — see HOPELESS 1
2 not capable of being repaired, regained, or undone ⟨It turned out that the flood damage was not *irremediable*.⟩ — see IRREPARABLE

irremovable *adj* incapable of moving or being moved ⟨The driveway had to be built to curve around an *irremovable* tree.⟩ — see IMMOVABLE 1

irreparable *adj* not capable of being repaired, regained, or undone ⟨*irreparable* damage to the car⟩
synonyms irrecoverable, irredeemable, irremediable, irretrievable, irreversible, unrecoverable, unredeemable
related words irreplaceable, irrevocable; unredeemed
near antonyms corrected, fixed, recovered, remedied, repaired
antonyms correctable, fixable, remediable, repairable, reparable, retrievable

irreproachable *adj* 1 free from guilt or blame ⟨The captain of the force is a police officer of absolutely *irreproachable* character.⟩ — see INNOCENT 2
2 being entirely without fault or flaw ⟨an *irreproachable* solution to the problem that should satisfy everyone⟩ — see PERFECT 1

irresolution *n* a state or an instance of temporary inaction because of uncertainty about the right course of action ⟨After a moment of anguished *irresolution*, I raised my hand and voted in favor of the proposal.⟩ — see HESITATION

irresponsible *adj* having or showing a lack of concern for the consequences of one's actions ⟨It was *irresponsible* to go off without telling anyone you were leaving.⟩ — see RECKLESS 1

irretrievable *adj* **1** not capable of being cured or reformed ⟨an *irretrievable* busybody⟩ — see HOPELESS 1
2 not capable of being repaired, regained, or undone ⟨This is just an *irretrievable* mess, so let's start all over again.⟩ — see IRREPARABLE
irreverence *n* an act of great disrespect shown to God or to sacred ideas, people, or things ⟨Taking the name of God in vain is considered an *irreverence* in some religions.⟩ — see BLASPHEMY
irreverent *adj* not showing proper reverence for the holy or sacred ⟨*irreverent* behavior during church services⟩
synonyms blasphemous, impious, profane, sacrilegious
related words agnostic, atheistic (*or* atheistical); godless, heretical (*also* heretic), irreligious, nonreligious, religionless, secular; ungodly, unholy; unconsecrated, unhallowed; heathen, pagan, paganish
near antonyms devout, God-fearing, godly, holy, prayerful, religious, saintly, worshipful, worshipping (*also* worshiping); consecrated, hallowed, sacred, sacrosanct, sanctified
antonyms pious, reverent
irreversible *adj* not capable of being repaired, regained, or undone ⟨Fortunately, the misprint wasn't an *irreversible* error since it was discovered early.⟩ — see IRREPARABLE
irrigate *vb* to pour liquid over or through in order to cleanse ⟨If you get the chemical in your eye, *irrigate* the eye thoroughly with water.⟩ — see FLUSH 1
irritability *n* readiness to show annoyance or impatience ⟨The librarian's well-known *irritability* makes students hesitant to ask questions.⟩ — see PETULANCE
irritable *adj* easily irritated or annoyed ⟨That *irritable* old man always yells at people to stay off of his lawn.⟩
synonyms choleric, crabby, cranky, cross, crotchety, fiery, grouchy, grumpy, irascible, peevish, perverse, pettish, petulant, prickly, quick-tempered, raspy, short-tempered, snappish, snappy, snippy, stuffy, testy, waspish
related words bearish, bilious, cantankerous, cross-grained, curmudgeonly, disagreeable, dyspeptic, ill-humored, ill-natured, ill-tempered, ornery, querulous, snarly, surly; argumentative, bellicose, belligerent, combative, contentious, disputatious, fractious, fretful, pugnacious, quarrelsome, scrappy, truculent; sensitive, short, sulky, sullen, touchy
phrases out of humor, out of sorts
near antonyms affable, companionable, cordial, extroverted (*also* extraverted), friendly, genial, gregarious, outgoing, sociable; agreeable, amiable, good-natured, good-tempered, sweet, well-disposed; carefree, easygoing, happy-go-lucky, relaxed; forbearing, long-suffering, obliging, patient, stoic (*or* stoical), tolerant, uncomplaining, understanding
irritableness *n* readiness to show annoyance or impatience ⟨The old man's chronic *irritableness* makes him the terror of the nursing home.⟩ — see PETULANCE
irritant *n* something that is a source of irritation ⟨The whining child was a constant *irritant* to his long-suffering parents.⟩ — see ANNOYANCE 3
irritate *vb* **1** to disturb the peace of mind of (someone) especially by repeated disagreeable acts ⟨Constant chatter *irritated* the student, who was trying to concentrate on a hard assignment.⟩
synonyms aggravate, annoy, bother, bug, chafe, eat, exasperate, frost, gall, get, grate, gripe, irk, nettle, peeve, persecute, pique, put out, rasp, rile, ruffle, spite, vex
related words hassle, heckle; nag; inflame (*also* enflame), provoke, rouse; badger, bait, devil, hagride, harry, pester, plague, tease; anger, antagonize, enrage, incense, infuriate, madden, rankle, roil; agitate, discomfort, discompose, disquiet, distress, exercise, freak (out), fret,

perturb, undo, unhinge, unsettle, upset, worry; affront, insult, offend, outrage; complicate, exacerbate, worsen
phrases get one's goat, get on one's nerves, get to, rub the wrong way, set one's teeth on edge, stick in one's craw, wear on
near antonyms appease, conciliate, mollify, oblige, pacify, placate, propitiate; delight, gladden, gratify, please, satisfy; assure, cheer, comfort, console, content, quiet, reassure, solace, soothe
2 to make sore by continued rubbing ⟨New shoes usually *irritate* my feet.⟩ — see CHAFE 1
irritating *adj* **1** causing annoyance ⟨his particularly *irritating* habit of leaving his dirty clothes on the floor⟩ — see ANNOYING
2 causing an unpleasant tingling sensation ⟨This soap leaves a residue that might be a little *irritating* if you have sensitive skin.⟩ — see SCRATCHY 2
irritation *n* the feeling of impatience or anger caused by another's repeated disagreeable acts ⟨Dad's general *irritation* at the incessant complaining coming from the back seat of the car⟩ — see ANNOYANCE 2
irruption *n* a sudden attack on and entrance into hostile territory ⟨the *irruptions* of the Goths into Italy in the fifth century⟩ — see RAID 1
island *n* a fairly small area of land completely surrounded by water ⟨The *island* of Hawaii is the largest in the Hawaiian archipelago.⟩
synonyms isle, islet
related words atoll, barrier reef, cay, coral reef, key
near antonyms continent, main, mainland
isle *n* a fairly small area of land completely surrounded by water ⟨The Australian seas abound in uninhabited *isles*.⟩ — see ISLAND
islet *n* a fairly small area of land completely surrounded by water ⟨We landed the boat on a tiny *islet* that we had all to ourselves.⟩ — see ISLAND
isolate *vb* to set or keep apart from others ⟨outlying villages that had been *isolated* from civilization⟩
synonyms cut off, insulate, seclude, segregate, separate, sequester
related words quarantine; confine, immure, incarcerate, intern, jail, lock (up), restrain, restrict; abstract, detach, disengage, remove; detain, hold, keep
near antonyms assimilate, associate, connect, join, link, unite; discharge, free, liberate, loose, release
antonyms desegregate, integrate, reintegrate
isolated *adj* **1** screened or sequestered from view ⟨The hikers unexpectedly came upon an *isolated* mountain cabin.⟩ — see SECLUDED
2 not often occurring or repeated ⟨Fortunately, the error was just an *isolated* incident.⟩ — see INFREQUENT
isolation *n* the state of being alone or kept apart from others ⟨After the long book tour, the author looked forward to the *isolation* of his office.⟩
synonyms insulation, secludedness, seclusion, segregation, sequestration, solitariness, solitude
related words loneliness, lonesomeness; confinement, incarceration, internment, quarantine
near antonyms camaraderie, companionship, company, comradeship, fellowship, society
issuance *n* the act or process of giving out something to each member of a group ⟨the *issuance* of an instruction sheet to each member of the class⟩ — see DISTRIBUTION 1
issue *n* **1** a condition or occurrence traceable to a cause ⟨One of the *issues* of the Civil War was a resolution to the question of states' rights.⟩ — see EFFECT 1
2 a place or means of going out ⟨Since the lake is the *issue* of the polluted river, it is becoming polluted as well.⟩ — see EXIT 1

3 the descendants of a person, animal, or plant ⟨Someone who dies without *issue* might have their estate turned over to the state.⟩ — see OFFSPRING

issue *vb* **1** to produce and release for distribution in printed form ⟨plans to *issue* a monthly newsletter⟩ — see PUBLISH 1
2 to throw or give off ⟨a volcano *issuing* vast clouds of hot ash⟩ — see EMIT 1

Italian sandwich *n* a large sandwich on a long split roll ⟨That restaurant makes a great *Italian sandwich*.⟩ — see SUBMARINE

itch *n* a strong wish for something ⟨Amy has an *itch* to travel to far-off and exciting places.⟩ — see DESIRE 1

itch (for) *vb* to have an earnest wish to own or enjoy ⟨kids who are just *itching for* summer vacation⟩ — see DESIRE 1

item *n* **1** a separate part in a list, account, or series ⟨I got all the *items* on my grocery list except cereal.⟩
  synonyms detail, particular, point
  related words article, object, stuff, thing; characteristic, component, constituent, element, factor, feature, member; ingredient; division, particle, partition, piece, portion, section, segment

near antonyms aggregate, composite, compound, conglomerate; sum, summation, total, totality, whole
2 a report of recent events or facts not previously known ⟨Our next *item* is about the blizzard blanketing the East Coast.⟩ — see NEWS

itemize *vb* **1** to make a list of ⟨*itemized* the expenses for the business trip⟩ — see ¹LIST 1
2 to specify one after another ⟨*itemized* the potential problems that might arise during the project⟩ — see ENUMERATE 1

itinerant *adj* traveling from place to place ⟨An *itinerant* musician can see a lot of the world.⟩
  synonyms errant, fugitive, gallivanting (*also* galavanting), nomad, peripatetic, ranging, roaming, roving, vagabond, vagrant, wandering, wayfaring
  related words drifting, footloose, rambling; sauntering, strolling, traipsing, walking; migrant, migratory
  phrases on the move
  near antonyms immobile, nonmoving, settled, standing, static, stationary; motionless, still

J

jab *n* a quick thrust ⟨I gave the jellyfish on the beach a cautious *jab* with my stick.⟩ — see ¹POKE 1

jab *vb* to penetrate or hold (something) with a pointed object ⟨*jabbed* a pickle and tossed it on the plate⟩ — see IMPALE

jabber *n* unintelligible or meaningless talk ⟨To me the baby's speech was simply *jabber*, but his mother claimed to know exactly what he was saying.⟩ — see GIBBERISH 1

jabber *vb* **1** to engage in casual or rambling conversation ⟨They *jabbered* away for hours.⟩ — see CHAT 1
2 to speak rapidly, inarticulately, and usually unintelligibly ⟨monkeys *jabbering* at each other in their cages⟩ — see BABBLE 1

jabberer *n* a person who talks constantly ⟨The teacher asked the two *jabberers* to change seats.⟩ — see CHATTERBOX

jabberwocky *n* unintelligible or meaningless talk ⟨When he gets angry, he talks in a sort of agitated *jabberwocky* that is really quite comical.⟩ — see GIBBERISH 1

jack *n* **1** *slang* something (as pieces of stamped metal or printed paper) customarily and legally used as a medium of exchange, a measure of value, or a means of payment ⟨I'd buy that watch, but I don't have the *jack* right now.⟩ — see MONEY
2 a piece of cloth with a special design that is used as an emblem or for signaling ⟨a Portuguese ship flying the national *jack*⟩ — see FLAG 1
3 one who operates or navigates a seagoing vessel ⟨a group of *jacks* returning to their ship⟩ — see SAILOR
4 the total of the bets at stake at one time ⟨Tension was mounting as the *jack* was getting bigger by the minute.⟩ — see POT 1
5 a person whose job is to cut down trees ⟨We'll need to hire more *jacks* to get this stand cut before winter.⟩ — see LUMBERJACK

jack (up) *vb* **1** to lift with effort ⟨*Jack up* the car so we can change that tire.⟩ — see HEAVE 1
2 to move from a lower to a higher place or position ⟨Local restaurants *jacked up* their prices for the summer tourist season.⟩ — see RAISE 1

jackass *n* a sturdy and patient domestic mammal that is used especially to carry things ⟨With our *jackasses* loaded with supplies, we slowly made our way down to the floor of the canyon.⟩ — see DONKEY 1

jacked (up) *adj* being at a higher level than average ⟨The convenience store had the item I needed but at a ridiculously *jacked up* price.⟩ — see HIGH 2

jacket *n* **1** something that encloses another thing especially to protect it ⟨Slip the art book into its *jacket* so it won't get dirty.⟩ — see ¹CASE 1
2 the hairy covering of a mammal especially when fine, soft, and thick ⟨Llamas are prized for their soft, lush *jackets*.⟩ — see FUR 1

jackpot *n* the total of the bets at stake at one time ⟨Once the *jackpot* hit $100 million, everybody was buying lottery tickets.⟩ — see POT 1

jack–tar *n* one who operates or navigates a seagoing vessel ⟨a *jack-tar* swabbing the deck under the critical eye of the first mate⟩ — see SAILOR

jade *vb* to make weary and restless by being dull or monotonous ⟨A steady diet of nothing but lobster would *jade* the palate of even the most ardent lobster lover.⟩ — see ²BORE

jaded *adj* **1** depleted in strength, energy, or freshness ⟨After that long bar exam, I'm too *jaded* for anything but a nap.⟩ — see WEARY 1
2 having one's patience, interest, or pleasure exhausted ⟨Even *jaded* sci-fi fans are finding this new space adventure fresh and exciting.⟩ — see WEARY 2

jading *adj* causing weariness, restlessness, or lack of interest ⟨the *jading* task of sorting and counting change⟩ — see BORING

jagged *adj* **1** having an uneven edge or outline ⟨It's going to be hard to repair the *jagged* tear in the tablecloth so that it doesn't show.⟩ — see RAGGED 1
2 not having a level or smooth surface ⟨We rode our

mountain bikes down the trail's *jagged* terrain, which made for a bumpy ride.⟩ — see UNEVEN 1

jail *n* a place of confinement for persons held in lawful custody ⟨sentenced to three years in *jail* for his crime⟩
synonyms brig, guardroom, hoosegow, jug, lockup, pen, penitentiary, prison, stockade
related words bull pen, cage, cell, hole; block, ward; guardhouse, hulk(s); concentration camp, labor camp, prison camp, work camp; dungeon, keep
near antonyms outside

jail *vb* to put in or as if in prison ⟨They were *jailed* for their part in the fraud.⟩ — see IMPRISON

jailbird *n* a person convicted as a criminal and serving a prison sentence ⟨a former *jailbird* trying to get a new lease on life⟩ — see CONVICT

jailed *adj* taken and held prisoner ⟨The *jailed* protestors were noisily demanding to see their lawyers.⟩ — see CAPTIVE

jam *n* **1** a crowded mass (as of cars) that impedes or blocks movement ⟨Thousands of cars trying to leave the stadium's parking lot at the same time are sure to create a *jam*.⟩
synonyms backup, bottleneck, snarl, tie-up
related words tangle; lock; congestion, traffic; crawl, delay, slowdown, stoppage
2 a difficult, puzzling, or embarrassing situation from which there is no easy escape ⟨The heavy rain puts us in a real *jam*: all of the preparations are for a garden wedding.⟩ — see PREDICAMENT

jam *vb* **1** to fit (people or things) into a tight space ⟨Tom *jammed* his clothes into the already bulging hamper.⟩ — see CROWD 1
2 to prevent passage through by filling with something ⟨Crumpled papers *jammed* the copier.⟩ — see CLOG 1
3 to put into (something) as much as can be held or contained ⟨The inn will *jam* a guest's picnic basket with an array of tempting foods.⟩ — see FILL 1
4 to force one's way ⟨Several more people *jammed* into the bus even though there was hardly room to stand.⟩ — see ²PRESS 4

jammed *adj* **1** containing or seeming to contain the greatest quantity or number possible ⟨Tour buses, *jammed* with eager sightseers, invariably stop at that spot.⟩ — see FULL 1
2 firmly positioned in place and difficult to dislodge ⟨This *jammed* door just won't budge!⟩ — see TIGHT 2

jam–pack *vb* to put into (something) as much as can be held or contained ⟨We *jam-packed* the box with goodies for our sick friend.⟩ — see FILL 1

jam–packed *adj* **1** containing or seeming to contain the greatest quantity or number possible ⟨a film *jam-packed* with spectacular action sequences⟩ — see FULL 1
2 having little space between items or parts ⟨The *jam-packed* placement of the chicken pieces in the frying pan prevented them from browning properly.⟩ — see CLOSE 1

janitor *n* a person who takes care of a property sometimes for an absent owner ⟨got a job as the night *janitor* at the elementary school⟩ — see CUSTODIAN 1

jar *n* **1** a forceful coming together of two things ⟨This padded case should protect your laptop from the *jars* normally experienced while traveling.⟩ — see IMPACT 1
2 something that makes a strong impression because it is so unexpected ⟨The flow of her day was interrupted with the *jar* of an unexpected crisis.⟩ — see SURPRISE 1
3 a harsh grating sound ⟨the *jar* of a stuck car door⟩ — see RASP

jar *vb* **1** to express different opinions about something often angrily ⟨Those two coworkers have such incompatible personalities that it's no wonder they constantly *jar*.⟩ — see ARGUE 2
2 to be out of harmony or agreement usually noticeably

⟨The bright orange of the walls *jars* with the light pastels of the furnishings.⟩ — see CLASH

jargon *n* the special terms or expressions of a particular group or field ⟨I don't understand a lot of computer *jargon*.⟩ — see TERMINOLOGY

jarring *adj* **1** causing a strong emotional reaction because of unexpectedness ⟨the *jarring* news that major financial institutions were on the verge of collapse⟩ — see SURPRISING 1
2 disagreeable to one's aesthetic or artistic sense ⟨The final chord of that song is too *jarring* for me.⟩ — see HARSH 2

jaundice *n* a deep-seated ill will ⟨the *jaundice* of the feuding neighbors⟩ — see ENMITY

jaundiced *adj* **1** having or showing mean resentment of another's possessions or advantages ⟨took a *jaundiced* view of his opponent's triumphs on the tennis court⟩ — see ENVIOUS
2 marked by opposition or ill will ⟨Environmentalists tend to cast a *jaundiced* eye on those oversized, gas-guzzling vehicles.⟩ — see HOSTILE 1

jaunt *n* a short trip for pleasure ⟨took a leisurely *jaunt* up to the mountains for the day⟩ — see EXCURSION 1

jaunty *adj* having much high-spirited energy and movement ⟨a *jaunty* dance step⟩ — see LIVELY 1

javelin *n* a weapon with a long straight handle and sharp head or blade ⟨From atop his horse the warrior hurled a *javelin*.⟩ — see SPEAR

jaw *n* friendly, informal conversation or an instance of this ⟨Now that he's retired, he's got all afternoon for a *jaw* with his friends at the senior center.⟩ — see CHAT 1

jaw *vb* **1** to criticize (someone) severely or angrily especially for personal failings ⟨You don't have to *jaw* me to death just because I bite my nails.⟩ — see SCOLD
2 to engage in casual or rambling conversation ⟨just a group of girls sitting around the locker room and *jawing* about the usual stuff⟩ — see CHAT 1

jazz *n* language, behavior, or ideas that are absurd and contrary to good sense ⟨Don't give me that *jazz* about how you didn't know how late it was.⟩ — see NONSENSE 1

jazz (up) *vb* to give life, vigor, or spirit to ⟨Your assignment is to *jazz up* the design of that Web page.⟩ — see ANIMATE

jazziness *n* the quality or state of having abundant or intense activity ⟨the surprising *jazziness* of the city's art scene⟩ — see VITALITY 1

jazzy *adj* **1** attractively eye-catching in style ⟨That's a *jazzy* bathing suit, with all those spangles.⟩
synonyms flashy, snazzy, splashy
related words cool, hip, neat; à la mode (*also* a la mode), chic, chichi; dapper, dashing, natty, sharp, smart, snappy, spruce; faddish, fashionable, in, modish, stylish, trendy; custom, designer; showy, striking; flamboyant, garish, gaudy, glittery, glitzy, loud, ostentatious, raffish, swank (*or* swanky), wild
near antonyms modest, plain, quiet, simple, unadorned; conservative, muted, restrained, subdued, toned-down, understated, unpretentious; styleless, unfashionable, unstylish
2 having much high-spirited energy and movement ⟨a *jazzy* little dance routine that the aerobics instructor created⟩ — see LIVELY 1

jealous *adj* **1** intolerant of rivalry or unfaithfulness ⟨a boyfriend who became *jealous* whenever she paid attention to anyone but him⟩
synonyms possessive
related words controlling, demanding, domineering, grasping; covetous, envious, invidious, jaundiced; distrustful, mistrustful, suspicious; overprotective, protective

near antonyms undemanding; permissive, tolerant, tolerating, trustful, trusting, understanding
2 having or showing mean resentment of another's possessions or advantages ⟨Ed was *jealous* of his friend's new car.⟩ — see ENVIOUS

jealousy *n* a painful awareness of another's possessions or advantages and a desire to have them too ⟨Her *jealousy* over her sister's singing career drove the two of them apart.⟩ — see ENVY

jeer *n* a vocal sound made to express scorn or disapproval ⟨ignored the *jeers* of the other team's fans and just focused on making her free throw shot⟩ — see CATCALL

jeer *vb* to make (someone or something) the object of unkind laughter ⟨The unforgiving crowd *jeered* the magician when the final trick went awry.⟩ — see RIDICULE

Jehovah *n* the being worshipped as the creator and ruler of the universe ⟨the Lord *Jehovah*⟩ — see DEITY 2

jell *vb* **1** to take on a definite form ⟨Our ideas for the marketing campaign are just beginning to *jell*.⟩ — see FORM 1
2 to turn from a liquid into a substance resembling jelly ⟨The sauce will *jell* once it cools down.⟩ — see COAGULATE

jelly *vb* to turn from a liquid into a substance resembling jelly ⟨This fruit juice is taking longer to *jelly* than I expected.⟩ — see COAGULATE

jeopardize *vb* to place in danger ⟨Don't do anything that will *jeopardize* your place on the advisory board.⟩ — see ENDANGER

jeopardizing *adj* involving potential loss or injury ⟨That stupid prank could turn out to be a *jeopardizing* event in your academic career.⟩ — see DANGEROUS 1

jeopardy *n* the state of not being protected from injury, harm, or evil ⟨The city's firefighters routinely put their lives in *jeopardy* by executing daring rescues.⟩ — see DANGER 1

jerk *n* **1** a person whose behavior is offensive to others ⟨I know it's not fair, but you don't have to be such a *jerk* about it.⟩
synonyms beast, boor, cad, churl, clown, creep, cur, dog, heel, joker, louse, lout, pill, rat, scum, skunk, slob, snake, stinker, swine
related words barbarian, brute, caveman, Neanderthal, savage; loudmouth, vulgarian; lowlife, miscreant, rascal, rogue, roughneck, scab, scamp, scoundrel, villain, wretch; booby, fool, nincompoop, ninny, nitwit, nut; blockhead, dolt, dope, dork [*slang*], goon, half-wit, idiot, imbecile, moron, turkey
phrases son of a gun
near antonyms hero, heroine, role model; gentleman, lady; angel, saint
2 the act or an instance of applying force on something so that it moves in the direction of the force ⟨guided the rowboat with a *jerk* of the rope⟩ — see PULL 1

jerk *vb* **1** to move or cause to move with a sharp quick motion ⟨I *jerked* to one side to avoid getting hit.⟩ ⟨*jerked* the leash to get the dog's attention⟩
synonyms buck, hitch, jolt, twitch, yank
related words bump, jounce, lurch, pitch, stagger; jig, jiggle, jog, joggle, shake; drag, lug, pull, tug; pluck, tweak; grab, rip, snap (up), snatch, tear, wrench, wrest, wring
2 to make jerky or restless movements ⟨You've got to quit *jerking*, or the barber will nick you by accident.⟩ — see FIDGET
3 to make a series of small irregular or violent movements ⟨The car *jerked* with every shift of the gear.⟩ — see SHAKE

jerky *adj* **1** marked by a series of sharp quick motions ⟨made *jerky* progress walking with the new crutches⟩
synonyms bumpy, choppy, rough
related words erratic, fitful, irregular, spasmodic, unsteady; jagged, ragged, uneven
near antonyms calm, placid, smooth, steady, still

2 showing or marked by a lack of good sense or judgment ⟨He's acting *jerky* just to get people's attention.⟩ — see FOOLISH 1

jerry–rigged *adj* hastily or roughly constructed ⟨a *jerry-rigged* switch to keep the machine in operation until it can be repaired⟩ — see RUDE 1

jest *n* **1** an attitude or manner not to be taken seriously ⟨You should know that our teasing was done entirely in *jest*.⟩ — see FUN 2
2 something said or done to cause laughter ⟨I laughed politely at his feeble *jest*.⟩ — see JOKE 1
3 a playful or mischievous act intended as a joke ⟨Putting a mouse in her desk drawer was intended to be a harmless *jest*.⟩ — see PRANK
4 a person or thing that is made fun of ⟨He became the *jest* of the town until he was proven right.⟩ — see LAUGHINGSTOCK

jest *vb* to make jokes ⟨When I asked my sister for a loan, she laughingly replied, "Surely you *jest*!"⟩ — see JOKE 1

jester *n* **1** a person (as a writer) noted for or specializing in humor ⟨A gentle *jester*, the cartoonist more often tries to evoke a broad smile than a hearty guffaw.⟩ — see HUMORIST
2 a person formerly kept in a royal or noble household to amuse with jests and pranks ⟨The king called for some much-needed entertainment from his *jester*.⟩ — see FOOL 2

jesting *adj* marked by or expressive of mild or good-natured teasing ⟨made *jesting* comments about my need for serious fashion advice⟩ — see QUIZZICAL

jesting *n* good-natured teasing or exchanging of clever remarks ⟨lots of laughter and elbow-nudging *jesting* at family reunions⟩ — see BANTER

jet *n* a usually forceful stream of fluid discharged from a narrow opening ⟨We bought a new showerhead that emits a superpowerful *jet* of water.⟩
synonyms spout, spurt, squirt
related words flush, gush, spew; spit, spray, spritz; geyser, spouter; blast, burst

jet *vb* **1** to flow out in great quantities or with force ⟨water *jetting* out of opened fire hydrants⟩ — see GUSH 1
2 to violently throw out or off (something from within) ⟨The volcano has been *jetting* out fiery lava.⟩ — see ERUPT 1
3 to proceed or move quickly ⟨The presidential candidates *jetted* through the state for a week before racing off to the next primary.⟩ — see HURRY 2

jettison *n* the getting rid of whatever is unwanted or useless ⟨With his ship rapidly sinking, the captain ordered a last-ditch *jettison* of much of its cargo.⟩ — see DISPOSAL 1

jettison *vb* to get rid of as useless or unwanted ⟨Let's just *jettison* that plan, because we know it won't work.⟩ — see DISCARD

jetty *n* a structure used by boats and ships for taking on or landing cargo and passengers ⟨He didn't see any passengers waiting for the ferry, so the captain sailed past the *jetty*.⟩ — see DOCK

jewel *n* **1** a usually valuable stone cut and polished for ornament ⟨a necklace set with priceless *jewels*⟩ — see GEM 1
2 an asset that brings praise or renown ⟨an illuminated medieval manuscript that is the *jewel* of the library's collection of rare books⟩ — see GLORY 2
3 someone or something unusually desirable ⟨a star athlete who would be a *jewel* for any team⟩ — see PRIZE 1

jibe *vb* to be in agreement on every point ⟨That doesn't *jibe* with what I know about his character.⟩ — see CHECK 1

jiffy *n* a very small space of time ⟨I'll be there in a *jiffy*!⟩ — see INSTANT

jig *n* a clever often underhanded means to achieve an end ⟨Okay, buster, the *jig* is up.⟩ — see TRICK 1

jig *vb* to make jerky or restless movements ⟨We could tell that the little boy had to use the bathroom because he was *jigging*.⟩ — see FIDGET

jigger *n* an interesting and often novel device with a practical use ⟨a kitchen store filled with neat little *jiggers* that you didn't know you needed⟩ — see GADGET

jiggle *vb* **1** to make a series of small irregular or violent movements ⟨The gelatin salad continued to *jiggle* after she set it on the table.⟩ — see SHAKE 1

2 to make jerky or restless movements ⟨The applicant's knees constantly *jiggled*, betraying her nervousness.⟩ — see FIDGET

jiggling *n* a series of slight movements by a body back and forth or from side to side ⟨the nerve-rattling *jiggling* we got when we drove over the railroad tracks⟩ — see VIBRATION 1

jim–dandy *n* something very good of its kind ⟨The brand new car was a *jim-dandy*.⟩

synonyms beauty, corker, crackerjack (*also* crackajack), dandy, dream, honey, knockout, nifty, pip, standout

related words marvel, phenomenon, prodigy, sensation, wonder; catch, diamond, gem, imperial, jewel, pearl, plum, treasure

phrases something else

near antonyms bust, disappointment, dud, failure, flop, lemon, letdown, loser, stinker, turkey

jim–dandy *adj* of the very best kind ⟨We had a *jim-dandy* vacation.⟩ — see EXCELLENT

jimmy *vb* to raise, move, or pull apart with or as if with a lever ⟨Let's try to *jimmy* the door lock with my credit card.⟩ — see ¹PRY 1

jingle *n* **1** a series of short high ringing sounds ⟨the *jingle* of change in my pocket⟩ — see TINKLE

2 a short musical composition for the human voice often with instrumental accompaniment ⟨loved that *jingle* in the commercial for the fast-food place⟩ — see SONG 1

jingle *vb* to make a repeated sharp light ringing sound ⟨The bell on the kitten's collar *jingled* as she walked.⟩

synonyms chink, clink, tingle, tinkle

related words clang, clangor, clank, clash, crash; clack, clatter, rattle; chime, ding, ding-dong, gong, ping, plink, ring

jingo *n* **1** one who shows excessive favoritism towards his or her country ⟨a *jingo* who thought other countries should automatically follow his country's policies⟩ — see NATIONALIST

2 one who urges or attempts to cause a war ⟨the often bitter rhetoric between the *jingoes* and the committed pacifists⟩ — see WARMONGER

jingoism *n* excessive favoritism towards one's own country ⟨Many people were caught up in a wave of *jingoism*.⟩ — see CHAUVINISM

jinx *n* something that brings bad luck ⟨believed the broken mirror was a *jinx*⟩

synonyms hex

related words Jonah; curse, evil eye, pox, spell, voodoo; augury, omen, portent

near antonyms amulet, charm, fetish (*also* fetich), talisman

jinxed *adj* having, prone to, or marked by bad luck ⟨This fishing rod must be *jinxed*, seeing as how I never catch anything.⟩ — see UNLUCKY 1

jitters *pl n* a sense of panic or extreme nervousness ⟨always got the *jitters* right before a test⟩

synonyms butterflies, dither, nerves, shakes, shivers, willies

related words cold sweat, creeps, fidgets, goose bumps; agitation, anxiety, fear, hysteria, uneasiness; frazzle; edginess, jumpiness, skittishness

near antonyms aplomb, calm, composure, equanimity,

imperturbability, self-possession, tranquillity (*or* tranquility)

jittery *adj* **1** easily excited by nature ⟨a *jittery* person who shouldn't even consider a career as an air traffic controller⟩ — see EXCITABLE

2 feeling or showing uncomfortable feelings of uncertainty ⟨feeling a little *jittery* before the flight⟩ — see NERVOUS 1

jive *n* the special terms or expressions of a particular group or field ⟨grew up talking street *jive*⟩ — see TERMINOLOGY

jive *vb* **1** to make fun of in a good-natured way ⟨good friends *jiving* each other⟩ — see TEASE 1

2 to make jokes ⟨Our team was laughing and *jiving* after our surprise win.⟩ — see JOKE 1

job *n* **1** an assignment at which one regularly works for pay ⟨a high-paying *job* as a banker⟩

synonyms appointment, berth, billet, capacity, connection, function, place, position, post, situation

related words business, employ, employment, occupation, profession; work; office, spot; calling, pursuit, trade, vocation; line, racket; engagement, gig, livelihood, living; career, lifework, practice (*also* practise); duty, mission, posting, service, task

near antonyms joblessness, unemployment

2 a piece of work that needs to be done regularly ⟨Taking the trash out is one of my *jobs*.⟩ — see CHORE 1

3 a specific task with which a person or group is charged ⟨Your *job* on this committee is to review the curriculum and suggest changes.⟩ — see MISSION

4 the action for which a person or thing is specially fitted or used or for which a thing exists ⟨A coffeemaker's *job* is to make coffee, and this overpriced machine doesn't do it very well.⟩ — see ROLE

5 a dull, unpleasant, or difficult piece of work ⟨Boy, doing all that filing was a real *job*!⟩ — see CHORE 2

jobholder *n* one who works for another for wages or a salary ⟨more *jobholders* than the state agency has ever had in the past⟩ — see EMPLOYEE

jocose *adj* indicative of or marked by high spirits or good humor ⟨The comedian's *jocose* introductions kept the awards ceremony from becoming a stodgy affair.⟩ — see MERRY

jocosely *adv* in a cheerful or happy manner ⟨a group of friends sitting around and commenting *jocosely* on the other wedding guests⟩ — see GAILY 1

jocular *adj* **1** given to or marked by mature intelligent humor ⟨He made the *jocular* observation that the best way to make a small fortune in the business is to start off with a large fortune.⟩ — see WITTY

2 indicative of or marked by high spirits or good humor ⟨The children at the library were charmed by the *jocular* storyteller.⟩ — see MERRY

jocund *adj* indicative of or marked by high spirits or good humor ⟨old friends engaged in *jocund* teasing⟩ — see MERRY

jog *vb* **1** to go at a pace faster than a walk ⟨I had to *jog* to catch up to them.⟩ — see RUN 1

2 to make short up-and-down movements ⟨Her purse was *jogging* against her hip as she walked.⟩ — see NOD

joggle *vb* to make a series of small irregular or violent movements ⟨The old bus *joggled* as it barreled down the dirt road.⟩ — see SHAKE 1

join *n* a place where two or more things are united ⟨a small crack in the chalice at the *join* of the stem and the bowl⟩ — see JOINT 1

join *vb* **1** to be adjacent to ⟨The condo complex *joins* the golf course.⟩ — see ADJOIN 1

2 to become a member of ⟨We're always looking for new people to *join* our book club.⟩ — see ENTER 2

3 to come together to form a single unit ⟨One oxygen atom and two hydrogen atoms *join* to make one water molecule.⟩ — see UNITE 1

4 to participate or assist in a joint effort to accomplish an end ⟨nations *joining* to bring aid to the earthquake-devastated region⟩ — see COOPERATE 1

5 to put or bring together so as to form a new and longer whole ⟨The plan is to *join* the various bike paths so that cyclists can travel from one end of the cape to the other.⟩ — see CONNECT 1

joining *adj* having a border in common ⟨Out of regard for your coworkers in the *joining* cubicles, please wear headphones when listening to electronic devices.⟩ — see ADJACENT

joining *n* a place where two or more things are united ⟨The *joining* of the original house and the later addition is barely noticeable.⟩ — see JOINT 1

joint *adj* used or done by a number of people as a group ⟨a *joint* effort to get the job done⟩ — see COLLECTIVE

joint *n* **1** a place where two or more things are united ⟨The leak was found at a *joint* in the pipe.⟩

synonyms connection, coupling, join, junction, juncture

related words link, tie; interconnection, intersection; abutment, articulation, attachment; seam; concourse, confluence, meeting; union

near antonyms cleft, crack, crevice, fissure, gap, rift, separation

2 a building, room, or suite of rooms occupied by a service business ⟨Let's go to the local burger *joint*.⟩ — see PLACE 2

jointly *adv* in or by combined action or effort ⟨We always purchase our mother's birthday present *jointly*.⟩ — see TOGETHER 2

joke *n* **1** something said or done to cause laughter ⟨He was known for his hilarious *jokes*.⟩

synonyms crack, funny, gag, jest, laugh, pleasantry, quip, rib, sally, waggery, wisecrack, witticism

related words funning, joking, wisecracking; panic [*slang*], riot, scream; antic, caper, monkeyshine(s), practical joke, prank, trick; burlesque, caricature, lampoon, mock, mockery, parody, put-on, riff; comedy, humor, wit, wordplay

2 a poor, insincere, or insulting imitation of something ⟨Her rendition of the national anthem is a *joke*.⟩ — see MOCKERY 1

3 a person or thing that is made fun of ⟨a company that became a *joke* in the industry⟩ — see LAUGHINGSTOCK

joke *vb* **1** to make jokes ⟨He was known for his ability to *joke* about his lack of anything resembling a social life.⟩

synonyms banter, chaff, fool, fun, gag, jest, jive, jolly, josh, kid, quip, wisecrack

related words gibe (*or* jibe), haze, jeer, mock, rally, razz, rib, ridicule, tease; caricature, lampoon, parody, satirize; amuse, divert, entertain

phrases crack wise

2 to make fun of in a good-natured way ⟨Oh, don't get offended, I was just *joking* you.⟩ — see TEASE 1

joker *n* **1** a person (as a writer) noted for or specializing in humor ⟨He's the *joker* of the family, always making us laugh.⟩ — see HUMORIST

2 a person whose behavior is offensive to others ⟨Just ignore that *joker* and his rude comments.⟩ — see JERK 1

3 an adult male human being ⟨sat next to some *joker* who snored during the entire flight home⟩ — see MAN 1

4 a danger or difficulty that is hidden or not easily recognized ⟨Read the contract carefully before signing to make sure there aren't any *jokers*.⟩ — see PITFALL 1

jokester *n* a person (as a writer) noted for or specializing

in humor ⟨hired the hot new Hollywood *jokester* to write the sitcom script⟩ — see HUMORIST

joking *adj* marked by or expressive of mild or good-natured teasing ⟨I grinned and gave him a *joking* nudge with my elbow.⟩ — see QUIZZICAL

jollification *n* joyful or festive activity ⟨Each year the mountain men of the Old West would gather for a week of carousing, tall tale-telling, and general *jollification*.⟩ — see MERRYMAKING

jollity *n* joyful or festive activity ⟨I love all of the warmhearted *jollity* of the holiday season.⟩ — see MERRYMAKING

jolly *adj* **1** indicative of or marked by high spirits or good humor ⟨an especially *jolly* crowd of well-wishers at their wedding reception⟩ — see MERRY

2 giving pleasure or contentment to the mind or senses ⟨We always have a *jolly* time at their seaside cottage.⟩ — see PLEASANT 1

jolly *adv* to a great degree ⟨I *jolly* well agree that you did the right thing.⟩ ⟨Ted has become a *jolly* careful driver since his recent accident.⟩ — see VERY 1

jolly *vb* to make jokes ⟨spent their nights around the campfire good-naturedly *jollying* and telling scary stories⟩ — see JOKE 1

jolt *n* **1** a forceful coming together of two things ⟨Please pack the glass vase so that it won't fall victim to any hard *jolts* in transit.⟩ — see IMPACT 1

2 something that makes a strong impression because it is so unexpected ⟨The news of the CEO's sudden retirement was a *jolt* to us all.⟩ — see SURPRISE 1

jolt *vb* **1** to make a series of small irregular or violent movements ⟨The roller coaster car jerked and *jolted* as it coursed along the old wooden tracks.⟩ — see SHAKE 1

2 to move or cause to move with a sharp quick motion ⟨She *jolted* the door open with her elbow.⟩ — see JERK 1

3 to cause an unpleasant surprise for ⟨The bad grade *jolted* me out of procrastinating in my studying.⟩ — see SHOCK 1

josh *vb* **1** to make fun of in a good-natured way ⟨I'm just *joshing* you!⟩ — see TEASE 1

2 to make jokes ⟨a very outgoing man who *joshes* with everyone he meets⟩ — see JOKE 1

joshing *adj* marked by or expressive of mild or good-natured teasing ⟨a *joshing* response to my earnest question⟩ — see QUIZZICAL

joshing *n* good-natured teasing or exchanging of clever remarks ⟨For all his *joshing*, he can be very serious when he needs to be.⟩ — see BANTER

jot *n* the smallest amount or part imaginable ⟨It's obvious that he doesn't have a *jot* of interest in history.⟩

synonyms darn (*also* durn), hoot, iota, lick, modicum, rap, tittle, whit, whoop

related words ace, bit, crumb, dab, driblet, glimmer, hint, little, mite, nip, ounce, particle, peanuts, pin, ray, scrap, scruple, semblance, shade, shadow, shred, smidgen (*also* smidgeon *or* smidgin *or* smidge), speck, spot, sprinkling, strain, streak, suspicion, touch, trace

jot (down) *vb* to make a written note of ⟨I'll *jot down* the message.⟩ — see RECORD 1

jounce *n* a forceful coming together of two things ⟨We felt a definite *jounce* every time the car hit a pothole.⟩ — see IMPACT 1

jounce *vb* **1** to make a series of small irregular or violent movements ⟨a rickety cart *jouncing* as it was being pulled over the cobblestoned streets⟩ — see SHAKE 1

2 to make short up-and-down movements ⟨Her head *jounced* as the horse began to gallop.⟩ — see NOD

journal *n* a publication that appears at regular intervals ⟨a monthly scientific *journal*⟩

synonyms bulletin, gazette, magazine, newspaper, organ, paper, periodical, review, serial

related words annual, bimonthly, biweekly, daily, monthly, quarterly, semimonthly, semiweekly, triweekly, weekly, yearbook; digest, little magazine; fanzine; pictorial, slick; newsletter, newsmagazine, newsweekly

journalist *n* a person employed by a newspaper, magazine, or radio or television station to gather, write, or report news ⟨a *journalist* who has won awards for two of his feature stories⟩ — see REPORTER

journey *n* a going from one place to another usually of some distance ⟨They were hungry and tired after their long *journey*.⟩
synonyms expedition, passage, peregrination, travel(s), trek, trip
related words commute, errand, excursion, flight, hop, jaunt, junket, outing, sally, sortie, tour; cruise, sail, voyage; drive, ride, spin; grand tour, odyssey, pilgrimage, progress, quest, safari; hike, slog, tramp, walk

journey *vb* to take a trip especially of some distance ⟨an intense yearning to *journey* to distant lands⟩ — see TRAVEL 1

jovial *adj* indicative of or marked by high spirits or good humor ⟨The trip to the amusement park put everyone in a *jovial* mood.⟩ — see MERRY

joviality *n* a mood characterized by high spirits and amusement and often accompanied by laughter ⟨The company's holiday parties often had an air of forced *joviality*.⟩ — see MIRTH

jovially *adv* in a cheerful or happy manner ⟨*jovially* waved good morning to us⟩ — see GAILY 1

joy *n* **1** a feeling or state of well-being and contentment ⟨the inexpressible *joy* that the couple are feeling upon the birth of their first child⟩ — see HAPPINESS 1
2 a source of great satisfaction ⟨My car is my pride and *joy*.⟩ — see DELIGHT 1

joy *vb* to feel or express joy or triumph ⟨The whole town is *joying* in the fact that its oldest house has been restored to its Victorian splendor.⟩ — see EXULT

joyful *adj* experiencing pleasure, satisfaction, or delight ⟨The news of the child's safe return made us all *joyful*.⟩ — see GLAD 1

joyless *adj* feeling unhappiness ⟨Dave was utterly *joyless* after his business failed.⟩ — see SAD 1

joylessness *n* a state or spell of low spirits ⟨the inescapable *joylessness* that marred Yuletide celebrations during the war years⟩ — see SADNESS

joyous *adj* experiencing pleasure, satisfaction, or delight ⟨a *joyous* crowd eagerly awaiting the countdown to midnight on New Year's Eve⟩ — see GLAD 1

jubilant *adj* having or expressing feelings of joy or triumph ⟨the nominee's *jubilant* acceptance speech before the cheering crowd⟩ — see EXULTANT

jubilee *n* a time or program of special events and entertainment in honor of something ⟨The town is planning a year-long *jubilee* in celebration of its founding 200 years ago.⟩ — see FESTIVAL

judge *n* **1** a person who impartially decides or resolves a dispute or controversy ⟨played the role of *judge* in their disagreement⟩
synonyms arbiter, arbitrator, referee, umpire
related words jurist, justice, magistrate; intermediary, intermediate, mediator, moderator, negotiator; conciliator, go-between, peacemaker, reconciler, troubleshooter; decider
2 a public official having authority to decide questions of law ⟨The *judge* gave the defendant a suspended sentence.⟩
synonyms bench, court, jurist, justice, magistrate
related words chief justice, circuit judge, justice of the peace, squire; auditor, master

judge *vb* **1** to give an opinion about (something at issue or in dispute) ⟨The committee will *judge* the case solely on the evidence.⟩
synonyms adjudge, adjudicate, arbitrate, decide, determine, referee, rule (on), settle, umpire
related words consider, deem, deliberate, hear, ponder, weigh; size up; mediate, moderate, negotiate; try; find (for *or* against); conclude, resolve
near antonyms equivocate, hedge, pussyfoot, skirt
2 to decide the size, amount, number, or distance of (something) without actual measurement ⟨Considering the amount of dough we have, I *judge* we'll get about six dozen cookies out of it.⟩ — see ESTIMATE 2
3 to form an opinion or reach a conclusion through reasoning and information ⟨You shouldn't always *judge* people by their appearance.⟩ — see INFER 1
4 to have as an opinion ⟨We *judged* that the chocolate pie was the best.⟩ — see BELIEVE 2

judgment *or* **judgement** *n* **1** a decision made by a court or tribunal regarding a case it has heard ⟨The court will give its *judgment* in this case tomorrow morning.⟩ — see SENTENCE
2 a position arrived at after consideration ⟨built her fortune by making intelligent *judgments* about the performance of stocks⟩ — see DECISION 1
3 an idea that is believed to be true or valid without positive knowledge ⟨Your *judgment* of the situation isn't a very good one.⟩ — see OPINION 1
4 an opinion on the nature, character, or quality of something ⟨Critical *judgment* on that new comedy has been overwhelmingly positive.⟩ — see ESTIMATION 1

judicious *adj* **1** having or showing good judgment and restraint especially in conduct or speech ⟨a good teacher who knows how to give *judicious* criticism as well as praise⟩ — see DISCREET 1
2 suitable for bringing about a desired result under the circumstances ⟨I'll ask for the raise at a time I deem most *judicious*.⟩ — see EXPEDIENT

jug *n* **1** a place of confinement for persons held in lawful custody ⟨told them to move along or they'd get thrown in the *jug*⟩ — see JAIL
2 a handled container for holding and pouring liquids that usually has a lip or a spout ⟨The host put a *jug* of milk on the table.⟩ — see PITCHER

jug *vb* to put in or as if in prison ⟨The luckless crooks got *jugged* before they knew what hit them.⟩ — see IMPRISON

jugglery *n* the use of clever underhanded actions to achieve an end ⟨You wouldn't believe the *jugglery* I have to resort to in order to get the cat in the carrier for a trip to the vet's.⟩ — see TRICKERY

juiciness *n* the quality or state of being full of juice ⟨the delicious *juiciness* of ripe pears⟩ — see SUCCULENCE

juicy *adj* full of juice ⟨She bit into the *juicy* orange.⟩
synonyms fleshy, pulpy, succulent
related words sappy, watery
near antonyms dehydrated, desiccated, dry, sere (*also* sear), shriveled (*or* shrivelled), withered
antonyms juiceless, sapless

jumble *n* **1** a state in which everything is out of order ⟨The house is always in a *jumble* before and after vacation trips.⟩ — see CHAOS
2 an unorganized collection or mixture of various things ⟨a *jumble* of rubber bands, batteries, and pencil stubs all stuffed into that drawer⟩ — see MISCELLANY 1

jumble *vb* to undo the proper order or arrangement of ⟨The contest editor has *jumbled* the letters of some common words.⟩ — see DISORDER

jumbled *adj* lacking in order, neatness, and often cleanliness ⟨a *jumbled* closet in which I can never find anything⟩ — see MESSY

jumbo *adj* unusually large ⟨a *jumbo* jet⟩ — see HUGE

jumbo *n* something that is unusually large and powerful ⟨The winner in the contest for biggest pumpkin was a *jumbo* that weighed in at over a thousand pounds.⟩ — see GIANT

jump *n* **1** an act of leaping into the air ⟨She took a small *jump* forward to avoid stepping in the puddle.⟩

synonyms bound, hop, leap, spring, vault

related words bounce, lope, skip; caper, gambol; attack, pounce; dive, pitch, plunge

2 the more favorable condition or position in a competition ⟨Let's get a *jump* on the competition by starting early.⟩ — see ADVANTAGE 1

jump *vb* **1** to propel oneself upward or forward into the air ⟨Jared *jumped* across the ditch.⟩

synonyms bound, hop, leap, spring, vault

related words bounce, hurdle, leapfrog, lope, skip; buck; caper, capriole, cavort, frolic, gambol, romp; attack, pounce; shoot, skyrocket

2 to move suddenly and sharply (as in surprise) ⟨The sudden appearance of a mouse scurrying across the floor made me *jump*.⟩ — see START 1

3 to proceed or move quickly ⟨When I tell you to do something, I expect you to *jump*.⟩ — see HURRY 2

jump (on) *vb* **1** to take sudden, violent action against ⟨*jumped on* the thief before he could flee⟩ — see ATTACK 1

2 to criticize harshly and usually publicly ⟨No need to *jump on* him just because he locked the keys in the car.⟩ — see ATTACK 2

jumpiness *n* a state of nervousness marked by sudden jerky movements ⟨The police detective interpreted the suspect's *jumpiness* as a sign of guilt.⟩

synonyms edginess, fidgets, flightiness, restiveness, skittishness

related words agitation, anxiety, anxiousness, apprehension, apprehensiveness, disquiet, restlessness, trepidation, uneasiness, upset, worry; nerves, tenseness, tension; butterflies, dither, jitters, shakes, shivers, willies

near antonyms confidence, self-assurance, self-confidence, sureness; control, self-control; aplomb, calm, calmness, collectedness, composure, coolness, ease, easiness, equanimity, equilibrium, imperturbability, poise, repose, self-possession, tranquillity (*or* tranquility)

jumpy *adj* **1** easily excited by nature ⟨a *jumpy* little terrier⟩ — see EXCITABLE

2 feeling or showing uncomfortable feelings of uncertainty ⟨Flight attendants had to calm *jumpy* passengers after the plane hit unexpected turbulence.⟩ — see NERVOUS 1

junction *n* **1** a place where two or more things are united ⟨Situated at the *junction* of several major railways, the city has long been a transportation hub.⟩ — see JOINT 1

2 the act or an instance of joining two or more things into one ⟨The *junction* of the coalition's two military forces has not been without problems.⟩ — see UNION 1

3 a place where roads meet ⟨The town finally installed a traffic light at that busy *junction*.⟩ — see CROSSROAD 1

juncture *n* **1** a particular and often important moment in time ⟨At the present *juncture*, I think the country is looking for a strong president.⟩ — see POINT 1

2 a place where two or more things are united ⟨The water is leaking at the *juncture* of those two pipes.⟩ — see JOINT 1

3 a time or state of affairs requiring prompt or decisive action ⟨We have now arrived at a *juncture* where something must be done.⟩ — see EMERGENCY

junior *adj* having not so great importance or rank as another ⟨*junior* advisers to the governor⟩ — see LESSER

junior *n* one who is of lower rank and typically under the authority of another ⟨She's my *junior* in the company.⟩ — see UNDERLING

junk *n* **1** that which is of low quality or worth ⟨I couldn't believe that such *junk* was chosen to be read for the book club.⟩ ⟨My car is *junk*—it spends more time in the shop than on the road!⟩

synonyms rubbish, trash

related words claptrap, humbug, nonsense; bomb, dud, lemon, stinker, turkey; mess, muddle, shambles

2 discarded or useless material ⟨*junk* on the side of the road waiting for the trash collection⟩ — see GARBAGE

junk *vb* to get rid of as useless or unwanted ⟨We'll have to *junk* this old car.⟩ — see DISCARD

junket *n* a short trip for pleasure ⟨We took a *junket* to the city for some sightseeing and shopping.⟩ — see EXCURSION 1

junket *vb* to entertain with a fancy meal ⟨a lobbyist who regularly *junkets* politicians who are friendly toward the oil industry⟩ — see FEAST 1

junkie *also* **junky** *n* a person with a strong and habitual liking for something ⟨a television cartoon *junkie*⟩ — see FAN

junking *n* the getting rid of whatever is unwanted or useless ⟨That old chair needs *junking*.⟩ — see DISPOSAL 1

junky *adj* **1** having no usefulness ⟨That broken watch you're wearing is *junky*.⟩ — see WORTHLESS

2 of low quality ⟨a *junky* coat that is sure to fall apart after one winter⟩ — see CHEAP 2

jurisdiction *n* lawful control over the affairs of a political unit (as a nation) ⟨The United States has no *jurisdiction* over Cuba.⟩ — see RULE 2

jurist *n* a public official having authority to decide questions of law ⟨earned a reputation as one of the most learned *jurists* in the federal courts⟩ — see JUDGE 2

just *adj* **1** being what is called for by accepted standards of right and wrong ⟨A *just* punishment should fit the crime.⟩

synonyms competent, deserved, due, fair, justified, merited, right, rightful, warranted

related words applicable, appropriate, apt, fit, fitting, meet, proper, requisite, suitable; lawful, legal, legitimate; accurate, correct, true; strict, stringent, uncompromising; equitable, impartial

near antonyms incoherent, incorrect, irrelative, irrelevant; improper, inapplicable, inappropriate, inapt, indefensible, unjustifiable, unreasonable, unsuitable; biased, inequitable, partial, unequal; arbitrary, despotic; illegitimate, unlawful

antonyms undeserved, undue, unfair, unjust, unjustified, unmerited, unwarranted

2 based on sound reasoning or information ⟨There are *just* reasons for the state's ban of the private use of fireworks.⟩ — see GOOD 1

3 conforming to a high standard of morality or virtue ⟨a *just* society⟩ — see GOOD 2

4 following the accepted rules of moral conduct ⟨the sort of *just* conduct that we expect of every soldier⟩ — see HONORABLE 1

5 guided by or in accordance with one's sense of right and wrong ⟨Stopping to help a stranded motorist is simply the *just* thing to do.⟩ — see CONSCIENTIOUS 1

6 marked by justice, honesty, and freedom from bias ⟨a *just* appraisal of the political situation⟩ — see FAIR 2

just *adv* **1** in the same manner ⟨You can do it *just* the way they do.⟩

synonyms exactly, precisely

related words even, expressly, faultlessly, perfectly; identically, uniformly; alike, likewise, similarly

phrases to a T

near antonyms slightly, somewhat, vaguely; differently, variably

2 by a very small margin ⟨I was *just* over the minimum height requirement for the amusement park ride.⟩
synonyms barely, hardly, marginally, scarcely, slightly
related words minimally, minutely, scantly; almost, closely, more or less, nearly, partly, roughly, somewhat
phrases by the skin of one's teeth
near antonyms definitely, easily, plainly, quite, unquestionably; abundantly, completely, copiously, fully, generously, greatly
antonyms considerably, significantly, substantially, vastly, well
3 nothing more than ⟨I was *just* kidding!⟩
synonyms but, merely, only, purely, simply
4 as stated or indicated without the slightest difference ⟨The length of the curtain is *just* right.⟩ — see EXACTLY 1
5 for nothing other than ⟨I got this present *just* for you.⟩ — see SOLELY 1
6 not long ago ⟨I *just* bought this dress.⟩ — see NEWLY

justice *n* **1** the practice of giving to others what is their due or an instance of this ⟨They felt that *justice* was done in court.⟩
synonyms equity, right
related words equitability, equitableness, fairness, impartiality; goodness, righteousness, virtue; honor, integrity, uprightness
near antonyms bias, one-sidedness, partiality, prejudice; unfairness, unjustness, wrongfulness; corruption, impropriety; crime, offense (*or* offence), wrongdoing; disservice, harm
antonyms inequity, injustice, raw deal, wrong
2 a public official having authority to decide questions of law ⟨a *justice* of the U.S. Supreme Court⟩ — see JUDGE 2
3 lack of favoritism toward one side or another ⟨With scrupulous *justice*, the mediator noted that both parties had a basis for their arguments.⟩ — see DETACHMENT 1

justifiable *adj* capable of being defended with good reasoning against verbal attack ⟨We had *justifiable* reasons for leaving early.⟩ — see TENABLE 2

justification *n* an explanation that frees one from fault or blame ⟨Steve offered a weak *justification* for why he was so late.⟩ — see EXCUSE

justified *adj* **1** based on sound reasoning or information ⟨In a well-*justified* ruling the court voted unanimously to overturn the law.⟩ — see GOOD 1
2 being what is called for by accepted standards of right and wrong ⟨The use of force to capture the armed fugitive was fully *justified*.⟩ — see JUST 1

justify *vb* **1** to be an acceptable reason for ⟨He tried to *justify* his behavior by saying everyone else was doing it too.⟩
synonyms excuse
related words account (for), explain, explain away, rationalize; brush (aside *or* off), condone, disregard, forgive, gloss (over), gloze (over), ignore, pardon, pass over, remit, shrug off, wink (at)
2 to continue to declare to be true or proper despite opposition or objections ⟨failed to *justify* the need for a war at this time⟩ — see MAINTAIN 2

jut *n* a part that sticks out from the general mass of something ⟨Cape Fear is one of the more colorfully named *juts* along the North Carolina coast.⟩ — see BULGE 1

jut *vb* to extend outward beyond a usual point ⟨The sandbar *juts* out into the ocean.⟩ — see BULGE 1

juvenile *adj* **1** being in the early stage of life, growth, or development ⟨a *juvenile* alligator just hatched from its egg⟩ — see YOUNG
2 having or showing the annoying qualities (as silliness) associated with children ⟨Throwing a tantrum is rather *juvenile* behavior for a person of your age.⟩ — see CHILDISH
3 lacking in adult experience or maturity ⟨a *juvenile* golfer who does not know how to win gracefully⟩ — see CALLOW

juvenile *n* a young person who is between infancy and adulthood ⟨a medical study that followed *juveniles* through adolescence and into adulthood⟩ — see CHILD 1

juxtaposed *adj* having a border in common ⟨The *juxtaposed* photographs of the country's richest and poorest areas are a telling commentary on inequality.⟩ — see ADJACENT

K

keelhaul *vb* to criticize (someone) severely or angrily especially for personal failings ⟨There's no need to *keelhaul* him—it was an honest mistake, and a small one at that.⟩ — see SCOLD

keen *adj* **1** able to sense slight impressions or differences ⟨pilots with especially *keen* eyesight⟩ — see ACUTE 1
2 causing intense discomfort to one's skin ⟨The *keen* wind gave me chapped lips.⟩ — see CUTTING 1
3 having an edge thin enough to cut or pierce something ⟨My doctor lanced the boil with a *keen* scalpel.⟩ — see SHARP 1
4 having or showing quickness of mind ⟨readers who were *keen* enough to realize that the writer was being satirical⟩ — see INTELLIGENT 1
5 showing urgent desire or interest ⟨a *keen* hunger for fame and fortune in the fashion industry⟩ — see EAGER
6 extreme in degree, power, or effect ⟨Movies gave him *keen* enjoyment like nothing else.⟩ — see INTENSE 1

keen *n* a crying out in grief ⟨the loud *keens* of the mourners⟩ — see LAMENT 1

keen *vb* to make a long loud mournful sound ⟨mourners *keening* for the dead⟩ — see HOWL 1

keenness *n* **1** a harsh or sharp quality ⟨The *keenness* of the knife should tell you that it was sharpened recently.⟩ ⟨a writer famous for the *keenness* of her wit⟩ — see EDGE 1
2 urgent desire or interest ⟨Grandpa was looking forward to his birthday party with the *keenness* of a youngster.⟩ — see EAGERNESS
3 exceptional discernment and judgment especially in practical matters ⟨had the financial *keenness* to know that the stock was overvalued⟩ — see ACUMEN
4 the state or quality of being able to sense slight impressions or differences ⟨There's an enhanced *keenness* of hearing that young mothers seem to develop.⟩ — see ACUITY

keep *vb* **1** to mark with an appropriate practice, rite, or ceremony ⟨*kept* the Sabbath by not working⟩
synonyms celebrate, commemorate, observe
related words bless, consecrate, sanctify, solemnize; fete (*or* fête), honor, laud, praise; memorialize, remember

near antonyms disregard, forget, ignore, neglect, overlook

antonyms break, transgress, violate

2 to continue to have in one's possession or power ⟨The money is yours to *keep*.⟩ ⟨*Keep* my secret and don't tell it to anyone!⟩

synonyms hold, reserve, retain, withhold

related words conserve, guard, preserve, protect, save; boast, enjoy, have, own, possess; command, control, detain, direct, manage, rule; bear, harbor; cherish, cling (to), hug, treasure

phrases hang on to, hold on to

near antonyms abandon, cede, drop; contribute, donate, give; discard, dump; decline, reject, repudiate, spurn; lose

antonyms give up, hand over, release, relinquish, surrender, yield

3 to do what is required by the terms of ⟨Make sure you *keep* your promise to help out at the homeless shelter.⟩ — see FULFILL 1

4 to place somewhere for safekeeping or ready availability ⟨I *keep* extra toothbrushes for unexpected overnight guests.⟩ — see STORE 1

5 to pay the living expenses of ⟨*keeping* foster children⟩ — see SUPPORT 2

6 to look after and make decisions about ⟨Sue enlisted a relative to *keep* the store while she was away.⟩ — see CONDUCT 1

7 to keep from exceeding a desirable degree or level (as of expression) ⟨Try to *keep* your composure no matter what happens.⟩ — see CONTROL 1

8 to drive danger or attack away from ⟨May God bless and *keep* you.⟩ — see DEFEND 1

keep (from) *vb* to resist the temptation of ⟨Try to *keep from* eating all the chocolate in one day!⟩ — see FORBEAR

keep (to) *vb* to give steadfast support to ⟨Dan always *keeps to* his political positions, even when they are unpopular.⟩ — see ADHERE (TO) 1

keeper *n* **1** a person or group that watches over someone or something ⟨How should I know where she is? I'm not her *keeper*!⟩ — see GUARD 1

2 a person who takes care of a property sometimes for an absent owner ⟨During the winter the *keeper* of the family's beach house is a local resident who looks after the place.⟩ — see CUSTODIAN 1

keeping *n* **1** responsibility for the safety and well-being of someone or something ⟨They put the house keys into a neighbor's secure *keeping* while they were on vacation.⟩ — see CUSTODY

2 the fact or state of having (something) at one's disposal ⟨My aunt has all of our family's old photographs in her *keeping*.⟩ — see POSSESSION 1

3 the following of a custom, rule, or law ⟨the *keeping* of religious laws and traditions⟩ — see OBSERVANCE 1

4 a state of being or fitness ⟨The estate hasn't been in good *keeping* since the owner suffered financial reverses.⟩ — see CONDITION 1

keepsake *n* something that serves to keep alive the memory of a person or event ⟨Emma saved the tassel from her mortarboard as a *keepsake* of her high school graduation.⟩ — see MEMORIAL

keep up *vb* **1** to continue to operate or to meet one's needs ⟨Let's hope that old air conditioner *keeps up* through this heat wave.⟩ — see HOLD OUT

2 to keep in good condition ⟨*kept* the house *up* while the owners were gone⟩ — see MAINTAIN 1

3 to remain indefinitely in existence or in the same state ⟨Let's hope this beautiful weather *keeps up* for the rest of our vacation.⟩ — see CONTINUE 1

keg *n* an enclosed wooden vessel for holding beverages ⟨a *keg* of beer⟩ — see CASK

kerchief *n* a scarf worn on the head ⟨tied the *kerchief* around her head to keep her hair out of her face⟩ — see BANDANNA

kerf *n* a V-shaped cut usually on an edge or a surface ⟨With a handsaw I made a *kerf* in the board to mark where I needed to cut.⟩ — see NOTCH 1

key *adj* **1** coming before all others in importance ⟨maintains that Sir Isaac Newton remains the *key* figure in physical science⟩ — see FOREMOST 1

2 of the greatest possible importance ⟨First—and this is *key*—I wasn't even there that evening!⟩ — see CRUCIAL

key *n* **1** an explanatory list of the symbols on a map or chart ⟨In order to know what those dotted lines represent, you'll need to look at the *key*.⟩ — see LEGEND 1

2 something that allows someone to achieve a desired goal ⟨A good education is the *key* to success.⟩ — see PASSPORT 1

3 the means or right of entering or participating in ⟨He had found the *key* to her heart.⟩ — see ENTRANCE 1

key *vb* to bring to a state free of conflicts, inconsistencies, or differences ⟨Her response was perfectly *keyed* to the situation.⟩ — see HARMONIZE 2

keystone *n* an immaterial thing upon which something else rests ⟨Tourism is the city's economic *keystone*.⟩ — see BASE 1

kibitzer *also* **kibbitzer** *n* a person who meddles in the affairs of others ⟨a nosy *kibitzer* who always knows who is dating whom⟩ — see BUSYBODY

kick *n* **1** a pleasurably intense stimulation of the feelings ⟨I get a *kick* out of downhill skiing.⟩ — see THRILL

2 a source of great satisfaction ⟨It was a *kick* for the parents to see their once-shy son star in a Broadway play.⟩ — see DELIGHT 1

3 a feeling or declaration of disapproval or dissent ⟨heard all sorts of *kicks* against the idea⟩ — see OBJECTION

4 a forceful coming together of two things ⟨I felt a *kick* in my hands as the jackhammer came roaring to life.⟩ — see IMPACT 1

kick *vb* to express dissatisfaction, pain, or resentment usually tiresomely ⟨He's been *kicking* all week about not getting the promotion.⟩ — see COMPLAIN

kick back *vb* **1** to refrain from labor or exertion ⟨I plan to spend the day *kicking back* and watching television.⟩ — see REST 1

2 to spend time doing nothing ⟨a good resort for people who want to *kick back* and relax⟩ — see IDLE

kick in *vb* to make a donation as part of a group effort ⟨If everyone in the department *kicks in*, we can give him an especially nice present for his retirement.⟩ — see CONTRIBUTE 1

kick off *vb* to take the first step in (a process or course of action) ⟨I'll *kick off* the discussion on ethics with this question.⟩ — see BEGIN 1

kid *n* a young person who is between infancy and adulthood ⟨a group of *kids* waiting for the school bus⟩ — see CHILD 1

kid *vb* **1** to make fun of in a good-natured way ⟨Everybody's *kidding* me about my new haircut.⟩ — see TEASE 1

2 to make jokes ⟨He always *kids* around about his "wild and crazy" life as an accountant.⟩ — see JOKE 1

kidding *adj* marked by or expressive of mild or good-natured teasing ⟨Jill made *kidding* remarks about my lack of skills in the kitchen.⟩ — see QUIZZICAL

kiddish *adj* having or showing the annoying qualities (as silliness) associated with children ⟨I didn't expect him to have such a *kiddish* response.⟩ — see CHILDISH

kiddo *n* a young person who is between infancy and adulthood ⟨Let's go out to a restaurant where there won't be any screaming *kiddos* running around.⟩ — see CHILD 1

kidnap *vb* to carry away (as a person) forcibly or unlawfully ⟨The wealthy industrialist was *kidnapped* and held for ransom.⟩

synonyms abduct

related words capture, impress, seize, shanghai, waylay; abscond (with), snatch, spirit; hijack (*also* highjack); catch, steal, take

phrases make away with, make off with, run off with

near antonyms deliver, ransom, redeem, rescue; restore, return

kill *vb* **1** to deprive of life ⟨During the war more soldiers were *killed* by disease than anything else.⟩

synonyms claim, croak [*slang*], destroy, dispatch, do in, fell, slay, take

related words butcher, cut down, finish, get, murder, rub out, scrag, take out, waste; annihilate, blot out, decimate, kill off, massacre, mow, slaughter, smite; execute, martyr, terminate

phrases do away with, make away with

near antonyms raise, restore, resurrect, resuscitate, revive; nurture

antonyms animate

2 to reject by or as if by a vote ⟨The Senate *killed* the bill by a single vote.⟩ — see NEGATIVE 1

3 to show (something written) to be no longer valid by drawing a cross over or a line through it ⟨I think that paragraph is irrelevant, so *kill* it.⟩ — see X (OUT)

4 to use up all the physical energy of ⟨The long hike up the mountain just about *killed* us.⟩ — see EXHAUST 1

5 to attract or delight as if by magic ⟨With his dark good looks he would positively *kill* the ladies.⟩ — see CHARM 1

6 to cause to stop functioning ⟨*Kill* the engine before it overheats.⟩ — see DEACTIVATE

killer *adj* **1** likely to cause or capable of causing death ⟨*killer* viruses that claimed millions of lives⟩ — see DEADLY 1

2 requiring considerable physical or mental effort ⟨a *killer* exercise program guaranteed to get you into shape⟩ — see HARD 2

killer *n* **1** a dull, unpleasant, or difficult piece of work ⟨Weeding out that overgrown garden is going to be a *killer*.⟩ — see CHORE 2

2 a person who kills another person ⟨Police captured the *killer*.⟩ — see ASSASSIN

killjoy *n* a person who spoils the pleasure of others ⟨His perpetually negative attitude made him a real *killjoy* when others were trying to have fun.⟩

synonyms drag, spoilsport, wet blanket

related words fuddy-duddy, goody-goody, Goody Two-shoes, old maid, stick-in-the-mud; defeatist, pessimist; complainer, crab, cynic, grouch, grump, sorehead, whiner; bore, downer, drip

near antonyms cutup, jester, live wire; carouser, celebrant, celebrator, merrymaker, rejoicer, reveler (*or* reveller), roisterer

kilter *n* a state of being or fitness ⟨Since I dropped my food processor, it's been all out of *kilter*.⟩ — see CONDITION 1

kin *n* **1** a group of persons who come from the same ancestor ⟨Tim invited all of his kith and *kin* to his graduation party.⟩ — see FAMILY 1

2 a person connected with another by blood or marriage ⟨Since she did not appear to be *kin* to either side, we've no idea what she was doing at the wedding.⟩ — see RELATIVE

kind *adj* **1** given to or made with heedful anticipation of the needs and happiness of others ⟨It was very *kind* of you to help out.⟩ — see THOUGHTFUL 1

2 having or marked by sympathy and consideration for

others ⟨a *kind* person who regularly volunteers at the homeless shelter⟩ — see HUMANE 1

kind *n* **1** a number of persons or things that are grouped together because they have something in common ⟨I like that *kind* of candy.⟩ — see SORT 1

2 one of the units into which a whole is divided on the basis of a common characteristic ⟨We looked at just about every *kind* of flooring before deciding which to use in the kitchen.⟩ — see CLASS 2

kindhearted *adj* having or marked by sympathy and consideration for others ⟨a *kindhearted* young man who shoveled his elderly neighbor's driveway after the blizzard⟩ — see HUMANE 1

kindheartedness *n* the capacity for feeling for another's unhappiness or misfortune ⟨Her natural *kindheartedness* is one reason why she's thinking about becoming a doctor.⟩ — see HEART 1

kindle *vb* to set (something) on fire ⟨worried that lightning will *kindle* the forest in the drought-stricken nature preserve⟩ — see BURN 2

kindled *adj* being on fire ⟨*Kindled* straw was responsible for the blaze that destroyed the barn.⟩ — see ABLAZE 1

kindliness *n* **1** kindly concern, interest, or support ⟨Doug was touched by the *kindliness* of his neighbors, who voluntarily took care of his dog while he was in the hospital.⟩ — see GOODWILL 1

2 the capacity for feeling for another's unhappiness or misfortune ⟨As a result of her *kindliness*, several poor families have the makings for a Thanksgiving feast.⟩ — see HEART 1

kindly *adj* **1** having or marked by sympathy and consideration for others ⟨brought homemade chicken soup out of *kindly* concern for my health⟩ — see HUMANE 1

2 promoting or contributing to personal or social well-being ⟨a *kindly* climate⟩ — see BENEFICIAL

kindly *adv* with good reason or courtesy ⟨Would you *kindly* hand me the scissors?⟩ — see WELL 4

kindness *n* **1** an act of kind assistance ⟨What a *kindness* to allow us to use your car for the trip!⟩ — see FAVOR 1

2 the capacity for feeling for another's unhappiness or misfortune ⟨Out of the *kindness* of your heart, would you at least consider adopting this stray cat?⟩ — see HEART 1

kind of *adv* to some degree or extent ⟨Those sheets are *kind of* new, so use something else to cover the floor while painting.⟩ — see FAIRLY 1

kindred *adj* **1** having a close connection like that between family members ⟨archaeology and the *kindred* science of anthropology⟩ — see RELATED

2 having or marked by agreement in feeling or action ⟨finally found people who were *kindred* spirits when she joined the hiking club⟩ — see HARMONIOUS 3

kindred *n* a group of persons who come from the same ancestor ⟨The kingdom's royal *kindred* actually numbers in the thousands.⟩ — see FAMILY 1

kinfolk *or* **kinfolks** *pl n* a group of persons who come from the same ancestor ⟨Let's invite all our *kinfolk* for the holidays.⟩ — see FAMILY 1

king *n* a person of rank, power, or influence in a particular field ⟨the undisputed *king* of automobile sales for the entire metropolitan area⟩ — see MAGNATE

kingdom come *n* a dwelling place of perfect happiness for the soul after death ⟨Be careful with that thing, or you'll send us all to *kingdom come*.⟩ — see HEAVEN 1

kingly *adj* fit for or worthy of a royal ruler ⟨a *kingly* gift of 50 million dollars to his old alma mater⟩ — see MONARCHICAL

kingpin *n* **1** one of high position or importance within a group ⟨*kingpins* of the tech industry⟩ — see BIG SHOT

2 the person (as an employer or supervisor) who tells

people and especially workers what to do ⟨finally nailed the mob *kingpin*⟩ — see BOSS

king–size *or* **king–sized** *adj* **1** unusually large ⟨built a *king-size* mansion⟩ — see HUGE
2 of great extent from end to end ⟨the *king-size* snake known as the anaconda⟩ — see LONG 1

king's ransom *n* a very large amount of money ⟨That enormous diamond ring must have cost a *king's ransom*.⟩ — see FORTUNE 2

kinsfolk *pl n* a group of persons who come from the same ancestor ⟨My *kinsfolk* all live in the East.⟩ — see FAMILY 1

kinship *n* the fact or state of having something in common ⟨She and I have a special *kinship* since we both grew up in England.⟩ — see CONNECTION 1

kinsman *n* a person connected with another by blood or marriage ⟨To protect the family honor, he sought to revenge the murder of his *kinsman*.⟩ — see RELATIVE

kirk *n, chiefly Scottish* a building for public worship and especially Christian worship ⟨left Edinburgh early in the morning for St. John's *Kirk* in Perth⟩ — see CHURCH 1

kiss *vb* **1** to touch one another with the lips as a sign of love ⟨It's traditional for couples to *kiss* under the mistletoe at Christmastime.⟩
synonyms smooch
related words buss, French-kiss, osculate, smack; canoodle, make out, pet, spoon; caress, embrace, fondle, hug, love; bill, cuddle, nestle, snuggle
2 to pass lightly across or touch gently especially in passing ⟨a gentle breeze *kissing* the water's surface⟩ — see ²BRUSH

kisser *n, slang* **1** the front part of the head ⟨His embarrassment was made known by his bright red *kisser*.⟩ — see FACE 1
2 the opening through which food passes into the body of an animal ⟨How'd you like a punch right in the *kisser*?⟩ — see MOUTH 1

kittenish *adj* affecting shyness or modesty ⟨the *kittenish* heroine of a nineteenth century romance⟩ — see COY 1

¹**kitty** *n* a small domestic animal known for catching mice ⟨delighted to adopt a stray *kitty* from the pound⟩ — see CAT

²**kitty** *n* a sum of money set aside for a particular purpose ⟨Why don't you get us all sodas and just take the money from the party *kitty*?⟩ — see FUND 1

knack *n* **1** a clever often underhanded means to achieve an end ⟨tried every *knack* to get him to spill the beans⟩ — see TRICK 1
2 a special and usually inborn ability ⟨a jazz musician with an incredible *knack* for improvisation⟩ — see TALENT

knapsack *n* a soft-sided case designed for carrying belongings especially on the back ⟨grabbed my *knapsack* from the hook and ran to catch my ride⟩ — see PACK 1

knave *n* a mean, evil, or unprincipled person ⟨He plays the role of the duplicitous *knave* who tries to foil the play's hero.⟩ — see VILLAIN

knavery *n* **1** a playful or mischievous act intended as a joke ⟨the sort of schoolboy *knaveries* that become the stuff of campus legend⟩ — see PRANK
2 playful, reckless behavior that is not intended to cause serious harm ⟨suspects some *knavery* going on in the political campaign⟩ — see MISCHIEF 1

knavish *adj* tending to or exhibiting reckless playfulness ⟨a *knavish* bunch of urchins racing pell-mell through the marketplace⟩ — see MISCHIEVOUS 1

knell *vb* to make the clear sound heard when metal vibrates ⟨The church bells *knelled* to mark the death of the nation's beloved leader.⟩ — see ²RING

knickknack *also* **nicknack** *n* a small object displayed for its attractiveness or interest ⟨A variety of pretty porcelain *knickknacks* adorned the mantel.⟩
synonyms bauble, curio, curiosity, gaud, gewgaw (*also* geegaw), novelty, ornamental; trinket

related words bagatelle, trifle; figurine, ornament; keepsake, memento, souvenir; conversation piece; collectible (*or* collectable), collector's item

knife *n* an instrument with a metal length that has a sharp edge for cutting ⟨Be careful in using the *knife* to split open the cardboard box.⟩
synonyms blade, cutter
related words cleaver, hack; bayonet, bodkin, bolo, bowie knife, cutlass, dagger, dirk, jackknife, machete, pocketknife, poniard, sheath knife, stiletto, stylet, switchblade, yataghan; rapier, saber (*or* sabre), steel, sword; scalpel

knob *n* a small uneven mass ⟨First, toss a *knob* of butter into the frying pan.⟩ — see LUMP 1

knock *n* **1** a hard strike with a part of the body or an instrument ⟨gave the door a good *knock*⟩ — see ¹BLOW
2 bad luck or an example of this ⟨Getting his college degree was a six year adventure not without its share of *knocks* along the way.⟩ — see MISFORTUNE
3 a change in status for the worse usually temporarily ⟨The geneticist's reputation took a *knock* when several of his peers were unable to confirm his research findings.⟩ — see REVERSE 1

knock *vb* **1** to come into usually forceful contact with something ⟨My knee *knocked* against the table leg when I tried to get up quickly.⟩ — see HIT 2
2 to deliver a blow to (someone or something) usually in a strong vigorous manner ⟨The gust of wind *knocked* him backwards.⟩ — see HIT 1
3 to express one's unfavorable opinion of the worth or quality of ⟨Hey, don't *knock* it until you've tried it!⟩ — see CRITICIZE

knock (about) *vb* to move about from place to place aimlessly ⟨We *knocked about* from town to town, looking for a place to stay.⟩ — see WANDER 1

knockabout *adj* being rough or noisy in a high-spirited way ⟨a *knockabout* game of football in the mud⟩ — see BOISTEROUS

knock down *vb* **1** to receive as return for effort ⟨She's *knocking down* a good salary.⟩ — see EARN 1
2 to take apart ⟨Right after the holidays the stores start to *knock down* the window displays.⟩ — see DISASSEMBLE 1
3 to strike (someone) so forcefully as to cause a fall ⟨The overexcited dog *knocked* the toddler *down*.⟩ — see FELL 1
4 to make smaller in amount, volume, or extent ⟨They'll have to *knock down* the price of those televisions if they expect to sell any.⟩ — see DECREASE 1

knock off *vb* **1** to bring (as an action or operation) to an immediate end ⟨*Knock* it *off*!⟩ — see STOP 1
2 to stop doing (something) permanently ⟨Jane decided it was time to *knock off* telling fibs about her family background.⟩ — see QUIT 2
3 to take away (an amount or number) from a total ⟨a proposal to *knock* 10 cents *off* the gasoline tax⟩ — see SUBTRACT

knockout *adj* very pleasing to look at ⟨a *knockout* sports car that's the talk of the neighborhood⟩ — see BEAUTIFUL 1

knockout *n* **1** a lovely woman ⟨The actress is a *knockout* with real talent.⟩ — see BEAUTY 2
2 a temporary state of unconsciousness ⟨A splash of cold water brought the boxer out of his *knockout*.⟩ — see FAINT
3 something very good of its kind ⟨The band's new album is a *knockout*.⟩ — see JIM-DANDY
4 a physically attractive person ⟨The lead singer of the boy band is a *knockout*.⟩ — see DOLL 2

knot *n* **1** a number of things considered as a unit ⟨From the summit we could see *knots* of houses up and down the river valley.⟩ — see GROUP 1

2 a small rounded mass of swollen tissue ⟨Jim felt a small *knot* on the back of his head.⟩ — see BUMP 1

3 a uniting or binding force or influence ⟨Their business partnership is strengthened by the *knot* of personal friendship.⟩ — see BOND 2

4 a usually small number of persons considered as a unit ⟨*Knots* of people were quietly chatting around the meeting hall.⟩ — see GROUP 2

5 something that requires thought and skill for resolution ⟨an issue fraught with legal and medical *knots*⟩ — see PROBLEM 1

knot *vb* to twist together into a usually confused mass ⟨The extension cords were hopelessly *knotted* together.⟩ — see ENTANGLE 1

knotty *adj* **1** having many parts or aspects that are usually interrelated ⟨the *knotty* problems that arise when every nation is part of the global marketplace⟩ — see COMPLEX 1

2 requiring exceptional skill or caution in performance or handling ⟨The candidates cautiously gave their views on an array of *knotty* issues.⟩ — see TRICKY 1

know *vb* **1** to have a practical understanding of ⟨a career diplomat who *knows* several languages⟩

synonyms comprehend, grasp, understand

related words appreciate, apprehend, fathom, follow, perceive; have, possess; catch on (to), pick up

near antonyms misapprehend, misconceive, misinterpret, misknow, misunderstand

2 to come to a knowledge of (something) by living through it ⟨I *know* full well how nerve-wracking it can be to speak in public.⟩ — see EXPERIENCE

3 to have a clear idea of ⟨I think I *know* what you're trying to say.⟩ — see COMPREHEND 1

know–how *n* knowledge gained by actually doing or living through something ⟨You'll gain some practical *know-how* in this auto mechanics class.⟩ — see EXPERIENCE 1

knowing *adj* **1** having inside information ⟨Amy exchanged a *knowing* look with her business partner during the sales presentation.⟩ — see WISE 2

2 having or showing a practical cleverness or judgment ⟨*Knowing* movie producers do not invest their own money in their risky ventures.⟩ — see SHREWD 1

3 made, given, or done with full awareness of what one is doing ⟨a *knowing* decision to go against my wishes⟩ — see INTENTIONAL

4 decided on as a result of careful thought ⟨With *knowing* disobedience, he refused to carry out the order.⟩ — see DELIBERATE 1

knowingly *adv* with full awareness of what one is doing ⟨cannot convict unless the defendant *knowingly* committed perjury⟩ — see INTENTIONALLY

knowledge *n* **1** a body of facts learned by study or experience ⟨The forest ranger shared some of his vast *knowledge* of the woods with us.⟩

synonyms lore, science, wisdom

related words dope, information, intelligence, know, lowdown, news; evidence, facts; acquaintance, awareness, familiarity; erudition, learning, scholarship; expertise, know-how

near antonyms ignorance, inexperience, innocence, unfamiliarity

2 the understanding and information gained from being educated ⟨Tests evaluate how much *knowledge* you have gained in a particular subject.⟩ — see EDUCATION 2

3 a state of being aware ⟨My *knowledge* that I was watching a true story made the film more compelling.⟩ — see ATTENTION 2

knowledgeable *adj* **1** having information especially as a result of study or experience ⟨I'm fairly *knowledgeable* about art.⟩ — see FAMILIAR 2

2 having or displaying advanced knowledge or education ⟨*Knowledgeable* historians regard that story as pure fiction.⟩ ⟨a *knowledgeable* report on the latest advances in cancer research⟩ — see EDUCATED 1

know–nothing *n* a stupid person ⟨disparaged her opponent as a *know-nothing* opportunist⟩ — see IDIOT

knuckle under *vb* **1** to cease resistance (as to another's arguments, demands, or control) ⟨encouraged her to stand firm and not *knuckle under* to political pressure⟩ — see YIELD 3

2 to yield to the control or power of enemy forces ⟨The remote outpost was overrun and forced to *knuckle under*.⟩ — see FALL 2

kook *n* a person of odd or whimsical habits ⟨a show about *kooks* looking for a yeti⟩ — see ECCENTRIC

kooky *also* **kookie** *adj* **1** different from the ordinary in a way that causes curiosity or suspicion ⟨He's got some pretty *kooky* ideas.⟩ — see ODD 2

2 showing or marked by a lack of good sense or judgment ⟨a *kooky* bicyclist who stubbornly refuses to wear a helmet⟩ ⟨That was a *kooky* thing to do.⟩ — see FOOLISH 1

kowtow *vb* to use flattery or the doing of favors in order to win approval especially from a superior ⟨You can try *kowtowing* to the boss, but he'll see right through you.⟩ — see FAWN

L

label *n* a slip (as of paper or cloth) that is attached to something to identify or describe it ⟨On its frame the painting had a *label* with its title and the name of the artist.⟩

synonyms marker, tag, ticket

related words caption, legend; brand, emblem, hallmark, logo, mark, symbol, trademark; badge, decal, plaque, seal, stamp, sticker

label *vb* **1** to attach an identifying slip to ⟨He *labeled* all of the poisonous materials with the familiar skull and crossbones.⟩

synonyms mark, tag, ticket

related words caption, earmark, hallmark, stamp; call, designate, identify, name, tab; entitle, style, term, title; brand, stigmatize

2 to give a name to ⟨The dictionary *labels* some words "archaic."⟩ — see NAME 1

labor *n* **1** a dull, unpleasant, or difficult piece of work ⟨One of the *labors* of Hercules in classical mythology was to clean out the stables of King Augeas.⟩ — see CHORE 2

2 the active use of energy in producing a result ⟨A superhuman amount of *labor* must have gone into designing and building the pyramids of Egypt.⟩ — see EFFORT

3 very hard or unpleasant work ⟨After years of *labor*, the Hoover Dam was completed.⟩ — see TOIL

4 the act or process of giving birth to children ⟨The mother's *labor* lasted for six hours.⟩ — see CHILDBIRTH
5 something produced by physical or intellectual effort ⟨a small, personal film that was clearly a *labor* of love for the director and actors⟩ — see PRODUCT 1
labor *vb* to devote serious and sustained effort ⟨He *labored* most of the day over the difficult legal brief.⟩
synonyms drudge, endeavor, grub, hump, hustle, moil, peg (away), plod, plow, plug, slog, strain, strive, struggle, sweat, toil, travail, tug, work
related words apply (oneself), buckle (down), dig in, hammer (away), knuckle down, pitch in; attack, drive; essay, try; exercise, exert, overexert, overwork; eke out, grind (out), put out, scrabble, scratch; trudge, wade
phrases sweat blood
near antonyms break, ease (up), let up, slacken; bum, chill, dally, dillydally, goof (off), idle, loaf, lounge, shirk, slack (off); bask, loll, relax, repose, rest, unwind; dabble, goof (around), hang, monkey (around), play, potter (around), putter (around), trifle
laborer *n* a person who does very hard or dull work ⟨Having no higher skills, the men could only find work as *laborers*.⟩ — see DRUDGE
laborious *adj* **1** involved in often constant activity ⟨The volunteers have been commendably *laborious* in their cleanup of the beach.⟩ — see BUSY 1
2 requiring considerable physical or mental effort ⟨the *laborious* task of cleaning up the oil spill⟩ — see HARD 2
3 requiring much time, effort, or careful attention ⟨That report is the product of months of *laborious* research.⟩ — see DEMANDING 1
laboriously *adv* with great effort or determination ⟨The farmer *laboriously* pruned all season long to produce the finest crop of grapes possible.⟩ — see HARD 1
laborsaving *adj* designed to replace or decrease human labor and especially physical labor ⟨A new *laborsaving* device let us clean the house in half the time.⟩
synonyms automated, automatic, robotic, self-acting
related words mechanical, motorized, nonmanual; computerized; aiding, helping; easing, relieving; time-saving; semiautomatic
antonyms nonautomated, nonautomatic
labyrinth *n* a confusing and complicated arrangement of passages ⟨We eventually realized that we were lost in the *labyrinth* of hallways in the museum.⟩ — see MAZE
labyrinthine *adj* having many parts or aspects that are usually interrelated ⟨The *labyrinthine* politics of the early twentieth century left us confounded.⟩ — see COMPLEX 1
lace *n* **1** a length of braided, flexible material that is used for tying or connecting things ⟨I had to replace the *lace* of my shoe because it kept breaking whenever I pulled the knot too tight.⟩ — see CORD 1
2 a length of something formed of three or more strands woven together ⟨There will be gold *lace* decorating both sleeves of the new uniform.⟩ — see BRAID
lace *vb* **1** to cause to twine about one another ⟨The gardener *laced* the shoots of ivy around the trellis to direct their growth.⟩ — see INTERTWINE 1
2 to scatter or set here and there among other things ⟨The decorator *laced* small mirrors among the knickknacks for added effect.⟩ — see THREAD 1
3 to strike repeatedly ⟨*laced* the seaman's back as punishment⟩ — see BEAT 1
4 to make more pleasant to the taste by adding something intensely flavored ⟨a savory dish *laced* with saffron and ginger⟩ — see SEASON 1
5 to alter (something) for the worse with the addition of foreign or lower-grade substances ⟨*laced* the juice with sugar⟩ — see ADULTERATE

laceration *n* a long deep cut ⟨The fall from the motocross bike left him with several *lacerations* from the sharp rocks.⟩ — see GASH
lachrymose *adj* given to expressing strong emotion (as sorrow) by readily shedding tears ⟨The more *lachrymose* mourners required a steady supply of tissues.⟩ — see TEARFUL 1
lacing *n* **1** a length of braided, flexible material that is used for tying or connecting things ⟨Mike stopped briefly to tighten the *lacing* on his shoe.⟩ — see CORD 1
2 a length of something formed of three or more strands woven together ⟨The *lacing* on the uniform gives it a smart look.⟩ — see BRAID
lack *n* **1** the fact or state of being absent ⟨The *lack* of news about the situation was frustrating.⟩
synonyms absence, dearth, want
related words deficiency, deficit, failure, famine, inadequacy, insufficiency, meagerness, paucity, poverty, scantiness, scantness, scarceness, scarcity, shortage, skimpiness; deprivation, loss, necessity, need, needfulness, omission
near antonyms abundance, amplitude, bounty, plenitude, plenteousness, plentifulness, plentitude, plenty, wealth; adequacy, sufficiency; excess, overabundance, oversupply, superabundance, surfeit, surplus; deluge, flood; bushel, deal, gobs, heap, loads, lot, mass, mountain, much, oodles, peck, pile, pot, quantity, raft, reams, scads, stack, volume, wad
antonyms presence
2 a falling short of an essential or desirable amount or number ⟨The *lack* of eligible candidates for the jury kept the trial from getting started.⟩ — see DEFICIENCY
3 a state of being without something necessary, desirable, or useful ⟨The *lack* of fresh water at the campsite definitely would be a problem.⟩ — see NEED 1
lackadaisical *adj* lacking bodily energy or motivation ⟨Feeling particularly *lackadaisical* in the summer heat, they lazily tossed a ball back and forth.⟩ — see LISTLESS
lacking *adj* **1** not coming up to an expected measure or meeting a particular need ⟨We felt the afternoon television offerings were somewhat *lacking* in entertainment value.⟩ — see SHORT 3
2 not present or in evidence ⟨For the moment anyway, wood for the fireplace is *lacking*.⟩ — see ABSENT 2
laconic *adj* **1** marked by the use of few words to convey much information or meaning ⟨The sportscaster's color commentary tends to be *laconic* but very much to the point.⟩ — see CONCISE
2 tending not to speak frequently (as by habit or inclination) ⟨*Laconic* by nature, he found the monastery's vow of silence was very much to his liking.⟩ — see SILENT 2
laconically *adv* in a few words ⟨The witness answered the prosecutor's questions rather *laconically* and had to be coaxed into giving more details.⟩ — see SHORTLY 1
lad *n* **1** a male person who has not yet reached adulthood ⟨Dad is fond of telling tall tales of the days when he was just a *lad*.⟩ — see BOY 1
2 an adult male human being ⟨Another day's work done, right, *lads*?⟩ — see MAN 1
ladder *n* a scheme of rank or order ⟨Their team placed third on the tournament *ladder*.⟩ — see ³SCALE 1
laddie *n* a male person who has not yet reached adulthood ⟨just a wee *laddie*⟩ — see BOY 1
lade *vb* **1** to lift out with something that holds liquid ⟨The cook *laded* the stew into small bowls.⟩ — see DIP 2
2 to place a weight or burden on ⟨The trucks were heavily *laden* with produce for the market.⟩ — see LOAD 1
lading *n* a mass or quantity of something taken up and carried, conveyed, or transported ⟨A bill of *lading* is a document issued by a carrier that lists goods being

shipped and specifies the terms of their transport.⟩ — see LOAD 1

ladle *n* a utensil with a bowl and a handle that is used especially in cooking and serving food ⟨The chef hunted for a *ladle* to add the chicken broth to the pot.⟩ — see SPOON

ladle *vb* to lift out with something that holds liquid ⟨The server *ladled* out the soup from a large tureen.⟩ — see DIP 2

lady *n* **1** an adult female human being ⟨"*Ladies* and gentlemen, please observe closely," said the magician.⟩ — see WOMAN 1

2 a female partner in a marriage ⟨What would you and your good *lady* like to drink?⟩ — see WIFE

3 a woman of high birth or social position ⟨The *ladies* of the royal court were all dressed extravagantly.⟩ — see GENTLEWOMAN

4 a female romantic companion ⟨I've been wanting to meet his new *lady*.⟩ — see GIRLFRIEND

ladylove *n* a female romantic companion ⟨Ever the gallant, he bought an enormous bouquet of flowers for his *ladylove*.⟩ — see GIRLFRIEND

lag *adj* following all others of the same kind in order or time ⟨We're now in the *lag* end of the project.⟩ — see LAST 1

lag *vb* **1** to lose bodily strength or vigor ⟨During the fourth quarter the whole team seemed to *lag*.⟩ — see WEAKEN 2

2 to move or act slowly ⟨The tired puppy was *lagging* behind the rest of the pack.⟩ — see DELAY 1

laggard *adj* moving or proceeding at less than the normal, desirable, or required speed ⟨I hate being stuck behind *laggard* drivers on the freeway.⟩ — see SLOW 1

laggard *n* someone who moves slowly or more slowly than others ⟨tried to spur on the *laggards* at the back of the line during the hike⟩ — see SLOWPOKE

laggardly *adv* at a pace that is less than usual, desirable, or expected ⟨Some students *laggardly* wandered in to class, obviously dreading the upcoming quiz.⟩ — see SLOW

lagger *n* someone who moves slowly or more slowly than others ⟨One of the bear cubs ran ahead while the mother waited for the *lagger*.⟩ — see SLOWPOKE

lagging *adj* moving or proceeding at less than the normal, desirable, or required speed ⟨The *lagging* pace of work on the project was worrisome.⟩ — see SLOW 1

lagniappe *n* **1** something given in addition to what is ordinarily expected or owed ⟨The meal was served with a *lagniappe* of freshly made cornbread.⟩ — see BONUS

2 something given to someone without expectation of a return ⟨The hotel threw in some free shampoo as a *lagniappe*.⟩ — see GIFT 1

laid–back *adj* having a relaxed, casual manner ⟨A *laid-back* fisherman, he didn't really care if he caught anything, being content to relax and enjoy the sunshine.⟩ — see EASYGOING 1

lair *n* **1** a place where a person goes to hide or to avoid others ⟨The detectives tracked the thieves to their *lair* and made immediate arrests.⟩ — see HIDEOUT

2 the shelter or resting place of a wild animal ⟨We found an abandoned fox's *lair* in the woods behind the barn.⟩ — see DEN 1

lam *n* the act or an instance of getting free from danger or confinement ⟨The prisoners were recaptured after only three days on the *lam*.⟩ — see ESCAPE 1

lam *vb* to get free from a dangerous or confining situation ⟨Let's *lam* out of here while there's still time.⟩ — see ESCAPE 1

lamb *n* an innocent or gentle person ⟨The new guys at football camp were *lambs* who hardly knew what awaited them.⟩

    synonyms angel, dove, innocent, sheep

    related words babe, colt, cub, fledgling, greenhorn, ingenue (*or* ingénue), naïf (*or* naif), newbie, tenderfoot,

virgin; cherub, saint; mollycoddle, sissy, softy (*or* softie), weakling, wimp; dupe, pigeon, sap, sucker

    near antonyms bully, roughneck, rowdy, tough; beast, boor, cad, churl, clown, creep, cur, heel, jerk, joker, louse, lout, slob; shark, skunk, snake, stinker; devil, knave, miscreant, no-good, rapscallion, rascal, reprobate, rogue, scalawag (*or* scallywag), scamp, scoundrel, varlet, villain

    antonyms wolf

lambaste *or* **lambast** *vb* **1** to criticize (someone) severely or angrily especially for personal failings ⟨The director *lambasted* them mercilessly for forgetting their lines during the final dress rehearsal.⟩ — see SCOLD

2 to criticize harshly and usually publicly ⟨Movie critics across the country *lambasted* the thriller for its unnecessary violence.⟩ — see ATTACK 2

lambent *adj* giving off or reflecting much light ⟨The *lambent* flames from our campfire cast a comforting glow.⟩ — see BRIGHT 1

lame *adj* **1** arousing or deserving of one's loathing and disgust ⟨That's a pretty *lame* way to treat someone.⟩ — see CONTEMPTIBLE 1

2 falling short of a standard ⟨The amenities at this hotel are *lame*; there's not even a television in the room.⟩ — see BAD 1

lame *vb* to cause severe or permanent injury to ⟨We were afraid that the horse would be *lamed* by its fall.⟩ — see MAIM

lamella *n* a small thin piece of material that resembles an animal scale ⟨The gemstone's distinctive iridescence is caused by light passing from one *lamella* of crystal to another.⟩ — see ²SCALE

lament *n* **1** a crying out in grief ⟨the national *lament* that was heard when President Kennedy was assassinated⟩

    synonyms groan, howl, keen, lamentation, moan, plaint, wail

    related words cry, sob, tears; agonizing, grieving, mourning, sorrowing, suffering, weeping; hand-wringing, regret; anguish, dolor, grief, heartache, heartbreak, sorrow, woe

    near antonyms cheering, laughing, smiling

    antonyms exultation, rejoicing

2 a composition expressing one's grief over a loss ⟨a poem that is her *lament* for her late grandmother⟩

    synonyms dirge, elegy, requiem

    near antonyms encomium, eulogy, paean, panegyric

3 an expression of dissatisfaction, pain, or resentment ⟨the actress's *lament* that there aren't enough good roles for women⟩ — see COMPLAINT 1

lament *vb* **1** to feel or express sorrow for ⟨She *lamented* her friend's decision to move across the country.⟩

    synonyms bemoan, bewail, deplore, grieve (for), mourn, wail (for)

    related words elegize; cry (for), keen, moan, weep; regret, rue; bawl, blubber, sob; agonize, bleed, hurt, sorrow, suffer

    near antonyms beam, cheer, grin, laugh, smile

    antonyms delight, exult (in), glory (in), joy

2 to feel sorry or dissatisfied about ⟨The youth *lamented* not having spent more time with his late grandfather.⟩ — see REGRET

lamentable *adj* **1** expressing or suggesting mourning ⟨a *lamentable* cry⟩ — see MOURNFUL 1

2 of a kind to cause great distress ⟨It's a *lamentable* situation, but I don't see how it can be fixed.⟩ — see REGRETTABLE

lamentation *n* a crying out in grief ⟨There was a great *lamentation* on Wall Street when the market surged downward.⟩ — see LAMENT 1

lamina *n* a small thin piece of material that resembles an animal scale ⟨The *laminae* of stratified rock were deposited separately, building upwards as time passed.〉 — see ²SCALE

lamp *n* something that provides illumination 〈I didn't realize it had gotten so dark in the room until my wife came in and turned on the *lamp*, momentarily blinding me.〉 — see LIGHT 2

lampoon *n* a creative work that uses sharp humor to point up the foolishness of a person, institution, or human nature in general 〈This classic musical is a *lampoon* of the movie business at the time when sound was introduced.〉 — see SATIRE

lance *n* a weapon with a long straight handle and sharp head or blade 〈The *lance* struck squarely on the knight's shield, knocking him from his horse.〉 — see SPEAR

lance *vb* to penetrate or hold (something) with a pointed object 〈Doctors used to *lance* infected sores, so that they could drain clean.〉 — see IMPALE

land *n* **1** a body of people composed of one or more nationalities usually with its own territory and government 〈The whole *land* rejoiced over their Olympic teams' victories.〉 — see NATION
2 a broad geographical area 〈The *land* to the west was said to have incredibly rich soil and plentiful water.〉 — see REGION 2
3 the solid part of our planet's surface as distinguished from the sea and air 〈It's always good to be back on dry *land* after a long boat ride.〉 — see EARTH 2

land *vb* **1** to stop at or near a place along the shore 〈The Pilgrims *landed* at Plymouth after exploring Cape Cod Bay.〉
synonyms anchor, dock
related words berth, moor, tie up; beach, ground; harbor; arrive, reach, show up, turn up; debark, disembark
phrases make port
near antonyms embark, launch, sail
2 to get to a destination 〈We *landed* at the hotel just before midnight.〉 — see COME 2
3 to go ashore from a ship 〈The passengers on the cruise *landed* at St. George in Bermuda.〉 — see DISEMBARK 1
4 to come to rest after descending from the air 〈Our plane is *landing* in 15 minutes, so we need to put all of our things away.〉 — see ALIGHT 1
5 to receive as return for effort 〈Because of his work on the boss's pet project, he *landed* a promotion as well as a raise.〉 — see EARN 1
6 to take physical control or possession of (something) suddenly or forcibly 〈After struggling for half an hour, the fisherman finally *landed* a 10-pound bass.〉 — see CATCH 1

landfill *n* a place where discarded materials (as trash) are dumped 〈We took all of our old, broken furniture to the *landfill*.〉 — see DUMP 1

landing *n* a structure used by boats and ships for taking on or landing cargo and passengers 〈Our families waved good-bye to us from the *landing* as we left on our honeymoon cruise.〉 — see DOCK

landlord *n* the owner of land or housing that is rented to another 〈We agreed to pay the *landlord* the rent on the first Monday of each month.〉
synonyms lessor, letter, renter
related words landlady; laird, landholder, landowner; proprietor; slumlord
antonyms lodger, roomer, tenant

landmark *n* a point in a chain of events at which an important change (as in one's fortunes) occurs 〈Typically, people feel that turning 21 is a *landmark* in one's life.〉 — see TURNING POINT

language *n* **1** the stock of words, pronunciation, and grammar used by a people as their basic means of communication 〈Great Britain, the United States, Australia, and other countries where English is the dominant *language*〉

synonyms lingo, mother tongue, speech, tongue, vocabulary
related words argot, cant, colloquial, dialect, idiolect, idiom, jargon, parlance, patois, patter, pidgin, slang, slanguage, vernacular; colloquialism, localism, provincialism, regionalism, shibboleth, vernacularism; terminology; coinage, modernism, neologism
2 the special terms or expressions of a particular group or field 〈"Love" means "nothing" in the *language* of tennis.〉 — see TERMINOLOGY
3 the way in which something is put into words 〈We're finding the *language* of the legal documents to be tough going.〉 — see WORDING 1

languid *adj* **1** lacking bodily energy or motivation 〈A few *languid* dancers swayed about on the dance floor without much enthusiasm.〉 — see LISTLESS
2 lacking bodily strength 〈the tired athlete's *languid* movements on the tennis court〉 — see WEAK 1
3 moving or proceeding at less than the normal, desirable, or required speed 〈The film's *languid* pace will not be to the taste of many moviegoers.〉 — see SLOW 1

languish *vb* to lose bodily strength or vigor 〈Older people, especially, were *languishing* during the prolonged heat wave.〉 — see WEAKEN 2

languishing *adj* lacking bodily energy or motivation 〈His lingering sickness left him *languishing* and uninterested in his usual activities.〉 — see LISTLESS

languor *n* the quality or state of lacking physical strength or vigor 〈The tropical heat sapped our strength, leaving us in a state of unaccustomed *languor*.〉 — see WEAKNESS 1

languorous *adj* lacking bodily energy or motivation 〈The drummer's *languorous* playing caused the rest of the band to keep missing the beat.〉 — see LISTLESS

lank *adj* not stiff in structure 〈Right after a shower, her *lank* hair hung down to her shoulders.〉 — see LIMP 1

lanky *adj* being tall, thin and usually loose-jointed 〈The *lanky* basketball star was great at slam-dunking.〉
synonyms gangling, gangly, rangy, spindling, spindly
related words angular, gaunt, lank, rawboned, scraggy, scrawny, skinny; lean, slender, slim, spare, thin; racy, reedy, spidery, stringy, twiggy, waspish, weedy, willowy, wiry
near antonyms beefy, bulky, chubby, chunky, heavyset, pudgy, squat, stocky, stout, stubby, stumpy, sturdy, thickset, weighty; muscle-bound; corpulent, fat, fleshy, full, gross, obese, overweight, plump, portly, roly-poly, rotund, round, tubby

lap *n* a portion of a trip 〈We were on the last *lap* of the journey, eagerly heading for home.〉 — see LEG 2

¹**lap** *vb* **1** to flow along or against 〈The waves gently *lapped* the sandy shore.〉 — see WASH 1
2 to flow in a broken irregular stream 〈The creek *lapped* along through the ravine before collecting in the pond.〉 — see GURGLE
3 to move with a splashing motion 〈a stiff breeze that was causing the lake waters to *lap* against the hull with some force〉 — see SLOSH 1

²**lap** *vb* **1** to lie over parts of one another 〈The armadillo's plates *lap* tightly so as to form a protective shield.〉 — see OVERLAP
2 to surround or cover closely 〈This recording of the symphony is sure to *lap* listeners in stereophonic bliss.〉 — see ENFOLD 1

lapping *n* a partial covering of one thing by an adjoining member 〈The *lapping* of the roofing shingles should be several inches in order to avoid leaks.〉 — see OVERLAP

lapse *n* **1** a change in status for the worse usually temporarily 〈The scandal caused the president to suffer a dramatic *lapse* in popularity.〉 — see REVERSE 1

2 an unintentional departure from truth or accuracy ⟨an atypical *lapse* in her usually meticulous accounting⟩ — see ERROR 1

3 the stopping of a process or activity ⟨Sara wasn't bothered by the *lapse* of her membership at the health club.⟩ — see END 1

lapse *vb* to come to an end ⟨The contract will *lapse* at the end of the year unless we renew.⟩ — see CEASE 1

larceny *n* the unlawful taking and carrying away of property without the consent of its owner ⟨arrested and charged with *larceny*⟩ — see THEFT 1

large *adj* of a size greater than average of its kind ⟨He was hungry, so he ordered the *large* pizza.⟩

synonyms big, bulky, considerable, goodly, grand, great, handsome, hefty, hulking, husky, largish, outsize (*also* outsized), oversize (*or* oversized), sizable (*or* sizeable), substantial, tidy, voluminous

related words astronomical (*also* astronomic), bumper, cavernous, colossal, cosmic (*also* cosmical), elephantine, enormous, gargantuan, gigantic, gross, herculean, heroic (*also* heroical), Himalayan, huge, immense, jumbo, king-size (*or* king-sized), leviathan, major, mammoth, massive, monolithic, monstrous, monumental, mountainous, prodigious, staggering, stupendous, super, super-duper, titanic, tremendous, vast, vasty, whacking, whopping; bloated

near antonyms diminutive, half-pint, infinitesimal, little-bitty, microscopic (*also* microscopical), mini, miniature, minuscule, minute, pint-size (*or* pint-sized), pocket-size (*also* pocket-sized), pygmy, teeny, teeny-weeny, tiny, wee

antonyms bantam, dinky, dwarf, dwarfish, little, puny, small, smallish, undersized (*also* undersize)

large *adv* in a luxurious manner ⟨I decided to go for it and live *large* while on vacation.⟩ — see HIGH

largely *adv* **1** for the most part ⟨The earth's surface is *largely* composed of water.⟩ — see CHIEFLY

2 to a large extent or degree ⟨With this land purchase, the corporation *largely* increases its holdings in the area.⟩ — see GREATLY 2

largeness *n* the quality or state of being large in size ⟨I was impressed by the *largeness* of the portions at the new restaurant.⟩

synonyms bigness, bulkiness, grandness, greatness, heftiness, voluminousness

related words enormity, enormousness, extensiveness, hugeness, immenseness, immensity, magnitude, massiveness, mightiness, mountainousness, stupendousness, vastness; extravagance, extremeness; abundance, ampleness, bountifulness, copiousness, generosity, liberality

near antonyms diminutiveness, minuteness, tininess; slightness, meagerness, poorness, scantiness, scarceness, scarcity, skimpiness, slenderness, slimness, spareness, sparseness, sparsity, stinginess; deficiency, inadequacy

antonyms fineness, littleness, puniness, smallness

largess *also* **largesse** *n* **1** something given to someone without expectation of a return ⟨The alumna's huge bequest was an unexpected *largess*.⟩ — see GIFT 1

2 the quality or state of being generous ⟨The philanthropist was known for his *largess* to all of the city's cultural institutions.⟩ — see LIBERALITY

largish *adj* **1** of a size greater than average of its kind ⟨She was hungry, so she took a somewhat *largish* portion of food from the buffet.⟩ — see LARGE

2 sufficiently large in size, amount, or number to merit attention ⟨A *largish* amount of media attention was paid to something that was a nonstory.⟩ — see CONSIDERABLE 1

lariat *n* a rope or long leather thong with a noose used especially for catching livestock ⟨The cowboy could throw

a *lariat* around a running steer's head from 20 yards away.⟩ — see LASSO

lark *n* a time or instance of carefree fun ⟨The kids will have a grand *lark* at the carnival.⟩ — see FLING 1

lark *vb* to play and run about happily ⟨We would rather *lark* about in the summer than get part-time jobs.⟩ — see FROLIC 1

lascivious *adj* **1** depicting or referring to sexual matters in a way that is unacceptable in polite society ⟨*lascivious* remarks⟩ — see OBSCENE 1

2 having a strong sexual desire ⟨*lascivious* lovers⟩ — see LUSTFUL

lasciviousness *n* the quality or state of being obscene ⟨The minister preached a sermon against the *lasciviousness* that pervades so much of popular culture.⟩ — see OBSCENITY

lash *n* **1** a hard strike with a part of the body or an instrument ⟨The pirate threatened the crew with 10 *lashes* for any disobedience.⟩ — see ¹BLOW

2 a long thin or flexible tool for striking ⟨The rider struck the horse with the *lash*.⟩ — see WHIP

lash *vb* **1** to strike repeatedly with something long and thin or flexible ⟨The cat's tail nervously *lashed* the table leg.⟩ — see WHIP 1

2 to strike repeatedly ⟨All night long sheets of rain *lashed* the windows.⟩ — see BEAT 1

lass *n* a female person who has not yet reached adulthood ⟨She's a sweet *lass*.⟩ — see GIRL 2

lassie *n* a female person who has not yet reached adulthood ⟨a *lassie* of 16 years⟩ — see GIRL 2

lassitude *n* a complete depletion of energy or strength ⟨Our *lassitude* was such that we couldn't even be bothered to get up from the couch.⟩ — see FATIGUE

lasso *n* a rope or long leather thong with a noose used especially for catching livestock ⟨The cowpuncher skillfully tossed the *lasso* around the calf's neck.⟩

synonyms lariat, reata, riata

last *adj* **1** following all others of the same kind in order or time ⟨*Last* one in the pool is a rotten egg!⟩

synonyms closing, concluding, final, hindmost, lag, latest, latter, rearmost, terminal, terminating, ultimate

related words consequent, ensuing, eventual, following, succeeding; conclusive, crowning, decisive, definitive; farthermost, farthest, furthermost, furthest, remotest; lowest; endmost, extreme, outermost, outmost, utmost; penultimate

near antonyms eminent, premier, superior

antonyms beginning, earliest, first, foremost, inaugural, initial, leadoff, maiden, opening, original, pioneer, primary, starting

2 serving to put an end to all debate or questioning ⟨a book on the Kennedy assassination that supposedly is the *last* statement on what happened that fateful day⟩ — see CONCLUSIVE 1

3 of the greatest or highest degree or quantity ⟨Our *last* praise should be reserved for those original thinkers who expand the frontiers of science.⟩ — see ULTIMATE 1

last *vb* **1** to continue to operate or to meet one's needs ⟨We were lucky that the batteries *lasted* until we could get to the store to buy more.⟩ — see HOLD OUT

2 to remain indefinitely in existence or in the same state ⟨This heavy drought has *lasted* all summer.⟩ — see CONTINUE 1

lasting *adj* having an existence or validity that does not change or diminish ⟨one of the few books published last year that is likely to have *lasting* significance⟩ — see ABIDING

last word *n* a practice or interest that is very popular for a short time ⟨running shoes that are the *last word* in sportswear this season⟩ — see FAD

late *adj* **1** not arriving, occurring, or settled at the due, usual, or proper time ⟨I ran as fast as I could, but was still *late* for class.⟩

synonyms behind, behindhand, belated, delinquent, latish, overdue, tardy

related words delayed, detained, postponed; dallying, dawdling, dilatory, dillydallying, dragging, laggard, lagging, poky (*or* pokey), slow, sluggish, unhurried

near antonyms opportune, seasonable, timely; prompt, punctual

antonyms early, inopportune, precocious, premature, unseasonable, untimely

2 having been such at some previous time ⟨The *late* musical director is missed by her students.⟩ — see FORMER 1

3 no longer living ⟨Our *late* granduncle remembered us in his will.⟩ — see DEAD 1

4 being far along in development ⟨*Late* impressionism gave rise to pointillism.⟩ — see ADVANCED

late *adv* **1** after the due, usual, or proper time ⟨She has a habit of arriving *late* for everything.⟩

synonyms tardily

related words afterward (*or* afterwards), anon, eventually, later, latterly, subsequently, thereafter; dilatorily, laggardly, slow, slowly, sluggishly

near antonyms immediately, promptly, punctually; pronto, quickly, rapidly, snappily, speedily, swiftly

antonyms beforehand, early, inopportunely, precociously, prematurely, unseasonably

2 not long ago ⟨The actress, *late* of New York but now of Los Angeles, is being eagerly sought for film roles.⟩ — see NEWLY

lately *adv* not long ago ⟨Have you been listening to the radio much *lately*?⟩ — see NEWLY

latency *n* a state of temporary inactivity ⟨The flower bulbs went from *latency* to full bloom in a matter of days.⟩ — see ABEYANCE

lateness *n* the quality or state of being late ⟨We were unable to get into the movie due to our *lateness* in arriving.⟩

synonyms belatedness, delinquency, tardiness

related words dilatoriness, sluggishness

near antonyms promptitude, promptness, punctuality

antonyms earliness, prematureness, prematurity

latent *adj* not being in a state of use, activity, or employment ⟨He has a *latent* talent for acting that he hasn't had a chance to express yet.⟩ — see INACTIVE 2

later *adj* being, occurring, or carried out at a time after something else ⟨The details of the plan will be filled in at a *later* date.⟩ — see SUBSEQUENT

later *adv* following in time or place ⟨We're going to go to the mall *later* on.⟩ — see AFTER

lateral *adj* of, relating to, or located on one side ⟨From the *lateral* view you can see how thick the wall really is.⟩ — see SIDE

latest *adj* following all others of the same kind in order or time ⟨The *latest* news reveals many details we didn't know before.⟩ — see LAST 1

latest *n* a practice or interest that is very popular for a short time ⟨That phone is the absolute *latest*!⟩ — see FAD

lather *n* **1** a light mass of fine bubbles formed in or on a liquid ⟨She worked the shampoo into a *lather* before rubbing it into her pet dog's coat.⟩ — see FOAM

2 a state of nervous or irritated concern ⟨He worked himself into a *lather* waiting for the results of the test.⟩ — see FRET

lathery *adj* covered with, consisting of, or resembling foam ⟨The *lathery* crests of the waves washed up and down the sandy beach.⟩ — see FOAMY

latish *adj* not arriving, occurring, or settled at the due, usual, or proper time ⟨The bus was often a little *latish*, but never more than by a few minutes.⟩ — see LATE 1

latitude *n* **1** an allowable margin of freedom or variation ⟨The regulations regarding the pasteurization of dairy products don't allow for much *latitude*.⟩ — see SLACK 1

2 the right to act or move freely ⟨The new laws gave the police more *latitude* in dealing with suspected criminals.⟩ — see FREEDOM 2

latrine *n* a room furnished with a fixture for flushing body waste ⟨Where's the nearest *latrine*, soldier?⟩ — see TOILET

latter *adj* following all others of the same kind in order or time ⟨The multiplex was showing a comedy and a horror film, and we decided that the *latter* would be more fun to watch.⟩ — see LAST 1

laud *vb* **1** to declare enthusiastic approval of ⟨The critics have *lauded* the best-selling author's newest novel.⟩ — see ACCLAIM

2 to proclaim the glory of ⟨The nation's people were expected to *laud* the dictator at every opportunity.⟩ — see PRAISE 1

laudable *adj* deserving of high regard or great approval ⟨You showed *laudable* restraint in dealing with that ridiculously demanding customer.⟩ — see ADMIRABLE

laugh *n* **1** an explosive sound that is a sign of amusement ⟨The child's frown turned into a *laugh* when he saw the clown.⟩

synonyms cackle, chortle, chuckle, giggle, guffaw, horselaugh, laughter, snicker, snigger, titter, twitter

related words crow, whoop; grin, simper, smile, smirk

near antonyms cry, groan, moan, sob, wail; face, frown, grimace, lower (*also* lour), mouth, pout, scowl

2 someone or something that is very funny ⟨That new sitcom is a *laugh*.⟩ — see SCREAM

3 something said or done to cause laughter ⟨The film comedy had a good *laugh* in just about every scene.⟩ — see JOKE 1

laugh *vb* **1** to show mirth with an explosive vocal sound ⟨Everyone *laughed* when the clown dramatically slipped and fell.⟩

synonyms break up, cackle, chortle, chuckle, crack up, giggle, roar, scream, snicker, titter, twitter

related words grin, smile

phrases split one's sides

near antonyms bawl, blubber, cry, sob, weep; howl, scream, squall, wail, yowl; pule, whimper, whine; sniffle, snivel; groan, moan, sigh

2 to express scornful amusement by means of facial contortions ⟨You think you're smarter than me? Don't make me *laugh*!⟩ — see SNEER

laugh (at) *vb* to make (someone or something) the object of unkind laughter ⟨Most viewers seem to tune in just to *laugh at* the self-deluded souls who think that they can actually sing.⟩ — see RIDICULE

laughable *adj* **1** causing or intended to cause laughter ⟨the *laughable*, boisterous antics of the circus clowns⟩ — see FUNNY 1

2 so foolish or pointless as to be worthy of scornful laughter ⟨The movie shows a *laughable* ignorance of history.⟩ — see RIDICULOUS 1

laughing *adj* indicative of or marked by high spirits or good humor ⟨The comedy put us in a *laughing* mood for the rest of the evening.⟩ — see MERRY

laughingstock *n* a person or thing that is made fun of ⟨The team has become the *laughingstock* of the league.⟩

synonyms butt, derision, jest, joke, mark, mock, mockery, sport, target

related words chump, dupe, fall guy, fool, gull, monkey, pigeon, sap, sucker, victim

near antonyms darling, favorite, pet

laughter *n* an explosive sound that is a sign of amusement

⟨The nervous producers were reassured by the sounds of *laughter* coming from the theater.⟩ — see LAUGH 1

launch *n* the point at which something begins ⟨We are at the *launch* of a new age of space exploration.⟩ — see BEGINNING

launch *vb* **1** to be responsible for the creation and early operation or use of ⟨After retiring, he *launched* a small company devoted to making medical devices.⟩ — see FOUND

2 to take the first step in (a process or course of action) ⟨She *launched* a career in journalism after quitting acting school.⟩ — see BEGIN 1

3 to send through the air especially with a quick forward motion of the arm ⟨The javelin thrower *launched* his spear.⟩ — see THROW 1

laurels *pl n* public acknowledgment or admiration for an achievement ⟨The medics received many *laurels* for their heroic actions during the disaster.⟩ — see GLORY 1

lavatory *n* a room furnished with a fixture for flushing body waste ⟨The school's filthy, broken-down *lavatories* were a disgrace.⟩ — see TOILET

lave *vb* to flow along or against ⟨The cold water from the stream gently *laved* her burned fingers.⟩ — see WASH 1

lavish *adj* **1** going beyond a normal or acceptable limit in degree or amount ⟨This *lavish* consumption of our natural resources simply cannot continue.⟩ — see EXCESSIVE

2 pouring forth in great amounts ⟨The *lavish* praise that the novel was receiving made me eager to read it.⟩ — see PROFUSE

3 showing obvious signs of wealth and comfort ⟨The *lavish* apartment even boasted a marble bathroom with gold-plated fixtures.⟩ — see LUXURIOUS

lavish *vb* **1** to give readily and in large quantities ⟨doting parents *lavishing* lots of attention on their children⟩ — see RAIN 2

2 to use up carelessly ⟨a great actor who *lavished* his talent in lousy movies⟩ — see WASTE 1

lavishly *adv* **1** in a generous manner ⟨complained that the university spends *lavishly* on the football program but underfunds other sports⟩ — see WELL 2

2 in a luxurious manner ⟨Hollywood celebrities are known for living *lavishly*.⟩ — see HIGH

lavishness *n* the quality or fact of being free or wasteful in the expenditure of money ⟨The lottery winner's friends were struck by the *lavishness* of his new lifestyle.⟩ — see EXTRAVAGANCE 1

law *n* **1** a rule of conduct or action laid down by a governing authority and especially a legislature ⟨A record number of *laws* were passed in that legislative session.⟩

synonyms act, bill, constitution, enactment, ordinance, statute

related words command, commandment, decree, dictate, directive, edict, fiat, ruling; bylaw, ground rule, regulation, rule; amendment, legislation; common law, martial law; prohibition, proscription, restriction

near antonyms higher law

2 a collection or system of rules of conduct ⟨It's important to obey the *law* at all times.⟩ — see CODE

3 the department of government that keeps order, fights crime, and enforces statutes ⟨a petty thief who had somehow managed to avoid the *law* for most of his life⟩ — see POLICE 1

law–abiding *adj* readily giving in to the command or authority of another ⟨*law-abiding* citizens⟩ — see OBEDIENT

lawbreaker *n* a person who has committed a crime ⟨legislation that mandates lengthy prison sentences for chronic *lawbreakers*⟩ — see CRIMINAL

lawbreaking *adj* not restrained by or under the control of legal authority ⟨Some sociologists specialize in studying the *lawbreaking* elements of society.⟩ — see LAWLESS 1

lawbreaking *n* **1** a breaking of a moral or legal code ⟨Even something as simple as littering is considered an example of *lawbreaking*.⟩ — see OFFENSE 1

2 activities that are in violation of the laws of the state ⟨He denied being involved in any *lawbreaking*.⟩ — see CRIME 1

lawful *adj* permitted by law ⟨Hunting is a *lawful* activity only if you have the proper license.⟩ — see LEGAL 1

lawfulness *n* the quality or state of being legal ⟨The lawyers had to work for weeks to determine the *lawfulness* of the proposed contract.⟩ — see LEGALITY

lawgiver *n* a member of an organized body of persons having the authority to make laws ⟨Political activists strenuously lobbied the state's *lawgivers* to expand the scope of the civil rights legislation.⟩ — see LEGISLATOR

lawless *adj* **1** not restrained by or under the control of legal authority ⟨a *lawless* mob⟩

synonyms anarchic (*also* anarchical), disorderly, lawbreaking, unruly

related words defiant, insubordinate, mutinous, rebellious, refractory, riotous; undisciplined; criminal, felonious, illegal, illegitimate, illicit, unlawful, wrongful; disobedient, froward, intractable, recalcitrant

near antonyms lawful, legal, legalized, legitimate; amenable, compliant, docile, obedient, submissive, tractable

antonyms law-abiding, orderly

2 contrary to or forbidden by law ⟨The level of *lawless* activity in the territory had reached the point where the authorities felt compelled to act.⟩ — see ILLEGAL 1

lawlessness *n* **1** a state in which there is widespread wrongdoing and disregard for rules and authority ⟨The western frontier was notorious for its *lawlessness*.⟩ — see ANARCHY

2 activities that are in violation of the laws of the state ⟨*Lawlessness* in the city had dropped in recent years.⟩ — see CRIME 1

lawmaker *n* a member of an organized body of persons having the authority to make laws ⟨The state's *lawmakers* worked long into the night drafting a bill that would be acceptable to everyone.⟩ — see LEGISLATOR

lawsuit *n* a court case for enforcing a right or claim ⟨The homeowner filed a *lawsuit* against the moving company that was refusing to be held responsible for damaging her furniture.⟩

synonyms action, proceeding, suit

related words litigation; case, cause, complaint; countersuit, cross action, cross-claim

lawyer *n* a person whose profession is to conduct lawsuits for clients or to advise about legal rights and obligations ⟨Their *lawyers* told them that they couldn't use the park for the concert without permission from the city.⟩

synonyms advocate, attorney, counsel, counselor (*or* counsellor)

related words cocounsel; district attorney, prosecuting attorney, prosecutor, solicitor; criminal lawyer, public defender, trial lawyer; solicitor; jurist; lawgiver, lawmaker, legislator, solon

lax *adj* **1** failing to give proper care and attention ⟨*lax* parents who let their kids stay out as late as they want⟩ — see NEGLIGENT

2 not bound by rigid standards ⟨The guidelines for the essay contest were fairly *lax*, permitting a wide variety of topics.⟩ — see EASYGOING 2

3 not tightly fastened, tied, or stretched ⟨The sheet on the foresail was *lax*, and so the sail was flapping wildly in the stiff wind.⟩ — see LOOSE 1

laxness *n* failure to take the care that a cautious person usually takes ⟨The mountain climber's uncharacteristic *laxness* almost caused an accident.⟩ — see NEGLIGENCE 1

lay *n* **1** a rhythmic series of musical tones arranged to give a pleasing effect ⟨The minstrel strummed a cheerful *lay* on his lute.⟩ — see MELODY

2 a short musical composition for the human voice often with instrumental accompaniment ⟨She sang a short *lay* in dedication to her husband.⟩ — see SONG 1

lay *vb* **1** to arrange something in a certain spot or position ⟨Just *lay* the book over there on the table for now.⟩ — see PLACE 1

2 to cause to come to rest at the bottom (as of a liquid) ⟨The rain was just hard enough to *lay* the dust in the air.⟩ — see SETTLE 1

3 to establish or apply as a charge or penalty ⟨State officials tried to *lay* a tax on merchandise sold over the Internet.⟩ — see IMPOSE

4 to make ready in advance ⟨She's *laying* plans for the charity auction months ahead of time.⟩ — see PREPARE 1

5 to put a layer of on a surface ⟨The mason *laid* mortar over the first row of bricks before starting the second.⟩ — see SPREAD 2

6 to risk (something) on the outcome of an uncertain event ⟨I'll *lay* five dollars that you can't do it!⟩ — see BET

7 to explain (something) as being the result of something else ⟨an electrical fire that was *laid* to faulty wiring⟩ — see CREDIT 1

8 to place (a dead body) in the earth, a tomb, or the sea ⟨Let's *lay* the corpse to rest.⟩ — see BURY 1

lay away *vb* to put (something of future use or value) in a safe or secret place ⟨The weather forecast warned of a severe storm, so we *laid away* a generous supply of bottled water and canned food just in case.⟩ — see HOARD

lay down *vb* **1** to put into effect through legislative or authoritative action ⟨The city council promises to *lay down* new ordinances that will force dog walkers to clean up after their animals.⟩ — see ENACT

2 to state clearly and strongly ⟨At the risk of their popularity, the parents *laid down* the rules for the party and wouldn't accept any arguments.⟩ — see ASSERT 1

3 to give the rules about (something) clearly and exactly ⟨The supervisor *laid down* the procedure for filing a complaint.⟩ — see PRESCRIBE

4 to give (something) over to the control or possession of another usually under duress ⟨commanded the surrounded troops to *lay down* their weapons⟩ — see SURRENDER 1

layoff *n* the termination of the employment of an employee or a work force often temporarily ⟨Even senior employees lost their jobs in the massive *layoff*.⟩

synonyms discharge, dismissal, furlough

related words pink slip; bum's rush, downsizing, firing, heave-ho, sack; closing, shutdown; shakeout, shake-up

near antonyms callback, recall, reemployment, rehire

lay off *vb* to bring (as an action or operation) to an immediate end ⟨I've got to *lay off* the late nights for a while.⟩ — see STOP 1

lay off (of) *vb* to stop doing (something) permanently ⟨We warned him to *lay off of* the cigarette smoking.⟩ — see QUIT 2

layout *n* **1** the way in which something is sized, arranged, or organized ⟨The decorator changed the *layout* of the living room three times before declaring it finished.⟩ — see FORMAT 1

2 the way in which the elements of something (as a work of art) are arranged ⟨The *layout* of his portraits typically consists of a finely drawn subject against a roughly sketched background.⟩ — see COMPOSITION 3

lay out *vb* **1** to hand over or use up in payment ⟨He *laid out* big bucks for a new lawnmower that runs by itself.⟩ — see SPEND 1

2 to work out the details of (something) in advance ⟨The transatlantic balloonists *laid out* a backup plan in case of an emergency.⟩ — see PLAN 1

3 to put into a particular arrangement ⟨Plants in the botanical gardens are *laid out* according to biogeographic region.⟩ — see ORDER 1

4 to present so as to invite notice or attention ⟨For the historic celebration, the museum *laid out* its full collection of Greek artifacts.⟩ — see SHOW 1

layover *n* a brief halt in a journey ⟨Our flight from New York to San Francisco made a *layover* in Chicago.⟩ — see STOP 1

lay up *vb* to put (something of future use or value) in a safe or secret place ⟨a farmer *laying up* grain for the winter⟩ — see HOARD

laziness *n* an inclination not to do work or engage in activities ⟨If not for my *laziness*, I could have gotten more done over the weekend.⟩

synonyms idleness, indolence, inertia, shiftlessness, sloth

related words apathy, languor, lassitude, listlessness, sluggishness; dallying, loafing, lolling, lounging

near antonyms ambition, enterprise, go, hustle, initiative; assiduity, assiduousness, diligence, perseverance; animation, briskness, energy, exuberance, jazziness, liveliness, lustiness, pep, peppiness, robustness, sprightliness, vibrancy, vigor, vim, vitality, vivacity

antonyms drive, industriousness, industry

lazy *adj* **1** not easily aroused to action or work ⟨The *lazy* dog just wanted to lie on the couch all day and sleep.⟩

synonyms idle, indolent, shiftless, slothful

related words apathetic, drowsy, inert, languorous, lethargic, listless, quiescent, sleepy, sluggish, torpid

near antonyms ambitious, diligent, enterprising, zealous; active, animated, bouncing, brisk, dynamic, energetic, exuberant, frisky, jaunty, jazzy, lively, peppy, perky, pert, snappy, spirited, sprightly, springy, vigorous, vivacious, zippy

antonyms industrious

2 failing to give proper care and attention ⟨That cookbook author can be *lazy* about giving cooking times and temperatures.⟩ — see NEGLIGENT

lazy *vb* to spend time doing nothing ⟨a good afternoon to spend *lazying* on the back porch⟩ — see IDLE

lazybones *pl n* a lazy person ⟨He's a *lazybones* who is never willing to do any work.⟩

synonyms drone, idler, loafer, slouch, slug, sluggard

related words bum; crawler, creeper, dawdler, laggard, putterer, slowpoke, snail, stick-in-the-mud, straggler; malingerer, shirker, slacker; dallier, lingerer, loiterer, loller, lounger, saunterer; delayer, procrastinator

near antonyms achiever, comer; live wire, powerhouse

antonyms doer, go-ahead, go-getter, hummer, hustler, rustler, self-starter

lea *or* **ley** *n* **1** a broad area of level or rolling treeless country ⟨Across the *lea* rolls a lonely wagon.⟩ — see PLAIN 1

2 open land over which livestock may roam and feed ⟨The cattle were free to range over the *lea*.⟩ — see RANGE 1

lead *adj* highest in rank or authority ⟨The *lead* diplomat is responsible for making policy for the entire embassy.⟩ — see HEAD

lead *n* **1** the person who has the most important role in a play, movie, or TV show ⟨The actor's career has really taken off since he became the *lead* in that prime-time drama.⟩ — see STAR 2

2 the space or amount of space between two points, lines, surfaces, or objects ⟨The runner maintained a *lead* of several meters all the way around the track.⟩ — see DISTANCE 1

3 a piece of advice or useful information especially from an expert ⟨My sister got a *lead* on the job opening from her neighbor, who is the human resources director for the company.⟩ — see ¹TIP 1

4 a slight or indirect pointing to something (as a solution or explanation) ⟨The police are now working on several *leads* generated by the evidence gathered at the crime scene.⟩ — see HINT 1

lead *vb* **1** to point out the way for (someone) especially from a position in front ⟨An enthusiastic docent *led* our group through the art museum.⟩

synonyms conduct, direct, guide, marshal (*also* marshall), pilot, route, show, steer, usher

related words precede; accompany, attend, chaperone (*or* chaperon), convoy, escort, see; control, manage

near antonyms dog, hound, shadow, tail, tailgate

antonyms follow, trail

2 to serve as leader of ⟨A senior programmer is *leading* the team that is developing the new accounting software.⟩

synonyms boss, captain, command, head, spearhead

related words control, dominate; direct, govern, handle, manage, oversee, regulate, run, superintend, supervise

near antonyms bow (to), comply (with), defer (to), follow, obey, serve, submit (to), yield (to)

3 to be at the front of ⟨The local high school's marching band *led* the parade.⟩

synonyms head

related words precede; announce, herald; accompany, attend, escort, usher

near antonyms conclude, end, finish, stop, terminate; tail, tailgate; dog, follow, trail

4 to be positioned along a certain course or in a certain direction ⟨This old road *leads* to an abandoned quarry.⟩ — see RUN 3

5 to give advice and instruction to (someone) regarding the course or process to be followed ⟨The salesclerk *led* us through the maze of options now available to television buyers.⟩ — see GUIDE 1

leaden *adj* **1** causing weariness, restlessness, or lack of interest ⟨a *leaden* performance of a classic American play that nearly put us to sleep⟩ — see BORING

2 of the color gray ⟨The *leaden* sky made everything seem dark and depressing.⟩ — see GRAY 1

leader *n* **1** a long hollow cylinder for carrying a substance (as a liquid or gas) ⟨The *leader* funnels water off of the roof and down into the cistern.⟩ — see PIPE 1

2 the person (as an employer or supervisor) who tells people and especially workers what to do ⟨The team *leader* is good at making sure that everyone keeps busy at their assigned tasks.⟩ — see BOSS

leading *adj* **1** coming before all others in importance ⟨They are the *leading* suppliers of auto accessories in the country.⟩ — see FOREMOST 1

2 highest in rank or authority ⟨served as the *leading* counsel on the defendant's legal team⟩ — see HEAD

leadoff *adj* coming before all others in time or order ⟨the *leadoff* batter⟩ — see FIRST 1

lead on *vb* to lead away from a usual or proper course by offering some pleasure or advantage ⟨a con man whose dupes are usually *led on* by their own greed and eagerness to turn an easy buck⟩ — see LURE

leafage *n* green leaves or plants ⟨The springtime *leafage* enveloping the park makes it seem much more private.⟩ — see GREENERY

leaflet *n* a short printed publication with no cover or with a paper cover ⟨The company hires college students to work the phones and distribute *leaflets* for its clients.⟩ — see PAMPHLET

leafy *adj* covered with a thick, healthy natural growth ⟨The backyard's *leafy* bushes look nice, but have a tendency to attract deer.⟩ — see LUSH 1

league *n* **1** a group of persons formally joined together for some common interest ⟨a *league* of concerned parents

who are seeking a greater voice in school affairs⟩ — see ASSOCIATION 2

2 an association of persons, parties, or states for mutual assistance and protection ⟨Created to avert future wars, the *League* of Nations was a forerunner of the United Nations.⟩ — see CONFEDERACY

3 one of the units into which a whole is divided on the basis of a common characteristic ⟨That falls into a different *league* of fiction—the popular novel.⟩ — see CLASS 2

league *vb* **1** to form or enter into an association that furthers the interests of its members ⟨The whole block *leagued* together to keep a park open in their neighborhood.⟩ — see ALLY

2 to participate or assist in a joint effort to accomplish an end ⟨Some unlikely political bedfellows *leagued* together to get the bill passed.⟩ — see COOPERATE 1

leak (out) *vb* to become known ⟨The candidate's campaign didn't want his choice of a running mate to *leak out* before an official announcement was made.⟩ — see GET OUT 1

lean *adj* having a noticeably small amount of body fat ⟨The marathoner is extremely *lean*.⟩ — see THIN 1

lean *n* the degree to which something rises up from a position level with the horizon ⟨The wall has enough of a *lean* that we can't set a bookcase against it.⟩ — see SLANT 1

lean *vb* **1** to set or cause to be at an angle ⟨Just *lean* the ladder against the tree and climb up it.⟩

synonyms angle, cant, cock, heel, incline, list, pitch, slant, slope, tilt, tip

related words bank; bend, deviate, swerve, veer; decline, descend, recline, retreat

near antonyms even, flatten, level, straighten

2 to show a liking or proneness (for something) ⟨The family's diet *leans* toward vegetarian.⟩

synonyms incline, run, tend, trend

related words go, gravitate; indicate, point, suggest

near antonyms avoid, shun, shy (from *or* away from)

3 to place reliance or trust ⟨You can always *lean* on me if you need help.⟩ — see DEPEND 2

leaning *adj* running in a slanting direction ⟨The *leaning* tower of Pisa is a popular tourist attraction in Italy.⟩ — see DIAGONAL

leaning *n* **1** a prevailing or general movement or inclination ⟨The news media are often accused of having liberal *leanings*.⟩ — see TREND 1

2 a habitual attraction to some activity or thing ⟨The two have similar musical *leanings*.⟩ — see INCLINATION 1

leap *n* an act of leaping into the air ⟨The horse cleared the hurdle with a tremendous *leap*.⟩ — see JUMP 1

leap *vb* to propel oneself upward or forward into the air ⟨The outfielder *leaped* into the air to catch the ball before it went over the fence.⟩ — see JUMP 1

leaping *adj* passing from one topic to another ⟨We had trouble following the lecturer's *leaping* look at archaeological discoveries around the world.⟩ — see DISCURSIVE

learn *vb* **1** to acquire complete knowledge, understanding, or skill in ⟨After months of trying, he finally *learned* the dance steps.⟩

synonyms get, master, pick up

related words apprehend, comprehend, grasp, know, understand; absorb, assimilate, digest, imbibe; major (in), study; memorize

phrases get the hang of

near antonyms forget; misunderstand; miss, overlook; disregard, ignore, neglect

antonyms unlearn

2 to come to an awareness of ⟨The directors have since *learned* that they should examine the company's financial reports a little more closely.⟩ — see DISCOVER 1

3 to come upon after searching, study, or effort ⟨We soon *learned* where the odd noise was coming from.⟩ — see FIND 1

4 to commit to memory ⟨He *learned* the words to the song while performing karaoke.⟩ — see MEMORIZE

learned *adj* **1** having or displaying advanced knowledge or education ⟨The *learned* professor can speak knowledgeably on a wide array of subjects.⟩ — see EDUCATED 1

2 suggestive of the vocabulary used in books ⟨a teaching assistant who tries to impress us with all of his *learned* words⟩ — see BOOKISH

learnedness *n* the understanding and information gained from being educated ⟨The university's head librarian exuded an aura of *learnedness*.⟩ — see EDUCATION 2

learning *n* the understanding and information gained from being educated ⟨The *learning* that you get from books is just as important as the experience you get from life.⟩ — see EDUCATION 2

lease *vb* **1** to give the possession and use of (something) in return for periodic payment ⟨The landlord was willing to *lease* the apartment for less than what we had expected.⟩ — see RENT 1

2 to take or get the temporary use of (something) for a set sum ⟨I couldn't afford to buy a car outright, so I decided to *lease* one instead.⟩ — see HIRE 1

leather *n* **1** the hairless natural covering of an animal prepared for use ⟨The company claims to use only the finest *leathers* for its shoes and handbags.⟩

synonyms hide, skin

related words coat, fleece, fur, pelt; alligator, antelope, buckskin, calfskin, chamois, cordovan, cowhide, crocodile, deerskin, doeskin, goatskin, horsehide, kid, kidskin, lambskin, morocco, ostrich, pigskin, seal, sharkskin, sheepskin, snakeskin; nubuck, patent leather, suede

2 the outer covering of an animal removed for its commercial value ⟨This jacket was made from real *leather*.⟩ — see HIDE 1

leather *vb* to strike repeatedly with something long and thin or flexible ⟨An expert rider will find almost no reason to *leather* a horse.⟩ — see WHIP 1

leathery *adj* not easily chewed ⟨The *leathery* meat served in the cafeteria drove many of us to start bringing our own lunches.⟩ — see TOUGH 1

leave *n* **1** a period during which the usual routine of school or work is suspended ⟨The soldier was on *leave* for three days before having to report back to base.⟩ — see VACATION

2 the approval by someone in authority for the doing of something ⟨The editor gave the reporters *leave* to follow up on their initial investigation of the senator's fund-raising practices.⟩ — see PERMISSION

3 the act of leaving a place ⟨The party was clearly dying down, and it was time to take our *leave*.⟩ — see DEPARTURE 1

leave *vb* **1** to cause to remain behind ⟨You can *leave* your lunch in the refrigerator while we're outside.⟩ ⟨starry-eyed lovers who promise never to *leave* one another⟩

synonyms abandon, desert, forsake, maroon, quit, strand

related words discard, ditch, dump, fling, jettison, junk, scrap, shed, shuck (off), throw away, throw out; deliver, give up, hand over, relinquish, surrender, yield; escape, retreat (from), take off (from), vacate, withdraw (from); abjure, cut off, disown, reject, renounce, repudiate, separate (from)

phrases walk away from, walk out on

near antonyms harbor, have, hold, keep, own, possess, reserve, retain, withhold; redeem, rescue, save

antonyms reclaim

2 to give by means of a will ⟨I'm going to *leave* all of my possessions to my children.⟩

synonyms bequeath, will

related words deed; hand down, hand on, pass (down); devise

3 to give up (a job or office) ⟨He *left* his job in the city and moved out into the country.⟩ — see QUIT 1

4 to put (something) into the possession or safekeeping of another ⟨Why don't you *leave* your watch with me while you swim?⟩ — see GIVE 2

5 to end a usually intimate relationship with ⟨didn't have the heart to *leave* him⟩ — see DITCH 1

6 to give permission to ⟨Aw, *leave* him come!⟩ — see ALLOW 2

leave off *vb* **1** to bring (as an action or operation) to an immediate end ⟨We usually *leave off* working as soon as the bell rings.⟩ — see STOP 1

2 to come to an end ⟨The snow should *leave off* around midnight.⟩ — see CEASE 1

leave–taking *n* **1** the act of leaving a place ⟨The *leave-taking* of the guest of honor was scheduled for 11 o'clock.⟩ — see DEPARTURE 1

2 the act or process of two or more persons going off in different directions ⟨The sweethearts' *leave-taking* was filled with tearful pauses and promises to meet again.⟩ — see PARTING 1

leavings *pl n* a remaining group or portion ⟨The *leavings* of the banquet were packed up and delivered to a shelter for the homeless.⟩ — see REMAINDER 1

lecture *vb* **1** to criticize (someone) severely or angrily especially for personal failings ⟨The frustrated manager *lectured* the waitstaff about its poor level of service.⟩ — see SCOLD

2 to give a formal often extended talk on a subject ⟨She often *lectures* on modern art at the local college.⟩ — see TALK 1

leech *n* a person who is supported by or seeks support from another without making an adequate return ⟨Whenever we go out for pizza, that *leech* always has an excuse for not paying his fair share.⟩

synonyms hanger-on, moocher, parasite, sponge, sponger

related words dependent; idler; flunky (*also* flunkey *or* flunkie), henchman, lackey; cheapskate, miser, niggard, piker, scrooge, skinflint, tightwad

near antonyms benefactor, philanthropist, supporter

leer (at) *vb* to look at in a flirtatious or desiring way ⟨a painting that shows a satyr *leering at* forest nymphs⟩ — see OGLE

leeward *adj* being in the direction that the wind is blowing ⟨We moved to the *leeward* side of the ship so that we wouldn't have the wind in our faces.⟩ — see DOWNWIND

left *n* a political belief stressing progress, the essential goodness of humankind, and individual freedom ⟨a rising politician who is being hailed as the new voice of the *left*⟩ — see LIBERALISM

left–handed *adj* **1** lacking or showing a lack of nimbleness in using one's hands ⟨I'd rather have no help at all than have his *left-handed* "assistance."⟩ — see CLUMSY 1

2 not being or expressing what one appears to be or express ⟨Jim failed to realize that he had received a *left-handed* compliment.⟩ — see INSINCERE

leftover *n* **1** an unused or unwanted piece or item typically of small size or value ⟨That doormat is just a *leftover* from when the new carpet was installed.⟩ — see ¹SCRAP 1

2 leftovers *pl* a remaining group or portion ⟨Take as many of these calendars as you want, and put the *leftovers* back on the shelf.⟩ — see REMAINDER 1

leg *n* **1** a lower limb of an animal ⟨He broke his *leg* when he accidentally stepped in that gopher hole.⟩

synonyms pin

related words member; foreleg, forelimb; calf, drumstick, ham, shank, shin, thigh

2 a portion of a trip ⟨On the first *leg* of the cruise they went south to the Caribbean.⟩

synonyms lap, stage

related words layover, stopover

leg (it) *vb* to go on foot ⟨The car was in the shop so we had to *leg it* to work for a couple of days.⟩ — see WALK 1

legacy *n* something that is or may be inherited ⟨The old locket was part of the *legacy* from my great-great-grandmother.⟩ — see INHERITANCE

legal *adj* **1** permitted by law ⟨Is it *legal* to build a campfire in the park?⟩

synonyms lawful, legitimate

related words allowable, authorized, noncriminal, permissible; justifiable, warrantable; constitutional; de jure, regulation, statutory; good, innocent, just, proper, right

near antonyms bad, corrupt, evil, immoral, iniquitous, reprobate, sinful, wicked, wrong; banned, criminal, forbidden, guilty, impermissible, outlawed, prohibited, unauthorized, unjust; under-the-counter, under-the-table; nonconstitutional, unconstitutional

antonyms illegal, illegitimate, illicit, lawless, unlawful, wrongful

2 following or according to the rules ⟨The referee declared it a *legal* play.⟩ — see FAIR 3

legality *n* the quality or state of being legal ⟨The senator questioned the *legality* of the proposed espionage operation.⟩

synonyms lawfulness, legitimacy

related words rightfulness, rightness; permissibility, permissibleness

near antonyms badness, immorality, iniquity, sinfulness, unjustness, wickedness, wrongness; criminality, unconstitutionality

antonyms illegality, illegitimacy, unlawfulness, wrongfulness

legal tender *n* something (as pieces of stamped metal or printed paper) customarily and legally used as a medium of exchange, a measure of value, or a means of payment ⟨Coins and bills are considered *legal tender*, but postage stamps are not.⟩ — see MONEY

legate *n* a person sent on a mission to represent another ⟨The *legate* was charged with a list of objectives to accomplish on behalf of his country.⟩ — see AMBASSADOR

legatee *n* a person who has the right to inherit property ⟨The couple had no children, so they declared their nephew their only *legatee*.⟩ — see HEIR

legend *n* **1** an explanatory list of the symbols on a map or chart ⟨The *legend* indicated that a large circle represented a major city, while a small circle stood for a small town.⟩

synonyms key

related words scale; caption; guide, table

2 an explanation or description accompanying a pictorial illustration ⟨The *legend* in the science textbook indicated that the accompanying picture had been enlarged by 1000%.⟩ — see CAPTION 1

3 a traditional but unfounded story that gives the reason for a current custom, belief, or fact of nature ⟨Some ancient civilizations had *legends* about spirits that inhabited trees and rocks.⟩ — see MYTH 1

4 the body of customs, beliefs, stories, and sayings associated with a people, thing, or place ⟨That story of how the world came to be has long been part of Greek *legend*.⟩ — see FOLKLORE

legendary *adj* based on, described in, or being a myth ⟨The unicorn is a *legendary* creature.⟩ — see MYTHICAL 1

legerdemain *n* **1** the art or skill of performing tricks or illusions for entertainment ⟨The illusionist's show is an entertaining blend of *legerdemain* and over-the-top showmanship.⟩ — see MAGIC 2

2 the use of clever underhanded actions to achieve an end ⟨The reduction of the deficit is due in part to financial *legerdemain*.⟩ — see TRICKERY

legion *adj* being of a large but indefinite number ⟨The obstacles that the programmers had to overcome have been *legion*.⟩ — see MANY

legion *n* **1** a large body of men and women organized for land warfare ⟨joined the French Foreign *Legion*⟩ — see ARMY 1

2 a great number of persons or creatures massed together ⟨*Legions* of fans crowded the stadium for the rock concert.⟩ — see CROWD 1

legionary *n* a person engaged in military service ⟨The daring exploits of the French *legionaries* have long been the stuff of literary and cinematic legend.⟩ — see SOLDIER

legionnaire *n* a person engaged in military service ⟨The *legionnaires* are well respected for their fighting prowess.⟩ — see SOLDIER

legislate *vb* to put into effect through legislative or authoritative action ⟨She wants the Congress to *legislate* new laws on certain imports.⟩ — see ENACT

legislator *n* a member of an organized body of persons having the authority to make laws ⟨The *legislators* met in an all-night session to hammer out the details of the bill.⟩

synonyms lawgiver, lawmaker, solon

related words assemblyman, assemblywoman; congressman, congresswoman; senator

legitimacy *n* the quality or state of being legal ⟨The *legitimacy* of the military dictatorship was not recognized by most other nations.⟩ — see LEGALITY

legitimate *adj* permitted by law ⟨The mistrust created among investors by the financial scandal has hurt even companies engaged in wholly *legitimate* business practices.⟩ — see LEGAL 1

lei *n* an ornamental chain or string (as of beads) worn around the neck ⟨We were presented with flowery *leis* as soon as we stepped off the plane in Hawaii.⟩ — see NECKLACE

leisure *n* freedom from activity or labor ⟨Upon retiring, the elderly couple looked forward to a life of well-deserved *leisure*.⟩ — see ¹REST 1

leisurely *adj* moving or proceeding at less than the normal, desirable, or required speed ⟨After buying our stuff, we just wandered around the mall at a *leisurely* pace.⟩ — see SLOW 1

leisurely *adv* at a pace that is less than usual, desirable, or expected ⟨The old hound dog *leisurely* sauntered over to his water bowl to take a drink.⟩ — see SLOW

lemon *n* something that has failed ⟨The used car he bought turned out to be a *lemon*, and he soon had trouble starting the thing.⟩ — see FAILURE 3

lend *vb* to give to another for temporary use with the understanding that it or a like thing will be returned ⟨I can *lend* you my copy of the textbook until the weekend.⟩ ⟨Can you *lend* me five dollars?⟩

synonyms advance, loan

related words furnish, give, grant; lease, rent

near antonyms take

antonyms borrow

length *n* **1** a wide space or area ⟨He vowed that he would journey the *lengths* of the earth to find her.⟩ — see EXPANSE

2 the space or amount of space between two points, lines, surfaces, or objects ⟨The *length* of a professional tennis court is 78 feet from baseline to baseline.⟩ — see DISTANCE 1

lengthen *vb* to make longer ⟨I had to *lengthen* the handle of the paint roller in order to reach the top of the wall.⟩ — see EXTEND 1

lengthening *n* the act of making longer ⟨A *lengthening* of the school year is favored by many of the parents in the school district.⟩ — see EXTENSION 1

lengthy *adj* **1** of great extent from end to end ⟨She used a *lengthy* piece of rope to tie her dog to a tree.⟩ — see LONG 1

2 lasting for a considerable time ⟨We got into a *lengthy* discussion.⟩ — see LONG 2

lenience *n* kind, gentle, or compassionate treatment especially towards someone who is undeserving of it ⟨a teacher's reputation for *lenience* towards his students⟩ — see MERCY 1

leniency *n* kind, gentle, or compassionate treatment especially towards someone who is undeserving of it ⟨The defense requested *leniency* in light of their client's lack of a prior criminal record.⟩ — see MERCY 1

lenity *n* kind, gentle, or compassionate treatment especially towards someone who is undeserving of it ⟨a judge's *lenity* toward first-time offenders⟩ — see MERCY 1

leprechaun *n* an imaginary being usually having a small human form and magical powers ⟨the story that if you follow a rainbow to its end, you'll find a *leprechaun's* pot of gold⟩ — see FAIRY

less *adj* having not so great importance or rank as another ⟨The restaurant's chowder has been declared the state's best by no *less* a person than the governor himself.⟩ — see LESSER

lessen *vb* **1** to make smaller in amount, volume, or extent ⟨We *lessened* our efforts as it became clear they weren't having an effect.⟩ — see DECREASE 1

2 to grow less in scope or intensity especially gradually ⟨The pain should begin to *lessen* within minutes of taking the medication.⟩ — see DECREASE 2

3 to lower in character, dignity, or quality ⟨blatant hypocrisy that *lessened* him in the eyes of the voters⟩ — see DEBASE 1

lesser *adj* having not so great importance or rank as another ⟨It was the *lesser* evil of the two choices.⟩

synonyms inferior, junior, less, lower, minor, smaller, subordinate

related words little, mean, small; minute, petty; jerkwater, one-horse, second-class, second-rate, two-bit; associate, auxiliary, secondary, subsidiary

near antonyms choice, exceptional, first-class, first-rate

antonyms greater, higher, major, more, primary, prime, senior, superior

lesson *n* something assigned to be read or studied ⟨Your *lesson* for tonight will be the chapter on chemical reactions.⟩

synonyms assignment, reading

related words homework, schoolwork; lecture; drill, exercise, practice (*also* practise); étude, study

lessor *n* the owner of land or housing that is rented to another ⟨*Lessors* are free to charge as much as they want for a house.⟩ — see LANDLORD

let *vb* **1** to give permission to ⟨My parents would not *let* me drive until I had a job and could pay for my own gas.⟩ — see ALLOW 2

2 to make able or possible ⟨The low gravity on the moon *lets* you make enormous leaps and jumps.⟩ — see ENABLE 1

3 to fail to prevent (some behavior on someone's part) especially from neglect or indifference ⟨They *let* their kids get away with everything.⟩ — see ALLOW 3

letdown *n* **1** the emotion felt when one's expectations are not met ⟨The museum exhibit was just so-so, and we returned home with a vague sense of *letdown*.⟩ — see DISAPPOINTMENT 1

2 something that disappoints ⟨The eagerly anticipated new movie starring our favorite actor turned out to be a big *letdown*.⟩ — see DISAPPOINTMENT 2

let down *vb* to fall short in satisfying the expectation or hope of ⟨With my poor performance I really felt that I had *let* my teammates *down*.⟩ — see DISAPPOINT

lethal *adj* likely to cause or capable of causing death ⟨The snake's venom isn't *lethal*.⟩ — see DEADLY 1

lethargic *adj* slow to move or act ⟨A big meal always makes me feel *lethargic* and sleepy.⟩ — see INACTIVE 1

let on *vb* to take on a false or deceptive appearance ⟨He knows more than he likes to *let on*.⟩ — see PRETEND 1

¹**letter** *n* a message on paper from one person or group to another ⟨He faithfully wrote her a *letter* every week they were apart.⟩

synonyms dispatch, epistle, memo, memorandum, missive, note

related words billet-doux, open letter; airmail, card, electronic mail, e-mail, junk mail, mail, postal card, postcard; communication, report; encyclical

²**letter** *n* the owner of land or housing that is rented to another ⟨It is the *letter* of the apartment—not the lessee—who is responsible for basic repair and upkeep.⟩ — see LANDLORD

letter carrier *n* a person who delivers mail ⟨We like to leave a little gift in the mailbox around Christmas for our *letter carrier*.⟩

synonyms mail carrier, mailman, postman

related words courier, messenger; postmaster, postmistress

letter–perfect *adj* being entirely without fault or flaw ⟨The actress's recitation was *letter-perfect*.⟩ — see PERFECT 1

letup *n* a usually gradual decrease in the pace or level of activity of something ⟨The downpour continued for hours without *letup*.⟩ — see SLOWDOWN

let up *vb* **1** to come to an end ⟨The rain *let up* just as we reached the house.⟩ — see CEASE 1

2 to grow less in scope or intensity especially gradually ⟨The windmill slowed down as the wind *let up*.⟩ — see DECREASE 2

levee *n* **1** a bank of earth constructed to control water ⟨A *levee* was built to control floodwaters.⟩ — see DAM

2 a structure used by boats and ships for taking on or landing cargo and passengers ⟨We tied the boat up at the *levee* and started unloading the fish we had caught.⟩ — see DOCK

level *adj* **1** having a surface without bends, breaks, or irregularities ⟨looked for a *level* place to land the plane⟩

synonyms even, flat, flush, plane, smooth

related words exact, uniform; aligned (*also* alined), regular, true; horizontal, tabular; plumb, straight, vertical

near antonyms inexact, irregular, unaligned, warped; undulating, undulatory, wavy; pitted, pockmarked

antonyms bumpy, coarse, lumpy, rough, uneven, unsmoothed

2 free from emotional or mental agitation ⟨in a much more *level* mood now that the worst is over⟩ — see CALM 2

level *n* the placement of someone or something in relation to others in a vertical arrangement ⟨a young karate student ready to rise to the next *level* in his chosen art of self-defense⟩ — see RANK 1

level *vb* **1** to make equal in amount, degree, or status ⟨We'll give both teams the same equipment so as to *level* the playing field.⟩ — see EQUALIZE

2 to make free from breaks, curves, or bumps ⟨The construction workers *leveled* the ground before laying a foundation for the new house.⟩ — see EVEN 1

3 to point or turn (something) toward a target or goal ⟨The marksman *leveled* his gun at the target and fired.⟩ — see AIM 1

4 to strike (someone) so forcefully as to cause a fall ⟨The boxer *leveled* his badly outclassed opponent with a single blow.⟩ — see FELL 1

5 to destroy (as a building) completely by knocking down or breaking to pieces ⟨an architectural gem that was *leveled* to build a parking lot⟩ — see DEMOLISH 1

levelheaded *adj* based on sound reasoning or information ⟨I've always appreciated my father's *levelheaded* advice.⟩ — see GOOD 1

levelheadedness *n* the ability to make intelligent decisions especially in everyday matters ⟨The judge had developed a reputation for no-nonsense *levelheadedness* in deciding cases.⟩ — see COMMON SENSE

lever *vb* to raise, move, or pull apart with or as if with a lever ⟨The workers used crowbars to *lever* the heavy stone block into its new position.⟩ — see ¹PRY 1

leviathan *adj* unusually large ⟨The Titanic was a *leviathan* ship by the standards of the time.⟩ — see HUGE

leviathan *n* something that is unusually large and powerful ⟨A *leviathan* of the seas, that cruise ship is said to be the largest passenger vessel afloat.⟩ — see GIANT

levity *n* a lack of seriousness often at an improper time ⟨inappropriate *levity* during the solemn ceremony⟩ — see FRIVOLITY

levy *n* a charge usually of money collected by the government from people or businesses for public use ⟨The legislators approved a new *levy* on imported cattle to help protect American ranchers.⟩ — see TAX

levy *vb* **1** to pick especially for required military service ⟨Unprepared for war, the government was forced to *levy* men on a scale that was unprecedented in its history.⟩ — see DRAFT 1

2 to establish or apply as a charge or penalty ⟨The baseball commissioner is *levying* a fine of $10,000 against every player involved in the fracas.⟩ — see IMPOSE

lewd *adj* **1** depicting or referring to sexual matters in a way that is unacceptable in polite society ⟨offended by some *lewd* comments⟩ — see OBSCENE 1

2 having a strong sexual desire ⟨a *lewd* 18th-century nobleman⟩ — see LUSTFUL

3 hinting at or intended to call to mind matters regarded as indecent ⟨*lewd* jokes⟩ — see SUGGESTIVE 1

lewdness *n* the quality or state of being obscene ⟨the *lewdness* of the remark⟩ — see OBSCENITY

lexical *adj* of or relating to words or language ⟨A dictionary provides *lexical* information—it tells you what the word "cat" means, not all there is to know about cats.⟩ — see VERBAL 1

lexicon *n* a reference book giving information about the meanings, pronunciations, uses, and origins of words listed in alphabetical order ⟨an avid word enthusiast who is compiling a *lexicon* of archaic and unusual words⟩ — see DICTIONARY

liability *n* **1** a feature of someone or something that creates difficulty for achieving success ⟨His small size was a *liability* as a football player.⟩ — see DISADVANTAGE 1

2 the state of being held as the cause of something that needs to be set right ⟨The *liability* for the accident is held by the person who was driving too fast.⟩ — see RESPONSIBILITY 1

3 the state of being left without shelter or protection against something harmful ⟨Failure to properly clean the wound could increase your *liability* to infection.⟩ — see EXPOSURE 1

4 the quality or state of being likely to occur ⟨What's the *liability* that he'll file a formal complaint if he's refused admission?⟩ — see PROBABILITY 1

5 *usually* **liabilities** *pl* something (as money) which is owed ⟨Your *liabilities* total about $200,000.⟩ — see DEBT 1

liable *adj* **1** being in a situation where one is likely to meet with harm ⟨Because of his frail constitution, he's *liable* to diseases.⟩

synonyms endangered, exposed, open, sensitive, subject (to), susceptible, vulnerable

related words likely, prone; uncovered, undefended, unguarded, unprotected, unscreened, unsecured

phrases at risk, in deep water, in jeopardy

near antonyms covered, guarded, protected, safeguarded, screened, secured, sheltered, shielded, warded

antonyms insusceptible, invulnerable, unexposed, unsusceptible

2 being the one who must meet an obligation or suffer the consequences for failing to do so ⟨The owner of a pet is *liable* for any damage that that pet might do.⟩ — see RESPONSIBLE 1

liaison *n* **1** the fact or state of having something in common ⟨A variety of political factions are attracted to that presidential contender, but there doesn't appear to be much of a *liaison* between them and the candidate.⟩ — see CONNECTION 1

2 the state of having shared interests or efforts (as in social or business matters) ⟨The strong *liaison* between the parents and teachers is based on the fact that both have the students' best interests at heart.⟩ — see ASSOCIATION 1

liar *n* a person who tells lies ⟨She knew he was a *liar* when he started claiming that he was an astronaut.⟩

synonyms fabricator, fibber, prevaricator, storyteller

related words exaggerator; calumniator, defamer, libeler, libelist, slanderer; perjurer; distorter, falsifier; equivocator, palterer; gossip, talebearer; charlatan, cheat, cheater, counterfeiter, cozener, deceiver, defrauder, dissembler, dissimulator, fraud, hustler, knave, mountebank, operator, pretender

near antonyms square shooter

libation *n* a liquid suitable for drinking ⟨A variety of *libations* will be available at the wedding reception.⟩ — see DRINK 1

libel *n* the making of false statements that damage another's reputation ⟨The governor's office issued a statement accusing the state's largest newspaper of *libel*.⟩ — see SLANDER

libel *vb* to make untrue and harmful statements about ⟨The court decided that the newspaper's reportage of the former mayor, while irresponsible, did not constitute an effort to *libel* him.⟩ — see SLANDER

libeling *or* **libelling** *n* the making of false statements that damage another's reputation ⟨The underhanded politician resorted to *libeling* when it became clear that that was the only way he was going to win the election.⟩ — see SLANDER

libelous *or* **libellous** *adj* causing or intended to cause unjust injury to a person's good name ⟨*libelous* statements about a celebrity for which the tabloid was sued⟩

synonyms defamatory, scandalous, slanderous

related words erroneous, false, inaccurate, incorrect, inexact, invalid, untrue, wrong; depreciative, depreciatory, derogatory, disparaging, uncomplimentary, unfavorable, unflattering; invidious, objectionable; maligning, traducing, vilifying; hateful, malevolent, malicious, spiteful

near antonyms appreciative, complimentary, favorable; adulatory, commendatory, eulogistic, laudatory; accurate, correct, errorless, factual, right, sound, true, valid

liberal *adj* **1** not bound by traditional ways or beliefs ⟨parents who take a very *liberal* attitude toward letting their children stay out late⟩

synonyms broad-minded, nonconventional, nonorthodox, nontraditional, open-minded, progressive, radical, unconventional, unorthodox

related words advanced, contemporary, modern; forbearing, indulgent, large-minded, lenient, permissive, tolerant; extreme; impartial, objective, unbiased

near antonyms hard, rigid, strict; doctrinal; bigoted, blinkered, intolerant, narrow-minded; reactionary, unreconstructed

antonyms conservative, conventional, hidebound, nonprogressive, old-fashioned, orthodox, stodgy, traditional

2 being more than enough without being excessive 〈He always puts *liberal* amounts of grated cheese on his pizza.〉 — see PLENTIFUL

3 giving or sharing in abundance and without hesitation 〈a doctor who has been very *liberal* in dispensing low-cost care to patients who could not otherwise afford it〉 — see GENEROUS 1

liberalism *n* a political belief stressing progress, the essential goodness of humankind, and individual freedom 〈*Liberalism* had always claimed to stand for the greatest social good.〉

synonyms left

related words neoliberalism; radicalism, socialism

near antonyms neoconservatism

antonyms right

liberality *n* the quality or state of being generous 〈Already known for his *liberality*, the billionaire continued to give away record amounts of money.〉

synonyms bountifulness, bounty, generosity, largess (*also* largesse), openhandedness, openheartedness, philanthropy, unselfishness

related words beneficence, charity, kindliness, selflessness; kindness; gift, gratuity, lagniappe; tribute; extravagance, improvidence, lavishness, prodigality, wastefulness; spendthrift; dissipating, squandering

near antonyms conserving, economizing, economy, frugality, husbandry, providence, scrimping, skimping, thrift; conservation, saving; husbanding, managing; scraping; cutting back

antonyms cheapness, closeness, meanness, miserliness, parsimony, penuriousness, pinching, selfishness, stinginess, tightness, ungenerosity

liberally *adv* in a generous manner 〈She spread frosting *liberally* over the cake until it oozed over the edges.〉 — see WELL 2

liberate *vb* **1** to release (as from slavery or confinement) 〈The animal rights activists snuck into the laboratory in the middle of the night to *liberate* all of the monkeys.〉 — see FREE 1

2 to set free from entanglement or difficulty 〈We were *liberated* from our financial woes when we hit the grand prize in the lottery.〉 — see EXTRICATE

liberation *n* the act of setting free from slavery 〈The *liberation* of enslaved people was one of the key results of the Civil War.〉

synonyms emancipation, enfranchisement, freeing, manumission

related words deliverance, redemption, salvation; autonomy, freedom, independence, liberty, self-government, sovereignty (*also* sovranty)

near antonyms bondage, serfdom, servitude, yoke; captivity, imprisonment, incarceration, internment; conquest, subjugation

antonyms enslavement

libertine *adj* having or showing lowered moral character or standards 〈The book about an infamous 19th-century *libertine* nobleman can still shock readers.〉 — see CORRUPT

libertine *n* a person who has sunk below the normal moral standard 〈The legend of Don Juan depicts him as a playboy and *libertine*.〉 — see DEGENERATE

liberty *n* **1** the power, right, or opportunity to choose 〈He doesn't want to go to the sales conference, but he doesn't have that *liberty*.〉 — see CHOICE 1

2 the state of being free from the control or power of another 〈the hope that the country's first-ever elections will usher in a new era of *liberty* and respect for the rule of law〉 — see FREEDOM 1

library *n* **1** a place where books, periodicals, and records are kept for use but not for sale 〈I went to the *library* to do some research for my report.〉

synonyms archive

2 an organized group of objects acquired and maintained for study, exhibition, or personal pleasure 〈a confirmed film freak with an impressive *library* of classic movies〉 — see COLLECTION 1

license *also* **licence** *vb* to give official or legal power to 〈A state statute *licenses* county sheriffs to choose their own deputies.〉 — see AUTHORIZE 1

license *or* **licence** *n* **1** the approval by someone in authority for the doing of something 〈The company is seeking *license* to operate several more power plants in the state.〉 — see PERMISSION

2 the granting of power to perform various acts or duties 〈A restaurant owner has to get a *license* to serve food and drink.〉 — see COMMISSION 1

3 the right to act or move freely 〈Military commanders on the ground must be granted considerable *license*, as wars cannot be micromanaged by people back in Washington.〉 — see FREEDOM 2

licentious *adj* having a strong sexual desire 〈the *licentious* main character of Mozart's *Don Giovanni*〉 — see LUSTFUL

licentiousness *n* immoral conduct or practices harmful or offensive to society 〈condemns the *licentiousness* portrayed in the film〉 — see VICE 1

lick *n* **1** a hard strike with a part of the body or an instrument 〈gave the ball a solid *lick* with the bat〉 — see ¹BLOW

2 a very small amount 〈The soup needs just a *lick* more of salt.〉 — see PARTICLE 1

3 the smallest amount or part imaginable 〈You haven't done a *lick* of work all day.〉 — see JOT

lick *vb* **1** to strike repeatedly 〈threatened to *lick* me〉 — see BEAT 1

2 to achieve a victory over 〈He's determined to do everything he can to *lick* the habit.〉 — see BEAT 2

licking *n* failure to win a contest 〈Our team took a *licking* last night, but we'll get them next time!〉 — see DEFEAT 1

lid *n* **1** a piece placed over an open container to hold in, protect, or conceal its contents 〈I had to get a screwdriver to pry the *lid* off of the paint can.〉 — see COVER 1

2 *slang* a covering for the head usually having a shaped crown 〈As he left the field, the pitcher tipped his *lid* to the cheering crowd.〉 — see HAT

lie *n* a statement known by its maker to be untrue and made in order to deceive 〈He wanted to deny the accusation, but he couldn't tell a *lie*.〉

synonyms fable, fabrication, fairy tale, falsehood, falsity, fib, mendacity, prevarication, story, tale, untruth, whopper

related words distortion, exaggeration, half-truth; ambiguity, equivocation; defamation, libel, slander; perjury; bluff, fiction, pose, pretense (*or* pretence); fallacy, misconception, myth; falsification, misinformation, misreport, misrepresentation, misstatement; deceit, deceitfulness, dishonesty, duplicity, fraudulence

near antonyms fact, truism, verity; honesty, truthfulness, veracity; authentication, confirmation, substantiation, validation, verification

antonyms truth

¹**lie** *vb* to make a statement one knows to be untrue 〈Would I *lie* to you about that?〉

synonyms fabricate, fib, prevaricate

related words perjure; equivocate, fudge, palter; beguile, cozen, deceive, delude, dupe, fool, gull, hoax, hoodwink, kid, take in, trick; defame, libel, slander, traduce; falsify, misreport, misrepresent, misstate; distort, garble; dissemble, dissimulate; misguide, misinform, mislead

near antonyms assert, swear, testify; authenticate, confirm, substantiate, validate, verify

²**lie** *vb* **1** to be positioned along a certain course or in a certain direction ⟨The train tracks *lie* just over that hill.⟩ — see RUN 3

2 to occupy a place or location ⟨I left the book *lying* on the counter.⟩ — see STAND 1

3 to remain out of sight ⟨Paparazzi were *lying* in wait outside the restaurant, a well-known celebrity hangout.⟩ — see ¹HIDE 3

lie detector *n* an instrument for detecting physical signs of the tension that goes with lying ⟨hooked the suspect up to a *lie detector* before interrogating him about the robbery⟩

synonyms polygraph

life *n* **1** a history of a person's life ⟨a renowned historian who has written *lives* of several early presidents⟩ — see BIOGRAPHY

2 a member of the human race ⟨Every day *lives* are saved by medical advances.⟩ — see HUMAN

3 active strength of body or mind ⟨Even though he's 86 years old, he still shows a lot of *life*.⟩ — see VIGOR 1

4 the period during which something exists, lasts, or is in progress ⟨The Egyptian civilization had an extremely long *life*.⟩ — see DURATION 1

5 the way people live at a particular time and place ⟨Frontier *life* must have been rugged, exciting, challenging, and more than a little dangerous.⟩ — see CIVILIZATION 1

lifeless *adj* no longer living ⟨a *lifeless* corpse⟩ — see DEAD 1

lifelessness *n* the state of being dead ⟨the *lifelessness* of the fish on the dock⟩ — see DEATH 2

lifelike *adj* closely resembling the object imitated ⟨The eyes of the *lifelike* portrait seem to follow visitors around the room.⟩ — see NATURAL 2

life span *n* the period during which something exists, lasts, or is in progress ⟨I saw no need to pay more for a better-built computer that would just grow obsolete before the end of its *life span*.⟩ — see DURATION 1

lifestyle *n* the way people live at a particular time and place ⟨retirees enjoying a more casual, stress-free *lifestyle*⟩ — see CIVILIZATION 1

lifetime *n* the period during which something exists, lasts, or is in progress ⟨The *lifetime* of the camera's batteries was so short we couldn't get through a day trip without having to replace them.⟩ — see DURATION 1

lift *n* **1** an act or instance of helping ⟨The company's senior vice president gave her son a much-needed *lift* up the corporate ladder.⟩ — see HELP 1

2 a means of getting to a destination in a vehicle driven by another ⟨I'll need a *lift* to work while my car is in the shop.⟩ — see RIDE

lift *vb* **1** to move from a lower to a higher place or position ⟨I needed help *lifting* the heavy globe back up to the top shelf.⟩ — see RAISE 1

2 to move or extend upward ⟨Once the sun started to cut through the morning fog, the colorful hot-air balloons began to *lift* off from the field.⟩ — see ASCEND

3 to take (something) without right and with an intent to keep ⟨She turned her back for just a moment, and somebody *lifted* her purse.⟩ — see STEAL 1

lifted *adj* being positioned above a surface ⟨With *lifted* heels and bent knees, the runners tensely waited for the starting pistol to go off.⟩ — see ELEVATED 1

ligature *n* **1** something that physically prevents free movement ⟨The surgeon tied a *ligature* around the tube to keep it in place.⟩ — see BOND 1

2 a uniting or binding force or influence ⟨A common language is often the *ligature* that unites the people of a nation.⟩ — see BOND 2

light *n* **1** the steady giving off of the form of radiation that makes vision possible ⟨He read poetry to her by the *light* of the moon.⟩

synonyms blaze, flare, fluorescence, glare, gleam, glow, illumination, incandescence, luminescence, radiance, shine

related words flash, glimmer, glint, glitter, scintillation, shimmer, sparkle, twinkle; daylight, moonlight, sunlight, sunshine; afterglow, aurora, beam, ray, shaft, streak, stream, sunbeam; glisten, gloss, luster (*or* lustre), polish, reflection, sheen

near antonyms blackness, dark, darkness, dimness, dusk, duskiness, gloom, night, shadow

2 something that provides illumination ⟨Please turn off the *light* when you go to bed.⟩

synonyms beacon, lamp

related words arc lamp (*also* arc light), candelabra, candelabrum, candle, chandelier, flare, flash, flashlight, floodlight, fluorescent lamp, gaslight, headlight, incandescent lamp, klieg light (*or* kleig light), lantern, light bulb, lighting, sconce, streetlight, sun lamp

3 a person who is widely known and usually much talked about ⟨a leading *light* in the acting profession⟩ — see CELEBRITY 1

4 the first appearance of light in the morning or the time of its appearance ⟨Things will look different by the *light* of day.⟩ — see DAWN 1

¹**light** *adj* **1** having little weight ⟨The suitcase was as *light* as a feather after all the clothes were removed.⟩

synonyms feathery, lightweight, underweight, weightless

related words bantam, diminutive, little, minute, puny, small, smallish, tiny, undersized (*also* undersize), wee; flimsy, fragile, insubstantial; petite, slender, slight, slim, thin

near antonyms big, considerable, extensive, goodly, great, handsome, huge, hulking, jumbo, king-size (*or* king-sized), large, largish, massive, overscale (*or* overscaled), oversize (*or* oversized), sizable (*or* sizeable), substantial, super, voluminous, whacking; bulky, cumbersome, unwieldy

antonyms heavy, hefty, leaden, overweight, ponderous, weighty

2 involving minimal difficulty or effort ⟨A little *light* work was all it took to straighten up the room.⟩ — see EASY 1

3 less plentiful than what is normal, necessary, or desirable ⟨Traffic on the highway seems to be very *light* today.⟩ — see MEAGER

4 moving easily ⟨The dancer was exceptionally *light* on her feet.⟩ — see GRACEFUL 1

5 not harsh or stern especially in nature or effect ⟨*light* punishment to fit a minor offense⟩ — see GENTLE 1

6 resembling air in lightness ⟨The waves had an especially *light* foam at their crests because of the strong breeze.⟩ — see AIRY 1

²**light** *adj* **1** filled with much light ⟨The *light*, airy room is exceptionally cheerful.⟩ — see BRIGHT 2

2 lacking intensity of color ⟨We painted the walls a *light* blue.⟩ — see PALE 1

3 of light complexion ⟨Her *light* skin tends to freckle easily in the sun.⟩ — see FAIR 4

¹**light** *vb* **1** to set (something) on fire ⟨We *lit* the kindling before adding the heavier logs.⟩ — see BURN 2

2 to supply with light ⟨The lights from the TV cameras will *light* this room as though it were high noon.⟩ — see ILLUMINATE 1

²**light** *vb* **1** to come to rest after descending from the air

⟨The bird *lit* on the branch and began to sing.⟩ — see ALIGHT 1

2 to come down from something (as a vehicle) ⟨He hurriedly *lighted* from the bus and started walking up the street.⟩ — see ALIGHT 2

light (on *or* upon) *vb* to come upon unexpectedly or by chance ⟨The novelist *lit upon* the plot for his latest thriller while visiting a remote lighthouse in Maine.⟩ — see HAPPEN (ON *or* UPON)

¹lighten *vb* to become glad or hopeful ⟨The patient *lightened* when he heard the disease responds well to treatment.⟩ — see CHEER (UP) 1

²lighten *vb* to supply with light ⟨The room was gradually *lightened* by the rising sun.⟩ — see ILLUMINATE 1

light–footed *also* **light–foot** *adj* moving easily ⟨The *light-footed* cat crept silently through the house.⟩ — see GRACEFUL 1

light–headed *adj* **1** having a feeling of being whirled about and in danger of falling down ⟨I always get *light-headed* after riding roller coasters, even when I'm standing still again.⟩ — see DIZZY 1

2 lacking in seriousness or maturity ⟨We couldn't concentrate on our work because we were feeling so *light-headed*.⟩ — see GIDDY 1

light–headedness *n* a lack of seriousness often at an improper time ⟨the *light-headedness* of giggling audience members during the emotional scene⟩ — see FRIVOLITY

lighthearted *adj* having or showing freedom from worries or troubles ⟨His *lighthearted* attitude in the face of danger was the source of some concern.⟩ — see CAREFREE

lightheartedness *n* carefree freedom from constraint ⟨He approaches his medical duties with a *lightheartedness* that some patients find disturbing.⟩ — see ABANDON

lighting out *n* the act of leaving a place ⟨his sudden *lighting out* for home⟩ — see DEPARTURE 1

lightly *adv* without difficulty ⟨You're not going to get off *lightly* if they catch you!⟩ — see EASILY 1

¹lightness *n* **1** the state or quality of having little weight ⟨The first thing I noticed about the little bird was its *lightness*; I could hardly tell I was holding it in my hand.⟩
synonyms slightness, weightlessness
related words airiness, delicacy, ethereality, etherealness; flimsiness, fluffiness, insubstantiality
near antonyms solidity, solidness, substantiality
antonyms heaviness, heftiness, massiveness, ponderousness, weightiness

2 a lack of seriousness often at an improper time ⟨We were shocked by the inappropriate *lightness* of the anchorman's tone.⟩ — see FRIVOLITY

²lightness *n* the quality or state of having or giving off light ⟨The photographer was concerned that the *lightness* of the background would cast the main subject into shadow.⟩ — see BRILLIANCE 1

lightning *adj* moving, proceeding, or acting with great speed ⟨He made a *lightning* dash for the goal.⟩ — see FAST 1

¹lightsome *adj* filled with much light ⟨a lovely and *lightsome* room with huge windows⟩ — see BRIGHT 1

²lightsome *adj* **1** having or showing a good mood or disposition ⟨lighthearted lovers skipping along the beach with a *lightsome* gait⟩ — see CHEERFUL 1

2 having or showing freedom from worries or troubles ⟨Greg set off on his grand tour of Europe with a *lightsome* heart.⟩ — see CAREFREE

3 moving easily ⟨Still *lightsome* despite her advancing years, the cat continued to ignore orders not to leap onto the kitchen table.⟩ — see GRACEFUL 1

lightweight *adj* having little weight ⟨It's going to be hot, so wear mostly *lightweight* clothing.⟩ — see ¹LIGHT 1

lightweight *n* a person of no importance or influence

⟨considered a *lightweight* among astronomers⟩ — see NOBODY

¹like *n* **1** a number of persons or things that are grouped together because they have something in common ⟨rules that make it hard for him and his *like*⟩ — see SORT 1

2 one that is equal to another in status, achievement, or value ⟨We'd never seen its *like* in any other shop in town.⟩ — see EQUAL

²like *n* positive regard for something ⟨She thought her new boyfriend was unusually interested in her *likes* and dislikes.⟩ — see LIKING

like *adj* having qualities in common ⟨You're not talking about *like* things when you compare football and golf.⟩ — see ALIKE

like *adv* to some degree or extent ⟨The cat would curl up, tightly *like*, and just go to sleep.⟩ — see FAIRLY 1

like *conj* the way it would be or one would do if ⟨It looks *like* it's going to rain at any moment.⟩ — see AS IF

like *vb* **1** to wish to have ⟨I'd *like* another slice of pizza, please.⟩
synonyms care (for), want
related words adore, delight (in), dig, enjoy, fancy, groove (on), love, relish, revel (in), welcome; covet, crave, desire, die (for), hanker (for *or* after), wish (for), yearn (for)
phrases feel like

2 to show partiality toward ⟨I *like* romantic comedies more than action movies.⟩ — see PREFER 1

3 to take pleasure in ⟨an adventuresome young woman who *likes* skydiving⟩ — see ENJOY 1

4 to see fit ⟨Please feel free to order whatever you *like* from the menu.⟩ — see CHOOSE 2

likelihood *n* the quality or state of being likely to occur ⟨The weatherman on TV said that the *likelihood* of rain today was fairly high.⟩ — see PROBABILITY 1

likely *adj* **1** having a high chance of occurring ⟨It's *likely* we'll see them at the party.⟩
synonyms probable
related words conceivable, earthly, imaginable, possible, potential, supposable; apt, bound, certain, doubtless, imminent, inescapable, inevitable, liable, necessary, sure, unavoidable
near antonyms impossible, inconceivable, unimaginable
antonyms doubtful, dubious, improbable, questionable, unlikely

2 having qualities which inspire hope ⟨This looks like a *likely* spot for good trout fishing.⟩ — see HOPEFUL 1

3 worthy of being accepted as true or reasonable ⟨We didn't find her excuse a very *likely* story.⟩ — see BELIEVABLE

likely *adv* by reasonable assumption ⟨The picnic will *likely* be cancelled if the storm continues.⟩ — see PROBABLY

liken *vb* **1** to describe as similar ⟨She *likened* her hall of fame visit to a pilgrimage.⟩ — see COMPARE 1

2 to regard or represent as equal or comparable ⟨I think that we can *liken* the two pianists, at least in terms of natural talent.⟩ — see EQUATE 1

likeness *n* **1** a two-dimensional design intended to look like a person or thing ⟨The wealthy businessman hired a leading artist to paint his *likeness*.⟩ — see PICTURE 1

2 something or someone that strongly resembles another ⟨Why, you're the very *likeness* of your mother!⟩ — see IMAGE 1

3 the quality or state of having many qualities in common ⟨The forgery was difficult to detect due to the pinpoint *likeness* it bore to the original.⟩ — see SIMILARITY 1

likewise *adv* **1** in addition to what has been said ⟨The owner of the restaurant is *likewise* the owner of the deli next door.⟩ — see MORE 1

2 in like manner ⟨I mind my own business, and you should do *likewise*.⟩ — see ALSO 1

liking *n* positive regard for something ⟨I have a *liking* for dark chocolate.⟩

synonyms appetite, fancy, favor, fondness, like, love, love affair, partiality, preference, relish, shine, taste, use

related words craving, desire, hankering, longing, thirst, yen; enthusiasm, interest, passion; bias, prejudice; bent, inclination, leaning, propensity, tendency; tooth; palate; weakness

near antonyms apathy, disinclination; indifference, unconcern

antonyms aversion, disfavor, disgust, dislike, distaste, hatred, loathing

lily–livered *adj* having or showing a shameful lack of courage ⟨accused him of being a *lily-livered* coward⟩ — see COWARDLY

limb *n* a major outgrowth from the main stem of a woody plant ⟨We hung the swing from the highest *limb* of the tree that we could reach.⟩ — see BRANCH 1

limber *adj* able to bend easily without breaking ⟨He shaped the basket out of *limber* branches that could bend easily around a frame.⟩ — see WILLOWY

limit *n* 1 a real or imaginary point beyond which a person or thing cannot go ⟨There was no *limit* to the number of challenges they faced.⟩

synonyms bound, boundary, cap, ceiling, confines, end, extent, limitation, line, termination

related words extremity, terminus; border, brim, edge, margin, rim, verge; outside; bar, barrier, fence, hedge, restraint, stop, wall

2 the most extreme or advanced point ⟨Those kids have pushed my patience to the *limit*!⟩ — see HEIGHT 2

limit *vb* 1 to set bounds or an upper limit for ⟨You should *limit* the note to a few words.⟩

synonyms cap, circumscribe, confine, restrict

related words bar, block, hamper, hinder, impede, obstruct; constrict, contract, lessen, narrow, pinch, squeeze; quell, repress, suppress; number; modify, qualify

near antonyms broaden, expand, widen; overextend, overreach

antonyms exceed

2 to mark the limits of ⟨Adjectives *limit* the meanings of nouns.⟩

synonyms bound, circumscribe, define, delimit, demarcate, terminate

related words control, determine, govern; delineate, describe

limitation *n* 1 a real or imaginary point beyond which a person or thing cannot go ⟨The bridge has a weight *limitation* that bars heavy trucks from crossing it.⟩ — see LIMIT 1

2 something that limits one's freedom of action or choice ⟨The country has some fairly strict *limitations* on the transport of plants over the border.⟩ — see RESTRICTION 1

3 the act or practice of keeping something (as an activity) within certain boundaries ⟨The *limitation* on the number of vehicles allowed on the island does not sit well with year-round residents.⟩ — see RESTRICTION 1

limited *adj* 1 having distinct or certain limits ⟨To avoid overcrowding, the number of tickets to the outdoor concerts is *limited*.⟩

synonyms bounded, circumscribed, defined, definite, determinate, finite, measured, narrow, restricted

related words modified, qualified; detailed, exact, precise, specific; constricted, moderate, modest; minute, puny, small, tiny; determined, fixed, settled

near antonyms bottomless, countless, incalculable, inexhaustible, innumerable, unfathomable; unqualified, unreserved; general, indeterminate, nebulous, vague; enlarged, escalated, expanded; copious, plenitudinous, plentiful

antonyms boundless, dimensionless, endless, illimitable,

immeasurable, indefinite, infinite, limitless, measureless, unbounded, undefined, unlimited, unmeasured

2 having a limit ⟨Competition for *limited* resources among growing populations is often a source of international conflict.⟩ — see FINITE 1

limitless *adj* being or seeming to be without limits ⟨The *limitless* nature of the universe is awe-inspiring.⟩ — see INFINITE

limp *adj* 1 not stiff in structure ⟨His broken arm was *limp* as he held it against his side.⟩

synonyms droopy, flaccid, floppy, lank, yielding

related words flabby, mushy, semisoft, soft, squashy, squishy; delicate, flimsy, insubstantial; elastic, flexible, lax, loose, pliant, relaxed, resilient, springy, stretchy, supple

near antonyms firm, hard, indurated, solid, sound, strong; brittle, crisp; compact, dense, substantial

antonyms inflexible, resilient, rigid, stiff, sturdy, tense

2 depleted in strength, energy, or freshness ⟨The *limp* runners just dropped to the ground after crossing the finish line.⟩ — see WEARY 1

3 lacking bodily energy or motivation ⟨The team's *limp* performance has many calling for the head coach's resignation.⟩ — see LISTLESS

limp *vb* 1 to walk while favoring one leg ⟨She *limped* all day after stubbing her toe on the lawn sprinkler.⟩

synonyms halt, hobble

related words hitch; blunder, falter, flounder, lurch, shamble, shuffle, stagger, stumble, teeter, totter, waver, wobble (*also* wabble); dodder

near antonyms breeze, glide, sail

antonyms stride

2 to proceed or act clumsily or ineffectually ⟨The damaged boat *limped* back into port.⟩ — see FLOUNDER 1

3 to move slowly ⟨We'll have to stop *limping* if we are ever going to make our destination in time.⟩ — see CRAWL 2

limpid *adj* 1 easily seen through ⟨Her eyes are the blue of a *limpid* stream of water.⟩ — see CLEAR 1

2 free from emotional or mental agitation ⟨the *limpid* days of my childhood⟩ — see CALM 2

limpidity *n* the state or quality of being easily seen through ⟨Crystal Lake was obviously named for the *limpidity* of its water.⟩ — see CLARITY 1

limpidness *n* the state or quality of being easily seen through ⟨The *limpidness* of the water allows visitors to actually see fish swimming along the bottom.⟩ — see CLARITY 1

line *n* 1 a series of persons or things arranged one behind another ⟨The *line* for tickets stretched around the block.⟩

synonyms column, cue, file, queue, range, string, train

related words echelon, rank, row; chain, progression, sequence, succession; array

2 a way of acting or proceeding ⟨Since the election, the president has taken a very conservative *line*.⟩ — see COURSE 2

3 the activity by which one regularly makes a living ⟨My *line* of business is "pre-owned" vehicles, and have I got a deal for you!⟩ — see OCCUPATION

4 a region of activity, knowledge, or influence ⟨Advanced mathematics is a little outside of my *line*, but I'll see what I can do to help.⟩ — see FIELD 1

5 a real or imaginary point beyond which a person or thing cannot go ⟨You really crossed the *line* with that remark.⟩ — see LIMIT 1

6 a long hollow cylinder for carrying a substance (as a liquid or gas) ⟨The workers rushed to fix the leak in the gas *line*.⟩ — see PIPE 1

7 a length of braided, flexible material that is used for tying or connecting things ⟨He made sure to bring extra fishing *line* in case a fish broke free.⟩ — see CORD 1

8 a group of vehicles traveling together or under one management ⟨She owns a *line* of limousines.⟩ — see FLEET

9 the direction along which something or someone moves ⟨The airplane took a southerly *line* toward the capital.⟩ — see PATH 1

10 a group of persons who come from the same ancestor ⟨A 10th of all island residents are members of the *line* of this early settler.⟩ — see FAMILY 1

11 the line of ancestors from whom a person is descended ⟨He comes from a noble *line* that goes back several centuries.⟩ — see ANCESTRY

lineage *n* **1** the line of ancestors from whom a person is descended ⟨His Italian *lineage* was very important to him.⟩ — see ANCESTRY

2 a group of persons who come from the same ancestor ⟨He was putting together a family tree to learn more about his *lineage*.⟩ — see FAMILY 1

linear *adj* free from irregularities or digressions in course ⟨The bullets from early firearms were notorious for not following a strictly *linear* path through the air.⟩ — see STRAIGHT 1

linger *vb* to move or act slowly ⟨They *lingered* over coffee after dinner.⟩ — see DELAY 1

lingerer *n* someone who moves slowly or more slowly than others ⟨He's known as a *lingerer*, always the last to arrive and the last to leave.⟩ — see SLOWPOKE

lingo *n* **1** the stock of words, pronunciation, and grammar used by a people as their basic means of communication ⟨It can be hard to travel in a foreign country if you don't know the *lingo*.⟩ — see LANGUAGE 1

2 the special terms or expressions of a particular group or field ⟨the shorthand medical *lingo* that the hospital staffers use with one another⟩ — see TERMINOLOGY

linguistic *also* **linguistical** *adj* of or relating to words or language ⟨the age at which children begin to acquire *linguistic* skills⟩ — see VERBAL 1

link *n* **1** a rod-shaped portion of seasoned ground meat in a casing ⟨I like to put maple syrup on my breakfast *links*.⟩ — see SAUSAGE

2 a uniting or binding force or influence ⟨Those old love letters were her only remaining *link* with her late grandparents.⟩ — see BOND 2

link *vb* **1** to put or bring together so as to form a new and longer whole ⟨She *linked* the flowers together to form a long chain.⟩ — see CONNECT 1

2 to think of (something) in combination ⟨Since childhood I have always *linked* trips to the beach with the discomforts of sunburn and sand in my clothes.⟩ — see ASSOCIATE 2

link (up) *vb* to come together to form a single unit ⟨Carbon atoms *link up* to form a diamond crystal.⟩ — see UNITE 1

linkage *n* the fact or state of having something in common ⟨The accountants noticed a *linkage* between the two supposedly independent companies.⟩ — see CONNECTION 1

linking *n* the act or an instance of joining two or more things into one ⟨the *linking* of state roads and highways into one interstate highway system⟩ — see UNION 1

linkup *n* the state of having shared interests or efforts (as in social or business matters) ⟨The *linkup* of the two art museums has proved beneficial to both institutions.⟩ — see ASSOCIATION 1

lint *n* a soft airy substance or covering ⟨It's important to clean the *lint* out of the dryer every time you use it.⟩ — see FUZZ

lionhearted *adj* feeling or displaying no fear by temperament ⟨Traditionally young Masai men are consigned to a period of isolation in the bush in order to turn them into strong, *lionhearted* warriors.⟩ — see BRAVE 1

liquefy *also* **liquify** *vb* to go from a solid to a liquid state ⟨The steel *liquefied* in the intense heat of the forge.⟩

synonyms deliquesce, flux, fuse, melt, run, thaw

related words dissolve, render; soften, thin

near antonyms clot, coagulate, congeal, gel, jell, jelly, thicken

antonyms harden, set, solidify

liquid *adj* **1** capable of moving like a liquid ⟨Always have in the kitchen a dispenser of *liquid* soap available for hand washing.⟩ — see FLUID 1

2 easily seen through ⟨the *liquid* air of the remote mountains⟩ — see CLEAR 1

liquidate *vb* **1** to destroy all traces of ⟨a decisive act that *liquidated* all doubts and fears about his governing abilities⟩ — see ANNIHILATE 1

2 to put to death deliberately ⟨mobsters *liquidating* their rivals⟩ — see MURDER 1

3 to give what is owed for ⟨We used our savings to *liquidate* our debts.⟩ — see PAY 2

liquor *n* a distilled beverage that can make a person drunk ⟨You can't buy *liquor* until you're 21 years old.⟩ — see ALCOHOL

lissome *also* **lissom** *adj* **1** moving easily ⟨The *lissome* actress's dance training is apparent in the way she moves on stage.⟩ — see GRACEFUL 1

2 able to bend easily without breaking ⟨Rattan is such a *lissome* material that it can be used for all manner of furniture and baskets.⟩ — see WILLOWY

¹list *n* a record of a series of items (as names or titles) usually arranged according to some system ⟨We put eggs, sour cream, tomatoes, roast beef, and cheddar cheese on the shopping *list*.⟩

synonyms canon, catalog (*or* catalogue), checklist, listing, menu, register, registry, roll, roster, schedule, table

related words agenda, bibliography, compilation, directory, docket, enumeration, glossary, index, inventory, manifest, payroll; calendar, timetable

²list *n* the act of positioning or an instance of being positioned at an angle ⟨The extreme *list* of the racing yacht made it hard for the untried crew to keep their balance.⟩ — see TILT

³list *n* a long narrow piece of material ⟨shaved a thin *list* from the side of the board⟩ — see STRIP 1

¹list *vb* **1** to make a list of ⟨The coach *listed* the people on the team.⟩

synonyms enumerate, inventory, itemize, numerate

related words count, mark, number; check (off), tick (off)

2 to put (someone or something) on a list ⟨Her number isn't *listed* in the phone book.⟩

synonyms catalog (*or* catalogue), enroll (*also* enrol), enter, index, inscribe, put down, record, register, schedule, slate

related words book, card, file, note; classify, compile, tabulate, tally; reschedule

near antonyms delete

3 to add (a person) to a list or roll as a participant or member ⟨Our grandfather is *listed* among the war dead honored by the memorial.⟩ — see ENROLL 1

4 to specify one after another ⟨Do I need to *list* all of the reasons why your idea won't work?⟩ — see ENUMERATE 1

²list *vb* to set or cause to be at an angle ⟨The sudden shift of the load in the hull *listed* the ship badly.⟩ — see LEAN 1

listen *vb* to pay attention especially through the act of hearing ⟨Would you *listen* to what I have to say?⟩

synonyms attend, hark, hear, hearken, heed, mind

phrases prick up one's ears

near antonyms discount, disregard

antonyms ignore, tune out

listen (to) *vb* to take notice of and be guided by ⟨You'd better *listen to* my advice!⟩ — see HEED 1

listen in (on) *vb* to listen to (another in private conversation) ⟨It's not polite to *listen in on* other people's private conversations.⟩ — see EAVESDROP (ON)

listing *adj* **1** inclined or twisted to one side ⟨The *listing* battleship limped back to port for repairs.⟩ — see AWRY

2 running in a slanting direction ⟨the *listing* lines of a poem scrawled on a chalkboard⟩ — see DIAGONAL

listing *n* a record of a series of items (as names or titles) usually arranged according to some system ⟨an alphabetical *listing* of all of the students currently enrolled in the school⟩ — see ¹LIST

listless *adj* lacking bodily energy or motivation ⟨When I had the flu, I felt *listless* and worn-out.⟩

synonyms enervated, lackadaisical, languid, languishing, languorous, limp, spiritless

related words indolent, lazy, slothful; dull, lethargic, logy (*also* loggy), sleepy, sluggish, torpid; exhausted, tired, weary; feeble, frail, weak; apathetic, impassive, indifferent, phlegmatic, stolid; inactive, inert

near antonyms active, dynamic, industrious; avid, eager, enthusiastic, keen, lively, vivacious; cheerful, chipper, perky, up; agog, alert, awake, open-eyed, sleepless, vigilant, watchful, wide-awake

antonyms ambitious, animated, energetic, enterprising, motivated

listlessness *n* **1** the state of being bored ⟨We searched desperately for something to jar us out of our *listlessness*.⟩ — see BOREDOM

2 the quality or state of lacking physical strength or vigor ⟨General *listlessness* is often a side effect of the medication.⟩ — see WEAKNESS 1

literal *adj* restricted to or based on fact ⟨A *literal* account of the explorer's adventures is actually a lot less interesting than his own exaggerated stories.⟩ — see FACTUAL 1

literary *adj* suggestive of the vocabulary used in books ⟨The novel's dialogue is a little too *literary* in flavor to be entirely convincing.⟩ — see BOOKISH

literate *adj* having or displaying advanced knowledge or education ⟨The columnist's witty and *literate* comments on current events make her a popular guest on political talk shows.⟩ — see EDUCATED 1

lithe *adj* **1** able to bend easily without breaking ⟨the *lithe* blade of a fencing foil⟩ — see WILLOWY

2 moving easily ⟨*Lithe* dancers glided across the stage.⟩ — see GRACEFUL 1

3 having a noticeably small amount of body fat ⟨She has the *lithe*, sinewy body of a distance runner.⟩ — see THIN 1

lithesome *adj* **1** able to bend easily without breaking ⟨stretching exercises designed to make the athlete's limbs more *lithesome*⟩ — see WILLOWY

2 moving easily ⟨The *lithesome* panther moved effortlessly and noiselessly through the rain forest.⟩ — see GRACEFUL 1

litter *n* **1** an unorganized collection or mixture of various things ⟨A *litter* of magazines covered the bedroom floor.⟩ — see MISCELLANY 1

2 discarded or useless material ⟨If you get caught throwing your *litter* on the sidewalk, you'll get slapped with a fine.⟩ — see GARBAGE

littered *adj* lacking in order, neatness, and often cleanliness ⟨Is there any wonder that you can never find anything in your *littered* desk?⟩ — see MESSY

little *adj* **1** having relatively little height ⟨There was a *little* hedge separating the two lawns.⟩ — see SHORT 1

2 lacking importance ⟨There were just a few *little* details left to take care of.⟩ — see UNIMPORTANT

3 not broad or open in views or opinions ⟨*little*-minded people who dislike the fact that human society is always progressing⟩ — see NARROW 2

4 not lasting for a considerable time ⟨Let's take a *little* pause to relax.⟩ — see SHORT 2

5 of a size that is less than average ⟨The petting zoo has a *little* horse in addition to all of the goats and sheep.⟩ — see SMALL 1

little *adv* **1** in a very small quantity or degree ⟨We had *little* more than we needed to survive in the wilderness.⟩

synonyms negligibly, nominally, slightly

related words meagerly, scantily; barely, hardly, just, marginally, minimally, scarcely

phrases a bit, a trifle

near antonyms completely, entirely, purely, thoroughly, totally, utterly; exceptionally; appreciably, discernibly, noticeably, palpably; abundantly, plentifully; generously, handsomely, liberally; grandly, hugely, monstrously

antonyms awfully, beastly, considerably, deadly, especially, exceedingly (*also* exceeding), extensively, extra, extremely, far, frightfully, full, greatly, heavily, highly, mightily, mighty, mortally, most, much, particularly, rattling, real, right, significantly, so, substantially, super, terribly, too, very, whacking

2 not often ⟨He's been studying very *little* for the bar exam.⟩ — see SELDOM

little *n* a very small amount ⟨There's just a *little* of the pie left.⟩ — see PARTICLE 1

little by little *adv* by small steps or amounts ⟨*Little by little*, we pieced together the jigsaw puzzle.⟩ — see GRADUALLY

littleness *n* the quality or state of being little in size ⟨The *littleness* of the painting hardly gives any indication of its price—which is a fortune.⟩ — see SMALLNESS

littlest *adj* being the least in amount, number, or size possible ⟨The *littlest* kitten in the litter was also the cutest.⟩ — see MINIMAL

livable *also* **liveable** *adj* suitable for living in ⟨After we added some furniture and painted the walls, the apartment was *livable*.⟩

synonyms habitable, inhabitable

related words comfortable, cozy, homelike, homey (*also* homy), intimate, snug; acceptable, bearable, endurable, sufferable, supportable, sustainable, tolerable

near antonyms uncomfortable; humble; insupportable, intolerable, unacceptable, unbearable, unendurable

antonyms uninhabitable, unlivable

live *adj* **1** being in effective operation ⟨He didn't realize that the microphone was *live* and proceeded to make some rather indiscreet comments.⟩ — see ACTIVE 1

2 having or showing life ⟨There is a tank of *live* lobsters sitting at the front of the restaurant.⟩ — see ALIVE 1

live *vb* **1** to have a home ⟨He *lives* next door to the hospital.⟩

synonyms abide, dwell, reside

related words lodge, settle, stay; frequent, haunt, visit; cohabit, inhabit, occupy; people; lease, rent, sublet, tenant

2 to have life ⟨Socrates was a philosopher who *lived* in ancient Greece.⟩ — see BE 1

liveliness *n* the quality or state of having abundant or intense activity ⟨We were surprised by the *liveliness* of the crowd at the restaurant despite the early hour.⟩ — see VITALITY 1

lively *adv* in a quick and spirited manner ⟨Now then, step *lively* there!⟩ — see GAILY 2

lively *adj* **1** having much high-spirited energy and movement ⟨The *lively* puppy was racing around the dining room floor chasing after people's shoelaces.⟩

synonyms active, airy, animate, animated, bouncing, brisk, energetic, frisky, jaunty, jazzy, mettlesome, peppy, perky, pert, racy, snappy, spanking, sparky, spirited, sprightly, springy, vital, vivacious, zippy

related words dapper, dashing, spiffy; agog, alert, awake, open-eyed, up, wide-awake; agile, nimble, spry; bright, buoyant, cheerful, chipper, chirpy, effervescent, sparkly, upbeat; eager, enthusiastic, keen; frolicsome, impish, pixieish, playful; boisterous, bubbly, ebullient, exuberant, high-spirited

phrases on the go

near antonyms indolent, lazy, unambitious; inert, lethargic, sleepy, sluggish, tired, torpid, weary; apathetic, impassive, phlegmatic, stolid; boring, dull, irksome, tedious

antonyms dead, inactive, lackadaisical, languid, languishing, languorous, leaden, lifeless, limp, listless, spiritless, vapid

2 marked by much life, movement, or activity ⟨The party was a *lively* affair that lasted into the small hours of the morning.⟩ — see ALIVE 2

liven (up) *vb* to give life, vigor, or spirit to ⟨The bandleader tried to *liven up* the party by playing more energetic music so people would dance.⟩ — see ANIMATE

livery *n* the distinctive clothing worn by members of a particular group ⟨The limousine chauffeur was easily distinguished from the cab drivers by his *livery*.⟩ — see UNIFORM

live wire *n* an ambitious person who eagerly goes after what is desired ⟨That new reporter on the police beat is a real *live wire*.⟩ — see GO-GETTER

livid *adj* **1** feeling or showing anger ⟨The boss was *livid* when yet another deadline was missed.⟩ — see ANGRY
2 lacking a healthy skin color ⟨His face was *livid* with fear.⟩ — see PALE 2

living *adj* **1** being in effective operation ⟨a *living* tradition of the holiday season⟩ ⟨a *living* culture that has survived a number of foreign invasions⟩ — see ACTIVE 1
2 having being at the present time ⟨There are fewer than a dozen *living* former presidents.⟩ — see EXTANT 1
3 having or showing life ⟨Is your hamster still *living*?⟩ — see ALIVE 1
4 closely resembling the object imitated ⟨an outdoor museum that is a *living* re-creation of a typical New England village circa 1840⟩ — see NATURAL 2

load *n* **1** a mass or quantity of something taken up and carried, conveyed, or transported ⟨hoisted a *load* of grain on the truck going to Florida⟩
synonyms burden, cargo, draft, freight, haul, lading, loading, payload, weight
related words consignment; boatload, shipload, trainload, truckload, wagonload; ballast, deadweight; overload, surcharge; bale, bundle, pack, package, packet, parcel, shipment; manifest; body, bulk, mass
2 loads *pl* a considerable amount ⟨There's no rush, since we've got *loads* of time left.⟩ — see LOT 2

load *vb* **1** to place a weight or burden on ⟨students complaining that their teachers were *loading* them with work⟩
synonyms burden, encumber, freight, lade, lumber, saddle, weight
related words clog, clutter, fill, pack; heap, mound, pile, stack; press, weigh; strain, tax; overburden, overload, overtax, surcharge; hamper, handicap; afflict, oppress
near antonyms alleviate, ease, lighten, relieve
antonyms disburden, discharge, disencumber, unburden, unlade, unload
2 to put into (something) as much as can be held or contained ⟨She *loaded* her plate at the buffet with as much food as it could carry.⟩ — see FILL 1

loaded *adj* **1** containing or seeming to contain the greatest quantity or number possible ⟨The department stores were *loaded* with goods for the holiday shopping season.⟩ — see FULL 1
2 having goods, property, or money in abundance ⟨The guy in the fancy foreign sports car obviously was *loaded*.⟩ — see RICH 1

loading *n* a mass or quantity of something taken up and carried, conveyed, or transported ⟨The accident was caused by an 18-wheeler with a *loading* in excess of the legal limit.⟩ — see LOAD 1

loaf *vb* to spend time doing nothing ⟨the kind of sultry August afternoon that makes you just want to *loaf*⟩ — see IDLE

loafer *n* a lazy person ⟨an incorrigible *loafer* who never accomplished anything⟩ — see LAZYBONES

loamy *adj* consisting or suggestive of earth ⟨That *loamy* section of the backyard is perfect for growing a garden.⟩ — see EARTHY 1

loan *vb* to give to another for temporary use with the understanding that it or a like thing will be returned ⟨Can you *loan* me your lawn mower this weekend?⟩ — see LEND

loath *also* **loth** *or* **lothe** *adj* slow to begin or proceed with a course of action because of doubts or uncertainty ⟨I was *loath* to accept his claim of having climbed Mount Everest.⟩ — see HESITANT

loathe *vb* to dislike strongly ⟨I simply *loathe* tapioca pudding.⟩ — see HATE

loathing *n* **1** a dislike so strong as to cause stomach upset or queasiness ⟨The sight of his nemesis getting that undeserved promotion filled him with *loathing*.⟩ — see DISGUST
2 a very strong dislike ⟨I have an uncompromising *loathing* for anyone who would deliberately harm an animal.⟩ — see HATE 1

loathsome *adj* causing intense displeasure, disgust, or resentment ⟨We traced the foul smell to a pile of *loathsome* garbage by the back wall.⟩ — see OFFENSIVE 1

lob *vb* to send through the air especially with a quick forward motion of the arm ⟨He lightly *lobbed* the errant ball over the fence to the waiting children.⟩ — see THROW 1

lobby *n* **1** a centrally located room in a building that serves as a gathering or waiting area or as a passageway into the interior ⟨Our tour group met downstairs in the *lobby* of the hotel before going out to dinner.⟩ — see FOYER 1
2 the entrance room of a building ⟨The ticket booth is located in the theater's outer *lobby*.⟩ — see HALL 1

local *n* **1** a local unit of an organization ⟨The truck drivers are members of *Local* 349 of the Teamsters' Union.⟩ — see CHAPTER 1
2 a usually longtime resident of a locality ⟨Few *locals* seem to patronize the city's touristy restaurants, leaving them to diners who prefer atmosphere over food.⟩ — see NATIVE

locale *n* **1** the area or space occupied by or intended for something ⟨We found an ideal *locale* for our annual picnic.⟩ — see PLACE 1
2 the place and time in which the action for a portion of a dramatic work (as a movie) is set ⟨The movie's *locale* is ambiguous, though the architecture and dress are suggestive of 19th-century Europe.⟩ — see SCENE 1

locality *n* the area or space occupied by or intended for something ⟨a *locality* filled with exotic plants⟩ — see PLACE 1

locate *vb* to come upon after searching, study, or effort ⟨We were finally able to *locate* the missing cat, who had been sleeping in the closet the whole time.⟩ — see FIND 1

location *n* the area or space occupied by or intended for something ⟨We chose the historic church on Main Street as the *location* for the ceremony.⟩ — see PLACE 1

loch *n, Scottish* a part of a body of water that extends beyond the general shoreline ⟨In his biography of Samuel Johnson, James Boswell tells of being conducted by a Scottish boatman "across one of the *lochs*, as they call them, or arms of the sea."⟩ — see GULF 1

lock (up) *vb* to put in or as if in prison ⟨If they catch you, they're going to *lock* you *up* and throw away the key!⟩ — see IMPRISON

locker *n* **1** a covered rectangular container for storing or transporting things ⟨The enlisted man usually stored his uniform in his *locker* at the foot of his bed.⟩ — see CHEST

2 a storage case typically having doors and shelves ⟨a down-at-the-heels health club where most of the *lockers* look to be unusable⟩ — see CABINET

lockup *n* a place of confinement for persons held in lawful custody ⟨talked to her client in the *lockup*⟩ — see JAIL

locus *n* **1** a thing or place that is of greatest importance to an activity or interest ⟨an area of the Southwest that has been the *locus* of a number of New Age movements⟩ — see CENTER 1

2 the area or space occupied by or intended for something ⟨The *locus* of brightness occurs where the rays of sunlight converge in front of the lens.⟩ — see PLACE 1

locution *n* a distinctive way of putting ideas into words ⟨In the poet's somewhat affected *locution*, word order is often reversed and so we have "the sea serene."⟩ — see STYLE 1

lodestone *also* **loadstone** *n* something that attracts interest ⟨The city is a *lodestone* for aspiring musicians.⟩ — see MAGNET

lodge *n* **1** a place that provides rooms and usually a public dining room for overnight guests ⟨When we go on our country vacation, we always stay at this little *lodge* in the middle of nowhere.⟩ — see HOTEL

2 an often small house for recreational or seasonal use ⟨Every summer we rent a small fishing *lodge* by the lake.⟩ — see COTTAGE

3 the meeting place of an organization ⟨The Masons meet at the *lodge* every Thursday evening.⟩ — see CLUB 2

4 the shelter or resting place of a wild animal ⟨The family of beavers built a *lodge* near the narrow point of the river.⟩ — see DEN 1

lodge *vb* **1** to provide with living quarters or shelter ⟨The landlord can legally *lodge* up to 20 people in his apartment building at one time.⟩ — see HOUSE 1

2 to establish or place comfortably or snugly ⟨Our pet guinea pig *lodged* himself in the far corner of his cage and simply refused to come out.⟩ — see ENSCONCE 1

3 to set solidly in or as if in surrounding matter ⟨*lodged* the head of the ax in the log⟩ — see ENTRENCH

lodged *adj* firmly positioned in place and difficult to dislodge ⟨The rusty, old bolts were so well *lodged* that a power wrench was needed to extract them.⟩ — see TIGHT 2

lodger *n* one who rents a room or apartment in another's house ⟨The mysterious *lodger* slept all day and only went out at night.⟩ — see TENANT 1

lodging *n* **1** the place where one lives ⟨Food and *lodging* are two of the largest expenses of living in the city.⟩ — see HOME 1

2 lodgings *pl* a room or set of rooms in a private house or a block used as a separate dwelling place ⟨I've rented *lodgings* in the old boardinghouse downtown.⟩ — see APARTMENT 1

3 a place to sleep and related amenities for the temporary use of a tourist or traveler ⟨*Lodging* was whatever budget motel we could find for each leg of our trip.⟩ — see ACCOMMODATION 1

loft *vb* to send through the air especially with a quick forward motion of the arm ⟨He *lofted* the ball down the center of the field toward a receiver.⟩ — see THROW 1

loftiest *adj* being at a point or level higher than all others ⟨From the *loftiest* part of the mountain ridge you could see all the way to the next state.⟩ — see TOP 1

loftiness *n* an exaggerated sense of one's importance that shows itself in the making of excessive or unjustified claims ⟨We were offended by the new club member's air of *loftiness*.⟩ — see ARROGANCE

lofty *adj* **1** extending to a great distance upward ⟨the ever-increasing *lofty* heights of the world's skyscrapers⟩ — see HIGH 1

2 having a feeling of superiority that shows itself in an overbearing attitude ⟨She acts all *lofty* and superior just because she went to an Ivy League college.⟩ — see ARROGANT

3 having or displaying feelings of scorn for what is regarded as beneath oneself ⟨His *lofty* attitude toward menial chores really rankles the other camp counselors.⟩ — see PROUD 1

4 having, characterized by, or arising from a dignified and generous nature ⟨He remained true to the cause's *lofty* ideals, regardless of the changing winds of popular opinion.⟩ — see NOBLE 2

5 very dignified in form, tone, or style ⟨the *lofty* nature of the coronation ceremony⟩ — see ELEVATED 2

log *vb* **1** to make a written note of ⟨The station captain *logged* the arrest and then left for home.⟩ — see RECORD 1

2 to obtain (as a goal) through effort ⟨an actor who has *logged* a record number of Academy Award nominations in the course of her career⟩ — see ACHIEVE 1

logger *n* a person whose job is to cut down trees ⟨The *loggers* were obliged to plant as many trees as they cut down.⟩ — see LUMBERJACK

logic *n* the thought processes that have been established as leading to valid solutions to problems ⟨I tried to use *logic* to figure out the solution to the puzzle.⟩

synonyms reason, reasoning, sense
related words cogency, coherence, logicality, logicalness, rationality, rationalness; persuasiveness; syllogism; analysis, dissection; deduction, induction; disputation
near antonyms illogic, incoherence; absurdity, brainlessness, insanity, irrationality, nonsensicalness, preposterousness, senselessness

logical *adj* **1** according to the rules of logic ⟨The lawyer won the case with a *logical* argument about the motives of the suspect.⟩

synonyms analytic (*or* analytical), coherent, consequent, good, rational, reasonable, sensible, sound, valid, well-founded
related words cognitive, empirical (*also* empiric); defendable, defensible, justifiable, maintainable, supportable, sustainable, tenable
near antonyms fallacious, misleading, sophistic (*or* sophistical), specious; unarticulated; unscientific; absurd, cockeyed, daffy, fatuous, half-baked, half-witted, harebrained, nonsensical, preposterous, simpleminded, stupid, weakminded, witless; senseless, thoughtless; unconvincing
antonyms illegitimate, illogical, incoherent, inconsequential, invalid, irrational, unreasonable, unsound, weak

2 based on sound reasoning or information ⟨That's the *logical* choice under the circumstances.⟩ — see GOOD 1

logo *n* a device, design, or figure used as an identifying mark ⟨The company's *logo* is instantly recognizable all over the world.⟩ — see EMBLEM

logy *also* **loggy** *adj* depleted in strength, energy, or freshness ⟨The next morning I was feeling *logy*, having stayed up half the night.⟩ — see WEARY 1

loiter *vb* to move or act slowly ⟨Patrons are requested not to *loiter* outside the theater.⟩ — see DELAY 1

loiterer *n* someone who moves slowly or more slowly than others ⟨She yelled at the *loiterers* at the end of the line to hurry up.⟩ — see SLOWPOKE

loll *vb* **1** to be limp from lack of water or vigor ⟨The heads of the flowers *lolled* on their stems in the blistering heat.⟩ — see DROOP 1

2 to refrain from labor or exertion ⟨farmhands *lolling* about in the shade and taking a break from the midday sun⟩ — see REST 1

3 to spend time doing nothing ⟨Some members of the decorating committee were hard at work, and others were just *lolling* about.⟩ — see IDLE

lone *adj* **1** being the one or ones of a class with no other members ⟨the *lone* ripe apple in the entire bag⟩ — see ONLY 2

2 not being in the company of others ⟨just one *lone* cow in the middle of the field⟩ — see ALONE 1

lonely *adj* **1** not being in the company of others ⟨a single *lonely* cactus in the desert⟩ — see ALONE 1

2 sad from lack of companionship or separation from others ⟨I was *lonely* when I first got to Los Angeles, but I soon made friends.⟩ — see LONESOME 1

3 causing or marked by an atmosphere lacking in cheer ⟨the *lonely* streets of a honky-tonk beach town in the off-season⟩ — see GLOOMY 1

lonesome *adj* **1** sad from lack of companionship or separation from others ⟨a *lonesome* kitten left at the pound⟩

synonyms desolate, forlorn, lonely, lorn

related words friendless; abandoned, deserted, forgotten, forsaken, neglected, rejected; alone, lone, solitary, solo, unaccompanied; only, sole

near antonyms accompanied, attended, escorted

2 not being in the company of others ⟨a *lonesome* cypress tree on a rocky, windswept point⟩ — see ALONE 1

3 causing or marked by an atmosphere lacking in cheer ⟨The playground seems especially *lonesome* now that there are no young children in the neighborhood.⟩ — see GLOOMY 1

lone wolf *n* a person who does not conform to generally accepted standards or customs ⟨A *lone wolf* in the art world, he has his own style and paints only to please himself.⟩ — see NONCONFORMIST 1

long *adj* **1** of great extent from end to end ⟨Giraffes have *long* necks to help them reach leaves on tall trees.⟩

synonyms elongate (*or* elongated), extended, king-size (*or* king-sized), lengthy

related words extensive, far-reaching, longish, outstretched; oblong, rectangular; big, considerable, hefty, hulking, jumbo, large, largish, overscale (*or* overscaled), oversize (*or* oversized), sizable (*or* sizeable), substantial, super

near antonyms abbreviated, abridged, curtailed, diminished, shortened; bitty, diminutive, little, miniature, minute, puny, small, smallish, teeny, tiny, undersized (*also* undersize), wee

antonyms brief, curt, short, shortish

2 lasting for a considerable time ⟨If it's boring, even a movie with a running time of 90 minutes can seem *long*.⟩

synonyms extended, far, great, lengthy, long-lived, long-term

related words endless, everlasting, interminable, persistent; longish, overlong, prolonged, protracted; permanent; all-day, all-night; multiday, multiyear

near antonyms abrupt, sudden; abbreviated, condensed, curtailed, shortened; ephemeral, fleeting, momentary, transient, transitory; impermanent; short-range

antonyms brief, little, mini, short, shortish, short-lived, short-term

long *n* a long or seemingly long period of time ⟨They should be here before *long*.⟩ — see AGE 2

long (for) *vb* to have an earnest wish to own or enjoy ⟨I *long for* the day when I see you again.⟩ — see DESIRE 1

longhand *n* writing done by hand ⟨My computer was down for most of the afternoon, so I wrote out my report in *longhand*.⟩ — see HANDWRITING 2

longing *n* a strong wish for something ⟨By four o'clock in the afternoon, I usually experience a strong *longing* for chocolate.⟩ — see DESIRE 1

long–lived *adj* **1** being of advanced years and especially past middle age ⟨That sequoia tree is especially *long-lived*, having reached an age generally estimated to be at least 3,000 years.⟩ — see ELDERLY

2 lasting for a considerable time ⟨Much to the relief of

his parents, the youth's interest in the piano proved to be *long-lived*.⟩ — see LONG 2

longshoreman *n* one who loads and unloads ships at a port ⟨The *longshoremen* moved all of the fish into cold storage for shipment to the market.⟩ — see DOCKWORKER

long–suffering *adj* accepting pains or hardships calmly or without complaint ⟨The *long-suffering* parents calmly waited until the tantrum had passed.⟩ — see PATIENT 1

long–suffering *n* the capacity to endure what is difficult or disagreeable without complaining ⟨a man known for his patience and *long-suffering*⟩ — see PATIENCE

long–term *adj* lasting for a considerable time ⟨Before approving a new drug, the government insists on some *long-term* research to determine any possible side effects.⟩ — see LONG 2

long–winded *adj* using or containing more words than necessary to express an idea ⟨His *long-winded* explanation could have been boiled down to two sentences.⟩ — see WORDY 1

long–windedness *n* the use of too many words to express an idea ⟨That professor's *long-windedness* has long been legendary on campus.⟩ — see VERBIAGE 1

look *n* **1** facial appearance regarded as an indication of mood or feeling ⟨You should have seen the *look* on your face when we yelled "Surprise!"⟩

synonyms cast, countenance, expression, face, visage

related words frown, grimace, lower (*also* lour), mouth, pout, scowl; grin, smile; air, appearance, aspect, bearing, demeanor, manner, mien, presence

2 an instance of looking especially briefly ⟨She gave the junk mail a quick *look* before throwing it in the wastebasket.⟩

synonyms cast, eye, gander, glance, glimpse, peek, peep, regard, sight, view

related words gape, gaze, glare, leer, ogle, stare

3 the outward form of someone or something especially as indicative of a quality ⟨He has the *look* of a prosperous businessman.⟩ — see APPEARANCE 1

4 looks *pl* the qualities in a person or thing that as a whole give pleasure to the senses ⟨He has boyish good *looks*.⟩ — see BEAUTY 1

look *vb* **1** to give the impression of being ⟨It *looks* like it might rain.⟩ — see SEEM

2 to make known (as an idea, emotion, or opinion) ⟨The music teacher *looked* her displeasure with a fierce frown.⟩ — see EXPRESS 1

3 to have in mind as a purpose or goal ⟨They were *looking* to make a fast buck.⟩ — see INTEND 1

look (at) *vb* to make note of (something) through the use of one's eyes ⟨I found him at the mall *looking at* the new model TVs.⟩ — see SEE 1

look (into) *vb* to search through or into ⟨The owner is *looking into* new options for promoting business.⟩ — see EXPLORE 1

look (toward) *vb* to stand or sit with the face or front toward ⟨The bay window *looks toward* the park.⟩ — see FACE 1

looking glass *n* a smooth or polished surface that forms images by reflection ⟨Always remember that the image is reversed in the *looking glass*.⟩ — see MIRROR

lookout *n* **1** a high place or structure from which a wide view is possible ⟨We went up to the *lookout* on the top of the hill to watch the fireworks.⟩

synonyms observatory, outlook, overlook

related words aerie, crow's nest, tower, watchtower

2 all that can be seen from a certain point ⟨We were struck by the amazing beauty of the *lookout* from the top of the tower.⟩ — see VIEW 1

3 a person or group that watches over someone or something ⟨Make sure to post a *lookout* so that no one can sneak up on us.⟩ — see GUARD 1

look up *vb* **1** to go in search of ⟨Be sure to *look* me *up* if you're ever in town.⟩ — see SEEK 1

2 to become glad or hopeful ⟨By the next morning, the skies had begun to clear and we were *looking up.*⟩ — see CHEER (UP) 1

loom *vb* to be about to happen ⟨He could tell that a storm was *looming* when the sky suddenly darkened.⟩
synonyms brew, impend
related words advance, approach, draw on, gather, near; hang, hover, lower (*also* lour), menace, overhang, threaten
near antonyms abate, decline, de-escalate, die down, diminish, disappear, dwindle, ebb, fade, fall, lessen, let up, lower, moderate, recede, relent, remit, shrink, subside, taper, taper off, vanish, wane; fall back, pass, recede, retreat, withdraw

looming *adj* giving signs of immediate occurrence ⟨Some economists see a *looming* collapse of the stock market.⟩ — see IMMINENT 1

loop *n* a circular strip ⟨Cut the paper into narrow strips, and then paste those into *loops.*⟩ — see ¹RING 2

loose *adj* **1** not tightly fastened, tied, or stretched ⟨Secure your neckerchief with a *loose* knot.⟩
synonyms insecure, lax, loosened, relaxed, slack, slackened, unsecured
related words detached, free, unattached, unbound, undone, unfastened, untied; baggy, blousy, saggy
near antonyms constrained, restrained; attached, bound, fastened, tied; fast, firm, jammed, snug, stuck, wedged
antonyms taut, tense, tight

2 consisting of particles that do not stick together ⟨The car wheels slipped on the *loose* gravel in the driveway.⟩
synonyms incoherent, unconsolidated
related words nonadhesive, nonviscous; disconnected, disjointed, separate, unconnected; coarse, granular, rough
near antonyms connected, solid; compacted, compressed; adhesive, gelatinous, gluey, glutinous, gooey, gummy, sticky, viscid, viscous
antonyms coherent, compact, dense, packed

3 not bound by rigid standards ⟨a *loose* interpretation of the law⟩ — see EASYGOING 2

4 not bound, confined, or detained by force ⟨There was a brief panic when the lion got *loose* from its cage at the zoo.⟩ — see FREE 3

5 not precisely correct ⟨a *loose* guess about the size of the crowd at the outdoor concert⟩ — see INEXACT 1

6 having or showing lowered moral character or standards ⟨He was accused of *loose* behavior.⟩ — see CORRUPT

loose *vb* **1** to cause (a projectile) to be driven forward with force ⟨The archers *loosed* a great volley of arrows at the foot soldiers charging towards them.⟩ — see SHOOT 1

2 to find emotional release for ⟨Do not *loose* your pent-up frustrations on the next person who happens by.⟩ — see TAKE OUT 1

3 to release (as from slavery or confinement) ⟨He opened the jar and *loosed* the fireflies.⟩ — see FREE 1

4 to set free (from a state of being held in check) ⟨The storm *loosed* its full fury when it hit the coastline at high tide.⟩ — see RELEASE 1

loosen *vb* **1** to make less taut ⟨The lead climber *loosened* the climbing rope so that the other climber could have more room to maneuver.⟩ — see SLACKEN 1

2 to release (as from slavery or confinement) ⟨The dentist *loosened* the impacted wisdom tooth from the gum.⟩ — see FREE 1

3 to set free (from a state of being held in check) ⟨Once he got to know us better, his inhibitions *loosened* a bit.⟩ — see RELEASE 1

loosen (up) *vb* to free from obstruction or difficulty ⟨asked the school administrators to *loosen up* the rules on what can be printed on T-shirts⟩ — see EASE 1

loosened *adj* not tightly fastened, tied, or stretched ⟨The *loosened* nuts finally dropped off of the screws.⟩ — see LOOSE 1

loot *n* valuables stolen or taken by force ⟨The burglar was caught when he foolishly stopped to examine the *loot* from the robbery.⟩
synonyms booty, pillage, plunder, spoil, swag
related words prize; catch, haul, take, treasure; pilferage; windfall

loot *vb* to search through with the intent of committing robbery ⟨The bandits *looted* the archaeological dig before riding off into the night.⟩ — see RANSACK 1

lop (off) *vb* to make (something) shorter or smaller with the use of a cutting instrument ⟨The hair stylist started by *lopping off* several inches from her long tresses, before beginning to shape what was left.⟩ — see CLIP 1

lope *vb* to move with a light springing step ⟨The jogger happily *loped* along, just enjoying the fresh morning air.⟩ — see SKIP 1

lopsided *adj* inclined or twisted to one side ⟨The portrait in the foyer was *lopsided*, so I straightened it while I was waiting.⟩ — see AWRY

loquacious *adj* fond of talking or conversation ⟨Sometimes the *loquacious* talk show host barely lets guests get a word in.⟩ — see TALKATIVE

lord (it over) *vb* to assume or treat with an air of superiority ⟨Waiters at that fancy restaurant like to *lord it over* the customers, acting like they're doing them a favor just being there.⟩ — see CONDESCEND 2

lordliness *n* an exaggerated sense of one's importance that shows itself in the making of excessive or unjustified claims ⟨The *lordliness* of his manner really got on his colleagues' nerves, as he had no real authority over them.⟩ — see ARROGANCE

lordly *adj* **1** having a feeling of superiority that shows itself in an overbearing attitude ⟨One dinner guest was a little *lordly*, requesting that the food be prepared in just a certain way.⟩ — see ARROGANT

2 having or displaying feelings of scorn for what is regarded as beneath oneself ⟨his *lordly* attitude toward people who enjoy popular music⟩ — see PROUD 1

3 having, characterized by, or arising from a dignified and generous nature ⟨Born to great wealth, he has always displayed a *lordly* generosity toward the less fortunate.⟩ — see NOBLE 2

lore *n* **1** a body of facts learned by study or experience ⟨The home gardener had acquired her herbal *lore* from many years of trial and error.⟩ — see KNOWLEDGE 1

2 the body of customs, beliefs, stories, and sayings associated with a people, thing, or place ⟨He set out to study the rich *lore* of the Cajun people of Louisiana before it all vanished.⟩ — see FOLKLORE

lorn *adj* sad from lack of companionship or separation from others ⟨The *lorn* puppy waited for the family to return home.⟩ — see LONESOME 1

lose *vb* **1** to be unable to find or have at hand ⟨I always *lose* my keys.⟩
synonyms mislay, misplace
related words forget, miss, overlook, pass over
near antonyms enjoy, have, hold, keep, occupy, own, possess, retain; descry, detect, find, locate, run down, scare up, scout (up), track (down)

2 to fail to win, gain, or obtain ⟨If the team *loses* this game, they're out of the play-offs.⟩
synonyms drop
related words forfeit
near antonyms conquer, prevail (over), triumph (over)
antonyms nail (down), win

3 to undergo defeat ⟨She really hates to *lose* at anything.⟩
synonyms fall

related words falter; throw; forfeit; bomb, collapse, crack (up), fail, flop, flunk, fold, founder, miss, strike out, wash out
phrases take the count
near antonyms flourish, prosper, succeed, thrive
antonyms conquer, prevail, triumph, win
4 to get rid of as useless or unwanted ⟨We told the recent grad to *lose* the flashy shirts and dress conservatively for the job interview.⟩ — see DISCARD
5 to use up carelessly ⟨We *lost* a good hour while he tried to find his keys.⟩ — see WASTE 1
loser *n* something that has failed ⟨The first movie in the series was good, but all the sequels have been *losers*.⟩ — see FAILURE 3
loss *n* **1** the act or an instance of not having or being able to find ⟨He was upset over the *loss* of his wedding ring.⟩
synonyms mislaying, misplacement
related words deprivation, dispossession, privation; forfeit, forfeiture, penalty; sacrifice; bereavement; absence, lack, need, want
near antonyms control, hands, having, keeping, possession
antonyms gain
2 a person or thing harmed, lost, or destroyed ⟨The platoon was able to accomplish its reconnaissance mission without any *losses*.⟩ — see CASUALTY 1
3 failure to win a contest ⟨We're discouraged by our *loss* on Friday, but we're training hard for next week's game nevertheless.⟩ — see DEFEAT 1
4 the amount by which something is lessened ⟨The stock market experienced a *loss* of four percentage points yesterday.⟩ — see DECREASE
5 the state of being robbed of something normally enjoyed ⟨Her *loss* of sleep meant that she would have trouble concentrating at work the next day.⟩ — see PRIVATION
6 the state or fact of being rendered nonexistent, physically unsound, or useless ⟨The *loss* of the oil tanker was more significant than the *loss* of its cargo.⟩ — see DESTRUCTION 1
lost *adj* no longer possessed ⟨We searched all over the house for the *lost* keys.⟩
synonyms gone, mislaid, misplaced, missing
related words absent, castaway; irrecoverable, irretrievable; forgotten, unknown
near antonyms cherished, loved, prized, protected, treasured, valued
antonyms owned, retained
lot *n* **1** a small piece of land that is developed or available for development ⟨The softball team often plays in the vacant *lot* down at the end of the street.⟩
synonyms parcel, plat, plot, property, tract
related words patch; lease; development; real estate
2 a considerable amount ⟨You'll need to do a *lot* of studying for the test.⟩ ⟨You sure bought a *lot* of clothing.⟩
synonyms abundance, barrel, boatload, bucket, bunch, bundle, bushel, chunk, deal, gobs, heap, loads, mass, mess, mountain, much, multiplicity, myriad, oodles, pack, passel, peck, pile, plenitude, plentitude, plenty, pot, profusion, quantity, raft, reams, scads, sight, spate, stack, store, volume, wad, wealth, yard
related words plague, rash; bonanza, embarrassment, excess, overabundance, overage, overkill, overmuch, oversupply, redundancy, superabundance, superfluity, surfeit, surplus; deluge, flood, overflow; army, bevy, cram, crowd, crush, drove, flock, herd, horde, host, legion, mob, multitude, press, score, sea, swarm, throng
phrases all kinds (of), quite a bit
near antonyms atom, crumb, dot, fleck, flyspeck, fragment, grain, granule, iota, jot, modicum, molecule, mote, nubbin, particle, ray, scrap, shred, tittle, whit; smattering

antonyms ace, bit, dab, driblet, glimmer, handful, hint, lick, little, mite, mouthful, nip, ounce, peanuts, pinch, pittance, scruple, shade, shadow, smidgen (*also* smidgeon *or* smidgin *or* smidge), speck, spot, sprinkle, sprinkling, strain, streak, tad, touch, trace
3 a small area of usually open land ⟨There were still plenty of Christmas trees available for sale in the *lot*.⟩ — see FIELD 1
4 a number of things considered as a unit ⟨The auctioneer next introduced a *lot* containing several pieces of fine china.⟩ — see GROUP 1
5 a state or end that seemingly has been decided beforehand ⟨Unhappy with her *lot*, she moved to a new city to start over.⟩ — see FATE 1
6 a group of people sharing a common interest and relating together socially ⟨You should stop hanging out with that *lot*, or you'll end up in trouble.⟩ — see GANG 2
7 a usually small number of persons considered as a unit ⟨The school is indeed fortunate in its science teachers, because there's not a bad one in the *lot*.⟩ — see GROUP 2
lot *vb* to give as a share or portion ⟨Everyone is *lotted* opportunities in life, and it's their responsibility to take them.⟩ — see ALLOT
loud *adj* **1** marked by a high volume of sound ⟨*loud* music that could be heard all over the neighborhood⟩
synonyms blaring, blasting, booming, clamorous, clangorous, deafening, earsplitting, piercing, resounding, roaring, sonorous, stentorian, thunderous
related words brazen, dinning, discordant, noisy, obstreperous, raucous, rip-roaring, vociferous; grating, harsh, overloud, sharp, shrill, squealing, strident
near antonyms dead, quiet, silent, still, stilly, ultraquiet; calm, dreamy, peaceful, restful, serene, soothing, tranquil; hushed, muffled, muted, softened, toned (down)
antonyms gentle, low, soft
2 excessively showy ⟨His *loud* Hawaiian shirt made him easy to pick out in the crowd.⟩ — see GAUDY
lounge *n* a long upholstered piece of furniture designed for several sitters ⟨The tired youth stretched out on the *lounge* and breathed a huge sigh of relief.⟩ — see COUCH
lounge *vb* **1** to refrain from labor or exertion ⟨decided to *lounge* in bed for a little while longer⟩ — see REST 1
2 to spend time doing nothing ⟨After putting in tons of overtime at the office, all we wanted to do on vacation was *lounge* around.⟩ — see IDLE
louse *n* a person whose behavior is offensive to others ⟨I can't believe you're willing to spend time with that lying *louse*!⟩ — see JERK 1
louse up *vb* **1** to make a mistake ⟨Everything is riding on this project, so we can't afford to *louse up*.⟩ — see ERR 1
2 to make or do (something) in a clumsy or unskillful way ⟨I *loused up* the wallpapering job in the bedroom—the seams show too much.⟩ — see BOTCH
lousy *adj* **1** arousing or deserving of one's loathing and disgust ⟨Why, you *lousy* cheater!⟩ — see CONTEMPTIBLE 1
2 falling short of a standard ⟨I actually play a pretty *lousy* game of tennis.⟩ — see BAD 1
3 extremely unsatisfactory ⟨a *lousy* meal that we shouldn't have had to pay for⟩ — see WRETCHED 1
4 of low quality ⟨a tacky store selling *lousy* souvenirs⟩ — see CHEAP 2
5 possessing or covered with great numbers or amounts of something specified ⟨a Manhattan neighborhood that is *lousy* with wannabe actors⟩ — see RIFE
lout *n* **1** a big clumsy often slow-witted person ⟨Watch where you're going, you big *lout*!⟩ — see OAF 1
2 a person whose behavior is offensive to others ⟨Howard's rude behavior at the country club earned him a reputation as a *lout*.⟩ — see JERK 1

loutish *adj* having or showing crudely insensitive or impolite manners ⟨temper tantrums and other *loutish* behavior⟩ — see CLOWNISH

lovable *also* **loveable** *adj* having qualities that tend to make one loved ⟨She was a *lovable* child, always helpful and kind.⟩
synonyms adorable, darling, dear, disarming, endearing, precious, sweet, winning, winsome
related words embraceable, kissable; beloved, cherished, favored, favorite, loved, treasured; attractive, beautiful, desirable, lovely; alluring, appealing, captivating, charming, enchanting, engaging, entrancing, fascinating, fetching; admirable, likable (*or* likeable), reputable, respectable; affable, agreeable, cheerful, cordial, friendly, genial, good-natured, good-tempered, gracious, kind, nice, pleasant; delightful, pleasing
near antonyms unloved; contemptible, disagreeable, distasteful, heinous, horrible, lousy, nasty, offensive, unlikable, unpleasant, wretched; frightful, grotesque, hideous, ill-favored, monstrous, repellent (*also* repellant), repugnant, repulsive; ugly, unattractive, unsightly, vile; appalling, awful, dreadful, foul, horrendous, horrid, nauseating, noisome, obnoxious, obscene, revolting, shocking, sickening
antonyms abhorrent, abominable, detestable, hateful, loathsome, odious, unlovable

love *n* **1** a feeling of strong or constant regard for and dedication to someone ⟨Her *love* for her children was truly selfless.⟩
synonyms affection, attachment, devotedness, devotion, fondness, passion
related words appetite, fancy, favor, like, liking, partiality, preference, relish, taste; craving, crush, desire, infatuation, longing, lust, yearning; ardor, eagerness, enthusiasm, fervor, zeal; appreciation, esteem, estimation, regard, respect; allegiance, faithfulness, fealty, fidelity, loyalty, steadfastness
near antonyms animosity, antagonism, antipathy, aversion, disfavor, dislike, enmity, hostility; abhorrence, disgust, repugnance, repulsion, revulsion
antonyms abomination, hate, hatred, loathing, rancor
2 a person with whom one is in love ⟨She is the *love* of my life!⟩ — see SWEETHEART
3 positive regard for something ⟨a *love* of chocolate, which I will pay anything to indulge⟩ — see LIKING
4 a brief romantic relationship ⟨He refused to discuss past *loves.*⟩ — see AFFAIR 1

love *vb* **1** to hold dear ⟨patriots who *loved* their country well enough to die for it⟩
synonyms appreciate, cherish, prize, treasure, value
related words delight (in), dig, enjoy, fancy, groove (on), like, relish, revel (in); admire, apprize, esteem, regard, respect, revere, reverence, venerate; enshrine, memorialize; adore, caress, dote (on), idolize, worship
phrases set store by (*or* set store on)
near antonyms abhor, abominate, despise, detest, execrate, hate, loathe; disdain, scorn, slight, sniff (at), snub; bad-mouth, belittle, cry down, decry, deprecate, depreciate, disparage, minimize, put down, write off
antonyms disvalue
2 to feel passion, devotion, or tenderness for ⟨a husband who *loves* his wife more than anything⟩
synonyms adore, cherish, worship
related words adulate, canonize, deify, idealize, idolize; revere, reverence, venerate; delight (in), dote (on)
phrases carry a torch for (*or* carry the torch for), fall for, lose one's heart (to)
near antonyms antagonize, displease; disapprove (of), disfavor, dislike; disgust, nauseate, repel, repulse, revolt, sicken, turn off

antonyms abhor, abominate, despise, detest, execrate, hate, loathe
3 to take pleasure in ⟨I *love* playing Frisbee in the summer rain.⟩ — see ENJOY 1
4 to touch or handle in a tender or loving manner ⟨The baby responded to my caresses and kisses by *loving* me right back.⟩ — see FONDLE

love affair *n* **1** a brief romantic relationship ⟨The tabloids feel obliged to keep us informed of the *love affairs* of celebrities, whether we care to know or not.⟩ — see AFFAIR 1
2 positive regard for something ⟨a group of young men united by their *love affair* with the muscle car⟩ — see LIKING

loved *adj* granted special treatment or attention ⟨Her grandparents' constant doting made her feel especially *loved.*⟩ — see DARLING 1

loveliness *n* the qualities in a person or thing that as a whole give pleasure to the senses ⟨Our daughter was a vision of *loveliness* in her prom dress.⟩ — see BEAUTY 1

lovely *adj* **1** of the very best kind ⟨thanked their hosts for the *lovely* time they had at the party⟩ — see EXCELLENT
2 very pleasing to look at ⟨a *lovely* painting of young girls in their summer dresses⟩ — see BEAUTIFUL 1

lover *n* a person with a strong and habitual liking for something ⟨an enthusiastic *lover* of all kinds of team sports⟩ — see FAN

loving *adj* **1** feeling or showing love ⟨They were a *loving* family, supporting each other when times were bad.⟩
synonyms adoring, affectionate, devoted, fond, tender, tenderhearted
related words caring, compassionate, considerate, cordial, doting, forgiving, kind, understanding, warmhearted; ardent, fervent, impassioned, passionate, warm; enamored, infatuated, lovesick; mushy, romantic, sappy, sentimental; brotherly, fatherly, motherly, sisterly
near antonyms aloof, antisocial, cool, detached, distant, dry, frosty, indifferent, pitiless, remote, reserved, standoffish, unbending, uncaring, unfeeling; disaffected, unconcerned, uninvolved; cold, frigid, unfriendly; callous, cold-blooded, heartless, pitiless, ruthless, unromantic, unsentimental
antonyms unloving
2 taking, showing, or involving great care and effort ⟨The homemade costume clearly showed the *loving* work that had gone into it.⟩ — see PAINSTAKING

low *adj* **1** being near the equator ⟨We took a cruise to the *low* northern latitudes.⟩
synonyms equatorial, tropical
related words semitropical (*also* semitropic), subtropical (*also* subtropic)
near antonyms temperate
antonyms polar
2 belonging to or characteristic of an early level of skill or development ⟨Once considered the latest thing, electric typewriters now look like *low* technology indeed.⟩ — see PRIMITIVE 1
3 belonging to the class of people of low social or economic rank ⟨People, both high and *low*, have been worshipping in this cathedral for centuries.⟩ — see IGNOBLE 1
4 feeling unhappiness ⟨I was feeling *low*, and wanted to do something exciting to cheer myself up.⟩ — see SAD 1
5 having a low musical pitch or range ⟨The tuba's *low* notes made the floor vibrate.⟩ — see DEEP 2
6 having relatively little height ⟨The *low* hedge surrounding the garden wasn't meant to keep anything out, just to look pretty.⟩ — see SHORT 1
7 lacking bodily strength ⟨The weeklong bout of the flu laid her *low*.⟩ — see WEAK 1

8 lacking in refinement or good taste ⟨Jokes about toilets are generally considered *low* humor.⟩ — see COARSE 2

9 not following or in accordance with standards of honor and decency ⟨*Low* tactics of that sort will not be tolerated on this hockey team.⟩ — see IGNOBLE 2

10 not loud in pitch or volume ⟨murmured her answer in a *low* voice⟩ — see SOFT 1

11 costing little ⟨Gas is *low* right now, but prices will inevitably rise this summer, when people start driving more.⟩ — see CHEAP 1

12 of, relating to, or located at the bottom ⟨currently enjoys a *low* standing in the polls⟩ — see BOTTOM

13 not coming up to an expected measure or meeting a particular need ⟨Levels for school volunteers remain *low*, at least compared to what was expected.⟩ — see SHORT 3

14 no longer living ⟨livestock laid *low* by the deadly virus⟩ — see DEAD 1

lowbred *adj* lacking in refinement or good taste ⟨offended by such *lowbred* behavior⟩ — see COARSE 2

lowbrow *adj* lacking in refinement or good taste ⟨audience members put off by the *lowbrow* humor⟩ — see COARSE 2

lowbrow *n* a person who is chiefly interested in material comfort and is hostile or indifferent to art and culture ⟨The town's *lowbrows* think that the school's music program is a complete waste of taxpayers' money.⟩ — see PHILISTINE

lowdown *n* information not generally available to the public ⟨Have you heard the *lowdown* on the new chairman of the department?⟩ — see DOPE 1

lower *adj* **1** having not so great importance or rank as another ⟨a *lower* position in the company⟩ — see LESSER

2 situated lower down ⟨This book goes on the *lower* shelf.⟩ — see INFERIOR 1

¹lower *vb* **1** to cause to fall intentionally or unintentionally ⟨Workmen slowly *lowered* the heavy statue into place.⟩ — see DROP 1

2 to go to a lower level especially abruptly ⟨Prices of the new type of televisions *lowered* considerably as competition and sales increased.⟩ — see DROP 2

3 to make smaller in amount, volume, or extent ⟨Tom decided to *lower* his career ambitions to something more achievable.⟩ — see DECREASE 1

4 to grow less in scope or intensity especially gradually ⟨The noise of the jet engine *lowered* as the plane disappeared in the distance.⟩ — see DECREASE 2

5 to reduce to a lower standing in one's own eyes or in others' eyes ⟨How could you *lower* yourself by passing off someone else's work as your own?⟩ — see HUMBLE 1

6 to diminish the price or value of ⟨Over time, inflation *lowers* incomes and savings in terms of actual buying power.⟩ — see DEPRECIATE 1

²lower *also* **lour** *vb* **1** to take on a gloomy or forbidding look ⟨The sky *lowered* overhead, threatening a fierce thunderstorm.⟩ — see DARKEN 1

2 to look with anger or disapproval ⟨The motorist *lowered* at the driver who had cut in front of her.⟩ — see FROWN 1

lower *also* **lour** *n* a twisting of the facial features in disgust or disapproval ⟨He turned to see the scornful *lower* on her face.⟩ — see GRIMACE

lower–class *adj* belonging to the class of people of low social or economic rank ⟨They were finally earning enough to get out of the *lower-class* tax bracket.⟩ — see IGNOBLE 1

lowered *adj* directed down ⟨She wouldn't look at me, preferring instead to just sit there with *lowered* eyes.⟩ — see DOWNCAST 1

lowering *also* **louring** *adj* **1** covered over by clouds ⟨The *lowering* sky made us think twice about going to the park.⟩ — see OVERCAST

2 harsh and threatening in manner or appearance ⟨We chose our next words carefully, mindful of the *lowering* expression on her face.⟩ — see GRIM 1

lowest *adj* being the least in amount, number, or size possible ⟨I play my radio at the *lowest* volume, but the neighbors still complain about the noise.⟩ — see MINIMAL

low–grade *adj* of low quality ⟨plumbing fixtures that were made out of *low-grade* materials⟩ — see CHEAP 2

lowliness *n* the absence of any feelings of being better than others ⟨That saint is often held up as a role model for her piety and unaffected *lowliness*.⟩ — see HUMILITY

lowly *adj* **1** belonging to the class of people of low social or economic rank ⟨a tycoon who struggled all his life to overcome his *lowly* origins⟩ — see IGNOBLE 1

2 not having or showing any feelings of superiority, self-assertiveness, or showiness ⟨a *lowly* blacksmith who lived in a small cottage at the edge of town⟩ — see HUMBLE 1

lowly *adv* in a manner showing no signs of pride or self-assertion ⟨*Lowly* bowing before his king, he accepted his knighthood.⟩

synonyms deferentially, humbly, meanly, meekly, modestly, sheepishly, submissively

related words obsequiously, servilely, subserviently; fearfully, timidly; bashfully, diffidently, self-deprecatingly, shyly, timorously; courteously, politely, respectfully

phrases cap in hand

near antonyms discourteously, disdainfully, disrespectfully, impertinently, rashly, recklessly, saucily; impolitely, impudently, rudely, ungraciously

antonyms arrogantly, audaciously, brashly, brazenly, contemptuously, haughtily, huffily, imperiously, loftily, pompously, presumptuously, pretentiously, pridefully, proudly, scornfully

low–lying *adj* having relatively little height ⟨The *low-lying* hills blocked our view of the sea only a little bit.⟩ — see SHORT 1

lowness *n* **1** the quality or state of lacking refinement or good taste ⟨The *lowness* of the comedian's humor is something movie fans either love or hate.⟩ — see VULGARITY 1

2 the quality or state of lacking physical strength or vigor ⟨Her lingering illness reduced her to a state of *lowness* she had never known before.⟩ — see WEAKNESS 1

low–pressure *adj* having a relaxed, casual manner ⟨a *low-pressure* boss who lets employees do their work without looking over their shoulders⟩ — see EASYGOING 1

low–spirited *adj* feeling unhappiness ⟨The captain tried to cheer up her *low-spirited* teammates after their big loss.⟩ — see SAD 1

loyal *adj* firm in one's allegiance to someone or something ⟨We remain *loyal* to the ideals for which this organization stands.⟩ — see FAITHFUL 1

loyalist *n* a person who loves his or her country and supports its interests and policies ⟨die-hard *loyalists* engaging in espionage against the revolutionaries⟩ — see PATRIOT

loyalty *n* adherence to something to which one is bound by a pledge or duty ⟨There was no denying that dog's *loyalty* to his owner.⟩ — see FIDELITY

lozenge *n* a small mass containing medicine to be taken orally ⟨Take one of these *lozenges* for your cold.⟩ — see PILL 1

lubber *n* a big clumsy often slow-witted person ⟨Although he's something of a *lubber*, everyone agrees that he has a kind heart.⟩ — see OAF 1

lubricate *vb* to coat (something) with a slippery substance in order to reduce friction ⟨It's not a good idea to use olive oil to *lubricate* the gears in an appliance.⟩

synonyms grease, oil, slick, wax

related words bathe, douse (*also* dowse), drench, soak, souse, wash, water, wet

near antonyms coarsen, rough, roughen; dehydrate, dry, parch, sear

lubricated *adj* having or being a surface so smooth as to greatly reduce traction ⟨The *lubricated* parts of the machine were whirring smoothly.⟩ — see SLICK 1

lucent *adj* **1** easily seen through ⟨the pristine waters of *lucent* mountain streams⟩ — see CLEAR 1

2 giving off or reflecting much light ⟨The moon was a *lucent* orb in the cloudless autumn sky.⟩ — see BRIGHT 1

lucid *adj* **1** giving off or reflecting much light ⟨those *lucid* bands that spread across the arctic sky and are known as the northern lights⟩ — see BRIGHT 1

2 having full use of one's mind and control over one's actions ⟨decided to make out her will while she was still *lucid*⟩ — see SANE

3 not subject to misinterpretation or more than one interpretation ⟨Our boss tried to make his instructions as *lucid* as possible so that everyone would understand what to do.⟩ — see CLEAR 2

lucidity *n* clearness of expression ⟨The *lucidity* of the recipe should ensure a minimum of confusion.⟩ — see SIMPLICITY 2

lucidness *n* clearness of expression ⟨She was impressed by the *lucidness* of her surgeon's explanation of the operation.⟩ — see SIMPLICITY 2

Lucifer *n* the supreme personification of evil often represented as the ruler of hell ⟨*Lucifer* is depicted as a powerful but proud angel who leads a revolt against heaven.⟩ — see DEVIL 1

luck *n* **1** success that is partly the result of chance ⟨Some people have all the *luck*.⟩

synonyms fortunateness, fortune, luckiness

related words blessing, boon, godsend, hit, serendipity, strike, windfall; break, chance, opportunity; coup, stroke

near antonyms knock, misadventure, mishap; adversity, curse, debacle (*also* débâcle), sorrow, tragedy, trouble; calamity, cataclysm, catastrophe, disaster; defeat, failure; accident, casualty; disappointment, lapse, letdown, reversal, reverse, setback, slipup; destiny, doom, fate, lot, portion; hex, jinx

antonyms mischance, misfortune, unluckiness

2 the uncertain course of events ⟨Let's plan our vacation rather than leave everything to *luck*.⟩ — see CHANCE 1

luckiness *n* success that is partly the result of chance ⟨The supposed *luckiness* of a rabbit's foot didn't do much for the rabbit.⟩ — see LUCK 1

luckless *adj* having, prone to, or marked by bad luck ⟨a *luckless* team with the worst record in the league⟩ — see UNLUCKY 1

lucky *adj* **1** having good luck ⟨The *lucky* contestant finished the game show with $10,000.⟩

synonyms fortunate, happy

related words blessed (*also* blest), favored, gifted, privileged; fair, golden, promising; hot

near antonyms disadvantaged

antonyms hapless, ill-fated, ill-starred, luckless, starcrossed, unfortunate, unhappy, unlucky

2 coming or happening by good luck especially unexpectedly ⟨Finding this $20 bill on the way to the candy store was a *lucky* break.⟩ — see FORTUNATE 1

lucrative *adj* yielding a profit ⟨The turnaround specialist's mission was to turn the failing store into a *lucrative* operation.⟩ — see PROFITABLE 1

lucre *n* **1** something (as pieces of stamped metal or printed paper) customarily and legally used as a medium of exchange, a measure of value, or a means of payment ⟨Foreign coins are not acceptable *lucre* in most vending machines in this country.⟩ — see MONEY

2 the amount of money left when expenses are subtracted from the total amount received ⟨The pursuit of *lucre* causes many people to make bad choices.⟩ — see PROFIT 1

ludicrous *adj* **1** causing or intended to cause laughter ⟨the *ludicrous* sight of their teacher in a Halloween costume⟩ — see FUNNY 1

2 so foolish or pointless as to be worthy of scornful laughter ⟨a *ludicrous* and easily detected attempt to forge his father's signature on a note to school⟩ — see RIDICULOUS 1

lug *n* a big clumsy often slow-witted person ⟨Get off of my feet, you big *lug*!⟩ — see OAF 1

lug *vb* **1** to cause to follow by applying steady force on ⟨*lugged* the lawn mower out into the backyard⟩ — see PULL 1

2 to support and take from one place to another ⟨I don't understand why he's always *lugging* all of his books around when his locker is right over there.⟩ — see CARRY 1

lugubrious *adj* **1** causing or marked by an atmosphere lacking in cheer ⟨The diner's dim lighting makes eating there a particularly *lugubrious* experience.⟩ — see GLOOMY 1

2 expressing or suggesting mourning ⟨In Victorian times, people who could affect particularly *lugubrious* expressions were hired to march in funeral processions as professional mourners.⟩ — see MOURNFUL 1

lukewarm *adj* **1** having or giving off heat to a moderate degree ⟨I left the bowl of soup sitting on the counter too long, and now it's *lukewarm*.⟩ — see WARM 1

2 showing little or no interest or enthusiasm ⟨The dentist's lecture on the merits of flossing got only a *lukewarm* response.⟩ — see TEPID 1

lukewarmness *n* the quality or state of being moderate in temperature ⟨The *lukewarmness* of the coffee did nothing for its taste.⟩ — see WARMTH 1

lull *n* a momentary halt in an activity ⟨We took the opportunity of a *lull* in the conversation to announce that we were engaged to be married.⟩ — see PAUSE 1

lull *vb* to free from distress or disturbance ⟨We were *lulled* into a false sense of security.⟩ — see CALM 1

lulling *adj* tending to calm the emotions and relieve stress ⟨The *lulling* sound of a gently flowing stream⟩ — see SOOTHING 1

lumber *n* tree logs as prepared for human use ⟨A huge amount of *lumber* will be needed to build the house.⟩ — see WOOD 1

lumber *vb* **1** to move heavily or clumsily ⟨The elephant *lumbered* through the jungle.⟩

synonyms barge, clump, flounder, lump, plod, pound, scuff, scuffle, shamble, shuffle, slog, slough, stamp, stomp, stumble, stump, tramp, tromp, trudge

related words drag, flop, haul; blunder, careen, dodder, lurch, reel, stagger, sway, teeter, totter, waddle, weave, wobble (*also* wabble)

near antonyms drift, float, hang, hover, poise, waft

antonyms breeze, coast, glide, slide, waltz, whisk

2 to proceed or act clumsily or ineffectually ⟨The novel's plot *lumbers* to its predictable conclusion after 500 long pages.⟩ — see FLOUNDER 1

3 to make a low heavy rolling sound ⟨The horse-drawn wagon *lumbered* along the trail.⟩ — see RUMBLE

4 to place a weight or burden on ⟨preparations that will *lumber* the expedition with unnecessary equipment and supplies⟩ — see LOAD 1

lumberjack *n* a person whose job is to cut down trees ⟨The sawmill gets most of its business from the *lumberjacks* up north.⟩

synonyms jack, logger

related words lumberer; sawyer; forester

luminary *n* **1** a ball-shaped gaseous celestial body that shines by its own light ⟨awed by the vast number of *luminaries* in the night sky⟩ — see STAR 1

2 a person who is widely known and usually much talked about ⟨*Luminaries* from the worlds of sports, entertainment, and politics were at the gala.⟩ — see CELEBRITY 1

luminescence *n* the steady giving off of the form of radiation that makes vision possible ⟨We could see inside the cave even without a flashlight because of the *luminescence* coming from some of the fungus on the walls.⟩ — see LIGHT 1

luminosity *n* the quality or state of having or giving off light ⟨The *luminosity* of the fireflies made for an enchanting nighttime show.⟩ — see BRILLIANCE 1

luminous *adj* **1** giving off or reflecting much light ⟨The *luminous* moon bathed the snow-covered fields with a pearly glow.⟩ — see BRIGHT 1

2 standing above others in rank, importance, or achievement ⟨Some of the most *luminous* writers in the nation's history have graced that magazine's pages.⟩ — see EMINENT

3 not subject to misinterpretation or more than one interpretation ⟨an author with a simple, *luminous* prose style that is free of affectation and pretention⟩ — see CLEAR 2

lump *n* **1** a small uneven mass ⟨She dumped a *lump* of clay on the table and started to sculpt.⟩

synonyms blob, chunk, clod, clot, clump, glob, gob, gobbet, hunk, knob, nub, nubble, nugget, wad

related words drop, globule; block, body, bulk; particle, piece, portion; bit, chip, crumb, granule, morsel, nubbin, patch, scrap

2 a small rounded mass of swollen tissue ⟨I got a good-sized *lump* on my head from that fall.⟩ — see BUMP 1

3 an abnormal mass of tissue ⟨She was advised by her doctor to get regular mammograms to detect unusual *lumps*.⟩ — see GROWTH 1

4 failure to win a contest ⟨You can't win all the time, so learn to take your *lumps* in stride.⟩ — see DEFEAT 1

5 a big clumsy often slow-witted person ⟨Standing next to those ballet dancers, with their delicate features and lithe bodies, I felt like a *lump*.⟩ — see OAF 1

lump *vb* **1** to bring together in one body or place ⟨When we *lumped* all of our pocket change together, we found that we had just enough to buy a carton of ice cream.⟩ — see GATHER 1

2 to move heavily or clumsily ⟨While I was on crutches, I was *lumping* about the house like an elephant.⟩ — see LUMBER 1

lumpy *adj* **1** having small pieces or lumps spread throughout ⟨The *lumpy* mashed potatoes were cold as well.⟩ — see CHUNKY 1

2 not having a level or smooth surface ⟨Before painting, we had to sand the *lumpy* surface to make it smooth.⟩ — see UNEVEN 1

lurch *vb* **1** to make a series of unsteady side-to-side motions ⟨The boat *lurched* with every crash of a wave.⟩ — see ROCK 1

2 to move forward while swaying from side to side ⟨Dressed in his zombie costume, the boy *lurched* down the street in his quest for Halloween candy.⟩ — see STAGGER 1

lure *n* **1** something that persuades one to perform an action for pleasure or gain ⟨The promise of easy money is always the *lure* for some people to try get-rich-quick schemes.⟩

synonyms allurement, bait, enticement, temptation, turn-on

related words appeal, call; attraction, encouragement, goad, impetus, impulse, incentive, inducement, motiva-

tion, persuasion, seducement, seduction, spur, stimulus; decoy, snare, trap

near antonyms alarm (*also* alarum), alert, caution, forewarning, notice, warning

2 something used to attract animals to a hook or into a trap ⟨The fish simply didn't seem to like the *lure* I was using, so I didn't catch a thing.⟩ — see BAIT 1

3 the act or pressure of giving in to a desire especially when ill-advised ⟨The *lure* of the video game was distracting me from my studies.⟩ — see TEMPTATION 1

lure *vb* to lead away from a usual or proper course by offering some pleasure or advantage ⟨*lured* the bear out of its den⟩

synonyms allure, bait, beguile, betray, decoy, entice, lead on, seduce, solicit, tempt

related words draw in, inveigle, persuade, rope (in), snow; catch, enmesh (*also* immesh), ensnare, entrap, mesh, snare, tangle, trap; bewitch, captivate, charm, enchant, fascinate, magnetize, wile

near antonyms alert, caution, forewarn, ward (off), warn; drive (away *or* off), repulse

lurid *adj* **1** extremely disturbing or repellent ⟨We quickly drove past the *lurid* scene of the crash.⟩ — see HORRIBLE 1

2 lacking a healthy skin color ⟨The doctor was alarmed by the patient's *lurid* complexion.⟩ — see PALE 2

3 arousing a strong and usually superficial interest or emotional reaction ⟨the *lurid* news reports about the romance between the two Hollywood stars⟩ — see SENSATIONAL 1

luring *adj* having an often mysterious or magical power to attract ⟨the *luring* sight of sparkling gemstones in a jewelry-store window⟩ — see FASCINATING 1

lurk *vb* **1** to move about in a sly or secret manner ⟨We caught a glimpse of someone *lurking* around the corner.⟩ — see SNEAK 1

2 to remain out of sight ⟨Watch out for snakes *lurking* in the tall grass!⟩ — see ¹HIDE 3

lurker *n* someone who acts in a sly and secret manner ⟨Suddenly, the mysterious *lurker* leapt out into the light!⟩ — see SNEAK

luscious *adj* **1** very pleasing to the sense of taste ⟨a *luscious* strawberry bursting with juice⟩ — see DELICIOUS 1

2 pleasing to the physical senses ⟨*luscious* silk fabric that slid across her hands⟩ — see SENSUAL

3 giving pleasure or contentment to the mind or senses ⟨the *luscious* thought that while she was basking on the beach she didn't need to do her usual tasks at the office⟩ — see PLEASANT 1

lusciousness *n* the quality of being delicious ⟨It was hard to resist the decadent *lusciousness* of the three-layer chocolate cake.⟩ — see DELICIOUSNESS

lush *adj* **1** covered with a thick, healthy natural growth ⟨They loved to go for picnics in the *lush* woodlands.⟩

synonyms green, leafy, luxuriant, overgrown, verdant

related words fat, fecund, fertile, fruitful, productive, prolific, rich; dense

near antonyms bleak, depleted, impoverished, infertile, poor, stark, unproductive; arid, dead, desert, dry, parched, sere (*also* sear), waterless

antonyms barren, leafless

2 growing thickly and vigorously ⟨*Lush* dandelions had turned the meadow into a sea of yellow.⟩ — see RANK 1

3 very pleasing to the sense of taste ⟨*lush* desserts that are well worth the calories⟩ — see DELICIOUS 1

4 marked by vigorous growth and well-being especially economically ⟨Those were *lush* times for the tech industry.⟩ — see PROSPEROUS 1

5 pleasing to the physical senses ⟨I could listen to the baritone's *lush* voice for hours.⟩ — see SENSUAL

6 producing abundantly ⟨His *lush* fields were the envy of neighboring farmers.⟩ — see FERTILE

lust *n* **1** intense sexual desire ⟨was filled with *lust*⟩
synonyms ardor, passion
related words lasciviousness, lewdness, libidinousness, licentiousness, salaciousness, wantonness
near antonyms frigidity

2 urgent desire or interest ⟨vacation tours for people with a *lust* for adventure⟩ — see EAGERNESS

lust (for *or* **after)** *vb* to have an earnest wish to own or enjoy ⟨I'm *lusting after* that job.⟩ — see DESIRE 1

luster *or* **lustre** *n* **1** brightness created by light reflected from a surface ⟨The Hope diamond is famous for its brilliant *luster*.⟩ — see SHINE 1

2 the quality or state of having or giving off light ⟨On a clear night at sea the stars seem to take on a magical *luster*.⟩ — see BRILLIANCE 1

luster *or* **lustre** *vb* to shoot forth bursts of light ⟨Her pearl necklace *lustered* softly in the candlelight of the restaurant.⟩ — see FLASH 1

lusterless *adj* lacking a surface luster or gloss ⟨A small tombstone of *lusterless* granite marks his modest grave.⟩ — see MATTE

lustful *adj* having a strong sexual desire ⟨had a *lustful* dream⟩
synonyms lascivious, lewd, licentious, passionate, wanton
related words aroused, excited; easy, fast, loose, promiscuous; dissipated, dissolute, libertine; corrupt, debased, debauched, decadent, degenerate, degraded, demoralized, depraved, dissipated, dissolute, immoral, indecent
near antonyms celibate, chaste, decent, immaculate, modest, moral, pure, virtuous; maidenly, virginal; innocent; priggish, prim, prudish, puritanical, straitlaced (*or* straightlaced)
antonyms frigid

lustiness *n* the quality or state of having abundant or intense activity ⟨campaign volunteers working for their candidate with a *lustiness* that is inspiring⟩ — see VITALITY 1

lustrous *adj* **1** giving off or reflecting much light ⟨The *lustrous* finish on the satin bedspread adds to the feeling of luxury.⟩ — see BRIGHT 1

2 having a shiny surface or finish ⟨*Lustrous* silver jewelry adorned her neck.⟩ — see GLOSSY

lusty *adj* **1** having active strength of body or mind ⟨the *lusty* young rowers on the college crew team⟩ — see VIGOROUS 1

2 not showing weakness or uncertainty ⟨a *lusty* spirit of adventure⟩ — see FIRM 1

3 having an abundance of some characteristic quality (as flavor) ⟨Such a *lusty* sauce calls for an equally hearty pasta.⟩ — see FULL-BODIED

luxuriant *adj* **1** covered with a thick, healthy natural growth ⟨an older man who still has a *luxuriant* head of hair⟩ — see LUSH 1

2 growing thickly and vigorously ⟨a *luxuriant* coat of fur⟩ — see RANK 1

3 producing abundantly ⟨*luxuriant* soil that yields endless fields of grain⟩ — see FERTILE

4 showing obvious signs of wealth and comfort ⟨The fashion model always wore the most *luxuriant* outfits.⟩ — see LUXURIOUS

luxurious *adj* showing obvious signs of wealth and comfort ⟨The *luxurious* apartment was filled with the latest electronic gadgets and fine works of art.⟩
synonyms deluxe, lavish, luxuriant, luxury, opulent, palatial, plush, sumptuous
related words costly, dear, expensive, precious, premium, rich; extravagant, grandiose, ostentatious, pretentious, showy; august, awesome, baronial, beautiful, gorgeous, grand, imposing, impressive, kingly, magnificent, majestic, monumental, noble, regal, royal, splendid, stately
near antonyms economical, frugal, meager (*or* meagre), spare, stingy, thrifty
antonyms ascetic (*also* ascetical), austere, humble

luxuriously *adv* in a luxurious manner ⟨We welcomed the opportunity to live *luxuriously* while on the ocean liner.⟩ — see HIGH

luxury *adj* showing obvious signs of wealth and comfort ⟨a *luxury* ski lodge for those who prefer not to rough it⟩ — see LUXURIOUS

luxury *n* **1** something adding to pleasure or comfort but not absolutely necessary ⟨A private yacht is a *luxury*.⟩
synonyms amenity, comfort, extra, frill, indulgence, superfluity
related words extravagance, nonessential; delicacy, nicety, treat; accessory (*also* accessary), accoutrement (*or* accouterment), bells and whistles, option
antonyms basic, essential, fundamental, must, necessity, requirement

2 something that adds to one's ease of living ⟨Having one's own bathroom is one of life's greatest *luxuries*.⟩ — see COMFORT 2

lying *adj* telling or containing lies ⟨That *lying* salesman told me that the used car had never been in an accident.⟩ — see DISHONEST 1

lynx–eyed *adj* having unusually keen vision ⟨The *lynx-eyed* copy editor never seemed to miss an error in the reporters' work.⟩ — see SHARP-EYED

lyric *adj* **1** having a pleasantly flowing quality suggestive of music ⟨They performed a slow, *lyric* dance for the audience.⟩
synonyms euphonious, lyrical, mellifluous, mellow, melodic, melodious, musical
related words golden, sweet
near antonyms disconnected, staccato; discordant, dissonant, grating, harsh, inharmonious, jarring, strident, unmelodious, unmusical
antonyms unlyrical

2 having qualities suggestive of poetry ⟨The film's *lyric* photography really enhanced its romantic mood.⟩ — see POETIC

lyric *n* **1** a composition using rhythm and often rhyme to create a lyrical effect ⟨Would you care to read your short *lyric* aloud?⟩ — see POEM

2 a short musical composition for the human voice often with instrumental accompaniment ⟨The guitarist sang a gentle *lyric* while playing.⟩ — see SONG 1

lyrical *adj* **1** having a pleasantly flowing quality suggestive of music ⟨The *lyrical* cadences of voice-over narration give the film a very poignant quality.⟩ — see LYRIC 1

2 having qualities suggestive of poetry ⟨The photographer achieves a very *lyrical* effect with her intentionally blurred images of flowers growing in the wild.⟩ — see POETIC

M

ma *n* a female human parent ⟨I told my *ma* that on Mother's Day we'd be dining at the town's fanciest restaurant.⟩ — see MOTHER

macabre *adj* extremely disturbing or repellent ⟨a *macabre* movie about animated corpses⟩ — see HORRIBLE 1

Machiavellian *adj* not guided by or showing a concern for what is right ⟨yet another tale of a power-mad dictator with a *Machiavellian* plan to take over the world⟩ — see UNPRINCIPLED

machinate *vb* **1** to engage in a secret plan to accomplish evil or unlawful ends ⟨a trio of courtiers who were discovered to be *machinating* against the queen⟩ — see PLOT

2 to plan out usually with subtle skill or care ⟨The hackers *machinated* a way to steal customer information from the company's website.⟩ — see ENGINEER

machination *n* a secret plan for accomplishing evil or unlawful ends ⟨His plans were defeated by the *machinations* of his enemies.⟩ — see PLOT 1

machine *n* **1** a device that changes energy into mechanical motion ⟨a *machine* that washes dishes for you⟩ — see ENGINE

2 a self-propelled passenger vehicle on four wheels ⟨That Corvette is a *machine* that anyone would love to own.⟩ — see CAR

machinery *n* something used to achieve an end ⟨sincerely believes that the *machinery* of government can be used to better people's lives⟩ — see AGENT 1

macrocosm *n* the whole body of things observed or assumed ⟨Almost the entirety of the vast *macrocosm* remains beyond our reach.⟩ — see UNIVERSE

mad *adj* **1** feeling or showing anger ⟨The constant harassment from telemarketers finally made her good and *mad*.⟩ — see ANGRY

2 marked by great and often stressful excitement or activity ⟨a *mad* rush to finish packing before the trip⟩ — see FURIOUS 1

mad *n* an intense emotional state of displeasure with someone or something ⟨Watch out, the boss has got a bit of a *mad* on just now.⟩ — see ANGER

mad (about) *adj* filled with an intense or excessive love for ⟨He's virtually inseparable from his new girlfriend and seems to be just *mad about* her.⟩ — see ENAMORED (OF)

madcap *adj* foolishly adventurous or bold ⟨a *madcap* scheme to go over Niagara Falls in a barrel⟩ — see FOOLHARDY 1

madcap *n* a person who seeks out very dangerous or foolhardy adventures with no apparent fear ⟨an incorrigible *madcap* who loves drag racing and white-water rafting⟩ — see DAREDEVIL

madden *vb* **1** to cause to go insane or as if insane ⟨The endless swarms of mosquitoes all but *maddened* the explorers.⟩ — see CRAZE

2 to make angry ⟨Her perpetual tardiness *maddened* her friends to no end.⟩ — see ANGER

maddening *adj* causing annoyance ⟨After a few days, she found the monotonous work to be absolutely *maddening*.⟩ — see ANNOYING

made–up *adj* not real and existing only in the imagination ⟨The bogeyman was one of those *made-up* monsters whose sole purpose was to threaten children.⟩ — see IMAGINARY

madhouse *n* a place of uproar or confusion ⟨Our house is always a *madhouse* on school mornings, with five kids and two dogs running around.⟩

synonyms babel, bedlam, circus, three-ring circus

related words bustle, commotion, pandemonium, racket, ruckus, tumult, turmoil; brouhaha, clamor, clatter, din, hubbub, noise; chaos, confusion, disarrangement, disarray, disorder, havoc, hell, mess, muss, shambles

near antonyms arcadia, heaven, paradise, utopia; calm, lull, peace, respite; hush, quiet, silence, stillness

madly *adv* **1** in a confused and reckless manner ⟨dashed *madly* around the house during last-minute preparations for the party⟩ — see HELTER-SKELTER 1

2 in an enthusiastic manner ⟨The young singer has been *madly* praised by the critics.⟩ — see SKY-HIGH

madman *n* a person who seeks out very dangerous or foolhardy adventures with no apparent fear ⟨As far as I'm concerned, anyone who likes skydiving is a *madman*.⟩ — see DAREDEVIL

madness *n* **1** lack of good sense or judgment ⟨To do something so reckless would be sheer *madness*.⟩ — see FOOLISHNESS 1

2 an intense emotional state of displeasure with someone or something ⟨The debating candidates tried to goad each other to *madness*.⟩ — see ANGER

maelstrom *n* water moving rapidly in a circle with a hollow in the center ⟨Our rubber raft got caught in a *maelstrom* in a particularly rough stretch of white water.⟩ — see WHIRLPOOL

maestro *n* a person with a high level of knowledge or skill in a field ⟨a *maestro* of the violin⟩ — see EXPERT

Mafia *n* a group involved in secret or criminal activities ⟨was accused of being a member of the local *Mafia*⟩ — see ¹RING 1

magazine *n* **1** a building for storing goods ⟨The village kept a *magazine* where people left common supplies.⟩ — see STOREHOUSE

2 a place where military arms are stored ⟨The *magazine* is heavily guarded to prevent theft.⟩ — see ARMORY

3 a publication that appears at regular intervals ⟨a weekly sports *magazine*⟩ — see JOURNAL

magic *adj* **1** being or appearing to be under a magic spell ⟨a *magic* castle in which even the furniture comes to life⟩ — see ENCHANTED

2 having seemingly supernatural qualities or powers ⟨Truth seekers of all sorts seem to be attracted to this *magic* spot in the desert.⟩ — see MYSTIC 1

magic *n* **1** the power to control natural forces through supernatural means ⟨He claimed that he could summon a storm through *magic*.⟩

synonyms bewitchment, conjuring, devilry (*or* deviltry), enchantment, mojo, necromancy, sorcery, witchcraft, witchery, wizardry

related words abracadabra, amulet, charm, fetish (*also* fetich), mascot, talisman; conjuration, incantation, spell; curse, hex, jinx; augury, crystal gazing, divining, forecasting, foreknowing, foreseeing, foretelling, fortunetelling, predicting, presaging, prognosticating, prophesying, soothsaying; occultism, spiritualism; augur, omen; exorcism; alchemy

near antonyms science

2 the art or skill of performing tricks or illusions for entertainment ⟨The couple hired an entertainer to perform *magic* for their child's 10th birthday party.⟩

synonyms conjuring, legerdemain, prestidigitation

related words trickery

phrases sleight of hand

3 the power of irresistible attraction ⟨a leader so charismatic that his appeal was like *magic*⟩ — see CHARM 2

magical *adj* **1** being or appearing to be under a magic spell ⟨The gym was decorated to resemble a *magical* wonderland for the party.⟩ — see ENCHANTED

2 being so extraordinary or abnormal as to suggest powers which violate the laws of nature ⟨Modern aviation must seem *magical* to someone who doesn't understand basic aeronautics.⟩ — see SUPERNATURAL 2

3 having seemingly supernatural qualities or powers ⟨The child prodigy's musical talent is so spectacular that it seems *magical*.⟩ — see MYSTIC 1

magician *n* **1** a person skilled in using supernatural forces ⟨The *magician* was able to summon the birds of the air and the beasts of the field with a simple spell.⟩

synonyms conjurer (*or* conjuror), enchanter, necromancer, sorcerer, witch, wizard

related words enchantress, hag, hex, sorceress; warlock; occultist; medicine man, shaman, shamanist, witch doctor; crystal gazer, diviner, foreseer, fortune-teller, prognosticator, prophesier, prophet, seer, soothsayer; medium; exorciser, exorcist

2 one who practices tricks and illusions for entertainment ⟨The famous *magician's* signature trick was pulling a rabbit out of a hat.⟩

synonyms conjurer (*or* conjuror), illusionist, prestidigitator, trickster

related words enchanter, enchantress

magistrate *n* a public official having authority to decide questions of law ⟨chose to take their case before the local *magistrate*⟩ — see JUDGE 2

magnanimous *adj* having, characterized by, or arising from a dignified and generous nature ⟨a *magnanimous* donation to the town's animal shelter⟩ — see NOBLE 2

magnanimously *adv* in a manner befitting a person of the highest character and ideals ⟨Jill *magnanimously* congratulated her opponent, who won the match with the aid of some obviously biased refereeing.⟩ — see GREATLY 1

magnate *n* a person of rank, power, or influence in a particular field ⟨a studio *magnate* who had the biggest stars in Hollywood at his beck and call⟩

synonyms baron, captain, czar (*also* tsar *or* tzar), king, mogul, monarch, prince, tycoon

related words big shot, bigwig, figure, nabob, notable, personage; celebrity, personality, star, superstar; deity, demigod, god

near antonyms lightweight, small-timer; inferior, subordinate, underling; nobody, nothing, zero

magnet *n* something that attracts interest ⟨The giant theme park is a *magnet* for tourists to the area.⟩

synonyms attraction, draw, lodestone (*also* loadstone)

related words capital, center, cynosure, mecca, pole; allure, allurement, bait, enticement, fascination, lure, temptation, turn-on; appeal, call; incentive, inducement, persuasion, spur, stimulus; curiosity, sight(s)

magnetic *adj* having an often mysterious or magical power to attract ⟨a cult leader who attracted followers with his *magnetic* gaze⟩ — see FASCINATING 1

magnetism *n* the power of irresistible attraction ⟨She managed to win the election by sheer personal *magnetism*.⟩ — see CHARM 2

magnetize *vb* to attract or delight as if by magic ⟨The store's gorgeous window displays never fail to *magnetize* shoppers and sightseers.⟩ — see CHARM 1

magnification *n* the representation of something in terms that go beyond the facts ⟨Most movies don't deal in reality but in a *magnification* of reality where everything is more intense.⟩ — see EXAGGERATION

magnificence *n* impressiveness of beauty on a large scale ⟨The *magnificence* of the great castle hallway is beyond description.⟩

synonyms augustness, brilliance, gloriousness, glory, gorgeousness, grandeur, grandness, majesty, nobility, nobleness, resplendence, splendor, stateliness, stupendousness, sublimeness, superbness

related words awesomeness, formidability, marvelousness, wonderfulness, wondrousness; dignity, elegance, grace; lavishness, luxuriance, luxuriousness, luxury, opulence, princeliness, richness, sumptuousness; grandiosity, ostentation, pretentiousness; elaborateness, flashiness, gaudiness, ornateness, poshness, ritziness, showiness, swankiness; extraordinariness, remarkableness

magnificent *adj* large and impressive in size, grandeur, extent, or conception ⟨a *magnificent* mansion that still takes away the breath of visitors⟩ — see GRAND 1

magnify *vb* **1** to add to the interest of by including made-up details ⟨There's no need to *magnify* the events of your trip in order to make it seem impressive.⟩ — see EMBROIDER

2 to assign a high status or value to ⟨His newfound fame as an actor has finally *magnified* him in the eyes of his perennially doubting family.⟩ — see EXALT 1

3 to make markedly greater in measure or degree ⟨The movie's sound effects *magnify* every crash and boom in the action scenes.⟩ — see INTENSIFY

4 to proclaim the glory of ⟨imposing cathedrals that were built to *magnify* the Lord and to inspire awe in worshippers⟩ — see PRAISE 1

magnitude *n* **1** the quality or state of being important ⟨The *magnitude* of the issue can scarcely be overstated.⟩ — see IMPORTANCE

2 the quality or state of being very large ⟨The mountain's sheer *magnitude* usually leaves tourists speechless.⟩ — see IMMENSITY

3 the total amount of measurable space or surface occupied by something ⟨The *magnitude* of the planned skyscraper is totally disproportionate with that of the other buildings on the block.⟩ — see ¹SIZE

magnum opus *n* something (as a work of art) that is a great achievement and often its creator's greatest achievement ⟨This symphony is usually considered Beethoven's *magnum opus*.⟩ — see MASTERPIECE

maid *n* **1** a person hired to perform household or personal services ⟨hired a *maid* to take care of the house⟩

synonyms charwoman, domestic, housekeeper, housemaid, maidservant

related words attendant, chambermaid; nursemaid; menial

2 a young unmarried woman ⟨a dance where the fair *maids* and handsome bucks of the village hoped to meet one another⟩ — see GIRL 1

maiden *adj* coming before all others in time or order ⟨The Titanic sank on its *maiden* voyage.⟩ — see FIRST 1

maiden *n* a young unmarried woman ⟨a story about a beautiful *maiden* and her mysterious father⟩ — see GIRL 1

maidservant *n* a person hired to perform household or personal services ⟨a large estate that once had many *maidservants*⟩ — see MAID 1

mail *n* communications or parcels sent or carried through the postal system ⟨Jed began receiving lots of *mail* after he became known as a frequent donor to charities.⟩

synonyms correspondence, matter, parcel post, snail mail

related words airmail, airpost, certified mail, registered mail, rural delivery, rural free delivery, special delivery, special handling; direct mail, junk mail, mailer; card, dispatch, epistle, letter, message, missive, note, postal card, postcard, printed matter

mail *vb* to send through the postal system ⟨If you don't *mail* that letter soon, it's going to arrive late.⟩

synonyms post

related words airmail, frank; address, consign; direct, dispatch, forward, remit, route, ship, transmit, transport; register

near antonyms get

mail carrier *n* a person who delivers mail ⟨Our *mail carrier* always delivers our mail before noon.⟩ — see LETTER CARRIER

mailman *n* a person who delivers mail ⟨The *mailman* usually leaves packages outside the mailbox.⟩ — see LETTER CARRIER

maim *vb* to cause severe or permanent injury to ⟨On-the-job accidents *maim* far too many workers every year.⟩

synonyms cripple, disable, incapacitate, lame, mutilate

related words dismember, hamstring, hobble, paralyze; batter, bruise, mangle, maul, rough (up); gore, lacerate, wing, wound; disfigure, scar; kneecap; break, damage, harm, hurt, impair, injure; bash, beat, belt, bludgeon, buffet, drub, hammer, lace, lambaste (*or* lambast), lick, paste, pelt, pommel, pound, pummel, thump; bang, box, hit, punch, slap, smack, smash, sock, spank, swat, swipe, thrash, thwack, whack; flog, lash, wallop, whip; kill, murder; torment, torture

near antonyms cure, heal, rehabilitate, remedy; doctor, fix, mend, patch; rejuvenate, renew, repair, restore

main *adj* coming before all others in importance ⟨This is the *main* point of the study—everything else is secondary.⟩ — see FOREMOST 1

main *n* **1** muscular strength ⟨All their might and *main* could not budge the stalled car.⟩ — see MUSCLE 1

2 one of the great divisions of land on the globe or the main part of such a division ⟨Islanders periodically traveled back to the *main* for supplies.⟩ — see MAINLAND

3 the main or greater part of something as distinguished from its subordinate parts ⟨The *main* of the tree is still healthy.⟩ — see BODY 1

mainland *n* one of the great divisions of land on the globe or the main part of such a division ⟨The boat back to the *mainland* leaves once every two days.⟩

synonyms continent, main

related words subcontinent, supercontinent

near antonyms island, isle, islet; atoll, barrier reef, cay, coral reef, key; cape, headland, peninsula, promontory

mainly *adv* for the most part ⟨You *mainly* need to focus on improving your golf swing.⟩ — see CHIEFLY

mainstay *n* something or someone to which one looks for support ⟨Mom has been our *mainstay* in this crisis.⟩ — see DEPENDENCE 2

maintain *vb* **1** to keep in good condition ⟨He repairs and *maintains* antique cars as a hobby.⟩

synonyms conserve, keep up, preserve, save

related words service; support, sustain; care (for), husband, manage; defend, guard, protect, safeguard, screen, shield; cure, fix, heal, remedy; mend, patch, rebuild, reconstruct, rehabilitate, rejuvenate, restore

near antonyms disregard, ignore, neglect; break, damage, destroy, harm, hurt, impair, injure, ruin, wreck

2 to continue to declare to be true or proper despite opposition or objections ⟨Part of debating is learning to *maintain* your position in the face of harsh challenges.⟩

synonyms defend, justify, support, uphold

related words advocate, champion, espouse; confirm, vindicate, warrant; affirm, assert, aver, avouch, avow, claim, contend, insist, plead, proclaim, profess, protest, state; argue, debate, discuss; emphasize, stress, underline, underscore

phrases stand up for, stick up for

near antonyms abandon, abjure, forsake, recant, retract, take back, withdraw; reverse, switch; disprove, rebut, refute

3 to pay the living expenses of ⟨We simply cannot afford to *maintain* a horse.⟩ — see SUPPORT 2

4 to state (something) as a reason in support of or against something under consideration ⟨She continued to *maintain* that a sewing machine would end up paying for itself since she could make her own clothes.⟩ — see ARGUE 1

5 to state as a fact usually forcefully ⟨He *maintains* that there is indeed hard evidence for extraterrestrial visitors.⟩ — see CLAIM 1

maintainable *adj* capable of being defended with good reasoning against verbal attack ⟨It is important to choose a *maintainable* position for your thesis.⟩ — see TENABLE 2

maintenance *n* the act or activity of keeping something in an existing and usually satisfactory condition ⟨I was hired to perform basic *maintenance* until the property could be sold.⟩

synonyms conservation, conserving, preservation, preserving, upkeep

related words support, sustaining; care, custody, guardianship; defense, guarding, protection, safeguarding, safekeeping

near antonyms dereliction, disregard, ignoring, inattention, neglect, negligence; damage, demolition, destruction, harm, hurt, injury, ruin, ruination

majestic *adj* **1** having or showing elegance ⟨a *majestic* pillar of society who continues to entertain in grand style⟩ — see ELEGANT 1

2 large and impressive in size, grandeur, extent, or conception ⟨a *majestic* Egyptian pyramid that has enthralled travelers for eons⟩ — see GRAND 1

3 very dignified in form, tone, or style ⟨the *majestic* language and beautiful cadences of the King James Version of the Bible⟩ — see ELEVATED 2

majesty *n* **1** a dignified bearing or appearance befitting someone of royal status ⟨Even as a child, the princess possessed a certain *majesty* that would later serve her well.⟩

synonyms augustness, stateliness

related words high-mindedness, magnanimity, nobility, nobleness; haughtiness, lordliness, pompousness; dignity, poise; gloriousness, grandeur, grandness, greatness, impressiveness, magnificence, resplendence, splendor; class, elegance, grace

2 dignified or restrained beauty of form, appearance, or style ⟨The eagle soared overhead with an impressive *majesty*.⟩ — see ELEGANCE

3 impressiveness of beauty on a large scale ⟨The *majesty* of the Roman Colosseum is breathtaking.⟩ — see MAGNIFICENCE

major *adj* **1** sufficiently large in size, amount, or number to merit attention ⟨With several blockbuster hits under her belt, the actress now commands some *major* cash for appearing in a movie.⟩ — see CONSIDERABLE 1

2 having great meaning or lasting effect ⟨a *major* change in how science is taught in our high schools⟩ — see IMPORTANT 1

majority *adj* held by or applicable to a majority of the people ⟨The *majority* opinion among the tour group members was that they should cancel the rest of the trip.⟩ — see GENERAL 3

majority *n* **1** the largest part or quantity of something ⟨A vast *majority* of the town's residents support the proposed tax reduction.⟩

synonyms bulk, generality, mass

related words plurality; maximum, most; abundance, heap, loads, lot, much, oodles, plenty, profusion, reams, scads, wealth

near antonyms couple, few, handful, smattering, sprinkling; least, minimum

2 the state of being fully grown or developed ⟨She will inherit a fortune upon her *majority*.⟩ — see MATURITY

make *vb* **1** to bring into being by combining, shaping, or transforming materials ⟨Will you help me *make* the dough for the cookies?⟩

synonyms fabricate, fashion, form, frame, manufacture, produce

related words assemble, build, construct, erect, make up, put up, raise, rear, set up, structure, throw up; craft, handcraft; hew; forge, shape; patch (together), throw up; prefabricate; create, invent, mint, originate; establish, father, institute, organize; concoct, contrive, cook (up), design, devise, imagine, think (up); conceive, envisage, picture, visualize; refashion, remake, remanufacture

phrases put together

near antonyms disassemble, dismantle, take apart; break up, dismember; flatten, pulverize, raze, ruin, shatter, smash, wreck; blow up, explode

2 to obtain (as a goal) through effort ⟨We finally *made* it!⟩ — see ACHIEVE 1

3 to be the cause of (a situation, action, or state of mind) ⟨The cats *made* quite a disturbance when they knocked the Christmas tree over.⟩ — see EFFECT

4 to carry through (as a process) to completion ⟨One person from each department will be asked to *make* a short presentation at the meeting.⟩ — see PERFORM 1

5 to cause (a person) to give in to pressure ⟨She *made* him do all the work while everyone else just lounged around.⟩ — see FORCE

6 to decide the size, amount, number, or distance of (something) without actual measurement ⟨I *make* that to be about six feet long.⟩ — see ESTIMATE 2

7 to form by putting together parts or materials ⟨Let's *make* a model airplane.⟩ — see BUILD

8 to give the impression of being ⟨The family *made* merry despite their financial worries.⟩ — see SEEM

9 to go on a specified course or in a certain direction ⟨The baby *made* straight for the toy lying on the rug.⟩ — see HEAD 1

10 to put into effect through legislative or authoritative action ⟨The legislature failed to *make* any new laws last session.⟩ — see ENACT

11 to receive as return for effort ⟨I *make* considerably more money now than I did when I first started working here.⟩ — see EARN 1

12 to have a clear idea of ⟨What do you *make* of the latest information?⟩ — see COMPREHEND 1

make–believe *adj* not real and existing only in the imagination ⟨zoomed around the house in a *make-believe* car⟩ — see IMAGINARY

make out *vb* **1** to meet one's day-to-day needs ⟨We're not rich, but we're *making out* all right.⟩ — see GET ALONG 1

2 to have a clear idea of ⟨I can't quite *make out* what she is trying to say.⟩ — see COMPREHEND 1

3 to take on a false or deceptive appearance ⟨He tried to *make out* that he didn't mind losing his job, but friends suspected he was desperately worried.⟩ — see PRETEND 1

4 to form an opinion or reach a conclusion through reasoning and information ⟨As best as I can *make out*, the police were informed of the incident but didn't think it was worth investigating.⟩ — see INFER 1

make over *vb* **1** to change in form, appearance, or use ⟨The old factory was completely *made over* and is now an upscale shopping center.⟩ — see CONVERT 2

2 to give over the legal possession or ownership of ⟨The owner *made* the deed *over* to his daughter.⟩ — see TRANSFER 1

3 to make different in some way ⟨We *made over* the whole house to look more up-to-date.⟩ — see CHANGE 1

Maker *n* the being worshipped as the creator and ruler of the universe ⟨Let us give thanks to our *Maker* for this meal.⟩ — see DEITY 2

makeshift *adj* taking the place of one that came before ⟨A large box served as a *makeshift* table.⟩ — see NEW 1

makeshift *n* a temporary replacement ⟨When his belt broke, he was forced to use string as a *makeshift*.⟩

synonyms expedient, stopgap

related words quick fix; recourse, refuge, resort; alternate, backup, standby, stand-in, substitute, understudy

makeup *n* **1** preparations intended to beautify the face ⟨She never left the house without applying her *makeup* and arranging her jewelry.⟩

synonyms cosmetics, paint

related words greasepaint; camo, camouflage; cold cream, cream, eye shadow, kohl, lipstick, lotion, mascara, oil, powder, rouge, vanishing cream

2 the way in which the elements of something (as a work of art) are arranged ⟨The *makeup* of the memorial is strikingly simple: a single massive globe signifying world unity.⟩ — see COMPOSITION 3

make up *vb* **1** to be all the substance of ⟨The book is *made up* of 20 chapters.⟩ — see CONSTITUTE 1

2 to create or think of by clever use of the imagination ⟨She keeps *making up* excuses as to why she hasn't yet finished the project.⟩ — see INVENT

3 to form by putting together parts or materials ⟨We'll have to *make up* the bookcase, which came in a box marked "some assembly required."⟩ — see BUILD

make up (for) *vb* to balance with an equal force so as to make ineffective ⟨The lavish present almost *made up for* her forgetting his birthday.⟩ — see OFFSET

making *n, often pl* **makings** the basic elements from which something can be developed ⟨She has all the *makings* of an excellent leader, but she needs some experience first.⟩

synonyms material, raw material, stuff, substance

related words possibility, potential, potentiality; matter, metal

maladroit *adj* **1** lacking or showing a lack of nimbleness in using one's hands ⟨Some *maladroit* steering on her part caused the bicycle to go crashing into the bushes.⟩ — see CLUMSY 1

2 showing or marked by a lack of skill and tact (as in dealing with a situation) ⟨The governor has been criticized for his *maladroit* handling of the budget crisis.⟩ — see AWKWARD 2

malady *n* an abnormal state that disrupts a plant's or animal's normal bodily functioning ⟨In the olden days people were always suffering from some unknown *malady*.⟩ — see DISEASE

malcontent *adj* having a feeling that one has been wronged or thwarted in one's ambitions ⟨She seems like a very *malcontent* person, always acting as if the entire world were out to get her.⟩ — see DISCONTENTED

male *adj* of, relating to, or marked by qualities traditionally associated with men ⟨There were more *male* than female students.⟩ — see MASCULINE

male *n* an adult male human being ⟨Research shows that more *males* than females are responding positively to the new ad campaign.⟩ — see MAN 1

malediction *n* a prayer that harm will come to someone ⟨The two old women began casting aspersions and heaping *maledictions* upon one another.⟩ — see CURSE 1

malefaction *n* a breaking of a moral or legal code ⟨The town treasurer has been linked to the kickback scheme and other financial *malefactions*.⟩ — see OFFENSE 1

malefactor *n* **1** a person who commits moral wrongs ⟨She regards anyone who would cause the breakup of a family as a *malefactor* of the worst sort.⟩ — see EVILDOER 1

2 a person who has committed a crime ⟨The victim was able to give a clear description of the *malefactor* to the police.⟩ — see CRIMINAL

malevolence *n* the desire to cause pain for the satisfaction of doing harm ⟨glared at us with *malevolence*⟩ — see MALICE

malevolent *adj* having or showing a desire to cause someone pain or suffering for the sheer enjoyment of it ⟨The novel grossly oversimplified the conflict as a struggle between relentlessly *malevolent* villains on one side and faultless saints on the other.⟩ — see HATEFUL

malevolently *adv* in a mean or spiteful manner ⟨"I'll get you yet!" she hissed *malevolently*.⟩ — see NASTILY

malfeasance *n* improper or illegal behavior ⟨a campaign to impeach the governor for *malfeasance* in office⟩ — see MISCONDUCT

malformed *adj* badly or imperfectly formed ⟨a dog with a *malformed* tail⟩
synonyms deformed, distorted, misshapen, monstrous, shapeless
related words defaced, disfigured; aberrant, abnormal, freakish, mutant; asymmetrical (*or* asymmetric), crooked, disproportionate, irregular, lopsided, nonsymmetrical, overbalanced, unbalanced, unequal; horrible, terrible; ugly, unattractive
near antonyms shapely; flawless, perfect
antonyms undeformed

malfunctioning *adj* not being in working order ⟨A *malfunctioning* computer cost us days of work.⟩ — see INOPERABLE 1

malice *n* the desire to cause pain for the satisfaction of doing harm ⟨She claimed that her criticisms were without *malice*.⟩
synonyms cattiness, despite, hatefulness, malevolence, maliciousness, malignancy, malignity, meanness, nastiness, spite, spitefulness, spleen, venom, viciousness
related words abusiveness, cruelty; abhorrence, abomination, execration, hate, hatred, loathing; animosity, antagonism, antipathy, bitterness, enmity, grudge, hostility, ill will, jaundice, mean-spiritedness, rancor, resentment; despicableness, invidiousness; vengefulness, vindictiveness; aversion, disgust, distaste, horror, repugnance, repulsion, revulsion; contempt, disdain; jealousy, pique, resentment, scorn; bile, rancor, virulence, vitriol
near antonyms devotion, love, passion; amiability, amicability, amity, civility, cordiality, friendliness, hospitality; adoration, ardor, infatuation, veneration, worship; affection, charity, kindliness, kindness; comity, empathy, friendship, goodwill, sympathy, understanding

malicious *adj* having or showing a desire to cause someone pain or suffering for the sheer enjoyment of it ⟨The neighborhood chatterbox has again been spreading *malicious* gossip.⟩ — see HATEFUL

maliciously *adv* in a mean or spiteful manner ⟨*maliciously* tried to ruin my reputation⟩ — see NASTILY

maliciousness *n* the desire to cause pain for the satisfaction of doing harm ⟨The rival team pranked us on game day, but there was no *maliciousness* involved.⟩ — see MALICE

malign *adj* having or showing a desire to cause someone pain or suffering for the sheer enjoyment of it ⟨He used his power for *malign* purposes.⟩ — see HATEFUL

malign *vb* to make untrue and harmful statements about ⟨a candidate who believes that it is possible to win an election without *maligning* anyone⟩ — see SLANDER

malignancy *n* the desire to cause pain for the satisfaction of doing harm ⟨Her irrepressible *malignancy* was such that she even attacked her friends behind their backs.⟩ — see MALICE

malignant *adj* having or showing a desire to cause someone pain or suffering for the sheer enjoyment of it ⟨a

malignant wish to lash out at everyone who was smarter, richer, or better-looking than he was⟩ — see HATEFUL

malignantly *adv* in a mean or spiteful manner ⟨She's *malignantly* conspiring to ruin her rival's career.⟩ — see NASTILY

maligning *n* the making of false statements that damage another's reputation ⟨Public *maligning* of a person can actually be grounds for a lawsuit.⟩ — see SLANDER

malignity *n* the desire to cause pain for the satisfaction of doing harm ⟨One of the characters in the novel is a scoundrel of such *malignity* that his name came to be synonymous with villain.⟩ — see MALICE

malleability *n* the quality or state of being easily molded ⟨The *malleability* and conductivity of gold makes it well-suited for use in electronic circuitry.⟩ — see PLASTICITY

malleable *adj* **1** capable of being easily molded or modeled ⟨*malleable* cookie dough⟩ — see PLASTIC 1
2 capable of being readily changed ⟨The cult leader took advantage of the *malleable*, compliant personalities of his followers.⟩ — see FLEXIBLE 1

malodorous *adj* having an unpleasant smell ⟨The cellar will need to be cleared of several *malodorous* piles of garbage.⟩
synonyms fetid, foul, fusty, musty, noisome, rank, reeking, reeky, ripe, smelly, stinking, stinky, strong
related words putrid, skunky, stale; bad, offensive, repulsive, revolting, vile; decayed, decaying, decomposed, decomposing, rotted, rotten, rotting, spoiled, spoiling; dirty, filthy, nasty, noxious; odiferous, odoriferous, odorous
near antonyms flowery, fruity, spicy, woodsy
antonyms ambrosial, aromatic, fragrant, perfumed, redolent, savory (*also* savoury), scented, sweet

maltreat *vb* **1** to inflict physical or emotional harm upon ⟨a manager fired for *maltreating* the staff⟩ — see ABUSE 1
2 to abuse physically ⟨If you *maltreat* the puppy, we will take it away immediately.⟩ — see MANHANDLE 1

mama *also* **mamma** *or* **momma** *n* a female human parent ⟨Can you read me a story, *mama*?⟩ — see MOTHER

mammoth *adj* unusually large ⟨a *mammoth* book with color plates of birds native to North America⟩ — see HUGE

mammoth *n* something that is unusually large and powerful ⟨Even as sport-utility vehicles go, that one is a *mammoth*.⟩ — see GIANT

mammy *n* a female human parent ⟨The toddler clung to her *mammy* and eyed the strangers fearfully.⟩ — see MOTHER

man *n* **1** an adult male human being ⟨Several *men* will be needed to dig up the old tree stump in the backyard.⟩
synonyms buck, dude, fellow, gent, gentleman, guy, hombre, joker, lad, male
related words sir; buddy, buster
2 a male romantic companion ⟨Who's the new *man* in your life?⟩ — see BOYFRIEND
3 a member of the human race ⟨Every *man* has a responsibility to safeguard the planet.⟩ — see HUMAN
4 the human race ⟨found evidence of early *man* in the valley⟩ — see MANKIND
5 a male partner in a marriage ⟨I now pronounce you *man* and wife.⟩ — see HUSBAND

manacle *n* **1** *usually* **manacles** *pl* something that physically prevents free movement ⟨*Manacles* prevented the bear from roaming beyond a very small area.⟩ — see BOND 1
2 something that makes movement or progress difficult ⟨The warring groups need to shake off the *manacle* of their troubled past and learn to live with one another in peace.⟩ — see ENCUMBRANCE

manacle *vb* **1** to confine or restrain with or as if with chains ⟨*manacled* the prisoner to the wall⟩ — see BIND 1
2 to create difficulty for the work or activity of ⟨an aid group *manacled* by regional politics⟩ — see HAMPER

manage *vb* **1** to deal with (something) usually skillfully or efficiently ⟨As usual, she *managed* the crisis with a minimum of fuss.⟩ — see HANDLE 1

2 to look after and make decisions about ⟨You'll have to *manage* your time wisely.⟩ — see CONDUCT 1

3 to meet one's day-to-day needs ⟨It'll be hard for a few weeks, but we'll *manage*.⟩ — see GET ALONG 1

management *n* the act or activity of looking after and making decisions about something ⟨Fiscal *management* of the city's sports facility can be challenging.⟩ — see CONDUCT 1

manager *n* a person who manages or directs something ⟨We wanted an exemption from the policy regarding refunds, but the store *manager* refused.⟩ — see EXECUTIVE

managerial *adj* suited for or relating to the directing of things ⟨Her *managerial* style is very direct and detail-oriented.⟩ — see EXECUTIVE

man–at–arms *n* a person engaged in military service ⟨The condottieri who served as *men-at-arms* for the Italian city-states often sold their allegiance to the highest bidder.⟩ — see SOLDIER

mandate *n* the granting of power to perform various acts or duties ⟨The committee has been given a *mandate* to reform the process for admitting applicants to the university.⟩ — see COMMISSION 1

mandate *vb* to request the doing of by virtue of one's authority ⟨The president of the sports league has *mandated* concussion testing for all active members.⟩ — see COMMAND 2

mandatory *adj* forcing one's compliance or participation by or as if by law ⟨The tests are *mandatory* for all students wishing to graduate.⟩

synonyms compulsory, forced, imperative, incumbent, involuntary, necessary, nonelective, obligatory, peremptory, required

related words all-important, essential, indispensable, needed, requisite; insistent, persistent, pressing, urgent; demanded, enforced; coercive

near antonyms chosen, discretionary; dispensable, unnecessary, unneeded, unwanted; inconsequential, insignificant, nonessential, unimportant

antonyms elective, optional, voluntary

maneuver *vb* **1** to deal with (something) usually skillfully or efficiently ⟨Debra *maneuvered* the conversation so as to avoid touchy subjects.⟩ — see HANDLE 1

2 to plan out usually with subtle skill or care ⟨Companies are *maneuvering* for position in the new market.⟩ — see ENGINEER

manful *adj* feeling or displaying no fear by temperament ⟨He made the *manful* decision to stick by his friends when everyone else had abandoned them.⟩ — see BRAVE 1

mangle *vb* to make or do (something) in a clumsy or unskillful way ⟨The cover band *mangled* the song.⟩ — see BOTCH

mangy *adj* showing signs of advanced wear and tear and neglect ⟨a *mangy* old rug⟩ — see SHABBY 1

manhandle *vb* **1** to abuse physically ⟨charges that the police *manhandled* peaceful protesters⟩

synonyms maltreat, maul, mishandle, rough (up)

related words abuse, ill-treat, ill-use, mistreat, misuse; roughhouse, wrestle; bash, batter, beat, buffet, drub, lambaste (*or* lambast), lick, pommel, pound, pummel, slap, thrash; harm, hurt, injure, wound; oppress, persecute, wrong; ambush, assail, attack; clobber, fight, gang up (on), hit, jump, knock; torment, torture

near antonyms caress, fondle, pet; coddle, mollycoddle, pamper; care (for), foster, nurture

2 to inflict physical or emotional harm upon ⟨a receiver *manhandled* by a defensive tackle⟩ — see ABUSE 1

manhood *n* the set of qualities traditionally considered appropriate for or characteristic of men ⟨a society that highly values *manhood* and courage⟩ — see VIRILITY

mania *n* something about which one is constantly thinking or concerned ⟨He has a *mania* for old comic books.⟩ — see FIXATION

maniac *n* a person with a strong and habitual liking for something ⟨I'm a *maniac* for anything flavored with peppermint.⟩ — see FAN

manifest *adj* not subject to misinterpretation or more than one interpretation ⟨Despite his *manifest* lack of leadership skills, the shift supervisor managed to keep his position.⟩ — see CLEAR 2

manifest *vb* **1** to make known (something abstract) through outward signs ⟨a frustration that is often *manifested* by a minor facial tic⟩ — see SHOW 2

2 to represent in visible form ⟨Graduates of the military academies *manifest*, we hope, the best that this country has to offer.⟩ — see EMBODY 2

manifestation *n* a visible representation of something abstract (as a quality) ⟨a portrait of a mother and child that is regarded as the very *manifestation* of maternal love⟩ — see EMBODIMENT

manifold *adj* being of many and various kinds ⟨The *manifold* attractions of that state make it an ideal destination for a family vacation.⟩

synonyms divers, multifarious, myriad

related words multiform, multiple, multiplex, multitudinous; heterogeneous, heterogenous, miscellaneous, mixed, sundry; different, diverse, unlike, varied

near antonyms homogeneous, homogenous, monolithic, unmixed, unvaried; alike, identical, same; distinct, distinctive, individual, separate; alone, lone, only, sole, solitary; singular, unique

manikin *also* **mannikin** *n* **1** a three-dimensional representation of the human body used especially for displaying clothes ⟨The store has *manikins* so lifelike that they have startled me on more than one occasion.⟩ — see MANNEQUIN 1

2 a person who poses with or wears merchandise (as clothes) often for pictorial advertising ⟨*manikins* strutting down the catwalk⟩ — see MODEL 2

manipulate *vb* **1** to control or take advantage of by artful, unfair, or insidious means ⟨The con man would slyly *manipulate* the emotions of his marks in order to win their sympathy and trust.⟩

synonyms exploit, play (upon)

related words engineer, finagle, jockey, maneuver; beguile, bluff, cozen, deceive, delude, dupe, fool, gull, hoax, hoodwink, kid, shanghai, snow, take in, trick; intrigue, machinate, plot, scheme; arrange, contrive, devise, finesse, mastermind; cheat, chisel, con, defraud, fleece, hustle, swindle

2 to deal with (something) usually skillfully or efficiently ⟨a scientist effortlessly *manipulating* a slew of statistics while testifying before Congress⟩ — see HANDLE 1

3 to plan out usually with subtle skill or care ⟨*manipulated* the schedule of presidential primaries so that the choice of the party elders would win the nomination⟩ — see ENGINEER

mankind *n* the human race ⟨All of *mankind* stands to gain if world peace is ever achieved.⟩

synonyms Homo sapiens, humanity, humankind, man

related words being, body, creature, fellowman, human, individual, mortal, party, person

manliness *n* the set of qualities traditionally considered appropriate for or characteristic of men ⟨a test of his *manliness*⟩ — see VIRILITY

manly *adj* of, relating to, or marked by qualities traditionally associated with men ⟨a deep *manly* voice⟩ — see MASCULINE

man–made *adj* **1** being such in appearance only and made with or manufactured from usually cheaper materials ⟨*man-made* diamonds that were really just glass⟩ — see IMITATION
2 produced by humans rather than natural processes ⟨The houses in the new development are built around a *man-made* lake.⟩ — see SYNTHETIC 1

manna *n* **1** a source of great satisfaction ⟨The announcement that there would be a sequel was *manna* to the many fans of the original movie.⟩ — see DELIGHT 1
2 something that provides happiness or does good for a person or thing ⟨The company's annual bonus was especially welcome *manna* this year.⟩ — see BLESSING 2

mannequin *n* **1** a three-dimensional representation of the human body used especially for displaying clothes ⟨The *mannequin* over there looks so real.⟩
synonyms dummy, figure, form, manikin (*also* mannikin)
related words doll
2 a person who poses with or wears merchandise (as clothes) often for pictorial advertising ⟨*mannequins* striding down the runway in the designer's spring collection⟩ — see MODEL 2

manner *n* **1** **manners** *pl* personal conduct or behavior as evaluated by an accepted standard of appropriateness for a social or professional setting ⟨The young man's impeccable *manners* are an unmistakable sign of a good upbringing.⟩
synonyms etiquette, form, mores, proprieties
related words amenities, civilities, pleasantries; bearing, demeanor, deportment, mien; courtesy, decorum, mannerliness, politeness; formalities, protocol, rules; air, carriage, poise, polish, pose, posture, presence
2 a distinctive way of putting ideas into words ⟨The former doctor writes his novels very much in the *manner* of someone who is used to observing the smallest details.⟩ — see STYLE 1
3 a number of persons or things that are grouped together because they have something in common ⟨fish and all *manner* of sea life on view at the aquarium⟩ — see SORT 1
4 the means or procedure for doing something ⟨You happened to reach the correct answer, but the *manner* by which you solved the problem was wrong.⟩ — see METHOD

mannerism *n* an odd or peculiar habit ⟨quirky *mannerisms* such as toying with her hair and tapping her toes⟩ — see IDIOSYNCRASY

mannerliness *n* speech or behavior that is a sign of good manners ⟨The elderly gentleman comported himself with old-world, old-school *mannerliness*.⟩ — see POLITENESS 1

mannerly *adj* showing consideration, courtesy, and good manners ⟨A *mannerly* child is welcome everywhere.⟩ — see POLITE 1

mannish *adj* **1** of, relating to, or marked by qualities traditionally associated with men ⟨a woman with a somewhat *mannish* voice⟩ — see MASCULINE
2 having qualities or traits that are traditionally considered inappropriate for a girl or woman ⟨For her first outing as a spelunker she wore the same *mannish* jeans as the guys.⟩ — see UNFEMININE

manor *n* a large impressive residence ⟨The old family *manor* has 117 rooms.⟩ — see MANSION

manor house *n* a large impressive residence ⟨entertained everyone at their *manor house* after the wedding ceremony⟩ — see MANSION

manpower *n* a body of persons at work or available for work ⟨We're a little short on *manpower* today, so we'll need you to do some extra tasks.⟩ — see FORCE 1

mansion *n* a large impressive residence ⟨If I ever win the lottery, I'm going to buy a *mansion* in the hills.⟩

synonyms castle, château, estate, hacienda, hall, manor, manor house, palace, villa
related words showplace; abode, domicile, dwelling, habitation, hearth, home, house, lodging(s), pad, place; housing, nest, quarter(s), roof; great house; country house, countryseat; aerie, penthouse; salon, suite, town house

man–size *or* **man–sized** *adj* of, relating to, or marked by qualities traditionally associated with men ⟨Tim worked up a *man-size* appetite playing soccer.⟩ — see MASCULINE

manta *n* any of several extremely large rays ⟨A *manta* glided along the sea bottom.⟩ — see DEVILFISH

manta ray *n* any of several extremely large rays ⟨The *manta ray* blended in beautifully with the sandy ocean floor.⟩ — see DEVILFISH

mantilla *n* a scarf worn on the head ⟨a beautiful Spanish lady with a lace *mantilla*⟩ — see BANDANNA

mantle *n* **1** a sleeveless garment worn so as to hang over the shoulders, arms, and back ⟨a long black velvet *mantle*⟩ — see ¹CAPE
2 something that covers or conceals like a piece of cloth ⟨the *mantle* of secrecy that surrounds the operations of the organization's hierarchy⟩ — see CLOAK 1

mantle *vb* to surround or cover closely ⟨Early-morning fog *mantled* the fields along the river.⟩ — see ENFOLD 1

manual *n* a book used for instruction in a subject ⟨An owner's *manual* comes with the camera.⟩ — see TEXTBOOK

manufactory *n* a building or set of buildings for the manufacturing of goods ⟨Recent years have seen a tremendous growth in *manufactories* all along the river.⟩ — see FACTORY

manufacture *vb* **1** to bring into being by combining, shaping, or transforming materials ⟨The company *manufactures* appliances and electronics.⟩ — see MAKE 1
2 to create or think of by clever use of the imagination ⟨He *manufactured* some story about how his car broke down and he was unable to call home and let anyone know that he would be late.⟩ — see INVENT

manumission *n* the act of setting free from slavery ⟨The official *manumission* of enslaved Africans in the U.S. came after the Civil War.⟩ — see LIBERATION

manumit *vb* to release (as from slavery or confinement) ⟨By the end of the Civil War, thousands of *manumitted* Africans had joined the Union army.⟩ — see FREE 1

manuscript *n* writing done by hand ⟨beautiful, careful *manuscript* on the school's diplomas⟩ — see HANDWRITING 2

many *adj* being of a large but indefinite number ⟨A journey of *many* miles begins with a single step.⟩
synonyms legion, multiple, multiplex, multitudinous, numerous
related words countless, innumerable, numberless, uncountable, unnumbered, untold; several; some; miscellaneous, mixed, sundry; divers, manifold, multifarious, myriad
phrases all kinds of, quite a few
near antonyms countable, limited
antonyms few

map *n* an illustration of certain features of a geographical area ⟨a wall *map* of the United States⟩
synonyms chart
related words ground plan, plan, plat, plot; relief map

map (out) *vb* to work out the details of (something) in advance ⟨*mapped out* a plan for the fledgling company to become profitable within two years⟩ — see PLAN 1

mar *n* something that spoils the appearance or completeness of a thing ⟨The Johnsons complained to the movers about broken dishes and *mars* on the furniture.⟩ — see BLEMISH

mar *vb* **1** to affect slightly with something morally bad or undesirable ⟨Don't *mar* a politician's reputation with scurrilous rumors.⟩ — see TAINT 1

2 to reduce the soundness, effectiveness, or perfection of ⟨The once glossy surface is now *marred* by numerous small pits and abrasions.⟩ — see DAMAGE 1

maraud *vb* to search through with the intent of committing robbery ⟨A raccoon *marauded* our trash cans.⟩ — see RANSACK 1

marble *vb* to mark with small spots especially unevenly ⟨Let's *marble* the paper with several different dyes to get a striking effect.⟩ — see SPOT 1

marbled *adj* having blotches of two or more colors ⟨a *marbled* chocolate and vanilla cake⟩ — see PIED

¹**march** *n* a region along the dividing line between two countries ⟨When it was first built, this castle protected what was then the country's northern *march*.⟩ — see FRONTIER 1

²**march** *n* forward movement in time or place ⟨the *march* of time⟩ — see ADVANCE 1

march *vb* **1** to move along with a steady regular step especially in a group ⟨The band had to practice for hours to be able to *march* in perfect step.⟩

synonyms file, pace, parade, stride

related words goose-step; step, traipse, tread; hike, tramp; lumber, plod, stamp, stomp, stride, trudge

near antonyms meander, ramble, stroll, wander

2 to move forward along a course ⟨bleary-eyed commuters *marching* off to the train station for the morning commute⟩ — see GO 1

margin *n* the line or relatively narrow space that marks the outer limit of something ⟨The *margins* of the paper should only be an inch wide.⟩ — see BORDER 1

margin *vb* to serve as a border for ⟨The riverbed is *margined* by a flat beach of smooth rocks.⟩ — see BORDER

marginally *adv* by a very small margin ⟨The team lost another game, but at least they performed *marginally* better this time out.⟩ — see JUST 2

marine *adj* **1** of or relating to the sea ⟨He loves collecting little *marine* creatures while at the beach.⟩

synonyms maritime, oceanic, pelagic

related words abyssal, deepwater, saltwater; benthic; nautical, naval; undersea, underwater; hydrographic, oceanographic (*also* oceanographical)

2 of or relating to navigation of the sea ⟨a collection of *marine* instruments, including a sextant⟩

synonyms maritime, nautical, navigational

related words naval; oceangoing, seafaring, seagoing; hydrographic, oceanographic (*also* oceanographical)

mariner *n* one who operates or navigates a seagoing vessel ⟨The ancient Phoenicians were outstanding *mariners* who explored and colonized much of the eastern Mediterranean.⟩ — see SAILOR

marital *adj* of or relating to marriage ⟨Neither of them ever forgot their *marital* vows, no matter how hard things sometimes got.⟩

synonyms conjugal, connubial, married, matrimonial, nuptial, wedded

related words espoused, matched, mated; bridal, prenuptial; spousal, wifely; affianced, betrothed, committed, engaged, pledged, promised

antonyms nonmarital

maritime *adj* **1** of or relating to navigation of the sea ⟨a rare *maritime* chart from the 17th century⟩ — see MARINE 2

2 of or relating to the sea ⟨The city's extraordinary boom is almost entirely due to the increase in *maritime* commerce.⟩ — see MARINE 1

mark *n* **1** a person or thing that is made fun of ⟨In the wake of his latest gaffe, the governor became the favorite *mark* of late-night comedians.⟩ — see LAUGHINGSTOCK

2 a person or thing that is the object of abuse, criticism,

or ridicule ⟨We knew our unpopular position would make us the *marks* of critics.⟩ — see TARGET 1

3 overall quality as seen or judged by people in general ⟨a brand of crystal that bears the *mark* of excellence⟩ — see REPUTATION

4 something set up as an example against which others of the same type are compared ⟨Lately his playing hasn't been up to the *mark* expected of a concert pianist.⟩ — see STANDARD 1

5 something that one hopes or intends to accomplish ⟨set *marks* for expected daily output⟩ — see GOAL

6 something that sets apart an individual from others of the same kind ⟨a sensitive expression that is the *mark* of a poet⟩ — see CHARACTERISTIC

7 something that spoils the appearance or completeness of a thing ⟨a small *mark* where the car had scraped a wall⟩ — see BLEMISH

8 the power to bring about a result on another ⟨a person of some *mark* in the field of evolutionary biology⟩ — see EFFECT 2

mark *vb* **1** to attach an identifying slip to ⟨*marked* each application with a numbered sticker⟩ — see LABEL 1

2 to be an important feature of ⟨an annual event *marked* mostly by noise and confusion⟩ — see CHARACTERIZE 2

3 to make a written note of ⟨*Mark* down the names of those who are planning to attend the dinner.⟩ — see RECORD 1

mark down *vb* to diminish the price or value of ⟨*marked down* all seasonal goods immediately after the holidays⟩ — see DEPRECIATE 1

marked *adj* likely to attract attention ⟨a *marked* improvement in her classwork⟩ — see NOTICEABLE

marker *n* **1** a slip (as of paper or cloth) that is attached to something to identify or describe it ⟨The *markers* on the rock and mineral specimens were old and faded.⟩ — see LABEL

2 something that sets apart an individual from others of the same kind ⟨The discovery of a *marker* for the virus has improved the accuracy of diagnosis.⟩ — see CHARACTERISTIC

market *n* the state of being sought after especially for purchase ⟨a great decline in the *market* for large cars⟩ — see DEMAND 2

market *vb* to offer for sale to the public ⟨Local farmers *market* their garden-fresh produce at roadside stands all over the valley.⟩

synonyms deal (in), merchandise (*also* merchandize), put up, retail, sell, vend

related words presell, wholesale; hawk, peddle; barter, distribute, exchange, export, handle, trade, traffic (in); advertise, ballyhoo, boost, plug, promote, tout; auction; provide, supply; carry, keep, stock

antonyms buy, purchase

marketable *adj* **1** fit to be offered for sale ⟨Bob realized that the birdhouses he enjoyed making were *marketable* and began selling them at craft fairs.⟩

synonyms salable (*or* saleable)

related words commercial, profitable; costly, fancy, fine, high-grade, precious, premium, prime, valuable

near antonyms damaged, shopworn; cheap, useless, worthless; bad, inferior, low-grade, substandard, unsatisfactory

antonyms nonsalable, unmarketable, unsalable, unsellable

2 fit or likely to be sold especially on a large scale ⟨trying to turn their invention into a *marketable* product⟩ — see COMMERCIAL

marketplace *n* the buying and selling of goods especially on a large scale and between different places ⟨nations struggling to compete in the global *marketplace*⟩ — see COMMERCE 1

marksman *n* a person skilled in shooting at a target ⟨Only the best *marksmen* can hit the bull's-eye at 500 feet.⟩
synonyms sharpshooter, shooter, shot
related words sniper; rifleman; trapshooter; gun, gunman, gunner; markswoman

maroon *vb* to cause to remain behind ⟨sailors *marooned* on a desert island⟩ — see LEAVE 1

marriage *n* **1** a union representing a special kind of social and legal partnership between two people ⟨They have a very happy *marriage*.⟩
synonyms match, matrimony, wedlock
related words monogamy; bigamy, polyandry, polygamy, polygyny; intermarriage, miscegenation, mixed marriage, remarriage; cohabitation, common-law marriage; civil union, domestic partnership; attachment, commitment, relationship; betrothal, engagement, espousal, hand, pledge, promise, proposal, troth
near antonyms divorce, separation
2 a ceremony in which two people are united in matrimony ⟨Just a small group of family and friends have been invited to witness the *marriage*.⟩ — see WEDDING

married *adj* of or relating to marriage ⟨a sermon on the joys and responsibilities of *married* love⟩ — see MARITAL

marry *vb* **1** to perform the ceremony of marriage for ⟨They chose a priest who was a family friend to *marry* them.⟩
synonyms wed
related words match, mate; conjoin, connect, unite; affiance
2 to give in marriage ⟨Once they *marry* off me and my siblings, my parents are selling their house.⟩
synonyms espouse, match, wed
related words commit, engage; affiance, betroth, pledge, promise
3 to take as a spouse ⟨He *married* his girlfriend three years ago, and they've been happy ever since.⟩
synonyms espouse, wed
related words affiance, betroth, commit, engage, pledge, promise, propose; remarry
near antonyms separate (from)
antonyms divorce
4 to take a spouse ⟨She had always believed she would never *marry*, but fate proved her wrong.⟩
synonyms wed
related words couple, mate; pair off, remarry
phrases tie the knot
near antonyms divorce, separate
5 to come together to form a single unit ⟨Cheese and tomatoes *marry* especially well.⟩ — see UNITE 1

marsh *n* spongy land saturated or partially covered with water ⟨The *marshes* along the coast support a remarkable profusion of plants and animals.⟩ — see SWAMP

marshal *also* **marshall** *vb* **1** to assemble and make ready for action ⟨*marshaled* their forces for battle⟩ — see MOBILIZE
2 to point out the way for (someone) especially from a position in front ⟨*marshaling* a small group of children on a tour of the science museum⟩ — see LEAD 1
3 to put into a particular arrangement ⟨You should *marshal* your arguments before you stand up to speak.⟩ — see ORDER 1

marshaling *or* **marshalling** *n* an act of gathering forces together to renew or attempt an effort ⟨The last-minute *marshaling* of the reserves repelled the onslaught.⟩ — see RALLY 1

marshland *n* spongy land saturated or partially covered with water ⟨Grasses, sedges, and rushes are the plant species most commonly found in *marshlands*.⟩ — see SWAMP

martial *adj* **1** of, relating to, or suitable for war or a warrior ⟨The marching band played "The Battle Hymn of the Republic" and several other *martial* airs.⟩
synonyms military, soldierly
related words aggressive, bellicose, combative, contentious, guerrilla, pugnacious, quarrelsome, scrappy, truculent, warlike; belligerent, militant, militarist, militaristic, warring
near antonyms civil, civilian, nonmilitary; conciliatory, nonviolent, pacific, peaceable, peaceful; affable, amiable, amicable, benevolent, complaisant, cordial, easygoing, friendly, genial, good-natured, obliging
antonyms unsoldierly
2 of or relating to the armed services ⟨one of the basic tenets of *martial* law⟩ — see MILITARY 1

marvel *n* something extraordinary or surprising ⟨That new self-driving car really is a *marvel*.⟩ — see WONDER 1

marveling *or* **marvelling** *adj* filled with amazement or wonder ⟨With *marveling* stares, onlookers gathered round the remarkable invention.⟩ — see OPENMOUTHED

marvelous *or* **marvellous** *adj* **1** causing wonder or astonishment ⟨The sheer immensity of the ancient ruin known as Stonehenge is *marvelous* to behold.⟩
synonyms amazing, astonishing, astounding, awesome, awful, eye-opening, fabulous, miraculous, portentous, prodigious, staggering, stunning, stupendous, sublime, surprising, wonderful, wondrous
related words incomprehensible, inconceivable, incredible, unbelievable, unimaginable, unthinkable; extraordinary, phenomenal, rare, sensational; singular, uncommon, unique, unusual, unwonted; conspicuous, notable, noticeable, outstanding, remarkable; impressive, smashing, striking; alluring, attracting, attractive, beguiling, bewitching, captivating, charming, enchanting, enthralling, fascinating, interesting
near antonyms unimpressive, uninspiring, unremarkable; boring, dull, jading, monotonous, tedious, tiring, uninspired, uninteresting, wearisome, weary, wearying; common, customary, mundane, normal, ordinary, typical, unexceptional, usual
2 excitingly or mysteriously unusual ⟨old seafarers' tales of *marvelous* lands⟩ — see EXOTIC
3 of the very best kind ⟨The novel is a *marvelous* example of a children's book which has not been dumbed down for its intended audience.⟩ — see EXCELLENT

mascot *n* something worn or kept to bring good luck or keep away evil ⟨She wears a *mascot* made of ebony and silver on a chain around her neck.⟩ — see CHARM 1

masculine *adj* of, relating to, or marked by qualities traditionally associated with men ⟨Some people consider a deep voice to be a particularly appealing *masculine* trait.⟩
synonyms male, manly, mannish, man-size (*or* man-sized), virile
related words ultramasculine; boyish, hoydenish, tomboyish
near antonyms effeminate, girlish; feminine, womanish, womanlike, womanly; emasculated, impotent, weakened; neuter
antonyms unmanly, unmasculine

masculinity *n* the set of qualities traditionally considered appropriate for or characteristic of men ⟨an advertisement trying to evoke *masculinity*⟩ — see VIRILITY

mash *vb* **1** to apply external pressure on so as to force out the juice or contents of ⟨This press can *mash* 10 bushels of apples at a time.⟩ — see ²PRESS 2
2 to cause to become a pulpy mass ⟨*Mash* the ripe banana before adding it to the mixture.⟩ — see CRUSH 1

mask *n* **1** a cover or partial cover for the face used to disguise oneself ⟨an elaborate *mask* that would be suitable for a fancy masquerade ball⟩
synonyms vizard
related words camouflage, costume, disguise, guise; bill, cloak, domino, hood, veil, visor (*also* vizor)

2 something that covers or conceals like a piece of cloth ⟨His unexpected friendliness is just a *mask*, for he always has an ulterior motive.⟩ — see CLOAK 1

mask *vb* **1** to change the dress or looks of so as to conceal true identity ⟨The federal agents *masked* their surveillance vehicle so that it looked like an ordinary moving van.⟩ — see DISGUISE 1
2 to keep secret or shut off from view ⟨*masked* his real motives for wanting to see the house that was for sale⟩ — see ¹HIDE 2

masquerade *n* a display of emotion or behavior that is insincere or intended to deceive ⟨Although she was deeply bored, she maintained a *masquerade* of polite interest as her guest droned on.⟩
synonyms act, airs, charade, disguise, facade (*also* façade), front, guise, pose, pretense (*or* pretence), put-on, semblance, show
related words impersonation, performance, portrayal; image, persona; appearance, color, gloss; camouflage, cloak; affectation, deceit, dissembling, dissimulation, double-dealing, duplicity, fakery, fraud, guile; betrayal, double cross, faithlessness, falseness, falsity, infidelity, perfidy, treachery, treason, unfaithfulness; excuse, pretext
near antonyms candidness, candor, directness, forthrightness, frankness, openheartedness, outspokenness, straightforwardness; artlessness, genuineness, naïveté (*also* naivete *or* naiveté)

masquerade (as) *vb* to pretend to be (what one is not) in appearance or behavior ⟨a story about a spy *masquerading* as a salesman⟩ — see IMPERSONATE 1

mass *n* **1** *masses pl* the body of the community as contrasted with the elite ⟨The *masses* demanded the elimination of tax breaks for the rich.⟩
synonyms commoners, crowd, herd, mob, multitude, people, plebeians, populace, public, rank and file
related words cattle, proletariat, rabble, riffraff, rout, trash, unwashed
near antonyms gentry, nobility, patriciate, peerage, society
antonyms A-list, aristocracy, best, choice, cream, elect, elite, fat, flower, pick, pride, upper crust
2 a considerable amount ⟨I have a *mass* of work to do tonight.⟩ — see LOT 2
3 a distinct and separate portion of matter ⟨a *mass* of leaves in a corner of the yard⟩ — see BODY 2
4 the main or greater part of something as distinguished from its subordinate parts ⟨When taking pictures, focus your attention on the *mass* of the main subject.⟩ — see BODY 1
5 the largest part or quantity of something ⟨He believes that the great *mass* of voters are in the political center and consider themselves neither conservative nor liberal.⟩ — see MAJORITY 1
6 a great number of persons or creatures massed together ⟨A huge *mass* of people had gathered in the park to protest.⟩ — see CROWD 1

mass *vb* to gradually form into a layer, pile, or mass ⟨clouds *massing* on the western side of the mountain range⟩ — see COLLECT 2

massacre *n* the killing of a large number of people ⟨the infamous *massacre* of more than 200 Lakota at Wounded Knee, South Dakota⟩
synonyms butchery, carnage, death, holocaust, slaughter
related words bloodletting, bloodshed, foul play, homicide, manslaughter, murder, slaying; annihilation, decimation, eradication, extermination; genocide, pogrom

massacre *vb* to kill on a large scale ⟨The country's rival ethnic groups began *massacring* one another.⟩
synonyms butcher, mow (down), slaughter

related words dispatch, do in, execute, fell, murder, slay, smite; annihilate, blot out, decimate, eradicate, exterminate, waste, wipe out

massive *adj* **1** having great weight ⟨a *massive* piece of furniture that was nearly impossible to move⟩ — see HEAVY 1
2 unusually large ⟨The *massive* statue took up most of the small yard.⟩ — see HUGE
3 large and impressive in size, grandeur, extent, or conception ⟨The war memorial's *massive* dignity moves most visitors to reflective silence.⟩ — see GRAND 1

massively *adv* to a large extent or degree ⟨I am *massively* irritated by this new development.⟩ — see GREATLY 2

massiveness *n* **1** the quality or state of being very large ⟨The *massiveness* of the puppy's paws suggested that this would be a very large dog.⟩ — see IMMENSITY
2 the state or quality of being heavy ⟨I need something with sufficient *massiveness* to block the wheels so this car won't roll down the ramp.⟩ — see WEIGHTINESS 1

mass–produced *adj* made beforehand in large numbers ⟨a cheap *mass-produced* plastic toy⟩ — see READY-MADE

master *adj* **1** coming before all others in importance ⟨the network's *master* computer⟩ — see FOREMOST 1
2 having or showing exceptional knowledge, experience, or skill in a field of endeavor ⟨a *master* craftsman who makes fine wood furniture of his own designs⟩ — see PROFICIENT

master *n* **1** a person with a high level of knowledge or skill in a field ⟨a *master* at chess⟩ — see EXPERT
2 one that defeats an enemy or opponent ⟨Little did the tennis pro know that his new student would someday become his *master*.⟩ — see VICTOR 1
3 the person (as an employer or supervisor) who tells people and especially workers what to do ⟨I'm the *master* of this operation, and I can answer any questions you have.⟩ — see BOSS

master *vb* **1** to achieve a victory over ⟨finally *mastered* her longtime opponent at chess⟩ — see BEAT 2
2 to acquire complete knowledge, understanding, or skill in ⟨I think I've *mastered* algebra at last.⟩ — see LEARN 1

masterful *adj* **1** accomplished with trained ability ⟨a *masterful* performance of a difficult piece for the violin⟩ — see SKILLFUL 1
2 fond of ordering people around ⟨a *masterful* coworker who liked to tell other people how to do their jobs⟩ — see BOSSY
3 having a feeling of superiority that shows itself in an overbearing attitude ⟨a *masterful* manager who pushed others aside in climbing the ladder of success⟩ — see ARROGANT
4 having or showing exceptional knowledge, experience, or skill in a field of endeavor ⟨a president who was celebrated as a *masterful* communicator of his administration's policies⟩ — see PROFICIENT

masterfully *adv* in a skillful or expert manner ⟨plays the violin *masterfully*, especially for a performer of her age⟩ — see WELL 3

masterfulness *n* **1** subtle or imaginative ability in inventing, devising, or executing something ⟨The sheer *masterfulness* of the thieves' plan could not be denied, even by the police.⟩ — see SKILL 1
2 an exaggerated sense of one's importance that shows itself in the making of excessive or unjustified claims ⟨His *masterfulness* was positively galling to his colleagues.⟩ — see ARROGANCE

masterly *adj* **1** accomplished with trained ability ⟨a *masterly* performance of one of the most difficult ballets in the repertory⟩ — see SKILLFUL 1
2 having or showing exceptional knowledge, experience, or skill in a field of endeavor ⟨a *masterly* handling of a complex topic in philosophy⟩ — see PROFICIENT

masterly *adv* in a skillful or expert manner ⟨a *masterly* executed somersault⟩ — see WELL 3

mastermind *n* a person who designs and guides a plan or undertaking ⟨the real *mastermind* behind the embezzlement scheme⟩ — see ENGINEER

mastermind *vb* to plan out usually with subtle skill or care ⟨He was charged with *masterminding* a plan to redecorate the suite of offices without seriously disrupting business operations.⟩ — see ENGINEER

masterpiece *n* something (as a work of art) that is a great achievement and often its creator's greatest achievement ⟨Michelangelo's frescoes in the Sistine Chapel are often considered to be his *masterpieces*.⟩

synonyms classic, magnum opus

related words masterstroke, pièce de résistance, showpiece; blockbuster, megahit, smash, success, winner; gem, jewel, prize, treasure

near antonyms bomb, catastrophe, debacle (*also* débâcle), disaster, dud, failure, fiasco, fizzle, flop, loser, turkey, washout

mastership *n* a highly developed skill in or knowledge of something ⟨We're still working on *mastership* of the new computer system.⟩ — see COMMAND 2

mastery *n* **1** a highly developed skill in or knowledge of something ⟨The exchange student returned from her year in Spain with a complete *mastery* of the language.⟩ — see COMMAND 2

2 the right or means to command or control others ⟨The British monarch has only token *mastery* over the citizens of the United Kingdom.⟩ — see POWER 1

masticate *vb* to crush or grind with the teeth ⟨mindlessly *masticated* peanuts while watching the baseball game on TV⟩ — see BITE (ON)

match *n* **1** a competitive encounter between individuals or groups carried on for amusement, exercise, or in pursuit of a prize ⟨a chess *match*⟩ — see GAME 1

2 a union representing a special kind of social and legal partnership between two people ⟨From all appearances those two have got a good *match* there.⟩ — see MARRIAGE 1

3 either of a pair matched in one or more qualities ⟨I can't find the *match* to this sock.⟩ — see MATE 1

4 one that is equal to another in status, achievement, or value ⟨a politician who has finally met his *match*⟩ — see EQUAL

5 something or someone that strongly resembles another ⟨Erin is so nearly my exact *match* you'd think she must be my twin and not just my cousin.⟩ — see IMAGE 1

6 an earnest effort for superiority or victory over another ⟨The discussion soon degenerated into a pointless shouting *match*.⟩ — see CONTEST 1

match *vb* **1** to be the exact counterpart of ⟨Your socks don't *match*.⟩ ⟨the rare blood type that exactly *matched* that of the transplant recipient⟩

synonyms correspond (to), equal, parallel

related words blend (with), conform (to), coordinate (with), go (with), harmonize (with); complement, supplement; counterbalance, counterpoise; echo, image, mirror, repeat; add up (to), amount (to), approach, come (to), near; measure (up), rival, suggest

2 to give in marriage ⟨They thought of *matching* their son with a young noblewoman.⟩ — see MARRY 2

3 to produce something equal to (as in quality or value) ⟨We were unable to *match* their offer.⟩ — see EQUAL 1

matching *adj* having qualities in common ⟨was fond of dressing the twins in *matching* outfits⟩ — see ALIKE

matchless *adj* having no equal or rival for excellence or desirability ⟨the *matchless* beauty and grandeur of Yosemite Valley⟩ — see ONLY 1

mate *n* **1** either of a pair matched in one or more qualities ⟨Have you seen the *mate* to this glove anywhere?⟩

synonyms companion, fellow, half, match, twin

related words coordinate; coequal, counterpart, equal, equivalent, like, parallel, peer, rival; carbon copy, double, duplicate, facsimile, identical twin, likeness, replica, ringer; analogue (*or* analog), similarity

near antonyms antipode, antithesis, contrary, converse, opposite, reverse

2 a person frequently seen in the company of another ⟨met his *mates* at the game⟩ — see ASSOCIATE 1

3 the person to whom another is married ⟨They vowed to each other that they would remain *mates* for life.⟩ — see SPOUSE

mate *vb* to engage in sexual intercourse ⟨Cats conceive almost every time they *mate*.⟩ — see COPULATE

material *adj* **1** relating to or composed of matter ⟨There's no *material* evidence that a crime has been committed.⟩

synonyms concrete, physical, substantial

related words bodily, carnal, corporal, corporeal, embodied, fleshly; apparent, appreciable, detectable, discernible (*also* discernable), noticeable, observable, palpable, perceptible, seeable, sensible, tangible, touchable, visible; objective, phenomenal; bulky, heavy, hefty, massive, ponderous, solid, weighty

near antonyms bodiless, disembodied, formless, incorporeal; ethereal, insubstantial, unsubstantial; impalpable, imperceptible, insensible, intangible, unnoticeable; metaphysical, spiritual

antonyms immaterial, nonmaterial, nonphysical

2 having great meaning or lasting effect ⟨There's no *material* difference between the two designs for the skyscraper.⟩ — see IMPORTANT 1

3 having to do with life on earth especially as opposed to that in heaven ⟨people who worry more about *material* concerns than about spiritual ones⟩ — see EARTHLY

4 having to do with the matter at hand ⟨That information, while fascinating, is not *material* to our discussion.⟩ — see PERTINENT

5 of or relating to the human body ⟨*material* needs such as food and warmth⟩ — see PHYSICAL 1

material *n* **1** the basic elements from which something can be developed ⟨She's clearly movie star *material*.⟩ — see MAKING

2 *usually* **materials** *pl* items needed for the performance of a task or activity ⟨I have all the *materials* to build the mobile.⟩ — see EQUIPMENT

materialist *n* a person who is chiefly interested in material comfort and is hostile or indifferent to art and culture ⟨a *materialist* who knows the price of everything and the value of nothing⟩ — see PHILISTINE

materiality *n* **1** something that actually exists ⟨The detective preferred a single *materiality* to a slew of hypotheticals.⟩ — see FACT 2

2 the fact or state of being pertinent ⟨The *materiality* of that fact is not in dispute.⟩ — see PERTINENCE

3 the quality of being actual ⟨seems to question the very *materiality* of the universe⟩ — see FACT 1

materialize *vb* **1** to come into existence ⟨The business speculator promised profits that never seemed to materialize.⟩ — see BEGIN 2

2 to come into view ⟨The train station *materialized* through the fog.⟩ — see APPEAR 1

3 to come to one's attention especially gradually or unexpectedly ⟨An unforeseen problem with this project seems to have *materialized*.⟩ — see ARISE 2

4 to represent in visible form ⟨a statue of a laughing child that seems to *materialize* the very concept of joy⟩ — see EMBODY 2

matériel *or* **materiel** *n* items needed for the performance of a task or activity ⟨The army is running short of clothing and other *matériel*.⟩ — see EQUIPMENT

maternal *adj* of, relating to, or characteristic of a mother ⟨Her *maternal* instincts told her that something was wrong.⟩ — see MOTHERLY

maternity *n* motherly character or qualities ⟨She had such *maternity* at such a young age that all her classmates went to her for comfort.⟩
synonyms motherliness
related words nurturance; fertility, fruitfulness

mathematical *adj* meeting the highest standard of accuracy ⟨produced an answer of *mathematical* precision⟩ — see PRECISE 1

matriarch *n* a dignified usually elderly woman of some rank or authority ⟨Even though she was 87, the *matriarch* of the family knew everything that was going on.⟩
synonyms dame, dowager, matron
related words grandam (*or* grandame); headmistress, mistress

matriculate *vb* to add (a person) to a list or roll as a participant or member ⟨The college *matriculated* 1000 students for the fall semester.⟩ — see ENROLL 1

matrimonial *adj* of or relating to marriage ⟨opened an office to practice *matrimonial* law⟩ — see MARITAL

matrimony *n* a union representing a special kind of social and legal partnership between two people ⟨We intend to be joined in *matrimony* until "death do us part."⟩ — see MARRIAGE 1

matron *n* a dignified usually elderly woman of some rank or authority ⟨The *matron* firmly ordered the rowdy little boys back to their seats.⟩ — see MATRIARCH

matte *also* **mat** *or* **matt** *adj* lacking a surface luster or gloss ⟨I chose a paint with a *matte* finish so the walls wouldn't be too shiny.⟩
synonyms dim, dull, dulled, flat, lusterless
related words tarnished, unpolished; cloudy, dingy, dirty, drab, lackluster, mousy (*or* mousey), muddy; gray (*also* grey), leaden, pale, palish; black, dark, darkened, darkish, dimmed, dusky, gloomy, murky, obscure
near antonyms buffed, burnished, glazed, lacquered, polished, rubbed, shellacked, varnished; satin, satiny; silken, silky; gleaming, glimmering, glinting, glistening, glittering, scintillating, shimmering, shining, sparkling, twinkling; beaming, bedazzling, bright, brightened, brilliant, dazzling, effulgent, glowing, incandescent, lambent, lucent, lucid, luminous, radiant, refulgent, resplendent
antonyms glossy, lustrous, shiny, sleek

matter *n* **1** a major object of interest or concern (as in a discussion or artistic composition) ⟨That is not relevant to the *matter* under discussion.⟩
synonyms content, motif, motive, question, subject, theme, topic
related words subject matter; talking point; count, idea, point, purpose; consideration, issue, problem; body, bulk, burden, core, crux, essence, fundamental, generality, gist, grist, heart, main, marrow, mass, net, nub, nubbin, nucleus, pith, pivot, purport, quick, staple, substance, sum
near antonyms digression, excursion, interjection, parenthesis, tangent
2 something to be dealt with ⟨We must take care of this *matter* before it becomes a real problem.⟩
synonyms affair, business, thing
related words consideration, issue, problem; crisis, crossroad(s), crunch, emergency, exigency, head, juncture, strait, zero hour; concern, trouble, worry; care, lookout, responsibility; corner, fix, hole, jam, pickle, pinch, predicament, scrape, spot
phrases ball of wax

3 communications or parcels sent or carried through the postal system ⟨first-class *matter*⟩ — see MAIL

4 something that requires thought and skill for resolution ⟨I've been thinking about the *matter* all night, and I believe I have a solution.⟩ — see PROBLEM 1

5 an approximate amount, extent, or degree ⟨a simple meal that can be prepared in a *matter* of 20 to 30 minutes⟩ — see NEIGHBORHOOD 1

matter *vb* to be of importance ⟨She believes that doing well in school really does *matter*.⟩
synonyms count, import, mean, signify, weigh
related words affect, concern, influence, sway; add up (to), amount (to)
phrases carry weight, cut ice

matter-of-fact *adj* **1** restricted to or based on fact ⟨a *matter-of-fact* recitation of the events of the last week⟩ — see FACTUAL 1
2 willing to see things as they really are and deal with them sensibly ⟨a *matter-of-fact* woman who didn't worry about "what ifs"⟩ — see REALISTIC 1

maturation *n* the process of becoming mature ⟨A flower's *maturation* from bud to full bloom can take weeks.⟩
synonyms development, growth, maturing, ripening
related words blossoming, flourishing, flowering; mellowing, softening; evolution, evolvement, expansion, progression; coming-of-age, maturity
near antonyms decadence, decay, decaying, declension, decline, declining, degeneration, descent, deterioration; ebbing, fading, shriveling (*or* shrivelling), waning, wilting, withering; death, decease, demise, dying, end, exit, expiration; regression, retrogression, reversion

mature *adj* **1** fully grown or developed ⟨I like pears when they're still hard, before they're *mature*.⟩
synonyms adult, full-blown, full-fledged, matured, ripe, ripened
related words aged, aging (*or* ageing), long-lived, old, older; golden, mellow
near antonyms blooming, blossoming, burgeoning, flourishing, flowering; undeveloped, unfinished, unfledged, unformed
antonyms adolescent, green, immature, juvenile, unripe, unripened, young, youngish, youthful
2 having reached the date at which payment is required ⟨*mature* bonds⟩ — see DUE 1
3 relating to or typical of adults; displaying proper maturity ⟨That wasn't a very *mature* response to my well-meaning criticism.⟩ — see ADULT 1

mature *vb* to become mature ⟨a young figure skater whose talent is still *maturing*⟩
synonyms age, develop, grow, grow up, progress, ripen
related words mellow, soften; bloom, blossom, burgeon (*also* bourgeon), flourish, flower; open, unfold; advance, evolve; get along, get on, gray (*also* grey)
near antonyms decay, decline, degenerate, deteriorate, sink, worsen; droop, dry, fade, flag, sag, shrivel, wane, waste (away), weaken, wilt, wither; regress, retrogress, revert; backslide, lapse, return

matured *adj* fully grown or developed ⟨a *matured* plant in full bloom⟩ — see MATURE 1

maturing *n* the process of becoming mature ⟨The *maturing* of young horses can take several years.⟩ — see MATURATION

maturity *n* the state of being fully grown or developed ⟨People are legally considered to have reached *maturity* at the age of 18 in the United States.⟩
synonyms adulthood, majority
related words manhood; bloom, flush, heyday, prime; middle age, midlife

near antonyms babyhood, infancy, toddlerhood; childhood, youth
antonyms immaturity

maudlin *adj* appealing to the emotions in an obvious and tiresome way ⟨a *maudlin* movie about a lovable tramp⟩ — see CORNY

maul *vb* **1** to abuse physically ⟨The hiker survived being *mauled* by a bear.⟩ — see MANHANDLE 1
2 to strike repeatedly ⟨two boxers *mauling* each other in the ring⟩ — see BEAT 1

maunder *vb* **1** to move about from place to place aimlessly ⟨*maundered* all over town on his day off⟩ — see WANDER 1
2 to talk at length without sticking to a topic or getting to a point ⟨Ask her a question and she'll *maunder* for half an hour.⟩ — see RAMBLE 1

maundering *adj* passing from one topic to another ⟨a long, *maundering* conversation about what was wrong with the world and how he could fix it⟩ — see DISCURSIVE

maverick *adj* deviating from commonly accepted beliefs or practices ⟨George Sand's *maverick* views on marriage scandalized 19th-century French society.⟩ — see HERETICAL

maverick *n* a person who does not conform to generally accepted standards or customs ⟨There's always one *maverick* who has to go his own way.⟩ — see NONCONFORMIST 1

mawkish *adj* appealing to the emotions in an obvious and tiresome way ⟨a *mawkish* plea for donations to the charity⟩ — see CORNY

mawkishness *n* the state or quality of having an excess of tender feelings (as of love, nostalgia, or compassion) ⟨the grating *mawkishness* of her poetry⟩ — see SENTIMENTALITY

maxim *n* an often stated observation regarding something from common experience ⟨It's a common *maxim* that "a watched pot never boils," but that's not literally true.⟩ — see SAYING

maximum *adj* **1** of the greatest or highest degree or quantity ⟨the *maximum* amount of time needed to complete the project⟩ — see ULTIMATE 1
2 of the highest degree ⟨He always puts out *maximum* effort.⟩ — see FULL 2

maximum *n* the greatest amount, number, or part ⟨achieved the *maximum*⟩ — see MOST

maybe *adv* it is possible ⟨*Maybe* we can make it to the concert, if we hurry.⟩ — see PERHAPS

mayhap *adv* it is possible ⟨*Mayhap* I could see you again next week? I so enjoyed our date tonight.⟩ — see PERHAPS

maze *n* a confusing and complicated arrangement of passages ⟨The mansion had a beautifully landscaped *maze* that was constructed of tall cypresses.⟩
synonyms labyrinth
related words meander; jungle, quagmire; catacomb, cat's cradle, knot, snarl, tangle, web; entanglement, entrapment, snare, trap

maze *vb* to throw into a state of mental uncertainty ⟨I'm completely *mazed* by the multitude of plans for health insurance.⟩ — see CONFUSE 1

meager *or* **meagre** *adj* less plentiful than what is normal, necessary, or desirable ⟨Everyday he eats a *meager* breakfast of toast and coffee.⟩
synonyms hand-to-mouth, light, niggardly, poor, scant, scanty, scarce, skimpy, slender, slim, spare, sparing, sparse, stingy
related words deficient, inadequate, insufficient, lacking, short, wanting; bare, bare-bones; least, littlest, lowest, mere, minimal, slightest
phrases thin on the ground
near antonyms adequate, enough, satisfactory, sufficient, tolerable; fat, fecund, fertile, fruitful, prolific, rich; lavish, luxuriant; excess, extra, surplus

antonyms abundant, ample, bountiful, copious, generous, liberal, plenteous, plentiful

meal *n* food eaten or prepared for eating at one time ⟨All she wants to do is sit quietly after the large Thanksgiving *meal*.⟩
synonyms chow, feed, menu, mess, repast, table
related words board; breakfast, buffet, collation, dinner, lunch, luncheon, refreshments, snack, supper, tea; banquet, feast, regale, spread; bake, barbecue (*also* barbeque), clambake, cookout, fry, luau, picnic, potluck, roast

mealy *adj* **1** lacking a healthy skin color ⟨Her *mealy* complexion might be an indication of a health condition.⟩ — see PALE 2
2 not being or expressing what one appears to be or express ⟨a *mealy* apology that was really no apology at all⟩ — see INSINCERE

mealymouthed *adj* not being or expressing what one appears to be or express ⟨a *mealymouthed* compliment from a jealous competitor⟩ — see INSINCERE

¹**mean** *adj* being about midway between extremes of amount or size ⟨For the state of Florida, what is the *mean* number of sunny days per month?⟩ — see MIDDLE 2

²**mean** *adj* **1** belonging to the class of people of low social or economic rank ⟨Alexander Hamilton seems to have had feelings of inferiority because of his *mean* origins.⟩ — see IGNOBLE 1
2 giving or sharing as little as possible ⟨a *mean* child who hoarded all her toys⟩ — see STINGY 1
3 having or showing a desire to cause someone pain or suffering for the sheer enjoyment of it ⟨Why are you being so *mean* to me?⟩ — see HATEFUL
4 not following or in accordance with standards of honor and decency ⟨a *mean* trick to play on a trusting person⟩ — see IGNOBLE 2
5 of little or less value or merit ⟨It's no *mean* feat to memorize that long poem.⟩ — see INFERIOR 2
6 of the very best kind ⟨I'm a *mean* dancer, so you could do worse than go to the prom with me.⟩ — see EXCELLENT
7 showing signs of advanced wear and tear and neglect ⟨He worked hard to escape the *mean* neighborhood of his youth.⟩ — see SHABBY 1
8 arousing or deserving of one's loathing and disgust ⟨That was no *mean* stunt to pull off, especially with so little advance preparation.⟩ — see CONTEMPTIBLE 1

mean *n* **1** a middle point between extremes ⟨That candidate's moderate views were seen as the *mean* that voters were looking for.⟩
synonyms golden mean, medium, middle, midpoint
related words arithmetic mean, average; median, norm, par, standard
phrases middle of the road
near antonyms maximum, utmost; minimum
2 means *pl* an action planned or taken to achieve a desired result ⟨She won the competition by fair and honest *means*.⟩ — see MEASURE 1
3 means *pl* something used to achieve an end ⟨The ends don't justify the *means*.⟩ — see AGENT 1
4 means *pl* the total of one's money and property ⟨a woman of considerable *means*⟩ — see WEALTH 1

mean *vb* **1** to communicate or convey (as an idea) to the mind ⟨The national anthem *means* various things to various people.⟩
synonyms denote, express, import, intend, signify, spell
related words connote, imply, suggest; hint, infer, insinuate, intimate; embody, epitomize, personify, represent, symbol, symbolize; advert, allude (to), cite, instance, mention, refer (to), specify, touch (on *or* upon); designate, indicate, signal
2 to be of importance ⟨Your presence at my graduation would *mean* a lot to me.⟩ — see MATTER

3 to have in mind as a purpose or goal ⟨I *mean* to win this race.⟩ — see INTEND 1

4 to serve as a sign or symptom of ⟨These colder nights *mean* autumn has truly arrived.⟩ — see INDICATE 1

meander *vb* to move about from place to place aimlessly ⟨theatergoers *meandering* around the lobby waiting for the play to start⟩ — see WANDER 1

meaning *adj* clearly conveying a special meaning (as one's mood) ⟨gave me a *meaning* look after I said that⟩ — see EXPRESSIVE

meaning *n* **1** the idea that is conveyed or intended to be conveyed to the mind by language, symbol, or action ⟨the unmistakable *meaning* of the skier's upraised arms as he finished his spectacular run⟩

synonyms content, denotation, drift, import, intent, intention, purport, sense, significance, signification

related words connotation; clue, cue, hint, implication, indication, inkling, intimation, suggestion; message, tenor, theme; bottom, essence, essentiality, nature, soul, spirit, stuff; acceptance, acceptation; burden, crux, gist; core, heart, marrow, nub, nucleus, pith, point, quick

2 something that one hopes or intends to accomplish ⟨The people have a right to know what the president's *meaning* is in getting the nation involved in this war.⟩ — see GOAL

meaningful *adj* **1** clearly conveying a special meaning (as one's mood) ⟨gave a *meaningful* sigh when I asked her how things were going⟩ — see EXPRESSIVE

2 having great meaning or lasting effect ⟨His time in office was too brief to accomplish anything *meaningful*.⟩ — see IMPORTANT 1

meaningless *adj* having no meaning ⟨This argument over seating arrangements is an utterly *meaningless* bit of nonsense.⟩

synonyms empty, inane, pointless, senseless

related words frivolous, inconsequential, inconsiderable, insignificant, minor, negligible, slight, trifling, trivial, unimportant; absurd, asinine, balmy, brainless, empty-headed, fatuous, foolish, half-witted, harebrained, mindless, nonsensical, preposterous, stupid, unintelligent, unwise, weak-minded, witless, zany; irrational, unreasonable; aimless, haphazard, purposeless

near antonyms eloquent, expressive, pregnant, revealing, suggestive, telling; logical, rational, reasonable, valid; consequential, eventful, important, key, major, momentous, substantial, weighty

antonyms meaningful, significant

meanly *adv* **1** in a manner showing no signs of pride or self-assertion ⟨*Meanly* silent up to that point, he now felt that fair criticism was turning into gratuitous insult.⟩ — see LOWLY

2 in a mean or spiteful manner ⟨In a *meanly* worded letter she told me that she never wanted to see me again.⟩ — see NASTILY

meanness *n* the desire to cause pain for the satisfaction of doing harm ⟨Nothing more than unprovoked *meanness* drove him to smash the child's toy.⟩ — see MALICE

measly *adj* so small or unimportant as to warrant little or no attention ⟨offered her guest only one *measly* cookie⟩ — see NEGLIGIBLE 1

measure *n* **1** an action planned or taken to achieve a desired result ⟨such new security *measures* as metal detectors at all the entrances⟩

synonyms expedient, means, move, shift, step

related words act, action, deed, doing, feat, thing; course, procedure, proceeding, process; activity, affair, business, dealing, enterprise, event; attempt, crack, endeavor, essay, fling, go, initiative, operation, pass, shot, stab, trial, try, undertaking, whack; effort, exertion, labor, pains, trouble, while, work; project, proposal, proposition; makeshift, resort, resource, stopgap; countermeasure, countermove, counterstep

2 a given or particular mass or aggregate of matter ⟨the *measure* of oil needed to make the dressing⟩ — see AMOUNT

3 something set up as an example against which others of the same type are compared ⟨During the Renaissance, man came to be viewed as the *measure* of all things.⟩ — see STANDARD 1

4 the recurrent pattern formed by a series of sounds having a regular rise and fall in intensity ⟨The song's soft, soothing *measures* make it a good lullaby.⟩ — see RHYTHM

5 the total amount of measurable space or surface occupied by something ⟨a slipcover for the couch that was made to *measure*⟩ — see ¹SIZE

measure *vb* **1** to find out the size, extent, or amount of ⟨For this experiment, you need to carefully *measure* all the chemicals before you mix them together.⟩

synonyms gauge (*also* gage), scale, span

related words weigh; calibrate, caliper; quantify, quantitate; lay off; calculate, cipher, compute, figure, reckon, work out; appraise, assess, conjecture, estimate, evaluate, guess, judge, suppose, value; add up, sum, tally, total

2 to keep from exceeding a desirable degree or level (as of expression) ⟨He carefully *measured* his response to the provocative question.⟩ — see CONTROL 1

measured *adj* **1** decided on as a result of careful thought ⟨a *measured* response to the situation⟩ — see DELIBERATE 1

2 having distinct or certain limits ⟨the *measured* authority of the mayor in running the town's affairs⟩ — see LIMITED 1

3 marked by or occurring with a noticeable regularity in the rise and fall of sound ⟨The procession moved along to the *measured* beating of a drum.⟩ — see RHYTHMIC

measureless *adj* being or seeming to be without limits ⟨the *measureless* universe⟩ — see INFINITE

measurement *n* the total amount of measurable space or surface occupied by something ⟨The *measurement* of the average house lot in that neighborhood is half an acre.⟩ — see ¹SIZE

measure up (to) *vb* to come near or nearer to in character or quality ⟨He always worried about *measuring up to* his older brother.⟩ — see APPROXIMATE

meat *n* **1** animal and especially mammal tissue used as food ⟨We need to go shopping: there's only enough *meat* in the freezer for one more dinner.⟩

synonyms flesh

related words game, poultry, red meat, variety meat

2 substances intended to be eaten ⟨offered his guests *meat* and drink⟩ — see FOOD

3 the central part or aspect of something under consideration ⟨He dances all around it without ever addressing the *meat* of the issue.⟩ — see CRUX

mecca *n* a thing or place that is of greatest importance to an activity or interest ⟨That region of Connecticut is a *mecca* for antique hunters.⟩ — see CENTER 1

mechanical *adj* **1** done instantly and without conscious thought or decision ⟨the waiter's *mechanical* reply of "Everything on the menu is good"⟩ — see AUTOMATIC 1

2 lacking in natural or spontaneous quality ⟨a somewhat *mechanical* vocal performance⟩ — see ARTIFICIAL 1

medal *n* a piece of metal given in honor of a special event, a person, or an achievement ⟨The display case held an impressive array of military *medals* from World War II.⟩

synonyms medallion, order

related words decoration, honor; crown, insignia, laurel, ribbon, title; bronze, gold, silver; badge, button, chevron, clasp, cockade, color, ensign, rosette, star; distinction; award, prize; citation, commendation

medallion *n* a piece of metal given in honor of a special event, a person, or an achievement ⟨The hockey team received a gold *medallion* at the Olympics.⟩ — see MEDAL

meddle *vb* to interest oneself in what is not one's concern ⟨Please stop *meddling* in your sister's life, even though you mean well.⟩ — see INTERFERE

meddler *n* a person who meddles in the affairs of others ⟨a *meddler* who stayed up all night watching the neighbors⟩ — see BUSYBODY

meddlesome *adj* thrusting oneself where one is not welcome or invited ⟨*Meddlesome* neighbors kept asking the couple when they were going to have children.⟩ — see INTRUSIVE

meddling *adj* thrusting oneself where one is not welcome or invited ⟨They promised not to be *meddling* in-laws.⟩ — see INTRUSIVE

medial *adj* occupying a position equally distant from the ends or extremes ⟨Four is the *medial* number between one and seven.⟩ — see MIDDLE 1

median *adj* **1** being about midway between extremes of amount or size ⟨the *median* price of a home in the area⟩ — see MIDDLE 2

2 occupying a position equally distant from the ends or extremes ⟨Find the *median* point between your speakers, and test the audio from there.⟩ — see MIDDLE 1

mediate *adj* occupying a position equally distant from the ends or extremes ⟨He has a black-and-white view of human nature, believing that there is no *mediate* state between good and evil.⟩ — see MIDDLE 1

mediate *vb* to act as a go-between for opposing sides ⟨Their middle child is often asked to *mediate* between the oldest and the youngest.⟩ — see INTERVENE

mediator *n* one who works with opposing sides in order to bring about an agreement ⟨If you two cannot resolve this argument on your own, we'll have to bring in a *mediator*.⟩
synonyms buffer, conciliator, go-between, intercessor, intermediary, intermediate, interposer, middleman, peacemaker
related words troubleshooter; moderator; bargainer, negotiant, negotiator; appeaser, pacificator, pacifier, reconciler; agent, attorney, deputy, factor, procurator, proxy; liaison, medium; arbiter, arbitrator, judge, referee, umpire; adviser (*also* advisor), counselor (*or* counsellor)

medic *n* a person specially trained in healing human medical disorders ⟨The wounded soldier called for a *medic*.⟩ — see DOCTOR

medication *n* a substance or preparation used to treat disease ⟨The doctor prescribed two different *medications* for the infection.⟩ — see MEDICINE

medicine *n* a substance or preparation used to treat disease ⟨If you don't take all the doses of your *medicine*, you might get sick again.⟩
synonyms cure, drug, medication, pharmaceutical, physic, remedy, specific
related words cure-all, panacea; botanical, patent medicine, prescription drug; cordial, potion, tonic; miracle drug, wonder drug; cap, capsule, pill, tablet; injection, shot; embrocation, liniment, lotion, ointment, potion, poultice; antibiotic, serum; cathartic, purgative

mediocre *adj* **1** of average to below average quality ⟨The entree was good, but the dessert was just *mediocre*.⟩
synonyms common, fair, indifferent, medium, middling, ordinary, passable, second-class, second-rate, so-so
related words acceptable, adequate, all right, alright, decent, OK (*or* okay), reasonable, satisfactory, sufficient, sufficing, tolerable; moderate, modest; presentable, respectable; minimal, unexceptional
near antonyms A1, capital, distinguished, excellent, exceptional, fine, first-class, first-rate, grand, great, match-less, maximum, number one (*also* No. 1), optimal, optimum, outstanding, par excellence, peerless, preeminent, prime, sensational, special, splendid, stellar, sterling, superb, superior, superlative, supreme, swell, terrific, tiptop, top, top-notch; unmatched, unparalleled, unsurpassed; deficient, inadequate, insufficient, lacking, unacceptable, unsatisfactory, wanting

2 of low quality ⟨*mediocre* souvenirs that are sold to tourists⟩ — see CHEAP 2

meditate *vb* **1** to give serious and careful thought to ⟨I've been *meditating* a career change for months.⟩ — see PONDER

2 to have in mind as a purpose or goal ⟨Gina had *meditated* a quick return to work after having the baby, but circumstances changed.⟩ — see INTEND 1

meditation *n* long or deep thinking about spiritual matters ⟨The busy executive devotes an hour a day to quiet *meditation*.⟩ — see CONTEMPLATION

meditative *adj* given to or marked by long, quiet thinking ⟨I've been in a *meditative* mood all day.⟩ — see CONTEMPLATIVE

medium *adj* **1** being about midway between extremes of amount or size ⟨taxpayers of *medium* income⟩ — see MIDDLE 2

2 occupying a position equally distant from the ends or extremes ⟨a politician who first reads the polls and then inevitably takes the *medium* stance on every issue⟩ — see MIDDLE 1

3 of average to below average quality ⟨another *medium* effort from a movie director who can do better⟩ — see MEDIOCRE 1

medium *n* **1** a middle point between extremes ⟨trying to achieve a happy *medium* as far as work and personal life are concerned⟩ — see MEAN 1

2 something used to achieve an end ⟨regards political activism on the local level as the best *medium* for effecting social change⟩ — see AGENT 1

3 the circumstances, conditions, or objects by which one is surrounded ⟨an artist who enjoys the cultural *medium* of the big city⟩ — see ENVIRONMENT

medley *n* an unorganized collection or mixture of various things ⟨a *medley* of snack foods available on the buffet table⟩ — see MISCELLANY 1

meek *adj* not having or showing any feelings of superiority, self-assertiveness, or showiness ⟨a *meek* girl who quietly went along with whatever her circle of friends wanted⟩ — see HUMBLE 1

meekly *adv* in a manner showing no signs of pride or self-assertion ⟨He asked *meekly* for help.⟩ — see LOWLY

meekness *n* the absence of any feelings of being better than others ⟨the *meekness* with which he obeyed the command⟩ — see HUMILITY

meet *adj* meeting the requirements of a purpose or situation ⟨In this case, splitting the winnings of the contested lottery ticket seems like a *meet* solution.⟩ — see FIT 1

meet *n* a competitive encounter between individuals or groups carried on for amusement, exercise, or in pursuit of a prize ⟨a swim *meet*⟩ — see GAME 1

meet *vb* **1** to come upon face-to-face or as if face-to-face ⟨We never once *met* another car on that lonely country road.⟩
synonyms catch, chance (upon), encounter, happen (upon), stumble (upon)
related words accost, confront; face, greet, salute; collide (with), crash (into); crisscross, cross, pass; hit (upon), light (upon), tumble (to); reencounter, remeet
phrases bump into, cross paths (with), run across, run into, run upon
near antonyms avoid, dodge, duck, elude, escape, evade, shake, shun

2 to come together into one body or place ⟨We'll *meet* for dinner, with a discussion to follow, next week.⟩ — see ASSEMBLE 1

3 to come upon unexpectedly or by chance ⟨*met* her future husband at a party⟩ — see HAPPEN (ON *or* UPON)

4 to do what is required by the terms of ⟨a financially struggling city trying to *meet* its loans⟩ — see FULFILL 1

5 to enter into contest or conflict with ⟨The up-and-coming boxer will *meet* the reigning champ for the first time tomorrow.⟩ — see ENGAGE 2

6 to produce something equal to (as in quality or value) ⟨I'll *meet* your bet, nay, I'll even raise it.⟩ — see EQUAL 1

7 to put up with (something painful or difficult) ⟨trying to *meet* the challenge of going to college while working at a full-time job⟩ — see BEAR 2

8 to give what is owed for ⟨I paid a portion of the bill to keep my provider from cutting off service until I can *meet* the remainder of the charges.⟩ — see PAY 2

meeting *n* **1** a coming together of a number of persons for a specified purpose ⟨There will be another committee *meeting* next week to discuss fundraising.⟩

synonyms assembly, congress, convention, convocation, council, gathering, get-together, huddle

related words clinic, workshop; caucus, conclave, synod; demonstration, rally; conversation, dialogue (*also* dialog), discourse, discussion, palaver, talk; negotiation, parley, summit; conference, forum, roundtable, seminar, symposium; session

2 a body of people come together in one place ⟨a *meeting* marked by no consensus of what needs to be done⟩ — see GATHERING 1

3 the coming together of two or more things to the same point ⟨a *meeting* of two railroad lines⟩ — see CONVERGENCE

meetly *adv* in a manner suitable for the occasion or purpose ⟨The governor *meetly* and rightly did his duty when he vetoed a bill that was clearly unconstitutional.⟩ — see PROPERLY

megahit *n* a person or thing that is successful ⟨The band's latest album is a *megahit*.⟩ — see HIT 1

megalopolis *n* a thickly settled, highly populated area ⟨What was once a series of discrete towns interspersed with countryside is now one vast *megalopolis*.⟩ — see CITY

melancholy *adj* **1** causing unhappiness ⟨the *melancholy* thought of having to say good-bye to all the friends he had made over the summer⟩ — see SAD 2

2 feeling unhappiness ⟨She was a bit *melancholy* after her youngest child left for college.⟩ — see SAD 1

3 given to or marked by long, quiet thinking ⟨a *melancholy* period in the artist's life that is reflected in his work⟩ — see CONTEMPLATIVE

melancholy *n* a state or spell of low spirits ⟨The bleakness of winter sometimes gives me cause for *melancholy*.⟩ — see SADNESS

mélange *n* an unorganized collection or mixture of various things ⟨a *mélange* of outfits for her workouts at the gym⟩ — see MISCELLANY 1

meld *n* a distinct entity formed by the combining of two or more different things ⟨Her music is a *meld* of rock and country.⟩ — see BLEND

meld *vb* to turn into a single mass or entity that is more or less the same throughout ⟨a cuisine that *melds* East and West into strikingly original flavor combinations⟩ — see BLEND 1

melee *n* a rough and often noisy fight usually involving several people ⟨A verbal disagreement at the football game soon turned into a general *melee* involving scores of spectators.⟩ — see BRAWL 1

meliorate *vb* to make better ⟨regulations that were intend-ed to *meliorate* the working conditions of migrant farm laborers⟩ — see IMPROVE

mellifluous *adj* having a pleasantly flowing quality suggestive of music ⟨a rich, *mellifluous* voice that gets her a lot of work in radio and TV commercials⟩ — see LYRIC 1

mellow *adj* **1** having a pleasantly flowing quality suggestive of music ⟨the *mellow* tones of an old violin⟩ — see LYRIC 1

2 not harsh or stern especially in nature or effect ⟨a teacher with a *mellow* approach to classroom discipline⟩ ⟨*mellow* soaps⟩ — see GENTLE 1

3 having an easygoing and pleasing manner especially in social situations ⟨*Mellow* and unflappable, the office manager greatly contributes to the work environment.⟩ — see AMIABLE

4 having a relaxed, casual manner ⟨a *mellow* crowd at the party⟩ — see EASYGOING 1

melodic *adj* having a pleasantly flowing quality suggestive of music ⟨a sweetly *melodic* chant⟩ — see LYRIC 1

melodious *adj* **1** having a pleasantly flowing quality suggestive of music ⟨He preferred the *melodious* sounds of the woodlands to anything produced in a concert hall.⟩ — see LYRIC 1

2 having a pleasing mixture of notes ⟨a particularly *melodious* ringtone that was instantly recognizable⟩ — see HARMONIOUS 1

melodramatic *adj* **1** given to or marked by attention-getting behavior suggestive of stage acting ⟨He yet again made the *melodramatic* declaration that he couldn't take it anymore and was resigning.⟩ — see THEATRICAL 1

2 having the general quality or effect of a stage performance ⟨He gave his usual *melodramatic* speech that he had learned his lesson and thereafter would always make sure his bills were paid on time.⟩ — see DRAMATIC 1

melody *n* a rhythmic series of musical tones arranged to give a pleasing effect ⟨This week, we'll learn to play a more complicated *melody* on the saxophone.⟩

synonyms air, lay, song, strain, tune, warble

related words descant (*also* discant); cadence, measure, meter, rhythm; ballad, ditty, hymn, lyric, madrigal

melt *vb* **1** to cease to be visible ⟨The fog soon *melted* away with the rising of the sun.⟩ — see DISAPPEAR

2 to go from a solid to a liquid state ⟨A forgotten carton of ice cream was *melting* away on the counter.⟩ — see LIQUEFY

member *n* **1** one of the parts that make up a whole ⟨You're only one *member* of this group effort.⟩ — see ELEMENT 1

2 one of the pieces from which something is designed to be assembled ⟨lost an indispensable *member* of the model airplane kit⟩ — see PART 1

memento *n* something that serves to keep alive the memory of a person or event ⟨The couple kept a seashell as a *memento* of their first meeting, which happened to be at the beach.⟩ — see MEMORIAL

memo *n* **1** a message on paper from one person or group to another ⟨a long series of *memos* between the two authors collaborating on the book⟩ — see ¹LETTER

2 a usually brief written reminder ⟨wrote a *memo* to herself about the upcoming meeting⟩ — see NOTE 1

3 a written communication giving information or directions ⟨*Memos* were the standard means of office communication before the arrival of e-mail.⟩ — see MEMORANDUM 1

memoir *n* a history of a person's life ⟨The ex-president has a lucrative contract to write his *memoirs*, in which he will supposedly set the record straight.⟩ — see BIOGRAPHY

memorandum *n* **1** a written communication giving information or directions ⟨I'm waiting for the *memorandum* that will explain the new vacation policy.⟩

synonyms directive, memo, notice

related words announcement, bulletin, declaration, notification, posting, proclamation, pronouncement, release; dispatch, report; charge, command, dictate; directions, instructions, orders, word

2 a message on paper from one person or group to another ⟨The studio executives depend on endless *memoranda* to keep track of what's going on at a movie shot on location.⟩ — see ¹LETTER

3 a usually brief written reminder ⟨dispatched a *memorandum* to her assistant about the assignment⟩ — see NOTE 1

memorial *adj* serving to preserve the memory of a person, thing, or an event ⟨a *memorial* plaque on the bridge for a diver who died in the line of duty⟩ — see COMMEMORATIVE

memorial *n* something that serves to keep alive the memory of a person or event ⟨The Vietnam War *Memorial* is a starkly beautiful testimonial to the bravery of the soldiers who served in Vietnam.⟩

synonyms commemorative, keepsake, memento, monument, remembrance, reminder, souvenir, token

related words memorabilia; relic, vestige; cairn, landmark, marker; tribute; cenotaph

memorialize *vb* to be a memorial of ⟨At the entrance to the park stands a statue *memorializing* the novelist Sir Walter Scott.⟩ — see COMMEMORATE 1

memorializing *adj* serving to preserve the memory of a person, thing, or an event ⟨a *memorializing* book on the sinking of the Titanic⟩ — see COMMEMORATIVE

memorize *vb* to commit to memory ⟨Everyone has to *memorize* a poem for next week's class.⟩

synonyms con, learn, study

related words hark back (to), recall, recollect, relive, remember, reminisce (about), retain, think (of); accept, apprehend, comprehend, grasp, know, understand; absorb, digest

near antonyms forget, misremember; disregard, ignore, neglect, overlook, overpass, pass over, slight, slur (over)

antonyms unlearn

memory *n* **1** the power or process of recalling what has been previously learned or experienced ⟨A photographic *memory* makes taking tests entirely too easy.⟩

synonyms mind, recollection, remembrance, reminiscence

related words contemplation, meditation, reflection, retrospection, thinking; awareness, cognizance; apprehension, comprehension, grasp, grip, perception, understanding

near antonyms amnesia, repression; forgetfulness

2 a particular act or instance of recalling or the thing remembered ⟨I have only the vaguest *memory* of the family vacation we took the year I turned three.⟩

synonyms recall, recollection, remembrance, reminiscence

related words flashback; memento, memorial, reminder, souvenir, token; association

menace *n* something that may cause injury or harm ⟨Those dogs are a *menace* to this neighborhood.⟩ — see DANGER 2

menace *vb* **1** to place in danger ⟨Poisonous lionfish *menaced* unwary divers.⟩ — see ENDANGER

2 to remain poised to inflict harm, danger, or distress on ⟨an invasive species that *menaces* the indigenous fish population⟩ — see THREATEN

menacing *adj* **1** being or showing a sign of evil or calamity to come ⟨The report warns that the emergence of new viruses is one of the most *menacing* developments we face.⟩ — see OMINOUS

2 involving potential loss or injury ⟨fears that the unemployment rate may be reaching *menacing* proportions⟩ — see DANGEROUS 1

ménage *n* those who live as a family in one house ⟨Getting the whole unruly *ménage* ready for an outing takes quite a while.⟩ — see HOUSEHOLD

mend *vb* **1** to put into good shape or working order again ⟨That shirt will be as good as new when I'm finished *mending* it.⟩

synonyms doctor, fix, patch, recondition, renovate, repair, revamp

related words fix up, overhaul, rebuild, reconstruct, refurbish; aid, cure, heal, help; condition, prepare, ready; care (for), maintain, service; freshen, refresh, refreshen, regenerate, rejuvenate, renew, restore, revitalize, revive; ameliorate, better, enhance, enrich, improve, meliorate

near antonyms blemish, break, damage, deface, disfigure, flaw, harm, hurt, impair, injure, mar, ruin, spoil, vandalize, wreck; cripple, disable, maim, mangle, mutilate

2 to become healthy and strong again after illness or weakness ⟨She's *mending* after a particularly nasty bout of the flu.⟩ — see CONVALESCE

3 to restore to a healthy condition ⟨*mended* the broken plant so that it was soon thriving again⟩ — see HEAL 1

4 to make up for (an offense) ⟨The proverb "least said, soonest *mended*" should be heeded by anyone tempted to angrily blurt out things they really don't mean.⟩ — see EXPIATE

5 to change one's behavior or character for the better ⟨Everyone's written her off as a liar, but I say it's never too late to *mend*.⟩ — see REFORM 2

6 to bring about recovery from ⟨the old adage that only time can *mend* a broken heart⟩ — see CURE 1

mendacious *adj* telling or containing lies ⟨That tabloid routinely publishes the most moronically *mendacious* stories about celebrities.⟩ — see DISHONEST 1

mendacity *n* **1** a statement known by its maker to be untrue and made in order to deceive ⟨highly fictionalized "memoirs" in which the facts were few and the *mendacities* many⟩ — see LIE

2 the tendency to tell lies ⟨You need to overcome this deplorable *mendacity*, or no one will ever believe anything you say.⟩ — see DISHONESTY 1

mendicant *n* a person who lives by public begging ⟨put change into the *mendicant's* can⟩ — see BEGGAR

mending *n* the process or period of gradually regaining one's health and strength ⟨It was a long slow *mending* of his injuries from the car crash, but he's fine now.⟩ — see CONVALESCENCE

menstruation *n* an occurrence of menstruating ⟨the discomforts of *menstruation*⟩ — see PERIOD 1

mental *adj* of or relating to the mind ⟨A funny *mental* image made him laugh out loud.⟩

synonyms cerebral, inner, intellectual, interior, internal, psychological (*also* psychologic)

related words cognitive, conscious; telepathic; brainy, clever, intelligent, quick-witted, rational, reasoning, sharp, sharp-witted, smart, thinking

near antonyms bodily, carnal, corporal, corporeal, fleshly, physical; unconscious; brainless, doltish, half-witted, mindless, obtuse, simple, slow-witted, stupid, thickheaded, unintelligent, weak-minded, witless

antonyms nonmental

mentality *n* the ability to learn and understand or to deal with problems ⟨hired a teacher with a good *mentality* for helping struggling students⟩ — see INTELLIGENCE 1

mention *n* a formal recognition of an achievement or praiseworthy deed ⟨Ava received a special *mention* for her submission to the exhibition of local artists.⟩ — see COMMENDATION 1

mention *vb* **1** to make reference to or speak about briefly but specifically ⟨You only *mentioned* in passing some of your accomplishments.⟩

synonyms advert (to), cite, drop, instance, name, note, notice, quote, refer (to), specify, touch (on *or* upon)

related words allude (to), hint (at), imply, indicate, infer, intend, intimate, suggest; point (out), signal, signify; denominate, designate; indicate; bring up, broach, interject, interpolate, interpose, introduce; infiltrate, insinuate, worm; advertise, announce, broadcast, declare, proclaim, pronounce, publicize, publish, sound

near antonyms disregard, forget, ignore, neglect, overlook, overpass, pass over, slight

2 to give as an example ⟨*mentioned* several legal precedents in support of her argument⟩ — see QUOTE 1

mentor *vb* to give advice and instruction to (someone) regarding the course or process to be followed ⟨We're looking for volunteers to *mentor* students in the theater arts.⟩ — see GUIDE 1

menu *n* **1** a list of foods served at or available for a meal ⟨The *menu* at the fancy restaurant listed many dishes that I had never heard of.⟩

synonyms card

related words chow, chuck [*chiefly West*], cuisine, fare, grub, provender, table

phrases bill of fare

2 a record of a series of items (as names or titles) usually arranged according to some system ⟨checked the *menu* of available books⟩ — see ¹LIST

3 food eaten or prepared for eating at one time ⟨a nine-course *menu* that consisted of pocket-size portions of the chef's specialties⟩ — see MEAL

mercenary *adj* having or marked by an eager and often selfish desire especially for material possessions ⟨They were a *mercenary* couple, who defined themselves not by what they were but by what they owned.⟩ — see GREEDY 1

merchandise *n* products that are bought and sold in business ⟨We stock only the finest-quality *merchandise* in this store.⟩

synonyms goods, wares

related words line; export, import; inventory, staples, stock, stuff, supply; job lot; domestics, durables (*also* durable goods), hard goods

merchandise *also* **merchandize** *vb* to offer for sale to the public ⟨the familiar practice of stores *merchandising* goods at dramatically lower prices on the day after Thanksgiving⟩ — see MARKET

merchandiser *n* **1** a buyer and seller of goods for profit ⟨The wholesale *merchandiser* makes a 15% profit on those toys.⟩ — see MERCHANT

2 the person in a business deal who hands over an item in exchange for money ⟨a scattering of small *merchandisers* selling souvenirs around the fairgrounds⟩ — see VENDOR

merchant *n* a buyer and seller of goods for profit ⟨free trade agreements that are favored by *merchants* on both sides of the border⟩

synonyms dealer, merchandiser, trader, tradesman, trafficker

related words businessman, enterprise, entrepreneur; buyer, marketer, purchaser; hawker, huckster, hustler, peddler (*also* pedlar); retailer, seller, shopkeeper, storekeeper, vendor (*also* vender); jobber, middleman, wholesaler; distributor, provider, provisioner, purveyor, supplier

mercifulness *n* kind, gentle, or compassionate treatment especially towards someone who is undeserving of it ⟨preached that the *mercifulness* of the Lord is without limit⟩ — see MERCY 1

merciless *adj* having or showing a lack of sympathy or

tender feelings ⟨She is a *merciless* competitor at board games of any kind.⟩ — see HARD 1

mercurial *adj* likely to change frequently, suddenly, or unexpectedly ⟨The boss's mood is so *mercurial* that we never know how he's going to react to anything.⟩ — see FICKLE 1

mercy *n* **1** kind, gentle, or compassionate treatment especially towards someone who is undeserving of it ⟨Always show your enemies *mercy*, because it makes you a better person.⟩

synonyms charity, clemency, forbearance, lenience, leniency, lenity, mercifulness, quarter

related words humanitarianism, philanthropy; empathy, pity, sympathy, understanding; commiseration, favor, grace; benevolence, care, compassion, gentleness, goodness, goodwill, kindliness, kindness; altruism, generosity, magnanimity, nobility

near antonyms hard-heartedness, mercilessness, pitilessness, ruthlessness, uncharitableness; reprisal, requital, retaliation, retribution, revenge, vengeance; venom, vindictiveness, virulence, vitriol; atrocity, barbarity, brutality, cruelty, sadism, savageness, savagery, truculence, viciousness, violence, wantonness; castigation, chastisement, discipline, punishment, scolding; abhorrence, abomination, execration, hate, hatred, loathing

2 an act of kind assistance ⟨did a *mercy* for the stranded motorist and was richly rewarded⟩ — see FAVOR 1

3 the capacity for feeling for another's unhappiness or misfortune ⟨The defendant threw himself on the *mercy* of the court.⟩ — see HEART 1

mere *adj* being this and no more ⟨His voice did not rise above a *mere* whisper.⟩

synonyms bare, very

related words absolute, all-out, arrant, out-and-out, outright, pure, sheer, simple, stark, total, unadulterated, unalloyed, unmitigated, unqualified, utter; alone, lone, only, singular, sole, solitary, solo, unique

merely *adv* nothing more than ⟨The outside noise was *merely* a raccoon knocking over the garbage can.⟩ — see JUST 3

merge *vb* to turn into a single mass or entity that is more or less the same throughout ⟨Their music *merges* different styles from around the world.⟩ — see BLEND 1

merging *n* the act or an instance of joining two or more things into one ⟨The *merging* of the two companies resulted in a corporation with a totally different configuration.⟩ — see UNION 1

meridian *n* the highest part or point ⟨a lawyer at the *meridian* of his career arguing a case before the U.S. Supreme Court⟩ — see HEIGHT 1

merit *n* **1** a quality that gives something special worth ⟨This mystery novel at least has the *merit* of an original plot.⟩ — see EXCELLENCE 2

2 the relative usefulness or importance of something as judged by specific qualities ⟨That idea has some *merit*, so let's explore it.⟩ — see WORTH 1

merit *vb* to be or make worthy of (as a reward or punishment) ⟨That selfless act of heroism *merited* a public ceremony to honor the young swimmer.⟩ — see EARN 2

merited *adj* being what is called for by accepted standards of right and wrong ⟨The punishment, although harsh, was entirely *merited*.⟩ — see JUST 1

meritorious *adj* **1** deserving of high regard or great approval ⟨worked all night with *meritorious* determination to get the project done on time⟩ — see ADMIRABLE

2 having sufficient worth or merit to receive one's honor, esteem, or reward ⟨All agreed that the most *meritorious* science project had won the competition.⟩ — see WORTHY

merrily *adv* in a cheerful or happy manner ⟨Our coworker *merrily* announced that it was her birthday, so we treated her to lunch.⟩ — see GAILY 1

merriment *n* **1** a mood characterized by high spirits and amusement and often accompanied by laughter ⟨Their unexpected *merriment* made him nervously inquire as to the reason for it.⟩ — see MIRTH

2 joyful or festive activity ⟨The wedding reception *merriment* lasted long into the night.⟩ — see MERRYMAKING

merriness *n* a mood characterized by high spirits and amusement and often accompanied by laughter ⟨The opening of the new playground was celebrated with joy and *merriness*.⟩ — see MIRTH

merry *adj* indicative of or marked by high spirits or good humor ⟨the traditional depiction of Santa Claus as a rotund man with *merry*, twinkling blue eyes⟩

synonyms blithesome, festive, gleeful, jocose, jocular, jocund, jolly, jovial, laughing, mirthful, sunny

related words amused, beaming, chuckling, giggling, smiling; bright, buoyant, carefree, cheerful, cheery, chipper, lighthearted, lightsome, upbeat; animated, bouncing, frisky, jaunty, lively, peppy, perky, spirited, sprightful, sprightly, vivacious, zippy; blessed (*also* blest), blissful, delighted, ecstatic, elated, enraptured, entranced, euphoric, exhilarated, exuberant, exultant, gladsome, happy, high, joyful, joyous, jubilant, overjoyed, radiant, rapturous, ravished, thrilled, tickled; amusing, facetious, flippant, frolicsome, funny, hilarious, jesting, joking, joshing, playful, sportive, witty

near antonyms aggrieved, anguished, blue, brokenhearted, crestfallen, dejected, depressed, despondent, disconsolate, disheartened, dispirited, downcast, downhearted, forlorn, glum, heartbroken, heartsick, low-spirited, melancholy, sad, saddened, sorrowful, unhappy; crying, groaning, moaning, sobbing, wailing, weeping; discontented, disgruntled, moody

merrymaker *n* one who engages in merrymaking especially in honor of a special occasion ⟨*Merrymakers* from the community celebrated New Year's Eve in an especially grand style.⟩ — see CELEBRANT

merrymaking *n* joyful or festive activity ⟨The Fourth of July is always an occasion of much *merrymaking* at our home.⟩

synonyms conviviality, festivity, gaiety (*also* gayety), jollification, jollity, merriment, rejoicing, reveling (*or* revelling), revelry

related words carousal, carouse; delight, diversion, entertainment, fun, mischief, pleasure, recreation; cheer, cheerfulness, cheeriness, glee, gleefulness, hilarity, joviality, merriness, mirth, mirthfulness; carnival, celebration, festival, party, revel; frolicking, gamboling (*or* gambolling), rollicking, romping; binge, fling, frolic, gambol, lark, rollick, romp, spree; frivolity, funning, jesting, jocularity, joking, joshing, levity, lightheartedness, playfulness, zaniness

near antonyms dolefulness, dolor, gloom, gloominess, grief, heartache, heartbreak, heartsickness, misery, mourning, woe, wretchedness; dejection, depression, despondency, disconsolateness, dispiritedness, doldrums, downheartedness, forlornness, joylessness, melancholy, sorrow, unhappiness

mesa *n* a broad flat area of elevated land ⟨a *mesa* in the Arizona desert⟩ — see PLATEAU

mesh *n* **1** *usually* **meshes** *pl* something that catches and holds ⟨a routine request that got hung up in the *meshes* of the state bureaucracy⟩ — see WEB 1

2 a fabric made of strands loosely twisted, knotted, or woven together at regular intervals ⟨spread a *mesh* across the doorway to keep out insects⟩ — see ¹NET 1

mesh *vb* to catch or hold as if in a net ⟨Dolphins sometimes become *meshed* in fishnets.⟩ — see ENTANGLE 2

mesmerism *n* the art or act of inducing in a person a sleeplike state during which he or she readily follows suggestions ⟨made a living at *mesmerism* and the selling of medical remedies of dubious value⟩ — see HYPNOSIS

mesmerize *vb* to hold the attention of as if by a spell ⟨discovered that the children were *mesmerized* by a video game⟩ — see ENTHRALL 1

mess *n* **1** a state in which everything is out of order ⟨The party had left the house in a total *mess*.⟩ — see CHAOS

2 food eaten or prepared for eating at one time ⟨a *mess* of oatmeal⟩ — see MEAL

3 something unpleasant to look at ⟨The car was a *mess* after the accident.⟩ — see EYESORE

4 a considerable amount ⟨an unexpected Super Bowl loss that unleashed a whole *mess* of finger-pointing and second-guessing⟩ — see LOT 2

mess *vb* to interest oneself in what is not one's concern ⟨Please don't *mess* with me while I'm trying to concentrate.⟩ — see INTERFERE

mess (up) *vb* **1** to make or do (something) in a clumsy or unskillful way ⟨I *messed up* the drawing and had to start over.⟩ — see BOTCH

2 to undo the proper order or arrangement of ⟨A nap had *messed up* her hair.⟩ — see DISORDER

3 to make a mistake ⟨If anyone *messes up* even once while we're recording, we have to start all over again.⟩ — see ERR 1

4 to strike repeatedly ⟨said he would *mess* him *up* if he cheated⟩ — see BEAT 1

mess (with) *vb* to handle thoughtlessly, ignorantly, or mischievously ⟨Please don't *mess with* the buttons on the camera.⟩ — see TAMPER (WITH)

message *n* a piece of conveyed information ⟨answered the phone and took a *message*⟩ — see COMMUNICATION 1

messed *adj* lacking in order, neatness, and often cleanliness ⟨Dad came home to find a *messed* basement with his tools scattered about.⟩ — see MESSY

messenger *n* one that carries a message or does an errand ⟨The *messenger* comes by twice a day to pick up packages.⟩

synonyms courier, go-between, page, runner

related words forerunner, harbinger, herald; agent, ambassador, delegate, deputy, emissary, envoy, representative; bearer, carrier, deliveryman, letter carrier, mail carrier, mailman

messiness *n* a state in which everything is out of order ⟨A professional chef would not tolerate such *messiness* in the kitchen.⟩ — see CHAOS

messy *adj* lacking in order, neatness, and often cleanliness ⟨a *messy* room⟩

synonyms chaotic, cluttered, confused, disarranged, disarrayed, disheveled (*or* dishevelled), disordered, disorderly, higgledy-piggledy, hugger-mugger, jumbled, littered, messed, muddled, mussed, mussy, pell-mell, rumpled, sloppy, topsy-turvy, tousled, tumbled, unkempt, untidy, upside-down

related words bedraggled, besmirched, blackened, dingy, dirty, filthy, foul, grimy, grubby, grungy, mucky, nasty, soiled, spotted, squalid, stained, sullied, unclean, uncleanly; dowdy, frowsy (*or* frowzy), shaggy, slatternly, sloven, slovenly

phrases at sixes and sevens, out of joint

near antonyms clean, cleaned, hygienic, immaculate, sparkling, spick-and-span (*or* spic-and-span), spotless, stainless, unsoiled, unsullied; methodical (*also* methodic), regular, systematic, systematized; careful, fastidious, finicky, fussy, meticulous; combed, groomed, manicured; taintless, undefiled, unpolluted, untainted, wholesome

antonyms crisp, neat, neatened, ordered, orderly, organized, shipshape, snug, tidied, tidy, trim, uncluttered, well-ordered

metamorphose *vb* to change in form, appearance, or use ⟨a science fiction story in which radiation *metamorphoses* people into giant bugs⟩ — see CONVERT 2

metamorphosis *n* a change in form, appearance, or use ⟨the *metamorphosis* of caterpillars into butterflies⟩ ⟨the *metamorphosis* of the abandoned factory into a mixed-use property⟩ — see CONVERSION 1

metaphor *n* an elaborate or fanciful way of expressing something ⟨"It's raining cats and dogs" is just a colorful *metaphor* and not a meteorological announcement.⟩ — see CONCEIT 1

metaphoric *or* **metaphorical** *adj* expressing one thing in terms normally used for another ⟨an author fond of such *metaphorical* phrases as "the desert was a fiery furnace"⟩ — see FIGURATIVE

metaphysical *adj* **1** dealing with or expressing a quality or idea ⟨a work that deals with such *metaphysical* questions as the very nature of knowledge⟩ — see ABSTRACT 1
2 of, relating to, or being part of a reality beyond the observable physical universe ⟨belief in a *metaphysical* world beyond the one in which we live⟩ — see SUPERNATURAL 1

mete (out) *vb* to give out (something) to appropriate individuals ⟨determined to *mete out* an appropriate punishment for the CEO guilty of insider trading⟩ — see ADMINISTER 1

meter *n* the recurrent pattern formed by a series of sounds having a regular rise and fall in intensity ⟨The poem's heavy *meter* is meant to reinforce the atmosphere of gloom.⟩ — see RHYTHM

method *n* the means or procedure for doing something ⟨The city council is stuck in the last century and needs to adopt more modern *methods* for doing things.⟩
synonyms approach, fashion, form, manner, strategy, style, system, tack, tactics, technique, way
related words mode, modus operandi; blueprint, design, game, ground plan, intrigue, layout, line, model, plan, plot, program, route, scheme; expedient, move, shift, step; practice (*also* practise), process, routine; policy

methodical *also* **methodic** *adj* following a set method, arrangement, or pattern ⟨a *methodical* study plan that included lists of points to memorize⟩
synonyms neat, orderly, organized, regular, systematic, systematized
related words ordered, regularized, standardized, structured; accurate, clocklike, correct, exact, precise; detailed, specific
near antonyms chaotic, disordered, disorderly
antonyms disorganized, haphazard, hit-or-miss, immethodical, irregular, nonsystematic, patternless, planless, systemless, unsystematic

meticulous *adj* taking, showing, or involving great care and effort ⟨did a *meticulous* job of restoring the painting⟩ — see PAINSTAKING

meticulousness *n* strict attentiveness to what one is doing ⟨He dressed himself with uncharacteristic *meticulousness*, which made us suspect he was going on an interview.⟩ — see CARE 1

metrical *or* **metric** *adj* marked by or occurring with a noticeable regularity in the rise and fall of sound ⟨The *metrical* chugging of the machinery had a hypnotic effect.⟩ — see RHYTHMIC

metropolis *n* a thickly settled, highly populated area ⟨a big, teeming *metropolis* where ambitious people from all over come to make their mark⟩ — see CITY

metropolitan *n* a person with the outlook, experience, and manners thought to be typical of big city dwellers ⟨a TV

series about the lives and loves of a group of young, attractive *metropolitans*⟩ — see COSMOPOLITAN

mettlesome *adj* **1** having much high-spirited energy and movement ⟨The *mettlesome* opening dance number got the audience all jazzed up.⟩ — see LIVELY 1
2 marked by a lively display of strong feeling ⟨a *mettlesome* debate on a thorny issue⟩ — see SPIRITED 1

mewl *vb* to utter feeble plaintive cries ⟨The tiny kitten *mewled* for its mother.⟩ — see WHIMPER 1

microscopic *also* **microscopical** *adj* very small in size ⟨Even a *microscopic* speck of dust in the eye will cause pain.⟩ — see TINY

mid *adj* occupying a position equally distant from the ends or extremes ⟨Her *mid* molar will have to be extracted and replaced by a bridge.⟩ — see MIDDLE 1

mid *prep* in or into the middle of ⟨*Mid* a tangle of weeds grew a perfect rose.⟩ — see AMONG

midday *n* the middle of the day ⟨By *midday* the sun and heat were unbearable.⟩ — see NOON 1

middle *adj* **1** occupying a position equally distant from the ends or extremes ⟨You must mark the exact *middle* point of each of these lines in order to solve the problem.⟩
synonyms central, halfway, intermediary, intermediate, medial, median, mediate, medium, mid, midmost
related words equidistant; inmost, inner, innermost, nearest; betwixt and between, gray (*also* grey), in-between
near antonyms outer, peripheral
antonyms extreme, farthest, farthermost, furthermost, furthest, outermost, outmost, remotest, utmost
2 being about midway between extremes of amount or size ⟨a house that is *middle*-sized for that neighborhood⟩ ⟨a man of *middle* height⟩
synonyms average, intermediate, mean, median, medium, middling, moderate, modest
related words reasonable; common, commonplace, conventional, normal, popular, regular, routine, standard, typical, usual; adequate, passable, tolerable
near antonyms excessive, extreme; exceptional, rare, strange, uncommon, unusual; distinctive, idiosyncratic, special, unique; individual, peculiar, private

middle *n* **1** a middle point between extremes ⟨His salary is exactly at the *middle* of the company's pay scale.⟩ — see MEAN 1
2 an area or point that is an equal distance from all points along an edge or outer surface ⟨Put the serving dish in the *middle* of the table.⟩ — see CENTER 2
3 the middle region of the human torso ⟨clutched the football tightly against her *middle*⟩ — see MIDRIFF
4 the most intense or characteristic phase of something ⟨I'm right in the *middle* of a phone conversation, so can you come back later?⟩ — see THICK

middleman *n* one who works with opposing sides in order to bring about an agreement ⟨The retired statesman is often asked to be a *middleman* in international disputes.⟩ — see MEDIATOR

middle–of–the–road *adj* avoiding major social change or extreme political ideas ⟨a candidate with *middle-of-the-road* views on most hot-button issues⟩ — see MODERATE 2

middling *adj* **1** being about midway between extremes of amount or size ⟨Tired of the city but not particularly interested in small-town life, he moved to a suburb of *middling* size.⟩ — see MIDDLE 2
2 of average to below average quality ⟨I was disappointed in the renowned historian's latest book, which is only *middling*.⟩ — see MEDIOCRE 1

midget *n* a living thing much smaller than others of its kind ⟨a breed that is the *midget* of the horse world⟩ — see DWARF 1

midmost *adj* occupying a position equally distant from the ends or extremes ⟨The *midmost* subway car is usually the most crowded one in the train, so try to avoid it.⟩ — see MIDDLE 1

midpoint *n* 1 a middle point between extremes ⟨I don't want the cheapest or the most expensive phone, but one that is at the *midpoint* in price.⟩ — see MEAN 1
2 an area or point that is an equal distance from all points along an edge or outer surface ⟨That house is the precise *midpoint* of the school district.⟩ — see CENTER 2

midriff *n* the middle region of the human torso ⟨*Midriff*-baring tops are popular this summer.⟩
synonyms middle, waist, waistline
related words trunk; abdomen, belly, gut, stomach

midst *n* 1 an area or point that is an equal distance from all points along an edge or outer surface ⟨stood in the *midst* of the crowd⟩ — see CENTER 2
2 the most intense or characteristic phase of something ⟨in the *midst* of illustrating a new book⟩ — see THICK

midst *prep* in or into the middle of ⟨gave a victory speech *midst* cheering supporters⟩ — see AMONG

mien *n* the outward form of someone or something especially as indicative of a quality ⟨The kindly *mien* of the librarian suggested that she would be willing to help me.⟩ — see APPEARANCE 1

might *n* the ability to exert effort for the accomplishment of a task ⟨Currently the President lacks the political *might* to push his programs through the Congress.⟩ — see POWER 2

mightily *adv* 1 to a great degree ⟨Every volunteer contributed *mightily* to the cause.⟩ — see VERY 1
2 with great effort or determination ⟨struggled *mightily* to climb up the steep cliff⟩ — see HARD 1
3 in a vigorous and forceful manner ⟨It is a foregone conclusion that the President's supporters will *mightily* applaud virtually every line of his speech.⟩ — see HARD 3

mighty *adj* 1 having great power or influence ⟨one of the *mighty* leaders of the U.S. financial world⟩ — see IMPORTANT 2
2 unusually large ⟨A *mighty* castle towered over everything nearby.⟩ — see HUGE

mighty *adv* to a great degree ⟨He was *mighty* hungry after raking leaves all afternoon.⟩ — see VERY 1

migrant *adj* having a way of life that involves moving from one region to another typically on a seasonal basis ⟨*migrant* laborers picking produce⟩ — see MIGRATORY

migrant *n* one that leaves one place to settle in another ⟨a nation of *migrants*⟩ — see EMIGRANT

migratory *adj* having a way of life that involves moving from one region to another typically on a seasonal basis ⟨Most of the apple crop is picked by *migratory* workers.⟩ ⟨*migratory* birds heading south for the winter⟩
synonyms migrant, mobile
related words errant, fugitive, itinerant, peripatetic, ranging, roaming, roving, traveling (*or* travelling), vagabond, vagrant, wandering, wayfaring; drifting, fiddle-footed, footloose, gadabout, gallivanting (*also* galavanting), rambling, sauntering, strolling, traipsing
near antonyms immobile, stationary; established, fast, fixed, rooted, sedentary, set, settled
antonyms nonmigrant, nonmigratory, resident

mild *adj* 1 marked by temperatures that are neither too high nor too low ⟨the *mild* weather that makes springtime such a delight⟩ — see CLEMENT 1
2 not harsh or stern especially in nature or effect ⟨a quiet gentleman with a kindly soul and a *mild* disposition⟩ — see GENTLE 1

milestone *n* a point in a chain of events at which an important change (as in one's fortunes) occurs ⟨The new drug was regarded as a *milestone* in the treatment of heart disease.⟩ — see TURNING POINT

milieu *n* the circumstances, conditions, or objects by which one is surrounded ⟨Young, innovative artists thrive in the freewheeling *milieu* that a big city offers.⟩ — see ENVIRONMENT

militancy *n* an inclination to fight or quarrel ⟨the *militancy* of the radical organization⟩ — see BELLIGERENCE

militant *adj* 1 feeling or displaying eagerness to fight ⟨an angry and *militant* speech⟩ — see BELLIGERENT
2 having or showing a bold forcefulness in the pursuit of a goal ⟨*militant* protestors refusing to disperse⟩ — see AGGRESSIVE 1

militant *n* one who is intensely or excessively devoted to a cause ⟨*Militants* within the movement insisted that there could be no compromise.⟩ — see ZEALOT

militarist *n* one who urges or attempts to cause a war ⟨a government dominated by *militarists*⟩ — see WARMONGER

military *adj* 1 of or relating to the armed services ⟨The colonel testified that revealing any more information would have required giving away *military* secrets.⟩
synonyms martial, service
related words naval; GI, gladiatorial, mercenary, soldierly; militant, militarist, militaristic, warlike; enlisted, regular; paramilitary
near antonyms civil, civilian
antonyms nonmilitary
2 of, relating to, or suitable for war or a warrior ⟨imposing *military* discipline⟩ — see MARTIAL 1

military *n* the combined army, air force, and navy of a nation ⟨had a long career in the *military*⟩ — see ARMED FORCES

mill *n* a building or set of buildings for the manufacturing of goods ⟨a steel *mill* that remains the town's principal employer⟩ — see FACTORY

mill *vb* to reduce to fine particles ⟨a demonstration of how dried kernels of corn were *milled* in colonial times⟩ — see POWDER

mime *n* 1 an actor in a story performed silently and entirely by body movements ⟨an internationally renowned *mime*⟩
synonyms mimic, mummer, pantomime, pantomimist
related words entertainer, performer, player, trouper; aper, imitator, impersonator, impressionist; clown, pantaloon
2 a movement of the body or limbs that expresses or emphasizes an idea or feeling ⟨The game is to communicate a phrase with *mime*.⟩ — see GESTURE 1

mime *vb* to use (someone or something) as the model for one's speech, mannerisms, or behavior ⟨As a joke, Eric knelt by the dinner table and began *miming* a dog begging for food.⟩ — see IMITATE 1

mimetic *adj* using or marked by the use of something else as a basis or model ⟨Children have a tendency toward *mimetic* behavior, often imitating their parents at a fairly early age.⟩ — see IMITATIVE 1

mimic *adj* 1 being such in appearance only and made with or manufactured from usually cheaper materials ⟨a *mimic* designer handbag⟩ — see IMITATION
2 using or marked by the use of something else as a basis or model ⟨a *mimic* rocket launch by kids pretending on a play structure⟩ — see IMITATIVE 1

mimic *n* 1 a person who imitates another's voice and mannerisms for comic effect ⟨a gifted *mimic* who can do a terrific imitation of anyone's voice⟩
synonyms imitator, impersonator, impressionist
related words burlesquer, caricaturist, lampooner, mocker, parodist, satirist; mime, mimer, mummer, pantomime, pantomimist; actor, player, trouper; ape, copycat, echo, parrot

2 an actor in a story performed silently and entirely by body movements ⟨a *mimic* in black clothes and white facial makeup⟩ — see MIME 1

mimic *vb* **1** to copy or exaggerate (someone or something) in order to make fun of ⟨The comedian was famous for *mimicking* the President's distinctive way of speaking.⟩
synonyms burlesque, caricature, do, imitate, mock, parody, spoof, travesty
related words lampoon, satirize; deride, gibe (*or* jibe), ridicule; ape, copycat, monkey, parrot; duplicate, emulate, replicate, reproduce; act, counterfeit, dissemble, fake, feign, pretend, sham, simulate; elaborate, embellish, embroider, exaggerate, magnify, pad, stretch; amplify, enhance, expand, flesh (out), overdraw, overstate, put on; mime, pantomime; impersonate, perform, play
2 to use (someone or something) as the model for one's speech, mannerisms, or behavior ⟨We began to learn their language by *mimicking* the sounds they made.⟩ — see IMITATE 1

mince *vb* to cut into small pieces ⟨*minced* some garlic and added it to the stew⟩ — see CHOP

mind *n* **1** the part of a person that feels, thinks, perceives, wills, and especially reasons ⟨I went for a walk to clear my *mind.*⟩
synonyms brain, cerebrum, head, psyche, thinker
related words gray matter, intellect, intelligence, reason, skull; acumen, alertness, astuteness, brilliance, insight, mentality, perception, perspicacity, sagacity, sapience, wisdom, wit
2 the normal or healthy condition of the mental abilities ⟨That noise is driving me out of my *mind.*⟩
synonyms daylights, head, reason, saneness, sanity, wit(s)
related words rationality, reasonableness, sense; clearheadedness, lucidity, lucidness, soundness; wisdom
near antonyms delusion, hallucination; delirium, frenzy, hysteria
antonyms dementia, unreason
3 an idea that is believed to be true or valid without positive knowledge ⟨Please speak your *mind* freely on this matter.⟩ — see OPINION 1
4 the power or process of recalling what has been previously learned or experienced ⟨Let's call to *mind* the events of last year.⟩ — see MEMORY 1

mind *vb* **1** to pay attention especially through the act of hearing ⟨You'll be in big trouble if you don't straighten up and *mind.*⟩ — see LISTEN
2 to act according to the commands of ⟨Tell the children to *mind* the babysitter.⟩ — see OBEY
3 to be cautious of or on guard against ⟨*Mind* the slippery steps!⟩ — see BEWARE (OF)
4 to have an interest or concern for ⟨Don't *mind* him; he's always complaining.⟩ — see CARE
5 to take charge of especially on behalf of another ⟨The salesperson will *mind* the store while the manager goes out to lunch.⟩ — see ²TEND 1
6 to take notice of and be guided by ⟨*Mind* the instructions that appear at the top of the first page of the exam.⟩ — see HEED 1

minded *adj* having a desire or inclination (as for a specified course of action) ⟨In most David vs. Goliath contests, people are generally *minded* to side with the underdog.⟩ — see WILLING 1

mindful *adj* having specified facts or feelings actively impressed on the mind ⟨a truly considerate person, always *mindful* of the needs of others⟩ — see CONSCIOUS 1

mindless *adj* **1** not having or showing an ability to absorb ideas readily ⟨underestimate the official as a *mindless* bureaucrat⟩ — see STUPID 1

2 not paying or showing close attention especially for the purpose of avoiding trouble ⟨*Mindless* of danger, the foolhardy skiers ignored the avalanche warnings.⟩ — see CARELESS 1

mindlessness *n* the quality or state of lacking intelligence or quickness of mind ⟨despised the sheer *mindlessness* of the movie's violence⟩ — see STUPIDITY 1

mine *n* **1** an abundant source ⟨a baseball fanatic who is a *mine* of fascinating trivia about the game⟩
synonyms cornucopia
related words repository, store, storehouse; cache, hoard, stash; bonanza
2 a usually concealed explosive device designed to go off when disturbed ⟨The soldiers were careful to disarm any *mines* they found in their path.⟩ — see BOOBY TRAP 1

mingle *vb* **1** to turn into a single mass or entity that is more or less the same throughout ⟨the site where the river and the ocean *mingle* their waters to form a broad estuary⟩ — see BLEND 1
2 to take part in social activities ⟨*mingling* at a cocktail party⟩ — see SOCIALIZE

miniature *adj* very small in size ⟨a dollhouse with *miniature* furnishings⟩ — see TINY

miniature *n* an exact representation of something in greatly reduced size ⟨a diorama filled with *miniatures* of town buildings as they looked in the 19th century⟩ — see MODEL 1

minimal *adj* being the least in amount, number, or size possible ⟨The repairs were made with *minimal* disruption to the workday.⟩
synonyms littlest, lowest, minimum, slightest
related words fewer, lesser, low, minor, modest, slight, small, smaller; infinitesimal, micro, subminimal, ultramicro; irreducible
near antonyms highest
antonyms biggest, full, greatest, hugest, largest, maximum, most, top, topmost, utmost

minimize *vb* to express scornfully one's low opinion of ⟨sore losers trying to *minimize* the other team's victory⟩ — see DECRY 1

minimum *adj* being the least in amount, number, or size possible ⟨They spent the *minimum* amount necessary to acquire the property.⟩ — see MINIMAL

minion *n* a person or thing that is preferred over others ⟨Most of the top appointments went to the new governor's personal *minions* and political cronies.⟩ — see FAVORITE

minister *n* a person sent on a mission to represent another ⟨the British *ministers* at the international peace conference⟩ — see AMBASSADOR

minister (to) *vb* to attend to the needs and comforts of ⟨volunteered to help *minister to* the sick at the local hospice⟩ — see NURSE 1

ministerial *adj* of, relating to, or characteristic of the clergy ⟨a priest conscientiously tending to his *ministerial* duties⟩ — see CLERICAL

minor *adj* **1** having not so great importance or rank as another ⟨some *minor* official who attends ceremonial events⟩ — see LESSER
2 of little or less value or merit ⟨a *minor* poet who is little read nowadays⟩ — see INFERIOR 2
3 lacking importance ⟨only a *minor* detail, which we can easily disregard for the moment⟩ — see UNIMPORTANT

minstrel *n* a person who writes poetry ⟨Edna St. Vincent Millay was unofficially the *minstrel* of Maine, as her poetry celebrates its coast and countryside.⟩ — see POET

minstrelsy *n* writing that uses rhythm, vivid language, and often rhyme to provoke an emotional response ⟨the traditional forms of German *minstrelsy*⟩ — see POETRY 1

mint *adj* being in an original and unused or unspoiled state ⟨a *mint* baseball card that should be worth a lot to a collector⟩ — see FRESH 1

mint *n* a very large amount of money ⟨She made a *mint* when the real estate market was hot.⟩ — see FORTUNE 2

minus *n* a feature of someone or something that creates difficulty for achieving success ⟨a plan with lots of pluses and only a few *minuses*⟩ — see DISADVANTAGE 1

minus *prep* not having ⟨The contraption was like a giant carousel *minus* the horses.⟩ — see WITHOUT 1

minuscule *adj* very small in size ⟨Public health officials have claimed that the chemical is harmless in such *minuscule* amounts.⟩ — see TINY

minute *adj* **1** including many small descriptive features ⟨a *minute* description of the setting of the story⟩ — see DETAILED 1
2 lacking importance ⟨a person who wastes time on the most *minute* aspects of everyday life⟩ — see UNIMPORTANT
3 so small or unimportant as to warrant little or no attention ⟨only *minute* differences between the two photographic prints⟩ — see NEGLIGIBLE 1
4 made or done with extreme care and accuracy ⟨a *minute* examination of the marine specimen⟩ — see FINE 2
5 very small in size ⟨We made some *minute* adjustments to the controls.⟩ — see TINY

minute *n* a very small space of time ⟨I'll be with you in just a *minute!*⟩ — see INSTANT

minutely *adv* with attention to all aspects or details ⟨a *minutely* detailed analysis of the series of glitches that resulted in the blackout⟩ — see THOROUGHLY 1

miracle *n* something extraordinary or surprising ⟨It's a *miracle* that you weren't hurt in the accident.⟩ — see WONDER 1

miraculous *adj* **1** being so extraordinary or abnormal as to suggest powers which violate the laws of nature ⟨the *miraculous* nature of the revelation⟩ — see SUPERNATURAL 2
2 causing wonder or astonishment ⟨his *miraculous* escape from the burning building⟩ — see MARVELOUS 1

mire *n* **1** soft wet earth ⟨We played on a football field that was thick with *mire*.⟩ — see MUD
2 spongy land saturated or partially covered with water ⟨Much of the land in that area is *mire* that cannot be developed.⟩ — see SWAMP
3 a difficult, puzzling, or embarrassing situation from which there is no easy escape ⟨The company is caught in a *mire* of legal problems.⟩ — see PREDICAMENT

mire *vb* **1** to make dirty ⟨The sight of the standard, which had emerged from the battle mangled and *mired*, still stirred the soldiers' hearts.⟩ — see DIRTY
2 to place in conflict or difficulties ⟨The case has been *mired* in probate court for years.⟩ — see EMBROIL

mirror *n* a smooth or polished surface that forms images by reflection ⟨Breaking a *mirror* is supposed to bring seven years of bad luck.⟩
synonyms looking glass
related words cheval glass, hand glass, pier glass

mirror *vb* to reproduce or show (an exact likeness) as a mirror would ⟨the still waters of the pond *mirroring* the cloudless sky above⟩ — see REFLECT 1

mirth *n* a mood characterized by high spirits and amusement and often accompanied by laughter ⟨Her unexpected visit provided much *mirth* in the office.⟩
synonyms cheer, cheerfulness, cheeriness, festivity, gaiety (*also* gayety), glee, gleefulness, hilarity, joviality, merriment, merriness, mirthfulness
related words frivolity, levity; jollification, jollity, reveling (*or* revelling), revelry; brightness, buoyancy, good-humoredness, good-naturedness, humor, sunniness; gamesomeness, insouciance, lightheartedness, playfulness, sport-

iveness; clownishness, flippancy, funning, jest, jesting, jocoseness, jocosity, jocularity, joking, joshing; frolicking, gamboling (*or* gambolling), rollicking, romping
near antonyms blues, dejection, depression, forlornness, sadness, sorrow, unhappiness; dolefulness, dolorousness, joylessness, plaintiveness, woe, woefulness; blackness, darkness, gloominess; desolateness, desolation; heartbreak, misery, mourning, wretchedness

mirthful *adj* indicative of or marked by high spirits or good humor ⟨the *mirthful* laughter of old teammates telling jokes and stories⟩ — see MERRY

mirthfully *adv* in a cheerful or happy manner ⟨a collection of holiday songs, *mirthfully* sung⟩ — see GAILY 1

mirthfulness *n* a mood characterized by high spirits and amusement and often accompanied by laughter ⟨The *mirthfulness* of the revelers was contagious, and pretty soon everyone was laughing and singing.⟩ — see MIRTH

miry *adj* full of or covered with soft wet earth ⟨*miry* fields that required a good pair of boots⟩ — see MUDDY 1

misadventure *n* bad luck or an example of this ⟨A string of financial *misadventures* eventually left him broke.⟩ — see MISFORTUNE

misanthrope *n* a person who distrusts other people and believes that everything is done for selfish reasons ⟨a former *misanthrope* who now professes a newly discovered love of mankind⟩ — see CYNIC

misanthropic *adj* having or showing a deep distrust of human beings and their motives ⟨She became increasingly *misanthropic* in her old age.⟩ — see CYNICAL

misapplication *n* incorrect or improper use ⟨This silly gossiping is a serious *misapplication* of your time.⟩ — see MISUSE

misapply *vb* to put to a bad or improper use ⟨You've *misapplied* the theorem to certain problems that require a different formula.⟩ ⟨public funds that were *misapplied*⟩
synonyms abuse, misuse, pervert, profane
related words degrade, twist; mismanage; corrupt, debase, desecrate
near antonyms apply, employ, use, utilize; respect

misapprehend *vb* to fail to understand the true or actual meaning of ⟨Unfortunately, the message that the artist was trying to convey has been *misapprehended* by many museum patrons.⟩ — see MISUNDERSTAND

misapprehension *n* **1** a failure to understand correctly ⟨Officials tried to eliminate all *misapprehensions* about the planned riverfront development.⟩ — see MISUNDERSTANDING 1
2 a wrong judgment ⟨a common *misapprehension* about how our language functions⟩ — see MISTAKE 1

misappropriate *vb* to take (something) without right and with an intent to keep ⟨a financial manager *misappropriating* funds from her clients' accounts⟩ — see STEAL 1

misbehave *vb* to behave badly ⟨scolded the children for *misbehaving*⟩
synonyms act out, act up, carry on
related words misconduct; disobey, rebel; clown (around), cut up, horse around, kid (around); show off; roughhouse
phrases raise Cain (*or* raise hell), run riot
near antonyms obey; acquit, act, bear, comport, conduct, demean, deport, quit; comply, conform; check, collect, compose, constrain, contain, control, curb, handle, inhibit, move, quiet, repress, restrain

misbehaving *adj* engaging in or marked by childish misbehavior ⟨a new approach for disciplining a chronically *misbehaving* child⟩ — see NAUGHTY

misbehavior *n* improper or illegal behavior ⟨Ms. Curry would not tolerate any *misbehavior* from her students.⟩ — see MISCONDUCT

misbelief *n* a false idea or belief ⟨the common *misbelief* that the Great Wall of China is visible from the moon⟩ — see FALLACY 1

miscalculate *vb* to make an incorrect judgment regarding ⟨They *miscalculated* how difficult the mountainous trek would be.⟩

  synonyms misconceive, misjudge, mistake

  related words misapprehend, misconstrue, misinterpret, misunderstand; overestimate, overrate, overvalue; miscount, misreckon

miscarry *vb* to go wrong ⟨The plan *miscarried* and we had to start all over.⟩

  synonyms misfire

  related words miss; break down, bust, conk (out), crash, die, fail, founder, stall; bomb, fizzle, flame out, flop, flunk, fold, wash out; flounder, struggle; decline, slip, slump, wane

  phrases come a cropper, come to grief, fall flat, fall short

  near antonyms prevail, succeed; flourish, prosper, thrive

miscellaneous *adj* consisting of many things of different sorts ⟨The bottom of the drawer was always a *miscellaneous* accumulation of odds and ends.⟩

  synonyms assorted, eclectic, heterogeneous, mixed, motley, patchwork, promiscuous, ragtag, varied

  related words manifold, multifarious; multiple, multiplex, myriad; disparate, divergent, diverse, sundry; amalgamated, blended, combined, commingled, commixed, conglomerated, fused, incorporated, intermingled, intermixed, merged, mingled; composite, conglomerate, hybrid; unclassified, unsorted

  near antonyms monolithic, uniform; alike, identical, like, same; distinct, distinctive, individual, separate

  antonyms homogeneous

miscellaneousness *n* the quality or state of being composed of many different elements or types ⟨The *miscellaneousness* of the store's merchandise makes it a browser's delight.⟩ — see VARIETY 1

miscellany *n* **1** an unorganized collection or mixture of various things ⟨The box from the attic contained a *miscellany* of old records, family photo albums, and long-forgotten love letters.⟩

  synonyms agglomerate, agglomeration, assortment, clutter, hash, hodgepodge, hotchpotch, jumble, litter, medley, mélange, mishmash, motley, muddle, patchwork, potpourri, ragbag, rummage, scramble, shuffle, tumble, variety, welter

  related words notions, oddments, odds and ends, sundries; admixture, amalgam, blend, combination, commixture, composite, compound, fusion, intermixture, mix-up; mess, morass, shambles

  2 a collection of writings ⟨The volume is a *miscellany* of tales and legends of the New England coast.⟩ — see ANTHOLOGY

mischance *n* **1** a chance and usually sudden event bringing loss or injury ⟨The smallest *mischance* could spell disaster for our plan.⟩ — see ACCIDENT 1

  2 bad luck or an example of this ⟨By *mischance* she took a wrong turn and became hopelessly lost in the city.⟩ — see MISFORTUNE

mischief *n* **1** playful, reckless behavior that is not intended to cause serious harm ⟨They are always up to some kind of *mischief*.⟩

  synonyms devilishness, devilment, devilry (*or* deviltry), hob, impishness, knavery, mischievousness, rascality, roguishness

  related words diabolicalness, misbehavior, misconduct, naughtiness, troublemaking; friskiness, playfulness,

sportiveness; chicanery, trickery; goings-on, hanky-panky, high jinks (*also* hijinks), monkeying, skylarking, tomfoolery; horseplay, roughhousing; antic, caper, practical joke, trick

  near antonyms gravity, seriousness, solemnity

  2 a natural disposition for playful behavior ⟨Your mother was full of *mischief* as a child, believe it or not.⟩ — see PLAYFULNESS

  3 an appealingly mischievous person ⟨He's a little *mischief* who means no harm.⟩ — see SCAMP 1

mischievous *adj* **1** tending to or exhibiting reckless playfulness ⟨The children had been so *mischievous* that we had to pay the babysitter extra to clean up the mess.⟩

  synonyms arch, devilish, elvish, impish, knavish, pixieish, prankish, rascally, roguish, sly, waggish

  related words antic, coltish, coy, frisky, frolicsome, kittenish, playful, sportive; happy, lighthearted, whimsical; energetic, lively, spirited, sprightly; artful, crafty, cunning, trickish, tricky, wily; misbehaving, naughty, troublemaking; pestering, riling, teasing

  near antonyms grave, grim, sedate, sober, solemn, staid, stern

  2 engaging in or marked by childish misbehavior ⟨punished for their *mischievous* tricks on the neighbors⟩ — see NAUGHTY

  3 causing or capable of causing harm ⟨*mischievous* gossip that ruined an innocent person's reputation⟩ — see HARMFUL

mischievousness *n* **1** a natural disposition for playful behavior ⟨As they grew older, they lost much of their youthful *mischievousness*.⟩ — see PLAYFULNESS

  2 playful, reckless behavior that is not intended to cause serious harm ⟨Bored kids often engage in a certain amount of *mischievousness* during the long summer vacation.⟩ — see MISCHIEF 1

misconceive *vb* to make an incorrect judgment regarding ⟨*misconceived* the scope of the nation's financial crisis⟩ — see MISCALCULATE

misconception *n* a false idea or belief ⟨It is a popular *misconception* that toilets flush in the opposite direction in the Southern Hemisphere.⟩ — see FALLACY 1

misconduct *n* improper or illegal behavior ⟨Some rough play got the hockey player fined for *misconduct* on the ice.⟩

  synonyms malfeasance, misbehavior, misdoing, wrongdoing

  related words crime, malefaction, misdeed, misdemeanor, sin, transgression, trespass, wrong; malpractice; goings-on, hanky-panky; familiarity, impropriety, indiscretion; blunder, flub, fumble, goof, lapse, miscue, misstep, mistake, slip, slipup, stumble

misconduct *vb* to manage badly ⟨Scott *misconducted* the polar expedition and paid for his mistakes with his life.⟩ — see MISMANAGE

misconstruction *n* a failure to understand correctly ⟨His *misconstruction* of the blueprints led to some costly and time-consuming repairs.⟩ — see MISUNDERSTANDING 1

misconstrue *vb* to fail to understand the true or actual meaning of ⟨claimed that the press had *misconstrued* her comments⟩ — see MISUNDERSTAND

misconstruing *n* a failure to understand correctly ⟨There are several words in English that are the result of the common *misconstruing* of singular forms as plurals.⟩ — see MISUNDERSTANDING 1

miscreant *n* **1** a mean, evil, or unprincipled person ⟨Halt, vile *miscreant*, and face justice!⟩ — see VILLAIN

  2 a person who has committed a crime ⟨hard-bitten *miscreants* serving time⟩ — see CRIMINAL

miscue *n* an unintentional departure from truth or accuracy

〈The slightest *miscue* could make the trapeze artist lose his grip and fall to the mat below.〉 — see ERROR 1

misdeed *n* a breaking of a moral or legal code 〈punished for his *misdeeds* by the church elders〉 — see OFFENSE 1

misdoing *n* 1 a breaking of a moral or legal code 〈The sordid *misdoings* of the city councilman were exposed as a result of an intense investigation by the local newspaper.〉 — see OFFENSE 1

2 improper or illegal behavior 〈kept a watchful eye for any *misdoing* by team members〉 — see MISCONDUCT

miser *n* a mean grasping person who is usually stingy with money 〈The *miser* liked to sit and play with his money.〉

synonyms cheapskate, niggard, piker, scrooge, skinflint, tightwad

related words hoarder, pack rat, saver

near antonyms prodigal, profligate, spender, spendthrift, squanderer, waster, wastrel

miserable *adj* 1 causing or marked by an atmosphere lacking in cheer 〈We've been having *miserable* weather.〉 — see GLOOMY 1

2 feeling unhappiness 〈The awful news made us *miserable*.〉 — see SAD 1

3 of low quality 〈had a *miserable* meal at some fast-food place〉 — see CHEAP 2

4 showing signs of advanced wear and tear and neglect 〈a *miserable* little apartment〉 — see SHABBY 1

5 deserving of one's pity 〈a *miserable* animal brought to the shelter〉 — see PATHETIC 1

6 deserving pitying scorn (as for inadequacy) 〈That ugly junk is one *miserable* excuse for a car.〉 — see PITIFUL 1

miserliness *n* the quality or practice of being overly sparing with money 〈Some kids like to grouse about the *miserliness* of their parents as far as allowances are concerned.〉 〈The company's misguided *miserliness* is the reason we're still using these inefficient, outdated computers.〉 — see PARSIMONY 1

misery *n* 1 a situation or state that causes great suffering and unhappiness 〈The flood brought *misery* to the towns along the river.〉 — see HELL 2

2 a state of great suffering of body or mind 〈a medical breakthrough that ended the *misery* of thousands〉 — see DISTRESS 1

misfire *vb* to go wrong 〈Their scheme to rob the bank *misfired* disastrously and landed them all in jail.〉 — see MISCARRY

misfortune *n* bad luck or an example of this 〈Through sheer *misfortune* our car got a flat tire and we were late for the ceremony.〉 〈Our *misfortunes* of the last year included the loss of a beloved pet.〉

synonyms adversity, ill, knock, misadventure, mischance, mishap, tragedy

related words calamity, cataclysm, catastrophe, disaster; affliction, hardship, trial, tribulation, woe; distress, misery, suffering, unhappiness; defeat, failure, fizzle, nonsuccess; curse, evil, sorrow, trouble; accident, casualty; blow, body blow, disappointment, letdown, setback; circumstance, destiny, doom, fate, lot, portion

near antonyms break, chance, godsend, hit, opportunity, strike, stroke, windfall; accomplishment, achievement, success

antonyms fortune, luck, serendipity

misgiving *n* 1 a feeling or attitude that one does not know the truth, truthfulness, or trustworthiness of someone or something 〈I had *misgivings* about the story, but I was afraid to speak up.〉 — see DOUBT

2 an uneasy feeling about the rightness of what one is doing or going to do 〈He was filled with *misgivings* about committing himself to such a huge loan.〉 — see QUALM

3 suspicion or fear of future harm or misfortune 〈over-

come by a sudden *misgiving* upon seeing the creepy old mansion〉 — see APPREHENSION 1

misgovern *vb* to manage badly 〈The party was soundly defeated at the polls for having disastrously *misgoverned* the country.〉 — see MISMANAGE

misguide *vb* to cause to believe what is untrue 〈We were *misguided* by the flashy advertisements for what turned out to be pretty lousy pizza.〉 — see DECEIVE

mishandle *vb* 1 to inflict physical or emotional harm upon 〈Many staffers were angry at how the boss *mishandled* employees who dared to complain.〉 — see ABUSE 1

2 to abuse physically 〈The musician brought her instrument on the plane so it would not be *mishandled* in baggage.〉 — see MANHANDLE 1

3 to manage badly 〈We took over as soon as we realized that the fill-in had been *mishandling* the situation.〉 — see MISMANAGE

mishap *n* 1 a chance and usually sudden event bringing loss or injury 〈the usual *mishaps* of a family vacation〉 — see ACCIDENT 1

2 bad luck or an example of this 〈*Mishap* followed wherever he went.〉 — see MISFORTUNE

mishmash *n* an unorganized collection or mixture of various things 〈The painting was just a *mishmash* of colors and abstract shapes as far as we could tell.〉 — see MISCELLANY 1

misinform *vb* to cause to believe what is untrue 〈She had been *misinformed* about the purpose of the meeting and walked in on what was a surprise birthday party.〉 — see DECEIVE

misinterpret *vb* 1 to change so much as to create a wrong impression or alter the meaning of 〈His note on this passage in the novel seriously *misinterprets* the author's meaning.〉 — see GARBLE

2 to fail to understand the true or actual meaning of 〈We *misinterpreted* the directions and ended up on the wrong side of town.〉 — see MISUNDERSTAND

misinterpretation *n* a failure to understand correctly 〈His *misinterpretation* of the ambiguously worded instructions was hardly his fault.〉 — see MISUNDERSTANDING 1

misjudge *vb* to make an incorrect judgment regarding 〈The gymnast *misjudged* her landing and sprained her ankle.〉 — see MISCALCULATE

misjudging *n* a wrong judgment 〈A series of small *misjudgings* along the way eventually amounted to a colossal mistake.〉 — see MISTAKE 1

misjudgment *n* a wrong judgment 〈One serious *misjudgment* at this point could cost the candidate the election.〉 — see MISTAKE 1

mislaid *adj* no longer possessed 〈a traveler looking for his *mislaid* passport〉 — see LOST

mislay *vb* to be unable to find or have at hand 〈I'm always *mislaying* my bus pass.〉 — see LOSE 1

mislaying *n* the act or an instance of not having or being able to find 〈Your *mislaying* of the car keys caused us to be late for work once again.〉 — see LOSS 1

mislead *vb* to cause to believe what is untrue 〈Some kingsnakes developed colors similar to venomous coral snakes to *mislead* predators into thinking they are dangerous.〉 — see DECEIVE

misleading *adj* tending or having power to deceive 〈The *misleading* text of the advertisement would like you to believe that you're getting something for nothing.〉 — see DECEPTIVE 1

mismanage *vb* to manage badly 〈The business was *mismanaged* so seriously that it eventually had to declare bankruptcy.〉

synonyms misconduct, misgovern, mishandle, misrule

related words abuse, ill-treat, ill-use, maltreat, mistreat, misuse; damage, harm, hurt, violate; botch, bungle

near antonyms govern, handle, husband, manage, rule; care (for), nurture; aid, help, protect, rescue

misplace *vb* to be unable to find or have at hand ⟨I seem to have *misplaced* my keys.⟩ — see LOSE 1

misplaced *adj* no longer possessed ⟨We eventually found the *misplaced* tickets in his coat pocket.⟩ — see LOST

misplacement *n* the act or an instance of not having or being able to find ⟨They worried that his *misplacement* of the invitation would keep them from getting in, but fortunately their names were on the list.⟩ — see LOSS 1

misread *vb* to fail to understand the true or actual meaning of ⟨I *misread* her body language and thought she was becoming confrontational.⟩ — see MISUNDERSTAND

misreading *n* a failure to understand correctly ⟨Your *misreading* of the definition of the word is what got you into trouble.⟩ — see MISUNDERSTANDING 1

misrepresent *vb* **1** to change so much as to create a wrong impression or alter the meaning of ⟨This summary seriously *misrepresents* the general tone and substance of the speech.⟩ — see GARBLE
2 to give a misleading impression of ⟨deliberately *misrepresented* the facts of the case⟩ — see BELIE 1

misrule *n* a state in which there is widespread wrongdoing and disregard for rules and authority ⟨a country with a long period of *misrule*⟩ — see ANARCHY

misrule *vb* to manage badly ⟨He was accused of *misruling* his island nation to the point of economic collapse.⟩ — see MISMANAGE

¹**miss** *n* **1** a female person who has not yet reached adulthood ⟨a talented young *miss*⟩ — see GIRL 2
2 a young unmarried woman ⟨Can I help you, *miss*?⟩ — see GIRL 1

²**miss** *n* something that has failed ⟨a television season with far fewer hits than *misses*⟩ — see FAILURE 3

miss *vb* **1** to fail to attend ⟨I had to *miss* work for a week because of the flu.⟩ — see CUT 2
2 to fail to understand the true or actual meaning of ⟨I think you're *missing* the point.⟩ — see MISUNDERSTAND
3 to be unsuccessful ⟨With a cast like that, the movie can't *miss*.⟩ — see FAIL 2

misshapen *adj* badly or imperfectly formed ⟨The returning camper proudly presented his mother with a *misshapen* clay bowl that he had made in crafts class.⟩ — see MALFORMED

missing *adj* **1** no longer possessed ⟨The *missing* socks turned up in the dog's special hiding place.⟩ — see LOST
2 not present or in evidence ⟨Any sense of how real people talk and act is *missing* from this novel.⟩ — see ABSENT 2
3 not at a certain place ⟨Our coach is *missing* this afternoon, so we'll have to have practice without her.⟩ — see ABSENT 1

mission *n* a specific task with which a person or group is charged ⟨Your *mission* is to clean up the house before company arrives.⟩
synonyms assignment, brief, business, charge, detail, job, operation, post
related words burden, chore, duty, need, obligation, office, requirement, responsibility; errand, labor, work; commitment, pledge, promise; appointment, commission, designation, nomination; compulsion, constraint, restraint

missive *n* a message on paper from one person or group to another ⟨The two old friends like to fire off *missives* filled with good-natured teasing and mock insults.⟩ — see ¹LETTER

misspend *vb* to use up carelessly ⟨lamented his *misspent* youth⟩ — see WASTE 1

misstate *vb* to change so much as to create a wrong impression or alter the meaning of ⟨a person who can be counted on to *misstate* even the simplest telephone message⟩ — see GARBLE

misstep *n* **1** a wrong judgment ⟨Another *misstep* like that, and the company could go belly-up.⟩ — see MISTAKE 1
2 an unintentional departure from truth or accuracy ⟨a *misstep* that could lead to disaster⟩ — see ERROR 1

mist *n* **1** a light or fine rain ⟨A *mist* was falling on the streets as we drove home.⟩ — see DRIZZLE
2 an atmospheric condition in which suspended particles in the air rob it of its transparency ⟨A heavy *mist* obscured our view of the city from the observatory.⟩ — see HAZE 1

mist *vb* to make dark, dim, or indistinct ⟨The damp air *misted* the window pane.⟩ — see CLOUD 1

mistake *n* **1** a wrong judgment ⟨I made a *mistake* when I believed him.⟩
synonyms misapprehension, misjudging, misjudgment, misstep, slip, slipup
related words blunder, errancy, error, fault, flub, fumble, gaffe, goof, inaccuracy, lapse, miscue, stumble, trip; foul-up, muff, misstatement; misconception, misconstruction, misconstruing, misinterpretation, misunderstanding
2 an unintentional departure from truth or accuracy ⟨Kay made a *mistake* on the exam that almost cost her a passing grade.⟩ — see ERROR 1

mistake *vb* **1** to fail to understand the true or actual meaning of ⟨The auctioneer *mistook* my nod for a bid, and I ended up buying a painting I don't even like.⟩ — see MISUNDERSTAND
2 to make an incorrect judgment regarding ⟨You seriously *mistake* me if you think I scare so easily.⟩ — see MISCALCULATE
3 to fail to differentiate (a thing) from something similar or related ⟨*mistook* wealth for happiness⟩ — see CONFUSE 3

mistaken *adj* having an opinion that does not agree with truth or the facts ⟨Tacos are on the cafeteria's menu today, if I'm not *mistaken*.⟩ — see INCORRECT 1

mistakenly *adv* in a mistaken or inappropriate way ⟨We *mistakenly* thought that this was our conference room.⟩ — see WRONGLY

mistreat *vb* to inflict physical or emotional harm upon ⟨a shelter for *mistreated* animals⟩ — see ABUSE 1

mistrust *n* a feeling or attitude that one does not know the truth, truthfulness, or trustworthiness of someone or something ⟨Granny had an unfortunate *mistrust* of doctors, so her medical condition was allowed to worsen.⟩ — see DOUBT

mistrust *vb* to have no trust or confidence in ⟨a recluse who *mistrusts* her neighbors and stays in her house all day⟩ — see DISTRUST

mistrustful *adj* **1** inclined to doubt or question claims ⟨We were *mistrustful* of the so-called "miracle cure."⟩ — see SKEPTICAL 1
2 not feeling sure about the truth, wisdom, or trustworthiness of someone or something ⟨Inhabitants of that remote community tend to be *mistrustful* of outsiders.⟩ — see DOUBTFUL 1

mistrustfully *adv* with distrust ⟨Our cat tends to view strangers *mistrustfully*.⟩ — see ASKANCE

mistrustfulness *n* a feeling or attitude that one does not know the truth, truthfulness, or trustworthiness of someone or something ⟨The man eyed the strange invention with his usual *mistrustfulness*.⟩ — see DOUBT

misty *adj* **1** filled with or dimmed by fine particles (as of dust or water) in suspension ⟨enjoyed the *misty* view of the thunderous falls from the deck of the sightseeing boat⟩ — see HAZY 1

2 not seen or understood clearly 〈I've a *misty* understanding of the issue but not so much that I could vote intelligently.〉 — see FAINT 1

misunderstand *vb* to fail to understand the true or actual meaning of 〈You *misunderstood* that poem because you took everything so literally.〉

synonyms misapprehend, misconstrue, misinterpret, misread, miss, mistake

related words misconceive, misjudge; mishear

antonyms appreciate, apprehend, catch, comprehend, conceive, fathom, get, grasp, know, make out, penetrate, perceive, see, seize, take in, understand

misunderstanding *n* **1** a failure to understand correctly 〈People once thought that there were canals on Mars because of a common *misunderstanding* of a report by an Italian astronomer.〉

synonyms misapprehension, misconstruction, misconstruing, misinterpretation, misreading

related words misconception, misperception, mistake

near antonyms appreciation, apprehension, comprehension, conception, grasp, knowledge, perception, understanding; awareness, realization

2 an often noisy or angry expression of differing opinions 〈tried to resolve their *misunderstandings* peacefully〉 — see ARGUMENT 1

misusage *n* incorrect or improper use 〈The teacher was appalled by the new student's *misusage* of some basic scientific terms.〉 — see MISUSE

misuse *n* incorrect or improper use 〈The warranty for this dryer is null and void if you subject the product to deliberate *misuse*.〉

synonyms abuse, misapplication, misusage, perversion

related words mishandling, mismanagement, mismanaging; ill-treatment, ill-usage, maltreatment, mistreatment; damage, destruction, ruin, spoiling, wrecking; corruption, debasement, desecration, prostitution

near antonyms application, employment, use, utilization

misuse *vb* **1** to put to a bad or improper use 〈an actor who *misused* his considerable talent by appearing in too many lousy movies〉 — see MISAPPLY

2 to inflict physical or emotional harm upon 〈sadly *misused* by the people he had trusted〉 — see ABUSE 1

mite *n* **1** a very small sum of money 〈I have only a *mite* left to buy lunch for the rest of the week.〉

synonyms peanuts, pittance, shoestring, song

related words petty cash, pocket money, spending money

near antonyms bankroll, capital, funds, means, wherewithal; opulence, riches, treasure, wealth; bonanza, mine, treasury

antonyms bundle, fortune, mint, wad

2 a living thing much smaller than others of its kind 〈The kitten was just a *mite*, hardly the size of my palm.〉 — see DWARF 1

3 a very small amount 〈That speech didn't make a *mite* of sense.〉 — see PARTICLE 1

mitigate *vb* to make more bearable or less severe 〈This medicine should *mitigate* the pain until the strained muscle heals itself.〉 — see HELP 2

mix *n* a distinct entity formed by the combining of two or more different things 〈Guacamole is usually a *mix* of avocado, tomato, onion, and spices.〉 — see BLEND

mix *vb* **1** to turn into a single mass or entity that is more or less the same throughout 〈Those ingredients should not be *mixed* until the last stage of the recipe.〉 — see BLEND 1

2 to take part in social activities 〈happily *mixing* with the other guests at the party〉 — see SOCIALIZE

mix (up) *vb* **1** to fail to differentiate (a thing) from something similar or related 〈You've *mixed* "there" up with "their."〉 — see CONFUSE 3

2 to undo the proper order or arrangement of 〈In my rush I had *mixed up* the files and had to sort them out later.〉 — see DISORDER

mixed *adj* **1** being offspring produced by parents of different races, breeds, species, or genera 〈Our *mixed* dog has a greyhound's body but the features of a collie.〉

synonyms cold-blooded (*or* coldblood), cross, crossbred, hybrid, mongrel

related words grade, half-bred; crossed, hybridized, interbred, outcrossed

near antonyms pedigreed (*or* pedigree); inbred, linebred, straightbred

antonyms full-blooded, purebred, thoroughbred

2 consisting of many things of different sorts 〈The continuing education program offers a very *mixed* selection of courses.〉 — see MISCELLANEOUS

mixture *n* a distinct entity formed by the combining of two or more different things 〈Next, add eggs to the *mixture* of dry ingredients.〉 — see BLEND

mix–up *n* an instance of confusion 〈There was a *mix-up* at the airport and our luggage was accidentally sent to Ohio.〉 — see FOUL-UP

moan *n* **1** a long low sound indicating pain or grief 〈She uttered an agonized *moan* and clutched her stomach.〉

synonyms groan, wail

related words blubbering, crying, sniveling, sobbing, weeping, whimpering, whining, yammering; keen, lament, lamentation, plaint; bawl, cry, howl, shriek, squall, whimper, whine, yelp, yowl

near antonyms cackle, chortle, chuckle, giggle, guffaw, laugh, snicker, snigger, titter, twitter

2 a crying out in grief 〈A great *moan* arose from the crowd when the awful news was announced.〉 — see LAMENT 1

3 an expression of dissatisfaction, pain, or resentment 〈not the sort of person who would accept without a *moan* unfair treatment at work〉 — see COMPLAINT 1

moan *vb* **1** to utter a moan 〈The child *moaned* and cried when it was discovered that his favorite toy was lost.〉

synonyms groan, wail

related words blubber, cry, sob, weep; sniff, snivel, whimper, whine; bemoan, bewail, deplore, keen, lament, rue; agonize, anguish, bleed, grieve, hurt, mourn, sorrow, suffer; bawl, howl, shriek, squall, yammer, yelp, yowl

near antonyms cackle, chortle, chuckle, crack up, giggle, guffaw, laugh, snicker, titter, twitter

2 to express dissatisfaction, pain, or resentment usually tiresomely 〈Their son *moaned* whenever anyone asked him to do some work.〉 — see COMPLAIN

mob *n* **1** a great number of persons or creatures massed together 〈A *mob* of pigeons soon flocked around us after they spied the bread crumbs.〉 — see CROWD 1

2 a group involved in secret or criminal activities 〈The club owner was accused of having connections with a *mob* of racketeers.〉 — see ¹RING 1

3 the body of the community as contrasted with the elite 〈political speeches designed to appeal to the *mob*〉 — see MASS 1

mob *vb* to move upon or fill (something) in great numbers 〈The snack bar was *mobbed* as soon as the meeting was over.〉 — see CROWD 2

mobile *adj* **1** capable of being moved especially with ease 〈a *mobile* electric generator〉 — see MOVABLE

2 having a way of life that involves moving from one region to another typically on a seasonal basis 〈*mobile* workers who work the New England resorts in the summer and the ones in Florida during the winter〉 — see MIGRATORY

mobilization *n* an act of gathering forces together to renew or attempt an effort ⟨Officials called for the prompt *mobilization* of all national resources to combat the epidemic.⟩ — see RALLY 1

mobilize *vb* to assemble and make ready for action ⟨We are prepared to *mobilize* the troops on very short notice.⟩

synonyms marshal (*also* marshall), muster, rally

related words arrange, group, line up, order, organize; call (up), convene, summon; activate; collect, round up

near antonyms disarrange, disorder, disorganize, disrupt, disturb; deactivate, dismiss; break up, disband, dissolve, split (up)

antonyms demobilize

mobster *n* a violent, brutal person who is often a member of an organized gang ⟨the spectacle of the well-known *mobster's* trial⟩ — see HOODLUM

mock *adj* **1** being such in appearance only and made with or manufactured from usually cheaper materials ⟨*mock* turtle soup⟩ — see IMITATION

2 lacking in natural or spontaneous quality ⟨Since I had inadvertently learned what I was getting, I opened the present with *mock* surprise.⟩ — see ARTIFICIAL 1

mock *n* **1** a person or thing that is made fun of ⟨They made a *mock* of my first attempt at driving.⟩ — see LAUGHINGSTOCK

2 something that is made to look exactly like something else ⟨Obviously, the "priceless" Grecian urn that is destroyed in the movie was a *mock*.⟩ — see COPY

mock *vb* **1** to copy or exaggerate (someone or something) in order to make fun of ⟨The team good-naturedly *mocked* their coach's familiar bellow.⟩ — see MIMIC 1

2 to make (someone or something) the object of unkind laughter ⟨Though they are now considered masterpieces, the artist's works were originally *mocked* by critics.⟩ — see RIDICULE

3 to go against the commands, prohibitions, or rules of ⟨She *mocked* the company's dress code by wearing jeans.⟩ — see DISOBEY

mocker *n* a person who causes repeated emotional pain, distress, or annoyance to another ⟨The players paid no attention to *mockers* in the stands.⟩ — see TORMENTOR

mockery *n* **1** a poor, insincere, or insulting imitation of something ⟨He argued that a failure to charge white-collar criminals makes a *mockery* of the rule of law.⟩

synonyms caricature, cartoon, farce, joke, parody, sham, travesty

related words burlesque, comedy; lampoon, takeoff; counterfeit, fake, feigning, forgery, hoax, humbug, knockoff, phony (*also* phoney), pretense (*or* pretence)

near antonyms homage, tribute

2 a person or thing that is made fun of ⟨You won't make a *mockery* of me!⟩ — see LAUGHINGSTOCK

3 the making of unkind jokes as a way of showing one's scorn for someone or something ⟨fans subjecting the team to *mockery* for their embarrassing loss⟩ — see RIDICULE

mod *adj* being or involving the latest methods, concepts, information, or styles ⟨The young artist's converted loft is decorated in a self-consciously *mod* style.⟩ — see MODERN

¹**mode** *n* **1** a distinctive way of putting ideas into words ⟨He uses a colloquial *mode* of expression for his informal essays.⟩ — see STYLE 1

2 a state of mind dominated by a particular emotion ⟨When I'm in my cooking *mode*, I just have to go into the kitchen and make something.⟩ — see MOOD 1

²**mode** *n* a practice or interest that is very popular for a short time ⟨Flaunting of bling is the *mode* at that resort.⟩ — see FAD

model *adj* constituting, serving as, or worthy of being a pattern to be imitated ⟨the university's *model* program⟩

synonyms archetypal (*also* archetypical), classic, definitive, exemplary, paradigmatic, quintessential, textbook

related words ideal, nonpareil, special, unique; absolute, flawless, impeccable, perfect; A1, bang-up, banner, capital, choice, crackerjack, dandy, excellent, fabulous, fantastic, fine, first-class, first-rate, grand, great, marvelous (*or* marvellous), nifty, par excellence, prime, sensational, splendid, stellar, sterling, superb, superior, superlative, swell, terrific, tip-top, top, top-notch, unsurpassed, wonderful

near antonyms bad, low-grade, poor, substandard, unsatisfactory; atrocious, execrable, vile, wretched; deficient, disappointing, failed, inadequate, inferior; average, normal, ordinary, representative, typical; mediocre, second-class, second-rate

model *n* **1** an exact representation of something in greatly reduced size ⟨The dollhouse was a tiny, perfect *model* of the family's actual house.⟩

synonyms miniature

related words carbon copy, copy, dummy, dupe, duplicate, duplication, facsimile, imitation, mock, reduplication, replica, replication, reproduction; dwarf, midget, mini, pocket edition, pygmy (*also* pigmy)

near antonyms archetype, original, prototype; blowup, enlargement

2 a person who poses with or wears merchandise (as clothes) often for pictorial advertising ⟨The most famous *models* can earn thousands of dollars an hour.⟩

synonyms manikin (*also* mannikin), mannequin

related words spokesmodel, supermodel

3 someone of such unequaled perfection as to deserve imitation ⟨She's the very *model* of the dedicated teacher.⟩ — see IDEAL 1

moderate *adj* **1** avoiding extremes in behavior or expression ⟨a *moderate* coffee drinker⟩

synonyms temperate

related words controlled, curbed, disciplined, inhibited, restrained, self-controlled, self-disciplined; calculated, deliberate, measured; levelheaded, rational, reasonable, sensible; average, mediocre, medium, modest, run-of-the-mill, so-so; normal, ordinary, regular, routine, typical, usual

near antonyms excessive, extreme, inordinate, radical; irrational, unreasonable, unreasoning; extremist, fanatic (*or* fanatical), rabid; unbridled, unchecked, uncontrolled, unrestrained

antonyms immoderate, intemperate

2 avoiding major social change or extreme political ideas ⟨The candidate attracts more *moderate* voters.⟩

synonyms central, middle-of-the-road

related words conventional, nonrevolutionary, orthodox, traditional; levelheaded, rational, reasonable, sensible; neutral

near antonyms excessive; conservative, reactionary, rightist; leftist, liberal, progressive; fanatic (*or* fanatical), rabid, subversive, violent; agitating, exciting, fomenting, incendiary, inciting, instigating, provocative, provoking; rabble-rousing; dissenting

antonyms extremist, radical, revolutionary, revolutionist, ultra

3 being about midway between extremes of amount or size ⟨A *moderate* snowfall was forecast for the region.⟩ — see MIDDLE 2

4 marked by temperatures that are neither too high nor too low ⟨a city that is celebrated for its *moderate* climate⟩ — see CLEMENT 1

moderate *vb* to grow less in scope or intensity especially gradually ⟨The wind began to *moderate* as the night wore on.⟩ — see DECREASE 2

moderately *adv* to some degree or extent ⟨It was raining *moderately* hard outside.⟩ — see FAIRLY 1

moderateness *n* an avoidance of extremes in one's actions, beliefs, or habits ⟨The *moderateness* of their enthusiasm for my idea suggested that they would rather do something else.⟩ — see TEMPERANCE

moderation *n* an avoidance of extremes in one's actions, beliefs, or habits ⟨the kind of person who does everything in *moderation*⟩ — see TEMPERANCE

moderator *n* a person in charge of a meeting ⟨The *moderator* should make sure that everyone gets a chance to speak.⟩ — see CHAIR 1

modern *adj* being or involving the latest methods, concepts, information, or styles ⟨changed the furniture for a more *modern* look⟩
synonyms contemporary, current, designer, hot, mod, modernistic, new, newfangled, new-fashioned, present-day, red-hot, space-age, ultramodern, up-to-date
related words fashionable, happening, in, modish, now, stylish; last, latest; modernized, updated; futuristic, high-tech (*also* hi-tech); latter-day, recent
near antonyms anachronistic; aged, age-old, ancient, antediluvian, hoary, old, venerable; bygone, former, late, olden, past; antique, historical; retro, retrograde; obsolete, outmoded, outworn, unmodernized; old-world; discarded, disused, moth-eaten; forgotten, remote
antonyms antiquated, archaic, dated, fusty, musty, old-fangled, old-fashioned, old-time, out-of-date, passé

modern *n* a person with very modern ideas ⟨considers himself a *modern* when it comes to certain issues⟩
synonyms ultramodernist
related words leftist, lefty, liberal, progressive; extremist, radical, reformer, reformist, revolutionary, revolutionist; bohemian
near antonyms conservative, rightist, right-winger, standpatter, Tory; old hand, old-timer, veteran; conformist; Bourbon, diehard; square
antonyms antediluvian, dodo, fogy (*also* fogey), fossil, fuddy-duddy, reactionary, stick-in-the-mud

modernistic *adj* being or involving the latest methods, concepts, information, or styles ⟨a trendy hotel with *modernistic* room lamps that required some figuring just to turn on⟩ — see MODERN

modest *adj* **1** being about midway between extremes of amount or size ⟨He was awarded a *modest* pension when he retired.⟩ — see MIDDLE 2
2 free from any trace of the coarse or indecent ⟨tended to wear more *modest* clothing⟩ — see CHASTE 1
3 not comfortable around people ⟨a *modest* winner who said a quick thank-you and promptly left the stage⟩ — see SHY 2
4 not having or showing any feelings of superiority, self-assertiveness, or showiness ⟨was *modest* about her success in the industry⟩ — see HUMBLE 1

modestly *adv* **1** in a manner showing no signs of pride or self-assertion ⟨spoke *modestly* about his accomplishments as an entrepreneur⟩ — see LOWLY
2 with purity of thought and deed ⟨a sect that encourages dressing *modestly*⟩ — see PURELY 1

modesty *n* **1** the absence of any feelings of being better than others ⟨His natural *modesty* makes him reluctant to run for public office.⟩ — see HUMILITY
2 the quality or state of being morally pure ⟨a historical period known for promoting *modesty* and formality⟩ — see CHASTITY

modicum *n* the smallest amount or part imaginable ⟨Only a *modicum* of skill is necessary to put the kit together.⟩ — see JOT

modifiable *adj* capable of being readily changed ⟨Architects designed the arena to be easily *modifiable* for staging a variety of events.⟩ — see FLEXIBLE 1

modification *n* the act, process, or result of making different ⟨The rough draft needed only a few *modifications* before it was ready to hand in.⟩ — see CHANGE 1

modify *vb* **1** to limit the meaning of (as a noun) ⟨Adjectives are words that *modify* nouns, while adverbs can *modify* adjectives and verbs.⟩ — see QUALIFY 1
2 to make different in some way ⟨He *modified* the appliance so that it would run more quietly.⟩ — see CHANGE 1

modish *adj* **1** being in the latest or current fashion ⟨the strikingly *modish* gowns that actresses wear to award shows⟩ — see STYLISH
2 enjoying widespread favor or approval ⟨a *modish* chef who is currently the darling of the restaurant reviewers⟩ — see POPULAR 1

modishness *n* **1** the quality or state of being fashionable ⟨When it comes to clothes, she prefers comfort to *modishness*.⟩ — see COOL 2
2 the state of enjoying widespread approval ⟨The *modishness* of that hairstyle is now so transparent that the really hip people have moved on to something else.⟩ — see POPULARITY

mogul *n* a person of rank, power, or influence in a particular field ⟨movie *moguls* promising to turn young actors into stars⟩ — see MAGNATE

moil *vb* to devote serious and sustained effort ⟨miners *moiling* all day in the sunless recesses of the earth⟩ — see LABOR

moist *adj* slightly or moderately wet ⟨Luckily, my new suede shoes are only a bit *moist* after I accidentally wore them in the rain.⟩
synonyms damp, dank
related words semimoist; dewy, misty; humid, muggy, sticky; sultry, summery, sweltering, torrid, tropical; awash, bathed, doused (*also* dowsed), drenched, dripping, saturate, saturated, soaked, soaking, sodden, soggy, sopping, soppy, soused, steeped, washed, watered, waterlogged
near antonyms arid, dry, waterless; baked, bone-dry, burned (*or* burnt), dehydrated, desert, droughty, dusty, parched, scorched, seared, sere (*also* sear), sunbaked

moisten *vb* to make or become slightly or moderately wet ⟨*Moisten* the cloth before cleaning with it.⟩
synonyms damp, dampen
related words bathe, lave; douse (*also* dowse), drench, impregnate, saturate, soak, souse, steep, wash, water, wet; humidify; dip, dunk, immerge, immerse; flush, irrigate, rinse, sluice; refresh, rehydrate, remoisten
near antonyms dehumidify, dehydrate, parch, scorch, sear
antonyms dry

moisture *n* the amount of water suspended in the air in tiny droplets ⟨Dew is really just *moisture* from the air that condenses and collects when the temperature drops at night.⟩
synonyms damp, dampness, humidity
related words mugginess, stickiness, stuffiness; sultriness; clamminess, dankness, soddenness, sogginess, wetness
near antonyms aridity, dryness

mojo *n* **1** something worn or kept to bring good luck or keep away evil ⟨A *mojo* is a type of voodoo charm.⟩ — see CHARM 1
2 the power to control natural forces through supernatural means ⟨He joked that he had worked his *mojo* to assure a sunny day for the picnic.⟩ — see MAGIC 1

molder *vb* to go through decomposition ⟨leaves *moldering* in the compost pile⟩ — see DECAY 1

molecule *n* a very small piece ⟨not a *molecule* of truth in that story⟩ — see BIT 1

mollify *vb* **1** to lessen the anger or agitation of ⟨An apology would probably *mollify* your friend.⟩ — see PACIFY 1
2 to make more bearable or less severe ⟨a friendly gesture that did a lot to *mollify* their suspicions about the new neighbor⟩ — see HELP 2

mollifying *adj* tending to lessen or avoid conflict or hostility ⟨a new roommate using *mollifying* flattery to overcome a bad first impression⟩ — see PACIFIC 1

mollycoddle *vb* to treat with great or excessive care ⟨She refused to *mollycoddle* her malingering son and sent him off to school.⟩ — see BABY

molt *vb* to cast (a natural bodily covering or appendage) aside ⟨A crab *molts* its shell as it grows larger.⟩ — see SHED 1

mom *n* a female human parent ⟨Be sure to tell your *mom* and dad that you'll be home late for supper.⟩ — see MOTHER

moment *n* **1** a particular point at which an event takes place ⟨At that *moment* he suddenly turned around and headed toward me.⟩ — see OCCASION 1
2 the quality or state of being important ⟨an event of great *moment*⟩ — see IMPORTANCE
3 a very small space of time ⟨I'll be there in just a *moment*.⟩ — see INSTANT
4 the time currently existing or in progress ⟨I'm not doing anything at the *moment*.⟩ — see ¹PRESENT

momentarily *adv* at or within a short time ⟨We'll be finished *momentarily*.⟩ — see SHORTLY 2

momentary *adj* lasting only for a short time ⟨The pain of the flu shot was only *momentary*.⟩
synonyms brief, ephemeral, evanescent, flash, fleeting, fugitive, impermanent, passing, short-lived, temporary, transient, transitory
related words little, short, shortish; acting, interim, provisional, short-term
near antonyms lifelong; continuing, durable, persistent; imperishable, indestructible
antonyms ceaseless, dateless, deathless, endless, enduring, eternal, everlasting, immortal, lasting, long-lived, permanent, perpetual, timeless, undying, unending

momentous *adj* having great meaning or lasting effect ⟨a *momentous* occasion that will go down in the history books⟩ — see IMPORTANT 1

momentum *n* something that arouses action or activity ⟨The former president's endorsement was all the *momentum* the campaign needed.⟩ — see IMPULSE 1

monarch *n* **1** one who rules over a people with a sole, supreme, and usually hereditary authority ⟨The ruling *monarch* of Britain at that time was Queen Elizabeth I.⟩
synonyms autocrat, potentate, ruler, sovereign (*also* sovran)
related words coruler; Caesar, czar (*also* tsar *or* tzar), emir (*or* amir *also* ameer), emperor, empress, kaiser, khan, king, mogul, prince, queen, satrap, shah, sultan, suzerain; authoritarian, despot, dictator, führer (*or* fuehrer), monocrat, overlord, tyrant
2 a person of rank, power, or influence in a particular field ⟨The glitzy gala was attended by most of the reigning *monarchs* of the recording industry.⟩ — see MAGNATE

monarchal *or* **monarchial** *adj* fit for or worthy of a royal ruler ⟨a political leader with a *monarchal* demeanor⟩ — see MONARCHICAL

monarchical *also* **monarchic** *adj* fit for or worthy of a royal ruler ⟨Guests who stay in the hotel's most expensive suite live in *monarchical* splendor.⟩
synonyms kingly, monarchal (*or* monarchial), princely, queenly, regal, royal
related words aristocratic, baronial, imperial, lordly, noble, patrician; grandiose, heroic (*also* heroical), imposing, magnificent, majestic, monumental, splendid, stately

monastery *n* a residence for men under religious vows ⟨Gregory Mendel worked out his concepts of genetics by doing breeding experiments using pea plants in the *monastery's* garden.⟩
synonyms abbey, cloister, friary, hermitage, priory
related words house; convent, nunnery; lamasery

monetary *adj* of or relating to money, banking, or investments ⟨an economist who is critical of this administration's *monetary* policies⟩ — see FINANCIAL

money *n* something (as pieces of stamped metal or printed paper) customarily and legally used as a medium of exchange, a measure of value, or a means of payment ⟨Are you sure you have enough *money* to buy all that?⟩
synonyms bread [*slang*], bucks, cash, change, chips, currency, dough, gold, green, jack [*slang*], legal tender, lucre, pelf, tender, wampum
related words coinage, specie; paper money, scrip; cashier's check, check, draft, money order, note, promissory note; bill, greenback; bankroll, capital, finances, funds, wad; mite, peanuts, pittance, shoestring; bundle, fortune, king's ransom, mint, pile, pot; opulence, riches, treasure, wealth; resources, wherewithal; petty cash, pin money, pocket money, spending money

moneyed *also* **monied** *adj* having goods, property, or money in abundance ⟨The shop sells luxury goods purchased mainly by *moneyed* tourists from abroad.⟩ — see RICH 1

mongrel *adj* being offspring produced by parents of different races, breeds, species, or genera ⟨a *mongrel* dog⟩ — see MIXED 1

mongrel *n* an offspring of parents with different genes especially when of different races, breeds, species, or genera ⟨*Mongrels* often suffer fewer health problems than purebreds.⟩ — see HYBRID

monitor *vb* to pay continued close attention to (something) for a particular purpose ⟨Police regularly *monitor* that road to record traffic density and to catch speeders.⟩
synonyms cover, watch
related words surveil; eye; behold, espy, look, note, notice, observe, regard, see, sight, spy, view, witness; gape, gawk, gaze, glare, goggle, peer, rubberneck, stare; glance, glimpse, peek, peep
phrases keep an eye on

monkey *n* an appealingly mischievous person ⟨Come back here, you little *monkey*!⟩ — see SCAMP 1

monkey (around) *vb* **1** to engage in attention-getting playful or boisterous behavior ⟨Stop *monkeying around* in the house or you'll break something!⟩ — see CUT UP
2 to spend time in aimless activity ⟨Sam would rather just *monkey around* instead of doing work.⟩ — see FIDDLE (AROUND)

monkey (with) *vb* to handle thoughtlessly, ignorantly, or mischievously ⟨Don't *monkey with* that broken lawnmower!⟩ — see TAMPER (WITH)

monkeying *n* wildly playful or mischievous behavior ⟨All that *monkeying* was sure to end in someone or something getting hurt.⟩ — see HORSEPLAY

monochromatic *adj* **1** having or consisting of a single color ⟨Although marble and bronze sculptures are *monochromatic*, they can be amazingly lifelike.⟩
synonyms solid
related words achromatic, neutral
near antonyms dappled (*also* dapple), marbled, shaded; mottled, parti-color (*or* parti-colored), piebald, pied, pinto, skewbald; barred, brindled (*or* brindle), streaked, striated; checkered, dotted, patterned, plaid, striped; flecked, speckled, spotted; bicolored (*or* bicolor), dichromatic, two-tone

antonyms colorful, motley, multicolored, polychromatic, polychrome, varicolored, varied, variegated
2 causing weariness, restlessness, or lack of interest ⟨a *monochromatic* portrayal of a hero seemingly without flaws or even distinctive traits⟩ — see BORING
monopolize *vb* to have complete control over ⟨It is illegal in the United States to *monopolize* an entire industry.⟩ ⟨You shouldn't *monopolize* the exercise equipment while others are waiting to use it.⟩
synonyms sew up
related words corner, hog; absorb, consume, engross; have, hold, own, possess; command, control, direct, govern, manage, reign (over), rule
monotonous *adj* causing weariness, restlessness, or lack of interest ⟨The lecturer's *monotonous* delivery threatened to put us to sleep.⟩ — see BORING
monotonousness *n* a tedious lack of variety ⟨detested the mind-numbing *monotonousness* of the task but knew that it had to be done⟩ — see MONOTONY
monotony *n* a tedious lack of variety ⟨The *monotony* of the cafeteria's selections was as bad as the quality.⟩
synonyms humdrum, monotonousness, sameness
related words uniformity; blahs, boredom, drabness, dullness (*also* dulness), ennui, restlessness, tediousness, tedium, tiresomeness, weariness, wearisomeness
near antonyms diversity, multiplicity, variety; variability, variation; absorption, engagement, engrossment, enthrallment, fascination, grip, interest, involvement; animation, enlivenment, invigoration, stimulation
monster *adj* unusually large ⟨a *monster* truck competition⟩ — see HUGE
monster *n* **1** a strange or horrible and often frightening creature ⟨Both children insisted that their parents check under the bed for *monsters* every night.⟩
synonyms grotesque, monstrosity, ogre
related words ogress; Frankenstein; banshee, bogeyman (*also* bogyman), demon (*or* daemon), devil, fiend, fright, imp, incubus; horror, terror; abomination, anathema; abnormality, freak; mutant, mutation
2 a person, thing, or event that is far from normal ⟨The gardener destroyed all of the *monsters* that mutated from his tomato plants.⟩ — see FREAK 1
3 a mean, evil, or unprincipled person ⟨You don't want to work for that *monster*.⟩ — see VILLAIN
4 something that is unusually large and powerful ⟨a *monster* of a sandwich that could easily feed two hearty eaters⟩ — see GIANT
monstrosity *n* **1** a person, thing, or event that is far from normal ⟨Mythologies are often filled with strange beasts and *monstrosities*.⟩ — see FREAK 1
2 a strange or horrible and often frightening creature ⟨filled the haunted house with all sorts of spooks and mechanical *monstrosities*⟩ — see MONSTER 1
3 something unpleasant to look at ⟨We were glad when the city tore down that *monstrosity* that used to stand across from the park.⟩ — see EYESORE
4 the quality of inspiring intense dread or dismay ⟨the *monstrosity* of the famine⟩ — see HORROR 1
5 the state or quality of being utterly evil ⟨the *monstrosity* of the crime⟩ — see ENORMITY 1
monstrous *adj* **1** badly or imperfectly formed ⟨a *monstrous* melon that was clearly not fit to eat⟩ — see MALFORMED
2 extremely disturbing or repellent ⟨the *monstrous* injustice perpetrated against them⟩ — see HORRIBLE 1
3 unusually large ⟨a *monstrous* tomato as big as a basketball⟩ — see HUGE
4 unpleasant to look at ⟨Some *monstrous* high-rises have begun to spoil that lovely residential neighborhood.⟩ — see UGLY 1

monstrously *adv* **1** beyond a normal or acceptable limit ⟨Our team wasn't merely bad—we were *monstrously* inept!⟩ — see TOO 1
2 to a large extent or degree ⟨a *monstrously* expensive movie that nearly bankrupted the studio⟩ — see GREATLY 2
Montezuma's revenge *n* abnormally frequent intestinal evacuations with more or less fluid stools ⟨The one person in the tour group who didn't drink the water was spared *Montezuma's revenge*.⟩ — see DIARRHEA
monument *n* **1** a shaped stone laid over or erected near a grave and usually bearing an inscription to identify and preserve the memory of the deceased ⟨The Quakers disapproved of *monuments*, regarding them as idolatrous, so thousands of Nantucketers spend their eternal rest in complete anonymity.⟩ — see TOMBSTONE
2 something that serves to keep alive the memory of a person or event ⟨a moving *monument* to the great war and a tribute to the untold millions who died in it⟩ — see MEMORIAL
monumental *adj* **1** large and impressive in size, grandeur, extent, or conception ⟨a *monumental* misunderstanding that had far-reaching consequences⟩ — see GRAND 1
2 unusually large ⟨serves a *monumental* sundae that usually requires three people to finish it⟩ — see HUGE
3 having great meaning or lasting effect ⟨The moon landing was seen as a *monumental* event in human history.⟩ — see IMPORTANT 1
mooch *vb* **1** to move about in a sly or secret manner ⟨I suspect she's *mooching* around in the background and keeping an eye on us.⟩ — see SNEAK 1
2 to move about from place to place aimlessly ⟨kids on vacation *mooching* about the house and looking for something to do⟩ — see WANDER 1
moocher *n* a person who is supported by or seeks support from another without making an adequate return ⟨My roommate's a *moocher* and always eating my food.⟩ — see LEECH
mood *n* **1** a state of mind dominated by a particular emotion ⟨Losing my favorite sweater left me in a bad *mood* for the rest of the day.⟩
synonyms cheer, feather, humor, mode, spirit, temper
related words angle, mind-set, outlook, perspective, slant, standpoint, viewpoint; emotion, feeling, heart, passion, sentiment; strain; expression, tone, vein; character, disposition, identity, individuality, makeup, mettle, personality, temper, temperament
phrases frame of mind
2 a special quality or impression associated with something ⟨There's a haunting *mood* of melancholy about the ruined old castle.⟩ — see AURA 1
moody *adj* frequently influenced by moods and especially bad moods ⟨a brilliant but *moody* artist⟩
synonyms temperamental
related words capricious, changeable, changeful, fickle, fluctuating, fluid, freakish, impulsive, inconstant, mercurial, mutable, uncertain, unsettled, unstable, unsteady, variable, volatile, whimsical; sulky; choleric, crabby, cranky, cross, crotchety, grouchy, grumpy, irascible, irritable, peevish, petulant, quick-tempered, short-tempered, snappish, snippety, snippy, testy, waspish
near antonyms equable, even; immutable, inflexible, invariable, unalterable, unchangeable; changeless, constant, settled, stable, steady, unchanging
moon *n* a long or seemingly long period of time ⟨We've been planning this big event for many *moons*.⟩ — see AGE 2
moonshine *n* **1** illegally produced liquor ⟨During Prohibition, *moonshine* and "bathtub gin" were made secretly.⟩
synonyms bootleg

related words bathtub gin, red-eye, rotgut; alcohol, booze, drink, firewater, grog, rum, spirits

2 a distilled beverage that can make a person drunk ⟨mountaineers who made their own *moonshine*⟩ — see ALCOHOL

3 language, behavior, or ideas that are absurd and contrary to good sense ⟨a book about the so-called good old days that's sentimental *moonshine*⟩ — see NONSENSE 1

moor *n* **1** a broad area of level or rolling treeless country ⟨As she wanders the windswept *moor*, the novel's heroine vows that she will never marry the vicar.⟩ — see PLAIN 1

2 spongy land saturated or partially covered with water ⟨a mysterious figure who was said to have haunted the *moors* of southwest England⟩ — see SWAMP

moor *vb* to put securely in place or in a desired position ⟨We *moored* the boat to the dock.⟩ — see FASTEN 2

moot *adj* open to question or dispute ⟨It's a *moot* question what might have happened if the American colonies had not broken away from Great Britain.⟩ — see DEBATABLE 1

moot *vb* **1** to present or bring forward for discussion ⟨Conservatives had shouted down the proposal when it was first *mooted*.⟩ — see INTRODUCE 2

2 to talk about (an issue) usually from various points of view and for the purpose of arriving at a decision or opinion ⟨The issue of whether a person's nature or upbringing is more important continues to be *mooted* by experts and laymen alike.⟩ — see DISCUSS

mope *vb* **1** to move or act slowly ⟨We were in a rush, and the Sunday driver in front of us was just *moping* along.⟩ — see DELAY 1

2 to silently go about in a bad mood ⟨She's been *moping* all weekend because her friends are away.⟩ — see SULK

mopes *pl n* a state or spell of low spirits ⟨He's got the *mopes* because his friend is mad at him.⟩ — see SADNESS

moppet *n* a young person who is between infancy and adulthood ⟨A host of adorable *moppets* were hired for the ad campaign.⟩ — see CHILD 1

moral *adj* **1** conforming to a high standard of morality or virtue ⟨We're confident she has the *moral* fiber to make the right decision.⟩ — see GOOD 2

2 guided by or in accordance with one's sense of right and wrong ⟨He feels it's his *moral* obligation to help the poor.⟩ — see CONSCIENTIOUS 1

moralist *n* a person who is greatly concerned with seemly behavior and morality especially regarding sexual matters ⟨A smattering of *moralists* around the country tried to get the songs banned from the radio.⟩ — see PRUDE

morality *n* **1** conduct that conforms to an accepted standard of right and wrong ⟨He has a reputation for unswerving *morality*.⟩

synonyms character, decency, goodness, honesty, integrity, probity, rectitude, righteousness, rightness, uprightness, virtue, virtuousness

related words high-mindedness, honor, incorruptibility, right-mindedness, scrupulosity, scrupulousness; appropriateness, correctness, decorousness, decorum, etiquette, fitness, propriety, seemliness; ethics, morals

near antonyms impropriety, indecency, indiscretion; debauchery, degeneracy, degradation, depravity, perversion, pervertedness, sinfulness; crookedness, dishonesty, underhandedness, unscrupulousness; lowness, meanness, viciousness, vileness; corruption

antonyms badness, evil, evildoing, immorality, iniquity, sin, villainy, wickedness

2 the code of good conduct for an individual or group ⟨the *morality* that members of the organization are expected to adhere to⟩ — see ETHICS

morally *adv* with purity of thought and deed ⟨a politician who is in the habit of acting legally without behaving *morally*⟩ — see PURELY 1

morals *pl n* the code of good conduct for an individual or group ⟨At issue were the doctor's professional ethics, not her private *morals*.⟩ — see ETHICS

morass *n* **1** something that catches and holds ⟨He advised against becoming involved in the foreign nation's civil war, warning that escape from that *morass* might prove nigh impossible.⟩ — see WEB 1

2 spongy land saturated or partially covered with water ⟨The distracted driver had driven his car off the road and into a *morass*.⟩ — see SWAMP

moratorium *n* a state of temporary inactivity ⟨The residents called for a *moratorium* on building.⟩ — see ABEYANCE

morbid *adj* causing or marked by an atmosphere lacking in cheer ⟨a pessimist who is given to *morbid* introspection⟩ — see GLOOMY 1

mordant *adj* marked by the use of wit that is intended to cause hurt feelings ⟨a *mordant* review of the movie that compared it to having one's teeth pulled for two hours⟩ — see SARCASTIC

more *adj* resulting in an increase in amount or number ⟨We bought *more* apples in order to make a bigger pie.⟩ — see ADDITIONAL

more *adv* **1** in addition to what has been said ⟨The sci-fi movie was totally unbelievable and, what's *more*, it was boring.⟩

synonyms additionally, again, also, besides, further, furthermore, likewise, moreover, then, too, withal, yet

phrases as well, for good measure, in addition to, into the bargain (*also* in the bargain), on top of, to boot, what's more

2 to a greater or higher extent ⟨The boxers for this bout are *more* evenly matched than the last two were.⟩

synonyms better

more *n* something added (as by growth) ⟨Let's add a little *more* to the mixture.⟩ — see INCREASE 1

more or less *adv* **1** very close to but not completely ⟨The lot is 16 acres *more or less*.⟩ — see ALMOST

2 to some degree or extent ⟨Most couples in the survey said that they were *more or less* happy in their marriage.⟩ — see FAIRLY 1

moreover *adv* in addition to what has been said ⟨Swimming alone is against the rules and, *moreover*, it's dangerous.⟩ — see MORE 1

mores *pl n* personal conduct or behavior as evaluated by an accepted standard of appropriateness for a social or professional setting ⟨the *mores* of academic life as opposed to those of the business world⟩ — see MANNER 1

moribund *adj* nearly dead ⟨With its run-down look and empty aisles, the grocery store appeared *moribund*.⟩

synonyms dying

related words expiring, fading, passing away, sinking; decadent, declining, deteriorating; dead, deceased, defunct, departed, fallen, gone, lifeless, passed away; terminal

phrases at death's door

near antonyms alive, animate, live, living, quick; being, breathing, existing, subsisting, surviving; booming, flourishing, prospering, roaring, thriving; animated, bouncing, energetic, frisky, jazzy, lively, peppy, perky, spirited, sprightful, sprightly, springy, vital, vivacious, zippy

morn *n* **1** the first appearance of light in the morning or the time of its appearance ⟨My herald of the *morn* is my cat, sticking his paw in my face to wake me up.⟩ — see DAWN 1

2 the time from sunrise until noon ⟨So, how are you this lovely *morn*?⟩ — see MORNING 1

morning *n* **1** the time from sunrise until noon ⟨After working in the fields all *morning*, we were ready for a hearty lunch.⟩

synonyms forenoon, morn

related words dawn, dawning, daybreak, daylight; cockcrow, sunrise, sunup; day, daytime, light

near antonyms dark, darkness, night, nighttime, twilight; dusk, evening, nightfall, sundown, sunset

2 the first appearance of light in the morning or the time of its appearance ⟨*Morning* has broken!⟩ — see DAWN 1

3 the point at which something begins ⟨The period when people in ancient Mesopotamia began living in cities is usually regarded as the *morning* of civilization.⟩ — see BEGINNING

moron *n* a stupid person ⟨Sorry I forgot to call you. I'm such a *moron!*⟩ — see IDIOT

morose *adj* causing or marked by an atmosphere lacking in cheer ⟨those *morose* job seekers who have grown accustomed to rejection⟩ — see GLOOMY 1

morsel *n* **1** a small piece or quantity of food ⟨The chef's cuisine is so good that diners will want to savor every *morsel*.⟩

synonyms bite, mouthful, nibble, nugget, taste, tidbit (*also* titbit)

related words nosh, snack; appetizer, canapé, hors d'oeuvre; bit, chew, crumb, dab, dribble, driblet, fleck, hint, mote, nubbin, particle, pinch, scrap, scruple, shred, smidgen (*also* smidgeon *or* smidgin *or* smidge), snip, snippet, speck, spot, sprinkling, suspicion, tittle, touch, trace

2 a very small piece ⟨searching for any *morsel* of useful information⟩ — see BIT 1

mortal *adj* **1** likely to cause or capable of causing death ⟨a *mortal* wound⟩ — see DEADLY 1

2 of, relating to, or suggestive of death ⟨a wounded soldier writhing in *mortal* agony⟩ — see DEATHLY 1

3 relating to or characteristic of human beings ⟨just an ordinary guy with all the usual *mortal* limitations⟩ — see HUMAN

4 marked by opposition or ill will ⟨have always had a *mortal* aversion to narcissistic people⟩ — see HOSTILE 1

mortal *n* a member of the human race ⟨just an ordinary *mortal* living an ordinary life⟩ — see HUMAN

mortally *adv* to a great degree ⟨I'm *mortally* certain that I've seen that guy before.⟩ — see VERY 1

mortician *n* a person who manages funerals and prepares the dead for burial or cremation ⟨The *mortician* will take care of all of the arrangements for the funeral.⟩ — see FUNERAL DIRECTOR

mortification *n* the emotional state of being made self-consciously uncomfortable ⟨She was filled with *mortification* when she realized her mistake.⟩ — see EMBARRASSMENT 1

mortify *vb* to throw into a state of self-conscious distress ⟨He was *mortified* when he had to admit he'd never actually read the book.⟩ — see EMBARRASS 1

¹**most** *adv* to a great degree ⟨a *most* careful driver, especially in bad weather⟩ — see VERY 1

²**most** *adv* very close to but not completely ⟨The cost of *most* everything is higher nowadays.⟩ — see ALMOST

most *adj* of the greatest or highest degree or quantity ⟨the player with the *most* ability on the tennis team⟩ — see ULTIMATE 1

most *n* the greatest amount, number, or part ⟨This room will accommodate 50 people at the *most*.⟩

synonyms maximum, outside

related words best, ultimate, utmost; extreme

antonyms least, minimum

mostly *adv* for the most part ⟨The weather this month has been *mostly* mild.⟩ — see CHIEFLY

mote *n* a very small piece ⟨There's not a *mote* of dirt in their house.⟩ — see BIT 1

moth–eaten *adj* **1** having passed its time of use or usefulness ⟨*moth-eaten* scientific theories that no one's believed in ages⟩ — see OBSOLETE

2 showing signs of advanced wear and tear and neglect ⟨a man who's been wearing the same *moth-eaten* clothes for decades⟩ — see SHABBY 1

3 used or heard so often as to be dull ⟨a cousin who tells the same *moth-eaten* stories every Thanksgiving⟩ — see STALE 1

mother *adj* of, relating to, or characteristic of a mother ⟨I have that *mother* instinct to look up anytime a child calls for their mom.⟩ — see MOTHERLY

mother *n* a female human parent ⟨He dreaded telling his *mother* that he'd put a dent in her car.⟩

synonyms ma, mama (*also* mamma *or* momma), mammy, mom, old lady

related words matriarch, matron; stepmother; supermom, superwoman

mother *vb* **1** to bring forth from the womb ⟨I hope to *mother* at least one child.⟩ — see BEAR 1

2 to attend to the needs and comforts of ⟨We *mothered* the patients with chicken soup.⟩ — see NURSE 1

motherland *n* **1** a place of origin ⟨For many oenophiles, France remains the *motherland* of fine wines.⟩ — see BIRTHPLACE

2 the land of one's birth, residence, or citizenship ⟨All his life he longed to return to his *motherland*.⟩ — see COUNTRY 1

motherliness *n* motherly character or qualities ⟨He cherished his foster parent for her *motherliness*.⟩ — see MATERNITY

motherly *adj* of, relating to, or characteristic of a mother ⟨She showed a sweet *motherly* tenderness toward the tiny kitten she was taking care of.⟩

synonyms maternal, mother

related words parental; female, feminine, womanish, womanlike, womanly; matriarchal, matronly; caring, giving, nurturing

mother tongue *n* the stock of words, pronunciation, and grammar used by a people as their basic means of communication ⟨He speaks English fluently, but his *mother tongue* is Chinese.⟩ — see LANGUAGE 1

motif *n* **1** a major object of interest or concern (as in a discussion or artistic composition) ⟨The *motif* of mute figures standing in lonely isolation is a recurrent one in the artist's works.⟩ — see MATTER 1

2 a unit of decoration that is repeated all over something (as a fabric) ⟨The fabric for the upholstery features a scallop shell *motif*.⟩ — see PATTERN 1

motion *n* the act or an instance of changing position ⟨We were instructed not to make any sudden *motions* or we might scare away the deer.⟩ — see MOVEMENT 1

motion *vb* to direct or notify by a movement or gesture ⟨The referee *motioned* the team captains to confer with him on the sideline.⟩

synonyms beckon, flag, gesture, signal, wave

related words nod; gesticulate, mime, pantomime, sign; signalize; acquaint, advise, inform, relate, tell; flourish, shrug

motionlessly *adv* without motion ⟨The model could sit *motionlessly* for hours.⟩ — see STILL 1

motion picture *n* **1** a story told by means of a series of continuously projected pictures and a sound track ⟨a popular novel that was made into a major *motion picture*⟩ — see MOVIE 1

2 motion pictures *pl* the art or business of making a movie ⟨To the industrialist, producing *motion pictures* seemed a lot more glamorous than manufacturing synthetics.⟩ — see MOVIE 2

motivation *n* something that arouses action or activity ⟨Fear of failing should be plenty of *motivation* to study for the test.⟩ — see IMPULSE 1

motive *n* **1** a major object of interest or concern (as in a discussion or artistic composition) ⟨The principal *motive* of the piece was introduced in the flute section.⟩ — see MATTER 1
2 a unit of decoration that is repeated all over something (as a fabric) ⟨decorated with a paisley *motive*⟩ — see PATTERN 1
3 something (as a belief) that serves as the basis for another thing ⟨The detective felt that the first suspect didn't have any *motive* for committing the crime.⟩ — see REASON 2

motley *adj* **1** consisting of many things of different sorts ⟨a ship with a *motley* crew of old salts, young adventurers, and shifty characters of all ages⟩ — see MISCELLANEOUS
2 marked by a variety of usually vivid colors ⟨a tropical bird with *motley* plumage⟩ — see COLORFUL

motley *n* **1** a person formerly kept in a royal or noble household to amuse with jests and pranks ⟨the *motleys* with their colorful outfits⟩ — see FOOL 2
2 an unorganized collection or mixture of various things ⟨a *motley* of old junk stored in the attic⟩ — see MISCELLANY 1

motor *n* **1** a device that changes energy into mechanical motion ⟨The device was equipped with a small electrical *motor* to make the gears spin.⟩ — see ENGINE
2 a self-propelled passenger vehicle on four wheels ⟨We went shopping for a new automobile at Valley *Motors*.⟩ — see CAR

motor *vb* **1** to proceed or move quickly ⟨effortlessly *motored* past the other runners for a first-place finish⟩ — see HURRY 1
2 to travel by a motorized vehicle ⟨*motoring* along the highway at the speed limit⟩ — see DRIVE 2

motorboat *n* a boat equipped with a motor ⟨*Motorboats* are banned on the lake because they are a hazard to swimmers.⟩
synonyms powerboat, speedboat
related words cabin cruiser, cruiser, hydrofoil, motor sailer, runabout, sedan

motorcade *n* a group of vehicles traveling together or under one management ⟨The next part of the parade was a *motorcade* of fire engines.⟩ — see FLEET

motorcar *n* a self-propelled passenger vehicle on four wheels ⟨a convention for those who love antique *motorcars*⟩ — see CAR

motor home *n* a motor vehicle that is specially equipped for living while traveling ⟨They lived out of their *motor home* until they found a suitable house.⟩ — see CAMPER

motorist *n* a person who travels by automobile ⟨Environmental organizations suggest that *motorists* get together and carpool to avoid adding to pollution levels.⟩
synonyms automobilist, driver
related words operator; codriver; chauffeur; carpooler
antonyms nondriver

motor vehicle *n* a self-propelled passenger vehicle on four wheels ⟨Emily got a license to drive a *motor vehicle* the minute she turned 16.⟩ — see CAR

mottle *n* a small area that is different (as in color) from the main part ⟨canvases covered with streaks and *mottles*⟩ — see SPOT 1

mottle *vb* to mark with small spots especially unevenly ⟨old papers that were *mottled* by mold⟩ — see SPOT 1

mottled *adj* **1** having blotches of two or more colors ⟨a *mottled* complexion⟩ — see PIED

2 marked with spots ⟨*mottled* leather upholstery that isn't supposed to look perfect⟩ — see SPOTTED 1

mound *n* **1** a pile or ridge of granular matter (as sand or snow) ⟨*mounds* of snow after the plow had passed⟩ — see ²BANK
2 a quantity of things thrown or stacked on one another ⟨an ever-growing *mound* of dirty laundry on the floor⟩ — see ¹PILE 1
3 an area of high ground ⟨a pitcher's *mound*⟩ — see HEIGHT 4

mound *vb* **1** to form into a pile or ridge of earth ⟨First, *mound* the mulch around the plants.⟩
synonyms bank, hill
related words heap, pile, pyramid, stack; embank; bunch, bundle, clump, lump, mass, wad; accumulate, amass, assemble, collect, conglomerate, gather, group
2 to lay or throw on top of one another ⟨*mounding* slices of cheese on top of her sandwich meat⟩ — see PILE 1

¹mount *n* an elevation of land higher than a hill ⟨*Mount* Everest⟩ — see MOUNTAIN 1

²mount *n* a structure that holds up or serves as a foundation for something else ⟨hammered together a *mount* for the cameras⟩ — see SUPPORT 1

mount *vb* **1** to become greater in extent, volume, amount, or number ⟨Medical expenses began to *mount*.⟩ — see INCREASE 2
2 to bring before the public in performance or exhibition ⟨the huge amount of money needed to *mount* a campaign⟩ — see PRESENT 1
3 to move or extend upward ⟨The cable car continues to *mount* to ever higher terrain until the moment when the entire valley comes into view.⟩ — see ASCEND

mountain *n* **1** an elevation of land higher than a hill ⟨My cousin likes to climb *mountains* just because she can.⟩
synonyms alp, hump, mount, peak
related words cordillera, mountain range, range, sierra; inselberg, knob, seamount; aiguille, horn, mountaintop, pinnacle, summit
near antonyms basin, bowl, depression, hollow, vale, valley
2 a considerable amount ⟨He receives a *mountain* of mail every year for the holidays.⟩ — see LOT 2
3 a quantity of things thrown or stacked on one another ⟨He piled a *mountain* of mashed potatoes on his plate.⟩ — see ¹PILE 1

mountain lion *n* a large tawny cat of the wild ⟨A *mountain lion* was spotted near the border of the conservation area.⟩ — see COUGAR

mountainous *adj* unusually large ⟨the seemingly *mountainous* obstacles he had to overcome while growing up⟩ — see HUGE

mountebank *n* one who makes false claims of identity or expertise ⟨claimed that many doctors were frauds and *mountebanks*⟩ — see IMPOSTOR

mounting *n* a structure that holds up or serves as a foundation for something else ⟨built a new *mounting* for the engine⟩ — see SUPPORT 1

mourn *vb* **1** to feel deep sadness or mental pain ⟨We *mourned* for weeks after our beloved pet's death.⟩ — see GRIEVE
2 to feel or express sorrow for ⟨an editorial that *mourns* the loss of the town's last movie theater⟩ — see LAMENT 1

mournful *adj* **1** expressing or suggesting mourning ⟨She had such a *mournful* expression that we wondered what could be wrong.⟩
synonyms aching, anguished, bemoaning, bewailing, bitter, deploring, doleful, dolorous, funeral, grieving, heartbroken, lamentable, lugubrious, plaintive, regretful, rueful, sorrowful, sorry, wailing, weeping, woeful
related words elegiac (*also* elegiacal), melancholy;

dejected, depressed, despondent, disconsolate, dispirited, downcast, downhearted, heartsick, heartsore, inconsolable, tearful; brokenhearted, careworn, crestfallen, downcast, downhearted, forlorn, gloomy, glum, low-spirited, miserable, sad, triste, unhappy, woebegone; bawling, crying, groaning, howling, keening, moaning, yammering; black, bleak, cheerless, comfortless, dark, darkening, desolate, dismal, dreary, funereal, gloomy, glum, gray (*also* grey), joyless, low, miserable, moody, morbid, morose, pathetic, pessimistic, piteous, saturnine, somber (*or* sombre), sullen

near antonyms delighted, exulting, glorying, happy, joyful, rejoicing, triumphant; bright, cheerful, cheering, cheery; laughing, smiling; blissful, blithe, blithesome, buoyant, jocund, jolly, joyous, lighthearted, merry, mirthful; encouraging, hopeful, optimistic; ecstatic, elated, euphoric, exhilarated, giddy, rapturous, rhapsodic (*also* rhapsodical)

2 feeling unhappiness ⟨the *mournful* relatives at the memorial service⟩ — see SAD 1

3 causing unhappiness ⟨the *mournful* death of a beloved entertainer⟩ — see SAD 2

mournfully *adv* with feelings of bitterness or grief ⟨spoke *mournfully* of his late mother⟩ — see HARD 2

mouse *vb* to move about in a sly or secret manner ⟨a cat *mousing* along in the shadows of the garden⟩ — see SNEAK 1

mousy *or* **mousey** *adj* easily frightened ⟨a *mousy* little girl who hid behind her mother the entire time we were there⟩ — see SHY 1

mouth *n* **1** the opening through which food passes into the body of an animal ⟨The baby chicks opened their *mouths* very wide and chirped piteously when their mother came back with worms.⟩

synonyms kisser [*slang*], mug

related words countenance, face, puss [*slang*], visage

2 a twisting of the facial features in disgust or disapproval ⟨The boy usually makes a *mouth* when he gets an injection.⟩ — see GRIMACE

3 disrespectful or argumentative talk given in response to a command or request ⟨I won't tolerate you giving me *mouth* about everything.⟩ — see BACK TALK

mouth *vb* **1** to distort one's face ⟨When her mother told her to mind, the little girl *mouthed* insolently and rolled her eyes.⟩ — see MUG 1

2 to speak softly and unclearly ⟨The prompter *mouthed* the forgotten words under his breath.⟩ — see MUMBLE

mouth (off) *vb* to talk as if giving an important and formal speech ⟨She was always *mouthing off* about how the company should be run.⟩ — see ORATE 1

mouthful *n* a small piece or quantity of food ⟨Kara took a small *mouthful* of the soup to see if she liked it.⟩ — see MORSEL 1

mouthpiece *n* a person who speaks for another or for a group ⟨a statement read by the official *mouthpiece* of the company⟩ — see SPOKESPERSON

movable *or* **moveable** *adj* capable of being moved especially with ease ⟨Any furniture that is not *movable* will be covered with protective cloths by the painters.⟩

synonyms mobile, portable

related words adjustable, flexible, modular; removable (*also* removeable), transferable (*also* transferrable), transportable; motile, moving; unbalanced, unstable, unsteady; manageable

near antonyms nonmotile, nonmoving; motionless, moveless, standing, static, stationary, still, stuck, wedged; fast, fixed, rooted, steadfast

antonyms immobile, immovable, irremovable, nonmobile, unmovable

movables *or* **moveables** *pl n* **1** the movable articles (such as tables and chairs) in a room ⟨When painting a room, you should first cover the big pieces and remove all of the *movables*.⟩ — see FURNITURE

2 transportable items that one owns ⟨We packed our *movables* into the van and headed off to our new home.⟩ — see POSSESSION 2

move *n* **1** an action planned or taken to achieve a desired result ⟨Retiring early was a smart *move*.⟩ — see MEASURE 1

2 the act or an instance of changing position ⟨Don't make a *move*!⟩ — see MOVEMENT 1

move *vb* **1** to change the place or position of ⟨I need you to *move* all your books off that chair before company gets here.⟩

synonyms budge, dislocate, displace, disturb, remove, shift, transfer, transpose

related words bear, carry, cart, convey, drive, haul, lug, tote, transmit, transplant, transport; replace, supersede, supplant; alter, make over, modify, redo, refashion, remake, remodel, revamp, revise, rework, vary

near antonyms anchor, fix, freeze, moor, secure, set, stabilize; embed (*also* imbed), entrench (*also* intrench), implant, ingrain (*also* engrain), lodge, root

2 to set or keep in motion ⟨The hands of the wall clock are *moved* by battery.⟩

synonyms actuate, drive, impel, propel, work

related words activate, motivate, provoke; abet, ferment, foment, incite, raise, stir (up), whip (up); set off, trigger, trip; arouse, excite, fire (up), galvanize, inflame (*also* enflame), inspire, instigate, rouse, stimulate

near antonyms bridle, check, constrain, contain, control, curb, inhibit, regulate, rein (in), restrain

3 to change one's position ⟨Don't *move* while I'm trying to draw your portrait.⟩

synonyms budge, shift, stir

related words fiddle, fidget, jiggle, squiggle, squirm, toss, twitch, wiggle, wriggle, writhe; rouse

near antonyms hang around, remain, stay, stick around, tarry; stabilize

antonyms freeze, still

4 to act upon (a person or a person's feelings) so as to cause a response ⟨We were deeply *moved* by the program of patriotic music.⟩ — see ¹AFFECT 1

5 to rouse to strong feeling or action ⟨The heartfelt appeal *moved* the people to reach into their pockets and donate generously.⟩ — see PROVOKE 1

6 to cause (someone) to agree with a belief or course of action by using arguments or earnest requests ⟨The report *moved* me to change my mind about the issue.⟩ — see PERSUADE

7 to cause to function ⟨This one button *moves* the whole machine.⟩ — see ACTIVATE

8 to leave a place often for another ⟨The police officer told the loiterers to *move* along.⟩ — see GO 2

movement *n* **1** the act or an instance of changing position ⟨A sudden *movement* in the far corner of the room made her turn in that direction.⟩

synonyms motion, move, shift, shifting, stir, stirring

related words dislocation, migration, relocation; locomotion, mobility, motility, motivity; fidgeting, squirm, squirming, twitching, wriggling, writhing; flailing, flapping, waving

near antonyms immobility; inertia, inertness, stillness; cessation, discontinuance, ending, expiration, finish, halt, lapse, pause, shutdown, shutoff, stop, stoppage, surcease, termination

antonyms motionlessness

2 a series of activities undertaken to achieve a goal ⟨a *movement* for political reform in the city⟩ — see CAMPAIGN

movie *n* **1** a story told by means of a series of continuously projected pictures and a sound track ⟨There was much excitement when it was announced that the popular children's book would be turned into a *movie*.⟩
synonyms film, flick, flicker, motion picture, moving picture, picture
related words animated cartoon, cartoon, docudrama, documentary, feature; silent, talkie
2 movies *pl* the art or business of making a movie ⟨Many a small-town girl has gone to Hollywood, dreaming of making it big in the *movies*.⟩
synonyms cinema, film, motion pictures, pictures, screen
related words showbiz, show business

moving *adj* having the power to affect the feelings or sympathies ⟨He gave a truly *moving* graduation speech that had some graduates in tears.⟩
synonyms affecting, emotional, impressive, poignant, stirring, touching
related words eloquent, expressive, meaningful, significant; demonstrative, excitable, feeling, passionate, responsive, sensitive; exciting, inspirational, provoking, rousing, stimulating; dramatic, histrionic, melodramatic, theatrical (*also* theatric); cathartic
near antonyms cold, cool, detached, dispassionate; deadpan
antonyms unaffecting, unemotional, unimpressive

moving picture *n* a story told by means of a series of continuously projected pictures and a sound track ⟨In the 20th century *moving pictures* became an important form of artistic expression.⟩ — see MOVIE 1

mow *vb* **1** to shorten the standing leafy plant cover of ⟨You really should *mow* the lawn before it gets much higher.⟩
synonyms cut
related words clip, crop, curtail, cut back, dock, hack, lop, manicure, nip, pare, prune, trim; bob, shave, shear, snip
2 to bring down by cutting ⟨an afternoon spent *mowing* hay⟩ — see FELL 2

mow (down) *vb* **1** to kill on a large scale ⟨Machine guns *mowed down* the advancing troops.⟩ — see MASSACRE
2 to strike (someone) so forcefully as to cause a fall ⟨The crowd rushing in for the sale *mowed down* the poor clerks standing at the front entrance.⟩ — see FELL 1

much *adj* having great meaning or lasting effect ⟨Actually, nothing *much* changed.⟩ — see IMPORTANT 1

much *adv* **1** to a great degree ⟨*much* gratified by the favorable response to her novel⟩ — see VERY 1
2 to a large extent or degree ⟨The new decorations made me *much* happier.⟩ — see GREATLY 2
3 very close to but not completely ⟨Today the old neighborhood looks *much* as it did years ago.⟩ — see ALMOST
4 many times ⟨I don't go that *much* anymore.⟩ — see OFTEN

much *n* a considerable amount ⟨*Much* of what people think they know about words is inaccurate or downright false.⟩ — see LOT 2

muck *n* **1** foul matter that mars the purity or cleanliness of something ⟨spattered with *muck* from the pigpen⟩ — see FILTH 1
2 soft wet earth ⟨Her shoes were covered with *muck* by the end of the soccer game.⟩ — see MUD

muck *vb* to make dirty ⟨You can't work in the garden and not expect to *muck* your clothes.⟩ — see DIRTY

mucky *adj* **1** full of or covered with soft wet earth ⟨The ground was very *mucky* after a night of pouring rain.⟩ — see MUDDY 1

2 not clean ⟨only too happy to remove those old *mucky* clothes⟩ — see DIRTY 1

mud *n* soft wet earth ⟨We cannot play softball today because the field turned to *mud* after last night's heavy rain.⟩
synonyms mire, muck, ooze, slime, slop, sludge, slush
related words gumbo, silt; clay, dirt, gravel, humus, loam, sand, soil; glop, slop, swill

muddle *n* **1** a state in which everything is out of order ⟨Things at the newly built school were all in a *muddle* on opening day.⟩ — see CHAOS
2 a state of mental confusion ⟨I was in such a *muddle* after the accident that I didn't know where I was.⟩ — see HAZE 2
3 a state of mental uncertainty ⟨The new, supposedly improved forms simply put taxpayers in a bigger *muddle*.⟩ — see CONFUSION 1
4 an unorganized collection or mixture of various things ⟨a *muddle* of old magazines piled on the shelves⟩ — see MISCELLANY 1

muddle *vb* **1** to throw into a state of mental uncertainty ⟨a car shopper thoroughly *muddled* by too much well-meaning advice⟩ — see CONFUSE 1
2 to undo the proper order or arrangement of ⟨I always get their names *muddled* up in my mind.⟩ — see DISORDER

muddled *adj* lacking in order, neatness, and often cleanliness ⟨a *muddled* arrangement of trophies in the display case⟩ — see MESSY

muddy *adj* **1** full of or covered with soft wet earth ⟨Please do not walk in the house with *muddy* boots on, as you will get the carpet dirty.⟩
synonyms miry, mucky, oozy, slimy, sludgy, slushy
related words clayey, loamy, silty; bedraggled; dirty, filthy, foul, grimy, grubby, gunky, impure, smutty, soiled, squalid, stained, sullied, unclean, uncleanly
near antonyms clean, immaculate, pristine, sparkling, spick-and-span (*or* spic-and-span), spotless, unsoiled, unstained, unsullied
2 having visible particles in liquid suspension ⟨Whether *muddy* or not, water taken from lakes and streams should be boiled by campers.⟩ — see CLOUDY 1
3 not clean ⟨We were all *muddy* after playing outside.⟩ — see DIRTY 1

muddy *vb* **1** to throw into a state of mental uncertainty ⟨My mind had been thoroughly *muddied* by the long hours of exacting work.⟩ — see CONFUSE 1
2 to make (something) unclear to the understanding ⟨That argument is irrelevant and will just *muddy* the issue we're trying to resolve.⟩ — see CONFUSE 2
3 to make dirty ⟨forgot to take off our shoes and accidentally *muddied* the kitchen floor⟩ — see DIRTY

muff *vb* to make or do (something) in a clumsy or unskillful way ⟨I *muffed* the repair job and had to do it again.⟩ — see BOTCH

muffle *vb* **1** to deaden the sound of ⟨The walls *muffled* their conversation so that only a low murmur was heard.⟩
synonyms mute, stifle
related words insulate, soundproof; pad; dampen, mellow, soften, subdue, tone (down); baffle; smother
near antonyms amplify, boost, deepen, enhance, heighten, increase, magnify, step up, strengthen
antonyms unmuffle
2 to surround or cover closely ⟨The airport had been *muffled* in fog all morning long.⟩ — see ENFOLD 1

mug *n* **1** a round vessel equipped with a handle and designed for drinking ⟨a coffee *mug*⟩ — see CUP
2 the front part of the head ⟨She joked about not having to see his ugly *mug* anymore.⟩ — see FACE 1

3 the opening through which food passes into the body of an animal ⟨Keep your *mug* shut and listen up!⟩ — see MOUTH 1

4 a twisting of the facial features in disgust or disapproval ⟨an involuntary *mug* at the revolting sight⟩ — see GRIMACE

mug *vb* **1** to distort one's face ⟨Every time their picture was snapped, both children *mugged* by sticking out their tongues or scrunching up their faces.⟩
synonyms grimace, mouth
related words pout; contort, deform, twist, warp; frown, glare, gloom, glower, lower (*also* lour), scowl; gape, gaze, ogle, stare; growl, snarl, sneer; simper, smirk
phrases make a face (*or* make faces), pull a face
near antonyms beam, grin, smile

2 to take a photograph of ⟨*mugging* captured criminals for the police records⟩ — see PHOTOGRAPH

muggy *adj* containing or characterized by an uncomfortable amount of moisture ⟨The air was so *muggy* we felt we just had to go for a swim.⟩ — see HUMID

mulct *n* a sum of money to be paid as a punishment ⟨The credit card company usually imposed a *mulct* of an additional $30 on overdue payments.⟩ — see FINE

mulct *vb* to rob by the use of trickery or threats ⟨trying to *mulct* the insurance company for an accident that never happened⟩ — see FLEECE

mulish *adj* sticking to an opinion, purpose, or course of action in spite of reason, arguments, or persuasion ⟨a *mulish* determination to have his own way⟩ — see OBSTINATE

mulishness *n* a steadfast adherence to an opinion, purpose, or course of action in spite of reason, arguments, or persuasion ⟨cursed their *mulishness* for failing to own up to what seemed like an obvious mistake to him⟩ — see OBSTINACY

mull (over) *vb* to give serious and careful thought to ⟨*Mull over* the idea for a while and then let me know.⟩ — see PONDER

multicolored *adj* marked by a variety of usually vivid colors ⟨displays of *multicolored* pottery from around the world⟩ — see COLORFUL

multifarious *adj* being of many and various kinds ⟨the *multifarious* interests and activities in which Benjamin Franklin immersed himself⟩ — see MANIFOLD

multiple *adj* **1** used or done by a number of people as a group ⟨*multiple* ownership of a vacation condo⟩ — see COLLECTIVE

2 being of a large but indefinite number ⟨the *multiple* achievements of her long career in public education⟩ — see MANY

multiplex *adj* being of a large but indefinite number ⟨He would sometimes experience *multiplex* moods in the course of a single day.⟩ — see MANY

multiplication *n* the act or process of becoming greater in number ⟨There's been a steady *multiplication* in our attic of old equipment since the revolution in consumer electronics.⟩
synonyms accumulating, accumulation, addition, increase, proliferation
related words doubling, quadrupling, tripling; creep, growth, rise, spread; enlargement, escalation, expansion; amplification, distension (*or* distention); accretion, accrual, augmentation; extension, lengthening, boost, gain, hike, increment, rise
near antonyms abatement, compressing, compression, condensation, constriction, contraction, diminishing, diminution, diminution, drop, fall, lessening, lowering, reduction, shrinkage, shrinking; retrenching, retrenchment, shortening
antonyms decrease

multiplicity *n* **1** a considerable amount ⟨a *multiplicity* of suggestions for turning the company around⟩ — see LOT 2

2 the quality or state of being composed of many different elements or types ⟨Shakespeare's works seem to encompass the full *multiplicity* of human experience.⟩ — see VARIETY 1

multiply *vb* **1** to bring forth offspring ⟨Rabbits *multiply* with proverbial rapidity.⟩ — see PROCREATE

2 to make greater in size, amount, or number ⟨The booming economy *multiplied* the wealth of investors.⟩ — see INCREASE 1

3 to become greater in extent, volume, amount, or number ⟨With each attempt the problems *multiplied*.⟩ — see INCREASE 2

multitude *n* **1** a great number of persons or creatures massed together ⟨awed by the *multitude* of stars in the night sky⟩ — see CROWD 1

2 the body of the community as contrasted with the elite ⟨a candidate who tried to appeal to the *multitude*⟩ — see MASS 1

multitudinous *adj* being of a large but indefinite number ⟨The new teacher fielded the *multitudinous* questions that seem to be an inevitable part of opening day at school.⟩ — see MANY

mum *adj* deliberately refraining from speech ⟨kept *mum* about the surprise bridal shower⟩ — see SILENT 1

mumble *n* speech that is not clear enough to be understood ⟨He spoke in a *mumble*.⟩
synonyms grunt, grunting, murmur, murmuring, mutter, muttering
related words rumor, undertone, whisper; babble, babbling, blab, blabbing, chatter, chattering, drivel, driveling (*or* drivelling), gabble, gabbling, jabber, jabbering, maundering, prattle, prattling, rambling

mumble *vb* to speak softly and unclearly ⟨I can't understand you if you *mumble*.⟩
synonyms grunt, mouth, murmur, mutter
related words babble, blab, chatter, drivel, gabble, gibber, jabber, maunder, prattle, ramble; breathe, gasp, pant, whisper; buzz
near antonyms articulate, enunciate
antonyms speak out, speak up

mumbo jumbo *n* unintelligible or meaningless talk ⟨The soothsayer's predictions were nothing but *mumbo jumbo*.⟩ — see GIBBERISH 1

mummer *n* **1** an actor in a story performed silently and entirely by body movements ⟨a street festival featuring *mummers* in a pantomime⟩ — see MIME 1

2 one who acts professionally (as in a play, movie, or television show) ⟨a *mummer* who repeatedly called out for his lines⟩ — see ACTOR 1

munchies *pl n* a need or desire for food ⟨I often get the *munchies* while watching TV late at night.⟩ — see HUNGER 1

mundane *adj* **1** having to do with the practical details of regular life ⟨They didn't want to be bothered with *mundane* concerns like doing the dishes while on vacation.⟩
synonyms everyday, prosaic, terrestrial, workaday
related words earthly, temporal, worldly; average, common, commonplace, customary, familiar, garden, generic, normal, ordinary, plain, popular, routine, run-of-the-mill, standard, typical, unexceptional, unremarkable, usual; frequent, habitual, regular
near antonyms high-minded, lofty, noble, sublime; aberrant, abnormal, atypical; exceptional, extraordinary, freak, peculiar, phenomenal, rare, singular, special, uncommon, uncustomary, unique, unusual, unwonted; bizarre, curious, far-out, odd, outlandish, out-of-the-way, quirky, remarkable, screwy, strange, weird, wild

2 having to do with life on earth especially as opposed to that in heaven ⟨a period for reflection and penitence, when spiritual concerns should take precedence over those that are *mundane*⟩ — see EARTHLY

municipality *n* a thickly settled, highly populated area ⟨a *municipality* with an excellent police department⟩ — see CITY

munificent *adj* giving or sharing in abundance and without hesitation ⟨a *munificent* host who has presided over many charitable events at his mansion⟩ — see GENEROUS 1

munificently *adv* in a generous manner ⟨The heiress has shared her wealth *munificently* on countless occasions.⟩ — see WELL 2

murder *n* **1** a situation or state that causes great suffering and unhappiness ⟨This weather is *murder* on my sinuses.⟩ — see HELL 2

2 the taking of another person's life ⟨arrested for attempting to commit *murder*⟩ — see HOMICIDE 1

murder *vb* **1** to put to death deliberately ⟨It is illegal to *murder* someone.⟩

synonyms croak [*slang*], dispatch, do in, execute, get, liquidate, rub out, slay, terminate

related words shoot; blot out, claim, cut down, destroy, fell, kill, smite, zap; butcher, massacre, mow (down), slaughter; annihilate, eliminate, eradicate, exterminate, wipe out

phrases do away with

near antonyms animate, raise, restore, resurrect, resuscitate, revive

2 to make or do (something) in a clumsy or unskillful way ⟨We listened in horror as she *murdered* our favorite song on stage.⟩ — see BOTCH

murderer *n* a person who kills another person ⟨The *murderer* was sentenced to life in prison without the possibility of parole.⟩ — see ASSASSIN

murdering *adj* eager for or marked by the shedding of blood, extreme violence, or killing ⟨a vow to bring down the *murdering* fiend who had destroyed his family⟩ — see BLOODTHIRSTY

murderous *adj* **1** difficult to endure ⟨the *murderous* heat of the desert⟩ — see HARSH 1

2 requiring considerable physical or mental effort ⟨Those exams were *murderous*.⟩ — see HARD 2

3 likely to cause or capable of causing death ⟨braved *murderous* machine-gun fire to capture the hill from the enemy⟩ — see DEADLY 1

4 eager for or marked by the shedding of blood, extreme violence, or killing ⟨Viking warriors became legendary for the *murderous* fury they displayed in battle.⟩ — see BLOODTHIRSTY

murk *n* **1** a time or place of little or no light ⟨a predator lying unseen in the *murk*⟩ — see DARK 1

2 an atmospheric condition in which suspended particles in the air rob it of its transparency ⟨I was stuck outside in the *murk* and the rain.⟩ — see HAZE 1

murkiness *n* the quality or state of having a veiled or uncertain meaning ⟨We had trouble understanding the passage because of its *murkiness*.⟩ — see OBSCURITY 1

murky *adj* **1** being without light or without much light ⟨I didn't like walking around the *murky* campground without a flashlight.⟩ — see DARK 1

2 causing or marked by an atmosphere lacking in cheer ⟨the *murky* shadows of the cemetery⟩ — see GLOOMY 1

3 filled with or dimmed by fine particles (as of dust or water) in suspension ⟨skies made *murky* from the smoke of forest fires that were many miles to the west⟩ — see HAZY 1

4 having an often intentionally veiled or uncertain meaning ⟨a *murky* reply to a question about his intentions⟩ — see OBSCURE 1

5 not seen or understood clearly ⟨a gubernatorial candidate with a *murky* position on the hot-button issue⟩ — see FAINT 1

murmur *n* **1** an expression of dissatisfaction, pain, or resentment ⟨She finished the tedious job without a *murmur*.⟩ — see COMPLAINT 1

2 speech that is not clear enough to be understood ⟨The actors could just barely hear the *murmurs* of the audience.⟩ — see MUMBLE

murmur *vb* **1** to express dissatisfaction, pain, or resentment usually tiresomely ⟨No prisoner dared *murmur* out loud.⟩ — see COMPLAIN

2 to speak softly and unclearly ⟨a college professor who tends to *murmur*⟩ — see MUMBLE

murmurer *n* an irritable and complaining person ⟨There were always a few *murmurers* in the crowd.⟩ — see GROUCH 1

murmuring *n* speech that is not clear enough to be understood ⟨His surprising announcement brought *murmurings* from the crowd.⟩ — see MUMBLE

muscle *n* **1** muscular strength ⟨I'm going to need someone with real *muscle* to help me move all this furniture.⟩

synonyms beef, brawn, main

related words force, might, potency, power, puissance, sinew; energy, vigor

near antonyms impotence, impotency, weakness; debilitation, debility, enfeeblement, faintness, feebleness, frailness, frailty, infirmity

2 the ability to exert effort for the accomplishment of a task ⟨He lacks the political *muscle* to get the policy changed.⟩ — see POWER 2

muscle *vb* **1** to cause (a person) to give in to pressure ⟨He was *muscled* out of command by his opponents at military headquarters.⟩ — see FORCE

2 to force one's way ⟨*muscling* straight through the packed crowd of people waiting to board the ship⟩ — see ²PRESS 4

muscular *adj* **1** marked by a well-developed musculature ⟨Olympic runners tend to have very *muscular* legs.⟩

synonyms brawny, sinewy

related words wiry; powerful, strong; beefy, burly, hefty, hulking, husky; able-bodied, athletic, herculean, mighty, robust, rugged, stalwart, stout, strapping, sturdy; muscle-bound; sculpted

near antonyms nonathletic; debilitated, delicate, effete, enervated, enfeebled, feeble, fragile, frail, weak, weakened, weakly, wimpy; light, lightweight, slight; lean, slender, slim, svelte, sylphlike, thin, willowy; emaciated, gaunt, lank, rawboned, scraggy, spare

antonyms scrawny, skinny

2 having muscles capable of exerting great physical force ⟨a *muscular* superhero who can easily lift a ton or more⟩ — see STRONG 1

3 marked by or uttered with forcefulness ⟨a presidential speech that promises to be a *muscular* enunciation of the nation's foreign policy⟩ — see EMPHATIC 1

4 having an abundance of some characteristic quality (as flavor) ⟨a *muscular* red wine that goes especially well with beef⟩ — see FULL-BODIED

museum *n* a building or part of a building in which objects of interest are displayed ⟨a trip to the *Museum* of Natural History⟩

synonyms gallery, salon

related words archives, assemblage, collection, library; display, exhibition; studio

mush *n* **1** something (as a work of literature or music) that is too sentimental ⟨an opera that is pure *mush*⟩ — see CORN

2 the state or quality of having an excess of tender feelings (as of love, nostalgia, or compassion) ⟨I couldn't stand all the *mush* in the movie's romantic scenes.⟩ — see SENTIMENTALITY

mushroom *vb* to become greater in extent, volume, amount, or number ⟨The suburb's population has *mushroomed* tremendously in the last decade.⟩ — see INCREASE 2

mushy *adj* **1** appealing to the emotions in an obvious and tiresome way ⟨a *mushy* love story⟩ — see CORNY
2 giving easily to the touch ⟨*mushy* fruit that was obviously overripe⟩ — see SOFT 3

musical *adj* **1** having a pleasantly flowing quality suggestive of music ⟨the *musical* sounds of the babbling brook⟩ — see LYRIC 1
2 having a pleasing mixture of notes ⟨The song of the skylark has been celebrated for being especially *musical*.⟩ — see HARMONIOUS 1

musicale *n* an entertainment featuring singing or the playing of musical instruments ⟨The neighbors gathered every month in someone's home for an informal *musicale*.⟩ — see CONCERT

musician *n* **1** a person who plays a musical instrument ⟨The violinist was a famous and exquisitely talented *musician*.⟩
synonyms instrumentalist, player
related words minstrel; artist, performer; maestro, virtuoso; accompanist, recitalist, soloist, symphonist; accordionist, bassoonist, clarinetist (*or* clarinettist), cornetist (*or* cornettist), drummer, fiddler, flautist, flutist, guitarist, harpist, hornist, keyboardist, oboist, organ-grinder, organist, percussionist, pianist, picker, piper, reedman, saxophonist, trombonist, trumpeter, violinist, violist
2 a person who writes musical compositions ⟨That *musician* is known for having written music that is very difficult to perform.⟩ — see COMPOSER

muskeg *n* spongy land saturated or partially covered with water ⟨Local farmers can make extra money by digging peat out of the nearby *muskeg*.⟩ — see SWAMP

muss *n* a state in which everything is out of order ⟨Careful planning had eliminated most of the *muss* that usually accompanies a move to a new house.⟩ — see CHAOS

muss *vb* to undo the proper order or arrangement of ⟨The wind *mussed* up my hair.⟩ — see DISORDER

mussed *adj* lacking in order, neatness, and often cleanliness ⟨a *mussed* look that was a change from his usual meticulous grooming⟩ — see MESSY

mussy *adj* lacking in order, neatness, and often cleanliness ⟨a *mussy* pile of papers and books⟩ — see MESSY

must *n* something necessary, indispensable, or unavoidable ⟨Exercise is a *must* if you want to stay healthy.⟩ — see ESSENTIAL 1

must *vb* to be under necessity or obligation to ⟨We *must* be quiet during the performance.⟩ — see NEED 2

muster *n* **1** a body of people come together in one place ⟨a *muster* of concerned citizens⟩ — see GATHERING 1
2 a number of things considered as a unit ⟨considering the *muster* of suggestions that were submitted for "word of the year"⟩ — see GROUP 1

muster *vb* **1** to assemble and make ready for action ⟨a command to *muster* the troops⟩ — see MOBILIZE
2 to bring together in assembly by or as if by command ⟨all the supporters that I could *muster* for the fund-raising campaign⟩ — see CONVOKE
3 to be made up of ⟨The corps of regular book-readers *musters* only about 30% of the population.⟩ — see COMPRISE 1

muster out *vb* to let go from office, service, or employ-

ment ⟨*mustered out* of the army at the end of the war⟩ — see DISMISS 1

musty *adj* **1** having an unpleasant smell ⟨*musty* old gym socks⟩ — see MALODOROUS
2 used or heard so often as to be dull ⟨the *musty* prose of writers who use the same expressions over and over⟩ — see STALE 1

mutable *adj* likely to change frequently, suddenly, or unexpectedly ⟨a politician with very *mutable* positions on all the issues⟩ — see FICKLE 1

mutate *vb* to pass from one form, state, or level to another ⟨colored lights that slowly *mutate* from green to blue and so on across the color spectrum⟩ — see CHANGE 2

mute *adj* **1** unable to speak ⟨The child is both deaf and *mute*.⟩
synonyms inarticulate, speechless, voiceless
related words closemouthed, laconic, reserved, reticent, taciturn, tight-lipped, uncommunicative; mum, nonspeaking, quiet, silent, wordless
near antonyms blabby, chatty, communicative, expansive, gabby, garrulous, loquacious, talkative, talky, vocal; expatiating, speaking out, speaking up; articulating, speaking, talking; articulate, eloquent, fluent, voluble
2 deliberately refraining from speech ⟨The child remained *mute* no matter how much we pleaded for an answer.⟩ — see SILENT 1

mute *n* a device on a musical instrument that deadens or softens its tone ⟨I was practicing my trumpet at three in the morning when the *mute* fell out, and I managed to wake everyone up.⟩
synonyms damper
related words muffler, quieter, softener, soft pedal

mute *vb* **1** to stop the noise or speech of ⟨*muted* the television while she was on the phone⟩ — see SILENCE 1
2 to deaden the sound of ⟨Closing the windows *muted* the traffic noise so we could get to sleep.⟩ — see MUFFLE 1

muted *adj* **1** mostly or entirely without sound ⟨the *muted* reaction of the shocked crowd⟩ — see SILENT 3
2 not excessively showy ⟨painted with *muted* colors⟩ — see QUIET 2
3 deliberately refraining from speech ⟨She was unexpectedly *muted* in the presence of her literary idol.⟩ — see SILENT 1

muteness *n* incapacity for or restraint from speaking ⟨We were baffled by his uncharacteristic *muteness*.⟩ — see SILENCE 1

mutilate *vb* to cause severe or permanent injury to ⟨was lucky not to be *mutilated* in the car crash⟩ — see MAIM

mutineer *n* a person who rises up against authority ⟨The *mutineers* were captured after they turned to piracy on the open seas.⟩ — see REBEL

mutinous *adj* taking part in a rebellion ⟨vowed that he would someday see the *mutinous* crew hang⟩ — see REBELLIOUS 1

mutiny *n* open fighting against authority (as one's own government) ⟨a *mutiny* led by the ship's cook⟩ — see REBELLION 1

mutiny *vb* to rise up against established authority ⟨The party's conservative faction *mutinied* just before the election.⟩ — see REBEL

mutter *n* speech that is not clear enough to be understood ⟨the distracting *mutter* of some member of the audience⟩ — see MUMBLE

mutter *vb* **1** to express dissatisfaction, pain, or resentment usually tiresomely ⟨a *muttering* group of workers⟩ — see COMPLAIN
2 to speak softly and unclearly ⟨*muttering* to himself under his breath⟩ — see MUMBLE

mutterer *n* an irritable and complaining person ⟨the usual *mutterers* about the food in the cafeteria⟩ — see GROUCH 1

muttering *n* speech that is not clear enough to be understood ⟨barely heard *mutterings* of discontent⟩ — see MUMBLE

mutual *adj* used or done by a number of people as a group ⟨Every film is a *mutual* effort by the director, writer, actors, and a host of others.⟩ — see COLLECTIVE

myopic *adj* **1** able to see near things more clearly than distant ones ⟨He became so *myopic* that he finally broke down and got contact lenses.⟩ — see NEARSIGHTED
2 not thinking about and providing for the future ⟨the *myopic* city designers who did not plan for growth⟩ — see IMPROVIDENT

myriad *adj* **1** being of many and various kinds ⟨the *myriad* problems that today's cities face⟩ — see MANIFOLD
2 too many to be counted ⟨the *myriad* influences that shape a person's character⟩ — see COUNTLESS

myriad *n* a considerable amount ⟨The car can be outfitted with a *myriad* of options.⟩ — see LOT 2

mysterious *adj* **1** being beyond one's powers to know, understand, or explain ⟨The huge stone statues on Easter Island are ancient, *mysterious*, and haunting.⟩
synonyms cryptic, deep, enigmatic (*also* enigmatical), impenetrable, inscrutable, mystic, occult, uncanny
related words dark, darkling, fuzzy, murky, obscure, shadowy, vague; ambiguous, equivocal; imponderable, incomprehensible, unfathomable, unintelligible, unsearchable; inexplicable, unaccountable, unexplainable; unanswerable, unknowable; metaphysical, mystical, numinous, supernatural; abstruse, esoteric, recondite; baffling, befuddling, bewildering, confounding, confusing, mystifying, perplexing, puzzling
near antonyms apparent, clear, evident, manifest, obvious, open-and-shut, palpable, patent, perspicuous, plain, straightforward, transparent, unambiguous, unequivocal, unmistakable
2 having an often intentionally veiled or uncertain meaning ⟨the stranger's *mysterious* prediction⟩ — see OBSCURE 1

mystery *n* something hard to understand or explain ⟨The cause of the disease is still a *mystery* to scientists.⟩
synonyms conundrum, enigma, mystification, puzzle, puzzlement, riddle, secret
related words brainteaser, case, challenge, knot, matter, perplexity, poser, problem, stumper, trouble

mystic *adj* **1** having seemingly supernatural qualities or powers ⟨The notion that a cat has nine lives is based upon the belief that nine is a *mystic* number.⟩
synonyms magic, magical, occult, weird
related words bewitched, enchanted, spellbound; bewitching, charming, conjuring, enchanting, wiling; amazing, astonishing, astounding, awesome, extraordinary, fabulous, marvelous (*or* marvellous), miraculous, portentous, stunning, stupendous, sublime, wondrous; di-

vining, forecasting, foreknowing, foreseeing, foretelling, predicting, presaging, prognosticating, prophesying, soothsaying; metaphysical, preternatural, unearthly
near antonyms commonplace, everyday, normal, ordinary, prosaic, routine, run-of-the-mill, unexceptional, unremarkable, usual, workaday
2 being beyond one's powers to know, understand, or explain ⟨the belief that there are *mystic* forces at work here⟩ — see MYSTERIOUS 1
3 having an often intentionally veiled or uncertain meaning ⟨*mystic* prophesies that are never understood until it is too late⟩ — see OBSCURE 1

mystification *n* **1** a state of mental uncertainty ⟨The new information did little to ease our *mystification*.⟩ — see CONFUSION 1
2 something hard to understand or explain ⟨an event that is one of the great *mystifications* in all of maritime history⟩ — see MYSTERY

mystify *vb* to throw into a state of mental uncertainty ⟨We were *mystified* by the sudden changes in the tax code.⟩ — see CONFUSE 1

myth *n* **1** a traditional but unfounded story that gives the reason for a current custom, belief, or fact of nature ⟨According to an ancient Greek *myth*, humans acquired fire from Prometheus, a Titan who had stolen it from heaven.⟩
synonyms fable, legend
related words allegory, parable; fabrication, fantasy (*also* phantasy), fiction, figment, invention; narrative, saga, story, tale, yarn
2 the body of customs, beliefs, stories, and sayings associated with a people, thing, or place ⟨Over the years Davy Crockett evolved from an actual person to one of the great figures of American *myth*.⟩ — see FOLKLORE
3 a false idea or belief ⟨The idea that alligators can live in the sewers of New York is just a *myth*.⟩ — see FALLACY 1

mythical *or* **mythic** *adj* **1** based on, described in, or being a myth ⟨For years the Spanish conquistadors searched for the *mythical* El Dorado, a place of unimaginable riches.⟩
synonyms fabled, fabulous, legendary
related words famed, romanticized, storied; chimerical (*also* chimeric), fabricated, fantastic (*also* fantastical), fictional, fictitious; fanciful, imaginary, imagined, invented, made-up, make-believe, pretend, unreal; allegorical, mythological (*also* mythologic); semilegendary
near antonyms actual, existent, real, real-world; historical; factual, true; attested, authenticated, confirmed, established, proven, substantiated, validated, verified; authentic, bona fide, genuine, real-life
2 not real and existing only in the imagination ⟨the *mythical* unicorn⟩ — see IMAGINARY

mythology *n* the body of customs, beliefs, stories, and sayings associated with a people, thing, or place ⟨Ares is the god of war in Greek *mythology*.⟩ — see FOLKLORE

N

nab *vb* **1** to take or keep under one's control by authority of law ⟨The officer *nabbed* the purse snatcher before he could escape.⟩ — see ARREST 1
2 to take physical control or possession of (something) suddenly or forcibly ⟨A pickpocket *nabbed* my wallet.⟩ — see CATCH 1

nabob *n* one of high position or importance within a group ⟨We dressed conservatively so as to make a good impression with the *nabobs* on the co-op's board.⟩ — see BIG SHOT

nag *n* a large hoofed domestic animal that is used for carrying or drawing loads and for riding ⟨a poor farmer who could only afford one old *nag*⟩ — see HORSE

nag *vb* **1** to subject (someone) to constant scoldings and sharp reminders ⟨My parents are always *nagging* me about my homework.⟩
synonyms dog, henpeck, hound, needle
related words carp (at), fuss (about *or* over), nitpick; annoy, badger, bait, bother, bug, chivy (*or* chivvy), harry, hassle, irk, pester, plague, ride, vex, yap (at); goad, incite, prod, prompt, spur, urge; exhort, insist, press, pressure, push; blandish, cajole, coax, wheedle; beg, importune, plead
phrases pick at
near antonyms compliment; commend, laud, praise, recommend, tout; acclaim, applaud, eulogize, extol (*also* extoll)
2 to express dissatisfaction, pain, or resentment usually tiresomely ⟨If all you can do is *nag*, then you are of no use to this organization at all.⟩ — see COMPLAIN

naiad *n* a mythical goddess represented as a young woman and said to live outdoors ⟨In Greek mythology, *naiads* supposedly drowned the young men with whom they became enamored.⟩ — see NYMPH

nail *vb* **1** to deliver a blow to (someone or something) usually in a strong vigorous manner ⟨The boxer *nailed* his opponent with a devastating left hook.⟩ — see HIT 1
2 to make final, definite, or beyond dispute ⟨We *nailed* down a date for the meeting.⟩ — see CLINCH
3 to reveal the true nature of ⟨*nailed* the source of the story and forced a retraction⟩ — see EXPOSE 1
4 to take or keep under one's control by authority of law ⟨The FBI *nailed* the hackers.⟩ — see ARREST 1
5 to take physical control or possession of (something) suddenly or forcibly ⟨The running back saw the pass coming in and *nailed* it.⟩ — see CATCH 1

naive *or* **naïve** *adj* **1** lacking in worldly wisdom or informed judgment ⟨a first-time buyer who was so *naive* that he believed the salesman's spiel and paid good money for the rusty and broken-down car⟩
synonyms green, ingenuous, innocent, simple, simpleminded, uncritical, unknowing, unsophisticated, unsuspecting, unsuspicious, unwary, unworldly, wide-eyed
related words callow, childish, immature, inexperienced, raw; childlike, impractical, unrealistic; believing, credulous, gullible (*also* gullable), susceptible, trustful, trusting, unguarded; beguiled, duped, gulled, tricked; careless, heedless, thoughtless
near antonyms critical, cynical, doubting, incredulous, skeptical, suspecting, suspicious, unconvinced; careful, cautious, guarded, leery (*also* leary), wary, watchful; down-to-earth, hardheaded, pragmatic (*also* pragmatical), realistic, sober; street-smart, streetwise

antonyms cosmopolitan, experienced, knowing, sophisticated, worldly, worldly-wise
2 free from any intent to deceive or impress others ⟨The young girl gave honest and *naive* answers to the social worker's probing questions.⟩ — see GUILELESS
3 readily taken advantage of ⟨We get piles of junk mail because you are *naive* enough to keep entering these dumb contests.⟩ — see EASY 2

naively *or* **naïvely** *adv* without any attempt to impress by deception or exaggeration ⟨She *naively* admitted to the job interviewer that she actually had little work experience.⟩ — see NATURALLY 3

naïveté *also* **naivete** *or* **naïveté** *n* **1** the quality or state of being simple and sincere ⟨Her *naïveté* led her to leave her new car unlocked while she shopped at the mall.⟩
synonyms artlessness, guilelessness, ingenuousness, innocence, naturalness, simpleness, simplicity, unsophistication, unworldliness
related words candor, frankness, genuineness, honesty, openness, sincerity, straightforwardness, unaffectedness, unpretentiousness; callowness, childishness, inexperience, rawness; insularity, parochialism, provincialism; carelessness, heedlessness, thoughtlessness; ignorance, obliviousness, unawareness; credulity, credulousness, gullibility, impressionability; idealism, impracticality, optimism
near antonyms affectedness, artificiality, pretentiousness; deviousness, dishonesty, insincerity; disbelief, doubtfulness, incredulity, suspiciousness; carefulness, caution, wariness; pessimism, skepticism; maturity
antonyms artfulness, cynicism, sophistication, worldliness
2 readiness to believe the claims of others without sufficient evidence ⟨Though he was streetwise, the investigative reporter regularly assumed an air of *naïveté* when he was interviewing confidence men, charlatans, counterfeiters, and other assorted swindlers of the general public.⟩ — see CREDULITY

naked *adj* **1** lacking or shed of clothing ⟨I had recurrent nightmares about being *naked* in public.⟩
synonyms bare, disrobed, nude, stripped, unclad, unclothed, undressed
related words topless; denuded, peeled
phrases in the altogether (*or* the buff *or* the nude *or* one's birthday suit *or* the raw), stark naked
near antonyms covered, veiled; arrayed, caparisoned, decked (out), rigged (out), tricked (out); vested; decent
antonyms appareled (*or* apparelled), attired, clothed, dressed, garbed, invested, robed, suited
2 lacking a usual or natural covering ⟨The winter trees now look so *naked* without their colorful fall foliage.⟩
synonyms bald, bare, denuded, exposed, open, peeled, stripped, uncovered
related words displayed, revealed; hairless, shaven; disrobed, unclad, unclothed, undressed; furless, skinned; divested; unprotected
near antonyms mantled; overgrown, overrun, overspread; bearded, hairy
antonyms covered
3 free from all additions or embellishment ⟨a *naked* room waiting for an interior decorator's inspired touch⟩ — see PLAIN 1

name *adj* having a good reputation especially in a field of knowledge ⟨The university's physics department boasts a number of *name* physicists.⟩ — see RESPECTABLE 1

name *n* **1** a word or combination of words by which a person or thing is regularly known ⟨The guy introduced himself and then asked what my *name* was.⟩

synonyms appellation, cognomen, denomination, denotation, designation, handle, title

related words baptismal name, Christian name, forename, given name; maiden name, middle name; diminutive, epithet, nickname, sobriquet (*also* soubriquet); banner, rubric, tag; alias, nom de plume, pen name, pseudonym; binomial, monomial; trivial name, vernacular; misnomer; brand name, label, trademark, trade name

2 an act or expression showing scorn and usually intended to hurt another's feelings ⟨Quit calling her *names*.⟩ — see INSULT

3 outward and often deceptive indication ⟨a celebrity who is the head of the charitable organization in *name* only⟩ — see APPEARANCE 2

4 overall quality as seen or judged by people in general ⟨has a good *name* among fellow marine biologists⟩ — see REPUTATION

5 a person who is widely known and usually much talked about ⟨managed to get several *names* to appear at the restaurant's opening⟩ — see CELEBRITY 1

name *vb* **1** to give a name to ⟨Amy decided to *name* her new puppy "Bubbles."⟩

synonyms baptize, call, christen, denominate, designate, dub, entitle, label, style, term, title

related words brand, stigmatize, tag; denote, specify; miscall, misname, mistitle; nickname

2 to make reference to or speak about briefly but specifically ⟨I don't want to *name* anyone in particular, but someone in this room fiddled with my phone.⟩ — see MENTION 1

3 to pick (someone) by one's authority for a specific position or duty ⟨was *named* the provost of the university⟩ — see APPOINT 2

4 to decide to accept (someone or something) from a group of possibilities ⟨You don't like my offer? Just *name* your price.⟩ — see CHOOSE 1

5 to decide upon (the time or date for an event) usually from a position of authority ⟨You *name* the date and I'll make sure I'm there.⟩ — see APPOINT 1

6 to come to a judgment about after discussion or consideration ⟨They finally *named* a date for the wedding.⟩ — see DECIDE 1

nameless *adj* **1** not named or identified by a name ⟨The victim of the crime will remain *nameless* to protect his privacy.⟩ ⟨those *nameless* editors who write the synopses for TV shows in the newspaper⟩

synonyms anonymous, faceless, incognito, unbaptized, unchristened, unidentified, unnamed, untitled

related words undetermined, unspecified; obscure, uncelebrated, unheard-of, unheralded, unknown, unsung; unexceptional, unremarkable

near antonyms denominated, designated, specified; labeled (*or* labelled), tabbed, titled; celebrated, famed, famous, known, notable, noted, noteworthy, remarkable, renowned, well-known; exceptional

antonyms baptized, christened, dubbed, named, termed

2 beyond the power to describe ⟨was seized with a *nameless*, vague fear that made her seek the companionship of another person⟩ — see INDESCRIBABLE

3 not widely known ⟨a *nameless* poet who has just been rediscovered by devotees of love poems⟩ — see OBSCURE 2

namer *n* someone with the right or responsibility for making a selection ⟨We can't start the ceremony until the

namer of the scholarship winners shows up.⟩ — see SELECTOR

nanny *also* **nannie** *n* a person employed to care for a young child or children ⟨wrote a memoir recounting her days as a *nanny* for the rich and often indiscreet⟩ — see NURSE

¹**nap** *n* a short sleep ⟨so tired that she needed to take a refreshing *nap* before soccer practice⟩

synonyms catnap, doze, drowse, forty winks, siesta, snooze, wink

related words repose, rest; slumber; bed

²**nap** *n* a soft airy substance or covering ⟨High-quality suede has a good, even *nap*.⟩ — see FUZZ

nap *vb* **1** to sleep lightly or briefly ⟨decided to let the kids *nap* for a few more minutes before waking them⟩

synonyms catnap, doze, drowse, slumber, snooze

related words relax, repose, rest; couch, lay, lie, roost; lull

near antonyms arise, arouse, awake, awaken, get up, rise, rouse, uprise, wake (up), waken

2 to be in a state of sleep ⟨I'm just going to *nap* the entire afternoon.⟩ — see SLEEP 1

napping *adj* being in a state of suspended consciousness ⟨The *napping* children looked so peaceful.⟩ — see ASLEEP 1

napping *n* a natural periodic loss of consciousness during which the body restores itself ⟨Some people think that *napping* in the afternoon will keep you from sleeping well at night.⟩ — see SLEEP 1

narcotic *adj* tending to cause sleep ⟨The lecturer droned on in a *narcotic* monotone that eventually had the entire class struggling to stay awake.⟩ — see HYPNOTIC

narcotic *n* something that soothes, calms, or induces passivity or a sense of security ⟨investors lulled by the *narcotic* of a long bull stock market⟩ — see OPIATE

narrate *vb* to give an oral or written account of in some detail ⟨Mom got an audio version of the best-selling children's story that happened to be *narrated* by the author herself.⟩ — see TELL 1

narration *n* a relating of events usually in the order in which they happened ⟨a *narration* that vastly overstates her minor role in this international affair⟩ — see ACCOUNT 1

narrative *n* **1** a relating of events usually in the order in which they happened ⟨wrote a witty, chatty *narrative* of all the happenings at the party⟩ — see ACCOUNT 1

2 a work with imaginary characters and events that is shorter and usually less complex than a novel ⟨In such *narratives* as "The Murders in the Rue Morgue" and "The Purloined Letter," Edgar Allan Poe essentially created the modern detective story.⟩ — see STORY 1

narrow *adj* **1** being of less than usual width ⟨The cat found a *narrow* opening in the fence that he was able to squeeze through.⟩

synonyms fine, hairline, needlelike, skinny, slender, slim, thin

related words attenuated, elongate (*or* elongated), linear; bottleneck, close, compressed, condensed, constricted, contracted, squeezed, tight, tightened; lanky, rangy, reedy, shoestring, spindly, stalky, stringy, twiggy, willowy, wispy; lank, spare

near antonyms chunky, squat, stocky, stumpy, thick, thickset; bulky, massive, voluminous; thickish, widish

antonyms broad, fat, wide

2 not broad or open in views or opinions ⟨a *narrow* person with outdated ideas⟩

synonyms insular, little, narrow-minded, parochial, petty, picayune, provincial, sectarian, small, small-minded

related words inflexible, ironbound, obdurate, obstinate, rigid, set, stubborn, unyielding, wrongheaded; bigoted, intolerant; biased, jaundiced, one-sided, partial, partisan, prejudiced; brass bound, hidebound, old-fashioned, reactionary, stodgy, straitlaced (*or* straight-laced), stuffy; opinionated

near antonyms impartial, nonpartisan, objective, unbiased, unprejudiced; freethinking

antonyms broad-minded, cosmopolitan, liberal, open, open-minded, receptive, tolerant

3 having distinct or certain limits ⟨a play about human suffering, but in a *narrower* sense, also about the modern struggles of the working-class poor⟩ — see LIMITED 1

4 showing little difference in the standing of the competitors ⟨a *narrow* gubernatorial contest, the outcome of which may depend upon a handful of votes⟩ — see CLOSE 3

5 unwilling to grant other people social rights or to accept other viewpoints ⟨a *narrow* society in which many suffered injustice⟩ — see INTOLERANT 2

narrow–minded *adj* **1** unwilling to grant other people social rights or to accept other viewpoints ⟨Integration of the public schools was once vigorously opposed by *narrow-minded* people who feared social change.⟩ — see INTOLERANT 2

2 not broad or open in views or opinions ⟨a *narrow-minded* person who only listens to those who agree with him⟩ — see NARROW 2

narrows *pl n* a narrow body of water between two land masses ⟨We had to cautiously navigate our dinghy through the *narrows* before reaching the open water of the bay.⟩ — see CHANNEL 2

nastily *adv* in a mean or spiteful manner ⟨He *nastily* stuck his foot out and tripped the front runner, simply because he couldn't stand to see her win.⟩

synonyms cattily, despitefully, hatefully, malevolently, maliciously, malignantly, meanly, spitefully, viciously, villainously, virulently, wickedly

related words contemptuously, deprecatingly, disdainfully, scornfully; acrimoniously, hostilely, invidiously, obnoxiously, rancorously, venomously, vindictively, vituperatively; bitterly, enviously, jealously, resentfully; callously, cruelly, hard-heartedly, heartlessly, inhumanely, kindlessly, mercilessly, pitilessly, ruthlessly, soullessly, unfeelingly; disagreeably, ill, ungraciously, unkindly; ill-naturedly, inconsiderately, insensitively, thoughtlessly

near antonyms affably, agreeably, amiably, cordially, genially, good-naturedly, nicely, pleasantly; altruistically, humanely; considerately, feelingly, lovingly, mercifully, sensitively, softheartedly, solicitously, thoughtfully; compassionately, sympathetically

antonyms benevolently, benignantly, good-heartedly, kindheartedly, kindly

nastiness *n* **1** the desire to cause pain for the satisfaction of doing harm ⟨the *nastiness* of the bitter political campaign⟩ — see MALICE

2 the quality or state of being obscene ⟨The *nastiness* of the post required that it be deleted immediately.⟩ — see OBSCENITY

3 the state or quality of being dirty ⟨the *nastiness* of the neglected restroom⟩ — see DIRTINESS

nasty *adj* **1** arousing or deserving of one's loathing and disgust ⟨Fortunately, the story's *nasty* characters are balanced by some truly good people.⟩ — see CONTEMPTIBLE 1

2 causing intense displeasure, disgust, or resentment ⟨a *nasty* video game that was so violent that I could hardly watch the opening scenes⟩ — see OFFENSIVE 1

3 causing or feeling bodily pain ⟨a *nasty* cut on my lip⟩ — see PAINFUL 1

4 depicting or referring to sexual matters in a way that is unacceptable in polite society ⟨a movie with *nasty* dialogue⟩ — see OBSCENE 1

5 having or showing a desire to cause someone pain or suffering for the sheer enjoyment of it ⟨posted *nasty* comments on the website⟩ — see HATEFUL

6 marked by wet and windy conditions ⟨Bring your raincoat, as the weather's supposed to be *nasty*.⟩ — see FOUL 1

7 not clean ⟨It's incredibly *nasty* inside that garbage bin, so stay away from there.⟩ — see DIRTY 1

8 not giving pleasure to the mind or senses ⟨The smell of those old leftovers is downright *nasty*.⟩ — see UNPLEASANT

9 causing worry or anxiety ⟨She had the *nasty* sense that she'd made a mistake somewhere.⟩ — see TROUBLESOME

10 not being in accordance with the rules or standards of what is fair in sport ⟨A *nasty* hit got the hockey player suspended.⟩ — see FOUL 2

11 not following or in accordance with standards of honor and decency ⟨That was a *nasty* trick to play on people who were so trusting.⟩ — see IGNOBLE 2

12 requiring exceptional skill or caution in performance or handling ⟨Given the high-ranking people involved, it will be a *nasty* job to hammer out a compromise.⟩ — see TRICKY 1

nation *n* a body of people composed of one or more nationalities usually with its own territory and government ⟨The American people became one *nation* when they adopted the Constitution in 1789.⟩

synonyms commonwealth, country, land, sovereignty (*also* sovranty), state

related words city-state, ministate, nation-state; domain, dominion, empire, realm, republic; democracy, dictatorship, monarchy, monocracy, oligarchy, sovereign (*also* sovran); theocracy; fatherland, homeland, motherland; great power, power, sea power, superpower, world power

national *adj* of or relating to a nation ⟨played the home team's *national* anthem before the start of the soccer game⟩

synonyms civil, public

related words civic, federal, municipal; government, governmental; democratic, republican; nationwide

near antonyms global; alien, external, foreign

antonyms nonnational

national *n* a person who owes allegiance to a government and is protected by it ⟨recommended that foreign *nationals* living in the region stay alert⟩ — see CITIZEN 1

nationalism *n* **1** excessive favoritism towards one's own country ⟨Nazism's almost epic *nationalism* appealed to downtrodden Germans still suffering the humiliation of being defeated in World War I.⟩ — see CHAUVINISM

2 love and support for one's country ⟨American *nationalism* is often most visible during Fourth of July celebrations.⟩ — see PATRIOTISM

nationalist *adj* **1** having or showing excessive favoritism towards one's own country ⟨a politician with a xenophobic, *nationalist* platform⟩

synonyms chauvinist, nationalistic

related words loyal, patriotic; antiforeign, anti-immigrant, nativist, nativistic, xenophobic

near antonyms internationalist

2 having or showing love and support for one's country ⟨*Nationalist* fervor is often at its highest when a country is at war.⟩ — see PATRIOTIC

nationalist *n* one who shows excessive favoritism towards his or her country ⟨a staunch *nationalist* who favored any policy that would give the country more power in the international arena⟩

synonyms chauvinist, jingo

related words loyalist, patriot; hawk, warmonger; nativist

near antonyms internationalist; neutralist

nationalistic *adj* **1** having or showing love and support for one's country ⟨a *nationalistic* display of the country's flag at all civic events⟩ — see PATRIOTIC

2 having or showing excessive favoritism towards one's own country ⟨a *nationalistic* economic policy that raises up enormous barriers against the importation of goods from other countries⟩ — see NATIONALIST 1

native *adj* **1** belonging to a particular place by birth or origin ⟨Though she now lived in the Northeast, she was a *native* Midwesterner.⟩

synonyms aboriginal, born, domestic, endemic, indigenous

related words local, regional; original

near antonyms imported, introduced, transplanted; alien, foreign, strange; expatriate, immigrant

antonyms nonindigenous, nonnative

2 being such as found in nature and not altered by processing or refining ⟨Diamonds in their *native* state are not the bright, flashy gems that one might imagine.⟩ — see CRUDE 1

3 being a part of the innermost nature of a person or thing ⟨a *native* energy and ambition that would allow him to rise above his humble beginnings⟩ — see INHERENT

native *n* a usually longtime resident of a locality ⟨The *natives* seem to resent the summer tourists even though they depend upon them for their livelihood.⟩

synonyms local, townie (*or* towny)

related words denizen, dweller, habitant, inhabitant, occupant, resident, resider

near antonyms excursionist, sightseer, traveler (*or* traveller); holidayer, vacationer, vacationist

nativity *n* the act or instance of being born ⟨the place of my *nativity*⟩ — see BIRTH 1

nattily *adv* in a strikingly neat and trim manner ⟨He's very *nattily* dressed in a new tailored suit.⟩ — see SMARTLY

natty *adj* being strikingly neat and trim in style or appearance ⟨A *natty* woman, she's usually impeccably dressed in tailored clothing from Europe.⟩ — see SMART 1

natural *adj* **1** being such from birth or by nature ⟨From his first visits to the wading pool, we could tell that our little boy loved water and was a *natural* swimmer.⟩

synonyms born, congenital

related words chronic, confirmed, habitual, incorrigible, ingrained (*also* engrained), inveterate, proper, regular, unreconstructed, unregenerate; constitutional, consummate; elemental, elementary, essential; connate, hereditary, inborn, inherent, innate, intimate, intrinsic, native; instinctual, intuitive

near antonyms cultivated, developed, trained; alien, foreign, unnatural

2 closely resembling the object imitated ⟨The diorama featuring stuffed birds and plastic plants actually looked very *natural*.⟩

synonyms lifelike, living, near, realistic

related words alike, like, matching, similar, verisimilar; akin, analogous, approximate, comparable, resembling; accurate, close, faithful, true; compelling, convincing, expressive, graphic (*also* graphical), vivid

near antonyms dissimilar, off, unalike, unlike; incomparable, unmatched; contrasted, contrasting, different, disparate; fake, mock, phony (*also* phoney), sham

antonyms nonrealistic, unnatural, unrealistic

3 being such by blood and not by adoption or marriage ⟨an adult adoptee who has decided to search for his *natural* parents⟩

synonyms birth

antonyms adopted, adoptive, nonbiological

4 being a part of the innermost nature of a person or thing ⟨Her *natural* talent for music first became apparent when, unbidden, she started banging on a toy piano.⟩ — see INHERENT

5 being such as found in nature and not altered by processing or refining ⟨*Natural* salts are not edible until they are washed and processed.⟩ — see CRUDE 1

6 existing without human habitation or cultivation ⟨photographs of animals in their *natural* habitat⟩ — see WILD 2

7 free from any intent to deceive or impress others ⟨She was completely *natural* in expressing her feelings for him, unafraid of how they would be received.⟩ — see GUILELESS

8 relating to or characteristic of human beings ⟨It's only *natural* to make mistakes—it's part of being human.⟩ — see HUMAN

naturally *adv* **1** by natural character or ability ⟨tour guides who are *naturally* outgoing and can easily approach and converse with strangers⟩

synonyms constitutionally, inherently, innately, intrinsically

related words basically, elementally, essentially, fundamentally; instinctively, intuitively

near antonyms artificially, unnaturally

2 according to the usual course of things ⟨We *naturally* like to be as comfortable as possible.⟩

synonyms commonly, generally, normally, ordinarily, typically, usually

related words customarily, habitually, regularly, routinely; familiarly; conventionally, traditionally

phrases as a rule, needless to say, of course, on the whole

near antonyms funnily, oddly, peculiarly, queerly, strangely, weirdly; anomalously, irregularly; radically

antonyms abnormally, atypically, extraordinarily, untypically, unusually

3 without any attempt to impress by deception or exaggeration ⟨a boy trying to act *naturally* around the girl he has a crush on⟩

synonyms artlessly, guilelessly, ingenuously, innocently, naively (*or* naïvely), sincerely, unaffectedly, unfeignedly, unpretentiously

related words genuinely, honestly, simply, truly; freely, openheartedly, openly; candidly, frankly, matter-of-factly; casually, coolly (*also* cooly), nonchalantly

near antonyms cannily, deceitfully, deceptively, deviously, dishonestly, falsely; calculatingly, craftily, cunningly, furtively, insidiously, sharply, slickly, slyly (*also* slily), underhand, underhanded, underhandedly; flatteringly, unctuously

antonyms affectedly, artificially, hypocritically, insincerely, pretentiously, unnaturally

naturalness *n* **1** carefree freedom from constraint ⟨The children danced with a *naturalness* born of the sheer enjoyment of music and movement.⟩ — see ABANDON

2 the quality or state of being simple and sincere ⟨He has always admired the very *naturalness* of the Amish lifestyle.⟩ — see NAÏVETÉ 1

nature *n* **1** the set of qualities that makes a person, a group of people, or a thing different from others ⟨His books have a humorous *nature*.⟩ ⟨Her *nature* was such that lying was never an option for her.⟩ ⟨The stoic *nature* of these people enables them to endure one calamity after another.⟩

synonyms character, colors, complexion, constitution, genius, personality, tone

related words distinctiveness, distinctness, individuality, singularity, uniqueness; attribute, characteristic, earmark, essentiality, feature, flavor, hallmark, mark, point, property, savor (*also* savour), stamp, trait; disposition, grain, sort, temper, temperament; composition, makeup;

essence, essentiality, interior, interiority, soul, spirit; metal, stuff, substance; habit, way
2 that part of the physical world that is removed from human habitation ⟨Bill needed to get out of the office and back to *nature* in order to clear his head.⟩
synonyms open, open air, outdoors, out-of-doors, wild, wilderness
related words backwoods, bush, country, frontier, hinterland, sticks, up-country; outside, without; badland, barren, desert, waste, wasteland
3 a number of persons or things that are grouped together because they have something in common ⟨Group together anything round: buttons, lids, coins, and other things of that *nature*.⟩ — see SORT 1
4 one's characteristic attitude or mood ⟨a boy of a quiet and shy *nature*⟩ — see DISPOSITION 1
5 the quality or qualities that make a thing what it is ⟨Some artists maintain that color, light, and shadow are the very *nature* of painting.⟩ — see ESSENCE 1
6 the whole body of things observed or assumed ⟨the belief that all of *nature* is controlled by an unseen Supreme Being⟩ — see UNIVERSE
naught *also* **nought** *n* the numerical symbol 0 or the absence of number or quantity represented by it ⟨My locker number is *naught*-seven-two.⟩ — see ZERO 1
naughty *adj* engaging in or marked by childish misbehavior ⟨The children were *naughty* at school today.⟩
synonyms bad, contrary, errant, froward, misbehaving, mischievous
related words defiant, disrespectful, ill-mannered, ill-natured, impolite, improper, impudent, indecorous, insolent, rude, uncouth, unmannerly; disobedient, headstrong, intractable, obstreperous, recalcitrant, refractory, transgressing, unruly, untoward, willful (*or* wilful); balky, restive, uncontrollable, ungovernable, wayward, wild; elfish, impish, knavish, monkeying, monkeyish, ornery, pixieish, prankish, rascally, roguish, waggish; disorderly, rowdy; babyish, childish, immature, infantile, juvenile, kiddish, puerile
near antonyms acquiescent, compliant, complying, dutiful, obedient, submissive; considerate, courteous, kindly, mannerly, polite, thoughtful; angelic (*or* angelical), cherubic, divine, heavenly; amenable, docile, governable, tractable; amiable, complaisant, good-natured, obliging, pleasant; discreet, modest; adult, grown-up, mature
antonyms behaved, behaving, nice, orderly
nausea *n* **1** a disturbed condition of the stomach in which one feels like vomiting ⟨Symptoms include fever accompanied by a loss of appetite and *nausea*.⟩
synonyms qualmishness, queasiness, queerness, sickness, squeamishness
related words qualm; airsickness, altitude sickness, car sickness, morning sickness, motion sickness, mountain sickness, seasickness
2 a dislike so strong as to cause stomach upset or queasiness ⟨Such graphic scenes of senseless violence fill me with *nausea*.⟩ — see DISGUST
nauseate *vb* to cause to feel disgust ⟨The way they flaunt their money *nauseates* me.⟩ — see DISGUST
nauseated *adj* **1** affected with nausea ⟨Being aboard ship during that storm would make anyone but the most experienced sailor *nauseated*.⟩ — see NAUSEOUS 1
2 filled with disgust ⟨*Nauseated* critics panned the movie comedy for its celebration of gross behavior.⟩ — see SICK 2
nauseating *adj* causing intense displeasure, disgust, or resentment ⟨Her relentlessly vicious gossiping is absolutely *nauseating*.⟩ — see OFFENSIVE 1

nauseous *adj* **1** affected with nausea ⟨After eating the last four pieces of the two-week-old pizza, he was feeling a little *nauseous*.⟩
synonyms ill, nauseated, qualmish, queasy (*also* queazy), queer, queerish, sick, sickish, squeamish
related words green, peaked, sickly; unsettled, upset
near antonyms settled; healthy, well
2 causing intense displeasure, disgust, or resentment ⟨It turned out that a dead mouse between the walls was causing the *nauseous* stench.⟩ — see OFFENSIVE 1
nautical *adj* of or relating to navigation of the sea ⟨collected sextants and other antique *nautical* equipment⟩ — see MARINE 2
navigable *adj* capable of being traveled on ⟨This map shows which rivers are *navigable* and which aren't.⟩ — see PASSABLE 1
navigate *vb* **1** to operate or control the course of ⟨the hours of training that are required before a student pilot is allowed to *navigate* an airplane solo⟩
synonyms helm, pilot, steer
related words commandeer, hijack (*also* highjack)
2 to travel on water in a vessel ⟨the months that were once required to *navigate* around South America in the days before the Panama Canal⟩ — see SAIL 1
3 to make one's way through, across, or over ⟨It will take some effort to *navigate* that stretch of hills, but we can do it.⟩ — see TRAVERSE
navigational *adj* of or relating to navigation of the sea ⟨the folly of trying to sail with outdated *navigational* maps⟩ — see MARINE 2
navigator *n* one who operates or navigates a seagoing vessel ⟨Our crew comprised a captain, a *navigator*, and a few deckhands.⟩ — see SAILOR
nay *adv* not merely this but also ⟨I was happy—*nay*, thrilled—at my acceptance into the college.⟩ — see EVEN 1
nay *n* **1** a vote or decision against something ⟨When the votes were tallied, it was 241 yeas and 54 *nays*.⟩ — see NO 1
2 an unwillingness to grant something asked for ⟨Dad gave a resounding *nay* to my request for a cell phone upgrade.⟩ — see DENIAL 1
Neanderthal *n* a big clumsy often slow-witted person ⟨He's actually a really great guy, not the *Neanderthal* I remember from high school.⟩ — see OAF 1
Neanderthal *or* **Neandertal** *adj* not civilized ⟨Her boyfriend's *Neanderthal* manners were often embarrassing.⟩ — see UNCIVILIZED
near *adj* **1** being the less far of two ⟨Grab the comforter from the *near* side of the bed and fold it in half.⟩
synonyms closer, hither, nigher, this
related words forward, front, inside
near antonyms distant, remote, remoter; back, outside
antonyms far, farther, further, opposite, other
2 being such only when compared to something else ⟨The incessant busyness of the family next-door makes us look like we live in *near* retirement.⟩ — see COMPARATIVE
3 closely resembling the object imitated ⟨The dress is made from a *near* silk that would fool anyone but an expert.⟩ — see NATURAL 2
4 not being distant in time, space, or significance ⟨the famous prediction that in the *near* future everyone will be famous for 15 minutes⟩ — see CLOSE 2
near *adv* **1** at, within, or to a short distance or time ⟨As the campers grew cold, they gravitated *nearer* to the campfire.⟩ ⟨As summer draws *near*, we usually start planning our annual vacation.⟩
synonyms around, by, close, hard, in, nearby, nigh
related words hereabouts (*or* hereabout), thereabouts

(*also* thereabout); along, alongside; accessibly, conveniently, handily

phrases at close quarters, at hand, on one's doorstep, within call

2 to a close degree ⟨Copy the artist's drawing into your own sketchbook as *near* as you can.⟩

synonyms closely, nearly

near antonyms distantly, remotely

3 very close to but not completely ⟨It's *near* six o'clock, so we should start preparing dinner.⟩ — see ALMOST

near *prep* close to ⟨Please don't cough *near* me!⟩ — see AROUND 1

near *vb* **1** to come near or nearer ⟨As the procession *nears*, you'll be able to take a better picture of the graduates.⟩ — see APPROACH 1

2 to move closer to ⟨As we *near* the church, you'll be able to see the bas-relief sculptures better.⟩ — see COME 1

nearby *adj* not being distant in time, space, or significance ⟨She grabbed the *nearby* quilt and gently laid it over the sleeping child.⟩ — see CLOSE 2

nearby *adv* at, within, or to a short distance or time ⟨I'll be *nearby* if you need anything.⟩ — see NEAR 1

nearing *adj* being soon to appear or take place ⟨teachers preparing for the fast-*nearing* school year⟩ — see FORTHCOMING 1

nearly *adv* **1** to a close degree ⟨Copy that design as *nearly* as you can.⟩ — see NEAR 2

2 very close to but not completely ⟨I *nearly* fell down the stairs.⟩ — see ALMOST

nearness *n* **1** the state of being in a very personal or private relationship ⟨My cousin and I have lost that *nearness* we had when we were kids.⟩ — see FAMILIARITY 1

2 the state or condition of being near ⟨Our *nearness* to the theme park has made us beloved by relatives from all over the country.⟩ — see PROXIMITY

nearsighted *adj* able to see near things more clearly than distant ones ⟨I am a little *nearsighted* and need to wear glasses to drive.⟩

synonyms myopic, shortsighted

related words astigmatic; purblind

near antonyms presbyopic

antonyms farsighted

neat *adj* **1** being clean and in good order ⟨Keep the kitchen *neat* so the cook doesn't have to work around piles of dirty dishes.⟩

synonyms crisp, groomed, orderly, shipshape, snug, tidied, tidy, trim, uncluttered

related words dapper, natty, saucy, smart, spiffy, spruce; immaculate, spick-and-span (*or* spic-and-span), spotless; sleek, streamlined, taut; organized, straight, systematic

near antonyms scruffy, seedy, shabby, slipshod, sloppy; dirty, filthy, foul, nasty, sordid, squalid; dowdy, frowsy (*or* frowzy), rumpled, tousled, tumbled; disorganized, unsystematic

antonyms disheveled (*or* dishevelled), disordered, disorderly, messy, mussed, mussy, sloven, slovenly, unkempt, untidy

2 free from added matter ⟨I like my soda *neat*, so skip the ice cubes.⟩ — see PURE 1

3 of the very best kind ⟨That new skateboard park is *neat!*⟩ — see EXCELLENT

4 following a set method, arrangement, or pattern ⟨a *neat* way of saving the data⟩ — see METHODICAL

nebulous *adj* **1** having an often intentionally veiled or uncertain meaning ⟨made *nebulous* references to some major changes the future may hold⟩ — see OBSCURE 1

2 not seen or understood clearly ⟨We could just make out the *nebulous* outline of a fishing shack in the dense fog.⟩ — see FAINT 1

nebulousness *n* the quality or state of having a veiled or uncertain meaning ⟨The *nebulousness* of the imagery in his poetry seems to be part of its attraction to some readers.⟩ — see OBSCURITY 1

necessarily *adv* because of necessity ⟨the argument that the existence of the universe *necessarily* implies the existence of an all-powerful being responsible for creating it⟩ — see NEEDS

necessary *adj* **1** forcing one's compliance or participation by or as if by law ⟨An emissions test is *necessary* before you can renew the registration for your car.⟩ — see MANDATORY

2 impossible to avoid or evade ⟨Taxes will always be a *necessary* evil.⟩ — see INEVITABLE

3 impossible to do without ⟨Food and water are *necessary* for survival.⟩ — see ESSENTIAL 1

necessary *n* something necessary, indispensable, or unavoidable ⟨a modest income that provided the family with only the *necessaries* of life⟩ — see ESSENTIAL 1

necessitate *vb* to have as a requirement ⟨Getting new shoes would *necessitate* another trip to the mall.⟩ — see NEED 1

necessity *n* **1** something necessary, indispensable, or unavoidable ⟨Sunscreen is a *necessity* for me on the beach.⟩ — see ESSENTIAL 1

2 the state of lacking sufficient money or material possessions ⟨Two years of unemployment had reduced the family to abject *necessity*.⟩ — see POVERTY 1

neck and neck *adj* showing little difference in the standing of the competitors ⟨a *neck and neck* finish in which only a fraction of a second separated the winner from the runner-up⟩ — see CLOSE 3

necklace *n* an ornamental chain or string (as of beads) worn around the neck ⟨found a lovely *necklace* to match the bracelet and ring her mother had given her⟩

synonyms choker, collar, lei

related words torque (*or* torc); beads, carcanet [*archaic*], rivière; rope, strand; bangle, lavaliere (*also* lavalliere), locket, pendant (*also* pendent)

necromancer *n* a person skilled in using supernatural forces ⟨In ancient times any kind of natural disaster was apt to be regarded as the work of some evil-minded *necromancer*.⟩ — see MAGICIAN 1

necromancy *n* the power to control natural forces through supernatural means ⟨In the conjuring of the souls of the dead, *necromancy* seemed to offer human beings a means of exerting some control over an uncertain world.⟩ — see MAGIC 1

need *n* **1** a state of being without something necessary, desirable, or useful ⟨When it came time to wrap the presents, he found he was in *need* of adhesive tape.⟩

synonyms absence, lack, needfulness, want

related words deficiency, deficit, inadequacy, insufficiency; dearth, meagerness, paucity, poverty, scantiness, scarceness, scarcity, shortage, skimpiness; defect, minus; deprivation, privation; demand, essential, necessity, requirement, requisite

near antonyms adequacy, enough, sufficiency; fund, pool, stock, supply; excess, fill, overabundance, oversupply, plenty, surfeit, surplus; hoard, stockpile

2 something necessary, indispensable, or unavoidable ⟨Ned got a job that barely provided for his basic *needs*.⟩ — see ESSENTIAL 1

3 something one must do because of prior agreement ⟨There's no *need* to apologize.⟩ — see OBLIGATION 1

4 the state of lacking sufficient money or material possessions ⟨donating money to help those in *need*⟩ — see POVERTY 1

need *vb* **1** to have as a requirement ⟨a national crisis that *needs* a strong leader to solve it⟩

synonyms bear, challenge, claim, demand, necessitate, require, take, want, warrant
related words entail, involve; ask, beg, claim, clamor (for), cry (for); hurt (for), lack; command, enjoin, exact, insist, press, quest, stipulate
phrases call for
near antonyms own, possess
antonyms have, hold
2 to be under necessity or obligation to ⟨You *need* not stand when she enters the room.⟩
synonyms have (to), must, ought (to), shall, should
related words will

needed *adj* impossible to do without ⟨Pack only what will be *needed*.⟩ — see ESSENTIAL 1

needful *adj* **1** impossible to do without ⟨purchased *needful* provisions⟩ — see ESSENTIAL 1
2 lacking money or material possessions ⟨Let's first help the *needful* families in our own community.⟩ — see POOR 1

needful *n* something necessary, indispensable, or unavoidable ⟨packed a warm jacket and other *needfuls* for an autumn weekend in the country⟩ — see ESSENTIAL 1

needfulness *n* a state of being without something necessary, desirable, or useful ⟨I can scarcely describe my *needfulness* for a hot shower after a hard-fought game of racquetball.⟩ — see NEED 1

neediness *n* the state of lacking sufficient money or material possessions ⟨A family's general level of *neediness* is the determining factor in the allocation of charitable donations.⟩ — see POVERTY 1

needle *n* **1** a slender hollow instrument by which material is put into or taken from the body through the skin ⟨The nurse inserted the *needle* into his vein and collected some blood for testing.⟩
synonyms hypodermic, hypodermic needle, hypodermic syringe, syringe
2 an arrow-shaped piece on a dial or scale for registering information ⟨Simply by reading the compass *needle* you should be able to figure out in which direction we're heading.⟩ — see POINTER 1

needle *vb* **1** to attack repeatedly with mean put-downs or insults ⟨We couldn't resist *needling* him about his childhood nickname, "Bubbles."⟩ — see TEASE 2
2 to subject (someone) to constant scoldings and sharp reminders ⟨Quit *needling* me! I'll take out the trash in a minute!⟩ — see NAG 1

needlelike *adj* being of less than usual width ⟨I need a *needlelike* piece of wire to finish making this wreath.⟩ — see NARROW 1

needler *n* a person who causes repeated emotional pain, distress, or annoyance to another ⟨If she wasn't such a *needler*, she might have more friends.⟩ — see TORMENTOR

needless *adj* not needed by the circumstances or to accomplish an end ⟨*needless* expenditures that pushed the construction project way over budget⟩ — see UNNECESSARY

needlework *n* decorative stitching done on cloth with the use of a needle ⟨a visit to the art museum to see an exhibition of 18th-century *needlework*⟩
synonyms embroidery
related words crewel, cross-stitch, needlepoint; hemstitch, smocking; fancywork

needs *adv* because of necessity ⟨The dangers of global warming must *needs* be recognized—and recognized soon—by the industrialized nations of the world.⟩
synonyms inescapably, inevitably, necessarily, perforce, unavoidably
related words involuntarily
antonyms unnecessarily

needy *adj* lacking money or material possessions ⟨those generous souls who regularly give money and donate clothes to help the *needy*⟩ — see POOR 1

ne'er *adv* at no time ⟨Fare thee well, for *ne'er* shall I return!⟩ — see NEVER 1

nefarious *adj* not conforming to a high moral standard; morally unacceptable ⟨the chaste heroines and *nefarious* villains of old-time melodramas⟩ — see BAD 2

negate *vb* **1** to declare not to be true ⟨This evidence *negates* his claim that he was not at the scene of the crime.⟩ — see DENY 1
2 to put an end to by formal action ⟨Prohibition was established by the 18th Amendment to the U.S. Constitution, only to be *negated* by the 21st Amendment 13 years later.⟩ — see ABOLISH 1
3 to think not to be true or real ⟨You simply can't *negate* your feelings for someone, even if they don't feel the same way about you.⟩ — see DISBELIEVE

negation *n* a refusal to confirm the truth of a statement ⟨issued specific *negations* of all of the accusations against her⟩ — see DENIAL 2

negative *adj* **1** marked by opposition or ill will ⟨There are no longer any *negative* feelings between us.⟩ — see HOSTILE 1
2 opposed to one's interests ⟨the almost universally *negative* reaction to the book⟩ — see ADVERSE 1

negative *n* **1** a vote or decision against something ⟨In the absence of an unambiguous *negative* from the commander, we decided to continue on the mission.⟩ — see NO 1
2 something that is as different as possible from something else ⟨The desire to control another person is actually the *negative* of real love.⟩ — see OPPOSITE
3 a feature of someone or something that creates difficulty for achieving success ⟨The main *negative* of this job is that I have to get up at 4:30 a.m.⟩ — see DISADVANTAGE 1

negative *vb* **1** to reject by or as if by a vote ⟨Although the rebuttal was very eloquent, the jury *negatived* it in favor of the prosecution's argument.⟩ ⟨We promptly *negatived* the idea of having pizza again for dinner, noting that we had already had it for three nights that week.⟩
synonyms blackball, down, kill, veto
related words decline, disallow, disapprove, dismiss, refuse; blacklist
near antonyms admit, allow, approve, assent (to), pass, sanction; elect, support
antonyms confirm, ratify
2 to declare not to be true ⟨The governor's press secretary promptly *negatived* the rumor that he was not intending to run for reelection.⟩ — see DENY 1
3 to show unwillingness to accept, do, engage in, or agree to ⟨Even though I had originally *negatived* the invitation, Mom thought I should go anyway.⟩ — see DECLINE 1
4 to be unwilling to grant ⟨Ultimately, we *negatived* the request for a personal loan.⟩ — see DENY 2

neglect *n* **1** the state of being unattended to or not cared for ⟨For years the barn sat in *neglect* until one day it finally fell down.⟩
synonyms desolation, dilapidation, disrepair, seediness
related words inattention, negligence; abandonment, desertion; decay, decrepitude, dereliction, deterioration, disintegration, dumpiness, ruin, ruination
near antonyms conservation, preservation, upkeep
antonyms keeping, repair
2 the nonperformance of an assigned or expected action ⟨Your ongoing *neglect* of your health is going to land you in the hospital someday.⟩ — see FAILURE 1

neglect *vb* **1** to fail to give proper attention to ⟨The news media *neglected* the real issues of the campaign and focused on personalities.⟩
synonyms bypass, disregard, forget, ignore, overlook, overpass, pass over, slight, slur (over)

related words fail; miss, omit; brush (aside *or* off), reject, shrug off; disdain, pooh-pooh (*also* pooh), scorn; scant, skimp

near antonyms appreciate, cherish, prize, treasure, value; cultivate, foster, nurse, nurture; pamper; remember; listen (to), watch; follow, mark, note, notice, observe, remark

antonyms attend (to), heed, mind, regard, tend (to)

2 to leave undone or unattended to especially through carelessness ⟨I've *neglected* my garden, and now it's overgrown with weeds.⟩

synonyms forget, shirk

related words slack (off)

near antonyms carry out, do, execute, perform; accomplish, achieve; keep up, maintain

antonyms attend (to), remember

3 to miss the opportunity or obligation ⟨Conveniently, the salesman *neglected* to mention that the car had been through a flood.⟩

synonyms fail, forget, omit

related words disregard, ignore, overlook, overpass, pass over, slight; slide, slip; default; skip

phrases miss out on

near antonyms heed, mind, remember; keep, observe; carry out, do, execute, perform, practice (*also* practise); discharge, fulfill (*or* fulfil), meet, satisfy; comply (with)

neglected *adj* showing signs of advanced wear and tear and neglect ⟨a *neglected* teddy bear, missing one eye and both ears, shoved into the closet⟩ — see SHABBY 1

neglectful *adj* failing to give proper care and attention ⟨He's certainly not a *neglectful* father as he takes very good care of his children.⟩ — see NEGLIGENT

neglecting *adj* failing to give proper care and attention ⟨Our chronically *neglecting* custodian has let trash accumulate around the warehouse.⟩ — see NEGLIGENT

negligence *n* **1** failure to take the care that a cautious person usually takes ⟨The accident was caused by the driver's *negligence*.⟩

synonyms carelessness, dereliction, heedlessness, incautiousness, laxness, slackness

related words foolhardiness, rashness, recklessness, wildness; neglect, omission; delinquency, irresponsibility, irresponsibleness, malfeasance, malpractice, misconduct; misdirection, mishandling, mismanagement; forgetfulness, inadvertence, inattention, inattentiveness, obliviousness, shortsightedness, unwariness

near antonyms alertness, attention, attentiveness, awareness; circumspection, observance, vigilance, watchfulness; responsibility, responsibleness

antonyms care, carefulness, caution, cautiousness, heedfulness

2 the nonperformance of an assigned or expected action ⟨The factory's owners are being charged with criminal *negligence* for the fire.⟩ — see FAILURE 1

negligent *adj* failing to give proper care and attention ⟨The youngster has been woefully *negligent* in taking care of the vacationing neighbor's dog, repeatedly forgetting to feed the poor animal.⟩

synonyms careless, derelict, lax, lazy, neglectful, neglecting, remiss, slack

related words heedless, incautious, irresponsible, reckless, wild; unguarded, unwary; forgetful; disregarding, inattentive, oblivious, thoughtless, unheeding, unmindful, unthinking; apathetic, indifferent, unconcerned, uninterested

near antonyms meticulous, painstaking, punctilious; cautious, circumspect, gingerly, guarded; alert, heedful, heeding, mindful, observant, regardful, regarding, vigilant, wary, watchful; foresighted, forethoughtful, provi-

dent, responsible; thinking, thoughtful; concerned, interested

antonyms attentive, careful, conscientious, nonnegligent

negligible *adj* **1** so small or unimportant as to warrant little or no attention ⟨The two cents in change was such a *negligible* sum that she left the store without bothering to take it.⟩

synonyms inconsequential, inconsiderable, insignificant, measly, minute, nominal, paltry, petty, picayune, piddling, slight, trifling, trivial

related words inferior, mean; imperceptible, inappreciable; little, puny, tiny; hairsplitting, nitpicking, pettifogging, quibbling; one-horse, small-fry, two-bit

near antonyms serious, substantial, weighty; eventful, momentous, pivotal; conspicuous, noteworthy, outstanding, prominent, remarkable, striking; appreciable, discernible (*also* discernable), measurable

antonyms big, consequential, considerable, important, material, significant

2 lacking importance ⟨The results from that small study of coffee drinkers are *negligible* and can be ignored.⟩ — see UNIMPORTANT

3 small in degree ⟨There's a *negligible* chance I may make it to the picnic, but don't count on it.⟩ — see REMOTE 1

negligibly *adv* in a very small quantity or degree ⟨This box is *negligibly* bigger than the other one, but it's such a slight difference I don't think it matters.⟩ — see LITTLE 1

negotiable *adj* **1** capable of being traveled on ⟨Some of the national park's roads are not *negotiable* in winter.⟩ — see PASSABLE 1

2 open to question or dispute ⟨The final judgment is not *negotiable*.⟩ — see DEBATABLE 1

negotiate *vb* **1** to bring about through discussion and compromise ⟨Ava wanted to *negotiate* a higher salary before she accepted the job offer.⟩

synonyms arrange, bargain, concert, conclude

related words settle (on *or* upon); chaffer, deal, dicker, haggle, horse-trade, palter; agree; contract, covenant; argue, debate, discuss, hash (over), reason, talk, talk over, work out; renegotiate

2 to deal with (something) usually skillfully or efficiently ⟨She's good at *negotiating* personality conflicts between coworkers.⟩ — see HANDLE 1

3 to plan out usually with subtle skill or care ⟨The prisoners *negotiated* their escape by using Morse code to tap messages to each other through the walls.⟩ — see ENGINEER

4 to talk over or dispute the terms of a purchase ⟨I told them I'd take $8,000 for the car and wasn't in the mood to *negotiate*.⟩ — see BARGAIN 1

5 to carry through (as a process) to completion ⟨Scores of experiments later, the chemists managed to *negotiate* the development of a more durable polymer.⟩ — see PERFORM 1

negotiation *n* the act or practice of each side giving up something in order to reach an agreement ⟨It will take some *negotiation*, but I think we can get each side to agree to a cease-fire.⟩ — see CONCESSION 1

neigh *vb* to make the cry typical of a horse ⟨The horses *neighed* when the rider came into the barn.⟩

synonyms nicker, whinny

neighbor *vb* to be adjacent to ⟨The baseball field *neighbors* a parking lot.⟩ — see ADJOIN 1

neighborhood *n* **1** an approximate amount, extent, or degree ⟨a movie that's said to have cost in the *neighborhood* of 100 million dollars⟩

synonyms matter, tune

related words nearness, proximity

2 an area (as of a city) set apart for some purpose or having some special feature ⟨a quiet residential *neighborhood*⟩ — see DISTRICT

3 the people living in a particular area ⟨We invited practically the whole *neighborhood* over for a big party.⟩ — see COMMUNITY 1

4 an adjoining region or space ⟨We were somewhere in the *neighborhood* of the Capitol because we could see the dome.⟩ — see ENVIRONS 2

neighboring *adj* **1** having a border in common ⟨He and his future wife grew up on *neighboring* farms.⟩ — see ADJACENT

2 not being distant in time, space, or significance ⟨the statehouse and its *neighboring* buildings⟩ — see CLOSE 2

neighborliness *n* kindly concern, interest, or support ⟨Showing uncommon *neighborliness*, one of my new coworkers took me out to lunch on my first day.⟩ — see GOODWILL 1

neighborly *adj* having or showing kindly feeling and sincere interest ⟨They were *neighborly* folks, always ready to lend a helping hand whenever necessary.⟩ — see FRIENDLY 1

nemesis *n* **1** one who inflicts punishment in return for an injury or offense ⟨Batman is the Joker's main *nemesis* and always foils his wicked plots.⟩

synonyms avenger, castigator, chastiser, punisher, scourge, vigilante

related words revenger; redresser, righter; requiter

near antonyms ransomer, redeemer, vindicator

2 suffering, loss, or hardship imposed in response to a crime or offense ⟨Since they were never caught, there was no *nemesis* for their transgressions.⟩ — see PUNISHMENT

3 a source of harm or misfortune ⟨Irrationality is the *nemesis* of democracy, for good government depends upon the wisdom of the electorate.⟩ — see BANE 1

neophyte *n* **1** a person who has recently been persuaded to join a religious sect ⟨*Neophytes* are assigned an experienced church member to guide them through their first year.⟩ — see CONVERT 1

2 a person who is just starting out in a field of activity ⟨a *neophyte* in snowboarding⟩ — see BEGINNER

neoplasm *n* an abnormal mass of tissue ⟨Surgeons removed a *neoplasm* from the patient's abdomen.⟩ — see GROWTH 1

nerd *n* **1** a person devoted to intellectual or academic pursuits ⟨The candidate accepted being characterized as a *nerd* and branded herself as smart and hardworking.⟩

synonyms bookworm, grind

related words egghead, highbrow, intellectual; brain, genius; academic, scholar

near antonyms slacker, underachiever; lowbrow

2 a person with strong intellectual interests ⟨a *nerd* who studies chemistry for fun⟩ — see INTELLECTUAL

nerdy *adj* much given to learning and thinking ⟨a fringe party of *nerdy* political activists⟩ — see INTELLECTUAL 1

nerve *n* **1** shameless boldness ⟨You've got a lot of *nerve* showing up here!⟩ — see EFFRONTERY

2 strength of mind to carry on in spite of danger ⟨That daring rescue took some *nerve*.⟩ — see COURAGE

3 nerves *pl* a sense of panic or extreme nervousness ⟨a veteran performer who still gets a case of the *nerves* before performances⟩ — see JITTERS

nerve *vb* to prepare (oneself) mentally or emotionally ⟨Jim needs to *nerve* himself for the big game tomorrow.⟩ — see FORTIFY 1

nerved *adj* inclined or willing to take risks ⟨a *nerved* and fearless driver of race cars⟩ — see BOLD 1

nerveless *adj* **1** lacking strength of will or character ⟨He's a *nerveless* pushover who'll be eaten alive by his own staff.⟩ — see WEAK 2

2 not easily panicked or upset ⟨To be a paramedic, you need to be calm, clearheaded, and *nerveless* in emergencies.⟩ — see UNFLAPPABLE

nerviness *n* shameless boldness ⟨I didn't appreciate her *nerviness* in redoing my work.⟩ — see EFFRONTERY

nervous *adj* **1** feeling or showing uncomfortable feelings of uncertainty ⟨He was *nervous* about how he would do at the varsity basketball tryouts.⟩

synonyms aflutter, anxious, dithery, edgy, het up, hung up, insecure, jittery, jumpy, nervy, perturbed, queasy (*also* queazy), tense, troubled, uneasy, unquiet, upset, uptight, worried

related words aggrieved, concerned, disquieted, distraught, distressed, disturbed, freaked, freaked-out, shook-up; foreboding, hesitant, misgiving; fretful, fretting, stewing; flustered, twittered, undone, unnerved, unstrung; obsessed, preoccupied, restless; flighty, fluttery, high-strung, skittish, spooky; annoyed, put out

phrases keyed up, on edge, on pins and needles, on tenterhooks

near antonyms confident, self-assured, self-confident, sure; controlled, self-controlled

antonyms calm, collected, cool, easy, happy-go-lucky, nerveless, relaxed

2 marked by or causing agitation or uncomfortable feelings ⟨A *nervous* silence filled the room as the teacher handed out the graded exams.⟩

synonyms agitating, anxious, creepy, disquieting, distressful, distressing, disturbing, fraught, hairy, restless, tense, uneasy, unnerving, unsettling, worrisome

related words bothersome, troublesome; foreboding, misgiving; discouraging, disheartening, strained; restive, restless, unrestful; awkward, embarrassing

near antonyms restful; pacific

antonyms calming, comfortable, easy, peaceful, quiet, quieting, tranquil

3 easily excited by nature ⟨A *nervous* sort of person, she's completely thrown by anything unexpected.⟩ — see EXCITABLE

nervousness *n* an uneasy state of mind usually over the possibility of an anticipated misfortune or trouble ⟨Your *nervousness* over your son's safety is only natural.⟩ — see ANXIETY 1

nervy *adj* **1** displaying or marked by rude boldness ⟨The *nervy* waiter held up the small tip and called out to the departing customers, "Hope it doesn't break the bank!"⟩

synonyms audacious, bold, bold-faced, brash, brassy, brazen, cheeky, cocksure, cocky, fresh, impertinent, impudent, insolent, sassy, saucy, wise

related words assertive, forward, obtrusive; audacious, defiant, disrespectful; shameless, unabashed, unblushing; bluff, blunt, curt; cute, facetious, flip, flippant, pert, smart, smart-alecky; lippy

near antonyms demure, humble, modest; courteous, genteel, mannerly, polite, proper; deferential, respectful; abashed, ashamed, blushing, embarrassed, shamefaced; gentle, mild; inconspicuous, unobtrusive

antonyms meek, mousy (*or* mousey), retiring, shy, timid

2 inclined or willing to take risks ⟨*nervy* rock climbers wanting to make gravity-defying ascents⟩ — see BOLD 1

3 feeling or showing uncomfortable feelings of uncertainty ⟨I'm a little *nervy* about my first job interview.⟩ — see NERVOUS 1

nest *n* a place where a person goes to hide or to avoid others ⟨headed back to her cozy *nest* in the mountains for a little rest and relaxation⟩ — see HIDEOUT

nest egg *n* a sum of money set aside for a particular purpose ⟨Tom paid for the computer out of his *nest egg*.⟩ — see FUND 1

nestle *vb* **1** to lie close ⟨*nestled* in next to the other kittens in the box⟩ — see NUZZLE

2 to sit or recline comfortably or cozily ⟨*nestling* with her children on the couch⟩ — see SNUGGLE 1

3 to establish or place comfortably or snugly ⟨We had scarcely *nestled* the children in their beds when there was a knock at the door.⟩ — see ENSCONCE 1

¹**net** *n* **1** a fabric made of strands loosely twisted, knotted, or woven together at regular intervals ⟨The basketball didn't go into the basket—it just hit the *net*.⟩

synonyms mesh, netting, network

related words web, webbing; grille (*also* grill), lattice, screen, screening, wirework; filigree, fishnet, lace

2 a device or scheme for capturing another by surprise ⟨identity thieves caught in an elaborate *net* set by the police⟩ — see TRAP 1

3 something that catches and holds ⟨caught in a *net* of palace intrigues⟩ — see WEB 1

²**net** *n* **1** the amount of money left when expenses are subtracted from the total amount received ⟨His *net* for the year was about 60% of his total income.⟩ — see PROFIT 1

2 the central part or aspect of something under consideration ⟨The *net* of the study is that things are better but more needs to be done.⟩ — see CRUX

¹**net** *vb* **1** to catch or hold as if in a net ⟨The kite was stubbornly *netted* in the branches of the willow tree.⟩ — see ENTANGLE 2

2 to take physical control or possession of (something) suddenly or forcibly ⟨an international sting operation that *netted* tax dodgers from all parts of the world⟩ — see CATCH 1

²**net** *vb* to receive after charges and deductions have been made ⟨The entrepreneur *netted* millions on that deal.⟩

synonyms clear

related words earn, gain, garner, get, make, realize; cash in (on), rake (in); clean up

near antonyms gross

nether *adj* situated lower down ⟨Most beginners skied the *nether* slope of the mountain.⟩ — see INFERIOR 1

netting *n* a fabric made of strands loosely twisted, knotted, or woven together at regular intervals ⟨wore a veil of *netting*⟩ — see ¹NET 1

nettle *vb* to disturb the peace of mind of (someone) especially by repeated disagreeable acts ⟨Don't *nettle* your brother while he's trying to do his homework.⟩ — see IRRITATE 1

nettling *adj* causing annoyance ⟨Your constant sniffling is extremely *nettling*.⟩ — see ANNOYING

network *n* **1** a fabric made of strands loosely twisted, knotted, or woven together at regular intervals ⟨She didn't like to embroider *network* as it tore so easily.⟩ — see ¹NET 1

2 something made up of many interdependent or related parts ⟨a computer *network*⟩ — see SYSTEM 1

3 a group of people sharing a common interest and relating together socially ⟨a *network* of community volunteers⟩ — see GANG 2

neuter *vb* to remove the sex organs of ⟨He agreed to let the children have the dog on the condition that they have her *neutered*.⟩

synonyms alter, desex, fix

related words emasculate, geld; spay; sterilize

neutral *adj* not favoring or joined to either side in a quarrel, contest, or war ⟨Sweden remained *neutral* during World War II, refusing to join either side in the conflict.⟩

synonyms nonpartisan

related words nonaligned; hands-off, noninterventionist; autonomous, independent, sovereign (*also* sovran), unaffiliated; nonbelligerent; individualistic; disinterested, evenhanded, fair, impartial, indifferent, unbiased, uninfluenced, unprejudiced; bipartisan

phrases on the fence

near antonyms biased, partial, partisan, prejudiced, unfair; affiliated, associated, federated; belligerent

antonyms allied, confederate

neutrality *n* lack of favoritism toward one side or another ⟨His unimpeachable *neutrality* makes him the ideal person to judge which of us is right.⟩ — see DETACHMENT 1

neutralize *vb* to balance with an equal force so as to make ineffective ⟨an impenetrable defensive line that *neutralized* the opposing team's offense⟩ — see OFFSET

neutralizer *n* a force or influence that makes an opposing force ineffective or less effective ⟨Sour cream was a cooling *neutralizer* of the hot and spicy chili.⟩ — see COUNTERBALANCE

never *adv* **1** at no time ⟨I have *never* been out of the country.⟩

synonyms ne'er

related words nevermore; not; infrequently, little, rarely, seldom

near antonyms eternally, everlastingly, evermore, invariably; frequently, often, recurrently, repeatedly

antonyms always, constantly, continuously, endlessly, ever, forever, perpetually

2 not in any degree, way, or under any condition ⟨Though she turned down his offer of marriage twice, he was *never* convinced that she did not love him.⟩

synonyms no, none, nothing, noway (*or* noways), nowise

related words nowhere near

phrases by no means, in no wise, nothing doing, on no account

near antonyms completely, extremely, full, fully, par excellence, right, very; altogether, exactly; somehow, someway (*also* someways); out

antonyms anyhow, anyway, anywise, at all, ever, half, however

nevertheless *adv* in spite of that ⟨I really don't want to; *nevertheless*, I will do it because you asked me to.⟩ — see HOWEVER

new *adj* **1** taking the place of one that came before ⟨After my bike was stolen, my scooter became my *new* mode of transportation.⟩

synonyms makeshift, substitute

related words alternate, alternative, pinch; different, other, separate; extra, spare; improvised, jury; another, second; utility; successive; equivalent

near antonyms first, former; equal, identical, same; lasting, permanent

antonyms original

2 not known or experienced before ⟨Spanish was a *new* course of study for her.⟩ ⟨I like to visit *new* places.⟩

synonyms fresh, novel, original, strange, unaccustomed, unfamiliar, unheard-of, unknown, unprecedented

related words innovative, unique; nontraditional, unconventional, untried, unused, unworn; pathbreaking, pioneering, trailblazing

near antonyms conventional, established, traditional, tried, tried-and-true; derivative, imitative

antonyms familiar, hackneyed, old, time-honored, tired, warmed-over

3 recently made and never used before ⟨That unique scent is the telltale sign of a *new* car.⟩

synonyms brand-new, spick-and-span (*or* spic-and-span), unused

related words clean, fresh, mint, pristine, unspoiled; untouched; newfangled, new-fashioned; natural, raw, unprocessed, untreated, unworked, virgin

near antonyms dirty, soiled, spoiled, stale; aged, old, shabby, shopworn, well-handled, worn

antonyms hand-me-down, second hand, used

4 made or become fresh in spirits or vigor ⟨A little rest made him a *new* man after the exhausting basketball game.⟩
synonyms energized, freshened, invigorated, newborn, reanimated, recreated, reenergized, refreshed, regenerated, renewed, resuscitated, revived
related words animated, enlivened, exhilarated, jazzed (up); resurrected; rested, untired, unwearied
near antonyms tired, weary; dampened, deadened; emasculated; demoralized, disheartened, dispirited
antonyms drained, enervate, enervated, exhausted, weakened
5 being or involving the latest methods, concepts, information, or styles ⟨*new* techniques in plastic surgery⟩ — see MODERN

new *adv* not long ago ⟨*new*-mown grass⟩ — see NEWLY

newbie *n* a person who is just starting out in a field of activity ⟨He is a *newbie* to the gaming community.⟩ — see BEGINNER

newborn *adj* made or become fresh in spirits or vigor ⟨Theo felt like a *newborn* supporter after that pep rally.⟩ — see NEW 4

newborn *n* a recently born person ⟨Joan intentionally bought clothes that were too big for her *newborn* but which undoubtedly would fit him in a few months.⟩ — see BABY 1

newcomer *n* a person who is just starting out in a field of activity ⟨He's a *newcomer* to ice hockey.⟩ — see BEGINNER

newfangled *adj* being or involving the latest methods, concepts, information, or styles ⟨We got one of those *newfangled* espresso makers.⟩ — see MODERN

new–fashioned *adj* being or involving the latest methods, concepts, information, or styles ⟨*new-fashioned* ways of keeping in touch⟩ — see MODERN

newly *adv* not long ago ⟨a *newly* married couple still getting to know one another⟩
synonyms freshly, just, late, lately, new, now, only, recently
related words latterly
phrases of late
near antonyms before, early, erstwhile, previously; heretofore, hitherto
antonyms anciently

newness *n* the quality or appeal of being new ⟨All that the skyscraper has going for it is its *newness*, for it's an ugly, poorly designed building.⟩ — see NOVELTY 1

news *pl n* a report of recent events or facts not previously known ⟨I heard the good *news* about your promotion.⟩
synonyms information, intelligence, item, story, tidings, word
related words announcement, bulletin, communication, correspondence, dispatch, message, reportage; dope, lowdown, scoop, tidbit (*also* titbit), tip; gossip, rumor, tale, tattle; feedback; disinformation, propaganda

newsman *n* a person employed by a newspaper, magazine, or radio or television station to gather, write, or report news ⟨Any *newsman* will tell you that if you talk to enough people, you'll eventually get a quote.⟩ — see REPORTER

newspaper *n* a publication that appears at regular intervals ⟨I like to read the *newspaper* every morning.⟩ — see JOURNAL

newsy *adj* having the style and content of everyday conversation ⟨a *newsy* TV program covering the local scene⟩ — see CHATTY 1

next *adj* being the one that comes immediately after another ⟨My house is the *next* one.⟩ ⟨Turn at the *next* street, not this one.⟩ ⟨She was *next* in line for concert tickets.⟩
synonyms coming, ensuing, following, succeeding

related words consecutive, sequential, successive; posterior, subsequent; immediate; second
phrases on deck
near antonyms anterior, former; past; last
antonyms antecedent, foregoing, precedent, preceding, previous, prior

next–door *adj* not being distant in time, space, or significance ⟨a *next-door* neighbor who is always helpful and friendly⟩ — see CLOSE 2

next to *adv* very close to but not completely ⟨We bought it for *next to* nothing.⟩ — see ALMOST

next to *prep* **1** close to ⟨Dan enjoys living *next to* the ocean.⟩ — see AROUND 1
2 subsequent to in time or order ⟨*Next to* science, math is my favorite subject at school.⟩ — see AFTER

nib *n* **1** the jaws of a bird together with their hornlike covering ⟨a finch cracking seeds in its *nib*⟩ — see BEAK 1
2 the last and usually sharp or tapering part of something long and narrow ⟨Make sure the *nib* has been sharpened before you try to cut anything.⟩ — see POINT 2

nibble *n* a small piece or quantity of food ⟨I don't want a whole dessert, so can I just have a *nibble* of yours?⟩ — see MORSEL 1

nibble *vb* **1** to eat reluctantly and in small bites ⟨Having no real appetite at all, I just *nibbled* during the party.⟩
synonyms peck, pick
related words graze, nosh, snack; taste
near antonyms gorge, gormandize, overeat, pig out, swill
2 to crush or grind with the teeth ⟨*nibbling* crackers⟩ — see BITE (ON)
3 to consume or wear away gradually ⟨discovered that inflation had steadily *nibbled* their savings⟩ — see EAT 2

nice *adj* **1** following the established traditions of refined society and good taste ⟨The children had *nice* manners.⟩ — see PROPER 1
2 giving pleasure or contentment to the mind or senses ⟨A cool glass of lemonade sure would be *nice*.⟩ — see PLEASANT 1
3 hard to please ⟨She's far too *nice* about her clothes for me to even consider giving her clothing for her birthday.⟩ — see FINICKY
4 having an easygoing and pleasing manner especially in social situations ⟨such a *nice* person to have as a party guest⟩ — see AMIABLE
5 made or done with extreme care and accuracy ⟨The noticeably *nice* folding of the dinner napkins told us that we were in the home of a domestic diva.⟩ — see FINE 2
6 conforming to a high standard of morality or virtue ⟨In those days *nice* people would not have been caught dead in a gambling casino.⟩ — see GOOD 2

nicely *adv* **1** in a pleasing way ⟨He's a *nicely* helpful child.⟩ — see WELL 5
2 in a satisfactory way ⟨I'm doing *nicely*, and thanks for asking.⟩ — see WELL 1
3 with good reason or courtesy ⟨Excuse yourself *nicely* and you should be fine.⟩ — see WELL 4

niceness *n* the state or quality of having a pleasant or agreeable manner in socializing with others ⟨His unfailing *niceness* makes him a great student to have in class.⟩ — see AMIABILITY 1

nicety *n* **1** a single piece of information ⟨knows all the *niceties* of diplomatic protocol⟩ — see FACT 3
2 something that adds to one's ease of living ⟨She's too fond of the *niceties* of urban living to become a farmer.⟩ — see COMFORT 2
3 the quality or state of being very accurate ⟨There's a *nicety* of detail in his meticulously painted landscapes.⟩ — see PRECISION

niche *n* **1** a hollowed-out space in a wall ⟨Statues of various saints occupy the *niches* lining the abbey's many corridors.⟩
synonyms alcove, nook, recess
related words corner, cranny, cubbyhole; cubicle; dent, embrasure, indentation
2 a situation or activity for which a person or thing is best suited ⟨After several false starts, she finally found her *niche* in the restaurant business.⟩
synonyms groove, place
related words appointment, berth, billet, capacity, function, job, position, post; rank, standing, station, status; forte, speciality, specialty, thing
3 the place where a plant or animal is usually or naturally found ⟨The platypus's *niche* is the waters of eastern Australia and Tasmania.⟩ — see HOME 2
nick *n* a V-shaped cut usually on an edge or a surface ⟨I made a *nick* in the frame when I accidentally dropped it.⟩ — see NOTCH 1
nicker *vb* to make the cry typical of a horse ⟨horses *nickering* in the barn⟩ — see NEIGH
nickname *n* a descriptive or familiar name given instead of or in addition to the one belonging to an individual ⟨His wavy hair earned him the *nickname* "Curly" early in life.⟩
synonyms alias, cognomen, epithet, handle, sobriquet (*also* soubriquet)
related words appellation, denomination, denotation, designation, label, tag, title; anonym, nom de plume, pen name, pseudonym
nifty *adj* of the very best kind ⟨That popcorn popper is *nifty*.⟩ — see EXCELLENT
nifty *n* something very good of its kind ⟨That joke was a *nifty*.⟩ — see JIM-DANDY
niggard *adj* giving or sharing as little as possible ⟨In Shakespeare's sonnet, the narrator begs his love to give him more praise "than *niggard* truth would willingly impart."⟩ — see STINGY 1
niggard *n* a mean grasping person who is usually stingy with money ⟨such a *niggard* that he refused to hand out candy at Halloween, saying it would cost too much money⟩ — see MISER
niggardly *adj* **1** giving or sharing as little as possible ⟨She's a *niggardly* woman, so don't expect a handout from her.⟩ — see STINGY 1
2 less plentiful than what is normal, necessary, or desirable ⟨*niggardly* portions of meat for dinner⟩ — see MEAGER
nigh *adj* not being distant in time, space, or significance ⟨The end is *nigh*.⟩ — see CLOSE 2
nigh *adv* **1** at, within, or to a short distance or time ⟨I have worked for them for *nigh* on 10 years.⟩ — see NEAR 1
2 very close to but not completely ⟨He has *nigh* completed his degree.⟩ — see ALMOST
nigh *prep* close to ⟨a field *nigh* the church⟩ — see AROUND 1
nigh *vb* **1** to come near or nearer ⟨as the hour of his departure was *nighing*⟩ — see APPROACH 1
2 to move closer to ⟨as he was *nighing* his hour of departure⟩ — see COME 1
nigher *adj* being the less far of two ⟨The town has only two motels, and the one *nigher* to the train station is actually the better one.⟩ — see NEAR 1
night *adj* of, relating to, or occurring in the night ⟨took a *night* flight out to the coast⟩ — see NOCTURNAL
night *n* **1** the time from sunset to sunrise when there is no visible sunlight ⟨The couple loved to sit outside at *night* and watch the stars.⟩
synonyms dark, darkness, nighttime
related words dusk, evening, gloaming, nightfall, twilight; midnight

near antonyms dawn, daybreak, sunrise, sunup; forenoon, morning; high noon, midday, noon, noonday, noontide, noontime
antonyms day, daytime
2 a time or place of little or no light ⟨snuck out of town under the cover of *night*⟩ — see DARK 1
3 the time from when the sun begins to set to the onset of total darkness ⟨We waited until *night* to begin lighting the candles in the windows.⟩ — see DUSK 1
nightclub *n* a bar or restaurant offering special nighttime entertainment (as music, dancing, or comedy acts) ⟨We decided to go dancing at a local *nightclub* after the long dinner and movie.⟩
synonyms cabaret, café (*also* cafe), club, roadhouse
related words disco; barroom, saloon, tavern; dive, honky-tonk, speakeasy
nightdress *n* a loose pullover garment worn in bed ⟨bought a long *nightdress* for the cold winter months ahead⟩ — see NIGHTGOWN
nightfall *n* the time from when the sun begins to set to the onset of total darkness ⟨Since you aren't taking a flashlight, make sure you're back at camp by *nightfall*.⟩ — see DUSK 1
nightgown *n* a loose pullover garment worn in bed ⟨decided to buy a flannel *nightgown* instead of pajamas⟩
synonyms gown, nightdress, nightshirt
related words nightclothes; pajamas, pj's; nightcap; lingerie, negligee (*also* negligé), nightie (*or* nighty)
nightly *adj* of, relating to, or occurring in the night ⟨the elderly couple's *nightly* walk around the neighborhood⟩ — see NOCTURNAL
nightmare *adj* extremely disturbing or repellent ⟨told a *nightmare* tale about getting lost in the desert⟩ — see HORRIBLE 1
nightmare *n* a situation or state that causes great suffering and unhappiness ⟨That 20-page exam was a *nightmare*.⟩ — see HELL 2
nightmarish *adj* extremely disturbing or repellent ⟨a photographic exhibit of *nightmarish* images from the wars of the 20th century⟩ — see HORRIBLE 1
nightshirt *n* a loose pullover garment worn in bed ⟨preferred *nightshirts* over pajama sets⟩ — see NIGHTGOWN
nightstick *n* a heavy rigid stick used as a weapon or for punishment ⟨police officers fitted out with *nightsticks* and handcuffs⟩ — see CLUB 1
nighttime *adj* of, relating to, or occurring in the night ⟨warnings about protecting household pets from *nighttime* predators in the outer reaches of suburbia⟩ — see NOCTURNAL
nighttime *n* the time from sunset to sunrise when there is no visible sunlight ⟨Before electricity, gas lamps were used for illumination during the *nighttime*.⟩ — see NIGHT 1
nil *n* the numerical symbol 0 or the absence of number or quantity represented by it ⟨The chances of that happening are practically *nil*.⟩ — see ZERO 1
nimble *adj* **1** having or showing quickness of mind ⟨Possessing a *nimble* wit, he always has a cutting comeback for any intended insult thrown his way.⟩ — see INTELLIGENT 1
2 moving easily ⟨Her *nimble* fingers make playing guitar look so easy.⟩ — see GRACEFUL 1
nimbleness *n* ease and grace in physical activity ⟨That dance routine requires a certain amount of *nimbleness* and flexibility.⟩ — see DEXTERITY 2
nincompoop *n* **1** a person who lacks good sense or judgment ⟨Quit acting like a *nincompoop*, because I know you are smarter than that!⟩ — see FOOL 1
2 a stupid person ⟨Who wants a *nincompoop* as a business partner?⟩ — see IDIOT

ninny *n* **1** a person who lacks good sense or judgment ⟨Only a *ninny* would try to cross a swollen, raging river.⟩ — see FOOL 1

2 a stupid person ⟨I'm not such a *ninny* that I'd turn down some help.⟩ — see IDIOT

¹**nip** *n* **1** the quality or state of being stimulating to the mind or senses ⟨The barbecue sauce has a *nip* to it that balances out the sweetness.⟩ — see PIQUANCY

2 a very small amount ⟨I'll have just a *nip* of your sandwich.⟩ — see PARTICLE 1

3 an uncomfortable degree of coolness ⟨There's a *nip* in the air today.⟩ — see CHILL

²**nip** *n* the portion of a serving of a beverage that is swallowed at one time ⟨Gve me just a *nip* of milk to help me swallow this pill.⟩ — see DRINK 2

nip *vb* **1** to make (something) shorter or smaller with the use of a cutting instrument ⟨I'm just going to *nip* these hedges, and then I'll be done with the work outside.⟩ — see CLIP 1

2 to squeeze tightly between two surfaces, edges, or points ⟨The puppy *nipped* her hand while playing.⟩ — see PINCH 1

3 to take (something) without right and with an intent to keep ⟨That guy *nipped* my wallet from the restaurant table when I turned away.⟩ — see STEAL 1

4 to proceed or move quickly ⟨I'll just *nip* off to the corner store for some milk.⟩ — see HURRY 2

nip and tuck *adj* showing little difference in the standing of the competitors ⟨The race was *nip and tuck* to the very end, with the judges needing to look at photos of the finish three times.⟩ — see CLOSE 3

nipper *n* a male person who has not yet reached adulthood ⟨The little *nipper* can't quite reach the cabinet.⟩ — see BOY 1

nipping *adj* **1** having a low or subnormal temperature ⟨a group of campers waking up to the *nipping* air of a Rocky Mountain morning⟩ — see COLD 1

2 uncomfortably cool ⟨Better wear a windbreaker if you're going sailing in this *nipping* wind.⟩ — see CHILLY 1

nippy *adj* **1** having a low or subnormal temperature ⟨Bring a jacket, as it's a little *nippy* outside.⟩ — see COLD 1

2 having a powerfully stimulating odor or flavor ⟨Blue cheese is a little too *nippy* for my taste.⟩ — see SHARP 2

3 moving, proceeding, or acting with great speed ⟨racing around the neighborhood on a *nippy* scooter⟩ — see FAST 1

4 uncomfortably cool ⟨a *nippy* wind that chilled parade watchers to the bone⟩ — see CHILLY 1

nitpick *vb* to make often peevish criticisms or objections about matters that are minor, unimportant, or irrelevant ⟨Stop *nitpicking* and just let me get this done.⟩ — see QUIBBLE 1

nitpicker *n* a person given to harsh judgments and to finding faults ⟨a tiresome *nitpicker* who seems to think that I can't do anything right⟩ — see CRITIC 1

nitwit *n* **1** a person who lacks good sense or judgment ⟨Don't be a *nitwit*—wear a seat belt!⟩ — see FOOL 1

2 a stupid person ⟨an absolute *nitwit* as far as geography is concerned⟩ — see IDIOT

no *adv* **1** not in any degree, way, or under any condition ⟨This cake is *no* better than the last one we made.⟩ — see NEVER 2

2 certainly not ⟨In *no* uncertain terms we were told to leave.⟩ — see HARDLY 2

no *interj* how surprising, doubtful, or unbelievable ⟨*No*—you can't possibly mean that I failed that test! I studied for days!⟩

synonyms ah, aha, fie, indeed, pshaw, well, what, why

related words gee, gee whiz, hello, lo, oh; fiddlesticks, pooh; there; oops (*or* whoops *also* woops); egad, gad, the devil, the dickens

no *n* **1** a vote or decision against something ⟨Though I wanted spaghetti for dinner, the consensus was a decisive *no*.⟩

synonyms nay, negative

related words con; blackball, veto; denial, negation, refusal

near antonyms pro; acceptance, approval, grace

antonyms positive, yea, yes

2 an unwillingness to grant something asked for ⟨I got a *no* when I asked for the day off.⟩ — see DENIAL 1

nobility *n* **1** impressiveness of beauty on a large scale ⟨was struck by the *nobility* of such an old, distinguished castle⟩ — see MAGNIFICENCE

2 the highest class in a society ⟨a member of the *nobility* who married a commoner⟩ — see ARISTOCRACY 1

noble *adj* **1** of high birth, rank, or station ⟨Despite his *noble* background, the prince is known for his unpretentious way with common people.⟩

synonyms aristocratic, genteel, gentle, grand, great, highborn, patrician, upper-class, wellborn

related words high, lofty, superior; elevated, ennobled, exalted; gentlemanly, kingly, knightly, ladylike, lordly, princely, queenly, regal, royal; high-level, senior

near antonyms inferior, knavish; ordinary, plain; abased, degraded; junior, subordinate

antonyms baseborn, common, humble, ignoble, low, lower-class, lowly, mean, nonaristocratic, plebeian, ungenteel

2 having, characterized by, or arising from a dignified and generous nature ⟨The factory owner had a kind, *noble* disposition that showed in his unstinting generosity toward the poor.⟩ ⟨Our country was founded on the *noble* ideas that are put forth in the Founding Fathers' writings.⟩

synonyms big, chivalrous, elevated, gallant, great, greathearted, high, high-minded, lofty, lordly, magnanimous, sublime

related words ennobled, exalted, glorified; heroic (*also* heroical), honorable, valiant, venerable, worthy; knightly, princely, regal; inspiring, moving, uplifting; august, magnificent, majestic

near antonyms sordid, squalid, vile, wretched; abominable, contemptible, despicable, detestable, hateful, offensive, repulsive, ugly, vicious; dastardly, dirty, lousy, sorry; little, mean, narrow, small-minded

antonyms base, debased, degenerate, degraded, ignoble, low

3 following the accepted rules of moral conduct ⟨his *noble* behavior even as he was being unjustly attacked by his political opponents⟩ — see HONORABLE 1

4 large and impressive in size, grandeur, extent, or conception ⟨Peter the Great's plan to build for Russia a capital city as *noble* as any in Europe⟩ — see GRAND 1

5 of the very best kind ⟨a *noble* racehorse⟩ — see EXCELLENT

6 standing above others in rank, importance, or achievement ⟨a *noble* professor known internationally for his medical research⟩ — see EMINENT

nobleman *n* a man of high birth or social position ⟨the household of a wealthy *nobleman*⟩ — see GENTLEMAN 1

nobleness *n* impressiveness of beauty on a large scale ⟨These snapshots just don't convey the breathtaking *nobleness* of St. Peter's basilica in Rome.⟩ — see MAGNIFICENCE

noblewoman *n* a woman of high birth or social position ⟨a portrait of a 16th century *noblewoman*⟩ — see GENTLEWOMAN

nobly *adv* in a manner befitting a person of the highest character and ideals ⟨civil rights activists *nobly* striving for justice and equality⟩ — see GREATLY 1

nobody *n* a person of no importance or influence ⟨Tired of feeling like a *nobody*, she decided to launch her own business.⟩
synonyms cipher, lightweight, nonentity, nothing, pipsqueak, pygmy (*also* pigmy), shrimp, twerp, whippersnapper, zero, zilch
related words noncelebrity; figurehead, puppet; nonperson
near antonyms chief, head, lead, leader; celebrity, luminary, notable, personality, star, superstar
antonyms big shot, bigwig, eminence, figure, kingpin, magnate, nabob, personage, somebody, VIP

nobody *pron* no person ⟨There is *nobody* home.⟩ ⟨*Nobody* wants to clean up that mess.⟩
synonyms none, no one
near antonyms anybody, anyone; somebody, someone
antonyms everybody, everyone

nocturnal *adj* of, relating to, or occurring in the night ⟨He bought a new telescope so he could pursue his favorite *nocturnal* hobby of astronomy.⟩
synonyms night, nightly, nighttime
related words late; midnight, overnight
near antonyms noon
antonyms daily, diurnal

nod *vb* to make short up-and-down movements ⟨Though she couldn't see the rain, she knew it had started because she could see the flowers *nod* as raindrops hit them.⟩
synonyms bob, bobble, jog, jounce, pump, seesaw, wag
related words jerk, jiggle, shake, wiggle, wobble (*also* wabble); oscillate, rock, sway, swing, undulate; drop, duck

nodding *adj* bending downward or forward ⟨Some students, with *nodding* heads, were helplessly falling asleep during the boring lecture.⟩
synonyms bowed, bowing, declined, declining, descendant (*also* descendent), descending, drooping, droopy, hanging, hung, inclining, pendulous, sagging, stooping, weeping
related words floppy, limp; dangling, falling, pendent (*or* pendant); dipping, sinking, slumping
near antonyms erect, inflexible, rigid, stiff; elevated, raised, upraised
antonyms unbending, upright

noddle *n* the upper or front part of the body that contains the brain, the major sense organs, and the mouth ⟨tapped his *noddle* to indicate he was thinking⟩ — see HEAD 1

node *n* a small rounded mass of swollen tissue ⟨The doctor examined the *node* on my knee before deciding it was the result of arthritis.⟩ — see BUMP 1

nodule *n* a small rounded mass of swollen tissue ⟨A *nodule* on the leaf indicated that a worm had laid eggs there.⟩ — see BUMP 1

Noel *n* the season celebrating Christmas ⟨For *Noel* the town puts on a festival of indoor and outdoor events, including strolling carolers in Victorian dress.⟩ — see YULETIDE

noggin *n* the upper or front part of the body that contains the brain, the major sense organs, and the mouth ⟨Watch the lintel above the door, unless you want to bang your *noggin*.⟩ — see HEAD 1

no–good *adj* having no usefulness ⟨That *no-good* chair should be thrown away.⟩ — see WORTHLESS

no–good *n* a mean, evil, or unprincipled person ⟨an actor as comfortable playing a hero as a *no-good*⟩ — see VILLAIN

noise *n* 1 loud, confused, and usually inharmonious sound ⟨The incessant *noise* of traffic on Fifth Avenue made normal conversation impossible.⟩
synonyms babel, blare, bluster, cacophony, chatter, clamor, clangor, din, discordance, racket, rattle, roar
related words discord; commotion, furor, hubbub, hullabaloo, hurly-burly, rumpus, tumult, uproar; clatter; bang, blast, boom, clap, crack, crash
near antonyms calm, hush, lull; quietude, serenity, tranquillity (*or* tranquility)
antonyms quiet, silence, silentness, still, stillness
2 a violent shouting ⟨Keep the *noise* down, you kids!⟩ — see CLAMOR 1

noiseless *adj* mostly or entirely without sound ⟨The new dishwasher is practically *noiseless*.⟩ — see SILENT 3

noisome *adj* 1 bad for the well-being of the body ⟨It's no fun having asthma and living in an area with *noisome* smog.⟩ — see UNHEALTHY 1
2 causing intense displeasure, disgust, or resentment ⟨a *noisome* remark that stuck with me for days⟩ — see OFFENSIVE 1
3 having an unpleasant smell ⟨the *noisome* air of the area of the city that was downwind of the dog food factory⟩ — see MALODOROUS

noisy *adj* 1 making loud, confused, and usually unharmonious sounds ⟨The *noisy* crowd marched up the street, shouting ever louder as they approached the palace.⟩
synonyms clangorous, dinning, discordant
related words cacophonous, dissonant; resounding, sonorous; clamorous, uproarious; blatant, obstreperous, strident, vociferous; blaring, booming, brassy, brazen, clanging, earsplitting, jangly
near antonyms calm, hushed
antonyms noiseless, quiet, silent, soundless, still
2 full of or characterized by the presence of noise ⟨The crowded auditorium was *noisy*, packed with excited theatergoers eager for the show to start.⟩ ⟨The manufacturing plant was a decidedly *noisy* place, so we wore ear protection while we toured it.⟩
synonyms clamorous, clangorous, clattering, clattery, resounding, uproarious
related words resonant, sonorous; buzzing, humming, murmuring; blustery, boisterous, raucous, rip-roaring, roaring, roistering, romping, rowdy; tumultuous, woolly (*also* wooly); obstreperous, vociferous
near antonyms calm, peaceful, serene, tranquil
antonyms hushed, noiseless, quiet, silent, soundless, stilled, stilly
3 excessively showy ⟨The wallpaper was far too *noisy* for what was supposed to be a restful bedroom.⟩ — see GAUDY
4 likely to attract attention ⟨The movie was preceded by months of *noisy* hype.⟩ — see NOTICEABLE

nomad *adj* traveling from place to place ⟨*nomad* caravans of Bedouins⟩ — see ITINERANT

nomad *n* a person who roams about without a fixed route or destination ⟨After college she became quite the *nomad*, backpacking through Europe with no particular destination.⟩
synonyms drifter, gadabout, rambler, roamer, rover, stroller, vagabond, wanderer, wayfarer
related words laggard, straggler; lingerer, loiterer, sojourner; bum, hobo, tramp; sightseer, traveler (*or* traveller); migrant, transient, vagrant; saunterer; hiker
near antonyms homebody; denizen, dweller, habitant, inhabitant, resident, settler

nominal *adj* 1 being something in name or form only ⟨He was the *nominal* head of state—everyone knew the country was actually run by one of his advisers.⟩
synonyms formal, paper, titular

related words so-called; phantom, virtual; apparent, assumed, evident, ostensible, presumed, seeming, supposed
near antonyms actual, real, true

2 so small or unimportant as to warrant little or no attention ⟨When you pay $400 for an airline ticket, a ticketing fee of five dollars seems *nominal*.⟩ — see NEGLIGIBLE 1

nominally *adv* in a very small quantity or degree ⟨Although the more expensive TV is *nominally* better than the other, it's not worth the big difference in price.⟩ — see LITTLE 1

nonaction *n* lack of action or activity ⟨Your *nonaction* on this matter will result in the commencement of legal proceedings.⟩ — see INACTION

nonbinding *adj* having no legal or binding force ⟨A verbal agreement is considered *nonbinding* in this state.⟩ — see NULL 1

nonchalance *n* lack of interest or concern ⟨With their usual *nonchalance* they arrived at the wedding ceremony half an hour late.⟩ — see INDIFFERENCE

nonchalant *adj* having or showing a lack of interest or concern ⟨You shouldn't be so *nonchalant* about something that is so important to your parents.⟩ — see INDIFFERENT 1

noncombustible *adj* incapable of being burned ⟨Firefighting gear is made of *noncombustible* material.⟩ — see INCOMBUSTIBLE

nonconflicting *adj* not having or showing any apparent conflict ⟨There are several *nonconflicting* reports on the effectiveness of the new drug.⟩ — see CONSISTENT

nonconformist *adj* deviating from commonly accepted beliefs or practices ⟨a *nonconformist* view on education⟩ — see HERETICAL

nonconformist *n* **1** a person who does not conform to generally accepted standards or customs ⟨Always the *nonconformist*, she insisted on wearing red on St. Patrick's Day and not green like everyone else.⟩
synonyms bohemian, deviant, heretic, individualist, lone wolf, maverick
related words freethinker; character, codger, crackbrain, crackpot, crank, eccentric, freak, kook, nut, oddball, screwball, weirdo; eight ball, misfit, outsider
near antonyms adherent, follower, supporter; sheep
antonyms conformer, conformist
2 a person who believes, teaches, or advocates something opposed to accepted beliefs ⟨a *nonconformist* who was excommunicated from her church for her teachings⟩ — see HERETIC 1

nonconformity *n* departure from a generally accepted theory, opinion, or practice ⟨an artistic movement that doesn't tolerate *nonconformity*⟩ — see HERESY

nonconventional *adj* not bound by traditional ways or beliefs ⟨His *nonconventional* cures were the subject of some controversy.⟩ — see LIBERAL 1

none *adv* **1** certainly not ⟨Your help comes *none* too soon.⟩ — see HARDLY 2
2 not in any degree, way, or under any condition ⟨I'll switch his mug with mine, and he'll be *none* the wiser.⟩ — see NEVER 2

none *pron* no person ⟨*None* will come to the party.⟩ — see NOBODY

nonelective *adj* forcing one's compliance or participation by or as if by law ⟨Language arts, math, and science are *nonelective* subjects taken by all students at the school.⟩ — see MANDATORY

nonentity *n* **1** a conception or image created by the imagination and having no objective reality ⟨The arctic circle is a *nonentity*—you won't see it on the way to the north pole.⟩ — see FANTASY 1
2 a person of no importance or influence ⟨The new guy

was so quiet he was almost a *nonentity* at the meeting.⟩ — see NOBODY

nonessential *adj* not needed by the circumstances or to accomplish an end ⟨Money's tight, so we'll have to skip *nonessential* purchases.⟩ — see UNNECESSARY

nonetheless *adv* in spite of that ⟨The hike was difficult, but fun *nonetheless*.⟩ — see HOWEVER

nonexistent *adj* not present or in evidence ⟨Our perennially *nonexistent* computer tech is, once again, not here today.⟩ — see ABSENT 2

nonfictional *adj* restricted to or based on fact ⟨a *nonfictional* account of a disastrous ascent of Mount Everest⟩ — see FACTUAL 1

nonflammable *adj* incapable of being burned ⟨children's pajamas made of *nonflammable* fabric⟩ — see INCOMBUSTIBLE

nonfunctional *adj* not being in working order ⟨That gas pump is *nonfunctional*, which is the reason for the plastic bag over the nozzle.⟩ — see INOPERABLE 1

nonfunctioning *adj* not being in working order ⟨The Ferris wheel is *nonfunctioning* at the moment.⟩ — see INOPERABLE 1

noninflammable *adj* incapable of being burned ⟨*noninflammable* materials used for bedding⟩ — see INCOMBUSTIBLE

nonliterary *adj* used in or suitable for speech and not formal writing ⟨Slang words are usually considered *nonliterary*.⟩ — see COLLOQUIAL 1

nonmaterial *adj* not composed of matter ⟨Newton's laws explain the effects of *nonmaterial* forces on bodies.⟩ — see IMMATERIAL 1

nonmotile *adj* incapable of moving or being moved ⟨an examination of the slides of *nonmotile* cells⟩ — see IMMOVABLE 1

nonmoving *adj* **1** fixed in a place or position ⟨The restaurant is actually in a *nonmoving* vessel permanently docked on the city's waterfront.⟩ — see STATIONARY 1
2 incapable of moving or being moved ⟨all of the machine's *nonmoving* parts⟩ — see IMMOVABLE 1

nonnative *adj* being, relating to, or characteristic of a country other than one's own ⟨classes for *nonnative* speakers⟩ — see FOREIGN 1

nonnative *n* a person who is not native to or known to a community ⟨markets that cater to *nonnatives*⟩ — see STRANGER

nonobjective *adj* using elements of form (as color, line, or texture) with little or no attempt at creating a realistic picture ⟨The real subject of his *nonobjective* paintings is color—and the intense emotional response it can provoke in the viewer.⟩ — see ABSTRACT 2

no–nonsense *adj* not joking or playful in mood or manner ⟨a *no-nonsense* gymnastics coach⟩ — see SERIOUS 1

nonoperating *adj* not being in working order ⟨fixed all *nonoperating* parts⟩ — see INOPERABLE 1

nonorthodox *adj* **1** deviating from commonly accepted beliefs or practices ⟨one of the few colonies to tolerate *nonorthodox* religious beliefs⟩ — see HERETICAL
2 not bound by traditional ways or beliefs ⟨a *nonorthodox* approach to teaching music⟩ — see LIBERAL 1

nonpareil *adj* having no equal or rival for excellence or desirability ⟨The bakery's cakes are *nonpareil*.⟩ — see ONLY 1

nonpareil *n* someone of such unequaled perfection as to deserve imitation ⟨Among the knights of the Round Table, Galahad stood alone as the *nonpareil* of nobility and selflessness.⟩ — see IDEAL 1

nonpartisan *adj* **1** marked by justice, honesty, and freedom from bias ⟨made a *nonpartisan* decision that satisfied all concerned⟩ — see FAIR 2
2 not favoring or joined to either side in a quarrel, con-

test, or war ⟨*nonpartisan* observers who were there to ensure a fair election⟩ — see NEUTRAL

nonphysical *adj* not composed of matter ⟨Ghosts are generally thought to be *nonphysical* in nature.⟩ — see IMMATERIAL 1

nonplus *vb* to throw into a state of self-conscious distress ⟨I was *nonplussed* by his openly expressed admiration of me.⟩ — see EMBARRASS 1

nonpractical *adj* not capable of being put to use or account ⟨an inventor who seemed to be able to create only *nonpractical* gadgets⟩ — see IMPRACTICAL

nonprofessional *adj* lacking or showing a lack of expert skill ⟨They didn't like the *nonprofessional* photos the wedding photographer did for them.⟩ — see AMATEURISH

nonprofessional *n* a person who regularly or occasionally engages in an activity as a pastime rather than as a profession ⟨One need not be a legal professional to join the bar association; it is open to professionals and *nonprofessionals* alike.⟩ — see AMATEUR 1

nonpublic *adj* not known or meant to be known by the general populace ⟨School records are regarded as *nonpublic* information.⟩ — see PRIVATE 1

nonrational *adj* not using or following good reasoning ⟨Dad was so upset that he was completely *nonrational* for a moment.⟩ — see ILLOGICAL

nonrealistic *adj* using elements of form (as color, line, or texture) with little or no attempt at creating a realistic picture ⟨a *nonrealistic* rendering of the chaos and destruction wreaked by war⟩ — see ABSTRACT 2

nonreligious *adj* 1 lacking religious emotions, principles, or practices ⟨grew up in a *nonreligious* family⟩ — see IRRELIGIOUS
2 not involving religion or religious matters ⟨a display of *nonreligious* holiday decorations on municipally owned property⟩ — see PROFANE 1

nonresistant *adj* receiving or enduring without offering resistance ⟨the *nonresistant* arrest of most of the demonstrators⟩ — see PASSIVE

nonsense *n* 1 language, behavior, or ideas that are absurd and contrary to good sense ⟨told him to stop his mischievous *nonsense* and start behaving properly⟩ ⟨The discussion about building a time machine was complete *nonsense*.⟩ ⟨A hundred years ago, the idea that man could walk on the moon was regarded as impractical *nonsense*.⟩
synonyms blarney, bull [*slang*], bunk, claptrap, drivel, folly, foolishness, fudge, hogwash, humbug, humbuggery, jazz, moonshine, piffle, rot, rubbish, senselessness, silliness, stupidity, trash, trumpery, twaddle
related words absurdity, asininity, foolery, idiocy, imbecility, inaneness, inanity, kookiness; absurdness, craziness, madness, senselessness, witlessness; monkeyshine(s), shenanigan(s), tomfoolery; gas, hot air, rigmarole (*also* rigamarole); double-talk
near antonyms levelheadedness, rationality, reasonability, reasonableness, sensibleness; common sense, horse sense, sense; discernment, judgment (*or* judgement), wisdom
2 unintelligible or meaningless talk ⟨Many of the words in the poem are *nonsense*.⟩ — see GIBBERISH 1

nonsensical *adj* 1 conceived or made without regard for reason or reality ⟨a *nonsensical* decision that doesn't face the facts⟩ — see FANTASTIC 1
2 showing or marked by a lack of good sense or judgment ⟨Your plan to lose weight through total starvation is completely *nonsensical*.⟩ — see FOOLISH 1

nonsensicalness *n* lack of good sense or judgment ⟨The *nonsensicalness* of your attempt to swim across the icy river is beyond words.⟩ — see FOOLISHNESS 1

nonspecific *adj* relating to the main elements and not to specific details ⟨His criticism of the picture is fairly *nonspecific*, but he clearly doesn't like it.⟩ — see GENERAL 2

nonsuccess *n* a falling short of one's goals ⟨Mia refused to let the *nonsuccess* of her bid for a seat in the state senate discourage her from a career in politics.⟩ — see FAILURE 2

nontraditional *adj* not bound by traditional ways or beliefs ⟨a *nontraditional* couple who are planning a very unconventional wedding⟩ — see LIBERAL 1

nonvalid *adj* 1 having no basis in reason or fact ⟨a *nonvalid* theory that most scientists rejected long ago⟩ — see GROUNDLESS
2 having no legal or binding force ⟨Failure to inform the suspect of his rights rendered his confession *nonvalid*.⟩ — see NULL 1

nonviolent *adj* not involving violence or force ⟨*nonviolent* protests⟩ — see PEACEFUL 2

nook *n* a hollowed-out space in a wall ⟨Books filled every *nook* in the house.⟩ — see NICHE 1

noon *n* 1 the middle of the day ⟨We eat a big lunch around *noon* then have dinner in the evening.⟩
synonyms high noon, midday, noonday, noontide, noontime
related words forenoon, morning; evening
2 the highest part or point ⟨reached the *noon* of her life⟩ — see HEIGHT 1

noonday *n* the middle of the day ⟨In the tropics the *noonday* heat can be overwhelming.⟩ — see NOON 1

no one *pron* no person ⟨*No one* is home.⟩ — see NOBODY

noontide *n* the middle of the day ⟨We like to work off lunch with a *noontide* ramble.⟩ — see NOON 1

noontime *n* 1 the highest part or point ⟨Far removed from the *noontime* of their popularity, when they had performed at sold-out arenas, the band now played at small clubs.⟩ — see HEIGHT 1
2 the middle of the day ⟨listening to the radio at *noontime* for news updates⟩ — see NOON 1

norm *n* 1 what is typical of a group, class, or series ⟨sales figures that are within the *norm* of a store of that size⟩ — see AVERAGE
2 norms *pl* the code of good conduct for an individual or group ⟨Societal *norms* dictate that murder is wrong.⟩ — see ETHICS

normal *adj* 1 being of the type that is encountered in the normal course of events ⟨That fateful day had begun just like any *normal* workday.⟩ — see ORDINARY 1
2 having full use of one's mind and control over one's actions ⟨If you run around screaming like that, no one will think you are *normal*.⟩ — see SANE
3 having or showing the qualities associated with the members of a particular group or kind ⟨She has *normal* reading abilities for a child her age.⟩ — see TYPICAL 1

normal *n* what is typical of a group, class, or series ⟨a temperature chart showing the *normals* and extremes for various regions⟩ — see AVERAGE

normalcy *n* the state or fact of being the way things usually are ⟨a combat-weary soldier longing for the *normalcy* of peacetime life⟩ — see NORMALITY

normality *n* the state or fact of being the way things usually are ⟨The county slowly has returned to *normality* after a week of flash flooding.⟩
synonyms normalcy, status quo
related words groove, routine, rut; currency, prevalence; conventionality; harmony, orderliness, peace
near antonyms irregularity, uncommonness, unusualness; disruptiveness; disruption, disturbance; anomalousness, deviance; exceptionalness, extraordinariness, noteworthiness, remarkableness
antonyms abnormality

normalize *vb* to make agree with a single established standard or model ⟨English spelling wasn't *normalized* until printed books became common.⟩ — see STANDARDIZE

normally *adv* according to the usual course of things ⟨*Normally* I go to my health club after work, but today I'm giving myself a break.⟩ — see NATURALLY 2

nose *n* 1 the part of the face bearing the nostrils and nasal cavity ⟨With that *nose*, the baby sure looks like his father.⟩
synonyms beak
related words pug, pugnose
2 the last and usually sharp or tapering part of something long and narrow ⟨bent the wire around the *nose* of the pliers⟩ — see POINT 2

nose *vb* 1 to become aware of by means of the sense organs in the nose ⟨I could *nose* the garbage from across the street.⟩ — see SMELL 1
2 to interest oneself in what is not one's concern ⟨a neighbor who likes to *nose* around and discover everyone's secrets⟩ — see INTERFERE
3 to move slowly ⟨The line to get tickets is just *nosing*, so we are going to be here for a while.⟩ — see CRAWL 2

nosedive *n* the act or process of going to a lower level or altitude ⟨The pilot struggled to pull his plane out of a *nosedive*.⟩ — see DESCENT 1

nose–dive *vb* to go to a lower level especially abruptly ⟨Prices on just about everything *nose-dived* right after the holidays.⟩ — see DROP 2

nosegay *n* a bunch of flowers ⟨a stately procession of bridesmaids holding small *nosegays*⟩ — see BOUQUET 1

nosiness *n* an eager desire to find out about things that are often none of one's business ⟨Your annoying *nosiness* isn't going to win you any friends.⟩ — see CURIOSITY 1

nosy *or* **nosey** *adj* 1 interested in what is not one's own business ⟨*nosy* in-laws asking about our finances⟩ — see CURIOUS 1
2 thrusting oneself where one is not welcome or invited ⟨A *nosy* coworker sat down right next to us as we were having an unmistakably private conversation.⟩ — see INTRUSIVE

notable *adj* 1 standing above others in rank, importance, or achievement ⟨a panel made up of *notable* authorities on the virus⟩ — see EMINENT
2 worth remembering or mentioning ⟨predicts trends in the stock market with *notable* accuracy⟩ — see NOTEWORTHY 1

notable *n* a person who is widely known and usually much talked about ⟨directors, actors, and other *notables* at the annual gathering for the Academy Awards⟩ — see CELEBRITY 1

notation *n* a usually brief written reminder ⟨He had scribbled his *notation* so quickly I couldn't read it.⟩ — see NOTE 1

notch *n* 1 a V-shaped cut usually on an edge or a surface ⟨lifted up the fence rail and positioned it in the *notch* cut into the post⟩
synonyms chip, hack, indentation, kerf, nick
related words groove, score, undercut; slit
2 a narrow opening between hillsides or mountains that can be used for passage ⟨Let's try to get through the *notch* before the storm blows in.⟩ — see CANYON
3 an individual part of a process, series, or ranking ⟨Sales for the album increased, and it moved up another *notch* on the music charts.⟩ — see DEGREE 1

notch (up) *vb* to obtain (as a goal) through effort ⟨a stunning performance that *notched up* a second Academy Award for the actor⟩ — see ACHIEVE 1

note *n* 1 a usually brief written reminder ⟨I'll make a *note* to myself so I don't forget to pick up some milk on the way home.⟩
synonyms memo, memorandum, notation

related words memoir, memorial, minutes, protocol, report; line; document, writing
2 a message on paper from one person or group to another ⟨Let's write a friendly *note* to the new neighbors welcoming them.⟩ — see ¹LETTER
3 a natural vocal sound made by an animal ⟨Can you distinguish between the *notes* of the whippoorwill and the mockingbird?⟩ — see CALL 1
4 a piece of printed paper used as money in the United States ⟨Will you be paying in coins or *notes*?⟩ — see ¹BILL 2
5 a special quality or impression associated with something ⟨spoke with a *note* of wistfulness in her voice⟩ — see AURA 1
6 overall quality as seen or judged by people in general ⟨a writer of *note* among readers of modern poetry⟩ — see REPUTATION
7 a briefly expressed opinion ⟨Let me read a few *notes* I jotted down while you were auditioning.⟩ — see REMARK
8 a state of being aware ⟨During my long convalescence I had taken *note* of which friends had helped me and which ones had found other things to do.⟩ — see ATTENTION 2
9 something that sets apart an individual from others of the same kind ⟨an intense, full-bodied red wine with all of the spicy *notes* for which that grape variety is famous⟩ — see CHARACTERISTIC

note *vb* 1 to make a statement of one's opinion ⟨I'd like to *note* that I'm happy with the way things turned out.⟩ — see REMARK 1
2 to make a written note of ⟨a waitress hurriedly *noting* our orders⟩ — see RECORD 1
3 to make note of (something) through the use of one's eyes ⟨*Note* the artist's rendering of the trees, how their leaves seem to dance in the wind.⟩ — see SEE 1
4 to make reference to or speak about briefly but specifically ⟨The lecturer *noted* several sources where listeners could go for further information.⟩ — see MENTION 1
5 to take notice of and be guided by ⟨Please *note* that the office will be closed tomorrow.⟩ — see HEED 1

noted *adj* widely known ⟨a serious play that needs a *noted* Broadway actor for the lead if it is to attract audiences⟩ — see FAMOUS 1

notepad *n* a number of sheets of writing paper glued together at one edge ⟨I used a different *notepad* for each class's notes.⟩ — see PAD 1

noteworthiness *n* the fact or state of being above others in rank or importance ⟨Her long-standing *noteworthiness* as a neurosurgeon gets her many referrals from doctors around the country.⟩ — see EMINENCE 1

noteworthy *adj* 1 worth remembering or mentioning ⟨Nothing *noteworthy* happened while you were gone.⟩
synonyms notable, observable, remarkable
related words quotable, repeatable; newsworthy
near antonyms average, ordinary, prosaic, routine, run-of-the-mill, standard, unexceptional
antonyms forgettable, unmemorable, unremarkable
2 standing above others in rank, importance, or achievement ⟨winner of the Nobel Prize for his *noteworthy* contributions to the field of genetics⟩ — see EMINENT

nothing *adv* not in any degree, way, or under any condition ⟨*Nothing* daunted by the poor reception his first novel received, he proceeded to write another one.⟩ — see NEVER 2

nothing *n* 1 a person of no importance or influence ⟨We used to care for each other, but she's *nothing* to me now.⟩ — see NOBODY
2 something of little importance ⟨You're always worrying about *nothing*.⟩ — see TRIFLE

3 the numerical symbol 0 or the absence of number or quantity represented by it ⟨Two minus two equals *nothing.*⟩ — see ZERO 1

notice *n* **1** a published statement informing the public of a matter of general interest ⟨a public safety *notice* regarding the need for a smoke detector in the home⟩ — see ANNOUNCEMENT
2 a state of being aware ⟨The group first came to public *notice* about five years ago.⟩ — see ATTENTION 2
3 a written communication giving information or directions ⟨received a *notice* of promotion from the head of the company⟩ — see MEMORANDUM 1
4 an essay evaluating or analyzing something ⟨She avidly reads the latest theater *notices* in the paper.⟩ — see CRITICISM
5 the act or an instance of telling beforehand of danger or risk ⟨The terms of service can be changed without *notice.*⟩ — see WARNING 1

notice *vb* **1** to make note of (something) through the use of one's eyes ⟨Did you *notice* what time it was?⟩ — see SEE 1
2 to make reference to or speak about briefly but specifically ⟨briefly *noticed* in his lecture the author's first published work⟩ — see MENTION 1

noticeable *adj* likely to attract attention ⟨The stain on the new carpet was quite *noticeable*, and nothing we did made it any lighter.⟩
synonyms arresting, bold, brilliant, catchy, commanding, conspicuous, dramatic, emphatic, eye-catching, flamboyant, marked, noisy, prominent, pronounced, remarkable, showy, splashy, striking
related words detectable, discernible (*also* discernable), observable, perceptible, recognizable, visible; outstanding, salient; distinguished, eminent, impressive, notable, noteworthy; highlighted, spotlighted; flagrant, glaring, howling, screaming; flashy, garish, gaudy, glitzy, jazzy, loud, meretricious, swank (*or* swanky), tawdry; highfalutin (*also* hifalutin), ostentatious, pretentious; extravagant, fancy, florid, glittery; opulent, ornate, overdone, overwrought
near antonyms subtle; concealed, shrouded; dim, faint, obscure; insignificant, undistinguished, unimportant; modest, unaffected, unassuming, unpretentious; conservative, plain, quiet, simple, understated; muted, restrained, subdued, toned-down
antonyms inconspicuous, unemphatic, unflamboyant, unnoticeable, unobtrusive, unremarkable, unshowy

notification *n* a published statement informing the public of a matter of general interest ⟨a *notification* posted by the health board that its inspectors had cited the restaurant for several violations⟩ — see ANNOUNCEMENT

notion *n* **1 notions** *pl* small useful items ⟨The fabric store had a wide variety of thread, pins, buttons, and other *notions.*⟩
synonyms novelties, odds and ends, sundries
related words baubles, bric-a-brac, gewgaws (*also* geegaws), knickknacks (*also* nicknacks), trinkets; gadgets, gimmicks, jiggers
2 a sudden impulsive and apparently unmotivated idea or action ⟨I have a *notion* to go swimming this afternoon.⟩ — see WHIM
3 an idea that is believed to be true or valid without positive knowledge ⟨Anne has a *notion* that most people are basically honest.⟩ — see OPINION 1
4 something imagined or pictured in the mind ⟨That modernistic building does not match my *notion* of what a country cottage should look like.⟩ — see IDEA 1
5 an idea or statement about all of the members of a group or all the instances of a situation ⟨The study disputes the *notion* that animals don't have emotions.⟩ — see GENERALIZATION

notoriety *n* **1** a person who is widely known and usually much talked about ⟨a television show featuring a rogues' gallery of *notorieties* from 20 years of overhyped scandals⟩ — see CELEBRITY 1
2 the fact or state of being known to the public ⟨a lawyer of *notoriety* for the huge awards he's won in medical malpractice cases⟩ — see FAME 1

notorious *adj* **1** not respectable ⟨a *notorious* mastermind of criminal activities⟩ — see DISREPUTABLE
2 widely known ⟨a book signing for a *notorious* author of tell-all celebrity biographies⟩ — see FAMOUS 1

notwithstanding *adv* in spite of that ⟨We've already started eating, but you're welcome to join us for dinner *notwithstanding.*⟩ — see HOWEVER

notwithstanding *conj* in spite of the fact that ⟨The man is little known to his neighbors, *notwithstanding* he has lived in the apartment complex for years.⟩ — see ALTHOUGH

notwithstanding *prep* without being prevented by ⟨We went to see the show, my objections *notwithstanding.*⟩ — see DESPITE

nourish *vb* **1** to help the growth or development of ⟨wanted to *nourish* her students' love of art⟩ — see FOSTER 1
2 to supply with nourishment ⟨We've always been *nourished* by such good food when staying at their house.⟩ — see SUSTAIN 1
3 to bring to maturity through care and education ⟨He willingly *nourished* a child that was not his own.⟩ — see BRING UP 1

nourishing *adj* providing the substances necessary for health and bodily growth ⟨Milk should be part of a *nourishing* breakfast.⟩ — see NUTRITIOUS

novel *adj* not known or experienced before ⟨That's a *novel* idea for a TV series!⟩ — see NEW 2

novelette *n* a work with imaginary characters and events that is shorter and usually less complex than a novel ⟨bought a collection of his novels and *novelettes*⟩ — see STORY 1

novella *n* a work with imaginary characters and events that is shorter and usually less complex than a novel ⟨Pressed for time, many English teachers have their students read the one *novella* among the novelist's works.⟩ — see STORY 1

novelty *n* **1** the quality or appeal of being new ⟨The *novelty* of having a cat wore off after the first time I had to change the litter box.⟩
synonyms freshness, newness, originality
related words bizarreness, strangeness, unfamiliarity, unusualness; progressiveness; currentness, recentness, up-to-dateness; departure, divergence, innovation, offshoot, shoot
near antonyms banality, commonness, familiarity; outdatedness, staleness
2 novelties *pl* small useful items ⟨travel kits filled with small bars of soap, a folding toothbrush, and other *novelties*⟩ — see NOTION 1
3 a small object displayed for its attractiveness or interest ⟨a shop selling souvenirs, T-shirts, and assorted *novelties* for tourists passing through⟩ — see KNICKKNACK

novice *n* a person who is just starting out in a field of activity ⟨a *novice* chess player⟩ — see BEGINNER

now *adv* **1** at the present time ⟨That company doesn't make those toys *now* because they are unsafe.⟩
synonyms anymore, currently, nowadays, presently, right now, today
related words here
phrases at present, for the time being
near antonyms away, far, farthest, remotest; heretofore, hitherto, since; previously
antonyms before, long, then
2 not long ago ⟨I was just *now* wondering what to do about those old clothes.⟩ — see NEWLY

3 on some occasions ⟨goes *now* here, *now* there—all seemingly without plan or purpose⟩ — see SOMETIMES

4 without delay ⟨Come here right *now!*⟩ — see IMMEDIATELY

now *conj* for the reason that ⟨I'll repeat my question *now* that you are paying attention.⟩ — see SINCE

now *n* the time currently existing or in progress ⟨I know I said you could go, but that was then and this is *now*.⟩ — see ¹PRESENT

nowadays *adv* at the present time ⟨People don't wear hats as much *nowadays*.⟩ — see NOW 1

noway *adv* **1** *or* **noways** not in any degree, way, or under any condition ⟨That will *noway* hurt your chances of getting on the team.⟩ — see NEVER 2

2 *usually* **no way** certainly not ⟨*No way* will I give up!⟩ — see HARDLY 2

nowise *adv* not in any degree, way, or under any condition ⟨Her romance novels are *nowise* different from those of scores of other writers.⟩ — see NEVER 2

noxious *adj* **1** bad for the well-being of the body ⟨Mixing bleach and ammonia can cause *noxious* fumes that can seriously harm you.⟩ — see UNHEALTHY 1

2 causing or capable of causing harm ⟨*noxious* smog that for years has been encrusting the historic cathedral with soot⟩ — see HARMFUL

3 causing intense displeasure, disgust, or resentment ⟨saw turning farms into housing developments as a *noxious* use of land⟩ — see OFFENSIVE 1

nth *adj* of the greatest or highest degree or quantity ⟨exaggerates to the *nth* degree about everything she ever did⟩ — see ULTIMATE 1

nub *n* **1** a small uneven mass ⟨First, throw a *nub* of butter into the frying pan.⟩ — see LUMP 1

2 the central part or aspect of something under consideration ⟨The *nub* of the problem is lack of funding.⟩ — see CRUX

nubbin *n* **1** a very small piece ⟨had only a *nubbin* of crayon left⟩ — see BIT 1

2 the central part or aspect of something under consideration ⟨The *nubbin* of the story is how they thrived under pressure.⟩ — see CRUX

nubble *n* a small uneven mass ⟨dropped a *nubble* of clay on the floor of the pottery⟩ — see LUMP 1

nubbly *adj* having small pieces or lumps spread throughout ⟨The walls were painted with a *nubbly* paint that was supposed to give them an interesting texture.⟩ — see CHUNKY 1

nubby *adj* having small pieces or lumps spread throughout ⟨a *nubby* yarn that produces bumpy fabrics when woven⟩ — see CHUNKY 1

nucleus *n* **1** a thing or place that is of greatest importance to an activity or interest ⟨a college campus that was a *nucleus* of opposition to the war⟩ — see CENTER 1

2 the central part or aspect of something under consideration ⟨The *nucleus* of the movement's methodology has always been passive resistance.⟩ — see CRUX

nude *adj* lacking or shed of clothing ⟨Picasso's paintings of *nude* art models⟩ — see NAKED 1

nudge *vb* **1** to pass lightly across or touch gently especially in passing ⟨accidentally *nudged* me as they squeezed past⟩ — see ²BRUSH

2 to try to persuade (someone) through earnest appeals to follow a course of action ⟨The car salesman *nudged* me into taking a test-drive, even though I had said that I was just looking.⟩ — see URGE

nugget *n* **1** a small piece or quantity of food ⟨*nuggets* of beef in the chow mein⟩ ⟨fried chicken *nuggets*⟩ — see MORSEL 1

2 a small uneven mass ⟨a *nugget* of gold⟩ — see LUMP 1

3 a very small piece ⟨a seemingly inconsequential *nugget* of information that proved to be the key to cracking the case⟩ — see BIT 1

nuisance *n* **1** one who is obnoxiously annoying ⟨The new neighbor is threatening to become a *nuisance*, dropping in on us several times a day.⟩

synonyms annoyance, annoyer, bother, gadfly, pain, persecutor, pest, tease, teaser

related words headache; harrier, heckler, interrupter (*also* interruptor); hassle, plague; molester, tormentor (*also* tormenter), torturer

phrases pain in the neck

near antonyms charmer, smoothy (*or* smoothie); comforter, solacer, soother

2 something that is a source of irritation ⟨Folding up this map correctly is such a *nuisance*.⟩ — see ANNOYANCE 3

null *adj* **1** having no legal or binding force ⟨The contract was *null* because one party forgot to sign it.⟩

synonyms bad, inoperative, invalid, nonbinding, nonvalid, null and void, void

related words illegal; useless, worthless; ineffective, ineffectual

near antonyms legal; working

antonyms binding, good, valid

2 having no usefulness ⟨That information is as *null* as no information at all.⟩ — see WORTHLESS

null *vb* to put an end to by formal action ⟨asked the state court to *null* the election results because of widespread voting irregularities⟩ — see ABOLISH 1

null and void *adj* having no legal or binding force ⟨Public disclosure of the terms of the out-of-court settlement renders it *null and void*.⟩ — see NULL 1

nullify *vb* to put an end to by formal action ⟨the constitutional amendment that *nullified* Prohibition⟩ — see ABOLISH 1

numb *adj* **1** lacking in sensation or feeling ⟨I've been sitting in the same position for too long and now my feet are *numb*.⟩

synonyms asleep, benumbed, dead, insensitive, numbed, torpid, unfeeling

related words chilled, nipped; anesthetized, deadened, drugged, stupefied; blunted, dulled; insensible, senseless, unconscious; insensate

near antonyms awake

antonyms feeling, sensible, sensitive

2 not expressing any emotion ⟨Apparently in shock, he answered the police officer's questions with a *numb* expression on his face.⟩ — see BLANK 1

3 not feeling or showing emotion ⟨After listening to his complaints for years, I've grown *numb* to them.⟩ — see IMPASSIVE 1

numb *vb* to reduce or weaken in strength or feeling ⟨Wait for the medication to *numb* your mouth.⟩ — see DULL 1

numbed *adj* lacking in sensation or feeling ⟨*numbed* fingers that needed warming by the fire⟩ — see NUMB 1

number *n* **1** a character used to represent a mathematical value ⟨asked him to write out the equation in *numbers*, not letters⟩

synonyms digit, figure, integer, numeral, whole number

related words decimal; cipher; symbol

2 a literary, musical, or artistic production ⟨a doomsday novel that turns out to be one of those it-was-all-a-dream *numbers*⟩ — see COMPOSITION 1

3 a performance regularly presented by an individual or group ⟨a modern dance *number*⟩ — see ACT 1

4 an act of notable skill, strength, or cleverness ⟨a stunning gymnastics *number* that really impressed the judges⟩ — see FEAT 1

5 numbers *pl* the act or process of performing mathematical operations to find a value ⟨If you believe the president's *numbers*, we can afford these new programs and still have tax cuts.⟩ — see CALCULATION

number *vb* **1** to find the sum of (a collection of things) by noting each one as it is being added ⟨*Number* those apples and tell me how many you have.⟩ — see COUNT 1

2 to have a total of ⟨The full-time staff *numbers* 30 people.⟩ — see AMOUNT (TO) 1

3 to have as part of a whole ⟨is *numbered* among the great minds of our times⟩ — see INCLUDE 1

number crunching *n* the act or process of performing mathematical operations to find a value ⟨He did a little *number crunching* and made an offer on the house.⟩ — see CALCULATION

numberless *adj* too many to be counted ⟨the *numberless* stars in the universe⟩ — see COUNTLESS

numbing *adj* **1** causing weariness, restlessness, or lack of interest ⟨an utterly *numbing* class in statistics⟩ — see BORING

2 having a low or subnormal temperature ⟨the *numbing* air of that wintry morning⟩ — see COLD 1

numbness *n* a lack of emotion or emotional expressiveness ⟨Some sufferers of stress disorder exhibit *numbness*.⟩ — see APATHY 1

numeral *n* a character used to represent a mathematical value ⟨Write the answer in Roman *numerals*.⟩ — see NUMBER 1

numerate *vb* **1** to make a list of ⟨Again *numerate* the dish's ingredients for me.⟩ — see ¹LIST 1

2 to specify one after another ⟨I don't have the time to *numerate* all the reasons, so I'll offer just a few.⟩ — see ENUMERATE 1

numerous *adj* being of a large but indefinite number ⟨received *numerous* complaints about that product⟩ — see MANY

numskull *or* **numbskull** *n* a stupid person ⟨Don't be such a *numskull*—you know he was only kidding.⟩ — see IDIOT

nuptial *adj* of or relating to marriage ⟨newlyweds still in a state of *nuptial* bliss⟩ — see MARITAL

nuptial *n, usually* **nuptials** *pl* a ceremony in which two people are united in matrimony ⟨Their *nuptials* will take place at the university chapel.⟩ — see WEDDING

nurse *n* a person employed to care for a young child or children ⟨In *Peter Pan*, the Darling children's *nurse*, Nana, was actually a large dog.⟩

synonyms babysitter, nanny (*also* nannie), nursemaid, sitter

related words duenna, governess

nurse *vb* **1** to attend to the needs and comforts of ⟨Jim willingly lent a hand to *nurse* his grandmother in her final years, helping her get from one room to the other and making sure she was warm.⟩

synonyms care (for), minister (to), mother

related words cure, heal, remedy; doctor, treat; aid, conserve, preserve, provide (for), support; baby, coddle, mollycoddle, pamper, spoil; cater (to), humor; indulge

phrases look after, look out for, look to, see to, take care of, wait on (*also* wait upon)

near antonyms brush (aside *or* off), forget, ignore, neglect, overlook, slight

2 to keep in one's mind or heart ⟨He continues to *nurse* a tender affection for his first girlfriend.⟩ — see HARBOR 1

3 to treat with great or excessive care ⟨*nursed* his sprained ankle for the rest of the week⟩ — see BABY

4 to bring to maturity through care and education ⟨As foster parents they accepted and *nursed* 16 needy children over the years.⟩ — see BRING UP 1

5 to help the growth or development of ⟨Her teachers did much to *nurse* her literary talent.⟩ — see FOSTER 1

6 to use or give out in stingy amounts ⟨He carefully *nursed* his energy during the marathon so that he would have something left for the final stretch.⟩ — see SPARE 1

nursemaid *n* a person employed to care for a young child or children ⟨sent the children to their *nursemaid*⟩ — see NURSE

nurture *vb* **1** to help the growth or development of ⟨Paul wanted to find the art school that would best *nurture* his artistic talent.⟩ — see FOSTER 1

2 to provide (someone) with moral or spiritual understanding ⟨She feels that her lifelong practice of helping the poor has *nurtured* her in ways she cannot describe.⟩ — see ENLIGHTEN 2

3 to supply with nourishment ⟨*nurtured* her children through the long winters with home-cooked soup⟩ — see SUSTAIN 1

nut *n* **1** a person of odd or whimsical habits ⟨a show devoted to those lovable *nuts* who collect the weirdest things just for fun⟩ — see ECCENTRIC

2 a person with a strong and habitual liking for something ⟨a baseball *nut* who waited 86 years for the Boston Red Sox to win the World Series⟩ — see FAN

nutrient *adj* providing the substances necessary for health and bodily growth ⟨a breakfast drink enriched with *nutrient* proteins and vitamins⟩ — see NUTRITIOUS

nutritional *adj* providing the substances necessary for health and bodily growth ⟨The doctor recommended *nutritional* supplements.⟩ — see NUTRITIOUS

nutritious *adj* providing the substances necessary for health and bodily growth ⟨Kate opted for a *nutritious* snack and bought an apple instead of a candy bar.⟩

synonyms nourishing, nutrient, nutritional, nutritive

related words enriched, fortified; dietary, dietetic; beneficial, healthful, healthy, restorative, salubrious, salutary, wholesome

near antonyms unhealthful, unhealthy, unwholesome

antonyms nonnutritious, nonnutritive

nutritive *adj* providing the substances necessary for health and bodily growth ⟨Nutritionists contend that whole wheat bread is significantly more *nutritive* than white bread.⟩ — see NUTRITIOUS

nuts *adj* showing urgent desire or interest ⟨I'm *nuts* for the homecoming game.⟩ — see EAGER

nuts (about) *adj* filled with an intense or excessive love for ⟨a group of old girlfriends fondly recalling teen heartthrobs that they were once *nuts about*⟩ — see ENAMORED (OF)

nuttiness *n* lack of good sense or judgment ⟨The plan worked despite its sheer *nuttiness*.⟩ — see FOOLISHNESS 1

nutty *adj* showing or marked by a lack of good sense or judgment ⟨That's a *nutty* idea that won't work at all!⟩ — see FOOLISH 1

nuzzle *vb* to lie close ⟨newborn puppies *nuzzling* against their mother to stay warm⟩

synonyms cuddle, nestle, snuggle

related words curl up; crouch, huddle

near antonyms blench, flinch, quail, recoil, shrink, shy, start, wince

nymph *n* a mythical goddess represented as a young woman and said to live outdoors ⟨She bought the book of fairy tales for the beautiful engravings of *nymphs* and fairies featured between the stories.⟩

synonyms dryad, naiad, oread

related words mermaid, Nereid, Oceanid, sea-maid (*or* sea-maiden), siren, water nymph

O

oaf *n* **1** a big clumsy often slow-witted person ⟨It's not nice to call your brother an *oaf*.⟩
synonyms clod, clodhopper, gawk, hulk, lout, lubber, lug, lump, Neanderthal
related words chump, turkey; blockhead, bonehead, dolt, dope, dork [*slang*], dumbbell, dumbhead, dumdum, dummy, dunce, dunderhead, fathead, galoot [*slang*], goof, goon, half-wit, hammerhead, hardhead, idiot, ignoramus, imbecile, know-nothing, lump, meathead, moron, nincompoop, ninny, numskull (*or* numbskull), pinhead, schnook [*slang*], simpleton, thickhead, woodenhead, yo-yo; boor, brute, cad, churl, clown, creep, cur, heel, louse, skunk, snake, stinker; fool, goose; klutz
near antonyms brain, egghead, genius, intellectual, sage, thinker, whiz, wizard
2 a stupid person ⟨Anyone who took him for an *oaf* and tried to cheat him would be in for a nasty surprise.⟩ — see IDIOT
oafish *adj* not having or showing an ability to absorb ideas readily ⟨Far from being *oafish*, the professional wrestler was in fact a college graduate.⟩ — see STUPID 1
oafishness *n* the quality or state of lacking intelligence or quickness of mind ⟨The *oafishness* of the investigators, who missed clues and mishandled physical evidence, is the reason why that crime was never solved.⟩ — see STUPIDITY 1
oar *n* a person who drives a boat forward by means of oars ⟨"All *oars* ho!" the boatswain ordered.⟩ — see OARSMAN
oar *vb* to move a boat by means of oars ⟨Since the wind had completely died, they had to *oar* the sailboat back to shore.⟩ — see ¹ROW
oarsman *n* a person who drives a boat forward by means of oars ⟨the only *oarsman* in a rowboat designed for two⟩
synonyms oar, rower, sculler
related words bowman, oarswoman; coxswain, crewman; puller; kayaker
oath *n* a person's solemn declaration that he or she will do or not do something ⟨I need your *oath* that you won't do anything until I've had time to make a decision.⟩ — see PROMISE
obduracy *n* a steadfast adherence to an opinion, purpose, or course of action in spite of reason, arguments, or persuasion ⟨The administrator was known for her unyielding *obduracy* even in the face of proof that she was wrong.⟩ — see OBSTINACY
obdurate *adj* **1** having or showing a lack of sympathy or tender feelings ⟨the *obdurate* refusal of the crotchety old man to let the neighborhood kids retrieve their stray ball from his backyard⟩ — see HARD 1
2 sticking to an opinion, purpose, or course of action in spite of reason, arguments, or persuasion ⟨The doctor was *obdurate*—the patient could have no visitors.⟩ — see OBSTINATE
obedience *n* **1** a bending to the authority or control of another ⟨The drill sergeant demanded complete and unquestioning *obedience* from the recruits.⟩
synonyms compliance, submission, subordination
related words abidance, amenability, tractability, trainability; acquiescence, capitulation, obeisance, obsequiousness, submissiveness, surrender, yielding; deference, docility, dutifulness, humility, meekness, modesty, servility, subordinateness, subservience; inhibition, repression, restraint, suppression; control, discipline, order

near antonyms disrespect, impudence, insolence, rudeness; insurgency, insurrection, mutiny, outbreak, revolt; hardheadedness, mulishness, mutinousness, obstinacy, perversity, stubbornness; misbehavior, mischievousness, naughtiness; dissent, dissidence
antonyms contrariness, contumacy, defiance, disobedience, frowardness, insubordination, intractability, noncompliance, rebelling, rebellion, rebelliousness, recalcitrance, refractoriness, self-will, unruliness, waywardness, willfulness
2 a readiness or willingness to yield to the wishes of others ⟨followed their leader with blind *obedience*⟩ — see COMPLIANCE 1
3 the following of a custom, rule, or law ⟨Expectations of strict *obedience* to the guidelines were soon dashed.⟩ — see OBSERVANCE 1
obedient *adj* readily giving in to the command or authority of another ⟨That boy is so *obedient* that he does everything the first time he is asked.⟩
synonyms amenable, compliant, conformable, docile, law-abiding, submissive, tractable
related words acquiescent, agreeable, amiable, dutiful, obliging, placable; fawning, kowtowing, obeisant, obsequious, subordinate, subservient; decorous, disciplined, mannerly, orderly; controllable, disciplinable, governable, handleable, manageable, tame, teachable, trainable; gentle, meek, mild
near antonyms insurgent, mutinous; dogged, hardheaded, headstrong, mulish, obdurate, obstinate, peevish, pigheaded, self-willed, stubborn, unyielding; uncontrollable, unmanageable, wild; perverse, resistant; disorderly, errant, misbehaving, mischievous, naughty; ill-bred, undisciplined; dissident, nonconformist; disrespectful, illmannered, impolite, impudent, insolent, rude
antonyms balky, contrary, defiant, disobedient, froward, insubordinate, intractable, noncompliant, obstreperous, rebel, rebellious, recalcitrant, refractory, restive, unamenable, ungovernable, unruly, untoward, wayward, willful (*or* wilful)
obese *adj* having an excess of body fat ⟨The basset hound was so *obese* that its stomach touched the floor.⟩ — see FAT 1
obesity *n* the condition of having an excess of body fat ⟨*Obesity* has been linked to a number of health risks, such as heart disease.⟩ — see CORPULENCE
obey *vb* to act according to the commands of ⟨She taught her dog to *obey* her when she said "Sit!"⟩ ⟨Most people *obey* the law and wear their seat belts.⟩
synonyms adhere (to), comply (with), conform (to), follow, mind, observe
related words defer (to), submit (to), surrender (to), yield (to); accede (to), acquiesce (to), agree (to), assent (to); attend, hear, heed, listen (to), mark, note, notice, regard, take, watch
phrases abide by, fall in with, keep to
near antonyms disoblige; challenge, dare; refuse, renounce, repudiate; brush off, disregard, ignore, overlook, overpass, pass over, tune out, wink (at); dismiss, pooh-pooh (*also* pooh), shrug off; breach, break, infringe, transgress, violate; deride, flout, mock, scoff (at), scorn; mutiny (against), revolt (against); buck, combat, contest, dispute, fight, oppose, resist, withstand
antonyms defy, disobey, rebel (against)
object *n* **1** something material that can be perceived by the

senses ⟨I kept tripping over countless little *objects* scattered about the darkened room.⟩

synonyms thing

related words article, item, piece; being, entity, substance; good; thingummy

2 one that has a real and independent existence ⟨trying to determine whether communication with the dead is an *object* for study, a hoax, or a figment of the imagination⟩ — see ENTITY

3 something that one hopes or intends to accomplish ⟨The *object* of this course is to teach you algebra.⟩ — see GOAL

object *vb* to present an opposing opinion or argument ⟨They *objected* to the conductor's insistence that their train tickets were not valid.⟩

synonyms demur, except, protest, remonstrate (with)

related words cavil, quibble; challenge, dare, defy, fight; conflict, debate, dispute, hassle, quarrel, squabble, wrangle; beef, bellyache, carp, complain, crab, croak, fuss, gripe, grouch, grouse, growl, grumble, grump, holler, keen, moan, murmur, mutter, nag, repine, scream, squawk, squeal, wail, whimper, whine, yammer, yowl; balk, gag, stick; censure, criticize, denounce; disobey, rebel, withstand; demonstrate

phrases take exception, take issue

near antonyms approve, sanction; accept; accede, acquiesce, agree, assent; adhere, comply, conform, follow, mind, obey, observe; advocate, champion, defend, maintain, support, sustain, uphold; applaud, cheer, commend

objection *n* a feeling or declaration of disapproval or dissent ⟨Pardon me, but I have an *objection* to any plan that requires staying out all night.⟩

synonyms challenge, complaint, demur, difficulty, expostulation, fuss, kick, protest, question, remonstrance, stink

related words compunction, doubt, misgiving, qualm, scruple; cavil, quibble; argument, conflict, debate, dispute, quarrel, squabble; censure, criticism; defiance, disobedience, rebellion; distrust, distrustfulness, incertitude, indetermination, mistrust, mistrustfulness, reservation, skepticism, suspicion, uncertainty; qualmishness, uneasiness; reluctance, unwillingness

near antonyms willingness; approval, sanction; acceptance, acquiescence, agreement, assent; compliance, obedience

objectionable *adj* provoking or likely to provoke protest ⟨found nothing *objectionable* about the TV show⟩

synonyms censurable, exceptionable, obnoxious, offensive, reprehensible

related words unacceptable, undesirable, unwanted, unwelcome; disagreeable, displeasing, distasteful, unpleasant; bad, execrable, lousy, miserable, terrible, unspeakable, wretched; atrocious, infamous; abhorrent, gross, loathsome, repellent (*also* repellant), repugnant, repulsive, revolting, sickening, vile; debasing, perverted, profane; off, racy, salty, suggestive; indecent, indecorous, unbecoming; earthy, unprintable; bawdy, coarse, crude, dirty, filthy, foul, gross, lewd, nasty, obscene, smutty, vulgar; lascivious, pornographic, ribald, scurrilous

near antonyms acceptable, agreeable, blessed (*also* blest), congenial, delectable, delicious, delightful, enjoyable, felicitous, good, grateful, gratifying, nice, palatable, pleasant, pleasing, pleasurable, satisfying, welcome; approved, endorsed (*also* indorsed), sanctioned; becoming, correct, decent, decorous, exemplary, proper, respectable, seemly; blameless, commendable, creditable; immaculate, perfect, pure, spotless; politically correct

antonyms inoffensive, unobjectionable

objective *adj* **1** based on observation or experience ⟨an

objective assessment based solely upon the results of the experiment⟩ — see EMPIRICAL 1

2 marked by justice, honesty, and freedom from bias ⟨The judge removed herself from the case because she doubted her ability to remain *objective*, given her friendship with one of the attorneys.⟩ — see FAIR 2

3 restricted to or based on fact ⟨The paper's news stories strive to be scrupulously *objective*, with opinions clearly labeled as commentary.⟩ — see FACTUAL 1

objective *n* something that one hopes or intends to accomplish ⟨The summer camp's stated *objective* is to produce tournament-level tennis players.⟩ — see GOAL

objectivity *n* lack of favoritism toward one side or another ⟨The teacher's *objectivity* would be seriously compromised if his own child were placed in the class.⟩ — see DETACHMENT 1

obligate *vb* to cause (a person) to give in to pressure ⟨The problem is of your own making, so don't think that you can *obligate* me to help.⟩ — see FORCE

obligated *adj* being under obligation for a favor or gift ⟨We have been their guests so many times that we feel *obligated* to return their hospitality.⟩ — see BEHOLDEN

obligation *n* **1** something one must do because of prior agreement ⟨Their financial *obligations* keep them from giving to charities as much as they would like.⟩

synonyms burden, charge, commitment, duty, imperative, need, office, responsibility

related words oath, pledge, promise, vow, word; arrangement, prearrangement, setup; compact, contract, covenant, pact, trust; debt, payment, tribute; compulsion, constraint, restraint; must, requirement; coercion, duress, force; appointment, engagement, reservation; burden

near antonyms grace, postponement, stay; discharge, ease, exemption, release, relief, waiver; loophole; alternative, choice, option, pick, preference, selection

2 something (as money) which is owed ⟨I have to pay off my current *obligations* before I can buy a new car.⟩ — see DEBT 1

obligatory *adj* forcing one's compliance or participation by or as if by law ⟨In this state, school attendance is *obligatory* until the age of 17.⟩ — see MANDATORY

oblige *vb* **1** to do a service or favor for ⟨I would appreciate it greatly if you could *oblige* me by bringing a dessert to the party.⟩

synonyms accommodate, favor

related words humor, indulge; coddle, mollycoddle, pamper; appease, conciliate, mollify, pacify, placate; delight, gladden, gratify, please, satisfy; abet, aid, assist, help, support; attend, care (for), comfort, minister (to), relieve, succor

near antonyms bother, discommode, disturb, incommode, inconvenience, trouble; burden, encumber, saddle, weigh; desert, disappoint, fail, let down; constrain, hamper, hamstring, hinder, hobble, hold back, impede, obstruct, restrain; frustrate, oppose, sabotage, thwart

antonyms disoblige

2 to cause (a person) to give in to pressure ⟨I know you're in a hurry, but you can't *oblige* me to drive any faster than the speed limit.⟩ — see FORCE

obliged *adj* **1** being under obligation for a favor or gift ⟨My new neighbor invited us to dinner, and now I feel *obliged* to reciprocate.⟩ — see BEHOLDEN

2 feeling or expressing gratitude ⟨I'd be much *obliged* if you could do me this favor.⟩ — see GRATEFUL 1

obliging *adj* willing to do a favor ⟨An *obliging* concierge used her pull to get us reservations at the town's hottest restaurant.⟩ — see ACCOMMODATING

oblique *adj* **1** inclined or twisted to one side ⟨Kim gave the eavesdropper an *oblique* glance out of the corner of her eye.⟩ — see AWRY

2 running in a slanting direction ⟨In the painting the artist repeats the *oblique* line of the path with the *oblique* line of the outstretched arm.⟩ — see DIAGONAL

obliquely *adv* in a line or direction running from corner to corner ⟨The photographer has framed the shot so that the river runs *obliquely* through it, creating a great sense of depth for the viewer.⟩ — see CROSSWISE

obliterate *vb* to destroy all traces of ⟨In a stroke, the March snowstorm *obliterated* our hopes for an early spring.⟩ — see ANNIHILATE 1

obliteration *n* the state or fact of being rendered nonexistent, physically unsound, or useless ⟨the ill-advised *obliteration* of the town's historic district in order to make way for a shopping mall⟩ — see DESTRUCTION 1

oblivion *n* a state of being disregardful or unconscious of one's surroundings, concerns, or obligations ⟨For two weeks each year the stressed-out couple enjoys the blissful *oblivion* that comes with a vacation at the beach.⟩
synonyms forgetfulness, obliviousness
related words ignorance, innocence, insensibility, unawareness, unconsciousness, unfamiliarity; absentmindedness, absorption, inattention, inattentiveness, preoccupation
near antonyms memory, recall, recollection, remembrance; alertness, awareness, cognizance

oblivious *adj* not informed about or aware of something ⟨The out-of-state motorist claimed to be *oblivious* of the local speed limit, even though the signs must have been hard to miss.⟩ — see IGNORANT 2

obliviousness *n* **1** a state of being disregardful or unconscious of one's surroundings, concerns, or obligations ⟨My *obliviousness* when reading often means I don't notice the time.⟩ — see OBLIVION
2 the state of being unaware or uninformed ⟨*Obliviousness* of a law is not an acceptable excuse for breaking it.⟩ — see IGNORANCE 1

obnoxious *adj* **1** causing intense displeasure, disgust, or resentment ⟨an *obnoxious* law that was widely flouted⟩ — see OFFENSIVE 1
2 provoking or likely to provoke protest ⟨an *obnoxious* comment for which there should be an immediate apology⟩ — see OBJECTIONABLE

obscene *adj* **1** depicting or referring to sexual matters in a way that is unacceptable in polite society ⟨an inappropriate and *obscene* gesture⟩
synonyms bawdy, blue, coarse, crude, dirty, filthy, foul, gross, impure, indecent, lascivious, lewd, nasty, ribald, smutty, vulgar, wanton
related words broad, coarse-grained, gamy (*or* gamey), off, racy, salty, suggestive; earthy, scatological; immodest, indecorous, low, unbecoming; depraved, kinky, naughty, perverse, perverted, wicked; exceptionable, objectionable, unacceptable, undesirable, unwanted, unwelcome; abhorrent, debasing, loathsome, offensive, repellent (*also* repellant), repugnant, repulsive, revolting; distasteful, obnoxious, unpleasant; abusive, scurrilous
near antonyms priggish, prim, prudish, puritanical, staid, straitlaced (*or* straightlaced); correct, decorous, genteel, nice, polite, proper, respectable, seemly; innocuous, inoffensive; appropriate, becoming, fit, meet, suitable; immaculate, perfect, pure, spotless, virginal
antonyms clean, decent, nonobscene, wholesome
2 causing intense displeasure, disgust, or resentment ⟨That ugly new store is really an *obscene* bit of architecture.⟩ — see OFFENSIVE 1

obscenity *n* the quality or state of being obscene ⟨arrested on *obscenity* charges⟩

synonyms bawdiness, coarseness, crudeness, filth, filthiness, foulness, grossness, impurity, indecency, lasciviousness, lewdness, nastiness, ribaldry, smut, smuttiness, vulgarity, wantonness
related words broadness, earthiness, gaminess, raciness, saltiness, suggestiveness; immodesty, indelicacy, indelicateness, lowness, unbecomingness; lechery; depravedness, depravity, kinkiness, naughtiness, perverseness, perversion, perversity, pervertedness, wickedness; abusiveness, scurrilousness; loathsomeness, offensiveness, repellency, repugnance, repulsiveness; distastefulness, obnoxiousness, unpleasantness
near antonyms priggery, priggishness, primness, prudery, prudishness, puritanism; correctness, decency, decorousness, decorum, seemliness; immaculateness, perfection, purity, spotlessness

obscure *adj* **1** having an often intentionally veiled or uncertain meaning ⟨a fantasy writer who likes to put lots of *obscure* references and images in her tales of wizards and warlocks⟩
synonyms ambiguous, cryptic, dark, deep, enigmatic (*also* enigmatical), equivocal, inscrutable, murky, mysterious, mystic, nebulous, occult, opaque
related words abstruse, esoteric, recondite; cloaked, concealed, disguised, masked, shrouded; cloudy, dim, faint, foggy, fuzzy, hazy, indistinct, indistinguishable, misty, muddy, shaded, shadowlike, shadowy, sphinxlike; indefinite, inexact, noncommittal, questionable, unclear, uncertain, undefined, undetermined, vague; impenetrable, incomprehensible, inexplicable; eerie (*also* eery), uncanny, weird; baffling, bewildering, confounding, confusing, mystifying, perplexing, puzzling, unfathomable; circuitous, indirect, roundabout
near antonyms knowable, pellucid; bright, distinct, evident, self-explanatory; certain, firm, strong, sure; defined, determined; direct, straightforward; definite, exact, explicit
antonyms accessible, clear, obvious, plain, unambiguous, unequivocal
2 not widely known ⟨He's an *obscure* artist now, but he's sure to be famous someday.⟩
synonyms nameless, uncelebrated, unknown, unsung
related words insignificant, minor, unimportant; undistinguished, unexceptional, unremarkable; unpopular; anonymous, faceless, unnoticeable, unrecognizable; unnoticed; forgotten, unremembered
near antonyms fabled, fabulous, legendary; infamous; distinguished, eminent, exceptional, great, illustrious, notable, outstanding, prestigious, remarkable; honorable, reputable, respectable; important, influential, leading, major, newsworthy, noteworthy, significant; favorite, popular, preferred
antonyms celebrated, famed, famous, noted, notorious, prominent, renowned, well-known
3 being without light or without much light ⟨hid in an *obscure* spot among the trees⟩ — see DARK 1
4 not seen or understood clearly ⟨a distinction so *obscure* that only the experts can really see it⟩ — see FAINT 1

obscure *vb* **1** to keep secret or shut off from view ⟨The investigative reporters *obscured* their real motives for visiting the company by pretending the story was about something else.⟩ — see ¹HIDE 2
2 to make dark, dim, or indistinct ⟨When it isn't *obscured* by smog, the view of the city from the observatory can be spectacular.⟩ — see CLOUD 1

obscured *adj* being without light or without much light ⟨an *obscured* area of the prison yard that was the perfect escape route⟩ — see DARK 1

obscurity *n* **1** the quality or state of having a veiled or uncertain meaning ⟨The 16th-century astrologer's predictions are so filled with *obscurity* that people can interpret them any way they want.⟩

synonyms ambiguity, ambiguousness, darkness, equivocalness, equivocation, murkiness, nebulousness, opacity
related words mystery, reconditeness; cloudiness, dimness, faintness, fogginess, fuzziness, haziness, indefiniteness, indistinctness, mistiness, shade, shadow, uncertainty, vagueness; incomprehensibility, incomprehensibleness; depth, profoundness; inscrutability
near antonyms comprehensibility, intelligibility, legibility; brightness, distinctness, self-evidence; certainty, surety; definiteness, exactness, explicitness, incision, incisiveness, lucidity, lucidness, perspicuity, perspicuousness; directness, forthrightness, straightforwardness
antonyms clarity, clearness, obviousness, plainness
2 the quality or state of being mostly or completely unknown ⟨The singer languished in relative *obscurity* for years before becoming famous.⟩
synonyms anonymity, silence
related words oblivion; inconspicuousness, invisibility, invisibleness; unpopularity
near antonyms mark, name, note, report, reputation, repute; favor, popularity; importance, significance; distinction, eminence, glory, greatness, honor, illustriousness, note, preeminence, prominence; position, prestige, rank, standing, stature; acclaim, acknowledgment (*or* acknowledgement), praise, recognition; adoration, idolization
antonyms celebrity, fame, notoriety, renown
observable *adj* **1** capable of being seen ⟨Scientists often work with phenomena that are not directly *observable*.⟩ — see VISIBLE 1
2 worth remembering or mentioning ⟨a man who apparently was devoid of any *observable* virtue⟩ — see NOTEWORTHY 1
observance *n* **1** the following of a custom, rule, or law ⟨The *observance* of this family tradition would make your grandmother very happy.⟩ ⟨*observance* of the smoking ban in public buildings⟩
synonyms abidance, adherence, compliance, conformity, keeping, obedience, observation
related words deference, honor, regard, respect, upholding; acquiescence, submission, surrender; attendance, attention, heed, notice
near antonyms brush-off, disregard, ignoring; delinquency, dereliction, forgetting, neglect, overlooking; challenge, defiance, flouting, rebellion
antonyms breach, infraction, infringement, nonobservance, transgression, trespass, violation
2 an oft-repeated action or series of actions performed in accordance with tradition or a set of rules ⟨Some religions require very specific *observances* on holy days.⟩ — see RITE
3 a state of being aware ⟨I'm sorry, but I was so busy that your presence escaped my *observance*.⟩ — see ATTENTION 2
observant *adj* **1** paying close attention usually for the purpose of anticipating approaching danger or opportunity ⟨If you were more *observant*, you would perceive that something is troubling her deeply.⟩ — see ALERT 1
2 having the mind fixed on something ⟨*Observant* viewers will notice that the position of the hero's facial wound changes in the course of the scene.⟩ — see ATTENTIVE 1
observation *n* **1** a state of being aware ⟨It has come to my *observation* that you've been missing a lot of school lately.⟩ — see ATTENTION 2
2 the following of a custom, rule, or law ⟨a society in which a strict *observation* of business etiquette is expected of visiting foreigners⟩ — see OBSERVANCE 1

observational *adj* based on observation or experience ⟨Her reports on the great apes were based on firsthand *observational* evidence.⟩ — see EMPIRICAL 1
observatory *n* a high place or structure from which a wide view is possible ⟨The *observatory* is located on a mountaintop.⟩ — see LOOKOUT 1
observe *vb* **1** to act according to the commands of ⟨You must *observe* all the rules of this school, not simply the ones that meet with your personal approval.⟩ — see OBEY
2 to mark with an appropriate practice, rite, or ceremony ⟨a time when few people in New England *observed* Christmas⟩ — see KEEP 1
3 to keep one's eyes on ⟨We happily spent many hours *observing* the birds at the backyard feeder.⟩ — see WATCH 1
4 to make a statement of one's opinion ⟨"I think you might be mistaken," he *observed*.⟩ — see REMARK 1
5 to make note of (something) through the use of one's eyes ⟨She *observed* that the weather had changed again.⟩ — see SEE 1
6 to take notice of and be guided by ⟨generally *observes* the suggestions of the experts regarding baby care⟩ — see HEED 1
obsessed *adj* having extreme or relentless concern ⟨The youngster was so *obsessed* with video games that he had little interest in playing outside.⟩ — see HUNG UP 1
obsession *n* something about which one is constantly thinking or concerned ⟨Her latest *obsession* is golf.⟩ — see FIXATION
obsessive *adj* caused by or suggestive of an irresistible urge ⟨intrigued by the man's *obsessive* counting of everyday objects⟩ — see COMPULSIVE
obsolete *adj* having passed its time of use or usefulness ⟨I was told my old printer is *obsolete* and I can't get replacement parts.⟩
synonyms antiquated, archaic, dated, moth-eaten, outdated, outmoded, out-of-date, outworn, passé, superannuated
related words aging (*or* ageing), obsolescent; discarded, disused, inoperable, unusable, unworkable, useless; dead, defunct, expired, extinct, vanished; dormant, fallow, idle, inactive, inert, inoperative, latent; ancient, antediluvian, antique, dateless, fusty, musty, old; oldfangled, old-fashioned, old-time, retro; aged, age-old, hoary, venerable; bygone, erstwhile, former, late, old-world, past
near antonyms contemporary, current, mod, modern, new, newfangled, new-fashioned, present-day, recent, ultramodern, up-to-date; fresh; modernized, refurbished, remodeled, renewed; functional, operable, operational, workable; active, alive, busy, employed, functioning, operating, operative
obstacle *n* something that makes movement or progress difficult ⟨stumbling on all the *obstacles* along the path⟩ — see ENCUMBRANCE
obstinacy *n* a steadfast adherence to an opinion, purpose, or course of action in spite of reason, arguments, or persuasion ⟨The *obstinacy* of the parties made negotiating a compromise difficult.⟩
synonyms bullheadedness, doggedness, hardheadedness, mulishness, obduracy, pertinaciousness, pertinacity, self-will, stubbornness, willfulness
related words perverseness, perversity, waywardness, wrongheadedness; adamancy (*also* adamance), determination, implacability, inexorability, inflexibility, inveteracy, perseverance, persistence, persistency, relentlessness, resolve, single-mindedness, steadfastness, tenaciousness, tenacity; firmness, hardness, rigor, rigorousness, sternness,

strictness; rigidity, rigidness; cantankerousness, contrariness, cussedness; defiance, disobedience, frowardness, insubordination, intractability, rebelliousness, recalcitrance, refractoriness, unruliness

near antonyms broad-mindedness, open-mindedness, reasonability, reasonableness, receptiveness, receptivity; acceptance, acquiescence, flexibility, pliability; compliance, docility, obedience, subordinateness, subordination; submission, surrender, willingness, yielding; subservience, subserviency

obstinate *adj* sticking to an opinion, purpose, or course of action in spite of reason, arguments, or persuasion ⟨The child was *obstinate* about wanting that specific toy, despite being offered several others.⟩

synonyms adamant, dogged, hard, hardened, hardheaded, headstrong, immovable, implacable, inflexible, mulish, obdurate, opinionated, ossified, pat, pertinacious, perverse, pigheaded, self-willed, stubborn, unbending, uncompromising, unrelenting, unyielding, willful (*or* wilful)

related words obsessive; wayward, wrongheaded; determined, hell-bent, inexorable, persistent, relentless, resolved, set, single-minded, steadfast, stouthearted, tenacious, unflinching; firm, hard-line, iron, severe, stern, strict; hidebound, narrow-minded, rigid; cantankerous; contrary; disobedient, froward, insubordinate, intractable, recalcitrant, refractory, uncooperative, ungovernable, unmanageable, unruly; defiant, insurgent, mutinous; indomitable, invincible, unconquerable; confirmed, inveterate, unregenerate; demanding, exacting; dogmatic

near antonyms docile, obedient, placable, submissive, tractable; accepting, persuadable, receptive, responsive, willing; governable, manageable, reasonable, temperate; subservient

antonyms acquiescent, agreeable, amenable, compliant, complying, flexible, pliable, pliant, relenting, yielding

obstreperous *adj* **1** engaging in or marked by loud and insistent cries especially of protest ⟨an *obstreperous* crowd protesting the referee's call⟩ — see VOCIFEROUS

2 given to resisting authority or another's control ⟨The club's president was at his wits' end with *obstreperous* members who refused to cooperate.⟩ — see DISOBEDIENT

obstruct *vb* **1** to create difficulty for the work or activity of ⟨This would go much faster if you would stop *obstructing* me with your constant interruptions.⟩ — see HAMPER

2 to prevent passage through by filling with something ⟨At the moment the city's only tunnel between downtown and the airport is *obstructed* by an overturned tanker truck.⟩ — see CLOG 1

obstruction *n* something that makes movement or progress difficult ⟨An *obstruction* in the drain has the water all backed up.⟩ — see ENCUMBRANCE

obtain *vb* to receive as return for effort ⟨After years of proving herself, she *obtained* recognition as a serious journalist.⟩ — see EARN 1

obtainable *adj* possible to get ⟨Gas was in such short supply that it was just not *obtainable* at any price.⟩ — see AVAILABLE 1

obtrude *vb* to interest oneself in what is not one's concern ⟨Please stop *obtruding* in your brother's affairs.⟩ — see INTERFERE

obtrusive *adj* thrusting oneself where one is not welcome or invited ⟨Meddling in other people's lives is both *obtrusive* and presumptuous.⟩ — see INTRUSIVE

obtuse *adj* **1** lacking sharpness of edge or point ⟨*obtuse* scissors designed so that young users will not cut themselves⟩ — see DULL 1

2 not having or showing an ability to absorb ideas readily ⟨Forgive me for being *obtuse*, but could you explain that to me again?⟩ — see STUPID 1

obtuseness *n* the quality or state of lacking intelligence or quickness of mind ⟨Our guest's *obtuseness* was such that he failed to take even the broadest hint that it was time to leave.⟩ — see STUPIDITY 1

obviate *vb* to keep from happening by taking action in advance ⟨Brushing regularly should *obviate* the need for frequent trips to the dentist.⟩ — see PREVENT

obvious *adj* **1** not subject to misinterpretation or more than one interpretation ⟨That remark was an *obvious* joke, so lighten up!⟩ — see CLEAR 2

2 very noticeable especially for being incorrect or bad ⟨*obvious* errors in the book that the editor or proofreader should have caught⟩ — see EGREGIOUS

occasion *n* **1** a particular point at which an event takes place ⟨On that *occasion*, I met your father.⟩

synonyms moment, time

related words flash, instant, jiffy, minute, second, shake, split second, trice, twinkle, wink; bit, space, spell, stretch, while

2 a favorable combination of circumstances, time, and place ⟨The substitute violinist rose to the *occasion* and performed the piece beautifully.⟩ — see OPPORTUNITY

3 someone or something responsible for a result ⟨The missing money proved to be the *occasion* of much strife between the two brothers.⟩ — see CAUSE 1

4 something that happens ⟨Weddings are generally happy *occasions*.⟩ — see EVENT 1

occasion *vb* to be the cause of (a situation, action, or state of mind) ⟨The announcement concerning the change in scheduling *occasioned* much confusion.⟩ — see EFFECT

occasional *adj* **1** lacking in steadiness or regularity of occurrence ⟨The weekend forecast is for *occasional* showers.⟩ — see FITFUL

2 not often occurring or repeated ⟨an *occasional* mechanical problem with our car, but nothing serious⟩ — see INFREQUENT

occasionally *adv* on some occasions ⟨We *occasionally* stop for ice cream on the way home.⟩ — see SOMETIMES

occlude *vb* to prevent passage through by filling with something ⟨A blood clot had *occluded* a major artery in his body.⟩ — see CLOG 1

occult *adj* **1** being beyond one's powers to know, understand, or explain ⟨the *occult* ways in which the human mind works⟩ — see MYSTERIOUS 1

2 having an often intentionally veiled or uncertain meaning ⟨an *occult* reference in the text that has puzzled scholars ever since⟩ — see OBSCURE 1

3 having seemingly supernatural qualities or powers ⟨Great Britain's Stonehenge is one of those *occult* places where people expect something of cosmic significance to happen.⟩ — see MYSTIC 1

occult *vb* to keep secret or shut off from view ⟨*occulted* their house from prying eyes by planting large trees around it⟩ ⟨The actor's private life had long been *occulted* by a contrived public persona.⟩ — see ¹HIDE 2

occupant *n* one who lives permanently in a place ⟨The only *occupants* of that house are an old lady and her cat.⟩ — see INHABITANT

occupation *n* the activity by which one regularly makes a living ⟨My primary *occupation* is stockbroker, but I'm a drummer in a rock band on the weekends.⟩

synonyms calling, employment, game, line, profession, trade, vocation, work

related words call, lifework; business, enterprise, field, livelihood, living, racket [*slang*]; assignment, engagement, gig, mission; art, craft, handcraft, handicraft; appointment, berth, billet, office, place, position, post, situation; duty, function, job, load, task, workload

near antonyms pursuit

occupied *adj* involved in often constant activity ⟨The boy is constantly *occupied*, usually with sports or schoolwork.⟩ — see BUSY 1

occupy *vb* to hold the attention of ⟨A puzzle will *occupy* that child for hours.⟩ — see ENGAGE 1

occur *vb* to take place ⟨Let me know when the lunar eclipse is scheduled to *occur*.⟩ — see HAPPEN

occur (to) *vb* to enter the mind of ⟨It didn't *occur to* me to ask until much later.⟩
 synonyms come (to), cross, dawn (on), strike
 related words recall, recollect, remember, reminisce; con, learn, memorize; appear, arrive, emerge, materialize
 near antonyms forget, unlearn; disregard, ignore, neglect, overlook

occurrence *n* something that happens ⟨Life is full of random *occurrences*.⟩ — see EVENT 1

ocean *n* 1 the whole body of salt water that covers nearly three-fourths of the earth ⟨The *ocean* still holds mysteries that we are only beginning to unravel.⟩
 synonyms blue, brine, deep, sea, seven seas
 related words blue water, high seas, main, waters; basin; Davy Jones's locker, depths
 2 an immeasurable depth or space ⟨With a single bound from the top of the cliff, he propelled the hang glider into the *ocean* of air over the valley.⟩ — see ABYSS

oceanic *adj* 1 of or relating to the sea ⟨the theory that ancient mariners took advantage of *oceanic* currents to roam the seas on primitive rafts⟩ — see MARINE 1
 2 unusually large ⟨an *oceanic* field of wheat that stretched as far as the eye could see⟩ — see HUGE

ocular *adj* of, relating to, or used in vision ⟨recommends regular eye examinations for the early detection of such *ocular* diseases as glaucoma⟩ — see VISUAL 1

odd *adj* 1 being one of a pair or set without a corresponding mate ⟨Somehow, there's always at least one *odd* sock that comes out of the dryer.⟩
 synonyms unmatched, unpaired
 related words alone, lone, only, single, singular, sole, solitary
 antonyms matched, paired
 2 different from the ordinary in a way that causes curiosity or suspicion ⟨There's something *odd* about his explanation.⟩
 synonyms bizarre, cranky, crazy, curious, eccentric, erratic, far-out, funny, kooky (*also* kookie), offbeat, outlandish, out-of-the-way, peculiar, quaint, queer, queerish, quirky, remarkable, screwy, strange, wacky (*also* whacky), way-out, weird, wild
 related words aberrant, abnormal, addlepated, flaky; extraordinary, fantastic (*also* fantastical), freak, freakish, freaky, phenomenal; atypical, rare, singular, uncommon, uncustomary, unique, unusual, unwonted; conspicuous, notable, noticeable, outstanding, prominent, salient, striking; atrocious, outrageous, shocking; out-there, unconventional, unorthodox; baffling, bewildering, confounding, mystifying, perplexing, puzzling
 near antonyms average, commonplace, everyday, garden, normal, ordinary, prosaic, routine, run-of-the-mill, standard, typical, unexceptional, unremarkable, usual, workaday; conformist, conservative, conventional; expected, familiar, predictable; common, customary, frequent, habitual, regular, wonted
 3 being out of the ordinary ⟨The only *odd* grade for the exam was the one perfect score.⟩ — see EXCEPTIONAL 1
 4 noticeably different from what is generally found or experienced ⟨The *odd* occurrences in the area attracted the attention of people interested in psychic phenomena.⟩ — see UNUSUAL 1
 5 not often occurring or repeated ⟨With the exception of the *odd* sick day, he never takes time off from work.⟩ — see INFREQUENT

oddball *n* a person of odd or whimsical habits ⟨an endearing *oddball* always dreaming up zany ideas⟩ — see ECCENTRIC

oddity *n* 1 an odd or peculiar habit ⟨His one *oddity* is collecting used pencil leads.⟩ — see IDIOSYNCRASY
 2 something strange or unusual that is an object of interest ⟨deep-sea *oddities* such as the anglerfish⟩ — see CURIOSITY 2
 3 something that is different from what is ordinary or expected ⟨His shyness makes him something of an *oddity* in the world of standup comedy.⟩ — see ANOMALY 1
 4 a person of odd or whimsical habits ⟨an *oddity* with a penchant for historical clothing⟩ — see ECCENTRIC

oddment *n* 1 an unused or unwanted piece or item typically of small size or value ⟨The fabric store sells *oddments* left over from cutting.⟩ — see ¹SCRAP 1
 2 something that is different from what is ordinary or expected ⟨one of those medical *oddments* that has perplexed and intrigued generations of medical historians⟩ — see ANOMALY 1
 3 something strange or unusual that is an object of interest ⟨an exhibit devoted to the incredible array of *oddments* that are collected by people the world over⟩ — see CURIOSITY 2

odds *pl n* a measure of how often an event will occur instead of another ⟨The *odds* of winning the lottery are currently 200 million to one.⟩ — see PROBABILITY 2

odds and ends *pl n* 1 small useful items ⟨She's always searching among the *odds and ends* in the drawer for some tool that she needs.⟩ — see NOTION 1
 2 a remaining group or portion ⟨Almost all of the piece of leather will be needed for upholstering the chair, so just throw away any *odds and ends*.⟩ — see REMAINDER 1

odious *adj* causing intense displeasure, disgust, or resentment ⟨an *odious* and unforgivable insult⟩ — see OFFENSIVE 1

odium *n* the state of having lost the esteem of others ⟨Time did nothing to diminish the *odium* in which the traitor lived out his days.⟩ — see DISGRACE 1

odor *n* 1 a special quality or impression associated with something ⟨There's an *odor* of decay about the mom-and-pop amusement park, which clearly has seen better days.⟩ — see AURA 1
 2 the quality of a thing that makes it perceptible to the sense organs in the nose ⟨Some people find the *odor* of skunk rather pleasant.⟩ — see SMELL 1
 3 overall quality as seen or judged by people in general ⟨Her movie career has not been in good *odor* since her latest box office failure.⟩ — see REPUTATION

of *prep* 1 earlier than ⟨It's ten minutes *of* two right now.⟩ — see BEFORE 1
 2 having to do with ⟨The librarian read stories *of* princes and princesses to the youngsters.⟩ — see ABOUT 1

off *adj* 1 falling short of a standard ⟨The milk tasted *off*.⟩ — see BAD 1
 2 not being in a state of use, activity, or employment ⟨The computer is *off*, so you'll have to turn it on in order to use it.⟩ — see INACTIVE 2
 3 not being in agreement with what is true ⟨That claim that everyone is actually related to everyone else seems a bit *off*.⟩ — see FALSE 1
 4 small in degree ⟨On the *off* chance that you do get straight A's, you can skip a grade.⟩ — see REMOTE 1

off *adv* from this or that place ⟨Move *off* a few yards before I throw the football.⟩ — see AWAY

offbeat *adj* 1 different from the ordinary in a way that causes curiosity or suspicion ⟨an *offbeat* approach to the task, but it gets the job done⟩ — see ODD 2

2 noticeably different from what is generally found or experienced ⟨This writer has an enjoyably *offbeat* sense of humor.⟩ — see UNUSUAL 1

offend *vb* **1** to commit an offense ⟨Since this is the first time you've *offended*, we'll let you off lightly.⟩
synonyms err, fall, sin, transgress, trespass, wander
related words breach, break, infringe, violate; backslide, lapse; mess up
phrases break the law, fall from grace
near antonyms forgive, justify, pardon; regret, repent, rue
2 to cause hurt feelings or deep resentment in ⟨The visitor unintentionally *offended* his hosts terribly by failing to compliment them on the elaborately prepared meal.⟩ — see INSULT
3 to fail to keep ⟨The careless job *offended* the standards she had set for herself.⟩ — see VIOLATE 1

offender *n* a person who has committed a crime ⟨a program for first-time *offenders*⟩ — see CRIMINAL

offense *or* **offence** *n* **1** a breaking of a moral or legal code ⟨was fined for a minor *offense*⟩
synonyms breach, crime, debt, error, lawbreaking, malefaction, misdeed, misdoing, sin, transgression, trespass, violation, wrongdoing
related words felony, misconduct, misdemeanor, misfeasance; fault, foible, peccadillo; break, infringement; immorality, iniquity, sinfulness, vice, wickedness; corruption, debauchery, depravity, licentiousness; abuse, criminality, illegality, lawlessness, unlawfulness; descent, downfall, fall
near antonyms blamelessness, faultlessness, guiltlessness, impeccability, innocence; goodness, morality, righteousness, virtue, virtuousness
antonyms noncrime
2 the act or action of setting upon with force or violence ⟨After three consecutive first downs, the *offense* stalled at the 30 yard line.⟩ — see ATTACK 1
3 an act or expression showing scorn and usually intended to hurt another's feelings ⟨A diplomat never deliberately gives *offense*.⟩ — see INSULT
4 the feeling of being offended or resentful after a slight or indignity ⟨My mother was prone to take *offense* even at the most innocent remark.⟩ — see PIQUE

offensive *adj* **1** causing intense displeasure, disgust, or resentment ⟨I find your disrespectful attitude toward your grandparents very *offensive*.⟩ ⟨The smell of rotting food is quite *offensive*.⟩
synonyms abhorrent, abominable, appalling, awful, distasteful, dreadful, evil, foul, fulsome, gross, hideous, horrendous, horrible, horrid, loathsome, nasty, nauseating, nauseous, noisome, noxious, obnoxious, obscene, odious, repellent (*also* repellant), repugnant, repulsive, revolting, scandalous, shocking, sickening, ugly
related words exceptionable, objectionable; disagreeable, dislikable (*also* dislikeable), unpleasant; contemptible, despicable, detestable, hard, hateful; unhealthy, unsavory, unwholesome; execrable, lousy, miserable; shocking, sick, sickish, sickly, terrible, unspeakable, vile; off-putting, undesirable, unwanted, unwelcome; distressing, disturbing, upsetting
near antonyms acceptable, agreeable, alluring, appealing, attractive, blessed (*also* blest), desirable, enjoyable, felicitous, gratifying, heavenly, inviting, likable (*or* likeable), luscious, nice, palatable, pleasant, pleasing, pleasurable, satisfying, savory (*also* savoury), sweet, welcome; unexceptionable, unobjectionable
antonyms innocuous, inoffensive
2 provoking or likely to provoke protest ⟨insensitive, *offensive* remarks⟩ — see OBJECTIONABLE

offensive *n* the act or action of setting upon with force or violence ⟨The primary *offensive* by the ground forces will commence at dawn tomorrow.⟩ — see ATTACK 1

offer *n* **1** an effort to do or accomplish something ⟨Dan made the usual halfhearted *offer* to grab the check before his dinner companion could.⟩ — see ATTEMPT 1
2 something which is presented for consideration ⟨a job *offer* that I couldn't refuse⟩ — see PROPOSAL

offer *vb* **1** to put before another for acceptance or consideration ⟨I *offered* my boss an alternative to the original plan, which would have required me to work overtime.⟩
synonyms extend, give, proffer, tender
related words pose, propose; hold out; give in, submit; volunteer
phrases run by (*or* run past)
near antonyms accept, take; accredit, approbate, approve, authorize, clear, confirm, finalize, formalize, OK (*or* okay), ratify, sanction, warrant; decline, deny, disallow, disapprove, negative, reject, turn down, veto; rebuff, rebut, refuse, spurn; retract, withdraw; disregard, ignore, neglect, overlook
2 to set before the mind for consideration ⟨I *offered* the idea of a vacation at a beach resort in the Caribbean.⟩ — see PROPOSE 1
3 to bring before the public in performance or exhibition ⟨a summer theater *offering* a full schedule of musicals to the vacationing public⟩ — see PRESENT 1
4 to give up as an offering to a god ⟨When fruits, flowers, or crops are *offered*, the offering is known as a bloodless sacrifice.⟩ — see SACRIFICE

offering *n* something offered to a god ⟨Some ancient gods were thought to demand burnt *offerings*.⟩ — see SACRIFICE

offhand *adj* made or done without previous thought or preparation ⟨an *offhand* comment that later caused the politician much embarrassment⟩ — see EXTEMPORANEOUS

offhanded *adj* made or done without previous thought or preparation ⟨a quick, *offhanded* suggestion that was actually much better than any of the prepared proposals⟩ — see EXTEMPORANEOUS

office *n* **1** a large unit of a governmental, business, or educational organization ⟨The company's main *office* is in Atlanta.⟩ — see DIVISION 2
2 something one must do because of prior agreement ⟨One of the chief *offices* of a friend is to be there in someone's hour of need.⟩ — see OBLIGATION 1

officeholder *n* a person who holds a public office ⟨The last *officeholder* was extremely conscientious about not using public funds for his personal gain.⟩ — see OFFICIAL

officer *n* **1** a member of a force charged with law enforcement at the local level ⟨If you are ever lost, find the nearest *officer* and ask for help.⟩
synonyms cop, policeman, police officer
related words patrolman, policewoman; detective, inspector, investigator, plainclothesman, sleuth; marshal (*also* marshall), sheriff, trooper; peace officer; captain, sergeant; constabulary, heat [*slang*], police, police force; operative
near antonyms civilian
2 a person who holds a public office ⟨an *officer* of the court⟩ — see OFFICIAL

official *adj* ordered or allowed by those in authority ⟨The *official* languages for those Olympic Games were French and English.⟩
synonyms authorized, sanctioned
related words lawful, legal, legitimate, permissible, regulation; approved, endorsed (*also* indorsed); abetted, encouraged, promoted, suggested, supported; licensed; authoritative, canonical, ex officio; semiofficial

near antonyms illegal, illegitimate, illicit, impermissible, lawless, unlawful, wrongful; unapproved, unlicensed

antonyms nonofficial, unauthorized, unofficial, unsanctioned

official *n* a person who holds a public office ⟨Some of our best public *officials* do their jobs quietly and are never in the news.⟩

synonyms functionary, officeholder, officer, public servant

related words bureaucrat; administrator, commissioner, director, executive, head, manager, regulator, superintendent, supervisor; chair, chairman; flunky (*also* flunkey *or* flunkie), minion, underling; co-official

officious *adj* thrusting oneself where one is not welcome or invited ⟨an *officious* little man who was always telling everyone else how to do their jobs⟩ — see INTRUSIVE

offing *n* time that is to come ⟨Major changes are in the *offing* for the company.⟩ — see FUTURE 1

offset *n* 1 a force or influence that makes an opposing force ineffective or less effective ⟨A better performance this time will be an *offset* to last year's dismal showing.⟩ — see COUNTERBALANCE

2 the stopping of a process or activity ⟨symptoms that were striking for their abrupt onset and their equally abrupt *offset*⟩ — see END 1

offset *vb* to balance with an equal force so as to make ineffective ⟨If you get a high grade on this quiz, it will *offset* the D from your last one.⟩

synonyms annul, cancel (out), compensate (for), correct, counteract, counterbalance, counterpoise, make up (for), neutralize

related words invalidate, negate, neuter, nullify; atone (for); outbalance, outweigh, redeem; redress, relieve, remedy; override, overrule

offshoot *n* 1 a branch of a main stem especially of a plant ⟨We knew the rosebush had survived the harsh winter when it began producing *offshoots* and turning green again.⟩

synonyms outgrowth, shoot

related words excrescence, growth; bough, branchlet, limb; floret; spray, sprig, spur

2 something that naturally develops or is developed from something else ⟨opened a shop selling fancy foods as an *offshoot* of their very successful restaurant⟩ — see DERIVATIVE

offspring *n* the descendants of a person, animal, or plant ⟨The racehorse's *offspring* all proved to be very good racers as well.⟩ ⟨The couple celebrated their 50th wedding anniversary surrounded by three generations of *offspring*.⟩

synonyms fruit, get, issue, posterity, progeny, seed, spawn

related words brood, hatch, litter, young; child, scion; family, kin; lineage, stock

near antonyms ancestor, antecedent, father, forebear (*also* forbear), forefather, grandfather, parent

oft *adv* many times ⟨As I have *oft* said, you need to look before you leap.⟩ — see OFTEN

often *adv* many times ⟨I seem to stumble *often* when I try to walk in high heels.⟩

synonyms constantly, continually, frequently, much, oft, oftentimes (*or* ofttimes), repeatedly

related words always, consistently, continuingly, continuously, perpetually, unceasingly; uninterruptedly; afresh, again, anew; commonly, habitually, ordinarily, regularly, routinely; intermittently, periodically, recurrently; generally, usually; consecutively

phrases a lot, time after time, time and again

near antonyms now, occasionally, sometimes, sporadically; ne'er, never

antonyms infrequently, little, rarely, seldom

oftentimes *or* **ofttimes** *adv* many times ⟨Children *oftentimes* don't realize how quickly time passes.⟩ — see OFTEN

ogle *vb* to look at in a flirtatious or desiring way ⟨I do wish you two would stop *ogling* each other during class.⟩

synonyms leer (at)

related words eye, gape, gawk, gaze, glare, goggle, peer, rubberneck, stare

phrases make eyes (at)

ogre *n* 1 a strange or horrible and often frightening creature ⟨a horror movie filled with *ogres* and demons of every description⟩ — see MONSTER 1

2 something or someone that causes fear or dread especially without reason ⟨The *ogre* of the standardized test keeps recurring.⟩ — see BOGEY 1

oh *n* the numerical symbol 0 or the absence of number or quantity represented by it ⟨The number is one-*oh*-two-four.⟩ — see ZERO 1

oil *n* a picture created with oil paint ⟨That artist is known to have created only *oils* and charcoal sketches.⟩ — see PAINTING

oil *vb* to coat (something) with a slippery substance in order to reduce friction ⟨If you *oil* the machinery on a regular basis, it will operate more efficiently.⟩ — see LUBRICATE

oiled *adj* having or being a surface so smooth as to greatly reduce traction ⟨Following the fuel spill, the resulting *oiled* stretch of roadway had to be closed to traffic.⟩ — see SLICK 1

oil painting *n* a picture created with oil paint ⟨We hung a beautiful *oil painting* of the bay on the living room wall.⟩ — see PAINTING

oilskin *n* a coat made of water-resistant material ⟨The *oilskins* worn by the fishing boat's crew gave them scant protection from the cold, driving rain.⟩ — see RAINCOAT

OK *or* **okay** *adj* 1 being to one's liking ⟨That dinner was *OK*, but I liked yesterday's better.⟩ — see SATISFACTORY 1

2 of a level of quality that meets one's needs or standards ⟨This latest draft of the essay is *OK* but could be better.⟩ — see ADEQUATE

OK *or* **okay** *adv* 1 in a satisfactory way ⟨You did *OK* on that last test.⟩ — see WELL 1

2 used to express agreement ⟨*OK*, fine, I'll go to the party!⟩ — see YES

OK *or* **okay** *n* an acceptance of something as satisfactory ⟨Our supervisor gave his *OK* on the project, so we can go ahead with it.⟩ — see APPROVAL

OK *or* **okay** *vb* 1 to give official acceptance of as satisfactory ⟨A judge will have to *OK* the search warrant.⟩ — see APPROVE

2 to have a favorable opinion of ⟨I'm glad that my parents *OK'd* my choice of colleges.⟩ — see APPROVE (OF)

old *adj* 1 being of advanced years and especially past middle age ⟨Every day the *old* fisherman set out in his small boat to brave the dangers of the sea.⟩ — see ELDERLY

2 dating or surviving from the distant past ⟨An extremely *old* piece of jewelry was discovered in the Egyptian ruins.⟩ — see ANCIENT 1

3 having been such at some previous time ⟨I ran into my *old* fourth-grade teacher yesterday.⟩ — see FORMER 1

4 causing weariness, restlessness, or lack of interest ⟨Even the most stirring speeches start to get *old* after you've heard them a few times.⟩ — see BORING

older *adj* being of advanced years and especially past middle age ⟨An *older* woman was the treasurer for the town.⟩ — see ELDERLY

oldfangled *adj* pleasantly reminiscent of an earlier time ⟨Those big solid-iron phones are an *oldfangled* reminder of the time when you had to rent a phone from the telephone company.⟩ — see OLD-FASHIONED 1

old–fashioned *adj* **1** pleasantly reminiscent of an earlier time ⟨an elegant, *old-fashioned* bun that was held in place with pearl hairpins⟩
synonyms antique, oldfangled, old-time, old-world, quaint, retro
related words antiquated, moldy, obsolete; historical, olden, traditional; old hat, outdated, outmoded, out-of-date, outworn, passé, superannuated; dated, fusty, moth-eaten, musty, stodgy; aged, age-old, ancient, antediluvian, hoary, venerable; bygone, erstwhile, former, late, past; forgotten, remote; anachronistic
near antonyms fresh, new; chic, designer, fashionable, smart, stylish; modernized, refurbished, remodeled, renewed, updated; last, latest; futuristic, high-tech (*also* hi-tech), latter-day, nontraditional; recent
antonyms contemporary, current, hot, mod, modern, modernistic, new age, newfangled, new-fashioned, present-day, red-hot, space-age, ultramodern, up-to-date
2 tending to favor established ideas, conditions, or institutions ⟨I'm so *old-fashioned* that I actually think people should use standard grammar and punctuation when composing e-mails.⟩ — see CONSERVATIVE 1
old hand *n* a person with long experience in a specified area ⟨With 25 years on the job, Vinnie was the *old hand* everyone went to with their problems.⟩ — see VETERAN
old lady *n* **1** a female human parent ⟨The story is that my *old lady* wanted to name me "Cecil," but the old man prevailed.⟩ — see MOTHER
2 a female partner in a marriage ⟨brought my *old lady* flowers on our anniversary⟩ — see WIFE
3 a female romantic companion ⟨went to the show with his *old lady*⟩ — see GIRLFRIEND
old man *n* **1** a male human parent ⟨I'll ask my *old man* if he's up for a round of golf this weekend.⟩ — see FATHER 1
2 a male partner in a marriage ⟨My *old man* and I have been together for 10 years now.⟩ — see HUSBAND
3 a male romantic companion ⟨My *old man* and I have decided to move in together.⟩ — see BOYFRIEND
oldster *n* a person of advanced years ⟨a family film that will appeal to youngsters and *oldsters* alike⟩ — see SENIOR CITIZEN
old–time *adj* pleasantly reminiscent of an earlier time ⟨an *old-time* song that took the long-married couple back to when they were first dating⟩ — see OLD-FASHIONED 1
old–timer *n* **1** a person of advanced years ⟨a group of *old-timers* playing shuffleboard⟩ — see SENIOR CITIZEN
2 a person with long experience in a specified area ⟨Old-timers in the fishing industry couldn't remember a time when catches were so low.⟩ — see VETERAN
old wives' tale *n* a false idea or belief ⟨The belief that going outside with wet hair will cause you to catch cold is just an *old wives' tale*.⟩ — see FALLACY 1
old–world *adj* pleasantly reminiscent of an earlier time ⟨The theater has been painstakingly restored to its *old-world* elegance.⟩ — see OLD-FASHIONED 1
omen *n* something believed to be a sign or warning of a future event ⟨Some people still believe that a black cat crossing your path is a bad *omen*.⟩
synonyms augury, auspice, boding, foreboding, foreshadowing, portent, prefiguring, presage
related words forerunner, harbinger, herald, precursor; foretaste, hint, inkling, intimation, suggestion; forewarning; forecast, foretelling, prediction, prognostication, prophecy (*also* prophesy)
phrases straw in the wind
ominous *adj* being or showing a sign of evil or calamity to come ⟨That comment about downsizing from the company president sounded *ominous*.⟩

synonyms baleful, dire, direful, foreboding, ill, inauspicious, menacing, portentous, sinister, threatening
related words black, bleak, cheerless, chill, cold, comfortless, dark, darkening, depressing, desolate, dim, disconsolate, dismal, drear, dreary, forlorn, funereal, gloomy, glum, godforsaken, gray (*also* grey), lonely, lonesome, lugubrious, miserable, morbid, morose, murky, saturnine, sepulchral, somber (*or* sombre), sullen, wretched; discouraging, disheartening, hopeless, unfavorable, unpromising, unpropitious; ill-fated, ill-starred, star-crossed, troubled, unfortunate, unlucky; evil, malign, malignant
near antonyms auspicious, benign, bright, encouraging, favorable, golden, heartening, hopeful, promising, propitious, prosperous
antonyms unthreatening
omission *n* something left out ⟨The disk contains a selection of deleted scenes, and a couple of the *omissions* greatly add to the intelligibility of the movie's plot.⟩
synonyms deletion
related words elimination; blank, skip; lapse, slip; deduction, reduction, subtraction; default, delinquency, dereliction, failure, neglect, negligence, oversight, pretermission; abbreviation, condensation
near antonyms inclusion; accretion, accrual, addendum, addition, augmentation, boost, expansion, gain, increase, increment
omit *vb* to miss the opportunity or obligation ⟨You must not *omit* mentioning the sources you used in researching your paper.⟩ — see NEGLECT 3
omnibus *adj* covering everything or all important points ⟨The president's state of the union speech is usually an *omnibus* look at the issues that the country is confronting.⟩ — see ENCYCLOPEDIC
omnipotent *adj* having unlimited power or authority ⟨the belief that God is *omnipotent* and omniscient⟩
synonyms all-powerful, almighty
related words great, sovereign (*also* sovran), supreme, towering; authoritative, majestic, master, masterful; mighty, potent, powerful, puissant, strong; divine, godlike; able, capable, competent, effective, efficient; authoritarian, autocratic (*also* autocratical), despotic, dictatorial, tyrannical (*also* tyrannic)
near antonyms helpless, impotent, powerless; limited, restricted; paralyzed, weak; incapable, incompetent, ineffective, ineffectual, inept, unfit, useless; feeble, frail, infirm
omnipresent *adj* present in all places and at all times ⟨seeking some much-needed relief from the *omnipresent* noise of the big city⟩
synonyms ubiquitous, universal
related words boundless, endless, horizonless, illimitable, immeasurable, indefinite, infinite, limitless, measureless, unbounded, unfathomable, unlimited; extensive, far-flung, widespread
near antonyms bounded, circumscribed, finite, limited, measured, narrow, restricted
on *adj* being in effective operation ⟨Please don't leave the sanding machine *on* if you're not going to be near it.⟩ — see ACTIVE 1
on *adv* **1** toward a point ahead in space or time ⟨We really must move *on* now if we're going to end this meeting before midnight.⟩ — see ONWARD 1
2 toward or at a point lying in advance in space or time ⟨He's getting *on* in years and doesn't see or hear as well as he used to.⟩ — see ALONG
on *prep* **1** having to do with ⟨Books *on* sports heroes are my favorite reading matter.⟩ — see ABOUT 1
2 in or into contact with ⟨Don't lean *on* that ladder—you'll knock it over.⟩ — see AGAINST

oncoming *adj* being soon to appear or take place ⟨We're looking forward to your *oncoming* visit.⟩ — see FORTH-COMING 1

one *adj* **1** being the one or ones of a class with no other members ⟨That's the *one* author I would stand in line for hours to get an autograph from.⟩ — see ONLY 2
2 known but not named ⟨*One* person that I know said that it was the best movie he had ever seen.⟩ — see CER-TAIN 1

one–dimensional *adj* having or showing a lack of depth of understanding or character ⟨a *one-dimensional* analy-sis of a novel that has a lot to say about personal cour-age⟩ — see SUPERFICIAL 2

onerous *adj* **1** difficult to endure ⟨He had an *onerous* and stressful job.⟩ — see HARSH 1
2 requiring much time, effort, or careful attention ⟨Building the scale model of the frigate was an *onerous* task.⟩ — see DEMANDING 1

one–sided *adj* inclined to favor one side over another ⟨My neighbor's account of how the feud got started was somewhat *one-sided*.⟩ — see PARTIAL 1

one–sidedness *n* an attitude that always favors one way of feeling or acting especially without considering any other possibilities ⟨The obvious *one-sidedness* of the host means that his radio talk show isn't the open forum that he pretends it is.⟩ — see BIAS 1

onetime *adj* having been such at some previous time ⟨The *onetime* English teacher now works for a newspaper.⟩ — see FORMER 1

ongoing *adj* **1** being in progress or development ⟨We do seem to be making some headway on that *ongoing* proj-ect.⟩ ⟨the ever *ongoing* quest for knowledge by men and women of science⟩
synonyms afoot, proceeding
related words functioning, happening, operating, work-ing; alive, going; advancing, continuing, gaining
near antonyms receding, regressing, retrogressing
antonyms arrested, ended, halted, stalled, stopped
2 existing or in progress right now ⟨the *ongoing* presiden-tial campaign⟩ — see PRESENT 1
3 having an existence or validity that does not change or diminish ⟨an *ongoing* commitment to improving their community⟩ — see ABIDING

only *adj* **1** having no equal or rival for excellence or desir-ability ⟨The *only* way to really appreciate the beauty of the forest is to walk through it.⟩
synonyms incomparable, inimitable, matchless, nonpa-reil, peerless, unequaled (*or* unequalled), unexampled, unmatched, unparalleled, unrivaled (*or* unrivalled), un-surpassable, unsurpassed
related words alone, singular, unique; exceptional, ex-traordinary, rare, uncommon, unusual; awesome, beau-tiful, brave, capital, choice, classic, dandy, divine, excel-lent, fabulous, fantastic, fine, first-class, first-rate, grand, great, lovely, marvelous (*or* marvellous), par excellence, quality, sensational, splendid, stellar, sterling, superb, su-perior, superlative, swell, terrific, tip-top, top, top-notch, wonderful; better, preferred; exceptional, fancy, high-grade, special
phrases out of sight
near antonyms common, commonplace, everyday, fa-miliar, frequent, normal, ordinary, routine, ubiquitous, usual; inferior, lesser, worse, worst; deficient, dissatisfac-tory, lame, lousy, low, lower, off, paltry, poor, punk, sub-standard, unacceptable, unsatisfactory, wanting; low-grade, substandard; mediocre, second-class, second-rate; atrocious, awful, execrable, pathetic, rotten, terrible, vile, wretched
2 being the one or ones of a class with no other members

⟨That is the *only* possible right answer.⟩ ⟨We were the *only* passengers on the tour bus.⟩
synonyms alone, lone, one, singular, sole, solitary, spe-cial, unique
related words single, solo, unaccompanied, unattended; incomparable, inimitable, matchless, peerless, unequaled (*or* unequalled), unmatched, unparalleled, unrivaled (*or* unrivalled), unsurpassable, unsurpassed; distinct, dis-tinctive, individual, separate; nonce
near antonyms divers, manifold, multifarious, myriad; assorted, heterogenous, miscellaneous, mixed, motley, patchwork, promiscuous, varied; popular, prevailing, prevalent, rampant; perennial, recurrent, repeated

only *adv* **1** for nothing other than ⟨You're doing that *only* to annoy me!⟩ — see SOLELY 1
2 not long ago ⟨We won the election *only* six days ago.⟩ — see NEWLY
3 nothing more than ⟨I was *only* fooling when I said I saw a shark in the water.⟩ — see JUST 3

only *conj* if it were not for the fact that ⟨That's a very nice idea, *only* it won't help.⟩ — see EXCEPT

onrush *n* forward movement in time or place ⟨a sudden *onrush* of development in an area that was rural until very recently⟩ — see ADVANCE 1

onset *n* **1** the act or action of setting upon with force or violence ⟨The walls withstood the *onset* of the first bat-talion.⟩ — see ATTACK 1
2 the point at which something begins ⟨the claim that if you take enough vitamin C at the *onset* of a cold, you'll often recover faster⟩ — see BEGINNING

onslaught *n* the act or action of setting upon with force or violence ⟨The massive *onslaught* of enemy troops caught the country by surprise.⟩ — see ATTACK 1

onward *also* **onwards** *adv* **1** toward a point ahead in space or time ⟨We must continue to move *onward*, or we will not get there in time.⟩
synonyms ahead, forth, forward, on
near antonyms backward (*or* backwards)
2 toward or at a point lying in advance in space or time ⟨Work on the project has been continuing *onward* at a steady pace.⟩ — see ALONG

oodles *pl n* a considerable amount ⟨The neighbors let us know that they bought *oodles* of candy for Halloween this year.⟩ — see LOT 2

ooze *n* soft wet earth ⟨Our car tires sank deep in the *ooze*.⟩ — see MUD

ooze *vb* **1** to flow forth slowly through small openings ⟨Maple sap *oozed* slowly from the cut in the tree and into the bucket.⟩ — see EXUDE
2 to move slowly ⟨The rush hour traffic *oozed* along the interstate.⟩ — see CRAWL 2

oozy *adj* full of or covered with soft wet earth ⟨lost a shoe in the *oozy* field⟩ — see MUDDY 1

opacity *n* the quality or state of having a veiled or uncer-tain meaning ⟨The *opacity* of the abstract painter's works simply baffles many gallery visitors.⟩ — see OBSCURITY 1

opaque *adj* **1** having an often intentionally veiled or un-certain meaning ⟨Somehow listeners seem to connect with the songwriter, despite his deeply personal, often *opaque* lyrics.⟩ — see OBSCURE 1
2 not seen or understood clearly ⟨an *opaque* remark that seemed to hint that there would be future retaliation⟩ — see FAINT 1
3 not having or showing an ability to absorb ideas read-ily ⟨too *opaque* to recognize an insult⟩ — see STUPID 1

open *adj* **1** allowing passage without obstruction ⟨Thank you for clearing out the hallway so that it's *open* again.⟩
synonyms clear, cleared, free, unclogged, unclosed, un-obstructed, unstopped

related words enterable, navigable, passable; emptied, empty, unoccupied, vacant; exposed, revealed; gaping, wide, yawning; unbarred, unbolted, unclasped, unfastened, unlatched, unlocked, unsealed

near antonyms impassable (*also* impassible); constricted, cramped, encumbered, hampered, hindered, impeded, interfered (with), trammeled (*or* trammelled); barricaded, blockaded, dammed, gated

antonyms blocked, clogged, closed, jammed, obstructed, plugged, shut, stopped, stuffed, uncleared

2 freely available for use or participation by all ⟨The lanes at the bowling alley will be *open* during the afternoon, but will be available only for league play in the evening.⟩

synonyms free-for-all, public, unrestricted

related words collective, common, communal, shared; accessible, available, free; unregulated, unreserved

near antonyms limited; inaccessible, unavailable

antonyms closed, exclusive, off-limits, private, restricted

3 being in a situation where one is likely to meet with harm ⟨By being secretive about the incident, he makes himself *open* to political attack.⟩ — see LIABLE 1

4 free in expressing one's true feelings and opinions ⟨a talkative and *open* child who tells people more than they want to know⟩ — see FRANK

5 lacking a usual or natural covering ⟨*open* wounds in his legs⟩ — see NAKED 2

6 not known by only a select few ⟨The two boxers have an *open* dislike for each other.⟩ — see PUBLIC 1

7 not yet settled or decided ⟨That issue will have to remain *open* until the supervisor can decide.⟩ — see PENDING 1

8 willing to consider new or different ideas ⟨She is always *open* and ready to listen to anyone's suggestions.⟩ — see OPEN-MINDED 1

9 giving or sharing in abundance and without hesitation ⟨He's very *open* with his opinions.⟩ — see GENEROUS 1

open *n* that part of the physical world that is removed from human habitation ⟨a daguerreotype of a cowboy whose face is roughened from a hard life in the *open*⟩ — see NATURE 2

open *vb* **1** to change from a closed to an open position ⟨Please *open* the door to let the cat out.⟩

synonyms unclose

related words unbar, unbolt, unclasp, unfasten, unlatch, unlock; unbutton, unclench, unfold, unzip; disengage, release, slip

near antonyms bar, bolt, clasp, fasten, latch, lock; button (up), zip (up)

antonyms close, shut

2 to make passage through (something) possible by removing obstructions ⟨We need to *open* this drain that's clogged with hair.⟩

synonyms clear, free, unclog, unstop

related words ease, facilitate, loosen (up), smooth

near antonyms constrict, encumber, hamper, hinder, impede, interfere (with), obstruct, trammel; barricade, blockade

antonyms block, clog (up), close, dam (up), plug (up), stop

3 to arrange the parts of (something) over a wider area ⟨When we got too close, the cardinal *opened* its wings and flew to a higher branch.⟩

synonyms expand, extend, fan (out), flare (out), outspread, outstretch, spread (out), stretch (out), unfold

related words overspread

near antonyms compact, compress, condense, reduce

antonyms close, contract, fold

4 to rid the surface of (as an area) from things in the way

⟨Snowplows *opened* the runway without much trouble.⟩ — see CLEAR 1

5 to take the first step in (a process or course of action) ⟨We will *open* the proceedings tomorrow with a short ceremony.⟩ — see BEGIN 1

open–air *adj* of, relating to, or held in the open air ⟨an *open-air* concert under the stars⟩ — see OUTDOOR

open air *n* that part of the physical world that is removed from human habitation ⟨a family of city dwellers who can't wait to go camping in the *open air*⟩ — see NATURE 2

open–and–shut *adj* not subject to misinterpretation or more than one interpretation ⟨an *open-and-shut* case⟩ — see CLEAR 2

open–eyed *adj* paying close attention usually for the purpose of anticipating approaching danger or opportunity ⟨An *open-eyed* deer cautiously grazed in the backyard.⟩ — see ALERT 1

openhanded *adj* giving or sharing in abundance and without hesitation ⟨In the aftermath of the disaster, many people were exceptionally *openhanded* with their donations to charity.⟩ — see GENEROUS 1

openhandedly *adv* in a generous manner ⟨The CEO *openhandedly* gave the intern advice about succeeding in the business.⟩ — see WELL 2

openhandedness *n* the quality or state of being generous ⟨The foundation has a reputation for *openhandedness* when it comes to environmental causes.⟩ — see LIBERALITY

openhearted *adj* free in expressing one's true feelings and opinions ⟨Many therapists believe that it is better to be *openhearted* than to repress one's feelings.⟩ — see FRANK

openheartedness *n* **1** the free expression of one's true feelings and opinions ⟨The *openheartedness* with which he discussed his private life often startled new acquaintances.⟩ — see CANDOR 1

2 the quality or state of being generous ⟨Their natural *openheartedness* made them easy prey for every trickster with a sad story.⟩ — see LIBERALITY

opening *n* **1** a favorable combination of circumstances, time, and place ⟨The talk show host's usual modus operandi is to talk over his guests, thereby denying them an *opening* to articulate their positions.⟩ — see OPPORTUNITY

2 a place in a surface allowing passage into or through a thing ⟨An *opening* in the roof is letting rain drip inside.⟩ — see HOLE 1

3 an open space in a barrier (as a wall or hedge) ⟨The rabbit found a little *opening* in the bushes and darted through it.⟩ — see GAP 1

open–minded *adj* **1** willing to consider new or different ideas ⟨All I ask is that you try to be *open-minded* when we present all our suggestions.⟩

synonyms broad-minded, open, receptive

related words impartial, neutral, objective, unbiased, unprejudiced; easygoing, nonjudgmental, tolerant; calm, detached, dispassionate; amenable, compliant; impressionable, suggestible, susceptible; persuadable, persuasible

near antonyms biased, narrow, one-sided, partial, partisan, prejudiced; bigoted, intolerant

antonyms narrow-minded, unreceptive

2 not bound by traditional ways or beliefs ⟨Younger people are often more *open-minded* on social and political issues.⟩ — see LIBERAL 1

openmouthed *adj* filled with amazement or wonder ⟨The stunning view from the mountaintop left us *openmouthed* and at a loss for words.⟩

synonyms amazed, astonished, astounded, awed, awestruck (*also* awestricken), dumbfounded (*also* dumfounded), flabbergasted, marveling (*or* marvelling), wondering

related words startled, surprised (*also* surprized); bewildered, puzzled; overwhelmed, staggered, stunned, stupefied

near antonyms unimpressed; disinterested, incurious, indifferent, unconcerned, uninterested; dispassionate, impassive, unemotional; bored, jaded

openness *n* **1** the free expression of one's true feelings and opinions ⟨Her *openness* was refreshing after the tiresome coyness of her friends.⟩ — see CANDOR 1

2 the state of being left without shelter or protection against something harmful ⟨Doctors are concerned about the population's *openness* to the new strain of the flu virus.⟩ — see EXPOSURE 1

open sesame *n* something that allows someone to achieve a desired goal ⟨It turned out that a simple "please" was the *open sesame* for charming the hotel manager into giving us a room with a better view.⟩ — see PASSPORT 1

operable *adj* capable of or suitable for being used for a particular purpose ⟨The historic wooden ship has been fully restored and is once again an *operable* seafaring vessel.⟩ — see USABLE 1

operate *vb* **1** to control the mechanical operation of ⟨Do not *operate* heavy machinery, including cars, after taking this medication.⟩

synonyms handle, run, work

related words use; maneuver, manipulate, ply, wield; command, control, direct, drive, guide, pilot, steer

2 to look after and make decisions about ⟨It takes years to learn how to *operate* that kind of business so that it makes money.⟩ — see CONDUCT 1

3 to produce a desired effect ⟨The medicine will take an hour or so to *operate* the first time you use it.⟩ — see ACT 2

4 to put into action or service ⟨Use protective eyewear when *operating* the machine.⟩ — see USE 1

operating *adj* being in effective operation ⟨the only *operating* nuclear power plant in the state⟩ — see ACTIVE 1

operation *n* **1** a specific task with which a person or group is charged ⟨a secret *operation* which, if it is discovered, the government will deny any knowledge of⟩ — see MISSION

2 a usually fixed or ordered series of actions or events leading to a result ⟨A specific mathematical *operation* is required in order to get the correct answer.⟩ — see PROCESS 1

3 the act or activity of looking after and making decisions about something ⟨*Operation* of the business fell to the founder's children.⟩ — see CONDUCT 1

4 the act or practice of employing something for a particular purpose ⟨A considerable amount of training is required for the *operation* of these new high-tech machines.⟩ — see USE 1

operational *adj* being in effective operation ⟨a fully *operational* oil refinery⟩ — see ACTIVE 1

operative *adj* **1** being in effective operation ⟨the last *operative* bookbinder of its kind in the business⟩ — see ACTIVE 1

2 producing or capable of producing a desired result ⟨Unfortunately, the *operative* amount of the medication and the lethal amount were too close for it to be used safely.⟩ — see EFFECTIVE 1

operative *n* **1** a person who tries secretly to obtain information for one country in the territory of another usually unfriendly country ⟨CIA *operatives* take terrible risks to find out the secrets of foreign countries.⟩ — see SPY

2 a person not on the police force who investigates criminal or illicit activity or searches for missing persons ⟨Set in the 1930s, the novel is about a washed-out *operative*

working for a third-rate detective agency.⟩ — see DETECTIVE

opiate *adj* tending to cause sleep ⟨Morphine is an *opiate* drug.⟩ — see HYPNOTIC

opiate *n* something that soothes, calms, or induces passivity or a sense of security ⟨a cultural critic who argues that the Internet has now joined television as an *opiate* of the American people⟩

synonyms narcotic

related words pacifier, palliative; hypnotic, sedative, tranquilizer (*also* tranquillizer)

opine *vb* to make a statement of one's opinion ⟨Some people *opined* that the coverage was biased.⟩ — see REMARK 1

opinion *n* **1** an idea that is believed to be true or valid without positive knowledge ⟨In my *opinion*, it's the best car on the market.⟩

synonyms belief, conviction, eye, feeling, judgment (*or* judgement), mind, notion, persuasion, sentiment, verdict, view

related words say; impression, perception, take; assumption, presumption, presupposition; conclusion, decision, determination; deliverance, estimate, estimation; credence, credit, faith; concept, conception, idea, thought; position, stance, stand; comment, observation, reflection, remark; conjecture, guess, hunch, hypothesis, surmise, theory; advice, input, recommendation, suggestion; angle, outlook, perspective, shoes, slant, standpoint, viewpoint; counterview

near antonyms fact, truth

2 a position arrived at after consideration ⟨After reviewing the evidence, the athletic board came to the *opinion* that the team be disqualified for recruiting violations.⟩ — see DECISION 1

opinionated *adj* sticking to an opinion, purpose, or course of action in spite of reason, arguments, or persuasion ⟨an *opinionated* professor who often clashes with students who dare to disagree with him⟩ — see OBSTINATE

opponent *n* **1** one that takes a position opposite another in a competition or conflict ⟨In martial arts, before the match begins, always bow to your *opponent*.⟩

synonyms adversary, antagonist, foe, rival

related words equal, match; enemy; archenemy, nemesis; competitor, contestant; combatant

near antonyms accomplice, ally, confederate, partner; advocate, champion, exponent, proponent, supporter, sympathizer

2 one that is hostile toward another ⟨The senator has many political *opponents* who would love to ruin his career.⟩ — see ENEMY

opportune *adj* especially suitable for a certain time ⟨An *opportune* rain shower gave them an excuse to leave the outdoor concert early.⟩ — see TIMELY 1

opportunist *n* **1** a person who dexterously and expediently changes or adopts opinions ⟨Ever the *opportunist*, she immediately set about becoming the incoming administrator's new best friend.⟩ — see ACROBAT 2

2 one who does things only for his own benefit and with little regard for right and wrong ⟨an *opportunist* who makes friends and then drops them as soon as they aren't useful anymore⟩ — see SELF-SEEKER

opportunity *n* a favorable combination of circumstances, time, and place ⟨This art school could be a wonderful *opportunity* for you to finally develop your talent for painting.⟩

synonyms break, chance, occasion, opening, room, shot

related words play, way; juncture, pass

oppose *vb* **1** to refuse to give in to ⟨I will continue to *oppose* any attempts to infringe upon our civil liberties.⟩ — see RESIST

2 to strive to reduce or eliminate ⟨We must *oppose* ignorance and prejudice wherever and whenever they arise.⟩ — see FIGHT 2

opposite *adj* being as different as possible ⟨Those two are fundamentally *opposite*—she being loquacious and outgoing where he is quiet and reserved.⟩

synonyms antipodal, antipodean, antithetical, contradictory, contrary, diametric (*or* diametrical), polar

related words adverse, negative, unfavorable; antagonistic, antipathetic, counter, cross, hostile; converse, inverse, reverse; alien, disparate, dissimilar, divergent, unalike, unlike

near antonyms alike, analogous, like, similar; equivalent, identical, same; synonymous

antonyms noncontradictory

opposite *n* something that is as different as possible from something else ⟨No matter what I say, you insist on the *opposite*.⟩

synonyms antipode, antithesis, contrary, counter, negative, reverse

related words negation; antonym; counterpoint; converse, inverse

near antonyms synonym; analogue (*or* analog), counterpart; carbon copy, copy, duplicate, replica

opposition *n* the inclination to resist ⟨The regulation faces *opposition* from the business community.⟩ — see RESISTANCE 1

oppress *vb* 1 to make sad ⟨This gloomy weather is *oppressing* all of us.⟩ — see DEPRESS 1

2 to subject to incapacitating emotional or mental stress ⟨a film about a man who is haunted and *oppressed* by the secrets of his past⟩ — see OVERWHELM 1

oppression *n* a state or spell of low spirits ⟨He suffered a lingering *oppression* of spirits in the weeks after his friend moved away.⟩ — see SADNESS

oppressive *adj* difficult to endure ⟨The country is ruled by an *oppressive* regime.⟩ — see HARSH 1

oppressively *adv* in a manner so as to cause loss or suffering ⟨forced to live under an *oppressively* cruel government⟩ — see HARDLY 1

oppressor *n* a person who uses power or authority in a cruel, unjust, or harmful way ⟨The dictatorship had scarcely been overthrown when the formerly oppressed suddenly abandoned their democratic ideals and became the *oppressors*.⟩ — see DESPOT

opprobrious *adj* marked by harsh insulting language ⟨an *opprobrious* comment posted on the website⟩ — see ABUSIVE

opprobrium *n* 1 a cause of shame ⟨cynically uses "optimist" as a term of *opprobrium*⟩ — see DISGRACE 2

2 the state of having lost the esteem of others ⟨the *opprobrium* that was long attached to the convicted embezzler's name⟩ — see DISGRACE 1

opt *vb* to come to a judgment about after discussion or consideration ⟨After that emergency, they *opted* to reinstate the telephone service.⟩ — see DECIDE 1

opt (for) *vb* to decide to accept (someone or something) from a group of possibilities ⟨I *opted for* the smaller car after I calculated how much money I would save on gas every week.⟩ — see CHOOSE 1

optic *adj* of, relating to, or used in vision ⟨the *optic* nerve⟩ — see VISUAL 1

optical *adj* of, relating to, or used in vision ⟨an *optical* illusion that fools most people⟩ — see VISUAL 1

optimism *n* an inclination to believe in the most favorable outcome ⟨your perpetual *optimism* even when things look bleak⟩

synonyms sanguinity

related words brightness, cheerfulness, perkiness, sunniness; hope, hopefulness, rosiness; idealism

near antonyms skepticism; apprehension, caution, concern; cynicism; despair, desperation, discouragement, disheartenment, hopelessness; bleakness, cheerlessness, dreariness, gloominess; pragmatism

antonyms bearishness, pessimism

optimistic *adj* having qualities which inspire hope ⟨The economic predictions for the coming year are actually quite *optimistic*.⟩ — see HOPEFUL 1

option *n* 1 something that is not necessary in itself but adds to the convenience or performance of the main piece of equipment ⟨a slew of *options* that would add several thousand dollars to the base price of the car⟩ — see ACCESSORY 1

2 the power, right, or opportunity to choose ⟨You will have the *option* to select one of several quite different health insurance plans.⟩ — see CHOICE 1

optional *adj* subject to one's freedom of choice ⟨At the resort all recreational activities are *optional*, and you may choose to participate in none of them.⟩

synonyms discretionary, elective, voluntary

related words alternate, alternative, chosen; dispensable, unnecessary, unneeded, unwanted

near antonyms essential, indispensable, necessary, requisite

antonyms compulsory, mandatory, nonelective, nonvoluntary, obligatory, required

opulence *n* the total of one's money and property ⟨In some parts of the city nearly unimaginable *opulence* can be found side by side with nearly unthinkable poverty.⟩ — see WEALTH 1

opulent *adj* 1 having goods, property, or money in abundance ⟨an *opulent* upper crust that liked to show off its possessions⟩ — see RICH 1

2 showing obvious signs of wealth and comfort ⟨an *opulent* mansion filled with priceless art and antiques⟩ — see LUXURIOUS

opulently *adv* in a luxurious manner ⟨an *opulently* furnished palace⟩ — see HIGH

opus *n* a literary, musical, or artistic production ⟨The composer's final *opus* was performed posthumously to great acclaim.⟩ — see COMPOSITION 1

oral *adj* 1 expressed or communicated by voice ⟨A baby's crying is usually interpreted as an *oral* expression of distress.⟩ — see VOCAL

2 made or carried on through speaking rather than in writing ⟨Lawyers for the plaintiff will be presenting *oral* arguments before the Supreme Court next week.⟩ — see VERBAL 2

orate *vb* 1 to talk as if giving an important and formal speech ⟨Given the opportunity, many politicians will *orate* at considerable length on just about any subject.⟩

synonyms declaim, discourse, harangue, mouth (off)

related words rant, rave; lecture, preach, sermonize; advertise, announce, broadcast, declare, proclaim, pronounce; speak, speechify, talk

2 to give a formal often extended talk on a subject ⟨The respected anthropologist is expected to *orate* about her latest research findings before a packed auditorium.⟩ — see TALK 1

oration *n* a usually formal discourse delivered to an audience ⟨the celebrated *orations* of Daniel Webster in unwavering support of the federal union⟩ — see SPEECH 1

oratorical *adj* marked by the use of impressive-sounding but mostly meaningless words and phrases ⟨a speech that was an *oratorical* endorsement of the value of education⟩ — see RHETORICAL 1

oratory *n* 1 the art of speaking in public eloquently and effectively ⟨a presidential hopeful with a gift for *oratory* and a highly charismatic personality⟩

synonyms elocution

related words bombast, grandiloquence; eloquence, rhetoric; discourse, speech, talk

2 language that is impressive-sounding but not meaningful or sincere ⟨The politician's *oratory* sounded good only to people who didn't bother to think.⟩ — see RHETORIC 1

orb *n* a more or less round body or mass ⟨Out of the countless celestial *orbs* twirling in space, the planet Earth remains the only one we can call home, so perhaps we should take care of it.⟩ — see ¹BALL 1

orbit *vb* to travel completely around ⟨The moon *orbits* the Earth.⟩ — see ENCIRCLE 1

orchestra *n* a usually large group of musicians playing together ⟨The *orchestra* will be performing a selection of Beethoven pieces tomorrow night.⟩ — see ²BAND 1

ordain *vb* **1** to determine the fate of in advance ⟨He is stoic in the face of adversity, bolstered by his faith that everything in life has been *ordained* by a higher power.⟩ — see DESTINE

2 to request the doing of by virtue of one's authority ⟨a new bill that would *ordain* the funding of public schools through state lottery revenues⟩ — see COMMAND 2

3 to put into effect through legislative or authoritative action ⟨The founders of the African republic *ordained* a form of government that was closely modeled on that of the United States.⟩ — see ENACT

ordeal *n* a test of faith, patience, or strength ⟨The hikers were finally rescued after a three-day *ordeal* in the wilderness.⟩ — see TRIAL 1

order *n* **1** the way objects in space or events in time are arranged or follow one another ⟨You always keep your books in perfect alphabetical *order*.⟩ ⟨We haven't found out the *order* of the speeches yet.⟩

synonyms arrangement, array, disposal, disposition, distribution, ordering, sequence, setup

related words precedence, priority; chain, procession, progression, succession; series; aligning (*also* alining), alignment (*also* alinement); lining up; design, layout, pattern, structure, system

near antonyms confusion, disorder, disorganization, disruption, upset; disconnection, disjointedness

2 a group of persons formally joined together for some common interest ⟨a religious *order*⟩ — see ASSOCIATION 2

3 a number of persons or things that are grouped together because they have something in common ⟨Don collects movie posters, photographs and autographs of the stars, and other memorabilia of that *order*.⟩ — see SORT 1

4 a piece of metal given in honor of a special event, a person, or an achievement ⟨a book with full-color illustrations of British *orders* and decorations⟩ — see MEDAL

5 a state of being or fitness ⟨We finally got the car back in working *order*.⟩ — see CONDITION 1

6 a statement of what to do that must be obeyed by those concerned ⟨The commander issued an *order* that the number of guards for the prisoner be doubled.⟩ — see COMMAND 1

7 one of the segments of society into which people are grouped ⟨The lower *orders* gradually gained a measure of equality.⟩ — see CLASS 1

8 one of the units into which a whole is divided on the basis of a common characteristic ⟨regards draftees as an entirely different *order* of soldier and less desirable than volunteers⟩ — see CLASS 2

order *vb* **1** to put into a particular arrangement ⟨I've *ordered* all of my books according to subject matter.⟩ ⟨He likes to *order* his life so that there are few surprises.⟩

synonyms arrange, array, classify, codify, dispose, draw up, lay out, marshal (*also* marshall), organize, range, systematize

related words make up, straighten (up); unscramble;

align (*also* aline), cue, line, line up, queue; alphabetize, file, prioritize, sequence; place, set; display, map (out)

antonyms derange, disarrange, disarray, disorder, mess (up), muss (up), rumple, upset

2 to give a request or demand for ⟨The players *ordered* hamburgers for lunch.⟩

synonyms ask (for), request, requisition

related words commission, solicit; charter, hire, license (*also* licence)

phrases call for

3 to request the doing of by virtue of one's authority ⟨The teacher *ordered* that everyone sit down immediately and be quiet.⟩ — see COMMAND 2

4 to issue orders to (someone) by right of authority ⟨The police officer *ordered* the crowd to back away from the accident.⟩ — see COMMAND 1

ordering *n* **1** a scheme of rank or order ⟨In the *ordering* of crimes, ripping the tags off upholstered furniture should rank fairly low.⟩ — see ³SCALE 1

2 the way objects in space or events in time are arranged or follow one another ⟨The *ordering* of the children in the procession was according to height.⟩ — see ORDER 1

orderly *adj* **1** being clean and in good order ⟨a small, unpretentious inn offering pleasant, *orderly* rooms⟩ — see NEAT 1

2 following a set method, arrangement, or pattern ⟨The consultant developed an *orderly* procedure that allows us to process our Internet sales much more quickly and efficiently.⟩ — see METHODICAL

ordinance *n* a rule of conduct or action laid down by a governing authority and especially a legislature ⟨A local *ordinance* forbids all street parking during snowstorms.⟩ — see LAW 1

ordinarily *adv* according to the usual course of things ⟨*Ordinarily*, I get off work at five, but this week I'm working late to meet a project deadline.⟩ — see NATURALLY 2

ordinary *adj* **1** being of the type that is encountered in the normal course of events ⟨It was a perfectly *ordinary* and undistinguished shirt.⟩

synonyms average, common, commonplace, everyday, normal, prosaic, routine, run-of-the-mill, standard, unexceptional, unremarkable, usual, workaday

related words regular, typical, unextraordinary; familiar, homely, plain, popular, vulgar; natural; customary, wonted; insignificant, trivial, unimportant; frequent, habitual; expected, predictable

phrases par for the course

near antonyms curious, funny, peculiar, quaint, queer; aberrant, anomalous, atypical, irregular, untypical; rare, scarce; fantastic (*also* fantastical), phenomenal; bizarre, far-out, outrageous, wacky (*also* whacky), way-out, weird, wild; eccentric, idiosyncratic, kooky (*also* kookie), nonconformist, oddball, offbeat, unconventional, unorthodox; freak, freakish; conspicuous, notable, outstanding, prominent, salient, signal, striking, unexampled, unprecedented; singular, unique, unparalleled

antonyms abnormal, exceptional, extraordinary, odd, out-of-the-way, strange, unusual

2 of average to below average quality ⟨The pizza at that restaurant is just *ordinary*—it's nothing to write home about.⟩ — see MEDIOCRE 1

3 often observed or encountered ⟨an *ordinary* hairstyle for boys of that age⟩ — see COMMON 1

ordnance *n* large firearms (as cannon or rockets) ⟨The army is waiting for the heavy *ordnance* to be brought in.⟩ — see ARTILLERY

oread *n* a mythical goddess represented as a young woman and said to live outdoors ⟨*Oreads* supposedly prefer to live in hills and mountains.⟩ — see NYMPH

organ *n* **1** a publication that appears at regular intervals ⟨That newspaper is intended as an *organ* for the whole university community.⟩ — see JOURNAL
2 something used to achieve an end ⟨She uses the business as an *organ* to fund a variety of political and social causes.⟩ — see AGENT 1
organization *n* a group of persons formally joined together for some common interest ⟨an *organization* of people devoted to promoting world peace⟩ — see ASSOCIATION 2
organize *vb* **1** to put into a particular arrangement ⟨carefully *organized* the hotel's silverware by pattern⟩ — see ORDER 1
2 to work out the details of (something) in advance ⟨We started *organizing* the anniversary party months in advance.⟩ — see PLAN 1
organized *adj* following a set method, arrangement, or pattern ⟨Our department is more *organized* and, therefore, more efficient in handling the tasks assigned to it.⟩ — see METHODICAL
orient *vb* to impart knowledge of a new thing or situation to ⟨a training program to *orient* new employees to the requirements and dimensions of the job⟩ — see ACQUAINT 1
orientate *vb* to impart knowledge of a new thing or situation to ⟨Guides will *orientate* all incoming freshmen to the layout of the campus.⟩ — see ACQUAINT 1
orifice *n* a place in a surface allowing passage into or through a thing ⟨The mouth is a bodily *orifice*.⟩ — see HOLE 1
origin *n* **1** a point or place at which something is invented or provided ⟨The *origins* of human language remain a matter of considerable debate.⟩ — see SOURCE 1
2 the source from which something grows or develops ⟨the *origin* of the tradition of giving presents on birthdays⟩ — see SEED 1
3 the line of ancestors from whom a person is descended ⟨They could trace their *origins* back 15 generations.⟩ — see ANCESTRY
original *adj* **1** coming before all others in time or order ⟨The *original* plan had to be discarded when the situation changed drastically.⟩ — see FIRST 1
2 having the skill and imagination to create new things ⟨an *original* artist who wanted his paintings to convey his emotional responses to the people, objects, and landscapes he painted⟩ — see CREATIVE 1
3 not known or experienced before ⟨separate categories for *original* and adapted screenplays⟩ — see NEW 2
original *n* something from which copies are made ⟨Please make copies to hand out, but keep the *original*.⟩
synonyms archetype, prototype
related words source; example, paradigm, pattern; beau ideal, classic, exemplar, ideal, model, nonpareil, paragon; blueprint, draft
near antonyms copy, imitation, replica, reproduction; counterfeit, fake, forgery, sham
originality *n* **1** the quality or appeal of being new ⟨The *originality* of the war memorial sparked a heated controversy, as most people had been expecting something more traditional.⟩ — see NOVELTY 1
2 the skill and imagination to create new things ⟨A poet of great *originality*, she brought a whole new range of subject matter and imagery to poetry.⟩ — see CREATIVITY 1
3 the ability to form mental images of things that either are not physically present or have never been conceived or created by others ⟨a graphic novel that shows a lot of *originality* on the part of its creator⟩ — see IMAGINATION 1

originally *adv* in the beginning ⟨We *originally* planned to go out tonight, but we changed our minds.⟩
synonyms firstly, initially, primarily
related words incipiently; primitively
phrases at first, to start with
near antonyms finally, lastly, ultimately
originate *vb* to come into existence ⟨The theory of relativity *originated* with Albert Einstein.⟩ — see BEGIN 2
originator *n* **1** one who creates or introduces something new ⟨Thomas Edison was the *originator* of the light bulb.⟩ — see INVENTOR
2 a person who establishes a whole new field of endeavor ⟨Copernicus is sometimes hailed as the *originator* of modern astronomy, for he overturned the notion of an earth-centered universe.⟩ — see FATHER 2
orison *n* an address to God or a deity ⟨a fervent *orison* asking for divine guidance in bringing about a peaceful solution to the grave international crisis⟩ — see PRAYER 1
ornament *n* something that decorates or beautifies ⟨a collection of plaster gnomes used as lawn *ornaments*⟩ — see DECORATION 1
ornament *vb* to make more attractive by adding something that is beautiful or becoming ⟨Delicate crystal figurines *ornament* the mantel over the fireplace.⟩ — see DECORATE
ornamental *adj* serving to add beauty ⟨The trim on Victorian houses is sometimes elaborately *ornamental*.⟩ — see DECORATIVE
ornamental *n* a small object displayed for its attractiveness or interest ⟨a collection of fragile *ornamentals* kept in a glass cabinet⟩ — see KNICKKNACK
ornate *adj* **1** elaborately and often excessively decorated ⟨an *ornate* gambling casino that is designed to look like an Italian palace⟩
synonyms bedizened, florid, fussy, gingerbread, overdecorated, overwrought
related words arabesque, rococo; extravagant, flamboyant, splashy; bedaubed, flashy, garish, gaudy, glitzy, loud, ostentatious, pretentious, showy, swank (*or* swanky), tawdry; elaborate, extreme; adorned, arrayed, beautified, bedecked, decorated, dressed, embellished, enriched, garnished, ornamented, trimmed; flowery, frilly, lacy, bejeweled (*or* bejewelled), bossed, chased, emblazoned, embossed, embroidered, flounced, fringed, garlanded, gilded (*or* gilt), laced, sequined (*or* sequinned), wreathed
near antonyms bare, denuded, exposed, naked, stripped, uncovered; modest, simple, unassuming, unpretentious; conservative, muted, quiet, restrained, subdued, tasteful, toned-down, understated, unobtrusive
antonyms austere, plain, severe, stark, unadorned
2 full of fine words and fancy expressions ⟨the *ornate* prose that was standard in all diplomatic correspondence in those days⟩ — see FLOWERY 1
ornery *adj* having or showing a habitually bad temper ⟨Our *ornery* neighbors blamed me for the trash on their lawn.⟩ — see ILL-TEMPERED
orthodox *adj* **1** following or agreeing with established form, custom, or rules ⟨Schoolteachers tended to favor poets who followed a very *orthodox* style of poetry.⟩ — see FORMAL 1
2 tending to favor established ideas, conditions, or institutions ⟨*Orthodox* in their view of the world, the Founding Fathers subscribed to the 18th-century notion that only men with property should be allowed to vote.⟩ — see CONSERVATIVE 1
oscillation *n* **1** the frequent and usually sudden passing from one condition to another ⟨fickle springtime weather in which there seemed to be an unceasing *oscillation*

between unseasonable heat and unseasonable cold⟩ — see FLUX 1

2 a series of slight movements by a body back and forth or from side to side ⟨the precise *oscillations* of the quartz crystal that allows a quartz watch to keep such accurate time⟩ — see VIBRATION 1

ossified *adj* sticking to an opinion, purpose, or course of action in spite of reason, arguments, or persuasion ⟨The company's *ossified* management team failed to see the technological revolution that was sweeping their own industry.⟩ — see OBSTINATE

ostensible *adj* appearing to be true on the basis of evidence that may or may not be confirmed ⟨The *ostensible* reason for the meeting turned out to be a trick to get him to the surprise party.⟩ — see APPARENT 1

ostensibly *adv* to all outward appearances ⟨*Ostensibly* a university student studying abroad, he was actually an espionage agent.⟩ — see APPARENTLY

ostentation *n* excessive or unnecessary display ⟨The sheer *ostentation* of the rock star's mansion was overwhelming.⟩
  synonyms flamboyance, flash, flashiness, garishness, gaudiness, glitz, ostentatiousness, pretentiousness, showiness, swank
  related words pretense (*or* pretence); pageant, parade, show; dazzle, fanfare, pageantry, pomp, razzmatazz; adornment, decoration, dressing, embellishment, garnishment, trimming; extravagance, fanciness, luxuriance, luxuriousness, magnificence, opulence, richness, sumptuousness; luridness; meretriciousness, tawdriness, vulgarity
  near antonyms moderation, modesty, restraint, simplicity, understatement; elegance, gracefulness, tastefulness; minimalism
  antonyms austerity, plainness, severity

ostentatious *adj* **1** excessively showy ⟨wears an *ostentatious* diamond ring on his little finger⟩ — see GAUDY
  2 self-consciously trying to present an appearance of grandeur or importance ⟨an *ostentatious* man who desperately wants to impress people with his newly acquired wealth⟩ — see PRETENTIOUS 1

ostentatiousness *n* excessive or unnecessary display ⟨the over-the-top *ostentatiousness* of the wedding banquet⟩ — see OSTENTATION

other *adj* **1** being not of the same kind ⟨No, I need the *other* pen, the blue one.⟩ — see DIFFERENT 1
  2 resulting in an increase in amount or number ⟨We'll be taking one *other* person on the trip.⟩ — see ADDITIONAL
  3 having been such at some previous time ⟨I was something of a celebrity in *other* days.⟩ — see FORMER 1

other than *prep* not including ⟨*Other than* a new jacket, I bought no special clothes for the wedding.⟩ — see EXCEPT

otherwise *adv* in a different way ⟨The candidate was gracious in his defeat, though he clearly wished the election had gone *otherwise*.⟩
  synonyms differently, else
  related words dissimilarly, diversely, variously
  near antonyms similarly
  antonyms likewise

ought (to) *vb* to be under necessity or obligation to ⟨You *ought to* buy him a new book to replace the one you lost.⟩ — see NEED 2

ounce *n* a very small amount ⟨An *ounce* of prevention is worth a pound of cure.⟩ — see PARTICLE 1

oust *vb* **1** to drive or force out ⟨She was *ousted* from her job after it was proven she'd been pilfering company supplies.⟩ — see EJECT 1
  2 to remove from a position of prominence or power (as a throne) ⟨The people finally rose up and *ousted* the corrupt dictator.⟩ — see DEPOSE 1

out *adj* **1** fully committed to achieving a goal ⟨He's *out* to get even with the guy who beat him last time around.⟩ — see DETERMINED 1
  2 not at a certain place ⟨Half the staff is *out* with the flu.⟩ — see ABSENT 1

out *adv* **1** in or into the open air ⟨You really should get *out* more.⟩ — see OUTDOORS
  2 with one's normal voice speaking the words ⟨The search parties were sent in different directions and told to cry *out* if they discovered anything.⟩ — see ALOUD
  3 to a full extent or degree ⟨When stretched *out*, the ribbon was just long enough.⟩ — see FULLY 1
  4 from this or that place ⟨People walked *out* of the darkened theater blinking their eyes.⟩ — see AWAY

out *n* the act or a means of getting or keeping away from something undesirable ⟨I really don't want to go to the party, and I've been searching for an *out*.⟩ — see ESCAPE 2

out *vb* **1** to become known ⟨The truth will *out* eventually.⟩ — see GET OUT 1
  2 to drive or force out ⟨Before moving in, we *outed* all the furry little creatures who had settled in the cabin over the winter.⟩ — see EJECT 1

out–and–out *adj* **1** having no exceptions or restrictions ⟨an *out-and-out* cheater at every game⟩ ⟨The story is not just an exaggeration, it's an *out-and-out* lie.⟩ — see ABSOLUTE 2
  2 trying all possibilities ⟨mounted an *out-and-out* effort to find the lost child⟩ — see EXHAUSTIVE 1

outbrave *vb* to oppose (something hostile or dangerous) with firmness or courage ⟨Completing the survival course is largely a matter of one's willingness to *outbrave* both the elements and the specter of total isolation.⟩ — see FACE 2

outbreak *n* **1** a sudden and usually temporary growth of activity ⟨There was an immediate *outbreak* of paper shuffling and a pretense of work when the supervisor passed through the room.⟩
  synonyms burst, flare, flare-up, flash, flicker, flurry, flutter, outburst, spurt
  related words recrudescence, recurrence, renewal; binge, jag, spree; boost, increase, pickup, upswing, upturn; eruption, explosion, paroxysm; deluge, flood, rush, spate, surge, volley; commotion, furor, uproar
  near antonyms calm, doldrums, slump
  2 open fighting against authority (as one's own government) ⟨The government quelled the *outbreak*.⟩ — see REBELLION 1

outburst *n* **1** a sudden intense expression of strong feeling ⟨The judge directed the courtroom spectators to refrain from any *outbursts* when the verdict was read.⟩
  synonyms agony, blaze, burst, eruption, explosion, fit, flare, flare-up, flash, flush, gale, gush, gust, paroxysm, spasm, storm
  related words blowup, grouch, rage, tantrum; ecstasy, rapture, transport; delirium, frenzy, furor
  2 a sudden and usually temporary growth of activity ⟨There was a remarkable *outburst* of work in the office as the visiting VIPs made their tour.⟩ — see OUTBREAK 1
  3 the act or an instance of exploding ⟨In the *outburst* known as a supernova, the star may reach an intrinsic luminosity one billion times that of the sun.⟩ — see EXPLOSION 1

outcast *n* one who is cast out or rejected by society ⟨The professor is something of an *outcast* in the halls of academe now that his former support of a dictatorial regime has become public.⟩
  synonyms castaway, castoff, pariah, reject
  related words untouchable; outsider; deportee, exile
  near antonyms insider

outclass *vb* to be greater, better, or stronger than ⟨a tennis player who *outclassed* the competition, breezing through the tournament without losing a set⟩ — see SURPASS 1

outcome *n* a condition or occurrence traceable to a cause ⟨One expected *outcome* of hard work is greater success.⟩ — see EFFECT 1

outcry *n* a violent shouting ⟨I went to the window to see what the sudden *outcry* from the street below was about.⟩ — see CLAMOR 1

outdated *adj* having passed its time of use or usefulness ⟨an *outdated* rotary telephone⟩ — see OBSOLETE

outdistance *vb* to be greater, better, or stronger than ⟨The new student rapidly *outdistanced* the rest of the class in math.⟩ — see SURPASS 1

outdo *vb* to be greater, better, or stronger than ⟨two vaccine developers who spent years vigorously trying to *outdo* one another's research⟩ — see SURPASS 1

outdoor *also* **outdoors** *adj* of, relating to, or held in the open air ⟨An *outdoor* picnic is always at the mercy of the weather, of course.⟩
synonyms open-air, out-of-door (*or* out-of-doors)
related words airy; exterior, external, outer, outside, outward; outermost, outmost
near antonyms inner, inside, interior, internal, inward; inmost, innermost
antonyms indoor

outdoors *adv* in or into the open air ⟨I can't wait to get *outdoors* and into the sunshine.⟩
synonyms out, outside
related words without
near antonyms in, inside, within
antonyms indoors

outdoors *n* that part of the physical world that is removed from human habitation ⟨Our family loves to hike and camp in the great *outdoors*.⟩ — see NATURE 2

outer *adj* situated on the outside or farther out ⟨The *outer* edge of the blade of your figure skate always wears out faster than the inner because you use it more.⟩
synonyms exterior, external, outside, outward
related words outermost, outlying, outmost; superficial, surface
near antonyms inmost, innermost; mid, middle, midmost
antonyms inner, inside, interior, internal, inward

outermost *adj* most distant from a center ⟨The *outermost* ring of listeners had trouble hearing the concert.⟩ — see EXTREME 1

outfit *n* **1** clothing chosen as appropriate for a specific situation ⟨The restaurant provides its waitstaff with themed *outfits*.⟩ ⟨Do you want to buy a new *outfit* for the Halloween party?⟩
synonyms costume, drag, dress, garb, getup, guise, togs
related words apparel, attire, clothes, duds, habiliment(s), raiment; fashion, mode, style; array, caparison
2 a commercial or industrial activity or organization ⟨They're an *outfit* specializing in travel tours for senior citizens.⟩ — see ENTERPRISE 1
3 a group of people working together on a task ⟨The whole *outfit* quit early for lunch.⟩ — see GANG 1
4 items needed for the performance of a task or activity ⟨For this class, you will need a professional camera *outfit* which includes at least one telephoto lens and one wide-angle lens.⟩ — see EQUIPMENT
5 the distinctive clothing worn by members of a particular group ⟨The highway patrol *outfit* includes jackboots and a high-crowned hat.⟩ — see UNIFORM

outfit *vb* to provide (someone) with what is needed for a task or activity ⟨*outfitted* the scuba instructors handsomely with all new gear⟩ — see FURNISH 1

outflow *n* a flowing or going out ⟨Over the last year the state experienced an unprecedented brain drain as the *outflow* of highly educated professionals exceeded the inflow.⟩
synonyms exodus, gush, outpouring
related words drain, flow; ebb, reflow, reflux; rush, stampede; diaspora, emigration, flight; discharge, effluence, emanation, emission
near antonyms deluge, flood, inundation, overflow, spate, torrent; river, stream, tide
antonyms flux, inflow, influx, inrush

outfox *vb* to get the better of through cleverness ⟨The prisoners *outfoxed* the guards by tunneling beneath the prison walls.⟩ — see OUTWIT

outgo *n* **1** a payment made in the course of achieving a result ⟨Last year the film company's *outgoes* exceeded its revenues by a wide margin.⟩ — see EXPENSE
2 the act of leaving a place ⟨The *outgo* of the town's only remaining manufacturing plant was hard on the local economy.⟩ — see DEPARTURE 1

outgoing *adj* likely to seek or enjoy the company of others ⟨a salesman whose aggressively *outgoing* personality could sometimes be overbearing⟩ — see CONVIVIAL

outgrowth *n* **1** a branch of a main stem especially of a plant ⟨trimmed back some of the tree's *outgrowths* so they wouldn't interfere with the power lines⟩ — see OFFSHOOT 1
2 a condition or occurrence traceable to a cause ⟨A predictable *outgrowth* of the suburb's ever growing population will be the need for more schools.⟩ — see EFFECT 1
3 something that naturally develops or is developed from something else ⟨an industry that is an *outgrowth* of the technology first developed for the U.S. space program⟩ — see DERIVATIVE

outing *n* a short trip for pleasure ⟨an *outing* to the zoo⟩ — see EXCURSION 1

outlander *n* a person who is not native to or known to a community ⟨Although we have lived in the village for years, to the families who have been here for generations, we are still *outlanders*.⟩ — see STRANGER

outlandish *adj* **1** different from the ordinary in a way that causes curiosity or suspicion ⟨an *outlandish* outfit made entirely out of bottle caps⟩ — see ODD 2
2 excitingly or mysteriously unusual ⟨the *outlandish* outfits on the people at the club⟩ — see EXOTIC

outlast *vb* to last longer than ⟨I truly hope this car will *outlast* our previous one.⟩ ⟨Your work will probably *outlast* you.⟩
synonyms outlive, outwear
related words survive; outstay; abide (beyond), endure (past), hold (past), hold out (past), last (beyond), persist (beyond); draw out, perpetuate; succeed

outlaw *vb* to order not to do or use or to be done or used ⟨Fed up with the constant interruptions, the physician has *outlawed* all cell phone use from his office.⟩ — see FORBID

outlawed *adj* that may not be permitted ⟨a pesticide that is *outlawed* in some states⟩ — see IMPERMISSIBLE

outlawing *n* the act of ordering that something not be done or used ⟨the *outlawing* of the use of plastic shopping bags by stores⟩ — see PROHIBITION 1

outlay *n* a payment made in the course of achieving a result ⟨The *outlays* for the couple's upcoming wedding seem to be multiplying at an incredible rate.⟩ — see EXPENSE

outlay *vb* to hand over or use up in payment ⟨The nation had *outlaid* nearly 20 billion dollars on social programs at that point.⟩ — see SPEND 1

outlet *n* a place or means of going out ⟨This road is the only *outlet* for traffic coming from the racetrack.⟩ — see EXIT 1

outline *n* **1** a line that traces the outer limits of an object or surface ⟨Place your hand on the paper and draw an *outline* around it.⟩
synonyms contour, figure, silhouette
related words delineation, sketch; profile, skyline; cast, configuration, conformation, form, geometry, shape; framework, skeleton
2 a short statement of the main points ⟨A printed *outline* of the lecture has been made available for all attendees.⟩ — see SUMMARY

outline *vb* **1** to draw or make apparent the outline of ⟨She carefully *outlined* the tree before she started drawing in the leaves.⟩
synonyms define, delineate, silhouette, sketch, trace
related words line; bound, fringe, margin, skirt; edge, hem, rim, trim; frame; circle, compass, encircle, girdle, girth, loop, ring, round, surround; chart, diagram, draw, map (out)
2 to make into a short statement of the main points (as of a report) ⟨*outlined* the important points in the introduction⟩ — see SUMMARIZE

outlive *vb* to last longer than ⟨Tortoises will *outlive* most people, as they live to be over 100 years old.⟩ — see OUTLAST

outlook *n* **1** a high place or structure from which a wide view is possible ⟨The cliff-top *outlook* provides an expansive view of the sleepy village down in the valley.⟩ — see LOOKOUT 1
2 a way of looking at or thinking about something ⟨I tried to keep a cheerful *outlook* on life.⟩ — see PERSPECTIVE 1
3 all that can be seen from a certain point ⟨The *outlook* from the tower is spectacular in all directions.⟩ — see VIEW 1

out loud *adv* with one's normal voice speaking the words ⟨registered their dissatisfaction with the meal *out loud* to the waiter⟩ — see ALOUD

outmaneuver *vb* to get the better of through cleverness ⟨*outmaneuvered* his congressional opponent by co-opting his call for change in Washington⟩ — see OUTWIT

outmoded *adj* having passed its time of use or usefulness ⟨*outmoded* computers that can be recycled⟩ — see OBSOLETE

outmost *adj* most distant from a center ⟨The *outmost* areas of the park, where few tourists venture, are still wilderness.⟩ — see EXTREME 1

out-of-date *adj* having passed its time of use or usefulness ⟨the sorely *out-of-date* information that one finds all too frequently online⟩ — see OBSOLETE

out-of-door *or* **out-of-doors** *adj* of, relating to, or held in the open air ⟨an *out-of-door* performance under the stars⟩ — see OUTDOOR

out-of-doors *n* that part of the physical world that is removed from human habitation ⟨Hiking in the *out-of-doors* can be a tremendous appetite builder.⟩ — see NATURE 2

out-of-the-way *adj* **1** different from the ordinary in a way that causes curiosity or suspicion ⟨a tell-all book that focuses obsessively on the *out-of-the-way* activities allegedly engaged in by the film star⟩ — see ODD 2
2 noticeably different from what is generally found or experienced ⟨There was nothing *out-of-the-way* about the suspect's appearance.⟩ — see UNUSUAL 1

outpouring *n* a flowing or going out ⟨an *outpouring* of affection and support for the high school athlete in need of an organ transplant⟩ — see OUTFLOW

output *n* something produced by physical or intellectual effort ⟨an author known for his prodigious literary *output*⟩ — see PRODUCT 1

outrage *n* **1** an act or expression showing scorn and usually intended to hurt another's feelings ⟨The booing during the graduation speech was an *outrage*.⟩ — see INSULT
2 an intense emotional state of displeasure with someone or something ⟨The actress could barely contain her *outrage* at being passed over for an Oscar yet again.⟩ — see ANGER

outrage *vb* **1** to cause hurt feelings or deep resentment in ⟨The spiteful comment *outraged* her so much that she's still holding a grudge.⟩ — see INSULT
2 to make angry ⟨The vandalism in the cemetery *outraged* the entire community.⟩ — see ANGER

outraged *adj* feeling or showing anger ⟨The judge was *outraged* to discover that several jurors had disregarded her orders not to speak with members of the press.⟩ — see ANGRY

outrank *vb* to be greater in importance than ⟨One hard fact *outranks* a mountain of speculation anytime.⟩ — see OUTWEIGH

outright *adj* having no exceptions or restrictions ⟨That's an *outright* lie!⟩ — see ABSOLUTE 2

outrun *vb* to go beyond the limit of ⟨Our expenses have been *outrunning* our revenues for some months now.⟩ — see EXCEED 1

outset *n* the point at which something begins ⟨I wish you'd mentioned this problem at the *outset*.⟩ — see BEGINNING

outshine *vb* to be greater, better, or stronger than ⟨The trumpeter *outshines* all of his fellow band members.⟩ — see SURPASS 1

outside *adj* **1** situated on the outside or farther out ⟨Slower moving vehicles should keep to the *outside* lane.⟩ — see OUTER
2 small in degree ⟨Though they haven't been playing at their best, they still have an *outside* chance of making it into the championship series.⟩ — see REMOTE 1
3 of the greatest or highest degree or quantity ⟨The *outside* cost for repairing the item will be a thousand dollars.⟩ — see ULTIMATE 1

outside *adv* in or into the open air ⟨Go *outside* and play.⟩ — see OUTDOORS

outside *n* **1** an outer part or layer ⟨painted the *outside* of the house⟩ — see EXTERIOR
2 the greatest amount, number, or part ⟨There were 300 people at the *outside* who attended the softball game.⟩ — see MOST
3 the outward form of someone or something especially as indicative of a quality ⟨On the *outside*, he was the self-assured star athlete.⟩ — see APPEARANCE 1

outside *prep* **1** not including ⟨*Outside* that one suggestion, I haven't heard any better ideas.⟩ — see EXCEPT
2 out of the reach or sphere of ⟨It is always refreshing to be assigned a project at work that is *outside* one's usual range of responsibility.⟩ — see BEYOND 2

outside of *prep* **1** not including ⟨*Outside of* that project you don't like, I don't think you have many choices.⟩ — see EXCEPT
2 out of the reach or sphere of ⟨Budget cuts will result in some teachers teaching courses *outside of* their primary areas of expertise.⟩ — see BEYOND 2

outsider *n* a person who is not native to or known to a community ⟨She seems to enjoy the odd distinction of being the only *outsider* in such a small community.⟩ — see STRANGER

outsize *also* **outsized** *adj* of a size greater than average of its kind ⟨She likes to make dramatic appearances wearing her trademark *outsize* sunglasses.⟩ — see LARGE

outskirts *pl n* the districts adjacent to a city ⟨Some people prefer to live on the *outskirts* and work inside the city.⟩ — see ENVIRONS 1

outsmart *vb* to get the better of through cleverness ⟨an inexpensive security system that would likely be *outsmarted* by anyone with a serious interest in circumventing it⟩ — see OUTWIT

outspoken *adj* free in expressing one's true feelings and opinions ⟨a newspaper columnist who has been very *outspoken* on a number of controversial issues⟩ — see FRANK

outspokenness *n* the free expression of one's true feelings and opinions ⟨Some people find the celebrated *outspokenness* of that talk show host to be rather offensive.⟩ — see CANDOR 1

outspread *vb* to arrange the parts of (something) over a wider area ⟨When it *outspread* its wings, a pteranodon would have had a wingspan in excess of 20 feet.⟩ — see OPEN 3

outstanding *adj* **1** not yet paid ⟨There are several *outstanding* bills left, but at least we paid the rest.⟩
synonyms overdue, owed, owing, payable, unpaid, unsettled
related words due, mature
near antonyms prepaid
antonyms cleared, liquidated, paid (off *or* up), repaid, settled
2 standing above others in rank, importance, or achievement ⟨The award goes to the most *outstanding* student in science.⟩ — see EMINENT

outstretch *vb* **1** to arrange the parts of (something) over a wider area ⟨The dog had *outstretched* his legs and was lying across the width of the doorway.⟩ — see OPEN 3
2 to make longer ⟨Having *outstretched* our lunch break beyond all reason, we reluctantly headed back to work.⟩ — see EXTEND 1

outstrip *vb* to be greater, better, or stronger than ⟨Before he had reached his teens, the child prodigy had *outstripped* his music teacher's abilities.⟩ — see SURPASS 1

out–there *adj* deviating from commonly accepted beliefs or practices ⟨The professor's *out-there* political views have made him a lightning rod for controversy on campus.⟩ — see HERETICAL

outward *adj* situated on the outside or farther out ⟨The wall's *outward* face is painted over with a colorful mural honoring illustrious members of the community.⟩ — see OUTER

outward *n* outward and often deceptive indication ⟨Never was there in a man such a fine, heroic *outward* and such a cowardly interior.⟩ — see APPEARANCE 2

outwear *vb* **1** to last longer than ⟨These running shoes have *outworn* any others that I have ever bought.⟩ — see OUTLAST
2 to use up all the physical energy of ⟨a daily grind that would *outwear* anybody⟩ — see EXHAUST 1

outweigh *vb* to be greater in importance than ⟨In most elections the state of the economy *outweighs* all other issues.⟩
synonyms outrank, overbalance, overshadow, overweigh
related words count, import, matter, mean, signify, weigh; dwarf; exceed, outstrip, surpass, transcend

outwit *vb* to get the better of through cleverness ⟨a plan to *outwit* their opponents at their own game⟩
synonyms fox, outfox, outmaneuver, outsmart, overreach
related words outguess, second-guess; baffle, balk, circumvent, foil, frustrate, thwart; cozen, deceive, dupe, fool, gull, trick; conquer, defeat, lick, overcome

outworn *adj* having passed its time of use or usefulness ⟨*outworn* clothes with holes in them⟩ — see OBSOLETE

oval *adj* having the shape of an egg ⟨the *Oval* Office in the White House⟩
synonyms ovate, ovoid (*also* ovoidal)

ovate *adj* having the shape of an egg ⟨The governor's bald, *ovate* head makes him an easy target for caricaturists.⟩ — see OVAL

ovation *n* enthusiastic and usually public expression of approval ⟨received a standing *ovation* for the masterly performance⟩ — see APPLAUSE 1

over *adj* brought or having come to an end ⟨The play is *over* now.⟩ — see COMPLETE 2

over *adv* **1** from one side to the other of an intervening space ⟨Let's swim *over* to that island.⟩
synonyms across, athwart, through
related words clear
2 yet another time ⟨Several executives missed the presentation and would like you to do it *over* for them later this afternoon.⟩ — see AGAIN 1
3 to or in a higher place ⟨I heard the noise and was startled to discover that the plane was directly *over*.⟩ — see ABOVE
4 from beginning to end ⟨Read it *over* until you understand it thoroughly.⟩ — see THROUGH 1
5 toward or in a lower position ⟨The baby toddled two steps and then fell *over*.⟩ — see DOWN 1

over *prep* **1** higher than ⟨The boy towered *over* his siblings.⟩ — see ABOVE
2 in the course of ⟨The students learned a lot *over* the summer.⟩ — see DURING
3 on or to the farther side of ⟨peered *over* the wall⟩ — see BEYOND 1
4 to the opposite side of ⟨hopped *over* the dropped ball⟩ — see ACROSS 1
5 in random positions within the boundaries of ⟨marbles scattered all *over* the room⟩ — see AROUND 2

overabundance *n* the state or an instance of going beyond what is usual, proper, or needed ⟨an *overabundance* of desserts at a potluck dinner⟩ — see EXCESS

overactive *adj* being in a state of increased activity or agitation ⟨The boy manages to panic himself by his own *overactive* imagination.⟩ — see FEVERISH 1

overage *n* the state or an instance of going beyond what is usual, proper, or needed ⟨Several selectmen argued that the town's cash *overage* was significant enough to warrant a reduction of the residential property tax.⟩ — see EXCESS

overall *adj* **1** belonging or relating to the whole ⟨The *overall* view seems to be that we're doing fine economically.⟩ — see GENERAL 1
2 relating to the main elements and not to specific details ⟨There's an *overall* similarity in the looks of the models for that chain of clothing stores.⟩ — see GENERAL 2
3 held by or applicable to a majority of the people ⟨The *overall* mind-set among the people in our town seems to be that any increase in taxes is bad.⟩ — see GENERAL 3

overall *adv* **1** with everyone or everything taken into account at the same time ⟨We'll reduce the budget *overall* by 15 percent.⟩ — see ALL AROUND
2 for the most part ⟨*Overall*, this is a good speech, but it could use a little humor.⟩ — see CHIEFLY

over and above *prep* in addition to ⟨We'll need another gallon of milk *over and above* what we already have.⟩ — see BESIDES 1

overbalance *vb* to be greater in importance than ⟨My determination to finish the job *overbalanced* my exhaustion.⟩ — see OUTWEIGH

overbear *vb* to achieve a victory over ⟨That year the football team simply *overbore* opponent after opponent with steamroller ruthlessness.⟩ — see BEAT 2

overbearing *adj* **1** coming before all others in importance ⟨the *overbearing* problem in our nation's schools⟩ — see FOREMOST

2 fond of ordering people around ⟨The doctor's *overbearing* attitude is resented by nurses and patients alike.⟩ — see BOSSY

overbold *adj* foolishly adventurous or bold ⟨One *overbold* tourist almost tumbled over the rocks and into the sea.⟩ — see FOOLHARDY 1

overburden *vb* to fill or load to excess ⟨It is important that you bring on the hike plenty of food and water, but don't *overburden* your pack with unnecessary gear.⟩ — see OVERLOAD

overcast *adj* covered over by clouds ⟨The dark, *overcast* sky made the whole day seem depressing.⟩

synonyms beclouded, clouded, cloudy, dull, hazed, hazy, heavy, lowering (*also* louring), overclouded

related words bedimmed, befogged, blackened, darkened, dim, dimmed, dulled, dusky, misty, murky, obscure, obscured, overshadowed; black, bleak, cheerless, dark, desolate, dismal, dreary, funereal, gloomy, glum, gray (*also* grey), somber (*or* sombre), sullen

near antonyms sunlit, sunny, sunshiny; brightened, brilliant, dazzling, illuminated, illumined, lightened, radiant, shiny

antonyms clear, cloudless

overcast *vb* to make dark, dim, or indistinct ⟨An impenetrable fog *overcast* our view of the harbor.⟩ — see CLOUD 1

overcharge *vb* **1** to charge (someone) too much for goods or services ⟨I think that store may have *overcharged* us for the shoes, which were supposed to be on sale.⟩

synonyms gouge, soak, sting, surcharge

related words cheat, defraud, stick; clip, fleece, skin; mischarge

antonyms undercharge

2 to fill or load to excess ⟨*overcharged* his thesis with long, fancy words⟩ — see OVERLOAD

overcloud *vb* to make dark, dim, or indistinct ⟨The eerie dusk of an approaching storm *overclouded* the plains.⟩ — see CLOUD 1

overclouded *adj* covered over by clouds ⟨*Overclouded* skies are a common feature in that Dutch artist's landscape paintings.⟩ — see OVERCAST

overcoat *n* a warm outdoor coat ⟨Put your *overcoat* on—it's freezing out there!⟩

synonyms greatcoat, surcoat, topcoat

related words chesterfield, frock coat, mackinaw, ulster; jacket, parka, surtout; oilskin, raincoat, sou'wester; wrap

near antonyms undercoat

overcome *vb* **1** to achieve a victory over ⟨The baseball team finally *overcame* their opponents in the 13th inning.⟩ — see BEAT 2

2 to subject to incapacitating emotional or mental stress ⟨Already under stress, she was *overcome* by the bad news.⟩ — see OVERWHELM 1

overconfident *adj* foolishly adventurous or bold ⟨The *overconfident* quarterback made some careless decisions that cost him the game.⟩ — see FOOLHARDY 1

overcritical *adj* given to making or expressing unfavorable judgments about things ⟨An *overcritical* teacher can discourage even the most dedicated of students.⟩ — see CRITICAL 1

overdecorated *adj* elaborately and often excessively decorated ⟨The room was so *overdecorated* that no one thing was shown to its best advantage.⟩ — see ORNATE 1

overdo *vb* to describe or express in too strong terms ⟨The

fashion designer's claim that his new line of clothing would revolutionize the way we dress was perhaps *overdoing* it just a bit.⟩ — see OVERSTATE

overdraw *vb* to describe or express in too strong terms ⟨Commentators have *overdrawn* the dangers of the sport in order to make it appear more exciting.⟩ — see OVERSTATE

overdue *adj* **1** not arriving, occurring, or settled at the due, usual, or proper time ⟨An *overdue* library book will be subject to daily fines.⟩ — see LATE 1

2 not yet paid ⟨an *overdue* bill that's started incurring interest charges⟩ — see OUTSTANDING 1

3 going beyond a normal or acceptable limit in degree or amount ⟨Steve spends an *overdue* percentage of his income on fishing equipment.⟩ — see EXCESSIVE

overeat *vb* to eat greedily or to excess ⟨Because he watches his diet for most of the year, he feels free to *overeat* during the holidays.⟩ — see GORGE 2

overeater *n* one who eats greedily or too much ⟨I tend to be an *overeater* when I'm stressed.⟩ — see GLUTTON

overestimate *vb* to place too high a value on ⟨The contractors *overestimated* their ability to do the work on such short notice.⟩

synonyms overrate, overvalue

related words appreciate, cherish, prize, treasure, value; admire, esteem, regard, respect; adore, idolize, revere, reverence, venerate, worship

near antonyms minimize, play down, soft-pedal; belittle, decry, depreciate, disparage; despise, disdain, scorn; abhor, abominate, detest, loathe

overfamiliar *adj* showing a lack of proper social reserve or modesty ⟨The commander cautioned the officers against fraternization and being *overfamiliar* with their subordinates.⟩ — see PRESUMPTUOUS 1

overfill *vb* **1** to fill or load to excess ⟨*overfilled* the wheelbarrow with bricks until finally no one could push it⟩ — see OVERLOAD

2 to flow over the brim or top of ⟨Water *overfilled* the tub and poured onto the floor.⟩ — see OVERFLOW 1

overflow *n* **1** a great flow of water or of something that overwhelms ⟨A great *overflow* of water from the heavy rains swept mud and silt down onto the highway.⟩ — see FLOOD

2 the state or an instance of going beyond what is usual, proper, or needed ⟨An *overflow* of help actually made the job more complicated.⟩ — see EXCESS

overflow *vb* **1** to flow over the brim or top of ⟨While the waiter stood there gawking at the nearby celebrity, my coffee was *overflowing* its cup and pouring onto our table.⟩

synonyms overfill

related words boil over, run over, spill, well (up); flow, flush, gush, pour, sluice, spout, spurt, stream; deluge, drown, engulf, flood, inundate, overwhelm, submerge, submerse, swamp; wash (over); brim, cascade, slop, slosh

near antonyms recede

2 to cover with a flood ⟨The swollen river *overflowed* the surrounding land.⟩ — see FLOOD

3 to be copiously supplied ⟨a magazine that usually *overflows* with home-repair tips for the do-it-yourselfer⟩ — see ABOUND

overgrown *adj* covered with a thick, healthy natural growth ⟨The trail has become so *overgrown* that it is nearly impassable in spots.⟩ — see LUSH 1

overhang *n* a part that sticks out from the general mass of something ⟨a recess in the face of the cliff that is hidden by the thick vines dangling from the jagged *overhang* above⟩ — see BULGE 1

overhang *vb* **1** to extend outward beyond a usual point

⟨The narrow streets of the old European city are lined with row houses often having *overhanging* second stories.⟩ — see BULGE 1

2 to remain poised to inflict harm, danger, or distress on ⟨I finished the assignment early because I was tired of having it *overhang* me.⟩ — see THREATEN

overhasty *adj* acting or done with excessive or careless speed ⟨An *overhasty* reading of the recipe resulted in the omission of a critical ingredient.⟩ — see HASTY 1

overhaul *vb* to move fast enough to get even with ⟨In the final moments of the race, the horse in the rear sped forward at a furious pace and *overhauled* the horse that had been leading.⟩ — see OVERTAKE

overhead *adv* to or in a higher place ⟨the majestic sight of eagles soaring *overhead*⟩ — see ABOVE

overhear *vb* to listen to (another in private conversation) ⟨It's not polite to try to *overhear* intimate friends sharing confidences.⟩ — see EAVESDROP (ON)

overkill *n* the state or an instance of going beyond what is usual, proper, or needed ⟨The song already borders on the maudlin—the addition of a syrupy string accompaniment would just be *overkill*.⟩ — see EXCESS

overlap *n* a partial covering of one thing by an adjoining member ⟨The orthodontist will try to fix that *overlap* of two of your upper incisors.⟩
synonyms lapping
related words shingling; overlaying, overlying, overspreading

overlap *vb* to lie over parts of one another ⟨The brochures on the display table should *overlap* but not so much that the titles are obscured.⟩
synonyms lap, overlay, overlie, overspread
related words shingle

overlay *vb* **1** to form a layer over ⟨You should apply a coat of primer first, and then *overlay* it with two coats of paint.⟩ — see COVER 2

2 to lie over parts of one another ⟨cedar shingles *overlaying* one another on the roof⟩ — see OVERLAP

overlie *vb* **1** to lie over parts of one another ⟨The puzzle pieces *overlay* one another in complete disarray on the floor.⟩ — see OVERLAP

2 to form a layer over ⟨There will be freezing rain tonight, so we can expect to find a thick layer of ice *overlying* the car windshield in the morning.⟩ — see COVER 2

overload *vb* to fill or load to excess ⟨Try not to *overload* your backpack, or you could end up with back problems.⟩
synonyms overburden, overcharge, overfill
related words stuff; burden, charge, encumber, lade, load, lumber, saddle, weight
near antonyms lighten, unburden, unload

overlook *n* a high place or structure from which a wide view is possible ⟨Just down the road there's a great *overlook* where you can get a panoramic view of the valley below.⟩ — see LOOKOUT 1

overlook *vb* **1** to look down on ⟨The fortress *overlooks* the city.⟩
synonyms command, dominate
related words face, front

2 to fail to give proper attention to ⟨You've *overlooked* your chores again this week.⟩ — see NEGLECT 1

3 to be in charge of ⟨You'll be asked to *overlook* larger projects in the future.⟩ — see BOSS 1

4 to cast a spell on ⟨an old belief in a remedy for livestock that has been *overlooked*⟩ — see BEWITCH 1

5 to look over closely (as for judging quality or condition) ⟨I quickly *overlooked* the table of used books to see if there was anything of value.⟩ — see INSPECT

6 to dismiss as of little importance ⟨The mistakes are so minor that I think we can *overlook* them.⟩ — see EXCUSE 1

7 to look after and make decisions about ⟨the engineer hired to *overlook* the construction of the canal⟩ — see CONDUCT 1

overly *adv* beyond a normal or acceptable limit ⟨There's no need to be *overly* careful about the rough draft, since we'll polish it afterwards.⟩ — see TOO 1

overmatch *vb* to achieve a victory over ⟨an indomitable spirit that no amount of adversity could *overmatch*⟩ — see BEAT 2

overmuch *adj* going beyond a normal or acceptable limit in degree or amount ⟨I think you're putting *overmuch* work into this party—relax!⟩ — see EXCESSIVE

overmuch *adv* beyond a normal or acceptable limit ⟨You worry *overmuch* about what other people think.⟩ — see TOO 1

overmuch *n* the state or an instance of going beyond what is usual, proper, or needed ⟨You must not expect an *overmuch* of gratitude from a very young child.⟩ — see EXCESS

overpass *vb* **1** to dismiss as of little importance ⟨He didn't mean anything by that comment, so try to *overpass* it.⟩ — see EXCUSE 1

2 to go beyond the limit of ⟨a filmmaker whose technical bravura *overpasses* his ability to tell a coherent story⟩ — see EXCEED 1

3 to fail to give proper attention to ⟨army officers who had been unjustly *overpassed* for promotion⟩ — see NEGLECT 1

overpower *vb* **1** to bring under one's control by force of arms ⟨The invading army *overpowered* the countryside with lightning speed.⟩ — see CONQUER 1

2 to subject to incapacitating emotional or mental stress ⟨*overpowered* by fear of the unknown⟩ — see OVERWHELM 1

overpowering *n* the act or process of bringing someone or something under one's control ⟨the *overpowering* of much of Europe by the Nazis during World War II⟩ — see CONQUEST

overpraise *n* excessive praise ⟨The piano instructor believes in encouraging her students but avoids any *overpraise* that might make them complacent.⟩ — see FLATTERY

overpraise *vb* to praise too much ⟨Proud parents sometimes *overpraise* their children.⟩ — see FLATTER 1

overrate *vb* to place too high a value on ⟨I think the critics seriously *overrated* that movie.⟩ — see OVERESTIMATE

overreach *vb* **1** to get the better of through cleverness ⟨a real estate developer who is always trying to *overreach* his competitors, fair means or foul⟩ — see OUTWIT

2 to go beyond the limit of ⟨The mountain climbers *overreached* their abilities and had to give up.⟩ — see EXCEED 1

overripe *adj* having lost forcefulness, courage, or spirit ⟨an *overripe* artist whose abstract paintings are no longer considered fresh or significant⟩ — see EFFETE 1

overrun *vb* **1** to enter for conquest or plunder ⟨Waves of barbarians *overran* the Roman Empire during its long decline.⟩ — see INVADE

2 to go beyond the limit of ⟨He must not *overrun* his authority as governor.⟩ — see EXCEED 1

3 to spread or swarm over in a troublesome manner ⟨Ants are *overrunning* the garden.⟩ — see INFEST

oversee *vb* **1** to look after and make decisions about ⟨Carter will *oversee* the new manufacturing division.⟩ — see CONDUCT 1

2 to be in charge of ⟨looking for someone to *oversee* the project from start to finish⟩ — see BOSS 1

3 to take charge of especially on behalf of another ⟨You'll *oversee* the household until Dad gets home.⟩ — see ²TEND 1

4 to look over closely (as for judging quality or condition) 〈Her job was to *oversee* each and every dish before it left the kitchen and was served to a customer.〉 — see INSPECT

overshadow *vb* **1** to make dark, dim, or indistinct 〈Large trees *overshadow* the yard and darken the house for much of the day.〉 — see CLOUD 1

2 to be greater in importance than 〈Later you'll find that verbal skills *overshadow* any skills you have at video games.〉 — see OUTWEIGH

overshoot *vb* to go beyond the limit of 〈Don't worry if you *overshoot* the length requirement by three pages.〉 — see EXCEED 1

oversight *n* **1** the act or activity of looking after and making decisions about something 〈*oversight* of the club's fund-raising activities〉 — see CONDUCT 1

2 an unintentional departure from truth or accuracy 〈Claiming "three billion" instead of "three million" was just an *oversight*.〉 — see ERROR 1

3 the duty or function of watching or guarding for the sake of proper direction or control 〈You'll have *oversight* of the troop until the scoutmaster returns.〉 — see SUPERVISION 1

4 the nonperformance of an assigned or expected action 〈Failing to lock the car can be an expensive *oversight* if it gets stolen.〉 — see FAILURE 1

oversize *or* **oversized** *adj* of a size greater than average of its kind 〈A softball is an *oversize* and less densely stuffed baseball.〉 — see LARGE

overspread *vb* **1** to form a layer over 〈The butter should evenly *overspread* the baking pan.〉 — see COVER 2

2 to lie over parts of one another 〈autumn leaves *overspreading* one another on the lawn to form a colorful mosaic〉 — see OVERLAP

overstate *vb* to describe or express in too strong terms 〈It appears you've somewhat *overstated* your computer skills, if you can't find the "on" button!〉

synonyms exaggerate, overdo, overdraw, put on

related words color, elaborate, embellish, embroider, magnify, pad, stretch; fudge, hedge; overemphasize, overplay, sensationalize

near antonyms belittle, minimize, play down

antonyms understate

overstatement *n* the representation of something in terms that go beyond the facts 〈A claim to worldwide fame is a bit of an *overstatement* on the part of that restaurant.〉 — see EXAGGERATION

overstep *vb* to go beyond the limit of 〈The principal *overstepped* her authority in ordering everyone to remain in the unheated school.〉 — see EXCEED 1

oversupply *n* the state or an instance of going beyond what is usual, proper, or needed 〈An *oversupply* of new homes is helping to drive down housing prices.〉 — see EXCESS

overtake *vb* to move fast enough to get even with 〈She had to hurry to *overtake* her friends, who had forgotten their umbrellas.〉 〈The thunderstorm *overtook* them suddenly.〉

synonyms catch, catch up (with), overhaul

related words chase, pursue; gain, reach; pass, surpass

near antonyms fall short

overthrow *n* failure to win a contest 〈the surprising *overthrow* of the world's top-ranked chess player〉 — see DEFEAT 1

overtop *vb* to be greater, better, or stronger than 〈a manager whose arrogance was *overtopped* only by his ineptitude〉 — see SURPASS 1

overturn *vb* to turn on one's side or upside down 〈afraid that my kayak would *overturn*〉 — see CAPSIZE

overvalue *vb* to place too high a value on 〈Some people *overvalue* material things.〉 — see OVERESTIMATE

overweening *adj* **1** having too high an opinion of oneself 〈a director who has little patience for *overweening* actors who think they are above taking advice and criticism〉 — see CONCEITED

2 going beyond a normal or acceptable limit in degree or amount 〈*overweening* desire for wealth and fame〉 — see EXCESSIVE

3 having a feeling of superiority that shows itself in an overbearing attitude 〈an *overweening* administrator who simply doesn't know how to manage people〉 — see ARROGANT

overweigh *vb* to be greater in importance than 〈The benefits of treatment *overweigh* the slight risks.〉 — see OUTWEIGH

overweight *adj* having an excess of body fat 〈an *overweight* dog that was put on a special diet〉 — see FAT 1

overwhelm *vb* **1** to subject to incapacitating emotional or mental stress 〈Just the thought of how much work there is to do *overwhelms* me.〉

synonyms crush, devastate, floor, oppress, overcome, overpower, prostrate, snow under, swamp, whelm

related words deluge, drown, sink; confute, defeat, refute; break, demoralize, distress, disturb, rock, shatter, stagger, throw, unman, unnerve, upset

2 to cover with a flood 〈That spring the massive runoff from melting snows *overwhelmed* the valley.〉 — see FLOOD

overwrought *adj* **1** being in a state of increased activity or agitation 〈became *overwrought* when she heard about the accident〉 — see FEVERISH 1

2 elaborately and often excessively decorated 〈The author's prose is *overwrought* with purple passages and florid metaphors.〉 — see ORNATE 1

ovoid *adj* having the shape of an egg 〈an *ovoid* toy that the baby couldn't tip over〉 — see OVAL

owed *adj* not yet paid 〈finally paid the *owed* amount〉 — see OUTSTANDING 1

owing *adj* not yet paid 〈There's one bill still *owing*.〉 — see OUTSTANDING 1

owing to *prep* as the result of 〈*Owing to* the extra snow days this year, we'll have to run an additional two days into June.〉 — see BECAUSE OF

own *vb* to keep, control, or experience as one's own 〈We *own* a modest house and an equally modest car.〉 — see HAVE 1

own (up to) *vb* to accept the truth or existence of (something) usually reluctantly 〈No one *owned up to* damaging the car.〉 — see ADMIT 1

owner *n* one who has a legal or rightful claim to ownership 〈The *owner* of the building will have to decide whether or not to sell.〉 — see PROPRIETOR

P

pa *n* a male human parent ⟨I cherish my memories of the times that I went fishing with my *pa*.⟩ — see FATHER 1

pace *vb* **1** to move along with a steady regular step especially in a group ⟨Six jugglers *paced* neatly alongside one another in the parade.⟩ — see MARCH 1

2 to move forward along a course ⟨The students *paced* through the graduation ceremony before the assembled family and friends.⟩ — see GO 1

pacific *adj* **1** tending to lessen or avoid conflict or hostility ⟨As a *pacific* gesture, we invited our feuding neighbors to our backyard barbecue.⟩

synonyms appeasing, conciliating, conciliatory, disarming, mollifying, pacifying, peacemaking, placating, propitiatory

related words endearing, ingratiating, winning, winsome; peaceable, peaceful; nonbelligerent, unaggressive, unassertive; calming, comforting, lulling, quieting, relaxing, soothing, tranquilizing (*also* tranquillizing); obliging, satisfying; affable, agreeable, amiable, amicable, benevolent, genial, gentle, good-natured, good-tempered, kind, kindly; passive, submissive, yielding

near antonyms aggravating, annoying, chafing, exasperating, frustrating, galling, irksome, irritating, nettling, provoking, rankling, riling, vexing; incensing, infuriating, maddening; antagonistic, antipathetic, hostile, inhospitable, inimical, unfriendly, unsympathetic; aggressive, agonistic, argumentative, assertive, bellicose, belligerent, combative, contentious, pugnacious, quarrelsome, scrappy, truculent; martial, militant, militaristic, warlike

antonyms antagonizing

2 inclined to live in peace and to avoid war ⟨a *pacific* nation that has managed to remain neutral even during times of world conflict⟩ — see PEACEFUL 1

pacifist *n* a person who opposes war or warlike policies ⟨A committed *pacifist*, Gandhi succeeded in bringing about Indian independence using only nonviolence.⟩ — see DOVE 1

pacifist *or* **pacifistic** *adj* inclined to live in peace and to avoid war ⟨The newspaper's editorial board has clearly staked out a *pacifist* position on the current conflict.⟩ — see PEACEFUL 1

pacify *vb* **1** to lessen the anger or agitation of ⟨I tried to *pacify* the crying child.⟩

synonyms appease, assuage, conciliate, disarm, gentle, mollify, placate, propitiate

related words calm, comfort, console, content, hush, quiet, soothe, tranquilize (*also* tranquillize); endear (to), ingratiate; delight, gladden, gratify, please; cater (to), humor, indulge; blandish, cajole, coax, wheedle; baby, coddle, mollycoddle, pamper, spoil

near antonyms aggravate, annoy, antagonize, bother, bug, chafe, cross, exasperate, gall, get, grate, irk, irritate, nettle, peeve, pique, put out, rankle, rile, roil, ruffle, vex; provoke, rouse; harry, persecute, pester; agitate, discomfort, distress, disturb, fret, perturb, unhinge, unsettle, upset, worry; affront, insult, offend, slight

antonyms anger, enrage, incense, inflame (*also* enflame), infuriate, ire, madden, outrage

2 to bring under one's control by force of arms ⟨Additional ground forces were needed to occupy those areas that had already been *pacified*.⟩ — see CONQUER 1

pacifying *adj* **1** tending to calm the emotions and relieve stress ⟨a *pacifying* treat of milk and cookies⟩ — see SOOTHING 1

2 tending to lessen or avoid conflict or hostility ⟨The referee adopted a *pacifying* tone to try to calm everyone down.⟩ — see PACIFIC 1

pack *n* **1** a soft-sided case designed for carrying belongings especially on the back ⟨Part of basic training is becoming accustomed to taking very long hikes with an 80-pound *pack*.⟩

synonyms backpack, knapsack, rucksack

related words haversack; carryall, grip, handbag, suitcase, traveling bag; fanny pack, school bag, seabag; overnight bag, overnight case, weekend bag

2 a wrapped or sealed case containing an item or set of items ⟨She tucked a small *pack* of lozenges into her bag.⟩ — see PACKAGE 1

3 a considerable amount ⟨It took a *pack* of courage to stand up before that crowd and tell the truth.⟩ — see LOT 2

4 a group of people sharing a common interest and relating together socially ⟨had run with a *pack* of hot-rodders when he was in high school⟩ — see GANG 2

pack *vb* **1** to close up so that no empty spaces remain ⟨Carefully *pack* the food containers so we'll have as much as possible for the picnic.⟩ — see FILL 2

2 to put into (something) as much as can be held or contained ⟨I had *packed* the suitcase so tightly that it wouldn't close.⟩ — see FILL 1

3 to support and take from one place to another ⟨Remember to *pack* several changes of clothing.⟩ — see CARRY 1

4 to wear or have on one's person ⟨a private detective *packing* a weapon⟩ — see CARRY 2

pack (off) *vb* to cause to go or be taken from one place to another ⟨*packed* the child *off* to a good boarding school⟩ — see SEND

package *n* **1** a wrapped or sealed case containing an item or set of items ⟨Bill got a job sorting *packages* in the mail room.⟩

synonyms bundle, pack, packet, parcel

related words bag, poke [*chiefly Southern & Midland*], pouch, sack; bale; box, container, crate

2 a number of things considered as a unit ⟨He ate a whole *package* of cookies at once.⟩ — see GROUP 1

packed *adj* **1** containing or seeming to contain the greatest quantity or number possible ⟨The auditorium was *packed*.⟩ — see FULL 1

2 having little space between items or parts ⟨a densely *packed* sequence of events⟩ — see CLOSE 1

packet *n* a wrapped or sealed case containing an item or set of items ⟨a *packet* of letters that were written while he was in the army⟩ — see PACKAGE 1

pact *n* **1** a formal agreement between two or more nations or peoples ⟨a *pact* between the two small nations to defend one another in case of attack⟩ — see TREATY

2 an arrangement about action to be taken ⟨They made a *pact* to meet every week at the same time.⟩ — see AGREEMENT 2

pad *n* **1** a number of sheets of writing paper glued together at one edge ⟨We'll need to buy a new *pad* for telephone messages soon.⟩

synonyms notepad, tablet

related words scratch pad; album, notebook, scrapbook; booklet, pamphlet

2 a place set aside for sleeping ⟨I went back to my *pad* to get some rest.⟩ — see BED 1

3 something that serves as a protective barrier ⟨a *pad* on the chair to keep it from getting scratched⟩ — see CUSHION

4 the place where one lives ⟨Welcome to my *pad*!⟩ — see HOME 1

¹pad *vb* to add to the interest of by including made-up details ⟨The journalist was fired for *padding* certain stories to make them more interesting.⟩ — see EMBROIDER

²pad *vb* to go on foot ⟨A cat *padded* silently by⟩ — see WALK 1

padding *n* **1** soft material that is used to fill the hollow parts of something ⟨The *padding* is leaking out of that pillow.⟩ — see FILLING

2 the representation of something in terms that go beyond the facts ⟨That feature writer is sometimes guilty of *padding*, but he keeps it from getting out of hand.⟩ — see EXAGGERATION

paddle *vb* **1** to move a boat by means of oars ⟨I like to *paddle* on the river for exercise and relaxation.⟩ — see ¹ROW

2 to strike repeatedly ⟨You come here or I'll *paddle* your behind.⟩ — see BEAT 1

paean *n* a formal expression of praise ⟨His retirement party featured many *paeans* for his long years of service to the company.⟩ — see ENCOMIUM

pagan *n* a person who does not worship the God of the Bible ⟨an iconic structure built by ancient *pagans*⟩ — see HEATHEN 1

page *n* one that carries a message or does an errand ⟨Please dispatch a *page* to bring coffee to the senator.⟩ — see MESSENGER

pageant *n* a staged presentation often with music that consists of a procession of narrated or enacted scenes ⟨We always put on a Christmas *pageant* every year.⟩

synonyms cavalcade

related words tableau; kaleidoscope, montage, panorama; drama, dramatization, play; demonstration, performance, presentation, production; exhibition, show; parade, procession, progress

pail *n* a round container that is open at the top and outfitted with a handle ⟨Fetch me a *pail* full of water, please.⟩

synonyms bucket

related words cauldron, kettle, pot; canteen, flagon, jar, jug, pitcher; hod; tub, vat; holder, receptacle, vessel

pain *n* **1** a sharp unpleasant sensation usually felt in some specific part of the body ⟨The child was crying because of a *pain* in her knee.⟩

synonyms ache, pang, prick, shoot, smart, sting, stitch, throe, tingle, twinge

related words discomfort, distress, soreness; affliction, agony, anguish, misery, sufferance, suffering, torment, torture; inflammation, sore, swelling; damage, detriment, harm, hurt, injury; backache, bellyache, charley horse, colic, complaint, earache, gripe, headache, stomachache, toothache

near antonyms comfort, ease, easiness

2 a state of great suffering of body or mind ⟨A sprained ankle caused him great *pain* for a week.⟩ — see DISTRESS 1

3 pains *pl* strict attentiveness to what one is doing ⟨Take *pains* to be sure that you don't damage anything while moving the furniture.⟩ — see CARE 1

4 pains *pl* the active use of energy in producing a result ⟨She was at *pains* to reassure us that everything would be fine.⟩ — see EFFORT

5 one who is obnoxiously annoying ⟨Sometimes that child, who apparently never tires of asking questions, can be such a *pain*.⟩ — see NUISANCE 1

pain *vb* to feel or cause physical pain ⟨My poor head was *paining* so from all that racket.⟩ — see HURT 1

painful *adj* **1** causing or feeling bodily pain ⟨Her broken arm was too *painful* for her to go on the trip.⟩

synonyms aching, achy, hurting, nasty, sore

related words agonizing, excruciating, torturous; dam-

aging, deleterious, detrimental, harmful, hurtful, injurious, noxious, pernicious; raw, tender; bleeding, burning, chafing, cramping; itching, pinching, pricking, prickling, smarting, stinging; inflamed (*also* enflamed); grievous, severe, threatening, wounding

near antonyms healing, helping, remedial

antonyms indolent, painless

2 hard to accept or bear especially emotionally ⟨It's been very *painful* to accept that my grandfather is gone forever.⟩ — see BITTER 2

painfully *adv* with feelings of bitterness or grief ⟨*Painfully* she recounted the difficult decision to put down her beloved but sick kitty.⟩ — see HARD 2

painkiller *n* something (as a drug) that relieves pain ⟨I took an over-the-counter *painkiller* for my headache.⟩

synonyms analgesic, anesthetic

related words sedative, tranquilizer (*also* tranquillizer); narcotic, opiate

painless *adj* involving minimal difficulty or effort ⟨Getting paid to watch and review movies seems like a *painless* way to earn a living.⟩ — see EASY 1

painlessly *adv* without difficulty ⟨The move to our new house was accomplished rather *painlessly*.⟩ — see EASILY 1

painstaking *adj* taking, showing, or involving great care and effort ⟨She was always *painstaking* about her work.⟩

synonyms careful, conscientious, fussy, loving, meticulous, scrupulous

related words assiduous, diligent, indefatigable, persevering, sedulous; exhaustive, thorough, thoroughgoing; alert, attentive, observant, vigilant, watchful; accurate, exact, precise, strict; critical, demanding, discriminating, exacting, fastidious, finicky, particular; cautious, circumspect, gingerly, guarded, heedful, mindful, wary; deliberate, plodding, slow; studied, thoughtful; all-out, determined, dogged, intensive, patient, tenacious, tireless, zealous

near antonyms cursory, halfhearted; heedless, inattentive, incautious, mindless, unguarded, unsafe, unwary; lax, neglectful, negligent, slipshod, sloppy, slovenly; imprecise; inaccurate, uncritical, undemanding, undiscriminating; bold, impetuous, rash, reckless; apathetic, indifferent, lackadaisical, lazy

antonyms careless

paint *n* preparations intended to beautify the face ⟨Let me just put on a little *paint* before we go out.⟩ — see MAKE-UP 1

paint *vb* **1** to give a representation or account of in words ⟨The description *painted* a perfect image of the sun setting over the ocean.⟩ — see DESCRIBE 1

2 to give color or a different color to ⟨I've decided to *paint* the bathroom walls purple.⟩ — see COLOR 1

painting *n* a picture created with oil paint ⟨The *Mona Lisa* is a haunting *painting* of a woman with a most mysterious smile.⟩

synonyms canvas (*also* canvass), oil, oil painting

related words fresco, mural, panorama; diptych, triptych; drawing, etching, finger painting, pastel, sketch, tempera; masterpiece; pièce de résistance, showpiece

pair *n* two things of the same or similar kind that match or are considered together ⟨a *pair* of blue socks⟩ ⟨The cheerleader and the computer nerd make quite a *pair* together.⟩

synonyms brace, couple, duo, twain, twosome

related words span, yoke; partnership, team; companion, complement, doublet, fellow, half, match, mate, twin; coordinate, counterpart, equal, equivalent, like, parallel, peer, rival

pal *n* a person who has a strong liking for and trust in another ⟨I always choose my best *pal* for my softball team first.⟩ — see FRIEND 1

pal (around) *vb* to come or be together as friends ⟨They began to *pal around* after discovering that they both had kids on the same soccer team.⟩ — see ASSOCIATE 1

palace *n* **1** a large impressive residence ⟨The billionaire's "summer cottage" turned out to be an over-the-top *palace*.⟩ — see MANSION

2 a large, magnificent, or massive building ⟨The governor's opponents have accused him of building *palaces* to house the state government.⟩ — see EDIFICE 1

3 the residence of a ruler ⟨Buckingham *Palace* flies a special flag to indicate when the monarch is in residence.⟩ — see COURT 1

paladin *n* a person who actively supports or favors a cause ⟨an idealistic *paladin* seeking better treatment for the homeless⟩ — see EXPONENT 1

palatability *n* the quality of being delicious ⟨military rations that were obviously chosen for their durability and not their *palatability*⟩ — see DELICIOUSNESS

palatable *adj* **1** being to one's liking ⟨I did not find the idea of moving again very *palatable*.⟩ — see SATISFACTORY 1

2 giving pleasure or contentment to the mind or senses ⟨I always associate the *palatable* aroma of roasting turkey with Thanksgiving.⟩ — see PLEASANT 1

3 very pleasing to the sense of taste ⟨The vegetarian version of that classic dish turned out to be very *palatable*.⟩ — see DELICIOUS 1

palatial *adj* showing obvious signs of wealth and comfort ⟨a *palatial* penthouse apartment⟩ — see LUXURIOUS

palatially *adv* in a luxurious manner ⟨A premium membership in the club gives you exclusive access to a *palatially* appointed locker room and spa.⟩ — see HIGH

palaver *n* **1** an exchange of views for the purpose of exploring a subject or deciding an issue ⟨seemingly endless *palaver* between the negotiating parties⟩ — see DISCUSSION 1

2 friendly, informal conversation or an instance of this ⟨We should get together and have a nice *palaver* sometime.⟩ — see CHAT 1

palaver *vb* **1** to engage in casual or rambling conversation ⟨parents *palavering* and drinking coffee while watching their children play soccer⟩ — see CHAT 1

2 to get (someone) to do something by gentle urging, special attention, or flattery ⟨I let the salesclerk at the electronics store *palaver* me into a service contract that I didn't need.⟩ — see COAX

pale *adj* **1** lacking intensity of color ⟨We chose a very *pale* pink for the walls of the room.⟩
synonyms dull, dulled, faded, light, pastel, washed-out
related words flat, lackluster, lusterless, matte (*also* mat *or* matt); dim, faint; dirty, muddy; achromatic, colorless, uncolored, undyed, unpainted, unstained; blanched, bleached, washed, white, whitened; gray (*also* grey), indistinct, neutral
near antonyms bright, brilliant, vibrant, vivid; dyed, painted, stained, tinged, tinted; colorful, motley, multicolored, polychromatic, polychrome, varicolored, variegated; flashy, garish, gaudy, loud, showy, splashy
antonyms dark, deep, rich

2 lacking a healthy skin color ⟨After a week with the flu, she was deathly *pale* and noticeably thinner.⟩
synonyms ashen, ashy, blanched, cadaverous, livid, lurid, mealy, paled, pallid, pasty, peaked, wan
related words sallow, sallowish, sick, sickly, waxen; white, whitened; anemic, bloodless; untanned; whey-faced, white-faced
near antonyms blushing, flushed
antonyms blooming, florid, flush, full-blooded, glowing, red, rosy, rubicund, ruddy, sanguine

3 not seen or understood clearly ⟨A *pale* outline off in the distance proved to be someone out for a walk.⟩ — see FAINT 1

pale *vb* to make white or whiter by removing color ⟨The

sun eventually *paled* the bright blue beach umbrella.⟩ — see WHITEN

paled *adj* lacking a healthy skin color ⟨The shock of the news left him *paled* and shaking.⟩ — see PALE 2

palisade *n* a steep wall of rock, earth, or ice ⟨the *palisades* that line the west bank of the Hudson River for about 15 miles⟩ — see CLIFF

pall *n* **1** a boxlike container for holding a dead body ⟨Bearing her husband's *pall* were her four brothers and two nephews.⟩ — see COFFIN

2 an overspreading element that produces an atmosphere of gloom ⟨The sad news cast a *pall* over the school.⟩ — see CLOUD

3 something that covers or conceals like a piece of cloth ⟨A *pall* of gloom overshadowed the failing theater's last production.⟩ — see CLOAK 1

pall *vb* to grow less in scope or intensity especially gradually ⟨Viewers' interest in the reality show eventually *palled*.⟩ — see DECREASE 2

palliate *vb* **1** to make (something) seem less bad by offering excuses ⟨Don't try to *palliate* your constant lying by claiming that everybody lies.⟩
synonyms excuse, explain away, extenuate, gloss (over), gloze (over), whitewash
related words sugarcoat, varnish; apologize, atone, confess; account (for), explain, justify, rationalize; minimize, play down, soft-pedal; alleviate, ease, lessen, lighten, mitigate, moderate, soften, temper; absolve, acquit, clear, exculpate, exonerate, vindicate

2 to make more bearable or less severe ⟨This medicine should *palliate* your cough at least a little.⟩ — see HELP 2

pallid *adj* lacking a healthy skin color ⟨a *pallid* man who looked as though he'd never seen the sun⟩ — see PALE 2

palm off *vb* to offer (something fake, useless, or inferior) as genuine, useful, or valuable ⟨Please stop trying to *palm off* your leftovers onto me.⟩ — see FOIST

palmy *adj* **1** having attained a desired end or state of good fortune ⟨They knew her in her *palmy* days when she was living high.⟩ — see SUCCESSFUL 1

2 marked by vigorous growth and well-being especially economically ⟨a *palmy* suburb with lots of new homes and shopping centers⟩ — see PROSPEROUS 1

palpable *adj* **1** able to be perceived by a sense or by the mind ⟨The tension in the negotiating room was *palpable*.⟩ — see PERCEPTIBLE

2 capable of being perceived by the sense of touch ⟨a small but *palpable* lump in my neck⟩ — see TANGIBLE

3 not subject to misinterpretation or more than one interpretation ⟨a *palpable* case of lying under oath⟩ — see CLEAR 2

palpitate *vb* to expand and contract in a rhythmic manner ⟨My heart began to *palpitate* when I was named the winner.⟩ — see PULSATE

palpitation *n* a rhythmic expanding and contracting ⟨a *palpitation* of the blood vessels⟩ — see PULSATION

palsy *adj* having or showing kindly feeling and sincere interest ⟨The salesman changed his *palsy* attitude when he realized that I wasn't buying.⟩ — see FRIENDLY 1

palsy *n* complete or partial loss of physical function (as motion or sensation) in a part of the body ⟨*Palsy* can sometimes be caused by a brain injury.⟩ — see PARALYSIS

palter *vb* to talk over or dispute the terms of a purchase ⟨unwilling to *palter* over the price of the car⟩ — see BARGAIN 1

paltry *adj* **1** arousing or deserving of one's loathing and disgust ⟨a *paltry*, underhanded scheme to get someone fired⟩ — see CONTEMPTIBLE 1

2 falling short of a standard ⟨The hotel's shabby, out-dated exercise room was its *paltry* attempt at a health spa.⟩ — see BAD 1

3 not following or in accordance with standards of honor and decency ⟨just some *paltry* ruse to bilk the system⟩ — see IGNOBLE 2

4 so small or unimportant as to warrant little or no attention ⟨The guy wanted me to sell him my old records for a *paltry* sum.⟩ — see NEGLIGIBLE 1

pamper *vb* to treat with great or excessive care ⟨Always *pamper* a sick child.⟩ — see BABY

pamphlet *n* a short printed publication with no cover or with a paper cover ⟨*pamphlets* about common safety precautions that we all can put into use⟩
synonyms booklet, brochure, circular, folder, leaflet
related words dodger, flysheet, handbill, handout, throwaway; advertisement, catalog (*or* catalogue), shopper; tract; paperback, paperbound, pocket book; guidebook, handbook, how-to, instructions, manual

pan *vb* to express one's unfavorable opinion of the worth or quality of ⟨Virtually all the movie critics have *panned* this latest sequel in a tired series.⟩ — see CRITICIZE

panacea *n* something that cures all ills or problems ⟨a woman who seems to believe that chicken soup is a *panacea* for nearly everything⟩ — see CURE-ALL

pancake *n* a flat cake made from thin batter and cooked on both sides (as on a griddle) ⟨Every Sunday morning, we have *pancakes* and bacon for breakfast.⟩
synonyms flapjack, griddle cake, hotcake, slapjack
related words oatcake, wheat cake; blin, blintze (*or* blintz), crepe (*or* crêpe)

pandemonium *n* **1** a state of noisy, confused activity ⟨Christmas morning at our house is always marked by *pandemonium*.⟩ — see COMMOTION
2 *cap* the place of punishment for the wicked after death ⟨a surrealist painting in which all the torments of *Pandemonium* are vividly depicted⟩ — see HELL 1

panegyric *n* a formal expression of praise ⟨wrote a *panegyric* on the centennial of the Nobel laureate's birth⟩ — see ENCOMIUM

panel *n* **1** a meeting featuring a group discussion ⟨There will be a discussion *panel* on Tuesday.⟩ — see FORUM 1
2 a select group of persons assigned to consider or take action on some matter ⟨assembled a prestigious *panel* to investigate ways to stem the rising cost of health care⟩ — see COMMITTEE

pang *n* a sharp unpleasant sensation usually felt in some specific part of the body ⟨those hunger *pangs* that strike you in the middle of the afternoon⟩ — see PAIN 1

panhandler *n* a person who lives by public begging ⟨a *panhandler* asking for money to buy food⟩ — see BEGGAR

panic *n* the emotion experienced in the presence or threat of danger ⟨The sudden sight of a grizzly bear filled the hiker with *panic*.⟩ — see FEAR 1

panic *vb* to strike with fear ⟨The car's headlights *panicked* the crossing deer.⟩ — see FRIGHTEN

panorama *n* all that can be seen from a certain point ⟨We admired the breathtaking *panorama* from the top of the mountain.⟩ — see VIEW 1

panoramic *adj* covering everything or all important points ⟨a *panoramic* look at America's fascination with the automobile⟩ — see ENCYCLOPEDIC

pan out *vb* **1** to come to be ⟨The eagerly anticipated kayaking trip never *panned out*.⟩ — see COME OUT 1
2 to turn out as planned or desired ⟨The investment scheme didn't quite *pan out*.⟩ — see SUCCEED 1

pant *vb* to breathe hard, quickly, or with difficulty ⟨The dog was *panting* heavily after his breakneck run across the field.⟩ — see GASP

pant (after) *vb* to have an earnest wish to own or enjoy ⟨teenage gamers *panting after* the latest video game⟩ — see DESIRE 1

pantaloons *pl n* an outer garment covering each leg separately from waist to ankle ⟨loose-fitting cotton *pantaloons* that are designed to be worn as loungewear⟩ — see PANTS

panther *n* a large tawny cat of the wild ⟨The *panther* is surprisingly difficult to spot.⟩ — see COUGAR

pantomime *n* **1** a movement of the body or limbs that expresses or emphasizes an idea or feeling ⟨The game requires that you use *pantomime* to communicate an idea.⟩ — see GESTURE 1
2 an actor in a story performed silently and entirely by body movements ⟨In ancient Rome *pantomimes* performed tragic love stories.⟩ — see MIME 1

pantomimist *n* an actor in a story performed silently and entirely by body movements ⟨an exquisitely graceful *pantomimist*⟩ — see MIME 1

pants *pl n* an outer garment covering each leg separately from waist to ankle ⟨You'll need a nice pair of *pants* for the job interview.⟩
synonyms breeches, britches, pantaloons, slacks, trousers
related words baggies, bell-bottoms, blue jeans, cargo pants, cords, corduroys, denims, jeans; hose, legging (*or* leggin), sweatpants; pants suit, pantsuit; bloomers, knee breeches, knickerbockers

papa *also* **poppa** *n* a male human parent ⟨a proud *papa* of newborn twins⟩ — see FATHER 1

paper *adj* being something in name or form only ⟨There's a *paper* boycott of that company's products that nobody seems to be honoring.⟩ — see NOMINAL 1

paper *n* **1** a piece of paper with information written or to be written on it ⟨handed in the correct *papers*⟩ — see FORM 2
2 a publication that appears at regular intervals ⟨We get the *paper* every morning.⟩ — see JOURNAL
3 a short piece of writing done as a school exercise ⟨Write a *paper* about your favorite author.⟩ — see COMPOSITION 2
4 a short piece of writing typically expressing a point of view ⟨the *papers* written by the Founding Fathers urging adoption of the federal constitution⟩ — see ESSAY 1

par *n* **1** something set up as an example against which others of the same type are compared ⟨That last dining experience was not quite up to *par*.⟩ — see STANDARD 1
2 the state or fact of being exactly the same in number, amount, status, or quality ⟨The food at this local restaurant is on a *par* with some I've had in the city.⟩ — see EQUIVALENCE
3 what is typical of a group, class, or series ⟨A pulse of 70 is *par* for people of that age group.⟩ — see AVERAGE

parable *n* a story intended to teach a basic truth or moral about life ⟨the *parable* in which the repentant sinner is compared to the returning prodigal son who is welcomed home⟩ — see ALLEGORY

parade *n* a body of individuals moving along in an orderly and often ceremonial way ⟨a Fourth of July *parade*⟩ — see CORTEGE 2

parade *vb* **1** to move along with a steady regular step especially in a group ⟨The marching band *paraded* past jubilant crowds.⟩ — see MARCH 1
2 to present so as to invite notice or attention ⟨Sara intends to *parade* her expensive new dress at the party.⟩ — see SHOW 1

paradigmatic *adj* constituting, serving as, or worthy of being a pattern to be imitated ⟨a *paradigmatic* essay in which the writer presents his point of view clearly and engagingly⟩ — see MODEL

paradise *n* **1** an often imaginary place or state of utter perfection and happiness ⟨an idealist who trotted the globe looking for *paradise*⟩
synonyms Eden, Elysium, heaven, promised land, utopia
related words arcadia; dreamland, dreamworld, fairyland, wonderland
phrases Garden of Eden
near antonyms fool's paradise
antonyms hell
2 a dwelling place of perfect happiness for the soul after death ⟨a firm belief that good people will be rewarded in *paradise*⟩ — see HEAVEN 1
3 a state of overwhelming usually pleasurable emotion ⟨that early stage of a romance when the couple is in *paradise*⟩ — see ECSTASY
paradox *n* someone or something with qualities or features that seem to conflict with one another ⟨the *paradox* of fighting a war for peace⟩ — see CONTRADICTION 1
paragon *n* someone of such unequaled perfection as to deserve imitation ⟨In Arthurian legend, Sir Galahad is depicted as the one knight who is a *paragon* of virtue.⟩ — see IDEAL 1
parallel *adj* having qualities in common ⟨*parallel* lives of two friends who first met in college⟩ — see ALIKE
parallel *n* **1** a point which two or more things share in common ⟨Her professor pointed out some *parallels* between the two novels.⟩ — see SIMILARITY 2
2 one that is equal to another in status, achievement, or value ⟨an advance that is without *parallel* in the history of virology⟩ — see EQUAL
parallel *vb* to be the exact counterpart of ⟨Developments in the television show *paralleled* those in the lead actor's real life.⟩ — see MATCH 1
parallelism *n* the quality or state of having many qualities in common ⟨The striking *parallelism* between the two poems got scholars to thinking that they were written by the same person.⟩ — see SIMILARITY 1
paralysis *n* complete or partial loss of physical function (as motion or sensation) in a part of the body ⟨a tick bite that can result in a dog's *paralysis*⟩
synonyms palsy
related words cerebral palsy, multiple sclerosis, poliomyelitis; debilitation, debility, decrepitude, enfeeblement, feebleness, frailness, frailty, weakness; infirmity, lameness; disability, impairment; paraplegia, paresis, quadriplegia, spastic paralysis
near antonyms mobility, motility, sensation
paralytic *adj* affected with paralysis ⟨Animals with rabies eventually enter a *paralytic* stage.⟩
synonyms paralyzed
related words challenged, crippled, disabled, maimed, mutilated; halt, hobbled, lame, lamed; impaired, incapacitated; paraplegic, paretic, quadriplegic; debilitated, decrepit, enfeebled, feeble, frail, infirm, wasted, weak, weakened
near antonyms able-bodied; fit, hale, healthy, hearty, robust, sound, well, whole
paralyze *vb* **1** to render powerless, ineffective, or unable to move ⟨A blizzard *paralyzed* the city for two days.⟩
synonyms cripple, disable, hamstring, immobilize, incapacitate, prostrate
related words debilitate, enervate, enfeeble, sap, tire, undercut, undermine, weaken; hobble, lame; maim, mutilate
near antonyms energize, galvanize, invigorate, vitalize; fortify, strengthen; empower; freshen, refresh, refreshen, regenerate, rejuvenate, restore, revitalize, revive
2 to deprive of courage or confidence ⟨The school board is *paralyzed* by the threat of lawsuits.⟩ — see UNNERVE 1

paralyzed *adj* **1** affected with paralysis ⟨an event in the Paralympics for *paralyzed* athletes⟩ — see PARALYTIC
2 unable to act or achieve one's purpose ⟨was *paralyzed* with indecision⟩ — see POWERLESS
paramount *adj* **1** coming before all others in importance ⟨The *paramount* goal is to restore the colonial-era house with complete historical accuracy.⟩ — see FOREMOST 1
2 of the greatest or highest degree or quantity ⟨Maintaining the secrecy of the agreement is of *paramount* importance.⟩ — see ULTIMATE 1
paraphernalia *n* **1** items needed for the performance of a task or activity ⟨mountain-climbing *paraphernalia*⟩ — see EQUIPMENT
2 transportable items that one owns ⟨The Browns packed up all of their *paraphernalia* for the move across the country.⟩ — see POSSESSION 2
paraphrase *n* an instance of expressing something in different words ⟨Your essays on human rights should have some original thought and not be simply a *paraphrase* of what's in the textbook.⟩
synonyms rephrasing, restatement, restating, rewording, translating, translation
related words rehash; abstract, recap, recapitulation, reiteration, summary
near antonyms copy, transcript, transcription
antonyms quotation, quote
paraphrase *vb* to express something (as a text or statement) in different words ⟨Could you *paraphrase* your diagnosis of my medical condition, using simpler language?⟩
synonyms rephrase, restate, reword, translate
related words recapitulate, reiterate, summarize, sum up
near antonyms echo, repeat; copy, reproduce, transcribe
antonyms quote
parasite *n* a person who is supported by or seeks support from another without making an adequate return ⟨a *parasite* who's always borrowing money⟩ — see LEECH
parboil *vb* to cook in a liquid heated to the point that it gives off steam ⟨First, *parboil* a lobster.⟩ — see BOIL 2
parcel *n* **1** a number of things considered as a unit ⟨Her absurd explanation for the collision was a *parcel* of lies.⟩ — see GROUP 1
2 a small area of usually open land ⟨wandered around the little *parcel* out back⟩ — see FIELD 1
3 a small piece of land that is developed or available for development ⟨subdivided the huge farm into smaller *parcels* for sale⟩ — see LOT 1
4 a usually small number of persons considered as a unit ⟨a *parcel* of kids trailing at their heels⟩ — see GROUP 2
5 a wrapped or sealed case containing an item or set of items ⟨We received a mysterious *parcel* in the mail.⟩ — see PACKAGE 1
parcel (out) *vb* to give out (something) to appropriate individuals ⟨*parceled out* the assignments for work on the science fair⟩ — see ADMINISTER 1
parcel post *n* communications or parcels sent or carried through the postal system ⟨Only *parcel post* bearing a return address and not exceeding size and weight limits will be accepted.⟩ — see MAIL
parch *vb* to make dry ⟨The heat has really *parched* my throat.⟩ — see DRY 1
pardon *n* release from the guilt or penalty of an offense ⟨The criminal is hoping for a presidential *pardon*.⟩
synonyms absolution, amnesty, forgiveness, remission, remittal
related words parole; acquittal, exculpation, exoneration, vindication; condonation; exemption, immunity,

impunity, indemnity; commutation, commuting, reprieve; clemency, leniency, mercy
near antonyms conviction, sentence; assessment, charge, fine, imposition, levying; castigation, chastening, chastisement, condemnation
antonyms penalty, punishment, retribution
pardon *vb* **1** to cease to have feelings of anger or bitterness toward ⟨He eventually *pardoned* his sister for her selfish behavior.⟩ — see FORGIVE 1
2 to dismiss as of little importance ⟨His tardiness should be *pardoned*, given that we changed the time to meet.⟩ — see EXCUSE 1
pardonable *adj* worthy of forgiveness ⟨The new parents' gushing pride was *pardonable*.⟩ — see VENIAL
pare *vb* to make (something) shorter or smaller with the use of a cutting instrument ⟨*pared* the stray branches on the tree⟩ — see CLIP 1
parentage *n* the line of ancestors from whom a person is descended ⟨She was born in Canada, but is of Korean *parentage*.⟩ — see ANCESTRY
parenthood *n* the caring for a child by its parents ⟨*Parenthood* is a difficult task requiring great commitment.⟩ — see PARENTING
parenting *n* the caring for a child by its parents ⟨As the big day approaches, the expectant couple are starting to get worried about their readiness for *parenting*.⟩
synonyms parenthood
related words raising, rearing, upbringing; fatherhood, fathering, paternity; maternity, motherhood, mothering; caregiving, caretaking
par excellence *adj* of the very best kind ⟨sophisticated cuisine that is obviously the work of a chef *par excellence*⟩ — see EXCELLENT
pariah *n* one who is cast out or rejected by society ⟨He's a talented player but his temperament has made him a *pariah* in the game.⟩ — see OUTCAST
parity *n* the state or fact of being exactly the same in number, amount, status, or quality ⟨rules requiring that there be *parity* in what schools spend on men's and women's sports⟩ — see EQUIVALENCE
park *n* the area around and belonging to a building ⟨The tycoon's country estate is surrounded by a 500-acre *park*.⟩ — see GROUND 1
parley *n* **1** a meeting featuring a group discussion ⟨held a *parley* to debate the proposed change in the town's zoning laws⟩ — see FORUM 1
2 an exchange of views for the purpose of exploring a subject or deciding an issue ⟨Can we meet for an informal *parley* to see if we can effect a compromise?⟩ — see DISCUSSION 1
parley *vb* to exchange viewpoints or seek advice for the purpose of finding a solution to a problem ⟨In an effort to win the goodwill of the locals, the developers *parleyed* with them before finalizing plans for the massive mall.⟩ — see CONFER 2
parliament *n* the highest lawmaking body of a political unit ⟨The treaty was referred to the nation's *parliament* for ratification.⟩ — see CONGRESS 1
parlor *n* a building, room, or suite of rooms occupied by a service business ⟨an ice cream *parlor* with a 1950s theme⟩ — see PLACE 2
parlous *adj* involving potential loss or injury ⟨Window washing can indeed be a *parlous* occupation on a skyscraper.⟩ — see DANGEROUS 1
parochial *adj* not broad or open in views or opinions ⟨the *parochial* outlook of the people in that town⟩ — see NARROW 2
parody *n* **1** a work that imitates and exaggerates another work for comic effect ⟨The musical is a *parody* of every biblical epic ever made.⟩

synonyms burlesque, caricature, put-on, spoof, takeoff, travesty
related words lampoon, mockery, satire; comedy, farce, humor, sketch, slapstick, squib; distortion, exaggeration; imitation, impersonation, mimicking
2 a poor, insincere, or insulting imitation of something ⟨The young man sported a feeble *parody* of a mustache in a vain attempt to make himself look older.⟩ — see MOCKERY 1
parody *vb* to copy or exaggerate (someone or something) in order to make fun of ⟨*Parodying* a public figure's distinctive mannerisms takes particular talent.⟩ — see MIMIC 1
paroxysm *n* **1** a sudden intense expression of strong feeling ⟨A *paroxysm* of laughter greeted the pratfall.⟩ — see OUTBURST 1
2 a violent disturbance (as of the political or social order) ⟨Darwin's introduction of the theory of evolution created *paroxysms* in both religion and science that are still being felt today.⟩ — see CONVULSION
parrot *vb* to say after another ⟨The toddler *parroted* everything her father said, often to the latter's embarrassment.⟩ — see REPEAT 3
parsimonious *adj* giving or sharing as little as possible ⟨a *parsimonious* woman who insists that charity begins—and ends—at home⟩ — see STINGY 1
parsimony *n* **1** the quality or practice of being overly sparing with money ⟨Her *parsimony* was so extreme that she'd walk five miles to the store to save a few cents on gas.⟩
synonyms cheapness, closeness, miserliness, penuriousness, pinching, stinginess, tightness
related words conserving, economizing, economy, frugality, husbandry, providence, scrimping, skimping, thrift; conservation, saving; husbanding, managing
near antonyms bountifulness, bounty, generosity, largesse (*also* largess), liberality, openhandedness, openheartedness, philanthropy, unselfishness; extravagance, lavishness; dissipation, improvidence, prodigality, squandering, wastefulness
2 careful management of material resources ⟨People often think that the good times will last forever and have little interest in *parsimony*.⟩ — see ECONOMY
part *adv* in some measure or degree ⟨Well, you're at least *part* right about her original name.⟩ — see PARTLY
part *n* **1** one of the pieces from which something is designed to be assembled ⟨The model car came in several small *parts* that had to be put together.⟩
synonyms member, partition, portion, section, segment
related words component, constituent, element, factor, ingredient, parcel; bit, fragment, particle, scrap
near antonyms whole; aggregate, composite, compound, sum, total, totality
2 something belonging to, due to, or contributed by an individual member of a group ⟨wanted no *part* of the profits⟩ — see SHARE 1
3 the action for which a person or thing is specially fitted or used or for which a thing exists ⟨I'll do my *part*, so don't worry.⟩ — see ROLE
4 *usually* **parts** *pl* a broad geographical area ⟨I'm not from around these *parts*.⟩ — see REGION 2
part *vb* **1** to go or move in different directions from a central point ⟨After traveling together for three weeks, we *parted* at Rome.⟩ — see SEPARATE 2
2 to leave a place often for another ⟨We *parted* with great ceremony but with little preparation for the dangers that lay ahead.⟩ — see GO 2
3 to set or force apart ⟨*parted* the prongs with pliers⟩ — see SEPARATE 1
4 to stop living ⟨Before I *part*, I hope I have the opportunity to say my good-byes.⟩ — see DIE 1

partake *vb* **1** to take a share or part ⟨We should all *partake* of the city's rich cultural offerings while we have the opportunity.⟩
synonyms participate, share
related words endure, experience, feel, know, see, taste, undergo; encounter, meet; accept
2 to take a meal ⟨"Let us *partake*," our minister declared, unfolding his napkin and eyeing the feast laid out before us.⟩ — see DINE 1

partaker *n* one who takes part in something ⟨*partakers* in the ceremony⟩ — see PARTICIPANT

partial *adj* **1** inclined to favor one side over another ⟨That judge is always *partial* to the defense, so be careful.⟩
synonyms biased, one-sided, partisan, prejudiced
related words hostile, inimical, jaundiced, unfriendly, unsympathetic; distorted, misrepresented, shaded, warped
near antonyms open, open-minded, persuasible, receptive; aloof, detached, dispassionate, hardheaded, impersonal, unemotional; cold, distant, remote; apathetic, incurious, indifferent, unconcerned, uncurious, unenthusiastic, uninterested
antonyms disinterested, equal, equitable, evenhanded, fair, impartial, neutral, nonpartisan, objective, unbiased, unprejudiced
2 having a liking or affection ⟨I'm *partial* to chocolate cake.⟩ — see FOND 1
3 lacking some necessary part ⟨a *partial* answer to the problem⟩ — see INCOMPLETE

partiality *n* **1** an attitude that always favors one way of feeling or acting especially without considering any other possibilities ⟨*Partiality* blinded the administrator to the benefits of the proposed system for distributing work.⟩ — see BIAS 1
2 a habitual attraction to some activity or thing ⟨a person with an unfortunate *partiality* for jumping to conclusions⟩ — see INCLINATION 1
3 positive regard for something ⟨a *partiality* toward outdoor sports of all kinds⟩ — see LIKING

partially *adv* in some measure or degree ⟨The construction project is only *partially* complete.⟩ — see PARTLY

participant *n* one who takes part in something ⟨He seemed to be a willing *participant* in the prank.⟩
synonyms actor, partaker, participator, party, player, sharer
related words accessory (*also* accessary), aide, assistant, helper; colleague, partner
near antonyms looker-on, watcher
antonyms nonparticipant

participate *vb* to take a share or part ⟨eager to *participate* in the city's cultural life⟩ — see PARTAKE 1

participator *n* one who takes part in something ⟨a willing *participator* in any activity anyone suggested⟩ — see PARTICIPANT

particle *n* **1** a very small amount ⟨There was not a *particle* of truth in what she said.⟩
synonyms ace, bit, crumb, dab, driblet, glimmer, hint, lick, little, mite, nip, ounce, peanuts, ray, scruple, shade, shadow, shred, smack, smidgen (*also* smidgeon *or* smidgin *or* smidge), snap, spark, spatter, speck, splash, spot, sprinkling, strain, streak, suspicion, tad, touch, trace
related words hoot, iota, jot, minim, minimum, modicum, semblance, tittle, vestige, whit; atom, dot, fleck, flyspeck, grain, granule, molecule, morsel, mote, nubbin, patch, scrap; dash, drop, pinch; part, portion, section; bite, nibble, taste; handful, scattering, smattering; dose, shot
phrases drop in the bucket
near antonyms abundance, barrel, boatload, bucket,

bundle, bushel, deal, gobs, heaps, loads, lot, mass, mess, mountain, much, oodles, passel, peck, pile, plenty, potful, profusion, quantity, raft, reams, scads, stack, wad, wealth; volume; chunk, hunk, lump, slab
2 a very small piece ⟨A *particle* of cookie fell on the carpet.⟩ — see BIT 1

particular *adj* **1** hard to please ⟨She's very *particular* about the cleanliness of her car.⟩ — see FINICKY
2 of, relating to, or belonging to a single person ⟨That *particular* mug is Mike's.⟩ — see INDIVIDUAL 1
3 tending to select carefully ⟨He's *particular* about the corn he buys.⟩ — see SELECTIVE
4 including many small descriptive features ⟨a very *particular* account of the trip⟩ — see DETAILED 1

particular *n* **1** a separate part in a list, account, or series ⟨Noah requested a bill of *particulars* for the care he received in the hospital.⟩ — see ITEM 1
2 a single piece of information ⟨Everyone wanted to know all the *particulars* about the forthcoming merger.⟩ — see FACT 3

particularity *n* **1** careful thoroughness of detail ⟨With great *particularity* she described the scene.⟩
synonyms explicitness, specificity
related words attentiveness, care, carefulness, conscientiousness, finicalness, finickiness, fussiness, meticulosity, meticulousness; alertness, cautiousness, circumspection, heedfulness, scrupulousness; discrimination, selectivity; accuracy, definitude, exactitude, exactness, fineness, preciseness, precision
near antonyms imprecision, inaccuracy, inexactness; indistinctness, vagueness
antonyms generality
2 a single piece of information ⟨I can't comment without knowing the *particularities* of the case before the court.⟩ — see FACT 3
3 something that sets apart an individual from others of the same kind ⟨a novel that gets the *particularities* of life in academia exactly right⟩ — see CHARACTERISTIC

particularized *adj* including many small descriptive features ⟨The hope is that from their *particularized* descriptions of the landscape we can retrace the explorers' route.⟩ — see DETAILED 1

particularly *adv* **1** in the specific case of one person or thing as distinguished from others ⟨All of you, but *particularly* anyone with a problem, should feel free to contact me at any time.⟩ — see ESPECIALLY 1
2 to a great degree ⟨a *particularly* good explanation⟩ — see VERY 1

parting *adj* given, taken, or performed at parting ⟨She gave him a *parting* gift to remember her by.⟩
synonyms farewell, valedictory
related words closing, concluding, final, last, ultimate; departing, leaving

parting *n* **1** the act or process of two or more persons going off in different directions ⟨Although their *parting* was sad, they knew they would see each other again.⟩
synonyms farewell, leave-taking, separation
related words departure, exit, exiting, exodus, going, leaving, quitting, running away; decamping, decampment, flight, withdrawal; abandonment, desertion, forsaking
near antonyms reunion; arrival, greeting, salutation, welcome; gathering, joining, meeting
2 the act of leaving a place ⟨Everyone waved goodbye at his *parting*.⟩ — see DEPARTURE 1

partisan *adj* inclined to favor one side over another ⟨a shamelessly *partisan* reporter covering the primary campaign⟩ — see PARTIAL 1

partisan *also* **partizan** *n* **1** one who follows the opinions or teachings of another ⟨*Partisans* of the charismatic leader refuse to tolerate any criticism of him at all.⟩ — see FOLLOWER 1

2 one who is intensely or excessively devoted to a cause ⟨a *partisan* of the revolution who devoted her life to achieving its aims⟩ — see ZEALOT

3 one who stubbornly or intolerantly adheres to his or her own opinions and prejudices ⟨She's too much of a political *partisan* to ever concede that the other side might have a valid point.⟩ — see BIGOT

partisanship *n* an attitude that always favors one way of feeling or acting especially without considering any other possibilities ⟨*Partisanship* can discourage any serious search for the truth.⟩ — see BIAS 1

partition *n* **1** one of the pieces from which something is designed to be assembled ⟨one of the *partitions* of a prefabricated house⟩ — see PART 1

2 something that divides, separates, or marks off ⟨Let's put up a *partition* to divide the room into two.⟩ — see DIVISION 1

3 the act or process of a whole separating into two or more parts or pieces ⟨the *partition* of Czechoslovakia into the Czech Republic and Slovakia⟩ — see SEPARATION 1

partly *adv* in some measure or degree ⟨You're only *partly* right.⟩
synonyms half, halfway, incompletely, part, partially
related words fairly, kind of, like, moderately, more or less, pretty, quite, rather, relatively, somewhat, sort of
phrases in part
near antonyms absolutely, dead, downright, plain; especially, exceedingly (*also* exceeding), exceptionally, extremely, greatly, highly, hugely, particularly, very
antonyms all, altogether, completely, entirely, fully, perfectly, quite, totally, utterly, wholly

partner *n* the person to whom another is married ⟨The family welcomed his new *partner* with open arms.⟩ — see SPOUSE

partnership *n* the state of having shared interests or efforts (as in social or business matters) ⟨The symphony orchestra is presenting the choral piece in *partnership* with the city's leading choral society.⟩ — see ASSOCIATION 1

parturition *n* the act or process of giving birth to children ⟨*Parturition* can sometimes proceed more quickly than anticipated.⟩ — see CHILDBIRTH

party *n* **1** a social gathering ⟨We're all invited to the big *party* to celebrate the end of the year.⟩
synonyms affair, bash, binge, blast, blowout, do, event, fete (*or* fête), function, get-together, reception, shindig
related words benefit, fund-raiser; celebration, gala, occasion; bake, clambake, cocktail party, hen party, house party, housewarming, icebreaker, meet and greet, mixer, salon, shower, social, soiree (*or* soirée), supper, symposium, tea, tea party

2 a group of people acting together within a larger group ⟨A small *party* got together to protest the new chairman's decision.⟩ — see FACTION

3 a group of people working together on a task ⟨a search *party*⟩ — see GANG 1

4 a member of the human race ⟨My grandfather's a determined old *party*, so don't underestimate him.⟩ — see HUMAN

5 a usually small number of persons considered as a unit ⟨For *parties* of more than six people the restaurant automatically adds a 20% service charge to the bill.⟩ — see GROUP 2

6 one who takes part in something ⟨a *party* to the agreement⟩ — see PARTICIPANT

¹**pass** *n* **1** a narrow opening between hillsides or mountains that can be used for passage ⟨a mountain *pass* that was impassable during the winter⟩ — see CANYON

2 a passage cleared for public vehicular travel ⟨Take the second *pass* on the right.⟩ — see WAY 1

²**pass** *n* **1** a small sheet of plastic, paper, or paperboard showing that the bearer has a claim to something (as admittance) ⟨a *pass* to leave the military base for the weekend⟩ — see TICKET 1

2 an effort to do or accomplish something ⟨a final *pass* at the assignment⟩ — see ATTEMPT 1

3 the state of being actual or complete ⟨Eventually, all their career goals came to *pass*.⟩ — see FRUITION

pass *vb* **1** to shift possession of (something) from one person to another ⟨Could you please *pass* me the phone?⟩
synonyms buck, hand, hand over, reach, transfer
related words relay; bear, carry; handle, paw; cede, deliver, give, give up, release, relinquish, render, surrender, turn over, yield

2 to come to an end ⟨Eventually, the storm *passed*.⟩ — see CEASE 1

3 to put (something) into the possession or safekeeping of another ⟨*Pass* your forms to the department head once they're filled out.⟩ — see GIVE 2

4 to put into effect through legislative or authoritative action ⟨Congress cannot *pass* any law restricting free speech.⟩ — see ENACT

5 to take place ⟨And the destruction of the town came to *pass*, just as the seer had predicted.⟩ — see HAPPEN

6 to come to a knowledge of (something) by living through it ⟨a presidential candidate who doesn't yet know how it feels to *pass* the scrutiny of the national press⟩ — see EXPERIENCE

7 to express (a thought or emotion) in words ⟨She'll occasionally *pass* some insightful comment, but in general she doesn't have much to contribute.⟩ — see SAY 1

8 to show unwillingness to accept, do, engage in, or agree to ⟨We appreciate the invitation to the party, but we'll have to *pass*.⟩ ⟨I'll *pass* on the coffee.⟩ — see DECLINE 1

9 to withstand scrutiny and gain acceptance or approval ⟨The finished product isn't perfect, but it will *pass*.⟩ — see WASH 2

pass (on) *vb* to stop living ⟨My grandfather *passed on* at the age of 92.⟩ — see DIE 1

pass (over) *vb* to make one's way through, across, or over ⟨*passed over* two bridges⟩ — see TRAVERSE

passable *adj* **1** capable of being traveled on ⟨After the snowstorm ends, the roads might not be *passable* for the morning ride to school.⟩
synonyms navigable, negotiable
related words clear, cleared, free, open, unclogged, unclosed, unobstructed, unstopped
near antonyms blocked, choked, clogged, closed, congested, dammed, jammed, obstructed, plugged (up), stopped (up), stuffed; barricaded, blockaded
antonyms impassable (*also* impassible), unnegotiable, unpassable

2 capable of being passed into or through ⟨The jungle is not *passable* without a machete.⟩ — see PENETRABLE

3 of a level of quality that meets one's needs or standards ⟨That's a *passable* paper.⟩ — see ADEQUATE

4 of average to below average quality ⟨The actor's Scottish accent is *passable* at best.⟩ — see MEDIOCRE 1

passably *adv* in a satisfactory way ⟨He speaks Chinese *passably*.⟩ — see WELL 1

passage *n* **1** an established course for traveling from one place to another ⟨the long *passage* down the Atlantic seaboard, around Cape Horn, and up the Pacific Coast to California⟩
synonyms approach, avenue, path, route, way
related words bypath, byway, lane; artery, boulevard, bypass, drive, expressway, freeway, highway, pass, pas-

sageway, pike, road, roadway, row, street, thoroughfare, turnpike; walk, walkway; trace, track, trail; airway; bikeway; channel, gat, watercourse, waterway; door

2 a going from one place to another usually of some distance ⟨an arduous *passage* across the country⟩ — see JOURNEY

3 a journey over water in a vessel ⟨The *passage* to Britain requires several days.⟩ — see SAIL

4 a part taken from a longer work ⟨The news report quoted a *passage* from the novel.⟩ — see EXCERPT

5 forward movement in time or place ⟨a swift *passage* from mere liking to actual love⟩ — see ADVANCE 1

6 the permanent stopping of all the vital bodily activities ⟨sent condolences for the *passage* of her uncle⟩ — see DEATH 1

passageway *n* a typically long narrow way connecting parts of a building ⟨the *passageway* to the other side of the office⟩ — see HALL 2

pass away *vb* to stop living ⟨The old woman *passed away* quietly.⟩ — see DIE 1

passé *adj* having passed its time of use or usefulness ⟨That literary style is a bit *passé* nowadays.⟩ — see OBSOLETE

passel *n* **1** a number of things considered as a unit ⟨Reporters had a whole *passel* of questions for the new basketball coach.⟩ — see GROUP 1

2 a usually small number of persons considered as a unit ⟨The young couple had a *passel* of babies in the span of a few years.⟩ — see GROUP 2

3 a considerable amount ⟨a whole *passel* of unauthorized software on his computer⟩ — see LOT 2

passing *adj* lasting only for a short time ⟨His parents were willing to buy him a piano if he demonstrated that his interest in music was more than a *passing* fancy.⟩ — see MOMENTARY

passing *adv* to a great degree ⟨a *passing* strange turn of events⟩ — see VERY 1

passing *n* the permanent stopping of all the vital bodily activities ⟨surrounded by family at the time of his *passing*⟩ — see DEATH 1

passion *n* **1** a feeling of strong or constant regard for and dedication to someone ⟨Married at the age of 25, they share a *passion* that has lasted for over half a century.⟩ — see LOVE 1

2 a strong but often short-lived liking for another person ⟨a *passion* that fizzled in a few months time⟩ — see CRUSH 1

3 a strong wish for something ⟨a *passion* to become a doctor⟩ — see DESIRE 1

4 a subjective response to a person, thing, or situation ⟨Sometimes people are not in control of their own *passions*.⟩ — see FEELING 1

5 depth of feeling ⟨Your *passion* for your cause is admirable, but you still should be respectful of people who disagree with you.⟩ — see ARDOR 1

6 **passions** *pl* general emotional condition ⟨people who are swayed by their *passions* and not by reason⟩ — see FEELING 2

7 intense sexual desire ⟨the *passion* of honeymooners⟩ — see LUST 1

passionate *adj* **1** having a strong sexual desire ⟨a *passionate* couple counting the days till they'd be reunited⟩ — see LUSTFUL

2 having or expressing great depth of feeling ⟨a *passionate* defense of the controversial play⟩ — see FERVENT 1

passive *adj* receiving or enduring without offering resistance ⟨The union rank and file were surprisingly *passive* about the givebacks in the new labor contract.⟩

synonyms acquiescent, nonresistant, resigned, tolerant, tolerating, unresistant, yielding

related words forbearing, impassive, long-suffering, patient, stoic (*or* stoical), uncomplaining; agreeable, amenable, compliant, complying, docile, guidable, obedient, pliable, pliant, subordinate, tractable, willing; obeisant, submissive, surrendering; amiable, obliging; subservient; disciplined, governable, manageable; apathetic, uncaring, unresponsive

near antonyms defiant; contrary, disobedient, froward, insubordinate, insurgent, intractable, rebellious, recalcitrant, refractory, restive, uncontrollable, ungovernable, unruly, untoward; balky, perverse, wayward, wrongheaded; headstrong, willful (*or* wilful); indomitable; undisciplined, unmanageable; dissident, nonconformist

antonyms protesting, resistant, resisting, unyielding

pass off *vb* to offer (something fake, useless, or inferior) as genuine, useful, or valuable ⟨The con man tried to *pass off* a piece of blue glass as a sapphire.⟩ — see FOIST

pass out *vb* to lose consciousness ⟨I *passed out* from the flu.⟩ — see FAINT

pass over *vb* **1** to fail to give proper attention to ⟨You seem to have *passed over* an important e-mail notice.⟩ — see NEGLECT 1

2 to dismiss as of little importance ⟨I'd be willing to *pass over* this latest episode of tardiness if there hadn't been so many before.⟩ — see EXCUSE 1

passport *n* **1** something that allows someone to achieve a desired goal ⟨Meeting that movie director could be your *passport* to a big acting career.⟩

synonyms gateway, key, open sesame, secret, ticket

related words password; accomplishment, achievement, attainment, coup, success, triumph; blueprint, design, ground plan, plan, program, scheme, strategy

2 the means or right of entering or participating in ⟨Your park admission ticket is a *passport* to fun.⟩ — see ENTRANCE 1

password *n* a word or phrase that must be spoken by a person in order to pass a guard ⟨No one gets in without the *password*.⟩

synonyms countersign, watchword, word

related words shibboleth, sign; signal; hint, indication; parole

past *adj* having been such at some previous time ⟨a *past* editor of the newspaper⟩ — see FORMER 1

past *n* the events or experience of former times ⟨We spent a pleasant evening recalling the *past* together.⟩

synonyms auld lang syne, history, yesterday, yesteryear, yore

related words bygone; flashback; annals, chronicle, record; memoir; long ago

near antonyms by-and-by, future, futurity, hereafter, offing; moment, now, present, today

past *prep* **1** on or to the farther side of ⟨I drive *past* the school every day.⟩ — see BEYOND 1

2 subsequent to in time or order ⟨It's ten minutes *past* six o'clock.⟩ — see AFTER

paste *vb* **1** to defeat by a large margin ⟨With the economy having gone south, it was hardly surprising that the incumbent party got *pasted* in the general election.⟩ — see WHIP 2

2 to deliver a blow to (someone or something) usually in a strong vigorous manner ⟨*pasted* the soccer ball halfway across the field⟩ — see HIT 1

pastel *adj* lacking intensity of color ⟨a *pastel* blue to go with the pale pink walls⟩ — see PALE 1

past master *n* a person with a high level of knowledge or skill in a field ⟨a movie director who was widely regarded as the *past master* of suspense⟩ — see EXPERT

pastoral *adj* **1** of, relating to, associated with, or typical of open areas with few buildings or people ⟨painted a *pastoral* scene of a flower-filled meadow⟩ — see RURAL

2 of, relating to, or characteristic of the clergy ⟨*pastoral* advice to a young couple preparing to marry⟩ — see CLERICAL

pasturage *n* open land over which livestock may roam and feed ⟨We put the cows out on the back *pasturage*.⟩ — see RANGE 1

pasture *n* open land over which livestock may roam and feed ⟨horses grazing in a fenced *pasture*⟩ — see RANGE 1

pasture *vb* to feed on grass or herbs ⟨*Pasturing* sheep on town lands was actually a cheaper alternative to mowing.⟩ — see ¹GRAZE

pasty *adj* lacking a healthy skin color ⟨She's *pasty* after a whole winter spent indoors.⟩ — see PALE 2

pat *adj* sticking to an opinion, purpose, or course of action in spite of reason, arguments, or persuasion ⟨Despite our objections, they are going to stand *pat* on the decision.⟩ — see OBSTINATE

pat *adv* without any flaws or errors ⟨After months of practicing for the competition, the cheerleaders have their moves down *pat*.⟩ — see PERFECTLY 1

pat *vb* to touch or handle in a tender or loving manner ⟨affectionately *patted* the baby on the head⟩ — see FONDLE

patch *n* **1** a small area that is different (as in color) from the main part ⟨a black cat with a small *patch* of white next to her nose⟩ — see SPOT 1

2 a very small piece ⟨a *patch* of land hardly big enough for a garden⟩ — see BIT 1

patch *vb* to put into good shape or working order again ⟨*Patch* the tire and it'll be as good as new.⟩ — see MEND 1

patchwork *adj* consisting of many things of different sorts ⟨a *patchwork* collection of antiques from different periods⟩ — see MISCELLANEOUS

patchwork *n* an unorganized collection or mixture of various things ⟨the state's *patchwork* of outdated laws regulating commercial activity on Sundays⟩ — see MISCELLANY 1

pate *n* the upper or front part of the body that contains the brain, the major sense organs, and the mouth ⟨plopped a cap on his bald *pate*⟩ — see HEAD 1

patent *adj* **1** not subject to misinterpretation or more than one interpretation ⟨Unfortunately, the *patent* infeasibility of the proposal did not deter the city council from putting it up for a vote.⟩ — see CLEAR 2

2 very noticeable especially for being incorrect or bad ⟨a *patent* error that should have been caught before the book was published⟩ — see EGREGIOUS

path *n* **1** the direction along which something or someone moves ⟨Try to stay out of the *path* of the golf balls while playing.⟩ ⟨I tripped over a rock directly in my *path*.⟩

synonyms course, line, pathway, route, steps, track, way

related words circle, loop, orbit; arc, flight path, trajectory; ascent, descent

2 a rough course or way formed by or as if by repeated footsteps ⟨a *path* worn through the library lawn by too many people walking over it⟩ — see TRAIL 1

3 an established course for traveling from one place to another ⟨The *path* along which ancient traders traveled from Europe to China was known as the Silk Road.⟩ — see PASSAGE 1

pathetic *adj* **1** deserving of one's pity ⟨The plight of the homeless animals was quite *pathetic*.⟩

synonyms heartbreaking, heartrending, miserable, piteous, pitiable, pitiful, poor, rueful, sorry, wretched

related words deplorable, lamentable, regrettable; emotional, impressive, inspiring; affecting, moving, poignant, stirring, touching; distressing, disturbing, upsetting; grievous, mournful, sad, sorrowful, woeful

near antonyms unimpressive, uninspiring

2 causing unhappiness ⟨a *pathetic* story that made her cry⟩ — see SAD 2

3 deserving pitying scorn (as for inadequacy) ⟨The crowd mercilessly booed the boxer's *pathetic* performance.⟩ — see PITIFUL 1

4 so foolish or pointless as to be worthy of scornful laughter ⟨The pundit's latest book is another *pathetic* jumble of factual errors, half-baked political views, and baseless accusations.⟩ — see RIDICULOUS 1

pathway *n* **1** a rough course or way formed by or as if by repeated footsteps ⟨We parked our car near a rambling *pathway* that led down to the pond.⟩ — see TRAIL 1

2 the direction along which something or someone moves ⟨the long, winding *pathway* of the river before it meets the sea⟩ — see PATH 1

patience *n* the capacity to endure what is difficult or disagreeable without complaining ⟨I don't have the *patience* to stand in line for so long.⟩

synonyms forbearance, long-suffering, sufferance, tolerance

related words acquiescence, resignation; passiveness, passivity; amenability, compliance, conformism, docility, obedience, subordination, tractability, willingness; discipline, self-control; submission, submissiveness

near antonyms defiance; contrariness, disobedience, insubordination, intractability, recalcitrance, resistance, willfulness

antonyms impatience

patient *adj* **1** accepting pains or hardships calmly or without complaint ⟨You were very *patient* about having to wait for me for so long.⟩

synonyms forbearing, long-suffering, stoic (*or* stoical), tolerant, uncomplaining

related words lenient; acquiescent, passive, resigned, unresistant, yielding; agreeable, amenable, compliant, complying, docile, obedient, placable, submissive, subordinate, tractable, willing; subservient; amiable, obliging; collected, composed; restrained; disciplined, self-contained, self-controlled

near antonyms defiant, resistant; contrary, disobedient, insubordinate, intractable, rebellious, recalcitrant, refractory, ungovernable, unmanageable, unruly

antonyms complaining, fed up, impatient, protesting

2 continuing despite difficulties, opposition, or discouragement ⟨a *patient* effort to finish college despite the mounting debts⟩ — see PERSISTENT

patient *n* an individual awaiting or under medical care and treatment ⟨The nurse asked the *patient* to change into a paper gown.⟩

synonyms case

related words inpatient, outpatient; rehabilitant; sufferer, victim; convalescent, nursling

patio *n* an open space wholly or partly enclosed (as by buildings or walls) ⟨There's a *patio* in the center of the apartment complex.⟩ — see COURT 2

patois *n* the special terms or expressions of a particular group or field ⟨The medical *patois* that the hospital staffers used among themselves was incomprehensible to me.⟩ — see TERMINOLOGY

patrician *adj* of high birth, rank, or station ⟨Todd came from a *patrician* family.⟩ — see NOBLE 1

patrimony *n* something that is or may be inherited ⟨Her *patrimony* was the family's newspaper business.⟩ — see INHERITANCE

patriot *n* a person who loves his or her country and supports its interests and policies ⟨the contention that true *patriots* would be willing to do anything for their country⟩

synonyms loyalist

related words chauvinist; nationalist, superpatriot; compatriot, countryman

near antonyms collaborator, quisling, spy, traitor; betrayer, deserter, recreant; renegade

patriotic *adj* having or showing love and support for one's country ⟨Hanging a flag outside one's home is a *patriotic* gesture.⟩

synonyms nationalist, nationalistic

related words chauvinist; superpatriotic; constant, devoted, faithful, loyal, staunch (*also* stanch), steadfast, steady, true; ardent, fervent, fervid, impassioned, passionate

near antonyms traitorous, treasonous; disaffected, disloyal, faithless, false, fickle, inconstant, perfidious, recreant, treacherous, unfaithful

antonyms unpatriotic

patriotism *n* love and support for one's country ⟨Her *patriotism* was so heartfelt that she quit her job to work for the war effort.⟩

synonyms nationalism

related words chauvinism; jingoism; allegiance, constancy, devotion, faithfulness, fealty, loyalty, staunchness, steadfastness; fervency, fervidness, passion

near antonyms desertion, treason; disaffection, disloyalty, faithlessness, falseness, fickleness, inconstancy, perfidiousness, treachery, unfaithfulness

patron *n* **1** a person who buys a product or uses a service from a business ⟨a restaurant *patron*⟩ — see CUSTOMER 1

2 a person who takes the responsibility for some other person or thing ⟨The wealthy philanthropist is one of the city's most generous *patrons* of its symphony orchestra.⟩ — see SPONSOR

3 one that helps another with gifts or money ⟨The *patron* for the museum's current blockbuster is the city's biggest banking institution.⟩ — see BENEFACTOR

patronize *vb* **1** to assume or treat with an air of superiority ⟨a director with an unpleasant habit of *patronizing* even his most gifted actors⟩ — see CONDESCEND 2

2 to promote the interests or cause of ⟨a company that loyally *patronizes* the arts⟩ — see SUPPORT 1

patter *n* **1** friendly, informal conversation or an instance of this ⟨Their incessant *patter* was getting on my nerves.⟩ — see CHAT 1

2 the special terms or expressions of a particular group or field ⟨the *patter* of highbrow criticism that one hears in fashionable art galleries⟩ — see TERMINOLOGY

patter *vb* to engage in casual or rambling conversation ⟨The toddler *pattered* on for what seemed like hours.⟩ — see CHAT 1

pattern *n* **1** a unit of decoration that is repeated all over something (as a fabric) ⟨a coverlet with a nosegay of tiny pink roses as the *pattern*⟩

synonyms design, figure, motif, motive

related words scheme; device; adornment, caparison, decoration, embellishment, frill, garnish, ornament, trim

2 a usual manner of behaving or doing ⟨Her daily *pattern* begins with coffee and a bagel every morning for breakfast.⟩ — see HABIT 1

3 an established and often automatic or monotonous series of actions followed when engaging in some activity ⟨With her, everything must be done strictly according to *pattern*.⟩ — see ROUTINE 1

4 the way in which the elements of something (as a work of art) are arranged ⟨Many of the artist's paintings use the same *pattern* of a lone figure surrounded by a vast landscape.⟩ — see COMPOSITION 3

patty *also* **pattie** *n* a small usually rounded mass of minced food that has been fried ⟨the enticing aroma of sausage *patties* sizzling in the skillet⟩ — see CAKE 1

paucity *n* a falling short of an essential or desirable amount or number ⟨a *paucity* of useful answers to the problem of traffic congestion at rush hour⟩ — see DEFICIENCY

paunch *n* an enlarged or bulging abdomen ⟨Santa is depicted as a white-bearded man with a big *paunch*.⟩ — see POTBELLY

pauperism *n* the state of lacking sufficient money or material possessions ⟨nineteenth century reforms that aimed to end *pauperism*⟩ — see POVERTY 1

pause *n* **1** a momentary halt in an activity ⟨There was a brief *pause* for applause in her speech.⟩

synonyms break, breath, breather, interruption, lull, recess

related words interim, interlude, intermission, interval, respite, rest; cessation, discontinuance, ending, expiration, finishing, hitch, lapse, stoppage, stopping, termination; abeyance, moratorium, surcease, suspension; discontinuity, gap, hiatus

near antonyms continuation, endurance, persistence, progress, progression; extension, prolongation

2 a state or an instance of temporary inaction because of uncertainty about the right course of action ⟨The question caught the professor off guard, and there was a *pause* before he responded.⟩ — see HESITATION

pause *vb* to come to a temporary halt in one's activity ⟨He *paused* for a moment to regain his composure.⟩

synonyms break

related words hesitate; break in, interrupt; cease, discontinue, end, finish, stop, terminate; knock off, lay off, quit; lapse, let up

phrases catch one's breath, hold one's horses

near antonyms continue, persist; advance, progress; extend, prolong, stretch

¹pawn *n* one that is or can be used to further the purposes of another ⟨Though he liked to play up his influence with city hall, he was really just another *pawn* of the political bosses.⟩

synonyms instrument, puppet, tool

related words chump, dupe, foil, gull, sucker, victim; minion, stooge; lap dog, yes-man

²pawn *n* something given or held to assure that the giver will keep a promise ⟨Kara offered her license as a *pawn* that she would bring back the rental canoe.⟩ — see PLEDGE 1

pawn *vb* to leave as a guarantee of repayment of a loan ⟨He *pawned* his antique watch in order to pay off his debt.⟩

synonyms hock, pledge

related words deposit; bond

near antonyms buy (back), redeem, win (back)

pay *n* **1** the money paid regularly to a person for labor or services ⟨The work is hard, but the *pay* is good.⟩ — see WAGE

2 something (as money) that is given or received in return for goods or services ⟨We should demand *pay* for all the overtime we're putting in.⟩ — see PAYMENT 2

pay *vb* **1** to give (someone) the sum of money owed for goods or services received ⟨We need to *pay* the cashier and then we can leave.⟩

synonyms compensate, recompense, remunerate

related words refund, reimburse, repay, requite; remit; pay off, pay up, prepay

near antonyms stiff

2 to give what is owed for ⟨You ought to *pay* that bill before it's overdue.⟩

synonyms balance, clear, discharge, foot, liquidate, meet, pay off, pay up, quit, recompense, settle, spring (for), stand

antonyms repudiate

3 to hand over or use up in payment ⟨Rock fans were willing to *pay* enormous sums to get into the concert.⟩ — see SPEND 1

4 to produce as revenue ⟨an investment *paying* six percent⟩ — see YIELD 2

5 to provide with a paying job ⟨We'll *pay* someone to mow the lawn for the summer.⟩ — see EMPLOY 1

payable *adj* not yet paid ⟨Keep the bills *payable* separate from the receipts⟩ — see OUTSTANDING 1

paying *adj* yielding a profit ⟨Jed finally found a *paying* job.⟩ — see PROFITABLE 1

paying *n* the act of offering money in exchange for goods or services ⟨The actual shopping was quick, but with the long lines, *paying* for the stuff seemed to take forever.⟩ — see PAYMENT 1

payload *n* a mass or quantity of something taken up and carried, conveyed, or transported ⟨The space shuttle can carry a maximum *payload* of approximately 50,000 pounds.⟩ — see LOAD 1

payment *n* **1** the act of offering money in exchange for goods or services ⟨They are very prompt in the *payment* of their credit card bills.⟩

synonyms compensation, disbursement, giving, paying, remittment, remittance, remuneration

related words tendering; reimbursement, repayment; paying off, paying up, prepayment; overpayment

near antonyms underpayment

antonyms nonpayment

2 something (as money) that is given or received in return for goods or services ⟨Our *payment* for all the work we did barely covered our expenses.⟩ ⟨We finally mailed our last car *payment* last week.⟩

synonyms compensation, consideration, pay, recompense, remittance, remuneration, requital

related words salary, stipend, wage(s); disbursement, expenditure, outlay; rebate, refund; indemnity, recoupment, redress, reparation, restitution; settlement; deposit; reimbursement, repayment; prepayment; overpayment; rent, rental

3 the money paid regularly to a person for labor or services ⟨Your *payment* will be issued as a weekly check.⟩ — see WAGE

payoff *n* the amount of money left when expenses are subtracted from the total amount received ⟨The *payoff* on the investment was only about $500.⟩ — see PROFIT 1

pay off *vb* **1** to give what is owed for ⟨I finally *paid off* the loan.⟩ — see PAY 2

2 to influence someone with a bribe ⟨was *paid off* to keep his mouth shut⟩ — see BRIBE

pay up *vb* to give what is owed for ⟨For once our bills are all *paid up*.⟩ — see PAY 2

peace *n* **1** a state without war ⟨After a long and bitter war, the troubled region finally achieved *peace*.⟩

synonyms peacefulness

related words accord, amity, concord, harmony; calm, quiet, serenity, tranquillity (*or* tranquility); order, stability; pacification

near antonyms conflict, contention, discord, dissidence, strife, trouble; tumult, turmoil, unrest, upheaval; fighting, warfare; action, battle, combat

antonyms war

2 freedom from disquieting or oppressive thoughts or emotions ⟨a light, humorous novel that is good for putting my mind at *peace* right before I go to sleep⟩

synonyms calm, calmness, peacefulness, placidity, sereneness, serenity, tranquillity (*or* tranquility)

related words content, contentment, ease; comfort, consolation, relief, solace; quiet, quietude, repose

near antonyms care, concern, perturbation; strain, stress, tenseness, tension; consternation, desperateness, desperation, discomfort, discomposure, dismay, distraction, distress, disturbance, edginess, jitters, jumpiness, nervousness; fear, fearfulness, torment, upset; doubt, dread, foreboding, incertitude, misgiving, presentiment, suspense, uncertainty

antonyms agitation, alarm (*also* alarum), anguish, anxiety, anxiousness, apprehension, apprehensiveness, uneasiness, vexation, worry

3 a state of freedom from storm or disturbance ⟨the eerie *peace* after a tornado⟩ — see CALM 1

4 peaceful coexistence ⟨Can't we all just live in *peace*?⟩ — see HARMONY 2

peaceable *adj* **1** inclined to live in peace and to avoid war ⟨a *peaceable* nation that has never had any interest in conquest⟩ — see PEACEFUL 1

2 not involving violence or force ⟨trying to find a *peaceable* resolution⟩ — see PEACEFUL 2

peaceful *adj* **1** inclined to live in peace and to avoid war ⟨a *peaceful* country that remained neutral during World War 2⟩

synonyms pacific, pacifist (*or* pacifistic), peaceable

related words irenic, nonaggressive, nonbelligerent, noncombative, unaggressive, unwarlike; antimilitarist, antimilitaristic, antiviolence, antiwar; calm, mild, neutral, quiet, relaxed, serene, tranquil; affable, amiable, amicable, benevolent, genial, gentle, kind, kindly; submissive, yielding

near antonyms militarist, militaristic; aggressive, bellicose, belligerent, combative, contentious, discordant, pugnacious, quarrelsome, scrappy, truculent; antagonistic, argumentative, fierce, gladiatorial, hostile, hot-tempered

antonyms bloodthirsty, hawkish, martial, warlike

2 not involving violence or force ⟨UN officials struggled to find a *peaceful* solution to the troublesome conflict.⟩

synonyms nonviolent, peaceable

related words bloodless; conciliatory, irenic, pacific, peacemaking; nonbelligerent, unaggressive, unassertive; appeasing, conciliating, mollifying, pacifying, placating; calming, quieting, soothing

near antonyms armed, martial, militant, military, warlike; aggressive, assertive, bellicose, belligerent, combative, contentious, quarrelsome; antagonistic, argumentative, fierce, gladiatorial, hostile; tempestuous, volcanic

antonyms forced, violent

3 free from disturbing noise or uproar ⟨a *peaceful* house, now that the kids are all grown and departed⟩ — see QUIET 1

4 free from storms or physical disturbance ⟨a *peaceful* lake⟩ — see CALM 1

5 free from emotional or mental agitation ⟨The patient is *peaceful* and resting comfortably.⟩ — see CALM 2

peacefulness *n* **1** a state of freedom from storm or disturbance ⟨The *peacefulness* of the secluded beach was refreshing.⟩ — see CALM 1

2 a state without war ⟨a period of *peacefulness* that remained unbroken until World War I⟩ — see PEACE 1

3 freedom from disquieting or oppressive thoughts or emotions ⟨After making the decision, he felt a *peacefulness* that he had never experienced before.⟩ — see PEACE 2

peacemaker *n* one who works with opposing sides in order to bring about an agreement ⟨The former diplomat is coming out of retirement to lend his talents as a *peacemaker* to these crucial negotiations.⟩ — see MEDIATOR

peacemaking *adj* tending to lessen or avoid conflict or hostility ⟨Efforts at *peacemaking* overtures in the region have largely been ignored by both sides.⟩ — see PACIFIC 1

peak *n* **1** an elevation of land higher than a hill ⟨The nearest *peak* worth climbing is hundreds of miles away.⟩ — see MOUNTAIN 1

2 the highest part or point ⟨a pop singer at the *peak* of her career⟩ — see HEIGHT 1

3 the projecting front part of a hat or cap ⟨accidentally stepped on the hat and crushed the *peak*⟩ — see VISOR

¹**peaked** *adj* tapering to a thin tip ⟨The church's *peaked* spire is a prominent feature of the town's skyline.⟩ — see POINTED 1

²**peaked** *adj* **1** lacking a healthy skin color ⟨You probably should go home, as you're looking awfully *peaked*.⟩ — see PALE 2

2 temporarily suffering from a disorder of the body ⟨I'm feeling a little *peaked*, so I'm going to lie down.⟩ — see SICK 1

peal *vb* to make the clear sound heard when metal vibrates ⟨The village bells *pealed* every hour in commemoration.⟩ — see ²RING

peanuts *pl n* **1** a very small amount ⟨That's *peanuts* compared to what I had to deal with yesterday.⟩ — see PARTICLE 1

2 a very small sum of money ⟨Employees working for *peanuts* went to their union to see what could be done.⟩ — see MITE 1

pearl *n* someone or something unusually desirable ⟨an island that is described as a *pearl* of the Pacific⟩ — see PRIZE 1

pebbly *adj* not having a level or smooth surface ⟨a jerky ride on a *pebbly* road⟩ ⟨The rubber handles have a *pebbly* texture that makes them easier to grip when they are wet.⟩ — see UNEVEN 1

peck *n* a considerable amount ⟨Now you're in a *peck* of trouble!⟩ — see LOT 2

peck *vb* **1** to eat reluctantly and in small bites ⟨The boy just *pecked* at his food and said he wasn't hungry.⟩ — see NIBBLE 1

2 to penetrate or hold (something) with a pointed object ⟨The bird continued to *peck* the suet cake intently.⟩ — see IMPALE

peculiar *adj* **1** being out of the ordinary ⟨a writer with a *peculiar* talent for capturing the feel of everyday conversation⟩ — see EXCEPTIONAL 1

2 different from the ordinary in a way that causes curiosity or suspicion ⟨a *peculiar* and catlike way of walking⟩ — see ODD 2

3 noticeably different from what is generally found or experienced ⟨a *peculiar* response to a polite query about his health⟩ — see UNUSUAL 1

4 of, relating to, or belonging to a single person ⟨his *peculiar* way of talking⟩ — see INDIVIDUAL 1

5 serving to identify as belonging to an individual or group ⟨The koala is *peculiar* to Australia.⟩ — see CHARACTERISTIC 1

6 of a particular or exact sort ⟨a matter of *peculiar* interest to us⟩ — see EXPRESS 1

peculiarity *n* **1** an odd or peculiar habit ⟨John had the *peculiarity* of constantly fussing with his hair.⟩ — see IDIOSYNCRASY

2 something that sets apart an individual from others of the same kind ⟨As its name indicates, the red-winged blackbird has the distinctive *peculiarity* of a red patch on its wings.⟩ — see CHARACTERISTIC

pecuniary *adj* of or relating to money, banking, or investments ⟨That makes good *pecuniary* sense.⟩ ⟨The judge recused himself from the case because he had a *pecuniary* interest in the company that was being sued.⟩ — see FINANCIAL

pedagogue *n* a person whose occupation is to give formal instruction in a school ⟨a *pedagogue* whose classroom lessons consisted entirely of reading directly from the textbook in a monotone⟩ — see TEACHER

peddle *vb* to sell from place to place usually in small quantities ⟨They *peddled* fruits and vegetables out of their truck.⟩

synonyms hawk

related words retail, wholesale; deal (in), distribute, high-pressure, hustle, market, merchandise (*also* merchandize), trade (in), vend

peddler *also* **pedlar** *n* one who sells things outdoors ⟨the *peddler* on the street corner selling baseball caps⟩

synonyms hawker, huckster

related words dealer, merchandiser, merchant, seller, vendor (*also* vender); concessionaire; black marketer (*or* black marketeer), bootlegger, fence, fencer, hustler, pusher, smuggler, trader

near antonyms buyer, purchaser; consumer, end user, user

pedestrian *adj* causing weariness, restlessness, or lack of interest ⟨a TV detective show filled with *pedestrian* plots stolen from older and better series⟩ — see BORING

pedigree *n* the line of ancestors from whom a person is descended ⟨a woman of good *pedigree*⟩ — see ANCESTRY

pedigreed *or* **pedigree** *adj* of unmixed ancestry ⟨A *pedigreed* puppy is expensive.⟩ — see PUREBRED

peek *n* an instance of looking especially briefly ⟨Emma took a *peek* at her Christmas gift hidden in the closet.⟩ — see LOOK 2

peek *vb* to take a quick or hasty look ⟨*Peek* out the window and see if it's raining.⟩ — see GLANCE 2

peel *vb* to remove the natural covering of ⟨She *peels* apples with lightning speed.⟩

synonyms bark, flay, hull, husk, shell, shuck, skin

related words bare, denude, expose, scale, strip; pare

peel (off) *vb* to rid oneself of (a garment) ⟨Jack *peeled off* the wet clothes and tossed them over the shower rod.⟩ — see REMOVE 1

peeled *adj* lacking a usual or natural covering ⟨a *peeled* banana⟩ — see NAKED 2

peep *n* an instance of looking especially briefly ⟨I stole a *peep* at our neighbor's new pool.⟩ — see LOOK 2

peep *vb* to make a short sharp sound like a small bird ⟨The baby *peeps* and burbles when her mother picks her up.⟩ — see CHIRP

peer *n* **1** a man of high birth or social position ⟨claims to be related to an English *peer*⟩ — see GENTLEMAN 1

2 one that is equal to another in status, achievement, or value ⟨a jury of one's *peers*⟩ — see EQUAL

peer *vb* to look long and hard in wonder or surprise ⟨Visitors seem mesmerized as they *peer* at the variety of marine life in the aquarium's huge tank.⟩ — see GAPE

peerless *adj* having no equal or rival for excellence or desirability ⟨The show's enduring success was a testimony to the *peerless* talents of its ensemble cast.⟩ — see ONLY 1

peeve *n* **1** something that is a source of irritation ⟨My main *peeve* with the organization is the endless stream of e-mails.⟩ — see ANNOYANCE 3

2 the feeling of being offended or resentful after a slight or indignity ⟨He holds on to a *peeve* until the offending person apologizes.⟩ — see PIQUE

peeve *vb* to disturb the peace of mind of (someone) especially by repeated disagreeable acts ⟨She is constantly *peeved* by his habit of asking questions while she is trying to focus on her work.⟩ — see IRRITATE 1

peeving *adj* causing annoyance ⟨a *peeving* insistence that everyone drop their work just to help him⟩ — see ANNOYING

peevish *adj* easily irritated or annoyed ⟨I would rather figure things out on my own than ask that *peevish* librarian for help.⟩ — see IRRITABLE

peevishness *n* readiness to show annoyance or impatience ⟨His constant *peevishness* made everyone around him cranky as well.⟩ — see PETULANCE

peewee *n* a living thing much smaller than others of its kind ⟨That particular species is the *peewee* of the salmon world.⟩ — see DWARF 1

peg *n* an individual part of a process, series, or ranking ⟨took the arrogant student down a *peg*⟩ — see DEGREE 1

peg *vb* **1** to arrange or assign according to type ⟨I *pegged* her as a hard worker right from the beginning.⟩ — see CLASSIFY 1
2 to send through the air especially with a quick forward motion of the arm ⟨*pegged* the ball to the second baseman⟩ — see THROW 1

peg (away) *vb* to devote serious and sustained effort ⟨The writer *pegged away* at his first novel for three years before he felt that it was ready to be published.⟩ — see LABOR

pelage *n* the hairy covering of a mammal especially when fine, soft, and thick ⟨color variation in the snow leopard's *pelage*⟩ — see FUR 1

pelagic *adj* of or relating to the sea ⟨Among *pelagic* animals the undisputed king is the blue whale, the largest creature currently roaming the face of the earth.⟩ — see MARINE 1

pelf *n* something (as pieces of stamped metal or printed paper) customarily and legally used as a medium of exchange, a measure of value, or a means of payment ⟨a politician who seems more interested in *pelf* than in policy⟩ — see MONEY

pellet *n* a usually round or cone-shaped little piece of lead made to be fired from a firearm ⟨the tightly packed *pellets* of a shotgun cartridge⟩ — see BULLET

pell–mell *adj* **1** acting or done with excessive or careless speed ⟨When the theater doors opened, there was a *pell-mell* rush for the best seats.⟩ — see HASTY 1
2 lacking in order, neatness, and often cleanliness ⟨*pell-mell* piles of books everywhere in the professor's library⟩ — see MESSY

pell–mell *adv* **1** in a confused and reckless manner ⟨My roommate tossed stuff *pell-mell* into the dorm room.⟩ — see HELTER-SKELTER 1
2 with excessive or careless speed ⟨ran *pell-mell* down the road to get help⟩ — see HASTILY 1

pellucid *adj* **1** easily seen through ⟨the *pellucid* waters that lap upon that island's beaches⟩ — see CLEAR 1
2 not subject to misinterpretation or more than one interpretation ⟨Her poetry has a *pellucid* simplicity that betrays none of the sweat that went into writing it.⟩ — see CLEAR 2

¹**pelt** *n* a hard strike with a part of the body or an instrument ⟨a blacksmith's *pelt* on the hot iron⟩ — see ¹BLOW

²**pelt** *n* the outer covering of an animal removed for its commercial value ⟨caught beavers and sold the *pelts*⟩ — see HIDE 1

pelt *vb* **1** to proceed or move quickly ⟨*pelted* away when the cops arrived⟩ — see HURRY 2
2 to send through the air especially with a quick forward motion of the arm ⟨*pelted* snowballs at each other while waiting for the bus⟩ — see THROW 1
3 to strike repeatedly ⟨Hail *pelted* the windows.⟩ — see BEAT 1

¹**pen** *n* a place of confinement for persons held in lawful custody ⟨earned six years in a federal *pen*⟩ — see JAIL

²**pen** *n* an enclosure with an open framework for keeping animals ⟨a goat *pen*⟩ — see CAGE

³**pen** *n* a person who creates a written work ⟨Alexander Hamilton is reckoned to be the pseudonymous *pen* behind two thirds of the *Federalist Papers*.⟩ — see AUTHOR 1

¹**pen** *vb* to close or shut in by or as if by barriers ⟨Remember to *pen* up the dogs when visitors come over.⟩ — see ENCLOSE 1

²**pen** *vb* to compose and set down on paper the words of ⟨Though relatively unknown at the time of his death, the composer had *penned* some of the most memorable show tunes of his era.⟩ — see WRITE 1

penal *adj* inflicting, involving, or serving as punishment ⟨Australia was once a *penal* colony.⟩ — see PUNITIVE

penalize *vb* to inflict a penalty on for a fault or crime ⟨The player was *penalized* for unsportsmanlike conduct.⟩ — see PUNISH

penalizing *adj* inflicting, involving, or serving as punishment ⟨forced to listen to a *penalizing* lecture on the consequences of lying⟩ — see PUNITIVE

penalty *n* **1** a sum of money to be paid as a punishment ⟨The *penalty* for speeding is doubled in construction zones.⟩ — see FINE
2 suffering, loss, or hardship imposed in response to a crime or offense ⟨The company was assessed a stiff *penalty* for the violation.⟩ — see PUNISHMENT
3 the negative result caused by something that creates difficulty for achieving success ⟨The teen suffered the *penalty* of his decision to leave school without graduating.⟩ — see DISADVANTAGE 2

penchant *n* a habitual attraction to some activity or thing ⟨Her *penchant* for math helped her to become an engineer.⟩ — see INCLINATION 1

pendant *also* **pendent** *n* an ornament worn on a chain around the neck or wrist ⟨Navajo necklaces with *pendants* finely crafted in genuine sky-blue turquoise⟩
synonyms bangle, charm
related words locket, teardrop

pendent *or* **pendant** *adj* extending freely from a support from above ⟨The dining area is lit by tasteful *pendent* lamps over the tables.⟩ — see DEPENDENT 1

pending *adj* **1** not yet settled or decided ⟨A decision is *pending* about whether to buy computers or sports equipment with this money.⟩
synonyms open, undecided, undetermined, unresolved, unsettled
related words hanging; debatable, disputable, moot, uncertain, unsure
phrases in hand
near antonyms confirmed, established; certain, sure
antonyms decided, determined, resolved, settled
2 being soon to appear or take place ⟨a *pending* review of your work so far this term⟩ — see FORTHCOMING 1
3 giving signs of immediate occurrence ⟨The sky darkened with a *pending* storm.⟩ — see IMMINENT 1

pending *prep* in the course of ⟨The government must continue to function *pending* negotiations for next year's budget.⟩ — see DURING

pendulous *adj* **1** bending downward or forward ⟨a cow with a *pendulous* udder⟩ — see NODDING
2 extending freely from a support from above ⟨A *pendulous* crystal chandelier dominated the ballroom.⟩ — see DEPENDENT 1

penetrable *adj* capable of being passed into or through ⟨Unfortunately, our netting proved to be a rather *penetrable* barrier that allowed in our cabin a steady stream of mosquitoes.⟩
synonyms passable, permeable, porous
related words absorbent; breathable
near antonyms airtight, watertight; close, compact, dense, thick
antonyms impassable (*also* impassible), impenetrable, impermeable, impervious, nonporous

penetrate vb to go or come in or into ⟨A needle penetrated the heavy canvas only with great effort.⟩ — see ENTER 1

penetrating adj causing intense discomfort to one's skin ⟨an icy, penetrating rain that made you feel really miserable⟩ — see CUTTING 1

peninsula n an area of land that juts out into a body of water ⟨The peninsula is constantly buffeted by storms.⟩ — see ²CAPE

penitence n a feeling of responsibility for wrongdoing ⟨The sincerity of the player's penitence is questionable—he began to express remorse only after the suspension was handed down.⟩ — see GUILT 1

penitent adj feeling sorrow for a wrong that one has done ⟨a penitent gossip who had come to ask for forgiveness⟩ — see CONTRITE

penitentiary n a place of confinement for persons held in lawful custody ⟨a sentence in the state penitentiary for robbery⟩ — see JAIL

penman n 1 a person who creates a written work ⟨the prolific penman of dozens of horror stories⟩ — see AUTHOR 1
2 one who writes from dictation or copies manuscripts ⟨an essay on Jacob Shallus, the penman who inked the United States Constitution⟩ — see SCRIBE 1

penmanship n 1 the form or style of a particular person's writing ⟨Doctors are famous for their illegible penmanship.⟩ — see HANDWRITING 1
2 writing done by hand ⟨In many schools, students no longer practice their penmanship.⟩ — see HANDWRITING 2

pennant n a piece of cloth with a special design that is used as an emblem or for signaling ⟨The stadium was festooned with pennants from past championships.⟩ — see FLAG 1

penniless adj lacking money or material possessions ⟨Kate went from being penniless to owning her own restaurant.⟩ — see POOR 1

pennon n a piece of cloth with a special design that is used as an emblem or for signaling ⟨Pennons flew from the yachts gathered in the harbor for the festival.⟩ — see FLAG 1

pensive adj given to or marked by long, quiet thinking ⟨Rainy days often put her in a pensive mood.⟩ — see CONTEMPLATIVE

penstock n a long hollow cylinder for carrying a substance (as a liquid or gas) ⟨A penstock carried water for the waterwheel.⟩ — see PIPE 1

penthouse n a smaller structure added to a main building ⟨had a small penthouse built to serve as a toolshed⟩ — see ANNEX

penumbra n partial darkness due to the obstruction of light rays ⟨The lunar eclipse began with a subtle darkening of the lunar surface as it passed within the Earth's penumbra.⟩ — see SHADE 1

penurious adj 1 giving or sharing as little as possible ⟨The company's penurious management could not be convinced of the need to earmark more money for research and development.⟩ — see STINGY 1
2 lacking money or material possessions ⟨The most penurious members of the community are forced to depend on the services of the food bank.⟩ — see POOR 1

penuriousness n 1 the quality or practice of being overly sparing with money ⟨He daily practiced such penuriousness that few would have guessed that he was one of the state's wealthiest residents.⟩ — see PARSIMONY 1
2 the state of lacking sufficient money or material possessions ⟨The abject penuriousness of so many of the city's inhabitants should be a cause for concern.⟩ — see POVERTY 1

penury n the state of lacking sufficient money or material possessions ⟨tried to work their way out of penury⟩ — see POVERTY 1

peon n a person who does very hard or dull work ⟨The new rules apply to the whole department, from management down to us peons.⟩ — see DRUDGE

people pl n 1 human beings in general ⟨Despite the horrors she witnessed, Anne Frank never lost her faith in people.⟩
synonyms folks, humanity, humankind, public, world
related words community, society; crowd, masses, mob, populace, proletariat, rabble, riffraff
2 the body of the community as contrasted with the elite ⟨Tensions mounted until the people rose up in rebellion.⟩ — see MASS 1
3 a group of persons who come from the same ancestor ⟨Where are your people from?⟩ — see FAMILY 1

people vb to supply with inhabitants ⟨a science-fiction novel about a mission to people Mars⟩ — see SETTLE 2

pep n active strength of body or mind ⟨The students always display considerably more pep during the weeks immediately prior to the holidays.⟩ — see VIGOR 1

pep (up) vb to give life, vigor, or spirit to ⟨The music at the party pepped everyone up.⟩ — see ANIMATE

pepper vb 1 to cover by or as if by scattering something over or on ⟨Let's pepper the costume with flecks of glitter.⟩ — see SCATTER 2
2 to mark with small spots especially unevenly ⟨Spilled flour peppered the kitchen floor.⟩ — see SPOT 1

peppery adj marked by a lively display of strong feeling ⟨the author of several peppery editorials on the election⟩ — see SPIRITED 1

peppiness n the quality or state of having abundant or intense activity ⟨The peppiness of the city's music scene in the last year has been encouraging.⟩ — see VITALITY 1

peppy adj 1 having active strength of body or mind ⟨a peppy and entertaining group of young musicians⟩ — see VIGOROUS 1
2 having much high-spirited energy and movement ⟨a peppy dance performance⟩ — see LIVELY 1

per adv for each one ⟨You can have them at 50 cents per or three for $1.25.⟩ — see APIECE

per prep using the means or agency of ⟨The infection is spread to the rest of the body per the bloodstream.⟩ — see BY 2

perambulation n a relaxed journey on foot for exercise or pleasure ⟨took an invigorating perambulation around the lake to get some fresh air⟩ — see WALK 1

per capita adv for each one ⟨We expect the students to receive less funding per capita this year due to a marked increase in the school-age population.⟩ — see APIECE

perceive vb 1 to have a vague awareness of ⟨I thought I perceived a problem, but I wasn't sure.⟩ — see FEEL 1
2 to make note of (something) through the use of one's eyes ⟨I perceived that it was going to be a nice day.⟩ — see SEE 1
3 to have a clear idea of ⟨I perceive your point, but I still disagree.⟩ — see COMPREHEND 1

percentage n a measure of how often an event will occur instead of another ⟨Even though the odds of winning the lottery are astronomical, people always hope to defy this percentage.⟩ — see PROBABILITY 2

perceptible adj able to be perceived by a sense or by the mind ⟨You should note a perceptible temperature change when you add the second element.⟩
synonyms appreciable, detectable, discernible (also discernable), distinguishable, palpable, sensible
related words audible, observable, tangible, visible; clear, conspicuous, evident, eye-catching, manifest, noticeable, obvious, plain, ponderable, prominent, striking; apparent, distinct, identifiable, significant
near antonyms inaudible, intangible; inconspicuous, in-

distinct, unnoticeable, unobtrusive; faint, insignificant, slight, trivial; buried, concealed, covert, disguised, obscure, shrouded, vague

antonyms impalpable, imperceptible, inappreciable, indistinguishable, insensible, undetectable

perception *n* **1** the ability to understand inner qualities or relationships ⟨A writer of considerable *perception*, she remembers how it feels to be confused and insecure.⟩ — see WISDOM 1

2 the knowledge gained from the process of coming to know or understand something ⟨a growing *perception* of the enormity of the problem⟩ — see COMPREHENSION

perceptive *adj* **1** able to sense slight impressions or differences ⟨Due to their ability to rotate their ears, cats are very *perceptive* when it comes to pinpointing the source of a sound.⟩ — see ACUTE 1

2 having or showing deep understanding and intelligent application of knowledge ⟨A *perceptive* therapist was able to discover what was really troubling the youth.⟩ — see WISE 1

perceptiveness *n* **1** the ability to understand inner qualities or relationships ⟨The author's keen *perceptiveness* allows her some unique insights into the lives of real-life heroes.⟩ — see WISDOM 1

2 the state or quality of being able to sense slight impressions or differences ⟨a drama critic who was much respected for the *perceptiveness* of his critical observations⟩ — see ACUITY

perch *vb* **1** to come to rest after descending from the air ⟨pigeons *perching* on the roof⟩ — see ALIGHT 1

2 to establish or place comfortably or snugly ⟨*perched* the baby in a basket⟩ — see ENSCONCE 1

perchance *adv* it is possible ⟨*Perchance* he is playing the devil's advocate, and the opinions he has expressed are not actually his own.⟩ — see PERHAPS

percolate *vb* to flow forth slowly through small openings ⟨water *percolating* through the coffee filter⟩ — see EXUDE

percolate (into) *vb* to spread throughout ⟨The closing shot of the film is one of those iconic images that has long since *percolated into* the cultural consciousness.⟩ — see PERMEATE

perdition *n* the place of punishment for the wicked after death ⟨Inadvertent wrongdoing is not enough to doom one to *perdition*.⟩ — see HELL 1

peregrinate *vb* **1** to make one's way through, across, or over ⟨Jack Kerouac's celebrated novel about penniless free spirits *peregrinating* the United States⟩ — see TRAVERSE

2 to take a trip especially of some distance ⟨a couple of backpacking college students who decided to spend the summer *peregrinating* around Ireland⟩ — see TRAVEL 1

peregrination *n* a going from one place to another usually of some distance ⟨planning a leisurely *peregrination* across Europe for our honeymoon⟩ — see JOURNEY

peremptory *adj* **1** fond of ordering people around ⟨The governor's *peremptory* personal assistant began telling the crowd of reporters and photographers exactly where they had to stand.⟩ — see BOSSY

2 forcing one's compliance or participation by or as if by law ⟨a *peremptory* summons to appear before the committee⟩ — see MANDATORY

3 having a feeling of superiority that shows itself in an overbearing attitude ⟨She had such a *peremptory* approach to running the club that people started to avoid her.⟩ — see ARROGANT

4 having or showing a tendency to force one's will on others without any regard to fairness or necessity ⟨a *peremptory* insistence that the staff wait on them first⟩ — see ARBITRARY 1

perennial *adj* having an existence or validity that does not change or diminish ⟨Hot dogs are a *perennial* favorite at barbeques.⟩ — see ABIDING

perfect *adj* **1** being entirely without fault or flaw ⟨A stunningly *perfect* performance—not the slightest mistake—won her the gold medal in women's figure skating.⟩

synonyms absolute, faultless, flawless, ideal, immaculate, impeccable, irreproachable, letter-perfect, picture-perfect, unblemished

related words consummate, expert, masterly; classic, excellent, fabulous, fine, first-class, first-rate, grand, great, superb, superior, superlative, terrific, top, top-notch, unsurpassed; mint, unbruised, undamaged, unimpaired, uninjured, unmarred, unspoiled; exceptional, fancy, high-grade, special; inerrant, infallible, unerring, unfailing

near antonyms deficient, inadequate, insufficient, wanting; fallible; blemished, blighted, broken, damaged, defaced, disfigured, impaired, injured, malformed, marred, misshapen, spoiled

antonyms amiss, bad, censurable, defective, faulty, flawed, imperfect, reproachable

2 having no exceptions or restrictions ⟨living in *perfect* happiness in the country⟩ — see ABSOLUTE 2

3 not lacking any part or member that properly belongs to it ⟨I have a *perfect* recollection of that conversation.⟩ — see COMPLETE 1

perfect *vb* **1** to bring (something) to a state where nothing remains to be done ⟨*perfected* the arrangements for their long-awaited European vacation⟩ — see FINISH 1

2 to make better ⟨an art teacher who seems to believe that you can always *perfect* a painting with some additional brush strokes⟩ — see IMPROVE

perfection *n* **1** exceptionally high quality ⟨Louis Comfort Tiffany produced art glass of such exquisite *perfection* that he has achieved cult status.⟩ — see EXCELLENCE 1

2 the most perfect type or example ⟨Rembrandt's portraits are the *perfection* of the art of using facial expression, pose, and gesture to reveal the subject's interior life.⟩ — see QUINTESSENCE 1

3 the quality or state of being very accurate ⟨Audio recordings were reaching a level of *perfection* that earlier technicians had never dreamt possible.⟩ — see PRECISION

perfectly *adv* **1** without any flaws or errors ⟨You did that handspring *perfectly* on your first try.⟩

synonyms faultlessly, flawlessly, ideally, impeccably, pat

related words excellently, finely, grandly, greatly, marvelously, superbly, superiorly, superlatively, terrifically; exceptionally, fancily

phrases to a nicety, to a T, to a turn, to the nines

near antonyms deficiently, inadequately, incompletely, insufficiently; fallibly; atrociously, execrably, wretchedly

antonyms badly, defectively, faultily, imperfectly

2 to a full extent or degree ⟨You know *perfectly* well what I'm talking about, so don't pretend.⟩ — see FULLY 1

perfidious *adj* not true in one's allegiance to someone or something ⟨a *perfidious* campaign worker revealed the senator's strategy to his leading rival for the nomination.⟩ — see FAITHLESS

perfidy *n* the act or fact of violating the trust or confidence of another ⟨The full amount of intelligence compromised by the double agent's *perfidy* is not yet known.⟩ — see BETRAYAL

perforate *vb* to make a hole or series of holes in ⟨He *perforated* the sheet with his pencil and put it in his binder.⟩

synonyms bore, drill, hole, pierce, punch, puncture, riddle

related words broach, tap; poke, prick, prickle; penetrate; burrow (into), excavate, gouge, groove, hollow; break, cut, gash, notch, rend, rupture, slash, slit, split

near antonyms fill, patch, plug, seal

perforation n **1** a mark or small hole made by a pointed instrument ⟨absentmindedly made *perforations* in his paper with his pencil⟩ — see PRICK 1
2 a place in a surface allowing passage into or through a thing ⟨poked the button through a *perforation* in the fabric⟩ — see HOLE 1
perforce adv because of necessity ⟨We must, *perforce*, deal with this issue immediately, as procrastination is not an option.⟩ — see NEEDS
perform vb **1** to carry through (as a process) to completion ⟨She *performed* the task quickly and expertly.⟩
synonyms accomplish, achieve, carry out, commit, compass, do, execute, fulfill (*or* fulfil), make, negotiate
related words bring about, effect, effectuate, implement; ace, nail; engage (in), practice (*also* practise); work (at); reduplicate, reenact, repeat; actualize, attain, realize; complete, end, finish, wind up
phrases go through
near antonyms fail; skimp, slight, slur
2 to have a certain purpose ⟨The kidneys *perform* as a filtering system for the blood.⟩ — see FUNCTION
3 to present a portrayal or performance of ⟨has always dreamed of *performing* Hamlet on stage⟩ — see ACT 1
4 to produce a desired effect ⟨The new medication *performed* surprisingly well.⟩ — see ACT 2
performance n **1** a presentation of an artistic work (as a piece of music) from a particular point of view ⟨a disappointing, lackluster *performance* of a classic of the musical theater⟩ — see ACCOUNT 2
2 the doing of an action ⟨The *performance* of her nightly ritual, the taking of a warm bath, calmed her.⟩ — see COMMISSION 2
perfume n a sweet or pleasant smell ⟨The *perfume* of fresh flowers filled the room.⟩ — see FRAGRANCE
perfume vb to fill or infuse with a pleasant odor or odor-releasing substance ⟨Roses *perfumed* the wedding chapel.⟩ — see SCENT 1
perfumed adj having a pleasant smell ⟨delicately *perfumed* stationery⟩ — see FRAGRANT
perfunctory adj having or showing a lack of interest or concern ⟨The violinist delivered a *perfunctory* performance that displayed none of the passion and warmth he was once known for.⟩ — see INDIFFERENT 1
perhaps adv it is possible ⟨*Perhaps* we will not have to take this exam, but I doubt it.⟩
synonyms conceivably, maybe, mayhap, perchance, possibly
related words likely, probably; certainly, doubtless, sure, surely, undoubtedly; presumably, presumedly, supposably, supposedly
peril n **1** something that may cause injury or harm ⟨Life is full of unexpected *perils*.⟩ — see DANGER 2
2 the state of not being protected from injury, harm, or evil ⟨They were unhappy about sending their son into *peril* overseas.⟩ — see DANGER 1
peril vb to place in danger ⟨a tribute to the men and women who, as firefighters, *peril* their lives daily⟩ — see ENDANGER
perilous adj involving potential loss or injury ⟨a *perilous* journey through hostile territory⟩ — see DANGEROUS 1
perimeter n the line or relatively narrow space that marks the outer limit of something ⟨soldiers guarding the *perimeter* of the camp⟩ — see BORDER 1
period n **1** an occurrence of menstruating ⟨began getting her *period*⟩
synonyms menstruation
related words menses
2 an extent of time associated with a particular person or thing ⟨the Romantic *period* in music⟩ — see AGE 1

periodic adj **1** appearing or occurring repeatedly from time to time ⟨sent out *periodic* reminders about the office dress code⟩ — see REGULAR 1
2 occurring or appearing at intervals ⟨*periodic* snow showers that might leave up to an inch⟩ — see INTERMITTENT 1
periodical adj **1** appearing in parts or numbers that follow regularly ⟨a *periodical* town newsletter that is supported by local advertisers⟩ — see SERIAL
2 occurring or appearing at intervals ⟨*periodical* announcements from airline personnel concerning the delay⟩ — see INTERMITTENT 1
3 appearing or occurring repeatedly from time to time ⟨*Periodical* visits to the dentist will help keep your teeth healthy.⟩ — see REGULAR 1
periodical n a publication that appears at regular intervals ⟨subscribed to three new *periodicals*⟩ — see JOURNAL
peripatetic adj traveling from place to place ⟨a *peripatetic* reporter for a cable news network⟩ — see ITINERANT
peripheral adj available to supply something extra when needed ⟨The IT consultant suggested that we update the drivers for all of the computer's *peripheral* devices.⟩ — see AUXILIARY
periphery n the line or relatively narrow space that marks the outer limit of something ⟨The dogs are confined by an invisible electronic fence that runs along the *periphery* of the yard.⟩ — see BORDER 1
perish vb to stop living ⟨About 1,500 of the Titanic's passengers *perished* at sea.⟩ — see DIE 1
perk (up) vb **1** to become glad or hopeful ⟨We *perked up* once the sun came out.⟩ — see CHEER (UP) 1
2 to move from a lower to a higher place or position ⟨The dog tilts her head and *perks up* her ears whenever someone speaks to her.⟩ — see RAISE 1
perky adj having much high-spirited energy and movement ⟨a *perky* cheerleader⟩ — see LIVELY 1
permanent adj lasting forever ⟨A temporary compromise has been accepted until a more *permanent* solution can be agreed upon.⟩ — see EVERLASTING 1
permanently adv for all time ⟨planned to stay there *permanently*⟩ — see EVER 1
permeable adj capable of being passed into or through ⟨A *permeable* fabric that allows your body heat to escape will be much more comfortable in the summertime.⟩ — see PENETRABLE
permeate vb to spread throughout ⟨The smell of freshly baked bread *permeated* the house.⟩
synonyms interpenetrate, percolate (into), pervade, riddle, suffuse, transfuse
related words diffuse (through), impregnate, pass (into), penetrate; fill (up); drench, imbue, infuse, saturate, soak, steep; flood, glut
permissible adj that may be permitted ⟨a *permissible* level of noise⟩
synonyms admissible, allowable
related words acceptable, bearable, endurable, tolerable; accredited, allowed, authorized, endorsed (*also* indorsed), licensed, OK (*or* okay), permitted, sanctioned, warranted; lawful, legal; mandatory, ordered, required
near antonyms intolerable, unacceptable, unbearable, unendurable; objectionable; denied, disallowed, refused, rejected, vetoed; suppressed; outlawed
antonyms banned, barred, forbidden, impermissible, inadmissible, interdicted, prohibited, proscribed
permission n the approval by someone in authority for the doing of something ⟨She asked for *permission* to have a piece of candy.⟩ ⟨The President granted *permission* for the foreign diplomats to have special quarters.⟩
synonyms allowance, authorization, clearance, concur-

rence, consent, granting, leave, license (*or* licence), sanction, sufferance, warrant
related words imprimatur, seal, stamp; accreditation; liberty, pass; concession, patent, permit; tolerance, toleration; acceptance, acquiescence, agreement, assent, OK (*or* okay); accord, grant
near antonyms denial, refusal, rejection, revocation; veto; deterrence, discouragement, repression, suppression; ban, embargo, exclusion
antonyms interdiction, prohibition, proscription
permit *vb* **1** to give permission for or to approve of ⟨The school won't *permit* such an activity on its grounds.⟩ — see ALLOW 1
2 to give permission to ⟨You are not *permitted* to swim at the town pond without a season pass.⟩ — see ALLOW 2
3 to make able or possible ⟨We'll have our picnic on Thursday, weather *permitting*.⟩ — see ENABLE 1
4 to fail to prevent (some behavior on someone's part) especially from neglect or indifference ⟨They *permitted* the children to stay up much too late.⟩ — see ALLOW 3
pernicious *adj* causing or capable of causing harm ⟨She thinks television has a *pernicious* effect on children.⟩ — see HARMFUL
perpendicular *adj* rising straight up ⟨river rafters staring awestruck at the canyon's nearly *perpendicular* cliffs⟩ — see ERECT
perpetration *n* the doing of an action ⟨the *perpetration* of a series of pranks that resulted in an expulsion from school⟩ — see COMMISSION 2
perpetual *adj* **1** going on and on without any interruptions ⟨the *perpetual* rise and fall of the sea⟩ — see CONTINUOUS
2 having an existence or validity that does not change or diminish ⟨Freedom of religion is a *perpetual* right that is guaranteed by the nation's constitution.⟩ — see ABIDING
3 lasting forever ⟨an immature guy who seemed to be in a state of *perpetual* adolescence⟩ — see EVERLASTING 1
perpetually *adv* **1** for all time ⟨asteroids hurtling *perpetually* through space⟩ — see EVER 1
2 on every relevant occasion ⟨the *perpetually* smiling host of the morning talk show⟩ — see ALWAYS 1
perpetuate *vb* to give eternal or lasting existence to ⟨We hope to *perpetuate* this holiday tradition.⟩
synonyms immortalize
related words commemorate, memorialize; celebrate, enshrine, honor; conserve, keep up, maintain, preserve, support, sustain; defend, guard, protect, safeguard
near antonyms extinguish, put out, snuff (out); annihilate, crush, decimate, demolish, destroy, devastate; eradicate, expunge, extirpate, obliterate, wipe out
perpetuity *n* endless time ⟨lands that should remain in their wild state in *perpetuity*⟩ — see ETERNITY 1
perplex *vb* **1** to make complex or difficult ⟨Let's not *perplex* the issue further with irrelevant concerns.⟩ — see COMPLICATE
2 to throw into a state of mental uncertainty ⟨The question *perplexed* me.⟩ — see CONFUSE 1
perplexity *n* a state of mental uncertainty ⟨Seeing her *perplexity*, the teacher stepped in with a helpful hint.⟩ — see CONFUSION 1
perquisite *n* **1** a small sum of money given for a service over and above what is due ⟨Give the movers a *perquisite* if they do a good job.⟩ — see ²TIP 1
2 something given in addition to what is ordinarily expected or owed ⟨The use of a company car is one *perquisite* of the job.⟩ — see BONUS
persecute *vb* **1** to cause persistent suffering to ⟨people who were *persecuted* simply for practicing their religious faith⟩ — see AFFLICT
2 to disturb the peace of mind of (someone) especially by

repeated disagreeable acts ⟨She likes to *persecute* her sister with pointless, annoying questions at very inopportune times.⟩ — see IRRITATE 1
persecutor *n* **1** a person who causes repeated emotional pain, distress, or annoyance to another ⟨turned on their *persecutors* in defense⟩ — see TORMENTOR
2 one who is obnoxiously annoying ⟨*persecutors* who call nightly with telemarketing calls⟩ — see NUISANCE 1
persevere *vb* to continue despite difficulties, opposition, or discouragement ⟨Although he was frustrated by the lack of financial resources and support, he *persevered* in his scientific research.⟩
synonyms carry on, persist
related words dig in, hang on, keep up; knuckle down
phrases gut it out, hang in there
near antonyms give up, knock off, quit; bow, give in, submit, succumb, surrender, yield; falter, hang back, hesitate, shilly-shally, vacillate, waver
persevering *adj* continuing despite difficulties, opposition, or discouragement ⟨At the end of the long, winding trail, *persevering* hikers will be rewarded with an inviting, secluded lake.⟩ — see PERSISTENT
persist *vb* **1** to continue despite difficulties, opposition, or discouragement ⟨She *persisted* in her efforts and eventually got the job she wanted.⟩ — see PERSEVERE
2 to remain indefinitely in existence or in the same state ⟨My headache *persisted* for almost the entire day.⟩ — see CONTINUE 1
persistence *n* uninterrupted or lasting existence ⟨The *persistence* of the fever for a week caused me great worry.⟩ — see CONTINUATION
persistent *adj* continuing despite difficulties, opposition, or discouragement ⟨Although his first attempts were unsuccessful, he was *persistent* in his pursuit of a career in music.⟩
synonyms dogged, insistent, patient, persevering, pertinacious, tenacious
related words assured, certain, determined, firm, hellbent, intent, positive, resolute, resolved, single-minded, sure; adamant, dogged, hardened, hardheaded, headstrong, implacable, mulish, obdurate, obstinate, opinionated, peevish, pertinacious, perverse, pigheaded, self-willed, stiff-necked, stubborn, unregenerate, unyielding, willful (*or* wilful); unfaltering, unhesitating, unwavering; resistant, wayward, wrongheaded; constant, devoted, faithful, good, loyal, staunch (*also* stanch), steadfast, steady, true; indomitable, unconquerable; hard, inflexible, relentless, stern, unbending, unflinching, unrelenting
near antonyms quitting, surrendering, yielding; faltering, hesitant, hesitating, irresolute, vacillating, wavering; disloyal, faithless, false, fickle, inconstant, perfidious, traitorous, treacherous
person *n* a member of the human race ⟨Is there any *person* here who knows how to speak Spanish?⟩ — see HUMAN
personableness *n* the state or quality of having a pleasant or agreeable manner in socializing with others ⟨Never exactly known for his *personableness*, our boss unexpectedly showed his warm side at the company picnic.⟩ — see AMIABILITY 1
personage *n* **1** a member of the human race ⟨These sci-fi conventions attract *personages* of every description.⟩ — see HUMAN
2 a person who is widely known and usually much talked about ⟨*Personages* from the fields of sports and entertainment will be special guests at the political convention.⟩ — see CELEBRITY 1
personal *adj* of, relating to, or belonging to a single person ⟨He kept *personal* items in a separate drawer.⟩ — see INDIVIDUAL 1

personality *n* **1** a person who is widely known and usually much talked about ⟨a local television *personality* who is beloved by area residents⟩ — see CELEBRITY 1
2 the set of qualities that make a person different from other people ⟨She's got a great *personality*!⟩ — see INDIVIDUALITY 1
3 the set of qualities that makes a person, a group of people, or a thing different from others ⟨It has never been in the nation's *personality* to adhere to a rigid class system.⟩ — see NATURE 1
4 an act or expression showing scorn and usually intended to hurt another's feelings ⟨Every debate that was supposedly about the issues quickly degenerated into a juvenile exchange of *personalities*.⟩ — see INSULT

personalize *vb* to represent in visible form ⟨In the character of the good-hearted, virtuous seaman, the author has *personalized* the concept of perfect innocence.⟩ — see EMBODY 2

personalized *adj* of, relating to, or belonging to a single person ⟨a *personalized* jewelry box that had been engraved with her initials⟩ — see INDIVIDUAL 1

personally *adv* in person and usually privately ⟨The hostess told me *personally* that I was invited.⟩ — see TÊTE-À-TÊTE

personalty *n* transportable items that one owns ⟨And I leave my *personalty* to my children.⟩ — see POSSESSION 2

personification *n* a visible representation of something abstract (as a quality) ⟨He's the *personification* of kindness.⟩ — see EMBODIMENT

personify *vb* to represent in visible form ⟨Through her many good works she just *personifies* the spirit of charity.⟩ — see EMBODY 2

personnel *n* a body of persons at work or available for work ⟨We finally have enough *personnel* to start that big project.⟩ — see FORCE 1

perspective *n* **1** a way of looking at or thinking about something ⟨Whether she was being rude or candid is all a matter of *perspective*.⟩
synonyms angle, outlook, shoes, slant, standpoint, viewpoint
related words interpretation, spin; belief, conviction, eye, feeling, judgment (*or* judgement), mind, mind-set, notion, opinion, perception, persuasion, sentiment, verdict, view; impression, take
phrases frame of reference, point of view
2 all that can be seen from a certain point ⟨The *perspective* from the hotel balcony was dominated by the lake and mountains.⟩ — see VIEW 1

perspicuity *n* clearness of expression ⟨The *perspicuity* of this author's prose is one of the reasons why her novels are still read and those of her contemporaries are gathering dust.⟩ — see SIMPLICITY 2

perspicuous *adj* not subject to misinterpretation or more than one interpretation ⟨Believing that poetry need not be as *perspicuous* as prose, he writes poems that are intentionally ambiguous.⟩ — see CLEAR 2

perspicuousness *n* clearness of expression ⟨the undeniable *perspicuousness* of the prosecutor's closing argument⟩ — see SIMPLICITY 2

persuade *vb* to cause (someone) to agree with a belief or course of action by using arguments or earnest requests ⟨He *persuaded* his teachers to grant an extension.⟩
synonyms argue, bring, convert, convince, gain, get, induce, move, prevail (on *or* upon), satisfy, talk (into), win (over)
related words blandish, blarney, cajole, coax, entreat, exhort, fast-talk, urge, wheedle; allure, beguile, lead on, lure, seduce, snow, tempt; brainwash, overpersuade; incline, influence, move, prompt, sell, sway; reason (with)
near antonyms deter, discourage, dissuade, unsell

persuading *n* the act of reasoning or pleading with someone to accept a belief or course of action ⟨No amount of *persuading* could make her change her mind.⟩ — see PERSUASION 1

persuasion *n* **1** the act of reasoning or pleading with someone to accept a belief or course of action ⟨the suffragists' gradual *persuasion* of the American people that voting rights had to be extended to women⟩
synonyms conversion, convincing, inducement, inducing, persuading, suasion
related words blandishment, cajolement, cajolery, coaxing, entreaty, exhortation, urging, wheedling; seduction, tempting; influencing, prompting, swaying; lobbying, pressuring; brainwashing, overpersuasion
2 a body of beliefs and practices regarding the supernatural and the worship of one or more deities ⟨debating theology with someone of a different *persuasion*⟩ — see RELIGION 1
3 an idea that is believed to be true or valid without positive knowledge ⟨He's of the *persuasion* that everything that happens in this world is part of a divine plan.⟩ — see OPINION 1
4 the capacity to persuade ⟨There was an inherent *persuasion* in his sonorous voice that made listeners put aside any misgivings about his message.⟩ — see COGENCY 1

persuasive *adj* having the power to persuade ⟨a *persuasive* argument for increasing funding of the city's library system⟩ — see COGENT

persuasiveness *n* the capacity to persuade ⟨The *persuasiveness* of her closing statement changed the minds of several jurors who had been leaning toward conviction.⟩ — see COGENCY 1

pert *adj* **1** having much high-spirited energy and movement ⟨a *pert* girl who is captain of the soccer team⟩ — see LIVELY 1
2 making light of something usually regarded as serious or sacred ⟨a *pert* retort that irritated the teacher⟩ — see FLIPPANT
3 sharp and pleasantly stimulating to the mind or senses ⟨a *pert* suggestion for a truly original marketing campaign⟩ — see PIQUANT

pertain *vb* **1** to be the property of a person or group of persons ⟨the belief that quality medical care is a right that *pertains* to everyone⟩ — see BELONG 2
2 to have a relation or connection ⟨a person who is an expert in anything *pertaining* to the history of the American theater⟩ — see APPLY 1

pertain (to) *vb* to have (something) as a subject matter ⟨Where would I find books *pertaining to* birds?⟩ — see CONCERN 1

pertinacious *adj* **1** continuing despite difficulties, opposition, or discouragement ⟨a *pertinacious* little boy who was determined to catch a fish⟩ — see PERSISTENT
2 sticking to an opinion, purpose, or course of action in spite of reason, arguments, or persuasion ⟨a *pertinacious* salesman who would simply not take "No!" for an answer⟩ — see OBSTINATE

pertinaciousness *n* a steadfast adherence to an opinion, purpose, or course of action in spite of reason, arguments, or persuasion ⟨Thanks to his *pertinaciousness*, he eventually succeeded where all others had failed.⟩ — see OBSTINACY

pertinacity *n* a steadfast adherence to an opinion, purpose, or course of action in spite of reason, arguments, or persuasion ⟨the *pertinacity* of the candidate's supporters⟩ — see OBSTINACY

pertinence *n* the fact or state of being pertinent ⟨Job applicants should question the *pertinence* of any questions about their personal lives.⟩

synonyms applicability, bearing, connection, materiality, relevance, relevancy

related words appropriateness, aptness, felicitousness, fitness, fittingness, rightness, seemliness, suitability, suitableness; importance, significance; usefulness

near antonyms inappropriateness, inaptness, infelicity, unfitness, unsuitability; meaninglessness, pointlessness, uselessness

antonyms extraneousness, inapplicability, irrelevance, irrelevancy

pertinent *adj* having to do with the matter at hand 〈He impressed the jury with his concise, *pertinent* answers to the attorney's questions.〉

synonyms applicable, apposite, apropos, germane, material, pointed, relative, relevant

related words appropriate, apt, fit, fitting, suitable; important, meaningful, significant; sensible, useful; admissible, allowable

phrases to the point

near antonyms frivolous, inconsequential, insignificant, little, minor, negligible, slight, trifling, trivial, unimportant; meaningless, purposeless, senseless, useless; inappropriate, inapt, unsuitable; inadmissible

antonyms extraneous, immaterial, impertinent, inapplicable, irrelative, irrelevant, pointless

pertly *adv* in a quick and spirited manner 〈The young girl *pertly* informed him that he was her favorite uncle.〉 — see GAILY 2

pertness *n* shameless boldness 〈the startling *pertness* with which the waitress responded to our request to make a substitution〉 — see EFFRONTERY

perturb *vb* to trouble the mind of; to make uneasy 〈The problem *perturbed* me enough to keep me awake that night.〉 — see DISTURB 1

perturbed *adj* feeling or showing uncomfortable feelings of uncertainty 〈A *perturbed* look betrayed her nervousness at her first job interview.〉 — see NERVOUS 1

perturbing *adj* causing worry or anxiety 〈The *perturbing* news meant that we'd have to end our vacation prematurely.〉 — see TROUBLESOME

peruse *vb* to go over and mentally take in the content of 〈*perused* the manuscript, checking for grammatical errors〉 — see READ 1

pervade *vb* to spread throughout 〈The delicious scent of roasting turkey *pervaded* the house.〉 — see PERMEATE

perverse *adj* 1 easily irritated or annoyed 〈How can you be so cheerful one day, and so *perverse* the next?〉 — see IRRITABLE

2 having or showing lowered moral character or standards 〈a historian's account of a civilization turned *perverse* in its waning years〉 — see CORRUPT

3 sticking to an opinion, purpose, or course of action in spite of reason, arguments, or persuasion 〈a fact so self-evident that not even the most *perverse* of opponents could deny it〉 — see OBSTINATE

4 not appropriate for a particular occasion or situation 〈a *perverse* choice of music for a solemn event〉 — see INAPPROPRIATE

perverseness *n* readiness to show annoyance or impatience 〈the kind of *perverseness* that makes you want to snap at anyone who makes the mistake of greeting you〉 — see PETULANCE

perversion *n* 1 a sinking to a state of low moral standards and behavior 〈the *perversion* of a once virtuous organization〉 — see CORRUPTION 2

2 incorrect or improper use 〈If there's a hidden charge for the service, then that's a *perversion* of the word "free."〉 — see MISUSE

perversity *n* readiness to show annoyance or impatience 〈A certain coworker's habitual *perversity* makes him unpleasant to be around.〉 — see PETULANCE

pervert *n* a person who has sunk below the normal moral standard 〈a nineteenth-century author defamed as a *pervert*〉 — see DEGENERATE

pervert *vb* 1 to change so much as to create a wrong impression or alter the meaning of 〈That summary really *perverts* the other candidate's views on taxes.〉 — see GARBLE

2 to lower in character, dignity, or quality 〈a movie that *perverted* the story by emphasizing the violence over the redemption〉 — see DEBASE 1

3 to put to a bad or improper use 〈accused of *perverting* the justice system〉 — see MISAPPLY

perverted *adj* having or showing lowered moral character or standards 〈the *perverted* values of a society that had taken materialism to the extreme〉 — see CORRUPT

pessimist *n* 1 one who emphasizes bad aspects or conditions and expects the worst 〈She's such a *pessimist* that she's convinced she'll fail every test.〉

synonyms defeatist

related words cynic, fatalist, nihilist; hardnose, pragmatist, realist; worrier, worrywart

near antonyms dreamer, idealist, idealizer, romantic, romanticist, utopian, visionary; sentimentalist

antonyms optimist, Pollyanna

2 a person who distrusts other people and believes that everything is done for selfish reasons 〈a *pessimist* who claims the contest was rigged〉 — see CYNIC

pessimistic *adj* 1 emphasizing or expecting the worst 〈With that *pessimistic* attitude, it's no wonder you're depressed!〉

synonyms bearish, defeatist, despairing, hopeless

related words cynical, fatalistic, nihilist, nihilistic; discouraging, disheartening, inauspicious, unlikely, unpromising; bleak, cheerless, comfortless, depressing, desolate, dismal, dreary, funereal, gloomy, morose, saturnine, sepulchral, somber (*or* sombre), sullen; grim; contrary, hostile, negative

near antonyms auspicious, bright, encouraging, fair, golden, heartening, likely, promising, propitious; cheering, comforting, reassuring; favorable, good, positive; idealist, romantic, utopian, visionary; cheerful, cheery, chipper, sunny

antonyms hopeful, optimistic, rose-colored, rosy, upbeat

2 having or showing a deep distrust of human beings and their motives 〈*pessimistic* about the prospects for an economic revival in the area〉 — see CYNICAL

pest *n* 1 a widespread disease resulting in a high rate of death 〈One of the great *pests* of the 20th century was the influenza epidemic of 1918, which killed millions across the globe.〉 — see PLAGUE

2 one who is obnoxiously annoying 〈Stop being a *pest* to your sister and go find something else to do!〉 — see NUISANCE 1

3 something that is a source of irritation 〈a never-ending construction project that continues to be a *pest* for motorists〉 — see ANNOYANCE 3

pester *vb* to thrust oneself upon (another) without invitation 〈One resident *pestered* the condo board about every little thing.〉 — see BOTHER 1

pestering *n* the act of making unwelcome intrusions upon another 〈The endless *pestering* finally drove me to study at the library.〉 — see ANNOYANCE 1

pestiferous *adj* causing annoyance 〈a *pestiferous* weed that has given gardeners no end of grief〉 — see ANNOYING

pestilence *n* a widespread disease resulting in a high rate of death 〈the fourteenth century *pestilence* known as the Black Death〉 — see PLAGUE

pestilent *adj* **1** capable of being passed by physical contact from one person to another ⟨Proper hand washing will help prevent the spread of most *pestilent* diseases.⟩ — see CONTAGIOUS 1

2 causing annoyance ⟨*pestilent* reporters hounding him night and day⟩ — see ANNOYING

3 likely to cause or capable of causing death ⟨*pestilent* diseases such as bubonic plague and smallpox⟩ — see DEADLY 1

pesty *adj* causing annoyance ⟨a *pesty* kid who never stopped asking questions⟩ — see ANNOYING

pet *adj* granted special treatment or attention ⟨spent my free time on my *pet* project⟩ — see DARLING 1

¹pet *n* a person or thing that is preferred over others ⟨The teacher's *pet* was always getting special privileges.⟩ — see FAVORITE

²pet *n* a state of resentful silence or irritability ⟨stalked off in a *pet* after being refused permission to go to the movies⟩ — see SULK

pet *vb* to touch or handle in a tender or loving manner ⟨a cat who loves to be *petted*⟩ — see FONDLE

petition *n* an earnest request ⟨a flurry of *petitions* from residents seeking exemption from the regulation⟩ — see PLEA 1

petition *vb* to make a request to (someone) in an earnest or urgent manner ⟨*petitioned* the judge to be excused from jury duty for financial hardship⟩ — see BEG

petitioner *n* one who asks earnestly for a favor or gift ⟨The lottery winner was beset by a horde of *petitioners*, all of whom thought that they were most deserving of his charity.⟩ — see SUPPLICANT

pettish *adj* easily irritated or annoyed ⟨a *pettish* baby who always seemed to be crying⟩ — see IRRITABLE

pettishness *n* readiness to show annoyance or impatience ⟨His self-indulgent *pettishness* is more than his coworkers should endure.⟩ — see PETULANCE

petty *adj* **1** not broad or open in views or opinions ⟨apologized for such a *petty* remark⟩ — see NARROW 2

2 so small or unimportant as to warrant little or no attention ⟨obsessed over even *petty* problems⟩ — see NEGLIGIBLE 1

petulance *n* readiness to show annoyance or impatience ⟨I do not appreciate your *petulance* and eagerness to argue.⟩

synonyms crankiness, crossness, crotchetiness, grouchiness, grumpiness, huffiness, irascibility, irritability, irritableness, peevishness, perverseness, perversity, pettishness, testiness, waspishness

related words cantankerousness, crustiness, curmudgeonliness, disagreeableness, dyspepsia, fretfulness, orneriness, sulkiness, surliness; aggression, aggressiveness, bellicosity, belligerence, combativeness, contentiousness, contrariness, disputatiousness, pugnacity, scrappiness, truculence, truculency; fussiness, querulousness, rudeness; oversensitiveness, sensitivity, touchiness; animosity, antagonism, antipathy, fierceness, hostility, jaundice, rancor, unfriendliness; anger, exasperation, fury, indignation, wrath; hot-bloodedness, passion

near antonyms forbearance, long-suffering, patience, tolerance, understanding; affability, agreeableness, amenity, amicability, cordiality, friendliness, geniality, sociability; amiability, amiableness, good-humoredness, good-naturedness, good-temperedness; coolness, serenity, tranquillity (*or* tranquility); easygoingness, gentleness, kindliness, mildness

petulant *adj* easily irritated or annoyed ⟨a *petulant* and fussy man who is always blaming everyone else for his problems⟩ — see IRRITABLE

phantasm *also* **fantasm** *n* **1** a conception or image created by the imagination and having no objective reality ⟨frightened by the *phantasms* of his own making⟩ — see FANTASY 1

2 the soul of a dead person thought of especially as appearing to living people ⟨Taylor believed that she'd seen the *phantasm* of her father on the anniversary of his death.⟩ — see GHOST 1

phantasmal *adj* not real and existing only in the imagination ⟨*phantasmal* fears that have prevented her from living a normal life⟩ — see IMAGINARY

phantom *adj* not real and existing only in the imagination ⟨suffering from a *phantom* illness⟩ — see IMAGINARY

phantom *n* the soul of a dead person thought of especially as appearing to living people ⟨Halloween is supposed to be a time when *phantoms* return to walk among us.⟩ — see GHOST 1

pharmaceutical *n* a substance or preparation used to treat disease ⟨Some *pharmaceuticals* can be quite risky unless taken correctly.⟩ — see MEDICINE

pharmacist *n* a person who prepares drugs according to a doctor's prescription ⟨The *pharmacist* caught an error in the prescription's dosage.⟩ — see DRUGGIST

pharmacy *n* a retail store where medicines and miscellaneous articles are sold ⟨I stopped at the *pharmacy* for tissues and cold medicine.⟩ — see DRUGSTORE

phase *n* **1** a certain way in which something appears or may be regarded ⟨The moral *phase* of the problem has yet to be considered.⟩ — see ASPECT 1

2 an individual part of a process, series, or ranking ⟨in the final *phase* of production⟩ — see DEGREE 1

phased *adj* proceeding or changing by steps or degrees ⟨a *phased* construction of the tunnel through the heart of the city⟩ — see GRADUAL

phenomenal *adj* **1** being out of the ordinary ⟨the *phenomenal* growth that the suburb has experienced over the last decade⟩ — see EXCEPTIONAL 1

2 being so extraordinary or abnormal as to suggest powers which violate the laws of nature ⟨the *phenomenal* ability to remember the names of thousands of people⟩ — see SUPERNATURAL 2

phenomenon *n* something extraordinary or surprising ⟨Our jaws dropped when we saw this basketball *phenomenon* play for the first time.⟩ — see WONDER 1

philanthropic *also* **philanthropical** *adj* having or showing a concern for the welfare of others ⟨a *philanthropic* society that has been doing good for over a century⟩ — see CHARITABLE 1

philanthropy *n* **1** a gift of money or its equivalent to a charity, humanitarian cause, or public institution ⟨Among the industrialist's *philanthropies* was a college scholarship fund for deserving lower-income students.⟩ — see CONTRIBUTION

2 the giving of necessities and especially money to the needy ⟨Much dedicated to *philanthropy*, the industrialist maintains a surprisingly modest lifestyle.⟩ — see CHARITY 1

3 the quality or state of being generous ⟨a business leader renowned for her *philanthropy*⟩ — see LIBERALITY

philharmonic *n* a usually large group of musicians playing together ⟨served as a conductor for the *philharmonic*⟩ — see ²BAND 1

philistine *n* a person who is chiefly interested in material comfort and is hostile or indifferent to art and culture ⟨the town's *philistines* who think that spending on the arts is a waste of taxpayers' money⟩

synonyms lowbrow, materialist

related words boor, bounder, cad, churl, clown, creep, heel, jerk, joker, louse, lout, rat, rotter, scum

near antonyms highbrow; middlebrow; egghead, intellectual, sage, thinker; brain, genius

philosophy *n* the basic beliefs or guiding principles of a person or group ⟨Our *philosophy* is to do no harm to anyone.⟩ — see CREED 1

phlegm *n* a lack of emotion or emotional expressiveness ⟨a man of remarkable *phlegm*, never showing enthusiasm nor displeasure⟩ — see APATHY 1

phlegmatic *adj* not feeling or showing emotion ⟨a strangely *phlegmatic* response to what should have been happy news⟩ — see IMPASSIVE 1

phone *vb* to make a telephone call to ⟨She *phoned* her friend to invite her over for dinner.⟩ — see CALL 2

phony *also* **phoney** *adj* **1** being such in appearance only and made or manufactured with the intention of committing fraud ⟨a *phony* watch with a designer logo⟩ — see COUNTERFEIT 1

2 lacking in natural or spontaneous quality ⟨He always has this *phony* smile.⟩ — see ARTIFICIAL 1

3 not being or expressing what one appears to be or express ⟨Her concern for our welfare is as *phony* as all get-out—she just wants to know our business.⟩ — see INSINCERE 1

phony *also* **phoney** *n* **1** an imitation that is passed off as genuine ⟨The fancy "emerald" ring turned out to be a *phony*.⟩ — see FAKE 1

2 one who makes false claims of identity or expertise ⟨a supposed health expert who turned out to be a *phony*⟩ — see IMPOSTOR

phony *vb* to imitate or copy especially in order to deceive ⟨used *phonied* names in their hotel reviews⟩ — see FAKE 1

photo *n* a picture created from an image recorded on a light-sensitive surface by a camera ⟨an album of wedding *photos*⟩ — see PHOTOGRAPH

photo *vb* to take a photograph of ⟨*photoed* the historic mansion for a decorating magazine⟩ — see PHOTOGRAPH

photograph *n* a picture created from an image recorded on a light-sensitive surface by a camera ⟨The old *photograph* was faded but still clear enough to make out.⟩

synonyms photo, print, shot, snap, snapshot
related words blowup, enlargement, still; telephoto; daguerreotype, tintype

photograph *vb* to take a photograph of ⟨We've been *photographing* the baby virtually nonstop.⟩

synonyms mug, photo, shoot, snap
related words image, picture, rephotograph, retake; film, videotape

photographer *n* one who takes photographs ⟨We'll need to choose a *photographer* for the wedding.⟩

synonyms shooter, shutterbug
related words cinematographer

phrase *n* a sequence of words having a specific meaning ⟨kids drawing literal representations of the *phrase* "to rain cats and dogs"⟩

synonyms expression, idiom
related words cliché (*also* cliche); locution, term; epithet, expletive, name; byword, cry, motto, shibboleth, slogan, watchword; archaism, colloquialism, euphemism, modernism, neologism, provincialism, vulgarism
phrases figure of speech

phrase *vb* to convey in appropriate or telling terms ⟨He had trouble thinking of how to *phrase* his question for the visiting dignitary.⟩

synonyms articulate, clothe, couch, express, formulate, put, say, state, word
related words craft, frame; hint, imply, insinuate, intimate, suggest; paraphrase, rephrase, restate, reword, summarize, translate; communicate, disclose, speak, talk, tell, utter, verbalize; describe, render, write up

phraseology *n* **1** a distinctive way of putting ideas into words ⟨I recognized the writer's distinctive *phraseology* even before I saw the name.⟩ — see STYLE 1

2 the way in which something is put into words ⟨The unique *phraseology* of the suspect's answer stuck in my mind.⟩ — see WORDING 1

phrasing *n* **1** an act, process, or means of putting something into words ⟨Research has shown that the *phrasing* of the question on certain hot-button issues greatly influences the response.⟩ — see EXPRESSION 1

2 the way in which something is put into words ⟨a particularly delicate and careful *phrasing* of the statement⟩ — see WORDING 1

phylactery *n* something worn or kept to bring good luck or keep away evil ⟨He wore a small *phylactery* on a cord around his neck.⟩ — see CHARM 1

physic *n* a substance or preparation used to treat disease ⟨The museum has an exhibit on some of the strange *physics* that were once used to cure disease.⟩ — see MEDICINE

physical *adj* **1** of or relating to the human body ⟨*physical* sensations such as heat and pain⟩

synonyms animal, bodily, carnal, corporal, corporeal, fleshly, material, somatic
related words anatomic (*or* anatomical), physiological (*or* physiologic); sensual, sensuous; hand-to-hand
near antonyms cerebral, inner, intellectual, mental, psychological (*also* psychologic); bodiless, immaterial, incorporeal, insubstantial, spiritual; ethereal, metaphysical
antonyms nonmaterial, nonphysical

2 relating to or composed of matter ⟨I couldn't tell the difference between a *physical* object and a shadow in the dim light.⟩ — see MATERIAL 1

physician *n* a person specially trained in healing human medical disorders ⟨You should always consult a *physician* if you develop a high fever.⟩ — see DOCTOR

physique *n* the type of body that a person has ⟨exercise equipment that can be adjusted to suit the user's *physique*⟩

synonyms build, constitution, figure, form, frame, habit, shape
related words structure

picayune *adj* **1** not broad or open in views or opinions ⟨the *picayune* ponderings of a commentator who steadfastly believes others cultures are inferior to our own⟩ — see NARROW 2

2 so small or unimportant as to warrant little or no attention ⟨irritatingly *picayune* complaints⟩ — see NEGLIGIBLE 1

picayune *n* something of little importance ⟨Our lives don't amount to a *picayune* in the great scheme of things.⟩ — see TRIFLE

pick *n* **1** a person or thing that is chosen ⟨That team is my *pick* to win the Super Bowl.⟩ — see CHOICE 2

2 individuals carefully selected as being the best of a class ⟨The *pick* of the contestants will go on to the next competition.⟩ — see ELITE 1

3 the power, right, or opportunity to choose ⟨You have first *pick* of your office mates for the softball team.⟩ — see CHOICE 1

pick *vb* **1** to catch or collect (a crop or natural resource) for human use ⟨We'll *pick* peas and beans from the garden for dinner.⟩ — see HARVEST

2 to decide to accept (someone or something) from a group of possibilities ⟨I *pick* you as my partner!⟩ — see CHOOSE 1

3 to bring (something volatile or intense) into being ⟨He seems to be trying to *pick* a fight.⟩ — see INCITE 1

4 to eat reluctantly and in small bites ⟨Still suffering from the flu, he could do no more than *pick* halfheartedly at his food.⟩ — see NIBBLE 1

5 to penetrate or hold (something) with a pointed object ⟨continued to *pick* the block of ice until she was able to extract the shrimp⟩ — see IMPALE

picked *adj* singled out from a number or group as more to one's liking ⟨a *picked* group of people for the project⟩ — see SELECT 1

picker *n* someone with the right or responsibility for making a selection ⟨a book reviewer who is one of the *pickers* of the Pulitzer Prize for fiction⟩ — see SELECTOR

picket *n* a person or group that watches over someone or something ⟨set out a *picket* to watch the camp⟩ — see GUARD 1

picking *n* the act or process of selecting ⟨The *picking* of new recruits went on for three days.⟩ — see SELECTION 1

pickle *n* a difficult, puzzling, or embarrassing situation from which there is no easy escape ⟨Well, this is a bit of a *pickle* we've gotten ourselves into.⟩ — see PREDICAMENT

pick up *vb* 1 to acquire complete knowledge, understanding, or skill in ⟨He has a knack for *picking up* a language in a few weeks.⟩ — see LEARN 1

2 to bring together in one body or place ⟨*Pick up* all of your things because we have to be off this beach before dark.⟩ — see GATHER 1

3 to get possession of (something) by giving money in exchange for ⟨Could you *pick up* some milk at the store?⟩ — see BUY 1

4 to gradually increase in ⟨The boat was just *picking up* speed when it was rammed by another boat.⟩ — see GAIN 1

5 to move from a lower to a higher place or position ⟨*Pick up* your feet while I vacuum in front of the sofa.⟩ — see RAISE 1

6 to take or keep under one's control by authority of law ⟨Police *picked up* the fugitive in a neighboring state.⟩ — see ARREST 1

7 to make a place neat and orderly by removing extraneous stuff ⟨I thought you said you had *picked up*, so why are these things still lying around the rec room?⟩ — see CLEAN (UP) 1

8 to begin again or return to after an interruption ⟨After the break, the speaker *picked up* his lecture right where he had left off.⟩ — see RESUME

picky *adj* 1 hard to please ⟨a *picky* cat who would only eat one particular kind of food, and only if it was served in his special dish⟩ — see FINICKY

2 tending to select carefully ⟨She's *picky*, but she always finds the best quality in fresh meat and fish.⟩ — see SELECTIVE

picnic *n* something that is easy to do ⟨This class is no *picnic*, but I've really been learning a lot.⟩ — see CINCH

pictorial *adj* 1 consisting of or relating to pictures ⟨That photojournalist is planning to do a primarily *pictorial* report on the wildlife sanctuaries in Africa.⟩

synonyms graphic (*also* graphical), visual

related words photographic, video; drawn, painted, represented; illustrational, illustrative

2 producing a mental picture through clear and impressive description ⟨She writes a very *pictorial* kind of poetry, using words the way a painter applies strokes of color.⟩ — see GRAPHIC 1

picture *n* 1 a two-dimensional design intended to look like a person or thing ⟨Using only watercolors, she produced a strikingly lifelike *picture* of her mother.⟩

synonyms icon (*also* ikon), illustration, image, likeness

related words delineation, depiction, representation, resemblance, view; portrait; daub, drawing, finger painting; etching, silhouette, sketch, watercolor; caricature, cartoon; montage, photograph; hieroglyph, hieroglyphic, ideogram, ideograph; pictograph; diagram

2 a story told by means of a series of continuously projected pictures and a sound track ⟨The actor's latest *picture* is another thriller.⟩ — see MOVIE 1

3 a vivid representation in words of someone or some-

thing ⟨The newspaper report gives a detailed *picture* of the current situation.⟩ — see DESCRIPTION 1

4 position with regard to conditions and circumstances ⟨When personal opinion becomes part of the *picture*, the journalist isn't just reporting the news.⟩ — see SITUATION 1

5 something or someone that strongly resembles another ⟨The young woman is the very *picture* of her mother.⟩ — see IMAGE 1

6 something imagined or pictured in the mind ⟨I think I get the *picture*: you want me to leave.⟩ — see IDEA 1

7 pictures *pl* the art or business of making a movie ⟨hoping for a career in *pictures*⟩ — see MOVIE 2

picture *vb* 1 to present a picture of ⟨the famous painting that *pictures* the Founding Fathers signing the Declaration of Independence⟩

synonyms depict, image, portray, represent

related words delineate, describe, document, render; outline, silhouette, sketch; illustrate, show; diagram; caricature

2 to form a mental picture of ⟨I could easily *picture* the mining town from the vivid description of it in the author's memoirs.⟩ — see IMAGINE 1

3 to give a representation or account of in words ⟨*pictured* the sailing ship in vivid language⟩ — see DESCRIBE 1

4 to make a representation of by producing lines on a surface ⟨The next assignment is to *picture* your own face using colored pencils.⟩ — see DRAW 1

picture–perfect *adj* being entirely without fault or flaw ⟨It was a *picture-perfect* day for a picnic—the sun was shining and a light breeze stirred the air.⟩ — see PERFECT 1

picturesque *adj* producing a mental picture through clear and impressive description ⟨wrote a *picturesque* tale of their journey across the country⟩ — see GRAPHIC 1

piddling *adj* so small or unimportant as to warrant little or no attention ⟨She raised one final, *piddling* objection to the plan.⟩ — see NEGLIGIBLE 1

piebald *adj* having blotches of two or more colors ⟨a *piebald* horse that looked like it had been splashed with black and white paint⟩ — see PIED

piece *n* 1 a broken or irregular part of something that often remains incomplete ⟨A *piece* of stone fell from the crumbling wall.⟩ — see FRAGMENT

2 a literary, musical, or artistic production ⟨presented a new interpretation of the *piece* by Mozart⟩ — see COMPOSITION 1

3 a portable weapon from which a shot is discharged by gunpowder ⟨set the safety on the *piece*⟩ — see GUN 1

4 something belonging to, due to, or contributed by an individual member of a group ⟨Ben believes his *piece* of the profits should be higher.⟩ — see SHARE 1

piece *vb* to form by putting together parts or materials ⟨You might want to *piece* together a quilt from those odd patches of cloth.⟩ — see BUILD

piece by piece *adv* by small steps or amounts ⟨worked out the solution *piece by piece*⟩ — see GRADUALLY

piecemeal *adj* proceeding or changing by steps or degrees ⟨a *piecemeal* attempt to remedy the traffic congestion⟩ — see GRADUAL

piecemeal *adv* 1 by small steps or amounts ⟨They remodeled their house *piecemeal* because of budgetary constraints.⟩ — see GRADUALLY

2 into parts or pieces ⟨One well-aimed blow ripped the piñata *piecemeal*.⟩ — see APART

pied *adj* having blotches of two or more colors ⟨Although the mother's was pure black, the foal's coat was *pied*.⟩

synonyms blotched, dappled (*also* dapple), marbled, mottled, piebald, pinto, splotched, spotted

related words shaded; checkered, motley, multicolored, polychromatic, polychrome, varicolored, variegated;

blotted, brindled (*or* brindle), calico, speckled, streaked; colorful, pigmented; dotted, peppered, sprinkled; stippled
near antonyms monochromatic, solid
pier *n* **1** a structure used by boats and ships for taking on or landing cargo and passengers ⟨Deckhands tied the boat up at the *pier*.⟩ — see DOCK
2 an upright shaft that supports an overhead structure ⟨a bridge *pier*⟩ — see PILLAR 1
pierce *vb* **1** to go or come in or into ⟨Thoughts of revenge relentlessly *pierced* her mind.⟩ — see ENTER 1
2 to make a hole or series of holes in ⟨*pierced* his ears with a needle⟩ — see PERFORATE
3 to penetrate or hold (something) with a pointed object ⟨The saber *pierced* his chest.⟩ — see IMPALE
piercing *adj* **1** causing intense discomfort to one's skin ⟨That light sweater will be no match for the *piercing* wind outside.⟩ — see CUTTING 1
2 marked by a high volume of sound ⟨The frightened child emitted a *piercing* shriek that could be heard all over the house.⟩ — see LOUD 1
piety *n* **1** belief and trust in and loyalty to God ⟨Her *piety* is quiet but profound.⟩ — see FAITH 1
2 the quality or state of being spiritually pure or virtuous ⟨Among fellow clerics he is respected and admired for his *piety*.⟩ — see HOLINESS
3 adherence to something to which one is bound by a pledge or duty ⟨Familial *piety* keeps me from refusing to help my brother in this financial crisis.⟩ — see FIDELITY
piffle *n* language, behavior, or ideas that are absurd and contrary to good sense ⟨The belief that soda is made out of acid is just *piffle*.⟩ — see NONSENSE 1
pig *n* one who eats greedily or too much ⟨The dinner was so good, I'm afraid we made *pigs* of ourselves.⟩ — see GLUTTON
pigeon *n* one who is easily deceived or cheated ⟨a confidence man in search of another *pigeon*⟩ — see ¹DUPE
piggish *adj* having a huge appetite ⟨a *piggish* dog who ate anything left within reach⟩ — see VORACIOUS 1
pigheaded *adj* sticking to an opinion, purpose, or course of action in spite of reason, arguments, or persuasion ⟨was quite *pigheaded* about the matter⟩ — see OBSTINATE
pigment *n* a substance used to color other materials ⟨I'm running out of the black *pigment*.⟩
synonyms color, coloring, dye, dyestuff, stain
related words tint, toner; cast, hue, shade, tinge
pigment *vb* to give color or a different color to ⟨*pigmented* varnishes⟩ — see COLOR 1
pig out *vb* to eat greedily or to excess ⟨one holiday when you're expected to *pig out* on junk food⟩ — see GORGE 2
pigpen *n* a dirty or messy place ⟨Your room is a *pigpen*—so clean it up!⟩
synonyms dump, hole, pigsty, shambles, sty
related words chaos, confusion, disarrangement, disarray, disorder, disorganization, mess, muddle, muss; havoc, hell; clutter, jumble, litter, mishmash, welter
pigsty *n* a dirty or messy place ⟨How did this place become such a *pigsty*?⟩ — see PIGPEN
¹pike *n* a passage cleared for public vehicular travel ⟨You can take the *pike* all the way to the city.⟩ — see WAY 1
²pike *n* a weapon with a long straight handle and sharp head or blade ⟨a foot soldier armed with a *pike*⟩ — see SPEAR
³pike *n* the last and usually sharp or tapering part of something long and narrow ⟨The spear's metal *pike* was designed to cause a gaping wound.⟩ — see POINT 2
piker *n* a mean grasping person who is usually stingy with money ⟨Don't be such a *piker*—live it up a little while you're on vacation!⟩ — see MISER
pikestaff *n* a weapon with a long straight handle and sharp

head or blade ⟨*Pikestaffs* were in use from the Middle Ages to the 18th century.⟩ — see SPEAR
pilaster *n* an upright shaft that supports an overhead structure ⟨The rectangular *pilasters* spaced along the building's facade lend an air of classical grandeur.⟩ — see PILLAR 1
¹pile *n* **1** a quantity of things thrown or stacked on one another ⟨a large *pile* of newspapers that needed to be disposed of⟩
synonyms cock, heap, hill, mound, mountain, stack
related words bank, bar, drift, embankment; bed, layer; mow, pyramid, rick; barrow, cairn, pyre; accumulation, aggregate, array, assemblage, collection, conglomeration, gathering, grouping, hoard, huddle, jumble, knot
2 a considerable amount ⟨a job that paid *piles* of money⟩ — see LOT 2
3 a very large amount of money ⟨She made a *pile* in the stock market just before it headed south.⟩ — see FORTUNE 2
²pile *n* **1** a soft airy substance or covering ⟨the lush *pile* of the carpeting⟩ — see FUZZ
2 the hairy covering of a mammal especially when fine, soft, and thick ⟨a dog with such a dense *pile* that he never minded the cold⟩ — see FUR 1
pile *vb* **1** to lay or throw on top of one another ⟨*piled* all the clothes on the chair before putting them away⟩
synonyms heap, mound, stack
related words bank; layer, pyramid; accumulate, amass, assemble, collect, concentrate, garner, gather, group, mass; bunch, clump, lump
antonyms unpile
2 to gather into a closely packed group ⟨The kids *piled* into the car.⟩ — see ²PRESS 3
pile (up) *vb* to gradually form into a layer, pile, or mass ⟨snow *piling up* in the driveway at a rapid pace⟩ — see COLLECT 2
pilfer *vb* to take (something) without right and with an intent to keep ⟨What sort of person would *pilfer* lunches from the office refrigerator?⟩ — see STEAL 1
pilgrimage *vb* to take a trip especially of some distance ⟨tourists *pilgrimaging* to all of the traditional destinations across Europe⟩ — see TRAVEL 1
pill *n* **1** a small mass containing medicine to be taken orally ⟨You'll have to take one of these *pills* every six hours for your flu.⟩
synonyms cap, capsule, lozenge, tablet
related words cure, drug, medication, pharmaceutical, physic, remedy, specific; miracle drug, wonder drug; potion, preparation; dosage, dose
2 a person whose behavior is offensive to others ⟨She can be such a *pill* when things don't go her way.⟩ — see JERK 1
pillage *n* valuables stolen or taken by force ⟨The pirate ship was laden with the *pillage* of merchant ships from across the Spanish Main.⟩ — see LOOT
pillage *vb* to search through with the intent of committing robbery ⟨soldiers *pillaging* the countryside for anything of value⟩ — see RANSACK 1
pillar *n* **1** an upright shaft that supports an overhead structure ⟨The ancient Greek temple boasted graceful marble *pillars* with richly ornamented tops.⟩
synonyms column, pier, pilaster, post, stanchion
related words caryatid, pedestal; buttress, flying buttress; needle, obelisk; pile, piling
2 something or someone to which one looks for support ⟨My father has been my *pillar* throughout this crisis.⟩ — see DEPENDENCE 2
pilot *adj* made or done as an experiment ⟨a new *pilot* program to train students for jobs in the tech sector⟩ — see EXPERIMENTAL 1

pilot *n* one who flies or is qualified to fly an aircraft or spacecraft ⟨The airline is seeking experienced *pilots* to fly the new airplane.⟩
synonyms airman, aviator, birdman, flier (*also* flyer)
related words ace, barnstormer, bush pilot, copilot, flyboy, test pilot; captain, skipper

pilot *vb* **1** to give advice and instruction to (someone) regarding the course or process to be followed ⟨Her coach *piloted* the figure skater through the national championships.⟩ — see GUIDE 1
2 to point out the way for (someone) especially from a position in front ⟨The lead rider *piloted* the rest of the team.⟩ — see LEAD 1
3 to operate or control the course of ⟨managed to *pilot* the plane to safety despite the failure of the left engine⟩ — see NAVIGATE 1

pin *n* a lower limb of an animal ⟨a cat that was still a little unsteady on its *pins* after anesthesia⟩ — see LEG 1

pinch *n* **1** an instance of theft ⟨The *pinch* of my favorite sweater really bugged me!⟩ — see THEFT 2
2 the act of taking into one's control by authority of law ⟨a successful *pinch* of a hacking ring⟩ — see ARREST 1
3 a falling short of an essential or desirable amount or number ⟨This labor *pinch* means that there'll be long lines at the checkouts.⟩ — see DEFICIENCY

pinch *vb* **1** to squeeze tightly between two surfaces, edges, or points ⟨The zipper on those jeans always *pinches* me.⟩
synonyms nip
related words crimp, tweak; clasp, clutch, grasp, grip, hold, take
near antonyms drop, free, loose, loosen, release, spring
2 to take (something) without right and with an intent to keep ⟨*pinched* the earrings while the boutique owner was distracted by another customer⟩ — see STEAL 1
3 to take or keep under one's control by authority of law ⟨got *pinched* for stealing⟩ — see ARREST 1
4 to avoid unnecessary waste or expense ⟨If we *pinch* hard for the upcoming year, we can probably afford the vacation at that fancy resort.⟩ — see ECONOMIZE

pincher *n* one who steals ⟨The *pincher* of the stolen electronics was caught by the police trying to sell them.⟩ — see THIEF

pinch–hit *vb* to serve as a replacement usually for a time only ⟨assigned to *pinch-hit* as a math teacher for the remainder of the semester⟩ — see COVER 1

pinch hitter *n* a person or thing that takes the place of another ⟨The business owners brought in a *pinch hitter* until a permanent manager could be hired.⟩ — see SUBSTITUTE

pinching *n* the quality or practice of being overly sparing with money ⟨This constant *pinching* is getting ridiculous—we can afford to turn on one or two lights!⟩ — see PARSIMONY 1

pine (for) *vb* to have an earnest wish to own or enjoy ⟨*pining for* a house in the mountains⟩ — see DESIRE 1

pinhead *n* a stupid person ⟨thought her boss was a *pinhead*⟩ — see IDIOT

pinhole *n* a mark or small hole made by a pointed instrument ⟨*Pinholes* in a bedsheet will look like stars if you shine a light from behind it.⟩ — see PRICK 1

pining *n* a strong wish for something ⟨a sudden *pining* to have steak for dinner⟩ — see DESIRE 1

pinnacle *n* the highest part or point ⟨a singer who has reached the *pinnacle* of success⟩ — see HEIGHT 1

pinpoint *adj* meeting the highest standard of accuracy ⟨The pitcher had *pinpoint* control over his fastball.⟩ — see PRECISE 1

pinpoint *vb* **1** to find out or establish the identity of ⟨*pinpointed* the culprit by tracking calls from his cell phone⟩ — see IDENTIFY 1

2 to point or turn (something) toward a target or goal ⟨Publishers like to be able to *pinpoint* publicity efforts where they will have the most effect.⟩ — see AIM 1

pinprick *n* a mark or small hole made by a pointed instrument ⟨The nurse kindly put a decorated bandage over the *pinprick* from the injection.⟩ — see PRICK 1

pinto *adj* having blotches of two or more colors ⟨Somehow, the pure white mare had a *pinto* foal.⟩ — see PIED

pint–size *or* **pint–sized** *adj* of a size that is less than average ⟨a *pint-size* wrestler who could defeat opponents twice his size⟩ — see SMALL 1

pioneer *adj* coming before all others in time or order ⟨the nation's *pioneer* institution for the education of African-Americans⟩ — see FIRST 1

pioneer *n* a person who settles in a new region ⟨the hardships that the *pioneers* endured while settling in the West⟩ — see FRONTIERSMAN

pioneer *vb* to be responsible for the creation and early operation or use of ⟨He single-handedly *pioneered* the university's institute for medical research.⟩ — see FOUND

pious *adj* **1** firm in one's allegiance to someone or something ⟨a *pious* supporter of his school's athletic teams, during winning and losing seasons alike⟩ — see FAITHFUL 1
2 showing a devotion to God and to a life of virtue ⟨a *pious* woman who decided to become a nun⟩ — see HOLY 1

piousness *n* **1** the pretending of having virtues, principles, or beliefs that one in fact does not have ⟨an outward *piousness* that was just a ploy to get him the support of religious-minded voters⟩ — see HYPOCRISY
2 the quality or state of being spiritually pure or virtuous ⟨the quiet *piousness* of the cleric's life⟩ — see HOLINESS

¹**pip** *n* a small area that is different (as in color) from the main part ⟨a black horse with white *pips*⟩ — see SPOT 1

²**pip** *n* something very good of its kind ⟨That new sports car is a real *pip*!⟩ — see JIM-DANDY

pip *vb* to make a short sharp sound like a small bird ⟨baby birds *pipping* loudly in their nest⟩ — see CHIRP

pipe *n* **1** a long hollow cylinder for carrying a substance (as a liquid or gas) ⟨The plumber came and fixed the water *pipe* that was leaking.⟩
synonyms channel, conduit, duct, leader, line, penstock, trough, tube
related words drain, drainpipe, funnel, hydrant, main, smokestack, spout, standpipe, stovepipe, tile, waste pipe, waterspout; pipage (*or* pipeage), pipeline, piping
2 an enclosed wooden vessel for holding beverages ⟨a full *pipe* of wine⟩ — see CASK

pipe *vb* **1** to cause to move to a central point or along a restricted pathway ⟨*piped* water into every house⟩ — see CHANNEL
2 to make a short sharp sound like a small bird ⟨The baby *piped* shrilly in his bed.⟩ — see CHIRP

pipe down *vb* **1** to become still and orderly ⟨If you don't *pipe down*, we're turning this car around and going straight home!⟩ — see QUIET 1
2 to stop talking ⟨The sergeant ordered the troops to *pipe down*.⟩ — see SHUT UP 1

pipe dream *n* a conception or image created by the imagination and having no objective reality ⟨Opening our own restaurant has long been a *pipe dream*.⟩ — see FANTASY 1

pipeline *n* a direct way of passing along information or supplies ⟨A roadie serves as the columnist's *pipeline* for news about the band.⟩ ⟨The enemy destroyed our *pipeline* for resupply.⟩
synonyms channel
related words avenue, conduit, route; grapevine, outlet; origin, source; supplier; connection, contact

piping *adj* having a high musical pitch or range ⟨The *piping* sound of the teakettle caught my attention.⟩ — see SHRILL

piping hot *adj* having a notably high temperature ⟨the appeal of *piping hot* cocoa after an afternoon of shoveling snow⟩ — see HOT 1

pip–squeak *n* a person of no importance or influence ⟨I'm not changing my job based on the advice of some *pip-squeak* who cornered me at a party.⟩ — see NOBODY

piquancy *n* the quality or state of being stimulating to the mind or senses ⟨a talk show host known for the quickness and *piquancy* of his wit⟩ ⟨I appreciated the *piquancy* of the peppers in the sauce.⟩

synonyms nip, pungency, spice, zest, zing

related words raciness, spiciness; fieriness, hotness; acuteness, keenness, sharpness; provocativeness; excitement, invigoration, stimulant, stimulation, stimulus, thrill; flavor, redolence, savor (*also* savour), savoriness, tastiness

near antonyms flatness, tastelessness; dullness (*also* dulness), insipidity, monotonousness, monotony, predictability, tediousness; blandness, thinness, weakness

antonyms insipidity

piquant *adj* sharp and pleasantly stimulating to the mind or senses ⟨a *piquant* tidbit of information about the new neighbors⟩ ⟨The *piquant* cuisine of India boasts some highly spiced dishes.⟩

synonyms pert, poignant, pungent, salty, savory (*also* savoury), zesty

related words racy, spicy; fiery, gingery, hot, peppery, vinegary; acute, keen; biting, bitter, cutting, mordant, trenchant; animating, energizing, exciting, galvanizing, invigorating, piquing, provocative, provoking; ambrosial, appetizing, delectable, delicious, luscious, palatable, scrumptious, toothsome; flavorful, savorous, tasty

near antonyms flat, flavorless, savorless, tasteless; arid, banal, barren, boring, colorless, drab, dreary, dry, dull, flat, humdrum, leaden, monotonous, numbing, pedestrian, ponderous, stale, stodgy, tedious, tiring, wearisome; bland, dilute, thin, watery, weak

antonyms insipid, zestless

pique *n* the feeling of being offended or resentful after a slight or indignity ⟨After a moment of *pique*, she responded calmly to the accusation.⟩

synonyms dudgeon, huff, offense (*or* offence), peeve, resentment, umbrage

related words aggravation, anger, annoyance, bother, discomfort, exasperation, frustration, irritation, vexation; agitation, angriness, displeasure, distress, disturbance, indignation, irateness, ire, outrage, upset; dander, temper; fit, pouts, sulk(s), tantrum, tizzy; affront, barb, dig, indignity, insult, put-down, slap, slight, slur

near antonyms satisfaction; appeasement, mollification, pacification; contentment, delight, gratification, happiness, pleasure

pique *vb* **1** to disturb the peace of mind of (someone) especially by repeated disagreeable acts ⟨Her seat companion *piqued* her by repeatedly poking her in the ribs.⟩ — see IRRITATE 1

2 to rouse to strong feeling or action ⟨Their sarcastic comments *piqued* him to respond in kind.⟩ — see PROVOKE 1

piquing *adj* serving or likely to arouse a strong reaction ⟨*piquing* remarks that were said mainly to get a rise out of the other guests at the party⟩ — see PROVOCATIVE

piracy *n* the act or pursuit of robbing ships at sea ⟨Many countries have harsh penalties for *piracy* now.⟩

synonyms pirating

related words depredation, despoilment, despoliation, looting, marauding, pillaging, plunder, plundering, raiding, robbery, sacking; privateering

pirate *n* someone who engages in robbery of ships at sea ⟨Sir Francis Drake was a British *pirate* who preyed on Spanish ships with the connivance of Elizabeth I.⟩

synonyms buccaneer, corsair, freebooter, rover

related words despoiler, looter, marauder, pillager, plunderer, raider, robber; privateer

pirate *vb* to take or make use of under a guise of authority but without actual right ⟨using *pirated* software that was subject to copyright⟩ — see APPROPRIATE 1

pirating *n* the act or pursuit of robbing ships at sea ⟨Officially sanctioned *pirating* used to be common among warring nations.⟩ — see PIRACY

pirouette *n* a rapid turning about on an axis or central point ⟨the ballerina's perfectly executed *pirouette*⟩ — see SPIN 1

pirouette *vb* to move in circles around an axis or center ⟨The ballerina *pirouetted* across the stage.⟩ — see SPIN 1

pit *n* a sunken area forming a separate space ⟨Removal of the tree stump left a gaping *pit* in the yard.⟩ — see HOLE 2

pit–a–pat *vb* to expand and contract in a rhythmic manner ⟨Her heart *pit-a-patted* with surprise.⟩ — see PULSATE

pitch *n* **1** an act or instance of diving ⟨the daring *pitch* of the diver into the swirling ocean waters at the base of the cliff⟩ — see DIVE 1

2 the degree to which something rises up from a position level with the horizon ⟨The steep *pitch* of the roof makes it too dangerous to walk on.⟩ — see SLANT 1

pitch *vb* **1** to fix in an upright position ⟨needed help *pitching* a tent⟩ — see ERECT 1

2 to cast oneself head first into deep water ⟨When a wave hit the float, I lost my balance and *pitched* into the lake.⟩ — see DIVE 1

3 to make a series of unsteady side-to-side motions ⟨The ship *pitched* in the choppy sea.⟩ — see ROCK 1

4 to send through the air especially with a quick forward motion of the arm ⟨*pitched* the baseball almost 50 feet⟩ — see THROW 1

5 to get rid of as useless or unwanted ⟨We decided to *pitch* that whole system and start over again.⟩ — see DISCARD 1

6 to provide publicity for ⟨The cutting-edge ad agency was hired to *pitch* our products to a younger generation of consumers.⟩ — see PUBLICIZE 1

7 to set or cause to be at an angle ⟨The roof should be *pitched* steeply enough to prevent an excessive accumulation of snow.⟩ — see LEAN 1

pitch–black *adj* **1** being without light or without much light ⟨Finding anything in a *pitch-black* room is almost impossible.⟩ — see DARK 1

2 having the color of soot or coal ⟨a *pitch-black* cat with green eyes⟩ — see BLACK 1

pitch–dark *adj* **1** being without light or without much light ⟨With its only light burned out, the closet was *pitch-dark*.⟩ — see DARK 1

2 having the color of soot or coal ⟨On a whim she bleached her *pitch-dark* hair blond.⟩ — see BLACK 1

pitched *adj* **1** inclined or twisted to one side ⟨*Pitched* and badly weathered, the fence looked ready to fall down at any moment.⟩ — see AWRY

2 running in a slanting direction ⟨a sharply *pitched* rooftop⟩ — see DIAGONAL

pitcher *n* a handled container for holding and pouring liquids that usually has a lip or a spout ⟨Please bring me the *pitcher* of lemonade from the table.⟩

synonyms ewer, flagon, jug

related words carafe, decanter; bucket, pail, pot; bottle, canteen, cup, fiasco, flask, jorum, mug, stein, stoup, tankard; kettle, teakettle

pitch in *vb* to make a donation as part of a group effort ⟨Everyone at the office *pitched in* to buy a gift for the soon-to-be-wed couple.⟩ — see CONTRIBUTE 1

pitchy *adj* **1** being without light or without much light ⟨We stood staring into the *pitchy* dark forest, trying to determine what had made the strange cry.⟩ — see DARK 1
2 having the color of soot or coal ⟨The soldiers couldn't see a thing in the *pitchy* darkness.⟩ — see BLACK 1

piteous *adj* deserving of one's pity ⟨a *piteous* beggar huddled in the doorway of an abandoned building⟩ — see PATHETIC 1

pitfall *n* **1** a danger or difficulty that is hidden or not easily recognized ⟨Buying a house can be full of *pitfalls* for the unwary.⟩
synonyms booby trap, catch, gimmick, hitch, joker, snag
related words snare, trap, trip wire, web; hazard, peril, risk; bomb, bombshell, kicker, surprise (*also* surprize); bait, decoy, lure
2 something that may cause injury or harm ⟨One of the *pitfalls* of having a credit card is the high interest rate charged for not paying on time.⟩ — see DANGER 2

pith *n* the central part or aspect of something under consideration ⟨We finally got to the *pith* of the discussion.⟩ — see CRUX

pithily *adv* in a few words ⟨The observation that "War is hell" is how General Sherman *pithily* summed up his experiences in combat.⟩ — see SHORTLY 1

pithiness *n* the quality or state of being marked by or using only few words to convey much meaning ⟨the memorable *pithiness* of Calvin Coolidge's campaign announcement: "I do not choose to run for President in 1928"⟩ — see SUCCINCTNESS

pithy *adj* marked by the use of few words to convey much information or meaning ⟨a fairly *pithy* criticism about a notably lengthy novel⟩ — see CONCISE

pitiable *adj* **1** arousing or deserving of one's loathing and disgust ⟨The sales presentation was a *pitiable* display of ineptitude and disorganization.⟩ — see CONTEMPTIBLE 1
2 deserving pitying scorn (as for inadequacy) ⟨a *pitiable* attempt at singing⟩ — see PITIFUL 1
3 deserving of one's pity ⟨a *pitiable* old dog⟩ — see PATHETIC 1

pitiful *adj* **1** deserving pitying scorn (as for inadequacy) ⟨That piece of junk is a *pitiful* excuse for a car.⟩
synonyms contemptible, despicable, miserable, pathetic, pitiable, sad, sorry, wretched
related words deplorable, discreditable, disgraceful, disreputable, ignominious, infamous, misbegotten, notorious, shameful; abhorrent, abominable, beastly, detestable, hateful, lousy, odious, stinking; bad, inferior, lame, poor; dishonorable, shameful; meritless, unworthy, worthless
near antonyms admirable, commendable, creditable, laudable, meritorious, praiseworthy, redoubtable; notable, noteworthy, noticeable, outstanding, reputable, worthy; excellent; flawless, perfect; honorable, noble
antonyms decent, presentable, respectable
2 arousing or deserving of one's loathing and disgust ⟨a *pitiful* coward⟩ — see CONTEMPTIBLE 1
3 deserving of one's pity ⟨*pitiful* orphans⟩ — see PATHETIC 1

pitiless *adj* having or showing a lack of sympathy or tender feelings ⟨gave the beggar in the street a *pitiless* look and kept on walking⟩ — see HARD 1

pittance *n* a very small sum of money ⟨The internship offers only a *pittance* for a salary, but it is a great opportunity to gain experience.⟩ — see MITE 1

pitter–patter *vb* to expand and contract in a rhythmic manner ⟨His heart *pitter-pattered* with excitement as he waited for the right moment to propose.⟩ — see PULSATE

pity *n* **1** a regrettable or blameworthy act ⟨It's a *pity* the woodchuck ate all the flowers after you put so much effort into the garden.⟩ — see CRIME 2
2 the capacity for feeling for another's unhappiness or misfortune ⟨a woman of boundless *pity* who tried to care for every abandoned animal she found⟩ — see HEART 1

pity *vb* to have sympathy for ⟨I always *pity* the people who have to work in this freezing weather.⟩
synonyms ache (for), bleed (for), commiserate (with), condole (with), feel (for), sympathize (with), yearn (over)
related words care (for); grieve (for), sorrow (for); love; empathize (with), identify (with); tolerate, understand
near antonyms disregard, ignore, neglect, overlook; dislike, hate, scorn

pivot *n* the central part or aspect of something under consideration ⟨an issue that is the real *pivot* of the controversy⟩ — see CRUX

pivot *vb* to move (something) in a curved or circular path on or as if on an axis ⟨The telescope is mounted on a tripod so you can easily *pivot* it for viewing in any direction.⟩ — see TURN 1

pivotal *adj* of the greatest possible importance ⟨The report was missing a *pivotal* piece of information.⟩ — see CRUCIAL

pixie *also* **pixy** *n* an imaginary being usually having a small human form and magical powers ⟨Leave a dish of milk and some bread out for the *pixies*.⟩ — see FAIRY

pixieish *adj* tending to or exhibiting reckless playfulness ⟨The actress had a *pixieish* quality that served her well in screwball comedies.⟩ — see MISCHIEVOUS 1

placard *n* a sheet bearing an announcement for posting in a public place ⟨a *placard* announcing a campaign rally at the downtown plaza⟩ — see POSTER

placard *vb* **1** to affix (as a notice) to or on a suitable place ⟨*placarded* the poster about the upcoming play to the bulletin board⟩ — see ¹POST 1
2 to make known openly or publicly ⟨*placarded* the news about the planned construction project all over the neighborhood⟩ — see ANNOUNCE

placate *vb* to lessen the anger or agitation of ⟨I attempted to *placate* the screaming child by offering him a story.⟩ — see PACIFY 1

placating *adj* tending to lessen or avoid conflict or hostility ⟨a *placating* comment that seemed to calm everyone down a bit⟩ — see PACIFIC 1

place *n* **1** the area or space occupied by or intended for something ⟨the *place* chosen for the picnic⟩ ⟨There's the *place* where I left my umbrella.⟩
synonyms locale, locality, location, locus, point, position, site, spot, where
related words scene; region, section, sector; here, there
2 a building, room, or suite of rooms occupied by a service business ⟨We're going to our favorite *place* to eat.⟩
synonyms establishment, joint, parlor, salon
related words spot, station; facility, installation; club, house; den, dive, hole
3 an assignment at which one regularly works for pay ⟨A friend got her a *place* in a department store's clothing department.⟩ — see JOB 1
4 an extent or area available for or used up by some activity or thing ⟨Let's make a *place* around our campfire for the newest member of our group.⟩ — see ROOM 1
5 the action for which a person or thing is specially fitted or used or for which a thing exists ⟨knew his *place* in the organization⟩ — see ROLE
6 the place where one lives ⟨They have a nice little *place* in the country.⟩ — see HOME 1
7 the placement of someone or something in relation to others in a vertical arrangement ⟨Tom came in fourth *place* in the marathon.⟩ — see RANK 1
8 a situation or activity for which a person or thing is best suited ⟨He was having a hard time finding a *place* in the business world.⟩ — see NICHE 2

9 an individual part of a process, series, or ranking ⟨Well, in the first *place*, you shouldn't even be here.⟩ — see DEGREE 1

place *vb* **1** to arrange something in a certain spot or position ⟨He carefully *placed* the flowers in a vase.⟩
synonyms depose, deposit, dispose, fix, lay, position, put, set, set up, situate, stick
related words move, rearrange, reorder, shift; orient; establish, locate, plant, settle; clap, flop, plop, plump, plunk (*or* plonk), plunk down, slap; ensconce, niche; assemble, collect; carry; berth, park; affix, anchor, lock, lodge, wedge; array, lay out, line up, queue, rank; set down
near antonyms remove, take; banish; dislodge, displace, replace, supersede, supplant
2 to arrange or assign according to type ⟨I'd *place* those cyclists in the advanced group for the training ride.⟩ — see CLASSIFY 1
3 to decide the size, amount, number, or distance of (something) without actual measurement ⟨I'd *place* that as roughly the third largest house in the neighborhood.⟩ — see ESTIMATE 2
4 to take or have a certain position within a group arranged in vertical classes ⟨Kim *placed* second in the competition.⟩ — see RANK 1
5 to pick (someone) by one's authority for a specific position or duty ⟨*placed* the recent college grad in the company's research and development division⟩ — see APPOINT 2
6 to present or bring forward for discussion ⟨Once again the issue of the congested intersection was *placed* before the town council.⟩ — see INTRODUCE 2
7 to provide with a paying job ⟨Most of the trainees at the TV station are *placed* in clerical positions.⟩ — see EMPLOY 1

placid *adj* **1** free from emotional or mental agitation ⟨exceptionally *placid* parents who were rarely upset by their six children⟩ — see CALM 2
2 free from storms or physical disturbance ⟨a *placid* lake⟩ — see CALM 1
3 free from disturbing noise or uproar ⟨a vacation in the *placid* lake community⟩ — see QUIET 1

placidity *n* **1** a state of freedom from storm or disturbance ⟨The *placidity* of the area makes it a perfect vacation spot for people who just want to relax.⟩ — see CALM 1
2 evenness of emotions or temper ⟨His evident lack of *placidity* makes him poorly suited for such a stressful job.⟩ — see EQUANIMITY
3 freedom from disquieting or oppressive thoughts or emotions ⟨Her apparent *placidity* belied an inner turmoil as she faced a life-altering decision.⟩ — see PEACE 2

plague *n* a widespread disease resulting in a high rate of death ⟨The Black Death was a *plague* that killed about one third of Europe's population in the Middle Ages.⟩
synonyms pest, pestilence
related words pandemic; affection, affliction, ailment, contagion, illness, infection, infirmity, malady, sickness; curse, scourge
plague *vb* to cause persistent suffering to ⟨*plagued* by a cough for all of last week⟩ — see AFFLICT

plain *adj* **1** free from all additions or embellishment ⟨I like my hamburgers *plain*, with no ketchup or relish.⟩ ⟨Just give us the *plain* facts.⟩
synonyms bald, bare, naked, simple, unadorned, undecorated, unvarnished
related words denuded, divested, stripped; au naturel, earthy, elemental, homely, natural, unsophisticated; clean; austere, bleak, severe, stark; minimalist; inconspicuous, muted, restrained, sober, subdued, toned (down), unobtrusive; conservative, quiet, understated; no-frills

near antonyms flamboyant, flashy, garish, gaudy, glittery, glitzy, loud, ostentatious, showy, splashy, swank (*or* swanky), tawdry; bedizened, florid, lurid, ornate; overdecorated, overdone, overwrought; elaborate, extravagant, ornate, rococo; appareled (*or* apparelled), arrayed, bedecked, decked-out, dressed, embroidered, garnished, trimmed
antonyms adorned, decorated, embellished, fancy, ornamented
2 free from added matter ⟨I'd prefer my pasta *plain*, not flavored with tomato or spinach or anything else.⟩ — see PURE 1
3 free in expressing one's true feelings and opinions ⟨Their piano teacher is honest and *plain*, if not always tactful.⟩ — see FRANK
4 going straight to the point clearly and firmly ⟨a *plain* report on the current situation⟩ — see STRAIGHTFORWARD 1
5 not subject to misinterpretation or more than one interpretation ⟨Let me make my meaning *plain*.⟩ — see CLEAR 2

plain *adv* in an honest and direct manner ⟨told her *plain* that he loved her⟩ — see STRAIGHTFORWARD

plain *n* **1** a broad area of level or rolling treeless country ⟨The first settlers in that area lived on the vast *plains* in lonely log cabins.⟩
synonyms down(s), grassland, lea (*or* ley), moor, prairie, savanna (*also* savannah), steppe, tundra, veld (*or* veldt)
related words field, meadow; floodplain; bottom, bottomland, flat, lowland; plateau, table, tableland, upland
2 a wide space or area ⟨the vast *plains* of snow-covered earth that seemed to stretch endlessly⟩ — see EXPANSE

plainly *adv* **1** in an honest and direct manner ⟨You'll have to tell your relatives very *plainly* that you don't like perfume, or they'll keep giving it to you.⟩ — see STRAIGHTFORWARD
2 without any question ⟨She is *plainly* upset about something.⟩ — see INDEED 1

plainness *n* **1** the free expression of one's true feelings and opinions ⟨His unabashed *plainness* in telling people exactly what he thought of them was often offensive.⟩ — see CANDOR 1
2 the quality or state of having a form or structure of few parts or elements ⟨The *plainness* and clean lines of that coffeemaker make it a piece of modern sculpture as well as a kitchen appliance.⟩ — see SIMPLICITY 1

plainspoken *adj* free in expressing one's true feelings and opinions ⟨a *plainspoken* woman who never hesitated to speak the unvarnished truth⟩ — see FRANK

plaint *n* **1** a crying out in grief ⟨the piteous *plaints* of mourners⟩ — see LAMENT 1
2 an expression of dissatisfaction, pain, or resentment ⟨That taxes are too high is perhaps the most perennial of *plaints*.⟩ — see COMPLAINT 1

plaintiff *n* the person in a legal proceeding who makes a charge of wrongdoing against another ⟨The judge ruled that the *plaintiff's* lawsuit was groundless, and it was dismissed.⟩ — see COMPLAINANT

plaintive *adj* expressing or suggesting mourning ⟨the puppy's *plaintive* expression after we put the toy away⟩ — see MOURNFUL 1

plait *n* a length of something formed of three or more strands woven together ⟨She wore a *plait* down her back that reached her waist.⟩ — see BRAID

plait *vb* to form into a braid ⟨*plaited* the doll's hair so it wouldn't tangle⟩ — see BRAID

plan *n* **1** a method worked out in advance for achieving some objective ⟨There is a contingency *plan* in the office for handling almost any emergency.⟩

synonyms arrangement, blueprint, design, game, ground plan, program, project, scheme, strategy, system

related words collusion, conspiracy, plot; contrivance, device, maneuver, ruse, stratagem, subterfuge, trick; counterplan, counterstrategy; means, tactic, technique, way; procedure, protocol; conception, idea, projet, proposal, specific(s), specification(s); aim, intent, intention, purpose; diagram, formula, layout, map, pattern, platform, policy, setup

2 something that one hopes or intends to accomplish ⟨Our *plan* is to finish up by next Friday.⟩ — see GOAL

plan *vb* **1** to work out the details of (something) in advance ⟨We *planned* the school dance down to the smallest detail.⟩

synonyms arrange, blueprint, budget, calculate, chart, design, frame, lay out, map (out), organize, prepare, project, scheme (out), shape

related words conspire, contrive, devise, intrigue, machinate, plot, put up; concert, get up; draft, outline, sketch; aim, figure, have on, intend, mean; contemplate, meditate, premeditate

2 to have in mind as a purpose or goal ⟨I *plan* to have a party for my birthday, even if I have to throw it myself!⟩ — see INTEND 1

plane *adj* having a surface without bends, breaks, or irregularities ⟨You can do these tracings on any *plane* surface.⟩ — see LEVEL 1

plane *n* a vehicle for traveling through the air that has fixed wings for lift ⟨A *plane* flew overhead.⟩ — see AIRPLANE

¹**plane** *vb* to make free from breaks, curves, or bumps ⟨*planed* the wood for the picnic table perfectly smooth so that no one would get splinters⟩ — see EVEN 1

²**plane** *vb* to move through the air with or as if with outstretched wings ⟨An eagle *planed* effortlessly overhead, gliding on an air current.⟩ — see FLY 1

planet *n* the celestial body on which we live ⟨our collective responsibility to conserve the *planet* and its natural resources for future generations⟩ — see EARTH 1

plant *n* a building or set of buildings for the manufacturing of goods ⟨a furniture *plant* that employs hundreds of people⟩ — see FACTORY

plant *vb* **1** to put or set into the ground to grow ⟨I'll *plant* the marigold seeds in the spring.⟩

synonyms drill, put in, seed, sow

related words bed; replant, transplant; broadcast, scatter; pot; overseed, reseed

near antonyms gather, harvest, reap

2 to be responsible for the creation and early operation or use of ⟨Soon the sect had *planted* churches across the breadth of the colony.⟩ — see FOUND

3 to set permanently in the consciousness or mind-set ⟨a profound respect for Mother Nature that had been *planted* by long experience with hurricanes⟩ — see IMPLANT 1

plantation *n* a settlement in a new country or region ⟨The struggling *plantation* almost failed during the first winter.⟩ — see COLONY 1

planter *n* a person who cultivates the land and grows crops on it ⟨The *planters* are too busy around harvest time to pay the tourists much mind.⟩ — see FARMER

plash *vb* **1** to flow in a broken irregular stream ⟨Water *plashed* down the drain.⟩ — see GURGLE

2 to move with a splashing motion ⟨a child happily *plashing* in the tub⟩ — see SLOSH 1

3 to wet or soil by striking with something liquid or mushy ⟨Passing cars *plashed* us with roadside slush.⟩ — see SPLASH 2

plaster *n* a medicated covering used to heal an injury ⟨Put a *plaster* on the burn and don't touch it.⟩ — see DRESSING 1

plastic *adj* **1** capable of being easily molded or modeled ⟨Silly Putty is famous for being very *plastic*.⟩

synonyms malleable

related words adaptable; bendable, ductile, pliable, pliant, supple, willowy; elastic, flexible, limber, resilient, workable; bending, giving, kneadable, tractable, yielding

near antonyms inflexible, intractable, rigid, stiff

2 lacking in natural or spontaneous quality ⟨There's usually a *plastic* cordiality at these corporate events.⟩ — see ARTIFICIAL 1

plasticity *n* the quality or state of being easily molded ⟨We chose that type of clay for its greater *plasticity*.⟩

synonyms malleability

related words adaptability; ductility, pliability, pliableness, pliancy, pliantness, suppleness; elasticity, flexibility, limberness, resilience, workability, workableness

near antonyms inflexibility, rigidity, stiffness

¹**plat** *n* a length of something formed of three or more strands woven together ⟨a *plat* of lace⟩ — see BRAID

²**plat** *n* **1** a small area of usually open land ⟨Each settler was granted a *plat* to farm.⟩ — see FIELD 1

2 a small piece of land that is developed or available for development ⟨plans to build a shopping center on the last undeveloped *plat* in town⟩ — see LOT 1

plat *vb* to form into a braid ⟨First, *plat* the yarn into a cord.⟩ — see BRAID

plate *n* **1** a small thin piece of material that resembles an animal scale ⟨The tiny silver *plates* on the brooch are arranged to look like fish scales.⟩ — see ²SCALE

2 something that visually explains or decorates a text ⟨The book's color *plate* illustrates the internal organs of the human body.⟩ — see ILLUSTRATION 1

plateau *n* a broad flat area of elevated land ⟨Indigenous peoples have inhabited the *plateau* for centuries.⟩

synonyms mesa, table, tableland

related words butte, height, highland, upland

platform *n* a level usually raised surface ⟨You'll have to stand up there on the *platform* for your speech.⟩

synonyms dais, podium, rostrum, stage, stand

related words altar, pulpit; riser, scaffold; gallery

platitude *n* an idea or expression that has been used by many people ⟨"Blondes have more fun" is a silly *platitude*.⟩ — see COMMONPLACE

plaudit *n, usually* **plaudits** *pl* enthusiastic and usually public expression of approval ⟨The proud parents bragged that their daughter had received many *plaudits* for her academic achievements.⟩ — see APPLAUSE 1

plausible *adj* worthy of being accepted as true or reasonable ⟨It's a *plausible* explanation for the demise of that prehistoric species.⟩ — see BELIEVABLE

play *n* **1** activity engaged in to amuse oneself ⟨It's such a delight to watch the children in their *play*.⟩

synonyms dalliance, frolic, frolicking, fun, recreation, relaxation, rollicking, sport

related words gamboling (*or* gambolling), romping; amusement, diversion, entertainment; pastime; friskiness, playfulness, sportiveness, wantonness; knavery, mischief, mischievousness, rascality, roguishness, waggery; binge, fling, kick, lark, revel, rollick, spree; hilarity, merriment, merrymaking, revelry; high jinks (*also* hijinks), horseplay, tomfoolery; avocation, pursuit

near antonyms drudgery, labor, work; duty, obligation, responsibility

2 a written work in which the story is told through speech and action that is intended to be acted out on stage ⟨We'll be putting on a school *play* using that stage.⟩

synonyms drama, dramatization

related words interlude, playlet; comedy, docudrama, melodrama, musical, musical comedy, tragedy, tragicomedy; magnum opus, opus, work

3 an attitude or manner not to be taken seriously ⟨I

didn't mean to insult anyone, for it was all just *play.*⟩ — see FUN 2

4 the act or practice of employing something for a particular purpose ⟨The host's sense of humor was obviously in *play* during the awards ceremony.⟩ — see USE 1

5 a clever often underhanded means to achieve an end ⟨made a *play* for the job⟩ — see TRICK 1

play *vb* **1** to engage in activity for amusement ⟨He needed some time to run and *play* in the yard after his hard work.⟩

synonyms dally, disport, frolic, recreate, rollick, skylark, sport

related words cavort, frisk, gambol, romp; dabble, trifle; amuse, divert, entertain; delight, please; fiddle (around), putter (around); bum (around), dawdle, idle, loaf, lounge (around *or* about), relax, rest, screw around, slack (off); jest, joke, tease

near antonyms drudge, labor, plod, plug (away), strain, strive, struggle, sweat, toil, work

2 to present a portrayal or performance of ⟨Josh *played* Hamlet in the campus production of the classic.⟩ — see ACT 1

3 to pretend to be (what one is not) in appearance or behavior ⟨Stop *playing* the innocent, because I know that you were behind that prank.⟩ — see IMPERSONATE 1

4 to spend time in aimless activity ⟨We just *played* around while we waited for the bus to arrive.⟩ — see FIDDLE (AROUND)

5 to deal with (something) usually skillfully or efficiently ⟨This is how we're going to *play* the situation.⟩ — see HANDLE 1

6 to risk (something) on the outcome of an uncertain event ⟨Figuring that she had little to lose, she *played* her last few bucks on the state lottery.⟩ — see BET

play (on *or* **upon)** *vb* to take unfair advantage of ⟨The candidate *played on* the voters' prejudices.⟩ — see EXPLOIT 1

play (upon) *vb* to control or take advantage of by artful, unfair, or insidious means ⟨*playing upon* parents' worries to sell their safety products⟩ — see MANIPULATE 1

play (with) *vb* to handle thoughtlessly, ignorantly, or mischievously ⟨Please don't *play with* the telephone!⟩ — see TAMPER (WITH)

play down *vb* to express scornfully one's low opinion of ⟨Out of sheer envy, she would always *play down* her sister's accomplishments.⟩ — see DECRY 1

played out *adj* depleted in strength, energy, or freshness ⟨I'm just *played out* after the week I've had.⟩ — see WEARY 1

player *n* **1** a person who plays a musical instrument ⟨a horn *player*⟩ — see MUSICIAN 1

2 one who acts professionally (as in a play, movie, or television show) ⟨A troupe of *players* used to give performances on the town green.⟩ — see ACTOR 1

3 one who takes part in something ⟨a significant *player* in the negotiations⟩ — see PARTICIPANT

playful *adj* given to good-natured joking or teasing ⟨The little girl was lighthearted and *playful.*⟩

synonyms antic, coltish, elfish, fay, frisky, frolicsome, rollicking, sportive

related words coy, kittenish; happy, lighthearted, whimsical; energetic, frolic, jocund, lively, merry, spirited, sprightly, spunky, vivacious; devilish, impish, knavish, mischievous, pixie (*also* pixy), rascally, roguish; amusing, diverting, enjoyable, entertaining, fun, pleasurable; dabbling, frivolous, goofy, silly, trifling; jesting, jocose, jocular, joking, prankish, teasing

near antonyms dutiful, responsible; grave, grim, serious, solemn, somber (*or* sombre), stern, stolid; no-nonsense,

priggish, starchy, stuffy; decorous, formal, proper, sedate, staid; guarded, inhibited, restrained

antonyms earnest, serious-minded, sober, sobersided

playfulness *n* a natural disposition for playful behavior ⟨The *playfulness* of the kitten can be quite amusing.⟩

synonyms friskiness, impishness, mischief, mischievousness, prankishness, sportiveness

related words coyness, kittenishness; archness, devilment, devilry (*or* deviltry), hob, rascality, roguishness, waggery; devilishness, diabolicalness, knavery; frivolousness; energy, liveliness, spiritedness, sprightliness, spunkiness, vivaciousness, vivacity; gaiety (*also* gayety), jocularity, lightheartedness, mirthfulness, whimsicality

near antonyms graveness, grimness, seriousness, solemnity, sternness; priggishness, starchiness, stuffiness; constraint, restraint, self-control

antonyms earnestness, soberness

playhouse *n* a building or part of a building where movies are shown ⟨They're renovating the old *playhouse* and adding extra screens.⟩ — see THEATER 1

play out *vb* to make complete use of ⟨We've finally *played out* the leftovers from that huge holiday meal.⟩ — see DEPLETE 1

plea *n* **1** an earnest request ⟨a *plea* for donations⟩

synonyms appeal, cry, desire, entreaty, petition, pleading, prayer, solicitation, suit, supplication

related words application, requisition; call, claim, demand, insistence

2 an explanation that frees one from fault or blame ⟨My only *plea* is that I've been overworked lately.⟩ — see EXCUSE

plead *vb* to state (something) as a reason in support of or against something under consideration ⟨Despite a plea bargain being on the table, he maintained he didn't do it and *pleaded* not guilty.⟩ — see ARGUE 1

plead (for) *vb* to make a request for ⟨The children *pleaded for* a kitten.⟩ — see ASK (FOR) 1

plead (to) *vb* to make a request to (someone) in an earnest or urgent manner ⟨charities *pleading to* people for help⟩ — see BEG

pleader *n* one who asks earnestly for a favor or gift ⟨The parents finally granted the persistent *pleader* his wish: a puppy.⟩ — see SUPPLICANT

pleading *adj* asking humbly ⟨a *pleading* class asking for a retake of the exam⟩ — see SUPPLIANT

pleading *n* an earnest request ⟨Despite our *pleadings* to be let out early, we had to work a full day.⟩ — see PLEA 1

pleasant *adj* **1** giving pleasure or contentment to the mind or senses ⟨The massage was extremely *pleasant* and relaxing.⟩

synonyms agreeable, blessed (*also* blest), congenial, darling, delectable, delicious, delightful, dreamy, enjoyable, felicitous, good, grateful, gratifying, heavenly, jolly, luscious, nice, palatable, pleasing, pleasurable, pretty, satisfying, savory (*also* savoury), sweet, tasty, welcome

related words alluring, attractive, desirable, enviable, inviting, relishable, tempting; charming, enchanting, fascinating; calming, comforting, soothing; amusing, diverting, entertaining, recreative; affable, amiable, cheerful, cheery, comfortable, genial, goodly, good-natured, gracious, hospitable, kindly, personable; glad, happy, joyous; elating, exhilarating; ecstatic, euphoric, rapturous

near antonyms abominable, ghastly, god-awful, hellish, horrid, miserable, wretched; distasteful, obnoxious, offensive, repellent (*also* repellant); repugnant, repulsive, unsavory, vile, yucky (*also* yukky); abhorrent, detestable, hateful, odious; displeasing, dissatisfying; depressing, disheartening, dismal, dreary, gloomy, heartbreaking, heartrending, joyless, sad, unhappy; deplorable, doleful, dolorous, lamentable, lugubrious, mournful, re-

grettable, sorrowful, tragic (*also* tragical); aggravating, annoying, exasperating, irritating, peeving, perturbing, vexing; forbidding; hostile, intimidating; angering, enraging, incensing, inflaming (*also* enflaming), infuriating, maddening, outraging, rankling, riling; distressing, disturbing, upsetting
antonyms disagreeable, unpalatable, unpleasant, unwelcome
2 having an easygoing and pleasing manner especially in social situations ⟨She has a reputation among the employees for being a demanding boss, but she's unexpectedly *pleasant* outside of work.⟩ — see AMIABLE
pleasantly *adv* in a pleasing way ⟨We were *pleasantly* surprised by their offer to put us up for the night.⟩ — see WELL 5
pleasantness *n* the state or quality of having a pleasant or agreeable manner in socializing with others ⟨His habitual *pleasantness* makes him everyone's first choice for a party guest.⟩ — see AMIABILITY 1
pleasantry *n* **1** an act or utterance that is a customary show of good manners ⟨"How are you" is merely a social *pleasantry*.⟩ — see CIVILITY 1
2 something said or done to cause laughter ⟨His afterdinner speeches usually include the sort of gentle *pleasantry* that raises a chuckle.⟩ — see JOKE 1
please *vb* **1** to give satisfaction to ⟨Fresh flowers *please* me greatly.⟩
synonyms content, delight, feast, gladden, gratify, rejoice, satisfy, suit, warm
related words appease, mollify, pacify, placate, soothe; assuage, quench, sate, satiate; excite, tickle, titillate; amuse, divert, entertain, treat; captivate, charm; galvanize, thrill; calm, comfort; cater (to), humor, indulge; coddle, mollycoddle, pamper, spoil
near antonyms aggravate, annoy, bother, chafe, cross, exasperate, gall, grate, irk, irritate, nettle, peeve, perturb, pique, ruffle, vex; anger, enrage, incense, inflame (*also* enflame), infuriate, madden, outrage, rankle, rile, roil; provoke, rouse; agitate, distress, disturb, fret, upset; harry, pester
antonyms displease
2 to see fit ⟨Clearly, you are going to do as you *please* no matter what I advise.⟩ — see CHOOSE 2
pleased *adj* **1** experiencing pleasure, satisfaction, or delight ⟨She looked *pleased* with the gift.⟩ — see GLAD 1
2 feeling that one's needs or desires have been met ⟨a sleepy, *pleased* cat⟩ — see CONTENT
pleasing *adj* giving pleasure or contentment to the mind or senses ⟨*pleasing* music in the background⟩ — see PLEASANT 1
pleasingly *adv* in a pleasing way ⟨The dining room at the inn has a *pleasingly* old-fashioned look to it.⟩ — see WELL 5
pleasurable *adj* **1** giving pleasure or contentment to the mind or senses ⟨a *pleasurable* hot bath after a tiring day⟩ — see PLEASANT 1
2 providing amusement or enjoyment ⟨a number of *pleasurable* additions to the state fair this year⟩ — see FUN
pleasure *n* **1** the feeling experienced when one's wishes are met ⟨Nothing gives me more *pleasure* than a hot meal after a long day.⟩
synonyms content, contentedness, contentment, delectation, delight, enjoyment, gladness, gratification, happiness, relish, satisfaction
related words afterglow; bliss, felicity, glee, gleefulness, joy; amusement, diversion, entertainment; elation, exhilaration, exultation, intoxication; ecstasy, euphoria, heaven, rapture; cheer, cheerfulness, exuberance, gaiety (*also* gayety), jollity, joyfulness, jubilation; comfort, ease, restfulness

near antonyms misery, sadness, unhappiness, wretchedness; anguish, desolation, joylessness, sorrow, woe; dejection, depression, despondency, dispiritedness, gloom, melancholy; aggravation, annoyance, exasperation, irritation, pique, vexation; anger, fury, rage; agitation, distress, disturbance, upset; discomfort, restlessness, uneasiness
antonyms discontent, discontentedness, discontentment, displeasure, dissatisfaction, unhappiness
2 a source of great satisfaction ⟨The new car is a real *pleasure* to drive.⟩ — see DELIGHT 1
3 someone or something that provides amusement or enjoyment ⟨a good-humored girl who's a *pleasure* to be around⟩ — see FUN 1
pleat *vb* to form into a braid ⟨*pleated* ribbons⟩ — see BRAID
plebeian *adj* belonging to the class of people of low social or economic rank ⟨Nick wondered what the people at the country club would think of his *plebeian* origins.⟩ — see IGNOBLE 1
plebeians *pl n* the body of the community as contrasted with the elite ⟨The current administration evidently believes that we *plebeians* cannot withstand a dose of harsh reality.⟩ — see MASS 1
pledge *n* **1** something given or held to assure that the giver will keep a promise ⟨I was required to leave my keys as a *pledge* that I would bring the car back.⟩
synonyms gage, guarantee, guaranty, pawn, security
related words bond; deposit, down payment, earnest; surety, warranty; assurance, oath, promise, troth, word; commitment, compact, contract, covenant; recognizance
2 a person's solemn declaration that he or she will do or not do something ⟨made a *pledge* to quit smoking⟩ — see PROMISE
pledge *vb* **1** to obligate by prior agreement ⟨I would love to go to dinner with you, but I've *pledged* myself to a play with my parents that night.⟩
synonyms commit, engage, troth
related words affiance, betroth, plight, promise, swear, vow; contract, enlist, enroll (*also* enrol), sign on, sign up; overcommit
near antonyms renege
2 to leave as a guarantee of repayment of a loan ⟨*pledged* their house against the loan⟩ — see PAWN
3 to make a solemn declaration of intent ⟨I *pledge* that I will abide by all of the rules of this organization.⟩ — see PROMISE 1
plenary *adj* not lacking any part or member that properly belongs to it ⟨The delegation to the international convention was given *plenary* authority to negotiate a treaty in the nation's best interest.⟩ — see COMPLETE 1
plenitude *n* **1** a considerable amount ⟨There's a *plenitude* of natural beauty in the state.⟩ — see LOT 2
2 an amount or supply more than sufficient to meet one's needs ⟨a *plenitude* of food for the dinner party⟩ — see PLENTY 1
plenteous *adj* being more than enough without being excessive ⟨a *plenteous* supply of napkins for the backyard barbecue⟩ — see PLENTIFUL
plentiful *adj* being more than enough without being excessive ⟨a *plentiful* amount of strawberries that will be more than enough for a couple of pies⟩
synonyms abundant, ample, bounteous, bountiful, comfortable, galore, generous, liberal, plenteous, plenty
related words extra, supernumerary, surplus; abounding, blooming, overflowing, plump, replete, rich, rife, teeming, wealthy; adequate, enough, sufficient; fat, fecund, fertile, fruitful, luxuriant, prodigal, prolific; copious, fulsome, lavish, profuse
phrases all kinds of, thick on the ground

near antonyms deficient, inadequate, insufficient, lacking, wanting; meager (*or* meagre), niggardly, stingy; skimpy; least, minimum; light, slight, small; barren, infertile, sterile, unfruitful, unproductive

antonyms bare, minimal, scant, spare

plentitude *n* **1** a considerable amount ⟨That new baby is in for a *plentitude* of love.⟩ — see LOT 2

2 an amount or supply more than sufficient to meet one's needs ⟨a *plentitude* of lumber for the current housing market⟩ — see PLENTY 1

plenty *adj* being more than enough without being excessive ⟨We've picked *plenty* blueberries, so there'll be some left over after we make the pie.⟩ — see PLENTIFUL

plenty *n* **1** an amount or supply more than sufficient to meet one's needs ⟨You'll have *plenty* of time to make your connecting flight.⟩

synonyms abundance, cornucopia, feast, plenitude, plentitude, superabundance, wealth

related words adequacy, competence, competency, sufficiency; ampleness, amplitude, liberality; excess, overdose, overflow, overkill, oversupply, redundancy, superfluity, superfluousness, surfeit, surplus; copiousness, fecundity, fertility, fruitfulness, opulence, richness; lavishness, luxuriance

phrases embarrassment of riches

near antonyms paucity, poverty, scarcity; barrenness, infertility, sterility

antonyms deficiency, inadequacy, insufficiency

2 a considerable amount ⟨*Plenty* of people showed up.⟩ — see LOT 2

pliable *adj* **1** able to bend easily without breaking ⟨The wooden strips become more *pliable* if they are first soaked in water.⟩ — see WILLOWY

2 capable of being readily changed ⟨With such iffy weather, we had to keep our vacation schedule fairly *pliable*.⟩ — see FLEXIBLE 1

pliant *adj* able to bend easily without breaking ⟨a *pliant* branch bent low with the weight of ripe fruit⟩ — see WILLOWY

plod *vb* **1** to devote serious and sustained effort ⟨We *plodded* night and day to get the assignment done.⟩ — see LABOR

2 to proceed or act clumsily or ineffectually ⟨oxen *plodding* through deep mud⟩ — see FLOUNDER 1

3 to move slowly ⟨*plodded* reluctantly off to work⟩ — see CRAWL 2

4 to move heavily or clumsily ⟨wayfarers *plodding* across the sandy wastes⟩ — see LUMBER 1

plop *vb* to throw or set down clumsily or casually ⟨*plopped* his backpack down on a chair⟩ — see FLOP 1

plot *n* **1** a secret plan for accomplishing evil or unlawful ends ⟨They hatched a *plot* to steal the famous painting.⟩

synonyms conspiracy, design, intrigue, machination, scheme

related words counterconspiracy, counterplot; frame-up; manipulation, subterfuge, trickery; artifice, contrivance, dodge, draft, maneuver, stratagem, trick; cabal, confederacy, ring; game, gimmick, racket; ground plan, program, strategy, system; collusion, complicity, connivance, conniving, conspiration

2 a small area of usually open land ⟨The family grew vegetables in a little *plot*.⟩ — see FIELD 1

3 a small piece of land that is developed or available for development ⟨subdivided the old farm into *plots* for tract houses⟩ — see LOT 1

4 the unfolding of events in a dramatic or literary work ⟨wrote novels in which the *plot* was always subordinate to the characterizations⟩ — see ACTION 2

plot *vb* to engage in a secret plan to accomplish evil or unlawful ends ⟨He *plotted* his revenge.⟩

synonyms connive, conspire, contrive, intrigue, machinate, put up, scheme

related words counterplot; brew, concoct, cook (up), devise, hatch; engineer, jockey, maneuver, manipulate; design, frame, lay out, map, plan, shape

plow *vb* **1** to cut into and turn over the sod of (a piece of land) using a bladed implement ⟨We'll have to get out there and *plow* and plant both fields before it rains.⟩

synonyms break, furrow

related words cultivate, till; fallow; harrow, hoe, list, rake, rototill

2 to devote serious and sustained effort ⟨*plowed* determinedly through the weighty tome⟩ — see LABOR

ploy *n* a clever often underhanded means to achieve an end ⟨Asking me to take her shopping turned out to be a *ploy* to get me to the surprise party.⟩ — see TRICK 1

pluck *n* **1** the act or an instance of applying force on something so that it moves in the direction of the force ⟨A quick *pluck* pulled the hair right out.⟩ — see PULL 1

2 the strength of mind that enables a person to endure pain or hardship ⟨It takes *pluck* to survive a crippling car accident and still go on to become successful.⟩ — see FORTITUDE

pluck *vb* to rob by the use of trickery or threats ⟨The Internet opened up a whole new medium for con artists to *pluck* the gullible.⟩ — see FLEECE

plug *vb* **1** to close up so that no empty spaces remain ⟨*plugged* the hole in the wall with putty⟩ — see FILL 2

2 to devote serious and sustained effort ⟨*plugged* away at solving the math problem⟩ — see LABOR

3 to provide publicity for ⟨The actress is giving lots of interviews to *plug* her latest movie.⟩ — see PUBLICIZE 1

plug (up) *vb* to prevent passage through by filling with something ⟨Hair *plugged up* the drain.⟩ — see CLOG 1

plugger *n* a person who does very hard or dull work ⟨The quiet *pluggers* are the ones who really keep this company going.⟩ — see DRUDGE

plum *n* someone or something unusually desirable ⟨That job is considered a real *plum* in the broadcasting business.⟩ — see PRIZE 1

plumb *adj* **1** having no exceptions or restrictions ⟨a horror movie that's *plumb* trash⟩ — see ABSOLUTE 2

2 rising straight up ⟨The wall was not *plumb*, so everything else in the room was out of kilter.⟩ — see ERECT

plumb *adv* **1** in a direct line or course ⟨The golf ball rolled *plumb* into the hole.⟩ — see DIRECTLY 1

2 *chiefly dialect* to a full extent or degree ⟨I'm *plumb* tuckered out!⟩ — see FULLY 1

3 without delay ⟨We had no sooner resolved that crisis than we *plumb* rushed into another one.⟩ — see IMMEDIATELY

plumb *vb* to measure the depth of (as a body of water) typically with a weighted line ⟨*plumbed* the bay to make sure it was deep enough for the ship⟩ — see ²SOUND 1

plume *n* something given in recognition of achievement ⟨The Nobel Prize for Literature is the *plume* that all authors covet.⟩ — see AWARD 1

plume *vb* to think highly of (oneself) ⟨He *plumes* himself on his supposed athletic skills.⟩ — see PRIDE

plummet *vb* to go to a lower level especially abruptly ⟨a week in which stock prices *plummeted*⟩ — see DROP 2

plump *adj* having an excess of body fat ⟨a *plump* puppy⟩ — see FAT 1

plump *adv* in a direct line or course ⟨There was a squirrel on the sidewalk *plump* in front of us.⟩ — see DIRECTLY 1

plump *n* a hard strike with a part of the body or an instrument ⟨angrily gave a *plump* of his fist against the door⟩ — see ¹BLOW

plump *vb* to throw or set down clumsily or casually ⟨Gale *plumped* herself down on the couch and turned on the TV.⟩ — see FLOP 1

plump (for) *vb* to promote the interests or cause of ⟨We will *plump for* any candidate who supports our cause.⟩ — see SUPPORT 1

plumpness *n* the condition of having an excess of body fat ⟨the adorable *plumpness* of the baby's feet⟩ — see CORPULENCE

plunder *n* valuables stolen or taken by force ⟨The thieves were promptly arrested when they tried to sell their *plunder.*⟩ — see LOOT

plunder *vb* to search through with the intent of committing robbery ⟨Pirates *plundered* the port town.⟩ — see RANSACK 1

plunge *n* **1** an act or instance of diving ⟨a *plunge* off a diving board⟩ — see DIVE 1
2 the act or process of going to a lower level or altitude ⟨An overnight *plunge* in temperature sent the thermometer to below the freezing mark.⟩ — see DESCENT 1

plunge *vb* **1** to cast oneself head first into deep water ⟨She took a deep breath and *plunged* from the side of the pool.⟩ — see DIVE 1
2 to go to a lower level especially abruptly ⟨Prices for those televisions have really *plunged* since they were first introduced.⟩ — see DROP 2
3 to lead or extend downward ⟨a stairway *plunging* into darkness⟩ — see DESCEND 1

plunk *or* **plonk** *vb* to throw or set down clumsily or casually ⟨*plunked* a battered hat on his head⟩ — see FLOP 1

plus *n* something added (as by growth) ⟨a recalculation of the year's income that resulted in a *plus* in the company's profits⟩ — see INCREASE 1

plush *adj* **1** having an abundance of some characteristic quality (as flavor) ⟨a particularly *plush* and creamy cheese⟩ — see FULL-BODIED
2 showing obvious signs of wealth and comfort ⟨a *plush* estate filled with priceless art and antiques⟩ — see LUXURIOUS

ply *n* an attitude that always favors one way of feeling or acting especially without considering any other possibilities ⟨Since taking a *ply* to sci-fi, he's hardly even looked at anything else in the bookstore.⟩ — see BIAS 1

¹ply *vb* to bring to bear especially forcefully or effectively ⟨She *plied* all of her charm and intelligence to convince everyone to volunteer as tutors.⟩ — see EXERT

²ply *vb* to cause to twine about one another ⟨Two single yarns were *plied* together to get the fabric that smooth, firm feel.⟩ — see INTERTWINE 1

poach *vb* to cook in a liquid heated to the point that it gives off steam ⟨I love my eggs *poached* and served on top of buttered toast.⟩ — see BOIL 2

po'boy *also* **poor boy** *n* a large sandwich on a long split roll ⟨ordered a fried catfish *po'boy*⟩ — see SUBMARINE

pocket *adj* **1** of a size that is less than average ⟨a *pocket* dictionary⟩ — see SMALL 1
2 of or relating to money, banking, or investments ⟨His *pocket* involvement in the company was minimal.⟩ — see FINANCIAL

pocket *n* available money ⟨The engagement ring I wanted to buy for her was beyond my *pocket*.⟩ — see FUND 2

pocket *vb* **1** to refrain from openly showing or uttering ⟨*pocketed* my anger and just let the insult pass⟩ — see SUPPRESS 2
2 to take (something) without right and with an intent to keep ⟨She casually *pocketed* the note from his desk to read later.⟩ — see STEAL 1
3 to put up with (something painful or difficult) ⟨*pocketed* the insult with a patient smile⟩ — see BEAR 2

pocketbook *n* a container for carrying money and small personal items ⟨She pulled some lip balm out of her *pocketbook*.⟩ — see PURSE

pocket-size *also* **pocket-sized** *adj* of a size that is less than average ⟨a *pocket-size* country in the Pyrenees⟩ — see SMALL 1

pockmark *n* something that spoils the appearance or completeness of a thing ⟨The hailstorm left *pockmarks* all over the car.⟩ — see BLEMISH

pod *n* something that encloses another thing especially to protect it ⟨a fuel *pod*⟩ — see ¹CASE 1

podium *n* a level usually raised surface ⟨The conductor on the *podium* tonight is one of the leading figures of classical music.⟩ — see PLATFORM

poem *n* a composition using rhythm and often rhyme to create a lyrical effect ⟨Your assignment is to write two *poems* about springtime.⟩
synonyms lyric, song, verse
related words ballad, lay; anacreontic, clerihew, eclogue, elegy, English sonnet, epigram, epode, epopee, epos, georgic, idyll (*also* idyl), jingle, lament, limerick, madrigal, ode, pastoral, pastorale, psalm, rondeau, rondel (*or* rondelle), rondelet, sonnet, triolet, villanelle; haiku, senryu, tanka; blank verse, free verse, minstrelsy, poesy, poetry, versification, vers libre

poet *n* a person who writes poetry ⟨Emily Dickinson is famous as the *poet* who rarely left the house but often journeyed to the depths of the human heart.⟩
synonyms bard, minstrel, versifier
related words poetess; poet laureate; epigrammatist, lyricist, rhymer, sonneteer

poetic *adj* having qualities suggestive of poetry ⟨Your description of the sun setting over the Grand Canyon was a particularly *poetic* piece of writing.⟩
synonyms bardic, lyric, lyrical, poetical
related words metrical (*or* metric), rhyming (*also* riming), rhythmic (*or* rhythmical); rhapsodic (*also* rhapsodical); florid, flowery, grandiloquent, highfalutin (*also* hifalutin), high-flown, ornate; glamorized (*also* glamourized), idealized, romanticized; figurative, metaphoric (*or* metaphorical), symbolic (*also* symbolical)
near antonyms factual, literal, matter-of-fact
antonyms prosaic, prose, unlyrical, unpoetic

poetical *adj* having qualities suggestive of poetry ⟨love letters that were filled with *poetical* phrases⟩ — see POETIC

poetry *n* **1** writing that uses rhythm, vivid language, and often rhyme to provoke an emotional response ⟨Not all *poetry* has to rhyme.⟩
synonyms minstrelsy, song, verse
related words blank verse, free verse
antonyms prose
2 the art or power of speaking or writing in a forceful and convincing way ⟨The speeches of Dr. Martin Luther King were filled with the kind of *poetry* that touches people from all walks of life.⟩ — see ELOQUENCE

poignancy *n* a harsh or sharp quality ⟨There was a *poignancy* to his wit that often left his targets smarting.⟩ — see EDGE 1

poignant *adj* **1** having the power to affect the feelings or sympathies ⟨a *poignant* story of a love affair that ends in tragedy⟩ — see MOVING
2 sharp and pleasantly stimulating to the mind or senses ⟨a *poignant* truthfulness to the author's observations⟩ — see PIQUANT

point *n* **1** a particular and often important moment in time ⟨It was at that *point* that I had to stop and check on the experiment.⟩
synonyms juncture
related words beat, crack, flash, instant, jiffy, minute, moment, nanosecond, second, split second, tick, trice,

twinkle, wink; bit, spell, stretch, while; cusp, nick, threshold, verge; crisis, crunch time
phrases moment of truth
2 the last and usually sharp or tapering part of something long and narrow ⟨Be careful with the *point* on that umbrella, or you could hurt someone.⟩
synonyms apex, cusp, end, nib, nose, pike, tip
related words pinpoint; prong, tine; barb, jag, prickle, snag, spike, sticker
3 an interval of time just before the onset of something ⟨Dan was at the *point* of accepting the new job when he realized he didn't want to leave his old one.⟩
synonyms cusp, edge, threshold, verge
related words nick
4 a separate part in a list, account, or series ⟨went down the list *point* by *point*⟩ — see ITEM 1
5 a single piece of information ⟨two *points* that are important to remember⟩ — see FACT 3
6 a small area that is different (as in color) from the main part ⟨The little *points* of gold in the blue ceiling are supposed to represent stars.⟩ — see SPOT 1
7 an area of high ground jutting out into a body of water beyond the line of the coast ⟨The racing yacht rounded the *point* far ahead of its closest rival.⟩ — see HEADLAND 1
8 an area of land that juts out into a body of water ⟨*Point Reyes, California*⟩ — see ²CAPE
9 an individual part of a process, series, or ranking ⟨At this *point* in your life, you should already be saving for retirement.⟩ — see DEGREE 1
10 something that sets apart an individual from others of the same kind ⟨Impeccable politeness has always been her strong *point*.⟩ — see CHARACTERISTIC
11 the area or space occupied by or intended for something ⟨Runners began lining up by the starting *point*.⟩ — see PLACE 1
12 the quality of an utterance that provokes interest and produces an effect ⟨It took a while before she got to the *point* of the joke.⟩ — see ¹PUNCH 1
13 something that one hopes or intends to accomplish ⟨What we're doing does have a *point*—doesn't it?⟩ — see GOAL
14 the central part or aspect of something under consideration ⟨That clueless reviewer seems to have missed the whole *point* of the book.⟩ — see CRUX
point (toward) *vb* to stand or sit with the face or front toward ⟨The town's monument to its lost fishermen *points toward* the sea, the source of its wealth as well as its sorrow.⟩ — see FACE 1
point (up) *vb* to indicate the importance of by centering attention on ⟨*pointed up* his warning by furiously wagging his finger at them⟩ — see EMPHASIZE 1
pointed *adj* **1** tapering to a thin tip ⟨The sansevieria's long *pointed* leaves make it an easily recognized houseplant.⟩
synonyms peaked, sharp, tipped
related words needlelike, spiny; jagged, pronged, spiked, spikelike, spiky (*also* spikey); bladelike, knifelike
near antonyms dull, rounded
antonyms blunt
2 having to do with the matter at hand ⟨He made a number of *pointed* remarks on the situation.⟩ — see PERTINENT
pointer *n* **1** an arrow-shaped piece on a dial or scale for registering information ⟨The *pointer* on the scale indicated the pumpkin weighed eight pounds.⟩
synonyms hand, index, indicator, needle
related words dial, face, gauge (*also* gage)
2 a piece of advice or useful information especially from an expert ⟨The instructor gave me a few *pointers* but otherwise let me do the cooking by myself.⟩ — see ¹TIP 1

pointless *adj* having no meaning ⟨a *pointless* remark that left everyone scratching their heads in confusion⟩ — see MEANINGLESS
poise *n* **1** a condition in which opposing forces are equal to one another ⟨There must be a *poise* between the rights of the individual and the rights of society.⟩ — see BALANCE 1
2 a general way of holding the body ⟨Strength and flexibility are important for good *poise*.⟩ — see POSTURE 1
poise *vb* **1** to prepare (oneself) mentally or emotionally ⟨The business executive *poised* herself for the difficult press conference.⟩ — see FORTIFY 1
2 to rest or move along the surface of a liquid or in the air ⟨The falcon *poised* in the air for an instant before diving to attack its prey.⟩ — see FLOAT 1
poison *adj* containing or contaminated with a substance capable of injuring or killing a living thing ⟨The witch gave Snow White a *poison* apple.⟩ — see POISONOUS
poison *n* a substance that by chemical action can kill or injure a living thing ⟨The only way to get rid of rats is to leave out *poison*.⟩
synonyms bane, toxin, venom
related words cancer, contagion, disease, virus; fungicide, germicide, herbicide, insecticide, pesticide
near antonyms antivenin, antivenom; cure; cure-all, elixir, panacea
poison *vb* **1** to affect slightly with something morally bad or undesirable ⟨Jealousy *poisoned* their friendship.⟩ — see TAINT 1
2 to make unfit for use by the addition of something harmful or undesirable ⟨exhaust fumes *poisoning* the air⟩ — see CONTAMINATE
3 to lower in character, dignity, or quality ⟨This party partisanship *poisons* the national debate we should be having about this urgent problem.⟩ — see DEBASE 1
4 to cause to have often negative opinions formed without sufficient knowledge ⟨Malicious rumors had *poisoned* many residents against the new police chief.⟩ — see PREJUDICE
poisoned *adj* containing or contaminated with a substance capable of injuring or killing a living thing ⟨leaving *poisoned* food to try to kill the roaches⟩ — see POISONOUS
poisonous *adj* containing or contaminated with a substance capable of injuring or killing a living thing ⟨Don't eat those mushrooms—they're *poisonous*.⟩
synonyms envenomed, poison, poisoned, toxic, venomous
related words contagious, infectious, infective, pathogenic, pestilent; baneful, deleterious, harmful, hurtful, injurious, malignant, noxious, virulent; unhealthful, unhealthy, unwholesome
near antonyms beneficial, healthful, healthy, helpful, palliative, remedial, salubrious, salutary, wholesome; benign, harmless, innocuous, inoffensive; nonfatal, nonlethal
antonyms nonpoisonous, nontoxic, nonvenomous
¹poke *n* **1** a quick thrust ⟨A *poke* at the fire sent sparks flying.⟩
synonyms dab, dig, jab
related words punch; stab, stick; push, shove; jam, jerk, jog, nudge
2 a hard strike with a part of the body or an instrument ⟨a *poke* on the nose⟩ — see ¹BLOW
3 an act or expression showing scorn and usually intended to hurt another's feelings ⟨She thanked everyone, but couldn't resist taking a *poke* at those who had doubted her.⟩ — see INSULT
²poke *n, chiefly Southern & Midland* a container made of a flexible material (as paper or plastic) ⟨the old warning against buying a pig in a *poke*⟩ — see BAG 1
poke *vb* **1** to extend outward beyond a usual point ⟨saw his head *poking* through the window⟩ — see BULGE 1

2 to interest oneself in what is not one's concern ⟨We told him to stop *poking* into other people's business.⟩ — see INTERFERE

3 to move or act slowly ⟨I just *poked* around all morning and didn't accomplish much.⟩ — see DELAY 1

4 to move slowly ⟨They were just *poking* along home.⟩ — see CRAWL 2

poking *adj* moving or proceeding at less than the normal, desirable, or required speed ⟨The *poking* pace of the repair work has put everything way behind schedule.⟩ — see SLOW 1

poky *or* **pokey** *adj* moving or proceeding at less than the normal, desirable, or required speed ⟨frustrated with the *poky* traffic during rush hour⟩ — see SLOW 1

polar *adj* **1** being as different as possible ⟨They're friends despite their *polar* positions on a number of issues.⟩ — see OPPOSITE

2 having a low or subnormal temperature ⟨A *polar* air mass seemed to have settled over our area in January.⟩ — see COLD 1

police *n* **1** the department of government that keeps order, fights crime, and enforces statutes ⟨If you have something to report, call the *police*.⟩

synonyms law

related words judiciary, jurisprudence, justice

2 a body of officers of the law ⟨*Police* blockaded the street for the parade.⟩

synonyms constabulary, force, heat [*slang*], police force

related words bobby [*British*], constable, cop, gendarme, officer, policeman, police officer, policewoman, shamus [*slang*], trooper

police force *n* a body of officers of the law ⟨mobilized practically the entire *police force* to track down the escaped criminal⟩ — see POLICE 2

policeman *n* a member of a force charged with law enforcement at the local level ⟨reported the crime to the nearest *policeman*⟩ — see OFFICER 1

police officer *n* a member of a force charged with law enforcement at the local level ⟨There were *police officers* directing traffic around the scene of the accident.⟩ — see OFFICER 1

policy *n* **1** a way of acting or proceeding ⟨It's always been my *policy* not to spread rumors.⟩ — see COURSE 1

2 the ability to make intelligent decisions especially in everyday matters ⟨You should have exercised greater *policy* in your use of websites and not divulged so much personal information.⟩ — see COMMON SENSE

polish *n* **1** a high level of taste and enlightenment as a result of extensive intellectual training and exposure to the arts ⟨acquired a great deal of *polish* during his year abroad⟩ — see CULTURE 1

2 brightness created by light reflected from a surface ⟨buffed the silver plate to a high *polish*⟩ — see SHINE 1

polish *vb* **1** to make smooth or glossy usually by repeatedly applying surface pressure ⟨You'll need to *polish* your shoes with a clean rag before the performance.⟩

synonyms buff, burnish, dress, gloss, grind, rub, shine, smooth

related words sleek, slick; coat, glaze, japan, lacquer, varnish; face, finish, veneer; brighten; file, rasp, sand, sandblast, sandpaper, scour, scrape, scrub; bob, bone, lap

near antonyms rough (up), roughen, ruffle, scuff (up)

2 to bring (something) to a state where nothing remains to be done ⟨Once you *polish* the article a bit, it'll be ready to submit.⟩ — see FINISH 1

polished *adj* **1** having a shiny surface or finish ⟨She could see her face reflected in the *polished* hood of the car.⟩ — see GLOSSY

2 having or showing a taste for the fine arts and gracious living ⟨showing the *polished* manners of a cosmopolitan woman⟩ — see CULTIVATED

polite *adj* **1** showing consideration, courtesy, and good manners ⟨It's only *polite* to hold the door for the person behind you.⟩

synonyms civil, courteous, genteel, gracious, mannerly, well-bred

related words attentive, careful, considerate, nice, solicitous, thoughtful; chivalrous, civilized, courtly, gallant, gentlemanlike, gentlemanly, ladylike; ceremonial, ceremonious, red-carpet; couth, formal, smooth, suave, unctuous, urbane; elegant, refined; deferential, dutiful, respectful, submissive, yielding; affable, cordial, friendly, genial, hospitable, pleasant, sociable; felicitous, graceful; demure, humble, meek, modest

near antonyms heedless, inconsiderate, thoughtless; audacious, bold, bold-faced, brash, brassy, disrespectful, impertinent, impudent, insolent, lippy, saucy, shameless; boorish, churlish, clownish, loutish, uncouth, vulgar; arrogant, conceited, presuming, presumptuous, pretentious

antonyms discourteous, ill-bred, ill-mannered, impolite, inconsiderate, mannerless, rude, thoughtless, uncivil, ungenteel, ungracious, unmannerly

2 following the established traditions of refined society and good taste ⟨such matters are never mentioned in *polite* conversation⟩ — see PROPER 1

politeness *n* **1** speech or behavior that is a sign of good manners ⟨The little girl's *politeness* greatly impressed her teacher.⟩

synonyms civility, courteousness, courtesy, gentility, graciousness, mannerliness

related words attentiveness, consideration, thoughtfulness; chivalrousness, chivalry, courtliness, gallantry, gentlemanliness, knightliness; breeding, manners; suaveness, unctuousness, urbanity; elegance, refinement; deference, respect; decency, decorousness, decorum, polish, propriety, respectability, seemliness; affability, cordiality, friendliness, geniality, hospitality, sociability; felicitousness, gracefulness; humility, meekness, modesty, shyness

near antonyms audacity, boldness, brashness, brassiness, disrespect, impertinence, impudence, insolence, sauciness, shamelessness; boorishness, churlishness, clownishness, loutishness, vulgarity; inconsiderateness, inconsideration, thoughtlessness; arrogance, conceit, presumption, pretentiousness

antonyms discourteousness, discourtesy, impoliteness, incivility, rudeness, surliness, ungraciousness

2 an act or utterance that is a customary show of good manners ⟨He asked about her family out of simple *politeness*.⟩ — see CIVILITY 1

politic *adj* **1** having or showing tact ⟨The actor is *politic* in discussing the cancelled film project, being content to say that there were "creative differences."⟩ — see TACTFUL

2 suitable for bringing about a desired result under the circumstances ⟨It probably would not be *politic* to tell your boss that his latest idea is the worst thing you've ever heard.⟩ — see EXPEDIENT

poll *n* the upper or front part of the body that contains the brain, the major sense organs, and the mouth ⟨A jaunty cap was perched on his *poll*.⟩ — see HEAD 1

poll *vb* **1** to go around and approach (people) with a request for opinions or information ⟨assigned to *poll* residents on their views about a program for recycling⟩ — see CANVASS 1

2 to make (something) shorter or smaller with the use of a cutting instrument ⟨time to *poll* the sheep's wool⟩ — see CLIP 1

pollutant *n* something that is or that makes impure ⟨filtered the *pollutants* out of the water⟩ — see IMPURITY 1

pollute *vb* to make unfit for use by the addition of something harmful or undesirable ⟨outmoded factories *polluting* the air⟩ — see CONTAMINATE

polluted *adj* containing foreign or lower-grade substances ⟨called in to clean up the *polluted* stream⟩ — see IMPURE 1

poltergeist *n* the soul of a dead person thought of especially as appearing to living people ⟨We thought a *poltergeist* was knocking dishes off the shelves, but it turned out to just be vibrations from passing trains.⟩ — see GHOST 1

poltroon *adj* having or showing a shameful lack of courage ⟨a military commander who was so *poltroon* that he surrendered without having fired so much as a single shot⟩ — see COWARDLY

poltroon *n* a person who shows a shameful lack of courage in the face of danger ⟨Those *poltroons* in the state legislature have caved in to bigotry on this important issue of basic civil rights.⟩ — see COWARD

polychromatic *adj* marked by a variety of usually vivid colors ⟨a *polychromatic* tropical bird⟩ — see COLORFUL

polychrome *adj* marked by a variety of usually vivid colors ⟨*polychrome* pottery featuring designs from the American Southwest⟩ — see COLORFUL

polygraph *n* an instrument for detecting physical signs of the tension that goes with lying ⟨Intelligence agents were trained to fool the *polygraph*.⟩ — see LIE DETECTOR

pommel *vb* to strike repeatedly ⟨The elderly woman *pommeled* the would-be thief with her handbag until he begged for mercy.⟩ — see BEAT 1

pompous *adj* **1** having a feeling of superiority that shows itself in an overbearing attitude ⟨The *pompous* waiter served us in the manner of a person doing some poor soul a great favor.⟩ — see ARROGANT
2 having too high an opinion of oneself ⟨a *pompous* piano teacher who thought that the music world was lucky to have her⟩ — see CONCEITED
3 self-consciously trying to present an appearance of grandeur or importance ⟨a *pompous* gambling casino decorated to look like a palace in ancient Rome⟩ — see PRETENTIOUS 1

pompousness *n* **1** an exaggerated sense of one's importance that shows itself in the making of excessive or unjustified claims ⟨offended by the *pompousness* of the minor official⟩ — see ARROGANCE
2 an often unjustified feeling of being pleased with oneself or with one's situation or achievements ⟨The *pompousness* of the billionaire was evident in the gaudy mansion he built for himself.⟩ — see COMPLACENCE 1

ponder *vb* to give serious and careful thought to ⟨I'm *pondering* whether or not I should join another committee.⟩
synonyms chew over, cogitate, consider, contemplate, debate, deliberate, entertain, eye, meditate, mull (over), pore (over), question, revolve, ruminate, study, think (about *or* over), turn, weigh
related words muse (upon), reflect (on *or* upon), reminisce; analyze, explore, review; conclude, reason; second-guess, speculate (about); brood (about *or* over), fixate (on *or* upon), fret (about *or* over), obsess (about *or* over); believe, conceive, opine; absorb, assimilate, digest
phrases beat one's brains out (about), chew on, cudgel one's brains (about), look at
near antonyms disregard, ignore, overlook, slight; dismiss, pooh-pooh (*also* pooh), reject

ponderous *adj* **1** causing weariness, restlessness, or lack of interest ⟨fell asleep during the *ponderous* speech⟩ — see BORING
2 having great weight ⟨those *ponderous* pachyderms more commonly known as elephants⟩ — see HEAVY 1

3 difficult to use or operate especially because of size, weight, or design ⟨lugged a *ponderous* movie camera all over China⟩ — see CUMBERSOME

ponderousness *n* the state or quality of being heavy ⟨The sheer *ponderousness* of each stone of the huge pyramid makes its construction all the more remarkable.⟩ — see WEIGHTINESS 1

pooch *n* a domestic mammal that is related to the wolves and foxes ⟨walking down the street with several *pooches* on leashes⟩ — see DOG 1

¹pool *n* a small often deep body of water ⟨a secluded *pool* that has long been a locally favored spot for cooling off⟩
synonyms puddle, well
related words basin, hole, sinkhole; swimming pool; lake, pond, water hole

²pool *n* **1** a body of persons at work or available for work ⟨a large *pool* of applicants for the summer internship⟩ — see FORCE 1
2 the number of individuals or amount of something available at any given time ⟨a *pool* of ideas ready to use whenever the cartoonist needs to meet a deadline⟩ — see SUPPLY
3 a sum of money set aside for a particular purpose ⟨office workers setting up a *pool* for the collective purchase of lottery tickets⟩ — see FUND 2
4 the total of the bets at stake at one time ⟨Two coworkers split last week's football *pool*.⟩ — see POT 1

pooled *adj* used or done by a number of people as a group ⟨*pooled* coverage of the congressional hearings by the major broadcast networks⟩ — see COLLECTIVE

poor *adj* **1** lacking money or material possessions ⟨Every year, we make up a basket of food at Thanksgiving for a *poor* family in the neighborhood.⟩
synonyms beggared, broke, destitute, famished, hard up, impecunious, impoverished, indigent, needful, needy, penniless, penurious, poverty-stricken
related words deprived, disadvantaged, dispossessed, underprivileged; bankrupt, bankrupted, bust (*or* busted), insolvent; possessionless; depressed, distressed, hand-to-mouth, pinched, reduced, straitened; cash-strapped, low, short
phrases down on one's luck, out at elbows (*or* out at the elbows), out of pocket
near antonyms comfortable, prosperous
antonyms affluent, deep-pocketed, fat, fat-cat, flush, moneyed (*also* monied), opulent, rich, wealthy, well-heeled, well-off, well-to-do
2 producing inferior or only a small amount of vegetation ⟨land that is too *poor* for farming⟩ — see BARREN 1
3 less plentiful than what is normal, necessary, or desirable ⟨a *poor* crop because of the drought this year⟩ — see MEAGER
4 falling short of a standard ⟨a pretty *poor* musician, even for a garage band⟩ — see BAD 1
5 of low quality ⟨the *poor* workmanship of the furniture⟩ — see CHEAP 2
6 deserving of one's pity ⟨Aw, the *poor* kitten hurt its paw.⟩ — see PATHETIC 1

poorly *adj* temporarily suffering from a disorder of the body ⟨She stayed home because she was feeling *poorly*.⟩ — see SICK 1

poorly *adv* in an unsatisfactory way ⟨He tends to perform *poorly* on standardized tests.⟩ — see BADLY 1

poorness *n* the state of lacking sufficient money or material possessions ⟨Each country has its own standard of *poorness*, and one nation's needy inhabitant can be another's fairly well-off citizen.⟩ — see POVERTY 1

pop *adj* enjoying widespread favor or approval ⟨uninterested in the *pop* fiction that most of the other publishing houses happily churned out⟩ — see POPULAR 1

¹**pop** n a loud explosive sound ⟨The soda can opened with a sharp *pop*.⟩ — see CLAP 1

²**pop** n a male human parent ⟨Ask your *pop* if he knows where the keys to the shed are.⟩ — see FATHER 1

pop vb **1** to break open or into pieces usually because of internal pressure ⟨A balloon *popped* suddenly and startled us all.⟩ — see EXPLODE 1

2 to break suddenly with an explosive sound ⟨The last strand *popped*, causing the chandelier to drop to the floor with a great crash.⟩ — see CRACK 1

3 to cause to break open or into pieces by or as if by an explosive ⟨*popping* popcorn over a campfire⟩ — see BLAST 1

pop (in) vb to make a brief visit ⟨I just *popped in* to say hello.⟩ — see CALL 3

populace n the body of the community as contrasted with the elite ⟨high officials awkwardly mingling with the general *populace*⟩ — see MASS 1

popular adj **1** enjoying widespread favor or approval ⟨an actor who was *popular* in the 1990s⟩
synonyms big, faddish, faddy, fashionable, favorite, happening, hot, in, modish, pop, popularized, red-hot, vogue
related words semipopular; preferred, selected; desirable, liked, wanted; celebrated, famed, famous, noted, notorious, prominent, renowned, well-known; fabled, fabulous, legendary; leading, notable, outstanding, prominent, remarkable
near antonyms washed-up; despised, detested, disliked, hated, rejected; anonymous, nameless, obscure, unknown; inconspicuous
antonyms out, unfashionable, unpopular
2 accepted, used, or practiced by most people ⟨the *popular* custom of exchanging greeting cards during the holiday season⟩ — see CURRENT 1
3 held by or applicable to a majority of the people ⟨*Popular* opinion on that issue has changed dramatically over the years.⟩ — see GENERAL 3
4 of, relating to, or favoring political democracy ⟨a truly *popular* revolution, not one that replaced one dictatorship with another⟩ — see DEMOCRATIC
5 being within the financial means of most people ⟨electronics being sold directly to consumers at *popular* prices⟩ — see ACCESSIBLE 1
6 costing little ⟨We also have the *popular* models, for those who prefer not to invest too much in a new TV.⟩ — see CHEAP 1

popularity n the state of enjoying widespread approval ⟨the *popularity* of low-heeled shoes this season⟩
synonyms fashionableness, favor, hotness, modishness, vogue
related words craze, fad, mode, rage, style, trend; bandwagon, boom; fame, notoriety, prominence, renown; enthusiasm, fervor, passion
near antonyms oblivion, obscurity
antonyms disfavor, unpopularity

popularized adj enjoying widespread favor or approval ⟨a recently *popularized* hobby among kids⟩ — see POPULAR 1

pore (over) vb **1** to give serious and careful thought to ⟨The committee will probably *pore over* the results of the study for a long time before making their decision.⟩ — see PONDER

2 to go over and mentally take in the content of ⟨He *pored over* the textbook for hours in preparation for the test.⟩ — see READ 1

porous adj capable of being passed into or through ⟨a cleaner that should not be used on *porous* surfaces⟩ — see PENETRABLE

port n a part of a body of water protected and deep enough to be a place of safety for ships ⟨The cruise ship stops at each *port* for one night only.⟩ — see HARBOR 1

portable adj capable of being moved especially with ease ⟨a *portable* stereo system⟩ — see MOVABLE

portal n a barrier by which an entry is closed and opened ⟨The main *portal* to the estate is an elaborate wrought iron gate on the side facing the road.⟩ — see DOOR 1

portent n **1** something believed to be a sign or warning of a future event ⟨A red sky in the morning can be a *portent* of a coming storm.⟩ — see OMEN
2 something extraordinary or surprising ⟨A scout was sent to have a look at this teenage pitcher who was supposed to be the latest *portent* of the baseball world.⟩ — see WONDER 1

portentous adj **1** being or showing a sign of evil or calamity to come ⟨An eerie and *portentous* stillness hung over the camp the night before the battle.⟩ — see OMINOUS
2 causing wonder or astonishment ⟨In 1969 people regarded the first landing on the moon as a truly *portentous* event.⟩ — see MARVELOUS 1

portion n **1** a state or end that seemingly has been decided beforehand ⟨He had always just assumed that fatherhood would be his *portion*.⟩ — see FATE 1
2 one of the pieces from which something is designed to be assembled ⟨Equal *portions* of the students' day are devoted to study, recreation, and sleep.⟩ — see PART 1
3 something belonging to, due to, or contributed by an individual member of a group ⟨Each camper gets an equal *portion* of the food.⟩ — see SHARE 1

portion vb to give out (something) to appropriate individuals ⟨*portioned* out the medical supplies equally⟩ — see ADMINISTER 1

portliness n the condition of having an excess of body fat ⟨a president renowned for his *portliness*⟩ — see CORPULENCE

portly adj **1** having an excess of body fat ⟨a *portly* woodchuck waddling across the road⟩ — see FAT 1
2 having or showing a formal and serious or reserved manner ⟨walked with the *portly* grace of the grande dame that she was⟩ — see DIGNIFIED

portmanteau n a bag carried by hand and designed to hold a traveler's clothing and personal articles ⟨carried her possessions with her in an old *portmanteau*⟩ — see TRAVELING BAG

portrait n a vivid representation in words of someone or something ⟨His account created in the jurors' heads a detailed *portrait* of an innocent old man.⟩ — see DESCRIPTION 1

portray vb **1** to give a representation or account of in words ⟨The author *portrays* her characters with lifelike vividness.⟩ — see DESCRIBE 1
2 to point out the chief quality or qualities of an individual or group ⟨The book *portrays* the town's residents as salt of the earth Midwesterners.⟩ — see CHARACTERIZE 1
3 to present a picture of ⟨a landscape that *portrays* the scenery near the town where the painter grew up⟩ — see PICTURE 1
4 to present a portrayal or performance of ⟨gained fame *portraying* Susan B. Anthony in a one-woman show⟩ — see ACT 1

portrayal n a vivid representation in words of someone or something ⟨His novel presents a moving *portrayal* of a woman searching for personal fulfillment and happiness.⟩ — see DESCRIPTION 1

pose n a display of emotion or behavior that is insincere or intended to deceive ⟨My cheerfulness was just a *pose*, for I was feeling miserable.⟩ — see MASQUERADE

pose vb to set before the mind for consideration ⟨One student *posed* an interesting question for the visiting astronomer.⟩ — see PROPOSE 1

pose (as) vb to pretend to be (what one is not) in appearance or behavior 〈*Posing as* a soldier, the spy sneaked onto the base with surprising ease.〉 — see IMPERSONATE 1

position *n* **1** an assignment at which one regularly works for pay 〈He holds the *position* of manager at the store.〉 — see JOB 1

2 the action for which a person or thing is specially fitted or used or for which a thing exists 〈humanity's *position* in the universe〉 — see ROLE

3 the area or space occupied by or intended for something 〈I knew that someone had been in the room because the chair was out of its usual *position*.〉 — see PLACE 1

4 the place where someone is assigned to stand or remain 〈The soldiers were commanded to hold their *position* on the hill at all costs.〉 — see STATION 1

5 the placement of someone or something in relation to others in a vertical arrangement 〈holds the lead *position* in the standings〉 — see RANK 1

position *vb* to arrange something in a certain spot or position 〈*positioned* the chairs around the room〉 — see PLACE 1

positive *adj* **1** expressing approval 〈hoped for a *positive* reaction from the audience〉 — see FAVORABLE 1

2 having or showing a mind free from doubt 〈I'm *positive* that this is the right direction.〉 — see CERTAIN 2

3 not capable of being challenged or proved wrong 〈seeks *positive* proof that ghosts exist〉 — see IRREFUTABLE

positiveness *n* a state of mind in which one is free from doubt 〈I can't state with any *positiveness* that I know what really happened.〉 — see CONFIDENCE 2

possess *vb* to keep, control, or experience as one's own 〈She *possesses* a keen insight into people.〉 — see HAVE 1

possession *n* **1** the fact or state of having (something) at one's disposal 〈The university has several old manuscripts in its *possession*.〉

synonyms control, enjoyment, hands, keeping

related words ownership, proprietorship; authority, command, dominion, mastery, power; repossession, retention; claiming, collaring, confiscation, procurement

near antonyms dispossession, relinquishment, surrendering, transferal

antonyms nonpossession

2 possessions *pl* transportable items that one owns 〈We packed up all of our *possessions* and excitedly moved into a new house.〉

synonyms chattels, duds, effects, gear, goods, holdings, movables (*or* moveables), paraphernalia, personalty, stuff, things

related words treasures, valuables; appointments, fixtures, furnishings; estate, property, tangibles; collateral

near antonyms immovables, real estate

possessive *adj* intolerant of rivalry or unfaithfulness 〈The child was very *possessive* of his mother's attention.〉 — see JEALOUS 1

possessor *n* one who has a legal or rightful claim to ownership 〈She was the *possessor* of several acres of land in the country.〉 — see PROPRIETOR

possibility *n* **1** something that can develop or become actual 〈There's a *possibility* for improvement in the situation.〉 — see POTENTIAL

2 something that might happen 〈Winning the championship is a real *possibility* for us.〉 — see EVENT 2

possible *adj* **1** capable of being done or carried out 〈I think that building the entire set in two days is *possible*, albeit difficult.〉

synonyms achievable, attainable, doable, feasible, practicable, realizable, viable, workable

related words practical, reasonable, sensible; contingent, likely, probable; acceptable, believable, conceivable, creditable, plausible, thinkable; available, usable (*also* useable)

near antonyms impractical, unrealistic; doubtful, dubious, far-fetched, improbable, unlikely; implausible, inconceivable, incredible, unbelievable; futile, useless, vain; absurd, fantastic (*also* fantastical), outlandish, preposterous, ridiculous; unthinkable

antonyms hopeless, impossible, impracticable, infeasible, nonviable, unattainable, unfeasible, unviable, unworkable

2 existing only as a possibility and not in fact 〈only one of several *possible* outcomes〉 — see POTENTIAL

possibly *adv* it is possible 〈He may *possibly* recover after such a serious mistake, but it doesn't seem likely.〉 — see PERHAPS

¹post *n* **1** a specific task with which a person or group is charged 〈Selling lemonade was my *post* at the town fair.〉 — see MISSION

2 the place where someone is assigned to stand or remain 〈He wisely stayed at his *post* during the emergency.〉 — see STATION 1

3 an assignment at which one regularly works for pay 〈She's held a number of teaching *posts* at local colleges.〉 — see JOB 1

²post *n* an upright shaft that supports an overhead structure 〈hung the hammock between a tree and a *post* in the fence〉 — see PILLAR 1

¹post *vb* **1** to affix (as a notice) to or on a suitable place 〈The student organizations generally *post* their announcements on the campus bulletin board.〉

synonyms placard

related words nail, plaster, tack (up); advertise, announce, bill, blaze, broadcast, call, declare, proclaim, promulgate, publicize, publish

near antonyms remove, take down

2 to make known openly or publicly 〈*posted* the students' grades〉 — see ANNOUNCE

²post *vb* to assign to a place or position 〈The police are planning to *post* an officer outside the hospital room of the witness.〉

synonyms detail, station

related words set; appoint; place, position

³post *vb* to send through the postal system 〈Be sure to *post* the letter this afternoon.〉 — see MAIL

postdate *vb* to come after in time 〈The inscription at the base actually *postdates* the statue itself by a number of years.〉 — see FOLLOW 1

poster *n* a sheet bearing an announcement for posting in a public place 〈We put up a hundred *posters* announcing the concert.〉

synonyms bill, placard

related words billboard, sign, signboard; broadside, handbill, handout, playbill, show bill; ad, advertisement, announcement, bulletin, dispatch, release

posterior *adj* **1** being at or in the part of something opposite the front part 〈The chapel's *posterior* location in the church serves to make it a quiet retreat.〉 — see BACK

2 being, occurring, or carried out at a time after something else 〈artifacts dating from a *posterior* historical period〉 — see SUBSEQUENT

posterior *n* the part of the body upon which someone sits 〈The baseball players were always slapping one another on the *posterior*.〉 — see BUTTOCKS

posterity *n* the descendants of a person, animal, or plant 〈hoped to pass the family history to his *posterity*〉 — see OFFSPRING

posthaste *adv* with great speed 〈ran *posthaste* for the doctor〉 — see FAST 1

posthumous *adj* occurring after one's death 〈The soldier was awarded a *posthumous* medal for valor.〉

synonyms postmortem

related words belated, delayed, late

posting *n* a published statement informing the public of a matter of general interest ⟨a *posting* in the local newspaper of the public auction of a house on which a bank had foreclosed⟩ — see ANNOUNCEMENT

postman *n* a person who delivers mail ⟨The *postman* comes at around nine every morning.⟩ — see LETTER CARRIER

postmortem *adj* occurring after one's death ⟨*postmortem* tests on the brain tissue of people who had been suffering from Alzheimer's disease⟩ — see POSTHUMOUS

postmortem *n* examination of a dead body especially to find out the cause of death ⟨The *postmortem* revealed that the cause of death had been an undetected heart defect.⟩ — see AUTOPSY

postmortem examination *n* examination of a dead body especially to find out the cause of death ⟨A coroner performed the *postmortem examination* with painstaking thoroughness.⟩ — see AUTOPSY

postpone *vb* to assign to a later time ⟨We'll have to *postpone* a decision until we have all the information.⟩
synonyms defer, delay, hold off (on), hold up, put off, remit, shelve
related words suspend; hesitate, pause, stay; detain, retard, slow; extend, lengthen, prolong, protract, stretch (out); wait
near antonyms act, deal (with), decide (upon), do, work (on)

postulate *n* something taken as being true or factual and used as a starting point for a course of action or reasoning ⟨Einstein's theory of relativity was deduced from two *postulates*.⟩ — see ASSUMPTION 1

postulate *vb* to take as true or as a fact without actual proof ⟨*postulates* that all people are born with certain rights that can never be taken away from them⟩ — see ASSUME 2

posture *n* **1** a general way of holding the body ⟨A good upright *posture* will prevent backaches.⟩
synonyms carriage, poise, stance, station
related words attention; body language; pose, seat; bearing, behavior, conduct, demeanor, deportment; air, poise, presence; aspect, look, mien
2 position with regard to conditions and circumstances ⟨claims that the country's defense *posture* is weak⟩ — see SITUATION 1

posy *n* a bunch of flowers ⟨gathered a *posy* of wildflowers to present to his girlfriend⟩ — see BOUQUET 1

pot *n* **1** the total of the bets at stake at one time ⟨Everyone got a bit nervous when the *pot* grew to more than a hundred dollars.⟩
synonyms jack, jackpot, pool
related words fund, kitty; bet, stake, wager
2 a considerable amount ⟨made a *pot* of money in the real estate market⟩ — see LOT 2

potable *adj* suitable for drinking ⟨Around here, the only *potable* water comes from wells.⟩
synonyms drinkable
related words clean, fresh, pure, uncontaminated, unpolluted; nonpoisonous
near antonyms contaminated, dirty, foul, polluted; poison, poisonous, toxic; unhealthful, unhealthy, unwholesome
antonyms undrinkable

potable *n* a liquid suitable for drinking ⟨The menu included a number of interesting *potables*.⟩ — see DRINK 1

potbelly *n* an enlarged or bulging abdomen ⟨an image of the Laughing Buddha with his *potbelly*⟩
synonyms beer belly, belly, gut, paunch
related words breadbasket [*slang*], stomach, tummy

potency *n* the ability to exert effort for the accomplish-

ment of a task ⟨vitamins of high *potency* that should be taken only in the proper dosage⟩ — see POWER 2

potent *adj* **1** having an abundance of some characteristic quality (as flavor) ⟨a *potent* tea that is the perfect morning pick-me-up⟩ — see FULL-BODIED
2 having great power or influence ⟨a *potent* argument for expanding our program of space exploration⟩ — see IMPORTANT 2
3 producing or capable of producing a desired result ⟨*potent* medicine that can be obtained through a doctor's prescription⟩ — see EFFECTIVE 1

potentate *n* one who rules over a people with a sole, supreme, and usually hereditary authority ⟨Charles inherited the position of *potentate* of the Holy Roman Empire from his grandfather, as well that of king of Spain from his father.⟩ — see MONARCH 1

potential *adj* existing only as a possibility and not in fact ⟨I can see a few *potential* problems with co-owning a beach house with another couple.⟩
synonyms implicit, possible
related words conceivable, imaginable, plausible, thinkable; likely, probable; conjectural, hypothetical, suppositional, theoretical (*also* theoretic); alleged, assumed, purported, reputed, supposed; achievable, attainable, doable, feasible, practicable, viable, workable
near antonyms authenticated, confirmed, demonstrated, established, proven, substantiated; authentic, bona fide, genuine, true
antonyms actual, existent, factual, real

potential *n* something that can develop or become actual ⟨a time when cloning was merely a *potential* and the stuff of science fiction⟩
synonyms capability, eventuality, possibility, potentiality, prospect
related words likelihood, probability; latency, potency
near antonyms actuality, reality; certainty

potentiality *n* something that can develop or become actual ⟨would like to see a colony on the moon as an actuality and not merely a *potentiality*⟩ — see POTENTIAL

pother *n* **1** a state of nervous or irritated concern ⟨always in a *pother* over the state of her garden⟩ — see FRET
2 a state of noisy, confused activity ⟨the *pother* of city traffic that commuters face every day⟩ — see COMMOTION

potpourri *n* an unorganized collection or mixture of various things ⟨a *potpourri* of hit songs from the last 10 years⟩ — see MISCELLANY 1

potter (around) *vb* to spend time in aimless activity ⟨*pottering around* indoors on a rainy day⟩ — see FIDDLE (AROUND)

potterer *n* a person who regularly or occasionally engages in an activity as a pastime rather than as a profession ⟨a camera designed for people who don't pretend to be anything more than *potterers* at photography⟩ — see AMATEUR 1

potter's field *n* a piece of land used for burying the dead ⟨Criminals and unidentified people are sometimes buried in a *potter's field*.⟩ — see CEMETERY

pottery *n* articles made of baked clay ⟨We picked up some ceramic vases in a *pottery* store.⟩ — see CROCKERY

potty *n* a room furnished with a fixture for flushing body waste ⟨The little girl announced loudly that she needed to go to the *potty*.⟩ — see TOILET

pouch *n* a container made of a flexible material (as paper or plastic) ⟨We sealed the catnip in a cloth *pouch* and tossed it to the cat.⟩ — see BAG 1

pouch *vb* to extend outward beyond a usual point ⟨As he grew older, the skin on his neck *pouched*.⟩ — see BULGE 1

poultice *n* a medicated covering used to heal an injury ⟨placed a *poultice* over the infected cut⟩ — see DRESSING 1

pounce (on *or* upon) *vb* to take sudden, violent action against ⟨The cat *pounced on* the cornered mouse.⟩ — see ATTACK 1

¹pound *n* a hard strike with a part of the body or an instrument ⟨Give the nail a final *pound* with the hammer.⟩ — see ¹BLOW

²pound *n* an enclosure with an open framework for keeping animals ⟨Stray dogs wearing tags are kept in that *pound* until their owners can be notified.⟩ — see CAGE

pound *vb* **1** to move heavily or clumsily ⟨*pounding* down the road as fast as he could run⟩ — see LUMBER 1
2 to deliver a blow to (someone or something) usually in a strong vigorous manner ⟨*pounding* nails into boards all day long⟩ — see HIT 1
3 to strike repeatedly ⟨During the storm the waves furiously *pounded* the beach.⟩ — see BEAT 1
4 to shape with a hammer ⟨*pounding* out a depression in the metal⟩ — see HAMMER 1
5 to reduce to fine particles ⟨The tablet may be *pounded* and mixed in with the animal's food.⟩ — see POWDER

pour *vb* **1** to cause to flow in a stream ⟨She lifted the teakettle and *poured* some hot water from the spout.⟩
synonyms stream
related words ladle, spoon; cascade, trickle; deluge, flood, inundate, overflow
2 to move in a stream ⟨water gently *pouring* down the canal toward the dam⟩ — see FLOW 1
3 to flow out in great quantities or with force ⟨There were tears *pouring* down his cheeks.⟩ — see GUSH 1
4 to fall as water in a continuous stream of drops from the clouds ⟨It's *pouring* outside, so you'd better take an umbrella.⟩ — see RAIN 1
5 to give readily and in large quantities ⟨repeatedly *poured* money into the revitalization of the downtown area⟩ — see RAIN 2

pouring *adj* marked by or abounding with rain ⟨a *pouring*, miserable day⟩ — see RAINY

pout *n* **1** a twisting of the facial features in disgust or disapproval ⟨That storekeeper's face seems to be in a permanent *pout*.⟩ — see GRIMACE
2 *pouts pl* a state of resentful silence or irritability ⟨She stayed in the *pouts* all day.⟩ — see SULK

pout *vb* **1** to extend outward beyond a usual point ⟨Her lips *pouted* as she glared at him silently.⟩ — see BULGE 1
2 to silently go about in a bad mood ⟨*pouted* and didn't say a word to anyone all morning⟩ — see SULK

pouting *adj* given to or displaying a resentful silence and often irritability ⟨I stayed in a *pouting* mood until they apologized.⟩ — see SULKY

poverty *n* **1** the state of lacking sufficient money or material possessions ⟨He dreamed of finding a good job and working his way out of *poverty* and debt.⟩
synonyms beggary, destitution, impecuniousness, impoverishment, indigence, necessity, need, neediness, pauperism, penuriousness, penury, poorness, want
related words gutter, misery, woe, wretchedness; exigency; emergency; austerity, deprivation, privation
near antonyms luxury, prosperity
antonyms opulence, richness, wealth, wealthiness
2 a falling short of an essential or desirable amount or number ⟨a *poverty* of information about the new policies⟩ — see DEFICIENCY

poverty–stricken *adj* lacking money or material possessions ⟨*poverty-stricken* families struggling to make ends meet⟩ — see POOR 1

powder *vb* to reduce to fine particles ⟨You have to *powder* the antibiotic tablet and mix it with food.⟩
synonyms atomize, beat, crush, disintegrate, grind, mill, pound, pulverize

related words grate; crumble, crunch; break, bust, dash, fracture, fragment; shatter, smash, splinter

powdery *adj* consisting of very small particles ⟨the kind of *powdery* snow that is perfect for skiing⟩ — see FINE 1

power *n* **1** the right or means to command or control others ⟨The emir has nearly complete *power* over the emirate.⟩
synonyms arm, authority, clutch, command, control, dominion, grip, hold, mastery, rein(s), sway
related words clout, influence, pull, voice, weight; jurisdiction; direction, management; dominance, imperium, predominance, sovereignty (*also* sovranty), supremacy; prerogative, privilege, right
near antonyms helplessness, weakness
antonyms impotence, impotency, powerlessness
2 the ability to exert effort for the accomplishment of a task ⟨The corporation has the *power* to accomplish almost anything.⟩ ⟨You'll need to build a bit more *power* in order to be a star pitcher.⟩
synonyms energy, force, might, muscle, potency, puissance, sinew, strength, vigor
related words aptitude, capability, capacity, competence, competency; adequacy, effectiveness, effectualness, usefulness
near antonyms disability, inability, inaptitude, incapability, incapableness, incapacity, incompetence; ineffectiveness, ineffectuality, ineffectualness, inefficaciousness, inefficacy, uselessness; helplessness, paralysis
antonyms impotence, impotency, powerlessness, weakness
3 a natural ability of the mind or body ⟨Dogs have a very highly developed *power* of smell.⟩
synonyms faculty
related words function; capability, capacity; aptitude, endowment, flair, genius, gift, instinct, knack, talent
near antonyms inability, incapability, incapacity; inaptitude, inaptness, ineptness
4 something with a usable capacity for doing work ⟨nuclear *power*⟩ — see FUEL

powerboat *n* a boat equipped with a motor ⟨His friend had a *powerboat* and took them out waterskiing.⟩ — see MOTORBOAT

powerful *adj* having great power or influence ⟨a *powerful* producer in the music business who is considered responsible for the careers of several superstars⟩ — see IMPORTANT 2

powerfully *adv* in a vigorous and forceful manner ⟨began to row *powerfully* toward the shore⟩ — see HARD 3

powerhouse *n* an ambitious person who eagerly goes after what is desired ⟨From the very start of her singing career, she had a reputation for being a very determined *powerhouse*.⟩ — see GO-GETTER

powerless *adj* unable to act or achieve one's purpose ⟨I wish I could help you, but I am *powerless* in this situation.⟩
synonyms helpless, impotent, paralyzed, weak
related words incapable, incompetent, ineffective, ineffectual, inept, unfit, useless; feeble, frail, infirm, passive, spineless, supine, unaggressive
near antonyms able, capable, competent, effective, efficient; autocratic, autocrat (*also* autocratical), despotic, dictatorial, tyrannical (*also* tyrannic); dominant, dynamic, energetic, forceful, robust, sturdy, tough, vigorous
antonyms mighty, potent, powerful, puissant, strong

powerlessness *n* the lack of sufficient ability, power, or means ⟨Dave cursed his *powerlessness* to affect the outcome of his friend's problems.⟩ — see INABILITY

practicable *adj* **1** capable of being done or carried out ⟨a solution that is not *practicable* in the time available to us⟩ — see POSSIBLE 1

2 capable of being put to use or account ⟨a *practicable* knowledge of carpentry that came in handy when he volunteered to build houses for underprivileged families⟩ — see PRACTICAL 1

3 capable of or suitable for being used for a particular purpose ⟨That flimsy little saw is not a very *practicable* tool for cutting heavy tree branches.⟩ — see USABLE 1

practical *adj* **1** capable of being put to use or account ⟨a *practical* and simple solution for the town's waste disposal⟩ ⟨She has some *practical* information on sightseeing in San Francisco.⟩

synonyms applicable, functional, practicable, serviceable, usable (*also* useable), useful, workable, working

related words down-to-earth, pragmatic (*also* pragmatical), utilitarian; accessible, available, obtainable, reachable; all-around (*also* all-round), handy; active, alive, busy, employed, functioning, operating, operative

near antonyms abstract, academic (*also* academical), armchair, theoretical (*also* theoretic); inaccessible, unattainable, unavailable, unobtainable, unreachable; unsuitable

antonyms impracticable, impractical, inapplicable, nonpractical, unusable, unworkable, useless

2 willing to see things as they really are and deal with them sensibly ⟨a *practical* caseworker who doesn't spend a lot of time philosophizing while doing social work⟩ — see REALISTIC 1

practical joke *n* a playful or mischievous act intended as a joke ⟨Friends had left the message about winning the lottery on his voice mail as a *practical joke*.⟩ — see PRANK

practically *adv* very close to but not completely ⟨*Practically* everyone agreed to help.⟩ — see ALMOST

practice *also* **practise** *n* **1** a private performance or session in preparation for a public appearance ⟨We held one last *practice* before the big concert.⟩ — see REHEARSAL

2 a usual manner of behaving or doing ⟨The store's *practice* has always been to honor all major credit cards.⟩ — see HABIT 1

3 something done over and over in order to develop skill ⟨*Practice* makes perfect.⟩ — see EXERCISE 2

practice *also* **practise** *vb* to do over and over so as to become skilled ⟨In order to play the guitar well, you need to *practice* fingering every single day.⟩

synonyms exercise, rehearse, run over

related words groove, perfect, refine; point (for), prepare (for), train (with); drill, repeat; work (at *or* on); review, study

practiced *also* **practised** *adj* **1** having or showing exceptional knowledge, experience, or skill in a field of endeavor ⟨a simple dish that any *practiced* chef should be able to produce even blindfolded⟩ — see PROFICIENT

2 accomplished with trained ability ⟨a highly *practiced* performance of a classic ballet⟩ — see SKILLFUL 1

pragmatic *also* **pragmatical** *adj* willing to see things as they really are and deal with them sensibly ⟨a *pragmatic* man, not given to grand, visionary schemes⟩ — see REALISTIC 1

prairie *n* a broad area of level or rolling treeless country ⟨You can see for miles in every direction on the *prairie*.⟩ — see PLAIN 1

praise *vb* **1** to proclaim the glory of ⟨hymns that *praise* God⟩

synonyms bless, carol, celebrate, exalt, extol (*also* extoll), glorify, hymn, laud, magnify, resound

related words adore, belaud, deify, idolize, worship; acclaim, applaud, commend, compliment, hail, renown, salute; chant, cheer, eulogize, rhapsodize

near antonyms blame, censure, reprehend, reprobate; criticize, reprove; admonish, chide, keelhaul, rebuke, reprimand, reproach; castigate, lambaste (*or* lambast)

2 to declare enthusiastic approval of ⟨The school volunteers were *praised* for their excellent work in the reading program.⟩ — see ACCLAIM

praiseworthy *adj* deserving of high regard or great approval ⟨a *praiseworthy* effort to introduce youths to the visual arts⟩ — see ADMIRABLE

prance *vb* to walk with exaggerated arm and leg movements ⟨*pranced* across the room dressed in an outrageous costume⟩ — see STRUT 1

prank *n* a playful or mischievous act intended as a joke ⟨As a *prank*, several students managed to change all the classroom clocks to different times.⟩

synonyms antic, caper, escapade, frolic, gag, jest, knavery, practical joke, trick, waggery

related words skylarking; high jinks (*also* hijinks), horseplay, play, roughhousing, rowdyism; shenanigan(s), tomfoolery; joking, kidding, teasing; hoax, maneuver, ploy; caprice, conceit, fancy, vagary, whim, whimsy (*also* whimsey); fraud, hanky-panky, hoodwinking, ruse, sham, stratagem, subterfuge, trickery, wile

prankish *adj* tending to or exhibiting reckless playfulness ⟨told the *prankish* lad that someone would eventually get hurt if he kept it up⟩ — see MISCHIEVOUS 1

prankishness *n* a natural disposition for playful behavior ⟨Her irrepressible *prankishness* sometimes got her into trouble when she was growing up.⟩ — see PLAYFULNESS

prate *vb* to engage in casual or rambling conversation ⟨The young executive gratingly *prated* on about his weekend spent hobnobbing with the rich.⟩ — see CHAT 1

prattle *n* unintelligible or meaningless talk ⟨Parents often claim to understand the *prattle* of their infant offspring.⟩ — see GIBBERISH 1

prattle *vb* **1** to engage in casual or rambling conversation ⟨We spent an hour on the phone *prattling* on about nothing in particular.⟩ — see CHAT 1

2 to speak rapidly, inarticulately, and usually unintelligibly ⟨Stop *prattling* and calmly tell us the news.⟩ — see BABBLE 1

prattler *n* a person who talks constantly ⟨Stuck next to a *prattler* in the doctor's waiting room, she found the wait interminable.⟩ — see CHATTERBOX

pray *vb* to make a request to (someone) in an earnest or urgent manner ⟨I *pray* you: tell me where they went.⟩ — see BEG

prayer *n* **1** an address to God or a deity ⟨He always said a *prayer* before going to sleep.⟩

synonyms orison

related words collect, grace, litany, thanksgiving; evensong, matins, vespers; appeal, begging, beseeching, entreaty, imploring, petition, pleading, request, soliciting, suit, supplication

2 an earnest request ⟨We hope that the governor will hear our *prayer* and do something about this pressing problem.⟩ — see PLEA 1

preamble *n* **1** a performance, activity, or event that precedes and sets the stage for the main event ⟨The round of hors d'oeuvres was merely the *preamble* to an evening of lavish feasting.⟩ — see PRELUDE 1

2 a short section (as of a book) that leads to or explains the main part ⟨an insightful analysis of the *preamble* to the Constitution of the United States⟩ — see INTRODUCTION

precariousness *n* the quality or state of not being firmly fixed in position ⟨She quickly moved the china teapot after noticing its *precariousness* on the shelf.⟩ — see INSTABILITY

precautionary *adj* concerned with or serving to keep

something from happening ⟨Prior to the game, we moved the furniture out of the way as a *precautionary* measure.⟩ — see PREVENTIVE

precede *vb* to go or come before in time ⟨There are two speeches which will *precede* yours.⟩
synonyms antedate, forego, predate
antonyms follow, postdate, succeed

precedence *n* the right to one's attention before other things considered less important ⟨His merchandise order takes *precedence* because we received it first.⟩ — see PRIORITY

precedent *adj* going before another in time or order ⟨behavior that may be explained by a *precedent* event in her troubled life⟩ — see PREVIOUS

preceding *adj* going before another in time or order ⟨I had not eaten since the *preceding* day.⟩ — see PREVIOUS

preceptor *n* a person whose occupation is to give formal instruction in a school ⟨a *preceptor* at a small English boarding school⟩ — see TEACHER

precious *adj* **1** commanding a large price ⟨diamonds and other *precious* stones⟩ — see COSTLY
2 granted special treatment or attention ⟨parents who refuse to hear the slightest criticism of their *precious* children⟩ — see DARLING 1
3 having qualities that tend to make one loved ⟨a *precious* friend for whom I would do anything⟩ — see LOVABLE

precipice *n* a steep wall of rock, earth, or ice ⟨The teen scaled the steep *precipice* with the ease of an experienced climber.⟩ — see CLIFF

precipitate *adj* acting or done with excessive or careless speed ⟨the army's *precipitate* withdrawal from the field of battle⟩ — see HASTY 1

precipitate *n* matter that settles to the bottom of a body of liquid ⟨The chemist filtered out the *precipitate* from the solution.⟩ — see DEPOSIT 1

precipitate *vb* to fall as water in a continuous stream of drops from the clouds ⟨The air mass was dry, as much of the moisture had *precipitated* out on the other side of the mountains.⟩ — see RAIN 1

precipitately *adv* with excessive or careless speed ⟨He tended to act *precipitately* when faced with an unexpected turn of events.⟩ — see HASTILY 1

precipitating *adj* marked by or abounding with rain ⟨thick, *precipitating* clouds that just stayed in our region for days⟩ — see RAINY

precipitation *n* excited and often showy or disorderly speed ⟨I fear that I may have acted with some *precipitation* on this matter, so I would like to reconsider.⟩ — see HURRY 1

precipitous *adj* **1** acting or done with excessive or careless speed ⟨soon regretted our *precipitous* actions in international affairs⟩ — see HASTY 1
2 having an incline approaching the perpendicular ⟨a *precipitous* ski slope that fully merits its triple diamond designation⟩ — see STEEP 1

precipitously *adv* with excessive or careless speed ⟨the sight of swimmers exiting the water *precipitously* when some joker shouted "Shark!"⟩ — see HASTILY 1

precipitousness *n* excited and often showy or disorderly speed ⟨The *precipitousness* with which he acted would soon be a cause for regret.⟩ — see HURRY 1

précis *n* a short statement of the main points ⟨a *précis* of the bill that the legislature is currently considering⟩ — see SUMMARY

precise *adj* **1** meeting the highest standard of accuracy ⟨a machine which takes very *precise* measurements⟩
synonyms accurate, close, delicate, exact, fine, hairline, mathematical, pinpoint, refined, rigorous
related words correct, right, strict, true; definite, definitive; nice, subtle; careful, fastidious, finicky, meticulous

near antonyms approximate, round; false, incorrect, untrue, wrong; careless, loose; indefinite, unclear, vague; doubtful, dubious, questionable, unreliable, untrustworthy
antonyms coarse, imprecise, inaccurate, inexact, rough
2 being in agreement with the truth or a fact or a standard ⟨gave very *precise* answers to the members of the investigative committee⟩ — see CORRECT 1
3 being neither more nor less than a certain amount, number, or extent ⟨We gave him the *precise* amount that we owed him.⟩ — see EVEN 1
4 following an original exactly ⟨a *precise* translation of the original Greek⟩ — see FAITHFUL 2
5 of a particular or exact sort ⟨At that *precise* moment the lights went out.⟩ — see EXPRESS 1

precisely *adv* **1** as stated or indicated without the slightest difference ⟨Our guests arrived *precisely* at noon.⟩ — see EXACTLY 1
2 in the same manner ⟨I feel *precisely* the same way as you do.⟩ — see JUST 1
3 without any relaxation of standards or precision ⟨measured the length of the board *precisely*⟩ — see STRICTLY

preciseness *n* the quality or state of being very accurate ⟨The final result will be determined by the *preciseness* of the measurements.⟩ — see PRECISION

precision *n* the quality or state of being very accurate ⟨The company that measures TV ratings prides itself on the *precision* of its calculations.⟩
synonyms accuracy, closeness, delicacy, exactitude, exactness, fineness, nicety, perfection, preciseness, rigor, rigorousness, veracity
related words correctness, fidelity, rightness, strictness, truth; definiteness, definitiveness, definitude, determinacy; nicety, subtlety; care, carefulness, fastidiousness, meticulousness, persnicketiness
near antonyms approximation, roundness; falseness, falsity, incorrectness, wrongness; carelessness, guesswork, looseness; indefiniteness, vagueness
antonyms coarseness, impreciseness, imprecision, inaccuracy, inexactitude, inexactness, roughness

preclude *vb* to keep from happening by taking action in advance ⟨Dad issued a strict schedule for doing household chores so as to *preclude* any arguments.⟩ — see PREVENT

precluding *n* the act or practice of keeping something from happening ⟨The *precluding* of any misunderstanding seemed to be her top priority.⟩ — see PREVENTION

precocious *adj* occurring before the usual or expected time ⟨a *precocious* ability to read at age 4⟩ — see EARLY 2

precociously *adv* before the usual or expected time ⟨a *precociously* mature child⟩ — see EARLY

preconception *n* an attitude, belief, or impression formed in advance of actual experience of something ⟨Kim tried to go into the training sessions without any *preconceptions*.⟩ — see PREPOSSESSION 1

precursor *n* **1** one that announces or indicates the later arrival of another ⟨18th-century lyric poets like Robert Burns were *precursors* of the Romantics.⟩ — see FORERUNNER 1
2 something belonging to an earlier time from which something else was later developed ⟨a *precursor* of the modern eggplant⟩ — see ANCESTOR 2

predaceous *or* **predacious** *adj* living by killing and eating other animals ⟨the *predaceous* animals of the jungle, with the tiger at the top of the food chain⟩ — see PREDATORY

predate *vb* to go or come before in time ⟨Gunpowder *predated* the invention of the gun by several centuries.⟩ — see PRECEDE

predatory *adj* living by killing and eating other animals ⟨Hawks are *predatory* and pose a danger to rabbits and other pets.⟩
synonyms predaceous (*or* predacious), rapacious
related words carnivorous; aggressive, deadly, ferocious, fierce, savage, violent; untamed, wild
near antonyms herbivorous, vegetarian; gentle, submissive, tame

predecessor *n* something belonging to an earlier time from which something else was later developed ⟨The once-ubiquitous typewriter was the *predecessor* of today's electronic keyboard.⟩ — see ANCESTOR 2

predestine *vb* to determine the fate of in advance ⟨Our victory in the tournament was seemingly *predestined*.⟩ — see DESTINE

predetermine *vb* to determine the fate of in advance ⟨religious sects that believe that an individual's salvation has been *predetermined* by God⟩ — see DESTINE

predicament *n* a difficult, puzzling, or embarrassing situation from which there is no easy escape ⟨If you had told the truth in the first place, we wouldn't be in this *predicament*.⟩
synonyms bind, corner, dilemma, fix, hole, impasse, jam, mire, pickle, quagmire, spot
related words difficulty, node; hot water, soup; pinch, plight, quandary, scrape, trouble; deadlock, halt, stalemate, standstill; clutch, crisis, crossroad, emergency, exigency, juncture, strait
phrases kettle of fish

predicate *vb* to find a basis ⟨She has *predicated* her theory on recent findings by other astronomers.⟩ — see BASE

predict *vb* to tell of or describe beforehand ⟨I can't even begin to *predict* what housing prices will be like 30 years from now.⟩ — see FORETELL

predicting *n* a declaration that something will happen in the future ⟨those annual *predictings* by self-styled psychics that grace the front pages of the tabloids⟩ — see PREDICTION

prediction *n* a declaration that something will happen in the future ⟨We were all amazed when the fortune-teller's *predictions* turned out to be true.⟩
synonyms auguring, augury, cast, forecast, forecasting, foretelling, predicting, presaging, prognosis, prognostication, prophecy (*also* prophesy), soothsaying
related words foreboding, harbinger, omen, portent, prospectus, sign; foreknowledge; foresight; conjecture, guess, surmise

predictive *adj* being a sign of a later course of events ⟨Unfortunately, the stock market crash of 1929 turned out to be a *predictive* event, for the next decade was consumed by the Great Depression.⟩ — see PROPHETIC

predilection *n* a habitual attraction to some activity or thing ⟨a young lad with a *predilection* for telling tall tales⟩ — see INCLINATION 1

predisposition *n* a habitual attraction to some activity or thing ⟨the young woman's *predisposition* to date men who are very much like her father⟩ — see INCLINATION 1

predominance *n* controlling power or influence over others ⟨the *predominance* of the Dutch in international trade during the 17th century⟩ — see SUPREMACY 1

predominant *adj* coming before all others in importance ⟨Red is the *predominant* color in that painting.⟩ — see FOREMOST 1

predominantly *adv* for the most part ⟨a *predominantly* middle-class neighborhood⟩ — see CHIEFLY

preeminence *n* **1** exceptionally high quality ⟨The restaurant is known for the *preeminence* of its seafood dishes.⟩ — see EXCELLENCE 1
2 controlling power or influence over others ⟨Some historians contended that no nation had attained such undisputed *preeminence* since the glory days of the Roman Empire.⟩ — see SUPREMACY 1
3 the fact or state of being above others in rank or importance ⟨his *preeminence* in the field of obstetrics⟩ — see EMINENCE 1

preeminent *adj* **1** coming before all others in importance ⟨the *preeminent* reason for the booming economy⟩ — see FOREMOST 1
2 highest in rank or authority ⟨the *preeminent* golfer of his generation⟩ — see HEAD
3 standing above others in rank, importance, or achievement ⟨a meeting of *preeminent* scientists from around the world⟩ — see EMINENT

preempt *vb* to take or make use of under a guise of authority but without actual right ⟨The thoughtless attendees had *preempted* front-row seats that were reserved for the guests of honor.⟩ — see APPROPRIATE 1

preface *n* a short section (as of a book) that leads to or explains the main part ⟨A noted critic has written a short *preface* to her story to explain some of the historical background.⟩ — see INTRODUCTION

prefer *vb* **1** to show partiality toward ⟨I generally *prefer* chocolate ice cream over vanilla.⟩
synonyms care (for), favor, like
related words adore, cotton (to), delight (in), dig, enjoy, fancy, groove (on), relish, revel (in); choose, cull, handpick, name, pick, select, single (out); take; covet, crave, desire, hanker (for *or* after), want, wish (for); incline (toward), tend (to)
phrases be partial to, go in for
near antonyms disfavor, dislike; abhor, abominate, detest, hate, loathe; decline, refuse, reject, turn down; discard, jettison, throw away, throw out
2 to decide to accept (someone or something) from a group of possibilities ⟨Most buyers of that vehicle have *preferred* the model with four-wheel drive.⟩ — see CHOOSE 1

preferably *adv* by choice or preference ⟨I like football, but *preferably* watching from the stands rather than being down on the field.⟩ — see RATHER 1

preference *n* **1** a person or thing that is preferred over others ⟨My *preference* is soul music.⟩ — see FAVORITE
2 positive regard for something ⟨a *preference* for cool weather⟩ — see LIKING
3 the power, right, or opportunity to choose ⟨He was promised his *preference* when the time came to repaint his bedroom.⟩ — see CHOICE 1
4 a raising or a state of being raised to a higher rank or position ⟨a long-sought *preference* to the position of naval commander⟩ — see ADVANCEMENT 1

preferment *n* a raising or a state of being raised to a higher rank or position ⟨anticipated her *preferment* to a better-paying position within the company⟩ — see ADVANCEMENT 1

preferred *adj* singled out from a number or group as more to one's liking ⟨My *preferred* means of communication is e-mail.⟩ — see SELECT 1

prefigure *vb* to give a slight indication of beforehand ⟨The first crocus traditionally *prefigures* the arrival of spring.⟩ — see FORESHADOW

prefiguring *n* something believed to be a sign or warning of a future event ⟨His style of painting is generally regarded as a *prefiguring* of modern art.⟩ — see OMEN

pregnancy *n* the state of containing unborn young within the body ⟨An elephant's *pregnancy* can last almost two years.⟩
synonyms gestation
related words conception; begetting, breeding, generation, procreation, siring, spawning
near antonyms barrenness, infertility

pregnant *adj* **1** containing unborn young within the body ⟨We only realized that our cat had been *pregnant* when she unexpectedly delivered three kittens.⟩
synonyms big, expectant, gone, gravid, heavy
related words parturient, prenatal; childbearing, gestational; brooding; conceiving, impregnated
phrases with child, with young
near antonyms barren, infertile; aborting, miscarrying; delivered
antonyms nonpregnant
2 clearly conveying a special meaning (as one's mood) ⟨A *pregnant* silence followed the ill-advised attempt at humor.⟩ — see EXPRESSIVE

prejudgment *n* an attitude, belief, or impression formed in advance of actual experience of something ⟨the general public's *prejudgment* of the accused before the trial had even started⟩ — see PREPOSSESSION 1

prejudice *n* **1** an attitude that always favors one way of feeling or acting especially without considering any other possibilities ⟨her lifelong *prejudice* against doing "dirty" jobs⟩ — see BIAS 1
2 hatred of or discrimination against a person or persons based on their race ⟨fought racial *prejudice* through education and activism⟩ — see RACISM

prejudice *vb* to cause to have often negative opinions formed without sufficient knowledge ⟨All the bad stories I had heard about the incoming CEO *prejudiced* me against him even before the first meeting.⟩
synonyms bias, poison, turn
related words dispose, incline, predispose; influence, prepossess; convince, persuade, suggest

prejudiced *adj* **1** inclined to favor one side over another ⟨an employer who is known to be *prejudiced* toward graduates from Ivy League schools⟩ — see PARTIAL 1
2 unwilling to grant other people social rights or to accept other viewpoints ⟨a change in the law that took place despite the opposition of *prejudiced* people⟩ — see INTOLERANT 2

prejudicial *adj* **1** causing or capable of causing harm ⟨pretrial publicity that may be extremely *prejudicial* to a defendant's right to a fair trial⟩ — see HARMFUL
2 opposed to one's interests ⟨The defense will try to counterbalance the mass of *prejudicial* evidence presented by the prosecution.⟩ — see ADVERSE 1

preliminary *adj* coming before the main part or item usually to introduce or prepare for what follows ⟨We need to do some *preliminary* research in order to properly focus the experiment.⟩
synonyms beginning, introductory, preparatory, primary
related words introducing, prefacing, preparing, readying; premonitory, warning; basic, elementary, fundamental
near antonyms following, subsequent

preliminary *n* a performance, activity, or event that precedes and sets the stage for the main event ⟨a meeting to discuss seating arrangements that was merely a *preliminary* to the formal negotiating sessions⟩ — see PRELUDE 1

prelude *n* **1** a performance, activity, or event that precedes and sets the stage for the main event ⟨Appetizers were offered as a *prelude* to dinner.⟩
synonyms preamble, preliminary, prologue (*also* prolog)
related words lead-in; start
2 a short section (as of a book) that leads to or explains the main part ⟨The musical had a brief *prelude* to get the audience in the proper mood.⟩ — see INTRODUCTION

premature *adj* occurring before the usual or expected time ⟨His *premature* arrival at his own surprise party almost ruined everything.⟩ — see EARLY 2

prematurely *adv* before the usual or expected time ⟨a baby born three weeks *prematurely*⟩ — see EARLY

premier *adj* **1** coming before all others in time or order ⟨a space shuttle on its *premier* voyage⟩ — see FIRST 1
2 highest in rank or authority ⟨the *premier* authority on butterflies⟩ — see HEAD
3 coming before all others in importance ⟨the *premier* social occasion of the summer season⟩ — see FOREMOST 1

premise *also* **premiss** *n* **1** something taken as being true or factual and used as a starting point for a course of action or reasoning ⟨Your conclusion is all wrong because you started out with a false *premise*.⟩ — see ASSUMPTION 1
2 premises *pl* the area around and belonging to a building ⟨Detectives painstakingly searched the *premises* for clues to the disappearance.⟩ — see GROUND 1

premise *vb* to take as true or as a fact without actual proof ⟨Let us *premise* certain things, such as every person's need for love, before beginning our line of reasoning.⟩ — see ASSUME 2

premium *adj* commanding a large price ⟨lavish feasts at which *premium* delicacies were served⟩ — see COSTLY

premium *n* something given in recognition of achievement ⟨encouraging Girl Scouts to sell more cookies by offering *premiums*⟩ — see AWARD 1

premonition *n* a feeling that something bad will happen ⟨She had a *premonition* that her cat would somehow get hurt that day.⟩
synonyms foreboding, presage, presentiment, prognostication
related words foreknowledge; feel, insight, intuition; augury, omen, portent, sign; agitation, alarm (*also* alarum), anxiety, anxiousness, apprehension, apprehensiveness, care, concern, disquiet, doubt, dread, fear, misgiving, nervousness, uneasiness, worry; foresight, prescience

premonitory *adj* serving as or offering a warning ⟨a moderate tremor that some seismologists have interpreted as a *premonitory* sign of a catastrophic quake in the future⟩ — see CAUTIONARY

preoccupation *n* something about which one is constantly thinking or concerned ⟨the future entomologist's *preoccupation* with insects from a very early age⟩ — see FIXATION

preoccupied *adj* lost in thought and unaware of one's surroundings or actions ⟨too *preoccupied* with her worries to enjoy the meal⟩ — see ABSENTMINDED 1

preordain *vb* to determine the fate of in advance ⟨My wife and I are such soulmates, I'm convinced that our marriage was *preordained*.⟩ — see DESTINE

preparatory *adj* coming before the main part or item usually to introduce or prepare for what follows ⟨a *preparatory* investigation to see if there is enough evidence to warrant bringing charges⟩ — see PRELIMINARY

prepare *vb* **1** to make ready in advance ⟨I think I have *prepared* myself well for this challenge.⟩ ⟨We *prepared* the classroom for the important visitors by getting rid of some unsightly clutter.⟩
synonyms fit, fix, lay, ready
related words brace, fortify, gird, steel; batten, gear up, mount; educate, indoctrinate, instruct, school, train, tutor; boot (up), prime; arrange, set, spread; arm, equip, forearm, furnish, outfit, provide, supply; draft, draw up, frame
2 to make competent (as by training, skill, or ability) for a particular office or function ⟨Basic training is intended to *prepare* raw recruits for active duty in the military.⟩ — see QUALIFY 2
3 to put (something) into proper and usually carefully worked out written form ⟨The CEO asked his assistant to *prepare* a statement for the press.⟩ — see COMPOSE 1

4 to work out the details of (something) in advance ⟨*preparing* an escape route in case of a fire⟩ — see PLAN 1

prepared *adj* being in a state of fitness for some experience or action ⟨a marathoner completely *prepared* for the grueling race⟩ — see READY 1

prepossession *n* **1** an attitude, belief, or impression formed in advance of actual experience of something ⟨The foreign tourists' *prepossessions* about life in the U.S. had been formed by many hours of American TV shows.⟩
synonyms preconception, prejudgment
related words bias, favor, partiality, prejudice; assumption, conjecture, hypothesis, imagining, predetermination, presumption, presupposition, speculation, supposition, theory, thesis; concept, conception, image, notion, picture, thought
near antonyms detachment, impartiality, neutrality, objectivity, open-mindedness, unbiasedness
2 something about which one is constantly thinking or concerned ⟨tried to cure him of his *prepossession* with money⟩ — see FIXATION

preposterous *adj* **1** conceived or made without regard for reason or reality ⟨The idea that extraterrestrials built the pyramids is *preposterous*.⟩ — see FANTASTIC 1
2 showing or marked by a lack of good sense or judgment ⟨a *preposterous* suggestion to go swimming in this freezing weather⟩ — see FOOLISH 1
3 so foolish or pointless as to be worthy of scornful laughter ⟨The movie thriller had such a *preposterous* plot that we couldn't help snickering.⟩ — see RIDICULOUS 1

preposterousness *n* lack of good sense or judgment ⟨laughed at the sheer *preposterousness* of the idea⟩ — see FOOLISHNESS 1

prerogative *n* something to which one has a just claim ⟨It's your *prerogative* to refuse to attend the school's orientation, but it's recommended.⟩ — see RIGHT 1

presage *n* **1** a feeling that something bad will happen ⟨I had a nagging *presage* that the results of my tests would not be good.⟩ — see PREMONITION
2 something believed to be a sign or warning of a future event ⟨The sight of the first robin is always a welcome *presage* of spring.⟩ — see OMEN

presage *vb* to tell of or describe beforehand ⟨People used to believe that a comet *presaged* a major event, such as the death of a king.⟩ — see FORETELL

presaging *n* a declaration that something will happen in the future ⟨the far-fetched *presagings* of self-styled seers about current celebrities⟩ — see PREDICTION

prescience *n* **1** the special ability to see or know about events before they actually occur ⟨Her *prescience* as an investor is impressive.⟩ — see FORESIGHT 1
2 concern or preparation for the future ⟨parents who had the *prescience* to make everything in their house childproof before the arrival of their first baby⟩ — see FORESIGHT 2

prescient *adj* having or showing awareness of and preparation for the future ⟨*prescient* environmentalists and politicians who long ago made sure that these beautiful areas would forever be spared from development⟩ — see FORESIGHTED

prescribe *vb* to give the rules about (something) clearly and exactly ⟨In chess, you can move the various pieces only in certain *prescribed* ways.⟩
synonyms define, lay down, specify
related words decree, dictate, ordain; assign, direct, fix, set, settle; arrange, order; choose, select; bid, charge, command, enjoin, instruct, tell; conduct, control, govern, lead, manage; coerce, compel, constrain, force; obligate, oblige, require

presence *n* **1** a position within view ⟨The will was signed in the *presence* of two witnesses.⟩
synonyms company, sight
related words closeness, contiguity, immediacy, nearness, proximity
2 the outward form of someone or something especially as indicative of a quality ⟨The orchestra's musical director has a very stately *presence*.⟩ — see APPEARANCE 1

present *adj* **1** existing or in progress right now ⟨I am very busy at the *present* moment.⟩
synonyms current, extant, immediate, instant, ongoing, present-day
related words contemporary, modern, modernistic, new, newfangled, new-fashioned, recent, red-hot, space-age, ultramodern, up-to-date; breathing, existent, living
near antonyms coming, future, unborn; completed, concluded, done, ended, finished, over, terminated, through, up; ancient, antediluvian, antiquated, antique, archaic, dated, fusty, musty, obsolete, old, oldfangled, old-fashioned, old-time, out-of-date, outworn, passé; bygone, erstwhile, former, past
2 being within the confines of a specified place ⟨All of you are required to be *present* for every meeting.⟩
synonyms attending, in
related words accompanying, observing, participating; available; abounding; latent; breathing, existent, existing, extant, live
phrases at hand, in attendance, on hand
near antonyms departed, gone, retired; nonexistent; AWOL, truant; dead, deceased, defunct; lost, vanished; belated, delayed, late, tardy
antonyms absent, away, missing, out

¹present *n* the time currently existing or in progress ⟨I cannot talk to you at *present*, but perhaps in a few minutes.⟩
synonyms moment, now, today
related words phase, stage, state
near antonyms history, past, yesterday, yesteryear, yore; by-and-by, future, futurity, hereafter, offing

²present *n* something given to someone without expectation of a return ⟨an impressive array of *presents* for the bride and groom⟩ — see GIFT 1

present *vb* **1** to bring before the public in performance or exhibition ⟨We will *present* a performance of *Our Town* tomorrow evening.⟩
synonyms carry, give, mount, offer, stage
related words display, exhibit, expose, parade, show, show off, unveil; preview; act, impersonate, perform, play, portray; depict, dramatize, enact, render, represent; extend, proffer, tender
phrases come out with
2 to make (one person) known (to another) socially ⟨May I *present* my niece Sarah?⟩ — see INTRODUCE 1
3 to make a present of ⟨The company *presented* a gold watch to him on the occasion of his retirement.⟩ — see GIVE 1

presentation *n* something given to someone without expectation of a return ⟨a *presentation* of much-needed money to the children's charity⟩ — see GIFT 1

present–day *adj* **1** being or involving the latest methods, concepts, information, or styles ⟨*Present-day* technology has rendered yesterday's marvels obsolete.⟩ — see MODERN
2 existing or in progress right now ⟨the *present-day* administration in Washington⟩ — see PRESENT 1

presentiment *n* a feeling that something bad will happen ⟨a nagging *presentiment* of danger⟩ — see PREMONITION

presently *adv* **1** at or within a short time ⟨I cannot attend to the matter this instant, but I will *presently*.⟩ — see SHORTLY 2

2 at the present time ⟨We are *presently* waiting in line for our turn.⟩ — see NOW 1

3 without delay ⟨The performance is starting *presently*.⟩ — see IMMEDIATELY

preservation *n* **1** the act or activity of keeping something in an existing and usually satisfactory condition ⟨Each curator is responsible for the *preservation* of the works of art within his or her department.⟩ — see MAINTENANCE

2 the careful maintaining and protection of something valuable especially in its natural or original state ⟨The *preservation* of the tropical rainforests is a global responsibility.⟩ — see CONSERVATION 1

preserve *vb* to keep in good condition ⟨vigilantly *preserving* the ancient statue for future generations to enjoy⟩ — see MAINTAIN 1

preserving *n* the act or activity of keeping something in an existing and usually satisfactory condition ⟨the *preserving* of our rights and civil liberties⟩ — see MAINTENANCE

preside (over) *vb* **1** to exercise authority or power over ⟨From 1923 to 1948 Palestine was *presided over* by Great Britain under a mandate granted by the League of Nations.⟩ — see GOVERN 1

2 to look after and make decisions about ⟨He *presides over* a vast communications empire.⟩ — see CONDUCT 1

president *n* a person in charge of a meeting ⟨the *president* of the international conference⟩ — see CHAIR 1

presiding *adj* highest in rank or authority ⟨a senator who is the *presiding* member of the armed services committee⟩ — see HEAD

press *n* **1** a built-in space for storage behind a door ⟨Please put the towels in the linen *press*.⟩ — see CLOSET 1

2 a great number of persons or creatures massed together ⟨He pushed his way through the *press* of people outside the courthouse.⟩ — see CROWD 1

3 a storage case typically having doors and shelves ⟨Originally designed as a *press* for clothes, it now serves to hide the bedroom TV.⟩ — see CABINET

¹**press** *vb* to take or make use of under a guise of authority but without actual right ⟨The fleeing bank robber *pressed* a nearby taxi into service as a getaway car.⟩ — see APPROPRIATE 1

²**press** *vb* **1** to push steadily against with some force ⟨an old doorbell that requires you to *press* the button hard⟩
synonyms bear (down on), depress, shove, weigh (on *or* upon)
related words compress, mash, punch, squash, squeeze, squish; compel, force, pressure; lean (on *or* against), muscle; drive, propel, thrust; compact, condense, constrict, contract, crush, scrunch, wring; cram, jam, jampack, pack, stuff, wedge

2 to apply external pressure on so as to force out the juice or contents of ⟨My family will only drink juice from freshly *pressed* oranges.⟩
synonyms crush, express, mash, squeeze
related words pulp, puree (*or* purée); extract, extrude

3 to gather into a closely packed group ⟨Everyone *pressed* around me to see the pictures.⟩
synonyms bunch, cluster, crowd, huddle, pile
related words assemble, collect, concentrate, congregate, convene, converge, flock, forgather (*or* foregather), herd, swarm, throng; encircle, mob, surround; embrace, hug
near antonyms break up, disband, disperse, split (up)

4 to force one's way ⟨We continued to *press* deeper and deeper into the tangled rain forest.⟩
synonyms bore, bull, bulldoze, crash, elbow, jam, muscle, push, shoulder, squeeze
related words ram, shove, thrust

5 to cause (a person) to give in to pressure ⟨a manager

pressed by a business crisis to return from his vacation ahead of schedule⟩ — see FORCE

6 to try to persuade (someone) through earnest appeals to follow a course of action ⟨*pressed* us to go with them to the school board meeting⟩ — see URGE

7 to indicate the importance of by centering attention on ⟨an office e-mail that *presses* the need for greater vigilance concerning building security⟩ — see EMPHASIZE 1

press (for) *vb* to ask for (something) earnestly or with authority ⟨workers *pressing for* higher wages and better working conditions⟩ — see DEMAND 1

pressing *adj* needing immediate attention ⟨She had *pressing* business on the other side of town.⟩ — see ACUTE 2

pressure *n* **1** the burden on one's emotional or mental well-being created by demands on one's time ⟨a business executive who works well under *pressure*⟩ — see STRESS 1

2 the use of power to impose one's will on another ⟨*Pressure* from their peers can often cause teens to do things that they normally wouldn't consider.⟩ — see FORCE 2

pressure *vb* to cause (a person) to give in to pressure ⟨His father *pressured* him to go out for the swim team.⟩ — see FORCE

prestidigitation *n* the art or skill of performing tricks or illusions for entertainment ⟨Houdini's powers of *prestidigitation* remain legendary to this very day.⟩ — see MAGIC 2

prestidigitator *n* one who practices tricks and illusions for entertainment ⟨A skilled *prestidigitator* can make entire buildings seem to disappear.⟩ — see MAGICIAN 2

prestigious *adj* **1** having a good reputation especially in a field of knowledge ⟨a nutritional study that has been published by a *prestigious* medical journal⟩ — see RESPECTABLE 1

2 standing above others in rank, importance, or achievement ⟨the most *prestigious* social club in town⟩ — see EMINENT

presto *adv* with great speed ⟨The hungry men dived into the food and, *presto*, it was gone.⟩ — see FAST 1

presumably *adv* **1** to all outward appearances ⟨*Presumably* he's going on the trip for business reasons.⟩ — see APPARENTLY

2 by reasonable assumption ⟨*Presumably* he'll come later.⟩ — see PROBABLY

presume *vb* **1** to form an opinion from little or no evidence ⟨I *presume* you'll fly if you do go.⟩ — see GUESS 1

2 to take as true or as a fact without actual proof ⟨We should *presume* that a person is innocent until proven guilty.⟩ — see ASSUME 2

presumed *adj* appearing to be true on the basis of evidence that may or may not be confirmed ⟨the *presumed* culprit⟩ — see APPARENT 1

presuming *adj* **1** having a feeling of superiority that shows itself in an overbearing attitude ⟨It's rather *presuming* of you to expect to be our first choice for the award.⟩ — see ARROGANT

2 showing a lack of proper social reserve or modesty ⟨I thought it *presuming* of him to think that we would invite him along.⟩ — see PRESUMPTUOUS 1

3 thrusting oneself where one is not welcome or invited ⟨Some *presuming* waiter thought that it was his business to tell me what I should or shouldn't eat.⟩ — see INTRUSIVE

presumption *n* **1** shameless boldness ⟨shocked by his *presumption* in insisting that we buy his raffle tickets⟩ — see EFFRONTERY

2 something taken as being true or factual and used as a starting point for a course of action or reasoning ⟨the *presumption* of innocence⟩ — see ASSUMPTION 1

presumptuous *adj* **1** showing a lack of proper social reserve or modesty ⟨It's a little *presumptuous* of you to as-

sume that I'm your new best friend just because I invited you along.⟩
synonyms bold, familiar, forward, free, immodest, over-familiar, presuming
related words arrogant, complacent, conceited, egoistic (*also* egoistical), egotistic (*or* egotistical), highfalutin (*also* hifalutin), high-hat, hoity-toity, important, overweening, pompous, prideful, proud, self-assertive, self-complacent, self-conceited, self-important, self-satisfied, smug, uppity, vain, vainglorious; cavalier, disdainful, haughty, lordly, pretentious, stuck-up, supercilious, superior; audacious, bold-faced, brash, brassy, brazen, cheeky, cocky, fresh, impertinent, impudent, insolent, overbold, pert, sassy, saucy; confident, self-assured, self-confident, sure; boastful, braggart, bragging; domineering, high-handed, imperious
near antonyms demure, down-to-earth, humble, lowly, meek, unassertive, unpretentious; bashful, mousy (*or* mousey), retiring, shy, timid, timorous; diffident, self-doubting
antonyms modest, unassuming
2 having a feeling of superiority that shows itself in an overbearing attitude ⟨The *presumptuous* doctor didn't even bother to explain to me the treatment that I would be receiving.⟩ — see ARROGANT
3 thrusting oneself where one is not welcome or invited ⟨The *presumptuous* salesclerk started picking out some very expensive accessories for the outfit I had just chosen.⟩ — see INTRUSIVE
presumptuousness *n* **1** an exaggerated sense of one's importance that shows itself in the making of excessive or unjustified claims ⟨Only a person of unparalleled *presumptuousness* would assert that she knows all there is to know about words.⟩ — see ARROGANCE
2 shameless boldness ⟨He found that a certain amount of *presumptuousness* could get you in trouble, but it could also get you into places where you normally weren't allowed.⟩ — see EFFRONTERY
presuppose *vb* to take as true or as a fact without actual proof ⟨The book *presupposes* its readers will already know something about the subject.⟩ — see ASSUME 2
presupposition *n* something taken as being true or factual and used as a starting point for a course of action or reasoning ⟨the cynic's *presupposition* that everyone acts out of purely selfish motives⟩ — see ASSUMPTION 1
pretend *adj* **1** being such in appearance only and made with or manufactured from usually cheaper materials ⟨If you were to see the movie's *pretend* jewels in real life, you wouldn't be fooled for a minute.⟩ — see IMITATION
2 not real and existing only in the imagination ⟨The children played on a *pretend* spaceship.⟩ — see IMAGINARY
pretend *vb* **1** to take on a false or deceptive appearance ⟨I *pretended* that I didn't care what other people had to say about me.⟩
synonyms dissemble, dissimulate, let on, make out
related words act, impersonate, masquerade, play, play-act, pose; affect, assume, counterfeit, fake, feign, profess, put on, sham, simulate; camouflage, conceal, disguise, mask; bluff, feint
phrases make a pretense, make a show, make believe, put on an act, put up a front
2 to present a false appearance of ⟨As if I would ever *pretend* illness just to take off a day from work!⟩ — see FEIGN
pretended *adj* **1** lacking in natural or spontaneous quality ⟨He shows a *pretended* affection for his girlfriend's cat.⟩ — see ARTIFICIAL 1
2 not being or expressing what one appears to be or express ⟨hoped that his *pretended* interest in classical music would impress the boss⟩ — see INSINCERE

pretender *n* one who makes false claims of identity or expertise ⟨a *pretender* to the throne⟩ — see IMPOSTOR
pretense *or* **pretence** *n* **1** the quality or state of appearing or trying to appear more important or more valuable than is the case ⟨She seemed to be a very down-to-earth woman who was completely free of *pretense*.⟩
synonyms affectation, affectedness, grandiosity, pretension, pretentiousness
related words arrogance, complacency, conceit, egotism, imperiousness, pompousness, presumptuousness, pride, self-aggrandizement, self-assertion, self-assumption, self-conceit, self-consequence, self-glorification, self-importance, self-satisfaction, smugness, vaingloriousness, vainglory, vainness, vanity; disdain, haughtiness, lordliness, snobbery, snobbishness, superciliousness, superiority; confidence, presumption, self-assurance, self-confidence, sureness; grandiloquence; flamboyance, flashiness, garishness, gaudiness, glitz, mummery, ostentation, ostentatiousness, show, showiness
near antonyms demureness, humbleness, humility, lowliness, meekness, modesty; bashfulness, diffidence, shyness, timidity; naturalness, sincerity
2 a display of emotion or behavior that is insincere or intended to deceive ⟨Her display of bravado was just a *pretense*.⟩ — see MASQUERADE
3 an entitlement to something ⟨This book on gardening makes no *pretense* at completeness.⟩ — see CLAIM 1
4 an exaggerated sense of one's importance that shows itself in the making of excessive or unjustified claims ⟨the *pretense* of that woman in thinking that the other hotel guests should be inconvenienced just for her⟩ — see ARROGANCE
pretension *n* **1** an entitlement to something ⟨a *pretension* of long standing to the throne of Hungary⟩ — see CLAIM 1
2 an exaggerated sense of one's importance that shows itself in the making of excessive or unjustified claims ⟨a woman full of *pretension* and pompousness⟩ — see ARROGANCE
3 the quality or state of appearing or trying to appear more important or more valuable than is the case ⟨The *pretension* of that French restaurant is more than I can bear.⟩ — see PRETENSE 1
4 something that one hopes or intends to accomplish ⟨Eric has serious *pretensions* of becoming a writer.⟩ — see GOAL
pretentious *adj* **1** self-consciously trying to present an appearance of grandeur or importance ⟨That *pretentious* couple always serves caviar at their parties, even though they themselves dislike it.⟩
synonyms affected, grandiose, highfalutin (*also* hifalutin), high-minded, ostentatious, pompous, snippy
related words airy, grandiloquent, high-flown, high-sounding, high-toned; arrogant, complacent, conceited, egoistic (*also* egoistical), egotistic (*or* egotistical), high-handed, high-hat, hoity-toity, imperious, important, overweening, presumptuous, prideful, proud, self-centered, self-complacent, self-conceited, self-important, self-obsessed, self-pleased, self-satisfied, smug, uppity, vain, vainglorious; self-aggrandizing, self-dramatizing, self-glorifying, self-promoting; cavalier, disdainful, haughty, lordly, stuck-up, supercilious, superior; flamboyant, flashy, flaunting, garish, gaudy, glitzy, showy, splashy
near antonyms demure, down-to-earth, homely, humble, lowly, meek, retiring, unassertive, unassuming; bashful, diffident, mousy (*or* mousey), overmodest, passive, quiet, reserved, shy, timid
antonyms modest, unpretentious
2 having a feeling of superiority that shows itself in an overbearing attitude ⟨a *pretentious* author whose books

only appeal to equally *pretentious* readers⟩ — see ARRO-
GANT

pretentiousness *n* **1** an exaggerated sense of one's importance that shows itself in the making of excessive or unjustified claims ⟨Everyone took her ingrained *pretentiousness* into account when considering her statements.⟩
— see ARROGANCE

2 excessive or unnecessary display ⟨the sheer *pretentiousness* of the debutante's wedding⟩ — see OSTENTATION

3 the quality or state of appearing or trying to appear
more important or more valuable than is the case ⟨The
utter *pretentiousness* of the movie is matched only by the
incomprehensibility of its story.⟩ — see PRETENSE 1

preternatural *adj* **1** of, relating to, or being part of a reality
beyond the observable physical universe ⟨an investigator
of *preternatural* phenomena⟩ — see SUPERNATURAL 1

2 being so extraordinary or abnormal as to suggest powers which violate the laws of nature ⟨a *preternatural* ability to predict how the stock market will perform⟩ — see
SUPERNATURAL 2

prettiness *n* the qualities in a person or thing that as a
whole give pleasure to the senses ⟨The sugary *prettiness*
of the knickknacks is sure to appeal to a certain type of
collector.⟩ — see BEAUTY 1

pretty *adj* **1** giving pleasure or contentment to the mind or
senses ⟨The kitchen wasn't a *pretty* sight after we made
all the food for the party.⟩ — see PLEASANT 1

2 meeting the requirements of a purpose or situation ⟨as
pretty an example of a creative solution as you're likely
to find⟩ — see FIT 1

3 very pleasing to look at ⟨a *pretty* young girl⟩ — see
BEAUTIFUL 1

pretty *adv* to some degree or extent ⟨We've had some *pretty* cold weather lately.⟩ — see FAIRLY 1

prevail *vb* **1** to achieve victory (as in a contest) ⟨We shall
prevail despite the overwhelming odds.⟩ — see WIN 1

2 to continue to operate or to meet one's needs ⟨a custom that still *prevails* in many areas of the country⟩ —
see HOLD OUT

prevail (on *or* **upon)** *vb* to cause (someone) to agree with a
belief or course of action by using arguments or earnest
requests ⟨We *prevailed on* him to sing in front of all his
friends.⟩ — see PERSUADE

prevail (over) *vb* to achieve a victory over ⟨*prevailed over* their
traditional rivals for the first time in years⟩ — see BEAT 2

prevailing *adj* **1** accepted, used, or practiced by most people ⟨The principal disagrees with the *prevailing* attitude
toward dress codes.⟩ — see CURRENT 1

2 held by or applicable to a majority of the people ⟨The
prevailing custom here is to leave one's doors unlocked.⟩
— see GENERAL 3

prevalence *n* the fact or state of happening often ⟨the
prevalence of rumors when hard information is withheld
from the public⟩ — see FREQUENCY

prevalent *adj* accepted, used, or practiced by most people
⟨the kinds of accidents seen in places where snowmo-
biles are *prevalent*⟩ — see CURRENT 1

prevaricate *vb* to make a statement one knows to be untrue ⟨During the hearings the witness was willing to *prevaricate* in order to protect his friend.⟩ — see ¹LIE

prevarication *n* a statement known by its maker to be untrue and made in order to deceive ⟨She knew that his
account was a pure *prevarication*.⟩ — see LIE

prevaricator *n* a person who tells lies ⟨She was clearly one
of the more practiced *prevaricators* ever to come before
the congressional committee.⟩ — see LIAR

prevent *vb* to keep from happening by taking action in
advance ⟨A lot of problems would have been *prevented* if
we'd just prepared better.⟩

synonyms avert, forestall, help, obviate, preclude, stave
off

related words anticipate, provide; negate, neutralize,
nullify; save; baffle, balk, checkmate, deter, foil, frustrate, thwart; bar, block, hamper, hinder, impede, interfere (with), retard, stall; deflect, fend (off), stop, ward
(off); avoid, circumvent, dodge, duck, elude, escape, eschew, evade, shake, shirk, shun; forbid, inhibit, prohibit;
arrest, check, halt, stop; compensate (for), counteract,
counterbalance, make up (for), offset

near antonyms abet, aid, assist; ease, facilitate, smooth,
unclog; advance, cultivate, encourage, forward, foster,
further, nurture, promote; allow, leave, let, permit

preventative *adj* concerned with or serving to keep something from happening ⟨the department in charge of taking *preventative* measures against cyber attacks⟩ — see
PREVENTIVE

prevention *n* the act or practice of keeping something
from happening ⟨Good hygiene is crucial to the *prevention* of illness.⟩

synonyms averting, forestallment, precluding

related words avoidance, circumvention; negation, neutralization; determent, deterrence, foiling, frustration,
thwarting; barring, enjoining, forbidding, interdicting,
interdiction, outlawing, prohibiting, prohibition, proscribing, proscription

near antonyms aid, assistance, backing, support; facilitation; advancement, cultivation, encouragement, nurture, promotion

preventive *adj* concerned with or serving to keep something from happening ⟨If you start taking this *preventive*
medicine now, you may not get sick after all.⟩

synonyms precautionary, preventative

related words deterrent, deterring; negating, neutraliz-
ing, nullifying; baffling, balking, foiling, frustrating,
thwarting; blocking, hampering, hindering, impeding

near antonyms abetting, aiding, assisting; easing, facilitating, smoothing; encouraging, forwarding, fostering,
furthering, nurturing, promoting

previous *adj* going before another in time or order ⟨The
new instructor should consult with the *previous* teacher
about the lesson plans.⟩ ⟨The *previous* math problem
also included a reference to store discounts.⟩

synonyms antecedent, anterior, foregoing, former,
precedent, preceding, prior

related words advance, early, premature; earliest, first,
inaugural, initial, maiden, original, pioneer; preexisting;
introductory, preliminary; erstwhile, whilom

near antonyms advanced, late; closing, concluding, final, last, latest, latter, terminal, ultimate

antonyms after, ensuing, following, later, posterior, subsequent, succeeding

previously *adv* so as to precede something in order of time
⟨He had prepared the meat stocks *previously* so as to
make things easier on the day of the big dinner.⟩ — see
AHEAD 1

previous to *prep* earlier than ⟨His passport arrived just
previous to his trip.⟩ — see BEFORE 1

prey *n* **1** an animal that is hunted or killed ⟨Rabbits are
common *prey* for owls and hawks.⟩

synonyms chase, quarry

related words game; kill, victim; beast, brute, creature,
critter; target

near antonyms chaser, hunter, pursuer

2 a person or thing harmed, lost, or destroyed ⟨He fell
prey to an online scam.⟩ — see CASUALTY 1

3 a person or thing that is the object of abuse, criticism,
or ridicule ⟨a snack food that is the common *prey* of
nutrition experts⟩ — see TARGET 1

prey (on *or* **upon)** *vb* to seize and eat (something) as prey ⟨A fox has been *preying on* the chickens.⟩
   synonyms feed (on, upon, *or* off)
   related words chase, hunt, pursue, stalk; destroy, dispatch, do in, fell, kill, slay
price *n* **1** the amount of money that is demanded as payment for something ⟨I really wanted to buy that shirt, but the *price* was more money than I had.⟩
   synonyms charge, cost, damage, fee, figure, freight
   related words market value, valuation, value; asking price, list price, sticker price; price point, rate, tariff, unit price; carrying charge, overcharge, service charge (*also* service fee), surcharge; account, bill, check, invoice, tab
   2 the loss or penalty involved in achieving a goal ⟨I finished the project, but the *price* was losing a night's sleep.⟩
   synonyms cost
   related words expense, toll; damages, forfeit, forfeiture, mulct, sacrifice; risk
   3 something offered or given in return for a service performed ⟨There was a *price* on the criminal's head.⟩ — see REWARD
prick *n* **1** a mark or small hole made by a pointed instrument ⟨The immunization shot left a *prick* on my arm that turned into a bruise.⟩
   synonyms perforation, pinhole, pinprick, punch, puncture, stab
   related words gouge, groove, hollow; break, cut, gash, incision, laceration, notch, rent, rip, rupture, slash, slit, tear
   2 a sharp unpleasant sensation usually felt in some specific part of the body ⟨She felt a sharp *prick* when the nurse gave her the shot.⟩ — see PAIN 1
prickly *adj* **1** causing an unpleasant tingling sensation ⟨She tried to ignore the feel of the *prickly* wool against her skin.⟩ — see SCRATCHY 2
   2 easily irritated or annoyed ⟨She dreaded having to deal with her *prickly* boss.⟩ — see IRRITABLE
   3 having leaves or branches which are likely to cause a scratch ⟨We waded carefully through the *prickly* bushes.⟩ — see SCRATCHY 1
   4 requiring exceptional skill or caution in performance or handling ⟨a *prickly* issue that will outrage at least one special interest if not handled delicately⟩ — see TRICKY 1
pride *n* **1** a reasonable or justifiable sense of one's worth or importance ⟨Finishing that survival course gave me a real sense of *pride* and confidence in my abilities.⟩
   synonyms ego, pridefulness, self-esteem, self-regard, self-respect
   related words aplomb, assurance, confidence, self-assurance, self-confidence, self-pride, self-worth; dignity, face, honor, prestige
   near antonyms discredit, disgrace, dishonor, disrepute, humiliation, ignominy, infamy, odium, opprobrium, shame; demureness, humbleness, humility, modesty; diffidence, meekness, shyness, timidity, timidness
   2 an asset that brings praise or renown ⟨An architectural and acoustical masterpiece, the concert hall is the *pride* of the whole city.⟩ — see GLORY 2
   3 an often unjustified feeling of being pleased with oneself or with one's situation or achievements ⟨so full of *pride* that they were ripe for a big comedown⟩ — see COMPLACENCE 1
   4 individuals carefully selected as being the best of a class ⟨crackerjack test pilots who are the *pride* of the navy's air arm⟩ — see ELITE 1
pride *vb* to think highly of (oneself) ⟨He *prides* himself on the quality of his writing.⟩
   synonyms flatter, plume
   related words boast, brag, crow, swagger; congratulate, felicitate

prideful *adj* **1** having or displaying feelings of scorn for what is regarded as beneath oneself ⟨*Prideful* intellectuals long considered rock music unworthy of serious study.⟩ — see PROUD 1
   2 having too high an opinion of oneself ⟨At the wedding the *prideful* snobs ignored their poor relations.⟩ — see CONCEITED
   3 having or expressing feelings of joy or triumph ⟨Amy flashed a *prideful* smile as she received her college diploma.⟩ — see EXULTANT
pridefulness *n* **1** a reasonable or justifiable sense of one's worth or importance ⟨Beaming with understandable *pridefulness*, the graduate accepted his college diploma.⟩ — see PRIDE 1
   2 an often unjustified feeling of being pleased with oneself or with one's situation or achievements ⟨an inordinate amount of *pridefulness* for someone who has much to be modest about⟩ — see COMPLACENCE 1
priestly *adj* of, relating to, or characteristic of the clergy ⟨majestically robed in *priestly* garments⟩ — see CLERICAL
prim *adj* given to or marked by very conservative standards regarding personal behavior or morals ⟨A very *prim* editor removed all the swear words from the article.⟩ — see STRAITLACED
primacy *n* the fact or state of being above others in rank or importance ⟨the *primacy* of calcium for building strong bones⟩ — see EMINENCE 1
primal *adj* **1** coming before all others in importance ⟨The *primal* theme of the essay is toleration of religious diversity.⟩ — see FOREMOST 1
   2 relating to or occurring near the beginning of a process, series, or time period ⟨There was a period of *primal* idealism after the founding of the republic and before the rise of partisan politics.⟩ — see EARLY 1
primarily *adv* **1** in the beginning ⟨The university was *primarily* an agricultural college when it was founded over two centuries ago.⟩ — see ORIGINALLY
   2 for the most part ⟨Ketchup is *primarily* made from tomatoes.⟩ — see CHIEFLY
primary *adj* **1** coming before all others in importance ⟨The *primary* concern for many house hunters is the asking price.⟩ — see FOREMOST 1
   2 done or working without something else coming in between ⟨a crop failure that was the *primary* cause of the famine⟩ — see DIRECT 1
   3 highest in rank or authority ⟨the movie's *primary* screenwriter⟩ — see HEAD
   4 coming before the main part or item usually to introduce or prepare for what follows ⟨a few minutes of *primary* instruction in the use of our diving gear before we actually got into the water⟩ — see PRELIMINARY
prime *adj* **1** highest in rank or authority ⟨the *prime* strategist in the senator's presidential campaign⟩ — see HEAD
   2 of the very best kind ⟨The family owns a thousand acres of *prime* farmland.⟩ — see EXCELLENT
prime *n* **1** a state or time of great activity, thriving, or achievement ⟨in the *prime* of her life⟩ — see BLOOM 1
   2 individuals carefully selected as being the best of a class ⟨chose the *prime* of the litter of pups⟩ — see ELITE 1
primer *n* a book used for instruction in a subject ⟨a *primer* of human anatomy⟩ — see TEXTBOOK
primeval *adj* relating to or occurring near the beginning of a process, series, or time period ⟨*primeval* forests slowly disappearing as the climate changed⟩ — see EARLY 1
primitive *adj* **1** belonging to or characteristic of an early level of skill or development ⟨*Primitive* wooden tools were used before the Iron Age.⟩
   synonyms crude, low, rude, rudimentary
   related words basic, simple, uncomplicated; homely, un-

sophisticated; early, embryonic, primeval, primordial; backward, underdeveloped, undeveloped; aged, ancient, antediluvian, antiquated, antique, dated, fusty, hoary, musty, obsolete, old, oldfangled, old-fashioned, old-time, out-of-date, outworn, passé, past, quaint, unmodernized
near antonyms complex, complicated, intricate, involved, sophisticated; full-blown, mature, matured, perfected, ripe, ripened; civilized, cultivated, enlightened, refined; contemporary, current, latest, mod, modern, modernistic, new, newfangled, new-fashioned, novel, now, present-day, space-age, state-of-the-art, supermodern, ultramodern, up-to-date
antonyms advanced, developed, evolved, high, higher, late
2 relating to or occurring near the beginning of a process, series, or time period ⟨a *primitive* period in the state's history⟩ — see EARLY 1

primordial *adj* relating to or occurring near the beginning of a process, series, or time period ⟨All life on Earth supposedly came from a *primordial* ooze in existence many millions of years ago.⟩ — see EARLY 1

prince *n* a person of rank, power, or influence in a particular field ⟨a neighborhood in which the city's merchant *princes* built palaces that shamelessly celebrated their wealth⟩ — see MAGNATE

princely *adj* fit for or worthy of a royal ruler ⟨set a *princely* meal before their guests⟩ — see MONARCHICAL

principal *adj* **1** coming before all others in importance ⟨our *principal* reason for coming here today⟩ — see FOREMOST 1
2 highest in rank or authority ⟨the *principal* researcher in the company's chemical division⟩ — see HEAD

principal *n* the person who has the most important role in a play, movie, or TV show ⟨My cousin is one of the *principals* in a new sitcom this fall.⟩ — see STAR 2

principally *adv* for the most part ⟨The tourists were *principally* concerned with the quantity of the food, and only secondarily with the quality.⟩ — see CHIEFLY

principled *adj* **1** following the accepted rules of moral conduct ⟨a high-*principled* art expert who always told clients what he honestly thought their items were worth⟩ — see HONORABLE 1
2 guided by or in accordance with one's sense of right and wrong ⟨a politician widely respected for her *principled* behavior in every office she ever held⟩ — see CONSCIENTIOUS 1

principles *pl n* **1** general or basic truths on which other truths or theories can be based ⟨If you don't learn the *principles* of algebra now, you won't understand much later on.⟩
synonyms basics, elements, essentials, fundamentals, rudiments
related words basis, bedrock, cornerstone, foundation, groundwork, keystone, underpinning; belief, canon, doctrine, dogma, faith, philosophy; axiom, law, precept, tenet; rule, standard; theorem
near antonyms details, trivia
2 the code of good conduct for an individual or group ⟨Ted stuck to his *principles* even in the face of extreme pressure.⟩ — see ETHICS

print *n* **1** a perceptible trace left by pressure ⟨One telltale sign that I had been napping was the *print* left by the chenille bedspread on my cheek.⟩
synonyms impress, impression, imprint, stamp
related words dent, hollow, indentation; mark, sign
2 a picture created from an image recorded on a light-sensitive surface by a camera ⟨We now get our *prints* developed online.⟩ — see PHOTOGRAPH

print *vb* to produce and release for distribution in printed form ⟨The newspaper's motto remains "All the News That's Fit to *Print*."⟩ — see PUBLISH 1

prior *adj* **1** coming before all others in importance ⟨This assignment will be *prior* to any other work you may have.⟩ — see FOREMOST 1
2 going before another in time or order ⟨We've made *prior* arrangements.⟩ — see PREVIOUS

priority *n* the right to one's attention before other things considered less important ⟨The committee has decided to give your request *priority*, so you'll have a meeting early tomorrow morning.⟩
synonyms precedence, right-of-way
related words preference; urgency; ascendancy (*also* ascendency), preeminence, primacy, supremacy; transcendence, transcendency; order, progression, sequence, succession; front burner
near antonyms back burner

prior to *prep* earlier than ⟨Make sure all revisions are approved by the author *prior to* publication.⟩ — see BEFORE 1

priory *n* a residence for men under religious vows ⟨You can hear the bells from the *priory* from the other side of the village.⟩ — see MONASTERY

prison *n* **1** a place of confinement for persons held in lawful custody ⟨in *prison* for fraud and embezzlement⟩ — see JAIL
2 the act of confining or the state of being confined ⟨the view that *prison* does nothing to cure the criminal⟩ — see INTERNMENT

prisoner *n* one that has been taken and held in confinement ⟨The *prisoners* were allowed a period of outdoor exercise each day.⟩ — see CAPTIVE

pristine *adj* **1** being in an original and unused or unspoiled state ⟨a *pristine* forest that has never been subjected to logging or development⟩ — see FRESH 1
2 free from dirt or stain ⟨I wouldn't dare spill anything on his car's *pristine* upholstery.⟩ — see CLEAN 1

private *adj* **1** not known or meant to be known by the general populace ⟨That he is planning to retire is *private* information until he makes a public announcement.⟩
synonyms confidential, esoteric, hushed, inside, intimate, nonpublic, privy, secret
related words classified, restricted, top secret; silent, unadvertised, unannounced, undisclosed, unmentioned, unsaid, untold; clandestine, closet, collusive, conspiratorial, covert; furtive, hugger-mugger, occult, sneak, sneaking, sneaky, stealthy, surreptitious, undercover, underground, underhand, underhanded; personal; closeted, concealed; silenced, stifled, suppressed; backstage, offscreen, offstage
near antonyms well-known; advertised, aired, announced, blazed, broadcast, declared, disclosed, divulged, enunciated, heralded, proclaimed, professed, promulgated, publicized, published, reported, spotlighted
antonyms common, open, public
2 undertaken or done so as to escape being observed or known by others ⟨a *private* investigation of the organization's activities⟩ — see SECRET 1
3 of, relating to, or belonging to a single person ⟨club lockers in which *private* property may be stored⟩ — see INDIVIDUAL 1

privation *n* the state of being robbed of something normally enjoyed ⟨The constant *privation* of sleep was starting to affect my work.⟩
synonyms deprivation, loss
related words absence, dearth, lack, need, want; dispossession; denial, forfeit, forfeiture, penalty, sacrifice; bereavement; deficiency, inadequacy, insufficiency, paucity, poverty, scarcity, shortage

near antonyms control, ownership, possession; accumulation, acquiring, gain

privilege *n* something granted as a special favor ⟨The town's oldest resident will have the *privilege* of leading the parade kicking off the Heritage Celebration.⟩
synonyms boon, concession, honor
related words courtesy; claim, right; birthright; perquisite, prerogative; charter, grant, patent; exemption, immunity, waiver
near antonyms burden, duty, obligation, responsibility

privilege *vb* to give a right to ⟨Only professionals who meet the education and experience requirements set by law are *privileged* to use the title "interior designer" in Oklahoma.⟩ — see ENTITLE 1

privy *adj* **1** not known or meant to be known by the general populace ⟨*privy* information on the current state of the peace negotiations⟩ — see PRIVATE 1
2 undertaken or done so as to escape being observed or known by others ⟨*privy* meetings between high-level representatives from both sides for the purpose of bringing about an armistice⟩ — see SECRET 1
3 of, relating to, or belonging to a single person ⟨a *privy* seal that can be used only by the British monarch⟩ — see INDIVIDUAL 1

prize *adj* of the very best kind ⟨delighted to be guests at one of her *prize* dinner parties⟩ — see EXCELLENT

prize *n* **1** someone or something unusually desirable ⟨The picture would be the *prize* of any museum's collection.⟩
synonyms catch, gem, jewel, pearl, plum, treasure
related words blessing, find, godsend, goody (*or* goodie), valuable, windfall; booty, loot, plunder, spoil, swag; brass ring; glory, pride; gold, jackpot, prize money
near antonyms lemon, loser
2 something given in recognition of achievement ⟨The Pritzker Architecture *Prize* is the world's most prestigious honor in the field of architecture.⟩ — see AWARD 1

¹**prize** *vb* **1** to draw out by force or with effort ⟨*prizing* the stubborn nails out of the board⟩ — see EXTRACT
2 to raise, move, or pull apart with or as if with a lever ⟨trying to *prize* apart the jammed gears⟩ — see ¹PRY 1

²**prize** *vb* to hold dear ⟨Veterinarians know that pets are highly *prized* by their owners.⟩ — see LOVE 1

prizefighter *n* one that engages in the sport of fighting with the fists ⟨a *prizefighter* who is generally acknowledged to be one of the ring's most dangerous men⟩ — see BOXER

proactive *adj* having or showing awareness of and preparation for the future ⟨*proactive* decision by the city leaders to plan for the eventual withering away of the region's manufacturing base⟩ — see FORESIGHTED

probability *n* **1** the quality or state of being likely to occur ⟨The plot of the movie thriller was exciting and surprising but woefully lacking in *probability*.⟩
synonyms liability, likelihood
related words credibility, plausibility, plausibleness; feasibility, possibility, potentiality, reasonability, reasonableness, viability
near antonyms doubtfulness, dubiousness; impracticability, impracticality; implausibility, incredibility, incredibleness
antonyms improbability, unlikelihood, unlikeliness
2 a measure of how often an event will occur instead of another ⟨The *probability* of flipping a coin and getting heads 50 times in a row is not good.⟩
synonyms chance, odds, percentage
related words outlook, prospect; contingency, possibility, potential, potentiality; conditional probability

probable *adj* **1** worthy of being accepted as true or reasonable ⟨His explanation of what happened is more *probable* than not.⟩ — see BELIEVABLE

2 having a high chance of occurring ⟨A *probable* outcome of the price increase will be lower consumption.⟩ — see LIKELY 1

probably *adv* by reasonable assumption ⟨We would *probably* win that bet.⟩
synonyms doubtless, likely, presumably
related words maybe, mayhap, perchance, perhaps, possibly; conceivably, imaginably, plausibly, practically, reasonably; potentially; assuredly, certainly, conclusively, decisively, definitely, definitively, indisputably, indubitably, really, surely, truly, undeniably, undoubtedly, unquestionably; presumedly, supposably, supposedly
phrases as like as not (*or* like as not)
near antonyms implausibly, inconceivably, incredibly, unbelievably, unthinkably
antonyms improbably

probe *n* a systematic search for the truth or facts about something ⟨a congressional *probe* into the accusations⟩ — see INQUIRY 1

probe *vb* **1** to search through or into ⟨tabloid reporters who seem determined to *probe* every detail of the singer's private life⟩ — see EXPLORE 1
2 to go into or range over for purposes of discovery ⟨*probing* the depths of the undersea trench⟩ — see EXPLORE 2

probing *n* a systematic search for the truth or facts about something ⟨questionings and *probings* by several committees into the affair⟩ — see INQUIRY 1

probity *n* **1** conduct that conforms to an accepted standard of right and wrong ⟨A person of indisputable *probity* must head the disciplinary panel.⟩ — see MORALITY 1
2 devotion to telling the truth ⟨The defense attorney questioned the *probity* of the witness.⟩ — see HONESTY 1
3 faithfulness to high moral standards ⟨ideals of fairness and *probity* in journalism⟩ — see HONOR 1

problem *n* **1** something that requires thought and skill for resolution ⟨the *problem* of habitat loss⟩
synonyms case, challenge, knot, matter, trouble
related words issue, question; corner, fix, hole, hot water, jam, mire, pickle, predicament, quagmire, spot; crux, toughie (*also* toughy); dilemma, quandary; catch, glitch, hitch, pitfall, snag; conundrum, enigma, mystery, puzzle, puzzlement, riddle; brainteaser, poser, stumper
near antonyms magic bullet, silver bullet; cure-all, panacea
antonyms answer, solution
2 an interrogative expression often used to test knowledge ⟨There were only 10 *problems* on the exam, but they were all challenging.⟩ — see QUESTION 1

problematic *also* **problematical** *adj* **1** requiring exceptional skill or caution in performance or handling ⟨the *problematic* situation of having two wedding invitations for the same date⟩ — see TRICKY 1
2 giving good reason for being doubted, questioned, or challenged ⟨Whether we should even bother finishing the project at this point is *problematic*.⟩ — see DOUBTFUL 2

procedure *n* **1** a usually fixed or ordered series of actions or events leading to a result ⟨followed the *procedure* for replacing the broken part exactly as the owner's manual instructed⟩ — see PROCESS 1
2 a way of acting or proceeding ⟨followed standard *procedure* for dealing with a consumer complaint⟩ — see COURSE 1

proceed *vb* to move forward along a course ⟨You may *proceed* with your plan.⟩ — see GO 1

proceed (along) *vb* to make one's way through, across, or over ⟨The hikers *proceeded along* the ridge for several hundred feet.⟩ — see TRAVERSE

proceeding *adj* being in progress or development ⟨Currently *proceeding* projects include construction of a new school gym.⟩ — see ONGOING 1

proceeding *n* **1** a court case for enforcing a right or claim ⟨a bankruptcy *proceeding*⟩ — see LAWSUIT

2 a usually fixed or ordered series of actions or events leading to a result ⟨This is not the haphazard *proceeding* that it may seem to the casual observer.⟩ — see PROCESS 1

proceeds *pl n* **1** an increase usually measured in money that comes from labor, business, or property ⟨estimated that the annual *proceeds* from an increase in the state sales tax would be enormous⟩ — see INCOME 1

2 the amount of money left when expenses are subtracted from the total amount received ⟨All *proceeds* from the special promotion will go to charity.⟩ — see PROFIT 1

process *n* **1** a usually fixed or ordered series of actions or events leading to a result ⟨the *process* by which the elastic fibers spun by silkworms are turned into soft, lustrous cloth⟩

synonyms course, operation, procedure, proceeding

related words drill, routine; fashion, form, manner, method, mode, style, system, technique, way; approach, arrangement, blueprint, design, formula, ground plan, layout, plan, plot, program, project, scheme, strategy

2 forward movement in time or place ⟨In the *process* of doing this project we all learned a lot.⟩ — see ADVANCE 1

procession *n* **1** a body of individuals moving along in an orderly and often ceremonial way ⟨a *procession* of mourners leaving the cemetery⟩ — see CORTEGE 2

2 forward movement in time or place ⟨watched the constant *procession* of cars headed out of the city at the start of the weekend⟩ — see ADVANCE 1

proclaim *vb* to make known openly or publicly ⟨loudly *proclaimed* her innocence⟩ — see ANNOUNCE

proclivity *n* a habitual attraction to some activity or thing ⟨The boy showed artistic *proclivities* at an early age.⟩ — see INCLINATION 1

procreate *vb* to bring forth offspring ⟨Animals have a natural instinct to *procreate*.⟩

synonyms breed, multiply, propagate, reproduce

related words bear, beget, engender, gender, generate, get, have, mother, parent, produce, sire; hatch, spawn

procurable *adj* possible to get ⟨The necessary ingredients should be *procurable* at almost any grocery store.⟩ — see AVAILABLE 1

procurator *n* a person who acts or does business for another ⟨He was appointed *procurator* of the church and was responsible for all of the financial arrangements.⟩ — see AGENT 2

procure *vb* to receive as return for effort ⟨a reputation for integrity and incorruptibility that has *procured* for him the universal respect and admiration of his colleagues⟩ — see EARN 1

prod *vb* **1** to urge or push forward with or as if with a pointed object ⟨The boy kept *prodding* the sheep with a staff to get them to move along faster.⟩

synonyms dig, goad, spur

related words chuck, jab, jog, knock, nudge, poke; bore, drill, perforate, pierce, prick, punch, puncture, stab, stick; drive, hale, propel

2 to try to persuade (someone) through earnest appeals to follow a course of action ⟨A public outcry eventually *prodded* the politicians into action.⟩ — see URGE

prodigal *adj* given to spending money freely or foolishly ⟨The *prodigal* child always spent her allowance the minute she got it.⟩

synonyms extravagant, profligate, spendthrift, squandering, thriftless, unthrifty, wasteful

related words improvident, myopic, shortsighted; unselfish, unsparing; careless, heedless, imprudent, incautious, injudicious, unwise; indulgent, reckless, splurging, wanton

near antonyms cheap, close, closefisted, mean, niggardly, parsimonious, penurious, pinching, spare, sparing, stingy, stinting, tight, tightfisted; careful, judicious, prudent, sensible, wise; farsighted, forehanded, foreseeing, foresighted, provident

antonyms conserving, economical, economizing, frugal, scrimping, skimping, thrifty

prodigal *n* someone who spends money freely or foolishly ⟨The million-dollar lottery winner was such a *prodigal* that his windfall was exhausted after only a few years.⟩

synonyms fritterer, profligate, spender, spendthrift, squanderer, waster, wastrel

related words dissipate

near antonyms cheapskate, miser, niggard, piker, scrooge, skinflint, tightwad; conserver, saver

antonyms economizer

prodigality *n* **1** an instance of spending money or resources without care or restraint ⟨His purchase of a new yacht was only one of a series of reckless *prodigalities*.⟩ — see WASTE 1

2 the quality or fact of being free or wasteful in the expenditure of money ⟨His *prodigality* eventually turned him into a pauper.⟩ — see EXTRAVAGANCE 1

prodigious *adj* **1** causing wonder or astonishment ⟨stage magicians performing *prodigious* feats for rapt audiences⟩ — see MARVELOUS 1

2 unusually large ⟨a *prodigious* supply of canned food kept in the basement for emergencies⟩ — see HUGE

prodigy *n* something extraordinary or surprising ⟨a new drug that is being hailed as the latest *prodigy* of the medical world⟩ — see WONDER 1

produce *n* something produced by physical or intellectual effort ⟨a book that was the *produce* of a lifetime of study on the subject⟩ — see PRODUCT 1

produce *vb* **1** to be the cause of (a situation, action, or state of mind) ⟨Hopefully, the new approach to securing websites will *produce* better results.⟩ — see EFFECT

2 to bring forth from the womb ⟨Rabbits can potentially *produce* many offspring at once.⟩ — see BEAR 1

3 to bring into being by combining, shaping, or transforming materials ⟨a factory *producing* steel⟩ — see MAKE 1

4 to present so as to invite notice or attention ⟨He *produced* his brand-new driver's license at every possible opportunity.⟩ — see SHOW 1

product *n* **1** something produced by physical or intellectual effort ⟨That biography is the *product* of years of work.⟩ ⟨a rebuilt car which is the *product* of several people's labor⟩

synonyms affair, fruit, handiwork, labor, output, produce, production, thing, work, yield

related words article, entry, object; goods, line, merchandise, wares; handcraft, handicraft; aftereffect, aftermath, conclusion, consequence, corollary, development, effect, issue, outcome, result, resultant, sequel, sequence, upshot; by-product, derivative, offshoot, offspring, outgrowth, residual, side effect (*also* side reaction), spin-off

2 a condition or occurrence traceable to a cause ⟨Her relentless ambition is a *product* of her home environment.⟩ — see EFFECT 1

production *n* something produced by physical or intellectual effort ⟨the total *production* of one week's intensive labor⟩ — see PRODUCT 1

productive *adj* **1** having a role in deciding something's final form ⟨Joe contributed several *productive* ideas to the project.⟩ — see FORMATIVE

2 producing abundantly ⟨Overfishing has depleted the stock of fish in these waters, which were once so *productive*.⟩ — see FERTILE

3 producing or capable of producing a desired result

⟨Panicking during a crisis is not *productive* behavior.⟩ — see EFFECTIVE 1

productiveness *n* the power to produce a desired result ⟨the prodigious *productiveness* of the nation's shipyards during World War II⟩ — see EFFICACY

profane *adj* 1 not involving religion or religious matters ⟨It was hard to juggle the requirements of church and our more *profane* duties.⟩

synonyms nonreligious, secular, temporal

related words atheistic, godless, irreligious, pagan, paganish, religionless; lay, nonclerical; nondenominational, nonsectarian; earthly, mundane, worldly; material, physical, substantial; bodily, carnal, corporal, fleshly; blasphemous, impious, irreverent, sacrilegious; unconsecrated, unhallowed

near antonyms divine, spiritual; consecrated, hallowed, holy, sacrosanct, sanctified; churchly, devout, godly, pious, prayerful, reverent, worshipful; ethereal, insubstantial, metaphysical, unsubstantial

antonyms religious, sacred

2 not showing proper reverence for the holy or sacred ⟨offended by the *profane* language that her coworkers used so casually⟩ — see IRREVERENT

profane *vb* 1 to lower in character, dignity, or quality ⟨The once-lovely landscape had been *profaned* by ugly factories.⟩ — see DEBASE 1

2 to put to a bad or improper use ⟨*profaned* his considerable acting talents by appearing in some wretched movies⟩ — see MISAPPLY

3 to treat (a sacred place or object) shamefully or with great disrespect ⟨Invading troops *profaned* the altar by playing poker on it.⟩ — see DESECRATE

profess *vb* 1 to present a false appearance of ⟨*professed* friendship while secretly plotting revenge⟩ — see FEIGN

2 to state clearly and strongly ⟨The woman *professed* her love in a series of letters to her husband deployed overseas.⟩ — see ASSERT 1

3 to state as a fact usually forcefully ⟨He *professed* his innocence to anyone who would listen.⟩ — see CLAIM 1

profession *n* 1 a solemn and often public declaration of the truth or existence of something ⟨the weekly *profession* of faith by the members of the congregation⟩ — see PROTESTATION

2 the activity by which one regularly makes a living ⟨A gifted communicator, he was very good at his chosen *profession*: teaching.⟩ — see OCCUPATION

proffer *n* something which is presented for consideration ⟨a generous *proffer* of his baronial estate for the charity gala⟩ — see PROPOSAL

proffer *vb* 1 to put before another for acceptance or consideration ⟨*proffered* his assistance in helping the two sides reach a compromise⟩ — see OFFER 1

2 to set before the mind for consideration ⟨*proffered* a novel solution for getting themselves out of debt⟩ — see PROPOSE 1

proficiency *n* 1 a highly developed skill in or knowledge of something ⟨surprised by his *proficiency* at the game after only the briefest explanation of the rules⟩ — see COMMAND 2

2 knowledge gained by actually doing or living through something ⟨Will acquired *proficiency* at golf through long hours of practice.⟩ — see EXPERIENCE 1

proficient *adj* having or showing exceptional knowledge, experience, or skill in a field of endeavor ⟨She is quite *proficient* at computer repair.⟩ ⟨a *proficient* rendition of a difficult piano piece.⟩

synonyms accomplished, ace, adept, complete, consummate, crack, crackerjack, educated, experienced, expert,

good, great, master, masterful, masterly, practiced (*also* practised), skilled, skillful, versed, veteran, virtuoso

related words adroit, clever, deft, dexterous (*also* dextrous), handy, sure-handed; gifted, talented; polished, refined; effective, effectual, efficient, workmanlike; able, capable, competent, fit, fitted, qualified; educated, knowledgeable, schooled, taught, trained, tutored; all-around (*also* all-round), well-rounded; multiskilled, multitalented

near antonyms incapable, incompetent, inept, unfit, unqualified, weak; artless, crude, rude; ineffective, ineffectual, inefficient; talentless, ungifted, untalented; ignorant, unschooled, untaught, untrained, untutored; beginning, green, inexperienced, new, raw, unseasoned, untested, untried, would-be; primitive, rough, unpolished; awkward, clumsy, heavy-handed

antonyms amateur, amateurish, inexperienced, inexpert, unprofessional, unseasoned, unskilled, unskillful

proficiently *adv* in a skillful or expert manner ⟨an administrator who can deal with the problems quickly and *proficiently*⟩ — see WELL 3

profit *n* 1 the amount of money left when expenses are subtracted from the total amount received ⟨After we deducted the cost of sugar, lemons, and paper cups, the *profit* from a day of lemonade sales was about $20.⟩

synonyms earnings, gain, lucre, net, payoff, proceeds, return

related words cleanup, windfall; gross, sales; compensation, emolument, income, pay, payment, remittal, requital, salary, wages; interest, return, revenue, yield

near antonyms charge, cost, disbursement, expenditure, expense, loss, outgo, outlay

2 an increase usually measured in money that comes from labor, business, or property ⟨She found that there was a *profit* in training dogs for rich people.⟩ — see INCOME 1

profit *vb* to provide with something useful or desirable ⟨an agreement that *profited* us all⟩ — see BENEFIT

profitable *adj* 1 yielding a profit ⟨Selling real estate on the side turned out to be a *profitable* venture.⟩

synonyms fat, gainful, lucrative, paying, remunerative

related words advantageous, beneficial, favorable, rewarding, useful, worthwhile; bankable

near antonyms disadvantageous, unfavorable

antonyms unprofitable

2 promoting or contributing to personal or social well-being ⟨I have always found honesty to be a *profitable* course of action.⟩ — see BENEFICIAL

profitless *adj* producing no results ⟨Trying to reason with her is always a *profitless* enterprise.⟩ — see FUTILE

profligacy *n* immoral conduct or practices harmful or offensive to society ⟨a religious leader who railed against the *profligacy* of the nation's decadent aristocrats⟩ — see VICE 1

profligate *adj* given to spending money freely or foolishly ⟨*profligate* movie producers hoping to create the next blockbuster⟩ — see PRODIGAL

profligate *n* 1 someone who spends money freely or foolishly ⟨In the early 1900s, fans didn't care that Babe Ruth was a *profligate*, as long as he kept making runs.⟩ — see PRODIGAL

2 a person who has sunk below the normal moral standard ⟨Friends of the *profligate* tried to help him change his ways.⟩ — see DEGENERATE

profound *adj* 1 difficult for one of ordinary knowledge or intelligence to understand ⟨a *profound* observation about good and evil that few listeners fully grasped⟩

synonyms abstruse, deep, esoteric, recondite

related words erudite, learned, scholarly; academic (*also* academical), pedantic; complex, complicated, hard; darkling, enigmatic (*also* enigmatical), inscrutable, mysterious, mystic, mystical, uncanny; impenetrable, incomprehensible, unfathomable, unintelligible; ambiguous, cryptic; unanswerable, unknowable; baffling, bewildering, confounding, confusing, disorienting, mystifying, perplexing, puzzling

near antonyms easy, facile, simple, straightforward; apparent, clear, clear-cut, distinct, evident, lucid, manifest, obvious, perspicuous, plain, transparent

antonyms shallow, superficial

2 extreme in degree, power, or effect ⟨A *profound* silence fell over the audience after the last note had sounded.⟩ — see INTENSE 1

3 having no exceptions or restrictions ⟨a *profound* dislike of frauds and phonies⟩ — see ABSOLUTE 2

4 extending far downward ⟨With eyes wide with disbelief, the explorers made their way through a canyon more *profound* than any they had ever imagined.⟩ — see DEEP 1

profoundness *n* the quality of being great in extent (as of insight) ⟨We were struck by the *profoundness* of his observations on the ultimate meaning of life.⟩ — see DEPTH 2

profundity *n* the quality of being great in extent (as of insight) ⟨a philosopher who is widely respected for the *profundity* of her thinking⟩ — see DEPTH 2

profuse *adj* pouring forth in great amounts ⟨We received *profuse* thanks for our efforts.⟩ ⟨a *profuse* rush of water from the collapsing dike⟩

synonyms copious, galore, gushing, lavish, riotous

related words abounding, abundant, ample, bounteous, bountiful, liberal, plenteous, plentiful; extravagant, luxuriant; fat, fecund, fertile; free, munificent, openhanded, unsparing; excessive, immoderate, redundant; adequate, enough, sufficient

near antonyms meager (*or* meagre), niggardly, poor, scant, scanty, spare, sparse, stingy; deficient, inadequate, incomplete, insufficient, lacking, scarce, unsatisfactory, wanting; bare, mere, minimal

antonyms dribbling, trickling

profusion *n* **1** a considerable amount ⟨Apples grow in *profusion* in this valley.⟩ — see LOT 2

2 the quality or fact of being free or wasteful in the expenditure of money ⟨In giving gifts, he was generous to the point of *profusion*.⟩ — see EXTRAVAGANCE 1

progeny *n* the descendants of a person, animal, or plant ⟨The rancher carefully examined the *progeny* of the new breed of cattle.⟩ — see OFFSPRING

prognosis *n* a declaration that something will happen in the future ⟨the securities analyst's *prognosis* for the stock market in the new year⟩ — see PREDICTION

prognosticate *vb* to tell of or describe beforehand ⟨using current trends to *prognosticate* what the workplace of the future will be like⟩ — see FORETELL

prognostication *n* **1** a declaration that something will happen in the future ⟨The complete fulfillment of his *prognostication* surprised even him.⟩ — see PREDICTION

2 a feeling that something bad will happen ⟨At the sight of the brooding mansion, her *prognostications* of ill fortune grew stronger.⟩ — see PREMONITION

prognosticator *n* one who predicts future events or developments ⟨one of the best *prognosticators* in the weather business⟩ — see PROPHET 1

program *n* **1** a listing of things to be presented or considered (as at a concert or play) ⟨The *program* will tell us the scheduled order of musical numbers.⟩

synonyms agenda, calendar, docket, schedule, timetable

related words card, dance card, exercises, plate; arrangement, order, ordering, organization, sequence, set-up

phrases bill of fare

2 a method worked out in advance for achieving some objective ⟨We need to come up with a *program* to retrain our workforce.⟩ — see PLAN 1

3 a way of acting or proceeding ⟨recommends a *program* of regular dental checkups⟩ — see COURSE 1

progress *n* **1** forward movement in time or place ⟨We're making slow *progress* against this stiff headwind.⟩ — see ADVANCE 1

2 the act or process of going from the simple or basic to the complex or advanced ⟨the rapid *progress* of medical science in the last century⟩ — see DEVELOPMENT 1

progress *vb* **1** to become mature ⟨Generally a species *progresses* from simple forms to more specialized forms.⟩ — see MATURE

2 to move forward along a course ⟨Our wedding plans are *progressing* nicely.⟩ — see GO 1

progression *n* **1** a series of things linked together ⟨a *progression* of events that ended in utter disaster for the arctic explorers⟩ — see CHAIN 1

2 forward movement in time or place ⟨Our *progression* was slow but steady.⟩ — see ADVANCE 1

3 the act or process of going from the simple or basic to the complex or advanced ⟨that civilization's gradual *progression* from simple bartering to a complex economy and monetary system⟩ — see DEVELOPMENT 1

progressive *adj* **1** being far along in development ⟨*progressive* forms of animal life⟩ — see ADVANCED

2 not bound by traditional ways or beliefs ⟨a *progressive* community that favored the educational reforms⟩ — see LIBERAL 1

prohibit *vb* to order not to do or use or to be done or used ⟨The city *prohibits* swimming in the lake after dark.⟩ — see FORBID

prohibited *adj* that may not be permitted ⟨There will be no toleration for smoking and other *prohibited* activities.⟩ — see IMPERMISSIBLE

prohibiting *n* the act of ordering that something not be done or used ⟨Not surprisingly, the *prohibiting* of the use of cell phones proved to be unpopular with patients visiting the doctor.⟩ — see PROHIBITION 1

prohibition *n* **1** the act of ordering that something not be done or used ⟨The principal's *prohibition* against the use of cell phones in the school building met with unanimous approval by the teachers.⟩

synonyms banning, barring, enjoining, forbidding, interdicting, interdiction, outlawing, prohibiting, proscribing, proscription

related words bidding, charging, decreeing, dictation, direction, instruction; deterrence, discouragement, dissuading; repression, suppression; coercion, compulsion, constraint, force

near antonyms allowance, permission, sufferance, toleration; approval, endorsement (*also* indorsement); authorization, clearance, license (*or* licence), sanction; encouragement, promotion, support; compliance, obedience, submission

2 an order that something not be done or used ⟨The city issued a *prohibition* against parking on the street during snowstorms.⟩

synonyms ban, embargo, interdict, interdiction, proscription, veto

related words no-no, taboo (*also* tabu); constraint, inhibition, limitation, restraint, restriction; deterrent, discouragement; repression, suppression; prevention; denial, disallowance, negation, refusal, rejection; objection, protest; caveat, warning; commandment, decree, dictate, edict, mandate

near antonyms sufferance, tolerance, toleration; allowance, allowing, authorization, clearance, consent, granting, leave, letting, license (*or* licence), licensing (*also* licencing), permission, permitting, sanction, sanctioning; approbation, approval, blessing, endorsement (*also* indorsement), imprimatur, OK (*or* okay); enabling, encouragement, facilitation, promotion, support; compliance, obedience, submission; acquiescence, agreement, assent

project *n* a method worked out in advance for achieving some objective ⟨an ambitious *project* to develop the city's waterfront⟩ — see PLAN 1

project *vb* **1** to extend outward beyond a usual point ⟨Some boulders *projected* dangerously out above the trail.⟩ — see BULGE 1

2 to work out the details of (something) in advance ⟨We must *project* next year's budget now.⟩ — see PLAN 1

projection *n* a part that sticks out from the general mass of something ⟨filed down all the *projections* until the surface was smooth⟩ — see BULGE 1

proletarian *adj* belonging to the class of people of low social or economic rank ⟨a self-made Internet magnate who is not at all ashamed of his *proletarian* background⟩ — see IGNOBLE 1

proletariat *n* people looked down upon as ignorant and of the lowest class ⟨The Bolsheviks believed that Russia's discontented *proletariat* made that nation ripe for revolution.⟩ — see RABBLE

proliferate *vb* to become greater in extent, volume, amount, or number ⟨Rumors about the incident *proliferated* on the Internet.⟩ — see INCREASE 2

proliferation *n* **1** something added (as by growth) ⟨A large *proliferation* in the number of electrical appliances was placing enormous demands upon the region's power supply.⟩ — see INCREASE 1

2 the act or process of becoming greater in number ⟨the *proliferation* of mistakes as both actors and crew became more and more tired⟩ — see MULTIPLICATION

prolific *adj* producing abundantly ⟨a famously *prolific* author who could produce several works of fiction and nonfiction a year⟩ — see FERTILE

prolix *adj* using or containing more words than necessary to express an idea ⟨a person known for habitually transforming brief anecdotes into *prolix* sagas that exhaust their listeners⟩ — see WORDY 1

prolixity *n* the use of too many words to express an idea ⟨*Prolixity* is one of the worst offenses that a writer of any age can commit.⟩ — see VERBIAGE 1

prologue *also* **prolog** *n* **1** a performance, activity, or event that precedes and sets the stage for the main event ⟨incidents that were a *prologue* to the American Revolution⟩ — see PRELUDE 1

2 a short section (as of a book) that leads to or explains the main part ⟨A brief *prologue* sets the scene for the story that follows.⟩ — see INTRODUCTION

prolong *vb* to make longer ⟨We would like to *prolong* our vacation by any means possible.⟩ — see EXTEND 1

prolongation *n* the act of making longer ⟨the indefinite *prolongation* of the cease-fire⟩ — see EXTENSION 1

prolonging *n* the act of making longer ⟨his habitual *prolonging* of any task so that it fills up an entire afternoon⟩ — see EXTENSION 1

prom *n* a social gathering for dancing ⟨He resolved to ask her to the school *prom* at the first opportunity.⟩ — see DANCE

prominence *n* an area of high ground ⟨a rocky *prominence* that commands a stunning view of the surrounding area⟩ — see HEIGHT 4

prominent *adj* **1** likely to attract attention ⟨an attorney who occupies a *prominent* position in the town⟩ — see NOTICEABLE

2 widely known ⟨*prominent* figures in the history of sports⟩ — see FAMOUS 1

promiscuous *adj* consisting of many things of different sorts ⟨Since I just collect stamps that I happen to like, my collection is pretty *promiscuous*.⟩ — see MISCELLANEOUS

promise *n* a person's solemn declaration that he or she will do or not do something ⟨He made a *promise* to arrive on time.⟩
synonyms oath, pledge, troth, vow, word
related words appointment, arrangement, commitment, engagement, obligation; agreement, compact, contract, covenant; assurance, guarantee, guaranty, undertaking; bond, deposit, gage, pawn, security, token, warranty

promise *vb* **1** to make a solemn declaration of intent ⟨They *promised* to keep in touch with us after they moved away.⟩
synonyms covenant, pledge, swear, vow
related words affiance, betroth, plight, troth; accede, agree, assent, consent; contract, engage, ensure, guarantee, undertake; affirm, assert, aver, avouch, avow, declare, insist, warrant
phrases give one's word

2 to show signs of a favorable or successful outcome ⟨Given the cast, the new sitcom *promises* to be an excellent show.⟩ — see BODE

promised land *n* an often imaginary place or state of utter perfection and happiness ⟨I finally realized that the *promised land* doesn't exist.⟩ — see PARADISE 1

promising *adj* **1** having qualities which inspire hope ⟨a *promising* writer who just may write the great American novel someday⟩ — see HOPEFUL 1

2 pointing toward a happy outcome ⟨All the signs for the new business are *promising*.⟩ — see FAVORABLE 2

promontory *n* **1** an area of high ground jutting out into a body of water beyond the line of the coast ⟨stood on the windswept *promontory* overlooking the bay⟩ — see HEADLAND 1

2 an area of land that juts out into a body of water ⟨Cape May is Delaware Bay's largest *promontory*.⟩ — see ²CAPE

promote *vb* **1** to move higher in rank or position ⟨The navy *promoted* her to captain for her record of outstanding performance.⟩
synonyms advance, elevate, raise, upgrade
related words forward, further; aggrandize, boost, heighten, improve, lift, uplift; commission, ennoble, knight; acclaim, applaud, celebrate, cite, commend, compliment, congratulate, decorate; eulogize, exalt, extol (*also* extoll), glorify, hail, honor, laud, praise, salute
phrases kick upstairs
near antonyms depose, dethrone, dismiss, expel, impeach, oust, overthrow, remove, unmake, unseat; demean, disgrace, dishonor, humble, humiliate, mortify, shame, take down; censure, condemn, denounce
antonyms abase, degrade, demote, downgrade, lower, reduce

2 to help the growth or development of ⟨a campaign *promoting* good dental hygiene⟩ — see FOSTER 1

3 to look after or assist the growth of by labor and care ⟨Meg spends all her time now *promoting* her new business.⟩ — see GROW 1

4 to provide publicity for ⟨*promoting* a new line of toys based on the popular movie⟩ — see PUBLICIZE 1

promoter *n* a person who actively supports or favors a cause ⟨a *promoter* of greater understanding and cooperation among churches⟩ — see EXPONENT 1

promotion *n* a raising or a state of being raised to a higher rank or position ⟨After 10 years at the company he was rewarded with a *promotion* to vice president.⟩ — see ADVANCEMENT 1

prompt *adj* **1** done, carried out, or given without delay ⟨*Prompt* treatment of snakebites is always advisable.⟩
synonyms immediate, punctual, speedy, timely
related words apt, quick, ready, swift, willing; opportune, seasonable; early
near antonyms delinquent, latish, overdue; behind, behindhand, delayed, detained; dilatory, laggard, slow
antonyms belated, late, tardy
2 having or showing the ability to respond without delay or hesitation ⟨Our waiter was *prompt* and courteous despite the fact that the restaurant was understaffed.⟩ — see QUICK 1

prompt *vb* **1** to be the cause of (a situation, action, or state of mind) ⟨Curiosity *prompted* her to ask a few questions.⟩ — see EFFECT
2 to try to persuade (someone) through earnest appeals to follow a course of action ⟨*prompted* the reluctant performer onto the stage with loud cheers and whistles⟩ — see URGE

promptitude *n* the quality or habit of arriving or being ready on time ⟨His chronic tardiness has put him in poor standing with his boss, who values hustle and *promptitude*.⟩
synonyms promptness, punctuality, timeliness
related words alacrity, aptness, quickness, readiness, willingness; earliness, prematurity
near antonyms belatedness, lateness; slowness
antonyms tardiness, unpunctuality

promptly *adv* without delay ⟨I shipped the package *promptly* so that it would arrive on time.⟩ — see IMMEDIATELY

promptness *n* the quality or habit of arriving or being ready on time ⟨The *promptness* of the local bus line has always been reassuring.⟩ — see PROMPTITUDE

promulgate *vb* to make known openly or publicly ⟨a story widely *promulgated* on the Internet⟩ — see ANNOUNCE

prone *adj* **1** having a tendency to be or act in a certain way ⟨He was *prone* to emotional outbursts under stress.⟩
synonyms apt, given, inclined, tending
related words choosing, preferring; disposed, liable, likely, minded, predisposed, willing
near antonyms averse, disinclined, indisposed, loath (*also* loth *or* loathe), unwilling
2 lying with the face downwards ⟨He was in a *prone* position on the floor.⟩
synonyms prostrate
related words flat, recumbent; reclining, reposing; horizontal
near antonyms erect, raised, standing, upright, upstanding, vertical
antonyms supine

proneness *n* an established pattern of behavior ⟨The quarterback's *proneness* to injury has prompted team owners to offer him less lucrative terms on his new contract.⟩ — see TENDENCY 1

pronounced *adj* **1** likely to attract attention ⟨a *pronounced* tendency to slurp her soup⟩ — see NOTICEABLE
2 very noticeable especially for being incorrect or bad ⟨walking with a *pronounced* limp⟩ — see EGREGIOUS

pronto *adv* **1** with great speed ⟨If they don't arrive *pronto*, we'll have to go to the movie without them.⟩ — see FAST 1
2 without delay ⟨the kind of boss who wants everything *pronto*⟩ — see IMMEDIATELY

proof *n* something presented in support of the truth or accuracy of a claim ⟨She presented *proof* that she had not cheated.⟩
synonyms attestation, confirmation, corroboration, documentation, evidence, substantiation, testament, testimony, validation, witness

related words (the) goods; certificate, document, exhibit; demonstration, illustration; authentication, identification, manifestation, verification
near antonyms rebuttal, refutation; accusation, allegation, charge; assumption, conjecture, guess, presumption, surmise, suspicion
antonyms disproof

prop (up) *vb* **1** to hold up or serve as a foundation for ⟨These beams are *propping up* the entire roof.⟩ — see SUPPORT 3
2 to provide (someone) with what is useful or necessary to achieve an end ⟨Invariably his strong religious faith *props* him *up* in times of crisis.⟩ — see HELP 1

propagate *vb* **1** to bring forth offspring ⟨The dams along the river are interfering with the salmon's ability to *propagate*.⟩ — see PROCREATE
2 to cause to be known over a considerable area or by many people ⟨the various ways in which candidates can *propagate* their positions on the issues⟩ — see SPREAD 1

propel *vb* **1** to apply force to (someone or something) so that it moves in front of one ⟨Playfully he *propelled* his rambunctious friend into the swimming pool to cool him off.⟩ — see PUSH 1
2 to set or keep in motion ⟨The aircraft is *propelled* by a pair of turboprop engines.⟩ — see MOVE 2

propensity *n* **1** an established pattern of behavior ⟨The family's *propensity* for athleticism extended over several generations.⟩ — see TENDENCY 1
2 a habitual attraction to some activity or thing ⟨a neighbor who has an unfortunate *propensity* for snooping⟩ — see INCLINATION 1

proper *adj* **1** following the established traditions of refined society and good taste ⟨The formal ball called for *proper* attire—tuxedos and full-length gowns only.⟩
synonyms befitting, correct, decent, decorous, genteel, nice, polite, respectable, seemly
related words acceptable, adequate, satisfactory, tolerable; dress, dressy, formal; dignified, elegant, gracious; priggish, prim, stiff, stuffy; apt, material, relevant; allowed, authorized, kosher, permitted
near antonyms intolerable, unacceptable, unsatisfactory; casual, grungy, informal; seedy, shabby, tacky; banned, barred, disallowed; forbidden, interdicted, outlawed, prohibited, proscribed
antonyms improper, inappropriate, incorrect, indecent, indecorous, unbecoming, ungenteel, unseemly
2 being in agreement with the truth or a fact or a standard ⟨There is really more than one *proper* way to pronounce that word in English.⟩ — see CORRECT 1
3 marked by or showing careful attention to set forms and details ⟨We had nodded and said hello to one another but had never had a *proper* introduction.⟩ — see CEREMONIOUS 1
4 meeting the requirements of a purpose or situation ⟨You'll need to have a *proper* diet if you want to lose weight.⟩ — see FIT 1
5 serving to identify as belonging to an individual or group ⟨malaria and other diseases that are *proper* to the tropics⟩ — see CHARACTERISTIC 1

properly *adv* in a manner suitable for the occasion or purpose ⟨The scouts were *properly* dressed for a week of camping.⟩
synonyms appropriately, congruously, correctly, fittingly, happily, meetly, right, rightly, suitably
related words well; acceptably, adequately, passably, satisfactorily, tolerably; decorously
near antonyms unacceptably, unsatisfactorily; inopportunely, unfortunately, unseasonably
antonyms improperly, inappropriately, incongruously, incorrectly, unseemly, unsuitably, wrongly

property *n* **1** a small piece of land that is developed or available for development ⟨We bought a secluded *property* in the mountains.⟩ — see LOT 1
2 something that sets apart an individual from others of the same kind ⟨The ability to be magnetized is a common *property* of metals.⟩ — see CHARACTERISTIC
prophecy *also* **prophesy** *n* a declaration that something will happen in the future ⟨The report on climate change included alarming *prophecies* of rising sea levels and increased storm activity.⟩ — see PREDICTION
prophesier *n* one who predicts future events or developments ⟨a *prophesier* of good things for the team in the coming season⟩ — see PROPHET 1
prophesy *vb* to tell of or describe beforehand ⟨The book claims that modern events were *prophesied* in ancient times.⟩ — see FORETELL
prophet *n* **1** one who predicts future events or developments ⟨an economist who is regarded by many as a reliable *prophet* of future developments in the global economy⟩
synonyms augur, diviner, forecaster, foreseer, foreteller, fortune-teller, futurist, prognosticator, prophesier, seer, soothsayer, visionary
related words prophetess, sibyl; mystic, oracle
2 a person who speaks for another or for a group ⟨In the 1960s Timothy Leary gained fame as the *prophet* of the psychedelic movement.⟩ — see SPOKESPERSON
prophetic *also* **prophetical** *adj* being a sign of a later course of events ⟨In retrospect, those lower-than-expected sales numbers were a *prophetic* indicator of the financial trouble the company would soon be in.⟩
synonyms predictive
related words baleful, dire, foreboding, menacing, portentous, sinister, threatening; inauspicious, unpromising; oracular; revelatory, telling
near antonyms auspicious, promising, propitious, rosy
propitiate *vb* to lessen the anger or agitation of ⟨The temple was once the site of sacrifices—both to honor the gods in times of plenty and to *propitiate* them in times of trouble.⟩ — see PACIFY 1
propitiatory *adj* tending to lessen or avoid conflict or hostility ⟨sent her flowers as a *propitiatory* gesture⟩ — see PACIFIC 1
propitious *adj* **1** having qualities which inspire hope ⟨The success of the first big movie in May was a *propitious* start for the summer season of blockbusters.⟩ — see HOPEFUL 1
2 pointing toward a happy outcome ⟨a *propitious* time for starting a business⟩ — see FAVORABLE 2
proponent *n* a person who actively supports or favors a cause ⟨a vocal *proponent* of the use of electric-powered cars⟩ — see EXPONENT 1
proportion *n* **1** a balanced, pleasing, or suitable arrangement of parts ⟨The head was drawn too large, being way out of *proportion* with the body.⟩ — see HARMONY 1
2 something belonging to, due to, or contributed by an individual member of a group ⟨The players argue that they aren't getting the *proportion* of the league's profits that are due to them.⟩ — see SHARE 1
3 the relationship in quantity, amount, or size between two or more things ⟨The *proportion* of length to width for those screens was usually three to two.⟩ — see RATIO
4 the total amount of measurable space or surface occupied by something ⟨The exact *proportions* of the room were critical.⟩ — see ¹SIZE
proportional *adj* corresponding in size, amount, extent, or degree ⟨The website's popularity increased exponentially, resulting in a *proportional* increase in advertising revenue.⟩
synonyms commensurate, proportionate

related words balanced, symmetrical (*or* symmetric); reciprocal; contingent, dependent, relative; akin, comparable, similar
phrases in proportion
near antonyms asymmetrical (*or* asymmetric), distorted, irregular, lopsided, nonsymmetrical, twisted, unsymmetrical; unbalanced
antonyms disproportionate
proportionate *adj* corresponding in size, amount, extent, or degree ⟨Expect financial returns *proportionate* to your efforts.⟩ — see PROPORTIONAL
proposal *n* something which is presented for consideration ⟨The city council is accepting *proposals* for ways to use that land.⟩
synonyms offer, proffer, proposition, suggestion
related words counteroffer, counterproposal, countersuggestion; feeler; motion; advancement, nomination, recommendation; bid, presentation, submission, submittal, tender; arrangement, game, ground plan, layout, line, plan, plot, project, strategy, system; conception, idea, notion, theory, thought
propose *vb* **1** to set before the mind for consideration ⟨He *proposed* that we go for a walk this afternoon.⟩
synonyms advance, bounce, offer, pose, proffer, propound, suggest, vote
related words move; recommend; present, submit, tender; file, lay, lodge; arrange, calculate, chart, contrive, cover, frame, map, plan, plot, shape
phrases put forth, put forward
2 to have in mind as a purpose or goal ⟨We *propose* to buy a new house within the next year.⟩ — see INTEND 1
proposition *n* **1** an idea that is the starting point for making a case or conducting an investigation ⟨We started the discussion with the simple *proposition* that no one ever does anything out of pure altruism.⟩ — see THEORY
2 something which is presented for consideration ⟨a neighbor with a business *proposition* to tell us about⟩ — see PROPOSAL
propound *vb* to set before the mind for consideration ⟨Her new book expands on the theory *propounded* in her first book.⟩ — see PROPOSE 1
proprietor *n* one who has a legal or rightful claim to ownership ⟨the *proprietor* of a used-car dealership⟩
synonyms holder, owner, possessor
related words co-owner, coproprietor; landlord, landowner
near antonyms squatter; renter, tenant
propriety *n* **1** socially acceptable behavior ⟨They acted with *propriety*.⟩ — see DECENCY 1
2 **proprieties** *pl* personal conduct or behavior as evaluated by an accepted standard of appropriateness for a social or professional setting ⟨an etiquette columnist who insists that traditional *proprieties* are necessary in order to maintain a civil society⟩ — see MANNER 1
3 the quality or state of being especially suitable or fitting ⟨I'm not sure about the *propriety* of serving champagne in these glasses.⟩ — see APPROPRIATENESS
prorate *vb* to give out (something) to appropriate individuals ⟨Shares in the company's profits were *prorated* according to the workers' length of service.⟩ — see ADMINISTER 1
prosaic *adj* **1** being of the type that is encountered in the normal course of events ⟨an author with a knack for finding something of interest in the most *prosaic* details of suburban life⟩ — see ORDINARY 1
2 having to do with the practical details of regular life ⟨My job at the TV station dealt with the much more *prosaic* business of cleaning the floors.⟩ — see MUNDANE 1
proscribe *vb* to order not to do or use or to be done or

used ⟨Regulations *proscribe* the use of electronic devices on board a plane while it is landing.⟩ — see FORBID

proscribed *adj* that may not be permitted ⟨The organization lost its nonprofit status after it was determined to have engaged in several *proscribed* fund-raising activities.⟩ — see IMPERMISSIBLE

proscribing *n* the act of ordering that something not be done or used ⟨The *proscribing* of the use of alcohol was to be expected.⟩ — see PROHIBITION 1

proscription *n* **1** the act of ordering that something not be done or used ⟨The *proscription* against bicycles and skateboards is intended to make the plaza a more pedestrian-friendly place.⟩ — see PROHIBITION 1
2 an order that something not be done or used ⟨a strongly worded *proscription* against smoking indoors⟩ — see PROHIBITION 2

proselyte *n* a person who has recently been persuaded to join a religious sect ⟨an adult *proselyte* who had only recently been baptized⟩ — see CONVERT 1

proselyte *vb* to persuade to change to one's religious faith ⟨She's been trying to *proselyte* everyone in the office ever since she joined that church.⟩ — see CONVERT 1

proselytize *vb* to persuade to change to one's religious faith ⟨He uses his position to *proselytize* others.⟩ — see CONVERT 1

prospect *n* **1** all that can be seen from a certain point ⟨gazing at the wide *prospect* spread out before me⟩ — see VIEW 1
2 one who seeks an office, honor, position, or award ⟨a good *prospect* for the position of auditor⟩ — see CANDIDATE
3 something that can develop or become actual ⟨One highly desirable *prospect* for the city is a major-league franchise.⟩ — see POTENTIAL

prospect *vb* to go into or range over for purposes of discovery ⟨Soon all manner of people had arrived in the valley to *prospect* it for gold.⟩ — see EXPLORE 2

prosper *vb* **1** to grow vigorously ⟨The plants seem to be *prospering* on the new fertilizers.⟩ — see THRIVE 1
2 to reach a desired level of accomplishment ⟨The company began to *prosper* after years of crushing setbacks.⟩ — see SUCCEED 2

prospering *adj* marked by vigorous growth and well-being especially economically ⟨selling a whole range of luxury products to the *prospering* middle class⟩ — see PROSPEROUS 1

prosperous *adj* **1** marked by vigorous growth and well-being especially economically ⟨a *prosperous* business that will soon be expanding⟩
synonyms booming, flourishing, golden, halcyon, healthy, lush, palmy, prospering, roaring, successful, thriving
related words affluent, moneyed (*also* monied), opulent, rich, substantial, wealthy, well-heeled, well-off, well-to-do; comfortable
near antonyms declining, dying, failing, floundering, languishing, struggling; bankrupt, bankrupted, insolvent
antonyms depressed, unprosperous, unsuccessful
2 having attained a desired end or state of good fortune ⟨one of the most *prosperous* families in the community⟩ — see SUCCESSFUL 1
3 growing thickly and vigorously ⟨Our neighbor has a real green thumb and a yard full of healthy, *prosperous* plants.⟩ — see RANK 1

prostrate *adj* **1** depleted in strength, energy, or freshness ⟨*Prostrate* marathoners typically spend the day after the race recovering.⟩ — see WEARY 1
2 lacking bodily strength ⟨*prostrate* with the heat⟩ — see WEAK 1

3 lying with the face downwards ⟨She was laying *prostrate* on the bed.⟩ — see PRONE 2

prostrate *vb* **1** to diminish the physical strength of ⟨an athlete *prostrated* for weeks by a bout of pneumonia⟩ — see WEAKEN 1
2 to render powerless, ineffective, or unable to move ⟨The huge increase in gas prices really *prostrated* the nation's economic engine.⟩ — see PARALYZE 1
3 to subject to incapacitating emotional or mental stress ⟨a widow *prostrated* by grief⟩ — see OVERWHELM 1
4 to strike (someone) so forcefully as to cause a fall ⟨The boxer bragged that he could *prostrate* any opponent with a single blow.⟩ — see FELL 1

prostrated *adj* lacking bodily strength ⟨Patients should expect to feel very *prostrated* after the surgery.⟩ — see WEAK 1

prostration *n* a complete depletion of energy or strength ⟨an outpatient suffering from fever, *prostration*, and nausea⟩ — see FATIGUE

protean *adj* able to do many different kinds of things ⟨a *protean* actor who is equally comfortable with light comedy and serious drama⟩ — see VERSATILE

protect *vb* to drive danger or attack away from ⟨The mother bear was just trying to *protect* her cubs.⟩ — see DEFEND 1

protection *n* **1** means or method of defending ⟨This small umbrella is adequate *protection* in a sudden shower.⟩ — see DEFENSE 1
2 someone that protects ⟨The bodyguard was her *protection* from overzealous fans.⟩ — see PROTECTOR
3 the state of not being exposed to danger ⟨The open boat offered no *protection* from the weather.⟩ — see SAFETY 1

protective *adj* intended to resist or prevent attack or aggression ⟨The cat drew back its ears and sank into a *protective* posture as the dog approached it.⟩ — see DEFENSIVE

protector *n* someone that protects ⟨saw his older brother as his *protector*⟩
synonyms custodian, defender, guard, guardian, protection
related words bodyguard, champion; lookout, sentinel, sentry, warden, warder, watch, watchdog, watchman; conserver, harborer, keeper, preserver, saver

protest *n* a feeling or declaration of disapproval or dissent ⟨submitted an official *protest* about her treatment⟩ — see OBJECTION

protest *vb* **1** to state as a fact usually forcefully ⟨He *protested* that he usually was very good at baseball, and all the strikeouts were just bad luck.⟩ — see CLAIM 1
2 to present an opposing opinion or argument ⟨plans to *protest* against the judge's ruling regarding admissible evidence⟩ — see OBJECT

protestation *n* a solemn and often public declaration of the truth or existence of something ⟨The governor went on television to make a passionate *protestation* of his innocence in the bribery scandal.⟩
synonyms affirmation, assertion, avouchment, avowal, claim, declaration, insistence, profession
related words allegation; announcement, proclamation, pronouncement; argument, justification, rationalization, reason; confirmation, reaffirmation, reconfirmation, vindication
near antonyms disclaimer; challenge, dispute, question; confutation, disproof, rebuttal, refutation; contradiction, denial, negation
antonyms disavowal

prototype *n* **1** one of a group or collection that shows what the whole is like ⟨a literary character who is universally regarded as the ultimate *prototype* of the spoiled, willful Southern belle⟩ — see EXAMPLE

2 something belonging to an earlier time from which something else was later developed ⟨the Greek epic that is the *prototype* of the hero myth⟩ — see ANCESTOR 2

3 something from which copies are made ⟨The manufacturer exhaustively tested the *prototype* of the vehicle before approving production.⟩ — see ORIGINAL

protract *vb* to make longer ⟨The highway project was *protracted* by years of litigation.⟩ — see EXTEND 1

protrude *vb* to extend outward beyond a usual point ⟨We spotted the kitten's tail *protruding* from beneath the dresser.⟩ — see BULGE 1

protrusion *n* a part that sticks out from the general mass of something ⟨the bizarrely shaped *protrusions* of a coral reef⟩ — see BULGE 1

protuberance *n* a part that sticks out from the general mass of something ⟨The tree trunk had several mossy *protuberances* where branches had once grown.⟩ — see BULGE 1

proud *adj* **1** having or displaying feelings of scorn for what is regarded as beneath oneself ⟨She was too *proud* to accept help from her family.⟩
synonyms disdainful, haughty, highfalutin (*also* hifalutin), lofty, lordly, prideful, superior
related words complacent, conceited, egoistic, egotistic (*also* egotistical), important, self-assertive, self-conceited, self-contented, self-important, self-satisfied, smug, uppity, vain, vainglorious; arrogant, pretentious, stuck-up, supercilious; cavalier, overbearing, overweening, peremptory, swaggering; high-sounding, pompous; condescending, patronizing; cocky, overconfident, presuming, presumptuous; boastful, bombastic, self-glorifying; audacious, bold, brash, brassy, cheeky, cocksure, forward, impertinent, impudent, saucy; confident, presuming, self-assured, self-confident, sure; bossy, domineering, high-handed, imperious; egocentric, self-centered, selfish
near antonyms demure, meek, unassuming, unpretentious; bashful, retiring, shy, timid; diffident, self-doubting; acquiescent, compliant, deferential, resigned, submissive, unassertive, yielding; cowering, cringing, shrinking; passive, quiet, reserved, subdued, unobtrusive
antonyms humble, lowly, modest

2 having too high an opinion of oneself ⟨a *proud* and opinionated person⟩ — see CONCEITED

3 large and impressive in size, grandeur, extent, or conception ⟨The old neighborhood was known for its stately trees and *proud* Victorian houses.⟩ — see GRAND 1

4 having or expressing feelings of joy or triumph ⟨In his acceptance letter he assured his soon-to-be boss that he was *proud* to be joining such a fine company.⟩ — see EXULTANT

provable *adj* capable of being proven as true or real ⟨The police have more than enough evidence to build a *provable* case against the accused.⟩ — see VERIFIABLE

prove *vb* **1** to show the existence or truth of by evidence ⟨The defense attorney used DNA evidence to *prove* the defendant's innocence.⟩
synonyms demonstrate, document, establish, substantiate, validate
related words back (up), buttress, corroborate; evidence, evince, record, support, uphold, witness; adduce, attest, authenticate, certify, identify; confirm, sustain, verify, vouch; clinch, nail, settle
near antonyms challenge, dispute, object; allege, assume, conjecture, guess, presume, surmise, suspect
antonyms disprove, rebut, refute

2 to come to be ⟨The new automobile engine design *proved* impractical.⟩ — see COME OUT 1

3 to gain full recognition or acceptance of ⟨Ruth *proved* herself a great actress on the Broadway stage.⟩ — see ESTABLISH 1

provender *n* substances intended to be eaten ⟨a chef who prides himself on creating all of his dishes from local *provender*⟩ — see FOOD

proverb *n* an often stated observation regarding something from common experience ⟨Her grandfather has a *proverb* for every occasion.⟩ — see SAYING

provide *vb* to put (something) into the possession of someone for use or consumption ⟨This luxury hotel *provides* all the comforts of home to well-heeled vacationers.⟩ — see FURNISH 2

provide (for) *vb* to pay the living expenses of ⟨sufficient income to *provide for* their ever-growing family⟩ — see SUPPORT 2

providence *n* **1** careful management of material resources ⟨Practicing its customary *providence*, the snowbound family was able to make the meager stores last until help arrived.⟩ — see ECONOMY

2 concern or preparation for the future ⟨We had the *providence* to lay in supplies before the storm hit.⟩ — see FORESIGHT 2

3 *cap* the being worshipped as the creator and ruler of the universe ⟨She trusted in *Providence* to see her through the crisis.⟩ — see DEITY 2

provident *adj* **1** careful in the management of money or resources ⟨It is possible to be *provident* without being miserly.⟩ — see FRUGAL

2 having or showing awareness of and preparation for the future ⟨Her *provident* measures kept us safe while we waited out the hurricane.⟩ — see FORESIGHTED

providential *adj* coming or happening by good luck especially unexpectedly ⟨Winning the lottery could not have come at a more *providential* time for the recently laid-off worker.⟩ — see FORTUNATE 1

province *n* a region of activity, knowledge, or influence ⟨a legal question outside the doctor's *province*⟩ — see FIELD 2

provincial *adj* not broad or open in views or opinions ⟨Some people regard a fear of new things as an unmistakable sign of a *provincial* attitude.⟩ — see NARROW 2

provincial *n* an awkward or simple person especially from a small town or the country ⟨The confidence man figured that fleecing these *provincials* would be easy.⟩ — see HICK

provision *n* **1** something upon which the carrying out of an agreement or offer depends ⟨We loaned them the car with the *provision* that they refill the gas tank before returning it.⟩ — see CONDITION 2

2 provisions *pl* substances intended to be eaten ⟨We gave them ample *provisions* so they would not get hungry on the trip.⟩ — see FOOD

provision *vb* **1** to provide (someone) with what is needed for a task or activity ⟨The climbers were sufficiently *provisioned* to withstand just about any mountaineering emergency.⟩ — see FURNISH 1

2 to provide food or meals for ⟨It was the quartermaster's job to properly equip and *provision* the troops.⟩ — see FEED 1

provisional *adj* **1** intended to last, continue, or serve for a limited time ⟨will form a *provisional* government until a new leader can be elected⟩ — see TEMPORARY 1

2 serving in a position for the time being ⟨He was appointed *provisional* executor of the industrialist's vast estate.⟩ — see ACTING

proviso *n* something upon which the carrying out of an agreement or offer depends ⟨I accepted the job with one *proviso*: I would work alone.⟩ — see CONDITION 2

provocation *n* **1** something that arouses a strong response from another ⟨a patient person who gets angry only from the greatest of *provocations*⟩
synonyms excitement, incitement, instigation

related words encouragement, goad, incentive, inducement, jog, prod, spur, stimulant, stimulation, stimulus; enticement, lure; induction, inspiration, motivation; aggravation, annoyance, bother, frustration, hassle, headache, irritant, nuisance, peeve, pest
near antonyms subduing
2 something that arouses action or activity ⟨ready to retaliate at the slightest *provocation*⟩ — see IMPULSE 1
provocative *adj* serving or likely to arouse a strong reaction ⟨a *provocative* editorial that sparked a heated discussion⟩
synonyms charged, edgy, exciting, inciting, instigating, piquing, provoking, stimulating
related words explosive, fiery, incendiary, triggering; inducing, inspirational, inspiring, motivating, motivational, motivative; jeering, taunting, teasing; activating, energizing, galvanizing, quickening, vitalizing; angering, enraging, maddening, upsetting; aggravating, annoying, bothersome, exasperating, galling, irksome, irritating, vexatious, vexing
near antonyms subduing
antonyms noninflammatory
provoke *vb* **1** to rouse to strong feeling or action ⟨The remarks finally *provoked* them to anger.⟩ ⟨Bees generally will not sting unless they are *provoked*.⟩
synonyms arouse, encourage, excite, fire (up), incite, instigate, move, pique, spark, stimulate, stir
related words fan, ignite, inflame (*also* enflame), kindle, trigger; activate, animate, drive, energize, galvanize, induce, inspire, key (up), motivate, quicken, set off, vitalize; abet, ferment, foment, raise, whip (up); anger, enrage, madden, upset; jeer, taunt, tease; annoy, bother, exasperate, gall, irritate, vex
phrases build a fire under
near antonyms calm, soothe, subdue, tranquilize (*also* tranquillize); appease, mollify, pacify, placate
2 to bring (something volatile or intense) into being ⟨rankings that are sure to *provoke* an argument among film buffs⟩ — see INCITE 1
provoking *adj* serving or likely to arouse a strong reaction ⟨The host's *provoking* opinions are the reason why people tune in to his radio talk show in the first place.⟩ — see PROVOCATIVE
proximity *n* the state or condition of being near ⟨The *proximity* of the curtains to the fireplace was a cause of concern for the safety inspector.⟩
synonyms closeness, contiguity, immediacy, nearness
related words abutment, juxtaposition
antonyms distance, remoteness
proxy *n* a person who acts or does business for another ⟨sent a *proxy* to the meeting to cast his vote for him⟩ — see AGENT 2
prude *n* a person who is greatly concerned with seemly behavior and morality especially regarding sexual matters ⟨too much of a *prude* to enjoy the movie⟩
synonyms moralist, puritan
related words moralizer; goody-goody, Goody Two-shoes; fuddy-duddy, old maid, prig
near antonyms libertarian, libertine; misbehaver
prudence *n* **1** a close attentiveness to avoiding danger ⟨You're advised to use some old-fashioned *prudence* when deciding how to manage your finances.⟩ — see CAUTION 1
2 the ability to make intelligent decisions especially in everyday matters ⟨In the long run, *prudence* will pay off more often than taking wild risks.⟩ — see COMMON SENSE
prudent *adj* **1** having or showing good judgment and restraint especially in conduct or speech ⟨Her calm response was very *prudent* under the circumstances.⟩ — see DISCREET 1

2 suitable for bringing about a desired result under the circumstances ⟨It wouldn't be *prudent* to ask for a raise while the company is having financial troubles.⟩ — see EXPEDIENT
3 having or showing deep understanding and intelligent application of knowledge ⟨Her many years of experience as a social worker have made her a *prudent* judge of character.⟩ — see WISE 1
prudery *n* a tendency to care a great deal about seemly behavior and morals especially in sexual matters ⟨the well-known *prudery* of the Victorians⟩
synonyms prudishness, puritanism
related words priggery, priggishness, primness
near antonyms lechery, prurience, pruriency; libertinage; libertarianism
prudish *adj* given to or marked by very conservative standards regarding personal behavior or morals ⟨By the *prudish* standards of the 19th century, the book was scandalous.⟩ — see STRAITLACED
prudishness *n* a tendency to care a great deal about seemly behavior and morals especially in sexual matters ⟨The *prudishness* of the people of the Victorian era was a hindrance to the dissemination of some basic information on human health and hygiene.⟩ — see PRUDERY
prune *vb* to make (something) shorter or smaller with the use of a cutting instrument ⟨I *pruned* the dead branches from the old apple tree.⟩ — see CLIP 1
¹**pry** *vb* **1** to raise, move, or pull apart with or as if with a lever ⟨It took some effort to *pry* up the trap door.⟩
synonyms jimmy, lever, prize
related words elevate, hoist, lift, uplift; break up, detach, disengage, disjoin, divide, part, pull, separate
near antonyms connect, join
2 to draw out by force or with effort ⟨a vain attempt to *pry* the cork out of a wine bottle⟩ — see EXTRACT
²**pry** *vb* to interest oneself in what is not one's concern ⟨Don't go *prying* into other people's business!⟩ — see INTERFERE
prying *adj* **1** interested in what is not one's own business ⟨As we moved into our new home, we could sense that there were *prying* eyes watching us.⟩ — see CURIOUS 1
2 thrusting oneself where one is not welcome or invited ⟨*prying* neighbors who refuse to mind their own business⟩ — see INTRUSIVE
psalm *n* a religious song ⟨After the sermon we sang a brief *psalm*.⟩ — see HYMN 1
psalmody *n* a book of hymns ⟨a *psalmody* containing many beloved hymns⟩ — see HYMNAL
pseudo *adj* lacking in natural or spontaneous quality ⟨the *pseudo* friendliness of a salesperson trying to sell you something⟩ — see ARTIFICIAL 1
pseudonym *n* a fictitious or assumed name ⟨The most notorious serial killer of the 19th century remains known only by the *pseudonym* of Jack the Ripper.⟩
synonyms alias
related words nom de plume, pen name; appellation, designation; epithet, nickname, sobriquet (*also* soubriquet)
pshaw *interj* how surprising, doubtful, or unbelievable ⟨*Pshaw*! Anyone else could have done that job in half the time.⟩ — see NO
psych (up) *vb* to prepare (oneself) mentally or emotionally ⟨I have to *psych* myself *up* before every swimming competition.⟩ — see FORTIFY 1
psyche *n* **1** an immaterial force within a human being thought to give the body life, energy, and power ⟨disturbing, enigmatic paintings that seem to embody the *psyche* of this brilliant but troubled artist⟩ — see SOUL 1
2 the part of a person that feels, thinks, perceives, wills,

and especially reasons ⟨a novel that explores the *psyche* of a teenager⟩ — see MIND 1

psychological *also* **psychologic** *adj* of or relating to the mind ⟨suffered from *psychological* disorders⟩ — see MENTAL

pub *n* a place of business where alcoholic beverages are sold to be consumed on the premises ⟨the convivial atmosphere of the Irish *pub*⟩ — see BARROOM

public *adj* **1** not known by only a select few ⟨information that is *public* knowledge⟩

synonyms open

related words general, popular; nonclassified, unclassified, well-known; advertised, aired, announced, broadcast, declared, disclosed, divulged, heralded, posted, proclaimed, promulgated, publicized, published, spotlighted; reported, reputed, rumored

phrases on record

near antonyms classified; unadvertised, unannounced, undisclosed; clandestine, collusive, conspiratorial, covert; surreptitious, undercover, underhand, underhanded; intimate, personal; concealed, reserved, silenced, stifled, suppressed, withheld; recanted, retracted, revoked

antonyms confidential, private, privy, secret

2 freely available for use or participation by all ⟨a *public* swimming pool⟩ — see OPEN 2

3 of or relating to a nation ⟨a trade agreement in the *public* interest⟩ — see NATIONAL

4 held by or applicable to a majority of the people ⟨*Public* sentiment was against the war.⟩ — see GENERAL 3

5 used or done by a number of people as a group ⟨*public* transportation⟩ — see COLLECTIVE

public *n* **1** human beings in general ⟨a lecture open to the *public*⟩ — see PEOPLE 1

2 the body of the community as contrasted with the elite ⟨The highbrows have always disdained his horror novels, but the *public* just eats them up.⟩ — see MASS 1

public house *n* a place that provides rooms and usually a public dining room for overnight guests ⟨He took lodging at a cheap *public house* in town.⟩ — see HOTEL

publicity *n* information released to the media that is designed to gain public attention or support for a person, business, or cause ⟨An endless flow of *publicity* for our charity event resulted in a great turnout.⟩

synonyms ballyhoo

related words ad, advertisement, commercial, message, plug, promotion, spot, word; advertising, marketing, propaganda; pronouncement, publication, release; broadcast, bulletin, dispatch, report, story; write-up

publicize *vb* **1** to provide publicity for ⟨The movie studios widely *publicized* their summer blockbusters.⟩

synonyms ballyhoo, pitch, plug, promote, tout

related words advertise, bark, merchandise (*also* merchandize), sell; push; acclaim, hail, laud, praise; endorse (*also* indorse), plump (for), plunk (for) *or* plonk (for); recommend, review; announce, broadcast, publish

phrases beat the drum (for)

2 to make known openly or publicly ⟨The city hasn't done a good job of *publicizing* the new regulations for its recycling operation.⟩ — see ANNOUNCE

public servant *n* **1** a person who holds a public office ⟨The new governor vowed that he would always remember why he was called a *public servant*.⟩ — see OFFICIAL

2 a worker in a government agency ⟨concerned that the new federal agency would just add another slew of *public servants* to the government payroll⟩ — see BUREAUCRAT

publish *vb* **1** to produce and release for distribution in printed form ⟨Our local animal shelter *publishes* a newsletter.⟩

synonyms get out, issue, print, put out

related words copublish; reissue, reprint, republish; serialize; contribute, edit, syndicate; distribute, market

phrases come out with

near antonyms censor, suppress

2 to make known openly or publicly ⟨will *publish* the exam scores as soon as they are available⟩ — see ANNOUNCE

puck *n* an imaginary being usually having a small human form and magical powers ⟨Sophia dreamed that her garden was the secret meeting place of *pucks* and sprites.⟩ — see FAIRY

puddle *n* a small often deep body of water ⟨splashing in the *puddles* on the way home from the bus stop⟩ — see ¹POOL

pudginess *n* the condition of having an excess of body fat ⟨the *pudginess* of the baby's cheeks⟩ — see CORPULENCE

pudgy *adj* having an excess of body fat ⟨The baby wrapped its *pudgy* little hand around my finger.⟩ — see FAT 1

puerile *adj* **1** having or showing the annoying qualities (as silliness) associated with children ⟨advised the class that *puerile* behavior would not be tolerated during the ceremony⟩ — see CHILDISH

2 lacking in adult experience or maturity ⟨allowed the company to be taken over by a bunch of *puerile* whippersnappers fresh out of business school⟩ — see CALLOW

3 lacking in seriousness or maturity ⟨a movie overloaded with *puerile* jokes⟩ — see GIDDY 1

puff *n* a slight or gentle movement of air ⟨felt a *puff* of wind on his face⟩ — see BREEZE 1

puff *vb* **1** to breathe hard, quickly, or with difficulty ⟨He came running up the stairs *puffing* and wheezing.⟩ — see GASP

2 to praise too much ⟨a talk show host who can be counted on to *puff* up the celebrities who readily consent to be interviewed⟩ — see FLATTER 1

pugilist *n* one that engages in the sport of fighting with the fists ⟨a *pugilist* with the trademark of the boxing ring: a nose that showed signs of having been broken on more than one occasion⟩ — see BOXER

pugnacious *adj* feeling or displaying eagerness to fight ⟨a movie reviewer who is spirited, even *pugnacious*, when defending her opinions⟩ — see BELLIGERENT

pugnacity *n* an inclination to fight or quarrel ⟨The players need to temper their *pugnacity* with a little self-restraint—their aggressive style of play too often results in penalties.⟩ — see BELLIGERENCE

puissance *n* the ability to exert effort for the accomplishment of a task ⟨The president pledged to put the full *puissance* of the nation into the war effort.⟩ — see POWER 2

puissant *adj* having great power or influence ⟨one of the nation's most respected and *puissant* advocates for equal rights⟩ — see IMPORTANT 2

puke *vb* to discharge the contents of the stomach through the mouth ⟨I was so nervous I thought I would *puke*.⟩ — see VOMIT

pule *vb* to utter feeble plaintive cries ⟨a distressed baby *puling* in its crib⟩ — see WHIMPER 1

pull *n* **1** the act or an instance of applying force on something so that it moves in the direction of the force ⟨I gave the door such a *pull* that when it suddenly opened, I nearly fell backwards.⟩

synonyms draw, haul, jerk, pluck, tug, wrench, yank

related words drag, tow; hitch, twitch; grab, snatch

near antonyms heave, shove, thrust

antonyms push

2 the power to direct the thinking or behavior of others usually indirectly ⟨Their lawyer supposedly has a lot of *pull* with the administration in Washington.⟩ — see INFLUENCE 1

3 the more favorable condition or position in a competition ⟨a political candidate with all of the *pull* that comes with a vast fortune and famous surname⟩ — see ADVANTAGE 1

pull *vb* **1** to cause to follow by applying steady force on ⟨a team of horses *pulling* a heavy wagon⟩
synonyms drag, draw, hale, haul, lug, tow, tug
related words attract; heave, jerk, yank; carry, convey, ferry, move, transport
near antonyms shove, thrust
antonyms drive, propel, push
2 to draw out by force or with effort ⟨The dentist had to struggle to *pull* the tooth.⟩ — see EXTRACT
3 to injure by overuse, misuse, or pressure ⟨Lift the crate carefully, or you'll *pull* a muscle.⟩ — see STRAIN 1

pulp *vb* to cause to become a pulpy mass ⟨*pulped* three oranges to get their juice⟩ — see CRUSH 1

pulpiness *n* the quality or state of being full of juice ⟨Select ripe peaches of sufficient *pulpiness* to readily yield the amount of juice required by the recipe.⟩ — see SUCCULENCE

pulpy *adj* **1** full of juice ⟨Good, ripe peaches will be *pulpy* and not mealy.⟩ — see JUICY
2 giving easily to the touch ⟨the *pulpy* flesh of ripe fruit⟩ — see SOFT 3

pulsate *vb* to expand and contract in a rhythmic manner ⟨The heart muscle *pulsates* regularly to pump blood.⟩
synonyms beat, palpitate, pit-a-pat, pitter-patter, pulse, throb
related words fluctuate, oscillate, vibrate; quiver, tremble

pulsation *n* a rhythmic expanding and contracting ⟨You should press against the artery in your wrist and count the *pulsations* to calculate your heart rate.⟩
synonyms beat, beating, palpitation, pulse, throb
related words oscillation, vibration; quiver, tremble, tremor

pulse *n* a rhythmic expanding and contracting ⟨His resting *pulse* rate is much lower than that of most men his age.⟩ — see PULSATION

pulse *vb* to expand and contract in a rhythmic manner ⟨blood vessels *pulsing* in time with the heartbeat⟩ — see PULSATE

pulverize *vb* **1** to bring to a complete end the physical soundness, existence, or usefulness of ⟨accidentally ran over the bicycle and *pulverized* it⟩ — see DESTROY 1
2 to reduce to fine particles ⟨*Pulverize* the cement into dust for reuse.⟩ — see POWDER

puma *n* a large tawny cat of the wild ⟨Adult *pumas* can sometimes weigh over 200 pounds.⟩ — see COUGAR

pummel *vb* to strike repeatedly ⟨*pummeled* the steering wheel with her fists⟩ — see BEAT 1

pump *vb* **1** to make short up-and-down movements ⟨The thighs of the bicyclists were *pumping* furiously as they neared the finish line.⟩ — see NOD
2 to put a series of questions to ⟨Prying neighbors *pumped* the guileless child for information about the family's new pool.⟩ — see EXAMINE 1
3 to remove (liquid) gradually or completely ⟨*pumped* water from the well⟩ — see DRAIN 1

¹**punch** *n* **1** the quality of an utterance that provokes interest and produces an effect ⟨The real *punch* of the speech came in its closing lines.⟩
synonyms cogency, effectiveness, force, forcefulness, impact, point
related words payoff; importance, significance; appeal, attraction, charm, fascination
2 active strength of body or mind ⟨We're going to need a candidate with real *punch* if voters are ever going to get excited about this election.⟩ — see VIGOR 1

3 a hard strike with a part of the body or an instrument ⟨The poor palooka wasn't able to land a single *punch* on his opponent.⟩ — see ¹BLOW

²**punch** *n* a mark or small hole made by a pointed instrument ⟨Old computers used to get information by reading the *punches* on a series of cards.⟩ — see PRICK 1

punch *vb* **1** to deliver a blow to (someone or something) usually in a strong vigorous manner ⟨*Punch* the risen dough and allow it to rise again.⟩ — see HIT 1
2 to make a hole or series of holes in ⟨The conductor *punched* my ticket.⟩ — see PERFORATE
3 to urge, push, or force onward ⟨cowboys *punching* cattle⟩ — see DRIVE 1

puncheon *n* an enclosed wooden vessel for holding beverages ⟨stored the *puncheons* of cider in the pantry⟩ — see CASK

punctilious *adj* marked by or showing careful attention to set forms and details ⟨old-money aristocrats with a *punctilious* sense of propriety⟩ — see CEREMONIOUS 1

punctual *adj* done, carried out, or given without delay ⟨the *punctual* delivery of the daily mail⟩ — see PROMPT 1

punctuality *n* the quality or habit of arriving or being ready on time ⟨Our boss is a real stickler for *punctuality*—he expects everyone to be at their desk by nine o'clock.⟩ — see PROMPTITUDE

puncture *n* a mark or small hole made by a pointed instrument ⟨a leak caused by several small *punctures* in the rubber gasket⟩ — see PRICK 1

puncture *vb* **1** to make a hole or series of holes in ⟨A nail *punctured* the tire.⟩ — see PERFORATE
2 to penetrate or hold (something) with a pointed object ⟨I could never *puncture* my own skin with a hypodermic needle.⟩ — see IMPALE

pungency *n* **1** a harsh or sharp quality ⟨The *pungency* of the vinegar gives the salad dressing the kick that it needs.⟩ — see EDGE 1
2 the quality or state of being stimulating to the mind or senses ⟨Theatergoers have long delighted in the *pungency* and wit of the play's dialogue.⟩ — see PIQUANCY

pungent *adj* **1** having a powerfully stimulating odor or flavor ⟨a *pungent* chili that is not for those with timid taste buds⟩ — see SHARP 2
2 marked by the use of wit that is intended to cause hurt feelings ⟨a *pungent* put-down that she will not soon forget⟩ — see SARCASTIC
3 sharp and pleasantly stimulating to the mind or senses ⟨a newspaper columnist known for his *pungent* observations on everyday life⟩ — see PIQUANT

puniness *n* the quality or state of being little in size ⟨outgrew his *puniness* in a spurt over the summer⟩ — see SMALLNESS

punish *vb* to inflict a penalty on for a fault or crime ⟨The child was *punished* for breaking the rules.⟩ ⟨If caught, the thief will be severely *punished*.⟩
synonyms castigate, chasten, chastise, correct, discipline, penalize
related words assess, charge, dock, fine, impose, levy, mulct; convict, sentence; condemn, damn, denounce; criticize, keelhaul, rebuke, reprimand, reprove; wreak
near antonyms forfeit; get off, ransom, release; commute, reprieve; absolve, acquit, exculpate, exonerate, vindicate
antonyms excuse, pardon, spare

punisher *n* one who inflicts punishment in return for an injury or offense ⟨the *punisher* of those who do wrong⟩ — see NEMESIS 1

punishment *n* suffering, loss, or hardship imposed in response to a crime or offense ⟨He is serving five years in prison as *punishment* for his crime.⟩

synonyms castigation, chastisement, correction, desert(s), discipline, nemesis, penalty, wrath

related words reprisal, retaliation, retribution, revenge, vengeance; assessment, charge, fine, mulct; example, sentence; confinement, imprisonment, incarceration; condemnation, damnation, denouncement; censure, criticism, rebuke, reprimand, reproof

near antonyms amnesty, indemnity, pardon, parole; acquittal, exculpation, exoneration, vindication; exemption, immunity, impunity; release; commutation, reprieve; absolution, forgiveness, remission, remitment; condonation, disregard, overlooking

punitive *adj* inflicting, involving, or serving as punishment ⟨Any misbehavior was immediately met with a *punitive* response.⟩ ⟨The company had to pay a million dollars in *punitive* damages.⟩

synonyms castigating, chastening, chastising, correcting, correctional, corrective, disciplinary, disciplining, penal, penalizing

related words retaliative, retaliatory, retributive, retributory, revengeful; vengeful, wrathful

near antonyms compensatory; acquitting, exculpating, exculpatory, exonerating, vindicating; absolving, condoning, pardoning, remitting; commuting, reprieving

antonyms nonpunitive

punk *adj* **1** falling short of a standard ⟨She plays a *punk* game of tennis, so you won't have any trouble beating her.⟩ — see BAD 1

2 extremely unsatisfactory ⟨The acting in the movie ranged all the way from poor to *punk*.⟩ — see WRETCHED 1

3 temporarily suffering from a disorder of the body ⟨I've been feeling *punk* today.⟩ — see SICK 1

punk *n* **1** a person who is just starting out in a field of activity ⟨an impertinent *punk* who was trying to tell senior colleagues how to do their jobs⟩ — see BEGINNER

2 a violent, brutal person who is often a member of an organized gang ⟨told the *punks* to move on before the cops came⟩ — see HOODLUM

puny *adj* of a size that is less than average ⟨a *puny*, wrinkled apple⟩ — see SMALL 1

pupil *n* **1** one who attends a school ⟨Generally there are 20 *pupils* in each class.⟩ — see STUDENT

2 one who follows the opinions or teachings of another ⟨To *pupils* of the philosopher Henry David Thoreau, the shores of Walden Pond are hallowed ground.⟩ — see FOLLOWER 1

puppet *n* **1** a small figure often of a human being used especially as a child's plaything ⟨gave her a *puppet* with strings for a gift⟩ — see DOLL 1

2 one that is or can be used to further the purposes of another ⟨accused the newspaper editor of being a *puppet* for the moneyed people of the town⟩ — see ¹PAWN

purchase *vb* to get possession of (something) by giving money in exchange for ⟨I need to *purchase* a new heavy coat.⟩ — see BUY 1

pure *adj* **1** free from added matter ⟨I'm allergic to any jewelry that isn't *pure* silver.⟩ ⟨The solution must be kept *pure* for the experiment to work.⟩

synonyms absolute, fine, neat, plain, purified, refined, straight, unadulterated, unalloyed, undiluted, unmixed

related words clarified, filtered; clean, fresh, taintless, uncontaminated, uncorrupted, undefiled, unpolluted, untainted; rendered, tried; concentrated, full-bodied, strong; uncombined

near antonyms besmirched, contaminated, corrupted, debased, defiled, fouled, polluted, soiled, spoiled, sullied, tainted; unclarified; cheapened, doctored, watered-down

antonyms adulterated, alloyed, diluted, impure, mixed

2 free from any trace of the coarse or indecent ⟨The

humor in the movie is *pure* and wholesome for the youngest viewers.⟩ — see CHASTE 1

3 free from sin ⟨In one beatitude those who are *pure* in heart are promised the sight of God.⟩ — see INNOCENT 1

4 having no exceptions or restrictions ⟨That story is *pure* nonsense.⟩ — see ABSOLUTE 2

purebred *adj* of unmixed ancestry ⟨That horse is a *purebred* Arabian.⟩

synonyms full-blooded, pedigreed (*or* pedigree), thoroughbred

related words well-bred; inbred

near antonyms crossbred, crossed, half-blood (*or* half-blooded), half-bred, hybridized, interbred, outcrossed

antonyms hybrid, mixed, mongrel

purely *adv* **1** with purity of thought and deed ⟨vowed to live *purely* and in the service of God⟩

synonyms chastely, innocently, modestly, morally, righteously, virtuously

related words decorously, properly; priggishly, primly, prudishly

near antonyms indecently, obscenely, vulgarly; lasciviously, lewdly, lustfully

antonyms evilly, immorally, impurely, sinfully, wickedly

2 for nothing other than ⟨I fish *purely* for the fun of it—I don't care if I end up with no fish to fry.⟩ — see SOLELY 1

3 nothing more than ⟨Her pleasantries were *purely* for show and masked her true feelings.⟩ — see JUST 3

purge *vb* to free from moral guilt or blemish especially ceremonially ⟨a day on which the faithful are expected to *purge* themselves of their sins through prayer and fasting⟩ — see PURIFY 1

purification *n* the act or fact of freeing from sin or moral guilt ⟨Some people must undergo a ritual *purification* after certain activities.⟩

synonyms cleansing, sanctification

related words rebirth, regeneration, restoration; grace, redemption, salvation; absolution, forgiveness, remission; acquittal, clearance, clearing, exoneration, vindication; atonement, expiation

near antonyms blasphemy, defilement, desecration, violation; corruption, debasement, perversion; pollution, sullying, tarnishing

purified *adj* free from added matter ⟨*purified* water that was now safe to drink⟩ — see PURE 1

purify *vb* **1** to free from moral guilt or blemish especially ceremonially ⟨She believed she could be *purified* through prayer.⟩

synonyms cleanse, purge, sanctify

related words amend, improve, refine; heal, regenerate, restore; elevate, ennoble, uplift; absolve, acquit, clear, exonerate, vindicate

near antonyms corrupt, debase, debauch, defile, degrade, demean, deprave, pervert, stain, warp; poison, profane; sully, tarnish

2 to remove usually visible impurities from ⟨*Purify* the water by distillation.⟩ — see CLARIFY 1

puritan *n* a person who is greatly concerned with seemly behavior and morality especially regarding sexual matters ⟨a *puritan* when it comes to the school's choices in literature⟩ — see PRUDE

puritanical *adj* given to or marked by very conservative standards regarding personal behavior or morals ⟨Some of the state laws are vestiges of a more *puritanical* time and are rarely, if ever, enforced.⟩ — see STRAITLACED

puritanism *n* a tendency to care a great deal about seemly behavior and morals especially in sexual matters ⟨The Victorian era was often characterized by a hypocritical *puritanism*.⟩ — see PRUDERY

purity *n* the quality or state of being morally pure ⟨struggling to live a life of *purity* while surrounded by wickedness⟩ — see CHASTITY

purloin *vb* to take (something) without right and with an intent to keep ⟨The studio stepped up security, fearing that someone might attempt to *purloin* a copy of the script for the show's season finale.⟩ — see STEAL 1

purloiner *n* one who steals ⟨She demanded that the pusillanimous *purloiner* of her chocolates step forward.⟩ — see THIEF

purport *n* the idea that is conveyed or intended to be conveyed to the mind by language, symbol, or action ⟨She was able to give the *purport* of the governor's speech in a few words.⟩ — see MEANING 1

purport *vb* **1** to have in mind as a purpose or goal ⟨Do you *purport* to spend the rest of your life on that couch, or do you think you might get a job someday?⟩ — see INTEND 1
2 to state as a fact usually forcefully ⟨He *purports* to be an expert in criminalistics.⟩ — see CLAIM 1

purpose *n* **1** something that one hopes or intends to accomplish ⟨The *purpose* of the research is to discover how the virus is transmitted.⟩ — see GOAL
2 the action for which a person or thing is specially fitted or used or for which a thing exists ⟨still trying to discover her *purpose* in life⟩ — see ROLE

purpose *vb* to have in mind as a purpose or goal ⟨I've been *purposing* to fix that thing for some time now.⟩ — see INTEND 1

purposeful *adj* **1** fully committed to achieving a goal ⟨a soft-spoken but *purposeful* criminal investigator⟩ — see DETERMINED 1
2 made, given, or done with full awareness of what one is doing ⟨There's a difference between a *purposeful* lie and an accidental untruth.⟩ — see INTENTIONAL

purposefully *adv* **1** with full awareness of what one is doing ⟨He *purposefully* chose the more difficult route to the mountain summit.⟩ — see INTENTIONALLY
2 with great effort or determination ⟨Peter strode *purposefully* into the boss's office, determined to ask for a raise.⟩ — see HARD 1

purposefulness *n* firm or unwavering adherence to one's purpose ⟨approached the challenge with grim *purposefulness*⟩ — see DETERMINATION 1

purposely *adv* with full awareness of what one is doing ⟨The real estate agent *purposely* withheld information that would have discouraged us from buying the property.⟩ — see INTENTIONALLY

purr *n* a monotonous sound like that of an insect in motion ⟨listened to the reassuring *purr* of the car engine⟩ — see HUM

purse *n* a container for carrying money and small personal items ⟨I left my *purse* at home, so I can't buy anything after all.⟩
synonyms bag, handbag, pocketbook
related words clutch, clutch bag; billfold; poke, pouch, sack; shoulder bag

pursuance *n* the doing of an action ⟨Until recently she has been fully engaged in *pursuance* of her duties as governor.⟩ — see COMMISSION 2

pursue *vb* **1** to go after or on the track of ⟨The police officer doggedly *pursued* the pickpocket through the crowded subway station.⟩ — see FOLLOW 2
2 to go in search of ⟨He urged the graduates to *pursue* personal fulfillment instead of financial success.⟩ — see SEEK 1

pursuing *n* the act of going after or in the tracks of another ⟨the controversy concerning the *pursuing* of criminals in speeding vehicles along busy highways⟩ — see PURSUIT

pursuit *n* the act of going after or in the tracks of another ⟨The cat ran down the street with a pair of dogs in *pursuit*.⟩
synonyms chase, chasing, dogging, following, hounding, pursuing, shadowing, tagging, tailing, tracing, tracking, trailing
related words hot pursuit; tagging along; path, track, trail; search, seeking

push *n* a series of activities undertaken to achieve a goal ⟨an unprecedented *push* for higher wages⟩ — see CAMPAIGN

push *vb* **1** to apply force to (someone or something) so that it moves in front of one ⟨I had to *push* my damaged bike all the way home.⟩
synonyms drive, propel, shove, thrust
related words impel, move; bear (down), compress, depress, jam, pressure, squash, squeeze, weigh (upon); bulldoze, compel, force, lean (on *or* against), muscle, ram
2 to force one's way ⟨We had to *push* our way through a crowd that was mostly headed in the opposite direction.⟩ — see ²PRESS 4

pushover *n* **1** a person without strength of character ⟨*pushovers* who don't stand up for themselves⟩ — see WEAKLING 2
2 one who is easily deceived or cheated ⟨scam artists mistakenly thinking that these farm families would be *pushovers*⟩ — see ¹DUPE
3 something that is easy to do ⟨Though the mountain is not especially high, the climb is very arduous and is definitely not a *pushover*.⟩ — see CINCH

pusillanimous *adj* having or showing a shameful lack of courage ⟨*pusillanimous* politicians who vote according to whichever way the political wind is blowing⟩ — see COWARDLY

¹puss *n, slang* the front part of the head ⟨The snowball smacked him right in the *puss*.⟩ — see FACE 1

²puss *n* a small domestic animal known for catching mice ⟨I don't want a purebred cat, just some playful *puss* in need of a good home.⟩ — see CAT

pussy *n* a small domestic animal known for catching mice ⟨Mike fed his *pussy* only the finest fish for her supper.⟩ — see CAT

pussyfoot *vb* **1** to avoid giving a definite answer or position ⟨politicians who try to *pussyfoot* around hot-button issues⟩ — see EQUIVOCATE
2 to move about in a sly or secret manner ⟨*pussyfooting* through the hallways in the middle of the night⟩ — see SNEAK 1

put *vb* **1** to arrange something in a certain spot or position ⟨You can *put* this box next to the bookshelf.⟩ — see PLACE 1
2 to convey in appropriate or telling terms ⟨tried to think of a good way of *putting* the news⟩ — see PHRASE
3 to decide the size, amount, number, or distance of (something) without actual measurement ⟨*put* the time of the photograph at about noon⟩ — see ESTIMATE 2
4 to establish or apply as a charge or penalty ⟨a proposal to *put* a special tax on luxuries⟩ — see IMPOSE
5 to change (something) so as to make it suitable for a new use or situation ⟨Key *put* the words of his patriotic poem to the tune of a well-known drinking song.⟩ — see ADAPT
6 to risk (something) on the outcome of an uncertain event ⟨Deciding to go for broke, he *put* $1000 on a horse that had 20 to 1 odds.⟩ — see BET

put by *vb* to put (something of future use or value) in a safe or secret place ⟨You should have money *put by* for an emergency.⟩ — see HOARD

put–down *n* **1** an act or expression showing scorn and usually intended to hurt another's feelings ⟨New hires always have to deal with *put-downs* and practical jokes from the older employees.⟩ — see INSULT

2 the act of making a person or a thing seem little or unimportant ⟨Your never-ending *put-down* of my musical talents is really starting to annoy me.⟩ — see DEPRECIATION

put down *vb* **1** to express scornfully one's low opinion of ⟨He has the annoying habit of *putting down* others under the guise of offering constructive criticism.⟩ — see DECRY 1

2 to make a written note of ⟨We had the whole agreement *put down* on paper.⟩ — see RECORD 1

3 to put (someone or something) on a list ⟨We'll *put* her *down* as one of the chaperones for the field trip.⟩ — see ¹LIST 2

4 to put a stop to (something) by the use of force ⟨a tyrant who ruthlessly *put down* uprisings⟩ — see QUELL 1

5 to explain (something) as being the result of something else ⟨a fender bender that probably can be *put down* to the driver's inexperience⟩ — see CREDIT 1

6 to take in as food ⟨football players *putting down* a big meal⟩ — see EAT 1

put in *vb* to put or set into the ground to grow ⟨*put in* a crop of winter wheat⟩ — see PLANT 1

put off *vb* **1** to assign to a later time ⟨Never *put off* until tomorrow what you can do today.⟩ — see POSTPONE

2 to rid oneself of (a garment) ⟨*Put off* your coat and stay awhile.⟩ — see REMOVE 1

3 to cause to feel disgust ⟨She was *put off* by his negative attitude.⟩ — see DISGUST

put–on *adj* lacking in natural or spontaneous quality ⟨a *put-on* goofy voice⟩ — see ARTIFICIAL 1

put–on *n* **1** a display of emotion or behavior that is insincere or intended to deceive ⟨My bravery was all a *put-on*—I was scared out of my wits.⟩ — see MASQUERADE

2 a work that imitates and exaggerates another work for comic effect ⟨For a moment, I couldn't tell if the commercial was serious or a deadpan *put-on* of ads by other insurance companies.⟩ — see PARODY 1

put on *vb* **1** to place on one's person ⟨I *put on* a coat and shoes to go outside.⟩

synonyms don, slip (on *or* into), throw (on)

related words apparel, array, attire, bedeck, bedizen, bundle up, caparison, clothe, doll up, dress, garb, rig, robe, suit, trick, uniform; overdress

near antonyms disrobe, strip, undress

antonyms doff, remove, take off

2 to describe or express in too strong terms ⟨Some critics are *putting* it *on* when they say it's the best comedy ever made.⟩ — see OVERSTATE

3 to present a false appearance of ⟨*put on* a show of anger just for fun⟩ — see FEIGN

put out *vb* **1** to bring to bear especially forcefully or effectively ⟨Despite *putting out* her best effort, she was unable to beat her longtime tennis rival.⟩ — see EXERT

2 to cause to cease burning ⟨Please *put out* the campfire before leaving.⟩ — see EXTINGUISH 1

3 to disturb the peace of mind of (someone) especially by repeated disagreeable acts ⟨My father was *put out* by all the street noise outside our house.⟩ — see IRRITATE 1

4 to cause discomfort to or trouble for ⟨If it wouldn't *put* you *out* too much, would you mind giving me a ride to the airport?⟩ — see INCONVENIENCE

5 to produce and release for distribution in printed form ⟨Though most of their sales are now transacted through the Internet, the company still *puts out* a mail-order catalog.⟩ — see PUBLISH 1

putrefaction *n* the process by which dead organic matter separates into simpler substances ⟨Clearing the refrigerator of what the previous tenant had left behind was like taking a course in the advanced *putrefaction* of leftovers.⟩ — see CORRUPTION 1

putrefied *adj* having undergone organic breakdown ⟨We had to throw out the *putrefied* tomatoes that had been sitting on the counter all week.⟩ — see ROTTEN 1

putrefy *vb* to go through decomposition ⟨We traced the bad smell to a dead skunk *putrefying* under the house.⟩ — see DECAY 1

putrid *adj* having undergone organic breakdown ⟨the *putrid* remains of a dead raccoon on the side of the highway⟩ — see ROTTEN 1

putter (around) *vb* to spend time in aimless activity ⟨I spent all weekend at home just *puttering around*.⟩ — see FIDDLE (AROUND)

putterer *n* a person who regularly or occasionally engages in an activity as a pastime rather than as a profession ⟨He is an inveterate *putterer*, and his garage is full of half-finished projects he has worked on over the years.⟩ — see AMATEUR 1

put up *vb* **1** to fix in an upright position ⟨The builders *put up* the walls before starting on the roof.⟩ — see ERECT 1

2 to form by putting together parts or materials ⟨plans to *put up* a pavilion in the public gardens⟩ — see BUILD

3 to offer for sale to the public ⟨*put* their possessions *up* for auction⟩ — see MARKET

4 to provide with living quarters or shelter ⟨The university *puts up* students in a variety of buildings.⟩ — see HOUSE 1

5 to engage in a secret plan to accomplish evil or unlawful ends ⟨*put up* an elaborate scheme to defraud insurance companies⟩ — see PLOT

6 to place somewhere for safekeeping or ready availability ⟨I need to clear out a space in the garage to *put up* my motorcycle for the winter.⟩ — see STORE 1

puzzle *n* something hard to understand or explain ⟨The final fate of the colonists at Roanoke remains a *puzzle* to this very day.⟩ — see MYSTERY

puzzle *vb* to throw into a state of mental uncertainty ⟨It is the cause of the disease that *puzzles* doctors.⟩ — see CONFUSE 1

puzzle (out) *vb* to find an answer for through reasoning ⟨I was able to *puzzle out* the riddle in a fairly short time.⟩ — see SOLVE

puzzlement *n* **1** a state of mental uncertainty ⟨Her explanation did little to relieve his *puzzlement*.⟩ — see CONFUSION 1

2 something hard to understand or explain ⟨The whole situation remains a *puzzlement* to everyone who was there.⟩ — see MYSTERY

pygmy *adj* of a size that is less than average ⟨a *pygmy* elephant⟩ — see SMALL 1

pygmy *also* **pigmy** *n* **1** a living thing much smaller than others of its kind ⟨Hummingbirds may be the *pygmies* of the avian world, but what they lack in size they make up for in beauty.⟩ — see DWARF 1

2 a person of no importance or influence ⟨Regrettably, most of the candidates for the party's nomination that year were political *pygmies*.⟩ — see NOBODY

Q

quack *n* one who makes false claims of identity or expertise ⟨Don't bother to see that guy, as I've heard he's a *quack* with no actual training.⟩ — see IMPOSTOR

quadrangle *n* an open space wholly or partly enclosed (as by buildings or walls) ⟨Since the weather was sunny, the convocation was held outside in the college's *quadrangle*.⟩ — see COURT 2

quaff *n* the portion of a serving of a beverage that is swallowed at one time ⟨She was so thirsty that she drank her iced tea in one long *quaff*.⟩ — see DRINK 2

quaff *vb* to swallow in liquid form ⟨After digging our car out of the snowdrift, we were ready to *quaff* some hot chocolate.⟩ — see DRINK 1

quagmire *n* **1** a difficult, puzzling, or embarrassing situation from which there is no easy escape ⟨He's caught in a *quagmire* of debt.⟩ — see PREDICAMENT
2 something that catches and holds ⟨The trial became a legal *quagmire*.⟩ — see WEB 1

quail *vb* **1** to draw back in fear, pain, or disgust ⟨We *quailed* when the waiter unexpectedly presented us with a hindquarter of frog's legs.⟩ — see FLINCH
2 to draw back or crouch down in fearful submission ⟨brave resisters who did not *quail* before the tyrant's iron hand⟩ — see COWER

quaint *adj* **1** different from the ordinary in a way that causes curiosity or suspicion ⟨The sudden appearance of a man dressed in *quaint* clothes immediately drew the notice of passersby.⟩ — see ODD 2
2 pleasantly reminiscent of an earlier time ⟨a *quaint* general store on one of the back roads of Vermont⟩ — see OLD-FASHIONED 1

quake *n* a shaking of the earth ⟨The *quake* registered 6.5 on the Richter scale.⟩ — see EARTHQUAKE 1

quake *vb* to make a series of small irregular or violent movements ⟨The horror film was so scary it left us *quaking* with fear for hours afterwards.⟩ — see SHAKE 1

quaking *adj* marked by or given to small uncontrollable bodily movements ⟨found the *quaking* stray dog wandering outside in the rain⟩ — see SHAKY 1

qualification *n* **1** a skill, an ability, or knowledge that makes a person able to do a particular job ⟨The fashion firm was looking for an applicant who could list superior sewing skills among his or her *qualifications*.⟩
synonyms capability, credentials, goods, stuff
related words command, expertise, know-how, mastership, mastery, proficiency; ability, capacity, competence, competency, facility, faculty; aptitude, endowment, flair, genius, gift, knack, talent; forte, specialty; fitness, suitability, suitableness; makings, potentiality
2 something upon which the carrying out of an agreement or offer depends ⟨He will give us his permission to go to the conference with the *qualification* that we make up the time later.⟩ — see CONDITION 2

qualified *adj* having the required skills for an acceptable level of performance ⟨The candidate has demonstrated that he is amply *qualified* for the position.⟩ — see COMPETENT 1

qualify *vb* **1** to limit the meaning of (as a noun) ⟨*Qualifying* the noun "adventure" in the title of your story with a descriptive adjective would make it more attention-grabbing.⟩
synonyms modify
related words alter, color, distort, misrepresent, misstate, pervert, twist, warp; narrow

near antonyms broaden, expand, widen
2 to make competent (as by training, skill, or ability) for a particular office or function ⟨Her career as a defense attorney has *qualified* her to be a legal analyst for the news show.⟩
synonyms equip, fit, prepare, ready, season, train
related words accustom, adapt, adjust, condition, shape, tailor; authorize, entitle; empower, enable; educate, indoctrinate, instruct, school, teach, tutor
3 to give a right to ⟨This coupon *qualifies* the bearer for an extra 15% off the discounted price.⟩ — see ENTITLE 1
4 to give official or legal power to ⟨Passing the state bar exam will *qualify* you to practice law.⟩ — see AUTHORIZE 1

quality *adj* of the very best kind ⟨an antiques dealer who handles nothing but *quality* pieces⟩ — see EXCELLENT

quality *n* **1** degree of excellence ⟨We expect a high *quality* of service in such a fancy restaurant.⟩
synonyms caliber (*or* calibre), class, grade, rate
related words hallmark; mark; footing, place, position, rank, standing, stature, status; benchmark, criterion, measure, par, standard, touchstone, yardstick
2 high position within society ⟨a glamorous invitation-only party for all the people of *quality* in the summer resort⟩ — see RANK 2
3 something that sets apart an individual from others of the same kind ⟨Unfailing kindness is one of her many fine *qualities*.⟩ — see CHARACTERISTIC

qualm *n* an uneasy feeling about the rightness of what one is doing or going to do ⟨She has no *qualms* about downloading pirated movies from the Internet.⟩
synonyms compunction, misgiving, scruple
related words conscience; distrust, doubt, incertitude, mistrust, reservation, skepticism, suspicion, uncertainness, uncertainty; qualmishness, uneasiness; reluctance, unwillingness; demur, fuss, objection, protest, question, remonstrance; aversion, disinclination, indisposition, reluctance, unwillingness; guilt, regret, remorse, self-reproach, shame
near antonyms aplomb, assurance, certainty, certitude, confidence, conviction, self-assurance, self-confidence, sureness

qualmish *adj* affected with nausea ⟨Some passengers felt a little *qualmish* after the bumpy landing on the airstrip.⟩ — see NAUSEOUS 1

qualmishness *n* **1** a disturbed condition of the stomach in which one feels like vomiting ⟨Her *qualmishness* subsided after she had sipped a little ginger ale.⟩ — see NAUSEA 1
2 the tendency to be or state of being squeamish ⟨I can't explain my *qualmishness* about spiders, but for some reason they really bother me.⟩ — see DELICACY 3

quandary *n* a situation in which one has to choose between two or more equally unsatisfactory choices ⟨I'm in a *quandary* about whether I should try to repair my car or buy a new one, even though I don't have the money to do either.⟩ — see DILEMMA 1

quantity *n* **1** a considerable amount ⟨I wish you *quantities* of happiness in the New Year!⟩ — see LOT 2
2 a given or particular mass or aggregate of matter ⟨They prepared a huge *quantity* of mashed potatoes for the feast.⟩ — see AMOUNT

quarrel *n* an often noisy or angry expression of differing opinions ⟨A loud *quarrel* erupted at the next table over.⟩ — see ARGUMENT 1

quarrel *vb* to express different opinions about something often angrily ⟨The coach and the referee *quarreled* about whether the ball was in bounds.⟩ — see ARGUE 2

quarreler *or* **quarreller** *n* a person who takes part in a dispute ⟨Known as the *quarreler* in the family, she never dropped an argument, no matter how pointless.⟩ — see DISPUTANT

quarrelsome *adj* **1** feeling or displaying eagerness to fight ⟨a *quarrelsome* student who was always being sent to the principal's office⟩ — see BELLIGERENT
2 given to arguing ⟨You're so *quarrelsome*: you can never do anything without a fuss!⟩ — see ARGUMENTATIVE 1

quarry *n* an animal that is hunted or killed ⟨a hunter relentlessly tracking his *quarry*⟩ — see PREY 1

quarter *n* **1** an area (as of a city) set apart for some purpose or having some special feature ⟨They lived on the edge of the central business *quarter*.⟩ — see DISTRICT
2 kind, gentle, or compassionate treatment especially towards someone who is undeserving of it ⟨The coach told the team to show their opponents no *quarter* during the championship game.⟩ — see MERCY 1
3 the place where someone is assigned to stand or remain ⟨called the crew to their *quarters* on deck to await further instruction⟩ — see STATION 1
4 quarters *pl* the place where one lives ⟨Our living *quarters* were very comfortable.⟩ — see HOME 1

quarter *vb* to provide with living quarters or shelter ⟨The militia is being *quartered* just outside the city.⟩ — see HOUSE 1

¹**quash** *vb* to put a stop to (something) by the use of force ⟨The dictator commanded the army to *quash* the uprising.⟩ — see QUELL 1

²**quash** *vb* to put an end to by formal action ⟨Attorneys asked the court to *quash* the indictment.⟩ — see ABOLISH 1

quaver *vb* to sing with the alternation of two musical tones ⟨Know-it-alls snickered as the opera singer *quavered* on the high note.⟩ — see WARBLE

quavery *adj* marked by or given to small uncontrollable bodily movements ⟨a *quavery* foal trying to stand for the first time⟩ — see SHAKY 1

quay *n* a structure used by boats and ships for taking on or landing cargo and passengers ⟨docked the ferry at the *quay* to let the passengers off⟩ — see DOCK

queasiness *n* **1** a disturbed condition of the stomach in which one feels like vomiting ⟨He still battled *queasiness*, even on large cruise ships.⟩ — see NAUSEA 1
2 the tendency to be or state of being squeamish ⟨a girl who has no *queasiness* about bugs at all⟩ — see DELICACY 3

queasy *also* **queazy** *adj* **1** affected with nausea ⟨The youngster felt a little *queasy* after eating too much candy.⟩ — see NAUSEOUS 1
2 feeling or showing uncomfortable feelings of uncertainty ⟨Since I don't know much about mechanical things, I'm always *queasy* when dealing with auto mechanics.⟩ — see NERVOUS 1

queen *n* a lovely woman ⟨In her lover's eyes she's a *queen*.⟩ — see BEAUTY 2

queenly *adj* fit for or worthy of a royal ruler ⟨a richly appointed, *queenly* bedroom, complete with a massive four-poster bed⟩ — see MONARCHICAL

queer *adj* **1** affected with nausea ⟨Eating all of that deep-fried food would make most people feel a little *queer*.⟩ — see NAUSEOUS 1
2 different from the ordinary in a way that causes curiosity or suspicion ⟨One competitor had a *queer* way of running that attracted a lot of attention from the spectators.⟩ — see ODD 2
3 noticeably different from what is generally found or experienced ⟨A lot of *queer* things started happening almost from the day that we moved into the house.⟩ — see UNUSUAL 1

4 giving good reason for being doubted, questioned, or challenged ⟨*queer* business practices that bear some looking into⟩ — see DOUBTFUL 2

queerish *adj* **1** affected with nausea ⟨If you don't take that antibiotic with food, you might feel a little *queerish* at first.⟩ — see NAUSEOUS 1
2 different from the ordinary in a way that causes curiosity or suspicion ⟨The drink left a *queerish* taste in my mouth.⟩ — see ODD 2

queerness *n* a disturbed condition of the stomach in which one feels like vomiting ⟨After the roller coaster ride, I had to rest to overcome the dizziness and *queerness* that I was feeling.⟩ — see NAUSEA 1

quell *vb* **1** to put a stop to (something) by the use of force ⟨The National Guard was called in to help *quell* the late-night disturbances downtown.⟩
synonyms clamp down (on), crack down (on), crush, put down, quash, repress, silence, snuff (out), squash, squelch, subdue, suppress
related words douse (*also* dowse), extinguish, put out, quench; smother, stifle, strangle, throttle; annihilate, decimate, demolish, desolate, destroy, devastate, rub out, ruin, smash, waste, wreck; exterminate, obliterate, wipe out; conquer, dominate, overcome, overpower, overwhelm, subdue, subjugate, vanquish
phrases sit on
near antonyms abet, aid, assist, back, help, prop up, support; foment, incite, instigate, provoke, stir, whip (up); advance, cultivate, encourage, forward, foster, further, nourish, nurture, promote
2 to stop the noise or speech of ⟨The principal held up her hand to *quell* the students so they could hear the urgent announcement.⟩ — see SILENCE 1

quench *vb* **1** to cause to cease burning ⟨We thoroughly *quenched* the campfire before we headed to bed.⟩ — see EXTINGUISH 1
2 to put a complete end to (a physical need or desire) ⟨This lemonade really *quenches* my thirst.⟩ — see SATISFY 1

quencher *n* a liquid suitable for drinking ⟨Marathon runners often find that plain water is the best *quencher* of all.⟩ — see DRINK 1

querulous *adj* given to complaining a lot ⟨car trips that were frequently spoiled by a couple of *querulous* passengers in the back⟩ — see FUSSY 1

query *n* **1** a feeling or attitude that one does not know the truth, truthfulness, or trustworthiness of someone or something ⟨Readers will likely have a *query* or two about some of the more remarkable episodes in the memoir.⟩ — see DOUBT
2 an act or instance of asking for information ⟨Please respond to my *query* at your earliest convenience.⟩ — see QUESTION 2

query *vb* **1** to demand proof of the truth or rightness of ⟨It seems odd that someone would want two stoves, so you'd better *query* that order.⟩ — see CHALLENGE 1
2 to put a question or questions to ⟨*queried* the professor about the assignment⟩ — see ASK 1
3 to put a series of questions to ⟨Once the statement was given, the press secretary allowed reporters to *query* the President.⟩ — see EXAMINE 1

quest *n* an act or process of looking carefully or thoroughly for someone or something ⟨The Holy Grail was the object of a mystical *quest* by the knights of the Round Table.⟩ — see SEARCH

quest *vb* **1** to ask for (something) earnestly or with authority ⟨I respectfully *quest* your assistance in this matter.⟩ — see DEMAND 1
2 to go in search of ⟨Many daydreamers trekked to Cali-

fornia *questing* riches during the great gold rush of 1849.⟩ — see SEEK 1

3 to make a request for ⟨Please wait until the lecturer specifically *quests* comments from the audience before chiming in.⟩ — see ASK (FOR) 1

question *n* **1** an interrogative expression often used to test knowledge ⟨Because I have missed so many classes, I had a hard time answering every *question* on today's surprise quiz.⟩

synonyms problem

related words brainteaser, conundrum, poser, puzzle, quiz, riddle, stickler, stumper, toughie (*also* toughy)

near antonyms answer, response, solution

2 an act or instance of asking for information ⟨After reading the brief statement to the reporters, the lawyer ended the press conference by saying, "No more *questions*, please!"⟩ ⟨the dozens of *questions* researched by the reference librarians⟩

synonyms call, inquiry, query, request

related words interrogatory; poll, questionnaire, survey; inquisition, interrogating, interrogation, questioning; examination, exploration, inquest, investigation, probe, probing, research, study

near antonyms answer, reply, response

3 a feeling or declaration of disapproval or dissent ⟨That these measurements are accurate is beyond *question*.⟩ — see OBJECTION

4 a major object of interest or concern (as in a discussion or artistic composition) ⟨It's a *question* of personal responsibility.⟩ — see MATTER 1

question *vb* **1** to demand proof of the truth or rightness of ⟨The teenager openly *questioned* the authority of the town's police force to impose a curfew on residents under the age of 18.⟩ — see CHALLENGE 1

2 to give serious and careful thought to ⟨*Question* your motives before you file the lawsuit: do you really care about the trees, or are you just trying to harass the neighbors?⟩ — see PONDER

3 to have no trust or confidence in ⟨It was apparent that voters were *questioning* the President's ability to manage the economy.⟩ — see DISTRUST

4 to put a question or questions to ⟨The press should be allowed to *question* public officials about any matter of general interest.⟩ — see ASK 1

5 to put a series of questions to ⟨The police *questioned* the suspect before deciding that there was insufficient evidence to hold him.⟩ — see EXAMINE 1

questionable *adj* **1** giving good reason for being doubted, questioned, or challenged ⟨The truth of the statements was highly *questionable*.⟩ — see DOUBTFUL 2

2 not likely to be true or to occur ⟨It's *questionable* that he will show up tonight considering all the bad weather we're having.⟩ — see IMPROBABLE

3 open to question or dispute ⟨Whether it will rain today or not is *questionable*.⟩ — see DEBATABLE 1

questioner *n* a person who is always ready to doubt or question the truth or existence of something ⟨Henry is always happy to debate any *questioner* of the theory.⟩ — see SKEPTIC

questioning *adj* inclined to doubt or question claims ⟨A naturally *questioning* person, she demands rock-solid proof before she believes anything.⟩ — see SKEPTICAL 1

queue *n* a series of persons or things arranged one behind another ⟨Join the *queue* to my left if you need to return merchandise.⟩ — see LINE 1

quibble *vb* **1** to make often peevish criticisms or objections about matters that are minor, unimportant, or irrelevant ⟨He spent the entire evening *quibbling* about the

historical inaccuracies in the television series on World War II.⟩

synonyms carp, cavil, fuss, nitpick

related words criticize, fault; beef, bellyache, complain, crab, gripe, grouse, growl, grumble, kick, moan, squawk, squeal, wail, whine, yammer, yowl

phrases split hairs

near antonyms applaud, commend, compliment, praise, recommend; approve, back, champion, endorse (*also* indorse), support

2 to express different opinions about something often angrily ⟨Don't *quibble* over who gets to sit in front!⟩ — see ARGUE 2

quick *adj* **1** having or showing the ability to respond without delay or hesitation ⟨She's a *quick* wit, always ready with a pun or joke when the moment calls for one.⟩

synonyms alacritous, alert, expeditious, prompt, ready, willing

related words receptive, responsive; immediate, instant, instantaneous, summary; breakneck, breathless, brisk, fast, fleet, fleet-footed, hit-and-run, lightning, rapid, rapid-fire, rattling, snappy, speedy, swift, whirlwind; eager, keen, sharp; apt, clever, quick, quick-witted, ready-witted, sharp-witted, smart

near antonyms unresponsive; crawling, creeping, dallying, dawdling, dilatory, dillydallying, dragging, laggard, lagging, lazy, lazyish, leisurely, logy (*also* loggy), poking, poky (*or* pokey), slothful, slow, slowish, sluggish, tardy, unhurried; dormant, idle, inactive, inert

2 having or showing quickness of mind ⟨A *quick* lad, he immediately caught on to how the gadget operated.⟩ — see INTELLIGENT 1

3 moving, proceeding, or acting with great speed ⟨A *quick* run through the car wash, and your vehicle will look as good as new!⟩ — see FAST 1

4 having or showing life ⟨After the battle, there was a hurried accounting of the *quick* and the dead.⟩ — see ALIVE 1

5 able to sense slight impressions or differences ⟨parlayed her *quick* sense of a person's emotions into a career in psychology⟩ — see ACUTE 1

quick *adv* with great speed ⟨Watch out, as the cars pass by here pretty *quick*.⟩ — see FAST 1

quick *n* the seat of one's deepest thoughts and emotions ⟨That nasty comment cut me to the *quick*.⟩ — see CORE 1

quicken *vb* **1** to cause to move or proceed fast or faster ⟨She eventually *quickened* her pace so she could keep up with the others.⟩ — see HURRY 1

2 to give life, vigor, or spirit to ⟨The news that we'd head to Florida for vacation *quickened* the children, who instantly began jumping for joy.⟩ — see ANIMATE

quickly *adv* with great speed ⟨*quickly* moved to block the goal⟩ — see FAST 1

quickness *n* a high rate of movement or performance ⟨His agility and overall *quickness* made him the football coach's top choice for receiver.⟩ — see SPEED 1

quick–tempered *adj* easily irritated or annoyed ⟨a *quick-tempered* man who invariably utters threats at any kids who wander into his yard⟩ — see IRRITABLE

quick–witted *adj* having or showing quickness of mind ⟨The *quick-witted* child easily figured out the trick to making the toy work.⟩ — see INTELLIGENT 1

quiescence *n* **1** a state of temporary inactivity ⟨The resort community's social scene is lively during the summer but undergoes a deep *quiescence* during the long winter.⟩ — see ABEYANCE

2 lack of action or activity ⟨was struck by the elk's *quiescence* as it just stood there in the clearing⟩ — see INACTION

quiescent *adj* slow to move or act ⟨a group of *quiescent* loungers recovering from the Thanksgiving feast⟩ — see INACTIVE 1

quiet *adj* **1** free from disturbing noise or uproar ⟨We left the din of the concert and went to a *quiet* restaurant where we could hear one another talk.⟩
synonyms calm, hushed, peaceful, placid, restful, serene, still, stilly, tranquil
related words noiseless, silent, soundless; mute, speechless, wordless; dead, motionless, quiescent; muffled, muted, quieted; dull, gentle, low, soft; ultraquiet
near antonyms tempestuous, wild; blaring, blasting, booming, earsplitting, piercing, roaring, thunderous
antonyms boisterous, clamorous, clattery, deafening, loud, noisy, raucous, rip-roaring, roistering, romping, rowdy, tumultuous, unquiet, uproarious
2 not excessively showy ⟨She decided that it would be best to wear a *quiet* business suit to the job interview.⟩
synonyms conservative, muted, restrained, sober, subdued, toned-down, understated, unpretentious
related words appropriate, becoming, fit, fitting, proper, suitable; modest, plain, simple, unadorned, undecorated; inconspicuous, unnoticeable, unobtrusive; graceful, handsome, refined, tasteful; drab, mousy (*or* mousey); practical, sensible
near antonyms meretricious; graceless, inelegant, tacky, tasteless, tawdry, trashy, vulgar; fancy, frilly, gilded (*or* gilt), ornate, rococo; overdecorated, overdone, overwrought
antonyms flamboyant, flashy, garish, gaudy, glitzy, loud, noisy, ostentatious, splashy, swank (*or* swanky)
3 free from storms or physical disturbance ⟨a *quiet* interlude as the eye of the storm passed over us⟩ — see CALM 1
4 screened or sequestered from view ⟨a *quiet* little house set far back from the street⟩ — see SECLUDED
5 mostly or entirely without sound ⟨a diver who loves to retreat to the *quiet* world beneath the surface of the sea⟩ — see SILENT 3
6 not loud in pitch or volume ⟨*Quiet* music is generally more relaxing.⟩ — see SOFT 1

quiet *adv* without motion ⟨Lie *quiet* and no one will guess you're hiding under the bed.⟩ — see STILL 1

quiet *n* **1** a state of freedom from storm or disturbance ⟨sailors enjoying the *quiet* of a clear evening at sea⟩ — see CALM 1
2 the near or complete absence of sound ⟨new parents appreciating the blessed *quiet* that comes when their baby finally falls asleep⟩ — see SILENCE 2

quiet *vb* **1** to become still and orderly ⟨The museum docent told the rowdy youngsters to *quiet* down for the tour.⟩
synonyms calm (down), chill out [*slang*], hush, pipe down, settle (down)
related words dry up; relax, tranquilize (*also* tranquilize), unwind, zone out
phrases cool it
near antonyms clown (around), horse around, monkey (around), show off, skylark
antonyms act up, carry on, cut up
2 to free from distress or disturbance ⟨*quieted* the crying toddler with a story⟩ — see CALM 1
3 to stop the noise or speech of ⟨The nanny could *quiet* unruly children with just a look.⟩ — see SILENCE 1

quiet (down) *vb* to stop talking ⟨The kids *quieted down* when they realized I was about to ask them if they wanted ice cream.⟩ — see SHUT UP 1

quieted *adj* mostly or entirely without sound ⟨One could hear a pin drop in the *quieted* concert hall as the conductor raised his baton.⟩ — see SILENT 3

quieting *adj* tending to calm the emotions and relieve stress ⟨a nice *quieting* cup of tea after a hard day at work⟩ — see SOOTHING 1

quietly *adv* without motion ⟨She stood *quietly* behind the curtains, hoping to scare her sister when she came into the room.⟩ — see STILL 1

quietness *n* **1** a state of freedom from storm or disturbance ⟨enjoyed the soothing *quietness* of the forest⟩ — see CALM 1
2 the near or complete absence of sound ⟨the tense *quietness* of the crowd as it anxiously awaited the announcement of the winner⟩ — see SILENCE 2

quietude *n* **1** a state of freedom from storm or disturbance ⟨After his tantrum, the toddler lapsed into an exhausted *quietude* and fell asleep.⟩ — see CALM 1
2 the near or complete absence of sound ⟨The *quietude* of the early morning was broken only by the occasional chirping of birds.⟩ — see SILENCE 2

quietus *n* **1** a freeing from an obligation or responsibility ⟨He was granted a *quietus* on the remainder of the debt in the old man's will.⟩ — see RELEASE 1
2 the permanent stopping of all the vital bodily activities ⟨Her unshakable belief in a blissful afterlife allowed her to meet her *quietus* without the slightest tinge of fear or regret.⟩ — see DEATH 1

quintessence *n* **1** the most perfect type or example ⟨The Parthenon in Greece was considered the *quintessence* of the perfectly proportioned building.⟩
synonyms acme, beau ideal, byword, classic, epitome, exemplar, ideal, perfection
related words archetype, model, prototype; paradigm, standard; nonpareil, paragon; abstract, embodiment, incarnation, manifestation, personification; height, meridian, ultimate, zenith; benchmark, criterion, touchstone, yardstick
2 the quality or qualities that make a thing what it is ⟨A selfless desire to help others is the *quintessence* of the virtue of charity.⟩ — see ESSENCE 1

quintessential *adj* constituting, serving as, or worthy of being a pattern to be imitated ⟨Helen of Troy was supposedly the *quintessential* beauty of the ancient world.⟩ — see MODEL

quip *n* something said or done to cause laughter ⟨The crowd laughed aloud at the author's clever *quip*.⟩ — see JOKE 1

quip *vb* to make jokes ⟨She rolled her eyes at her brother's bragging and *quipped*, "You're a legend in your own mind, all right!"⟩ — see JOKE 1

quirk *n* an odd or peculiar habit ⟨Wearing red shoes every day is just one of her *quirks*.⟩ — see IDIOSYNCRASY

quirky *adj* different from the ordinary in a way that causes curiosity or suspicion ⟨He has a *quirky* sense of humor.⟩ — see ODD 2

quisling *n* one who betrays a trust or an allegiance ⟨warned that all *quislings* would be found out and punished⟩ — see TRAITOR

quit *adj* no longer burdened with something unpleasant or painful ⟨I am finally *quit* of that terrible task.⟩ — see FREE 2

quit *vb* **1** to give up (a job or office) ⟨He decided to *quit* his job at the fast-food restaurant.⟩
synonyms bag, chuck, leave, resign (from), retire (from), step down (from)
related words abandon, vacate; drop out (of), throw up
phrases give notice
near antonyms hire (out *or* on)
antonyms stay (at)
2 to stop doing (something) permanently ⟨Her doctor told her it was high time she *quit* smoking.⟩
synonyms abandon, discontinue, drop, give up, knock off, lay off (of)
related words break off, break up, cease, close, conclude, end, expire, finish, halt, leave off, shut off; pause,

taper off; throw up; round (off *or* out), terminate, wind up, wrap up

phrases hang it up, have done (with)

near antonyms go, run on; hang in, hang on, hold on, persevere, persist; renew, reopen, restart, resume; preserve, stay; begin, commence, start

antonyms carry on, continue, keep, keep up, maintain

3 to bring (as an action or operation) to an immediate end ⟨*Quit* pestering your coworkers with pointless questions!⟩ — see STOP 1

4 to cause to remain behind ⟨He *quit* the house sometime around nine this morning and hasn't been seen since.⟩ — see LEAVE 1

5 to cease resistance (as to another's arguments, demands, or control) ⟨tried to persuade his daughter to remain at home, but eventually he just *quit* and let her go out on her own⟩ — see YIELD 3

6 to come to an end ⟨Will this tomfoolery ever *quit*?⟩ — see CEASE 1

7 to give what is owed for ⟨eager to *quit* all debts before starting married life⟩ — see PAY 2

8 to leave a place often for another ⟨We plan to *quit* the amusement park around seven tonight and then head to the diner for some food.⟩ — see GO 2

9 to manage the actions of (oneself) in a particular way ⟨I thought the kids *quitted* themselves quite well at the concert tonight.⟩ — see BEHAVE

quite *adv* **1** to a full extent or degree ⟨Are you *quite* sure you have permission to go?⟩ — see FULLY 1

2 to some degree or extent ⟨We camped *quite* near Mount Rushmore.⟩ — see FAIRLY 1

quittance *n* **1** a freeing from an obligation or responsibility ⟨The employee obtained a *quittance* from his contract and was no longer required to work for the company.⟩ — see RELEASE 1

2 payment to another for a loss or injury ⟨The court awarded the plaintiff a substantial *quittance* for bodily injury and emotional distress.⟩ — see COMPENSATION 1

quitting *n* the act of leaving a place ⟨We simply didn't know what to make of the couple's sudden *quitting* of the party.⟩ — see DEPARTURE 1

quiver *n* an instance of shaking involuntarily with fear or cold ⟨A *quiver* ran through the audience when the monster cornered the movie's hero.⟩ — see SHIVER 1

quiver *vb* to make a series of small irregular or violent movements ⟨aspen leaves *quivering* in the breeze⟩ — see SHAKE 1

quivering *adj* marked by or given to small uncontrollable bodily movements ⟨Our *quivering* dog tried to hide under the bed during the thunderstorm.⟩ — see SHAKY 1

quivering *n* a series of slight movements by a body back and forth or from side to side ⟨The kids were amused by the *quivering* of the gelatin and kept poking it to see it wiggle.⟩ — see VIBRATION 1

quiz *n* **1** a person who causes repeated emotional pain, distress, or annoyance to another ⟨Always eager to put everything down, he had to be a *quiz* and make fun of the actors and costumes in our local theater troupe's latest production.⟩ — see TORMENTOR

2 a set of questions or problems designed to assess knowledge, skills, or intelligence ⟨According to the magazine's financial *quiz*, the chances that we'll ever be able to retire are just about nil!⟩ — see EXAMINATION 1

quiz *vb* **1** to put a question or questions to ⟨quickly *quizzed* her about the assignment before heading off to class⟩ — see ASK 1

2 to put a series of questions to ⟨I hated the way those relatives would *quiz* me about my partner and our living arrangements.⟩ — see EXAMINE 1

quizzical *adj* marked by or expressive of mild or good-natured teasing ⟨My puns are usually greeted with loud *quizzical* groans by my so-called friends.⟩

synonyms bantering, chaffing, fooling, funning, jesting, joking, joshing, kidding, rallying, razzing, ribbing

related words bandying, quipping; baiting, deriding, derisive, derisory, hassling, heckling, jeering, mocking, needling, ridiculing, taunting; contemptuous, disdainful, sarcastic, scornful

quota *n* something belonging to, due to, or contributed by an individual member of a group ⟨You need to meet your sales *quota*, or you'll be put on probation.⟩ — see SHARE 1

quotation *n* a passage referred to, repeated, or offered as an example ⟨The beautiful autumn day brought to mind this *quotation* from Thoreau: "So live in each season as it passes; breathe the air, drink the drink, taste the fruit, and resign yourself to the influences of each."⟩

synonyms citation, quote

related words allusion, reference; excerpt, extract; line, part, section; snippet

quote *n* a passage referred to, repeated, or offered as an example ⟨He got a book of *quotes* from his favorite author for his birthday.⟩ — see QUOTATION

quote *vb* **1** to give as an example ⟨I could *quote* to you a hundred instances in the past when you've lied to me.⟩

synonyms adduce, cite, instance, mention

related words exemplify, represent; advert (to), illustrate, instance, name, refer (to), specify, touch (on *or* upon); bear out, corroborate, document, substantiate, validate; reference, source

2 to make reference to or speak about briefly but specifically ⟨Emma *quoted* Thomas Jefferson's views on liberty in her paper on the American Revolution.⟩ — see MENTION 1

3 to say after another ⟨Don't *quote* this to anyone, but I think we're going to Veracruz for winter vacation.⟩ — see REPEAT 3

R

rabble *n* people looked down upon as ignorant and of the lowest class ⟨The crown prince was reminded that even the *rabble* of the realm deserved his attention and compassion.⟩

synonyms proletariat, riffraff, rout, scum, trash

related words dregs; commoners, herd, masses, mob, multitude, people, plebeians, populace, public, rank and file; bourgeoisie, middle class, working class

near antonyms elect, establishment; nobility, peerage

antonyms aristocracy, elite, gentry, society, upper class, upper crust

rabble–rouser *n* a person who stirs up public feelings especially of discontent ⟨*rabble-rousers* inciting hungry people in breadlines to demand social justice⟩ — see AGITATOR

rabid *adj* **1** being very far from the center of public opinion ⟨soccer fans whose *rabid* enthusiasm makes them go berserk when their team wins⟩ — see EXTREME 2

2 feeling or showing anger ⟨He became *rabid* when the bank manager told him he would lose the family farm if he didn't pay the mortgage.⟩ — see ANGRY

3 marked by bursts of destructive force or intense activity ⟨a *rabid* nationalism that led to turbulent protests⟩ — see VIOLENT 1

4 marked by great and often stressful excitement or activity ⟨the *rabid* witch hunts that occurred in Salem in 1692, when 150 people were accused of witchcraft and imprisoned⟩ — see FURIOUS 1

race *n* a group of persons who come from the same ancestor ⟨a man born of noble *race*⟩ — see FAMILY 1

race *vb* **1** to engage in a contest ⟨Just how many candidates are *racing* for the senatorial seat this year?⟩ — see COMPETE

2 to proceed or move quickly ⟨Liz was *racing* around trying to get everything done before her big trip to India.⟩ — see HURRY 2

raceway *n* an open man-made passageway for water ⟨The child who fell through the ice was helplessly swept along the *raceway* by the current until rescued.⟩ — see CHANNEL 1

racial *adj* of, relating to, or reflecting the traits exhibited by a group of people with a common ancestry and culture ⟨an optional question about *racial* identity⟩

synonyms ethnic, tribal

related words familial; folk; kin, kindred; cultural, multicultural, national

antonyms nonracial

racism *n* hatred of or discrimination against a person or persons based on their race ⟨The 1963 bombing of the Sixteenth Street Baptist Church in Birmingham, Alabama, was one of the most deplorable incidents of *racism* that occurred during the Civil Rights Movement of the 1960s.⟩

synonyms prejudice

related words race-baiting; apartheid, Jim Crow, segregation, separatism; narrowness

near antonyms antidiscrimination, antiracism, antisegregation; assimilationism

rack *n* **1** a place set aside for sleeping ⟨The clock struck midnight, signaling that it was time to hit the *rack*.⟩ — see BED 1

2 a state of great suffering of body or mind ⟨a hiker suffering the *rack* of a sprained ankle⟩ — see DISTRESS 1

rack *vb* **1** to cause persistent suffering to ⟨The young man was *racked* with guilt over the lie he had told to his parents.⟩ — see AFFLICT

2 to injure by overuse, misuse, or pressure ⟨She *racked* her brain trying to remember where she'd put the money.⟩ — see STRAIN 1

racket *n* loud, confused, and usually inharmonious sound ⟨If all the *racket* on the stairs is any indication, someone must be moving into apartment 3B.⟩ — see NOISE 1

racketeer *n* a person who gets money from another by using force or threats ⟨a *racketeer* serving time in prison⟩

synonyms blackmailer, extortioner, extortionist

related words blackhander, gangster, hoodlum, mafioso, mobster; bully, ruffian, thug; gouger, hustler, profiteer, shark, sharper, sharpie (*or* sharpy), swindler

racking *adj* intensely or unbearably painful ⟨A *racking* cough kept him awake all night.⟩ — see EXCRUCIATING 1

rack up *vb* **1** to gain (as points or runs in a game) as credit towards one's total number of points ⟨Having *racked up* a huge number of points in the short program, the figure skater would have to have a disastrous long program in order to miss out on a medal.⟩ — see SCORE 2

2 to obtain (as a goal) through effort ⟨*racked up* their second consecutive Super Bowl victory⟩ — see ACHIEVE 1

racy *adj* **1** having much high-spirited energy and movement ⟨vivid writing and a *racy* plot that keeps readers turning the pages⟩ — see LIVELY 1

2 hinting at or intended to call to mind matters regarded as indecent ⟨a comedy with language that was a little too *racy* for an eight-year-old child⟩ — see SUGGESTIVE 1

radiance *n* **1** the quality or state of having or giving off light ⟨The *radiance* of the midday sun created a harsh glare for the skiers.⟩ — see BRILLIANCE 1

2 the steady giving off of the form of radiation that makes vision possible ⟨Kelly had a dream in which she was steadily moving down a dark tunnel toward a *radiance* at the far end.⟩ — see LIGHT 1

radiant *adj* **1** having or being an outward sign of good feelings (as of love, confidence, or happiness) ⟨She left the interview with a *radiant* smile on her face, confident she had gotten the job.⟩ ⟨a *radiant* bride⟩

synonyms aglow, beaming, bright, glowing, sunny

related words brilliant, dazzling, effulgent, gleaming, luminous, refulgent, shining, starry; blithe, blithesome, bright, cheerful, cheery, chipper, gladsome, lightsome, merry, mirthful, optimistic, upbeat; jocund, jovial, laughing, smiling; blooming, rosy; blissful, delighted, gratified, happy, joyful, joyous

near antonyms blank, flat, listless, stoic (*or* stoical), unemotional; black, dark, darkening, depressing, dismal, gloomy, glum, gray (*also* grey), melancholy, sullen; frowning, glaring, glowering, lowering (*also* louring), scowling

2 giving off or reflecting much light ⟨From the plane we could see the statehouse's *radiant* gold dome.⟩ — see BRIGHT 1

radiate *vb* **1** to extend outwards from or as if from a central point ⟨the heat *radiating* from the fire⟩ ⟨The spokes of a bicycle wheel *radiate* from the hub towards the rim.⟩

synonyms branch, fan (out), ray

related words diffuse, dispel, disperse, dissipate; fork, stem; diverge, divide, part, ramify, separate, split, uncouple, unlink, unyoke; scatter, splay, spread

near antonyms approach, close in (on), near; center (on), centralize; connect, couple, join, link, unite

antonyms concentrate, converge, focus, funnel, meet

2 to emit rays of light ⟨Fireflies give off their light by means of a chemical reaction that causes their abdomens to *radiate*.⟩ — see SHINE 1

3 to throw or give off ⟨The sun *radiates* tiny amounts of energy in the form of microwaves.⟩ — see EMIT 1

radical *adj* **1** being very far from the center of public opinion ⟨has some pretty *radical* ideas about education⟩ — see EXTREME 2

2 not bound by traditional ways or beliefs ⟨*Radical* proponents of spelling reform would have every word spelled "just the way it sounds."⟩ — see LIBERAL 1

radical *n* a person who favors rapid and sweeping changes especially in laws and methods of government ⟨He was a *radical* in his youth, but now he's pretty moderate.⟩

synonyms extremist, revolutionary, revolutionist

related words young Turk; leftist, lefty, red; progressive, reformer, reformist; anarchist, subversive; agitator, insurgent, insurrectionist, rebel; secessionist, separationist, separatist

near antonyms conservative, fuddy-duddy, reactionary, rightist, standpatter, Tory

antonyms moderate

raffish *adj* lacking in refinement or good taste ⟨a strip lined by *raffish* motels⟩ — see COARSE 2

raffishness *n* the quality or state of lacking refinement or good taste ⟨the *raffishness* of the burger joint⟩ — see VULGARITY 1

raft *n* a considerable amount ⟨The babysitter had to listen to a whole *raft* of rules before she was allowed to even pick up the baby.⟩ — see LOT 2

ragbag *n* an unorganized collection or mixture of various things ⟨a *ragbag* of souvenirs and trinkets she had accumulated over the years⟩ — see MISCELLANY 1

rage *n* **1** a state of wildly excited activity or emotion ⟨The children were in a *rage* of excitement when the bell finally rang and school was out for the summer.⟩ — see FRENZY
2 an intense emotional state of displeasure with someone or something ⟨Boiling with *rage* at the sales clerk's insult, he demanded to see the manager.⟩ — see ANGER
3 a practice or interest that is very popular for a short time ⟨There was time when playing with Frisbees was all the *rage*.⟩ — see FAD

rage *vb* **1** to express one's anger usually violently ⟨The bad call prompted the coach to *rage* about the refereeing.⟩
synonyms bristle, fume, storm
related words blow up, flare (up); bluster, carry on, fulminate, rampage, rant, rave, take on; burn, foam, seethe, smolder (*or* smoulder), steam; chafe, fret, stew
phrases make a scene, run amok (*or* run amuck)
near antonyms allay, appease, pacify, soothe; check, choke (back), collect, compose, contain, curb, pocket, rein, repress, restrain, smother, stifle, strangle, subdue, suppress, swallow; moderate, temper, tone (down); ease, let up, relax; calm, cool, hush, quell, quiet, settle, still
2 to be excited or emotionally stirred up with anger ⟨Still *raging* about his assistant's burnt pies, the pastry cook forgot to add the egg whites to his cake batter.⟩ — see BOIL 1

ragged *adj* **1** having an uneven edge or outline ⟨The Rocky Mountains cut an angular, *ragged* profile against the sky, in contrast to the rounded silhouette of the rolling, green Adirondack Mountains.⟩
synonyms broken, craggy, jagged, scraggly, scraggy
related words saw-toothed, serrate, serrated; harsh, rough, roughened, rugged; bumpy, coarse, irregular, nonuniform
near antonyms regular, uniform; flat, flush, level, plane
antonyms clean, even, smooth, soft, unbroken
2 worn or torn into or as if into rags ⟨We finally convinced her to throw away her favorite pair of jeans, *ragged* from decades of yard work.⟩
synonyms frayed, raggedy, ratty, seedy, shabby, tattered, threadbare, worn-out
related words dowdy, scruffy, tatterdemalion; dingy, faded; lacerate (*or* lacerated), shredded; holey, patchy; broken-down, decrepit, dilapidated, dog-eared, grungy, mangy, moth-eaten, run-down, scuzzy [*slang*], tacky
near antonyms brand-new, new, spick-and-span (*or* spic-and-span), unused
3 not having a level or smooth surface ⟨She cut herself on the *ragged* edge of the tin can's lid.⟩ — see UNEVEN 1
4 wearing torn or worn-out clothes ⟨the *ragged* soldiers of General Washington's army⟩ — see TATTERED 1

raggedy *adj* **1** wearing torn or worn-out clothes ⟨*raggedy* urchins playing in the village streets⟩ — see TATTERED 1
2 worn or torn into or as if into rags ⟨wears *raggedy* old T-shirts and jeans around the house⟩ — see RAGGED 2

ragtag *adj* **1** consisting of many things of different sorts ⟨The team was a *ragtag* bunch who had only one thing in common: a lack of skill.⟩ — see MISCELLANEOUS
2 wearing torn or worn-out clothes ⟨A *ragtag* and weary regiment arrived back at headquarters with the latest news from the front.⟩ — see TATTERED 1

raid *n* **1** a sudden attack on and entrance into hostile territory ⟨Repeated Viking *raids* wore down the defenses of the seaside village.⟩

synonyms descent, foray, incursion, inroad, invasion, irruption
related words pillage, plunder; aggression, assault, offense (*or* offence), offensive, onset, onslaught, rush, siege, storm, strike; charge, sally, sortie; ambuscade, ambush, surprise (*also* surprize), trap; air raid, blitz, blitzkrieg, bombardment; counterattack, counteroffensive
2 the act or action of setting upon with force or violence ⟨An early morning *raid* by Federal agents took the smugglers in their hideout by surprise.⟩ — see ATTACK 1

raid *vb* **1** to enter for conquest or plunder ⟨A fox has been *raiding* the chicken coop, and now we're down to eight hens.⟩ — see INVADE
2 to take sudden, violent action against ⟨The enemy *raided* the village just before dawn, taking everyone by surprise.⟩ — see ATTACK 1

raider *n* one that starts armed conflict against another especially without reasonable cause ⟨Villagers lived in constant fear of the *raiders*, who pillaged their homes.⟩ — see AGGRESSOR

rail *n* **1** a protective barrier consisting of a horizontal bar and its supports ⟨The stairs are icy, so hold onto the *rail*.⟩ — see RAILING
2 a roadway overlaid with parallel steel rails over which trains travel ⟨an abandoned stretch of *rail* that was overgrown with brush⟩ — see RAILROAD

rail (at *or* against) *vb* to criticize (someone) severely or angrily especially for personal failings ⟨We could hear the cook in the kitchen *railing against* his assistant and wondered if we'd ever get our food.⟩ — see SCOLD

railing *n* a protective barrier consisting of a horizontal bar and its supports ⟨They had to put a childproof *railing* on the balcony when the baby started walking.⟩
synonyms balustrade, banister (*also* bannister), guardrail, rail
related words handrail; taffrail; fender

raillery *n* good-natured teasing or exchanging of clever remarks ⟨Luke had to put up with a lot of *raillery* from his sister the first time he asked a girl for a date.⟩ — see BANTER

railroad *n* a roadway overlaid with parallel steel rails over which trains travel ⟨That *railroad* hasn't been used for passenger trains for decades.⟩
synonyms rail, railway, road
related words el, elevated, elevated railroad; monorail

railway *n* a roadway overlaid with parallel steel rails over which trains travel ⟨a system of *railways* that crisscrosses the whole nation⟩ — see RAILROAD

raiment *n* covering for the human body ⟨The prince exchanged his silken *raiment* for the pauper's humble homespun.⟩ — see CLOTHING

rain *n* **1** a steady falling of water from the sky in significant quantity ⟨The *rain* continued for most of the day.⟩
synonyms cloudburst, deluge, downfall, downpour, rainfall, rainstorm, storm, wet
related words precipitation, shower; thundershower, thunderstorm, weather
near antonyms drizzle, mist, scud, sprinkle
2 a heavy fall of objects ⟨The Norman invaders fled when the castle's defenders threw a *rain* of stones down upon them.⟩
synonyms hail, shower, storm
related words barrage, bombardment, broadside, cannonade, fusillade, salvo, volley; flood, gush, rush, spate, torrent; eruption, outbreak, outburst

rain *vb* **1** to fall as water in a continuous stream of drops from the clouds ⟨It started *raining* early this morning and hasn't let up since.⟩
synonyms pour, precipitate, storm

related words shower; hail, squall; deluge, drown, engulf, flood, inundate, swamp

phrases rain cats and dogs

near antonyms drizzle, mist, sprinkle

2 to give readily and in large quantities ⟨She *rained* praise upon her graduating students.⟩ ⟨The squadron *rained* bombs on the enemy's fortifications.⟩

synonyms heap, lavish, pour, shower

related words gush, stream; flood, inundate, overflow, overwhelm, swamp; bombard, hail

near antonyms hold back, keep, reserve, retain, withhold

raincoat *n* a coat made of water-resistant material ⟨I grabbed my umbrella and *raincoat* before going out in the thunderstorm.⟩

synonyms oilskin, slicker

related words rain gear, rainwear; poncho, sou'wester, trench, trench coat

rainfall *n* a steady falling of water from the sky in significant quantity ⟨A torrential *rainfall* washed away most of the little sprouts in our vegetable garden.⟩ — see RAIN 1

rainstorm *n* a steady falling of water from the sky in significant quantity ⟨We ran into a big *rainstorm* on Highway 6, and the visibility was so poor we had to pull over.⟩ — see RAIN 1

rainy *adj* marked by or abounding with rain ⟨found that the cold, *rainy* weather made his joints swell and ache⟩

synonyms pouring, precipitating, stormy, wet

related words drizzling, drizzly, misty, sprinkling

near antonyms dry

raise *n* something added (as by growth) ⟨a *raise* in salary⟩ — see INCREASE 1

raise *vb* **1** to move from a lower to a higher place or position ⟨He asked members of the audience to *raise* their hands if they had been to his show before.⟩

synonyms boost, crane, elevate, heave, heft, heighten, hike, hoist, jack (up), lift, perk (up), pick up, take up, up, uphold, uplift, upraise

related words ascend, mount, rise; rear, upend

near antonyms descend, dip, fall, pitch, plunge, slip; bear, depress, press, push; sink, submerge

antonyms drop, lower

2 to bring to maturity through care and education ⟨Since she was only two when her mother died, the girl was *raised* mainly by her aunt.⟩ — see BRING UP 1

3 to bring (something volatile or intense) into being ⟨A proposal to cover the library's red brick with vinyl siding *raised* a mighty ruckus with those favoring historical preservation.⟩ — see INCITE 1

4 to draw out (something hidden, latent, or reserved) ⟨The lawsuit *raised* old resentments that had never been completely extinguished.⟩ — see EDUCE

5 to fix in an upright position ⟨The mattress will fit into the moving truck only if we *raise* it on its side.⟩ — see ERECT 1

6 to form by putting together parts or materials ⟨*raised* a memorial on the site of the historic battlefield⟩ — see BUILD

7 to look after or assist the growth of by labor and care ⟨*raises* ducks, geese, and other exotic fowl ultimately destined for the dinner table⟩ — see GROW 1

8 to make greater in size, amount, or number ⟨The multiplex *raised* the minimum age for paid admissions from four to six.⟩ — see INCREASE 1

9 to move higher in rank or position ⟨He was recently *raised* to lieutenant in the fire department.⟩ — see PROMOTE 1

10 to present or bring forward for discussion ⟨One member of the tour *raised* the subject of appropriate attire for travel.⟩ — see INTRODUCE 2

11 to make known (as an idea, emotion, or opinion) ⟨too afraid to *raise* an objection⟩ — see EXPRESS 1

raised *adj* **1** being at a higher level than average ⟨Due to *raised* levels of mercury in the water, there is a warning against eating the local shrimp.⟩ — see HIGH 2

2 being positioned above a surface ⟨directed the filming of the movie's battle scene from a *raised* platform⟩ — see ELEVATED 1

3 rising straight up ⟨The 63 Braille characters are made up of one to six *raised* dots arranged in a matrix.⟩ — see ERECT

¹rake *n* a person who has sunk below the normal moral standard ⟨had a reputation as one of the city's most notorious *rakes*⟩ — see DEGENERATE

²rake *n* the degree to which something rises up from a position level with the horizon ⟨The floor of the auditorium doesn't have much of a *rake*, so sightlines for spectators in the rear are not good.⟩ — see SLANT 1

rake *vb* to look through (as a place) carefully or thoroughly in an effort to find or discover something ⟨He *raked* through his suitcase looking for his passport.⟩ — see SEARCH 1

¹rally *vb* **1** to assemble and make ready for action ⟨*rallied* the Red Cross workers to help the distressed areas⟩ — see MOBILIZE

2 to become healthy and strong again after illness or weakness ⟨After several days of rest I was able to *rally* from the flu.⟩ — see CONVALESCE

3 to regain a former or normal state ⟨After wavering a moment on the balance beam, she quickly *rallied* and finished with a fine dismount.⟩ — see RECOVER 2

²rally *vb* to make fun of in a good-natured way ⟨His friends *rallied* him for missing an easy putt.⟩ — see TEASE 1

rally *n* **1** an act of gathering forces together to renew or attempt an effort ⟨In a state-wide *rally* the community was able to provide aid to everyone affected by the storm.⟩

synonyms marshaling (*also* marshalling), mobilization, rallying

related words call, call-up, summons; convening, convocation, muster, mustering

phrases call to arms

2 a mass meeting for the purpose of displaying or arousing support for a cause or person ⟨a huge *rally* for the candidate on the eve of the election⟩

synonyms demonstration

related words assembly, conference, congress, convention, convocation, council, gathering; march; protest, sit-down, sit-in, strike; counterdemonstration, counterprotest, counterrally

3 the process or period of gradually regaining one's health and strength ⟨The doctors were amazed at the sick child's unexpected *rally*, which was apparently due to the new drug.⟩ — see CONVALESCENCE

rallying *adj* marked by or expressive of mild or good-natured teasing ⟨He took his friends' *rallying* remarks good-naturedly.⟩ — see QUIZZICAL

rallying *n* an act of gathering forces together to renew or attempt an effort ⟨The *rallying* of students to support our petition for better bus service was made a lot easier by this morning's subzero temperatures.⟩ — see RALLY 1

ram *vb* **1** to come into usually forceful contact with something ⟨The truck suddenly swerved and *rammed* into the side of a building.⟩ — see HIT 2

2 to fit (people or things) into a tight space ⟨The boy *rammed* as many candies into his mouth as he could fit.⟩ — see CROWD 1

3 to proceed or move quickly ⟨I threw myself out of the way as a car *rammed* through the crosswalk.⟩ — see HURRY 2

ramble *n* **1** a short trip for pleasure ⟨the couple's weekend *rambles* up and down the valley in search of interesting antiques⟩ — see EXCURSION 1

2 a relaxed journey on foot for exercise or pleasure ⟨Our usual practice is to take a *ramble* around the neighborhood after dinner.⟩ — see WALK 1

ramble *vb* **1** to talk at length without sticking to a topic or getting to a point ⟨The teenagers sat around the pizza parlor, *rambling* on about dating, homework, movies, and the local football team.⟩

synonyms maunder, rattle, run on

related words deviate, digress, stray, wander; sidetrack; blab, blabber, chat, chatter, drivel, drool, gab, gibber, jabber, patter, prate, prattle

phrases run one's mouth

2 to move about from place to place aimlessly ⟨By tirelessly *rambling* around San Francisco for a week we probably saw more of it than many residents ever have.⟩ — see WANDER 1

3 to travel by foot for exercise or pleasure ⟨We're planning to *ramble* all over the highland moors when we're in Dartmoor.⟩ — see HIKE 1

rambler *n* a person who roams about without a fixed route or destination ⟨A *rambler* her whole life, my aunt is likely to send me a postcard from just about any corner of the world.⟩ — see NOMAD

rambling *adj* **1** passing from one topic to another ⟨I listened patiently to Mrs. Parsifal's *rambling* reminiscences, though I had no idea who "Dorothy" and "the stepson" were.⟩ — see DISCURSIVE

2 using or containing more words than necessary to express an idea ⟨I sat through another of his *rambling* lectures.⟩ — see WORDY 1

rambunctious *adj* being rough or noisy in a high-spirited way ⟨That beach is often taken over by packs of *rambunctious* young people, so don't go there expecting peace and quiet.⟩ — see BOISTEROUS

ramify *vb* to set or force apart ⟨The rise of streaming television shows *ramified* the audience, creating ever smaller segments for an ever growing array of programming choices.⟩ — see SEPARATE 1

rampage *n* a state of wildly excited activity or emotion ⟨Some guy went on a *rampage* in the public library and started grabbing books off the shelves and tossing them around.⟩ — see FRENZY

rampant *adj* **1** showing no signs of being under control ⟨Rumors of their engagement ran *rampant*.⟩

synonyms abandoned, intemperate, raw, unbounded, unbridled, unchecked, uncontrolled, unhampered, unhindered, unrestrained

related words uncontrollable, ungovernable; barbaric, hog wild, riotous, uninhibited, wild

near antonyms moderate, tempered

antonyms bridled, checked, constrained, controlled, curbed, governed, hampered, hindered, restrained, temperate

2 growing thickly and vigorously ⟨Try to avoid the patch of *rampant* poison ivy near the resting spot on the trail.⟩ — see RANK 1

ramrod *adj* given to exacting standards of discipline and self-restraint ⟨a *ramrod* camp director who's been known to send kids home for a minor infraction of the rules⟩ — see SEVERE 1

ranch *n* a piece of land and its buildings used to grow crops or raise livestock ⟨The family lives on a cattle *ranch* in Texas that's as big as the whole state of Rhode Island.⟩ — see FARM

rancor *n* a deep-seated ill will ⟨The controversy over use of pesticides has caused a lot of *rancor* in this agricultural community.⟩ — see ENMITY

rancorous *adj* having or showing deep-seated resentment ⟨a *rancorous* autobiography in which the author heaps blame on just about everyone who had the misfortune of knowing him⟩ — see BITTER 1

random *adj* lacking a definite plan, purpose, or pattern ⟨Since we were new in town, our choice of a vet for our dog was entirely *random*.⟩

synonyms aimless, arbitrary, desultory, erratic, haphazard, helter-skelter, hit-or-miss, scattered, slapdash, stray

related words accidental, casual, chance, chancy, contingent, fluky (*also* flukey), fortuitous, inadvertent, incidental, lucky, unconsidered, unintended, unintentional, unplanned, unpremeditated; scattershot, shotgun; irregular, odd, sporadic, spot; directionless, objectless, purposeless; unsystematic; undirected; disorderly, disorganized; undiscriminating, unselective

near antonyms established, fixed, regular, set, stable, steady; constant, continuous, even; arranged, managed, orchestrated, ordered, planned; aware, conscious, deliberate, purposeful, thoughtful, willful (*or* wilful)

antonyms methodical (*also* methodic), nonrandom, orderly, organized, regular, systematic, systematized

randomly *adv* without definite aim, direction, rule, or method ⟨The winner will be *randomly* chosen from among all of the entries.⟩ — see HIT OR MISS

range *n* **1** open land over which livestock may roam and feed ⟨knew exactly how many head of cattle were turned out on the *range* that morning to graze⟩

synonyms lea (*or* ley), pasturage, pasture

related words ranch, station; feedlot, stockyard, yard; grassland, pampas, prairie, savanna (*also* savannah), steppe

2 an area over which activity, capacity, or influence extends ⟨I didn't know she had such a wide *range* of knowledge until I talked to her.⟩

synonyms amplitude, breadth, compass, confines, dimension(s), extent, reach, realm, scope, sweep, width

related words gamut, spectrum, spread; circle, demesne, department, discipline, domain, element, field, province, region, specialty, sphere; frontier; horizon, panorama

3 the distance or extent between possible extremes ⟨an actor who can go through the full *range* of emotion, from joy to sorrow, in mere minutes⟩

synonyms gamut, scale, spectrum, spread, stretch

related words measure, pitch, scale; ambit, amplitude, compass, dimension(s), extent, reach, realm, scope, sweep, width

4 a relaxed journey on foot for exercise or pleasure ⟨They were stopped by security personnel while taking an innocent *range* through the palace grounds.⟩ — see WALK 1

5 a series of persons or things arranged one behind another ⟨From the air, the mountain *range* stretched as far as we could see in both directions.⟩ — see LINE 1

6 an appliance that prepares food for consumption by heating it ⟨The high-end appliances include a professional-quality gas *range*.⟩ — see COOKER 1

7 the place where a plant or animal is usually or naturally found ⟨The American robin's winter *range* has steadily extended farther and farther north.⟩ — see HOME 2

range *vb* **1** to arrange or assign according to type ⟨The campers were *ranged* in patrols, each patrol consisting of girls in a certain age group.⟩ — see CLASSIFY 1

2 to move about from place to place aimlessly ⟨She let her dog off the leash and whistled for him every now and then to make sure he didn't *range* out of hearing.⟩ — see WANDER 1

3 to occur within a continuous range of variation ⟨The

color of Florida grapefruit can *range* anywhere from pale pink to ruby red.⟩ — see RUN 4

4 to put into a particular arrangement ⟨Chairs were *ranged* round the perimeter of the room.⟩ — see ORDER 1

ranging *adj* traveling from place to place ⟨A *ranging* bear has been spotted at bird feeders in different parts of town.⟩ — see ITINERANT

rangy *adj* **1** being tall, thin and usually loose-jointed ⟨We could use a *rangy* girl like you on our basketball team.⟩ — see LANKY

2 having considerable extent ⟨a speech that took a *rangy* look at the problems facing the university⟩ — see EXTENSIVE

rank *adj* **1** growing thickly and vigorously ⟨The wall was covered with trumpet vines so *rank* you couldn't see the trellis beneath them.⟩

synonyms lush, luxuriant, prosperous, rampant, weedy

related words lavish, profuse; overgrown, overrun, verdant; close, dense, thick

near antonyms dormant; blighted, stunted

antonyms sparse

2 having an unpleasant smell ⟨smokes *rank* cigars that usually send me running for fresh air⟩ — see MALODOROUS

3 very noticeable especially for being incorrect or bad ⟨The article about fairy tales was full of *rank* errors, such as a reference to "Cinderella biting into the poisoned apple."⟩ — see EGREGIOUS

4 having no exceptions or restrictions ⟨a sidewalk sale of art works by *rank* amateurs⟩ — see ABSOLUTE 2

rank *n* **1** the placement of someone or something in relation to others in a vertical arrangement ⟨attained the highest *rank* in the Freemasons⟩

synonyms degree, echelon, footing, level, place, position, ranking, reach(es), situation, standing, station, status, stratum

related words condition, estate, order, walk; capacity, function; rating

2 high position within society ⟨remembered as a woman of *rank* who socialized only with other members of the elite⟩

synonyms class, dignity, fashion, quality, standing, state

related words gentility, gentleness, nobility, nobleness; grandness, highness, loftiness; distinction, dominance, precedence, preeminence, primacy, superiority; caste, station, status; preferment

near antonyms debasement, degradation; subordinateness, subordination; baseness, commonness, inferiority, lowliness, lowness

3 a series of people or things arranged side by side ⟨*Rank* upon *rank* of cavalry came thundering down the hill.⟩ — see ¹ROW 1

4 *usually* **ranks** *pl* one of the units into which a whole is divided on the basis of a common characteristic ⟨This book will someday join the *ranks* of the world's great novels.⟩ — see CLASS 2

rank *vb* **1** to take or have a certain position within a group arranged in vertical classes ⟨My favorite pitcher *ranks* first in the league for number of consecutive outs.⟩

synonyms be, grade, place, rate, stand

related words seed; count; categorize, class, classify, codify, group, separate, set, sort; install, instate

2 to arrange or assign according to type ⟨Most critics would *rank* him among our best actors.⟩ — see CLASSIFY 1

rank and file *n* the body of the community as contrasted with the elite ⟨The chosen few might have the opportunity for a trip in the space shuttle, but it will be a while before the *rank and file* are taking space trips.⟩ — see MASS 1

ranking *n* **1** a scheme of rank or order ⟨In one *ranking* of the best places to live, San Francisco surpassed all the other cities in the U.S.⟩ — see ³SCALE 1

2 the placement of someone or something in relation to others in a vertical arrangement ⟨The President's *ranking* in the polls is at its highest level since he took office.⟩ — see RANK 1

rankle *vb* **1** to be excited or emotionally stirred up with anger ⟨That kind of rude treatment makes me *rankle*.⟩ — see BOIL 1

2 to make angry ⟨It *rankles* me when some schools can't even afford supplies for the students.⟩ — see ANGER

rankled *adj* feeling or showing anger ⟨Our supervisor was *rankled* by all the unexpected delays and problems we ran into.⟩ — see ANGRY

rankling *adj* causing annoyance ⟨For some air travelers, the most *rankling* aspect of the boarding process seems to be the long lines.⟩ — see ANNOYING

ransack *vb* **1** to search through with the intent of committing robbery ⟨It was clear that the thieves who had *ransacked* the museum were professionals—they bypassed most of the exhibits and went straight for the vaults.⟩

synonyms despoil, loot, maraud, pillage, plunder, sack

related words break in, burglarize, rip off, steal (from); comb, hunt, rake, rifle, rummage; harry, raid; ravish

2 to look through (as a place) carefully or thoroughly in an effort to find or discover something ⟨I've *ransacked* the whole house for that bracelet you lent me and it's nowhere to be found.⟩ — see SEARCH 1

ransom *vb* to free from captivity or punishment by paying a price ⟨The prince emptied the treasury to *ransom* his son from the kidnappers.⟩

synonyms redeem

related words deliver, rescue, save; emancipate, liberate; recover, regain, retrieve; release; buy; salvage

rant *n* **1** a long angry speech or scolding ⟨After complaining about the hotel's lousy service, the woman went off on another *rant* about the condition of her room.⟩ — see TIRADE

2 boastful speech or writing ⟨Instead of addressing the current crisis, the mayor's speech was a lot of *rant* emphasizing his accomplishments.⟩ — see BOMBAST 1

rant *vb* to talk loudly and wildly ⟨When the salesclerk gave him incorrect change, he began *ranting* about the poor service.⟩

synonyms bluster, fulminate, huff, rave, spout

related words sound off, speak out, speak up; blare, blurt (out), bolt; declaim, harangue, mouth (off), orate, pontificate; carry on, rage, storm, take on

near antonyms grunt, murmur, mutter, slur; breathe, whisper

¹rap *n* **1** a formal claim of criminal wrongdoing against a person ⟨The headlines in the paper today are all about the mayor facing an embezzlement *rap*.⟩ — see CHARGE 1

2 a hard strike with a part of the body or an instrument ⟨The doctor used a little hammer to give me a *rap* on the knee to test my reflexes.⟩ — see ¹BLOW 1

3 responsibility for wrongdoing or failure ⟨He would sooner take the *rap* for the missing money than tell on his friend.⟩ — see BLAME 1

²rap *n* friendly, informal conversation or an instance of this ⟨After our pickup softball game, I had a friendly *rap* with a couple of the guys in the park.⟩ — see CHAT 1

³rap *n* the smallest amount or part imaginable ⟨I don't care a *rap* about losing that old jacket.⟩ — see JOT

¹rap *vb* **1** to deliver a blow to (someone or something) usually in a strong vigorous manner ⟨a childhood memory of the time he got his knuckles *rapped* for trying to steal candy from the corner store⟩ — see HIT 1

2 to strike or cause to strike lightly and usually rhythmically ⟨The impatient man was *rapping* his knuckles on the door, hoping to wake up the sleeping attendant.⟩ — see ¹TAP

²**rap** *vb* to engage in casual or rambling conversation ⟨The guys at the gym never seem to tire of *rapping* about basketball.⟩ — see CHAT 1

³**rap** *vb* **1** to fill with overwhelming emotion (as wonder or delight) ⟨Concertgoers were utterly *rapped* by the power of Handel's oratorio.⟩ — see ENTRANCE
2 to take physical control or possession of (something) suddenly or forcibly ⟨Suddenly the hawk swooped down and *rapped* the unwary rodent.⟩ — see CATCH 1

rapacious *adj* **1** having a huge appetite ⟨Nothing livens things up like a whole team of *rapacious* basketball players descending upon the pizza parlor.⟩ — see VORACIOUS 1
2 living by killing and eating other animals ⟨*rapacious* mammals, such as coyotes, foxes, and bobcats⟩ — see PREDATORY
3 having or marked by an eager and often selfish desire especially for material possessions ⟨*rapacious* plunderers who despoiled the tombs in the ancient pyramids⟩ — see GREEDY 1

rapaciousness *n* an intense selfish desire for wealth or possessions ⟨The land developer's *rapaciousness* knew no bounds, and if what she wanted wasn't for sale, she would force the owner into selling it.⟩ — see GREED

rapacity *n* an intense selfish desire for wealth or possessions ⟨The *rapacity* of the Spanish conquistadors was such that they were undeterred by the very preposterousness of the legend of El Dorado.⟩ — see GREED

rapid *adj* moving, proceeding, or acting with great speed ⟨The *rapid* descent of the roller coaster made me feel very queasy.⟩ — see FAST 1

rapid–fire *adj* moving, proceeding, or acting with great speed ⟨The witness stayed unruffled all through the prosecutor's *rapid-fire* questioning.⟩ — see FAST 1

rapidity *n* a high rate of movement or performance ⟨The *rapidity* with which she can do mental math calculations is amazing.⟩ — see SPEED 1

rapidly *adv* with great speed ⟨Summer vacation has gone by way too *rapidly*.⟩ — see FAST 1

rapidness *n* a high rate of movement or performance ⟨The *rapidness* of the response to a call for assistance is critical in saving the victim of a heart attack.⟩ — see SPEED 1

rapport *n* a friendly relationship marked by ready communication and mutual understanding ⟨His good *rapport* with his students was one of the reasons why the school board named him Teacher of the Year.⟩
synonyms communion, fellowship, rapprochement
related words accord, agreement, concord, harmony; oneness, solidarity, togetherness, unity; affinity, empathy, sympathy, understanding; amity, chumminess, companionship, friendliness, friendship; reciprocity, symbiosis
near antonyms alienation, disaffection, disgruntlement, estrangement; cold shoulder, distance, iciness; animosity, antagonism, antipathy, bitterness, enmity, hostility, jaundice, rancor, spite

rapprochement *n* a friendly relationship marked by ready communication and mutual understanding ⟨an era of *rapprochement* between Mexico and the U.S. that was highlighted by a new trade agreement⟩ — see RAPPORT

rapscallion *n* **1** a mean, evil, or unprincipled person ⟨The city's run-down waterfront was frequented by *rapscallions*.⟩ — see VILLAIN
2 an appealingly mischievous person ⟨That little *rapscallion* kept hiding my shoes and making me go look for them.⟩ — see SCAMP 1

rapt *adj* **1** experiencing or marked by overwhelming usually pleasurable emotion ⟨a rock band that still attracts *rapt* crowds of aging baby boomers⟩ — see ECSTATIC
2 having the mind fixed on something ⟨With a mixture of delight and awe, the *rapt* children stared at the chick in the incubator breaking out of its shell.⟩ — see ATTENTIVE 1

rapture *n* a state of overwhelming usually pleasurable emotion ⟨In *The Nutcracker* Clara gazes in *rapture* as the Christmas tree grows before her very eyes.⟩ — see ECSTASY

rapture *vb* to fill with overwhelming emotion (as wonder or delight) ⟨Nature lovers will be *raptured* by the documentary's breathtaking cinematography.⟩ — see ENTRANCE

rapturous *adj* experiencing or marked by overwhelming usually pleasurable emotion ⟨We heard the whoops of the *rapturous* fan whose quest for an autograph had met with success.⟩ — see ECSTATIC

rare *adj* **1** being out of the ordinary ⟨Even among the prize-winning roses, this one is a *rare* beauty.⟩ — see EXCEPTIONAL 1
2 having qualities that appeal to a refined taste ⟨*rare* specialty wools, such as cashmere, prized for their fineness, lightness and exceptional warmth⟩ — see CHOICE 1
3 not often occurring or repeated ⟨The French pronunciation of the family's name is *rare*, except in Louisiana.⟩ — see INFREQUENT
4 noticeably different from what is generally found or experienced ⟨"Such good manners are *rare* these days," remarked Mrs. Denby, as the young man let her go ahead of him in line.⟩ — see UNUSUAL 1

rarely *adv* not often ⟨Summer thunderstorms occur only *rarely* along the Oregon coast.⟩ — see SELDOM

raring *adj* showing urgent desire or interest ⟨We'd gotten up so early that by the time eight o'clock rolled around, we were *raring* to get started on the hike.⟩ — see EAGER

rarity *n* **1** something strange or unusual that is an object of interest ⟨An American visitor in that remote Chinese village is a *rarity*.⟩ — see CURIOSITY 2
2 something that is different from what is ordinary or expected ⟨Snow is a *rarity* in this part of the world.⟩ — see ANOMALY 1

rascal *n* **1** a mean, evil, or unprincipled person ⟨Some cold-blooded *rascal* had set the barn afire.⟩ — see VILLAIN
2 an appealingly mischievous person ⟨You little *rascal*, I saw you snitching some hors d'oeuvres even though our guests haven't even arrived yet!⟩ — see SCAMP 1

rascality *n* playful, reckless behavior that is not intended to cause serious harm ⟨Switching the entrance and exits signs in the school parking lot may seem like harmless *rascality*, if you're not the one involved in an accident.⟩ — see MISCHIEF 1

rascally *adj* tending to or exhibiting reckless playfulness ⟨Those *rascally* boys had let all of the lab mice out of their cages.⟩ — see MISCHIEVOUS 1

rash *adj* acting or done with excessive or careless speed ⟨That was too *rash* a move, for now I've lost my bishop and probably the whole chess game.⟩ — see HASTY 1

rashly *adv* with excessive or careless speed ⟨I *rashly* agreed to babysit for the Franklin family, completely forgetting that the last time had been awful.⟩ — see HASTILY 1

rasp *n* a harsh grating sound ⟨The rusted lock opened with a *rasp*.⟩
synonyms creak, grind, jar, scrape
related words clang, clangor, clank, clash; scuff; croak, gargle; blast, bray, screech

rasp *vb* **1** to make smooth by friction ⟨After sawing the board in half, *rasp* the ends to remove any splinters.⟩ — see GRIND 1

2 to pass roughly and noisily over or against a surface ⟨The sound of fingernails *rasping* on the blackboard makes me cringe.⟩ — see SCRAPE 1

3 to disturb the peace of mind of (someone) especially by repeated disagreeable acts ⟨The two siblings seemed intent on *rasping* each other for the entire car trip.⟩ — see IRRITATE 1

4 to damage or diminish by continued friction ⟨During the last ice age, glaciers *rasped* the surface, leaving the deeply scarred rock.⟩ — see ABRADE 1

raspberry *n* a vocal sound made to express scorn or disapproval ⟨There were *raspberries* from the audience when the hapless actress kept forgetting her lines.⟩ — see CATCALL

rasping *adj* harsh and dry in sound ⟨a patient beset by a *rasping* cough from years of smoking⟩ — see HOARSE

raspy *adj* **1** easily irritated or annoyed ⟨Overwork tends to make him *raspy*.⟩ — see IRRITABLE

2 harsh and dry in sound ⟨The man spoke in a barely audible, *raspy* voice.⟩ — see HOARSE

rat *n* **1** a person who provides information about another's wrongdoing ⟨The drug mule refused to turn *rat* without a guarantee of immunity.⟩ — see INFORMER

2 someone who regularly spends time in a particular place ⟨On Saturday morning the gym *rats* were out in full force.⟩ — see DENIZEN 1

3 a person whose behavior is offensive to others ⟨I'm done hanging around with that *rat*.⟩ — see JERK 1

rat (on) *vb* **1** to give information (as to the authorities) about another's improper or unlawful activities ⟨Someone must have *ratted on* us to the police.⟩ — see SQUEAL 1

2 to leave (a cause or party) often in order to take up another ⟨Many party operatives *ratted on* the senator's candidacy once her poll numbers started to slip.⟩ — see DEFECT (FROM)

¹**rate** *vb* **1** to be or make worthy of (as a reward or punishment) ⟨How does a summer intern *rate* a new computer when I've been told to make do with this clunker?⟩ — see EARN 2

2 to make an approximate or tentative judgment regarding ⟨Most people would probably *rate* their cell phone as an essential piece of electronic equipment.⟩ — see ESTIMATE 1

3 to take or have a certain position within a group arranged in vertical classes ⟨a restaurant that consistently *rates* high in all the standard categories⟩ — see RANK 1

4 to think of in a particular way ⟨I would *rate* her my best friend; after all, she's always been there when I needed her.⟩ — see CONSIDER 1

²**rate** *vb* to criticize (someone) severely or angrily especially for personal failings ⟨got *rated* for being late yet again⟩ — see SCOLD

rate *n* **1** degree of excellence ⟨Not being of the first *rate*, these apples are usually sold as food for livestock.⟩ — see QUALITY 1

2 the relationship in quantity, amount, or size between two or more things ⟨The exchange *rate* against the dollar was trending down.⟩ — see RATIO

rather *adv* **1** by choice or preference ⟨I would *rather* go to the movies than stay at home.⟩

synonyms first, preferably, readily, soon, willingly

related words alternately, alternatively, instead; desirably, gladly, wishfully; obligingly, voluntarily

near antonyms reluctantly; forcibly, willy-nilly

antonyms involuntarily, unwillingly

2 as a substitute ⟨Don't think of the placement test as torture but *rather* as a chance to show off how much you know.⟩ — see INSTEAD

3 to some degree or extent ⟨I say, don't you think that's *rather* expensive for a hamburger?⟩ — see FAIRLY 1

ratify *vb* to give official acceptance of as satisfactory ⟨Lincoln's home state of Illinois was the first to *ratify* the 13th Amendment to the U.S. Constitution, which provided for the abolition of slavery.⟩ — see APPROVE

ratio *n* the relationship in quantity, amount, or size between two or more things ⟨The *ratio* of students to teachers in the school is nine to one.⟩

synonyms proportion, rate

related words average; frequency; correspondence; percentage

near antonyms disproportion

ration *vb* to give as a share or portion ⟨The region has had to *ration* water during times of drought.⟩ — see ALLOT

rational *adj* **1** having the ability to reason ⟨Human beings are *rational* creatures.⟩

synonyms intelligent, reasonable, reasoning, thinking

related words analytic (*or* analytical), logical; brainy, cerebral, highbrow, intellectual; cognitional, cognitive, mental; levelheaded, practical, sane, sensible, sober

near antonyms brainless, dense, doltish, dopey (*also* dopy), dull, dumb, fatuous, half-witted, mindless, obtuse, senseless, slow, stupid, thickheaded; fallacious, groundless, illogical, invalid, nonsensical

antonyms irrational, nonrational, nonthinking, unintelligent, unreasonable, unreasoning, unthinking

2 according to the rules of logic ⟨insisted there was a *rational* explanation for the strange creaking noises and that there were no such things as ghosts⟩ — see LOGICAL 1

3 based on sound reasoning or information ⟨Betting all of your savings on the lottery is not a *rational* move.⟩ — see GOOD 1

rationale *n* a statement given to explain a belief or act ⟨The *rationale* for starting the school day an hour later is that kids will supposedly get an extra hour of sleep.⟩ — see REASON 1

rationalize *vb* to give the reason for or cause of ⟨Tom *rationalized* his decision to buy the new car by noting that it was more fuel efficient than his old vehicle.⟩ — see EXPLAIN 2

rattle *n* loud, confused, and usually inharmonious sound ⟨They could hear the *rattle* of the crowd as they neared the stadium.⟩ — see NOISE 1

rattle *vb* **1** to make a series of short sharp noises ⟨The children tromped through the kitchen, making the plates on the shelf *rattle*.⟩

synonyms clack, clatter

related words chink, chirp, clank, click, clink; clang, clash, crash; spatter, sputter; racket

2 to engage in casual or rambling conversation ⟨Busily *rattling* away about our vacation plans, we didn't listen to the announcements and missed our flight.⟩ — see CHAT 1

3 to talk at length without sticking to a topic or getting to a point ⟨She *rattled* on and on about all her European shopping trips, but I wasn't really listening.⟩ — see RAMBLE 1

4 to throw into a state of self-conscious distress ⟨Don't let a little mistake *rattle* you while you're playing during the piano recital.⟩ — see EMBARRASS 1

rattling *adj* moving, proceeding, or acting with great speed ⟨We drove off at a *rattling* pace.⟩ — see FAST 1

ratty *adj* **1** showing signs of advanced wear and tear and neglect ⟨Some *ratty* old magazines were the only reading material in the mountaintop cabin.⟩ — see SHABBY 1

2 worn or torn into or as if into rags ⟨Can I use this *ratty* old T-shirt to wipe up some paint?⟩ — see RAGGED 2

raucous *adj* being rough or noisy in a high-spirited way ⟨The partying neighbors kept up their *raucous* laughter half the night.⟩ — see BOISTEROUS

ravage *vb* to bring destruction to (something) through violent action ⟨The forest was *ravaged* by fire.⟩

synonyms destroy, devastate, ruin, scourge

related words despoil, foray, harry, loot, maraud, pillage, plunder, sack, strip; annihilate, desolate, eradicate, expunge, extinguish, extirpate, obliterate, rub out, shatter, smash, total, waste, wipe out, wreck; decimate, mow; demolish, raze; crush, overpower, overrun, overthrow, overwhelm

near antonyms recondition, recover, redeem, rehabilitate, restore; fix, mend, patch, repair, revamp

rave *vb* **1** to make an exaggerated display of affection or enthusiasm ⟨Just to be polite, our guest *raved* about the canned beans and franks we'd set before him.⟩ — see GUSH 2

2 to talk loudly and wildly ⟨A man stood outside city hall waving his arms and *raving* about his tax bill.⟩ — see RANT

rave *n, often* **raves** *pl* enthusiastic and usually public expression of approval ⟨The books have received even more *raves* from parents than from the kids they were written for.⟩ — see APPLAUSE 1

ravel (out) *vb* to separate the various strands of ⟨Since the sweater is too small, you could *ravel* the yarn *out* and make something else with it.⟩ — see UNRAVEL 1

raven *adj* having the color of soot or coal ⟨had dark eyes and *raven* hair⟩ — see BLACK 1

ravenous *adj* having a huge appetite ⟨We were *ravenous* after our canoe paddling, and the chili bubbling over the campfire smelled heavenly.⟩ — see VORACIOUS 1

ravine *n* a narrow opening between hillsides or mountains that can be used for passage ⟨He urged his horse down into the *ravine* where there was a thin stream of water flowing.⟩ — see CANYON

ravish *vb* to fill with overwhelming emotion (as wonder or delight) ⟨Travelers have long been *ravished* with wonder and awe by the immensity of the Great Pyramid at Giza.⟩ — see ENTRANCE

ravishing *adj* very pleasing to look at ⟨The hotel offers a *ravishing* view of the ocean.⟩ — see BEAUTIFUL 1

raw *adj* **1** not cooked ⟨You should wash your hands after handling *raw* chicken.⟩

synonyms uncooked

related words unheated; rare; half-baked, underdone

near antonyms well-done; overdone; baked, boiled, braised, broiled, fried, grilled, heated, roasted, sautéed (*also* sauteed); burned (*or* burnt), charred, scorched

antonyms cooked

2 being such as found in nature and not altered by processing or refining ⟨*Raw* sugar is honey-colored because the crystals retain cane juices, minerals, and other impurities that haven't been refined out.⟩ — see CRUDE 1

3 lacking in adult experience or maturity ⟨Recruiters like to say the military turns *raw* youths into responsible men and women.⟩ — see CALLOW

4 marked by wet and windy conditions ⟨one of those bleak, blustery, *raw* winter days⟩ — see FOUL 1

5 uncomfortably cool ⟨Evenings in those mountains, even during the summer, tend to be a little *raw*.⟩ — see CHILLY 1

6 causing intense discomfort to one's skin ⟨Bundle up if you're going sailing, as there's a *raw* wind out there in the bay.⟩ — see CUTTING 1

7 showing no signs of being under control ⟨a frightening display of *raw* anger⟩ — see RAMPANT 1

raw deal *n* unfair or inadequate treatment of someone or something or an instance of this ⟨Customers felt they were getting a *raw deal*.⟩ — see DISSERVICE

raw material *n* the basic elements from which something can be developed ⟨Canada now converts most of its *raw materials* into manufactured goods such as automobiles and auto parts.⟩ — see MAKING

rawness *n* **1** an uncomfortable degree of coolness ⟨I lit a fire in the hearth to combat the *rawness* of that blustery March morning.⟩ — see CHILL

2 the quality or state of lacking refinement or good taste ⟨the *rawness* of the movie's language⟩ — see VULGARITY 1

ray *n* **1** a narrow sharply defined line of light radiating from an object ⟨Two red eyes were reflected in the *ray* of light from the flashlight.⟩ — see SHAFT 1

2 a very small amount ⟨The new treatment brings a *ray* of hope to all who suffer from the condition.⟩ — see PARTICLE 1

ray *vb* **1** to emit rays of light ⟨Klieg lights were *raying* against the nighttime sky at the Hollywood premiere.⟩ — see SHINE 1

2 to extend outwards from or as if from a central point ⟨Laugh wrinkles *rayed* out from the corners of the old man's eyes.⟩ — see RADIATE 1

raze *vb* **1** to bring to a complete end the physical soundness, existence, or usefulness of ⟨an entire city block *razed* by a terrible fire⟩ — see DESTROY 1

2 to destroy (as a building) completely by knocking down or breaking to pieces ⟨The developer *razed* the old school building and built a high-rise condominium complex.⟩ — see DEMOLISH 1

razz *vb* to make fun of in a good-natured way ⟨got *razzed* all day for wearing mismatched sneakers⟩ — see TEASE 1

razzing *adj* marked by or expressive of mild or good-natured teasing ⟨His little sister made *razzing* kissing noises whenever he was on the phone with his girlfriend.⟩ — see QUIZZICAL

reach *n* **1** a wide space or area ⟨a wide *reach* of woods⟩ — see EXPANSE

2 an area over which activity, capacity, or influence extends ⟨Buying a new car is beyond our *reach* right now.⟩ — see RANGE 2

3 *usually* **reaches** *pl* the placement of someone or something in relation to others in a vertical arrangement ⟨the upper *reaches* of the profession⟩ — see RANK 1

reach *vb* **1** to shift possession of (something) from one person to another ⟨Would you *reach* me the potatoes, please?⟩ — see PASS 1

2 to transmit information or requests to ⟨You can *reach* me by phone after 3:00 p.m. most days.⟩ — see CONTACT

3 to act upon (a person or a person's feelings) so as to cause a response ⟨The movie adaptation just didn't *reach* me the way the novel did.⟩ — see ¹AFFECT 1

reachable *adj* situated within easy reach ⟨placed the book at a *reachable* distance from the bed⟩ — see CONVENIENT

reacquire *vb* to get again in one's possession ⟨The hockey team is hoping to *reacquire* the Stanley Cup this year.⟩ — see RECOVER 1

react *vb* to act or behave in response (as to a stimulus or influence) ⟨It was my first touchdown, and I didn't know how to *react* to the cheers of the crowd.⟩

synonyms reply, respond

related words answer, return; retaliate; construe, interpret, read, take, understand; contend (with), cope (with), grapple (with), handle, manage, negotiate

near antonyms act, behave; affect, cause, draw, effect

reaction *n* action or behavior that is done in return to other action or behavior ⟨Their *reaction* to the news was positive.⟩

synonyms answer, reply, response, take

related words backlash, kickback; rebound; recoil, reflex; revulsion, rise; counterreaction, counterresponse

near antonyms action, behavior; cause, effect

reactionary *adj* tending to favor established ideas, conditions, or institutions ⟨*Reactionary* guardians of proper

English usage invariably regard every new coinage that comes along as a nonword.⟩ — see CONSERVATIVE 1

reactionary *n* **1** a person whose political beliefs are centered on tradition and keeping things the way they are ⟨*Reactionaries* tried to stop the passage of the legislation.⟩ — see CONSERVATIVE

2 a person with old-fashioned ideas ⟨tended to be a *reactionary* in his views⟩ — see FOGY

read *vb* **1** to go over and mentally take in the content of ⟨He always *reads* the newspaper in the morning as he eats breakfast.⟩

synonyms peruse, pore (over)

related words browse, dip (into), leaf (through), scan, skim, speed-read, thumb (through), turn over; devour, gobble (up); slog (through), wade (through); reread; proofread; decipher; review, study; apprehend, comprehend, grasp, make, make out, perceive, understand

2 to tell of or describe beforehand ⟨The psychic claimed to be able to *read* his future.⟩ — see FORETELL

readdress *vb* to consider again especially with the possibility of change or reversal ⟨The Senate will *readdress* the pending legislation in their next session.⟩ — see RECONSIDER

readily *adv* **1** by choice or preference ⟨She would *readily* give up piano lessons for a season ticket at her local ski area.⟩ — see RATHER 1

2 without difficulty ⟨always gives directions that are *readily* understood⟩ — see EASILY 1

reading *n* **1** a presentation of an artistic work (as a piece of music) from a particular point of view ⟨a very bizarre *reading* of one of Shakespeare's greatest tragedies by an alternative theater company⟩ — see ACCOUNT 2

2 something assigned to be read or studied ⟨Make sure you do the assigned *reading* for tonight.⟩ — see LESSON

ready *adj* **1** being in a state of fitness for some experience or action ⟨After studying for months, she felt *ready* for the bar exam.⟩

synonyms fit, go, prepared, set

related words conditioned, primed, ripe; armed, braced, fortified, steeled; qualified, trained

near antonyms unqualified, untrained

antonyms half-baked, half-cocked, underprepared, unprepared, unready

2 having a desire or inclination (as for a specified course of action) ⟨I'm *ready* to help, if I can.⟩ — see WILLING 1

3 having or showing the ability to respond without delay or hesitation ⟨He had a *ready* response to every one of her objections regarding the feasibility of the plan.⟩ — see QUICK 1

4 involving minimal difficulty or effort ⟨We're hoping you have a *ready* solution to our networking problem.⟩ — see EASY 1

ready *vb* **1** to make competent (as by training, skill, or ability) for a particular office or function ⟨This advanced course should *ready* him for college.⟩ — see QUALIFY 2

2 to make ready in advance ⟨We can *ready* the desserts for the party a day in advance.⟩ — see PREPARE 1

3 to prepare (oneself) mentally or emotionally ⟨The basketball players sat quietly in the locker room, *readying* themselves for the final game of the season.⟩ — see FORTIFY 1

ready–made *adj* made beforehand in large numbers ⟨The store carries mostly inexpensive *ready-made* clothing.⟩

synonyms mass-produced, store

related words ready-to-wear; prefabricated

near antonyms homemade

antonyms custom, customized, custom-made, tailored, tailor-made

real *adj* **1** being exactly as appears or as claimed ⟨This shirt is *real* silk, not polyester.⟩ — see AUTHENTIC 1

2 existing in fact and not merely as a possibility ⟨asked her parents if the Tooth Fairy was *real*⟩ — see ACTUAL

3 free from any intent to deceive or impress others ⟨*real* folk who don't put on airs⟩ — see GUILELESS

real *adv* to a great degree ⟨This fish tastes *real* good.⟩ — see VERY 1

realistic *adj* **1** willing to see things as they really are and deal with them sensibly ⟨high schoolers who need to be more *realistic* in their career choices, as so few people end up as pro athletes⟩

synonyms down-to-earth, earthy, hardheaded, matter-of-fact, practical, pragmatic (*also* pragmatical)

related words idealless, philistine, utilitarian; grounded, levelheaded, logical, no-nonsense, rational, reasonable, sane, sensible, sober, sobersided, sound; bottom-line, hard, hard-boiled, hard-edged, tough-minded, unromantic, unsentimental

near antonyms fanciful, fantastic (*also* fantastical), imaginative, romantic, sentimental; cheerful, optimistic, rose-colored; trustful, trusting, unsuspicious; half-baked, illogical, irrational, unreasonable; theoretical (*also* theoretic)

antonyms blue-sky, impractical, unrealistic, utopian, visionary

2 closely resembling the object imitated ⟨Those special effects look really *realistic*—I'd never guess they were all computer-generated.⟩ — see NATURAL 2

reality *n* **1** something that actually exists ⟨the ambition to make his dreams a *reality*⟩ — see FACT 2

2 the fact of being or of being real ⟨No one denies the *reality* of electricity, though few people understand it fully.⟩ — see EXISTENCE

3 the quality of being actual ⟨The *reality* of the situation finally dawned on her and she sat down in stunned silence.⟩ — see FACT 1

4 one that has a real and independent existence ⟨You'll need to cope with a whole new set of *realities* once you've become a parent.⟩ — see ENTITY

realizable *adj* capable of being done or carried out ⟨The spies waited until their goal was *realizable* and then acted.⟩ — see POSSIBLE 1

realization *n* the state of being actual or complete ⟨This research paper is the *realization* of an entire year's work.⟩ — see FRUITION

realize *vb* **1** to come to an awareness of ⟨I just *realized* that I can't go out to dinner tonight because I'm supposed to babysit for our neighbor.⟩ — see DISCOVER 1

2 to receive as return for effort ⟨If you deposit your paycheck in a savings account, you'll *realize* a little interest on it.⟩ — see EARN 1

really *adv* **1** in actual fact ⟨I'm *really* sorry I upset you.⟩ — see VERY 2

2 to tell the truth ⟨Well, *really*, I'd rather go to the movies than go to dinner.⟩ — see ACTUALLY 1

3 without any question ⟨That was *really* a sweet gesture on your part.⟩ — see INDEED 1

4 to a great degree ⟨*really* tired after staying up all night⟩ — see VERY 1

realm *n* **1** a region of activity, knowledge, or influence ⟨Medieval history is really Professor Jones' *realm*, so I'll let her answer your question.⟩ — see FIELD 2

2 an area over which activity, capacity, or influence extends ⟨a medical breakthrough that is within the *realm* of possibility⟩ — see RANGE 2

reams *pl n* a considerable amount ⟨I have *reams* of paperwork to do before I can leave today.⟩ — see LOT 2

reanalyze *vb* to consider again especially with the possibility of change or reversal ⟨You need to *reanalyze* the data, because the numbers don't tally.⟩ — see RECONSIDER

reanimate *vb* to bring back to life, practice, or activity ⟨The new multiplex has begun to *reanimate* the old neighborhood.⟩ — see REVIVE 1

reanimated *adj* made or become fresh in spirits or vigor ⟨The hikers were *reanimated* and ready to go after their brief rest along the side of the trail.⟩ — see NEW 4

reanimation *n* the act or an instance of bringing something back to life, public attention, or vigorous activity ⟨a call for the *reanimation* of curfew ordinances that were discarded decades ago⟩ — see REVIVAL

reap *vb* 1 to catch or collect (a crop or natural resource) for human use ⟨My great-grandfather had to *reap* the wheat on his family farm with a hand scythe.⟩ — see HARVEST
2 to receive as return for effort ⟨If you continue to work hard at musicianship, you will *reap* the rewards of being a concert pianist.⟩ — see EARN 1

reappraisal *n* a usually critical look at a past event ⟨Teachers are undertaking a *reappraisal* of the current grading system, as the consensus is that A's have been given out too easily of late.⟩ — see REVIEW 1

rear *adj* being at or in the part of something opposite the front part ⟨Go to the back of the building and look out the *rear* window and you'll see the eagle.⟩ — see BACK

rear *n* 1 a behind part or surface ⟨The *rear* of the car was sleekly designed.⟩
synonyms back, reverse, tail
antonyms face, forehead, forepart, front
2 the part of the body upon which someone sits ⟨Amy fell off her skates onto her *rear*.⟩ — see BUTTOCKS

rear *vb* 1 to bring to maturity through care and education ⟨watched a documentary on how wolves *rear* their young⟩ — see BRING UP 1
2 to fix in an upright position ⟨It took all the men in the village to *rear* the frame for the barn, pulling hard at the ropes until all the sides were standing.⟩ — see ERECT 1
3 to form by putting together parts or materials ⟨The city has plans for *rearing* a new convention center over the next two years.⟩ — see BUILD
4 to look after or assist the growth of by labor and care ⟨an amateur who *rears* rare orchids in a professional-grade greenhouse⟩ — see GROW 1

rearmost *adj* following all others of the same kind in order or time ⟨The *rearmost* people in the cafeteria line often get the dregs that nobody else wants.⟩ — see LAST 1

rearward *adj* 1 being at or in the part of something opposite the front part ⟨got *rearward* quarters aboard the ship⟩ — see BACK
2 directed, turned, or done toward the back ⟨gave a *rearward* glance toward home⟩ — see BACKWARD 1

rearward *also* **rearwards** *adv* toward the rear ⟨I turned *rearward* for a moment, just for one final look at the haunting scene.⟩ — see BACKWARD 1

reason *n* 1 a statement given to explain a belief or act ⟨She gave a good *reason* for her seemingly suspicious behavior.⟩
synonyms account, argument, case, explanation, rationale
related words alibi, apologia, defense, excuse, justification, vindication; appeal, plea; guise, pretense (*or* pretence), pretext, rationalization
2 something (as a belief) that serves as the basis for another thing ⟨A firm belief that we are here on earth to help others is the *reason* for her tireless volunteer work.⟩
synonyms account, authority, grounds, motive, subject, wherefore, why
related words antecedent, cause, consideration, impetus, incentive, inspiration, instigation, occasion, stimulus
3 an explanation that frees one from fault or blame ⟨What *reason* do you have for being in such a bad mood?⟩ — see EXCUSE

4 someone or something responsible for a result ⟨What's the meteorological *reason* for tornadoes?⟩ — see CAUSE 1
5 the ability to learn and understand or to deal with problems ⟨You'll need to use all of your *reason* to get out of this tight spot.⟩ — see INTELLIGENCE 1
6 the normal or healthy condition of the mental abilities ⟨I was afraid that with all the stress he was under, he'd lose all *reason*.⟩ — see MIND 2
7 the thought processes that have been established as leading to valid solutions to problems ⟨In a time of national crisis we need to listen to the voice of *reason*.⟩ — see LOGIC

reason *vb* 1 to form an opinion or reach a conclusion through reasoning and information ⟨She *reasoned* that since all of the cakes were on sale for the same price, she might as well pick the biggest one.⟩ — see INFER 1
2 to state (something) as a reason in support of or against something under consideration ⟨He tried to *reason* that no one in their right mind would buy his brother's old video games, but they were put on the online auction anyway.⟩ — see ARGUE 1

reasonable *adj* 1 according to the rules of logic ⟨His answer is perfectly *reasonable*.⟩ — see LOGICAL 1
2 based on sound reasoning or information ⟨Those playing rules sound *reasonable* to me.⟩ — see GOOD 1
3 costing little ⟨desperately trying to find *reasonable* hotel rates for the holiday weekend⟩ — see CHEAP 1
4 having the ability to reason ⟨found their counterparts in the negotiation to be *reasonable* people⟩ — see RATIONAL 1

reasonably *adv* with good reason or courtesy ⟨I expect to be treated *reasonably* by the clerks when I shop at a store.⟩ — see WELL 4

reasoned *adj* 1 based on sound reasoning or information ⟨a candidate with a *reasoned* stance on this important issue⟩ — see GOOD 1
2 being or provable by reasoning in which the conclusion follows necessarily from given information ⟨Given the information you have, that is the only *reasoned* solution to the problem.⟩ — see DEDUCTIVE
3 decided on as a result of careful thought ⟨Refusing to be swayed by the passions of the moment, the president consulted with his advisers before making a *reasoned* response to this unprovoked act of aggression.⟩ — see DELIBERATE 1

reasoning *adj* having the ability to reason ⟨judged by the courts not to be a *reasoning* being who could be held accountable for his crimes⟩ — see RATIONAL 1

reasoning *n* the thought processes that have been established as leading to valid solutions to problems ⟨Your *reasoning* here is faulty, for although all wives are spouses, not all spouses are wives.⟩ — see LOGIC

reassure *vb* to ease the grief or distress of ⟨We tried to *reassure* her that the dog would come back home by nightfall.⟩ — see COMFORT

reata *n* a rope or long leather thong with a noose used especially for catching livestock ⟨The gauchos tied their *reatas* and rode out onto the pampas to rope calves.⟩ — see LASSO

rebel *adj* given to resisting authority or another's control ⟨Today's *rebel* chefs feel free to ignore the dictates of classic French cuisine.⟩ — see DISOBEDIENT

rebel *n* a person who rises up against authority ⟨The *rebel* would not submit peacefully, even after he was captured.⟩
synonyms insurgent, insurrectionary, insurrectionist, mutineer, red, revolter, revolutionary, revolutionist
related words challenger, defier, insubordinate, oppositionist, resister; anarchist; discontent, extremist, malcontent, radical

near antonyms loyalist, patriot, supporter; counterinsurgent, counterrevolutionary, counterrevolutionist

rebel *vb* to rise up against established authority ⟨The colonists *rebelled* in the wake of an onslaught of abuses.⟩
synonyms mutiny, revolt
related words defy, disobey, mock; revolutionize; buck, combat, contest, fight, oppose, resist, withstand
near antonyms comply (with), follow, mind, obey, submit; attend, serve

rebel (against) *vb* to go against the commands, prohibitions, or rules of ⟨Experts tell parents that if their once-compliant children *rebel against* them, then they should take it as a sign the kids are growing up and becoming their own persons.⟩ — see DISOBEY

rebellion *n* 1 open fighting against authority (as one's own government) ⟨The *rebellion* would have failed if not for the aid sent by other countries.⟩
synonyms insurgency, insurrection, mutiny, outbreak, revolt, revolution, rising, uprising
related words coup, coup d'état (*or* coup d'etat), overthrow; sedition, treachery, treason; subversion
near antonyms counterinsurgency, counterrevolution
2 refusal to obey ⟨the period of *rebellion* that two-year-olds often go through⟩ — see DISOBEDIENCE

rebellious *adj* 1 taking part in a rebellion ⟨The *rebellious* troops fought a pitched battle with divisions still loyal to the government.⟩
synonyms insurgent, insurrectionary, mutinous, revolutionary
related words traitorous, treacherous, treasonous; agitating, demagogic, rabble-rousing; defiant, disobedient, insubordinate, intractable, recalcitrant, refractory, restive, ungovernable, unruly
near antonyms constant, devoted, loyal, staunch (*also* stanch), steadfast, true, true-blue; compliant, obedient, submissive, tractable
2 given to resisting authority or another's control ⟨She expected her son to grow a little more *rebellious* as he got older, but she knew he understood when he pushed it too far.⟩ — see DISOBEDIENT

rebelliousness *n* refusal to obey ⟨tried to cope with the horse's *rebelliousness*⟩ — see DISOBEDIENCE

rebirth *n* the act or an instance of bringing something back to life, public attention, or vigorous activity ⟨A renewed interest in long-playing records led to the *rebirth* of the turntable among audiophiles.⟩ — see REVIVAL

rebound *vb* 1 to regain a former or normal state ⟨The economy will *rebound* from this latest slump.⟩ — see RECOVER 2
2 to strike and fly off at an angle ⟨The ball *rebounded* off the rim.⟩ — see GLANCE 1

rebuff *n* treatment that is deliberately unfriendly ⟨Lisa took her *rebuff* in stride, and still greeted her cousin with a friendly smile.⟩ — see COLD SHOULDER

rebuke *n* an often public or formal expression of disapproval ⟨delivered a stinging *rebuke* to the Congress, calling for an end to partisanship⟩ — see CENSURE

rebuke *vb* 1 to criticize (someone) so as to correct a fault ⟨The father was forced to *rebuke* his son for the spendthrift ways he had adopted since arriving at college.⟩
synonyms admonish, chide, reprimand, reproach, reprove
related words berate, castigate, chew out, dress down, flay, harangue, jaw, keelhaul, lambaste (*or* lambast), lecture, rail (at *or* against), rate, scold, score, upbraid; abuse, assail, attack, bad-mouth, blame, blast, censure, condemn, criticize, crucify, denounce, excoriate, reprehend, slam; mock, put down; deride, ridicule, scoff, scorn
phrases burn one's ears, get after, get on

near antonyms approve, endorse (*also* indorse), OK (*or* okay), sanction; applaud, extol (*also* extoll), hail, laud, praise, salute, tout
2 to criticize (someone) severely or angrily especially for personal failings ⟨strongly *rebuked* the girl for playing with matches⟩ — see SCOLD
3 to express public or formal disapproval of ⟨In a rare move, the state's supreme court *rebuked* the governor for trying to circumvent one of its recent rulings.⟩ — see CENSURE 1

rebut *vb* 1 to drive back ⟨Stalingrad's defenders were finally able to *rebut* the besiegers, but only after a horrendous loss of life.⟩ — see REPEL 1
2 to prove to be false ⟨Magellan's circumnavigation of the globe effectively *rebutted* any lingering notions that the earth is flat.⟩ — see DISPROVE

rebuttal *n* something (as an argument) that serves to disprove ⟨an effective *rebuttal* to her claim of having the gift of clairvoyance⟩ — see CONFUTATION

recalcitrance *n* refusal to obey ⟨We punished her *recalcitrance* by taking away her driving privileges.⟩ — see DISOBEDIENCE

recalcitrant *adj* 1 given to resisting authority or another's control ⟨The manager worried that the *recalcitrant* employee would try to undermine his authority.⟩ — see DISOBEDIENT
2 given to resisting control or discipline by others ⟨a *recalcitrant* dog sent to obedience school⟩ — see UNCONTROLLABLE

recall *n* 1 a particular act or instance of recalling or the thing remembered ⟨His *recall* of the events of that turbulent time is significantly different from the accounts of other eyewitnesses.⟩ — see MEMORY 2
2 the act of putting an end to something planned or previously agreed to ⟨We can't get a refund on the plane tickets, so the trip is beyond *recall*.⟩ — see CANCELLATION

recall *vb* 1 to bring back to mind ⟨I don't *recall* meeting you before.⟩ — see REMEMBER
2 to put an end to (something planned or previously agreed to) ⟨I'll *recall* my purchase order if the company refuses to guarantee that it'll arrive on time.⟩ — see CANCEL 1

recant *vb* to solemnly or formally reject or go back on (as something formerly adhered to) ⟨The Inquisition forced Galileo to *recant* his support of the Copernican observation that the earth revolves around the sun.⟩ — see ABJURE 1

recap *n* a short statement of the main points ⟨After a *recap* of this morning's meeting, we can discuss the issues that were raised.⟩ — see SUMMARY

recap *vb* to make into a short statement of the main points (as of a report) ⟨Please *recap* the highlights of the game for me.⟩ — see SUMMARIZE

recapitulate *vb* to make into a short statement of the main points (as of a report) ⟨The professor told the students that their papers should not *recapitulate* the whole plot but should rather discuss in detail one particular incident.⟩ — see SUMMARIZE

recapitulation *n* a short statement of the main points ⟨Bill will begin his presentation with a *recapitulation* of the research done on the disease up to this point.⟩ — see SUMMARY

recapture *n* the act or process of getting something back ⟨The *recapture* of the territory may take longer than expected.⟩ — see RECOVERY 1

recapture *vb* to get again in one's possession ⟨Our team managed to *recapture* the ball after the fumble.⟩ — see RECOVER 1

recast *vb* to make different in some way ⟨Once he *recast* the question in different terms, I understood what he was asking.⟩ — see CHANGE 1

recede *vb* **1** to grow less in scope or intensity especially gradually ⟨The sound of sirens *receded* as the fire engines roared off into the distance.⟩ — see DECREASE 2

2 to move back or away (as from something difficult, dangerous, or disagreeable) ⟨After the rain stops, the floodwaters should gradually *recede*.⟩ — see RETREAT 1

recently *adv* not long ago ⟨I *recently* purchased a car.⟩ ⟨Have you seen her *recently*?⟩ — see NEWLY

receptacle *n* something into which a liquid or smaller objects can be put for storage or transportation ⟨Place all wrappers in the trash *receptacles* at the entrances of the theater.⟩ — see CONTAINER

reception *n* a social gathering ⟨a wedding *reception*⟩ — see PARTY 1

receptive *adj* willing to consider new or different ideas ⟨I needed a partner who was *receptive* to new ways of managing the business.⟩ — see OPEN-MINDED 1

recess *n* **1** a hollowed-out space in a wall ⟨The curator placed the large vase in one of the *recesses* of the gallery wall.⟩ — see NICHE 1

2 a period during which the usual routine of school or work is suspended ⟨The couple goes to Florida every January for a month-long *recess* from the rigors of winter.⟩ — see VACATION

3 a momentary halt in an activity ⟨The judge called for a brief *recess* so that the witness could regain her composure.⟩ — see PAUSE 1

4 a sunken area forming a separate space ⟨decided to camp in a sandy *recess* where the beach met the forest⟩ — see HOLE 2

recess *vb* to bring to a formal close for a period of time ⟨The judge *recessed* the court for lunch.⟩ — see ADJOURN

recessed *adj* curved inward ⟨displayed the decorative plate on a *recessed* shelf in the wall⟩ — see HOLLOW

recession *n* **1** a period of decreased economic activity ⟨The country is just coming out of a *recession*, so expect to see fewer layoffs and more new jobs in the coming year.⟩ — see DEPRESSION 1

2 an act of moving away especially from something difficult, dangerous, or disagreeable ⟨a retiring CEO making a gradual *recession* from the daily rigors of running a major corporation⟩ — see RETREAT 1

reciprocal *adj* related to each other in such a way that one completes the other ⟨The two nations agreed to give *reciprocal* work rights to each other's citizens, thus facilitating the daily border crossings of workers from both countries.⟩ — see COMPLEMENTARY

recite *vb* **1** to give an oral or written account of in some detail ⟨John *recited* the funny story of how he and his girlfriend met.⟩ — see TELL 1

2 to give from memory ⟨After all these years, she's still able to *recite* the poems she learned as a child.⟩ — see REPEAT 2

3 to specify one after another ⟨The Declaration of Independence *recites* a long list of grievances against King George III.⟩ — see ENUMERATE 1

reckless *adj* **1** having or showing a lack of concern for the consequences of one's actions ⟨The *reckless* skiers were making everyone nervous by schussing down the mountainside at lightning speed.⟩

synonyms daredevil, devil-may-care, foolhardy, harum-scarum, irresponsible

related words adventurous, audacious, bold, daring, venturesome; hasty, headlong, hotheaded, impetuous, precipitate, rash, wild; blithe, carefree, happy-go-lucky,

madcap, slaphappy; nonchalant, unconcerned, unworried; careless, freewheeling, heedless, inattentive, incautious, mindless, regardless, unheeding, unmindful; inconsiderate, thoughtless, unthinking

near antonyms careful, cautious, circumspect, heedful; overcareful, overcautious, timid

antonyms responsible

2 foolishly adventurous or bold ⟨a *reckless* driver who cut off other cars on the road⟩ — see FOOLHARDY 1

reckon *vb* **1** to decide the size, amount, number, or distance of (something) without actual measurement ⟨Police tried to *reckon* the size of the crowd at the stadium.⟩ — see ESTIMATE 2

2 *chiefly dialect* to have as an opinion ⟨I *reckon* you must be new to these parts.⟩ — see BELIEVE 2

3 to determine (a value) by doing the necessary mathematical operations ⟨*reckoned* the runner's pace by dividing her finishing time by the race distance⟩ — see CALCULATE 1

4 to place reliance or trust ⟨Don't *reckon* on being provided with low-cost housing if you take a summer job there.⟩ — see DEPEND 2

5 to think of in a particular way ⟨He was *reckoned* among the great heroes of his time.⟩ — see CONSIDER 1

reckoning *n* **1** the act of placing a value on the nature, character, or quality of something ⟨That old chest isn't worth much by my *reckoning*, but an antiques dealer might think otherwise.⟩ — see ESTIMATE 1

2 the act or process of performing mathematical operations to find a value ⟨You forgot about the decimal point, so your *reckoning* was way off.⟩ — see CALCULATION

reclaim *vb* **1** to get again in one's possession ⟨She *reclaimed* the championship title after losing it last year.⟩ — see RECOVER 1

2 to make better in behavior or character ⟨Environmental groups have been *reclaiming* contaminated sites.⟩ — see REFORM 1

3 to obtain (a raw material) by separating it from a by-product or waste product ⟨After *reclaiming* the glycerin from used vegetable oil, you can use the oil to create a fuel that burns cleaner than regular gasoline.⟩ — see RECYCLE

reclamation *n* the act or process of getting something back ⟨pumped water out of the field as part of the land *reclamation* program designed to provide farmers with more farmland⟩ — see RECOVERY 1

recluse *n* a person who lives away from others ⟨He was sick of cities and crowds, so he decided to go live by himself in the woods as a *recluse*.⟩

synonyms hermit, solitary

related words homebody, shut-in

near antonyms socialite; socializer

recognize *vb* **1** to have a clear idea of ⟨We finally *recognized* that we were hopelessly lost.⟩ — see COMPREHEND 1

2 to show appreciation, respect, or affection for (someone) with a public celebration ⟨an awards banquet to *recognize* local heroes⟩ — see HONOR

recoil *vb* to draw back in fear, pain, or disgust ⟨*recoiled* at the sight of the spider⟩ — see FLINCH

recollect *vb* to bring back to mind ⟨I can't *recollect* if I turned the stove off or not before leaving the house.⟩ — see REMEMBER

re–collect *vb* **1** to gain emotional or mental control of ⟨She had to calm down and *re-collect* herself after being told she had won the lottery.⟩ — see COLLECT 1

2 to get again in one's possession ⟨I struggled to *re-collect* the papers the wind had torn from my hands.⟩ — see RECOVER 1

recollection *n* **1** a particular act or instance of recalling or the thing remembered ⟨I have no *recollection* of ever saying that.⟩ — see MEMORY 2

2 the power or process of recalling what has been previously learned or experienced ⟨The gradual *recollection* of that long-ago romance brought back both happy and painful feelings.⟩ — see MEMORY 1

recommend *vb* **1** to put (something) into the possession or safekeeping of another ⟨Serious gastronomes should *recommend* their stomachs to the restaurant's chef, giving full rein to his culinary prowess and imagination.⟩ — see GIVE 2
2 to put (something) forward as one's choice for a wise or proper course of action ⟨I would *recommend* you look into that option a little more closely because I don't think it will work nearly as well as you think.⟩ — see ADVISE 2

recompense *n* **1** payment to another for a loss or injury ⟨The jury awarded an additional $5,000 in *recompense* for physical pain and suffering.⟩ — see COMPENSATION 1
2 something (as money) that is given or received in return for goods or services ⟨The volunteer expects nothing more than sincere thanks as *recompense* for his efforts.⟩ — see PAYMENT 2

recompense *vb* **1** to give (someone) the sum of money owed for goods or services received ⟨The cash-strapped museum can *recompense* lecturers with only token honorariums.⟩ — see PAY 1
2 to give what is owed for ⟨That company still needs to *recompense* the work that the contractor finished last month.⟩ — see PAY 2
3 to provide (someone) with a just payment for loss or injury ⟨The government has yet to adequately *recompense* the property owners for the land taken for the new highway.⟩ — see COMPENSATE 1

reconceive *vb* to consider again especially with the possibility of change or reversal ⟨I will have to *reconceive* my earlier opinion about him in light of his recent behavior.⟩ — see RECONSIDER

reconcile *vb* to bring to a state free of conflicts, inconsistencies, or differences ⟨Historians have never been able to *reconcile* the two eyewitness accounts of the battle.⟩ — see HARMONIZE 2

recondite *adj* difficult for one of ordinary knowledge or intelligence to understand ⟨Geochemistry is a *recondite* subject.⟩ — see PROFOUND 1

recondition *vb* to put into good shape or working order again ⟨asked my neighbor to help me *recondition* the old tractor for use on the family farm⟩ — see MEND 1

reconsider *vb* to consider again especially with the possibility of change or reversal ⟨The new intelligence forced the general to *reconsider* his plan of attack.⟩
synonyms readdress, reanalyze, reconceive, reevaluate, reexamine, rethink, review, reweigh
related words rehear; reconceptualize, reenvision, reimagine; reappraise, reassess, reinvestigate, restudy; amend, correct, emend, rectify, reform, remedy, revise
phrases change one's mind (about), go over, think better of
near antonyms assert, defend, maintain, uphold

reconsideration *n* a usually critical look at a past event ⟨The discovery of new evidence calls for a *reconsideration* of the case.⟩ — see REVIEW 1

record *n* **1** a relating of events usually in the order in which they happened ⟨The town paper published a *record* of the debate, as well as a synopsis of each candidate's stance on the major questions.⟩ — see ACCOUNT 1
2 an account of important events in the order in which they happened ⟨Historical *records* on the rise of the Roman Empire are plentiful.⟩ — see HISTORY 1

record *vb* **1** to make a written note of ⟨The reporter *recorded* the events of the evening in her tablet for later reference.⟩

synonyms jot (down), log, mark, note, put down, register, report, set down, take down
related words chronicle, minute, transcribe; enter, inscribe; chalk (up), notch, score
2 to put (someone or something) on a list ⟨He was *recorded* as having been a passenger on that ill-fated ship, but his body was never recovered.⟩ — see ¹LIST 2

recount *vb* to give an oral or written account of in some detail ⟨a novel that *recounted* an American soldier's adventures among the samurai warriors of 19th-century Japan⟩ — see TELL 1

recoup *vb* **1** to get again in one's possession ⟨Dan tried to *recoup* the $1,000 he had when he walked into the casino by risking his last dollar on a slot machine.⟩ — see RECOVER 1
2 to provide (someone) with a just payment for loss or injury ⟨You will have to submit the proper paperwork before the insurance company will *recoup* you for the damage to your vehicle.⟩ — see COMPENSATE 1
3 to become healthy and strong again after illness or weakness ⟨He's *recouping* at home after a bout of the flu.⟩ — see CONVALESCE

recoupment *n* **1** payment to another for a loss or injury ⟨The jury's award included a *recoupment* for emotional distress.⟩ — see COMPENSATION 1
2 the act or process of getting something back ⟨Almost immediately after the new contract was signed, the company began the *recoupment* of revenue lost during the strike.⟩ — see RECOVERY 1

recourse *n* something that one uses to accomplish an end especially when the usual means is not available ⟨His only *recourse* is to file a complaint with the manager.⟩ — see RESOURCE 1

recover *vb* **1** to get again in one's possession ⟨After fishing around in the garbage for 10 minutes, I was able to *recover* my lost keys.⟩
synonyms reacquire, recapture, reclaim, re-collect, recoup, regain, repossess, retake, retrieve
related words recruit, replenish; redeem, repurchase; rescue
near antonyms lose, mislay, misplace
2 to regain a former or normal state ⟨After a disastrous first half, the team was able to *recover* and pull off a victory.⟩
synonyms bounce (back), rally, rebound, snap back
related words reanimate, revitalize, revive
phrases make (or stage) a comeback
near antonyms decline, fail, worsen
3 to become healthy and strong again after illness or weakness ⟨I see you're *recovering* well from the accident.⟩ — see CONVALESCE
4 to obtain (a raw material) by separating it from a byproduct or waste product ⟨the process of *recovering* aluminum from old cans⟩ — see RECYCLE

recovery *n* **1** the act or process of getting something back ⟨The *recovery* of the sunken boat took over a week.⟩
synonyms recapture, reclamation, recoupment, repossession, retrieval
related words recruitment, replenishment; redemption, rescue
near antonyms loss, misplacement
2 the process or period of gradually regaining one's health and strength ⟨His *recovery* from the flu was remarkably quick.⟩ — see CONVALESCENCE

recreant *adj* **1** having or showing a shameful lack of courage ⟨The victors had only contempt for the *recreant* enemy soldiers who surrendered without firing a shot.⟩ — see COWARDLY
2 not true in one's allegiance to someone or something

⟨*recreant* campaign workers who walked out as soon as their candidate began dropping in the polls⟩ — see FAITHLESS

recreant *n* **1** a person who abandons a cause or organization usually without right ⟨Traditionally armies have dealt harshly with *recreants*.⟩ — see RENEGADE

2 a person who shows a shameful lack of courage in the face of danger ⟨The historian reserved his greatest contempt for those *recreants* who opposed the witch hunt but lacked the courage to speak out against it.⟩ — see COWARD

3 one who betrays a trust or an allegiance ⟨a spy and *recreant* to his country⟩ — see TRAITOR

recreate *vb* **1** to bring back to a former condition or vigor ⟨Supporters of preservation hope to *recreate* the architectural splendor that the old movie theater had when it first opened.⟩ — see RENEW 1

2 to engage in activity for amusement ⟨an old summer resort where families have been *recreating* for over a century⟩ — see PLAY 1

recreated *adj* made or become fresh in spirits or vigor ⟨The club finally got some new, enthusiastic members, and the *recreated* organization actually began contributing to the community.⟩ — see NEW 4

recreation *n* **1** activity engaged in to amuse oneself ⟨We decided to take a bike tour of the island for *recreation* and relaxation.⟩ — see PLAY 1

2 someone or something that provides amusement or enjoyment ⟨Bowling is great *recreation* on a rainy afternoon.⟩ — see FUN 1

3 the act or activity of providing pleasure or amusement especially for the public ⟨Water parks have become a significant part of the *recreation* business.⟩ — see ENTERTAINMENT 1

recreational vehicle *n* a motor vehicle that is specially equipped for living while traveling ⟨Sales of *recreational vehicles* typically go down when gas prices go up.⟩ — see CAMPER

recruit *n* a person who is just starting out in a field of activity ⟨The skydiving instructor and other experienced jumpers tried to encourage the new *recruits* on their first jump.⟩ — see BEGINNER

recruit *vb* to provide with a paying job ⟨Thousands of recent immigrants were *recruited* to build the nation's rail system.⟩ — see EMPLOY 1

rectify *vb* to remove errors, defects, deficiencies, or deviations from ⟨Let me get the store manager, and he'll *rectify* the invoice for your order.⟩ — see CORRECT 1

rectifying *adj* serving to raise or adjust something to some standard or proper condition ⟨The company is taking *rectifying* measures to address the lack of access to the building for people with disabilities.⟩ — see CORRECTIVE 1

rectitude *n* **1** conduct that conforms to an accepted standard of right and wrong ⟨She encouraged the graduates to go on to live lives of unimpeachable *rectitude* and integrity.⟩ — see MORALITY 1

2 faithfulness to high moral standards ⟨Joe has a finely honed sense of *rectitude* that keeps him from cheating on exams.⟩ — see HONOR 1

recuperate *vb* to become healthy and strong again after illness or weakness ⟨Half the office was out today, many employees being sick or *recuperating* from the flu.⟩ — see CONVALESCE

recuperation *n* the process or period of gradually regaining one's health and strength ⟨The older you get, the longer *recuperation* takes.⟩ — see CONVALESCENCE

recurrent *adj* occurring or appearing at intervals ⟨I had *recurrent* problems with the computer for months and finally junked it.⟩ — see INTERMITTENT 1

recurring *adj* occurring or appearing at intervals ⟨Death and spirituality are *recurring* themes throughout the whole of this author's work.⟩ — see INTERMITTENT 1

recycle *vb* to obtain (a raw material) by separating it from a by-product or waste product ⟨*Recycling* the aluminum from soft drink cans is environmentally sound.⟩
synonyms reclaim, recover
related words reuse; process, reprocess

red *adj* **1** having a healthy reddish skin tone ⟨the merry, *red*, smiling face of Santa Claus⟩ — see RUDDY

2 having a notably high temperature ⟨The streams of *red* lava were especially spectacular at night.⟩ — see HOT 1

red *n* a person who rises up against authority ⟨The *reds* demanded a violent overthrow of the government.⟩ — see REBEL

red–blooded *adj* having active strength of body or mind ⟨a *red-blooded* rugby player who always plays to win⟩ — see VIGOROUS 1

redden *vb* to develop a rosy facial color (as from excitement or embarrassment) ⟨His face *reddened* when he realized his mistake.⟩ — see BLUSH

redeem *vb* **1** to do what is required by the terms of ⟨The Little League coach *redeemed* his promise to take the players out for ice cream if they improved their fielding over the season.⟩ — see FULFILL 1

2 to free from captivity or punishment by paying a price ⟨The government has consistently refused to *redeem* hostages captured by terrorists.⟩ — see RANSOM

3 to free from the penalties or consequences of sin ⟨the belief that sinners are *redeemed* by their faith in God⟩ — see SAVE 1

4 to make better in behavior or character ⟨The struggling team *redeemed* itself with two wins in a row.⟩ — see REFORM 1

5 to make up for (an offense) ⟨He quickly *redeemed* the offending remark with a sincere and unconditional apology.⟩ — see EXPIATE

redeemer *n* one that saves from danger or destruction ⟨The rescued hostages profusely thanked their camouflage-clad *redeemers*.⟩ — see SAVIOR

red–hot *adj* **1** being or involving the latest methods, concepts, information, or styles ⟨This *red-hot* sports car uses the latest technology for its engine design.⟩ — see MODERN

2 having a notably high temperature ⟨Don't touch the stove—it's *red-hot*!⟩ — see HOT 1

3 having or expressing great depth of feeling ⟨*red-hot* calls to action from both supporters and opponents of the war⟩ — see FERVENT 1

4 enjoying widespread favor or approval ⟨a show that is this year's *red-hot* sitcom⟩ — see POPULAR 1

redo *n* the act of saying or doing over again ⟨As a way of celebrating our silver wedding anniversary, we're planning a *redo* of the trip we took on our honeymoon.⟩ — see REPEAT

redo *vb* **1** to make different in some way ⟨We desperately wanted to *redo* the red living room in soothing shades of green.⟩ — see CHANGE 1

2 to make or do again ⟨The conductor kept asking the violinist to *redo* that passage until he was completely satisfied.⟩ — see REPEAT 4

redoing *n* the act, process, or result of making different ⟨Some residents objected to the *redoing* of the historic school building.⟩ — see CHANGE 1

redolence *n* **1** a sweet or pleasant smell ⟨breathed in the *redolence* of the apple orchard⟩ — see FRAGRANCE

2 the quality of a thing that makes it perceptible to the sense organs in the nose ⟨The *redolence* of sunscreen always reminds me of the beach.⟩ — see SMELL 1

redolent *adj* having a pleasant smell ⟨My grandmother's house always seemed to be *redolent* with the aroma of baking bread.⟩ — see FRAGRANT

redouble *vb* **1** to make markedly greater in measure or degree ⟨They *redoubled* their efforts to finish the work on time.⟩ — see INTENSIFY

2 to make twice as great or as many ⟨If we *redouble* the recipe, we'll have enough cookies for everyone.⟩ — see DOUBLE 1

redoubtable *adj* **1** causing fear ⟨His next opponent, the reigning champion, would be by far the most *redoubtable* adversary the young boxer had ever faced.⟩ — see FEARFUL 1

2 standing above others in rank, importance, or achievement ⟨a surprising discovery by one of the most *redoubtable* figures in Egyptian archaeology⟩ — see EMINENT

redraft *vb* to prepare for publication by correcting, rewriting, or updating ⟨If you *redraft* that paper and include more recent data, I think we could publish it.⟩ — see EDIT 1

redress *n* payment to another for a loss or injury ⟨The new skis were certainly an adequate *redress* for the lost snowboard.⟩ — see COMPENSATION 1

redress *vb* to punish in kind the wrongdoer responsible for ⟨must either forget or *redress* the wrong⟩ — see AVENGE

reduce *vb* **1** to bring to a lower grade or rank ⟨was *reduced* from team captain to team member as punishment for his misbehavior on the court⟩ — see DEMOTE

2 to make smaller in amount, volume, or extent ⟨You'll have to *reduce* the amount of money you spend on unnecessary purchases if you want to have any money left for retirement.⟩ — see DECREASE 1

3 to diminish the price or value of ⟨a mortgage crisis that *reduced* homes to their lowest level in a decade⟩ — see DEPRECIATE 1

reduction *n* **1** something that is or may be subtracted ⟨There was a sizable *reduction* in her weekly pay when she decided to buy health insurance.⟩ — see DEDUCTION 1

2 the amount by which something is lessened ⟨Officials saw an 11% *reduction* in the number of students applying to the school.⟩ — see DECREASE

3 the act or an instance of bringing to a lower grade or rank ⟨The captain was punished with a *reduction* to lieutenant.⟩ — see BUMP 2

redundancy *n* **1** the use of too many words to express an idea ⟨Even though the phrase "free gift" is a *redundancy*, many retailers still use it to assure customers that an item is really free.⟩ — see VERBIAGE 1

2 the state or an instance of going beyond what is usual, proper, or needed ⟨There's a *redundancy* of high-priced restaurants in the area.⟩ — see EXCESS

redundant *adj* being over what is needed ⟨This area is already chockablock with shopping malls; another one would be *redundant*.⟩ — see SPARE 1

reduplicate *vb* **1** to make an exact likeness of ⟨*reduplicated* a recording of the concert for my friend⟩ — see COPY 1

2 to make or do again ⟨We found out halfway through the project that I was *reduplicating* another team member's efforts, so we had to figure out who was going to do what.⟩ — see REPEAT 4

reduplication *n* **1** something that is made to look exactly like something else ⟨That old-looking colonial mansion is actually a 20th-century *reduplication* of the original, which was destroyed many years ago.⟩ — see COPY

2 the act of saying or doing over again ⟨Ever since I was forced to do a *reduplication* of a day's work, I've been more conscientious about hitting my computer's "save" button.⟩ — see REPEAT

reecho *vb* **1** to continue or be repeated in a series of reflected sound waves ⟨thunder *reechoing* through the canyon⟩ — see REVERBERATE

2 to say after another ⟨She *reechoed* an earlier speaker's points, only with a slightly different emphasis.⟩ — see REPEAT 3

reek *n* **1** a strong unpleasant smell ⟨a terrible *reek* coming from the garbage can⟩ — see STINK 1

2 an atmospheric condition in which suspended particles in the air rob it of its transparency ⟨We couldn't see through the *reek* of smog and smoke surrounding the steel plant.⟩ — see HAZE 1

reek *vb* to give off an extremely unpleasant smell ⟨Those old sneakers *reek* something awful.⟩ — see STINK

reeking *adj* having an unpleasant smell ⟨I would rather not be the one to wash your *reeking* gym clothes.⟩ — see MALODOROUS

reeky *adj* having an unpleasant smell ⟨a *reeky* riverbank that at low tide smells of rotting fish⟩ — see MALODOROUS

reel *n* a rapid turning about on an axis or central point ⟨She slipped and, after an out-of-control *reel*, fell on her backside.⟩ — see SPIN 1

reel *vb* **1** to be in a confused state as if from being twirled around ⟨His mind *reeled* upon hearing the news.⟩ — see SPIN 2

2 to move forward while swaying from side to side ⟨I got off the amusement park ride *reeling* and barely able to stand.⟩ — see STAGGER 1

reeling *adj* having a feeling of being whirled about and in danger of falling down ⟨The blood donor experienced a *reeling* sensation after standing up too quickly.⟩ — see DIZZY 1

reel off *vb* **1** to give from memory ⟨He's able to *reel off* the names of all the U.S. presidents, in historical order and without pausing.⟩ — see REPEAT 2

2 to specify one after another ⟨Her friend proceeded to *reel off* the right answers without hesitation.⟩ — see ENUMERATE 1

reenergized *adj* made or become fresh in spirits or vigor ⟨was *reenergized* after a short nap⟩ — see NEW 4

reevaluate *vb* to consider again especially with the possibility of change or reversal ⟨The senator is arguing that the government needs to *reevaluate* its budget in light of the committee's findings.⟩ — see RECONSIDER

reexamination *n* a usually critical look at a past event ⟨the safety board's *reexamination* of the accident to see if it could have been prevented⟩ — see REVIEW 1

reexamine *vb* to consider again especially with the possibility of change or reversal ⟨In light of your broken leg, we should *reexamine* our decision to go on a hiking vacation this summer.⟩ — see RECONSIDER

refashion *vb* to make different in some way ⟨*refashioned* my old pair of jeans into a cover for my scrapbook⟩ — see CHANGE 1

refashioning *n* the act, process, or result of making different ⟨The *refashioning* of the theater will make it more up-to-date and expand the seating capacity.⟩ — see CHANGE 1

refer *vb* to have a relation or connection ⟨I don't think that rule of play *refers* to this particular situation.⟩ — see APPLY 1

refer (to) *vb* **1** to make reference to or speak about briefly but specifically ⟨Try not to *refer to* the incident when you meet.⟩ — see MENTION 1

2 to use or seek out as a source of aid, relief, or advantage ⟨She studied so she wouldn't have to *refer to* the book during the exam.⟩ — see RESORT (TO) 1

referee *n* a person who impartially decides or resolves a dispute or controversy ⟨served as the unofficial *referee* in disputes over the family business⟩ — see JUDGE 1

referee *vb* to give an opinion about (something at issue or in dispute⟩ ⟨I usually end up *refereeing* any disputes concerning use of the car.⟩ — see JUDGE 1

reference *n* **1** something mentioned in a text as providing related and especially supporting information ⟨The author's argument is interesting, but the lack of *references* makes me wonder if it can be proven.⟩
synonyms authority, source
related words citation, excerpt, extract, quotation; caption, cross-reference, footnote, note
2 relation to or concern with something specified ⟨This reply is in *reference* to your last question.⟩ — see RESPECT 1

refine *vb* to make better ⟨worked on *refining* her backhand before the big tennis match⟩ — see IMPROVE

refined *adj* **1** being far along in development ⟨a *refined* analysis of the factors that produce economic wealth in the new global economy⟩ — see ADVANCED
2 free from added matter ⟨*refined* gold⟩ — see PURE 1
3 having or showing a taste for the fine arts and gracious living ⟨a *refined* couple who have hosted many elegant benefits for organizations promoting the arts⟩ — see CULTIVATED
4 having or showing elegance ⟨a *refined* woman with gracious manners⟩ — see ELEGANT 1
5 made or done with extreme care and accuracy ⟨The dressmaker took a set of quite *refined* measurements before actually starting work.⟩ — see FINE 2
6 satisfying or pleasing because of fineness or mildness ⟨The chef's *refined* cuisine is one that true gourmets will appreciate.⟩ — see DELICATE 1
7 meeting the highest standard of accuracy ⟨This is not a *refined* calculation of the total number of calories in the dish—just a rough estimate.⟩ — see PRECISE 1

refinement *n* **1** an instance of notable progress in the development of knowledge, technology, or skill ⟨the recent *refinements* in this area of medical technology⟩ — see ADVANCE 2
2 a high level of taste and enlightenment as a result of extensive intellectual training and exposure to the arts ⟨Anna had a sense of *refinement* that her small hometown couldn't satisfy, so she moved to New York City to be closer to great museums and concert halls.⟩ — see CULTURE 1
3 dignified or restrained beauty of form, appearance, or style ⟨Although she can afford all the jewelry that money can buy, she dresses with the gentle *refinement* that only taste can bestow.⟩ — see ELEGANCE

reflect *vb* **1** to reproduce or show (an exact likeness) as a mirror would ⟨Her face was *reflected* in the waters of the still pond.⟩
synonyms image, mirror
related words copy, duplicate, imitate, reduplicate, repeat, replicate, reproduce
2 to make a statement of one's opinion ⟨*reflected* on the huge influence that the electronic media have on our national elections⟩ — see REMARK 1

reflection *n* **1** a briefly expressed opinion ⟨Does anyone want to share their *reflections* on the passage we just read?⟩ — see REMARK
2 a cause of shame ⟨Your constant lying is a serious *reflection* on your character.⟩ — see DISGRACE 2
3 a careful weighing of the reasons for or against something ⟨After *reflection*, they decided to refuse the offer on the house.⟩ — see CONSIDERATION 1

reflective *adj* **1** given to or marked by long, quiet thinking ⟨One of the twins was outgoing and talkative while the other was withdrawn and *reflective*.⟩ — see CONTEMPLATIVE
2 indicating something ⟨This new policy is *reflective* of the company's desire to improve customer relations.⟩ — see INDICATIVE

reform *vb* **1** to make better in behavior or character ⟨an effort to *reform* repeat offenders⟩
synonyms reclaim, redeem, regenerate, rehabilitate
related words reeducate; amend, improve, refine; cleanse, purify, restore
near antonyms abase, canker, corrupt, debauch, degrade, demean, demoralize, deprave, lower, pervert, poison, profane, subvert, warp
2 to change one's behavior or character for the better ⟨a cheating athlete who *reformed* after getting caught⟩
synonyms amend, mend
related words behave, regenerate; better, improve
phrases clean up one's act
near antonyms backslide, regress
3 to remove errors, defects, deficiencies, or deviations from ⟨He had better *reform* his ways if he wants any of us to trust him.⟩ — see CORRECT 1

reformative *adj* serving to raise or adjust something to some standard or proper condition ⟨Lawmakers took *reformative* measures to curb abuses in campaign financing.⟩ — see CORRECTIVE 1

reformatory *adj* serving to raise or adjust something to some standard or proper condition ⟨the belief that a summer job would be a *reformatory* experience for his spoiled children⟩ — see CORRECTIVE 1

refractoriness *n* refusal to obey ⟨the *refractoriness* of a two-year-old⟩ — see DISOBEDIENCE

refractory *adj* **1** given to resisting authority or another's control ⟨*Refractory* players will be ejected from the game.⟩ — see DISOBEDIENT
2 given to resisting control or discipline by others ⟨Believing that rules are only for other people, he's been *refractory* virtually his entire life.⟩ — see UNCONTROLLABLE

refrain *n* a part of a song or hymn that is repeated every so often ⟨I didn't know the verses of the song, so I only sang on the *refrain*.⟩ — see CHORUS 2

refrain (from) *vb* to resist the temptation of ⟨couldn't *refrain from* ruffling her nephew's neatly combed hair whenever she saw him⟩ — see FORBEAR

refresh *vb* **1** to bring back to a former condition or vigor ⟨brought out some iced tea to *refresh* the spirits of the folks working out in the sun⟩ — see RENEW 1
2 to take a meal ⟨We were looking for a family-friendly restaurant where we could sit down and *refresh* before continuing.⟩ — see DINE 1

refreshed *adj* made or become fresh in spirits or vigor ⟨woke the next morning *refreshed* and ready for the day⟩ — see NEW 4

refreshen *vb* to bring back to a former condition or vigor ⟨I *refreshened* the wilting flowers by cutting the stems again and putting them in a vase with water.⟩ — see RENEW 1

refreshing *adj* having a renewing effect on the state of the body or mind ⟨The cool wind off the ocean is *refreshing* on such a hot day.⟩ — see TONIC 1

refrigerate *vb* to cause to lose heat ⟨*Refrigerate* the cake after you frost it so that the frosting doesn't melt.⟩ — see COOL

refuge *n* something (as a building) that offers cover from the weather or protection from danger ⟨Hunting is strictly forbidden in the wildlife *refuge*.⟩ — see SHELTER

refuge *vb* to be or provide a shelter for ⟨a nation with a long, honorable history of *refuging* political asylum seekers⟩ — see SHELTER 1

refugee *n* a person forced to emigrate for political reasons ⟨*Refugees* began returning to their homeland after years of political unrest and war.⟩ — see ÉMIGRÉ 1

refulgence *n* the quality or state of having or giving off light ⟨the *refulgence* of a full moon on a clear autumn night⟩ — see BRILLIANCE 1

refulgent *adj* giving off or reflecting much light ⟨*Refulgent* sunlight broke through the clouds, creating huge swaths of light in the valley below us.⟩ — see BRIGHT 1

refund *vb* to make a return payment to ⟨We will *refund* you your money.⟩ — see REPAY

refusal *n* an unwillingness to grant something asked for ⟨His flat *refusal* of our reasonable request was rather startling.⟩ — see DENIAL 1

refuse *n* discarded or useless material ⟨*Refuse* had littered the playground until our volunteer group cleaned it up.⟩ — see GARBAGE

refuse *vb* **1** to be unwilling to grant ⟨The reclusive movie star usually *refuses* requests for interviews.⟩ — see DENY 2
2 to show unwillingness to accept, do, engage in, or agree to ⟨*refused* the award, citing the hard work of others who deserved the recognition more⟩ — see DECLINE 1

refutation *n* something (as an argument) that serves to disprove ⟨These are hard scientific facts against which there can be no reasonable *refutation*.⟩ — see CONFUTATION

refute *vb* **1** to declare not to be true ⟨While publicly *refuting* rumors of a merger, behind the scenes the CEO was working to effect that very outcome.⟩ — see DENY 1
2 to prove to be false ⟨The victories of African American athlete Jesse Owens in the 1936 Olympics effectively *refuted* the racial views of the Nazis.⟩ — see DISPROVE

regain *vb* to get again in one's possession ⟨Our team *regained* the ball with just two minutes left on the clock.⟩ — see RECOVER 1

regal *adj* **1** fit for or worthy of a royal ruler ⟨The actress's *regal* bearing makes her a perfect choice to play royalty on the screen.⟩ — see MONARCHICAL
2 large and impressive in size, grandeur, extent, or conception ⟨They envisioned a *regal* wedding with hundreds of guests, a full choir, and a reception at the fanciest hotel in town.⟩ — see GRAND 1

regale *vb* **1** to cause (someone) to pass the time agreeably occupied ⟨*regaled* his grandchildren with stories of his time in Morocco⟩ — see AMUSE
2 to entertain with a fancy meal ⟨an inn that nightly *regales* its guests with five-course meals prepared by a master chef⟩ — see FEAST 1

regalia *n* dressy clothing ⟨a monarch in full *regalia*⟩ — see FINERY

regard *n* **1** a feeling of great approval and liking ⟨I have a deep *regard* for humanitarian aid workers who risk everything to help the poor.⟩ — see ADMIRATION 1
2 an instance of looking especially briefly ⟨flashed the young man an imperial *regard* that clearly indicated such behavior was out of line⟩ — see LOOK 2
3 relation to or concern with something specified ⟨With *regard* to your request for time off, go ahead and take the whole week for vacation.⟩ — see RESPECT 1
4 regards *pl* best wishes ⟨Please give your parents my *regards*.⟩ — see COMPLIMENT 2
5 a fixed intent look ⟨fixed the same magisterial *regard* on all the miscreants who appeared before her in court⟩ — see GAZE

regard *vb* **1** to make note of (something) through the use of one's eyes ⟨She *regarded* him with astonishment when he announced he had gotten engaged.⟩ — see SEE 1
2 to take notice of and be guided by ⟨As a traveler, you should *regard* the laws and customs of whatever country you are visiting.⟩ — see HEED 1
3 to think of in a particular way ⟨I wouldn't *regard* that offhand comment as an insult.⟩ — see CONSIDER 1
4 to think very highly or favorably of ⟨an astronomer who is highly *regarded* by his peers⟩ — see ADMIRE

regardful *adj* marked by or showing proper regard for another's higher status ⟨his *regardful* willingness to let his

elderly father carve the turkey this year⟩ — see RESPECTFUL

regarding *prep* having to do with ⟨We wanted to talk to the company's vice president *regarding* a new product line.⟩ — see ABOUT 1

regardless *adv* in spite of everything ⟨The weather looked bad, but they were resolved to go on with their picnic *regardless*.⟩
synonyms anyhow, anyway
related words after all, however, nevertheless; always
phrases at all events, at any rate, in any case, in any event, no matter, whether or no (*or* whether or not)

regenerate *vb* **1** to bring back to a former condition or vigor ⟨The neighborhood was *regenerated* thanks to a government grant for restoring all the old buildings and creating studio spaces for artists.⟩ — see RENEW 1
2 to bring back to life, practice, or activity ⟨Dairy farming in the area was *regenerated* when new arrivals bought the old creamery.⟩ — see REVIVE 1
3 to make better in behavior or character ⟨The ex-convict credits his newfound faith with *regenerating* him beyond anything that he could have imagined.⟩ — see REFORM 1

regenerated *adj* made or become fresh in spirits or vigor ⟨After a cool dip in the river, the *regenerated* hikers continued on their way.⟩ — see NEW 4

regeneration *n* the act or an instance of bringing something back to life, public attention, or vigorous activity ⟨The *regeneration* of knitting and crocheting is in full bloom, with Hollywood stars admitting they knit and crochet on movie sets.⟩ — see REVIVAL

regime *also* **régime** *n* lawful control over the affairs of a political unit (as a nation) ⟨The *regime* of the dictator collapsed with surprising abruptness.⟩ — see RULE 2

regimen *n* lawful control over the affairs of a political unit (as a nation) ⟨With the start of the new year, a new party will have *regimen* over the nation.⟩ — see RULE 2

region *n* **1** a part or portion having no fixed boundaries ⟨If you look in the upper left *region* of the sky, you can see the constellation Orion.⟩
synonyms area, demesne, field, zone
related words corner, section; locale, locality, location, locus, place, point, position, site, space, spot
2 a broad geographical area ⟨Corn is mostly grown in the central *regions* of the country.⟩
synonyms belt, corridor, land, part(s), tract, zone
related words district, domain, latitude(s), range, realm, territory; neighborhood

¹**register** *n* an official whose job is to keep records ⟨Ask the county *register* for a copy of your birth certificate.⟩ — see CLERK 1

²**register** *n* a record of a series of items (as names or titles) usually arranged according to some system ⟨Check the voter *register* to see if it has my current party affiliation.⟩ — see ¹LIST

register *vb* **1** to add (a person) to a list or roll as a participant or member ⟨Please *register* me for the yoga class.⟩ — see ENROLL 1
2 to make a written note of ⟨The management *registered* her complaint in their log and promised to get back to her in a week.⟩ — see RECORD 1
3 to put (someone or something) on a list ⟨I have to *register* my new car when I renew my driver's license.⟩ — see ¹LIST 2
4 to have a clear idea of ⟨I'm not *registering* what you're saying.⟩ — see COMPREHEND 1

registrar *n* an official whose job is to keep records ⟨Will got a copy of his transcript from the school's *registrar*.⟩ — see CLERK 1

registration *n* the number of individuals registered ⟨There was a large *registration* for the popular swim classes at the community center.⟩

synonyms enrollment (*also* enrolment), registry

related words class, roster; count, membership

registry *n* **1** a record of a series of items (as names or titles) usually arranged according to some system ⟨We got a copy of the couple's bridal *registry* from the store's computer and scanned it for items we could afford.⟩ — see ¹LIST

2 the number of individuals registered ⟨Has the *registry* for the professional development seminar reached its limit yet?⟩ — see REGISTRATION

regress *vb* **1** to go back to a previous and usually lower state or level ⟨In extreme circumstances, people sometimes *regress* to the behavior they exhibited in childhood.⟩

synonyms retrogress, return, revert

related words backslide, lapse, relapse; throw back; ebb; decline, degenerate, drop, fall, retrograde, worsen

near antonyms grow, mature, ripen

antonyms advance, develop, evolve, progress

2 to become worse or of less value ⟨After months without practice, the team *regressed* to the previous year's level.⟩ — see DETERIORATE 1

regression *n* the act or an instance of going back to an earlier and lower level especially of intelligence or behavior ⟨*regression* to childish behavior⟩

synonyms retrogression, reversion

related words backslide, lapse, relapse; atavism, return; nondevelopment; decline, degeneration\

near antonyms gestation, growth, maturation, ripening

antonyms advancement, development, evolution, progression

regret *n* a feeling of responsibility for wrongdoing ⟨She was consumed with *regret* for belittling him in public and felt much better once she had apologized.⟩ — see GUILT 1

regret *vb* to feel sorry or dissatisfied about ⟨We *regret* any inconvenience that we may have caused you.⟩

synonyms bemoan, deplore, lament, repent, rue

related words ache (for), bewail, grieve (for), mourn, sorrow (for)

near antonyms delight (in), enjoy, relish, revel (in), savor (*also* savour)

regretful *adj* **1** expressing or suggesting mourning ⟨gave me a *regretful* look when I told him we had to move my mother to a nursing home⟩ — see MOURNFUL 1

2 feeling sorrow for a wrong that one has done ⟨Kim was truly *regretful* that she had yelled at him.⟩ — see CONTRITE

regretfully *adv* with feelings of bitterness or grief ⟨I must *regretfully* inform you that you are not among those who have been accepted for our internship program.⟩ — see HARD 2

regrettable *adj* of a kind to cause great distress ⟨The explorers forged ahead despite the *regrettable* loss of some of their companions.⟩

synonyms deplorable, distressful, distressing, grievous, heartbreaking, heartrending, lamentable, tragic (*also* tragical), unfortunate, unlucky, woeful

related words troublesome, vexatious; affecting, doleful, moving, piteous, poignant, ruthful, touching; awful, dire, dreadful, fearful, severe, terrible; alarming, disturbing, perturbing, traumatic, unsettling; crushing, excruciating, harrowing, horrible, horrifying, intolerable, overwhelming, shocking, sickening, unbearable; miserable, pitiful, sad, wretched; calamitous, disastrous

near antonyms gratifying, pleasing, rewarding, satisfying; comforting, encouraging, heartening; cheering, heartwarming, inspiring; fortunate, happy, lucky

regular *adj* **1** appearing or occurring repeatedly from time to time ⟨What with one or another of our pets having

problems, we've been *regular* visitors at the animal hospital.⟩

synonyms constant, frequent, habitual, periodic, periodical, repeated, steady

related words continual, intermittent, recurrent, recurring; cyclic (*or* cyclical); around-the-clock, round-the-clock; chronic, confirmed, inveterate; expected, usual

near antonyms episodic (*also* episodical), occasional; unexpected, unusual

antonyms inconstant, infrequent, irregular

2 following a set method, arrangement, or pattern ⟨He's followed a *regular* schedule for almost 20 years: up by 5, in bed by 10.⟩ — see METHODICAL

3 following or agreeing with established form, custom, or rules ⟨We thought about having a nontraditional wedding but in the end went with a *regular* ceremony instead.⟩ — see FORMAL 1

4 having no exceptions or restrictions ⟨Your room is a *regular* sty, and you need to clean it before you can go to the movies.⟩ — see ABSOLUTE 2

5 having or showing the qualities associated with the members of a particular group or kind ⟨Tantrums aren't his *regular* behavior.⟩ ⟨was just a *regular* guy who preferred hanging out with friends⟩ — see TYPICAL 1

regular *n* **1** a person engaged in military service ⟨Throughout the war, the *regulars* were supplemented by corps of volunteers and militiamen.⟩ — see SOLDIER

2 someone who regularly spends time in a particular place ⟨The coffeehouse *regulars* were put out by the interlopers occupying their usual table.⟩ — see DENIZEN 1

regularize *vb* to make agree with a single established standard or model ⟨The garment industry agreed to *regularize* clothing sizes.⟩ — see STANDARDIZE

regulate *vb* **1** to keep from exceeding a desirable degree or level (as of expression) ⟨You would be well advised to *regulate* your enthusiasm for the venture and pause to consider the risk involved.⟩ — see CONTROL 1

2 to look after and make decisions about ⟨the government agency that *regulates* the nuclear power industry in this country⟩ — see CONDUCT 1

regulation *n* **1** a statement spelling out the proper procedure or conduct for an activity ⟨It's against community *regulations* to leave your trash on the curb for more than two days.⟩ — see RULE 1

2 the act or activity of looking after and making decisions about something ⟨The owner seldom visited the plant and did not take an active part in the *regulation* of the company.⟩ — see CONDUCT 1

3 the duty or function of watching or guarding for the sake of proper direction or control ⟨The *regulation* of the soccer team was left entirely to the head coach and her assistants.⟩ — see SUPERVISION 1

regulator *n* a mechanism for adjusting the operation of a device, machine, or system ⟨The voltage *regulator* will make sure your car's alternator gets the right amount of electricity.⟩ — see CONTROL 1

rehabilitate *vb* **1** to make better in behavior or character ⟨an organization that *rehabilitates* criminals so they can reenter society⟩ — see REFORM 1

2 to restore to a healthy condition ⟨Holly underwent physical therapy to help *rehabilitate* her broken elbow.⟩ — see HEAL 1

rehabilitation *n* the process or period of gradually regaining one's health and strength ⟨His *rehabilitation* from the flu was brief, and he was up and working again within a few days.⟩ — see CONVALESCENCE

rehearsal *n* a private performance or session in preparation for a public appearance ⟨We made a few mistakes in

rehearsal, but we were pretty sure that we'd be OK on opening night.⟩
synonyms dry run, practice (*also* practise), trial
related words dress rehearsal; preview; drill, exercise

rehearse *vb* **1** to do over and over so as to become skilled ⟨The orchestra *rehearsed* the symphony until they finally got it to the conductor's satisfaction.⟩ — see PRACTICE
2 to give an oral or written account of in some detail ⟨wrote a letter to the management *rehearsing* in lurid detail our terrible stay at their hotel⟩ — see TELL 1
3 to say or state again ⟨Beth *rehearsed* her story about why she was late as she walked into the meeting.⟩ — see REPEAT 1
4 to specify one after another ⟨*rehearsed* the list of things he wanted for his birthday so that there would be no doubt in my mind⟩ — see ENUMERATE 1

reimburse *vb* to make a return payment to ⟨Make sure you keep your receipts so we can *reimburse* you for your expenses.⟩ — see REPAY

rein *n* **1** *usually* **reins** *pl* the place of leadership or command ⟨After the president resigned, the vice president stepped in and took the *reins* of the company.⟩ — see HEAD 2
2 the act or practice of keeping something (as an activity) within certain boundaries ⟨The oversight committee called on the state to keep a much tighter *rein* on the activities of its contractors.⟩ — see RESTRICTION 2
3 *usually* **reins** *pl* the right or means to command or control others ⟨A peaceful transfer of the *reins* of government has always been a hallmark of our nation.⟩ — see POWER 1

rein (in) *vb* to keep from exceeding a desirable degree or level (as of expression) ⟨Try to *rein in* your spending, so you have some money left for saving.⟩ — see CONTROL 1

reiterate *vb* **1** to make or do again ⟨The pianist's valedictory concert will *reiterate* the program he played on the national tour.⟩ — see REPEAT 4
2 to say or state again ⟨I want to *reiterate* that under no circumstances are you to leave the house.⟩ — see REPEAT 1

reiteration *n* the act of saying or doing over again ⟨There's no need for the *reiteration* of the rules, as I know them already.⟩ — see REPEAT

reiterative *adj* marked by repetition ⟨The novelist's *reiterative* style really bores some readers.⟩ — see REPETITIVE

reject *n* **1** one who is cast out or rejected by society ⟨people who were once social *rejects* but are now valued members of the community⟩ — see OUTCAST
2 something separated from a group or lot for not being as good as the others ⟨That apple has a mushy spot on it, so it's a *reject*.⟩ — see CULL

reject *vb* **1** to be unwilling to grant ⟨*rejected* his request for time off⟩ — see DENY 2
2 to declare not to be true ⟨I *reject* the claim that I have ever lied about that.⟩ — see DENY 1
3 to get rid of as useless or unwanted ⟨We sorted through the nuts and *rejected* any that had cracked shells or were shattered.⟩ — see DISCARD
4 to show unwillingness to accept, do, engage in, or agree to ⟨*rejected* the proposal⟩ — see DECLINE 1

rejected *adj* left unoccupied or unused ⟨Tara picked up the *rejected* toy to see what was wrong with it.⟩ — see ABANDONED 1

rejection *n* **1** a refusal to confirm the truth of a statement ⟨made a flat *rejection* of the charges against him⟩ — see DENIAL 2
2 an unwillingness to grant something asked for ⟨the judge's swift *rejection* of the lawyer's request for a recess⟩ — see DENIAL 1
3 something separated from a group or lot for not being

as good as the others ⟨That pile is for *rejections*, and this one is for applications we'll be accepting.⟩ — see CULL

rejoice *vb* **1** to feel or express joy or triumph ⟨*rejoiced* over our unexpected victory on the soccer field⟩ — see EXULT
2 to give satisfaction to ⟨News of the enemy's surrender *rejoiced* a nation weary of war.⟩ — see PLEASE 1

rejoicing *adj* having or expressing feelings of joy or triumph ⟨the *rejoicing* parents of the valedictorian⟩ — see EXULTANT

rejoicing *n* joyful or festive activity ⟨There was great *rejoicing* at the launch party for the book.⟩ — see MERRYMAKING

rejoin *vb* to speak or write in reaction to a question or to another reaction ⟨"Oh, yeah? Well, same to you," she *rejoined*.⟩ — see ANSWER 1

rejoinder *n* something spoken or written in reaction especially to a question ⟨He always has a smart-aleck *rejoinder* to everything.⟩ — see ANSWER 1

rejuvenate *vb* **1** to bring back to a former condition or vigor ⟨The shower *rejuvenated* me after a long day of cleaning out the garage.⟩ — see RENEW 1
2 to bring back to life, practice, or activity ⟨That designer has *rejuvenated* '80s fashion for a whole new generation.⟩ — see REVIVE 1

rejuvenation *n* the act or an instance of bringing something back to life, public attention, or vigorous activity ⟨Hollywood was seeing the *rejuvenation* of kung fu movies.⟩ — see REVIVAL

rekindle *vb* to bring back to life, practice, or activity ⟨The trip to Ireland *rekindled* her interest in learning Gaelic.⟩ — see REVIVE 1

relate *vb* **1** to form a close personal relationship ⟨She and I *relate* so well it's almost like we're siblings.⟩ — see COMMUNE
2 to give an oral or written account of in some detail ⟨We asked our uncle to *relate* the story of his visit to Russia many years ago.⟩ — see TELL 1
3 to have a relation or connection ⟨How does your comment *relate* to what the rest of us have been talking about for the last hour?⟩ — see APPLY 1
4 to think of (something) in combination ⟨Most Americans probably *relate* tea to the United Kingdom and coffee to the U.S.⟩ — see ASSOCIATE 2

related *adj* having a close connection like that between family members ⟨the *related* fields of anthropology and archaeology⟩
synonyms affiliated, akin, allied, kindred
related words associated, connected, interconnected, interrelated, joined; alike, analogous, cognate, comparable, connate, correspondent, corresponding, matching, parallel, resemblant, resembling, similar, suchlike; apropos, cogent, germane, material, pertinent, relevant
near antonyms different, disparate, dissimilar, distinct, distinctive, diverse, other, unalike, unlike; discriminable, distinguishable
antonyms unrelated

relation *n* **1** **relations** *pl* doings between individuals or groups ⟨*Relations* between the rival newspapers remained friendly despite their competition for the same stories.⟩
synonyms commerce, dealings, interaction, intercourse
related words interrelationship; cross-fertilization, cross-pollination; companionship, company
antonyms nonintercourse
2 a person connected with another by blood or marriage ⟨He and I are *relations* on my mother's side.⟩ — see RELATIVE
3 the fact or state of having something in common ⟨There's no *relation* between you losing your favorite baseball hat and your team losing the game.⟩ — see CONNECTION 1
4 the state of having shared interests or efforts (as in so-

cial or business matters) ⟨Our intramural baseball team had a *relation* with the other baseball teams in the area.⟩ — see ASSOCIATION 1

5 relations *pl* sexual union involving penetration of the vagina by the penis ⟨opposes *relations* outside of marriage⟩ — see SEXUAL INTERCOURSE

relationship *n* **1** the fact or state of having something in common ⟨studied the *relationship* between the phases of the moon and ocean tides⟩ — see CONNECTION 1

2 the state of having shared interests or efforts (as in social or business matters) ⟨The street's shopkeepers have a good business *relationship*.⟩ — see ASSOCIATION 1

relative *adj* **1** being such only when compared to something else ⟨After being crammed into a one-bedroom apartment, they lived in *relative* comfort in a two-bedroom house.⟩ — see COMPARATIVE

2 having to do with the matter at hand ⟨I don't need the whole story, just the details that are *relative* to the case.⟩ — see PERTINENT

relative *n* a person connected with another by blood or marriage ⟨It's always fun to see all your *relatives* at a big family gathering.⟩

synonyms kin, kinsman, relation

related words in-law; kinswoman; blood, clan, family, folk, house, kindred, kinfolk (*or* kinfolks), kinsfolk, line, lineage, people, race, stock, tribe

antonyms nonrelative

relatively *adv* to some degree or extent ⟨These newly acquired in-laws felt *relatively* comfortable at our family reunion.⟩ — see FAIRLY 1

relax *vb* **1** to get rid of nervous tension or anxiety ⟨She took deep breaths to *relax* before going on stage.⟩

synonyms chill, chill out [*slang*], de-stress, unwind

related words unbend; bask, kick back, loll, lounge, repose, rest; bum, dally, dawdle, dillydally, drone, footle, goof (off), idle, loaf, vegetate, zone out; alleviate, comfort, ease, relieve; calm, compose, cool, quiet, settle

phrases hang loose

antonyms tense (up)

2 to make less taut ⟨*Relax* the rope a bit so I can pick up the slack and tie this knot.⟩ — see SLACKEN 1

3 to refrain from labor or exertion ⟨I just want to kick back and *relax* after mowing that huge lawn.⟩ — see REST 1

relaxation *n* **1** activity engaged in to amuse oneself ⟨What do people around here do for *relaxation*?⟩ — see PLAY 1

2 freedom from activity or labor ⟨meditating in a state of total *relaxation*⟩ — see ¹REST 1

relaxed *adj* **1** enjoying physical comfort ⟨The frazzled executive was totally *relaxed* after the warm bath.⟩ — see COMFORTABLE 2

2 not bound by rigid standards ⟨We're having a very *relaxed* staff meeting, and then everyone can get an early start on the long holiday weekend.⟩ — see EASYGOING 2

3 not tightly fastened, tied, or stretched ⟨The fishing line was *relaxed* and looped lazily into the pond.⟩ — see LOOSE 1

relaxing *adj* tending to calm the emotions and relieve stress ⟨a *relaxing* cup of chamomile tea⟩ — see SOOTHING 1

release *n* **1** a freeing from an obligation or responsibility ⟨Because they had legally declared bankruptcy, they received *release* from their debt.⟩

synonyms delivery, discharge, quietus, quittance

related words dispensation, exemption, immunity, waiver

2 a document containing a declaration of an intentional giving up of a right, claim, or privilege ⟨We had to sign a liability *release* before they'd let us go rock climbing on their property.⟩ — see WAIVER

3 a published statement informing the public of a matter

of general interest ⟨a press *release* announcing that the governor would not run for a second term⟩ — see ANNOUNCEMENT

4 reduction of or freedom from pain ⟨Only sleep offered any *release* from the agony of the migraine.⟩ — see EASE 1

release *vb* **1** to set free (from a state of being held in check) ⟨The losing player *released* his anger with a great yell of frustration.⟩

synonyms loose, loosen, uncork, unleash, unlock, unloose, unloosen

related words discharge, emancipate, enfranchise, free, liberate, manumit, spring, unbind, uncage, unchain, unfetter, unmoor, unshackle; air, express, vent

phrases let go

near antonyms handcuff, manacle, shackle, trammel; bind, confine, enchain, fetter; halter, hamper

antonyms bridle, check, constrain, contain, control, curb, govern, hold, inhibit, regulate, rein (in), restrain, smother, tame

2 to find emotional release for ⟨Gail tried to find other ways of *releasing* tension than by chewing her fingernails.⟩ — see TAKE OUT 1

3 to release (as from slavery or confinement) ⟨*Release* the prisoners immediately!⟩ — see FREE 1

4 to set free from entanglement or difficulty ⟨The new governor finally managed to *release* himself from his rash campaign promise.⟩ — see EXTRICATE

5 to throw or give off ⟨an air freshener that *releases* a pleasing scent into the room⟩ — see EMIT 1

6 to make known openly or publicly ⟨The panel of nutritionists *released* their findings on the safety and effectiveness of various diets.⟩ — see ANNOUNCE

7 to let go from office, service, or employment ⟨They *released* the workers who couldn't handle the new technology.⟩ — see DISMISS 1

relent *vb* **1** to cease resistance (as to another's arguments, demands, or control) ⟨The supervisor finally *relented* in the face of the petition, and allowed employees to take longer lunch breaks.⟩ — see YIELD 3

2 to grow less in scope or intensity especially gradually ⟨The fury of the storm *relented*, and the next day the sun finally broke through the clouds.⟩ — see DECREASE 2

relentless *adj* showing no signs of slackening or yielding in one's purpose ⟨The team's offense was *relentless* in trying to score a touchdown.⟩ — see UNYIELDING 1

relevance *n* the fact or state of being pertinent ⟨The question had no *relevance* to the topic being discussed.⟩ — see PERTINENCE

relevancy *n* the fact or state of being pertinent ⟨This new information has no *relevancy* to the case.⟩ — see PERTINENCE

relevant *adj* having to do with the matter at hand ⟨Make sure your comments during the interview are short and *relevant*.⟩ — see PERTINENT

reliability *n* worthiness as the recipient of another's trust or confidence ⟨We never had reason to question the *reliability* of the park rangers in the event of an emergency.⟩

synonyms dependability, reliableness, responsibility, solidity, solidness, sureness, trustworthiness

related words inerrancy, infallibility; credibility, creditability, creditableness

near antonyms doubtfulness, dubiousness, questionableness, shakiness, uncertainness

antonyms unreliability

reliable *adj* worthy of one's trust ⟨I need a *reliable* car that's not going to break down constantly.⟩ — see DEPENDABLE

reliableness *n* worthiness as the recipient of another's trust or confidence ⟨the proven *reliableness* of that brand of household appliances⟩ — see RELIABILITY

reliance *n* **1** something or someone to which one looks for support ⟨He's been the family's foremost *reliance* in times of trouble many times.⟩ — see DEPENDENCE 2
2 the quality or state of needing something or someone ⟨a baby's *reliance* on her parents⟩ ⟨his *reliance* on his next-door neighbor for all the local gossip⟩ — see DEPENDENCE 1

relic *n* **1** a tiny often physical indication of something lost or vanished ⟨a crude stone ax and other *relics* of the Neanderthals⟩ — see VESTIGE 1
2 something belonging to or surviving from an earlier period ⟨In my grandparents' attic are many "groovy" *relics* from the 1960s.⟩ — see ANTIQUE

relief *n* **1** a feeling of ease from grief or trouble ⟨I felt such *relief* when final exams were over.⟩ — see COMFORT 1
2 a person or thing that takes the place of another ⟨I can't go home from my nursing shift until my *relief* shows up to take over.⟩ — see SUBSTITUTE
3 reduction of or freedom from pain ⟨The aspirin gave him some *relief* from the headache.⟩ — see EASE 1

relieve *vb* **1** to make more bearable or less severe ⟨An ice pack will *relieve* the swelling.⟩ — see HELP 2
2 to set (a person or thing) free of something that encumbers ⟨The bellhop *relieved* him of his luggage and led him to the elevator.⟩ — see RID
3 to take the place of ⟨At daybreak a soldier arrived to *relieve* the one who had spent the night on guard duty.⟩ — see REPLACE 1

religion *n* **1** a body of beliefs and practices regarding the supernatural and the worship of one or more deities ⟨The Jewish *religion* has followers in many parts of the globe.⟩
synonyms credo, creed, cult, faith, persuasion
related words church, communion, denomination, sect; doctrine, dogma, theology; deism, heathenism, monotheism, paganism, pantheism, polytheism, theism
near antonyms agnosticism, know-nothingism; atheism, godlessness, secularism
2 belief and trust in and loyalty to God ⟨Without his *religion*, he would not have been able to survive all the difficulties he has faced over the years.⟩ — see FAITH 1

religious *adj* **1** of, relating to, or used in the practice or worship services of a religion ⟨Johann Sebastian Bach wrote some of the most beautiful *religious* music in the world.⟩
synonyms devotional, sacred, spiritual
related words blessed (*also* blest), consecrated, hallowed, holy, sacrosanct, sanctified; solemn; liturgical, ritual, sacramental; semireligious, semisacred
near antonyms earthly, mundane, terrestrial, worldly
antonyms nonreligious, profane, secular
2 showing a devotion to God and to a life of virtue ⟨a deeply *religious* woman who eventually decided to quit her job and to become a nun⟩ — see HOLY 1
3 having or expressing great depth of feeling ⟨a person known for embracing various causes with a *religious* enthusiasm⟩ — see FERVENT 1

relinquish *vb* **1** to give (something) over to the control or possession of another usually under duress ⟨The boy reluctantly *relinquished* the illegal fireworks to the police officer.⟩ — see SURRENDER 1
2 to give up (as a position of authority) formally ⟨The retiring CEO *relinquished* his position to the company's vice president with very mixed feelings.⟩ — see ABDICATE

relinquishment *n* the usually forced yielding of one's person or possessions to the control of another ⟨*relinquishment* of command over the unit⟩ — see SURRENDER

relish *n* **1** positive regard for something ⟨She has great *relish* for early morning walks, which she takes nearly every day.⟩ — see LIKING

2 the feeling experienced when one's wishes are met ⟨Tim ate the bowl of ice cream with *relish*.⟩ — see PLEASURE 1

relish *vb* to take pleasure in ⟨Please visit again real soon, for I *relish* your company.⟩ — see ENJOY 1

reluctance *n* a lack of willingness or desire to do or accept something ⟨The mice showed an odd *reluctance* to eat the cheese we had put out for them.⟩
synonyms disinclination, hesitance, hesitancy, reticence, unwillingness
related words faltering, hesitation, indecision, irresolution, shilly-shallying, staggering, vacillation, wavering, wobbling (*also* wabbling); distrust, distrustfulness, doubt, incertitude, misgiving, mistrust, mistrustfulness, skepticism, suspicion, uncertainness, uncertainty
near antonyms assurance, assuredness, certainty, certitude, conviction, positiveness, sureness, surety
antonyms inclination, willingness

reluctant *adj* slow to begin or proceed with a course of action because of doubts or uncertainty ⟨I'm *reluctant* to get involved with their scheme.⟩ — see HESITANT

rely *vb* to place reliance or trust ⟨rigorously tested the rope before starting out, for the rock climbers would be *relying* on it with their very lives⟩ — see DEPEND 2

remain *vb* **1** to continue to be in a place for a significant amount of time ⟨One of the three bridges known as "the London Bridge," it was moved in the late 1960s to Lake Havasu City, Arizona, where it *remains* today.⟩ — see ¹STAY 1
2 to remain indefinitely in existence or in the same state ⟨The fact *remains*: it's still impossible to be in two places at once.⟩ — see CONTINUE 1

remainder *n* **1** a remaining group or portion ⟨The *remainder* of the water was saved in case it was needed later.⟩
synonyms balance, leavings, leftovers, odds and ends, remains, remnant, residue, rest
related words fragment, scrap, vestige; butt, oddment, scraping(s), stub, stump; excess, fat, overabundance, overage, overflow, overkill, overmuch, oversupply, superabundance, superfluity, surfeit, surplus
near antonyms body, bulk, main, mass, most, weight
2 an unused or unwanted piece or item typically of small size or value ⟨The *remainder* of the dough can be used to make a tartlet.⟩ — see ¹SCRAP 1

remains *pl n* **1** the portion or bits of something left over or behind after it has been destroyed ⟨The *remains* of the tree ripped apart by the tornado littered the street for weeks afterward.⟩
synonyms ashes, debris, residue, rubble, ruins, wreck, wreckage
related words jetsam, leavings, remnant; chaff, deadwood, dross, dust, garbage, junk, litter, refuse, riffraff, rubbish, scrap, trash, waste
2 a dead body ⟨Archaeologists discovered the *remains* of an Incan woman and carefully excavated her burial site, which promised to yield important clues about her status.⟩ — see CORPSE
3 a remaining group or portion ⟨We gathered up the *remains* of the buffet and delivered them to a local homeless shelter.⟩ — see REMAINDER 1

remake *vb* **1** to make different in some way ⟨one of those people who left the security and conformity of a small town to *remake* their lives in the big city⟩ — see CHANGE 1
2 to make or do again ⟨Yesterday's soup was so good that we decided to *remake* it for today's lunch.⟩ — see REPEAT 4

remaking *n* the act, process, or result of making different ⟨thought that the room looked no better for all the *remaking* and rearranging we did⟩ — see CHANGE 1

remark *n* a briefly expressed opinion ⟨The director made some short *remarks* about the new museum before officially opening the doors to visitors.⟩
synonyms comment, note, reflection
related words analysis, commentary, exposition; belief, conviction, eye, feeling, judgment (*or* judgement), mind, notion, persuasion, sentiment, verdict, view; advice, input
remark *vb* 1 to make a statement of one's opinion ⟨The mayor *remarked* on how quickly the building project was progressing.⟩
synonyms allow, comment, note, observe, opine, reflect
related words commentate; articulate, express, say, speak, state, talk, tell, utter, verbalize, vocalize; conjecture, guess, speculate, suppose, surmise
2 to make note of (something) through the use of one's eyes ⟨I *remarked* how much the child had grown.⟩ — see SEE 1
remarkable *adj* 1 different from the ordinary in a way that causes curiosity or suspicion ⟨One participant in the race had a *remarkable* walk that was half-run, half-skip.⟩ — see ODD 2
2 likely to attract attention ⟨There's a *remarkable* fixation with vanity of earthly pleasures in this author's poetry.⟩ — see NOTICEABLE
3 worth remembering or mentioning ⟨just your average suburban ranch house, with nothing *remarkable* about it⟩ — see NOTEWORTHY 1
remediable *adj* capable of being corrected ⟨The problems with the local transportation system were severe but still *remediable*.⟩
synonyms correctable, fixable, repairable, reparable
related words amendable, emendable, improvable, resolvable; reversible, reformable, regenerable; corrected, fixed, remedied, repaired
near antonyms irretrievable, unrecoverable; irreplaceable, irreversible, irrevocable
antonyms incorrigible, irrecoverable, irredeemable, irremediable, irreparable, unredeemable
remedial *adj* serving to raise or adjust something to some standard or proper condition ⟨took a *remedial* math course over the summer so he'd be ready for algebra the following school year⟩ — see CORRECTIVE 1
remedy *n* 1 a substance or preparation used to treat disease ⟨preferred to treat colds with a homemade *remedy* made from garlic⟩ — see MEDICINE
2 something that corrects or counteracts something undesirable ⟨The mayor was desperately searching for a *remedy* to the city's problem with crumbling infrastructure.⟩ — see CURE 1
remedy *vb* 1 to bring about recovery from ⟨A little extra studying should *remedy* your poor performance in history thus far this year.⟩ — see CURE 1
2 to remove errors, defects, deficiencies, or deviations from ⟨Tonya needed to wear glasses to *remedy* her bad vision.⟩ — see CORRECT 1
remedying *adj* serving to raise or adjust something to some standard or proper condition ⟨I've given the engine a *remedying* tune-up that should put an end to that knocking.⟩ — see CORRECTIVE 1
remember *vb* to bring back to mind ⟨I *remember* very clearly the fun we had that long-ago summer, but I can't *remember* what I had for lunch yesterday.⟩
synonyms hark back (to), recall, recollect, reminisce (about), think (of)
related words recapture, recur; educe, elicit, evoke, extract, raise, remind; relive; represent
near antonyms misremember; disregard, ignore, neglect, overlook; lose, miss; blank (out)
antonyms forget, unlearn
remembrance *n* 1 a particular act or instance of recalling

or the thing remembered ⟨a happy couple with many fond *remembrances* of when they were dating in college⟩ — see MEMORY 2
2 something that serves to keep alive the memory of a person or event ⟨a dinner held in *remembrance* of their grandmother⟩ — see MEMORIAL
3 the power or process of recalling what has been previously learned or experienced ⟨*Remembrance* will wane with age.⟩ — see MEMORY 1
reminder *n* something that serves to keep alive the memory of a person or event ⟨The peach tree in our front yard is a living *reminder* of my late grandfather, who owned an orchard.⟩ — see MEMORIAL
reminisce (about) *vb* to bring back to mind ⟨two friends *reminiscing about* those proverbial good old days⟩ — see REMEMBER
reminiscence *n* 1 a particular act or instance of recalling or the thing remembered ⟨His *reminiscences* about the war were painful to hear.⟩ — see MEMORY 2
2 the power or process of recalling what has been previously learned or experienced ⟨We wondered whether she could trust her *reminiscence* of events that happened so long ago.⟩ — see MEMORY 1
reminiscent *adj* provoking a memory or mental association ⟨a sparkling winter day that was oddly *reminiscent* of summer in its cheering sunniness⟩ — see SUGGESTIVE 2
remiss *adj* failing to give proper care and attention ⟨I would be *remiss* if I didn't tell you how much I appreciated the lovely gift.⟩ — see NEGLIGENT
remissible *adj* worthy of forgiveness ⟨only guilty of *remissible* sins⟩ — see VENIAL
remission *n* release from the guilt or penalty of an offense ⟨the *remission* of sins⟩ — see PARDON
remit *vb* 1 to grow less in scope or intensity especially gradually ⟨I waited until the rain *remitted* a little and ran to the car.⟩ — see DECREASE 2
2 to dismiss as of little importance ⟨The judge refused to *remit* the young man's cavalier disregard for his pile of unpaid speeding tickets and summarily revoked his driver's license.⟩ — see EXCUSE 1
3 to assign to a later time ⟨The legislature has *remitted* the matter to the next session, where it will most likely die in committee.⟩ — see POSTPONE
remitment *n* the act of offering money in exchange for goods or services ⟨The charge account will be closed upon the *remitment* of the outstanding balance.⟩ — see PAYMENT 1
remittable *adj* worthy of forgiveness ⟨Forgetting a doctor's appointment that was made months in advance is a *remittable* offense.⟩ — see VENIAL
remittal *n* release from the guilt or penalty of an offense ⟨a king who was once obliged to do public penance for the *remittal* of his sins⟩ — see PARDON
remittance *n* 1 something (as money) that is given or received in return for goods or services ⟨She always mails in her *remittance* on time so she won't ever be charged a late fee on her electric bill.⟩ — see PAYMENT 2
2 the act of offering money in exchange for goods or services ⟨The *remittance* of your outstanding balance is required before you can make more purchases.⟩ — see PAYMENT 1
remnant *n* 1 a remaining group or portion ⟨sailed home with just a *remnant* of the colony's original population aboard⟩ — see REMAINDER 1
2 an unused or unwanted piece or item typically of small size or value ⟨Beth gathered together her fabric *remnants* to see if she had enough of them to sew a quilt.⟩ — see ¹SCRAP 1
remodel *vb* to make different in some way ⟨We completely

remodeled the house right after we moved in.⟩ — see CHANGE 1

remodeling *n* the act, process, or result of making different ⟨We moved out of the apartment and into a motel during the *remodeling.*⟩ — see CHANGE 1

remonstrance *n* a feeling or declaration of disapproval or dissent ⟨Over the vociferous *remonstrances* of my parents I decided to drop my music lessons.⟩ — see OBJECTION

remonstrate (with) *vb* to present an opposing opinion or argument ⟨I discouraged her from *remonstrating with* her father, whose mind was obviously made up.⟩ — see OBJECT

remorse *n* a feeling of responsibility for wrongdoing ⟨He felt a deep *remorse* for having neglected his friend over the years.⟩ — see GUILT 1

remorseful *adj* feeling sorrow for a wrong that one has done ⟨Don was *remorseful* about all the trouble that he had caused in the family.⟩ — see CONTRITE

remorsefulness *n* a feeling of responsibility for wrongdoing ⟨She was gnawed by an unrelenting *remorsefulness* for the pain that she had caused people.⟩ — see GUILT 1

remorseless *adj* **1** not sorry for having done wrong ⟨The *remorseless* criminal was sentenced to life in prison without chance of parole.⟩

synonyms impenitent, shameless, unashamed, unrepentant

related words cruel, merciless, pitiless, ruthless, unmerciful; evil, immoral, iniquitous, nefarious, reprobate, unregenerate, vicious, vile, villainous, wicked; callous, cold-blooded, heartless, inhuman, inhumane, soulless, unfeeling

near antonyms hangdog, shamefaced; charitable, compassionate, humane, merciful, sensitive, softhearted, sympathetic, tender, tenderhearted, warm, warmhearted

antonyms apologetic, ashamed, contrite, guilty, penitent, regretful, remorseful, repentant, rueful, shamed, sorry

2 having or showing a lack of sympathy or tender feelings ⟨In *Les Miserables,* Inspector Javert engaged in a *remorseless* pursuit of Jean Valjean for stealing a loaf of bread.⟩ — see HARD 1

remote *adj* **1** small in degree ⟨There's a *remote* chance that it'll rain today, so I brought an umbrella.⟩

synonyms fragile, frail, negligible, off, outside, slight, slim, small

related words minimal, minor; little, tiny

near antonyms great, large; distinct, significant; considerable, goodly, healthy, largish, respectable, significant, sizable (*or* sizeable), substantial, tidy

antonyms good

2 having or showing a lack of friendliness or interest in others ⟨His grandfather had been a somewhat *remote* figure, at least until they got to spend a summer together.⟩ — see COOL 1

3 screened or sequestered from view ⟨a *remote* cottage on the far side of the mountain⟩ — see SECLUDED

4 not close in time or space ⟨A permanent base on Mars is likely to happen only in the *remote* future.⟩ — see DISTANT 1

remotest *adj* most distant from a center ⟨News of the emperor's death had spread even to the *remotest* corners of the empire.⟩ — see EXTREME 1

removal *n* the getting rid of whatever is unwanted or useless ⟨a product for the *removal* of warts⟩ — see DISPOSAL 1

remove *n* the space or amount of space between two points, lines, surfaces, or objects ⟨Their farm is just a *remove* of two miles from the town center.⟩ — see DISTANCE 1

remove *vb* **1** to rid oneself of (a garment) ⟨I *removed* my coat as soon as I got inside.⟩

synonyms doff, douse, peel (off), put off, shrug off, take off

related words husk, shed; kick (off); disrobe, strip, undress

near antonyms wear; apparel, array, attire, bedeck, clothe, dress, garb, rig, robe, suit

antonyms don, put on, slip (into), throw (on)

2 to take away from a place or position ⟨He carefully *removed* the old manuscript from the shelf.⟩

synonyms clear, draw, take out, withdraw

related words demount, dislodge; abstract, cut, draw off, draw out, extract, pull; budge, dislocate, displace, disturb, move, shift, transfer, transpose

near antonyms mount; anchor, clamp, fix, hitch, moor, secure, set; embed (*also* imbed), entrench (*also* intrench), implant, ingrain (*also* engrain), lodge, root; set up, site, situate, stick

antonyms place, position, put

3 to change the place or position of ⟨Please *remove* that chair to the other room.⟩ — see MOVE 1

4 to let go from office, service, or employment ⟨Voters *removed* the selectman from office the first chance they got.⟩ — see DISMISS 1

removed *adj* not close in time or space ⟨an island far *removed* from the mainland⟩ — see DISTANT 1

remunerate *vb* **1** to give (someone) the sum of money owed for goods or services received ⟨We promptly *remunerated* the repair company for fixing the dryer.⟩ — see PAY 1

2 to provide (someone) with a just payment for loss or injury ⟨The negligent landlord must *remunerate* those made homeless by the fire by finding and paying for new housing for them.⟩ — see COMPENSATE 1

remuneration *n* **1** the act of offering money in exchange for goods or services ⟨Customers who are tardy in their *remuneration* will be subject to extra charges.⟩ — see PAYMENT 1

2 payment to another for a loss or injury ⟨The vandals were ordered to pay the property owners thousands of dollars in *remuneration.*⟩ — see COMPENSATION 1

3 something (as money) that is given or received in return for goods or services ⟨We can't accept your *remuneration* for services provided until we officially bill you.⟩ — see PAYMENT 2

remunerative *adj* yielding a profit ⟨I made a highly *remunerative* investment that will end up paying my college tuition.⟩ — see PROFITABLE 1

rend *vb* to cause (something) to separate into jagged pieces by violently pulling at it ⟨people *rending* their garments in mourning⟩ — see TEAR 1

render *vb* **1** to give (something) over to the control or possession of another usually under duress ⟨a gentleman bandit who graciously asked his victims to *render* their wallets to his safe possession⟩ — see SURRENDER 1

2 to make an exact likeness of ⟨*rendered* Thomas Jefferson's signature for use on an array of gift items⟩ — see COPY 1

3 to give a representation or account of in words ⟨The witness convincingly *rendered* her version of events in just a few words.⟩ — see DESCRIBE 1

rendezvous *n* **1** a place for spending time or for socializing ⟨The arcade was the *rendezvous* of choice for most of the teenagers in town.⟩ — see HANGOUT

2 an agreement to be present at a specified time and place ⟨I have a *rendezvous* with him at lunchtime.⟩ — see ENGAGEMENT 2

rendezvous *vb* to come together into one body or place ⟨We'll *rendezvous* at the entrance to the park at 6:00 p.m.⟩ — see ASSEMBLE 1

renegade *n* a person who abandons a cause or organization usually without right ⟨a band of *renegades* who had deserted their infantry units⟩
synonyms apostate, defector, deserter, recreant
related words betrayer, double-crosser, quisling, traitor, traitress (*or* traitoress), turncoat; abandoner, dropout, leaver; defier, insurgent, insurrectionary, insurrectionist, mutineer, rebel, red, revolter, revolutionary, revolutionist; discontent, malcontent
near antonyms adherent, disciple, follower, supporter; fanatic, militant, partisan (*also* partizan), zealot
antonyms loyalist

renege *vb* **1** to break a promise or agreement ⟨My so-called best friend promised to help me move, only to *renege* come Saturday morning.⟩
synonyms back down, back off, cop out
related words chicken (out), wimp out; backpedal, backtrack; disavow, recall, recant, repudiate, retract, take back, unsay, withdraw; beg off
phrases go back on
near antonyms adhere (to); comply (with); fulfill (*or* fulfil), honor, keep, satisfy
2 to solemnly or formally reject or go back on (as something formerly adhered to) ⟨refused to *renege* the principles by which she had always lived her life, even if it resulted in losing her business⟩ — see ABJURE 1

renew *vb* **1** to bring back to a former condition or vigor ⟨The trip to New York *renewed* our enthusiasm for travel.⟩
synonyms freshen, recreate, refresh, refreshen, regenerate, rejuvenate, repair, restore, resuscitate, revitalize, revive
related words make over, overhaul, reclaim, recondition, reconstitute, redesign, redevelop, redo, reengineer, refurbish, rehab, rehabilitate, remake, remodel, renovate; refill, replenish, resupply
2 to begin again or return to after an interruption ⟨With daybreak, the rescue team will *renew* its efforts to reach the stranded mountain climbers.⟩ — see RESUME
3 to bring back to life, practice, or activity ⟨The spate of recent movies based on classic comic book characters has *renewed* interest in the comics themselves.⟩ — see REVIVE 1
4 to make or do again ⟨I can only *renew* my offer to help—it's up to them to accept it.⟩ — see REPEAT 4

renewal *n* **1** the act of saying or doing over again ⟨a campaign season that witnessed the endless *renewal* of the same stupid charges and countercharges⟩ — see REPEAT
2 the act or an instance of bringing something back to life, public attention, or vigorous activity ⟨Roller-skating experienced a major *renewal* after the introduction of in-line skates.⟩ — see REVIVAL

renewed *adj* made or become fresh in spirits or vigor ⟨I was a *renewed* reader after that short nap.⟩ — see NEW 4

renounce *vb* **1** to give up (as a position of authority) formally ⟨In wake of the corruption scandal, the congressman was forced to *renounce* his seat in the House.⟩ — see ABDICATE
2 to solemnly or formally reject or go back on (as something formerly adhered to) ⟨He *renounced* his old way of life.⟩ — see ABJURE 1

renouncement *n* the act or practice of giving up or rejecting something once enjoyed or desired ⟨her *renouncement* of her inheritance⟩ — see RENUNCIATION

renovate *vb* to put into good shape or working order again ⟨We will have to *renovate* the house extensively before we can move in.⟩ — see MEND 1

renown *n* the fact or state of being known to the public ⟨a basketball icon whose *renown* is truly international⟩ — see FAME 1

renowned *adj* widely known ⟨the *renowned* painter, sculp-

tor, architect, and engineer, Leonardo da Vinci⟩ — see FAMOUS 1

rent *n* **1** a long deep cut ⟨Getting her skirt caught on a nail resulted in a four-inch *rent* that she couldn't possibly repair.⟩ — see GASH
2 an open space in a barrier (as a wall or hedge) ⟨peered through the *rent* in the old garden wall for a glimpse of her mysterious new neighbor⟩ — see GAP 1

rent *vb* **1** to give the possession and use of (something) in return for periodic payment ⟨We *rented* the apartment to a college student for $500 a month.⟩
synonyms lease
related words charter, engage, hire; lodge; sublease, sublet
2 to take or get the temporary use of (something) for a set sum ⟨We will need to *rent* a car while we're in Europe.⟩ — see HIRE 1

renter *n* **1** one who rents a room or apartment in another's house ⟨One of the *renters* called to tell us the hot water heater was broken.⟩ — see TENANT 1
2 the owner of land or housing that is rented to another ⟨left our apartment keys at the *renter's* office just before leaving in the moving truck⟩ — see LANDLORD

renunciation *n* the act or practice of giving up or rejecting something once enjoyed or desired ⟨His sudden *renunciation* of his smoking habit pleased his whole family.⟩
synonyms renouncement, repudiation, self-denial
related words denial, refusal; relinquishment, resignation, surrender; self-abnegation, self-renunciation
near antonyms acceptance; adoption, embrace, embracement, espousal
antonyms indulgence, self-indulgence

reopen *vb* to begin again or return to after an interruption ⟨Court will *reopen* after a brief recess.⟩ — see RESUME

rep *n* a person who acts or does business for another ⟨The company dispatched three *reps* to the annual marketing fair.⟩ — see AGENT 2

repair *n* a state of being or fitness ⟨The dining table is in good *repair*, so you won't need to refinish it.⟩ — see CONDITION 1

repair *vb* **1** to bring back to a former condition or vigor ⟨It will take some time to *repair* your energy after a bout with the flu.⟩ — see RENEW 1
2 to put into good shape or working order again ⟨having trouble finding someone who *repairs* audio components⟩ — see MEND 1

repairable *adj* capable of being corrected ⟨The damage to her career from this performance may not be *repairable*.⟩ — see REMEDIABLE

reparable *adj* capable of being corrected ⟨Whether the harm your lying has done to our friendship is *reparable* or irreparable depends a lot on you.⟩ — see REMEDIABLE

reparation *n* payment to another for a loss or injury ⟨The company paid millions in *reparations*.⟩ — see COMPENSATION 1

repartee *n* **1** a quick witty response ⟨That *repartee* to the reporter's question drew laughs from the bystanders.⟩ — see RETORT 1
2 good-natured teasing or exchanging of clever remarks ⟨The late night host and his guest engaged in witty *repartee*.⟩ — see BANTER

repast *n* food eaten or prepared for eating at one time ⟨monks taking their evening *repast* in silence⟩ — see MEAL

repay *vb* to make a return payment to ⟨I *repaid* my friend the $20 he had lent me.⟩
synonyms refund, reimburse
related words give back, render (to); compensate, recompense, remunerate; liquidate, pay down, pay off, pay up, quit, satisfy, settle; reciprocate, requite
phrases pay back

repeal *n* the act of putting an end to something planned or previously agreed to ⟨the *repeal* of archaic laws⟩ — see CANCELLATION

repeal *vb* **1** to put an end to (something planned or previously agreed to) ⟨The company called the furniture store to *repeal* the order for six new desks.⟩ — see CANCEL 1
2 to put an end to by formal action ⟨In 1933, Congress passed the 21st Amendment which *repealed* the Prohibition Amendment of 1919, thus making the sale, distribution, and use of alcohol legal once again.⟩ — see ABOLISH 1
3 to solemnly or formally reject or go back on (as something formerly adhered to) ⟨If I find that you have been lying about this, I'll instantly *repeal* every promise I made to you.⟩ — see ABJURE 1

repeat *n* the act of saying or doing over again ⟨If we don't want a *repeat* of last year's disastrous celebration, we had better do some more planning.⟩
synonyms duplication, redo, reduplication, reiteration, renewal, repetition, replication
related words rebroadcast, rerun; recitation, rehearsal

repeat *vb* **1** to say or state again ⟨I *repeated* the address over and over until I had it memorized.⟩
synonyms chime, din, rehearse, reiterate
related words paraphrase, reword; echo, reecho; mouth, parrot; abstract, encapsulate, epitomize, outline, recap, recapitulate, summarize, sum up
phrases come again
2 to give from memory ⟨Kate *repeated* correctly all the verses she had memorized.⟩
synonyms recite, reel off, say
related words con, learn, memorize, study; declaim, mouth, orate, speak
near antonyms read
3 to say after another ⟨Now *repeat* the oath after me.⟩
synonyms echo, parrot, quote, reecho
related words mouth; ape, copy, copycat, emulate, imitate, mime, mimic
4 to make or do again ⟨Try not to *repeat* your mistakes.⟩
synonyms duplicate, redo, reduplicate, reiterate, remake, renew, replicate
related words recreate, reenact, reinvent

repeated *adj* appearing or occurring repeatedly from time to time ⟨I made *repeated* attempts to get in touch with her.⟩ — see REGULAR 1

repeatedly *adv* many times ⟨I've told him *repeatedly* not to do that.⟩ — see OFTEN

repel *vb* **1** to drive back ⟨The defenders *repelled* the attacking army after several hours of fierce fighting.⟩
synonyms fend (off), rebut, repulse, stave off
related words defy, fight, hold off, oppose, resist, stand off, withstand; deflect, ward (off); rebuff, snub, spurn
near antonyms embrace, hail, welcome
2 to cause to feel disgust ⟨The idea of chocolate-covered grasshoppers *repels* me.⟩ — see DISGUST
3 to refuse to give in to ⟨*repelled* the temptation to stay out late and call in sick the next day⟩ — see RESIST

repelled *adj* filled with disgust ⟨*Repelled* reviewers couldn't believe how violent the movie was.⟩ — see SICK 2

repellent *also* **repellant** *adj* causing intense displeasure, disgust, or resentment ⟨Your snobbish behavior towards my friends is so *repellent* I can't stand to be around you anymore.⟩ — see OFFENSIVE 1

repent *vb* to feel sorry or dissatisfied about ⟨After hearing what a great time you guys had at the party, I am *repenting* my decision to stay home.⟩ — see REGRET

repentance *n* a feeling of responsibility for wrongdoing ⟨preached that *repentance* was the first step on the path of redemption⟩ — see GUILT 1

repentant *adj* feeling sorrow for a wrong that one has done ⟨*repentant* sinners⟩ — see CONTRITE

repercussion *n* the power to bring about a result on another ⟨Your decision not to go to college will have *repercussions* you'll feel for years to come.⟩ — see EFFECT 2

repetition *n* the act of saying or doing over again ⟨The *repetition* of the honor society's oath at the initiation ceremonies got old really quickly.⟩ — see REPEAT

repetitious *adj* marked by repetition ⟨At a real trial, *repetitious* questioning by the attorneys makes the whole affair less than thrilling.⟩ — see REPETITIVE

repetitive *adj* marked by repetition ⟨the *repetitive* lyrics of so many rock songs⟩
synonyms reiterative, repetitious
related words redundant

rephrase *vb* to express something (as a text or statement) in different words ⟨I don't understand what you're asking—could you *rephrase* your question?⟩ — see PARAPHRASE

rephrasing *n* an instance of expressing something in different words ⟨A more polite *rephrasing* of your request might get better results.⟩ — see PARAPHRASE

repine (for) *vb* to have an earnest wish to own or enjoy ⟨During the deep cold of winter, I *repine for* warm tropical beaches.⟩ — see DESIRE 1

replace *vb* **1** to take the place of ⟨The old street lights were *replaced* by more energy-efficient models.⟩
synonyms cut out, displace, relieve, substitute, supersede, supplant
related words preempt, usurp
2 to bring, send, or put back to a former or proper place ⟨He took the fragile vase down to look at it and then gently *replaced* it on the shelf.⟩ — see RETURN 1

replacement *n* a person or thing that takes the place of another ⟨Seeing that the starting quarterback was unable to play, the coach immediately called in his *replacement*.⟩ — see SUBSTITUTE

replete *adj* **1** having an excess of body fat ⟨The merchant was a richly *replete* gentleman, clearly enjoying the fruits of his success.⟩ — see FAT 1
2 possessing or covered with great numbers or amounts of something specified ⟨a gym that is *replete* with the very latest in exercise equipment⟩ — see RIFE
3 having one's appetite completely satisfied ⟨Everyone settled back and relaxed, completely *replete* after the huge meal.⟩ — see FULL 3

replica *n* **1** something or someone that strongly resembles another ⟨Filled with the usual chain stores, the new mall is a too-familiar *replica* of hundreds of other malls.⟩ — see IMAGE 1
2 something that is made to look exactly like something else ⟨assembled a small-scale *replica* of the Queen Mary ocean liner⟩ — see COPY

replicate *vb* **1** to make an exact likeness of ⟨*replicated* the famous painting in our art class⟩ — see COPY 1
2 to make or do again ⟨I can't *replicate* your results when I do the experiment myself.⟩ — see REPEAT 4

replication *n* **1** something that is made to look exactly like something else ⟨bought a smaller and cheaper *replication* of the marble statue for his garden⟩ — see COPY
2 the act of saying or doing over again ⟨We'll need to do a *replication* of that experiment so we can collect more data.⟩ — see REPEAT

reply *n* **1** action or behavior that is done in return to other action or behavior ⟨I asked what was wrong, and in *reply* she handed me the letter.⟩ — see REACTION
2 something spoken or written in reaction especially to a question ⟨I look forward to your *reply* to my request.⟩ — see ANSWER 1

reply *vb* **1** to act or behave in response (as to a stimulus or influence) ⟨Anna *replied* to the news that she had won the scholarship by jumping around the room and cheering.⟩ — see REACT

2 to speak or write in reaction to a question or to another reaction ⟨Please *reply* to my question at your earliest convenience.⟩ — see ANSWER 1

report *n* **1** a loud explosive sound ⟨startled by the *report* of a gun⟩ — see CLAP 1

2 a relating of events usually in the order in which they happened ⟨The Browns gave a full *report* of their trip to London.⟩ — see ACCOUNT 1

3 overall quality as seen or judged by people in general ⟨He's a player of good *report* in golfing circles.⟩ — see REPUTATION

4 information or opinion that is widely disseminated without any authority or confirmation of accuracy ⟨The *report* is that she was caught embezzling, but no one has any evidence.⟩ — see RUMOR

report *vb* **1** to give an oral or written account of in some detail ⟨will *report* the progress of the reform efforts before a congressional committee on Monday⟩ — see TELL 1

2 to make a written note of ⟨*reported* the lawyer's closing statement⟩ — see RECORD 1

reporter *n* a person employed by a newspaper, magazine, or radio or television station to gather, write, or report news ⟨The *reporter* was careful to ask as many questions as possible without annoying anyone.⟩

synonyms correspondent, journalist, newsman

related words broadcaster, newspaperman, newswoman; anchor, anchorman, anchorperson, anchorwoman; columnist, commentator; copyreader, editor; muckraker, photojournalist, police reporter, sportswriter

repose *n* **1** a natural periodic loss of consciousness during which the body restores itself ⟨Typically the wealthy socialite spends most of the morning in *repose*, is served lunch, and then embarks on an exhaustive afternoon of shopping.⟩ — see SLEEP 1

2 a state of freedom from storm or disturbance ⟨We enjoyed the *repose* of a serene summer evening.⟩ — see CALM 1

3 freedom from activity or labor ⟨The doctor ordered a period of *repose* for the patient recovering from pneumonia.⟩ — see ¹REST 1

4 evenness of emotions or temper ⟨Her *repose* in the face of the screaming demonstrators was impressive.⟩ — see EQUANIMITY

¹repose *vb* **1** to remain out of sight ⟨a little-explored region beneath which vast mineral reserves are said to *repose*⟩ — see ¹HIDE 3

2 to refrain from labor or exertion ⟨Mia *reposed* in the Caribbean sun, enjoying her break from the world of work.⟩ — see REST 1

²repose *vb* to put (something) into the possession or safekeeping of another ⟨The Constitution *reposes* the power to declare war to Congress, and to that body alone.⟩ — see GIVE 2

repository *n* a building for storing goods ⟨nurses going back and forth to the medication *repository*⟩ — see STOREHOUSE

repossess *vb* to get again in one's possession ⟨If you don't pay off the loan, the bank will come and *repossess* your car.⟩ — see RECOVER 1

repossession *n* the act or process of getting something back ⟨an account of France's loss of the Louisiana Territory to Spain and its brief *repossession* of the area before selling it to the U.S. in 1803⟩ — see RECOVERY 1

reprehend *vb* **1** to declare to be morally wrong or evil ⟨*reprehends* the taking of life in any form⟩ — see CONDEMN 1

2 to express one's unfavorable opinion of the worth or quality of ⟨Without exception, book reviewers *reprehended* the novel's tired plot.⟩ — see CRITICIZE

reprehensible *adj* **1** deserving reproach or blame ⟨A *reprehensible* tyrant, who oppressed his country for decades, has finally been brought to justice.⟩ — see BLAMEWORTHY

2 provoking or likely to provoke protest ⟨Your behavior towards the other team was truly *reprehensible*, so you're being suspended from the next three games.⟩ — see OBJECTIONABLE

represent *vb* **1** to point out the chief quality or qualities of an individual or group ⟨The writer of the magazine article *represented* the students at the academy as a bunch of rich kids.⟩ — see CHARACTERIZE 1

2 to present a picture of ⟨a painting *representing* the ocean at sunrise⟩ — see PICTURE 1

3 to serve as a material counterpart of ⟨This orange *represents* the sun and this pea *represents* the Earth.⟩ — see SYMBOLIZE

representative *adj* **1** having or showing the qualities associated with the members of a particular group or kind ⟨a *representative* example of what that talented chef can do with even simple ingredients⟩ — see TYPICAL 1

2 having the function or meaning of an object or figure that stands for something else ⟨A red cross on this map is *representative* of a hospital or other medical facility.⟩ — see SYMBOLIC

representative *n* **1** a person who acts or does business for another ⟨A *representative* from the car dealership called to ask how we were enjoying the new car.⟩ — see AGENT 2

2 a person sent on a mission to represent another ⟨I speak on this matter as a *representative* of the people of the U.S.⟩ — see AMBASSADOR

3 one of a group or collection that shows what the whole is like ⟨This song is a fairly good *representative* of the other songs on the album.⟩ — see EXAMPLE

repress *vb* **1** to put a stop to (something) by the use of force ⟨quickly *repressed* the rebellion in the provincial city and restored order⟩ — see QUELL 1

2 to refrain from openly showing or uttering ⟨You can't *repress* your feelings forever, so tell her how you feel about her.⟩ — see SUPPRESS 2

repression *n* the checking of one's true feelings and impulses when dealing with others ⟨psychologists talking about the *repression* of anger and how it affects one's health⟩ — see CONSTRAINT 1

reprimand *n* an often public or formal expression of disapproval ⟨While reviewing the troops, the officer delivered a curt *reprimand* to one of the soldiers.⟩ — see CENSURE

reprimand *vb* **1** to criticize (someone) severely or angrily especially for personal failings ⟨*reprimanded* the summer intern for her constant tardiness⟩ — see SCOLD

2 to criticize (someone) so as to correct a fault ⟨*reprimanded* the student for using the lax grammar and punctuation of text messaging in a term paper⟩ — see REBUKE 1

3 to express public or formal disapproval of ⟨The president was forced to *reprimand* the general for publicly voicing his disagreements with the nation's foreign policy.⟩ — see CENSURE 1

reprisal *n* **1** *usually* **reprisals** *pl* payment to another for a loss or injury ⟨a peace agreement that was rejected because it contained no provisions for *reprisals*⟩ — see COMPENSATION 1

2 the act or an instance of responding to an injury with an injury ⟨After defeating them last year in the finals, our team nervously awaited the expected *reprisal* by our archrivals in this year's tournament.⟩ — see REVENGE

reproach *n* **1** a cause of shame ⟨Your public display of bad behavior is a *reproach* to this entire school.⟩ — see DIS-GRACE 2

2 an often public or formal expression of disapproval ⟨A letter of *reproach* was added to her dossier.⟩ — see CENSURE

3 the state of having lost the esteem of others ⟨Nothing the traitor did in later life lessened the *reproach* in which he was universally held.⟩ — see DISGRACE 1

reproach *vb* **1** to criticize (someone) severely or angrily especially for personal failings ⟨Our neighbor loudly *reproached* us for tromping through his yard.⟩ — see SCOLD

2 to criticize (someone) so as to correct a fault ⟨She cleared her throat as a way of *reproaching* us for having our elbows on the table.⟩ — see REBUKE 1

3 to express public or formal disapproval of ⟨The governor *reproached* the legislature for failing to pass the budget on time and once again throwing the state into fiscal chaos.⟩ — see CENSURE 1

reproachable *adj* deserving reproach or blame ⟨There are only a few *reproachable* lapses in a generally well-researched book.⟩ — see BLAMEWORTHY

reprobate *adj* having or showing lowered moral character or standards ⟨a *reprobate* judge who could be bribed⟩ — see CORRUPT

reprobate *n* a mean, evil, or unprincipled person ⟨a program for rehabilitating *reprobates* and turning them into hard-working, law-abiding citizens⟩ — see VILLAIN

reprobate *vb* **1** to be unwilling to grant ⟨The board will most likely *reprobate* the request for parole.⟩ — see DENY 2

2 to show unwillingness to accept, do, engage in, or agree to ⟨Without hesitation she *reprobated* such a repellant idea.⟩ — see DECLINE 1

3 to declare to be morally wrong or evil ⟨She spent much of her talk *reprobating* the callous indifference of a materialistic society to the suffering of people in the third world.⟩ — see CONDEMN 1

reproduce *vb* **1** to bring forth offspring ⟨Mice *reproduce* at a much faster rate than humans do.⟩ — see PROCREATE

2 to make an exact likeness of ⟨You'll have to *reproduce* that design on every tile in the bathroom.⟩ — see COPY 1

reproduction *n* something that is made to look exactly like something else ⟨We walked through a *reproduction* of the interior of the Parthenon as it must have looked when it was first built.⟩ — see COPY

reproof *n* an often public or formal expression of disapproval ⟨The fear of *reproof* prevented them from complaining.⟩ — see CENSURE

reprove *vb* **1** to criticize (someone) so as to correct a fault ⟨My piano teacher often *reproves* me for slouching while playing, observing that good posture helps one play better.⟩ — see REBUKE 1

2 to express public or formal disapproval of ⟨The principal *reproved* the hockey team for their display of poor sportsmanship on the ice.⟩ — see CENSURE 1

3 to hold an unfavorable opinion of ⟨The older generation has always *reproved* the younger generation's taste in music.⟩ — see DISAPPROVE (OF)

republic *n* government in which the supreme power is held by the people and used by them directly or indirectly through representation ⟨When asked by a passer-by what sort of government the constitutional convention had formulated for the new nation, Benjamin Franklin memorably replied, "A *republic*, if you can keep it."⟩ — see DEMOCRACY

republican *adj* of, relating to, or favoring political democracy ⟨a small but well-organized *republican* movement working quietly to overthrow the military dictatorship⟩ — see DEMOCRATIC

repudiate *vb* **1** to declare not to be true ⟨Ava vigorously *repudiated* the charge that she had lied on her résumé.⟩ — see DENY 1

2 to refuse to acknowledge as one's own or as one's responsibility ⟨The angry mother bitterly *repudiated* her daughter.⟩ — see DISCLAIM 1

3 to show unwillingness to accept, do, engage in, or agree to ⟨We didn't like the terms, so we *repudiated* the proposal.⟩ — see DECLINE 1

4 to solemnly or formally reject or go back on (as something formerly adhered to) ⟨The producers of the hit TV show threatened to take the disgruntled actor to court if he attempted to *repudiate* his contract.⟩ — see ABJURE 1

repudiation *n* **1** a refusal to confirm the truth of a statement ⟨Voters seemed satisfied by the candidate's public *repudiation* of the beliefs of an organization to which he had briefly belonged as a youth.⟩ — see DENIAL 2

2 the act or practice of giving up or rejecting something once enjoyed or desired ⟨New Year's resolutions typically include the *repudiation* of sweets and other indulgences and the promise to resume working out at the gym.⟩ — see RENUNCIATION

repugnance *n* a dislike so strong as to cause stomach upset or queasiness ⟨Kara could barely contain her *repugnance* of frogs and nearly threw up when she found out we'd have to dissect one in science class.⟩ — see DISGUST

repugnant *adj* **1** causing intense displeasure, disgust, or resentment ⟨The suggestion was completely *repugnant* to us.⟩ — see OFFENSIVE 1

2 not being in agreement or harmony ⟨Technically speaking, it may not be a violation, but it is certainly *repugnant* to the spirit of the law.⟩ — see INCONSISTENT 1

repulse *n* treatment that is deliberately unfriendly ⟨The waiter's incredibly rude *repulse* of our polite request for a better table—one that wasn't right next to the kitchen—prompted us to walk out.⟩ — see COLD SHOULDER

repulse *vb* **1** to cause to feel disgust ⟨The smell of that town's paper mill totally *repulses* me.⟩ — see DISGUST

2 to drive back ⟨The defense repeatedly *repulsed* all of the offense's attempts to move the ball forward, keeping them firmly planted on the 20-yard line.⟩ — see REPEL 1

repulsed *adj* filled with disgust ⟨I am *repulsed* that you think it's OK to cheat on your taxes.⟩ — see SICK 2

repulsion *n* a dislike so strong as to cause stomach upset or queasiness ⟨We giggled at my father, who was overcome with *repulsion* when he realized he was eating octopus.⟩ — see DISGUST

repulsive *adj* causing intense displeasure, disgust, or resentment ⟨a *repulsive* display of shameless flattery that made the embarrassed actor wrinkle his nose in disgust⟩ — see OFFENSIVE 1

repulsiveness *n* the quality of inspiring intense dread or dismay ⟨horror films that seem to be trying to outdo one another in the *repulsiveness* of their monsters⟩ — see HORROR 1

reputable *adj* having a good reputation especially in a field of knowledge ⟨Make sure you buy your used car from a *reputable* dealer.⟩ — see RESPECTABLE 1

reputation *n* overall quality as seen or judged by people in general ⟨The college's athletic department has a good *reputation*, but the school's science facilities are a bit lacking.⟩
   synonyms character, fame, mark, name, note, odor, report, repute
   related words credit, honor; celebrity, notoriety, renown; image, persona; admiration, regard, reverence
   near antonyms discredit, disgrace, dishonor, disrepute, ignominy, infamy, odium, opprobrium, reproach, shame

repute *n* overall quality as seen or judged by people in general ⟨That's a repair shop of good *repute*.⟩ — see REPUTATION

reputed *adj* **1** appearing to be true on the basis of evidence that may or may not be confirmed ⟨This treatment is a *reputed* cure for the condition, but studies haven't confirmed that claim.⟩ — see APPARENT 1

2 having a good reputation especially in a field of knowledge ⟨a *reputed* oceanographer whose excellent work is known internationally⟩ — see RESPECTABLE 1

request *n* **1** an act or instance of asking for information ⟨The medical columnist is unable to answer individual *requests* for specific information on various disorders.⟩ — see QUESTION 2

2 the state of being sought after especially for purchase ⟨Reliable babysitters are much in *request*, especially on weekends.⟩ — see DEMAND 2

request *vb* **1** to give a request or demand for ⟨a notice *requesting* that I report for jury duty on Monday morning⟩ — see ORDER 2

2 to make a request for ⟨I *requested* extra ketchup for my fries.⟩ — see ASK (FOR) 1

3 to make a request of ⟨a letter from the First Lady graciously *requesting* the chorus to perform at the White House⟩ — see ASK 2

requiem *n* a composition expressing one's grief over a loss ⟨The choir will sing Mozart's *Requiem*.⟩ — see LAMENT 2

require *vb* to have as a requirement ⟨The toy *requires* four batteries, which are not included.⟩ — see NEED 1

required *adj* **1** forcing one's compliance or participation by or as if by law ⟨Formal instruction in driving is *required* in this state before you can get your driver's license.⟩ — see MANDATORY

2 impossible to do without ⟨With these frigid winds, hats, scarves, and good mittens are *required* equipment for heading outside.⟩ — see ESSENTIAL 1

requirement *n* something necessary, indispensable, or unavoidable ⟨This science course is a *requirement* for graduation.⟩ — see ESSENTIAL 1

requisite *adj* impossible to do without ⟨This new album is the *requisite* recording of the year for classical music lovers.⟩ — see ESSENTIAL 1

requisite *n* something necessary, indispensable, or unavoidable ⟨Art 101 is a *requisite* for Art 201.⟩ — see ESSENTIAL 1

requisition *n* something that someone insists upon having ⟨A brand-new, top-notch computer was the new science teacher's first *requisition*.⟩ — see DEMAND 1

requisition *vb* to give a request or demand for ⟨The invading soldiers *requisitioned* food and gasoline from the townspeople.⟩ — see ORDER 2

requital *n* **1** payment to another for a loss or injury ⟨The judge ordered the landlord to pay his former tenants $100,000 each as *requital* for goods lost or damaged in the apartment fire.⟩ — see COMPENSATION 1

2 something (as money) that is given or received in return for goods or services ⟨The electrician's *requital* for the used car was in the form of work on the dealer's house.⟩ — see PAYMENT 2

3 the act or an instance of responding to an injury with an injury ⟨"An eye for an eye" is a form of *requital* that is still legal in some countries.⟩ — see REVENGE

requite *vb* **1** to provide (someone) with a just payment for loss or injury ⟨The company *requited* the employee who had fallen on the ice while leaving work by promptly paying all his medical bills, hoping that would stave off a lawsuit.⟩ — see COMPENSATE 1

2 to punish in kind the wrongdoer responsible for ⟨The writer would later *requite* the harsh treatment his family suffered when he was a child by creating scathing portraits of the upper classes in his novels.⟩ — see AVENGE

rescind *vb* **1** to put an end to (something planned or previ-

ously agreed to) ⟨The library refused to *rescind* its decision to include the controversial book in its collection.⟩ — see CANCEL 1

2 to put an end to by formal action ⟨The new mayor vowed not to seek to *rescind* existing laws prohibiting smoking in the city's public places.⟩ — see ABOLISH 1

rescission *n* the act of putting an end to something planned or previously agreed to ⟨The judge ruled that the town's *rescission* of the contract was justified due the contractor's repeated failures to meet its obligations.⟩ — see CANCELLATION

rescue *n* the saving from danger or evil ⟨stranded people hoping for *rescue* from the rising floodwaters⟩ — see SALVATION

rescue *vb* to remove from danger or harm ⟨an all-out effort to *rescue* a beached whale⟩ — see SAVE 2

rescuer *n* one that saves from danger or destruction ⟨*Rescuers* went out immediately in search of the lost dog.⟩ — see SAVIOR

research *n* a systematic search for the truth or facts about something ⟨I'll have to do some *research* for this project.⟩ — see INQUIRY 1

research *vb* to search through or into ⟨Bella *researched* the public record for more information about her great-grandparents.⟩ — see EXPLORE 1

resemblance *n* **1** a point which two or more things share in common ⟨I see a family *resemblance* between you and your brother.⟩ — see SIMILARITY 2

2 the quality or state of having many qualities in common ⟨The look of the director's latest film bears a strong *resemblance* to the look of his last film.⟩ — see SIMILARITY 1

resembling *adj* having qualities in common ⟨*Resembling* Impressionist landscapes were hung side by side so that visitors could compare how fellow artists treated the same subject matter.⟩ — see ALIKE

resentful *adj* **1** having or showing deep-seated resentment ⟨He is still *resentful* about being passed over for a promotion.⟩ — see BITTER 1

2 having or showing mean resentment of another's possessions or advantages ⟨*resentful* of her cousin's wealth⟩ — see ENVIOUS

resentfully *adv* with feelings of bitterness or grief ⟨She apologized later, but it was clear she did so *resentfully*.⟩ — see HARD 2

resentment *n* **1** a lingering ill will towards a person for a real or imagined wrong ⟨If you continue to harbor *resentment* toward your father, you'll never be able to move on with your life.⟩ — see GRUDGE 1

2 a painful awareness of another's possessions or advantages and a desire to have them too ⟨I don't have any *resentment* over my friend's luxurious house.⟩ — see ENVY

3 the feeling of being offended or resentful after a slight or indignity ⟨my *resentment* at being spoken to like I'm stupid⟩ — see PIQUE

reservation *n* **1** a feeling or attitude that one does not know the truth, truthfulness, or trustworthiness of someone or something ⟨Despite my *reservations*, we hired the young teen as a babysitter.⟩ — see DOUBT

2 something upon which the carrying out of an agreement or offer depends ⟨gave us his approval without any *reservations*⟩ — see CONDITION 2

reserve *n* **1** the checking of one's true feelings and impulses when dealing with others ⟨The salesclerk showed great *reserve* in dealing with the unreasonable demands of the angry customer.⟩ — see CONSTRAINT 1

2 a collection of things kept available for future use or need ⟨Our fuel *reserves* are low.⟩ — see STORE 1

3 a person or thing that takes the place of another ⟨When the first brigade fell back in retreat, the commander sent out the *reserves* to try to hold the line of battle.⟩ — see SUBSTITUTE

4 an interchangeable part or piece of equipment that is kept on hand for replacement of an original ⟨Don't throw that extra bike chain away, as I want to keep it as a *reserve* in case the current one breaks.⟩ — see SPARE

reserve *vb* **1** to arrange to have something (as a hotel room) held for one's future use ⟨We made sure to *reserve* a kennel for our dog several months before the start of the family vacation.⟩
synonyms bespeak, book
related words earmark; contract, engage, hire, retain

2 to continue to have in one's possession or power ⟨I'm *reserving* the right to work by myself if you don't do your share of the project.⟩ — see KEEP 2

3 to keep or intend for a special purpose ⟨We must *reserve* this cup for ceremonial use only.⟩ — see DEVOTE 1

reserved *adj* tending not to speak frequently (as by habit or inclination) ⟨A *reserved* and shy person who was wrongly thought to be stuck-up until someone finally got into a conversation with her.⟩ — see SILENT 2

reside *vb* to have a home ⟨He's a freelance writer who *resides* in the Midwest.⟩ — see LIVE 1

residence *n* the place where one lives ⟨Police stopped by his *residence* to question him.⟩ — see HOME 1

resident *n* one who lives permanently in a place ⟨a *resident* of Atlanta⟩ — see INHABITANT

resider *n* one who lives permanently in a place ⟨Karl was born in the U.S. but is now a *resider* of Dresden, Germany.⟩ — see INHABITANT

residue *n* **1** the portion or bits of something left over or behind after it has been destroyed ⟨The detective noticed an ashy *residue* in the sink and deduced that a piece of paper had been burned there.⟩ — see REMAINS 1

2 a remaining group or portion ⟨The *residue* of our Thanksgiving feast consisted of a denuded turkey carcass and a couple rolls.⟩ — see REMAINDER 1

resign *vb* to give up (as a position of authority) formally ⟨Following the election, the incumbent cabinet members *resigned* their positions so the president could feel free to pick a new administration.⟩ — see ABDICATE

resign (from) *vb* to give up (a job or office) ⟨He *resigned from* the company after the news broke that he had been falsifying financial statements for years.⟩ — see QUIT 1

resigned *adj* receiving or enduring without offering resistance ⟨I am *resigned* to the fact that I'll never be rich.⟩ — see PASSIVE

resilient *adj* able to revert to original size and shape after being stretched, squeezed, or twisted ⟨After being dipped in liquid nitrogen, the rubber ball's normally *resilient* surface is as brittle as ceramic.⟩ — see ELASTIC 1

resist *vb* to refuse to give in to ⟨It is important to *resist* the temptation to run away from your problems.⟩
synonyms buck, defy, fight, oppose, repel, withstand
related words battle, combat, contend (with); challenge, contest, contradict, dispute; baffle, balk, foil, frustrate, thwart; check, counter, hinder, obstruct, stem
antonyms bow (to), capitulate (to), give in (to), knuckle under (to), stoop (to), submit (to), succumb (to), surrender (to), yield (to)

resistance *n* **1** the inclination to resist ⟨After some initial *resistance*, the city council warmed up to the proposed development plan.⟩
synonyms defiance, opposition
related words demur, objection, protest, remonstrance; compunction, misgiving, reservation; disobedience, noncompliance, recalcitrance; contrariety, contrariness

near antonyms compliance, obedience; acceptance, approval
antonyms acquiescence

2 a secret organization in a conquered country fighting against enemy forces ⟨Soldiers from the *resistance* were captured after a skirmish outside the foreign ministry.⟩
synonyms underground
related words cabal, conspiracy

resolute *adj* fully committed to achieving a goal ⟨Despite the risks involved, she was *resolute* in her decision to undergo the experimental operation.⟩ — see DETERMINED 1

resoluteness *n* firm or unwavering adherence to one's purpose ⟨With a *resoluteness* that was admirable, the losing team continued to play hard until the bitter end.⟩ — see DETERMINATION 1

resolution *n* **1** a position arrived at after consideration ⟨Her *resolution* to become a vegetarian is based on what she recently learned about modern farming practices.⟩ — see DECISION 1

2 firm or unwavering adherence to one's purpose ⟨That athlete's *resolution* to win is amazing.⟩ — see DETERMINATION 1

resolvable *adj* capable of having the reason for or cause of determined ⟨I have no doubt that this mystery will turn out to be *resolvable*.⟩ — see SOLVABLE

resolve *n* firm or unwavering adherence to one's purpose ⟨a naval pilot who has been unwavering in his *resolve* to become an astronaut⟩ — see DETERMINATION 1

resolve *vb* **1** to come to a judgment about after discussion or consideration ⟨I *resolved* to eat more healthily and to exercise regularly.⟩ — see DECIDE 1

2 to find an answer for through reasoning ⟨*resolved* the apparent contradictions in the collected data⟩ — see SOLVE

3 to set or force apart ⟨A prism will *resolve* a beam of light into an array of colors.⟩ — see SEPARATE 1

resolved *adj* fully committed to achieving a goal ⟨Only the most *resolved* of explorers had any chance of finding the source of the Nile.⟩ — see DETERMINED 1

resonant *adj* marked by conspicuously full and rich sounds or tones ⟨The orator's *resonant* voice filled the hall.⟩
synonyms golden, resounding, reverberant, reverberating, rotund, round, sonorous, vibrant
related words deep, full, mellifluous, mellow, rich; loud, powerful, stentorian, thunderous
near antonyms cavernous, hollow; faint, low, murmurous, muted, smothered, soft, weak; thin, tinny

resonate *vb* to continue or be repeated in a series of reflected sound waves ⟨The deep sounds of the bassoon *resonated* through the concert hall.⟩ — see REVERBERATE

resort *n* **1** a place for spending time or for socializing ⟨The island port was once the *resort* of smugglers, pirates, and other unsavory characters.⟩ — see HANGOUT

2 something that one uses to accomplish an end especially when the usual means is not available ⟨Use this money only as a last *resort*.⟩ — see RESOURCE 1

resort (to) *vb* **1** to use or seek out as a source of aid, relief, or advantage ⟨He had to *resort to* asking his parents for money.⟩
synonyms consult, go (to), refer (to), turn (to)
related words employ, use, utilize; depend (on), rely (on)
phrases fall back on

2 to go to or spend time in often ⟨Tom *resorted to* the library whenever he felt the need for a little peace and quiet.⟩ — see FREQUENT

resound *vb* **1** to proclaim the glory of ⟨folk songs that *resound* the noble deeds of the nation's heroes of yore⟩ — see PRAISE 1

2 to continue or be repeated in a series of reflected sound waves ⟨Thunder *resounded* across the plain.⟩ — see RE-VERBERATE

resounding *adj* **1** full of or characterized by the presence of noise ⟨the *resounding* hubbub of the streets of New York City⟩ — see NOISY 2

2 marked by a high volume of sound ⟨The emcee announced the winner in a *resounding* voice that could be heard all the way to the back of the hall.⟩ — see LOUD 1

3 marked by conspicuously full and rich sounds or tones ⟨a *resounding* chord⟩ — see RESONANT

4 marked by or uttered with forcefulness ⟨a *resounding* defeat for the opposition party⟩ — see EMPHATIC 1

resource *n* **1** something that one uses to accomplish an end especially when the usual means is not available ⟨We used every possible *resource* to raise the funds needed to save our town's oldest house.⟩

synonyms expedient, recourse, resort

related words hope, opportunity, possibility, relief; makeshift, replacement, stopgap, substitute

2 resources *pl* available money ⟨Do you have the *resources* to buy a new car or even a used car?⟩ — see FUND 2

respect *n* **1** relation to or concern with something specified ⟨with *respect* to your application⟩

synonyms reference, regard

2 a feeling of great approval and liking ⟨I have a lot of *respect* for Martin Luther King, Jr.'s steadfast courage.⟩ — see ADMIRATION 1

3 respects *pl* best wishes ⟨Please give your mother my *respects*.⟩ — see COMPLIMENT 2

respect *vb* to think very highly or favorably of ⟨an upstanding senator who is *respected* by political allies and foes alike⟩ — see ADMIRE

respectable *adj* **1** having a good reputation especially in a field of knowledge ⟨No *respectable* dietician would advise people to eat just one kind of food.⟩

synonyms esteemed, name, prestigious, reputable, reputed, respected

related words honorable, venerable, worthy; creditable, good, praiseworthy; celebrated, distinguished, famed, famous, honored, illustrious, notable, prominent, redoubtable, renowned, well-known

near antonyms seedy, shadowy, shady; obscure, undistinguished, unknown

antonyms disreputable

2 following the accepted rules of moral conduct ⟨Cheating is not a *respectable* thing to do under any circumstances.⟩ — see HONORABLE 1

3 following the established traditions of refined society and good taste ⟨Tim has the *respectable* manners of someone who was well brought up.⟩ — see PROPER 1

4 of a level of quality that meets one's needs or standards ⟨The artwork that we commissioned from the muralist turned out to be *respectable* but was not quite what we had hoped for.⟩ — see ADEQUATE

5 sufficiently large in size, amount, or number to merit attention ⟨got paid a *respectable* sum for speaking at our graduation⟩ — see CONSIDERABLE 1

respected *adj* having a good reputation especially in a field of knowledge ⟨a *respected* oncologist whose reputation brought her patients from all over the world⟩ — see RESPECTABLE 1

respectful *adj* marked by or showing proper regard for another's higher status ⟨The children were remarkably *respectful* while in the president's office.⟩

synonyms deferential, dutiful, regardful

related words reverent, reverential, venerating, worshipful; fawning, groveling (*or* grovelling), kowtowing, obsequious, subservient, sycophantic, toadying; civil, courteous, gracious, polite

near antonyms abusive, insulting, offensive; belittling, demeaning, depreciative, depreciatory, derogatory, disparaging; contemptuous, impudent, irreverent, scornful; discourteous, insolent, rude, uncivil

antonyms disrespectful, undutiful

respecting *prep* having to do with ⟨*Respecting* your earlier question, I'd like to make an additional comment.⟩ — see ABOUT 1

respective *adj* not the same or shared ⟨It was late when the concert let out, so we all went our *respective* ways.⟩ — see SEPARATE 1

respire *vb* to inhale and exhale air ⟨Though unconscious, the patient is still *respiring*.⟩ — see BREATHE 1

resplendence *n* impressiveness of beauty on a large scale ⟨the fabled *resplendence* of the Taj Mahal⟩ — see MAGNIFICENCE

respond *vb* **1** to act or behave in response (as to a stimulus or influence) ⟨doctors studying how the brain *responds* to pain⟩ — see REACT

2 to speak or write in reaction to a question or to another reaction ⟨The students energetically participated in the discussion, *responding* to the teacher's questions and comments with alacrity and enthusiasm.⟩ — see ANSWER 1

response *n* **1** action or behavior that is done in return to other action or behavior ⟨My *response* to my first boxing defeat was to train even harder.⟩ — see REACTION

2 something spoken or written in reaction especially to a question ⟨the real estate office's unhelpful *response* to my question about what houses in the area are renting for⟩ — see ANSWER 1

responsibility *n* **1** the state of being held as the cause of something that needs to be set right ⟨*Responsibility* for the accident lies with the driver who was speeding.⟩

synonyms blame, fault, liability

related words accountability, answerability

2 something one must do because of prior agreement ⟨I had the *responsibility* of closing up the shop at night.⟩ — see OBLIGATION 1

3 worthiness as the recipient of another's trust or confidence ⟨The newspaper publisher hires kids of *responsibility* to deliver its papers.⟩ — see RELIABILITY

responsible *adj* **1** being the one who must meet an obligation or suffer the consequences for failing to do so ⟨The state laws hold pet owners *responsible* for any damage or injury done by improperly restrained animals.⟩

synonyms accountable, amenable, answerable, liable

related words beholden, indebted, obligated, obliged

near antonyms exempt, immune

antonyms irresponsible, nonaccountable, unaccountable

2 worthy of one's trust ⟨Our regular babysitter is very *responsible*.⟩ — see DEPENDABLE

¹rest *n* **1** freedom from activity or labor ⟨The coming weekend will provide some much needed *rest*.⟩

synonyms ease, leisure, relaxation, repose

related words catnapping, dozing, lazing, napping, resting, sleep, slumber, slumbering, snoozing; quiet, silence, stillness; calm, peace, peacefulness, placidity, respite, restfulness, sereneness, serenity, tranquillity (*or* tranquility)

near antonyms pressure, strain, stress, tenseness, tension

antonyms exertion, labor, toil, work

2 a natural periodic loss of consciousness during which the body restores itself ⟨After a long day, I lay down on the couch for a little *rest* before dinner.⟩ — see SLEEP 1

²rest *n* a remaining group or portion ⟨Can you hand me the *rest* of those papers?⟩ — see REMAINDER 1

rest *vb* **1** to refrain from labor or exertion ⟨a beach resort that caters to fitness enthusiasts and adventurers as well as vacationers who just want to *rest*⟩

synonyms bask, kick back, loll, lounge, relax, repose
related words bum, hang, hang around, idle, loaf, slack (off)
near antonyms drudge, grub, hump, hustle, labor, moil, peg (away), plod, plow, plug, slog, strain, strive, struggle, sweat, toil, travail, work; exercise, work out
2 to be in a state of sleep ⟨The patient is currently *resting*, but as soon as he awakes, I'll tell him you called.⟩ — see SLEEP 1
3 to find a basis ⟨You're *resting* your argument on a faulty premise.⟩ — see BASE

restart *vb* to begin again or return to after an interruption ⟨After being shut down for three years, the power plant will *restart* operations this week.⟩ — see RESUME

restate *vb* to express something (as a text or statement) in different words ⟨Though I couldn't remember the exact words he used, I *restated* his message as accurately as I could.⟩ — see PARAPHRASE

restatement *n* an instance of expressing something in different words ⟨The press release provides no new details—it is merely a *restatement* of information we already have.⟩ — see PARAPHRASE

restating *n* an instance of expressing something in different words ⟨I think the intent of the passage comes through better in the editor's *restating*.⟩ — see PARAPHRASE

restaurant *n* a public establishment where meals are served to paying customers for consumption on the premises ⟨When we get sick of cooking dinner at home, we like to go out to eat at a nice *restaurant*.⟩
synonyms café (*also* cafe), diner, grill
related words cafeteria, lunch counter, luncheonette, lunchroom, snack bar; pizzeria; coffeehouse, coffee shop, teahouse, tearoom; bar, barroom, inn, tavern

restful *adj* free from disturbing noise or uproar ⟨I hope you had a relaxing and *restful* weekend.⟩ — see QUIET 1

restfulness *n* a state of freedom from storm or disturbance ⟨I enjoyed the bucolic *restfulness* of the retreat center.⟩ — see CALM 1

resting *adj* being in a state of suspended consciousness ⟨The *resting* cat was curled up in my favorite chair.⟩ — see ASLEEP 1

resting *n* a natural periodic loss of consciousness during which the body restores itself ⟨The hyena is ready to scavenge again after its brief *resting*.⟩ — see SLEEP 1

restitution *n* payment to another for a loss or injury ⟨sought *restitution* from the other driver's insurance company for lost wages⟩ — see COMPENSATION 1

restive *adj* **1** given to resisting authority or another's control ⟨The *restive* horse threw its head and refused to move when the rider urged it forward.⟩ — see DISOBEDIENT
2 lacking or denying rest ⟨I spent a *restive* night worrying about the next day's exam.⟩ — see RESTLESS 1

restiveness *n* **1** a disturbed or uneasy state ⟨The warnings of drought were the likely source of the *restiveness* that could be felt all over town.⟩ — see UNREST
2 a state of nervousness marked by sudden jerky movements ⟨I sensed that his *restiveness* at breakfast probably had something to do with the big presentation he would be making at the sales conference.⟩ — see JUMPINESS

restless *adj* **1** lacking or denying rest ⟨The worried mother spent a *restless* night, tossing and turning in bed for hours.⟩
synonyms restive, uneasy, unquiet, unrestful
related words agitated, distressed, disturbed, perturbed, troubled, unsettled; aflutter, anxious, dithery, edgy, het up, hung up, jittery, jumpy, nervous, nervy, tense, upset, uptight, worried
near antonyms calm, easy, peaceful, quiet, relaxing, tranquil
antonyms restful

2 marked by or causing agitation or uncomfortable feelings ⟨The figure skater was visibly *restless* as she waited for her scores to be posted.⟩ — see NERVOUS 2

restlessness *n* **1** a disturbed or uneasy state ⟨The *restlessness* of the crowd was apparent as it waited to learn whether the football player was seriously injured.⟩ — see UNREST
2 the state of being bored ⟨She began to pick at the grass near her hammock out of sheer *restlessness*.⟩ — see BOREDOM

restorative *adj* **1** beneficial to the health of body or mind ⟨Jim took a *restorative* vitamin mix to improve his immune system.⟩ — see HEALTHFUL
2 having a renewing effect on the state of the body or mind ⟨I am in need of a long, *restorative* vacation.⟩ — see TONIC 1

restore *vb* **1** to bring back to a former condition or vigor ⟨*restored* an old car⟩ — see RENEW 1
2 to bring, send, or put back to a former or proper place ⟨The maid *restored* the trophy to its proper place at the center of the shelf.⟩ — see RETURN 1

restrain *vb* **1** to keep from exceeding a desirable degree or level (as of expression) ⟨The manufacturer took measures to *restrain* costs.⟩ — see CONTROL 1
2 to take or keep under one's control by authority of law ⟨The suspect was *restrained* and taken to the police station.⟩ — see ARREST 1

restrained *adj* not excessively showy ⟨a *restrained* but elegant black purse⟩ — see QUIET 2

restraint *n* **1** the checking of one's true feelings and impulses when dealing with others ⟨It will take a great deal of *restraint* to keep from spilling the real story.⟩ — see CONSTRAINT 1
2 something that limits one's freedom of action or choice ⟨Civil libertarians contend that the new laws place too many *restraints* on our constitutionally guaranteed rights.⟩ — see RESTRICTION 1
3 the power to control one's actions, impulses, or emotions ⟨He shows very little *restraint* or tact when expressing his opinions about others.⟩ — see WILL 1

restrict *vb* to set bounds or an upper limit for ⟨will *restrict* access to the laboratory⟩ — see LIMIT 1

restricted *adj* having distinct or certain limits ⟨The public is allowed some *restricted* access to the government-owned land.⟩ — see LIMITED 1

restriction *n* **1** something that limits one's freedom of action or choice ⟨The logging company decided to relocate to another state where there would be fewer *restrictions* on its operations.⟩
synonyms check, condition, constraint, curb, fetter, limitation, restraint
related words proviso, qualification, reservation, stipulation, strings; ban, prohibition, proscription
near antonyms freedom, latitude
2 the act or practice of keeping something (as an activity) within certain boundaries ⟨The *restriction* of surfing to the southern end of the beach rankled some surfers.⟩
synonyms confinement, limitation, rein, stint
related words constraint, restraint; containment, isolation, segregation

result *n* **1** a condition or occurrence traceable to a cause ⟨The frequent computer crashes are an unexpected *result* of the new security software we installed.⟩ — see EFFECT 1
2 something attained by mental effort and especially by computation ⟨A nonpartisan panel of experts did the math on the proposed tax cuts and spending programs and the *result* was an $800 billion federal deficit.⟩ — see ANSWER 2

result (in) *vb* to be the cause of (a situation, action, or state of mind) ⟨The mix of icy conditions and rush-hour traffic *resulted in* a number of accidents on the interstate.⟩ — see EFFECT

resultant *adj* coming as a result ⟨She deserves credit for the increase in sales and the *resultant* increase in profit.⟩
synonyms attendant, consequent, consequential, due (to)
related words accompanying, coincident, concomitant
near antonyms causal

resultant *n* a condition or occurrence traceable to a cause ⟨A person's decision to purchase a certain automobile is often the *resultant* of an array of factors, ranging from the actual performance of the vehicle to the buyer's self-image.⟩ — see EFFECT 1

resume *vb* to begin again or return to after an interruption ⟨We *resumed* the game as soon as the rain had passed.⟩
synonyms continue, pick up, renew, reopen, restart
related words resuscitate, revive
near antonyms complete, conclude, consummate, end, finalize, finish; belay, break, can [*slang*], cease, check, cut, desist, discontinue, drop, halt, knock off, leave off, quit, scuttle, shut off, stay, stop, terminate

résumé *or* **resume** *also* **resumé** *n* a short statement of the main points ⟨a brief *résumé* of the news⟩ — see SUMMARY

resurgence *n* the act or an instance of bringing something back to life, public attention, or vigorous activity ⟨The downtown has experienced a *resurgence* since the commercial revitalization project was completed.⟩ — see REVIVAL

resurrect *vb* to bring back to life, practice, or activity ⟨Attempts are being made to *resurrect* the stalled arms negotiations.⟩ — see REVIVE 1

resurrection *n* the act or an instance of bringing something back to life, public attention, or vigorous activity ⟨a general *resurrection* of patriotism after the war began⟩ — see REVIVAL

resuscitate *vb* **1** to bring back to a former condition or vigor ⟨She hopes to *resuscitate* the currently defunct charity organization.⟩ — see RENEW 1
2 to bring back to life, practice, or activity ⟨The withered plants were *resuscitated* by rain.⟩ — see REVIVE 1

resuscitated *adj* made or become fresh in spirits or vigor ⟨After the gloom of winter, I felt *resuscitated* by the unexpected gift of a bouquet of tulips.⟩ — see NEW 4

resuscitation *n* the act or an instance of bringing something back to life, public attention, or vigorous activity ⟨The actor's appearance in a hit movie has led to the *resuscitation* of a career that had been on life support.⟩ — see REVIVAL

retail *vb* to offer for sale to the public ⟨The textile manufacturer doesn't *retail* its fabrics to consumers, offering them only to wholesalers and garment makers.⟩ — see MARKET

retain *vb* **1** to continue to have in one's possession or power ⟨I plan to *retain* the family heirlooms until my own children are mature enough to appreciate them, and then I will lovingly pass them on.⟩ — see KEEP 2
2 to keep, control, or experience as one's own ⟨That author *retains* the right to veto any changes in his books suggested by his publisher's notoriously intrusive editor.⟩ — see HAVE 1
3 to provide with a paying job ⟨Her neighbor *retained* her as a nanny for the summer, thus giving her something to do until school started again.⟩ — see EMPLOY 1

retainer *n* one who works for another for wages or a salary ⟨lifelong civil service *retainers*⟩ — see EMPLOYEE

retake *vb* to get again in one's possession ⟨After some fierce fighting, government forces have *retaken* the capital.⟩ — see RECOVER 1

retaliate *vb* to punish in kind the wrongdoer responsible

for ⟨He *retaliated* his neighbor's malicious destruction of his flower garden by cutting down the man's prize apple tree.⟩ — see AVENGE

retaliation *n* the act or an instance of responding to an injury with an injury ⟨The union threatened a strike in *retaliation* for the company's reduction in benefits.⟩ — see REVENGE

retard *vb* to cause to move or proceed at a less rapid pace ⟨an herbicide to *retard* the growth of weeds⟩ — see SLOW

retardation *n* a usually gradual decrease in the pace or level of activity of something ⟨Scientists discovered that they could achieve the *retardation* of light if they shined it through a variety of substances.⟩ — see SLOWDOWN

retch *vb* to discharge the contents of the stomach through the mouth ⟨The smell of rotten cabbage makes me *retch*.⟩ — see VOMIT

rethink *vb* to consider again especially with the possibility of change or reversal ⟨Since my efforts to solve this problem aren't working, I need to *rethink* my approach.⟩ — see RECONSIDER

reticence *n* a lack of willingness or desire to do or accept something ⟨the publisher's *reticence* to make content available online for free⟩ — see RELUCTANCE

reticent *adj* **1** given to keeping one's activities hidden from public observation or knowledge ⟨The panel decided to investigate the fraud charges against the company, which has always been *reticent* about its internal operations.⟩ — see SECRETIVE
2 tending not to speak frequently (as by habit or inclination) ⟨He is by nature a *reticent* and thoughtful person.⟩ — see SILENT 2
3 slow to begin or proceed with a course of action because of doubts or uncertainty ⟨Understandably, she's *reticent* about quitting her job to start her own business.⟩ — see HESITANT

retinue *n* a body of employees or attendants who accompany and wait on a person ⟨a campaign bus carrying the candidate, her *retinue*, and a gaggle of reporters and bloggers⟩ — see CORTEGE 1

retire *vb* **1** to go to one's bed in order to sleep ⟨I'm exhausted, so I think I'll *retire* for the evening.⟩ — see BED 1
2 to let go from office, service, or employment ⟨As a part of its restructuring, the company has begun to *retire* its older employees.⟩ — see DISMISS 1
3 to move back or away (as from something difficult, dangerous, or disagreeable) ⟨The army was forced to *retire* from the battlefield.⟩ — see RETREAT 1

retire (from) *vb* to give up (a job or office) ⟨At the age of 72, she finally *retired from* the job she had held at the shoe factory for over 50 years.⟩ — see QUIT 1

retired *adj* screened or sequestered from view ⟨We hiked out to a *retired* beach and fished in the surf.⟩ — see SECLUDED

retirement *n* an act of moving away especially from something difficult, dangerous, or disagreeable ⟨Military historians have blamed the defeat on that battalion's *retirement* from the front lines.⟩ — see RETREAT 1

retiring *adj* not comfortable around people ⟨One *retiring* young girl was sitting alone quietly in a corner during the party.⟩ — see SHY 2

retort *n* **1** a quick witty response ⟨She responded to the heckler with a scathing but hilarious *retort* that instantly won over the audience.⟩
synonyms comeback, repartee, riposte
related words squelch; back talk; crack, quip, sally, wisecrack, witticism, zinger; cut, insult, put-down
2 something spoken or written in reaction especially to a question ⟨The salesclerk responded to my query about the price with a brusque *retort*.⟩ — see ANSWER 1

retort *vb* to speak or write in reaction to a question or to another reaction ⟨When told she couldn't have it, she *retorted*, "Fine, I didn't want it anyway!"⟩ — see ANSWER 1

retract *vb* to solemnly or formally reject or go back on (as something formerly adhered to) ⟨The newspaper was forced to *retract* the story, which turned out to be based on fabricated reporting.⟩ — see ABJURE 1

retreat *n* **1** an act of moving away especially from something difficult, dangerous, or disagreeable ⟨We made a strategic *retreat* when we realized that we were outnumbered.⟩
  synonyms recession, retirement, withdrawal
  related words rout; flinch, recoil, revulsion, shrinking; disengagement, disentanglement
  antonyms advance, advancement
  2 something (as a building) that offers cover from the weather or protection from danger ⟨The abandoned cabin was a welcome *retreat* from the storm.⟩ — see SHELTER

retreat *vb* **1** to move back or away (as from something difficult, dangerous, or disagreeable) ⟨We *retreated* to the safety of the cellar at the first sign of the tornado.⟩
  synonyms back away, fall back, recede, retire, withdraw
  related words flee, fly; flinch, recoil, shrink; chicken (out); back down, backpedal, backtrack, climb down; detach, disengage, disentangle, pull away; abandon, depart, evacuate, go, leave, quit, vacate
  phrases give ground, give way, lose ground
  near antonyms beard, brave, brazen, breast, confront, dare, defy, face, outbrave
  antonyms advance
  2 to hasten away from something dangerous or frightening ⟨When the enemy attacked, our troops were forced to *retreat*.⟩ — see RUN 2

retribution *n* the act or an instance of responding to an injury with an injury ⟨seeking *retribution* for the wrong⟩ — see REVENGE

retrieval *n* the act or process of getting something back ⟨a law firm that has been involved in the *retrieval* of artworks that were plundered during the war⟩ — see RECOVERY 1

retrieve *vb* to get again in one's possession ⟨I needed to *retrieve* the book from my friend so I could return it to the library.⟩ — see RECOVER 1

retro *adj* pleasantly reminiscent of an earlier time ⟨*retro* fashions that seek to capture the lost glamour of Hollywood in the 1930s⟩ — see OLD-FASHIONED 1

retrograde *adj* directed, turned, or done toward the back ⟨*Retrograde* pedaling will engage the brakes on that bike.⟩ — see BACKWARD 1

retrograde *vb* to become worse or of less value ⟨the Dark Ages, the period following the fall of the Roman Empire when Western civilization seriously *retrograded*⟩ — see DETERIORATE 1

retrogress *vb* to go back to a previous and usually lower state or level ⟨The quality of research at the university lab has begun to *retrogress* since the massive budget cuts went into effect.⟩ — see REGRESS 1

retrogression *n* the act or an instance of going back to an earlier and lower level especially of intelligence or behavior ⟨the *retrogression* of a once advancing nation⟩ — see REGRESSION

retrospect *n* a usually critical look at a past event ⟨In *retrospect*, we should have saved more money for college.⟩ — see REVIEW 1

retrospection *n* a usually critical look at a past event ⟨The president is confident that future *retrospections* will cast his actions in a more favorable light.⟩ — see REVIEW 1

return *n* **1** something spoken or written in reaction especially to a question ⟨I was moved by my grandfather's lengthy *return* to my casual question about his experiences in the Vietnam War.⟩ — see ANSWER 1
  2 an increase usually measured in money that comes from labor, business, or property ⟨If we buy better equipment, we'll be able to make the product faster, thus getting a better *return* on our investment.⟩ — see INCOME 1
  3 the amount of money left when expenses are subtracted from the total amount received ⟨The *return* on each unit sold has increased since we streamlined the production process.⟩ — see PROFIT 1

return *vb* **1** to bring, send, or put back to a former or proper place ⟨When I'm done reading a book, I always *return* it to the very shelf I got it from.⟩
  synonyms replace, restore
  related words reconvey
  near antonyms remove, take
  2 to produce as revenue ⟨This technology stock is expected to *return* a healthy profit.⟩ — see YIELD 2
  3 to speak or write in reaction to a question or to another reaction ⟨When I asked him to sit down to dinner, he *returned* that he would come in just a minute.⟩ — see ANSWER 1
  4 to go back to a previous and usually lower state or level ⟨The neglected farmland began to *return* to its uncultivated state.⟩ — see REGRESS 1

revamp *vb* **1** to make different in some way ⟨The automaker is *revamping* a number of its cars in an effort to make them more appealing to younger consumers.⟩ — see CHANGE 1
  2 to prepare for publication by correcting, rewriting, or updating ⟨She *revamped* the short story so that it would fit better with the magazine's other offerings.⟩ — see EDIT 1
  3 to put into good shape or working order again ⟨It will be cheaper to replace the old machinery than it would be to *revamp* it.⟩ — see MEND 1

revamping *n* the act, process, or result of making different ⟨Despite the extensive *revamping*, much of the factory's equipment is still obsolete.⟩ — see CHANGE 1

reveal *vb* **1** to make known (as information previously kept secret) ⟨At the end of the book, the detective *reveals* the identity of the mysterious stranger.⟩
  synonyms bare, disclose, discover, divulge, expose, spill, tell, unbosom, uncloak, uncover, unmask, unveil
  related words share; debunk, show up; unclothe, undrape; advertise, announce, blaze, broadcast, declare, placard, post, proclaim, promulgate, publicize, publish, sound; betray, blab, give away, leak; inform, squeal, talk; communicate, impart, relate; disinter, rake up, smoke out, unearth
  phrases bring to light, go public (with), let the cat out of the bag (about), spill the beans (about)
  near antonyms camouflage, disguise, gild, gloss (over), varnish, whitewash; becloud, bedim, befog, cloud, darken, eclipse, obscure, overcast, overshadow, shade
  antonyms cloak, conceal, cover (up), enshroud, hide, mask, shroud, veil
  2 to make known (something abstract) through outward signs ⟨a habitual smile that *reveals* his contentment⟩ — see SHOW 2

revealing *adj* clearly conveying a special meaning (as one's mood) ⟨The pundit's comments were particularly *revealing* and exposed some of his more distasteful prejudices.⟩ — see EXPRESSIVE

revel *n* a time or instance of carefree fun ⟨In Finland, Midsummer Day ushers in a nationwide *revel* as the Finns celebrate the endless hours of sunlight with bonfires and parties.⟩ — see FLING 1

revel (in) *vb* to take pleasure in ⟨winter-weary residents *reveling in* the warm spring weather⟩ — see ENJOY 1

revelation *n* the act or an instance of making known something previously unknown or concealed ⟨the *revelation* of the movie star's secret marriage by the tabloids⟩ ⟨a new biography of the former president that contains several shocking *revelations*⟩
synonyms disclosure, divulgence, exposure
related words bombshell, kick, kicker, surprise (*also* surprize); acknowledgment (*or* acknowledgement), admission, avowal, concession, confession
near antonyms concealment

revelatory *adj* clearly conveying a special meaning (as one's mood) ⟨He ended his tall tale with a *revelatory* wink that indicated that it had all been an elaborate put-on.⟩ — see EXPRESSIVE

reveler *or* **reveller** *n* one who engages in merrymaking especially in honor of a special occasion ⟨wedding *revelers* whooping it up until dawn⟩ — see CELEBRANT

reveling *or* **revelling** *n* joyful or festive activity ⟨The *reveling* was too much for her, so she went to bed early even though the party was still going strong.⟩ — see MERRYMAKING

revelry *n* joyful or festive activity ⟨The lottery winner was exhausted after a long night of *revelry*.⟩ — see MERRYMAKING

revenge *n* the act or an instance of responding to an injury with an injury ⟨Both sides were determined to get *revenge* for perceived wrongs and showed little interest in ending the feud.⟩
synonyms reprisal, requital, retaliation, retribution, vengeance
related words counter, counterattack, counteroffensive; castigation, chastisement, correction; desert(s), discipline, nemesis, penalty, punishment, wrath
near antonyms clemency, grace, leniency, lenity, mercy; forgiveness, pardon, remission

revenge *vb* to punish in kind the wrongdoer responsible for ⟨a man who took matters into his own hands and *revenged* the death of his brother⟩ — see AVENGE

revengeful *adj* likely to seek revenge ⟨The minister urged his congregation to be less *revengeful* and more forgiving in spirit.⟩ — see VINDICTIVE

revenue *n* an increase usually measured in money that comes from labor, business, or property ⟨The struggling business didn't create much *revenue* during its first year of operation.⟩ — see INCOME 1

reverberant *adj* marked by conspicuously full and rich sounds or tones ⟨The professor's *reverberant* voice could be heard all over the large lecture hall.⟩ — see RESONANT

reverberate *vb* to continue or be repeated in a series of reflected sound waves ⟨The sound of thunder *reverberated* from one end of the mountain pass to the other.⟩
synonyms echo, reecho, resonate, resound, sound
related words ring, roll
near antonyms damp, dampen, deaden, dull, quiet

reverberating *adj* marked by conspicuously full and rich sounds or tones ⟨The temple was filled with the *reverberating* sound of the gong.⟩ — see RESONANT

revere *vb* to offer honor or respect to (someone) as a divine power ⟨In some cultures people *revere* their ancestors, even leaving food offerings for them.⟩ — see WORSHIP 1

revered *adj* deserving honor and respect especially by reason of age ⟨a professor who is highly *revered* at the college where she has taught for the last four decades⟩ — see VENERABLE 1

reverence *vb* to offer honor or respect to (someone) as a divine power ⟨devotees coming to *reverence* their god⟩ — see WORSHIP 1

reverend *adj* deserving honor and respect especially by reason of age ⟨Our *reverend* elders should be accorded a special place of honor at the ceremonies.⟩ — see VENERABLE 1

reverie *also* **revery** *n* the state of being lost in thought ⟨I was lost in *reverie* and didn't realize my flight was boarding until it was almost too late.⟩
synonyms daydreaming, study, trance, woolgathering
related words contemplation, meditation; absentmindedness, absorption, preoccupation; chimera, conceit, daydream, delusion, dream, fancy, fantasy (*also* phantasy), figment, hallucination, illusion, phantasm (*also* fantasm), pipe dream

reversal *n* a change in status for the worse usually temporarily ⟨The company's long-term strategy is sound, and they should be able to weather this latest *reversal*.⟩ — see REVERSE 1

reverse *n* 1 a change in status for the worse usually temporarily ⟨The party has suffered some major *reverses* as a result of the corruption scandal.⟩
synonyms knock, lapse, reversal, setback
related words disappointment, frustration, letdown; comedown, decline, descent, down, downfall, fall; recession, regression, retrogression, reversion; relapse; breakdown, collapse, crash, meltdown, ruin
near antonyms status quo
2 something that is as different as possible from something else ⟨How could you think I don't like pizza, when it's just the *reverse*: I love pizza!⟩ — see OPPOSITE
3 a behind part or surface ⟨On the *reverse* of the ticket you'll find the notice that it's nontransferable.⟩ — see REAR 1

reverse *vb* 1 to change (as an opinion) to the contrary ⟨The appeals court *reversed* the district court's decision.⟩
synonyms switch
related words abrogate, annul, overturn, repeal, rescind, revoke; backtrack, countermand, revert
near antonyms maintain, support, uphold
2 to change the position of (an object) so that the opposite side or end is showing ⟨When one side of the cleaning cloth gets dirty, just *reverse* it.⟩ ⟨You can *reverse* the jacket for a whole new look.⟩
synonyms flip, invert, turn over
related words transpose; exchange, interchange, shift, switch; overturn, upset

reversion *n* the act or an instance of going back to an earlier and lower level especially of intelligence or behavior ⟨After the birth of his baby brother, the toddler temporarily underwent a kind of *reversion*, acting like a baby himself.⟩ — see REGRESSION

revert *vb* to go back to a previous and usually lower state or level ⟨After the national emergency had passed, the political parties abandoned their shotgun unity and *reverted* to their partisan squabbling.⟩ — see REGRESS 1

review *n* 1 a usually critical look at a past event ⟨A *review* of yesterday's football game gave us a lot of good ideas on how to improve for the next one.⟩
synonyms reappraisal, reconsideration, reexamination, retrospect, retrospection
related words recap, recapitulation, rehash
near antonyms preview
2 a close look at or over someone or something in order to judge condition ⟨Jess took the car to her mechanic for a complete mechanical *review* before she decided to sell it.⟩ — see INSPECTION
3 a publication that appears at regular intervals ⟨Our son had his poetry published in a literary *review*.⟩ — see JOURNAL
4 an essay evaluating or analyzing something ⟨a harsh movie *review* of an expected summer blockbuster⟩ — see CRITICISM

5 the act, process, or result of making different ⟨The company decided that the 100-year-old office building could use a *review*.⟩ — see CHANGE 1

review *vb* **1** to consider again especially with the possibility of change or reversal ⟨Since we can't follow that plan, we'll have to *review* our options and decide on something else.⟩ — see RECONSIDER
2 to look over closely (as for judging quality or condition) ⟨A consultant was brought in to *review* our security procedures.⟩ — see INSPECT

reviewer *n* a person who makes or expresses a judgment on the quality of offerings in some field of endeavor ⟨Many *reviewers* were unhappy with the movie's cryptic ending.⟩ — see CRITIC 2

revise *n* the act, process, or result of making different ⟨That paper needs one more *revise*, and then I think it's ready to turn in.⟩ — see CHANGE 1

revise *vb* **1** to make different in some way ⟨With the snow, we'll need to *revise* our travel plans.⟩ — see CHANGE 1
2 to prepare for publication by correcting, rewriting, or updating ⟨*Revise* the article and add more up-to-date information so we can reprint it.⟩ — see EDIT 1

revision *n* the act, process, or result of making different ⟨a finicky author who makes countless *revisions* before submitting a work for publication⟩ — see CHANGE 1

revitalization *n* the act or an instance of bringing something back to life, public attention, or vigorous activity ⟨the *revitalization* of the old industrial neighborhood as a new center for art galleries and lofts⟩ — see REVIVAL

revitalize *vb* **1** to bring back to a former condition or vigor ⟨a new cream that claims to *revitalize* sun-damaged skin⟩ — see RENEW 1
2 to bring back to life, practice, or activity ⟨The bowling alley, eager to *revitalize* business, started offering free pizza every Friday night.⟩ — see REVIVE 1

revival *n* the act or an instance of bringing something back to life, public attention, or vigorous activity ⟨There was a *revival* of interest in the author's classic horror stories after a film version of his best-known tale was released.⟩
synonyms reanimation, rebirth, regeneration, rejuvenation, renewal, resurgence, resurrection, resuscitation, revitalization
related words renascence; reinvention; reactivation; rally, recovery, recuperation; restoral, restoration
near antonyms death, expiration, extinction

revive *vb* **1** to bring back to life, practice, or activity ⟨an effort to *revive* the once-common custom of celebrating May 1 as a springtime festival of games and dances⟩
synonyms reanimate, regenerate, rejuvenate, rekindle, renew, resurrect, resuscitate, revitalize
related words kick-start; reactivate, restart; reinvent; refresh, refreshen
near antonyms extinguish, kill, quench, suppress
2 to bring back to a former condition or vigor ⟨Around mid-morning, I usually need to *revive* myself with a cup of strong coffee.⟩ — see RENEW 1
3 to gain consciousness again ⟨The patient eventually *revived* and was able to give us her name and address.⟩ — see COME TO

revived *adj* made or become fresh in spirits or vigor ⟨The farmers felt *revived* as they headed back to the fields after a hearty lunch.⟩ — see NEW 4

reviving *adj* having a renewing effect on the state of the body or mind ⟨The Carters took a *reviving* vacation in the Caribbean.⟩ — see TONIC 1

revocation *n* the act of putting an end to something planned or previously agreed to ⟨He threatened the *revocation* of his son's driving privileges.⟩ — see CANCELLATION

revoke *vb* to put an end to (something planned or previ-

ously agreed to) ⟨The judge *revoked* the jail sentence when the defendant promised to do community service instead.⟩ — see CANCEL 1

revolt *n* open fighting against authority (as one's own government) ⟨Soon the *revolt* had spread to every corner of the country.⟩ — see REBELLION 1

revolt *vb* **1** to cause to feel disgust ⟨The smell of fried foods *revolts* me first thing in the morning.⟩ — see DISGUST
2 to rise up against established authority ⟨The students practically *revolted* when the school cancelled the championship football game.⟩ — see REBEL

revolted *adj* filled with disgust ⟨We were *revolted* when we learned about the wasteful disposal of the leftover banquet food.⟩ — see SICK 2

revolter *n* a person who rises up against authority ⟨Spartacus, who led a revolt in ancient Rome, has served as an inspiration for a number of other *revolters* over the centuries.⟩ — see REBEL

revolting *adj* causing intense displeasure, disgust, or resentment ⟨the *revolting* sight of animals being slaughtered for no good reason⟩ — see OFFENSIVE 1

revolution *n* **1** a rapid turning about on an axis or central point ⟨revved the engine to 3000 *revolutions* per minute⟩ — see SPIN 1
2 open fighting against authority (as one's own government) ⟨The *revolution* by which the American colonies gained their independence from Great Britain necessitated going up against the world's most powerful army.⟩ — see REBELLION 1

revolutionary *adj* **1** being very far from the center of public opinion ⟨a candidate with a lot of *revolutionary* ideas that she believes will help women and children all over the country⟩ — see EXTREME 2
2 taking part in a rebellion ⟨*revolutionary* forces that were soundly defeated before reaching the capital⟩ — see REBELLIOUS 1

revolutionary *n* **1** a person who favors rapid and sweeping changes especially in laws and methods of government ⟨After the collapse of the Russian monarchy, the moderate socialists briefly governed until being overthrown by the Bolshevik *revolutionaries*.⟩ — see RADICAL
2 a person who rises up against authority ⟨At first the government was not worried about this small band of unarmed *revolutionaries*.⟩ — see REBEL

revolutionist *adj* being very far from the center of public opinion ⟨His *revolutionist* ideas won't get him elected.⟩ — see EXTREME 2

revolutionist *n* **1** a person who favors rapid and sweeping changes especially in laws and methods of government ⟨After a troubled period, the people were ready for a *revolutionist* who promised to bring sweeping change to the nation.⟩ — see RADICAL
2 a person who rises up against authority ⟨Historically, *revolutionists* have generally been young men willing to risk everything, even their lives, in the pursuit of their cause.⟩ — see REBEL

revolve *vb* **1** to move (something) in a curved or circular path on or as if on an axis ⟨The salesclerk *revolved* the glass display case so I could see the watchbands on the reverse side.⟩ — see TURN 1
2 to move in circles around an axis or center ⟨The sidereal day measures the time it takes the Earth to *revolve* completely about its axis with respect to the fixed stars.⟩ — see SPIN 1
3 to give serious and careful thought to ⟨For the next several hours he kept *revolving* the cryptic message in his mind, trying to make sense of it.⟩ — see PONDER

revulsion *n* a dislike so strong as to cause stomach upset or queasiness ⟨The publication of the graphic photos prompted expressions of outrage and *revulsion.*⟩ — see DISGUST

reward *n* something offered or given in return for a service performed ⟨There was a *reward* of $50 for the return of the missing cat.⟩
synonyms bounty, price
related words bonus, lagniappe, premium; bonanza, jackpot; award, decoration, distinction, honor, prize; gratuity, tip; desert(s), wages

reward *vb* to give something as a token of gratitude or admiration for a service or achievement ⟨The firefighters were *rewarded* by the city for their heroic actions.⟩
synonyms award
related words cite, decorate, honor, remember; compensate, pay, recompense, requite; reimburse, repay; acclaim, applaud, commend, compliment, hail, praise, salute

rewarding *adj* making one feel good inside ⟨Tom pursued a *rewarding* career providing medical care to poor children in rural areas.⟩ — see HEARTWARMING

reweigh *vb* to consider again especially with the possibility of change or reversal ⟨The new study is leading doctors and nutritionists to *reweigh* the benefits of some dietary supplements.⟩ — see RECONSIDER

reword *vb* to express something (as a text or statement) in different words ⟨I'll *reword* the question for you so you can better understand it.⟩ — see PARAPHRASE

rewording *n* an instance of expressing something in different words ⟨I like your *rewording* of that paragraph better than the original.⟩ — see PARAPHRASE

rework *vb* **1** to make different in some way ⟨The sculptor *reworked* the clay into another shape.⟩ — see CHANGE 1
2 to prepare for publication by correcting, rewriting, or updating ⟨The magazine will publish your poem if you *rework* it so that it's a little shorter.⟩ — see EDIT 1

reworking *n* the act, process, or result of making different ⟨The contract will need some *reworking* before it is acceptable to both parties.⟩ — see CHANGE 1

rhapsodic *also* **rhapsodical** *adj* experiencing or marked by overwhelming usually pleasurable emotion ⟨The jingle used in the commercial is a humorously *rhapsodic* celebration of fast food.⟩ — see ECSTATIC

rhapsodically *adv* in an enthusiastic manner ⟨*rhapsodically* described the glittering party at the billionaire's mansion⟩ — see SKY-HIGH

rhapsodize *vb* to make an exaggerated display of affection or enthusiasm ⟨They *rhapsodized* about the food so as not to hurt their host's feelings.⟩ — see GUSH 2

rhapsody *n* a state of overwhelming usually pleasurable emotion ⟨Listening to Mozart always left him in a *rhapsody* that lingered for the remainder of the evening.⟩ — see ECSTASY

rhetoric *n* **1** language that is impressive-sounding but not meaningful or sincere ⟨The mayor's promise was just *rhetoric*, since there was no money in the city budget to fulfill it.⟩
synonyms bombast, gas, grandiloquence, hot air, oratory, verbiage, wind
related words claptrap, drivel, gibberish, hogwash, humbug, jabberwocky, jazz, moonshine, nonsense; affectedness, floweriness, grandiosity, loftiness, pretension, pretentiousness; verboseness, verbosity, windiness, wordiness
2 the art or power of speaking or writing in a forceful and convincing way ⟨Great leaders have often been masters of *rhetoric*, which they have used for both good and ill.⟩ — see ELOQUENCE

rhetorical *also* **rhetoric** *adj* **1** marked by the use of impressive-sounding but mostly meaningless words and phrases ⟨You can skip over the *rhetorical* passages and still get the gist of the essay.⟩

synonyms bombastic, gaseous, grandiloquent, oratorical, windy
related words elevated, florid, flowery, grandiose, highfalutin (*also* hifalutin), high-flown, high-sounding, lofty, ornate, pompous, pretentious, stilted; overdone, verbose, wordy
near antonyms eloquent, well-spoken; bald, direct, matter-of-fact, plain, plainspoken, simple, stark, straightforward, unadorned, unaffected, unpretentious
antonyms unrhetorical
2 full of fine words and fancy expressions ⟨The new governor delivered a long *rhetorical* speech about our state's bright future but laid out no specific programs for ensuring it.⟩ — see FLOWERY 1
3 of or relating to words or language ⟨a poet who employed a range of *rhetorical* devices⟩ — see VERBAL 1

rhythm *n* the recurrent pattern formed by a series of sounds having a regular rise and fall in intensity ⟨the steady *rhythm* of the rain falling on the roof⟩
synonyms beat, cadence, measure, meter
related words accent, accentuation, emphasis, stress; backbeat; drum, throb; lilt, movement, sway, swing; hexameter, pentameter, tetrameter, trimeter

rhythmic *or* **rhythmical** *adj* marked by or occurring with a noticeable regularity in the rise and fall of sound ⟨lulled to sleep by the *rhythmic* sound of her mother's voice reading the beloved childhood classic⟩
synonyms cadenced, measured, metrical (*or* metric)
related words even, regular, steady, uniform; lilting, musical, swaying
antonyms arrhythmic, nonmetrical, unmeasured, unrhythmic

riata *n* a rope or long leather thong with a noose used especially for catching livestock ⟨The cowboy neatly tossed a *riata* over the head of the escaping cow.⟩ — see LASSO

rib *n* something said or done to cause laughter ⟨Joe began to lose his sense of humor after being the butt of his friends' *ribs* once too often.⟩ — see JOKE 1

rib *vb* to make fun of in a good-natured way ⟨*ribbed* him a bit about fumbling such an easy play⟩ — see TEASE 1

ribald *adj* **1** depicting or referring to sexual matters in a way that is unacceptable in polite society ⟨some *ribald* scenes in the movie⟩ — see OBSCENE 1
2 hinting at or intended to call to mind matters regarded as indecent ⟨a *ribald* tale rife with double entendres and innuendo⟩ — see SUGGESTIVE 1

ribaldry *n* the quality or state of being obscene ⟨There's a *ribaldry* in the works of Chaucer that generations of students of English literature have enjoyed.⟩ — see OBSCENITY

ribbing *adj* marked by or expressive of mild or good-natured teasing ⟨The lightly *ribbing* tone tipped me off that this wasn't a serious reprimand.⟩ — see QUIZZICAL

ribbon *n* a long narrow piece of material ⟨tied a silk *ribbon* in her hair⟩ — see STRIP 1

rich *adj* **1** having goods, property, or money in abundance ⟨You would have to be quite *rich* to be able to afford a home in that neighborhood.⟩
synonyms affluent, flush, loaded, moneyed (*also* monied), opulent, wealthy, well-fixed, well-heeled, well-off, well-to-do
related words better-off, comfortable, propertied, prosperous, substantial, successful; flourishing, prospering, thriving; advantaged, blessed (*also* blest), privileged
phrases in the chips
near antonyms unaffluent; deprived, disadvantaged, hand-to-mouth, underprivileged; bankrupt, bankrupted, beggared, broke, indebted, insolvent; depressed, pinched, reduced, straitened; low, short

antonyms destitute, impecunious, impoverished, indigent, needy, penniless, penurious, poor, poverty-stricken
2 containing much seasoning, fat, or sugar ⟨Stay away from *rich* foods before you sleep.⟩
synonyms heavy
related words buttery, fat, fatty, greasy; caloric, calorific, fattening; oversweet; filling, overfilling, satiating, sating; spicy, sugary, sweet; creamy, sauced
near antonyms natural, plain, simple; unseasoned; diet, nonfattening, slimming; nonfat
antonyms light, lite
3 having an abundance of some characteristic quality (as flavor) ⟨a *rich* tomato soup⟩ — see FULL-BODIED
4 producing abundantly ⟨*rich* farmland⟩ — see FERTILE
riches *pl n* the total of one's money and property ⟨industrialists who had amassed *riches* of a magnitude that few had dreamed possible⟩ — see WEALTH 1
richly *adv* in a luxurious manner ⟨a *richly* decorated penthouse that showed off the owner's art collection to its best advantage⟩ — see HIGH
richness *n* the amusing quality or element in something ⟨The *richness* of the irony—I had just contributed to the political campaign of a multimillionaire—was too much for me to ignore.⟩ — see HUMOR 1
ricochet *vb* to strike and fly off at an angle ⟨The ball *ricocheted* off the fielder's glove and went over the fence for a home run.⟩ — see GLANCE 1
rid *vb* to set (a person or thing) free of something that encumbers ⟨worked two jobs to *rid* himself of debt⟩
synonyms clear, disburden, disencumber, free, relieve, unburden
related words discharge, emancipate, enfranchise, liberate, loose, loosen, manumit, release, spring, unbind, uncage, unchain, unfetter; bail (out), deliver, redeem, rescue; disengage, disentangle, extricate
near antonyms bog (down), fetter, hamper, restrain, shackle, subject, weight (down)
antonyms burden, encumber, saddle
riddance *n* the getting rid of whatever is unwanted or useless ⟨The *riddance* of all the fleas from the house was a relief to everyone concerned.⟩ — see DISPOSAL 1
riddle *n* something hard to understand or explain ⟨His motives for starting an argument with the coach were a complete *riddle*.⟩ — see MYSTERY
riddle *vb* **1** to make a hole or series of holes in ⟨The awnings were *riddled* by the hailstorm.⟩ — see PERFORATE
2 to spread throughout ⟨The book is *riddled* with mistakes.⟩ — see PERMEATE
ride *n* a means of getting to a destination in a vehicle driven by another ⟨an organization that provides *rides* for senior citizens⟩
synonyms lift, transportation
related words drive, spin, turn; joyride; conveyance, passage, transport
ride *vb* **1** to attack repeatedly with mean put-downs or insults ⟨That supervisor is always *riding* everyone for every little thing.⟩ — see TEASE 2
2 to make fun of in a good-natured way ⟨His wife couldn't resist *riding* him for forgetting his own birthday.⟩ — see TEASE 1
3 to rest or move along the surface of a liquid or in the air ⟨a condor *riding* high in the sky⟩ — see FLOAT 1
4 to be determined by, based on, or subject (to) ⟨Our plan for the party *rides* on whether he can come.⟩ — see DEPEND 1
ride (out) *vb* to come safely through ⟨Just as we always have in the past, we'll *ride out* this latest crisis.⟩ — see SURVIVE 1
ridge *n* the line formed when two sloping surfaces come

together along their topmost edge ⟨pigeons roosting along the *ridge* of the roof⟩
synonyms crest
related words divide; backbone, ridgepole, spine; eminence, peak, prominence, promontory, rise
ridicule *n* the making of unkind jokes as a way of showing one's scorn for someone or something ⟨Though initially an object of *ridicule*, the theory turned out to be correct.⟩
synonyms derision, mockery, sport
related words contempt, disdain, scorn; belittlement, deprecation, disparagement; catcall, insult, put-down; laughter, snickering; burlesque, caricature, mimicry, satire
near antonyms applause, approval, commendation, praise
ridicule *vb* to make (someone or something) the object of unkind laughter ⟨The term "big bang theory" was originally coined to *ridicule* the belief that the universe was created by a giant explosion.⟩
synonyms deride, gibe (*or* jibe), jeer, laugh (at), mock, scout, skewer
related words scoff (at), scorn, sneer (at); bad-mouth, belittle, decry, disparage, pooh-pooh (*also* pooh), put down; jive, josh, kid, quiz, razz, rib, ride, tease, tweak, twit; bait, bug, catcall, harry, hassle, heckle, needle, pester, target, taunt, torment; ape, burlesque, caricature, imitate, lampoon, mimic, parody, parrot, pillory, satirize, take off (on), travesty
phrases make fun of, make sport of, poke fun at, rag on
near antonyms applaud, approve, commend, endorse (*also* indorse), sanction
ridiculer *n* a person who causes repeated emotional pain, distress, or annoyance to another ⟨Any person of great vision has his or her *ridiculers*, who inevitably fail to appreciate genius and originality.⟩ — see TORMENTOR
ridiculous *adj* **1** so foolish or pointless as to be worthy of scornful laughter ⟨a movie thriller with such a *ridiculous* plot that it gets only guffaws from audiences⟩
synonyms absurd, comical, derisive, derisory, farcical, laughable, ludicrous, pathetic, preposterous, risible, silly
related words asinine, brainless, dumb, fatuous, foolish, half-baked, half-witted, harebrained, idiotic (*also* idiotical), imbecile (*or* imbecilic), inane, jerky, moronic, nonsensical, simpleminded, stupid, unwise, weak-minded, witless; balmy, cockeyed, daffy, daft, dotty, kooky (*also* kookie), screwball, senseless, wacky (*also* whacky); fantastic (*also* fantastical), far-fetched, inconceivable, incredible, unbelievable, unreal, unrealistic, unreasonable; illogical, irrational
phrases for the birds
near antonyms earnest, serious, solemn; believable, conceivable, credible, logical, rational, realistic, reasonable, sensible
2 causing or intended to cause laughter ⟨a movie comedian who has perfected the *ridiculous* pratfall⟩ — see FUNNY 1
rife *adj* possessing or covered with great numbers or amounts of something specified ⟨The school was *rife* with rumors.⟩
synonyms abounding, abundant, awash, flush, fraught, lousy, replete, swarming, teeming, thick, thronging
related words brimming, bulging, bursting, chock-full (*or* chockful), crammed, crowded, fat, filled, full, jammed, jam-packed, loaded, packed, saturated, stuffed; clogged, congested, overcrowded, overfilled, overflowing, overfull, overladen, overloaded, overstuffed, surfeited; alive, animated, astir, bustling, busy, buzzing, humming, lively
near antonyms bare, barren, blank, devoid, empty, stark, vacant, void; depleted, drained, exhausted; deficient, incomplete, insufficient, short

riffraff *n* **1** discarded or useless material ⟨The sight of piles and piles of *riffraff* at the town dump was a sobering reminder that we are indeed a society of consumers.⟩ — see GARBAGE

2 people looked down upon as ignorant and of the lowest class ⟨local ordinances that are intended to keep the *riffraff* out of the town⟩ — see RABBLE

rifle *vb* to look through (as a place) carefully or thoroughly in an effort to find or discover something ⟨Macy *rifled* the desk drawer in search of the insurance policy.⟩ — see SEARCH 1

rift *n* **1** an irregular usually narrow break in a surface created by pressure ⟨A small *rift* opened in the earth's crust.⟩ — see CRACK 1

2 an open space in a barrier (as a wall or hedge) ⟨It was possible to peek through the *rift* in the fence and see the ball game.⟩ — see GAP 1

rig *n* **1** a horse-drawn wheeled vehicle for carrying passengers ⟨Romantic couples enjoy being driven in the old-fashioned *rig* through the park.⟩ — see CARRIAGE 1

2 covering for the human body ⟨Most of the celebrants of the town's bicentennial will be in festive *rig*.⟩ — see CLOTHING

rig *vb* to provide (someone) with what is needed for a task or activity ⟨We carefully *rigged* each diver with the required equipment before starting out.⟩ — see FURNISH 1

rig (out) *vb* to outfit with clothes and especially fine or special clothes ⟨Everyone was *rigged out* for the prom.⟩ — see CLOTHE 1

right *adj* **1** following an original exactly ⟨a modern replica of an 18th-century British warship that is *right* in all of its details⟩ — see FAITHFUL 2

2 being exactly as appears or as claimed ⟨Despite the name, New York's East River is a strait and not a *right* river.⟩ — see AUTHENTIC 1

3 being in agreement with the truth or a fact or a standard ⟨The obvious answer is not always the *right* one.⟩ — see CORRECT 1

4 being what is called for by accepted standards of right and wrong ⟨trying to do what is *right*⟩ — see JUST 1

5 conforming to a high standard of morality or virtue ⟨a *right* man, honest and true⟩ — see GOOD 2

6 free from irregularities or digressions in course ⟨the first city in America laid out with broad, *right* avenues⟩ — see STRAIGHT 1

7 having full use of one's mind and control over one's actions ⟨He hasn't been *right* since he suffered serious brain injury in the accident.⟩ — see SANE

8 meeting the requirements of a purpose or situation ⟨the *right* tool for the job⟩ — see FIT 1

right *adv* **1** as stated or indicated without the slightest difference ⟨Stay *right* where you are!⟩ — see EXACTLY 1

2 in a direct line or course ⟨Walk *right* over here now!⟩ — see DIRECTLY 1

3 to a great degree ⟨A *right* beautiful day we're having!⟩ — see VERY 1

4 without delay ⟨We'll leave *right* after dinner.⟩ — see IMMEDIATELY

5 in a manner suitable for the occasion or purpose ⟨You're not dressed *right* for an interview with a big-time law firm.⟩ — see PROPERLY

right *n* **1** something to which one has a just claim ⟨Everyone has the *right* to life, liberty, and the pursuit of happiness.⟩

synonyms birthright, prerogative

related words call, due, perquisite, pretense (*or* pretence), pretension, privilege

2 an entitlement to something ⟨What *right* do you have to tell us what to do?⟩ — see CLAIM 1

3 the practice of giving to others what is their due or an instance of this ⟨activists who have fought all their lives for *right*⟩ — see JUSTICE 1

right away *adv* without delay ⟨You need to have this fixed *right away*.⟩ — see IMMEDIATELY

righteous *adj* **1** conforming to a high standard of morality or virtue ⟨A *righteous* man can be trusted to act honorably regardless of the circumstances.⟩ — see GOOD 2

2 following the accepted rules of moral conduct ⟨*Righteous* behavior is its own reward.⟩ — see HONORABLE 1

righteously *adv* with purity of thought and deed ⟨If you have acted *righteously*, you have nothing to fear.⟩ — see PURELY 1

righteousness *n* **1** conduct that conforms to an accepted standard of right and wrong ⟨The laws do not always dictate *righteousness*, for what is legal is not always moral.⟩ — see MORALITY 1

2 faithfulness to high moral standards ⟨A life lived with *righteousness* guarantees that you will always respect yourself.⟩ — see HONOR 1

rightful *adj* being what is called for by accepted standards of right and wrong ⟨fighting for a *rightful* cause⟩ — see JUST 1

rightist *n* a person whose political beliefs are centered on tradition and keeping things the way they are ⟨*Rightists* opposed the new social programs.⟩ — see CONSERVATIVE

rightly *adv* in a manner suitable for the occasion or purpose ⟨Marveling at the awesome sight, we had to agree that the Grand Canyon was *rightly* named.⟩ — see PROPERLY

right–minded *adj* conforming to a high standard of morality or virtue ⟨a group of *right-minded* people working for social change⟩ — see GOOD 2

rightness *n* **1** conduct that conforms to an accepted standard of right and wrong ⟨She seems to confuse *rightness* with self-righteousness.⟩ — see MORALITY 1

2 the quality or state of being especially suitable or fitting ⟨The irrefutable *rightness* of the criticism didn't make it any more pleasant to hear.⟩ — see APPROPRIATENESS

right now *adv* **1** at the present time ⟨*Right now* we are in the middle of a major home renovation.⟩ — see NOW 1

2 without delay ⟨Answer my question *right now*!⟩ — see IMMEDIATELY

right–of–way *n* the right to one's attention before other things considered less important ⟨The bill for emergency aid was immediately granted *right-of-way*.⟩ — see PRIORITY

rigid *adj* **1** not allowing for any exceptions or loosening of standards ⟨*rigid* enforcement of drug laws⟩

synonyms exacting, inflexible, rigorous, strict, stringent, uncompromising

related words close, conscientious, exact, fussy, meticulous, painstaking, punctilious, scrupulous, undeviating; adamant, adamantine, determined, dogged, firm, relentless, resolved, single-minded, steadfast, stubborn, tenacious, unbending, unflinching; immovable, implacable, unappeasable, unrelenting, unsparing, unyielding; austere, demanding, flinty, grim, hard, hardened, harsh, severe, stern, tough

near antonyms acquiescent, compliant, compromising, pliable, pliant, relenting, yielding; easy, easygoing, gentle, indulgent, kindly, lenient, merciful, mild, pampering, soft, spoiling, tolerant; neglectful, negligent, remiss, slipshod, sloppy, slovenly, unfussy

antonyms flexible, lax, loose, relaxed, slack

2 given to exacting standards of discipline and self-restraint ⟨a *rigid* man who cannot seem to relax⟩ — see SEVERE 1

3 having a consistency that does not easily yield to pressure ⟨*rigid* steel bars that should be able to hold the weight⟩ — see FIRM 2

4 incapable of or highly resistant to bending ⟨the mineral that gives bone its *rigid* structure⟩ — see STIFF 1

5 stretched with little or no give ⟨Make sure that the clothesline is *rigid* so that the longer garments don't drag on the ground.⟩ — see TAUT

rigidity *n* the quality or state of being demanding or unyielding (as in discipline or criticism) ⟨Sometimes the *rigidity* of the headmaster's discipline was deemed excessive by even much of the faculty.⟩ — see SEVERITY

rigidly *adv* without any relaxation of standards or precision ⟨The judge stuck *rigidly* to the letter of the law.⟩ — see STRICTLY

rigidness *n* the quality or state of being demanding or unyielding (as in discipline or criticism) ⟨No one even asked anymore, as their father's *rigidness* regarding bedtime was legendary.⟩ — see SEVERITY

rigmarole *also* **rigamarole** *n* language marked by abstractions, jargon, euphemisms, and circumlocutions ⟨The security guard gave me some kind of *rigmarole* about passes and authorizations.⟩ — see GIBBERISH 2

rigor *n* **1** something that is a cause for suffering or special effort especially in the attainment of a goal ⟨hard-bitten folk who survived many *rigors* on the way to the promised land⟩ — see DIFFICULTY 1

2 the quality or state of being demanding or unyielding (as in discipline or criticism) ⟨After being coddled by his former coach, the swimmer was shocked at the *rigor* of the new training program.⟩ — see SEVERITY

3 the quality or state of being very accurate ⟨They conducted the experiments with scientific *rigor*.⟩ — see PRECISION

rigorous *adj* **1** given to exacting standards of discipline and self-restraint ⟨a *rigorous* football coach who pushes his players to their physical and mental limits⟩ — see SEVERE 1

2 meeting the highest standard of accuracy ⟨a *rigorous* analysis of the data⟩ — see PRECISE 1

3 not allowing for any exceptions or loosening of standards ⟨a *rigorous* diet and exercise regimen⟩ — see RIGID 1

4 requiring considerable physical or mental effort ⟨She studied for umpteen months for the *rigorous* exam.⟩ — see HARD 2

rigorously *adv* without any relaxation of standards or precision ⟨a *rigorously* accurate accounting of expenses⟩ — see STRICTLY

rigorousness *n* **1** the quality or state of being demanding or unyielding (as in discipline or criticism) ⟨The *rigorousness* of the training paid off when the dance students performed brilliantly at the recital.⟩ — see SEVERITY

2 the quality or state of being very accurate ⟨These days the *rigorousness* of electronic timing is necessary to measure the minute differences in the performances of Olympic athletes.⟩ — see PRECISION

rile *vb* **1** to disturb the peace of mind of (someone) especially by repeated disagreeable acts ⟨One sure way to *rile* me is to keep yelling for me.⟩ — see IRRITATE 1

2 to make angry ⟨He isn't easily *riled*, but once he is, he stays that way for days.⟩ — see ANGER

riled *adj* feeling or showing anger ⟨The woman was obviously *riled*, as she was raising her voice.⟩ — see ANGRY

riling *adj* causing annoyance ⟨a *riling* habit that really gets on my nerves⟩ — see ANNOYING

rill *n* a natural body of running water smaller than a river ⟨There are a few tiny fish in the *rill*.⟩ — see CREEK 1

rim *n* the line or relatively narrow space that marks the outer limit of something ⟨the *rim* of a glass⟩ — see BORDER 1

rim *vb* to serve as a border for ⟨Long lashes *rimmed* his eyes.⟩ — see BORDER

rime *n* a covering of tiny ice crystals on a cold surface ⟨*rime* on the bedroom window after a bitterly cold night⟩ — see FROST 1

rime *vb* to cover with a hardened layer ⟨frost *riming* the doorknob⟩ — see ENCRUST

¹ring *n* **1** a group involved in secret or criminal activities ⟨a *ring* of counterfeiters passing phony $20 bills⟩

synonyms cabal, conspiracy, crew, gang, Mafia, mob, syndicate

related words bunch, circle, clan, clique, coterie, crowd, galère, lot, network, pack, set; junta, oligarchy

2 a circular strip ⟨A metal *ring* encircled the barrel.⟩

synonyms band, circle, eye, hoop, loop, round

related words belt, cincture, collar, girdle; wreath; annulet, becket, coil, curl, furl, hank, spiral, spire, twirl, whorl

3 a group of people sharing a common interest and relating together socially ⟨a gaming *ring* that meets once a week to play⟩ — see GANG 2

4 something with a perfectly round circumference ⟨The coffee cup left a *ring* on the table.⟩ — see CIRCLE 1

²ring *n* a communication by telephone ⟨Give me a *ring* when you're ready to go.⟩ — see CALL 3

¹ring *vb* **1** to form a circle around ⟨tall cypress trees *ringing* the park⟩ — see SURROUND

2 to travel completely around ⟨The line of season ticket buyers *ringed* the block.⟩ — see ENCIRCLE 1

²ring *vb* to make the clear sound heard when metal vibrates ⟨I didn't hear the doorbell *ring*.⟩

synonyms chime, knell, peal, toll

related words chink, clang, clank, clash, clink, ding, ding-dong, gong, jingle, ping, plink, plunk (*or* plonk), tingle, tinkle; echo, resonate, resound, reverberate

ringer *n* **1** one who makes false claims of identity or expertise ⟨One of the players on the opposing team was a *ringer*.⟩ — see IMPOSTOR

2 something or someone that strongly resembles another ⟨He's a dead *ringer* for his grandfather.⟩ — see IMAGE 1

ringlet *n* a length of hair that forms a loop or series of loops ⟨a little child with a head of perfect *ringlets*⟩ — see CURL

rinse *vb* to pour liquid over or through in order to cleanse ⟨*Rinse* that shirt immediately, or the paint will set.⟩ — see FLUSH 1

riot *n* someone or something that is very funny ⟨She's such a *riot* at parties.⟩ — see SCREAM

riotous *adj* **1** causing or intended to cause laughter ⟨His *riotous* mugging always has everyone in hysterics.⟩ — see FUNNY 1

2 pouring forth in great amounts ⟨A painting by that artist is usually a *riotous* display of color.⟩ — see PROFUSE

rip *n* a long deep cut ⟨The hoe left *rips* in the lawn.⟩ — see GASH

rip *vb* **1** to cause (something) to separate into jagged pieces by violently pulling at it ⟨The dog *ripped* the sleeve of my shirt by grabbing it with his teeth.⟩ — see TEAR 1

2 to penetrate with a sharp edge (as a knife) ⟨You can see where someone *ripped* the painting with a penknife.⟩ — see CUT 1

3 to proceed or move quickly ⟨The car went *ripping* down the road.⟩ — see HURRY 2

4 to separate or remove by forceful pulling ⟨*Rip* a sheet off the pad of paper.⟩ — see TEAR 2

ripe *adj* **1** fully grown or developed ⟨a *ripe* tomato⟩ — see MATURE 1

2 having an unpleasant smell ⟨The clothes of the field hands were sweaty and *ripe* after a hard day's work.⟩ — see MALODOROUS

ripen *vb* to become mature ⟨pears *ripening* on the tree⟩ — see MATURE

ripened *adj* fully grown or developed ⟨a fully *ripened* musical talent⟩ — see MATURE 1

ripening *n* the process of becoming mature ⟨The *ripening* of a pumpkin can take a whole season.⟩ — see MATURATION

rip–off *n* an instance of theft ⟨a daring burglary of the art museum that resulted in one of the greatest *rip-offs* in history⟩ — see THEFT 2

rip off *vb* **1** to remove valuables from (a place) unlawfully ⟨an employee who was fired for *ripping off* the office⟩ — see ROB

2 to take (something) without right and with an intent to keep ⟨The thief *ripped off* some jewelry as soon as no one was looking.⟩ — see STEAL 1

3 to rob by the use of trickery or threats ⟨An investigation revealed that a whole slew of suppliers had been *ripping off* the defense department.⟩ — see FLEECE

riposte *n* a quick witty response ⟨He's known for having a brilliant *riposte* to nearly any insult.⟩ — see RETORT 1

riposte *vb* to speak or write in reaction to a question or to another reaction ⟨At cocktail parties she could *riposte* with lightning speed to even the most unexpected quip.⟩ — see ANSWER 1

ripple *vb* to flow in a broken irregular stream ⟨water *rippling* gently over the tiers of the fountain⟩ — see GURGLE

rip–roaring *adj* causing great emotional or mental stimulation ⟨a *rip-roaring* tale of the Old West⟩ — see EXCITING 1

rise *n* **1** a raising or a state of being raised to a higher rank or position ⟨a rapid *rise* to the position of president of the company⟩ — see ADVANCEMENT 1

2 an area of high ground ⟨If we can get to the top of that *rise*, we'll be able to see for miles.⟩ — see HEIGHT 4

3 an upward slope ⟨The *rise* of the hill was relatively gentle.⟩ — see ASCENT 2

4 something added (as by growth) ⟨an unexpected *rise* in prices⟩ — see INCREASE 1

5 the act or an instance of rising or climbing up ⟨Unfortunately, the descent of the balloon was just as swift as its *rise*.⟩ — see ASCENT 1

rise *vb* **1** to become greater in extent, volume, amount, or number ⟨The snow accumulation is *rising* at an alarming rate.⟩ — see INCREASE 2

2 to leave one's bed ⟨I generally *rise* around six and leave for work by seven.⟩ — see ARISE 1

3 to move or extend upward ⟨mountains majestically *rising* towards the sky⟩ — see ASCEND

risible *adj* **1** causing or intended to cause laughter ⟨a *risible* comment that made the whole class laugh⟩ — see FUNNY 1
2 so foolish or pointless as to be worthy of scornful laughter ⟨The idea that people are meant to have wings is *risible*.⟩ — see RIDICULOUS 1

rising *n* **1** open fighting against authority (as one's own government) ⟨A great *rising* of the people was all it took to bring down a regime that imagined that it would endure for a thousand years.⟩ — see REBELLION 1

2 the act or an instance of rising or climbing up ⟨the *rising* of the sun⟩ — see ASCENT 1

risk *n* **1** something that may cause injury or harm ⟨Mountain climbing is a *risk*, but the thrill and challenge are worth it.⟩ — see DANGER 2

2 the state of not being protected from injury, harm, or evil ⟨The first responders put their lives at *risk*.⟩ — see DANGER 1

risk *vb* **1** to take a chance on ⟨Colette didn't want to *risk* running out of food for her party, so she bought twice what she thought she would actually need.⟩
synonyms adventure, chance, gamble (on), hazard, tempt, venture
related words beard, brave, brazen, breast, challenge, confront, dare, defy, face, outbrave; compromise, endan-

ger, imperil, jeopardize, menace; expose, subject; bet (on), wager
phrases run the risk of

2 to place in danger ⟨We refuse to *risk* our life savings on this investment scheme.⟩ — see ENDANGER

risky *adj* involving potential loss or injury ⟨a *risky* new adventure⟩ — see DANGEROUS 1

rite *n* an oft-repeated action or series of actions performed in accordance with tradition or a set of rules ⟨the annual summer *rite* of loading up the car for the big family vacation⟩
synonyms ceremonial, ceremony, form, formality, observance, ritual, solemnity
related words amenities, civility, decorum, etiquette, graces, proprieties; protocol; convention, custom, habit, manners, mores, practice (*also* practise), standard, tradition, way; celebration, service

ritual *n* **1** a usual manner of behaving or doing ⟨Her morning *ritual* is to enjoy a bracing cup of coffee while reading the newspaper.⟩ — see HABIT 1

2 an oft-repeated action or series of actions performed in accordance with tradition or a set of rules ⟨a *ritual* that the ancient peoples of that country believed would bring rain⟩ — see RITE

rival *n* **1** one that is equal to another in status, achievement, or value ⟨a design that is a *rival* to any produced by a professional graphic artist⟩ — see EQUAL

2 one that takes a position opposite another in a competition or conflict ⟨the boxer's toughest *rival* thus far⟩ — see OPPONENT 1

3 one who strives for the same thing as another ⟨the four cities that are the top *rivals* for the site of the next Olympic Games⟩ — see COMPETITOR

rival *vb* to engage in a contest ⟨two longtime friends who have *rivaled* for the same things at every stage of their lives⟩ — see COMPETE

rivalry *n* an earnest effort for superiority or victory over another ⟨a healthy *rivalry* in sports between the two schools⟩ — see CONTEST 1

rive *vb* **1** to cause to separate into pieces usually suddenly or forcibly ⟨road pavement that had been *riven* by the annual freeze-and-thaw cycle⟩ — see BREAK 1

2 to cause (something) to separate into jagged pieces by violently pulling at it ⟨The bitter disappointment threatened to *rive* my heart in two.⟩ — see TEAR 1

rivet *vb* to fix (as one's attention) steadily toward a central objective ⟨Everyone *riveted* their eyes on the trick that the magician was performing on stage.⟩ — see CONCENTRATE 2

riveting *adj* holding the attention or provoking interest ⟨a *riveting* explanation of light waves that fascinated the class⟩ — see INTERESTING

rivulet *n* a natural body of running water smaller than a river ⟨Small *rivulets* trickled down the side of the cliff.⟩ — see CREEK 1

road *n* **1** a passage cleared for public vehicular travel ⟨I think we should take one of the less congested *roads*.⟩ — see WAY 1

2 a roadway overlaid with parallel steel rails over which trains travel ⟨The railway companies are continually repairing their *roads*.⟩ — see RAILROAD

roadhouse *n* a bar or restaurant offering special nighttime entertainment (as music, dancing, or comedy acts) ⟨While at the *roadhouse* we enjoyed some line dancing.⟩ — see NIGHTCLUB

roadway *n* a passage cleared for public vehicular travel ⟨A cow wandered into the *roadway*.⟩ — see WAY 1

roam *vb* to move about from place to place aimlessly ⟨He took a year off and *roamed* over Europe before going on to college.⟩ — see WANDER 1

roamer *n* a person who roams about without a fixed route or destination ⟨The couple retired, sold their house, and became carefree *roamers* in an RV.⟩ — see NOMAD

roaming *adj* traveling from place to place ⟨a *roaming* circus that plays small towns across the country⟩ — see ITINERANT

roar *n* **1** a violent shouting ⟨A *roar* went up from the crowd when the verdict was read.⟩ — see CLAMOR 1

2 loud, confused, and usually inharmonious sound ⟨the *roar* of the machinery in the factory⟩ — see NOISE 1

roar *vb* **1** to make a long loud deep noise or cry ⟨The car's engine *roared* as it sped away.⟩

synonyms bellow, boom, growl, thunder

related words grumble, roll, rumble; bang, blare, blast, peal, scream, screech, shriek, squall; bawl, call, cry, holler, hoot, shout, whoop, yell; howl, wail, yowl

near antonyms grunt, mouth, mumble, murmur, mutter, whisper; mewl, pule, squeak, whimper

2 to speak so as to be heard at a distance ⟨The sergeant *roared* orders at the recruits.⟩ — see CALL 1

3 to show mirth with an explosive vocal sound ⟨a madcap comedy that had movie audiences *roaring* all summer long⟩ — see LAUGH 1

roaring *adj* **1** marked by a high volume of sound ⟨a *roaring* party that woke the whole neighborhood⟩ — see LOUD 1

2 marked by vigorous growth and well-being especially economically ⟨The *roaring* mining town attracted job seekers eager to share in the boom.⟩ — see PROSPEROUS 1

roaring *adv* to a great degree ⟨We had a *roaring* good time at the party.⟩ — see VERY 1

roast *vb* to make fun of in a good-natured way ⟨playfully *roasting* their mother for her choice of hat⟩ — see TEASE 1

roasting *adj* having a notably high temperature ⟨Turn on the air conditioner—the house is *roasting* today!⟩ — see HOT 1

rob *vb* to remove valuables from (a place) unlawfully ⟨in jail for *robbing* a bank⟩

synonyms burglarize, rip off, steal (from)

related words ransack, rifle; despoil, loot, pillage, plunder, ravish, sack, spoil, strip; bleed, break in, cheat, chisel, cozen, defraud, exploit, fleece, hustle, mulct, pluck, rook, shortchange, skin, squeeze, stick, sting, swindle; hold up, mug, roll, stick up

robber *n* one who steals ⟨The *robber* was caught not far from the bank.⟩ — see THIEF

robbery *n* the unlawful taking and carrying away of property without the consent of its owner ⟨The first sign that there had been a *robbery* was the broken door lock.⟩ — see THEFT 1

robe *n* something that covers or conceals like a piece of cloth ⟨With the coming of spring the hills will once again don their *robes* of green.⟩ — see CLOAK 1

robe *vb* to outfit with clothes and especially fine or special clothes ⟨Attendants *robed* the queen in her ceremonial garments.⟩ — see CLOTHE 1

robotic *adj* **1** designed to replace or decrease human labor and especially physical labor ⟨The dishwasher is one of the greatest *robotic* devices ever invented.⟩ — see LABORSAVING

2 done instantly and without conscious thought or decision ⟨She gave *robotic* answers to the questions.⟩ — see AUTOMATIC 1

robust *adj* **1** enjoying health and vigor ⟨a *robust* and sturdy toddler⟩ — see HEALTHY 1

2 having active strength of body or mind ⟨a *robust* older man who still bicycles 10 miles a day⟩ — see VIGOROUS 1

3 having an abundance of some characteristic quality (as flavor) ⟨freshly ground the beans for a *robust* coffee⟩ — see FULL-BODIED

4 not showing weakness or uncertainty ⟨a *robust* slap on the back welcoming me to the company⟩ — see FIRM 1

robustness *n* **1** the condition of being sound in body ⟨She has the *robustness* of a woman half her age.⟩ — see HEALTH 1

2 the quality or state of having abundant or intense activity ⟨The relentless *robustness* of the city has always inspired writers and artists.⟩ — see VITALITY 1

rock *n, slang* a usually valuable stone cut and polished for ornament ⟨millionaires dressed by designers and dripping with *rocks*⟩ — see GEM 1

rock *vb* **1** to make a series of unsteady side-to-side motions ⟨The boat was *rocking* so much that several passengers felt seasick.⟩

synonyms careen, lurch, pitch, roll, seesaw, sway, toss, wobble (*also* wabble)

related words blunder, buck, dodder, falter, flounder, halt, hitch, hobble, jerk, jolt, reel, shake, stagger, stumble, teeter, toddle, totter, tumble, vacillate, vibrate, waddle, waver, weave; oscillate, undulate, wag, waggle

2 to swing unsteadily back and forth or from side to side ⟨The toddler *rocked* on his heels for a moment and then took another faltering step.⟩ — see TEETER 1

3 to make senseless or dizzy by a blow ⟨She *rocked* her opponent with a single punch.⟩ — see STUN 1

4 to make a strong impression on (someone) with something unexpected ⟨The news of the mayor's sudden resignation *rocked* the city.⟩ — see SURPRISE 1

rock bottom *n* the lowest part, place, or point ⟨When the stock market was at its *rock bottom* was the time to buy in.⟩ — see BOTTOM 3

rocket *vb* **1** to proceed or move quickly ⟨The startled cat *rocketed* out of the room.⟩ — see HURRY 2

2 to rise abruptly and rapidly ⟨The child actor *rocketed* to stardom at the age of eight.⟩ — see SKYROCKET

rod *n* **1** a heavy rigid stick used as a weapon or for punishment ⟨Contrary to the old saying, she did not believe that sparing the *rod* would spoil the child.⟩ — see CLUB 1

2 a straight piece (as of wood or metal) that is longer than it is wide ⟨a curtain *rod*⟩ — see BAR 1

rogue *adj* given to or marked by cheating and deception ⟨a *rogue* administrator who took bribes to falsify paperwork⟩ — see DISHONEST 2

rogue *n* **1** a mean, evil, or unprincipled person ⟨I could tell when we met that he was an unscrupulous *rogue*.⟩ — see VILLAIN

2 an appealingly mischievous person ⟨The little *rogue* always seems to end up being forgiven for his pranks.⟩ — see SCAMP 1

roguish *adj* tending to or exhibiting reckless playfulness ⟨A *roguish* grin was the only sign that she had something up her sleeve for the office party.⟩ — see MISCHIEVOUS 1

roguishness *n* playful, reckless behavior that is not intended to cause serious harm ⟨a bit of childish *roguishness* that ended up with a window being broken⟩ — see MISCHIEF 1

roil *vb* **1** to be in a state of violent rolling motion ⟨The waters of the gulf tossed and *roiled* as the hurricane surged toward the shore.⟩ — see SEETHE 1

2 to make angry ⟨The clerk's brusque refusal of her request *roiled* her enough to prompt a complaint to his supervisor.⟩ — see ANGER

roiled *adj* **1** feeling or showing anger ⟨He waited until he wasn't so obviously *roiled* before voicing a complaint to the manager.⟩ — see ANGRY

2 having visible particles in liquid suspension ⟨The *roiled* water made more difficult the work of the divers searching for the ancient shipwreck.⟩ — see CLOUDY 1

roisterer *n* one who engages in merrymaking especially in honor of a special occasion ⟨the rowdy *roisterers* who fill the streets of New Orleans during Mardi Gras⟩ — see CELEBRANT

role *also* **rôle** *n* the action for which a person or thing is specially fitted or used or for which a thing exists ⟨studying the *role* of sunlight in the body's production of vitamin D⟩
synonyms business, capacity, function, job, part, place, position, purpose, task, work
related words affair, concern, hand, involvement, participation; niche, office, post, situation; calling, occupation, pursuit, vocation; activity, assignment, charge, commission, duty, employ, mission, responsibility, service, use

¹roll *n* a record of a series of items (as names or titles) usually arranged according to some system ⟨called the *roll* of people supposed to be in the class⟩ — see ¹LIST

²roll *n* a rapid turning about on an axis or central point ⟨The squirrel did a quick *roll* and vanished up a tree.⟩ — see SPIN 1

roll *vb* **1** to form into a round compact mass ⟨*rolled* up the wrapper from the straw and threw it⟩ — see WAD
2 to make a low heavy rolling sound ⟨thunder *rolling* in the distance⟩ — see RUMBLE
3 to make a series of unsteady side-to-side motions ⟨The car suddenly was *rolling* as high winds swept across the bridge.⟩ — see ROCK 1
4 to move (something) in a curved or circular path on or as if on an axis ⟨In order to knock your opponent off balance, you have to *roll* the log when he least expects it.⟩ — see TURN 1
5 to move in a stream ⟨just lying on the beach, watching the clouds *roll* by⟩ — see FLOW 1
6 to move in circles around an axis or center ⟨*rolled* her head around her shoulders to loosen herself up⟩ — see SPIN 1
7 to move or proceed smoothly and readily ⟨Once we started *rolling*, everything went perfectly.⟩ — see FLOW 2

rollick *n* a time or instance of carefree fun ⟨enjoying a summer *rollick* before knuckling down in medical school⟩ — see FLING 1

rollick *vb* **1** to engage in activity for amusement ⟨an educator who realized that children need to *rollick* as well as to study and learn⟩ — see PLAY 1
2 to play and run about happily ⟨children *rollicking* during recess⟩ — see FROLIC 1

rollicking *adj* **1** being rough or noisy in a high-spirited way ⟨Reunions with his friends from college were usually *rollicking* affairs.⟩ — see BOISTEROUS
2 given to good-natured joking or teasing ⟨a *rollicking* boy who quickly charms everyone he meets⟩ — see PLAYFUL

rollicking *n* activity engaged in to amuse oneself ⟨Ted likes to indulge in mindless *rollicking* after a day at work in order to relax.⟩ — see PLAY 1

roly–poly *adj* having an excess of body fat ⟨a *roly-poly* puppy who stole our hearts⟩ — see FAT 1

romance *n* a brief romantic relationship ⟨a summer *romance* that ended once school started again⟩ — see AFFAIR 1

romantic *adj* excitingly or mysteriously unusual ⟨An unexplored island provided the setting for a perfect *romantic* adventure.⟩ — see EXOTIC

romantic *n* one whose conduct is guided more by the image of perfection than by the real world ⟨She's a hopeless *romantic* who believes that her one true love is somewhere waiting to be found.⟩ — see IDEALIST

romanticize *vb* to represent or think of as better than reality would warrant ⟨He *romanticized* what life in a small town would be like, only to be later disappointed when reality intruded.⟩ — see IDEALIZE

romp *n* a time or instance of carefree fun ⟨one last *romp* before starting their new life as parents⟩ — see FLING 1

romp *vb* to play and run about happily ⟨The kids *romped* on the lawn until dinner was ready.⟩ — see FROLIC 1

roof *n* **1** a raised covering over something for decoration or protection ⟨The *roof* of the pavilion leaks when it rains.⟩ — see CANOPY
2 the place where one lives ⟨As long as you're living under my *roof*, you'll obey my rules!⟩ — see HOME 1

roof *vb* to provide with living quarters or shelter ⟨fed and *roofed* the emergency volunteers for a week⟩ — see HOUSE 1

rook *vb* to rob by the use of trickery or threats ⟨Once you learn to recognize these swindler's tricks, no one will be able to use them to *rook* you.⟩ — see FLEECE

rookie *n* a person who is just starting out in a field of activity ⟨Although a star in his old sport of basketball, he was still just a *rookie* as far as baseball was concerned.⟩ — see BEGINNER

room *n* **1** an extent or area available for or used up by some activity or thing ⟨I need more *room* to do a cartwheel.⟩ ⟨They made *room* for him on the bench.⟩
synonyms place, space, way
related words capacity, compass, range, scope; berth, clearance, freedom, latitude, play
2 an area within a building that has been set apart from surrounding space by a wall ⟨Tim finally had a *room* to himself when his older brother went off to college.⟩
synonyms apartment, cell, chamber, closet
related words accommodation, bay, berth, booth, cabin, compartment, cubicle; alcove, niche, nook, recess; snuggery [*chiefly British*]
3 a favorable combination of circumstances, time, and place ⟨There's still *room* for improvement.⟩ — see OPPORTUNITY

room *vb* to provide with living quarters or shelter ⟨We can *room* up to four visitors in our two guest bedrooms.⟩ — see HOUSE 1

roomer *n* one who rents a room or apartment in another's house ⟨The new owners took in *roomers* to help pay for the house.⟩ — see TENANT 1

roomy *adj* more than adequate or average in capacity ⟨a small car that's surprisingly *roomy* inside⟩ — see SPACIOUS

roost *vb* **1** to come to rest after descending from the air ⟨pigeons flying home to *roost* on the roof⟩ — see ALIGHT 1
2 to establish or place comfortably or snugly ⟨A group of friends had *roosted* themselves around the ski lodge's massive fireplace.⟩ — see ENSCONCE 1

root *n* **1** a point or place at which something is invented or provided ⟨He insists that insecurity is the *root* of all jealousy.⟩ — see SOURCE 1
2 the source from which something grows or develops ⟨One would need to go back at least several hundred years to find the *root* of the entrenched hostility between the neighboring nations.⟩ — see SEED 1
3 an immaterial thing upon which something else rests ⟨An implicit trust in the wisdom of the people is the *root* of democracy.⟩ — see BASE 1
4 the central part or aspect of something under consideration ⟨At *root*, it's a question of the proper limits, if any, of free speech.⟩ — see CRUX

root *vb* to set solidly in or as if in surrounding matter ⟨*rooted* the post securely in the dirt⟩ — see ENTRENCH

root (out) *vb* **1** to destroy all traces of ⟨a concerted effort to *root out* prejudice of any kind in the armed services⟩ — see ANNIHILATE 1
2 to draw out by force or with effort ⟨a dog *rooting out* a buried toy⟩ — see EXTRACT

3 to come upon after searching, study, or effort ⟨a journalist seeking to *root out* and expose corruption⟩ — see FIND 1

rooted *adj* firmly established over time ⟨a popular, *rooted* misconception that has proved very resistant to correction⟩ — see INVETERATE 1

rope *n* a length of braided, flexible material that is used for tying or connecting things ⟨We used a *rope* to tie the boat to the dock.⟩ — see CORD 1

ropy *also* **ropey** *adj* being of a consistency that resists flow ⟨Because the paint was so old, it was *ropy* and couldn't be smoothly applied to the wood.⟩ — see THICK 2

rose–colored *adj* having qualities which inspire hope ⟨An incurable optimist sees the world through a *rose-colored* perspective.⟩ — see HOPEFUL 1

roster *n* a record of a series of items (as names or titles) usually arranged according to some system ⟨the *roster* of subscribers to the journal⟩ — see ¹LIST

rostrum *n* a level usually raised surface ⟨stood on a *rostrum* to address the huge crowd⟩ — see PLATFORM

rosy *adj* **1** having a healthy reddish skin tone ⟨*rosy* and cheerful after a day outside in the snow⟩ — see RUDDY

2 having qualities which inspire hope ⟨That's a particularly *rosy* view of the economic situation.⟩ — see HOPEFUL 1

rot *n* **1** language, behavior, or ideas that are absurd and contrary to good sense ⟨I won't stand here and listen to such *rot*.⟩ — see NONSENSE 1

2 the process by which dead organic matter separates into simpler substances ⟨The *rot* begins shortly after the fish are killed.⟩ — see CORRUPTION 1

rot *vb* **1** to become worse or of less value ⟨The house slowly fell into disrepair and *rotted*.⟩ — see DETERIORATE 1

2 to go through decomposition ⟨*rotting* vegetation on the bank of the river⟩ — see DECAY 1

rotate *vb* **1** to move (something) in a curved or circular path on or as if on an axis ⟨*Rotate* the mirror 180 degrees.⟩ — see TURN 1

2 to move in circles around an axis or center ⟨The Earth *rotates* around its axis.⟩ — see SPIN 1

rotation *n* a rapid turning about on an axis or central point ⟨The Earth completes a single *rotation* around its axis in approximately 24 hours.⟩ — see SPIN 1

rote *n* an established and often automatic or monotonous series of actions followed when engaging in some activity ⟨learned the *rote* for the exercise warm-up but not the reasoning behind it⟩ — see ROUTINE 1

rotten *adj* **1** having undergone organic breakdown ⟨*rotten*, smelly meat that should have been thrown out⟩

synonyms addled, bad, corrupted, decayed, decomposed, putrefied, putrid, spoiled

related words curdled, fermented, off, rank, sour, soured, turned; contaminated, defiled, fouled, impure, polluted, tainted; corroded, crumbled, degenerated, deteriorated, disintegrated; decaying, decomposing, disintegrating, mildewy, moldering, moldy, putrefying, putrescent, rotting; gangrenous

near antonyms fresh, good, sweet; preserved, pristine, uncontaminated, undefiled, unpolluted, unspoiled, untainted, untouched

antonyms undecomposed

2 not conforming to a high moral standard; morally unacceptable ⟨The boy played a *rotten* trick.⟩ — see BAD 2

3 not giving pleasure to the mind or senses ⟨I had a *rotten* time while on vacation.⟩ — see UNPLEASANT

4 extremely unsatisfactory ⟨*rotten* housing conditions that no one should be forced to tolerate⟩ — see WRETCHED 1

5 of low quality ⟨I can't do anything with these *rotten* tools.⟩ — see CHEAP 1

rotund *adj* **1** having an excess of body fat ⟨The costume made him appear *rotund*, perfect for his role as Santa Claus.⟩ — see FAT 1

2 marked by conspicuously full and rich sounds or tones ⟨The actor's distinct baritone and his clear and *rotund* elocution are especially effective in dramatic readings.⟩ — see RESONANT

rotundity *n* the condition of having an excess of body fat ⟨the famous *rotundity* of our 27th president⟩ — see CORPULENCE

rough *adj* **1** covered with or as if with hair ⟨a face *rough* with a couple days' worth of beard⟩ — see HAIRY 1

2 marked by bursts of destructive force or intense activity ⟨*rough* waters that made sailing our sloop a little risky⟩ — see VIOLENT 1

3 marked by wet and windy conditions ⟨At least wear a raincoat if you're going out into that *rough* weather.⟩ — see FOUL 1

4 not having a level or smooth surface ⟨A *rough* board can give you splinters.⟩ — see UNEVEN 1

5 requiring considerable physical or mental effort ⟨a forensics expert who willingly takes on *rough* assignments⟩ — see HARD 2

6 difficult to endure ⟨I've had a *rough* time of it since I lost my job.⟩ — see HARSH 1

7 harsh and threatening in manner or appearance ⟨the *rough* faces of hardened criminals who had spent most of their lives behind bars⟩ — see GRIM 1

8 hastily or roughly constructed ⟨They made a *rough* camp as darkness fell over the forest.⟩ — see RUDE 1

9 lacking in refinement or good taste ⟨He learned polite words to replace the *rough* language he used in his youth.⟩ — see COARSE 2

10 made of or resembling hair ⟨a *rough*-coated dog who was always shedding his fur⟩ — see HAIRY 2

11 marked by a series of sharp quick motions ⟨a *rough* flight that left some passengers nauseated⟩ — see JERKY 1

12 marked by turmoil or disturbance especially of natural elements ⟨After a *rough* week on the high seas, we were happy to sail through the gulf's more tranquil waters.⟩ — see WILD 3

rough (up) *vb* **1** to strike repeatedly ⟨a hockey player penalized for *roughing up* an opponent with his stick⟩ — see BEAT 1

2 to abuse physically ⟨The photographer claimed that he had been *roughed up* by the actor's bodyguards outside the club.⟩ — see MANHANDLE 1

roughened *adj* not having a level or smooth surface ⟨*roughened* hands from hard work⟩ — see UNEVEN 1

roughhouse *n* wildly playful or mischievous behavior ⟨Their parents simply wouldn't tolerate any *roughhouse* in the living room.⟩ — see HORSEPLAY

roughhousing *n* wildly playful or mischievous behavior ⟨*Roughhousing* was simply part of growing up in a family with four kids.⟩ — see HORSEPLAY

roughly *adv* in a manner so as to cause loss or suffering ⟨If you treat the phone *roughly*, it will of course break.⟩ — see HARDLY 1

roughneck *adj* lacking in refinement or good taste ⟨a team whose *roughneck* antics often made the headlines⟩ — see COARSE 2

roughneck *n* a violent, brutal person who is often a member of an organized gang ⟨a group of *roughnecks* who had frequent run-ins with the police⟩ — see HOODLUM

roughness *n* **1** a harsh or sharp quality ⟨a *roughness* to his guitar playing⟩ — see EDGE 1

2 the quality or state of lacking refinement or good taste ⟨The *roughness* of pioneer life is not glossed over in the documentary.⟩ — see VULGARITY 1

round *adj* **1** having every part of the surface the same dis-

tance from the center 〈*round* ping pong balls〉 〈The earth is not perfectly *round*.〉
synonyms global, spherical
related words annular, circular, discoid, discoidal, disk-like, ringlike; curved, looped, spiral; bulbous, rotund, rounded, roundish; cylindrical (*also* cylindric), oblong, oval, ovate, ovoid (*also* ovoidal)
antonyms nonspherical
2 having an excess of body fat 〈I patted the piglet's little *round* belly.〉 — see FAT 1
3 marked by conspicuously full and rich sounds or tones 〈an organ with a beautifully *round* sound〉 — see RESONANT
4 being neither more nor less than a certain amount, number, or extent 〈a *round* dozen eggs〉 — see EVEN 1
round *adv* **1** from beginning to end 〈people working there all year *round*〉 — see THROUGH 1
2 on all sides or in every direction 〈Kids, gather *round* and listen to my story.〉 — see AROUND 1
3 toward the opposite direction 〈I turned *round* to see who was calling out.〉 — see AROUND 2
round *n* **1** a circular strip 〈a *round* of steel to reinforce the wooden beam〉 — see ¹RING 2
2 a series of events or actions that repeat themselves regularly and in the same order 〈a busy *round* of parties during the holiday season〉 — see CYCLE 1
3 something with a perfectly round circumference 〈Use a cookie cutter to make the *rounds* of dough.〉 — see CIRCLE 1
round *prep* in random positions within the boundaries of 〈talked to voters *round* the city〉 — see AROUND 2
round *vb* **1** to form into a round compact mass 〈The baker carefully *rounded* the dough and placed it on a cookie tray.〉 — see WAD
2 to travel completely around 〈a monorail for visitors that *rounds* the park〉 — see ENCIRCLE 1
3 to turn away from a straight line or course 〈*rounded* on the track and headed for the finish line〉 — see CURVE 1
round (off *or* **out)** *vb* **1** to bring (an event) to a natural or appropriate stopping point 〈I'll *round off* the meeting here and let everyone get an early start on the weekend.〉 — see CLOSE 3
2 to serve as a completing element to 〈Coffee and dessert *rounded out* the meal.〉 — see COMPLEMENT
roundabout *adj* not straightforward or direct 〈took a *roundabout* route to the beach〉 — see INDIRECT
roundly *adv* **1** in a vigorous and forceful manner 〈She *roundly* attacked the proposal to raise the state's gas tax.〉 — see HARD 3
2 with attention to all aspects or details 〈Few sitcoms were as *roundly* disliked as that one.〉 — see THOROUGHLY 1
roundtable *n* a meeting featuring a group discussion 〈an international *roundtable* of medical experts on the disease〉 — see FORUM 1
roundup *n* a short statement of the main points 〈I can't read 500 pages by tomorrow, so just give me the *roundup*.〉 — see SUMMARY
round up *vb* to bring together in one body or place 〈*rounded* everyone *up* for one final training session〉 — see GATHER 1
rouse *vb* **1** to cause to stop sleeping 〈The honking horns *roused* her from a deep sleep.〉 — see WAKE 1
2 to cease to be asleep 〈I finally *roused* around noon, after going to bed very late.〉 — see WAKE 2
rousing *adj* **1** causing great emotional or mental stimulation 〈a *rousing* rendition of our national anthem〉 — see EXCITING 1
2 marked by much life, movement, or activity 〈During the heat wave stores were doing a *rousing* business in air conditioners.〉 — see ALIVE 2

¹**rout** *n* **1** a great number of persons or creatures massed together 〈A great *rout* of onlookers had gathered around the scene.〉 — see CROWD 1
2 people looked down upon as ignorant and of the lowest class 〈At first the protests were dismissed as nothing more than the doings of the restless *rout*.〉 — see RABBLE
²**rout** *n* **1** failure to win a contest 〈The championship game was a humiliating *rout* for the team that had been favored to win.〉 — see DEFEAT 1
2 the act or an instance of getting free from danger or confinement 〈put the enemy to *rout*〉 — see ESCAPE 1
rout *vb* **1** to defeat by a large margin 〈As expected, the professional team had no trouble *routing* the amateurs.〉 — see WHIP 2
2 to drive or force out 〈The Roman legion quickly *routed* the would-be invaders.〉 — see EJECT 1
route *n* **1** a passage cleared for public vehicular travel 〈Take *Route* 190 for six miles, then get off.〉 — see WAY 1
2 an established course for traveling from one place to another 〈We're going to get stuck in traffic if we take the usual *route*.〉 — see PASSAGE 1
3 the direction along which something or someone moves 〈Hurricanes generally take a northerly *route* up the Atlantic seaboard.〉 — see PATH 1
route *vb* to point out the way for (someone) especially from a position in front 〈The guide *routed* us smoothly through the jungle.〉 — see LEAD 1
routine *adj* **1** being of the type that is encountered in the normal course of events 〈This is just a *routine* inspection.〉 — see ORDINARY 1
2 following or agreeing with established form, custom, or rules 〈the *routine* procedure for filing a complaint with the board〉 — see FORMAL 1
3 often observed or encountered 〈The movie is a *routine* thriller that has little to recommend it.〉 — see COMMON 1
routine *n* **1** an established and often automatic or monotonous series of actions followed when engaging in some activity 〈Part of my morning *routine* is drinking a cup of coffee while reading the news.〉
synonyms drill, grind, groove, pattern, rote, rut, treadmill
related words regimen; custom, fashion, habit, practice (*also* practise), trick, wont; approach, manner, method, procedure, strategy, style, tack, technique, way
2 something done over and over in order to develop skill 〈a training *routine*〉 — see EXERCISE 2
3 a performance regularly presented by an individual or group 〈The stand-up did a tired *routine* that's been around since the days of vaudeville.〉 — see ACT 1
rove *vb* to move about from place to place aimlessly 〈buffalo *roving* over the vast plains〉 — see WANDER 1
rover *n* **1** a person who roams about without a fixed route or destination 〈Ever since he developed a strong case of wanderlust in college, he's been a *rover*.〉 — see NOMAD 1
2 someone who engages in robbery of ships at sea 〈a story of the days when sea *rovers* plied the Caribbean〉 — see PIRATE
roving *adj* traveling from place to place 〈a *roving* substitute teacher who works in a different district every day〉 — see ITINERANT
¹**row** *n* **1** a series of people or things arranged side by side 〈stood in a *row* to have their picture taken〉 〈Three *rows* of eight jelly beans equals 24 jelly beans.〉
synonyms bank, rank
related words chain, column, cue, file, line, procession, queue, range, string, train; echelon; sequence
2 a passage cleared for public vehicular travel 〈Drive up Market *Row* and turn left.〉 — see WAY 1
²**row** *n* **1** a rough and often noisy fight usually involving

several people ⟨police breaking up a *row* at the game⟩ — see BRAWL 1

2 a state of noisy, confused activity ⟨The combination of drums and shouting contributed to the awful *row*.⟩ — see COMMOTION

3 an often noisy or angry expression of differing opinions ⟨They had a *row* yesterday, and now they aren't speaking.⟩ — see ARGUMENT 1

¹row *vb* to move a boat by means of oars ⟨*rowed* around the lake⟩

synonyms oar, paddle, scull

related words canoe, kayak; pole, punt; feather, pull

²row *vb* to express different opinions about something often angrily ⟨The couple *rows* all the time, and yet they seem happy together.⟩ — see ARGUE 2

rowdy *adj* being rough or noisy in a high-spirited way ⟨a *rowdy* but good-natured group of teenagers⟩ — see BOISTEROUS

rowdy *n* a violent, brutal person who is often a member of an organized gang ⟨a couple of *rowdies* ejected from the concert⟩ — see HOODLUM

rower *n* a person who drives a boat forward by means of oars ⟨The racing shell carries four *rowers* and a coxswain.⟩ — see OARSMAN

royal *adj* **1** fit for or worthy of a royal ruler ⟨The school superintendent received a *royal* welcome.⟩ — see MONARCHICAL

2 large and impressive in size, grandeur, extent, or conception ⟨My little brother is a *royal* pain.⟩ — see GRAND 1

3 involving minimal difficulty or effort ⟨Unfortunately, there is no *royal* way for a person to achieve maturity.⟩ — see EASY 1

rub *n* something that is a source of irritation ⟨Even what seems to be a dream job usually turns out to have its fair share of *rubs*.⟩ — see ANNOYANCE 3

rub *vb* **1** to damage or diminish by continued friction ⟨The brake pads were *rubbed* away as a result of years of use.⟩ — see ABRADE 1

2 to make smooth by friction ⟨The furniture restorer *rubbed* the board perfectly smooth with sandpaper.⟩ — see GRIND 1

3 to make smooth or glossy usually by repeatedly applying surface pressure ⟨The butler *rubbed* the silver tea set until it gleamed.⟩ — see POLISH 1

rubbed *adj* having a shiny surface or finish ⟨The *rubbed* brass of the wall sconce showed my reflection.⟩ — see GLOSSY

rubberlike *adj* able to revert to original size and shape after being stretched, squeezed, or twisted ⟨a *rubberlike* material that is used for household products⟩ — see ELASTIC 1

rubberneck *n* a person who travels for pleasure ⟨Every year raucous *rubbernecks* by the busload descend upon the city for its famed Mardi Gras.⟩ — see TOURIST

rubberneck *vb* to look long and hard in wonder or surprise ⟨thoughtless drivers pausing on the highway to *rubberneck* at the accident⟩ — see GAPE

rubbery *adj* able to revert to original size and shape after being stretched, squeezed, or twisted ⟨Mozzarella is a *rubbery* cheese known to every pizza lover.⟩ — see ELASTIC 1

rubbish *n* **1** discarded or useless material ⟨It's illegal to throw *rubbish* out of your car on the highway.⟩ — see GARBAGE

2 that which is of low quality or worth ⟨regarded most romance novels as the lowest form of literary *rubbish*⟩ — see JUNK 1

3 language, behavior, or ideas that are absurd and contrary to good sense ⟨You're obviously no economist because what you're saying is absolute *rubbish*.⟩ — see NONSENSE 1

rubbishy *adj* of low quality ⟨*rubbishy* merchandise that is mainly bought by tourists⟩ — see CHEAP 2

rubble *n* the portion or bits of something left over or behind after it has been destroyed ⟨clearing the *rubble* after the earthquake⟩ — see REMAINS 1

rubicund *adj* having a healthy reddish skin tone ⟨the *rubicund* face of a man who clearly got a lot of fresh air and exercise⟩ — see RUDDY

rub out *vb* **1** to bring to a complete end the physical soundness, existence, or usefulness of ⟨Aerial bombs *rubbed out* the oil refinery.⟩ — see DESTROY 1

2 to put to death deliberately ⟨an elaborate setup to *rub out* rival mobsters⟩ — see MURDER 1

3 to destroy all traces of ⟨a promise to *rub out* government waste⟩ — see ANNIHILATE 1

rubric *n* **1** a word or series of words often in larger letters placed at the beginning of a passage or at the top of a page in order to introduce or categorize ⟨The *rubrics* at the beginning of the chapters are intended to be humorous.⟩ — see HEADING

2 an inherited or established way of thinking, feeling, or doing ⟨the *rubric*, popular among jewelers anyway, that a man should spend a month's salary on his fiancée's engagement ring⟩ — see TRADITION 1

3 one of the units into which a whole is divided on the basis of a common characteristic ⟨All of these books fall under the *rubric* of historical fiction.⟩ — see CLASS 2

rucksack *n* a soft-sided case designed for carrying belongings especially on the back ⟨hikers carrying their food and water in *rucksacks*⟩ — see PACK 1

ruckus *n* **1** a rough and often noisy fight usually involving several people ⟨The *ruckus* was quickly ended.⟩ — see BRAWL 1

2 a state of noisy, confused activity ⟨Quit creating such a *ruckus*—I'm trying to sleep!⟩ — see COMMOTION

ruction *n* **1** a rough and often noisy fight usually involving several people ⟨unintentionally started a *ruction*⟩ — see BRAWL 1

2 a state of noisy, confused activity ⟨The *ruction* outside the door prompted me to investigate what was going on.⟩ — see COMMOTION

ruddy *adj* having a healthy reddish skin tone ⟨*Ruddy* complexions run in the family.⟩

synonyms blooming, florid, flush, full-blooded, glowing, red, rosy, rubicund, sanguine

related words bronzed, brown, suntanned, tanned; bloomy, blushing, flushed, warm; cherubic

near antonyms waxen; blanched, white, whitened; anemic, sick, sickly; white-faced

antonyms ashen, ashy, livid, lurid, mealy, pale, paled, palish, pallid, pasty, peaked, sallow, sallowish, wan

rude *adj* **1** hastily or roughly constructed ⟨a *rude* shelter built from unfinished logs by some forgotten pioneer⟩

synonyms artless, clumsy, crude, jerry-rigged, rough, unrefined

related words defective, faulty, flawed, imperfect; imprecise, inexact; inartistic, undressed, unfinished, unpolished, unworked; amateur, amateurish, inexpert, unprofessional, unskilled, unskillful; primitive, rudimentary; unshaped, unshapen

near antonyms faultless, finished, flawless, meticulous, perfect, perfected, polished, well-done; adept, adroit, dexterous (*also* dextrous), expert, masterful, masterly, neat, practiced (*also* practised), skillful, workmanlike; artful, artistic, sophisticated; exact, precise

antonyms refined

2 belonging to or characteristic of an early level of skill or development ⟨*rude* stone tools⟩ — see PRIMITIVE 1

3 lacking in refinement or good taste ⟨a comedian who uses a lot of *rude* language in his act⟩ — see COARSE 2

4 not civilized ⟨a *rude* period in history⟩ — see UNCIVILIZED

5 showing a lack of manners or consideration for others ⟨made a *rude* comment⟩ — see IMPOLITE

6 lacking in education or the knowledge gained from books ⟨*Rude* folks they might have been, but they produced music with real poignancy.⟩ — see IGNORANT 1

7 being such as found in nature and not altered by processing or refining ⟨*rude* pelts that were sent to Europe to be fashioned into elegant hats and coats⟩ — see CRUDE 1

rudeness *n* **1** rude behavior ⟨Such *rudeness* will not be tolerated in this office.⟩ — see DISCOURTESY

2 the quality or state of lacking refinement or good taste ⟨The *rudeness* of frontier life gradually diminished with time.⟩ — see VULGARITY 1

rudimentary *adj* **1** belonging to or characteristic of an early level of skill or development ⟨*rudimentary* shelters built by prehistoric peoples⟩ — see PRIMITIVE 1

2 of or relating to the simplest facts or theories of a subject ⟨They had only a *rudimentary* knowledge of science.⟩ — see ELEMENTARY

rudiments *pl n* general or basic truths on which other truths or theories can be based ⟨learned the *rudiments* of mathematics⟩ — see PRINCIPLES 1

rue *n* a feeling of responsibility for wrongdoing ⟨a soul filled with pain and *rue*⟩ — see GUILT 1

rue *vb* to feel sorry or dissatisfied about ⟨I *rue* the day I agreed to this stupid plan.⟩ — see REGRET

rueful *adj* **1** expressing or suggesting mourning ⟨the *rueful* faces of friends and family who had gathered to pay their last respects⟩ — see MOURNFUL 1

2 feeling sorrow for a wrong that one has done ⟨a *rueful* youth who had come to ask for forgiveness⟩ — see CONTRITE

3 deserving of one's pity ⟨the *rueful* poverty of people in parts of the world⟩ — see PATHETIC 1

ruefully *adv* with feelings of bitterness or grief ⟨"I still have a scar from the accident," he said *ruefully*.⟩ — see HARD 2

ruffian *n* a violent, brutal person who is often a member of an organized gang ⟨played the role of a *ruffian* and petty criminal⟩ — see HOODLUM

ruffle *n* **1** a strip of fabric gathered or pleated on one edge and used as trimming ⟨likes lace curtains without *ruffles* and chintz curtains with *ruffles*⟩

synonyms flounce, frill, furbelow

related words border, fringe, trim; plait, pleat, ruff; bunting, skirting

2 something that is a source of irritation ⟨A spouse's snoring is one *ruffle* that many couples must eventually come to terms with.⟩ — see ANNOYANCE 3

ruffle *vb* to disturb the peace of mind of (someone) especially by repeated disagreeable acts ⟨The stream of minor complaints finally *ruffled* him into snapping, "If you don't like the way I'm doing it, do it yourself!"⟩ — see IRRITATE 1

rugged *adj* **1** able to withstand hardship, strain, or exposure ⟨a *rugged* construction that survived for hundreds of years⟩ — see HARDY 1

2 difficult to endure ⟨the incredibly *rugged* conditions that the polar explorers faced⟩ — see HARSH 1

3 harsh and threatening in manner or appearance ⟨The warrior's *rugged* features frightened the child.⟩ — see GRIM 1

4 having muscles capable of exerting great physical force ⟨a *rugged* athlete who's competing in weight lifting in the Olympics⟩ — see STRONG 1

5 not having a level or smooth surface ⟨*rugged* terrain that made for slow going⟩ — see UNEVEN 1

6 requiring considerable physical or mental effort ⟨Even more *rugged* than most ultramarathons, this one crosses a desert.⟩ — see HARD 2

7 marked by turmoil or disturbance especially of natural elements ⟨New Hampshire's Mount Washington has some of the *ruggedest* weather in all of North America.⟩ — see WILD 3

8 lacking in refinement or good taste ⟨enjoyed a kind of *rugged* humor⟩ — see COARSE 2

ruin *n* **1** the state or fact of being rendered nonexistent, physically unsound, or useless ⟨The building lay in *ruins*.⟩ — see DESTRUCTION 1

2 ruins *pl* the portion or bits of something left over or behind after it has been destroyed ⟨the *ruins* of an abandoned abbey⟩ — see REMAINS 1

3 something that is the cause of one's ultimate failure or loss of life ⟨The politician's eventual *ruin* would be a financial scandal.⟩ — see DOWNFALL 1

ruin *vb* **1** to cause to lose one's fortune and become unable to pay one's debts ⟨After he was *ruined* by the Great Chicago Fire of 1871, the industrialist was forced to sell his mansion and start all over again.⟩

synonyms bankrupt, break, bust

related words beggar, impoverish, pauperize; reduce, straiten; clean (out), wipe out

near antonyms enrich, richen

2 to bring destruction to (something) through violent action ⟨Tornadoes *ruined* a wide swath of the forest.⟩ — see RAVAGE

3 to bring to a complete end the physical soundness, existence, or usefulness of ⟨I burned dinner and *ruined* it.⟩ — see DESTROY 1

ruination *n* **1** something that is the cause of one's ultimate failure or loss of life ⟨In some places, water pollution is causing the *ruination* of the fishing industry.⟩ — see DOWNFALL 1

2 the state or fact of being rendered nonexistent, physically unsound, or useless ⟨Although this is a setback, it isn't complete *ruination* for the company.⟩ — see DESTRUCTION 1

ruinous *adj* **1** bringing about ruin or misfortune ⟨A *ruinous* miscalculation of the financial markets left them bankrupt.⟩ — see FATAL 1

2 causing or tending to cause destruction ⟨A *ruinous* windstorm destroyed the crops.⟩ — see DESTRUCTIVE 1

rule *n* **1** a statement spelling out the proper procedure or conduct for an activity ⟨Read the *rules* that are posted before you use the pool.⟩

synonyms bylaw, ground rule, regulation

related words code, constitution, decalogue, directory; act, law, ordinance, statute; behest, charge, command, commandment, decree, dictate, direction, directive, edict, fiat, instruction, order; axiom, fundamental, maxim, precept; moral, principle, value; ban, interdiction, prohibition, proscription, restriction; blueprint, canon, formula, guide, guideline, standard

2 lawful control over the affairs of a political unit (as a nation) ⟨the years during which Russia was under Communist *rule*⟩

synonyms administration, authority, governance, government, jurisdiction, regime (*also* régime), regimen

related words dominion, power, sovereignty (*also* sovranty), supremacy, sway; command, leadership; direction, management, regulation, superintendence, supervision; autocracy, dictatorship, mastery, oppression, subjugation, tyranny

3 an inherited or established way of thinking, feeling, or doing ⟨One of the sacred *rules* of that ancient society was respect for the elderly.⟩ — see TRADITION 1

rule *vb* **1** to exercise authority or power over ⟨a sea captain who *ruled* his ship sternly but justly⟩ — see GOVERN 1

2 to keep from exceeding a desirable degree or level (as of expression) ⟨a monarch who is known for *ruling* her emotions with an iron hand⟩ — see CONTROL 1

rule (on) *vb* to give an opinion about (something at issue or in dispute) ⟨The coach *ruled on* the question of whether the player ought to be disqualified from the team.⟩ — see JUDGE 1

rule out *vb* to prevent the participation, consideration, or inclusion of ⟨Another loss would *rule* them *out* of the tournament.⟩ — see EXCLUDE

ruler *n* one who rules over a people with a sole, supreme, and usually hereditary authority ⟨The aging *ruler* agonized over the choice of an heir.⟩ — see MONARCH 1

ruling *adj* held by or applicable to a majority of the people ⟨the *ruling* view on privacy issues⟩ — see GENERAL 3

ruling *n* **1** a decision made by a court or tribunal regarding a case it has heard ⟨The controversial *ruling* by the state's supreme court caused an uproar.⟩ — see SENTENCE
2 an order publicly issued by an authority ⟨the FCC's *ruling* regarding the broadcasting of political messages⟩ — see EDICT 1

rumble *vb* to make a low heavy rolling sound ⟨When thunder *rumbled* in the distant sky, we wisely began packing up our picnic.⟩
synonyms growl, grumble, lumber, roll
related words boom, drum, thunder; bellow

ruminant *adj* given to or marked by long, quiet thinking ⟨I wandered around campus all day in a *ruminant* mood.⟩ — see CONTEMPLATIVE

ruminate *vb* to give serious and careful thought to ⟨The minister hoped that the congregation would spend the remainder of the week *ruminating* the message of his sermon.⟩ — see PONDER

rummage *n* an unorganized collection or mixture of various things ⟨a *rummage* of textbooks, notebooks, and old school papers all over the desk⟩ — see MISCELLANY 1

rummage *vb* **1** to come upon after searching, study, or effort ⟨At the last minute she *rummaged* a costume from the attic.⟩ — see FIND 1
2 to look through (as a place) carefully or thoroughly in an effort to find or discover something ⟨He *rummaged* the desk drawer trying to find the spare keys.⟩ — see SEARCH 1

rumor *n* information or opinion that is widely disseminated without any authority or confirmation of accuracy ⟨*Rumor* has it that she's planning to shut down the company.⟩
synonyms buzz, dish, gossip, report, talk, tattle, word
related words tale, whisper, whispering; hint, intimation, rumbling; propaganda; dirt, scandal

rumor *vb* to make (as a piece of information) the subject of common talk without any authority or confirmation of accuracy ⟨For years people have been *rumoring* the CEO's imminent retirement.⟩
synonyms bruit (about), circulate, whisper
related words bandy (about), blab, gossip, tattle; bare, disclose, divulge, expose, report, reveal, spill, tell; hint, imply, insinuate, intimate, suggest; broadcast, proclaim, propagate, publicize, spread

rump *n* the part of the body upon which someone sits ⟨I plopped down on my *rump* to listen to the campfire story.⟩ — see BUTTOCKS

rumple *vb* **1** to create (as by crushing) an irregular mass of creases in ⟨The guest *rumpled* the antique bedspread by lying down on it.⟩ — see CRUMPLE 1
2 to develop creases or folds ⟨The linen skirt *rumpled* as soon as she started wearing it.⟩ — see WRINKLE 1
3 to undo the proper order or arrangement of ⟨The aunt would invariably *rumple* the little boy's hair whenever she came to visit.⟩ — see DISORDER

rumpled *adj* lacking in order, neatness, and often cleanliness ⟨a *rumpled* room that suited its teenage occupant just fine⟩ — see MESSY

rumpus *n* a state of noisy, confused activity ⟨The kids made such a *rumpus* that they woke up everyone else in the house.⟩ — see COMMOTION

run *n* **1** a prevailing or general movement or inclination ⟨The company's stock has remained consistent with the overall *run* of the market.⟩ — see TREND 1
2 *chiefly Midland* a natural body of running water smaller than a river ⟨a *run* full of catfish⟩ — see CREEK 1
3 the period during which something exists, lasts, or is in progress ⟨The actor has been assigned the part for the *run* of the show.⟩ — see DURATION 1
4 the right to act or move freely ⟨The owner gave the dogs the *run* of the place.⟩ — see FREEDOM 2
5 runs *pl* abnormally frequent intestinal evacuations with more or less fluid stools ⟨a bad case of the *runs*⟩ — see DIARRHEA

run *vb* **1** to go at a pace faster than a walk ⟨We *ran* all the way to the bus stop, but still missed the bus.⟩
synonyms dash, gallop, jog, sprint, trip, trot
related words bound, canter, leap, lope, skip, spring; barrel, belt, blast, blaze, blow, bolt, bowl, breeze, bustle, buzz, careen, course, foot (it), hasten, hie, hoof (it), hotfoot (it), hump, hurl, hurry, hurtle, hustle, jet, leg (it), pelt, race, ram, rip, rocket, rush, rustle, shoot, speed, tear, whirl, whisk, zip, zoom; scoot, scurry, scuttle, step (along)
near antonyms saunter, shamble, shuffle, stroll; crawl, creep, dally, dawdle, dillydally, drag, lag, linger, loiter, poke, tarry; lumber, plod, trudge; hobble, limp
2 to hasten away from something dangerous or frightening ⟨Rather than *run* from a black bear, it's better to hold your ground and make lots of noise.⟩
synonyms bolt, break, flee, fly, retreat, run away, run off
related words abscond, clear out, decamp, elope, escape, get (away), get out, light out, make off, scram, skip (out), skirr
phrases beat a retreat, beat it, make tracks, turn tail
near antonyms beard, brave, confront, dare, defy, face; abide, dwell, hang around, linger, remain, stay, stick around, tarry
3 to be positioned along a certain course or in a certain direction ⟨The road *runs* along the river for a while.⟩
synonyms bear, extend, go, head, lead, lie
related words cross, cut, pass; course, follow, span, traverse
4 to occur within a continuous range of variation ⟨The electric bill *runs* between 30 and 50 dollars a month.⟩
synonyms go, range, vary
related words alternate, fluctuate, move, shift; change, mutate; extend, reach, stretch, sweep
5 to move in a stream ⟨water *running* down the window⟩ — see FLOW 1
6 to proceed or move quickly ⟨*Run* and get the nurse!⟩ — see HURRY 2
7 to show a liking or proneness (for something) ⟨This tree *runs* to quite tart fruit.⟩ — see LEAN 2
8 to urge, push, or force onward ⟨They *ran* the horses hard in order to get to the ranch quickly.⟩ — see DRIVE 1
9 to control the mechanical operation of ⟨I know how to *run* that machine.⟩ — see OPERATE 1
10 to eventually have as a state or quality ⟨The poor woman *ran* herself ragged trying to get everything done.⟩ — see BECOME
11 to go from a solid to a liquid state ⟨The icing on the cake began to *run*.⟩ — see LIQUEFY
12 to look after and make decisions about ⟨learning to *run* the family business⟩ — see CONDUCT 1

13 to cause to function ⟨In olden days mills were *run* by flowing water.⟩ — see ACTIVATE

14 to have a price of ⟨That sort of computer *runs* at least several hundred dollars.⟩ — see COST

15 to come or be together as friends ⟨They've been *running* with a bad crowd lately.⟩ — see ASSOCIATE 1

16 to go after or on the track of ⟨If that dog continues to *run* cars, he's going to get seriously hurt.⟩ — see FOLLOW 2

run away *vb* **1** to get free from a dangerous or confining situation ⟨*ran away* and joined the circus⟩ — see ESCAPE 1

2 to hasten away from something dangerous or frightening ⟨The child *runs away* from large dogs.⟩ — see RUN 2

run–down *adj* **1** showing signs of advanced wear and tear and neglect ⟨a *run-down* old house that really should be torn down⟩ — see SHABBY 1

2 temporarily suffering from a disorder of the body ⟨I'm afraid I'll be staying home today as I'm feeling *run-down*.⟩ — see SICK 1

run down *vb* **1** to come upon after searching, study, or effort ⟨I finally *ran down* the answer after hours of research.⟩ — see FIND 1

2 to express scornfully one's low opinion of ⟨Constantly *running down* the city's cultural life won't do anything to improve it.⟩ — see DECRY 1

run–in *n* a brief clash between enemies or rivals ⟨had a *run-in* with her old nemesis⟩ — see ENCOUNTER

runner *n* one that carries a message or does an errand ⟨The king sent a *runner* to tell them that all was ready for the feast.⟩ — see MESSENGER

running *adj* **1** being in effective operation ⟨The car has been *running* for almost an entire day.⟩ — see ACTIVE 1

2 going on and on without any interruptions ⟨a *running* struggle just to make ends meet⟩ — see CONTINUOUS

running *n* the act or activity of looking after and making decisions about something ⟨left the *running* of the corporation to his subordinates⟩ — see CONDUCT 1

runny *adj* having an overly soft liquid consistency ⟨*runny* scrambled eggs⟩

  synonyms soupy, watery

  related words flowing, fluent, fluid, liquefied; dilute, diluted, thin, thinned, watered-down, weak, weakened; sloshy, slushy, soggy, waterlogged, wet

  near antonyms ropy (*also* ropey), syrupy, viscid, viscous; creamy, heavy, thick, thickened, thickish; gelatinous, gluey, glutinous, gooey, gummy, sticky

run off *vb* **1** to drive or force out ⟨The dog often *ran off* cats and other animals that had intruded upon his owner's property.⟩ — see EJECT 1

2 to get free from a dangerous or confining situation ⟨took all the money and *ran off*⟩ — see ESCAPE 1

3 to hasten away from something dangerous or frightening ⟨The mouse *ran off* as soon as it saw us.⟩ — see RUN 2

run–of–the–mill *adj* being of the type that is encountered in the normal course of events ⟨just another *run-of-the-mill* suburb with its shopping malls and fast-food restaurants⟩ — see ORDINARY 1

run on *vb* **1** to engage in casual or rambling conversation ⟨We were just *running on* about how neither of us has aged a bit after all these years.⟩ — see CHAT 1

2 to remain indefinitely in existence or in the same state ⟨Allow the savings account to *run on* for now.⟩ — see CONTINUE 1

3 to talk at length without sticking to a topic or getting to a point ⟨tended to *run on* and never get the message across⟩ — see RAMBLE 1

run over *vb* to do over and over so as to become skilled ⟨Let's *run over* this dance number one more time.⟩ — see PRACTICE

runt *n* a living thing much smaller than others of its kind ⟨One kitten was definitely the *runt*, weighing only six ounces at birth.⟩ — see DWARF 1

run through *vb* **1** to penetrate or hold (something) with a pointed object ⟨The dastardly villain *ran* him *through* with a sword.⟩ — see IMPALE

2 to use up carelessly ⟨How did you manage to *run through* $300 in one day?⟩ — see WASTE 1

rural *adj* of, relating to, associated with, or typical of open areas with few buildings or people ⟨grew up in a *rural* community where more than half the people were farmers⟩ ⟨a painter noted for his *rural* landscapes⟩

  synonyms bucolic, country, pastoral, rustic (*also* rustical)

  related words backwoods, backwoodsy, countrified (*also* countryfied), provincial; agrarian, agricultural; nonurban, semirural

  near antonyms citified, urbanized; metropolitan, municipal; nonagricultural, nonfarm

  antonyms urban

rush *n* **1** excited and often showy or disorderly speed ⟨What's the reason for all this *rush*?⟩ — see HURRY 1

2 the act or action of setting upon with force or violence ⟨The regiment recaptured the hill with a single *rush*.⟩ — see ATTACK 1

rush *vb* **1** to cause to move or proceed fast or faster ⟨I wouldn't make so many mistakes if you'd stop *rushing* me.⟩ — see HURRY 1

2 to flow out in great quantities or with force ⟨In the spring the stream's *rushing* waters make crossing treacherous.⟩ — see GUSH 1

3 to proceed or move quickly ⟨*Rushing* is a good way to slip and fall.⟩ — see HURRY 2

4 to take sudden, violent action against ⟨One goat suddenly *rushed* the other and knocked it down.⟩ — see ATTACK 1

rushed *adj* acting or done with excessive or careless speed ⟨a *rushed* job with a number of errors⟩ — see HASTY 1

rustic *n* an awkward or simple person especially from a small town or the country ⟨a *rustic* who was awed by the prices that city dwellers had to pay⟩ — see HICK

rustic *also* **rustical** *adj* **1** lacking social grace and assurance ⟨*rustic* visitors who weren't quite sure what to say⟩ — see AWKWARD 1

2 of, relating to, associated with, or typical of open areas with few buildings or people ⟨a *rustic* area that has a refreshing lack of billboards and shopping malls⟩ — see RURAL

rustle *vb* **1** to feed on grass or herbs ⟨Just take the steer out to pasture and let it *rustle* for itself.⟩ — see ¹GRAZE

2 to proceed or move quickly ⟨*rustled* around enthusiastically on the morning of the big trip⟩ — see HURRY 2

3 to make small sounds usually by rubbing or moving ⟨My pet peeve is candy wrappers *rustling* during a movie.⟩ — see CRINKLE 1

rustler *n* an ambitious person who eagerly goes after what is desired ⟨The job requires a *rustler* who doesn't always need to be told what to do.⟩ — see GO-GETTER

rut *n* an established and often automatic or monotonous series of actions followed when engaging in some activity ⟨I've fallen into a *rut*, watching television and then going to bed every night.⟩ — see ROUTINE 1

ruthless *adj* having or showing a lack of sympathy or tender feelings ⟨an office supervisor with a *ruthless* disregard for others' feelings⟩ — see HARD 1

RV *n* a motor vehicle that is specially equipped for living while traveling ⟨The *RV* parked in the driveway is a sure sign that their relatives from Florida have arrived.⟩ — see CAMPER

S

sable *adj* having the color of soot or coal ⟨a beautiful *sable* cat⟩ — see BLACK 1

saccharine *adj* appealing to the emotions in an obvious and tiresome way ⟨The movie was funny, but it had a *saccharine* ending in which everyone lives happily ever after.⟩ — see CORNY

sacerdotal *adj* of, relating to, or characteristic of the clergy ⟨*sacerdotal* garments such as a cassock⟩ — see CLERICAL

sack *n* **1** a container made of a flexible material (as paper or plastic) ⟨asked the bagger to put all the loaves of bread in the same *sack*⟩ — see BAG 1
2 a place set aside for sleeping ⟨I think I'm ready to hit the *sack*.⟩ — see BED 1

¹sack *vb* to let go from office, service, or employment ⟨He was *sacked* for showing up late once too often.⟩ — see DISMISS 1

²sack *vb* to search through with the intent of committing robbery ⟨Thieves *sacked* the house in search of the diamond necklace.⟩ — see RANSACK 1

sacred *adj* **1** not to be violated, criticized, or tampered with ⟨the *sacred* trust that exists between elected officials and the electorate⟩
synonyms hallowed, holy, inviolable, sacrosanct, unassailable, untouchable
related words inviolate, pure; privileged, protected, secure, shielded; exempt, immune
near antonyms blasphemous, irreverent, profane, sacrilegious
2 of, relating to, or being God ⟨a *sacred* name that must not be uttered in vain⟩ — see HOLY 3
3 of, relating to, or used in the practice or worship services of a religion ⟨a *sacred* chalice⟩ — see RELIGIOUS 1
4 set apart or worthy of veneration by association with God ⟨the *sacred* bones of a saint⟩ — see HOLY 2
5 deserving honor and respect especially by reason of age ⟨The alumni procession at graduation is one of the college's most *sacred* traditions, dating back over a hundred years.⟩ — see VENERABLE 1

sacrifice *n* something offered to a god ⟨The herders selected their best lamb as a *sacrifice* in order to receive blessings from their god.⟩
synonyms immolation, offering, victim
related words libation, propitiation; holocaust; contribution, donation

sacrifice *vb* to give up as an offering to a god ⟨an ancient ritual that involved *sacrificing* an animal⟩
synonyms immolate, offer
related words consecrate, dedicate, devote; give, hand over, surrender, yield

sacrilege *n* an act of great disrespect shown to God or to sacred ideas, people, or things ⟨Spitting on the temple floor would be a great *sacrilege*.⟩ — see BLASPHEMY

sacrilegious *adj* not showing proper reverence for the holy or sacred ⟨a *sacrilegious*, obscene joke⟩ — see IRREVERENT

sacristy *n* a room in a church building for sacred furnishings (as vestments) ⟨Our choir robes were stored in the *sacristy*.⟩
synonyms vestry
related words cloakroom

sacrosanct *adj* **1** not to be violated, criticized, or tampered with ⟨The teacher's book of grades is *sacrosanct*, and someone could be expelled for changing anything in it.⟩ — see SACRED 1

2 set apart or worthy of veneration by association with God ⟨Believers eventually built a shrine on the *sacrosanct* spot where the miracle was thought to have taken place.⟩ — see HOLY 2

sad *adj* **1** feeling unhappiness ⟨Movies in which the hero dies always make us feel *sad*.⟩
synonyms bad, blue, brokenhearted, crestfallen, dejected, depressed, despondent, disconsolate, doleful, down, downcast, downhearted, droopy, forlorn, gloomy, glum, hangdog, heartbroken, heartsick, heartsore, inconsolable, joyless, low, low-spirited, melancholy, miserable, mournful, saddened, sorrowful, sorry, unhappy, woebegone, woeful, wretched
related words aggrieved, distressed, troubled, uneasy, upset, worried; despairing, hopeless, sunk; disappointed, discouraged, disheartened, dispirited; suicidal; dolorous, lachrymose, lugubrious, plaintive, tearful; regretful, rueful; anguished, grieving, wailing, weeping; black, bleak, cheerless, comfortless, dark, darkening, depressing, desolate, dismal, dreary, elegiac (*also* elegiacal), funereal, gray (*also* grey), morbid, morose, saturnine, somber (*or* sombre), sullen
near antonyms ecstatic, elated, enraptured, entranced, euphoric, exhilarated, exuberant, exultant, overjoyed, rapturous, rhapsodic (*also* rhapsodical); blithe, blithesome, jocose, jocular, jocund, jolly, jovial, lightsome, merry, mirthful; excited, thrilled; hopeful, optimistic, rosy, sanguine; encouraged, heartened; animated, bouncing, energetic, frisky, jaunty, lively, peppy, perky, spirited, sprightly, springy, vital, vivacious, zippy; content, gratified, pleased, satisfied; beaming, grinning, laughing, smiling
antonyms blissful, buoyant, buoyed, cheerful, cheery, chipper, delighted, glad, gladdened, gladsome, gleeful, happy, joyful, joyous, jubilant, sunny, upbeat
2 causing unhappiness ⟨The *sad* news about our uncle's death made my father cry.⟩
synonyms depressing, dismal, dreary, heartbreaking, heartrending, melancholy, mournful, pathetic, saddening, sorry, tearful, teary
related words deplorable, distressful, grievous, lamentable, unfortunate, woeful; discomforting, discomposing, disquieting, distressing, disturbing, perturbing; discouraging, disheartening, dispiriting
near antonyms heartening, heartwarming, inspiring, stimulating, stirring, uplifting; agreeable, delightful, enjoyable, pleasant, pleasing, pleasurable, satisfying, welcome; exhilarating, thrilling
antonyms cheering, cheery, glad, happy
3 deserving pitying scorn (as for inadequacy) ⟨That's a pretty *sad*-looking birthday cake.⟩ — see PITIFUL 1

sadden *vb* to make sad ⟨The arrival of winter always *saddens* me.⟩ — see DEPRESS 1

saddened *adj* feeling unhappiness ⟨We were all *saddened* when our doctor retired.⟩ — see SAD 1

saddening *adj* causing unhappiness ⟨the *saddening* discovery that something is threatening the birds in the area⟩ — see SAD 2

saddle *vb* to place a weight or burden on ⟨It seemed as though her supervisor had once again *saddled* her with a truly impossible task.⟩ — see LOAD 1

sadism *n* disposition to willfully inflict pain and suffering on others ⟨It isn't *sadism* when Kitty plays with her prey, just her nature.⟩ — see CRUELTY

sadistic *adj* having or showing the desire to inflict severe pain and suffering on others 〈called the teacher *sadistic* for assigning another project〉 — see CRUEL 1

sadly *adv* with feelings of bitterness or grief 〈She *sadly* said goodbye.〉 — see HARD 2

sadness *n* a state or spell of low spirits 〈She was filled with *sadness* at the thought of having to leave her family.〉

synonyms blues, dejection, depression, desolation, despond, despondency, disconsolateness, dispiritedness, doldrums, dolefulness, downheartedness, dreariness, dumps, forlornness, gloom, gloominess, heartsickness, joylessness, melancholy, mopes, oppression, unhappiness

related words melancholia, self-pity; anguish, dolor, grief, mourning, somberness, sorrow, woefulness; agony, distress, pain; misery, woe, wretchedness; discouragement, disheartenment; moodiness; despair, desperation, hopelessness; dismalness, morbidness, moroseness

near antonyms gaiety (*also* gayety), glee, gleefulness, humor, jollity, joviality, lightheartedness, merriment, mirth, mirthfulness; cheer, cheerfulness, cheeriness, hopefulness, optimism, sunniness; contentedness, contentment, satisfaction; delight, gratification

antonyms bliss, blissfulness, ecstasy, elation, euphoria, exhilaration, exuberance, exultation, felicity, gladness, happiness, joy, joyfulness, joyousness, jubilation, rapture, rapturousness

safe *adj* **1** not exposed to the threat of loss or injury 〈The minute the rain started, we looked for a place where we would be *safe* from a drenching downpour.〉

synonyms all right, alright, secure

related words hale, healthy, intact, sound, well, whole; unharmed, unhurt, uninjured, unscathed

near antonyms damaged, harmed, hurt, injured, scathed, wounded

antonyms endangered, exposed, imperiled (*or* imperilled), insecure, liable, open, subject (to), susceptible, threatened, unsafe, violable, vulnerable

2 providing safety 〈We tried to find a *safe* place to hide our valuables while we went swimming.〉

synonyms secure, snug

related words guarding, protecting, safeguarding, sheltering, shielding; defended, guarded, protected, sheltered, shielded; impregnable, inviolable, invulnerable, unassailable, unconquerable

near antonyms menacing, perilous, threatening; undefended, unguarded, unprotected, vulnerable; precarious, treacherous, uncertain

antonyms dangerous, hazardous, insecure, risky, unsafe

3 having or showing a close attentiveness to avoiding danger or trouble 〈rewarded *safe* drivers with lower insurance rates〉 — see CAREFUL 1

4 not causing or being capable of causing injury or hurt 〈That pain reliever is *safe* for most people to take.〉 — see HARMLESS

5 worthy of one's trust 〈She always offers *safe* advice.〉 — see DEPENDABLE

safe *n* a specially reinforced container to keep valuables safe 〈The hotel recommended that we keep all our valuables in its *safe* during our stay.〉

synonyms coffer, safe-deposit box, strongbox

related words vault; locker, storeroom, treasury; box, caddy, case, casket, chest, footlocker, locker, trunk

safe–deposit box *n* a specially reinforced container to keep valuables safe 〈We kept the deed to the house in a *safe-deposit box* at the bank.〉 — see SAFE

safeguard *n* means or method of defending 〈With these *safeguards* in place, no one should be able to break into our computers.〉 — see DEFENSE 1

safeguard *vb* to drive danger or attack away from 〈Sheep-

dogs *safeguard* the flock from attacks by wolves.〉 — see DEFEND 1

safekeeping *n* responsibility for the safety and well-being of someone or something 〈While they were away on vacation, the family entrusted their dog into their neighbor's *safekeeping*.〉 — see CUSTODY

safeness *n* the state of not being exposed to danger 〈The *safeness* of her children was something that she worried about constantly.〉 — see SAFETY 1

safety *n* **1** the state of not being exposed to danger 〈We were lucky to make it to *safety* just as the lions broke loose from their cage at the zoo.〉

synonyms protection, safeness, security

related words aegis (*also* egis), cover, defense, guardianship, ward; guard, safeguard, screen, shield; asylum, harbor, haven, refuge, retreat, shelter; impregnability, impregnableness, invincibility, invincibleness, inviolability, inviolableness, invulnerability, invulnerableness

near antonyms hazard, risk, threat; instability, precariousness; exposure, liability, openness, violability, vulnerability, vulnerableness; susceptibility, susceptibleness

antonyms danger, distress, endangerment, imperilment, jeopardy, peril, trouble

2 a protective device (as on a weapon) to prevent accidental operation 〈The gun couldn't be fired as long as the *safety* was on.〉

synonyms guard

related words lock; defense, protection, safeguard, shield

sag *vb* **1** to be limp from lack of water or vigor 〈The plant's leaves were *sagging* feebly in the intense heat.〉 — see DROOP 1

2 to decline gradually from a standard level 〈Sales figures have *sagged* slightly over the past six months.〉 — see SLIP 1

3 to lose bodily strength or vigor 〈After a whole day of working in the hot sun, he began to *sag*.〉 — see WEAKEN 2

sag *n* the extent to which something hangs or dips below a straight line 〈If there's too much *sag* in the rod, the curtains will drag on the floor.〉

synonyms droop, hang, slack, slackness

related words floppiness, laxity, laxness, limpness, looseness

near antonyms rigidity, rigidness, tautness, tenseness, tension, tightness

sagacious *adj* having or showing deep understanding and intelligent application of knowledge 〈a *sagacious* critique of the current social climate in our nation〉 — see WISE 1

sagaciousness *n* the ability to understand inner qualities or relationships 〈a woman of such down-to-earth *sagaciousness* that she ought to be writing an advice column for the newspaper〉 — see WISDOM 1

sagacity *n* the ability to understand inner qualities or relationships 〈a novelist of surprising *sagacity* considering his youthfulness〉 — see WISDOM 1

sage *adj* having or showing deep understanding and intelligent application of knowledge 〈a *sage* suggestion that they think long and hard before deciding to marry at such a young age〉 — see WISE 1

sage *n* a person of deep wisdom or learning 〈The young prince made a pilgrimage to the *sage*, hoping to learn the meaning of life.〉

synonyms savant, scholar

related words seer, wise man; brain, egghead, genius, highbrow, intellect, intellectual, thinker, whiz, wizard; rabbi; master, mentor, teacher

near antonyms blockhead, dodo, dolt, dope, dumbbell,

dummy, dunce, fool, goon, half-wit, idiot, ignoramus, imbecile, know-nothing, moron, nincompoop, ninny, nitwit, numskull (*or* numbskull), pinhead, simpleton

sageness *n* the ability to understand inner qualities or relationships ⟨Her father has always shown an unpretentious *sageness* about the practicalities of life.⟩ — see WISDOM 1

sagging *adj* bending downward or forward ⟨*sagging* branches that were weighted down with snow⟩ — see NODDING

sail *n* a journey over water in a vessel ⟨We went for a brief *sail* on the bay to relax.⟩
  synonyms crossing, cruise, passage, voyage

sail *vb* **1** to travel on water in a vessel ⟨I can't *sail* when there's any breeze at all because I get seasick easily.⟩
  synonyms boat, cruise, ferry, navigate, voyage
  related words canoe, kayak, yacht; coast
  phrases make sail, take ship
  2 to move or proceed smoothly and readily ⟨*sailed* through the latest assignment⟩ — see FLOW 2
  3 to rest or move along the surface of a liquid or in the air ⟨A leaf *sailed* by, carried by the breeze.⟩ — see FLOAT 1

sailboat *n* a boat equipped with one or more sails ⟨We were stuck in the *sailboat* for an hour until the wind came up and we could move again.⟩
  synonyms bark, dinghy, windjammer
  related words brigantine, caravel, catamaran, catboat, clipper, corvette, cutter, frigate, galleon, galley, junk, keelboat, ketch, knockabout, lugger, outrigger, schooner, ship, sloop, square-rigger, xebec, yacht, yawl; bottom, craft, vessel

sailor *n* one who operates or navigates a seagoing vessel ⟨The *sailors* were glad to be arriving in port after their long voyage.⟩
  synonyms gob, hearty, jack, jack-tar, mariner, navigator, salt, sea dog, seafarer, seaman, swab, tar
  related words crewman, deckhand, shipmate; ablebodied seaman, able seaman, lubber

sainted *adj* showing a devotion to God and to a life of virtue ⟨Renowned as a theologian as well as for his work as a medical missionary in Africa, Dr. Albert Schweitzer was widely regarded as one of the most *sainted* individuals of his time.⟩ — see HOLY 1

sainthood *n* the quality or state of being spiritually pure or virtuous ⟨always admired the *sainthood* of my kind and patient grandmother⟩ — see HOLINESS

saintliness *n* the quality or state of being spiritually pure or virtuous ⟨True *saintliness* requires utter selflessness and devotion to others.⟩ — see HOLINESS

saintly *adj* showing a devotion to God and to a life of virtue ⟨a *saintly* man who devoted his life to caring for the ill⟩ — see HOLY 1

saintship *n* the quality or state of being spiritually pure or virtuous ⟨a man who always maintained that his mother's *saintship* was beyond question⟩ — see HOLINESS

salable *or* **saleable** *adj* **1** fit or likely to be sold especially on a large scale ⟨an item that would be too expensive to produce, and attractive to too few people, to ever be considered a *salable* commodity⟩ — see COMMERCIAL
  2 fit to be offered for sale ⟨The car has to be put in better condition before it will be at all *salable*.⟩ — see MARKETABLE 1

salary *n* the money paid regularly to a person for labor or services ⟨signed a contract for a new job with a *salary* of $60,000 per year⟩ — see WAGE

sale *n* the transfer of ownership of something from one person to another for a price ⟨My neighbor tried to make a *sale*, but no one was interested in buying his old car.⟩
  synonyms deal, trade, transaction
  related words auction, haggle, horse-trading, negotiation; bargain, buy, steal; purchase; clearance, closeout, fire sale; fair; rummage sale

salesclerk *n* a person employed to sell goods or services especially in a store ⟨The *salesclerk* told us where to find the jewelry department.⟩ — see SALESPERSON

salesman *n* a person employed to sell goods or services especially in a store ⟨A furniture *salesman* followed us around the whole time we looked for a new couch.⟩ — see SALESPERSON

salesperson *n* a person employed to sell goods or services especially in a store ⟨We asked the *salesperson* to see if there were any shoes in our size in the stockroom.⟩
  synonyms clerk, salesclerk, salesman
  related words salespeople; salesgirl, saleslady, saleswoman, shopgirl; pitchman, pitchwoman; floorwalker

saline *adj* of, relating to, or containing salt ⟨Tears are *saline*.⟩ — see SALTY 1

salinity *n* the quality or state of being salty ⟨Distilling will eliminate the *salinity* of seawater.⟩ — see SALTINESS

saliva *n* the fluid that is secreted into the mouth by certain glands ⟨Our mouths filled with *saliva* when we smelled the delicious dinner.⟩
  synonyms drool, slaver, slobber, spit, spittle
  related words foam, froth; expectoration, salivation, sputum

salivate *vb* to let saliva or some other substance flow from the mouth ⟨The dog *salivated* at the sight of the raw meat.⟩ — see DROOL 1

sally *n* **1** a short trip for pleasure ⟨a morning *sally* out to see the historic monuments around the city⟩ — see EXCURSION 1
  2 something said or done to cause laughter ⟨The final *sally* made her laugh, and that ended the argument.⟩ — see JOKE 1

sally (forth) *vb* to leave a place often for another ⟨He eagerly *sallied forth* from his small town to seek a new life in the bustling city.⟩ — see GO 2

salon *n* **1** a building or part of a building in which objects of interest are displayed ⟨At its headquarters the company maintains a fashionable *salon* filled with works of modern art.⟩ — see MUSEUM
  2 a building, room, or suite of rooms occupied by a service business ⟨a hair *salon*⟩ — see PLACE 2

saloon *n* a place of business where alcoholic beverages are sold to be consumed on the premises ⟨cowboys drinking in the *saloon* after their work was done for the day⟩ — see BARROOM

salt *adj* of, relating to, or containing salt ⟨The oceans are *salt* water.⟩ — see SALTY 1

salt *n* one who operates or navigates a seagoing vessel ⟨an old *salt* who taught me everything I know about sailing and the sea⟩ — see SAILOR

salt *vb* to scatter or set here and there among other things ⟨The old sailor *salted* his tale of the voyage with crude anecdotes and rough language.⟩ — see THREAD 1

salt away *vb* to put (something of future use or value) in a safe or secret place ⟨*salted away* some jewels in a safe-deposit box for the lean times⟩ — see HOARD

saltiness *n* the quality or state of being salty ⟨the *saltiness* of the pretzels⟩
  synonyms brininess, salinity, saltness
  near antonyms freshness, purity; sweetness

saltness *n* the quality or state of being salty ⟨The excessive *saltness* of the soup made it inedible.⟩ — see SALTINESS

salty *adj* **1** of, relating to, or containing salt ⟨*Salty* sea water is safe to swim in, but you really shouldn't swallow it.⟩

  synonyms brackish, briny, saline, salt

  related words hard

  near antonyms sweet; clear, pure; freshwater

  antonyms nonsaline

  2 hinting at or intended to call to mind matters regarded as indecent ⟨*salty* language that earned the movie an R rating⟩ — see SUGGESTIVE 1

  3 sharp and pleasantly stimulating to the mind or senses ⟨a *salty* biography of a provocative personality⟩ — see PIQUANT

salubrious *adj* beneficial to the health of body or mind ⟨Fresh air and exercise are always *salubrious*.⟩ — see HEALTHFUL

salutary *adj* **1** promoting or contributing to personal or social well-being ⟨The low interest rates should have a *salutary* effect on business.⟩ — see BENEFICIAL

  2 beneficial to the health of body or mind ⟨increasing scientific evidence that dark chocolate is quite *salutary*⟩ — see HEALTHFUL

salutation *n* **1** a formal expression of praise ⟨The speaker introduced the evening's honored guest with a lavish *salutation*.⟩ — see ENCOMIUM

  2 an expression of goodwill upon meeting ⟨He began the discussion with a gracious *salutation* to the distinguished assembly.⟩ — see HELLO

salute *n* an expression of goodwill upon meeting ⟨offered a cheery *salute* as they passed the soldiers on the street⟩ — see HELLO

salute *vb* to declare enthusiastic approval of ⟨I *salute* the idea of healthier lunch options for our students.⟩ — see ACCLAIM

salvation *n* the saving from danger or evil ⟨We hoped that rain would bring *salvation* from the heat wave.⟩

  synonyms deliverance, rescue

  related words ransom, recovery, redemption; extrication; defense, guard, protection, safeguard, safeguarding, security; conservation, guardianship, preservation, safekeeping

salvo *n* a rapid or overwhelming outpouring of many things at once ⟨He attacked the manager with a *salvo* of complaints before she even managed to say "hello."⟩ — see BARRAGE

same *adj* **1** resembling another in every respect ⟨I bought the *same* shirt online for five dollars less.⟩

  synonyms coequal, duplicate, equal, even, identical, indistinguishable

  related words akin, alike, analogous, comparable, coordinate, correspondent, corresponding, equivalent, like, matching, parallel, similar, such, suchlike, synonymous, tantamount

  near antonyms divers, miscellaneous, sundry, varied

  antonyms different, disparate, dissimilar, distant, distinct, distinctive, distinguishable, diverse, other, unalike, unlike

  2 being one and not another ⟨That's the *same* guy I saw down at the beach yesterday.⟩

  synonyms identical, selfsame, very

  near antonyms disparate, dissimilar, distinct, distinctive, distinguishable, diverse, unalike, unlike, varied

  antonyms another, different, other

sameness *n* **1** a tedious lack of variety ⟨The endless *sameness* of what we keep having for dinner is starting to bore me.⟩ — see MONOTONY

  2 the state of being exactly alike ⟨The *sameness* of the two essays made the teacher immediately suspect plagiarism.⟩ — see IDENTITY 1

3 the state or fact of being exactly the same in number, amount, status, or quality ⟨The striking *sameness* of the results for both experiments suggests that this is a real discovery.⟩ — see EQUIVALENCE

sample *vb* to put (something) to a test ⟨I *sampled* the soup to see if it tasted good.⟩ — see TRY (OUT)

sample *n* **1** a number of things selected from a group to stand for the whole ⟨Based on a *sample* of the menu items, we decided that this was the best restaurant in town.⟩

  synonyms cross section, selection, slice

  related words case, example, exemplar, exemplification, illustration, instance, representative, specimen; archetype, classic, paradigm, prototype; microcosm

  2 one of a group or collection that shows what the whole is like ⟨This vase is a *sample* of the high-quality glassware that the glassblowers can produce.⟩ — see EXAMPLE

sanctification *n* **1** the act of making something holy through religious ritual ⟨The sacred site required another *sanctification* after it had been defiled by the invaders.⟩ — see CONSECRATION

  2 the act or fact of freeing from sin or moral guilt ⟨preached about a way of life that led to *sanctification*⟩ — see PURIFICATION

sanctified *adj* set apart or worthy of veneration by association with God ⟨a site believed by the faithful to be *sanctified*⟩ — see HOLY 2

sanctify *vb* **1** to free from moral guilt or blemish especially ceremonially ⟨received the sacrament of penance, whereby they were *sanctified* and restored to divine grace⟩ — see PURIFY 1

  2 to make holy through prayers or ritual ⟨a ceremony to *sanctify* the site⟩ — see BLESS 1

sanction *n* the approval by someone in authority for the doing of something ⟨You cannot make a student video without your faculty advisor's *sanction* of its subject matter prior to shooting.⟩ — see PERMISSION

sanction *vb* to give official acceptance of as satisfactory ⟨The administration will *sanction* almost any field trip with educational value.⟩ — see APPROVE

sanctioned *adj* ordered or allowed by those in authority ⟨a *sanctioned* use of company property⟩ — see OFFICIAL

sanctity *n* the quality or state of being spiritually pure or virtuous ⟨The *sanctity* of the elderly cleric shone through in his every word and gesture.⟩ — see HOLINESS

sanctuary *n* **1** a place that is considered sacred (as within a religion) ⟨By law, anyone who sought refuge in a religious *sanctuary* was safe from arrest by the civil authorities.⟩ — see SHRINE

  2 something (as a building) that offers cover from the weather or protection from danger ⟨The marshland has been set aside as a *sanctuary* for shorebirds along that section of the coast.⟩ — see SHELTER

sanctum *n* **1** a place that is considered sacred (as within a religion) ⟨The city of Jerusalem is an important *sanctum* for Christians, Jews, and Muslims alike.⟩ — see SHRINE

  2 something (as a building) that offers cover from the weather or protection from danger ⟨John used the cabin in the woods as a *sanctum* from the commotion and interference of his family.⟩ — see SHELTER

sand *vb* to make smooth by friction ⟨We painstakingly *sanded* down the wooden floors of the old house.⟩ — see GRIND 1

sand *n*, *often* **sands** *pl* the usually sandy or gravelly land bordering a body of water ⟨We went for a moonlight walk on the *sands*.⟩ — see BEACH

sandwich *vb* to fit (people or things) into a tight space ⟨We *sandwiched* six kids into the tent somehow.⟩ — see CROWD 1

sandy *adj* of a pale yellow or yellowish brown color ⟨The child with *sandy* hair really stood out among the brunettes.⟩ — see BLOND

sane *adj* having full use of one's mind and control over one's actions ⟨The court ruled that the woman was indeed *sane* when she made out her will.⟩
synonyms balanced, clearheaded, lucid, normal, right, stable
related words analytic (*or* analytical), clear, coherent, logical, rational, reasonable; even-keeled, judicious, levelheaded, sensible, wise; healthy, sound, unneurotic; well-adjusted, well-balanced
near antonyms daft, wacky (*also* whacky); foolish, senseless, witless; irrational, unreasonable; distracted, distraught, frantic, frenzied; fixated, obsessed
antonyms insane, unsound

saneness *n* the normal or healthy condition of the mental abilities ⟨Our teacher recommended getting a good night's sleep before finals if only to maintain our *saneness*.⟩ — see MIND 2

sanguinary *adj* eager for or marked by the shedding of blood, extreme violence, or killing ⟨a movie so *sanguinary* that I covered my eyes during at least half of it⟩ — see BLOODTHIRSTY

sanguine *adj* **1** eager for or marked by the shedding of blood, extreme violence, or killing ⟨The Civil War remains America's most *sanguine* conflict.⟩ — see BLOODTHIRSTY
2 having a healthy reddish skin tone ⟨A baby with a *sanguine* complexion is more likely to leave the hospital early than a sickly-looking one.⟩ — see RUDDY
3 having or showing a mind free from doubt ⟨I'm reasonably *sanguine* about the adoption of the latest proposal.⟩ — see CERTAIN 2

sanguinity *n* an inclination to believe in the most favorable outcome ⟨Pollyanna had so great a tendency to look for the good in everyone and everything that her name has become a synonym for someone of irrepressible *sanguinity*.⟩ — see OPTIMISM

sanitary *adj* free from filth, infection, or dangers to health ⟨The nurse made sure that everything in the room was *sanitary* so that the baby wouldn't get sick.⟩
synonyms aseptic, germfree, hygienic, sterile
related words germproof; antibacterial, antibiotic, germicidal, microbicidal; clean, immaculate, pristine, spick-and-span (*or* spic-and-span), spotless, stainless, unsoiled, unstained, unsullied; pure, taintless, undefiled, unpolluted, untainted; bleached, cleansed, purified, scrubbed, washed, whitened
near antonyms infectious, pathogenic, poisonous, sickening, toxic; bedraggled, besmirched, dingy, dirty, dusty, filthy, foul, grimy, grubby, grungy, mucky, muddy, nasty, smirched, soiled, sordid, stained, sullied, unclean, uncleanly, unwashed; defiled, polluted, tainted, unsterilized
antonyms germy, insanitary, unhygienic, unsanitary, unsterile

sanitary landfill *n* a place where discarded materials (as trash) are dumped ⟨Even after many years in *sanitary landfills*, plastic bags have proven to be resistant to decomposition.⟩ — see DUMP 1

sanity *n* the normal or healthy condition of the mental abilities ⟨I meditate daily for my *sanity*.⟩ — see MIND 2

sans *prep* not having ⟨Anyone *sans* shirt will not be allowed in the restaurant.⟩ — see WITHOUT 1

sap *n* **1** active strength of body or mind ⟨a child full of *sap* and vivacity⟩ — see VIGOR 1
2 one who is easily deceived or cheated ⟨Some poor *sap* would probably fall for that telephone scam.⟩ — see ¹DUPE

3 the condition of being sound in body ⟨I may no longer have the *sap* of youth, but I do have the sapience that comes only with advanced years.⟩ — see HEALTH 1

sap *vb* to diminish the physical strength of ⟨Weeks of hard work had *sapped* her and left her exhausted.⟩ — see WEAKEN 1

sapience *n* the ability to understand inner qualities or relationships ⟨the kind of *sapience* that comes from a lifetime of experience as an educator⟩ — see WISDOM 1

sapient *adj* having or showing deep understanding and intelligent application of knowledge ⟨an uncle who is always good for valuable insights and some *sapient* advice⟩ — see WISE 1

sapped *adj* lacking bodily strength ⟨I was completely *sapped* after the first day of hauling logs.⟩ — see WEAK 1

sappiness *n* the state or quality of having an excess of tender feelings (as of love, nostalgia, or compassion) ⟨the over-the-top *sappiness* of the verse on the Valentine's Day card⟩ — see SENTIMENTALITY

sappy *adj* **1** appealing to the emotions in an obvious and tiresome way ⟨a *sappy* letter filled with silly romantic clichés⟩ — see CORNY
2 showing or marked by a lack of good sense or judgment ⟨a *sappy* plan that somehow managed to succeed⟩ — see FOOLISH 1

sarcasm *n* an act or expression showing scorn and usually intended to hurt another's feelings ⟨I know you're not happy, but there's no need to resort to petty *sarcasms* to make your point.⟩ — see INSULT

sarcastic *adj* marked by the use of wit that is intended to cause hurt feelings ⟨Her *sarcastic* comments didn't do anything to help the situation.⟩
synonyms acid, acidic, acrid, biting, caustic, cutting, mordant, pungent, sardonic, satiric (*or* satirical), scalding, scathing, sharp, smart-alecky, tart
related words brisk, cross, sharp-tongued, sour, spiky (*also* spikey), tartish; incisive, keen, poignant, trenchant; cynical, dry, ironic (*also* ironical), wry; facetious, flippant, tongue-in-cheek; acrimonious, bitter, resentful; harsh, rough, severe, stringent; abrupt, blunt, brusque (*also* brusk), concise, crisp, curt, gruff, pithy, snippety, snippy, succinct, terse; backhanded, insincere
near antonyms amusing, droll, merry, playful, sportive, waggish; gentle, mild; bland; good-humored, good-natured; diplomatic, polite, smooth, suave, urbane; affable, cordial, genial, gracious, hospitable, sociable

sardonic *adj* marked by the use of wit that is intended to cause hurt feelings ⟨a *sardonic* little jab that made her visitor quiet and subdued for the rest of the night⟩ — see SARCASTIC

sash *n* a strip of flexible material (as leather) worn around the waist ⟨a dress with a flowered silk *sash*⟩ — see ²BELT 1

sass *n* disrespectful or argumentative talk given in response to a command or request ⟨an old-fashioned diner where getting *sass* from the waitstaff is part of the experience⟩ — see BACK TALK

sassy *adj* displaying or marked by rude boldness ⟨gave a *sassy* answer to the question⟩ — see NERVY 1

Satan *n* the supreme personification of evil often represented as the ruler of hell ⟨Some people believe that *Satan* can successfully tempt almost anyone with lies and flattery.⟩ — see DEVIL 1

satanic *adj* of, relating to, or worthy of an evil spirit ⟨The cat's eyes reflected a *satanic* red in the dark.⟩ — see FIENDISH 1

sate *vb* **1** to fill with food to capacity ⟨I *sated* myself with an array of offerings from the dessert table.⟩ — see GORGE 1
2 to put a complete end to (a physical need or desire) ⟨a

huge meal that should have *sated* everyone's hunger⟩ — see SATISFY 1

sated *adj* having one's appetite completely satisfied ⟨The *sated* baby fell instantly to sleep.⟩ — see FULL 3

satiate *adj* having one's appetite completely satisfied ⟨A couple of *satiate* dinner guests had ensconced themselves on the living room sofa.⟩ — see FULL 3

satiate *vb* to put a complete end to (a physical need or desire) ⟨A long drink of water at last *satiated* my thirst.⟩ — see SATISFY 1

satiated *adj* having one's appetite completely satisfied ⟨He was too *satiated* even to consider the proffered cookie.⟩ — see FULL 3

satin *adj* **1** having a shiny surface or finish ⟨*satin* paint⟩ — see GLOSSY

2 smooth or delicate in appearance or feel ⟨the *satin* petals of a rose⟩ — see SOFT 2

satiny *adj* **1** having a shiny surface or finish ⟨the *satiny* short coat of an Arabian horse⟩ — see GLOSSY

2 smooth or delicate in appearance or feel ⟨a lovely *satiny* fabric that feels so good next to the skin⟩ — see SOFT 2

satire *n* a creative work that uses sharp humor to point up the foolishness of a person, institution, or human nature in general ⟨a *satire* about the music industry in which a handsome but untalented youth is turned into a rock star⟩

synonyms lampoon

related words burlesque, caricature, parody, spoof, takeoff; comedy, farce, sketch, skit, slapstick, squib; derision, ridicule; cartoon, mockery, travesty

satiric *or* **satirical** *adj* marked by the use of wit that is intended to cause hurt feelings ⟨a *satiric* story about the movie business⟩ — see SARCASTIC

satisfaction *n* **1** the feeling experienced when one's wishes are met ⟨Readers will close the covers of this mystery novel with complete *satisfaction*.⟩ — see PLEASURE 1

2 payment to another for a loss or injury ⟨He's demanding *satisfaction* from his neighbor for running over his prize rose bush.⟩ — see COMPENSATION 1

3 a state of mind in which one is free from doubt ⟨He proved to my *satisfaction* that he could not have done it.⟩ — see CONFIDENCE 2

satisfactorily *adv* **1** in a satisfactory way ⟨The matter has been resolved *satisfactorily*.⟩ — see WELL 1

2 in or to a degree or quantity that meets one's requirements or satisfaction ⟨supplied us *satisfactorily*, if not lavishly, with meals during our stay⟩ — see ENOUGH 1

satisfactoriness *n* the quality or state of meeting one's needs adequately ⟨The overall *satisfactoriness* of the service led us to leave a reasonable tip.⟩ — see SUFFICIENCY

satisfactory *adj* **1** being to one's liking ⟨We found the meal most *satisfactory*.⟩

synonyms agreeable, all right, alright, copacetic (*also* copasetic *or* copesetic), fine, good, OK (*or* okay), palatable

related words delectable, delicious, delightful, dreamy, felicitous, gratifying, nice, pleasant, pleasing, scrumptious, welcome; acceptable, adequate, decent, passable, tolerable

near antonyms bad, deficient, inferior, lousy, poor, punk, substandard, unacceptable, wanting, wretched; mediocre, middling, second-class, second-rate

antonyms disagreeable, unsatisfactory

2 of a level of quality that meets one's needs or standards ⟨The newlyweds' first attempt at cooking dinner was actually quite *satisfactory*.⟩ — see ADEQUATE

satisfied *adj* **1** experiencing pleasure, satisfaction, or delight ⟨*Satisfied* customers tend to come back over and over.⟩ — see GLAD 1

2 feeling that one's needs or desires have been met ⟨A *satisfied* vacationer is one who has spent the time doing exactly what he or she wanted.⟩ — see CONTENT

satisfy *vb* **1** to put a complete end to (a physical need or desire) ⟨The players *satisfied* their hunger after the game with a big pasta dinner.⟩

synonyms assuage, quench, sate, satiate

related words cater (to), gratify, humor, indulge; alleviate, lighten, relieve; cloy, saturate, surfeit

near antonyms arouse, excite, pique, stimulate; tantalize, tease

2 to cause (someone) to agree with a belief or course of action by using arguments or earnest requests ⟨It took me a while to *satisfy* my attorney that I had good grounds for a lawsuit.⟩ — see PERSUADE

3 to do what is required by the terms of ⟨The contractor had clearly failed to *satisfy* the terms of the agreement.⟩ — see FULFILL 1

4 to give satisfaction to ⟨A hot dinner at the end of the day never fails to *satisfy* me.⟩ — see PLEASE 1

5 to provide (someone) with a just payment for loss or injury ⟨The owners of the restaurant were generously *satisfied* for any business lost during the filming.⟩ — see COMPENSATE 1

satisfying *adj* **1** giving pleasure or contentment to the mind or senses ⟨a *satisfying* and relaxing bubble bath after a long day⟩ — see PLEASANT 1

2 having the power to persuade ⟨"I don't feel like it" is not a *satisfying* reason for skipping your chores.⟩ — see COGENT

3 making one feel good inside ⟨Julia received many *satisfying* compliments on her gardening efforts.⟩ — see HEARTWARMING

satisfyingly *adv* in a pleasing way ⟨capped the story with a *satisfyingly* happy ending⟩ — see WELL 5

saturate *vb* to wet thoroughly with liquid ⟨*Saturate* your hair with water before applying the dye.⟩ — see SOAK 1

saturate *adj* containing, covered with, or thoroughly penetrated by water ⟨The test will only work if the sample cloth is *saturate* with solution.⟩ — see WET 1

saturated *adj* containing, covered with, or thoroughly penetrated by water ⟨The carpet should be damp but not entirely *saturated*.⟩ — see WET 1

saturnine *adj* causing or marked by an atmosphere lacking in cheer ⟨wore a *saturnine* expression that discouraged conversation⟩ — see GLOOMY 1

sauce *n* **1** a savory fluid food used as a topping or accompaniment to a main dish ⟨The chef poured *sauce* over the meat just before he served it.⟩

synonyms dressing, gravy

related words condiment, relish, seasoning; fixing(s), garnish, topping; dip, marinade

2 disrespectful or argumentative talk given in response to a command or request ⟨If you put up with any *sauce* from them, they'll only get worse.⟩ — see BACK TALK

3 shameless boldness ⟨The woman was shocked by the *sauce* of the child who ran right up to her and asked for money.⟩ — see EFFRONTERY

sauciness *n* shameless boldness ⟨was offended by the boy's *sauciness*⟩ — see EFFRONTERY

saucy *adj* displaying or marked by rude boldness ⟨Eric irritated his fellow travelers with *saucy* questions and comments.⟩ — see NERVY 1

saunter *n* a relaxed journey on foot for exercise or pleasure ⟨tourists on a morning *saunter* around the old section of the city⟩ — see WALK 1

saunter *vb* to travel by foot for exercise or pleasure ⟨He lazily *saunters* about the French countryside, mostly photographing birds and flowers.⟩ — see HIKE 1

sausage *n* a rod-shaped portion of seasoned ground meat in a casing ⟨A couple of *sausages* and eggs make a good breakfast.⟩
synonyms link
related words bologna, frank, frankfurter, kielbasa, knockwurst (*also* knackwurst), liver sausage (*also* liver pudding), liverwurst, pepperoni, salami, Vienna sausage, weenie, wiener (*also* weiner), wienerwurst; blood sausage (*also* blood pudding)

savage *n* a mean, evil, or unprincipled person ⟨What kind of *savage* would do such a thing?⟩ — see VILLAIN

savage *adj* **1** having or showing the desire to inflict severe pain and suffering on others ⟨a *savage* attack on a helpless person⟩ — see CRUEL 1
2 living outdoors without taming or domestication by humans ⟨*savage* beasts that seemed threatening to the tourists⟩ — see WILD 1
3 violently unfriendly or aggressive in disposition ⟨a novel about schoolboys who become *savage* while marooned on an island⟩ — see FIERCE 1

savage *vb* to criticize harshly and usually publicly ⟨Book reviewers mercilessly *savaged* his latest novel.⟩ — see ATTACK 2

savageness *n* disposition to willfully inflict pain and suffering on others ⟨a quote from an ancient Greek writer about taming the *savageness* of man⟩ — see CRUELTY

savagery *n* disposition to willfully inflict pain and suffering on others ⟨a condemnation of the *savagery* of war⟩ — see CRUELTY

savanna *also* **savannah** *n* a broad area of level or rolling treeless country ⟨lions roaming the *savanna*⟩ — see PLAIN 1

savant *n* a person of deep wisdom or learning ⟨a *savant* in the field of medical ethics⟩ — see SAGE

save *prep* not including ⟨Everyone *save* me is going to the party!⟩ — see EXCEPT

save *vb* **1** to free from the penalties or consequences of sin ⟨believes the Lord will *save* him⟩
synonyms deliver, redeem
related words reclaim, reform; forgive, pardon, remit, shrive; bless, hallow; consecrate, purify, sanctify
2 to remove from danger or harm ⟨The firefighters managed to *save* the family's dogs.⟩
synonyms bail out, deliver, rescue
related words salvage; emancipate, free, liberate, release; disentangle, extricate; recover
antonyms adventure, compromise, endanger, gamble (with), hazard, imperil, jeopardize, peril, risk, venture
3 to avoid unnecessary waste or expense ⟨We'll have to scrimp and *save* to be able to afford college.⟩ — see ECONOMIZE
4 to keep in good condition ⟨lovingly *saved* the classic car and even upgraded its engine⟩ — see MAINTAIN 1
5 to keep or intend for a special purpose ⟨I'm *saving* this dress for a formal occasion.⟩ — see DEVOTE 1

saver *n* one that saves from danger or destruction ⟨Of all the *savers* of Jews during the Holocaust, none was more heroic than the Swedish diplomat Raoul Wallenberg.⟩ — see SAVIOR

saving *conj* if it were not for the fact that ⟨I would be ready, *saving* the fact that I can't find my missing shoe.⟩ — see EXCEPT

saving *prep* not including ⟨*Saving* three members, the club is now fully committed to the fund-raising project.⟩ — see EXCEPT

savior *or* **saviour** *n* one that saves from danger or destruction ⟨The highway patrol officer proved to be our *savior*, arriving on the scene just as the car broke down.⟩
synonyms deliverer, redeemer, rescuer, saver
related words custodian, defender, guard, guardian,

keeper, lookout, protector, sentinel, sentry, warden, warder, watch, watcher, watchman; ransomer; salvager

savor *also* **savour** *n* **1** the property of a substance that can be identified by the sense of taste ⟨a gourmet who can identify the ingredients in any dish solely by their *savor*⟩ — see TASTE 1
2 the quality of being delicious ⟨the wonderful *savor* of Mom's apple pie⟩ — see DELICIOUSNESS

savor *also* **savour** *vb* **1** to make more pleasant to the taste by adding something intensely flavored ⟨cuisine that has been generously *savored* with southern India's rich array of spices⟩ — see SEASON 1
2 to take pleasure in ⟨It's my dream vacation, and I intend to *savor* every moment.⟩ — see ENJOY 1

savoriness *n* the quality of being delicious ⟨The *savoriness* of freshly baked bread simply cannot be overrated.⟩ — see DELICIOUSNESS

savorless *adj* lacking in taste or flavor ⟨The white rice was filling, but rather *savorless*.⟩ — see INSIPID 1

savory *also* **savoury** *adj* **1** having a pleasant smell ⟨Cedar is one of the most *savory* of all woods.⟩ — see FRAGRANT
2 very pleasing to the sense of taste ⟨a *savory* beef stew that really hit the spot⟩ — see DELICIOUS 1
3 giving pleasure or contentment to the mind or senses ⟨Having to fire someone was not a task that the manager found at all *savory*.⟩ — see PLEASANT 1
4 sharp and pleasantly stimulating to the mind or senses ⟨a *savory* new book on a subject that seemingly had been done to death⟩ — see PIQUANT

savvy *n* knowledge gained by actually doing or living through something ⟨She's an excellent scholar of political science, but lacks the kind of *savvy* needed to run for public office.⟩ — see EXPERIENCE 1

savvy *adj* having or showing a practical cleverness or judgment ⟨*Savvy* investors quickly saw the potential in tech stocks.⟩ — see SHREWD 1

savvy *vb* to have a clear idea of ⟨The man growled, "I'll deal with this myself—you *savvy*?"⟩ — see COMPREHEND 1

saw *n* an often stated observation regarding something from common experience ⟨It's an old *saw* that a red sunset presages fair skies the next day.⟩ — see SAYING

saw–toothed *adj* notched or toothed along the edge ⟨a dandelion's *saw-toothed* leaves⟩ — see SERRATED

say *n* the right to express a wish, choice, or opinion ⟨Even if they decide otherwise, at least I had my *say*.⟩ — see VOICE 1

say *vb* **1** to express (a thought or emotion) in words ⟨Why don't you just *say* what's on your mind?⟩
synonyms articulate, enunciate, pass, speak, state, talk, tell, utter, verbalize, vocalize
related words air, discuss, share, sound, vent, ventilate, voice; blabber, blurt, get off, shoot; advertise, announce, blaze, broadcast, declare, post, proclaim, promulgate, publicize, publish; affirm, allege, assert, aver, avouch, avow; breathe, chirp, drawl, gasp, mouth, murmur, purr, shout, spout, whisper; clothe, couch, formulate, phrase, word; comment, pipe up (with), remark
phrases put into words
near antonyms stifle, suppress
2 to convey in appropriate or telling terms ⟨I'm not quite sure how to *say* this, but I'm going to have to quit the group.⟩ — see PHRASE
3 to give from memory ⟨*Say* your prayers before going to bed.⟩ — see REPEAT 2
4 to take as true or as a fact without actual proof ⟨Let's *say*, for the sake of argument, that this is true.⟩ — see ASSUME 2

saying *n* an often stated observation regarding something from common experience ⟨There's an old *saying* that you should let sleeping dogs lie.⟩

synonyms adage, aphorism, byword, epigram, maxim, proverb, saw, word

related words cliché (*also* cliche), commonplace, platitude, wheeze; expression, felicity; axiom, motto, precept, truism, truth; formula; comment, note, reflection, remark

say–so *n* the right to express a wish, choice, or opinion ⟨Some of the members complained they didn't have any *say-so* in how the organization spent its funds.⟩ — see VOICE 1

scabby *adj* arousing or deserving of one's loathing and disgust ⟨That's a *scabby* trick to play on someone trying to help.⟩ — see CONTEMPTIBLE 1

scads *pl n* a considerable amount ⟨*Scads* of people showed up for the party.⟩ — see LOT 2

scalawag *or* **scallywag** *n* a mean, evil, or unprincipled person ⟨called him a *scalawag* and a cheat⟩ — see VILLAIN

scalding *adj* **1** having a notably high temperature ⟨the *scalding* water of a geyser⟩ — see HOT 1

2 marked by the use of wit that is intended to cause hurt feelings ⟨*scalding* reviews for the overproduced horror movie⟩ — see SARCASTIC

¹scale *n* a device for measuring weight ⟨The vet had a special *scale* for weighing the biggest dogs.⟩

synonyms balance

related words gravimeter

²scale *n* a small thin piece of material that resembles an animal scale ⟨*Scales* of mica were embedded in the granite.⟩

synonyms lamella, lamina, plate

related words chip, flake, sliver, splint, splinter; sheet, slice

³scale *n* **1** a scheme of rank or order ⟨a student who scored very highly on a standard intelligence *scale*⟩

synonyms graduation, ladder, ordering, ranking

related words food chain, pecking order (*also* peck order); arrangement, array, disposal, disposition, distribution, sequence, series, setup; degree, echelon, footing, level, place, position, reaches, situation, spot, standing, station, status

2 the distance or extent between possible extremes ⟨With the *scale* going from one to ten, what did you think of the movie?⟩ — see RANGE 3

scale *vb* to find out the size, extent, or amount of ⟨We *scaled* the logs to get a rough idea of the amount of usable lumber they were likely to yield.⟩ — see MEASURE 1

scaly *adj* composed of or covered with scales ⟨The snake's *scaly* skin was dry to the touch.⟩

synonyms squamous

related words scalelike

near antonyms smooth

antonyms scaleless

scam *n* an instance of the use of dishonest methods to acquire something of value ⟨That's just a *scam* to bilk insurance companies for staged accidents.⟩ — see FRAUD 1

scamp *n* **1** an appealingly mischievous person ⟨Those little *scamps* are always getting into trouble, but no one has the heart to punish them.⟩

synonyms devil, hellion, imp, mischief, monkey, rapscallion, rascal, rogue, urchin

related words cutup, madcap, skylarker; brat, nuisance; juvenile delinquent; gamin, gamine

near antonyms beast, boor, cad, churl, clown, creep, cur, heel, joker, louse, lout, skunk, snake, stinkard, stinker; knave, miscreant, reprobate, scalawag (*or* scallywag), scoundrel, varlet, villain

2 a mean, evil, or unprincipled person ⟨an insincere and ruthlessly ambitious *scamp* who was willing to do anything to win the reality show's grand prize⟩ — see VILLAIN

scan *n* a close look at or over someone or something in order to judge condition ⟨I gave the car a good *scan* to see if it was worth buying.⟩ — see INSPECTION

scan *vb* to look over closely (as for judging quality or condition) ⟨*scanned* the manuscript carefully for any overlooked errors⟩ — see INSPECT

scandal *n* a cause of shame ⟨a *scandal* that for many years haunted the family of the banker convicted of embezzlement⟩ — see DISGRACE 2

scandalous *adj* **1** causing intense displeasure, disgust, or resentment ⟨the *scandalous* news that the study's research had been fabricated⟩ — see OFFENSIVE 1

2 causing or intended to cause unjust injury to a person's good name ⟨spread a *scandalous* rumor about a coworker that almost cost him his job⟩ — see LIBELOUS

scant *adj* less plentiful than what is normal, necessary, or desirable ⟨Jobs for teenagers were *scant* that summer.⟩ — see MEAGER

scant *vb* to use or give out in stingy amounts ⟨Don't *scant* the peanut butter on those sandwiches!⟩ — see SPARE 1

scantiness *n* a falling short of an essential or desirable amount or number ⟨The *scantiness* of grass meant that we had to feed the cows extra hay.⟩ — see DEFICIENCY

scanty *adj* less plentiful than what is normal, necessary, or desirable ⟨The camera's *scanty* instructions left me somewhat confused.⟩ — see MEAGER

scapegoat *n* a person or thing taking the blame for others ⟨Companies often use the economy as a *scapegoat* to avoid taking responsibility for dropping sales.⟩

synonyms fall guy, goat, whipping boy

related words victim; butt, dupe, fool, laughingstock, mark, mockery, monkey; excuse

¹scar *n* something that spoils the appearance or completeness of a thing ⟨the *scars* left by carelessly scratching the car door with one's keys⟩ — see BLEMISH

²scar *n* a steep wall of rock, earth, or ice ⟨At the next bend in the river, a *scar* of red sandstone steeply rises to over 100 feet.⟩ — see CLIFF

scarce *adj* **1** less plentiful than what is normal, necessary, or desirable ⟨Food was a bit *scarce* last winter.⟩ — see MEAGER

2 not coming up to an expected measure or meeting a particular need ⟨Help is always *scarce* in the resort town during the busy summer season.⟩ — see SHORT 3

scarcely *adv* **1** by a very small margin ⟨He could *scarcely* contain his joy.⟩ — see JUST 2

2 certainly not ⟨I *scarcely* think that one person being sick is an "epidemic."⟩ — see HARDLY 2

scarceness *n* a falling short of an essential or desirable amount or number ⟨The continuing *scarceness* of supplies means that we will have to ration ourselves.⟩ — see DEFICIENCY

scarcity *n* a falling short of an essential or desirable amount or number ⟨The *scarcity* of good restaurants around here is surprising.⟩ — see DEFICIENCY

scare *vb* to strike with fear ⟨Thunderstorms have always *scared* her.⟩ — see FRIGHTEN

scare *n* the emotion experienced in the presence or threat of danger ⟨You gave me quite a *scare* coming home so late.⟩ — see FEAR 1

scared *adj* filled with fear or dread ⟨At the sight of the grizzly bear he froze, being too *scared* to even run away.⟩ — see AFRAID

scare up *vb* to come upon after searching, study, or effort ⟨I can probably *scare up* my old textbooks if you need them.⟩ — see FIND 1

scarf *vb* to swallow or eat greedily ⟨The college students *scarfed* the entire contents of the care package in one sitting.⟩ — see GOBBLE

scarp *n* a steep wall of rock, earth, or ice 〈Years of violent ocean storms had heavily eroded the beach, creating a *scarp* along one end of it.〉 — see CLIFF

scary *adj* **1** causing fear 〈a *scary* movie that gave the child nightmares for weeks afterwards〉 — see FEARFUL 1
2 easily frightened 〈a *scary* horse who spooked and kicked at its own shadow〉 — see SHY 1
3 filled with fear or dread 〈I got a little *scary* when I heard the noise in the basement.〉 — see AFRAID

scathe *vb* to criticize harshly and usually publicly 〈Newspaper cartoonists *scathed* the governor with a series of caricatures.〉 — see ATTACK 2

scathing *adj* marked by the use of wit that is intended to cause hurt feelings 〈a *scathing* rebuttal of the latest accusations〉 — see SARCASTIC

scatter *n* a small number 〈played before only a *scatter* of spectators in that huge stadium〉 — see FEW

scatter *vb* **1** to cause (members of a group) to move widely apart 〈The noise of the backfiring car *scattered* the pigeons.〉
synonyms clear out, disband, dispel, disperse, dissipate, squander
related words break up, isolate, part, segregate, separate, split (up); diffuse, disseminate, diverge, spread
near antonyms agglutinate, conglomerate; unify, unite
antonyms assemble, cluster, collect, concentrate, congregate, gather, ingather
2 to cover by or as if by scattering something over or on 〈The hillside was *scattered* with boulders deposited by the last ice age.〉
synonyms bestrew, dot, pepper, sow, spray, sprinkle, strew
related words blanket, drizzle, dust; stud; dapple, fleck, speckle, stipple; bespatter, spatter
3 to go off in different directions and cease to exist as a body or unified whole 〈The crowd at the beach *scattered* when it started to rain.〉 — see DISPERSE 1

scatterbrained *adj* lacking in seriousness or maturity 〈a *scatterbrained* child who couldn't seem to stop fooling around〉 — see GIDDY 1

scattered *adj* lacking a definite plan, purpose, or pattern 〈a hodgepodge of *scattered* ideas that didn't add up to a clear hypothesis〉 — see RANDOM

scattering *n* **1** an act or process in which something scatters or is scattered 〈the *scattering* of the leaves by the wind〉
synonyms disbandment, dispersal, dispersion, dissipation
related words diffusion, dissemination; breakup, dissolution, disunion, separation, split
near antonyms assembly, collection, concentration, gathering
2 a small number 〈a *scattering* of people in the mostly empty theater〉 — see FEW

scenario *n* the written form of a story prepared for film production 〈submitted a *scenario* to the producers〉 — see SCREENPLAY

scene *n* **1** the place and time in which the action for a portion of a dramatic work (as a movie) is set 〈The first *scene* was the kitchen of a fancy restaurant during dinner.〉
synonyms background, locale, setting
related words backdrop, scenery, set; tableau
2 an outburst or display of excited anger 〈Please don't make a *scene* while we're at the restaurant.〉 — see TANTRUM
3 position with regard to conditions and circumstances 〈one of the leading figures in the current political *scene*〉 — see SITUATION 1
4 the array of painted backgrounds and furnishings used to establish the setting in a stage production 〈Noah

helped build and paint *scenes* for the school play.〉 — see SCENERY

scenery *n* the array of painted backgrounds and furnishings used to establish the setting in a stage production 〈The musical was worth seeing just for the elaborate *scenery*.〉
synonyms scene, set
related words backdrop, drop; background; set piece; property

scent *n* **1** a sweet or pleasant smell 〈the delightful *scent* of her perfume〉 — see FRAGRANCE
2 the quality of a thing that makes it perceptible to the sense organs in the nose 〈Dogs are able to detect *scents* that are far below the threshold detectable by the human nose.〉 — see SMELL 1

scent *vb* **1** to fill or infuse with a pleasant odor or odor-releasing substance 〈fancy bars of soap *scented* with lavender〉
synonyms incense, perfume
near antonyms deodorize
antonyms stink up
2 to become aware of by means of the sense organs in the nose 〈The dog *scented* a rabbit and suddenly took off.〉 — see SMELL 1
3 to have a vague awareness of 〈He *scented* danger.〉 — see FEEL 1

scented *adj* having a pleasant smell 〈a bowl of *scented* petals used to perfume a room〉 — see FRAGRANT

schedule *n* **1** a listing of things to be presented or considered (as at a concert or play) 〈the *schedule* of events for the conference〉 — see PROGRAM 1
2 a record of a series of items (as names or titles) usually arranged according to some system 〈a *schedule* of arrivals and departures〉 — see ¹LIST

schedule *vb* to put (someone or something) on a list 〈I've *scheduled* you for an appointment tomorrow.〉 — see ¹LIST 2

scheduled *adj* being in accordance with the prescribed, normal, or logical course of events 〈a *scheduled* stop for the train〉 — see DUE 2

scheme *n* **1** a clever often underhanded means to achieve an end 〈an e-mail *scheme* to trick unwary Internet users into disclosing passwords and financial information〉 — see TRICK 1
2 a secret plan for accomplishing evil or unlawful ends 〈a *scheme* to rob a bank〉 — see PLOT 1
3 a method worked out in advance for achieving some objective 〈a *scheme* to upgrade the city's mass transit system〉 — see PLAN 1

scheme *vb* to engage in a secret plan to accomplish evil or unlawful ends 〈They *schemed* to take control of the company.〉 — see PLOT

scheme (out) *vb* to work out the details of (something) in advance 〈The campaign operatives *schemed out* a plan for dealing with bombshells about the candidate's past.〉 — see PLAN 1

schism *n* **1** a lack of agreement or harmony 〈*Schism* within the charitable organization was preventing it from achieving its goals.〉 — see DISCORD
2 the act or process of a whole separating into two or more parts or pieces 〈the *schism* in 1054 of the Christian church into the Roman Catholic and Eastern Orthodox churches〉 — see SEPARATION 1

schmaltz *also* **schmalz** *n* something (as a work of literature or music) that is too sentimental 〈The love song was a typical example of overproduced *schmaltz*.〉 — see CORN

schmaltzy *adj* appealing to the emotions in an obvious and tiresome way 〈a *schmaltzy* television commercial featuring a photogenic, perfect family〉 — see CORNY

schmooze *n* friendly, informal conversation or an instance of this ⟨had to master the art of the *schmooze* in order to get ahead in the business⟩ — see CHAT 1

schmooze *or* **shmooze** *vb* to engage in casual or rambling conversation ⟨Emily spent every spare minute of the conference *schmoozing* with the industry's power players.⟩ — see CHAT 1

scholar *n* **1** a person of deep wisdom or learning ⟨*Scholars* have long debated whether there is ever such a thing as a truly selfless act.⟩ — see SAGE
2 a person with a high level of knowledge or skill in a field ⟨a *scholar* who is a specialist in the history of ancient Greece⟩ — see EXPERT
3 one who attends a school ⟨a competition for promising young *scholars* from across the country⟩ — see STUDENT

scholarly *adj* **1** having or displaying advanced knowledge or education ⟨a *scholarly* analysis of the historical document⟩ — see EDUCATED 1
2 of or relating to schooling or learning especially at an advanced level ⟨a *scholarly* essay making comparisons between 18th-century French authors and their Germanic counterparts⟩ — see ACADEMIC 1

scholarship *n* the understanding and information gained from being educated ⟨The historian's new book displays a remarkable level of *scholarship*.⟩ — see EDUCATION 2

scholastic *adj* of or relating to schooling or learning especially at an advanced level ⟨a college that gives a higher priority to *scholastic* endeavors than to athletic pursuits⟩ — see ACADEMIC 1

school *vb* to cause to acquire knowledge or skill in some field ⟨*schooled* their children in proper etiquette for formal occasions⟩ — see TEACH

school *n* a place or establishment for teaching and learning ⟨one of the first *schools* in the country to offer online courses⟩
synonyms academy, seminary
related words boarding school, preparatory school, prep school; elementary school, grammar school, high school, junior high school, kindergarten, middle school, primary school, public school, secondary school, senior high school, trade school, training school; charter school, magnet school, minischool

schooling *n* the act or process of imparting knowledge or skills to another ⟨the extended *schooling* needed for a horse to be able to make those precision movements⟩ — see EDUCATION 1

schoolteacher *n* a person whose occupation is to give formal instruction in a school ⟨*Schoolteachers* don't always get the summers off, for some teach during that period as well.⟩ — see TEACHER

science *n* a body of facts learned by study or experience ⟨The *science* of medicine grew tremendously in the course of the 19th century.⟩ — see KNOWLEDGE 1

scintillate *vb* **1** to give off sparks ⟨We watched contentedly as our campfire *scintillated* in the darkness.⟩ — see SPARK 1
2 to shoot forth bursts of light ⟨The diamond ring *scintillated* in the sunlight.⟩ — see FLASH 1

scoff *vb* to swallow or eat greedily ⟨*scoffed* dinner before running off to the basketball game⟩ — see GOBBLE

scold *vb* to criticize (someone) severely or angrily especially for personal failings ⟨He *scolded* the kids for not cleaning up the mess they had made in the kitchen.⟩
synonyms bawl out, berate, castigate, chastise, chew out, dress down, flay, hammer, jaw, keelhaul, lambaste (*or* lambast), lecture, rail (at *or* against), rate, rebuke, reprimand, reproach, score, upbraid
related words admonish, chide, remonstrate (with), reprove; abuse, assail, attack, bad-mouth, blame, blast, censure, condemn, criticize, crucify, denounce, dis (*also*

diss) [*slang*], excoriate, fault, harangue, knock, lace (into), lash, pan, reprehend, revile, scourge, slam, vituperate; belittle, disparage, mock, put down; ridicule, scoff, scorn
phrases lay into, read the riot act (to), take to task
near antonyms approve, endorse (*also* indorse), sanction; extol (*also* extoll), laud, praise

scoop *n* **1** a utensil with a bowl and a handle that is used especially in cooking and serving food ⟨an ice cream *scoop*⟩ — see SPOON
2 information not generally available to the public ⟨Come on, I know you've got the *scoop* on the story!⟩ — see DOPE 1

scoop *vb* to lift out with something that holds liquid ⟨*scooped* broth out of the pan with a spoon⟩ — see DIP 2

scoot *vb* to proceed or move quickly ⟨Now we've got to *scoot*, or we'll be late.⟩ — see HURRY 2

scope *n* an area over which activity, capacity, or influence extends ⟨The company's *scope* of operations now spans two continents.⟩ — see RANGE 2

scorch *vb* **1** to burn on the surface ⟨The picnickers kept *scorching* their marshmallows, deliberately sticking their skewers into the licking flames of the campfire.⟩
synonyms char, sear, singe
related words fire, ignite, inflame (*also* enflame), kindle, light; bake, cremate, incinerate; scald, scathe
2 to make dry ⟨Weeks of drought had badly *scorched* the soil.⟩ — see DRY 1

scorching *adj* having a notably high temperature ⟨We keep indoors as much as possible during the day so as to avoid the *scorching* summer heat.⟩ — see HOT 1

score *n* **1** a lingering ill will towards a person for a real or imagined wrong ⟨a whistle-blower who was more interested in settling a *score* with his employers than in exposing an injustice⟩ — see GRUDGE 1
2 something (as money) which is owed ⟨We'll pay the full *score* next week.⟩ — see DEBT 1

score *vb* **1** to mark with or as if with a line or groove ⟨The glassblower *scored* the glass rod first so that it would break cleanly.⟩
synonyms groove, scribe, seam
related words abrade, file, graze, mill, rasp, scarify, scratch; bevel, chamfer, flute
2 to gain (as points or runs in a game) as credit towards one's total number of points ⟨He *scored* the winning goal in the final minute of play.⟩
synonyms rack up, tally
related words triumph, win; best, defeat
near antonyms lose
3 to obtain (as a goal) through effort ⟨finally *scored* a good job after years of hard work⟩ — see ACHIEVE 1
4 to criticize (someone) severely or angrily especially for personal failings ⟨*scored* her for failing to report the security breach immediately⟩ — see SCOLD

scorn *n* open dislike for someone or something considered unworthy of one's concern or respect ⟨The old man has nothing but *scorn* for new ideas of any kind.⟩ — see CONTEMPT

scorn *vb* **1** to show contempt for ⟨*scorned* the traditions of their ancestors⟩
synonyms disdain, disrespect, high-hat, slight, sniff (at), snub
related words scout; abhor, abominate, despise, detest, execrate, hate, loathe; belittle, deplore, deprecate, disparage; disapprove (of), discountenance, disfavor
phrases look down one's nose (at), sneeze at, thumb one's nose (at), walk over
near antonyms cherish, prize, treasure, value; admire, esteem, lionize; hallow, revere, venerate, worship; ac-

cept, appreciate, approve (of), care (for), countenance, favor, OK (*or* okay), subscribe (to)

antonyms honor, respect

2 to ignore in a disrespectful manner ⟨She *scorned* the advice of her ophthalmologist and had the laser eye surgery anyway.⟩

synonyms despise, disregard, flout

related words dismiss, forget, neglect, overlook, overpass, pass over, slur (over); belittle, deprecate, disparage, slight

near antonyms accept, approve; use

scornful *adj* **1** feeling or showing open dislike for someone or something regarded as undeserving of respect or concern ⟨The actress gave the paparazzi a *scornful* glare before breezing on by them.⟩ — see CONTEMPTUOUS 1

2 intended to make a person or thing seem of little importance or value ⟨The tenant's complaints were met with the *scornful* observation that he expected too much for the rent he was paying.⟩ — see DEROGATORY

scoundrel *n* a mean, evil, or unprincipled person ⟨Some *scoundrel* stole my wallet!⟩ — see VILLAIN

scour *vb* to look through (as a place) carefully or thoroughly in an effort to find or discover something ⟨I *scoured* the tag sale for collectible toys.⟩ — see SEARCH 1

scourge *n* **1** a long thin or flexible tool for striking ⟨The museum display included a *scourge*, thumbscrews, and other notorious instruments of torture.⟩ — see WHIP

2 one who inflicts punishment in return for an injury or offense ⟨The attorney general, who just happens to be a candidate for governor, is a self-proclaimed *scourge* of white-collar crime.⟩ — see NEMESIS 1

3 a source of harm or misfortune ⟨the robocallers that are the *scourge* of dinnertime⟩ — see BANE 1

scourge *vb* **1** to bring destruction to (something) through violent action ⟨Barbarians *scourged* the countryside.⟩ — see RAVAGE

2 to strike repeatedly with something long and thin or flexible ⟨*scourged* the tree with a whip to loosen the bark⟩ — see WHIP 1

scout *n* a member of the human race ⟨You're a good *scout*.⟩ — see HUMAN

scout *vb* to make (someone or something) the object of unkind laughter ⟨The actor's attempt to try a more serious role was roundly *scouted* by the critics.⟩ — see RIDICULE

scout (up) *vb* to come upon after searching, study, or effort ⟨I think I've *scouted up* a way for us to manage this.⟩ — see FIND 1

scowl *n* a twisting of the facial features in disgust or disapproval ⟨The man across the street never seems to wear anything but a *scowl*.⟩ — see GRIMACE

scowl *vb* to look with anger or disapproval ⟨*scowled* down at the misbehaving child⟩ — see FROWN

scrabble *n* a forceful effort to reach a goal or objective ⟨It'll be a long *scrabble* to pull ourselves out of bankruptcy.⟩ — see STRUGGLE 1

scrabble *vb* **1** to move (as up or over something) often with the help of the hands in holding or pulling ⟨We *scrabbled* up a sand dune to get a better view of the sea.⟩ — see CLIMB 1

2 to search for something blindly or uncertainly ⟨He frantically *scrabbled* through the storage chest looking for the needed documents.⟩ — see GROPE

scraggly *adj* having an uneven edge or outline ⟨a *scraggly* little tree⟩ — see RAGGED 1

scraggy *adj* **1** having an uneven edge or outline ⟨a *scraggy* beard⟩ — see RAGGED 1

2 not having a level or smooth surface ⟨Climbers badly scraped their limbs on the *scraggy* cliffs.⟩ — see UNEVEN 1

scramble *n* an unorganized collection or mixture of vari-

ous things ⟨a *scramble* of pens and pencils in the desk drawer⟩ — see MISCELLANY 1

scramble *vb* **1** to move (as up or over something) often with the help of the hands in holding or pulling ⟨The toddler *scrambled* up the stairs.⟩ — see CLIMB 1

2 to undo the proper order or arrangement of ⟨*scrambled* the letters of the word⟩ — see DISORDER

¹scrap *n* **1** an unused or unwanted piece or item typically of small size or value ⟨Only a *scrap* of silk was left on the sewing table after they had finished the project.⟩

synonyms end, leftover, oddment, remainder, remnant, stub

related words leavings, odds and ends, pickings, refuse, remains, residual, residue, scraping(s), stump, vestige; balance, rest; chip, flake, fragment, piece, sliver, splinter; ribbon(s), shred, tatter

near antonyms whole

2 a broken or irregular part of something that often remains incomplete ⟨A *scrap* of paper fluttered to the floor.⟩ — see FRAGMENT

3 a very small piece ⟨brushed away a *scrap* of lint⟩ — see BIT 1

4 discarded or useless material ⟨The rest of this stuff is just *scrap*, so sweep it up and throw it away.⟩ — see GARBAGE

²scrap *n* **1** an often noisy or angry expression of differing opinions ⟨the state legislature's annual *scrap* over the budget⟩ — see ARGUMENT 1

2 a physical dispute between opposing individuals or groups ⟨Several fans got into a *scrap* with the other team's supporters.⟩ — see FIGHT 1

¹scrap *vb* to express different opinions about something often angrily ⟨The siblings *scrapped* about which movie to see.⟩ — see ARGUE 2

²scrap *vb* **1** to get rid of as useless or unwanted ⟨We've decided to *scrap* the second car.⟩ — see DISCARD 1

2 to put an end to (something planned or previously agreed to) ⟨We *scrapped* our plans to go to Paris, and set out the next day for Prague.⟩ — see CANCEL 1

scrape *n* **1** a brief clash between enemies or rivals ⟨He's had his share of *scrapes* with the law in the past.⟩ — see ENCOUNTER

2 a harsh grating sound ⟨the *scrape* of a shovel on concrete⟩ — see RASP

3 an area of skin roughened or worn away by harsh rubbing against another surface ⟨*scrapes* that were caused by a too-tight harness⟩ — see ABRASION

scrape *vb* **1** to pass roughly and noisily over or against a surface ⟨The rusty old gate *scrapes* against the pavement whenever anyone opens it.⟩

synonyms grate, grind, rasp, scratch

related words rub; groan, whine

near antonyms glide, skate, slide

2 to damage by rubbing against a sharp or rough surface ⟨She *scraped* her knee when she fell down.⟩

synonyms abrade, graze, scratch, scuff

related words bark, skin; chafe, fret, gall; claw, cut, lacerate; bruise, contuse

near antonyms polish, smooth, soften, wax

3 to press or strike against or together so as to make a scraping sound ⟨She *scraped* her fingernails across the chalkboard to get everyone's attention.⟩ — see GRIND 2

scrappiness *n* an inclination to fight or quarrel ⟨His natural *scrappiness* serves him well as an aggressive defense attorney.⟩ — see BELLIGERENCE

scrapping *n* the getting rid of whatever is unwanted or useless ⟨The *scrapping* of the park's last horse-drawn carriage marks the end of an era.⟩ — see DISPOSAL 1

scrappy *adj* **1** feeling or displaying eagerness to fight ⟨She was a *scrappy* girl despite—or, perhaps, because of—her small size.⟩ — see BELLIGERENT

2 given to arguing ⟨a pair of *scrappy* movie critics who can never agree on anything⟩ — see ARGUMENTATIVE 1

scratch *vb* **1** to damage by rubbing against a sharp or rough surface ⟨*scratched* his arm on a branch⟩ — see SCRAPE 2

2 to pass roughly and noisily over or against a surface ⟨The branches of the willow tree *scratch* against the windowpane whenever the wind blows.⟩ — see SCRAPE 1

3 to write or draw hastily or carelessly ⟨*scratched* a quick doodle in the margins⟩ — see SCRIBBLE 1

scratch (out) *vb* **1** to compose and set down on paper the words of ⟨*scratched out* a poem for his beloved⟩ — see WRITE 1

2 to show (something written) to be no longer valid by drawing a cross over or a line through it ⟨I *scratched out* the old phone number and wrote in the new one.⟩ — see X (OUT)

scratchy *adj* **1** having leaves or branches which are likely to cause a scratch ⟨*scratchy* shrubbery that's intended to keep his dogs in the yard⟩

synonyms brambly, prickly, thistly, thorny

related words burred; bristly, coarse, jagged, rough

2 causing an unpleasant tingling sensation ⟨The wool pants are so *scratchy* that I can't stand to wear them.⟩

synonyms irritating, prickly

related words coarse, harsh, rough

near antonyms silken, silky, soft, soothing

3 harsh and dry in sound ⟨Her voice was *scratchy* from a cold.⟩ — see HOARSE

scrawl *vb* to write or draw hastily or carelessly ⟨I *scrawled* a quick note, stuck it in their mailbox, and hurried off.⟩ — see SCRIBBLE 1

scream *n* someone or something that is very funny ⟨That new comedy is a *scream*!⟩

synonyms hoot, laugh, riot

related words crack, gag, jest, joke, pleasantry, quip, sally, waggery, wisecrack, witticism; caution, sight

near antonyms bummer, downer

scream *vb* **1** to cry out loudly and emotionally ⟨We *screamed* when the roller coaster began its 30-foot plunge.⟩

synonyms howl, screech, shriek, shrill, squall, squeal, yell, yelp

related words bay, keen, squawk, wail, yowl; bawl, call, cry, holler, shout, thunder, vociferate

near antonyms murmur, mutter, whisper

2 to show mirth with an explosive vocal sound ⟨The crowd *screamed* at the performer's spot-on impression of the President.⟩ — see LAUGH 1

3 to express dissatisfaction, pain, or resentment usually tiresomely ⟨Angry residents *screamed* that their neighborhood still hadn't been plowed a week after the snowstorm.⟩ — see COMPLAIN

screaming *adj* **1** arousing a strong and usually superficial interest or emotional reaction ⟨*screaming* headlines about the latest showbiz scandal⟩ — see SENSATIONAL 1

2 causing or intended to cause laughter ⟨a *screaming* picture of everyone making silly faces⟩ — see FUNNY 1

screech *vb* to cry out loudly and emotionally ⟨The toddler *screeched* in anger when her stuffed rabbit was taken away.⟩ — see SCREAM 1

screeching *adj* having a high musical pitch or range ⟨The *screeching* blast of the factory whistle hurt my ears.⟩ — see SHRILL

screen *n* **1** the art or business of making a movie ⟨He was a star of both stage and *screen*.⟩ — see MOVIE 2

2 means or method of defending ⟨The target will be difficult to reach as it is behind a *screen* of anti-aircraft batteries.⟩ — see DEFENSE 1

screen *vb* **1** to drive danger or attack away from ⟨Helicopters were called in to help *screen* the troops from further attacks.⟩ — see DEFEND 1

2 to keep secret or shut off from view ⟨Bushes *screened* the swimming pool from passersby on the street.⟩ — see ¹HIDE 2

3 to pass through a filter ⟨You should *screen* the cooking oil to remove impurities.⟩ — see STRAIN 2

4 to place a protective layer over ⟨*screened* his eyes with his hand to block the sun⟩ — see COVER 3

screenplay *n* the written form of a story prepared for film production ⟨Each actor will be given a copy of the *screenplay* to study.⟩

synonyms scenario, script

related words story, text

screw *vb* **1** to twist (something) out of a natural or normal shape or condition ⟨Billy *screwed* up his face at the taste of the medicine.⟩ — see CONTORT

2 to rob by the use of trickery or threats ⟨The company *screwed* investors out of thousands of dollars.⟩ — see FLEECE

screwball *adj* showing or marked by a lack of good sense or judgment ⟨a *screwball* plan⟩ — see FOOLISH 1

screwball *n* a person of odd or whimsical habits ⟨a *screwball* who tried every get-rich-quick scheme⟩ — see ECCENTRIC

screwing *n* the twisting of something out of its natural or normal shape or condition ⟨You'll regret the constant *screwing* of your face—someday it's going to freeze in that position!⟩ — see CONTORTION

screwlike *adj* turning around an axis like the thread of a screw ⟨performed a *screwlike* dive into the pool⟩ — see SPIRAL

screwup *n* **1** an unintentional departure from truth or accuracy ⟨Clearly, there's been some sort of *screwup* about what time we were supposed to meet.⟩ — see ERROR 1

2 someone who bungles an effort ⟨a *screwup* who gave me the wrong information⟩ — see BUTCHER

screw up *vb* **1** to make a mistake ⟨We all *screw up* from time to time, so don't sweat it.⟩ — see ERR 1

2 to make or do (something) in a clumsy or unskillful way ⟨Oh, no! I totally *screwed up* the spreadsheet!⟩ — see BOTCH

screwy *adj* different from the ordinary in a way that causes curiosity or suspicion ⟨The counterfeit bills are poorly done and would look *screwy* to even the untrained eye.⟩ — see ODD 2

scribble *vb* **1** to write or draw hastily or carelessly ⟨She *scribbled* a quick note on the pad by the door before leaving.⟩

synonyms scratch, scrawl

related words jot (down); inscribe, letter, pen, pencil, print, write

2 to compose and set down on paper the words of ⟨He *scribbled* a quick note to his wife and taped it to the front door.⟩ — see WRITE 1

scribe *n* **1** one who writes from dictation or copies manuscripts ⟨Variations between the different manuscripts attest to the fallibility of the *scribes* who transmitted them.⟩

synonyms copyist, penman

2 an official whose job is to keep records ⟨The *scribe* keeps the minutes of the club's meetings.⟩ — see CLERK 1

3 a person who creates a written work ⟨a book of dusty poems by some now-forgotten *scribe*⟩ — see AUTHOR 1

scribe *vb* to mark with or as if with a line or groove ⟨carefully *scribed* two lines into the wood⟩ — see SCORE 1

scrimmage *n* a physical dispute between opposing individuals or groups ⟨The two players got into a *scrimmage* off the court and got suspended.⟩ — see FIGHT 1

scrimmage (with) *vb* to oppose (someone) in physical conflict ⟨a cat *scrimmaging with* another in the alley⟩ — see FIGHT 1

scrimp *vb* to avoid unnecessary waste or expense ⟨We had to *scrimp* and save for years in order to be able to afford a house.⟩ — see ECONOMIZE

scrimping *adj* careful in the management of money or resources ⟨a *scrimping* chief financial officer⟩ — see FRUGAL

scrimping *n* careful management of material resources ⟨She had grown tired of *scrimping* and was glad to finally have a job with a decent paycheck.⟩ — see ECONOMY

script *n* **1** the form or style of a particular person's writing ⟨Joan has a neat, careful *script* with delicate loops.⟩ — see HANDWRITING 1
2 the written form of a story prepared for film production ⟨sold two *scripts* to the movie studio⟩ — see SCREENPLAY
3 writing done by hand ⟨Sending a thank-you note in *script*—and not just an e-mail—is a more personal way to express one's gratitude.⟩ — see HANDWRITING 2

Scripture *n* a book made up of the writings accepted by Christians as coming from God ⟨One of the greatest commandments from *Scripture* is "Love thy neighbor."⟩ — see BIBLE

scrooge *n* a mean grasping person who is usually stingy with money ⟨a *scrooge* who never participates in our fundraisers⟩ — see MISER

scrub *n* a living thing much smaller than others of its kind ⟨That *scrub* of a mutt turned out to be the smartest dog we ever had.⟩ — see DWARF 1

scrub *vb* to put an end to (something planned or previously agreed to) ⟨The outdoor art project was *scrubbed* when the organizers found out they needed permission from city hall.⟩ — see CANCEL 1

scruffy *adj* showing signs of advanced wear and tear and neglect ⟨Gail dressed in *scruffy* old clothes to clean out the garage.⟩ — see SHABBY 1

scrumptious *adj* very pleasing to the sense of taste ⟨baked a *scrumptious* chocolate cake⟩ — see DELICIOUS 1

scrunch *vb* **1** to create (as by crushing) an irregular mass of creases in ⟨*scrunched* up the shirt and tossed it in the laundry⟩ — see CRUMPLE 1
2 to lie low with the limbs close to the body ⟨The climbers *scrunched* down on the leeward side of a large boulder and waited for the storm to pass.⟩ — see CROUCH
3 to press or strike against or together so as to make a scraping sound ⟨*scrunched* loose gravel with every footstep⟩ — see GRIND 2

¹scruple *n* **1** a very small amount ⟨went about her business without even a *scruple* of hesitation⟩ — see PARTICLE 1
2 a very small piece ⟨left just a *scruple* of asparagus on the plate⟩ — see BIT 1

²scruple *n* an uneasy feeling about the rightness of what one is doing or going to do ⟨They seem to have no *scruples* about exaggerating the truth.⟩ — see QUALM

scruple *vb* to show uncertainty about the right course of action ⟨a tabloid journalist who has never *scrupled* to reveal the most intimate details about the lives of celebrities⟩ — see HESITATE

scrupulous *adj* **1** guided by or in accordance with one's sense of right and wrong ⟨an exemplar of morality who was *scrupulous* in all of his dealings⟩ — see CONSCIENTIOUS 1
2 taking, showing, or involving great care and effort ⟨A *scrupulous* attention to detail is evident in all of his reporting.⟩ — see PAINSTAKING

scrupulousness *n* strict attentiveness to what one is doing ⟨the admirable *scrupulousness* with which they performed every step of the experiment⟩ — see CARE 1

scrutinize *vb* to look over closely (as for judging quality or condition) ⟨The project's time constraints make it impossible for the programmers to *scrutinize* every line of code, so some bugs should be expected.⟩ — see INSPECT

scrutiny *n* **1** a close look at or over someone or something in order to judge condition ⟨His performance on the football field is seemingly unaffected by the media's intense *scrutiny* of his tumultuous personal life.⟩ — see INSPECTION
2 a fixed intent look ⟨He began to squirm under the penetrating *scrutiny* of the judge.⟩ — see GAZE

scuff *vb* **1** to damage by rubbing against a sharp or rough surface ⟨*scuffed* up her shoes by rubbing her feet under the rung of the chair⟩ — see SCRAPE 2
2 to move heavily or clumsily ⟨The miners *scuffed* past in heavy boots.⟩ — see LUMBER 1

scuffle *n* a physical dispute between opposing individuals or groups ⟨Several chairs were knocked over in the *scuffle*.⟩ — see FIGHT 1

scuffle *vb* **1** to move heavily or clumsily ⟨She *scuffled* along in shoes that were much too large for her.⟩ — see LUMBER 1
2 to seize and attempt to unbalance one another for the purpose of achieving physical mastery ⟨The boys *scuffled* till one knocked the other into the pool.⟩ — see WRESTLE

scull *vb* to move a boat by means of oars ⟨A couple *sculled* past in a racing shell.⟩ — see ¹ROW

sculler *n* a person who drives a boat forward by means of oars ⟨*Scullers* tend to have well-developed arm muscles.⟩ — see OARSMAN

sculpt *vb* to create a three-dimensional representation of (something) using solid material ⟨The colossal statue was *sculpted* from a single block of marble.⟩
synonyms carve, sculpture
related words chisel, engrave, etch, grave, incise, inscribe; knap; cast, form, model, shape

sculpture *vb* to create a three-dimensional representation of (something) using solid material ⟨The artist used a hammer and chisel to *sculpture* the horse out of ice.⟩ — see SCULPT

scum *n* **1** people looked down upon as ignorant and of the lowest class ⟨claimed that the townspeople were *scum*⟩ — see RABBLE
2 a person whose behavior is offensive to others ⟨Ignore the heckler—he's complete *scum*.⟩ — see JERK 1

scummy *adj* arousing or deserving of one's loathing and disgust ⟨The jury was disgusted by the defense attorney's *scummy* attempt to blame the victim.⟩ — see CONTEMPTIBLE 1

scurrilous *adj* marked by harsh insulting language ⟨a *scurrilous* satire on the scandal that enveloped Washington⟩ — see ABUSIVE

scurry *vb* to proceed or move quickly ⟨Everyone *scurried* back to work as soon as they saw the boss's car pull into the parking lot.⟩ — see HURRY 2

scurvy *adj* arousing or deserving of one's loathing and disgust ⟨After winning the lottery, she was beset by a whole *scurvy* swarm of con artists, ne'er-do-wells, and hangers-on.⟩ — see CONTEMPTIBLE 1

scuttle *vb* to proceed or move quickly ⟨mice *scuttling* across the barn floor to escape the cats⟩ — see HURRY 2

sea *n* the whole body of salt water that covers nearly three-fourths of the earth ⟨Millions of plants and animals live in the *sea*.⟩ — see OCEAN 1

sea devil *n* any of several extremely large rays ⟨A *sea devil* glided along the ocean floor.⟩ — see DEVILFISH

sea dog *n* one who operates or navigates a seagoing vessel ⟨the tale of a grizzled old *sea dog* who sets out for one last voyage⟩ — see SAILOR

seafarer *n* one who operates or navigates a seagoing vessel ⟨Ships and the intrepid *seafarers* who serve on them remain a vital part of the world economy.⟩ — see SAILOR

seam *vb* to mark with or as if with a line or groove ⟨In fencing circles it is a mark of honor to have one's face *seamed* with saber cuts.⟩ — see SCORE 1

seaman *n* one who operates or navigates a seagoing vessel ⟨a weathered old *seaman* who now captains a tour boat⟩ — see SAILOR

sear *vb* **1** to burn on the surface ⟨Lightly *sear* the steaks, but don't cook them all the way through.⟩ — see SCORCH 1
2 to make dry ⟨The clear desert air is *seared* by the summer sun.⟩ — see DRY 1

search *n* an act or process of looking carefully or thoroughly for someone or something ⟨The *search* for the missing hikers lasted several days.⟩
synonyms hunt, quest
related words shakedown; sweep; chase, pursuit; reconnaissance, scout; canvass (*also* canvas), survey; exploration, probe; forage

search *vb* **1** to look through (as a place) carefully or thoroughly in an effort to find or discover something ⟨Archaeologists have begun to *search* the southern end of the valley, where they believe the underground tombs are located.⟩
synonyms comb, dig (through), dredge, hunt (through), rake, ransack, rifle, rummage, scour
related words frisk, pat down; audit, check (out), examine, inspect, investigate, review, scan, scrutinize, survey; ascertain, descry, detect, determine, discover, ferret (out), find, find out, get, hit (on *or* upon), learn, locate, run down, scare up, track (down); grub (about), poke (around); explore, probe, snoop; browse, glance (over), look over; peruse, study
near antonyms hide; abandon, lose; ignore, neglect
2 to go into or range over for purposes of discovery ⟨the Spanish conquistadors *searched* vast areas of the Southwest in their quest for the fabled cities of gold⟩ — see EXPLORE 2

search (for *or* **out)** *vb* to go in search of ⟨Every year major league scouts crisscross the country to *search for* young players with promising talent.⟩ — see SEEK 1

searing *adj* **1** having a notably high temperature ⟨In our air-conditioned office, we were oblivious to the *searing* heat outside.⟩ — see HOT 1
2 difficult to endure ⟨The undersecretary looked chastened as he listened to the congressman's *searing* rebuke.⟩ — see HARSH 1

season *vb* **1** to make more pleasant to the taste by adding something intensely flavored ⟨The chef *seasoned* the vegetables as soon as they came out of the oven.⟩
synonyms flavor, lace, savor (*also* savour), spice
related words enhance, enrich, sauce; pepper, salt; aromatize, perfume
2 to bring to a proper or desired state of fitness ⟨carefully *seasoned* the cast iron pan with vegetable oil before using it for the first time⟩ — see CONDITION 1
3 to make able to withstand physical hardship, strain, or exposure ⟨troops that had been *seasoned* by months of heavy fighting⟩ — see HARDEN 2
4 to make competent (as by training, skill, or ability) for a particular office or function ⟨Her campaign manager has been *seasoned* by several hotly contested gubernatorial campaigns.⟩ — see QUALIFY 2

seasonable *adj* especially suitable for a certain time ⟨*Seasonable* advice is more likely to be listened to.⟩ — see TIMELY 1

seasoning *n* **1** something (as an herb) that adds an agreeable or interesting taste to food ⟨The stew was too bland before they added the *seasoning*.⟩
synonyms flavor, flavoring, spice
related words sauce
2 something used to enhance the flavor of cooked or prepared food ⟨She thinks salt is the ideal *seasoning* for all batter-fried foods.⟩ — see CONDIMENT

seat *n* **1** a place from which authority is exercised ⟨All applications had to be submitted at the county *seat* for proper processing.⟩
synonyms command, headquarters
related words high command; center, home; capital
2 the part of the body upon which someone sits ⟨fell down on his *seat*⟩ — see BUTTOCKS
3 a thing or place that is of greatest importance to an activity or interest ⟨a capital that is the *seat* of culture for the whole nation⟩ — see CENTER 1

seat *vb* **1** to cause to sit down ⟨The usher *seated* them in the third row.⟩
synonyms set down, sit
related words ensconce, settle; lay, lie, rest; place, put; recline, repose
2 to put into an office or welcome into an organization with special ceremonies ⟨one of the first appointments that he made after being *seated* as president of the state senate⟩ — see INSTALL 1

seclude *vb* to set or keep apart from others ⟨The patients will be *secluded* until they are no longer contagious.⟩ — see ISOLATE

secluded *adj* screened or sequestered from view ⟨We stayed in a *secluded* resort, far away from the regular tourist crowds.⟩
synonyms cloistered, covert, isolated, quiet, remote, retired, secret, sheltered
related words lone, lonely, lonesome, reclusive, solitary; private
near antonyms obvious, visible; exposed

secludedness *n* the state of being alone or kept apart from others ⟨The inn's greatest appeal for guests was its woodland *secludedness*.⟩ — see ISOLATION

seclusion *n* the state of being alone or kept apart from others ⟨She went into *seclusion* in order to focus entirely on writing her book.⟩ — see ISOLATION

¹second *n* a very small space of time ⟨I'll be ready in a *second*!⟩ — see INSTANT

²second *n* something separated from a group or lot for not being as good as the others ⟨The slightly flawed linens were sold as *seconds*.⟩ — see CULL

secondary *adj* **1** taken or created from something original or basic ⟨History textbooks are *secondary* sources for historical information and do not represent original research.⟩
synonyms derivative, secondhand
related words unoriginal; consequent, resultant
near antonyms fundamental, nonderivative; first, primary
antonyms basic, original
2 of little or less value or merit ⟨We need to focus on getting the groceries bought and the rent paid—everything else is *secondary*.⟩ — see INFERIOR 2

second–class *adj* **1** of little or less value or merit ⟨a playwright who produced only *second-class* work when he turned his hand to poetry⟩ — see INFERIOR 2
2 of average to below average quality ⟨It's only a *second-class* restaurant and not worth the high prices.⟩ — see MEDIOCRE 1

secondhand *adj* taken or created from something original or basic ⟨memoirs filled with *secondhand* stories about show-business celebrities⟩ — see SECONDARY 1

second–rate *adj* **1** of average to below average quality ⟨a *second-rate* song from a songwriter who has done much better⟩ — see MEDIOCRE 1
2 of little or less value or merit ⟨a *second-rate* company that was never considered among the top manufacturers of televisions⟩ — see INFERIOR 2

3 of low quality ⟨*second-rate* goods specifically manufactured for the low end of the market⟩ — see CHEAP 2

secrecy *n* the practice or habit of keeping secrets or keeping one's affairs secret ⟨She swore him to *secrecy*.⟩
synonyms closeness, secretiveness
related words confidentiality; discreetness, discretion, prudence; circumspection, wariness; reserve, reticence, silence, taciturnity; furtiveness, shiftiness, slyness, sneakiness, underhandedness; concealment, covertness, subterfuge
near antonyms candor, frankness, honesty, openness; imprudence, indiscretion

secret *adj* **1** undertaken or done so as to escape being observed or known by others ⟨a *secret* operation to rescue captive soldiers behind enemy lines⟩
synonyms clandestine, covert, furtive, hugger-mugger, private, privy, sneak, sneaking, sneaky, stealthy, surreptitious, undercover, underground, underhand, underhanded
related words off-the-record; classified, confidential, restricted, top secret, undisclosed; concealed, secreted
near antonyms acknowledged, avowed; aboveboard, straightforward, unconcealed, undisguised; unclassified, unrestricted; clear, evident, manifest, obvious, patent, plain
antonyms open, overt, public
2 working on missions in which one's objectives, activities, or true identity are not publicly revealed ⟨*secret* agents whose wartime exploits were known only by top government officials⟩
synonyms undercover
related words covert, private, secretive
near antonyms overt
3 screened or sequestered from view ⟨a *secret* cave that is screened by trees⟩ — see SECLUDED
4 not known or meant to be known by the general populace ⟨proprietary information that the company does its best to keep *secret*⟩ — see PRIVATE 1

secret *n* **1** information shared only with another or with a select few ⟨You didn't really expect him to keep a *secret* from me, did you?⟩
synonyms confidence
related words dope, lowdown
near antonyms open secret
2 something hard to understand or explain ⟨The *secrets* of the Egyptian pyramids include the construction methods used to lift the huge blocks of stone in place.⟩ — see MYSTERY
3 something that allows someone to achieve a desired goal ⟨The *secret* to advancement in this company is to appear dedicated.⟩ — see PASSPORT 1

secretary *n* an official whose job is to keep records ⟨File your intent to run for office with the city *secretary*.⟩ — see CLERK 1

secrete *vb* to put into a hiding place ⟨Treasure hunters found the hoard *secreted* in a cave.⟩ — see ¹HIDE 1

secretion *n* the placing of something out of sight ⟨The *secretion* of their money in the backyard turned out to be a huge mistake.⟩ — see CONCEALMENT 1

secretive *adj* given to keeping one's activities hidden from public observation or knowledge ⟨The intelligence agency remained *secretive* despite the media's demands for more openness in government.⟩
synonyms close, closemouthed, dark, reticent, uncommunicative
related words quiet, reserved, silent, taciturn, tight-lipped; discreet, prudent; clandestine, covert, furtive, hugger-mugger, secret, sneak, sneaky, stealthy, surreptitious, undercover, underhand, underhanded

near antonyms candid, frank, honest; blunt, outspoken, tactless
antonyms communicative, open

secretiveness *n* the practice or habit of keeping secrets or keeping one's affairs secret ⟨His *secretiveness* about his past always made some people suspicious of what he might be hiding.⟩ — see SECRECY

sect *n* a group of people acting together within a larger group ⟨One *sect* of medical researchers holds the minority view that the disease is not caused by that virus.⟩ — see FACTION

sectarian *adj* not broad or open in views or opinions ⟨There are people on both the left and the right who have staked out unyielding *sectarian* positions in this debate.⟩ — see NARROW 2

sectarian *n* one who stubbornly or intolerantly adheres to his or her own opinions and prejudices ⟨He charged that the work of Congress has been stymied by *sectarians* who are indifferent to reason and intolerant of compromise.⟩ — see BIGOT

section *n* **1** an area (as of a city) set apart for some purpose or having some special feature ⟨Several abandoned warehouses in the city's industrial *section* are being converted into art galleries and artists' lofts.⟩ — see DISTRICT
2 one of the pieces from which something is designed to be assembled ⟨We had trouble fitting the *sections* of the bookcase together.⟩ — see PART 1

secular *adj* not involving religion or religious matters ⟨That's an issue for the *secular* authorities, not the church.⟩ — see PROFANE 1

secure *adj* **1** having or showing great faith in oneself or one's abilities ⟨He's so *secure* about winning the marathon that he's practically spent the prize money.⟩ — see CONFIDENT 1
2 not exposed to the threat of loss or injury ⟨The fortress was thought to be *secure* against attack.⟩ — see SAFE 1
3 providing safety ⟨escaped to a *secure* location⟩ — see SAFE 2
4 worthy of one's trust ⟨a fund that should provide them with a *secure* income in their retirement⟩ — see DEPENDABLE

secure *vb* **1** to drive danger or attack away from ⟨sent troops to *secure* the city⟩ — see DEFEND 1
2 to make sure, certain, or safe ⟨a retirement account that will help to *secure* our future⟩ — see ENSURE
3 to put securely in place or in a desired position ⟨Candidates for admission are asked to *secure* a recent photo to their application forms.⟩ — see FASTEN 2
4 to receive as return for effort ⟨finally *secured* a job after sending out dozens of applications⟩ — see EARN 1

security *n* **1** means or method of defending ⟨measures taken to beef up our national *security*⟩ — see DEFENSE 1
2 something given or held to assure that the giver will keep a promise ⟨Their house will serve as *security* for the loan.⟩ — see PLEDGE 1
3 the state of not being exposed to danger ⟨After the burglaries, police presence in the neighborhood was enhanced to give residents a stronger sense of *security*.⟩ — see SAFETY 1

sedate *adj* **1** not joking or playful in mood or manner ⟨While not exactly cold, the doctor does maintain a *sedate* and purely professional demeanor with his patients.⟩ — see SERIOUS 1
2 free from emotional or mental agitation ⟨Her expression remained *sedate* as I told her the bad news.⟩ — see CALM 2

sedative *adj* tending to calm the emotions and relieve stress ⟨Some people find a cup of tea to be a civilized and *sedative* addition to an evening meal.⟩ — see SOOTHING 1

sediment *vb* to cause to come to rest at the bottom (as of a liquid) ⟨The water flowing into the reservoir is *sedimenting* silt faster than was originally expected.⟩ — see SETTLE 1

sediment *n* matter that settles to the bottom of a body of liquid ⟨The *sediment* at the bottom of the river needs to be routinely dredged so that it doesn't interfere with barge traffic.⟩ — see DEPOSIT 1

seduce *vb* to lead away from a usual or proper course by offering some pleasure or advantage ⟨I wasn't going to buy the car, but was *seduced* by the low-interest payment plan.⟩ — see LURE

seducer *n* one that tries to get a person to give in to a desire ⟨Fabled as a land of endless opportunity, California continues to be a *seducer* of dreamers and doers.⟩ — see TEMPTER

seduction *n* the act or pressure of giving in to a desire especially when ill-advised ⟨the swift *seduction* of the home buyers into a bigger house than they could afford⟩ — see TEMPTATION 1

seductive *adj* having an often mysterious or magical power or to attract ⟨People always remarked on the cult leader's *seductive* personality.⟩ — see FASCINATING 1

seductiveness *n* the power of irresistible attraction ⟨the *seductiveness* of the advertising⟩ — see CHARM 2

seductress *n* a woman whom men find irresistibly attractive ⟨In the movie she played Mata Hari, one of history's most infamous *seductresses*.⟩ — see SIREN

sedulous *adj* involved in often constant activity ⟨the judge's *sedulous* clerk⟩ — see BUSY 1

sedulously *adv* with great effort or determination ⟨*sedulously* devoted herself to completing the project on time⟩ — see HARD 1

see *vb* 1 to make note of (something) through the use of one's eyes ⟨Out of the corner of my eye I *saw* the deer run into the woods.⟩
  synonyms behold, catch, descry, discern, distinguish, espy, eye, look (at), note, notice, observe, perceive, regard, remark, sight, spot, spy, view, witness
  related words identify, make out, pick out, pick up; attend (to), consider, heed, mark, mind; study, watch; examine, inspect, scan, scrutinize, survey; glance (at), glimpse, peer (at)
  phrases get a load of [*slang*], lay eyes on, set eyes on
  near antonyms disregard, ignore, neglect, overpass, pass over; miss, overlook
2 to come to a knowledge of (something) by living through it ⟨a writer who *saw* World War II through the eyes of a common soldier⟩ — see EXPERIENCE
3 to come to an awareness of ⟨I bought the best seller just to *see* what all the fuss was about.⟩ — see DISCOVER 1
4 to have a vague awareness of ⟨I *see* a certain sadness in his letters to his relatives back home.⟩ — see FEEL 1
5 to make a social call upon ⟨You should go and *see* Father at the hospital this afternoon.⟩ — see VISIT 1
6 to have a clear idea of ⟨I *see* your point.⟩ — see COMPREHEND 1
7 to go along with in order to provide assistance, protection, or companionship ⟨Thanks for coming, and I'll *see* you to the door.⟩ — see ACCOMPANY 1
8 to form a mental picture of ⟨I can't *see* Grandma as a little girl.⟩ — see IMAGINE 1

seeable *adj* capable of being seen ⟨a *seeable* flaw in the windowpane⟩ — see VISIBLE 1

seed *n* 1 the source from which something grows or develops ⟨Ancient Greece provided the *seed* for much of Western civilization's political and philosophical thought.⟩
  synonyms origin, root
  related words spring, well, wellhead; beginning, birth, commencement, dawn, genesis, inception, incipiency,

launch, morning, onset, outset, start, threshold; creation, inauguration, origination
2 the descendants of a person, animal, or plant ⟨The famous stallion's *seed* can be found on racetracks all over the world.⟩ — see OFFSPRING

seed *vb* to put or set into the ground to grow ⟨*seeded* grass in the backyard⟩ — see PLANT 1

seediness *n* the state of being unattended to or not cared for ⟨The general *seediness* of the hotel made us decide to find another.⟩ — see NEGLECT 1

seedy *adj* 1 showing signs of advanced wear and tear and neglect ⟨an area of *seedy* warehouses and old mill buildings⟩ — see SHABBY 1
2 worn or torn into or as if into rags ⟨chose old, *seedy* clothes to wear while painting the bathroom⟩ — see RAGGED 2

seeing *conj* for the reason that ⟨*Seeing* as we're already running late, there's no reason to waste any more time.⟩ — see SINCE

seek *vb* 1 to go in search of ⟨Henry Hudson was set adrift by mutinous crewmen while *seeking* the Northwest Passage to the Pacific Ocean.⟩
  synonyms cast about (for), cast around (for), forage (for), hunt, look up, pursue, quest, search (for *or* out)
  related words ferret (out), root (out)
  phrases look for
  near antonyms hide, lose; ignore, neglect
2 to make a request for ⟨came *seeking* financial advice⟩ — see ASK (FOR) 1
3 to make an effort to do ⟨*seek* to find the best solution⟩ — see ATTEMPT

seeker *n* one who seeks an office, honor, position, or award ⟨predicted a tough year for summer job *seekers*⟩ — see CANDIDATE

seem *vb* to give the impression of being ⟨I tried to cheer them up because they *seemed* depressed.⟩
  synonyms act, appear, feel, look, make, sound
  related words dissemble, pretend; recall, resemble, suggest; hint, imply, insinuate

seeming *adj* appearing to be true on the basis of evidence that may or may not be confirmed ⟨a *seeming* contradiction that disappeared upon closer analysis of the text⟩ — see APPARENT 1

seeming *n* outward and often deceptive indication ⟨I was fooled by the *seeming* simplicity of the instructions.⟩ — see APPEARANCE 2

seemingly *adv* to all outward appearances ⟨a *seemingly* contented baby who was fast asleep in his crib⟩ — see APPARENTLY

seemliness *n* the quality or state of being especially suitable or fitting ⟨questioned the *seemliness* of the timing for the announcement⟩ — see APPROPRIATENESS

seemly *adj* 1 following the established traditions of refined society and good taste ⟨It would not be *seemly* to use the memorial service as a forum for your political views.⟩ — see PROPER 1
2 very pleasing to look at ⟨a young man of *seemly* appearance, robust health, and keen intelligence⟩ — see BEAUTIFUL 1

seep *vb* to flow forth slowly through small openings ⟨water *seeping* through the basement walls⟩ — see EXUDE

seer *n* one who predicts future events or developments ⟨Several leading Wall Street *seers* have cautioned investors to prepare for a downturn in the economy.⟩ — see PROPHET 1

seesaw *vb* 1 to make a series of unsteady side-to-side motions ⟨Their boat *seesawed* in the rough water.⟩ — see ROCK 1
2 to make short up-and-down movements ⟨The price of the stock has been *seesawing* all week.⟩ — see NOD

seethe *vb* **1** to be in a state of violent rolling motion ⟨The water *seethed* with schools of feeding piranha.⟩
synonyms boil, churn, roil
related words reel, spin, swirl, whirl; agitate, stir
near antonyms abate, calm, subside
2 to be excited or emotionally stirred up with anger ⟨She *seethed* at the injustice of it all.⟩ — see BOIL 1

segment *n* one of the pieces from which something is designed to be assembled ⟨I think I lost one *segment* of this model kit.⟩ — see PART 1

segregate *vb* to set or keep apart from others ⟨The sick cows were *segregated* from the remainder of the herd.⟩ — see ISOLATE

segregation *n* the state of being alone or kept apart from others ⟨a Supreme Court case that ended *segregation* in public schools⟩ — see ISOLATION

seize *vb* **1** to have a clear idea of ⟨a critic with a sharp intellect that is able to *seize* the most subtle nuances of a work of art⟩ — see COMPREHEND 1
2 to take or keep under one's control by authority of law ⟨Police *seized* the leaders of the hacking community.⟩ — see ARREST 1
3 to take physical control or possession of (something) suddenly or forcibly ⟨She *seized* the escaping balloon just before it got out of reach.⟩ — see CATCH 1
4 to take or make use of under a guise of authority but without actual right ⟨Richard III *seized* the English throne from his nephew Edward in 1483.⟩ — see APPROPRIATE 1

seizure *n* **1** a sudden experiencing of a physical or mental disorder ⟨an epileptic *seizure*⟩ — see ATTACK 2
2 the unlawful taking or withholding of something from the rightful owner under a guise of authority ⟨secret intrigues with the czar's ministers that culminated in the czarina's *seizure* of the throne⟩ — see APPROPRIATION 2

seldom *adv* not often ⟨We *seldom* go to the theater downtown because its prices are so high.⟩
synonyms infrequently, little, rarely
related words ne'er, never; irregularly, occasionally, sometimes, sporadically
phrases once in a blue moon
near antonyms customarily, generally, habitually, ordinarily, routinely, usually; always, constantly, continually, continuously, endlessly, eternally, ever, everlastingly, evermore, forever, invariably, perennially, perpetually, unceasingly; chronically, recurrently, repeatedly
antonyms frequently, oft, often, oftentimes (*or* ofttimes)

select *vb* to decide to accept (someone or something) from a group of possibilities ⟨They *selected* only two people out of 300 applicants for the summer internship.⟩ — see CHOOSE 1

select *adj* **1** singled out from a number or group as more to one's liking ⟨The company claims to use only *select* beans to make its coffee.⟩
synonyms choice, chosen, elect, favored, favorite, picked, preferred, selected
related words fashionable; exclusive; culled, picked over, screened, weeded (out), winnowed (out)
phrases of choice
near antonyms average, common, commonplace, ordinary, run-of-the-mill
2 having qualities that appeal to a refined taste ⟨*select* fabrics that the shop makes into expensive suits for its well-heeled clientele⟩ — see CHOICE 1

selected *adj* singled out from a number or group as more to one's liking ⟨a *selected* brand of ice cream with an exceptionally high butterfat content⟩ — see SELECT 1

selecting *n* the act or process of selecting ⟨The *selecting* of the party's nominee took three days and half a dozen votes.⟩ — see SELECTION 1

selection *n* **1** the act or process of selecting ⟨Her *selection* of a running mate was a long, tedious affair.⟩
synonyms choice, choosing, election, picking, selecting
related words option; appointment, assignment, designation, naming, nomination; decision
2 a person or thing that is chosen ⟨Our *selection* was the third entrant in the dog show.⟩ — see CHOICE 2
3 the power, right, or opportunity to choose ⟨The inn's table d'hôte is excellent, but there's very limited *selection*.⟩ — see CHOICE 1
4 a number of things selected from a group to stand for the whole ⟨a *selection* of the company's latest line of products for display at the trade show⟩ — see SAMPLE 1

selective *adj* tending to select carefully ⟨We were highly *selective* about the music we listened to.⟩
synonyms choosy (*or* choosey), particular, picky
related words nice; fastidious, finicky, fussy; discerning, discriminating, judicious
near antonyms indiscriminating
antonyms nonselective, unselective

selector *n* someone with the right or responsibility for making a selection ⟨the librarians who are the *selectors* of the annual award for best children's book⟩
synonyms chooser, namer, picker
related words elector, voter; nominator; decider

self–acting *adj* designed to replace or decrease human labor and especially physical labor ⟨*self-acting* machines that were ushered in with the industrial revolution⟩ — see LABORSAVING

self–admiration *n* an often unjustified feeling of being pleased with oneself or with one's situation or achievements ⟨His overweening *self-admiration* blinded him to constructive criticism of any kind.⟩ — see COMPLACENCE 1

self–assertive *adj* **1** having or showing a bold forcefulness in the pursuit of a goal ⟨We need to hire *self-assertive* salespeople who don't require constant supervision.⟩ — see AGGRESSIVE 1
2 having a feeling of superiority that shows itself in an overbearing attitude ⟨We chose a less *self-assertive* and more self-effacing applicant.⟩ — see ARROGANT

self–assurance *n* great faith in oneself or one's abilities ⟨Her *self-assurance* led her to quit her dead-end job and start her own company.⟩ — see CONFIDENCE 1

self–assured *adj* having or showing great faith in oneself or one's abilities ⟨He's a *self-assured* yachtsman who's not at all intimidated by the competition.⟩ — see CONFIDENT 1

self–centered *adj* overly concerned with one's own desires, needs, or interests ⟨a group of *self-centered* residents with no interest or involvement in their community⟩ — see EGOCENTRIC

self–centeredness *n* excessive interest in oneself ⟨In her extreme *self-centeredness* she hadn't even noticed that her friend was depressed.⟩ — see EGOISM

self–conceit *n* an often unjustified feeling of being pleased with oneself or with one's situation or achievements ⟨The movie star became a victim of her own *self-conceit*, having deluded herself into believing that she was as great as her press agent said she was.⟩ — see COMPLACENCE 1

self–conceited *adj* having too high an opinion of oneself ⟨*self-conceited* medical researchers who never acknowledged their colleagues' contributions⟩ — see CONCEITED

self–confidence *n* great faith in oneself or one's abilities ⟨For so young a pianist, he has remarkable composure and *self-confidence* on stage.⟩ — see CONFIDENCE 1

self–confident *adj* having or showing great faith in oneself or one's abilities ⟨Only a *self-confident* person can win the trust of the people and serve as an effective leader.⟩ — see CONFIDENT 1

self–containment *n* the power to control one's actions, impulses, or emotions ⟨A man of extraordinary *self-containment*, he refused to lose his temper even in the most trying of circumstances.⟩ — see WILL 1

self–control *n* **1** the power to control one's actions, impulses, or emotions ⟨Toddlers have very little *self-control*.⟩ — see WILL 1
2 the checking of one's true feelings and impulses when dealing with others ⟨She could be passionate and intense, but generally exercised steely *self-control* in the company of strangers.⟩ — see CONSTRAINT 1

self–denial *n* the act or practice of giving up or rejecting something once enjoyed or desired ⟨Dieting is an endless exercise in *self-denial*.⟩ — see RENUNCIATION

self–destruction *n* the act of deliberately killing oneself ⟨a story of *self-destruction* through excess⟩ — see SUICIDE

self–determination *n* **1** the act or power of making one's own choices or decisions ⟨The United States officially recognizes 18 as the age at which someone is entitled to *self-determination*.⟩ — see FREE WILL
2 the state of being free from the control or power of another ⟨rebels fighting for the territory's *self-determination*⟩ — see FREEDOM 1

self–discipline *n* the power to control one's actions, impulses, or emotions ⟨It takes *self-discipline* not to yell out when someone makes you angry.⟩ — see WILL 1

self–esteem *n* **1** a reasonable or justifiable sense of one's worth or importance ⟨Friends and family have tried to help the child develop some *self-esteem*.⟩ — see PRIDE 1
2 an often unjustified feeling of being pleased with oneself or with one's situation or achievements ⟨His towering *self-esteem* made praise from other people entirely unnecessary.⟩ — see COMPLACENCE 1
3 great faith in oneself or one's abilities ⟨the kind of *self-esteem* that a struggling actor needs to keep going in the face of constant discouragement and rejection⟩ — see CONFIDENCE 1

self–governing *adj* **1** not being under the rule or control of another ⟨She left home and became entirely *self-governing* and financially independent at the age of 18.⟩ — see FREE 1
2 of, relating to, or favoring political democracy ⟨a *self-governing* nation that could be a role model for other countries in the region⟩ — see DEMOCRATIC

self–government *n* **1** government in which the supreme power is held by the people and used by them directly or indirectly through representation ⟨*Self-government* implies faith in the wisdom and essential goodness of the people.⟩ — see DEMOCRACY
2 the power to control one's actions, impulses, or emotions ⟨Steely *self-government* was all that kept her from lashing out at the rude customer.⟩ — see WILL 1
3 the state of being free from the control or power of another ⟨championed *self-government* for the nation's indigenous peoples⟩ — see FREEDOM 1

selfhood *n* the set of qualities that make a person different from other people ⟨He spent a gap year determining the core of his *selfhood*.⟩ — see INDIVIDUALITY 1

self–identity *n* the set of qualities that make a person different from other people ⟨twins making an effort to establish their separate *self-identities*⟩ — see INDIVIDUALITY 1

self–importance *n* **1** an exaggerated sense of one's importance that shows itself in the making of excessive or unjustified claims ⟨The boxer's flamboyant *self-importance* often made for a colorful prefight press conference.⟩ — see ARROGANCE

2 an often unjustified feeling of being pleased with oneself or with one's situation or achievements ⟨Her overbearing *self-importance* has given her a sense of entitlement.⟩ — see COMPLACENCE 1

self–important *adj* having too high an opinion of oneself ⟨a *self-important* businessman who believed his schedule mattered more than anyone else's⟩ — see CONCEITED

self–imposed *adj* done, made, or given with one's own free will ⟨If the candidates all follow *self-imposed* campaign-spending limits, government oversight is unnecessary.⟩ — see VOLUNTARY 1

self–interest *n* excessive interest in oneself ⟨Her degree of *self-interest* is perhaps best reflected in her favorite topic of conversation—herself.⟩ — see EGOISM

selfish *adj* overly concerned with one's own desires, needs, or interests ⟨a *selfish* desire to succeed at the expense of others⟩ — see EGOCENTRIC

selfishness *n* excessive interest in oneself ⟨The only reason for constantly ignoring everyone else's problems is *selfishness*.⟩ — see EGOISM

self–possessed *adj* free from emotional or mental agitation ⟨a supremely *self-possessed* teacher who could handle any crisis⟩ — see CALM 2

self–possession *n* **1** evenness of emotions or temper ⟨That neurosurgeon's *self-possession* in the operating room is legendary.⟩ — see EQUANIMITY
2 the power to control one's actions, impulses, or emotions ⟨The little girl's *self-possession* very occasionally gave way to crying fits.⟩ — see WILL 1

self–regard *n* **1** excessive interest in oneself ⟨Her *self-regard* meant that she assumed everyone wanted to hear about every tiny detail of her life.⟩ — see EGOISM
2 a reasonable or justifiable sense of one's worth or importance ⟨people with enough *self-regard* to keep their modest home in spotless condition⟩ — see PRIDE 1

self–reliance *n* the ability to care for one's self ⟨Some people don't achieve *self-reliance* until they're over 30 years old.⟩ — see SELF-SUFFICIENCY

self–reliant *adj* able to take care of oneself or itself without outside help ⟨a surprisingly calm and *self-reliant* child⟩ — see SELF-SUFFICIENT

self–reproach *n* a feeling of responsibility for wrongdoing ⟨He was filled with *self-reproach* for causing the accident.⟩ — see GUILT 1

self–respect *n* a reasonable or justifiable sense of one's worth or importance ⟨Getting a job did a lot to increase his *self-respect*.⟩ — see PRIDE 1

self–restraint *n* **1** the power to control one's actions, impulses, or emotions ⟨She demonstrated an almost unnatural *self-restraint* during the trial.⟩ — see WILL 1
2 the checking of one's true feelings and impulses when dealing with others ⟨We must practice *self-restraint* even with people who are deliberately rude.⟩ — see CONSTRAINT 1

self–rule *n* government in which the supreme power is held by the people and used by them directly or indirectly through representation ⟨The newly created United States opted for *self-rule* rather than monarchy.⟩ — see DEMOCRACY

self–ruling *adj* **1** of, relating to, or favoring political democracy ⟨Having rid itself of the yoke of colonialism, the new nation chose to be a *self-ruling* state.⟩ — see DEMOCRATIC
2 not being under the rule or control of another ⟨was granted special status as a *self-ruling* province⟩ — see FREE 1

selfsame *adj* being one and not another ⟨That's the *selfsame* man who once helped me.⟩ — see SAME 2

self–satisfaction *n* an often unjustified feeling of being pleased with oneself or with one's situation or achievements 〈felt a smug *self-satisfaction* at having been proven right〉 — see COMPLACENCE 1

self–satisfied *adj* having too high an opinion of oneself 〈a *self-satisfied* woman who thought that if she could balance two careers, everyone else should too〉 — see CONCEITED

self–seeker *n* one who does things only for his own benefit and with little regard for right and wrong 〈He's a *self-seeker* who is nice only to people who can do him favors.〉

synonyms opportunist, temporizer

related words egocentric; conniver, machinator, plotter, schemer; hanger-on, leech

near antonyms altruist

self–seeking *adj* **1** having a strong desire for personal advancement 〈a *self-seeking* schemer who claimed others' ideas and achievements as his own〉 — see AMBITIOUS 1

2 overly concerned with one's own desires, needs, or interests 〈a *self-seeking* woman who could be counted on to sidetrack all conversation into a discussion of her problems〉 — see EGOCENTRIC

self–starter *n* an ambitious person who eagerly goes after what is desired 〈hired a *self-starter* who instantly saw what needed to be done, and did it〉 — see GO-GETTER

self–sufficiency *n* the ability to care for one's self 〈*Self-sufficiency* is a goal that all teenagers should work towards.〉

synonyms independence, self-reliance, self-support

related words autonomy, freedom, self-determination; potency, power, resilience, strength

near antonyms helplessness, impotence, impotency, inadequacy, weakness

antonyms dependence (*also* dependance), reliance

self–sufficient *adj* able to take care of oneself or itself without outside help 〈The college student worked nights so that he would be *self-sufficient*.〉

synonyms independent, self-reliant, self-supporting

related words autonomous, free, self-determining; potent, powerful, resilient, strong

near antonyms helpless, inadequate, incompetent, insufficient; impotent, weak

antonyms dependent, reliant

self–support *n* the ability to care for one's self 〈hopes to achieve full *self-support* within a year of graduating from college〉 — see SELF-SUFFICIENCY

self–supporting *adj* able to take care of oneself or itself without outside help 〈She had to take a higher-paying job in order to be *self-supporting*.〉 — see SELF-SUFFICIENT

self–will *n* a steadfast adherence to an opinion, purpose, or course of action in spite of reason, arguments, or persuasion 〈a schoolboy with a streak of *self-will* and rebellion〉 — see OBSTINACY

self–willed *adj* sticking to an opinion, purpose, or course of action in spite of reason, arguments, or persuasion 〈a *self-willed* toddler who refused to take her shoes off in the examining room〉 — see OBSTINATE

sell *vb* to offer for sale to the public 〈used to *sell* groceries in a small neighborhood market〉 — see MARKET

sell (for) *vb* to have a price of 〈The house is *selling for* $200,000.〉 — see COST

sell (out) *vb* to be unfaithful or disloyal to 〈The band *sold out* its faithful followers, abandoning its edgy style for a more commercial sound.〉 — see BETRAY 1

seller *n* the person in a business deal who hands over an item in exchange for money 〈The *seller* ceremoniously gave me the title to the car when I handed him my check.〉 — see VENDOR

sellout *n* the act or fact of violating the trust or confidence of another 〈The *sellout* makes it much harder for me to trust you ever again.〉 — see BETRAYAL

semblance *n* **1** a display of emotion or behavior that is insincere or intended to deceive 〈Eve tried to project some *semblance* of confidence even though public speaking terrified her.〉 — see MASQUERADE

2 outward and often deceptive indication 〈a used-car dealer with only a *semblance* of honesty〉 — see APPEARANCE 2

semidarkness *n* a time or place of little or no light 〈fumbling around in the *semidarkness*〉 — see DARK 1

seminar *n* a meeting featuring a group discussion 〈a *seminar* bringing together the world's leading epidemiologists〉 — see FORUM 1

seminary *n* a place or establishment for teaching and learning 〈a *seminary* exclusively for women〉 — see SCHOOL

send *vb* to cause to go or be taken from one place to another 〈They promised to *send* the package in the morning.〉

synonyms consign, dispatch, pack (off), ship, shoot, transfer, transmit, transport

related words convey, deliver, hand over, pass, render; advance, drop, launch; address, forward; export, import; bestow, contribute, donate, give, present; resend, return

near antonyms acquire, draw, earn, gain, garner, get, obtain, procure, secure

antonyms accept

senior *adj* being of advanced years and especially past middle age 〈We bought special food intended for *senior* dogs.〉 — see ELDERLY

senior *n* **1** one who is older than another 〈Since the man next door is my *senior* by a number of years, I always address him as "Mr. Barton."〉

synonyms elder

related words ancestor, forerunner, predecessor

near antonyms contemporary, peer; descendant (*also* descendent), successor

antonyms junior

2 one who is above another in rank, station, or office 〈The young attorney benefited from the mentorship of one of his *seniors* at the firm.〉 — see SUPERIOR

3 the senior member of a group 〈When he retires, she will be the *senior* on the faculty.〉 — see DEAN

4 a person of advanced years 〈Weekday movie matinees are often popular with *seniors*.〉 — see SENIOR CITIZEN

senior citizen *n* a person of advanced years 〈More and more *senior citizens* are living active, rewarding lives.〉

synonyms ancient, elder, golden-ager, oldster, old-timer, senior

related words graybeard, patriarch; beldam (*or* beldame), dowager, grandam (*or* grandame); adult, grown-up

near antonyms adolescent, minor; child, cub, juvenile, kid

antonyms youngster, youth

sensation *n* **1** an indefinite physical response to a stimulus 〈We felt just the smallest *sensation* of warmth when we leaned against the radiator.〉

synonyms feel, feeling, sense

related words impression, perception; hint, suggestion, touch

2 a practice or interest that is very popular for a short time 〈The satirical video was a short-lived online *sensation*.〉 — see FAD

3 something extraordinary or surprising 〈The first clone was considered a *sensation*.〉 — see WONDER 1

sensational *adj* **1** arousing a strong and usually superficial interest or emotional reaction 〈The *sensational* news story caused a stir, but after a few days everyone forgot about it.〉

synonyms lurid, screaming

related words catchy; colorful, juicy, racy, suggestive; dramatic, histrionic, melodramatic, theatrical (*also* theatric); coarse, vulgar; gory, shocking
near antonyms innocuous, inoffensive, tame; dignified, formal, proper, restrained
antonyms nonsensational
2 of or relating to physical sensation or the senses ⟨*sensational* hallucinations⟩ — see SENSORY
3 of the very best kind ⟨This ice cream is *sensational*!⟩ — see EXCELLENT

sense *n* **1** an indefinite physical response to a stimulus ⟨a strange *sense* of discomfort brought on by the room's strong colors⟩ — see SENSATION 1
2 the ability to learn and understand or to deal with problems ⟨Although he has little formal education, he is a man of considerable practical *sense*.⟩ — see INTELLIGENCE 1
3 the ability to make intelligent decisions especially in everyday matters ⟨You have the *sense* to handle anything that comes up.⟩ — see COMMON SENSE
4 the idea that is conveyed or intended to be conveyed to the mind by language, symbol, or action ⟨I got the general *sense* of the poem.⟩ — see MEANING 1
5 the thought processes that have been established as leading to valid solutions to problems ⟨Your argument simply shows no *sense*.⟩ — see LOGIC
sense *vb* **1** to have a vague awareness of ⟨The deer seemed to *sense* danger.⟩ — see FEEL 1
2 to have a clear idea of ⟨I did not *sense* the full meaning of his cryptic warning until much later.⟩ — see COMPREHEND 1

senseless *adj* **1** having lost consciousness ⟨She collapsed, *senseless*, after hitting her head.⟩ — see UNCONSCIOUS 1
2 having no meaning ⟨a pretty but *senseless* phrase⟩ — see MEANINGLESS
3 not having or showing an ability to absorb ideas readily ⟨He may be a little absentminded, but he's really not as *senseless* as he seems.⟩ — see STUPID 1
4 showing or marked by a lack of good sense or judgment ⟨a *senseless* decision to risk his life on a practical joke⟩ — see FOOLISH 1
5 lacking animate awareness or sensation ⟨Even the *senseless* sea seemed determined to swamp the storm-tossed ship.⟩ — see INSENSATE 1

senselessness *n* **1** lack of good sense or judgment ⟨Who had the *senselessness* to mix these dangerous chemicals together?⟩ — see FOOLISHNESS 1
2 language, behavior, or ideas that are absurd and contrary to good sense ⟨babbled some *senselessness* while talking in his sleep⟩ — see NONSENSE 1
3 the quality or state of lacking intelligence or quickness of mind ⟨the *senselessness* of the decision to quit college⟩ — see STUPIDITY 1

sensibilities *pl n* general emotional condition ⟨The violent movie upset their *sensibilities*.⟩ — see FEELING 2
sensible *adj* **1** able to be perceived by a sense or by the mind ⟨a *sensible* change in temperature⟩ — see PERCEPTIBLE
2 according to the rules of logic ⟨This is the only *sensible* conclusion.⟩ — see LOGICAL 1
3 based on sound reasoning or information ⟨a *sensible* decision to delay marriage until they knew one another better⟩ — see GOOD 1
4 having specified facts or feelings actively impressed on the mind ⟨*sensible* of the shift in attitude by the general public on the issue⟩ — see CONSCIOUS 1
sensibleness *n* the ability to make intelligent decisions especially in everyday matters ⟨proud of their teenage daughter's unfailing *sensibleness* and maturity⟩ — see COMMON SENSE

sensitive *adj* **1** able to sense slight impressions or differences ⟨a scale that is *sensitive* to the smallest change in weight⟩ — see ACUTE 1
2 being in a situation where one is likely to meet with harm ⟨She's very *sensitive* to the sun and will burn if she's outside for any amount of time.⟩ — see LIABLE 1
3 easily injured without careful handling ⟨the *sensitive* skin of a newborn mouse⟩ — see TENDER 1
4 of or relating to physical sensation or the senses ⟨*sensitive* data⟩ — see SENSORY
5 requiring exceptional skill or caution in performance or handling ⟨Pointing out to the boss that she's wrong is always a *sensitive* task.⟩ — see TRICKY 1

sensitiveness *n* the state or quality of being able to sense slight impressions or differences ⟨The extreme *sensitiveness* of the detection mechanism means that the alarm is always going accidentally.⟩ — see ACUITY
sensitivity *n* the state or quality of being able to sense slight impressions or differences ⟨the *sensitivity* needed for a microphone that will be used in a recording studio⟩ — see ACUITY
sensor *n* a device that detects some physical quantity and responds usually with a transmitted signal ⟨The thief accidentally triggered the motion *sensor*, which set off the alarm.⟩
synonyms detector
related words eye; electric eye, photoelectric cell; alarm (*also* alarum), trigger

sensory *adj* of or relating to physical sensation or the senses ⟨Trying to listen to music while watching the TV and eating dinner caused a sort of *sensory* overload.⟩
synonyms sensational, sensitive, sensuous
related words afferent, receptive; sensate, sensual
near antonyms extrasensory, intuitional

sensual *adj* pleasing to the physical senses ⟨the *sensual* feel of a velvet shirt against the skin⟩
synonyms carnal, fleshly, luscious, lush, sensuous, voluptuous
related words bodily, corporeal; agreeable, delectable, delicious, delightful, dreamy, gratifying, palatable, pleasant, pleasing, pleasurable, scrumptious; epicurean, luxurious
near antonyms harsh, painful, uncomfortable; foul, hideous

sensuous *adj* **1** of or relating to physical sensation or the senses ⟨the *sensuous* pleasure of a massage⟩ — see SENSORY
2 pleasing to the physical senses ⟨a gentle, *sensuous* breeze⟩ — see SENSUAL

sentence *n* a decision made by a court or tribunal regarding a case it has heard ⟨Because it was a first offense, the defendant was given a suspended *sentence*.⟩
synonyms finding, holding, judgment (*or* judgement), ruling
related words inquest, verdict; authority; decree, edict, order; declaration, deliverance, dictum, pronouncement; conclusion, decision, determination, opinion, resolution; discipline, penalty, punishment
sentence *vb* to impose a judicial punishment on ⟨The judge *sentenced* him to a fine and time served.⟩
synonyms condemn, damn, doom
related words adjudge, judge; castigate, censure, chasten, chastise, correct, discipline, penalize, punish; conclude, decide, decree, determine, find, opine, resolve, rule
near antonyms pardon, reprieve
sentient *adj* having specified facts or feelings actively impressed on the mind ⟨*sentient* of the danger posed by the approaching storm⟩ — see CONSCIOUS 1

sentiment *n* **1** a subjective response to a person, thing, or situation ⟨a *sentiment* of happiness and goodwill⟩ — see FEELING 1
2 an idea that is believed to be true or valid without positive knowledge ⟨antiwar *sentiments*⟩ — see OPINION 1
sentimental *adj* appealing to the emotions in an obvious and tiresome way ⟨a *sentimental* story about unrequited love⟩ — see CORNY
sentimentalism *n* the state or quality of having an excess of tender feelings (as of love, nostalgia, or compassion) ⟨The novel's *sentimentalism* bored me.⟩ — see SENTIMENTALITY
sentimentality *n* the state or quality of having an excess of tender feelings (as of love, nostalgia, or compassion) ⟨The *sentimentality* of the story of star-crossed lovers only made it even more popular with moviegoers.⟩
synonyms mawkishness, mush, sappiness, sentimentalism, sloppiness
related words emotion; sentiment; corn, corniness, hokeyness (*or* hokiness), schmaltz (*also* schmalz)
near antonyms cynicism, hardheadedness, hard-heartedness
sentinel *n* a person or group that watches over someone or something ⟨A lone *sentinel* kept watch over the fort.⟩ — see GUARD 1
sentry *n* a person or group that watches over someone or something ⟨a *sentry* posted to watch for intruders⟩ — see GUARD 1
separable *adj* capable of being split into two or more parts or pieces ⟨the outdated belief that the atom is the smallest particle of matter and is not *separable*⟩
synonyms divisible
related words detachable
near antonyms combinable, joinable
antonyms indivisible
separate *adj* **1** not the same or shared ⟨We stayed in *separate* apartments on our vacation.⟩
synonyms different, individual, respective
related words disparate, dissimilar, distinct, distinctive, distinguishable, divergent, diverse, unalike, varied
near antonyms identical, selfsame, very
antonyms same
2 not physically attached to another unit ⟨The housing development has 200 *separate* homes, each with its own enclosed yard.⟩
synonyms detached, disconnected, discrete, free, freestanding, single, unattached, unconnected
related words independent, self-contained; individual, private
near antonyms adjoining
antonyms attached, connected, joined, linked
3 not being under the rule or control of another ⟨The former colony became a *separate* country.⟩ — see FREE 1
4 of, relating to, or belonging to a single person ⟨The siblings each have *separate* interests.⟩ — see INDIVIDUAL 1
separate *vb* **1** to set or force apart ⟨We tried to *separate* the gluey pages, but they were stuck tight.⟩
synonyms break up, disconnect, disjoin, disjoint, dissever, dissociate, disunite, divide, divorce, part, ramify, resolve, sever, split, sunder, uncouple, unlink, unyoke
related words break down, decompose, disassemble, disintegrate, dissolve; bisect, cleave, dissect, halve, partition, quarter, segment, subdivide, trisect; break, fracture, pull, rend, rift, rip, rive, rupture, tear; cut off, insulate, isolate, seclude, segregate, sequester; detach, disengage, disentangle, unravel, untie
near antonyms assemble, associate, blend, combine, mingle, mix; connect, couple; accumulate, agglutinate, attach, bind, cement, close, fasten, fuse, knit, stick, weld
antonyms join, link, unify, unite

2 to go or move in different directions from a central point ⟨The searchers *separated* in order to cover more ground.⟩
synonyms branch (out), diverge, divide, fork, part, spread
related words bestrew, break up, broadcast, clear out, disband, dispel, disperse, dissipate, distribute, scatter, sow; distance, recede, retreat
near antonyms assemble, gather, meet
antonyms converge, join
3 to arrange or assign according to type ⟨*separated* the students by age⟩ — see CLASSIFY 1
4 to set or keep apart from others ⟨*separated* the injured calf from the herd⟩ — see ISOLATE
5 to understand or point out the difference in ⟨trying to *separate* fact from fiction on one specific point⟩ — see DISTINGUISH 1
separation *n* **1** the act or process of a whole separating into two or more parts or pieces ⟨the *separation* of Norway and Sweden into two independent nations in 1905⟩
synonyms breakup, dissolution, disunion, division, fractionation, partition, schism, split
related words breach, rupture; divorce, severance; decomposition, disassembly, dismemberment, segmentation, subdivision; diffusion, dispersal, dispersion, scattering; administration, apportionment, distribution; isolation, seclusion, segregation, sequestration
near antonyms assemblage, association; attachment, conjunction, connection, link, linkage, linkup; aggregation, combination, consolidation, fusion
antonyms unification, union
2 the state of being kept distinct ⟨The *separation* of church and state is an important concept in the United States.⟩
synonyms demarcation, discreteness, discrimination, distinction
related words differentiation; isolation, segregation
near antonyms blurring, confusion
3 a movement in different directions away from a common point ⟨a sudden *separation* of the herd of deer when they were startled⟩ — see DIVERGENCE 1
4 an open space in a barrier (as a wall or hedge) ⟨the narrow *separation* between posts in the fence⟩ — see GAP 1
5 the act or process of two or more persons going off in different directions ⟨friends who dreaded the inevitable *separation* after graduation⟩ — see PARTING 1
6 something that divides, separates, or marks off ⟨a filing cabinet with lots of adjustable *separations*⟩ — see DIVISION 1
sepulchral *adj* causing or marked by an atmosphere lacking in cheer ⟨The decrepit mansion had a *sepulchral* tone that gave everyone a chill.⟩ — see GLOOMY 1
sepulture *n* **1** a final resting place for a dead person ⟨opened the *sepulture* and examined the mummy⟩ — see GRAVE 1
2 the act or ceremony of putting a dead body in its final resting place ⟨the final *sepulture* of the body⟩ — see BURIAL 1
sequel *n* a condition or occurrence traceable to a cause ⟨Higher prices are a logical *sequel* to higher costs for manufacturers.⟩ — see EFFECT 1
sequence *n* **1** a condition or occurrence traceable to a cause ⟨The attempt to help was a natural *sequence* to her charitable nature.⟩ — see EFFECT 1
2 a series of things linked together ⟨a *sequence* of events that no one predicted⟩ — see CHAIN 1
3 the way objects in space or events in time are arranged or follow one another ⟨Police are trying to reconstruct the *sequence* of events.⟩ — see ORDER 1

sequential *adj* following one after another without others coming in between ⟨I explained that if the two required algebra semesters weren't *sequential*, the students would likely forget the material.⟩ — see CONSECUTIVE

sequester *vb* 1 to set or keep apart from others ⟨*sequestered* the patient until she was no longer contagious⟩ — see ISOLATE

2 to take ownership or control of (something) by right of one's authority ⟨*sequestering* the debtor's property⟩ — see CONFISCATE

sequestration *n* the state of being alone or kept apart from others ⟨What would you bring for *sequestration* on a desert island?⟩ — see ISOLATION

sere *also* **sear** *adj* marked by little or no precipitation or humidity ⟨a *sere* region that can't support agriculture⟩ — see DRY 1

serene *adj* 1 free from disturbing noise or uproar ⟨a *serene* vacation spot⟩ — see QUIET 1

2 free from emotional or mental agitation ⟨a *serene* woman who was everyone's source of support⟩ — see CALM 2

3 free from storms or physical disturbance ⟨a *serene* lake⟩ — see CALM 1

sereneness *n* 1 a state of freedom from storm or disturbance ⟨the inviting *sereneness* of the secluded monastery⟩ — see CALM 1

2 freedom from disquieting or oppressive thoughts or emotions ⟨a quite afternoon providing the *sereneness* for reflection⟩ — see PEACE 2

serenity *n* 1 a state of freedom from storm or disturbance ⟨The *serenity* in the aftermath of the tornado was remarkable.⟩ — see CALM 1

2 evenness of emotions or temper ⟨His *serenity* calmed those around him.⟩ — see EQUANIMITY

3 freedom from disquieting or oppressive thoughts or emotions ⟨The momentary *serenity* experienced during his lunchtime rambles gets him through the rest of the workday.⟩ — see PEACE 2

serial *adj* appearing in parts or numbers that follow regularly ⟨"The Count of Monte Cristo" first appeared as a *serial* novel from 1844 to 1846.⟩

synonyms episodic (*also* episodical), periodical

related words sequential; successive; periodic, recurrent, recurring, regular

serial *n* a publication that appears at regular intervals ⟨The university library has a vast collection of *serials*.⟩ — see JOURNAL

serious *adj* 1 not joking or playful in mood or manner ⟨I'm *serious* when I say that you need to be aware of your surroundings when driving.⟩

synonyms earnest, grave, humorless, no-nonsense, sedate, severe, sober, solemn, staid, uncomic, unsmiling, weighty

related words harsh, stern, strict; businesslike, professional; dignified, distinguished, elevated, serious-minded; gloomy, grim

near antonyms antic, comic, comical, droll, farcical, funny, hilarious, hysterical (*also* hysteric), laughable, light, light-headed, ludicrous, ridiculous, riotous, risible, screaming, uproarious; featherbrained, flighty, frivolous, goofy, harebrained, lighthearted, puerile, scatterbrained

antonyms facetious, flip, flippant, humorous, jesting, jocular, joking, playful

2 having a matter of importance as its topic ⟨a very *serious* film that deals with our justice system⟩

synonyms grave, heavy, weighty

related words big, consequential, eventful, important, major, material, meaningful, momentous, portentous, significant, solid, substantial

near antonyms frivolous, insignificant, little, minor, silly, slight, small, trivial, unimportant

antonyms light, unserious

3 involving potential loss or injury ⟨a *serious* accident⟩ — see DANGEROUS 1

seriousness *n* a mental state free of jesting or trifling ⟨We knew from the doctor's *seriousness* that she didn't have good news.⟩ — see EARNESTNESS

sermon *n* a public speech usually by a member of the clergy for the purpose of giving moral guidance or uplift ⟨a *sermon* whose message was that we should love our neighbors as much as we love ourselves⟩

synonyms homily

related words address, lecture, speech, talk; exhortation; lesson

serpent *n* 1 a limbless reptile with a long body ⟨an Aztec carving of a feathered *serpent* representing the god Quetzalcoatl⟩ — see SNAKE 1

2 the supreme personification of evil often represented as the ruler of hell ⟨Beware the temptations of the *serpent!*⟩ — see DEVIL 1

3 one who betrays a trust or an allegiance ⟨A *serpent* in their midst had betrayed the revolutionaries to the authorities.⟩ — see TRAITOR

serpentine *adj* marked by a long series of irregular curves ⟨The country inn lies at the end of a rather *serpentine* road, but it's worth the trip.⟩ — see CROOKED 1

serrate *adj* notched or toothed along the edge ⟨a *serrate* saw⟩ — see SERRATED

serrated *adj* notched or toothed along the edge ⟨You should use a *serrated* knife when cutting bread, so you don't squash the loaf.⟩

synonyms saw-toothed, serrate

related words serried; jagged, ragged; wavy

near antonyms flat, smooth

serve *vb* 1 to be an employee for ⟨a butler who *served* several prime ministers⟩

synonyms work (for)

related words attend, minister (to), tend (to)

phrases wait on (*also* wait upon)

2 to be enough ⟨They made the pasta *serve* for eight guests.⟩

synonyms do, suffice

related words answer, suit; assuage, content, quench, sate, satiate, satisfy

3 to be fitting or proper ⟨Those old riding boots will *serve* for now, but you'll need newer ones for the horse show.⟩ — see DO 1

4 to behave toward in a stated way ⟨My parents *served* me well in preparing me for life.⟩ — see TREAT 1

5 to have a certain purpose ⟨The punishment *served* to teach everyone a lesson.⟩ — see FUNCTION

6 to provide with something useful or desirable ⟨an excellent college that *served* her with the skills necessary to make it in today's job market⟩ — see BENEFIT

server *n* a person who serves food or drink ⟨We had barely finished ordering when the *server* brought our salads.⟩

synonyms waiter, waitperson

related words waitress; barkeep (*also* barkeeper), bartender; sommelier; steward, stewardess; headwaiter

service *adj* of or relating to the armed services ⟨spent his time in the army as a correspondent for *service* newspapers⟩ — see MILITARY 1

service *n* 1 an act of kind assistance ⟨performed many *services* for the charitable organization⟩ — see FAVOR 1

2 the capacity for being useful for some purpose ⟨That broom is worn-out beyond all *service*.⟩ — see USE 2

3 the combined army, air force, and navy of a nation ⟨At the time the country had about a million men and women in the *service*.⟩ — see ARMED FORCES

4 a large unit of a governmental, business, or educational organization ⟨the OSS, the nation's wartime intelligence *service*⟩ — see DIVISION 2

serviceability *n* the capacity for being useful for some purpose ⟨I have doubts about the *serviceability* of some of the junk we've accumulated.⟩ — see USE 2

serviceable *adj* **1** capable of being put to use or account ⟨Be sure to wear *serviceable* shoes if you're going to be walking on the rocks along the shore.⟩ — see PRACTICAL 1
2 capable of or suitable for being used for a particular purpose ⟨A perfectly *serviceable*, if old, set of screwdrivers worked fine for repairing the door.⟩ — see USABLE 1
3 of a level of quality that meets one's needs or standards ⟨The acting was *serviceable*, although not particularly inspired.⟩ — see ADEQUATE

serviceableness *n* the capacity for being useful for some purpose ⟨The *serviceableness* of most of the junk that my grandfather had been hoarding was very doubtful.⟩ — see USE 2

serviceman *n* a person engaged in military service ⟨wishing our *servicemen* overseas the best of luck⟩ — see SOLDIER

servility *n* the state of being enslaved ⟨the joy that emancipation must have brought to people who had known only *servility* since birth⟩ — see SLAVERY

servitude *n* the state of being enslaved ⟨The Fugitive Slave Act had the effect of returning Africans who had made it to freedom in the North to a brutal life of *servitude* in the South.⟩ — see SLAVERY

set *adj* **1** being in a state of fitness for some experience or action ⟨We're all *set* to go!⟩ — see READY 1
2 firmly positioned in place and difficult to dislodge ⟨That rock is really *set* in the hillside.⟩ — see TIGHT 2
3 fully committed to achieving a goal ⟨*set* on being the first in her family to graduate from college⟩ — see DETERMINED 1
4 having been established and usually not subject to change ⟨The library is only open during *set* hours.⟩ — see FIXED 1
5 of a particular or exact sort ⟨International law has *set* rules for the treatment of prisoners of war.⟩ — see EXPRESS 1
6 made, given, or done with full awareness of what one is doing ⟨It was not my *set* purpose to cause trouble for anyone.⟩ — see INTENTIONAL

set *n* **1** a group of people acting together within a larger group ⟨music that is popular with the college *set*⟩ — see FACTION
2 a group of people sharing a common interest and relating together socially ⟨They rarely associate with anyone outside their social *set*.⟩ — see GANG 2
3 a number of things considered as a unit ⟨a *set* of tools⟩ — see GROUP 1
4 one of the units into which a whole is divided on the basis of a common characteristic ⟨The next *set* of job applicants had far more education and practical experience.⟩ — see CLASS 2
5 the array of painted backgrounds and furnishings used to establish the setting in a stage production ⟨built *sets* for the play⟩ — see SCENERY

set *vb* **1** to cover and warm eggs as the young inside develop ⟨The hen *set* for days.⟩
synonyms brood, hatch, incubate, sit
related words lay, spawn
2 to decide upon (the time or date for an event) usually from a position of authority ⟨Let's *set* a date for the wedding.⟩ — see APPOINT 1
3 to make an approximate or tentative judgment regarding ⟨Fire losses were *set* at a million dollars.⟩ — see ESTIMATE 1

4 *chiefly dialect* to rest on the buttocks or haunches ⟨Come over and *set* for a spell.⟩ — see SIT 1
5 to point or turn (something) toward a target or goal ⟨Determined to see the West, she *set* her car towards the sun and drove off.⟩ — see AIM 1
6 to come to an agreement or decision concerning the details of ⟨finally *set* some plans for the luncheon⟩ — see ARRANGE 1
7 to put securely in place or in a desired position ⟨had the jeweler *set* the diamond again⟩ — see FASTEN 2
8 to turn from a liquid into a substance resembling jelly ⟨The gelatin is just starting to *set* now.⟩ — see COAGULATE
9 to arrange something in a certain spot or position ⟨*set* a book on the table⟩ — see PLACE 1
10 to become physically firm or solid ⟨The concrete must *set* completely before anyone can walk on it.⟩ — see HARDEN 1

setback *n* a change in status for the worse usually temporarily ⟨The colonists persevered despite suffering *setbacks* that would have discouraged lesser souls.⟩ — see REVERSE 1

set down *vb* **1** to cause to sit down ⟨*set* the toddler *down* in her seat⟩ — see SEAT 1
2 to make a written note of ⟨*set down* the names of those in attendance⟩ — see RECORD 1
3 to think of in a particular way ⟨Early in the campaign, voters *set* the senator *down* as an opportunist, and the perception stuck.⟩ — see CONSIDER 1

set in *vb* to come into existence ⟨A cold spell *set in* sometime last week.⟩ — see BEGIN 2

set off *vb* to cause to function ⟨*set off* the fireworks⟩ — see ACTIVATE

settee *n* a long upholstered piece of furniture designed for several sitters ⟨The young couple snuggled on the *settee*.⟩ — see COUCH

setting *n* **1** the circumstances, conditions, or objects by which one is surrounded ⟨The novice camper felt lost outside of his familiar urban *setting*.⟩ — see ENVIRONMENT
2 the place and time in which the action for a portion of a dramatic work (as a movie) is set ⟨The *setting* for the novel is Victorian England.⟩ — see SCENE 1

settle *vb* **1** to cause to come to rest at the bottom (as of a liquid) ⟨The light rain will *settle* the dust in the air.⟩ ⟨Allowing a few moments of rest will *settle* the grounds in the coffee.⟩
synonyms lay, sediment
related words filter, screen, sieve, sift, strain; clarify, clear; resettle
near antonyms agitate, disturb, mix, stir
antonyms raise
2 to supply with inhabitants ⟨The region was originally *settled* by farmers.⟩
synonyms people
related words inhabit; move (to), relocate (to)
antonyms depopulate
3 to give an opinion about (something at issue or in dispute) ⟨*settled* the lawsuit in favor of the defendant⟩ — see JUDGE 1
4 to come to an agreement or decision concerning the details of ⟨They *settled* their wedding plans without any major disagreements.⟩ — see ARRANGE 1
5 to come to rest after descending from the air ⟨birds *settling* on the branches of the maple tree⟩ — see ALIGHT 1
6 to establish or place comfortably or snugly ⟨*settled* the sleeping baby into her crib⟩ — see ENSCONCE 1
7 to free from distress or disturbance ⟨A hot meal *settled* the children down.⟩ — see CALM 1
8 to gain emotional or mental control of ⟨Dave *settled* himself only with visible effort after the outburst.⟩ — see COLLECT 1

9 to give what is owed for ⟨*settle* a debt⟩ — see PAY 2

10 to make final, definite, or beyond dispute ⟨This information should *settle* the question of who is right.⟩ — see CLINCH

11 to stop the noise or speech of ⟨She *settled* the class with a firm "Quiet!"⟩ — see SILENCE 1

settle (down) *vb* to become still and orderly ⟨*Settle down* and get to work, please!⟩ — see QUIET 1

settle (on *or* **upon)** *vb* to come to a judgment about after discussion or consideration ⟨The car buyer *settled on* that brand only after a lot of research.⟩ — see DECIDE 1

settled *adj* **1** firmly established over time ⟨a remote village with a *settled* way of doing things⟩ — see INVETERATE 1

2 having been established and usually not subject to change ⟨*settled* rules that cannot be disregarded when it is convenient to do so⟩ — see FIXED 1

settlement *n* an arrangement about action to be taken ⟨We eventually reached a peace *settlement*.⟩ — see AGREEMENT 2

settler *n* **1** a person who settles in a new region ⟨*settlers* learning to live in their new environment⟩ — see FRONTIERSMAN

2 one that leaves one place to settle in another ⟨In 1889 Jane Addams, in an effort to provide Chicago's latest wave of *settlers* with much-needed services, founded the city's first settlement house.⟩ — see EMIGRANT

setup *n* **1** the way in which something is sized, arranged, or organized ⟨The textbook's *setup* calls for a list of questions at the end of each chapter.⟩ — see FORMAT 1

2 the way objects in space or events in time are arranged or follow one another ⟨We changed the *setup* of the living room furniture several times before being satisfied.⟩ — see ORDER 1

set up *vb* **1** to arrange something in a certain spot or position ⟨We *set up* tables in the living room for the party.⟩ — see PLACE 1

2 to be responsible for the creation and early operation or use of ⟨*set up* a scholarship fund for deserving students⟩ — see FOUND

3 to fix in an upright position ⟨He *set up* a post from which to hang the sign.⟩ — see ERECT 1

4 to form by putting together parts or materials ⟨First, *set up* the prefabricated shed by following the instructions.⟩ — see BUILD

5 to restore to a healthy condition ⟨Don't worry, the doctor will *set* you *up* in no time.⟩ — see HEAL 1

seven seas *pl n* the whole body of salt water that covers nearly three-fourths of the earth ⟨sailing the *seven seas* in search of adventure⟩ — see OCEAN 1

sever *vb* to set or force apart ⟨*severed* ties with former friends⟩ — see SEPARATE 1

severe *adj* **1** given to exacting standards of discipline and self-restraint ⟨a *severe*, uncompromising teacher who closed the classroom door precisely when the bell rang and let no one in afterward⟩

synonyms austere, authoritarian, flinty, hard, harsh, heavy-handed, ramrod, rigid, rigorous, stern, strict, tough

related words demanding, exacting; uncharitable, unforgiving; adamant, callous, hardened, hard-line, immovable, implacable, inflexible, merciless, pitiless, relentless, rock-ribbed, stiff, unbending, uncompromising, unrelenting, unsparing, unyielding; dour, gruff; ascetic (*also* ascetical), monastic, monkish; browbeating, bullying

near antonyms easy, easygoing, laid-back, undemanding; charitable, kind, merciful, mild, patient, soft, softhearted; accepting, compromising, yielding; responsive, willing; acquiescent, agreeable, amenable, complaisant, compliant, flexible, pliable, pliant

antonyms clement, forbearing, gentle, indulgent, lax, lenient, tolerant

2 harsh and threatening in manner or appearance ⟨clergymen who dressed in *severe* clothing⟩ — see GRIM 1

3 not joking or playful in mood or manner ⟨The judge maintained a *severe* expression throughout the trial.⟩ — see SERIOUS 1

4 difficult to endure ⟨a *severe* winter that was among the coldest on record⟩ — see HARSH 1

5 requiring considerable physical or mental effort ⟨a *severe* test of courage⟩ — see HARD 2

severely *adv* **1** in a manner so as to cause loss or suffering ⟨The trees were *severely* damaged by the strong winds.⟩ — see HARDLY 1

2 to a great degree ⟨The rescued mountain climbers were *severely* dehydrated.⟩ — see VERY 1

severity *n* the quality or state of being demanding or unyielding (as in discipline or criticism) ⟨Even though no one expected the film to be a hit with the critics, the director was taken aback by the *severity* of the criticism.⟩

synonyms hardness, harshness, inflexibility, rigidity, rigidness, rigor, rigorousness, sternness, strictness

related words callousness, hard-heartedness, implacability, obduracy, pitilessness; dourness, gruffness; asceticism, austereness, austerity, monasticism; determination, firmness, resolve, steadfastness

near antonyms forbearance, indulgence, kindness, lenience, patience, softness, tolerance; responsiveness, willingness

antonyms flexibility, gentleness, laxness, mildness

sew *vb* to close up with a series of interlacing stitches ⟨Luckily, I was able to *sew* the tear so skillfully that my pants looked as good as new.⟩

synonyms darn, stitch

related words mend, patch, repair; baste, ease, fell, finish, overcast; cross-stitch, embroider; crochet, knit

near antonyms unsew

sew up *vb* to have complete control over ⟨*sewed up* the available tee times so that no one else had a chance to play golf⟩ — see MONOPOLIZE

sex *n* sexual union involving penetration of the vagina by the penis ⟨learning about *sex* and reproduction in health class⟩ — see SEXUAL INTERCOURSE

sexual intercourse *n* sexual union involving penetration of the vagina by the penis ⟨had a talk with his son about *sexual intercourse*⟩

synonyms coitus, copulation, intercourse, relations, sex, sexual relations

related words fornication; safe sex; sexuality; breeding, insemination

phrases making love

sexual relations *pl n* sexual union involving penetration of the vagina by the penis ⟨not emotionally ready for *sexual relations*⟩ — see SEXUAL INTERCOURSE

sexy *adj* of, relating to, exciting, or expressing sexual attraction or desire ⟨a *sexy* new cologne⟩ — see EROTIC

shabby *adj* **1** showing signs of advanced wear and tear and neglect ⟨*shabby* wallpaper that was peeling from the walls⟩

synonyms dilapidated, dog-eared, dumpy, grungy, mangy, mean, miserable, moth-eaten, neglected, ratty, run-down, scruffy, seedy, tacky, threadbare, tumbledown

related words abandoned, uncared-for, unkept; desolate, forlorn, godforsaken; broken-down, decrepit, tired, worn-out; bedraggled, dingy, ragged, tattered; decaying, deteriorated, deteriorating, ramshackle, rattletrap, rickety; broken, damaged, harmed, hurt, impaired, injured, wrecked

phrases gone to seed

near antonyms brand-new, fresh, new; kept-up, maintained; mended, patched, rebuilt, reconstructed; smart, spiffy, spruce

2 worn or torn into or as if into rags ⟨*shabby*, stained clothes that are barely better than rags⟩ — see RAGGED 2

shack *n* a small, simply constructed, and often temporary dwelling ⟨a farmer's *shack* out in the fields that's used for lambing and as a shelter from storms⟩

synonyms cabin, camp, hovel, hut, hutch, shanty

related words lean-to, shed; cot, cottage, lodge; cabana; bungalow, chalet; hogan, wickiup, wigwam; tent

shackle *n* **1** something that physically prevents free movement ⟨placed *shackles* on the legs of the prisoners⟩ — see BOND 1

2 shackles *pl* something that makes movement or progress difficult ⟨the *shackles* of illiteracy⟩ — see ENCUMBRANCE

shackle *vb* **1** to confine or restrain with or as if with chains ⟨unwilling to *shackle* the dogs⟩ — see BIND 1

2 to create difficulty for the work or activity of ⟨*shackled* by poverty⟩ — see HAMPER

shade *n* **1** partial darkness due to the obstruction of light rays ⟨It was hard to see in the *shade* after being in the brilliant sunlight.⟩ ⟨The trees cast *shade*.⟩

synonyms dusk, penumbra, shadiness, shadow, umbra

related words blackness, dimness, duskiness, gloom, gloominess, murkiness, obscurity, semidarkness, somberness; cloudiness

near antonyms brightness, brilliance, effulgence, illumination, incandescence, light, lightness, lucidity, lucidness, luminosity, radiance, radiancy

2 a time or place of little or no light ⟨enjoying the cool *shade* of the evening⟩ — see DARK 1

3 a property that becomes apparent when light falls on an object and by which things that are identical in form can be distinguished ⟨a lovely *shade* of blue⟩ — see COLOR 1

4 a very small amount ⟨just a *shade* taller than his dance partner⟩ — see PARTICLE 1

5 the soul of a dead person thought of especially as appearing to living people ⟨spirits and *shades* haunting the night⟩ — see GHOST 1

shade *vb* to shelter (something) from light and heat ⟨The trees *shaded* us quite nicely from the noonday sun.⟩

synonyms shadow

related words cloud, darken, dim, dull, overcast, overshadow; canopy, cover, protect, screen

near antonyms illuminate, light, lighten; expose

shaded *adj* protected from the sun's rays ⟨walking along the park's *shaded* pathway⟩ — see SHADY 1

shadiness *n* partial darkness due to the obstruction of light rays ⟨the inviting *shadiness* of a woodland grove⟩ — see SHADE 1

shadow *n* **1** partial darkness due to the obstruction of light rays ⟨The valley was in *shadow*.⟩ — see SHADE 1

2 shadows *pl* a time or place of little or no light ⟨lurking in the *shadows*⟩ — see DARK 1

3 a tiny often physical indication of something lost or vanished ⟨a run-down mansion that is only a *shadow* of its former glory⟩ — see VESTIGE 1

4 a very small amount ⟨not even a *shadow* of a doubt about the defendant's guilt⟩ — see PARTICLE 1

5 the soul of a dead person thought of especially as appearing to living people ⟨rumors of a *shadow* haunting the castle⟩ — see GHOST 1

6 an overspreading element that produces an atmosphere of gloom ⟨The disquieting news had cast a *shadow* over the dinner party.⟩ — see CLOUD

shadow *vb* **1** to go after or on the track of ⟨*shadowing* the suspect to see what he was up to⟩ — see FOLLOW 2

2 to make dark, dim, or indistinct ⟨Thickening clouds *shadowed* the countryside.⟩ — see CLOUD 1

3 to shelter (something) from light and heat ⟨a pathway *shadowed* by a canopy of arching branches⟩ — see SHADE

shadowed *adj* protected from the sun's rays ⟨I sat in a *shadowed* corner of the garden.⟩ — see SHADY 1

shadowing *n* the act of going after or in the tracks of another ⟨the submarine's relentless *shadowing* of the destroyer⟩ — see PURSUIT

shadowy *adj* **1** not seen or understood clearly ⟨He had only a *shadowy* idea of what they wanted him to do.⟩ — see FAINT 1

2 protected from the sun's rays ⟨a *shadowy* lane that is a mosaic of colors during the autumn foliage season⟩ — see SHADY 1

shady *adj* **1** protected from the sun's rays ⟨a lovely *shady* spot in the park that was pleasantly cool⟩

synonyms shaded, shadowed, shadowy

related words canopied, covered, sheltered; cloudy; dark, darkened, darkish, darkling, darksome, dim, dimmed, dusky, gloomy, inky, moonless, murky, obscure, obscured, penumbral, pitch-black, pitch-dark, somber (*or* sombre)

near antonyms bedazzling, bright, brightened, brilliant, dazzling, effulgent, illuminated, illumined, incandescent, light, lucent, lucid, luminary, luminous; beaming, lambent, radiant, shining; lustrous

antonyms exposed, shadeless, sunny

2 given to or marked by cheating and deception ⟨a *shady* business deal⟩ — see DISHONEST 2

3 giving good reason for being doubted, questioned, or challenged ⟨cited some *shady* statistics to back up his argument⟩ — see DOUBTFUL 2

4 given to acting in secret and to concealing one's intentions ⟨He seems like a pretty *shady* character.⟩ — see SNEAKY 1

5 not respectable ⟨had a *shady* reputation⟩ — see DISREPUTABLE

shaft *n* **1** a narrow sharply defined line of light radiating from an object ⟨*Shafts* of late-afternoon sunlight pierced the blinds and streaked the floor.⟩

synonyms beam, ray

related words moonbeam, sunbeam, sunburst; laser

2 a weapon with a long straight handle and sharp head or blade ⟨The footmen set their *shafts* so as to form a bank of steel against the enemy's charging cavalry.⟩ — see SPEAR

3 unfair or inadequate treatment of someone or something or an instance of this ⟨The homeowners who were bought out are convinced they got the *shaft* in that deal.⟩ — see DISSERVICE

shaggy *adj* **1** covered with or as if with hair ⟨A big, *shaggy* dog kept trying to lick my face.⟩ — see HAIRY 1

2 made of or resembling hair ⟨a *shaggy* carpet that was a relic of the 1970s⟩ — see HAIRY 2

shake *n* **1** a very small space of time ⟨I'll be there in two *shakes*!⟩ — see INSTANT

2 shakes *pl* a sense of panic or extreme nervousness ⟨I get the *shakes* every time I hear her voice.⟩ — see JITTERS

3 a shaking of the earth ⟨The *shake* was a modest 3.1 on the Richter scale.⟩ — see EARTHQUAKE 1

shake *vb* **1** to make a series of small irregular or violent movements ⟨The bus rattled and *shook* as it barreled down a rutted road.⟩

synonyms agitate, convulse, jerk, jiggle, joggle, jolt, jounce, quake, quiver, shudder, vibrate, wobble (*also* wabble)

related words rock, sway, swing; chatter, quaver, shiver, thrill, tremble; twitch; dodder, waver; flicker, fluctuate, flutter, oscillate, undulate, wave; beat, palpitate, pit-a-pat, pitter-patter, pulsate, pulse, throb

2 to get or keep away from (as a responsibility) through cleverness or trickery ⟨They *shook* their pursuers by cutting through the abandoned lot.⟩ — see ESCAPE 2

shake up *vb* to cause an unpleasant surprise for ⟨The news that we had failed the auto inspection *shook* us *up*.⟩ — see SHOCK 1

shakiness *n* the quality or state of not being firmly fixed in position ⟨We added a couple more ropes to help reduce the *shakiness* of the footbridge.⟩ — see INSTABILITY

shaking *adj* marked by or given to small uncontrollable bodily movements ⟨suffered a *shaking* chill during his bout with the flu⟩ — see SHAKY 1

shaking *n* **1** a series of slight movements by a body back and forth or from side to side ⟨gave the bottle of salad dressing a good *shaking*⟩ — see VIBRATION 1

2 the act or a means of getting or keeping away from something undesirable ⟨He credited a couple of days of rest for his quick *shaking* of the flu.⟩ — see ESCAPE 2

shaky *adj* **1** marked by or given to small uncontrollable bodily movements ⟨The old man's hands were so *shaky* that I was afraid he'd drop the glass.⟩

synonyms quaking, quavery, quivering, shaking, shuddering, shuddery, tottery, trembling, tremulous, wobbling (*also* wabbling), wobbly (*also* wabbly)

related words convulsive; shivery; rocky, unstable, unsteady, wavering, wavery; palpitating, pulsating, throbbing

near antonyms controlled, firm, settled, stable, steady

2 giving good reason for being doubted, questioned, or challenged ⟨results that were arrived at using some *shaky* experimental procedures⟩ — see DOUBTFUL 2

shall *vb* to be under necessity or obligation to ⟨You *shall* do as I say.⟩ — see NEED 2

shallow *n*, *usually* **shallows** *pl* a place where a body of water (as a sea or river) is shallow ⟨We waded through the *shallows* looking for tadpoles.⟩ — see SHOAL

shallow *adj* **1** lacking significant physical depth ⟨The dog quickly dug a *shallow* hole that was barely deep enough to accommodate his bone.⟩

synonyms depthless, shoal

related words skin-deep, superficial, surface; measurable; finite, limited, measured, restricted; even, flat, flush, horizontal, level, plane, smooth; two-dimensional

near antonyms abysmal, abyssal, bottomless, boundless, endless, immeasurable, infinite, limitless, measureless, profound, unfathomable, unlimited, vast; navigable

antonyms deep

2 having or showing a lack of depth of understanding or character ⟨It was *shallow* of the driver to be worrying about his car while the pedestrian was in need of medical attention.⟩ — see SUPERFICIAL 2

sham *adj* **1** being such in appearance only and made with or manufactured from usually cheaper materials ⟨a sofa upholstered in *sham* leather⟩ — see IMITATION

2 being such in appearance only and made or manufactured with the intention of committing fraud ⟨street vendors selling *sham* designer handbags to gullible tourists⟩ — see COUNTERFEIT 1

3 lacking in natural or spontaneous quality ⟨the *sham* friendliness of a salesman trying to sell you something⟩ — see ARTIFICIAL 1

sham *n* **1** a poor, insincere, or insulting imitation of something ⟨condemned the rigged election as a total *sham*⟩ — see MOCKERY 1

2 an imitation that is passed off as genuine ⟨The sup-

posed Renaissance masterpiece turned out to be a *sham*.⟩ — see FAKE 1

3 one who makes false claims of identity or expertise ⟨That supposed French movie star was a *sham*.⟩ — see IMPOSTOR

sham *vb* to present a false appearance of ⟨*shammed* a most unconvincing limp just to get sympathy⟩ — see FEIGN

shamble *vb* to move heavily or clumsily ⟨Disconsolate and exhausted after losing the match, the wrestler *shambled* toward the locker room.⟩ — see LUMBER 1

shambles *pl n* **1** a dirty or messy place ⟨This room is a *shambles*—clean it up right now!⟩ — see PIGPEN

2 a state in which everything is out of order ⟨The party left the whole house in a *shambles*.⟩ — see CHAOS

shame *n* **1** a feeling of responsibility for wrongdoing ⟨racked with *shame* over her actions of the previous week⟩ — see GUILT 1

2 a regrettable or blameworthy act ⟨It's a *shame* you won't be able to come to the party.⟩ — see CRIME 2

3 the state of having lost the esteem of others ⟨The teen left the room in *shame* after his angry outburst.⟩ — see DISGRACE 1

shame *vb* to reduce to a lower standing in one's own eyes or in others' eyes ⟨*shamed* the family name with his behavior⟩ — see HUMBLE

shamed *adj* suffering from or expressive of a feeling of responsibility for wrongdoing ⟨the *shamed* look of someone who knows that he is being given credit he doesn't deserve⟩ — see GUILTY

shamefaced *adj* suffering from or expressive of a feeling of responsibility for wrongdoing ⟨The newspaper offered a *shamefaced* apology for having published photographs that were later exposed as fakes.⟩ — see GUILTY

shameful *adj* not respectable ⟨*shameful* behavior by a bunch of poor losers⟩ — see DISREPUTABLE

shameless *adj* **1** not embarrassed or ashamed ⟨She's truly *shameless* in the seemingly endless self-promotion of herself.⟩ — see UNABASHED

2 not sorry for having done wrong ⟨a *shameless* exploiter of impoverished workers in overseas sweatshops⟩ — see REMORSELESS 1

shanty *n* a small, simply constructed, and often temporary dwelling ⟨lived just off the beach in a crude *shanty*⟩ — see SHACK

shape *n* **1** a state of being or fitness ⟨She was in good *shape* after having worked outdoors all summer long.⟩ — see CONDITION 1

2 the outward appearance of something as distinguished from its substance ⟨That part of the state is known as the panhandle because of its *shape*.⟩ — see FORM 1

3 the type of body that a person has ⟨a style of jacket that suits any *shape*⟩ — see PHYSIQUE

shape *vb* **1** to change (something) so as to make it suitable for a new use or situation ⟨a suit *shaped* to the customer's particular frame⟩ — see ADAPT

2 to work out the details of (something) in advance ⟨Over the winter the committee *shaped* the company's new marketing strategy.⟩ — see PLAN 1

shape (up) *vb* to take on a definite form ⟨This group of summer interns is *shaping up* to be one of the best we've ever hired.⟩ — see FORM 1

shapeless *adj* **1** badly or imperfectly formed ⟨a *shapeless* old hat⟩ — see MALFORMED

2 having no definite or recognizable form ⟨Right now this clay is just a *shapeless* lump, but wait until I'm done sculpting it.⟩ — see FORMLESS 1

share *vb* to take a share or part ⟨Everyone in the enterprise will *share* in the profits.⟩ — see PARTAKE 1

share *n* **1** something belonging to, due to, or contributed by an individual member of a group ⟨My *share* of the lottery winnings is over a million dollars.⟩ ⟨Her *share* of the bill comes to $13.44.⟩
synonyms allotment, allowance, cut, end, part, piece, portion, proportion, quota, slice, take
related words lot, ration; commission, percentage; member, partition, section, segment
near antonyms aggregate, composite, compound, pool, sum, total, totality; whole
2 a legal right to participation in the advantages, profits, and responsibility of something ⟨She sold her *share* in the business to her partner.⟩ — see INTEREST 1

shared *adj* used or done by a number of people as a group ⟨*shared* resources⟩ — see COLLECTIVE

sharer *n* one who takes part in something ⟨All pilots are *sharers* of the same air space.⟩ — see PARTICIPANT

shark *n* **1** a dishonest person who uses clever means to cheat others out of something of value ⟨a card *shark*⟩ — see TRICKSTER 1
2 a person with a high level of knowledge or skill in a field ⟨a *shark* at calculus⟩ — see EXPERT

sharp *adv* as stated or indicated without the slightest difference ⟨Be there at four o'clock *sharp*!⟩ — see EXACTLY 1

sharp *adj* **1** having an edge thin enough to cut or pierce something ⟨Be careful, as that knife is *sharp* enough to slice off a finger.⟩
synonyms cutting, edged, edgy, ground, honed, keen, sharpened, stropped, trenchant, whetted
related words clawlike, daggerlike, knifelike; jabbing, jagged, lacerating, piercing, scratching, stabbing; pointed, spiky (*also* spikey)
near antonyms rounded, smooth; soft
antonyms blunt, blunted, dull, dulled, obtuse
2 having a powerfully stimulating odor or flavor ⟨a *sharp* cheese⟩
synonyms nippy, pungent, strong, tangy
related words acid, acidic; acrid, bitter, harsh; gingery, hot, peppery, piquant, spicy, tart, zesty; putrid, rank, skunky; appetizing, delectable, delicious, palatable, toothsome; flavorful, savory (*also* savoury), tasty; aromatic, redolent
near antonyms aged, mellow, ripe; gentle, soft; flat, flavorless, insipid; savorless, tasteless, zestless; dilute, thin, watery, weak
antonyms bland, mild, smooth
3 tapering to a thin tip ⟨tipped with a *sharp* arrowhead⟩ — see POINTED 1
4 being in the latest or current fashion ⟨wore a *sharp* suit to his first big job interview⟩ — see STYLISH
5 being strikingly neat and trim in style or appearance ⟨a television personality who's known as a *sharp* dresser⟩ — see SMART 1
6 causing intense discomfort to one's skin ⟨I got chapped lips from sailing all day in that *sharp* wind.⟩ — see CUTTING 1
7 given to or marked by cheating and deception ⟨*sharp* business practices that are being investigated by the state's consumer protection agency⟩ — see DISHONEST 2
8 having or showing a practical cleverness or judgment ⟨a *sharp* customer who wasn't about to be taken in by that smooth-tongued salesman⟩ — see SHREWD 1
9 having or showing quickness of mind ⟨Any *sharp* student would have noticed the error immediately.⟩ — see INTELLIGENT 1
10 marked by the use of wit that is intended to cause hurt feelings ⟨an unnecessarily *sharp* retort to a perfectly civil question⟩ — see SARCASTIC
11 able to sense slight impressions or differences ⟨You have *sharp* eyes!⟩ — see ACUTE 1

12 uncomfortably cool ⟨a spell of unusually *sharp* weather for this time of year⟩ — see CHILLY 1

sharpen *vb* to make sharp or sharper ⟨You need to *sharpen* your penknife's blade frequently in order to be able to whittle properly.⟩
synonyms edge, grind, hone, strop, whet
related words file
near antonyms buff, burnish, gloss, polish, round, smooth
antonyms blunt, dull

sharpened *adj* having an edge thin enough to cut or pierce something ⟨the *sharpened* blade of a lawn mower⟩ — see SHARP 1

sharper *n* a dishonest person who uses clever means to cheat others out of something of value ⟨carnival *sharpers* eager to relieve people of their money⟩ — see TRICKSTER 1

sharp—eyed *adj* having unusually keen vision ⟨A very *sharp-eyed* child found the last Easter egg, which was hidden in the flower arrangement.⟩
synonyms clear-sighted, lynx-eyed
related words sighted; alert, attentive, aware, observant, observing, vigilant, watchful
near antonyms blind, eyeless, sightless, stone-blind; astigmatic, myopic, nearsighted, shortsighted; purblind

sharply *adv* in a strikingly neat and trim manner ⟨*sharply* dressed groomsmen at a formal wedding⟩ — see SMARTLY

sharpness *n* **1** a harsh or sharp quality ⟨He found that the bland crackers helped cut the *sharpness* of the cheese.⟩ — see EDGE 1
2 an uncomfortable degree of coolness ⟨Dress warmly; there's a bit of *sharpness* in the air today.⟩ — see CHILL
3 exceptional discernment and judgment especially in practical matters ⟨possesses a political *sharpness* that most campaign managers would envy⟩ — see ACUMEN
4 the state or quality of being able to sense slight impressions or differences ⟨He possesses the proverbial *sharpness* of an eagle's eye.⟩ — see ACUITY

sharpshooter *n* a person skilled in shooting at a target ⟨trained as a police *sharpshooter*⟩ — see MARKSMAN

sharp—witted *adj* **1** having or showing a practical cleverness or judgment ⟨Her *sharp-witted* questions always cut right to the core of the issue.⟩ — see SHREWD 1
2 having or showing quickness of mind ⟨a TV game show that allows *sharp-witted* contestants to show their stuff⟩ — see INTELLIGENT 1

shatter *vb* **1** to bring to a complete end the physical soundness, existence, or usefulness of ⟨tried to restore their *shattered* hopes⟩ — see DESTROY 1
2 to cause to break open or into pieces by or as if by an explosive ⟨*shattered* the sealed clay pot to find out what was inside⟩ — see BLAST 1
3 to cause to break with violence and much noise ⟨The visitor *shattered* the priceless vase in one clumsy fall.⟩ — see SMASH 1

shave *vb* **1** to make (something) shorter or smaller with the use of a cutting instrument ⟨He always *shaves* most of his hair off when the weather starts getting warmer.⟩ — see CLIP 1
2 to pass lightly across or touch gently especially in passing ⟨I just *shaved* the concrete post as the car turned the corner.⟩ — see ²BRUSH

shaver *n* a male person who has not yet reached adulthood ⟨back in the old days when my dad was just a little *shaver*⟩ — see BOY 1

shear *vb* **1** to make (something) shorter or smaller with the use of a cutting instrument ⟨It took almost a week to *shear* all the wool off the flock of sheep.⟩ — see CLIP 1
2 to penetrate with a sharp edge (as a knife) ⟨The shark's

razor-sharp teeth *sheared* the swimmer's flesh.⟩ — see CUT 1

sheath *n* something that encloses another thing especially to protect it ⟨He removed his knife from its *sheath* and started to whittle.⟩ — see ¹CASE 1

sheathe *also* **sheath** *vb* to cover with something that protects ⟨Sometimes shipbuilders *sheathe* a ship's bottom with copper for extra protection from barnacles and other threats.⟩

synonyms face

related words apparel, array, clothe, dress, garb, robe; encase, enclose (*also* inclose), enshroud, envelop, enwrap, invest, lap, mantle, shroud, surround, swathe, veil, wrap; blanket, overlay, overspread

near antonyms bare, denude, expose, strip; unswathe

shed *vb* **1** to cast (a natural bodily covering or appendage) aside ⟨A snake's skin doesn't grow as the snake does, so every so often the snake will *shed* its old skin.⟩

synonyms exfoliate, molt, slip, slough (*also* sluff)

related words flake, peel, scale; chuck, discard, ditch, fling (off *or* away), jettison, junk, scrap, shuck (off), throw away, throw out, unload

2 to get rid of as useless or unwanted ⟨couldn't *shed* the reputation as a troublemaker⟩ — see DISCARD

sheen *n* brightness created by light reflected from a surface ⟨He polished the metal until it had an even *sheen*.⟩ — see SHINE 1

sheep *n* an innocent or gentle person ⟨He came to see that the members of the cult were *sheep* who naively went along with whatever their leader dictated.⟩ — see LAMB

sheepish *adj* not comfortable around people ⟨a *sheepish* scholar who is most comfortable when surrounded by books⟩ — see SHY 2

sheepishly *adv* in a manner showing no signs of pride or self-assertion ⟨The younger boy, who idolized the older one, would *sheepishly* follow him around.⟩ — see LOWLY

sheer *vb* **1** to change one's course or direction ⟨The cruise ship *sheered* to the northwest, putting it safely out of the path of the hurricane.⟩ — see TURN 3

2 to depart abruptly from a straight line or course ⟨The car *sheered* to avoid hitting the dog.⟩ — see SWERVE 1

sheer *adj* **1** very thin and easy to see through ⟨We had to get window shades because passersby could see right through our *sheer* curtains.⟩

synonyms filmy, gauzy, gossamer, gossamery, transparent

related words clear, crystalline, limpid, liquid, lucent, pellucid; lucid, translucent; dainty, delicate, flimsy, fragile, frail, insubstantial, unsubstantial; colorless, uncolored

near antonyms opaque; cloudy, foggy, hazy, misty, murky, nebulous, smoky (*also* smokey); drab, dull, lackluster, lusterless

2 having no exceptions or restrictions ⟨That story is *sheer* nonsense.⟩ — see ABSOLUTE 2

3 having an incline approaching the perpendicular ⟨the *sheer* slopes of the ravine⟩ — see STEEP 1

sheet *vb* to form a layer over ⟨Dust *sheeted* the floors of the old, abandoned house⟩ — see COVER 2

sheet *n* a wide space or area ⟨From the bow of our ship all we could see was an impenetrable *sheet* of fog.⟩ — see EXPANSE

shell *n* **1** something that encloses another thing especially to protect it ⟨eating oysters straight out of their *shells*⟩ — see ¹CASE 1

2 the arrangement of parts that gives something its basic form ⟨Workers at the shipyard have thus far erected the *shell* of the ship.⟩ — see FRAME 1

3 an outer part or layer ⟨The *shell* of the building is all

glass, making it conspicuous on a street with mostly limestone facades.⟩ — see EXTERIOR

shell *vb* **1** to remove the natural covering of ⟨*shelling* peanuts⟩ — see PEEL

2 to use bombs or artillery against ⟨The enemy *shelled* the city.⟩ — see BOMBARD 1

shellacking *n* failure to win a contest ⟨suffered a *shellacking* at the hands of a vastly superior opposition⟩ — see DEFEAT 1

shell–shocked *adj* **1** suffering from high levels of physical and especially psychological stress ⟨Even after the long furlough, the returning soldiers still felt a little *shell-shocked*.⟩ — see STRESSED-OUT

2 suffering from mental confusion ⟨They were *shell-shocked* by the onslaught of media attention.⟩ — see DIZZY 2

shelter *n* something (as a building) that offers cover from the weather or protection from danger ⟨The sudden fierce storm forced us to run to the nearest *shelter*.⟩

synonyms asylum, harbor, harborage, haven, refuge, retreat, sanctuary, sanctum

related words oasis; anchorage, mooring, port; cover, screen; housing, lodging, quarters, residence, rest, roof; cloister, closet, covert, den, hermitage, hideaway, hideout, lair; lean-to, lee, shed, windbreak

shelter *vb* **1** to be or provide a shelter for ⟨The abandoned barn *shelters* a colony of stray cats.⟩

synonyms harbor, refuge

related words cover, defend, protect, safeguard, screen, secure, shield, ward; domicile, house, place, quarter; shade, shadow

near antonyms expose

2 to provide with living quarters or shelter ⟨*sheltered* the troops in tents until permanent barracks could be built⟩ — see HOUSE 1

sheltered *adj* screened or sequestered from view ⟨moored the sailboat in a *sheltered* cove⟩ — see SECLUDED

shelve *vb* to assign to a later time ⟨Let's *shelve* the project for now.⟩ — see POSTPONE

shepherd *vb* to give advice and instruction to (someone) regarding the course or process to be followed ⟨*shepherding* her through the procedure of taking out a loan⟩ — see GUIDE 1

shibboleth *n* **1** an attention-getting word or phrase used to publicize something (as a campaign or product) ⟨We knew that their claim of giving "the best deal in town" was just a *shibboleth*.⟩ — see SLOGAN

2 an idea or expression that has been used by many people ⟨There's a lot of truth in the *shibboleth* that if you give some people an inch, they'll take a mile.⟩ — see COMMONPLACE

shield *n* means or method of defending ⟨Exercise and good nutrition are a *shield* against disease.⟩ — see DEFENSE 1

shield *vb* **1** to drive danger or attack away from ⟨celebrities who are *shielded* by a cluster of bodyguards whenever they appear in public⟩ — see DEFEND 1

2 to place a protective layer over ⟨She *shielded* her eyes from the sun with her hand.⟩ — see COVER 3

shift *n* **1** an action planned or taken to achieve a desired result ⟨desperate *shifts* to stave off financial disaster⟩ — see MEASURE 1

2 the act or an instance of changing position ⟨We made a small *shift* to the left to make more room on the bench.⟩ — see MOVEMENT 1

shift *vb* **1** to change the place or position of ⟨He *shifted* the vase closer to the wall so that it wouldn't get knocked over.⟩ — see MOVE 1

2 to change one's position ⟨She *shifted* uncomfortably in her seat throughout the interview.⟩ — see MOVE 3

3 to pass from one form, state, or level to another ⟨She watched the aurora in fascination as its colors *shifted* from green to blue.⟩ — see CHANGE 2

4 to give up (something) and take something else in return ⟨My brother and I *shifted* seats just before takeoff so that he could sit by the window.⟩ — see CHANGE 3

5 to meet one's day-to-day needs ⟨I left the others to *shift* for themselves.⟩ — see GET ALONG 1

shifting *n* the act or an instance of changing position ⟨The *shifting* of the toys to the front of the display was a direct result of their sudden popularity.⟩ — see MOVEMENT 1

shiftless *adj* not easily aroused to action or work ⟨*shiftless* spongers who never thought to do anything for themselves⟩ — see LAZY 1

shiftlessness *n* an inclination not to do work or engage in activities ⟨With the start of the warm weather, combating the students' *shiftlessness* was a constant ordeal.⟩ — see LAZINESS

shifty *adj* **1** given to acting in secret and to concealing one's intentions ⟨*shifty* characters involved in fraud⟩ — see SNEAKY 1

2 given to or marked by cheating and deception ⟨*shifty* practices such as turning back the odometers on used cars⟩ — see DISHONEST 2

shillelagh *also* **shillalah** *n* a heavy rigid stick used as a weapon or for punishment ⟨kept an authentic Irish *shillelagh* near the hearth⟩ — see CLUB 1

shilly–shally *vb* **1** to show uncertainty about the right course of action ⟨I didn't *shilly-shally* but instead raced to the hospital as soon as I heard the news.⟩ — see HESITATE 1

2 to move or act slowly ⟨With dinner guests due in two hours, there was no time to *shilly-shally* in front of the TV set.⟩ — see DELAY 1

shilly–shally *n* a state or an instance of temporary inaction because of uncertainty about the right course of action ⟨The construction project was once again delayed by the bureaucratic *shilly-shally* of regulatory agencies.⟩ — see HESITATION

shilly–shallying *n* a state or an instance of temporary inaction because of uncertainty about the right course of action ⟨Fortunately, during the crisis there was no *shilly-shallying* on the part of the president.⟩ — see HESITATION

shimmer *vb* to shoot forth bursts of light ⟨a sequined dress *shimmering* under the studio lights⟩ — see FLASH 1

shindig *n* a social gathering ⟨We're hosting a little *shindig* this weekend for some friends.⟩ — see PARTY 1

shindy *n* a state of noisy, confused activity ⟨The prime minister created a brief *shindy* with his unexpected appearance.⟩ — see COMMOTION

shine *n* **1** brightness created by light reflected from a surface ⟨The troop inspector insisted on nothing less than a dazzling *shine* from every pair of shoes in the line of review.⟩

synonyms burnish, gloss, luster (*or* lustre), polish, sheen

related words glare, gleam, glimmer, glint, glisten, glow, shimmer; blink, flicker, sparkle, twinkle; illumination, irradiation; iridescence, luminescence; brilliance, luminosity, radiance, radiancy; refulgence; finish, glaze

near antonyms dimness, dinginess, dirtiness, drabness, dullness (*also* dulness), flatness; grayness, paleness; cloudiness, gloom, murkiness, obscureness, obscurity, somberness

2 the steady giving off of the form of radiation that makes vision possible ⟨By the *shine* of the full moon we could see the rabbit helping himself to our garden vegetables.⟩ — see LIGHT 1

3 positive regard for something ⟨He took quite a *shine* to the new neighbors.⟩ — see LIKING

shine *vb* **1** to emit rays of light ⟨The sun appears to *shine* particularly brightly in summer because that is when it's closest to the Earth.⟩

synonyms beam, radiate, ray

related words blaze, burn, fire, flame, gleam, glimmer, glint, glisten, glister, glitter, glow, luminesce, sheen, shimmer; blink, flare, flash, flicker, luster (*or* lustre), scintillate, sparkle, twinkle; beat (down), glare; brighten, illuminate, illumine, irradiate, light, lighten; bedazzle, blind, daze, dazzle

near antonyms blacken, darken; lower (*also* lour)

2 to make smooth or glossy usually by repeatedly applying surface pressure ⟨The salesman *shined* his shoes every morning before leaving the house.⟩ — see POLISH 1

shining *adj* giving off or reflecting much light ⟨The *shining* moon formed a nice backdrop for our outdoor concert.⟩ — see BRIGHT 1

shiny *adj* giving off or reflecting much light ⟨We could see our reflections in the *shiny* surface of the marble walls.⟩ — see BRIGHT 1

ship *n* a large craft for travel by water ⟨a cruise *ship* plying the warm waters of the Caribbean⟩

synonyms boat, vessel

related words aircraft carrier, argosy, barge, containership, corvette, cruiser, cutter, destroyer, ferryboat, flagship, freighter, icebreaker, ironclad, lightship, liner, man-of-war (*also* man-o'-war), merchantman, merchant ship, motor ship, packet, steamer, steamship, superliner, supertanker, tanker, trader, tramp, transport, warship; bark (*or* barque), brig, brigantine, caravel, clipper, junk, ketch, sailboat, schooner, square-rigger, tall ship, windjammer, xebec, yacht

ship *vb* to cause to go or be taken from one place to another ⟨We *shipped* those books out yesterday.⟩ — see SEND

shippable *adj* capable of being taken from one place to another by public carrier ⟨Only boxes of five pounds and under are *shippable* by the postal service.⟩

synonyms transferable (*also* transferrable), transmittable, transportable

related words addressable; mailable

antonyms nontransferable, receivable

shipshape *adj* being clean and in good order ⟨made everything *shipshape* for the inspection⟩ — see NEAT 1

shipwreck *n* the destruction or loss of a ship ⟨The *shipwreck* of much of the Spanish Armada ended Spain's plans for invading England.⟩

synonyms shipwrecking, wreck, wreckage, wrecking

related words beaching, grounding, stranding; foundering, sinking; scuttling

near antonyms recovery, salvage, salvaging

shipwreck *vb* to cause irreparable damage to (a ship) by running aground or sinking ⟨The yachtsman fell asleep at the wheel and *shipwrecked* his ketch on the rocks.⟩

synonyms strand, wreck

related words beach; founder; scuttle

near antonyms recover, salvage

shipwrecking *n* the destruction or loss of a ship ⟨The *shipwrecking* of the Titanic by an iceberg ranks as one of the greatest disasters in the annals of the sea.⟩ — see SHIPWRECK

shirk *vb* **1** to get or keep away from (as a responsibility) through cleverness or trickery ⟨You always try to *shirk* paying your fair share of the bill by claiming you "forgot" your wallet.⟩ — see ESCAPE 2

2 to leave undone or unattended to especially through carelessness ⟨He's too conscientious to *shirk* his duties.⟩ — see NEGLECT 2

3 to move about in a sly or secret manner ⟨managed to *shirk* out of the meeting for a break⟩ — see SNEAK 1

shirker *n* one who deliberately avoids work or duty ⟨Even before we weighed anchor, the captain forcefully served notice that there would be no *shirkers* on his ship.⟩ — see SLACKER

shiver *n* **1** an instance of shaking involuntarily with fear or cold ⟨experienced a sudden *shiver* when the wind blew the door open⟩
synonyms quiver, shudder, tremble
related words agitation, convulsing, jolt, quake, shake, tremor, vibration, wobble (*also* wabble); flutter, oscillation, wave; beat, palpitation, pulsation, pulse, throb
2 shivers *pl* a sense of panic or extreme nervousness ⟨Looking down from the window ledge sent *shivers* up my spine.⟩ — see JITTERS

shivery *adj* having a low or subnormal temperature ⟨those *shivery* days of January⟩ — see COLD 1

shoal *adj* lacking significant physical depth ⟨*Shoal* waters of the bay meant that our ship had to be moored a considerable distance from shore.⟩ — see SHALLOW 1

shoal *n* a place where a body of water (as a sea or river) is shallow ⟨The *shoals* off Nantucket Island are famous as the final resting places of many ill-fated ships.⟩
synonyms ford, shallow(s)
related words bank, bar, sandbank, sandbar, towhead
near antonyms trench; abyss, deep, depth, gulf

shock *n* **1** a forceful coming together of two things ⟨The whole railway platform shook from the *shock* of the two trains colliding.⟩ — see IMPACT 1
2 the state of being strongly impressed by something unexpected or unusual ⟨Prepare yourself for a *shock* because the place has changed a lot.⟩ — see SURPRISE 2

shock *vb* **1** to cause an unpleasant surprise for ⟨Mom was *shocked* by the news that her coworker had been fired.⟩ ⟨I was *shocked* to find out that I was the victim of identity theft.⟩
synonyms appall (*also* appal), floor, jolt, shake up
related words astonish, dumbfound (*also* dumfound), flabbergast, freak (out), stun, stupefy; affright, alarm (*also* alarum), dismay, fright, frighten, horrify, panic, scare, scarify, spook, startle, terrify, terrorize; disgust, nauseate, repel, revolt, sicken, turn off; displease, offend, outrage, scandalize; amaze, astound, awe; chill, daunt, demoralize, dispirit, emasculate, undo, unman, unnerve, unstring; discomfort, discompose, disconcert, disquiet, distress, disturb, perturb, shake, unsettle, upset; crush, overpower, overwhelm
phrases knock for a loop
near antonyms buffer, cushion; delight, gratify, please, rejoice, tickle; charm, entice, tempt; assure, cheer, comfort, console, solace, soothe; reassure
2 to make a strong impression on (someone) with something unexpected ⟨Residents were *shocked* by the way the law against improperly dumping trash was constantly being broken.⟩ — see SURPRISE 1
3 to strike with fear ⟨The sudden appearance of the ghost *shocked* us to the core.⟩ — see FRIGHTEN

shocked *adj* **1** affected with sudden and great wonder or surprise ⟨The magician bid farewell to the *shocked* audience members as he disappeared.⟩ — see THUNDERSTRUCK
2 filled with disgust ⟨We were *shocked* at the appalling conditions in the prison.⟩ — see SICK 2
3 filled with fear or dread ⟨The hikers were so *shocked* at the sight of a bear that they didn't dare move.⟩ — see AFRAID

shocking *adj* **1** causing a strong emotional reaction because of unexpectedness ⟨We all clustered around to hear the *shocking* news.⟩ — see SURPRISING 1
2 causing fear ⟨the *shocking* appearance of a shark just a few yards off shore⟩ — see FEARFUL 1

3 causing intense displeasure, disgust, or resentment ⟨the *shocking* behavior of some fans at the game⟩ — see OFFENSIVE 1
4 extremely disturbing or repellent ⟨a soldier who had witnessed the *shocking* sight of his best friend being injured⟩ — see HORRIBLE 1

shoddy *adj* **1** of low quality ⟨*shoddy* merchandise that soon fell to pieces⟩ — see CHEAP 2
2 not respectable ⟨a businessman with a reputation for making *shoddy* deals⟩ — see DISREPUTABLE

shoes *pl n* a way of looking at or thinking about something ⟨What would you do if you were in your friend's *shoes*?⟩ — see PERSPECTIVE 1

shoestring *n* a very small sum of money ⟨trying to start a business on a *shoestring*⟩ — see MITE 1

shoot *n* **1** a branch of a main stem especially of a plant ⟨collected the most tender *shoots* for the vegetable dish he was making⟩ — see OFFSHOOT 1
2 a sharp unpleasant sensation usually felt in some specific part of the body ⟨a *shoot* of pain from that molar whenever I bit down.⟩ — see PAIN 1

shoot *vb* **1** to cause (a projectile) to be driven forward with force ⟨BB guns *shoot* small round metal pellets.⟩
synonyms blast, discharge, fire, loose
related words launch, project; blaze (at), snipe (at); cast, catapult, fling, heave, hurl, hurtle, lob, pelt, pitch, sling, throw, toss
2 to cause a weapon to release a missile with great force ⟨Soldiers train extensively to learn to *shoot* accurately and quickly.⟩
synonyms blast, discharge, fire
related words blaze, pepper; plink, snipe
3 to strike with a missile from a gun ⟨Hunters can *shoot* turkeys only during the legally specified open season.⟩
synonyms drill, gun
related words bring down, drop; blaze, pepper, snipe (at); blast (at), fire (at); shotgun; machine-gun, tommygun
4 to proceed or move quickly ⟨Some show-off *shot* past all the other skiers on the slope.⟩ — see HURRY 2
5 to take a photograph of ⟨*shooting* the lakeside scene while the light lasted⟩ — see PHOTOGRAPH
6 to throw or give off ⟨Suddenly the old, broken-down toaster began *shooting* out sparks.⟩ — see EMIT 1
7 to voice one's opinions freely with force ⟨You've been wanting to say something since this meeting started, so *shoot*.⟩ — see SPEAK UP
8 to cause to go or be taken from one place to another ⟨Tom *shot* a congratulatory e-mail to his friend as soon as he heard the good news.⟩ — see SEND

shoot (up) *vb* to rise abruptly and rapidly ⟨Gas prices *shot* up seemingly overnight.⟩ — see SKYROCKET

shooter *n* **1** a person skilled in shooting at a target ⟨There were eight *shooters* taking turns at the same target in the final competition.⟩ — see MARKSMAN
2 one who takes photographs ⟨He's one of the best *shooters* of wildlife in all of professional photography.⟩ — see PHOTOGRAPHER

shop *n* **1** *also* **shoppe** an establishment where goods are sold to consumers ⟨The only *shop* that has that video game in stock is halfway across the state.⟩
synonyms bazaar, emporium, store
related words market, marketplace, outlet, showroom; boutique, chain store, department store, dime store, exchange, five-and-ten (*also* five-and-dime), mart, thrift shop, variety store
2 a building or set of buildings for the manufacturing of goods ⟨a machine *shop*⟩ — see FACTORY
3 the special terms or expressions of a particular group

or field ⟨The patient impressed her cardiologist with her ability to talk *shop*.⟩ — see TERMINOLOGY

shopworn *adj* used or heard so often as to be dull ⟨the *shopworn* suggestion to job applicants to "just be yourself"⟩ — see STALE 1

shore *n* a structure that holds up or serves as a foundation for something else ⟨The carpenter placed a *shore* underneath the sagging roof of the porch.⟩ — see SUPPORT 1

shore (up) *vb* **1** to hold up or serve as a foundation for ⟨a highway tunnel *shored up* by massive columns of concrete⟩ — see SUPPORT 3
2 to provide evidence or information for (as a claim or idea) ⟨The governor used an avalanche of statistics to *shore up* his claim that the state's economy is in fine shape.⟩ — see SUPPORT 4

short *adj* **1** having relatively little height ⟨He is *short* for his age.⟩
synonyms little, low, low-lying
related words dwarf, dwarfish; compact, petite, slight; diminutive, half-pint, pint-size (*or* pint-sized), pocket, pocket-size (*also* pocket-sized), pygmy, small, smallish; bantam, bitty, dinky, mini, miniature, minute, puny, teeny, teeny-weeny, tiny, undersized (*also* undersize), wee; stubby, stumpy, stunted
near antonyms elevated, lifted, raised, uplifted, upswept; high-rise, statuesque; gangling, gangly, lanky, rangy; big, bulky, hefty, hulking, large, largish, outsize (*also* outsized), oversize (*or* oversized), sizable (*or* sizeable), voluminous
antonyms high, lofty, tall, towering
2 not lasting for a considerable time ⟨Fortunately for those of us in the hot sun, the graduation speech was *short* and to the point.⟩
synonyms brief, fast, little
related words shortish; abbreviated, abridged, curtailed, cut-back, shortened, syncopated; compact, condensed; abrupt, sudden; ephemeral, fleeting, momentary, short-lived, transient, transitory; impermanent; compendious, concise, pithy, succinct, summary, terse; short-range, short-term
near antonyms endless, everlasting, interminable, persistent, unending; longish, overlong, prolonged, protracted; permanent; enlarged, expanded, supplemented; long-range, long-term
antonyms extended, far, great, lengthy, long, long-lived
3 not coming up to an expected measure or meeting a particular need ⟨Regrettably, the art supplies are *short* this year, so you'll have to share.⟩
synonyms deficient, inadequate, insufficient, lacking, low, scarce, shy, wanting
related words substandard, unacceptable, unsatisfactory; hand-to-mouth, lean, light, meager (*or* meagre), poor, scant, scanty, skimp, skimpy, slender, slim, spare, sparse, stingy; bare, minimum; slight, small
near antonyms abundant, ample, bounteous, bountiful, copious, generous, liberal, plenteous, plentiful; enlarged, expanded, supplemented; abounding, overflowing, teeming; satisfactory, tolerable; big, considerable, hefty, jumbo, king-size (*or* king-sized), large, largish, oversize (*or* oversized), sizable (*or* sizeable)
antonyms adequate, enough, sufficient
4 having a texture that readily breaks into little pieces under pressure ⟨*short* pastry⟩ — see CRISP 1
5 being or characterized by direct, brief, and potentially rude speech or manner ⟨I didn't mean to be so *short* with you by responding to your request with a snippy "I'm busy!"⟩ — see BLUNT 1

short *adv* with great suddenness ⟨The bicyclist ahead of me unexpectedly pulled up *short* and I almost plowed into him.⟩
synonyms abruptly, suddenly
related words surprisingly, unexpectedly; directly, immediately, instantly, promptly, pronto, right, right away, straightaway; fast, full-tilt, posthaste, quick, quickly, rapidly, readily, snappily, speedily, swift, swiftly; hastily, impetuously, impulsively, rashly, recklessly
phrases all of a sudden (*also* on a sudden)
near antonyms gradually, slowly; hesitantly

short *vb* to rob by the use of trickery or threats ⟨charged that the used-car dealer had been *shorting* customers for years⟩ — see FLEECE

shortage *n* a falling short of an essential or desirable amount or number ⟨There was a troubling *shortage* of supplies for the troops overseas this year.⟩ — see DEFICIENCY

shortchange *vb* to rob by the use of trickery or threats ⟨was *shortchanged* out of a promotion⟩ — see FLEECE

shortcoming *n* a defect in character ⟨He has many more strengths than *shortcomings*.⟩ — see FAULT 1

shorten *vb* to make less in extent or duration ⟨We decided to *shorten* the distance we had to walk home by cutting across the neighbor's lawn.⟩ ⟨If Grandma has to go shopping today, you'll need to *shorten* your visit.⟩
synonyms abbreviate, abridge, curtail, cut back, dock, truncate
related words abstract, digest, encapsulate, epitomize, recapitulate, summarize, sum up; abate, compress, constrict, contract, cut, cut down, pare, prune, trim; decrease, de-escalate, deflate, diminish, downsize, dwindle, lessen, lower, moderate, modify, reduce, retrench, shrink, slash, subtract (from), taper
near antonyms enlarge, expand, supplement; add, aggrandize, amplify, augment, balloon, boost, dilate, escalate, heighten, increase, maximize, raise; blow up, distend, inflate, swell
antonyms elongate, extend, lengthen, prolong, protract

short–lived *adj* lasting only for a short time ⟨The skier's triumph turned out to be *short-lived*, as the next competitor bested her time.⟩ — see MOMENTARY

shortly *adv* **1** in a few words ⟨The sudden closing of the restaurant was announced only with a *shortly* worded sign: "Out of Business."⟩
synonyms briefly, compactly, concisely, crisply, laconically, pithily, succinctly, summarily, tersely
related words exactly, precisely; abruptly, bluffly, bluntly, brusquely
phrases in a nutshell, in a word, in brief, in short, in sum
near antonyms redundantly, repetitiously
antonyms diffusely, long-windedly, verbosely, wordily
2 at or within a short time ⟨The meeting will begin *shortly*, so don't go too far away.⟩
synonyms anon, directly, momentarily, presently, soon
related words forthwith, immediately, instantly, now, promptly, pronto, right away, right now, straightaway, straightway

shortness *n* the condition of being short ⟨The *shortness* of the commencement speech was much appreciated by the impatient graduates.⟩ — see BREVITY 1

shortsighted *adj* **1** able to see near things more clearly than distant ones ⟨She wears glasses because she's *shortsighted*.⟩ — see NEARSIGHTED
2 not thinking about and providing for the future ⟨*shortsighted* investors who failed to see that the boom couldn't last⟩ — see IMPROVIDENT

short story *n* a work with imaginary characters and events that is shorter and usually less complex than a novel ⟨Her very first *short story* was accepted for publication in a local journal.⟩ — see STORY 1

short–tempered *adj* easily irritated or annoyed ⟨Shop customers learned not to bother the *short-tempered* dog on their way out.⟩ — see IRRITABLE

short–term *adj* intended to last, continue, or serve for a limited time ⟨This is only a *short-term* solution to a long-term problem.⟩ — see TEMPORARY 1

shot *n* **1** a directed propelling of a missile by a firearm or artillery piece ⟨Cannon operators often had to use several *shots* to figure out the range of their targets.⟩
synonyms blasting, discharge, firing
related words barrage, blitz, blitzkrieg, bombardment, broadside, burst, cannonade, fusillade, hail, salvo, shower, storm, volley
2 an effort to do or accomplish something ⟨Let's take another *shot* at the puzzle.⟩ — see ATTEMPT 1
3 a picture created from an image recorded on a light-sensitive surface by a camera ⟨Ed took a *shot* of his family for the scrapbook.⟩ — see PHOTOGRAPH
4 a person skilled in shooting at a target ⟨a soldier who's an excellent *shot* with a rifle⟩ — see MARKSMAN
5 the portion of a serving of a beverage that is swallowed at one time ⟨woke herself up with a *shot* of espresso⟩ — see DRINK 2
6 an opinion or judgment based on little or no evidence ⟨I have no idea what's different about you, but I'll take a *shot*: you cut your hair?⟩ — see CONJECTURE
7 a favorable combination of circumstances, time, and place ⟨We have a real *shot* at getting into the championship if we win this next match.⟩ — see OPPORTUNITY

should *vb* to be under necessity or obligation to ⟨You *should* stop by more often.⟩ — see NEED 2

shoulder *vb* **1** to take to or upon oneself ⟨agreed to *shoulder* the burden of caring for their elderly father⟩ — see ASSUME 1
2 to force one's way ⟨I *shouldered* through the crowd at the concert and found my friends.⟩ — see ²PRESS 4

shout *vb* to speak so as to be heard at a distance ⟨Well-wishers *shouted* to departing passengers from the dock.⟩ — see CALL 1

shout *n* a loud vocal expression of strong emotion ⟨I gave a sudden *shout* of surprise when the shower abruptly turned ice-cold.⟩
synonyms cry, holler, hoot, howl, whoop, yell, yowl
related words ejaculation, interjection; scream, screech, shriek, shrill, squall, squeak, squeal, yelp; bawl, bellow, clamor, outcry, roar; wail
near antonyms mumble, murmur, mutter; gasp, whimper, whisper

shove *vb* **1** to apply force to (someone or something) so that it moves in front of one ⟨I had to keep *shoving* my heavy suitcase as I slowly made my way to the head of the line.⟩ — see PUSH 1
2 to push steadily against with some force ⟨She *shoved* the papers into her backpack.⟩ — see ²PRESS 1

shove (off) *vb* to leave a place often for another ⟨time to *shove off* for home⟩ — see GO 2

shovel *vb* to hollow out or form (something) by removing earth ⟨The troops quickly *shoveled* a trench.⟩ — see DIG 1

show *n* **1** an outward and often exaggerated indication of something abstract (as a feeling) for effect ⟨The children made a *show* of disgust when confronted with asparagus.⟩
synonyms demonstration, display, exhibition, flaunting
related words act, charade, facade (*also* façade), front, guise, pretense (*or* pretence), put-on, semblance, simulation; affectation, pose, sham; betrayal, disclosure
2 a display of emotion or behavior that is insincere or intended to deceive ⟨Her "concern" for the less fortunate is all just a big *show*.⟩ — see MASQUERADE

3 outward and often deceptive indication ⟨a false *show* of strength that fooled the enemy⟩ — see APPEARANCE 2
4 a public showing of objects of interest ⟨a boat *show* at the convention center⟩ — see EXHIBITION 1

show *vb* **1** to present so as to invite notice or attention ⟨Fishing for compliments, the neighbors *showed* their new car to everyone on the block.⟩
synonyms display, disport, exhibit, expose, flash, flaunt, lay out, parade, produce, show off, sport, strut, unveil
related words brandish, flourish, wave; advertise, air, announce, blaze, broadcast, herald, placard, post, proclaim, publicize, sound, trumpet; divulge, talk (about); bare, discover, reveal, uncloak, uncover, unmask
near antonyms camouflage, disguise, mask; conceal, cover, curtain, enshroud, hide, obscure, occlude, occult, shroud, veil
2 to make known (something abstract) through outward signs ⟨The actor's expressive face *shows* his every thought and emotion clearly.⟩
synonyms bespeak, betray, communicate, declare, demonstrate, display, evince, expose, give away, manifest, reveal
related words bare, disclose, uncloak, uncover; advertise, air, announce, blaze, broadcast, placard, proclaim, publicize, sound, trumpet; project
near antonyms belie, misrepresent; distort, falsify, garble, twist; camouflage, disguise; gild, gloss (over), varnish, whitewash; conceal, counterfeit, cover, hide, mask, obscure, occlude, veil
3 to gain full recognition or acceptance of ⟨That *shows* we're right!⟩ — see ESTABLISH 1
4 to give advice and instruction to (someone) regarding the course or process to be followed ⟨*showed* me how to play the guitar⟩ — see GUIDE 1
5 to point out the way for (someone) especially from a position in front ⟨*showed* them the way to get home⟩ — see LEAD 1
6 to come into view ⟨Another car *showed* just as we were thinking we'd have the whole place to ourselves.⟩ — see APPEAR 1

shower *n* **1** a heavy fall of objects ⟨A *shower* of books fell from the collapsing shelves.⟩ — see RAIN 2
2 a rapid or overwhelming outpouring of many things at once ⟨A *shower* of insults and curses rained down on the criminal as he was led through the crowd.⟩ — see BARRAGE

shower *vb* to give readily and in large quantities ⟨*showered* gifts on the guests of honor⟩ — see RAIN 2

showiness *n* excessive or unnecessary display ⟨We were somewhat put off by the saber-rattling *showiness* of the military parade.⟩ — see OSTENTATION

show off *vb* **1** to engage in attention-getting playful or boisterous behavior ⟨The athletes warmed up, happily *showing off* for the crowd before the match officially started.⟩ — see CUT UP
2 to present so as to invite notice or attention ⟨She just wants to *show off* her new car.⟩ — see SHOW 1

show up *vb* **1** to come into view ⟨The flaws in the repair job *show up* under the light.⟩ — see APPEAR 1
2 to get to a destination ⟨The band *showed up* an hour late.⟩ — see COME 2
3 to reveal the true nature of ⟨The bullies were *shown up* for what they really are.⟩ — see EXPOSE 1

showy *adj* likely to attract attention ⟨Orchid plants are known for their huge *showy* flowers.⟩ — see NOTICEABLE

shred *n* a very small amount ⟨The vandals showed not a *shred* of decency.⟩ — see PARTICLE 1

shred *vb* to cause (something) to separate into jagged pieces by violently pulling at it 〈*shredded* some cooked chicken for the soup〉 — see TEAR 1

shrew *n* a bad-tempered scolding woman 〈the famous Shakespearean play about a *shrew* and the suitor who reforms her〉

synonyms fury, virago

related words gorgon; carper, faultfinder, nitpicker, scold

shrewd *adj* **1** having or showing a practical cleverness or judgment 〈a *shrewd* used car dealer who knew how to make the best possible deal〉 〈*shrewd* investments that paid off big〉

synonyms astute, canny, clear-sighted, hard-boiled, hardheaded, knowing, savvy, sharp, sharp-witted, smart

related words artful, cagey (*also* cagy), crafty, cunning, devious, foxy, guileful, slick, sly, subtle, tricky, wily; discerning, insightful, perceptive, percipient, perspicacious, sagacious, sage, sapient, wise; agile, alert, brainy, bright, brilliant, clever, intelligent, keen, nimble, quick, quick-witted, sharp-eyed; apt, ingenious, resourceful; calculating

near antonyms artless, guileless, ingenuous, innocent, naive (*or* naïve); exploitable, gullible (*also* gullable); dense, dull, obtuse; brainless, dim-witted, dopey (*also* dopy), dumb, empty-headed, feebleminded, half-witted, knuckleheaded, simple, slow, slow-witted, softheaded, stupid, thickheaded, thick-witted, unintelligent, weak-minded; foolish, idiotic (*also* idiotical), imbecile (*or* imbecilic), moronic, silly, thoughtless, witless; ignorant, uninformed

antonyms unknowing

2 causing intense discomfort to one's skin 〈She pulled her coat tighter against the *shrewd* breeze whipping down the alley.〉 — see CUTTING 1

3 clever at attaining one's ends by indirect and often deceptive means 〈A *shrewd* operator in the real estate game, she made every buyer think they were getting the deal of the century.〉 — see ARTFUL 1

shrewdness *n* exceptional discernment and judgment especially in practical matters 〈a woman with the thick-skinned *shrewdness* to survive in a tough business〉 — see ACUMEN

shriek *vb* to cry out loudly and emotionally 〈The children *shrieked* with excitement.〉 — see SCREAM 1

shrieking *adj* having a high musical pitch or range 〈*shrieking* horns of impatient drivers stuck in a traffic jam〉 — see SHRILL

shrill *vb* to cry out loudly and emotionally 〈The mud-splattered bystanders were *shrilling* with outrage at the inconsiderate motorist.〉 — see SCREAM 1

shrill *adj* having a high musical pitch or range 〈the *shrill* sound of a policeman's whistle〉

synonyms high-pitched, piping, screeching, shrieking, squeaking, squeaky, treble, whistling

related words peeping, thin, tinny; earsplitting, nasal, penetrating, piercing, sharp, strident; squealing, whining, whiny (*also* whiney), yapping, yelping

near antonyms gruff, hoarse, husky, rough, smoky (*also* smokey)

antonyms bass, deep, grave, low, throaty

shrimp *n* **1** a living thing much smaller than others of its kind 〈My brother was just a *shrimp* until his teens, when he had a growth spurt.〉 — see DWARF 1

2 a person of no importance or influence 〈You have no business telling me what to do, you little *shrimp*!〉 — see NOBODY

shrine *n* a place that is considered sacred (as within a religion) 〈For centuries pilgrims have traveled to the *shrine* of Saint Thomas à Becket in Canterbury, England.〉

synonyms sanctuary, sanctum

related words reliquary

shrink *vb* **1** to become smaller in size or volume through the drawing together of particles of matter 〈The sweater will *shrink* a little when washed.〉 — see CONTRACT 2

2 to draw back in fear, pain, or disgust 〈*shrinking* back from the approaching flames〉 — see FLINCH

3 to grow less in scope or intensity especially gradually 〈It's just a fad, and interest in it will soon start to *shrink*.〉 — see DECREASE 2

shrinkage *n* the amount by which something is lessened 〈The *shrinkage* contributions is significant.〉 — see DECREASE

shroud *n* something that covers or conceals like a piece of cloth 〈The truth of the affair will always be hidden under a *shroud* of secrecy.〉 — see CLOAK 1

shroud *vb* **1** to keep secret or shut off from view 〈Their work was *shrouded* in secrecy.〉 — see ¹HIDE 2

2 to make dark, dim, or indistinct 〈The smog *shrouded* our aerial view of the city.〉 — see CLOUD 1

3 to surround or cover closely 〈During rainy season the summit of the mountain is *shrouded* in mist.〉 — see ENFOLD 1

shrug off *vb* **1** to dismiss as of little importance 〈an administration that was willing to *shrug off* the problem〉 — see EXCUSE 1

2 to rid oneself of (a garment) 〈She *shrugged off* her coat and hung it up neatly.〉 — see REMOVE 1

shuck *n, usually* **shucks** *pl* something of little importance 〈It doesn't matter *shucks* to her what anyone else earns.〉 — see TRIFLE

shuck *vb* to remove the natural covering of 〈*shucking* peas〉 — see PEEL

shuck (off) *vb* to get rid of as useless or unwanted 〈Bad habits are hard to *shuck off*.〉 — see DISCARD

shudder *n* an instance of shaking involuntarily with fear or cold 〈A *shudder* ran through him as he stepped outside into the snow.〉 — see SHIVER 1

shudder *vb* to make a series of small irregular or violent movements 〈I *shuddered* when I thought of what could have happened.〉 — see SHAKE 1

shuddering *adj* marked by or given to small uncontrollable bodily movements 〈With a *shuddering* extension of his hand, the elderly man asked for help to stand up.〉 — see SHAKY 1

shuddering *n* a series of slight movements by a body back and forth or from side to side 〈tried to control the *shuddering* of his hand〉 — see VIBRATION 1

shuddery *adj* marked by or given to small uncontrollable bodily movements 〈With a few *shuddery* strokes of a pen, she signed her last will and testament.〉 — see SHAKY 1

shuffle *n* **1** an unorganized collection or mixture of various things 〈The paper got lost in the *shuffle* on his desk.〉 — see MISCELLANY 1

2 deliberate evasion in speech 〈No matter how directly we asked the question, all we got was *shuffle* in return.〉 — see CIRCUMLOCUTION 1

shuffle *vb* **1** to move heavily or clumsily 〈The old man *shuffled* across the floor in his slippers.〉 — see LUMBER 1

2 to undo the proper order or arrangement of 〈*Shuffle* the cards and deal five to each player.〉 — see DISORDER

shun *vb* to get or keep away from (as a responsibility) through cleverness or trickery 〈just a ruse to *shun* the debt collectors〉 — see ESCAPE 2

shunning *n* the act or a means of getting or keeping away from something undesirable 〈This *shunning* of your financial responsibilities cannot continue indefinitely.〉 — see ESCAPE 2

shush *vb* to stop the noise or speech of 〈*shushed* the crying baby〉 — see SILENCE 1

shut *vb* **1** to position (something) so as to prevent passage through an opening ⟨Please *shut* the door when you leave.⟩ — see CLOSE 1

2 to stop the operations of ⟨*shut* both stores for a week⟩ — see CLOSE 2

shutdown *n* the stopping of a process or activity ⟨The factory resumed operation after a brief *shutdown* for repairs.⟩ — see END 1

shutoff *n* the stopping of a process or activity ⟨The utility company threatened them with the *shutoff* of electricity if the bills weren't paid.⟩ — see END 1

shut off *vb* **1** to bring (as an action or operation) to an immediate end ⟨They threatened to *shut off* peace talks if the other side kept making unreasonable demands.⟩ — see STOP 1

2 to cause to stop functioning ⟨*shut off* the computer to save electricity⟩ — see DEACTIVATE

shut out *vb* to prevent the participation, consideration, or inclusion of ⟨Local residents feel that they have been *shut out* of the debate for expanding the airport.⟩ — see EXCLUDE

shutterbug *n* one who takes photographs ⟨an avid *shutterbug* who takes her camera with her everywhere⟩ — see PHOTOGRAPHER

shut up *vb* **1** to stop talking ⟨You have no right to tell the rest of us to *shut up*.⟩
synonyms clam up, hush, pipe down, quiet (down)
related words calm (down), cool (down), settle (down)
phrases hold one's tongue (*or* hold one's peace)
near antonyms sound off, speak out, speak up, spout (off)
antonyms speak, talk

2 to stop the noise or speech of ⟨Nothing I said would *shut* them *up*.⟩ — see SILENCE 1

shy *adj* **1** easily frightened ⟨a *shy* cat who hid under the bed every time she heard any loud noise⟩
synonyms fainthearted, fearful, fearsome, mousy (*or* mousey), scary, skittish, timid, timorous, tremulous
related words chicken, chickenhearted, cowardly, craven, dastardly, lily-livered, spineless, yellow; jittery, jumpy, spooky; anxious, nervous; afraid, alarmed, horrified, panicked, panicky, panic-stricken, scared, shocked, spooked, startled, terrified, terrorized, unnerved
near antonyms brave, courageous, dauntless, doughty, fearless, gallant, greathearted, heroic (*also* heroical), intrepid, lionhearted, stalwart, stout, stouthearted, undaunted, valiant, valorous; assured, confident, self-assured, self-confident; determined, firm, game, plucky, resolute, undeterred, unflinching, unswerving; mettlesome, spirited, spunky
antonyms adventuresome, adventurous, audacious, bold, daring, dashing, gutsy, hardy, venturesome, venturous

2 not comfortable around people ⟨a *shy* person who finds talking to anyone but a close friend to be an awkward and unpleasant experience⟩
synonyms backward, bashful, coy, demure, diffident, introverted, modest, retiring, sheepish, withdrawn
related words antisocial, unsociable, unsocial; awkward, embarrassed, self-conscious, unadventurous, unassertive, unenterprising; inhibited, reserved, uneasy, uptight
near antonyms boon, companionable, convivial, gregarious, sociable, social; bold, dashing, forceful; brash, forward, overbold, uninhibited, unreserved
antonyms extroverted (*also* extraverted), immodest, outgoing

3 not coming up to an expected measure or meeting a particular need ⟨The team is *shy* a couple of players because of illness.⟩ — see SHORT 3

4 not respectable ⟨a *shy* casino⟩ — see DISREPUTABLE

sick *adj* **1** temporarily suffering from a disorder of the body ⟨He is at home *sick* in bed.⟩
synonyms ailing, bad, down, ill, indisposed, peaked, poorly, punk, run-down, sickened, unhealthy, unsound, unwell
related words lousy, sickish; nauseated, nauseous, qualmish, queasy (*also* queazy), squeamish; airsick, carsick, seasick; dizzy, light-headed, shaky; achy, feverish; diseased, disordered; decrepit, feeble, fragile, frail, infirm, invalid, sickly, weak, weakly; afflicted, troubled; challenged, debilitated, disabled, halt, incapacitated, lame; hypochondriac, hypochondriacal
phrases out of sorts, under the weather
near antonyms able-bodied, conditioned, fit; cured; better, convalescing, improved, mending, recovering, recuperating, rehabilitated; hardy, hearty, lusty, robust, rugged, stalwart, strong, tough; blooming, bouncing, chipper, flourishing, flush, thriving
antonyms hale, healthful, healthy, sound, well, whole, wholesome

2 filled with disgust ⟨It makes me *sick* to think of someone hurting a helpless animal.⟩
synonyms disgusted, nauseated, repelled, repulsed, revolted, shocked, sickened
related words fed up, weary; angered, angry, displeased, enraged, fuming, furious, incensed, indignant, infuriated, irate, livid, mad, outraged, rankled, riled, roiled, sore, steaming, upset, worked up, wrought (up)
near antonyms delighted, gratified, pleased, satisfied, thankful, thrilled, tickled; beguiled, bewitched, captivated, charmed, enchanted, enthralled, entranced, fascinated, mesmerized, spellbound

3 affected with nausea ⟨The bumpy ride made her *sick* to her stomach.⟩ — see NAUSEOUS 1

4 having one's patience, interest, or pleasure exhausted ⟨I'm *sick* of listening to this radio station!⟩ — see WEARY 2

5 having or showing lowered moral character or standards ⟨Some people insisted that only a *sick* soul could enjoy such a violent movie.⟩ — see CORRUPT

sicken *vb* to cause to feel disgust ⟨*sickened* by the awful news⟩ — see DISGUST

sicken (with) *vb* to become affected with (a disease or disorder) ⟨A number of the passengers on the cruise ship were *sickened with* food poisoning.⟩ — see CONTRACT 1

sickened *adj* **1** temporarily suffering from a disorder of the body ⟨The *sickened* passengers were rushed to the emergency room for treatment.⟩ — see SICK 1

2 filled with disgust ⟨Many audience members, *sickened* by the movie's graphic nature, left the theater.⟩ — see SICK 2

sickening *adj* causing intense displeasure, disgust, or resentment ⟨a *sickening* display of selfishness⟩ — see OFFENSIVE 1

sickish *adj* affected with nausea ⟨The fumes from the freshly applied paint made her feel *sickish*.⟩ — see NAUSEOUS 1

sickly *adj* **1** chronically or repeatedly suffering from poor health ⟨a *sickly* foal that seemed to catch everything that the other horses had⟩
synonyms ailing, invalid, weakly
related words bedfast, bedridden; delicate, fragile, frail; dying, fading, incurable, moribund; challenged, debilitated, incapacitated, lame; decrepit, enfeebled, feeble, infirm, weak, weakened, worn-out; ill, indisposed, peaked, poorly, run-down, sick, unhealthy, unsound, unwell
near antonyms able-bodied, fit, hale, hearty, sound, whole, wholesome
antonyms healthy, well

2 bad for the well-being of the body ⟨lungs scarred by years of exposure to the *sickly* air of the coal mines⟩ — see UNHEALTHY 1

sickness *n* **1** the condition of not being in good health ⟨She was plagued by *sickness* most of her adult life.⟩
synonyms illness, indisposition, unhealthiness, unsoundness
related words malaise; affliction, ailment, condition, disease, disorder, dysfunction (*also* disfunction), malady, trouble, upset; debility, decrepitude, feebleness, frailness, infirmity, invalidism, weakness; hypochondria
near antonyms comeback, convalescence, healing, mending, rally, recovery, recuperation, rehab, rehabilitation, snapback; fettle, fitness, shape; hardiness, heartiness, lustiness, robustness, ruggedness, stamina, strength, toughness, vigor, vigorousness, vitality; bloom, flush, flushness; weal, welfare, well-being
antonyms health, healthiness, soundness, wellness, wholeness, wholesomeness
2 an abnormal state that disrupts a plant's or animal's normal bodily functioning ⟨a *sickness* that resulted in the death of millions of the nation's elm trees⟩ — see DISEASE
3 a disturbed condition of the stomach in which one feels like vomiting ⟨the *sickness* that women often feel during the early months of a pregnancy⟩ — see NAUSEA 1

side *adj* of, relating to, or located on one side ⟨Please bring all deliveries to the *side* door.⟩
synonyms lateral
related words left, right; one-sided
side *n* **1** a place, space, or direction away from or beyond a central point or line ⟨Will everyone who wants to sign up for volleyball please stand off to this *side* of the gym?⟩
synonyms flank, hand
related words outside; face, top; bottom, foot, underbelly, underbody, underpart, underside, undersurface; lee, leeward, windward; left, right
near antonyms center, inside, interior, middle, midway
2 a certain way in which something appears or may be regarded ⟨examined the problem from all *sides*⟩ — see ASPECT 1
3 a group of people acting together within a larger group ⟨Our *side* won, and the club will have a holiday party after all.⟩ — see FACTION

sideboard *n* a storage case typically having doors and shelves ⟨All of the silverware was kept in the *sideboard*.⟩ — see CABINET

sidekick *n* a person who helps a more skilled person ⟨Movie heroes invariably have a trusty *sidekick*, who often provides comic relief.⟩ — see HELPER

sidestep *vb* **1** to avoid having to comply with (something) especially through cleverness ⟨The eager enlistee *sidestepped* the regulations by lying about his age.⟩ — see CIRCUMVENT 1
2 to move suddenly aside or to and fro ⟨The startled spectator *sidestepped* away from the oncoming ball.⟩ — see DODGE 1

sideways *adv* **1** with one side faced forward ⟨I had to walk *sideways* to get between the two towering piles of boxes.⟩
synonyms broadside, edgewise, sidewise
related words aslant, indirectly, obliquely; laterally, sideward (*or* sidewards)
near antonyms direct, right, straight
2 with distrust ⟨She glanced at us *sideways* when she heard us claim we weren't there that night.⟩ — see ASKANCE

sidewise *adv* with one side faced forward ⟨standing *sidewise* in the doorway⟩ — see SIDEWAYS 1

siege *n* **1** a sudden experiencing of a physical or mental disorder ⟨A devastating *siege* of typhoid fever hit the city.⟩ — see ATTACK 2
2 the cutting off of an area by military means to stop the flow of people or supplies ⟨After a *siege* of six weeks, the city of Vicksburg surrendered to General Grant and his Union forces.⟩ — see BLOCKADE

siesta *n* a short sleep ⟨He typically takes a *siesta* after lunch, waiting for it to become a little cooler until resuming work.⟩ — see ¹NAP

sigh (for) *vb* to have an earnest wish to own or enjoy ⟨People have always been *sighing for* the "good old days."⟩ — see DESIRE 1

sight *n* **1** a position within view ⟨Get out of my *sight*!⟩ — see PRESENCE 1
2 an instance of looking especially briefly ⟨He always fainted at the merest *sight* of blood.⟩ — see LOOK 2
3 something unpleasant to look at ⟨The house was a *sight* the morning after the party.⟩ — see EYESORE
4 the ability to see ⟨Bill lost his *sight* in an accident when he was young.⟩ — see EYESIGHT
5 a considerable amount ⟨This place sure is a good *sight* better than that last motel.⟩ — see LOT 2
sight *vb* to make note of (something) through the use of one's eyes ⟨The crew felt a rush of excitement upon hearing that the lookout had *sighted* land.⟩ — see SEE 1

sightless *adj* lacking the power of sight ⟨Bats are often thought to be completely *sightless*, but this is not really true.⟩ — see BLIND

sightliness *n* the qualities in a person or thing that as a whole give pleasure to the senses ⟨Never known for their *sightliness*, landfills are unwelcome in most communities.⟩ — see BEAUTY 1

sightly *adj* very pleasing to look at ⟨The calligrapher's *sightly* handwriting would be desirable on the diplomas.⟩ — see BEAUTIFUL 1

sightseer *n* a person who travels for pleasure ⟨We shared the bus with a group of *sightseers* from out of town.⟩ — see TOURIST

sign *n* **1** a movement of the body or limbs that expresses or emphasizes an idea or feeling ⟨made a *sign* for the audience to be quiet⟩ — see GESTURE 1
2 a written or printed mark that is meant to convey information to the reader ⟨an "and" *sign*⟩ — see CHARACTER 1
sign *vb* to write one's name on (as a document) ⟨You'll have to *sign* the contract for it to be legal.⟩
synonyms autograph
related words sign up; cosign, countersign, endorse (*also* indorse), register, sign on; inscribe; author, pen, pencil (in), scratch (out), scrawl, scribble; notarize

signal *adj* standing above others in rank, importance, or achievement ⟨The Louisiana Purchase is cited by many historians as one of the most *signal* events in American history.⟩ — see EMINENT
signal *vb* to direct or notify by a movement or gesture ⟨*signaled* the oncoming traffic to stop while the wrecked car was being towed away⟩ — see MOTION
signal *n* **1** an object intended to give public notice or warning ⟨Stop signs are *signals* for vehicles to come to a full stop.⟩
synonyms flag, tocsin
related words red light; knell
2 a movement of the body or limbs that expresses or emphasizes an idea or feeling ⟨quietly waiting for the *signal* to advance⟩ — see GESTURE 1

significance *n* **1** the idea that is conveyed or intended to be conveyed to the mind by language, symbol, or action ⟨The *significance* of that word is much debated by biblical scholars.⟩ — see MEANING 1

2 the quality or state of being important ⟨the political *significance* of the special commission's report⟩ — see IMPORTANCE

significant *adj* **1** clearly conveying a special meaning (as one's mood) ⟨After remarking that tardiness was on the rise, our boss cast a *significant* glance my way.⟩ — see EXPRESSIVE

2 indicating something ⟨The town's generous library budget is *significant* of the value its residents place on learning.⟩ — see INDICATIVE

3 having great meaning or lasting effect ⟨made a *significant* change in the procedure for applying for citizenship⟩ — see IMPORTANT 1

4 having great power or influence ⟨a producer who is playing a *significant* role in the creation of the new film⟩ — see IMPORTANT 2

5 sufficiently large in size, amount, or number to merit attention ⟨paid a *significant* amount of money for the movie rights to the book⟩ — see CONSIDERABLE 1

signification *n* the idea that is conveyed or intended to be conveyed to the mind by language, symbol, or action ⟨We should assume that the author is using the word in its ordinary *signification*.⟩ — see MEANING 1

signify *vb* **1** to be of importance ⟨Never mind, as the color of the room doesn't *signify* in the least.⟩ — see MATTER

2 to communicate or convey (as an idea) to the mind ⟨The symbol failed to *signify* anything to me—until I realized that it was upside down.⟩ — see MEAN 1

3 to serve as a sign or symptom of ⟨The opening of the new business *signifies* the city's overdue emergence from economic depression.⟩ — see INDICATE 1

signifying *adj* indicating something ⟨His tendency to use weasel words is seen as a *signifying* character trait.⟩ — see INDICATIVE

sign on (for) *vb* to become a member of ⟨I *signed on for* the crew team simply as a lark.⟩ — see ENTER 2

sign up (for) *vb* to become a member of ⟨They both *signed up for* a Spanish class.⟩ — see ENTER 2

silence *n* **1** incapacity for or restraint from speaking ⟨The violinist expects complete *silence* from the audience during his concerts.⟩

synonyms dumbness, muteness, speechlessness, stillness
related words reserve, reticence, reticency, taciturnity
near antonyms communication, speaking, talking; eloquence, fluency, volubility; chattiness, loquaciousness, loquacity, talkativeness; verboseness, verbosity, windiness, wordiness

2 the near or complete absence of sound ⟨The *silence* of the garden was refreshing after the din of the party inside.⟩
synonyms hush, quiet, quietness, quietude, still, stillness
related words calm, lull, peace, peacefulness, tranquillity (*or* tranquility)
near antonyms cacophony, chatter, clamor, clangor, din, hubbub, racket, rattle, roar, tumult, uproar
antonyms noise, sound

3 the quality or state of being mostly or completely unknown ⟨The book soon vanished into the *silence* that awaits best sellers whose time has passed.⟩ — see OBSCURITY 2

silence *vb* **1** to stop the noise or speech of ⟨The instructor quickly *silenced* anyone who tried to interrupt.⟩ ⟨We need to have a repairman come and *silence* that door alarm.⟩
synonyms hush, mute, quell, quiet, settle, shush, shut up, squelch, still
near antonyms agitate, stir

2 to put a stop to (something) by the use of force ⟨*silenced* all political dissent in the country⟩ — see QUELL 1

silent *adj* **1** deliberately refraining from speech ⟨The suddenly *silent* child had to be prompted to say hello.⟩

synonyms dumb, mum, mute, muted, speechless, uncommunicative, wordless
related words inarticulate, tongue-tied; nonvocal, voiceless; sulking, sulky, sullen
near antonyms articulate, eloquent, fluent, voluble, well-spoken; gabby, garrulous, loquacious, talkative, talky; outspoken, unreserved, vocal; facile, glib, smooth-tongued
antonyms communicative, speaking, talking

2 tending not to speak frequently (as by habit or inclination) ⟨A naturally *silent* boy, he was often overshadowed by his louder siblings.⟩
synonyms closemouthed, dumb, laconic, reserved, reticent, taciturn, tight-lipped, uncommunicative
related words aloof, inhibited, introverted, reserved, restrained; sedate, self-contained, sober, staid; backward, bashful, coy, demure, diffident, modest, retiring, sheepish
near antonyms free-spoken, outspoken, vocal; long-winded, prolix, rambling, verbose, windy, wordy; extroverted (*also* extraverted), gregarious, outgoing, sociable
antonyms blabby, chatty, gabby, garrulous, loquacious, talkative, talky, unreserved

3 mostly or entirely without sound ⟨The room was so *silent* that you could have heard the proverbial pin drop.⟩
synonyms hushed, muted, noiseless, quiet, quieted, soundless, still, stilly
related words calm, peaceable, peaceful, serene, tranquil
near antonyms boisterous, clamorous, clangorous, clattering, clattery, raucous, rip-roaring, roaring, roistering, tumultuous
antonyms noisy, unquiet, uproarious

silent treatment *n* treatment that is deliberately unfriendly ⟨Ever since our run-in at the party she's been giving me the *silent treatment*.⟩ — see COLD SHOULDER

silhouette *n* a line that traces the outer limits of an object or surface ⟨Cartoonists often try to give their characters recognizable *silhouettes*.⟩ — see OUTLINE 1

silhouette *vb* to draw or make apparent the outline of ⟨In the photograph the majestic mountain is strikingly *silhouetted* against the setting sun.⟩ — see OUTLINE 1

silken *adj* smooth or delicate in appearance or feel ⟨the *silken* texture of the synthetic fabric⟩ — see SOFT 2

silky *adj* **1** smooth or delicate in appearance or feel ⟨The plant's fibers feel *silky* to the touch.⟩ — see SOFT 2

2 covered with or as if with hair ⟨The tops of the leaves are a dark glossy green, but the undersides are light and *silky*.⟩ — see HAIRY 1

silliness *n* **1** lack of good sense or judgment ⟨She was both amused and irritated by the *silliness* of his comments regarding the movie they has just seen.⟩ — see FOOLISHNESS 1

2 language, behavior, or ideas that are absurd and contrary to good sense ⟨Stop this *silliness* at once!⟩ — see NONSENSE 1

3 a lack of seriousness often at an improper time ⟨This inability to refrain from *silliness* is a distressing sign of professional immaturity.⟩ — see FRIVOLITY

silly *adj* **1** lacking in seriousness or maturity ⟨The matinee show was filled with a bunch of *silly* children making noise.⟩ — see GIDDY 1

2 showing or marked by a lack of good sense or judgment ⟨those *silly* movie producers who thought that audiences would fall for that gimmick all over again⟩ — see FOOLISH 1

3 so foolish or pointless as to be worthy of scornful laughter ⟨Ask a *silly* question, get a *silly* answer.⟩ — see RIDICULOUS 1

4 suffering from mental confusion ⟨stunning news that knocked me *silly*⟩ — see DIZZY 2

silver *adj* of the color gray ⟨a distinguished-looking gentleman with *silver* hair⟩ — see GRAY 1

silver *n* eating and serving utensils ⟨laid out the *silver* for the dinner guests⟩ — see TABLEWARE 1

silverware *n* eating and serving utensils ⟨We keep the *silverware* in a separate drawer.⟩ — see TABLEWARE 1

silvery *adj* of the color gray ⟨a *silvery* metal of some kind⟩ — see GRAY 1

similar *adj* having qualities in common ⟨The two actresses accidentally wore *similar* outfits to the same gala.⟩ — see ALIKE

similarity *n* 1 the quality or state of having many qualities in common ⟨The *similarity* between the two essays is too great to be coincidental—one author virtually copied the other.⟩

synonyms alikeness, community, correspondence, likeness, parallelism, resemblance, similitude

related words semblance; affinity, analogousness; equation, equivalence, equivalency, par, parity; identicalness, identity, sameness; correlation, relationship; exchangeability, interchangeability; accordance, agreement, compatibility, conformity, congruity

near antonyms inequality; conflict; incompatibility, incongruence, incongruity, incongruousness, nonconformity; disproportion, imbalance, inequality, nonequivalence

antonyms difference, disagreement, discrepancy, disparateness, disparity, dissimilarity, distinctiveness, distinctness, unlikeness

2 a point which two or more things share in common ⟨The only *similarity* between this project and the last one is that both will involve some lab work.⟩

synonyms congruity, correspondence, parallel, resemblance, similitude

related words counterpart, equal, equivalent; analogy; homology

near antonyms difference, discrepancy; deviance, divergence, incongruence, incongruity; change, modification, variation

antonyms dissimilarity

similarly *adv* in like manner ⟨All the other men were removing their ties, so I did *similarly*.⟩ — see ALSO 1

similitude *n* 1 the quality or state of having many qualities in common ⟨the striking *similitude* between that modern city and the Rome of ancient times⟩ — see SIMILARITY 1

2 a point which two or more things share in common ⟨The two robberies, committed on opposite ends of the country, show some curious *similitudes*.⟩ — see SIMILARITY 2

simmer *vb* to cook in a liquid heated to the point that it gives off steam ⟨I gently *simmered* the chili for an hour.⟩ — see BOIL 2

simple *adj* 1 free from all additions or embellishment ⟨a *simple* design, and one that never goes out of fashion⟩ — see PLAIN 1

2 free from any intent to deceive or impress others ⟨growing up in *simple* innocence⟩ — see GUILELESS

3 having no exceptions or restrictions ⟨That's the *simple* truth!⟩ — see ABSOLUTE 2

4 involving minimal difficulty or effort ⟨I got all of the answers right because it was such a *simple* test.⟩ — see EASY 1

5 lacking in worldly wisdom or informed judgment ⟨Developers mistakenly thought that the local residents were *simple* people who would sell their land for practically nothing.⟩ — see NAIVE 1

6 lacking in education or the knowledge gained from books ⟨The fact that he didn't go to college doesn't mean he's *simple*.⟩ — see IGNORANT 1

7 not having or showing an ability to absorb ideas readily ⟨Don't be so quick to characterize people who have trouble with computers as *simple*.⟩ — see STUPID 1

simpleminded *adj* 1 lacking in worldly wisdom or informed judgment ⟨a *simpleminded* view of a complex problem⟩ — see NAIVE 1

2 showing or marked by a lack of good sense or judgment ⟨a *simpleminded* mistake⟩ — see FOOLISH 1

simpleness *n* 1 the quality or state of being simple and sincere ⟨The *simpleness* of the villagers was so disarming that she temporarily abandoned her natural cynicism.⟩ — see NAÏVETÉ 1

2 the quality or state of lacking intelligence or quickness of mind ⟨misjudged his lack of interest as *simpleness*⟩ — see STUPIDITY 1

3 readiness to believe the claims of others without sufficient evidence ⟨There's a good-hearted *simpleness* about her that makes her easy prey for scams.⟩ — see CREDULITY

simpleton *n* 1 a person who lacks good sense or judgment ⟨His silly antics at the office have earned him a reputation as a *simpleton*.⟩ — see FOOL 1

2 a stupid person ⟨She felt like such a *simpleton* for needing help to install her home theater.⟩ — see IDIOT

simplicity *n* 1 the quality or state of having a form or structure of few parts or elements ⟨The *simplicity* of this machine should ensure ease of use by almost anyone.⟩

synonyms plainness, unsophistication

related words homogeneity, homogeneousness, uniformity, unity

antonyms complexity, complicacy, complicatedness, complication, elaborateness, intricacy, sophistication

2 clearness of expression ⟨The *simplicity* of this poem is beautiful.⟩

synonyms clarity, explicitness, lucidity, lucidness, perspicuity, perspicuousness

related words incision, incisiveness; directness, forthrightness, openness, straightforwardness; comprehensibility, intelligibility, legibility

near antonyms ambiguity, ambiguousness, equivocalness, equivocation, obliquity, opacity; incomprehensibility, incomprehensibleness, unintelligibility, unintelligibleness; circuitousness, deviousness, indirectness, indistinctness; dimness, disjointedness, incoherence; faintness, fuzziness, muddiness, nebulousness, vagueness

antonyms obscureness, obscurity, unclarity

3 lack of good sense or judgment ⟨the *simplicity* of the generals who thought that war would be over in a month⟩ — see FOOLISHNESS 1

4 the quality or state of being simple and sincere ⟨She answered the judge's questions with childlike *simplicity*.⟩ — see NAÏVETÉ 1

simplify *vb* 1 to make less complex ⟨You need to *simplify* this process somewhat or you'll never finish it today.⟩

synonyms streamline

related words dumb down, oversimplify; prune, strip (down), trim; purify, refine

near antonyms elaborate

antonyms complex, complicate, perplex, sophisticate

2 to make plain or understandable ⟨The book *simplifies* for the layman some concepts of economics.⟩ — see EXPLAIN 1

simply *adv* 1 for nothing other than ⟨Uninterested in food, she eats *simply* to keep alive.⟩ — see SOLELY 1

2 nothing more than ⟨It's *simply* smart to shop around before buying an item.⟩ — see JUST 3

simulate *vb* to present a false appearance of ⟨cosmetics that *simulate* a suntan⟩ — see FEIGN

simulated *adj* 1 being such in appearance only and made with or manufactured from usually cheaper materials ⟨a *simulated* leopard skin rug⟩ — see IMITATION

2 lacking in natural or spontaneous quality ⟨the *simulated* friendliness in public of two politicians who can't stand each other in private⟩ — see ARTIFICIAL 1

simultaneous *adj* existing or occurring at the same period of time ⟨a *simultaneous* release of the movie and its soundtrack⟩ — see CONTEMPORARY 1

simultaneously *adv* at one and the same time ⟨Fires broke out *simultaneously* in several parts of town.⟩ — see TOGETHER 1

sin *n* **1** a breaking of a moral or legal code ⟨a child old enough to know that lying is a *sin*⟩ — see OFFENSE 1

2 that which is morally unacceptable ⟨a minister who worries that modern society has abandoned the concept of *sin*⟩ — see EVIL

3 immoral conduct or practices harmful or offensive to society ⟨a sordid section of the city that is mainly known for *sin* and degradation⟩ — see VICE 1

4 a regrettable or blameworthy act ⟨It's a *sin* to waste food when people are starving.⟩ — see CRIME 2

5 a defect in character ⟨My besetting *sin* is impatience—I hate to wait for anything.⟩ — see FAULT 1

sin *vb* to commit an offense ⟨Forgive me, for I have *sinned*.⟩ — see OFFEND 1

since *conj* for the reason that ⟨*Since* you are already here, we might as well get the meeting started.⟩

   synonyms as, because, for, inasmuch as, now, seeing, whereas

sincere *adj* free from any intent to deceive or impress others ⟨done out of a *sincere* desire to help others⟩ — see GUILELESS

sincerely *adv* without any attempt to impress by deception or exaggeration ⟨I thanked them *sincerely* for their help.⟩ — see NATURALLY 3

sinew *n* the ability to exert effort for the accomplishment of a task ⟨The justices displayed great intellectual depth and *sinew* in writing their opinion on this case.⟩ — see POWER 2

sinewy *adj* **1** having muscles capable of exerting great physical force ⟨the lithe, *sinewy* body of the ballet company's leading male dancer⟩ — see STRONG 1

2 marked by a well-developed musculature ⟨the *sinewy* arms of the weight lifter⟩ — see MUSCULAR 1

sinful *adj* not conforming to a high moral standard; morally unacceptable ⟨chastised by his minister for his *sinful* behavior⟩ — see BAD 2

sinfulness *n* the state or quality of being utterly evil ⟨Private diaries reveal that the perpetrators came to realize the *sinfulness* of their actions and were ever afterwards regretful.⟩ — see ENORMITY 1

sing *vb* **1** to produce musical sounds with the voice ⟨It's relatively rare to find actors who can also *sing* well.⟩

   synonyms carol, chant, descant, vocalize

   related words belt, croon, harmonize, hum, lilt, quaver, trill, warble, yodel; serenade

2 to utter in musical or drawn out tones ⟨The cantor *sang* the prayers before the entire congregation.⟩ — see CHANT 1

3 to utter one's distinctive animal sound ⟨I can hear a bird *singing* in the distance.⟩ — see CRY 2

4 to give information (as to the authorities) about another's improper or unlawful activities ⟨Once he saw the kind of jail time he was facing, the suspect was *singing* loud and clear to the police.⟩ — see SQUEAL 1

singe *vb* to burn on the surface ⟨The marshmallows got a bit *singed* over the campfire, but we like them that way.⟩ — see SCORCH 1

singer *n* one who sings ⟨A famous opera *singer* will be performing at the gala opening of the arts center.⟩

   synonyms caroler (*or* caroller), songster, vocalist, vocalizer, voice

   related words belter; crooner, harmonizer, hummer, warbler, yodeler; serenader; cantor, chanter, chorister; songstress; bard, troubadour

single *adj* **1** not married ⟨posted his status as *single*⟩

   synonyms unattached, unmarried, unwed

   related words fancy-free, footloose; marriageable, unpaired; divorced, separated

   near antonyms mated, paired; affianced, betrothed, committed, engaged, pledged, promised; remarried

   antonyms attached, espoused, hitched, married, wedded (*also* wed)

2 belonging only to the one person, unit, or group named ⟨Any view expressed on the newspaper's editorial pages is the *single* opinion of the writer of the column.⟩ — see SOLE 1

3 not physically attached to another unit ⟨the average price of *single* homes in the area⟩ — see SEPARATE 2

4 not being in the company of others ⟨a restaurant where the *single* diner is made to feel welcome and given the same level of service as couples or groups⟩ — see ALONE 1

single (out) *vb* **1** to decide to accept (someone or something) from a group of possibilities ⟨She quickly *singled out* the most qualified candidate from the pool of the applicants.⟩ — see CHOOSE 1

2 to find out or establish the identity of ⟨Through careful reasoning and the process of elimination, neighbors *singled* her *out* as the writer of the anonymous letter.⟩ — see IDENTIFY 1

single-handedly *adv* without aid or support ⟨The team's star slugger hit three home runs, effectively winning the game *single-handedly*.⟩ — see ALONE 1

single-minded *adj* fully committed to achieving a goal ⟨Every successful reform movement has been spearheaded by a *single-minded* activist who refused to accept defeat.⟩ — see DETERMINED 1

singly *adv* without aid or support ⟨Either *singly* or with the cooperation of other nations, we must do something about this pressing environmental issue.⟩ — see ALONE 1

singular *adj* **1** being out of the ordinary ⟨The novelist's *singular* command of the language makes her a compelling voice in contemporary fiction.⟩ — see EXCEPTIONAL 1

2 noticeably different from what is generally found or experienced ⟨Appearing on the game show has been the most *singular* experience of my life.⟩ — see UNUSUAL 1

3 of, relating to, or belonging to a single person ⟨Preserving our national heritage is not a *singular* responsibility but our collective duty.⟩ — see INDIVIDUAL 1

4 being the one or ones of a class with no other members ⟨This crime was a *singular* case, and using it as a reason for revising the criminal code would be ill-advised.⟩ — see ONLY 2

singularity *n* an odd or peculiar habit ⟨a college professor with *singularities* of dress and speech that have long endeared him to his students⟩ — see IDIOSYNCRASY

sinister *adj* being or showing a sign of evil or calamity to come ⟨The movie relies too much on *sinister* background music to create the suspense that the plot sorely lacks.⟩ — see OMINOUS

sink *vb* **1** to become worse or of less value ⟨His fortunes have steadily *sunk* since his business failed.⟩ — see DETERIORATE 1

2 to go to a lower level especially abruptly ⟨I had just bought a bundle of shares of the stock when its price *sank* like a rock.⟩ — see DROP 2

3 to cease to be visible ⟨That evening we sat on the beach, dreamily watching the sun *sink* beneath the horizon.⟩ — see DISAPPEAR

4 to diminish the price or value of ⟨The slightest nick will *sink* the price of a piece of Tiffany glass.⟩ — see DEPRECIATE 1

5 to reduce to a lower standing in one's own eyes or in others' eyes ⟨The revelation that he has been lying for years definitely *sinks* him in my opinion.⟩ — see HUMBLE

6 to lead or extend downward ⟨The road *sinks* abruptly after that curve.⟩ — see DESCEND 1

7 to lose bodily strength or vigor ⟨The old woman only *sunk* further after she was moved to the nursing home.⟩ — see WEAKEN 2

sinner *n* a person who commits moral wrongs ⟨Even the worst *sinner* can be redeemed.⟩ — see EVILDOER 1

sinuous *adj* marked by a long series of irregular curves ⟨The river flowed in a *sinuous* path through the lush valley.⟩ — see CROOKED 1

sip *vb* to swallow in liquid form ⟨slowly *sipping* the hot soup⟩ — see DRINK 1

sip *n* the portion of a serving of a beverage that is swallowed at one time ⟨There are a few *sips* left in the glass.⟩ — see DRINK 2

siphon *also* **syphon** *vb* **1** to remove (liquid) gradually or completely ⟨I let the stranded motorist *siphon* some of my gas so he could be on his way.⟩ — see DRAIN 1

2 to cause to move to a central point or along a restricted pathway ⟨Funds were *siphoned* from the school to build a new stadium.⟩ — see CHANNEL

sire *vb* to become the father of ⟨The champion racehorse went on to *sire* a long line of winners.⟩ — see FATHER

sire *n* **1** a male human parent ⟨His *sire* had been a renowned Wall Street lawyer.⟩ — see FATHER 1

2 a person who establishes a whole new field of endeavor ⟨the revered *sire* of the impressionist movement in art⟩ — see FATHER 2

siren *n* a woman whom men find irresistibly attractive ⟨In addition to being a brilliant writer, Anaïs Nin had a reputation as a *siren*.⟩

synonyms enchantress, seductress, temptress

related words beguiler, charmer, seducer, vamp

sissy *n* a person who shows a shameful lack of courage in the face of danger ⟨Don't be such a *sissy*—it's just a frog.⟩ — see COWARD

sit *vb* **1** to rest on the buttocks or haunches ⟨Everybody needs to *sit* down, or no one will be able to see the movie.⟩

synonyms set [*chiefly dialect*]

related words perch; lounge, slouch, sprawl, squat, straddle

near antonyms arise, get up, rise, stand

2 to cause to sit down ⟨The host had to *sit* some of the guests on the porch.⟩ — see SEAT 1

3 to cover and warm eggs as the young inside develop ⟨We didn't want to disturb the hens, as they were *sitting*.⟩ — see SET 1

4 to occupy a place or location ⟨the large monument that *sits* at the entrance to the battlefield⟩ — see STAND 1

site *n* the area or space occupied by or intended for something ⟨This field is the intended *site* for a new shopping mall.⟩ — see PLACE 1

sitter *n* a person employed to care for a young child or children ⟨We'll be going to the movie if we can get a *sitter* for the kids.⟩ — see NURSE

sitting duck *n* a person or thing that is the object of abuse, criticism, or ridicule ⟨Those tone-deaf comments just made him a *sitting duck* for comedians.⟩ — see TARGET 1

situate *vb* to arrange something in a certain spot or position ⟨The new industrial complex is *situated* near the highway.⟩ — see PLACE 1

situation *n* **1** position with regard to conditions and circumstances ⟨The school's *situation* is improving with additional financial help.⟩

synonyms deal, footing, picture, posture, scene, status, story

related words rank, standing; place, spot, state; score, status quo

2 an assignment at which one regularly works for pay ⟨There were the usual "*situation* wanted" postings in the local newspaper.⟩ — see JOB 1

3 the placement of someone or something in relation to others in a vertical arrangement ⟨In earlier times when there was less upward mobility, people were unable to alter their *situation* in life.⟩ — see RANK 1

sixth sense *n* the power of seeing or knowing about things that are not present to the senses ⟨a filmmaker with a *sixth sense* for knowing which stories the general public will find irresistible⟩ — see CLAIRVOYANCE

sizable *or* **sizeable** *adj* **1** of a size greater than average of its kind ⟨a *sizable* sum of money⟩ — see LARGE

2 sufficiently large in size, amount, or number to merit attention ⟨a *sizable* increase in attendance since the team began its winning streak⟩ — see CONSIDERABLE 1

sizably *adv* to a large extent or degree ⟨We need to *sizably* increase production if we want to finish this project on time.⟩ — see GREATLY 2

¹**size** *n* the total amount of measurable space or surface occupied by something ⟨We worried that the immense *size* of the sofa would make getting it through the doorway impossible.⟩

synonyms bulk, dimension, extent, magnitude, measure, measurement, proportion

related words area; capaciousness, commodiousness, roominess, spaciousness; ampleness, amplitude, bigness, bulkiness, enormousness, heftiness, hugeness, immenseness, immensity, largeness, mass, massiveness, monstrousness, stupendousness, tremendousness, vastness, volume, voluminousness

²**size** *n* a substance used to stick things together ⟨coated the fabric with *size* before applying it to the wall⟩ — see GLUE

sizzle *n* a sound similar to the speech sound \s\ stretched out ⟨There was a brief *sizzle* as the moth flew into the flame.⟩ — see HISS 1

sizzle *vb* **1** to make a sound like that of stretching out the speech sound \s\ ⟨From my bed I could hear the bacon *sizzling* in the frying pan.⟩ — see HISS

2 to be excited or emotionally stirred up with anger ⟨She was really *sizzling* about being passed over for the promotion, and nearly quit.⟩ — see BOIL 1

skeletal *adj* suffering extreme weight loss as a result of hunger or disease ⟨The stray kitten's *skeletal* body was pitiful to look at.⟩ — see EMACIATED

skeleton *n* the arrangement of parts that gives something its basic form ⟨Even though their new house was still only a *skeleton* they could picture what it would look like finished.⟩ — see FRAME 1

skeptic *n* a person who is always ready to doubt or question the truth or existence of something ⟨the demand by *skeptics* that believers in Bigfoot produce some hard evidence of that hairy humanoid⟩

synonyms disbeliever, doubter, questioner, unbeliever

related words agnostic; cynic, misanthrope, pessimist; derider, ridiculer, scoffer

near antonyms chump, dupe, gull, pigeon, sucker

skeptical *adj* **1** inclined to doubt or question claims ⟨It's good to be *skeptical* about what you see on TV.⟩

synonyms disbelieving, distrustful, doubting, incredulous, mistrustful, questioning, suspecting, suspicious, unbelieving

related words paranoid (*also* paranoidal); critical, puzzled, quizzical; careful, cautious, guarded, gun-shy, leery (*also* leary), wary, watchful; cynical, experienced, knowing, sophisticated, worldly, worldly-wise; curious, inquiring, inquisitive, nosy (*or* nosey), snoopy; uncertain, unconvinced, undecided, undetermined, unsettled, unsure; hesitant

near antonyms ingenuous, innocent, naive (*or* naïve), simple, simpleminded, unknowing, unsophisticated, unworldly, wide-eyed; certain, confident, positive, sure; deceived, duped, gulled, tricked; careless, heedless, unsuspecting, unsuspicious, unwary

antonyms credulous, gullible (*also* gullable), trustful, trusting, uncritical, unquestioning

2 not feeling sure about the truth, wisdom, or trustworthiness of someone or something ⟨I'm a little *skeptical* of this low bid, since it's way below what the other contractors said that they would charge.⟩ — see DOUBTFUL 1

skeptically *adv* with distrust ⟨The researchers' findings should be received *skeptically* until they can be replicated by other scientists.⟩ — see ASKANCE

skepticism *n* a feeling or attitude that one does not know the truth, truthfulness, or trustworthiness of someone or something ⟨Our alibi was met with *skepticism* at first, but we gradually convinced them of the truth.⟩ — see DOUBT

sketch *n* **1** a picture using lines to represent the chief features of an object or scene ⟨The artist made a quick *sketch* from which she would create a more detailed painting later.⟩ — see DRAWING

2 a vivid representation in words of someone or something ⟨Liz gave her boss quick *sketches* of the personalities of the clients he was about to meet.⟩ — see DESCRIPTION 1

sketch *vb* **1** to draw or make apparent the outline of ⟨*sketched* the garden pavilion on a pad of paper so the homeowners would have a rough idea of how it was going to look⟩ — see OUTLINE 1

2 to give a representation or account of in words ⟨briefly *sketched* the intent of the reorganization plan⟩ — see DESCRIBE 1

skewed *adj* inclined or twisted to one side ⟨He could see that the ropes had gotten all *skewed* in the collision.⟩ — see AWRY

skewer *vb* **1** to penetrate or hold (something) with a pointed object ⟨Let's *skewer* our marshmallows on these sticks and start toasting.⟩ — see IMPALE

2 to make (someone or something) the object of unkind laughter ⟨The satirical comic strip gleefully *skewers* many of society's sacred cows.⟩ — see RIDICULE

skill *n* **1** subtle or imaginative ability in inventing, devising, or executing something ⟨With unbelievable *skill*, the expert in origami transformed a few sheets of paper into a menagerie of exotic animals.⟩

synonyms adeptness, adroitness, art, artfulness, artifice, artistry, cleverness, craft, cunning, deftness, masterfulness, skillfulness

related words dexterity, ease, finesse, handiness; experience, expertise, expertness, know-how, proficiency; creativity, ingenuity, inventiveness, knowledge, learning; aptitude, bent, flair, gift, knack, talent

near antonyms awkwardness, clumsiness, klutziness; inability, inadequacy, incapability, incapacity, incompetence, ineffectiveness, ineffectuality, ineffectualness, inefficacy, inefficiency

antonyms artlessness, ineptitude, ineptness, maladroitness

2 skills *pl* knowledge gained by actually doing or living through something ⟨He had acquired valuable *skills* during his life at sea.⟩ — see EXPERIENCE 1

skilled *adj* having or showing exceptional knowledge, experience, or skill in a field of endeavor ⟨a delicate brain operation requiring the services of a highly *skilled* surgeon⟩ — see PROFICIENT

skillful *adj* **1** accomplished with trained ability ⟨The ice skater performed a *skillful* and graceful series of jumps.⟩

synonyms adroit, artful, deft, delicate, dexterous (*also* dextrous), expert, masterful, masterly, practiced (*also* practised), virtuoso, workmanlike

related words facile, smooth; artistic, creative, fancy, ingenious, neat; adept, clever, cunning; able, adequate, capable, competent

near antonyms awkward, clumsy, crude; ineffective, ineffectual; incompetent, inept

antonyms amateur, amateurish, artless, rude, unprofessional, unskillful

2 having or showing exceptional knowledge, experience, or skill in a field of endeavor ⟨performance testing of automobiles that should be done only by *skillful* drivers on a closed course⟩ — see PROFICIENT

skillfully *adv* in a skillful or expert manner ⟨*skillfully* guided the powerboat around the obstacles⟩ — see WELL 3

skillfulness *n* subtle or imaginative ability in inventing, devising, or executing something ⟨The *skillfulness* with which she handled that touchy situation is indeed admirable.⟩ — see SKILL 1

skim *vb* **1** to turn over pages in an idle or cursory manner ⟨I'll just *skim* through a few styling magazines and see if something interesting catches my eye.⟩

synonyms flip, thumb

related words browse, dip; glance (at), look over, scan

near antonyms pore (over); study

2 to move or proceed smoothly and readily ⟨a lone hang glider *skimming* along just above the treetops⟩ — see FLOW 2

3 to pass lightly across or touch gently especially in passing ⟨Her hand just barely *skimmed* the wall as she ran down the hallway.⟩ — see ²BRUSH

4 to strike and fly off at an angle ⟨The rock just *skimmed* the surface of the water.⟩ — see GLANCE 1

5 to take a quick or hasty look ⟨He impatiently *skimmed* through the book, looking for the specific passage he remembered seeing.⟩ — see GLANCE 2

skimp *vb* to avoid unnecessary waste or expense ⟨We must *skimp* and save if we are going to afford a vacation this summer.⟩ — see ECONOMIZE

skimp (on) *vb* to use or give out in stingy amounts ⟨I'd like a baked potato, and don't *skimp on* the sour cream.⟩ — see SPARE 1

skimping *n* careful management of material resources ⟨After years of *skimping* and saving, he was finally able to afford the sports car he had always wanted.⟩ — see ECONOMY

skimpy *adj* less plentiful than what is normal, necessary, or desirable ⟨The information in the user's manual for the microwave is *skimpy* and not particularly helpful.⟩ — see MEAGER

skin *n* **1** an outer part or layer ⟨space-age materials used on the *skin* of the aircraft⟩ — see EXTERIOR

2 the outer covering of an animal removed for its commercial value ⟨Hats made from beaver *skins* were once fashionable.⟩ — see HIDE 1

3 the hairless natural covering of an animal prepared for use ⟨calf*skin* gloves⟩ — see LEATHER 1

skin *vb* **1** to remove the natural covering of ⟨I prefer not to *skin* potatoes before mashing them.⟩ — see PEEL

2 to rob by the use of trickery or threats ⟨Joe got his revenge on the dirty swindler who had *skinned* him.⟩ — see FLEECE

3 to defeat by a large margin ⟨We simply got *skinned* in the interoffice softball tournament.⟩ — see WHIP 2

skin–deep *adj* **1** lying on or affecting only the outer layer of something ⟨Fortunately, the cut was only *skin-deep*.⟩ — see SUPERFICIAL 1

2 having or showing a lack of depth of understanding or character ⟨The book provides some interesting anecdotes but only offers a *skin-deep* analysis of the events it chronicles.⟩ — see SUPERFICIAL 2

skinflint *n* a mean grasping person who is usually stingy with money ⟨The team's owner is a *skinflint* whose penny-pinching ways keeps the team from acquiring any real talent.⟩ — see MISER

skinny *adj* **1** being of less than usual width ⟨The tree swing was supported only by a couple of *skinny* branches.⟩ — see NARROW 1

2 having a noticeably small amount of body fat ⟨Her grandmother was always insisting that she was too *skinny* and never tired of trying to force more food on her.⟩ — see THIN 1

skip *vb* **1** to move with a light springing step ⟨children *skipping* along the woodland path⟩
synonyms bounce, bound, hop, lope, trip
related words caper, frisk, gambol, romp; skim, skitter; jump, leap, vault
near antonyms lumber, plod, trudge

2 to fail to attend ⟨It was a tradition for the seniors to *skip* class on their last day and go to the beach.⟩ — see CUT 2

3 to strike and fly off at an angle ⟨The soap slipped out of my hand and went *skipping* across the bathroom floor.⟩ — see GLANCE 1

skipper *n* a person in overall command of a ship ⟨We asked the *skipper* how long it would be before we reached port.⟩ — see CAPTAIN 1

skirmish *n* **1** a brief clash between enemies or rivals ⟨The candidates' first debate was only a *skirmish* in a very long campaign.⟩ — see ENCOUNTER

2 a physical dispute between opposing individuals or groups ⟨rebel groups *skirmishing* in the outskirts⟩ — see FIGHT 1

skirmish (with) *vb* to oppose (someone) in physical conflict ⟨For years the Apache leader had been *skirmishing with* the Mexicans, who were responsible for his nickname, Geronimo.⟩ — see FIGHT 1

skirt *n* the line or relatively narrow space that marks the outer limit of something ⟨an old shack on the *skirts* of the town⟩ — see BORDER 1

skirt *vb* **1** to avoid by going around ⟨*skirted* the construction zone⟩ — see DETOUR 1

2 to avoid having to comply with (something) especially through cleverness ⟨The new bill would make it harder for companies to *skirt* environmental regulations.⟩ — see CIRCUMVENT 1

3 to be adjacent to ⟨The commercial district *skirts* the river's edge.⟩ — see ADJOIN 1

4 to serve as a border for ⟨the wooden fence that *skirts* the construction site⟩ — see BORDER

skirting *adj* having a border in common ⟨The house hunters loved the property, but they were a bit leery of the *skirting* swamp.⟩ — see ADJACENT

skirting *n* the line or relatively narrow space that marks the outer limit of something ⟨The *skirting* on the saddle was a slightly darker shade of leather.⟩ — see BORDER 1

skittish *adj* **1** easily excited by nature ⟨The *skittish* colt leapt up when we approached.⟩ — see EXCITABLE

2 easily frightened ⟨The cat is *skittish* around people she doesn't know.⟩ — see SHY 1

3 likely to change frequently, suddenly, or unexpectedly ⟨A *skittish* housing market had both buyers and sellers on edge.⟩ — see FICKLE 1

skittishness *n* a state of nervousness marked by sudden jerky movements ⟨Because of the horse's *skittishness* and

temperamental nature, only experienced riders should ride him.⟩ — see JUMPINESS

skulduggery *or* **skullduggery** *n* the use of clever underhanded actions to achieve an end ⟨The company's apparently healthy bottom line was merely an illusion, the result of years of accounting *skulduggery*.⟩ — see TRICKERY

skulk *vb* **1** to move about in a sly or secret manner ⟨I thought I saw someone *skulking* about in the shadows⟩ — see SNEAK 1

2 to remain out of sight ⟨The officers caught the hapless robber *skulking* behind some trash cans.⟩ — see ¹HIDE 3

skulk *n* someone who acts in a sly and secret manner ⟨What is that *skulk* up to now?⟩ — see SNEAK

skulker *n* someone who acts in a sly and secret manner ⟨We kept guard to keep any *skulkers* from passing through the city gate.⟩ — see SNEAK

skull *n* the case of bone that encloses the brain and supports the jaws of vertebrates ⟨Paleoanthropologists recently found the *skull* of a prehistoric man in a remote area of the desert.⟩
synonyms cranium
related words braincase; death's-head; head, noddle, noggin, pate, poll; crown, scalp

skunk *n* a person whose behavior is offensive to others ⟨He's nothing but a dirty, rotten *skunk*!⟩ — see JERK 1

skunk *vb* **1** to defeat by a large margin ⟨We ended up *skunking* them, as our goalie was able to prevent the other team from scoring a single goal.⟩ — see WHIP 2

2 to achieve a victory over ⟨Our football team consistently *skunks* our traditional rivals Thanksgiving after Thanksgiving.⟩ — see BEAT 2

sky *n* **1** the expanse of air surrounding the earth ⟨The *sky* usually looks deep blue on a bright clear day.⟩
synonyms blue, firmament, heaven(s), high
related words midair; horizon, skyline

2 a dwelling place of perfect happiness for the soul after death ⟨a belief that warriors felled in battle will be raised to the *sky*⟩ — see HEAVEN 1

sky–high *adv* in an enthusiastic manner ⟨Some reviewers had praised the movie *sky-high*, but we thought that it was just a so-so comedy.⟩
synonyms enthusiastically, exuberantly, madly, rhapsodically
related words avidly, eagerly, excitedly, impatiently, keenly; fanatically, rabidly, warmly, zealously
near antonyms aloofly, disinterestedly, impassively, incuriously; hesitantly, reluctantly, unwillingly
antonyms apathetically, indifferently, lukewarmly, perfunctorily

skylark *vb* **1** to engage in attention-getting playful or boisterous behavior ⟨Some of the graduates couldn't resist the temptation to *skylark* as commencement ceremonies came to a close.⟩ — see CUT UP

2 to engage in activity for amusement ⟨He spends his time joking and *skylarking*, but his brother is serious and industrious.⟩ — see PLAY 1

skylarking *n* wildly playful or mischievous behavior ⟨The players often engaged in a bit of roughhousing and *skylarking* before big games.⟩ — see HORSEPLAY

skyrocket *vb* to rise abruptly and rapidly ⟨The crisis has caused oil prices to *skyrocket*.⟩
synonyms rocket, shoot (up), soar, zoom
related words accumulate, appreciate, balloon, burgeon (*also* bourgeon), enlarge, escalate, expand, increase, mount, multiply, mushroom, proliferate, snowball, swell, wax; crest, peak, surge; heighten, intensify
near antonyms collapse, fall; contract, decrease, diminish, drop, lessen, wane
antonyms nose-dive, plummet, plunge, slump, tumble

slack *adj* **1** failing to give proper care and attention ⟨a building contractor known mainly for his firm's *slack* workmanship and slipshod construction⟩ — see NEGLIGENT

2 not bound by rigid standards ⟨*slack* supervision on the project⟩ — see EASYGOING 2

3 not tightly fastened, tied, or stretched ⟨left the ropes *slack*⟩ — see LOOSE 1

slack *n* **1** an allowable margin of freedom or variation ⟨Our boss doesn't cut us any *slack* when it comes to being back from lunch on time.⟩

synonyms latitude, space

related words license (*or* licence), rein, swing

2 the extent to which something hangs or dips below a straight line ⟨take up the *slack* of a rope⟩ — see SAG

3 slacks *pl* an outer garment covering each leg separately from waist to ankle ⟨dressed in a polo shirt and *slacks*⟩ — see PANTS

slack *vb* to make less taut ⟨The skipper ordered the crew to *slack* off the sheets on the mainsail.⟩ — see SLACKEN 1

slacken *vb* **1** to make less taut ⟨You'll need to *slacken* the rope a bit to get it free of that post.⟩

synonyms ease, loosen, relax, slack

related words detach, free, unbind, undo, unfasten, untie

near antonyms attach, bind, fasten, tie; constrain, restrain

antonyms strain, stretch, tense, tension

2 to cause to move or proceed at a less rapid pace ⟨Drivers need to *slacken* their speed as they approach the sharp curve.⟩ — see SLOW

slackened *adj* not tightly fastened, tied, or stretched ⟨*slackened* lines⟩ — see LOOSE 1

slacker *n* one who deliberately avoids work or duty ⟨There will be no *slackers* tolerated in this group—anyone who doesn't do their share will get booted out.⟩

synonyms shirker

related words malingerer; dropout, quitter, drone, idler, lazybones, loafer, slouch, slug, sluggard; dallier, lingerer, loiterer, lounger, saunterer; dawdler, laggard, putterer, slowpoke; bum, derelict, ne'er-do-well, no-good

near antonyms live wire, powerhouse; doer, go-getter, hustler, rustler, self-starter

slackness *n* **1** failure to take the care that a cautious person usually takes ⟨Considering the company's *slackness* when it comes to safety, it's a wonder there hasn't been an accident.⟩ — see NEGLIGENCE 1

2 the extent to which something hangs or dips below a straight line ⟨There's simply too much *slackness* in this clothesline.⟩ — see SAG

slam *n* **1** a hard strike with a part of the body or an instrument ⟨I gave the stubborn nail one last *slam* with the hammer.⟩ — see ¹BLOW

2 a loud explosive sound ⟨shut the door with a loud *slam*⟩ — see CLAP 1

3 a forceful coming together of two things ⟨the sudden *slam* of my head against the low hanging branch⟩ — see IMPACT 1

slam *vb* **1** to shove into a closed position with force and noise ⟨Please don't *slam* the door every time you step out.⟩

synonyms bang

related words close, shut, stop; bar, batten (down), bolt, chain, fasten, latch, lock, seal, secure

near antonyms open; unbar, unbolt, unfasten, unlatch, unlock, unseal

2 to deliver a blow to (someone or something) usually in a strong vigorous manner ⟨She *slammed* the ball deep into center field.⟩ — see HIT 1

3 to come into usually forceful contact with something ⟨The car *slammed* into the wall with a fearful crunch.⟩ — see HIT 2

4 to criticize harshly and usually publicly ⟨*slammed* the

cast members for forgetting their lines on opening night⟩ — see ATTACK 2

slander *n* the making of false statements that damage another's reputation ⟨Instead of resorting to *slander*, the candidates should be outlining their plans for the future.⟩

synonyms aspersing, blackening, defamation, defaming, libel, libeling (*or* libelling), maligning, smearing, traducing, vilification, vilifying

related words aspersion, smear; backbiting, detraction; abuse, invective, vituperation; attack, censure, criticism, denunciation; contempt, disdain, scorn; belittlement, disparagement; hatefulness, malevolence, malice, maliciousness, malignancy, malignity, meanness, nastiness, spite, spitefulness, spleen, venom, viciousness

near antonyms acclaim, accolade, applause, commendation, praise; esteem, honor, respect; adulation, flattery; adoration, reverence, veneration, worship

slander *vb* to make untrue and harmful statements about ⟨For some reason, that newspaper seems determined to *slander* one particular celebrity.⟩

synonyms asperse, blacken, defame, libel, malign, smear, traduce, vilify

related words belittle, disparage; discredit, disgrace, dishonor, shame; abase, debase, degrade, humble, humiliate; disdain, scorn

near antonyms exalt, glorify, honor; acclaim, applaud, commend, praise; esteem, respect; admire, regard; adore, revere, venerate, worship

slanderous *adj* causing or intended to cause unjust injury to a person's good name ⟨made *slanderous* comments about his opponent's military record⟩ — see LIBELOUS

slang *n* the special terms or expressions of a particular group or field ⟨Paul tends to use too much hacker's *slang* when talking to coworkers about their computer problems.⟩ — see TERMINOLOGY

slant *adj* running in a slanting direction ⟨As they poked through the blinds, the *slant* rays of the setting sun created interesting patterns on the room's far wall.⟩ — see DIAGONAL

slant *n* **1** the degree to which something rises up from a position level with the horizon ⟨The road has just enough of a *slant* to make bicycling up it a little strenuous.⟩

synonyms cant, diagonal, grade, gradient, inclination, incline, lean, pitch, rake, slope, upgrade

related words ascent, bank, climb, rise

near antonyms declension, decline, descent, dip, downgrade, fall, hang, hanging, receding

2 a way of looking at or thinking about something ⟨an interesting *slant* on the events of the era⟩ — see PERSPECTIVE 1

slant *vb* **1** to change so much as to create a wrong impression or alter the meaning of ⟨reporters who *slant* the truth in order to push a political agenda⟩ — see GARBLE

2 to set or cause to be at an angle ⟨a ramp *slanted* at a 20 degree angle⟩ — see LEAN 1

slanted *adj* **1** inclined or twisted to one side ⟨a *slanted* fence post⟩ — see AWRY

2 running in a slanting direction ⟨*slanted* stripes⟩ — see DIAGONAL

slanting *adj* inclined or twisted to one side ⟨an old, torn flag hanging from a *slanting* flagpole⟩ — see AWRY

slantways *adv* so as to slant ⟨The temporary supports were placed *slantways* against the side of the sagging wall.⟩ — see SLANTWISE

slantwise *adj* **1** inclined or twisted to one side ⟨a hodgepodge of *slantwise* postcards tacked to the wall of his cubicle⟩ — see AWRY

2 running in a slanting direction ⟨The *slantwise* cables that run between the roadway and the towers give the bridge a cathedral-like appearance.⟩ — see DIAGONAL

slantwise *adv* so as to slant ⟨Be careful not to lay the first boards *slantwise*, or the whole bookcase will be crooked.⟩
synonyms slantways
related words down, downward (*or* downwards), up, upward (*or* upwards)

slap *n* 1 a hard strike with a part of the body or an instrument ⟨Doctors used to give newborns a light *slap* to get them to start breathing.⟩ — see ¹BLOW
2 an act or expression showing scorn and usually intended to hurt another's feelings ⟨That comment is a *slap* to anyone who has ever served in the military.⟩ — see INSULT

slap *vb* 1 to deliver a blow to (someone or something) usually in a strong vigorous manner ⟨She called the dog by *slapping* her thigh with her hand and whistling.⟩ — see HIT 1
2 to cause hurt feelings or deep resentment in ⟨tired of jokes that *slap* people of faith⟩ — see INSULT

slapdash *adj* lacking a definite plan, purpose, or pattern ⟨The investigation of the charges against the mayor was *slapdash* and not very thorough.⟩ — see RANDOM

slapjack *n* a flat cake made from thin batter and cooked on both sides (as on a griddle) ⟨had a big plate of *slapjacks* with syrup for breakfast⟩ — see PANCAKE

slapstick *n* humorous entertainment ⟨an actor whose roles range from *slapstick* to serious drama⟩ — see COMEDY 1

slash *n* a long deep cut ⟨made a *slash* in the fabric with a knife⟩ — see GASH

slash *vb* 1 to penetrate with a sharp edge (as a knife) ⟨The tire appears to have been deliberately *slashed*.⟩ — see CUT 1
2 to strike repeatedly with something long and thin or flexible ⟨wildly *slashing* the ground with his club and never once hitting the golf ball he was aiming at⟩ — see WHIP 1

slate *adj* of the color gray ⟨The *slate* sky was a sure sign of rain.⟩ — see GRAY 1

¹**slate** *vb* to put (someone or something) on a list ⟨You've been *slated* for a three o'clock interview.⟩ — see ¹LIST 2

²**slate** *vb* to strike repeatedly ⟨ready to *slate* anyone who disagreed⟩ — see BEAT 1

slated *adj* being in accordance with the prescribed, normal, or logical course of events ⟨*slated* to arrive at five o'clock⟩ — see DUE 2

slaty *also* **slatey** *adj* of the color gray ⟨*slaty* stones in the riverbed⟩ — see GRAY 1

slaughter *n* the killing of a large number of people ⟨the *slaughter* of the Meuse-Argonne Offensive during World War I⟩ — see MASSACRE

slaughter *vb* to kill on a large scale ⟨Modern poultry farms *slaughter* a vast number of chickens every day.⟩ — see MASSACRE

slaver *vb* to let saliva or some other substance flow from the mouth ⟨a dog *slavering* over a bone⟩ — see DROOL 1

slaver *n* the fluid that is secreted into the mouth by certain glands ⟨*Slaver* dripped from the snarling dog's jaws.⟩ — see SALIVA

slavery *n* the state of being enslaved ⟨discovered the stories of ancestors who had endured *slavery*⟩
synonyms bondage, enslavement, servility, servitude, thrall, thralldom (*or* thraldom), yoke
related words peonage, serfdom; dependence (*also* dependance), subjection, subjugation; captivity, enchainment, imprisonment, incarceration
near antonyms emancipation, enfranchisement, liberation, manumission; autonomy, independence, self-government, sovereignty (*also* sovranty)
antonyms freedom, liberty

slay *vb* 1 to deprive of life ⟨Millions have been *slain* worldwide by this dreadful disease.⟩ — see KILL 1
2 to put to death deliberately ⟨The knight *slew* the dragon.⟩ — see MURDER 1

slaying *n* the taking of another person's life ⟨Police have arrested a suspect in connection with the *slaying* that happened last week.⟩ — see HOMICIDE 1

sleazy *adj* 1 of low quality ⟨a *sleazy* yellow coat that was marked down to practically nothing and not worth even that⟩ — see CHEAP 2
2 being of a material lacking in sturdiness or substance ⟨These cheap, *sleazy* curtains would do a poor job of blocking those wintertime blasts of cold air.⟩ — see FLIMSY 1

sleek *adj* having a shiny surface or finish ⟨a horse's *sleek* black coat⟩ — see GLOSSY

sleep *n* 1 a natural periodic loss of consciousness during which the body restores itself ⟨Neither of them has been getting much *sleep* since the baby was born.⟩
synonyms bed, catnapping, dozing, napping, repose, rest, resting, slumber, slumbering, snoozing
related words catnap, doze, drowse, forty winks, nap, siesta, snooze, wink; oversleeping; dreaming, rapid eye movement
2 the state of being dead ⟨The troubador sang a mournful song about joining his beloved in eternal *sleep*.⟩ — see DEATH 2
3 the permanent stopping of all the vital bodily activities ⟨regretfully put their terminally ill dog to *sleep*⟩ — see DEATH 1

sleep *vb* 1 to be in a state of sleep ⟨The baby *slept* for the entire length of the car trip.⟩
synonyms catnap, doze, nap, rest, slumber, snooze
related words drop off, drowse (off), nod off; oversleep, sleep in; dream, hibernate
near antonyms arise, arouse, awake, rise, wake
2 to engage in sexual intercourse ⟨weren't *sleeping* together⟩ — see COPULATE

sleeper *n* one who sleeps ⟨She's a light *sleeper* and usually wakes up when I get in late.⟩
synonyms dozer, slumberer
related words nodder
near antonyms riser, waker

sleepiness *n* the quality or state of desiring or needing sleep ⟨The truck driver keeps a thermos of coffee with him to stave off *sleepiness*.⟩
synonyms drowsiness, somnolence
related words fatigue, tiredness, weariness; lassitude, sluggishness, torpidity; dozing, resting, sleeping, slumbering; oversleeping
near antonyms awareness

sleeping *adj* being in a state of suspended consciousness ⟨a roomful of *sleeping* preschoolers at a daycare center⟩ — see ASLEEP 1

sleepless *adj* not sleeping or able to sleep ⟨lay *sleepless* with worry⟩ — see WAKEFUL

sleepy *adj* 1 desiring or needing sleep ⟨The *sleepy* children were carried up to bed.⟩
synonyms drowsy, slumberous (*or* slumbrous), somnolent
related words asleep, dormant, dozing, resting, sleeping, slumbering; nodding, yawning
near antonyms restive, restless, sleepless
antonyms alert, awake, conscious, wakeful, wide-awake
2 slow to move or act ⟨a *sleepy* little town on the coast⟩ — see INACTIVE 1

sleight *n* 1 a clever often underhanded means to achieve an end ⟨He must have employed some sophisticated *sleight* to con that wary couple out of their money.⟩ — see TRICK 1
2 mental skill or quickness ⟨a brilliant new theory that pays tribute to his remarkable *sleight* of mind⟩ — see DEXTERITY 1

3 ease and grace in physical activity ⟨a muscle-bound weight lifter known more for his might than his *sleight*⟩ — see DEXTERITY 2

slender *adj* **1** being of less than usual width ⟨graceful, *slender* table legs⟩ — see NARROW 1

2 having a noticeably small amount of body fat ⟨The aerobics instructor is *slender* and athletic.⟩ — see THIN 1

3 less plentiful than what is normal, necessary, or desirable ⟨People of *slender* means simply can't afford those prices.⟩ — see MEAGER

sleuth *n* a person not on the police force who investigates criminal or illicit activity or searches for missing persons ⟨The popular TV *sleuth* lives a much more action-packed life than do his real-world counterparts.⟩ — see DETECTIVE

slice *vb* **1** to cut into long slender pieces ⟨*Slice* the carrot into tiny strips.⟩ — see SLIVER

2 to penetrate with a sharp edge (as a knife) ⟨The shard of glass *sliced* my hand, and I started bleeding profusely.⟩ — see CUT 1

slice *n* **1** a number of things selected from a group to stand for the whole ⟨The novel's multitudinous array of characters constitute a veritable *slice* of humanity.⟩ — see SAMPLE 1

2 a piece that has been separated from the whole by cutting ⟨Joe took a *slice* from the cake before passing it down the table.⟩ — see CUT 1

3 something belonging to, due to, or contributed by an individual member of a group ⟨There's a pile of money to be made on this land deal, and everybody's trying to get their *slice*.⟩ — see SHARE 1

slick *vb* to coat (something) with a slippery substance in order to reduce friction ⟨*slicking* the bottom of their skis with wax⟩ — see LUBRICATE

slick *adj* **1** having or being a surface so smooth as to greatly reduce traction ⟨Roads are often *slick* during the first hour of a rainstorm.⟩

synonyms greased, greasy, lubricated, oiled, slicked, slippery, slithery

related words brushed, buffed, burnished, glossed, ground, polished, rubbed, shined; coated, glazed, waxed; soapy; rasped, sandblasted, sanded, sandpapered, scoured, scraped, scrubbed

near antonyms coarsened, rough, roughened, scuffed, uneven

2 clever at attaining one's ends by indirect and often deceptive means ⟨a *slick* ad campaign that made the little car look cool⟩ — see ARTFUL 1

slicked *adj* having or being a surface so smooth as to greatly reduce traction ⟨Area roadways, *slicked* with ice, were absolutely treacherous for driving.⟩ — see SLICK 1

slicker *n* **1** a coat made of water-resistant material ⟨He put on his *slicker* and boots and headed out into the rain.⟩ — see RAINCOAT

2 a person with the outlook, experience, and manners thought to be typical of big city dwellers ⟨Dressed in their designer duds, the out-of-state *slickers* stood out amongst the locals at the harvest supper.⟩ — see COSMOPOLITAN

slickness *n* skill in achieving one's ends through indirect, subtle, or underhanded means ⟨We were both impressed and outraged by the expert *slickness* with which the swindler fooled us.⟩ — see CUNNING 1

slide *vb* **1** to move or proceed in a sly or secret manner ⟨Ted *slid* gently into his seat without anyone else in the meeting noticing.⟩ — see SNEAK 1

2 to move or proceed smoothly and readily ⟨At this point the river *slides* along its banks with barely a ripple.⟩ — see FLOW 2

3 to move slowly with the body close to the ground ⟨The convict escaped by *sliding* through the prison's ductwork.⟩ — see CRAWL 1

slight *adj* **1** lacking bodily strength ⟨a small child with a *slight* build⟩ — see WEAK 1

2 lacking importance ⟨a *slight* comedy that did nothing to further her career⟩ — see UNIMPORTANT

3 of a size that is less than average ⟨The *slight* youth packed a surprisingly solid punch.⟩ — see SMALL 1

4 so small or unimportant as to warrant little or no attention ⟨Apart from a *slight* fishy taste, the dish was fine.⟩ — see NEGLIGIBLE 1

5 small in degree ⟨only a *slight* chance of success⟩ — see REMOTE 1

slight *n* an act or expression showing scorn and usually intended to hurt another's feelings ⟨I refused to respond to their petty *slights*.⟩ — see INSULT

slight *vb* **1** to cause hurt feelings or deep resentment in ⟨The dancers felt *slighted* by the harsh comments of the judges.⟩ — see INSULT

2 to deliberately ignore or treat rudely ⟨As a temp worker, she often feels *slighted* by the people she has to work with.⟩ — see SNUB 1

3 to show contempt for ⟨music critics who *slight* any style of music that doesn't fit their personal taste⟩ — see SCORN 1

4 to fail to give proper attention to ⟨*slighted* several major authors in her survey of 20th-century fiction⟩ — see NEGLECT 1

slightest *adj* being the least in amount, number, or size possible ⟨There's not the *slightest* chance that your plan will work.⟩ — see MINIMAL

slighting *adj* intended to make a person or thing seem of little importance or value ⟨*slighting* remarks about the general lack of musical talent among the contestants⟩ — see DEROGATORY

slightly *adv* **1** by a very small margin ⟨I thought the first one was *slightly* better.⟩ — see JUST 2

2 in a very small quantity or degree ⟨He was *slightly* curious about the visitors, but not enough to bother asking.⟩ — see LITTLE 1

slightness *n* **1** the quality or state of being little in size ⟨The old photograph shows a man whose *slightness* of build seems at variance with his reputation as a robust outdoorsman.⟩ — see SMALLNESS

2 the state or quality of having little weight ⟨His *slightness* will serve him well if he ever decides to become a jockey.⟩ — see ¹LIGHTNESS 1

slim *adj* **1** being of less than usual width ⟨a *slim* volume of poetry⟩ — see NARROW 1

2 having a noticeably small amount of body fat ⟨the pressure on ballet dancers to remain gracefully *slim*⟩ — see THIN 1

3 less plentiful than what is normal, necessary, or desirable ⟨*slim* pickings at the garage sale⟩ — see MEAGER

4 small in degree ⟨A *slim* chance is still better than none.⟩ — see REMOTE 1

slime *n* soft wet earth ⟨She picked her steps carefully so as not to get any *slime* on her new shoes.⟩ — see MUD

slimy *adj* full of or covered with soft wet earth ⟨Please remove your *slimy* boots before coming into the house.⟩ — see MUDDY 1

¹sling *vb* **1** to place on an elevated point without support from below ⟨Let's *sling* a hammock between the trees.⟩ — see HANG 1

²sling *vb* to send through the air especially with a quick forward motion of the arm ⟨*slinging* stones at the fence post⟩ — see THROW 1

slink *vb* to move about in a sly or secret manner ⟨like a thief *slinking* about in the middle of the night⟩ — see SNEAK 1

¹**slip** *n* a long narrow piece of material ⟨baskets woven from *slips* of wicker⟩ — see STRIP 1

²**slip** *n* 1 an unintentional departure from truth or accuracy ⟨a careless *slip* of the tongue⟩ — see ERROR 1
2 the act of going down from an upright position suddenly and involuntarily ⟨The girl had a nasty *slip* on the ice.⟩ — see FALL 1
3 the act or an instance of getting free from danger or confinement ⟨gave their pursuers the *slip*⟩ — see ESCAPE 1
4 a wrong judgment ⟨That's not the sort of *slip* that a prudent person would have made.⟩ — see MISTAKE 1

slip *vb* 1 to decline gradually from a standard level ⟨The store's quality of service began to *slip* after the new owners took over.⟩
synonyms sag
related words drop, fall, slump; flag, sink, slacken, slow (down), weaken; abate, contract, decrease, de-escalate, die (down), diminish, dwindle, ebb, lessen, let up, lower, moderate, recede, relent, shrink, subside, taper, taper off, wane
near antonyms rocket, shoot (up), soar; balloon, burgeon (*also* bourgeon), enlarge, escalate, expand, increase, mount, multiply, mushroom, proliferate, snowball, swell, wax; crest, peak, surge
2 to go down from an upright position suddenly and involuntarily ⟨Be careful not to *slip* on the spilled oil.⟩ — see FALL 1
3 to introduce in a gradual, secret, or clever way ⟨casually *slipped* it into the conversation⟩ — see INSINUATE 1
4 to move about in a sly or secret manner ⟨*slipped* behind the cover of the trees⟩ — see SNEAK 1
5 to move or proceed smoothly and readily ⟨jumped into the car and *slipped* behind the wheel⟩ — see FLOW 2
6 to cast (a natural bodily covering or appendage) aside ⟨Periodically crabs *slip* their shells and grow new ones.⟩ — see SHED 1

slip (on *or* **into)** *vb* to place on one's person ⟨Wait here while I *slip into* something more comfortable.⟩ — see PUT ON 1

slippery *adj* 1 given to acting in secret and to concealing one's intentions ⟨a place where a lot of *slippery* characters were known to hang out⟩ — see SNEAKY 1
2 having or being a surface so smooth as to greatly reduce traction ⟨I had trouble keeping upright on the *slippery* ice.⟩ — see SLICK 1

slipup *n* 1 an unintentional departure from truth or accuracy ⟨The marketing director made sure there were no *slipups* for the important presentation.⟩ — see ERROR 1
2 a wrong judgment ⟨He ran a flawless campaign—not a single *slipup*.⟩ — see MISTAKE 1

slit *n* a long deep cut ⟨made a *slit* in the fabric about nine inches long⟩ — see GASH

slit *vb* to penetrate with a sharp edge (as a knife) ⟨I *slit* my finger open while cleaning up the broken glass.⟩ — see CUT 1

slither *vb* to move slowly with the body close to the ground ⟨a snake *slithering* through the garden⟩ — see CRAWL 1

slithery *adj* having or being a surface so smooth as to greatly reduce traction ⟨Low tide exposes a stretch of beach strewn with seaweed and *slithery* rocks.⟩ — see SLICK 1

sliver *n* a small flat piece separated from a whole ⟨I got a *sliver* of wood stuck in my finger.⟩ — see CHIP 1

sliver *vb* to cut into long slender pieces ⟨carefully *slivered* the rattan stems into strips for basketry⟩
synonyms slice, splinter
related words chip, chop, dice, hash, julienne, mince, saw, scissor; cleave, rive, split; gash, incise, rip, slash, slit

slob *n* 1 a dirty or sloppy person ⟨a *slob* of a professor whose office was littered with a decade's worth of notes and student papers⟩
synonyms sloven
antonyms neatnik
2 a person whose behavior is offensive to others ⟨a loud-mouthed *slob*⟩ — see JERK 1

slobber *n* the fluid that is secreted into the mouth by certain glands ⟨The dog got *slobber* all over our tennis ball.⟩ — see SALIVA

slobber *vb* 1 to let saliva or some other substance flow from the mouth ⟨Our dog always starts to *slobber* whenever we open a can of food.⟩ — see DROOL 1
2 to make an exaggerated display of affection or enthusiasm ⟨Right on cue, his entourage of sycophants began to *slobber* over every inane thing he said.⟩ — see GUSH 2

slobby *adj* lacking neatness in dress or person ⟨a classic movie about a *slobby* sportswriter and his neat-freak roommate⟩ — see SLOPPY 1

slog *vb* 1 to deliver a blow to (someone or something) usually in a strong vigorous manner ⟨The two boxers were so exhausted they just *slogged* each other indiscriminately.⟩ — see HIT 1
2 to devote serious and sustained effort ⟨*slogging* their way through a pile of paperwork⟩ — see LABOR
3 to strike repeatedly ⟨*slogging* at ants coming out of the picnic basket⟩ — see BEAT 1
4 to move heavily or clumsily ⟨Gramps never tired of telling how he had to *slog* through the snow in order to get to school.⟩ — see LUMBER 1

slogan *n* an attention-getting word or phrase used to publicize something (as a campaign or product) ⟨Within days, virtually everyone was familiar with the newest advertising *slogan* for that brand of soda.⟩
synonyms banner, cry, shibboleth, watchword
related words expression, idiom; catchword, cliché (*also* cliche); maxim, motto; battle cry, war cry

slogger *n* a person who does very hard or dull work ⟨nothing but respect for the *sloggers* who work in the basement archives⟩ — see DRUDGE

slop *n* 1 soft wet earth ⟨slipped and fell in the *slop* behind the shed⟩ — see MUD
2 slops *pl* solid matter discharged from an animal's alimentary canal ⟨cleaned the *slops* out of the cow barn⟩ — see DROPPING 1

slop *vb* to cause (something liquid or mushy) to move along in sheets ⟨She *slopped* water everywhere when she picked up the full pan.⟩ — see SPLASH 1

slope *n* the degree to which something rises up from a position level with the horizon ⟨The next stretch of the trail had a gentle *slope* which made it easier to climb.⟩ — see SLANT 1

slope *vb* to set or cause to be at an angle ⟨They *sloped* our new driveway too steeply and now my car scrapes bottom whenever I back out onto the street.⟩ — see LEAN 1

sloped *adj* running in a slanting direction ⟨The *sloped* arrangement of the pictures along the staircase wall should follow the line of the banister.⟩ — see DIAGONAL

sloping *adj* running in a slanting direction ⟨A *sloping* ray of light that illuminates the painting's central figure is symbolic of heavenly inspiration.⟩ — see DIAGONAL

sloppily *adv* in a careless or unfashionable manner ⟨a *sloppily* arranged desk⟩
synonyms dowdily, slovenly
related words slatternly; messily, untidily; shabbily, sleazily; dingily, dirtily, filthily, foully
near antonyms neatly, orderly, tidily; fashionably, modishly; carefully, fastidiously, fussily, meticulously; spotlessly
antonyms nattily, sharply, smart, smartly, sprucely

sloppiness *n* the state or quality of having an excess of tender feelings (as of love, nostalgia, or compassion) ⟨the tearful *sloppiness* that you find in so many country-and-western songs⟩ — see SENTIMENTALITY

sloppy *adj* 1 lacking neatness in dress or person ⟨a *sloppy* child who always seems to have spilled something on his clothes⟩

synonyms dowdy, frowsy (*or* frowzy), slobby, slovenly, unkempt, untidy

related words slatternly; chaotic, cluttered, confused, disarranged, disheveled (*or* dishevelled), disordered, messed, messy, muddled, mussed, mussy, rumpled, shaggy, uncombed, wrinkled; shabby, sleazy; besmirched, blackened, dingy, dirty, filthy, foul, grimy, grubby, grungy, mucky, nasty, soiled, spotted, squalid, stained, sullied, unclean, uncleanly

near antonyms chic, fashionable, modish, stylish; combed, groomed; neat, ordered, orderly, tidy; careful, fastidious, fussy, meticulous; clean, cleaned, immaculate, spotless, stainless, unsoiled, unsullied

antonyms dapper, dashing, dolled up, sharp, smart, spruce

2 lacking in order, neatness, and often cleanliness ⟨She dumped the papers in a *sloppy* pile on the desk.⟩ — see MESSY

3 appealing to the emotions in an obvious and tiresome way ⟨a cinematic romance with a *sloppy* musical score that will have audiences reaching for their handkerchiefs⟩ — see CORNY

slosh *vb* 1 to move with a splashing motion ⟨The baby gurgled contentedly as the water *sloshed* gently around him in the bathtub.⟩

synonyms lap, plash, splash, swash

related words babble, bubble, gurgle, ripple

2 to cause (something liquid or mushy) to move along in sheets ⟨While painting the chair, he carelessly *sloshed* paint all over the adjacent wall.⟩ — see SPLASH 1

sloth *n* an inclination not to do work or engage in activities ⟨a youth inclined more toward *sloth* than athletics⟩ — see LAZINESS

slothful *adj* not easily aroused to action or work ⟨His overly lax managerial style has resulted in a department that is *slothful* and unproductive.⟩ — see LAZY 1

slouch *n* a lazy person ⟨Dan is no *slouch* when it comes to cooking.⟩ — see LAZYBONES

slouch *vb* to move slowly ⟨*slouched* towards the school⟩ — see CRAWL 2

slough *also* **slew** *or* **slue** *n* spongy land saturated or partially covered with water ⟨The land for miles around the lake is strewn with ponds, *sloughs*, and mudflats.⟩ — see SWAMP

¹**slough** *vb* to move heavily or clumsily ⟨the unpleasant task of *sloughing* through the muck to retrieve the ball⟩ — see LUMBER 1

²**slough** *also* **sluff** *vb* to cast (a natural bodily covering or appendage) aside ⟨The snake is *sloughing* its old skin.⟩ — see SHED 1

sloven *n* a dirty or sloppy person ⟨I'm not a complete *sloven*, but I could try to be neater.⟩ — see SLOB 1

slovenly *adj* lacking neatness in dress or person ⟨For the sake of their image, the band members began dressing in a more *slovenly* manner.⟩ — see SLOPPY 1

slovenly *adv* in a careless or unfashionable manner ⟨an employee who went overboard on dress-down day and came in dressed *slovenly* for work⟩ — see SLOPPILY

slow *adj* 1 moving or proceeding at less than the normal, desirable, or required speed ⟨Because of the holiday, traffic to the beach was particularly *slow*.⟩ ⟨*slow* readers⟩

synonyms crawling, creeping, dallying, dawdling, dilatory, dillydallying, dragging, laggard, lagging, languid, leisurely, poking, poky (*or* pokey), sluggish, tardy, unhurried

related words deliberate, measured; inactive, inert, lethargic; lingering, loitering, tarrying; ambling, heavy-footed, inching, plodding, shuffling, slow-footed; strolling; decelerating, slowing; procrastinating, stalling

near antonyms expeditious, prompt, ready; accelerated, hastened, quickened; hurried, rushed

antonyms barreling, bolting, breakneck, breathless, brisk, careering, dizzy, fast, fleet, flying, hasty, hurrying, lightning, meteoric, quick, racing, rapid, rocketing, running, rushing, speeding, speedy, swift, warp-speed, whirling, whirlwind, whisking, zipping

2 not having or showing an ability to absorb ideas readily ⟨We love our bulldog, though he's a little *slower* than our German Shepherd.⟩ — see STUPID 1

3 lacking in gaiety, movement, or animation ⟨a *slow* day on Wall Street⟩ — see DEAD 2

4 causing weariness, restlessness, or lack of interest ⟨The first half of the movie is *slow*, but then it gets exciting.⟩ — see BORING

slow *adv* at a pace that is less than usual, desirable, or expected ⟨You need to go *slow* with this experiment, or you'll make mistakes.⟩

synonyms laggardly, leisurely, slowly, sluggishly, tardily

related words carefully, cautiously, deliberately, purposefully; heavily, ploddingly

near antonyms immediately, posthaste, presto, promptly, pronto, readily, soon; impetuously, impulsively, rashly, recklessly; abruptly, suddenly

antonyms apace, briskly, fast, fleetly, full tilt, hastily, quick, quickly, rapidly, snappily, speedily, swift, swiftly

slow *vb* to cause to move or proceed at a less rapid pace ⟨If you don't *slow* your delivery down a bit, your speech will be over too soon.⟩

synonyms brake, decelerate, retard, slacken

related words halt, stop; encumber, hamper, handicap, hinder, hobble, hold back, hold up, impede, inhibit, obstruct, set back, tie up; arrest, check, constrain, curb, rein, restrain; baffle, foil, frustrate, thwart

near antonyms drive, encourage, goad, propel, push, spur, stir, urge; advance, aid, dispatch, ease, expedite, facilitate, forward, further, help

antonyms accelerate, hasten, hurry, quicken, rush, speed (up), step up

slowdown *n* a usually gradual decrease in the pace or level of activity of something ⟨Disease experts are encouraged by the recent *slowdown* in the spread of the virus.⟩

synonyms braking, deceleration, letup, retardation

related words decline, drop, slump; ebb, remission, retreat, wane; flagging, weakening; arrest, check, halt, stoppage; collapse, crash, fall, plunge

antonyms acceleration, hastening, quickening

slowly *adv* at a pace that is less than usual, desirable, or expected ⟨walked *slowly* toward the ringing phone⟩ — see SLOW

slowness *n* the quality or state of lacking intelligence or quickness of mind ⟨a condition sometimes manifested by mild forms of physical disability and mental *slowness*⟩ — see STUPIDITY 1

slowpoke *n* someone who moves slowly or more slowly than others ⟨Quit being such a *slowpoke* this morning, or you'll be late.⟩

synonyms crawler, dallier, dawdler, dragger, laggard, lagger, lingerer, loiterer, snail, straggler

related words latecomer; idler, lazybones, loafer, lounger, slouch, slug, sluggard; delayer, procrastinator

near antonyms go-getter, hustler, scrambler; hurrier, rusher, speeder

antonyms speedster

sludge *n* **1** soft wet earth ⟨After a day of heavy rain, the fairgrounds had turned into pure *sludge*.⟩ — see MUD
2 something (as a work of literature or music) that is too sentimental ⟨I can't bring myself to read that *sludge*.⟩ — see CORN

sludgy *adj* full of or covered with soft wet earth ⟨a *sludgy* riverbed⟩ — see MUDDY 1

¹slug *n* a hard strike with a part of the body or an instrument ⟨One well aimed *slug* ended the boxing match with a knockout.⟩ — see ¹BLOW

²slug *n* **1** a lazy person ⟨He's always a *slug* in the morning, which is why he prefers to sleep late.⟩ — see LAZYBONES
2 the portion of a serving of a beverage that is swallowed at one time ⟨forced down another *slug* of the horrible medicine⟩ — see DRINK 2

slug *vb* to deliver a blow to (someone or something) usually in a strong vigorous manner ⟨She got so angry that she *slugged* the back of the chair and knocked it over.⟩ — see HIT 1

sluggard *n* a lazy person ⟨I tried to wake up the *sluggards* who were still sleeping at that late hour.⟩ — see LAZY-BONES

sluggish *adj* **1** moving or proceeding at less than the normal, desirable, or required speed ⟨The *sluggish* pace of the project is worrisome.⟩ — see SLOW 1
2 slow to move or act ⟨Reptiles are naturally *sluggish* at low temperatures.⟩ — see INACTIVE 1

sluggishly *adv* at a pace that is less than usual, desirable, or expected ⟨The car responds *sluggishly* until it warms up.⟩ — see SLOW

sluice *vb* to pour liquid over or through in order to cleanse ⟨He *sluiced* the gutters with lots of water in order to make sure they were clear.⟩ — see FLUSH 1

slumber *n* a natural periodic loss of consciousness during which the body restores itself ⟨a toddler looking so innocent and peaceful in *slumber*⟩ — see SLEEP 1

slumber *vb* **1** to be in a state of sleep ⟨She *slumbered* for hours while the train rolled on.⟩ — see SLEEP 1
2 to sleep lightly or briefly ⟨*slumbering* restlessly in the tropical heat⟩ — see NAP 1

slumberer *n* one who sleeps ⟨Rip Van Winkle is one of literature's most famous *slumberers*.⟩ — see SLEEPER

slumbering *adj* being in a state of suspended consciousness ⟨made a comparison between the inattentive nation and a *slumbering* giant⟩ — see ASLEEP 1

slumbering *n* a natural periodic loss of consciousness during which the body restores itself ⟨My peaceful *slumbering* was interrupted by a ring of the doorbell.⟩ — see SLEEP 1

slumberous *or* **slumbrous** *adj* **1** desiring or needing sleep ⟨parents putting their *slumberous* children to bed⟩ — see SLEEPY 1
2 tending to cause sleep ⟨the *slumberous* murmur of the wind in the trees⟩ — see HYPNOTIC

slump *n* a period of decreased economic activity ⟨The stock market is in a bit of a *slump*, but analysts expect things to pick up in the next fiscal quarter.⟩ — see DEPRESSION 1

slur *n* **1** an act or expression showing scorn and usually intended to hurt another's feelings ⟨a word that is a hateful *slur*⟩ — see INSULT
2 a mark of guilt or disgrace ⟨Your behavior has cast a *slur* on this family.⟩ — see STAIN 1

slur (over) *vb* to fail to give proper attention to ⟨a documentary that *slurs over* certain important facts as it offers a very biased case for a conspiracy theory⟩ — see NEGLECT 1

slurp *vb* to swallow in liquid form ⟨His dinner companion *slurped* soup directly from the bowl.⟩ — see DRINK 1

slush *n* **1** soft wet earth ⟨He paused in front of the doorway to wipe the *slush* off of his boots.⟩ — see MUD
2 something (as a work of literature or music) that is too sentimental ⟨a musical that has been reviled as pure *slush* by the New York critics⟩ — see CORN

slushy *adj* **1** full of or covered with soft wet earth ⟨The *slushy* racetrack resulted in a significantly slower time for the winning horse.⟩ — see MUDDY 1
2 appealing to the emotions in an obvious and tiresome way ⟨*Slushy* music underscores the movie's emotional scenes.⟩ — see CORNY

sly *adj* **1** clever at attaining one's ends by indirect and often deceptive means ⟨The movie pairs a *sly*, dissembling ex-con with an upstanding, straight-arrow cop.⟩ — see ARTFUL 1
2 given to acting in secret and to concealing one's intentions ⟨Why, you *sly* fellow! I had no idea you were planning my birthday party!⟩ — see SNEAKY 1
3 tending to or exhibiting reckless playfulness ⟨a *sly* sense of humor⟩ — see MISCHIEVOUS 1

slyness *n* skill in achieving one's ends through indirect, subtle, or underhanded means ⟨The *slyness* with which the FBI agent infiltrated the subversive organization was indeed impressive.⟩ — see CUNNING 1

¹smack *n* a very small amount ⟨Add just a *smack* of vanilla to the whipped cream.⟩ — see PARTICLE 1

²smack *n* a hard strike with a part of the body or an instrument ⟨The cook gave him a *smack* on the wrist when he tried to sneak an early taste of the sauce.⟩ — see ¹BLOW

smack *vb* to deliver a blow to (someone or something) usually in a strong vigorous manner ⟨He *smacked* the punching bag one final time before heading to the showers.⟩ — see HIT 1

smack–dab *adv* as stated or indicated without the slightest difference ⟨a restaurant that's *smack-dab* in the center of town⟩ — see EXACTLY 1

small *adj* **1** of a size that is less than average ⟨a *small* cat who never weighed more than five pounds⟩
synonyms bantam, diminutive, dinky, dwarfish, fine, little, pint-size (*or* pint-sized), pocket, pocket-size (*also* pocket-sized), puny, pygmy, slight, smallish, undersized (*also* undersize)
related words dwarf; runtish, runty, scrubby, stunted; bitty, infinitesimal, micro, microscopic (*also* microscopical), mini, miniature, miniaturized, minuscule, minute, teeny, teeny-weeny, tiny, wee
near antonyms bulky, hefty, hulking, massive, voluminous; cavernous, colossal, elephantine, enormous, gargantuan, giant, gigantic, gross, herculean, heroic (*also* heroical), huge, immense, jumbo, mammoth, monstrous, monumental, mountainous, prodigious, staggering, stupendous, titanic, tremendous, vast
antonyms big, considerable, goodly, grand, great, handsome, husky, king-size (*or* king-sized), large, largish, outsize (*also* outsized), overscale (*or* overscaled), oversize (*or* oversized), sizable (*or* sizeable), substantial, tidy, whacking, whopping
2 small in degree ⟨Your chances of winning the lottery are so *small* that it's best not to count on it.⟩ — see REMOTE 1
3 lacking importance ⟨reluctant to bring such a *small* matter to the boss's attention⟩ — see UNIMPORTANT
4 not broad or open in views or opinions ⟨townspeople who were helpful to one another but who also could be *small* and intolerant⟩ — see NARROW 2

small arm *n* a portable weapon from which a shot is discharged by gunpowder ⟨The soldiers keep their *small arms* securely in their holsters when not on patrol.⟩ — see GUN 1

smaller *adj* having not so great importance or rank as another ⟨a *smaller* task but one that needs to be done nevertheless⟩ — see LESSER

small–fry *adj* lacking importance ⟨some *small-fry* official in the state government with a big-time ego⟩ — see UNIMPORTANT

smallish *adj* of a size that is less than average ⟨a *smallish* row of bushes lining the yard⟩ — see SMALL 1

small–minded *adj* 1 unwilling to grant other people social rights or to accept other viewpoints ⟨a *small-minded* man only concerned with his own well-being⟩ — see INTOLERANT 2

2 not broad or open in views or opinions ⟨resented the *small-minded* people who automatically opposed every new idea⟩ — see NARROW 2

smallness *n* the quality or state of being little in size ⟨My grandmother was surprised by the *smallness* of the latest electronic devices.⟩

synonyms diminutiveness, fineness, littleness, puniness, slightness

related words petiteness; minuteness, tininess; meagerness, poorness, scantiness, scantness, scarceness, scarcity, skimpiness, slenderness, slimness, spareness, sparseness

near antonyms enormity, enormousness, grossness, hugeness, immenseness, immensity, mountainousness, stupendousness; extensiveness, vastness; heaviness, heftiness, weightiness; bulkiness, massiveness, voluminousness

antonyms bigness, grandness, greatness, largeness, magnitude

small talk *n* friendly, informal conversation or an instance of this ⟨At the corporate get-together we made the obligatory *small talk* with some people from the home office.⟩ — see CHAT 1

smart *n* a sharp unpleasant sensation usually felt in some specific part of the body ⟨The toddler was whining over the *smart* from the cut.⟩ — see PAIN 1

smart *vb* to feel or cause physical pain ⟨The injection only *smarted* for a moment.⟩ — see HURT 1

smart *adj* 1 being strikingly neat and trim in style or appearance ⟨Dressed in their *smart* new uniforms, the cadets proudly paraded around the grounds of the military school.⟩

synonyms dapper, natty, sharp, snappy, spruce

related words dolled up, dressy, elegant, formal, spiffed-up; orderly, tidy; à la mode (*also* a la mode), chic, fashionable, in, modish, stylish; careful, fastidious, fussy, meticulous; combed, groomed

near antonyms messy, mussed, rumpled, uncombed, untidy, wrinkled; shabby, sleazy; dowdy, inelegant, unfashionable, unstylish

antonyms disheveled (*or* dishevelled), frowsy (*or* frowzy), sloppy, slovenly, unkempt

2 being in the latest or current fashion ⟨boutiques specializing in *smart* clothes⟩ — see STYLISH

3 given to or marked by mature intelligent humor ⟨a welcome addition to the lineup on TV: a *smart* sitcom⟩ — see WITTY

4 making light of something usually regarded as serious or sacred ⟨The boys just joked and made *smart* comments during the ceremony.⟩ — see FLIPPANT

5 having or showing a practical cleverness or judgment ⟨a *smart* investment that has really paid off⟩ — see SHREWD 1

6 having or showing quickness of mind ⟨a *smart* child who will do well in school⟩ — see INTELLIGENT 1

7 having a wide and refined knowledge of the world especially from personal experience ⟨a novelist who got much of the material for his works by hanging out with the *smart* set⟩ — see WORLDLY-WISE

smart aleck *also* **smart alec** *n* a person who likes to show off in a clever but annoying way ⟨Some *smart aleck* in the audience kept shouting clever insults at the nervous speaker.⟩

synonyms smarty (*or* smartie), wiseacre, wise guy

related words know-it-all; wisecracker; hotshot, show-off

smart–alecky *adj* 1 making light of something usually regarded as serious or sacred ⟨You wouldn't be so *smart-alecky* if you were in my situation.⟩ — see FLIPPANT

2 marked by the use of wit that is intended to cause hurt feelings ⟨was irritated by *smart-alecky* comments from a coworker⟩ — see SARCASTIC

smarting *adj* causing intense discomfort to one's skin ⟨We had to press on, despite the *smarting* sleet that was blowing in our faces.⟩ — see CUTTING 1

smartly *adv* in a strikingly neat and trim manner ⟨The *smartly* dressed scouts marched at the head of the Memorial Day parade.⟩

synonyms dashingly, nattily, sharply, snappily, sprucely

related words neatly, orderly, tidily, trimly; elegantly, fashionably, modishly, stylishly, swankily

near antonyms dowdily, inelegantly; slatternly; messily, untidily

antonyms sloppily, slovenly

smarty *or* **smartie** *n* a person who likes to show off in a clever but annoying way ⟨Think so, *smarty*? Well, you're wrong, and I can prove it!⟩ — see SMART ALECK

smash *n* 1 a forceful coming together of two things ⟨the awful *smash* when his dreams got hit by reality⟩ — see IMPACT 1

2 the violent coming together of two bodies into destructive contact ⟨The sound of the *smash* made all of the bystanders immediately whip their heads around.⟩ — see CRASH 1

3 a hard strike with a part of the body or an instrument ⟨She gave the tennis ball a *smash* and sent it flying over the other side of the net.⟩ — see ¹BLOW

4 a loud explosive sound ⟨The bikes collided with a huge *smash*.⟩ — see CLAP 1

5 a person or thing that is successful ⟨The new Broadway musical is a *smash*.⟩ — see HIT 1

smash *vb* 1 to cause to break with violence and much noise ⟨The ball *smashed* the window.⟩

synonyms break down, crash, shatter

related words bust, fracture, fragment; bash, demolish, destroy, devastate, pulverize, ruin, tear down, total, waste, wreck; shiver, splinter, split; crack, crunch, crush, snap

2 to cause to break open or into pieces by or as if by an explosive ⟨The firecracker *smashed* the clay pot.⟩ — see BLAST 1

3 to bring to a complete end the physical soundness, existence, or usefulness of ⟨The invading troops *smashed* the resistance and went on to conquer the country.⟩ — see DESTROY 1

4 to come into usually forceful contact with something ⟨We nearly *smashed* into each other on the skating rink.⟩ — see HIT 2

smashup *n* the violent coming together of two bodies into destructive contact ⟨Three cars were involved in a *smashup* on my street last night.⟩ — see CRASH 1

smattering *n* a small number ⟨a *smattering* of guests at the art exhibit⟩ — see FEW

smear *vb* 1 to rub an oily or sticky substance over ⟨The toddler gleefully *smeared* her hair and face with maple syrup.⟩

synonyms anoint, bedaub, besmear, daub

related words coat, paint, plaster; grease, oil; gum, lard; pitch, tar; befoul, begrime, besmirch, blacken, dirty, foul, grime, mire, muck, muddy, smirch, smudge, soil, stain, sully

2 to make untrue and harmful statements about ⟨He is willing to *smear* his opponent if doing so would win the election.⟩ — see SLANDER

smearing *n* the making of false statements that damage another's reputation ⟨This *smearing* has got to stop, or the voters will conclude that there's absolutely no one worth voting for.⟩ — see SLANDER

smell *n* **1** the quality of a thing that makes it perceptible to the sense organs in the nose ⟨The *smell* of vanilla is supposed to be very soothing.⟩

synonyms aroma, odor, redolence, scent, sniff

related words whiff; bouquet, fragrance, perfume; ambrosia, lusciousness, savor (*also* savour), savoriness, spice; acridness, fetidness, foulness, gaminess, noisomeness, rancidity, rankness, reek, stench, stink

2 a special quality or impression associated with something ⟨a law firm with a mahogany-lined boardroom that has the discernible *smell* of money and power⟩ — see AURA 1

smell *vb* **1** to become aware of by means of the sense organs in the nose ⟨We *smelled* the aroma of freshly baked cookies as soon as we walked in the house.⟩

synonyms nose, scent, sniff, whiff

related words breathe, respire; snort, snuffle; savor (*also* savour)

2 to have a vague awareness of ⟨I *smell* something fishy about this situation.⟩ — see FEEL 1

smelly *adj* having an unpleasant smell ⟨Your *smelly* sneakers are enough to raise the dead.⟩ — see MALODOROUS

smidgen *also* **smidgeon** *or* **smidgin** *or* **smidge** *n* a very small amount ⟨We cleaned the house until there wasn't even a *smidgen* of dust left.⟩ — see PARTICLE 1

smile *vb* **1** to express an emotion (as amusement) by curving the lips upward ⟨The soldier *smiled* in pleasure when he saw the giant sign welcoming him home.⟩

synonyms beam, grin

related words laugh, simper; smirk, sneer

near antonyms grimace; frown, glare, gloom, glower, lower (*also* lour), scowl; pout, sulk

2 to express scornful amusement by means of facial contortions ⟨I just *smiled* and shook my head at the mess the kids left again.⟩ — see SNEER

smirch *n* a mark of guilt or disgrace ⟨corruption charges that were a *smirch* on her reputation⟩ — see STAIN 1

smirch *vb* **1** to make dirty ⟨Their clothes were *smirched* by dust from the trail.⟩ — see DIRTY

2 to reduce to a lower standing in one's own eyes or in others' eyes ⟨This scandal will forever *smirch* the name of a once-great family.⟩ — see HUMBLE

smite *vb* to deliver a blow to (someone or something) usually in a strong vigorous manner ⟨He shall *smite* his enemies with a mighty fist.⟩ — see HIT 1

smog *n* an atmospheric condition in which suspended particles in the air rob it of its transparency ⟨The city's *smog* was once so bad that darkness often prevailed, even at noon.⟩ — see HAZE 1

smoggy *adj* filled with or dimmed by fine particles (as of dust or water) in suspension ⟨It was hard to see through the *smoggy* afternoon sky.⟩ — see HAZY 1

smooch *vb* to touch one another with the lips as a sign of love ⟨I hugged and *smooched* my dog after being away for a week.⟩ — see KISS 1

smooth *adj* **1** having or showing very polished and worldly manners ⟨a *smooth* salesman of expensive jewelry⟩ — see SUAVE

2 involving minimal difficulty or effort ⟨It should be *smooth* going from this point on.⟩ — see EASY 1

3 having a surface without bends, breaks, or irregularities ⟨a *smooth* skating rink⟩ — see LEVEL 1

4 free from emotional or mental agitation ⟨His *smooth* disposition and leadership qualities lend themselves well to the position.⟩ — see CALM 2

smooth *vb* **1** to free from obstruction or difficulty ⟨A willingness to compromise will *smooth* the way to an early agreement.⟩ — see EASE 1

2 to make free from breaks, curves, or bumps ⟨The workers *smoothed* the surface of the concrete before letting it dry.⟩ — see EVEN 1

3 to make smooth or glossy usually by repeatedly applying surface pressure ⟨He used fine sandpaper to *smooth* the face of the wood.⟩ — see POLISH 1

smoothly *adv* without difficulty ⟨We proceeded *smoothly* to the next stage of the project.⟩ — see EASILY 1

smother *vb* **1** to be or cause to be killed by lack of breathable air ⟨Children should never play inside discarded appliances because they could become entrapped and *smother*.⟩

synonyms choke, stifle, strangle, suffocate

related words garrote (*or* garotte), throttle; asphyxiate

near antonyms breathe, exhale, expire, inspire; resuscitate, revive

2 to refrain from openly showing or uttering ⟨He quickly *smothered* his inappropriate laughter at the funeral ceremony.⟩ — see SUPPRESS 2

smudge *vb* to make dirty ⟨She accidentally *smudged* the phone's screen.⟩ — see DIRTY

smudge *n* a mark of guilt or disgrace ⟨had not the slightest *smudge* to damage her reputation⟩ — see STAIN 1

smug *adj* having too high an opinion of oneself ⟨a winner who was so *smug* that he lost the goodwill of the crowd⟩ — see CONCEITED

smugness *n* an often unjustified feeling of being pleased with oneself or with one's situation or achievements ⟨the sense of *smugness* that can come with too many easy victories⟩ — see COMPLACENCE 1

smut *n* **1** foul matter that mars the purity or cleanliness of something ⟨Once a year they cleaned all of the *smut* out of the chimney.⟩ — see FILTH 1

2 the quality or state of being obscene ⟨The talk-show host is famous for shows filled with *smut* and scandal.⟩ — see OBSCENITY

smuttiness *n* **1** the quality or state of being obscene ⟨We were offended by the *smuttiness* of the jokes that the comedian was telling.⟩ — see OBSCENITY

2 the state or quality of being dirty ⟨appalled by the *smuttiness* of the rental apartments that they were shown⟩ — see DIRTINESS

smutty *adj* **1** depicting or referring to sexual matters in a way that is unacceptable in polite society ⟨The movie was rated R because of some *smutty* dialogue.⟩ — see OBSCENE 1

2 not clean ⟨a street urchin with a *smutty* face⟩ — see DIRTY 1

snag *n* a danger or difficulty that is hidden or not easily recognized ⟨We ran into a slight *snag* the night before the show.⟩ — see PITFALL 1

snag *vb* to take physical control or possession of (something) suddenly or forcibly ⟨Often late for work, I generally *snag* a bagel as I run out the door in the morning.⟩ — see CATCH 1

snail *n* someone who moves slowly or more slowly than others ⟨Go and tell the *snails* in the back to hurry up!⟩ — see SLOWPOKE

snail mail *n* communications or parcels sent or carried through the postal system ⟨I still communicate with some of my friends and family by *snail mail*.⟩ — see MAIL

snake *vb* **1** to move about in a sly or secret manner ⟨*snaking* softly through the brush⟩ — see SNEAK 1

2 to move slowly with the body close to the ground ⟨commandos *snaking* through the grass toward the compound⟩ — see CRAWL 1

snake *n* **1** a limbless reptile with a long body ⟨*Snakes* are cold-blooded, so they regulate their body temperature by alternately basking in sunlight and seeking shade.⟩

synonyms serpent, viper

related words adder, anaconda, asp, blacksnake, boa, bull snake, bushmaster, cobra, constrictor, copperhead, coral snake, cottonmouth moccasin, diamondback rattlesnake, fer-de-lance, garter snake, gopher snake, green snake, hognose snake, indigo snake, king cobra, king snake, krait, mamba, milk snake, moccasin, pit viper, puff adder, python, racer, rat snake, rattlesnake, sea serpent, sidewinder, water moccasin, water snake

2 a person whose behavior is offensive to others ⟨Why, that dirty, rotten *snake!*⟩ — see JERK 1

3 one who betrays a trust or an allegiance ⟨I should have known she was a *snake* who couldn't be trusted.⟩ — see TRAITOR

snap *adj* **1** involving minimal difficulty or effort ⟨a *snap* course that anyone could pass⟩ — see EASY 1

2 made or done without previous thought or preparation ⟨made a *snap* decision⟩ — see EXTEMPORANEOUS

snap *n* **1** a loud explosive sound ⟨The plastic coat hook broke off with a loud *snap* when he tried to hang the heavy bag on it.⟩ — see CLAP 1

2 a picture created from an image recorded on a light-sensitive surface by a camera ⟨took several *snaps* of his family for the scrapbook⟩ — see PHOTOGRAPH

3 active strength of body or mind ⟨The team is showing a lot of *snap* tonight.⟩ — see VIGOR 1

4 a weather condition marked by low temperatures ⟨a prolonged cold *snap*⟩ — see COLD

5 a very small amount ⟨I don't care a *snap* about gossip!⟩ — see PARTICLE 1

6 something that is easy to do ⟨This test will be a *snap*.⟩ — see CINCH

snap *vb* **1** to speak sharply or irritably ⟨The shopkeeper finally *snapped* at one customer who couldn't seem to make up his mind.⟩

synonyms bark, snarl

related words growl, grumble; roar, scream, shout, shriek, yell; fulminate, rage, rant, rave, sputter, storm, tee off, vent, vituperate; blow up, explode, flare (up)

near antonyms calm (down), simmer down

2 to break suddenly with an explosive sound ⟨The fragile twig *snapped* in her hands.⟩ — see CRACK 1

3 to take a photograph of ⟨Be sure to *snap* everything you see on your vacation, and then you can show us.⟩ — see PHOTOGRAPH

4 to pass from one form, state, or level to another ⟨She abruptly *snapped* alert.⟩ — see CHANGE 2

snap (up) *vb* to take physical control or possession of (something) suddenly or forcibly ⟨I *snapped up* the last remaining cupcake before anyone else could get their mitts on it.⟩ — see CATCH 1

snapback *n* the process or period of gradually regaining one's health and strength ⟨The doctor predicted a quick *snapback* for the rugged young soldier.⟩ — see CONVALESCENCE

snap back *vb* **1** to become healthy and strong again after illness or weakness ⟨Teenagers will often *snap back* remarkably quickly.⟩ — see CONVALESCE

2 to regain a former or normal state ⟨Analysts hoped that the economy would *snap back* over the next few months.⟩ — see RECOVER 2

snappily *adv* **1** with great speed ⟨She *snappily* completed the job application and handed it to the receptionist.⟩ — see FAST 1

2 in a strikingly neat and trim manner ⟨The *snappily* attired dancers wore top hats and tails.⟩ — see SMARTLY

snappish *adj* easily irritated or annoyed ⟨I always start feeling *snappish* whenever I get really hungry.⟩ — see IRRITABLE

snappy *adj* **1** being in the latest or current fashion ⟨That's a really *snappy* outfit.⟩ — see STYLISH

2 easily irritated or annoyed ⟨We tried to avoid her when she was acting *snappy*.⟩ — see IRRITABLE

3 having a low or subnormal temperature ⟨typically *snappy* weather for March⟩ — see COLD 1

4 having much high-spirited energy and movement ⟨much *snappy* repartee at the party celebrating the new art gallery's opening⟩ — see LIVELY 1

5 moving, proceeding, or acting with great speed ⟨Bring us some more french fries, and make it *snappy!*⟩ — see FAST 1

6 being strikingly neat and trim in style or appearance ⟨He's a *snappy* dresser.⟩ — see SMART 1

snapshot *n* a picture created from an image recorded on a light-sensitive surface by a camera ⟨Fans excitedly took *snapshots* of the rock star as he dashed into the hotel.⟩ — see PHOTOGRAPH

snare *n* **1** a device or scheme for capturing another by surprise ⟨You fell for my clever *snare*, you fool!⟩ — see TRAP 1

2 something that catches and holds ⟨Someday you'll find that your lies are a *snare* from which you can't escape.⟩ — see WEB 1

snare *vb* **1** to catch or hold as if in a net ⟨easily distracted by any bright object that *snared* his eye⟩ — see ENTANGLE 2

2 to take physical control or possession of (something) suddenly or forcibly ⟨campers trying to *snare* brook trout for supper⟩ — see CATCH 1

¹**snarl** *vb* to speak sharply or irritably ⟨She *snarled* at me after I kept badgering her with questions.⟩ — see SNAP 1

²**snarl** *vb* to twist together into a usually confused mass ⟨You'll be awfully sorry if you *snarl* your fishing line.⟩ — see ENTANGLE 1

snarl *n* a crowded mass (as of cars) that impedes or blocks movement ⟨To no avail, the city promotes carpooling to help ease the traffic *snarls* that always accompany rush hour.⟩ — see JAM 1

snatch *vb* to take physical control or possession of (something) suddenly or forcibly ⟨The brazen seagull *snatched* the french fry right from my hand.⟩ — see CATCH 1

snatching *n* an instance of theft ⟨an industry in which the *snatching* of trade secrets is greatly feared⟩ — see THEFT 2

snazzy *adj* attractively eye-catching in style ⟨fond of tooling around town in a *snazzy* car⟩ — see JAZZY 1

sneak *adj* undertaken or done so as to escape being observed or known by others ⟨I took a *sneak* peek at the birthday presents hidden in the closet.⟩ — see SECRET 1

sneak *n* someone who acts in a sly and secret manner ⟨"Why, you little *sneak*," the mother exclaimed, "you made my birthday present right under my nose!"⟩

synonyms lurker, skulk, skulker

related words skunk, snake; sharper, slicker, swindler; snoop, snooper, spy; stalker

sneak *vb* **1** to move about in a sly or secret manner ⟨The little kids *sneak* around upstairs when they're supposed to be in bed.⟩

synonyms lurk, mooch, mouse, pussyfoot, shirk, skulk, slide, slink, slip, snake, steal

related words crawl, creep, inch, worm; pad, tiptoe

2 to introduce in a gradual, secret, or clever way ⟨*Sneak* the topic into the conversation any way you can.⟩ — see INSINUATE 1

sneakiness *n* skill in achieving one's ends through indirect, subtle, or underhanded means ⟨She was impressed by the *sneakiness* with which they had planned the surprise party.⟩ — see CUNNING 1

sneaking *adj* 1 given to acting in secret and to concealing one's intentions ⟨Never let one of those *sneaking* salespeople into your house.⟩ — see SNEAKY 1

2 undertaken or done so as to escape being observed or known by others ⟨harbored a *sneaking* admiration for his chief business rival⟩ — see SECRET 1

3 arousing or deserving of one's loathing and disgust ⟨a *sneaking* eavesdropper⟩ — see CONTEMPTIBLE 1

sneaky *adj* 1 given to acting in secret and to concealing one's intentions ⟨His opponent's *sneaky* campaign manager was clearly up to something.⟩

synonyms furtive, shady, shifty, slippery, sly, sneaking, stealthy

related words artful, crafty, cunning, devious, foxy, guileful, slick, wily; close, closemouthed, reticent, secretive; clandestine, covert, dark; deceitful, deceiving, deceptive, devious, trickish, tricky, underhand, underhanded; crooked, defrauding, dishonest, dissembling, double-dealing, knavish, two-faced; lying, mendacious, untrustworthy, untruthful; insidious, perfidious, serpentine, treacherous

near antonyms aboveboard, forthright, plainspoken, straightforward; candid, direct, foursquare, frank, open, plain; honest, trustworthy, truthful

2 undertaken or done so as to escape being observed or known by others ⟨a *sneaky* plan to replace the priceless painting with a copy⟩ — see SECRET 1

sneer *vb* to express scornful amusement by means of facial contortions ⟨She *sneered* at me in disgust.⟩

synonyms laugh, smile, snicker, snigger

related words sniff, snort; catcall, deride, gibe (*or* jibe), hoot, insult, jeer, mock, ridicule; decry, despise, disdain; scoff (at), scorn; bad-mouth, belittle, disparage, pooh-pooh (*also* pooh), put down; heckle, jive, razz, rib, ride, taunt, tease, torment

snicker *n* an explosive sound that is a sign of amusement ⟨His unlikely story drew *snickers*.⟩ — see LAUGH 1

snicker *vb* 1 to express scornful amusement by means of facial contortions ⟨He *snickered* at the puzzled look on her face.⟩ — see SNEER

2 to show mirth with an explosive vocal sound ⟨I *snickered* at the silly joke.⟩ — see LAUGH 1

snide *adj* not following or in accordance with standards of honor and decency ⟨a *snide* trick to get the old woman to sell her antiques for practically nothing⟩ — see IGNOBLE 2

sniff *n* the quality of a thing that makes it perceptible to the sense organs in the nose ⟨We took a good *sniff* of the sauce, trying to guess its ingredients.⟩ — see SMELL 1

sniff *vb* to become aware of by means of the sense organs in the nose ⟨a curious cat *sniffing* the flowers in the garden⟩ — see SMELL 1

sniff (at) *vb* to show contempt for ⟨Her carpentry skills are nothing to *sniff at*.⟩ — see SCORN 1

snigger *n* an explosive sound that is a sign of amusement ⟨a love scene that unintentionally drew *sniggers* from the audience⟩ — see LAUGH 1

snigger *vb* to express scornful amusement by means of facial contortions ⟨We *sniggered* as the actor kept forgetting his lines.⟩ — see SNEER

snip *vb* to make (something) shorter or smaller with the use of a cutting instrument ⟨*snipped* the loose ends⟩ — see CLIP 1

snip *n* a very small piece ⟨cleared out the *snips* of paper that had been clogging the machine⟩ — see BIT 1

snippet *n* a very small piece ⟨Will read them a *snippet* of his latest poem.⟩ — see BIT 1

snippy *adj* 1 being or characterized by direct, brief, and potentially rude speech or manner ⟨*snippy* remarks about the quality of the food at the potluck⟩ — see BLUNT 1

2 easily irritated or annoyed ⟨feeling *snippy* after a long day of work⟩ — see IRRITABLE

3 self-consciously trying to present an appearance of grandeur or importance ⟨I get tired of his *snippy* insistence that emulating the rich and famous is the only way to appear successful.⟩ — see PRETENTIOUS 1

¹snitch *vb* to give information (as to the authorities) about another's improper or unlawful activities ⟨Someone must have *snitched* to the police.⟩ — see SQUEAL 1

²snitch *vb* to take (something) without right and with an intent to keep ⟨Joan *snitched* some paper from the office supply room for use with her printer at home.⟩ — see STEAL 1

snitch *n* a person who provides information about another's wrongdoing ⟨Several men were sentenced to prison based on the now-questionable testimony of a jailhouse *snitch*.⟩ — see INFORMER

snitcher *n* a person who provides information about another's wrongdoing ⟨The prison inmate swore that he'd get revenge if he ever found out who the *snitcher* was.⟩ — see INFORMER

snoop *vb* to interest oneself in what is not one's concern ⟨a private investigator *snooping* around the abandoned warehouse⟩ — see INTERFERE

snoopy *adj* 1 interested in what is not one's own business ⟨She feels that being *snoopy* is a desirable, even essential, trait in a reporter.⟩ — see CURIOUS 1

2 thrusting oneself where one is not welcome or invited ⟨We put a fence around the yard to keep out *snoopy* neighbors.⟩ — see INTRUSIVE

snooze *n* a short sleep ⟨Paul took a *snooze* after lunch to refresh himself.⟩ — see ¹NAP

snooze *vb* 1 to be in a state of sleep ⟨I *snoozed* through those long winter nights under a thick down comforter.⟩ — see SLEEP 1

2 to sleep lightly or briefly ⟨She was just *snoozing* when she heard the knock at the door.⟩ — see NAP 1

snoozing *n* a natural periodic loss of consciousness during which the body restores itself ⟨All that *snoozing* should have you well rested and ready for some hard work.⟩ — see SLEEP 1

snort *n* 1 a vocal sound made to express scorn or disapproval ⟨She made a *snort* of derision at the suggestion.⟩ — see CATCALL

2 the portion of a serving of a beverage that is swallowed at one time ⟨The old cowpoke asked for a *snort* of whiskey.⟩ — see DRINK 2

snow *vb* to cause to believe what is untrue ⟨easily *snowed* by her glib talk⟩ — see DECEIVE

snowball *vb* to become greater in extent, volume, amount, or number ⟨The little problems we had ignored began to *snowball* into huge headaches.⟩ — see INCREASE 2

snow under *vb* 1 to defeat by a large margin ⟨The challenger *snowed* the incumbent *under* in a big upset.⟩ — see WHIP 2

2 to subject to incapacitating emotional or mental stress ⟨*snowed under* by the huge pile of paperwork⟩ — see OVERWHELM 1

snub *n* treatment that is deliberately unfriendly ⟨He tolerated the *snubs* from his in-laws because the holidays come but once a year, thankfully.⟩ — see COLD SHOULDER

snub *vb* 1 to deliberately ignore or treat rudely ⟨The snob in town always *snubbed* anyone she thought was beneath her.⟩

synonyms cold-shoulder, cut, high-hat, slight

related words isolate, ostracize; brush (aside *or* off), disdain, rebuff, reject, repel, repulse, scorn, spurn; disregard, forget, neglect, overlook, shrug off

2 to show contempt for ⟨a social set that *snubs* anyone below their income bracket⟩ — see SCORN 1

snuff (out) *vb* **1** to cause to cease burning ⟨*Snuff out* the candle before you leave.⟩ — see EXTINGUISH 1

2 to destroy all traces of ⟨The forest fire *snuffed out* all of the animal life in the immediate area.⟩ — see ANNIHILATE 1

3 to put a stop to (something) by the use of force ⟨*snuffed out* the movement for democratic rule⟩ — see QUELL 1

snug *adj* **1** being clean and in good order ⟨a *snug* soldier in dress uniform⟩ — see NEAT 1

2 providing physical comfort ⟨a *snug* cottage that's the perfect retreat for a rustic vacation⟩ — see COMFORTABLE 1

3 enjoying physical comfort ⟨While *snug* in our warm beds, we listened to the winter storm raging outside.⟩ — see COMFORTABLE 2

4 firmly positioned in place and difficult to dislodge ⟨Make sure that all screws and nuts in the shelving unit are *snug*.⟩ — see TIGHT 2

5 providing safety ⟨yachtsmen looking for a *snug* harbor in which to anchor for the night⟩ — see SAFE 2

snug *vb* to sit or recline comfortably or cozily ⟨The farmhand *snugged* down in the hay and proceeded to go to sleep.⟩ — see SNUGGLE 1

snuggle *vb* **1** to sit or recline comfortably or cozily ⟨It's particularly nice to *snuggle* next to the fire on a snowy day.⟩
synonyms curl up, nestle, snug
related words burrow; couch, crouch, huddle, hunch, scrunch, squat, squinch

2 to lie close ⟨I love to *snuggle* up to a friendly cat.⟩ — see NUZZLE

so *adj* being in agreement with the truth or a fact or a standard ⟨I'm afraid that some of what you've said just isn't *so*.⟩ — see CORRECT 1

so *adv* **1** for this or that reason ⟨It was raining, *so* we stayed inside.⟩ — see THEREFORE

2 in like manner ⟨The boss works very hard, and *so* does everyone else.⟩ — see ALSO 1

3 to a great degree ⟨It's *so* cold outside!⟩ — see VERY 1

4 without any question ⟨You are *so* in trouble if I catch you again.⟩ — see INDEED 1

soak *vb* **1** to wet thoroughly with liquid ⟨We ran for home as soon as the rain started, but our clothes still ended up *soaked*.⟩
synonyms drench, drown, impregnate, saturate, sop, souse, steep
related words marinate, seethe; presoak; dip, immerse, inundate, submerge, swamp; bathe, douse (*also* dowse), hydrate, swill, wash, water; infiltrate, penetrate, permeate; damp, dampen, humidify, moisten
near antonyms dehydrate, dry, parch, sear; drain, empty, void; dehumidify
antonyms wring (out)

2 to charge (someone) too much for goods or services ⟨a merchant who *soaks* the tourists every summer⟩ — see OVERCHARGE 1

3 to make wet ⟨That downpour *soaked* my hair, and now I look like a sight!⟩ — see WET 1

soak (up) *vb* to take in (something liquid) through small openings ⟨This sponge should *soak up* the spilled juice very nicely.⟩ — see ABSORB 1

soaked *adj* containing, covered with, or thoroughly penetrated by water ⟨a miserable, *soaked* cat who looked like a drowned rat⟩ — see WET 1

soaking *adj* containing, covered with, or thoroughly penetrated by water ⟨The fisherman couldn't wait to take off his *soaking* socks.⟩ — see WET 1

soap *n* a substance used for cleaning ⟨A little *soap* and water should clean this in no time.⟩ — see CLEANER

soar *n* the act or an instance of rising or climbing up ⟨The *soar* of the space shuttle never failed to inspire.⟩ — see ASCENT 1

soar *vb* **1** to move or extend upward ⟨the Eiffel Tower *soaring* into the skies above Paris⟩ — see ASCEND

2 to move through the air with or as if with outstretched wings ⟨bats *soaring* and swooping through the night air⟩ — see FLY 1

3 to rise abruptly and rapidly ⟨Gas prices *soared* overnight because of the shortage.⟩ — see SKYROCKET

sob *vb* to shed tears often while making meaningless sounds as a sign of pain or distress ⟨The child *sobbed* when she found the dead frog.⟩ — see CRY 1

sober *adj* **1** not having one's mind affected by alcohol ⟨was *sober* to drive home⟩
synonyms clearheaded, straight
related words abstemious, abstinent, dry, temperate; cool, level, steady
near antonyms alcoholic, bibulous; maudlin; befuddled, besotted, dopey (*also* dopy); debauched, dissipated, dissolute
antonyms drunk, drunken, high, inebriate, inebriated, intoxicated, soused, tipsy

2 based on sound reasoning or information ⟨a *sober* assessment of the situation⟩ — see GOOD 1

3 not joking or playful in mood or manner ⟨a *sober* reply to what was only a teasing comment⟩ — see SERIOUS 1

4 not excessively showy ⟨He wore *sober* clothing to the funeral.⟩ — see QUIET 2

5 given to or marked by restraint in the satisfaction of one's appetites ⟨Cruise passengers of *sober* dispositions will be put off by the focus on nonstop dining.⟩ — see ABSTEMIOUS

soberness *n* a mental state free of jesting or trifling ⟨The unexpected *soberness* of the class clown at the memorial service was startling.⟩ — see EARNESTNESS

sobriety *n* a mental state free of jesting or trifling ⟨An abrupt *sobriety* fell over the group when they heard the news.⟩ — see EARNESTNESS

sobriquet *also* **soubriquet** *n* a descriptive or familiar name given instead of or in addition to the one belonging to an individual ⟨tagged her with the *sobriquet* "peanut" because of her diminutive size⟩ — see NICKNAME

sociability *n* the quality or state of being social ⟨Her *sociability* was called into question when she said she hated parties.⟩
synonyms conviviality, gregariousness
related words amiability, cordiality, folksiness, friendliness, neighborliness; camaraderie, companionship, fellowship
near antonyms bashfulness, coyness, diffidence, shyness, timidity, timidness; introversion; modesty, retiringness
antonyms unsociability, unsociableness

sociable *adj* **1** likely to seek or enjoy the company of others ⟨He's an intensely *sociable* child, and often has friends staying over.⟩ — see CONVIVIAL

2 showing a natural kindness and courtesy especially in social situations ⟨a pleasant and *sociable* hostess who puts everyone instantly at ease⟩ — see GRACIOUS 1

social *adj* likely to seek or enjoy the company of others ⟨Not exactly the *social* sort, our boss generally stays in his office and keeps to himself.⟩ — see CONVIVIAL

socialize *vb* to take part in social activities ⟨He likes to *socialize* with his coworkers after work ends.⟩
synonyms associate, fraternize, hobnob, mingle, mix
related words carouse, party, revel; circulate
phrases rub elbows (*or* rub shoulders)
near antonyms avoid, eschew, shun; slight, snub

society *n* **1** a group of persons formally joined together for some common interest ⟨a debate *society*⟩ — see ASSOCIATION 2

2 the feeling of closeness and friendship that exists between companions ⟨an evening marked by a lovely dinner and the *society* of our closest friends⟩ — see COMPANIONSHIP

3 the way people live at a particular time and place ⟨a pre-automobile *society* in which ordinary people rarely strayed far from home⟩ — see CIVILIZATION 1

¹**sock** *n* a close-fitting covering for the foot and leg ⟨black *socks* to go with black pants and shoes⟩ — see STOCKING

²**sock** *n* a hard strike with a part of the body or an instrument ⟨gave the pillow a few *socks* to plump it up⟩ — see ¹BLOW

sock *vb* to deliver a blow to (someone or something) usually in a strong vigorous manner ⟨kept *socking* the punching bag until he was exhausted⟩ — see HIT 1

sod *n* the land of one's birth, residence, or citizenship ⟨a sentimental journey back to the old *sod*⟩ — see COUNTRY 1

sodality *n* **1** a group of persons formally joined together for some common interest ⟨A 19th-century observer of American society noted that Americans had a fondness for forming *sodalities.*⟩ — see ASSOCIATION 2

2 the body of people in a profession or field of activity ⟨a pride that was felt throughout the *sodality* of firefighters⟩ — see CORPS

sodden *adj* containing, covered with, or thoroughly penetrated by water ⟨eyes peering out between strands of *sodden* hair⟩ — see WET 1

sofa *n* a long upholstered piece of furniture designed for several sitters ⟨I curled up on the *sofa* with a book.⟩ — see COUCH

soft *adj* **1** not loud in pitch or volume ⟨*Soft* music played in the background while we ate.⟩
synonyms dull, gentle, low, quiet
related words dead, silent, still; calm, dreamy, hushed, peaceful, restful, serene, soothing, stilly, tranquil; muffled, muted, softened, toned (down)
near antonyms brazen, dinning, discordant, noisy, obstreperous, raucous, rip-roaring, vociferous; grating, harsh, shrill, squealing, strident; clarion, clear, trumpet-like
antonyms blaring, blasting, booming, clamorous, clangorous, deafening, earsplitting, loud, overloud, piercing, resounding, ringing, roaring, sonorous, stentorian, thunderous

2 smooth or delicate in appearance or feel ⟨I like this sweater the best because it is so *soft* and comfortable.⟩
synonyms cottony, downy, satin, satiny, silken, silky, velvety
related words creamy; chiffon, delicate, fine, slick; ultrasoft
near antonyms bumpy, irregular, jagged, lumpy, pebbly; broken, jagged, ragged, roughened, rugged, scraggy; grainy, granular, gritty
antonyms coarse, harsh, rough, scratchy

3 giving easily to the touch ⟨*Soft* mattresses make it very easy to fall asleep, but they have a tendency to get lumpy.⟩
synonyms flabby, mushy, pulpy, spongy, squashy, squishy
related words fleshy; droopy, flaccid, floppy, lank, limp, slack, yielding; bendable, compressible, crushable, elastic, flexible, kneadable, malleable, pliable, pliant, resilient, supple, willowy, workable; airy, light
near antonyms inelastic, inflexible, rigid, stiff, tense, unbending, unyielding; resistant, sound, strong, sturdy, tough; hardened, indurated, stiffened, tempered; com-

pacted, compressed, condensed; adamantine, rock, rock-like; sturdy, substantial
antonyms firm, hard, solid

4 involving minimal difficulty or effort ⟨looking for a *soft* job in local government⟩ — see EASY 1

5 lacking bodily strength ⟨*soft* recruits who will get toughened up in the army⟩ — see WEAK 1

6 lacking strength of will or character ⟨a *soft* person who tends to yield to stronger personalities⟩ — see WEAK 2

7 not harsh or stern especially in nature or effect ⟨a *soft* breeze coming off the lake⟩ — see GENTLE 1

8 providing physical comfort ⟨a warm, *soft* bed to rest my weary bones⟩ — see COMFORTABLE 1

9 tolerant and kind in the judgment of and expectations for others ⟨thought they were too *soft* with their children⟩ — see INDULGENT 1

10 marked by temperatures that are neither too high nor too low ⟨It was a lovely *soft* spring evening.⟩ — see CLEMENT 1

soften *vb* **1** to diminish the physical strength of ⟨Three weeks of being sick in bed had noticeably *softened* her.⟩ — see WEAKEN 1

2 to lessen the shock of ⟨The author's agent tried to *soften* the blow of the publisher's rejection.⟩ — see CUSHION

softened *adj* lacking bodily strength ⟨The athlete, *softened* by the long period of convalescence, had to begin his training program almost from scratch.⟩ — see WEAK 1

softhearted *adj* having or marked by sympathy and consideration for others ⟨a *softhearted* person who never hesitates to help anyone in trouble⟩ — see HUMANE 1

softheartedness *n* the capacity for feeling for another's unhappiness or misfortune ⟨the kind of *softheartedness* that makes him an easy target for anyone with a tale of woe⟩ — see HEART 1

softness *n* the quality or state of lacking strength of will or character ⟨*Softness* is not a typical quality of military leaders.⟩ — see WEAKNESS 2

soft–soap *vb* **1** to get (someone) to do something by gentle urging, special attention, or flattery ⟨She cunningly *soft-soaped* her parents into letting her go on the trip.⟩ — see COAX

2 to praise too much ⟨shrewd voters who know when a politician is trying to *soft-soap* them⟩ — see FLATTER 1

soft soap *n* excessive praise ⟨a salesman who knows the value of *soft soap* in making a sale⟩ — see FLATTERY

softy *or* **softie** *n* a person lacking in physical strength ⟨a *softy* who usually needs someone else's strong hands to open bottles and jars⟩ — see WEAKLING 1

soggy *adj* containing, covered with, or thoroughly penetrated by water ⟨We'll spread the *soggy* papers out to dry.⟩ — see WET 1

¹**soil** *n* foul matter that mars the purity or cleanliness of something ⟨I got some sort of *soil* on my white pants.⟩ — see FILTH 1

²**soil** *n* **1** the loose surface material in which plants naturally grow ⟨bought rich *soil* to plant flowers in⟩ — see DIRT 1

2 the solid part of our planet's surface as distinguished from the sea and air ⟨happy to have *soil* under my feet after that long sea voyage⟩ — see EARTH 2

soil *vb* to make dirty ⟨Oil and grease *soiled* the mechanic's shirt.⟩ — see DIRTY

soilage *n* the state or quality of being dirty ⟨The fee for cleaning the carpet will depend upon the extent of the *soilage.*⟩ — see DIRTINESS

soiled *adj* not clean ⟨a *soiled* carpet in need of a good shampooing⟩ — see DIRTY 1

sojourn *n* a temporary residing as another's guest ⟨Alex spent a relaxing *sojourn* in her friend's summer home.⟩ — see VISIT 1

sojourn *vb* to reside as a temporary guest ⟨began their retirement by leisurely *sojourning* with friends and relatives scattered across the country⟩ — see VISIT 2

solace *n* **1** a feeling of ease from grief or trouble ⟨The kind words brought a little *solace*.⟩ — see COMFORT 1
2 the giving of hope and strength in times of grief, distress, or suffering ⟨the selfless *solace* of the sick by the workers at the hospice⟩ — see CONSOLATION 1

solace *vb* **1** to ease the grief or distress of ⟨Counselors did their best to *solace* the bereaved.⟩ — see COMFORT
2 to cause (someone) to pass the time agreeably occupied ⟨I *solaced* myself with a book while I waited for the bus.⟩ — see AMUSE

solacing *n* the giving of hope and strength in times of grief, distress, or suffering ⟨I will be forever grateful for my friend's *solacing* of me when I was down.⟩ — see CONSOLATION 1

solar plexus *n* the part of the body between the chest and the pelvis ⟨felt a sharp pain in the *solar plexus*⟩ — see STOMACH 1

soldier *n* a person engaged in military service ⟨a platoon of *soldiers*⟩
synonyms fighter, legionary, legionnaire, man-at-arms, regular, serviceman, warrior
related words servicewoman; cavalier, cavalryman, cuirassier; doughboy, footman, foot soldier, infantryman; commando, raider; marine, ranger; artilleryman, cannoneer, gunner, musketeer, rifleman; GI, guardsman, militiaman, minuteman; conscript, draftee, enrollee, recruit; reservist
antonyms civilian

soldierly *adj* of, relating to, or suitable for war or a warrior ⟨Noah Webster's brief contribution to the Revolutionary cause suggests that his *soldierly* skills were few.⟩ — see MARTIAL 1

sole *adj* **1** belonging only to the one person, unit, or group named ⟨The landowner has *sole* rights to the property, so he can do whatever he wants to with it.⟩
synonyms exclusive, single, unshared
related words proprietary; personal, private
near antonyms common, communal, conjoint, cooperative, joint, multiple, mutual, pooled, public, shared, united
antonyms nonexclusive
2 being the one or ones of a class with no other members ⟨The eldest son became the family's *sole* support.⟩ — see ONLY 2

solecism *n* a socially improper or unsuitable act or remark ⟨the *solecism* of asking one's hosts how much something in their house cost them⟩ — see IMPROPRIETY 2

solely *adv* **1** for nothing other than ⟨The promotion was based *solely* on merit.⟩
synonyms alone, exclusively, just, only, purely, simply
related words basically, by and large, chiefly, generally, largely, mainly, mostly, predominantly, primarily, principally, substantially
near antonyms additionally, also, besides, likewise
2 without aid or support ⟨You undertook that project *solely* on your own, and you will finish it likewise.⟩ — see ALONE 1

solemn *adj* **1** having or showing a formal and serious or reserved manner ⟨The director of the funeral home has a fittingly *solemn* demeanor.⟩ — see DIGNIFIED
2 not joking or playful in mood or manner ⟨*solemn* as a judge⟩ — see SERIOUS 1
3 causing or marked by an atmosphere lacking in cheer ⟨The Capitol's rotunda was draped in *solemn* decorations of a state funeral.⟩ — see GLOOMY 1

solemnity *n* **1** a mental state free of jesting or trifling ⟨The coronation ceremony requires absolute *solemnity*.⟩ — see EARNESTNESS
2 an oft-repeated action or series of actions performed in accordance with tradition or a set of rules ⟨Elaborate *solemnities* marked the 100th anniversary of the event.⟩ — see RITE

solicit *vb* **1** to go around and approach (people) with a request for opinions or information ⟨*solicited* several opinions about which job he should accept⟩ — see CANVASS 1
2 to make a request for ⟨always ready to *solicit* donations for a charity⟩ — see ASK (FOR) 1
3 to make a request of ⟨I personally *solicited* him to join the team.⟩ — see ASK 2
4 to make a request to (someone) in an earnest or urgent manner ⟨*solicited* the President for relief funds⟩ — see BEG
5 to lead away from a usual or proper course by offering some pleasure or advantage ⟨was *solicited* into purchasing high-yield but risky stocks⟩ — see LURE

solicitation *n* an earnest request ⟨The mail is always full of *solicitations* from worthy causes.⟩ — see PLEA 1

soliciting *adj* asking humbly ⟨A *soliciting* tone is better when asking for lenient treatment you don't deserve.⟩ — see SUPPLIANT

solicitor *n* **1** one that tries to get a person to give in to a desire ⟨money, that great *solicitor* that has often succeeded in persuading people to sell their very souls⟩ — see TEMPTER
2 one who asks earnestly for a favor or gift ⟨Even a billionaire doesn't have the wherewithal to grant the wish of every deserving *solicitor* who comes his way.⟩ — see SUPPLIANT

solicitous *adj* **1** given to or made with heedful anticipation of the needs and happiness of others ⟨I appreciated the *solicitous* offer of help during my recovery.⟩ — see THOUGHTFUL 1
2 showing urgent desire or interest ⟨a family that is *solicitous* to put this whole unfortunate affair behind them and to move on with their lives⟩ — see EAGER

solicitude *n* **1** an uneasy state of mind usually over the possibility of an anticipated misfortune or trouble ⟨a growing *solicitude* over the possible results of the criminal investigation⟩ — see ANXIETY 1
2 attention accompanied by protectiveness and responsibility ⟨She shows much more *solicitude* toward her aging parents than any of her siblings do.⟩ — see CARE 2

solid *adj* **1** based on sound reasoning or information ⟨the only *solid* conclusion that the jury could have reached⟩ — see GOOD 1
2 having a consistency that does not easily yield to pressure ⟨The ice cream is too *solid* to scoop right now.⟩ — see FIRM 2
3 having or consisting of a single color ⟨Both kittens are black, but one has a *solid* coat and the other has a few white patches.⟩ — see MONOCHROMATIC 1
4 not showing weakness or uncertainty ⟨Some people see a *solid* handshake as a sign of strong character.⟩ — see FIRM 1
5 worthy of one's trust ⟨a *solid* source of information to reporters⟩ — see DEPENDABLE

solidify *vb* **1** to become physically firm or solid ⟨water *solidifying* into ice⟩ — see HARDEN 1
2 to take on a definite form ⟨My ideas on this topic are just starting to *solidify*.⟩ — see FORM 1

solidity *n* worthiness as the recipient of another's trust or confidence ⟨The *solidity* of his word is such that I don't need a written contract—or anything else.⟩ — see RELIABILITY

solidness *n* worthiness as the recipient of another's trust or confidence ⟨Her proven *solidness* as a friend is something that I can't even begin to describe.⟩ — see RELIABILITY

solitariness *n* the state of being alone or kept apart from others ⟨It was the overwhelming *solitariness* of his existence that caused the marooned sailor the most distress.⟩ — see ISOLATION

solitary *adj* **1** being the one or ones of a class with no other members ⟨A *solitary* example of truth-stretching is hardly grounds for branding the man a congenital liar.⟩ — see ONLY 2

2 not being in the company of others ⟨A *solitary* sailboat was the only object on the horizon.⟩ — see ALONE 1

solitary *n* a person who lives away from others ⟨Weary of European civilization, the painter Paul Gauguin famously abandoned France to become a *solitary* in the South Seas.⟩ — see RECLUSE

solitude *n* the state of being alone or kept apart from others ⟨sought the kind of *solitude* where his thoughts would be his only companions⟩ — see ISOLATION

solo *adj* not being in the company of others ⟨a *solo* flight in a hot-air balloon⟩ — see ALONE 1

solon *n* a member of an organized body of persons having the authority to make laws ⟨one of the most politically adept *solons* in the state legislature⟩ — see LEGISLATOR

soluble *adj* capable of having the reason for or cause of determined ⟨one murder case that proved to be *soluble* after all⟩ — see SOLVABLE

solution *n* something attained by mental effort and especially by computation ⟨the *solution* to a math problem⟩ — see ANSWER 2

solvable *adj* capable of having the reason for or cause of determined ⟨I'm sure that the mystery of what happened to the missing pizza is *solvable*.⟩

synonyms answerable, explainable, explicable, resolvable, soluble

related words analyzable, decipherable; feasible, workable

near antonyms difficult, inextricable, knotty; impossible, insuperable; absurd, fantastic (*also* fantastical), outlandish, preposterous, ridiculous

antonyms hopeless, inexplicable, insoluble, unexplainable, unresolvable, unsolvable

solve *vb* to find an answer for through reasoning ⟨It took me half an hour to *solve* the logic puzzle.⟩

synonyms answer, break, crack, dope (out), figure out, puzzle (out), resolve, unravel, work, work out

related words conclude, decide, deduce, gather, infer, judge, reason; clear (up), iron out, straighten (out), unscramble, untangle, untie; assume, conjecture, divine, guess, presume, speculate; decipher, decode

somatic *adj* of or relating to the human body ⟨a *somatic* disorder that was once thought to be "all in the patient's head"⟩ — see PHYSICAL 1

somber *or* **sombre** *adj* **1** being without light or without much light ⟨a *somber* courtroom⟩ — see DARK 1

2 causing or marked by an atmosphere lacking in cheer ⟨the *somber* occasion of an old comrade's memorial service⟩ — see GLOOMY 1

some *adj* known but not named ⟨*Some* people won't be able to come.⟩ — see CERTAIN 1

somebody *n* a person who is widely known and usually much talked about ⟨a small-town girl who hopes to become a *somebody* someday⟩ — see CELEBRITY 1

someday *adv* at a later time ⟨the dream that we'll get to the other planets *someday*⟩ — see YET 1

something *adv* to some degree or extent ⟨a person of *something* less than total honesty⟩ — see FAIRLY 1

something *n* one that has a real and independent existence ⟨I heard *something* fall off the counter.⟩ — see ENTITY

sometime *adj* having been such at some previous time ⟨a *sometime* athlete who retired long ago⟩ — see FORMER 1

sometime *adv* at a later time ⟨We'll get around to it *sometime*.⟩ — see YET 1

sometimes *adv* on some occasions ⟨*Sometimes* I like to go skiing, and *sometimes* I prefer to stay inside where it's warm.⟩

synonyms now, occasionally

related words intermittently, off and on, periodically, recurrently; infrequently, little, rarely, seldom; irregularly, sporadically, variously

phrases at times, every now and then (*or* every now and again *or* every so often), from time to time, once in a while, on occasion

near antonyms frequently, much, oft, often, oftentimes (*or* ofttimes); commonly, ordinarily, regularly, routinely, usually; always, consistently, constantly, invariably; continually, continuingly, continuously, incessantly, perpetually, unceasingly, uninterruptedly; endlessly, ever, interminably

somewhat *adv* to some degree or extent ⟨Wear a jacket as it's *somewhat* chilly today.⟩ — see FAIRLY 1

somnolence *n* the quality or state of desiring or needing sleep ⟨*Somnolence* is likely to be the most typical and telling reaction to this novel.⟩ — see SLEEPINESS

somnolent *adj* **1** desiring or needing sleep ⟨trying to teach *somnolent* students on a very hot day⟩ — see SLEEPY 1

2 tending to cause sleep ⟨the *somnolent* hum of insects in the grass⟩ — see HYPNOTIC

song *n* **1** a short musical composition for the human voice often with instrumental accompaniment ⟨She sang a little-known *song* for the talent show.⟩

synonyms ballad, ditty, jingle, lay, lyric, vocal

related words anthem, cantata, canticle, carol, chorale, hymn, noel, psalm, spiritual; dirge, lament, requiem, threnody; paean; aria, barcarole (*or* barcarolle), chant, chantey (*or* chanty *or* shanty), folk song, glee, madrigal, motet, part-song, round, roundelay, serenade

2 a composition using rhythm and often rhyme to create a lyrical effect ⟨the *songs* of Shakespeare⟩ — see POEM

3 a rhythmic series of musical tones arranged to give a pleasing effect ⟨Why not whistle a *song* as accompaniment to your work?⟩ — see MELODY

4 a very small sum of money ⟨Developers bought the land for a *song*.⟩ — see MITE 1

5 writing that uses rhythm, vivid language, and often rhyme to provoke an emotional response ⟨a hero honored in *song* and story⟩ — see POETRY 1

songster *n* one who sings ⟨one of the most popular *songsters* during the World War II era⟩ — see SINGER

sonny *n* a male person who has not yet reached adulthood ⟨Come over here, *sonny*, and help me clean up.⟩ — see BOY 1

sonorous *adj* **1** marked by a high volume of sound ⟨a *sonorous* waterfall that can be heard from a considerable distance⟩ — see LOUD 1

2 marked by conspicuously full and rich sounds or tones ⟨a baritone with a particularly *sonorous* voice⟩ — see RESONANT

soon *adv* **1** at or within a short time ⟨We'll be done *soon*.⟩ — see SHORTLY 2

2 by choice or preference ⟨I'd *sooner* do it now than wait till tomorrow.⟩ — see RATHER 1

3 with great speed ⟨as *soon* as possible⟩ — see FAST 1

soothe *vb* **1** to ease the grief or distress of ⟨The manager tried to *soothe* the angry customer.⟩ — see COMFORT

2 to free from distress or disturbance ⟨*soothed* the baby with a bottle⟩ — see CALM 1

3 to make more bearable or less severe ⟨Hot tea with honey will *soothe* a sore throat.⟩ — see HELP 2

soothing *adj* **1** tending to calm the emotions and relieve stress ⟨The *soothing* music eventually put the entire yoga class in the proper mood.⟩

synonyms calming, comforting, dreamy, lulling, pacifying, quieting, relaxing, sedative, tranquilizing (*also* tranquillizing)

related words analgesic, anesthetic, deadening, depressant, numbing

near antonyms painful, stressful, tiresome, troubling, trying, unsettling, worrisome; energizing, invigorating, stimulant, stimulating; aggravating, annoying, bothersome, disturbing, exasperating, frustrating, galling, grating, harassing, irksome, irritating, maddening, troublesome, vexatious, vexing

2 not harsh or stern especially in nature or effect ⟨spoke to the boy in a *soothing* voice⟩ — see GENTLE 1

soothsayer *n* one who predicts future events or developments ⟨In Shakespeare's play, a *soothsayer* warns Caesar to "beware the ides of March."⟩ — see PROPHET 1

soothsaying *n* a declaration that something will happen in the future ⟨I took the *soothsayings* published in the tabloids with a grain of salt.⟩ — see PREDICTION

sop *n* something given or promised in order to improperly influence a person's conduct or decision ⟨As a *sop* to the teachers' union for supporting his reelection campaign, the mayor promised to push for the abolition of the residency requirement.⟩ — see BRIBE

sop *vb* **1** to wet thoroughly with liquid ⟨I *sopped* the sponge with the detergent and began scrubbing the floor vigorously.⟩ — see SOAK 1

2 to make wet ⟨My book fell in the swimming pool and was thoroughly *sopped* before I could fish it out.⟩ — see WET

3 to sink or push (something) briefly into or as if into a liquid ⟨hesitant to *sop* his bread in gravy, no matter how delicious, at such a formal banquet⟩ — see DIP 1

sophisticate *n* a person with the outlook, experience, and manners thought to be typical of big city dwellers ⟨young urban *sophisticates* moving into the neighborhood⟩ — see COSMOPOLITAN

sophisticate *vb* **1** to make complex or difficult ⟨There's no need to *sophisticate* something that is beautiful in its simplicity.⟩ — see COMPLICATE

2 to alter (something) for the worse with the addition of foreign or lower-grade substances ⟨vanilla extract that has been *sophisticated* with corn syrup⟩ — see ADULTERATE

sophisticated *adj* **1** having a wide and refined knowledge of the world especially from personal experience ⟨a surprisingly *sophisticated* and widely traveled child⟩ — see WORLDLY-WISE

2 having many parts or aspects that are usually interrelated ⟨a very *sophisticated* machine that is a marvel of modern design⟩ — see COMPLEX 1

3 having or showing very polished and worldly manners ⟨A *sophisticated* gentleman, he is a welcomed guest at dinner parties all over town.⟩ — see SUAVE

4 made or done with great care or with much detail ⟨a *sophisticated* plan for totally redesigning the city's complicated traffic patterns⟩ — see ELABORATE 1

sophistication *n* the state or quality of having many interrelated parts or aspects ⟨The engine's *sophistication* requires that all repairs be done by an experienced mechanic.⟩ — see COMPLEXITY 1

sopping *adj* containing, covered with, or thoroughly penetrated by water ⟨My hair and clothes were absolutely *sopping* after the unexpected downpour.⟩ — see WET 1

soppy *adj* containing, covered with, or thoroughly penetrated by water ⟨trudging over *soppy* ground at the county fair⟩ — see WET 1

sorcerer *n* a person skilled in using supernatural forces ⟨a *sorcerer* who used his power for evil ends⟩ — see MAGICIAN 1

sorceress *n* a woman believed to have often harmful supernatural powers ⟨He asked the *sorceress* to cast an evil spell over the village.⟩ — see WITCH 1

sorcery *n* the power to control natural forces through supernatural means ⟨suspected the old man of *sorcery*⟩ — see MAGIC 1

sordid *adj* **1** not clean ⟨He managed to rise above the *sordid* streets upon which he grew up.⟩ — see DIRTY 1

2 not following or in accordance with standards of honor and decency ⟨a *sordid* affair involving bribery and corruption in high places⟩ — see IGNOBLE 2

sore *adj* **1** causing or feeling bodily pain ⟨My legs are *sore* after that long walk yesterday.⟩ — see PAINFUL 1

2 feeling or showing anger ⟨The coach was *sore* at the ref's call.⟩ — see ANGRY

3 having or showing deep-seated resentment ⟨Are you still *sore* about what happened?⟩ — see BITTER 1

sore *adv* to a great degree ⟨I was *sore* afraid we'd never make it home.⟩ — see VERY 1

sorely *adv* **1** with feelings of bitterness or grief ⟨Our company president, who is retiring at the end of the year, will be *sorely* missed.⟩ — see HARD 2

2 to a great degree ⟨completed some *sorely* needed repairs to the boat⟩ — see VERY 1

sorrow *vb* to feel deep sadness or mental pain ⟨a *sorrowing* family, grieving over the loss of their grandmother⟩ — see GRIEVE

sorrow *n* deep sadness especially for the loss of someone or something loved ⟨He felt great *sorrow* at the loss of his beloved dog.⟩

synonyms affliction, anguish, dolefulness, dolor, grief, heartache, heartbreak, woe

related words agony, distress, pain, suffering, torment; blues, dejection, depression, desolateness, desolation, despair, despondency, disconsolateness, dispiritedness, distress, doldrums, downheartedness, dreariness, dumps, forlornness, gloom, gloominess, heartsickness, joylessness, melancholy, misery, mopes, oppression, unhappiness, woefulness, wretchedness; contrition, guilt, regret, remorse, rue, self-reproach, shame; melancholia, self-pity

near antonyms gaiety (*also* gayety), humor, jollity, joviality, lightheartedness, merriment, merrymaking, mirth, mirthfulness; hopefulness, optimism, sunniness; enjoyment; content, contentedness, contentment

antonyms bliss, blissfulness, cheer, cheerfulness, cheeriness, delight, ecstasy, elation, euphoria, exhilaration, exuberance, exultation, gladness, gladsomeness, glee, gleefulness, happiness, joy, joyfulness, joyousness, jubilation, pleasure, rapture, rapturousness

sorrowful *adj* **1** expressing or suggesting mourning ⟨adopted a *sorrowful* tone of voice to read the news story about the former governor's death⟩ — see MOURNFUL 1

2 feeling unhappiness ⟨a *sorrowful* assemblage of bereaved fans⟩ — see SAD 1

sorrowfully *adv* with feelings of bitterness or grief ⟨In a *sorrowfully* worded statement she announced that she was dropping out of the race for mayor.⟩ — see HARD 2

sorry *adj* **1** arousing or deserving of one's loathing and disgust ⟨One more *sorry* stunt like that and you'll be fired.⟩ — see CONTEMPTIBLE 1

2 causing unhappiness ⟨We have *sorry* news to report tonight.⟩ — see SAD 2

3 deserving pitying scorn (as for inadequacy) ⟨The ragtag circus was a *sorry* spectacle indeed.⟩ — see PITIFUL 1

4 feeling sorrow for a wrong that one has done ⟨She's genuinely *sorry* for hurting his feelings.⟩ — see CONTRITE

5 feeling unhappiness ⟨He was *sorry* to see the family farm being sold.⟩ — see SAD 1

6 expressing or suggesting mourning ⟨Those *sorry* rituals that we go through when somebody dies are not for the dead but for the living.⟩ — see MOURNFUL 1

7 deserving of one's pity ⟨Some *sorry* wretch had the task of putting all of those files back in order.⟩ — see PATHETIC 1

sort *n* **1** a number of persons or things that are grouped together because they have something in common ⟨I prefer jackets with zippers to the *sort* that close with buttons.⟩
synonyms breed, class, description, feather, ilk, kind, like, manner, nature, order, species, strain, stripe, type, variety
related words model; sample, specimen; bracket, bunch, category, division, family, grade, group, grouping, lot, persuasion, rank(s), set, suite
2 a member of the human race ⟨He's a decent *sort*.⟩ — see HUMAN

sort *vb* **1** to come or be together as friends ⟨You should be careful about whom you *sort* with.⟩ — see ASSOCIATE 1
2 to be in agreement on every point ⟨That doesn't *sort* with what you said the last time.⟩ — see CHECK 1
3 to arrange or assign according to type ⟨We *sorted* the mail into bills to be paid and junk to be thrown out.⟩ — see CLASSIFY 1

sort of *adv* to some degree or extent ⟨You've been acting *sort of* funny all week.⟩ — see FAIRLY 1

so–so *adj* of average or below average quality ⟨a *so-so* production of a great play⟩ — see MEDIOCRE 1

so–so *adv* in a satisfactory way ⟨I think I did *so-so* on the test.⟩ — see WELL 1

soul *n* **1** an immaterial force within a human being thought to give the body life, energy, and power ⟨Many religions teach that the *soul* is immortal.⟩
synonyms psyche, spirit
related words life, vitality; being, essence, quintessence
near antonyms body, flesh
2 a member of the human race ⟨I promise I won't tell another *soul*.⟩ — see HUMAN
3 the quality or qualities that make a thing what it is ⟨a kind act that was the very *soul* of charity⟩ — see ESSENCE 1
4 the seat of one's deepest thoughts and emotions ⟨knew in her *soul* that it was true⟩ — see CORE 1

soulless *adj* having or showing a lack of sympathy or tender feelings ⟨a company that was a *soulless* money-making machine⟩ — see HARD 1

¹sound *vb* **1** to continue or be repeated in a series of reflected sound waves ⟨The stranded hiker's cries for help *sounded* throughout the canyon.⟩ — see REVERBERATE
2 to give the impression of being ⟨The idea at least *sounds* plausible.⟩ — see SEEM
3 to make known (as an idea, emotion, or opinion) ⟨a person who certainly isn't shy about *sounding* her opinions⟩ — see EXPRESS 1
4 to make known openly or publicly ⟨They *sounded* the news far and wide.⟩ — see ANNOUNCE

²sound *vb* **1** to measure the depth of (as a body of water) typically with a weighted line ⟨The pilot *sounded* the river to make sure we weren't in any danger of running aground.⟩
synonyms fathom, plumb
related words gauge (*also* gage), scale, span; remeasure, replumb
2 to cast oneself head first into deep water ⟨A whale suddenly surfaced and then, just as suddenly, *sounded*.⟩ — see DIVE 1

¹sound *n* range of hearing ⟨wandered off, out of her parents' sight and *sound*⟩ — see EARSHOT

²sound *n* a narrow body of water between two land masses ⟨Long Island *Sound* is between Long Island, New York, and Connecticut.⟩ — see CHANNEL 2

sound *adj* **1** according to the rules of logic ⟨*Sound* reasoning alone should tell you that the result is invalid.⟩ — see LOGICAL 1
2 enjoying health and vigor ⟨The horse is getting along in years, but still perfectly *sound*.⟩ — see HEALTHY 1
3 marked by the ability to withstand stress without structural damage or distortion ⟨The shed looks flimsy, but it's actually surprisingly *sound*.⟩ — see STABLE 1

soundless *adj* mostly or entirely without sound ⟨crept in on *soundless* little feet⟩ — see SILENT 3

soundness *n* **1** the ability to withstand force or stress without being distorted, dislodged, or damaged ⟨The car manufacturer tested the *soundness* of the new model in various types of collisions.⟩ — see STABILITY 1
2 the condition of being sound in body ⟨His athletic *soundness* is open to question since he's been away from the sport for so long.⟩ — see HEALTH 1

sound off *vb* **1** to voice one's opinions freely with force ⟨She never missed a chance to *sound off* about the latest political decisions.⟩ — see SPEAK UP
2 to speak so as to be heard at a distance ⟨The guard captain commanded each sentry to *sound off*.⟩ — see CALL 1

soup *n* an atmospheric condition in which suspended particles in the air rob it of its transparency ⟨In *soup* like this, amateur pilots can easily become disoriented.⟩ — see HAZE 1

soupy *adj* **1** filled with or dimmed by fine particles (as of dust or water) in suspension ⟨The *soupy* skies over the island make a nighttime landing a very risky business.⟩ — see HAZY 1
2 having an overly soft liquid consistency ⟨*soupy* ice cream that had been left out on the counter⟩ — see RUNNY

sour *vb* to cause to change from friendly or loving to unfriendly or uncaring ⟨a misunderstanding that *soured* their relationship for a long time⟩ — see ESTRANGE

sour *adj* **1** causing or characterized by the one of the basic taste sensations that is produced chiefly by acids ⟨The *sour* candy made our mouths all wrinkly inside.⟩
synonyms acid, acidic, tart, vinegary
related words dry, soured, unsweetened; pungent, sharp, tangy, zestful, zesty; astringent, puckery; hyperacid
near antonyms sweet; bland, smooth; flat, flavorless, insipid, savorless, tasteless, zestless; dilute, thin, watery, weak
2 not giving pleasure to the mind or senses ⟨You'll have to face up to the *sour* truth of the matter.⟩ — see UNPLEASANT
3 falling short of a standard ⟨Things started off well, but now it's all gone *sour*.⟩ — see BAD 1

source *n* **1** a point or place at which something is invented or provided ⟨We were uncertain as to the *source* of the rumors.⟩ ⟨a *source* of inspiration⟩
synonyms cradle, origin, root, spring, well
related words beginning, commencement, dawn, genesis, inception, launch, onset, outset, start, threshold; ground zero, square one
2 the beginning part of a stream ⟨19th-century explorers who sought the *source* of the Nile⟩ — see HEADWATER
3 something mentioned in a text as providing related and especially supporting information ⟨The professor asked the students to have at least five different *sources* for their papers.⟩ — see REFERENCE 1

souring *n* the loss of friendship or affection ⟨The *souring* of the business partnership led to an ugly legal battle.⟩ — see ESTRANGEMENT

souse *vb* **1** to make wet ⟨A passing car barreled through the puddle and *soused* us good.⟩ — see WET

2 to sink or push (something) briefly into or as if into a liquid ⟨repeatedly *soused* the tools in the tub to get the dirt off⟩ — see DIP 1

3 to wet thoroughly with liquid ⟨Firefighters *soused* the neighboring houses so that they wouldn't catch fire as well.⟩ — see SOAK 1

soused *adj* containing, covered with, or thoroughly penetrated by water ⟨peeled off his *soused* socks and instantly felt much more comfortable⟩ — see WET 1

souvenir *n* something that serves to keep alive the memory of a person or event ⟨kept their love letters as *souvenirs* of their courtship⟩ — see MEMORIAL

sovereign *also* **sovran** *adj* **1** coming before all others in importance ⟨The *sovereign* issue for voters is the performance of the local schools.⟩ — see FOREMOST 1

2 not being under the rule or control of another ⟨a *sovereign* state whose domestic policies are its own business⟩ — see FREE 1

sovereign *also* **sovran** *n* one who rules over a people with a sole, supreme, and usually hereditary authority ⟨After the current *sovereign* dies, the monarchy may be abolished.⟩ — see MONARCH 1

sovereignty *also* **sovranty** *n* **1** the state of being free from the control or power of another ⟨Upon leaving home she felt that she had achieved *sovereignty* for the first time in her life.⟩ — see FREEDOM 1

2 a body of people composed of one or more nationalities usually with its own territory and government ⟨As parts of the same *sovereignty*, the states should not enact laws intended to harm one another economically.⟩ — see NATION

3 controlling power or influence over others ⟨the gradual *sovereignty* of English as the language of international communication⟩ — see SUPREMACY 1

sow *vb* **1** to cover by or as if by scattering something over or on ⟨*Sow* the fields with maize in early spring, and the crop should be ready by late summer.⟩ — see SCATTER 2

2 to put or set into the ground to grow ⟨First *sow* the seeds in potting soil.⟩ — see PLANT 1

3 to set permanently in the consciousness or mind-set ⟨They *sowed* suspicion in our minds.⟩ — see IMPLANT 1

spa *n* a building or room used for sports activities and exercising ⟨a six-month membership in a health *spa*⟩ — see GYM

space *n* **1** an extent or area available for or used up by some activity or thing ⟨How much *space* will you need for the art project?⟩ — see ROOM 1

2 an indefinite but usually short period of time ⟨In the *space* of a few minutes the room had filled up.⟩ — see WHILE 1

3 an incomplete or deficient area ⟨The cancellation created a huge *space* in the dentist's schedule for that day.⟩ — see GAP 3

4 an allowable margin of freedom or variation ⟨The children should be given some *space* to express themselves in their schoolwork.⟩ — see SLACK 1

space-age *adj* being or involving the latest methods, concepts, information, or styles ⟨*space-age* technology that totally transformed the news-gathering business⟩ — see MODERN

spacing *n* the space or amount of space between two points, lines, surfaces, or objects ⟨The *spacing* of the houses was a little tight.⟩ — see DISTANCE 1

spacious *adj* more than adequate or average in capacity ⟨Almost all of the guests were able to fit into the *spacious* living room.⟩

synonyms ample, capacious, commodious, roomy

related words cavernous, voluminous; broad, wide; big, bulky, considerable, generous, goodly, grand, great, handsome, hefty, hulking, large, largish, outsize (*also* outsized), overscale (*or* overscaled), oversize (*or* oversized), sizable (*or* sizeable), substantial, tidy; expansive, extended, extensive, vast; boundless, limitless, unbounded

near antonyms cramped, incommodious, limited, narrow, restricted; small, snug, tight, tiny

span *vb* to find out the size, extent, or amount of ⟨I tried to *span* the distance between the two trees by eye alone.⟩ — see MEASURE 1

spank *n* a hard strike with a part of the body or an instrument ⟨The oar hit the water with a loud *spank*.⟩ — see ¹BLOW

spanking *adj* having much high-spirited energy and movement ⟨a *spanking* and speedy little horse⟩ — see LIVELY 1

spanking *adv* to a great degree ⟨The bathroom tiles were *spanking* white when she finished cleaning them.⟩ — see VERY 1

spare *adj* **1** being over what is needed ⟨I had some *spare* time to kill, so I cleaned up my cubicle a bit.⟩

synonyms excess, extra, redundant, superfluous, supernumerary, surplus

related words accessory, additional, supplemental, supplementary; dispensable, extraneous, gratuitous, needless, nonessential, uncalled-for, unessential, unnecessary, unneeded, unwanted; abundant, ample, bountiful, copious, plenteous, plentiful

near antonyms deficient, inadequate, insufficient, meager (*or* meagre), niggardly, poor, scant, scanty, scarce, short, skimpy, sparse

2 giving or sharing as little as possible ⟨a man who is kind and gentle but definitely *spare* of speech⟩ — see STINGY 1

3 having a noticeably small amount of body fat ⟨a tall, *spare* man⟩ — see THIN 1

4 less plentiful than what is normal, necessary, or desirable ⟨*spare* vegetation that made foraging very difficult⟩ — see MEAGER

spare *n* an interchangeable part or piece of equipment that is kept on hand for replacement of an original ⟨We promptly replaced the burnt-out lightbulb with a *spare*.⟩

synonyms extra, reserve

related words backup, substitute; stock; carbon copy, copy, double, dummy, dupe, duplicate, replacement, replica, replication, reproduction

near antonyms archetype, original, prototype

spare *vb* **1** to use or give out in stingy amounts ⟨I'll have a banana split—and don't *spare* the whipped cream!⟩

synonyms nurse, scant, skimp (on), stint (on)

related words mete (out), portion (out), ration (out); pinch, shortchange; conserve, preserve

near antonyms heap, lavish, pour, rain, shower

2 to avoid unnecessary waste or expense ⟨She had grown up during the Great Depression, so she was no stranger to *sparing*.⟩ — see ECONOMIZE

sparing *adj* **1** careful in the management of money or resources ⟨a *sparing* couple who are trying to save up enough for a house⟩ — see FRUGAL

2 giving or sharing as little as possible ⟨a government agency that has always been *sparing* of public information⟩ — see STINGY 1

3 less plentiful than what is normal, necessary, or desirable ⟨Unfortunately, the explanation of the health insurance plan was somewhat *sparing* on details.⟩ — see MEAGER

spark *n* a very small amount ⟨not a *spark* of interest in the actress's memoirs⟩ — see PARTICLE 1

spark *vb* **1** to give off sparks ⟨The broken radio *sparked* and smoked the instant it was plugged in.⟩
synonyms scintillate, sparkle
related words flash, shine, twinkle; blaze, burn, combust, flame, flare (up), glow, light (up), radiate, scintillate
2 to cause to function ⟨interesting questions that are designed to *spark* the reader's brain⟩ — see ACTIVATE
3 to rouse to strong feeling or action ⟨President Kennedy's inspirational speeches *sparked* a generation of young idealists to enter the public arena.⟩ — see PROVOKE 1

sparkle *vb* **1** to give off sparks ⟨While fireworks that *sparkle* may be entertaining to look at, they can be highly dangerous when used indoors.⟩ — see SPARK 1
2 to shoot forth bursts of light ⟨The crystal *sparkled* in the sunlight.⟩ — see FLASH 1

sparky *adj* having much high-spirited energy and movement ⟨That *sparky* little kid tires me out just looking at him!⟩ — see LIVELY 1

sparse *adj* less plentiful than what is normal, necessary, or desirable ⟨Open land is *sparse* around here.⟩ — see MEAGER

spasm *n* **1** a painful sudden tightening of a muscle ⟨He suffers terribly from back *spasms*.⟩ — see ¹CRAMP
2 a sudden intense expression of strong feeling ⟨a *spasm* of love that he had never experienced before⟩ — see OUTBURST 1

spasmodic *adj* **1** lacking in steadiness or regularity of occurrence ⟨*spasmodic* problems that we will have to deal with as they crop up⟩ — see FITFUL
2 easily excited by nature ⟨a talk show host who was famed for his edgy, *spasmodic* manner⟩ — see EXCITABLE

spat *n* an often noisy or angry expression of differing opinions ⟨Like any couple, they have their *spats*.⟩ — see ARGUMENT 1

spat *vb* to express different opinions about something often angrily ⟨We tend to *spat* over money more than anything else.⟩ — see ARGUE 2

spate *n* **1** a great flow of water or of something that overwhelms ⟨A *spate* of words has been published on this controversial topic.⟩ — see FLOOD
2 a considerable amount ⟨a remark that drew a *spate* of complaints from viewers⟩ — see LOT 2

spatter *vb* **1** to cause (something liquid or mushy) to move along in sheets ⟨A passing car *spattered* mud on her clothes.⟩ — see SPLASH 1
2 to wet or soil by striking with something liquid or mushy ⟨The dog vigorously shook himself, *spattering* the carpet and walls with water.⟩ — see SPLASH 2

spatter *n* a very small amount ⟨A *spatter* of praise for her work was mixed in with quite a lot of criticism.⟩ — see PARTICLE 1

spawn *n* the descendants of a person, animal, or plant ⟨fingerlings that are the *spawn* of adult salmon⟩ — see OFFSPRING

spawn *vb* to be the cause of (a situation, action, or state of mind) ⟨These artists *spawned* a whole new movement in painting.⟩ — see EFFECT

speak *vb* **1** to express (a thought or emotion) in words ⟨finally *spoke* her fears⟩ — see SAY 1
2 to give a formal often extended talk on a subject ⟨The Mayanists have been invited to *speak* about their latest archaeological discoveries.⟩ — see TALK 1

speak (to *or* with) *vb* to communicate with by means of spoken words ⟨We *spoke to* the mall's leasing agent about opening a shop.⟩ — see TALK (TO)

speaker *n* **1** a person in charge of a meeting ⟨The *speaker* announced that it was time for the club to move on to another matter.⟩ — see CHAIR 1

2 a person who speaks for another or for a group ⟨unofficially chose a *speaker* to broach the subject with the supervisor of the department⟩ — see SPOKESPERSON

speak out *vb* to voice one's opinions freely with force ⟨It's a free country, so anyone can *speak out*.⟩ — see SPEAK UP

speak up *vb* to voice one's opinions freely with force ⟨She's never been afraid to *speak up* at town meetings.⟩
synonyms shoot, sound off, speak out, spout (off)
related words bawl, bay, bellow, call, cry, holler, roar, shout, sing (out), thunder, vociferate, yell; articulate, enunciate
phrases speak one's mind
near antonyms clam up, dummy up, hush, shut up, suppress; quiet

spear *vb* to penetrate or hold (something) with a pointed object ⟨*speared* a pickle with her fork⟩ — see IMPALE

spear *n* a weapon with a long straight handle and sharp head or blade ⟨The Roman gladiator thrust his *spear* triumphantly into the lion's side.⟩
synonyms javelin, lance, pike, pikestaff, shaft
related words dart, spike; gaff, halberd (*also* halbert), harpoon, trident

spearhead *vb* to serve as leader of ⟨Martin Luther King, Jr. was among those who *spearheaded* the civil rights movement.⟩ — see LEAD 2

special *adj* **1** being the one or ones of a class with no other members ⟨This is a *special* case and I want you to handle it personally.⟩ — see ONLY 2
2 granted special treatment or attention ⟨one student who was treated as *special* by the teacher⟩ — see DARLING 1
3 of a particular or exact sort ⟨You'll need *special* permission from the fire department to do that.⟩ — see EXPRESS 1

speciality *n* something for which a person shows a special talent ⟨My *speciality* is linguistics.⟩ — see FORTE

specialized *adj* used by or intended for experts in a particular field of knowledge ⟨highly *specialized* terms that have very specific meanings in legal documents⟩ — see TECHNICAL

specialty *n* **1** a region of activity, knowledge, or influence ⟨a doctor with a *specialty* in internal medicine⟩ — see FIELD 2
2 something for which a person shows a special talent ⟨Singing operatic works is my *specialty*.⟩ — see FORTE

species *n* **1** one of the units into which a whole is divided on the basis of a common characteristic ⟨a music that is now generally regarded as a distinct *species* of rap⟩ — see CLASS 2
2 a number of persons or things that are grouped together because they have something in common ⟨In the late 1960s there emerged a new *species* of actor: edgy and not conventionally handsome.⟩ — see SORT 1

specific *adj* **1** of a particular or exact sort ⟨We need a *specific* type of pen to sign the diplomas.⟩ — see EXPRESS 1
2 so clearly expressed as to leave no doubt about the meaning ⟨*specific* instructions regarding the handling of the chemical⟩ — see EXPLICIT

specific *n* **1** a substance or preparation used to treat disease ⟨Quinine is a *specific* for malaria.⟩ — see MEDICINE
2 a single piece of information ⟨Although the speech was long on rhetoric and platitudinous generalities, it lacked *specifics*.⟩ — see FACT 3
3 something that sets apart an individual from others of the same kind ⟨The two submissions differ only in certain *specifics*.⟩ — see CHARACTERISTIC

specificity *n* careful thoroughness of detail ⟨The *specificity* of your description of the medical condition helped in the diagnosis.⟩ — see PARTICULARITY 1

specify *vb* **1** to give the rules about (something) clearly and exactly ⟨The document *specifies* precisely how you may use the information it contains.⟩ — see PRESCRIBE **2** to make reference to or speak about briefly but specifically ⟨Police reports didn't *specify* the model of car the robbers were driving.⟩ — see MENTION 1

specimen *n* **1** a member of the human race ⟨He's a particularly fine *specimen*.⟩ — see HUMAN **2** one of a group or collection that shows what the whole is like ⟨chose one frog as a good *specimen* of the breed⟩ — see EXAMPLE

specious *adj* tending or having power to deceive ⟨a *specious* argument that really does not stand up under close examination⟩ — see DECEPTIVE 1

speck *n* **1** a small area that is different (as in color) from the main part ⟨a lizard with *specks* of white against a green body⟩ — see SPOT 1 **2** a very small amount ⟨not a *speck* of explanation to accompany the book's pictures⟩ — see PARTICLE 1 **3** a very small piece ⟨A *speck* of dust was preventing the laser from reading the disc.⟩ — see BIT 1

speck *vb* to mark with small spots especially unevenly ⟨dirt that had *specked* the windows of the factory for ages⟩ — see SPOT 1

speckle *n* a small area that is different (as in color) from the main part ⟨The cat has a *speckle* of orange right at her whiskers.⟩ — see SPOT 1

speckle *vb* to mark with small spots especially unevenly ⟨*speckled* the cookies with colored sugar⟩ — see SPOT 1

speckled *adj* marked with spots ⟨a *speckled* dog⟩ — see SPOTTED 1

specter *or* **spectre** *n* the soul of a dead person thought of especially as appearing to living people ⟨feeling so terrified that every shadow became a *specter*⟩ — see GHOST 1

spectrum *n* the distance or extent between possible extremes ⟨the complete *spectrum* of opinions on this hotly debated subject⟩ — see RANGE 3

speculate *vb* to form an opinion from little or no evidence ⟨I *speculate* that some animal has been in the cabin.⟩ — see GUESS 1

speculation *n* a risky undertaking ⟨The couple lost all their money in real estate *speculations*.⟩ — see GAMBLE

speculative *adj* existing only as an assumption or speculation ⟨a *speculative* explanation of why this ancient pottery was found hundreds of miles from where it was made⟩ — see THEORETICAL 1

speech *n* **1** a usually formal discourse delivered to an audience ⟨The guest of honor gave a short *speech* in appreciation of the award.⟩
synonyms address, declamation, harangue, oration, talk
related words diatribe, rant, tirade; eulogy, panegyric, tribute; keynote address (*or* keynote speech), lecture, salutatory; homily, sermon; monologue (*also* monolog), soliloquy; pitch, presentation, spiel
2 the stock of words, pronunciation, and grammar used by a people as their basic means of communication ⟨Wanting to develop a writing system for his people, Sequoya created a system of 86 symbols representing all the syllables of Cherokee *speech*.⟩ — see LANGUAGE 1

speechless *adj* **1** deliberately refraining from speech ⟨He remained *speechless*, even in the face of outrageous accusations.⟩ — see SILENT 1 **2** unable to speak ⟨If only this poor, *speechless* animal could tell us what's wrong with it.⟩ — see MUTE 1

speechlessness *n* incapacity for or restraint from speaking ⟨The *speechlessness* of our cat never seemed so frustrating as the time that it was seriously sick.⟩ — see SILENCE 1

speed *n* **1** a high rate of movement or performance ⟨We dashed off the remaining paperwork with as much *speed* as possible so we could leave for the long weekend.⟩
synonyms celerity, fastness, fleetness, haste, hurry, quickness, rapidity, rapidness, speediness, swiftness, velocity
related words clip, gait, pace, rate, tempo; drive, hustle; acceleration, hastiness, precipitation, precipitousness, rush; alacrity, dispatch, expedition, expeditiousness, promptitude, promptness
near antonyms languor, leisureliness, torpidity; deliberateness, deliberation; dilatoriness, lateness, pokiness, procrastination
antonyms slowness, sluggishness
2 a person or thing that is preferred over others ⟨That kind of old-fashioned horror movie is just my *speed*.⟩ — see FAVORITE

speed *vb* to proceed or move quickly ⟨a bullet train *speeding* across the lush countryside⟩ — see HURRY 2

speed (up) *vb* to cause to move or proceed fast or faster ⟨We have to *speed up* production if we are ever going to make the deadline.⟩ — see HURRY 1

speedboat *n* a boat equipped with a motor ⟨*speedboats* leaving wakes that cause damage to docked vessels and the shoreline⟩ — see MOTORBOAT

speedily *adv* with great speed ⟨He *speedily* finished the yard work and left to play ball.⟩ — see FAST 1

speediness *n* a high rate of movement or performance ⟨The *speediness* with which she calculates is simply amazing.⟩ — see SPEED 1

speedy *adj* **1** moving, proceeding, or acting with great speed ⟨a *speedy* worker but not a very careful one, unfortunately⟩ — see FAST 1 **2** done, carried out, or given without delay ⟨I was surprised by and pleased with the company's *speedy* response to my complaints.⟩ — see PROMPT 1

spell *vb* **1** to cast a spell on ⟨It was as if he had *spelled* the public into believing his ridiculous claims.⟩ — see BEWITCH 1 **2** to communicate or convey (as an idea) to the mind ⟨Her boss's resignation *spelled* the end to her troubles.⟩ — see MEAN 1

spell *n* **1** a spoken word or set of words believed to have magic power ⟨The witch cast a *spell* that turned the prince into a toad.⟩
synonyms abracadabra, bewitchment, charm, conjuration, enchantment, hex, incantation
related words curse, jinx; conjuring, magic, mojo, necromancy, sorcery, voodoo, voodooism, witchcraft, witchery, wizardry; amulet, charm, fetish (*also* fetich), phylactery, talisman
2 a sudden experiencing of a physical or mental disorder ⟨a dizzy *spell* that caused me to fall⟩ — see ATTACK 2 **3** an indefinite but usually short period of time ⟨Come rest a *spell*.⟩ — see WHILE 1

spellbind *vb* to hold the attention of as if by a spell ⟨The tale about pirates and their buried treasure had completely *spellbound* the children.⟩ — see ENTHRALL 1

spellbound *adj* being or appearing to be under a magic spell ⟨She's a storyteller that will keep you *spellbound*.⟩ — see ENCHANTED

spell out *vb* to make plain or understandable ⟨The contract *spelled out* the terms of the deal.⟩ — see EXPLAIN 1

spend *vb* **1** to hand over or use up in payment ⟨I always end up *spending* too much money at the store.⟩
synonyms disburse, drop, expend, give, lay out, outlay, pay
related words lavish, rain; blow, dissipate, fritter (away), run through, squander, throw away, waste
near antonyms cache, hoard, lay up, save; acquire, earn, gain, garner, make, procure, realize, secure, win

2 to make complete use of ⟨The town has already *spent* its budget for snow removal, and it's only January.⟩ — see DEPLETE 1

3 to use up carelessly ⟨*spent* all his energy on impractical schemes⟩ — see WASTE 1

spender *n* someone who spends money freely or foolishly ⟨The restaurant gives big *spenders* special treatment.⟩ — see PRODIGAL

spendthrift *adj* given to spending money freely or foolishly ⟨*Spendthrift* consumers had amassed a mountain of debt on their credit cards.⟩ — see PRODIGAL

spendthrift *n* someone who spends money freely or foolishly ⟨The *spendthrift* managed to blow all of his inheritance in a single year.⟩ — see PRODIGAL

spent *adj* depleted in strength, energy, or freshness ⟨He plopped down in his chair, completely *spent*, and then fell asleep.⟩ — see WEARY 1

spew *vb* **1** to flow out in great quantities or with force ⟨water *spewing* violently from the broken pipe⟩ — see GUSH 1

2 to violently throw out or off (something from within) ⟨a volcano *spewing* out lava⟩ — see ERUPT 1

3 to discharge the contents of the stomach through the mouth ⟨"I'm going to *spew* right here in the car if you don't pull over!" she wailed to her friend.⟩ — see VOMIT

sphere *n* **1** a more or less round body or mass ⟨This *sphere* that we live on is just a tiny speck in the universe.⟩ — see ¹BALL 1

2 a region of activity, knowledge, or influence ⟨Higher mathematics is a little outside my *sphere*.⟩ — see FIELD 2

3 a ball-shaped gaseous celestial body that shines by its own light ⟨Perhaps there is indeed life on planets circling *spheres* in galaxies far, far away.⟩ — see STAR 1

spherical *adj* having every part of the surface the same distance from the center ⟨The planet Earth is not, in fact, perfectly *spherical*.⟩ — see ROUND 1

spice *n* **1** a sweet or pleasant smell ⟨a cologne for men that captures all of the *spice* of the sea⟩ — see FRAGRANCE

2 something (as an herb) that adds an agreeable or interesting taste to food ⟨She used several different *spices* in her secret chili recipe.⟩ — see SEASONING 1

3 the quality or state of being stimulating to the mind or senses ⟨A new hobby will add *spice* to your life.⟩ — see PIQUANCY

spice *vb* to make more pleasant to the taste by adding something intensely flavored ⟨*Spice* the stew with more pepper.⟩ — see SEASON 1

spick–and–span *or* **spic–and–span** *adj* **1** free from dirt or stain ⟨Let's make the house *spick-and-span* for our visitors.⟩ — see CLEAN 1

2 recently made and never used before ⟨Breakfast came from a *spick-and-span* waffle iron that our host was obviously using for the first time.⟩ — see NEW 3

spicy *adj* hinting at or intended to call to mind matters regarded as indecent ⟨a *spicy* story⟩ — see SUGGESTIVE 1

spigot *n* a fixture for controlling the flow of a liquid ⟨The plumber has installed a new *spigot* over the kitchen sink.⟩ — see FAUCET

spike *vb* **1** to penetrate or hold (something) with a pointed object ⟨Scorpions use their stinger-equipped tails to *spike* their prey.⟩ — see IMPALE

2 to give life, vigor, or spirit to ⟨He *spiked* what otherwise would have been a dry economic lecture with some jokes and anecdotes.⟩ — see ANIMATE

spill *n* the act of going down from an upright position suddenly and involuntarily ⟨She tripped over the toy and had a nasty *spill* on the stairs.⟩ — see FALL 1

spill *vb* to make known (as information previously kept secret) ⟨The actor's butler *spilled* the secret to a tabloid for $40,000.⟩ — see REVEAL 1

spin *n* **1** a rapid turning about on an axis or central point ⟨The ice skater moved into a tight *spin* at the end of her routine.⟩

synonyms gyration, pirouette, reel, revolution, roll, rotation, twirl, wheel, whirl

related words circulation, ring, round; coil, curl, curve, spiral, twist, whorl; circle, orbit; eddy, swirl

2 a state of mental confusion ⟨The news left me all in a *spin*.⟩ — see HAZE 2

3 a short trip for pleasure ⟨a family out for a *spin* on a beautiful Sunday afternoon⟩ — see EXCURSION 1

spin *vb* **1** to move in circles around an axis or center ⟨*Spinning* on its axis, the Earth makes one complete rotation every 23 hours 56 minutes 4 seconds.⟩

synonyms gyrate, pirouette, revolve, roll, rotate, turn, twirl, wheel, whirl

related words coil, curl, curve, round, spiral, swirl, twine, twist, wind; circle, circulate, encircle, orbit, ring; pivot

2 to be in a confused state as if from being twirled around ⟨My head *spun* as I contemplated all the possible problems this restructuring could cause.⟩

synonyms reel, swim, turn, whirl

related words swirl

near antonyms calm, collect; settle, steady

3 to move (something) in a curved or circular path on or as if on an axis ⟨*spun* the child around until he was hopelessly dizzy⟩ — see TURN 1

spinal column *n* a column of bones supporting the trunk of a vertebrate animal ⟨a diagram of the *spinal column*⟩ — see SPINE

spindling *adj* being tall, thin and usually loose-jointed ⟨a sickly, *spindling* child who spent most of his time indoors⟩ — see LANKY

spindly *adj* being tall, thin and usually loose-jointed ⟨*Spindly* water birds waded through the reeds.⟩ — see LANKY

spine *n* a column of bones supporting the trunk of a vertebrate animal ⟨He hurt his *spine* in the accident, but the doctor says he'll be walking again in no time.⟩

synonyms backbone, chine, spinal column, vertebral column

related words back, spinal cord, vertebra

spineless *adj* **1** lacking strength of will or character ⟨a *spineless* manager who never stands up for the members of his staff⟩ — see WEAK 2

2 having or showing a shameful lack of courage ⟨*spineless* seamen who trembled at the first roar of the cannon⟩ — see COWARDLY

spinelessness *n* **1** the quality or state of lacking strength of will or character ⟨The organization's members assailed the *spinelessness* of the leadership.⟩ — see WEAKNESS 2

2 a shameful lack of courage in the face of danger ⟨accused the midshipman of *spinelessness* under fire⟩ — see COWARDICE

spin–off *n* something that naturally develops or is developed from something else ⟨a *spin-off* of the popular television series⟩ — see DERIVATIVE

spiny *adj* requiring exceptional skill or caution in performance or handling ⟨This promises to be a *spiny* problem to negotiate.⟩ — see TRICKY 1

spiral *vb* to follow a circular or spiral course ⟨a narrow road *spiraling* up the mountain to the summit⟩ — see WIND 1

spiral *adj* turning around an axis like the thread of a screw ⟨A *spiral* staircase takes visitors up into the Statue of Liberty.⟩

synonyms coiling, corkscrew, helical, screwlike, winding

related words circular; curling, curving, swirly, twisting

near antonyms lineal, linear, right, straight

spirit *n* **1** an immaterial force within a human being thought to give the body life, energy, and power ⟨the theological and philosophical belief that the *spirit* is superior to the body⟩ — see SOUL 1
2 a state of mind dominated by a particular emotion ⟨had been in a combative *spirit* all week⟩ — see MOOD 1
3 the soul of a dead person thought of especially as appearing to living people ⟨Hamlet's late father appears to him in the form of a *spirit* and with the revelation that he was in fact murdered.⟩ — see GHOST 1
4 spirits *pl* a distilled beverage that can make a person drunk ⟨a store selling *spirits*⟩ — see ALCOHOL
spirited *adj* **1** marked by a lively display of strong feeling ⟨The town meeting featured a *spirited* debate about the proposed ban on skateboarding in the plaza downtown.⟩
synonyms fiery, gingery, high-spirited, mettlesome, peppery, spunky
related words aggressive, ambitious, assertive, high-pressure, in-your-face, militant; animate, animated, bouncing, brisk, energetic, frisky, jaunty, jazzy, peppy, perky, pert, racy, scrappy, snappy, spanking, sparky, sprightly, springy, vital, vivacious, zippy; ardent, fervent, impassioned, passionate; emphatic, obtrusive
near antonyms bloodless, boring, dull, lifeless; dead, lackadaisical, languid, languorous, limp, listless; inert, lethargic, sleepy, sluggish, tired, torpid; low-pressure, nonassertive, unaggressive, unambitious, unassertive, unenterprising
antonyms halfhearted, leaden, spiritless
2 having much high-spirited energy and movement ⟨a team known for its *spirited* and in-your-face basketball⟩ — see LIVELY 1
spiritedly *adv* in a quick and spirited manner ⟨The two spaniels ran *spiritedly* into the surf.⟩ — see GAILY 2
spiritless *adj* lacking bodily energy or motivation ⟨He was *spiritless* and depressed for weeks after being fired.⟩ — see LISTLESS
spiritual *adj* **1** not composed of matter ⟨A staunch skeptic and realist, he scoffs at the very notion of ghosts and other *spiritual* entities.⟩ — see IMMATERIAL 1
2 of, relating to, or used in the practice or worship services of a religion ⟨*spiritual* songs that have been sung by generations of worshippers⟩ — see RELIGIOUS 1
spiritual *n* a religious song ⟨sang a *spiritual* at the funeral⟩ — see HYMN 1
¹spit *n* an area of land that juts out into a body of water ⟨At the northeast end of the island is a long *spit* whose terminal is crowned by a towering lighthouse.⟩ — see ²CAPE
²spit *n* **1** something or someone that strongly resembles another ⟨the *spit* and image of his father⟩ — see IMAGE 1
2 the fluid that is secreted into the mouth by certain glands ⟨so dry that he felt as if he had no *spit* left in his mouth⟩ — see SALIVA
spit *vb* to penetrate or hold (something) with a pointed object ⟨*spitting* shrimp and placing them over the coals⟩ — see IMPALE
spite *n* the desire to cause pain for the satisfaction of doing harm ⟨spread cruel lies out of pure *spite*⟩ — see MALICE
spite *vb* to disturb the peace of mind of (someone) especially by repeated disagreeable acts ⟨Sometimes, I swear, she keeps doing that just to *spite* me.⟩ — see IRRITATE 1
spiteful *adj* having or showing a desire to cause someone pain or suffering for the sheer enjoyment of it ⟨a *spiteful* gossip⟩ — see HATEFUL
spitefully *adv* in a mean or spiteful manner ⟨She *spitefully* refused my request.⟩ — see NASTILY
spitefulness *n* the desire to cause pain for the satisfaction of doing harm ⟨cut down their neighbors' tree out of sheer *spitefulness*⟩ — see MALICE

spittle *n* the fluid that is secreted into the mouth by certain glands ⟨unaware that *spittle* was leaking out of his mouth while he slept⟩ — see SALIVA
spit up *vb* to discharge the contents of the stomach through the mouth ⟨The baby finished nursing and promptly *spit up*.⟩ — see VOMIT
splash *n* a very small amount ⟨I like just a *splash* of milk in my coffee.⟩ — see PARTICLE 1
splash *vb* **1** to cause (something liquid or mushy) to move along in sheets ⟨rowdy teenagers *splashing* water at each other in the community pool⟩
synonyms dash, slop, slosh, spatter, swash
related words dabble, lap, plash, wash; spray, sprinkle, spritz; squirt
2 to wet or soil by striking with something liquid or mushy ⟨The bus *splashed* us as it barrelled through the puddles.⟩
synonyms bespatter, dash, plash, spatter, splatter
related words drench, drown, impregnate, saturate, soak, sop, souse, steep; bathe, douse (*also* dowse), wash, water; slop, slush, spray, sprinkle, squirt
3 to flow along or against ⟨Water constantly *splashing* the wooden pilings eventually weakened them.⟩ — see WASH 1
4 to flow in a broken irregular stream ⟨The spilled juice *splashed* over the counter and onto the floor.⟩ — see GURGLE
5 to move with a splashing motion ⟨a baby *splashing* about in the tub⟩ — see SLOSH 1
splashy *adj* **1** likely to attract attention ⟨a *splashy* new restaurant that's currently the in place to go⟩ — see NOTICEABLE
2 attractively eye-catching in style ⟨a *splashy* ad for the new brand of blue jeans⟩ — see JAZZY 1
3 excessively showy ⟨*splashy* Hawaiian shirts⟩ — see GAUDY
splatter *vb* to wet or soil by striking with something liquid or mushy ⟨The house painters accidentally *splattered* my car with paint.⟩ — see SPLASH 2
spleen *n* **1** an intense emotional state of displeasure with someone or something ⟨vented her *spleen* and felt much better for having done so⟩ — see ANGER
2 the desire to cause pain for the satisfaction of doing harm ⟨The bill's failure to pass in the legislature was due to nothing more than partisan *spleen*.⟩ — see MALICE
splendid *adj* **1** large and impressive in size, grandeur, extent, or conception ⟨a *splendid* mansion in the Georgian style⟩ — see GRAND 1
2 of the very best kind ⟨The restaurant's chef can always be relied upon to prepare a *splendid* dinner.⟩ — see EXCELLENT
3 giving off or reflecting much light ⟨a *splendid* diamond that must have been worth a king's ransom⟩ — see BRIGHT 1
splendidly *adv* in a pleasing way ⟨The graduation party went *splendidly*.⟩ — see WELL 5
splendor *n* **1** impressiveness of beauty on a large scale ⟨The *splendor* of the ancient monument awed us into silence.⟩ — see MAGNIFICENCE
2 the quality or state of having or giving off light ⟨The *splendor* of the huge diamond can scarcely be described.⟩ — see BRILLIANCE 1
3 something extraordinary or surprising ⟨Some of the many *splendors* of the reign of Tutankhamen are on display in this new travelling exhibition.⟩ — see WONDER 1
splenetic *adj* having or showing a habitually bad temper ⟨The newspaper publisher's *splenetic* editorials often struck fear into local politicians.⟩ — see ILL-TEMPERED
splint *n* a small flat piece separated from a whole ⟨a *splint* off the board⟩ — see CHIP 1

splinter *n* a small flat piece separated from a whole ⟨She got a *splinter* from the unfinished wall.⟩ — see CHIP 1

splinter *vb* to cut into long slender pieces ⟨*splintered* the carrots into little sticks⟩ — see SLIVER

split *adj* disagreeing with each other ⟨Opinions are *split* on the subject.⟩ — see DIVIDED

split *n* **1** an irregular usually narrow break in a surface created by pressure ⟨An earthquake left a *split* in the ground.⟩ — see CRACK 1
2 the act or process of a whole separating into two or more parts or pieces ⟨The *split* of the group into two factions marked the beginning of the end of the organization.⟩ — see SEPARATION 1

split *vb* to set or force apart ⟨*split* logs for the winter's supply of wood⟩ — see SEPARATE 1

split–second *adj* done or occurring without any noticeable lapse in time ⟨a day trader who is used to making *split-second* decisions⟩ — see INSTANTANEOUS

split second *n* a very small space of time ⟨In a *split second* it was all over.⟩ — see INSTANT

splotch *n* a small area that is different (as in color) from the main part ⟨The bleach left a small white *splotch* on my shirt.⟩ — see SPOT 1

splotch *vb* to mark with small spots especially unevenly ⟨Ink from a leaking pen had badly *splotched* his shirt pocket.⟩ — see SPOT 1

splotched *adj* having blotches of two or more colors ⟨a *splotched* tan and white puppy⟩ — see PIED

splotchy *adj* marked with spots ⟨a country road *splotchy* with patches of snow⟩ — see SPOTTED 1

spoil *n* valuables stolen or taken by force ⟨The bandits escaped with their lives but not with the *spoils*.⟩ — see LOOT

spoil *vb* **1** to affect slightly with something morally bad or undesirable ⟨The grandparents tended to *spoil* their only grandchild.⟩ — see TAINT 1
2 to go through decomposition ⟨The meat has *spoiled*.⟩ — see DECAY 1
3 to reduce the soundness, effectiveness, or perfection of ⟨Know when to stop, for an unnecessary brushstroke can *spoil* a painted portrait.⟩ — see DAMAGE 1
4 to treat with great or excessive care ⟨The hotel *spoils* their guests with fine dining and excellent service.⟩ — see BABY

spoilage *n* the process by which dead organic matter separates into simpler substances ⟨In the days before refrigeration, *spoilage* was a constant problem.⟩ — see CORRUPTION 1

spoiled *adj* having undergone organic breakdown ⟨*spoiled* milk⟩ — see ROTTEN 1

spoilsport *n* a person who spoils the pleasure of others ⟨If you don't want to play, at least don't be a *spoilsport*.⟩ — see KILLJOY

spoken *adj* **1** made or carried on through speaking rather than in writing ⟨A *spoken* agreement is too easily broken.⟩ — see VERBAL 2
2 expressed or communicated by voice ⟨a politician who knows the power of the *spoken* word⟩ — see VOCAL

spokesman *n* a person who speaks for another or for a group ⟨a *spokesman* for the cattle industry⟩ — see SPOKESPERSON

spokesperson *n* a person who speaks for another or for a group ⟨The *spokesperson* for the protesting students presented their demands to the administration.⟩
synonyms mouthpiece, prophet, speaker, spokesman
related words spokesmodel, spokeswoman; front, promoter; communicator, sayer, talker; agent, ambassador, delegate, emissary, envoy, representative

sponge *n* a person who is supported by or seeks support from another without making an adequate return ⟨finally told the *sponge* to move out of their house and to get a job⟩ — see LEECH

sponge *vb* to take in (something liquid) through small openings ⟨The ground quickly *sponged* up the much-needed rain.⟩ — see ABSORB 1

sponger *n* a person who is supported by or seeks support from another without making an adequate return ⟨a spoiled *sponger* who, after college, moved back in with her parents and seems to be in no hurry to get a job⟩ — see LEECH

spongy *adj* **1** giving easily to the touch ⟨*Spongy* moss covered the ground.⟩ — see SOFT 3
2 able to soak up liquids especially readily ⟨Generously pour the syrup over the cake, which is so *spongy* that it will absorb most of the liquid.⟩ — see ABSORBENT

sponsor *n* a person who takes the responsibility for some other person or thing ⟨You'll need a *sponsor* to recommend you in order to get into the exclusive country club.⟩
synonyms backer, guarantor, patron, surety
related words chaperone (*or* chaperon); advocate, champion, supporter; angel, benefactor, underwriter; coach, mentor, teacher; cosponsor

spontaneity *n* carefree freedom from constraint ⟨The couple sacrificed some of the *spontaneity* in their lives when they had a baby.⟩ — see ABANDON

spontaneous *adj* done instantly and without conscious thought or decision ⟨Hugging a crying child is simply a *spontaneous* reaction.⟩ — see AUTOMATIC 1

spontaneousness *n* carefree freedom from constraint ⟨Her friends loved her for her natural *spontaneousness*.⟩ — see ABANDON

spoof *n* a work that imitates and exaggerates another work for comic effect ⟨Many viewers thought that the *spoof* of a television newscast was the real thing.⟩ — see PARODY 1

spoof *vb* **1** to copy or exaggerate (someone or something) in order to make fun of ⟨*spoofed* overly competitive parents in a mockumentary about tryouts for a national T-ball team⟩ — see MIMIC 1
2 to cause to believe what is untrue ⟨The newspaper was *spoofed* by a supposedly plausible claim of a UFO encounter.⟩ — see DECEIVE

spook *n* **1** a person who tries secretly to obtain information for one country in the territory of another usually unfriendly country ⟨a novel about a *spook* during the Cold War⟩ — see SPY
2 the soul of a dead person thought of especially as appearing to living people ⟨Halloween is the night when *spooks* and goblins are said to roam abroad.⟩ — see GHOST 1

spook *vb* to strike with fear ⟨The sudden noise *spooked* her out of her skin.⟩ — see FRIGHTEN

spooked *adj* filled with fear or dread ⟨Ichabod Crane was so *spooked* that he left Sleepy Hollow for good.⟩ — see AFRAID

spooky *adj* **1** easily excited by nature ⟨a *spooky* horse shying at shadows⟩ — see EXCITABLE
2 fearfully and mysteriously strange or fantastic ⟨a *spooky* tale of strange hauntings and mysterious reincarnations⟩ — see EERIE

spoon *vb* to lift out with something that holds liquid ⟨My mom lovingly *spooned* the homemade stew out of the pot.⟩ — see DIP 2

spoon *n* a utensil with a bowl and a handle that is used especially in cooking and serving food ⟨An assortment of metal and wooden *spoons* should be part of every cook's culinary arsenal.⟩
synonyms dipper, ladle, scoop

related words skimmer; dessertspoon, soupspoon, tablespoon, teaspoon

sporadic *adj* **1** lacking in steadiness or regularity of occurrence ⟨*Sporadic* loud noises kept startling everyone.⟩ — see FITFUL

2 not often occurring or repeated ⟨So long as the complaints remain *sporadic*, we're doing fine.⟩ — see INFREQUENT

sport *n* **1** activity engaged in to amuse oneself ⟨I don't care whether I actually catch any fish, as I'm just doing this for *sport*.⟩ — see PLAY 1

2 an attitude or manner not to be taken seriously ⟨Arm wrestling that began in *sport* suddenly turned serious.⟩ — see FUN 2

3 the making of unkind jokes as a way of showing one's scorn for someone or something ⟨got in trouble for making *sport* of his little brother's security blanket⟩ — see RIDICULE

4 a person or thing that is made fun of ⟨The old junker he drove became the *sport* of his group even though they all rode in it.⟩ — see LAUGHINGSTOCK

sport *vb* **1** to engage in activity for amusement ⟨From sailing to snorkeling, each day we *sported* at a different activity offered by the beach resort.⟩ — see PLAY 1

2 to play and run about happily ⟨the millionaire's grandchildren *sporting* on the estate's spacious grounds⟩ — see FROLIC 1

3 to present so as to invite notice or attention ⟨Jake *sported* his flashy new car by driving it all over town.⟩ — see SHOW 1

sportive *adj* given to good-natured joking or teasing ⟨a *sportive* professor who began every lecture with a joke⟩ — see PLAYFUL

sportiveness *n* a natural disposition for playful behavior ⟨Her high-spirited *sportiveness* can sometimes distract her and others from serious work.⟩ — see PLAYFULNESS

sportsmanlike *adj* following or according to the rules ⟨admired by the fans for his *sportsmanlike* conduct on the ice⟩ — see FAIR 3

sportsmanly *adj* following or according to the rules ⟨In wrestling, biting is not *sportsmanly*, and will result in a forfeit.⟩ — see FAIR 3

spot *n* **1** a small area that is different (as in color) from the main part ⟨In summer the white coat of the snow leopard is studded with brownish black *spots*.⟩

synonyms blotch, dapple, dot, eyespot, fleck, mottle, patch, pip, point, speck, speckle, splotch

related words birthmark, freckle, mole; blob, blot, smear, smudge, stain; spatter, splash; polka dot

2 a difficult, puzzling, or embarrassing situation from which there is no easy escape ⟨We're in a bit of a *spot* right now with our mortgage payments.⟩ — see PREDICAMENT

3 a mark of guilt or disgrace ⟨scandalous conduct that will forever be a *spot* upon the family name⟩ — see STAIN 1

4 a very small amount ⟨Tom had only a *spot* of stew for dinner, as he wasn't very hungry.⟩ — see PARTICLE 1

5 the area or space occupied by or intended for something ⟨The cat grabbed my *spot* on the couch the minute I stood up.⟩ — see PLACE 1

spot *vb* **1** to mark with small spots especially unevenly ⟨To give the effect of sunlight on water, the artist *spotted* the lake in his painting with flecks of gold paint.⟩

synonyms blotch, dapple, dot, fleck, freckle, marble, mottle, pepper, speck, speckle, splotch, sprinkle, stipple

related words blot, dye, stain; band, bar, streak, stripe; intersperse, set, stud; bespatter, spatter

2 to make note of (something) through the use of one's eyes ⟨I *spotted* both of them as they tried to sneak out the back door.⟩ — see SEE 1

spotless *adj* free from dirt or stain ⟨a *spotless* white dress⟩ — see CLEAN 1

spotted *adj* **1** marked with spots ⟨The *spotted* tablecloth clashed with the stripes on the wallpaper.⟩

synonyms dappled (*also* dapple), dotted, flecked, freckled, mottled, speckled, splotchy, spotty, stippled, variegated

related words spangled; marbled, moiré (*or* moire), veined; colorful, motley, multicolored, polychromatic, polychrome, varicolored, variegated; blotched, piebald, pinto, roan

near antonyms solid

antonyms unspotted

2 having blotches of two or more colors ⟨Not surprisingly, the white cow and black bull had a *spotted* calf.⟩ — see PIED

spotting *n* the act or process of sighting or learning the existence of something for the first time ⟨The *spotting* of a new bird is always a thrill for an avid bird-watcher.⟩ — see DISCOVERY 1

spotty *adj* **1** lacking in steadiness or regularity of occurrence ⟨Only *spotty* business failures marred the economic boom.⟩ — see FITFUL

2 marked with spots ⟨Dalmatians are *spotty* dogs.⟩ — see SPOTTED 1

spouse *n* the person to whom another is married ⟨Employees and their *spouses* are covered by the health plan.⟩

synonyms better half, consort, mate, partner

related words soul mate; bridegroom, husband, man, old man; bride, helpmate, helpmeet, lady, wife

near antonyms ex; single; bachelor; bachelorette, maid, maiden, spinster

spout *n* **1** a pipe or channel for carrying off water from a roof ⟨During the winter, runoff from the *spout* tends to freeze over and form a dangerous patch of ice on the walkway.⟩ — see GUTTER 1

2 a usually forceful stream of fluid discharged from a narrow opening ⟨kids cooling off under the *spout* of water from an opened fire hydrant⟩ — see JET

spout *vb* **1** to flow out in great quantities or with force ⟨water *spouting* from the hose⟩ — see GUSH 1

2 to talk loudly and wildly ⟨a self-important loudmouth who is always *spouting* about the mess that politicians have made of everything⟩ — see RANT

3 to violently throw out or off (something from within) ⟨The drain suddenly *spouted* water and debris.⟩ — see ERUPT 1

spout (off) *vb* to voice one's opinions freely with force ⟨got in trouble for *spouting off* in class in a disrespectful way⟩ — see SPEAK UP

spray *vb* to cover by or as if by scattering something over or on ⟨*sprayed* the lawn with pesticides⟩ — see SCATTER 1

spread *n* **1** a decorative cloth used as a top covering for a bed ⟨bought a brightly colored *spread* for summer⟩ — see COUNTERPANE

2 a large fancy meal often accompanied by ceremony or entertainment ⟨They really know how to put out a good *spread*.⟩ — see FEAST 1

3 a wide space or area ⟨a vast *spread* of land just waiting to be settled⟩ — see EXPANSE

4 the distance or extent between possible extremes ⟨The *spread* of grades was from 15 to 79 on that quiz.⟩ — see RANGE 3

5 the space or amount of space between two points, lines, surfaces, or objects ⟨a *spread* of nearly 100 miles between farms⟩ — see DISTANCE 1

spread *vb* **1** to cause to be known over a considerable area or by many people ⟨*Spread* the news!⟩

synonyms broadcast, circulate, disseminate, propagate

related words radiate, sprawl; diffuse, dispense, disperse, dissipate, scatter, sow; communicate, convey, impart, pass (on), transmit
near antonyms cloak, conceal, enshroud, hide, mask, obscure, secrete, shroud, veil; contain, limit, restrict
2 to put a layer of on a surface ⟨We *spread* the fertilizer over the lawn evenly until it was fully covered.⟩
synonyms apply, lay
related words anoint, bedaub, besmear, dab, daub, plaster, slather, smear; blanket, carpet, coat, cover, layer, mantle, overlay, overspread, sheet, surface
near antonyms bare, expose, peel, strip, uncover
3 to become known ⟨Once news of the war's end had *spread*, spontaneous celebrations broke out everywhere.⟩ — see GET OUT 1
4 to cause (something) to pass from one to another ⟨living conditions that help to *spread* the disease⟩ — see COMMUNICATE 1
5 to go or move in different directions from a central point ⟨The walls of the old barn *spread* under the weight of the snow on the roof.⟩ — see SEPARATE 2
6 to become greater in extent, volume, amount, or number ⟨The popularity of the style *spread* quickly.⟩ — see INCREASE 2
spread (out) *vb* to arrange the parts of (something) over a wider area ⟨Let's *spread* the puzzle *out* on the floor and see what we've got.⟩ — see OPEN 3
spreading *adj* exciting a similar feeling or reaction in others ⟨*spreading* enthusiasm that got our club rolling again⟩ — see CONTAGIOUS 2
spree *n* a time or instance of carefree fun ⟨went on a spending *spree*⟩ — see FLING 1
sprightliness *n* the quality or state of having abundant or intense activity ⟨The *sprightliness* of the young girl made us tired just watching her.⟩ — see VITALITY 1
sprightly *adj* having much high-spirited energy and movement ⟨a *sprightly* child who often claims to be too tired to move when it's time to do chores⟩ — see LIVELY 1
sprightly *adv* in a quick and spirited manner ⟨Every morning the elderly couple *sprightly* sets out on a walk.⟩ — see GAILY 2
spring *n* **1** an act of leaping into the air ⟨The deer gave a sudden *spring* and disappeared into the woods.⟩ — see JUMP 1
2 a point or place at which something is invented or provided ⟨The *springs* of this time-honored tradition run too deep to allow for easy explanation.⟩ — see SOURCE 1
spring *vb* **1** to come into existence ⟨When it comes to love and romance, hope *springs* eternally.⟩ — see BEGIN 2
2 to propel oneself upward or forward into the air ⟨The cat *sprang* and pounced on the mouse.⟩ — see JUMP 1
3 to release (as from slavery or confinement) ⟨had to spend a night in jail until their lawyer could come to *spring* them⟩ — see FREE 1
spring (for) *vb* to give what is owed for ⟨offered to *spring for* dinner for the whole gang⟩ — see PAY 2
spring (up) *vb* to come to one's attention especially gradually or unexpectedly ⟨A new issue *sprang up* at yesterday's meeting of the school board.⟩ — see ARISE 2
springy *adj* **1** able to revert to original size and shape after being stretched, squeezed, or twisted ⟨pillows made with *springy* foam that bounces right back⟩ — see ELASTIC 1
2 having much high-spirited energy and movement ⟨walks with a *springy* step⟩ — see LIVELY 1
sprinkle *n* **1** a light or fine rain ⟨decided it was not worth carrying an umbrella for just a *sprinkle*⟩ — see DRIZZLE
2 a small number ⟨received only a *sprinkle* of suggestions for the name of the school mascot⟩ — see FEW
sprinkle *vb* **1** to cover by or as if by scattering something

over or on ⟨You need to *sprinkle* the newly seeded lawn with water.⟩ — see SCATTER 2
2 to mark with small spots especially unevenly ⟨*sprinkled* the cake with bits of coconut⟩ — see SPOT 1
sprinkling *n* **1** a small number ⟨A *sprinkling* of fans showed up at the airport.⟩ — see FEW
2 a very small amount ⟨just a *sprinkling* of experience with the computer program⟩ — see PARTICLE 1
sprint *vb* to go at a pace faster than a walk ⟨He *sprinted* off to class so as to avoid being late.⟩ — see RUN 1
sprite *n* **1** an imaginary being usually having a small human form and magical powers ⟨The child insisted that he'd seen a *sprite* hiding in the garden.⟩ — see FAIRY
2 the soul of a dead person thought of especially as appearing to living people ⟨told hair-raising stories of *sprites* and spectral ships⟩ — see GHOST 1
spruce *adj* being strikingly neat and trim in style or appearance ⟨a *spruce* man in a tailor-made business suit⟩ — see SMART 1
sprucely *adv* in a strikingly neat and trim manner ⟨*Sprucely* dressed, I set out for my first job interview.⟩ — see SMARTLY
spry *adj* moving easily ⟨an older woman who's still surprisingly *spry*⟩ — see GRACEFUL 1
spryness *n* ease and grace in physical activity ⟨has the *spryness* and flexibility of a professional athlete⟩ — see DEXTERITY 2
spume *n* a light mass of fine bubbles formed in or on a liquid ⟨*spume* floating on the ocean⟩ — see FOAM
spunk *n* the strength of mind that enables a person to endure pain or hardship ⟨He had the *spunk* to overcome a severe physical disability.⟩ — see FORTITUDE
spunky *adj* marked by a lively display of strong feeling ⟨a *spunky* determination to make the best of a bad situation⟩ — see SPIRITED 1
spur *n* **1** something that arouses action or activity ⟨The threat of losing its only sports franchise was the *spur* the city council needed to finally do something about the old arena.⟩ — see IMPULSE 1
2 a structure that holds up or serves as a foundation for something else ⟨a weak wall that might need a *spur*⟩ — see SUPPORT 1
spur *vb* to urge or push forward with or as if with a pointed object ⟨gently *spurred* the horse with his heels⟩ — see PROD 1
spurious *adj* being such in appearance only and made or manufactured with the intention of committing fraud ⟨a *spurious* Picasso painting that wouldn't have fooled an art expert for a second⟩ — see COUNTERFEIT 1
spurn *vb* to show unwillingness to accept, do, engage in, or agree to ⟨Fiercely independent, the elderly couple *spurned* all offers of financial help.⟩ — see DECLINE 1
spur–of–the–moment *adj* made or done without previous thought or preparation ⟨a *spur-of-the-moment* trip to the zoo⟩ — see EXTEMPORANEOUS
spurt *n* **1** a sudden and usually temporary growth of activity ⟨a *spurt* of economic growth for the first quarter of the year⟩ — see OUTBREAK 1
2 a usually forceful stream of fluid discharged from a narrow opening ⟨A sudden *spurt* of water rushed out from the cracked pipe.⟩ — see JET
spurt *vb* **1** to flow out in great quantities or with force ⟨Water *spurted* from the garden hose just as I was checking the nozzle.⟩ — see GUSH 1
2 to violently throw out or off (something from within) ⟨The pipe suddenly cracked and began *spurting* water.⟩ — see ERUPT 1
sputter *vb* to speak rapidly, inarticulately, and usually unintelligibly ⟨She was so shocked that, for a moment, all she could do was *sputter*.⟩ — see BABBLE 1

spy *vb* to make note of (something) through the use of one's eyes ⟨I *spy* a motel off in the distance, so let's spend the night there.⟩ — see SEE 1

spy *n* a person who tries secretly to obtain information for one country in the territory of another usually unfriendly country ⟨The government *spy* risked his life every day.⟩

synonyms agent, emissary, operative, spook

related words courier; counterspy; infiltrator, informer, stool pigeon

phrases secret agent, undercover agent

spying *n* the secret gathering of information on others ⟨a secret group engaged in *spying* during the war⟩ — see ESPIONAGE

squabble *n* an often noisy or angry expression of differing opinions ⟨Frightened by noise of the *squabble*, the cat hid under the couch.⟩ — see ARGUMENT 1

squabble *vb* to express different opinions about something often angrily ⟨The children *squabbled* loudly over who got to play with the toy first.⟩ — see ARGUE 2

squabbler *n* a person who takes part in a dispute ⟨A couple of *squabblers* sat at the table next to us.⟩ — see DISPUTANT

squad *n* a group of people working together on a task ⟨The cleaning *squad* usually arrives after regular business hours.⟩ — see GANG 1

squalidness *n* the state or quality of being dirty ⟨The *squalidness* of the showers made us leave the campground.⟩ — see DIRTINESS

squall *n* **1** a disturbance of the atmosphere accompanied by wind and often by precipitation (as rain or snow) ⟨A snow *squall* is expected tonight.⟩ — see STORM 1

2 a state of noisy, confused activity ⟨The annual *squall* created when the store holds its biggest sale of the year.⟩ — see COMMOTION

squall *vb* to cry out loudly and emotionally ⟨The baby *squalled* in pain.⟩ — see SCREAM 1

squally *adj* **1** marked by wet and windy conditions ⟨Be careful driving in this *squally* weather.⟩ — see FOUL 1

2 marked by strong wind or more wind than usual ⟨This coastal region often experiences wet, *squally* weather.⟩ — see ¹WINDY 1

squamous *adj* composed of or covered with scales ⟨a *squamous* plant bulb⟩ — see SCALY

squander *vb* **1** to use up carelessly ⟨*squandered* all her money on a get-rich-quick scheme⟩ — see WASTE 1

2 to cause (members of a group) to move widely apart ⟨A single blast of the shotgun *squandered* the herd of deer.⟩ — see SCATTER 1

squanderer *n* someone who spends money freely or foolishly ⟨The elderly woman refused to leave any money to the family's most notorious *squanderer*.⟩ — see PRODIGAL

squandering *adj* given to spending money freely or foolishly ⟨The store's ridiculous prices seem geared to *squandering* shoppers with more money than sense.⟩ — see PRODIGAL

square *adj* **1** having four equal sides and four right angles ⟨a *square* room⟩

synonyms foursquare

related words blocky, boxlike, boxy, cubic, cubical; squarish; rectangular

2 marked by justice, honesty, and freedom from bias ⟨The student received a *square* hearing from the disciplinary panel.⟩ — see FAIR 2

square *vb* **1** to be in agreement on every point ⟨That explanation *squares* entirely with the evidence that we've seen.⟩ — see CHECK 1

2 to influence someone with a bribe ⟨tried to *square* the police officer⟩ — see BRIBE

squarely *adv* as stated or indicated without the slightest difference ⟨a line that is *squarely* in the middle⟩ — see EXACTLY 1

squash *vb* **1** to cause to become a pulpy mass ⟨the sort of person who couldn't even *squash* a bug⟩ — see CRUSH 1

2 to put a stop to (something) by the use of force ⟨*squashed* any effort to bring about reform⟩ — see QUELL 1

squashy *adj* giving easily to the touch ⟨a bed covered in big *squashy* pillows⟩ — see SOFT 3

squat *adj* being compact and broad in build and often short in stature ⟨a short, *squat* bulldog⟩ — see STOCKY

squat *vb* to lie low with the limbs close to the body ⟨a detective *squatting* to examine something on the ground⟩ — see CROUCH

squatty *adj* being compact and broad in build and often short in stature ⟨a *squatty* little wrestler⟩ — see STOCKY

squawk *n* an expression of dissatisfaction, pain, or resentment ⟨If we don't receive any *squawks*, we can assume the change was acceptable.⟩ — see COMPLAINT 1

squawk *vb* to express dissatisfaction, pain, or resentment usually tiresomely ⟨She *squawked* on for hours about how salespeople were always rude to her.⟩ — see COMPLAIN

squeaking *adj* having a high musical pitch or range ⟨a baby bird making little *squeaking* cries⟩ — see SHRILL

squeaky *adj* having a high musical pitch or range ⟨a child with a *squeaky* voice⟩ — see SHRILL

squeal *vb* **1** to give information (as to the authorities) about another's improper or unlawful activities ⟨That stool pigeon *squealed* to the police about the whole operation.⟩

synonyms inform, rat (on), sing, snitch, talk, tell (on)

related words betray, give away, turn in; cross, double-cross, sell (out); blab, tattle; tip (off)

2 to cry out loudly and emotionally ⟨The child *squealed* with frustration.⟩ — see SCREAM 1

3 to express dissatisfaction, pain, or resentment usually tiresomely ⟨We hoped that portable game players would keep the kids from *squealing* about long car rides.⟩ — see COMPLAIN

squealer *n* a person who provides information about another's wrongdoing ⟨He assured them he was no *squealer* and wouldn't talk to the police.⟩ — see INFORMER

squeamish *adj* affected with nausea ⟨The rolling of the ship made her *squeamish*.⟩ — see NAUSEOUS 1

squeamishness *n* **1** a disturbed condition of the stomach in which one feels like vomiting ⟨An ever-rising *squeamishness* suddenly overwhelmed her, and she ran for the bathroom.⟩ — see NAUSEA 1

2 the tendency to be or state of being squeamish ⟨His general *squeamishness* makes him a terrible choice as a lab partner for a dissection.⟩ — see DELICACY 3

squeeze *vb* **1** to apply external pressure on so as to force out the juice or contents of ⟨She kept *squeezing* the bottle until the ketchup squirted all over the table.⟩ — see ²PRESS 2

2 to fit (people or things) into a tight space ⟨I think we can *squeeze* a bit more into the washing machine.⟩ — see CROWD 1

3 to reduce in size or volume by or as if by pressing parts or members together ⟨*squeezed* the blanket until it fit into the box⟩ — see COMPRESS 1

4 to rob by the use of trickery or threats ⟨a blackmailer *squeezing* them for more money⟩ — see FLEECE

5 to force one's way ⟨I was able to *squeeze* through the people clustered around the luggage carousel.⟩ — see ²PRESS 4

squeeze *n* **1** the act or process of reducing the size or volume of something by or as if by pressing ⟨He gave the plastic bag a *squeeze* and then folded it up for storage.⟩ — see COMPRESSION

2 *slang* a person with whom one is in love ⟨She and her main *squeeze* are spending Valentine's Day at a romantic country inn.⟩ — see SWEETHEART

squeezing *n* the act or process of reducing the size or volume of something by or as if by pressing ⟨The *squeezing* of all the lemons produced about a cup of juice.⟩ — see COMPRESSION

squelch *vb* **1** to put a stop to (something) by the use of force ⟨immediately *squelched* any signs of rebellion⟩ — see QUELL 1

2 to stop the noise or speech of ⟨His irritated glare *squelched* any other potential objectors.⟩ — see SILENCE 1

squinch *vb* **1** to lie low with the limbs close to the body ⟨*squinched* down to fit under the table⟩ — see CROUCH

2 to twist (something) out of a natural or normal shape or condition ⟨*squinched* up her eyes in disgust⟩ — see CONTORT

3 to draw back in fear, pain, or disgust ⟨My uncle didn't *squinch* a bit when he saw the snake.⟩ — see FLINCH

squinching *n* the twisting of something out of its natural or normal shape or condition ⟨Mom warned him that the constant *squinching* of his face would someday leave him with a permanently deformed look.⟩ — see CONTORTION

squire *vb* to go along with in order to provide assistance, protection, or companionship ⟨Her father *squired* her to the freshman dorm.⟩ — see ACCOMPANY 1

squirm *vb* to make jerky or restless movements ⟨The toddler *squirmed* the whole time we were in the waiting room.⟩ — see FIDGET

squirrel (away) *vb* to put (something of future use or value) in a safe or secret place ⟨I *squirreled* the information *away* for future reference.⟩ — see HOARD

squirt *vb* to flow out in great quantities or with force ⟨water *squirting* out of the faucet⟩ — see GUSH 1

squirt *n* **1** a usually forceful stream of fluid discharged from a narrow opening ⟨I added a *squirt* of lemon juice to the baked haddock.⟩ — see JET

2 a young person who is between infancy and adulthood ⟨I am fond of the little *squirt*, I'll admit.⟩ — see CHILD 1

squishy *adj* giving easily to the touch ⟨a *squishy* beanbag chair⟩ — see SOFT 3

stab *n* **1** a mark or small hole made by a pointed instrument ⟨The injection left a small *stab* on her upper arm.⟩ — see PRICK 1

2 an effort to do or accomplish something ⟨Everybody will get a *stab* at solving the problem.⟩ — see ATTEMPT 1

stab *vb* to penetrate or hold (something) with a pointed object ⟨*stabbed* the pesky leaf with the tines of the rake⟩ — see IMPALE

stability *n* **1** the ability to withstand force or stress without being distorted, dislodged, or damaged ⟨The bridge was designed with such great *stability* that it supposedly will not collapse even under the harshest weather conditions.⟩

synonyms firmness, soundness, strength, sturdiness

related words dependability, durability, reliability; solidity, solidness; cohesion, toughness

near antonyms insubstantiality, unsoundness, unsubstantiality; weakness

antonyms insecurity, instability, precariousness, shakiness, unsteadiness

2 the state of continuing without change ⟨The *stability* of the regime is in jeopardy.⟩ — see CONSTANCY 1

stable *adj* **1** marked by the ability to withstand stress without structural damage or distortion ⟨The observation tower is *stable* enough to withstand the strongest winds without collapsing.⟩

synonyms fast, firm, sound, strong, sturdy

related words dependable, durable, reliable; unbreakable; beefy, solid; cohesive, tough

near antonyms infirm, insecure, weak; shaky, tottery, unbalanced, wobbly (*also* wabbly); unsubstantial

antonyms rickety, unsound, unstable, unsteady

2 having been established and usually not subject to change ⟨a troubled nation badly in need of a *stable* government⟩ — see FIXED 1

3 having full use of one's mind and control over one's actions ⟨the last will and testament made by a person of sound and *stable* mind⟩ — see SANE

4 not undergoing a change in condition ⟨A *stable* economic climate is best for business.⟩ — see CONSTANT 1

stack *n* **1** a considerable amount ⟨earned a *stack* of money for writing the screenplay⟩ — see LOT 2

2 a quantity of things thrown or stacked on one another ⟨a *stack* of playing cards⟩ — see ¹PILE 1

stack *vb* to lay or throw on top of one another ⟨*stacked* the split logs by the house⟩ — see PILE 1

stack up (against *or* **with)** *vb* to come near or nearer to in character or quality ⟨How does the new car *stack up against* your old one?⟩ — see APPROXIMATE

stadium *n* a large usually roofless building for sporting events with tiers of seats for spectators ⟨The football game will be held at the new *stadium*, which seats 100,000 people.⟩

synonyms bowl, circus, coliseum, colosseum

related words park; gym, gymnasium, spa; arena, hippodrome

staff *n* **1** a body of persons at work or available for work ⟨We're working with a short *staff* at the office today.⟩ — see FORCE 1

2 a heavy rigid stick used as a weapon or for punishment ⟨I carried a *staff* when walking.⟩ — see CLUB 1

stage *n* **1** a level usually raised surface ⟨spoke to the audience from a small *stage* in front⟩ — see PLATFORM

2 a portion of a trip ⟨This is only the first *stage* of the journey.⟩ — see LEG 2

3 an individual part of a process, series, or ranking ⟨in the last *stage* of the project⟩ — see DEGREE 1

4 the public performance of plays ⟨drawn to the *stage* as a career⟩ — see DRAMA 1

stage *vb* to bring before the public in performance or exhibition ⟨*staged* the full body of Shakespeare's plays in the course of a year⟩ — see PRESENT 1

stagger *vb* **1** to move forward while swaying from side to side ⟨I was so tired last night that I just *staggered* upstairs to bed without eating dinner.⟩

synonyms careen, dodder, lurch, reel, teeter, totter, waddle

related words rock, roll, seesaw, swag, sway, waver, weave, wobble (*also* wabble); clomp, clump, flounder, lumber, lump, pound, scuffle, shamble, shuffle, stamp, stomp, stumble, tramp, tromp

2 to show uncertainty about the right course of action ⟨a daunting problem that would make even the most decisive person *stagger* just a bit⟩ — see HESITATE

staggering *adj* causing wonder or astonishment ⟨the *staggering* scope of the new construction on campus⟩ — see MARVELOUS 1

staggeringly *adv* to a large extent or degree ⟨a *staggeringly* huge advancement in technology⟩ — see GREATLY 2

staid *adj* **1** not joking or playful in mood or manner ⟨Everyone was surprised by the funny comments from the usually *staid* professor.⟩ — see SERIOUS 1

2 having or showing a formal and serious or reserved manner ⟨*staid* colors that would be good for business attire⟩ — see DIGNIFIED

staidness *n* a mental state free of jesting or trifling ⟨The *staidness* of the Quaker meeting was surprising to those accustomed to more exuberant services.⟩ — see EARNESTNESS

stain *vb* **1** to affect slightly with something morally bad or undesirable ⟨Her poor choice of companions *stained* her reputation somewhat.⟩ — see TAINT 1
2 to give color or a different color to ⟨*stained* the table to look like cherry⟩ — see COLOR 1
3 to make dirty ⟨Oil *stained* his work pants.⟩ — see DIRTY

stain *n* **1** a mark of guilt or disgrace ⟨The *stain* of this cowardly act would haunt him for the rest of his career.⟩
synonyms blot, brand, slur, smirch, smudge, spot, stigma, taint
related words discredit, disgrace, dishonor, disrepute, guilt, ignominy, infamy, odium, opprobrium, reproach, shame; corruption, depravity, immorality, iniquity, sin, vice
near antonyms award, credit, honor; chasteness, chastity, modesty, purity, stainlessness; honesty, integrity, probity, rectitude, uprightness; goodness, righteousness, virtuousness; fame
2 a substance used to color other materials ⟨applied several coats of *stain* to the wood⟩ — see PIGMENT

stained *adj* not clean ⟨always seen wearing *stained* clothes, which he apparently hoped would mark him as a bohemian⟩ — see DIRTY 1

stainless *adj* free from dirt or stain ⟨Nothing less than a perfectly *stainless* sheet of parchment would do for a diploma.⟩ — see CLEAN 1

stake *n* **1** a legal right to participation in the advantages, profits, and responsibility of something ⟨If I invest in your business, I expect a *stake* in it in return.⟩ — see INTEREST 1
2 the money or thing risked on the outcome of an uncertain event ⟨lost his entire *stake* in the business in one week⟩ — see BET 1

stake *vb* **1** to provide money for ⟨The actor *staked* the entire production of the film with his own money.⟩ — see FINANCE 1
2 to risk (something) on the outcome of an uncertain event ⟨I'd *stake* a year's salary that she'll win the general election.⟩ — see BET

stale *adj* **1** used or heard so often as to be dull ⟨Viewers were bored by the *stale* story lines of the new crop of sitcoms.⟩
synonyms banal, cliché, commonplace, hack, hackney, hackneyed, moth-eaten, musty, shopworn, stereotyped, threadbare, tired, trite
related words twice-told; canned, derivative, imitative, tried-and-true, unimaginative, uninspired, unoriginal; boring, colorless, drab, dreary, dry, dull, dusty, flat, heavy, humdrum, leaden, monotonous, numbing, old, pedestrian, ponderous, prosaic, stodgy, stuffy, tame, tedious, tiresome, tiring, uninteresting, vapid, wearisome, weary, wearying
near antonyms animating, energizing, enlivening, exciting, galvanizing, invigorating, stimulating; absorbing, engaging, engrossing, gripping, interesting, intriguing, involving, riveting; pathbreaking, pioneering, trailblazing
antonyms fresh, new, novel, original
2 causing weariness, restlessness, or lack of interest ⟨The sequel is basically a *stale* remake of the first movie.⟩ — see BORING

stalemate *n* **1** a point in a struggle where neither side is capable of winning or willing to give in ⟨A new negotiator finally got both sides past the *stalemate*.⟩ — see IMPASSE 1
2 a situation in which neither participant in a contest, competition, or struggle comes out ahead of the other ⟨After playing chess for 16 hours, we ended the game in a *stalemate*.⟩ — see TIE 1

stalk *vb* **1** to seek out (game) for food or sport ⟨lions *stalking* gazelles on the plains⟩ — see HUNT 1
2 to walk with exaggerated arm and leg movements ⟨The irate customer *stalked* off in a huff.⟩ — see STRUT 1

stall *vb* **1** to bring (something) to a standstill ⟨Endless complaints *stalled* the process of selecting the winning design for the memorial.⟩ — see ¹HALT 1
2 to stop functioning ⟨The engine *stalls* sometimes when it's very cold outside.⟩ — see FAIL 1

stalwart *adj* **1** feeling or displaying no fear by temperament ⟨the *stalwart* soldiers in the army of Alexander the Great, who willingly followed him to the ends of the known world⟩ — see BRAVE 1
2 having muscles capable of exerting great physical force ⟨a *stalwart* yet lithe athlete⟩ — see STRONG 1

stamp *n* **1** a perceptible trace left by pressure ⟨a *stamp* left in the mud by some prehistoric beast⟩ — see PRINT 1
2 something that sets apart an individual from others of the same kind ⟨Virtually without exception Van Gogh's portraits bear the *stamp* of genius.⟩ — see CHARACTERISTIC

stamp *vb* **1** to move heavily or clumsily ⟨*stamping* around in oversized boots⟩ — see LUMBER 1
2 to tread on heavily so as to crush or injure ⟨*stamped* the grass down in a circle⟩ — see TRAMPLE

stamp (out) *vb* to destroy all traces of ⟨working to *stamp out* racism in this country⟩ — see ANNIHILATE 1

stance *n* a general way of holding the body ⟨a slightly aggressive *stance*⟩ — see POSTURE 1

stanchion *n* an upright shaft that supports an overhead structure ⟨the *stanchion* of an arch⟩ — see PILLAR 1

stand *n* a level usually raised surface ⟨Marchers passed by the reviewing *stand*.⟩ — see PLATFORM

stand *vb* **1** to occupy a place or location ⟨The monument *stands* in the middle of the town plaza.⟩
synonyms be, bear, lie, sit
related words command, overlook; hang around, remain, rest, stay, stick around, tarry; await, wait; post, station; dwell, reside
2 to put up with (something painful or difficult) ⟨I don't know how you can *stand* that job.⟩ — see BEAR 2
3 to give what is owed for ⟨I'll *stand* lunch, and you can pay me back later.⟩ — see PAY 2
4 to take or have a certain position within a group arranged in vertical classes ⟨If the city's baseball team wins today, they will *stand* first in the league.⟩ — see RANK 1

standard *adj* **1** being of the type that is encountered in the normal course of events ⟨A *standard* bandage is all that that wound needs.⟩ — see ORDINARY 1
2 having or showing the qualities associated with the members of a particular group or kind ⟨He's pretty much your *standard* high-school jock.⟩ — see TYPICAL 1
3 accepted, used, or practiced by most people ⟨*standard* procedure⟩ — see CURRENT 1

standard *n* **1** something set up as an example against which others of the same type are compared ⟨The animation in that movie set the *standard* against which all later animated cartoons were judged.⟩
synonyms bar, benchmark, criterion, grade, mark, measure, par, touchstone, yardstick
related words case, example, instance; average, norm, rule; acme, apex, meridian, peak, pinnacle, summit, zenith
near antonyms aberration, abnormality
2 a piece of cloth with a special design that is used as an emblem or for signaling ⟨a ship flying the queen's *standard*⟩ — see FLAG 1
3 what is typical of a group, class, or series ⟨somewhat shorter than the *standard* for boys that age⟩ — see AVERAGE

4 standards *pl* the code of good conduct for an individual or group ⟨a life guided by high *standards*⟩ — see ETHICS

standardize *vb* to make agree with a single established standard or model ⟨The plan is to *standardize* the test for reading comprehension so that we can see how students across the state compare.⟩

synonyms formalize, homogenize, normalize, regularize

related words codify, marshal (*also* marshall); methodize, order, organize, systematize, systemize; average, equalize, even; square; accredit, certify; control, govern, regulate, rule; conciliate, conform, coordinate, harmonize, integrate, reconcile, synthesize

near antonyms customize, individualize, tailor

standby *n* something or someone to which one looks for support ⟨our old *standby* in times of trouble⟩ — see DEPENDENCE 2

stand by *vb* to give steadfast support to ⟨No matter how much people object, I will *stand by* my decision.⟩ — see ADHERE (TO) 1

stand–in *n* a person or thing that takes the place of another ⟨We hired him at the last minute as a *stand-in* for the person who quit.⟩ — see SUBSTITUTE

stand in *vb* to serve as a replacement usually for a time only ⟨She will be *standing in* for the regular teacher for a week.⟩ — see COVER 1

standing *adj* rising straight up ⟨All *standing* timbers are in sound condition.⟩ — see ERECT

standing *n* **1** high position within society ⟨a man of *standing* in his community⟩ — see RANK 2

2 the period during which something exists, lasts, or is in progress ⟨a tradition of long *standing*⟩ — see DURATION 1

3 the placement of someone or something in relation to others in a vertical arrangement ⟨my *standing* in the class at the time of graduation⟩ — see RANK 1

standoff *n* **1** a situation in which neither participant in a contest, competition, or struggle comes out ahead of the other ⟨After two hours they had played to a 5-5 *standoff*.⟩ — see TIE 1

2 a point in a struggle where neither side is capable of winning or willing to give in ⟨The *standoff* continued for three days before the fugitive gave himself up to the authorities.⟩ — see IMPASSE 1

standoffish *adj* having or showing a lack of friendliness or interest in others ⟨She proved to be simply shy, not *standoffish*.⟩ — see COOL 1

standout *n* **1** a person who is widely known and usually much talked about ⟨Several *standouts* from showbiz were at the gala.⟩ — see CELEBRITY 1

2 something very good of its kind ⟨His debut novel was a *standout* in an otherwise lackluster year.⟩ — see JIM-DANDY

stand out *vb* to extend outward beyond a usual point ⟨The relief figures *stand out* from the wall quite strikingly.⟩ — see BULGE 1

standpoint *n* a way of looking at or thinking about something ⟨I never thought about it from that *standpoint* before.⟩ — see PERSPECTIVE 1

standstill *n* a point in a struggle where neither side is capable of winning or willing to give in ⟨battled each other to a *standstill*⟩ — see IMPASSE 1

staple *n* the main or greater part of something as distinguished from its subordinate parts ⟨Reading is the very *staple* of a person's education.⟩ — see BODY 1

star *adj* **1** of or relating to the stars ⟨*star* observations⟩ — see STELLAR 1

2 standing above others in rank, importance, or achievement ⟨the teacher's *star* pupil⟩ — see EMINENT

3 widely known ⟨They're looking for *star* actors to play the leads.⟩ — see FAMOUS 1

star *n* **1** a ball-shaped gaseous celestial body that shines by its own light ⟨It's difficult to see the *stars* at night in the middle of the city because of all the streetlights.⟩

synonyms luminary, sphere, sun

related words cluster; binary star, brown dwarf, dwarf, fixed star, giant star, neutron star, nova, pulsar, quasar, red dwarf, red giant, red star, supergiant, supernova, variable star, white dwarf

2 the person who has the most important role in a play, movie, or TV show ⟨When the *star* of the school play came down with the flu on opening night, her understudy got to go on.⟩

synonyms lead, principal

related words leading lady, leading man; superstar; ingenue (*or* ingénue), starlet

near antonyms extra, supernumerary

3 a person who is widely known and usually much talked about ⟨the public's endless fascination with *stars*⟩ — see CELEBRITY 1

starch *n* active strength of body or mind ⟨a middle-aged woman who has retained the *starch* of youth⟩ — see VIGOR 1

starchy *adj* marked by or showing careful attention to set forms and details ⟨a *starchy* and demanding teacher⟩ — see CEREMONIOUS 1

star–crossed *adj* having, prone to, or marked by bad luck ⟨Romeo and Juliet are among literature's most famous *star-crossed* lovers.⟩ — see UNLUCKY 1

stare *vb* to look long and hard in wonder or surprise ⟨Her friends *stared* in disbelief upon seeing her in a bit role on TV.⟩ — see GAPE

stare *n* a fixed intent look ⟨caught the child's wide-eyed *stare* on film⟩ — see GAZE

stark *adj* **1** harsh and threatening in manner or appearance ⟨*stark* and forbidding mountains that the settlers knew that they would have to cross⟩ — see GRIM 1

2 having no exceptions or restrictions ⟨the school's *stark* prohibition against cell phones in the classroom⟩ — see ABSOLUTE 2

3 lacking contents that could or should be present ⟨house buyers trying to imagine what those *stark* rooms would look like when filled with furniture⟩ — see EMPTY 1

4 producing inferior or only a small amount of vegetation ⟨a once-lush landscape rendered depressingly *stark* by strip-mining and deforestation⟩ — see BARREN 1

starry *adj* of or relating to the stars ⟨the *starry* light of the firmament on a clear night⟩ — see STELLAR 1

start *n* the point at which something begins ⟨Tom knew from the *start* of the game that he would win easily.⟩ — see BEGINNING

start *vb* **1** to move suddenly and sharply (as in surprise) ⟨I *started* from my chair when I heard the sudden scream.⟩

synonyms bolt, jump, startle

related words jerk, jolt, twitch; blench, cringe, flinch, quail, recoil, shrink, spook, squinch, wince; bound, leap, spring; react, respond

2 to be responsible for the creation and early operation or use of ⟨*started* the impressionist movement in art⟩ — see FOUND

3 to cause to function ⟨trying to *start* the car on a frigid morning⟩ — see ACTIVATE

4 to come into existence ⟨The fire *started* in the laboratory.⟩ — see BEGIN 2

5 to extend outward beyond a usual point ⟨frightened horses with *starting* eyes⟩ — see BULGE 1

6 to take the first step in (a process or course of action) ⟨We'll be ready to *start* the concert in a moment.⟩ — see BEGIN 1

startle *vb* **1** to make a strong impression on (someone) with something unexpected ⟨The lightning *startled* the children and sent them scurrying for cover.⟩ — see SURPRISE 1

2 to move suddenly and sharply (as in surprise) ⟨The cat *startled* when the door slammed shut with a bang.⟩ — see START 1

3 to strike with fear ⟨Loud noises always *startle* her.⟩ — see FRIGHTEN

startling *adj* causing a strong emotional reaction because of unexpectedness ⟨The *startling* news that my sister will be having a baby.⟩ — see SURPRISING 1

starved *adj* feeling a desire or need for food ⟨After that long soccer practice, the children were really *starved*.⟩ — see HUNGRY 1

starving *adj* feeling a desire or need for food ⟨I missed lunch, and now I'm *starving!*⟩ — see HUNGRY 1

stash *n* a supply stored up and often hidden away ⟨Debbie keeps a *stash* of tissues in her desk in case anyone needs one.⟩ — see HOARD 1

stash *vb* to put (something of future use or value) in a safe or secret place ⟨*stashed* the extra antifreeze in the trunk of the car⟩ — see HOARD

stashing *n* the placing of something out of sight ⟨The *stashing* of the title to the house in a strongbox that wasn't fireproof was foolish.⟩ — see CONCEALMENT 1

state *n* **1** a body of people composed of one or more nationalities usually with its own territory and government ⟨The British monarch is the head of *state*, while the prime minister is the head of the government.⟩ — see NATION

2 high position within society ⟨The dignitaries were given a welcome befitting their *state*.⟩ — see RANK 2

state *vb* **1** to convey in appropriate or telling terms ⟨Please *state* the vehicle's mechanical problem as clearly and briefly as possible.⟩ — see PHRASE

2 to express (a thought or emotion) in words ⟨"I believe this theory is wrong," she *stated*.⟩ — see SAY 1

3 to make known (as an idea, emotion, or opinion) ⟨Everyone has a right to *state* his or her opinion, no matter how unpopular it may be.⟩ — see EXPRESS 1

statehouse *n* the building in which a state legislature meets ⟨a field trip to the *statehouse* to see the legislature in session⟩ — see CAPITOL

stateliness *n* **1** a dignified bearing or appearance befitting someone of royal status ⟨The princess has a *stateliness* that will serve her well when she becomes queen.⟩ — see MAJESTY 1

2 dignified or restrained beauty of form, appearance, or style ⟨the refined *stateliness* of the mansion that has served as the official home of the state's governors since the 18th century⟩ — see ELEGANCE

3 impressiveness of beauty on a large scale ⟨The *stateliness* of this mountain range is best appreciated from one of its summits.⟩ — see MAGNIFICENCE

stately *adj* **1** having or showing a formal and serious or reserved manner ⟨The monarch watched the ceremony with *stately* aloofness.⟩ — see DIGNIFIED

2 having or showing elegance ⟨a *stately* procession down the aisle⟩ — see ELEGANT 1

3 large and impressive in size, grandeur, extent, or conception ⟨*stately* mansions that are now open to the public as museums⟩ — see GRAND 1

4 very dignified in form, tone, or style ⟨a *stately* composition that has served as the musical accompaniment for countless graduations and other ceremonial occasions⟩ — see ELEVATED 2

statement *n* **1** a record of goods sold or services performed together with the costs due ⟨received a *statement* from the plumber in the mail⟩ — see ¹BILL 1

2 an act, process, or means of putting something into

words ⟨a careful *statement* of the legal case before the court⟩ — see EXPRESSION 1

3 something that is said ⟨Her *statement* was met with considerable skepticism.⟩ — see WORD 2

static *adj* fixed in a place or position ⟨The *static* installation of the statue in that niche means that no one will ever see its back, which is also of interest.⟩ — see STATIONARY 1

station *vb* to assign to a place or position ⟨*stationed* guards around the perimeter of the encampment⟩ — see ²POST

station *n* **1** the place where someone is assigned to stand or remain ⟨The soldiers remained at their *station* even though a huge enemy force was approaching.⟩

synonyms position, post, quarter

related words assignment, brief, business, charge, detail, job, operation

2 a regular stopping place ⟨The historic house was once a *station* on the Underground Railroad, the network that helped Africans escaping enslavement reach freedom in the North.⟩

synonyms stop, way station

related words depot, terminal; layover, stopover

3 the placement of someone or something in relation to others in a vertical arrangement ⟨worked hard to improve their *station* in life⟩ — see RANK 1

4 a general way of holding the body ⟨The palace guards are required to maintain a rigid *station*.⟩ — see POSTURE 1

stationary *adj* **1** fixed in a place or position ⟨A *stationary* bicycle is good for exercise, but you won't enjoy the scenery very much.⟩

synonyms immobile, nonmoving, static

related words immovable, irremovable, nonmotile, unmovable; frozen, motionless, moveless, stagnant, still; stuck, unbudging, wedged; fast, rooted, steadfast

phrases in place

near antonyms motile; adjustable, flexible, modular; displaceable, portable, removable (*also* removeable), transferable (*also* transferrable), transportable; unbalanced, unstable, unsteady

antonyms mobile, movable (*or* moveable), moving, nonstationary

2 not undergoing a change in condition ⟨Auction prices for that artist's works have been *stationary* for some time.⟩ — see CONSTANT 1

statuette *n* a small statue ⟨won a gold-plated *statuette* as the prize⟩ — see FIGURINE

stature *n* the distance of something or someone from bottom to top ⟨a man of surprisingly great *stature*⟩ — see HEIGHT 3

status *n* **1** position with regard to conditions and circumstances ⟨Let me know if your *status* changes and you're available to work.⟩ — see SITUATION 1

2 the placement of someone or something in relation to others in a vertical arrangement ⟨resented her lowly *status* in the organization⟩ — see RANK 1

status quo *n* the state or fact of being the way things usually are ⟨civic leaders who are afraid to do anything that might change the town's *status quo*⟩ — see NORMALITY

statute *n* a rule of conduct or action laid down by a governing authority and especially a legislature ⟨a new anti-littering *statute*⟩ — see LAW 1

staunch *also* **stanch** *adj* firm in one's allegiance to someone or something ⟨a *staunch* believer in the democratic system⟩ — see FAITHFUL 1

stave off *vb* **1** to drive back ⟨managed to *stave off* the invaders⟩ — see REPEL 1

2 to keep from happening by taking action in advance ⟨The quartermaster *staved off* a shortage by requisitioning more than enough supplies.⟩ — see PREVENT

¹stay *n* **1** a temporary residing as another's guest ⟨My mother-in-law is coming for a brief *stay* next week.⟩ — see VISIT 1

2 the stopping of a process or activity ⟨We must work without *stay* if we are ever to reach our goal of equal rights for everyone.⟩ — see END 1

²stay *n* a structure that holds up or serves as a foundation for something else ⟨A free press is one of the principal *stays* of a democratic society.⟩ — see SUPPORT 1

¹stay *vb* **1** to continue to be in a place for a significant amount of time ⟨Let's *stay* inside this pavilion until it stops raining.⟩

synonyms abide, dwell, hang around, remain, stick around, tarry

related words await, hang on, hold on, wait; dally, dawdle, linger, loiter; outstay, overstay

near antonyms abscond, decamp, escape, evacuate, flee, fly, get out, run away, scram, skip; abandon, desert, forsake, vacate

antonyms bail out, clear out, cut out, depart, exit, get off, go, go off, leave, move, quit, shove (off), take off, walk out

2 to bring (something) to a standstill ⟨*Stay* the trial until this new evidence has been processed.⟩ — see ¹HALT 1

3 to remain in place in readiness or expectation of something ⟨We'll *stay* for a while longer and see if anyone shows up.⟩ — see WAIT

4 to reside as a temporary guest ⟨Let's *stay* at a quaint inn rather than at some generic motel.⟩ — see VISIT 2

²stay *vb* to hold up or serve as a foundation for ⟨beams being used to *stay* the bridge while it is undergoing repairs⟩ — see SUPPORT 3

stead *n* the more favorable condition or position in a competition ⟨A summer internship will stand you in good *stead* when applying to college.⟩ — see ADVANTAGE 1

steadfast *adj* firm in one's allegiance to someone or something ⟨a *steadfast* supporter of the president⟩ — see FAITHFUL 1

steadfastness *n* adherence to something to which one is bound by a pledge or duty ⟨His refusal to be swayed on this issue is more the result of stubbornness than principled *steadfastness*.⟩ — see FIDELITY

steadiness *n* the state of continuing without change ⟨The *steadiness* of the weather is something that every New Englander knows not to trust.⟩ — see CONSTANCY 1

steady *adj* **1** firm in one's allegiance to someone or something ⟨Even as wild accusations were circulating, she remained *steady* in her support for the candidate.⟩ — see FAITHFUL 1

2 appearing or occurring repeatedly from time to time ⟨a popular author who produces a *steady* output of best sellers year after year⟩ — see REGULAR 1

3 not undergoing a change in condition ⟨a *steady* breeze from the west⟩ — see CONSTANT 1

4 not varying ⟨support for her presidential bid has been *steady*⟩ — see UNIFORM

5 worthy of one's trust ⟨a quiet but *steady* man who is one of the pillars of the community⟩ — see DEPENDABLE

steal *n* something bought or offered for sale at a desirable price ⟨At 50% off, that shirt is a real *steal*.⟩ — see BARGAIN 1

steal *vb* **1** to take (something) without right and with an intent to keep ⟨The guy who tried to *steal* my car was sentenced to a year in jail.⟩

synonyms appropriate, filch, heist, hook, lift, misappropriate, nip, pilfer, pinch, pocket, purloin, rip off, snitch, swipe, thieve

related words burglarize, rob; loot, pillage, plunder, sack; carjack, hijack (*also* highjack); pick, rifle; poach,

rustle, shoplift; collar, grab, grasp, nail, seize, snatch, take; mooch, sponge

phrases make away with, make off with, run off with, walk off with

near antonyms buy, purchase; bestow, contribute, donate, give, hand over, present

2 to move about in a sly or secret manner ⟨They *stole* out of the room.⟩ — see SNEAK 1

steal (from) *vb* to remove valuables from (a place) unlawfully ⟨There's little wonder that the store went out of business, as its employees had been *stealing from* it for years.⟩ — see ROB

stealer *n* one who steals ⟨The Internet has simply provided *stealers* and scammers with a new venue for their crimes.⟩ — see THIEF

stealing *n* the unlawful taking and carrying away of property without the consent of its owner ⟨In those days the *stealing* of a horse was a very serious crime.⟩ — see THEFT 1

stealthy *adj* **1** given to acting in secret and to concealing one's intentions ⟨Cats are among the *stealthiest* of stalkers.⟩ — see SNEAKY 1

2 undertaken or done so as to escape being observed or known by others ⟨constantly harassed the enemy with *stealthy* raids⟩ — see SECRET 1

steam *vb* to be excited or emotionally stirred up with anger ⟨The bank's new fees made a lot of customers *steam*.⟩ — see BOIL 1

steaming *adj* feeling or showing anger ⟨She was *steaming* after hearing that she was being slandered by someone who had once been her best friend.⟩ — see ANGRY

steed *n* a large hoofed domestic animal that is used for carrying or drawing loads and for riding ⟨The knight mounted his trusty *steed*.⟩ — see HORSE

steel *n* a hand weapon with a length of metal sharpened on one or both sides and usually tapered to a sharp point ⟨The swordsman drew *steel* on the knaves, who immediately fled for their lives.⟩ — see SWORD

steel *vb* **1** to fill with courage or strength of purpose ⟨hoped that his inspirational talk would *steel* the youths in the pursuit of their dreams⟩ — see ENCOURAGE 1

2 to make able to withstand physical hardship, strain, or exposure ⟨Years of running a farm had *steeled* the hard-bitten woman.⟩ — see HARDEN 2

3 to prepare (oneself) mentally or emotionally ⟨He had spent the previous night *steeling* himself for the moment when he would demand a raise.⟩ — see FORTIFY 1

steely *adj* **1** harsh and threatening in manner or appearance ⟨pinned them with a *steely* gaze and demanded to know what they were doing⟩ — see GRIM 1

2 of the color gray ⟨*steely* eyes that are the color of a stormy sky⟩ — see GRAY 1

steep *adj* **1** having an incline approaching the perpendicular ⟨a very *steep* rock face that is nearly impossible to climb⟩

synonyms abrupt, bold, precipitous, sheer

related words perpendicular, plumb, straight, vertical; craggy, hillocky, hilly, mountainous, scarped; angled, canted, cocked, heeled, inclined, listed, slanted, sloped, tilted, tipped

near antonyms gentle, gradual, moderate, soft; even, flat, flush, horizontal, level, plane

antonyms easy

2 going beyond a normal or acceptable limit in degree or amount ⟨We would like to hire him, but his salary demands are just too *steep*.⟩ — see EXCESSIVE

steep *vb* **1** to cause (as a person) to become filled or saturated with a certain quality or principle ⟨grew up *steeped* in the ways of his ancestors⟩ ⟨a town *steeped* in history⟩ — see INFUSE

2 to wet thoroughly with liquid ⟨Chew fresh ginger that has been *steeped* in hot water to aid digestion.⟩ — see SOAK 1

steer *vb* **1** to point out the way for (someone) especially from a position in front ⟨The man in the train station was able to *steer* us in the right direction.⟩ — see LEAD 1
2 to operate or control the course of ⟨first needed to learn how to *steer* her personal watercraft before going out on the crowded lake⟩ — see NAVIGATE 1

stellar *adj* **1** of or relating to the stars ⟨Humankind's dream of *stellar* navigation is hampered by the vast distances between the stars, even in our own galaxy.⟩
synonyms astral, star, starry
related words celestial, empyrean, heavenly; intergalactic, interstellar; astronomical (*also* astronomic), astrophysical; astronautic (*or* astronautical); starlike, star-spangled
2 of the very best kind ⟨This miniature palm tree is a *stellar* example of the art of bonsai.⟩ — see EXCELLENT

stench *n* a strong unpleasant smell ⟨We finally discovered the dead rat that was causing the *stench* in the basement.⟩ — see STINK 1

stentorian *adj* marked by a high volume of sound ⟨The professor's *stentorian* voice was enough to keep even the drowsiest student awake.⟩ — see LOUD 1

step *n* **1** an action planned or taken to achieve a desired result ⟨took *steps* to ensure that there would be no more incidences of food poisoning⟩ — see MEASURE 1
2 an individual part of a process, series, or ranking ⟨The manual enumerates every *step* in the procedure for shutting down the assembly line.⟩ — see DEGREE 1
3 the mark or impression made by a foot ⟨*steps* in the sand leading into the water and back out again⟩ — see FOOTPRINT
4 steps *pl* the direction along which something or someone moves ⟨Their *steps* led them through a long corridor.⟩ — see PATH 1
5 a very small distance or degree ⟨He lives just a *step* away from his elderly mother, so he's there if she needs him for any reason.⟩ — see HAIR 1

step *vb* **1** to go on foot ⟨I *stepped* across the street for a quick lunch at the new diner.⟩ — see WALK 1
2 to perform a series of usually rhythmic bodily movements to music ⟨She was in her element, happily *stepping* around the dance floor.⟩ — see DANCE 1
3 to proceed or move quickly ⟨Many people wanted to linger before the president's bier, but guards kept the line of mourners *stepping* forward.⟩ — see HURRY 2

step (along) *vb* to leave a place often for another ⟨Now that my ride's here, I'll be *stepping along*.⟩ — see GO 2

step–by–step *adj* proceeding or changing by steps or degrees ⟨The incessant *step-by-step* advance of the enemy's troops could no longer be resisted.⟩ — see GRADUAL

step down (from) *vb* **1** to give up (a job or office) ⟨He could no longer resist calls for him to *step down from* chairmanship of the department.⟩ — see QUIT 1
2 to give up (as a position of authority) formally ⟨Even in the face of a palace revolt, Queen Elizabeth I refused to *step down from* the throne.⟩ — see ABDICATE

steppe *n* a broad area of level or rolling treeless country ⟨Nomads have long grazed yaks on the *steppes* of Mongolia.⟩ — see PLAIN 1

step up *vb* to make markedly greater in measure or degree ⟨candidates *stepping up* their campaigns as election day draws near⟩ ⟨*stepped up* the pace to catch up with the others⟩ — see INTENSIFY

stereotype *n* an idea or statement about all of the members of a group or all the instances of a situation ⟨the *stereotype* of the absent-minded professor⟩ — see GENERALIZATION

stereotype *vb* to use so much as to make less appealing ⟨Movies have *stereotyped* the domineering mother-in-law ad nauseam.⟩ — see HACKNEY

stereotyped *adj* used or heard so often as to be dull ⟨the wacky neighbor and other *stereotyped* characters seen on TV sitcoms⟩ — see STALE 1

sterile *adj* **1** not able to produce fruit or offspring ⟨*Sterile* couples sometimes choose to adopt needy children.⟩ ⟨The apple tree turned out to be *sterile*, never yielding a crop of apples.⟩
synonyms barren, fruitless, impotent, infertile, unfruitful
related words altered, desexed, neutered, sterilized; castrated, emasculated, gelded; spayed; unproductive
near antonyms fecund, luxuriant, productive, prolific; enriched, fertilized, rich; impregnated, pregnant; potent; bearing, producing, yielding; blooming, bursting, flourishing, swarming, teeming
antonyms fat, fertile, fruitful
2 free from filth, infection, or dangers to health ⟨*sterile* surgical supplies⟩ — see SANITARY

sterling *adj* of the very best kind ⟨credited the win to the pitcher's *sterling* performance on the mound⟩ — see EXCELLENT

stern *adj* **1** given to exacting standards of discipline and self-restraint ⟨The army post's *stern* commander always had the utmost respect of those who served under him.⟩ — see SEVERE 1
2 harsh and threatening in manner or appearance ⟨A *stern* receptionist took our names without even looking up.⟩ — see GRIM 1

sternly *adv* in a manner so as to cause loss or suffering ⟨The judge *sternly* reprimanded the prosecuting attorney for making comments that never should have been heard by the jury.⟩ — see HARDLY 1

sternness *n* the quality or state of being demanding or unyielding (as in discipline or criticism) ⟨The company's new president has a reputation for granitelike *sternness* and monkish austerity.⟩ — see SEVERITY

stevedore *n* one who loads and unloads ships at a port ⟨On the wharves, *stevedores* were unloading cargo from the far corners of the world.⟩ — see DOCKWORKER

stew *n* **1** a state of nervous or irritated concern ⟨Many in town are in a *stew* about the proposed plan to close at least one of the elementary schools.⟩ — see FRET
2 a state of noisy, confused activity ⟨The audience went into a *stew* when the performance was abruptly cancelled.⟩ — see COMMOTION

stew *vb* **1** to cook in a liquid heated to the point that it gives off steam ⟨*Stew* the chicken till tender, and then remove the meat from the bones.⟩ — see BOIL 2
2 to experience concern or anxiety ⟨Stop *stewing* over that game and just try to do better next time.⟩ — see WORRY 1

steward *vb* to look after and make decisions about ⟨will *steward* the city's library programs⟩ — see CONDUCT 1

stewardship *n* **1** the act or activity of looking after and making decisions about something ⟨Generally the dean left the day-to-day *stewardship* of the college to the assistant dean.⟩ — see CONDUCT 1
2 the duty or function of watching or guarding for the sake of proper direction or control ⟨She believes that *stewardship* of the environment is everyone's responsibility.⟩ — see SUPERVISION 1

stick *vb* **1** to hold to something firmly as if by adhesion ⟨Those magnets are strong enough to *stick* to the refrigerator without any problems.⟩
synonyms adhere, cleave, cling, hew
related words bind, cohere, fasten, fuse, glue, unite
near antonyms loosen; drop, fall

2 to arrange something in a certain spot or position ⟨You can *stick* that box in the corner until I figure out where to put everything.⟩ — see PLACE 1

3 to penetrate or hold (something) with a pointed object ⟨I could hardly feel the needle when the nurse *stuck* my arm with it.⟩ — see IMPALE

4 to rob by the use of trickery or threats ⟨She got *stuck* by an unscrupulous seller while using the online auction site.⟩ — see FLEECE

stick (to *or* **with)** *vb* to give steadfast support to ⟨Thanks for *sticking with* me after all my other so-called friends turned their backs.⟩ ⟨The governor has sworn to *stick to* his campaign promises.⟩ — see ADHERE (TO) 1

stick around *vb* to continue to be in a place for a significant amount of time ⟨We *stuck around* afterwards to help clean up.⟩ — see ¹STAY 1

stick–in–the–mud *n* a person with old-fashioned ideas ⟨The committee is dominated by old *stick-in-the-muds* who have little interest in bringing new ideas to the table.⟩ — see FOGY

stick out *vb* **1** to extend outward beyond a usual point ⟨No feet *sticking out* in the aisles, please!⟩ — see BULGE 1

2 to put up with (something painful or difficult) ⟨managed to *stick out* the whole race despite her bad knee⟩ — see BEAR 2

sticks *pl n* the open rural area outside of big towns and cities ⟨grew up in the *sticks* and is used to traveling miles just to get a loaf of bread⟩ — see COUNTRY 2

sticky *adj* **1** tending to adhere to objects upon contact ⟨Both sides of the tape are *sticky*, making it a little tricky to work with.⟩

synonyms adherent, adhesive, gluey, glutinous, gummy, tacky, tenacious, viscid

related words gelatinous, gooey, ropy (*also* ropey), syrupy, viscous; pitchy, tarry

near antonyms nonviscous

antonyms nonadhesive

2 containing or characterized by an uncomfortable amount of moisture ⟨a warm *sticky* day when all we wanted to do was sit somewhere with air-conditioning⟩ — see HUMID

3 requiring exceptional skill or caution in performance or handling ⟨an especially *sticky* conversation about money matters⟩ — see TRICKY 1

stiff *adj* **1** incapable of or highly resistant to bending ⟨Use a *stiff* piece of paper for the project.⟩

synonyms inflexible, rigid, stiffened, unyielding

related words inelastic; firm, hard, solid, sound, strong; nonelastic, nonmalleable

near antonyms elastic, resilient, springy, stretchy, workable; malleable, plastic; droopy, flabby, flaccid, mushy, semisoft, soft, squashy, squishy; lank, limber, limp, lissome (*also* lissom), lithe, lithesome, willowy

antonyms flexible, floppy, pliable, pliant, supple, yielding

2 difficult to endure ⟨*stiff* winds⟩ — see HARSH 1

3 going beyond a normal or acceptable limit in degree or amount ⟨Don't you think that's a pretty *stiff* fine for such a minor infraction?⟩ — see EXCESSIVE

4 having a consistency that does not easily yield to pressure ⟨Stir two cups of flour with the remaining ingredients to make a *stiff* dough.⟩ — see FIRM 2

5 lacking social grace and assurance ⟨Tara felt *stiff* and ill-at-ease whenever she was introduced to her father's friends.⟩ — see AWKWARD 1

6 requiring considerable physical or mental effort ⟨We'll have a *stiff* climb to actually reach the summit.⟩ — see HARD 2

7 marked by or showing careful attention to set forms and details ⟨The *stiff* politeness with which I was greeted

suggested that they weren't truly happy to see me.⟩ — see CEREMONIOUS 1

stiff *n* **1** a dead body ⟨To the mortician, a *stiff* was a *stiff* and they were all pretty much alike.⟩ — see CORPSE

2 a member of the human race ⟨One lucky *stiff* will get the biggest jackpot in the lottery's history.⟩ — see HUMAN

stiff *vb* to rob by the use of trickery or threats ⟨customers who were too embarrassed to admit that they had been *stiffed* by an Internet company selling counterfeit designer watches⟩ — see FLEECE

stiffened *adj* incapable of or highly resistant to bending ⟨*stiffened* corpses⟩ ⟨an old-fashioned dress with a *stiffened* lace collar⟩ — see STIFF 1

stiffly *adv* **1** in a manner so as to cause loss or suffering ⟨*stiffly* criticized for making such indiscreet comments in public⟩ — see HARDLY 1

2 in a vigorous and forceful manner ⟨a *stiffly* fought battle⟩ — see HARD 3

stifle *vb* **1** to be or cause to be killed by lack of breathable air ⟨We were almost *stifled* by the smoke.⟩ — see SMOTHER 1

2 to refrain from openly showing or uttering ⟨*stifled* a yawn⟩ — see SUPPRESS 2

3 to deaden the sound of ⟨He *stifled* a cough with his hand.⟩ — see MUFFLE 1

stifling *adj* lacking fresh air ⟨The lecture hall was *stifling* until we opened several windows.⟩ — see STUFFY 1

stigma *n* a mark of guilt or disgrace ⟨The *stigma* of mental illness often harms those seeking care.⟩ — see STAIN 1

still *adj* **1** free from disturbing noise or uproar ⟨The town's streets are usually *still* and peopleless in the early morning hours.⟩ — see QUIET 1

2 free from storms or physical disturbance ⟨The air was ominously *still* as dark clouds gathered in the distance.⟩ — see CALM 1

3 mostly or entirely without sound ⟨In his paintings Paul Gauguin depicts a *still* tropical paradise.⟩ — see SILENT 3

still *n* **1** a state of freedom from storm or disturbance ⟨In the *still* of the forest he could relax and forget his worries.⟩ — see CALM 1

2 the near or complete absence of sound ⟨A loud noise shattered the *still* of the night.⟩ — see SILENCE 2

still *vb* **1** to bring (something) to a standstill ⟨The report has not *stilled* debate over the procedure.⟩ — see ¹HALT 1

2 to free from distress or disturbance ⟨Reading a book helps me to relax and *still* my mind before going to bed.⟩ — see CALM 1

3 to stop the noise or speech of ⟨The conversation was abruptly *stilled* by a loud crash from the next room.⟩ — see SILENCE 1

still *adv* **1** without motion ⟨The cat sat absolutely *still*, watching as the mouse began to make its way across the floor.⟩

synonyms motionlessly, quiet, quietly

related words immovably; inactively

near antonyms movably

2 in spite of that ⟨Their star player was injured in yesterday's game; *still*, it looks like he will be able to play today.⟩ — see HOWEVER

stillness *n* **1** a state of freedom from storm or disturbance ⟨dozing in the warm *stillness* of a summer afternoon⟩ — see CALM 1

2 incapacity for or restraint from speaking ⟨From the tense *stillness* in the room I sensed that something had happened before I arrived.⟩ — see SILENCE 1

3 the near or complete absence of sound ⟨The only thing that broke the *stillness* of the garden was the droning of a bee.⟩ — see SILENCE 2

stilly *adj* **1** free from disturbing noise or uproar ⟨bats taking flight in the *stilly* summer evening⟩ — see QUIET 1

2 free from storms or physical disturbance ⟨Dipping my

paddle into the *stilly* water, I began canoeing across the pond.⟩ — see CALM 1

3 mostly or entirely without sound ⟨the blissful peace of a star-filled, *stilly* night⟩ — see SILENT 3

stilted *adj* **1** lacking social grace and assurance ⟨The conversation was somewhat *stilted* as we didn't seem to share any interests.⟩ — see AWKWARD 1

2 marked by or showing careful attention to set forms and details ⟨a *stilted* letter of apology that was written and accepted with equal measures of insincerity⟩ — see CEREMONIOUS 1

stimulant *n* something that arouses action or activity ⟨The relaxed zoning regulations should serve as a *stimulant* for development in the area.⟩ — see IMPULSE 1

stimulate *vb* **1** to give life, vigor, or spirit to ⟨Research into alternative energy sources has been *stimulated* by this funding increase.⟩ — see ANIMATE

2 to rouse to strong feeling or action ⟨Their discussion *stimulated* him to learn more about the subject.⟩ — see PROVOKE 1

stimulating *adj* **1** causing great emotional or mental stimulation ⟨enjoys the good food and *stimulating* conversation at his best friend's house⟩ — see EXCITING 1

2 having a renewing effect on the state of the body or mind ⟨a brisk, *stimulating* walk on a bright, clear wintry day⟩ — see TONIC 1

3 serving or likely to arouse a strong reaction ⟨an article containing a *stimulating* argument for raising, not lowering, the tax on gasoline⟩ — see PROVOCATIVE

stimulative *adj* having a renewing effect on the state of the body or mind ⟨the supposed *stimulative* power of herbal teas⟩ — see TONIC 1

stimulus *n* something that arouses action or activity ⟨Seeing a Broadway play for the first time was the *stimulus* for her career in the theater.⟩ — see IMPULSE 1

sting *vb* **1** to charge (someone) too much for goods or services ⟨a business that's been *stinging* patrons for years⟩ — see OVERCHARGE 1

2 to rob by the use of trickery or threats ⟨swindlers who *sting* unwary tourists⟩ — see FLEECE

sting *n* **1** an instance of the use of dishonest methods to acquire something of value ⟨The pawn shop operation turned out to be a *sting* by undercover police officers to catch the ring of burglars.⟩ — see FRAUD 1

2 a sharp unpleasant sensation usually felt in some specific part of the body ⟨the *sting* of cold air against my face⟩ — see PAIN 1

stinger *n* a hard strike with a part of the body or an instrument ⟨In the eighth round he delivered a *stinger* that knocked his opponent flat.⟩ — see ¹BLOW

stinginess *n* the quality or practice of being overly sparing with money ⟨Refusing to tip poorly paid restaurant servers is a particularly petty form of *stinginess*.⟩ — see PARSIMONY 1

stinging *adj* causing intense discomfort to one's skin ⟨These cold, *stinging* winds are not just a discomfort—they can be dangerous to exposed flesh.⟩ — see CUTTING 1

stingy *adj* **1** giving or sharing as little as possible ⟨Until his redemption, Ebenezer Scrooge is the classic example of a very *stingy*, heartless miser.⟩

synonyms cheap, close, closefisted, mean, niggard, niggardly, parsimonious, penurious, spare, sparing, stinting, tight, tightfisted, uncharitable

related words careful, conserving, economical, economizing, frugal, saving, scrimping, skimping, thrifty; acquisitive, avaricious, covetous, grasping, greedy, hoggish, mercenary, rapacious; begrudging, envious, grudging, resentful; inhospitable

near antonyms altruistic, selfless, unselfish; extrava-

gant, lavish, overgenerous, profuse; beneficent, benevolent, hospitable, humanitarian, philanthropic (*also* philanthropical); compassionate, good-hearted, greathearted, kindly, magnanimous, openhearted; thriftless, unthrifty; dissipating, frittering, prodigal, profligate, spendthrift, splurging, squandering, wasteful, wasting

antonyms bounteous, bountiful, charitable, freehanded, generous, liberal, munificent, openhanded, unsparing

2 less plentiful than what is normal, necessary, or desirable ⟨a *stingy* serving of mashed potatoes⟩ — see MEAGER

stink *n* **1** a strong unpleasant smell ⟨The *stink* of burned plastic lingered in the kitchen for days after we accidentally melted a spatula on the stove.⟩

synonyms funk, reek, stench

related words acridness, fetidness, foulness, fustiness, malodorousness, mustiness, rancidity, rankness, staleness; badness, vileness; dirtiness, filthiness, nastiness; odor, redolence, scent

near antonyms floweriness, lusciousness, savoriness, spiciness, sweetness

antonyms aroma, fragrance, perfume

2 a feeling or declaration of disapproval or dissent ⟨Many town residents raised an unholy *stink* about the proposal to increase taxes yet again.⟩ — see OBJECTION

stink *vb* to give off an extremely unpleasant smell ⟨The dog *stinks* because she tangled with a skunk again.⟩

synonyms reek

related words exhale, savor (*also* savour), smell; decay, decompose, rot, spoil; disgust, offend, repulse, revolt

stinker *n* a person whose behavior is offensive to others ⟨Some *stinker* nearly crashed his car into me because he was yakking on his cell phone.⟩ — see JERK 1

stinking *adj* having an unpleasant smell ⟨came home from their trip to find *stinking* garbage that had been left in the kitchen⟩ — see MALODOROUS

stinky *adj* having an unpleasant smell ⟨a *stinky* plant that attracts certain insects and then devours them⟩ — see MALODOROUS

stint *n* **1** a fixed period of time during which a person holds a job or position ⟨signed up for a three-year *stint* in the army⟩ — see TERM 1

2 the act or practice of keeping something (as an activity) within certain boundaries ⟨His parents have always supported him without *stint*, no matter what interests he has chosen to pursue.⟩ — see RESTRICTION 2

stint (on) *vb* to use or give out in stingy amounts ⟨The entrées would be worth these prices if the restaurant didn't *stint on* the side dishes so much.⟩ — see SPARE 1

stinting *adj* giving or sharing as little as possible ⟨a *stinting* boss who doesn't give regular raises⟩ — see STINGY 1

stipend *n* the money paid regularly to a person for labor or services ⟨The *stipend* you'll receive as an intern will just barely cover your housing costs.⟩ — see WAGE

stipple *vb* to mark with small spots especially unevenly ⟨The sunlight falling through the lace curtain *stippled* her face.⟩ — see SPOT 1

stippled *adj* marked with spots ⟨create a *stippled* effect by dabbing a contrasting color of paint over an undercoat with a rag or sponge⟩ — see SPOTTED 1

stipulate (for) *vb* to ask for (something) earnestly or with authority ⟨The contract *stipulates for* a renegotiation of the terms after two years.⟩ — see DEMAND 1

stipulation *n* something upon which the carrying out of an agreement or offer depends ⟨Their proposal for a baseball franchise includes several *stipulations* that are unacceptable.⟩ — see CONDITION 2

stir *n* **1** a state of noisy, confused activity ⟨The plane's first jolt caused a *stir* among the passengers, and by the third one they were in a panic.⟩ — see COMMOTION

2 the act or an instance of changing position ⟨We were warned that the slightest *stir* would scare the mother bird so we hardly dared to breathe.⟩ — see MOVEMENT 1

stir *vb* **1** to cause (as a liquid) to move about in a circle especially repeatedly ⟨The recipe says to *stir* the mixture carefully until it's properly blended.⟩
synonyms agitate, churn, swirl, wash, whirl
related words beat, paddle, whip, whisk; reel, shake, wheel
2 to change one's position ⟨The cat *stirred*, then opened its eyes and slowly got to its feet.⟩ — see MOVE 3
3 to rouse to strong feeling or action ⟨News coverage of the fire *stirred* many to send donations to a fund for the families who had lost their homes.⟩ — see PROVOKE 1

stir (up) *vb* to bring (something volatile or intense) into being ⟨I couldn't *stir up* any interest in a Saturday morning outing to the art museum.⟩ — see INCITE 1

stirring *adj* **1** causing great emotional or mental stimulation ⟨The message of brotherhood in Martin Luther King's *stirring* "I Have a Dream" speech still resonates today.⟩ — see EXCITING 1
2 having the power to affect the feelings or sympathies ⟨a *stirring* rendition of the national anthem⟩ — see MOVING
3 marked by much life, movement, or activity ⟨Spring has arrived, and the meadow is *stirring* with life.⟩ — see ALIVE 2

stirring *n* the act or an instance of changing position ⟨I thought I detected a slight *stirring* of the leaves, and yet there wasn't a breath of wind.⟩ — see MOVEMENT 1

stitch *n* a sharp unpleasant sensation usually felt in some specific part of the body ⟨Joe had to drop out of the race when the *stitch* in his side became too painful.⟩ — see PAIN 1

stitch *vb* to close up with a series of interlacing stitches ⟨The doctor *stitched* the wound so adroitly that the scar was barely visible after the stitches were removed.⟩ — see SEW

stock *adj* accepted, used, or practiced by most people ⟨The conversation became interesting once we got beyond the *stock* niceties and observations about the weather.⟩ — see CURRENT 1

stock *n* **1** a group of persons who come from the same ancestor ⟨The brothers come from good *stock*.⟩ — see FAMILY 1
2 a stupid person ⟨just sat there like a *stock*, staring at me blankly whenever I asked him a question⟩ — see IDIOT
3 firm belief in the integrity, ability, effectiveness, or genuineness of someone or something ⟨Don't put any *stock* in her promises—she'll just tell you what she thinks you want to hear.⟩ — see TRUST 1
4 the line of ancestors from whom a person is descended ⟨His family is of mixed northern European *stock*.⟩ — see ANCESTRY
5 the number of individuals or amount of something available at any given time ⟨The new study adds to the general *stock* of knowledge about genetic disorders.⟩ — see SUPPLY

stockade *n* a place of confinement for persons held in lawful custody ⟨prisoners of war confined in a *stockade*⟩ — see JAIL

stocking *n* a close-fitting covering for the foot and leg ⟨thick wool *stockings* designed to be worn with hiking boots⟩
synonyms hose, sock
related words hosiery; support hose; anklet, bobby socks, bootee

stockpile *n* a supply stored up and often hidden away ⟨an emergency *stockpile* of potable water and canned goods in the cellar⟩ — see HOARD 1

stockpile *vb* to put (something of future use or value) in a safe or secret place ⟨We should be able to *stockpile* enough vaccine for the upcoming flu season.⟩ — see HOARD

stocky *adj* being compact and broad in build and often short in stature ⟨The *stocky* boxer's strength and speed more than make up for his opponent's longer reach.⟩

synonyms chunky, dumpy, heavyset, squat, squatty, stout, stubby, stumpy, thickset
related words beefy, brawny, bulky, burly, husky, sturdy, thick, thickish, weighty; chubby, heavy, plump, portly, pudgy, roly-poly, rotund, round, tubby
near antonyms delicate, fragile, frail, puny; lean, skinny, slender, slim, spare, thin; angular, gaunt, lank, lanky, rawboned, sinewy; scraggy, scrawny, slight; spindly, twiggy, waspish, weedy, willowy, wiry

stodgy *adj* causing weariness, restlessness, or lack of interest ⟨The sitcom was offbeat and interesting in its first season, but has since become predictable and *stodgy*.⟩ — see BORING

stoic *or* **stoical** *adj* **1** accepting pains or hardships calmly or without complaint ⟨Years of misfortune had made them *stoic* in the face of adversity.⟩ — see PATIENT 1
2 not feeling or showing emotion ⟨At her husband's funeral she remained *stoic*, and only a few imagined the depth of her grief.⟩ — see IMPASSIVE 1

stolid *adj* **1** not expressing any emotion ⟨The butler responded to the duchess's constant demands with *stolid* indifference.⟩ — see BLANK 1
2 not feeling or showing emotion ⟨The actor's turn as a *stolid*, impersonal bureaucrat was an interesting departure from his more impassioned roles.⟩ — see IMPASSIVE 1

stomach *vb* to put up with (something painful or difficult) ⟨I could no longer *stomach* working for such a petty tyrant.⟩ — see BEAR 2

stomach *n* **1** the part of the body between the chest and the pelvis ⟨Please don't lean on my *stomach*—I just had a big meal!⟩
synonyms abdomen, belly, breadbasket [*slang*], gut, solar plexus, tummy
related words middle, midriff, waist; paunch, potbelly; thorax
2 a need or desire for food ⟨The cake looks delicious, but I'm afraid that I have no *stomach* for sweets right now.⟩ — see HUNGER 1

stomachache *n* abdominal pain especially when focused in the digestive organs ⟨All that fried food gave me a *stomachache*.⟩
synonyms bellyache
related words colic, cramps, gripes

stomp *vb* **1** to move heavily or clumsily ⟨The girl came *stomping* up the stairs and tossed her backpack on the bed.⟩ — see LUMBER 1
2 to tread on heavily so as to crush or injure ⟨*stomping* the burning leaves in a vain attempt to put out the fire⟩ — see TRAMPLE

stone–blind *adj* lacking the power of sight ⟨He's so oblivious to everything around him that you'd think he was *stone-blind*.⟩ — see BLIND

stone's throw *n* a very small distance or degree ⟨The cottage is a *stone's throw* from the beach.⟩ — see HAIR 1

stoneware *n* articles made of baked clay ⟨collects 19th-century English *stoneware*, especially soup tureens⟩ — see CROCKERY

stony *also* **stoney** *adj* having or showing a lack of sympathy or tender feelings ⟨The judge's *stony* demeanor didn't raise the defendant's hopes for a more lenient sentence.⟩ — see HARD 1

stool pigeon *n* a person who provides information about another's wrongdoing ⟨The FBI finally got a break when a *stool pigeon* talked.⟩ — see INFORMER

stoop *vb* to descend to a level that is beneath one's dignity ⟨The debate would be more enlightening if both sides didn't *stoop* to name-calling.⟩ — see CONDESCEND 1

stooping *adj* bending downward or forward ⟨rested under the *stooping* branches of the willow tree⟩ — see NODDING

stop *n* **1** a brief halt in a journey ⟨Our guide called for a *stop* at the trail hut so we could eat and rest a bit.⟩
synonyms layover, stopover
related words break, pause, rest
2 a regular stopping place ⟨had lunch on a picnic table at a shady rest *stop* along the highway⟩ — see STATION 2
3 something that makes movement or progress difficult ⟨pulled out all the *stops* and presented the most spectacular show ever⟩ — see ENCUMBRANCE
4 the stopping of a process or activity ⟨Let's put a *stop* to this nonsense.⟩ — see END 1
stop *vb* **1** to bring (as an action or operation) to an immediate end ⟨The manufacturer will *stop* selling the toy and will immediately recall all the units that have already been sold.⟩
synonyms break, break off, break up, can [*slang*], cease, cut off, cut out, desist (from), discontinue, drop, end, halt, knock off, lay off, leave off, quit, shut off
related words complete, conclude, finish; deactivate; block, blockade, dam, delay, detain, hinder, hold, hold back, impede, kibosh, obstruct, stem; call, suspend; arrest, brake, check, clamp down, rein (in), squash, squelch, stamp, stanch (*or* staunch), stunt, suppress; pause, stay, suspend
phrases have done with, put the kibosh on
near antonyms carry on, continue, keep up, run on; advance, proceed, progress
2 to bring (something) to a standstill ⟨Traffic was *stopped* for over an hour by the overturned truck.⟩ — see ¹HALT 1
3 to close up so that no empty spaces remain ⟨I *stopped* the mouse hole with plaster.⟩ — see FILL 2
4 to come to an end ⟨The music *stopped* but we kept on dancing.⟩ — see CEASE 1
stop (by *or* **in)** *vb* to make a brief visit ⟨*Stop by* on your way to the game so we can go there together.⟩ — see CALL 3
stop (up) *vb* to prevent passage through by filling with something ⟨Clear the leaves out of the rain gutters so they don't *stop up* the downspouts again.⟩ — see CLOG 1
stopcock *n* a fixture for controlling the flow of a liquid ⟨a mechanical engineer who designs industrial valves and *stopcocks*⟩ — see FAUCET
stopgap *n* a temporary replacement ⟨The coach we have now was only hired as a *stopgap* until someone with more experience is found.⟩ — see MAKESHIFT
stopover *n* a brief halt in a journey ⟨I've been to Belgium—if you count a *stopover* in Brussels on my way to Istanbul.⟩ — see STOP 1
stoppage *n* the stopping of a process or activity ⟨yet another *stoppage* in play for some unexplained reason⟩ — see END 1
storage *n* a building for storing goods ⟨In colonial times the granary was one of the community's most important *storages*.⟩ — see STOREHOUSE
store *adj* made beforehand in large numbers ⟨preferred homemade bread to *store* brands⟩ — see READY-MADE
store *n* **1** a collection of things kept available for future use or need ⟨He has a *store* of old magazines that he has been collecting for years.⟩
synonyms cache, deposit, hoard, reserve
related words budget, fund, nest egg; armory, arsenal, bank, pool, stock, stockpile, supply; accumulation, assemblage, collection, gathering
2 a supply stored up and often hidden away ⟨keeps a *store* of napkins in the glove compartment⟩ — see HOARD 1
3 an establishment where goods are sold to consumers ⟨I need to go to the grocery *store* for orange juice and eggs.⟩ — see SHOP 1

4 a considerable amount ⟨We laid by a *store* of food for the party.⟩ — see LOT 2
store *vb* **1** to place somewhere for safekeeping or ready availability ⟨We decided to *store* the lawn mower in the shed instead of the garage.⟩
synonyms keep, put up, stow
related words cellar, garage, hangar, house, warehouse; file, pack, shelve
2 to put (something of future use or value) in a safe or secret place ⟨Squirrels commonly *store* nuts in the hollows of trees and other places to prepare for the winter.⟩ — see HOARD
storehouse *n* a building for storing goods ⟨The company has a large *storehouse* filled with lumber for manufacturing its line of furniture.⟩
synonyms depository, depot, magazine, repository, storage, warehouse
related words cache, stockroom, storeroom; bank, bin, container, locker, safe-deposit box, strongbox; arsenal, dump; stowage
storm *vb* **1** to express one's anger usually violently ⟨The chef spent the morning *storming* at his staff about the ruined sauces.⟩ — see RAGE 1
2 to fall as water in a continuous stream of drops from the clouds ⟨It *storms* so frequently up in the mountains that the peaks are rarely visible from the valley below.⟩ — see RAIN 1
3 to take sudden, violent action against ⟨The pirates *stormed* the ship.⟩ — see ATTACK 1
4 to be excited or emotionally stirred up with anger ⟨By the time we arrived, our hostess was *storming* because dinner was ruined.⟩ — see BOIL 1
storm *n* **1** a disturbance of the atmosphere accompanied by wind and often by precipitation (as rain or snow) ⟨a winter *storm* bringing about six inches of snow⟩
synonyms squall, tempest
related words blizzard, ice storm, snowstorm; cloudburst, hailstorm, rainstorm, thundershower, thunderstorm, weather, windstorm; northeaster (*or* nor'easter), norther, southeaster, southwester; cyclone, hurricane, typhoon; sandstorm
2 a heavy fall of objects ⟨Police had to endure a *storm* of rocks and bricks hurled by the rioters.⟩ — see RAIN 2
3 a rapid or overwhelming outpouring of many things at once ⟨The army's spokesperson faced a *storm* of questions from reporters.⟩ — see BARRAGE
4 a state of noisy, confused activity ⟨a few minutes of calm before the *storm*, when the store would open its doors on the busiest day of the year⟩ — see COMMOTION
5 a steady falling of water from the sky in significant quantity ⟨The *storm* caused major damage to our barn.⟩ — see RAIN 1
6 a sudden intense expression of strong feeling ⟨A *storm* of indignation and demands for his resignation arose when the mayor's dishonesty was exposed.⟩ — see OUTBURST 1
7 a violent disturbance (as of the political or social order) ⟨the *storms* of unrest that swept through Europe prior to World War I⟩ — see CONVULSION
stormy *adj* **1** marked by bursts of destructive force or intense activity ⟨a small nation, but one with a long and *stormy* history⟩ — see VIOLENT 1
2 marked by or abounding with rain ⟨*Stormy* weather was forecast for the next three days, so we cancelled our camping trip.⟩ — see RAINY
3 marked by sudden or violent disturbance ⟨They have a *stormy* relationship.⟩ — see CONVULSIVE 1
4 marked by turmoil or disturbance especially of natural elements ⟨Neptune has the *stormiest* atmosphere of any

planet, with winds of up to 900 miles per hour.⟩ — see WILD 3

5 marked by wet and windy conditions ⟨*Stormy* seas forced the schooner far off its intended course.⟩ — see FOUL 1

story *n* **1** a work with imaginary characters and events that is shorter and usually less complex than a novel ⟨He's a talented writer, but his quirky *stories* will never find a wide readership.⟩

synonyms narrative, novelette, novella, short story, tale, yarn

related words bedtime story; exemplum, fable, parable; anecdote, joke; fairy tale, folktale, legend, myth, romance; account, annals, chronicle, history, record, report

2 a brief account of something interesting that happened especially to one personally ⟨Grandpa is always telling *stories* about what it was like growing up on a farm.⟩

synonyms anecdote, tale, yarn

related words episode, event, happening, incident, occurrence; recital, recitation

3 a report of recent events or facts not previously known ⟨a *story* in the morning paper about plans for a new library⟩ — see NEWS

4 a relating of events usually in the order in which they happened ⟨gave us the whole *story* of the accident⟩ — see ACCOUNT 1

5 a rumor or report of a personal or sensational nature ⟨*stories* going around that the old man had died with thousands of dollars hidden under his mattress⟩ — see TALE 1

6 a statement known by its maker to be untrue and made in order to deceive ⟨She tells *stories* just to get attention, so don't believe that stuff about her father being somebody important.⟩ — see LIE

7 the unfolding of events in a dramatic or literary work ⟨The *story* proceeds at a pace that many readers will find a bit too leisurely.⟩ — see ACTION 2

8 position with regard to conditions and circumstances ⟨Management is trying to figure out what the *story* is with the accident down in the warehouse.⟩ — see SITUATION 1

storyteller *n* a person who tells lies ⟨He's something of a *storyteller*, so I wouldn't put too much stock in anything he says.⟩ — see LIAR

stout *adj* **1** able to withstand hardship, strain, or exposure ⟨erected a *stout* wooden fence to keep the wild animals out⟩ — see HARDY 1

2 being compact and broad in build and often short in stature ⟨The wrestler is *stout* in build, so he is frequently underestimated by his opponents.⟩ — see STOCKY

3 feeling or displaying no fear by temperament ⟨*stout* souls who boldly ventured forward, not knowing what kinds of danger they faced⟩ — see BRAVE 1

4 having muscles capable of exerting great physical force ⟨covered wagons drawn by *stout* oxen⟩ — see STRONG 1

5 not showing weakness or uncertainty ⟨a *stout* defender of women's rights around the world⟩ — see FIRM 1

stouthearted *adj* feeling or displaying no fear by temperament ⟨*stouthearted* men and women who served in the army medical corps⟩ — see BRAVE 1

stoutly *adv* in a vigorous and forceful manner ⟨a settler *stoutly* defending his right to be on the land⟩ — see HARD 3

stoutness *n* strength of mind to carry on in spite of danger ⟨Even in the face of insurmountable odds, the troops displayed a *stoutness* of heart that was inspiring.⟩ — see COURAGE

stow *vb* **1** to place somewhere for safekeeping or ready availability ⟨*Stow* the extra life jackets in the chest.⟩ — see STORE 1

2 to put (something of future use or value) in a safe or secret place ⟨*stowed* some extra protein bars in her backpack⟩ — see HOARD

straggler *n* someone who moves slowly or more slowly than others ⟨The cowboy had to round up a few *stragglers*.⟩ — see SLOWPOKE

straight *adv* **1** in a direct line or course ⟨When we got to the airport, we went *straight* to the baggage claim area.⟩ — see DIRECTLY 1

2 in an honest and direct manner ⟨We gave it to him *straight*: his performance would have to improve—or he was out.⟩ — see STRAIGHTFORWARD

straight *adj* **1** free from irregularities or digressions in course ⟨In the wide, open spaces of the West some rural roads are incredibly *straight*.⟩

synonyms direct, linear, right, straightaway, straightforward

related words unbent, uncurled, untwisted; undeviating, unswerving

near antonyms bowed, rounded; entwined, kinked, swirled, turned, turning, twined, twining, twisted, twisting, veering, warped; bending, coiled, coiling, corkscrew, curled, curling, curved, curving, looped, looping, spiral, spiraling (*or* spiralling), wavy, winding; devious, serpentine, sinuous; crooked, zigzag, zigzagging

2 conforming to a high standard of morality or virtue ⟨a store owner known and trusted for his *straight* dealings⟩ — see GOOD 2

3 free from added matter ⟨poured *straight* vinegar on the salad⟩ — see PURE 1

4 free in expressing one's true feelings and opinions ⟨You should be *straight* with your boss and tell him that you're not happy with the current situation.⟩ — see FRANK

5 going straight to the point clearly and firmly ⟨a politician who can never give a *straight* answer to questions about his positions⟩ — see STRAIGHTFORWARD 1

6 not having one's mind affected by alcohol ⟨has been *straight* for two years now⟩ — see SOBER 1

7 following one after another without others coming in between ⟨I was awake for two *straight* days.⟩ — see CONSECUTIVE

straightaway *adj* **1** done or occurring without any noticeable lapse in time ⟨Her first novel was a *straightaway* success.⟩ — see INSTANTANEOUS

2 free from irregularities or digressions in course ⟨The doomed ship was headed on a *straightaway* course in the path of the iceberg.⟩ — see STRAIGHT 1

straightaway *adv* without delay ⟨He got to the hospital, and *straightaway* he was admitted and given intravenous fluids.⟩ — see IMMEDIATELY

straighten *vb* to cause to follow a line that is without bends or curls ⟨*Straighten* that extension cord—it should be just long enough to reach the wall outlet.⟩

synonyms unbend, uncurl

related words uncoil, unroll, unwind; disentangle, untangle, untwine, untwist

near antonyms arc, bend, bow, hook, round; entwine, swirl, turn, twine, twist; coil, loop, spiral, wind

antonyms bend, crook, curl, curve

straightforward *adj* **1** going straight to the point clearly and firmly ⟨a *straightforward* account of the football game with no digressions or personal comments⟩

synonyms direct, forthright, foursquare, plain, straight

related words aboveboard, candid, frank, free-spoken, honest, open, openhearted, outspoken, plainspoken, unguarded, unreserved; artless, earnest, sincere; uninhibited, unrestrained; abrupt, bluff, blunt, brusque (*also* brusk), curt, gruff, point-blank, sharp; impolite, inconsiderate, rude, tactless

near antonyms circumlocutory, long-winded, prolix,

verbose, wordy; inhibited, reserved, restrained; civil, courteous, polite, tactful; ambiguous, equivocal, evasive, misleading; double-dealing, hypocritical, two-faced
antonyms circuitous, indirect, roundabout
2 free from irregularities or digressions in course ⟨took a *straightforward* route home⟩ — see STRAIGHT 1
3 free in expressing one's true feelings and opinions ⟨I want you to be *straightforward* with me and tell me if this sounds like a bad idea.⟩ — see FRANK
4 not subject to misinterpretation or more than one interpretation ⟨The distinction between the two types of offenses is pretty *straightforward*.⟩ — see CLEAR 2
straightforward *also* **straightforwards** *adv* in an honest and direct manner ⟨She finally told him *straightforward* that he wasn't going to get the job.⟩
synonyms directly, forthrightly, foursquare, plain, plainly, straight, straightforwardly
related words candidly, frankly, honestly, openheartedly, openly, unguardedly, unreservedly; artlessly, earnestly, simply, sincerely; abruptly, bluntly, brusquely, gruffly, point-blank, sharply; impolitely, inconsiderately, rudely, tactlessly
near antonyms long-windedly, verbosely, wordily; civilly, courteously, diplomatically, politely, tactfully; ambiguously, circuitously, equivocally, evasively, indirectly
straightforwardly *adv* in an honest and direct manner ⟨*Straightforwardly* yet compassionately, the doctor tells his patients what their options are.⟩ — see STRAIGHTFORWARD
straightforwardness *n* the free expression of one's true feelings and opinions ⟨Not all of her voice students appreciate the *straightforwardness* with which she tells them that they're not going to make it as professional singers.⟩ — see CANDOR 1
straightway *adv* **1** without delay ⟨*Straightway*, the decorator told us that the old couch had to go.⟩ — see IMMEDIATELY
2 in a direct line or course ⟨She went *straightway* to the main office to turn in the cell phone she'd found.⟩ — see DIRECTLY 1
¹strain *n* **1** the line of ancestors from whom a person is descended ⟨descended from a *strain* of Irish seafarers⟩ — see ANCESTRY
2 a rhythmic series of musical tones arranged to give a pleasing effect ⟨The *strain* of an old Irish ballad rose up from the revelers downstairs.⟩ — see MELODY
3 a very small amount ⟨I detected a *strain* of panic in her voice when she asked if the substance was poisonous.⟩ — see PARTICLE 1
4 a number of persons or things that are grouped together because they have something in common ⟨writes mystery novels of a more sophisticated *strain*⟩ — see SORT 1
²strain *n* the burden on one's emotional or mental well-being created by demands on one's time ⟨The family's constant moving is putting a real *strain* on the children.⟩ — see STRESS 1
strain *vb* **1** to injure by overuse, misuse, or pressure ⟨In order to lift something heavy, squat down and lift with your legs, or you'll *strain* your back.⟩
synonyms pull, rack, stretch, wrench
related words fray, tax, weaken; damage, harm, hurt, impair, wound; batter, bruise, tear; cripple, lame, mangle, mutilate
2 to pass through a filter ⟨Better *strain* that coffee thoroughly to get all the grounds out.⟩
synonyms filter, screen
related words leach, percolate
3 to devote serious and sustained effort ⟨The whole department is *straining* to complete the project before the deadline.⟩ — see LABOR

4 to flow forth slowly through small openings ⟨Put the cooked fruit in a cheesecloth bag and let the juice *strain* into a pan.⟩ — see EXUDE
5 to subject (a personal quality or faculty) to often excessive stress ⟨*strained* her memory but the name just wouldn't come to her⟩ — see TRY 1
6 to put one's arms around and press tightly ⟨The woman tenderly *strained* to her breast the child that she had missed so badly.⟩ — see EMBRACE 1
strained *adj* lacking in natural or spontaneous quality ⟨I took the complaint manager's *strained* smile to mean I wasn't a welcome sight.⟩ — see ARTIFICIAL 1
strait *n* **1** a narrow body of water between two land masses ⟨As the ship headed east through the *Strait* of Gibraltar, Spain was on our left and Africa on our right.⟩ — see CHANNEL 2
2 *often* **straits** *pl* a state of great suffering of body or mind ⟨She was in great *straits* over the loss of her mother's cherished necklace.⟩ — see DISTRESS 1
straitlaced *or* **straightlaced** *adj* given to or marked by very conservative standards regarding personal behavior or morals ⟨In the movie, she plays a teacher whose forthrightness with her students shocks her more *straitlaced* colleagues.⟩
synonyms prim, prudish, puritanical
related words priggish, staid, stuffy; genteel, proper, refined; decent, honest, moral, right, righteous, upright, virtuous
near antonyms liberated, permissive; bad, immoral, improper, indecent, lax, loose, prurient, wicked; slatternly, sleazy; debauched, degenerate, degraded, depraved, perverted
strand *n* the usually sandy or gravelly land bordering a body of water ⟨the wishful dream of living an indolent, idyllic existence on some far-off *strand*⟩ — see BEACH
strand *vb* **1** to cause irreparable damage to (a ship) by running aground or sinking ⟨the ghostly remains of ships that had been *stranded* by the reef⟩ — see SHIPWRECK
2 to cause to remain behind ⟨She missed her flight and was *stranded* at the airport.⟩ — see LEAVE 1
stranded *adj* resting on the shore or bottom of a body of water ⟨discovered a *stranded* dolphin on the beach⟩ — see AGROUND
strange *adj* **1** different from the ordinary in a way that causes curiosity or suspicion ⟨The *strange* smell we'd noticed turned out, unhappily, to be from the dinner our host was making.⟩ — see ODD 2
2 excitingly or mysteriously unusual ⟨*strange* fruits from faraway lands⟩ — see EXOTIC
3 not known or experienced before ⟨Using public transportation was all very *strange* to a rural girl like her.⟩ — see NEW 2
4 noticeably different from what is generally found or experienced ⟨a rather *strange* story about a garden filled with poisonous plants⟩ — see UNUSUAL 1
stranger *n* a person who is not native to or known to a community ⟨The people of the island are quick to make *strangers* feel at home.⟩
synonyms foreigner, nonnative, outlander, outsider
related words alien, nonresident; outcast, pariah; drifter, transient, wanderer
near antonyms buddy, chum, comrade, confidant, crony, familiar, friend, intimate, pal; acquaintance, associate, cohort, colleague, companion, fellow, hearty, hobnobber, mate, partner, peer; citizen, habitant, inhabitant, resident
antonyms native
strangle *vb* **1** to be or cause to be killed by lack of breathable air ⟨The gull got tangled in a piece of fishing line on the beach and was *strangled*.⟩ — see SMOTHER 1

2 to keep (someone) from breathing by exerting pressure on the windpipe ⟨The boy complained that he was being *strangled* by his tie.⟩ — see CHOKE 1

3 to refrain from openly showing or uttering ⟨*strangled* a gasp of surprise upon hearing the news⟩ — see SUPPRESS 2

stratagem *n* a clever often underhanded means to achieve an end ⟨I tried various *stratagems* to get the cat into the carrier, but the feisty feline was wise to them all.⟩ — see TRICK 1

strategy *n* **1** a method worked out in advance for achieving some objective ⟨a statewide *strategy* to raise students' achievement test scores over the next three years⟩ — see PLAN 1

2 the means or procedure for doing something ⟨You'll need a better *strategy* than just knocking on doors if you want to sell that many magazines.⟩ — see METHOD

stratum *n* **1** one of the segments of society into which people are grouped ⟨The lower *strata* of society have been hit especially hard by this economic downturn.⟩ — see CLASS 1

2 the placement of someone or something in relation to others in a vertical arrangement ⟨The level of writing in that pop novel is several *strata* beneath that of serious fiction.⟩ — see RANK 1

straw *adj* of a pale yellow or yellowish brown color ⟨The cheese maker told us that the best Parmesan cheeses are *straw*, not white, in color.⟩ — see BLOND

stray *adj* lacking a definite plan, purpose, or pattern ⟨*stray* sightings of UFO's, none of which have been rigorously analyzed by scientists⟩ — see RANDOM

streak *n* **1** a line or long narrow section differing in color from the background ⟨The flower has white petals with red *streaks*.⟩ — see ¹STRIPE 1

2 a very small amount ⟨There's just a *streak* of stubbornness in that child.⟩ — see PARTICLE 1

streak *vb* to make stripes on ⟨Light from the setting sun *streaked* the clouds in brilliant bands of pink and orange.⟩ — see STRIPE

streaked *adj* having stripes ⟨hair *streaked* with gray⟩ — see STRIPED

stream *vb* **1** to cause to flow in a stream ⟨His eyes were *streaming* tears.⟩ — see POUR 1

2 to move in a stream ⟨water *streaming* out of a hose⟩ — see FLOW 1

3 to move or proceed smoothly and readily ⟨cars *streaming* along the freeway⟩ — see FLOW 2

streamer *n* a piece of cloth with a special design that is used as an emblem or for signaling ⟨*Streamers* in the team's colors hung from the top of the stadium.⟩ — see FLAG 1

streamlet *n* a natural body of running water smaller than a river ⟨The raging brook of last spring is a mere *streamlet* now that it's July.⟩ — see CREEK 1

streamline *vb* to make less complex ⟨*Streamline* the work of mailing out flyers by using computer-generated labels.⟩ — see SIMPLIFY 1

street *n* a passage cleared for public vehicular travel ⟨going the wrong way on a one-way *street*⟩ — see WAY 1

strength *n* **1** the ability to exert effort for the accomplishment of a task ⟨I found the *strength* to do what had to be done.⟩ — see POWER 2

2 the ability to withstand force or stress without being distorted, dislodged, or damaged ⟨This cheap shelving unit doesn't have the *strength* to hold all those books.⟩ — see STABILITY 1

strengthen *vb* **1** to increase the ability of (as a muscle) to exert physical force ⟨Lifting weights every day will eventually *strengthen* your muscles.⟩ ⟨The army makes new recruits run for miles in order to *strengthen* them.⟩

synonyms beef (up), fortify, harden, toughen

related words anneal, temper; firm (up), tone (up); energize, invigorate, vitalize; restrengthen

near antonyms cripple, incapacitate, paralyze; damage, harm, hurt, impair, injure; break down, wear out; sap, undercut, undermine

antonyms debilitate, enervate, enfeeble, weaken

2 to make able to withstand physical hardship, strain, or exposure ⟨Tim required weeks of physical therapy to *strengthen* his arm enough to pitch for the team again.⟩ — see HARDEN 2

3 to make markedly greater in measure or degree ⟨encouraged the boarding school students to *strengthen* their ties with the community by doing public service⟩ — see INTENSIFY

4 to prepare (oneself) mentally or emotionally ⟨*strengthened* herself for the moment she'd have to tell her friend that she had lost the borrowed necklace⟩ — see FORTIFY 1

strenuous *adj* **1** marked by or uttered with forcefulness ⟨parents who voiced *strenuous* objections to the new textbooks⟩ — see EMPHATIC 1

2 requiring considerable physical or mental effort ⟨a *strenuous* workout on the obstacle course⟩ — see HARD 2

strenuously *adv* **1** in a vigorous and forceful manner ⟨The coach argued *strenuously* in favor of easing the academic requirements for participation in school sports.⟩ — see HARD 3

2 with great effort or determination ⟨The IT staff worked *strenuously* to get the network back online.⟩ — see HARD 1

stress *n* **1** the burden on one's emotional or mental well-being created by demands on one's time ⟨With a full-time job and her college courses, the young woman is under a lot of *stress* right now.⟩

synonyms pressure, strain, tension

related words load, weight; anxiety, concern, uneasiness, worry; aggravation, anger, annoyance, exasperation, irritation, persecution, trouble

near antonyms comfort, consolation

2 a special notice or importance given to something ⟨The company's orientation program places considerable *stress* on workplace safety.⟩ — see EMPHASIS 1

stress *vb* **1** to experience concern or anxiety ⟨The restaurant manager has a tendency to *stress* about every little thing that goes wrong.⟩ — see WORRY 1

2 to make more apparent ⟨His bad performance only *stressed* what I'd been saying all along.⟩ — see EMPHASIZE 2

3 to indicate the importance of by centering attention on ⟨The doctor *stressed* the importance of exercise.⟩ — see EMPHASIZE 1

stressed–out *adj* suffering from high levels of physical and especially psychological stress ⟨The demands of this job are enough to make anyone *stressed-out*.⟩

synonyms shell-shocked

related words burned-out (*or* burnt-out), exhausted, tired, worn-out; undone, unnerved, unstrung; edgy, nervous, tense, uneasy

near antonyms laid-back, relaxed, rested; carefree, devil-may-care, happy-go-lucky, lighthearted, unconcerned

stretch *adj* able to revert to original size and shape after being stretched, squeezed, or twisted ⟨*stretch* fabrics that don't wrinkle or sag⟩ — see ELASTIC 1

stretch *n* **1** a wide space or area ⟨a narrow *stretch* of beach below the cliffs⟩ — see EXPANSE

2 an indefinite but usually short period of time ⟨There was a cardinal at our bird feeder for a short *stretch* last spring.⟩ — see WHILE 1

3 the distance or extent between possible extremes ⟨The stories were written over a considerable *stretch* of time.⟩ — see RANGE 3

4 the space or amount of space between two points, lines, surfaces, or objects ⟨the longest *stretch* of the drive without any place to get gas⟩ — see DISTANCE 1

stretch *vb* **1** to add to the interest of by including made-up details ⟨It was *stretching* the truth to say she'd been in the movies: she was once an extra whose scene was cut in the final version.⟩ — see EMBROIDER

2 to injure by overuse, misuse, or pressure ⟨I *stretched* a back muscle, and the pain is killing me.⟩ — see STRAIN 1

3 to make longer ⟨The time it would take to fix the car got *stretched* from three hours to two days when the part we needed had to be ordered.⟩ — see EXTEND 1

4 to subject (a personal quality or faculty) to often excessive stress ⟨Your whining is *stretching* my patience to the limit.⟩ — see TRY 1

stretch (out) *vb* to arrange the parts of (something) over a wider area ⟨You can't *stretch out* your legs to the point where you're blocking the aisle.⟩ — see OPEN 3

stretchable *adj* able to revert to original size and shape after being stretched, squeezed, or twisted ⟨*stretchable* gloves⟩ ⟨*stretchable* bandages⟩ — see ELASTIC 1

stretching *n* **1** the act of making longer ⟨Excessive *stretching* can cause the fabric to tear or lose its elasticity.⟩ — see EXTENSION 1

2 the representation of something in terms that go beyond the facts ⟨Your constant *stretching* of the truth is going to get you in trouble someday.⟩ — see EXAGGERATION

strew *vb* to cover by or as if by scattering something over or on ⟨sidewalks *strewed* with trash left by the parade watchers⟩ — see SCATTER 2

strict *adj* **1** following an original exactly ⟨not a *strict* translation, because a lot of the humor is in the wordplay⟩ — see FAITHFUL 2

2 given to exacting standards of discipline and self-restraint ⟨That piano teacher is notoriously *strict*, but students make great strides under her tutelage.⟩ — see SEVERE 1

3 not allowing for any exceptions or loosening of standards ⟨on a *strict* diet⟩ ⟨*strict* adherence to the letter of the law⟩ — see RIGID 1

strictly *adv* without any relaxation of standards or precision ⟨*Strictly* speaking, Columbus did not discover America—the people living there had long known about it.⟩ ⟨The rules must be *strictly* obeyed.⟩

synonyms exactly, precisely, rigidly, rigorously

related words carefully, conscientiously, meticulously, scrupulously

antonyms imprecisely, inexactly, loosely

strictness *n* the quality or state of being demanding or unyielding (as in discipline or criticism) ⟨His stoic temperament suited him well to the demands and *strictness* of military life.⟩ — see SEVERITY

stricture *n* an often public or formal expression of disapproval ⟨I don't agree with all her *strictures* on the state of modern theater.⟩ — see CENSURE

stride *vb* to move along with a steady regular step especially in a group ⟨He *strode* across the room toward me.⟩ — see MARCH 1

strife *n* **1** a lack of agreement or harmony ⟨In order to avoid family *strife*, the children spend equal time during the holidays with both sets of grandparents.⟩ — see DISCORD

2 an earnest effort for superiority or victory over another ⟨bitter *strife* between the two political factions⟩ — see CONTEST 1

strike *n* **1** a work stoppage by a body of workers intended to force an employer to meet their demands ⟨The nurses will go on *strike* tomorrow unless they're finally given a pay raise.⟩

synonyms walkout

related words sit-down, sit-in, slowdown; lockout

2 the act or action of setting upon with force or violence ⟨The first *strike* was directed at a munitions warehouse.⟩ — see ATTACK 1

3 a feature of someone or something that creates difficulty for achieving success ⟨Kids born into poverty already have a *strike* against them.⟩ — see DISADVANTAGE 1

4 a forceful coming together of two things ⟨The *strike* of a hammer against a nail always has a satisfying sound when you're building something yourself.⟩ — see IMPACT 1

strike *vb* **1** to refuse to work in order to force an employer to meet demands ⟨The union is calling for its members to *strike* until the mining company agrees to meet safety standards.⟩

synonyms walk, walk out

related words sit in; lock out

2 to act upon (a person or a person's feelings) so as to cause a response ⟨We were *struck* by the willingness of total strangers to go out of their way to help us.⟩ — see ¹AFFECT 1

3 to enter the mind of ⟨It *struck* her later that no one at the bank had asked for identification.⟩ — see OCCUR (TO)

4 to come into usually forceful contact with something ⟨the thump of hailstones *striking* the cars in the parking lot⟩ — see HIT 2

5 to deliver a blow to (someone or something) usually in a strong vigorous manner ⟨The driver of the car behind me applied his brakes too late and *struck* my car from the rear.⟩ — see HIT 1

6 to take sudden, violent action against ⟨A rattlesnake *strikes* its prey with lightning speed.⟩ — see ATTACK 1

strike (into) *vb* to take the first step in (a process or course of action) ⟨Before you actually *strike into* your speech, you should introduce yourself.⟩ — see BEGIN 1

strike (out) *vb* to show (something written) to be no longer valid by drawing a cross over or a line through it ⟨The editor *struck out* the last few sentences of the article.⟩ — see X (OUT)

striking *adj* **1** likely to attract attention ⟨You'd be amazed what a *striking* difference a new paint job can make in a room.⟩ — see NOTICEABLE

2 very noticeable especially for being incorrect or bad ⟨several *striking* contradictions in her argument⟩ — see EGREGIOUS

string *n* **1** a length of braided, flexible material that is used for tying or connecting things ⟨A piece of *string* won't hold that gate shut if a big wind comes along.⟩ — see CORD 1

2 a series of persons or things arranged one behind another ⟨a *string* of cars stretching as far as we could see⟩ — see LINE 1

3 a series of things linked together ⟨recounted the *string* of events that led to the discovery⟩ — see CHAIN 1

string *vb* to put together into a series by means of or as if by means of a thread ⟨The prosecuting attorney *strung* the evidence together so that the accused man really did look guilty.⟩ — see THREAD 2

string along *vb* to cause to believe what is untrue ⟨The student succeeded in *stringing* even his teachers *along* with his tales of family hardships.⟩ — see DECEIVE

stringent *adj* not allowing for any exceptions or loosening of standards ⟨*stringent* rules against unauthorized persons being in the building⟩ — see RIGID 1

stringy *adj* resembling or having the texture of a mass of strings ⟨*stringy* hair that clearly needs a good washing⟩

synonyms fibrous

related words knotty, ropy (*also* ropey), thready; sinewy, wiry

strip *vb* to remove clothing from ⟨The baby was *stripped* down to his diaper for the examination.⟩ — see UNDRESS 1

strip *n* **1** a long narrow piece of material ⟨Now tear the paper into *strips* and fold them up carefully.⟩
synonyms list, ribbon, slip
related words slat; band, bandage, belt, binding, girth, strap, swatch, swath (*or* swathe), tape
2 a series of drawings that tell a story or part of a story ⟨a cartoonist who uses his daily *strip* to make his political points⟩ — see COMIC STRIP

¹**stripe** *n* **1** a line or long narrow section differing in color from the background ⟨The United States flag has seven red *stripes*.⟩
synonyms band, bar, streak
related words blaze, crossbar, pinstripe
2 a number of persons or things that are grouped together because they have something in common ⟨Singers of every *stripe* will perform at the benefit concert.⟩ — see SORT 1

²**stripe** *n* a hard strike with a part of the body or an instrument ⟨The pirate received 10 *stripes*.⟩ — see ¹BLOW

stripe *vb* to make stripes on ⟨The children carefully *striped* the paper with red and blue paint.⟩
synonyms band, bar, streak
related words blaze

striped *adj* having stripes ⟨The zebra is a black-and-white *striped* animal.⟩
synonyms barred, streaked
related words corded, tabby

stripling *n* a male person who has not yet reached adulthood ⟨The young boxer looked like a mere *stripling* next to his larger, more seasoned opponent.⟩ — see BOY 1

stripped *adj* **1** lacking a usual or natural covering ⟨bought matching end tables of *stripped* pine⟩ — see NAKED 2
2 lacking or shed of clothing ⟨Highway construction workers, *stripped* to the waist, toiled away in the sweltering heat.⟩ — see NAKED 1

strive *vb* **1** to devote serious and sustained effort ⟨Not only must we *strive* for peace in time of war, we must *strive* mightily to maintain that peace.⟩ — see LABOR
2 to make an effort to do ⟨Let us *strive* to make the most of this opportunity.⟩ — see ATTEMPT

stroke *n* a hard strike with a part of the body or an instrument ⟨All it took was one hard *stroke* to knock the ball out of the tree.⟩ — see ¹BLOW

stroke *vb* **1** to touch or handle in a tender or loving manner ⟨The young mother gently *stroked* the sleeping child's brow and then leaned over and kissed him.⟩ — see FONDLE
2 to praise too much ⟨a politician with a special gift for *stroking* fat-cat donors⟩ — see FLATTER 1

stroke (out) *vb* to show (something written) to be no longer valid by drawing a cross over or a line through it ⟨If you make a mistake on the form, just *stroke* it *out*.⟩ — see X (OUT)

stroll *n* a relaxed journey on foot for exercise or pleasure ⟨We arrived early and took a *stroll* through the park before dinner.⟩ — see WALK 1

stroll *vb* to travel by foot for exercise or pleasure ⟨People who like to *stroll* along the beach would love this place.⟩ — see HIKE 1

stroller *n* a person who roams about without a fixed route or destination ⟨back in olden days when *strollers* and vagabonds wandered the Scottish countryside⟩ — see NOMAD

strong *adj* **1** having muscles capable of exerting great physical force ⟨I need some *strong* people to help me move furniture.⟩
synonyms brawny, muscular, rugged, sinewy, stalwart, stout
related words forceful, forcible, mighty, potent, powerful, puissant; able-bodied, athletic, fit, trim; beefy, burly, husky, strapping; masculine, virile; hard, inured, strengthened, sturdy, tough, toughened; energetic, energized, invigorated, lusty, red-blooded, robust, vigorous, vitalized; hale, healthy, hearty, sound
near antonyms challenged, disabled, incapacitated, paralyzed; impotent, powerless; puny, slight, small, unathletic, unfit, unhealthy
antonyms delicate, feeble, frail, weak, weakling, wimpy
2 able to withstand hardship, strain, or exposure ⟨The doctor soon declared her *strong* enough to go home from the hospital.⟩ — see HARDY 1
3 having a powerfully stimulating odor or flavor ⟨The garlic in the sauce is almost too *strong*.⟩ ⟨That's mighty *strong* perfume you're wearing.⟩ — see SHARP 2
4 having an abundance of some characteristic quality (as flavor) ⟨*strong* coffee⟩ — see FULL-BODIED
5 having an unpleasant smell ⟨The dog's *strong* breath nearly bowled me over.⟩ — see MALODOROUS
6 having great power or influence ⟨She proved to be a *strong* leader.⟩ — see IMPORTANT 2
7 having the power to persuade ⟨made a *strong* argument for starting school an hour later each day⟩ — see COGENT
8 marked by the ability to withstand stress without structural damage or distortion ⟨buildings *strong* enough to withstand an earthquake⟩ — see STABLE 1
9 not showing weakness or uncertainty ⟨a *strong* belief in the value of hard work⟩ — see FIRM 1

strongbox *n* a specially reinforced container to keep valuables safe ⟨keeps her jewelry in a *strongbox*⟩ — see SAFE

stronghold *n* a structure or place from which one can resist attack ⟨The island was the pirates' last *stronghold* in the West Indies.⟩ — see FORT

strongly *adv* in a vigorous and forceful manner ⟨In the past, the senator has always *strongly* opposed any suggested increase in taxes.⟩ — see HARD 3

strop *vb* to make sharp or sharper ⟨At the museum they showed us how men used to *strop* razors with leather bands before the days of disposable blades.⟩ — see SHARPEN

stropped *adj* having an edge thin enough to cut or pierce something ⟨I was surprised at how sharp the *stropped* razor was.⟩ — see SHARP 1

structure *n* **1** something built as a dwelling, shelter, or place for human activity ⟨The only *structure* on the island is an old Spanish fort—or what's left of it.⟩ — see BUILDING
2 something put together by arranging or connecting an array of parts ⟨The Egyptian pyramids are among the most remarkable *structures* ever built.⟩ — see CONSTRUCTION 1
3 the arrangement of parts that gives something its basic form ⟨The basic *structure* of all those tract houses is the same: basically, a box.⟩ — see FRAME 1

struggle *n* **1** a forceful effort to reach a goal or objective ⟨the child's determined *struggle* to make straight A's in school⟩
synonyms battle, fight, fray, scrabble, throes
related words effort, exertion, labor, pains, trouble, work; drudgery, grind, sweat, toil, travail; combat, conflict, contest, strife, tussle, war, warfare; attempt, endeavor, essay, try
2 a physical dispute between opposing individuals or groups ⟨a *struggle* between a bison and a wolf pack⟩ — see FIGHT 1
3 an earnest effort for superiority or victory over another ⟨her staunchest supporters in her *struggle* for the office⟩ — see CONTEST 1

struggle *vb* **1** to proceed or act clumsily or ineffectually ⟨Each week I would *struggle* through my piano lesson, keenly aware that I wasn't getting any better.⟩ — see FLOUNDER 1

2 to devote serious and sustained effort ⟨The financially strapped couple *struggled* to make ends meet.⟩ — see LABOR

strut *vb* **1** to walk with exaggerated arm and leg movements ⟨The cat *strutted* proudly onto the porch with a bird in its mouth.⟩
synonyms prance, stalk, swagger
related words flounce, mince, traipse; pussyfoot, tiptoe; sweep; parade; pad, step, tread; pace, stride; lumber, lurch, pound, shamble, shuffle, stagger
2 to present so as to invite notice or attention ⟨*strutting* his blue ribbon for all to see⟩ — see SHOW 1

stub *n* an unused or unwanted piece or item typically of small size or value ⟨ticket *stubs*⟩ — see ¹SCRAP 1

stubborn *adj* sticking to an opinion, purpose, or course of action in spite of reason, arguments, or persuasion ⟨He's just being *stubborn*, refusing even to try the new toothpaste.⟩ — see OBSTINATE

stubbornness *n* a steadfast adherence to an opinion, purpose, or course of action in spite of reason, arguments, or persuasion ⟨Between my brother's *stubbornness* and my own, it's amazing when we come to an agreement about anything.⟩ — see OBSTINACY

stubby *adj* being compact and broad in build and often short in stature ⟨Seven *stubby* little fellows carried the sleeping Snow White back to their home in a cave.⟩ — see STOCKY

stuck *adj* firmly positioned in place and difficult to dislodge ⟨The car was hopelessly *stuck* in the mud.⟩ — see TIGHT 2

stuck-up *adj* having too high an opinion of oneself ⟨Noah thought that the kids at his new school were snobbish and *stuck-up*.⟩ — see CONCEITED

student *n* one who attends a school ⟨a straight-A *student* at the local high school⟩
synonyms pupil, scholar
related words schoolboy, schoolchild, schoolgirl; schoolfellow, schoolmate; coed, collegian, postgraduate, undergraduate; high schooler, kindergartner (*also* kindergartener); middle schooler; freshman, junior, senior, sophomore; underclassman, undergrad, upperclassman; exchange student
antonyms nonstudent

studied *adj* decided on as a result of careful thought ⟨a *studied* move by the company that was designed to put the competition out of business⟩ — see DELIBERATE 1

study *n* **1** a systematic search for the truth or facts about something ⟨conducted a *study* to determine the sleep needs of adolescents⟩ — see INQUIRY 1
2 the state of being lost in thought ⟨I found her staring at the fire in a deep *study*.⟩ — see REVERIE
3 a careful weighing of the reasons for or against something ⟨The idea is under *study* by the city council.⟩ — see CONSIDERATION 1

study *vb* **1** to use the mind to acquire knowledge ⟨You'll have to *study* hard and learn all about the Revolutionary War in order to pass the history test.⟩
synonyms bone (up)
related words cram; analyze, deduce, find out; con, learn, memorize, read; research, restudy; apprehend, comprehend, grasp, know, understand; absorb, digest
phrases go over, go through
2 to commit to memory ⟨Having carefully *studied* the document, he could repeat what it said exactly.⟩ — see MEMORIZE
3 to give serious and careful thought to ⟨scientists who *study* the origin of the universe⟩ — see PONDER

stuff *n* **1** a skill, an ability, or knowledge that makes a person able to do a particular job ⟨a guy who has the

stuff it takes to be head of a major corporation⟩ — see QUALIFICATION 1
2 the basic elements from which something can be developed ⟨reading, writing, and arithmetic—the *stuff* of an education⟩ — see MAKING
3 the quality or qualities that make a thing what it is ⟨The real *stuff* of nobility of character isn't riches or a title, but honor and integrity.⟩ — see ESSENCE 1
4 transportable items that one owns ⟨Gather up your *stuff* so that we can get going.⟩ — see POSSESSION 2
5 items needed for the performance of a task or activity ⟨I missed a great photo opportunity because all of my camera *stuff* was at home.⟩ — see EQUIPMENT

stuff *vb* **1** to close up so that no empty spaces remain ⟨She *stuffed* the box with tissue paper so the contents wouldn't rattle around.⟩ — see FILL 2
2 to fill with food to capacity ⟨kids who *stuff* themselves with junk food after school and then don't have any room for supper⟩ — see GORGE 1
3 to fit (people or things) into a tight space ⟨*stuffed* all the groceries into the back of the car⟩ — see CROWD 1
4 to prevent passage through by filling with something ⟨I can't smell anything, as my nose is all *stuffed*.⟩ — see CLOG 1
5 to put into (something) as much as can be held or contained ⟨*stuffed* a whole suitcase with gifts for her relatives in Mexico⟩ — see FILL 1

stuffed *adj* **1** containing or seeming to contain the greatest quantity or number possible ⟨I had never seen shelves so *stuffed* with books.⟩ — see FULL 1
2 having one's appetite completely satisfied ⟨We were still *stuffed* from our huge breakfast and didn't want lunch.⟩ — see FULL 3

stuffing *n* soft material that is used to fill the hollow parts of something ⟨never heard of using goose down as *stuffing* for comforters until she moved to a cold climate⟩ — see FILLING

stuffy *adj* **1** lacking fresh air ⟨The house was very *stuffy* after being closed up for a month.⟩
synonyms breathless, close, stifling, suffocating
related words airless, unventilated; heavy, oppressive, thick
near antonyms bracing, brisk, invigorating, refreshed, refreshing, restorative, reviving, sweet
antonyms airy, breezy, unstuffy
2 causing weariness, restlessness, or lack of interest ⟨There's nothing *stuffy* about this science museum—it's all interactive and fun.⟩ — see BORING
3 easily irritated or annoyed ⟨a *stuffy* clerk at the Registry of Motor Vehicles⟩ — see IRRITABLE

stumble *n* **1** an unintentional departure from truth or accuracy ⟨Was his hurtful remark a regrettable *stumble*, or was it made with artful intention?⟩ — see ERROR 1
2 the act of going down from an upright position suddenly and involuntarily ⟨has bones so brittle that a minor *stumble* could result in a serious break⟩ — see FALL 1

stumble *vb* **1** to go down from an upright position suddenly and involuntarily ⟨The bride *stumbled* on the altar steps.⟩ — see FALL 1
2 to proceed or act clumsily or ineffectually ⟨Jill *stumbled* twice while she was reciting the "Gettysburg Address."⟩ — see FLOUNDER 1
3 to move heavily or clumsily ⟨The exhausted hikers wearily *stumbled* through the tangled undergrowth.⟩ — see LUMBER 1
4 to make a mistake ⟨That network announcer rarely *stumbles* when he's on the air.⟩ — see ERR 1

stumble (on *or* **onto)** *vb* to come upon unexpectedly or by chance ⟨Mom *stumbled on* some old family photos when she was cleaning out a drawer.⟩ — see HAPPEN (ON or UPON)

stumble (upon) *vb* to come upon face-to-face or as if face-to-face ⟨*stumbled upon* an old acquaintance at the airport⟩ — see MEET 1

stumbling block *n* something that makes movement or progress difficult ⟨The only *stumbling block* to our move across the country was finding someone to adopt our cats.⟩ — see ENCUMBRANCE

stump *vb* **1** to move heavily or clumsily ⟨The seemingly endless parade finally ended, and the drummers and tuba players *stumped* wearily to their buses.⟩ — see LUMBER 1
2 to invite (someone) to take part in a contest or to perform a feat ⟨When my grandfather was a kid, he and his friends would *stump* one another to dive into the local swimming hole.⟩ — see CHALLENGE 2

stumpy *adj* being compact and broad in build and often short in stature ⟨*Stumpy* penguins become agile swimmers the moment they hit the water.⟩ — see STOCKY

stun *vb* **1** to make senseless or dizzy by a blow ⟨A powerful uppercut to the jaw *stunned* the boxer and sent him crashing to the canvas.⟩
synonyms daze, rock
related words deaden, paralyze; benumb, numb, stupefy; knock down; bang, bash, belt, bludgeon, clobber, clout, hammer, hit, paste, pound, punch, rap, slam, slap, slug, smack, smite, sock, strike, swat, thump, thwack, wallop, whack, whale; batter, beat, buffet, bung, chop, cuff, drub, pelt, pummel
phrases knock for a loop, knock silly
2 to make a strong impression on (someone) with something unexpected ⟨News of the forgery *stunned* the art world.⟩ — see SURPRISE 1

stunned *adj* **1** affected with sudden and great wonder or surprise ⟨Realizing that they had been left out of the will, the billionaire's relatives just sat there, *stunned*.⟩ — see THUNDERSTRUCK
2 suffering from mental confusion ⟨The loud blast left her momentarily *stunned*.⟩ — see DIZZY 2

stunner *n* **1** a lovely woman ⟨Not only is she smart, she's a real *stunner*!⟩ — see BEAUTY 2
2 something that makes a strong impression because it is so unexpected ⟨As expected, the box-office champ was another superhero actioner, but the real *stunner* was the second-place finish for the low-budget comedy.⟩ — see SURPRISE 1

stunning *adj* **1** causing a strong emotional reaction because of unexpectedness ⟨We suffered a *stunning* defeat at the hands of the bottom-ranked team in the division.⟩ — see SURPRISING 1
2 causing wonder or astonishment ⟨the *stunning* beauty of the star-filled sky on a cloudless night⟩ — see MARVELOUS 1
3 very pleasing to look at ⟨How *stunning* the performers look in their costumes!⟩ — see BEAUTIFUL 1

stunt *n* an act of notable skill, strength, or cleverness ⟨performs mental *stunts*, such as pronouncing words backwards as soon as you say them⟩ — see FEAT 1

stunt *vb* to hold back the normal growth of ⟨Unfortunately, an unusually dry summer seems to have permanently *stunted* the tree.⟩
synonyms dwarf, suppress
related words arrest, catch, check, halt, hold up, stall, stay, still, stop; balk, block, hold back, impede, obstruct, stem; diminish, downsize, shrink
near antonyms advance, boost, encourage, forward, foster, nourish, nurture, promote

stupefied *adj* **1** affected with sudden and great wonder or surprise ⟨gazed, *stupefied*, as humanoids with large heads

emerged from the crashed UFO⟩ — see THUNDERSTRUCK
2 suffering from mental confusion ⟨When the plane finally righted itself after a terrifying nose-dive, the *stupefied* passengers were unsure how to act.⟩ — see DIZZY 2

stupefy *vb* to make a strong impression on (someone) with something unexpected ⟨*stupefied* by the ruling that he could not compete because he missed the qualifying age by two days⟩ — see SURPRISE 1

stupefying *adj* causing a strong emotional reaction because of unexpectedness ⟨a *stupefying* turn of events⟩ — see SURPRISING 1

stupendous *adj* causing wonder or astonishment ⟨the *stupendous* engineering feats achieved by the ancient Romans⟩ — see MARVELOUS 1

stupendously *adv* to a large extent or degree ⟨a *stupendously* successful Broadway debut⟩ — see GREATLY 2

stupendousness *n* impressiveness of beauty on a large scale ⟨For stunning *stupendousness* the world had never seen anything the equal of the Palace of Versailles.⟩ — see MAGNIFICENCE

stupid *adj* **1** not having or showing an ability to absorb ideas readily ⟨The instructor assured us that there are no *stupid* questions.⟩
synonyms brainless, dense, doltish, dopey (*also* dopy), dorky [*slang*], dull, dumb, fatuous, half-witted, mindless, oafish, obtuse, opaque, senseless, simple, slow, thick, thickheaded, unintelligent, vacuous, weak-minded, witless
related words feebleminded, simpleminded; foolish, idiotic, imbecile (*or* imbecilic); moronic; ignorant, illiterate, lowbrow, uneducated, uninformed, unintellectual, untaught, unthinking; absurd, asinine, balmy, cockeyed, daffy, daft, half-baked, harebrained, nonsensical, wacky, zany; imperceptive, unwise
near antonyms ingenious, resourceful; acute, astute, discerning, insightful, keen, knowing, perceptive, sagacious, sage, sapient, savvy, wise; cerebral, erudite, highbrow, intellectual, knowledgeable, learned, literate, scholarly, thinking, well-read; crafty, cunning, foxy, shrewd, wily; judicious, prudent, sane, sensible, sound
antonyms apt, brainy, bright, brilliant, clever, fast, intelligent, keen, nimble, quick, quick-witted, sharp, sharp-witted, smart
2 causing weariness, restlessness, or lack of interest ⟨I can't believe we sat through the whole *stupid* movie!⟩ — see BORING
3 showing or marked by a lack of good sense or judgment ⟨Not liking the captain is a *stupid* reason to quit the team.⟩ — see FOOLISH 1

stupidity *n* **1** the quality or state of lacking intelligence or quickness of mind ⟨The *stupidity* of the dialogue between the two romantic leads had movie audiences giggling uncontrollably.⟩
synonyms brainlessness, denseness, density, doltishness, dopiness, dullness (*also* dulness), dumbness, fatuity, foolishness, mindlessness, oafishness, obtuseness, senselessness, simpleness, slowness, stupidness, thickness, vacuity, witlessness
related words feeblemindedness; absurdity, asininity, balminess, daftness, folly, idiocy, inaneness, inanity, madness, nonsensicalness, nuttiness, preposterousness, silliness, wackiness, zaniness
near antonyms acumen, alertness, astuteness, discernment, insight, judgment (*or* judgement), perception; sagacity, sageness, sapience, wisdom, wit; logicalness, rationality, reasonableness, soundness, validity
antonyms braininess, brightness, brilliance, cleverness, intelligence, quick-wittedness, smartness
2 a foolish act or idea ⟨The succession of *stupidities* by

the company's owners was bound to result in bankruptcy.⟩ — see FOLLY 1

3 language, behavior, or ideas that are absurd and contrary to good sense ⟨Never repaying you was just sheer *stupidity* on my part.⟩ — see NONSENSE 1

stupidness *n* the quality or state of lacking intelligence or quickness of mind ⟨I'm not sure if he leaves his front door unlocked from carelessness or just plain *stupidness*.⟩ — see STUPIDITY 1

sturdily *adv* in a vigorous and forceful manner ⟨no longer so *sturdily* maintained his innocence when his alibi proved to be a fabrication⟩ — see HARD 3

sturdiness *n* the ability to withstand force or stress without being distorted, dislodged, or damaged ⟨demonstrated the suitcase's *sturdiness* by dropping it from a third-floor window⟩ — see STABILITY 1

sturdy *adj* **1** able to withstand hardship, strain, or exposure ⟨It took a *sturdy* person to endure the life of a pioneer.⟩ — see HARDY 1

2 marked by the ability to withstand stress without structural damage or distortion ⟨Wear *sturdy* boots because we will be going over sharp rocks and uneven terrain.⟩ — see STABLE 1

3 not showing weakness or uncertainty ⟨You'll need a *sturdy* grasp of the concepts of algebra before you can take calculus.⟩ — see FIRM 1

sty *n* a dirty or messy place ⟨"This house is a *sty*," she said disgustedly.⟩ — see PIGPEN

style *vb* to give a name to ⟨Although nowadays he's often *styled* a biologist, he's probably better thought of as a classic 19th-century naturalist.⟩ — see NAME 1

style *n* **1** a distinctive way of putting ideas into words ⟨I correctly identified the quotation because I recognized Mark Twain's inimitable *style*.⟩

synonyms fashion, locution, manner, mode, phraseology, tone, vein

related words address, delivery, elocution; archaism, colloquialism, regionalism; acceptation, connotation, denotation, expression, idiom

2 the means or procedure for doing something ⟨Unfortunately, the club president's usual *style* is to make decisions without asking anyone's advice or approval.⟩ — see METHOD

3 a practice or interest that is very popular for a short time ⟨parents who were very relieved when the *style* for having one's nose pierced faded⟩ — see FAD

styleless *adj* marked by an obvious lack of style or good taste ⟨They are forced to wear *styleless* uniforms for the restaurant job.⟩ — see ¹TACKY 1

stylish *adj* being in the latest or current fashion ⟨a pretty, *stylish* dress⟩

synonyms à la mode (*also* a la mode), chic, cool [*slang*], exclusive, fashionable, happening, hip, in, modish, sharp, smart, snappy, supercool, swell, trendy

related words dapper, dashing, dressy, natty, sassy, saucy, spiffy, spruce; chichi, classy, nobby, posh, swank (*or* swanky); elegant, graceful, handsome, majestic, refined, sophisticated, stately, tasteful, understated; flashy, gallant; dandyish, dudish, foppish

near antonyms cheesy, tacky, unattractive, unbecoming; graceless, inelegant, tasteless, trashy; frowsy (*or* frowzy), sloppy, slovenly, unkempt, untidy; disheveled (*or* dishevelled), messy, mussy, rumpled, wrinkled; shabby, sleazy

antonyms dowdy, out, outmoded, styleless, unfashionable, unstylish

stymie *vb* to create difficulty for the work or activity of ⟨The raging blizzard *stymied* the rescuers' attempts to find the stranded mountain climbers.⟩ — see HAMPER

suasion *n* the act of reasoning or pleading with someone to accept a belief or course of action ⟨A defense lawyer uses not only legal arguments but also moral *suasion* to appeal to a jury's sense of right and wrong.⟩ — see PERSUASION 1

suave *adj* having or showing very polished and worldly manners ⟨The *suave* gentleman charmed everyone who attended parties at the embassy.⟩

synonyms debonair, smooth, sophisticated, urbane

related words cavalier, glib, slick, unctuous; civilized, couth, cultivated, cultured, genteel, graceful, gracious, poised, polished, refined, well-bred; cosmopolitan, metropolitan, smart, worldly-wise; assured, calm, collected, composed, confident, cool, placid, secure, self-assured, self-confident, self-possessed, serene, tranquil, undisturbed, unperturbed

near antonyms awkward, clumsy, gauche, graceless, stiff, stilted, uncomfortable, uneasy, ungraceful, wooden; hick, parochial, provincial, rustic (*also* rustical); uncivilized, uncultured, unrefined; unsophisticated, unworldly; gawky, lubberly, stodgy, ungainly; diffident, insecure

antonyms boorish, churlish, classless, clownish, loutish, uncouth

¹sub *n* a large sandwich on a long split roll ⟨We shared a tuna *sub* at lunch.⟩ — see SUBMARINE

²sub *n* a person or thing that takes the place of another ⟨We had a *sub* in English today, so we didn't get our test results back.⟩ — see SUBSTITUTE

sub *vb* to serve as a replacement usually for a time only ⟨The weekend anchor is *subbing* for the TV station's main anchor all this week.⟩ — see COVER 1

subdue *vb* **1** to achieve a victory over ⟨Kate *subdued* her fear of the dark by joining a club for spelunkers.⟩ — see BEAT 2

2 to bring under one's control by force of arms ⟨*subdued* the rebels and sent their leaders to the gallows⟩ — see CONQUER 1

3 to put a stop to (something) by the use of force ⟨labored through the night to *subdue* the river's rising waters by building a wall of sandbags around their property⟩ — see QUELL 1

subdued *adj* not excessively showy ⟨The wedding was a *subdued* affair, with only close family and friends attending.⟩ — see QUIET 2

subduer *n* one that defeats an enemy or opponent ⟨the Norman *subduers* of the English⟩ — see VICTOR 1

subduing *n* the act or process of bringing someone or something under one's control ⟨the *subduing* of his irrational fears⟩ — see CONQUEST

subject *n* **1** a major object of interest or concern (as in a discussion or artistic composition) ⟨The *subject* of our discussion switched from who would be the next president to who was the greatest president in the nation's history.⟩ — see MATTER 1

2 a person who owes allegiance to a government and is protected by it ⟨My dad was born in England and is still a British *subject*.⟩ — see CITIZEN 1

3 something (as a belief) that serves as the basis for another thing ⟨He has no *subject* to protest this time, but that's never stopped him before.⟩ — see REASON 2

subject *vb* to bring under one's control by force of arms ⟨Attila the Hun *subjected* most of Europe to his barbaric pillage.⟩ — see CONQUER 1

subject (to) *adj* **1** determined by something else ⟨Your extra piano lesson on Tuesdays is *subject to* the availability of the music room.⟩ — see DEPENDENT 2

2 being in a situation where one is likely to meet with harm ⟨This type of wound is highly *subject to* infection.⟩ — see LIABLE 1

subjecting *n* the act or process of bringing someone or something under one's control ⟨The *subjecting* of patients to major surgery should only be done after getting a second opinion.⟩ — see CONQUEST

subjection *n* the act or process of bringing someone or something under one's control ⟨a holy man for whom the *subjection* of earthly desires is the path to spiritual perfection⟩ — see CONQUEST

subjugate *vb* to bring under one's control by force of arms ⟨The Romans *subjugated* subjected surrounding lands.⟩ — see CONQUER 1

subjugating *n* the act or process of bringing someone or something under one's control ⟨the *subjugating* of a country by a larger nation⟩ — see CONQUEST

subjugation *n* the act or process of bringing someone or something under one's control ⟨the *subjugation* of much of Europe by Napoléon⟩ — see CONQUEST

sublime *adj* **1** causing wonder or astonishment ⟨the *sublime* beauty of the firmament⟩ — see MARVELOUS 1
2 having, characterized by, or arising from a dignified and generous nature ⟨the *sublime* virtue of having given all one's worldly goods to the poor⟩ — see NOBLE 2

sublimeness *n* impressiveness of beauty on a large scale ⟨the awe-inspiring *sublimeness* of Yosemite Valley⟩ — see MAGNIFICENCE

submarine *adj* living, lying, or occurring below the surface of the water ⟨the *submarine* fossils that are to be found in coral reefs⟩ — see UNDERWATER

submarine *n* a large sandwich on a long split roll ⟨always orders a roast beef *submarine* with the works⟩
synonyms grinder, hero, hoagie (*also* hoagy), Italian sandwich, po'boy (*also* poor boy), sub

submerge *vb* **1** to cover with a flood ⟨*submerged* by requests to speak after she received a favorable write-up in a popular news blog⟩ — see FLOOD
2 to sink or push (something) briefly into or as if into a liquid ⟨*Submerge* the tomatoes in boiling hot water for a few seconds and they will be easier to peel.⟩ — see DIP 1
3 to refrain from openly showing or uttering ⟨learned to *submerge* her ego and became a better teammate for doing so⟩ — see SUPPRESS 2

submerged *adj* living, lying, or occurring below the surface of the water ⟨*Submerged* local roadways made for hazardous driving.⟩ — see UNDERWATER

submerse *vb* **1** to cover with a flood ⟨a week of nonstop rain that *submersed* the cornfields and delayed planting for days⟩ — see FLOOD
2 to sink or push (something) briefly into or as if into a liquid ⟨those hardy souls who daily *submerse* themselves in icy cold water for its invigorating effect⟩ — see DIP 1

submission *n* **1** a bending to the authority or control of another ⟨Not given to unquestioning *submission*, he often came in conflict with his superiors.⟩ — see OBEDIENCE 1
2 the usually forced yielding of one's person or possessions to the control of another ⟨The judge ordered the *submission* of all of the company's records to the prosecutors.⟩ — see SURRENDER

submissive *adj* readily giving in to the command or authority of another ⟨It's not in her nature to be *submissive*.⟩ — see OBEDIENT

submissively *adv* in a manner showing no signs of pride or self-assertion ⟨All of the extended family was expected to be *submissively* amenable to the matriarch's wishes.⟩ — see LOWLY

submissiveness *n* a readiness or willingness to yield to the wishes of others ⟨His uncharacteristic *submissiveness* to the doctor's advice must mean he's really sick.⟩ — see COMPLIANCE 1

submit *vb* **1** to cease resistance (as to another's arguments, demands, or control) ⟨In the end he *submitted* and agreed to take that awful-tasting medicine.⟩ — see YIELD 3
2 to give up and cease resistance (as to a liking, temptation, or habit) ⟨Refusing to *submit* to sleep, she stayed by her son's hospital bed the whole night.⟩ — see YIELD 1
3 to yield to the control or power of enemy forces ⟨The fort's commander received orders not to *submit* under any circumstances, as reinforcements were on the way.⟩ — see FALL 2

submitting *n* the usually forced yielding of one's person or possessions to the control of another ⟨Public pressure resulted in his *submitting* of financial records to investigators.⟩ — see SURRENDER

subordinate *adj* having not so great importance or rank as another ⟨His contention is that environment plays a *subordinate* role to heredity in determining what we become.⟩ — see LESSER

subordinate *n* one who is of lower rank and typically under the authority of another ⟨*Subordinates* do most of the actual creation of the famous designer's clothing designs.⟩ — see UNDERLING

subordinate *vb* to bring under one's control by force of arms ⟨It is one of the lessons of history that more powerful civilizations often *subordinate* weaker ones.⟩ — see CONQUER 1

subordination *n* a bending to the authority or control of another ⟨An oligarchy requires *subordination* by the masses to the will of a tiny elite.⟩ — see OBEDIENCE 1

subscribe (to) *vb* to have a favorable opinion of ⟨I *subscribe to* the idea that voting is a civic duty.⟩ — see APPROVE (OF)

subsequent *adj* being, occurring, or carried out at a time after something else ⟨I'll do the first problem as an example, but all *subsequent* efforts must be done on your own.⟩
synonyms after, ensuing, later, posterior
related words behind, belated, delayed, late, slow; closing, concluding, eventual, final, last, latest, latter, terminal, ultimate; following
near antonyms advance, advanced, early, premature
antonyms antecedent, anterior, foregoing, former, precedent, preceding, previous, prior

subsequently *adv* following in time or place ⟨*subsequently* found the missing glove⟩ — see AFTER

subside *vb* to grow less in scope or intensity especially gradually ⟨As the noise of the siren *subsided*, I was able to fall back to sleep.⟩ — see DECREASE 2

subsidize *vb* **1** to furnish (as an institution) with a regular source of income ⟨The museum is annually *subsidized* by funds from several major corporations.⟩ — see ENDOW 2
2 to provide money for ⟨housing for the elderly that was *subsidized* by the federal government⟩ — see FINANCE 1

subsidy *n* a sum of money allotted for a specific use by official or formal action ⟨government *subsidies* for farmers in case of crop failure⟩ — see APPROPRIATION 1

subsist *vb* to have life ⟨a love that was as great as any that ever did *subsist*⟩ — see BE 1

subsistence *n* **1** the fact of being or of being real ⟨He believes in the *subsistence* of a soul as a separate entity from the body.⟩ — see EXISTENCE
2 uninterrupted or lasting existence ⟨The *subsistence* of the patient's infection, even after the use of antibiotics, had the doctors puzzled.⟩ — see CONTINUATION

substance *n* **1** the basic elements from which something can be developed ⟨Many thought that the mayor's speech lacked *substance* because specific proposals for solving the city's problems were few.⟩ — see MAKING
2 the quality or qualities that make a thing what it is ⟨tireless caring and nurturing that was the very *substance* of maternal love⟩ — see ESSENCE 1

3 the total of one's money and property ⟨Measure the worth of a person not by earthly *substance* but by good deeds.⟩ — see WEALTH 1

4 one that has a real and independent existence ⟨the question of whether the soul is a *substance* entirely independent of the body⟩ — see ENTITY

substandard *adj* falling short of a standard ⟨a teacher who rejects *substandard* work without hesitation⟩ — see BAD 1

substantial *adj* **1** having great meaning or lasting effect ⟨*substantial* changes to the school dress code that made a lot of people unhappy⟩ — see IMPORTANT 1

2 of a size greater than average of its kind ⟨The amount he inherited was quite *substantial*, so he quit his job and set out to see the world.⟩ — see LARGE

3 relating to or composed of matter ⟨The Land of Oz turned out to be a world of dreams, even less *substantial* than a rainbow.⟩ — see MATERIAL 1

4 sufficiently large in size, amount, or number to merit attention ⟨There's been a *substantial* increase in attendance at girls' volleyball games ever since the start of their winning streak.⟩ — see CONSIDERABLE 1

substantially *adv* for the most part ⟨The *Little House* books are *substantially* based on the memories of Laura Ingalls Wilder.⟩ — see CHIEFLY

substantiate *vb* **1** to gain full recognition or acceptance of ⟨*substantiated* his claim to local mountaineering fame with a photo of himself on the summit of Mount Denali⟩ — see ESTABLISH 1

2 to give evidence or testimony to the truth or factualness of ⟨Mr. MacGregor couldn't *substantiate* that it was Peter, and not some other rabbit, in the cabbage patch.⟩ — see CONFIRM 1

3 to represent in visible form ⟨The artist's intense feelings are *substantiated* by his paintings' bold colors and broad brush strokes.⟩ — see EMBODY 2

4 to show the existence or truth of by evidence ⟨*substantiated* the need for a tuition increase with some concrete figures⟩ — see PROVE 1

5 to provide evidence or information for (as a claim or idea) ⟨Darwin spent the rest of his life gathering evidence to *substantiate* his theory of the origin of species.⟩ — see SUPPORT 4

substantiating *adj* serving to give support to the truth or factualness of something ⟨Without some *substantiating* evidence, such as a stub from a bus ticket, who's going to believe your alibi?⟩ — see CORROBORATIVE

substantiation *n* something presented in support of the truth or accuracy of a claim ⟨The signature of a witness provides *substantiation* that a person's will is genuine.⟩ — see PROOF

substitute *adj* **1** being such in appearance only and made with or manufactured from usually cheaper materials ⟨*substitute* wools that supposedly have the look and feel of cashmere⟩ — see IMITATION

2 taking the place of one that came before ⟨We had to find *substitute* transportation during the bus strike.⟩ — see NEW 1

substitute *vb* **1** to give up (something) and take something else in return ⟨Can I *substitute* coleslaw for potato salad if I order the chicken?⟩ — see CHANGE 3

2 to serve as a replacement usually for a time only ⟨*substituting* for the talk show host while she is on vacation⟩ — see COVER 1

3 to take the place of ⟨"John Doe," "Jane Doe," and "Baby Doe" *substituted* the real names of the parties involved to preserve their privacy.⟩ — see REPLACE 1

substitute *n* a person or thing that takes the place of another ⟨You'll be getting a *substitute* until your regular

teacher is feeling better.⟩ ⟨If you like, you can use nuts as a *substitute* for coconut in that recipe.⟩

synonyms backup, pinch hitter, relief, replacement, reserve, stand-in, sub

related words alternate, understudy; makeshift, stopgap; agent, attorney, commissary, delegate, deputy, envoy, factor, proxy, representative, surrogate; assistant, reliever, second; successor, superseder

subsume *vb* to have as part of a whole ⟨Games and team sports are *subsumed* under the classification of "recreation."⟩ — see INCLUDE 1

subterfuge *n* the use of clever underhanded actions to achieve an end ⟨propagandists who use a kind of photographic *subterfuge*, superimposing one image on another to create a false "reality"⟩ — see TRICKERY

subtle *adj* **1** clever at attaining one's ends by indirect and often deceptive means ⟨used *subtle* methods of persuasion⟩ — see ARTFUL 1

2 made or done with extreme care and accuracy ⟨the *subtle* strokes of the painter's brush⟩ — see FINE 2

3 satisfying or pleasing because of fineness or mildness ⟨a *subtle* suggestion of the Near East in the soup's flavoring⟩ — see DELICATE 1

subtleness *n* skill in achieving one's ends through indirect, subtle, or underhanded means ⟨the *subtleness* with which the boutique owner convinces you that you have to have that outrageously priced article of clothing⟩ — see CUNNING 1

subtlety *n* skill in achieving one's ends through indirect, subtle, or underhanded means ⟨We appreciated the *subtlety* with which our host indicated that it was time to leave: he volunteered to pack us a little lunch for the road.⟩ — see CUNNING 1

subtract *vb* to take away (an amount or number) from a total ⟨If you *subtract* 10 from 23, you get 13.⟩ ⟨You can *subtract* the amount you spent on groceries from the total you owe for room and board.⟩

synonyms abate, deduct, knock off, take off

related words decrease, diminish, discount, downsize, dwindle, knock down, lessen, lower, reduce; abbreviate, abridge, clip, crop, curtail, cut, cut back, cut down, dock, pare, prune, retrench, shorten, slash, trim, truncate, whittle

near antonyms adjoin, annex, append; complement, supplement; enhance, heighten, intensify, magnify; aggrandize, amplify, augment, beef (up), boost, compound, enlarge, escalate, expand, increase, multiply

antonyms add, tack (on)

subtraction *n* the act or an instance of taking away from a total ⟨The restaurant may not have raised the price, but there's definitely been a *subtraction* in the number of fries in a side order.⟩

synonyms deduction

related words discount, kickback, rebate; abatement, decline, diminishment, diminution, drop, fall, loss, reduction, shrinkage; curtailment, cut, cutback

near antonyms boost, enlargement, gain, increase, increment, raise, rise; accretion, accrual, accumulation, addendum, augmentation, supplement, supplementation

antonyms addition

suburbia *n* the districts adjacent to a city ⟨families moving out of *suburbia*⟩ — see ENVIRONS 1

subvert *vb* to lower in character, dignity, or quality ⟨By insisting that she pay me for helping her, she *subverted* my noble desire to do a good deed without reward.⟩ — see DEBASE 1

succeed *vb* **1** to turn out as planned or desired ⟨The advertising campaign that finally *succeeded* used humor to sell the product.⟩

synonyms click, deliver, go, go over, pan out, work out

related words catch on; flourish, prosper, thrive; cook, percolate

phrases bear fruit, catch fire, deliver the goods, do the trick, go like clockwork

near antonyms languish; flounder, struggle; decline, sink, slip, slump, wane; crash, crumble, flame out; choke, crack up, miscarry, misfire; fall down, go under; implode, self-destruct

antonyms bomb, collapse, fail, flop, flunk, fold, founder, miss, strike out, wash out

2 to reach a desired level of accomplishment ⟨If you want to *succeed* in show business, you have to feel comfortable in front of an audience.⟩

synonyms arrive, flourish, prosper, thrive

related words prevail, triumph, win; excel

phrases come into one's own, cut it, cut the mustard, get ahead, get somewhere, get there, hack it, hit it big, make good, make it, make one's mark, make the grade

near antonyms flounder, struggle

antonyms fail

3 to come after in time ⟨Only the results on election day will tell who will *succeed* the current president.⟩ — see FOLLOW 1

succeeding *adj* **1** being the one that comes immediately after another ⟨The couple purchased some land, and in the course of the *succeeding* year built a house on it.⟩ — see NEXT

2 following one after another without others coming in between ⟨That land remained in the family for five *succeeding* generations.⟩ — see CONSECUTIVE

success *n* **1** a person or thing that is successful ⟨Their homemade jellies have been such a *success* that they are now distributed nationwide.⟩ — see HIT 1

2 a successful result brought about by hard work ⟨a long list of *successes* that the retiring president of the college can point to with pride⟩ — see ACCOMPLISHMENT 1

successful *adj* **1** having attained a desired end or state of good fortune ⟨The play had a *successful* run on Broadway.⟩

synonyms flourishing, going, palmy, prosperous, thriving, triumphant

related words coming, promising; booming, growing, roaring, robust

phrases in clover (*also* in the clover)

near antonyms futureless, hopeless, inauspicious, nogood, unpromising; collapsing, failing, flopping, flunking, folding, washing-out; declining, slipping, slumping, waning; destroyed, wrecked

antonyms failed, unsuccessful

2 marked by vigorous growth and well-being especially economically ⟨sold their *successful* dry-cleaning business and retired to Hawaii⟩ — see PROSPEROUS 1

successional *adj* following one after another without others coming in between ⟨the *successional* stages that an area goes through following a forest fire⟩ — see CONSECUTIVE

successive *adj* following one after another without others coming in between ⟨made the honor roll for three *successive* school terms⟩ — see CONSECUTIVE

succinct *adj* marked by the use of few words to convey much information or meaning ⟨a pocket guide that provides *succinct* explanations for rules of grammar and punctuation⟩ — see CONCISE

succinctly *adv* in a few words ⟨We found it difficult to explain *succinctly* to the technician the nature of the problems we were having with the computer.⟩ — see SHORTLY 1

succinctness *n* the quality or state of being marked by or using only few words to convey much meaning ⟨Caesar's observation, "I came, I saw, I conquered," is famous for its *succinctness*.⟩

synonyms brevity, briefness, compactness, conciseness, crispness, pithiness, terseness

related words abruptness, brusqueness, curtness, shortness

near antonyms redundancy, repetitiousness, repetitiveness, tautology

antonyms diffuseness, long-windedness, prolixity, verbosity, wordiness

succulence *n* the quality or state of being full of juice ⟨The *succulence* of the apple was such that the first bite sent juice running down my chin.⟩

synonyms fleshiness, juiciness, pulpiness

related words sap, sappiness

near antonyms dryness

succulent *adj* **1** full of juice ⟨vines weighted down with plump, *succulent* grapes⟩ — see JUICY

2 very pleasing to the sense of taste ⟨a buffet table set with an array of *succulent* roasts⟩ — see DELICIOUS 1

succumb *vb* **1** to cease resistance (as to another's arguments, demands, or control) ⟨He finally *succumbed* to the designer's suggestions and got rid of his dilapidated easy chair.⟩ — see YIELD 3

2 to give up and cease resistance (as to a liking, temptation, or habit) ⟨refused to *succumb* to her fears and defiantly walked through the dark cemetery⟩ — see YIELD 1

3 to stop living ⟨The patient lay so still and pale that everyone thought he had *succumbed*, and then he opened his eyes.⟩ — see DIE 1

4 to yield to the control or power of enemy forces ⟨The doctor worked tirelessly until finally he, too, *succumbed* to the fever.⟩ — see FALL 2

such *adj* having qualities in common ⟨All *such* questions should be saved until the end of the class.⟩ — see ALIKE

such *adv* to a great degree ⟨I have never seen *such* a large cat!⟩ — see VERY 1

suchlike *adj* having qualities in common ⟨He kept asking me how long I'd lived here, and how I liked it, and *suchlike* questions.⟩ — see ALIKE

suck (up) *vb* **1** to use flattery or the doing of favors in order to win approval especially from a superior ⟨a young lieutenant constantly *sucking up* to the commanding officer⟩ — see FAWN

2 to take in (something liquid) through small openings ⟨These lilacs *sucked up* all the water I added to the vase yesterday.⟩ — see ABSORB 1

sucker *n* **1** one who is easily deceived or cheated ⟨I was a *sucker* and believed them when they said the only tickets they could get were double the price.⟩ — see ¹DUPE

2 a person with a strong and habitual liking for something ⟨I'm a *sucker* for cheesy horror movies.⟩ — see FAN

sudden *adj* not expected ⟨The *sudden* snowstorm resulted in thousands of evening commuters abandoning their cars on impassable highways.⟩ — see UNEXPECTED

suddenly *adv* **1** with great suddenness ⟨The bus stopped *suddenly*, and somebody's lunch landed in the aisle.⟩ — see SHORT

2 without warning ⟨*Suddenly*, something fell out of the sky and landed in the field a few feet away.⟩ — see UNAWARES

suds *pl n* a light mass of fine bubbles formed in or on a liquid ⟨I can't seem to get any *suds* to form with this cheap dish detergent.⟩ — see FOAM

sudsy *adj* covered with, consisting of, or resembling foam ⟨Kara came out of the bathroom with her hair all *sudsy* because someone had turned off the water.⟩ — see FOAMY

sue (for) *vb* to make a request for ⟨The nation *sued for* peace.⟩ — see ASK (FOR) 1

suffer *vb* **1** to come to a knowledge of (something) by living through it ⟨willingly *suffered* hardships so that their children would have a better life⟩ — see EXPERIENCE
2 to feel deep sadness or mental pain ⟨It made him *suffer* to see his elderly parents' struggle with age.⟩ — see GRIEVE
3 to give permission for or to approve of ⟨Cell phone use is something our school does not *suffer*.⟩ — see ALLOW 1
4 to fail to prevent (some behavior on someone's part) especially from neglect or indifference ⟨I will not *suffer* you to insult me so!⟩ — see ALLOW 3
sufferable *adj* capable of being endured ⟨The only thing that makes finals *sufferable* is that school vacation will follow.⟩ — see BEARABLE
sufferance *n* **1** the approval by someone in authority for the doing of something ⟨was pointedly reminded that he was at the private beach on *sufferance* and could be kicked out at any time⟩ — see PERMISSION
2 the capacity to endure what is difficult or disagreeable without complaining ⟨We found working inside all day without some fresh air beyond *sufferance*.⟩ — see PATIENCE
suffice *vb* to be enough ⟨I was told I have to wear shoes—will sandals *suffice*?⟩ — see SERVE 2
sufficiency *n* the quality or state of meeting one's needs adequately ⟨The *sufficiency* of the portions is such that you will leave the restaurant with a full stomach but without doggie bags.⟩
synonyms acceptability, adequacy, satisfactoriness
related words bountifulness, copiousness; excess, overabundance, oversupply, surfeit, surplus; abundance, amplitude, opulence, plenitude, plenteousness, plentifulness, plentitude, plenty
near antonyms lack, want; crunch, dearth, deficit, famine, lack, shortage; meagerness, paucity, poorness, poverty, rareness, rarity, scantiness, scantness, scarceness, scarcity, skimpiness; necessity, need, privation
antonyms inadequacy, insufficiency, unsatisfactoriness
sufficiently *adv* **1** in or to a degree or quantity that meets one's requirements or satisfaction ⟨After eight tutoring sessions, I felt *sufficiently* prepared for the entrance exam.⟩ — see ENOUGH 1
2 in a satisfactory way ⟨It's not great literature, but this whodunit is *sufficiently* suspenseful.⟩ — see WELL 1
suffocate *vb* **1** to be or cause to be killed by lack of breathable air ⟨The law requires the owner of a discarded refrigerator to remove its door so that a child won't get trapped inside and *suffocate*.⟩ — see SMOTHER 1
2 to keep (someone) from breathing by exerting pressure on the windpipe ⟨temporarily *suffocated* by the seat belt⟩ — see CHOKE 1
3 to experience complete or partial blockage of the windpipe ⟨*suffocating* in the thick, black smoke of the burning building⟩ — see CHOKE 2
suffocating *adj* lacking fresh air ⟨Inside the bunker it was *suffocating*.⟩ — see STUFFY 1
suffrage *n* the right to formally express one's position or will in an election ⟨The 19th Amendment to the U. S. Constitution granted women *suffrage*.⟩ — see VOTE 1
suffuse *vb* **1** to cause (as a person) to become filled or saturated with a certain quality or principle ⟨She was *suffused* with an overwhelming feeling of liberation as her horse broke into a gallop.⟩ — see INFUSE
2 to spread throughout ⟨a living room *suffused* with warm sunlight⟩ — see PERMEATE
sugarcoated *adj* appealing to the emotions in an obvious and tiresome way ⟨those *sugarcoated* versions of family life that old TV sitcoms portrayed⟩ — see CORNY
sugary *adj* appealing to the emotions in an obvious and

tiresome way ⟨writes *sugary* lyrics for singers of country music⟩ — see CORNY
suggest *vb* **1** to convey an idea indirectly ⟨This letter *suggests* that there's more going on than she's telling us.⟩ — see HINT
2 to put (something) forward as one's choice for a wise or proper course of action ⟨I *suggested* that they talk to their counselors about college.⟩ — see ADVISE 2
3 to set before the mind for consideration ⟨Might I *suggest*, for an appetizer, our jumbo shrimp cocktail?⟩ — see PROPOSE 1
suggestion *n* **1** a slight or indirect pointing to something (as a solution or explanation) ⟨If you don't want to give the *suggestion* that you're evading the truth, you must look your questioner in the eye.⟩ — see HINT 1
2 something which is presented for consideration ⟨No one had any better *suggestions*, so as usual we spent the afternoon at the basketball court.⟩ — see PROPOSAL
3 an almost imperceptible sign of something ⟨We took care to avoid so much as even a *suggestion* of impropriety.⟩ — see HINT 2
suggestive *adj* **1** hinting at or intended to call to mind matters regarded as indecent ⟨was offended by the *suggestive* comment⟩
synonyms bawdy, lewd, racy, ribald, salty, spicy
related words leering; coarse, crude, earthy, foul, gross, vulgar; dirty, filthy, lascivious, nasty, obscene, pornographic, prurient, smutty; immodest, indecorous, naughty
near antonyms clean, decent; innocuous, inoffensive; priggish, prim, prudish, puritanical, staid, straitlaced (*or* straightlaced); correct, decorous, genteel, proper, respectable, seemly
2 provoking a memory or mental association ⟨a haunting and *suggestive* song about a long-lost love⟩
synonyms evocative, reminiscent
related words eloquent, expressive, meaningful, pregnant, revealing, significant; affecting, emotional, impressive, moving, poignant, stirring, touching; exciting, provocative, provoking, rousing, stimulating
3 clearly conveying a special meaning (as one's mood) ⟨The baby's behavior is *suggestive* of a growing sense of empathy.⟩ — see EXPRESSIVE
suicide *n* the act of deliberately killing oneself ⟨a *suicide* hotline⟩
synonyms self-destruction
related words martyrdom; homicide, murder, slaying; dispatch, manslaughter; assassination, execution; euthanasia, mercy killing
suit *n* **1** a court case for enforcing a right or claim ⟨She filed a *suit* against the company that had manufactured the faulty heater.⟩ — see LAWSUIT
2 an earnest request ⟨brought their *suit* for justice to the queen⟩ — see PLEA 1
3 the series of social engagements shared by a couple looking to get married ⟨A rather old-fashioned fellow, he first sought the approval of his girlfriend's parents for the *suit*.⟩ — see COURTSHIP
suit *vb* **1** to be fitting or proper ⟨If you want only the fundamentals, that class should *suit*.⟩ — see DO 1
2 to give satisfaction to ⟨The location of our hotel *suited* us just fine.⟩ — see PLEASE 1
3 to outfit with clothes and especially fine or special clothes ⟨Rob went to the party *suited* in a strange getup that he'd picked out himself.⟩ — see CLOTHE 1
4 to change (something) so as to make it suitable for a new use or situation ⟨A bohemian by nature, she would have to *suit* her behavior to the corporate culture.⟩ — see ADAPT
suitability *n* the quality or state of being especially suitable

or fitting ⟨The *suitability* of the accommodations will ultimately depend on whether they're accessible for someone in a wheelchair.⟩ — see APPROPRIATENESS

suitable *adj* **1** having the required skills for an acceptable level of performance ⟨With only one *suitable* candidate it's not difficult to decide for whom to vote.⟩ — see COMPETENT 1

2 meeting the requirements of a purpose or situation ⟨I don't have anything *suitable* to wear to a bar mitzvah.⟩ — see FIT 1

suitableness *n* the quality or state of being especially suitable or fitting ⟨questioned the *suitableness* of bringing a dog to a wedding⟩ — see APPROPRIATENESS

suitably *adv* **1** in a manner suitable for the occasion or purpose ⟨We tried to appear *suitably* amused by his well-intentioned anecdote.⟩ — see PROPERLY

2 in or to a degree or quantity that meets one's requirements or satisfaction ⟨I need someone who's *suitably* versed in computers to help me decide what to buy.⟩ — see ENOUGH 1

suitcase *n* a bag carried by hand and designed to hold a traveler's clothing and personal articles ⟨It'll be much easier to carry a backpack than to lug that *suitcase* all over the place.⟩ — see TRAVELING BAG

suite *n* **1** a body of employees or attendants who accompany and wait on a person ⟨an athlete accompanied everywhere by a *suite* of attendants, including his personal trainer, a dietician, and a massage therapist⟩ — see CORTEGE 1

2 a number of things considered as a unit ⟨We replaced the mismatched bed and chests of drawers with a handsome new bedroom *suite*.⟩ — see GROUP 1

3 a room or set of rooms in a private house or a block used as a separate dwelling place ⟨Whenever he visits the city, he stays in his uncle's 10th-floor *suite*.⟩ — see APARTMENT 1

suitor *n* **1** a man who courts a woman usually with the goal of marrying her ⟨My sister married her *suitor* of six years on Sunday.⟩

synonyms gallant, swain, wooer

related words beau, boyfriend, fellow, man, old man, squeeze [*slang*]; admirer, crush, steady; beloved, darling, dear, favorite, flame, honey, love, lover, sweetheart, valentine; date, escort; fiancé, intended

2 one who asks earnestly for a favor or gift ⟨The inventors had several *suitors* for their patent, but they weren't interested in dealing with a big company.⟩ — see SUPPLICANT

sulk *n* a state of resentful silence or irritability ⟨a child sitting in a *sulk* over a minor disagreement⟩

synonyms grouch, pet, pouts, sulkiness, sullenness

related words blues, dumps, mopes; surliness; biliousness, crankiness, crossness, crotchetiness, grouchiness, grumpiness, huffiness, irascibility, irritability, irritableness, peevishness, perverseness, perversity, pettishness, petulance, surliness, testiness, waspishness; cantankerousness, disagreeableness, fretfulness, orneriness

near antonyms cheerfulness, gaiety (*also* gayety), gladsomeness, high-spiritedness, lightheartedness, perkiness; affability, agreeableness, amenity, amicability, cordiality, friendliness, geniality, graciousness, pleasantness, sociability, sociality; amiability, amiableness, good-humoredness, good-naturedness, good-temperedness

sulk *vb* to silently go about in a bad mood ⟨The toddler would *sulk* for hours whenever he didn't get his way.⟩

synonyms grump, mope, pout

related words brood, dwell (on), mull (over), muse (over), ponder; frown, glower, lower (*also* lour), scowl

sulkiness *n* a state of resentful silence or irritability ⟨Liz was fun to be with when she finally got over her *sulkiness*.⟩ — see SULK

sulky *adj* given to or displaying a resentful silence and often irritability ⟨The cancellation of the trip made him *sulky*.⟩

synonyms glum, pouting, sullen, surly

related words dour, gloomy, morose; choleric, crabby, cranky, cross, crotchety, grouchy, grumpy, irascible, irritable, peevish, perverse, pettish, petulant, prickly, quick-tempered, short-tempered, snappish, snappy, snippety, snippy, testy, waspish; brooding, moping; bilious, cantankerous, disagreeable, dyspeptic, ill-humored, ill-natured, ill-tempered, ornery; temperamental, touchy

near antonyms sociable; cheerful, cheery, gladsome, good-humored, good-natured, good-tempered, perky, sunny; carefree, easygoing, happy-go-lucky, relaxed

sullen *adj* **1** causing or marked by an atmosphere lacking in cheer ⟨*sullen* skies that matched our mood⟩ — see GLOOMY 1

2 given to or displaying a resentful silence and often irritability ⟨He sat in *sullen* silence.⟩ — see SULKY

sullenness *n* a state of resentful silence or irritability ⟨Her friends managed to dispel her *sullenness*.⟩ — see SULK

sullied *adj* not clean ⟨lying in *sullied* bed linens that had not seen the inside of a washing machine for some time⟩ — see DIRTY 1

sully *vb* to make dirty ⟨people that *sully* our state parks with their trash⟩ ⟨a once-gleaming marble facade *sullied* by decades of exposure to the elements⟩ — see DIRTY

sultry *adj* **1** containing or characterized by an uncomfortable amount of moisture ⟨On really *sultry* days we go to the pool to cool off.⟩ — see HUMID

2 having a notably high temperature ⟨the incredibly dry, *sultry* desert air⟩ — see HOT 1

sum *n* **1** a complete amount of something ⟨the *sum* of human knowledge on that subject⟩ — see WHOLE

2 a short statement of the main points ⟨The district attorney delivered a *sum* of the evidence against the accused that was simply staggering.⟩ — see SUMMARY

3 the central part or aspect of something under consideration ⟨The *sum* of the issue is: who will pay for this?⟩ — see CRUX

sum *vb* to combine (numbers) into a single sum ⟨Jim can *sum* figures in his head faster than I can punch them into a calculator.⟩ — see ADD 2

sum (to *or* **into)** *vb* to have a total of ⟨a lifetime of charitable contributions that *sum into* the millions⟩ — see AMOUNT (TO) 1

summarily *adv* in a few words ⟨*summarily* informed us that our help was not welcome⟩ — see SHORTLY 1

summarization *n* a short statement of the main points ⟨What you wrote goes way beyond a *summarization* of the speech.⟩ — see SUMMARY

summarize *vb* to make into a short statement of the main points (as of a report) ⟨The closing minute of the newscast *summarizes* the main story of the day.⟩

synonyms abstract, digest, encapsulate, epitomize, outline, recap, recapitulate, sum up, wrap up

related words abridge, condense, curtail, cut back, shorten; downsize, shrink; concentrate, consolidate; simplify, streamline

near antonyms elongate, extend, lengthen, prolong, protract; amplify, elaborate (on *or* upon), expand, supplement

summary *adj* marked by the use of few words to convey much information or meaning ⟨Obviously the slim book can offer only a very *summary* account of the American Civil War.⟩ — see CONCISE

summary *n* a short statement of the main points ⟨Many book reports choose to begin with a *summary* of the book.⟩

synonyms abstract, brief, digest, encapsulation, epitome, outline, précis, recap, recapitulation, résumé (or resume *also* resumé), roundup, sum, summarization, synopsis, wrap-up

related words abbreviation, abridgment (or abridgement), compend, condensation, curtailment, shortening; simplification, streamlining; rehash; conclusion, epilogue (*also* epilog)

near antonyms amplification, enlargement, expansion; addendum, supplement

summation *n* a complete amount of something ⟨the *summation* of climatic conditions that affect plant growth⟩ — see WHOLE

summit *n* the highest part or point ⟨a new movie that some enthusiastic reviewers are already calling the *summit* of cinematic achievement⟩ — see HEIGHT 1

summon *vb* **1** to demand or request the presence or service of ⟨Without explanation, the managing editor *summoned* me to his office.⟩

synonyms call, hail

related words cite, subpoena; assemble, call out, call up, convene, convoke, muster; ask, bid, invite; command, order, request, requisition; beckon, demand; buzz, knell, page, ring, whistle

phrases send for

near antonyms dismiss, send (away); banish, boot (out), drum (out), eject, expel, oust, out, rout, run off, throw out

2 to call into being through the use of one's inner resources or powers ⟨She managed to *summon* a bright smile despite the gloomy day.⟩

synonyms conjure (up), gather, get up

related words educe, elicit, evoke, raise

3 to bring together in assembly by or as if by command ⟨*summoned* a special session of parliament⟩ — see CONVOKE

sumptuous *adj* showing obvious signs of wealth and comfort ⟨The cruise ship claims to offer *sumptuous* furnishings, exquisitely prepared cuisine, and stellar entertainment.⟩ — see LUXURIOUS

sumptuously *adv* in a luxurious manner ⟨a history book *sumptuously* illustrated with maps, drawings, and photographs⟩ — see HIGH

sum up *vb* to make into a short statement of the main points (as of a report) ⟨In *summing up* the evidence against the defendant, the district attorney presented fact after damning fact.⟩ — see SUMMARIZE

sun *n* **1** the light given off by the star around which the planet Earth revolves ⟨Be sure to wear sunscreen if you plan to spend more than a few minutes in the *sun*.⟩

synonyms sunlight, sunshine

related words sunburst; daylight; glare, shine

near antonyms cloudiness; penumbra, shade, shadiness, shadow, umbra

2 a ball-shaped gaseous celestial body that shines by its own light ⟨the incomprehensible vastness of a universe filled with billions of *suns*⟩ — see STAR 1

3 the first appearance of light in the morning or the time of its appearance ⟨I'm afraid that for this long trip we shall have to leave with the *sun*.⟩ — see DAWN 1

4 public acknowledgment or admiration for an achievement ⟨Olympians basking in the *sun* of athletic achievement⟩ — see GLORY 1

sunder *vb* to set or force apart ⟨During the cold war East and West Berlin were *sundered* by an impenetrable wall.⟩ — see SEPARATE 1

sundown *n* the time from when the sun begins to set to the onset of total darkness ⟨We were told that the best time to see elk is at *sundown*.⟩ — see DUSK 1

sundries *pl n* small useful items ⟨The only things she

needed for her overnight stay were her carryall and a small bag for *sundries*.⟩ — see NOTION 1

sunken *adj* **1** curved inward ⟨The convalescing patient's *sunken* cheeks soon filled out.⟩ — see HOLLOW

2 living, lying, or occurring below the surface of the water ⟨diving for *sunken* treasure⟩ — see UNDERWATER

sunlight *n* the light given off by the star around which the planet Earth revolves ⟨Let's raise the shades and let in some *sunlight*.⟩ — see SUN 1

sunny *adj* **1** having or being an outward sign of good feelings (as of love, confidence, or happiness) ⟨Her *sunny* laughter filled the house with joy.⟩ — see RADIANT 1

2 having or showing a good mood or disposition ⟨momentarily forgot their worries at the sight of the baby's *sunny* smile⟩ — see CHEERFUL 1

3 indicative of or marked by high spirits or good humor ⟨The good-natured waitresses enhance the restaurant's *sunny* and cheery atmosphere.⟩ — see MERRY

4 not stormy or cloudy ⟨We are hoping for a *sunny* weekend so we can spend time at the beach.⟩ — see FAIR 1

sunrise *n* the first appearance of light in the morning or the time of its appearance ⟨a job that requires him to get up before *sunrise*⟩ — see DAWN 1

sunset *n* the time from when the sun begins to set to the onset of total darkness ⟨the glow of the western sky at *sunset*⟩ — see DUSK 1

sunshine *n* the light given off by the star around which the planet Earth revolves ⟨spent a week at the shore soaking up the *sunshine* and salt air⟩ — see SUN 1

sunshiny *adj* not stormy or cloudy ⟨We're due for a *sunshiny* weekend after all the rain we've had.⟩ — see FAIR 1

sunup *n* the first appearance of light in the morning or the time of its appearance ⟨Have you actually heard a rooster crow at *sunup*?⟩ — see DAWN 1

sup *n* the portion of a serving of a beverage that is swallowed at one time ⟨The old mariner took a *sup* of grog and began his tale.⟩ — see DRINK 2

sup *vb* to swallow in liquid form ⟨Dan *supped* the broth slowly.⟩ — see DRINK 1

super *adj* unusually large ⟨Drinks come in three sizes: medium, large, or *super*.⟩ — see HUGE

super *adv* to a great degree ⟨My computer is *super* slow this morning.⟩ — see VERY 1

superabundance *n* **1** an amount or supply more than sufficient to meet one's needs ⟨A *superabundance* of donations flowed in after the family's plight was seen on national TV.⟩ — see PLENTY 1

2 the state or an instance of going beyond what is usual, proper, or needed ⟨a *superabundance* of applicants for a limited number of jobs⟩ — see EXCESS

superannuated *adj* having passed its time of use or usefulness ⟨a periodical that insists on using largely *superannuated* terms like "aviatrix"⟩ — see OBSOLETE

superb *adj* of the very best kind ⟨The restaurant's baker makes a *superb* chocolate cake.⟩ — see EXCELLENT

superbness *n* **1** exceptionally high quality ⟨The *superbness* of the orchestra's performance was such that the music critics were straining for superlatives.⟩ — see EXCELLENCE 1

2 impressiveness of beauty on a large scale ⟨Climbers rave about the *superbness* of the view from the mountain's summit.⟩ — see MAGNIFICENCE

supercilious *adj* having a feeling of superiority that shows itself in an overbearing attitude ⟨The *supercilious* art dealer rolled her eyes when we asked if she had anything for under $1,000.⟩ — see ARROGANT

superciliousness *n* an exaggerated sense of one's importance that shows itself in the making of excessive or unjustified claims ⟨can't bear the *superciliousness* of her cousin, who lives in the city and thinks everybody who doesn't is a hick⟩ — see ARROGANCE

supercool *adj* being in the latest or current fashion ⟨He picked out some *supercool*, superexpensive sneakers.⟩ — see STYLISH

superficial *adj* **1** lying on or affecting only the outer layer of something ⟨a *superficial* scratch that barely even broke the skin⟩
synonyms skin-deep, surface
related words depthless, shallow, shoal; two-dimensional; external
near antonyms deep, deep-seated
2 having or showing a lack of depth of understanding or character ⟨a *superficial* analysis of how the violence in video games affects young people⟩
synonyms facile, one-dimensional, shallow, skin-deep
related words cursory, hasty, oversimple, passing, sketchy; aimless, desultory, haphazard, hit-or-miss, random; limited, narrow, restricted
near antonyms discerning, penetrating; broad, complete, comprehensive, exhaustive, extensive, far-reaching, wide; general, global, inclusive; detailed, in-depth; critical
antonyms deep, profound

superfluity *n* **1** something adding to pleasure or comfort but not absolutely necessary ⟨The car came with heated seats and other *superfluities*.⟩ — see LUXURY 1
2 the state or an instance of going beyond what is usual, proper, or needed ⟨a *superfluity* of wire coat hangers from all of those trips to the dry cleaner⟩ — see EXCESS

superfluous *adj* being over what is needed ⟨cleared off all the *superfluous* stuff on his desk to make room for the new computer⟩ — see SPARE 1

superheated *adj* having a notably high temperature ⟨Certain *superheated* liquids change to gas with almost explosive violence.⟩ — see HOT 1

superhuman *adj* being so extraordinary or abnormal as to suggest powers which violate the laws of nature ⟨In his dreams the boy can always perform *superhuman* feats.⟩ — see SUPERNATURAL 2

superintend *vb* **1** to be in charge of ⟨*superintends* the construction of all scenery at the summer theater⟩ — see BOSS 1
2 to look after and make decisions about ⟨homeschooling parents who *superintend* their children's education⟩ — see CONDUCT 1
3 to take charge of especially on behalf of another ⟨Whoever's *superintending* the warehouse will know what's been delivered today.⟩ — see ²TEND 1

superintendence *n* **1** the act or activity of looking after and making decisions about something ⟨Under her *superintendence* the company undertook some overdue restructuring.⟩ — see CONDUCT 1
2 the duty or function of watching or guarding for the sake of proper direction or control ⟨The *superintendence* of the local music festival is handled jointly by the city and the county.⟩ — see SUPERVISION 1

superintendency *n* **1** the duty or function of watching or guarding for the sake of proper direction or control ⟨*Superintendency* of the polling places is largely carried out by retired citizens.⟩ — see SUPERVISION 1
2 the act or activity of looking after and making decisions about something ⟨Currently a faculty member is needed for *superintendency* of the program.⟩ — see CONDUCT 1

superintendent *n* a person who manages or directs something ⟨The office of the *superintendent* of parks issues camping permits.⟩ — see EXECUTIVE

superior *adj* **1** having a feeling of superiority that shows itself in an overbearing attitude ⟨That *superior* sports-

caster lets it be known which baseball teams he thinks are second-rate.⟩ — see ARROGANT
2 having or displaying feelings of scorn for what is regarded as beneath oneself ⟨His parents taught him never to have a *superior* attitude towards people who don't have the privileges he has.⟩ — see PROUD 1
3 of the very best kind ⟨a five-star restaurant known for its *superior* wine list⟩ — see EXCELLENT
4 standing above others in rank, importance, or achievement ⟨a university known for attracting *superior* scientists and mathematicians⟩ — see EMINENT

superior *n* one who is above another in rank, station, or office ⟨If a customer is rude to you, report it to your *superior* and she'll handle it.⟩
synonyms better, elder, senior
related words boss, chief, head, leader, master
near antonyms assistant, deputy
antonyms inferior, subordinate, underling

superiority *n* **1** an exaggerated sense of one's importance that shows itself in the making of excessive or unjustified claims ⟨Their success has given them a false sense of *superiority*.⟩ — see ARROGANCE
2 exceptionally high quality ⟨The *superiority* of tree-ripened mangoes might make you want to spend the rest of your life in a tropical climate.⟩ — see EXCELLENCE 1
3 the fact or state of being above others in rank or importance ⟨the *superiority* of the nation in military might⟩ — see EMINENCE 1

superlative *adj* of the very best kind ⟨The New England town meeting is a *superlative* example of grassroots democracy.⟩ — see EXCELLENT

supernal *adj* **1** of the very best kind ⟨an absolutely *supernal* performance of the concerto by a 16-year old prodigy⟩ — see EXCELLENT
2 of, relating to, or suggesting heaven ⟨a couple enjoying the *supernal* joys of parenthood for the first time⟩ — see CELESTIAL

supernatural *adj* **1** of, relating to, or being part of a reality beyond the observable physical universe ⟨The man believes in ghosts, guardian angels, and other *supernatural* beings.⟩
synonyms metaphysical, preternatural, unearthly
related words mystic, mystical, occult; extrasensory; celestial, divine, ethereal, heavenly, spiritual, unworldly
near antonyms earthly, mundane
antonyms natural
2 being so extraordinary or abnormal as to suggest powers which violate the laws of nature ⟨He seems to read books with *supernatural* speed.⟩
synonyms magical, miraculous, phenomenal, preternatural, superhuman, uncanny, unearthly
related words bizarre, curious, eerie (*also* eery), far-out, grotesque, outlandish, out-of-the-way, outrageous, outré, peculiar, quaint, queer, quirky, screwy, strange, wacky (*also* whacky), way-out, weird, wild; baffling, bewildering, confounding, mystifying, perplexing, puzzling, shocking; aberrant, atypical, fantastic (*also* fantastical), flaky, freak, freakish, idiosyncratic, marvelous (*or* marvellous), prodigious, rare, singular, uncommon, unique, unnatural, unusual
near antonyms average, commonplace, everyday, ordinary, prosaic, routine, run-of-the-mill, typical, unexceptional, unremarkable, usual, workaday; expected, familiar, predictable; common, customary, frequent, habitual, regular, wonted
3 of, relating to, or being God ⟨believed he had a *supernatural* calling to join the ministry⟩ — see HOLY 3

supernumerary *adj* being over what is needed ⟨a third, *supernumerary* witness to the signing of the will⟩ — see SPARE 1

supersede *vb* to take the place of ⟨That edition of the dictionary that you have has been *superseded* by a more recent one.⟩ — see REPLACE 1

superstar *n* a person who is widely known and usually much talked about ⟨a basketball *superstar*⟩ — see CELEBRITY 1

supervene *vb* to come after in time ⟨It was not the faulty brakes that caused the accident but a *supervening* act of negligent driving.⟩ — see FOLLOW 1

supervise *vb* **1** to be in charge of ⟨For each sailboat an experienced hand is assigned to *supervise* a novice seaman.⟩ — see BOSS 1
2 to look after and make decisions about ⟨*supervises* all the affairs of the athletic club, including hiring someone to run the summer tennis camp⟩ — see CONDUCT 1
3 to take charge of especially on behalf of another ⟨We need someone to *supervise* the construction project while the foreman is in the hospital.⟩ — see ²TEND 1

supervision *n* **1** the duty or function of watching or guarding for the sake of proper direction or control ⟨One of your responsibilities will be the *supervision* of all fund-raising activities for the club.⟩
synonyms care, charge, guidance, headship, oversight, regulation, stewardship, superintendence, superintendency, surveillance
related words monitoring, observance, observing, policing; administration, control, direction, generalship, hand(s), management, running; leadership, piloting, shepherding, steering; government, rule; aegis (*also* egis), auspices, guardianship, protection, trusteeship, tutelage
2 the act or activity of looking after and making decisions about something ⟨One of the senior editors took over *supervision* of the project while the editor-in-chief was on maternity leave.⟩ — see CONDUCT 1

supervisor *n* a person who manages or directs something ⟨If you need to change your schedule, speak to your *supervisor*.⟩ — see EXECUTIVE

supervisory *adj* suited for or relating to the directing of things ⟨Jake was promoted to a *supervisory* position with several assistants working under him.⟩ — see EXECUTIVE

supplant *vb* to take the place of ⟨old traditions that were fading away and being *supplanted* by modern ways⟩ — see REPLACE 1

supple *adj* **1** able to bend easily without breaking ⟨a dome tent outfitted with *supple* fiberglass tent poles⟩ — see WILLOWY
2 able to revert to original size and shape after being stretched, squeezed, or twisted ⟨shoes made from *supple* leather⟩ — see ELASTIC 1

supplement *n* **1** something added (as by growth) ⟨This new rule restricting e-mail to job-related activity is only a *supplement* to the preexisting policy regarding personal use of company resources.⟩ — see INCREASE 1
2 something that serves to complete or make up for a deficiency in something else ⟨recommends taking a vitamin C *supplement* to prevent colds⟩ — see COMPLEMENT 1
3 a part added at the end of a book or periodical ⟨a *supplement* containing updated information⟩ — see ADDENDUM 1

supplemental *adj* **1** available to supply something extra when needed ⟨The new program will provide *supplemental* health insurance to thousands of workers.⟩ — see AUXILIARY
2 related to each other in such a way that one completes the other ⟨*supplemental* courses like algebra and calculus⟩ — see COMPLEMENTARY

supplementary *adj* **1** available to supply something extra when needed ⟨The teacher's edition of the textbook comes with a lot of *supplementary* material.⟩ — see AUXILIARY
2 related to each other in such a way that one completes the other ⟨regards anthropology and archaeology as *supplementary* fields of study⟩ — see COMPLEMENTARY

suppliant *n* one who asks earnestly for a favor or gift ⟨Amy didn't like being in the position of a *suppliant*, having to ask her parents to help her pay the rent on her apartment.⟩ — see SUPPLICANT

suppliant *adj* asking humbly ⟨The *suppliant* thief pleaded for a second chance.⟩
synonyms beseeching, entreating, imploring, pleading, soliciting, supplicant, supplicating
related words begging, insistent, persistent

supplicant *adj* asking humbly ⟨Ed hated having to go before his boss like a *supplicant* beggar whenever he needed some time off to attend to personal matters.⟩ — see SUPPLIANT

supplicant *n* one who asks earnestly for a favor or gift ⟨The new governor soon had to deal with a long line of *supplicants* asking for jobs and other political favors.⟩
synonyms petitioner, pleader, solicitor, suitor, suppliant
related words beggar, mendicant, panhandler

supplicate *vb* to make a request to (someone) in an earnest or urgent manner ⟨They knelt and *supplicated* the king to protect them.⟩ — see BEG

supplicating *adj* asking humbly ⟨In a *supplicating* gesture, he got down on his knees and asked, "Will you marry me?"⟩ — see SUPPLIANT

supplication *n* an earnest request ⟨The Red Cross made an urgent *supplication* for donations of food and blankets.⟩ — see PLEA 1

supply *vb* **1** to provide (someone) with what is needed for a task or activity ⟨Be sure to pack your own towels in case the hostel doesn't *supply* them.⟩ — see FURNISH 1
2 to put (something) into the possession of someone for use or consumption ⟨The stable will *supply* safety helmets, but we need to bring our own riding boots.⟩ — see FURNISH 2

supply *n* the number of individuals or amount of something available at any given time ⟨The *supply* of parents willing to coach youth soccer seems to be shrinking.⟩
synonyms budget, force, fund, inventory, pool, stock
related words reserve, resource; cache, hoard, stockpile; refill, renewal, replacement; kitty, nest egg, pot, purse; mine, source, spring, well

support *n* **1** a structure that holds up or serves as a foundation for something else ⟨If you don't add a couple more *supports* to that tower of blocks, it's going to fall down.⟩
synonyms brace, buttress, mount, mounting, shore, spur, stay, underpinning
related words shoring; column, pedestal, pilaster, pillar; arch, bolster, bracket, cantilever, girder; bearing; crutch, peg, post, stake, stanchion, stand, stilt, strut, truss; base, foundation, frame
2 an act or instance of helping ⟨The team's victory owes a lot to Joe's strong *support* in left field.⟩ — see HELP 1

support *vb* **1** to promote the interests or cause of ⟨Though childless themselves, they *support* the local schools both by volunteering and by fiercely opposing funding cuts.⟩
synonyms advocate, back, champion, endorse (*also* indorse), patronize, plump (for)
related words adopt, embrace, espouse; abet, aid, assist, help, prop (up), second, side (with); bolster, boost, buttress; advance, forward, further; plug, preach
phrases go in for, go to bat for, hold a brief for, stand up for, stick up for
near antonyms baffle, foil, frustrate, interfere, oppose, sabotage, thwart; desert, disappoint, fail, let down

2 to pay the living expenses of ⟨They have three children to *support*.⟩
synonyms keep, maintain, provide (for)
related words finance, fund, patronize, set up, sponsor, stake, underwrite
phrases foot the bill (for), take care of
3 to hold up or serve as a foundation for ⟨pillars *supporting* the bridge⟩
synonyms bear, bolster, brace, buttress, carry, prop (up), shore (up), stay, sustain, underpin, uphold
related words steady, truss, underlie
4 to provide evidence or information for (as a claim or idea) ⟨studies that *support* the claim that eating dark chocolate lowers the risk of cardiovascular disease⟩
synonyms back, bolster, buttress, corroborate, shore (up), substantiate
related words confirm, establish, prove, verify; affirm, avouch, validate
near antonyms undercut, undermine, weaken
5 to continue to declare to be true or proper despite opposition or objections ⟨We *support* the students' right to speak out on local issues that affect them.⟩ — see MAINTAIN 2
6 to give evidence or testimony to the truth or factualness of ⟨New evidence *supports* the original researchers' unexpected conclusions.⟩ — see CONFIRM 1
7 to provide (someone) with what is useful or necessary to achieve an end ⟨sent reinforcements to *support* the troops deployed overseas⟩ — see HELP 1
8 to put up with (something painful or difficult) ⟨He simply cannot *support* the thought of having to go on alone.⟩ — see BEAR 2
supportable *adj* **1** capable of being defended with good reasoning against verbal attack ⟨Are there ever circumstances where laws that restrict a person's freedom of speech are *supportable*?⟩ — see TENABLE 2
2 capable of being endured ⟨Her beloved cat had been rescued from the burning house, making her other losses at least *supportable*.⟩ — see BEARABLE
3 capable of being proven as true or real ⟨The news editor simply assumed the facts of the story were *supportable* and did not assign it to a fact checker.⟩ — see VERIFIABLE
supporter *n* **1** a person who actively supports or favors a cause ⟨President Lyndon B. Johnson was a strong *supporter* of civil rights.⟩ — see EXPONENT 1
2 someone associated with another to give assistance or moral support ⟨Even the President's *supporters* acknowledge that some of the criticism is justified.⟩ — see ALLY
supporting *adj* serving to give support to the truth or factualness of something ⟨scientists looking for direct *supporting* evidence of microscopic black holes, the existence of which is theoretical⟩ — see CORROBORATIVE
supportive *adj* serving to give support to the truth or factualness of something ⟨The jimmied window latch is *supportive* of the theory that there was forced entry into the house.⟩ — see CORROBORATIVE
suppose *vb* **1** to decide the size, amount, number, or distance of (something) without actual measurement ⟨If we *suppose* a minimum profit of $10,000 from the charity auction, we should be able to pay for the family's medical expenses.⟩ — see ESTIMATE 2
2 to form an opinion from little or no evidence ⟨What do you *suppose* he's going to do with the prize money he won?⟩ — see GUESS 1
3 to have as an opinion ⟨Voters wrongly *supposed* that the new mayor would be opposed to letting hazardous waste be transported through the city.⟩ — see BELIEVE 2
4 to take as true or as a fact without actual proof ⟨Kay

had always *supposed* that her father would bequeath the family farm to her.⟩ — see ASSUME 2
supposed *adj* appearing to be true on the basis of evidence that may or may not be confirmed ⟨This new computer program is a *supposed* improvement over the old one.⟩ — see APPARENT 1
supposedly *adv* to all outward appearances ⟨She's *supposedly* too sick to come.⟩ — see APPARENTLY
supposition *n* **1** an idea that is the starting point for making a case or conducting an investigation ⟨My *supposition* is that we are reading this essay because there will be a quiz on it next week.⟩ — see THEORY
2 an opinion or judgment based on little or no evidence ⟨It's pure *supposition* on your part that there's something illegal going on next door.⟩ — see CONJECTURE
3 something taken as being true or factual and used as a starting point for a course of action or reasoning ⟨worthless genetic research that was based on the erroneous *supposition* that acquired characteristics can be passed on to offspring⟩ — see ASSUMPTION 1
suppositional *adj* existing only as an assumption or speculation ⟨Concepts regarding the origin and structure of the universe must perforce be *suppositional*.⟩ — see THEORETICAL 1
suppress *vb* **1** to keep from being publicly known ⟨The governor tried to *suppress* the news.⟩
synonyms cover (up), hush (up)
related words black out, censor, gag, muzzle, silence; quash, repress, smother, spike, squash, squelch, stifle, strangle, throttle
near antonyms debunk, expose, reveal, show up, uncloak, uncover, unmask; blab, disclose, divulge, spill, tell, unveil; broadcast, circulate, publish, spread; describe, narrate, recite, recount, rehearse, relate, report
2 to refrain from openly showing or uttering ⟨He managed to *suppress* a laugh.⟩ ⟨*suppressed* her anger⟩
synonyms choke (back), hold back, pocket, repress, smother, stifle, strangle, submerge, swallow
related words control, govern, manage; bridle, check, curb, quash, quell; bottle up, contain; muffle, squelch
near antonyms express, loose, release, take out, unleash, vent
3 to hold back the normal growth of ⟨Pruning helps *suppress* buds at the ends of developed branches and encourages new growth elsewhere.⟩ — see STUNT
4 to put a stop to (something) by the use of force ⟨Nothing could *suppress* the rising tide of protest against the dictator's latest injustices.⟩ — see QUELL 1
5 to keep secret or shut off from view ⟨The defense attorney is openly accusing the prosecutor of attempting to *suppress* vital evidence.⟩ — see ¹HIDE 2
suppression *n* the checking of one's true feelings and impulses when dealing with others ⟨learned that *suppression* of her angry feelings didn't necessarily make them go away⟩ — see CONSTRAINT 1
supremacy *n* **1** controlling power or influence over others ⟨The Roman empire had *supremacy* over the entire Mediterranean world.⟩
synonyms ascendancy (*also* ascendency), dominance, domination, dominion, predominance, preeminence, sovereignty (*also* sovranty)
related words primacy, superiority; lordship, scepter; arm, authority, choke hold, clutch, command, control, grip, hold, mastery, sway; direction, management; clout, might, pull, weight; eminence, importance, moment; prerogative, privilege, right
near antonyms helplessness, weakness; impotence, impotency, powerlessness
2 exceptionally high quality ⟨The *supremacy* of cash-

mere among wools accounts for its high price.⟩ — see EXCELLENCE 1

3 the fact or state of being above others in rank or importance ⟨England's maritime *supremacy* in the 18th century⟩ — see EMINENCE 1

supreme *adj* **1** highest in rank or authority ⟨the *supreme* commander of the multinational force⟩ — see HEAD

2 coming before all others in importance ⟨In our house, watching baseball reigns *supreme* as the activity of choice on summer evenings.⟩ — see FOREMOST 1

3 of the greatest or highest degree or quantity ⟨considers a letter of gratitude from a former student the *supreme* reward for his years of teaching⟩ — see ULTIMATE 1

Supreme Being *n* the being worshipped as the creator and ruler of the universe ⟨Anthropologists have found that most cultures around the world believe in a *Supreme Being.*⟩ — see DEITY 2

supremely *adv* to a great degree ⟨Climbing Mount Everest is *supremely* difficult.⟩ — see VERY 1

surcease *n* the stopping of a process or activity ⟨hoping the new medicine would bring *surcease* to his pain⟩ — see END 1

surcharge *vb* to charge (someone) too much for goods or services ⟨contends that with the present tax structure, the state's lower-income residents are being *surcharged* and the wealthiest residents are getting off too lightly⟩ — see OVERCHARGE 1

surcoat *n* a warm outdoor coat ⟨A knight in a fur-lined and hooded *surcoat* over a long tunic stood in the forest clearing.⟩ — see OVERCOAT 1

sure *adj* **1** having or showing a mind free from doubt ⟨Are you absolutely *sure* that she said she was coming today?⟩ — see CERTAIN 2

2 impossible to avoid or evade ⟨The joke's a *sure* dud if you don't pause in the right places.⟩ — see INEVITABLE 1

3 not likely to fail ⟨a *sure* cure for the winter blues—a week in the Bahamas⟩ — see INFALLIBLE 2

4 worthy of one's trust ⟨A sister is a *sure* friend for life.⟩ — see DEPENDABLE 1

5 not capable of being challenged or proved wrong ⟨no *sure* evidence that life exists on other planets⟩ — see IRREFUTABLE

sure *adv* without any question ⟨We *sure* could use your help here!⟩ — see INDEED 1

surefire *adj* not likely to fail ⟨Pizza seems like a *surefire* choice for a food that everyone at the party will be happy with.⟩ — see INFALLIBLE 2

surely *adv* without any question ⟨*Surely* there's something I can do to help!⟩ — see INDEED 1

sureness *n* **1** a state of mind in which one is free from doubt ⟨Unfortunately, he lacked the *sureness* of his opponent in the tennis match.⟩ — see CONFIDENCE 2

2 worthiness as the recipient of another's trust or confidence ⟨Investors in those risky foreign enterprises were gambling on the *sureness* of their instincts.⟩ — see RELIABILITY

surety *n* **1** a formal agreement to fulfill an obligation ⟨gave his *surety* that he would pay back the loan if his sister was unable to for any reason⟩ — see GUARANTEE 1

2 a person who takes the responsibility for some other person or thing ⟨A mutual friend agreed to act as *surety* if I lent my cousin some money, since I wasn't certain that he'd be able to pay it back.⟩ — see SPONSOR

3 a state of mind in which one is free from doubt ⟨I can't tell you the year in which that event happened with any great *surety*.⟩ — see CONFIDENCE 2

surf *n* a light mass of fine bubbles formed in or on a liquid ⟨beachgoers romping in the swirling *surf*⟩ — see FOAM

surface *adj* lying on or affecting only the outer layer of something ⟨a *surface* stain on the wood that can easily be removed with a mild detergent⟩ — see SUPERFICIAL 1

surface *n* an outer part or layer ⟨The *surface* of just about everything in the kitchen was covered with soot after we put the grease fire out.⟩ — see EXTERIOR

surface *vb* **1** to come to one's attention especially gradually or unexpectedly ⟨No information regarding the stolen car has *surfaced* since the police found it abandoned on a country road.⟩ — see ARISE 2

2 to penetrate the surface (as of water) from below ⟨A submarine *surfaced* on the starboard side of the aircraft carrier.⟩ — see BROACH 1

surfeit *n* the state or an instance of going beyond what is usual, proper, or needed ⟨ended up with a *surfeit* of volunteers⟩ — see EXCESS

surfeit *vb* to fill with food to capacity ⟨Having *surfeited* ourselves on appetizers, we had to decline the rest of the restaurant's offerings.⟩ — see GORGE 1

surfeited *adj* having one's appetite completely satisfied ⟨*Surfeited* by the Thanksgiving repast, the grown-ups dozed off in front of the TV.⟩ — see FULL 3

surge *n* a moving ridge on the surface of water ⟨A huge *surge* nearly capsized the boat and drenched the hapless fishermen.⟩ — see WAVE

surly *adj* **1** given to or displaying a resentful silence and often irritability ⟨Keith went about his chores in a *surly* huff, totally annoyed that he was stuck at home on this beautiful Saturday.⟩ — see SULKY

2 having or showing a habitually bad temper ⟨The *surly* receptionist told us we'd have to wait outside in the rain.⟩ — see ILL-TEMPERED

surmise *n* an opinion or judgment based on little or no evidence ⟨My *surmise* is that the couple's "good news" is the announcement that they are going to have a baby.⟩ — see CONJECTURE

surmise *vb* to form an opinion from little or no evidence ⟨They must have *surmised* that I wasn't interested.⟩ — see GUESS 1

surmount *vb* to achieve a victory over ⟨an Olympic swimmer who *surmounted* endless obstacles to achieve her goals⟩ — see BEAT 2

surpass *vb* **1** to be greater, better, or stronger than ⟨She always tried to *surpass* her older brother at anything he did.⟩

synonyms beat, better, eclipse, exceed, excel, outclass, outdistance, outdo, outshine, outstrip, overtop, top, transcend

related words outpace, outrun, overpass; best, clobber, conquer, crush, defeat, drub, lick, master, overcome, overmatch, prevail (over), rout, shame, skunk, subdue, surmount, thrash, trim, triumph (over), trounce, wallop, whip, win (against), worst; outbalance, outweigh, overbear, overshadow, trump

phrases go one better, run circles around (*or* run rings around)

near antonyms lose (to)

2 to go beyond the limit of ⟨The sales of the band's newest album have *surpassed* the combined sales of its last two albums.⟩ — see EXCEED 1

surplus *adj* being over what is needed ⟨*Surplus* stock gets shipped to the warehouse and is eventually sold at auction.⟩ — see SPARE 1

surplus *n* the state or an instance of going beyond what is usual, proper, or needed ⟨We have a *surplus* of plastic knives, but we're short on forks and spoons for the picnic.⟩ — see EXCESS

surprise *also* **surprize** *n* **1** something that makes a strong impression because it is so unexpected ⟨The anniversary party was such a complete *surprise* that the couple was speechless for a moment.⟩

synonyms bombshell, jar, jolt, stunner

related words shock, thunderclap; eye-opener, revelation, shocker; amazement, marvel, wonder
phrases bolt from the blue (*also* bolt out of the blue)
2 the state of being strongly impressed by something unexpected or unusual ⟨stared in utter *surprise* at the deer in his cabin⟩
synonyms amazement, astonishment, shock
related words awe, wonder, wonderment; startle; bewilderment, confusion, consternation, discomfiture, dismay
3 a setup in which hidden attackers lie in wait ⟨waited under cover of darkness and took the enemy encampment by *surprise* at dawn⟩ — see AMBUSH 1
surprise *also* **surprize** *vb* **1** to make a strong impression on (someone) with something unexpected ⟨I was very *surprised* when my parents offered to pay the down payment on our house.⟩
synonyms amaze, astonish, astound, dumbfound (*also* dumfound), flabbergast, floor, rock, shock, startle, stun, stupefy
related words befuddle, bewilder, confound, confuse, daze, discomfit, disconcert, dismay, jar, muddle, nonplus, perplex, shake up
phrases knock for a loop, take aback, take by surprise
2 to lie in wait for and attack by surprise ⟨FBI agents *surprised* the counterfeiters in their own base of operations.⟩ — see AMBUSH
surprising *adj* **1** causing a strong emotional reaction because of unexpectedness ⟨The *surprising* news that they were going to have a baby had them rushing to buy nursery furniture.⟩
synonyms amazing, astonishing, astounding, dumbfounding (*also* dumfounding), eye-opening, flabbergasting, jarring, shocking, startling, stunning, stupefying
related words unannounced, unanticipated, unexpected, unforeseen; awesome, awful, breathtaking, fabulous, marvelous (*or* marvellous), miraculous, portentous, prodigious, staggering, stupendous, sublime, wonderful, wondrous; befuddling, bewildering, confounding, confusing, discomfiting, disconcerting, dismaying, flustering, muddling, nonplussing (*also* nonplusing), perplexing, upsetting; incomprehensible, inconceivable, incredible, unbelievable, unimaginable, unlikely, unthinkable
near antonyms common, customary, normal, ordinary, typical, unexceptional, unremarkable, usual
antonyms unsurprising
2 causing wonder or astonishment ⟨It's *surprising* how much knowledge of physics the architects of those immense medieval cathedrals must have had.⟩ — see MARVELOUS 1
surrender *n* the usually forced yielding of one's person or possessions to the control of another ⟨*surrendered* the territory to the invaders⟩
synonyms capitulating, capitulation, relinquishment, submission, submitting
related words acceptance, acquiescence, concession; compromise; appeasement, conciliation, reconcilement, reconciliation; capture, fall
near antonyms resistance
surrender *vb* **1** to give (something) over to the control or possession of another usually under duress ⟨The toddler *surrendered* the doll to her mother after a brief struggle.⟩ ⟨The commander *surrendered* the garrison without having fired a single shot.⟩
synonyms cede, deliver, give up, hand over, lay down, relinquish, render, turn in, turn over, yield
related words commit, consign, entrust (*also* intrust), transfer; forfeit, release, waive; abnegate, renounce, resign; abandon, desert, discard, forsake, part (with), shed
near antonyms keep, retain, withhold

2 to cease resistance (as to another's arguments, demands, or control) ⟨The father refused to *surrender* to his son's constant begging for a smartphone.⟩ — see YIELD 3
3 to give up (as a position of authority) formally ⟨The aging queen refused to *surrender* the throne to her increasingly impatient heir.⟩ — see ABDICATE
4 to give up and cease resistance (as to a liking, temptation, or habit) ⟨Determined to give up smoking, she so far has not *surrendered* to her incessant desire to have a cigarette.⟩ — see YIELD 1
5 to yield to the control or power of enemy forces ⟨General Robert E. Lee *surrendered* to General Ulysses S. Grant on April 9, 1865, thus ending the Civil War.⟩ — see FALL 2
6 to give (oneself) over to something especially unrestrainedly ⟨They refused to *surrender* themselves to despair.⟩ — see ABANDON 1
surreptitious *adj* undertaken or done so as to escape being observed or known by others ⟨a private investigator adept at taking *surreptitious* pictures⟩ — see SECRET 1
surround *n* the circumstances, conditions, or objects by which one is surrounded ⟨The vast, featureless *surround* of the desert was strangely appealing to him.⟩ — see ENVIRONMENT
surround *vb* to form a circle around ⟨She was *surrounded* by cheering fans within moments of scoring the winning goal.⟩
synonyms circle, compass, embrace, encircle, enclose (*also* inclose), encompass, gird, girdle, ring, wreathe
related words circumscribe, cordon (off), fence (in), wall; beset, besiege, entrench (*also* intrench), invest, swarm
surroundings *pl n* the circumstances, conditions, or objects by which one is surrounded ⟨We relaxed and forgot our worries for a while in the plush *surroundings* of the hotel.⟩ — see ENVIRONMENT
surveillance *n* the duty or function of watching or guarding for the sake of proper direction or control ⟨a neutral country charged with the *surveillance* of the post-war rebuilding effort⟩ — see SUPERVISION 1
survey *n* a close look at or over someone or something in order to judge condition ⟨A *survey* of the premises revealed some safety violations.⟩ — see INSPECTION
survey *vb* **1** to go around and approach (people) with a request for opinions or information ⟨*surveyed* the medical residents and found out that 60% of them don't think they get enough sleep⟩ — see CANVASS 1
2 to look over closely (as for judging quality or condition) ⟨I *surveyed* the books at the estate sale, fondly hoping to find a rare first edition.⟩ — see INSPECT
survive *vb* **1** to come safely through ⟨The cat miraculously *survived* a two-story fall.⟩
synonyms ride (out), weather
related words outlast, outlive, wear out; pull through; abide, continue, endure, hang on, hold on, hold out, hold up, last, lead, persist, stand, stick out, withstand; be, breathe, exist, live, subsist; flourish, prosper, thrive
phrases make it (through)
near antonyms decease, depart, die, expire, pass (on), pass away, perish, succumb; disappear, evaporate, fade, vanish; cease, end, stop
2 to continue to operate or to meet one's needs ⟨Some old-world customs still *survive* in modern-day America.⟩ — see HOLD OUT
susceptibility *n* the quality or state of having little resistance to some outside agent ⟨His aunt's unfortunate *susceptibility* to viruses meant she was nearly always sick.⟩ ⟨a country doctor who had a well-known *susceptibility* to anyone with a hard-luck story⟩
synonyms defenselessness, vulnerability, weakness

related words helplessness, powerlessness; passiveness, passivity; feebleness, frailness, frailty, infirmity; exposure, liability, openness, predisposition, proneness, sensitivity; receptiveness, receptivity

near antonyms immunity; indomitability, indomitableness, invincibility

antonyms invulnerability

susceptible *adj* **1** being in a situation where one is likely to meet with harm ⟨Some people are more *susceptible* to depression during the winter because of reduced exposure to sunlight.⟩ — see LIABLE 1

2 lacking protection from danger or resistance against attack ⟨completely *susceptible* and totally defenseless against the imploring eyes of the puppy in the pet store⟩ — see HELPLESS 1

3 readily taken advantage of ⟨Having recently lost his job, he was more *susceptible* to the illusory promises of get-rich-quick schemes.⟩ — see EASY 2

suspect *adj* giving good reason for being doubted, questioned, or challenged ⟨Her story about why she was late was *suspect*.⟩ — see DOUBTFUL 2

suspect *vb* **1** to form an opinion from little or no evidence ⟨I *suspected* that you'd forget our appointment.⟩ — see GUESS 1

2 to have no trust or confidence in ⟨I *suspected* him from the moment he claimed to be an expert.⟩ — see DISTRUST

suspecting *adj* inclined to doubt or question claims ⟨*Suspecting* consumers probably wouldn't fall for a scam like that.⟩ — see SKEPTICAL 1

suspend *vb* **1** to bring to a formal close for a period of time ⟨The judge *suspended* the hearing to give the district attorney more time to process evidence.⟩ — see ADJOURN

2 to place on an elevated point without support from below ⟨*suspended* a banner proclaiming the town's "Heritage Days" from the archway⟩ — see HANG 1

suspense *n* a state of temporary inactivity ⟨The lawsuit is in *suspense* until the court makes a decision concerning a related lawsuit.⟩ — see ABEYANCE

suspension *n* a state of temporary inactivity ⟨Trading with that nation is in *suspension* until it improves its record on human rights.⟩ — see ABEYANCE

suspicion *n* **1** a feeling or attitude that one does not know the truth, truthfulness, or trustworthiness of someone or something ⟨All his promises were received with well-deserved *suspicion*.⟩ — see DOUBT

2 a very small amount ⟨new parents who were alarmed by just a *suspicion* of a rash on their baby's chest⟩ — see PARTICLE 1

suspicious *adj* **1** giving good reason for being doubted, questioned, or challenged ⟨*suspicious* claims of being the rightful owner of the property⟩ — see DOUBTFUL 2

2 inclined to doubt or question claims ⟨*suspicious* of any menu dish having a name she can't pronounce⟩ — see SKEPTICAL 1

3 not feeling sure about the truth, wisdom, or trustworthiness of someone or something ⟨You should be very *suspicious* of those telephone calls from people telling you that you're the winner of a contest you never entered.⟩ — see DOUBTFUL 1

suspiciously *adv* with distrust ⟨eyed me *suspiciously* when I snapped my book shut and hurriedly stuffed it into my bag⟩ — see ASKANCE

sustain *vb* **1** to supply with nourishment ⟨A granola bar should *sustain* you long enough to last until lunch.⟩

synonyms nourish, nurture

related words sate, satiate, satisfy; nurse; cloy, fill, surfeit; fortify, replenish, strengthen; feed; board, cater, provision, victual

2 to come to a knowledge of (something) by living through it ⟨*sustained* serious injuries in the car crash⟩ — see EXPERIENCE

3 to put up with (something painful or difficult) ⟨I won't *sustain* such insolence!⟩ — see BEAR 2

4 to hold up or serve as a foundation for ⟨no oxygen to *sustain* life⟩ — see SUPPORT 3

sustainable *adj* **1** capable of being defended with good reasoning against verbal attack ⟨a line of argument that is probably not *sustainable* in a public forum against skilled debaters⟩ — see TENABLE 2

2 capable of being proven as true or real ⟨He has no *sustainable* claim to the property without a deed or some other document.⟩ — see VERIFIABLE

3 capable of being endured ⟨had set a pace that was too fast to be *sustainable*⟩ — see BEARABLE

svelte *adj* having a noticeably small amount of body fat ⟨The *svelte* dancer seemed to float across the stage.⟩ — see THIN 1

swab *n* one who operates or navigates a seagoing vessel ⟨old *swabs* swapping sea stories as they spend their last days in the veterans' home⟩ — see SAILOR

swag *n* valuables stolen or taken by force ⟨robbed a bank and hid the *swag* under the floorboards⟩ — see LOOT

swagger *vb* **1** to praise or express pride in one's own possessions, qualities, or accomplishments often to excess ⟨I, too, would *swagger* if I'd won first place in the bowling tournament.⟩ — see BOAST 1

2 to walk with exaggerated arm and leg movements ⟨He *swaggered* into the room like he owned the place.⟩ — see STRUT 1

swaggerer *n* someone who boasts ⟨Despite his reputation for being a swellheaded *swaggerer*, he's actually quite insecure.⟩ — see BRAGGART

swain *n* **1** a male romantic companion ⟨fair maidens and their gallant *swains*⟩ — see BOYFRIEND

2 a man who courts a woman usually with the goal of marrying her ⟨Grandma claims that she had several *swains* pursuing her, but it was only Grandpa who won her heart.⟩ — see SUITOR 1

swallow *n* the portion of a serving of a beverage that is swallowed at one time ⟨The girl drank the cool refreshing water in two *swallows* and held out her cup for more.⟩ — see DRINK 2

swallow *vb* **1** to take into the stomach through the mouth and throat ⟨Try not to *swallow* the toothpaste.⟩

synonyms down, ingest

related words drink, guzzle, imbibe, sip; bolt, devour, gobble (up *or* down), gulp; consume, eat, mouth (down), sup; gorge, scarf, scoff, wolf; chew, gnaw (at *or* on), lap, lick, munch, nibble (on); dispatch, finish, polish off

2 to refrain from openly showing or uttering ⟨*swallowed* his pride and asked for help⟩ — see SUPPRESS 2

3 to regard as right or true ⟨My little niece *swallows* everything I tell her.⟩ — see BELIEVE 1

swamp *vb* **1** to cover with a flood ⟨The boat was *swamped* by the huge wave.⟩ ⟨Sue has been *swamped* with paperwork since she returned from vacation.⟩ — see FLOOD

2 to subject to incapacitating emotional or mental stress ⟨parents feeling *swamped* by work and family obligations⟩ — see OVERWHELM 1

swamp *n* spongy land saturated or partially covered with water ⟨You can't build there because the area is mostly *swamp*.⟩

synonyms bog, fen, marsh, marshland, mire, moor, morass, muskeg, slough (*also* slew *or* slue), swampland, wash

related words swale; quagmire

swampland *n* spongy land saturated or partially covered with water ⟨Much of the county's *swampland* was drained for agriculture.⟩ — see SWAMP

swank *n* excessive or unnecessary display ⟨They deliver service that is the essence of *swank*: the waiters pull out your chair for you and even place your napkin on your lap.⟩ — see OSTENTATION

swank *or* **swanky** *adj* excessively showy ⟨They drove up in a red sports car, the *swank* interior of which was decorated in silver and black.⟩ — see GAUDY

swap *n* a giving or taking of one thing of value in return for another ⟨We made a *swap*: I'll do the dishes tonight and she'll do them for me tomorrow.⟩ — see EXCHANGE 1

swap *vb* to give up (something) and take something else in return ⟨We *swapped* our other lawn mower for our neighbors' old snowblower.⟩ — see CHANGE 3

swarm *n* a great number of persons or creatures massed together ⟨A *swarm* of tourists descends upon the island every summer.⟩ — see CROWD 1

¹**swarm** *vb* **1** to move upon or fill (something) in great numbers ⟨Meeting little resistance, the pirates *swarmed* the decks of the merchant ship.⟩ — see CROWD 2

2 to be copiously supplied ⟨At this time of year that Mexican resort *swarms* with college students on spring break.⟩ — see ABOUND

²**swarm** *vb* to move (as up or over something) often with the help of the hands in holding or pulling ⟨One of the physical challenges had competitors *swarming* over a pile of logs.⟩ — see CLIMB 1

swarming *adj* possessing or covered with great numbers or amounts of something specified ⟨The museum was *swarming* with schoolchildren on a field trip.⟩ — see RIFE

swash *vb* **1** to move with a splashing motion ⟨waves gently *swashing* against the shore⟩ — see SLOSH 1

2 to cause (something liquid or mushy) to move along in sheets ⟨Every bump in the road *swashed* a little more of my soda on the car's upholstery.⟩ — see SPLASH 1

swat *n* a hard strike with a part of the body or an instrument ⟨killed the fly with a sharp *swat*⟩ — see ¹BLOW

swat *vb* to deliver a blow to (someone or something) usually in a strong vigorous manner ⟨Megan didn't sleep a wink all night because she was too busy *swatting* mosquitoes.⟩ — see HIT 1

swathe *vb* **1** to surround or cover closely ⟨handed me an odd-shaped package *swathed* in bright pink tissue paper⟩ — see ENFOLD 1

2 to cover with a bandage ⟨A nurse tenderly *swathed* the soldier's wounds.⟩ — see BANDAGE

sway *n* **1** the power to bring about a result on another ⟨Under the *sway* of euphoria, she offered to take us all out to dinner in celebration of her new job.⟩ — see EFFECT 2

2 the power to direct the thinking or behavior of others usually indirectly ⟨outdated attitudes that still hold *sway* in some communities⟩ — see INFLUENCE 1

3 the right or means to command or control others ⟨a time when Rome held *sway* over a vast empire that stretched from Britain to the Near East⟩ — see POWER 1

sway *vb* **1** to act upon (a person or a person's feelings) so as to cause a response ⟨How can you not be *swayed* by that precious kitten, meowing as if to say, "Please take me home with you?"⟩ — see ¹AFFECT 1

2 to make a series of unsteady side-to-side motions ⟨The way the ski lift was *swaying* in the wind made me nervous.⟩ — see ROCK 1

swear *vb* **1** to use offensive or indecent language ⟨No one is allowed to *swear* in this house.⟩

synonyms blaspheme, curse, cuss

related words confound, damn, execrate, imprecate; fulminate, rail, rant, revile

2 to make a solemn declaration of intent ⟨Do you *swear* to tell the truth, the whole truth, and nothing but the truth?⟩ — see PROMISE 1

3 to make a solemn declaration under oath for the purpose of establishing a fact ⟨The *sworn* statement of the witness was presented as evidence.⟩ — see TESTIFY

sweat *n* **1** the active use of energy in producing a result ⟨Buying gifts online didn't take long and saved us a lot of *sweat*.⟩ — see EFFORT

2 very hard or unpleasant work ⟨It took years of *sweat* to bring the farm to the point where it is now.⟩ — see TOIL

3 an uneasy state of mind usually over the possibility of an anticipated misfortune or trouble ⟨My boss told me not to get in a *sweat* about the accident—she'd make sure I wasn't blamed for it.⟩ — see ANXIETY 1

sweat *vb* **1** to devote serious and sustained effort ⟨Cora spent the afternoon *sweating* over her tax returns.⟩ — see LABOR

2 to experience concern or anxiety ⟨Don't *sweat* over getting the application in a day late, as it probably doesn't matter.⟩ — see WORRY 1

3 to flow forth slowly through small openings ⟨The oil coat may *sweat* through this varnish.⟩ — see EXUDE

sweat out *vb* to put up with (something painful or difficult) ⟨I can *sweat* out one more year of this job before I retire.⟩ — see BEAR 2

sweep *n* an area over which activity, capacity, or influence extends ⟨Mrs. Griswold has been a teacher for so long that the *sweep* of her influence extends across three generations of the townspeople.⟩ — see RANGE 2

sweep *vb* **1** to move or proceed smoothly and readily ⟨The wind *swept* across the plain without respite.⟩ — see FLOW 2

2 to turn away from a straight line or course ⟨From this point the mountain range *sweeps* to the northeast and extends into the next state.⟩ — see CURVE 1

sweepstakes *also* **sweep–stake** *pl n* **1** an earnest effort for superiority or victory over another ⟨In last week's box office *sweepstakes* a quirky little comedy handily bested Hollywood's latest special effects extravaganza.⟩ — see CONTEST 1

2 a competitive encounter between individuals or groups carried on for amusement, exercise, or in pursuit of a prize ⟨regards the music awards as nothing more than a popularity *sweepstakes*⟩ — see GAME 1

sweet *adj* **1** granted special treatment or attention ⟨Dan promised his *sweet* sister that he would always look out for her.⟩ — see DARLING 1

2 having a pleasant smell ⟨breathed in the *sweet* air of the azalea garden⟩ — see FRAGRANT

3 having an easygoing and pleasing manner especially in social situations ⟨A very *sweet* man directed us to the lost and found.⟩ — see AMIABLE

4 having qualities that tend to make one loved ⟨a *sweet* little kitten⟩ — see LOVABLE

5 giving pleasure or contentment to the mind or senses ⟨The glowing reviews of his novel were the *sweetest* things the writer had ever read.⟩ — see PLEASANT 1

sweet *n* **1** a food having a high sugar content ⟨Remember to brush your teeth after eating *sweets*.⟩

synonyms confection, sweetmeat

related words confectionery, dessert, pastry

2 a person with whom one is in love ⟨My darling, my *sweet*, won't you be mine?⟩ — see SWEETHEART

sweetheart *n* a person with whom one is in love ⟨I married my high-school *sweetheart* as soon as we both finished college.⟩

synonyms beloved, darling, dear, flame, honey, love, squeeze [*slang*], sweet

related words beau, boy, boyfriend, fellow, man, swain; gal, girl, girlfriend, ladylove, lass; amour, lover, paramour; date, escort, steady; admirer, gallant, suitor, wooer; husband; bride, wife; fiancé, intended; crush, heartthrob

sweetmeat *n* a food having a high sugar content ⟨16th-century Naples carried on a vast export trade in silks and *sweetmeats*.⟩ — see SWEET 1

sweetness *n* the state or quality of having a pleasant or agreeable manner in socializing with others ⟨a guy well-known for the *sweetness* of his nature⟩ — see AMIABILITY 1

swell *adj* **1** of the very best kind ⟨What a *swell* time we had at the dance.⟩ — see EXCELLENT

2 being in the latest or current fashion ⟨In its heyday as a summer resort, the town was known for its swanky hotels and *swell* restaurants.⟩ — see STYLISH

swell *vb* **1** to become greater in extent, volume, amount, or number ⟨The club membership has really *swelled* in recent months.⟩ — see INCREASE 2

2 to make greater in size, amount, or number ⟨More layoffs will *swell* the ranks of the unemployed to unprecedented levels.⟩ — see INCREASE 1

3 to extend outward beyond a usual point ⟨At that point the Congo River *swells* and forms Malebo Pool.⟩ — see BULGE 1

swell *n* **1** a part that sticks out from the general mass of something ⟨the graceful *swell* of the vase⟩ — see BULGE 1

2 a moving ridge on the surface of water ⟨Huge *swells* overwhelmed the tiny craft.⟩ — see WAVE

swelling *n* a small rounded mass of swollen tissue ⟨The *swelling* from the injury has gone down.⟩ — see BUMP 1

sweltering *adj* having a notably high temperature ⟨The air conditioning was broken, and it was *sweltering* in the office.⟩ — see HOT 1

swerve *vb* **1** to depart abruptly from a straight line or course ⟨The car *swerved* sharply to avoid the squirrel in the road.⟩

synonyms break, cut, sheer, veer, yaw

related words skew; arc, arch, bend, bow, crook, curve, hook, round, sweep, wheel; pivot; circle, coil, curl, loop, spiral; turn, twist, wind; weave, zigzag; deviate, stray, wander, waver

antonyms straighten

2 to turn away from a straight line or course ⟨The bike path gently *swerves* to the right.⟩ — see CURVE 1

3 to cause to turn away from a straight line ⟨A dog dashed out in front of me and made me *swerve* my bike almost into the path of an oncoming car.⟩ — see BEND 1

4 to change one's course or direction ⟨The hurricane had been following the coastline before it *swerved* and headed out to sea.⟩ — see TURN 3

swift *adj* moving, proceeding, or acting with great speed ⟨the sleekest, *swiftest* boat ever to have sailed in the regatta⟩ — see FAST 1

swift *adv* with great speed ⟨tried to cross the *swift*-flowing river⟩ — see FAST 1

swiftly *adv* with great speed ⟨*swiftly* established himself as a star in Hollywood⟩ — see FAST 1

swiftness *n* a high rate of movement or performance ⟨With amazing *swiftness*, the airline agent got our ticket changed, and we boarded the plane just as it was about to leave.⟩ — see SPEED 1

swig *n* the portion of a serving of a beverage that is swallowed at one time ⟨Can I have just a *swig* of your lemonade to wash down these french fries?⟩ — see DRINK 2

swig *vb* to swallow in liquid form ⟨The only way he can stay awake at his night job is by constantly *swigging* drinks containing caffeine.⟩ — see DRINK 1

swill *n* the portion of a serving of a beverage that is swallowed at one time ⟨took his daily *swill* of the foul-tasting medicine⟩ — see DRINK 2

swill *vb* **1** to eat greedily or to excess ⟨They can spend hours chatting and *swilling*.⟩ — see GORGE 2

2 to swallow in liquid form ⟨The runners *swilled* sports drinks after the race.⟩ — see DRINK 1

swiller *n* one who eats greedily or too much ⟨The largest puppy was a *swiller* who crowded the others out.⟩ — see GLUTTON

swim *vb* **1** to be in a confused state as if from being twirled around ⟨I felt weak and my head was *swimming*.⟩ — see SPIN 2

2 to rest or move along the surface of a liquid or in the air ⟨There appeared to be an oily film *swimming* on the water.⟩ — see FLOAT 1

swim *n* a temporary state of unconsciousness ⟨The heat sent him into a *swim*.⟩ — see FAINT

swimmingly *adv* in a pleasing way ⟨The rehearsals were going *swimmingly* until half the cast came down with the flu.⟩ — see WELL 5

swindle *n* an instance of the use of dishonest methods to acquire something of value ⟨Identity theft has become one of the most frequent and feared *swindles* of our time.⟩ — see FRAUD 1

swindle *vb* to rob by the use of trickery or threats ⟨Hundreds of people were *swindled* out of their savings, and all they had to show for it were fake land deeds.⟩ — see FLEECE

swindler *n* a dishonest person who uses clever means to cheat others out of something of value ⟨The *swindlers*, representing themselves as land developers, produced a glossy brochure showing beaches, palm trees, and golf links.⟩ — see TRICKSTER 1

swine *n* a person whose behavior is offensive to others ⟨You really are a *swine*—you have no sense of decency at all!⟩ — see JERK 1

swing *vb* **1** to change one's course or direction ⟨Not sure where we were going, we abruptly *swung* to the left at the next intersection.⟩ — see TURN 3

2 to change the course or direction of (something) ⟨At the sound of gunfire, the cavalry officer *swung* his horse around and galloped rapidly back to the fort.⟩ — see TURN 2

3 to deal with (something) usually skillfully or efficiently ⟨a man who's able to *swing* two full-time jobs⟩ — see HANDLE 1

4 to move (something) in a curved or circular path on or as if on an axis ⟨*swung* the bat and missed the ball⟩ ⟨Don't let the wind *swing* that gate shut.⟩ — see TURN 1

5 to place on an elevated point without support from below ⟨beach towels *swung* up to dry on the lifeguard's high chair⟩ — see HANG 1

6 to have enough money for ⟨I don't think that we can *swing* that hefty a mortgage.⟩ — see AFFORD

swinish *adj* having a huge appetite ⟨an eating contest for *swinish* competitors⟩ — see VORACIOUS 1

swipe *n* a hard strike with a part of the body or an instrument ⟨One *swipe* of a grizzly's paw can do a person in.⟩ — see ¹BLOW

swipe *vb* **1** to come into usually forceful contact with something ⟨a blindfolded partygoer *swiping* at the piñata with a stick⟩ — see HIT 2

2 to deliver a blow to (someone or something) usually in a strong vigorous manner ⟨That car just *swiped* the fender of our car!⟩ — see HIT 1

3 to take (something) without right and with an intent to keep ⟨Somebody *swiped* the stop sign that used to be on the corner.⟩ — see STEAL 1

swiping *n* an instance of theft ⟨When the cheese *swipings* abruptly stopped, we wondered if the mouse had met his end elsewhere.⟩ — see THEFT 2

swirl *vb* **1** to cause (as a liquid) to move about in a circle especially repeatedly ⟨Fay kept *swirling* her lemonade with her straw.⟩ — see STIR 1

2 to move (something) in a curved or circular path on or as if on an axis ⟨*swirled* her skirts as she danced the tango⟩ — see TURN 1

swish *n* **1** a sound similar to the speech sound \s\ stretched out ⟨the steady *swish* of the windshield wipers⟩ — see HISS 1

2 a quick jerky movement from side to side or up and down ⟨The mare brushed away the flies with a sweeping *swish* of her tail.⟩ — see ¹WAG

swish *vb* **1** to make a sound like that of stretching out the speech sound \s\ ⟨With their satin costumes *swishing*, the little ballerinas pirouetted onto the stage.⟩ — see HISS

2 to move from side to side or up and down with quick jerky motions ⟨The horse's tail *swishes* after every jump.⟩ — see WAG 1

switch *n* **1** a long thin or flexible tool for striking ⟨He struck the horse's hide with a leather *switch*, and it took off at a gallop.⟩ — see WHIP

2 a quick jerky movement from side to side or up and down ⟨That telltale *switch* of the cat's tail meant there was a mouse under the piano.⟩ — see ¹WAG

3 a hard strike with a part of the body or an instrument ⟨In frustration, he gave the mule a sharp *switch* on the rump, but it still wouldn't budge.⟩ — see ¹BLOW

switch *vb* **1** to give up (something) and take something else in return ⟨*switched* the real grapes for fake ones⟩ ⟨*switched* the day of his flight from Thursday to Friday⟩ — see CHANGE 3

2 to move from side to side or up and down with quick jerky motions ⟨cows lazily *switching* their tails and chewing their cud⟩ — see WAG 1

3 to strike repeatedly with something long and thin or flexible ⟨The cow *switched* at flies with its tail.⟩ — see WHIP 1

4 to change (as an opinion) to the contrary ⟨a politician who has *switched* his position on a number of issues⟩ — see REVERSE 1

5 to strike repeatedly ⟨a prank for which the youngsters were soundly *switched*⟩ — see BEAT 1

swoon *vb* to lose consciousness ⟨She almost *swooned* from the heat.⟩ — see FAINT

swoon *n* **1** a state of mental confusion ⟨She wandered about in a *swoon* for several days after receiving the tragic news.⟩ — see HAZE 2

2 a temporary state of unconsciousness ⟨I fell into a *swoon* at the sight of the ghost.⟩ — see FAINT

3 a state of overwhelming usually pleasurable emotion ⟨The good news sent her into a joyous *swoon*.⟩ — see ECSTASY

sword *n* a hand weapon with a length of metal sharpened on one or both sides and usually tapered to a sharp point ⟨Once upon a time dueling with *swords* was the gentlemanly way to settle a point of honor.⟩
synonyms blade, brand, steel
related words broadsword, cutlass, rapier, saber (*or* sabre), scimitar, smallsword

sycophant *n* a person who flatters another in order to get ahead ⟨When her career was riding high, the self-deluded actress often mistook *sycophants* for true friends.⟩
synonyms fawner, flunky (*also* flunkey *or* flunkie), toady
related words yes-man; hanger-on, leech, parasite, sponge, sponger; henchman, lackey, minion, stooge; groveler, idol-

ater (*or* idolator), worshipper (*or* worshiper), zealot; adherent, convert, disciple, follower, partisan (*also* partizan), pupil, votary

symbol *n* **1** a device, design, or figure used as an identifying mark ⟨the traditional physician's *symbol* of a staff entwined with a snake⟩ — see EMBLEM

2 a written or printed mark that is meant to convey information to the reader ⟨The *symbol* ∼ indicates where a new paragraph should begin.⟩ — see CHARACTER 1

symbolic *also* **symbolical** *adj* having the function or meaning of an object or figure that stands for something else ⟨The butterfly in the poem is *symbolic* of the impermanence of youth.⟩
synonyms emblematic (*also* emblematical), representative
related words figurative, metaphoric (*or* metaphorical); allegorical
near antonyms actual, literal
antonyms nonsymbolic

symbolize *vb* to serve as a material counterpart of ⟨The flag *symbolizes* our country.⟩
synonyms represent
related words embody, epitomize, incarnate, manifest, materialize, objectify, personalize, personify; exemplify, illustrate
phrases stand for

symmetry *n* a balanced, pleasing, or suitable arrangement of parts ⟨planted azalea bushes on both sides of the front steps for *symmetry*⟩ — see HARMONY 1

sympathetic *adj* **1** having or showing the capacity for sharing the feelings of another ⟨a *sympathetic* smile⟩ ⟨She needed a *sympathetic* listener who would understand her problem.⟩
synonyms compassionate, humane, understanding
related words feeling, perceptive, sensitive; considerate, gentle, softhearted, tender, tenderhearted, warm, warmhearted; benevolent, benignant, charitable, kind, kindhearted, kindly, magnanimous; clement, lenient, merciful, tolerant; pitying
near antonyms inconsiderate, insensitive, thoughtless, unthinking; aloof, cool, indifferent, uncaring, uninterested; unaffectionate, unfriendly, unloving; merciless, pitiless, ruthless; bigoted, narrow-minded, small-minded; brutal, grim, harsh, oppressive, rough, severe, stern, tough, unrelenting; abusive, acrimonious, hateful, hostile, ill-natured, ill-tempered, malevolent, malicious, mean, rancorous, spiteful, surly, unkind, virulent
antonyms callous, cold-blooded, coldhearted, hard, heartless, inhuman, inhumane, obdurate, unfeeling, unsympathetic

2 having or marked by sympathy and consideration for others ⟨a *sympathetic* store manager who let us use the telephone⟩ ⟨*sympathetic* letters from supporters after the disappointing verdict⟩ — see HUMANE 1

sympathize (with) *vb* to have sympathy for ⟨Don't expect me to *sympathize with* you—each month you should have paid off your credit card in full.⟩ — see PITY

sympathizer *n* someone associated with another to give assistance or moral support ⟨Tom doesn't have many *sympathizers* since everyone knows he brought his troubles on himself.⟩ — see ALLY

sympathy *n* **1** sorrow or the capacity to feel sorrow for another's suffering or misfortune ⟨Since losing her own brother, the nurse has had greater *sympathy* for families going through the same agony.⟩
synonyms commiseration, compassion, feeling
related words condolence, regret; humanity, kindheartedness, kindliness, kindness, mercy, pity, softheartedness, warmheartedness; affinity, empathy, rapport, sensi-

tivity, understanding; altruism, benevolence, charity, generosity, goodwill, humanitarianism, largesse (*also* largess), magnanimity
near antonyms indifference, insensitivity, unconcern; cruelty, harshness, inhumanity; animosity, antipathy, dislike, hatred, hostility
antonyms callousness, coldheartedness, hard-heartedness, heartlessness
2 the capacity for feeling for another's unhappiness or misfortune ⟨The least you could do is have some *sympathy* for me if I have to stay home.⟩ — see HEART 1

symphonic *adj* having a pleasing mixture of notes ⟨the *symphonic* chorus of frogs in the spring⟩ — see HARMONIOUS 1

symphony *n* **1** a balanced, pleasing, or suitable arrangement of parts ⟨the satisfying *symphony* of color in Renoir's canvases⟩ — see HARMONY 1
2 a usually large group of musicians playing together ⟨a performance of a Bach concerto by the San Antonio *Symphony*⟩ — see ²BAND 1

symphony orchestra *n* a usually large group of musicians playing together ⟨plays oboe in the local *symphony orchestra*⟩ — see ²BAND 1

symposium *n* a meeting featuring a group discussion ⟨recently attended a daylong *symposium* on new methods of chromatography⟩ — see FORUM 1

symptomatic *adj* serving to identify as belonging to an individual or group ⟨A fever's refusal to respond to antibiotics is *symptomatic* of a viral infection.⟩ — see CHARACTERISTIC 1

synchronous *adj* existing or occurring at the same period of time ⟨The *synchronous* arrival of a baby sister and moving to a new school affected the child.⟩ — see CONTEMPORARY 1

syndicate *n* **1** a group involved in secret or criminal activities ⟨a *syndicate* of counterfeiters⟩ — see ¹RING 1
2 a number of businesses or enterprises united for commercial advantage ⟨a powerful banking *syndicate* that controls loans in the small country⟩ — see CARTEL

synopsis *n* a short statement of the main points ⟨I don't need to know every little plot twist; just give me a *synopsis* of the movie.⟩ — see SUMMARY

synthetic *adj* **1** produced by humans rather than natural processes ⟨That organic farm doesn't use any pesticides or *synthetic* fertilizers.⟩
synonyms artificial, man-made
related words fabricated, manufactured; cultivated, processed, refined; industrial, mechanical; faux, imitation
near antonyms crude, raw
antonyms natural
2 being such in appearance only and made with or manufactured from usually cheaper materials ⟨*synthetic* fur collars⟩ ⟨boots of waterproof *synthetic* leather⟩ — see IMITATION

syringe *n* a slender hollow instrument by which material is put into or taken from the body through the skin ⟨The *syringe* the nurse was leveling at my arm looked to me to be at least 10 inches long.⟩ — see NEEDLE 1

syrupy *adj* being of a consistency that resists flow ⟨Instead of neat squares of fudge we had *syrupy* goo.⟩ — see THICK 2

system *n* **1** something made up of many interdependent or related parts ⟨The national highway *system* allows travel from one end of the country to the other.⟩ ⟨the democratic *system* of checks and balances in government⟩
synonyms complex, network
related words interlacement, mesh, meshwork, net, plexus, web; aggregate, conglomeration, totality, whole; sequence, series
2 a method worked out in advance for achieving some objective ⟨If you're going to wrap all these presents in one afternoon, you'll need a *system*.⟩ — see PLAN 1
3 the means or procedure for doing something ⟨It's not the best *system* perhaps, but it gets the job done.⟩ — see METHOD

systematic *adj* following a set method, arrangement, or pattern ⟨*systematic* elimination and reintroduction of certain foods to determine what he's allergic to⟩ — see METHODICAL

systematize *vb* to put into a particular arrangement ⟨Carl Linnaeus was the first to *systematize* the plant and animal kingdoms by creating a uniform system for naming genera and species of organisms.⟩ — see ORDER 1

systematized *adj* following a set method, arrangement, or pattern ⟨a *systematized* arrangement of books⟩ — see METHODICAL

T

tab *n* **1** a record of goods sold or services performed together with the costs due ⟨I don't have any cash on me, so can you put this on my *tab*?⟩ — see ¹BILL 1
2 the amount owed at a bar or restaurant or the slip of paper stating the amount ⟨We asked the server to put our dinners on separate *tabs* so we could each pay for our own meal.⟩ — see CHECK 1

tabernacle *n* a building for public worship and especially Christian worship ⟨worshippers gathering at the Baptist *tabernacle* on a bright Sunday morning⟩ — see CHURCH 1

table *n* **1** a leg-mounted piece of furniture with a broad flat top designed for the serving of food ⟨We sat at the kitchen *table*, playing cards for hours on end.⟩
synonyms board
related words coffee table, refectory table, tea table; bar, counter; buffet, sideboard, side table; bed table, card table
2 food eaten or prepared for eating at one time ⟨always offers a well-prepared *table* for his guests⟩ — see MEAL
3 a broad flat area of elevated land ⟨The area between the two canyons forms one broad *table*.⟩ — see PLATEAU
4 a record of a series of items (as names or titles) usually arranged according to some system ⟨the periodic *table* of chemical elements⟩ — see ¹LIST
5 substances intended to be eaten ⟨The *table* that the innkeeper set out each morning made for a bountiful breakfast indeed.⟩ — see FOOD

tableland *n* a broad flat area of elevated land ⟨To the east of the valley lies a vast, fertile *tableland*.⟩ — see PLATEAU

tablet *n* **1** a number of sheets of writing paper glued together at one edge ⟨You'll need to use your writing *tablet* to record all the information that the real estate agent is likely to reel off.⟩ — see PAD 1
2 a small mass containing medicine to be taken orally ⟨Take two *tablets* of the medication every eight hours.⟩ — see PILL 1

table talk *n* friendly, informal conversation or an instance of this ⟨He thought he weathered the *table talk* over dinner with his future in-laws rather well.⟩ — see CHAT 1

tableware *n* **1** eating and serving utensils ⟨During the party we ran short of *tableware*, so I went next door and borrowed some forks and knives.⟩
synonyms flatware, silver, silverware
related words place setting, setting, setup; silver plate; cutlery; chopstick, fork, knife, spoon, tablespoon, teaspoon
2 dishes used for eating or serving food or drink ⟨The couple would take out their good *tableware* only on special occasions.⟩
synonyms dinnerware
related words place setting, setting, setup; china, chinaware, crockery, earthenware, porcelain, pottery, stoneware; glassware; plate, saucer; cup, demitasse, goblet, mug, teacup; bowl, casserole, charger, platter, tureen

taboo *also* **tabu** *adj* that may not be permitted ⟨Asking a guest how much money he or she makes is strictly *taboo* because it's a rude question to ask a stranger.⟩ — see IMPERMISSIBLE

tacit *adj* understood although not put into words ⟨We have a *tacit* agreement that if I wash the dishes, she dries them and puts them away.⟩ — see IMPLICIT 1

taciturn *adj* tending not to speak frequently (as by habit or inclination) ⟨A *taciturn* man, he almost never initiates a conversation.⟩ — see SILENT 2

tack *n* the means or procedure for doing something ⟨This clearly isn't working, so let's take a different *tack* in trying to solve the problem.⟩ — see METHOD

tack (on) *vb* to join (something) to a mass, quantity, or number so as to bring about an overall increase ⟨The ticket agency *tacked on* a hefty surcharge to what was already a hefty price for the theater tickets.⟩ — see ADD 1

tackle *n* items needed for the performance of a task or activity ⟨I grabbed my fishing *tackle* and headed out early one morning.⟩ — see EQUIPMENT

tackle *vb* to start work on energetically ⟨Once I have cleaned the kitchen, I think I'll *tackle* the bathroom.⟩ — see ATTACK 3

¹tacky *adj* **1** marked by an obvious lack of style or good taste ⟨It was *tacky* to wear sneakers to the wedding.⟩ ⟨*tacky* plastic flowers⟩
synonyms cheesy, dowdy, inelegant, styleless, tasteless, trashy, unfashionable, unstylish
related words graceless, inappropriate, incorrect, unbecoming, unseemly, unsuitable, wrong; coarse, crude, unrefined, vulgar; cheap, common, inferior, junky, lousy, low-grade, second-rate, shoddy, sleazy, tawdry; flashy, garish, gaudy, glitzy, grotesque, loud, ostentatious, showy, splashy
near antonyms appropriate, becoming, correct, fitting, proper, right, seemly, suitable; conservative, genteel, handsome, quiet, refined, restrained, simple, understated
antonyms chic, classic, classy, elegant, exquisite, fashionable, fine, posh, smart, sophisticated, stylish, tasteful
2 showing signs of advanced wear and tear and neglect ⟨a *tacky* old couch that needed new upholstery⟩ — see SHABBY 1

²tacky *adj* tending to adhere to objects upon contact ⟨Don't touch the walls while the fresh paint is still *tacky*.⟩ — see STICKY 1

tact *n* the ability to deal with others in touchy situations without offending them ⟨With supreme *tact*, Isabel suggested to her neighbor that her flower garden was probably not the best place for his dog to use as a bathroom.⟩
synonyms diplomacy, tactfulness
related words considerateness, consideration, courteousness, courtesy, delicacy, graciousness, sensitivity, thoughtfulness; civility, etiquette, manneriness, manners, politeness; charm, gallantry, gentility, grace, gracefulness, poise, suaveness, suavity; adroitness, deftness, dexterity, finesse; deference, regard, respect
near antonyms discourteousness, discourtesy, impoliteness, inconsiderateness, inconsideration, indelicacy, thoughtlessness, ungraciousness; impoliteness, incivility; boorishness, brashness, brassiness, loutishness; awkwardness, gaucheness, gracelessness, maladroitness; disrespect, impertinence, impudence, insolence, rudeness
antonyms clumsiness, insensitivity, tactlessness

tactful *adj* having or showing tact ⟨Amy tried to be *tactful* when asked to critique her friend's singing.⟩
synonyms diplomatic, politic
related words considerate, courteous, delicate, graceful, gracious, thoughtful; civil, mannerly, polite; charming, gallant, genteel, suave; affable, cordial, friendly, genial, kind, kindhearted
near antonyms discourteous, inconsiderate, thoughtless,

ungracious; ill-bred, ill-mannered, impolite, uncalled-for, uncivil, unmannerly; boorish, brash, brassy, caddish, churlish, clownish, loutish, uncouth; disrespectful, impertinent, impudent, insolent, rude

antonyms gauche, impolitic, tactless, untactful

tactfulness *n* the ability to deal with others in touchy situations without offending them ⟨The *tactfulness* with which the secretary of state has handled that diplomatic crisis is commendable.⟩ — see TACT

tactical *adj* suitable for bringing about a desired result under the circumstances ⟨Tom made the *tactical* move of becoming friendly with the journalism teacher, hoping that this would get him appointed editor of the school newspaper.⟩ — see EXPEDIENT

tactics *pl n* the means or procedure for doing something ⟨used dishonest *tactics* to win election to the town council⟩ — see METHOD

tactless *adj* showing poor judgment especially in personal relationships or social situations ⟨He made a *tactless* remark about how the woman's dress had that "homemade" look.⟩ — see INDISCREET

tad *n* 1 a very small amount ⟨It was a *tad* windy, but not too cold.⟩ — see PARTICLE 1
2 a male person who has not yet reached adulthood ⟨Grandfather never tires of telling us about the days when he was just a *tad*.⟩ — see BOY 1

tag *n* a slip (as of paper or cloth) that is attached to something to identify or describe it ⟨I read the *tag* on the shirt to find out if I could wash it or if it had to be dry-cleaned.⟩ — see LABEL

tag *vb* 1 to attach an identifying slip to ⟨We *tagged* all the dresses with sale stickers before putting them on the rack.⟩ — see LABEL 1
2 to go after or on the track of ⟨Wildlife experts surreptitiously *tagged* the timber wolf, carefully keeping a safe distance so the wolf wouldn't catch their scent and run.⟩ — see FOLLOW 2

tagging *n* the act of going after or in the tracks of another ⟨After a weeklong *tagging* of the suspect, the detective had all the evidence he needed.⟩ — see PURSUIT

tail *n* 1 the part of the body upon which someone sits ⟨Get your *tail* in here!⟩ — see BUTTOCKS
2 a behind part or surface ⟨the *tail* of the ship⟩ — see REAR 1

tail *vb* to go after or on the track of ⟨Detectives *tailed* the suspect.⟩ — see FOLLOW 2

tailing *n* the act of going after or in the tracks of another ⟨the reporter's constant *tailing* of the candidates⟩ — see PURSUIT

tailor *vb* to change (something) so as to make it suitable for a new use or situation ⟨The stand-up comic refused to *tailor* his routine for network television.⟩ — see ADAPT

tailored *adj* made or fitted to the needs or preferences of a specific customer ⟨Pants bought off the rack never fit me so I have to buy *tailored* ones instead.⟩ — see CUSTOM-MADE

tailor–made *adj* made or fitted to the needs or preferences of a specific customer ⟨took my measurements for the *tailor-made* bridal gown⟩ — see CUSTOM-MADE

taint *n* a mark of guilt or disgrace ⟨that rare political campaign that wasn't marred by the *taint* of false accusations⟩ — see STAIN 1

taint *vb* 1 to affect slightly with something morally bad or undesirable ⟨criticism of her sister's singing that was *tainted* by envy⟩ ⟨A tendency toward conceitedness *taints* that athlete's status as a role model.⟩
synonyms blemish, darken, mar, poison, spoil, stain, tarnish, touch, vitiate
related words begrime, besmear, besmirch, blacken,

blur, cloud, dirty, discolor, pollute, smear, smirch, smudge, soil, sully, tar; abase, cheapen, debase, degrade, demean, discredit, disgrace, dishonor, foul, lower, shame, sink; bastardize, corrupt, debauch, demoralize, deprave, pervert, subvert
near antonyms cleanse, purify; dignify, elevate, ennoble, enshrine, glorify, hallow, magnify, uplift
2 to make unfit for use by the addition of something harmful or undesirable ⟨Smog has long *tainted* the air of that city, making it difficult to breathe.⟩ — see CONTAMINATE

tainted *adj* containing foreign or lower-grade substances ⟨*tainted* groundwater that is unfit to drink⟩ — see IMPURE 1

take *n* 1 action or behavior that is done in return to other action or behavior ⟨What's your *take* on the announcement that the senior vice president is taking an early retirement?⟩ — see REACTION
2 the total amount collected or obtained especially at one time ⟨Who will win the poker tournament and collect the whole *take*?⟩ — see HAUL 1
3 something belonging to, due to, or contributed by an individual member of a group ⟨Because there were so many winners of the jackpot, each person's *take* will be smaller than expected.⟩ — see SHARE 1

take *vb* 1 to reach for and take hold of by embracing with the fingers or arms ⟨*Take* my hand, or we'll get separated in this crowd.⟩
synonyms clasp, grasp, grip, hold
related words clench, cling (to), clutch, hold on (to); catch, nab, seize, snatch
phrases hang on to, lay hold of
near antonyms discharge, drop, free, liberate, release; deliver, entrust (*also* intrust), give, hand, hand over, pass, relinquish, transfer, transmit, turn over, unhand
2 to agree to receive whether willingly or reluctantly ⟨Will you *take* that call?⟩ ⟨Ed *took* a cut in pay.⟩
synonyms accept, have
related words accede (to), assent (to), concede (to), confirm, consent (to), OK (*or* okay), ratify, sanction, warrant; acquiesce (to), bow (to), capitulate (to), give in (to), submit (to), succumb (to), surrender (to), yield (to); abide, bear, brook, countenance, endure, shoulder, stand, stick out, stomach, support, sustain, swallow, sweat out, tolerate; adopt, embrace, welcome
near antonyms dissent (to), object (to), oppose, protest; hold off, resist, withstand; combat, contest, fight
antonyms decline, deny, disallow, disapprove, negative, refuse, reject, spurn, turn down, veto
3 to become affected with (a disease or disorder) ⟨If you don't cover your head in this weather, you'll *take* cold and be stuck inside all weekend.⟩ — see CONTRACT 1
4 to decide to accept (someone or something) from a group of possibilities ⟨You can *take* the white side this time, since I got to be white for our last chess game.⟩ — see CHOOSE 1
5 to get possession of (something) by giving money in exchange for ⟨I'll *take* two cheeseburgers to go, please!⟩ — see BUY 1
6 to have as a requirement ⟨It will *take* a lot of courage to stand up for what is right.⟩ — see NEED 1
7 to make or have room for ⟨I think we can *take* two more in this elevator.⟩ — see ACCOMMODATE 1
8 to produce a desired effect ⟨It will be a few hours before this medication *takes*.⟩ — see ACT 2
9 to put up with (something painful or difficult) ⟨I can't *take* any more of your whining.⟩ — see BEAR 2
10 to regard as right or true ⟨I think we can *take* his word for it.⟩ — see BELIEVE 1

11 to achieve a victory over ⟨I know we can *take* that team.⟩ — see BEAT 2

12 to deal with (something) usually skillfully or efficiently ⟨Let's *take* each problem separately.⟩ — see HANDLE 1

13 to offer entrance (as to a place, school, or privilege) to ⟨The school *takes* only a small percentage of the thousands of applicants.⟩ — see ADMIT 2

14 to deprive of life ⟨The 1918 flu pandemic *took* millions around the world.⟩ — see KILL 1

take back *vb* to solemnly or formally reject or go back on (as something formerly adhered to) ⟨I *take back* what I said about her: she's not the fool I thought she was.⟩ — see ABJURE 1

take down *vb* **1** to reduce to a lower standing in one's own eyes or in others' eyes ⟨a braggart who needed to be *taken down* a bit⟩ — see HUMBLE

2 to take apart ⟨Electricians will *take down* all the lights for the set after the play has finished its run.⟩ — see DISASSEMBLE 1

3 to make a written note of ⟨We *took down* the customer's contact information.⟩ — see RECORD 1

take in *vb* **1** to cause to believe what is untrue ⟨A fellow passenger on the cruise completely *took* me *in* when he claimed to be the owner of a major software company.⟩ — see DECEIVE

2 to have as part of a whole ⟨This report *takes in* all the latest information on the subject.⟩ — see INCLUDE 1

3 to provide with living quarters or shelter ⟨We *took in* the stray dog.⟩ — see HOUSE 1

take–no–prisoners *adj* having or showing a lack of sympathy or tender feelings ⟨a theater critic with a *take-no-prisoners* approach to reviewing Broadway's latest offerings⟩ — see HARD 1

takeoff *n* a work that imitates and exaggerates another work for comic effect ⟨a movie that's a *takeoff* of an old TV show from the 1960s⟩ — see PARODY 1

take off *vb* **1** to leave a place often for another ⟨I can only stay for a few minutes, and then I'll need to *take off* again.⟩ — see GO 2

2 to rid oneself of (a garment) ⟨*Take off* your coat and stay awhile.⟩ — see REMOVE 1

3 to take away (an amount or number) from a total ⟨The store will *take* an additional 20% *off* if you bring in this coupon.⟩ — see SUBTRACT

take on *vb* **1** to enter into contest or conflict with ⟨The mayor will *take on* his chief opponent in the next political debate.⟩ — see ENGAGE 2

2 to provide with a paying job ⟨I decided to *take* her *on* as store manager.⟩ — see EMPLOY 1

3 to take for one's own use (something originated by another) ⟨recently arrived immigrants who are eager to *take on* the language and culture of their adopted homeland⟩ — see ADOPT

take out *vb* **1** to find emotional release for ⟨He *took out* his frustrations by splitting a cord of firewood.⟩

synonyms loose, release, unleash, vent
related words act out; air, express, state, ventilate, voice
phrases give way (to)
near antonyms control, govern, handle, manage; bridle, check, constrain, contain, curb, hold back, quell, rein (in), restrain, smother, tame; allay, lull, quiet, soothe, still; choke, inhibit, muffle, pocket, repress, stifle, strangle, swallow
antonyms bottle (up), repress, suppress

2 to go on a social engagement with ⟨She'd like to *take* the new boy *out* to the movies sometime.⟩ — see DATE 1

3 to take away from a place or position ⟨The airline passenger *took* his tablet *out* of its carrying case.⟩ — see REMOVE 2

take over *vb* **1** to serve as a replacement usually for a time only ⟨I'll *take over* for her until she gets back from her morning break.⟩ — see COVER 1

2 to take to or upon oneself ⟨*took over* the responsibility of caring for the animals⟩ — see ASSUME 1

3 to take or make use of under a guise of authority but without actual right ⟨Students protesting the war *took over* the college's radio station.⟩ — see APPROPRIATE 1

take up *vb* **1** to move from a lower to a higher place or position ⟨Please *take up* the blanket so I can look underneath it.⟩ — see RAISE 1

2 to take in (something liquid) through small openings ⟨The soil was so dry that the plant seemed to *take up* the much-needed water instantly.⟩ — see ABSORB 1

3 to take for one's own use (something originated by another) ⟨One cluster of fans started chanting the team name of the champions, and the crowd quickly *took up* the cry.⟩ — see ADOPT

taking *adj* very pleasing to look at ⟨We had never seen such a *taking* city as Venice.⟩ — see BEAUTIFUL 1

tale *n* **1** a rumor or report of a personal or sensational nature ⟨Don't believe the *tales* you hear about our neighbor's kid.⟩

synonyms story, whisper
related words dirt, gossip, talebearing, talk, tattle; defamation, libel, slander; fable, fabrication, fairy tale, falsehood, falsity, fib, lie, mendacity, prevarication, untruth, whopper

2 a brief account of something interesting that happened especially to one personally ⟨We asked Dad to tell once again the *tale* of how, as a kid, he broke his arm jumping out of a tree.⟩ — see STORY 2

3 a statement known by its maker to be untrue and made in order to deceive ⟨Anne told tall *tales* in an attempt to impress me with her supposedly upper-crust background.⟩ — see LIE

4 a work with imaginary characters and events that is shorter and usually less complex than a novel ⟨the oft-told *tale* of Sleeping Beauty⟩ — see STORY 1

5 a total number obtained or recorded by noting each thing as it was being added ⟨the *tale* of those who walked this trail⟩ — see COUNT 1

talebearer *n* **1** a person who habitually reveals personal or sensational facts about others ⟨*talebearers* of the secrets of celebrities⟩ — see GOSSIP 1

2 a person who provides information about another's wrongdoing ⟨The teacher told him not to be such a *talebearer*, as she was quite capable of detecting student misbehavior on her own.⟩ — see INFORMER

talent *n* a special and usually inborn ability ⟨Liza's musical *talent* was already apparent by the time she was five.⟩ ⟨a *talent* for coming up with really funny answers to stupid questions⟩

synonyms aptitude, bent, endowment, faculty, flair, genius, gift, head, knack
related words affinity, bias, disposition, impulse, inclination, leaning, partiality, penchant, predilection, predisposition, proclivity, propensity, tendency, turn; ear, eye, mind, nose; feel, hang, instinct, touch, way; capability, competence, facility, proficiency, skill; capacity, potential, power; forte, specialty
near antonyms disability, handicap, inability, incapacity; shortcoming, weakness

talisman *n* something worn or kept to bring good luck or keep away evil ⟨She wears a special pendant as a *talisman* for good luck.⟩ — see CHARM 1

talk *n* **1** a usually formal discourse delivered to an audience ⟨the noted author's *talk* on the state of the modern novel⟩ — see SPEECH 1

2 an exchange of views for the purpose of exploring a subject or deciding an issue ⟨What good will all this *talk* do when we need to take action now?⟩ — see DISCUSSION 1

3 friendly, informal conversation or an instance of this ⟨We sat down by the fire and had a nice little *talk* about what was new in the village.⟩ — see CHAT 1

4 information or opinion that is widely disseminated without any authority or confirmation of accuracy ⟨Her behavior is exciting some lurid *talk*.⟩ — see RUMOR

talk *vb* **1** to give a formal often extended talk on a subject ⟨The fire chief often *talks* at school assemblies about fire safety.⟩

synonyms declaim, descant, discourse, expatiate, harangue, lecture, orate, speak

related words recite, soliloquize; expound, pontificate; mouth, spout; filibuster

phrases hold forth, take the floor

2 to engage in casual or rambling conversation ⟨We *talked* with our neighbor as we unloaded the groceries from the car.⟩ — see CHAT 1

3 to express (a thought or emotion) in words ⟨You're *talking* nonsense: take a minute and think about what you are trying to say, and then start speaking.⟩ — see SAY 1

4 to give information (as to the authorities) about another's improper or unlawful activities ⟨The eyewitness *talked* at length about what he had seen in the alley.⟩ — see SQUEAL 1

5 to relate sometimes questionable or secret information of a personal nature ⟨I don't *talk* about my friends behind their backs.⟩ — see GOSSIP

talk (into) *vb* to cause (someone) to agree with a belief or course of action by using arguments or earnest requests ⟨The salesman *talked* us *into* buying a new vacuum.⟩ — see PERSUADE

talk (to) *vb* to communicate with by means of spoken words ⟨I had never *talked to* a real live cowboy before.⟩

synonyms chat (with), converse (with), speak (to *or* with)

related words accost, address, board, greet, hail, herald; inform, notify, tell

phrases engage in conversation

talkative *adj* fond of talking or conversation ⟨A *talkative* outgoing tour guide showed our school group around the city.⟩

synonyms blabby, chatty, conversational, gabby, garrulous, loquacious, talky

related words communicative, expansive; demonstrative, effusive, gushing; free-spoken, outspoken, unreserved, vocal; articulate, fluent, glib, voluble, well-spoken; gossipy, talebearing, tale-telling; long-winded, prolix, rambling, verbose, windy, wordy; extroverted (*also* extraverted), gregarious, outgoing, sociable

near antonyms quiet, shy; mum, mute, silent, speechless, tongue-tied, wordless; evasive, nonvocal, secretive, self-contained; aloof, indrawn, inhibited, introverted, retiring, unsociable, withdrawn

antonyms closemouthed, laconic, reserved, reticent, taciturn, tight-lipped, uncommunicative

talk down (to) *vb* to assume or treat with an air of superiority ⟨Just because I don't have extensive experience in the field is no reason to *talk down to* me as if I were a child.⟩ — see CONDESCEND 2

talker *n* a person who talks constantly ⟨Your brother is quite a *talker*—he wouldn't let me get a word in edgewise!⟩ — see CHATTERBOX

talk over *vb* to talk about (an issue) usually from various points of view and for the purpose of arriving at a decision or opinion ⟨Your father and I will have to *talk over* before agreeing to let you go on the class trip.⟩ — see DISCUSS

talky *adj* fond of talking or conversation ⟨a *talky* coworker who will corner you at your desk for hours with stories about his vacation⟩ — see TALKATIVE

tall *adj* **1** extending to a great distance upward ⟨*tall* skyscrapers that cast long shadows over the park⟩ — see HIGH 1

2 requiring considerable physical or mental effort ⟨That's a pretty *tall* order.⟩ — see HARD 2

tally *n* a total number obtained or recorded by noting each thing as it was being added ⟨The final *tally* for attendees at the convention was over 2,000.⟩ — see COUNT 1

tally *vb* **1** to be in agreement on every point ⟨Our lists for best movies of the year *tally* perfectly.⟩ — see CHECK 1

2 to gain (as points or runs in a game) as credit towards one's total number of points ⟨Our team *tallied* four touchdowns and gained a total of 435 yards last game.⟩ — see SCORE 2

tame *adj* **1** changed from the wild state so as to become useful and obedient to humans ⟨Every evening, a wild Canada goose is at the food trough with our *tame* geese.⟩

synonyms domestic, domesticated, tamed

related words housebroken, trained; docile, gentle, semidomesticated; subdued, submissive

near antonyms unbroken, untrained

antonyms feral, undomesticated, untamed, wild

2 causing weariness, restlessness, or lack of interest ⟨That action movie was so *tame* I fell asleep about 20 minutes into it.⟩ — see BORING

tame *vb* to keep from exceeding a desirable degree or level (as of expression) ⟨Try to *tame* your language when you're in front of the kids.⟩ — see CONTROL 1

tamed *adj* changed from the wild state so as to become useful and obedient to humans ⟨Circus trainers work with *tamed* tigers and elephants.⟩ — see TAME 1

tamper (with) *vb* to handle thoughtlessly, ignorantly, or mischievously ⟨Someone has *tampered with* my computer files.⟩

synonyms fiddle (with), fool (with), mess (with), monkey (with), play (with), tinker (with)

related words abuse, alter, doctor, manhandle, manipulate, mistreat, misuse; butt in, interfere, intrude, meddle

tan *vb* to strike repeatedly ⟨Grandpa told us that when he was a kid, if he misbehaved, his father would *tan* his hide.⟩ — see BEAT 1

tangent *n* a departure from the subject under consideration ⟨In the middle of her description of her dog's symptoms, she went off on a *tangent* about its cute behavior.⟩

synonyms digression, excursion

related words circuitousness, circumlocution, diffuseness, prolixity, verbosity, windiness, wordiness

tangible *adj* capable of being perceived by the sense of touch ⟨a firm belief in the existence of the soul, even though it is not at all *tangible*⟩

synonyms palpable, touchable

related words tactile; corporeal, physical; actual, concrete, embodied, existent, material, real, substantial; appreciable, detectable, discernible (*also* discernable), noticeable, observable, perceptible, seeable, sensible, visible

near antonyms bodiless, formless, immaterial, incorporeal, insubstantial, nonmaterial, nonphysical, unsubstantial; abstract, ethereal, spiritual, unreal, virtual; imperceptible, insensible

antonyms impalpable, intangible

tangle *n* a state of mental uncertainty ⟨My mind's been in a *tangle* ever since I learned some disturbing information about an acquaintance.⟩ — see CONFUSION 1

tangle *vb* **1** to catch or hold as if in a net ⟨He was at last *tangled* in the web of lies that he had told to everyone.⟩ — see ENTANGLE 2

2 to twist together into a usually confused mass ⟨That

darn cat *tangled* the yarn I was trying to knit with.⟩ — see ENTANGLE 1

tangy *adj* having a powerfully stimulating odor or flavor ⟨a *tangy* sauce with a strong aftertaste⟩ — see SHARP 2

tantrum *n* an outburst or display of excited anger ⟨Billy had a *tantrum* when he found his little sister using his model paints.⟩
synonyms blowup, explosion, fireworks, fit, hissy fit, huff, scene
related words eruption, flare-up, outburst, storm, uproar; agitation, delirium, distraction, frenzy, furor, furore, fury, hysteria, rage, rampage; convulsion(s), paroxysm, seizure, spasm, upheaval; angriness, indignation, irateness, ire, spleen, wrath, wrathfulness; reaction, rise; dander, temper; pet, pouts, sulk(s), sulkiness, sullenness

¹**tap** *vb* to strike or cause to strike lightly and usually rhythmically ⟨Meg *tapped* her foot in time to the music.⟩ ⟨kept *tapping* the desk with his pencil⟩
synonyms beat, drum, rap
related words bang, bash, bat, bop, hammer, hit, knock, paste, pound, slam, smack, sock, strike, swat, thud, thump, thwack, wallop, whack; pat, pit-a-pat, pitter-patter

²**tap** *vb* to remove (liquid) gradually or completely ⟨The oil company *tapped* that first well completely dry.⟩ — see DRAIN 1

tap *n* a fixture for controlling the flow of a liquid ⟨Turn the *tap* to the right for cold water and to the left for hot water.⟩ — see FAUCET

taper *vb* to grow less in scope or intensity especially gradually ⟨You'll find the symptoms begin *tapering* gradually about 24 hours after you take the medicine.⟩ — see DECREASE 2

taper off *vb* to grow less in scope or intensity especially gradually ⟨At this time of the year, light begins to *taper off* a little earlier each day.⟩ — see DECREASE 2

tar *n* one who operates or navigates a seagoing vessel ⟨a book about the adventurous lives of *tars*, skippers, and pirates of the 18th century⟩ — see SAILOR

tardily *adv* **1** after the due, usual, or proper time ⟨She submitted her scholarship application *tardily*, so she was not considered.⟩ — see LATE 1
2 at a pace that is less than usual, desirable, or expected ⟨Repayment of the money I owed him came *tardily*.⟩ — see SLOW

tardiness *n* the quality or state of being late ⟨Habitual *tardiness* will be recorded in your personnel file.⟩ — see LATENESS

tardy *adj* **1** moving or proceeding at less than the normal, desirable, or required speed ⟨Thus far progress on the project has been *tardy*.⟩ — see SLOW 1
2 not arriving, occurring, or settled at the due, usual, or proper time ⟨explained that I was *tardy* because my car had broken down on the way to work⟩ — see LATE 1

target *n* **1** a person or thing that is the object of abuse, criticism, or ridicule ⟨The hapless vice president quickly became the favorite *target* of late-night comedians.⟩
synonyms butt, mark, prey, sitting duck, victim
related words laughingstock, mockery; fall guy, goat, scapegoat, whipping boy
near antonyms defamer, libeler, libelist, traducer; baiter, heckler, needler, ribber, taunter, tease, teaser, tormentor (*also* tormenter), torturer; derider, insulter, mocker, ridiculer, scoffer, scorner; caricaturist, lampooner, parodist, satirist
2 a person or thing that is made fun of ⟨a TV commercial that was the *target* of lots of jokes⟩ — see LAUGHINGSTOCK
3 something that one hopes or intends to accomplish ⟨Our *target* is to raise $100,000 for a new playground by August.⟩ — see GOAL

tarnish *vb* to affect slightly with something morally bad or undesirable ⟨a false accusation that nonetheless *tarnished* her reputation⟩ — see TAINT 1

tarry *vb* **1** to continue to be in a place for a significant amount of time ⟨Upon seeing the sun beginning to sink in the sky, we realized we had *tarried* too long on the summit of the mountain.⟩ — see ¹STAY 1
2 to move or act slowly ⟨The dean *tarried* in making his decision of who should win the award.⟩ — see DELAY 1
3 to reside as a temporary guest ⟨He *tarried* with us all summer, sleeping on the screened-in porch most nights.⟩ — see VISIT 2

tart *adj* **1** causing or characterized by the one of the basic taste sensations that is produced chiefly by acids ⟨I didn't add enough sugar to the lemonade, and now it's way too *tart*.⟩ — see SOUR 1
2 marked by the use of wit that is intended to cause hurt feelings ⟨responded with a *tart* comeback⟩ — see SARCASTIC

tartness *n* **1** a harsh or sharp quality ⟨There's a *tartness* to this movie critic's reviews that's a little tiresome.⟩ — see EDGE 1
2 biting sharpness of feeling or expression ⟨There's a telltale *tartness* between these two teams that nobody could miss.⟩ — see ACRIMONY 1

task *n* **1** a piece of work that needs to be done regularly ⟨One of my *tasks* in the morning is to make lunches for everyone in the family.⟩ — see CHORE 1
2 the action for which a person or thing is specially fitted or used or for which a thing exists ⟨The forklift's *task* is to stack pallets of goods in the warehouse.⟩ — see ROLE

task *vb* to give a task, duty, or responsibility to ⟨I have been *tasked* by the host with bringing the pies for Thanksgiving this year.⟩ — see ENTRUST 1

taskmaster *n* the person (as an employer or supervisor) who tells people and especially workers what to do ⟨known as a tough but fair *taskmaster*⟩ — see BOSS

taste *n* **1** the property of a substance that can be identified by the sense of taste ⟨I can't stand the *taste* of cherry-flavored cough syrup.⟩
synonyms flavor, savor (*also* savour)
related words relish, smack; savoriness, tastiness; aftertaste
near antonyms tastelessness
2 a small piece or quantity of food ⟨I'll just have a *taste* of your dessert.⟩ — see MORSEL 1
3 positive regard for something ⟨trying to develop a *taste* for classical music⟩ — see LIKING

taste *vb* **1** to come to a knowledge of (something) by living through it ⟨an adventurer who has *tasted* danger and lived to tell the tale⟩ — see EXPERIENCE
2 to have a vague awareness of ⟨By your language I can *taste* that something is wrong.⟩ — see FEEL 1

tasteful *adj* **1** having or showing elegance ⟨a *tasteful* arrangement of white flowers and dark greenery⟩ — see ELEGANT 1
2 very pleasing to the sense of taste ⟨a line of microwavable frozen entrées that are surprisingly *tasteful*⟩ — see DELICIOUS 1

tasteless *adj* **1** lacking in refinement or good taste ⟨a completely *tasteless* comment about the recent tragedy⟩ — see COARSE 2
2 lacking in taste or flavor ⟨Breakfast was usually plain, *tasteless* oatmeal.⟩ — see INSIPID 1
3 marked by an obvious lack of style or good taste ⟨a *tasteless* suit that he wore to the party as a joke⟩ — see ¹TACKY 1

tastelessness *n* the quality or state of lacking refinement or good taste ⟨The *tastelessness* of his comments was appalling.⟩ — see VULGARITY 1

tastiness *n* the quality of being delicious ⟨the *tastiness* of homemade bread⟩ — see DELICIOUSNESS

tasty *adj* **1** giving pleasure or contentment to the mind or senses ⟨the *tasty* prospect of getting his dream job after all those years⟩ — see PLEASANT 1

2 very pleasing to the sense of taste ⟨a selection of *tasty* doughnuts from the corner bakery⟩ — see DELICIOUS 1

tatter *vb* to cause (something) to separate into jagged pieces by violently pulling at it ⟨The kids will *tatter* that doll beyond repair if they don't quit yanking on it.⟩ — see TEAR 1

tattered *adj* **1** wearing torn or worn-out clothes ⟨arrived at the refugee camp *tattered* and exhausted⟩
synonyms ragged, raggedy, ragtag
related words bedraggled, scruffy, shabby, threadbare
near antonyms decked (out), dolled up, dressed up; spiffy

2 worn or torn into or as if into rags ⟨a hobo in *tattered* old clothes and worn-out shoes⟩ — see RAGGED 2

tattle *n* information or opinion that is widely disseminated without any authority or confirmation of accuracy ⟨Don't believe the *tattle* you hear about them.⟩ — see RUMOR

tattle *vb* to relate sometimes questionable or secret information of a personal nature ⟨those neighborhood busybodies, constantly *tattling* and whispering over their backyard fences⟩ — see GOSSIP

tattler *n* a person who provides information about another's wrongdoing ⟨As the office's resident *tattler*, she can be counted on to report any unauthorized use of the photocopiers.⟩ — see INFORMER

tattletale *n* a person who provides information about another's wrongdoing ⟨Don't be such a *tattletale* and tell me about every little thing your sister does!⟩ — see INFORMER

taunt *vb* to attack repeatedly with mean put-downs or insults ⟨The coach reprimanded the players for *taunting* their opponents.⟩ — see TEASE 2

taunter *n* a person who causes repeated emotional pain, distress, or annoyance to another ⟨Tired of always being the butt of their jokes, he decided to get back at his *taunters*.⟩ — see TORMENTOR

taut *adj* stretched with little or no give ⟨a *taut* clothesline⟩
synonyms rigid, tense, tight
related words firm, inflexible, stiff, tightened, unrelaxed, unyielding
near antonyms drooping, droopy, flaccid, floppy, hanging, lank, limp, loosened, relaxed, sagging, slackened, yielding; elastic, flexible, pliant, resilient, springy, stretchy, supple
antonyms lax, loose, slack

tavern *n* **1** a place of business where alcoholic beverages are sold to be consumed on the premises ⟨a *tavern* serving food as well as drink⟩ — see BARROOM

2 a place that provides rooms and usually a public dining room for overnight guests ⟨a colonial-era *tavern* that has been serving weary travelers for two and a half centuries⟩ — see HOTEL

tawny *adj* of a pale yellow or yellowish brown color ⟨the *tawny* coat of a lion⟩ — see BLOND

tax *n* a charge usually of money collected by the government from people or businesses for public use ⟨The state sales *tax* boosted the final cost of my new computer.⟩
synonyms assessment, duty, imposition, impost, levy
related words direct tax, personal tax; capitation, custom(s), excise, hidden tax, income tax, poll tax, property tax, sales tax, single tax, sin tax, tariff, toll, tribute, value-added tax, withholding tax; supertax, surcharge, surtax

tax *vb* to subject (a personal quality or faculty) to often excessive stress ⟨Your constant arguing is starting to *tax* my patience.⟩ — see TRY 1

taxi *n* an automobile that carries passengers for a fare usually determined by the distance traveled ⟨couldn't hail a *taxi* so I had to run in the rain to make my appointment⟩ — see TAXICAB

taxicab *n* an automobile that carries passengers for a fare usually determined by the distance traveled ⟨took a *taxicab* to the airport⟩
synonyms cab, hack, taxi
related words hackney; limousine; rickshaw (*also* ricksha)

taxing *adj* requiring much time, effort, or careful attention ⟨a very *taxing* workload that is taking a lot of time to finish⟩ — see DEMANDING 1

teach *vb* to cause to acquire knowledge or skill in some field ⟨*taught* us about the basics of organic gardening⟩
synonyms educate, indoctrinate, instruct, school, train, tutor
related words coach, mentor; drill, fit, ground, prepare, prime, qualify; direct, guide, lead, rear; lecture, moralize, preach; implant, inculcate; homeschool; edify, enlighten; brief, familiarize, impart (to), inform, verse; initiate, introduce, show; reeducate, reschool, reteach, retrain

teacher *n* a person whose occupation is to give formal instruction in a school ⟨a young man who ardently wants to become a *teacher* and teach first grade⟩
synonyms educator, instructor, pedagogue (*also* pedagog), preceptor, schoolteacher
related words headmaster, master, rector, schoolmaster; headmistress, schoolmarm (*or* schoolma'am), schoolmistress; coach, guide, guru, preparer, trainer; mentor, tutor; dean, doctor, don, professor; governess, homeschooler

teaching *n* the act or process of imparting knowledge or skills to another ⟨The biologist devoted her career to *teaching* in the hope of encouraging science-minded students.⟩ — see EDUCATION 1

team *n* a group of people working together on a task ⟨asked the Boy Scouts to split into *teams* and begin pitching their tents⟩ — see GANG 1

team (up) *vb* to participate or assist in a joint effort to accomplish an end ⟨The television broadcast networks will be *teaming up* for joint coverage of the event.⟩ — see COOPERATE 1

teamwork *n* the work and activity of a number of persons who individually contribute toward the efficiency of the whole ⟨It takes *teamwork* to pull off a successful fundraiser.⟩
synonyms collaboration, cooperation, coordination
related words fellowship, partnership; community, mutualism, reciprocity, symbiosis; synergism; communion, cooperativeness, kinship, oneness, solidarity, togetherness, unity
antonyms noncooperation

tear *n* a long deep cut ⟨repaired a *tear* in the theater curtain just before the start of the show⟩ — see GASH

tear *vb* **1** to cause (something) to separate into jagged pieces by violently pulling at it ⟨angrily *tore* the letter to shreds⟩
synonyms rend, rip, rive, shred, tatter
related words break, cleave, rupture, split; cut, gash, incise, lacerate, slash; butcher, dismember, dissect, hack, mangle

2 to separate or remove by forceful pulling ⟨*tore* the book from his hand⟩
synonyms rip, wrench, wrest, yank
related words grab, nab, seize, snap (up), snatch; lop (off), nip; amputate, cut (off), dissever, sever; extract, force, jerk, prize, pry, pull, root (out), uproot
near antonyms reattach

3 to proceed or move quickly ⟨She *tore* out of the room as soon as the phone started to ring.⟩ — see HURRY 2

tear (out) *vb* to draw out by force or with effort ⟨You'll never *tear* that secret *out* of me!⟩ — see EXTRACT

tear down *vb* **1** to bring to a complete end the physical soundness, existence, or usefulness of ⟨We *tore down* the wooden fence between the two yards.⟩ — see DESTROY 1

2 to destroy (as a building) completely by knocking down or breaking to pieces ⟨The new owners apparently bought the house just to *tear* it *down* and build a lavish mansion in its place.⟩ — see DEMOLISH 1

tearful *adj* **1** given to expressing strong emotion (as sorrow) by readily shedding tears ⟨a *tearful* woman who can be counted on to cry at every wedding, anniversary, and funeral⟩

synonyms lachrymose, teary

related words demonstrative, effusive, emotional; maudlin, mawkish, sentimental; bawling, blubbering, crying, keening, sniffling, sniveling, sobbing, wailing, weeping, whimpering; bemoaning, bewailing; doleful, grieving, mournful, plaintive; brokenhearted, dejected, depressed, despondent, disconsolate, downcast, downhearted, heartbroken, heartsick, inconsolable, miserable, sad, sorrowful, woebegone, woeful, wretched

near antonyms beaming, laughing, smiling; blithe, blithesome, cheerful, cheery, happy, jocose, jovial, lighthearted, lightsome, merry, mirthful, sunny

2 causing unhappiness ⟨the *tearful* end to what had once been a close friendship⟩ — see SAD 2

teary *adj* **1** causing unhappiness ⟨a *teary* ending to what had been up to that point a lighthearted movie⟩ — see SAD 2

2 given to expressing strong emotion (as sorrow) by readily shedding tears ⟨He is a *teary* man who regularly tells sad stories.⟩ — see TEARFUL 1

tease *n* **1** a person who causes repeated emotional pain, distress, or annoyance to another ⟨Leave your little sister alone—don't be such a *tease*.⟩ — see TORMENTOR

2 one who is obnoxiously annoying ⟨My youngest brother is a complete *tease*, following me around everywhere and aping my every move.⟩ — see NUISANCE 1

tease *vb* **1** to make fun of in a good-natured way ⟨Pam likes to *tease* her twin brother about his seemingly endless string of girlfriends.⟩

synonyms chaff, jive, joke, josh, kid, rally, razz, rib, ride, roast

related words banter; fool, fun, string along; jest, quip, wisecrack

2 to attack repeatedly with mean put-downs or insults ⟨He was *teased* for being so tall at such a young age.⟩

synonyms bait, hassle, haze, heckle, needle, ride, taunt

related words deride, gibe (*or* jibe), jeer, mock, ridicule; annoy, bother, bug, chafe, fret, frost, gall, get, gnaw (at), grate, gripe, irk, irritate, nettle, peeve, pester, pique, put out, rasp, rile, ruffle, spite, trouble, vex; aggravate, exasperate, goad, test, try; aggrieve, agitate, bedevil, beleaguer, discomfort, disturb, perturb; badger, dog, hound; browbeat, bully, hector; harry, persecute, plague, terrorize, torment, torture

phrases make game of, pick on

teaser *n* **1** a person who causes repeated emotional pain, distress, or annoyance to another ⟨*Teasers* were not tolerated in the preschool classroom.⟩ — see TORMENTOR

2 one who is obnoxiously annoying ⟨He was by nature a *teaser*, someone who kept testing people to see if they could calmly bear his put-downs.⟩ — see NUISANCE 1

teasing *n* the act of making unwelcome intrusions upon another ⟨Stop that *teasing* before you make the baby cry.⟩ — see ANNOYANCE 1

technical *adj* used by or intended for experts in a particular field of knowledge ⟨Although the owner's manual was supposedly written for the average consumer, it's filled with *technical* language.⟩

synonyms specialized

related words esoteric, limited, narrow, peculiar, restricted, special, specific, unique; authoritative, expert, professional, specialist (*or* specialistic)

near antonyms common, generalized, generic, nonexclusive, nonspecific, ordinary, overall, universal; inexpert, lay, nonprofessional, unprofessional; self-explanatory, straightforward

antonyms general, nontechnical, untechnical

technique *n* the means or procedure for doing something ⟨My aunt showed me a different knitting *technique*.⟩ — see METHOD

tedious *adj* causing weariness, restlessness, or lack of interest ⟨a long and *tedious* staff meeting⟩ — see BORING

tedium *n* the state of being bored ⟨the *tedium* of spending a hot afternoon trapped inside the house⟩ — see BOREDOM

teem *vb* to be copiously supplied ⟨The area *teems* with entrepreneurs hoping to hit upon the next big thing.⟩ — see ABOUND

teeming *adj* possessing or covered with great numbers or amounts of something specified ⟨oceans *teeming* with life⟩ — see RIFE

teeny *adj* very small in size ⟨I had to look closely to see the *teeny* splinter in her foot.⟩ — see TINY

teeny–weeny *adj* very small in size ⟨kept losing the *teeny-weeny* coffee mugs for the kitchen in her dollhouse⟩ — see TINY

teeter *vb* **1** to swing unsteadily back and forth or from side to side ⟨He nervously *teetered* at the edge of the pool.⟩

synonyms falter, rock, totter, waver, wobble (*also* wabble)

related words flounder, lurch, stumble, toddle; quake, quaver, quiver, shake, shudder, tremble, vibrate; careen, reel, stagger, weave

2 to move forward while swaying from side to side ⟨The toddler *teetered* down the rink on her new skates.⟩ — see STAGGER 1

3 to show uncertainty about the right course of action ⟨Jim was *teetering* on the brink of making a decision about college.⟩ — see HESITATE

telephone *vb* to make a telephone call to ⟨I'll try to *telephone* the office and make an appointment today.⟩ — see CALL 2

tell *vb* **1** to give an oral or written account of in some detail ⟨They *told* the story of how they had met.⟩

synonyms chart, chronicle, describe, narrate, recite, recount, rehearse, relate, report

related words deliver, give, reel off, state, utter, voice; detail, enumerate, itemize, particularize; bare, disclose, divulge, expose, reveal; delineate, depict, express, render, sketch

phrases set forth

2 to express (a thought or emotion) in words ⟨Just *tell* us what is in your heart.⟩ — see SAY 1

3 to find the sum of (a collection of things) by noting each one as it is being added ⟨Who can *tell* the number of grains of sand in the world?⟩ — see COUNT 1

4 to give information to ⟨*Tell* me, when did you begin playing the violin?⟩ — see ENLIGHTEN 1

5 to issue orders to (someone) by right of authority ⟨told us to sit still and wait⟩ — see COMMAND 1

6 to make known (as information previously kept secret) ⟨I won't *tell* your secret to anyone.⟩ — see REVEAL 1

tell (on) *vb* **1** to act upon (a person or a person's feelings) so as to cause a response ⟨The pressure of final exams is

beginning to *tell on* the students in the dorm.⟩ — see
¹**AFFECT** 1
2 to give information (as to the authorities) about another's improper or unlawful activities ⟨The detective
convinced the thief to *tell on* her associates.⟩ — see
SQUEAL 1

telling *adj* having the power to persuade ⟨presented us
with *telling* evidence that convinced us he was right⟩ —
see COGENT

telltale *adj* indicating something ⟨I know you've been eating chocolate because of the *telltale* smudges on your
face.⟩ — see INDICATIVE

telltale *n* **1** a person who habitually reveals personal or
sensational facts about others ⟨The media's professional
telltales have basically decided that today's celebrities
have no right to privacy.⟩ — see GOSSIP 1
2 a person who provides information about another's
wrongdoing ⟨The department *telltale* told the boss that
his coworkers were taking extra long breaks.⟩ — see IN-
FORMER

temerity *n* shameless boldness ⟨She had the *temerity* to ask
my boyfriend if she could go out with him should he and
I ever break up.⟩ — see EFFRONTERY

temper *n* **1** a special quality or impression associated with
something ⟨There's a *temper* of tranquillity about the retreat that visitors find very inviting.⟩ — see AURA 1
2 a state of mind dominated by a particular emotion
⟨Tim was in quite a bad *temper* after spilling his juice all
over his new shirt.⟩ — see MOOD 1
3 one's characteristic attitude or mood ⟨She has an even
temper and a calm manner that sets everyone at ease.⟩ —
see DISPOSITION 1

temperament *n* one's characteristic attitude or mood
⟨looking for a dog with a sweet *temperament*⟩ — see DIS-
POSITION 1

temperamental *adj* **1** frequently influenced by moods and
especially bad moods ⟨one of those *temperamental* actresses who can make life difficult for everyone around
her⟩ — see MOODY
2 likely to change frequently, suddenly, or unexpectedly
⟨Stock prices have been pretty *temperamental* lately, often fluctuating wildly.⟩ — see FICKLE 1

temperance *n* an avoidance of extremes in one's actions,
beliefs, or habits ⟨My father attributes his ripe old age to
temperance in all things, especially eating and drinking.⟩
synonyms moderateness, moderation, temperateness
related words constraint, control, discipline, restraint,
self-control, self-discipline; asceticism, austerity, frugality, mortification, sacrifice, self-containment, self-denial;
abnegation, abstention, avoidance, eschewal, forbearance; rationality, reasonability, reasonableness, sensibility, sensibleness; sobriety
near antonyms unrestraint; extremism, radicalness; irrationality, unreasonableness

temperate *adj* **1** avoiding extremes in behavior or expression ⟨rather *temperate* in his appraisal of the movie, calling it good but not great⟩ — see MODERATE 1
2 marked by temperatures that are neither too high nor
too low ⟨We escaped a cold Midwestern winter by vacationing in a more *temperate* climate down south.⟩ — see
CLEMENT 1
3 given to or marked by restraint in the satisfaction of
one's appetites ⟨a soft-spoken, serious-minded person of
temperate habits⟩ — see ABSTEMIOUS

temperateness *n* an avoidance of extremes in one's actions, beliefs, or habits ⟨There was a steadfast *temperateness* about every aspect of his life.⟩ — see TEMPERANCE

tempest *n* **1** a disturbance of the atmosphere accompanied by wind and often by precipitation (as rain or snow)

⟨The sudden summertime *tempest* drove us off the golf
course and into the clubhouse.⟩ — see STORM 1
2 a violent disturbance (as of the political or social order)
⟨The town council handled the *tempest* over cuts to the
school budget as well as could be expected.⟩ — see CON-
VULSION

tempestuous *adj* **1** marked by bursts of destructive force
or intense activity ⟨Order was restored to the court after
the judge put a stop to the defendant's *tempestuous* outburst.⟩ — see VIOLENT 1
2 marked by sudden or violent disturbance ⟨In terms of
social change, the 1960s are generally considered the
most *tempestuous* decade in recent American history.⟩
— see CONVULSIVE 1
3 marked by turmoil or disturbance especially of natural
elements ⟨We spent a *tempestuous* night stranded on the
summit of the mountain.⟩ — see WILD 3
4 marked by wet and windy conditions ⟨Stay indoors this
weekend as the weather promises to be *tempestuous*.⟩ —
see FOUL 1

temple *n* a building for public worship and especially
Christian worship ⟨the largest *temple* in the Gothic style
in the country⟩ — see CHURCH 1

temporal *adj* **1** having to do with life on earth especially as
opposed to that in heaven ⟨Do not worry about *temporal*
concerns, but instead focus on spiritual matters.⟩ — see
EARTHLY
2 not involving religion or religious matters ⟨Administra-
tors on campus are in place to deal with students' *temporal* needs, and spiritual advisors are available to help students with their nontemporal needs.⟩ — see PROFANE 1

temporary *adj* **1** intended to last, continue, or serve for a
limited time ⟨summer workers looking for *temporary* accommodations in private homes⟩
synonyms impermanent, interim, provisional, short-term
related words acting; alternate, proxy, substitute; expedient, improvised, makeshift; intermediary, intermediate,
transitional; ephemeral, fleeting, fugitive, short-lived,
transitory; conditional, contingent, limited, qualified,
short-range, tentative; replaceable, terminable, terminate
near antonyms final, fixed, set, settled; extended, lasting, long-range, standing; dateless, deathless, endless, enduring, eternal, everlasting, immortal, perpetual, timeless, undying, unending
antonyms long-term, permanent
2 lasting only for a short time ⟨a *temporary* lapse of
memory⟩ — see MOMENTARY
3 serving in a position for the time being ⟨the *temporary*
head of the sales division⟩ — see ACTING

temporizer *n* **1** a person who dexterously and expediently
changes or adopts opinions ⟨the kind of *temporizer* who
determines his position on a political issue by taking a
look at the polls⟩ — see ACROBAT 2
2 one who does things only for his own benefit and with
little regard for right and wrong ⟨A lifelong *temporizer*,
he was for the war as long as it was popular and against
it the minute the tide of public opinion went the other
way.⟩ — see SELF-SEEKER

tempt *vb* **1** to lead away from a usual or proper course by
offering some pleasure or advantage ⟨That chocolate
dessert sure *tempts* me, but I should stick with my diet.⟩
— see LURE
2 to take a chance on ⟨Refusing to lay in enough food for
the long winter *tempts* the dangers of starvation.⟩ — see
RISK 1

temptation *n* **1** the act or pressure of giving in to a desire
especially when ill-advised ⟨He felt the *temptation* to go
sailing, but did his chores instead.⟩
synonyms allurement, enticement, lure, seduction

related words allure, appeal, attraction, attractiveness, charm, enchantment, glamour (*also* glamor); beckoning, invitation; bait, inducement, influence, persuasion, power, sway

2 something that persuades one to perform an action for pleasure or gain ⟨Money and power are always *temptations*.⟩ — see LURE 1

tempter *n* one that tries to get a person to give in to a desire ⟨There is no greater *tempter* to put off studying than my dog when he wants to play.⟩

synonyms baiter, seducer, solicitor

related words beguiler, enchantress, siren, temptress; tantalizer; briber, inducer, inveigler, persuader; corrupter (*also* corruptor), debaser, debaucher, degrader, perverter, undoer

temptress *n* a woman whom men find irresistibly attractive ⟨Greta Garbo was one of the most famous *temptresses* ever to appear on screen.⟩ — see SIREN

tenable *adj* **1** capable of being defended against physical attack ⟨The soldiers' encampment on the open plain was not *tenable*, so they retreated to higher ground.⟩

synonyms defendable, defensible

related words defended, guarded, protected, safeguarded, secure, secured, shielded; impregnable, indomitable, invincible, inviolable, invulnerable, unassailable, unbeatable, unconquerable, untouchable

near antonyms vincible, vulnerable; assailable, exposed, imperiled (*or* imperilled), insecure, liable, open, susceptible, undefended, unguarded, unprotected, unsecured; defenseless, helpless, powerless, weak

antonyms indefensible, untenable

2 capable of being defended with good reasoning against verbal attack ⟨the *tenable* theory that a giant meteor strike set off a chain of events resulting in the demise of the dinosaurs⟩

synonyms defendable, defensible, justifiable, maintainable, supportable, sustainable

related words rational, reasonable, sensible; acceptable, admissible, allowable, legitimate, passable, unobjectionable, viable, warrantable; confirmable, provable, verifiable; explainable, explicable

near antonyms absurd, illogical, irrational, ridiculous, unsound; extreme, outrageous, unreasonable; groundless, objectionable, unacceptable, unfounded; inexplicable, unexplainable

antonyms indefensible, insupportable, unjustifiable, unsustainable, untenable

tenacious *adj* **1** continuing despite difficulties, opposition, or discouragement ⟨A *tenacious* trainer, she adheres to her grueling swimming schedule no matter what.⟩ — see PERSISTENT

2 tending to adhere to objects upon contact ⟨You'll have a devil of a time getting those *tenacious* burrs off of your wool sweater.⟩ — see STICKY 1

tenant *n* **1** one who rents a room or apartment in another's house ⟨The laundry in the basement is for *tenants* only.⟩

synonyms boarder, lodger, renter, roomer

related words roommate (*also* roomie); occupant, occupier, resident, resider

near antonyms landholder, landowner, proprietor; landlady; slumlord

antonyms landlord, lessor, letter

2 one who lives permanently in a place ⟨The abandoned warehouse's only *tenants* are a band of squatters.⟩ — see INHABITANT

¹tend *vb* to show a liking or proneness (for something) ⟨Her wardrobe *tends* toward dark colors and heavy fabrics.⟩ — see LEAN 2

²tend *vb* **1** to take charge of especially on behalf of another ⟨*Tend* the store while I run an errand.⟩

synonyms attend, care (for), mind, oversee, superintend, supervise, watch

related words conduct, control, direct, govern, guide, manage, operate, preside (over), regulate, run, steward; guard, patrol, protect, safeguard, shield; baby, babysit, chaperone (*or* chaperon), mother, shepherd

phrases look after, see after, see to, take care of

near antonyms abandon, disregard, forget, ignore, neglect, pass over

2 to look after or assist the growth of by labor and care ⟨Lately I haven't been doing a good job of *tending* my garden.⟩ — see GROW 1

3 to work by plowing, sowing, and raising crops on ⟨plots that are *tended* by city dwellers as vegetable gardens⟩ — see FARM

4 to look after and make decisions about ⟨The aging man wondered who would *tend* the family business after he was gone.⟩ — see CONDUCT 1

tendency *n* **1** an established pattern of behavior ⟨a *tendency* to drop things⟩ ⟨a *tendency* to make snap judgments⟩

synonyms aptness, proneness, propensity, way

related words affinity, aptitude, bent, disposition, inclination, leaning, partiality, penchant, predilection, predisposition, proclivity, turn; custom, habit, pattern, practice (*also* practise), routine, wont; eccentricity, idiosyncrasy, oddity, peculiarity, quirk, singularity, trick

near antonyms averseness, disinclination, dislike, indisposition

2 a prevailing or general movement or inclination ⟨We'll be seeing a *tendency* for cars to get smaller this year.⟩ — see TREND 1

3 a habitual attraction to some activity or thing ⟨a youth with a natural *tendency* toward the arts⟩ — see INCLINATION 1

tender *adj* **1** easily injured without careful handling ⟨a *tender* wound⟩ ⟨*tender* plants that cannot take the cold⟩ ⟨*tender* pride that got bruised⟩

synonyms delicate, fragile, frail, sensitive

related words breakable, brittle, crushable, friable; feeble, flimsy, puny, slight, soft, tenuous, weak; perishable, resistless, susceptible, unresistant, vulnerable, yielding

near antonyms durable, firm, flinty, hard, hardy, resistant, robust, rugged, solid, sound, stiff, stout, strong, sturdy, substantial; infrangible, nonbreakable, unbreakable; hardened, inured, strengthened, tempered, toughened

antonyms tough

2 feeling or showing love ⟨a *tender* embrace between father and daughter⟩ — see LOVING 1

3 having or marked by sympathy and consideration for others ⟨an especially *tender* teacher who loves having kids with special educational needs in her class⟩ — see HUMANE 1

4 lacking bodily strength ⟨a very *tender* child who always seems to be sick⟩ — see WEAK 1

5 not harsh or stern especially in nature or effect ⟨His *tender* comments on how to improve her writing style were gratefully received.⟩ — see GENTLE 1

tender *n* something (as pieces of stamped metal or printed paper) customarily and legally used as a medium of exchange, a measure of value, or a means of payment ⟨Money from that board game is not legal *tender* and can't be exchanged for goods or services.⟩ — see MONEY

tender *vb* to put before another for acceptance or consideration ⟨The coach *tendered* his resignation and started a new career as a physical therapist.⟩ — see OFFER 1

tenderfoot *n* a person who is just starting out in a field of activity ⟨Skateboarders who are *tenderfeet* will inevitably fall as they learn their first moves.⟩ — see BEGINNER

tenderhearted *adj* **1** feeling or showing love ⟨a *tender-hearted* new mother⟩ — see LOVING 1
2 having or marked by sympathy and consideration for others ⟨a *tenderhearted* offer of help for the victims of the earthquake⟩ — see HUMANE 1

tending *adj* having a tendency to be or act in a certain way ⟨Men *tending* toward daily exercise will significantly reduce their risk of cardiac arrest.⟩ — see PRONE 1

tenement *n* a room or set of rooms in a private house or a block used as a separate dwelling place ⟨an exhibit of pictures showing the *tenements* of the New York City neighborhood of Hell's Kitchen during the 1920s⟩ — see APARTMENT 1

tense *adj* **1** feeling or showing uncomfortable feelings of uncertainty ⟨Lori was *tense* about the upcoming bar exam.⟩ — see NERVOUS 1
2 marked by or causing agitation or uncomfortable feelings ⟨A *tense* relationship existed between the two teachers.⟩ — see NERVOUS 2
3 stretched with little or no give ⟨a *tense* rope⟩ — see TAUT

tension *n* the burden on one's emotional or mental well-being created by demands on one's time ⟨under a lot of *tension* right now about her decision not to go to college⟩ — see STRESS 1

tent *n* a raised covering over something for decoration or protection ⟨A huge *tent* was erected for the outdoor wedding reception.⟩ — see CANOPY

tentative *adj* determined by something else ⟨Our plans are only *tentative* at this point and will depend on whether you can come.⟩ — see DEPENDENT 2

tenure *n* a fixed period of time during which a person holds a job or position ⟨During his *tenure* as president the college experienced steady growth.⟩ — see TERM 1

tepid *adj* **1** showing little or no interest or enthusiasm ⟨The proposed table tennis club met with only a *tepid* response.⟩
synonyms halfhearted, lukewarm, uneager, unenthusiastic
related words apathetic, disinterested, dispassionate, impassive, indifferent, neutral, uncaring, uninterested; lackadaisical, languid, listless, perfunctory, undemonstrative, unemotional, unresponsive; unfeeling, unsympathetic; chill, chilly, cold, cool, frigid, frosty, glacial, icy, unfriendly, wintry (*also* wintery)
near antonyms agog, ardent, avid, exuberant, fervid, feverish, fiery, gung ho, hot-blooded, impassioned, intense, raring, red-hot, vehement; engaged, engrossed, interested; ready, willing; cordial, friendly, genial, warmhearted
antonyms eager, enthusiastic, hearty, keen, passionate, warm, wholehearted
2 having or giving off heat to a moderate degree ⟨Make sure the water for the footbath is just *tepid* or you'll burn yourself.⟩ — see WARM 1

term *n* **1** a fixed period of time during which a person holds a job or position ⟨elected for a two-year *term* as mayor⟩
synonyms hitch, stint, tenure, tour
related words shift, watch; go, turn; duration, standing, time; cycle, span, spell, stretch; life, life span, lifetime, run
2 a pronounceable series of letters having a distinct meaning especially in a particular field ⟨What's the *term* for the odd feeling that you've experienced an event before?⟩ — see WORD 1

term *vb* to give a name to ⟨The armed forces began a rescue mission termed Operation In and Out.⟩ — see NAME 1

terminal *adj* **1** following all others of the same kind in order or time ⟨took me to the *terminal* point of that bus route⟩ — see LAST 1

2 likely to cause or capable of causing death ⟨a condition that can be *terminal*⟩ — see DEADLY 1

terminate *vb* **1** to bring (an event) to a natural or appropriate stopping point ⟨We need to *terminate* the discussion for this evening, but we'll resume tomorrow morning.⟩ — see CLOSE 3
2 to come to an end ⟨This class will *terminate* with the arrival of Memorial Day.⟩ — see CEASE 1
3 to mark the limits of ⟨*terminated* the area set aside for the runners to change their clothes with a series of folding screens⟩ — see LIMIT 2
4 to put to death deliberately ⟨The operative's covert mission was to *terminate* the leader of the opposition.⟩ — see MURDER 1
5 to let go from office, service, or employment ⟨He was *terminated* for constantly coming in to work late.⟩ — see DISMISS 1

terminated *adj* brought or having come to an end ⟨There is an effort to restart the *terminated* negotiations.⟩ — see COMPLETE 2

terminating *adj* following all others of the same kind in order or time ⟨The *terminating* speech of the political convention turned out to be the most inspiring.⟩ — see LAST 1

termination *n* **1** a real or imaginary point beyond which a person or thing cannot go ⟨I've reached the *termination* of my patience with you kids!⟩ — see LIMIT 1
2 the act of ceasing to exist ⟨He feels that the voluntary *termination* of one's life should be left entirely up to the patient.⟩ — see DEATH 3
3 the stopping of a process or activity ⟨At the *termination* of the movie, please throw away any empty food containers in the appropriate bins.⟩ — see END 1

terminology *n* the special terms or expressions of a particular group or field ⟨the *terminology* favored by sportscasters⟩ ⟨medical *terminology* that can be hard for the patient to understand⟩
synonyms argot, cant, dialect, jargon, jive, language, lingo, patois, patter, shop, slang, vocabulary
related words colloquialism, idiom, localism, parlance, pidgin, provincialism, regionalism, speech, vernacular; journalese

terra firma *n* the solid part of our planet's surface as distinguished from the sea and air ⟨After that nightmarish storm, the sailors were grateful to reach *terra firma*.⟩ — see EARTH 2

terrestrial *adj* **1** having to do with life on earth especially as opposed to that in heaven ⟨Scientists haven't even found all the *terrestrial* life on our planet.⟩ — see EARTHLY
2 having to do with the practical details of regular life ⟨Let's focus on *terrestrial* issues—such as how to pay the bills.⟩ — see MUNDANE 1

terrible *adj* **1** causing fear ⟨a *terrible* nightmare that woke me up⟩ — see FEARFUL 1
2 extreme in degree, power, or effect ⟨I have a *terrible* headache.⟩ — see INTENSE 1
3 extremely disturbing or repellent ⟨That is a *terrible* movie to let your six-year-old watch.⟩ — see HORRIBLE 1
4 extremely unsatisfactory ⟨This nonfat ice cream is *terrible*!⟩ — see WRETCHED 1
5 of low quality ⟨manufactures *terrible* clothes that often tear after a single wash⟩ — see CHEAP 2

terribly *adv* to a great degree ⟨I'm *terribly* sorry to bother you.⟩ — see VERY 1

terrific *adj* **1** of the very best kind ⟨You've done a *terrific* job on this report.⟩ — see EXCELLENT
2 extremely disturbing or repellent ⟨The jackhammers made a *terrific* noise.⟩ — see HORRIBLE 1

terrified *adj* filled with fear or dread ⟨a *terrified* cat hiding under the couch⟩ — see AFRAID

terrify *vb* to strike with fear ⟨The prospect of speaking in front of a huge crowd of people absolutely *terrifies* me.⟩ — see FRIGHTEN

terrifying *adj* causing fear ⟨heard a *terrifying* noise coming from the next room⟩ — see FEARFUL 1

territory *n* the place where a plant or animal is usually or naturally found ⟨That plant's *territory* extends from Georgia all the way north to Maine.⟩ — see HOME 2

terror *n* 1 a source of persistent emotional distress ⟨With his fear of flying, traveling for business became one of the *terrors* of his life.⟩ — see DEMON 2
2 the emotion experienced in the presence or threat of danger ⟨They lived in *terror* of being discovered.⟩ — see FEAR 1

terrorize *vb* to strike with fear ⟨Thunderstorms *terrorize* our cats, who all scamper downstairs when lightning flashes.⟩ — see FRIGHTEN

terrorized *adj* filled with fear or dread ⟨a movie about a *terrorized* village fighting off attack by vampires⟩ — see AFRAID

terse *adj* marked by the use of few words to convey much information or meaning ⟨I could tell from his *terse* replies to my questions that he was in no mood to talk.⟩ — see CONCISE

tersely *adv* in a few words ⟨She stated her dissatisfaction rather *tersely* with a simple "I don't approve."⟩ — see SHORTLY 1

terseness *n* the quality or state of being marked by or using only few words to convey much meaning ⟨The *terseness* of my replies simply meant that I was too busy to talk at that time.⟩ — see SUCCINCTNESS

test *n* 1 a procedure or operation carried out to resolve an uncertainty ⟨We will need to run some *tests* on the blood sample to rule out blood poisoning.⟩ — see EXPERIMENT
2 a set of questions or problems designed to assess knowledge, skills, or intelligence ⟨Applicants for the cashier's position must first take a simple math *test*.⟩ — see EXAMINATION 1

test *vb* 1 to put (something) to a test ⟨Please *test* this sample for the presence of lead.⟩ — see TRY (OUT)
2 to subject (a personal quality or faculty) to often excessive stress ⟨All of these unnecessary questions are *testing* my patience.⟩ — see TRY 1

testament *n* 1 something presented in support of the truth or accuracy of a claim ⟨The "before" and "after" pictures are a *testament* to the effectiveness of the weight loss program.⟩ — see PROOF
2 the basic beliefs or guiding principles of a person or group ⟨Jefferson's collected writings constitute his political *testament*.⟩ — see CREED 1

testify *vb* to make a solemn declaration under oath for the purpose of establishing a fact ⟨Several witnesses *testified* that they had seen the accused in the vicinity of the crime scene.⟩
synonyms attest, depose, swear, witness
related words verify; vouch; promise, vow
phrases bear witness

testify (to) *vb* to declare (something) to be true or genuine ⟨That auction house will always *testify to* a painting's authenticity.⟩ — see CERTIFY 1

testimony *n* something presented in support of the truth or accuracy of a claim ⟨The plaintiff's case rests largely on the *testimony* of several scientists with no known expertise in that field.⟩ — see PROOF

testiness *n* readiness to show annoyance or impatience ⟨attributed his unusual *testiness* this morning to being hungry⟩ — see PETULANCE

testy *adj* easily irritated or annoyed ⟨That coworker would be easier to get along with if she weren't so *testy* all the time.⟩ — see IRRITABLE

tête-à-tête *adv* in person and usually privately ⟨met *tête-à-tête* with the student's parents to discuss his academic progress⟩
synonyms face-to-face, personally
related words familiarly; directly, immediately
phrases in private, in secret
near antonyms distantly, indirectly; openly, publicly

tête-à-tête *n* friendly, informal conversation or an instance of this ⟨I had a quick *tête-à-tête* with my neighbor before heading off to work.⟩ — see CHAT 1

text *n* a book used for instruction in a subject ⟨The school's science curriculum suffers from a serious lack of up-to-date *texts*.⟩ — see TEXTBOOK

textbook *adj* constituting, serving as, or worthy of being a pattern to be imitated ⟨a *textbook* example of a film that captures the feel of the novel on which it is based⟩ — see MODEL

textbook *n* a book used for instruction in a subject ⟨One shelf in my bookcase is crammed full of my old college *textbooks*.⟩
synonyms handbook, manual, primer, text
related words schoolbook; grammar, speller; tract, treatise; dictionary, lexicon, vocabulary, wordbook; casebook, encyclopedia, reference; bible, guide, guidebook

textile *n* a woven or knitted material (as of cotton or nylon) ⟨brought back a whole suitcase of beautiful *textiles* from India⟩ — see CLOTH

thankful *adj* 1 experiencing pleasure, satisfaction, or delight ⟨We were *thankful* that someone else was footing the bill for the lavish wedding banquet.⟩ — see GLAD 1
2 feeling or expressing gratitude ⟨I am *thankful* for all your help.⟩ — see GRATEFUL 1

thankfulness *n* acknowledgment of having received something good from another ⟨Pat expressed her *thankfulness* for helping her move by taking us all out for dinner.⟩ — see THANKS

thankless *adj* 1 not showing gratitude ⟨a *thankless* boss who seems oblivious to the extra effort his subordinates have made⟩
synonyms unappreciative, ungrateful
related words rude, thoughtless, ungracious
near antonyms beholden, indebted; gratified, pleased; courteous, gracious, thoughtful
antonyms appreciative, grateful, obliged, thankful
2 not likely to be appreciated by those who benefit ⟨the *thankless* job of cleaning up after a party⟩
synonyms unappreciated, ungrateful
related words uncredited, underappreciated, underrated, undervalued, unnoticed, unrewarded, unsung, unvalued
near antonyms credited, esteemed, honored, prized, regarded, rewarded, valued; creditable, meritorious, praiseworthy
antonyms appreciated

thanks *pl n* acknowledgment of having received something good from another ⟨To express our *thanks*, we'd like to present you with this plaque.⟩
synonyms appreciation, appreciativeness, gratefulness, gratitude, thankfulness
related words thanksgiving; gratification, satisfaction; acknowledgment (*or* acknowledgement), recognition, tribute
antonyms unappreciation

thaw *vb* to go from a solid to a liquid state ⟨You will have to let the apple juice concentrate *thaw* before you can mix it with water.⟩ — see LIQUEFY

thawed *adj* freed from a frozen state by exposure to warmth ⟨recommends cooking *thawed* fish within 24 hours⟩
synonyms defrosted, unfrozen

related words liquefied, melted, molten; deiced; heated, warmed

near antonyms chilled, iced, refrigerated; quick-frozen, refrozen, supercooled; congealed, glaciated, semisolid; frostbitten, frosty, icy

antonyms frozen

theater *or* **theatre** *n* **1** a building or part of a building where movies are shown ⟨There's still one *theater* in town that shows independent films.⟩

synonyms cinema, playhouse

related words nickelodeon; megaplex, multiplex

2 the public performance of plays ⟨I have been fascinated by the *theater* ever since I was a child.⟩ — see DRAMA 1

3 a large room or building for enclosed public gatherings ⟨The lecturer waited until the *theater* was full before beginning.⟩ — see HALL 3

theatrical *also* **theatric** *adj* **1** given to or marked by attention-getting behavior suggestive of stage acting ⟨After stepping out of their hired limousine, the prom couple made a *theatrical* entrance in their evening clothes.⟩

synonyms dramatic, histrionic, melodramatic

related words overacted, overdone, sensational, staged; conspicuous, elaborate, flamboyant, grandiose, ostentatious, showy; affected, artificial, mannered, pretentious, self-conscious, studied, unnatural

near antonyms nondramatic, nontheatrical, unaffected, underplayed, unpretentious; muted, restrained, subdued, toned (down); conservative, discreet, inconspicuous; modest, plain, quiet, simple

antonyms undramatic

2 having the general quality or effect of a stage performance ⟨In a very *theatrical* voice the actress announced to the gathering that she did not sign autographs.⟩ — see DRAMATIC 1

theatricals *pl n* the public performance of plays ⟨Ben has been involved in amateur *theatricals* for most of his adult life.⟩ — see DRAMA 1

theft *n* **1** the unlawful taking and carrying away of property without the consent of its owner ⟨While violent crime in the city has decreased dramatically, the rate of *theft* has risen slightly.⟩

synonyms larceny, robbery, stealing, thievery

related words burglary, housebreaking; embezzlement, embezzling, graft, misapplication, misappropriation; filching, pilferage, pilfering, purloining, shoplifting; carjacking, hijacking (*also* highjacking), shanghaiing

2 an instance of theft ⟨The police found the stolen car an hour after the *theft* was reported.⟩

synonyms grab, heist, pinch, rip-off, snatching, swiping

related words break-in, burglary, holdup, mugging, stickup

theme *n* **1** a major object of interest or concern (as in a discussion or artistic composition) ⟨This dance piece deals with the timeless *themes* of birth and death.⟩ — see MATTER 1

2 a short piece of writing done as a school exercise ⟨Please write a one page *theme* on the main character of this book.⟩ — see COMPOSITION 2

3 a short piece of writing typically expressing a point of view ⟨The magazine will award a scholarship to the student who writes the best *theme* on the concept of personal freedom.⟩ — see ESSAY 1

then *adv* in addition to what has been said ⟨There's the cost of the car itself, and *then* there's the cost of insurance and maintenance.⟩ — see MORE 1

theoretical *also* **theoretic** *adj* **1** existing only as an assumption or speculation ⟨The merits of the new testing procedures are purely *theoretical*, since no one has ever used them before.⟩

synonyms academic (*also* academical), conjectural, hypothetical, speculative, suppositional

related words alleged, assumed, presumed, presupposed, proposed, supposed, unproved, unproven, untested; debatable, moot; abstract, conceptual, intellectual, metaphysical; nonclinical, nonpractical; nonempirical

near antonyms clinical, practical; concrete, defined, definite, distinct; attested, authenticated, confirmed, demonstrated, established, proven, substantiated, tested, time-tested, validated, verified; empirical (*also* empiric), nonspeculative, nontheoretical, observational

antonyms actual, factual, real

2 dealing with or expressing a quality or idea ⟨The *theoretical* musings in his new book are less engaging than the anecdote-driven arguments of his previous works.⟩ — see ABSTRACT 1

theory *n* an idea that is the starting point for making a case or conducting an investigation ⟨She set out to prove her *theory* that people can't really taste any difference between colas, so they buy according to the product's image.⟩

synonyms hypothesis, proposition, supposition, thesis

related words assumption, concession, premise (*also* premiss), presumption, presupposition, theorem; conjecture, generalization, guess, guesswork, inference, speculation, surmise; proffer, proposal, suggestion; feeling, hunch, impression, inkling, notion, suspicion; concept, conception, construct

near antonyms assurance, certainty, fact, knowledge

thereafter *adv* following in time or place ⟨gave his farewell speech and left the room shortly *thereafter*⟩ — see AFTER

therefore *adv* for this or that reason ⟨It's snowing hard; *therefore* I think we should stay home.⟩

synonyms accordingly, consequently, ergo, hence, so, thereupon, thus

phrases in consequence

theretofore *adv* up to this or that time ⟨*Theretofore* the team had been on a losing streak, but when a new player joined, she brought them to victory.⟩ — see HITHERTO

thereupon *adv* for this or that reason ⟨She didn't get into the college of her choice and *thereupon* decided to study for a year before retaking the college entrance exams.⟩ — see THEREFORE

thesis *n* **1** an idea or opinion that is put forth in a discussion or debate ⟨put forth the *thesis* that the media's coverage of politics trivializes the workings of our democracy⟩ — see CONTENTION 1

2 an idea that is the starting point for making a case or conducting an investigation ⟨It is not clear how the arguments you make actually support your *thesis*.⟩ — see THEORY

thick *adj* **1** having or being of relatively great depth or extent from one surface to its opposite ⟨A *thick* board was laid across the pit.⟩

synonyms chunky, fat

related words blockish, blocky, bulky, dense, hefty, thickish; broad, deep, wide

near antonyms narrow, shallow

antonyms skinny, slender, slim, thin

2 being of a consistency that resists flow ⟨*thick* maple syrup for pancakes⟩

synonyms ropy (*also* ropey), syrupy, viscid, viscous

related words creamy, heavy, slushy, thickened, thickish, turbid, undiluted; semifluid, semiliquid; gluey, glutinous, sticky; gelatinous, gooey, gummy, jellylike; concentrated, condensed

near antonyms flowing, fluid; dilute, diluted, liquid, watered-down, weak

antonyms runny, soupy, thin, watery

3 closely acquainted ⟨Those two have been *thick* since grade school.⟩ — see FAMILIAR 1

4 having a greater than usual measure across ⟨Cross your name off the list with a really *thick* line so I can see it.⟩ — see WIDE 1

5 having little space between items or parts ⟨a hedge *thick* with gorse bushes⟩ — see CLOSE 1

6 not having or showing an ability to absorb ideas readily ⟨I'm not *thick* enough to fall for such a scam.⟩ — see STUPID 1

7 possessing or covered with great numbers or amounts of something specified ⟨a meadow *thick* with wildflowers⟩ — see RIFE

thick *n* the most intense or characteristic phase of something ⟨In the *thick* of winter many Northerners are dreaming of tropical islands.⟩

synonyms deep, depth, height, middle, midst

related words center, heart

thicket *n* a thick patch of shrubbery, small trees, or underbrush ⟨flushed a pheasant from a *thicket* of willows⟩

synonyms brake, brushwood, chaparral, coppice, copse, covert

related words canebrake; brush, bush, scrub, scrubland; bramble, jungle, tangle; grove, hedge, stand, woodlot; forest, greenwood, wildwood, wood, woodland

thickheaded *adj* not having or showing an ability to absorb ideas readily ⟨Don't suppose that he's *thickheaded* just because he doesn't say a lot.⟩ — see STUPID 1

thickness *n* **1** the degree to which a fluid can resist flowing ⟨Beat the eggs and sugar until the mixture has the *thickness* of heavy cream.⟩ — see CONSISTENCY

2 the quality or state of lacking intelligence or quickness of mind ⟨It's not because of *thickness* that he gets poor grades, it's because he doesn't care.⟩ — see STUPIDITY 1

thickset *adj* being compact and broad in build and often short in stature ⟨a short, *thickset* bulldog⟩ — see STOCKY

thick–skinned *adj* having or showing a lack of sympathy or tender feelings ⟨Meg was so *thick-skinned* that she was clueless about the fact that the joke had hurt her friend's feelings.⟩ — see HARD 1

thief *n* one who steals ⟨A *thief* has been stealing wallets and valuables from the lockers at the gym.⟩

synonyms pincher, purloiner, robber, stealer

related words burglar, cat burglar, housebreaker, safecracker; embezzler, grafter; kleptomaniac; pickpocket, pilferer, shoplifter; abductor, carjacker, hijacker, kidnapper (*also* kidnaper), skyjacker

thieve *vb* to take (something) without right and with an intent to keep ⟨Someone's been *thieving* my cookies!⟩ — see STEAL 1

thievery *n* the unlawful taking and carrying away of property without the consent of its owner ⟨a man who has a history of petty *thievery*⟩ — see THEFT 1

thin *adj* **1** having a noticeably small amount of body fat ⟨After her bout with pneumonia, she looked *thinner*.⟩

synonyms lean, lithe, skinny, slender, slim, spare, svelte

related words clean-limbed, trim; sylphlike, willowy; angular, rawboned, scraggy, scrawny, sinewy, wiry; lank, lanky, rangy, reedy, spindling, spindly, stringy, twiggy, waspish, weedy; anorexic, cadaverous, emaciated, gaunt, haggard, pinched, skeletal, wasted, wizened; meager (*or* meagre), puny, slight

near antonyms beefy, bulky, chunky, fleshy, heavy, heavyset, stocky, stout, thick, thickset, weighty; brawny, burly, husky; pudgy, roly-poly, squat, stubby; flabby, soft; full, hippy, round

antonyms chubby, corpulent, fat, obese, overweight, plump, portly, rotund, tubby

2 being of less than usual width ⟨the *thin* threads of a cobweb⟩ — see NARROW 1

3 not containing very much of some important element

⟨The evidence for that oddball theory is pretty *thin*.⟩ — see WEAK 3

thin *vb* to alter (something) for the worse with the addition of foreign or lower-grade substances ⟨*thinned* the cream with milk but didn't tell anyone⟩ — see ADULTERATE

thing *n* **1** a member of the human race ⟨You poor *thing*, you must be exhausted!⟩ — see HUMAN

2 one that has a real and independent existence ⟨the *thing* to which the subject of the sentence refers⟩ — see ENTITY

3 something done by someone ⟨One of the *things* you can do is to help me clean up.⟩ — see ACTION 1

4 something material that can be perceived by the senses ⟨Can you hand me that *thing* over there?⟩ — see OBJECT 1

5 something produced by physical or intellectual effort ⟨just the latest *thing* from her fertile imagination⟩ — see PRODUCT 1

6 something that happens ⟨The accident was just one of those *things* that can happen anywhere.⟩ — see EVENT 1

7 something that one hopes or intends to accomplish ⟨The important *thing* is that we get the project back on schedule.⟩ — see GOAL

8 something to be dealt with ⟨I have lots of *things* to do this afternoon.⟩ — see MATTER 2

9 things *pl* transportable items that one owns ⟨Gather your *things* and get out!⟩ — see POSSESSION 2

10 something for which a person shows a special talent ⟨Math just isn't my *thing*.⟩ — see FORTE

think *vb* to have as an opinion ⟨I *think* we should wait for someone to come help us out.⟩ — see BELIEVE 2

think (about *or* **over)** *vb* to give serious and careful thought to ⟨I'll have to *think over* everything you've said before deciding what to do.⟩ — see PONDER

think (of) *vb* to bring back to mind ⟨That postcard from Florida makes me *think of* all the fun we used to have there as kids.⟩ — see REMEMBER

think (up) *vb* to create or think of by clever use of the imagination ⟨The marketing department is trying to *think up* better ways to pitch our product to younger consumers.⟩ — see INVENT

thinker *n* **1** a very smart person ⟨She's a very nice person and she's a great *thinker*.⟩ — see GENIUS 1

2 the part of a person that feels, thinks, perceives, wills, and especially reasons ⟨Granny loves crossword puzzles, bridge, and other pastimes that makes her use the old *thinker*.⟩ — see MIND 1

thinking *adj* having the ability to reason ⟨It's surprising to find *thinking* people who believe such nonsense.⟩ — see RATIONAL 1

thinned *adj* **1** containing foreign or lower-grade substances ⟨genuine maple syrup *thinned* with corn syrup⟩ — see IMPURE 1

2 not containing very much of some important element ⟨The *thinned* iced tea that the restaurant serves is barely distinguishable from water.⟩ — see WEAK 3

thirst *n* **1** a strong wish for something ⟨His *thirst* for knowledge is evident in his book-filled house.⟩ — see DESIRE 1

2 urgent desire or interest ⟨an unquenchable *thirst* for travel that has led her to the far corners of the globe⟩ — see EAGERNESS

thirst (for) *vb* to have an earnest wish to own or enjoy ⟨She has always *thirsted for* a more affluent lifestyle than her salary would allow.⟩ — see DESIRE 1

thirsty *adj* **1** marked by little or no precipitation or humidity ⟨struggling to survive in that hot and *thirsty* climate⟩ — see DRY 1

2 showing urgent desire or interest ⟨young athletes *thirsty* for a chance to prove themselves⟩ — see EAGER

3 able to soak up liquids especially readily ⟨Guest bathrooms are furnished with luxuriously thick, *thirsty* towels.⟩ — see ABSORBENT

this *adj* being the less far of two ⟨Some of the best restaurants are on *this* side of town.⟩ — see NEAR 1

thistly *adj* having leaves or branches which are likely to cause a scratch ⟨caught her sleeve on a *thistly* bush⟩ — see SCRATCHY 1

thorn *n* something that is a source of irritation ⟨Your constant questions are a *thorn* in my side.⟩ — see ANNOYANCE 3

thorny *adj* **1** having leaves or branches which are likely to cause a scratch ⟨Stay out of the *thorny* brambles unless you want a ton of scratches.⟩ — see SCRATCHY 1
2 requiring exceptional skill or caution in performance or handling ⟨The candidate tried to avoid discussing his views on *thorny* issues.⟩ — see TRICKY 1

thorough *adj* **1** having no exceptions or restrictions ⟨had *thorough* access to the files for her research⟩ — see ABSOLUTE 2
2 including many small descriptive features ⟨*thorough* analysis of the data⟩ — see DETAILED 1
3 trying all possibilities ⟨a *thorough* search of the office that turned up no evidence of wrongdoing⟩ — see EXHAUSTIVE 1
4 covering everything or all important points ⟨a very *thorough* textbook on respiratory disorders⟩ — see ENCYCLOPEDIC

thoroughbred *adj* of unmixed ancestry ⟨a *thoroughbred* dog⟩ — see PUREBRED

thoroughfare *n* a passage cleared for public vehicular travel ⟨one of the city's main *thoroughfares*⟩ — see WAY 1

thoroughgoing *adj* **1** having no exceptions or restrictions ⟨Civil rights advocates are hoping for a *thoroughgoing* rejection of the proposed bill.⟩ — see ABSOLUTE 2
2 trying all possibilities ⟨a *thoroughgoing* attempt to solve the puzzle and still no luck⟩ — see EXHAUSTIVE 1

thoroughly *adv* **1** with attention to all aspects or details ⟨They searched the grounds *thoroughly* for any sign of the intruder.⟩
synonyms completely, comprehensively, exhaustively, fully, minutely, roundly, totally
related words meticulously, microscopically; all-out, full blast, intensively; broadly, encyclopedically, extensively, generally, globally, widely; conclusively, definitely, perfectly
phrases at length, from stem to stern, from the ground up, in detail
near antonyms aimlessly, desultorily, haphazardly, hit-or-miss, randomly; cursorily, imperfectly, inadequately, shallowly, summarily, superficially; indeterminately, nebulously, vaguely
2 to a full extent or degree ⟨I am *thoroughly* satisfied with her explanation of the events of that evening.⟩ — see FULLY 1

though *adv* in spite of that ⟨I know we didn't win. I was happy with how we played, *though*.⟩ — see HOWEVER

though *conj* in spite of the fact that ⟨*Though* it has no well-known actors in it, the movie has become the sleeper hit of the summer.⟩ — see ALTHOUGH

thought *n* **1** a careful weighing of the reasons for or against something ⟨I'll give your request some *thought* and then let you know what my decision is.⟩ — see CONSIDERATION 1
2 something imagined or pictured in the mind ⟨I just had a *thought*: what if we both pitched in and bought him one big present instead of two smaller presents for his birthday?⟩ — see IDEA 1

thoughtful *adj* **1** given to or made with heedful anticipation of the needs and happiness of others ⟨a *thoughtful* offer to watch the neighbors' children on moving day⟩ ⟨a *thoughtful* manager who understands that people's families should be more important than their jobs⟩
synonyms attentive, considerate, kind, solicitous
related words brotherly, good, good-hearted, helpful, hospitable, kindhearted, kindly, neighborly, nice; caring, compassionate, sympathetic, tender; chivalrous, courteous, courtly, gallant, gracious, polite; diplomatic, tactful; deferential, dutiful, obliging, regardful, respectful; altruistic, beneficent, benevolent, benignant, humane, selfless, unselfish; charitable, generous, magnanimous
near antonyms inattentive, uncaring, unheeding; inhospitable, unkind, unkindly; ill-bred, ill-mannered, impolite, rude, uncivil, unmannerly; unhelpful; malevolent, malicious, mean, spiteful
antonyms heedless, inconsiderate, thoughtless, unthinking
2 decided on as a result of careful thought ⟨a *thoughtful* argument for military action⟩ — see DELIBERATE 1
3 given to or marked by long, quiet thinking ⟨Ben was a quiet and *thoughtful* child who rarely spoke but when he did, he almost always had something worthwhile to say.⟩ — see CONTEMPLATIVE

thoughtfully *adv* with good reason or courtesy ⟨a restaurant that *thoughtfully* provides the diners with a basket of bread while they await their meals⟩ — see WELL 4

thoughtless *adj* showing a lack of manners or consideration for others ⟨always making *thoughtless* comments that hurt other people's feelings⟩ — see IMPOLITE

thought–out *adj* decided on as a result of careful thought ⟨a well *thought-out* presentation on alternative energy sources⟩ — see DELIBERATE 1

thrall *n* the state of being enslaved ⟨a people who still bear the scars of having been in *thrall* for so many years⟩ — see SLAVERY

thralldom *or* **thraldom** *n* the state of being enslaved ⟨Newly emancipated from *thralldom*, the people rejoiced.⟩ — see SLAVERY

thrash *vb* **1** to defeat by a large margin ⟨The incumbent has been *thrashing* his opponents for so long that there's never any real contest for the Senate seat.⟩ — see WHIP 2
2 to strike repeatedly with something long and thin or flexible ⟨*thrashed* the poor horse with a riding crop⟩ — see WHIP 1
3 to strike repeatedly ⟨The tree branches *thrashed* the sides of the house as the storm continued to rage.⟩ — see BEAT 1
4 to make jerky or restless movements ⟨In obvious pain, the wounded soldier *thrashed* about his cot.⟩ — see FIDGET

thread *n* **1** a thin, flexible structure that resembles a hair ⟨The unwary bug was snared in the sticky *threads* of the spider's web.⟩ — see HAIR 2
2 threads *pl* covering for the human body ⟨A number of people at the prom complimented me on my "nice *threads*."⟩ — see CLOTHING

thread *vb* **1** to scatter or set here and there among other things ⟨This history book *threads* excerpts from the diaries of pioneer women into its account of the settlement of the West.⟩
synonyms interlace, intersperse, interweave, lace, salt, weave, wreathe
related words insert, intermingle, mingle, mix; alternate, juxtapose; amalgamate, assimilate, blend, combine, commingle, embody, fuse, incorporate, integrate, merge
2 to put together into a series by means of or as if by means of a thread ⟨The reporter *threaded* his newspaper articles about the basketball team into a book that was essentially a chronicle of their championship season.⟩
synonyms concatenate, string

related words chain, connect, join, link, unite; interlace, intersperse, intertwine, interweave, lace, weave, wreathe

threadbare *adj* **1** showing signs of advanced wear and tear and neglect ⟨We bought a *threadbare* couch at a garage sale.⟩ — see SHABBY 1

2 used or heard so often as to be dull ⟨a novel filled with nothing but *threadbare* clichés⟩ — see STALE 1

3 worn or torn into or as if into rags ⟨I loved that *threadbare* shirt, but after 10 years of wear, it was time to throw it away.⟩ — see RAGGED 2

threat *n* something that may cause injury or harm ⟨He perceived the question as a *threat* to his authority.⟩ — see DANGER 2

threaten *vb* to remain poised to inflict harm, danger, or distress on ⟨The powerful hurricane continues to *threaten* the southern coastline.⟩

synonyms hang (over), hover (over), impend (over), menace, overhang

related words endanger, hazard, imperil, jeopardize, peril

threatening *adj* **1** giving signs of immediate occurrence ⟨economists warning of a *threatening* recession⟩ — see IMMINENT 1

2 being or showing a sign of evil or calamity to come ⟨A *threatening* silence followed the loud thump in the adjoining motel room.⟩ — see OMINOUS

3 involving potential loss or injury ⟨*Threatening* rocks lined that narrow stretch of the river through which we would be rafting.⟩ — see DANGEROUS 1

threefold *adj* having three units or parts ⟨a *threefold* approach to solving the problem⟩ — see TRIPLE

three–ring circus *n* a place of uproar or confusion ⟨The house has been a *three-ring circus* ever since the kids got back from summer camp.⟩ — see MADHOUSE

threesome *n* a group of three ⟨The *threesome* has been playing music together since all three were in high school.⟩

synonyms triad, trinity, trio, triple, triplet, triumvirate

related words trilogy, triptych; triple crown; triplicate; triplex

threshold *n* **1** an interval of time just before the onset of something ⟨on the *threshold* of a new age of green technology⟩ — see POINT 3

2 the point at which something begins ⟨At the *threshold* of the new year, it's time to look back and make resolutions for the future.⟩ — see BEGINNING

thrift *n* careful management of material resources ⟨Through hard work and *thrift* our father was able to raise the money to put all four of us through college.⟩ — see ECONOMY

thriftless *adj* given to spending money freely or foolishly ⟨a *thriftless* couple who didn't keep track of their finances and overspent constantly⟩ — see PRODIGAL

thrifty *adj* careful in the management of money or resources ⟨If you are *thrifty*, you can find ways to decorate your room stylishly yet inexpensively.⟩ — see FRUGAL

thrill *n* a pleasurably intense stimulation of the feelings ⟨Everyone gets a real *thrill* out of the Independence Day fireworks.⟩

synonyms bang, charge, exhilaration, kick, titillation, wallop

related words jolt, shock, surprise (*also* surprize); delectation, delight, enjoyment, joy, lift, pleasure; amusement, diversion, entertainment, fun, treat

thrill *vb* to cause a pleasurable stimulation of the feelings of ⟨I was *thrilled* to hear that you got the promotion that you'd been so desperately wanting.⟩

synonyms charge, electrify, excite, exhilarate, galvanize, intoxicate, titillate, turn on

related words arouse, incite, inspire, provoke, stimulate;

bewitch, captivate, charm, delight, enchant, enthrall (*or* enthral), hypnotize, mesmerize, rivet, spellbind; interest, intrigue, tantalize

near antonyms bore, jade, pall, tire, weary; demoralize, discourage, dishearten, dispirit

thrilling *adj* causing great emotional or mental stimulation ⟨a *thrilling* adventure movie⟩ — see EXCITING 1

thrive *vb* **1** to grow vigorously ⟨These plants *thrive* with relatively little sunlight.⟩

synonyms burgeon (*also* bourgeon), flourish, prosper

related words luxuriate, overgrow, proliferate, shoot up; germinate, root; bloom, flower, fruit, produce, propagate, regenerate, seed

2 to reach a desired level of accomplishment ⟨Going to a school for gifted students will help him *thrive* as a musical prodigy.⟩ — see SUCCEED 2

thriving *adj* **1** having attained a desired end or state of good fortune ⟨Our new landscaping business is *thriving*.⟩ — see SUCCESSFUL 1

2 marked by much life, movement, or activity ⟨The once *thriving* bookstore fell into steep decline.⟩ — see ALIVE 2

3 marked by vigorous growth and well-being especially economically ⟨a *thriving* manufacturing community that is experiencing a tremendous growth in new jobs⟩ — see PROSPEROUS 1

throaty *adj* **1** harsh and dry in sound ⟨had a bad cold and a *throaty* cough to go with it⟩ — see HOARSE

2 having a low musical pitch or range ⟨a *throaty* alto⟩ — see DEEP 2

throb *n* a rhythmic expanding and contracting ⟨I could feel each *throb* of my heart.⟩ — see PULSATION

throb *vb* to expand and contract in a rhythmic manner ⟨the car's stereo speakers *throbbing* with the song's bass line⟩ — see PULSATE

throe *n* **1** a sharp unpleasant sensation usually felt in some specific part of the body ⟨collapsed in the *throes* of agony⟩ — see PAIN 1

2 throes *pl* a forceful effort to reach a goal or objective ⟨That country is caught up in the *throes* of a democratic revolution.⟩ — see STRUGGLE 1

throng *n* a great number of persons or creatures massed together ⟨grabbed a megaphone and addressed the vast *throng*⟩ — see CROWD 1

throng *vb* to move upon or fill (something) in great numbers ⟨Fans *thronged* the field to celebrate the win.⟩ — see CROWD 2

thronging *adj* possessing or covered with great numbers or amounts of something specified ⟨The theme park is *thronging* with tourists during the summer.⟩ — see RIFE

throttle *vb* to keep (someone) from breathing by exerting pressure on the windpipe ⟨felt as if the scarf was *throttling* her⟩ — see CHOKE 1

through *adj* brought or having come to an end ⟨a standing ovation for the cast when the play was *through*⟩ — see COMPLETE 2

through *adv* **1** from beginning to end ⟨I read the letter *through* twice.⟩ ⟨never once missed class the whole year *through*⟩

synonyms around, over, round, throughout

2 from one side to the other of an intervening space ⟨The rock struck the window and went right *through*.⟩ — see OVER 1

through *prep* **1** in or into the middle of ⟨tried to make their way *through* the crowd⟩ — see AMONG

2 in random positions within the boundaries of ⟨the numerous small towns scattered *through* these hills⟩ — see AROUND 2

3 in the course of ⟨thoughtless people talking *through* the whole movie⟩ — see DURING

4 to the opposite side of ⟨walked *through* the room⟩ — see ACROSS 1

5 along the way of ⟨The quickest way out of the building is *through* that hall there.⟩ — see BY 1

6 as the result of ⟨won the tournament *through* practice and hard work⟩ — see BECAUSE OF

7 using the means or agency of ⟨apparently got his money *through* hard work and smart decisions⟩ — see BY 2

throughout *adv* **1** from beginning to end ⟨While some fans deserted the singer during her troubled years, others remained loyal *throughout*.⟩ — see THROUGH 1

2 in every place or in all places ⟨a cake studded *throughout* with raisins⟩ — see EVERYWHERE

throughout *prep* **1** in random positions within the boundaries of ⟨We saw red-tailed hawks *throughout* the game preserve.⟩ — see AROUND 2

2 in the course of ⟨It rained *throughout* the day.⟩ — see DURING

throw *n* a risky undertaking ⟨a desperate *throw*, that could jump-start his presidential campaign or end it right there⟩ — see GAMBLE

throw *vb* **1** to send through the air especially with a quick forward motion of the arm ⟨She *threw* a life preserver to the drowning man.⟩
   synonyms cast, catapult, chuck, dash, fire, fling, heave, hurl, hurtle, launch, lob, loft, peg, pelt, pitch, sling, toss
   related words bowl, dart, flip, gun, hook, pass, roll, shoot; buck, eject, impel, precipitate, project, propel, rifle, thrust
   phrases let fly

2 to cause to fall intentionally or unintentionally ⟨The quarterback *threw* his helmet to the ground.⟩ — see DROP 1

throw (on) *vb* to place on one's person ⟨*threw on* a sweater and headed outside⟩ — see PUT ON 1

throw away *vb* **1** to get rid of as useless or unwanted ⟨I should *throw away* that torn shirt.⟩ — see DISCARD

2 to use up carelessly ⟨If you buy a high-end computer, you'll just be *throwing away* money on a bunch of features you'll never use.⟩ — see WASTE 1

throwing away *n* the getting rid of whatever is unwanted or useless ⟨The *throwing away* of her old stuffed animals marked the beginning of her mental preparation for an independent life as a college student.⟩ — see DISPOSAL 1

throw out *vb* **1** to drive or force out ⟨The player was *thrown out* of the game after arguing with the ref.⟩ — see EJECT 1

2 to get rid of as useless or unwanted ⟨Would you mind if I *threw out* that leftover pizza that's been in the fridge for two weeks?⟩ — see DISCARD

3 to throw or give off ⟨The charcoal grill is *throwing out* big billows of black smoke.⟩ — see EMIT 1

4 to show unwillingness to accept, do, engage in, or agree to ⟨He'll *throw out* any acting offers that don't meet his standards.⟩ — see DECLINE 1

throw up *vb* to discharge the contents of the stomach through the mouth ⟨She must have eaten something that didn't agree with her because she *threw up* right after dinner.⟩ — see VOMIT

thrum *n* a monotonous sound like that of an insect in motion ⟨the steady *thrum* of the turbines in the power plant⟩ — see HUM

thrust *vb* **1** to apply force to (someone or something) so that it moves in front of one ⟨The cat *thrust* her paw under the couch, trying to reach her toy mouse.⟩ — see PUSH 1

2 to move or extend upward ⟨The butte *thrusts* up 300 feet from the floor of the valley.⟩ — see ASCEND

thud *n* a hard strike with a part of the body or an instru-

ment ⟨The *thud* of his head against the cabinet door brought tears to his eyes.⟩ — see ¹BLOW

thud *vb* to come into usually forceful contact with something ⟨The snowball *thudded* against the side of my car.⟩ — see HIT 2

thumb *vb* **1** to travel by securing free rides ⟨He *thumbed* his way to New York in the 1960s.⟩ — see HITCHHIKE

2 to turn over pages in an idle or cursory manner ⟨I *thumbed* through the book during the flight but was too distracted to really read it.⟩ — see SKIM 1

thump *n* a hard strike with a part of the body or an instrument ⟨She was punished when she gave her brother a *thump* on the head.⟩ — see ¹BLOW

thump *vb* **1** to deliver a blow to (someone or something) usually in a strong vigorous manner ⟨*thumped* the desk with his hand as he delivered his speech⟩ — see HIT 1

2 to strike repeatedly ⟨playfully knocked his younger brother down and began to *thump* him with a foam bat⟩ — see BEAT 1

thunder *vb* **1** to make a long loud deep noise or cry ⟨As we got closer, the waterfall *thundered* louder and louder.⟩ — see ROAR 1

2 to speak so as to be heard at a distance ⟨a hotheaded man who was always *thundering* about the incompetents running the government⟩ — see CALL 1

thunderclap *n* a loud explosive sound ⟨awakened by the *thunderclap* of a large branch falling on the roof⟩ — see CLAP 1

thunderous *adj* marked by a high volume of sound ⟨The last *thunderous* chord of the symphony rang throughout the hall.⟩ — see LOUD 1

thunderstruck *adj* affected with sudden and great wonder or surprise ⟨She was *thunderstruck* to learn that she had been adopted.⟩
   synonyms amazed, astonished, astounded, awestruck (*also* awestricken), bowled over, dumbfounded (*also* dumfounded), flabbergasted, shocked, stunned, stupefied
   related words blindsided, startled, surprised (*also* surprized); aghast, appalled, dismayed, horrified; bewildered, confused, dazed, overwhelmed; agape, awed, awesome, openmouthed, wide-eyed, widemouthed
   near antonyms blasé (*also* blase), casual, nonchalant, unruffled

thus *adv* for this or that reason ⟨We didn't have room for all seven of us in my car and *thus* took two cars to go to the movies.⟩ — see THEREFORE

thwack *n* **1** a hard strike with a part of the body or an instrument ⟨He gave the ball a hard *thwack* with the bat and sent it deep into the outfield.⟩ — see ¹BLOW

2 a loud explosive sound ⟨Even from the top of the bleachers we could hear the loud *thwack* of the ball being hit.⟩ — see CLAP 1

thwack *vb* to deliver a blow to (someone or something) usually in a strong vigorous manner ⟨*thwacked* the growling dog on the nose with a rolled-up newspaper⟩ — see HIT 1

thwart *vb* to prevent from achieving a goal ⟨A coalition of grassroots organizations *thwarted* the company's efforts to get approval for a new power plant.⟩ — see FRUSTRATE 1

tic *n* an odd or peculiar habit ⟨Constantly playing with her hair is one of her more annoying *tics*.⟩ — see IDIOSYNCRASY

tick (off) *vb* to specify one after another ⟨*ticked off* everything she would need to buy while her daughter wrote the items down on a list⟩ — see ENUMERATE 1

ticket *n* **1** a small sheet of plastic, paper, or paperboard showing that the bearer has a claim to something (as admittance) ⟨Only people with *tickets* will be allowed past the front gates.⟩

synonyms check, coupon, pass

related words certificate, note, token

2 a slip (as of paper or cloth) that is attached to something to identify or describe it ⟨The price on the *ticket* is $20 more than the advertised price.⟩ — see LABEL

3 the means or right of entering or participating in ⟨believed that a college diploma was a *ticket* to a better life⟩ — see ENTRANCE 1

4 something that allows someone to achieve a desired goal ⟨That entry-level job could be her *ticket* to a career in big-time advertising.⟩ — see PASSPORT 1

ticket *vb* to attach an identifying slip to ⟨The attendant quickly *ticketed* my coat and handed the claim stub back to me.⟩ — see LABEL 1

tickled *adj* experiencing pleasure, satisfaction, or delight ⟨I'm *tickled* that you like the present so much!⟩ — see GLAD 1

ticklish *adj* **1** easily offended ⟨He's *ticklish* about his new haircut, so it's wisest to avoid the subject altogether.⟩ — see TOUCHY 1

2 requiring exceptional skill or caution in performance or handling ⟨Trying to tell him that his zipper is down without embarrassing him will be a *ticklish* task.⟩ — see TRICKY 1

tidbit *also* **titbit** *n* **1** something that is pleasing to eat because it is rare or a luxury ⟨He gave her an expensive box of chocolate *tidbits*.⟩ — see DELICACY 1

2 a small piece or quantity of food ⟨I'll just have a *tidbit* of the dessert, nothing too big.⟩ — see MORSEL 1

tide *n* a prevailing or general movement or inclination ⟨The *tide* of the battle turned suddenly, and the would-be invaders were forced to retreat.⟩ — see TREND 1

tidied *adj* being clean and in good order ⟨a teenager who keeps a nicely-*tidied* room⟩ — see NEAT 1

tidings *pl n* a report of recent events or facts not previously known ⟨Any *tidings* from the front, soldier?⟩ — see NEWS

tidy *adj* **1** being clean and in good order ⟨could easily find everything on her *tidy* desk⟩ — see NEAT 1

2 of a size greater than average of its kind ⟨They paid a *tidy* sum for a painting that may not even be a genuine Titian.⟩ — see LARGE

3 sufficiently large in size, amount, or number to merit attention ⟨signed a three-year contract for a *tidy* amount⟩ — see CONSIDERABLE 1

tie *n* **1** a situation in which neither participant in a contest, competition, or struggle comes out ahead of the other ⟨The competition for first place in the dessert division ended in a *tie* between the chocolate pecan pie and the walnut fudge tart.⟩

synonyms dead heat, draw, stalemate, standoff

related words deadlock, impasse; seesaw; photo finish; toss-up

2 a uniting or binding force or influence ⟨Their marriage will serve to form a very strong *tie* between our families.⟩ — see BOND 2

tie *vb* **1** to gather into a tight mass by means of a line or cord ⟨*tied* the newspapers into a bundle⟩

synonyms band, bind, truss

related words cinch, cord, rope, strap, thread, wire; gird, girt; lash, leash, tether; interlace, intertwine, interweave, lace; entangle, knot, snarl, tangle, twist; coil, wind

near antonyms undo, unfasten, unlace, unlash, unloose, unloosen, unstrap, unstring, unthread; unleash, untether; disentangle, unravel, unsnarl, untangle, untwine, untwist; uncoil, unspool, unwind

antonyms unbind, untie

2 to produce something equal to (as in quality or value) ⟨At the class reunion we learned that he had won the Nobel Prize in medicine—how could the rest of us *tie* that?⟩ — see EQUAL 1

tie–up *n* **1** a crowded mass (as of cars) that impedes or blocks movement ⟨A *tie-up* at the junction of Main and Central has slowed traffic to a crawl.⟩ — see JAM 1

2 the state of having shared interests or efforts (as in social or business matters) ⟨In a *tie-up* with the film studio, the toy company is producing a whole line of figures featuring characters from the animated movie.⟩ — see ASSOCIATION 1

tie up *vb* to create difficulty for the work or activity of ⟨An accident is *tying up* traffic at 5th and Broadway.⟩ — see HAMPER

tiff *n* an often noisy or angry expression of differing opinions ⟨They got into a little *tiff* about what color sheets to buy for their bed.⟩ — see ARGUMENT 1

tiff *vb* to express different opinions about something often angrily ⟨Like any couple, they occasionally *tiff*, but it's never anything serious.⟩ — see ARGUE 2

tight *adj* **1** not allowing penetration (as by gas, liquid, or light) ⟨The lid forms a *tight* seal with the canister that will keep the spices fresh.⟩

synonyms impenetrable, impermeable, impervious

related words close, compact, dense, snug, thick; airtight, hermetic (*also* hermetical), watertight; lightproof, soundproof, waterproof

near antonyms absorbent, leaky, porous, unsealed

antonyms penetrable, permeable

2 firmly positioned in place and difficult to dislodge ⟨a *tight* screw that won't come loose⟩ ⟨a jar with a *tight* lid⟩

synonyms fast, firm, frozen, jammed, lodged, set, snug, stuck, wedged

related words bonded, cemented, glued; anchored, clamped; embedded (*also* imbedded), entrenched (*also* intrenched), impacted, implanted; attached, bound, fastened, secured; immovable, unyielding

near antonyms detached, dislodged, freed, loosened, unattached, unbound, undone, unfastened, unsecured; movable (*or* moveable), yielding

antonyms insecure, loose

3 giving or sharing as little as possible ⟨Bob is fairly *tight* with his money.⟩ — see STINGY 1

4 having little space between items or parts ⟨The traffic on the freeway was so *tight* we couldn't get over to the exit we wanted.⟩ — see CLOSE 1

5 showing little difference in the standing of the competitors ⟨a *tight* race for governor⟩ — see CLOSE 3

6 stretched with little or no give ⟨The rope was pulled *tight*.⟩ — see TAUT

7 closely acquainted ⟨Supposedly he and the rock star have been totally *tight* since they went to high school together.⟩ — see FAMILIAR 1

tightfisted *adj* giving or sharing as little as possible ⟨The company is pretty *tightfisted* when it comes to bonuses.⟩ — see STINGY 1

tight–lipped *adj* tending not to speak frequently (as by habit or inclination) ⟨The cabinet official is usually *tight-lipped* about her private life.⟩ — see SILENT 2

tightness *n* the quality or practice of being overly sparing with money ⟨A man of legendary *tightness*, he has plenty of money in his savings account.⟩ — see PARSIMONY 1

tightwad *n* a mean grasping person who is usually stingy with money ⟨You're always such a *tightwad* when charity comes calling.⟩ — see MISER

till *vb* to work by plowing, sowing, and raising crops on ⟨farmers *tilling* the soil from sunup to sunset⟩ — see FARM

tiller *n* a person who cultivates the land and grows crops on it ⟨In his paintings farmers are invariably depicted as brawny yet noble *tillers* of the land.⟩ — see FARMER

tilt *n* the act of positioning or an instance of being positioned at an angle ⟨Kate indicated her approval with a slight *tilt* of her head.⟩

   synonyms angling, bend, cock, inclination, list, tip

   related words turn, twist, veer; bow, dip, nod

tilt *vb* to set or cause to be at an angle ⟨The robin *tilts* its head as it hunts for worms in the grass.⟩ — see LEAN 1

tilted *adj* **1** inclined or twisted to one side ⟨stared at me with a *tilted* head and a quizzical look⟩ — see AWRY

   2 running in a slanting direction ⟨The floors of the old house were *tilted* slightly.⟩ — see DIAGONAL

tilting *adj* running in a slanting direction ⟨a rickety, *tilting* staircase that did not look safe⟩ — see DIAGONAL

timber *n* **1** a dense growth of trees and shrubs covering a large area ⟨Upon our approach the deer disappeared back into the *timber* from whence it had come.⟩ — see FOREST

   2 tree logs as prepared for human use ⟨needed a new load of *timber* to finish building the house⟩ — see WOOD 1

timberland *n* a dense growth of trees and shrubs covering a large area ⟨The wildfire burned through a large swath of *timberland*.⟩ — see FOREST

time *n* **1** a particular point at which an event takes place ⟨Remember that one *time* you tried to wash the dog in the sink?⟩ — see OCCASION 1

   2 an exciting or noteworthy event that one experiences firsthand ⟨enjoys telling us about the *times* he had while he was in the army⟩ — see ADVENTURE 1

   3 an extent of time associated with a particular person or thing ⟨Back in my parents' *time*, families usually had only one car.⟩ — see AGE 1

   4 the period during which something exists, lasts, or is in progress ⟨How much *time* will the project take?⟩ — see DURATION 1

timeless *adj* having an existence or validity that does not change or diminish ⟨views the church's message and mission as *timeless*⟩ — see ABIDING

timeliness *n* the quality or habit of arriving or being ready on time ⟨Your *timeliness* will make a good impression on the person interviewing you for the job.⟩ — see PROMPTITUDE

timely *adj* **1** especially suitable for a certain time ⟨a *timely* invitation to lunch that came just as I was starting to feel hungry⟩

   synonyms opportune, seasonable

   related words appropriate, apt, fit, fitting, meet, pat, proper, suitable; pertinent, relative, relevant; fortunate, lucky, propitious; anticipated, expected; prompt, punctual

   near antonyms improper, inappropriate, irrelative, irrelevant, unfit, unseemly, unsuitable; unfortunate, unlucky; behind, behindhand, belated, delayed, delinquent, late, latish, overdue, postponed, slow, tardy; anticipatory, early, precocious, premature; abrupt, sudden, unanticipated, unexpected

   antonyms inopportune, unseasonable, untimely

   2 done, carried out, or given without delay ⟨When I order a pizza, I expect it to be delivered in a *timely* manner.⟩ — see PROMPT 1

timepiece *n* a device to measure time ⟨The only *timepiece* she used at the cabin was a garden sundial.⟩

   synonyms chronometer, clock, timer

   related words alarm clock, atomic clock, cuckoo clock, grandfather clock, time clock; hourglass, sandglass, sundial, water clock; chronograph, stopwatch, watch

timer *n* a device to measure time ⟨Set the kitchen *timer* to 30 minutes.⟩ — see TIMEPIECE

timetable *n* a listing of things to be presented or considered (as at a concert or play) ⟨I checked the *timetable* of events to see if I'd be able to get something to eat beforehand.⟩ — see PROGRAM 1

timid *adj* easily frightened ⟨A *timid* rabbit hopped cautiously out of the hedge.⟩ — see SHY 1

timidity *n* lack of willingness to assert oneself and take risks ⟨None of the scouts showed the least *timidity* about rappeling down the cliff.⟩

   synonyms faintheartedness, timidness, timorousness

   related words bashfulness, constraint, embarrassment, inhibition, restraint, shyness, skittishness; hesitation, indecision, indecisiveness, irresoluteness, irresolution; cowardice, cowardliness, cravenness, spinelessness

   near antonyms assurance, confidence, self-assertiveness, self-assurance, self-confidence; composure, coolness, insouciance, nonchalance, unconcern; backbone, decisiveness, determination, firmness, fortitude, grit, mettle, resoluteness, resolution, spunk; bravery, courage, courageousness, daring, dauntlessness, doughtiness, fearlessness, intrepidity, intrepidness, valor; brazenness, effrontery, gall, temerity

   antonyms audacity, boldness, nerve

timidness *n* lack of willingness to assert oneself and take risks ⟨Such *timidness* is surprising in a man as physically imposing as he is.⟩ — see TIMIDITY

timorous *adj* easily frightened ⟨sensational news stories that seem designed to needlessly alarm an already *timorous* public⟩ — see SHY 1

timorousness *n* lack of willingness to assert oneself and take risks ⟨the *timorousness* with which so many politicians approach hot-button issues⟩ — see TIMIDITY

tin *n* a metal container in the shape of a cylinder ⟨row upon row of *tins* containing food for an emergency that never happened⟩ — see CAN 1

tincture *n* a property that becomes apparent when light falls on an object and by which things that are identical in form can be distinguished ⟨a ragged shirt that seemed to be stained with the *tincture* of grass⟩ — see COLOR 1

tincture *vb* to give color or a different color to ⟨clouds *tinctured* by the rays of the setting sun⟩ — see COLOR 1

tinge *n* a property that becomes apparent when light falls on an object and by which things that are identical in form can be distinguished ⟨There's a bluish *tinge* to your lips—you must be freezing!⟩ — see COLOR 1

tinge *vb* to give color or a different color to ⟨Just slightly *tinge* the frosting with yellow food coloring to give it a lemony look.⟩ — see COLOR 1

tingle *n* a sharp unpleasant sensation usually felt in some specific part of the body ⟨can't stand those funny *tingles* I get when my foot falls asleep⟩ — see PAIN 1

tingle *vb* to make a repeated sharp light ringing sound ⟨I awoke to the steady pitter-patter of raindrops *tingling* on the rooftop.⟩ — see JINGLE

tinker (with) *vb* to handle thoughtlessly, ignorantly, or mischievously ⟨The camera hasn't worked properly ever since our son *tinkered with* it.⟩ — see TAMPER (WITH)

tinkle *n* a series of short high ringing sounds ⟨the soothing *tinkle* of the wind chime on the back porch⟩

   synonyms chime(s), jingle, tintinnabulation

   related words clatter, rattle; chink, clang, clank, clink, ding-dong, ping, ring; chirr, ripple, trill, warble

tinkle *vb* to make a repeated sharp light ringing sound ⟨The bell around the cat's neck *tinkled* as he ran across the yard.⟩ — see JINGLE

tint *n* a property that becomes apparent when light falls on an object and by which things that are identical in form can be distinguished ⟨Her eyes have a greenish *tint*.⟩ — see COLOR 1

tint *vb* to give color or a different color to ⟨If you *tint* that blue paint with this yellow paint, you should get a nice shade of green.⟩ — see COLOR 1

tintinnabulation *n* a series of short high ringing sounds ⟨the merry *tintinnabulation* of church bells⟩ — see TINKLE

tiny *adj* very small in size ⟨The forest ranger showed us how every square foot of forest is alive with *tiny* creatures.⟩

synonyms atomic, bitty, infinitesimal, microscopic (*also* microscopical), miniature, minuscule, minute, teeny, teeny-weeny, wee

related words baby, diminutive, dwarf, elfin, half-pint, little, micro, model, petite, pocket, pocket-size (*also* pocket-sized), pygmy, small, smallish; dinky, dwarfish, insignificant, pint-size (*or* pint-sized), puny, scrubby, undersized (*also* undersize)

near antonyms big, bulky, bumper, considerable, extensive, good, goodly, grand, great, gross, handsome, hefty, hulking, jumbo, king-size (*or* king-sized), large, largish, major, outsize (*also* outsized), overgrown, overscale (*or* overscaled), oversize (*or* oversized), sizable (*or* sizeable), substantial, super, whacking, whopping

antonyms astronomical (*also* astronomic), colossal, cosmic, elephantine, enormous, giant, gigantic, herculean, heroic, huge, immense, mammoth, massive, monster, monstrous, monumental, mountainous, prodigious, titanic, tremendous

¹tip *n* **1** a piece of advice or useful information especially from an expert ⟨I got some *tips* from a horticulturist on how to get my violets to bloom.⟩

synonyms hint, lead, pointer

related words advisement, assistance, counsel, guidance, recommendation, suggestion; caution, cautioning, sign, signal, telltale, tip-off, warning; brief, direction, feedback, instruction

2 information not generally available to the public ⟨Investigators are trying to determine whether the investor illegally received a *tip* that the company's stock was about to plunge.⟩ — see DOPE 1

²tip *n* **1** a small sum of money given for a service over and above what is due ⟨We gave our waiter an extra large *tip* for such fantastic service.⟩

synonyms gratuity, perquisite

related words donation, gift, lagniappe, largesse (*also* largess), present; bonus, favor, reward; contribution, offering

2 something given in addition to what is ordinarily expected or owed ⟨a customer who always gives his paper carrier a very generous *tip* at Christmastime⟩ — see BONUS

³tip *n* the act of positioning or an instance of being positioned at an angle ⟨She didn't say anything but just acknowledged our presence with a *tip* of her head.⟩ — see TILT

⁴tip *n* the last and usually sharp or tapering part of something long and narrow ⟨the *tip* of a knitting needle⟩ — see POINT 2

tip *vb* to set or cause to be at an angle ⟨Be careful because if you *tip* your cup any more, you'll spill your tea.⟩ — see LEAN 1

tip–off *n* something that tells of approaching danger or risk ⟨The retreat of the island's wildlife to higher ground was a *tip-off* that a tsunami was about to strike.⟩ — see WARNING 2

tipped *adj* tapering to a thin tip ⟨a round-*tipped* needle⟩ — see POINTED 1

tipping *adj* inclined or twisted to one side ⟨a boat *tipping* under the weight of a lopsided load⟩ — see AWRY

tip–top *adj* of the very best kind ⟨The doctor told me I was in *tip-top* shape.⟩ — see EXCELLENT

tip–top *n* the highest part or point ⟨This trail will take you to the fire tower at the *tip-top* of that hill.⟩ — see HEIGHT 1

tirade *n* a long angry speech or scolding ⟨After the inspection by the health department, we had to listen to the manager's *tirade* about keeping the restaurant's kitchen cleaner.⟩

synonyms diatribe, harangue, rant

related words assault, attack, broadside, invective, lambasting, lashing, tongue-lashing, vituperation; berating, chewing out, rebuke, reprimand, reproach, reproof; abuse, castigation, censure, condemnation, denunciation; excoriation, execration, revilement; admonishment, admonition, lecture, sermon

near antonyms encomium, eulogy, panegyric, rhapsody, tribute; acclaim, acclamation, accolade, citation, homage, honor, praise; approval, blessing, commendation, endorsement (*also* indorsement), sanction; ovation, plaudit, rave

tire *vb* **1** to diminish the physical strength of ⟨I don't want our walk to *tire* you too much.⟩ — see WEAKEN 1

2 to make weary and restless by being dull or monotonous ⟨This long dry lecture will *tire* the audience if you don't insert some jokes into it.⟩ — see ²BORE

3 to use up all the physical energy of ⟨This pentathlon will *tire* all but the hardiest athletes.⟩ — see EXHAUST 1

tired *adj* **1** depleted in strength, energy, or freshness ⟨I'm usually *tired* after a long day of working in the yard.⟩ — see WEARY 1

2 having one's patience, interest, or pleasure exhausted ⟨I'm sick and *tired* of your antics!⟩ — see WEARY 2

3 used or heard so often as to be dull ⟨Such *tired* phrases won't hold your reader's interest.⟩ — see STALE 1

tiredness *n* a complete depletion of energy or strength ⟨Your *tiredness* will go away after a good rest.⟩ — see FATIGUE

tireless *adj* showing no signs of weariness even after long hard effort ⟨a *tireless* advocate for human rights⟩

synonyms indefatigable, inexhaustible, unflagging, untiring, weariless

related words assiduous, conscientious, diligent, meticulous, painstaking, sedulous; determined, dogged, patient, persevering, persistent, pertinacious, plodding, relentless, steadfast, steady, stubborn, tenacious, unabated, unfailing, unfaltering, unflinching, unrelenting, unremitting, unwavering; industrious, intense, laborious, strenuous

near antonyms indolent, lackadaisical, laggard, lazy, listless, shiftless, slothful, sluggish; apathetic, casual, desultory, languid, spiritless; beat, broken, burned-out (*or* burnt-out), done in, drained, enervated, jaded, overtaxed, overworked, played out, sapped, spent, tuckered (out), wearied, worn-out

tiresome *adj* causing weariness, restlessness, or lack of interest ⟨What a *tiresome* meeting that turned out to be.⟩ — see BORING

tiring *adj* causing weariness, restlessness, or lack of interest ⟨The seminar was *tiring* and not particularly helpful or informative.⟩ — see BORING

titan *n* something that is unusually large and powerful ⟨This newest ocean liner is a true *titan* of the sea.⟩ — see GIANT

titanic *adj* unusually large ⟨The *titanic* new skyscraper dwarfs every other building around it.⟩ — see HUGE

titillate *vb* to cause a pleasurable stimulation of the feelings of ⟨Tabloids *titillate* their readers with details about the private lives of media-created celebrities.⟩ — see THRILL

titillation *n* a pleasurably intense stimulation of the feelings ⟨a cultural critic who argues that people have become too dependent upon the instant gratification and *titillation* that television and the Internet provide⟩ — see THRILL

title *n* **1** a word or combination of words by which a person or thing is regularly known ⟨About the only thing the book and the movie have in common are their *titles*.⟩ — see NAME 1

2 a word or series of words often in larger letters placed at the beginning of a passage or at the top of a page in order to introduce or categorize ⟨A humorous illustration appears above the *title* of every chapter in the book.⟩ — see HEADING

3 the position occupied by the one who comes in first in a competition ⟨won the singles *title* three years in a row⟩ — see CROWN 2

title *vb* to give a name to ⟨What do you plan on *titling* your latest album?⟩ — see NAME 1

titter *n* an explosive sound that is a sign of amusement ⟨A *titter* swept through the crowd at his verbal slip.⟩ — see LAUGH 1

titter *vb* to show mirth with an explosive vocal sound ⟨Even as students in the sex ed class continued to *titter*, the lecturer plowed ahead.⟩ — see LAUGH 1

tittle *n* **1** a very small piece ⟨We have examined every last *tittle* of evidence available and can find nothing to support his claims.⟩ — see BIT 1

2 the smallest amount or part imaginable ⟨There's not a *tittle* of sense in that book!⟩ — see JOT

titular *adj* being something in name or form only ⟨He's the *titular* head of the department, though it's the assistant managers who largely run things around here.⟩ — see NOMINAL 1

tizzy *n* a state of nervous or irritated concern ⟨all in a *tizzy* because she can't find her car keys⟩ — see FRET

to *prep* earlier than ⟨Right now it's 25 minutes *to* 10:00.⟩ — see BEFORE 1

toady *n* a person who flatters another in order to get ahead ⟨No one liked the office *toady*, who spent most of her time complimenting the boss on what a great job he was doing.⟩ — see SYCOPHANT

toady *vb* to use flattery or the doing of favors in order to win approval especially from a superior ⟨a satirical novel about an amoral go-getter who *toadies* his way to the top of the corporate ladder⟩ — see FAWN

toast *vb* to cause to have or give off heat to a moderate degree ⟨Come over and *toast* your toes by the fire!⟩ — see WARM 1

toasty *adj* having or giving off heat to a moderate degree ⟨I'm nice and *toasty* in front of the fire.⟩ — see WARM 1

tocsin *n* **1** an object intended to give public notice or warning ⟨The *tocsin* rang out, warning us of the approaching storm.⟩ — see SIGNAL 1

2 something that tells of approaching danger or risk ⟨noted that a sudden change in a cat's behavior may be a *tocsin* of a serious health issue⟩ — see WARNING 2

today *adv* at the present time ⟨*Today*, more than a million people live there.⟩ — see NOW 1

today *n* the time currently existing or in progress ⟨Live for *today* and let tomorrow worry about itself.⟩ — see ¹PRESENT

to–do *n* a state of noisy, confused activity ⟨There was such a *to-do* when the mice got loose from the science room that I thought the principal was going to close the school.⟩ — see COMMOTION

together *adv* **1** at one and the same time ⟨The two packages, although sent on different days, arrived *together*.⟩

synonyms coincidentally, coincidently, concurrently, contemporaneously, simultaneously

related words close, immediately, near

phrases at once, in unison

near antonyms apart, independently, individually, singly

antonyms separately

2 in or by combined action or effort ⟨Working *together*, we can get this project done on time.⟩

synonyms conjointly, jointly

related words collectively, mutually, reciprocally, unanimously, unitedly; cooperatively, symbiotically

phrases in concert

antonyms apart, independently, individually, separately, severally, single-handedly, singly, solely, unaided, unassisted, unilaterally

3 with everyone or everything taken into account at the same time ⟨*Together*, the properties are worth more than five million.⟩ — see ALL AROUND

togs *pl n* **1** clothing chosen as appropriate for a specific situation ⟨Put on your party *togs* and come over to our place for an all-night dance party!⟩ — see OUTFIT 1

2 covering for the human body ⟨Hey, those are some snazzy *togs* you're wearing!⟩ — see CLOTHING

toil *n* very hard or unpleasant work ⟨After years of *toil* in a sweatshop, Kim was finally able to start her own business.⟩

synonyms drudgery, grind, labor, sweat, travail

related words spadework; effort, exertion, pains, struggle, trouble; chore, duty, job, obligation, responsibility; routine, tedium, treadmill

near antonyms decompression, ease, leisure, relaxation, repose, rest; amusement, dalliance, diversion, entertainment, recreation, sport; dormancy, idleness, inactivity, inertia, inertness; dallying, goldbricking, loafing, lolling, lounging

antonyms fun, play

toil *vb* to devote serious and sustained effort ⟨*toiled* for many years on the mammoth outdoor sculpture⟩ — see LABOR

toiler *n* a person who does very hard or dull work ⟨On Labor Day we should give a thought to those *toilers* who work long hours at low-paying jobs.⟩ — see DRUDGE

toilet *n* a room furnished with a fixture for flushing body waste ⟨We were directed to the *toilets* in the church basement.⟩

synonyms bath, bathroom, head, latrine, lavatory, potty, washroom, water closet

related words commode; outhouse, privy

toilsome *adj* **1** requiring considerable physical or mental effort ⟨faced with the *toilsome* task of cleaning out her deceased father's homestead⟩ — see HARD 2

2 requiring much time, effort, or careful attention ⟨This is the most *toilsome* part of the construction, so we'll go slowly to make sure we're doing it right.⟩ — see DEMANDING 1

token *n* something that serves to keep alive the memory of a person or event ⟨Please accept this parting gift as a *token* of our lasting affection.⟩ — see MEMORIAL

tolerable *adj* **1** capable of being endured ⟨Stubbing your toe is at least a more *tolerable* pain than breaking your foot.⟩ — see BEARABLE

2 of a level of quality that meets one's needs or standards ⟨The accommodations are *tolerable* though not exactly luxurious.⟩ — see ADEQUATE

tolerably *adv* in a satisfactory way ⟨I'm doing *tolerably*, thanks for asking.⟩ — see WELL 1

tolerance *n* the capacity to endure what is difficult or disagreeable without complaining ⟨They showed great *tolerance* in dealing with the child's tantrums.⟩ — see PATIENCE

tolerant *adj* **1** accepting pains or hardships calmly or without complaint ⟨This job requires a *tolerant* person who is used to dealing with complaints and angry customers.⟩ — see PATIENT 1

2 receiving or enduring without offering resistance

⟨These plants are *tolerant* of hot climates.⟩ — see PASSIVE

tolerate *vb* **1** to fail to prevent (some behavior on someone's part) especially from neglect or indifference ⟨My boss simply doesn't *tolerate* tardiness.⟩ — see ALLOW 3
2 to put up with (something painful or difficult) ⟨Suffering a terrible headache, the poor woman couldn't *tolerate* all the noise the neighbors were making.⟩ — see BEAR 2

tolerating *adj* receiving or enduring without offering resistance ⟨old pictures of a graciously *tolerating* father letting his young children climb all over him⟩ — see PASSIVE

toll *vb* to make the clear sound heard when metal vibrates ⟨Let the church bells joyously *toll* on this most happy occasion!⟩ — see ²RING

tomb *n* a final resting place for a dead person ⟨explored the historic graveyard and saw *tombs* that dated back two centuries⟩ — see GRAVE 1

tomboyish *adj* having qualities or traits that are traditionally considered inappropriate for a girl or woman ⟨Her father thought that ice hockey was a little too *tomboyish* for her, but her mother and older brother encouraged her to take it up.⟩ — see UNFEMININE

tombstone *n* a shaped stone laid over or erected near a grave and usually bearing an inscription to identify and preserve the memory of the deceased ⟨The historic cemetery's many *tombstones* marking the graves of children are telling reminders of the harshness of pioneer life.⟩
synonyms gravestone, headstone, monument
related words cross, marker, plaque, table, tablet; monolith, obelisk, pillar; memorial, shrine; burial, sepulture, tomb

tome *n* a set of printed sheets of paper bound together between covers and forming a work of fiction or nonfiction ⟨picked up a thick *tome* on the Roman Empire at a used book store⟩ — see BOOK 1

tomfoolery *n* wildly playful or mischievous behavior ⟨The best man may have had something to do with the *tomfoolery* at the wedding reception.⟩ — see HORSEPLAY

tone *n* **1** a distinctive way of putting ideas into words ⟨The angry *tone* of his letter makes it clear he doesn't want to speak to me ever again.⟩ — see STYLE 1
2 a property that becomes apparent when light falls on an object and by which things that are identical in form can be distinguished ⟨fall fashions in deep jewel *tones*⟩ — see COLOR 1
3 the set of qualities that makes a person, a group of people, or a thing different from others ⟨All that showbiz glitz is out of keeping with the *tone* of the college.⟩ — see NATURE 1

toned–down *adj* not excessively showy ⟨After such a heated argument, it was a relief to hear someone use *toned-down* language to state their position.⟩ — see QUIET 2

tongue *n* the stock of words, pronunciation, and grammar used by a people as their basic means of communication ⟨He spoke in a *tongue* that I didn't understand.⟩ — see LANGUAGE 1

tonic *adj* **1** having a renewing effect on the state of the body or mind ⟨Never underestimate the *tonic* power of humor on a sick person.⟩
synonyms bracing, cordial, invigorating, refreshing, restorative, reviving, stimulating, stimulative, vital, vitalizing
related words conditioning, strengthening; animating, exhilarating, quickening, sharp; corrective, curing, rectifying, recuperative, rehabilitating, remedial, remedying, reparative; beneficial, healthful, healthy, helpful, salubrious, salutary, wholesome; healing, medicinal
near antonyms deadening, debilitating, draining, ener-

vating, enfeebling, exhausting, numbing, sapping, weakening, wearying; deleterious, injurious, pernicious; noxious, unhealthful, unhealthy, unwholesome
2 beneficial to the health of body or mind ⟨The *tonic* air of the mountains is just what you need after being cooped up in the city for so long.⟩ — see HEALTHFUL

too *adv* **1** beyond a normal or acceptable limit ⟨Ticket prices for the concert are simply *too* high.⟩
synonyms devilishly, excessively, exorbitantly, inordinately, monstrously, overly, overmuch, unacceptably, unduly
related words extravagantly, immoderately, intemperately; inexcusably, obscenely, unbearably, unconscionably, unreasonably; improperly, inappropriately; abnormally, extraordinarily, freakishly, singularly, unusually; astronomically, considerably, especially, exceedingly (*also* exceeding), exceptionally, extra, extremely, greatly, highly, hugely, incredibly, mightily, remarkably, significantly, substantially, super, terribly, very
phrases to a fault, to death, with a vengeance
near antonyms acceptably, moderately, modestly, reasonably, temperately; barely, hardly, just, marginally, meagerly, minimally, scantily, scarcely, slightly
antonyms deficiently, inadequately, insufficiently
2 in addition to what has been said ⟨I want to buy this sweater—and that sweater *too*!⟩ — see MORE 1
3 to a great degree ⟨The audience didn't seem *too* interested in what the speaker had to say.⟩ — see VERY 1

tool *n* **1** an article intended for use in work ⟨needed a special *tool* to remove the screen on the phone⟩ — see IMPLEMENT
2 one that is or can be used to further the purposes of another ⟨a ruthless leader using his trusting followers as *tools* in his quest for power⟩ — see ¹PAWN
3 one who is easily deceived or cheated ⟨You're just a pathetic *tool* of the advertising industry if you believe everything you see in TV commercials.⟩ — see ¹DUPE

tool *vb* to travel by a motorized vehicle ⟨I spent some time *tooling* around town today.⟩ — see DRIVE 2

tooth and nail *adv* with all power or resources being used ⟨I'll fight *tooth and nail* to win the finals.⟩ — see FULL BLAST

toothsome *adj* very pleasing to the sense of taste ⟨a *toothsome* chocolate dessert⟩ — see DELICIOUS 1

top *adj* **1** being at a point or level higher than all others ⟨an office in the *top* story of the building⟩ ⟨the *top* student in our graduating class⟩
synonyms highest, loftiest, topmost, upmost, uppermost
related words higher, loftier, upper; consummate, maximal, maximized, maximum, peaked, supreme, utmost, uttermost; chief, dominant, first, foremost, head, leading, predominant, preeminent, premier, principal; dominant, dominating, eminent, prominent, towering
near antonyms below, lower, nether, under, underneath; low, lowered, low-lying, sunken
antonyms lowest
2 of the greatest or highest degree or quantity ⟨Your safety is our *top* priority.⟩ — see ULTIMATE 1
3 of the highest degree ⟨going at *top* speed⟩ — see FULL 2
4 of the very best kind ⟨He's one of the tennis club's *top* players.⟩ — see EXCELLENT
5 highest in rank or authority ⟨Nearly all of the *top* officials in the state's department of corrections resigned after the scandal.⟩ — see HEAD

top *n* **1** a piece placed over an open container to hold in, protect, or conceal its contents ⟨Make sure the *top* is on the juice blender before you turn it on.⟩ — see COVER 1
2 the highest part or point ⟨a hawk's nest at the very *top* of the tree⟩ — see HEIGHT 1

top *vb* to be greater, better, or stronger than ⟨The next contender's javelin throw *topped* the reigning champion's and set a new world record.⟩ — see SURPASS 1

topcoat *n* a warm outdoor coat ⟨threw on a wool *topcoat* and headed out into the snow⟩ — see OVERCOAT

topic *n* a major object of interest or concern (as in a discussion or artistic composition) ⟨The *topic* of his poem is the bitter conflict in Northern Ireland.⟩ — see MATTER 1

topmost *adj* **1** being at a point or level higher than all others ⟨His kite got tangled in the *topmost* branches of the tree.⟩ — see TOP 1
2 of the highest degree ⟨Our *topmost* goal is to help students learn foreign languages in an easy and natural way.⟩ — see FULL 2

top–notch *adj* of the very best kind ⟨a *top-notch* violinist who had no trouble getting a position with the symphony⟩ — see EXCELLENT

top–of–the–line *adj* of the very best kind ⟨gourmet chefs who insist on *top-of-the-line* cookware and are willing to pay for it⟩ — see EXCELLENT

topper *n* something (as a fact or argument) that is decisive or overwhelming ⟨There are lots of good reasons we can't go to the concert, but the fact that the tickets are all sold out is the *topper*.⟩ — see CLINCHER

topple *vb* to go down from an upright position suddenly and involuntarily ⟨The tower of blocks *toppled* even though I bumped into it ever so slightly.⟩ — see FALL 1

topsy–turvy *adj* lacking in order, neatness, and often cleanliness ⟨The office is still *topsy-turvy* even though we moved in months ago.⟩ — see MESSY

torment *n* **1** a situation or state that causes great suffering and unhappiness ⟨The released soldiers gave interviews trying to explain to civilians the *torment* that prisoners of war experience.⟩ — see HELL 2
2 a state of great suffering of body or mind ⟨Jay was in *torment* for weeks after he broke up with his girlfriend.⟩ — see DISTRESS 1
3 a source of persistent emotional distress ⟨insomnia that was caused by a host of nighttime *torments*⟩ — see DEMON 2

torment *vb* to cause persistent suffering to ⟨He was *tormented* by nightmares about the accident.⟩ — see AFFLICT

tormenting *adj* **1** hard to accept or bear especially emotionally ⟨It was a *tormenting* moment as they helplessly watched the other team score in the final seconds of the game.⟩ — see BITTER 2
2 intensely or unbearably painful ⟨a *tormenting* injury⟩ — see EXCRUCIATING 1

tormentor *also* **tormenter** *n* a person who causes repeated emotional pain, distress, or annoyance to another ⟨He was shocked to learn that his childhood *tormentor* had written a book about the dangers of bullying.⟩
synonyms baiter, heckler, mocker, needler, persecutor, quiz, ridiculer, taunter, tease, teaser, torturer
related words belittler, derider, detractor, giber (*or* jiber), insulter, jeerer, scoffer, scorner; smart aleck (*also* smart alec), smarty (*or* smartie), smarty-pants, wiseacre, wiseguy; kidder, lampooner, satirist; bother, disturber, pest
near antonyms defender, deliverer, guard, protector, rescuer, savior (*or* saviour); comforter, solace, soother; bodyguard, champion

torpid *adj* **1** slow to move or act ⟨a *torpid* sloth that refused to budge off its tree branch⟩ — see INACTIVE 1
2 lacking in sensation or feeling ⟨My tongue and throat remained *torpid* for a time following the endoscopy.⟩ — see NUMB 1

torrent *n* a great flow of water or of something that over-whelms ⟨The dam broke, unleashing a *torrent* down the dry riverbed.⟩ — see FLOOD

torrid *adj* **1** having a notably high temperature ⟨the dry, *torrid* summers in southern Arizona⟩ — see HOT 1
2 having or expressing great depth of feeling ⟨a *torrid* love affair⟩ — see FERVENT 1

tortuous *adj* marked by a long series of irregular curves ⟨a *tortuous* mountain road marked by numerous hairpin turns⟩ — see CROOKED 1

torture *n* **1** a situation or state that causes great suffering and unhappiness ⟨It's *torture* for me to see you so unhappy.⟩ — see HELL 2
2 a state of great suffering of body or mind ⟨Liz spent an afternoon in *torture* waiting to hear whether her brother had made it home safely.⟩ — see DISTRESS 1

torture *vb* **1** to cause persistent suffering to ⟨The neighbor's dog constantly *tortures* our cat, barking at him and chasing him down the street.⟩ — see AFFLICT
2 to twist (something) out of a natural or normal shape or condition ⟨*tortured* her naturally straight hair into curls⟩ — see CONTORT

torturer *n* a person who causes repeated emotional pain, distress, or annoyance to another ⟨At the health club, one trainer in particular was known as a *torturer* who always demanded more.⟩ — see TORMENTOR

torturing *adj* intensely or unbearably painful ⟨We watched the final *torturing* moments of the game as the lead constantly shifted between the two teams.⟩ — see EXCRUCIATING 1

torturing *n* the twisting of something out of its natural or normal shape or condition ⟨Fans of the natural look frown on the *torturing* of garden trees and shrubs into fantastic shapes.⟩ — see CONTORTION

torturous *adj* **1** hard to accept or bear especially emotionally ⟨Relatives had to make the *torturous* decision to call off the search.⟩ — see BITTER 2
2 intensely or unbearably painful ⟨The post-infection treatment for rabies was as notoriously *torturous* as the disease itself.⟩ — see EXCRUCIATING 1

Tory *n* a person whose political beliefs are centered on tradition and keeping things the way they are ⟨a small-town *Tory* who saw that society was changing, much to his regret⟩ — see CONSERVATIVE

toss *vb* **1** to make a series of unsteady side-to-side motions ⟨The boat *tossed* to and fro in the heavy seas.⟩ — see ROCK 1
2 to make jerky or restless movements ⟨I *tossed* and turned in bed all night, unable to sleep in the heat.⟩ — see FIDGET
3 to send through the air especially with a quick forward motion of the arm ⟨*Toss* that football over here.⟩ — see THROW 1
4 to get rid of as useless or unwanted ⟨We need to go through the basement and *toss* whatever we don't use.⟩ — see DISCARD

toss (down *or* **off)** *vb* to swallow in liquid form ⟨*tossed* off the last of the medicine⟩ — see DRINK 1

total *adj* **1** having no exceptions or restrictions ⟨had *total* power over the people of that country⟩ — see ABSOLUTE 2
2 not lacking any part or member that properly belongs to it ⟨gave us a *total* rundown of the events⟩ — see COMPLETE 1
3 trying all possibilities ⟨This was *total* war as far as the military was concerned.⟩ — see EXHAUSTIVE 1

total *n* a complete amount of something ⟨That's the *total* for our wheat harvest this year.⟩ — see WHOLE

total *vb* **1** to have a total of ⟨Two and two *total* four.⟩ — see AMOUNT (TO) 1
2 to combine (numbers) into a single sum ⟨*Total* all the receipts and tell me how much I owe you.⟩ — see ADD 2
3 to bring to a complete end the physical soundness,

existence, or usefulness of ⟨He *totaled* the car and managed to walk away without a scratch.⟩ — see DESTROY 1

totalitarianism *n* a system of government in which the ruler has unlimited power ⟨In times of crisis, when a nation's people are frightened, there are often calls for *totalitarianism*.⟩ — see DESPOTISM

totality *n* a complete amount of something ⟨The *totality* of the stars in the universe can only be loosely guessed at.⟩ — see WHOLE

totally *adv* 1 to a full extent or degree ⟨I am *totally* upset you can't make it to the celebration.⟩ — see FULLY 1
2 with attention to all aspects or details ⟨He made *totally* sure the door was locked when he left the house.⟩ — see THOROUGHLY 1

tote *vb* to support and take from one place to another ⟨Jon *toted* his dog from the muddy backyard to the bathtub for a thorough washing.⟩ — see CARRY 1

totter *vb* 1 to move forward while swaying from side to side ⟨The baby *tottered* for a few steps and fell into his father's arms.⟩ — see STAGGER 1
2 to swing unsteadily back and forth or from side to side ⟨The figurine *tottered* precariously for a moment before falling off the shelf.⟩ — see TEETER 1

tottery *adj* marked by or given to small uncontrollable bodily movements ⟨With a *tottery* gait the frail, elderly woman slowly climbed the steps of the church.⟩ — see SHAKY 1

touch *n* 1 the state or fact of being able to exchange information regarding one's current situation ⟨Everyone promised to keep in *touch* over the summer.⟩
synonyms communication, contact, hold
related words commerce, communion, intercommunication, intercourse
2 a very small amount ⟨added just a *touch* of parsley to the dish⟩ — see PARTICLE 1
3 something that sets apart an individual from others of the same kind ⟨Each designer has his or her own personal *touches*.⟩ — see CHARACTERISTIC
4 an almost imperceptible sign of something ⟨A *touch* of irritation tinged his voice as the candidate fielded yet another question about his personal finances.⟩ — see HINT 2

touch *vb* 1 to come into bodily contact with (something) so as to perceive a slight pressure on the skin ⟨Be careful not to *touch* this pan—it's still hot!⟩
synonyms feel
related words caress, embrace, fondle, hug, kiss, nose, nudge, nuzzle, paw, rub, stroke; palp, palpate; brush, graze, shave, skim; clasp, clench, cling (to), clutch, grasp, grip, handle, hold; chuck, clap, dab, flick, pat, tag, tap, tip; hit, knock, pound, rap, whack
2 to act upon (a person or a person's feelings) so as to cause a response ⟨Your speech on the true meaning of patriotism *touched* me deeply.⟩ — see ¹AFFECT 1
3 to affect slightly with something morally bad or undesirable ⟨Unfortunately, his insufferable arrogance tends to *touch* even the good deeds that he does.⟩ — see TAINT 1
4 to be adjacent to ⟨Our property *touches* theirs right where that big elm tree is.⟩ — see ADJOIN 1
5 to be the business or affair of ⟨This is an issue that *touches* everyone.⟩ — see CONCERN 2

touch (on *or* **upon)** *vb* to make reference to or speak about briefly but specifically ⟨I do want to briefly *touch upon* the medieval view of the world before talking about Gothic architecture.⟩ — see MENTION 1

touchable *adj* capable of being perceived by the sense of touch ⟨Not very comfortable with abstractions, I usually relate better to *touchable* things.⟩ — see TANGIBLE

touch down *vb* to come to rest after descending from the air ⟨The plane will *touch down* in about 30 minutes.⟩ — see ALIGHT 1

touching *adj* 1 having a border in common ⟨*Touching* lots in the housing development will eventually be separated by hedges for privacy.⟩ — see ADJACENT
2 having the power to affect the feelings or sympathies ⟨a *touching* movie about two lost animals who try to find their way home⟩ — see MOVING

touching *prep* having to do with ⟨There has been an objection *touching* the last of the proposed new bylaws.⟩ — see ABOUT 1

touch off *vb* to cause to function ⟨His comment *touched off* a heated debate about what constitutes slander.⟩ — see ACTIVATE

touchstone *n* something set up as an example against which others of the same type are compared ⟨His book has long been a *touchstone* for travel writing that aspires to be literature.⟩ — see STANDARD 1

touchy *adj* 1 easily offended ⟨Watch what you say around him, as he's very *touchy* about every little thing.⟩
synonyms ticklish
related words hypersensitive, oversensitive, sensitive, supersensitive, tender; choleric, crabby, cranky, cross, crotchety, grouchy, grumpy, irascible, irritable, peevish, perverse, pettish, petulant, prickly, quick-tempered, short-tempered, snappish, snappy, snippy, stuffy, testy, waspish; bearish, bilious, cantankerous, curmudgeonly, disagreeable, dyspeptic, ill-humored, ill-natured, ill-tempered, ornery, querulous, surly
near antonyms agreeable, amiable, good-natured, good-tempered, well-disposed; carefree, easygoing, happy-go-lucky, relaxed, unconcerned; forbearing, long-suffering, obliging, understanding
antonyms thick-skinned
2 requiring exceptional skill or caution in performance or handling ⟨Money is a *touchy* subject for many people and shouldn't be discussed casually.⟩ — see TRICKY 1
3 capable of catching or being set on fire ⟨The experiment involves the use of some *touchy* chemicals, so caution is required.⟩ — see COMBUSTIBLE

tough *adj* 1 not easily chewed ⟨Her steak was so *tough* that she suggested the waiter use it as a hockey puck.⟩
synonyms chewy, leathery
related words fibrous, gristly, sinewy, stringy; brittle, crunchy, hard
near antonyms mushy, soft
antonyms tender
2 able to withstand hardship, strain, or exposure ⟨This is a *tough* plant that easily withstands harsh winters.⟩ — see HARDY 1
3 difficult to endure ⟨*tough* weather conditions on the top of the mountain all year long⟩ — see HARSH 1
4 requiring considerable physical or mental effort ⟨Even if you study for it, it's still a *tough* exam.⟩ — see HARD 2
5 requiring exceptional skill or caution in performance or handling ⟨You handled a *tough* situation with the aplomb and tact of a true diplomat.⟩ — see TRICKY 1
6 given to exacting standards of discipline and self-restraint ⟨a *tough* supervisor who docked the pay of anyone who punched in late, no matter what the reason⟩ — see SEVERE 1

tough *n* a violent, brutal person who is often a member of an organized gang ⟨didn't want her son hanging out with the neighborhood *toughs*⟩ — see HOODLUM

toughen *vb* 1 to increase the ability of (as a muscle) to exert physical force ⟨Weight lifting will help *toughen* those flabby muscles of yours.⟩ — see STRENGTHEN 1
2 to make able to withstand physical hardship, strain, or exposure ⟨Hiking every morning through snow and ice *toughened* him considerably.⟩ — see HARDEN 2

toughened *adj* able to withstand hardship, strain, or

exposure ⟨a group of *toughened* mountain bikers barreling up the hill⟩ — see HARDY 1

tour *n* a fixed period of time during which a person holds a job or position ⟨asked the soldiers to consider signing up for a second *tour* of duty⟩ — see TERM 1

tour *vb* to take a trip especially of some distance ⟨thought it would be lots of fun to *tour* all over Europe this summer⟩ — see TRAVEL 1

tourist *n* a person who travels for pleasure ⟨*Tourists* from all over like to take pictures of the alligators in the bayou.⟩
synonyms excursionist, rubberneck, sightseer, traveler (*or* traveller)
related words holidayer, vacationer, vacationist; guest, hosteler (*or* hosteller), visitor; transient; journeyer, pilgrim, wayfarer

tournament *n* a competitive encounter between individuals or groups carried on for amusement, exercise, or in pursuit of a prize ⟨a golf *tournament* in which professionals compete against amateurs⟩ — see GAME 1

tourney *n* a competitive encounter between individuals or groups carried on for amusement, exercise, or in pursuit of a prize ⟨progressed to the final round of the tennis *tourney*⟩ — see GAME 1

tousle *vb* to undo the proper order or arrangement of ⟨His grandfather would always *tousle* the boy's neatly combed hair.⟩ — see DISORDER

tousled *adj* lacking in order, neatness, and often cleanliness ⟨a *tousled* pile of yarn and material scraps at the bottom of her craft box⟩ — see MESSY

tout *vb* **1** to praise or publicize lavishly and often excessively ⟨a new cleaning agent *touted* as the only product a homeowner needs for all his or her cleaning chores⟩
synonyms ballyhoo, crack up, glorify, trumpet
related words acclaim, applaud, extol (*also* extoll), laud, magnify; commend, compliment, eulogize; advance, advertise, announce, blare, blaze, boost, herald, offer, plug, promote, publicize; assert, aver, claim, declare, lay down, make out, proclaim, pronounce
2 to declare enthusiastic approval of ⟨statements from several former patients *touting* the doctor's alleged cure⟩ — see ACCLAIM
3 to provide publicity for ⟨an avalanche of ads *touting* the new movie⟩ — see PUBLICIZE 1

tow *vb* to cause to follow by applying steady force on ⟨*towed* the car into the shop for repair⟩ — see PULL 1

toward *or* **towards** *prep* having to do with ⟨I didn't know what his attitude *toward* the issue was.⟩ — see ABOUT 1

tower *n* a large, magnificent, or massive building ⟨a hill from which one can gaze upon the *towers* of that great and historic city⟩ — see EDIFICE 1

towering *adj* **1** extending to a great distance upward ⟨the *towering* mountain peaks of the Rockies⟩ — see HIGH 1
2 going beyond a normal or acceptable limit in degree or amount ⟨doting parents who tend to give their children *towering* praise for very minor accomplishments⟩ — see EXCESSIVE
3 very dignified in form, tone, or style ⟨an article that in *towering* language decries the evils of modern society⟩ — see ELEVATED 2

town *n* a thickly settled, highly populated area ⟨After driving for miles with nothing but corn and wheat fields to look at, we were relieved to roll into a small *town* and have a bite to eat at the local diner.⟩ — see CITY

townie *or* **towny** *n* **1** a usually longtime resident of a locality ⟨The *townies* are dismayed that all the venerable manses around the village green are being bought as vacation homes by rich interlopers.⟩ — see NATIVE
2 a person who lives in a town on a permanent basis ⟨The university board met with an association representing the *townies* to figure out a solution to the problems created by off-campus parties.⟩ — see BURGHER

toxic *adj* containing or contaminated with a substance capable of injuring or killing a living thing ⟨Certain plants are *toxic* if eaten.⟩ — see POISONOUS

toxin *n* a substance that by chemical action can kill or injure a living thing ⟨a pamphlet on the *toxin* responsible for botulism, a food poisoning that can cause paralysis and even death in some cases⟩ — see POISON

trace *n* **1** a mark or series of marks left on a surface by something that has passed along it ⟨The wolf came and went without leaving a *trace* on the hard, dry ground.⟩ — see TRACK 1
2 a passage cleared for public vehicular travel ⟨an old *trace* that dates back to the days of the covered wagon⟩ — see WAY 1
3 a rough course or way formed by or as if by repeated footsteps ⟨Stay on the *trace*, or you'll get lost in these thick woods.⟩ — see TRAIL 1
4 a tiny often physical indication of something lost or vanished ⟨a ship that appears to have vanished without a *trace* on the high seas⟩ — see VESTIGE 1
5 a very small amount ⟨Doctors detected only a *trace* of bacteria in the blood sample but put the patient on antibiotics just in case.⟩ — see PARTICLE 1
6 an almost imperceptible sign of something ⟨There didn't seem to be so much as a *trace* of the truth to anything he said.⟩ — see HINT 2
7 the mark or impression made by a foot ⟨The hunter followed the *traces* of the deer into the deep woods.⟩ — see FOOTPRINT

trace *vb* **1** to draw or make apparent the outline of ⟨*Trace* your hand onto this piece of paper.⟩ — see OUTLINE 1
2 to go after or on the track of ⟨Police *traced* the burglar back to his apartment, where they discovered a ton of stolen loot.⟩ — see FOLLOW 2

tracing *n* the act of going after or in the tracks of another ⟨The *tracing* of this mountain lion is going to be difficult if the rain washes away all of the tracks.⟩ — see PURSUIT

track *n* **1** a mark or series of marks left on a surface by something that has passed along it ⟨a muddy *track* across the kitchen floor⟩
synonyms imprint, trace, trail
related words footprint, footstep, hoofprint, path, rut, step, tread; artifact, leavings, relic, remain(s), remainder, remnant, residual, residue, sign, spoor, token, vestige; clue, cue, hint, indication, inkling, intimation, lead, suggestion; scent, shadow, whiff
2 a rough course or way formed by or as if by repeated footsteps ⟨There was still a faint *track* through the underbrush that indicated where the path used to be.⟩ — see TRAIL 1
3 the direction along which something or someone moves ⟨I followed the *track* of the thief's eyes as he watched the woman put the money into her purse and walk away.⟩ — see PATH 1

track *vb* **1** to go after or on the track of ⟨predators stealthily *tracking* their prey⟩ — see FOLLOW 2
2 to make one's way through, across, or over ⟨Once upon a time, millions of buffalo *tracked* the wide open plains.⟩ — see TRAVERSE

track (down) *vb* to come upon after searching, study, or effort ⟨I'll try to *track down* his last known address.⟩ — see FIND 1

tracking *n* the act of going after or in the tracks of another ⟨Jed took a class in the *tracking* of game that the hunters' association offers.⟩ — see PURSUIT

tract *n* **1** a broad geographical area ⟨a vast and fertile *tract* of farmland⟩ — see REGION 2

2 a small area of usually open land ⟨The town had planned on turning that *tract* of meadow into a park.⟩ — see FIELD 1

3 a small piece of land that is developed or available for development ⟨A number of small *tracts* were for sale, but we couldn't afford to buy land and then build a house.⟩ — see LOT 1

tractable *adj* readily giving in to the command or authority of another ⟨We put the dog in obedience classes, with the hopes of making her a little more *tractable*.⟩ — see OBEDIENT

trade *n* **1** a giving or taking of one thing of value in return for another ⟨When the other team unexpectedly offered to hand over its top pitcher for our star shortstop, our coach agreed to the *trade*.⟩ — see EXCHANGE 1

2 an occupation requiring skillful use of the hands ⟨a youth eager to learn the *trade* of cabinetmaking⟩ — see CRAFT 1

3 the activity by which one regularly makes a living ⟨Writing is my *trade*.⟩ — see OCCUPATION

4 the buying and selling of goods especially on a large scale and between different places ⟨a bill regulating *trade* with that country⟩ — see COMMERCE 1

5 the transfer of ownership of something from one person to another for a price ⟨The *trade* of all of her holdings in the company just before the stock plunged in value immediately aroused suspicions.⟩ — see SALE

trade *vb* **1** to carry on the business of buying and selling goods or other property ⟨The U.S. agreed to *trade* with China.⟩

synonyms deal, traffic

related words bargain, barter, horse-trade, negotiate, transact; auction, exchange, merchandise (*also* merchandize), rebuy, resell, swap; buy, pick up, purchase, take; distribute, market, peddle, retail, sell, supply, vend, wholesale; bootleg, fence, smuggle; corner, monopolize, undersell; invest, speculate

near antonyms blackball, boycott

2 to give up (something) and take something else in return ⟨I'll *trade* my chocolate chip cookie for your bag of chips.⟩ — see CHANGE 3

trademark *n* **1** a device (as a word) identifying the maker of a piece of merchandise and legally reserved for the exclusive use of that person or company ⟨"Kleenex" is a *trademark* for a cleansing tissue.⟩

synonyms brand

related words brand name, trade name; collective mark, emblem, hallmark, imprint, label, logo, mark, service mark, stamp; copyright, patent

2 a device, design, or figure used as an identifying mark ⟨The golden arches are a *trademark* of McDonald's.⟩ — see EMBLEM

trade–off *n* a giving or taking of one thing of value in return for another ⟨a *trade-off* in which a company got a celebrity spokesperson and a fading star got some much-needed cash⟩ — see EXCHANGE 1

trader *n* a buyer and seller of goods for profit ⟨a coffee *trader*⟩ — see MERCHANT

tradesman *n* **1** a buyer and seller of goods for profit ⟨an antique dealer who's known as a good *tradesman*, buying his items cheaply and selling them for a hefty profit⟩ — see MERCHANT

2 a person whose occupation requires skill with the hands ⟨carpenters joining the *tradesmen's* union⟩ — see ARTISAN

tradition *n* **1** an inherited or established way of thinking, feeling, or doing ⟨the town *tradition* of having the oldest resident ride at the head of the parade⟩

synonyms convention, custom, heritage, rubric, rule

related words ethic, form, mode, mores, norm, principles, standards, values; birthright, inheritance, legacy; folklore, lore, superstition; culture, lifestyle

2 the body of customs, beliefs, stories, and sayings associated with a people, thing, or place ⟨According to *tradition*, kissing the Blarney Stone bestows the gift of gab.⟩ — see FOLKLORE

traditional *adj* **1** based on customs usually handed down from a previous generation ⟨a *traditional* Passover meal at his grandparents' house⟩

synonyms classical, conventional, customary

related words authentic, established, fixed, historical; common, habitual, orthodox, usual; ancestral, old-time, old-world; aged, age-old, ancient, antediluvian, hoary, old, venerable; ageless, dateless, immemorial, timeless

near antonyms contemporary, current, modern, modernized, new, new-age, present-day, updated, up-to-date; futuristic, high-tech (*also* hi-tech), hot, latest, mod, modernistic, newfangled, new-fashioned, red-hot, space-age, state-of-the-art, supermodern, ultramodern; nonconformist, nonorthodox, original, progressive, revolutionary, unorthodox, unprecedented, unusual

antonyms nontraditional, unconventional, uncustomary, untraditional

2 tending to favor established ideas, conditions, or institutions ⟨a family that is very *traditional* when it comes to institutions like marriage⟩ — see CONSERVATIVE 1

traduce *vb* **1** to fail to keep ⟨a law that *traduces* one of our most cherished rights: the right to privacy⟩ — see VIOLATE 1

2 to make untrue and harmful statements about ⟨My opponent in this campaign may villainously *traduce* me, but I will not stoop to his level.⟩ — see SLANDER

traducing *n* the making of false statements that damage another's reputation ⟨This endless *traducing* of candidates has got to stop, or the public will lose all faith in the electoral process.⟩ — see SLANDER

traffic *n* the buying and selling of goods especially on a large scale and between different places ⟨the *traffic* of exotic wildlife⟩ — see COMMERCE 1

traffic *vb* to carry on the business of buying and selling goods or other property ⟨arrested him for *trafficking* in drugs⟩ — see TRADE 1

trafficker *n* a buyer and seller of goods for profit ⟨a *trafficker* who sold pirated DVDs from the back of his car⟩ — see MERCHANT

tragedy *n* **1** a sudden violent event that brings about great loss or destruction ⟨The earthquake was only the latest in a series of *tragedies* for the city.⟩ — see DISASTER 1

2 bad luck or an example of this ⟨It's the *tragedy* of many great artists not to be recognized for their genius until after they're dead.⟩ — see MISFORTUNE

tragic *also* **tragical** *adj* of a kind to cause great distress ⟨In a *tragic* turn of events the area's sole remaining steel mill suddenly closed.⟩ — see REGRETTABLE

trail *n* **1** a rough course or way formed by or as if by repeated footsteps ⟨We took a *trail* through the woods to get to the main road.⟩

synonyms footpath, path, pathway, trace, track

related words bridle path; towpath; alley, alleyway, bypath, byroad, bystreet, byway, passageway, walkway; shortcut; lane, pass, passage, road, roadway, route, row, run, runway, street, thoroughfare

2 a mark or series of marks left on a surface by something that has passed along it ⟨The slugs left a slimy *trail* on the sidewalk.⟩ — see TRACK 1

trail *vb* to go after or on the track of ⟨We *trailed* our friend into the woods, inadvertently spoiling his plans for a solitary hike.⟩ — see FOLLOW 2

trailer *n* a motor vehicle that is specially equipped for living while traveling ⟨The band packed their equipment back into their *trailer* and headed off to their next gig.⟩ — see CAMPER

trailing *n* the act of going after or in the tracks of another ⟨Did you think I didn't know about your constant *trailing* of me?⟩ — see PURSUIT

train *n* **1** a body of employees or attendants who accompany and wait on a person ⟨a millionaire who never goes anywhere without a *train* of personal assistants⟩ — see CORTEGE 1

2 a group of vehicles traveling together or under one management ⟨a *train* of supply trucks making its way to the army encampment⟩ — see FLEET

3 a series of persons or things arranged one behind another ⟨already a long *train* of ticket buyers waiting outside the stadium⟩ — see LINE 1

4 a series of things linked together ⟨You've broken my *train* of thought—now what were we talking about?⟩ — see CHAIN 1

train *vb* **1** to bring to a proper or desired state of fitness ⟨The coach has been *training* track-and-field athletes at the school for years.⟩ — see CONDITION 1

2 to cause to acquire knowledge or skill in some field ⟨will *train* the students in good study habits⟩ — see TEACH

3 to fix (as one's attention) steadily toward a central objective ⟨*Train* all your thoughts on imagining how you'd score the winning goal in the game.⟩ — see CONCENTRATE 2

4 to point or turn (something) toward a target or goal ⟨*trained* his eyes on the distant bull's-eye⟩ — see AIM 1

5 to make competent (as by training, skill, or ability) for a particular office or function ⟨He's so experienced that they usually use him to *train* new recruits.⟩ — see QUALIFY 2

trainer *n* a person who trains performers or athletes ⟨hired a personal *trainer* to help her get in shape⟩ — see COACH

training *n* **1** something done over and over in order to develop skill ⟨a boxer who's been doing a lot of *training* with his footwork⟩ — see EXERCISE 2

2 the act or process of imparting knowledge or skills to another ⟨*Training* was going well with the new puppy.⟩ — see EDUCATION 1

traipse *vb* **1** to go on foot ⟨*traipsed* down the hall to get a cup of coffee⟩ — see WALK 1

2 to move about from place to place aimlessly ⟨a group of friends *traipsing* around the country the summer after graduation⟩ — see WANDER 1

trait *n* something that sets apart an individual from others of the same kind ⟨Honesty is one of her defining *traits*.⟩ — see CHARACTERISTIC

traitor *n* one who betrays a trust or an allegiance ⟨accused by her family of being a *traitor* when she sold their traditionally animal-friendly business to a competitor known to use animals for testing its products⟩
synonyms apostate, betrayer, double-crosser, quisling, recreant, serpent, snake, turncoat
related words collaborationist, collaborator, subversive, subverter; coconspirator, conspirator, intriguer, plotter, schemer; defector, deserter, renegade; informant, informer, rat, snitch, snitcher, squealer, stool pigeon, talebearer, tattler, tattletale

traitorous *adj* not true in one's allegiance to someone or something ⟨When our coach took a job at a rival college, a few *traitorous* players went right along with him.⟩ — see FAITHLESS

trammel *n* something that makes movement or progress difficult ⟨students and parents who want to throw off the *trammels* of outdated school policies⟩ — see ENCUMBRANCE

trammel *vb* **1** to confine or restrain with or as if with chains ⟨He was *trammeled* by fear of failure.⟩ — see BIND 1

2 to create difficulty for the work or activity of ⟨The new paperwork requirements will only *trammel* us and lower our productivity.⟩ — see HAMPER

tramp *n* a homeless wanderer who may beg or steal for a living ⟨The police encouraged the *tramps* who were sleeping in the park to spend the bitterly cold night in the homeless shelter.⟩
synonyms bum, hobo, vagabond, vagrant
related words drifter, roamer, transient; beggar, derelict, mendicant, panhandler; dodger, malingerer, shirker, slacker; gamine, ragamuffin, urchin, waif

tramp *vb* **1** to move heavily or clumsily ⟨*tramped* wearily up the stairs after a long day at work⟩ — see LUMBER 1

2 to tread on heavily so as to crush or injure ⟨I didn't mean to *tramp* your toes as I was running past you.⟩ — see TRAMPLE

3 to travel by foot for exercise or pleasure ⟨We would have happily *tramped* through the forest for the rest of the day if it hadn't started to rain.⟩ — see HIKE 1

trample *vb* to tread on heavily so as to crush or injure ⟨Isabel looked out her window and beheld the neighbor's Labrador retriever *trampling* her begonias.⟩
synonyms stamp, stomp, tramp, tromp
related words override, run down, run over, step (on); mash, pulp, smash, squash, squelch; hoof, kick

trance *n* the state of being lost in thought ⟨Lulled by the sound of the train, she stared out the window in a *trance*, oblivious to the fact that the conductor was taking tickets.⟩ — see REVERIE

tranquil *adj* **1** free from disturbing noise or uproar ⟨The house was once again *tranquil* after the kids moved outside to play.⟩ — see QUIET 1

2 free from emotional or mental agitation ⟨Though she should have been upset, she felt oddly *tranquil* upon learning that she would not be receiving the scholarship.⟩ — see CALM 2

3 free from storms or physical disturbance ⟨drifting dreamily through *tranquil* seas⟩ — see CALM 1

tranquilize *also* **tranquillize** *vb* to free from distress or disturbance ⟨At long last the crying baby was *tranquilized* by the steady rocking of her cradle.⟩ — see CALM 1

tranquilizing *also* **tranquillizing** *adj* tending to calm the emotions and relieve stress ⟨a woman who put a lot of faith in the *tranquilizing* effects of a cup of tea⟩ — see SOOTHING 1

tranquillity *or* **tranquility** *n* **1** a state of freedom from storm or disturbance ⟨enjoyed the *tranquillity* of the snow-covered field at dusk⟩ — see CALM 1

2 evenness of emotions or temper ⟨a psychotherapist valued for her *tranquillity* and ability to listen⟩ — see EQUANIMITY

3 freedom from disquieting or oppressive thoughts or emotions ⟨a mountain climber who finds inner *tranquillity* as he looks out from the edge of some lofty precipice⟩ — see PEACE 2

transaction *n* the transfer of ownership of something from one person to another for a price ⟨If you want to return any merchandise, make sure you keep the receipt for the initial sales *transaction*.⟩ — see SALE

transcend *vb* **1** to be greater, better, or stronger than ⟨a man whose practical knowledge of botany *transcends* that of his more educated colleagues⟩ — see SURPASS 1

2 to go beyond the limit of ⟨music that *transcends* cultural boundaries⟩ — see EXCEED 1

transcendence *n* the fact or state of being above others in rank or importance ⟨makes a case for the *transcendence* of Louis Armstrong's contributions to the field of jazz⟩ — see EMINENCE 1

transfer *vb* **1** to give over the legal possession or ownership of ⟨Claire's grandfather agreed to *transfer* certain stocks to her when she turned 18.⟩

synonyms alienate, assign, cede, convey, deed, make over

related words bequeath, hand down, leave, pass (down), will; bestow, commend, commit, confer, contribute, deliver, donate, grant, hand over, move, pass, present, release, relinquish, surrender, transmit, turn in, turn over, vest, yield; consign, entrust (*also* intrust), trust; lease, lend, loan, rent

phrases dispose of

near antonyms expropriate

2 to cause (something) to pass from one to another ⟨They used Morse Code to *transfer* the message from one ship to another.⟩ — see COMMUNICATE 1

3 to cause to go or be taken from one place to another ⟨I will have to *transfer* you from our San Francisco office to our New York headquarters.⟩ — see SEND

4 to change the place or position of ⟨*transferred* the car keys from my pocket to my purse⟩ — see MOVE 1

5 to put (something) into the possession or safekeeping of another ⟨Before she left the country, she *transferred* all her record books and important papers to her mother.⟩ — see GIVE 2

6 to shift possession of (something) from one person to another ⟨*transferred* the ball to the running back⟩ — see PASS 1

transferable *also* **transferrable** *adj* capable of being taken from one place to another by public carrier ⟨supplemental charges for oversized *transferable* goods like pianos⟩ — see SHIPPABLE

transfiguration *n* a change in form, appearance, or use ⟨After his *transfiguration* into a Buddhist monk, all his family and friends were amazed by his newly found patience and tranquillity.⟩ — see CONVERSION 1

transfigure *vb* to change in form, appearance, or use ⟨Married life has seemingly *transfigured* his formerly aimless existence.⟩ — see CONVERT 2

transfix *vb* to penetrate or hold (something) with a pointed object ⟨*transfixed* the inanimate butterfly specimens to the collection board⟩ — see IMPALE

transform *vb* to change in form, appearance, or use ⟨By clicking a few buttons, this toy car can be *transformed* into a robot.⟩ — see CONVERT 2

transformation *n* a change in form, appearance, or use ⟨a raven-haired starlet who underwent an attention-getting *transformation* and showed up at the awards ceremony as a blonde⟩ — see CONVERSION 1

transfuse *vb* **1** to cause (something) to pass from one to another ⟨a teacher who is able to *transfuse* his enthusiasm and passion for history to his students⟩ — see COMMUNICATE 1

2 to spread throughout ⟨Light *transfused* the room as the sun rose.⟩ — see PERMEATE

transgress *vb* **1** to commit an offense ⟨I didn't realize I was *transgressing* when I told your sister she looked like she had lost weight.⟩ — see OFFEND 1

2 to fail to keep ⟨Don't even think about *transgressing* the law when traveling abroad.⟩ — see VIOLATE 1

transgression *n* **1** a breaking of a moral or legal code ⟨acts that are *transgressions* against the laws of civilized societies everywhere⟩ — see OFFENSE 1

2 a failure to uphold the requirements of law, duty, or obligation ⟨a dying woman asking for divine forgiveness for a lifetime of *transgressions*⟩ — see BREACH 1

transient *adj* lasting only for a short time ⟨had *transient* thoughts of dying his hair blue but never acted upon them⟩ — see MOMENTARY

transitory *adj* lasting only for a short time ⟨A *transitory* panic struck me when I thought that I had left my wallet in the car.⟩ — see MOMENTARY

translate *vb* to express something (as a text or statement) in different words ⟨Would you mind *translating* this German article for me?⟩ — see PARAPHRASE

translate (into) *vb* to be the cause of (a situation, action, or state of mind) ⟨It remains to be seen whether the policy changes will *translate into* true progress.⟩ — see EFFECT

translating *n* an instance of expressing something in different words ⟨His insightful *translating* of that passage really captured the tone of the original.⟩ — see PARAPHRASE

translation *n* an instance of expressing something in different words ⟨I had to read Dante's *Divine Comedy* in *translation* since I don't know Italian.⟩ — see PARAPHRASE

transmit *vb* **1** to cause (something) to pass from one to another ⟨Sneezing and coughing can *transmit* disease.⟩ — see COMMUNICATE 1

2 to cause to go or be taken from one place to another ⟨I'll *transmit* this information over the airwaves.⟩ — see SEND

3 to put (something) into the possession or safekeeping of another ⟨*transmitted* the deed of his house to his lawyer⟩ — see GIVE 2

transmittable *adj* **1** capable of being passed by physical contact from one person to another ⟨That disease is only *transmittable* through direct contact with an infected person, not through contact with something the infected person has touched.⟩ — see CONTAGIOUS 1

2 capable of being taken from one place to another by public carrier ⟨I doubt that animals are legally *transmittable* through the mail.⟩ — see SHIPPABLE

transparency *n* the state or quality of being easily seen through ⟨Because of the *transparency* of the Caribbean waters, we could see sharks and tropical fish swimming 20 or 30 feet below the surface.⟩ — see CLARITY 1

transparent *adj* **1** easily seen through ⟨bottles of blue *transparent* glass⟩ — see CLEAR 1

2 not subject to misinterpretation or more than one interpretation ⟨His meaning in leaving the conversation is *transparent*: he doesn't want to talk about his combat experiences.⟩ — see CLEAR 2

3 very thin and easy to see through ⟨I froze the vegetables in *transparent* containers.⟩ — see SHEER 1

transpire *vb* to take place ⟨Please tell me what *transpired* on the night of October 1.⟩ — see HAPPEN

transport *n* **1** a state of overwhelming usually pleasurable emotion ⟨Jon was in *transports* of joy after winning the championship.⟩ — see ECSTASY

2 something used to carry goods or passengers ⟨Rising gas prices will impel more people to use public *transport*.⟩ — see CONVEYANCE

transport *vb* **1** to cause to go or be taken from one place to another ⟨I'll have to *transport* the car to our new home overseas by public carrier.⟩ — see SEND

2 to fill with great joy ⟨Anne was absolutely *transported* when she heard that her brother was getting married.⟩ — see ELATE

3 to fill with overwhelming emotion (as wonder or delight) ⟨Ava was *transported* with wonder when she saw the Matterhorn for the first time.⟩ — see ENTRANCE

4 to force to leave a country ⟨The offending journalist was *transported* out of the country and ordered to never return.⟩ — see BANISH 1

5 to support and take from one place to another ⟨Will

you *transport* this heavy casserole dish to the dining room for me?⟩ — see CARRY 1

transportable *adj* capable of being taken from one place to another by public carrier ⟨You'll need to see if that food is *transportable* overseas before you send boxes of it to your relatives in the military.⟩ — see SHIPPABLE

transportation *n* **1** a means of getting to a destination in a vehicle driven by another ⟨I'm without *transportation* tonight, so I can't meet you at the movies.⟩ — see RIDE
2 something used to carry goods or passengers ⟨Right now my bike is my only *transportation*.⟩ — see CONVEYANCE

transpose *vb* to change the place or position of ⟨I accidentally *transposed* two numbers when I wrote down the phone number.⟩ — see MOVE 1

transversely *adv* in a line or direction running from corner to corner ⟨The coat of arms had a line of white horses running *transversely* from one corner to another on a blue background.⟩ — see CROSSWISE

trap *n* **1** a device or scheme for capturing another by surprise ⟨Undercover agents devised a *trap* to catch the counterfeiters.⟩ ⟨a bear *trap*⟩
synonyms ambush, net, snare, web
related words enmeshment, entanglement, entrapment, envelopment; booby trap, catch, hazard, land mine, pitfall, snag; artifice, cheat, double-dealing, duplicity, ploy, ruse, subterfuge, trick
2 a setup in which hidden attackers lie in wait ⟨an overland route to the Far East that was once notorious for the many robbers who laid *traps* for unsuspecting wayfarers⟩ — see AMBUSH 1
3 something that catches and holds ⟨The promotion is really just a *trap* to keep her from taking a new job elsewhere.⟩ — see WEB 1

trap *vb* **1** to catch or hold as if in a net ⟨an ambitious young man who was now *trapped* in a series of shady business deals⟩ — see ENTANGLE 2
2 to take physical control or possession of (something) suddenly or forcibly ⟨Tim finally *trapped* the annoying fly in the palm of his hand.⟩ — see CATCH 1

trash *n* **1** discarded or useless material ⟨The neighbor's dog was rooting around in our *trash* this morning.⟩ — see GARBAGE
2 language, behavior, or ideas that are absurd and contrary to good sense ⟨Don't talk *trash* to me!⟩ — see NONSENSE 1
3 people looked down upon as ignorant and of the lowest class ⟨snooty people who thought that we were *trash* because we were in the cleaning business⟩ — see RABBLE
4 that which is of low quality or worth ⟨The souvenirs in the gift shop are nothing but *trash*.⟩ — see JUNK 1

trashy *adj* **1** marked by an obvious lack of style or good taste ⟨I know that sequined shirt cost a lot of money, but I still think it looks kind of *trashy*.⟩ — see ¹TACKY 1
2 of low quality ⟨*trashy* furniture that fell apart after a few weeks⟩ — see CHEAP 2

travail *n* **1** a state of great suffering of body or mind ⟨no greater *travail* than that of parents who have suffered the death of a child⟩ — see DISTRESS 1
2 very hard or unpleasant work ⟨We succeeded after months of *travail*.⟩ — see TOIL
3 the act or process of giving birth to children ⟨A midwife assisted her throughout her long *travail*.⟩ — see CHILDBIRTH

travail *vb* to devote serious and sustained effort ⟨Labor Day is the day on which we recognize those men and women who daily *travail* with little appreciation or compensation.⟩ — see LABOR

travel *n, often* **travels** *pl* a going from one place to another usually of some distance ⟨In all his *travels* he never met

pleasanter people than he had in that village.⟩ — see JOURNEY

travel *vb* **1** to take a trip especially of some distance ⟨The couple loves to *travel* and has been to 34 countries.⟩
synonyms journey, peregrinate, pilgrimage, tour, trek, voyage
related words gallivant (*also* galavant), hop, jaunt, knock (about), ramble, roam, rove, traipse, wander; migrate, road-trip; cab, coach, cruise, drive, fly, gig, jet, motor, navigate, ride, roll, sail, trundle; barnstorm
2 to make one's way through, across, or over ⟨We will *travel* the river for a while and then continue on land.⟩ — see TRAVERSE
3 to proceed or move quickly ⟨That racehorse can definitely *travel*.⟩ — see HURRY 2
4 to come or be together as friends ⟨He *traveled* with a fast crowd when he was in college.⟩ — see ASSOCIATE 1

traveler *or* **traveller** *n* a person who travels for pleasure ⟨a company that offers guidebooks and maps for *travelers*⟩ — see TOURIST

traveling bag *n* a bag carried by hand and designed to hold a traveler's clothing and personal articles ⟨*traveling bags* made of lightweight but tough fabrics⟩
synonyms carryall, grip, handbag, portmanteau, suitcase
related words overnight bag (*also* overnight case); carpetbag, duffel bag, kit; backpack, haversack, knapsack, rucksack; attaché, attaché case, briefcase, valise; baggage, bags, luggage

traverse *vb* to make one's way through, across, or over ⟨The spider *traversed* the wall from end to end.⟩
synonyms course, cover, cross, cut (across), follow, go, navigate, pass (over), peregrinate, proceed (along), track, travel
related words hike, traipse, tramp, tread, walk; ride, run; crisscross

travesty *n* **1** a poor, insincere, or insulting imitation of something ⟨Rigged from the start, his trial was a *travesty* of justice.⟩ — see MOCKERY 1
2 a work that imitates and exaggerates another work for comic effect ⟨The big-screen version of the classic sitcom is actually a good-natured *travesty* of the TV series.⟩ — see PARODY 1

travesty *vb* to copy or exaggerate (someone or something) in order to make fun of ⟨This comedy sketch mindlessly *travesties* the hard work of relief workers around the world.⟩ — see MIMIC 1

treacherous *adj* not true in one's allegiance to someone or something ⟨A *treacherous* "friend," she's been known to turn against people in the blink of an eye.⟩ — see FAITHLESS

treachery *n* the act or fact of violating the trust or confidence of another ⟨Steve was furious that she revealed his secret and never forgave her for the *treachery*.⟩ — see BETRAYAL

tread *vb* to go on foot ⟨To protect the fragile environment of the beach dunes, we must *tread* cautiously and lightly.⟩ — see WALK 1

treadmill *n* an established and often automatic or monotonous series of actions followed when engaging in some activity ⟨the *treadmill* of the morning commute to work⟩ — see ROUTINE 1

treason *n* the act or fact of violating the trust or confidence of another ⟨Reading a friend's diary without permission would have to be regarded as the ultimate act of personal *treason*.⟩ — see BETRAYAL

treasure *n* **1** an asset that brings praise or renown ⟨ancient archaeological *treasures* that today would never be allowed out of the country of origin⟩ — see GLORY 2

2 someone or something unusually desirable 〈In thanking them for their contributions, the mayor referred to the volunteers as the city's greatest *treasures*.〉 — see PRIZE 1

treasure *vb* **1** to hold dear 〈I'll always *treasure* the time my friend and I spent together this past summer.〉 — see LOVE 1

2 to put (something of future use or value) in a safe or secret place 〈a trove of old coins that he had lovingly *treasured* over the years〉 — see HOARD

treat *n* **1** a source of great satisfaction 〈Spending a long weekend at a ski resort is a real *treat*.〉 — see DELIGHT 1

2 something that is pleasing to eat because it is rare or a luxury 〈For us sushi is a real *treat* since no restaurant around here makes it.〉 — see DELICACY 1

treat *vb* **1** to behave toward in a stated way 〈She tries to *treat* all of her students fairly and equally, regardless of her personal feelings toward them.〉

   synonyms act (toward), be (to), deal (with), handle, serve, use

   related words consider, esteem, rate, reckon, regard, view; engage (with), react (to), respond (to)

   phrases do by

2 to deal with (something) usually skillfully or efficiently 〈School officials *treated* the vandalism of the students' artwork as a very serious matter.〉 — see HANDLE 1

3 to exchange viewpoints or seek advice for the purpose of finding a solution to a problem 〈I will *treat* with my lawyer and let you know what we decide.〉 — see CONFER 2

4 to give medical treatment to 〈a nurse *treating* a patient〉 — see DOCTOR 1

treat (of) *vb* to have (something) as a subject matter 〈His paper *treats of* the ethical dilemmas that doctors face every day in the emergency rooms of hospitals.〉 — see CONCERN 1

treaty *n* a formal agreement between two or more nations or peoples 〈In accordance with a *treaty* between the United States and the tribes of the Pacific Northwest, commercial fishing of certain kinds of salmon is limited to Indigenous people.〉

   synonyms accord, alliance, compact, convention, covenant, pact

   related words entente; bargain, bond, charter, concord, contract, deal, settlement, understanding

treble *adj* **1** having a high musical pitch or range 〈the *treble* shrieks of children at play〉 — see SHRILL

2 having three units or parts 〈a *treble* painting, with each panel telling a different part of the story of Icarus〉 — see TRIPLE

trek *n* a going from one place to another usually of some distance 〈We started on our *trek* up the mountain before the sun rose.〉 — see JOURNEY

trek *vb* to take a trip especially of some distance 〈adventurers *trekking* across the desert in search of a fabled city of gold〉 — see TRAVEL 1

tremble *n* an instance of shaking involuntarily with fear or cold 〈With a *tremble*, she ventured out into the snow.〉 — see SHIVER 1

trembling *adj* marked by or given to small uncontrollable bodily movements 〈*trembling* from the cold〉 — see SHAKY 1

trembling *n* a series of slight movements by a body back and forth or from side to side 〈We felt the *trembling* of the house each time a train passed by.〉 — see VIBRATION 1

tremendous *adj* unusually large 〈That's a *tremendous* amount of work for one person.〉 — see HUGE

tremendously *adv* to a large extent or degree 〈I'm *tremendously* upset I didn't get into that university.〉 — see GREATLY 2

tremor *n* a shaking of the earth 〈Smaller *tremors* continued for days after the major earthquake.〉 — see EARTHQUAKE 1

tremulous *adj* **1** easily frightened 〈A *tremulous* girl somehow mustered up the courage to ask a question of the governor.〉 — see SHY 1

2 marked by or given to small uncontrollable bodily movements 〈The frail woman extended a *tremulous* hand in welcome.〉 — see SHAKY 1

trench *n* a long narrow channel dug in the earth 〈dug a *trench* and filled it with water in an attempt to keep the forest fire off her property〉 — see DITCH

trenchant *adj* having an edge thin enough to cut or pierce something 〈Even the most *trenchant* sword could not sever the bonds of loyalty between them.〉 — see SHARP 1

trend *n* **1** a prevailing or general movement or inclination 〈According to the survey, there's a growing *trend* for companies to offer flexible hours.〉

   synonyms current, direction, drift, leaning, run, tendency, tide, wind

   related words curve, shift, swing, turn, upside; custom, habit, propensity, tenor, way; countercurrent, countertrend; undercurrent, undertow

2 a practice or interest that is very popular for a short time 〈Still had a coat from the last *trend* for fake fur, when the material lined everything from boots to coats to bracelets.〉 — see FAD

trend *vb* **1** to show a liking or proneness (for something) 〈During the winter our school system *trends* toward canceling school at the drop of a hat—or at least a snowflake.〉 — see LEAN 2

2 to turn away from a straight line or course 〈The river *trends* east, then west again, forming an oxbow.〉 — see CURVE 1

trendy *adj* being in the latest or current fashion 〈If what's in the stores is any indication, bright colors are *trendy* again this year.〉 — see STYLISH

trepidation *n* the emotion experienced in the presence or threat of danger 〈Shaking with *trepidation*, I stepped into the old abandoned house.〉 — see FEAR 1

trespass *n* **1** a breaking of a moral or legal code 〈Forgive us our *trespasses* as we forgive those who trespass against us.〉 — see OFFENSE 1

2 a failure to uphold the requirements of law, duty, or obligation 〈Plagiarism is a serious *trespass* of academic integrity.〉 — see BREACH 1

trespass *vb* to commit an offense 〈I consider him to be *trespassing* against all of us when he *trespasses* against any one of us.〉 — see OFFEND 1

triad *n* a group of three 〈a *triad* of candlesticks on the mantle〉 — see THREESOME

triadic *adj* having three units or parts 〈The application to this music school is *triadic* in structure: there's the written application, then the audition, and finally an interview with the admissions board.〉 — see TRIPLE

trial *adj* made or done as an experiment 〈a *trial* medical procedure that should be considered only after all other options have been exhausted〉 — see EXPERIMENTAL 1

trial *n* **1** a test of faith, patience, or strength 〈Living with her insufferable relatives was a real *trial*.〉

   synonyms cross, crucible, fire, gauntlet (*also* gantlet), ordeal

   related words baptism, initiation; adversity, affliction, asperity, misadventure, mischance, misfortune, mishap, privation, tragedy, tribulation, trouble, vicissitude, woe; challenge, complication, difficulty, hardship, rigor; annoyance, discomfort, inconvenience, nuisance

   phrases baptism of fire

2 a private performance or session in preparation for a

public appearance ⟨ran another *trial* of the aerial performance before opening night⟩ — see REHEARSAL

3 a procedure or operation carried out to resolve an uncertainty ⟨*Trials* by medical researchers haven't determined whether the medication is safe or not.⟩ — see EXPERIMENT

4 an effort to do or accomplish something ⟨The group will rest and make another *trial* at climbing the mountain.⟩ — see ATTEMPT 1

5 something that is a source of irritation ⟨The office renovations taking place during work hours were a real *trial*.⟩ — see ANNOYANCE 3

tribal *adj* of, relating to, or reflecting the traits exhibited by a group of people with a common ancestry and culture ⟨a *tribal* solidarity that transcends all other loyalties or bonds⟩ — see RACIAL

tribe *n* a group of persons who come from the same ancestor ⟨The Wichita *tribes* are indigenous to Texas, Oklahoma, and Kansas.⟩ — see FAMILY 1

tribulation *n* a state of great suffering of body or mind ⟨a documentary chronicling the lasting *tribulation* of Holocaust survivors⟩ — see DISTRESS 1

tribunal *n* an assembly of persons for the administration of justice ⟨He was tried before a military *tribunal* and found not guilty of the charges.⟩ — see COURT 3

tribute *n* a formal expression of praise ⟨*Tributes* were received from all over the world at the opera singer's farewell concert.⟩ — see ENCOMIUM

trice *n* a very small space of time ⟨It's just a scrape on the knee—we'll have you fixed up in a *trice*.⟩ — see INSTANT

trick *n* **1** a clever often underhanded means to achieve an end ⟨He used every *trick* in the book to get out of appearing in the charity's fashion show.⟩

synonyms artifice, device, dodge, gimmick, jig, knack, play, ploy, scheme, sleight, stratagem, wile

related words bluff, feint; chicanery, craft, cunning, duplicity, fakery, jugglery, legerdemain, skulduggery (*or* skullduggery), subterfuge, swindling, trickery; fraud, hoax, sham, swindle; blind, front, smoke screen

phrases sleight of hand

2 a playful or mischievous act intended as a joke ⟨I thought that gluing the silver dollar to the floor and watching him struggle to pick it up would be a good *trick*.⟩ — see PRANK

3 a usual manner of behaving or doing ⟨That deadbeat is up to his usual *tricks*: once again he's claiming the check is in the mail.⟩ — see HABIT 1

4 an act of notable skill, strength, or cleverness ⟨It'd be quite a *trick* to hit that target from here.⟩ — see FEAT 1

5 an odd or peculiar habit ⟨a dog with the *trick* of eating cabbage⟩ — see IDIOSYNCRASY

trick *vb* to cause to believe what is untrue ⟨You *tricked* me into thinking this wasn't a surprise party for me.⟩ — see DECEIVE

trickery *n* the use of clever underhanded actions to achieve an end ⟨Delia resorted to *trickery*—even loading up the fishing equipment—to induce her dog into the car for his vet appointment.⟩

synonyms artifice, chicanery, hanky-panky, jugglery, legerdemain, skulduggery (*or* skullduggery), subterfuge, wile

related words artfulness, caginess (*also* cageyness), craftiness, cunning, deviousness, foxiness, oiliness, shadiness, sharpness, shiftiness, shrewdness, slickness, slipperiness, slyness, sneakiness, treachery, underhandedness, wiliness; crookedness, deceit, deceitfulness, dishonesty, dissimulation, double-dealing, duplicity, guile, hypocrisy, insincerity; fakery, humbuggery, imposture, quackery; design, plotting

near antonyms artlessness, forthrightness, guilelessness, ingenuousness, sincerity; candidness, candor, directness, openness, plainness

trickle *vb* **1** to fall or let fall in or as if in drops ⟨*trickled* a little honey into her tea⟩ — see DRIP

2 to flow in a broken irregular stream ⟨The brook *trickled* along the glade.⟩ — see GURGLE

trickster *n* **1** a dishonest person who uses clever means to cheat others out of something of value ⟨A heartless *trickster* swindled the elderly woman out of her life savings.⟩

synonyms cheat, cheater, cozener, defrauder, dodger, hoaxer, shark, sharper, swindler

related words double-crosser; bluffer, charlatan, fake, faker, humbug, impostor (*or* imposter), mountebank, phony (*also* phoney), pretender, quack, ringer, sham; adventurer, fox, knave, prankster, rascal, rogue; slicker, smoothy (*or* smoothie), wheeler-dealer; plotter, schemer, sneak

2 one who practices tricks and illusions for entertainment ⟨a very adept *trickster* who used mirrors to make huge items—even buildings—seem to disappear⟩ — see MAGICIAN 2

tricky *adj* **1** requiring exceptional skill or caution in performance or handling ⟨a *tricky* musical passage for the woodwind section⟩

synonyms catchy, delicate, difficult, hairy, knotty, nasty, prickly, problematic (*also* problematical), sensitive, spiny, sticky, thorny, ticklish, touchy, tough

related words abstract, abstruse, complex, complicated, hard, intricate, involved, recondite, serious; problem, troublesome, troublous, vexatious, vexing, worrisome; burdensome, demanding, exacting, inconvenient, onerous, oppressive, painful, stressful

near antonyms easy, effortless, manageable, simple, straightforward, uncomplicated, undemanding

2 clever at attaining one's ends by indirect and often deceptive means ⟨He's a *tricky* one, so be careful when dealing with him.⟩ — see ARTFUL 1

tried *adj* worthy of one's trust ⟨a *tried* method for catching sport fish⟩ — see DEPENDABLE

tried–and–true *adj* worthy of one's trust ⟨a *tried-and-true* friend who has always been there for me⟩ — see DEPENDABLE

trifle *n* something of little importance ⟨Let us not speak of *trifles* when our nation may be going to war.⟩

synonyms child's play, nothing, picayune, shuck(s), triviality

related words naught (*also* nought), smoke, zero; peanuts, pittance, song, straw, two bits; bunk, claptrap, drivel, folly, fudge, hogwash, humbug, humbuggery, nonsense, piffle, rot, trash

trifle *vb* **1** to show a sexual attraction for someone just for fun ⟨Do not *trifle* with me unless you really care for me.⟩ — see FLIRT 1

2 to spend time in aimless activity ⟨We spent a lazy afternoon *trifling* on the front porch.⟩ — see FIDDLE (AROUND)

trifle (away) *vb* to use up carelessly ⟨*trifled away* his hard-earned professional respect with a single act of plagiarism⟩ — see WASTE 1

trifling *adj* **1** lacking importance ⟨Deciding what you want to do for a living is no *trifling* matter.⟩ — see UNIMPORTANT

2 so small or unimportant as to warrant little or no attention ⟨*trifling* differences between the theatrical and DVD versions of the movie⟩ — see NEGLIGIBLE 1

trigger *vb* to cause to function ⟨Mold *triggers* my allergies.⟩ — see ACTIVATE

trill *vb* to sing with the alternation of two musical tones ⟨A bluebird *trilled* outside our window.⟩ — see WARBLE

trim *adj* being clean and in good order ⟨kept his journal entries *trim*, never crossing out words or scribbling, but printing exactly and nicely⟩ — see NEAT 1

trim *n* **1** a state of being or fitness ⟨The doctor declared her to be in good *trim* for the race.⟩ — see CONDITION 1
2 something that decorates or beautifies ⟨Eva added a little *trim* to her cocktail dress to make it a little fancier.⟩ — see DECORATION 1

trim *vb* **1** to achieve a victory over ⟨a speed skater who consistently *trimmed* all his competition⟩ — see BEAT 2
2 to defeat by a large margin ⟨They *trimmed* our team by 40 points.⟩ — see WHIP 2
3 to make (something) shorter or smaller with the use of a cutting instrument ⟨*trimmed* her bangs⟩ — see CLIP 1
4 to make more attractive by adding something that is beautiful or becoming ⟨Let's *trim* a tree for Christmas!⟩ — see DECORATE

trimmer *n* one that defeats an enemy or opponent ⟨Last year's winner of the tournament unexpectedly got trimmed in the first round, and the *trimmer* was a young player that no one had ever heard of.⟩ — see VICTOR 1

trimming *n* failure to win a contest ⟨Our football team suffered a pretty severe *trimming*.⟩ — see DEFEAT 1

trinity *n* a group of three ⟨read novels and poetry produced by that sisterly *trinity* of English literature: Charlotte, Anne, and Emily Brontë⟩ — see THREESOME

trinket *n* a small object displayed for its attractiveness or interest ⟨The top of his desk was littered with *trinkets* that were collected as souvenirs from various vacations.⟩ — see KNICKKNACK

trio *n* a group of three ⟨The band was just a *trio* of musicians on piano, drums, and saxophone.⟩ — see THREESOME

trip *n* **1** a going from one place to another usually of some distance ⟨I'd like to book a *trip* to Greece with your travel agency.⟩ — see JOURNEY
2 an unintentional departure from truth or accuracy ⟨A *trip* in her calculations meant that she hadn't brought quite enough cash.⟩ — see ERROR 1

trip *vb* **1** to go at a pace faster than a walk ⟨They went *tripping* up the steps of city hall in their eagerness to get married.⟩ — see RUN 1
2 to go down from an upright position suddenly and involuntarily ⟨*tripped* over a chair and landed on her face⟩ — see FALL 1
3 to move with a light springing step ⟨dancers *tripping* lightly across the stage⟩ — see SKIP 1
4 to make a mistake ⟨The press has had it in for the new governor, and they are just waiting for her to *trip*.⟩ — see ERR 1

tripartite *adj* having three units or parts ⟨negotiated a *tripartite* agreement with its trading partner, with the first and second parts coming into effect immediately and the last part five years later⟩ — see TRIPLE

triple *adj* having three units or parts ⟨a *triple* scoop of chocolate ice cream⟩
  synonyms threefold, treble, triadic, tripartite, triplex
  related words triplicate

triple *n* a group of three ⟨that *triple* of terrors for the wintertime driver: snow, ice, and sleet⟩ — see THREESOME

triplet *n* a group of three ⟨The theater piece is actually a *triplet* of comedy sketches, all of them having romantic love as their theme.⟩ — see THREESOME

triplex *adj* having three units or parts ⟨a *triplex* house that features a separate apartment on each floor⟩ — see TRIPLE

trippingly *adv* in a quick and spirited manner ⟨loves words that roll *trippingly* off the tongue⟩ — see GAILY 2

trite *adj* used or heard so often as to be dull ⟨By the time the receiving line had ended, the bride and groom's thanks sounded *trite* and tired.⟩ — see STALE 1

triumph *n* **1** a successful result brought about by hard work ⟨Getting into Harvard is quite a *triumph*.⟩ — see ACCOMPLISHMENT 1
2 an instance of defeating an enemy or opponent ⟨Our stunning *triumph* on the field won us the title of regional champs.⟩ — see VICTORY

triumph *vb* **1** to achieve victory (as in a contest) ⟨Despite an accident early on, the runner persevered and ultimately *triumphed*.⟩ — see WIN 1
2 to feel or express joy or triumph ⟨In that part of the world it's customary for people to *triumph* by shooting off fireworks.⟩ — see EXULT

triumph (over) *vb* to achieve a victory over ⟨With teamwork, we can *triumph over* anything.⟩ — see BEAT 2

triumphant *adj* **1** having attained a desired end or state of good fortune ⟨the *triumphant* bidder on the house⟩ — see SUCCESSFUL 1
2 having or expressing feelings of joy or triumph ⟨He was positively *triumphant* when his country's team won the Olympic gold medal.⟩ — see EXULTANT

triumvirate *n* a group of three ⟨Among the city's cultural institutions, the art museum, the symphony orchestra, and the opera company reign as the supreme *triumvirate*.⟩ — see THREESOME

trivial *adj* **1** lacking importance ⟨Why spend so much time on *trivial* decisions?⟩ — see UNIMPORTANT
2 so small or unimportant as to warrant little or no attention ⟨figured that restaurant customers wouldn't notice such a *trivial* surcharge on their bill⟩ — see NEGLIGIBLE 1

triviality *n* something of little importance ⟨overlooked such *trivialities* as haphazardly folded napkins when rating the quality of restaurants⟩ — see TRIFLE

troll *n* an imaginary being usually having a small human form and magical powers ⟨"The Three Billy Goats Gruff" is the story of three goats trying to cross a bridge guarded by a nasty *troll* living beneath it.⟩ — see FAIRY

tromp *vb* **1** to move heavily or clumsily ⟨He sleepily *tromped* into the kitchen to get some coffee.⟩ — see LUMBER 1
2 to tread on heavily so as to crush or injure ⟨The kids *tromped* my flowers to smithereens.⟩ — see TRAMPLE
3 to travel by foot for exercise or pleasure ⟨The scouts *tromped* through the dell, mostly just following the course of the creek.⟩ — see HIKE 1

troop *n* **1** an organized group of stage performers ⟨A celebrated acting *troop* will be coming to town next month to perform one of Shakespeare's plays.⟩ — see COMPANY 1
2 **troops** *pl* the combined army, air force, and navy of a nation ⟨The *troops* overseas are grateful for the support of so many at home.⟩ — see ARMED FORCES

tropical *adj* being near the equator ⟨wanted to escape winter and visit some *tropical* location where freezing to death would not be a possibility⟩ — see LOW 1

trot *vb* **1** to go at a pace faster than a walk ⟨had to *trot* to keep up with the tour guide's quick pace⟩ — see RUN 1
2 to proceed or move quickly ⟨Now *trot* along and get washed up for supper.⟩ — see HURRY 2

troth *n* **1** a person's solemn declaration that he or she will do or not do something ⟨By my *troth*, I will not trespass on your precious property!⟩ — see PROMISE
2 adherence to something to which one is bound by a pledge or duty ⟨The knight pledged his eternal *troth* to the defense of the kingdom.⟩ — see FIDELITY

troth *vb* to obligate by prior agreement ⟨I *troth* myself eternally to your service.⟩ — see PLEDGE 1

trouble *n* **1** an abnormal state that disrupts a plant's or animal's normal bodily functioning ⟨I'm hoping that the doctor will be able to accurately diagnose my *trouble*.⟩ — see DISEASE

2 something that may cause injury or harm ⟨That wild dog is *trouble*, so stay away.⟩ — see DANGER 2

3 something that requires thought and skill for resolution ⟨The police officers first broke up the fight and then asked what the *trouble* was.⟩ — see PROBLEM 1

4 the active use of energy in producing a result ⟨Please, don't go to all that *trouble* just for me.⟩ — see EFFORT

5 the state of not being protected from injury, harm, or evil ⟨If you think your brother might be in *trouble*, then let's go check up on him.⟩ — see DANGER 1

trouble *vb* **1** to experience concern or anxiety ⟨Don't *trouble* about me—I'll be fine!⟩ — see WORRY 1

2 to cause discomfort to or trouble for ⟨I hate to *trouble* you, but would you mind moving for a minute so I can sweep under your chair?⟩ — see INCONVENIENCE

troubled *adj* feeling or showing uncomfortable feelings of uncertainty ⟨The *troubled* looks on their faces showed that they were still waiting for news about the accident.⟩ — see NERVOUS 1

troublesome *adj* causing worry or anxiety ⟨the *troublesome* news that there will be more cuts in the school budget⟩

synonyms discomforting, discomposing, disquieting, distressing, disturbing, nasty, perturbing, troubling, troublous, unsettling, upsetting, worrisome

related words daunting, demoralizing, discomfiting, disconcerting, discouraging, disheartening, dismaying, dispiriting; chilling, frightening, scary; alarming, dire, direful, dread, dreadful, fearful, fearsome, forbidding, formidable, frightening, frightful, ghastly, hair-raising, horrendous, horrible, horrifying, intimidating, scary, shocking, terrible, terrifying

near antonyms calming, quieting, settling, soothing; comforting, consoling, lulling, narcotic, pacifying, relaxing, sedative, tranquilizing (*also* tranquillizing)

antonyms reassuring

troubling *adj* causing worry or anxiety ⟨The most *troubling* sign of all is that he's stopped returning my phone calls.⟩ — see TROUBLESOME

troublous *adj* causing worry or anxiety ⟨They lived in *troublous* times.⟩ — see TROUBLESOME

trough *n* **1** a long hollow cylinder for carrying a substance (as a liquid or gas) ⟨All of the wiring for the converted residential loft is concealed in a vertical *trough*.⟩ — see PIPE 1

2 a long narrow channel dug in the earth ⟨I slid and fell into the *trough* by the side of the road, scraping my leg.⟩ — see DITCH

3 a pipe or channel for carrying off water from a roof ⟨The *troughs* on the eaves of the house were clogged with leaves.⟩ — see GUTTER 1

trounce *vb* to defeat by a large margin ⟨Our candidate *trounced* her opponent in the election, winning with 76% of the vote.⟩ — see WHIP 2

trouncing *n* failure to win a contest ⟨We took a serious *trouncing* during the last three minutes of the game.⟩ — see DEFEAT 1

troupe *n* an organized group of stage performers ⟨I desperately want to join our regional theater's acting *troupe* and perhaps get a lead role.⟩ — see COMPANY 1

trouper *n* one who acts professionally (as in a play, movie, or television show) ⟨had been a well-known Broadway *trouper* before making his screen debut⟩ — see ACTOR 1

trousers *pl n* an outer garment covering each leg separately from waist to ankle ⟨Dan picked up his *trousers* from the dry cleaners.⟩ — see PANTS

truce *n* a temporary stopping of fighting ⟨Both sides agreed to a 24-hour *truce* beginning at midnight on Christmas Eve.⟩

synonyms armistice, cease-fire

related words accord, reconcilement, reconciliation; détente (*or* detente); peace, peacetime

near antonyms conflict, hostilities, hot war, war

truck *n* **1** a giving or taking of one thing of value in return for another ⟨In medieval Europe, furs and forest products from the north were sold in *truck* for luxury products from the south.⟩ — see EXCHANGE 1

2 discarded or useless material ⟨filled a dozen large garbage bags with all the *truck* we collected when we cleaned the place out⟩ — see GARBAGE

truculence *n* **1** an inclination to fight or quarrel ⟨a *truculence* that resulted in his spending a good amount of time in the principal's office⟩ — see BELLIGERENCE

2 disposition to willfully inflict pain and suffering on others ⟨The sergeant's *truculence* was revealed when she made the recruits run even farther in the heat wave.⟩ — see CRUELTY

truculent *adj* **1** feeling or displaying eagerness to fight ⟨die-hard fans who became *truculent* and violent after their team's loss⟩ — see BELLIGERENT

2 marked by harsh insulting language ⟨a theater critic who was notorious for his titanically *truculent* reviews⟩ — see ABUSIVE

3 having or showing the desire to inflict severe pain and suffering on others ⟨played the role of a disturbed and *truculent* villain⟩ — see CRUEL 1

trudge *vb* **1** to move heavily or clumsily ⟨flooded residents who were forced to *trudge* through waist-deep water⟩ — see LUMBER 1

2 to proceed or act clumsily or ineffectually ⟨No expert on taxes, I spent the whole weekend *trudging* through Form 1040.⟩ — see FLOUNDER 1

true *adj* **1** being exactly as appears or as claimed ⟨His claim that he's the heir to the throne of Greece can't be *true*.⟩ — see AUTHENTIC 1

2 being in agreement with the truth or a fact or a standard ⟨If that is *true*, then we can't get in without a key.⟩ — see CORRECT 1

3 existing in fact and not merely as a possibility ⟨The *true* scope of this environmental problem is far greater than anyone imagined.⟩ — see ACTUAL

4 firm in one's allegiance to someone or something ⟨He will be *true* to his word.⟩ — see FAITHFUL 1

5 following an original exactly ⟨It's not a *true* reproduction of the painting because the original is much larger.⟩ — see FAITHFUL 2

6 free from any intent to deceive or impress others ⟨May our love for one another always be *true*!⟩ — see GUILELESS

7 restricted to or based on fact ⟨That news story is completely *true*, for the station released a list of its sources to back it up.⟩ — see FACTUAL 1

8 worthy of one's trust ⟨a *true* friend when you need one⟩ — see DEPENDABLE

9 having or showing the qualities associated with the members of a particular group or kind ⟨Paleontologists are still debating whether the fossil is that of a *true* dinosaur or a precursor.⟩ — see TYPICAL 1

true–blue *adj* firm in one's allegiance to someone or something ⟨a *true-blue* patriot even during the revolution's darkest hours⟩ — see FAITHFUL 1

truism *n* an idea or expression that has been used by many people ⟨ended his letter with the overused *truism*, "You can't win them all!"⟩ — see COMMONPLACE

truly *adv* **1** not merely this but also ⟨He is a kind, *truly* generous man.⟩ — see EVEN 1

2 to tell the truth ⟨*Truly*, I had no idea you were throwing me a party!⟩ — see ACTUALLY 1

3 without any question ⟨I very much appreciate your gift—*truly*, I can't thank you enough!⟩ — see INDEED 1

4 in actual fact ⟨This is *truly* the nicest thing anyone has done for me.⟩ — see VERY 2

trumpery *adj* of low quality ⟨*trumpery* knickknacks from some souvenir shop⟩ — see CHEAP 2

trumpery *n* language, behavior, or ideas that are absurd and contrary to good sense ⟨claims for health products that are based much more on manufacturers' *trumpery* than on science⟩ — see NONSENSE 1

trumpet *vb* **1** to make known openly or publicly ⟨The losing party lost no time in *trumpeting* allegations of election fraud.⟩ — see ANNOUNCE

2 to praise or publicize lavishly and often excessively ⟨Critics *trumpeted* the band's latest album as the best of the decade.⟩ — see TOUT 1

truncate *vb* to make less in extent or duration ⟨A *truncated* version of the 11 o'clock newscast followed the awards show, which ran over its time slot—as it always does.⟩ — see SHORTEN

truncheon *n* a heavy rigid stick used as a weapon or for punishment ⟨Police officers got ready to use their *truncheons*.⟩ — see CLUB 1

trunk *n* a covered rectangular container for storing or transporting things ⟨Jo threw the rest of her books and notebooks in the *trunk* and closed the lid.⟩ — see CHEST

truss *vb* to gather into a tight mass by means of a line or cord ⟨After stuffing the turkey, the chef quickly *trussed* it so the forcemeat wouldn't fall out during roasting.⟩ — see TIE 1

trust *n* **1** firm belief in the integrity, ability, effectiveness, or genuineness of someone or something ⟨a relationship of mutual *trust* between lawyer and client⟩
synonyms confidence, credence, faith, stock
related words acceptance, assurance, assuredness, certainty, certitude, conviction, positiveness, sureness, surety; credit, dependence (*also* dependance), hope, reliance
near antonyms disbelief, incredulity, unbelief; distrustfulness, doubt, dubiousness, incertitude, misgiving, mistrustfulness, nonconfidence, skepticism, suspicion, uncertainness, uncertainty; disenchantment, disillusion, disillusionment
antonyms distrust, mistrust

2 a number of businesses or enterprises united for commercial advantage ⟨Government lawyers argued against allowing the telephone companies to merge, asserting that such a merger would result in a *trust* that would stifle competition.⟩ — see CARTEL

3 responsibility for the safety and well-being of someone or something ⟨left her cat in the *trust* of her neighbors while she was on vacation⟩ — see CUSTODY

4 the right to take possession of goods before paying for them ⟨As his customers are sometimes short on money, the neighborhood grocer frequently has to sell on *trust*.⟩ — see CREDIT 1

trust *vb* **1** to give a task, duty, or responsibility to ⟨*trusted* the eldest child with walking the dog every morning⟩ — see ENTRUST 1

2 to put (something) into the possession or safekeeping of another ⟨I wouldn't *trust* my wallet with a complete stranger if I were you.⟩ — see GIVE 2

3 to regard as right or true ⟨Don't *trust* everything you read on the Internet.⟩ — see BELIEVE 1

trustful *adj* having or showing trust in another ⟨a *trustful* child quietly sleeping, sure in the knowledge that his parents would be there when he woke⟩ — see TRUSTING 1

trusting *adj* **1** having or showing trust in another ⟨Delia couldn't look into her dog's *trusting* eyes as she drove him to the vet.⟩
synonyms confiding, trustful
related words artless, childlike, credulous, guileless, gullible (*also* gullable), innocent, naive (*or* naïve), simple, unsophisticated; dependent, hopeful, reliant; accepting, believing, certain, confident, convinced, overconfident, secure, sure, unquestioning, unsuspecting, unsuspicious, unwary
near antonyms disbelieving, incredulous, unbelieving, unconvinced, undecided, unpersuaded; dubious, hesitant, leery (*also* leary), oversuspicious, skeptical, suspicious, uncertain, unsure, wary
antonyms distrustful, doubtful, doubting, mistrustful, trustless, untrusting

2 readily taken advantage of ⟨a corrupt stockbroker who preyed upon *trusting* customers⟩ — see EASY 2

trustworthiness *n* worthiness as the recipient of another's trust or confidence ⟨You have to prove your *trustworthiness* before I will tell you my secrets.⟩ — see RELIABILITY

trustworthy *adj* worthy of one's trust ⟨a *trustworthy* bodyguard who would never blab to the tabloids⟩ — see DEPENDABLE

trusty *adj* worthy of one's trust ⟨Movie cowboys always get on their *trusty* horses and ride off into the sunset.⟩ — see DEPENDABLE

truth *n* agreement with fact or reality ⟨There is no *truth* to the rumor that the business is moving to another state.⟩
synonyms factuality, verity
related words accuracy, actuality, authenticity, correctness; credibility, honesty, trustiness, trustworthiness, truthfulness, veracity; dependability, reliability
near antonyms erroneousness, fallaciousness, fallacy; falsehood, fiction, half-truth, lie; impreciseness, imprecision, inaccuracy, incorrectness, inexactitude, inexactness; deceit, dishonesty, equivocation, lying, mendacity, prevarication, untruthfulness
antonyms falseness, falsity, untruth

truthful *adj* being in the habit of telling the truth ⟨a *truthful* youngster who wouldn't just make up a story like that⟩
synonyms honest, veracious
related words candid, direct, forthcoming, forthright, foursquare, frank, free-spoken, open, openhearted, outfront, outspoken, plain, plainspoken; believable, credible, true, veritable; artless, earnest, genuine, guileless, unaffected, unpretending, unpretentious; conscientious, moral, principled, scrupulous; aboveboard, dependable, reliable, trustworthy, trusty
near antonyms fallacious, false, untrue; unbelievable, undependable, unreliable, unscrupulous, untrustworthy; bluffing, dissembling, dissimulating, equivocating, hypocritical, insincere, posing, pretending; artful, deceitful, deceptive, devious, evasive, slick, slippery, sly, sneaky, treacherous, tricky, underhanded, wily
antonyms dishonest, fibbing, lying, mendacious, prevaricating, untruthful

truthfully *adv* to tell the truth ⟨*Truthfully*, I'd rather go to the amusement park than to the museum, but I'll go along with the rest of the group.⟩ — see ACTUALLY 1

truthfulness *n* devotion to telling the truth ⟨Given the fact that used-car dealers are not renowned for their *truthfulness*, I had an independent mechanic check out the vehicle.⟩ — see HONESTY 1

try *n* an effort to do or accomplish something ⟨was granted another *try* at the field goal⟩ — see ATTEMPT 1

try *vb* **1** to subject (a personal quality or faculty) to often excessive stress ⟨You're *trying* my patience!⟩
synonyms strain, stretch, tax, test
related words demand, exact, importune, press,

pressure, push; aggravate, agitate, annoy, bother, exasperate, gall, get (to), gnaw (at), grate, harry, hassle, irk, irritate, nettle, pain, peeve, pester, rile, spite, vex
2 to make an effort to do ⟨*Try* to unlock the door.⟩ ⟨I will *try* to call later tonight.⟩ — see ATTEMPT

try (out) *vb* to put (something) to a test ⟨Want to *try out* my new skateboard?⟩ ⟨*tried out* his skill at archery⟩
synonyms sample, test
related words check (out), examine, experiment (with), explore, feel (out), investigate, research, study; resample, retest

trying *adj* difficult to endure ⟨They have been through some *trying* times together.⟩ — see HARSH 1

tryst *n* an agreement to be present at a specified time and place ⟨Both lovers had to hurry to keep their noontime *tryst* in the park.⟩ — see ENGAGEMENT 2

tsk–tsk *vb* to hold an unfavorable opinion of ⟨Some guests *tsk-tsked* the fact that the bride and groom were taking selfies.⟩ — see DISAPPROVE (OF)

tubby *adj* having an excess of body fat ⟨In America, Santa Claus is portrayed as a jolly and *tubby* older gentleman.⟩ — see FAT 1

tube *n* a long hollow cylinder for carrying a substance (as a liquid or gas) ⟨watched the liquid move through the *tube* between the flasks and recorded the movement in his chemistry notebook⟩ — see PIPE 1

tucker (out) *vb* to use up all the physical energy of ⟨We're hoping that the mountain bike ride will *tucker* the kids *out* so they'll sleep well tonight.⟩ — see EXHAUST 1

tuckered (out) *adj* depleted in strength, energy, or freshness ⟨*tuckered out* after a long day of playing tennis⟩ — see WEARY 1

tug *n* the act or an instance of applying force on something so that it moves in the direction of the force ⟨I gave the man in front a *tug* on his shirtsleeve as a sign that he was supposed to step aside.⟩ — see PULL 1

tug *vb* **1** to cause to follow by applying steady force on ⟨*tugged* on the door until it opened⟩ — see PULL 1
2 to devote serious and sustained effort ⟨She's *tugged* all her life to get to where she is now in the business world.⟩ — see LABOR

tug–of–war *n* an earnest effort for superiority or victory over another ⟨The effort to get their son to keep his room clean is a constant *tug-of-war*.⟩ — see CONTEST 1

tumble *n* **1** an unorganized collection or mixture of various things ⟨I cleaned a *tumble* of buttons, hair bands, loose change, and old candy wrappers out from the couch cushions.⟩ — see MISCELLANY 1
2 the act of going down from an upright position suddenly and involuntarily ⟨took a little *tumble* on the ice⟩ — see FALL 1
3 a state in which everything is out of order ⟨Her office is a *tumble* of books and papers, but somehow she can find everything.⟩ — see CHAOS

tumble *vb* **1** to go down from an upright position suddenly and involuntarily ⟨The infant stood for a moment and then *tumbled* on the carpet.⟩ — see FALL 1
2 to go to a lower level especially abruptly ⟨Prices for those stocks have really *tumbled*.⟩ — see DROP 2
3 to undo the proper order or arrangement of ⟨*tumbled* all the clothes in her closet as she furiously searched for her favorite pair of jeans⟩ — see DISORDER
4 to fall down or in as a result of physical pressure ⟨All we need is one strong wind, and that old barn is going to *tumble*.⟩ — see COLLAPSE 1

tumble (to) *vb* to have a clear idea of ⟨I finally *tumbled to* the fact that I had been duped into getting involved in a phony investment scheme.⟩ — see COMPREHEND 1

tumbled *adj* lacking in order, neatness, and often cleanliness ⟨a *tumbled* entryway filled with the usual jumble of sports equipment, backpacks, papers, and shoes⟩ — see MESSY

tumbledown *adj* showing signs of advanced wear and tear and neglect ⟨He lived alone on a *tumbledown* farm that had seen better days.⟩ — see SHABBY 1

tummy *n* the part of the body between the chest and the pelvis ⟨tickled the toddler's *tummy*⟩ — see STOMACH 1

tumor *n* an abnormal mass of tissue ⟨The scan showed a small *tumor* in her abdomen.⟩ — see GROWTH 1

tumult *n* **1** a state of noisy, confused activity ⟨In the *tumult* of our rush to the airport, we accidentally left on the lights.⟩ — see COMMOTION
2 a violent disturbance (as of the political or social order) ⟨the political *tumult* that swept the American colonies in the late 1700s⟩ — see CONVULSION
3 a violent shouting ⟨went to the window to see what the great *tumult* was and discovered a crowd of demonstrators marching down the street⟩ — see CLAMOR 1

tumultuous *adj* **1** marked by sudden or violent disturbance ⟨one of the most *tumultuous* periods in the history of the region⟩ — see CONVULSIVE 1
2 marked by turmoil or disturbance especially of natural elements ⟨We watched the *tumultuous* weather from the dry safety of our house.⟩ — see WILD 3
3 marked by bursts of destructive force or intense activity ⟨After a *tumultuous* day of trading, the stock market was down 500 points.⟩ — see VIOLENT 1

tundra *n* a broad area of level or rolling treeless country ⟨a report on the arctic *tundra* of Alaska and the polar bears that inhabit that vast, frozen plain⟩ — see PLAIN 1

tune *n* **1** a rhythmic series of musical tones arranged to give a pleasing effect ⟨hummed a little *tune* while I sorted the laundry⟩ — see MELODY
2 a state of consistency ⟨Your negative assessment of the restaurant seems to be in *tune* with the opinions of the critics.⟩ — see CONFORMITY 1
3 an approximate amount, extent, or degree ⟨Retail rents on the fashionable street can run to the *tune* of $100,000 a year.⟩ — see NEIGHBORHOOD 1

tuneful *adj* having a pleasing mixture of notes ⟨Some especially *tuneful* songs have been written for this new animated film.⟩ — see HARMONIOUS 1

turbid *adj* having visible particles in liquid suspension ⟨The pond water became *turbid* from our swimming and splashing.⟩ — see CLOUDY 1

turbulent *adj* **1** marked by bursts of destructive force or intense activity ⟨the *turbulent* struggle for civil rights that shook up American society in the 1960s⟩ — see VIOLENT 1
2 marked by turmoil or disturbance especially of natural elements ⟨The *turbulent* rapids of the river were certainly daunting to those of us who were new to river rafting.⟩ — see WILD 3
3 marked by wet and windy conditions ⟨Expect *turbulent* weather as the cold front brings rain and sleet.⟩ — see FOUL 1
4 marked by sudden or violent disturbance ⟨These are *turbulent*, dangerous times in a region known for being a powder keg.⟩ — see CONVULSIVE 1

turkey *n* **1** a person who lacks good sense or judgment ⟨He called me a *turkey* for playing golf during the thunderstorm.⟩ — see FOOL 1
2 a stupid person ⟨You *turkey*, that wasn't my boyfriend—it was my brother!⟩ — see IDIOT
3 something that has failed ⟨His business venture ended up being a *turkey*, and he lost quite a bit of money on it.⟩ — see FAILURE 3

turmoil *n* **1** a disturbed or uneasy state ⟨Don was in *turmoil* most of the night, trying to convince himself he had made the right decision.⟩ — see UNREST

2 a state of noisy, confused activity ⟨avoided the *turmoil* of the stores during the holiday season⟩ — see COMMOTION

turn *n* **1** a relaxed journey on foot for exercise or pleasure ⟨Would you care to take a *turn* around the garden?⟩ — see WALK 1

2 an act of kind assistance ⟨One good *turn* deserves another.⟩ — see FAVOR 1

3 a habitual attraction to some activity or thing ⟨an adventurous *turn* of mind that led him toward more physical activities like biking and skateboarding⟩ — see INCLINATION 1

4 something that curves or is curved ⟨Right after this *turn* in the road you'll find the antiques shop on the right.⟩ — see BEND 1

5 a sudden experiencing of a physical or mental disorder ⟨a sudden *turn* of dizziness that may have been brought on by a change in her medication⟩ — see ATTACK 2

6 a performance regularly presented by an individual or group ⟨Between the show's two major musical acts, there was a short *turn* by a juggling troupe.⟩ — see ACT 1

turn *vb* **1** to move (something) in a curved or circular path on or as if on an axis ⟨*turned* the doorknob as quietly as possible⟩
synonyms pivot, revolve, roll, rotate, spin, swing, swirl, twirl, twist, wheel, whirl
related words screw, unscrew; twiddle; coil, crank, reel, wind; circulate

2 to change the course or direction of (something) ⟨The dog *turned* the stampeding flock of sheep around.⟩ ⟨He *turned* his cart uphill.⟩
synonyms deflect, divert, swing, veer, wheel, whip
related words avert, deviate, move, rechannel, shift, shunt, sidetrack, swerve, switch, transfer; twist, whirl, zigzag; bend, curve, sway; reverse

3 to change one's course or direction ⟨We *turned* left at the light.⟩ ⟨The storm unexpectedly *turned* south and missed our area.⟩
synonyms detour, deviate, diverge, sheer, swerve, swing, turn off, veer, wheel
related words tack, zigzag; double (back)

4 to eventually have as a state or quality ⟨will *turn* 12 in six months⟩ — see BECOME

5 to move in circles around an axis or center ⟨The wheels *turned*, but the car was hopelessly stuck and wasn't moving.⟩ — see SPIN 1

6 to give serious and careful thought to ⟨We *turned* the question every which way but could find no answer.⟩ — see PONDER

7 to be determined by, based on, or subject (to) ⟨What we do next *turns* on your answer to the following question.⟩ — see DEPEND 1

8 to be in a confused state as if from being twirled around ⟨All the new information made his head *turn*.⟩ — see SPIN 2

9 to cause to have often negative opinions formed without sufficient knowledge ⟨He tried to *turn* his new friends against us.⟩ — see PREJUDICE

turn (to) *vb* to use or seek out as a source of aid, relief, or advantage ⟨no need to *turn to* violence when we can talk things out peacefully⟩ — see RESORT (TO) 1

turncoat *n* one who betrays a trust or an allegiance ⟨The plot of the story revolved around the gangster's relentless determination to learn the identity of the *turncoat*.⟩ — see TRAITOR

turn down *vb* to show unwillingness to accept, do, engage in, or agree to ⟨I'm afraid that I will have to *turn down* your invitation.⟩ — see DECLINE 1

turn in *vb* **1** to give (something) over to the control or possession of another usually under duress ⟨*turned in* the stolen items to the police⟩ — see SURRENDER 1

2 to go to one's bed in order to sleep ⟨It's almost midnight, so it's time to *turn in*.⟩ — see BED 1

turning point *n* a point in a chain of events at which an important change (as in one's fortunes) occurs ⟨The *turning point* came when Victor finally admitted he was a werewolf.⟩
synonyms climax, corner, landmark, milestone
related words break, clincher, crusher, highlight, topper; conversion, metamorphosis, transfiguration, transformation; clutch, crisis, crossroad(s), crunch, emergency, head, juncture, zero hour

turn off *vb* **1** to cause to feel disgust ⟨That memorably bad meal *turned* me *off* from restaurant food for a while.⟩ — see DISGUST

2 to change one's course or direction ⟨*Turn off* at the third exit and follow the ramp to your left.⟩ — see TURN 3

3 to let go from office, service, or employment ⟨Eventually, the supervisor *turned off* the insubordinate employee.⟩ — see DISMISS 1

4 to cause to stop functioning ⟨Please *turn off* the fan when you're done.⟩ — see DEACTIVATE

turn–on *n* something that persuades one to perform an action for pleasure or gain ⟨knew the offer of free pizza would be a major *turn-on* to the friends she had just asked to help her move⟩ — see LURE 1

turn on *vb* **1** to cause a pleasurable stimulation of the feelings of ⟨Unsurprisingly, the fanboys were *turned on* by the movie's amazing special effects and slam-bang plot.⟩ — see THRILL

2 to cause to function ⟨Would you *turn on* the TV?⟩ — see ACTIVATE

turn out *vb* **1** to leave one's bed ⟨We *turn out* early on workdays.⟩ — see ARISE 1

2 to remove the dirt from ⟨It's our practice to *turn out* the room after guests stay over.⟩ — see CLEAN 1

3 to drive or force out ⟨*turned* the dog *out* of the garden for digging up the plants⟩ — see EJECT 1

4 to come to be ⟨Everything will *turn out* fine in the end.⟩ — see COME OUT 1

turn over *vb* **1** to give (something) over to the control or possession of another usually under duress ⟨reluctantly *turned* the ship *over* to the first mate while he went below to try to stop the leak⟩ — see SURRENDER 1

2 to put (something) into the possession or safekeeping of another ⟨We *turned* the evidence *over* to the police.⟩ — see GIVE 2

3 to turn on one's side or upside down ⟨Don't try to tell me the bucket *turned over* all by itself!⟩ — see CAPSIZE

4 to change the position of (an object) so that the opposite side or end is showing ⟨Would you mind *turning* the picture *over* so I can see if the backing needs to be replaced?⟩ — see REVERSE 2

turnpike *n* a passage cleared for public vehicular travel ⟨The *turnpike* was jammed with people heading south for the long weekend.⟩ — see WAY 1

turn up *vb* **1** to come into view ⟨My missing car keys *turned up* just in time.⟩ — see APPEAR 1

2 to get to a destination ⟨When do you think our guests will *turn up*?⟩ — see COME 2

3 to come upon after searching, study, or effort ⟨It took days to *turn up* the original documents.⟩ — see FIND 1

tussle *n* a physical dispute between opposing individuals or groups ⟨A small *tussle* on the basketball court was quickly broken up.⟩ — see FIGHT 1

tussle *vb* to seize and attempt to unbalance one another for the purpose of achieving physical mastery ⟨puppies *tussling* with one another, rolling over and over on the carpet⟩ — see WRESTLE

tutelage *n* the act or process of imparting knowledge or skills to another ⟨a governess overseeing the *tutelage* of the family's children⟩ — see EDUCATION 1

tutor *vb* **1** to cause to acquire knowledge or skill in some field ⟨*tutored* me in Spanish⟩ — see TEACH
2 to give advice and instruction to (someone) regarding the course or process to be followed ⟨watched a video designed to *tutor* a person in the fine art of decorating cakes⟩ — see GUIDE 1

tutoring *n* the act or process of imparting knowledge or skills to another ⟨David found his calling in the *tutoring* of children with special educational needs.⟩ — see EDUCATION 1

twaddle *n* language, behavior, or ideas that are absurd and contrary to good sense ⟨The novel's elaborate theory detailing a supposed 2,000-year-old conspiracy is mostly tiresome *twaddle*.⟩ — see NONSENSE 1

twain *n* two things of the same or similar kind that match or are considered together ⟨I like rap and my parents like country music, and never the *twain* shall meet in our house.⟩ — see PAIR

tweet *vb* to make a short sharp sound like a small bird ⟨The computer *tweeted* again, signaling another error.⟩ — see CHIRP

twerp *n* a person of no importance or influence ⟨In high school he was just a little *twerp*, and now he's a big tech entrepreneur.⟩ — see NOBODY

twice *adv* to two times the amount or degree ⟨Having been turned down before, he is *twice* shy about making any more marriage proposals.⟩ — see DOUBLY

twilight *n* **1** a time or place of little or no light ⟨stumbled around the *twilight* of the shuttered room, unable to see where she was going⟩ — see DARK 1
2 the time from when the sun begins to set to the onset of total darkness ⟨The camper watched as *twilight* descended and the woods fell silent.⟩ — see DUSK 1

twin *adj* consisting of two members or parts that are usually joined ⟨a *twin*-cylinder engine⟩ — see DOUBLE 1

twin *n* **1** either of a pair matched in one or more qualities ⟨I've found one sock but can't find its *twin*.⟩ — see MATE 1
2 something or someone that strongly resembles another ⟨Some of these people who think that they're a given movie star's *twin* are kidding themselves.⟩ — see IMAGE 1

twine *vb* to follow a circular or spiral course ⟨The snake silently *twined* around the tree trunk.⟩ — see WIND 1

twinge *n* a sharp unpleasant sensation usually felt in some specific part of the body ⟨felt a *twinge* in her knee on that cold, rainy morning⟩ — see PAIN 1

twinkle *n* a very small space of time ⟨In just a *twinkle*, the shooting star was gone.⟩ — see INSTANT

twinkle *vb* **1** to shine with light at regular intervals ⟨Holiday decorations *twinkled* in the shop windows.⟩ — see BLINK 1
2 to shoot forth bursts of light ⟨stars *twinkling* on a crisp September night⟩ — see FLASH 1

twinkling *n* a very small space of time ⟨In a *twinkling*, the rabbit had disappeared.⟩ — see INSTANT

twirl *n* a rapid turning about on an axis or central point ⟨The *twirl* of the dancer's skirt mesmerized me.⟩ — see SPIN 1

twirl *vb* **1** to move (something) in a curved or circular path on or as if on an axis ⟨absentmindedly *twirled* a lock of her hair around her finger⟩ — see TURN 1
2 to move in circles around an axis or center ⟨an ice-skater *twirling* in place⟩ — see SPIN 1

twist *n* **1** a forceful rotating or pulling motion for the purpose of dislodging something ⟨With a forceful *twist* she loosened the bolt.⟩ — see WRENCH 1

2 an odd or peculiar habit ⟨My roommate has his little *twists*, and I have mine, so things should balance out.⟩ — see IDIOSYNCRASY

twist *vb* **1** to change so much as to create a wrong impression or alter the meaning of ⟨My enemies will *twist* my words, but you'll only hear the truth out of me.⟩ — see GARBLE
2 to follow a circular or spiral course ⟨The path gently *twisted* down the hill.⟩ — see WIND 1
3 to move (something) in a curved or circular path on or as if on an axis ⟨I *twisted* my wrist around to stretch it.⟩ — see TURN 1
4 to move by or as if by a forceful rotation ⟨kept *twisting* the cap until it came free⟩ — see WRENCH 1
5 to make jerky or restless movements ⟨The dental patient *twisted* nervously in the chair.⟩ — see FIDGET
6 to cause to twine about one another ⟨She has the habit of idly *twisting* the strands of her hair while daydreaming.⟩ — see INTERTWINE 1

twisted *adj* marked by a long series of irregular curves ⟨a *twisted* walking stick made from a blackthorn sapling⟩ — see CROOKED 1

twisting *adj* marked by a long series of irregular curves ⟨a *twisting* mountain road that requires extra careful driving⟩ — see CROOKED 1

twisting *n* a forceful rotating or pulling motion for the purpose of dislodging something ⟨It took some *twisting*, but I finally got the top off the jar.⟩ — see WRENCH 1

twitch *vb* **1** to make jerky or restless movements ⟨The dog *twitched* in her sleep.⟩ — see FIDGET
2 to move or cause to move with a sharp quick motion ⟨The rabbit *twitched* its nose.⟩ — see JERK 1

twitching *n* a series of slight movements by a body back and forth or from side to side ⟨The *twitching* of my cat's ears was a signal that I should stop petting her before she got any angrier.⟩ — see VIBRATION 1

twitter *n* **1** a state of nervous or irritated concern ⟨Our grandmother gets all in a *twitter* if she doesn't get her weekly phone call right on time.⟩ — see FRET
2 an explosive sound that is a sign of amusement ⟨the sort of lame double entendres that invariably provoke *twitters* among the immature⟩ — see LAUGH 1

twitter *vb* **1** to engage in casual or rambling conversation ⟨a local diner where the town gossips like to *twitter*⟩ — see CHAT 1
2 to make a short sharp sound like a small bird ⟨His two-way radio *twittered* as he answered it.⟩ — see CHIRP
3 to show mirth with an explosive vocal sound ⟨The class *twittered* at her jokes.⟩ — see LAUGH 1

two-faced *adj* not being or expressing what one appears to be or express ⟨a *two-faced* friend who was just using me to advance her career⟩ — see INSINCERE

twofold *adj* **1** being twice as great or as many ⟨My reasons for buying the condo are *twofold*: first, it will serve as my vacation home, and second, it should turn out to be a good investment.⟩ — see DOUBLE 2
2 consisting of two members or parts that are usually joined ⟨The mission of the campaign is *twofold*: to reduce underage drinking and to reduce alcohol-related traffic accidents.⟩ — see DOUBLE 1

twofold *adv* to two times the amount or degree ⟨With the start of the recession, home foreclosures began increasing *twofold*.⟩ — see DOUBLY

twosome *n* two things of the same or similar kind that match or are considered together ⟨Those sisters are a constant *twosome*, going everywhere together.⟩ — see PAIR

tycoon *n* a person of rank, power, or influence in a particular field ⟨an oil *tycoon* who's widely considered the richest person in the county⟩ — see MAGNATE

type *n* **1** a number of persons or things that are grouped together because they have something in common ⟨What *type* of people do you generally hang out with?⟩ — see SORT 1

2 one of the units into which a whole is divided on the basis of a common characteristic ⟨a music store that has a good selection of all *types* of music, not just pop, rock, and rap⟩ — see CLASS 2

type *vb* to arrange or assign according to type ⟨*Type* the birds by geographical range.⟩ — see CLASSIFY 1

typical *adj* **1** having or showing the qualities associated with the members of a particular group or kind ⟨*typical* behavior for a two-year-old⟩

synonyms archetypal (*also* archetypical), average, characteristic, normal, regular, representative, standard, true

related words common, commonplace, conventional, customary, everyday, ordinary, usual, wonted, workaday; classic, textbook; expected, familiar, habitual, predictable, routine, unexceptional, unremarkable; predominant, preponderant

near antonyms uncommon, unconventional, uncustomary, unusual, unwonted; distinctive, especial, exceptional, extraordinary, infrequent, noteworthy, rare, remarkable, singular, special, unexpected, unfamiliar, unique, unpredictable; eccentric, idiosyncratic, peculiar, unorthodox; curious, odd, oddball, offbeat, outlandish, quirky, screwy, strange, wacky (*also* whacky), way-out; bizarre, fantastic (*also* fantastical), far-out, freak, freakish, kooky (*also* kookie), out-of-the-way, outrageous, rare, unnatural, weird, wild

antonyms aberrant, abnormal, anomalous, atypical, deviant, irregular, nonrepresentative, nontypical, untypical

2 serving to identify as belonging to an individual or group ⟨When I asked what he had learned in school that day, he gave me his *typical* answer: "I don't know."⟩ — see CHARACTERISTIC 1

typically *adv* according to the usual course of things ⟨Prairie dogs *typically* live in open spaces.⟩ — see NATURALLY 2

tyrannical *also* **tyrannic** *adj* **1** exercising power or authority without interference by others ⟨a *tyrannical* ruler whose terrible reign was marked by oppression⟩ — see ABSOLUTE 1

2 fond of ordering people around ⟨Even when he was still a toddler, he tended to be a *tyrannical* playmate.⟩ — see BOSSY

tyrannizer *n* a person who uses power or authority in a cruel, unjust, or harmful way ⟨A petty *tyrannizer*, the manager made her employees' work lives miserable.⟩ — see DESPOT

tyrannous *adj* **1** exercising power or authority without interference by others ⟨We studied the *tyrannous* rule of Stalin, communist dictator of the Soviet Union.⟩ — see ABSOLUTE 1

2 fond of ordering people around ⟨My older sister is a *tyrannous* boor who isn't happy unless she's in charge.⟩ — see BOSSY

tyranny *n* a system of government in which the ruler has unlimited power ⟨A popular uprising replaced that nation's *tyranny* with freedom and democracy.⟩ — see DESPOTISM

tyrant *n* a person who uses power or authority in a cruel, unjust, or harmful way ⟨The people universally feared the *tyrant*, who was notorious for cruelly suppressing opposition.⟩ — see DESPOT

tyro *n* a person who is just starting out in a field of activity ⟨He's a good musician, but at 14, he's still a *tyro* and has a lot to learn.⟩ — see BEGINNER

U

ubiquitous *adj* **1** often observed or encountered ⟨By that time cell phones had become *ubiquitous*, and people had long ceased to be impressed by the sight of one.⟩ — see COMMON 1

2 present in all places and at all times ⟨I was weary of the *ubiquitous* noise of the big city and longed for the quiet of the country.⟩ — see OMNIPRESENT

ugly *adj* **1** unpleasant to look at ⟨Her first attempt at painting was pretty *ugly*—a portrait of her sister that was not at all flattering.⟩

synonyms grotesque, hideous, homely, ill-favored, monstrous, unappealing, unattractive, unbeautiful, unhandsome, unlovely, unpleasing, unpretty, unsightly, vile

related words abhorrent, abominable, appalling, awful, distasteful, dreadful, gross, horrible, horrid, loathsome, nauseating, nauseous, noisome, repellent (*also* repellant), repugnant, repulsive, revolting, sickening

near antonyms shapely; imposing, impressive, prepossessing

antonyms aesthetic (*also* esthetic *or* aesthetical *or* esthetical), attractive, beauteous, beautiful, bonny (*also* bonnie) [*chiefly British*], comely, cute, fair, fetching, goodly, gorgeous, handsome, knockout, lovely, pretty, ravishing, seemly, sightly, stunning, taking

2 causing intense displeasure, disgust, or resentment ⟨an *ugly* suggestion for controlling the overpopulation of deer in the area⟩ — see OFFENSIVE 1

ultimate *adj* **1** of the greatest or highest degree or quantity ⟨the *ultimate* speed yet attained by a land-based vehicle⟩

synonyms consummate, last, maximum, most, nth, outside, paramount, supreme, top, utmost, uttermost

related words unequaled (*or* unequalled), unmatched, unparalleled, unrivaled (*or* unrivalled), unsurpassed; biggest, hugest, largest; topmost, upmost, uppermost

near antonyms littlest; lowest

antonyms least, minimal, minimum, slightest

2 following all others of the same kind in order or time ⟨the *ultimate* speaker at today's meeting⟩ — see LAST 1

3 most distant from a center ⟨the *ultimate* edges of the universe⟩ — see EXTREME 1

ultimately *adv* at a later time ⟨We'll *ultimately* renovate this section of the house, but for now it will stay as it is.⟩ — see YET 1

ultimatum *n* something that someone insists upon having ⟨I issued the *ultimatum* that the project be finished by the following week, or it would be terminated.⟩ — see DEMAND 1

ultra *adj* being very far from the center of public opinion ⟨espoused a kind of *ultra* individualism⟩ — see EXTREME 2

ultramodern *adj* being or involving the latest methods, concepts, information, or styles ⟨an *ultramodern* design for the company's new line of automobiles⟩ — see MODERN

ultramodernist *n* a person with very modern ideas ⟨An *ultramodernist* in interior decoration, she freely uses materials that are recognizably man-made to achieve a look that enthusiastically embraces the 21st century.⟩ — see MODERN

umbra *n* **1** a time or place of little or no light ⟨Strange noises were coming from the wooded *umbra* beyond our campfire.⟩ — see DARK 1
2 partial darkness due to the obstruction of light rays ⟨During a solar eclipse observers located within the *umbra* experience a complete blocking of the sun by the moon.⟩ — see SHADE 1

umbrage *n* the feeling of being offended or resentful after a slight or indignity ⟨She took *umbrage* at the slightest suggestion of disrespect.⟩ — see PIQUE

umpire *n* a person who impartially decides or resolves a dispute or controversy ⟨Tom usually acts as *umpire* in the all-too-frequent squabbles between the two other roommates.⟩ — see JUDGE 1

umpire *vb* to give an opinion about (something at issue or in dispute) ⟨In our family disputes regarding the use of our home entertainment system are *umpired* by Dad.⟩ — see JUDGE 1

unabashed *adj* not embarrassed or ashamed ⟨*Unabashed* by their booing and hissing, he continued with his musical performance.⟩
synonyms shameless, unashamed, unblushing, unembarrassed
related words prideful, proud; bold, brassy, brazen, cheeky, impudent, insolent, saucy; unapologetic, undaunted, undeterred, undismayed; unblinking, unflinching; impenitent, remorseless, unrepentant
near antonyms confused, discomfited, disconcerted, discountenanced, fazed, flustered, mortified, rattled; apologetic, contrite, penitent, remorseful, repentant, sorry
antonyms abashed, ashamed, embarrassed, hangdog, shamed, shamefaced, sheepish

unacceptable *adj* falling short of a standard ⟨This work is entirely *unacceptable*.⟩ — see BAD 1

unacceptably *adv* **1** beyond a normal or acceptable limit ⟨The ski lodge was *unacceptably* cold.⟩ — see TOO 1
2 in an unsatisfactory way ⟨She does her chores quickly but usually *unacceptably*.⟩ — see BADLY 1

unacclimated *adj* not having acquired a habit or tolerance ⟨*unacclimated* to the intense heat of the tropics⟩ — see UNUSED 1

unaccompanied *adj* not being in the company of others ⟨an *unaccompanied* child on the airplane flight⟩ — see ALONE 1

unaccountable *adj* impossible to explain ⟨The decorator's client has an *unaccountable* dislike for that color.⟩ — see INEXPLICABLE

unaccustomed *adj* **1** not having acquired a habit or tolerance ⟨pampered youngsters who were *unaccustomed* to such hard work⟩ — see UNUSED 1
2 not known or experienced before ⟨the *unaccustomed* friendliness of my relatives after I won the lottery⟩ — see NEW 2
3 noticeably different from what is generally found or experienced ⟨*unaccustomed* styles of cooking that the tourists had to be persuaded to try⟩ — see UNUSUAL 1

unacquainted *adj* not informed about or aware of something ⟨*unacquainted* with the latest developments in the field of astronomy⟩ — see IGNORANT 2

unadapted *adj* not having acquired a habit or tolerance ⟨The animals that were *unadapted* to extreme cold quickly died out during the Ice Age.⟩ — see UNUSED 1

unadjusted *adj* not having acquired a habit or tolerance ⟨still *unadjusted* to the lifestyle of an air force cadet⟩ — see UNUSED 1

unadorned *adj* free from all additions or embellishment ⟨the completely *unadorned* clothing favored by members of that religious sect⟩ — see PLAIN 1

unadulterated *adj* **1** free from added matter ⟨An *unadulterated* solution is required for the experiment.⟩ — see PURE 1
2 having no exceptions or restrictions ⟨the *unadulterated* nonsense that you sometimes hear from political pundits on TV⟩ — see ABSOLUTE 1

unaesthetic *adj* disagreeable to one's aesthetic or artistic sense ⟨believes that even industrial buildings need not have *unaesthetic* designs⟩ — see HARSH 2

unaffected *adj* free from any intent to deceive or impress others ⟨a relaxed and *unaffected* style of public speaking⟩ — see GUILELESS

unaffectedly *adv* without any attempt to impress by deception or exaggeration ⟨She writes *unaffectedly* simple love poems.⟩ — see NATURALLY 3

unaided *adv* without aid or support ⟨The couple took pictures of the first time that the baby was able to walk *unaided*.⟩ — see ALONE 1

unalike *adj* being not of the same kind ⟨Our opinions of the movie couldn't have been more *unalike*.⟩ — see DIFFERENT 1

unalloyed *adj* **1** free from added matter ⟨*unalloyed* chemicals⟩ — see PURE 1
2 having no exceptions or restrictions ⟨the *unalloyed* happiness that marriage has brought them⟩ — see ABSOLUTE 1

unalterable *adj* not capable of changing or being changed ⟨The rules of the game are *unalterable*, regardless of who is playing.⟩ — see INFLEXIBLE 1

unambiguous *adj* **1** not subject to misinterpretation or more than one interpretation ⟨looked at his neighbor's new car with *unambiguous* envy⟩ — see CLEAR 2
2 so clearly expressed as to leave no doubt about the meaning ⟨an *unambiguous* declaration of his love for her⟩ — see EXPLICIT

unanimity *n* the state of being of one opinion about something ⟨In a rare moment of *unanimity* the club members decided to throw a party for themselves.⟩ — see AGREEMENT 1

unanimous *adj* having or marked by agreement in feeling or action ⟨a *unanimous* vote to upgrade the school's computer facilities⟩ — see HARMONIOUS 3

unanswerable *adj* not capable of being challenged or proved wrong ⟨the *unanswerable* assertion that she didn't know much about art but she knew what she liked⟩ — see IRREFUTABLE

unanticipated *adj* not expected ⟨We ran into some *unanticipated* difficulties with the computer program.⟩ — see UNEXPECTED

unappealing *adj* unpleasant to look at ⟨an *unappealing* mess of dirt and trash in the corner of the room⟩ — see UGLY 1

unappeasable *adj* showing no signs of slackening or yielding in one's purpose ⟨He warned that the nation was dealing with an *unappeasable* enemy.⟩ — see UNYIELDING 1

unappetizing *adj* disagreeable or disgusting to the sense of taste ⟨the array of *unappetizing* foods that we encountered at that cheap roadside restaurant⟩ — see DISTASTEFUL 1

unappreciated *adj* not likely to be appreciated by those who benefit ⟨a number of *unappreciated* little favors that we had done for the neighbors⟩ — see THANKLESS 2

unappreciative *adj* not showing gratitude ⟨vowed that his *unappreciative* niece would never receive another birthday present from him⟩ — see THANKLESS 1

unapproachable *adj* hard or impossible to get to or get at ⟨a nearly *unapproachable* fortress in the mountains⟩ — see INACCESSIBLE

unapt *adj* **1** not appropriate for a particular occasion or situation ⟨has a knack for saying the most *unapt* things at the worst possible moments⟩ — see INAPPROPRIATE
2 not likely to be true or to occur ⟨At this point an admission of guilt from him would be most *unapt*.⟩ — see IMPROBABLE

unashamed *adj* **1** not embarrassed or ashamed ⟨*unashamed* of her religious beliefs and values⟩ — see UNABASHED
2 not sorry for having done wrong ⟨Even after being convicted of housing violations, the slumlord remained as *unashamed* as ever.⟩ — see REMORSELESS 1

unasked *adj* not searched or asked for ⟨received a lot of *unasked* advice on the project⟩ — see UNSOUGHT

unassailable *adj* not to be violated, criticized, or tampered with ⟨one of the *unassailable* beliefs of that political party⟩ — see SACRED 1

unassisted *adv* without aid or support ⟨managed to do the group project *unassisted* after his partners got sick⟩ — see ALONE 1

unassuming *adj* not having or showing any feelings of superiority, self-assertiveness, or showiness ⟨a talented but surprisingly *unassuming* musician⟩ — see HUMBLE 1

unattached *adj* **1** not married ⟨My brother is currently *unattached*.⟩ — see SINGLE 1
2 not physically attached to another unit ⟨preferred an *unattached* house to a townhome⟩ — see SEPARATE 2

unattainable *adj* **1** hard or impossible to get to or get at ⟨an eagle's nest in an *unattainable* location⟩ — see INACCESSIBLE
2 incapable of being solved or accomplished ⟨She feels that, unfortunately, world peace is probably an *unattainable* ideal.⟩ — see IMPOSSIBLE

unattractive *adj* unpleasant to look at ⟨an *unattractive*, awkward baby bird⟩ — see UGLY 1

unauthentic *adj* being such in appearance only and made or manufactured with the intention of committing fraud ⟨trying to sell *unauthentic* autographs of American presidents⟩ — see COUNTERFEIT 1

unavailable *adj* hard or impossible to get to or get at ⟨The commander is *unavailable* right now.⟩ — see INACCESSIBLE

unavailing *adj* producing no results ⟨an *unavailing* effort to finish on time⟩ — see FUTILE

unavoidable *adj* impossible to avoid or evade ⟨Unfortunately, kitchen duty will be *unavoidable* tonight.⟩ — see INEVITABLE

unavoidably *adv* because of necessity ⟨We'll be *unavoidably* late this evening.⟩ — see NEEDS

unaware *adj* not informed about or aware of something ⟨She was *unaware* of the change in travel plans.⟩ — see IGNORANT 2

unaware *adv* without warning ⟨The predawn attack took the airmen completely *unaware*.⟩ — see UNAWARES

unawareness *n* the state of being unaware or uninformed ⟨He claimed *unawareness* of the problem.⟩ — see IGNORANCE 1

unawares *adv* without warning ⟨The thunderstorm caught us *unawares*, and we scrambled to get off the ridge as lightning started to flash.⟩
synonyms aback, suddenly, unaware, unexpectedly
related words abruptly, short; amazingly, astoundingly, surprisingly
phrases all of a sudden, off base
near antonyms laggardly, leisurely, slowly, sluggishly; tardily; obviously

unbalance *vb* to cause to go insane or as if insane ⟨The shock of the experience seems to have *unbalanced* him.⟩ — see CRAZE

unbalanced *adj* not being in or able to maintain a state of balance ⟨an *unbalanced* budget⟩ — see UNSTABLE 1

unbaptized *adj* not named or identified by a name ⟨Thus far the novel I've been working on remains *unbaptized*.⟩ — see NAMELESS 1

unbearable *adj* more than can be put up with ⟨This heat is *unbearable*—when are we going to get air-conditioning?⟩
synonyms insufferable, insupportable, intolerable, unendurable, unsupportable
related words unacceptable; crushing, overwhelming; comfortless, hard, harsh, painful, uncomfortable; appalling, dreadful, excruciating, gruesome (*also* grewsome), harrowing, horrendous, horrible, horrid, horrifying, nightmarish, shocking, terrible; tormenting, torturous, vile, wretched
near antonyms livable (*also* liveable); acceptable; adequate, admissible, allowable, reasonable, satisfactory
antonyms endurable, sufferable, supportable, sustainable, tolerable

unbeatable *adj* incapable of being defeated, overcome, or subdued ⟨a seemingly *unbeatable* baseball team⟩ — see INVINCIBLE

unbeautiful *adj* unpleasant to look at ⟨a makeshift shelter that was *unbeautiful* perhaps, but it kept us out of the rain⟩ — see UGLY 1

unbecoming *adj* not appropriate for a particular occasion or situation ⟨boorish behavior that is *unbecoming* to an officer⟩ — see INAPPROPRIATE

unbeknownst *also* **unbeknown** *adj* happening or existing without one's knowledge ⟨*Unbeknownst* to me, my mother was planning a party.⟩ — see UNKNOWN 1

unbelief *n* refusal to accept something as true ⟨A natural-born skeptic, she typically greets the latest conspiracy theory with head-shaking *unbelief*.⟩ — see DISBELIEF

unbelievable *adj* too extraordinary or improbable to believe ⟨a completely *unbelievable* story about why he was late⟩ — see INCREDIBLE

unbeliever *n* a person who is always ready to doubt or question the truth or existence of something ⟨a hard-headed *unbeliever* who demanded to see concrete evidence of any alleged UFO activity⟩ — see SKEPTIC

unbelieving *adj* inclined to doubt or question claims ⟨*unbelieving* scientists who demand that all phenomena be subjected to rigorous scientific scrutiny⟩ — see SKEPTICAL 1

unbend *vb* to cause to follow a line that is without bends or curls ⟨The new highway will largely *unbend* that twisting path that the old road used to follow.⟩ — see STRAIGHTEN

unbending *adj* **1** having or showing a lack of friendliness or interest in others ⟨the commanding officer's *unbending* reserve when dealing with subordinates⟩ — see COOL 1
2 sticking to an opinion, purpose, or course of action in spite of reason, arguments, or persuasion ⟨The school's new headmaster is reputed to be an *unbending* disciplinarian.⟩ — see OBSTINATE

unbiased *adj* marked by justice, honesty, and freedom from bias ⟨She offered an *unbiased* judgment of the dancer's performance.⟩ — see FAIR 2

unbidden *also* **unbid** *adj* not searched or asked for ⟨She arrived, *unbidden*, to help out at the Red Cross center.⟩ — see UNSOUGHT

unbind *vb* **1** to disengage the knotted parts of ⟨*unbind* a rope⟩ — see UNTIE
2 to release (as from slavery or confinement) ⟨a newly

elected democratic government whose first act was to *unbind* the nation's political prisoners⟩ — see FREE 1

unblemished *adj* being entirely without fault or flaw ⟨a modeling agency looking for people with *unblemished* complexions⟩ — see PERFECT 1

unblock *vb* to rid the surface of (as an area) from things in the way ⟨Let's *unblock* the road so that the convoy can proceed.⟩ — see CLEAR 1

unblushing *adj* not embarrassed or ashamed ⟨an *unblushing* patriotism that is manifested in the family's public display of the flag⟩ — see UNABASHED

unborn *adj* of a time after the present ⟨a home entertainment system that can be adapted for products as yet *unborn*⟩ — see FUTURE

unbosom *vb* to make known (as information previously kept secret) ⟨*unbosomed* his fears only to his closest friends⟩ — see REVEAL 1

unbound *adj* not bound, confined, or detained by force ⟨a dog left *unbound* in the yard⟩ — see FREE 3

unbounded *adj* 1 being or seeming to be without limits ⟨the *unbounded* enthusiasm shown by the new club members⟩ — see INFINITE

2 showing no signs of being under control ⟨*unbounded* speculation in the market⟩ — see RAMPANT 1

unbraid *vb* to separate the various strands of ⟨*unbraided* the line⟩ — see UNRAVEL 1

unbridled *adj* showing no signs of being under control ⟨a case that was solved only because of one detective's *unbridled* determination⟩ — see RAMPANT 1

unbroken *adj* 1 going on and on without any interruptions ⟨just mile after mile of *unbroken* woodland⟩ — see CONTINUOUS

2 living outdoors without taming or domestication by humans ⟨a young, *unbroken* horse⟩ — see WILD 1

unbudging *adj* incapable of moving or being moved ⟨The massive old bed was simply *unbudging*, despite our best efforts.⟩ — see IMMOVABLE 1

unburden *vb* 1 to empty or rid of cargo ⟨The crew was frantically *unburdening* the ship in an attempt to save it.⟩ — see UNLOAD 1

2 to set (a person or thing) free of something that encumbers ⟨A generous friend *unburdened* her of that particular financial worry.⟩ — see RID

unburdened *adj* no longer burdened with something unpleasant or painful ⟨Now *unburdened* of his painful secret, he felt free for the first time in years.⟩ — see FREE 2

uncage *vb* to release (as from slavery or confinement) ⟨*uncaged* the bird and let it fly away⟩ — see FREE 1

uncalled–for *adj* 1 not needed by the circumstances or to accomplish an end ⟨*uncalled-for* restrictions on freedom of the press during the national emergency⟩ — see UNNECESSARY

2 showing a lack of manners or consideration for others ⟨hurtful remarks that are simply *uncalled-for*⟩ — see IMPOLITE

uncanny *adj* 1 being beyond one's powers to know, understand, or explain ⟨a number of *uncanny* parallels in the lives of the twins who had been separated at birth⟩ — see MYSTERIOUS 1

2 being so extraordinary or abnormal as to suggest powers which violate the laws of nature ⟨an *uncanny* gift for knowing when someone, no matter how distant, needed help⟩ — see SUPERNATURAL 2

3 fearfully and mysteriously strange or fantastic ⟨*uncanny* and unexpected shadows along the mountainsides⟩ — see EERIE

uncataloged *adj* not appearing on a list ⟨Hundreds of *uncataloged* runners ran in the marathon.⟩ — see UNLISTED

unceasing *adj* going on and on without any interruptions ⟨This *unceasing* rain will turn me into a mushroom!⟩ — see CONTINUOUS

uncelebrated *adj* not widely known ⟨a gifted but *uncelebrated* poet⟩ — see OBSCURE 2

unceremonious *adj* 1 being or characterized by direct, brief, and potentially rude speech or manner ⟨My polite request was met with an *unceremonious* refusal.⟩ — see BLUNT 1

2 not rigidly following established form, custom, or rules ⟨Her *unceremonious* approach to her hosting duties puts party guests immediately at ease.⟩ — see INFORMAL 1

uncertain *adj* 1 likely to change frequently, suddenly, or unexpectedly ⟨The stifling heat would occasionally be relieved by an *uncertain* breeze.⟩ — see FICKLE 1

2 not feeling sure about the truth, wisdom, or trustworthiness of someone or something ⟨Never *uncertain* of her political beliefs or judgment, she was a decisive and fearless leader.⟩ — see DOUBTFUL 1

uncertainty *n* a feeling or attitude that one does not know the truth, truthfulness, or trustworthiness of someone or something ⟨*Uncertainty* about her job prospects has her worried.⟩ — see DOUBT

unchain *vb* to release (as from slavery or confinement) ⟨activists for animal rights who would like to *unchain* zoo animals and return them to the wild⟩ — see FREE 1

unchangeable *adj* not capable of changing or being changed ⟨I'm afraid that my opinion on this matter is *unchangeable*.⟩ — see INFLEXIBLE 1

unchangeableness *n* the state of continuing without change ⟨The endless days of sunshine were certainly pleasant, but the *unchangeableness* of the weather got to be boring after a while.⟩ — see CONSTANCY 1

unchanging *adj* 1 not undergoing a change in condition ⟨took comfort in *unchanging* family traditions⟩ — see CONSTANT 1

2 not varying ⟨wore an *unchanging* expression of boredom throughout the entire lecture⟩ — see UNIFORM

uncharitable *adj* 1 giving or sharing as little as possible ⟨an *uncharitable* couple who wouldn't even donate food to needy families at Thanksgiving⟩ — see STINGY 1

2 having or showing a lack of sympathy or tender feelings ⟨an *uncharitable* attitude towards people who struggle to make ends meet⟩ — see HARD 1

unchecked *adj* showing no signs of being under control ⟨*unchecked* corruption in the state's prison system⟩ — see RAMPANT 1

unchristened *adj* not named or identified by a name ⟨some *unchristened* dog that we just adopted from the local pound⟩ — see NAMELESS 1

uncivil *adj* 1 not civilized ⟨the *uncivil* and wild land that the pioneers tamed and settled⟩ — see UNCIVILIZED

2 showing a lack of manners or consideration for others ⟨Such *uncivil* behavior will not be tolerated!⟩ — see IMPOLITE

uncivilized *adj* not civilized ⟨Inaccurately characterized as *uncivilized* by early historians, the Indigenous peoples of the region had a sophisticated and advanced culture.⟩

synonyms barbarian, barbaric, barbarous, heathen, heathenish, Neanderthal (*or* Neandertal), rude, uncivil, uncultivated, wild

related words coarse, crude, primitive, rough; uncouth, uncultured

near antonyms cultured, enlightened, humane, sophisticated; genteel, polished, polite, refined, urbane, well-bred; semicivilized

antonyms civilized

unclad *adj* lacking or shed of clothing ⟨ancient sculptures of the *unclad* human figure⟩ — see NAKED 1

unclean *adj* **1** having or showing lowered moral character or standards ⟨There's something *unclean* about this whole business.⟩ — see CORRUPT

2 not clean ⟨a lackadaisical waiter who tried to set our table with smudged glasses and *unclean* silverware⟩ — see DIRTY 1

uncleanliness *n* the state or quality of being dirty ⟨The *uncleanliness* of the restaurant's windows wasn't very appetizing either.⟩ — see DIRTINESS

uncleanly *adj* not clean ⟨the *uncleanly* uniforms of the restaurant's staff⟩ — see DIRTY 1

uncleanness *n* the state or quality of being dirty ⟨The general *uncleanness* of the doctor's office turned my stomach.⟩ — see DIRTINESS

unclear *adj* **1** not expressed in precise terms ⟨Their suggestion for correcting the problem is a bit *unclear*.⟩ — see VAGUE 1

2 not seen or understood clearly ⟨obtained at best an *unclear* glimpse of the rarely seen bird from across the road⟩ — see FAINT 1

uncloak *vb* **1** to make known (as information previously kept secret) ⟨*uncloaked* the latest plan for improvements to the state capitol⟩ — see REVEAL 1

2 to reveal the true nature of ⟨Investigative reporters *uncloaked* the real estate tycoon, revealing him to be nothing more than a slumlord.⟩ — see EXPOSE 1

unclog *vb* **1** to make passage through (something) possible by removing obstructions ⟨tried *unclogging* a bathroom drain with a cleaner⟩ — see OPEN 2

2 to free from obstruction or difficulty ⟨*unclogged* the way for more people to take advantage of the government program⟩ — see EASE 1

unclogged *adj* allowing passage without obstruction ⟨An *unclogged* pipe works much more efficiently.⟩ — see OPEN 1

unclose *vb* to change from a closed to an open position ⟨One nurse closed the window in my room, and a minute later another nurse *unclosed* it.⟩ — see OPEN 1

unclosed *adj* allowing passage without obstruction ⟨We escaped through the one remaining *unclosed* passageway.⟩ — see OPEN 1

unclothe *vb* to remove clothing from ⟨partially *unclothed* the patient for treatment⟩ — see UNDRESS 1

unclothed *adj* lacking or shed of clothing ⟨an artist's drawings of clothed and *unclothed* figures⟩ — see NAKED 1

unclouded *adj* not stormy or cloudy ⟨campers awaking to the sight of a completely *unclouded* blue sky⟩ — see FAIR 1

uncluttered *adj* being clean and in good order ⟨I work better with an *uncluttered* desk.⟩ — see NEAT 1

uncolored *adj* lacking an addition of color ⟨The walls will be left *uncolored*, so you can choose your own color scheme.⟩ — see COLORLESS 1

uncomfortable *adj* **1** causing discomfort ⟨Unfortunately, dressing up for the dance meant wearing an *uncomfortable* shirt.⟩

synonyms comfortless, discomforting, harsh

related words aching, hurting, miserable, nasty, painful, sore; agonizing, excruciating, torturous; distressing, disturbing, upsetting; awkward, cumbersome, inconvenient, ungainly; uneasy; chafing, cramping, itching, pinching, pricking, prickling, smarting, stinging

near antonyms easy, soothing; cozy, cushy, snug, soft; easeful, relaxing, reposeful, restful

antonyms comfortable

2 causing embarrassment ⟨the *uncomfortable* situation of running into an ex-friend at a social gathering⟩ — see AWKWARD 3

3 lacking social grace and assurance ⟨a person who is *uncomfortable* at parties with lots of strangers⟩ — see AWKWARD 1

uncomic *adj* not joking or playful in mood or manner ⟨The movie takes a very *uncomic* approach to alcohol addiction.⟩ — see SERIOUS 1

uncommon *adj* **1** being out of the ordinary ⟨a landscape of *uncommon* beauty⟩ — see EXCEPTIONAL 1

2 noticeably different from what is generally found or experienced ⟨Backyard swimming pools are not an *uncommon* sight in that neighborhood.⟩ — see UNUSUAL 1

uncommunicative *adj* **1** deliberately refraining from speech ⟨They've been *uncommunicative* with us about their plans.⟩ — see SILENT 1

2 given to keeping one's activities hidden from public observation or knowledge ⟨Intelligence agencies must be *uncommunicative* about their operations if they are to be at all effective.⟩ — see SECRETIVE

3 tending not to speak frequently (as by habit or inclination) ⟨My freshman roommate turned out to be rather *uncommunicative*.⟩ — see SILENT 2

uncomplaining *adj* accepting pains or hardships calmly or without complaint ⟨an *uncomplaining* hardworking employee⟩ — see PATIENT 1

uncomplimentary *adj* intended to make a person or thing seem of little importance or value ⟨an *uncomplimentary* description of the town in which the writer grew up⟩ — see DEROGATORY

uncompromising *adj* **1** not allowing for any exceptions or loosening of standards ⟨an *uncompromising* adherence to the rules⟩ — see RIGID 1

2 sticking to an opinion, purpose, or course of action in spite of reason, arguments, or persuasion ⟨The professor is generally an *uncompromising* stickler for deadlines, but he will make exceptions for genuine need.⟩ — see OBSTINATE

unconcern *n* lack of interest or concern ⟨He wore an expression of general *unconcern* throughout the trial.⟩ — see INDIFFERENCE

unconcerned *adj* **1** having or showing freedom from worries or troubles ⟨playful and *unconcerned* despite his medical emergency⟩ — see CAREFREE

2 having or showing a lack of interest or concern ⟨an oblivious person who was completely *unconcerned* about the important issues of the day⟩ — see INDIFFERENT 1

unconditional *adj* having no exceptions or restrictions ⟨demanded an *unconditional* surrender⟩ — see ABSOLUTE 2

unconfined *adj* not bound, confined, or detained by force ⟨wild horses roaming *unconfined* over the plain⟩ — see FREE 3

uncongenial *adj* not giving pleasure to the mind or senses ⟨a dank and *uncongenial* castle that makes one question just how merry old England really was⟩ — see UNPLEASANT

unconnected *adj* **1** not clearly or logically connected ⟨a delirious patient whose *unconnected* ramblings confounded the staff⟩ — see INCOHERENT 1

2 not physically attached to another unit ⟨The *unconnected* houses in the private development have common areas and share certain facilities.⟩ — see SEPARATE 2

unconquerable *adj* incapable of being defeated, overcome, or subdued ⟨an *unconquerable* spirit that got the family through some hard times⟩ — see INVINCIBLE

unconscionable *adj* **1** going beyond a normal or acceptable limit in degree or amount ⟨an *unconscionable* number of errors for an important government report⟩ — see EXCESSIVE

2 not guided by or showing a concern for what is right ⟨a politician with an *unconscionable* disregard for the truth⟩ — see UNPRINCIPLED

unconscious *adj* **1** having lost consciousness ⟨The guard was knocked *unconscious* by a blow to the head.⟩

synonyms cold, insensible, senseless

related words semiconscious; anesthetized; collapsed

near antonyms alert, awake, aware, up; resuscitated, revived

antonyms conscious

2 not informed about or aware of something ⟨*unconscious* of the somber expression she wore⟩ — see IGNORANT 2

unconsidered *adj* made or done without previous thought or preparation ⟨regretted some *unconsidered* comments that she made during a live TV interview⟩ — see EXTEMPORANEOUS

unconsolidated *adj* consisting of particles that do not stick together ⟨*unconsolidated* soil⟩ — see LOOSE 2

uncontrollable *adj* given to resisting control or discipline by others ⟨The *uncontrollable* child kept throwing tantrums in public and creating scenes.⟩

synonyms froward, headstrong, intractable, recalcitrant, refractory, ungovernable, unmanageable, unruly, untoward, wayward, willful (*or* wilful)

related words contrary, difficult, hardheaded, incorrigible, mulish, obdurate, obstinate, opinionated, perverse, pigheaded, self-willed, stiff, stiff-necked, stubborn; undisciplined, unpunished; uncontrolled, wild; boisterous, irrepressible, rambunctious, rowdy; disobedient, insubordinate, rebellious

phrases out of hand

near antonyms docile, obedient, well-behaved; compliant, placable, pliable, submissive, yielding; accepting, persuadable, receptive, responsive, willing; reasonable, temperate, trainable

antonyms controllable, governable, manageable, tractable

uncontrolled *adj* showing no signs of being under control ⟨a tirade filled with *uncontrolled* anger about what the government was doing⟩ — see RAMPANT 1

unconventional *adj* **1** deviating from commonly accepted beliefs or practices ⟨The Shakers acquired their name because of their *unconventional* practice of dancing with shaking movements during worship.⟩ — see HERETICAL

2 not bound by traditional ways or beliefs ⟨had *unconventional* opinions on the raising of children⟩ — see LIBERAL 1

3 not rigidly following established form, custom, or rules ⟨young, creative people who lead *unconventional* but fulfilling lifestyles⟩ — see INFORMAL 1

unconvinced *adj* not feeling sure about the truth, wisdom, or trustworthiness of someone or something ⟨*unconvinced* that the prosecution had proven guilt beyond a reasonable doubt⟩ — see DOUBTFUL 1

unconvincing *adj* too extraordinary or improbable to believe ⟨The excuse for her tardiness was too *unconvincing* to be accepted.⟩ — see INCREDIBLE

uncooked *adj* not cooked ⟨crunching on *uncooked* carrots⟩ — see RAW 1

uncork *vb* to set free (from a state of being held in check) ⟨*uncorked* her emotions once she was alone in her room⟩ — see RELEASE 1

uncountable *adj* too many to be counted ⟨an *uncountable* number of mosquitoes in the yard⟩ — see COUNTLESS

uncounted *adj* too many to be counted ⟨gazed in wonder at the *uncounted* stars of the sky⟩ — see COUNTLESS

uncouple *vb* to set or force apart ⟨*uncoupled* the two railroad cars⟩ — see SEPARATE 1

uncouth *adj* **1** having or showing crudely insensitive or impolite manners ⟨Mom will not tolerate any *uncouth* behavior, such as eating with one's mouth open.⟩ — see CLOWNISH

2 lacking in refinement or good taste ⟨The movie's *uncouth* humor seemed to be purposely offensive.⟩ — see COARSE 2

uncover *vb* **1** to make known (as information previously kept secret) ⟨*uncovered* the location of the secret documents⟩ — see REVEAL 1

2 to reveal the true nature of ⟨a magazine article that purports to *uncover* the inner operations of a business that many regard as a scam⟩ — see EXPOSE 1

uncovered *adj* lacking a usual or natural covering ⟨The famed snows of Mount Kilimanjaro are receding, leaving behind much *uncovered* ground.⟩ — see NAKED 2

uncritical *adj* lacking in worldly wisdom or informed judgment ⟨had an *uncritical* trust in the nation's leaders⟩ — see NAIVE 1

uncrown *vb* to remove from a position of prominence or power (as a throne) ⟨Edward VIII effectively *uncrowned* himself when he insisted upon marrying an American divorcée.⟩ — see DEPOSE 1

unctuous *adj* **1** not being or expressing what one appears to be or express ⟨an *unctuous* effort to appear religious to the voters⟩ — see INSINCERE

2 overly or insincerely flattering ⟨an *unctuous* appraisal of the musical talent shown by the boss's daughter⟩ — see FULSOME 1

uncultivated *adj* **1** existing without human habitation or cultivation ⟨miles of *uncultivated* land that had never been touched by a plow or an ax⟩ — see WILD 2

2 lacking in refinement or good taste ⟨an *uncultivated* and ignorant philistine who cared only about money⟩ — see COARSE 2

3 not civilized ⟨an *uncultivated* age when people lived just to meet their day-to-day needs⟩ — see UNCIVILIZED

uncultured *adj* lacking in refinement or good taste ⟨an unlettered and *uncultured* society that still had the manners of the frontier⟩ — see COARSE 2

uncurious *adj* having or showing a lack of interest or concern ⟨How can you be so *uncurious* about the world around you?⟩ — see INDIFFERENT 1

uncurl *vb* to cause to follow a line that is without bends or curls ⟨*uncurled* the ribbon and flattened it out⟩ — see STRAIGHTEN

uncustomary *adj* **1** being out of the ordinary ⟨Emma has *uncustomary* grace and poise for a girl of her age.⟩ — see EXCEPTIONAL 1

2 noticeably different from what is generally found or experienced ⟨anger that was very *uncustomary* for such an even-tempered man⟩ — see UNUSUAL 1

undaunted *adj* feeling or displaying no fear by temperament ⟨*undaunted* despite their repeated failures at starting a business⟩ — see BRAVE 1

undeceive *vb* to free from mistaken beliefs or foolish hopes ⟨I promptly *undeceived* the shoppers about the sincerity of the salesman's claims.⟩ — see DISILLUSION

undecided *adj* **1** not yet settled or decided ⟨a number of *undecided* matters still before the committee⟩ — see PENDING 1

2 not feeling sure about the truth, wisdom, or trustworthiness of someone or something ⟨Voters still seem to be *undecided* about that candidate's fitness for the office of president.⟩ — see DOUBTFUL 1

undecorated *adj* free from all additions or embellishment ⟨Karen left the room simple and *undecorated* so that she'd be able to concentrate when she studied there.⟩ — see PLAIN 1

undefended *adj* lacking protection from danger or resistance against attack ⟨The cowardly soldiers fled, leaving the palace *undefended*.⟩ — see HELPLESS 1

undefined *adj* not seen or understood clearly ⟨plagued by *undefined* worries that kept her awake at night⟩ — see FAINT 1

undemonstrative *adj* not feeling or showing emotion ⟨An *undemonstrative* person by nature, he nevertheless loved his wife very much.⟩ — see IMPASSIVE 1

undeniable *adj* not capable of being challenged or proved wrong ⟨*undeniable* evidence of guilt⟩ — see IRREFUTABLE

undeniably *adv* without any question ⟨She is *undeniably* the best tennis player of her time.⟩ — see INDEED 1

under *adv* in or to a lower place ⟨Crouch down *under* where they won't see you.⟩ — see BELOW 1

under *prep* in a lower position than ⟨The cat is hiding *under* the bed.⟩ — see BELOW 1

underbelly *n* **1** the side or part facing downward from something ⟨The *underbelly* of the old submarine is in bad shape.⟩ — see BOTTOM 1

2 a vulnerable point ⟨The vast, thinly guarded southern border was obviously the *underbelly* of the nation's line of defense.⟩ — see ACHILLES' HEEL

underbody *n* the side or part facing downward from something ⟨The *underbody* of the car was starting to rust.⟩ — see BOTTOM 1

underclothes *pl n* clothing intended to be worn underneath other clothing ⟨I keep my *underclothes* in a separate drawer.⟩ — see UNDERWEAR

underclothing *n* clothing intended to be worn underneath other clothing ⟨He changes his *underclothing* every day.⟩ — see UNDERWEAR

undercover *adj* **1** undertaken or done so as to escape being observed or known by others ⟨an *undercover* operation to infiltrate the criminal organization⟩ — see SECRET 1

2 working on missions in which one's objectives, activities, or true identity are not publicly revealed ⟨For months she's been an *undercover* agent pretending to be a stock broker.⟩ — see SECRET 2

undergarments *pl n* clothing intended to be worn underneath other clothing ⟨Pack plenty of warm *undergarments* for the ski vacation.⟩ — see UNDERWEAR

undergo *vb* to come to a knowledge of (something) by living through it ⟨Some people *undergo* a complete transformation while away at college.⟩ — see EXPERIENCE

underground *adj* undertaken or done so as to escape being observed or known by others ⟨an *underground* operation to smuggle ancient artifacts out of the country⟩ — see SECRET 1

underground *n* a secret organization in a conquered country fighting against enemy forces ⟨joined the *underground* while still a teenager⟩ — see RESISTANCE 2

underhand *adj* **1** given to or marked by cheating and deception ⟨willing to stoop to *underhand* methods in order to win⟩ — see DISHONEST 2

2 undertaken or done so as to escape being observed or known by others ⟨the congressman's *underhand* attempt to slip several pork barrel items into the bill⟩ — see SECRET 1

underhanded *adj* **1** given to or marked by cheating and deception ⟨The commercial is a part of an *underhanded* PR campaign to whitewash the company's environmental record.⟩ — see DISHONEST 2

2 undertaken or done so as to escape being observed or known by others ⟨an *underhanded* attempt at infiltrating the other party's headquarters⟩ — see SECRET 1

underline *vb* to make more apparent ⟨a report that *underlines* the contributions of fathers to successful, happy families⟩ — see EMPHASIZE 2

underling *n* one who is of lower rank and typically under the authority of another ⟨The real estate tycoon has a whole army of *underlings* to attend to the details.⟩

synonyms inferior, junior, subordinate

related words attendant, follower, retainer; domestic, menial, steward; flunky (*also* flunkey *or* flunkie), henchman, lackey, minion; adjutant, aid, aide, assistant, coadjutor, deputy, second, second fiddle; helpmate, helpmeet, mate, sidekick

near antonyms boss, captain, chief, foreman, head, headman, helmsman, kingpin, leader, master, taskmaster

antonyms senior, superior

underlying *adj* of or relating to the simplest facts or theories of a subject ⟨the *underlying* differences between democracy and dictatorship⟩ — see ELEMENTARY

underneath *adv* in or to a lower place ⟨The ball rolled under the porch, so you'll have to crawl *underneath* to get it.⟩ — see BELOW 1

underpart *n* the side or part facing downward from something ⟨The bird's *underparts* were white.⟩ — see BOTTOM 1

underpin *vb* to hold up or serve as a foundation for ⟨the central beliefs that *underpin* a free society⟩ — see SUPPORT 3

underpinning *n* **1** an immaterial thing upon which something else rests ⟨The *underpinnings* of the theory have recently been called into question.⟩ — see BASE 1

2 a structure that holds up or serves as a foundation for something else ⟨The *underpinnings* of the bridge were seriously damaged in the collision.⟩ — see SUPPORT 1

underprivileged *adj* kept from having the necessities of life or a healthful environment ⟨The school department tried to focus more resources on serving the needs of *underprivileged* children.⟩ — see DEPRIVED

underscore *vb* to make more apparent ⟨a history of the Old West that *underscores* the role that pioneer women had in bringing order and stability to the wild frontier⟩ — see EMPHASIZE 2

underside *n* the side or part facing downward from something ⟨The *underside* of the cat's coat is pure white.⟩ — see BOTTOM 1

undersized *also* **undersize** *adj* of a size that is less than average ⟨Though a football all-star in high school, he was just a mediocre, *undersized* player at the college level.⟩ — see SMALL 1

understand *vb* **1** to form an opinion or reach a conclusion through reasoning and information ⟨As I *understand* it, this is the best plan that we have.⟩ — see INFER 1

2 to have a practical understanding of ⟨I think I *understand* how an engine works now.⟩ — see KNOW 1

3 to have a clear idea of ⟨After a few weeks in Russia I began to *understand* the language a little bit.⟩ — see COMPREHEND 1

understanding *adj* having or showing the capacity for sharing the feelings of another ⟨a kind and *understanding* teacher who often helps troubled students⟩ — see SYMPATHETIC 1

understanding *n* **1** an arrangement about action to be taken ⟨The landlord came to an *understanding* with the tenants about his obligations for maintaining the property.⟩ — see AGREEMENT 2

2 the knowledge gained from the process of coming to know or understand something ⟨a social observer with a deep *understanding* of the problems that the nation's cities face in the 21st century⟩ — see COMPREHENSION

understated *adj* not excessively showy ⟨The actor's *understated* interpretation of the lead role is surprisingly compelling.⟩ — see QUIET 2

undersurface *n* the side or part facing downward from something ⟨painted the *undersurface* of the plane blue⟩ — see BOTTOM 1

undertake *vb* to take to or upon oneself ⟨*undertook* the responsibility of raising the orphaned children as their own⟩ — see ASSUME 1

undertaker *n* a person who manages funerals and prepares the dead for burial or cremation ⟨The *undertaker* wore black clothes and a solemn expression.⟩ — see FUNERAL DIRECTOR

underwater *adj* living, lying, or occurring below the surface

of the water ⟨*Underwater* plants don't require as much light to grow as surface plants.⟩ ⟨a vessel designed for *underwater* exploration⟩
synonyms aquatic, submarine, submerged, sunken
related words oceanic; undersea; abysmal, abyssal, deep, deepwater
underwear *n* clothing intended to be worn underneath other clothing ⟨*Underwear* has got to be the most boring thing that one could ever receive as a birthday present!⟩
synonyms underclothes, underclothing, undergarments, undies
related words lingerie; panties; slip, underskirt; boxers, boxer shorts, briefs, drawers, long johns, pants, shorts, underdrawers, underpants, undershirt, undershorts, union suit; nightdress, nightgown, nightshirt, pajamas, pj's
near antonyms outerwear
underweight *adj* having little weight ⟨The long illness left him frail and *underweight*.⟩ — see ¹LIGHT 1
underwrite *vb* to provide money for ⟨a university willing to *underwrite* an archaeological expedition⟩ — see FINANCE 1
undetermined *adj* 1 not seen or understood clearly ⟨an *undetermined* form seen only from a distance⟩ — see FAINT 1
2 not yet settled or decided ⟨The fate of the proposal is still *undetermined*.⟩ — see PENDING 1
undeviating *adj* not varying ⟨an *undeviating* dedication to duty⟩ — see UNIFORM
undies *pl n* clothing intended to be worn underneath other clothing ⟨It was such a hot night that the little boy slept in just his *undies*.⟩ — see UNDERWEAR
undiluted *adj* free from added matter ⟨*Undiluted* cranberry juice would be too strong for anyone to drink.⟩ — see PURE 1
undisturbed *adj* free from emotional or mental agitation ⟨We didn't tell him the sad news until after the test, so he would remain *undisturbed*.⟩ — see CALM 2
undivided *adj* not divided or scattered among several areas of interest or concern ⟨a teacher who insists on the *undivided* attention of her students⟩ — see WHOLE 1
undo *vb* 1 to deprive of courage or confidence ⟨The sudden shriek *undid* the campers.⟩ — see UNNERVE 1
2 to disengage the knotted parts of ⟨I need to *undo* a tangled shoelace.⟩ — see UNTIE
3 to trouble the mind of; to make uneasy ⟨The mere mention of the home invasion still had the power to *undo* her.⟩ — see DISTURB 1
undomesticated *adj* living outdoors without taming or domestication by humans ⟨Domesticated rats are more tolerable companions than are their *undomesticated* cousins.⟩ — see WILD 1
undoubtedly *adv* without any question ⟨We will *undoubtedly* have to do some editing of our home video.⟩ — see INDEED 1
undress *vb* 1 to remove clothing from ⟨I quickly *undressed* myself and pulled on a set of dry clothes.⟩
synonyms disrobe, strip, unclothe
related words bare, denude, expose, uncover, undrape, unveil; bark, flay, peel, skin
near antonyms apparel, array, attire, caparison, clothe, costume, cover, deck, dress, feather, garb, garment, invest, rig (out), vest; cloak, mantle; swaddle, swathe; accoutre (*or* accouter), equip, furnish, outfit
antonyms dress, gown, robe
2 to reveal the true nature of ⟨a self-styled financial investor who was eventually *undressed* as a con artist running a pyramid scheme⟩ — see EXPOSE 1
undressed *adj* 1 being such as found in nature and not altered by processing or refining ⟨*undressed* animal hides⟩ — see CRUDE 1

2 lacking or shed of clothing ⟨an *undressed* patient waiting to be examined by the doctor⟩ — see NAKED 1
undue *adj* going beyond a normal or acceptable limit in degree or amount ⟨Try to avoid *undue* delay responding to e-mails.⟩ — see EXCESSIVE
unduly *adv* beyond a normal or acceptable limit ⟨*unduly* upset by the slight delay of our departure⟩ — see TOO 1
undyed *adj* lacking an addition of color ⟨pieces of *undyed* leather⟩ — see COLORLESS 1
undying *adj* 1 having an existence or validity that does not change or diminish ⟨His *undying* devotion to her is truly inspiring.⟩ — see ABIDING
2 lasting forever ⟨a duet in which the singers swear *undying* love for one another⟩ — see EVERLASTING 1
uneager *adj* showing little or no interest or enthusiasm ⟨received the usual *uneager* response when she asked for volunteers to help clean up⟩ — see TEPID 1
unearth *vb* to remove from place of burial ⟨*unearthed* a hoard of treasures from the Egyptian tomb⟩ — see EXHUME
unearthing *n* the act or process of sighting or learning the existence of something for the first time ⟨The *unearthing* of a prehistoric man who had been preserved in an Alpine glacier proved to be a great boon to science.⟩ — see DISCOVERY 1
unearthly *adj* 1 being so extraordinary or abnormal as to suggest powers which violate the laws of nature ⟨an *unearthly* knack for picking winning lottery numbers⟩ — see SUPERNATURAL 2
2 fearfully and mysteriously strange or fantastic ⟨An *unearthly* wail came from out of the darkness.⟩ — see EERIE
3 of, relating to, or being part of a reality beyond the observable physical universe ⟨*unearthly* messages that she believed were coming from her deceased father⟩ — see SUPERNATURAL 1
uneasiness *n* 1 a disturbed or uneasy state ⟨A general *uneasiness* has settled over the city in the wake of the crime.⟩ — see UNREST
2 an uneasy state of mind usually over the possibility of an anticipated misfortune or trouble ⟨His *uneasiness* lasted until his son's plane had returned safely to the ground.⟩ — see ANXIETY 1
uneasy *adj* 1 feeling or showing uncomfortable feelings of uncertainty ⟨I'm a bit *uneasy* about taking a baby on such a long trip.⟩ — see NERVOUS 1
2 lacking or denying rest ⟨spent an *uneasy* night sleeping in his car⟩ — see RESTLESS 1
3 lacking social grace and assurance ⟨A shy lad, he's always a bit *uneasy* at parties.⟩ — see AWKWARD 1
4 marked by or causing agitation or uncomfortable feelings ⟨An *uneasy* calm descended over the city as inhabitants waited for the mayor's announcement.⟩ — see NERVOUS 2
uneducated *adj* lacking in education or the knowledge gained from books ⟨a literary reference that could not be grasped by an *uneducated* person⟩ — see IGNORANT 1
unembarrassed *adj* not embarrassed or ashamed ⟨He seemed thoroughly *unembarrassed* by his sycophantic behavior at the company party.⟩ — see UNABASHED
unemotional *adj* not feeling or showing emotion ⟨a surprisingly *unemotional* expression for someone who was just informed that he'd won the lottery⟩ — see IMPASSIVE 1
unending *adj* lasting forever ⟨The writer's latest memoir is a seemingly *unending* exercise in narcissistic rambling.⟩ — see EVERLASTING 1
unendurable *adj* more than can be put up with ⟨People used to travel along this stretch of the highway by night so as to avoid the *unendurable* heat of the day.⟩ — see UNBEARABLE
unenthusiastic *adj* showing little or no interest or

enthusiasm ⟨My suggestion that we go to see the new action flick was greeted with an *unenthusiastic* shrug.⟩ — see TEPID 1

unequal *adj* not staying constant ⟨*unequal* pulsations of the heart that might be a sign of trouble⟩ — see UNEVEN 2

unequaled *or* **unequalled** *adj* having no equal or rival for excellence or desirability ⟨a horse of *unequaled* beauty⟩ — see ONLY 1

unequivocal *adj* **1** not subject to misinterpretation or more than one interpretation ⟨Few of the candidates have yet staked out *unequivocal* positions on the hot-button issues.⟩ — see CLEAR 2
2 so clearly expressed as to leave no doubt about the meaning ⟨The directions on the vial state in clear and *unequivocal* language that the drug should not be taken by pregnant women.⟩ — see EXPLICIT

unerring *adj* not being or likely to be wrong ⟨an *unerring* taste in interior decoration⟩ — see INFALLIBLE 1

unescapable *adj* impossible to avoid or evade ⟨You will make some mistakes—that is just one of the *unescapable* realities of this job.⟩ — see INEVITABLE

unessential *adj* not needed by the circumstances or to accomplish an end ⟨Don't pack any *unessential* items until we're sure we have room for everything we'll actually need.⟩ — see UNNECESSARY

unethical *adj* **1** not conforming to a high moral standard; morally unacceptable ⟨*unethical* treatment of animals⟩ — see BAD 2
2 not guided by or showing a concern for what is right ⟨a medical procedure that she considered *unethical*⟩ — see UNPRINCIPLED

uneven *adj* **1** not having a level or smooth surface ⟨The driveway is *uneven* and collects water in several large puddles whenever it rains.⟩
synonyms broken, bumpy, coarse, irregular, jagged, lumpy, pebbly, ragged, rough, roughened, rugged, scraggy
related words lopsided, unbalanced; inexact, unaligned; rutted, rutty, undulating, wavy; pitted, pocked; knobby, knurled, knurly, nubbly, nubby; burred, harsh, sandpapery, scraggly, scratchy
near antonyms exact, uniform; aligned (*also* alined), regular, true; horizontal, tabular; plumb, straight, vertical; flush
antonyms even, flat, level, plane, smooth
2 not staying constant ⟨The level of attendance at the ballpark has been very *uneven* this season.⟩
synonyms changing, erratic, fluctuating, irregular, unequal, unstable, unsteady, varying
related words capricious, changeable, changeful, choppy, fickle, fluid, inconsistent, inconstant, mercurial, mutable, uncertain, unsettled, variable, volatile
near antonyms regular
antonyms changeless, constant, stable, steady, unchanging, unvarying
3 inclined or twisted to one side ⟨a goofy guy with an *uneven* grin⟩ — see AWRY

unexampled *adj* having no equal or rival for excellence or desirability ⟨Her performance in the Olympics was an *unexampled* display of athletic prowess.⟩ — see ONLY 1

unexceptional *adj* being of the type that is encountered in the normal course of events ⟨The physicist, now regarded as one of the brightest minds in science, was an *unexceptional* student as a child.⟩ — see ORDINARY 1

unexpected *adj* not expected ⟨The failure of the backup generator was *unexpected* and a contingency for which we weren't prepared.⟩
synonyms abrupt, sudden, unanticipated, unforeseen, unlooked-for

related words unintended, unplanned; improbable, unlikely; startling, surprising
near antonyms predicted, prophesied; unsurprising
antonyms anticipated, expected, foreseen

unexpectedly *adv* without warning ⟨The snow started *unexpectedly*.⟩ — see UNAWARES

unexplainable *adj* impossible to explain ⟨a series of *unexplainable* weather events⟩ — see INEXPLICABLE

unexpressed *adj* understood although not put into words ⟨They shared an *unexpressed* but nevertheless deep affection.⟩ — see IMPLICIT 1

unfailing *adj* **1** not being or likely to be wrong ⟨an *unfailing* judge of personal character⟩ — see INFALLIBLE 1
2 not likely to fail ⟨The writer's *unfailing* sense of humor is again evident in his newest book.⟩ — see INFALLIBLE 2

unfailingly *adv* on every relevant occasion ⟨She has been *unfailingly* optimistic throughout this ordeal.⟩ — see ALWAYS 1

unfair *adj* not being in accordance with the rules or standards of what is fair in sport ⟨a team that is notorious throughout the league for its record of *unfair* play⟩ — see FOUL 2

unfairness *n* **1** the state of being unfair or unjust ⟨The transparent *unfairness* of the referee's decision made her furious.⟩ — see INJUSTICE 1
2 unfair or inadequate treatment of someone or something or an instance of this ⟨It would be no *unfairness* to the article's second author to characterize his contributions as minimal.⟩ — see DISSERVICE

unfaithful *adj* not true in one's allegiance to someone or something ⟨colonists who later proved to be *unfaithful* to the cause of independence⟩ — see FAITHLESS

unfaithfulness *n* **1** lack of faithfulness especially to one's husband or wife ⟨Though they each traveled extensively for work, neither spouse worried about the other's *unfaithfulness*.⟩ — see INFIDELITY 1
2 the act or fact of violating the trust or confidence of another ⟨The jaw-dropping *unfaithfulness* of the person she had considered her best friend was deeply hurtful.⟩ — see BETRAYAL
3 a sexual encounter or relationship between a married person and someone other than their spouse ⟨They both promised never to betray the other with *unfaithfulness*.⟩ — see ADULTERY

unfamiliar *adj* not known or experienced before ⟨The book was full of *unfamiliar* words.⟩ — see NEW 2

unfamiliarity *n* the state of being unaware or uninformed ⟨Some intense studying rapidly remedied my *unfamiliarity* with the subject.⟩ — see IGNORANCE 1

unfashionable *adj* marked by an obvious lack of style or good taste ⟨an old and *unfashionable* jacket that someone had donated to charity⟩ — see ¹TACKY 1

unfasten *vb* to disengage the knotted parts of ⟨gently *unfastened* the strings of the baby's hood⟩ — see UNTIE

unfathomable *adj* **1** being or seeming to be without limits ⟨the *unfathomable* reaches of space⟩ — see INFINITE
2 impossible to understand ⟨For some *unfathomable* reason the family decided to venture out into the blizzard.⟩ — see INCOMPREHENSIBLE

unfavorable *adj* opposed to one's interests ⟨The company chose to accept the *unfavorable* settlement rather than spend more money on legal fees.⟩ — see ADVERSE 1

unfeeling *adj* **1** having or showing a lack of sympathy or tender feelings ⟨gave the homeless people on the street only an *unfeeling* glance⟩ — see HARD 1
2 lacking in sensation or feeling ⟨Her heart was as cold and hard as the *unfeeling* marble statue in her garden.⟩ — see NUMB 1
3 lacking animate awareness or sensation ⟨She spoke

politely even to the *unfeeling* virtual assistant on her phone.⟩ — see INSENSATE 1

unfeignedly *adv* without any attempt to impress by deception or exaggeration ⟨parents who are *unfeignedly* enthusiastic about their child's wedding plans⟩ — see NATURALLY 3

unfeminine *adj* having qualities or traits that are traditionally considered inappropriate for a girl or woman ⟨In bygone days pants were considered *unfeminine*, and even women bicycling were expected to wear skirts.⟩

synonyms mannish, tomboyish, unladylike

related words gentlemanly, male, manly, masculine

near antonyms effeminate, girlish, sissified, sissy, unmanly, unmasculine, womanish, womanlike; distaff, petticoat

antonyms female, feminine, ladylike, womanly

unfetter *vb* to release (as from slavery or confinement) ⟨Authorities eventually *unfettered* the menagerie of wild animals that had been kept illegally as pets.⟩ — see FREE 1

unfit *adj* **1** lacking qualities (as knowledge, skill, or ability) required to do a job ⟨Just because I don't have actual work experience doesn't mean I'm *unfit* for the job.⟩ — see INCOMPETENT

2 not appropriate for a particular occasion or situation ⟨Those flimsy shoes are *unfit* for the hike we're about to take.⟩ — see INAPPROPRIATE

unfitness *n* the quality or state of being unsuitable or unfitting ⟨His *unfitness* for a managerial position is apparent in the way he treats his subordinates.⟩ — see INAPPROPRIATENESS 1

unflagging *adj* showing no signs of weariness even after long hard effort ⟨She's being rewarded for the *unflagging* zeal with which she led the fund-raising campaign.⟩ — see TIRELESS

unflappable *adj* not easily panicked or upset ⟨The *unflappable* teacher never even blinked when the whiteboard came crashing down.⟩

synonyms imperturbable, nerveless, unshakable

related words calm, collected, composed, cool, coolheaded, icy, nonchalant, placid, self-collected, self-possessed, serene, steely, tranquil, undisturbed, unperturbed, unruffled, unshaken, untroubled, unworried

near antonyms panicky; aflutter, anxious, dithery, edgy, het up, hung up, jittery, jumpy, nervous, nervy, perturbed, shaky, tense, troubled, uneasy, upset, uptight, worried

antonyms perturbable, shakable (*or* shakeable)

unfledged *adj* lacking in adult experience or maturity ⟨the kind of mistake in judgment that an *unfledged* youth could be expected to make⟩ — see CALLOW

unflinching *adj* showing no signs of slackening or yielding in one's purpose ⟨He was *unflinching* in his determination to see that justice was done.⟩ — see UNYIELDING 1

unfold *vb* **1** to arrange the parts of (something) over a wider area ⟨Carefully *unfold* that antique map so that it doesn't tear.⟩ — see OPEN 3

2 to gradually become clearer or more detailed ⟨As the situation *unfolded*, it became clear that more help would be needed.⟩ — see DEVELOP 1

3 to produce flowers ⟨The rosebud *unfolded* literally overnight.⟩ — see BLOOM 1

4 to come into view ⟨The majestic landscape *unfolded* before us.⟩ — see APPEAR 1

unforced *adj* done, made, or given with one's own free will ⟨The participation of the people on the project must be *unforced*, or it really isn't a volunteer effort.⟩ — see VOLUNTARY 1

unforeseen *adj* not expected ⟨There are almost always *unforeseen* consequences for any major endeavor.⟩ — see UNEXPECTED

unforgivable *adj* too bad to be excused or justified ⟨an *unforgivable* crime that society must seek just punishment for⟩ — see INEXCUSABLE

unformed *adj* **1** having no definite or recognizable form ⟨What was once an *unformed* lump of clay is now an attractive, useful bowl.⟩ — see FORMLESS 1

2 lacking in adult experience or maturity ⟨Under his care and tutelage, young men and women, *unformed* in mind and body, became battle-worthy soldiers.⟩ — see CALLOW

unfortunate *adj* **1** bringing about ruin or misfortune ⟨An *unfortunate* chain of events destroyed the business.⟩ — see FATAL 1

2 having, prone to, or marked by bad luck ⟨She was *unfortunate* enough to be chosen to present her project first.⟩ — see UNLUCKY 1

3 of a kind to cause great distress ⟨an *unfortunate* choice of words that would later prove to be embarrassing for the talk show host⟩ — see REGRETTABLE

unfounded *adj* having no basis in reason or fact ⟨The accusation proved to be *unfounded*.⟩ — see GROUNDLESS

unfriendly *adj* **1** lacking in friendliness or warmth of feeling ⟨The *unfriendly* looks quickly warmed when we were recognized as long-unseen relatives.⟩ — see COLD 2

2 marked by opposition or ill will ⟨an *unfriendly* nation⟩ — see HOSTILE 1

3 opposed to one's interests ⟨the claim that the state's numerous regulations create a climate *unfriendly* to small businesses⟩ — see ADVERSE 1

unfrozen *adj* freed from a frozen state by exposure to warmth ⟨There should be a couple of *unfrozen* chicken breasts in the refrigerator.⟩ — see THAWED

unfruitful *adj* not able to produce fruit or offspring ⟨disappointed to discover that the mare was *unfruitful*⟩ — see STERILE 1

ungainly *adj* **1** difficult to use or operate especially because of size, weight, or design ⟨Getting the *ungainly* couch up the stairs was a real chore.⟩ — see CUMBERSOME

2 having or showing an inability to move in a graceful manner ⟨The large dog was crushing any unlucky petunias that lay in the path of his *ungainly* tread.⟩ — see CLUMSY 2

ungentle *adj* harsh and threatening in manner or appearance ⟨a demanding and *ungentle* land that was not for the fainthearted⟩ — see GRIM 1

ungovernable *adj* **1** given to resisting authority or another's control ⟨A handful of *ungovernable* students are disrupting the learning environment for everyone else.⟩ — see DISOBEDIENT

2 given to resisting control or discipline by others ⟨I'm resigned to the fact that my cat is basically an *ungovernable* beast with a will of his own.⟩ — see UNCONTROLLABLE

ungraceful *adj* lacking social grace and assurance ⟨an *ungraceful* but well-meaning hostess⟩ — see AWKWARD 1

ungracious *adj* showing a lack of manners or consideration for others ⟨We were taken aback by our aunt's *ungracious* reply to the invitation we had sent her.⟩ — see IMPOLITE

ungraciousness *n* rude behavior ⟨the former champion's unbecoming *ungraciousness* in defeat, refusing to shake the new champion's hand⟩ — see DISCOURTESY

ungrateful *adj* **1** not likely to be appreciated by those who benefit ⟨The park's custodial staff has the *ungrateful* job of cleaning up after the Independence Day party is over.⟩ — see THANKLESS 2

2 not showing gratitude ⟨Although the food was being provided for free, the *ungrateful* recipients could not refrain from complaining that it was not to their liking.⟩ — see THANKLESS 1

unguarded *adj* **1** free in expressing one's true feelings and opinions ⟨The swimming coach quickly regretted his *unguarded* comments about the young swimmer's limitations.⟩ — see FRANK
2 lacking protection from danger or resistance against attack ⟨an *unguarded* gate that would later prove to be the fatal weakness in the city's defenses⟩ — see HELPLESS 1
3 not paying or showing close attention especially for the purpose of avoiding trouble ⟨In an *unguarded* moment I let my mind wander and smashed my car into a tree.⟩ — see CARELESS 1

unhampered *adj* showing no signs of being under control ⟨The freeway system needs to be expanded to meet the demands of the city's *unhampered* growth.⟩ — see RAMPANT 1

unhandsome *adj* **1** unpleasant to look at ⟨a character actor with a distinctively craggy, *unhandsome* face⟩ — see UGLY 1
2 showing a lack of manners or consideration for others ⟨In an interview the free-spoken actor made some *unhandsome* remarks about his costars.⟩ — see IMPOLITE

unhandy *adj* **1** difficult to use or operate especially because of size, weight, or design ⟨The large vehicle is particularly *unhandy* and difficult to maneuver in parking lots and narrow streets.⟩ — see CUMBERSOME
2 lacking or showing a lack of nimbleness in using one's hands ⟨An *unhandy* person should be kept away from knives and other sharp objects.⟩ — see CLUMSY 1

unhappily *adv* with feelings of bitterness or grief ⟨an *unhappily* employed worker looking for a new job⟩ — see HARD 2

unhappiness *n* a state or spell of low spirits ⟨With time the young woman got over the *unhappiness* caused by the breakup.⟩ — see SADNESS

unhappy *adj* **1** feeling unhappiness ⟨He's been *unhappy* ever since his family's move, which took him away from all his friends.⟩ — see SAD 1
2 having, prone to, or marked by bad luck ⟨She's trying to forget that whole *unhappy* attempt to start a business.⟩ — see UNLUCKY 1
3 not appropriate for a particular occasion or situation ⟨A guest unintentionally made *unhappy* reference to what is a painful situation for the family.⟩ — see INAPPROPRIATE

unhealthful *adj* bad for the well-being of the body ⟨the *unhealthful* level of smog in the city⟩ — see UNHEALTHY 1

unhealthiness *n* the condition of not being in good health ⟨Sam remedied his general *unhealthiness* with a long-overdue change to a healthy diet and exercise.⟩ — see SICKNESS 1

unhealthy *adj* **1** bad for the well-being of the body ⟨We knew that the junk food at the carnival was *unhealthy*, but it tasted so good!⟩
synonyms noisome, noxious, sickly, unhealthful, unwholesome
related words germy, insanitary, unhygienic, unsanitary; nonnutritious; poisonous, toxic; fatal, lethal, mortal
near antonyms hygienic, sanitary; nutritious
antonyms healthful, healthy
2 involving potential loss or injury ⟨Criticism of the military dictatorship has proved to be *unhealthy* for several of that nation's journalists.⟩ — see DANGEROUS 1
3 temporarily suffering from a disorder of the body ⟨She's been *unhealthy* for almost a week now.⟩ — see SICK 1

unheard–of *adj* not known or experienced before ⟨houses selling at *unheard-of* prices⟩ — see NEW 2

unheroic *adj* having or showing a shameful lack of courage ⟨The new biography casts the romanticized outlaw in a much more vicious and *unheroic* light.⟩ — see COWARDLY

unhindered *adj* showing no signs of being under control ⟨In the absence of appropriate oversight, the *unhindered* deforestation of the region continues.⟩ — see RAMPANT 1

unhinge *vb* **1** to cause to go insane or as if insane ⟨The pressure of that job could *unhinge* anyone.⟩ — see CRAZE
2 to trouble the mind of; to make uneasy ⟨I was momentarily *unhinged* by the unexpected question.⟩ — see DISTURB 1

unhurried *adj* moving or proceeding at less than the normal, desirable, or required speed ⟨We cycled at an *unhurried* pace and saved our strength for the hills up ahead.⟩ — see SLOW 1

unidentified *adj* **1** known but not named ⟨An *unidentified* worker reported the security breach.⟩ — see CERTAIN 1
2 not named or identified by a name ⟨Some *unidentified* person helped them and then left quietly.⟩ — see NAMELESS 1

unification *n* the act or an instance of joining two or more things into one ⟨the political *unification* of several regions into an empire⟩ — see UNION 1

uniform *adj* not varying ⟨Using cookie cutters will make the cookies *uniform* in size.⟩
synonyms even, invariant, steady, unchanging, undeviating, unvarying, unwavering
related words fixed, immutable, invariable, set, unalterable, unchangeable
antonyms changing, deviating, nonuniform, unsteady, varying

uniform *n* the distinctive clothing worn by members of a particular group ⟨The band *uniform* was brown with red and white stripes.⟩
synonyms livery, outfit
related words fatigues, full dress, regimentals; costume, finery, regalia

unify *vb* **1** to bring (something) to a central point or under a single control ⟨will *unify* the several departments into a single operation⟩ — see CENTRALIZE
2 to come together to form a single unit ⟨The two labor unions *unified* in order to strengthen their bargaining position with the manufacturers.⟩ — see UNITE 1

unimaginable *adj* too extraordinary or improbable to believe ⟨a nearly *unimaginable* string of coincidences⟩ — see INCREDIBLE

unimportant *adj* lacking importance ⟨We figured that the details were *unimportant* as long as we got the basic design correct.⟩
synonyms foolish, frivolous, incidental, inconsequential, inconsiderable, insignificant, little, minor, minute, negligible, slight, small, small-fry, trifling, trivial
related words jerkwater, one-horse; nickel-and-dime, paltry, petty, small-time, worthless; anonymous, nameless, obscure, uncelebrated, unknown
phrases neither here nor there
near antonyms decisive, fatal, fateful; chief, dominant, overbearing, overmastering, principal; distinctive, exceptional, impressive, outstanding, prominent, remarkable; valuable, worthwhile, worthy; distinguished, eminent, great, illustrious, preeminent, prestigious; famous, notorious, renowned; all-important, basic, essential, fundamental, key
antonyms big, consequential, eventful, important, major, material, meaningful, momentous, significant, substantial, unfrivolous, weighty

uninformed *adj* not informed about or aware of something ⟨The mayor is clearly *uninformed* when it comes to the state of the city's schools.⟩ — see IGNORANT 2

uninhibited *adj* showing feeling freely ⟨an *uninhibited* child who laughed and cried with equal abandon⟩ — see DEMONSTRATIVE 1

uninstructed *adj* lacking in education or the knowledge gained from books ⟨gathered the village's children, who were *uninstructed* for the most part, and formed a school⟩ — see IGNORANT 1

unintelligent *adj* not having or showing an ability to absorb ideas readily ⟨You're not *unintelligent*, so you must just be stubbornly resisting all attempts to teach you something.⟩ — see STUPID 1

unintelligible *adj* impossible to understand ⟨uttered only a string of *unintelligible* murmurs⟩ — see INCOMPREHENSIBLE

unintended *adj* 1 happening by chance ⟨backyard digging that resulted in *unintended* damage to buried phone wires⟩ — see ACCIDENTAL 1
2 not made or done willingly or by choice ⟨a response that yielded an *unintended* insight into her personal character⟩ — see INVOLUNTARY 1

unintentional *adj* 1 happening by chance ⟨an *unintentional* encounter with an old classmate⟩ — see ACCIDENTAL 1
2 not made or done willingly or by choice ⟨an *unintentional* insult that nevertheless was very hurtful⟩ — see INVOLUNTARY 1

uninterested *adj* having or showing a lack of interest or concern ⟨She seems *uninterested* in the idea.⟩ — see INDIFFERENT 1

uninteresting *adj* causing weariness, restlessness, or lack of interest ⟨The tour guide's spiel was *uninteresting* and not particularly informative.⟩ — see BORING

uninterrupted *adj* going on and on without any interruptions ⟨a movie comedy that is 90 minutes of *uninterrupted* hilarity⟩ — see CONTINUOUS

uninvited *adj* not searched or asked for ⟨I always ignore *uninvited* advice.⟩ — see UNSOUGHT

union *n* 1 the act or an instance of joining two or more things into one ⟨The *union* of the two smaller student groups provided new opportunities for collaboration.⟩
synonyms combination, combining, connecting, connection, consolidation, coupling, junction, linking, merging, unification
related words agglomeration, amalgamation, blend, coalescence, commingling, compounding, fusion, intermingling, intermixture, mingling, mix, mixture; reunification, reunion
near antonyms detachment, divorcement, separation, severance
antonyms breakup, disconnection, dissolution, disunion, division, parting, partition, schism, scission, split
2 an association of persons, parties, or states for mutual assistance and protection ⟨joined the European *Union*⟩ — see CONFEDERACY
3 the state of having shared interests or efforts (as in social or business matters) ⟨The movie studio is producing the blockbuster in *union* with another studio because of the tremendous cost involved.⟩ — see ASSOCIATION 1

unique *adj* 1 of, relating to, or belonging to a single person ⟨a comedian who brings a *unique* and twisted perspective to contemporary social issues⟩ — see INDIVIDUAL 1
2 being out of the ordinary ⟨The restaurant, specializing in fusion cuisine, provides a truly *unique* dining experience for those who can afford it.⟩ — see EXCEPTIONAL 1
3 being the one or ones of a class with no other members ⟨The Mapparium, a huge glass globe that visitors can walk through, is *unique*—there's not another one like it anywhere.⟩ — see ONLY 2
4 noticeably different from what is generally found or experienced ⟨a *unique* ability to add large sums in his head⟩ — see UNUSUAL 1

unison *n* the state of being of one opinion about something ⟨The members of the committee are in *unison* on this point.⟩ — see AGREEMENT 1

unite *vb* 1 to come together to form a single unit ⟨Using the microscope, we watched the water droplets *unite* into a single pool.⟩
synonyms associate, coalesce, combine, conjoin, conjugate, connect, couple, fuse, join, link (up), marry, unify
related words mate, yoke; ally, confederate, league; chain, compound, hitch, hook, splice; assemble, cluster, congregate, convene, gather, meet; recombine, reconnect, rejoin, reunify, reunite
near antonyms detach, disaffiliate, disconnect, disjoin, disjoint, dissociate, disunite, divide, divorce, fractionate, isolate, resolve, uncouple, unyoke; disband, disperse, scatter
antonyms break up, dissever, part, section, separate, sever, split, sunder, unlink
2 to bring (something) to a central point or under a single control ⟨*united* several teams under the reorganization plan⟩ — see CENTRALIZE
3 to form or enter into an association that furthers the interests of its members ⟨Parents *united* to reform the school's curriculum.⟩ — see ALLY
4 to participate or assist in a joint effort to accomplish an end ⟨Only if private investors and public officials *unite* for the common good, will this city experience an economic revival.⟩ — see COOPERATE 1

united *adj* 1 having or marked by agreement in feeling or action ⟨The party must present a *united* front if it hopes to win the election.⟩ — see HARMONIOUS 3
2 used or done by a number of people as a group ⟨When a campaign to raise funds is this successful, it's only because of the *united* effort of all concerned.⟩ — see COLLECTIVE

unity *n* a balanced, pleasing, or suitable arrangement of parts ⟨There's an aesthetic *unity* to the sculpture garden that makes it an ideal spot for quiet relaxing.⟩ — see HARMONY 1

universal *adj* 1 able to do many different kinds of things ⟨a *universal* wrench⟩ — see VERSATILE
2 belonging or relating to the whole ⟨mankind's *universal* need for affection⟩ — see GENERAL 1
3 covering everything or all important points ⟨The genius of Leonardo da Vinci was *universal*: he was an artist, an architect, an engineer, and a scientist, among other things.⟩ — see ENCYCLOPEDIC
4 present in all places and at all times ⟨After the home team won the national championship, throughout the city a sense of pride was as *universal* as the air.⟩ — see OMNIPRESENT

universe *n* the whole body of things observed or assumed ⟨questioning the theory that the *universe* is constantly expanding⟩
synonyms cosmos, creation, macrocosm, nature, world
related words existence, reality
near antonyms void

unjustifiable *adj* too bad to be excused or justified ⟨an *unjustifiable* accusation that must be rebutted⟩ — see INEXCUSABLE

unjustness *n* 1 the state of being unfair or unjust ⟨The sheer *unjustness* of the accusation infuriated her beyond words.⟩ — see INJUSTICE 1
2 unfair or inadequate treatment of someone or something or an instance of this ⟨Life seemed to treat him with an *unjustness* that was immensely frustrating.⟩ — see DISSERVICE

unkempt *adj* 1 lacking in order, neatness, and often cleanliness ⟨an *unkempt* and cluttered room⟩ — see MESSY
2 lacking neatness in dress or person ⟨the stereotype of the *unkempt* but brilliant scientist⟩ — see SLOPPY 1

unknowing *adj* 1 lacking in worldly wisdom or informed

judgment ⟨Those *unknowing* people who think that the world is a kindly place are in for a rude awakening.⟩ — see NAIVE 1

2 not informed about or aware of something ⟨The poor woman has been the *unknowing* target of some pretty vicious gossip.⟩ — see IGNORANT 2

unknown *adj* **1** happening or existing without one's knowledge ⟨*Unknown* to me was the fact that while I was out, my family was hurriedly preparing a surprise birthday party.⟩

synonyms unbeknownst (*also* unbeknown)

related words unperceived, unsuspected; unaware, unconscious, unmindful; unknowing, unsuspecting, unwitting; ignorant, unacquainted, unfamiliar

2 not known or experienced before ⟨Becoming a father brought *unknown* joy to his life.⟩ — see NEW 2

3 not widely known ⟨looking for a relatively *unknown* singer to record the song⟩ — see OBSCURE 2

unlade *vb* to empty or rid of cargo ⟨Permission will not be given to *unlade* the ship until it can be thoroughly inspected.⟩ — see UNLOAD 1

unladylike *adj* having qualities or traits that are traditionally considered inappropriate for a girl or woman ⟨The hockey player rolled her eyes when her grandfather suggested that figure skating might be less *unladylike*.⟩ — see UNFEMININE

unlash *vb* to disengage the knotted parts of ⟨*unlashed* the ropes which secured the crate in the bed of the truck⟩ — see UNTIE

unlawful *adj* **1** contrary to or forbidden by law ⟨It is *unlawful* to set off fireworks within the city limits.⟩ — see ILLEGAL 1

2 not conforming to a high moral standard; morally unacceptable ⟨the allure of *unlawful* temptations⟩ — see BAD 2

unlearn *vb* to be unable to recall or think of ⟨Let's hope that over the summer I don't *unlearn* everything I learned over the course of this past year.⟩ — see FORGET 1

unlearned *adj* lacking in education or the knowledge gained from books ⟨a wise though *unlearned* man⟩ — see IGNORANT 1

unleash *vb* **1** to set free (from a state of being held in check) ⟨He *unleashed* all of his feelings in a long letter.⟩ — see RELEASE 1

2 to find emotional release for ⟨Lifting weights is a way for me to *unleash* all the frustrations of the workday.⟩ — see TAKE OUT 1

unlettered *adj* lacking in education or the knowledge gained from books ⟨*Unlettered* moviegoers were unaware of how little resemblance the film bore to the novel on which it was supposedly based.⟩ — see IGNORANT 1

unlike *adj* being not of the same kind ⟨You're trying to compare very *unlike* things—like those proverbial apples and oranges.⟩ — see DIFFERENT 1

unlikely *adj* not likely to be true or to occur ⟨In the *unlikely* event that the file is deleted or corrupted, you will want to have backup copies available.⟩ — see IMPROBABLE

unlikeness *n* the quality or state of being different ⟨Because of the general *unlikeness* of their features, most new acquaintances are surprised to learn that they are brothers.⟩ — see DIFFERENCE 1

unlimited *adj* **1** being or seeming to be without limits ⟨No ruler should ever be given *unlimited* power.⟩ — see INFINITE

2 not limited or specialized in application or purpose ⟨an insurance policy that offers *unlimited* coverage in case of loss⟩ — see GENERAL 4

unlink *vb* to set or force apart ⟨*unlinked* the railroad cars⟩ — see SEPARATE 1

unlisted *adj* not appearing on a list ⟨She kept her phone number *unlisted* so as to reduce the number of unwanted calls.⟩

synonyms uncataloged, unrecorded, unregistered

related words unwritten; unidentified, unspecified; undisclosed, unknown, unrevealed

antonyms cataloged (*or* catalogued), listed, recorded, registered

unliterary *adj* used in or suitable for speech and not formal writing ⟨poems written in a natural, *unliterary* voice⟩ — see COLLOQUIAL 1

unload *vb* **1** to empty or rid of cargo ⟨The dockworkers *unloaded* the ship.⟩

synonyms disburden, discharge, disencumber, unburden, unlade, unpack

related words free, lighten, relieve; clear, empty, evacuate, vacate, void

near antonyms charge, cram, fill, heap, jam, jam-pack, stuff

antonyms load, pack

2 to get rid of as useless or unwanted ⟨I can't seem to *unload* this stuff—even the charities won't take it!⟩ — see DISCARD

unlock *vb* to set free (from a state of being held in check) ⟨That last insult *unlocked* her tongue, and she finally said what she really thought.⟩ — see RELEASE 1

unlooked–for *adj* not expected ⟨The interesting stuff found in the attic was an *unlooked-for* bonus for the new homeowners.⟩ — see UNEXPECTED

unloose *vb* to set free (from a state of being held in check) ⟨The familiar scent *unloosed* a flood of pleasant memories from her childhood.⟩ — see RELEASE 1

unloosen *vb* to set free (from a state of being held in check) ⟨A relaxing bath *unloosened* all the mental and physical tension that had been building throughout the day.⟩ — see RELEASE 1

unlovely *adj* **1** not giving pleasure to the mind or senses ⟨Sunday night is often spoiled by the *unlovely* thought of having to go back to school or work the next morning.⟩ — see UNPLEASANT

2 unpleasant to look at ⟨an *unlovely* but efficient little machine⟩ — see UGLY 1

unlucky *adj* **1** having, prone to, or marked by bad luck ⟨The *unlucky* campers had rain all week.⟩ ⟨I'm so *unlucky* I don't bother to play the lottery.⟩ ⟨an *unlucky* throw of the dice⟩

synonyms hapless, hard-luck, ill-fated, ill-starred, jinxed, luckless, star-crossed, unfortunate, unhappy

related words adverse, ill, inauspicious, unfavorable, unpromising, untoward; calamitous, catastrophic, disastrous; damned, tragic (*also* tragical)

near antonyms blessed (*also* blest), favored, gifted, privileged; auspicious, fair, favorable, golden, promising, propitious

antonyms fortunate, happy, lucky

2 of a kind to cause great distress ⟨The settlers made the *unlucky* decision to cross the dangerous mountain pass in the middle of winter.⟩ — see REGRETTABLE

unmake *vb* to remove from a position of prominence or power (as a throne) ⟨a movie studio chief who likes to boast that he can *unmake* any star in Hollywood if he wishes⟩ — see DEPOSE 1

unmanageable *adj* given to resisting control or discipline by others ⟨an *unmanageable* dog who had to be returned to the breeder⟩ — see UNCONTROLLABLE

unmannerly *adj* showing a lack of manners or consideration for others ⟨In an *unmannerly* disregard for anyone else's comfort, she turned up the heat without saying a word.⟩ — see IMPOLITE

unmarried *adj* not married ⟨They decided to remain *unmarried* until they both finished their degrees.⟩ — see SINGLE 1

unmask *vb* **1** to make known (as information previously kept secret) ⟨In the season's final episode, the killer's identity was *unmasked*.⟩ — see REVEAL 1
2 to reveal the true nature of ⟨*unmasked* the motives of the people advocating the sale of the publicly owned land⟩ — see EXPOSE 1

unmatched *adj* **1** being one of a pair or set without a corresponding mate ⟨a drawer full of *unmatched* socks⟩ — see ODD 1
2 having no equal or rival for excellence or desirability ⟨The house cat is a mouse-hunting machine of *unmatched* efficiency.⟩ — see ONLY 1

unmelodious *adj* marked by or producing a harsh combination of sounds ⟨I awoke to the *unmelodious* clatter of jackhammers at the construction site next door.⟩ — see DISSONANT

unmerciful *adj* **1** going beyond a normal or acceptable limit in degree or amount ⟨She went into an *unmerciful* level of detail about her latest health problems.⟩ — see EXCESSIVE
2 having or showing a lack of sympathy or tender feelings ⟨The critics were *unmerciful* in their assessments of the young actress's performance.⟩ — see HARD 1

unmindful *adj* not informed about or aware of something ⟨*unmindful* of the consequences of such a rash decision⟩ — see IGNORANT 2

unmistakable *adj* not subject to misinterpretation or more than one interpretation ⟨a glint in his eye that was an *unmistakable* expression of greed⟩ — see CLEAR 2

unmitigated *adj* having no exceptions or restrictions ⟨It looks like another one of your get-rich-quick schemes has ended in *unmitigated* failure.⟩ — see ABSOLUTE 2

unmixed *adj* free from added matter ⟨Chocolate has a great taste, but I prefer my milk *unmixed*.⟩ — see PURE 1

unmovable *adj* incapable of moving or being moved ⟨The tree was *unmovable*, so we designed the garden pond around it.⟩ — see IMMOVABLE 1

unmusical *adj* marked by or producing a harsh combination of sounds ⟨a very *unmusical* chorus of squawks from the angry ravens⟩ — see DISSONANT

unnamed *adj* **1** known but not named ⟨used some *unnamed* procedure for testing the accuracy of the device⟩ — see CERTAIN 1
2 not named or identified by a name ⟨The newspaper article quoted several *unnamed* sources.⟩ — see NAMELESS 1

unnatural *adj* **1** departing from some accepted standard of what is normal ⟨an *unnatural* obsession with zombie movies⟩ — see DEVIANT
2 lacking in natural or spontaneous quality ⟨Just before the debate, the candidates flashed *unnatural* smiles for the cameras.⟩ — see ARTIFICIAL 1

unnecessary *adj* not needed by the circumstances or to accomplish an end ⟨That large suitcase is *unnecessary*—we are only going to be away for a couple of days!⟩
synonyms dispensable, gratuitous, needless, nonessential, uncalled-for, unessential, unwarranted
related words discretionary, elective, optional; extra, extraneous, irrelative, irrelevant, redundant, superfluous
near antonyms all-important, crucial, important, vital; imperative, pressing, urgent
antonyms essential, indispensable, necessary, needed, needful, required

unnerve *vb* **1** to deprive of courage or confidence ⟨The riding accident so *unnerved* me that for a while I was afraid to get back on a horse.⟩
synonyms demoralize, emasculate, paralyze, undo, unstring
related words debilitate, enervate, enfeeble, neuter, weaken; prostrate, sap, soften, tire, waste; frighten, intimidate, psych (out); scare, terrify, terrorize; daunt, discourage, dishearten, dismay, dispirit; craze, derange, madden, unbalance, unhinge; discompose, disquiet, disturb, faze, perturb, unsettle, upset
near antonyms fortify, strengthen; embolden, encourage, hearten
antonyms nerve
2 to lessen the courage or confidence of ⟨A figure skater can't afford to be *unnerved* by an occasional slipup.⟩ — see DISCOURAGE 1

unnerving *adj* marked by or causing agitation or uncomfortable feelings ⟨the *unnerving* news of yet another round of layoffs⟩ — see NERVOUS 2

unnoticeable *adj* not readily seen or noticed ⟨a nearly *unnoticeable* change in the color⟩ — see UNOBTRUSIVE

unnumbered *adj* too many to be counted ⟨The *unnumbered* stars wheeled overhead.⟩ — see COUNTLESS

unobstructed *adj* allowing passage without obstruction ⟨Only one road remained *unobstructed* after the storm.⟩ — see OPEN 1

unobtainable *adj* hard or impossible to get to or get at ⟨That information is *unobtainable* as long as my computer is down.⟩ — see INACCESSIBLE

unobtrusive *adj* not readily seen or noticed ⟨The notice that an 18% tip would be automatically added was so *unobtrusive* we almost didn't see it at the bottom of the menu.⟩
synonyms discreet, inconspicuous, unnoticeable
related words unnoticed, unremarked, unseen; impalpable, imperceptible, inappreciable, indistinguishable, insensible; faint, indistinct, obscure; concealed
near antonyms arresting, eye-catching, showy, striking; flashy, loud, noisy; apparent, clear, discernible (*also* discernable), distinct, evident, manifest, obvious, patent, plain, prominent, unmistakable; blatant, flagrant, glaring, gross, screaming
antonyms conspicuous, noticeable, visible

unoriginal *adj* using or marked by the use of something else as a basis or model ⟨Critics faulted the novel for having a painfully *unoriginal* plot.⟩ — see IMITATIVE 1

unorthodox *adj* **1** deviating from commonly accepted beliefs or practices ⟨a time when people with *unorthodox* religious views were banished from the colony⟩ — see HERETICAL
2 not bound by traditional ways or beliefs ⟨raised by an aunt, whose *unorthodox* parenting practices made for an unusual but fun childhood⟩ — see LIBERAL 1
3 not rigidly following established form, custom, or rules ⟨an *unorthodox* but effective procedure for opening a wine bottle without a corkscrew⟩ — see INFORMAL 1

unpack *vb* to empty or rid of cargo ⟨The Browns *unpacked* the car the minute they got back from vacation.⟩ — see UNLOAD 1

unpaid *adj* not yet paid ⟨My goal is to have no *unpaid* balances on my credit cards.⟩ — see OUTSTANDING 1

unpainted *adj* lacking an addition of color ⟨The wooden shingles on the island's houses are usually left *unpainted*, and over time the salt air turns them a soft gray.⟩ — see COLORLESS 1

unpaired *adj* being one of a pair or set without a corresponding mate ⟨I found an *unpaired* shoe in the back of the closet.⟩ — see ODD 1

unpalatable *adj* **1** disagreeable or disgusting to the sense of taste ⟨Pasta and honey is an *unpalatable* combination.⟩ — see DISTASTEFUL 1

2 not giving pleasure to the mind or senses ⟨hesitated before sharing some of the more *unpalatable* details of the experience⟩ — see UNPLEASANT

unparalleled *adj* having no equal or rival for excellence or desirability ⟨an antique vase of *unparalleled* beauty⟩ — see ONLY 1

unpardonable *adj* too bad to be excused or justified ⟨regards cruelty to animals as an *unpardonable* sin⟩ — see INEXCUSABLE

unperturbed *adj* free from emotional or mental agitation ⟨remained *unperturbed* despite the latest problems in the construction of their new house⟩ — see CALM 2

unplanned *adj* **1** happening by chance ⟨There was an *unplanned* change in our itinerary—we got lost!⟩ — see ACCIDENTAL 1
2 made or done without previous thought or preparation ⟨stumbled through a completely *unplanned* acceptance speech⟩ — see EXTEMPORANEOUS

unpleasant *adj* not giving pleasure to the mind or senses ⟨The burnt pot roast had a very *unpleasant* odor.⟩
synonyms bad, bitter, disagreeable, displeasing, distasteful, harsh, nasty, rotten, sour, uncongenial, unlovely, unpalatable, unpleasing, unsavory, unwelcome, wicked, yucky (*also* yukky)
related words abhorrent, abominable, appalling, awful, beastly, bilious, dreadful, foul, ghastly, hideous, horrendous, horrible, horrid, invidious, loathsome, nauseating, nauseous, noisome, obnoxious, obscene, odious, offensive, repellent (*also* repellant), repugnant, repulsive, revolting, scandalous, seamy, shocking, sick, sickening, ugly, vile, villainous; aggravating, annoying, galling, irritating, vexing; crummy (*also* crumby), lousy, miserable, wretched
near antonyms delectable, delicious, delightful, dreamy, felicitous; amiable, charming, cheery, friendly, jolly, kindly, sweet
antonyms agreeable, congenial, good, grateful, gratifying, nice, palatable, pleasant, pleasing, pleasurable, satisfying, welcome

unpleasing *adj* **1** not giving pleasure to the mind or senses ⟨an *unpleasing* combination of flavors in the dish⟩ — see UNPLEASANT
2 unpleasant to look at ⟨an *unpleasing* combination of fuchsia and orange⟩ — see UGLY 1

unpolished *adj* lacking in refinement or good taste ⟨an *unpolished* but well-meaning young man⟩ — see COARSE 2

unprecedented *adj* not known or experienced before ⟨This is an *unprecedented* request for the reference desk.⟩ — see NEW 2

unpredictable *adj* likely to change frequently, suddenly, or unexpectedly ⟨*Unpredictable* spring weather that makes it really hard to know what to wear.⟩ — see FICKLE 1

unprejudiced *adj* marked by justice, honesty, and freedom from bias ⟨an *unprejudiced* judicial opinion⟩ — see FAIR 2

unpremeditated *adj* **1** happening by chance ⟨an *unpremeditated* encounter with an old friend⟩ — see ACCIDENTAL 1
2 made or done without previous thought or preparation ⟨an *unpremeditated* verbal attack that was prompted by an unexpected question at the press conference⟩ — see EXTEMPORANEOUS

unprepared *adj* made or done without previous thought or preparation ⟨an obviously *unprepared* acceptance speech by the surprise winner⟩ — see EXTEMPORANEOUS

unpretending *adj* free from any intent to deceive or impress others ⟨an *unpretending* manner that makes her quite a winning performer⟩ — see GUILELESS

unpretentious *adj* **1** free from any intent to deceive or impress others ⟨a simple and *unpretentious* account about growing up in the rural South⟩ — see GUILELESS
2 not excessively showy ⟨lives in a rather *unpretentious* house for someone so wealthy⟩ — see QUIET 2
3 not having or showing any feelings of superiority, self-assertiveness, or showiness ⟨the *unpretentious* disposition of an award-winning scientist who has nothing to prove to anyone⟩ — see HUMBLE 1

unpretentiously *adv* without any attempt to impress by deception or exaggeration ⟨that rare restaurant reviewer who writes engagingly but *unpretentiously* about food⟩ — see NATURALLY 3

unpretty *adj* unpleasant to look at ⟨an *unpretty* accumulation of trash right next to the entrance to the restaurant⟩ — see UGLY 1

unprincipled *adj* not guided by or showing a concern for what is right ⟨an *unprincipled* businessman who made a lot of money—and didn't care how he did it⟩
synonyms cutthroat, immoral, Machiavellian, unconscionable, unethical, unscrupulous
related words merciless, pitiless, remorseless, ruthless; crooked, deceitful, dishonest, knavish; corrupt, debased, debauched, decadent, degenerate, degraded, demoralized, depraved, dissipated, libertine, licentious, profligate; dog-eat-dog, opportunistic; calculating, sharp
near antonyms conscientious, good, honorable, just, noble, righteous, virtuous
antonyms ethical, moral, principled, scrupulous

unprocessed *adj* being such as found in nature and not altered by processing or refining ⟨*unprocessed* foods that still have much of their original flavor⟩ — see CRUDE 1

unproductive *adj* **1** producing inferior or only a small amount of vegetation ⟨Crop rotation had prevented the farmland from becoming *unproductive*.⟩ — see BARREN 1
2 producing no results ⟨Her attempts to write a novel have been *unproductive*.⟩ — see FUTILE

unprofessional *adj* lacking or showing a lack of expert skill ⟨an *unprofessional* carelessness about the accuracy of the news story⟩ — see AMATEURISH

unprofitable *adj* producing no results ⟨an *unprofitable* effort to find the information⟩ — see FUTILE

unprogressive *adj* tending to favor established ideas, conditions, or institutions ⟨a candidate with *unprogressive* ideas about public education⟩ — see CONSERVATIVE 1

unprotected *adj* lacking protection from danger or resistance against attack ⟨I was uncomfortable about leaving my house *unprotected*, so I bought a dog.⟩ — see HELPLESS 1

unqualified *adj* **1** having no exceptions or restrictions ⟨The new play is an *unqualified* success.⟩ — see ABSOLUTE 2
2 lacking qualities (as knowledge, skill, or ability) required to do a job ⟨If we hire an *unqualified* candidate, we'll just be wasting our time.⟩ — see INCOMPETENT
3 not limited or specialized in application or purpose ⟨an *unqualified* denial of the charges⟩ — see GENERAL 4

unquestionable *adj* not capable of being challenged or proved wrong ⟨a person of *unquestionable* integrity⟩ — see IRREFUTABLE

unquestionably *adv* without any question ⟨Given his experience, he is *unquestionably* the right person for this job.⟩ — see INDEED 1

unquiet *adj* **1** feeling or showing uncomfortable feelings of uncertainty ⟨plagued with an *unquiet* mind the whole time her son was stationed overseas⟩ — see NERVOUS 1
2 lacking or denying rest ⟨an *unquiet* curiosity that impelled him to study the world about him relentlessly⟩ — see RESTLESS 1

unravel *vb* **1** to separate the various strands of ⟨It took us forever to *unravel* the jumbled mass of Christmas tree lights.⟩

synonyms disentangle, ravel (out), unbraid, unsnarl, untangle, untwine, untwist

related words fray, fret; smooth, straighten (out); uncoil, undo, unknot, unlace, unroll, unstring, unthread, untie, unwind

near antonyms braid, knot, lace, plait, ply, splice, tie, wind

antonyms entangle, snarl, tangle

2 to find an answer for through reasoning ⟨*unraveled* the mystery⟩ — see SOLVE

unreachable *adj* hard or impossible to get to or get at ⟨bothered by an *unreachable* itch on her back⟩ — see INACCESSIBLE

unread *adj* lacking in education or the knowledge gained from books ⟨an officer who seemed to be completely *unread* in military theory⟩ — see IGNORANT 1

unreal *adj* **1** conceived or made without regard for reason or reality ⟨an *unreal* claim that is distant from the slightest hint of truth⟩ — see FANTASTIC 1

2 not real and existing only in the imagination ⟨the *unreal* world of TV sitcoms⟩ — see IMAGINARY

unreality *n* a conception or image created by the imagination and having no objective reality ⟨a sci-fi author who seems to have preferred the *unrealities* of his own fiction to the realities of the world about him⟩ — see FANTASY 1

unreasonable *adj* **1** having no basis in reason or fact ⟨an *unreasonable* assumption⟩ — see GROUNDLESS

2 not using or following good reasoning ⟨an *unreasonable* respect for a man who did not deserve it⟩ — see ILLOGICAL

unreasoning *adj* not using or following good reasoning ⟨an *unreasoning* argument based on some false assumptions⟩ — see ILLOGICAL

unrecorded *adj* not appearing on a list ⟨an *unrecorded* contribution to the scholarship fund⟩ — see UNLISTED

unrecoverable *adj* **1** not capable of being cured or reformed ⟨She believed that there was no such thing as an *unrecoverable* criminal.⟩ — see HOPELESS 1

2 not capable of being repaired, regained, or undone ⟨The flood caused *unrecoverable* damage to our home.⟩ — see IRREPARABLE

unredeemable *adj* **1** not capable of being cured or reformed ⟨*unredeemable* sinners⟩ — see HOPELESS 1

2 not capable of being repaired, regained, or undone ⟨assured the computer science class that there was no such thing as an *unredeemable* error when operating a computer⟩ — see IRREPARABLE

unrefined *adj* **1** being such as found in nature and not altered by processing or refining ⟨*unrefined* sugar⟩ — see CRUDE 1

2 hastily or roughly constructed ⟨an *unrefined* mountaineer's hut⟩ — see RUDE 1

3 lacking in refinement or good taste ⟨guilty of such *unrefined* behavior as eating with their mouths open⟩ — see COARSE 2

unregistered *adj* not appearing on a list ⟨an *unregistered* car⟩ — see UNLISTED

unrehearsed *adj* made or done without previous thought or preparation ⟨an *unrehearsed* speech of thanks⟩ — see EXTEMPORANEOUS

unrelenting *adj* **1** sticking to an opinion, purpose, or course of action in spite of reason, arguments, or persuasion ⟨That professor tends to be *unrelenting* about deadlines.⟩ — see OBSTINATE

2 showing no signs of slackening or yielding in one's purpose ⟨*unrelenting* in the pursuit of gender equality for all people⟩ — see UNYIELDING 1

unremarkable *adj* being of the type that is encountered in the normal course of events ⟨a quiet and *unremarkable* child⟩ — see ORDINARY 1

unremitting *adj* going on and on without any interruptions ⟨*unremitting* rain that lasted for six days⟩ — see CONTINUOUS

unrepentant *adj* not sorry for having done wrong ⟨She was *unrepentant* about getting rid of her ex-roommate's junk.⟩ — see REMORSELESS 1

unreserved *adj* **1** free in expressing one's true feelings and opinions ⟨The politician was criticized for being too *unreserved* in his pronouncements on touchy subjects.⟩ — see FRANK

2 showing feeling freely ⟨an *unreserved* family that expressed both anger and love openly⟩ — see DEMONSTRATIVE 1

unresistant *adj* **1** lacking protection from danger or resistance against attack ⟨a weakened immune system that rendered him *unresistant* to pneumonia⟩ — see HELPLESS 1

2 receiving or enduring without offering resistance ⟨The kitten was surprisingly *unresistant* when the vet examined her.⟩ — see PASSIVE

unresolved *adj* not yet settled or decided ⟨We have to deal with several *unresolved* issues.⟩ — see PENDING 1

unrest *n* a disturbed or uneasy state ⟨a period of civil *unrest*⟩ ⟨His stomach *unrest* was just a sign of stage fright.⟩

synonyms disquiet, ferment, restiveness, restlessness, turmoil, uneasiness

related words fidgets; agitation, commotion, confusion, excitement, hubbub, stir, storm, trouble, tumult, tumultuousness, turbulence, upheaval, uproar, unsettlement; disruption, perturbation; agitation, anxiety, inquietude, queasiness, tension; anarchy, chaos, disorder, welter

near antonyms order, orderliness

antonyms calm, ease, peace, peacefulness, quiet, tranquillity (*or* tranquility)

unrestful *adj* lacking or denying rest ⟨spent an *unrestful* night worrying about their children⟩ — see RESTLESS 1

unrestrained *adj* **1** not bound by rigid standards ⟨He believed his children would do best in an *unrestrained* learning environment.⟩ — see EASYGOING 2

2 not bound, confined, or detained by force ⟨*unrestrained* dogs⟩ — see FREE 3

3 showing feeling freely ⟨very reserved when she's around strangers, but quite *unrestrained* in the company of friends⟩ — see DEMONSTRATIVE 1

4 showing no signs of being under control ⟨*unrestrained* laughter that rang through the cafeteria⟩ — see RAMPANT 1

unrestraint *n* carefree freedom from constraint ⟨the cheerful *unrestraint* of children⟩ — see ABANDON

unrestricted *adj* **1** freely available for use or participation by all ⟨It's an *unrestricted* marathon—anyone can run in it.⟩ — see OPEN 2

2 not bound by rigid standards ⟨The author of the book has an *unrestricted* view of what qualifies as "art."⟩ — see EASYGOING 2

3 not limited or specialized in application or purpose ⟨an *unrestricted* license to operate a motor vehicle⟩ — see GENERAL 4

unrighteous *adj* not conforming to a high moral standard; morally unacceptable ⟨an *unrighteous* act that cannot go unpunished⟩ — see BAD 2

unripe *adj* lacking in adult experience or maturity ⟨*unripe* freshmen nervously navigating their first days of college life⟩ — see CALLOW

unripened *adj* lacking in adult experience or maturity ⟨the *unripened* thoughts of a young writer with limited life experiences⟩ — see CALLOW

unrivaled *or* **unrivalled** *adj* having no equal or rival for excellence or desirability ⟨a violinist who is hailed for his *unrivaled* musicianship⟩ — see ONLY 1

unruffled *adj* free from emotional or mental agitation ⟨He remained *unruffled* by the news that stocks were in a free fall.⟩ — see CALM 2

unruliness *n* refusal to obey ⟨Frustrated by the boys' *unruliness*, the lifeguard asked them to leave the pool.⟩ — see DISOBEDIENCE

unruly *adj* 1 given to resisting authority or another's control ⟨a mother dog trying to look after her *unruly* litter of pups⟩ — see DISOBEDIENT
2 given to resisting control or discipline by others ⟨had a mop of *unruly* hair⟩ — see UNCONTROLLABLE
3 not restrained by or under the control of legal authority ⟨Police tried to eject *unruly* fans.⟩ — see LAWLESS 1

unsafe *adj* 1 involving potential loss or injury ⟨Workers are forbidden from engaging in *unsafe* activities on company time.⟩ — see DANGEROUS 1
2 not paying or showing close attention especially for the purpose of avoiding trouble ⟨People who have a record of being *unsafe* drivers usually have to pay higher insurance premiums.⟩ — see CARELESS 1

unsatisfactorily *adv* in an unsatisfactory way ⟨*Unsatisfactorily* prepared entrées should be immediately returned to the kitchen and replaced with something more acceptable.⟩ — see BADLY 1

unsatisfactory *adj* falling short of a standard ⟨an *unsatisfactory* first attempt at building a birdhouse⟩ — see BAD 1

unsavory *adj* 1 disagreeable or disgusting to the sense of taste ⟨an *unsavory* blend of spices that simply overwhelmed the fish's delicate flavor⟩ — see DISTASTEFUL 1
2 not conforming to a high moral standard; morally unacceptable ⟨*unsavory* doings that ruined the law firm's good name in the community⟩ — see BAD 2
3 not giving pleasure to the mind or senses ⟨hated the whole *unsavory* business of firing people⟩ — see UNPLEASANT
4 lacking in taste or flavor ⟨The *unsavory* food dished up at the rest area's restaurant should be consumed only by the truly desperate.⟩ — see INSIPID 1

unsay *vb* to solemnly or formally reject or go back on (as something formerly adhered to) ⟨The witness tried to *unsay* the very testimony that he had given a few days earlier.⟩ — see ABJURE 1

unschooled *adj* lacking in education or the knowledge gained from books ⟨an *unschooled* but nevertheless intelligent woman who desperately wanted to learn how to read⟩ — see IGNORANT 1

unscrupulous *adj* not guided by or showing a concern for what is right ⟨An *unscrupulous* businessman manipulated them into selling their land for practically nothing.⟩ — see UNPRINCIPLED

unseasonable *adj* occurring before the usual or expected time ⟨an *unseasonable* snowstorm in early November⟩ — see EARLY 2

unseasonably *adv* before the usual or expected time ⟨It's been *unseasonably* hot this spring.⟩ — see EARLY

unseat *vb* to remove from a position of prominence or power (as a throne) ⟨a governor who was *unseated* by the first successful recall in the state's history⟩ — see DEPOSE 1

unsecured *adj* not tightly fastened, tied, or stretched ⟨an *unsecured* luggage rack on top of the car that was a hazard to other vehicles on the road⟩ — see LOOSE 1

unseemly *adj* not appropriate for a particular occasion or situation ⟨an *unseemly* interest in their host's income and expenses⟩ — see INAPPROPRIATE

unselfish *adj* giving or sharing in abundance and without hesitation ⟨an *unselfish* man who spends much of his time helping his community⟩ — see GENEROUS 1

unselfishness *n* the quality or state of being generous

⟨Her natural *unselfishness* sometimes attracts those who would take advantage.⟩ — see LIBERALITY

unsettle *vb* to trouble the mind of; to make uneasy ⟨The news that the local grocery store had sold contaminated produce *unsettled* many shoppers.⟩ — see DISTURB 1

unsettled *adj* 1 likely to change frequently, suddenly, or unexpectedly ⟨We've been having a lot of *unsettled* weather lately.⟩ — see FICKLE 1
2 not yet paid ⟨I keep *unsettled* bills next to the checkbook.⟩ — see OUTSTANDING 1
3 not yet settled or decided ⟨We can't move on as long as this important question remains *unsettled*.⟩ — see PENDING 1
4 not feeling sure about the truth, wisdom, or trustworthiness of someone or something ⟨I'm still *unsettled* about whether I should take that job.⟩ — see DOUBTFUL 1

unsettling *adj* 1 causing worry or anxiety ⟨*unsettling* news that left him unable to concentrate⟩ — see TROUBLESOME
2 marked by or causing agitation or uncomfortable feelings ⟨Jon had the *unsettling* task of helping his grandparents sell their home of 50 years.⟩ — see NERVOUS 2

unshakable *adj* not easily panicked or upset ⟨We need the kind of leader who will be *unshakable* in a national crisis.⟩ — see UNFLAPPABLE

unshaken *adj* free from emotional or mental agitation ⟨The witness remained *unshaken* throughout the cross-examination.⟩ — see CALM 2

unshaped *adj* having no definite or recognizable form ⟨an *unshaped* mass of clay that was just in need of some inspiration from the modeler⟩ — see FORMLESS 1

unshared *adj* belonging only to the one person, unit, or group named ⟨With her older sister off to college, she was thrilled to have an *unshared* bedroom for the first time in her life.⟩ — see SOLE 1

unshorn *adj* covered with or as if with hair ⟨the campers' *unshorn* beards⟩ — see HAIRY 1

unsightly *adj* unpleasant to look at ⟨Strip-mining leaves an *unsightly* gash in the landscape.⟩ — see UGLY 1

unskilled *adj* 1 lacking or showing a lack of expert skill ⟨An *unskilled* handling of the facial features in the portrait explains why it is attributed to "school of Velàzquez" and not to the master himself.⟩ — see AMATEURISH
2 lacking qualities (as knowledge, skill, or ability) required to do a job ⟨training *unskilled* workers for higher paying positions⟩ — see INCOMPETENT

unskillful *adj* 1 lacking qualities (as knowledge, skill, or ability) required to do a job ⟨An *unskillful* editor can be worse than none at all.⟩ — see INCOMPETENT
2 lacking or showing a lack of expert skill ⟨some painfully *unskillful* playing by the band's guitarist⟩ — see AMATEURISH

unsmiling *adj* not joking or playful in mood or manner ⟨Mr. Bart delivered the reprimand with a harsh and *unsmiling* face.⟩ — see SERIOUS 1

unsnarl *vb* to separate the various strands of ⟨*unsnarled* the fishing lines⟩ — see UNRAVEL 1

unsociable *adj* having or showing a lack of friendliness or interest in others ⟨an *unsociable* but not an overtly rude child⟩ — see COOL 1

unsoiled *adj* free from dirt or stain ⟨I never managed to make it through a day at the packing plant with *unsoiled* shoes.⟩ — see CLEAN 1

unsolicited *adj* not searched or asked for ⟨Pam tired of the *unsolicited* advice from friends and family regarding her career.⟩ — see UNSOUGHT

unsolvable *adj* incapable of being solved or accomplished ⟨an apparently *unsolvable* problem⟩ — see IMPOSSIBLE

unsophisticated *adj* lacking in worldly wisdom or

informed judgment ⟨mistakenly believed that the family was *unsophisticated* and would sell their land for a fraction of its worth⟩ — see NAIVE 1

unsophistication *n* **1** the quality or state of being simple and sincere ⟨The *unsophistication* of the plea touched his heart.⟩ — see NAÏVETÉ 1
2 the quality or state of having a form or structure of few parts or elements ⟨The *unsophistication* of the coffeemaker's design is part of its appeal.⟩ — see SIMPLICITY 1

unsought *adj* not searched or asked for ⟨The meddling neighbor insisted on giving us *unsought* advice.⟩
synonyms unasked, unbidden (*also* unbid), uninvited, unsolicited
related words undesired, unwanted, unwelcome; objectionable, offensive, unacceptable, undesirable; uncalledfor, unnecessary
near antonyms necessary, needed, required; desired, wanted, welcome
antonyms requested, solicited

unsound *adj* **1** not being in agreement with what is true ⟨an *unsound* and pernicious stereotype⟩ — see FALSE 1
2 not using or following good reasoning ⟨It is clearly *unsound* to argue that just because a scientific explanation for that phenomenon does not currently exist, no such explanation is possible.⟩ — see ILLOGICAL
3 temporarily suffering from a disorder of the body ⟨an *unsound* horse that will have to be disqualified from the race⟩ — see SICK 1

unsoundness *n* the condition of not being in good health ⟨The overall *unsoundness* of her health in her last years greatly limited what she could do.⟩ — see SICKNESS 1

unsparing *adj* **1** giving or sharing in abundance and without hesitation ⟨Neighbors were *unsparing* in their charity when a local family was rendered homeless by a fire.⟩ — see GENEROUS 1
2 having or showing a lack of sympathy or tender feelings ⟨*unsparing* in the punishment of even petty offenses⟩ — see HARD 1

unspeakable *adj* beyond the power to describe ⟨continually encountered *unspeakable* beauty in their travels through the Alps⟩ — see INDESCRIBABLE

unspecialized *adj* not limited or specialized in application or purpose ⟨They preferred to have one *unspecialized* tool rather than buy 16 specialized ones.⟩ — see GENERAL 4

unspecified *adj* known but not named ⟨Some *unspecified* person is expected to replace the retiring CFO.⟩ — see CERTAIN 1

unspoken *adj* understood although not put into words ⟨an *unspoken* promise to remain faithful to one another⟩ — see IMPLICIT 1

unsportsmanlike *adj* not being in accordance with the rules or standards of what is fair in sport ⟨was suspended for *unsportsmanlike* conduct⟩ — see FOUL 2

unstable *adj* **1** not being in or able to maintain a state of balance ⟨The minute we put the books down on the *unstable* desk, the whole stack went crashing to the floor.⟩
synonyms unbalanced, unsteady
related words rocky, shaky, tippy, tipsy, wavery, wobbly (*also* wabbly); infirm, insecure, precarious, unsound; doddering, doddery, jiggling, jiggly, rickety, teetering, tottery; askew, awry, cockeyed, lopsided, uneven
near antonyms even, level, straight; sound, sturdy, substantial
antonyms balanced, equilibrated, stabilized, stable, steady
2 likely to change frequently, suddenly, or unexpectedly ⟨Financial investors don't like an *unstable* economy.⟩ — see FICKLE 1
3 not staying constant ⟨*Unstable* temperatures are not ideal growing conditions for orchids.⟩ — see UNEVEN 2

unstained *adj* **1** free from dirt or stain ⟨You should be wearing a tie, preferably an *unstained* one.⟩ — see CLEAN 1
2 lacking an addition of color ⟨The Krays bought an *unstained* picnic table that they planned to finish themselves.⟩ — see COLORLESS 1

unsteadiness *n* the quality or state of not being firmly fixed in position ⟨blamed the poor quality of the video on the tripod's *unsteadiness*⟩ — see INSTABILITY

unsteady *adj* **1** lacking in steadiness or regularity of occurrence ⟨a year of *unsteady* economic growth⟩ — see FITFUL
2 likely to change frequently, suddenly, or unexpectedly ⟨In the days of sailing ships, mariners were constantly at the mercy of *unsteady* winds.⟩ — see FICKLE 1
3 not being in or able to maintain a state of balance ⟨cautiously climbed up the *unsteady* ladder⟩ — see UNSTABLE 1
4 not staying constant ⟨*unsteady* business conditions that rattled investors⟩ — see UNEVEN 2

unstintingly *adv* in a generous manner ⟨Donors gave *unstintingly* to the relief fund.⟩ — see WELL 2

unstop *vb* to make passage through (something) possible by removing obstructions ⟨The plumber *unstopped* the drain.⟩ — see OPEN 2

unstopped *adj* allowing passage without obstruction ⟨An *unstopped* hole was the cause of the leakage.⟩ — see OPEN 1

unstring *vb* **1** to cause to go insane or as if insane ⟨the kind of fierce combat that can *unstring* even hardened soldiers⟩ — see CRAZE
2 to deprive of courage or confidence ⟨a little *unstrung* by the fact that he was on his first job interview⟩ — see UNNERVE 1

unstructured *adj* having no definite or recognizable form ⟨writes *unstructured* compositions that some people might not even regard as poems⟩ — see FORMLESS 1

unstudied *adj* made or done without previous thought or preparation ⟨has an *unstudied* effervescence that is rare in show business⟩ — see EXTEMPORANEOUS

unstylish *adj* marked by an obvious lack of style or good taste ⟨an *unstylish* restaurant that hadn't changed in 40 years⟩ — see ¹TACKY 1

unsubstantial *adj* **1** not composed of matter ⟨as thin and *unsubstantial* as the wind⟩ — see IMMATERIAL 1
2 being of a material lacking in sturdiness or substance ⟨*unsubstantial* wisps of lace⟩ — see FLIMSY 1
3 lacking bodily strength ⟨an *unsubstantial* child who was unfit to play sports of any kind⟩ — see WEAK 1

unsubstantiated *adj* having no basis in reason or fact ⟨an *unsubstantiated* claim that was thrown out of court⟩ — see GROUNDLESS

unsuccessful *adj* producing no results ⟨an *unsuccessful* attempt to fix the faucet ourselves⟩ — see FUTILE

unsuitable *adj* not appropriate for a particular occasion or situation ⟨All the movies playing now are violent or otherwise *unsuitable* for a child's birthday party.⟩ — see INAPPROPRIATE

unsuitably *adv* in a mistaken or inappropriate way ⟨dressed *unsuitably* for the unexpectedly cold weather⟩ — see WRONGLY

unsullied *adj* free from dirt or stain ⟨Only *unsullied* vestments are ever appropriate for church services.⟩ — see CLEAN 1

unsung *adj* not widely known ⟨an *unsung* hero of the Holocaust⟩ — see OBSCURE 2

unsupportable *adj* more than can be put up with ⟨These high taxes are just *unsupportable*.⟩ — see UNBEARABLE

unsupported *adj* having no basis in reason or fact ⟨an *unsupported* claim that the structure was built by Vikings⟩ — see GROUNDLESS

unsure *adj* not feeling sure about the truth, wisdom, or trustworthiness of someone or something ⟨*unsure* of her ability to handle the pressure of competing in the Olympic Games⟩ — see DOUBTFUL 1

unsurpassable *adj* having no equal or rival for excellence or desirability ⟨the *unsurpassable* splendor of the palace⟩ — see ONLY 1

unsurpassed *adj* **1** having no equal or rival for excellence or desirability ⟨an artist who is *unsurpassed* at painting portraits that reveal the subject's inner life⟩ — see ONLY 1
2 of the very best kind ⟨a French restaurant known for its *unsurpassed* cuisine⟩ — see EXCELLENT

unsuspecting *adj* lacking in worldly wisdom or informed judgment ⟨sidewalk vendors selling bogus gems to *unsuspecting* tourists⟩ — see NAIVE 1

unsuspicious *adj* lacking in worldly wisdom or informed judgment ⟨a happy-go-lucky, *unsuspicious* fellow who was easy prey for scam artists⟩ — see NAIVE 1

unsympathetic *adj* **1** having or showing a lack of sympathy or tender feelings ⟨He gave them an *unsympathetic* look and pointed out that they'd brought the problem on themselves.⟩ — see HARD 1
2 lacking in friendliness or warmth of feeling ⟨an aloof and *unsympathetic* man who does not engage in small talk⟩ — see COLD 2
3 marked by opposition or ill will ⟨a bohemian artist who found the *unsympathetic* environment of the small town too much to bear⟩ — see HOSTILE 1
4 opposed to one's interests ⟨an *unsympathetic* reaction to her proposal to ban sugar from the company cafeteria⟩ — see ADVERSE 1

untamed *adj* **1** existing without human habitation or cultivation ⟨a dangerous and *untamed* land⟩ — see WILD 2
2 living outdoors without taming or domestication by humans ⟨tried to capture the *untamed* horse⟩ — see WILD 1

untangle *vb* **1** to separate the various strands of ⟨gently *untangled* the baby's hair⟩ — see UNRAVEL 1
2 to set free from entanglement or difficulty ⟨I was finally able to *untangle* myself from my credit problems.⟩ — see EXTRICATE

untaught *adj* lacking in education or the knowledge gained from books ⟨an *untaught* artist whose primitive paintings are now prized by collectors⟩ — see IGNORANT 1

unthinkable *adj* too extraordinary or improbable to believe ⟨To most of the players it seemed *unthinkable* that their teammate could play for another team.⟩ — see INCREDIBLE

unthrifty *adj* given to spending money freely or foolishly ⟨The *unthrifty* couple ended up having to declare bankruptcy.⟩ — see PRODIGAL

unthrone *vb* to remove from a position of prominence or power (as a throne) ⟨The board of directors *unthroned* the CEO when it became clear that he was not going to reverse the company's sagging fortunes anytime soon.⟩ — see DEPOSE 1

untidy *adj* **1** lacking in order, neatness, and often cleanliness ⟨I can never find anything in this *untidy* office!⟩ — see MESSY
2 lacking neatness in dress or person ⟨Neighbors gossiped about the couple's rumpled and *untidy* children.⟩ — see SLOPPY 1

untie *vb* to disengage the knotted parts of ⟨She always makes sure to *untie* her shoelaces before removing her shoes.⟩
synonyms unbind, undo, unfasten, unlash
related words unbraid, undo, unlace; disentangle, ravel, unravel, unsnarl, untangle, unwind; loose, loosen
near antonyms braid, interlace, interweave, lace, wind; entangle, snarl, tangle
antonyms bind, fasten, knot, lash, tie

untimely *adj* occurring before the usual or expected time ⟨The *untimely* arrival of our guests caught us by surprise.⟩ — see EARLY 2

untiring *adj* showing no signs of weariness even after long hard effort ⟨the camel's reputation as an *untiring* beast of burden⟩ ⟨The detective's *untiring* investigation of the crime finally led to several arrests.⟩ — see TIRELESS

untitled *adj* not named or identified by a name ⟨The band is working on a new album which is still *untitled*.⟩ — see NAMELESS 1

untold *adj* too many to be counted ⟨*Untold* generations have lived and died in this ancient land.⟩ — see COUNTLESS

untouchable *adj* **1** hard or impossible to get to or get at ⟨*untouchable* oil lying deep within the earth⟩ — see INACCESSIBLE
2 not to be violated, criticized, or tampered with ⟨an *untouchable* target for criticism as far as the local newspaper was concerned⟩ — see SACRED 1

untoward *adj* **1** given to resisting authority or another's control ⟨tried to reason with the *untoward* child⟩ — see DISOBEDIENT
2 given to resisting control or discipline by others ⟨dogs trying to drive the *untoward* flock through the gate⟩ — see UNCONTROLLABLE
3 opposed to one's interests ⟨reassured me that the medication had no *untoward* side effects⟩ — see ADVERSE 1
4 not appropriate for a particular occasion or situation ⟨There was nothing *untoward* about his remarks.⟩ — see INAPPROPRIATE

untreated *adj* being such as found in nature and not altered by processing or refining ⟨*untreated* wool⟩ — see CRUDE 1

untroubled *adj* **1** free from emotional or mental agitation ⟨She remains *untroubled* despite the chaos around her.⟩ — see CALM 2
2 free from storms or physical disturbance ⟨quietly canoeing on the *untroubled* waters of the lake⟩ — see CALM 1

untrue *adj* **1** not being in agreement with what is true ⟨"The sky is purple" is an *untrue* statement.⟩ — see FALSE 1
2 not true in one's allegiance to someone or something ⟨*untrue* to his country in its time of need⟩ — see FAITHLESS

untruth *n* **1** a false idea or belief ⟨Their argument rests on a fundamental *untruth* which has long been discredited.⟩ — see FALLACY 1
2 a statement known by its maker to be untrue and made in order to deceive ⟨The website is rife with *untruths* and misleading information.⟩ — see LIE
3 the quality or state of being false ⟨There is an element of *untruth* in all forms of art: works of art provide only a semblance of reality.⟩ — see FALLACY 2

untruthful *adj* **1** not being in agreement with what is true ⟨an unintentionally *untruthful* statement that the candidate later corrected⟩ — see FALSE 1
2 telling or containing lies ⟨The political action committee was slammed for spreading *untruthful* smears about the candidate.⟩ — see DISHONEST 1

untruthfulness *n* the tendency to tell lies ⟨Consistent *untruthfulness* on your part will result in consistent distrustfulness on other people's part.⟩ — see DISHONESTY 1

untutored *adj* lacking in education or the knowledge gained from books ⟨To the *untutored* observer these works of art must seem strange indeed.⟩ — see IGNORANT 1

untwine *vb* to separate the various strands of ⟨*untwined* his shoelaces⟩ — see UNRAVEL 1

untwist *vb* to separate the various strands of ⟨*untwisted* the ball of thread⟩ — see UNRAVEL 1

untypical *adj* departing from some accepted standard of what is normal ⟨The plant displays some *untypical* characteristics.⟩ — see DEVIANT

unusable *adj* not capable of being put to use or account ⟨a completely *unusable* gadget that's just taking up space in the drawer⟩ — see IMPRACTICAL

unused *adj* **1** not having acquired a habit or tolerance ⟨The runner's performance suffered because he was *unused* to running at such high elevations.⟩

synonyms unacclimated, unaccustomed, unadapted, unadjusted

related words unseasoned

near antonyms unaffected, uninfluenced

antonyms acclimated, accustomed, adapted, adjusted, habituated, used

2 recently made and never used before ⟨preferred to start with *unused* pencils⟩ — see NEW 3

3 not being in a state of use, activity, or employment ⟨Is there an *unused* cubicle that the temp could work out of?⟩ — see INACTIVE 2

unusual *adj* **1** noticeably different from what is generally found or experienced ⟨We found some *unusual* shells by the high-tide mark while combing the beach.⟩

synonyms curious, extraordinary, funny, odd, offbeat, out-of-the-way, peculiar, queer, rare, singular, strange, unaccustomed, uncommon, uncustomary, unique, weird

related words bizarre, eccentric, far-out, kooky (*also* kookie), oddball, outlandish, way-out; aberrant, abnormal, atypical, exceptional, irregular; newsworthy, notable, noteworthy, noticeable, particular, remarkable, special

near antonyms unexceptional; expected, predictable; familiar, normal, regular, typical

antonyms common, ordinary, plain, usual

2 being out of the ordinary ⟨The famously arrogant actor accepted his award with *unusual* grace and humility.⟩ — see EXCEPTIONAL 1

unutterable *adj* beyond the power to describe ⟨the *unutterable* joy that a baby can bring to a household⟩ ⟨the *unutterable* suffering brought on by the war⟩ — see INDESCRIBABLE

unvarnished *adj* free from all additions or embellishment ⟨I'm telling the *unvarnished* truth.⟩ — see PLAIN 1

unvarying *adj* **1** not undergoing a change in condition ⟨an *unvarying* dedication to the welfare of her community⟩ — see CONSTANT 1

2 not varying ⟨*Unvarying* temperatures and humidity are best for the preservation of ancient artifacts.⟩ — see UNIFORM

unveil *vb* **1** to make known (as information previously kept secret) ⟨*unveiled* the techniques that the self-styled clairvoyant used to trick her clients⟩ — see REVEAL 1

2 to present so as to invite notice or attention ⟨*unveiled* the new sculpture before a gathering of dignitaries⟩ — see SHOW 1

unvoiced *adj* understood although not put into words ⟨an *unvoiced* promise to be waiting for him when he returned from the war⟩ — see IMPLICIT 1

unwarrantable *adj* too bad to be excused or justified ⟨the *unwarrantable* arrogance of that man⟩ — see INEXCUSABLE

unwarranted *adj* **1** not needed by the circumstances or to accomplish an end ⟨The committee concluded that any further revisions to the regulations were currently *unwarranted*.⟩ — see UNNECESSARY

2 having no basis in reason or fact ⟨Don't leap to *unwarranted* conclusions.⟩ — see GROUNDLESS

unwary *adj* **1** lacking in worldly wisdom or informed judgment ⟨e-mail scams that take advantage of *unwary* computer users⟩ — see NAIVE 1

2 not paying or showing close attention especially for the purpose of avoiding trouble ⟨a dangerous stretch of desert that has claimed many *unwary* travelers⟩ — see CARELESS 1

3 readily taken advantage of ⟨*unwary* consumers who unquestioningly swallow the dubious claims of TV pitchmen⟩ — see EASY 2

unwavering *adj* not varying ⟨an *unwavering* commitment to social justice⟩ — see UNIFORM

unwed *adj* not married ⟨chose to remain *unwed* while finishing a Ph.D.⟩ — see SINGLE 1

unwelcome *adj* not giving pleasure to the mind or senses ⟨The *unwelcome* news ruined what had been a fine day.⟩ — see UNPLEASANT

unwell *adj* temporarily suffering from a disorder of the body ⟨She missed work because she was *unwell*.⟩ — see SICK 1

unwholesome *adj* **1** bad for the well-being of the body ⟨Health inspectors shut down several food stands that were using tainted and *unwholesome* meat.⟩ — see UNHEALTHY 1

2 having or showing lowered moral character or standards ⟨The company has engaged in *unwholesome* business practices.⟩ — see CORRUPT

unwieldy *adj* difficult to use or operate especially because of size, weight, or design ⟨an *unwieldy* machine that requires two people to operate it⟩ — see CUMBERSOME

unwilling *adj* not made or done willingly or by choice ⟨*unwilling* contributions from city employees who felt pressured to make them⟩ — see INVOLUNTARY 1

unwillingness *n* a lack of willingness or desire to do or accept something ⟨Your *unwillingness* to help with the cooking means that you won't be sharing in the eating.⟩ — see RELUCTANCE

unwind *vb* to get rid of nervous tension or anxiety ⟨Soft music and a good book help me *unwind*.⟩ — see RELAX 1

unwise *adj* **1** showing or marked by a lack of good sense or judgment ⟨Jon made the *unwise* decision to invest in a brand-new company.⟩ — see FOOLISH 1

2 showing poor judgment especially in personal relationships or social situations ⟨an *unwise* urge to confide in total strangers⟩ — see INDISCREET

unwitting *adj* **1** happening by chance ⟨an *unwitting* mistake made in copying the material⟩ — see ACCIDENTAL 1

2 not informed about or aware of something ⟨an *unwitting* accomplice to the crime⟩ — see IGNORANT 2

unwonted *adj* being out of the ordinary ⟨honored for *unwonted* courage in battle⟩ — see EXCEPTIONAL 1

unworkable *adj* not capable of being put to use or account ⟨The company decided that the proposed reorganization of its operations was *unworkable* due to high costs.⟩ — see IMPRACTICAL

unworldliness *n* the quality or state of being simple and sincere ⟨The sweet *unworldliness* about the child made us want to protect him.⟩ — see NAÏVETÉ 1

unworldly *adj* lacking in worldly wisdom or informed judgment ⟨The guy's *unworldly* enough to think that anything he reads online is true.⟩ — see NAIVE 1

unworried *adj* free from emotional or mental agitation ⟨remained *unworried* despite the panic all around her⟩ — see CALM 2

unwritten *adj* made or carried on through speaking rather than in writing ⟨An *unwritten* contract may not be enforceable.⟩ — see VERBAL 1

unyielding *adj* **1** showing no signs of slackening or yielding in one's purpose ⟨The pioneers faced the challenge of settling the frontier with *unyielding* courage.⟩

synonyms determined, dogged, grim, implacable, relentless, unappeasable, unflinching, unrelenting

related words persevering, persistent, tenacious; hard, hardheaded, headstrong, intractable, mulish, obdurate, opinionated, peevish, pertinacious, perverse, pigheaded, self-willed, stubborn, uncooperative, willful (*or* wilful); merciless, ruthless, unforgiving; inextinguishable, insatiable
near antonyms slackening, softening, yielding; impotent, invertebrate, slack, spineless, weak; complaisant, obliging, pliable, pliant
2 having a consistency that does not easily yield to pressure ⟨Knead the dough until it feels reasonably *unyielding*.⟩ — see FIRM 2
3 incapable of or highly resistant to bending ⟨an *unyielding* steel bar⟩ — see STIFF 1
4 sticking to an opinion, purpose, or course of action in spite of reason, arguments, or persuasion ⟨Despite studies showing that limits on development would hurt the local economy, the town council remained *unyielding* in their support for these limits.⟩ — see OBSTINATE
unyoke *vb* to set or force apart ⟨*Unyoke* these two boats and tie them to the dock separately.⟩ — see SEPARATE 1
up *adj* **1** being at a higher level than average ⟨The level of the lake is *up* this spring.⟩ — see HIGH 2
2 brought or having come to an end ⟨Okay, time is *up!*⟩ — see COMPLETE 2
3 having information especially as a result of study or experience ⟨She's always *up* on the latest developments in her field.⟩ — see FAMILIAR 2
up *vb* **1** to make greater in size, amount, or number ⟨Climbing fuel prices have forced the delivery company to *up* its prices.⟩ — see INCREASE 1
2 to move from a lower to a higher place or position ⟨*upped* the catboat's sail⟩ — see RAISE 1
3 to move or extend upward ⟨The road constantly *ups* and downs as it makes its way over the hills.⟩ — see ASCEND
upbeat *adj* **1** having or showing a good mood or disposition ⟨an *upbeat* attitude about life⟩ — see CHEERFUL 1
2 having qualities which inspire hope ⟨several *upbeat* signs that the economy is improving⟩ — see HOPEFUL 1
upbraid *vb* to criticize (someone) severely or angrily especially for personal failings ⟨Mom *upbraided* me for not offering to help my grandparents.⟩ — see SCOLD
upcoming *adj* being soon to appear or take place ⟨an *upcoming* election⟩ — see FORTHCOMING 1
up–country *n* a rural region that forms the edge of the settled or developed part of a country ⟨built a cabin in the *up-country*⟩ — see FRONTIER 2
upend *vb* **1** to achieve a victory over ⟨The team won the division play-offs, but was *upended* in the final championship game.⟩ — see BEAT 2
2 to fix in an upright position ⟨We had to *upend* the sofa in order to fit it into the elevator.⟩ — see ERECT 1
upgrade *n* **1** an upward slope ⟨We had to walk our bicycles on the *upgrades* on our ride through the hills.⟩ — see ASCENT 1
2 a raising or a state of being raised to a higher rank or position ⟨received an *upgrade* to lieutenant⟩ — see ADVANCEMENT 1
3 the degree to which something rises up from a position level with the horizon ⟨There's a steep *upgrade* to some of the hills on that route.⟩ — see SLANT 1
upgrade *vb* **1** to move higher in rank or position ⟨*upgraded* them to first class⟩ — see PROMOTE 1
2 to make better ⟨That restaurant had better *upgrade* its service—and fast—if it wants to stay in business!⟩ — see IMPROVE
upheaval *n* a violent disturbance (as of the political or social order) ⟨The government can no longer control the

social *upheaval* brought about by the collapse of the country's economy.⟩ — see CONVULSION
uphill *adj* requiring considerable physical or mental effort ⟨an *uphill* battle to eradicate poverty in an area of the state that has never known anything else⟩ — see HARD 2
uphill *n* an upward slope ⟨No matter where you go bicycle touring, the *uphills* always seem to outnumber the downhills.⟩ — see ASCENT 2
uphold *vb* **1** to continue to declare to be true or proper despite opposition or objections ⟨determined to *uphold* her views in the face of all challenges⟩ — see MAINTAIN 2
2 to hold up or serve as a foundation for ⟨an entablature *upheld* by a series of gracefully slender columns⟩ — see SUPPORT 3
3 to move from a lower to a higher place or position ⟨Worshippers *upheld* their joined hands and sang the praises of the Lord.⟩ — see RAISE 1
upkeep *n* the act or activity of keeping something in an existing and usually satisfactory condition ⟨The *upkeep* of the old place was costing a fortune.⟩ — see MAINTENANCE
upland *n* an area of high ground ⟨The animals huddled on the *upland* as the floodwater rose.⟩ — see HEIGHT 4
uplift *vb* to move from a lower to a higher place or position ⟨a mountain range that was *uplifted* millions of years ago by the collision of continental plates⟩ — see RAISE 1
uplifted *adj* being positioned above a surface ⟨an *uplifted* area of ground⟩ — see ELEVATED 1
upmost *adj* being at a point or level higher than all others ⟨the *upmost* floor of the building⟩ — see TOP 1
upon *prep* in or into contact with ⟨leaned *upon* the desk⟩ — see AGAINST
upper–class *adj* of high birth, rank, or station ⟨*upperclass* boys who had attended a private academy⟩ — see NOBLE 1
upper class *n* the highest class in a society ⟨a school founded to educate the children of the *upper class*⟩ — see ARISTOCRACY 1
upper crust *n* **1** individuals carefully selected as being the best of a class ⟨The conference was a gathering of the *upper crust* of the computer programming industry.⟩ — see ELITE 1
2 the highest class in a society ⟨a specialty clothing store for the *upper crust*⟩ — see ARISTOCRACY 1
upper hand *n* the more favorable condition or position in a competition ⟨finally gained the *upper hand* in the argument⟩ — see ADVANTAGE 1
uppermost *adj* being at a point or level higher than all others ⟨The *uppermost* floor of the house gets very hot in the summer.⟩ — see TOP 1
uppish *adj* having a feeling of superiority that shows itself in an overbearing attitude ⟨The new employee's *uppish* airs aren't winning him many friends among his colleagues.⟩ — see ARROGANT
uppity *adj* having a feeling of superiority that shows itself in an overbearing attitude ⟨an *uppity* sales clerk who barely gave us any help⟩ — see ARROGANT
upraise *vb* **1** to move from a lower to a higher place or position ⟨The runner's arms were *upraised* in a sign of victory as he crossed the finish line.⟩ — see RAISE 1
2 to fix in an upright position ⟨Archaeologists are still not sure how the mysterious statues on Easter Island were *upraised*.⟩ — see ERECT 1
upraised *adj* being positioned above a surface ⟨This *upraised* platform will be used as a small stage for next week's community concert.⟩ — see ELEVATED 1
upright *adj* **1** conforming to a high standard of morality or virtue ⟨an honest and *upright* people⟩ — see GOOD 2
2 following the accepted rules of moral conduct ⟨Informing the clerk that he had just given me back too

much in change was the only *upright* thing to do.⟩ — see HONORABLE 1

3 rising straight up ⟨Only one pillar of the ruined temple remained *upright*.⟩ — see ERECT

uprightness *n* **1** conduct that conforms to an accepted standard of right and wrong ⟨The *uprightness* of our cause is not what is being called into question here.⟩ — see MORALITY 1

2 faithfulness to high moral standards ⟨The members of this special investigative committee must be personages of unquestionable *uprightness*.⟩ — see HONOR 1

uprise *n* an upward slope ⟨The sharp *uprise* leading up to the fortress would make an assault extremely difficult.⟩ — see ASCENT 2

uprise *vb* **1** to leave one's bed ⟨*Uprise*! We have lots of work to do today!⟩ — see ARISE 1

2 to move or extend upward ⟨As we went from the coast into the state's interior, the land gradually began *uprising* and eventually we were on mountainous terrain.⟩ — see ASCEND

uprising *n* open fighting against authority (as one's own government) ⟨The *uprising* was quickly and brutally suppressed.⟩ — see REBELLION 1

uproar *n* **1** a state of noisy, confused activity ⟨The house is always in a jubilant *uproar* during the holidays.⟩ — see COMMOTION

2 a state of wildly excited activity or emotion ⟨The ref's controversial call sent the crowd into an *uproar*.⟩ — see FRENZY

3 a violent disturbance (as of the political or social order) ⟨The *uproar* following the corrupt election nearly toppled the government.⟩ — see CONVULSION

4 a violent shouting ⟨An *uproar* arose from the crowd when it was announced that the concert was cancelled and refunds might not be available.⟩ — see CLAMOR 1

uproarious *adj* **1** causing or intended to cause laughter ⟨The movie follows the comic duo through a series of outrageous and *uproarious* escapades.⟩ — see FUNNY 1

2 full of or characterized by the presence of noise ⟨visited the site where the action movie was being filmed only to find a chaotic, *uproarious* set⟩ — see NOISY 2

uproot *vb* to draw out by force or with effort ⟨*uprooted* the old bridge's pilings upon the completion of its replacement⟩ — see EXTRACT

upset *adj* feeling or showing uncomfortable feelings of uncertainty ⟨She was *upset* by the unexplained change in plans.⟩ — see NERVOUS 1

upset *n* an act or instance of the order of things being disturbed ⟨The move to a new town is just the latest in a series of *upsets* for my family over the last year.⟩

synonyms derangement, dislocation, disruption, disturbance
related words convulsion, revolution, unsettledness, unsettlement, upheaval

upset *vb* **1** to trouble the mind of; to make uneasy ⟨The smallest things can *upset* us if we're already stressed.⟩ — see DISTURB 1

2 to turn on one's side or upside down ⟨The narrow boat *upsets* easily and should be handled with care.⟩ — see CAPSIZE

3 to undo the proper order or arrangement of ⟨The change in the bus schedule *upset* our daily routine.⟩ — see DISORDER

upsetting *adj* causing worry or anxiety ⟨The constant arguing is *upsetting* to a sensitive person like your grandmother.⟩ — see TROUBLESOME

upshot *n* a condition or occurrence traceable to a cause ⟨The *upshot* of the court's ruling is that a number of communities will now have to change their zoning laws.⟩ — see EFFECT 1

upside–down *adj* lacking in order, neatness, and often cleanliness ⟨The frantic search left the room *upside-down*.⟩ — see MESSY

upstanding *adj* **1** following the accepted rules of moral conduct ⟨a fine, *upstanding* woman who deserves to be nominated to the state's highest court⟩ — see HONORABLE 1

2 rising straight up ⟨a stiff, *upstanding* collar⟩ — see ERECT

uptight *adj* feeling or showing uncomfortable feelings of uncertainty ⟨He has a tendency to fret and get *uptight* whenever his usual routine is disrupted.⟩ — see NERVOUS 1

up–to–date *adj* **1** being or involving the latest methods, concepts, information, or styles ⟨demanded the most *up-to-date* computer system available⟩ — see MODERN

2 having information especially as a result of study or experience ⟨I'm afraid that I'm not *up-to-date* on that issue.⟩ — see FAMILIAR 2

upturn *vb* to move or extend upward ⟨At this point the road *upturns* steeply, the trees become scarcer, and the valley unfolds before you.⟩ — see ASCEND

urbane *adj* having or showing very polished and worldly manners ⟨a gentlemanly and *urbane* host of elegant dinner parties⟩ — see SUAVE

urbanize *vb* to accustom to the ways of the city ⟨Every September the city of Boston *urbanizes* a new crop of college students from small towns across the country.⟩ — see CITIFY

urchin *n* an appealingly mischievous person ⟨We could never resist the little *urchin's* pleas to come and play.⟩ — see SCAMP 1

urge *n* a strong wish for something ⟨I'm trying to resist the *urge* to eat another piece of cake.⟩ — see DESIRE 1

urge *vb* to try to persuade (someone) through earnest appeals to follow a course of action ⟨The public service announcement *urges* pet owners to spay or neuter their pets.⟩

synonyms egg (on), encourage, exhort, goad, nudge, press, prod, prompt
related words drive, propel, spur, stimulate; hurry, hustle, push, rush; adjure, beseech, implore, importune; blandish, cajole, coax, soft-soap, wheedle; high-pressure, nag, needle, pressure; foment, incite, instigate, provoke, stir (up)
near antonyms deter, discourage, dissuade; brake, check, constrain, curb, hold back, inhibit, restrain

urgent *adj* needing immediate attention ⟨I will need to put off everything but the most *urgent* issues.⟩ — see ACUTE 2

usable *also* **useable** *adj* **1** capable of or suitable for being used for a particular purpose ⟨Although the spade is *usable* as a snow shovel, it doesn't do a very good job.⟩

synonyms available, employable, exploitable, fit, functional, operable, practicable, serviceable, useful
related words applicable, relevant; doable, feasible, viable, workable; reusable
antonyms impracticable, inoperable, nonfunctional, unavailable, unemployable, unusable

2 capable of being put to use or account ⟨There's not a scrap of *usable* information in that article on finding the right pet for one's family.⟩ — see PRACTICAL 1

usage *n* the act or practice of employing something for a particular purpose ⟨The machine's warranty does not cover malfunctions that result from improper *usage*.⟩ — see USE 1

use *n* **1** the act or practice of employing something for a particular purpose ⟨The *use* of cell phones is strictly prohibited in the doctor's office.⟩

synonyms application, employment, exercise, operation, play, usage
related words exertion; reuse
near antonyms disuse, nonuse

2 the capacity for being useful for some purpose ⟨The broken grill isn't going to be of much *use* in cooking the hamburgers.⟩

synonyms account, avail, service, serviceability, serviceableness, usefulness, utility

related words advantage, benefit, gain; aid, assistance, help; applicability, appropriateness, fitness, relevance; profit, value, worth

near antonyms inapplicability, inappropriateness

antonyms uselessness, worthlessness

3 positive regard for something ⟨I have no *use* for slackers!⟩ — see LIKING

use *vb* **1** to put into action or service ⟨I will need to *use* the large hammer for this project.⟩

synonyms apply, employ, exercise, exploit, harness, operate, utilize

related words handle, manipulate, wield; direct, run, work; cannibalize, recycle, reuse

phrases bring to bear, draw on (*or* upon), make use of

near antonyms ignore, neglect; misapply, misuse

2 to behave toward in a stated way ⟨The factory workers were underpaid and poorly *used* by their employers.⟩ — see TREAT 1

3 to take unfair advantage of ⟨I was paying for everything on our little outing, and I was starting to feel like I was being *used*.⟩ — see EXPLOIT 1

used *adj* being in the habit or custom ⟨My grandmother has spent her whole life on the farm and is *used* to working hard.⟩ — see ACCUSTOMED

useful *adj* **1** capable of being put to use or account ⟨*useful* suggestions for limiting the amount of fuel we use⟩ — see PRACTICAL 1

2 capable of or suitable for being used for a particular purpose ⟨I've found this tool really *useful* for making sure all my pictures are hung straight.⟩ — see USABLE 1

3 providing service or assistance ⟨Hopefully, the consultant's financial advice will prove *useful* in planning for our retirement.⟩ — see HELPFUL 1

usefulness *n* the capacity for being useful for some purpose ⟨the well-known *usefulness* of thick phone books as seat boosters for short diners⟩ — see USE 2

useless *adj* **1** not capable of being put to use or account ⟨a garage full of *useless* junk⟩ — see IMPRACTICAL

2 producing no results ⟨a *useless* attempt to reach an agreement⟩ — see FUTILE

user *n* a person who regularly uses drugs especially illegally ⟨a person who started out as a *user* and is now a drug dealer as well⟩ — see ADDICT 1

use up *vb* to make complete use of ⟨We *used up* the last of the flour when we made the waffles.⟩ — see DEPLETE 1

usher *vb* to point out the way for (someone) especially from a position in front ⟨*ushered* the job applicant into the room and then left⟩ — see LEAD 1

usual *adj* **1** accepted, used, or practiced by most people ⟨That's not the *usual* method, but it works!⟩ — see CURRENT 1

2 being of the type that is encountered in the normal course of events ⟨The characters in this novel are drawn with greater depth than is *usual* for a work of science fiction.⟩ — see ORDINARY 1

3 often observed or encountered ⟨The *usual* reaction to

the sight of the falls is one of absolute awe.⟩ — see COMMON 1

usually *adv* according to the usual course of things ⟨We *usually* go out to eat on Fridays.⟩ — see NATURALLY 2

usurp *vb* to take or make use of under a guise of authority but without actual right ⟨The mayor *usurped* the school board's authority when he fired the principal.⟩ — see APPROPRIATE 1

utensil *n* an article intended for use in work ⟨Participants in the class must supply their own writing *utensils*.⟩ — see IMPLEMENT

utility *n* the capacity for being useful for some purpose ⟨The store specializes in gee-whiz gadgetry of dubious *utility*.⟩ — see USE 2

utilize *vb* to put into action or service ⟨We must *utilize* all the tools at our disposal.⟩ — see USE 1

utmost *adj* **1** most distant from a center ⟨supreme power that extended to the *utmost* points of the empire⟩ — see EXTREME 1

2 of the greatest or highest degree or quantity ⟨I have the *utmost* respect for the teachers here.⟩ — see ULTIMATE 1

3 of the highest degree ⟨an intelligence operation that must be conducted with the *utmost* secrecy⟩ — see FULL 2

utopia *n* an often imaginary place or state of utter perfection and happiness ⟨dreamed of one day retiring to a tropical *utopia*⟩ — see PARADISE 1

utopian *n* one whose conduct is guided more by the image of perfection than by the real world ⟨In the 19th century *utopians* founded a number of short-lived socialist communities.⟩ — see IDEALIST

utter *adj* **1** having no exceptions or restrictions ⟨It's hard to believe we were *utter* strangers just a few short months ago.⟩ — see ABSOLUTE 2

2 of the highest degree ⟨spoke with *utter* certainty⟩ — see FULL 2

utter *vb* **1** to send forth using the vocal chords ⟨She tried not to *utter* a sound as the doctor gave her a flu shot.⟩

synonyms emit

related words deliver; blurt (out), ejaculate, exclaim; gasp, groan, heave, hoot, moan, pant, quaver, snarl, sob, sputter, squawk, squeak, squeal, stammer, stutter, whimper, yowl; mouth, whisper

2 to express (a thought or emotion) in words ⟨never *uttered* a single comment at the meeting⟩ — see SAY 1

utterance *n* **1** an act, process, or means of putting something into words ⟨Many writers have used poetry as a means to give *utterance* to their deepest thoughts.⟩ — see EXPRESSION 1

2 something that is said ⟨celebrities whose every *utterance* is treated as though it were newsworthy⟩ — see WORD 2

uttered *adj* expressed or communicated by voice ⟨her first *uttered* complaint since the start of the ordeal⟩ — see VOCAL

utterly *adv* **1** to a full extent or degree ⟨We are in fact *utterly* out of food.⟩ — see FULLY 1

2 to a large extent or degree ⟨was *utterly* overwhelmed by the demands on her time⟩ — see GREATLY 2

uttermost *adj* of the greatest or highest degree or quantity ⟨I have the *uttermost* faith in your abilities.⟩ — see ULTIMATE 1

V

vacancy *n* **1** empty space ⟨the vast *vacancy* that exists between our solar system and the nearest star having its own orbiting planets⟩
synonyms blank, blankness, emptiness, vacuity, void
related words inane, vacuum; air, open, waste; bareness, barrenness, bleakness, desolateness, hollowness; cavity, gap, hole, hollow
near antonyms repleteness
2 the quality or state of being empty ⟨The *vacancy* of the cavernous gymnasium was eerily apparent to me as I shot baskets alone.⟩
synonyms bareness, emptiness, vacuity
related words hollowness; blankness, vacuum, void; barrenness, bleakness, desolateness; availability, clearness, openness; dryness, exhaustion
near antonyms abundance, fatness, repleteness

vacant *adj* **1** lacking contents that could or should be present ⟨a *vacant* room that could be converted into a classroom⟩ — see EMPTY 1
2 not being in a state of use, activity, or employment ⟨looking for *vacant* land on which to build a house⟩ — see INACTIVE 2
3 not expressing any emotion ⟨He had a *vacant* and distracted expression.⟩ — see BLANK 1
4 left unoccupied or unused ⟨Police discovered that vagrants had been sleeping in the *vacant* warehouse.⟩ — see ABANDONED 1

vacate *vb* **1** to put an end to by formal action ⟨The appeals court *vacated* the lower court's order.⟩ — see ABOLISH 1
2 to remove the contents of ⟨*vacated* the house⟩ — see EMPTY

vacated *adj* left unoccupied or unused ⟨a *vacated* cottage on the lake that was for sale⟩ — see ABANDONED 1

vacation *n* a period during which the usual routine of school or work is suspended ⟨Area schools are on *vacation* that week in February so local ski resorts do a booming business.⟩
synonyms break, leave, recess
related words sabbatical; furlough, liberty; breather, relaxation, respite, rest; interim, intermission, interval; feast, holy day, legal holiday; idling, loafing, lounging, slacking; downtime

vacillate *vb* to show uncertainty about the right course of action ⟨*vacillated* for so long that someone else stepped in and made the decision⟩ — see HESITATE

vacillation *n* a state or an instance of temporary inaction because of uncertainty about the right course of action ⟨The president was soundly criticized for his *vacillation* before responding to the crisis.⟩ — see HESITATION

vacuity *n* **1** empty space ⟨the seemingly endless *vacuity* between settlements in the desert⟩ — see VACANCY 1
2 the quality or state of being empty ⟨The *vacuity* of the house after everyone had moved out was both striking and depressing.⟩ — see VACANCY 2
3 the quality or state of lacking intelligence or quickness of mind ⟨I grew tired of the *vacuity* of their conversation.⟩ — see STUPIDITY 1

vacuous *adj* **1** lacking contents that could or should be present ⟨a great *vacuous* space that should have been filled with an audience⟩ — see EMPTY 1
2 not having or showing an ability to absorb ideas readily ⟨a movie that was enthusiastically derided for its *vacuous* dialogue⟩ — see STUPID 1

vagabond *adj* traveling from place to place ⟨a *vagabond* group of entertainers⟩ — see ITINERANT

vagabond *n* **1** a homeless wanderer who may beg or steal for a living ⟨an author who had once been a *vagabond* living on the street⟩ — see TRAMP
2 a person who roams about without a fixed route or destination ⟨After they retired, the couple bought an RV and became footloose *vagabonds*.⟩ — see NOMAD

vagary *n* a sudden impulsive and apparently unmotivated idea or action ⟨the *vagaries* of a rather eccentric new acquaintance⟩ — see WHIM

vagrant *adj* traveling from place to place ⟨a *vagrant* poet capturing the essence of the nation⟩ — see ITINERANT

vagrant *n* a homeless wanderer who may beg or steal for a living ⟨*vagrants* sleeping in cardboard boxes on the sidewalk⟩ — see TRAMP

vague *adj* **1** not expressed in precise terms ⟨He gave as *vague* a reply as he could, hoping not to give away the surprise.⟩
synonyms fuzzy, indefinite, unclear
related words ambiguous, cryptic, dark, enigmatic (*also* enigmatical), equivocal, murky, nebulous, obscure, unintelligible; bleary, blurry, dim, faint, foggy, gauzy, hazy, misty; indeterminate, indistinct, indistinguishable, uncertain, undefinable, undefined, undetermined; inexplicable, inscrutable, mysterious; baffling, bewildering, confounding, confusing, mystifying, obfuscatory, perplexing, puzzling, unfathomable
near antonyms candid, direct, forthright, foursquare, frank, honest, open, openhearted, outspoken, plainspoken, straight, straightforward, unguarded; obvious, plain, unambiguous, unequivocal; defined, distinct, well-defined; blatant, patent, unmistakable
antonyms clear, definite, explicit, specific
2 not seen or understood clearly ⟨I have only a *vague* idea of what you're talking about!⟩ — see FAINT 1

vain *adj* **1** having too high an opinion of oneself ⟨a man so *vain* that he spent hours admiring himself in the mirror⟩ — see CONCEITED
2 producing no results ⟨All their efforts to escape proved *vain*.⟩ — see FUTILE
3 having no usefulness ⟨Having tired of the *vain* pleasures of life in the fast lane, he returned to the small town he had grown up in.⟩ — see WORTHLESS

vainglorious *adj* having too high an opinion of oneself ⟨a *vainglorious* woman who always insists on being the center of attention⟩ — see CONCEITED

vaingloriousness *n* an often unjustified feeling of being pleased with oneself or with one's situation or achievements ⟨a tiresome *vaingloriousness* that manifested itself in the old general's incessant boasting about his battlefield victories⟩ — see COMPLACENCE 1

vainglory *n* an often unjustified feeling of being pleased with oneself or with one's situation or achievements ⟨the *vainglory* that nations have historically shown after they have achieved military supremacy⟩ — see COMPLACENCE 1

vainness *n* an often unjustified feeling of being pleased with oneself or with one's situation or achievements ⟨the vexing *vainness* that seemed to fill every page of his memoirs⟩ — see COMPLACENCE 1

vale *n* an area of lowland between hills or mountains ⟨settled in a lush *vale* in the shadow of the mountains⟩ — see VALLEY

valedictory *adj* given, taken, or performed at parting ⟨a *valedictory* address given by the college president upon his retirement⟩ — see PARTING

valiant *adj* feeling or displaying no fear by temperament ⟨*valiant* soldiers marching off to war⟩ — see BRAVE 1

valid *adj* 1 according to the rules of logic ⟨Your argument isn't *valid* because you're taking what should be the conclusion and using it as a premise.⟩ — see LOGICAL 1

2 based on sound reasoning or information ⟨Only further investigation will show whether your theory is *valid*.⟩ — see GOOD 1

validate *vb* 1 to give evidence or testimony to the truth or factualness of ⟨A witness independently *validated* the policeman's version of events.⟩ — see CONFIRM 1

2 to show the existence or truth of by evidence ⟨The booming economy in and of itself *validated* the soundness of the government's economic policies.⟩ — see PROVE 1

validation *n* something presented in support of the truth or accuracy of a claim ⟨I'm afraid we cannot act on your claim without *validation*.⟩ — see PROOF

valley *n* an area of lowland between hills or mountains ⟨The *valley* will be the first to flood if the river rises.⟩
synonyms dale, hollow, vale
related words canyon (*also* cañon), dell, depression, dingle, glen, gorge, gulch, gully (*also* gulley), ravine, rift valley; basin, bowl
near antonyms alp, mount, mountain, peak; height, mountaintop, pinnacle, summit; plateau, tableland

valor *n* strength of mind to carry on in spite of danger ⟨She received the nation's highest award for *valor*.⟩ — see COURAGE

valorous *adj* feeling or displaying no fear by temperament ⟨*valorous* deeds that will be long remembered⟩ — see BRAVE 1

valuable *adj* commanding a large price ⟨an extremely *valuable* diamond necklace⟩ — see COSTLY

valuation *n* 1 the act of placing a value on the nature, character, or quality of something ⟨My *valuation* of your musical talent has nothing to do with our friendship.⟩ — see ESTIMATE 1

2 the amount of money for which something will find a buyer ⟨The final auction bid was still less than the minimum *valuation* that we had specified as acceptable, so the painting was withdrawn.⟩ — see VALUE 1

3 the relative usefulness or importance of something as judged by specific qualities ⟨the low *valuation* that society places on knowledge for the sake of knowledge⟩ — see WORTH 1

value *n* 1 the amount of money for which something will find a buyer ⟨The real *value* of that house is close to a million dollars.⟩
synonyms valuation, worth
related words charge, cost, fee, figure, price, rate; appraisal, assessment, estimate, estimation, evaluation; face value, list price, unit price

2 a quality that gives something special worth ⟨defending the democratic system's intrinsic *values*⟩ — see EXCELLENCE 2

3 the relative usefulness or importance of something as judged by specific qualities ⟨The *value* of a good education cannot be overstated.⟩ — see WORTH 1

value *vb* 1 to hold dear ⟨a nation that *values* individualism and self-reliance⟩ — see LOVE 1

2 to make an approximate or tentative judgment regarding ⟨*values* his stocks at $150,000 or thereabouts⟩ — see ESTIMATE 1

valueless *adj* having no usefulness ⟨a fish that was once regarded as *valueless* and routinely thrown away by fishermen⟩ — see WORTHLESS

valve *n* a fixture for controlling the flow of a liquid ⟨a hot water *valve*⟩ — see FAUCET

van *n* the leading or most important part of a movement ⟨a company that is considered by some to be in the *van* of the latest technology for renewable energy⟩ — see FOREFRONT

vandal *n* a person who damages or destroys property on purpose ⟨A group of *vandals* broke several gravestones in the cemetery.⟩
synonyms defacer
related words graffitist, tagger; demolisher, desecrater (*or* desecrator), despoiler, destroyer, ravager, ruiner, saboteur, waster, wrecker; depredator, looter, marauder, pillager, plunderer, ransacker, sacker, spoiler, spoliator
near antonyms conserver, preserver, protector, saver; conservator, preservationist

vandalism *n* deliberate damaging or destroying of another's property ⟨Anyone guilty of *vandalism* to university property will be expelled.⟩
synonyms defacement
related words demolishing, demolishment, desecrating, desecration, destruction, ravage, ravaging, ruin, ruination, wrecking; sabotage; depredation, despoiling, despoilment, looting, marauding, pillage, pillaging, plunder, plundering, predation, ransacking, sacking, spoliation
near antonyms conservation, preservation, protection, salvage, saving

vandalize *vb* to deliberately cause the damage or destruction of another's property ⟨My car was *vandalized* in the parking lot.⟩
synonyms deface
related words desecrate, violate; graffiti, tag; bang up, break, damage, harm, hurt, impair, mar, shatter, spoil; annihilate, demolish, destroy, devastate, ravage, raven, raze, ruin, scourge, smash, tear down, total, waste, wipe out, wreck; sabotage; depredate, despoil, loot, maraud, pillage, plunder, ransack, sack, spoliate
near antonyms conserve, preserve, protect, save; salvage; build, rebuild

vanguard *n* the leading or most important part of a movement ⟨They are in the *vanguard* of a revolution in medical research.⟩ — see FOREFRONT

vanish *vb* to cease to be visible ⟨The house *vanished* into the fog as we drove away.⟩ — see DISAPPEAR

vanished *adj* no longer existing ⟨the *vanished* tradition of the maypole as the center for May Day festivities⟩ — see EXTINCT

vanity *n* an often unjustified feeling of being pleased with oneself or with one's situation or achievements ⟨an all-consuming *vanity* that made him hunger for constant praise from others⟩ — see COMPLACENCE 1

vanquish *vb* to bring under one's control by force of arms ⟨*vanquished* nation after nation in his relentless conquest of Europe⟩ — see CONQUER 1

vanquisher *n* one that defeats an enemy or opponent ⟨a parade for the triumphal return of the empire's most celebrated *vanquisher*⟩ — see VICTOR 1

vanquishing *n* the act or process of bringing someone or something under one's control ⟨a movie about the *vanquishing* of Egypt by Rome⟩ — see CONQUEST

vantage *n* the more favorable condition or position in a competition ⟨The *vantage* had all been ours for the first half of the contest.⟩ — see ADVANTAGE 1

variable *adj* 1 capable of being readily changed ⟨a *variable* expense that we could reduce if we needed to⟩ — see FLEXIBLE 1

2 likely to change frequently, suddenly, or unexpectedly ⟨highly *variable* income from his job as a real estate agent⟩ — see FICKLE 1

variance *n* a lack of agreement or harmony ⟨Persistent *variance* within the band eventually caused it to break up.⟩ — see DISCORD

variation *n* the act, process, or result of making different ⟨the latest in a long line of *variations* in her hair color⟩ — see CHANGE 1

varicolored *adj* marked by a variety of usually vivid colors ⟨a brilliantly *varicolored* tapestry⟩ — see COLORFUL

varied *adj* **1** consisting of many things of different sorts ⟨the museum's highly *varied* collection of works of art⟩ — see MISCELLANEOUS

2 marked by a variety of usually vivid colors ⟨an annual springtime event during which birders get to observe these migratory birds in their *varied* breeding plumage⟩ — see COLORFUL

variegated *adj* **1** marked by a variety of usually vivid colors ⟨the *variegated* costumes of the dancers⟩ — see COLORFUL

2 marked with spots ⟨a variety of *variegated* tulip that is highly prized by gardeners⟩ — see SPOTTED 1

variety *n* **1** the quality or state of being composed of many different elements or types ⟨The sheer *variety* of the city's restaurants was dazzling.⟩

synonyms assortment, diverseness, diversity, heterogeneousness, miscellaneousness, multiplicity, variousness
related words disparateness, disparity, dissimilarity, distinction, distinctiveness, distinctness, unlikeness
near antonyms homogeneity, homogeneousness, likeness, sameness, similarity; fewness, paucity

2 an unorganized collection or mixture of various things ⟨Every kitchen has a drawer crammed with a *variety* of things for which there just doesn't seem to be any other place.⟩ — see MISCELLANY 1

3 a number of persons or things that are grouped together because they have something in common ⟨I prefer movies of the horror *variety*.⟩ — see SORT 1

variousness *n* the quality or state of being composed of many different elements or types ⟨The outfits that he wears are always interesting for their *variousness* and unpredictability.⟩ — see VARIETY 1

varlet *n* a mean, evil, or unprincipled person ⟨challenged the dastardly *varlet* to a duel⟩ — see VILLAIN

vary *vb* **1** to be unlike; to not be the same ⟨Opinions by experts on the subject *vary*.⟩ — see DIFFER 1

2 to make different in some way ⟨*varied* the method occasionally for the sake of experimentation⟩ — see CHANGE 1

3 to occur within a continuous range of variation ⟨The appliance store is offering discounts that *vary* from 10 to 40 percent, depending upon the brand.⟩ — see RUN 4

4 to pass from one form, state, or level to another ⟨terrain that constantly *varied* as we traveled from the coast to the interior⟩ — see CHANGE 2

varying *adj* not staying constant ⟨a *varying* commitment to the cause that meant that one could never be sure if the volunteers would show up⟩ — see UNEVEN 2

vast *adj* unusually large ⟨a *vast* expanse of land just waiting to be settled⟩ — see HUGE

vastly *adv* **1** to a great degree ⟨The team has *vastly* improved in the course of the season.⟩ — see VERY 1

2 to a large extent or degree ⟨*vastly* underestimated the cost of advertising the new product⟩ — see GREATLY 2

vastness *n* the quality or state of being very large ⟨awed by the *vastness* of the prairie⟩ — see IMMENSITY

vasty *adj* unusually large ⟨the days when intrepid explorers sailed the *vasty* deep in small vessels⟩ — see HUGE

¹**vault** *n* an underground burial chamber ⟨Archaeologists were thrilled to discover an ancient *vault* that hadn't been looted by grave robbers.⟩ — see CRYPT

²**vault** *n* an act of leaping into the air ⟨a *vault* over the car's hood by the frightened deer⟩ — see JUMP 1

vault *vb* to propel oneself upward or forward into the air ⟨*vaulted* over the obstacle with ease⟩ — see JUMP 1

veer *vb* **1** to change one's course or direction ⟨At this point the river *veers* to the southwest before finally emptying into the Atlantic Ocean.⟩ — see TURN 3

2 to change the course or direction of (something) ⟨*veered* the ship abruptly to the right to avoid a collision⟩ — see TURN 2

3 to depart abruptly from a straight line or course ⟨Without warning the car *veered* to the left and into an oncoming truck.⟩ — see SWERVE 1

vegetation *n* green leaves or plants ⟨The local *vegetation* is flourishing as a result of the recent rains.⟩ — see GREENERY

vehemence *n* **1** the quality or state of being forceful (as in expression) ⟨The *vehemence* in her voice when she insisted that she never gossiped surprised me.⟩

synonyms aggressiveness, assertiveness, emphasis, fierceness, forcefulness, intensity, vigorousness, violence
related words potency, power, strength; eloquence; ardor, fervency, fervidness, fervor, insistence, passion, warmth; stridency, vociferousness; clearness, directness, incision, incisiveness, plainness, straightforwardness, vividness
near antonyms ambiguity, equivocation; delicacy, lightness, subtlety
antonyms feebleness, mildness, weakness

2 depth of feeling ⟨Every cause that she pursues is pursued with great *vehemence*.⟩ — see ARDOR 1

vehement *adj* **1** marked by or uttered with forcefulness ⟨*vehement* complaints about the restaurant's poor service⟩ — see EMPHATIC 1

2 extreme in degree, power, or effect ⟨Despite the *vehement* opposition of the club's treasurer, the motion was passed.⟩ — see INTENSE 1

3 having or expressing great depth of feeling ⟨a *vehement* defender of human and civil rights⟩ — see FERVENT 1

vehicle *n* **1** something used to achieve an end ⟨used organized protests as a *vehicle* for change⟩ — see AGENT 1

2 something used to carry goods or passengers ⟨bought a larger *vehicle* after they had a third baby⟩ — see CONVEYANCE

veil *n* something that covers or conceals like a piece of cloth ⟨Under the *veil* of descending darkness the thieves began their operation.⟩ — see CLOAK 1

veil *vb* **1** to keep secret or shut off from view ⟨A thicket of bushes *veils* the private beach from the road.⟩ — see ¹HIDE 2

2 to surround or cover closely ⟨Morning fog *veiled* the fields.⟩ — see ENFOLD 1

vein *n* a distinctive way of putting ideas into words ⟨The author goes on in that sarcastic *vein* for pages.⟩ — see STYLE 1

veld *or* **veldt** *n* a broad area of level or rolling treeless country ⟨lions prowling the African *veld*⟩ — see PLAIN 1

velocity *n* a high rate of movement or performance ⟨The *velocity* of light is about 186,000 miles per second.⟩ — see SPEED 1

velvety *adj* smooth or delicate in appearance or feel ⟨a dog's *velvety* ears⟩ — see SOFT 2

venal *adj* open to improper influence and especially bribery ⟨That judge is known for being *venal* and easily bought.⟩

synonyms bribable, corruptible, dirty
related words temptable; hack, mercenary; crooked, cutthroat, dishonest, Machiavellian, unethical, unmoral, unprincipled, unscrupulous; corrupt, corrupted, debased, debauched, defiled, degenerate, degraded, demoralized, depraved, dissipated, dissolute, perverse, perverted,

reprobate, sleazy, vitiated, warped; bad, evil, immoral, iniquitous, nefarious, sinful, vicious, wicked
near antonyms ethical, honest, principled, scrupulous; good, moral, righteous, upright, virtuous
antonyms incorruptible

vend *vb* to offer for sale to the public ⟨*vends* snack foods and novelties at fairs⟩ — see MARKET

vendor *also* **vender** *n* the person in a business deal who hands over an item in exchange for money ⟨We're thinking of making a deal with that other software *vendor*.⟩
synonyms dealer, merchandiser, seller
related words merchant, trader, tradesman; auctioneer, concessionaire; black marketer (*or* black marketeer), bootlegger, fence, fencer, hustler, scalper, smuggler, trafficker; discounter, distributor, e-tailer, exporter, jobber, reseller, retailer, wholesaler; chapman [*British*], hawker, huckster, peddler (*also* pedlar); salesclerk, salesman, salesperson, saleswoman, shopgirl; bargainer, haggler, horse trader, palterer
near antonyms consumer, end user, user
antonyms buyer, purchaser

veneer *n* **1** a deceptively attractive external appearance ⟨The *veneer* of civility that the neighbors had maintained over the years disappeared with the filing of the first lawsuit.⟩ — see GLOSS 1
2 an outer part or layer ⟨The top and sides of the desk are overlaid with cherry *veneers*, while the interior wood is white pine.⟩ — see EXTERIOR

venerable *adj* **1** deserving honor and respect especially by reason of age ⟨The *venerable* old man was a cherished source of advice and wisdom for the villagers.⟩
synonyms hallowed, revered, reverend, sacred, venerated
related words honorable, reputable, respectable; considered, esteemed, honored, respected, reverenced; admirable, distinguished, redoubtable, worthy; good, moral, noble, righteous
near antonyms bad, discreditable, disgraceful, dishonorable, disreputable, ignominious, infamous, loose, notorious, shameful; immoral, seamy, shadowy, shady, sordid, unsavory, vile, wicked; base, contemptible, despicable, detestable, dirty, low, mean, wretched
2 dating or surviving from the distant past ⟨a *venerable* tradition that colleges have been maintaining for centuries⟩ — see ANCIENT 1

venerate *vb* to offer honor or respect to (someone) as a divine power ⟨a proper setting in which to *venerate* God⟩ — see WORSHIP 1

venerated *adj* deserving honor and respect especially by reason of age ⟨a beloved and *venerated* professor who has been a fixture on campus for decades⟩ — see VENERABLE 1

vengeance *n* the act or an instance of responding to an injury with an injury ⟨swore *vengeance* against their enemies⟩ — see REVENGE

vengeful *adj* likely to seek revenge ⟨A *vengeful* person never lets go of a grudge.⟩ — see VINDICTIVE

venial *adj* worthy of forgiveness ⟨Taking the restaurant's menu as a souvenir seems like a *venial* offense.⟩
synonyms excusable, forgivable, pardonable, remissible, remittable
related words justifiable; allowable, permissible; insignificant, minor, petty, trifling, trivial, unimportant; harmless, ignorable, tolerable
near antonyms abominable, criminal, evil, heinous; sinful, vile, wicked
antonyms indefensible, inexcusable, mortal, unforgivable, unjustifiable, unpardonable

venom *n* **1** a substance that by chemical action can kill or injure a living thing ⟨an antidote to snake *venom*⟩ — see POISON

2 the desire to cause pain for the satisfaction of doing harm ⟨a neighborhood gossip of such *venom* that she was disliked by everyone⟩ — see MALICE

venomous *adj* containing or contaminated with a substance capable of injuring or killing a living thing ⟨a *venomous* arrow⟩ — see POISONOUS

vent *vb* **1** to find emotional release for ⟨*vented* her anger and then quickly calmed down⟩ — see TAKE OUT 1
2 to make known (as an idea, emotion, or opinion) ⟨*vented* his opinions freely and loudly at town meetings⟩ — see EXPRESS 1
3 to throw or give off ⟨a clothes dryer *venting* steam⟩ — see EMIT 1

ventilate *vb* to make known (as an idea, emotion, or opinion) ⟨a person who tends to *ventilate* opinions without first thinking them through⟩ — see EXPRESS 1

venture *n* a risky undertaking ⟨Their latest business *venture* failed big-time.⟩ — see GAMBLE

venture *vb* **1** to place in danger ⟨Don't *venture* more money than you can afford to lose.⟩ — see ENDANGER
2 to take a chance on ⟨*ventured* to speak plainly at the meeting⟩ — see RISK 1

venturesome *adj* **1** inclined or willing to take risks ⟨A *venturesome* child tried to climb the huge tree.⟩ — see BOLD 1
2 involving potential loss or injury ⟨the first solo pilot to undertake the *venturesome* crossing of the Atlantic Ocean by air⟩ — see DANGEROUS 1

venturous *adj* inclined or willing to take risks ⟨was *venturous* enough to want to be an astronaut⟩ — see BOLD 1

veracious *adj* **1** being in the habit of telling the truth ⟨He has a reputation for being *veracious*, so people generally take his word for things.⟩ — see TRUTHFUL
2 following an original exactly ⟨Most readers have accepted the book as a *veracious* account of Samuel Johnson's table talk.⟩ — see FAITHFUL 2
3 being in agreement with the truth or a fact or a standard ⟨a novel that presents a fairly *veracious* and unvarnished picture of the lives of affluent suburbanites⟩ — see CORRECT 1

veracity *n* **1** devotion to telling the truth ⟨Her innate *veracity* is beyond question.⟩ — see HONESTY 1
2 the quality or state of being very accurate ⟨I challenge the *veracity* of many of the quotations in his memoirs, for he recreates conversations that occurred decades ago.⟩ — see PRECISION

verbal *adj* **1** of or relating to words or language ⟨The child didn't yet have the *verbal* skills needed to tell the doctor about the pain he was experiencing.⟩
synonyms lexical, linguistic (*also* linguistical), rhetorical (*also* rhetoric), wordy
related words communicative, conversational
antonyms nonlexical, nonlinguistic, nonverbal
2 made or carried on through speaking rather than in writing ⟨A *verbal* agreement carries less force than a written contract.⟩
synonyms oral, spoken, unwritten
related words consensual, implicit, informal; articulated, verbalized; given, pronounced, sounded, stated, told, voiced
near antonyms explicit, formal
antonyms paper, written

verbalize *vb* to express (a thought or emotion) in words ⟨couldn't quite *verbalize* his feelings⟩ — see SAY 1

verbatim *adv* in the same words ⟨You can't just copy the encyclopedia article *verbatim* for your report—that's plagiarism!⟩
synonyms directly, exactly, word for word
related words accurately, precisely; identically; literally

near antonyms basically, essentially, virtually; carelessly, freely, imprecisely, inaccurately, loosely
antonyms inexactly

verbiage *n* **1** the use of too many words to express an idea ⟨Teachers discourage the *verbiage* that students resort to in order to lengthen their reports.⟩
synonyms circumlocution, diffuseness, long-windedness, prolixity, redundancy, verboseness, verbosity, windiness, wordiness
related words circuitousness, circularity, digressiveness; pleonasm, tautology; reiteration, repetition, repetitiousness, repetitiveness; embellishment, embroidering, exaggeration, hyperbole, overstatement
near antonyms brevity, briefness, compactness, conciseness, crispness, pithiness, succinctness, terseness
2 language that is impressive-sounding but not meaningful or sincere ⟨the pretentious *verbiage* that one finds in the reviews of self-important art critics⟩ — see RHETORIC 1
3 the way in which something is put into words ⟨As per the standard *verbiage* of military reports, the assault was launched at "0700 hours."⟩ — see WORDING 1

verbose *adj* using or containing more words than necessary to express an idea ⟨had to wade through a *verbose* letter of complaint⟩ — see WORDY 1

verboseness *n* the use of too many words to express an idea ⟨The *verboseness* of the essay is obviously the result of being forced to meet a minimum-page requirement.⟩ — see VERBIAGE 1

verbosity *n* the use of too many words to express an idea ⟨Your ideas are good, but your penchant for *verbosity* is unfortunate.⟩ — see VERBIAGE 1

verdant *adj* covered with a thick, healthy natural growth ⟨a beautiful, *verdant* field⟩ — see LUSH 1

verdict *n* **1** a position arrived at after consideration ⟨The marketing consultant's *verdict* was that we were doing just fine.⟩ — see DECISION 1
2 an idea that is believed to be true or valid without positive knowledge ⟨was anxious to hear her best friend's *verdict* on her new apartment⟩ — see OPINION 1

verdure *n* green leaves or plants ⟨A good time to tour the valley is when it is clothed with the *verdure* of midsummer.⟩ — see GREENERY

verge *n* **1** an interval of time just before the onset of something ⟨The suspect was on the *verge* of confessing when the officers realized that he hadn't been read his rights.⟩ — see POINT 3
2 the line or relatively narrow space that marks the outer limit of something ⟨the southern *verge* of the national park⟩ — see BORDER 1

verge (on) *vb* **1** to be adjacent to ⟨Our land *verges on* a wildlife refuge.⟩ — see ADJOIN 1
2 to come very close to being ⟨a comment that *verged on* an insult⟩ — see BORDER (ON) 1

verging *adj* having a border in common ⟨The two brothers bought *verging* properties.⟩ — see ADJACENT

verifiable *adj* capable of being proven as true or real ⟨We're not sure whether that's a *verifiable* hypothesis.⟩ ⟨You need a *verifiable* letter from your doctor to file a claim for short-term disability.⟩
synonyms confirmable, demonstrable, empirical (*also* empiric), provable, supportable, sustainable
related words documentable, well-founded; defensible, excusable, justifiable, vindicable, warrantable; alleged, assumed, conjectured, guessed, presumed, surmised, suspected
near antonyms debatable, disprovable, disputable, refutable
antonyms indemonstrable, insupportable, unprovable, unsupportable, unsustainable

verify *vb* to give evidence or testimony to the truth or factualness of ⟨The dispatcher was able to *verify* the caller's location.⟩ — see CONFIRM 1

verifying *adj* serving to give support to the truth or factualness of something ⟨failed to produce any *verifying* evidence⟩ — see CORROBORATIVE

verily *adv* **1** to tell the truth ⟨*Verily*, I don't remember a single thing about that course.⟩ — see ACTUALLY 1
2 not merely this but also ⟨I shall pay back your loan and *verily* do so with considerable interest.⟩ — see EVEN 1

veritably *adv* in actual fact ⟨The view from the summit of the mountain is *veritably* breathtaking.⟩ — see VERY 2

verity *n* **1** agreement with fact or reality ⟨The local tourist bureau is less concerned with the *verity* of the legend than the fact that it attracts visitors to the area.⟩ — see TRUTH
2 devotion to telling the truth ⟨No one is questioning your *verity*—just your memory of events that happened long ago.⟩ — see HONESTY 1

vernacular *adj* used in or suitable for speech and not formal writing ⟨writes essays in a very easy-to-read, *vernacular* style⟩ — see COLLOQUIAL 1

versatile *adj* able to do many different kinds of things ⟨A *versatile* baseball player can play any position.⟩ ⟨This tool is *versatile* enough to serve as a wrench or pliers.⟩
synonyms adaptable, all-around (*also* all-round), protean, universal
related words mixed-use, multipurpose; well-rounded; able, ace, adept, experienced, expert, masterful, proficient, skilled, skillful; adjustable, alterable, changeable, elastic, flexible, fluid, malleable, modifiable, plastic, pliable, pliant, supple, variable
near antonyms limited; amateur, inexperienced

verse *n* **1** a composition using rhythm and often rhyme to create a lyrical effect ⟨composed a short *verse* for his mother's birthday⟩ — see POEM
2 writing that uses rhythm, vivid language, and often rhyme to provoke an emotional response ⟨skilled at *verse*⟩ — see POETRY 1

verse *vb* to give information to ⟨While living overseas, he *versed* himself in local customs.⟩ — see ENLIGHTEN 1

versed *adj* **1** having information especially as a result of study or experience ⟨*versed* in the latest developments in aeronautics⟩ — see FAMILIAR 2
2 having or showing exceptional knowledge, experience, or skill in a field of endeavor ⟨well *versed* in the techniques of laser surgery⟩ — see PROFICIENT

versifier *n* a person who writes poetry ⟨I may not be a great poet, but I'm as good as those *versifiers* hired by the greeting card companies.⟩ — see POET

vertebral column *n* a column of bones supporting the trunk of a vertebrate animal ⟨carefully reconstructed the *vertebral column* of the dinosaur⟩ — see SPINE

vertical *adj* rising straight up ⟨a *vertical* cliff face⟩ — see ERECT

verve *n* active strength of body or mind ⟨The actor plays the part of the superhero with tremendous *verve* and obvious enjoyment.⟩ — see VIGOR 1

very *adj* **1** being one and not another ⟨We stayed in the *very* hotel my parents stayed in for their honeymoon.⟩ — see SAME 2
2 being this and no more ⟨The *very* thought of having to go through that again is scary.⟩ — see MERE
3 existing in fact and not merely as a possibility ⟨Tourism is the *very* lifeblood of this community—the town would surely die without it.⟩ — see ACTUAL
4 having no exceptions or restrictions ⟨The *very* nerve of that woman—telling me how to raise my own children!⟩ — see ABSOLUTE 2

very *adv* **1** to a great degree ⟨That was a *very* brave thing to do.⟩
  synonyms almighty, awful, awfully, badly, beastly, bone, colossally, deadly, enormously, especially, ever, exceedingly (*also* exceeding), extra, extremely, far, filthy, frightfully, full, greatly, heavily, highly, hugely, incredibly, intensely, jolly, mightily, mighty, mortally, most, much, particularly, passing, real, really, right, roaring, severely, so, sore, sorely, spanking, such, super, supremely, terribly, too, vastly, way, whacking, wicked, wildly
  related words absolutely, altogether, completely, downright, entirely, fully, purely, radically, thoroughly, totally, utterly, wholly; deeply, profoundly; exceptionally, remarkably; considerably, extensively, significantly, substantially; appreciably, discernibly, markedly, noticeably, obviously, palpably, plainly, visibly; abundantly, plentifully; astronomically, grandly, monstrously; excessively, obscenely, overmuch; amazingly, astonishingly, staggeringly
  phrases a lot, as all get-out, good and
  near antonyms meagerly, scantily; barely, hardly, just, marginally, minimally, scarcely
  antonyms little, negligibly, nominally, slightly, somewhat
  2 in actual fact ⟨The *very* same thing happened to me.⟩
  synonyms actually, authentically, genuinely, really, truly, veritably
  related words accurately, exactly, just, precisely, right, sharp, smack-dab, squarely; almost, nearly, practically, virtually; literally, simply
  phrases in actuality, in reality, in truth
  near antonyms apparently, ostensibly, outwardly, plausibly, seemingly
  antonyms professedly, supposedly

vessel *n* **1** a large craft for travel by water ⟨a new ocean liner that claims to be the largest commercial *vessel* afloat⟩ — see SHIP
  2 a small buoyant structure for travel on water ⟨Any *vessel* that is buoyant and steerable can be entered in the annual race down the river.⟩ — see BOAT 1
  3 a usually circular utensil for holding something (as food) ⟨uses a large copper *vessel* for beating egg whites⟩ — see DISH 1
  4 something into which a liquid or smaller objects can be put for storage or transportation ⟨Any watertight *vessel* can be used for mixing the paints.⟩ — see CONTAINER

vest *vb* **1** to give official or legal power to ⟨"By the power *vested* in me by the state," intoned the officiant, "I now pronounce that you are married!"⟩ — see AUTHORIZE 1
  2 to put (something) into the possession or safekeeping of another ⟨*vested* the power to access their retirement accounts with their attorney⟩ — see GIVE 2
  3 to give the ownership or benefit of (something) formally or publicly ⟨The U.S. Constitution *vests* the power to declare war with Congress.⟩ — see CONFER 1

vestibule *n* the entrance room of a building ⟨Please leave your wet boots in the *vestibule*.⟩ — see HALL 1

vestige *n* **1** a tiny often physical indication of something lost or vanished ⟨A few strange words carved on a tree were the only *vestige* of the lost colony of Roanoke.⟩
  synonyms echo, ghost, relic, shadow, trace
  related words memento, remembrance, reminder; artifact; afterimage, aftertaste; balance, corpse, hangover, leftover, oddment, remainder, remnant, scrap; dreg(s), leavings, remain(s), residual, residue, rest
  2 the mark or impression made by a foot ⟨the fossilized *vestige* of a dinosaur that traversed that muddy landscape millions of years ago⟩ — see FOOTPRINT

vestry *n* a room in a church building for sacred furnishings (as vestments) ⟨The priest returned the chalice to the *vestry*.⟩ — see SACRISTY

vet *n* a person with long experience in a specified area ⟨He's a hardened *vet* of many political campaigns.⟩ — see VETERAN

veteran *adj* having or showing exceptional knowledge, experience, or skill in a field of endeavor ⟨a *veteran* teacher who mentors new teachers⟩ — see PROFICIENT

veteran *n* a person with long experience in a specified area ⟨As a *veteran* of overseas travel, she gave us solid advice about planning our trip.⟩
  synonyms old hand, old-timer, vet
  related words doyenne; adept, dab hand [*chiefly British*], expert, guru, hand, master, past master, pro, professional
  near antonyms apprentice, cub; amateur, dilettante; learner, student, trainee; candidate, entrant, probationer
  antonyms beginner, colt, fledgling, freshman, greenhorn, neophyte, newbie, newcomer, novice, recruit, rookie, tenderfoot, tyro

veto *n* an order that something not be done or used ⟨management's *veto* of our suggestion about allowing casual dress on Fridays⟩ — see PROHIBITION 2

veto *vb* to reject by or as if by a vote ⟨He quickly *vetoed* my suggestion that we adopt the stray dog.⟩ — see NEGATIVE 1

vex *vb* **1** to disturb the peace of mind of (someone) especially by repeated disagreeable acts ⟨My coworkers' loud, endless conversations *vexed* me.⟩ — see IRRITATE 1
  2 to throw into a state of mental uncertainty ⟨a mystery novel that is sure to *vex* even the canniest readers⟩ — see CONFUSE 1

vexation *n* **1** the act of making unwelcome intrusions upon another ⟨The repeated *vexations* guaranteed that she wouldn't get any work done.⟩ — see ANNOYANCE 1
  2 the feeling of impatience or anger caused by another's repeated disagreeable acts ⟨He suppressed his rising *vexation* and answered as politely as he could.⟩ — see ANNOYANCE 2
  3 something that is a source of irritation ⟨Add cell phones to the list of *vexations* that theatergoers have to contend with.⟩ — see ANNOYANCE 3

vexatious *adj* causing annoyance ⟨those *vexatious* phone calls from telemarketers during the dinner hour⟩ — see ANNOYING

vexing *adj* causing annoyance ⟨The constantly changing schedule was somewhat *vexing*, but I coped.⟩ — see ANNOYING

via *prep* **1** along the way of ⟨We're going to their house *via* the back roads.⟩ — see BY 1
  2 using the means or agency of ⟨contacted her *via* telephone⟩ — see BY 2

viable *adj* capable of being done or carried out ⟨More research will be required to see if this is a *viable* solution.⟩ — see POSSIBLE 1

viand *n* **1** something that is pleasing to eat because it is rare or a luxury ⟨a shop selling caviar, foie gras, designer chocolates, and other pricey *viands*⟩ — see DELICACY 1
  2 viands *pl* substances intended to be eaten ⟨The inn serves its choice *viands* on delicate china and its selection of vintage wines in the finest crystal available.⟩ — see FOOD

vibrancy *n* the quality or state of having abundant or intense activity ⟨The addition of several new stores enhances the *vibrancy* of the town.⟩ — see VITALITY 1

vibrant *adj* **1** marked by much life, movement, or activity ⟨I was rather overwhelmed by the *vibrant* environment of the big city.⟩ — see ALIVE 2
  2 marked by conspicuously full and rich sounds or tones ⟨a throaty, *vibrant* singing voice⟩ — see RESONANT

vibrate *vb* to make a series of small irregular or violent movements ⟨The glasses and knickknacks on the shelves *vibrated* whenever a train passed by.⟩ — see SHAKE 1

vibration *n* 1 a series of slight movements by a body back and forth or from side to side ⟨the *vibration* of the floor caused by thundering feet in the hallway⟩
synonyms jiggling, oscillation, quivering, shaking, shuddering, trembling, twitching
related words juddering [*chiefly British*], quaking, rocking; jiggle, palpitation, quiver, shake, shiver, shudder, tremble, tremor, twitch
2 *often* **vibrations** *pl* a spiritual force that is held to emanate from or give animation to living beings ⟨the Eastern holistic philosophy that unhappy thoughts disrupt the *vibrations* from one's energy field, causing illness⟩ — see ENERGY 1
3 *usually* **vibrations** *pl* a special quality or impression associated with something ⟨The tour guide claimed that although the murders happened long ago, the house still gives off unsettling *vibrations*.⟩ — see AURA 1

vice *n* 1 immoral conduct or practices harmful or offensive to society ⟨a unit in the police department assigned to focus on *vice*⟩
synonyms corruption, debauchery, depravity, immorality, iniquity, licentiousness, profligacy, sin
related words bad, badness, evil, evildoing, ill, villainy, wickedness, wrong; atrociousness, evilness, heinousness, sinfulness, unscrupulousness, viciousness, vileness, villainousness; devilry (*or* deviltry); corruptness, debasement, degeneracy, degeneration, depravedness, dissoluteness, dissolution; indecency, lasciviousness, lechery, lewdness, looseness, perversion, pervertedness, wantonness; abomination, anathema, taboo (*also* tabu); criminality, reprehensibleness; baseness, despicableness, dirtiness, lowness, meanness; lousiness, wretchedness
near antonyms good, right; honesty, honor, integrity, legitimacy, probity, rectitude, scrupulosity, scrupulousness, uprightness; goodness, righteousness, virtuousness; blamelessness; chastity, innocence, perfection, pureness, purity, spotlessness; cleanness, correctness, decency, decorousness, propriety, rightness, seemliness
antonyms morality, virtue
2 a defect in character ⟨Curiosity in children is not a *vice*, but something to be encouraged.⟩ — see FAULT 1

vicious *adj* 1 extreme in degree, power, or effect ⟨A *vicious* winter storm ripped through the region.⟩ — see INTENSE 1
2 having or showing the desire to inflict severe pain and suffering on others ⟨She made a *vicious* effort to destroy the lives of the people who had wronged her.⟩ — see CRUEL 1
3 not conforming to a high moral standard; morally unacceptable ⟨Even among the other inmates, this convict's crime was considered *vicious*.⟩ — see BAD 2
4 violently unfriendly or aggressive in disposition ⟨a *vicious* dog that has already bitten several people⟩ — see FIERCE 1
5 having or showing a desire to cause someone pain or suffering for the sheer enjoyment of it ⟨He spread *vicious* rumors about his former partner after their bitter falling out.⟩ — see HATEFUL

viciously *adv* in a mean or spiteful manner ⟨The administrator *viciously* denied me the time off that I needed to attend my dear aunt's funeral.⟩ — see NASTILY

viciousness *n* 1 the desire to cause pain for the satisfaction of doing harm ⟨Simple *viciousness* can be the only reason for spreading such vile, unfounded rumors.⟩ — see MALICE
2 disposition to willfully inflict pain and suffering on others ⟨the unspeakable *viciousness* of the architects of the Holocaust⟩ — see CRUELTY

victim *n* 1 a person or thing harmed, lost, or destroyed ⟨helped the *victims* of the fire⟩ — see CASUALTY 1
2 a person or thing that is the object of abuse, criticism, or ridicule ⟨the *victims* of the comic's sharp skewering⟩ — see TARGET 1
3 something offered to a god ⟨The Aztecs are believed to have sacrificed thousands of *victims* annually to the sun.⟩ — see SACRIFICE

victimize *vb* to rob by the use of trickery or threats ⟨*victimized* by a scam artist with a slick story⟩ — see FLEECE

victor *n* 1 one that defeats an enemy or opponent ⟨The computer is usually the *victor* in a chess match against a human opponent.⟩
synonyms beater, conqueror, master, subduer, trimmer, vanquisher, whipper, winner
related words champ, champion, finalist, placer; dominator, overdog, ruler, subjugator, top dog
near antonyms punching bag, pushover, quitter; failure, flop, washout; underdog
antonyms loser
2 the person who comes in first in a competition ⟨The *victor* in the science fair had constructed a functioning telescope.⟩ — see CHAMPION 1

victory *n* an instance of defeating an enemy or opponent ⟨With great effort, our team managed an upset *victory* in the final moments.⟩
synonyms triumph, win
related words capture, conquest, mastery, subjugation, vanquishing; blowout, landslide, laugher, romp, shutout, sweep, walkaway, walkover; squeaker; success
near antonyms upset; collapse, debacle (*also* débâcle), disaster, failure, fizzle, flop, nonsuccess, washout; decline, slip, slump, wane; lurch, setback
antonyms beating, defeat, drubbing, licking, loss, overthrow, rout, shellacking, trimming, whipping

victual *vb* to provide food or meals for ⟨The navy was usually equipped, clothed and *victualled* by the Crown.⟩ — see FEED 1

victuals *pl n* substances intended to be eaten ⟨sat down with a plate of hearty *victuals*⟩ — see FOOD

vie *vb* to engage in a contest ⟨*vied* with his colleagues for the coveted promotion⟩ — see COMPETE

view *n* 1 all that can be seen from a certain point ⟨The *view* of the mountains from the inn's porch is spectacular.⟩
synonyms command, lookout, outlook, panorama, perspective, prospect, vista
related words scene, scenery; ken, sight; visual field
2 an idea that is believed to be true or valid without positive knowledge ⟨That's one *view*, but I happen to disagree.⟩ — see OPINION 1
3 an instance of looking especially briefly ⟨Ed took a quick *view* of the Web page and decided that it didn't have what he was looking for.⟩ — see LOOK 2
4 a close look at or over someone or something in order to judge condition ⟨Upon closer *view* the painting was an obvious forgery.⟩ — see INSPECTION

view *vb* 1 to look over closely (as for judging quality or condition) ⟨I'll have to *view* all of the evidence before making a decision.⟩ — see INSPECT
2 to make note of (something) through the use of one's eyes ⟨*viewed* the latest changes and approved them⟩ — see SEE 1
3 to think of in a particular way ⟨I *view* housework as a necessary evil.⟩ — see CONSIDER 1

viewpoint *n* a way of looking at or thinking about something ⟨From my *viewpoint* the rule against slogans on

T-shirts infringes on my right to free speech.⟩ — see PERSPECTIVE 1

vigilance *n* the state of being constantly attentive and responsive to signs of opportunity, activity, or danger ⟨Eternal *vigilance* is the price of freedom.⟩

synonyms alert, alertness, attentiveness, watch, watchfulness

related words aliveness, awareness, receptiveness, receptivity, sensitivity; care, carefulness, cautiousness, chariness, heedfulness, wariness; preparation, readiness; vigil

near antonyms absentmindedness, daydreaming, daze, distraction; absorption, engrossment, obliviousness, preoccupation; unawareness, unconsciousness; carelessness, heedlessness, inattention, inattentiveness, inobservance; unwariness

vigilant *adj* paying close attention usually for the purpose of anticipating approaching danger or opportunity ⟨The night watchman, who was usually *vigilant*, apparently dozed off and didn't notice the vandals sneaking in.⟩ — see ALERT 1

vigilante *n* one who inflicts punishment in return for an injury or offense ⟨The danger of these self-appointed *vigilantes* is that they sometimes go after innocent people.⟩ — see NEMESIS 1

vignette *n* a vivid representation in words of someone or something ⟨The general's memoirs are filled with revealing *vignettes* of some of the war's most compelling personalities.⟩ — see DESCRIPTION 1

vigor *n* 1 active strength of body or mind ⟨She was picked to lead the volunteer group because of her *vigor* and enthusiasm.⟩

synonyms bounce, dash, drive, energy, esprit, gas, ginger, go, hardihood, life, pep, punch, sap, snap, starch, verve, vim, vitality, zing, zip

related words animal spirits, animation, briskness, jauntiness, liveliness, snappiness, spirit, spiritedness, sprightliness, spunk, spunkiness, vibrancy, vivaciousness, vivacity; ardor, élan, fervor, fire, passion, zeal; main, metal, mettle, might, muscle, potency, power, puissance, stamina, strength; brawniness, fitness, hardiness, huskiness, sturdiness, virility; health, healthiness, soundness, verdure, wellness

near antonyms indolence, laziness; debilitation, debility, delicacy, disablement, enfeeblement, faintness, feebleness, frailness, frailty, impotence, impotency, infirmity, powerlessness, puniness, slightness, softness, weakness; exhaustion, inanition, prostration

antonyms listlessness, sluggishness, torpidity

2 the ability to exert effort for the accomplishment of a task ⟨a drug for lowering cholesterol that acts with proven *vigor*⟩ — see POWER 2

vigorous *adj* 1 having active strength of body or mind ⟨He remains healthy and *vigorous* despite being over 80 years old.⟩

synonyms dynamic, energetic, flush, gingery, lusty, peppy, red-blooded, robust, vital

related words animated, brisk, dashing, lively, spirited, sprightly, vivacious; energized, enlivened, invigorated, vitalized; firm, fortified, mettlesome, mighty, powerful, puissant, strong; refreshed, rejuvenated, revitalized; ablebodied, athletic, beefy, brawny, burly, fit, hardy, husky, muscular, robustious, rugged, stalwart, stout, strapping, sturdy, tough, virile; hale, healthy, hearty, sound; capable, competent

near antonyms delicate, effete, enervated, faint, feeble, frail, infirm, wan, weak, weakened; impotent, powerless, prostrate, prostrated, sapped, tired; indolent, lackadaisical, languid, lazy; invertebrate, nerveless, soft, spineless,

wimpy; ill, unhealthy, unsound, unwell; broken-down, debilitated, decrepit, disabled, wasted, worn-out

antonyms dull, lethargic, listless, sluggish, torpid

2 able to withstand hardship, strain, or exposure ⟨*vigorous* and sturdy little sheep bred to live in mountainous regions⟩ — see HARDY 1

3 marked by or uttered with forcefulness ⟨offered a *vigorous* dissent to the proposal⟩ — see EMPHATIC 1

4 not showing weakness or uncertainty ⟨gave the bottle of sauce a *vigorous* shaking⟩ — see FIRM 1

vigorously *adv* in a vigorous and forceful manner ⟨Ian *vigorously* shook my hand and told me how happy he was to be there.⟩ — see HARD 3

vigorousness *n* 1 the quality or state of being forceful (as in expression) ⟨The *vigorousness* of the ideas in the essay was surpassed only by the vibrancy of its language.⟩ — see VEHEMENCE 1

2 the quality or state of having abundant or intense activity ⟨The record-breaking holiday sales reflect the *vigorousness* of the economy.⟩ — see VITALITY 1

vile *adj* 1 not conforming to a high moral standard; morally unacceptable ⟨a *vile* and cowardly act⟩ — see BAD 2

2 not following or in accordance with standards of honor and decency ⟨a *vile* trick to play on someone⟩ — see IGNOBLE 2

3 unpleasant to look at ⟨an outfit with a truly *vile* combination of colors⟩ — see UGLY 1

vileness *n* the state or quality of being utterly evil ⟨No one can question the sheer *vileness* of this act.⟩ — see ENORMITY 1

vilification *n* the making of false statements that damage another's reputation ⟨Pundits warned that the constant *vilification* of candidates for public office was undermining the people's faith in the political system.⟩ — see SLANDER

vilify *vb* to make untrue and harmful statements about ⟨claimed that she had been *vilified* by the press because of her views⟩ — see SLANDER

vilifying *n* the making of false statements that damage another's reputation ⟨The nonstop *vilifying* had the effect of making some people lose their impartiality.⟩ — see SLANDER

villa *n* a large impressive residence ⟨a millionaire with a luxurious *villa* in Mexico⟩ — see MANSION

villager *n* a person who lives in a town on a permanent basis ⟨The *villagers* have a reputation for being polite and helpful to the tourists.⟩ — see BURGHER

villain *n* a mean, evil, or unprincipled person ⟨Only a heartless *villain* would do something so cruel.⟩

synonyms beast, brute, devil, evildoer, fiend, heavy, hound, knave, miscreant, monster, no-good, rapscallion, rascal, reprobate, rogue, savage, scalawag (*or* scallywag), scamp, scoundrel, varlet, wretch

related words villainess; blackguard; criminal, crook, culprit, felon, lawbreaker, malefactor, offender, perp, perpetrator, transgressor; sinner, trespasser, wrongdoer; cad, heel, serpent, snake, viper; bandit, bravo, desperado, outlaw; con, convict, jailbird; assassin, cutthroat, gangster, goon, gunman, hoodlum, hooligan, racketeer, ruffian, thug; rough, rowdy, tough; loser, lowlife, stinker, trash

near antonyms angel, innocent, saint; hero

villainous *adj* not conforming to a high moral standard; morally unacceptable ⟨*villainous* behavior that made him one of the most notorious figures in history and gave rise to the legend of Dracula⟩ — see BAD 2

villainously *adv* in a mean or spiteful manner ⟨The robber *villainously* snatched the necklace from the old woman's throat.⟩ — see NASTILY

villainy *n* that which is morally unacceptable ⟨Psychologists and sociologists have tried to discover the roots of such *villainy.*⟩ — see EVIL

vim *n* active strength of body or mind ⟨Some food and a little rest should give me back some of my *vim.*⟩ — see VIGOR 1

vindicate *vb* 1 to free from a charge of wrongdoing ⟨vowed that the evidence would completely *vindicate* him⟩ — see EXCULPATE

2 to give evidence or testimony to the truth or factualness of ⟨Recent discoveries have generally *vindicated* the physicist's theories.⟩ — see CONFIRM 1

vindicating *adj* serving to give support to the truth or factualness of something ⟨*Vindicating* documents have turned up only recently.⟩ — see CORROBORATIVE

vindication *n* a setting free from a charge of wrongdoing ⟨recanted testimony that resulted in a long-overdue *vindication*⟩ — see ACQUITTAL

vindictive *adj* likely to seek revenge ⟨Be careful not to annoy the *vindictive* old woman who lives down the street.⟩
synonyms revengeful, vengeful
related words avenging, retaliatory; resentful, uncharitable, unforgiving; catty, cruel, despiteful, hateful, malevolent, malicious, malign, malignant, mean, nasty, sadistic, spiteful, venomous, vicious, viperish, virulent; narrow-minded, petty, small-minded; grim, implacable, merciless, pitiless, relentless, unrelenting; baleful, baneful, evil; harsh, hostile, inimical, wrathful
near antonyms charitable, forgiving, merciful, relenting; benevolent, benign, benignant, loving; brotherly, compassionate, good, good-hearted, kind, kindhearted, kindly, sympathetic, warm, warmhearted; altruistic, humane, humanitarian, philanthropic (*also* philanthropical); sweet, tender, tenderhearted; high-minded, magnanimous, noble

vinegary *adj* causing or characterized by the one of the basic taste sensations that is produced chiefly by acids ⟨*vinegary* potato salad⟩ — see SOUR 1

violate *vb* 1 to fail to keep ⟨You've *violated* the company's new rule against smoking on the premises.⟩
synonyms breach, break, fracture, offend, traduce, transgress
related words disobey, rebel; brush (off), disregard, flout, ignore, neglect, overlook, overpass, pass over, slight, tune out, wink (at); dismiss, pooh-pooh (*also* pooh), scorn, shrug off; defy, resist, withstand
near antonyms defer (to), serve, submit (to), surrender (to), yield (to); attend, hear, heed, listen (to), mark, note, notice, regard, watch
antonyms comply (with), conform (to), follow, mind, obey, observe

2 to treat (a sacred place or object) shamefully or with great disrespect ⟨The invaders *violated* the temple by using it to stable their horses.⟩ — see DESECRATE

violation *n* 1 a breaking of a moral or legal code ⟨In colonial times blasphemy was considered a serious civil *violation* that merited harsh punishment.⟩ — see OFFENSE 1

2 a failure to uphold the requirements of law, duty, or obligation ⟨a military action that must be regarded as a *violation* of the treaty⟩ — see BREACH 1

violence *n* 1 the use of brute strength to cause harm to a person or property ⟨They settled their disagreement without resorting to *violence.*⟩
synonyms force, foul play
related words coercion, compulsion, constraint, duress, pressure; barbarity, brutality, savagery; damage, detriment, harm, hurt, impairment, injury; crippling, maiming, mayhem, mutilation; assault, attack, bashing, battering, battery, beating, belting, bludgeoning, buffeting,

clubbing, cudgeling (*or* cudgelling), drubbing, flogging, hammering, lacing, licking, mauling, paddling, pelting, pommeling (*or* pommelling), pounding, pummeling (*also* pummelling), smashing, socking, thrashing, tromping, whaling, whipping; frenzy, fury, onslaught, outbreak, outrage, paroxysm, rage, rampage, revolt, riot, rupture, shock, storm, terror, threat, tumult, turbulence, upheaval, uproar; browbeating, bulldozing, bullying, hectoring, strong-arming
near antonyms pacificism, pacifism
antonyms nonviolence

2 the quality or state of being forceful (as in expression) ⟨the *violence* of her denial of any wrongdoing⟩ — see VEHEMENCE 1

3 depth of feeling ⟨Some people were taken aback by the *violence* with which the magazine's art critic attacked the exhibition.⟩ — see ARDOR 1

violent *adj* 1 marked by bursts of destructive force or intense activity ⟨the volcano's *violent* eruptions⟩
synonyms convulsive, explosive, ferocious, fierce, furious, hot, rabid, rough, stormy, tempestuous, tumultuous, turbulent, volcanic
related words barbarous, brutal, savage, vicious; antagonistic, hostile; aggressive, assertive, bellicose, belligerent, combative, contentious, gladiatorial, pugnacious, quarrelsome, truculent; combustible, volatile; agitated, frantic, frenzied, mad; cataclysmal (*or* cataclysmic), destructive, ruinous
near antonyms calm, halcyon, pacific, serene, tranquil; nonbelligerent, unaggressive
antonyms nonviolent, peaceable, peaceful

2 extreme in degree, power, or effect ⟨a *violent* thunderstorm⟩ — see INTENSE 1

3 marked by great and often stressful excitement or activity ⟨Our guest's imminent arrival provoked a *violent* effort to get the place cleaned up.⟩ — see FURIOUS 1

4 marked by or uttered with forcefulness ⟨prone to *violent* denunciation of anyone who disagrees with her⟩ — see EMPHATIC 1

VIP *n* a person who is widely known and usually much talked about ⟨The *VIPs* insisted on being seated in the restaurant's private dining room.⟩ — see CELEBRITY 1

viper *n* a limbless reptile with a long body ⟨a *viper* sliding silently through the field⟩ — see SNAKE 1

virago *n* a bad-tempered scolding woman ⟨fairy tales that typically portray stepmothers as *viragoes*⟩ — see SHREW

virgin *adj* 1 never having had sexual relations ⟨young people who are *virgin*⟩
synonyms virginal
related words chaste, modest, pure, vestal; innocent, untouched; abstinent, celibate, continent; unmarried, unwed
antonyms deflowered

2 being in an original and unused or unspoiled state ⟨the state's only remaining *virgin* forest⟩ — see FRESH 1

3 free from any trace of the coarse or indecent ⟨a scene of innocence and *virgin* sweetness⟩ — see CHASTE 1

4 existing without human habitation or cultivation ⟨a vast expanse of *virgin* territory⟩ — see WILD 2

5 coming before all others in time or order ⟨the author's *virgin* effort at a cloak-and-dagger thriller⟩ — see FIRST 1

virginal *adj* 1 being in an original and unused or unspoiled state ⟨one of the state's few remaining tracts of *virginal* prairie⟩ — see FRESH 1

2 never having had sexual relations ⟨a *virginal* couple who chose not to rush into a sexual relationship⟩ — see VIRGIN 1

3 free from any trace of the coarse or indecent ⟨The romance between the young boy and girl is portrayed with

virginal innocence that is touching in this day and age.〉
— see CHASTE 1

virile *adj* of, relating to, or marked by qualities traditionally associated with men 〈Men were once expected to be interested only in such *virile* activities as hunting.〉 — see MASCULINE

virility *n* the set of qualities traditionally considered appropriate for or characteristic of men 〈an actor known for playing roles evincing *virility*〉
synonyms manhood, manliness, masculinity
related words maleness; boyishness, mannishness, tomboyishness
near antonyms girlishness; girlhood, maidenhood; effeminacy, effeteness; emasculation
antonyms muliebrity

virtually *adv* very close to but not completely 〈fell in love with a man who was *virtually* penniless〉 — see ALMOST

virtue *n* **1** a quality that gives something special worth 〈The *virtue* of wool as a clothing material is that it can provide insulation from the cold even when wet.〉 — see EXCELLENCE 2
2 conduct that conforms to an accepted standard of right and wrong 〈a family of honor and *virtue*〉 — see MORALITY 1
3 strength of mind to carry on in spite of danger 〈a mili­tary hero whose *virtue* inspired a nation〉 — see COURAGE

virtuoso *adj* **1** accomplished with trained ability 〈a virtuo­so performance of a piano concerto〉 — see SKILLFUL 1
2 having or showing exceptional knowledge, experience, or skill in a field of endeavor 〈a *virtuoso* director, he is known for using every resource and technique known to film to tell a story〉 — see PROFICIENT

virtuoso *n* a person with a high level of knowledge or skill in a field 〈a violin *virtuoso*〉 — see EXPERT

virtuous *adj* conforming to a high standard of morality or virtue 〈*virtuous* behavior is its own reward〉 — see GOOD 2

virtuously *adv* with purity of thought and deed 〈lived sim­ply and *virtuously*〉 — see PURELY 1

virtuousness *n* conduct that conforms to an accepted standard of right and wrong 〈I admire the *virtuousness* of those who volunteered.〉 — see MORALITY 1

virulence *n* biting sharpness of feeling or expression 〈I was surprised by the *virulence* of the criticism.〉 — see ACRIMONY 1

virulent *adj* having or showing a desire to cause someone pain or suffering for the sheer enjoyment of it 〈The *viru­lent* look on her face warned me that she was about to say something unkind.〉 — see HATEFUL

virulently *adv* in a mean or spiteful manner 〈an organiza­tion that is even more *virulently* opposed to the candidate than others of its kind〉 — see NASTILY

visage *n* **1** facial appearance regarded as an indication of mood or feeling 〈an old man with a noticeably happy *visage*〉 — see LOOK 1
2 the front part of the head 〈Visitors to the mountain range had long noted that the natural rock formation bore a striking resemblance to the *visage* of a man.〉 — see FACE 1

viscera *pl n* the internal organs of the body 〈The research­ers examined the *viscera* of the infected rat.〉 — see GUT 1

viscid *adj* **1** being of a consistency that resists flow 〈honey that turned even more *viscid* in the cold〉 — see THICK 2
2 tending to adhere to objects upon contact 〈*viscid* tree resin〉 — see STICKY 1

viscosity *n* the degree to which a fluid can resist flowing 〈conducted an experiment to determine the *viscosity* of motor oil〉 — see CONSISTENCY

viscous *adj* being of a consistency that resists flow 〈vis-

cous syrup that takes forever to pour from a narrowneck bottle〉 — see THICK 2

visible *adj* **1** capable of being seen 〈The *visible* light spec­trum runs from red to violet.〉
synonyms apparent, observable, seeable, visual
related words viewable; detectable, discernible (*also* discernable), noticeable, perceptible; clear, conspicuous, evident, eye-catching, manifest, obvious, overt, patent, perceivable, plain, prominent, striking; exposed, external, outer, outward, superficial
near antonyms disappeared, dissolved, evanesced, evaporated, melted, vanished, vaporized; imperceptible, indiscernible, indistinct, unnoticeable, unobservable; faint, inconspicuous, insignificant, slight, unobtrusive, vague; buried, concealed, covert, disguised, latent, obscure, shrouded
antonyms sightless, viewless
2 widely known 〈Although he had been kicking around Hollywood for years, he only became a highly *visible* ac­tor after his starring role in that year's biggest movie.〉 — see FAMOUS 1

vision *n* **1** a conception or image created by the imagination and having no objective reality 〈a *vision* of the fu­ture that no other film director had ever created〉 — see FANTASY 1
2 the ability to see 〈the bright light temporarily robbed me of *vision*〉 — see EYESIGHT
3 the soul of a dead person thought of especially as appearing to living people 〈believed he'd seen a *vision* of his mother〉 — see GHOST 1
4 concern or preparation for the future 〈a company president with the long-range *vision* that his firm needs to survive in the global economy〉 — see FORESIGHT 2

vision *vb* to form a mental picture of 〈*visioned* her idea of the perfect meal〉 — see IMAGINE 1

visionary *adj* **1** not real and existing only in the imagination 〈a prophet who wrote of *visionary* experiences of hell〉 — see IMAGINARY
2 having or showing awareness of and preparation for the future 〈In a *visionary* move, the developer bought large tracts of the waterfront just before property values skyrocketed.〉 — see FORESIGHTED

visionary *n* **1** one who predicts future events or developments 〈According to Greek myth, Cassandra was a *vi­sionary* who was endowed with the gift of inerrant proph­ecy but fated to never be believed.〉 — see PROPHET 1
2 one whose conduct is guided more by the image of perfection than by the real world 〈19th-century *visionar­ies* who founded short-lived communities in which ev­eryone was supposed to live in perfect peace and har­mony〉 — see IDEALIST

visit *n* **1** a temporary residing as another's guest 〈My aunt always looks forward to her weeklong annual *visit* with her mother.〉
synonyms sojourn, stay
related words field trip, homestay, sleepover; layover, stop, stopover
2 a coming to see another briefly for social or business reasons 〈came by for a quick *visit*〉 — see CALL 2

visit *vb* **1** to make a social call upon 〈The community lead­ers make a point of *visiting* everyone who moves into the neighborhood.〉
synonyms call (on *or* upon), see
related words look up, seek (out)
near antonyms brush (aside *or* off), cold-shoulder, ignore, snub
2 to reside as a temporary guest 〈an old friend who comes to *visit* for a month every summer〉
synonyms crash [*slang*], sojourn, stay, tarry

related words come by, stop (by); frequent, haunt; inhabit, occupy

near antonyms abide, dwell, live, reside

3 to engage in casual or rambling conversation ⟨tries to *visit* with her best friend on the phone at least once a week⟩ — see CHAT 1

4 to go to or spend time in often ⟨*visit* Ireland for a few weeks every year⟩ — see FREQUENT

5 to make a brief visit ⟨stopped to *visit* with my father on the way out of town⟩ — see CALL 3

visitant *n* **1** a person who visits another ⟨the groundless theory that these ancient monuments were built by extraterrestrial *visitants*⟩ — see GUEST 1

2 the soul of a dead person thought of especially as appearing to living people ⟨a nocturnal *visitant* that must have been the shade of his late brother⟩ — see GHOST 1

visitation *n* a coming to see another briefly for social or business reasons ⟨The pastor could hardly express how honored he was to receive this *visitation* from the bishop.⟩ — see CALL 2

visitor *n* a person who visits another ⟨put nicer clothes on because they had *visitors* coming⟩ — see GUEST 1

visor *also* **vizor** *n* the projecting front part of a hat or cap ⟨The *visor* on your baseball cap should provide adequate shade for your eyes.⟩

synonyms bill, brim, peak

related words shade

vista *n* all that can be seen from a certain point ⟨a gorgeous *vista* of the mountains from the front window⟩ — see VIEW 1

visual *adj* **1** of, relating to, or used in vision ⟨The eyes are the primary *visual* organs in humans.⟩

synonyms ocular, optic, optical

related words seeing, sighted; focusing (*also* focussing)

antonyms nonvisual

2 capable of being seen ⟨That funny expression was a *visual* hint that she was getting bored.⟩ — see VISIBLE 1

3 consisting of or relating to pictures ⟨*visual* evidence that could be presented in court⟩ — see PICTORIAL 1

4 producing a mental picture through clear and impressive description ⟨accounts of Civil War battles that are grippingly *visual*⟩ — see GRAPHIC 1

visual *n* something that visually explains or decorates a text ⟨The strong *visuals* in the beginning biology book compensate somewhat for the weak text.⟩ — see ILLUSTRATION 1

visualize *vb* to form a mental picture of ⟨*visualized* herself executing a perfect dive⟩ — see IMAGINE 1

vital *adj* **1** having active strength of body or mind ⟨a man who remained *vital* well into his 90s⟩ — see VIGOROUS 1

2 having much high-spirited energy and movement ⟨The child is *vital* and active again after being sick.⟩ — see LIVELY 1

3 impossible to do without ⟨I forgot one *vital* ingredient, and now the biscuits taste strange.⟩ — see ESSENTIAL 1

4 likely to cause or capable of causing death ⟨received a *vital* wound in the abdomen⟩ — see DEADLY 1

5 of the greatest possible importance ⟨a matter that is *vital* to our national security⟩ — see CRUCIAL

6 having a renewing effect on the state of the body or mind ⟨After the long, dreary winter, we welcomed the *vital* rays of the summer sun.⟩ — see TONIC 1

vitality *n* **1** the quality or state of having abundant or intense activity ⟨a city known for the *vitality* of its music scene⟩

synonyms animation, briskness, exuberance, jazziness, liveliness, lustiness, peppiness, robustness, sprightliness, vibrancy, vigorousness

related words buoyancy, jauntiness, springiness; bright-

ness, cheer, cheerfulness, chirpiness, effervescence, friskiness, sparkle, spirit, verve, vivaciousness, vivacity; eagerness, ebullience, ebulliency, enthusiasm, keenness, spiritedness; friskiness, impishness, pertness, playfulness

near antonyms indolence, laziness; anemia, bloodlessness; languor, limpness, listlessness, sleepiness, sluggishness, spiritlessness, torpidity, weariness; apathy, impassivity; dullness (*also* dulness), pallidness, tediousness, tedium, vapidity, vapidness

antonyms inactivity, lifelessness

2 active strength of body or mind ⟨Her *vitality* seemed to spread to everyone around her.⟩ — see VIGOR 1

vitalize *vb* to give life, vigor, or spirit to ⟨A hearty lunch and a long nap afterwards *vitalized* him again.⟩ — see ANIMATE

vitalizing *adj* having a renewing effect on the state of the body or mind ⟨a *vitalizing* steam bath⟩ — see TONIC 1

vitals *pl n* the internal organs of the body ⟨Remember to wear a full vest to protect your *vitals* while sparring.⟩ — see GUT 1

vitiate *vb* **1** to affect slightly with something morally bad or undesirable ⟨believed that luxury *vitiates* even the most principled person⟩ — see TAINT 1

2 to reduce the soundness, effectiveness, or perfection of ⟨Numerous grammatical errors *vitiate* the effectiveness of your writing.⟩ — see DAMAGE 1

3 to lower in character, dignity, or quality ⟨A penchant for coarse language *vitiates* what is otherwise a refined literary style.⟩ — see DEBASE 1

vitriol *n* **1** biting sharpness of feeling or expression ⟨a film critic noted for the *vitriol* and sometimes outright cruelty of his pronouncements⟩ — see ACRIMONY 1

2 harsh insulting language ⟨The review was more than just unfavorable—it was loaded with *vitriol*.⟩ — see ABUSE 1

vittles *pl n* substances intended to be eaten ⟨claimed that the beans were just about the tastiest *vittles* he ever ate⟩ — see FOOD

vituperate *vb* to criticize harshly and usually publicly ⟨Every week the minister would ascend the pulpit and *vituperate* the parishioners for a litany of vices.⟩ — see ATTACK 2

vituperation *n* harsh insulting language ⟨Sick of the *vituperation* coming from ungrateful visitors, the put-upon webmaster took down the site's free webcam, which had afforded views of the town's picturesque harbor.⟩ — see ABUSE 1

vivacious *adj* **1** having much high-spirited energy and movement ⟨an outgoing, *vivacious* woman who became a successful sales rep⟩ — see LIVELY 1

2 joyously unrestrained ⟨The poem is a *vivacious* expression of his love for her.⟩ — see EXUBERANT

vivaciously *adv* in a quick and spirited manner ⟨a night of traditional songs that were sung lustily and *vivaciously*⟩ — see GAILY 2

vivid *adj* producing a mental picture through clear and impressive description ⟨*vivid* language that made the scene come alive in my mind⟩ — see GRAPHIC 1

vivify *vb* to give life, vigor, or spirit to ⟨This re-creation of a town in the Old West really *vivifies* the history that visitors learned in school.⟩ — see ANIMATE

vizard *n* a cover or partial cover for the face used to disguise oneself ⟨In those days, it was not uncommon for both men and women to wear *vizards* while in questionable company.⟩ — see MASK 1

vocabulary *n* **1** the special terms or expressions of a particular group or field ⟨scientific *vocabulary*⟩ — see TERMINOLOGY

2 the stock of words, pronunciation, and grammar used

by a people as their basic means of communication ⟨Children learn enough of the common *vocabulary* to make themselves understood by around the age of two.⟩ — see LANGUAGE 1

vocal *adj* expressed or communicated by voice ⟨Our cat is given to making strange *vocal* noises in the dead of night.⟩
synonyms oral, spoken, uttered, voiced
related words articulated, enunciated, pronounced, sonant; breathed, chirped, drawled, gasped, intoned, mouthed, mumbled, murmured, muttered, purred, shouted, spluttered, sputtered, squeaked, whispered
near antonyms inarticulate; mute, quiet, silent; unexpressed, unsaid, unspoken, unuttered, unvoiced; surd, voiceless
antonyms nonvocal

vocal *n* a short musical composition for the human voice often with instrumental accompaniment ⟨a recording artist who arranges his own *vocals*⟩ — see SONG 1

vocalist *n* one who sings ⟨hired a *vocalist* for their jazz band⟩ — see SINGER

vocalize *vb* 1 to express (a thought or emotion) in words ⟨She's not one to *vocalize* her worries.⟩ — see SAY 1
2 to produce musical sounds with the voice ⟨spent some time *vocalizing* before the concert⟩ — see SING 1

vocalizer *n* one who sings ⟨The song can be arranged according to the *vocalizer's* expression and ability.⟩ — see SINGER

vocation *n* 1 the activity by which one regularly makes a living ⟨finally made sculpting her *vocation* instead of just a hobby⟩ — see OCCUPATION
2 the body of people in a profession or field of activity ⟨She says that although she respects certain journalists, she despises the *vocation*.⟩ ⟨Politics has its honest and its dishonest practitioners, just like any other *vocation*.⟩ — see CORPS

vociferate *vb* to speak so as to be heard at a distance ⟨He can never seem to voice his opinions at a decent decibel level; he has to *vociferate*.⟩ — see CALL 1

vociferous *adj* engaging in or marked by loud and insistent cries especially of protest ⟨*Vociferous* opponents of the bill protested angrily outside the chambers of the legislature.⟩
synonyms blatant, clamorous, obstreperous
related words clangorous, dinning, discordant, noisy; loudmouthed, outspoken, vocal; boisterous, raucous, robustious, rowdy, uproarious; cacophonous, dissonant, earsplitting, grating, shrill, strident; blaring, blustering, booming, brassy, brazen
near antonyms noiseless, quiet, silent, soundless, still; calm, hushed, subdued

vogue *adj* enjoying widespread favor or approval ⟨always tries to use the *vogue* words of the moment so as to appear cool⟩ — see POPULAR 1

vogue *n* 1 a practice or interest that is very popular for a short time ⟨It was then the *vogue* to wear dark lipstick and thinly plucked brows.⟩ — see FAD
2 the state of enjoying widespread approval ⟨When did Thai food come into *vogue*?⟩ — see POPULARITY

voice *n* 1 the right to express a wish, choice, or opinion ⟨Everyone will have a *voice* in the decision of where to go for our vacation.⟩
synonyms say, say-so, vote
related words part, role (*also* rôle), share; ballot, enfranchisement, franchise, suffrage; belief, conviction, judgment (*or* judgement), opinion, sentiment, view
2 an act, process, or means of putting something into words ⟨a publisher who used his newspaper as a *voice* for his extreme conservatism⟩ — see EXPRESSION 1

3 one who sings ⟨one of the great *voices* of her generation⟩ — see SINGER

voice *vb* to make known (as an idea, emotion, or opinion) ⟨*voiced* a suggestion about where to go⟩ — see EXPRESS 1

voiced *adj* expressed or communicated by voice ⟨a loudly *voiced* expression of pain⟩ — see VOCAL

voiceless *adj* unable to speak ⟨believes that animals deserve basic rights even though they are *voiceless*⟩ — see MUTE 1

void *adj* 1 having no legal or binding force ⟨An agreement is *void* if obtained by force.⟩ — see NULL 1
2 lacking contents that could or should be present ⟨a *void* and lifeless landscape⟩ — see EMPTY 1
3 utterly lacking in something needed, wanted, or expected ⟨entirely *void* of common sense⟩ — see DEVOID 1
4 left unoccupied or unused ⟨The cornfields lay *void* under a blanket of snow.⟩ — see ABANDONED 1

void *n* 1 an incomplete or deficient area ⟨After she retires, it will be hard to fill the *void*.⟩ — see GAP 3
2 empty space ⟨those ancient travelers who traversed those vast watery *voids* between the islands of Oceania⟩ — see VACANCY 1
3 an open space in a barrier (as a wall or hedge) ⟨The client wanted an old-fashioned stone wall and did not want the *voids* filled in with mortar.⟩ — see GAP 1

void *vb* 1 to put an end to by formal action ⟨The court's decision *voided* the will.⟩ — see ABOLISH 1
2 to remove the contents of ⟨The seller has promised to *void* the house of all furniture.⟩ — see EMPTY

volatile *adj* likely to change frequently, suddenly, or unexpectedly ⟨A boss of *volatile* moods is frustrating to work for.⟩ — see FICKLE 1

volcanic *adj* marked by bursts of destructive force or intense activity ⟨a man with a *volcanic* temper that could go off at any moment⟩ — see VIOLENT 1

volition *n* 1 the act or power of making one's own choices or decisions ⟨Tourette's syndrome is a neurological disorder marked by recurrent tics and vocalizations that are beyond the sufferer's *volition* or control.⟩ — see FREE WILL
2 the power, right, or opportunity to choose ⟨left the job of her own *volition*, not because she was fired⟩ — see CHOICE 1

volitional *adj* done, made, or given with one's own free will ⟨believes in destiny and doubts that most decisions are truly *volitional*⟩ — see VOLUNTARY 1

volley *n* a rapid or overwhelming outpouring of many things at once ⟨surprised by the *volley* of complaints about cable service in the area⟩ — see BARRAGE

volume *n* 1 a considerable amount ⟨We can only make money if we sell our goods in *volume*.⟩ — see LOT 2
2 a given or particular mass or aggregate of matter ⟨produces great *volumes* of work each day⟩ — see AMOUNT
3 a set of printed sheets of paper bound together between covers and forming a work of fiction or nonfiction ⟨reissued the trilogy in a single *volume*⟩ — see BOOK 1
4 the largest number or amount that something can hold ⟨State the barrel's *volume* in terms of gallons.⟩ — see CAPACITY 1

voluminous *adj* of a size greater than average of its kind ⟨decorating tips to help make *voluminous* rooms feel cozy⟩ — see LARGE

voluminousness *n* the quality or state of being large in size ⟨The awesome *voluminousness* of the garment made it look more like a tent than a dress.⟩ — see LARGENESS

voluntarily *adv* of one's own free will ⟨You took part in this *voluntarily*, so you have no cause to complain.⟩
synonyms freely, willingly
related words consciously, deliberately, intentionally,

knowingly, wittingly; acquiescently, consentingly; electively, optionally

phrases of one's own accord

near antonyms unconsciously, unintentionally, unknowingly, unwittingly; reluctantly

antonyms involuntarily, unwillingly

voluntary *adj* **1** done, made, or given with one's own free will ⟨a *voluntary* contribution to the school's fund-raising drive⟩

synonyms freewill, self-imposed, unforced, volitional, volunteer, willing

related words discretionary, elective, optional; impulsive, instinctive, spontaneous, unpremeditated; conscious, deliberate, intentional, knowing, willful (*or* willful)

near antonyms compulsory, enforced, mandatory, necessary, nonelective, obligatory, ordered, required

antonyms coerced, compelled, forced, involuntary, nonvoluntary, unwilled

2 subject to one's freedom of choice ⟨Participation in the resort's recreational activities is strictly *voluntary*.⟩ — see OPTIONAL

3 made, given, or done with full awareness of what one is doing ⟨the legal distinctions between *voluntary* and involuntary manslaughter⟩ — see INTENTIONAL

volunteer *adj* done, made, or given with one's own free will ⟨*volunteer* work at the hospital⟩ — see VOLUNTARY 1

volunteer *vb* to make a present of ⟨trained tax consultants who *volunteer* their services at tax time⟩ — see GIVE 1

voluptuous *adj* pleasing to the physical senses ⟨the *voluptuous* richness of the music⟩ — see SENSUAL

vomit *vb* to discharge the contents of the stomach through the mouth ⟨The children with the flu *vomited* every time they tried to eat something.⟩

synonyms barf, gag, heave, hurl, puke, retch, spew, spit up, throw up

related words disgorge, regurgitate; eject, expel; nauseate

phrases lose one's lunch [*slang*], toss one's cookies

voracious *adj* **1** having a huge appetite ⟨It seemed like the *voracious* kitten was eating her weight in food every day.⟩

synonyms gluttonous, greedy, hoggish, piggish, rapacious, ravenous, swinish

related words hearty, wolfish; devouring, gobbling, gorging, gormandizing, gulping; empty, famished, hungry, starved, starving; malnourished, underfed, undernourished

near antonyms content, full, glutted, sated, satiated, satisfied, stuffed

2 showing urgent desire or interest ⟨a *voracious* reader⟩ — see EAGER

vortex *n* water moving rapidly in a circle with a hollow in the center ⟨a boat sucked down into the *vortex*⟩ — see WHIRLPOOL

votary *n* one who follows the opinions or teachings of another ⟨a *votary* of the religious leader⟩ — see FOLLOWER 1

vote *n* **1** the right to formally express one's position or will in an election ⟨In the United States, women were granted the *vote* by the 19th Amendment in 1920.⟩

synonyms ballot, enfranchisement, franchise, suffrage

related words say, say-so, voice

antonyms disenfranchisement

2 a piece of paper indicating a person's preferences in an election ⟨dropped her *vote* into the ballot box⟩ — see BALLOT 1

3 the right to express a wish, choice, or opinion ⟨He argued for a *vote* in the matter, since he was going to be affected by the final decision.⟩ — see VOICE 1

vote *vb* to set before the mind for consideration ⟨I *vote* we quit working and go out for lunch.⟩ — see PROPOSE 1

vouch (for) *vb* to declare (something) to be true or genuine ⟨a scientist who can *vouch for* the accuracy of the results⟩ — see CERTIFY 1

vow *n* a person's solemn declaration that he or she will do or not do something ⟨We need your *vow* that you won't damage anything while we're gone.⟩ — see PROMISE

vow *vb* to make a solemn declaration of intent ⟨She *vowed* to love him forever.⟩ — see PROMISE 1

voyage *n* a journey over water in a vessel ⟨the long, perilous *voyage* down the Atlantic seaboard, around Cape Horn, and up South America's Pacific coast⟩ — see SAIL

voyage *vb* **1** to take a trip especially of some distance ⟨*voyaged* to the ends of the earth in search of adventure⟩ — see TRAVEL 1

2 to travel on water in a vessel ⟨*voyaging* on a cruise ship for the first time⟩ — see SAIL 1

vulgar *adj* **1** belonging to the class of people of low social or economic rank ⟨paintings that appeal to *vulgar* tastes⟩ — see IGNOBLE 1

2 depicting or referring to sexual matters in a way that is unacceptable in polite society ⟨a warning about the movie's *vulgar* language⟩ — see OBSCENE 1

3 held by or applicable to a majority of the people ⟨The *vulgar* opinion is that there is a need for change.⟩ — see GENERAL 3

4 lacking in refinement or good taste ⟨*vulgar* behavior shown by someone who's made a lot of money and wants everyone to know it⟩ — see COARSE 2

5 used in or suitable for speech and not formal writing ⟨Latin was once the language of scholars, and English the *vulgar* language used by the common people.⟩ — see COLLOQUIAL 1

vulgarity *n* **1** the quality or state of lacking refinement or good taste ⟨Our cousins' general *vulgarity* and poor manners irritate me.⟩

synonyms coarseness, commonness, crassness, crudeness, grossness, indelicacy, indelicateness, lowness, raffishness, rawness, roughness, rudeness, tastelessness

related words boorishness, churlishness, clownishness, loutishness, rowdiness, rusticity, uncouthness; artlessness, gracelessness, inelegance, unsophistication; insensitiveness, insensitivity, thoughtlessness; kitsch, tackiness

near antonyms courtliness, urbanity; elegance, grace, graciousness; consideration, sensitivity, thoughtfulness

antonyms cultivation, gentility, polish, refinement, tastefulness

2 the quality or state of being obscene ⟨The pointless *vulgarity* of the joke was offensive.⟩ — see OBSCENITY

vulnerability *n* **1** the quality or state of having little resistance to some outside agent ⟨*vulnerability* to infection⟩ — see SUSCEPTIBILITY

2 the state of being left without shelter or protection against something harmful ⟨the *vulnerability* of the car to the elements when it's parked outside⟩ — see EXPOSURE 1

vulnerable *adj* **1** being in a situation where one is likely to meet with harm ⟨I'm *vulnerable* to sunburn whenever I go out in the sun.⟩ — see LIABLE 1

2 lacking protection from danger or resistance against attack ⟨*vulnerable* baby chicks⟩ — see HELPLESS 1

W

wackiness *n* lack of good sense or judgment ⟨the *wacki-ness* of the idea⟩ — see FOOLISHNESS 1

wacky *also* **whacky** *adj* **1** different from the ordinary in a way that causes curiosity or suspicion ⟨raised by an uncle with a rather *wacky* philosophy of parenting⟩ — see ODD 2 **2** showing or marked by a lack of good sense or judgment ⟨one club member whose *wacky* ideas for fundraisers usually produced groans⟩ — see FOOLISH 1

wad *n* **1** a considerable amount ⟨a star who usually gets a big *wad* of publicity for her outspokenness⟩ — see LOT 2 **2** a small uneven mass ⟨a *wad* of gum stuck to the desk⟩ — see LUMP 1 **3** a very large amount of money ⟨amassed—and lost—a *wad* playing the stock market⟩ — see FORTUNE 2

wad *vb* to form into a round compact mass ⟨Disgusted, she *wadded* up the paper and threw it in the wastebasket.⟩
synonyms agglomerate, ball, roll, round
related words bunch, clump, lump; pearl, pellet, pelletize; sphere
near antonyms flatten, open, smooth, spread, unfold
antonyms unroll

waddle *vb* to move forward while swaying from side to side ⟨The duck *waddled* back into the water.⟩ — see STAGGER 1

waft *n* a slight or gentle movement of air ⟨*wafts* carrying the scent of spring flowers⟩ — see BREEZE 1

waft *vb* to rest or move along the surface of a liquid or in the air ⟨a feather *wafted* past us and settled on the grass⟩ — see FLOAT 1

¹**wag** *n* a quick jerky movement from side to side or up and down ⟨The dog gave its tail a single *wag* before it flopped back down.⟩
synonyms swish, switch, waggle, whisk
related words oscillation, rock, sway, swing, waver; flap, flutter, wave, whip; flick, jerk, jolt, snap, twitch; jiggle, shake, wiggle; bob, nod

²**wag** *n* a person (as a writer) noted for or specializing in humor ⟨Some *wag* wrote a hilarious satire on the scandal for the newspaper.⟩ — see HUMORIST

wag *vb* **1** to move from side to side or up and down with quick jerky motions ⟨The cat's tail *wagged* back and forth in annoyance.⟩
synonyms swish, switch, waggle
related words oscillate, rock, sway, swing, waver; beat, flail, flap, flop, lash, whip; flick, flicker, flutter, wave; jerk, jolt; jig, jiggle, joggle, shake, twitch, wiggle; bob, jog, nod **2** to relate sometimes questionable or secret information of a personal nature ⟨Tongues will *wag* as soon as word of the house's selling price gets around.⟩ — see GOSSIP **3** to make short up-and-down movements ⟨The bird's head *wagged* jerkily as it looked for worms.⟩ — see NOD

wage *n, often* **wages** *pl* the money paid regularly to a person for labor or services ⟨The *wage* you earn is more than enough to support us comfortably.⟩
synonyms emolument, hire, pay, payment, salary, stipend
related words living wage, minimum wage, nominal wages, take-home pay; double time, overtime, time and a half; compensation, recompense, remittance, remuneration, requital, return; recoupment, redress, reparation, restitution; reimbursement, repayment; earnings, profit, takings, yield

wager *n* the money or thing risked on the outcome of an uncertain event ⟨lost her *wager* when the horse dropped out of the race⟩ — see BET 1

wager *vb* to risk (something) on the outcome of an uncertain event ⟨*wagered* 20 dollars that his favorite team would win⟩ — see BET

wagerer *n* one that bets (as on the outcome of a contest or sports event) ⟨As a *wagerer* of very small amounts, my uncle regards a visit to the racetrack as simply a pleasant way to spend the afternoon.⟩ — see BETTOR

waggery *n* **1** something said or done to cause laughter ⟨Will Rogers' homespun *waggeries* struck a chord with audiences during the Great Depression.⟩ — see JOKE 1 **2** a playful or mischievous act intended as a joke ⟨Her innocent little *waggeries* included sending funny e-mails to coworkers.⟩ — see PRANK

waggish *adj* tending to or exhibiting reckless playfulness ⟨a *waggish* disposition that often got him into trouble as a child⟩ — see MISCHIEVOUS 1

waggle *n* a quick jerky movement from side to side or up and down ⟨a quick *waggle* of her head to indicate "no"⟩ — see ¹WAG

waggle *vb* to move from side to side or up and down with quick jerky motions ⟨The rabbit *waggled* its ears and hopped away.⟩ — see WAG 1

wagon *n* a wheeled usually horse-drawn vehicle used for hauling ⟨Harness the horses up to the *wagon* so I can bring in the hay.⟩ — see CART

wail *n* **1** a crying out in grief ⟨He let out a *wail* as he read the letter.⟩ — see LAMENT 1 **2** a long low sound indicating pain or grief ⟨The little girl let out a *wail* after she fell off her bike.⟩ — see MOAN 1 **3** an expression of dissatisfaction, pain, or resentment ⟨a transit fare increase that is sure to bring *wails* from the straphangers⟩ — see COMPLAINT 1

wail *vb* **1** to express dissatisfaction, pain, or resentment usually tiresomely ⟨The state's residents are always *wailing* about their high taxes.⟩ — see COMPLAIN **2** to make a long loud mournful sound ⟨The little boy *wailed* when told his family's old dog had died.⟩ — see HOWL 1 **3** to utter a moan ⟨The patient lay in his bed, occasionally softly *wailing* in pain.⟩ — see MOAN 1

wail (for) *vb* to feel or express sorrow for ⟨Her grandfather asked her not to *wail for* him, saying that he had had a good life and was at peace.⟩ — see LAMENT 1

wailing *adj* expressing or suggesting mourning ⟨a *wailing* quality in her voice that makes her a natural for country music⟩ — see MOURNFUL 1

wain *n* a wheeled usually horse-drawn vehicle used for hauling ⟨an antique *wain* that was once used for delivering milk⟩ — see CART

waist *n* the middle region of the human torso ⟨bent at the *waist* to catch his breath⟩ — see MIDRIFF

waistline *n* the middle region of the human torso ⟨wore a belt around her *waistline*⟩ — see MIDRIFF

wait *n* an instance or period of being prevented from going about one's business ⟨There was a long *wait* for the manager to come and help us.⟩ — see DELAY

wait *vb* to remain in place in readiness or expectation of something ⟨Please *wait* here, and we'll seat you shortly.⟩
synonyms await, bide, hold on, stay
related words hang around, linger, remain, stick around, tarry; stand by; anticipate, expect, watch (for)
phrases bide one's time, cool one's heels, hold one's breath, sit tight

waiter *n* a person who serves food or drink ⟨*Waiters* at that elegant restaurant must go through an extended training program before being allowed to serve customers.〉 — see SERVER

waitperson *n* a person who serves food or drink 〈asked the *waitperson* what she would recommend on the menu〉 — see SERVER

waiver *n* a document containing a declaration of an intentional giving up of a right, claim, or privilege 〈Before you can participate in the athletic program, you have to sign a *waiver* in which you give up your right to sue.〉
synonyms disclaimer, release
related words dispensation, exemption, indemnity; abdication, relinquishment, renouncement; renunciation, surrender

wake *vb* **1** to cause to stop sleeping 〈My banging around in the kitchen *woke* my wife.〉
synonyms arouse, awake, awaken, rouse, waken
related words roust, rout; raise, revive; reawaken; agitate, bestir, disturb, excite, provoke, stimulate, stir
near antonyms hypnotize, mesmerize
antonyms lull
2 to cease to be asleep 〈I *woke* with a start when the door slammed.〉
synonyms arouse, awake, awaken, rouse, waken
related words arise, get up, rise, turn out, uprise; watch; revive; reawaken; shift, stir
near antonyms catnap, conk (off *or* out), doze, drop off, nap, nod, rest, sleep, slumber, snooze; bed (down), couch, flop, retire, sack out, turn in; lie up, sleep in; oversleep
3 to give notice to beforehand especially of danger or risk 〈a public service announcement designed to *wake* people to the dangers of aggressive driving〉 — see WARN

wakeful *adj* not sleeping or able to sleep 〈The mother remained *wakeful* until her child returned home.〉
synonyms awake, sleepless, wide-awake
related words aroused, awakened, roused, rousted, wakened; about, astir, up; aware, conscious; revived; reawakened
near antonyms drowsy, nodding, sleepy, slumberous (*or* slumbrous), somnolent; dreaming; hypnotized, mesmerized
antonyms asleep, dormant, dozing, napping, resting, sleeping, slumbering, unawakened

waken *vb* **1** to cause to stop sleeping 〈A sudden loud noise *wakened* us.〉 — see WAKE 1
2 to cease to be asleep 〈She usually *wakens* when sunlight begins to stream through the windows.〉 — see WAKE 2

wake–up call *n* something that tells of approaching danger or risk 〈His high blood pressure was a *wake-up call* that he needed to do something about his health.〉 — see WARNING 2

walk *n* **1** a relaxed journey on foot for exercise or pleasure 〈We went for a long *walk* outside because it was such a nice night.〉
synonyms constitutional, perambulation, ramble, range, saunter, stroll, turn, wander
related words parade, paseo; expedition, hike, march, peregrination, traipse, tramp, travel, traversal, traverse, trek, trip, walkabout; excursion, jaunt, junket, outing, sally, spin, tour; pilgrimage, progress, safari
2 a region of activity, knowledge, or influence 〈a nondenominational church that attracts worshippers from every *walk* of life〉 — see FIELD 2

walk *vb* **1** to go on foot 〈I *walked* slowly to school.〉
synonyms foot (it), hoof (it), leg (it), pad, step, traipse, tread
related words parade; march, pace, stride, troop; power walk; hike, peregrinate, trek; mosey, ramble, saunter, stroll, wander; clump, stomp, stump, tramp, trample, tromp; footslog, plod, trudge; gimp, hobble, limp; mince,

prance, pussyfoot, tiptoe; bounce, stalk, strut, swagger; falter, lumber, lurch, pound, scuff, shamble, shuffle, stagger, stumble, toddle, waddle; nip, tap, trip, trot
2 to refuse to work in order to force an employer to meet demands 〈Workers threatened to *walk* unless management agreed to shoulder more of the cost of health insurance.〉 — see STRIKE 1

walking out *n* the act of leaving a place 〈Your unexplained *walking out* like that was rude.〉 — see DEPARTURE 1

walkout *n* a work stoppage by a body of workers intended to force an employer to meet their demands 〈After four weeks of the *walkout*, management gave in.〉 — see STRIKE 1

walk out *vb* **1** to leave a place often for another 〈We simply *walked out* after waiting half an hour for someone to come and serve us.〉 — see GO 2
2 to refuse to work in order to force an employer to meet demands 〈The salesclerks *walked out* upon learning of the second pay cut in six months.〉 — see STRIKE 1

wall *n* **1** a physical object that blocks the way 〈an ancient *wall* that was built to block the invading barbarians〉 — see BARRIER
2 means or method of defending 〈Investigators faced a *wall* of silence when they began asking questions.〉 — see DEFENSE 1

wall (in) *vb* to close or shut in by or as if by barriers 〈a lake almost entirely *walled in* by mountains〉 — see ENCLOSE 1

wallop *n* **1** a forceful coming together of two things 〈felt the *wallop* of a car crashing into their front porch〉 — see IMPACT 1
2 a hard strike with a part of the body or an instrument 〈gave the ball a good *wallop* with the bat〉 — see ¹BLOW
3 a pleasurably intense stimulation of the feelings 〈She really got a *wallop* out of finding a rare first edition by her favorite author.〉 — see THRILL

wallop *vb* **1** to strike repeatedly 〈*walloped* the branches of the pear tree with a stick in an effort to knock down some fruit〉 — see BEAT 1
2 to defeat by a large margin 〈*walloped* their traditional rivals 20 to nothing〉 — see WHIP 2
3 to deliver a blow to (someone or something) usually in a strong vigorous manner 〈*walloped* the ball right out of the park〉 — see HIT 1

wampum *n* something (as pieces of stamped metal or printed paper) customarily and legally used as a medium of exchange, a measure of value, or a means of payment 〈made some real *wampum* on that last business deal〉 — see MONEY

wan *adj* lacking a healthy skin color 〈She looks a little *wan* after all that tiring work.〉 — see PALE 2

wander *n* a relaxed journey on foot for exercise or pleasure 〈a *wander* through the woods〉 — see WALK 1

wander *vb* **1** to move about from place to place aimlessly 〈We just went outside and *wandered* around until it was time to go.〉
synonyms bat, cruise, drift, float, gad (about), gallivant (*also* galavant), knock (about), maunder, meander, mooch, ramble, range, roam, rove, traipse
related words saunter, stroll; dawdle, mope; hobo, tramp, vagabond; mill (about *or* around); straggle, stray
2 to commit an offense 〈We have all *wandered* from the path of righteousness at least once in our lives.〉 — see OFFEND 1

wanderer *n* a person who roams about without a fixed route or destination 〈a *wanderer* who reasoned that he could never be lost, as he didn't care where he was going〉 — see NOMAD

wandering *adj* **1** passing from one topic to another 〈Your decidedly *wandering* essay loses its punch—stick to one theme.〉 — see DISCURSIVE

2 traveling from place to place 〈a *wandering* carnival that visited small towns all over the South〉 — see ITINERANT

wane *vb* to grow less in scope or intensity especially gradually 〈Over the course of the evening the storm steadily *waned*.〉 — see DECREASE 2

wangle *vb* to plan out usually with subtle skill or care 〈*wangled* a way to get free tickets to the show〉 — see ENGINEER

want *n* **1** the fact or state of being absent 〈the proverb that begins, "for *want* of a nail, the shoe was lost"〉 — see LACK 1

2 a falling short of an essential or desirable amount or number 〈There's a notable *want* of teachers in that rural school district.〉 — see DEFICIENCY

3 a state of being without something necessary, desirable, or useful 〈The house is in *want* of some repairs.〉 — see NEED 1

4 the state of lacking sufficient money or material possessions 〈grew up in extreme *want*〉 — see POVERTY 1

5 a defect in character 〈She's well-meaning and kind, but her besetting *want* is a complete lack of tact.〉 — see FAULT 1

want *vb* **1** to have an earnest wish to own or enjoy 〈I *want* a new car so badly!〉 — see DESIRE 1

2 to have as a requirement 〈That stray cat *wants* food and a clean place to sleep.〉 — see NEED 1

3 to see fit 〈Do what you *want*.〉 — see CHOOSE 2

4 to wish to have 〈I *want* some ice cream for dessert, please.〉 — see LIKE 1

wanting *adj* **1** falling short of a standard 〈We tried the restaurant's food and found it to be very *wanting*.〉 — see BAD 1

2 not coming up to an expected measure or meeting a particular need 〈At this time of year food for many wild animals is *wanting*.〉 — see SHORT 3

3 not present or in evidence 〈Grass is almost entirely *wanting* in that arid wasteland.〉 — see ABSENT 2

wanting *prep* not having 〈a mitten *wanting* its mate〉 — see WITHOUT 1

wanton *adj* **1** depicting or referring to sexual matters in a way that is unacceptable in polite society 〈That novel was once regarded as a *wanton* tale of forbidden love.〉 — see OBSCENE 1

2 having a strong sexual desire 〈*wanton* lovers〉 — see LUSTFUL

3 having or showing the desire to inflict severe pain and suffering on others 〈a *wanton* attack〉 — see CRUEL 1

wantonness *n* **1** disposition to willfully inflict pain and suffering on others 〈the *wantonness* with which the punishment was carried out〉 — see CRUELTY

2 the quality or state of being obscene 〈novels characterized chiefly by their sheer *wantonness*〉 — see OBSCENITY

war *n* **1** a state of armed violent struggle between states, nations, or groups 〈The *war* was the result of ethnic tensions that had been building in the region for decades.〉 — see *synonyms* conflagration, conflict, hostilities, hot war *related words* civil war, cold war, holy war, limited war, police action, world war; action, battle, engagement, skirmish; combat, fighting, warfare *near antonyms* demilitarization, demobilization, disarmament; pacification; cease-fire, truce; calm, peacefulness, tranquility (*or* tranquillity) *antonyms* peace

2 a lack of agreement or harmony 〈The siblings always seemed to be at *war* with one another.〉 — see DISCORD

3 an earnest effort for superiority or victory over anoth-er 〈only the latest round in the never-ending class *war*〉 — see CONTEST 1

war (against) *vb* to oppose (someone) in physical conflict 〈continually *warring against* their neighbors in an effort to expand their territory〉 — see FIGHT 1

warble *n* a rhythmic series of musical tones arranged to give a pleasing effect 〈whistled a cheerful *warble* as he strolled down the street〉 — see MELODY

warble *vb* to sing with the alternation of two musical tones 〈The skylark *warbled* prettily outside our window.〉 *synonyms* quaver, trill *related words* slur; yodel; belt, carol, chant, chorus, croon, descant, harmonize, troll, vocalize; lilt

ward *n* **1** means or method of defending 〈Frequent hand washing is an oft-recommended *ward* against the spread of common germs.〉 — see DEFENSE 1

2 responsibility for the safety and well-being of someone or something 〈gained the *ward* of his cousin upon the death of her parents〉 — see CUSTODY

ward *vb* to drive danger or attack away from 〈vowed that she would take whatever measures were necessary to *ward* the nation's people〉 — see DEFEND 1

warden *n* **1** a person or group that watches over someone or something 〈As *warden* of the school, a principal must provide a safe environment for the students.〉 — see GUARD 1

2 a person who takes care of a property sometimes for an absent owner 〈served as *warden* for the country estate〉 — see CUSTODIAN 1

warder *n* a person or group that watches over someone or something 〈As *warder* of the velvet rope, he decides who gets into the fashionable nightclub and who doesn't.〉 — see GUARD 1

warehouse *n* a building for storing goods 〈When the *warehouse* burned down, we lost most of our merchandise.〉 — see STOREHOUSE

wares *pl n* products that are bought and sold in business 〈a merchant proudly displaying his *wares*〉 — see MERCHANDISE

warfare *n* **1** a lack of agreement or harmony 〈Growing up, my sister and I seemed to be in a constant state of *warfare*.〉 — see DISCORD

2 an earnest effort for superiority or victory over another 〈companies engaged in constant *warfare* for dominance in the market for mobile phones〉 — see CONTEST 1

wariness *n* a close attentiveness to avoiding danger 〈Only his unceasing *wariness* saved the party of skiers from an avalanche.〉 — see CAUTION 1

warlike *adj* feeling or displaying eagerness to fight 〈a seafarer's legend that the remote island was inhabited by *warlike* people〉 — see BELLIGERENT

warm *adj* **1** having or giving off heat to a moderate degree 〈The pan was still *warm*, but no longer too hot to touch.〉 *synonyms* heated, lukewarm, tepid, toasty, warmed *related words* thawed; broiling, burning, fiery, hot, piping, red-hot, roasting, scalding, scorching, searing, steamy, sultry, sweltering, torrid; overheated, roasted, superheated, sweltering; blazing, glowing, molten, sizzling; reheated, rewarmed, warmed-over *near antonyms* arctic, bitter, bleak, chill, chilly, cold, freezing, frigid, frosty, glacial, ice-cold, iced, icy, nippy, polar, raw, sharp, snappy, snowy, subfreezing, subzero, ultracold, winterly, wintry (*also* wintery); frosted; benumbed, nipped, numb *antonyms* chilled, cool, cooled, coolish, refrigerated, unheated

2 having or expressing great depth of feeling 〈a *warm* hug of welcome from our grandmother〉 — see FERVENT 1

3 having or showing kindly feeling and sincere interest 〈a *warm* inquiry after his parents' health〉 — see FRIENDLY 1

warm *vb* **1** to cause to have or give off heat to a moderate degree ⟨You'll need to *warm* the food in the microwave.⟩
synonyms heat, toast
related words overheat, superheat; reheat, rewarm; thaw; bake, cook, roast; burn, char, fire, parch, scald, scorch, sear
near antonyms freeze, frost, supercool
antonyms chill, cool, refrigerate
2 to give satisfaction to ⟨My dance instructor's generous praise *warmed* my heart.⟩ — see PLEASE 1

warm–blooded *adj* having or expressing great depth of feeling ⟨a *warm-blooded* defense of everyone's right to free speech⟩ — see FERVENT 1

warmed *adj* having or giving off heat to a moderate degree ⟨The *warmed* towels that the attendant handed us were a nice touch.⟩ — see WARM 1

warmhearted *adj* **1** having or marked by sympathy and consideration for others ⟨a *warmhearted*, understanding teacher from whom many sought guidance⟩ — see HUMANE 1
2 having or showing kindly feeling and sincere interest ⟨a *warmhearted* welcome from the staff on my first day at work⟩ — see FRIENDLY 1

warmheartedness *n* the capacity for feeling for another's unhappiness or misfortune ⟨When we moved into our new house we were overwhelmed by the *warmheartedness* of the neighbors.⟩ — see HEART 1

warmness *n* the quality or state of being moderate in temperature ⟨The cozy *warmness* of a house can be so nice after an hour spent shoveling snow.⟩ — see WARMTH 1

warmonger *n* one who urges or attempts to cause a war ⟨The *warmongers* met with overwhelming opposition.⟩
synonyms hawk, jingo, militarist
related words agitator, firebrand, fomenter, instigator, rabble-rouser; belligerent, combatant, militant; chauvinist
near antonyms peacemaker; peacekeeper
antonyms dove, pacifist

warmth *n* **1** the quality or state of being moderate in temperature ⟨The cozy *warmth* of the inn's parlor was a welcome relief from the wintry weather outside.⟩
synonyms lukewarmness, warmness
related words balminess, mildness, temperateness; glow, radiance, radiancy; heat, hotness, stuffiness, sultriness, torridity, torridness
near antonyms bitterness, bleakness, cold, frigidity, frigidness, frostiness, iciness, rawness, sharpness; frost
antonyms chill, chilliness, coolness
2 depth of feeling ⟨I was surprised by the *warmth* of the greeting.⟩ — see ARDOR 1

warn *vb* to give notice to beforehand especially of danger or risk ⟨The lifeguard *warned* the boys that if they continued playing so rough, someone was sure to get hurt.⟩
synonyms advise, alert, caution, forewarn, wake
related words augur, forecast, foretell, harbinger, predict, presage, prognosticate, prophesy; apprise, inform, notify, tip (off); admonish, bode, forebode (*also* forbode), foreshadow, foretoken, portend
near antonyms imperil, risk

warning *adj* serving as or offering a warning ⟨usually gave her trademark *warning* look when the children were getting out of hand⟩ — see CAUTIONARY

warning *n* **1** the act or an instance of telling beforehand of danger or risk ⟨She delivered a strict *warning* that anyone who was caught stealing would be fired.⟩
synonyms admonishment, admonition, alarm (*also* alarum), alert, caution, forewarning, notice
related words auguring, augury, forecasting, foretelling, predicting, prediction, premonition, presaging, prognosticating, prophecy (*also* prophesy), prophesying; apprising, informing, notification, notifying, tip-off; advice, counsel, guidance, recommendation, suggestion, tip; announcement, declaration
2 something that tells of approaching danger or risk ⟨The ominously darkening sky was a *warning* that a storm was approaching.⟩
synonyms caution, tip-off, tocsin, wake-up call
related words omen, portent, premonition, presage; notice, notification; buoy, indicator, knell, sign, signal; foretaste, foretoken; announcement, declaration
phrases handwriting on the wall
near antonyms all clear

warp *n* an immaterial thing upon which something else rests ⟨An unshakable belief in the essential goodness of humankind is the *warp* of his philosophy.⟩ — see BASE 1

warp *vb* **1** to change so much as to create a wrong impression or alter the meaning of ⟨The faulty English translation really *warps* the meaning of the original Russian text.⟩ — see GARBLE
2 to lower in character, dignity, or quality ⟨claims that violent movies *warp* the values of viewers⟩ — see DEBASE 1
3 to twist (something) out of a natural or normal shape or condition ⟨Freezing *warped* the plastic, and now the cover won't fit.⟩ — see CONTORT

warped *adj* having or showing lowered moral character or standards ⟨tired of his sick jokes and *warped* sense of humor⟩ — see CORRUPT

warping *n* the twisting of something out of its natural or normal shape or condition ⟨The *warping* of the door frame over the years means there's always a draft now.⟩ — see CONTORTION

warrant *n* the approval by someone in authority for the doing of something ⟨Some employees suspected that the supervisor had no *warrant* from the CEO for instituting the draconian work rules.⟩ — see PERMISSION

warrant *vb* **1** to assume responsibility for the satisfactory quality or performance of ⟨The computer company unconditionally *warrants* all of its products for one full year.⟩
synonyms guarantee, guaranty
related words attest, authenticate, avouch, certify, testify (to), vouch (for), witness; assure, bond, contract, covenant; pledge, plight, stipulate, swear, undertake, vow; adhere, assert, aver, avow, declare, insist; insure
2 to give official acceptance of as satisfactory ⟨The state constitution *warrants* these measures.⟩ — see APPROVE
3 to have as a requirement ⟨The situation *warrants* your immediate attention.⟩ — see NEED 1
4 to state as a fact usually forcefully ⟨We'll all be gone before that happens, I *warrant*.⟩ — see CLAIM 1
5 to give official or legal power to ⟨Bailiffs are *warranted* to enforce the subpoena.⟩ — see AUTHORIZE 1

warranted *adj* being what is called for by accepted standards of right and wrong ⟨a *warranted* use of force⟩ — see JUST 1

warranty *n* a formal agreement to fulfill an obligation ⟨a one-year *warranty* for the refrigerator⟩ — see GUARANTEE 1

warrior *n* a person engaged in military service ⟨a program of tough training and discipline that turns untried civilians into *warriors*⟩ — see SOLDIER

wary *adj* having or showing a close attentiveness to avoiding danger or trouble ⟨kept a *wary* eye out for signs of the enemy⟩ — see CAREFUL 1

wash *n* spongy land saturated or partially covered with water ⟨an invasive species threatening the plants native to the region's *washes*⟩ — see SWAMP

wash *vb* **1** to flow along or against ⟨Crystal-clear waters gently *wash* the island's unspoiled beaches.⟩
synonyms bathe, lap, lave, splash
related words bubble, gurgle, plash, ripple, slosh

2 to withstand scrutiny and gain acceptance or approval ⟨The employee's story about missing the bus didn't *wash* with her manager.⟩
synonyms fly, hold up, pass
related words go down, go over, go through, play, take, work
phrases hold water, pass muster
3 to flow in a broken irregular stream ⟨soapy water *washing* down the drain⟩ — see GURGLE
4 to make wet ⟨Rain *washed* the countryside for days on end.⟩ — see WET
5 to pour liquid over or through in order to cleanse ⟨*washed* the baby's hair⟩ — see FLUSH 1
6 to cause (as a liquid) to move about in a circle especially repeatedly ⟨She absentmindedly *washed* her tea by tipping her cup, until the honey was at last mixed in.⟩ — see STIR 1

washed *adj* containing, covered with, or thoroughly penetrated by water ⟨*washed* city streets glistened with the light of the lampposts⟩ — see WET 1

washed–out *adj* **1** lacking intensity of color ⟨*washed-out* blond hair⟩ — see PALE 1
2 depleted in strength, energy, or freshness ⟨Feeling *washed-out* after the endless primary season, the party's nominee needs a vacation more than anything.⟩ — see WEARY 1

washed–up *adj* having lost forcefulness, courage, or spirit ⟨He felt rather *washed-up* after this latest business failure.⟩ — see EFFETE 1

washout *n* something that has failed ⟨The fashion designer's last showing was a complete *washout*.⟩ — see FAILURE 3

wash out *vb* **1** to be unsuccessful ⟨Most of the participants in the tough training program *washed out*.⟩ — see FAIL 2
2 to make white or whiter by removing color ⟨After several days, the sun *washed out* the clothes that had been left hanging outside.⟩ — see WHITEN
3 to use up all the physical energy of ⟨That last illness *washed* the child *out* completely.⟩ — see EXHAUST 1
4 to pour liquid over or through in order to cleanse ⟨*Wash out* your bathing suit in the sink.⟩ — see FLUSH 1

washroom *n* a room furnished with a fixture for flushing body waste ⟨Could you tell me where the *washroom* is?⟩ — see TOILET

waspish *adj* easily irritated or annoyed ⟨Extremely *waspish*, she uses her wit viciously when irritated.⟩ — see IRRITABLE

waspishness *n* readiness to show annoyance or impatience ⟨His perpetual *waspishness* only served to make those around him cranky as well.⟩ — see PETULANCE

wassail *vb* to take part in drunken revelry ⟨The knights feasted and *wassailed* for three days after the battlefield victory.⟩ — see CAROUSE

wastage *n* the state or fact of being rendered nonexistent, physically unsound, or useless ⟨the slash-and-burn *wastage* of the surrounding countryside as the army made its way to the sea⟩ — see DESTRUCTION 1

waste *adj* producing inferior or only a small amount of vegetation ⟨*waste* acreage that was not fit for anything⟩ — see BARREN 1

waste *n* **1** an instance of spending money or resources without care or restraint ⟨It seems like a *waste* to spend my entire paycheck on a bigger TV.⟩
synonyms extravagance, prodigality
related words indulgence, luxury, splurge; loss, wastage; dissipation, profligacy, profusion, squandering, wastefulness; overindulgence, self-indulgence; excess, overkill
near antonyms necessity; belt-tightening, conservation, economizing, economy, frugality, parsimony, saving,

scrimping, skimping, thrift; austerity, moderation, restraint, temperance, temperateness
2 discarded or useless material ⟨gathered up the *waste* when he was finished sewing⟩ — see GARBAGE
3 land that is uninhabited or not fit for crops ⟨an area that was a barren *waste* after the strip-mining had ended⟩ — see WASTELAND
4 solid matter discharged from an animal's alimentary canal ⟨a local ordinance requiring dog owners to properly dispose of their pet's *waste*⟩ — see DROPPING 1
5 a wide space or area ⟨a legendary mariner doomed to sail the watery *wastes* of the world until Judgment Day⟩ — see EXPANSE
6 a gradual weakening, loss, or destruction ⟨the slow *waste* of the once broad beach by the relentless tide⟩ — see CORROSION

waste *vb* **1** to use up carelessly ⟨He *wasted* his lottery winnings on more lottery tickets that were worthless.⟩
synonyms blow, dissipate, fritter (away), lavish, lose, misspend, run through, spend, squander, throw away, trifle (away)
related words splurge; consume, deplete, exhaust, impoverish, overspend, shoot; indulge, overindulge; disburse, expend, lay out
phrases play ducks and drakes with (*or* make ducks and drakes of)
near antonyms economize, scrimp, skimp; preserve, protect, save; hoard, lay up
antonyms conserve
2 to bring to a complete end the physical soundness, existence, or usefulness of ⟨one country attempting to *waste* another⟩ — see DESTROY 1
3 to diminish the physical strength of ⟨endless months of inactivity *wasted* him⟩ — see WEAKEN 1

waste (away) *vb* to lose bodily strength or vigor ⟨The tuberculosis resulted in her simply *wasting away*.⟩ — see WEAKEN 2

wasted *adj* **1** lacking bodily strength ⟨a *wasted* frame—a shadow of the man he once was⟩ — see WEAK 1
2 suffering extreme weight loss as a result of hunger or disease ⟨a frail and *wasted* famine victim⟩ — see EMACIATED

wasteful *adj* given to spending money freely or foolishly ⟨My one *wasteful* child always seemed to run out of money by midweek.⟩ — see PRODIGAL

wastefulness *n* the quality or fact of being free or wasteful in the expenditure of money ⟨Considering he has a family, his *wastefulness* is downright irresponsible.⟩ — see EXTRAVAGANCE 1

wasteland *n* land that is uninhabited or not fit for crops ⟨With proper irrigation and fertilizer, they turned the desert *wasteland* into a fertile plain.⟩
synonyms barren, desert, desolation, waste
related words badland; brush, bush; dust bowl; open, open air, outdoors, out-of-doors; nature, wild, wilderness

waster *n* someone who spends money freely or foolishly ⟨We want you to get a job so that you'll be a *waster* of your own money and not ours.⟩ — see PRODIGAL

wastrel *n* someone who spends money freely or foolishly ⟨a reformed *wastrel* who now has direct deposit of his paycheck⟩ — see PRODIGAL

watch *n* **1** a person or group that watches over someone or something ⟨the neighborhood crime *watch*⟩ — see GUARD 1
2 the state of being constantly attentive and responsive to signs of opportunity, activity, or danger ⟨kept a *watch* over the sick baby⟩ — see VIGILANCE

watch *vb* **1** to keep one's eyes on ⟨I turned my head to continue *watching* the bird as it flew away.⟩
synonyms eye, follow, observe

related words behold, look, perceive, regard, see, view; gape, gawk, gaze, glare, goggle, look on, peer, rubberneck, stare; guard, wake, ward; monitor, study; spy; espy, glance, glimpse, peek, peep

phrases have one's eye on

near antonyms blink, wink

2 to take notice of and be guided by ⟨*Watch* what I do when I run into that kind of problem.⟩ — see HEED 1

3 to pay continued close attention to (something) for a particular purpose ⟨*watched* the situation to see if it improved⟩ — see MONITOR

4 to have an interest or concern for ⟨You should *watch* what you eat if you want a long, healthy life.⟩ — see CARE

5 to take charge of especially on behalf of another ⟨hired a high school girl to *watch* their daughter until they got home from work⟩ — see ²TEND 1

watch (for) *vb* to believe in the future occurrence of (something) ⟨*Watch for* all the latest news on this website.⟩ — see EXPECT

watcher *n* a person or group that watches over someone or something ⟨The inexperienced babysitter turned out to be a naturally talented *watcher* of young children.⟩ — see GUARD 1

watchful *adj* paying close attention usually for the purpose of anticipating approaching danger or opportunity ⟨The toddler played under the *watchful* eye of her parents.⟩ — see ALERT 1

watchfulness *n* the state of being constantly attentive and responsive to signs of opportunity, activity, or danger ⟨It was only her motherly *watchfulness* that saved the boy from an accident.⟩ — see VIGILANCE

watchman *n* **1** a person or group that watches over someone or something ⟨hired a *watchman* to patrol the factory at night⟩ — see GUARD 1

2 a person who takes care of a property sometimes for an absent owner ⟨A *watchman* lives next door to scare off prowlers.⟩ — see CUSTODIAN 1

watch out (for) *vb* to be cautious of or on guard against ⟨*Watch out for* hazards in the road.⟩ — see BEWARE (OF)

watchword *n* **1** a word or phrase that must be spoken by a person in order to pass a guard ⟨The *watchword* is changed every day.⟩ — see PASSWORD

2 an attention-getting word or phrase used to publicize something (as a campaign or product) ⟨Their latest *watchword* turns up in every ad from that company.⟩ — see SLOGAN

water *vb* to make wet ⟨*watered* the plants⟩ — see WET

water closet *n* a room furnished with a fixture for flushing body waste ⟨the first house in town to have an indoor *water closet*⟩ — see TOILET

watercourse *n* an open man-made passageway for water ⟨The Erie Canal was the first *watercourse* to connect the Hudson River with the Great Lakes.⟩ — see CHANNEL 1

watercraft *n* a small buoyant structure for travel on water ⟨Just about any kind of *watercraft* can be seen on the lake during the summer.⟩ — see BOAT 1

watered *adj* containing, covered with, or thoroughly penetrated by water ⟨a heavily *watered* lawn⟩ — see WET 1

waterfall *n* a fall of water usually from a great height ⟨I used to like to throw sticks in the stream and watch them go over the *waterfall*.⟩

synonyms cascade, cataract, fall(s)

related words flume; chute (*also* shute), rapid(s), shoot, white water

waterless *adj* marked by little or no precipitation or humidity ⟨Cacti prefer a nearly *waterless* environment.⟩ — see DRY 1

waterlogged *adj* containing, covered with, or thoroughly

penetrated by water ⟨*waterlogged* soil that caused the roots of the potted plant to rot⟩ — see WET 1

waterproof *adj* made of or treated with material that does not allow water to penetrate ⟨Luckily, my backpack is *waterproof*, so my clothes didn't get wet.⟩

synonyms waterproofed

related words rainproof; water-repellent, water-resistant; staunch (*also* stanch), watertight; nonabsorbent, nonporous; weatherproof

near antonyms absorbent, porous; leaky

waterproofed *adj* made of or treated with material that does not allow water to penetrate ⟨a *waterproofed* fabric that is used for outerwear⟩ — see WATERPROOF

waterspout *n* a pipe or channel for carrying off water from a roof ⟨The *waterspout* became clogged, and then the roof leaked.⟩ — see GUTTER 1

waterway *n* an open man-made passageway for water ⟨The Erie Canal was superseded by a much larger *waterway*, the New York State Barge Canal.⟩ — see CHANNEL 1

watery *adj* **1** containing, covered with, or thoroughly penetrated by water ⟨the soft, *watery* earth of the marshland⟩ — see WET 1

2 having an overly soft liquid consistency ⟨*watery* oatmeal⟩ — see RUNNY

3 not containing very much of some important element ⟨a *watery* lemonade⟩ — see WEAK 3

4 lacking in qualities that make for spirit and character ⟨a *watery* writing style⟩ — see WISHY-WASHY 1

wave *n* a moving ridge on the surface of water ⟨The toddler was almost knocked down by the *waves* created by the speedboat.⟩

synonyms billow, surge, swell

related words sea(s); surf; breaker, whitecap; comber, curl; ripple, wavelet; ground swell, roller; tidal wave, tsunami

wave *vb* to direct or notify by a movement or gesture ⟨*waved* them over to the side of the road⟩ — see MOTION

waver *vb* **1** to show uncertainty about the right course of action ⟨He's still *wavering* about whether to take the job.⟩ — see HESITATE

2 to swing unsteadily back and forth or from side to side ⟨The steel tower *wavered* for a moment before falling over.⟩ — see TEETER 1

wavering *n* a state or an instance of temporary inaction because of uncertainty about the right course of action ⟨After a moment's *wavering*, she accepted the job.⟩ — see HESITATION

¹wax *vb* **1** to coat (something) with a slippery substance in order to reduce friction ⟨*waxing* a surfboard⟩ — see LUBRICATE

2 *slang* to defeat by a large margin ⟨I can't believe I bet on a football team that ended up getting *waxed* 45-0.⟩ — see WHIP 2

²wax *vb* **1** to become greater in extent, volume, amount, or number ⟨The commitment of the young volunteers to the cause seems to *wax* and wane.⟩ — see INCREASE 2

2 to eventually have as a state or quality ⟨*waxed* poetic whenever he wrote home⟩ — see BECOME

way *adv* to a great degree ⟨"Oh, I'm just *way* thrilled to be here!" the game show contestant gushed.⟩ — see VERY 1

way *n* **1** a passage cleared for public vehicular travel ⟨The town honored the local sports hero by naming after him a short *way* connecting two shopping centers.⟩

synonyms artery, avenue, boulevard, drag, drive, expressway, freeway, highway, pass, pike, road, roadway, route, row, street, thoroughfare, trace, turnpike

related words causeway; autoroute, interstate, superhighway; beltway, bypass, parkway; corniche, switchback; through street; Main Street; backstreet, branch, bystreet, byway, crossroad, secondary road, shunpike, side road, side street; alley, alleyway; circle, lane, place; cul-de-sac, dead end; corridor; track, trail; promenade, walk

2 a usual manner of behaving or doing ⟨She's set in her *ways* and is not about to change.⟩ — see HABIT 1

3 an established course for traveling from one place to another ⟨took the regular *way* to work⟩ — see PASSAGE 1

4 an established pattern of behavior ⟨That's just his *way*, so pay him no mind.⟩ — see TENDENCY 1

5 an extent or area available for or used up by some activity or thing ⟨made *way* for them to pass⟩ — see ROOM 1

6 the direction along which something or someone moves ⟨Go the same *way* that the school bus does.⟩ — see PATH 1

7 the means or procedure for doing something ⟨figured out the best *way* to accomplish the task⟩ — see METHOD

8 the opening through which one can enter or leave a structure ⟨We came in the back *way*.⟩ — see DOOR 2

9 the power, right, or opportunity to choose ⟨Have it your *way*.⟩ — see CHOICE 1

10 the space or amount of space between two points, lines, surfaces, or objects ⟨It's just a little *way* down the road.⟩ — see DISTANCE 1

wayfarer *n* a person who roams about without a fixed route or destination ⟨One of the great *wayfarers* of American folklore, Johnny Appleseed wandered across the country, always planting apple seeds.⟩ — see NOMAD

wayfaring *adj* traveling from place to place ⟨a *wayfaring* folksinger⟩ — see ITINERANT

waylay *vb* to lie in wait for and attack by surprise ⟨Outside the courthouse she was *waylaid* by reporters shouting questions.⟩ — see AMBUSH

way–out *adj* different from the ordinary in a way that causes curiosity or suspicion ⟨some new and *way-out* suggestions for naming the baby⟩ — see ODD 2

way station *n* a regular stopping place ⟨a *way station* for truck drivers⟩ — see STATION 2

wayward *adj* **1** given to resisting authority or another's control ⟨had always been the most *wayward* of their three children⟩ — see DISOBEDIENT

2 given to resisting control or discipline by others ⟨teachers who could work wonders with *wayward* teens⟩ — see UNCONTROLLABLE

waywardness *n* refusal to obey ⟨The unremitting *waywardness* of the child frustrated her parents at times.⟩ — see DISOBEDIENCE

weak *adj* **1** lacking bodily strength ⟨The little boy was simply too *weak* to lift the box.⟩

synonyms debilitated, delicate, effete, enervated, enfeebled, faint, feeble, frail, infirm, languid, low, prostrate, prostrated, sapped, slight, soft, softened, tender, unsubstantial, wasted, weakened, wimpy

related words challenged, disabled, incapacitated, invalid; paralyzed; broken-down, decrepit; impotent, powerless; breakable, flimsy, fragile; dizzy, groggy, rocky, unsteady; drained, exhausted, flagging, tired, weary, worn-out; damaged, harmed, hurt, impaired, injured, lame, unsound; resistless, susceptible, unresistant, vulnerable, yielding

near antonyms able-bodied, athletic, beefy, brawny, fit, husky, muscular, sinewy, strapping, virile; hard, hardy, lusty, red-blooded, robust, sturdy, tough; fortified, hardened, inured, strengthened, toughened; energetic, energized, invigorated, vigorous, vitalized; hale, healthy, sound; capable, competent; convalescing, recovering, recuperating

antonyms mighty, powerful, rugged, stalwart, stout, strong

2 lacking strength of will or character ⟨He proved to be a *weak* leader.⟩

synonyms characterless, effete, frail, invertebrate, nerveless, soft, spineless, weakened, weakling, wimpy, wishy-washy

related words flabby, flaccid, forceless, ineffective, ineffectual; impotent, powerless; emasculated, unnerved; lamblike, meek, pliable, submissive; corrupt, dastardly, unprincipled, unscrupulous, villainous; cowardly, craven, fainthearted, lily-livered, nebbishy, poltroon, pusillanimous, sissy, timid; infirm, irresolute, vacillating

near antonyms ethical, good, moral, principled, right, righteous, upright, virtuous; determined, mettlesome, resolute, unrelenting; courageous, stalwart, stouthearted

antonyms backboned, firm, hard, strong, tough

3 not containing very much of some important element ⟨The coffee came out too *weak* because I didn't use enough ground beans.⟩

synonyms dilute, diluted, thin, thinned, watery, weakened

related words adulterated, watered-down

near antonyms enriched, fortified; concentrated, condensed, evaporated

antonyms full-bodied, rich, strong

4 not using or following good reasoning ⟨Your argument is *weak*.⟩ — see ILLOGICAL

5 unable to act or achieve one's purpose ⟨The office of the vice president is relatively *weak*.⟩ — see POWERLESS

weaken *vb* **1** to diminish the physical strength of ⟨Weeks of hardship in the desert had greatly *weakened* them.⟩

synonyms debilitate, enervate, enfeeble, prostrate, sap, soften, tire, waste

related words cripple, disable, hamstring, incapacitate; deplete, depress, exhaust, impoverish, unman, wash out; damage, harm, hurt, impair, injure, invalid, lay up; break down, wear down, wear out; paralyze

near antonyms energize, invigorate, recruit, rejuvenate, vitalize; harden, season, toughen

antonyms beef (up), fortify, strengthen

2 to lose bodily strength or vigor ⟨The bodybuilder *weakened* once she eased off on her workouts.⟩

synonyms decay, droop, fade, fail, flag, go, lag, languish, sag, sink, waste (away), wilt, wither

related words break down, wear out; yield; degenerate, deteriorate, rot, run down

near antonyms convalesce, rally, rebound, recover, recuperate; gain

3 to alter (something) for the worse with the addition of foreign or lower-grade substances ⟨*weakened* the juice with too much water⟩ — see ADULTERATE

weakened *adj* **1** containing foreign or lower-grade substances ⟨All the melting ice resulted in a *weakened* punch.⟩ — see IMPURE 1

2 lacking bodily strength ⟨left *weakened* by a prolonged illness⟩ — see WEAK 1

3 lacking strength of will or character ⟨The resignation of its founder left the organization *weakened*.⟩ — see WEAK 2

4 not containing very much of some important element ⟨Some experts recommend that runners drink a *weakened* mixture of juice and water.⟩ — see WEAK 3

weakening *n* a gradual sinking and wasting away of mind or body ⟨The all-too-apparent *weakening* of our grandfather was hard on our mother.⟩ — see DECLINE 1

weakling *adj* lacking strength of will or character ⟨argues that in a time of crisis, the city can't afford to have a *weakling* mayor⟩ — see WEAK 2

weakling *n* **1** a person lacking in physical strength ⟨a puppy that was the *weakling* of the litter⟩

synonyms softy (*or* softie), wimp

related words pushover; milksop, mollycoddle, sissy

antonyms powerhouse

2 a person without strength of character ⟨Only a *weakling* would be willing to lie to save himself from punishment.⟩

synonyms pushover, wimp

related words coward, milquetoast, mouse, nebbish, nervous Nellie (*or* nervous Nelly); sheep

near antonyms mensch

antonyms stalwart

weakly *adj* chronically or repeatedly suffering from poor health ⟨a *weakly* baby who required repeated hospitalizations⟩ — see SICKLY 1

weak–minded *adj* **1** not having or showing an ability to absorb ideas readily ⟨Far from *weak-minded*, the very quiet girl proved to be of above-average intelligence.⟩ — see STUPID 1

2 showing or marked by a lack of good sense or judgment ⟨a *weak-minded* decision to use all of their savings to buy lottery tickets in the hopes of hitting the jackpot⟩ — see FOOLISH 1

weakness *n* **1** the quality or state of lacking physical strength or vigor ⟨The flu left me with such overwhelming *weakness* that I could hardly stand.⟩

synonyms debilitation, debility, delicacy, enfeeblement, faintness, feebleness, fragility, frailness, frailty, infirmity, languor, listlessness, lowness

related words decay, decrepitude; breakdown, collapse, prostration; exhaustion, fatigue, lassitude, weariness; defenselessness, helplessness, impotence, impuissance, powerlessness; effeteness, softness; disablement, incapacitation, invalidism; damage, harm, hurt, impairment, injury

near antonyms energy, vitality; brawniness, fitness, heftiness, huskiness, lustiness, muscularity, virility; hardness, ruggedness, stoutness, sturdiness, toughness; health, healthiness, soundness, wellness

antonyms hardihood, hardiness, robustness, strength, vigor

2 the quality or state of lacking strength of will or character ⟨In a moment of *weakness* he told them the secret.⟩

synonyms frailness, frailty, softness, spinelessness

related words collapse; failing, flaw, foible, peccadillo; evil, immorality, wickedness; corruption, corruptness

near antonyms discipline, self-discipline; goodness, integrity, morality, rectitude, righteousness, rightness, uprightness, virtuousness

antonyms backbone, chutzpah (*also* chutzpa *or* hutzpah *or* hutzpa), firmness, fortitude, hardihood, mettle, nerve, resoluteness, strength, toughness

3 a defect in character ⟨His one *weakness* is his unwarranted optimism about everything.⟩ — see FAULT 1

4 the quality or state of having little resistance to some outside agent ⟨the devastating *weakness* of the immune system that is experienced by people with AIDS⟩ — see SUSCEPTIBILITY

weal *n* the state of doing well especially in relation to one's happiness or success ⟨the belief that somehow it is the nation's president who is responsible for the *weal* or woe of the people⟩ — see WELFARE

wealth *n* **1** the total of one's money and property ⟨Her *wealth* increased to the point where she could afford several luxurious homes.⟩

synonyms capital, fortune, means, opulence, riches, substance, wherewithal, worth

related words belongings, chattels, effects, holdings, paraphernalia, possessions, things; bankroll, deep pockets, finances, funds, money; abundance, prosperity, success; treasure, valuables; personalty, property; nest egg, reserve, resources, savings, treasury

near antonyms debts, liabilities

2 a considerable amount ⟨a *wealth* of advice from all quarters on how they should spend their lottery winnings⟩ — see LOT 2

3 an amount or supply more than sufficient to meet one's needs ⟨a *wealth* of documentation to support her thesis⟩ — see PLENTY 1

wealthy *adj* having goods, property, or money in abundance ⟨a *wealthy* man who likes to collect antique cars⟩ — see RICH 1

wear *n* **1** the result of long and hard use ⟨After several years, the carpet was finally showing *wear*.⟩

synonyms wear and tear

related words abrasion, corrosion, erosion; decomposition, deterioration, disintegration; fatigue

near antonyms fixing, mending, patching, rebuilding, reconditioning, reconstruction, renovation, repair, revamping

2 covering for the human body ⟨the latest in fashionable *wear*⟩ — see CLOTHING

wear *vb* **1** to use up all the physical energy of ⟨The job of running their own business *wears* them sometimes.⟩ — see EXHAUST 1

2 to damage or diminish by continued friction ⟨All that walking every day *wore* the soles of my shoes very quickly.⟩ — see ABRADE 1

wear and tear *n* the result of long and hard use ⟨My favorite jeans finally succumbed to *wear and tear* and had to be replaced.⟩ — see WEAR 1

wearied *adj* **1** depleted in strength, energy, or freshness ⟨fell into bed *wearied* and desperate for sleep⟩ — see WEARY 1

2 having one's patience, interest, or pleasure exhausted ⟨*wearied* by her son's endless excuses for not having cleaned his room⟩ — see WEARY 2

weariless *adj* showing no signs of weariness even after long hard effort ⟨the *weariless* efforts to achieve peace⟩ — see TIRELESS

weariness *n* **1** a complete depletion of energy or strength ⟨the kind of satisfying *weariness* that comes from a good day's labor⟩ — see FATIGUE

2 the state of being bored ⟨faces showing *weariness* and irritation at the long graduation speech⟩ — see BOREDOM

wearisome *adj* causing weariness, restlessness, or lack of interest ⟨a *wearisome* lecture on civic responsibility⟩ — see BORING

wear out *vb* to use up all the physical energy of ⟨Keeping up with twin toddlers *wears* me *out*.⟩ — see EXHAUST 1

weary *adj* **1** depleted in strength, energy, or freshness ⟨I am just too *weary* to do any more work tonight.⟩

synonyms beat, bleary, burned-out (*or* burnt-out), bushed, dead, done, drained, exhausted, fatigued, jaded, limp, logy (*also* loggy), played out, prostrate, spent, tired, tuckered (out), washed-out, wearied, worn, worn-out

related words overfatigued, overtaxed, overworked; broken-down, run-down; debilitated, enervate, enervated, enfeebled, sapped, weakened; drowsy, heavy, sleepy; lethargic, sluggish

phrases worn to a frazzle

near antonyms fresh, refreshed, rejuvenated, relaxed, rested, revitalized; active, energetic, invigorated, peppy, strengthened, strong, tireless, vitalized, weariless

antonyms unwearied

2 having one's patience, interest, or pleasure exhausted ⟨I am totally *weary* of this constant bickering.⟩

synonyms bored, fed up, jaded, sick, tired, wearied

related words apathetic, disinterested, uninterested; glutted, sated, satiated, surfeited; dejected, demoralized, discouraged, disheartened, dispirited; beat, burned-out (*or* burnt-out), bushed, done in, drained, enervated, exhausted, fatigued, limp, played out, tuckered (out), worn-out; frustrated; disgusted, nauseated, repulsed; blasé (*also* blase), world-weary

near antonyms animated, energized, enlivened, excited, galvanized, invigorated, stimulated, vitalized; amused, entertained; beguiled, bewitched, captivated, charmed, enchanted, enthralled, fascinated, hypnotized, mesmerized; delighted, pleased, thrilled

antonyms absorbed, engaged, engrossed, interested, intrigued, rapt

3 causing weariness, restlessness, or lack of interest ⟨a *weary* march through a lot of boring facts and figures⟩ — see BORING

weary *vb* **1** to make weary and restless by being dull or monotonous ⟨These constant complaints are really *wearying* me.⟩ — see ²BORE

2 to use up all the physical energy of ⟨A whole day of hard physical labor had thoroughly *wearied* her.⟩ — see EXHAUST 1

wearying *adj* causing weariness, restlessness, or lack of interest ⟨a *wearying* effort to sort through years of records⟩ — see BORING

weather *vb* to come safely through ⟨We've *weathered* worse crises, and so we'll survive this one.⟩ — see SURVIVE 1

weave *vb* **1** to cause to twine about one another ⟨As they have for the past two centuries, crafters continue to *weave* osiers into the distinctive baskets that are the island's trademark.⟩ — see INTERTWINE 1

2 to scatter or set here and there among other things ⟨The story *weaves* myths into the plot in surprising ways.⟩ — see THREAD 1

3 to move suddenly aside or to and fro ⟨a van *weaving* through traffic with reckless speed⟩ — see DODGE 1

web *n* **1** something that catches and holds ⟨He was caught in the *web* of branches.⟩ ⟨She was trapped by her own *web* of lies.⟩

synonyms entanglement, mesh(es), morass, net, quagmire, snare, trap

related words knot, snarl, tangle; cat's cradle, labyrinth, maze; cobweb, spiderweb

2 a device or scheme for capturing another by surprise ⟨an ingenious *web* that was spun by undercover agents going after the criminals⟩ — see TRAP 1

wed *vb* **1** to give in marriage ⟨The king wished to *wed* his favorite daughter to the bravest knight in the realm.⟩ — see MARRY 2

2 to perform the ceremony of marriage for ⟨The priest usually *weds* six to eight couples a month.⟩ — see MARRY 1

3 to take a spouse ⟨She *wed* right after college.⟩ — see MARRY 4

4 to take as a spouse ⟨A true romantic, he intends to *wed* her on Valentine's Day.⟩ — see MARRY 3

wedded *adj* of or relating to marriage ⟨living in *wedded* bliss⟩ — see MARITAL

wedding *n* a ceremony in which two people are united in matrimony ⟨The couple chose to have a garden *wedding*.⟩

synonyms bridal, espousal, marriage, nuptial(s)

related words match, matrimony, wedlock; union

wedge *vb* to fit (people or things) into a tight space ⟨managed to *wedge* one last book onto the bookshelf⟩ — see CROWD 1

wedged *adj* firmly positioned in place and difficult to dislodge ⟨The pebble in the heel of his shoe was pretty well *wedged*.⟩ — see TIGHT 2

wedlock *n* a union representing a special kind of social and legal partnership between two people ⟨joined the happy couple in holy *wedlock*⟩ — see MARRIAGE 1

wee *adj* very small in size ⟨a *wee* baby⟩ — see TINY

weedy *adj* growing thickly and vigorously ⟨*weedy* vegetation in the abandoned lot⟩ — see RANK 1

weep *vb* **1** to flow forth slowly through small openings ⟨water *weeping* through the basement wall⟩ — see EXUDE

2 to shed tears often while making meaningless sounds as a sign of pain or distress ⟨The child was *weeping* over the loss of his toy.⟩ — see CRY 1

weeping *adj* **1** bending downward or forward ⟨With its long, *weeping* fronds, this plant makes a nice ornamental.⟩ — see NODDING

2 expressing or suggesting mourning ⟨a *weeping* song about a long-lost love⟩ — see MOURNFUL 1

weigh *vb* **1** to be of importance ⟨evidence that will *weigh* heavily against the defendant⟩ — see MATTER

2 to give serious and careful thought to ⟨*weighed* the options for weeks before making a decision⟩ — see PONDER

weigh (on *or* **upon)** *vb* to push steadily against with some force ⟨The bulky backpack *weighed* upon my back uncomfortably.⟩ — see ²PRESS 1

weighed *adj* decided on as a result of careful thought ⟨a carefully *weighed* decision to take the company in a new direction⟩ — see DELIBERATE 1

weight *n* **1** the amount that something weighs ⟨Because of a back condition, I'm not allowed to lift anything with a *weight* of over 10 pounds.⟩

synonyms avoirdupois, heaviness, heft

related words bulk, mass; poundage, tonnage; deadweight; heftiness, massiveness, ponderousness, weightiness; solidity, solidness, substantiality, substantialness

2 the quality or state of being important ⟨a matter of little *weight* that is a preoccupation solely of the news media⟩ — see IMPORTANCE

3 a mass or quantity of something taken up and carried, conveyed, or transported ⟨Those books are a heavy *weight* to have to carry around all day.⟩ — see LOAD 1

4 a special notice or importance given to something ⟨put extra *weight* on the matter by putting it at the top of the agenda⟩ — see EMPHASIS 1

5 the main or greater part of something as distinguished from its subordinate parts ⟨The *weight* of the evidence supports my conclusion.⟩ — see BODY 1

6 the power to direct the thinking or behavior of others usually indirectly ⟨As a critic he has great *weight* in the theater world.⟩ — see INFLUENCE 1

7 the condition of having an excess of body fat ⟨a doctor's recommendation to watch his *weight* and quit smoking⟩ — see CORPULENCE

weight *vb* to place a weight or burden on ⟨*weighted* the car with a ton of furniture and then headed off for college⟩ — see LOAD 1

weightiness *n* **1** the state or quality of being heavy ⟨the *weightiness* of the bookcase made it difficult to move⟩

synonyms heaviness, heftiness, massiveness, ponderousness

related words overweight; solidity, solidness, substantiality, substantialness; bulk, bulkiness, hugeness; cumbersomeness

near antonyms airiness, delicacy, ethereality, etherealness; flimsiness, fluffiness, insubstantiality, slightness

antonyms lightness, weightlessness

2 the quality or state of being important ⟨first judged the *weightiness* of a case before deciding to hear it⟩ — see IMPORTANCE

weightless *adj* having little weight ⟨The kitten seemed nearly *weightless* when I picked her up.⟩ — see ¹LIGHT 1

weightlessness *n* the state or quality of having little weight ⟨The relative *weightlessness* of the suitcase surprised me.⟩ — see ¹LIGHTNESS 1

weighty *adj* **1** having a matter of importance as its topic ⟨interrupted a *weighty* discussion with a silly question⟩ — see SERIOUS 2

2 having great meaning or lasting effect ⟨Choosing a college is a *weighty* decision.⟩ — see IMPORTANT 1

3 having great weight ⟨lifted the *weighty* sack and wondered what was in it⟩ — see HEAVY 1

4 not joking or playful in mood or manner ⟨The police office looked at me with a rather *weighty* expression.⟩ — see SERIOUS 1

5 having power over the minds or behavior of others ⟨one of the *weightiest* figures in the field of pediatric medicine⟩ — see INFLUENTIAL 1

weird *adj* **1** different from the ordinary in a way that causes curiosity or suspicion ⟨always has a somewhat *weird* opinion of what's happening in the news⟩ — see ODD 2

2 fearfully and mysteriously strange or fantastic ⟨*weird* sounds from the woods just beyond our campsite⟩ — see EERIE

3 having seemingly supernatural qualities or powers ⟨A self-styled, contemporary witch, she sells herbal mixtures that she claims are *weird* potions.⟩ — see MYSTIC 1

4 noticeably different from what is generally found or experienced ⟨a *weird* little plant that we found growing in the garden⟩ — see UNUSUAL 1

weirdo *n* a person of odd or whimsical habits ⟨a *weirdo* that the rest of the town always seemed to be talking about⟩ — see ECCENTRIC

welcome *adj* giving pleasure or contentment to the mind or senses ⟨a *welcome* chance to rest after a long journey⟩ — see PLEASANT 1

welcome *n* an expression of goodwill upon meeting ⟨offered a warm *welcome* to the stranger⟩ — see HELLO

welcome *vb* to receive or accept gladly or readily ⟨The eager recruits *welcomed* every new project with which they were presented.⟩

synonyms eat (up), embrace

related words adopt, espouse, take up; greet, hail; enjoy, like, prefer; choose, cull, decide (on), elect, handpick, name, opt (for), pick, select, single (out), take

near antonyms decline, refuse, reject, spurn, turn down; demur (to), object (to)

welfare *n* the state of doing well especially in relation to one's happiness or success ⟨I have your *welfare* at heart.⟩

synonyms good, interest, weal, well-being

related words fortune, prosperity, prosperousness, success, successfulness; fitness, health, healthiness, robustness, soundness, wellness, wholeness, wholesomeness; bliss, felicity, happiness, joy; advantage, benefit, gain, sake; content, contentedness, gratification, satisfaction

near antonyms unhealthiness, unsoundness; misery, sadness, suffering, unhappiness, wretchedness

antonyms ill-being

well *adj* enjoying health and vigor ⟨My mother is quite *well*, thank you.⟩ — see HEALTHY 1

well *adv* **1** in a satisfactory way ⟨Our current system for dividing household chores works *well*, so let's keep it.⟩

synonyms acceptably, adequately, all right, alright, fine, good, nicely, OK (*or* okay), passably, satisfactorily, so-so, sufficiently, tolerably

related words appropriately, aptly, congruously, correctly, decorously, felicitously, fittingly, happily, meetly, rightly, seemly, suitably; satisfyingly; effectively, effectually, efficiently, neatly, tidily

near antonyms unbearably; inappropriately, incorrectly, indecently, unsuitably; awfully, deplorably, disastrously, dreadfully, horrendously, horribly, horridly, miserably, terribly

antonyms bad, badly, deficiently, ill, inadequately, insufficiently, poorly, unacceptably, unsatisfactorily

2 in a generous manner ⟨a warm and gracious host who always treats guests *well*⟩

synonyms amply, bountifully, generously, handsomely, lavishly, liberally, munificently, openhandedly, unstintingly

related words considerately, courteously, hospitably, kindly, nicely, reasonably, thoughtfully; affably, amiably, cheerfully, cheerily, congenially, cordially, friendlily, genially, good-heartedly, good-naturedly; selflessly, ungrudgingly, unselfishly; altruistically, beneficently, benevolently, bigheartedly, charitably, humanely, kindheartedly, magnanimously, philanthropically

near antonyms contemptuously, disdainfully, rudely, scornfully; obnoxiously, provocatively; coldly, coolly (*also* cooly), frigidly, hostilely; angrily, belligerently; begrudgingly, grudgingly

antonyms parsimoniously, stingily, ungenerously

3 in a skillful or expert manner ⟨She plays the piano very *well*.⟩

synonyms ably, adeptly, adroitly, capably, competently, expertly, masterfully, masterly, proficiently, skillfully

related words aptly, fluently; cleverly, dexterously, neatly, nimbly; easily, facilely, handily

near antonyms inaptly; awkwardly, clumsily, crudely

antonyms amateurishly, artlessly, incapably, incompetently, inefficiently, ineptly, inexpertly, poorly, unskillfully

4 with good reason or courtesy ⟨We cannot *well* refuse the invitation.⟩

synonyms considerately, courteously, kindly, nicely, reasonably, thoughtfully

related words pleasantly; excusably, fairly, justifiably, validly; discreetly, judiciously, prudently, sensibly, wisely; chivalrously, decorously, deferentially, gallantly, politely, respectfully, solicitously; compassionately, humanely, kindheartedly, sympathetically

near antonyms contemptuously, disdainfully, disrespectfully, impolitely, rudely, scornfully, snootily; cruelly, heartlessly, nastily, viciously; shabbily, unfairly

antonyms discourteously, inconsiderately, thoughtlessly

5 in a pleasing way ⟨The day went *well*, despite the rough beginning.⟩

synonyms agreeably, delectably, deliciously, delightfully, dreamily, favorably, felicitously, gloriously, great, nicely, pleasantly, pleasingly, satisfyingly, splendidly, swimmingly

related words finely, grandly, magnificently; advantageously, helpfully; blessedly, fortunately, happily, luckily; excellently, superbly; marvelously, sensationally, wonderfully; attractively, beautifully, handsomely; appealingly, appetizingly, enticingly, invitingly, temptingly

near antonyms abominably, appallingly, awfully, dreadfully, horrendously, horribly, horridly, shockingly, sickeningly, terribly, vilely; annoyingly, disgustingly, distressingly, irritatingly, vexingly

antonyms badly, disagreeably, ill, unpleasantly

6 to a full extent or degree ⟨We are *well* aware that this home renovation is going to be costly.⟩ — see FULLY 1

7 without difficulty ⟨He can *well* afford to spare the time.⟩ — see EASILY 1

well *interj* how surprising, doubtful, or unbelievable ⟨*Well*, that is odd!⟩ — see NO

well *n* **1** a point or place at which something is invented or provided ⟨His quirky family proved to be a bottomless *well* of inspiration for the novelist.⟩ — see SOURCE 1

2 a small often deep body of water ⟨the spot where the spring bubbles up to the surface and forms a deep *well*⟩ — see ¹POOL

well-being *n* the state of doing well especially in relation to one's happiness or success ⟨We're only doing this for your own *well-being*.⟩ — see WELFARE

wellborn *adj* of high birth, rank, or station ⟨The *wellborn* men among the colonists had no experience with physical labor.⟩ — see NOBLE 1

well–bred *adj* showing consideration, courtesy, and good manners ⟨a *well-bred* young woman who is unfailingly polite to everyone⟩ — see POLITE 1

well–disposed *adj* having an easygoing and pleasing manner especially in social situations ⟨an actor who has a reputation for being *well-disposed*, especially when approached by fans⟩ — see AMIABLE

well–fixed *adj* having goods, property, or money in abundance ⟨She was always hitting up her *well-fixed* relatives for "loans."⟩ — see RICH 1

well–founded *adj* **1** according to the rules of logic ⟨Even a *well-founded* argument can lead to an erroneous conclusion if one of the premises is incorrect.⟩ — see LOGICAL 1

2 based on sound reasoning or information ⟨a *well-founded* complaint about the business's treatment of its customers⟩ — see GOOD 1

well–heeled *adj* having goods, property, or money in abundance ⟨The resort caters to a *well-heeled* clientele that demands the best and has the money to pay for it.⟩ — see RICH 1

well–known *adj* widely known ⟨an anchorwoman so *well-known* that she passes for a local celebrity⟩ — see FAMOUS 1

wellness *n* the condition of being sound in body ⟨Discounted gym memberships are part of the company's employee *wellness* program.⟩ — see HEALTH 1

well–nigh *adv* very close to but not completely ⟨It was *well-nigh* dark, but I could still see a little.⟩ — see ALMOST

well–off *adj* having goods, property, or money in abundance ⟨A *well-off* couple adopted the baby.⟩ — see RICH 1

well–read *adj* having or displaying advanced knowledge or education ⟨Any *well-read* person would recognize the quotation.⟩ — see EDUCATED 1

well–spoken *adj* able to express oneself clearly and well ⟨a *well-spoken* advocate for the legal rights of the underprivileged⟩ — see ARTICULATE

well–to–do *adj* having goods, property, or money in abundance ⟨a doctor who is now quite *well-to-do* as a result of his successful medical practice⟩ — see RICH 1

welter *n* **1** a state of noisy, confused activity ⟨There was a *welter* of pushing and shoving as people rushed to grab the best seats for the outdoor concert.⟩ — see COMMOTION

2 an unorganized collection or mixture of various things ⟨a *welter* of junk in the closet, most of which needed to be thrown out⟩ — see MISCELLANY 1

3 a state in which everything is out of order ⟨the claim that a change of course would plunge the company into a *welter* of confusion⟩ — see CHAOS

wet *adj* **1** containing, covered with, or thoroughly penetrated by water ⟨I left the car windows open while it rained, and the seats got all *wet*.⟩

synonyms awash, bathed, bedraggled, doused (*also* dowsed), drenched, dripping, saturate, saturated, soaked, soaking, sodden, soggy, sopping, soppy, soused, washed, watered, waterlogged, watery

related words deluged, drowned, flooded, inundated, overflowed; submerged, swamped; hydrated; dipped, dunked, splashed; aqueous; steeped; flushed, irrigated,

laved, rinsed, sluiced; damp, dank, humid, moist, semimoist; boggy, miry, seepy, sloppy, squashy

near antonyms bone-dry, hyperarid, ultradry; waterproof, water-repellent, water-resistant, watertight; baked, dehydrated, freeze-dried; droughty, parched, sere (*also* sear), sunbaked, thirsty; wrung

antonyms arid, dry, unwatered, waterless

2 marked by or abounding with rain ⟨a *wet* and dreary day⟩ — see RAINY

3 appealing to the emotions in an obvious and tiresome way ⟨Things get more than a little *wet* during the opera's big death scene.⟩ — see CORNY

wet *n* a steady falling of water from the sky in significant quantity ⟨winced as he walked out into the *wet* without any protection⟩ — see RAIN 1

wet *vb* to make wet ⟨You need to *wet* your hair thoroughly first.⟩

synonyms bathe, douse (*also* dowse), drench, drown, soak, sop, souse, wash, water

related words asperse, damp, dampen, drizzle, humidify, hydrate, mist, moisten, moisturize, shower, sprinkle; deluge, flood, hose (down), inundate, overflow; submerge, swamp; splash; impregnate, saturate, steep; flush, irrigate, lave, rinse, slosh, sluice; dip, duck, dunk; rehydrate, rewash, rewet

near antonyms dewater, evaporate, freeze-dry; drip-dry, wring; dehumidify

antonyms dehydrate, dry, parch, scorch, sear

wet blanket *n* a person who spoils the pleasure of others ⟨I'd love to go to the party, but with my cold, I'm afraid I'd just be a *wet blanket*.⟩ — see KILLJOY

whack *n* **1** an effort to do or accomplish something ⟨took a *whack* at solving the math problem⟩ — see ATTEMPT 1

2 a hard strike with a part of the body or an instrument ⟨gave the wasp's nest a good *whack* with the bat⟩ — see ¹BLOW

3 a loud explosive sound ⟨The *whack* echoed around the field.⟩ — see CLAP 1

whack *vb* to deliver a blow to (someone or something) usually in a strong vigorous manner ⟨*whacked* the vending machine to get the candy bar to fall⟩ — see HIT 1

whacking *adj* unusually large ⟨harvested a *whacking* number of zucchini from the garden⟩ — see HUGE

whacking *adv* to a great degree ⟨The clown wore a *whacking* big pair of shoes.⟩ — see VERY 1

whale *n* something that is unusually large and powerful ⟨a *whale* of a pickup truck⟩ — see GIANT

whale *vb* **1** to deliver a blow to (someone or something) usually in a strong vigorous manner ⟨*whaled* the ball so hard that it sailed over the fence and into the neighbor's yard⟩ — see HIT 1

2 to strike repeatedly with something long and thin or flexible ⟨*whaled* the rug with a broom to knock the dirt out of it⟩ — see WHIP 1

3 to strike repeatedly ⟨lacrosse players *whaling* each others' sticks⟩ — see BEAT 1

wharf *n* a structure used by boats and ships for taking on or landing cargo and passengers ⟨tied the rowboat up at the *wharf*⟩ — see DOCK

what *interj* how surprising, doubtful, or unbelievable ⟨*What*! I can't believe we won!⟩ — see NO

wheedle *vb* to get (someone) to do something by gentle urging, special attention, or flattery ⟨*wheedled* him into doing their work for them⟩ — see COAX

wheel *n* **1** a rapid turning about on an axis or central point ⟨the *wheel* of the tape reel⟩ — see SPIN 1

2 one of high position or importance within a group ⟨She's a major *wheel* in that state's Democratic Party.⟩ — see BIG SHOT

3 a series of events or actions that repeat themselves regularly and in the same order ⟨The *wheel* of time turns: the children are now the parents, and their children have taken their place at the school desks.⟩ — see CYCLE 1

4 wheels *pl, slang* a self-propelled passenger vehicle on four wheels ⟨Now that I've got *wheels*, I can get myself to school.⟩ — see CAR

wheel *vb* **1** to change the course or direction of (something) ⟨*wheeled* the bike around sharply to see what had fallen off⟩ — see TURN 2

2 to move (something) in a curved or circular path on or as if on an axis ⟨*wheeled* the bicycle's tires around to see if they were balanced⟩ — see TURN 1

3 to move in circles around an axis or center ⟨She *wheeled* around and around until finally she got dizzy and fell down.⟩ — see SPIN 1

4 to turn away from a straight line or course ⟨The highway *wheels* to the west as it forms an arc that bypasses the city.⟩ — see CURVE 1

5 to change one's course or direction ⟨Upon hearing her friends' voices, she *wheeled* around to greet them.⟩ — see TURN 3

wheeze *vb* to breathe hard, quickly, or with difficulty ⟨He was *wheezing* rapidly after a hard run.⟩ — see GASP

whelm *vb* to subject to incapacitating emotional or mental stress ⟨The news so *whelmed* them that they were stunned into silence.⟩ — see OVERWHELM 1

whelp *n* a young person who is between infancy and adulthood ⟨Playtime's over; it's time to gather up the *whelps* and head home.⟩ — see CHILD 1

when *conj* **1** at or during the time that ⟨She complained that no one was paying attention to her *when* she gave her speech.⟩
synonyms as, while
near antonyms after

2 just at the moment that ⟨You should say hello *when* you answer the phone.⟩
synonyms instantly
near antonyms after, since

3 in spite of the fact that ⟨She quit writing *when* she could have been a fine author.⟩ — see ALTHOUGH

where *adv* at, in, or to what place ⟨*Where* will you be tonight?⟩
synonyms whereabouts (*also* whereabout), whither
related words wherever
near antonyms whence

where *n* the area or space occupied by or intended for something ⟨We've decided on the when, but we still haven't resolved the *where* for the party.⟩ — see PLACE 1

whereabouts *also* **whereabout** *adv* at, in, or to what place ⟨*Whereabouts* do you expect to be on your journey tonight?⟩ — see WHERE

whereas *conj* **1** for the reason that ⟨*Whereas* you chose to participate in this stupid prank, you will be held responsible as well.⟩ — see SINCE

2 in spite of the fact that ⟨*Whereas* there are many good reasons to switch to Plan B, we must stick with Plan A as long as it is feasible.⟩ — see ALTHOUGH

wherefore *n* something (as a belief) that serves as the basis for another thing ⟨demanded to know the whys and *wherefores* for the decision⟩ — see REASON 2

wherewithal *n* **1** available money ⟨had the *wherewithal* to pay cash for the car⟩ — see FUND 2

2 the total of one's money and property ⟨people with the *wherewithal* to be able to afford such a lavish lifestyle⟩ — see WEALTH 1

whet *vb* to make sharp or sharper ⟨*whetted* the knife with the grindstone⟩ — see SHARPEN

whetted *adj* having an edge thin enough to cut or pierce

something ⟨I'll need a well-*whetted* axe to split the wood.⟩ — see SHARP 1

whiff *n* an almost imperceptible sign of something ⟨Even a *whiff* of appreciation for everything I've done for her would have been nice.⟩ — see HINT 2

whiff *vb* to become aware of by means of the sense organs in the nose ⟨*whiffed* the pot of chili on the stove and announced that he was staying for dinner⟩ — see SMELL 1

while *conj* **1** at or during the time that ⟨Pay attention *while* I'm explaining how the new phone system works.⟩ — see WHEN 1

2 in spite of the fact that ⟨*While* this term paper is very well done, it's still late.⟩ — see ALTHOUGH

while *n* **1** an indefinite but usually short period of time ⟨We stayed at the fair for a *while* longer.⟩
synonyms bit, space, spell, stretch
related words lapse; season, span; day, epoch, era; beat, flash, instant, jiffy, minute, moment, nanosecond, New York minute, second, shake, split second, spurt, trice, twinkle, twinkling, wink; eon (*or* aeon), age, eternity, infinity, perpetuity; interim, interlude, intermission, interval

2 the active use of energy in producing a result ⟨It's not worth my *while* to fix it, so we'll get a new one.⟩ — see EFFORT

whilom *adj* having been such at some previous time ⟨pointedly ignored the *whilom* friends who had turned on her⟩ — see FORMER 1

whim *n* a sudden impulsive and apparently unmotivated idea or action ⟨On a *whim*, we stopped at the roadside stand to get ice cream.⟩
synonyms caprice, crank, fancy, freak, humor, notion, vagary, whimsy (*also* whimsey)
related words capriciousness, fancifulness, fantasy (*also* phantasy), freakishness, impetuosity, whimsicality; conceit; concept, conception, image, impression, picture, thought; brainstorm, inspiration
phrases bee in one's bonnet

whimper *n* an expression of dissatisfaction, pain, or resentment ⟨patiently posed for dozens of photographs without so much as a *whimper*⟩ — see COMPLAINT 1

whimper *vb* **1** to utter feeble plaintive cries ⟨The dog *whimpered* to be let in.⟩
synonyms mewl, pule
related words fuss, sniffle, snivel, snuffle, whine; bawl, blubber, cry, sob, weep; peep, squeak; yelp; mumble, murmur, mutter; groan, moan, sigh
near antonyms scream, screech, shriek, squeal; howl, squall, wail, yowl; call, squawk; bellow, roar

2 to express dissatisfaction, pain, or resentment usually tiresomely ⟨a good-hearted person, but given to *whimpering* about trifles⟩ — see COMPLAIN

whimsical *adj* prone to sudden illogical changes of mind, ideas, or actions ⟨It's hard to make plans with such a *whimsical* best friend.⟩
synonyms capricious, impulsive
related words impetuous, mercurial, moody, temperamental, volatile; crankish, eccentric, flaky, quirky; arbitrary, erratic, fickle, inconstant, irregular, shaky, willful (*or* wilful); impractical, quixotical, romantic, unrealistic, utopian, visionary
near antonyms equable; down-to-earth, earthy, hardboiled, hardheaded, levelheaded, matter-of-fact, practical, pragmatic (*also* pragmatical), reasonable, sensible, tough-minded; grounded, logical, no-nonsense, rational, sane, sober, sobersided, sound; fast, fixed, hard-and-fast, immutable, inflexible, invariable, unalterable, unbending, unchangeable, uncompromising, unrelenting, unyielding; changeless, constant, established, set, settled, stable, steadfast, steady, unchanging, unvarying

whimsicality *n* an inclination to sudden illogical changes of mind, ideas, or actions ⟨His *whimsicality* made him an unpredictable companion.⟩

synonyms caprice, capriciousness, impulsiveness

related words mercurialness, moodiness, unpredictability, willfulness; eccentricity, flakiness; arbitrariness, fickleness, inconstancy, irregularity, volatileness, volatility; changeability, flexibility, mutability, variability, variableness

near antonyms levelheadedness, practicality, reasonability, reasonableness; fastness, firmness, fixedness, immovability, immovableness, immutability, inflexibility, invariability; changelessness, constancy, stability, steadfastness, steadiness

whimsy *also* **whimsey** *n* a sudden impulsive and apparently unmotivated idea or action ⟨The pop singer's latest *whimsy* is that she has acting talent.⟩ — see WHIM

whine *n* an expression of dissatisfaction, pain, or resentment ⟨the perennial *whine* that movies aren't as good as they used to be⟩ — see COMPLAINT 1

whine *vb* to express dissatisfaction, pain, or resentment usually tiresomely ⟨For the whole of our vacation, the kids *whined* on and on about the weather.⟩ — see COMPLAIN

whiner *n* **1** a person who makes frequent complaints usually about little things ⟨Don't be a *whiner*—the hike's not that difficult.⟩ — see CRYBABY

2 an irritable and complaining person ⟨Among the hospital staff the patient in 504 had acquired a reputation for being a *whiner*.⟩ — see GROUCH 1

whinny *vb* to make the cry typical of a horse ⟨Pretending to be a horse, the father *whinnied* and reared as his young daughter sat on his back.⟩ — see NEIGH

whip *n* a long thin or flexible tool for striking ⟨The vacuum cleaner's cord rewound suddenly and hit him on the leg like a *whip*.⟩

synonyms flogger, lash, scourge, switch

related words birch, blacksnake, bullwhip, cat-o'-nine-tails, cowhide, crop, hickory, knout, quirt, rattan, rawhide, strap; bastinado (*or* bastinade), bat, billy, billy club, bludgeon, cane, club, cudgel, flail, nightstick, staff

whip *vb* **1** to strike repeatedly with something long and thin or flexible ⟨a jockey *whipping* his horse with a riding crop⟩

synonyms birch, cowhide, flagellate, flail, flog, hide, horsewhip, lash, leather, scourge, slash, switch, thrash, whale

related words knout, quirt, strap; cut; flick, touch up; cane, club, cudgel, fustigate; pistol-whip; bang, bop, box, bust, clap, clip, clobber, clout, crack, cuff, hit, knock, lam, paste, punch, slap, slug, smack, smite, sock, spank, swat, swipe, thwack, wallop, whack; bash, baste, bat, batter, beat, belabor, belt, bludgeon, buffet, bung, drub, hammer, lace, lambaste (*or* lambast), lather, lick, mangle, maul, paddle, pelt, pommel, pound, pummel, rough, slate, slog, thump, tromp

2 to defeat by a large margin ⟨We *whipped* them 13–0 in the last game.⟩

synonyms annihilate, bomb, bury, clobber, cream, drub, dust, flatten, paste, rout, skin, skunk, snow under, thrash, trim, trounce, wallop, wax [*slang*]

related words sweep, upset; beat, best, conquer, dispatch, hurdle, lick, master, overbear, overcome, overmatch, prevail (over), subdue, surmount, take, throw, triumph (over), win (against), worst; crush, knock off, overpower, overthrow, overwhelm, subjugate, upend, vanquish; ace (out), better, eclipse, exceed, outdistance, outdo, outfight, outshine, outstrip, overtop, surpass, top, transcend; edge (out); cap, excel, flourish, score, succeed; break, destroy, do in, finish, sink, slaughter

phrases beat the pants off, eat alive, run circles around

(*or* run rings around), wipe the floor with (*or* wipe the ground with)

3 to change the course or direction of (something) ⟨Any more complaints and I'm *whipping* this car around and heading back home.⟩ — see TURN 2

4 to move or cause to move with a striking motion ⟨Her hair *whipped* in the wind.⟩ — see FLAP

5 to strike repeatedly ⟨Rain *whipped* the pavement.⟩ — see BEAT 1

whip (up) *vb* to bring (something volatile or intense) into being ⟨*whipped up* protests against the proposed amendment to the state's constitution⟩ — see INCITE 1

whipper *n* one that defeats an enemy or opponent ⟨As the *whippers* of teams from much larger schools, our players have much to be proud of.⟩ — see VICTOR 1

whippersnapper *n* a person of no importance or influence ⟨Some young *whippersnapper* piped up with a pointless comment.⟩ — see NOBODY

whipping *n* failure to win a contest ⟨suffered a *whipping* that took them out of competition⟩ — see DEFEAT 1

whipping boy *n* a person or thing taking the blame for others ⟨used the government's economic policies as the *whipping boy* for every bad decision the company made⟩ — see SCAPEGOAT

whir *also* **whirr** *n* a monotonous sound like that of an insect in motion ⟨a *whir* coming from the refrigerator⟩ — see HUM

whir *also* **whirr** *vb* to fly, turn, or move rapidly with a fluttering or vibratory sound ⟨The hummingbird *whirred* as it hovered over a flower.⟩ ⟨Our tires *whirred* as we traveled over the rough road.⟩

synonyms buzz, drone, hum, whish, whiz (*or* whizz), zip, zoom

related words chirr; thrum; fizz, hiss, murmur, purr, rustle, sigh, sizzle, swish, whisper; coo, curr; wheeze, whistle, whoosh

whirl *n* **1** a rapid turning about on an axis or central point ⟨The *whirl* of the mechanical ride made him dizzy.⟩ — see SPIN 1

2 a state of mental uncertainty ⟨So many changes at once had them all in a *whirl*.⟩ — see CONFUSION 1

3 a state of noisy, confused activity ⟨lost an earring in the *whirl* of the party⟩ — see COMMOTION

4 an effort to do or accomplish something ⟨I'm pretty good at fixing things, so how about if I give it a *whirl*?⟩ — see ATTEMPT 1

whirl *vb* **1** to cause (as a liquid) to move about in a circle especially repeatedly ⟨*whirled* the chocolate syrup into the milk with a spoon⟩ — see STIR 1

2 to move (something) in a curved or circular path on or as if on an axis ⟨The figure skater *whirled* his partner with effortless grace.⟩ — see TURN 1

3 to move in circles around an axis or center ⟨The gambler held his breath as the roulette wheel *whirled*.⟩ — see SPIN 1

4 to proceed or move quickly ⟨cars *whirling* by on the highway⟩ — see HURRY 2

5 to be in a confused state as if from being twirled around ⟨My mind *whirled* from all of the excitement.⟩ — see SPIN 2

whirling *adj* having a feeling of being whirled about and in danger of falling down ⟨Still *whirling* from the amusement park ride, I needed to sit down.⟩ — see DIZZY 1

whirlpool *n* water moving rapidly in a circle with a hollow in the center ⟨In *The Odyssey*, Ulysses is trapped between the six-headed monster Scylla and Charybdis, a deadly *whirlpool* that threatens to suck in his ship.⟩

synonyms gulf, maelstrom, vortex

related words tourbillion (*or* tourbillon); eddy, swirl, whirl

whirlwind *adj* moving, proceeding, or acting with great speed ⟨After a *whirlwind* romance of only a few weeks, the couple decided to get married.⟩ — see FAST 1

whish *n* a sound similar to the speech sound \\ʃ\\ stretched out ⟨the *whish* of tires on wet pavement⟩ — see HISS 1

whish *vb* 1 to fly, turn, or move rapidly with a fluttering or vibratory sound ⟨Seemingly out of nowhere, a baseball *whished* past my head.⟩ — see WHIR

2 to make a sound like that of stretching out the speech sound \\ʃ\\ ⟨The match *whished* as it burst into flame.⟩ — see HISS

whisk *n* a quick jerky movement from side to side or up and down ⟨With a *whisk* of the broom, the dirt was gone.⟩ — see ¹WAG

whisk *vb* 1 to cause to move or proceed fast or faster ⟨The museum guide kept *whisking* us along, telling us there was much more we had to see.⟩ — see HURRY 1

2 to move or proceed smoothly and readily ⟨Now that the highway has been widened, traffic just *whisks* along.⟩ — see FLOW 2

3 to proceed or move quickly ⟨*whisked* through the crowd and delivered the urgent message⟩ — see HURRY 2

whisper *n* a rumor or report of a personal or sensational nature ⟨There were *whispers* that the star was secretly married.⟩ — see TALE 1

whisper *vb* to make (as a piece of information) the subject of common talk without any authority or confirmation of accuracy ⟨Assistants *whispered* that the two singers were having a secret relationship.⟩ — see RUMOR

whistling *adj* having a high musical pitch or range ⟨the *whistling* sound of missiles as they sped toward their targets⟩ — see SHRILL

whit *n* the smallest amount or part imaginable ⟨I care not a *whit* about what other people think.⟩ — see JOT

white *adj* lacking an addition of color ⟨dazzlingly *white* paint on the walls of the new house⟩ — see COLORLESS 1

whiten *vb* to make white or whiter by removing color ⟨Years of sunlight had almost completely *whitened* the flag.⟩

synonyms blanch, bleach, blench, decolorize, dull, fade, pale, wash out

related words brighten, lighten; dim, mat (*also* matte *or* matt); whitewash; frost, silver

near antonyms blacken; blotch, checker, dapple, daub, discolor, fleck, marble, mottle, pattern, polychrome, shade, speck, speckle, splotch, spot, streak, striate, stripe, tarnish, variegate; color, dye, paint, pigment, stain, tincture, tinge, tint; burnish, polish, shine

antonyms darken, deepen, embrown

whitewash *vb* 1 to dismiss as of little importance ⟨refused to *whitewash* the governor's chronic disregard for the truth⟩ — see EXCUSE 1

2 to make (something) seem less bad by offering excuses ⟨Don't try to *whitewash* your rudeness by claiming that you were having a bad day.⟩ — see PALLIATE 1

whither *adv* at, in, or to what place ⟨*Whither* are you going, my lady?⟩ — see WHERE

¹**whiz** *or* **whizz** *n* 1 a sound similar to the speech sound \\ʃ\\ stretched out ⟨the *whiz* of an arrow flying by at an uncomfortably close range⟩ — see HISS 1

2 a monotonous sound like that of an insect in motion ⟨the irritating *whiz* of a bee in the room⟩ — see HUM

²**whiz** *n* 1 a person with a high level of knowledge or skill in a field ⟨the computer *whiz* to whom we all go when we're having problems, which is fairly often⟩ — see EXPERT

2 a very smart person ⟨one of those *whizzes* who does very well in every subject⟩ — see GENIUS 1

whiz *or* **whizz** *vb* 1 to make a sound like that of stretching out the speech sound \\ʃ\\ ⟨Just hearing the bullets *whiz* as

they fly by their heads must be terrifying for soldiers.⟩ — see HISS

2 to fly, turn, or move rapidly with a fluttering or vibratory sound ⟨Many vehicles were *whizzing* past us at breakneck speeds.⟩ — see WHIR

whole *adj* 1 not divided or scattered among several areas of interest or concern ⟨You'll need to put your *whole* effort into this project.⟩

synonyms all, concentrated, entire, exclusive, focused (*also* focussed), undivided

related words absolute, complete, full, lump, teetotal, thorough, total, unadulterated, unalloyed, unqualified, utter; comprehensive, intact, integral, perfect, unbroken; entireness, wholeness

near antonyms deficient, fragmental, fragmentary, halfway, incomplete, partial

antonyms diffuse, divided, scattered

2 enjoying health and vigor ⟨*whole* and happy again after months of recuperation⟩ — see HEALTHY 1

3 not lacking any part or member that properly belongs to it ⟨The puzzle isn't quite *whole*, but close enough.⟩ — see COMPLETE 1

whole *n* a complete amount of something ⟨The landlord eventually refunded the *whole* of our deposit.⟩

synonyms aggregate, full, sum, summation, total, totality

related words gross; comprehensiveness, cumulativeness; bulk, mass; enchilada, schmear

phrases grand total, the whole bit, the whole kit and caboodle, the whole nine yards, the whole shebang

near antonyms net

wholehearted *adj* characterized by unqualified enthusiasm ⟨*wholehearted* praise for the novel by the leading critics⟩ — see HEARTY 1

wholeness *n* the condition of being sound in body ⟨young people who don't appreciate their *wholeness* and youthfulness while they have it⟩ — see HEALTH 1

whole number *n* a character used to represent a mathematical value ⟨Since percentages have been rounded off to *whole numbers*, the total will not be exactly equal to 100%.⟩ — see NUMBER 1

wholesome *adj* 1 enjoying health and vigor ⟨a *wholesome* young woman in the prime of her life⟩ — see HEALTHY 1

2 beneficial to the health of body or mind ⟨trying to eat a more *wholesome* diet⟩ — see HEALTHFUL

wholesomeness *n* the condition of being sound in body ⟨After the physical exam the doctor declared that I appeared to be enjoying the *wholesomeness* of a man half my age.⟩ — see HEALTH 1

wholly *adv* to a full extent or degree ⟨not *wholly* convinced by the evidence that the prosecutor presented⟩ — see FULLY 1

whoop *n* 1 a loud vocal expression of strong emotion ⟨let out a *whoop* of joy⟩ — see SHOUT

2 the smallest amount or part imaginable ⟨He acts so rudely that I doubt he gives a *whoop* about other people's feelings.⟩ — see JOT

whopper *n* 1 a statement known by its maker to be untrue and made in order to deceive ⟨told a *whopper* to get out of jury duty⟩ — see LIE

2 something that is unusually large and powerful ⟨a *whopper* of a fish that won first prize in the derby⟩ — see GIANT

whopping *adj* unusually large ⟨delivered a *whopping* 10-pound baby⟩ — see HUGE

why *interj* how surprising, doubtful, or unbelievable ⟨*Why*, what a strange thing to say!⟩ — see NO

why *n* something (as a belief) that serves as the basis for another thing ⟨asked the *whys* behind the surprising decision⟩ — see REASON 2

wicked *adj* **1** not conforming to a high moral standard; morally unacceptable ⟨a *wicked* deed⟩ — see BAD 2
2 not giving pleasure to the mind or senses ⟨rotting eggs create a truly *wicked* stench⟩ — see UNPLEASANT
3 causing or capable of causing harm ⟨a *wicked* storm⟩ — see HARMFUL

wicked *adv* to a great degree ⟨We were *wicked* excited when our team finally won the pennant after so many years.⟩ — see VERY 1

wickedly *adv* in a mean or spiteful manner ⟨She *wickedly* whispered amusing but snide comments about the other performers in the talent show.⟩ — see NASTILY

wickedness *n* the state or quality of being utterly evil ⟨The movie featured a villain of unadulterated *wickedness*.⟩ — see ENORMITY 1

wide *adj* **1** having a greater than usual measure across ⟨The river is so *wide* that building a bridge across it would be impractical.⟩
synonyms broad, fat, thick
related words expansive, extensive; commodious, roomy, spacious; outsize (*also* outsized), oversize (*or* oversized), sizable (*or* sizeable), substantial, tidy, voluminous
near antonyms fine, hairlike, reedlike; elongate (*or* elongated), needlelike; bottleneck, close, compressed, condensed, constricted, contracted, squeezed, tight, tightened; attenuated; small, smallish, undersized (*also* undersize)
antonyms hairline, narrow, skinny, slender, slim, thin
2 having considerable extent ⟨a *wide* and detailed knowledge of the issue⟩ — see EXTENSIVE

wide *adv* to a full extent or degree ⟨The door was *wide* open.⟩ — see FULLY 1

wide–awake *adj* **1** not sleeping or able to sleep ⟨was *wide-awake* with worry for most of the night⟩ — see WAKEFUL
2 paying close attention usually for the purpose of anticipating approaching danger or opportunity ⟨investors who were *wide-awake* bought the stock as soon as it was offered⟩ — see ALERT 1

wide–eyed *adj* **1** lacking in worldly wisdom or informed judgment ⟨a *wide-eyed* and trusting child⟩ — see NAIVE 1
2 readily taken advantage of ⟨the sort of phony UFO "artifacts" that *wide-eyed* tourists fall for⟩ — see EASY 2

widespread *adj* having considerable extent ⟨a *widespread* area of drought⟩ — see EXTENSIVE

width *n* an area over which activity, capacity, or influence extends ⟨surprised by the *width* of his power and influence in the oil business⟩ — see RANGE 2

wield *vb* to bring to bear especially forcefully or effectively ⟨*wields* considerable influence in her field⟩ — see EXERT

wife *n* a female partner in a marriage ⟨I was pleased to meet your *wife*⟩
synonyms lady, old lady
related words bride; better half, companion, consort, mate, partner, significant other, soul mate, spouse; dowager, matron; hausfrau, homemaker, housewife; widow

wiggle *vb* to make jerky or restless movements ⟨The baby *wiggled* in her sleep.⟩ — see FIDGET

wight *n* a member of the human race ⟨What unfortunate *wight* would be out and about in such foul weather?⟩ — see HUMAN

wild *adj* **1** living outdoors without taming or domestication by humans ⟨*Wild* animals can be shy or aggressive when confronted by humans.⟩
synonyms feral, savage, unbroken, undomesticated, untamed
related words uncontrolled, undocile, unsubdued, untrained; brutal, brute; barbarous, uncivilized

near antonyms controlled, docile, familiar, semidomesticated, subdued, submissive; halterbroken, housebroken, trained; civilized, semicivilized, socialized
antonyms broken, domestic, domesticated, gentled, tame, tamed
2 existing without human habitation or cultivation ⟨That land has been completely *wild* since the owners abandoned it.⟩
synonyms natural, uncultivated, untamed, virgin
related words uninhabited, unpeopled, unsettled; overgrown, spontaneous, untended; waste; undeveloped; desolate, forlorn, howling
near antonyms inhabited; developed; seminatural
antonyms cultivated, tamed
3 marked by turmoil or disturbance especially of natural elements ⟨a *wild* night, full of wind and rain⟩
synonyms rough, rugged, stormy, tempestuous, tumultuous, turbulent
related words blustering, blustery, violent; brutal, harsh, severe; roily, unquiet, unsettled; bleak, inclement, nasty, raw, squally
near antonyms calm, halcyon, peaceful, placid, quiet, serene, tranquil; bright, clear, clement, cloudless, fair, sunny, sunshiny, unclouded
4 conceived or made without regard for reason or reality ⟨some *wild* claim that he was abducted by aliens⟩ — see FANTASTIC 1
5 different from the ordinary in a way that causes curiosity or suspicion ⟨Comments on the website sometimes offer some *wild* ideas.⟩ — see ODD 2
6 marked by great and often stressful excitement or activity ⟨The holidays were especially *wild* around here this year.⟩ — see FURIOUS 1
7 not civilized ⟨ancient traces of a *wild* people who lived in mountain caves⟩ — see UNCIVILIZED
8 showing urgent desire or interest ⟨They're just *wild* to go on the ecotour through the Amazon rain forest.⟩ — see EAGER

wild *adv* in a confused and reckless manner ⟨As soon as the doors opened, early-morning bargain hunters ran *wild* through the store.⟩ — see HELTER-SKELTER 1

wild *n* that part of the physical world that is removed from human habitation ⟨Some animals aren't meant to live outside of the *wild*.⟩ — see NATURE 2

wilderness *n* that part of the physical world that is removed from human habitation ⟨released the wolf back into the *wilderness*⟩ — see NATURE 2

wildly *adv* **1** in a confused and reckless manner ⟨Upon being dismissed, the students dashed *wildly* off in all directions.⟩ — see HELTER-SKELTER 1
2 to a great degree ⟨Trespassers make the recluse *wildly* angry.⟩ — see VERY 1

wile *n* **1** a clever often underhanded means to achieve an end ⟨had to use all of her *wiles* to convince her guests to stay for dinner⟩ — see TRICK 1
2 the use of clever underhanded actions to achieve an end ⟨It took both *wile* and cajolery to talk him into it.⟩ — see TRICKERY

wile *vb* to attract or delight as if by magic ⟨Her stories could *wile* anyone.⟩ — see CHARM 1

wiliness *n* **1** skill in achieving one's ends through indirect, subtle, or underhanded means ⟨admired the negotiator's *wiliness* in closing the deal⟩ — see CUNNING 1
2 the inclination or practice of misleading others through lies or trickery ⟨the *wiliness* of the scammers who concocted the fraudulent scheme⟩ — see DECEIT 1

will *n* **1** the power to control one's actions, impulses, or emotions ⟨She kept her face still by sheer force of *will*.⟩
synonyms restraint, self-containment, self-control,

self-discipline, self-government, self-possession, self-restraint, willpower

related words self-abnegation, self-denial; moderateness, moderation, temperance, temperateness; determination, nerve; command, control, discipline, mastery; abnegation, abstinence, abstention, avoidance, eschewal, forbearance; soberness, sobriety; aplomb, assurance, composure, confidence, coolness, equanimity, poise, self-confidence; discretion

near antonyms gratification, indulgence, self-indulgence; overindulgence; demerit, failing, fault, feebleness, foible, frailty, shortcoming, vice, weakness; indiscipline, unrestraint

2 the act or power of making one's own choices or decisions ⟨You cannot force me to do anything against my own *will*.⟩ — see FREE WILL

will *vb* **1** to give by means of a will ⟨*willed* their house to their adult children⟩ — see LEAVE 2

2 to see fit ⟨Do as you *will*—I wash my hands of the whole affair.⟩ — see CHOOSE 2

willful *or* **wilful** *adj* **1** given to resisting authority or another's control ⟨a particularly *willful* horse that took weeks to break to saddle⟩ — see DISOBEDIENT

2 given to resisting control or discipline by others ⟨Finally the parents sought professional counseling for the *willful* child.⟩ — see UNCONTROLLABLE

3 having or showing a tendency to force one's will on others without any regard to fairness or necessity ⟨a *willful* disregard for the rights of others⟩ — see ARBITRARY 1

4 made, given, or done with full awareness of what one is doing ⟨a *willful* attempt to cheat her siblings out of their rightful inheritance⟩ — see INTENTIONAL

5 sticking to an opinion, purpose, or course of action in spite of reason, arguments, or persuasion ⟨the kind of *willful* person who can never bring himself to admit that he made a mistake⟩ — see OBSTINATE

willfully *adv* with full awareness of what one is doing ⟨*willfully* chose to risk pneumonia by jumping into a freezing lake on a dare⟩ — see INTENTIONALLY

willfulness *n* **1** a steadfast adherence to an opinion, purpose, or course of action in spite of reason, arguments, or persuasion ⟨Her unceasing *willfulness* eventually wore down her critics and opponents.⟩ — see OBSTINACY

2 refusal to obey ⟨The dog trainer was able to tame our dog's *willfulness*.⟩ — see DISOBEDIENCE

willies *pl n* a sense of panic or extreme nervousness ⟨Spiders give me the *willies* for some reason.⟩ — see JITTERS

willing *adj* **1** having a desire or inclination (as for a specified course of action) ⟨I'm a little confused, but perfectly *willing* to do as you ask.⟩

synonyms amenable, disposed, game, glad, inclined, minded, ready

related words predisposed, prone; accommodating, agreeable, compliant, cooperative, obedient, obliging, submissive; favorable, receptive; prepared, prompt, quick, responsive, swift; desirous, eager, enthusiastic, excited

near antonyms averse, loath (*also* loth *or* loathe), reluctant, reticent

antonyms disinclined, unamenable, unwilling

2 having or showing the ability to respond without delay or hesitation ⟨She's always lent a *willing* hand whenever a neighbor needed help.⟩ — see QUICK 1

3 done, made, or given with one's own free will ⟨a *willing* sacrifice of her limited free time for a good cause⟩ — see VOLUNTARY 1

willingly *adv* **1** by choice or preference ⟨I would not *willingly* eat liver, but sometimes I have no choice.⟩ — see RATHER 1

2 of one's own free will ⟨I *willingly* made the campaign contribution; no one pressured me into doing so.⟩ — see VOLUNTARILY

willingness *n* cheerful readiness to do something ⟨His unhesitating *willingness* to take on the tough assignments has earned him the status of the president's right-hand man.⟩ — see ALACRITY

williwaw *n* **1** a state of noisy, confused activity ⟨The surprise verdict of the jury created a wild *williwaw* as reporters rushed to file their stories.⟩ — see COMMOTION

2 a sudden brief rush of wind ⟨A *williwaw* rose up seemingly out of nowhere and wreaked havoc with our campsite.⟩ — see GUST 1

willowy *adj* able to bend easily without breaking ⟨The rattan's stems are split into *willowy* staves that are woven together to produce exquisite baskets.⟩

synonyms flexible, limber, lissome (*also* lissom), lithe, lithesome, pliable, pliant, supple

related words adaptable, ductile, elastic, fluid, kneadable, malleable, modifiable, plastic, variable, yielding; droopy, flaccid, floppy, limp; semiflexible

near antonyms inelastic, nonmalleable, unyielding; breakable, brittle, fragile

antonyms inflexible, rigid, stiff, stiffened

willpower *n* the power to control one's actions, impulses, or emotions ⟨trying to summon the *willpower* to resist eating a huge piece of cake⟩ — see WILL 1

willy–nilly *adv* without definite aim, direction, rule, or method ⟨They were in a hurry, so they just tossed everything into the room *willy-nilly*, leaving it to be all sorted out later.⟩ — see HIT OR MISS

wilt *vb* **1** to be limp from lack of water or vigor ⟨The plants *wilted* after I forgot to water them for three whole days.⟩ — see DROOP 1

2 to lose bodily strength or vigor ⟨She had *wilted* a bit after walking around the hot and humid city.⟩ — see WEAKEN 2

3 to lose liveliness, force, or freshness ⟨After six solid hours of painting, his energy was starting to *wilt*.⟩ — see WITHER 1

wily *adj* clever at attaining one's ends by indirect and often deceptive means ⟨A *wily* judge of character, she takes advantage of car buyers' insecurities to sell them a bigger machine than they really need.⟩ — see ARTFUL 1

wimp *n* **1** a person lacking in physical strength ⟨Just because you can't lift 300 pounds doesn't mean you're a *wimp*.⟩ — see WEAKLING 1

2 a person without strength of character ⟨What kind of *wimp* would just give in to peer pressure?⟩ — see WEAKLING 2

wimpy *adj* **1** lacking bodily strength ⟨A *wimpy* person is not the best choice for a job with a moving company.⟩ — see WEAK 1

2 lacking strength of will or character ⟨a *wimpy* effort to change the law that was doomed to failure⟩ — see WEAK 2

win *n* an instance of defeating an enemy or opponent ⟨a team with 12 *wins* and two losses⟩ — see VICTORY

win *vb* **1** to achieve victory (as in a contest) ⟨the kind of person who always has to *win*—even if the game is just for fun⟩

synonyms conquer, prevail, triumph

related words overcome, sweep; squeak, squeeze; contend, vie; succeed; breeze, romp

phrases carry the day; kick butt

near antonyms collapse, fail, flop, fold, wash out; flounder, struggle; decline, slip, slump, wane

antonyms lose

2 to receive as return for effort ⟨*win* a gold medal in swimming⟩ — see EARN 1

3 to obtain (as a goal) through effort ⟨*won* a substantial victory in the struggle for civil rights for all⟩ — see ACHIEVE 1

win (against) *vb* to achieve a victory over ⟨a child prodigy who has already *won against* a number of more experienced chess players⟩ — see BEAT 2

win (over) *vb* to cause (someone) to agree with a belief or course of action by using arguments or earnest requests ⟨A combination of solid reasoning and outright begging *won* my parents *over*, and I became an exchange student for a year.⟩ — see PERSUADE

wince *vb* to draw back in fear, pain, or disgust ⟨*winced* at the movie's graphic depiction of combat injuries⟩ — see FLINCH

¹wind *n* **1** noticeable movement of air in a particular direction ⟨There's a *wind* coming from underneath the front door.⟩

synonyms current, draft

related words blast, blow, flurry, gale, gust, headwind, squall, tailwind, tempest, tornado, windstorm; breath, breeze, puff, waft, zephyr

2 a prevailing or general movement or inclination ⟨The *winds* of public opinion are changing on this issue.⟩ — see TREND 1

3 language that is impressive-sounding but not meaningful or sincere ⟨The speech contained nothing of substance and was just a lot of *wind*.⟩ — see RHETORIC 1

²wind *n* something that curves or is curved ⟨There's one last easterly *wind* to the river before it empties into the sea.⟩ — see BEND 1

wind *vb* **1** to follow a circular or spiral course ⟨Flowering vines *wind* around the porch's graceful columns.⟩

synonyms coil, corkscrew, curl, entwine, spiral, twine, twist

related words arc, arch, bend, crook, curve, hook, sweep, swerve, turn, veer, wheel; swirl, whirl; circle, encircle, loop; interlace, intertwine, lace; bow, bulge; meander, weave, zigzag

near antonyms straighten

2 to introduce in a gradual, secret, or clever way ⟨Self-interest *winds* itself into everything that he does—even his alleged favors for other people.⟩ — see INSINUATE 1

windbag *n* a person who talks constantly ⟨a *windbag* who used up his own time as well as the time allotted to the other speakers⟩ — see CHATTERBOX

windfall *n* something that provides happiness or does good for a person or thing ⟨Hitting the lottery jackpot was an incredible *windfall* for the recently laid-off worker.⟩ — see BLESSING 2

windiness *n* the use of too many words to express an idea ⟨He's a brilliant thinker, but his *windiness* tends to overwhelm his ideas.⟩ — see VERBIAGE 1

winding *adj* **1** marked by a long series of irregular curves ⟨a long and *winding* path through the woods⟩ — see CROOKED 1

2 turning around an axis like the thread of a screw ⟨a *winding* staircase leads to the top of the lighthouse⟩ — see SPIRAL

windjammer *n* a boat equipped with one or more sails ⟨With no set course to follow, a *windjammer* sails wherever the wind and the captain's whim takes it.⟩ — see SAILBOAT

windup *n* the last part of a process or action ⟨Wait until the *windup* of your sales pitch before giving up any information about the product's price point.⟩ — see FINALE

wind up *vb* **1** to bring (an event) to a natural or appropriate stopping point ⟨Try to *wind up* the performance, as we're almost out of time.⟩ — see CLOSE 3

2 to come to an end ⟨Her speeches usually *wind up* with one last joke.⟩ — see CEASE 1

¹windy *adj* **1** marked by strong wind or more wind than usual ⟨One particularly *windy* day should shake the last of the autumn leaves from the trees.⟩

synonyms blowy, blustery, breezy, gusty, squally

related words drafty; stormy, tempestuous

near antonyms breathless, calm, motionless, still

2 marked by the use of impressive-sounding but mostly meaningless words and phrases ⟨gave his usual *windy* speech about working for the common people⟩ — see RHETORICAL 1

3 using or containing more words than necessary to express an idea ⟨a *windy* saleswoman who told us a lot more than we wanted to know about the car⟩ — see WORDY 1

²windy *adj* marked by a long series of irregular curves ⟨a *windy* little creek⟩ — see CROOKED 1

wing *n* a group of people acting together within a larger group ⟨the conservative *wing* of the party⟩ — see FACTION

wing *vb* to move through the air with or as if with outstretched wings ⟨watched the flocks of birds as they *winged* southward for the winter⟩ — see FLY 1

wink *n* **1** a short sleep ⟨I wasn't able to catch a *wink* during the entire flight.⟩ — see ¹NAP

2 a very small space of time ⟨I turned to look away, and in a *wink* he was gone.⟩ — see INSTANT

wink *vb* **1** to rapidly open and close one's eyes ⟨She *winked* several times to get the dust and grit out of her eyes.⟩

synonyms blink

related words bat, flutter; squint

2 to shine with light at regular intervals ⟨a lighthouse was *winking* in the distance⟩ — see BLINK 1

3 to shoot forth bursts of light ⟨fireflies *winking* in the darkness beyond our campfire⟩ — see FLASH 1

4 to secretly sympathize with or pretend ignorance of something improper or unlawful ⟨The whole sporting world seems to *wink* as untold sums are bet on the outcome of the Super Bowl.⟩ — see CONNIVE 1

wink (at) *vb* to dismiss as of little importance ⟨The refs seemed to just *wink at* some illegal plays.⟩ — see EXCUSE 1

winner *n* **1** a person or thing that is successful ⟨The movie was panned by the critics but has been a *winner* at the box office.⟩ — see HIT 1

2 one that defeats an enemy or opponent ⟨The *winner* of any given war is usually the one who gets to write the history of that war.⟩ — see VICTOR 1

3 the person who comes in first in a competition ⟨The other finalists graciously congratulated the *winner*.⟩ — see CHAMPION 1

winning *adj* **1** having qualities that tend to make one loved ⟨a particularly *winning* child⟩ — see LOVABLE

2 likely or intended to win one's affection ⟨flashed a *winning* smile that soon had fans swooning⟩ — see INGRATIATING

winsome *adj* **1** having or showing a good mood or disposition ⟨He was a bright, *winsome* young man who could draw a smile out of anyone.⟩ — see CHEERFUL 1

2 likely or intended to win one's affection ⟨In her new role, the actress again displays the *winsome* charm that has made her an audience favorite.⟩ — see INGRATIATING

3 having qualities that tend to make one loved ⟨an actress who specialized in playing *winsome* ingenues in romantic comedies⟩ — see LOVABLE

wintry *also* **wintery** *adj* **1** having a low or subnormal temperature ⟨a *wintry* and snowy day⟩ — see COLD 1

2 lacking in friendliness or warmth of feeling ⟨The doorman gave the uninvited visitors a *wintry* smile and escorted them out.⟩ — see COLD 2

wipe out *vb* to destroy all traces of ⟨A bad financial decision nearly *wiped out* their entire life savings.⟩ — see ANNIHILATE 1

wire *n* a length of braided, flexible material that is used for tying or connecting things ⟨a telephone *wire*⟩ — see CORD 1

wisdom *n* **1** the ability to understand inner qualities or relationships ⟨With age and experience comes *wisdom*—hopefully.⟩ ⟨Neither book learning nor simple intelligence should be confused with *wisdom*.⟩
synonyms discernment, insight, perception, perceptiveness, sagaciousness, sagacity, sageness, sapience
related words acuity, acumen, astuteness, keenness, penetration, perspicacity, sensitivity, understanding; appreciation, apprehension, comprehension, grasp; brain(s), braininess, brightness, brilliance, canniness, cleverness, gray matter, intellect, intelligence, judgment (*or* judgement), mentality, power, reason, sense, smartness, wit; discrimination, foresight, foresightedness, prudence, sanity; logic, rationality
near antonyms density, dullness (*also* dulness), obtuseness; brainlessness, folly, foolishness, idiocy, imbecility, mindlessness, silliness, simpleness, stupidity, witlessness; illogic, irrationality, unreasonableness, unsoundness; preposterousness, senselessness, silliness, zaniness
2 a body of facts learned by study or experience ⟨The orientation meetings will provide the company's old hands with an opportunity to pass on their *wisdom* to the new employees.⟩ — see KNOWLEDGE 1
3 the ability to make intelligent decisions especially in everyday matters ⟨had overstayed her welcome and lacked the *wisdom* to know it⟩ — see COMMON SENSE

wise *adj* **1** having or showing deep understanding and intelligent application of knowledge ⟨a respected and *wise* old judge famous for her sensible rulings⟩
synonyms discerning, insightful, perceptive, prudent, sagacious, sage, sapient
related words acute, penetrating, percipient, perspicacious; experienced; discriminating, discriminative; brainy, bright, brilliant, clever, intelligent, keen, nimble, quick, quick-witted, smart; cerebral, erudite, knowledgeable, learned, literate, scholarly; astute, clearheaded, piercing, sharp, shrewd; contemplative, reflective, thoughtful
near antonyms dense, dull, obtuse, purblind, woodenheaded; brainless, dumb, feebleminded, foolish, idiotic (*also* idiotical), imbecile (*or* imbecilic), knuckleheaded, moronic, silly, simple, slow, slow-witted, stupid, thoughtless, unintelligent, witless; undiscriminating
antonyms unwise
2 having inside information ⟨They fooled everyone else, but I'd heard them talking and was *wise* to their true intentions.⟩
synonyms hip, knowing
related words alerted, aware, clued (in), forewarned, informed, prepared, ready, warned; observant, observing, sharp, sharp-eyed; alert, attentive, open-eyed, vigilant, watchful; plugged-in, with-it
phrases in the know
near antonyms oblivious, unaware, unconscious, uninformed, unwitting; heedless, unmindful; unprepared, unready, unwary
antonyms unknowing
3 suitable for bringing about a desired result under the circumstances ⟨Selling the stock just before it plunged in value was a *wise* move on your part.⟩ — see EXPEDIENT
4 making light of something usually regarded as serious or sacred ⟨You wouldn't be so *wise* if you were in my situation.⟩ — see FLIPPANT

5 displaying or marked by rude boldness ⟨She is competent, but she's always getting *wise* with the boss.⟩ — see NERVY 1

wise (up) *vb* **1** to give information to ⟨*wised* him *up* to some of the more effective tricks of salesmanship⟩ — see ENLIGHTEN 1
2 to come to an awareness of ⟨She eventually *wised up* to the fact that he was taking advantage of her.⟩ — see DISCOVER 1

wiseacre *n* a person who likes to show off in a clever but annoying way ⟨a loudmouthed *wiseacre* who thinks he is more amusing than he really is⟩ — see SMART ALECK

wisecrack *n* something said or done to cause laughter ⟨A whispered *wisecrack* doubled them over in laughter.⟩ — see JOKE 1

wisecrack *vb* to make jokes ⟨*wisecracked* to hide his nervousness during the auditions⟩ — see JOKE 1

wise guy *n* a person who likes to show off in a clever but annoying way ⟨If you weren't such a *wise guy* all the time, people might be more interested in hearing what you have to say.⟩ — see SMART ALECK

wish *vb* **1** to offer (something fake, useless, or inferior) as genuine, useful, or valuable ⟨Despite my protestations, the dreaded position of club secretary was *wished* on me.⟩ — see FOIST
2 to see fit ⟨You're free to sit wherever you *wish*.⟩ — see CHOOSE 2

wish (for) *vb* to have an earnest wish to own or enjoy ⟨Having her own home was something she had *wished for* since she was a child.⟩ — see DESIRE 1

wishy-washy *adj* **1** lacking in qualities that make for spirit and character ⟨This story is too *wishy-washy*; you need to add some verve to it.⟩
synonyms banal, flat, insipid, watery
related words unexciting, uninspiring, unrewarding; bland, boring, drab, dreary, dry, dull, heavy, humdrum, jading, leaden, lifeless, monotonous, pedestrian, ponderous, tedious, tiresome, tiring, uninteresting, vapid, wearisome, weary, wearying; inane; innocuous, inoffensive; mild, soft, subdued, tame, weak; common, commonplace, ordinary, stale, unexceptional
near antonyms piquant, poignant, pungent, racy, spicy; meaty, substantial; entertaining, exciting, galvanizing, inspiring, invigorating, thrilling
2 lacking strength of will or character ⟨In a time of crisis the nation can ill afford *wishy-washy* leaders.⟩ — see WEAK 2

wit *n* **1** a person (as a writer) noted for or specializing in humor ⟨The pundits and political *wits* will get a lot of mileage out of the senator's latest gaffe.⟩ — see HUMORIST
2 the ability to make intelligent decisions especially in everyday matters ⟨He doesn't even have the *wit* to know when to come in out of the rain.⟩ — see COMMON SENSE
3 *usually* **wits** *pl* the normal or healthy condition of the mental abilities ⟨scared out of her *wits*⟩ — see MIND 2
4 exceptional discernment and judgment especially in practical matters ⟨lacked the *wit* to see that the war was unwinnable⟩ — see ACUMEN

witch *n* **1** a woman believed to have often harmful supernatural powers ⟨The 17th-century house had once belonged to a woman who was hanged as a *witch*.⟩
synonyms enchantress, hag, hex, sorceress
related words charmer, conjurer (*or* conjuror), enchanter, necromancer; magician, sorcerer, warlock, wizard
2 a person skilled in using supernatural forces ⟨freakish storms that were once thought to be the work of *witches*⟩ — see MAGICIAN 1

witchcraft *n* the power to control natural forces through supernatural means ⟨The villagers blamed their problems on *witchcraft*.⟩ — see MAGIC 1

witchery *n* **1** the power of irresistible attraction ⟨The many interesting alleys and byways are frequently cited as the source of the historic town's *witchery* with travelers.⟩ — see CHARM 2

2 the power to control natural forces through supernatural means ⟨a tale of horror replete with eerie hauntings and evil *witchery*⟩ — see MAGIC 1

with *prep* **1** as the result of ⟨The young man was overcome *with* gratitude.⟩ — see BECAUSE OF

2 using the means or agency of ⟨was able to finish the project *with* her help⟩ — see BY 2

3 without being prevented by ⟨*With* all his tough talk, he is still a very gentle person.⟩ — see DESPITE

withal *adv* **1** in addition to what has been said ⟨a successful businessman and *withal* a major contributor to local charities⟩ — see MORE 1

2 in spite of that ⟨a rough singing voice that was *withal* rather compelling⟩ — see HOWEVER

withdraw *vb* **1** to move back or away (as from something difficult, dangerous, or disagreeable) ⟨The army was forced to *withdraw* from the line of battle.⟩ — see RETREAT 1

2 to solemnly or formally reject or go back on (as something formerly adhered to) ⟨*withdrew* the offer of surrender upon hearing the terms⟩ — see ABJURE 1

3 to take away from a place or position ⟨*withdrew* her hand from the table⟩ — see REMOVE 2

withdrawal *n* an act of moving away especially from something difficult, dangerous, or disagreeable ⟨The high command ordered the army's *withdrawal* from the city.⟩ — see RETREAT 1

withdrawn *adj* not comfortable around people ⟨a therapist who is especially good with *withdrawn* children⟩ — see SHY 2

wither *vb* **1** to lose liveliness, force, or freshness ⟨Shortly after the moon landing, interest in the space program *withered*.⟩ ⟨The old man seemed to *wither* suddenly upon turning 80.⟩

synonyms dry, wilt

related words mummify, shrivel, wizen; decline, fade, wane; decrease, diminish, lessen

near antonyms freshen, revive; bloom, flourish, prosper, thrive; develop, grow, increase, wax; crest, peak, surge

2 to lose bodily strength or vigor ⟨If you don't water the plant, it will just *wither* and die.⟩ — see WEAKEN 2

withhold *vb* **1** to be unwilling to grant ⟨must *withhold* official approval until all the proper forms have been submitted⟩ — see DENY 2

2 to continue to have in one's possession or power ⟨*withhold* some money for your own expenses⟩ — see KEEP 2

within *n* an interior or internal part ⟨Structural decay had started from *within*.⟩ — see INSIDE 1

without *prep* **1** not having ⟨spent two days *without* food⟩

synonyms absent, minus, sans, wanting

2 out of the reach or sphere of ⟨a goal *without* our grasp⟩ — see BEYOND 2

withstand *vb* to refuse to give in to ⟨trying to *withstand* the temptation to use the beautiful weather as an excuse to skip practice⟩ — see RESIST

witless *adj* **1** not having or showing an ability to absorb ideas readily ⟨a dog so *witless* that it is barely trainable⟩ — see STUPID 1

2 showing or marked by a lack of good sense or judgment ⟨a *witless* decision to relocate to the other side of the country without even the prospect of a job⟩ — see FOOLISH 1

witlessness *n* **1** lack of good sense or judgment ⟨His *witlessness* is the stuff of family legend.⟩ — see FOOLISHNESS 1

2 the quality or state of lacking intelligence or quickness of mind ⟨For sheer *witlessness* the movie's dialogue deserves some sort of award.⟩ — see STUPIDITY 1

witness *n* something presented in support of the truth or accuracy of a claim ⟨The ruins are a compelling *witness* of the ancient civilization's cultural and aesthetic achievements.⟩ — see PROOF

witness *vb* **1** to declare (something) to be true or genuine ⟨a notary public *witnessing* wills and other important documents⟩ — see CERTIFY 1

2 to make note of (something) through the use of one's eyes ⟨*witnessed* the crime⟩ — see SEE 1

3 to make a solemn declaration under oath for the purpose of establishing a fact ⟨I *witnessed* to the fact that I had seen them together that night.⟩ — see TESTIFY

4 to come to a knowledge of (something) by living through it ⟨War changes anyone who has ever *witnessed* it firsthand.⟩ — see EXPERIENCE

witticism *n* something said or done to cause laughter ⟨a drama critic who is best remembered for his biting *witticisms*⟩ — see JOKE 1

witting *adj* **1** having specified facts or feelings actively impressed on the mind ⟨She was a *witting* partner; he had told her about the risk involved.⟩ — see CONSCIOUS 1

2 made, given, or done with full awareness of what one is doing ⟨Your *witting* assistance in helping the robber escape makes you an accessory after the fact.⟩ — see INTENTIONAL

wittingly *adv* with full awareness of what one is doing ⟨Whether he hurt her feelings *wittingly* or unwittingly isn't important; he should still apologize.⟩ — see INTENTIONALLY

witty *adj* given to or marked by mature intelligent humor ⟨a *witty* and sardonic blogger who never fails to amuse her legion of readers⟩ ⟨He's well-known for his *witty* retorts.⟩

synonyms clever, facetious, humorous, jocular, smart

related words cerebral, highbrow, intellectual; bantering, frivolous, jesting, joking, joshing, teasing; antic, comic, comical, droll, farcical, funny, hysterical, laughable, ludicrous, ridiculous, riotous, risible, rollicking, screaming, uproarious; amusing, diverting, entertaining; mischievous, playful, prankish; jocose, jocund, jolly, jovial, laughing, merry, mirthful, sunny; scintillating, sparkling; flip, flippant, pert, smart-alecky, waggish; whimsical

near antonyms brainless, lowbrow, stupid, witless; corny, hackney, hackneyed, lame; humorless, unamusing, uncomic, unfunny; earnest, grave, serious, serious-minded, sober, solemn, somber (*or* sombre); doleful, dolorous, lachrymose, plaintive, sorry, tearful, woeful

wizard *n* **1** a person skilled in using supernatural forces ⟨The old *wizard* who introduces the young naïf to a life of adventure is one of the most overworked tropes in fantasy literature.⟩ — see MAGICIAN 1

2 a person with a high level of knowledge or skill in a field ⟨a *wizard* at fixing cars⟩ — see EXPERT

3 a very smart person ⟨a *wizard* who never studied for tests⟩ — see GENIUS 1

wizardry *n* the power to control natural forces through supernatural means ⟨a movie about *wizardry* and bizarre creatures⟩ — see MAGIC 1

wobble *also* **wabble** *vb* **1** to make a series of small irregular or violent movements ⟨The patient's hand *wobbles* so much that he can scarcely hold a glass of water.⟩ — see SHAKE 1

2 to make a series of unsteady side-to-side motions ⟨The table *wobbled* whenever I leaned on it.⟩ — see ROCK 1

3 to show uncertainty about the right course of action ⟨We cannot afford to have the governor *wobble* at this critical time.⟩ — see HESITATE

4 to swing unsteadily back and forth or from side to side ⟨The vase *wobbled* for a moment, and fell off the shelf.⟩ — see TEETER 1

wobbling *also* **wabbling** *adj* marked by or given to small uncontrollable bodily movements ⟨the old woman's *wobbling* gait⟩ — see SHAKY 1

wobbling *also* **wabbling** *n* a state or an instance of temporary inaction because of uncertainty about the right course of action ⟨the mayor's apparent *wobbling* on the issue of increased property taxes⟩ — see HESITATION

wobbly *also* **wabbly** *adj* marked by or given to small uncontrollable bodily movements ⟨all *wobbly* from the chills associated with the flu⟩ — see SHAKY 1

woe *n* **1** a state of great suffering of body or mind ⟨a tale of misery and *woe*⟩ — see DISTRESS 1

2 deep sadness especially for the loss of someone or something loved ⟨the incessant *woe* that she has felt since she lost her friend⟩ — see SORROW

woebegone *adj* feeling unhappiness ⟨the most *woebegone* people that I had ever seen in my life⟩ — see SAD 1

woeful *adj* **1** expressing or suggesting mourning ⟨the *woeful* expressions of the players after the humiliating loss⟩ — see MOURNFUL 1

2 feeling unhappiness ⟨I never saw a more *woeful*-looking bunch than those campers sitting there in the drenching rain.⟩ — see SAD 1

3 of a kind to cause great distress ⟨The restaurant patron made the *woeful* discovery that he had left his wallet at home.⟩ — see REGRETTABLE

woefully *adv* with feelings of bitterness or grief ⟨*woefully* recounted the many injustices that the family had endured at the hands of the dictator⟩ — see HARD 2

wolf *vb* to swallow or eat greedily ⟨The way you *wolfed* your food it's no wonder you have a stomachache.⟩ — see GOBBLE

woman *n* **1** an adult female human being ⟨the first *woman* to become governor of the state⟩
synonyms female, lady
related words dame, gentlewoman; madame, senora (*or* señora); beauty, belle, damsel, gal, girl, ingenue (*or* ingénue), lass, lassie, mademoiselle, maid, maiden, miss, senorita (*or* señorita)

2 a female romantic companion ⟨wanted to give his *woman* all the finer things in life⟩ — see GIRLFRIEND

womanish *adj* **1** of or relating to a man who has or displays qualities traditionally considered more suitable for women ⟨had *womanish* hands⟩ — see EFFEMINATE

2 of, relating to, or marked by qualities traditionally associated with women ⟨He admired her *womanish* gentleness, especially when she cared for her animals.⟩ — see FEMININE

womanlike *adj* of, relating to, or marked by qualities traditionally associated with women ⟨The photograph shows the silhouette of a *womanlike* figure framed against the backlight from an open farmhouse door.⟩ — see FEMININE

womanly *adj* of, relating to, or marked by qualities traditionally associated with women ⟨The novelist displays a *womanly* sensitivity when it comes to the characters' psyches.⟩ — see FEMININE

wonder *n* **1** something extraordinary or surprising ⟨The cunningly crafted miniature of our house is a *wonder*, perfect in every detail.⟩
synonyms caution, flash, marvel, miracle, phenomenon, portent, prodigy, sensation, splendor

related words curiosity, sight; beauty, corker, crackerjack (*also* crackajack), dandy, jim-dandy, knockout; apparition, appearance

2 the rapt attention and deep emotion caused by the sight of something extraordinary ⟨When we first saw the pyramids of Egypt, we gazed with openmouthed *wonder*.⟩
synonyms admiration, amazement, astonishment, awe, wonderment

related words dread; fear; respect, reverence, veneration; curiosity, interest; shock, surprise; disbelief, incredulity; beguilement, bewitchment, captivation, enchantment, fascination; animation, enlightenment, enlivenment, excitement, invigoration, stimulation; absorption, engagement, engrossment, enthrallment, immersion, involvement

near antonyms apathy, indifference, unconcern; boredom, doldrums, ennui, listlessness, restlessness, tedium, tiredness, weariness, weltschmerz; cheerlessness, dispiritedness, joylessness, melancholy

wonderful *adj* **1** causing wonder or astonishment ⟨The mountaintop city of Machu Picchu is unquestionably a *wonderful* sight to behold.⟩ — see MARVELOUS 1

2 of the very best kind ⟨That bakery makes *wonderful* cannoli.⟩ — see EXCELLENT

wondering *adj* filled with amazement or wonder ⟨With *wondering* expressions on our faces, we watched the acrobats perform their daring feats.⟩ — see OPENMOUTHED

wonderment *n* the rapt attention and deep emotion caused by the sight of something extraordinary ⟨gazed in *wonderment* at the holiday decorations⟩ — see WONDER 2

wondrous *adj* causing wonder or astonishment ⟨What a *wondrous* discovery fire must have been.⟩ — see MARVELOUS 1

wont *adj* being in the habit or custom ⟨She paced about the room, as she is *wont* to do whenever she is agitated.⟩ — see ACCUSTOMED

wont *n* a usual manner of behaving or doing ⟨He got up early, as is his *wont*.⟩ — see HABIT 1

woo *vb* to act so as to make (something) more likely ⟨His attempts to *woo* approval from working-class voters has not met with much success.⟩ — see COURT 1

wood *n* **1** tree logs as prepared for human use ⟨a huge load of *wood* outside the furniture maker's factory⟩
synonyms lumber, timber
related words beam, brace, pile, post, ridgepole, sill, splint, stake, stave, stick; bar, billet, block; cordwood, firewood

2 *often* **woods** *pl* a dense growth of trees and shrubs covering a large area ⟨Deer and mountain lions live in those *woods*.⟩ — see FOREST

wooden *adj* lacking social grace and assurance ⟨an eminent scientist who was *wooden* in front of television cameras⟩ — see AWKWARD 1

woodland *n* a dense growth of trees and shrubs covering a large area ⟨The house is perched atop a hill amid a stretch of dense *woodland*.⟩ — see FOREST

wooer *n* a man who courts a woman usually with the goal of marrying her ⟨Of all her *wooers*, he was the only one who was liked by all members of her family.⟩ — see SUITOR 1

wool *n* the hairy covering of a mammal especially when fine, soft, and thick ⟨The *wool* from cashmere goats is considered by many to be the finest available.⟩ — see FUR 1

woolgathering *n* the state of being lost in thought ⟨My *woolgathering* was abruptly interrupted by a question from the flight attendant.⟩ — see REVERIE

woolly *also* **wooly** *adj* **1** made of or resembling hair ⟨The dog's *woolly* coat will require a lot of grooming.⟩ — see HAIRY 2

2 covered with or as if with hair ⟨kept a *woolly* blanket on the bed⟩ — see HAIRY 1

word *n* **1** a pronounceable series of letters having a distinct meaning especially in a particular field ⟨My doctor used all of these medical *words* that I didn't understand.⟩
synonyms expression, term
related words linguistic form, monosyllable, morpheme, speech form; polysyllable; collocation, idiom, locution, phrase; archaism, coinage, colloquialism, euphemism, loanword, modernism, neologism, vernacularism
2 something that is said ⟨I agreed with every *word* she said.⟩
synonyms statement, utterance
related words communication, message; announcement, declamation, declaration, manifesto, proclamation, pronouncement; verbalization, vocalization
3 a report of recent events or facts not previously known ⟨What's the latest *word* on the stock market?⟩ — see NEWS
4 a person's solemn declaration that he or she will do or not do something ⟨I give you my *word* that I won't forget.⟩ — see PROMISE
5 a statement of what to do that must be obeyed by those concerned ⟨The troops waited for their commanding officer to give the *word*.⟩ — see COMMAND 1
6 information or opinion that is widely disseminated without any authority or confirmation of accuracy ⟨Don't tell anyone I told you about the layoffs, but that's the *word* right now.⟩ — see RUMOR
7 a word or phrase that must be spoken by a person in order to pass a guard ⟨"What's the *word*?" demanded the sentry.⟩ — see PASSWORD
8 an often stated observation regarding something from common experience ⟨Are there truer *words* than "never look a gift horse in the mouth"?⟩ — see SAYING

word *vb* to convey in appropriate or telling terms ⟨tried to *word* the declaration exactly right⟩ — see PHRASE

wordbook *n* a reference book giving information about the meanings, pronunciations, uses, and origins of words listed in alphabetical order ⟨a *wordbook* of nautical slang⟩ — see DICTIONARY

word for word *adv* in the same words ⟨You don't have to record the professor's comments *word for word* in your notes.⟩ — see VERBATIM

wordiness *n* the use of too many words to express an idea ⟨*Wordiness* will only detract from what you are trying to say.⟩ — see VERBIAGE 1

wording *n* **1** the way in which something is put into words ⟨It's important to get the *wording* of this law precisely correct.⟩
synonyms diction, language, phraseology, phrasing, verbiage
related words expression, formulation, locution; enunciation, phrase, speech, style, utterance, voice
2 an act, process, or means of putting something into words ⟨The *wording* of the pollster's questions seemed to reflect a built-in bias.⟩ — see EXPRESSION 1

wordless *adj* **1** deliberately refraining from speech ⟨He stood *wordless* before his accusers.⟩ — see SILENT 1
2 understood although not put into words ⟨a *wordless* fondness for each other⟩ — see IMPLICIT 1

wordy *adj* **1** using or containing more words than necessary to express an idea ⟨Her writing style is far too *wordy* for my tastes.⟩
synonyms circuitous, circumlocutory, diffuse, garrulous, long-winded, prolix, rambling, verbose, windy
related words chatty, communicative, conversational, gabby, loquacious, talkative, talky, voluble; periphrastic; redundant, repetitious, tautological, tautologous; embel-

lished, embroidered; bombastic, gaseous, gassy, grandiloquent, highfalutin (*also* hifalutin)
near antonyms brief, short; aphoristic, epigrammatic; compendious, summary; abbreviated, abridged, condensed, shortened; abrupt, blunt, brusque (*also* brusk), curt, laconic, snippy
antonyms compact, concise, crisp, pithy, succinct, terse
2 of or relating to words or language ⟨The neighborhood dispute escalated into a *wordy* war conducted through angry letters to the editor in the local paper.⟩ — see VERBAL 1

work *n* **1** a literary, musical, or artistic production ⟨Unfortunately, many of her *works* are now out of print.⟩ — see COMPOSITION 1
2 something produced by physical or intellectual effort ⟨The new app is the *work* of a pair of young but highly gifted programmers.⟩ — see PRODUCT 1
3 the action for which a person or thing is specially fitted or used or for which a thing exists ⟨The *work* of a movie director is to tell a story through a series of striking images.⟩ — see ROLE
4 the active use of energy in producing a result ⟨put a lot of *work* into the project⟩ — see EFFORT
5 the activity by which one regularly makes a living ⟨What line of *work* are you in?⟩ — see OCCUPATION
6 works *pl* a building or set of buildings for the manufacturing of goods ⟨a glass *works* where high quality glassware is made⟩ — see FACTORY

work *vb* **1** to be the cause of (a situation, action, or state of mind) ⟨This new drug can really *work* wonders.⟩ — see EFFECT
2 to find an answer for through reasoning ⟨finally figured out how to *work* the math problem⟩ — see SOLVE
3 to have a certain purpose ⟨The human kidneys *work* as a filtering system for the blood.⟩ — see FUNCTION
4 to produce a desired effect ⟨This headache remedy takes half an hour to *work*.⟩ — see ACT 2
5 to set or keep in motion ⟨This pump is *worked* by hand.⟩ — see MOVE 2
6 to control the mechanical operation of ⟨Show me how to *work* the machine.⟩ — see OPERATE 1
7 to devote serious and sustained effort ⟨The organization has *worked* for years to raise people's awareness of human rights issues.⟩ — see LABOR
8 to take unfair advantage of ⟨a man not afraid to *work* his family name in order to get ahead⟩ — see EXPLOIT 1

work (for) *vb* to be an employee for ⟨*worked for* a rich and powerful family⟩ — see SERVE 1

workable *adj* **1** capable of being done or carried out ⟨a *workable* plan for attracting a minor league team to the city⟩ — see POSSIBLE 1
2 capable of being put to use or account ⟨a *workable* solution to the state's growing financial woes⟩ — see PRACTICAL 1

workaday *adj* **1** being of the type that is encountered in the normal course of events ⟨just a *workaday* guy living a *workaday* life⟩ — see ORDINARY 1
2 having to do with the practical details of regular life ⟨wished that they could afford help so as not to be bothered with such *workaday* matters as housework⟩ — see MUNDANE 1
3 not designed to be worn only on special occasions ⟨a *workaday* outfit that I could afford to get dirty⟩ — see CASUAL 1

worker *n* **1** a person who does very hard or dull work ⟨a champion of the rights of the farm *workers* who pick the nation's fruits and vegetables⟩ — see DRUDGE
2 one who works for another for wages or a salary ⟨a factory owner who is known for fair and generous treatment of the *workers*⟩ — see EMPLOYEE

workforce *n* a body of persons at work or available for work ⟨The office's entire *workforce* is devoted to a single project right now.⟩ — see FORCE 1

working *adj* **1** being in effective operation ⟨the only *working* coal mine in the area⟩ — see ACTIVE 1

2 capable of being put to use or account ⟨As a would-be independent filmmaker, you'll need a *working* knowledge of motion picture photography and editing.⟩ — see PRACTICAL 1

3 involved in often constant activity ⟨a boss who is of the opinion that a *working* employee is a needed employee, as idleness is a sign of dispensability⟩ — see BUSY 1

workmanlike *adj* accomplished with trained ability ⟨The pitcher gave a *workmanlike* performance, allowing the other team to score only a single run.⟩ — see SKILLFUL 1

workout *n* something done over and over in order to develop skill ⟨a *workout* with dumbbells for building the muscles of the hands⟩ — see EXERCISE 2

work out *vb* **1** to find an answer for through reasoning ⟨By putting our heads together, we were able to *work out* the problem.⟩ — see SOLVE

2 to turn out as planned or desired ⟨Our plans for a ski vacation just didn't *work out*.⟩ — see SUCCEED 1

3 to determine (a value) by doing the necessary mathematical operations ⟨After *working out* the cost of a college education, we've decided that it's never too early to start saving.⟩ — see CALCULATE 1

workshop *n* a building or set of buildings for the manufacturing of goods ⟨a *workshop* for making high-end furniture⟩ — see FACTORY

world *n* **1** human beings in general ⟨The whole *world* is waiting to see how this situation will play out.⟩ — see PEOPLE 1

2 the celestial body on which we live ⟨worried about the effects of pollution on the *world*⟩ — see EARTH 1

3 the whole body of things observed or assumed ⟨theories about the origin of the *world*⟩ — see UNIVERSE

worldly *adj* **1** having a wide and refined knowledge of the world especially from personal experience ⟨She returned from her year as an exchange student a much more *worldly* person.⟩ — see WORLDLY-WISE

2 having to do with life on earth especially as opposed to that in heaven ⟨preoccupied with *worldly* concerns⟩ — see EARTHLY

worldly–wise *adj* having a wide and refined knowledge of the world especially from personal experience ⟨Her long career as a globe-trotting journalist has made her very *worldly-wise* and even a little jaded.⟩

synonyms cosmopolitan, smart, sophisticated, worldly

related words suave, urbane; civilized, cultivated, cultured, polished, refined; experienced, knowing, practiced, schooled, seasoned; bored, cynical, jaded, skeptical; down-to-earth, pragmatic (*also* pragmatical), realistic, sober

near antonyms callow, green, inexperienced, raw; parochial, provincial, rustic (*also* rustical); philistine, uncivilized, uncultured, unrefined; childlike, simple, simpleminded; impractical; uncritical, unknowing

antonyms guileless, ingenuous, innocent, naive (*or* naïve), unsophisticated, untutored, unworldly, wide-eyed

worm *vb* **1** to advance gradually beyond the usual or desirable limits ⟨neighborhoods *worming* into lands reserved for wildlife⟩ — see ENCROACH

2 to introduce in a gradual, secret, or clever way ⟨I *wormed* my way into his confidence.⟩ — see INSINUATE 1

3 to move slowly with the body close to the ground ⟨The cat silently *wormed* along the ground as it snuck up on the bird.⟩ — see CRAWL 1

worn *adj* depleted in strength, energy, or freshness ⟨She was feeling very *worn* after a long day at work.⟩ — see WEARY 1

worn–out *adj* **1** depleted in strength, energy, or freshness ⟨*worn-out* tourists heading back to their hotel after a long day of sightseeing⟩ — see WEARY 1

2 worn or torn into or as if into rags ⟨used a *worn-out* T-shirt for dusting the furniture⟩ — see RAGGED 2

worried *adj* feeling or showing uncomfortable feelings of uncertainty ⟨The soldier's father had a *worried* expression as he listened to the news.⟩ — see NERVOUS 1

worrisome *adj* **1** causing worry or anxiety ⟨The patient's erratic behavior has become increasingly *worrisome*.⟩ — see TROUBLESOME

2 marked by or causing agitation or uncomfortable feelings ⟨*Worrisome* looks passed between the two coworkers as the personnel manager began to enumerate the company's financial woes.⟩ — see NERVOUS 2

worry *n* an uneasy state of mind usually over the possibility of an anticipated misfortune or trouble ⟨She can only concentrate on something when she is free of *worry*.⟩ — see ANXIETY 1

worry *vb* **1** to experience concern or anxiety ⟨They *worried* for days about whether the loan would be approved.⟩

synonyms bother, fear, fret, fuss, stew, stress, sweat, trouble

related words agonize; long, pine, yearn; chafe; despair

phrases give a hang (*or* care a hang), sweat blood

near antonyms accept; abide, bear, endure, stick out, stomach, sustain, take, tolerate

2 to trouble the mind of; to make uneasy ⟨Those strange noises outside the house *worry* me.⟩ — see DISTURB 1

worsen *vb* to become worse or of less value ⟨The condition of the house *worsened* with every year of neglect.⟩ — see DETERIORATE 1

worship *n* excessive admiration of or devotion to a person ⟨the *worship* of professional athletes who often turn out to be all too fallible⟩

synonyms adulation, deification, idolatry, idolization, worshipping (*also* worshiping)

related words adoration, deference, glorification, reverence, veneration; idealization, romanticization; affection, fancy, favor, fondness, like, liking, love; appreciation, esteem, regard, respect; approval

near antonyms condemnation, disapproval, disfavor, dislike, dismissal, disregard, hatred, loathing, scorn

worship *vb* **1** to offer honor or respect to (someone) as a divine power ⟨The ancient Greeks *worshipped* many different gods.⟩

synonyms adore, deify, glorify, revere, reverence, venerate

related words admire, honor, love, regard, respect; apotheosize, canonize, dignify, exalt, lionize, magnify; extol (*also* extoll), laud, praise; delight, gratify, please, satisfy

near antonyms blaspheme, desecrate, profane, violate; affront, dishonor, disrespect, insult, offend, outrage, pique, ridicule, scorn, slight; displease; defame, disparage, libel, malign, slander, slur, smear

2 to feel passion, devotion, or tenderness for ⟨The new father *worships* his young daughter, and would do anything for her.⟩ — see LOVE 2

3 to love or admire too much ⟨thought that some of her fellow senior citizens *worshipped* the old days too much, observing that they weren't all good⟩ — see IDOLIZE

worshipful *adj* reflecting great admiration or devotion ⟨a movie fan's *worshipful* stare upon finally meeting her idol⟩ ⟨a teacher surrounded by *worshipful* little children⟩

synonyms adoring, adulatory, deifying, idolizing, worshipping (*also* worshiping) *related words* glorifying, reverent, reverential, venerating; hagiographic (*also* hagiographical); affectionate, fond, loving; appreciative, deferential, respectful; approving

near antonyms condemning, contemptuous, disapproving, hateful, loathing, scornful

worshipping *also* **worshiping** *adj* reflecting great admiration or devotion ⟨impressionable young men with a *worshipping* regard for professional athletes⟩ — see WORSHIPFUL

worshipping *also* **worshiping** *n* excessive admiration of or devotion to a person ⟨feels that there is just too much *worshipping* of celebrities⟩ — see WORSHIP

worst *vb* to achieve a victory over ⟨How humiliating for a tennis champ to be *worsted* by a player no one had ever heard of.⟩ — see BEAT 2

worth *n* 1 the relative usefulness or importance of something as judged by specific qualities ⟨Money alone cannot determine the true *worth* of some things.⟩

synonyms account, merit, valuation, value

related words assessment, estimation, evaluation; excellence, greatness, perfection; consequence, importance, significance, weight

near antonyms emptiness, valuelessness, worthlessness; baseness, cheapness, crumminess, inferiority, lousiness, meanness, paltriness, poorness; deficiency, inadequacy, insufficiency, unacceptability

2 the amount of money for which something will find a buyer ⟨One surefire way to determine the actual *worth* of a painting is to sell it at auction.⟩ — see VALUE 1

3 the total of one's money and property ⟨The entrepreneur's *worth* is well over 100 million dollars.⟩ — see WEALTH 1

worthless *adj* having no usefulness ⟨That expensive toy is *worthless* now that it's broken.⟩

synonyms empty, junky, no-good, null, vain, valueless

related words base, cheap, inferior, lousy, low-grade, second-rate; bad, defective, dud, flawed, imperfect, substandard, unsatisfactory; deficient, inadequate, insufficient, unacceptable

near antonyms precious; cherished, esteemed, prized, treasured; choice, exceptional, fancy, high-grade, special

antonyms useful, valuable, worthy

worthy *adj* having sufficient worth or merit to receive one's honor, esteem, or reward ⟨made charitable contributions to the American Red Cross and other *worthy* causes⟩ ⟨a *worthy* opponent in a tennis match⟩

synonyms deserving, good, meritorious

related words admirable, commendable, creditable, laudable, praiseworthy; cherished, prized, treasured; choice, excellent, exceptional, fancy, high-grade, primary, prime, special

near antonyms base, cheap, inferior, second-rate, substandard; bad, defective, flawed, imperfect; deficient, inadequate, insufficient, unacceptable, unsatisfactory

antonyms no-good, undeserving, valueless, worthless

wound *vb* 1 to cause bodily damage to ⟨A trap had *wounded* the animal, but the vet was able to save it.⟩ — see INJURE 1

2 to cause hurt feelings or deep resentment in ⟨That callous comment really *wounded* me.⟩ — see INSULT

wraith *n* the soul of a dead person thought of especially as appearing to living people ⟨The people who once lived here believed that their world was populated by *wraiths* and witches.⟩ — see GHOST 1

wrangle *n* an often noisy or angry expression of differing opinions ⟨There was a bit of a *wrangle* over how much money to give the high school for its sports programs.⟩ — see ARGUMENT 1

wrangle *vb* to express different opinions about something often angrily ⟨a town meeting at which local residents *wrangled* for hours about property taxes⟩ — see ARGUE 2

wrangler *n* 1 a hired hand who tends cattle or horses at a ranch or on the range ⟨a rough-hewn *wrangler* who never says much⟩ — see COWBOY

2 a person who takes part in a dispute ⟨known as a petty, unrelenting *wrangler* who likes argument for the sake of argument⟩ — see DISPUTANT

wrap *vb* 1 to encircle or bind with or as if with a belt ⟨*wrapped* her waist with a colorful silk sash⟩ — see GIRD 1

2 to surround or cover closely ⟨A sinister darkness seemed to *wrap* the lonely cabin.⟩ — see ENFOLD 1

wraps *pl n* something that covers or conceals like a piece of cloth ⟨kept the whole plan under *wraps* until they were ready to make a public announcement⟩ — see CLOAK 1

wrap–up *n* 1 a short statement of the main points ⟨a post-election *wrap-up* of the campaign's high points and many low points⟩ — see SUMMARY

2 the last part of a process or action ⟨The opening of the museum's modern art wing marks the *wrap-up* of its decade-long expansion plan.⟩ — see FINALE

wrap up *vb* 1 to bring (an event) to a natural or appropriate stopping point ⟨A grand parade will *wrap up* the weeklong celebration.⟩ — see CLOSE 3

2 to make into a short statement of the main points (as of a report) ⟨A reporter *wrapped up* the mayor's speech in a few sentences.⟩ — see SUMMARIZE

wrath *n* 1 an intense emotional state of displeasure with someone or something ⟨waited until my initial *wrath* had eased before voicing my complaint⟩ — see ANGER

2 suffering, loss, or hardship imposed in response to a crime or offense ⟨The evangelist warned the gathering that unrepentant sinners would suffer the *wrath* of God.⟩ — see PUNISHMENT

wrathful *adj* feeling or showing anger ⟨In a *wrathful* voice she demanded to know what had happened.⟩ — see ANGRY

wrathfulness *n* an intense emotional state of displeasure with someone or something ⟨The *wrathfulness* with which he voiced his complaint was shocking.⟩ — see ANGER

wreathe *vb* 1 to cause to twine about one another ⟨decided to *wreathe* the grapevines into a beribboned swag to give the room a "country look"⟩ — see INTERTWINE 1

2 to scatter or set here and there among other things ⟨*wreathed* small flowers into the design for the wallpaper⟩ — see THREAD 1

3 to form a circle around ⟨Pretty ribbons *wreathed* the flower girl's braided bun.⟩ — see SURROUND

wreck *n* 1 the portion or bits of something left over or behind after it has been destroyed ⟨found the *wreck* of the ship lying on the floor of the ocean⟩ — see REMAINS 1

2 the destruction or loss of a ship ⟨The *wreck* cost the insurance company millions of dollars.⟩ — see SHIPWRECK

3 the violent coming together of two bodies into destructive contact ⟨a dangerous stretch of roadway that has been the scene of numerous car *wrecks*⟩ — see CRASH 1

wreck *vb* 1 to cause irreparable damage to (a ship) by running aground or sinking ⟨Many unwary captains have *wrecked* their ships on the shoals that surround the island.⟩ — see SHIPWRECK

2 to bring to a complete end the physical soundness, existence, or usefulness of ⟨Most of the furniture on the ground floor was *wrecked* by the floodwaters.⟩ — see DESTROY 1

wreckage *n* 1 the state or fact of being rendered nonexistent, physically unsound, or useless ⟨The *wreckage* of those ancient statues represents a great loss to the art world.⟩ — see DESTRUCTION 1

2 the portion or bits of something left over or behind after it has been destroyed ⟨They cleared the *wreckage* from the racetrack.⟩ — see REMAINS 1

3 the destruction or loss of a ship ⟨Debris floated ashore for weeks after the *wreckage*.⟩ — see SHIPWRECK

wrecking *n* the destruction or loss of a ship ⟨The *wrecking* of the freighter was one of the worst disasters ever on the Great Lakes.⟩ — see SHIPWRECK

wrench *n* **1** a forceful rotating or pulling motion for the purpose of dislodging something ⟨With a sharp *wrench* of the hammer I pulled the nail from the board.⟩

synonyms twist, twisting, wrenching, wresting, wringing
related words draft, draw, extraction, pull, tug, yank; dislocation, displacement

2 the act or an instance of applying force on something so that it moves in the direction of the force ⟨With one final hard *wrench* I was able to pull the cork from the bottle.⟩ — see PULL 1

wrench *vb* **1** to move by or as if by a forceful rotation ⟨With one last sharp yank, he *wrenched* the lid off the bottle of ketchup.⟩

synonyms twist, wrest, wring
related words draw, dredge (up), extract, jerk, lug, pluck, pull, tug, tweak, yank; jimmy, lever, pry; budge, dislocate, displace, disturb, remove; shift, transfer, transpose

2 to injure by overuse, misuse, or pressure ⟨*wrenched* her shoulder by all of that heavy lifting⟩ — see STRAIN 1

3 to separate or remove by forceful pulling ⟨*wrenched* the post out of the ground⟩ — see TEAR 2

wrenching *adj* intensely or unbearably painful ⟨forced to make an emotionally *wrenching* decision⟩ — see EXCRUCIATING 1

wrenching *n* a forceful rotating or pulling motion for the purpose of dislodging something ⟨After a lot of *wrenching* and tugging, the plumber managed to pull the stubborn pipe free.⟩ — see WRENCH 1

wrest *vb* **1** to draw out by force or with effort ⟨The boy *wrested* the book out of his sister's hands.⟩ — see EXTRACT

2 to get (as money) by the use of force or threats ⟨debt collectors *wresting* money from intimidated debtors⟩ — see EXTORT

3 to move by or as if by a forceful rotation ⟨I need a strong arm to *wrest* the lid off this pickle jar.⟩ — see WRENCH 1

4 to separate or remove by forceful pulling ⟨*wrested* open the stuck door of the cabinet⟩ — see TEAR 2

wresting *n* a forceful rotating or pulling motion for the purpose of dislodging something ⟨No amount of *wresting* could loosen the rusted bolt.⟩ — see WRENCH 1

wrestle *vb* to seize and attempt to unbalance one another for the purpose of achieving physical mastery ⟨The young sisters *wrestled* on the floor over the toy.⟩

synonyms grapple, scuffle, tussle
related words battle, clash (with), combat, contend, duel, fight, war (against); bash, batter, beat, buffet, hit, punch, slug, strike; box, spar; brawl, skirmish

wretch *n* a mean, evil, or unprincipled person ⟨The clerk was an ungrateful *wretch* who stole money from his employer's cash register.⟩ — see VILLAIN

wretched *adj* **1** extremely unsatisfactory ⟨This report is simply *wretched*—you'll have to rewrite it.⟩

synonyms atrocious, awful, dismal, execrable, horrible, lousy, punk, rotten, terrible
related words bad, deficient, inferior, off, poor, substandard, wanting; contemptible, miserable, shameful; defective, faulty, flawed; low-grade, mediocre, reprehensible, second-rate; bum, useless, valueless, worthless; inadequate, insufficient, lacking; abominable, fiendish, odious, vile
near antonyms choice, excellent, exceptional, first-class, first-rate, premium, prime, superior; adequate, sufficient; acceptable, satisfactory
antonyms great, marvelous (*or* marvellous), wonderful

2 arousing or deserving of one's loathing and disgust ⟨a *wretched* lie⟩ — see CONTEMPTIBLE 1

3 causing or marked by an atmosphere lacking in cheer ⟨lived alone in a *wretched* apartment⟩ — see GLOOMY 1

4 falling short of a standard ⟨a *wretched* attempt at writing an original song⟩ — see BAD 1

5 feeling unhappiness ⟨She was *wretched* for weeks after her friend moved away.⟩ — see SAD 1

6 not following or in accordance with standards of honor and decency ⟨His *wretched* treatment of his employees earned him a bad reputation.⟩ — see IGNOBLE 2

7 of low quality ⟨*wretched* goods that aren't even worth half of what the store is charging for them⟩ — see CHEAP 2

8 deserving of one's pity ⟨those *wretched* souls who cannot even afford a decent roof over their heads⟩ — see PATHETIC 1

9 deserving pitying scorn (as for inadequacy) ⟨The pampered socialite complained that the only room available was in a *wretched* little motel by the highway.⟩ — see PITIFUL 1

wretchedly *adv* **1** in an unsatisfactory way ⟨The whole hockey team played *wretchedly* that night.⟩ — see BADLY 1

2 with feelings of bitterness or grief ⟨We're *wretchedly* disappointed in you for behaving so irresponsibly.⟩ — see HARD 2

wriggle *vb* **1** to make jerky or restless movements ⟨a toddler *wriggling* in his seat throughout the whole meal⟩ — see FIDGET

2 to move slowly with the body close to the ground ⟨A worm slowly *wriggled* across the sidewalk.⟩ — see CRAWL 1

3 to introduce in a gradual, secret, or clever way ⟨Within a month of moving, he had *wriggled* himself into his neighbors' good graces.⟩ — see INSINUATE 1

wring *vb* **1** to get (as money) by the use of force or threats ⟨That bill collector is willing to do anything to *wring* money out of deadbeats.⟩ — see EXTORT

2 to move by or as if by a forceful rotation ⟨Be sure to *wring* out the towel before you hang it back up.⟩ — see WRENCH 1

3 to draw out by force or with effort ⟨used every interrogation technique in order to *wring* the information out of the criminal⟩ — see EXTRACT

wringing *n* a forceful rotating or pulling motion for the purpose of dislodging something ⟨a firm *wringing* of the shoe got it off⟩ — see WRENCH 1

wrinkle *n* **1** a small fold in a soft and otherwise smooth surface ⟨The old woman's face creased into *wrinkles* as she smiled.⟩ ⟨The curtains cascaded onto the floor in ripples and *wrinkles*.⟩

synonyms crease, crimp, crinkle, furrow
related words corrugation, layer, loop, plait, pleat, ply, pucker, seam, tuck; crow's-foot

2 something (as a device) created for the first time through the use of the imagination ⟨the latest *wrinkle* in digital photography⟩ — see INVENTION 1

wrinkle *vb* **1** to develop creases or folds ⟨If you don't fold clothes promptly after drying, they'll *wrinkle*.⟩

synonyms crease, crinkle, furrow, rumple
related words collapse, crumple, double, fold

2 to create (as by crushing) an irregular mass of creases in ⟨Sitting down on the bedspread *wrinkled* it.⟩ — see CRUMPLE 1

write *vb* **1** to compose and set down on paper the words of ⟨A staunch supporter of the old school, he prefers to *write* all of his letters by hand.⟩
synonyms author, pen, scratch (out), scribble
related words cast, compose, craft, draft, draw up, formulate, frame, prepare; recast, redraft, revise, rewrite; letter, print, type, typewrite; record, take down, transcribe; autograph, pencil (in), register, sign; couch, express, phrase, put, word
2 to engage in an exchange of written messages ⟨Promise you'll *write* while you're away.⟩ — see CORRESPOND 1

write off *vb* **1** to express scornfully one's low opinion of ⟨Most critics have already *written off* that director as a hack incapable of turning out anything but schlock.⟩ — see DECRY 1
2 to diminish the price or value of ⟨That one blunder will *write off* to nothing all the goodwill we've been building up.⟩ — see DEPRECIATE 1

writer *n* a person who creates a written work ⟨a *writer* who is still trying to get published⟩ — see AUTHOR 1

writhe *vb* **1** to cause to twine about one another ⟨He tends to *writhe* his fingers together when he's nervous or upset.⟩ — see INTERTWINE 1
2 to make jerky or restless movements ⟨*writhing* in pain from his injuries⟩ — see FIDGET

wrong *adj* **1** falling short of a standard ⟨There is something *wrong* with this cake—it has a funny taste.⟩ — see BAD 1
2 having an opinion that does not agree with truth or the facts ⟨I'm sorry, but the latest research proves you *wrong*.⟩ — see INCORRECT 1
3 not appropriate for a particular occasion or situation ⟨He has a knack for saying just the *wrong* thing.⟩ — see INAPPROPRIATE
4 not being in agreement with what is true ⟨Her answer that Thomas Jefferson was the second president of the United States is *wrong*—it was John Adams, of course.⟩ — see FALSE 1
5 not conforming to a high moral standard; morally unacceptable ⟨was caught doing something *wrong*⟩ — see BAD 2

wrong *adv* off the desired or intended path or course ⟨All of our carefully laid plans have gone *wrong*.⟩
synonyms afield, amiss, astray, awry

related words badly; faultily, improperly, inappropriately, incorrectly, mistakenly, wrongly; inadequately, insufficiently, unpromisingly
near antonyms perfectly; auspiciously, favorably, promisingly; correctly, properly, rightly; appropriately, fittingly, suitably
antonyms aright, right, well

wrong *n* **1** that which is morally unacceptable ⟨Any reasonable person should be expected to know the difference between right and *wrong*.⟩ — see EVIL
2 unfair or inadequate treatment of someone or something or an instance of this ⟨trying to right all the *wrongs* in the world⟩ — see DISSERVICE

wrongdoer *n* a person who commits moral wrongs ⟨Anticorruption crusaders are going after *wrongdoers* at every level of the nation's government.⟩ — see EVILDOER 1

wrongdoing *n* **1** a breaking of a moral or legal code ⟨A local newspaper exposed the contractor's elaborate attempts to cover up his *wrongdoings*.⟩ — see OFFENSE 1
2 improper or illegal behavior ⟨The police officer was found to be completely innocent of any *wrongdoing*.⟩ — see MISCONDUCT

wrongful *adj* contrary to or forbidden by law ⟨suing his employer for *wrongful* termination⟩ — see ILLEGAL 1

wrongly *adv* in a mistaken or inappropriate way ⟨You have *wrongly* interpreted this line of the poem.⟩
synonyms amiss, erroneously, faultily, improperly, inaccurately, inappropriately, inaptly, incorrectly, mistakenly, unsuitably
related words misguidedly; fallibly, imperfectly; extraneously, irrelevantly, meaninglessly, pointlessly, senselessly; inadequately, insufficiently; undesirably, unsatisfactorily; foolishly, unwisely
near antonyms infallibly, perfectly; germanely, meaningfully, pertinently, relevantly, sensibly; acceptably, adequately, satisfactorily, sufficiently; prudently, sagely, wisely
antonyms appropriately, aptly, correctly, fittingly, properly, right, rightly, suitably, well

wrongness *n* the quality or state of being unsuitable or unfitting ⟨Arguments about the rightness or *wrongness* of the satirical skit drowned out any discussion of the points it attempted to raise.⟩ — see INAPPROPRIATENESS 1

wroth *adj* feeling or showing anger ⟨I've been waxing *wroth* all afternoon!⟩ — see ANGRY

XYZ

x (out) *vb* to show (something written) to be no longer valid by drawing a cross over or a line through it ⟨You can *x out* the names of the people who have already left.⟩
synonyms cancel, cross (out), delete, kill, scratch (out), strike (out), stroke (out)
related words blot out, efface, eradicate, expunge, obliterate, root (out), rub out, wipe out; bleep, blip, clip, cut, excise, remove; censor, clean (up), expurgate, redact; abbreviate, crop, shorten; black out, repress, silence, suppress
near antonyms stet

yammer *n* an expression of dissatisfaction, pain, or resentment ⟨a soccer coach having to endure the endless *yammers* from parents that their kids weren't getting enough time on the field⟩ — see COMPLAINT 1

yammer *vb* to express dissatisfaction, pain, or resentment usually tiresomely ⟨Customers *yammered* on for what seemed like days about the billing mistake.⟩ — see COMPLAIN

yank *n* the act or an instance of applying force on something so that it moves in the direction of the force ⟨I had to give the shoe a good *yank* to get it off.⟩ — see PULL 1

yank *vb* 1 to move or cause to move with a sharp quick motion ⟨I *yanked* the door shut.⟩ — see JERK 1
2 to draw out by force or with effort ⟨*yanked* out a tooth with a pair of pliers⟩ — see EXTRACT
3 to separate or remove by forceful pulling ⟨Grab the other one, and let's see if we can't *yank* these two grocery carriages apart.⟩ — see TEAR 2

¹yard *n* 1 an open space wholly or partly enclosed (as by buildings or walls) ⟨Inmates are allowed an hour of exercise in the prison's inner *yard*.⟩ — see COURT 2
2 the area around and belonging to a building ⟨We're looking for a house with a big *yard*.⟩ — see GROUND 1

²yard *n* a considerable amount ⟨a composer who produced *yards* of gorgeous music over the course of a long career⟩ — see LOT 2

yardstick *n* something set up as an example against which others of the same type are compared ⟨This essay will be the *yardstick* by which I grade the others.⟩ — see STANDARD 1

yarn *n* 1 a brief account of something interesting that happened especially to one personally ⟨Grandpa likes to tell *yarns* about when he was young.⟩ — see STORY 2
2 a work with imaginary characters and events that is shorter and usually less complex than a novel ⟨a ripping *yarn* about space travel and alien monsters⟩ — see STORY 1

yaw *vb* to depart abruptly from a straight line or course ⟨The ship *yawed* hard to the right when the rogue wave hit it broadside.⟩ — see SWERVE 1

yea *adv* 1 not merely this but also ⟨We will go to the new land, and, *yea*, we will pursue our dreams!⟩ — see EVEN 1
2 used to express agreement ⟨I vote *yea* on the proposed increase in the school budget.⟩ — see YES

yea *n* a vote or decision for something ⟨The measure passed with 50 *yeas* and 17 nays.⟩ — see YES

yeah *adv* used to express agreement ⟨*Yeah*, we'll be there.⟩ — see YES

yearn (for) *vb* to have an earnest wish to own or enjoy ⟨*yearned for* a little house in the country⟩ — see DESIRE 1

yearn (over) *vb* to have sympathy for ⟨Who wouldn't *yearn over* the poor little lost kitten?⟩ — see PITY

yearning *n* a strong wish for something ⟨had a sudden *yearning* for something sweet⟩ — see DESIRE 1

yeast *n* something that arouses action or activity ⟨Taxation without representation proved to be the *yeast* of rebellion.⟩ — see IMPULSE 1

yell *n* a loud vocal expression of strong emotion ⟨The crowd gave a *yell* of approval.⟩ — see SHOUT

yell *vb* 1 to cry out loudly and emotionally ⟨*yelled* with alarm when the baseball came flying toward them⟩ — see SCREAM 1
2 to speak so as to be heard at a distance ⟨I *yelled* to the kids in the backyard that it was time for dinner.⟩ — see CALL 1

yellow *adj* having or showing a shameful lack of courage ⟨You'll come with us into the cave, unless you're *yellow*.⟩ — see COWARDLY

yelp *vb* to cry out loudly and emotionally ⟨He *yelped* with surprise when everything fell off the closet shelf and onto his head.⟩ — see SCREAM 1

yen *n* a strong wish for something ⟨I have a strange *yen* to take the day off from work.⟩ — see DESIRE 1

yes *adv* used to express agreement ⟨*Yes*, I'll be ready for the test tomorrow.⟩
synonyms all right, alright, aye (*also* ay), exactly, OK (*or* okay), yea, yeah
related words absolutely, assuredly, certainly, indeed, indisputably, undoubtedly, unquestionably
antonyms nay, no, no way, scarcely

yes *n* a vote or decision for something ⟨The bill passed with 50 "*yeses*" and 12 "noes."⟩
synonyms yea
related words pro; acceptance, acquiescence, agreement, approval, assent, concurrence, consent, permission, sanction
near antonyms con; blackball, veto; denial, disallowance, negation, refusal, rejection
antonyms nay, negative, no, non placet

yesterday *n* the events or experience of former times ⟨My grandparents are always reminiscing about *yesterday*.⟩ — see PAST

yesteryear *n* the events or experience of former times ⟨the simple games of *yesteryear* that kept children entertained for hours⟩ — see PAST

yet *adv* 1 at a later time ⟨We may *yet* figure it out.⟩
synonyms eventually, finally, someday, sometime, ultimately
related words anon, directly, imminently, momentarily, presently, shortly, soon; forthwith, immediately, promptly, pronto, right away, right now, straightaway, straightway
phrases at last (*or* at long last), at length, in the end, in the fullness of time, in time
near antonyms ne'er, never, nevermore
2 in addition to what has been said ⟨The travel agent offered *yet* another option for our planned tour of Europe.⟩ — see MORE 1
3 in spite of that ⟨The hikers were scared, and *yet* they continued to go deeper into the cave.⟩ — see HOWEVER
4 up to this or that time ⟨We have *yet* to win a single game.⟩ ⟨She had *yet* to accomplish a single thing.⟩ — see HITHERTO

yet *conj* if it were not for the fact that ⟨It feels like summer, *yet* according to the calendar we're still in early spring.⟩ — see EXCEPT

yield *n* 1 an increase usually measured in money that

comes from labor, business, or property ⟨The stock's *yield* has increased over the years.⟩ — see INCOME 1

2 something produced by physical or intellectual effort ⟨Wheat farmers were able to increase the *yield* per acre substantially.⟩ — see PRODUCT 1

3 the total amount collected or obtained especially at one time ⟨The *yield* from the fund drive was beyond our expectations.⟩ — see HAUL 1

yield *vb* **1** to give up and cease resistance (as to a liking, temptation, or habit) ⟨I finally *yielded* to temptation and had a bowl of ice cream.⟩

synonyms bow, cave (in), give in, submit, succumb, surrender

related words cater (to), gratify, indulge, wallow; acquiesce (to), concede (to); buckle (under), knuckle under; give over (to)

near antonyms battle, breast, combat, confront, counter, defy, face, fight, meet, object, oppose, repel; thwart, withstand; reject; bridle, check, constrain, curb, inhibit, restrain, stifle

antonyms hold off, resist

2 to produce as revenue ⟨I expect that stock to *yield* at least 14% profit this year.⟩

synonyms bear, give, pay, return

related words net; afford, furnish, provide, supply; pay off

3 to cease resistance (as to another's arguments, demands, or control) ⟨After initially balking at the order, the soldier *yielded* when the commanding officer threatened a formal charge of insubordination.⟩

synonyms blink, bow, budge, capitulate, concede, give in, knuckle under, quit, relent, submit, succumb, surrender

related words acquiesce; defer

phrases say uncle, throw in the towel (*also* throw in the sponge)

near antonyms contend, fight, hold off; battle, breast, combat, confront, counter, defy, face, meet, object, oppose, repel; thwart, withstand

antonyms resist

4 to be the cause of (a situation, action, or state of mind) ⟨It was the sort of embarrassing question that seldom *yields* an honest answer.⟩ — see EFFECT

5 to fall down or in as a result of physical pressure ⟨The door soon *yielded* to the battering ram.⟩ — see COLLAPSE 1

6 to give (something) over to the control or possession of another usually under duress ⟨refusing to *yield* the city to enemy troops⟩ — see SURRENDER 1

7 to give (oneself) over to something especially unrestrainedly ⟨She *yielded* herself to every new social media fad and then complained about having no privacy.⟩ — see ABANDON 1

yielding *adj* **1** receiving or enduring without offering resistance ⟨a person too *yielding* to even stand up for his own rights⟩ — see PASSIVE

2 not stiff in structure ⟨After sitting on a hard bench for hours, I was happy to sink into the sofa's *yielding* cushions.⟩ — see LIMP 1

yoke *n* the state of being enslaved ⟨a people able at last to throw off the *yoke* and to embrace freedom⟩ — see SLAVERY

yoke *vb* to put or bring together so as to form a new and longer whole ⟨*yoked* several ideas together to come up with a new theory⟩ — see CONNECT 1

yokel *n* an awkward or simple person especially from a small town or the country ⟨a lame comedy about the misadventures of *yokels* in the big city⟩ — see HICK

yon *adv* at or to a greater distance or more advanced point

⟨the belief that it is the destiny of the human race to explore our solar system and *yon*⟩ — see FARTHER

yonder *adv* at or to a greater distance or more advanced point ⟨Look *yonder* and you'll see the skyline of the city.⟩ — see FARTHER

yore *n* the events or experience of former times ⟨My favorite stories are about gallant knights and fair maidens in the days of *yore*.⟩ — see PAST

young *adj* being in the early stage of life, growth, or development ⟨A *young* cat requires more food than an older one.⟩ ⟨a *young* tree that will eventually reach 50 feet tall⟩

synonyms adolescent, immature, juvenile, youngish, youthful

related words ephebic, minor, preteen, subadult, teenage (*or* teenaged), underage; embryonic; callow, green, inexperienced, puerile, raw; babyish, childish, childlike, infantile, infantine, kiddish; undeveloped, unfinished, unfledged, unformed, unripe, unripened; blooming, blossoming, burgeoning, flourishing, flowering

near antonyms aged, aging (*or* ageing), ancient, elderly, geriatric, long-lived, old, older, oldish, senior; full-blown, full-fledged; golden, mellow, ripe, ripened; middle-aged; anile, decrepit, doddering, over-the-hill, senile, spavined, tottery

antonyms adult, grown-up, mature, matured

youngish *adj* being in the early stage of life, growth, or development ⟨A *youngish* but surprisingly mature audience showed up to watch the serious film.⟩ — see YOUNG

youngster *n* a young person who is between infancy and adulthood ⟨a herd of *youngsters* following their nature guide like ducklings after a mother duck⟩ — see CHILD 1

youth *n* **1** a male person who has not yet reached adulthood ⟨He was a big, strapping *youth* who, even at his relatively young age, knew the meaning of hard work.⟩ — see BOY 1

2 a young person who is between infancy and adulthood ⟨They rounded up the neighborhood *youths* and organized them into a softball team.⟩ — see CHILD 1

3 the state or time of being a child ⟨She told the young people to enjoy their *youth* while they could.⟩ — see CHILDHOOD

youthful *adj* being in the early stage of life, growth, or development ⟨It's still a *youthful* nation with a lot of promise and potential.⟩ — see YOUNG

yowl *n* a loud vocal expression of strong emotion ⟨The cat gave a *yowl* of anger.⟩ — see SHOUT

yowl *vb* **1** to express dissatisfaction, pain, or resentment usually tiresomely ⟨a bitterly cold winter that had people *yowling* about their heating bills⟩ — see COMPLAIN

2 to make a long loud mournful sound ⟨coyotes *yowling* at the moon⟩ — see HOWL 1

yo-yo *n* **1** a person who lacks good sense or judgment ⟨Some *yo-yo* cut the electricity off while I still had unsaved data.⟩ — see FOOL 1

2 a stupid person ⟨those *yo-yos* who insist upon using their cell phones while speeding down the highway⟩ — see IDIOT

yucky *also* **yukky** *adj* **1** disagreeable or disgusting to the sense of taste ⟨a child at that age where every unfamiliar and untried food is preemptively dismissed as "*yucky*"⟩ — see DISTASTEFUL 1

2 not giving pleasure to the mind or senses ⟨The weather is supposed to be *yucky*, so bring your jacket and umbrella.⟩ — see UNPLEASANT

yuletide *n* the season celebrating Christmas ⟨These days, as far as the stores are concerned, *yuletide* starts in September.⟩

synonyms Christmastide, Christmastime, Noel

related words Advent; Christmas, nativity, Xmas, yule

yummy *adj* very pleasing to the sense of taste ⟨a *yummy* meal that is also nutritious⟩ — see DELICIOUS 1

zaniness *n* lack of good sense or judgment ⟨What *zaniness* possessed you to attempt such a dangerous jump on your bike?⟩ — see FOOLISHNESS 1

zany *adj* showing or marked by a lack of good sense or judgment ⟨a *zany* plan to drive cross-country on a motorized scooter⟩ — see FOOLISH 1

zany *n* 1 a comically dressed performer (as at a circus) who entertains with playful tricks and ridiculous behavior ⟨hired a *zany* to entertain the children at the birthday party⟩ — see CLOWN 1

2 a person of odd or whimsical habits ⟨One of the challenges of hosting a radio call-in program is preventing the *zanies* from completely taking over the discussion.⟩ — see ECCENTRIC

zap *vb* to deliver a blow to (someone or something) usually in a strong vigorous manner ⟨She *zapped* the annoying bug with a swatter.⟩ — see HIT 1

zealot *n* one who is intensely or excessively devoted to a cause ⟨*Zealots* on both sides of the issue resorted to name-calling and scare tactics.⟩

synonyms crusader, fanatic, militant, partisan (*also* partizan)

related words activist; dreamer, idealist, visionary; cultist, disciple, follower, hanger-on, idolizer, votary; addict, aficionado (*also* afficionado), buff, bug, devotee, enthusiast, fan, fancier, fiend, fool, freak, head, hound, junkie (*also* junky), lover, maniac, nut, sucker; advocate, apostle, backer, champion, evangelist, patron, promoter, stalwart, supporter; booster, rooter, well-wisher; faddist

near antonyms dabbler, dilettante

antonyms nonmilitant

zenith *n* the highest part or point ⟨at the *zenith* of her career as a dancer⟩ — see HEIGHT 1

zephyr *n* a slight or gentle movement of air ⟨A summer *zephyr* gently stirred her hair.⟩ — see BREEZE 1

zero *n* 1 the numerical symbol 0 or the absence of number or quantity represented by it ⟨Anything multiplied by *zero* comes out to *zero*.⟩

synonyms aught, cipher, goose egg, naught (*also* nought), nil, nothing, oh, zilch, zip

related words blank, void

2 a person of no importance or influence ⟨Those snobs on the cruise ship tried to make me feel like a complete *zero*.⟩ — see NOBODY

zero hour *n* a time or state of affairs requiring prompt or decisive action ⟨We're at the *zero hour*, so someone has to make a decision.⟩ — see EMERGENCY

zest *n* the quality or state of being stimulating to the mind or senses ⟨I dumped in more spices to add some *zest* to the marinade.⟩ — see PIQUANCY

zesty *adj* sharp and pleasantly stimulating to the mind or senses ⟨bland pasta that needs a *zesty* sauce⟩ — see PIQUANT

zigzag *vb* to move suddenly aside or to and fro ⟨The fleeing car *zigzagged* down the highway at breakneck speed.⟩ — see DODGE 1

zilch *n* 1 a person of no importance or influence ⟨He complained that to team owners, a fan is just a *zilch*.⟩ — see NOBODY

2 the numerical symbol 0 or the absence of number or quantity represented by it ⟨The amount of money that we have coming in right now is *zilch*.⟩ — see ZERO 1

zing *n* 1 active strength of body or mind ⟨has the youthful, adventurous *zing* to go out and conquer mountains⟩ — see VIGOR 1

2 the quality or state of being stimulating to the mind or senses ⟨The razor-sharp repartee puts some *zing* into the movie.⟩ ⟨An addition of ginger gave the marmalade a little extra *zing*.⟩ — see PIQUANCY

¹zip *n* active strength of body or mind ⟨He has surprising *zip* for a man his age.⟩ — see VIGOR 1

²zip *n* the numerical symbol 0 or the absence of number or quantity represented by it ⟨I've got *zip* as far as new ideas go.⟩ — see ZERO 1

zip *vb* 1 to fly, turn, or move rapidly with a fluttering or vibratory sound ⟨A dragonfly *zipped* by my ear.⟩ — see WHIR

2 to make an irregular series of quick, sudden movements ⟨The fly *zipped* around the room, trying to find a way to the outside.⟩ — see FLIT

3 to proceed or move quickly ⟨Knowing that she was already late, she went *zipping* off to meet her next client.⟩ — see HURRY 2

zip (up) *vb* to give life, vigor, or spirit to ⟨The newscaster asked the writer if there was a way to *zip up* the story a little.⟩ — see ANIMATE

zippy *adj* 1 having much high-spirited energy and movement ⟨a crowd of *zippy* children who'd been cooped up all day⟩ — see LIVELY 1

2 moving, proceeding, or acting with great speed ⟨She just bought a *zippy* new computer that should enable her to work more efficiently.⟩ — see FAST 1

zone *n* 1 a broad geographical area ⟨a tropical *zone*⟩ — see REGION 2

2 a part or portion having no fixed boundaries ⟨at that point we were out of the danger *zone* for avalanches⟩ — see REGION 1

zoom *n* a monotonous sound like that of an insect in motion ⟨the *zoom* of a motorboat off in the distance⟩ — see HUM

zoom *vb* 1 to fly, turn, or move rapidly with a fluttering or vibratory sound ⟨A squadron of fighter planes *zoomed* over our heads to start the airshow.⟩ — see WHIR

2 to proceed or move quickly ⟨race cars *zooming* around a track at breakneck speeds⟩ — see HURRY 2

3 to rise abruptly and rapidly ⟨She *zoomed* to a supervisory position after only a few short months.⟩ — see SKYROCKET